Economic Indicators Handbook

Third Edition

Economic Indicators Handbook

TIME SERIES • CONVERSIONS • DOCUMENTATION

Third Edition

Compiled and Edited by
Arsen J. Darnay

GALE

an International Thomson Publishing company I(T)P®

Arsen J. Darnay, *Editor*

Editorial Code & Data Inc. Staff

Marlita A. Reddy, *Research*
Nancy Ratliff, *Data Entry*
Ken Muth, *Data Processing*

Gale Research Staff

Lynn M. Osborn, *Assistant Editor and Project Coordinator*
Mary Beth Trimper, *Production Director*
Deborah Milliken, *Production Assistant*
C. J. Jonik, *Desktop Publisher*
Pursuit Studios, *Cover Designers*

Library of Congress Cataloging-in-Publication Data

Economic indicators handbook: time series, conversions, documentation / compiled and edited by
Arsen J. Darnay. - 3d ed.

p. cm.

Includes index.

ISBN 0-8103-9064-7

1. Economic indicators - United States 2. United States - Economic conditions. I. Darnay, Arsen
HC103.E26 1994

330.973 - dc20

92-13545
CIP

Gale Research
835 Penobscot Building
Detroit, Mi 48226-4094
ISBN 0-8103-6427-1
Printed in the United States of America
Published simultaneously in the United Kingdom
by Gale Research International Limited
(An affiliated company of Gale Research)

I(T)P™   Gale Research, an ITP Information/Reference Group Company.
ITP logo is a trademark under license.

TABLE OF CONTENTS

INTRODUCTION

SUMMARY

Economic Indicators Handbook (EIH) is now in its third edition. It presents a wide range of statistical series commonly used for measuring the economy of the United States. Featured are national income and product accounts, including Gross National Product (GNP) and Gross Domestic Product (GDP); the composite indexes of leading, lagging, and coincident indicators and their subcomponents; other cyclic indicators; selected economic series; a comprehensive presentation of the Consumer Price Index (CPI) in the aggregate and for 27 cities; a substantial selection from Producer Price Index (PPI); and selected stock market indexes. *EIH* covers 254 series; most are shown with detailed subdivisions or in constant and actual dollars so that, in total, 792 tables are presented. In all cases where data were available, series begin with the earliest date for which statistics were collected or estimated by the government or other sources, ranging from 1864-67 for GNP, 1913 for the CPI, and the 1940s for most business cycle indicators. *EIH* also features descriptive text; each major category is introduced and brief explanations, including an indication of significance, are provided for each series. Texts and tables are thoroughly indexed.

NEW IN THE THIRD EDITION

The third edition of *EIH* updates all series from their beginning to 1995. Some series were dropped because they have become obsolete. Others were added. Specific changes include the following:

- All series have been completely updated. Typically, two years of new data have been added to series that reach back to historical beginnings.

- Completely updated Gross Domestic Product (GDP) data are featured in current and in chained (1992) dollars from 1959 forward. Restatement of these series to 1929 will take place at a later date.

- A comprehensive explanation of the new chain-type indexing methods to deflate GDP and component results is presented as a new section in this Introduction.

- Gross National Product (GNP) is presented from 1929 to 1993 in 1987 constant dollars to preserve continuity back to the 19th century. A new GNP presentation, from 1959 forward in current and in chained (1992) dollars is also shown.

- The Implicit Price Deflators, presented in the last edition, have been replaced by tables with identical function based on chain-type price indexes.

- The Producer Price Index section has been enlarged by the addition of new product tables.

SCOPE

EIH presents statistical series grouped by major categories.

GNP and GDP. The fundamental measure of the U.S. economy—at least until the fall of 1991—has been GNP. For that reason, *EIH* begins with a presentation of aggregate GNP beginning with data for the 1869-1928 period and ending with data for 1995. This section is followed by a comprehensive presentation of GDP and all of its components, from 1959 to 1995. At the time of publication (early 1996), the government had not yet calculated its revised National Income and Product Accounts (NIPA) back to periods earlier than 1959.

1995 was the year for one of the government's comprehensive, benchmark revisions of NIPA and thus of the GDP and its components. This edition fully reflects those changes and presents summaries of what has changed in this Introduction and in chapter texts.

Constant dollar data have been replaced by chained dollar data in the NIPA accounts. This change is fully reflected in this edition and complete explanations for the changed indexes, and how they work, are incorporated.

Business Cycle Indicators. The federal government attempts to predict business cycles— recurring brief periods of decline in GNP/GDP followed by recovery and periods of growth—by using a number of economic series that lead the economy, coincide with it, or lag it (see Chapter 3). The composite indexes of leading, coincident, and lagging indicators are presented in full from the earliest period for which they are available; the series that make up these composite indexes are also presented.

Cyclic Indicators. Not all series classified as cyclic in behavior are included in the leading, coincident, and lagging indexes. A selection of others is presented under headings of Employment; Production and Income; Consumption, Trade, Orders, and Deliveries; Fixed Capital Investment; Inventories and Inventory Investment; Prices, Costs, and Profits; and Money and Credit. The selection was based in part on a review of series normally published in the business press (hence indicating usage by the public) and editorial judgment.

Economic Series. Many statistical measures of the economy are not classified as cyclic in nature and are not used to *predict* but to *measure* economic activity. The series included in *EIH* were, again, selected because they are commonly reported in the press or, in the editor's opinion, provide interesting insight into the functioning of the economy. Series on GDP implicit deflators were added in the second edition.

Prices. Chapters 6 and 7 present consumer and producer price indexes in considerable detail. The CPI is shown for both "all urban consumers" and the "urban wage earners" categories. Furthermore, major subcomponents categories (food, apparel, housing, etc.) are shown. Data for 27 cities/metro areas are then presented in the same detail. All CPI data are shown back to the earliest year for which they were collected or estimated by the Department of Labor.

The Producer Price Index is presented in Chapter 7 for 120 major categories and subcategories in monthly format; annual average data are also shown.

Selected Stock Market Indexes. The final chapter shows selected index data from the American Stock Exchange, NASDAQ (National Association of Securities Dealers Automated Quotation system), and the New York Stock Exchange. Another stock index series, the Standard & Poor's 500 index—which is used by the Bureau of Economic Analysis, U.S. Department of Commerce (BEA) as a leading indicator—is presented in Chapter 3.

SOURCES

The information included in *EIH* came from the U.S. Department of Commerce, the U.S. Department of Labor, the American Stock Exchange, the National Association of Securities Dealers, and the New York Stock Exchange. With a few exceptions, data were obtained by special arrangement rather than by being extracted from published sources.

Most federal data series, of course, are built from multiple sources, public and private. The majority rely on surveys, some of which are voluntary and some of which, such as the quadrennial censuses of business, are mandated by law. GNP and GDP data; the indicator series built into the leading, coincident, and lagging indexes; and the CPI and PPI all require substantial statistical work by the federal agencies that prepare them. They are, in a very real sense, statistical "products" of the agencies (or consortia of agencies): they are built from a diverse number of statistical "raw materials" and the methods of constructing the final series are continuously being refined.

ORGANIZATION AND PRESENTATION

EIH is organized into eight chapters as follows:

Chapter 1 - Gross National Product
Chapter 2 - Gross Domestic Product
Chapter 3 - Business Cycle Indicators
Chapter 4 - Cyclic Indicators
Chapter 5 - Economic Series
Chapter 6 - Consumer Price Index
Chapter 7 - Producer Price Index
Chapter 8 - Selected Stock Market Indexes

A keyword index holds references to text and table contents.

Each chapter begins with an introductory text. The subject to be covered in the chapter is outlined in general terms. A bibliography is provided. Chapters 1, 3, 4, and 5 are further subdivided. Each subdivision is separately introduced. Each series covered is separately discussed under its own heading in the chapter or section introductions.

STATISTICAL CONVENTIONS

Many statistical series presented in *EIH* make use of conventions which may be unfamiliar to the casual user. While most of these are discussed in context in the chapter and section notes, a general discussion of *Indexing, Base Periods, Constant and Current Dollars, Chained Dollars, Annualized Rates,* and *Seasonal Adjustments* is presented here.

Indexing. Statistical information in *EIH* is presented in the form of raw information (dollars, hours, weeks, etc.) or in the form of indexes. Index numbers are used to present information relative to data obtained for a specific period. A typical example is an index defined to have the value of 100 for the average outcome of a series in the year 1982. The following example illustrates the method used.

Year	Raw Value in Dollar	Index Value
1985	345	83.7
1986	356	86.4
1987	412	100.0
1988	436	105.8
1989	489	118.7

In the illustration above, 1987 is "the base period," discussed further below. It is assigned an arbitrary index value. In this case the value is 100, but it can be any number. Indexes of 10 or 50 are also commonly used, but 100 is the usual index base. The index for any year is calculated by the following formula:

(Current Year Raw Data / Base Year Raw Data) x 100.

Changes from one period to another may be calculated in index points or as a percent change. In the example above, the index point change between 1988 and 1989 is 12.9. The percentage change is 12.2, obtained by the formula:

((Current Index / Previous Index) - 1) x 100.

Measuring the percentage change between two index values produces the same result as measuring the percentage change in the raw data for the same periods.

Base Periods. Statistical series expressed as indexes or in constant dollars (see below) have base periods. A base period can be a day, a month, a year, or a range of years. The Consumer

Price Index, for instance, is based on the 1982-1984 period; the average prices for these years are defined as 100.

The government periodically changes the base periods of indexes. The year chosen is typically the year of one of the quadrennial business censuses. The most recent such census was held in 1992. Many series are still expressed with a base of 1982 or 1987. Rebasing of a series (shifting to a more recent base period) is usually associated with a significant reworking of the statistical machinery which produces the numbers; hence there tends to be a lag time between the most recent business census and the base period in use. For example, the Gross Domestic Product was rebased (to chained dollars) in 1995, three years following the 1992 economic censuses.

Constant and Current Dollars. The measurement of dollar-denominated values from one period to the next can produce inaccurate results, for some purposes, if changes due *only* to increasing or dropping prices are not taken into account. For this reason, many series are reported both in current dollars (also called "actual" dollars) and in constant dollars (also called "real" dollars). Constant dollars are current dollars that have been adjusted for the effects of inflation relative to a base period. Because a base period is used, people sometimes use phrases like "1982 dollars" or "1987 dollars." They mean constant dollars with a 1982 or a 1987 base year. The purchasing power of the dollar in the base year is arbitrarily defined as "real." And today's dollars are adjusted to that value by using series such as the Consumer Price Index and the Producer's Price Index. These indexes record changes in prices by surveying the actual prices charged for identical products and services two periods apart. If the same loaf of bread costs 89 cents in 1991 and 92 cents in 1992, inflation accounts for 3 cents: it took 3 cents more to get the same loaf in the second period. Constant dollar calculations, of course, use a wide range of representative products and services measured in a systematic manner across the nation.

Chained Dollars. A new measurement of national accounts (new in U.S. usage, at any rate), involves the calculation of chain-type indexes. An explanation of what these are and how they work is presented in this chapter under the heading of NIPA Changes, 1995. In essence, chained dollar indexes work by averaging price changes in the prices of two adjacent periods and using the resulting change from one period to the next as the current dollar deflator. Chain-type indexes are definitely "in." They are used by the majority of other countries for national accounting. They have now been adopted by the Bureau of Economic Analysis for the same purpose. They are expected soon to be used by the Bureau of Labor Statistics as well in calculating the CPI and the PPI price indexes.

Annualized Rates. National production and income data—as well as some other series— report some figures quarterly at "annualized rates." This means that data developed for the quarter are multiplied by four to show what the year would be like if results in this quarter continued. The data, typically, are seasonally adjusted (see below) before they are expressed at annualized rates.

Seasonal Adjustments. Economic activity is by nature seasonal. More heating oil will be used in the winter, more people seek employment in the summer as college students come home. Retailers sell proportionally more goods in December than in other months. Many series are seasonally adjusted to take such fluctuations into account. Other series are shown as "not seasonally adjusted." Seasonal adjustments are made by statisticians in and out of government by using experience factors developed over time. Data are recalculated using these experience factors so that heavy fuel oil sales in the fall and winter are "distributed" evenly across the entire year.

NIPA CHANGES, 1995

This edition of *EIH* reflects the 1995 comprehensive (benchmark) changes in the National Income and Product Accounts (NIPA), the source of the GDP and GNP reporting by the U.S. Department of Commerce. One major change concerns the manner in which account measurements are translated from "current" into constant or "real" dollars. That change is discussed under the general heading of Indexing Changes. As in every major revision cycle, the government has again introduced a number of changes in the way it accounts for national income. These will be summarized in this section under the heading of Component Changes.

Indexing Changes

A significant change in the measurement of "real" GDP (and its components) was implemented as part of the comprehensive NIPA revisions of 1995. This change, in preparation for some years now, replaces measurement of GDP in fixed-year constant dollars with a measurement using chained-type indexes. A before and after presentation of the two approaches follows:

Fixed-Year Indexes

Calculating Fixed-Year Constant Dollars. Why does the government report GDP in both current (actual) dollars and in constant dollars? The answer is that Americans want to know whether or not GDP has grown or declined; we want to know the "real" change in the "quantity" of the GDP in order to know how the economy is doing. The current dollar measurement of GDP does not tell us what the *real* change is since the last quarter or year. The GDP may have grown in dollars, but how much of that growth is the result of price changes only (potatoes up by 13 cents a pound)? How much is due to increased output of goods and services (10 percent more potatoes were produced)? To see the "real" changes in the economy, we need to remove that portion of the change due only to changes in prices.

A simple way of doing this is to select one year as the base year for measurement and then to apply the prices that prevailed in the base year to the quantities produced in the current year:

Base year price per unit	95.00	1
Current year price per unit	135.00	2
Units produced in current year	15	3
Current dollar results (135 x 15)	2,025	4
Constant dollar results (95 x 15)	1,425	5

In the example above, current dollars of $2,025 are deflated to $1,425 in constant dollars by using base year prices and applying them to current year quantities.

For large aggregates like the GDP or its components, quantity measures (line 3 above) cannot be obtained conveniently. Instead, as the smallest subcomponents of GDP are added to GDP, price indexes are used to deflate current to constant dollars at the point where the characteristics of the component are still clearly visible, e.g., indexes are applied to Food Consumption Expenditures before the totals are added to Personal Consumption Expenditures.

Price indexes measure change in prices *only*, from one period to the next. Examples are the Consumer Price Index and the Producer Price Index, each of which is built up of many detailed categories. In the example above, the price index for the current year for our unnamed commodity is the current price per unit divided by the base year price per unit:

| Price index in current year (135 / 95) | 1.421 | 6 |
| Constant dollar result (2,025 / 1.421) | 1,425 | 7 |

The constant dollar result can be calculated by dividing current dollars by the index. Notice that line 5 and line 7 produce identical "deflated" values—one by using a price-quantity multiplication, the other by dividing current dollars by a price index.

The actual construction of GDP deflators must, of course, correctly blend many price indexes into a single number. This is done by applying weights to individual indexes. What percentage of total consumption is food? If that percentage is 5.5, the food index contributes only 5.5 percent to the deflator. Weights needed to create accurate deflators are obtained by surveys.

Pros and Cons of the Fixed-Year Measure. The fixed-year constant dollar measure is simple to calculate and is well understood by the public.

The chief disadvantage of the measure is that it distorts results the farther we move from the base year. Another way to put this is that moving the base period forward causes a lower growth rate when the new constant dollar GDP is calculated: "We thought we were growing at 3.5 percent a year; now they tell us it was only 3.3 percent."

This well-known effect, known as the "substitution bias," is due to the natural tendency of the price structure to change. On the whole, products and services that grow most are those with prices that grow least. The inverse is also true. Using the higher "old" prices and applying them to the larger "new" quantities artificially overstates real growth. When the base year is moved forward, the old high prices are replaced by the new low prices; these are applied to the lower old quantities. Now growth between the periods is artificially understated. The following example makes the point arithmetically:

	YEAR 1					YEAR 2				
	Total in Year 1 Dollars - D x E	Total in Year 2 Dollars - D x J	Total in Current Dollars - D x E	Quantity	Price	Total in Year 1 Dollars - I x E	Total in Year 2 Dollars - I x J	Total in Current Dollars - I x J	Quantity	Price
Apples	3.00	6.00	3.00	30	.10	2.00	4.00	4.00	20	.20
Oranges	2.00	2.50	2.00	10	.20	4.00	5.00	5.00	20	.25
Fruit	5.00	8.50	5.00			6.00	9.00	9.00		
Growth						1.20	1.06	1.80		
	A	B	C	D	E	F	G	H	I	J

In the above table, change between Years 1 and 2 in Year 1 dollars is 1.20 and in Year 2 dollars 1.06. These results are due to the shift in the price structure of this mini-economy.

Using either Year 1 or Year 2 dollars is legitimate, despite the obvious distortions. Neither index is more correct than the other. The only "real" measure is in current dollars—because, in reality, price-quantity relationships (including inflationary effects) are inseparable. Constant dollar measures are analytical attempts at isolating quantitative change and are always correct if calculated correctly.

But what if we took the two results above and averaged them? Would that get us closer to a more accurate, less biased measure? The answer is Yes. And that introduces the topic of chained indexes.

Chain-Type Indexes

Chain-type indexes are created by obtaining the geometrical mean of two growth calculations. The first growth value is obtained using Period 1 dollars for both Period 1 and Period 2. The second is obtained using Period 2 dollars in both periods. These are the rates shown in Columns F and G above. The periods must be adjacent (adjacent years, quarters, months). Using the example above, the calculation is:

chained growth value = square root of (1.20 x 1.06)
chained growth value = 1.13

In the example above, growth between Year 1 and Year 2 in chained dollars would be 13 percent (rather than 20 or 6 percent using one valuation period only). Year 2 results in chained dollars would be $5.56 (Year 1 result of $5 times the 1.13 calculated rate).

In more technical terminology, the annual change in real GDP is calculated using the Fisher Ideal Index formula, defined as the geometric mean of a Laspeyres and a Paasche index. Year 2 values in Year 1 prices (Column F) are the Laspeyres index; Year 2 values in Year 2 prices (Column G) are the Paasche index.

How a Chained Index is Created. To create a hypothetical chain-type index, growth rates for each period are calculated using the Fisher Ideal Index formula, as shown above. For a series of GDP (or component) measurements, this will produce individual growth rates of "real" GDP based on the price weights of the year and the year before, as shown below. Note, please, that the growth rates shown are not those between the current dollar values shown but between constant dollar expressions of these values. The actual step of moving from line 2 values to line 3 values is not illustrated.

	1989	1990	1991	1992	1993	1994	1
Assumed Current $ Values	555	580	719	741	778	708	2
Fisher Ideal growth rates (%)	-	13.0	21.1	5.0	4.0	-7.3	3

The percentages in line 3 are next expressed as multipliers by dividing the cells of line 3 by 100 and adding one (the result is shown in line 4 below). Next, the multipliers are "chained," i.e., multiplied together—hence the name of this type of index. Column A is multiplied by Column B, and the result is placed back in Column B. Column B is then multiplied by Column C and the result placed back in Column C. And so on. Results are shown in line 5 below:

	A	B	C	D	E	F	
Expressed as multipliers	1.000	1.130	1.210	1.050	1.040	.927	4
Chained into Index	1.000	1.130	1.367	1.436	1.493	1.384	5

The chained values of line 5 can now be converted into an index of any desired base year. The method is to divide each cell's value by the base year value and to multiply the result by 100. In what follows, two indexes are created with base 1989 (line 6) and 1992 (line 7). Then the dollar values from line 2, above, will be translated into chained dollars of the base year (lines 8 and 9).

	A	B	C	D	E	F	
Index with 1989 Base	**100.0**	113.0	136.7	143.6	149.3	138.4	6
Index with 1992 Base	69.7	78.7	95.2	**100.0**	104.0	96.4	7
Chained (1989) Dollars	**555**	627	759	797	829	829	8
Chained (1992) Dollars	516	583	705	**741**	770	714	9

The chained dollar conversions are done by dividing the index with the appropriate base by 100 and multiplying the base year value (line 1 above) by the result.

Notice that the dollar magnitudes are different when expressed in different base year dollars. The growth relationships between the dollars, however, remain the same. The base year can be moved at will without affecting the growth relationships. Thus the growth from 1989 to 1990 in either chained (1989) dollars or chained (1992) dollars is 13 percent. Note, also, that as in the "old days," when fixed year constant dollars were used, so in chained dollar series, the base year's "current" dollars and "chained" dollars are identical.

In preparing this exposition, the author drew heavily on the wisdom presented in two papers in the *Survey of Current Business*. The first of these, by Allan H. Young, is titled "Alternative Measures of Change in Real Output and Prices," Volume 72, Number 4, April 1992, pp. 32-48. The second is by J. Steven Landefeld and Robert P. Parker, titled "Preview of the Comprehensive Revision of the National Income and Product Accounts: BEA's New Featured Measures of Output and Prices," Volume 75, Number 7, July 1995, pp. 31-38. Particularly useful was a note, appended to this article, written by Jack E. Triplett, titled "Note on Calculating Output and Price Indexes." Whatever merits this presentation has are due largely to these experts. Whatever it lacks is due to the author's failure of grasp.

Component Changes

Comprehensive benchmark revisions of the National Income and Product Accounts take place at intervals of 5 years, roughly 3 years after the last complete economic census of the U.S. (last in 1992). In the past, benchmark revisions typically resulted in the movement of the "constant dollar" base year to the year of the most recent economic census. This time, "constant dollar" indexing has been retired in favor of the chain-type indexing of GDP and its components (see last subhead). Other important changes will be summarized below.

Changed Treatment of Government Investments. Until this revision, expenditures by government on structures and equipment (highways, schools, office buildings, motor vehicles, computers) were classified, along with other purchases, as Government Purchases, with their value assumed to be consumed in the year the expenditures were made. Analogous expenditures by the private sector were treated differently and classified as either "gross private domestic investment" or "net foreign investment." Beginning with the 1995 revisions, a new category of investment, "gross government investment," will be added. The depreciation associated with this investment will be shown as part of "government consumption expenditures," the new category that replaces "government purchases."

Changed Treatment of Depreciation. Successive NIPA revisions have attempted to approximate better the real character of depreciation. In the most recent revision, the government is abandoning a methodology based on straight-line depreciation and adopting a methodology which assumes that depreciation takes place at a constant percentage rate of the residual value of the depreciated object rather than a constant dollar amount. This change is based on a number of empirical studies conducted by the government. Detailed articles on this subject were promised by the BEA for 1996 in the *Survey of Current Business*.

Other Changes. New estimating procedures and new and revised data have been introduced. These changes include such items as the use of a new Input-Output table (1987), incorporation of the results of the 1991 Residential Finance Survey, incorporation of revised estimates of employer contributions to private health insurance, and other estimating and methodological changes.

To review in more detail all changes to the NIPA, it is suggested that the user consult the September 1995, November/December 1995, and the January/February 1996 issues of *Survey of Current Business*.

ACKNOWLEDGMENTS

Economic Indicators Handbook is based on the hard work and intellectual rigor of many individuals in government, academia, associations, and industry. Some of them took of their valuable time to help in the preparation of this book by providing data and patient explanations of sometimes very difficult concepts. In particular, the editor is indebted to the staff of the Bureau of Economic Analysis, U.S. Department of Commerce and staff of the Bureau of Labor Statistics, U.S. Department of Labor. The continuing cooperation of the Media Relations staff of the American Stock Exchange, the research staff of the New York Stock Exchange, and of the computer support folks at National Association of Securities Dealers Automated Quotation System (NASDAQ) is much appreciated.

COMMENTS AND SUGGESTIONS

Comments on *EIH* or suggestion for its improvement are always welcome. Although every effort is made to maintain accuracy, errors may occasionally occur; the editor will be grateful if these are called to his attention. Please contact:

> Editor
> *Economic Indicators Handbook*
> Gale Research
> 835 Penobscot Building
> Detroit, MI 48226-4094
> Phone: (313) 961-2242 or (800) 347-GALE
> Fax: (313) 961-6741

CHAPTER 1

GROSS NATIONAL PRODUCT

GROSS NATIONAL PRODUCT

The Gross National Product (GNP) is the sum of all purchases of goods and services by individuals and government; the value of gross domestic investment, including changes in business inventories; and exports less imports (net exports). GNP is thus a measure of the productivity of the nation. GNP can be summarized by the following formula:

$$GNP = Consumption + Investment + Government + Exports - Imports.$$

Only final purchases are measured to avoid double counting. The value of unfinished goods purchased by companies and not resold as finished product is reflected in changed business inventories.

GNP measures goods and services *produced by labor and property supplied by U.S. residents*. The labor and property may be located *in* the U.S. or abroad. Conversely, goods and services produced by foreign labor and property are excluded, even if located on U.S. soil. The next chapter covers Gross Domestic Product (GDP) which measures goods and services *produced by labor and property located in the U.S.* GDP has been selected by the U.S. Department of Commerce as the new measure of U.S. production, displacing GNP. However, since GNP accounting has been the dominant method until recently (November 1991), GNP tables are provided here for retrospective reference.

Modern GNP reporting began in 1929 and is the product of a comprehensive statistical system (the National Income and Product Accounts, NIPA) managed by the Department of Commerce, Bureau of Economic Analysis (BEA). GNP estimates were extended back to 1909 based on limited statistical sources by the government; and estimates based on even less information have been made back to colonial times. Data in *EIH* are reported from 1929 forward when possible or from whatever year the Bureau of Economic Analysis, Department of Commerce, makes available. In this edition, for instance, data in the revised formats (1995 revisions) are presented back to 1959 only. *EIH* presents those data and also the earlier GNP series back to 1929 (1991 revisions).

GNP data are *estimates* based on a large number of surveys conducted by the federal government for other purposes or obtained from private industry or association sources. Precise measurement of economic activity on a scale such as that of the United States is virtually impossible; hence partial data, estimates, and statistical methods are necessary to approximate actual economic activity. During the years of the economic censuses, which recur at 5-year intervals, detailed data are collected for many GNP components which serve as "benchmarks" for estimates.

Presentation of Data

The first table is a summary of GNP for the period 1869-1928. Data were obtained, courtesy of the Bureau of Economic Analysis, for aggregate GNP for this period, in actual and in constant (1982) dollars.

Two tables for the GNP, one in actual and one in 1987 constant dollars, are presented for the 1929 through 1993 period. Detailed component tables are no longer included. The government has now completely shifted emphasis to Gross Domestic Product (GDP) and all data have been restated using GDP definitions. These tables show data in the 1991 revision format. Two additional tables, showing GNP data in the 1995 revision format, but only back to 1959, are presented next.

Historical Data. The historical data are presented in decade averages for the 1869-1878 and the 1879-1888 periods and then annually thereafter to 1928. Data are shown in actual and in constant dollars, permitting the calculation of growth and decline rates year to year and the implicit price deflator. The implicit price deflator shows the relationship of prices, in a given year, as they compare to those of a base year—in this case 1982. The deflator is calculated by the formula:

(Actual Dollar Value / Constant Dollar Value) x 100.

With the implicit price deflator known, constant dollar value can be calculated, if unknown, by the formula:

(Current Dollar Value x 100) / Implicit Price Deflator.

And current value, if unknown, can be calculated from constant dollar value by the formula:

(Constant Dollar Value / 100) x Implicit Price Deflator.

Quarterly Data. Data for quarters, when available, represent seasonally adjusted, annualized quarterly estimates. This means that the results for the quarter are projected for the entire year; for example, if 2 million cars were sold in the quarter, the annual rate would be 8 million cars; therefore, the production value of 8 million cars is reflected in that quarter's estimate. Seasonal adjustments are made to reflect conditions that are due to well known, recurring, seasonal phenomena. For example, fuel oil consumption is known to be much higher in winter than in summer; fuel consumption, therefore, is increased in summer quarters and decreased in winter quarters to "smooth" the data. Each quarter, in other words, shows what GNP would be for the entire year if the conditions in that quarter, as adjusted, were to continue for the balance of the year.

Growth or decline between any two quarters is also annualized, showing a compounded growth rate reached by the formula:

(This Quarter / Last Quarter)^4 *- 1 x 100* = percent growth rate of GNP.

If this quarter is \$4,118.9 billion and last quarter was \$4,124.1 billion, the formula results in - 0.503 percent because the quarterly growth rate was compounded and annualized—rather than a rate of - 0.12 percent, which is the simple percentile difference between the two numbers.

Annual Data. Annual figures show final estimates for GNP. Since GNP estimates are revised as better and better data become available, data for recent years are subject to revision and results for the most recent year tend to be preliminary estimates. Annual growth or decline figures show simple percentile changes between the two years reached by the formula:

(This Year / Last Year) - 1 x 100.

If this year is \$4,157.3 billion and last year was \$4,117.7 billion, the growth is 0.96 percent.

GNP in Constant Dollars. Constant dollars (also referred to as "real" dollars) are used to measure GNP in order to account for inflationary or deflationary price changes; inflation is believed to come about because prices are raised in response to unusually high demand; deflation (a much rarer phenomenon) results when prices drop because demand is soft; in both cases, products or services sold remain unchanged; only prices change; constant dollar expression of GNP permits direct comparison of one period with another. In the 20-year period 1970 to 1989, for instance, GNP showed positive growth in every year in actual dollars; measured in constant dollars, the years 1970, 1974-75, 1980, 1982, and 1991 showed negative growth.

GNP in Chained (1992) Dollars. Beginning in 1995, the BEA has adopted a new indexing method to express "real" dollar values—values that remove the effect of inflation. Tables using this method of "normalization" are shown to be in "chained (1992) dollars." A full explanation of this method is presented in the Introduction under the subheading, *NIPA Changes, 1995*. In essence, the "chained dollar" measure is a more sensitive indicator of changes in the quantities of dollars reported. For purposes of analysis, they are essentially equivalent to the "constant dollar" indexing methods of the recent past. Thus values expressed in chained (1992) dollars normalize today's ("current") dollars in terms of 1992 purchasing power—but with greater accuracy.

GNP Revisions

Changes in GNP methodologies and allocation of items to national accounts are continuous. These changes typically involve (1) changes in the classification of certain items from one GNP account to another; for example, in 1985, railroad track replacement costs were shifted from business expenditures to investment; (2) the inclusion or exclusion of areas (e.g., Puerto Rico and U.S. territories were excluded from GNP in 1985); and (3) changes in methodology, especially for estimating categories not fully covered by surveys; for example, in 1985, improved adjustments were made for misreporting on tax returns, the so-called "underground economy adjustments." Major changes in recent decades were introduced in 1976, 1980, 1985, 1991, and 1995.

For a full discussion of the 1995 revisions, please consult the November/December 1995 issue of *Survey of Current Business* (reference 4 below). The following are the major changes: (1) changes relating to the government's investment and contributions to retirement programs; (2) statistical changes, including (a) improved estimates of changes in output and prices; (b) new estimating procedures (especially for depreciation); (c) new and revised data from regular sources that become available less often than annually; (d) new and revised data from regular sources; and (e) updated seasonal factors for quarterly estimates.

These changes produce *increases* in current-dollar GNP—so that data for earlier years, in revised format, are higher. In other words, the comprehensive revisions of the national income accounts can, in effect, *revise financial history*.

For a bibliography of major and annual changes, see p. 23-30, reference 3, below, and Fall issues of the *Survey of Current Business* (reference 4).

Bibliography

1. Carnes, W. Stansbury and Stephen D. Slifer, *The Atlas of Economic Indicators*. Harper Collins, 1991.

2. U.S. Department of Commerce, Bureau of Economic Analysis. *GNP: An Overview of Source Data and Estimating Methods*. Methodology Paper Series MP-4. Washington, DC: U.S. Government Printing Office, September 1987.

3. U.S. Department of Commerce, Bureau of Economic Analysis. *An Introduction to National Economic Accounting*. Methodology Paper Series MP-1. Washington, DC: U.S. Government Printing Office, March 1985.

4. U.S. Department of Commerce, Bureau of Economic Analysis. *Survey of Current Business*. Superintendent of Documents, U.S. Government Printing Office, Washington, DC 20302.

Historical Gross National Product
1869-1928

Historial GNP estimates, 1869-1928, shown in billions of actual and constant 1982 dollars. 1869-78 and 1879-88 values are decade averages.

Year	Current Dollars (Billions)	Change from Previous Year - %	Constant 82 Dol. (Billions)	Change from Previous Year - %	Implicit Price Deflator 82=100	Year	Current Dollars (Billions)	Change from Previous Year - %	Constant 82 Dol. (Billions)	Change from Previous Year - %	Implicit Price Deflator 82=100
1869-78	7.7	-	84.6	-	9.102	1908	29.0	-8.8	366.4	-8.3	7.915
1879-88	11.7	-	154.5	-	7.573	1909	33.7	16.2	411.3	12.3	8.194
1889	13.1	-	179.5	-	7.298	1910	35.7	5.9	423.3	2.9	8.434
1890	13.7	4.6	192.8	7.4	7.106	1911	36.1	1.1	436.3	3.1	8.274
1891	14.1	2.9	201.6	4.6	6.994	1912	39.7	10.0	457.2	4.8	8.683
1892	15.0	6.4	220.7	9.5	6.797	1913	39.9	0.5	462.4	1.1	8.629
1893	14.4	-4.0	210.4	-4.7	6.844	1914	38.9	-2.5	444.4	-3.9	8.753
1894	13.2	-8.3	204.5	-2.8	6.455	1915	40.3	3.6	439.6	-1.1	9.167
1895	14.5	9.8	228.8	11.9	6.337	1916	48.6	20.6	472.8	7.6	10.279
1896	13.9	-4.1	223.7	-2.2	6.214	1917	60.7	24.9	481.7	1.9	12.601
1897	15.3	10.1	245.0	9.5	6.245	1918	76.8	26.5	570.0	18.3	13.474
1898	16.1	5.2	250.9	2.4	6.417	1919	84.7	10.3	528.3	-7.3	16.033
1899	18.2	13.0	273.7	9.1	6.650	1920	92.2	8.9	487.1	-7.8	18.928
1900	19.6	7.7	281.1	2.7	6.973	1921	70.2	-23.9	452.8	-7.0	15.504
1901	21.7	10.7	313.4	11.5	6.924	1922	74.8	6.6	519.6	14.8	14.396
1902	22.6	4.1	316.4	1.0	7.143	1923	85.9	14.8	576.9	11.0	14.890
1903	24.0	6.2	331.8	4.9	7.233	1924	85.5	-0.5	582.7	1.0	14.673
1904	24.0	0.0	328.2	-1.1	7.313	1925	94.0	9.9	625.0	7.3	15.040
1905	26.3	9.6	352.4	7.4	7.463	1926	97.9	4.1	662.3	6.0	14.782
1906	30.0	14.1	392.9	11.5	7.636	1927	95.8	-2.1	661.2	-0.2	14.489
1907	31.8	6.0	399.5	1.7	7.960	1928	97.7	2.0	667.7	1.0	14.632

Sources: National Bureau of Economic Research and U.S. Department of Commerce. Obtained as handwritten communication from Bureau of Economic Analysis.

Gross National Product - Actual Dollars

In billions of actual dollars and percent. Quarterly data are seasonally adjusted and annualized. Growth rates for quarters are compound annual growth rates; changes from year to year are percentage changes.

Year	1st Quarter	% Change	2nd Quarter	% Change	3rd Quarter	% Change	4th Quarter	% Change	TOTAL	% Change
1929	-	-	-	-	-	-	-	-	103.9	-
1930	-	-	-	-	-	-	-	-	91.1	-12.3
1931	-	-	-	-	-	-	-	-	76.3	-16.2
1932	-	-	-	-	-	-	-	-	58.3	-23.6
1933	-	-	-	-	-	-	-	-	55.9	-4.1
1934	-	-	-	-	-	-	-	-	65.4	17.0
1935	-	-	-	-	-	-	-	-	72.7	11.2
1936	-	-	-	-	-	-	-	-	83.0	14.2
1937	-	-	-	-	-	-	-	-	91.2	9.9
1938	-	-	-	-	-	-	-	-	85.3	-6.5
1939	-	-	-	-	-	-	-	-	91.3	7.0
1940	-	-	-	-	-	-	-	-	100.4	10.0
1941	-	-	-	-	-	-	-	-	125.5	25.0
1942	-	-	-	-	-	-	-	-	159.0	26.7
1943	-	-	-	-	-	-	-	-	192.8	21.3
1944	-	-	-	-	-	-	-	-	211.5	9.7
1945	-	-	-	-	-	-	-	-	213.5	0.9
1946	200.3	-	208.4	17.2	218.6	21.1	223.0	8.3	212.6	-0.4
1947	227.8	8.9	231.7	7.0	236.1	7.8	246.3	18.4	235.5	10.8
1948	252.6	10.6	259.9	12.1	266.8	11.0	268.1	2.0	261.8	11.2
1949	263.0	-7.4	259.5	-5.2	261.2	2.6	258.9	-3.5	260.7	-0.4
1950	269.6	17.6	279.3	15.2	296.9	27.7	308.4	16.4	288.5	10.7
1951	323.2	20.6	331.1	10.1	337.9	8.5	342.3	5.3	333.6	15.6
1952	345.3	3.6	345.9	0.7	351.7	6.9	364.2	15.0	351.8	5.5
1953	371.0	7.7	374.5	3.8	373.7	-0.9	368.7	-5.2	372.0	5.7
1954	368.4	-0.3	368.7	0.3	373.4	5.2	381.9	9.4	373.1	0.3
1955	394.8	14.2	403.1	8.7	411.4	8.5	417.8	6.4	406.8	9.0
1956	420.5	2.6	426.0	5.3	430.8	4.6	439.2	8.0	429.1	5.5
1957	448.1	8.4	450.1	1.8	457.2	6.5	451.7	-4.7	451.8	5.3
1958	444.4	-6.3	448.6	3.8	461.8	12.3	475.0	11.9	457.5	1.3
1959	486.2	9.8	498.9	10.9	499.3	0.3	503.6	3.5	497.0	8.6
1960	517.0	11.1	516.0	-0.8	519.0	2.3	514.2	-3.6	516.6	3.9
1961	518.8	3.6	529.4	8.4	540.2	8.4	553.2	10.0	535.4	3.6
1962	565.7	9.3	573.5	5.6	580.3	4.8	583.7	2.4	575.8	7.5
1963	592.7	6.3	601.1	5.8	613.9	8.8	623.0	6.1	607.7	5.5
1964	639.9	11.3	648.5	5.5	659.2	6.8	664.5	3.3	653.0	7.5
1965	685.3	13.1	697.7	7.4	713.7	9.5	735.6	12.9	708.1	8.4
1966	758.2	12.9	767.3	4.9	780.3	7.0	793.9	7.2	774.9	9.4
1967	803.0	4.7	809.0	3.0	826.2	8.8	841.0	7.4	819.8	5.8
1968	865.5	12.2	889.8	11.7	906.6	7.8	920.0	6.0	895.5	9.2
1969	943.7	10.7	957.3	5.9	976.7	8.4	984.8	3.4	965.6	7.8
1970	996.0	4.6	1,010.4	5.9	1,029.4	7.7	1,032.5	1.2	1,017.1	5.3
1971	1,077.3	18.5	1,096.2	7.2	1,115.7	7.3	1,130.2	5.3	1,104.9	8.6
1972	1,169.2	14.5	1,200.8	11.3	1,226.8	8.9	1,265.9	13.4	1,215.7	10.0
1973	1,315.1	16.5	1,346.2	9.8	1,372.3	8.0	1,415.6	13.2	1,362.3	12.1
1974	1,428.1	3.6	1,460.7	9.4	1,490.2	8.3	1,518.3	7.8	1,474.3	8.2
1975	1,525.2	1.8	1,564.0	10.6	1,627.6	17.3	1,679.5	13.4	1,599.1	8.5
1976	1,733.7	13.5	1,763.3	7.0	1,797.2	7.9	1,847.7	11.7	1,785.5	11.7
1977	1,902.7	12.4	1,973.8	15.8	2,036.2	13.3	2,065.8	5.9	1,994.6	11.7
1978	2,112.4	9.3	2,232.8	24.8	2,295.9	11.8	2,377.1	14.9	2,254.5	13.0
1979	2,425.2	8.3	2,483.0	9.9	2,559.6	12.9	2,615.3	9.0	2,520.8	11.8
1980	2,687.7	11.5	2,679.4	-1.2	2,739.8	9.3	2,861.5	19.0	2,742.1	8.8
1981	2,985.5	18.5	3,023.5	5.2	3,112.4	12.3	3,133.7	2.8	3,063.8	11.7
1982	3,123.7	-1.3	3,179.2	7.3	3,193.8	1.8	3,222.6	3.7	3,179.8	3.8
1983	3,283.8	7.8	3,394.0	14.1	3,481.6	10.7	3,578.4	11.6	3,434.4	8.0
1984	3,694.2	13.6	3,778.3	9.4	3,843.3	7.1	3,890.2	5.0	3,801.5	10.7
1985	3,955.7	6.9	4,012.9	5.9	4,089.5	7.9	4,156.2	6.7	4,053.6	6.6
1986	4,231.4	7.4	4,239.1	0.7	4,300.0	5.9	4,340.5	3.8	4,277.7	5.5
1987	4,412.4	6.8	4,497.5	7.9	4,577.7	7.3	4,690.5	10.2	4,544.5	6.2
1988	4,764.3	6.4	4,862.7	8.5	4,951.6	7.5	5,054.3	8.6	4,908.2	8.0
1989	5,164.0	9.0	5,243.3	6.3	5,294.7	4.0	5,365.0	5.4	5,266.8	7.3
1990	5,482.1	9.0	5,559.3	5.8	5,599.9	3.0	5,630.0	2.2	5,567.8	5.7
1991	5,656.1	1.9	5,710.6	3.9	5,766.2	4.0	5,815.5	3.5	5,737.1	3.0
1992	5,927.6	7.9	5,996.3	4.7	6,067.3	4.8	6,191.9	8.5	6,045.8	5.4
1993	6,262.1	4.6	6,327.1	4.2	-	-	-	-	-	-

Source: "The National Income and Product Accounts of the United States, 1929-82: Statistical Tables," and subsequent July issues of the *Survey of Current Business*. - indicates that data are unavailable or zero.

Gross National Product - 1987 Dollars

In billions of 1987 dollars and percent. Quarterly data are seasonally adjusted and annualized. Growth rates for quarters are compound annual growth rates; changes from year to year are percentage changes.

Year	1st Quarter	% Change	2nd Quarter	% Change	3rd Quarter	% Change	4th Quarter	% Change	TOTAL	% Change
1929	-	-	-	-	-	-	-	-	827.4	-
1930	-	-	-	-	-	-	-	-	754.2	-8.8
1931	-	-	-	-	-	-	-	-	695.5	-7.8
1932	-	-	-	-	-	-	-	-	603.0	-13.3
1933	-	-	-	-	-	-	-	-	589.9	-2.2
1934	-	-	-	-	-	-	-	-	634.8	7.6
1935	-	-	-	-	-	-	-	-	684.1	7.8
1936	-	-	-	-	-	-	-	-	780.0	14.0
1937	-	-	-	-	-	-	-	-	814.5	4.4
1938	-	-	-	-	-	-	-	-	782.2	-4.0
1939	-	-	-	-	-	-	-	-	844.2	7.9
1940	-	-	-	-	-	-	-	-	908.8	7.7
1941	-	-	-	-	-	-	-	-	1,074.4	18.2
1942	-	-	-	-	-	-	-	-	1,288.4	19.9
1943	-	-	-	-	-	-	-	-	1,543.6	19.8
1944	-	-	-	-	-	-	-	-	1,673.3	8.4
1945	-	-	-	-	-	-	-	-	1,605.0	-4.1
1946	-	-	-	-	-	-	-	-	1,276.0	-20.5
1947	1,244.9	-	1,252.9	2.6	1,260.7	2.5	1,275.6	4.8	1,258.5	-1.4
1948	1,290.9	4.9	1,302.9	3.8	1,310.9	2.5	1,323.5	3.9	1,307.0	3.9
1949	1,312.1	-3.4	1,308.6	-1.1	1,318.9	3.2	1,307.6	-3.4	1,311.8	0.4
1950	1,357.0	16.0	1,400.1	13.3	1,451.7	15.6	1,490.3	11.1	1,425.6	8.7
1951	1,509.2	5.2	1,557.1	13.3	1,594.9	10.1	1,606.2	2.9	1,567.4	9.9
1952	1,617.3	2.8	1,621.8	1.1	1,631.3	2.4	1,666.8	9.0	1,634.3	4.3
1953	1,696.2	7.2	1,704.8	2.0	1,696.2	-2.0	1,679.6	-3.9	1,694.2	3.7
1954	1,669.9	-2.3	1,667.5	-0.6	1,686.9	4.7	1,708.8	5.3	1,683.3	-0.6
1955	1,753.3	10.8	1,769.1	3.7	1,788.8	4.5	1,804.8	3.6	1,779.0	5.7
1956	1,799.2	-1.2	1,810.6	2.6	1,814.6	0.9	1,837.4	5.1	1,815.5	2.1
1957	1,849.3	2.6	1,848.8	-0.1	1,864.6	3.5	1,841.0	-5.0	1,850.9	1.9
1958	1,800.8	-8.5	1,815.4	3.3	1,851.4	8.2	1,891.2	8.9	1,839.7	-0.6
1959	1,915.1	5.2	1,947.7	7.0	1,941.8	-1.2	1,953.6	2.5	1,939.6	5.4
1960	1,988.1	7.3	1,983.3	-1.0	1,985.8	0.5	1,974.0	-2.4	1,982.8	2.2
1961	1,991.1	3.5	2,018.9	5.7	2,048.4	6.0	2,090.1	8.4	2,037.1	2.7
1962	2,117.3	5.3	2,140.6	4.5	2,157.7	3.2	2,157.6	-0.0	2,143.3	5.2
1963	2,187.4	5.6	2,215.3	5.2	2,253.6	7.1	2,271.0	3.1	2,231.8	4.1
1964	2,329.3	10.7	2,347.3	3.1	2,375.4	4.9	2,380.6	0.9	2,358.1	5.7
1965	2,429.1	8.4	2,462.5	5.6	2,503.8	6.9	2,560.3	9.3	2,488.9	5.5
1966	2,613.8	8.6	2,618.5	0.7	2,642.7	3.7	2,657.8	2.3	2,633.2	5.8
1967	2,674.2	2.5	2,685.5	1.7	2,717.9	4.9	2,732.8	2.2	2,702.6	2.6
1968	2,770.3	5.6	2,815.6	6.7	2,836.0	2.9	2,840.6	0.7	2,815.6	4.2
1969	2,883.6	6.2	2,886.0	0.3	2,901.7	2.2	2,892.2	-1.3	2,890.9	2.7
1970	2,885.5	-0.9	2,877.9	-1.0	2,913.0	5.0	2,889.7	-3.2	2,891.5	0.0
1971	2,959.7	10.0	2,965.4	0.8	2,981.2	2.1	2,997.4	2.2	2,975.9	2.9
1972	3,058.4	8.4	3,110.5	7.0	3,148.4	5.0	3,197.8	6.4	3,128.8	5.1
1973	3,279.4	10.6	3,295.6	2.0	3,297.2	0.2	3,322.1	3.1	3,298.6	5.4
1974	3,298.4	-2.8	3,304.3	0.7	3,272.2	-3.8	3,254.6	-2.1	3,282.4	-0.5
1975	3,177.3	-9.2	3,213.9	4.7	3,275.5	7.9	3,323.6	6.0	3,247.6	-1.1
1976	3,386.8	7.8	3,400.5	1.6	3,412.7	1.4	3,448.9	4.3	3,412.2	5.1
1977	3,503.9	6.5	3,561.7	6.8	3,610.8	5.6	3,599.3	-1.3	3,569.0	4.6
1978	3,629.1	3.4	3,737.9	12.5	3,769.8	3.5	3,819.0	5.4	3,739.0	4.8
1979	3,821.2	0.2	3,829.8	0.9	3,862.0	3.4	3,868.3	0.7	3,845.3	2.8
1980	3,884.6	1.7	3,782.3	-10.1	3,780.5	-0.2	3,846.2	7.1	3,823.4	-0.6
1981	3,901.6	5.9	3,882.8	-1.9	3,904.9	2.3	3,848.5	-5.7	3,884.4	1.6
1982	3,793.0	-5.6	3,810.3	1.8	3,789.4	-2.2	3,791.7	0.2	3,796.1	-2.3
1983	3,816.5	2.6	3,916.7	10.9	3,978.8	6.5	4,046.6	7.0	3,939.6	3.8
1984	4,119.1	7.4	4,169.4	5.0	4,193.0	2.3	4,216.4	2.3	4,174.5	6.0
1985	4,238.1	2.1	4,270.5	3.1	4,321.8	4.9	4,349.5	2.6	4,295.0	2.9
1986	4,406.4	5.3	4,394.6	-1.1	4,422.3	2.5	4,430.8	0.8	4,413.5	2.8
1987	4,463.9	3.0	4,517.8	4.9	4,563.6	4.1	4,633.0	6.2	4,544.5	3.0
1988	4,667.1	3.0	4,710.3	3.8	4,738.7	2.4	4,789.0	4.3	4,726.3	4.0
1989	4,830.7	3.5	4,851.6	1.7	4,853.4	0.1	4,875.1	1.8	4,852.7	2.7
1990	4,916.4	3.4	4,933.4	1.4	4,920.9	-1.0	4,895.4	-2.1	4,916.5	1.3
1991	4,859.3	-2.9	4,867.5	0.7	4,880.3	1.1	4,890.9	0.9	4,874.5	-0.9
1992	4,939.0	4.0	4,962.2	1.9	5,006.4	3.6	5,068.4	5.0	4,994.0	2.5
1993	5,080.7	1.0	5,104.1	1.9	-	-	-	-	-	-

Source: "The National Income and Product Accounts of the United States, 1929-82: Statistical Tables," and subsequent July issues of the *Survey of Current Business*. - indicates that data are unavailable or zero.

Gross National Product - 1995 Revisions - Actual Dollars

In billions of actual dollars and percent. Quarterly data are seasonally adjusted and annualized. Growth rates for quarters are compound annual growth rates; changes from year to year are percentage changes.

Year	1st Quarter	% Change	2nd Quarter	% Change	3rd Quarter	% Change	4th Quarter	% Change	TOTAL	% Change
1959	499.0	-	512.0	10.8	512.5	0.4	516.9	3.5	510.1	-
1960	530.3	10.8	529.2	-0.8	532.2	2.3	527.3	-3.6	529.8	3.9
1961	531.8	3.5	542.4	8.2	553.2	8.2	566.3	9.8	548.4	3.5
1962	579.0	9.3	586.9	5.6	594.1	5.0	597.7	2.4	589.4	7.5
1963	606.8	6.2	615.3	5.7	628.2	8.7	637.5	6.1	621.9	5.5
1964	654.5	11.1	663.4	5.6	674.3	6.7	679.9	3.4	668.0	7.4
1965	701.2	13.1	713.9	7.4	730.4	9.6	752.6	12.7	724.5	8.5
1966	775.6	12.8	785.2	5.0	798.6	7.0	812.5	7.1	793.0	9.5
1967	822.2	4.9	828.2	3.0	844.7	8.2	861.2	8.0	839.1	5.8
1968	886.5	12.3	910.8	11.4	926.0	6.8	943.6	7.8	916.7	9.2
1969	966.3	10.0	979.9	5.7	999.3	8.2	1,008.0	3.5	988.4	7.8
1970	1,020.3	5.0	1,035.7	6.2	1,053.8	7.2	1,058.4	1.8	1,042.0	5.4
1971	1,104.2	18.5	1,124.9	7.7	1,144.4	7.1	1,158.8	5.1	1,133.1	8.7
1972	1,198.5	14.4	1,231.8	11.6	1,256.7	8.3	1,297.0	13.5	1,246.0	10.0
1973	1,347.9	16.6	1,379.4	9.7	1,404.4	7.4	1,449.7	13.5	1,395.4	12.0
1974	1,463.9	4.0	1,496.8	9.3	1,526.4	8.1	1,563.2	10.0	1,512.6	8.4
1975	1,571.3	2.1	1,608.3	9.8	1,670.6	16.4	1,725.3	13.8	1,643.9	8.7
1976	1,783.5	14.2	1,814.0	7.0	1,847.9	7.7	1,899.0	11.5	1,836.1	11.7
1977	1,954.5	12.2	2,026.4	15.5	2,088.7	12.9	2,120.4	6.2	2,047.5	11.5
1978	2,166.8	9.0	2,293.7	25.6	2,356.2	11.4	2,437.0	14.4	2,313.5	13.0
1979	2,491.4	9.2	2,552.9	10.2	2,629.7	12.6	2,687.5	9.1	2,590.4	12.0
1980	2,761.7	11.5	2,756.1	-0.8	2,818.8	9.4	2,941.5	18.6	2,819.5	8.8
1981	3,076.6	19.7	3,105.4	3.8	3,197.7	12.4	3,222.8	3.2	3,150.6	11.7
1982	3,211.0	-1.5	3,270.3	7.6	3,287.8	2.2	3,323.8	4.5	3,273.2	3.9
1983	3,388.2	8.0	3,501.0	14.0	3,596.8	11.4	3,700.3	12.0	3,546.5	8.3
1984	3,824.4	14.1	3,911.3	9.4	3,975.6	6.7	4,022.7	4.8	3,933.5	10.9
1985	4,100.4	8.0	4,158.7	5.8	4,238.8	7.9	4,306.2	6.5	4,201.0	6.8
1986	4,376.6	6.7	4,399.4	2.1	4,455.8	5.2	4,508.5	4.8	4,435.1	5.6
1987	4,573.1	5.9	4,655.5	7.4	4,731.4	6.7	4,845.2	10.0	4,701.3	6.0
1988	4,914.5	5.8	5,013.7	8.3	5,105.3	7.5	5,217.1	9.1	5,062.6	7.7
1989	5,329.2	8.9	5,423.9	7.3	5,501.3	5.8	5,557.0	4.1	5,452.8	7.7
1990	5,681.4	9.3	5,767.8	6.2	5,796.8	2.0	5,813.6	1.2	5,764.9	5.7
1991	5,849.0	2.5	5,904.5	3.8	5,959.4	3.8	6,016.6	3.9	5,932.4	2.9
1992	6,138.3	8.3	6,212.2	4.9	6,281.1	4.5	6,390.5	7.2	6,255.5	5.4
1993	6,458.4	4.3	6,512.3	3.4	6,584.8	4.5	6,684.5	6.2	6,560.0	4.9
1994	6,773.6	5.4	6,876.3	6.2	6,977.6	6.0	7,062.2	4.9	6,922.4	5.5
1995	7,140.5	4.5	7,187.0	2.6	7,281.3	5.4	-	-	-	-

Source: The National Income and Product Accounts of the United States, 1959-95. Published on diskettes, January 1996, Bureau of Economic Analysis, U.S. Department of Commerce, Washington, D.C. - indicates that data are unavailable or zero.

Gross National Product - 1995 Revisions - Chained (1992) Dollars

In billions of chained (1992) dollars and percent. Quarterly data are seasonally adjusted and annualized. Growth rates for quarters are compound annual growth rates; changes from year to year are percentage changes.

Year	1st Quarter	% Change	2nd Quarter	% Change	3rd Quarter	% Change	4th Quarter	% Change	TOTAL	% Change
1959	-	-	-	-	2,237.7	-	2,238.7	0.2	2,224.3	-
1960	2,295.7	10.6	2,281.2	-2.5	2,279.1	-0.4	2,243.4	-6.1	2,274.8	2.3
1961	2,260.7	3.1	2,300.3	7.2	2,342.8	7.6	2,394.3	9.1	2,324.6	2.2
1962	2,435.3	7.0	2,456.4	3.5	2,481.8	4.2	2,489.9	1.3	2,465.9	6.1
1963	2,520.4	5.0	2,550.4	4.8	2,599.1	7.9	2,618.0	2.9	2,572.0	4.3
1964	2,681.9	10.1	2,711.7	4.5	2,743.8	4.8	2,751.9	1.2	2,722.3	5.8
1965	2,821.9	10.6	2,866.1	6.4	2,909.4	6.2	2,983.3	10.6	2,895.2	6.4
1966	3,053.1	9.7	3,065.0	1.6	3,085.8	2.7	3,111.7	3.4	3,078.9	6.3
1967	3,138.5	3.5	3,140.5	0.3	3,167.5	3.5	3,191.1	3.0	3,159.4	2.6
1968	3,250.2	7.6	3,307.2	7.2	3,332.3	3.1	3,347.3	1.8	3,309.2	4.7
1969	3,397.9	6.2	3,405.3	0.9	3,423.3	2.1	3,404.6	-2.2	3,407.8	3.0
1970	3,397.7	-0.8	3,402.4	0.6	3,432.9	3.6	3,397.7	-4.0	3,407.7	-0.0
1971	3,493.5	11.8	3,514.7	2.4	3,534.9	2.3	3,545.8	1.2	3,522.2	3.4
1972	3,617.2	8.3	3,699.1	9.4	3,738.9	4.4	3,802.1	6.9	3,714.3	5.5
1973	3,906.1	11.4	3,934.7	3.0	3,930.0	-0.5	3,973.5	4.5	3,936.0	6.0
1974	3,947.3	-2.6	3,962.1	1.5	3,916.1	-4.6	3,882.9	-3.3	3,927.1	-0.2
1975	3,820.0	-6.3	3,852.3	3.4	3,926.2	7.9	3,979.6	5.6	3,894.5	-0.8
1976	4,073.3	9.8	4,104.7	3.1	4,124.0	1.9	4,165.6	4.1	4,116.9	5.7
1977	4,224.8	5.8	4,310.1	8.3	4,378.0	6.5	4,367.7	-0.9	4,320.2	4.9
1978	4,383.9	1.5	4,536.6	14.7	4,579.5	3.8	4,637.7	5.2	4,534.4	5.0
1979	4,644.6	0.6	4,661.6	1.5	4,702.6	3.6	4,714.3	1.0	4,680.8	3.2
1980	4,738.3	2.1	4,621.6	-9.5	4,615.1	-0.6	4,695.9	7.2	4,667.7	-0.3
1981	4,789.9	8.3	4,747.1	-3.5	4,806.8	5.1	4,752.8	-4.4	4,774.1	2.3
1982	4,661.5	-7.5	4,685.6	2.1	4,654.4	-2.6	4,660.2	0.5	4,665.4	-2.3
1983	4,707.0	4.1	4,812.1	9.2	4,897.8	7.3	4,987.8	7.6	4,851.2	4.0
1984	5,092.4	8.7	5,169.3	6.2	5,206.2	2.9	5,236.6	2.4	5,176.1	6.7
1985	5,284.3	3.7	5,317.8	2.6	5,385.9	5.2	5,422.8	2.8	5,352.7	3.4
1986	5,485.7	4.7	5,482.7	-0.2	5,511.7	2.1	5,533.3	1.6	5,503.4	2.8
1987	5,568.2	2.5	5,627.5	4.3	5,674.7	3.4	5,758.5	6.0	5,657.2	2.8
1988	5,799.9	2.9	5,855.1	3.9	5,887.3	2.2	5,962.8	5.2	5,876.2	3.9
1989	6,020.8	3.9	6,063.5	2.9	6,099.9	2.4	6,111.7	0.8	6,074.0	3.4
1990	6,174.3	4.2	6,190.8	1.1	6,158.8	-2.1	6,113.4	-2.9	6,159.4	1.4
1991	6,074.8	-2.5	6,085.8	0.7	6,098.3	0.8	6,118.7	1.3	6,094.4	-1.1
1992	6,191.6	4.9	6,225.1	2.2	6,270.4	2.9	6,334.8	4.2	6,255.5	2.6
1993	6,342.7	0.5	6,362.9	1.3	6,404.0	2.6	6,465.1	3.9	6,393.7	2.2
1994	6,506.2	2.6	6,573.9	4.2	6,631.1	3.5	6,675.4	2.7	6,596.6	3.2
1995	6,695.7	1.2	6,701.2	0.3	6,749.5	2.9	-	-	-	-

Source: The National Income and Product Accounts of the United States, 1959-95. Published on diskettes, January 1996, Bureau of Economic Analysis, U.S. Department of Commerce, Washington, D.C. - indicates that data are unavailable or zero.

CHAPTER 2

GROSS DOMESTIC PRODUCT

GROSS DOMESTIC PRODUCT

In November 1995, the U.S. Department of Commerce's Bureau of Economic Analysis (BEA) introduced revisions to the National Income and Product Accounts (NIPA) which (1) changed the NIPA basing year for constant dollars from 1987 dollars to "chained (1992) dollars", (2) introduced new definitional changes, and (3) introduced a number of statistical changes. An earlier comprehensive revision, in 1991, had already shifted emphasis from the Gross National Product (GNP) to the Gross Domestic Product (GDP) as the principal measure of U.S. production. For more discussion of these issues, please see below and read the Introduction, the text accompanying the GNP chapter, and the November/December 1995 and January/February 1996 issues of the *Survey of Current Business* (reference 3).

The net effect of the 1995 NIPA revisions is that GDP is retrospectively *increased* and the accuracy of the GDP is improved by shifting from fixed base (1987) dollars to chained (1992) dollars to index quantitative changes in GDP and its components.

GDP versus GNP

The GDP and GNP differ in the following manner:

GNP measures goods and services produced by labor and property *supplied* by U.S. residents—wherever the goods and services are produced.

GDP measures goods and services produced by labor and property *located* in the U.S.—regardless of the nationality of the persons supplying the labor and property.

The difference between the two measures is *net factor income*; this is income produced by U.S. residents abroad less income produced by foreign residents in the United States. GNP is a better measure of *income* available to U.S. citizens by reason of their contribution to production. Savings are naturally expressed in relation to GNP; and estimating the availability of total resources (e.g., for education) is more appropriately made by looking at GNP.

GDP is a better measurement of *production* within the borders of the United States.

BEA's reasons for the shift may be summarized as follows:

1. GDP is the "appropriate measure for much of the short-term monitoring and analysis of the U.S. economy." It is "consistent in coverage with indicators such as employment, productivity, industry output, and investment in equipment and structures."

2. GDP is the measuring unit used by other countries; hence country-to-country comparisons will be easier. The U.S., in fact, is late in adopting the international System of National Accounts, the set of international guidelines for economic accounting.

3. The GDP measure makes quarterly estimates more accurate because BEA need not estimate factor income (which is received late and requires many adjustments for exchange rates, inflation, etc.) to obtain measures of the economy.

The 1995 Benchmark Revision

In January 1996, BEA released a comprehensive revision to the National Income and Product Accounts. The 1995 revision (delayed in reaching the public by the "government shutdowns" of 1995) was the 10th comprehensive "benchmark" revision of NIPA. These revisions involve changes in definitions and classifications to reflect better the character of the U.S. economy and its evolving structure as well as statistical changes to incorporate new and revised data. A full discussion of the changes is beyond the scope of this book. Readers are referred to the November/December 1995 edition of *Survey of Current Business*, reference 3 in the Bibliography. Highlights follow:

Government expenditures on certain classes of capital goods were recognized as an "investment".

Government contributions to both civilian and military retirement programs were recognized.

Fixed-year indexing (e.g. 1987=100) was replaced using chained (1992) dollar indexing to express "real" GDP changes from year to year. For a full discussion of this subject, see the Introduction.

New estimating procedures, especially relating to depreciation, are used.

Other statistical changes were made.

Presentation of Data

BEA has issued its revised GDP data from 1959 to 1995. All tables, therefore, show data for the 1959-1991 period only. It is expected that data back to 1929 will be available for the next edition.

The chapter consists of 24 series shown in current and in chained (1992) dollars—a total of 48 tables. Explanatory texts are provided for subsections on Personal Consumption Expenditures, Gross Private Domestic Investment, Net Exports of Goods and Services, and Government Purchases.

Uses of GDP

Since 1991, the GDP is used as the instrument for measuring the output of the U.S. economy as a whole (its magnitude, growth, or decline) and to determine the economic processes or mechanisms which accounts for the national product (what proportion of it is accounted for by government spending, investment in structures and capital goods, by personal consumption expenditures—and subcategories of these such as durable goods, nondurable goods, services, etc.).

GDP, Business Cycles, and Markets. The best-known use of GDP is as an indicator of economic growth or decline. A sustained period of decline in real GDP is defined as a recession. A sustained period of growth is called an expansion. The period from the trough of a recession to the peak of an expansion is a business cycle. Various economic indicators, covered in this part of *EIH*, have in the past proved capable of predicting the onset of recessions and recoveries.

Since recession invariably means increased unemployment, dropping demand, and slowing production . . . and rapid expansions can result in shortages and inflation, GDP is closely watched by government and private sector alike. Stock and bond market behavior is closely correlated with GDP's behavior as well: the stock market tends to rise and decline with GDP; the bond market behaves "counter cyclically," meaning that it rises when GDP drops and drops when GDP rises.

Bibliography

1. U.S. Department of Commerce. Bureau of Economic Analysis. *An Introduction to National Economic Accounting*. Methodology Paper Series MP-1. Washington, DC: U.S. Government Printing Office, March 1985.

2. U.S. Department of Commerce. Bureau of Economic Analysis. *GNP: An Overview of Source Data and Estimating Methods*. Methodology Paper Series MP-4. Washington, DC: U.S. Government Printing Office, September 1987.

3. U.S. Department of Commerce. Bureau of Economic Analysis. *Survey of Current Business*. Superintendent of Documents, U.S. Government Printing Office, Washington, DC 20302.

Gross Domestic Product - Actual Dollars

In billions of actual dollars and percent. Quarterly data are seasonally adjusted and annualized. Growth rates for quarters are compound annual growth rates; changes from year to year are percentage changes.

Year	1st Quarter	% Change	2nd Quarter	% Change	3rd Quarter	% Change	4th Quarter	% Change	TOTAL	% Change
1959	496.3	-	509.3	10.9	509.6	0.2	513.8	3.3	507.2	-
1960	527.3	10.9	526.1	-0.9	529.0	2.2	523.9	-3.8	526.6	3.8
1961	528.1	3.2	538.9	8.4	549.6	8.2	562.6	9.8	544.8	3.5
1962	575.3	9.3	582.8	5.3	589.9	5.0	592.9	2.0	585.2	7.4
1963	602.2	6.4	610.9	5.9	623.7	8.6	632.8	6.0	617.4	5.5
1964	649.4	10.9	658.4	5.7	669.2	6.7	675.1	3.6	663.0	7.4
1965	695.6	12.7	708.2	7.4	725.0	9.8	747.7	13.1	719.1	8.5
1966	770.5	12.8	780.0	5.0	793.6	7.2	807.1	7.0	787.8	9.6
1967	816.9	4.9	823.0	3.0	838.9	8.0	855.6	8.2	833.6	5.8
1968	880.6	12.2	904.7	11.4	919.7	6.8	937.3	7.9	910.6	9.2
1969	959.9	10.0	973.7	5.9	993.3	8.3	1,002.0	3.5	982.2	7.9
1970	1,014.0	4.9	1,029.0	6.0	1,047.2	7.3	1,052.3	2.0	1,035.6	5.4
1971	1,096.7	18.0	1,116.8	7.5	1,137.1	7.5	1,150.9	4.9	1,125.4	8.7
1972	1,190.1	14.3	1,223.5	11.7	1,247.6	8.1	1,287.9	13.6	1,237.3	9.9
1973	1,337.2	16.2	1,367.7	9.4	1,390.5	6.8	1,435.3	13.5	1,382.6	11.7
1974	1,446.6	3.2	1,480.2	9.6	1,510.9	8.6	1,549.7	10.7	1,496.9	8.3
1975	1,559.6	2.6	1,596.4	9.8	1,657.3	16.2	1,709.1	13.1	1,630.6	8.9
1976	1,767.4	14.4	1,797.1	6.9	1,830.5	7.6	1,880.8	11.5	1,819.0	11.6
1977	1,933.4	11.7	2,005.3	15.7	2,067.5	13.0	2,101.2	6.7	2,026.9	11.4
1978	2,144.4	8.5	2,274.6	26.6	2,334.8	11.0	2,411.7	13.8	2,291.4	13.0
1979	2,464.9	9.1	2,522.4	9.7	2,592.6	11.6	2,650.1	9.2	2,557.5	11.6
1980	2,722.9	11.4	2,719.4	-0.5	2,783.2	9.7	2,911.6	19.8	2,784.2	8.9
1981	3,043.2	19.3	3,073.3	4.0	3,163.2	12.2	3,183.9	2.6	3,115.9	11.9
1982	3,179.6	-0.5	3,234.7	7.1	3,258.5	3.0	3,295.5	4.6	3,242.1	4.1
1983	3,359.5	8.0	3,469.4	13.7	3,563.8	11.3	3,665.4	11.9	3,514.5	8.4
1984	3,792.8	14.6	3,879.2	9.4	3,943.3	6.8	3,994.4	5.3	3,902.4	11.0
1985	4,080.3	8.9	4,135.4	5.5	4,221.9	8.6	4,285.1	6.1	4,180.7	7.1
1986	4,358.2	7.0	4,386.7	2.6	4,442.4	5.2	4,501.4	5.4	4,422.2	5.8
1987	4,565.6	5.8	4,644.9	7.1	4,722.6	6.9	4,836.2	10.0	4,692.3	6.1
1988	4,898.5	5.3	5,000.5	8.6	5,094.5	7.7	5,204.9	9.0	5,049.6	7.6
1989	5,316.9	8.9	5,413.1	7.4	5,486.8	5.6	5,537.9	3.8	5,438.7	7.7
1990	5,660.4	9.1	5,751.0	6.6	5,782.4	2.2	5,781.5	-0.1	5,743.8	5.6
1991	5,822.1	2.8	5,892.3	4.9	5,950.0	4.0	6,002.3	3.6	5,916.7	3.0
1992	6,121.8	8.2	6,201.2	5.3	6,271.7	4.6	6,383.0	7.3	6,244.4	5.5
1993	6,442.8	3.8	6,503.2	3.8	6,571.3	4.3	6,683.7	7.0	6,550.2	4.9
1994	6,772.8	5.4	6,885.0	6.8	6,987.6	6.1	7,080.0	5.4	6,931.4	5.8
1995	7,147.8	3.9	7,196.5	2.8	7,297.2	5.7	-	-	-	-

Source: "National Income and Product Account Tables: Selected NIPA Tables," *Survey of Current Business*, November 1995, U.S. Department of Commerce, Bureau of Economic Analysis, National Income and Wealth Division. - indicates that no data are available.

Gross Domestic Product - Chained (1992) Dollars

In billions of chained (1992) dollars and percent. Quarterly data are seasonally adjusted and annualized. Growth rates for quarters are compound annual growth rates; changes from year to year are percentage changes.

Year	1st Quarter	% Change	2nd Quarter	% Change	3rd Quarter	% Change	4th Quarter	% Change	TOTAL	% Change
1959	-	-	-	-	2,225.6	-	2,225.8	0.0	2,212.3	-
1960	2,283.3	10.7	2,268.5	-2.6	2,265.8	-0.5	2,229.1	-6.3	2,261.7	2.2
1961	2,245.6	3.0	2,286.1	7.4	2,328.2	7.6	2,379.4	9.1	2,309.8	2.1
1962	2,420.4	7.1	2,440.0	3.3	2,465.2	4.2	2,470.7	0.9	2,449.1	6.0
1963	2,502.3	5.2	2,532.9	5.0	2,581.4	7.9	2,599.7	2.9	2,554.0	4.3
1964	2,661.8	9.9	2,692.5	4.7	2,723.9	4.7	2,733.6	1.4	2,702.9	5.8
1965	2,800.8	10.2	2,844.2	6.3	2,889.2	6.5	2,965.2	10.9	2,874.8	6.4
1966	3,034.4	9.7	3,046.2	1.6	3,067.6	2.8	3,092.6	3.3	3,060.2	6.4
1967	3,119.7	3.6	3,122.3	0.3	3,147.3	3.2	3,171.6	3.1	3,140.2	2.6
1968	3,230.2	7.6	3,286.6	7.2	3,311.1	3.0	3,326.3	1.8	3,288.6	4.7
1969	3,376.9	6.2	3,385.2	1.0	3,404.3	2.3	3,385.6	-2.2	3,388.0	3.0
1970	3,378.1	-0.9	3,382.1	0.5	3,412.9	3.7	3,379.6	-3.8	3,388.2	0.0
1971	3,471.5	11.3	3,491.3	2.3	3,514.0	2.6	3,523.6	1.1	3,500.1	3.3
1972	3,593.9	8.2	3,676.3	9.5	3,713.8	4.1	3,777.2	7.0	3,690.3	5.4
1973	3,876.9	11.0	3,903.3	2.8	3,892.8	-1.1	3,936.2	4.5	3,902.3	5.7
1974	3,903.0	-3.3	3,920.4	1.8	3,878.4	-4.2	3,850.9	-2.8	3,888.2	-0.4
1975	3,793.6	-5.8	3,825.6	3.4	3,897.0	7.7	3,944.2	4.9	3,865.1	-0.6
1976	4,039.1	10.0	4,068.9	3.0	4,087.7	1.9	4,128.4	4.0	4,081.1	5.6
1977	4,181.8	5.3	4,268.0	8.5	4,336.3	6.6	4,331.0	-0.5	4,279.3	4.9
1978	4,340.8	0.9	4,501.3	15.6	4,540.5	3.5	4,592.3	4.6	4,493.7	5.0
1979	4,597.7	0.5	4,608.6	1.0	4,638.8	2.6	4,651.0	1.1	4,624.0	2.9
1980	4,674.3	2.0	4,562.6	-9.2	4,559.6	-0.3	4,651.1	8.3	4,611.9	-0.3
1981	4,741.3	8.0	4,701.3	-3.3	4,758.4	4.9	4,698.6	-4.9	4,724.9	2.5
1982	4,618.9	-6.6	4,637.4	1.6	4,615.3	-1.9	4,622.8	0.7	4,623.6	-2.1
1983	4,669.8	4.1	4,771.3	9.0	4,855.5	7.2	4,943.6	7.5	4,810.0	4.0
1984	5,053.4	9.2	5,129.8	6.2	5,167.0	2.9	5,202.7	2.8	5,138.2	6.8
1985	5,261.3	4.6	5,290.8	2.3	5,367.0	5.9	5,398.9	2.4	5,329.5	3.7
1986	5,465.4	5.0	5,469.6	0.3	5,497.6	2.1	5,527.0	2.2	5,489.9	3.0
1987	5,561.4	2.5	5,616.8	4.0	5,666.0	3.6	5,749.4	6.0	5,648.4	2.9
1988	5,782.9	2.4	5,841.7	4.1	5,876.5	2.4	5,950.7	5.1	5,862.9	3.8
1989	6,008.7	4.0	6,053.4	3.0	6,086.2	2.2	6,093.0	0.4	6,060.4	3.4
1990	6,154.1	4.1	6,174.4	1.3	6,145.2	-1.9	6,081.0	-4.1	6,138.7	1.3
1991	6,047.9	-2.2	6,074.1	1.7	6,089.3	1.0	6,104.4	1.0	6,079.0	-1.0
1992	6,175.3	4.7	6,214.2	2.5	6,260.9	3.0	6,327.3	4.3	6,244.4	2.7
1993	6,327.0	-0.0	6,353.7	1.7	6,390.4	2.3	6,463.9	4.7	6,383.8	2.2
1994	6,504.6	2.5	6,581.5	4.8	6,639.5	3.6	6,691.3	3.2	6,604.2	3.5
1995	6,701.6	0.6	6,709.4	0.5	6,763.2	3.2	-	-	-	-

Source: "National Income and Product Account Tables: Selected NIPA Tables," *Survey of Current Business*, November 1995, U.S. Department of Commerce, Bureau of Economic Analysis, National Income and Wealth Division. - indicates that no data are available.

PERSONAL CONSUMPTION EXPENDITURES
Component of Gross Domestic Product

Personal Consumption Expenditures is the largest component of Gross Domestic Product (GDP). In 1994, it accounted for 67.2 percent of real GDP. The measure includes all expenditures by individuals on goods and services; goods are divided into durable and nondurable goods; services are reported as a single category.

The category is labeled "personal" consumption because it reflects all purchases by individuals. The category also incorporates goods and services that the private sector purchases in order to make final products. Paper clips purchased by an automobile producers, for instance, are accounted for in the ultimate price of cars sold to consumers. The measure excludes government purchases of goods and services and private purchases of goods (such as tooling) which are considered to be capital investments.

Note that Personal Consumption Expenditures do *not* include imported goods; these are measured as a separate category in the national accounts.

Sources for the data included in Personal Consumption Expenditures are many and varied. Typically, different sources are used for "benchmark" years (the years of the economic censuses), for other years, and for the most recent period in order to obtain the best and most accurate information. Where partial data only are available, estimates are made using a variety of procedures, including judgement based on trends.

All explanations are provided in this section, followed by tables showing Personal Consumption Expenditure totals and tables showing the subcomponents of the measure. Each item is shown in actual and in constant 1987 dollars.

Durable and Nondurable Goods

The Bureau of Economic Affairs bases its estimates on six distinct categories, each handled in a different way (reference 1). Most goods are based on census surveys in benchmark years and on annual and monthly retail surveys conducted in other years by the Census Bureau. Other distinct categories, using distinct estimating methodologies, are new trucks, new and used autos, gasoline and oil, and food furnished employees (including the military).

In 1994, durable goods accounted for 8.5 percent and nondurable goods for 21.1 percent of real GDP. Durable goods are products expected to last three years or longer; nondurables for a lesser time period.

Services

The category measures expenditures on services by individuals. The grouping of categories includes (1) rent paid for housing; (2) medical services; (3) expenditures on education from whatever sources; (4) financial, banking, brokerage services; (5) insurance, hospital expenses, religious activities, cable TV, utilities, and local transportation; (6) water and sanitary services; lotteries, (7) foreign travel by U.S. citizens less foreign visitors' spending in the U.S., and (8) a variety of other services, including repairs, tools, club memberships, etc. Estimating methods differ for each of these groupings.

The Services category of Personal Consumption Expenditures should not be viewed as equivalent to the "services" sector of the economy. The category includes rentals, insurance, banking, and financial services, which are classified elsewhere in the Standard Industrial Classification (SIC) system. And the category excludes services purchased by corporations and by government; services purchased by the private sector are "hidden" in the price of goods sold or services rendered; those purchased by government appear under the governmental category.

Presentation of Data

Data are shown from 1959 to 1995 in quarterly and in annual increments. Changes from one period to the next are shown. Changes from quarter to quarter are annualized, compounded growth rates as explained in the previous section on Gross National Product. Changes from year to year are simple percentile changes.

Analytical Uses

Personal consumption expenditures measure the allocation of individual resources between consumable products (food, clothing, etc.), durable goods (automobiles, appliances, etc.), and services (medical, entertainment, etc.) over time. As in all GDP series, significance appears when results for different periods are compared. Nondurable goods are the most essential; durable goods purchases can be deferred. Growth in one and decline in the other can thus signal a lack of consumer confidence. Strong growth in durables output, conversely, shows confidence in the future. The shift of expenditures from goods to services or from services to goods indicates, over time, changes in economic structure.

Gross Domestic Product

Personal consumption expenditures: Total - Actual Dollars

In billions of actual dollars and percent. Quarterly data are seasonally adjusted and annualized. Growth rates for quarters are compound annual growth rates; changes from year to year are percentage changes.

Year	1st Quarter	% Change	2nd Quarter	% Change	3rd Quarter	% Change	4th Quarter	% Change	TOTAL	% Change
1959	310.4	-	316.4	8.0	321.7	6.9	323.8	2.6	318.1	-
1960	327.3	4.4	333.2	7.4	333.1	-0.1	335.0	2.3	332.2	4.4
1961	335.7	0.8	340.6	6.0	343.5	3.4	350.7	8.7	342.6	3.1
1962	355.3	5.4	361.3	6.9	365.4	4.6	371.7	7.1	363.4	6.1
1963	375.1	3.7	379.4	4.7	386.4	7.6	391.1	5.0	383.0	5.4
1964	400.5	10.0	408.3	8.0	417.1	8.9	419.8	2.6	411.4	7.4
1965	430.6	10.7	437.8	6.9	447.2	8.9	461.5	13.4	444.3	8.0
1966	472.0	9.4	477.1	4.4	486.4	8.0	492.0	4.7	481.9	8.5
1967	496.8	4.0	506.2	7.8	513.7	6.1	521.2	6.0	509.5	5.7
1968	539.5	14.8	553.2	10.6	569.1	12.0	577.5	6.0	559.8	9.9
1969	588.8	8.1	599.4	7.4	609.2	6.7	621.1	8.0	604.7	8.0
1970	632.4	7.5	642.7	6.7	655.2	8.0	662.1	4.3	648.1	7.2
1971	681.6	12.3	695.8	8.6	708.2	7.3	724.5	9.5	702.5	8.4
1972	741.9	10.0	759.9	10.1	778.1	9.9	802.9	13.4	770.7	9.7
1973	827.2	12.7	842.1	7.4	860.8	9.2	876.1	7.3	851.6	10.5
1974	894.4	8.6	922.4	13.1	950.1	12.6	957.8	3.3	931.2	9.3
1975	982.7	10.8	1,012.4	12.6	1,046.3	14.1	1,075.1	11.5	1,029.1	10.5
1976	1,110.2	13.7	1,130.2	7.4	1,159.8	10.9	1,195.0	12.7	1,148.8	11.6
1977	1,230.7	12.5	1,259.1	9.6	1,290.3	10.3	1,328.1	12.2	1,277.1	11.2
1978	1,358.3	9.4	1,417.4	18.6	1,450.6	9.7	1,488.7	10.9	1,428.8	11.9
1979	1,529.3	11.4	1,563.9	9.4	1,617.4	14.4	1,663.5	11.9	1,593.5	11.5
1980	1,713.1	12.5	1,716.9	0.9	1,774.9	14.2	1,836.8	14.7	1,760.4	10.5
1981	1,890.3	12.2	1,923.5	7.2	1,967.4	9.4	1,983.9	3.4	1,941.3	10.3
1982	2,021.4	7.8	2,046.1	5.0	2,091.1	9.1	2,148.7	11.5	2,076.8	7.0
1983	2,185.0	6.9	2,257.2	13.9	2,316.8	11.0	2,374.7	10.4	2,283.4	9.9
1984	2,422.5	8.3	2,475.6	9.1	2,510.5	5.8	2,560.6	8.2	2,492.3	9.1
1985	2,623.8	10.2	2,673.4	7.8	2,742.3	10.7	2,779.6	5.6	2,704.8	8.5
1986	2,823.3	6.4	2,855.6	4.7	2,926.2	10.3	2,965.6	5.5	2,892.7	6.9
1987	3,002.4	5.1	3,070.0	9.3	3,134.2	8.6	3,171.3	4.8	3,094.5	7.0
1988	3,247.1	9.9	3,310.2	8.0	3,382.3	9.0	3,459.2	9.4	3,349.7	8.2
1989	3,506.1	5.5	3,569.7	7.5	3,627.3	6.6	3,676.1	5.5	3,594.8	7.3
1990	3,759.2	9.4	3,811.8	5.7	3,879.2	7.3	3,907.0	2.9	3,839.3	6.8
1991	3,910.7	0.4	3,961.0	5.2	4,001.6	4.2	4,027.1	2.6	3,975.1	3.5
1992	4,127.6	10.4	4,183.0	5.5	4,238.9	5.5	4,329.6	8.8	4,219.8	6.2
1993	4,367.8	3.6	4,424.7	5.3	4,481.0	5.2	4,543.0	5.7	4,454.1	5.6
1994	4,599.2	5.0	4,665.1	5.9	4,734.4	6.1	4,796.0	5.3	4,698.7	5.5
1995	4,836.3	3.4	4,908.7	6.1	4,965.1	4.7	-	-	-	-

Source: "National Income and Product Account Tables: Selected NIPA Tables," *Survey of Current Business*, November 1995, U.S. Department of Commerce, Bureau of Economic Analysis, National Income and Wealth Division. - indicates that no data are available.

Gross Domestic Product

Personal consumption expenditures: Total - Chained (1992) Dollars

In billions of chained (1992) dollars and percent. Quarterly data are seasonally adjusted and annualized. Growth rates for quarters are compound annual growth rates; changes from year to year are percentage changes.

Year	1st Quarter	% Change	2nd Quarter	% Change	3rd Quarter	% Change	4th Quarter	% Change	TOTAL	% Change
1959	-	-	-	-	1,407.2	-	1,409.5	0.7	1,394.6	-
1960	1,422.5	3.7	1,439.6	4.9	1,433.5	-1.7	1,434.8	0.4	1,432.6	2.7
1961	1,434.2	-0.2	1,455.7	6.1	1,463.5	2.2	1,492.8	8.3	1,461.5	2.0
1962	1,508.4	4.2	1,526.7	4.9	1,539.6	3.4	1,560.6	5.6	1,533.8	4.9
1963	1,571.2	2.7	1,586.3	3.9	1,607.6	5.5	1,621.1	3.4	1,596.6	4.1
1964	1,653.6	8.3	1,683.1	7.3	1,713.9	7.5	1,718.6	1.1	1,692.3	6.0
1965	1,756.2	9.0	1,776.1	4.6	1,806.1	6.9	1,858.0	12.0	1,799.1	6.3
1966	1,885.6	6.1	1,890.9	1.1	1,912.4	4.6	1,919.1	1.4	1,902.0	5.7
1967	1,931.2	2.5	1,957.5	5.6	1,967.1	2.0	1,978.5	2.3	1,958.6	3.0
1968	2,025.1	9.8	2,056.4	6.3	2,095.1	7.7	2,104.4	1.8	2,070.2	5.7
1969	2,128.0	4.6	2,141.4	2.5	2,152.0	2.0	2,168.8	3.2	2,147.5	3.7
1970	2,182.3	2.5	2,192.9	2.0	2,211.6	3.5	2,204.6	-1.3	2,197.8	2.3
1971	2,246.5	7.8	2,266.5	3.6	2,283.9	3.1	2,321.1	6.7	2,279.5	3.7
1972	2,352.0	5.4	2,394.9	7.5	2,430.6	6.1	2,486.1	9.5	2,415.9	6.0
1973	2,530.4	7.3	2,527.5	-0.5	2,539.9	2.0	2,532.6	-1.1	2,532.6	4.8
1974	2,512.7	-3.1	2,522.7	1.6	2,532.4	1.5	2,490.9	-6.4	2,514.7	-0.7
1975	2,513.2	3.6	2,556.3	7.0	2,591.8	5.7	2,618.7	4.2	2,570.0	2.2
1976	2,674.2	8.8	2,697.9	3.6	2,724.4	4.0	2,760.8	5.5	2,714.3	5.6
1977	2,794.3	4.9	2,810.3	2.3	2,836.9	3.8	2,877.6	5.9	2,829.8	4.3
1978	2,893.1	2.2	2,954.6	8.8	2,968.2	1.9	2,990.6	3.1	2,951.6	4.3
1979	3,008.1	2.4	3,003.5	-0.6	3,028.7	3.4	3,040.2	1.5	3,020.2	2.3
1980	3,037.2	-0.4	2,968.8	-8.7	2,998.5	4.1	3,034.2	4.8	3,009.7	-0.3
1981	3,045.6	1.5	3,045.8	0.0	3,058.8	1.7	3,035.3	-3.0	3,046.4	1.2
1982	3,054.0	2.5	3,062.1	1.1	3,080.1	2.4	3,129.7	6.6	3,081.5	1.2
1983	3,156.5	3.5	3,220.0	8.3	3,267.1	6.0	3,318.6	6.5	3,240.6	5.2
1984	3,354.0	4.3	3,397.5	5.3	3,418.4	2.5	3,460.6	5.0	3,407.6	5.2
1985	3,511.2	6.0	3,540.8	3.4	3,602.1	7.1	3,612.1	1.1	3,566.5	4.7
1986	3,644.0	3.6	3,683.0	4.4	3,742.8	6.7	3,764.8	2.4	3,708.7	4.0
1987	3,765.7	0.1	3,814.0	5.2	3,852.9	4.1	3,856.5	0.4	3,822.3	3.1
1988	3,924.2	7.2	3,952.2	2.9	3,985.1	3.4	4,029.1	4.5	3,972.7	3.9
1989	4,032.8	0.4	4,047.4	1.5	4,083.2	3.6	4,095.0	1.2	4,064.6	2.3
1990	4,128.9	3.4	4,134.7	0.6	4,148.5	1.3	4,116.4	-3.1	4,132.2	1.7
1991	4,084.5	-3.1	4,110.0	2.5	4,119.5	0.9	4,109.1	-1.0	4,105.8	-0.6
1992	4,173.8	6.4	4,196.4	2.2	4,226.7	2.9	4,282.3	5.4	4,219.8	2.8
1993	4,290.0	0.7	4,319.0	2.7	4,359.7	3.8	4,390.0	2.8	4,339.7	2.8
1994	4,418.8	2.7	4,457.7	3.6	4,485.8	2.5	4,522.3	3.3	4,471.1	3.0
1995	4,530.9	0.8	4,568.8	3.4	4,601.1	2.9	-	-	-	-

Source: "National Income and Product Account Tables: Selected NIPA Tables," *Survey of Current Business*, November 1995, U.S. Department of Commerce, Bureau of Economic Analysis, National Income and Wealth Division. - indicates that no data are available.

Gross Domestic Product
Personal consumption expenditures
Durable goods - Actual Dollars

In billions of actual dollars and percent. Quarterly data are seasonally adjusted and annualized. Growth rates for quarters are compound annual growth rates; changes from year to year are percentage changes.

Year	1st Quarter	% Change	2nd Quarter	% Change	3rd Quarter	% Change	4th Quarter	% Change	TOTAL	% Change
1959	41.5	-	43.2	17.4	44.1	8.6	41.8	-19.3	42.7	-
1960	43.2	14.1	44.1	8.6	43.6	-4.5	42.4	-10.6	43.3	1.4
1961	39.9	-21.6	40.9	10.4	42.1	12.3	44.2	21.5	41.8	-3.5
1962	45.2	9.4	46.4	11.0	46.9	4.4	48.9	18.2	46.9	12.2
1963	50.0	9.3	51.3	10.8	52.0	5.6	53.1	8.7	51.6	10.0
1964	55.2	16.8	56.6	10.5	58.4	13.3	56.4	-13.0	56.7	9.9
1965	61.9	45.1	61.7	-1.3	63.6	12.9	65.9	15.3	63.3	11.6
1966	68.9	19.5	66.3	-14.3	68.8	16.0	69.1	1.8	68.3	7.9
1967	67.6	-8.4	71.0	21.7	71.1	0.6	72.0	5.2	70.4	3.1
1968	77.1	31.5	79.1	10.8	83.3	23.0	83.6	1.4	80.8	14.8
1969	85.5	9.4	85.9	1.9	86.1	0.9	86.2	0.5	85.9	6.3
1970	84.9	-5.9	86.0	5.3	86.9	4.3	82.1	-20.3	85.0	-1.0
1971	92.7	62.5	95.5	12.6	97.8	10.0	101.5	16.0	96.9	14.0
1972	104.9	14.1	108.1	12.8	111.4	12.8	117.0	21.7	110.4	13.9
1973	125.2	31.1	124.1	-3.5	123.8	-1.0	121.1	-8.4	123.5	11.9
1974	118.9	-7.1	123.0	14.5	128.8	20.2	118.6	-28.1	122.3	-1.0
1975	123.2	16.4	128.3	17.6	138.0	33.8	144.4	19.9	133.5	9.2
1976	154.1	29.7	156.3	5.8	159.6	8.7	165.3	15.1	158.9	19.0
1977	173.6	21.6	178.7	12.3	183.0	10.0	189.0	13.8	181.1	14.0
1978	186.8	-4.6	204.4	43.4	204.8	0.8	209.8	10.1	201.4	11.2
1979	211.1	2.5	209.9	-2.3	218.4	17.2	216.3	-3.8	213.9	6.2
1980	219.4	5.9	199.2	-32.0	212.4	29.3	223.0	21.5	213.5	-0.2
1981	232.6	18.4	227.4	-8.6	238.4	20.8	223.6	-22.6	230.5	8.0
1982	233.2	18.3	235.6	4.2	238.1	4.3	250.1	21.7	239.3	3.8
1983	254.6	7.4	274.7	35.5	286.8	18.8	303.3	25.1	279.8	16.9
1984	315.0	16.3	324.4	12.5	324.9	0.6	336.0	14.4	325.1	16.2
1985	349.8	17.5	354.4	5.4	376.8	27.8	363.2	-13.7	361.1	11.1
1986	370.3	8.1	384.7	16.5	422.0	44.8	417.6	-4.1	398.7	10.4
1987	394.2	-20.6	413.8	21.4	434.7	21.8	424.1	-9.4	416.7	4.5
1988	444.2	20.3	448.2	3.7	447.1	-1.0	464.5	16.5	451.0	8.2
1989	462.5	-1.7	472.5	8.9	484.6	10.6	471.7	-10.2	472.8	4.8
1990	493.3	19.6	477.6	-12.1	473.2	-3.6	461.9	-9.2	476.5	0.8
1991	449.0	-10.7	452.7	3.3	462.0	8.5	457.3	-4.0	455.2	-4.5
1992	474.1	15.5	481.3	6.2	492.5	9.6	506.2	11.6	488.5	7.3
1993	508.3	1.7	525.2	14.0	536.7	9.1	552.3	12.1	530.7	8.6
1994	562.6	7.7	573.1	7.7	585.3	8.8	602.7	12.4	580.9	9.5
1995	593.0	-6.3	604.0	7.6	616.0	8.2	-	-	-	-

Source: "National Income and Product Account Tables: Selected NIPA Tables," *Survey of Current Business*, November 1995, U.S. Department of Commerce, Bureau of Economic Analysis, National Income and Wealth Division. - indicates that no data are available.

Gross Domestic Product

Personal consumption expenditures
Durable goods - Chained (1992) Dollars

In billions of chained (1992) dollars and percent. Quarterly data are seasonally adjusted and annualized. Growth rates for quarters are compound annual growth rates; changes from year to year are percentage changes.

Year	1st Quarter	% Change	2nd Quarter	% Change	3rd Quarter	% Change	4th Quarter	% Change	TOTAL	% Change
1959	-	-	-	-	106.5	-	101.0	-19.1	103.1	-
1960	104.5	14.6	106.9	9.5	106.1	-3.0	103.2	-10.5	105.2	2.0
1961	97.1	-21.6	99.2	8.9	101.7	10.5	106.8	21.6	101.2	-3.8
1962	109.1	8.9	111.9	10.7	113.0	4.0	118.2	19.7	113.0	11.7
1963	120.7	8.7	123.4	9.3	124.9	5.0	127.0	6.9	124.0	9.7
1964	131.7	15.6	135.3	11.4	139.7	13.7	135.2	-12.3	135.5	9.3
1965	148.1	44.0	148.4	0.8	153.7	15.1	160.3	18.3	152.6	12.6
1966	168.0	20.6	161.0	-15.7	166.5	14.4	166.6	0.2	165.5	8.5
1967	163.3	-7.7	170.7	19.4	169.1	-3.7	169.4	0.7	168.1	1.6
1968	180.1	27.8	183.6	8.0	192.0	19.6	190.8	-2.5	186.6	11.0
1969	194.1	7.1	193.7	-0.8	193.2	-1.0	192.1	-2.3	193.3	3.6
1970	188.7	-6.9	190.7	4.3	191.3	1.3	177.6	-25.7	187.0	-3.3
1971	197.3	52.3	201.9	9.7	207.3	11.1	216.4	18.7	205.7	10.0
1972	221.7	10.2	227.2	10.3	233.2	11.0	245.3	22.4	231.9	12.7
1973	261.7	29.5	257.4	-6.4	255.4	-3.1	248.8	-9.9	255.8	10.3
1974	242.1	-10.3	244.3	3.7	246.4	3.5	220.0	-36.4	238.2	-6.9
1975	225.4	10.2	230.2	8.8	244.9	28.1	252.0	12.1	238.1	-0.0
1976	265.7	23.6	266.2	0.8	268.7	3.8	273.4	7.2	268.5	12.8
1977	284.7	17.6	291.9	10.5	295.9	5.6	301.0	7.1	293.4	9.3
1978	293.9	-9.1	316.3	34.2	311.4	-6.1	313.7	3.0	308.8	5.2
1979	310.5	-4.0	303.5	-8.7	311.9	11.5	303.3	-10.6	307.3	-0.5
1980	299.3	-5.2	265.8	-37.8	278.2	20.0	287.0	13.3	282.6	-8.0
1981	295.7	12.7	283.7	-15.3	292.8	13.5	271.2	-26.4	285.8	1.1
1982	280.5	14.4	281.4	1.3	283.3	2.7	296.7	20.3	285.5	-0.1
1983	299.9	4.4	322.7	34.1	334.9	16.0	352.1	22.2	327.4	14.7
1984	365.9	16.6	374.4	9.6	373.7	-0.7	385.8	13.6	374.9	14.5
1985	399.3	14.7	404.0	4.8	429.6	27.9	412.6	-14.9	411.4	9.7
1986	420.3	7.7	435.4	15.2	472.6	38.8	465.4	-6.0	448.4	9.0
1987	435.8	-23.1	453.5	17.3	472.1	17.4	458.3	-11.2	454.9	1.4
1988	480.9	21.2	482.6	1.4	477.9	-3.8	492.7	13.0	483.5	6.3
1989	488.4	-3.4	496.8	7.1	507.4	8.8	492.2	-11.5	496.2	2.6
1990	511.2	16.4	495.4	-11.8	490.4	-4.0	476.3	-11.0	493.3	-0.6
1991	458.6	-14.1	460.5	1.7	467.3	6.0	461.5	-4.9	462.0	-6.3
1992	476.1	13.3	481.1	4.3	491.9	9.3	505.0	11.1	488.5	5.7
1993	506.0	0.8	519.6	11.2	528.9	7.4	541.9	10.2	524.1	7.3
1994	549.6	5.8	555.4	4.3	563.0	5.6	579.9	12.6	562.0	7.2
1995	566.9	-8.7	576.6	7.0	589.8	9.5	-	-	-	-

Source: "National Income and Product Account Tables: Selected NIPA Tables," *Survey of Current Business*, November 1995, U.S. Department of Commerce, Bureau of Economic Analysis, National Income and Wealth Division. - indicates that no data are available.

Gross Domestic Product
Personal consumption expenditures
Nondurable goods - Actual Dollars

In billions of actual dollars and percent. Quarterly data are seasonally adjusted and annualized. Growth rates for quarters are compound annual growth rates; changes from year to year are percentage changes.

Year	1st Quarter	% Change	2nd Quarter	% Change	3rd Quarter	% Change	4th Quarter	% Change	TOTAL	% Change
1959	146.1	-	147.7	4.5	149.3	4.4	150.9	4.4	148.5	-
1960	150.8	-0.3	153.6	7.6	153.0	-1.6	153.9	2.4	152.9	3.0
1961	155.2	3.4	156.0	2.1	156.5	1.3	158.6	5.5	156.6	2.4
1962	160.6	5.1	161.9	3.3	163.4	3.8	165.3	4.7	162.8	4.0
1963	166.3	2.4	167.0	1.7	169.4	5.9	169.9	1.2	168.2	3.3
1964	174.1	10.3	177.3	7.6	181.0	8.6	182.3	2.9	178.7	6.2
1965	185.0	6.1	188.7	8.2	192.6	8.5	200.0	16.3	191.6	7.2
1966	204.3	8.9	208.0	7.4	211.0	5.9	211.7	1.3	208.8	9.0
1967	213.9	4.2	215.6	3.2	218.0	4.5	220.9	5.4	217.1	4.0
1968	228.1	13.7	233.3	9.4	239.4	10.9	242.0	4.4	235.7	8.6
1969	246.4	7.5	251.1	7.9	255.2	6.7	259.9	7.6	253.2	7.4
1970	266.2	10.1	269.8	5.5	273.7	5.9	278.4	7.0	272.0	7.4
1971	280.3	2.8	284.1	5.5	286.7	3.7	291.0	6.1	285.5	5.0
1972	295.9	6.9	304.3	11.8	311.5	9.8	320.5	12.1	308.0	7.9
1973	330.3	12.8	337.0	8.4	347.6	13.2	357.4	11.8	343.1	11.4
1974	369.1	13.8	380.3	12.7	391.7	12.5	396.7	5.2	384.5	12.1
1975	404.4	8.0	415.5	11.4	427.7	12.3	435.0	7.0	420.6	9.4
1976	445.3	9.8	452.6	6.7	462.4	8.9	472.4	8.9	458.2	8.9
1977	483.7	9.9	492.0	7.0	498.5	5.4	513.5	12.6	496.9	8.4
1978	524.1	8.5	542.6	14.9	558.1	11.9	574.9	12.6	549.9	10.7
1979	593.5	13.6	610.1	11.7	635.3	17.6	657.1	14.4	624.0	13.5
1980	679.2	14.1	686.0	4.1	698.9	7.7	717.8	11.3	695.5	11.5
1981	745.1	16.1	755.5	5.7	762.5	3.8	769.5	3.7	758.2	9.0
1982	775.5	3.2	777.8	1.2	792.2	7.6	801.9	5.0	786.8	3.8
1983	805.3	1.7	823.1	9.1	841.4	9.2	851.1	4.7	830.3	5.5
1984	865.4	6.9	882.7	8.2	888.6	2.7	897.5	4.1	883.6	6.4
1985	909.3	5.4	923.0	6.2	931.7	3.8	946.3	6.4	927.6	5.0
1986	956.1	4.2	949.4	-2.8	955.6	2.6	967.8	5.2	957.2	3.2
1987	992.9	10.8	1,010.4	7.2	1,020.7	4.1	1,031.9	4.5	1,014.0	5.9
1988	1,045.4	5.3	1,067.8	8.9	1,094.0	10.2	1,117.1	8.7	1,081.1	6.6
1989	1,132.3	5.6	1,159.6	10.0	1,173.6	4.9	1,189.8	5.6	1,163.8	7.6
1990	1,220.7	10.8	1,230.2	3.1	1,256.2	8.7	1,274.1	5.8	1,245.3	7.0
1991	1,268.3	-1.8	1,279.7	3.6	1,283.4	1.2	1,279.0	-1.4	1,277.6	2.6
1992	1,303.1	7.8	1,308.4	1.6	1,326.3	5.6	1,349.5	7.2	1,321.8	3.5
1993	1,354.1	1.4	1,364.2	3.0	1,371.4	2.1	1,386.1	4.4	1,368.9	3.6
1994	1,399.7	4.0	1,416.6	4.9	1,443.5	7.8	1,459.0	4.4	1,429.7	4.4
1995	1,471.6	3.5	1,486.9	4.2	1,491.3	1.2	-	-	-	-

Source: "National Income and Product Account Tables: Selected NIPA Tables," *Survey of Current Business*, November 1995, U.S. Department of Commerce, Bureau of Economic Analysis, National Income and Wealth Division. - indicates that no data are available.

Gross Domestic Product

Personal consumption expenditures
Nondurable goods - Chained (1992) Dollars

In billions of chained (1992) dollars and percent. Quarterly data are seasonally adjusted and annualized. Growth rates for quarters are compound annual growth rates; changes from year to year are percentage changes.

Year	1st Quarter	% Change	2nd Quarter	% Change	3rd Quarter	% Change	4th Quarter	% Change	TOTAL	% Change
1959	-	-	-	-	608.1	-	612.2	2.7	606.3	-
1960	612.1	-0.1	619.3	4.8	615.0	-2.7	615.4	0.3	615.4	1.5
1961	619.5	2.7	625.9	4.2	626.3	0.3	635.3	5.9	626.7	1.8
1962	640.7	3.4	643.9	2.0	648.7	3.0	652.7	2.5	646.5	3.2
1963	655.3	1.6	658.0	1.7	663.2	3.2	663.7	0.3	660.0	2.1
1964	676.3	7.8	688.8	7.6	701.3	7.5	703.7	1.4	692.5	4.9
1965	711.9	4.7	719.9	4.6	730.1	5.8	755.4	14.6	729.3	5.3
1966	762.4	3.8	769.0	3.5	774.2	2.7	771.2	-1.5	769.2	5.5
1967	777.3	3.2	781.0	1.9	781.5	0.3	785.8	2.2	781.4	1.6
1968	802.9	9.0	813.1	5.2	825.8	6.4	825.7	-0.0	816.9	4.5
1969	833.5	3.8	837.6	2.0	839.1	0.7	844.2	2.5	838.6	2.7
1970	853.1	4.3	854.9	0.8	860.7	2.7	867.5	3.2	859.1	2.4
1971	870.4	1.3	873.5	1.4	873.5	-	880.7	3.3	874.5	1.8
1972	886.2	2.5	908.0	10.2	920.7	5.7	936.7	7.1	912.9	4.4
1973	946.5	4.3	938.5	-3.3	945.3	2.9	941.3	-1.7	942.9	3.3
1974	929.5	-4.9	926.3	-1.4	927.5	0.5	914.6	-5.4	924.5	-2.0
1975	919.1	2.0	938.3	8.6	946.2	3.4	949.5	1.4	938.3	1.5
1976	968.4	8.2	981.6	5.6	990.1	3.5	999.1	3.7	984.8	5.0
1977	1,005.6	2.6	1,005.0	-0.2	1,006.5	0.6	1,024.4	7.3	1,010.4	2.6
1978	1,029.9	2.2	1,040.5	4.2	1,050.3	3.8	1,062.1	4.6	1,045.7	3.5
1979	1,066.7	1.7	1,061.6	-1.9	1,070.8	3.5	1,079.7	3.4	1,069.7	2.3
1980	1,076.1	-1.3	1,061.7	-5.2	1,058.6	-1.2	1,063.8	2.0	1,065.1	-0.4
1981	1,073.3	3.6	1,075.2	0.7	1,074.0	-0.4	1,074.6	0.2	1,074.3	0.9
1982	1,075.5	0.3	1,075.9	0.1	1,080.9	1.9	1,090.2	3.5	1,080.6	0.6
1983	1,095.4	1.9	1,104.7	3.4	1,120.0	5.7	1,129.5	3.4	1,112.4	2.9
1984	1,135.7	2.2	1,153.8	6.5	1,156.4	0.9	1,161.2	1.7	1,151.8	3.5
1985	1,167.7	2.3	1,175.0	2.5	1,181.5	2.2	1,189.3	2.7	1,178.3	2.3
1986	1,204.0	5.0	1,215.5	3.9	1,217.0	0.5	1,227.0	3.3	1,215.9	3.2
1987	1,233.3	2.1	1,240.6	2.4	1,239.8	-0.3	1,243.2	1.1	1,239.3	1.9
1988	1,254.9	3.8	1,266.8	3.8	1,281.0	4.6	1,294.8	4.4	1,274.4	2.8
1989	1,295.3	0.2	1,295.6	0.1	1,308.2	3.9	1,315.0	2.1	1,303.5	2.3
1990	1,319.2	1.3	1,316.9	-0.7	1,319.8	0.9	1,308.4	-3.4	1,316.1	1.0
1991	1,300.6	-2.4	1,308.0	2.3	1,307.1	-0.3	1,295.7	-3.4	1,302.9	-1.0
1992	1,314.4	5.9	1,312.0	-0.7	1,321.1	2.8	1,339.8	5.8	1,321.8	1.5
1993	1,336.9	-0.9	1,344.7	2.4	1,354.2	2.9	1,359.8	1.7	1,348.9	2.1
1994	1,372.7	3.8	1,383.7	3.2	1,397.2	4.0	1,408.4	3.2	1,390.5	3.1
1995	1,416.8	2.4	1,423.5	1.9	1,425.3	0.5	-	-	-	-

Source: "National Income and Product Account Tables: Selected NIPA Tables," *Survey of Current Business*, November 1995, U.S. Department of Commerce, Bureau of Economic Analysis, National Income and Wealth Division. - indicates that no data are available.

Gross Domestic Product
Personal consumption expenditures
Services - Actual Dollars

In billions of actual dollars and percent. Quarterly data are seasonally adjusted and annualized. Growth rates for quarters are compound annual growth rates; changes from year to year are percentage changes.

Year	1st Quarter	% Change	2nd Quarter	% Change	3rd Quarter	% Change	4th Quarter	% Change	TOTAL	% Change
1959	122.8	-	125.5	9.1	128.4	9.6	131.1	8.7	127.0	-
1960	133.3	6.9	135.5	6.8	136.5	3.0	138.7	6.6	136.0	7.1
1961	140.6	5.6	143.7	9.1	144.9	3.4	147.9	8.5	144.3	6.1
1962	149.5	4.4	152.9	9.4	155.0	5.6	157.5	6.6	153.7	6.5
1963	158.8	3.3	161.1	5.9	165.0	10.0	168.0	7.5	163.2	6.2
1964	171.2	7.8	174.4	7.7	177.7	7.8	181.1	7.9	176.1	7.9
1965	183.7	5.9	187.4	8.3	191.0	7.9	195.7	10.2	189.4	7.6
1966	198.7	6.3	202.8	8.5	206.6	7.7	211.2	9.2	204.8	8.1
1967	215.3	8.0	219.6	8.2	224.5	9.2	228.3	6.9	222.0	8.4
1968	234.3	10.9	240.9	11.8	246.3	9.3	251.9	9.4	243.4	9.6
1969	256.9	8.2	262.4	8.8	267.9	8.7	275.0	11.0	265.5	9.1
1970	281.4	9.6	286.8	7.9	294.6	11.3	301.6	9.8	291.1	9.6
1971	308.6	9.6	316.1	10.1	323.7	10.0	332.1	10.8	320.1	10.0
1972	341.1	11.3	347.5	7.7	355.2	9.2	365.3	11.9	352.3	10.1
1973	371.6	7.1	381.0	10.5	389.4	9.1	397.6	8.7	384.9	9.3
1974	406.3	9.0	419.1	13.2	429.7	10.5	442.4	12.4	424.4	10.3
1975	455.1	12.0	468.6	12.4	480.6	10.6	495.7	13.2	475.0	11.9
1976	510.7	12.7	521.4	8.6	537.7	13.1	557.3	15.4	531.8	12.0
1977	573.4	12.1	588.3	10.8	608.8	14.7	625.5	11.4	599.0	12.6
1978	647.5	14.8	670.4	14.9	687.7	10.7	704.0	9.8	677.4	13.1
1979	724.7	12.3	743.9	11.0	763.7	11.1	790.1	14.6	755.6	11.5
1980	814.5	12.9	831.7	8.7	863.6	16.2	895.9	15.8	851.4	12.7
1981	912.6	7.7	940.6	12.8	966.6	11.5	990.8	10.4	952.6	11.9
1982	1,012.8	9.2	1,032.7	8.1	1,060.8	11.3	1,096.7	14.2	1,050.7	10.3
1983	1,125.1	10.8	1,159.4	12.8	1,188.5	10.4	1,220.2	11.1	1,173.3	11.7
1984	1,242.0	7.3	1,268.5	8.8	1,297.1	9.3	1,327.0	9.5	1,283.6	9.4
1985	1,364.7	11.9	1,395.9	9.5	1,433.8	11.3	1,470.1	10.5	1,416.1	10.3
1986	1,496.9	7.5	1,521.5	6.7	1,548.7	7.3	1,580.2	8.4	1,536.8	8.5
1987	1,615.2	9.2	1,645.8	7.8	1,678.9	8.3	1,715.3	9.0	1,663.8	8.3
1988	1,757.5	10.2	1,794.2	8.6	1,841.2	10.9	1,877.6	8.1	1,817.6	9.2
1989	1,911.4	7.4	1,937.6	5.6	1,969.1	6.7	2,014.5	9.5	1,958.1	7.7
1990	2,045.3	6.3	2,104.1	12.0	2,149.8	9.0	2,171.0	4.0	2,117.5	8.1
1991	2,193.5	4.2	2,228.6	6.6	2,256.3	5.1	2,290.7	6.2	2,242.3	5.9
1992	2,350.4	10.8	2,393.3	7.5	2,420.1	4.6	2,473.9	9.2	2,409.4	7.5
1993	2,505.3	5.2	2,535.4	4.9	2,572.9	6.0	2,604.6	5.0	2,554.6	6.0
1994	2,636.8	5.0	2,675.4	6.0	2,705.6	4.6	2,734.4	4.3	2,688.1	5.2
1995	2,771.7	5.6	2,817.9	6.8	2,857.8	5.8	-	-	-	-

Source: "National Income and Product Account Tables: Selected NIPA Tables," *Survey of Current Business*, November 1995, U.S. Department of Commerce, Bureau of Economic Analysis, National Income and Wealth Division. - indicates that no data are available.

Gross Domestic Product

Personal consumption expenditures
Services - Chained (1992) Dollars

In billions of chained (1992) dollars and percent. Quarterly data are seasonally adjusted and annualized. Growth rates for quarters are compound annual growth rates; changes from year to year are percentage changes.

Year	1st Quarter	% Change	2nd Quarter	% Change	3rd Quarter	% Change	4th Quarter	% Change	TOTAL	% Change
1959	-	-	-	-	692.9	-	702.6	5.7	687.4	-
1960	711.0	4.9	717.3	3.6	717.1	-0.1	724.3	4.1	717.4	4.4
1961	731.5	4.0	744.7	7.4	748.3	1.9	761.5	7.2	746.5	4.1
1962	768.6	3.8	780.5	6.3	787.6	3.7	797.0	4.9	783.4	4.9
1963	801.2	2.1	810.1	4.5	826.0	8.1	837.3	5.6	818.7	4.5
1964	850.4	6.4	862.6	5.9	874.4	5.6	886.2	5.5	868.4	6.1
1965	894.6	3.8	907.5	5.9	919.8	5.5	936.3	7.4	914.6	5.3
1966	945.2	3.9	956.8	5.0	965.1	3.5	976.8	4.9	961.0	5.1
1967	989.7	5.4	1,002.0	5.1	1,015.6	5.5	1,023.0	2.9	1,007.6	4.8
1968	1,036.2	5.3	1,053.6	6.9	1,067.4	5.3	1,080.9	5.2	1,059.6	5.2
1969	1,092.5	4.4	1,104.1	4.3	1,115.5	4.2	1,130.8	5.6	1,110.8	4.8
1970	1,141.8	3.9	1,148.4	2.3	1,161.9	4.8	1,169.8	2.7	1,155.4	4.0
1971	1,179.7	3.4	1,191.0	3.9	1,201.3	3.5	1,219.5	6.2	1,197.9	3.7
1972	1,239.1	6.6	1,252.1	4.3	1,267.4	5.0	1,291.2	7.7	1,262.5	5.4
1973	1,302.7	3.6	1,316.5	4.3	1,325.3	2.7	1,333.0	2.3	1,319.4	4.5
1974	1,335.9	0.9	1,348.2	3.7	1,354.5	1.9	1,366.1	3.5	1,351.2	2.4
1975	1,377.6	3.4	1,395.2	5.2	1,402.5	2.1	1,418.0	4.5	1,398.3	3.5
1976	1,436.1	5.2	1,445.7	2.7	1,461.7	4.5	1,484.7	6.4	1,457.1	4.2
1977	1,497.2	3.4	1,504.8	2.0	1,527.1	6.1	1,543.6	4.4	1,518.2	4.2
1978	1,565.4	5.8	1,587.6	5.8	1,598.5	2.8	1,605.7	1.8	1,589.3	4.7
1979	1,625.0	4.9	1,636.8	2.9	1,641.5	1.2	1,656.2	3.6	1,639.8	3.2
1980	1,663.0	1.7	1,653.0	-2.4	1,672.8	4.9	1,694.0	5.2	1,670.7	1.9
1981	1,682.1	-2.8	1,697.6	3.7	1,700.8	0.8	1,703.9	0.7	1,696.1	1.5
1982	1,710.7	1.6	1,718.1	1.7	1,729.3	2.6	1,754.6	6.0	1,728.2	1.9
1983	1,773.4	4.4	1,801.6	6.5	1,819.1	3.9	1,841.8	5.1	1,809.0	4.7
1984	1,855.2	2.9	1,870.5	3.3	1,890.9	4.4	1,915.5	5.3	1,883.0	4.1
1985	1,945.2	6.3	1,962.8	3.7	1,989.3	5.5	2,011.8	4.6	1,977.3	5.0
1986	2,020.1	1.7	2,030.5	2.1	2,047.0	3.3	2,067.8	4.1	2,041.4	3.2
1987	2,097.0	5.8	2,118.5	4.2	2,138.0	3.7	2,154.1	3.0	2,126.9	4.2
1988	2,185.8	6.0	2,200.4	2.7	2,224.6	4.5	2,238.9	2.6	2,212.4	4.0
1989	2,247.0	1.5	2,252.2	0.9	2,264.4	2.2	2,285.8	3.8	2,262.3	2.3
1990	2,295.7	1.7	2,321.1	4.5	2,337.3	2.8	2,331.2	-1.0	2,321.3	2.6
1991	2,325.3	-1.0	2,341.5	2.8	2,345.0	0.6	2,352.0	1.2	2,341.0	0.8
1992	2,383.2	5.4	2,403.2	3.4	2,413.6	1.7	2,437.6	4.0	2,409.4	2.9
1993	2,447.0	1.6	2,454.9	1.3	2,476.7	3.6	2,488.6	1.9	2,466.8	2.4
1994	2,497.0	1.4	2,519.0	3.6	2,526.3	1.2	2,535.1	1.4	2,519.4	2.1
1995	2,548.1	2.1	2,569.6	3.4	2,586.9	2.7	-	-	-	-

Source: "National Income and Product Account Tables: Selected NIPA Tables," *Survey of Current Business*, November 1995, U.S. Department of Commerce, Bureau of Economic Analysis, National Income and Wealth Division. - indicates that no data are available.

GROSS PRIVATE DOMESTIC INVESTMENT
Component of Gross Domestic Product

Gross Private Domestic Investment (GPDI) accounts for all expenditures on building and structures by corporations and individuals, all durable equipment ("capital goods") used in the production of goods and services (e.g., tooling, refineries, power plants, transmission lines, etc.), and change in business inventories. Excluded from this category are investments made by government (accounted for under *Government Purchases of Goods and Services*) and capital goods exports less imports (accounted for under *Net Exports of Goods and Services*).

The category is subdivided into Fixed Investment and Change in Business Inventories as follows:

> *Fixed Investment*
>> Nonresidential
>>> Structures
>>> Producers' durable equipment
>> Residential
> *Change in business inventories*
>> Nonfarm
>> Farm

GPDI represented 14.8 percent of real GDP in 1994, up substantially from the 1992 level (12.7 percent).

Fixed Investment

Nonresidential. Nonresidential fixed investment represents expenditures on permanent production facilities and equipment used by the private sector—the engine of economic activity. The category includes farm structures and farm machinery but excludes all investments made by government at all level, e.g., highways and bridges or government owned and operated production facilities. BEA estimates for the category are obtained under the headings of nonfarm buildings, public utilities, mining, other nonfarm structures, farm buildings, equipment except autos, and new and used autos; autos included in this category are used for business purposes; trucks are included under "equipment except autos." Each category has different sources of data and methods for obtaining estimates.

Residential. Residential fixed investments include permanent-site single-family housing units; multifamily housing units; mobile homes; and additions, alterations, and major replacements. Brokers commissions are also included under this category, as are purchases of capital equipment, used in production in a residential environment (e.g. a small printing press, apartment laundromat equipment, etc.).

Change in Business Inventories

Inventories are universally treated as capital investment—although not as fixed investment. Inventories "turn," meaning that stocks are withdrawn for use or sale while new stocks are added from purchases or production. For this reason, inventories, viewed as investments, are measured by comparing inventory levels at two points in time and measuring the change. The value can well be (1) negative if inventory levels have dropped from the first to the second period, (2) zero if no change took place, or (3) positive if inventory level has increased. Inventories may include finished goods (an automobile), work in process (an engine block), and raw materials in various stages (sheet steel, ingots). They may also be commodities like oil or gasoline stocks, grains or potatoes, or livestock.

The BEA subdivides the category into manufacturing and trade, other nonfarm industries, and farm; for each, different sources and estimating methods are used to arrive at quarterly and annual GDP estimates.

Presentation of Data

Data are shown from 1959 to 1995 in quarterly and in annual increments. Changes from one period to the next are shown for each category except Change in Business Inventories, which is already a change from one period to another. Changes from quarter to quarter are annualized, compounded growth rates as explained in the section on Gross National Product. Changes from year to year are simple percentile changes.

Analytical Uses

At the highest level of abstraction, GPDI is a measure, over time, of the relative proportion of national income that is reinvested to provide future productivity. A long-term decline in GPDI as a percentage of GDP indicates erosion of the nation's productive tooling and private infrastructure. A long-term growth in this measure may herald strong investment with benefits to be reaped in the future. The measure's chief limitation, for such analysis, is that it excludes public investment in infrastructure.

Change in business inventories can be used to evaluate the confidence of producers (signaled by inventory build-ups) or their vulnerability (unusually high inventories as the economy begins to decline). The measure will also reflect the likelihood of economic overheating (when inventories are low and demand is showing strong, sustained growth).

Gross Domestic Product
Gross private domestic investment: Total - Actual Dollars

In billions of actual dollars and percent. Quarterly data are seasonally adjusted and annualized. Growth rates for quarters are compound annual growth rates; changes from year to year are percentage changes.

Year	1st Quarter	% Change	2nd Quarter	% Change	3rd Quarter	% Change	4th Quarter	% Change	TOTAL	% Change
1959	76.7	-	82.7	35.2	76.3	-27.5	79.4	17.3	78.8	-
1960	89.1	58.6	79.4	-36.9	78.4	-4.9	68.1	-43.1	78.8	-
1961	70.1	12.3	75.4	33.8	82.2	41.3	84.0	9.1	77.9	-1.1
1962	89.3	27.7	87.9	-6.1	89.1	5.6	85.4	-15.6	87.9	12.8
1963	90.3	25.0	91.8	6.8	94.7	13.2	96.6	8.3	93.4	6.3
1964	100.6	17.6	100.4	-0.8	101.5	4.5	104.4	11.9	101.7	8.9
1965	115.8	51.4	115.8	-	119.1	11.9	121.3	7.6	118.0	16.0
1966	130.5	34.0	129.9	-1.8	129.4	-1.5	132.0	8.3	130.4	10.5
1967	127.1	-14.0	122.7	-13.1	128.5	20.3	133.9	17.9	128.0	-1.8
1968	135.8	5.8	141.7	18.5	138.3	-9.3	144.0	17.5	139.9	9.3
1969	154.5	32.5	154.0	-1.3	158.7	12.8	153.0	-13.6	155.0	10.8
1970	148.6	-11.0	150.5	5.2	153.3	7.7	148.6	-11.7	150.2	-3.1
1971	169.2	68.1	176.2	17.6	180.9	11.1	177.8	-6.7	176.0	17.2
1972	191.8	35.4	203.3	26.2	209.6	13.0	217.9	16.8	205.6	16.8
1973	232.6	29.8	240.6	14.5	239.4	-2.0	258.8	36.6	242.9	18.1
1974	241.3	-24.4	245.2	6.6	242.0	-5.1	254.0	21.4	245.6	1.1
1975	211.5	-51.9	209.8	-3.2	234.6	56.3	245.6	20.1	225.4	-8.2
1976	271.4	49.1	285.0	21.6	289.6	6.6	300.3	15.6	286.6	27.2
1977	320.4	29.6	353.4	48.0	378.1	31.0	374.5	-3.8	356.6	24.4
1978	389.6	17.1	426.5	43.6	444.4	17.9	462.7	17.5	430.8	20.8
1979	471.4	7.7	482.6	9.8	486.2	3.0	483.2	-2.4	480.9	11.6
1980	493.5	8.8	449.7	-31.0	430.6	-15.9	489.9	67.5	465.9	-3.1
1981	553.0	62.4	537.7	-10.6	571.7	27.8	562.5	-6.3	556.2	19.4
1982	512.1	-31.3	517.2	4.0	508.6	-6.5	466.3	-29.3	501.1	-9.9
1983	479.8	12.1	526.2	44.7	562.2	30.3	620.2	48.1	547.1	9.2
1984	697.3	59.8	715.6	10.9	732.8	10.0	716.5	-8.6	715.6	30.8
1985	704.8	-6.4	711.9	4.1	706.7	-2.9	737.0	18.3	715.1	-0.1
1986	752.1	8.5	730.9	-10.8	698.5	-16.6	708.7	6.0	722.5	1.0
1987	729.5	12.3	732.2	1.5	734.0	1.0	793.1	36.3	747.2	3.4
1988	756.8	-17.1	767.4	5.7	776.4	4.8	795.1	10.0	773.9	3.6
1989	829.1	18.2	835.9	3.3	831.8	-1.9	820.0	-5.6	829.2	7.1
1990	822.5	1.2	835.2	6.3	804.9	-13.7	736.1	-30.1	799.7	-3.6
1991	723.6	-6.6	716.2	-4.0	743.9	16.4	760.9	9.5	736.2	-7.9
1992	755.2	-3.0	790.8	20.2	799.7	4.6	816.1	8.5	790.4	7.4
1993	843.6	14.2	855.9	6.0	873.8	8.6	911.2	18.3	871.1	10.2
1994	957.6	22.0	1,016.5	27.0	1,033.6	6.9	1,050.1	6.5	1,014.4	16.5
1995	1,072.0	8.6	1,050.3	-7.9	1,067.1	6.6	-	-	-	-

Source: "National Income and Product Account Tables: Selected NIPA Tables," *Survey of Current Business*, November 1995, U.S. Department of Commerce, Bureau of Economic Analysis, National Income and Wealth Division. - indicates that no data are available.

Gross Domestic Product

Gross private domestic investment: Total - Chained (1992) Dollars

In billions of chained (1992) dollars and percent. Quarterly data are seasonally adjusted and annualized. Growth rates for quarters are compound annual growth rates; changes from year to year are percentage changes.

Year	1st Quarter	% Change	2nd Quarter	% Change	3rd Quarter	% Change	4th Quarter	% Change	TOTAL	% Change
1959	-	-	-	-	269.5	-	272.4	4.4	274.2	-
1960	308.1	63.7	275.1	-36.4	268.3	-9.5	230.5	-45.5	270.5	-1.3
1961	238.3	14.2	255.2	31.5	279.7	44.3	287.7	11.9	265.2	-2.0
1962	304.3	25.2	296.4	-10.0	302.0	7.8	291.3	-13.4	298.5	12.6
1963	308.8	26.3	313.0	5.6	324.3	15.2	326.6	2.9	318.1	6.6
1964	342.8	21.4	340.9	-2.2	345.2	5.1	349.6	5.2	344.6	8.3
1965	385.7	48.2	390.3	4.9	393.4	3.2	400.4	7.3	392.5	13.9
1966	429.7	32.6	422.5	-6.5	419.7	-2.6	422.2	2.4	423.5	7.9
1967	410.4	-10.7	394.4	-14.7	406.7	13.1	416.1	9.6	406.9	-3.9
1968	421.2	5.0	439.1	18.1	427.0	-10.6	431.8	4.6	429.8	5.6
1969	459.9	28.7	455.5	-3.8	464.5	8.1	437.8	-21.1	454.4	5.7
1970	421.8	-13.8	420.6	-1.1	428.6	7.8	407.1	-18.6	419.5	-7.7
1971	457.7	59.8	473.2	14.2	476.5	2.8	462.3	-11.4	467.4	11.4
1972	493.9	30.3	523.9	26.6	532.2	6.5	538.3	4.7	522.1	11.7
1973	575.6	30.7	587.6	8.6	571.1	-10.8	599.9	21.7	583.5	11.8
1974	561.7	-23.1	559.7	-1.4	529.5	-19.9	526.9	-1.9	544.4	-6.7
1975	426.3	-57.2	413.4	-11.6	455.4	47.3	467.0	10.6	440.5	-19.1
1976	515.9	48.9	538.4	18.6	540.0	1.2	551.9	9.1	536.6	21.8
1977	582.8	24.3	629.5	36.1	658.6	19.8	637.7	-12.1	627.1	16.9
1978	646.8	5.8	683.4	24.6	701.3	10.9	712.3	6.4	686.0	9.4
1979	711.4	-0.5	717.3	3.4	703.4	-7.5	686.1	-9.5	704.5	2.7
1980	686.1	-	611.7	-36.8	569.1	-25.1	638.0	58.0	626.2	-11.1
1981	701.8	46.4	666.4	-18.7	709.1	28.2	681.3	-14.8	689.7	10.1
1982	608.6	-36.3	604.1	-2.9	596.8	-4.7	551.9	-26.9	590.4	-14.4
1983	570.1	13.9	624.5	44.0	667.2	30.3	729.2	42.7	647.8	9.7
1984	812.0	53.8	832.7	10.6	847.7	7.4	834.0	-6.3	831.6	28.4
1985	820.1	-6.5	827.4	3.6	822.6	-2.3	846.5	12.1	829.2	-0.3
1986	859.3	6.2	826.3	-14.5	782.4	-19.6	786.9	2.3	813.8	-1.9
1987	808.1	11.2	806.0	-1.0	805.1	-0.4	862.9	32.0	820.5	0.8
1988	815.5	-20.2	821.0	2.7	827.9	3.4	839.7	5.8	826.0	0.7
1989	868.3	14.3	871.0	1.2	862.4	-3.9	845.9	-7.4	861.9	4.3
1990	844.1	-0.8	856.1	5.8	820.8	-15.5	748.1	-31.0	817.3	-5.2
1991	725.5	-11.5	718.0	-4.1	744.9	15.8	762.4	9.7	737.7	-9.7
1992	757.9	-2.3	792.8	19.7	798.6	3.0	812.4	7.1	790.4	7.1
1993	834.8	11.5	843.2	4.1	857.6	7.0	893.4	17.8	857.3	8.5
1994	933.5	19.2	984.6	23.8	994.1	3.9	1,006.3	5.0	979.6	14.3
1995	1,024.2	7.3	998.3	-9.7	1,008.9	4.3	-	-	-	-

Source: "National Income and Product Account Tables: Selected NIPA Tables," *Survey of Current Business*, November 1995, U.S. Department of Commerce, Bureau of Economic Analysis, National Income and Wealth Division. - indicates that no data are available.

Gross Domestic Product
Gross private domestic investment
Fixed investment - Actual Dollars

In billions of actual dollars and percent. Quarterly data are seasonally adjusted and annualized. Growth rates for quarters are compound annual growth rates; changes from year to year are percentage changes.

Year	1st Quarter	% Change	2nd Quarter	% Change	3rd Quarter	% Change	4th Quarter	% Change	TOTAL	% Change
1959	72.3	-	74.9	15.2	76.1	6.6	75.1	-5.2	74.6	-
1960	77.8	15.2	76.3	-7.5	74.2	-10.6	73.8	-2.1	75.5	1.2
1961	72.7	-5.8	73.8	6.2	75.5	9.5	78.0	13.9	75.0	-0.7
1962	79.8	9.6	82.2	12.6	82.9	3.5	82.4	-2.4	81.8	9.1
1963	83.3	4.4	86.9	18.4	88.8	9.0	91.8	14.2	87.7	7.2
1964	95.0	14.7	95.6	2.6	97.2	6.9	99.0	7.6	96.7	10.3
1965	103.5	19.5	106.6	12.5	109.6	11.7	113.4	14.6	108.3	12.0
1966	117.0	13.3	117.4	1.4	117.3	-0.3	114.9	-7.9	116.7	7.8
1967	112.7	-7.4	116.2	13.0	118.1	6.7	123.3	18.8	117.6	0.8
1968	127.5	14.3	128.0	1.6	130.7	8.7	137.0	20.7	130.8	11.2
1969	142.7	17.7	144.8	6.0	148.3	10.0	146.2	-5.5	145.5	11.2
1970	146.5	0.8	146.5	-	148.6	5.9	150.6	5.5	148.1	1.8
1971	156.8	17.5	165.7	24.7	170.7	12.6	176.8	15.1	167.5	13.1
1972	187.2	25.7	191.7	10.0	195.8	8.8	208.1	27.6	195.7	16.8
1973	219.0	22.7	224.7	10.8	228.7	7.3	229.1	0.7	225.4	15.2
1974	228.0	-1.9	231.2	5.7	235.9	8.4	231.0	-8.1	231.5	2.7
1975	223.9	-11.7	225.9	3.6	234.4	15.9	242.6	14.7	231.7	0.1
1976	255.2	22.5	264.0	14.5	270.4	10.1	288.9	30.3	269.6	16.4
1977	306.4	26.5	330.2	34.9	341.8	14.8	355.7	17.3	333.5	23.7
1978	364.8	10.6	398.8	42.8	417.1	19.7	433.9	17.1	403.6	21.0
1979	446.8	12.4	455.1	7.6	474.9	18.6	479.2	3.7	464.0	15.0
1980	484.6	4.6	450.1	-25.6	464.6	13.5	494.8	28.6	473.5	2.0
1981	511.6	14.3	525.3	11.1	533.6	6.5	541.8	6.3	528.1	11.5
1982	531.5	-7.4	517.8	-9.9	505.0	-9.5	507.9	2.3	515.6	-2.4
1983	514.6	5.4	534.0	16.0	563.4	23.9	596.0	25.2	552.0	7.1
1984	616.0	14.1	645.4	20.5	659.3	8.9	671.6	7.7	648.1	17.4
1985	680.0	5.1	686.9	4.1	685.8	-0.6	702.8	10.3	688.9	6.3
1986	707.0	2.4	710.9	2.2	712.6	1.0	721.1	4.9	712.9	3.5
1987	705.3	-8.5	719.3	8.2	732.0	7.3	735.1	1.7	722.9	1.4
1988	744.3	5.1	760.9	9.2	766.8	3.1	780.3	7.2	763.1	5.6
1989	790.1	5.1	794.2	2.1	808.1	7.2	797.5	-5.1	797.5	4.5
1990	813.9	8.5	794.0	-9.4	791.2	-1.4	767.5	-11.5	791.6	-0.7
1991	739.7	-13.7	736.2	-1.9	738.6	1.3	739.5	0.5	738.5	-6.7
1992	755.4	8.9	780.5	14.0	788.1	4.0	809.7	11.4	783.4	6.1
1993	823.8	7.1	834.3	5.2	851.8	8.7	892.3	20.4	850.5	8.6
1994	917.4	11.7	942.0	11.2	968.9	11.9	991.4	9.6	954.9	12.3
1995	1,013.9	9.4	1,016.3	1.0	1,036.5	8.2	-	-	-	-

Source: "National Income and Product Account Tables: Selected NIPA Tables," *Survey of Current Business*, November 1995, U.S. Department of Commerce, Bureau of Economic Analysis, National Income and Wealth Division. - indicates that no data are available.

Gross Domestic Product

Gross private domestic investment
Fixed investment - Chained (1992) Dollars

In billions of chained (1992) dollars and percent. Quarterly data are seasonally adjusted and annualized. Growth rates for quarters are compound annual growth rates; changes from year to year are percentage changes.

Year	1st Quarter	% Change	2nd Quarter	% Change	3rd Quarter	% Change	4th Quarter	% Change	TOTAL	% Change
1959	-	-	-	-	272.1	-	269.0	-4.5	267.1	-
1960	277.8	13.7	271.7	-8.5	264.2	-10.6	263.0	-1.8	269.2	0.8
1961	259.9	-4.6	263.2	5.2	269.6	10.1	278.7	14.2	267.9	-0.5
1962	284.5	8.6	293.6	13.4	295.9	3.2	294.1	-2.4	292.0	9.0
1963	297.2	4.3	310.5	19.1	318.4	10.6	328.5	13.3	313.7	7.4
1964	341.3	16.5	340.2	-1.3	345.5	6.4	347.7	2.6	343.7	9.6
1965	364.0	20.1	373.8	11.2	383.7	11.0	392.2	9.2	378.5	10.1
1966	406.8	15.7	401.2	-5.4	400.5	-0.7	387.7	-12.2	399.1	5.4
1967	378.3	-9.4	388.4	11.1	392.6	4.4	404.9	13.1	391.0	-2.0
1968	414.3	9.6	412.0	-2.2	417.9	5.9	428.1	10.1	418.1	6.9
1969	441.2	12.8	442.8	1.5	449.9	6.6	437.9	-10.2	442.9	5.9
1970	435.5	-2.2	425.6	-8.8	433.2	7.3	434.1	0.8	432.1	-2.4
1971	444.0	9.4	462.3	17.5	470.5	7.3	482.7	10.8	464.9	7.6
1972	504.7	19.5	513.6	7.2	519.2	4.4	543.6	20.2	520.3	11.9
1973	566.8	18.2	571.2	3.1	569.1	-1.5	562.7	-4.4	567.5	9.1
1974	549.4	-9.1	541.0	-6.0	530.9	-7.3	499.6	-21.6	530.2	-6.6
1975	467.8	-23.1	461.1	-5.6	473.0	10.7	482.2	8.0	471.0	-11.2
1976	502.4	17.8	510.6	6.7	515.5	3.9	541.9	22.1	517.6	9.9
1977	564.1	17.4	595.2	23.9	602.3	4.9	613.1	7.4	593.7	14.7
1978	616.6	2.3	660.2	31.4	676.8	10.4	689.5	7.7	660.8	11.3
1979	695.1	3.3	690.4	-2.7	702.6	7.3	694.1	-4.8	695.6	5.3
1980	685.5	-4.9	622.5	-32.0	629.3	4.4	656.3	18.3	648.4	-6.8
1981	660.7	2.7	662.6	1.2	661.5	-0.7	657.6	-2.3	660.6	1.9
1982	636.0	-12.5	612.8	-13.8	595.0	-11.1	597.7	1.8	610.4	-7.6
1983	608.4	7.4	633.4	17.5	668.9	24.4	706.1	24.2	654.2	7.2
1984	729.3	13.8	760.7	18.4	773.9	7.1	785.7	6.2	762.4	16.5
1985	792.9	3.7	800.1	3.7	794.9	-2.6	809.1	7.3	799.3	4.8
1986	809.3	0.1	806.6	-1.3	800.4	-3.0	803.9	1.8	805.0	0.7
1987	784.2	-9.4	797.7	7.1	809.5	6.0	806.3	-1.6	799.4	-0.7
1988	807.1	0.4	819.0	6.0	820.6	0.8	826.4	2.9	818.3	2.4
1989	831.9	2.7	830.9	-0.5	840.5	4.7	824.7	-7.3	832.0	1.7
1990	834.7	4.9	811.2	-10.8	803.1	-3.9	774.4	-13.5	805.8	-3.1
1991	742.6	-15.4	739.4	-1.7	741.0	0.9	742.0	0.5	741.3	-8.0
1992	758.3	9.1	782.4	13.3	787.3	2.5	805.8	9.7	783.4	5.7
1993	815.4	4.9	821.1	2.8	835.4	7.2	873.5	19.5	836.4	6.8
1994	892.4	8.9	911.4	8.8	930.8	8.8	949.7	8.4	921.1	10.1
1995	969.6	8.6	966.1	-1.4	980.6	6.1	-	-	-	-

Source: "National Income and Product Account Tables: Selected NIPA Tables," *Survey of Current Business*, November 1995, U.S. Department of Commerce, Bureau of Economic Analysis, National Income and Wealth Division. - indicates that no data are available.

Gross Domestic Product
Gross private domestic investment
Fixed investment - Nonresidential - Actual Dollars

In billions of actual dollars and percent. Quarterly data are seasonally adjusted and annualized. Growth rates for quarters are compound annual growth rates; changes from year to year are percentage changes.

Year	1st Quarter	% Change	2nd Quarter	% Change	3rd Quarter	% Change	4th Quarter	% Change	TOTAL	% Change
1959	44.5	-	46.1	15.2	47.8	15.6	47.6	-1.7	46.5	-
1960	49.4	16.0	50.2	6.6	48.9	-10.0	48.5	-3.2	49.2	5.8
1961	47.4	-8.8	48.3	7.8	48.6	2.5	50.2	13.8	48.6	-1.2
1962	51.4	9.9	53.0	13.0	53.7	5.4	53.2	-3.7	52.8	8.6
1963	53.1	-0.7	54.7	12.6	56.3	12.2	58.1	13.4	55.6	5.3
1964	59.6	10.7	61.4	12.6	63.5	14.4	65.2	11.1	62.4	12.2
1965	69.7	30.6	72.4	16.4	75.3	17.0	78.9	20.5	74.1	18.8
1966	82.2	17.8	84.2	10.1	85.3	5.3	85.7	1.9	84.4	13.9
1967	84.3	-6.4	84.5	1.0	84.7	1.0	87.2	12.3	85.2	0.9
1968	90.6	16.5	89.9	-3.1	91.8	8.7	96.0	19.6	92.1	8.1
1969	99.5	15.4	101.4	7.9	105.1	15.4	105.6	1.9	102.9	11.7
1970	105.8	0.8	107.1	5.0	108.2	4.2	105.7	-8.9	106.7	3.7
1971	108.2	9.8	111.1	11.2	112.4	4.8	115.3	10.7	111.7	4.7
1972	120.6	19.7	123.5	10.0	126.3	9.4	133.8	26.0	126.1	12.9
1973	141.2	24.0	149.0	24.0	153.7	13.2	156.4	7.2	150.0	19.0
1974	159.0	6.8	163.7	12.4	168.5	12.3	171.0	6.1	165.6	10.4
1975	166.3	-10.5	166.0	-0.7	169.7	9.2	173.9	10.3	169.0	2.1
1976	179.1	12.5	183.4	10.0	189.8	14.7	196.4	14.7	187.2	10.8
1977	208.8	27.7	218.5	19.9	226.8	16.1	238.8	22.9	223.2	19.2
1978	243.8	8.6	268.2	46.5	281.3	21.0	294.8	20.6	272.0	21.9
1979	308.2	19.5	314.2	8.0	331.4	23.8	338.0	8.2	323.0	18.8
1980	350.0	15.0	338.9	-12.1	348.7	12.1	363.5	18.1	350.3	8.5
1981	379.7	19.1	396.4	18.8	413.4	18.3	432.2	19.5	405.4	15.7
1982	426.7	-5.0	415.0	-10.5	402.6	-11.4	395.1	-7.2	409.9	1.1
1983	383.7	-11.1	385.8	2.2	400.9	16.6	427.4	29.2	399.4	-2.6
1984	440.4	12.7	464.0	23.2	478.4	13.0	490.3	10.3	468.3	17.3
1985	496.6	5.2	504.1	6.2	498.2	-4.6	508.9	8.9	502.0	7.2
1986	502.4	-5.0	492.6	-7.6	488.6	-3.2	495.6	5.9	494.8	-1.4
1987	480.0	-12.0	490.1	8.7	504.6	12.4	506.8	1.8	495.4	0.1
1988	515.9	7.4	529.4	10.9	533.2	2.9	543.7	8.1	530.6	7.1
1989	553.0	7.0	562.0	6.7	579.0	12.7	570.9	-5.5	566.2	6.7
1990	581.2	7.4	571.6	-6.4	580.3	6.2	570.6	-6.5	575.9	1.7
1991	555.4	-10.2	550.2	-3.7	544.3	-4.2	539.2	-3.7	547.3	-5.0
1992	544.1	3.7	556.8	9.7	561.0	3.1	569.6	6.3	557.9	1.9
1993	580.3	7.7	591.1	7.7	599.2	5.6	624.6	18.1	598.8	7.3
1994	638.8	9.4	653.5	9.5	678.5	16.2	697.9	11.9	667.2	11.4
1995	723.6	15.6	734.4	6.1	746.3	6.6	-		-	-

Source: "National Income and Product Account Tables: Selected NIPA Tables," *Survey of Current Business*, November 1995, U.S. Department of Commerce, Bureau of Economic Analysis, National Income and Wealth Division. - indicates that no data are available.

Gross Domestic Product
Gross private domestic investment
Fixed investment - Nonresidential - Chained (1992) Dollars

In billions of chained (1992) dollars and percent. Quarterly data are seasonally adjusted and annualized. Growth rates for quarters are compound annual growth rates; changes from year to year are percentage changes.

Year	1st Quarter	% Change	2nd Quarter	% Change	3rd Quarter	% Change	4th Quarter	% Change	TOTAL	% Change
1959	-	-	-	-	151.6	-	151.4	-0.5	147.7	-
1960	156.7	14.8	158.7	5.2	154.6	-9.9	153.6	-2.6	155.9	5.6
1961	150.6	-7.6	153.2	7.1	154.5	3.4	159.8	14.4	154.5	-0.9
1962	163.3	9.1	168.6	13.6	170.8	5.3	169.2	-3.7	168.0	8.7
1963	168.7	-1.2	173.7	12.4	178.8	12.3	184.5	13.4	176.4	5.0
1964	189.4	11.1	194.1	10.3	200.6	14.1	204.5	8.0	197.1	11.7
1965	218.7	30.8	226.6	15.3	235.0	15.7	244.9	17.9	231.3	17.4
1966	255.6	18.7	259.3	5.9	262.0	4.2	260.8	-1.8	259.4	12.1
1967	255.0	-8.6	254.4	-0.9	253.4	-1.6	258.6	8.5	255.3	-1.6
1968	266.4	12.6	261.6	-7.0	264.9	5.1	272.7	12.3	266.4	4.3
1969	280.4	11.8	283.2	4.1	290.6	10.9	288.4	-3.0	285.6	7.2
1970	285.9	-3.4	284.3	-2.2	285.8	2.1	275.3	-13.9	282.8	-1.0
1971	277.9	3.8	281.8	5.7	282.3	0.7	287.7	7.9	282.4	-0.1
1972	297.6	14.5	302.5	6.8	307.3	6.5	323.6	23.0	307.7	9.0
1973	339.0	20.4	352.5	16.9	358.2	6.6	360.5	2.6	352.5	14.6
1974	360.2	-0.3	359.2	-1.1	354.5	-5.1	343.6	-11.7	354.4	0.5
1975	321.5	-23.4	312.8	-10.4	315.9	4.0	319.1	4.1	317.3	-10.5
1976	324.9	7.5	328.4	4.4	335.4	8.8	341.6	7.6	332.6	4.8
1977	357.6	20.1	367.8	11.9	374.6	7.6	387.1	14.0	371.8	11.8
1978	389.1	2.1	421.0	37.1	433.8	12.7	446.5	12.2	422.6	13.7
1979	456.8	9.6	455.9	-0.8	470.3	13.2	470.2	-0.1	463.3	9.6
1980	475.8	4.8	450.4	-19.7	454.1	3.3	464.3	9.3	461.1	-0.5
1981	471.3	6.2	479.5	7.1	490.7	9.7	501.4	9.0	485.7	5.3
1982	488.0	-10.3	469.6	-14.3	454.2	-12.5	445.5	-7.4	464.3	-4.4
1983	435.9	-8.3	440.6	4.4	459.2	18.0	490.0	29.7	456.4	-1.7
1984	505.5	13.3	530.8	21.6	546.3	12.2	558.8	9.5	535.4	17.3
1985	564.6	4.2	572.7	5.9	563.5	-6.3	572.9	6.8	568.4	6.2
1986	563.8	-6.2	548.0	-10.7	538.7	-6.6	543.4	3.5	548.5	-3.5
1987	526.2	-12.1	537.5	8.9	553.8	12.7	552.0	-1.3	542.4	-1.1
1988	556.1	3.0	567.1	8.2	568.0	0.6	572.9	3.5	566.0	4.4
1989	579.5	4.7	586.6	5.0	600.5	9.8	588.8	-7.6	588.8	4.0
1990	595.3	4.5	583.4	-7.8	588.1	3.3	573.9	-9.3	585.2	-0.6
1991	555.1	-12.5	550.9	-3.0	545.3	-4.0	539.5	-4.2	547.7	-6.4
1992	544.4	3.7	557.5	10.0	560.6	2.2	569.1	6.2	557.9	1.9
1993	577.5	6.0	586.4	6.3	593.1	4.6	617.6	17.6	593.6	6.4
1994	628.6	7.3	639.5	7.1	660.4	13.7	679.7	12.2	652.1	9.9
1995	704.4	15.3	710.6	3.6	719.8	5.3	-	-	-	-

Source: "National Income and Product Account Tables: Selected NIPA Tables," *Survey of Current Business*, November 1995, U.S. Department of Commerce, Bureau of Economic Analysis, National Income and Wealth Division. - indicates that no data are available.

Gross Domestic Product
Gross private domestic investment
Fixed investment - Nonresidential - Structures - Actual Dollars

In billions of actual dollars and percent. Quarterly data are seasonally adjusted and annualized. Growth rates for quarters are compound annual growth rates; changes from year to year are percentage changes.

Year	1st Quarter	% Change	2nd Quarter	% Change	3rd Quarter	% Change	4th Quarter	% Change	TOTAL	% Change
1959	17.4	-	18.0	14.5	18.6	14.0	18.5	-2.1	18.1	-
1960	19.4	20.9	19.5	2.1	19.4	-2.0	20.0	13.0	19.6	8.3
1961	19.9	-2.0	19.6	-5.9	19.7	2.1	19.6	-2.0	19.7	0.5
1962	20.0	8.4	20.8	17.0	21.4	12.0	20.9	-9.0	20.8	5.6
1963	20.2	-12.7	21.2	21.3	21.4	3.8	21.9	9.7	21.2	1.9
1964	22.4	9.4	23.4	19.1	24.3	16.3	24.8	8.5	23.7	11.8
1965	26.1	22.7	28.2	36.3	28.5	4.3	30.4	29.5	28.3	19.4
1966	31.1	9.5	31.2	1.3	31.9	9.3	31.2	-8.5	31.3	10.6
1967	31.7	6.6	30.9	-9.7	31.5	8.0	32.0	6.5	31.5	0.6
1968	33.1	14.5	33.2	1.2	33.2	-	34.8	20.7	33.6	6.7
1969	35.8	12.0	36.7	10.4	38.9	26.2	39.4	5.2	37.7	12.2
1970	39.5	1.0	40.3	8.4	40.6	3.0	40.8	2.0	40.3	6.9
1971	41.5	7.0	42.3	7.9	43.1	7.8	43.8	6.7	42.7	6.0
1972	45.8	19.6	46.6	7.2	47.3	6.1	49.0	15.2	47.2	10.5
1973	51.3	20.1	54.1	23.7	56.8	21.5	57.7	6.5	55.0	16.5
1974	59.0	9.3	61.3	16.5	61.4	0.7	63.2	12.3	61.2	11.3
1975	61.7	-9.2	60.4	-8.2	61.3	6.1	62.0	4.6	61.4	0.3
1976	64.1	14.3	65.1	6.4	66.7	10.2	67.8	6.8	65.9	7.3
1977	69.7	11.7	73.6	24.3	76.4	16.1	78.5	11.5	74.6	13.2
1978	79.2	3.6	88.6	56.6	95.8	36.7	102.0	28.5	91.4	22.5
1979	104.8	11.4	110.0	21.4	119.1	37.4	125.7	24.1	114.9	25.7
1980	130.3	15.5	129.8	-1.5	133.6	12.2	141.9	27.3	133.9	16.5
1981	147.5	16.7	158.3	32.7	166.8	23.3	185.7	53.6	164.6	22.9
1982	183.8	-4.0	179.6	-8.8	170.4	-19.0	166.2	-9.5	175.0	6.3
1983	156.7	-21.0	147.8	-20.9	151.0	8.9	155.5	12.5	152.7	-12.7
1984	164.5	25.2	174.4	26.3	181.0	16.0	184.2	7.3	176.0	15.3
1985	193.5	21.8	194.1	1.2	191.0	-6.2	194.6	7.8	193.3	9.8
1986	190.9	-7.4	173.9	-31.1	168.3	-12.3	170.1	4.3	175.8	-9.1
1987	165.4	-10.6	167.3	4.7	175.3	20.5	180.3	11.9	172.1	-2.1
1988	177.4	-6.3	182.5	12.0	181.9	-1.3	183.3	3.1	181.3	5.3
1989	188.3	11.4	188.0	-0.6	196.4	19.1	196.6	0.4	192.3	6.1
1990	201.9	11.2	202.4	1.0	203.5	2.2	195.4	-15.0	200.8	4.4
1991	192.3	-6.2	187.6	-9.4	176.1	-22.4	170.8	-11.5	181.7	-9.5
1992	171.6	1.9	170.4	-2.8	167.6	-6.4	167.1	-1.2	169.2	-6.9
1993	170.2	7.6	169.7	-1.2	171.4	4.1	175.8	10.7	171.8	1.5
1994	171.8	-8.8	179.1	18.1	181.0	4.3	188.8	18.4	180.2	4.9
1995	194.5	12.6	197.6	6.5	202.3	9.9	-	-	-	-

Source: "National Income and Product Account Tables: Selected NIPA Tables," *Survey of Current Business*, November 1995, U.S. Department of Commerce, Bureau of Economic Analysis, National Income and Wealth Division. - indicates that no data are available.

Gross Domestic Product
Gross private domestic investment
Fixed investment - Nonresidential - Structures - Chained (1992) Dollars

In billions of chained (1992) dollars and percent. Quarterly data are seasonally adjusted and annualized. Growth rates for quarters are compound annual growth rates; changes from year to year are percentage changes.

Year	1st Quarter	% Change	2nd Quarter	% Change	3rd Quarter	% Change	4th Quarter	% Change	TOTAL	% Change
1959	-	-	-	-	87.8	-	87.2	-2.7	85.8	-
1960	90.8	17.6	91.9	4.9	92.1	0.9	95.6	16.1	92.6	7.9
1961	95.2	-1.7	93.6	-6.6	93.6	-	93.1	-2.1	93.9	1.4
1962	94.8	7.5	98.2	15.1	100.9	11.5	98.4	-9.5	98.1	4.5
1963	95.0	-13.1	99.4	19.9	100.1	2.8	102.1	8.2	99.2	1.1
1964	104.8	11.0	108.4	14.5	111.9	13.6	112.8	3.3	109.5	10.4
1965	118.6	22.2	126.9	31.1	128.2	4.2	134.1	19.7	126.9	15.9
1966	137.3	9.9	134.6	-7.6	137.6	9.2	133.0	-12.7	135.6	6.9
1967	134.3	4.0	130.5	-10.8	131.8	4.0	132.1	0.9	132.2	-2.5
1968	134.7	8.1	133.5	-3.5	132.6	-2.7	135.4	8.7	134.1	1.4
1969	137.4	6.0	138.5	3.2	145.1	20.5	144.1	-2.7	141.3	5.4
1970	143.0	-3.0	141.5	-4.1	142.1	1.7	140.4	-4.7	141.7	0.3
1971	140.0	-1.1	139.7	-0.9	139.2	-1.4	138.8	-1.1	139.4	-1.6
1972	142.4	10.8	143.2	2.3	143.5	0.8	145.7	6.3	143.7	3.1
1973	150.5	13.8	155.2	13.1	158.7	9.3	157.3	-3.5	155.4	8.1
1974	156.4	-2.3	155.8	-1.5	149.1	-16.1	147.3	-4.7	152.2	-2.1
1975	139.8	-18.9	134.4	-14.6	135.3	2.7	135.4	0.3	136.2	-10.5
1976	139.1	11.4	138.6	-1.4	140.1	4.4	140.5	1.1	139.6	2.5
1977	141.8	3.8	146.3	13.3	148.3	5.6	149.2	2.4	146.4	4.9
1978	147.1	-5.5	159.8	39.3	168.3	23.0	174.3	15.0	162.3	10.9
1979	174.3	-	177.6	7.8	186.5	21.6	192.5	13.5	182.7	12.6
1980	195.8	7.0	191.1	-9.3	193.5	5.1	199.8	13.7	195.0	6.7
1981	198.6	-2.4	205.8	15.3	210.7	9.9	226.4	33.3	210.4	7.9
1982	219.2	-12.1	211.9	-12.7	200.9	-19.2	197.0	-7.5	207.2	-1.5
1983	189.0	-15.3	179.9	-17.9	184.2	9.9	189.9	13.0	185.7	-10.4
1984	200.8	25.0	210.8	21.5	217.4	13.1	219.9	4.7	212.2	14.3
1985	229.3	18.2	229.5	0.3	224.6	-8.3	227.6	5.5	227.8	7.4
1986	222.3	-9.0	201.4	-32.6	194.2	-13.6	195.2	2.1	203.3	-10.8
1987	190.0	-10.2	191.3	2.8	199.4	18.0	202.8	7.0	195.9	-3.6
1988	195.9	-12.9	199.1	6.7	196.4	-5.3	195.9	-1.0	196.8	0.5
1989	199.8	8.2	197.2	-5.1	204.6	15.9	203.2	-2.7	201.2	2.2
1990	206.5	6.7	205.5	-1.9	205.2	-0.6	196.0	-16.8	203.3	1.0
1991	192.2	-7.5	187.2	-10.0	175.5	-22.8	171.4	-9.0	181.6	-10.7
1992	172.7	3.1	171.0	-3.9	167.4	-8.2	165.6	-4.2	169.2	-6.8
1993	167.0	3.4	164.8	-5.2	165.1	0.7	168.2	7.7	166.3	-1.7
1994	163.0	-11.8	169.0	15.6	169.1	0.2	174.3	12.9	168.8	1.5
1995	178.5	10.0	180.0	3.4	182.4	5.4	-	-	-	-

Source: "National Income and Product Account Tables: Selected NIPA Tables," *Survey of Current Business*, November 1995, U.S. Department of Commerce, Bureau of Economic Analysis, National Income and Wealth Division. - indicates that no data are available.

Gross Domestic Product
Gross private domestic investment
Fixed investment - Nonresidential - Producers' durable equipment - Actual Dollars

In billions of actual dollars and percent. Quarterly data are seasonally adjusted and annualized. Growth rates for quarters are compound annual growth rates; changes from year to year are percentage changes.

Year	1st Quarter	% Change	2nd Quarter	% Change	3rd Quarter	% Change	4th Quarter	% Change	TOTAL	% Change
1959	27.1	-	28.1	15.6	29.1	15.0	29.1	-	28.3	-
1960	30.1	14.5	30.7	8.2	29.5	-14.7	28.4	-14.1	29.7	4.9
1961	27.5	-12.1	28.7	18.6	28.9	2.8	30.6	25.7	28.9	-2.7
1962	31.4	10.9	32.2	10.6	32.3	1.2	32.3	-	32.1	11.1
1963	32.9	7.6	33.5	7.5	34.9	17.8	36.2	15.8	34.4	7.2
1964	37.2	11.5	38.0	8.9	39.3	14.4	40.3	10.6	38.7	12.5
1965	43.5	35.7	44.3	7.6	46.8	24.6	48.5	15.3	45.8	18.3
1966	51.1	23.2	53.0	15.7	53.4	3.1	54.5	8.5	53.0	15.7
1967	52.7	-12.6	53.6	7.0	53.2	-3.0	55.3	16.7	53.7	1.3
1968	57.6	17.7	56.7	-6.1	58.6	14.1	61.3	19.7	58.5	8.9
1969	63.7	16.6	64.7	6.4	66.1	8.9	66.2	0.6	65.2	11.5
1970	66.4	1.2	66.8	2.4	67.6	4.9	64.9	-15.0	66.4	1.8
1971	66.7	11.6	68.8	13.2	69.3	2.9	71.5	13.3	69.1	4.1
1972	74.9	20.4	76.9	11.1	78.9	10.8	84.9	34.1	78.9	14.2
1973	89.9	25.7	94.9	24.2	96.8	8.3	98.6	7.6	95.1	20.5
1974	100.0	5.8	102.3	9.5	107.1	20.1	107.8	2.6	104.3	9.7
1975	104.6	-11.4	105.6	3.9	108.4	11.0	111.8	13.1	107.6	3.2
1976	115.0	12.0	118.3	12.0	123.1	17.2	128.6	19.1	121.2	12.6
1977	139.1	36.9	144.8	17.4	150.4	16.4	160.3	29.0	148.7	22.7
1978	164.5	10.9	179.6	42.1	185.6	14.0	192.8	16.4	180.6	21.5
1979	203.4	23.9	204.3	1.8	212.2	16.4	212.3	0.2	208.1	15.2
1980	219.7	14.7	209.1	-17.9	215.1	12.0	221.6	12.6	216.4	4.0
1981	232.1	20.3	238.1	10.7	246.6	15.1	246.5	-0.2	240.9	11.3
1982	242.9	-5.7	235.4	-11.8	232.2	-5.3	228.9	-5.6	234.9	-2.5
1983	227.0	-3.3	238.0	20.8	249.9	21.6	272.0	40.3	246.7	5.0
1984	275.9	5.9	289.6	21.4	297.5	11.4	306.1	12.1	292.3	18.5
1985	303.1	-3.9	310.0	9.4	307.2	-3.6	314.3	9.6	308.7	5.6
1986	311.5	-3.5	318.7	9.6	320.3	2.0	325.5	6.7	319.0	3.3
1987	314.6	-12.7	322.8	10.8	329.3	8.3	326.5	-3.4	323.3	1.3
1988	338.5	15.5	346.9	10.3	351.3	5.2	360.4	10.8	349.3	8.0
1989	364.7	4.9	374.0	10.6	382.5	9.4	374.3	-8.3	373.9	7.0
1990	379.3	5.5	369.2	-10.2	376.7	8.4	375.1	-1.7	375.1	0.3
1991	363.1	-12.2	362.6	-0.5	368.2	6.3	368.4	0.2	365.6	-2.5
1992	372.5	4.5	386.3	15.7	393.4	7.6	402.5	9.6	388.7	6.3
1993	410.1	7.8	421.3	11.4	427.7	6.2	448.8	21.2	427.0	9.9
1994	467.0	17.2	474.4	6.5	497.5	20.9	509.1	9.7	487.0	14.1
1995	529.0	16.6	536.8	6.0	544.0	5.5	-	-	-	-

Source: "National Income and Product Account Tables: Selected NIPA Tables," *Survey of Current Business*, November 1995, U.S. Department of Commerce, Bureau of Economic Analysis, National Income and Wealth Division. - indicates that no data are available.

Gross Domestic Product

Gross private domestic investment

Fixed investment - Nonresidential - Producers' durable equipment - Chained (1992) Dollars

In billions of chained (1992) dollars and percent. Quarterly data are seasonally adjusted and annualized. Growth rates for quarters are compound annual growth rates; changes from year to year are percentage changes.

Year	1st Quarter	% Change	2nd Quarter	% Change	3rd Quarter	% Change	4th Quarter	% Change	TOTAL	% Change
1959	-	-	-	-	73.0	-	73.1	0.5	71.4	-
1960	75.6	14.4	76.8	6.5	73.7	-15.2	71.2	-12.9	74.3	4.1
1961	68.7	-13.3	71.7	18.6	72.7	5.7	77.1	26.5	72.5	-2.4
1962	79.0	10.2	81.4	12.7	81.7	1.5	81.8	0.5	81.0	11.7
1963	83.2	7.0	84.7	7.4	88.4	18.7	92.0	17.3	87.1	7.5
1964	94.4	10.9	96.2	7.8	99.5	14.4	102.1	10.9	98.1	12.6
1965	110.4	36.7	112.1	6.3	118.2	23.6	122.9	16.9	115.9	18.1
1966	129.7	24.0	134.3	15.0	134.7	1.2	136.5	5.5	133.8	15.4
1967	130.9	-15.4	132.7	5.6	131.0	-5.0	135.2	13.5	132.5	-1.0
1968	140.1	15.3	136.8	-9.1	140.2	10.3	145.0	14.4	140.5	6.0
1969	150.2	15.1	151.8	4.3	153.9	5.6	152.7	-3.1	152.2	8.3
1970	151.4	-3.4	150.9	-1.3	151.8	2.4	143.9	-19.2	149.5	-1.8
1971	146.3	6.8	149.9	10.2	150.7	2.2	155.7	13.9	150.7	0.8
1972	161.7	16.3	165.5	9.7	169.6	10.3	182.5	34.1	169.8	12.7
1973	192.7	24.3	201.4	19.3	203.8	4.9	207.0	6.4	201.2	18.5
1974	207.4	0.8	206.9	-1.0	207.9	1.9	199.4	-15.4	205.4	2.1
1975	185.0	-25.9	181.2	-8.0	183.3	4.7	186.1	6.3	183.9	-10.5
1976	188.6	5.5	192.2	7.9	197.4	11.3	202.7	11.2	195.2	6.1
1977	216.3	29.7	222.1	11.2	226.8	8.7	237.5	20.2	225.6	15.6
1978	241.0	6.0	260.3	36.1	265.2	7.7	272.1	10.8	259.6	15.1
1979	281.6	14.7	278.1	-4.9	284.1	8.9	279.0	-7.0	280.7	8.1
1980	281.5	3.6	261.5	-25.5	262.9	2.2	267.1	6.5	268.2	-4.5
1981	274.9	12.2	276.4	2.2	282.7	9.4	278.7	-5.5	278.2	3.7
1982	272.3	-8.9	261.2	-15.3	256.3	-7.3	251.5	-7.3	260.3	-6.4
1983	249.5	-3.1	262.5	22.5	276.5	23.1	301.1	40.6	272.4	4.6
1984	306.2	6.9	321.5	21.5	330.5	11.7	340.3	12.4	324.6	19.2
1985	337.3	-3.5	345.0	9.4	340.6	-5.0	346.9	7.6	342.4	5.5
1986	343.0	-4.4	347.2	5.0	344.8	-2.7	348.5	4.4	345.9	1.0
1987	336.7	-12.9	346.5	12.2	354.7	9.8	349.6	-5.6	346.9	0.3
1988	360.3	12.8	368.0	8.8	371.6	4.0	377.0	5.9	369.2	6.4
1989	379.7	2.9	389.4	10.6	395.9	6.8	385.6	-10.0	387.6	5.0
1990	388.8	3.4	377.8	-10.8	383.0	5.6	377.9	-5.2	381.9	-1.5
1991	362.9	-15.0	363.8	1.0	369.8	6.8	368.1	-1.8	366.2	-4.1
1992	371.7	4.0	386.4	16.8	393.1	7.1	403.5	11.0	388.7	6.1
1993	410.5	7.1	421.7	11.4	428.2	6.3	449.8	21.8	427.6	10.0
1994	466.5	15.7	471.2	4.1	492.4	19.2	506.4	11.9	484.1	13.2
1995	527.1	17.4	531.9	3.7	538.6	5.1	-	-	-	-

Source: "National Income and Product Account Tables: Selected NIPA Tables," *Survey of Current Business*, November 1995, U.S. Department of Commerce, Bureau of Economic Analysis, National Income and Wealth Division. - indicates that no data are available.

Gross Domestic Product

Gross private domestic investment
Fixed investment - Residential - Actual Dollars

In billions of actual dollars and percent. Quarterly data are seasonally adjusted and annualized. Growth rates for quarters are compound annual growth rates; changes from year to year are percentage changes.

Year	1st Quarter	% Change	2nd Quarter	% Change	3rd Quarter	% Change	4th Quarter	% Change	TOTAL	% Change
1959	27.8	-	28.8	15.2	28.3	-6.8	27.5	-10.8	28.1	-
1960	28.4	13.7	26.1	-28.7	25.3	-11.7	25.3	-	26.3	-6.4
1961	25.3	-	25.5	3.2	26.9	23.8	27.8	14.1	26.4	0.4
1962	28.4	8.9	29.2	11.8	29.2	-	29.1	-1.4	29.0	9.8
1963	30.2	16.0	32.2	29.2	32.5	3.8	33.7	15.6	32.1	10.7
1964	35.4	21.8	34.2	-12.9	33.7	-5.7	33.8	1.2	34.3	6.9
1965	33.9	1.2	34.2	3.6	34.3	1.2	34.5	2.4	34.2	-0.3
1966	34.8	3.5	33.2	-17.2	31.9	-14.8	29.2	-29.8	32.3	-5.6
1967	28.3	-11.8	31.6	55.5	33.4	24.8	36.0	35.0	32.4	0.3
1968	36.9	10.4	38.2	14.9	38.9	7.5	40.9	22.2	38.7	19.4
1969	43.2	24.5	43.4	1.9	43.2	-1.8	40.7	-21.2	42.6	10.1
1970	40.7	-	39.4	-12.2	40.4	10.5	45.0	53.9	41.4	-2.8
1971	48.6	36.0	54.6	59.3	58.3	30.0	61.5	23.8	55.8	34.8
1972	66.6	37.5	68.2	10.0	69.6	8.5	74.3	29.9	69.7	24.9
1973	77.9	20.8	75.8	-10.4	75.0	-4.2	72.7	-11.7	75.3	8.0
1974	69.0	-18.9	67.5	-8.4	67.4	-0.6	60.0	-37.2	66.0	-12.4
1975	57.7	-14.5	59.9	16.1	64.6	35.3	68.7	27.9	62.7	-5.0
1976	76.2	51.4	80.7	25.8	80.6	-0.5	92.5	73.5	82.5	31.6
1977	97.6	23.9	111.7	71.6	115.0	12.4	116.9	6.8	110.3	33.7
1978	121.1	15.2	130.5	34.9	135.8	17.3	139.1	10.1	131.6	19.3
1979	138.6	-1.4	140.9	6.8	143.5	7.6	141.2	-6.3	141.0	7.1
1980	134.5	-17.7	111.2	-53.3	115.9	18.0	131.3	64.7	123.2	-12.6
1981	132.0	2.1	128.9	-9.1	120.2	-24.4	109.6	-30.9	122.6	-0.5
1982	104.8	-16.4	102.8	-7.4	102.3	-1.9	112.8	47.8	105.7	-13.8
1983	130.9	81.4	148.2	64.3	162.6	44.9	168.5	15.3	152.5	44.3
1984	175.6	18.0	181.4	13.9	180.8	-1.3	181.3	1.1	179.8	17.9
1985	183.4	4.7	182.8	-1.3	187.7	11.2	193.9	13.9	186.9	3.9
1986	204.5	23.7	218.3	29.8	224.1	11.1	225.6	2.7	218.1	16.7
1987	225.3	-0.5	229.2	7.1	227.4	-3.1	228.4	1.8	227.6	4.4
1988	228.4	-	231.4	5.4	233.6	3.9	236.6	5.2	232.5	2.2
1989	237.2	1.0	232.2	-8.2	229.1	-5.2	226.6	-4.3	231.3	-0.5
1990	232.7	11.2	222.4	-16.6	210.9	-19.1	196.9	-24.0	215.7	-6.7
1991	184.3	-23.2	185.9	3.5	194.3	19.3	200.3	12.9	191.2	-11.4
1992	211.3	23.8	223.7	25.6	227.1	6.2	240.1	24.9	225.6	18.0
1993	243.5	5.8	243.2	-0.5	252.6	16.4	267.7	26.1	251.7	11.6
1994	278.5	17.1	288.5	15.2	290.4	2.7	293.5	4.3	287.7	14.3
1995	290.4	-4.2	281.9	-11.2	290.2	12.3	-	-	-	-

Source: "National Income and Product Account Tables: Selected NIPA Tables," *Survey of Current Business*, November 1995, U.S. Department of Commerce, Bureau of Economic Analysis, National Income and Wealth Division. - indicates that no data are available.

Gross Domestic Product
Gross private domestic investment
Fixed investment - Residential - Chained (1992) Dollars

In billions of chained (1992) dollars and percent. Quarterly data are seasonally adjusted and annualized. Growth rates for quarters are compound annual growth rates; changes from year to year are percentage changes.

Year	1st Quarter	% Change	2nd Quarter	% Change	3rd Quarter	% Change	4th Quarter	% Change	TOTAL	% Change
1959	-	-	-	-	132.0	-	128.1	-11.3	131.1	-
1960	131.8	12.1	121.0	-29.0	117.3	-11.7	117.2	-0.3	121.8	-7.1
1961	117.6	1.4	118.0	1.4	124.4	23.5	128.6	14.2	122.2	0.3
1962	130.9	7.3	135.0	13.1	134.9	-0.3	134.7	-0.6	133.9	9.6
1963	139.6	15.4	149.6	31.9	152.4	7.7	157.0	12.6	149.6	11.7
1964	166.6	26.8	158.2	-18.7	155.6	-6.4	152.8	-7.0	158.3	5.8
1965	153.4	1.6	154.6	3.2	155.2	1.6	151.8	-8.5	153.7	-2.9
1966	155.2	9.3	142.8	-28.3	138.2	-12.3	123.7	-35.8	140.0	-8.9
1967	119.9	-11.7	133.6	54.2	140.3	21.6	148.4	25.2	135.6	-3.1
1968	149.3	2.4	153.1	10.6	155.9	7.5	157.8	5.0	154.0	13.6
1969	163.5	15.3	161.7	-4.3	160.5	-2.9	148.7	-26.3	158.6	3.0
1970	149.0	0.8	139.1	-24.0	146.4	22.7	161.9	49.6	149.1	-6.0
1971	170.6	23.3	187.8	46.8	197.0	21.1	204.6	16.3	190.0	27.4
1972	218.3	29.6	222.6	8.1	223.1	0.9	231.1	15.1	223.7	17.7
1973	238.8	14.0	226.6	-18.9	217.0	-15.9	206.8	-17.5	222.3	-0.6
1974	191.6	-26.3	183.2	-16.4	177.1	-12.7	153.9	-43.0	176.4	-20.6
1975	144.3	-22.7	147.4	8.9	157.7	31.0	164.6	18.7	153.5	-13.0
1976	181.4	47.5	186.6	12.0	183.6	-6.3	207.0	61.6	189.7	23.6
1977	212.8	11.7	236.6	52.8	236.4	-0.3	233.5	-4.8	229.8	21.1
1978	235.1	2.8	246.2	20.3	249.7	5.8	249.0	-1.1	245.0	6.6
1979	243.2	-9.0	238.9	-6.9	235.7	-5.3	226.4	-14.9	236.0	-3.7
1980	210.3	-25.6	169.9	-57.4	173.0	7.5	191.3	49.5	186.1	-21.1
1981	188.0	-6.7	180.8	-14.5	166.5	-28.1	149.6	-34.8	171.2	-8.0
1982	141.1	-20.9	136.5	-12.4	134.8	-4.9	147.8	44.5	140.1	-18.2
1983	170.8	78.3	192.9	62.7	210.5	41.8	216.3	11.5	197.6	41.0
1984	224.0	15.0	229.6	10.4	226.6	-5.1	225.5	-1.9	226.4	14.6
1985	226.9	2.5	225.7	-2.1	230.2	8.2	235.1	8.8	229.5	1.4
1986	245.1	18.1	259.2	25.1	262.5	5.2	261.2	-2.0	257.0	12.0
1987	258.8	-3.6	260.8	3.1	256.2	-6.9	254.7	-2.3	257.6	0.2
1988	251.3	-5.2	252.2	1.4	252.9	1.1	253.7	1.3	252.5	-2.0
1989	252.6	-1.7	244.3	-12.5	240.1	-6.7	236.0	-6.7	243.2	-3.7
1990	239.4	5.9	227.8	-18.0	214.9	-20.8	200.3	-24.5	220.6	-9.3
1991	187.4	-23.4	188.3	1.9	195.6	16.4	202.4	14.6	193.4	-12.3
1992	213.9	24.7	224.9	22.2	226.7	3.2	236.7	18.8	225.6	16.6
1993	237.9	2.0	234.8	-5.1	242.2	13.2	255.8	24.4	242.7	7.6
1994	263.6	12.8	271.6	12.7	270.3	-1.9	270.3	-	268.9	10.8
1995	265.9	-6.4	256.6	-13.3	261.8	8.4	-	-	-	-

Source: "National Income and Product Account Tables: Selected NIPA Tables," *Survey of Current Business*, November 1995, U.S. Department of Commerce, Bureau of Economic Analysis, National Income and Wealth Division. - indicates that no data are available.

Gross Domestic Product
Gross private domestic investment
Change in business inventories - Actual Dollars

In billions of actual dollars. Quarterly data are seasonally adjusted and annualized.

Year	1st Quarter	2nd Quarter	3rd Quarter	4th Quarter	TOTAL
1959	4.4	7.8	0.2	4.3	4.2
1960	11.3	3.1	4.2	-5.7	3.2
1961	-2.6	1.6	-6.7	6.0	2.9
1962	9.5	5.6	6.2	3.1	6.1
1963	7.0	4.9	5.9	4.8	5.7
1964	5.6	4.8	4.3	5.4	5.0
1965	12.3	9.2	9.5	7.8	9.7
1966	13.5	12.5	12.2	17.0	13.8
1967	14.4	6.5	10.4	10.6	10.5
1968	8.3	13.7	7.6	7.0	9.1
1969	11.8	9.2	10.4	6.7	9.5
1970	2.0	4.1	4.7	-2.0	2.2
1971	12.4	10.5	10.1	1.0	8.5
1972	4.5	11.6	13.8	9.8	9.9
1973	13.6	15.9	10.7	29.7	17.5
1974	13.4	14.0	6.1	22.9	14.1
1975	-12.4	-16.1	0.2	3.0	-6.3
1976	16.2	21.0	19.2	11.4	16.9
1977	14.0	23.2	36.2	18.8	23.1
1978	24.8	27.8	27.3	28.9	27.2
1979	24.6	27.5	11.3	4.0	16.9
1980	9.0	-0.4	-34.1	-5.0	-7.6
1981	41.3	12.5	38.1	20.8	28.2
1982	-19.4	-0.6	3.7	-41.6	-14.5
1983	-34.8	-7.9	-1.2	24.2	-4.9
1984	81.3	70.2	73.5	44.9	67.5
1985	24.7	25.0	20.9	34.2	26.2
1986	45.1	20.0	-14.1	-12.4	9.6
1987	24.2	12.8	2.0	58.0	24.2
1988	12.5	6.6	9.6	14.8	10.9
1989	39.0	41.6	23.7	22.5	31.7
1990	8.6	41.2	13.8	-31.4	8.0
1991	-16.1	-19.9	5.3	21.4	-2.3
1992	-0.3	10.2	11.6	6.4	7.0
1993	19.9	21.6	22.0	18.8	20.6
1994	40.2	74.5	64.7	58.7	59.5
1995	58.1	34.0	30.6	-	-

Source: "National Income and Product Account Tables: Selected NIPA Tables," *Survey of Current Business*, November 1995, U.S. Department of Commerce, Bureau of Economic Analysis, National Income and Wealth Division. - indicates that no data are available.

Gross Domestic Product
Gross private domestic investment
Change in business inventories - Chained (1992) Dollars

In billions of chained 1992 dollars. Quarterly data are seasonally adjusted and annualized.

Year	1st Quarter	2nd Quarter	3rd Quarter	4th Quarter	TOTAL
1959	-	-	4.2	7.6	0.0
1960	33.6	10.5	14.5	-16.1	13.5
1961	-6.5	4.6	19.9	17.6	10.6
1962	30.0	15.6	21.1	13.3	8.9
1963	25.9	16.5	19.2	11.0	20.0
1964	15.6	15.8	14.5	16.6	18.1
1965	35.7	31.6	26.7	26.7	15.6
1966	41.1	38.2	37.8	52.1	30.2
1967	47.3	23.3	29.7	27.9	42.3
1968	22.0	39.7	24.2	21.6	32.1
1969	35.8	30.1	30.3	12.7	26.9
1970	0.8	11.2	15.1	-4.3	27.2
1971	34.5	31.6	25.3	-0.5	5.7
1972	11.4	32.8	36.7	19.7	22.7
1973	32.0	39.9	24.7	59.2	25.2
1974	29.1	28.5	9.3	29.0	39.0
1975	-27.1	-25.3	2.9	5.3	24.0
1976	29.5	38.0	32.2	16.3	-11.0
1977	22.2	36.6	59.0	34.1	29.0
1978	42.3	40.4	41.8	44.5	38.0
1979	36.8	39.9	14.6	1.2	42.3
1980	8.1	-2.1	-44.2	-1.7	23.1
1981	48.0	12.8	48.7	22.8	-10.0
1982	-24.7	-4.3	8.1	-41.5	33.1
1983	-36.2	-8.4	-2.5	23.6	-15.6
1984	84.0	76.1	80.2	58.8	-5.9
1985	33.8	29.9	24.1	31.4	74.8
1986	48.7	21.0	-15.3	-10.8	29.8
1987	29.7	14.4	0.8	59.9	10.9
1988	13.3	6.0	11.5	15.8	26.2
1989	41.9	44.2	24.9	22.3	11.6
1990	11.0	43.8	14.9	-28.2	33.3
1991	-17.5	-20.8	4.9	21.4	10.4
1992	-0.1	11.3	12.1	5.8	-3.0
1993	18.5	20.8	19.5	17.4	7.3
1994	40.1	74.1	64.0	57.3	19.1
1995	54.5	30.6	27.1	-	-

Source: "National Income and Product Account Tables: Selected NIPA Tables," *Survey of Current Business*, November 1995, U.S. Department of Commerce, Bureau of Economic Analysis, National Income and Wealth Division. - indicates that no data are available.

NET EXPORTS OF GOODS AND SERVICES
Component of Gross Domestic Product

Net exports of goods and services—the trade balance—account for the United States' trade with the rest of the world. This measure presents exports less imports of all goods and services; hence it can be a negative value. The category is subdivided into Exports and Imports. BEA estimates are developed from three categories: (1) merchandise exports and imports, (2) receipts from abroad and payments made abroad, including investment earnings, and (3) receipts and payments for other services; federal purchases and sales abroad are included in this category.

Presentation of Data

Data are shown from 1959 to 1995 in quarterly and in annual increments. Changes from one period to the next are shown for Exports and Imports but not for Net Exports, which can and do exhibit negative values. Changes from quarter to quarter are annualized, compounded growth rates as explained in the section on Gross National Product. Changes from year to year are simple percentile changes.

Analytical Uses

Net exports are, generally, an indicator of the national vigor in trading with the rest of the world. The category measures the U.S. trade balance directly; the trade balance, in turn, has a direct impact on GDP. Indirectly, net exports reflect (1) the strength of the dollar, (2) U.S. vulnerability in commodity categories, and (3) U.S. competitiveness in manufacturing and services.

A positive net exports figure adds to GDP; a negative figure subtracts from GDP and, consequently, can contribute to or even cause negative GDP growth rate. In national product accounting, exports, manufactured domestically, are part of GDP; imports, manufactured elsewhere, and therefore in another nation's GDP, are taken from GDP.

The trade balance is significantly influenced by the strength of the dollar as measured against other currencies. When the dollar is strong relative to other currencies, it can buy more abroad; at the same time, dollar-denominated goods are more expensive abroad and discourage sales. The value of the dollar, however, is controlled in part by national and international policies and the relative performance of other economies rather than by pure market forces. A negative trade balance, therefore, does not invariably signal economic weakness.

The trade balance was negative in all but 2 of the 36 years in the 1959-1994 period. As an indicator of economic prospects, the fact that net exports are negative is not as meaningful as the trend: is the trade deficit growing or decreasing. A growing deficit may signal problems; a shrinking deficit may signal a stronger economy because the ratio of exports to imports is changing favorably.

Net exports indicate, indirectly, U.S. dependence on important commodities, e.g. petroleum. An artificial increase in the price of crude oil can produce large trade deficits and also increase prices domestically. Similarly, net exports are influenced by the competitiveness of other economies in selling their goods to us. In recent years attention has focused on Japan, for instance.

Gross Domestic Product

Net exports of goods and services - Actual Dollars

In billions of actual dollars. Quarterly data are seasonally adjusted and annualized.

Year	1st Quarter	2nd Quarter	3rd Quarter	4th Quarter	TOTAL
1959	-1.7	-2.5	-1.1	-1.4	-1.7
1960	0.9	1.7	3.0	4.0	2.4
1961	4.4	3.3	2.8	2.9	3.4
1962	2.3	3.2	2.9	1.5	2.4
1963	2.0	3.7	3.1	4.4	3.3
1964	5.9	4.9	5.4	5.7	5.5
1965	3.0	4.7	3.7	4.1	3.9
1966	3.2	2.0	0.8	1.5	1.9
1967	2.3	2.1	1.1	0.2	1.4
1968	-1.2	-0.6	-1.3	-1.9	-1.3
1969	-1.9	-1.8	-1.3	0.1	-1.2
1970	1.1	2.4	0.9	0.4	1.2
1971	0.8	-3.8	-3.1	-6.0	-3.0
1972	-8.6	-8.3	-7.9	-7.1	-8.0
1973	-4.4	-1.1	3.2	4.7	0.6
1974	4.3	-5.6	-9.1	-2.2	-3.1
1975	13.1	16.6	11.6	12.9	13.6
1976	4.2	-1.1	-5.0	-7.2	-2.3
1977	-21.6	-21.7	-21.1	-30.3	-23.7
1978	-39.3	-23.3	-24.6	-17.3	-26.1
1979	-19.2	-23.4	-24.4	-29.0	-24.0
1980	-37.2	-16.7	3.3	-8.9	-14.9
1981	-17.0	-16.4	-10.2	-16.3	-15.0
1982	-17.2	-5.0	-30.3	-29.7	-20.5
1983	-24.6	-45.5	-65.2	-71.3	-51.7
1984	-94.3	-103.5	-103.1	-107.1	-102.0
1985	-91.4	-114.7	-117.2	-133.6	-114.2
1986	-126.9	-128.8	-138.0	-132.3	-131.5
1987	-139.4	-144.7	-142.4	-142.0	-142.1
1988	-120.9	-103.3	-95.8	-104.2	-106.1
1989	-83.7	-81.2	-79.3	-77.5	-80.4
1990	-74.3	-60.3	-78.5	-72.0	-71.3
1991	-32.9	-12.3	-22.0	-14.8	-20.5
1992	-8.9	-29.0	-37.6	-42.7	-29.5
1993	-47.4	-62.0	-77.1	-73.2	-64.9
1994	-80.3	-97.4	-108.4	-99.7	-96.4
1995	-106.6	-122.4	-100.6	-	-

Source: "National Income and Product Account Tables: Selected NIPA Tables," *Survey of Current Business*, November 1995, Department of Commerce, Bureau of Economic Analysis, National Income and Wealth Division. - indicates that no data are available

Gross Domestic Product
Net exports of goods and services - Chained (1992) Dollars

In billions of chained 1992 dollars. Quarterly data are seasonally adjusted and annualized.

Year	1st Quarter	2nd Quarter	3rd Quarter	4th Quarter	TOTAL
1959	-	-	-33.6	-33.8	-34.8
1960	-27.3	-24.5	-19.1	-14.1	-21.3
1961	-13.0	-18.6	-21.8	-23.0	-19.1
1962	-27.0	-23.6	-25.4	-30.2	-26.5
1963	-27.0	-21.4	-23.7	-18.7	-22.7
1964	-12.8	-16.5	-16.6	-17.6	-15.9
1965	-26.9	-26.0	-28.7	-27.8	-27.4
1966	-33.2	-38.0	-46.3	-45.9	-40.9
1967	-46.6	-46.8	-50.4	-56.6	-50.1
1968	-64.4	-65.2	-68.9	-70.2	-67.2
1969	-65.1	-75.8	-74.8	-69.6	-71.3
1970	-65.6	-64.6	-64.3	-65.6	-65.0
1971	-64.3	-81.5	-78.1	-79.5	-75.8
1972	-95.6	-88.3	-85.7	-86.1	-88.9
1973	-81.2	-64.7	-55.9	-50.3	-63.0
1974	-34.1	-34.7	-41.1	-32.3	-35.6
1975	-6.8	2.5	-11.9	-12.7	-7.2
1976	-29.2	-38.3	-42.8	-49.2	-39.9
1977	-67.0	-63.2	-56.9	-69.9	-64.2
1978	-84.9	-59.6	-62.0	-55.6	-65.6
1979	-55.7	-56.1	-40.2	-29.1	-45.3
1980	-20.0	11.3	33.4	15.7	10.1
1981	8.3	9.5	5.5	-0.9	5.6
1982	-5.3	2.6	-26.5	-27.3	-14.1
1983	-29.8	-54.6	-78.0	-90.8	-63.3
1984	-115.5	-125.5	-130.5	-137.7	-127.3
1985	-127.3	-151.6	-152.6	-160.0	-147.9
1986	-149.7	-167.1	-173.9	-164.9	-163.9
1987	-161.2	-160.2	-152.2	-151.3	-156.2
1988	-125.9	-106.9	-110.6	-114.3	-114.4
1989	-88.7	-79.8	-84.5	-77.9	-82.7
1990	-67.1	-66.7	-71.2	-42.5	-61.9
1991	-24.3	-17.1	-29.8	-17.9	-22.3
1992	-14.8	-32.5	-30.8	-40.0	-29.5
1993	-55.2	-67.0	-89.1	-86.2	-74.4
1994	-101.3	-112.2	-113.3	-105.8	-108.1
1995	-119.0	-126.8	-114.1	-	-

Source: "National Income and Product Account Tables: Selected NIPA Tables," *Survey of Current Business*, November 1995, U.S. Department of Commerce, Bureau of Economic Analysis, National Income and Wealth Division. - indicates that no data are available.

Gross Domestic Product
Net exports of goods and services
Exports: Total - Actual Dollars

In billions of actual dollars. Quarterly data are seasonally adjusted and annualized.

Year	1st Quarter	2nd Quarter	3rd Quarter	4th Quarter	TOTAL
1959	19.7	20.0	21.8	21.1	20.6
1960	24.2	25.2	25.9	25.8	25.3
1961	26.1	25.2	26.1	26.8	26.0
1962	26.6	28.1	28.0	27.0	27.4
1963	27.2	29.6	29.8	31.1	29.4
1964	32.9	32.6	33.9	35.0	33.6
1965	31.5	36.3	35.7	38.0	35.4
1966	38.2	38.2	39.0	40.4	38.9
1967	41.7	41.1	40.7	41.9	41.4
1968	43.2	44.8	47.0	46.2	45.3
1969	41.9	50.9	51.0	53.2	49.3
1970	54.7	57.6	57.3	58.3	57.0
1971	59.5	59.5	62.4	56.0	59.3
1972	63.5	63.1	66.2	72.1	66.2
1973	81.0	88.3	94.3	103.4	91.8
1974	114.6	123.8	124.5	134.4	124.3
1975	138.0	131.8	133.7	141.7	136.3
1976	143.1	146.0	150.9	155.4	148.9
1977	154.8	161.3	161.8	157.1	158.8
1978	164.0	185.6	190.5	204.5	186.1
1979	210.7	219.7	232.9	251.5	228.7
1980	267.1	275.9	282.5	290.3	278.9
1981	302.8	305.5	299.7	303.2	302.8
1982	292.3	294.2	279.0	265.1	282.6
1983	270.6	272.5	278.2	286.7	277.0
1984	293.7	303.0	306.5	309.2	303.1
1985	305.9	303.9	297.0	305.3	303.0
1986	312.2	314.5	320.5	335.4	320.7
1987	337.4	356.9	373.9	394.7	365.7
1988	421.1	442.1	456.2	469.3	447.2
1989	492.6	512.8	509.7	522.1	509.3
1990	541.6	554.8	555.5	577.3	557.3
1991	577.4	602.7	602.6	624.4	601.8
1992	632.4	635.9	640.2	649.1	639.4
1993	649.4	662.5	648.5	679.4	660.0
1994	681.5	708.6	734.2	763.6	722.0
1995	778.6	796.9	813.2	-	-

Source: "National Income and Product Account Tables: Selected NIPA Tables," *Survey of Current Business*, November 1995, U.S. Department of Commerce, Bureau of Economic Analysis, National Income and Wealth Division. - indicates that no data are available.

Gross Domestic Product
Net exports of goods and services
Exports: Total - Chained (1992) Dollars

In billions of chained 1992 dollars. Quarterly data are seasonally adjusted and annualized.

Year	1st Quarter	2nd Quarter	3rd Quarter	4th Quarter	TOTAL
1959	-	-	75.8	72.9	71.9
1960	83.2	86.7	88.7	88.7	86.8
1961	89.3	85.0	88.6	90.1	88.3
1962	89.5	95.4	95.2	91.9	93.0
1963	92.1	100.6	101.3	106.0	100.0
1964	111.7	110.8	114.2	116.6	113.3
1965	102.5	118.7	116.6	124.7	115.6
1966	123.1	122.2	123.0	125.1	123.4
1967	127.0	125.6	124.4	127.3	126.1
1968	130.3	132.5	140.7	137.6	135.3
1969	123.2	149.5	147.7	150.4	142.7
1970	153.8	159.0	158.7	160.9	158.1
1971	159.6	159.4	168.1	149.7	159.2
1972	167.4	164.8	172.4	183.5	172.0
1973	200.3	209.0	210.3	218.8	209.6
1974	226.4	236.4	225.0	231.1	229.8
1975	230.5	220.9	224.7	236.7	228.2
1976	235.9	238.1	244.7	247.7	241.6
1977	243.8	250.1	252.2	243.6	247.4
1978	249.5	275.5	278.3	289.1	273.1
1979	288.9	289.7	299.7	317.8	299.0
1980	327.7	333.9	332.8	331.1	331.4
1981	336.7	338.9	331.4	334.1	335.3
1982	320.4	322.8	308.2	294.3	311.4
1983	298.9	299.8	304.3	310.2	303.3
1984	317.5	325.7	332.0	338.3	328.4
1985	338.7	337.3	332.0	341.4	337.3
1986	351.3	355.9	364.1	377.5	362.2
1987	377.7	393.5	411.1	425.7	402.0
1988	448.8	461.4	469.4	483.5	465.8
1989	502.0	522.0	521.3	535.5	520.2
1990	555.2	566.8	561.8	573.9	564.4
1991	572.3	600.3	603.6	623.5	599.9
1992	633.0	635.8	639.7	649.1	639.4
1993	649.8	662.3	648.9	681.4	660.6
1994	680.4	704.3	724.8	751.0	715.1
1995	755.8	764.3	779.7	-	-

Source: "National Income and Product Account Tables: Selected NIPA Tables," *Survey of Current Business*, November 1995, U.S. Department of Commerce, Bureau of Economic Analysis, National Income and Wealth Division. - indicates that no data are available.

Gross Domestic Product
Net exports of goods and services
Exports - Goods - Actual Dollars

In billions of actual dollars. Quarterly data are seasonally adjusted and annualized.

Year	1st Quarter	2nd Quarter	3rd Quarter	4th Quarter	TOTAL
1959	15.6	15.9	17.5	16.9	16.5
1960	19.5	20.5	20.9	20.9	20.5
1961	21.2	20.1	21.0	21.5	20.9
1962	21.2	22.3	22.3	21.1	21.7
1963	21.3	23.4	23.8	24.9	23.3
1964	26.1	26.0	26.9	27.8	26.7
1965	24.4	28.8	27.9	30.1	27.8
1966	30.4	30.1	30.6	31.9	30.7
1967	32.5	32.3	31.6	32.3	32.2
1968	33.6	34.9	36.6	35.9	35.3
1969	31.6	39.9	39.5	42.0	38.3
1970	43.0	45.0	44.8	45.4	44.5
1971	45.9	45.7	48.4	42.2	45.6
1972	49.7	48.9	51.8	56.8	51.8
1973	64.4	70.9	75.6	84.8	73.9
1974	93.1	100.6	101.2	109.0	101.0
1975	112.0	105.9	107.1	113.4	109.6
1976	113.5	116.3	119.0	122.3	117.8
1977	121.3	126.2	126.1	121.0	123.7
1978	125.0	146.1	149.3	161.2	145.4
1979	167.0	175.7	188.0	205.4	184.0
1980	217.8	224.2	226.9	234.2	225.8
1981	242.2	242.0	234.2	238.0	239.1
1982	224.9	226.0	211.6	197.6	215.0
1983	200.7	202.8	207.4	218.3	207.3
1984	218.3	224.6	228.4	231.2	225.6
1985	225.7	223.5	217.4	222.4	222.2
1986	220.5	223.0	224.5	235.9	226.0
1987	234.3	248.7	264.2	283.0	257.5
1988	304.6	321.4	331.6	345.5	325.8
1989	359.3	377.8	370.2	379.4	371.7
1990	391.6	399.8	394.6	408.2	398.5
1991	414.8	428.8	423.9	438.1	426.4
1992	442.1	445.9	447.7	459.0	448.7
1993	451.2	461.8	448.3	477.0	459.5
1994	476.0	497.7	517.2	545.4	509.1
1995	558.9	574.7	588.3	-	-

Source: "National Income and Product Account Tables: Selected NIPA Tables," *Survey of Current Business*, November 1995, U.S. Department of Commerce, Bureau of Economic Analysis, National Income and Wealth Division. - indicates that no data are available.

Gross Domestic Product
Net exports of goods and services
Exports - Goods - Chained (1992) Dollars

In billions of chained 1992 dollars. Quarterly data are seasonally adjusted and annualized.

Year	1st Quarter	2nd Quarter	3rd Quarter	4th Quarter	TOTAL
1959	-	-	55.2	52.7	51.7
1960	61.0	64.0	65.1	65.2	63.8
1961	65.6	61.2	64.4	65.5	64.2
1962	64.7	68.9	69.0	65.4	67.0
1963	65.7	72.5	73.8	77.2	72.3
1964	80.7	80.6	82.9	84.5	82.2
1965	72.1	85.6	82.9	89.9	82.6
1966	88.9	87.4	87.7	89.5	88.4
1967	89.2	89.1	87.7	89.2	88.8
1968	92.1	93.5	100.0	97.6	95.8
1969	84.4	106.9	104.2	107.8	100.8
1970	109.8	112.5	112.8	114.2	112.3
1971	112.1	111.9	119.9	103.7	111.9
1972	120.5	117.6	124.6	133.0	123.9
1973	145.1	152.2	151.9	160.3	152.4
1974	163.3	170.1	160.9	163.6	164.5
1975	162.8	155.2	158.1	166.5	160.7
1976	164.6	166.9	170.0	171.6	168.3
1977	168.2	172.5	174.2	167.0	170.5
1978	169.3	192.8	194.1	201.9	189.5
1979	202.0	203.6	213.0	229.1	211.9
1980	236.2	240.6	236.4	235.6	237.2
1981	237.6	237.5	230.1	233.8	234.7
1982	220.1	222.8	211.5	199.5	213.5
1983	202.5	203.9	207.3	215.4	207.3
1984	214.4	219.8	226.6	233.8	223.7
1985	231.9	231.6	228.6	234.9	231.7
1986	235.7	240.5	244.3	254.0	243.6
1987	251.1	261.9	278.0	290.9	270.5
1988	308.8	317.5	322.1	337.1	321.4
1989	347.2	365.6	361.1	372.9	361.7
1990	386.8	394.8	388.0	397.0	391.6
1991	403.3	419.8	420.0	433.7	419.2
1992	440.3	445.1	448.3	461.0	448.7
1993	454.3	465.8	453.3	484.5	464.5
1994	481.5	501.8	518.3	543.9	511.4
1995	548.9	557.8	571.1	-	-

Source: "National Income and Product Account Tables: Selected NIPA Tables," *Survey of Current Business*, November 1995, U.S. Department of Commerce, Bureau of Economic Analysis, National Income and Wealth Division. - indicates that no data are available.

Gross Domestic Product
Net exports of goods and services
Exports - Services - Actual Dollars

In billions of actual dollars and percent. Quarterly data are seasonally adjusted and annualized. Growth rates for quarters are compound annual growth rates; changes from year to year are percentage changes.

Year	1st Quarter	% Change	2nd Quarter	% Change	3rd Quarter	% Change	4th Quarter	% Change	TOTAL	% Change
1959	4.1	-	4.1	-	4.3	21.0	4.3	-	4.2	-
1960	4.7	42.7	4.7	-	4.9	18.1	4.9	-	4.8	14.3
1961	4.9	-	5.1	17.4	5.2	8.1	5.2	-	5.1	6.2
1962	5.4	16.3	5.8	33.1	5.7	-6.7	5.9	14.8	5.7	11.8
1963	5.9	-	6.2	21.9	6.0	-12.3	6.3	21.6	6.1	7.0
1964	6.8	35.7	6.6	-11.3	6.9	19.5	7.1	12.1	6.9	13.1
1965	7.1	-	7.5	24.5	7.8	17.0	8.0	10.7	7.6	10.1
1966	7.8	-9.6	8.1	16.3	8.4	15.7	8.5	4.8	8.2	7.9
1967	9.2	37.2	8.9	-12.4	9.0	4.6	9.6	29.5	9.2	12.2
1968	9.6	-	9.9	13.1	10.3	17.2	10.3	-	10.0	8.7
1969	10.3	-	11.0	30.1	11.5	19.5	11.2	-10.0	11.0	10.0
1970	11.6	15.1	12.6	39.2	12.6	-	12.9	9.9	12.4	12.7
1971	13.6	23.5	13.8	6.0	13.9	2.9	13.8	-2.8	13.8	11.3
1972	13.8	-	14.2	12.1	14.3	2.8	15.3	31.0	14.4	4.3
1973	16.6	38.6	17.4	20.7	18.7	33.4	18.6	-2.1	17.8	23.6
1974	21.6	81.9	23.1	30.8	23.2	1.7	25.4	43.7	23.3	30.9
1975	26.0	9.8	25.9	-1.5	26.5	9.6	28.3	30.1	26.7	14.6
1976	29.6	19.7	29.7	1.4	31.9	33.1	33.1	15.9	31.1	16.5
1977	33.5	4.9	35.2	21.9	35.7	5.8	36.1	4.6	35.1	12.9
1978	38.9	34.8	39.5	6.3	41.2	18.4	43.3	22.0	40.7	16.0
1979	43.7	3.7	44.0	2.8	44.9	8.4	46.1	11.1	44.7	9.8
1980	49.3	30.8	51.7	20.9	55.6	33.8	56.1	3.6	53.2	19.0
1981	60.6	36.2	63.5	20.6	65.5	13.2	65.1	-2.4	63.7	19.7
1982	67.5	15.6	68.2	4.2	67.4	-4.6	67.5	0.6	67.6	6.1
1983	69.9	15.0	69.7	-1.1	70.8	6.5	68.4	-12.9	69.7	3.1
1984	75.4	47.7	78.4	16.9	78.1	-1.5	78.0	-0.5	77.5	11.2
1985	80.2	11.8	80.4	1.0	79.6	-3.9	82.9	17.6	80.8	4.3
1986	91.7	49.7	91.5	-0.9	96.0	21.2	99.5	15.4	94.7	17.2
1987	103.1	15.3	108.2	21.3	109.8	6.0	111.7	7.1	108.2	14.3
1988	116.5	18.3	120.7	15.2	124.5	13.2	123.9	-1.9	121.4	12.2
1989	133.3	34.0	135.0	5.2	139.5	14.0	142.7	9.5	137.6	13.3
1990	150.0	22.1	155.1	14.3	160.9	15.8	169.1	22.0	158.8	15.4
1991	162.7	-14.3	173.9	30.5	178.7	11.5	186.3	18.1	175.4	10.5
1992	190.3	8.9	190.0	-0.6	192.5	5.4	190.1	-4.9	190.7	8.7
1993	198.3	18.4	200.8	5.1	200.2	-1.2	202.4	4.5	200.4	5.1
1994	205.5	6.3	210.9	10.9	216.9	11.9	218.2	2.4	212.9	6.2
1995	219.7	2.8	222.2	4.6	224.9	4.9	-	-	-	-

Source: "National Income and Product Account Tables: Selected NIPA Tables," *Survey of Current Business*, November 1995, U.S. Department of Commerce, Bureau of Economic Analysis, National Income and Wealth Division. - indicates that no data are available.

Gross Domestic Product
Net exports of goods and services
Exports - Services - Chained (1992) Dollars

In billions of chained (1992) dollars and percent. Quarterly data are seasonally adjusted and annualized. Growth rates for quarters are compound annual growth rates; changes from year to year are percentage changes.

Year	1st Quarter	% Change	2nd Quarter	% Change	3rd Quarter	% Change	4th Quarter	% Change	TOTAL	% Change
1959	-	-	-	-	18.8	-	18.7	-2.1	18.6	-
1960	20.0	30.8	20.3	6.1	21.2	18.9	21.1	-1.9	20.6	10.8
1961	21.2	1.9	22.1	18.1	22.2	1.8	22.5	5.5	22.0	6.8
1962	22.8	5.4	24.5	33.3	24.0	-7.9	24.8	14.0	24.0	9.1
1963	24.8	-	26.0	20.8	25.2	-11.8	26.2	16.8	25.5	6.3
1964	28.6	42.0	27.6	-13.3	28.7	16.9	29.4	10.1	28.6	12.2
1965	28.9	-6.6	30.6	25.7	31.6	13.7	32.2	7.8	30.8	7.7
1966	31.5	-8.4	32.5	13.3	33.2	8.9	33.3	1.2	32.6	5.8
1967	36.1	38.1	34.5	-16.6	34.8	3.5	36.5	21.0	35.5	8.9
1968	36.0	-5.4	36.9	10.4	38.3	16.1	37.8	-5.1	37.3	5.1
1969	37.8	-	39.7	21.7	41.2	16.0	39.7	-13.8	39.6	6.2
1970	41.2	16.0	44.0	30.1	43.2	-7.1	44.0	7.6	43.1	8.8
1971	45.2	11.4	45.3	0.9	45.3	-	44.3	-8.5	45.0	4.4
1972	43.7	-5.3	44.3	5.6	44.3	-	46.6	22.4	44.7	-0.7
1973	51.0	43.5	52.1	8.9	54.3	18.0	53.0	-9.2	52.6	17.7
1974	58.8	51.5	62.0	23.6	60.6	-8.7	64.9	31.5	61.6	17.1
1975	65.4	3.1	64.1	-7.7	64.8	4.4	68.2	22.7	65.6	6.5
1976	70.3	12.9	69.7	-3.4	74.0	27.1	75.7	9.5	72.5	10.5
1977	75.7	-	77.8	11.6	78.0	1.0	77.2	-4.0	77.2	6.5
1978	81.9	26.7	81.2	-3.4	83.1	9.7	85.9	14.2	83.0	7.5
1979	85.4	-2.3	84.0	-6.4	83.2	-3.8	82.9	-1.4	83.9	1.1
1980	85.6	13.7	87.5	9.2	92.5	24.9	91.4	-4.7	89.2	6.3
1981	96.1	22.2	99.3	14.0	100.4	4.5	98.4	-7.7	98.5	10.4
1982	100.7	9.7	99.9	-3.1	97.2	-10.4	96.3	-3.7	98.5	-
1983	98.0	7.3	97.1	-3.6	98.0	3.8	94.2	-14.6	96.8	-1.7
1984	104.8	53.2	107.7	11.5	106.3	-5.1	104.6	-6.2	105.9	9.4
1985	107.6	12.0	106.3	-4.7	103.9	-8.7	106.9	12.1	106.1	0.2
1986	117.4	45.5	116.8	-2.0	121.7	17.9	125.2	12.0	120.3	13.4
1987	128.9	12.4	134.0	16.8	134.8	2.4	136.0	3.6	133.4	10.9
1988	140.8	14.9	144.7	11.5	148.3	10.3	146.4	-5.0	145.0	8.7
1989	155.4	27.0	156.1	1.8	160.5	11.8	162.8	5.9	158.7	9.4
1990	168.6	15.0	172.2	8.8	174.3	5.0	177.3	7.1	173.1	9.1
1991	168.9	-17.6	180.6	30.7	183.8	7.3	189.8	13.7	180.8	4.4
1992	192.8	6.5	190.7	-4.3	191.3	1.3	188.2	-6.3	190.7	5.5
1993	195.5	16.4	196.5	2.1	195.6	-1.8	197.0	2.9	196.2	2.9
1994	199.0	4.1	202.7	7.6	206.8	8.3	207.7	1.8	204.1	4.0
1995	207.6	-0.2	207.4	-0.4	209.6	4.3	-	-	-	-

Source: "National Income and Product Account Tables: Selected NIPA Tables," *Survey of Current Business*, November 1995, U.S. Department of Commerce, Bureau of Economic Analysis, National Income and Wealth Division. - indicates that no data are available.

Gross Domestic Product
Net exports of goods and services
Imports: Total - Actual Dollars

In billions of actual dollars and percent. Quarterly data are seasonally adjusted and annualized. Growth rates for quarters are compound annual growth rates; changes from year to year are percentage changes.

Year	1st Quarter	% Change	2nd Quarter	% Change	3rd Quarter	% Change	4th Quarter	% Change	TOTAL	% Change
1959	21.4	-	22.5	22.2	22.9	7.3	22.5	-6.8	22.3	-
1960	23.3	15.0	23.5	3.5	22.9	-9.8	21.7	-19.4	22.8	2.2
1961	21.7	-	21.9	3.7	23.3	28.1	23.9	10.7	22.7	-0.4
1962	24.3	6.9	24.9	10.2	25.1	3.3	25.6	8.2	25.0	10.1
1963	25.2	-6.1	25.9	11.6	26.7	12.9	26.8	1.5	26.1	4.4
1964	27.0	3.0	27.7	10.8	28.4	10.5	29.3	13.3	28.1	7.7
1965	28.5	-10.5	31.7	53.1	32.0	3.8	33.9	26.0	31.5	12.1
1966	35.0	13.6	36.2	14.4	38.2	24.0	38.8	6.4	37.1	17.8
1967	39.4	6.3	39.0	-4.0	39.5	5.2	41.7	24.2	39.9	7.5
1968	44.4	28.5	45.4	9.3	48.2	27.0	48.2	-	46.6	16.8
1969	43.8	-31.8	52.7	109.6	52.4	-2.3	53.1	5.5	50.5	8.4
1970	53.5	3.0	55.2	13.3	56.4	9.0	57.9	11.1	55.8	10.5
1971	58.7	5.6	63.3	35.2	65.5	14.6	61.9	-20.2	62.3	11.6
1972	72.2	85.1	71.4	-4.4	74.1	16.0	79.2	30.5	74.2	19.1
1973	85.4	35.2	89.5	20.6	91.1	7.3	98.7	37.8	91.2	22.9
1974	110.3	56.0	129.4	89.4	133.6	13.6	136.6	9.3	127.5	39.8
1975	124.9	-30.1	115.2	-27.6	122.1	26.2	128.7	23.4	122.7	-3.8
1976	138.9	35.7	147.1	25.8	155.8	25.8	162.7	18.9	151.1	23.1
1977	176.4	38.2	183.0	15.8	182.9	-0.2	187.4	10.2	182.4	20.7
1978	203.3	38.5	208.8	11.3	215.1	12.6	221.8	13.1	212.3	16.4
1979	229.8	15.2	243.1	25.2	257.3	25.5	280.5	41.2	252.7	19.0
1980	304.3	38.5	292.6	-14.5	279.2	-17.1	299.2	31.9	293.8	16.3
1981	319.7	30.4	322.0	2.9	309.9	-14.2	319.4	12.8	317.8	8.2
1982	309.5	-11.8	299.1	-12.8	309.3	14.4	294.9	-17.4	303.2	-4.6
1983	295.3	0.5	318.0	34.5	343.4	36.0	358.0	18.1	328.6	8.4
1984	388.0	38.0	406.5	20.5	409.6	3.1	416.4	6.8	405.1	23.3
1985	397.3	-17.1	418.6	23.2	414.2	-4.1	438.9	26.1	417.2	3.0
1986	439.1	0.2	443.4	4.0	458.5	14.3	467.7	8.3	452.2	8.4
1987	476.9	8.1	501.6	22.4	516.4	12.3	536.7	16.7	507.9	12.3
1988	542.0	4.0	545.4	2.5	552.0	4.9	573.5	16.5	553.2	8.9
1989	576.3	2.0	594.0	12.9	589.0	-3.3	599.7	7.5	589.7	6.6
1990	615.9	11.3	615.1	-0.5	634.1	12.9	649.2	9.9	628.6	6.6
1991	610.3	-21.9	615.0	3.1	624.5	6.3	639.3	9.8	622.3	-1.0
1992	641.3	1.3	664.9	15.6	677.8	8.0	691.8	8.5	669.0	7.5
1993	696.8	2.9	724.6	16.9	725.6	0.6	752.6	15.7	724.9	8.4
1994	761.7	4.9	806.0	25.4	842.6	19.4	863.3	10.2	818.4	12.9
1995	885.1	10.5	919.3	16.4	913.7	-2.4	-	-	-	-

Source: "National Income and Product Account Tables: Selected NIPA Tables," *Survey of Current Business*, November 1995, U.S. Department of Commerce, Bureau of Economic Analysis, National Income and Wealth Division. - indicates that no data are available.

Gross Domestic Product
Net exports of goods and services
Imports: Total - Chained (1992) Dollars

In billions of chained (1992) dollars and percent. Quarterly data are seasonally adjusted and annualized. Growth rates for quarters are compound annual growth rates; changes from year to year are percentage changes.

Year	1st Quarter	% Change	2nd Quarter	% Change	3rd Quarter	% Change	4th Quarter	% Change	TOTAL	% Change
1959	-	-	-	-	109.4	-	106.7	-9.5	106.6	-
1960	110.5	15.0	111.2	2.6	107.8	-11.7	102.7	-17.6	108.1	1.4
1961	102.3	-1.5	103.6	5.2	110.4	29.0	113.1	10.1	107.3	-0.7
1962	116.5	12.6	119.0	8.9	120.5	5.1	122.0	5.1	119.5	11.4
1963	119.1	-9.2	122.0	10.1	125.0	10.2	124.7	-1.0	122.7	2.7
1964	124.5	-0.6	127.4	9.6	130.8	11.1	134.2	10.8	129.2	5.3
1965	129.4	-13.6	144.7	56.4	145.3	1.7	152.5	21.3	143.0	10.7
1966	156.3	10.3	160.2	10.4	169.3	24.7	171.1	4.3	164.2	14.8
1967	173.6	6.0	172.4	-2.7	174.8	5.7	184.0	22.8	176.2	7.3
1968	194.7	25.4	197.7	6.3	209.6	26.3	207.8	-3.4	202.5	14.9
1969	188.3	-32.6	225.3	104.9	222.4	-5.1	220.0	-4.2	214.0	5.7
1970	219.4	-1.1	223.6	7.9	223.0	-1.1	226.5	6.4	223.1	4.3
1971	223.9	-4.5	240.9	34.0	246.1	8.9	229.2	-24.8	235.0	5.3
1972	263.0	73.4	253.1	-14.2	258.2	8.3	269.6	18.9	261.0	11.1
1973	281.5	18.9	273.7	-10.6	266.2	-10.5	269.1	4.4	272.6	4.4
1974	260.6	-12.0	271.1	17.1	266.1	-7.2	263.4	-4.0	265.3	-2.7
1975	237.3	-34.1	218.4	-28.3	236.6	37.7	249.3	23.3	235.4	-11.3
1976	265.2	28.1	276.5	18.2	287.5	16.9	296.8	13.6	281.5	19.6
1977	310.8	20.2	313.3	3.3	309.1	-5.3	313.4	5.7	311.6	10.7
1978	334.4	29.6	335.1	0.8	340.3	6.4	344.7	5.3	338.6	8.7
1979	344.6	-0.1	345.7	1.3	340.0	-6.4	346.9	8.4	344.3	1.7
1980	347.8	1.0	322.7	-25.9	299.4	-25.9	315.4	23.2	321.3	-6.7
1981	328.5	17.7	329.4	1.1	325.9	-4.2	334.9	11.5	329.7	2.6
1982	325.7	-10.5	320.2	-6.6	334.7	19.4	321.7	-14.7	325.5	-1.3
1983	328.8	9.1	354.5	35.1	382.2	35.1	401.0	21.2	366.6	12.6
1984	433.0	35.9	451.2	17.9	462.5	10.4	476.1	12.3	455.7	24.3
1985	466.0	-8.2	489.0	21.3	484.6	-3.6	501.3	14.5	485.2	6.5
1986	501.0	-0.2	523.0	18.8	538.1	12.1	542.3	3.2	526.1	8.4
1987	538.8	-2.6	553.7	11.5	563.2	7.0	577.0	10.2	558.2	6.1
1988	574.8	-1.5	568.3	-4.4	580.0	8.5	597.8	12.9	580.2	3.9
1989	590.7	-4.7	601.9	7.8	605.8	2.6	613.5	5.2	603.0	3.9
1990	622.3	5.9	633.5	7.4	633.0	-0.3	616.4	-10.1	626.3	3.9
1991	596.6	-12.2	617.4	14.7	633.4	10.8	641.4	5.1	622.2	-0.7
1992	647.8	4.1	668.3	13.3	670.5	1.3	689.1	11.6	669.0	7.5
1993	705.1	9.6	729.4	14.5	738.1	4.9	767.6	17.0	735.0	9.9
1994	781.7	7.6	816.5	19.0	838.1	11.0	856.8	9.2	823.3	12.0
1995	874.9	8.7	891.2	7.7	893.9	1.2	-	-	-	-

Source: "National Income and Product Account Tables: Selected NIPA Tables," *Survey of Current Business*, November 1995, U.S. Department of Commerce, Bureau of Economic Analysis, National Income and Wealth Division. - indicates that no data are available.

Gross Domestic Product
Net exports of goods and services
Imports - Goods - Actual Dollars

In billions of actual dollars and percent. Quarterly data are seasonally adjusted and annualized. Growth rates for quarters are compound annual growth rates; changes from year to year are percentage changes.

Year	1st Quarter	% Change	2nd Quarter	% Change	3rd Quarter	% Change	4th Quarter	% Change	TOTAL	% Change
1959	14.5	-	15.5	30.6	15.8	8.0	15.4	-9.7	15.3	-
1960	15.7	8.0	15.9	5.2	15.1	-18.7	14.2	-21.8	15.2	-0.7
1961	14.1	-2.8	14.3	5.8	15.8	49.0	16.1	7.8	15.1	-0.7
1962	16.4	7.7	16.9	12.8	17.1	4.8	17.0	-2.3	16.9	11.9
1963	16.9	-2.3	17.6	17.6	18.2	14.3	18.2	-	17.7	4.7
1964	18.3	2.2	19.1	18.7	19.7	13.2	20.4	15.0	19.4	9.6
1965	19.6	-14.8	22.4	70.6	22.8	7.3	24.2	26.9	22.2	14.4
1966	24.9	12.1	25.6	11.7	27.2	27.4	27.7	7.6	26.3	18.5
1967	27.7	-	26.8	-12.4	27.0	3.0	29.5	42.5	27.8	5.7
1968	32.1	40.2	33.2	14.4	35.4	29.3	35.1	-3.3	33.9	21.9
1969	30.8	-40.7	39.1	159.7	38.5	-6.0	38.8	3.2	36.8	8.6
1970	39.3	5.3	40.1	8.4	41.2	11.4	42.8	16.5	40.9	11.1
1971	43.4	5.7	47.4	42.3	49.6	19.9	45.7	-27.9	46.6	13.9
1972	55.1	111.3	54.1	-7.1	57.3	25.8	61.3	31.0	56.9	22.1
1973	66.5	38.5	70.0	22.8	72.1	12.6	78.8	42.7	71.8	26.2
1974	88.8	61.3	106.4	106.1	110.6	16.7	112.3	6.3	104.5	45.5
1975	100.9	-34.8	92.3	-30.0	98.8	31.3	104.0	22.8	99.0	-5.3
1976	113.5	41.9	121.3	30.5	128.9	27.5	134.7	19.3	124.6	25.9
1977	147.6	44.2	153.2	16.1	153.2	-	156.6	9.2	152.6	22.5
1978	170.3	39.9	175.1	11.8	179.4	10.2	184.8	12.6	177.4	16.3
1979	192.2	17.0	204.1	27.2	216.8	27.3	238.1	45.5	212.8	20.0
1980	259.7	41.5	248.5	-16.2	234.1	-21.2	252.0	34.3	248.6	16.8
1981	270.2	32.2	271.8	2.4	260.5	-15.6	268.8	13.4	267.8	7.7
1982	257.6	-15.7	245.8	-17.1	257.2	19.9	241.5	-22.3	250.5	-6.5
1983	242.5	1.7	262.8	37.9	285.9	40.1	299.6	20.6	272.7	8.9
1984	322.5	34.3	337.9	20.5	339.9	2.4	345.0	6.1	336.3	23.3
1985	325.4	-20.9	344.4	25.5	340.5	-4.5	362.8	28.9	343.3	2.1
1986	357.7	-5.5	365.1	8.5	374.8	11.1	382.5	8.5	370.0	7.8
1987	389.5	7.5	409.1	21.7	422.8	14.1	437.7	14.9	414.8	12.1
1988	441.5	3.5	445.7	3.9	451.1	4.9	470.2	18.0	452.1	9.0
1989	473.0	2.4	490.3	15.5	483.1	-5.7	491.5	7.1	484.5	7.2
1990	500.4	7.4	497.4	-2.4	511.3	11.7	522.9	9.4	508.0	4.9
1991	488.3	-24.0	493.5	4.3	504.6	9.3	516.5	9.8	500.7	-1.4
1992	516.8	0.2	541.1	20.2	557.2	12.4	564.4	5.3	544.9	8.8
1993	569.7	3.8	593.8	18.0	593.7	-0.1	613.8	14.2	592.7	8.8
1994	622.4	5.7	665.7	30.9	699.9	22.2	720.9	12.6	677.3	14.3
1995	740.3	11.2	771.0	17.6	765.4	-2.9	-	-	-	-

Source: "National Income and Product Account Tables: Selected NIPA Tables," *Survey of Current Business*, November 1995, U.S. Department of Commerce, Bureau of Economic Analysis, National Income and Wealth Division. - indicates that no data are available.

Gross Domestic Product
Net exports of goods and services
Imports - Goods - Chained (1992) Dollars

In billions of chained (1992) dollars and percent. Quarterly data are seasonally adjusted and annualized. Growth rates for quarters are compound annual growth rates; changes from year to year are percentage changes.

Year	1st Quarter	% Change	2nd Quarter	% Change	3rd Quarter	% Change	4th Quarter	% Change	TOTAL	% Change
1959	-	-	-	-	73.7	-	71.1	-13.4	71.1	-
1960	72.3	6.9	73.0	3.9	69.0	-20.2	65.7	-17.8	70.0	-1.5
1961	65.0	-4.2	66.2	7.6	73.3	50.3	75.0	9.6	69.9	-0.1
1962	77.7	15.2	80.1	12.9	81.6	7.7	81.4	-1.0	80.2	14.7
1963	80.4	-4.8	83.1	14.1	85.2	10.5	85.1	-0.5	83.5	4.1
1964	84.4	-3.2	87.4	15.0	90.6	15.5	93.5	13.4	89.0	6.6
1965	89.3	-16.8	103.3	79.1	104.3	3.9	109.4	21.0	101.6	14.2
1966	112.2	10.6	114.0	6.6	121.4	28.6	122.8	4.7	117.6	15.7
1967	123.0	0.7	119.6	-10.6	120.7	3.7	131.9	42.6	123.8	5.3
1968	142.4	35.9	145.8	9.9	155.9	30.7	153.3	-6.5	149.4	20.7
1969	133.6	-42.3	169.2	157.3	165.8	-7.8	161.6	-9.8	157.5	5.4
1970	161.9	0.7	163.2	3.3	162.6	-1.5	167.2	11.8	163.7	3.9
1971	166.4	-1.9	182.5	44.7	188.9	14.8	172.0	-31.3	177.4	8.4
1972	202.4	91.7	192.8	-17.7	201.0	18.1	210.2	19.6	201.6	13.6
1973	220.7	21.5	215.1	-9.8	212.2	-5.3	215.2	5.8	215.8	7.0
1974	205.5	-16.8	214.9	19.6	211.3	-6.5	207.5	-7.0	209.8	-2.8
1975	183.7	-38.6	168.0	-30.0	185.6	49.0	196.1	24.6	183.4	-12.6
1976	210.0	31.5	220.5	21.6	230.3	19.0	238.4	14.8	224.8	22.6
1977	251.3	23.5	253.2	3.1	250.3	-4.5	253.9	5.9	252.2	12.2
1978	271.4	30.6	272.3	1.3	276.0	5.5	279.4	5.0	274.8	9.0
1979	279.3	-0.1	280.7	2.0	275.6	-7.1	282.4	10.2	279.5	1.7
1980	282.8	0.6	261.0	-27.4	239.0	-29.7	252.3	24.2	258.7	-7.4
1981	262.6	17.4	263.4	1.2	260.9	-3.7	269.3	13.5	264.0	2.0
1982	259.4	-13.9	251.9	-11.1	266.1	24.5	252.1	-19.4	257.4	-2.5
1983	259.6	12.4	281.7	38.7	305.6	38.5	322.7	24.3	292.4	13.6
1984	346.3	32.6	360.6	17.6	368.0	8.5	377.5	10.7	363.1	24.2
1985	366.0	-11.6	387.6	25.8	386.9	-0.7	403.3	18.1	385.9	6.3
1986	400.5	-2.7	426.3	28.4	436.3	9.7	438.9	2.4	425.5	10.3
1987	431.4	-6.7	440.8	9.0	450.2	8.8	458.6	7.7	445.2	4.6
1988	457.1	-1.3	452.9	-3.6	463.7	9.9	479.0	13.9	463.2	4.0
1989	471.7	-6.0	482.4	9.4	485.2	2.3	491.4	5.2	482.7	4.2
1990	494.2	2.3	504.0	8.2	503.2	-0.6	487.9	-11.6	497.3	3.0
1991	472.2	-12.3	490.8	16.7	509.4	16.0	515.9	5.2	497.1	-0.0
1992	521.2	4.2	543.6	18.3	552.8	6.9	561.8	6.7	544.9	9.6
1993	577.3	11.5	598.6	15.6	605.1	4.4	629.1	16.8	602.5	10.6
1994	643.0	9.1	676.4	22.5	698.1	13.5	718.6	12.3	684.0	13.5
1995	732.8	8.1	750.5	10.0	752.4	1.0	-	-	-	-

Source: "National Income and Product Account Tables: Selected NIPA Tables," *Survey of Current Business*, November 1995, U.S. Department of Commerce, Bureau of Economic Analysis, National Income and Wealth Division. - indicates that no data are available.

Gross Domestic Product

Net exports of goods and services
Imports - Services - Actual Dollars

In billions of actual dollars and percent. Quarterly data are seasonally adjusted and annualized. Growth rates for quarters are compound annual growth rates; changes from year to year are percentage changes.

Year	1st Quarter	% Change	2nd Quarter	% Change	3rd Quarter	% Change	4th Quarter	% Change	TOTAL	% Change
1959	6.9	-	7.0	5.9	7.1	5.8	7.1	-	7.0	-
1960	7.6	31.3	7.6	-	7.8	10.9	7.5	-14.5	7.6	8.6
1961	7.6	5.4	7.6	-	7.6	-	7.7	5.4	7.6	-
1962	7.9	10.8	8.0	5.2	8.0	-	8.5	27.4	8.1	6.6
1963	8.3	-9.1	8.3	-	8.6	15.3	8.5	-4.6	8.4	3.7
1964	8.6	4.8	8.6	-	8.7	4.7	8.9	9.5	8.7	3.6
1965	8.9	-	9.2	14.2	9.2	-	9.8	28.8	9.3	6.9
1966	10.1	12.8	10.6	21.3	11.0	16.0	11.1	3.7	10.7	15.1
1967	11.7	23.4	12.2	18.2	12.5	10.2	12.1	-12.2	12.2	14.0
1968	12.3	6.8	12.3	-	12.8	17.3	13.1	9.7	12.6	3.3
1969	13.0	-3.0	13.6	19.8	13.8	6.0	14.3	15.3	13.7	8.7
1970	14.2	-2.8	15.1	27.9	15.3	5.4	15.1	-5.1	14.9	8.8
1971	15.3	5.4	15.9	16.6	15.8	-2.5	16.2	10.5	15.8	6.0
1972	17.1	24.1	17.3	4.8	16.8	-11.1	17.9	28.9	17.3	9.5
1973	18.9	24.3	19.4	11.0	19.0	-8.0	19.9	20.3	19.3	11.6
1974	21.5	36.3	23.0	31.0	23.0	-	24.3	24.6	22.9	18.7
1975	24.0	-4.8	23.0	-15.7	23.3	5.3	24.7	26.3	23.7	3.5
1976	25.4	11.8	25.8	6.4	26.9	18.2	27.9	15.7	26.5	11.8
1977	28.8	13.5	29.9	16.2	29.7	-2.6	30.8	15.7	29.8	12.5
1978	32.9	30.2	33.7	10.1	35.7	25.9	37.1	16.6	34.8	16.8
1979	37.6	5.5	39.0	15.7	40.5	16.3	42.4	20.1	39.9	14.7
1980	44.7	23.5	44.1	-5.3	45.1	9.4	47.2	20.0	45.3	13.5
1981	49.5	21.0	50.2	5.8	49.4	-6.2	50.6	10.1	49.9	10.2
1982	51.9	10.7	53.3	11.2	52.1	-8.7	53.4	10.4	52.6	5.4
1983	52.7	-5.1	55.2	20.4	57.5	17.7	58.4	6.4	56.0	6.5
1984	65.5	58.2	68.6	20.3	69.7	6.6	71.3	9.5	68.8	22.9
1985	71.9	3.4	74.1	12.8	73.6	-2.7	76.0	13.7	73.9	7.4
1986	81.4	31.6	78.3	-14.4	83.8	31.2	85.3	7.4	82.2	11.2
1987	87.3	9.7	92.5	26.0	93.6	4.8	99.0	25.2	93.1	13.3
1988	100.5	6.2	99.7	-3.1	100.8	4.5	103.3	10.3	101.1	8.6
1989	103.3	-	103.8	2.0	105.9	8.3	108.1	8.6	105.3	4.2
1990	115.5	30.3	117.8	8.2	122.7	17.7	126.4	12.6	120.6	14.5
1991	122.1	-12.9	121.6	-1.6	119.9	-5.5	122.7	9.7	121.6	0.8
1992	124.5	6.0	123.8	-2.2	120.6	-9.9	127.4	24.5	124.1	2.1
1993	127.1	-0.9	130.8	12.2	131.9	3.4	138.8	22.6	132.1	6.4
1994	139.3	1.4	140.3	2.9	142.6	6.7	142.3	-0.8	141.1	6.8
1995	144.8	7.2	148.3	10.0	148.3	-	-	-	-	-

Source: "National Income and Product Account Tables: Selected NIPA Tables," *Survey of Current Business*, November 1995, U.S. Department of Commerce, Bureau of Economic Analysis, National Income and Wealth Division. - indicates that no data are available.

Gross Domestic Product

Net exports of goods and services
Imports - Services - Chained (1992) Dollars

In billions of chained (1992) dollars and percent. Quarterly data are seasonally adjusted and annualized. Growth rates for quarters are compound annual growth rates; changes from year to year are percentage changes.

Year	1st Quarter	% Change	2nd Quarter	% Change	3rd Quarter	% Change	4th Quarter	% Change	TOTAL	% Change
1959	-	-	-	-	35.1	-	35.1	-	34.9	-
1960	37.8	34.5	37.7	-1.1	38.5	8.8	36.7	-17.4	37.7	8.0
1961	36.9	2.2	37.0	1.1	36.7	-3.2	37.5	9.0	37.0	-1.9
1962	38.3	8.8	38.3	-	38.4	1.0	40.0	17.7	38.8	4.9
1963	38.2	-16.8	38.3	1.1	39.2	9.7	39.0	-2.0	38.7	-0.3
1964	39.6	6.3	39.5	-1.0	39.6	1.0	40.1	5.1	39.7	2.6
1965	39.6	-4.9	40.8	12.7	40.5	-2.9	42.5	21.3	40.9	3.0
1966	43.5	9.7	45.6	20.8	47.3	15.8	47.7	3.4	46.0	12.5
1967	49.9	19.8	52.0	17.9	53.3	10.4	51.4	-13.5	51.7	12.4
1968	51.8	3.1	51.4	-3.1	53.2	14.8	54.0	6.2	52.6	1.7
1969	53.9	-0.7	55.7	14.0	56.2	3.6	57.9	12.7	55.9	6.3
1970	57.0	-6.1	59.9	22.0	59.8	-0.7	58.8	-6.5	58.8	5.2
1971	57.0	-11.7	58.0	7.2	57.0	-6.7	56.7	-2.1	57.2	-2.7
1972	60.2	27.1	60.0	-1.3	57.0	-18.5	59.3	17.1	59.1	3.3
1973	60.8	10.5	58.7	-13.1	53.8	-29.4	53.6	-1.5	56.7	-4.1
1974	55.1	11.7	56.1	7.5	54.5	-10.9	55.9	10.7	55.4	-2.3
1975	54.3	-11.0	51.3	-20.3	51.2	-0.8	53.4	18.3	52.5	-5.2
1976	55.0	12.5	55.5	3.7	56.7	8.9	57.7	7.2	56.2	7.0
1977	58.3	4.2	59.1	5.6	57.6	-9.8	58.4	5.7	58.4	3.9
1978	61.6	23.8	61.4	-1.3	62.9	10.1	64.0	7.2	62.5	7.0
1979	63.9	-0.6	63.6	-1.9	63.1	-3.1	62.9	-1.3	63.4	1.4
1980	63.4	3.2	60.6	-16.5	60.4	-1.3	63.0	18.4	61.8	-2.5
1981	65.8	19.0	65.9	0.6	64.7	-7.1	65.1	2.5	65.4	5.8
1982	66.4	8.2	69.3	18.6	68.9	-2.3	70.8	11.5	68.9	5.4
1983	70.0	-4.4	73.2	19.6	76.6	19.9	77.8	6.4	74.4	8.0
1984	86.7	54.2	90.7	19.8	94.9	19.8	99.3	19.9	92.9	24.9
1985	101.3	8.3	101.9	2.4	98.0	-14.5	97.8	-0.8	99.7	7.3
1986	100.7	12.4	95.9	-17.7	101.1	23.5	103.0	7.7	100.2	0.5
1987	107.4	18.2	113.1	23.0	113.1	-	118.8	21.7	113.1	12.9
1988	118.0	-2.7	115.6	-7.9	116.3	2.4	118.6	8.1	117.1	3.5
1989	119.1	1.7	119.3	0.7	120.6	4.4	122.0	4.7	120.2	2.6
1990	128.5	23.1	129.8	4.1	130.2	1.2	129.0	-3.6	129.4	7.7
1991	124.8	-12.4	126.8	6.6	124.1	-8.2	125.6	4.9	125.3	-3.2
1992	126.7	3.5	124.7	-6.2	117.7	-20.6	127.4	37.3	124.1	-1.0
1993	127.8	1.3	130.8	9.7	133.0	6.9	138.5	17.6	132.5	6.8
1994	138.8	0.9	140.2	4.1	140.2	-	138.5	-4.8	139.4	5.2
1995	142.4	11.7	141.1	-3.6	141.8	2.0	-	-	-	-

Source: "National Income and Product Account Tables: Selected NIPA Tables," *Survey of Current Business*, November 1995, U.S. Department of Commerce, Bureau of Economic Analysis, National Income and Wealth Division. - indicates that no data are available.

GOVERNMENT CONSUMPTION EXPENDITURES AND GROSS INVESTMENT
Component of Gross Domestic Product

Government—federal, state, and local—represented nearly 19.1 percent of real GDP in 1994, down from 20.2 percent in 1992. The category includes purchases of durable and nondurable goods, expenditures on structures (such as highways and bridges), purchases of services, and compensation of government employees. This category *excludes* transfer payments such as entitlements, transactions in land, grants-in-aid, and financial transactions. The effect of these excluded budgetary items are accounted for in purchases made by those who receive the money. In constant dollars, state and local purchases account for well over half of the total (61.1 percent and growing), the federal government for the rest.

The category is divided as follows:

> *Federal*
>> National defense
>> Nondefense
> *State and local*

Estimates are prepared by BEA under four categories: (1) federal expenditures, derived from the *Budget of the United States* and other sources, with categories such as transfer payments removed; (2) state and local compensation, (3) state and local expenditures for structures, and (4) state and local purchases other than compensation and structures. Each category is governed by its own estimating procedures and analytical methodologies.

Presentation of Data

Data are shown from 1959 to 1995 in quarterly and in annual increments. Changes from one period to the next are shown for each category covered. Changes from quarter to quarter are annualized, compounded growth rates as explained in the section on Gross National Product. Changes from year to year are simple percentile changes.

Analytical Uses

The total category best depicts the importance of government as a customer and employer—in that it includes what governmental bodies purchase and what they pay. It is not a good measure of total governmental activity because it excludes money the government collects for redistribution in transfer payments. Government activity has shown sharp rise during periods of war.

Gross Domestic Product
Government consumption expenditures and gross investment: Total - Actual Dollars

In billions of actual dollars and percent. Quarterly data are seasonally adjusted and annualized. Growth rates for quarters are compound annual growth rates; changes from year to year are percentage changes.

Year	1st Quarter	% Change	2nd Quarter	% Change	3rd Quarter	% Change	4th Quarter	% Change	TOTAL	% Change
1959	110.9	-	112.6	6.3	112.6	-	111.9	-2.5	112.0	-
1960	110.0	-6.6	111.8	6.7	114.5	10.0	116.7	7.9	113.2	1.1
1961	117.8	3.8	119.7	6.6	121.0	4.4	124.9	13.5	120.9	6.8
1962	128.4	11.7	130.4	6.4	132.6	6.9	134.3	5.2	131.4	8.7
1963	134.7	1.2	135.9	3.6	139.5	11.0	140.7	3.5	137.7	4.8
1964	142.4	4.9	144.8	6.9	145.1	0.8	145.3	0.6	144.4	4.9
1965	146.2	2.5	149.9	10.5	155.0	14.3	160.9	16.1	153.0	6.0
1966	164.8	10.1	171.1	16.2	176.9	14.3	181.6	11.1	173.6	13.5
1967	190.8	21.9	191.9	2.3	195.6	7.9	200.3	10.0	194.6	12.1
1968	206.6	13.2	210.4	7.6	213.6	6.2	217.7	7.9	212.1	9.0
1969	218.4	1.3	222.0	6.8	226.7	8.7	227.8	2.0	223.8	5.5
1970	231.8	7.2	233.4	2.8	237.9	7.9	241.2	5.7	236.1	5.5
1971	245.1	6.6	248.7	6.0	251.1	3.9	254.6	5.7	249.9	5.8
1972	265.2	17.7	268.6	5.2	267.9	-1.0	274.1	9.6	268.9	7.6
1973	281.8	11.7	286.0	6.1	287.1	1.5	295.6	12.4	287.6	7.0
1974	306.6	15.7	318.2	16.0	328.0	12.9	340.1	15.6	323.2	12.4
1975	352.3	15.1	357.7	6.3	364.9	8.3	375.5	12.1	362.6	12.2
1976	381.7	6.8	383.0	1.4	386.0	3.2	392.8	7.2	385.9	6.4
1977	403.9	11.8	414.6	11.0	420.2	5.5	428.9	8.5	416.9	8.0
1978	435.8	6.6	453.9	17.7	464.4	9.6	477.5	11.8	457.9	9.8
1979	483.3	4.9	499.3	13.9	513.4	11.8	532.3	15.6	507.1	10.7
1980	553.4	16.8	569.5	12.2	574.5	3.6	593.8	14.1	572.8	13.0
1981	616.9	16.5	628.5	7.7	634.4	3.8	653.7	12.7	633.4	10.6
1982	663.4	6.1	676.3	8.0	689.1	7.8	710.3	12.9	684.8	8.1
1983	719.4	5.2	731.5	6.9	750.0	10.5	741.9	-4.3	735.7	7.4
1984	767.4	14.5	791.4	13.1	803.1	6.0	824.5	11.1	796.6	8.3
1985	843.1	9.3	864.8	10.7	890.0	12.2	902.1	5.6	875.0	9.8
1986	909.7	3.4	929.1	8.8	955.7	12.0	959.5	1.6	938.5	7.3
1987	973.2	5.8	987.4	6.0	996.8	3.9	1,013.8	7.0	992.8	5.8
1988	1,015.5	0.7	1,026.2	4.3	1,031.5	2.1	1,054.8	9.3	1,032.0	3.9
1989	1,065.3	4.0	1,088.7	9.1	1,107.0	6.9	1,119.4	4.6	1,095.1	6.1
1990	1,153.0	12.6	1,164.3	4.0	1,176.9	4.4	1,210.4	11.9	1,176.1	7.4
1991	1,220.6	3.4	1,227.4	2.2	1,226.5	-0.3	1,229.2	0.9	1,225.9	4.2
1992	1,247.9	6.2	1,256.4	2.8	1,270.7	4.6	1,280.0	3.0	1,263.8	3.1
1993	1,278.8	-0.4	1,284.6	1.8	1,293.6	2.8	1,302.7	2.8	1,289.9	2.1
1994	1,296.4	-1.9	1,300.8	1.4	1,328.0	8.6	1,333.5	1.7	1,314.7	1.9
1995	1,346.0	3.8	1,359.9	4.2	1,365.5	1.7	-	-	-	-

Source: "National Income and Product Account Tables: Selected NIPA Tables," *Survey of Current Business*, November 1995, U.S. Department of Commerce, Bureau of Economic Analysis, National Income and Wealth Division. - indicates that no data are available.

Gross Domestic Product

Government consumption expenditures and gross investment: Total - Chained (1992) Dollars

In billions of chained (1992) dollars and percent. Quarterly data are seasonally adjusted and annualized. Growth rates for quarters are compound annual growth rates; changes from year to year are percentage changes.

Year	1st Quarter	% Change	2nd Quarter	% Change	3rd Quarter	% Change	4th Quarter	% Change	TOTAL	% Change
1959	-	-	-	-	624.2	-	618.5	-3.6	618.5	-
1960	605.5	-8.1	613.6	5.5	621.6	5.3	627.9	4.1	617.2	-0.2
1961	635.6	5.0	641.2	3.6	648.0	4.3	663.9	10.2	647.2	4.9
1962	674.8	6.7	682.4	4.6	691.4	5.4	695.4	2.3	686.0	6.0
1963	691.1	-2.5	694.5	2.0	713.3	11.3	708.6	-2.6	701.9	2.3
1964	712.5	2.2	721.4	5.1	714.9	-3.6	714.7	-0.1	715.9	2.0
1965	713.8	-0.5	728.4	8.4	746.3	10.2	761.7	8.5	737.6	3.0
1966	776.3	7.9	799.9	12.7	812.5	6.5	829.5	8.6	804.6	9.1
1967	864.3	17.9	860.2	-1.9	865.4	2.4	872.5	3.3	865.6	7.6
1968	887.3	7.0	892.2	2.2	893.6	0.6	896.6	1.3	892.4	3.1
1969	891.6	-2.2	890.8	-0.4	888.7	-0.9	878.8	-4.4	887.5	-0.5
1970	871.8	-3.1	863.2	-3.9	866.7	1.6	865.5	-0.6	866.8	-2.3
1971	856.4	-4.1	852.5	-1.8	848.8	-1.7	846.4	-1.1	851.0	-1.8
1972	858.8	6.0	859.9	0.5	848.4	-5.2	849.2	0.4	854.1	0.4
1973	854.6	2.6	852.3	-1.1	839.1	-6.1	847.7	4.2	848.4	-0.7
1974	857.5	4.7	866.9	4.5	861.8	-2.3	865.6	1.8	862.9	1.7
1975	875.7	4.7	871.6	-1.9	875.7	1.9	882.2	3.0	876.3	1.6
1976	886.1	1.8	876.8	-4.1	872.8	-1.8	871.5	-0.6	876.8	0.1
1977	878.1	3.1	887.6	4.4	887.4	-0.1	885.8	-0.7	884.7	0.9
1978	887.5	0.8	910.9	11.0	917.8	3.1	925.9	3.6	910.6	2.9
1979	916.2	-4.1	924.8	3.8	925.6	0.3	932.9	3.2	924.9	1.6
1980	946.5	6.0	948.3	0.8	936.4	-4.9	934.4	-0.9	941.4	1.8
1981	946.1	5.1	947.7	0.7	945.5	-0.9	951.7	2.6	947.7	0.7
1982	949.0	-1.1	954.7	2.4	961.2	2.8	975.5	6.1	960.1	1.3
1983	978.4	1.2	985.0	2.7	1,001.8	7.0	984.1	-6.9	987.3	2.8
1984	994.1	4.1	1,016.6	9.4	1,022.5	2.3	1,040.4	7.2	1,018.4	3.2
1985	1,053.2	5.0	1,072.8	7.7	1,095.7	8.8	1,098.9	1.2	1,080.1	6.1
1986	1,108.3	3.5	1,129.6	7.9	1,154.5	9.1	1,147.7	-2.3	1,135.0	5.1
1987	1,153.4	2.0	1,162.8	3.3	1,165.9	1.1	1,181.5	5.5	1,165.9	2.7
1988	1,172.5	-3.0	1,177.0	1.5	1,176.1	-0.3	1,198.1	7.7	1,180.9	1.3
1989	1,193.5	-1.5	1,211.1	6.0	1,222.6	3.9	1,228.4	1.9	1,213.9	2.8
1990	1,246.5	6.0	1,248.2	0.5	1,246.8	-0.4	1,259.9	4.3	1,250.4	3.0
1991	1,262.6	0.9	1,263.8	0.4	1,255.1	-2.7	1,250.7	-1.4	1,258.0	0.6
1992	1,258.5	2.5	1,257.5	-0.3	1,266.5	2.9	1,272.5	1.9	1,263.8	0.5
1993	1,257.2	-4.7	1,257.9	0.2	1,261.1	1.0	1,265.7	1.5	1,260.5	-0.3
1994	1,252.3	-4.2	1,249.7	-0.8	1,271.0	7.0	1,266.6	-1.4	1,259.9	-0.0
1995	1,263.0	-1.1	1,265.8	0.9	1,264.4	-0.4	-	-	-	-

Source: "National Income and Product Account Tables: Selected NIPA Tables," *Survey of Current Business*, November 1995, U.S. Department of Commerce, Bureau of Economic Analysis, National Income and Wealth Division. - indicates that no data are available.

Gross Domestic Product
Government consumption expenditures and gross investment
Federal: Total - Actual Dollars

In billions of actual dollars and percent. Quarterly data are seasonally adjusted and annualized. Growth rates for quarters are compound annual growth rates; changes from year to year are percentage changes.

Year	1st Quarter	% Change	2nd Quarter	% Change	3rd Quarter	% Change	4th Quarter	% Change	TOTAL	% Change
1959	66.2	-	67.8	10.0	67.7	-0.6	67.1	-3.5	67.2	-
1960	64.0	-17.2	64.5	3.2	66.2	11.0	67.7	9.4	65.6	-2.4
1961	67.1	-3.5	68.7	9.9	69.3	3.5	71.3	12.1	69.1	5.3
1962	74.5	19.2	75.9	7.7	77.3	7.6	78.1	4.2	76.5	10.7
1963	76.9	-6.0	77.3	2.1	79.1	9.6	79.0	-0.5	78.1	2.1
1964	79.4	2.0	80.1	3.6	79.4	-3.5	78.6	-4.0	79.4	1.7
1965	78.3	-1.5	79.9	8.4	82.4	13.1	86.5	21.4	81.8	3.0
1966	88.5	9.6	92.9	21.4	96.7	17.4	98.4	7.2	94.1	15.0
1967	105.1	30.1	105.0	-0.4	107.0	7.8	109.1	8.1	106.6	13.3
1968	112.4	12.7	113.1	2.5	114.2	3.9	115.5	4.6	113.8	6.8
1969	114.1	-4.8	114.8	2.5	117.6	10.1	116.7	-3.0	115.8	1.8
1970	117.1	1.4	115.5	-5.4	115.3	-0.7	115.7	1.4	115.9	0.1
1971	116.2	1.7	116.8	2.1	117.3	1.7	117.8	1.7	117.1	1.0
1972	125.2	27.6	127.3	6.9	123.1	-12.6	124.7	5.3	125.1	6.8
1973	128.3	12.1	129.1	2.5	126.0	-9.3	129.6	11.9	128.2	2.5
1974	133.7	13.3	137.2	10.9	140.9	11.2	147.8	21.1	139.9	9.1
1975	150.5	7.5	153.0	6.8	154.7	4.5	159.7	13.6	154.5	10.4
1976	159.3	-1.0	160.8	3.8	163.1	5.8	167.7	11.8	162.7	5.3
1977	172.7	12.5	177.8	12.3	179.5	3.9	183.7	9.7	178.4	9.6
1978	186.3	5.8	192.5	14.0	196.1	7.7	202.9	14.6	194.4	9.0
1979	206.5	7.3	212.0	11.1	216.0	7.8	225.6	19.0	215.0	10.6
1980	236.3	20.4	247.8	20.9	248.5	1.1	261.1	21.9	248.4	15.5
1981	271.3	16.6	282.8	18.1	285.4	3.7	296.9	17.1	284.1	14.4
1982	301.5	6.3	307.6	8.3	314.8	9.7	328.9	19.2	313.2	10.2
1983	334.5	7.0	343.8	11.6	355.5	14.3	344.0	-12.3	344.5	10.0
1984	358.1	17.4	372.6	17.2	373.3	0.8	386.3	14.7	372.6	8.2
1985	395.2	9.5	404.4	9.6	418.6	14.8	422.2	3.5	410.1	10.1
1986	418.6	-3.4	431.1	12.5	448.4	17.0	442.8	-4.9	435.2	6.1
1987	447.9	4.7	454.9	6.4	456.5	1.4	463.4	6.2	455.7	4.7
1988	456.3	-6.0	454.6	-1.5	453.5	-1.0	465.0	10.5	457.3	0.4
1989	465.5	0.4	476.5	9.8	484.9	7.2	482.0	-2.4	477.2	4.4
1990	496.4	12.5	500.1	3.0	501.2	0.9	516.7	13.0	503.6	5.5
1991	525.6	7.1	528.2	2.0	520.9	-5.4	515.5	-4.1	522.6	3.8
1992	521.8	5.0	523.2	1.1	532.0	6.9	535.0	2.3	528.0	1.0
1993	525.0	-7.3	519.6	-4.1	520.8	0.9	522.9	1.6	522.1	-1.1
1994	511.3	-8.6	509.4	-1.5	523.6	11.6	520.9	-2.0	516.3	-1.1
1995	519.9	-0.8	522.6	2.1	517.3	-4.0	-	-	-	-

Source: "National Income and Product Account Tables: Selected NIPA Tables," *Survey of Current Business*, November 1995, U.S. Department of Commerce, Bureau of Economic Analysis, National Income and Wealth Division. - indicates that no data are available.

Gross Domestic Product

Government consumption expenditures and gross investment
Federal: Total - Chained (1992) Dollars

In billions of chained (1992) dollars and percent. Quarterly data are seasonally adjusted and annualized. Growth rates for quarters are compound annual growth rates; changes from year to year are percentage changes.

Year	1st Quarter	% Change	2nd Quarter	% Change	3rd Quarter	% Change	4th Quarter	% Change	TOTAL	% Change
1959	-	-	-	-	365.6	-	361.4	-4.5	360.5	-
1960	345.0	-17.0	347.1	2.5	351.1	4.7	354.5	3.9	349.4	-3.1
1961	353.6	-1.0	360.6	8.2	364.9	4.9	373.0	9.2	363.0	3.9
1962	386.2	14.9	391.7	5.8	397.0	5.5	398.0	1.0	393.2	8.3
1963	388.3	-9.4	388.8	0.5	399.5	11.5	390.5	-8.7	391.8	-0.4
1964	389.5	-1.0	391.6	2.2	381.7	-9.7	377.9	-3.9	385.2	-1.7
1965	374.2	-3.9	380.2	6.6	388.2	8.7	398.3	10.8	385.2	-
1966	407.7	9.8	428.1	21.6	436.6	8.2	444.2	7.1	429.1	11.4
1967	474.4	30.1	468.3	-5.0	471.8	3.0	472.3	0.4	471.7	9.9
1968	480.5	7.1	477.7	-2.3	473.6	-3.4	473.5	-0.1	476.3	1.0
1969	466.3	-5.9	462.5	-3.2	459.8	-2.3	451.0	-7.4	459.9	-3.4
1970	439.7	-9.7	428.5	-9.8	422.0	-5.9	418.3	-3.5	427.2	-7.1
1971	406.6	-10.7	399.7	-6.6	394.8	-4.8	386.8	-7.9	397.0	-7.1
1972	397.0	11.0	399.7	2.7	384.7	-14.2	379.3	-5.5	390.2	-1.7
1973	381.8	2.7	378.6	-3.3	360.6	-17.7	363.6	3.4	371.1	-4.9
1974	367.6	4.5	370.7	3.4	366.6	-4.4	370.4	4.2	368.8	-0.6
1975	368.5	-2.0	368.2	-0.3	366.9	-1.4	368.1	1.3	367.9	-0.2
1976	365.2	-3.1	364.4	-0.9	363.6	-0.9	363.8	0.2	364.3	-1.0
1977	366.0	2.4	372.3	7.1	372.2	-0.1	369.8	-2.6	370.1	1.6
1978	370.7	1.0	378.6	8.8	379.3	0.7	382.2	3.1	377.7	2.1
1979	381.3	-0.9	384.8	3.7	383.1	-1.8	384.0	0.9	383.3	1.5
1980	395.1	12.1	403.7	9.0	399.3	-4.3	399.2	-0.1	399.3	4.2
1981	406.7	7.7	418.4	12.0	418.1	-0.3	420.5	2.3	415.9	4.2
1982	420.2	-0.3	424.3	4.0	431.0	6.5	442.1	10.7	429.4	3.2
1983	444.6	2.3	452.5	7.3	465.1	11.6	448.4	-13.6	452.7	5.4
1984	450.8	2.2	465.9	14.1	463.1	-2.4	475.1	10.8	463.7	2.4
1985	482.3	6.2	491.5	7.9	505.2	11.6	503.4	-1.4	495.6	6.9
1986	500.1	-2.6	514.8	12.3	533.9	15.7	524.8	-6.6	518.4	4.6
1987	526.9	1.6	534.3	5.7	534.2	-0.1	542.2	6.1	534.4	3.1
1988	527.6	-10.3	522.2	-4.0	517.9	-3.3	530.6	10.2	524.6	-1.8
1989	521.4	-6.8	532.0	8.4	537.7	4.4	535.0	-2.0	531.5	1.3
1990	542.9	6.0	543.0	0.1	538.2	-3.5	543.5	4.0	541.9	2.0
1991	547.3	2.8	547.1	-0.1	536.3	-7.7	526.9	-6.8	539.4	-0.5
1992	525.1	-1.4	523.3	-1.4	529.6	4.9	534.0	3.4	528.0	-2.1
1993	515.7	-13.0	509.2	-4.9	505.4	-3.0	504.5	-0.7	508.7	-3.7
1994	489.8	-11.2	483.3	-5.2	496.6	11.5	489.1	-5.9	489.7	-3.7
1995	481.3	-6.2	479.9	-1.2	473.2	-5.5	-	-		

Source: "National Income and Product Account Tables: Selected NIPA Tables," *Survey of Current Business*, November 1995, U.S. Department of Commerce, Bureau of Economic Analysis, National Income and Wealth Division. - indicates that no data are available.

Gross Domestic Product

Government consumption expenditures and gross investment
Federal - National defense - Actual Dollars

In billions of actual dollars and percent. Quarterly data are seasonally adjusted and annualized. Growth rates for quarters are compound annual growth rates; changes from year to year are percentage changes.

Year	1st Quarter	% Change	2nd Quarter	% Change	3rd Quarter	% Change	4th Quarter	% Change	TOTAL	% Change
1959	56.1	-	55.6	-3.5	55.7	0.7	55.4	-2.1	55.7	-
1960	54.2	-8.4	54.2	-	55.2	7.6	55.8	4.4	54.9	-1.4
1961	56.6	5.9	57.3	5.0	57.6	2.1	59.3	12.3	57.7	5.1
1962	61.9	18.7	62.3	2.6	62.4	0.6	62.5	0.6	62.3	8.0
1963	62.0	-3.2	62.3	1.9	62.2	-0.6	62.4	1.3	62.2	-0.2
1964	62.0	-2.5	61.8	-1.3	61.2	-3.8	60.3	-5.8	61.3	-1.4
1965	59.5	-5.2	60.8	9.0	62.0	8.1	65.9	27.6	62.0	1.1
1966	68.0	13.4	71.4	21.6	75.9	27.7	78.5	14.4	73.4	18.4
1967	83.1	25.6	84.3	5.9	86.7	11.9	87.9	5.7	85.5	16.5
1968	90.9	14.4	92.1	5.4	92.0	-0.4	92.8	3.5	92.0	7.6
1969	91.1	-7.1	91.5	1.8	93.4	8.6	93.4	-	92.4	0.4
1970	92.6	-3.4	89.9	-11.2	89.9	-	90.1	0.9	90.6	-1.9
1971	90.1	-	88.5	-6.9	87.4	-4.9	88.8	6.6	88.7	-2.1
1972	94.0	25.6	95.3	5.6	91.2	-16.1	92.4	5.4	93.2	5.1
1973	94.9	11.3	95.8	3.8	92.4	-13.5	95.7	15.1	94.7	1.6
1974	97.7	8.6	102.0	18.8	101.9	-0.4	106.1	17.5	101.9	7.6
1975	108.6	9.8	109.9	4.9	111.0	4.1	114.2	12.0	110.9	8.8
1976	113.5	-2.4	115.0	5.4	116.8	6.4	119.2	8.5	116.1	4.7
1977	122.8	12.6	126.1	11.2	126.5	1.3	127.7	3.8	125.8	8.4
1978	130.2	8.1	134.4	13.5	136.9	7.7	140.9	12.2	135.6	7.8
1979	144.2	9.7	149.1	14.3	151.9	7.7	159.7	22.2	151.2	11.5
1980	166.7	18.7	171.4	11.8	174.2	6.7	184.6	26.1	174.2	15.2
1981	191.2	15.1	199.7	19.0	203.6	8.0	213.3	20.5	202.0	16.0
1982	219.0	11.1	227.8	17.1	233.7	10.8	243.3	17.5	230.9	14.3
1983	245.8	4.2	253.3	12.8	256.6	5.3	264.5	12.9	255.0	10.4
1984	275.5	17.7	280.8	7.9	281.1	0.4	293.4	18.7	282.7	10.9
1985	298.8	7.6	306.5	10.7	320.0	18.8	324.4	5.6	312.4	10.5
1986	320.2	-5.1	330.6	13.6	343.7	16.8	335.0	-9.7	332.4	6.4
1987	341.7	8.2	349.9	10.0	355.5	6.6	354.4	-1.2	350.4	5.4
1988	354.6	0.2	353.2	-1.6	351.5	-1.9	356.7	6.1	354.0	1.0
1989	352.8	-4.3	360.6	9.1	367.6	8.0	361.3	-6.7	360.6	1.9
1990	369.7	9.6	370.6	1.0	368.9	-1.8	383.3	16.6	373.1	3.5
1991	389.7	6.8	389.3	-0.4	382.1	-7.2	373.0	-9.2	383.5	2.8
1992	372.8	-0.2	374.1	1.4	380.9	7.5	375.3	-5.8	375.8	-2.0
1993	365.2	-10.3	362.2	-3.2	360.7	-1.6	360.8	0.1	362.2	-3.6
1994	346.7	-14.7	349.3	3.0	362.1	15.5	349.6	-13.1	352.0	-2.8
1995	347.7	-2.2	352.3	5.4	346.2	-6.7	-	-	-	-

Source: "National Income and Product Account Tables: Selected NIPA Tables," *Survey of Current Business*, November 1995, U.S. Department of Commerce, Bureau of Economic Analysis, National Income and Wealth Division. - indicates that no data are available.

Gross Domestic Product
Government consumption expenditures and gross investment
Federal - National defense - Chained (1992) Dollars

In billions of chained (1992) dollars and percent. Quarterly data are seasonally adjusted and annualized. Growth rates for quarters are compound annual growth rates; changes from year to year are percentage changes.

Year	1st Quarter	% Change	2nd Quarter	% Change	3rd Quarter	% Change	4th Quarter	% Change	TOTAL	% Change
1959	-	-	-	-	309.8	-	306.9	-3.7	307.6	-
1960	300.8	-7.7	300.1	-0.9	302.6	3.4	301.6	-1.3	301.3	-2.0
1961	308.8	9.9	311.1	3.0	314.1	3.9	321.3	9.5	313.8	4.1
1962	332.5	14.7	333.5	1.2	332.0	-1.8	331.5	-0.6	332.4	5.9
1963	324.5	-8.2	325.4	1.1	326.5	1.4	319.6	-8.2	324.0	-2.5
1964	316.0	-4.4	314.6	-1.8	306.9	-9.4	302.2	-6.0	309.9	-4.4
1965	296.3	-7.6	300.7	6.1	303.7	4.1	314.4	14.9	303.8	-2.0
1966	326.0	15.6	342.8	22.3	355.4	15.5	368.5	15.6	348.2	14.6
1967	390.6	26.2	391.5	0.9	397.3	6.1	394.5	-2.8	393.5	13.0
1968	404.6	10.6	405.0	0.4	397.6	-7.1	396.4	-1.2	400.9	1.9
1969	387.9	-8.3	383.3	-4.7	380.0	-3.4	375.4	-4.8	381.6	-4.8
1970	363.1	-12.5	349.1	-14.6	343.9	-5.8	339.9	-4.6	349.0	-8.5
1971	328.5	-12.8	316.1	-14.3	307.2	-10.8	303.2	-5.1	313.7	-10.1
1972	307.5	5.8	309.1	2.1	294.7	-17.4	289.9	-6.4	300.3	-4.3
1973	291.3	1.9	288.8	-3.4	270.0	-23.6	274.5	6.8	281.2	-6.4
1974	273.9	-0.9	280.5	10.0	269.3	-15.0	270.5	1.8	273.5	-2.7
1975	271.2	1.0	270.1	-1.6	268.9	-1.8	268.7	-0.3	269.7	-1.4
1976	265.2	-5.1	265.2	-	265.0	-0.3	263.2	-2.7	264.7	-1.9
1977	265.5	3.5	269.9	6.8	268.1	-2.6	262.1	-8.7	266.4	0.6
1978	263.0	1.4	267.9	7.7	267.7	-0.3	268.5	1.2	266.7	0.1
1979	267.9	-0.9	272.1	6.4	271.0	-1.6	273.1	3.1	271.0	1.6
1980	279.8	10.2	279.2	-0.9	280.9	2.5	283.1	3.2	280.7	3.6
1981	287.3	6.1	295.9	12.5	298.6	3.7	302.2	4.9	296.0	5.5
1982	304.9	3.6	313.7	12.1	320.0	8.3	327.5	9.7	316.5	6.9
1983	326.8	-0.9	333.2	8.1	335.4	2.7	343.1	9.5	334.6	5.7
1984	342.8	-0.3	347.3	5.4	345.3	-2.3	356.9	14.1	348.1	4.0
1985	361.9	5.7	369.9	9.1	382.2	14.0	382.4	0.2	374.1	7.5
1986	379.0	-3.5	392.1	14.6	407.2	16.3	395.2	-11.3	393.4	5.2
1987	399.7	4.6	408.9	9.5	414.7	5.8	413.3	-1.3	409.2	4.0
1988	409.3	-3.8	405.6	-3.6	401.1	-4.4	406.1	5.1	405.5	-0.9
1989	394.4	-11.0	402.4	8.4	407.4	5.1	402.1	-5.1	401.6	-1.0
1990	404.1	2.0	402.8	-1.3	396.1	-6.5	403.1	7.3	401.5	-0.0
1991	408.4	5.4	405.0	-3.3	395.0	-9.5	381.7	-12.8	397.5	-1.0
1992	374.2	-7.6	373.3	-1.0	378.7	5.9	376.8	-2.0	375.8	-5.5
1993	361.2	-15.6	356.4	-5.2	351.2	-5.7	350.8	-0.5	354.9	-5.6
1994	334.8	-17.0	335.5	0.8	346.1	13.2	331.3	-16.0	336.9	-5.1
1995	325.3	-7.0	326.1	1.0	319.8	-7.5	-	-	-	-

Source: "National Income and Product Account Tables: Selected NIPA Tables," *Survey of Current Business*, November 1995, U.S. Department of Commerce, Bureau of Economic Analysis, National Income and Wealth Division. - indicates that no data are available.

Gross Domestic Product

Government consumption expenditures and gross investment
Federal - Nondefense - Actual Dollars

In billions of actual dollars and percent. Quarterly data are seasonally adjusted and annualized. Growth rates for quarters are compound annual growth rates; changes from year to year are percentage changes.

Year	1st Quarter	% Change	2nd Quarter	% Change	3rd Quarter	% Change	4th Quarter	% Change	TOTAL	% Change
1959	10.1	-	12.2	112.9	12.0	-6.4	11.8	-6.5	11.5	-
1960	9.8	-52.4	10.3	22.0	11.0	30.1	11.9	37.0	10.8	-6.1
1961	10.5	-39.4	11.4	39.0	11.7	10.9	12.0	10.7	11.4	5.6
1962	12.6	21.6	13.6	35.7	14.9	44.1	15.5	17.1	14.2	24.6
1963	15.0	-12.3	14.9	-2.6	16.9	65.5	16.6	-6.9	15.9	12.0
1964	17.4	20.7	18.4	25.0	18.2	-4.3	18.4	4.5	18.1	13.8
1965	18.7	6.7	19.1	8.8	20.4	30.1	20.6	4.0	19.7	8.8
1966	20.5	-1.9	21.5	21.0	20.8	-12.4	19.9	-16.2	20.7	5.1
1967	22.0	49.4	20.6	-23.1	20.3	-5.7	21.2	18.9	21.0	1.4
1968	21.5	5.8	20.9	-10.7	22.2	27.3	22.6	7.4	21.8	3.8
1969	22.9	5.4	23.3	7.2	24.2	16.4	23.3	-14.1	23.4	7.3
1970	24.5	22.2	25.6	19.2	25.4	-3.1	25.6	3.2	25.3	8.1
1971	26.1	8.0	28.3	38.2	29.9	24.6	29.0	-11.5	28.3	11.9
1972	31.2	34.0	32.0	10.7	32.0	-	32.3	3.8	31.9	12.7
1973	33.3	13.0	33.3	-	33.6	3.7	33.8	2.4	33.5	5.0
1974	36.0	28.7	35.3	-7.6	39.0	49.0	41.7	30.7	38.0	13.4
1975	41.9	1.9	43.1	12.0	43.7	5.7	45.5	17.5	43.6	14.7
1976	45.8	2.7	45.9	0.9	46.3	3.5	48.6	21.4	46.6	6.9
1977	49.9	11.1	51.6	14.3	52.9	10.5	56.0	25.6	52.6	12.9
1978	56.1	0.7	58.2	15.8	59.2	7.1	62.0	20.3	58.9	12.0
1979	62.3	1.9	62.9	3.9	64.0	7.2	65.9	12.4	63.8	8.3
1980	69.6	24.4	76.4	45.2	74.3	-10.5	76.5	12.4	74.2	16.3
1981	80.1	20.2	83.2	16.4	81.8	-6.6	83.6	9.1	82.2	10.8
1982	82.5	-5.2	79.9	-12.0	81.1	6.1	85.6	24.1	82.3	0.1
1983	88.7	15.3	90.4	7.9	98.9	43.3	79.6	-58.0	89.4	8.6
1984	82.6	15.9	91.8	52.6	92.2	1.8	93.0	3.5	89.9	0.6
1985	96.4	15.4	97.9	6.4	98.6	2.9	97.8	-3.2	97.7	8.7
1986	98.5	2.9	100.5	8.4	104.7	17.8	107.7	12.0	102.9	5.3
1987	106.2	-5.5	105.0	-4.4	100.9	-14.7	109.0	36.2	105.3	2.3
1988	101.7	-24.2	101.4	-1.2	102.0	2.4	108.2	26.6	103.3	-1.9
1989	112.7	17.7	115.9	11.9	117.3	4.9	120.7	12.1	116.7	13.0
1990	126.7	21.4	129.5	9.1	132.3	8.9	133.3	3.1	130.4	11.7
1991	136.0	8.4	138.9	8.8	138.8	-0.3	142.6	11.4	139.1	6.7
1992	149.0	19.2	149.1	0.3	151.1	5.5	159.7	24.8	152.2	9.4
1993	159.8	0.3	157.4	-5.9	160.1	7.0	162.2	5.4	159.9	5.1
1994	164.6	6.1	160.0	-10.7	161.5	3.8	171.2	26.3	164.3	2.8
1995	172.1	2.1	170.3	-4.1	171.1	1.9	-	-	-	-

Source: "National Income and Product Account Tables: Selected NIPA Tables," *Survey of Current Business*, November 1995, U.S. Department of Commerce, Bureau of Economic Analysis, National Income and Wealth Division. - indicates that no data are available.

Gross Domestic Product
Government consumption expenditures and gross investment
Federal - Nondefense - Chained (1992) Dollars

In billions of chained (1992) dollars and percent. Quarterly data are seasonally adjusted and annualized. Growth rates for quarters are compound annual growth rates; changes from year to year are percentage changes.

Year	1st Quarter	% Change	2nd Quarter	% Change	3rd Quarter	% Change	4th Quarter	% Change	TOTAL	% Change
1959	-	-	-	-	61.6	-	60.3	-8.2	58.8	-
1960	50.3	-51.6	53.0	23.3	54.4	11.0	58.6	34.6	54.1	-8.0
1961	51.2	-41.7	55.7	40.1	57.0	9.7	58.0	7.2	55.5	2.6
1962	60.2	16.1	64.4	31.0	70.6	44.4	71.9	7.6	66.8	20.4
1963	69.3	-13.7	68.9	-2.3	77.7	61.7	75.6	-10.4	72.9	9.1
1964	77.8	12.2	80.9	16.9	78.7	-10.4	79.3	3.1	79.2	8.6
1965	81.1	9.4	82.7	8.1	87.3	24.2	87.2	-0.5	84.6	6.8
1966	85.6	-7.1	89.4	19.0	86.1	-14.0	81.6	-19.3	85.7	1.3
1967	89.7	46.0	83.4	-25.3	81.5	-8.8	84.3	14.5	84.7	-1.2
1968	83.1	-5.6	80.2	-13.2	82.8	13.6	83.8	4.9	82.5	-2.6
1969	84.8	4.9	85.2	1.9	85.7	2.4	81.7	-17.4	84.3	2.2
1970	82.2	2.5	84.2	10.1	82.9	-6.0	82.9	-	83.0	-1.5
1971	82.3	-2.9	86.7	23.2	90.0	16.1	86.2	-15.8	86.3	4.0
1972	91.7	28.1	92.8	4.9	92.0	-3.4	91.2	-3.4	91.9	6.5
1973	92.1	4.0	91.5	-2.6	91.8	1.3	90.5	-5.5	91.5	-0.4
1974	94.8	20.4	91.7	-12.5	98.3	32.0	100.8	10.6	96.4	5.4
1975	98.3	-9.6	99.1	3.3	98.9	-0.8	100.2	5.4	99.1	2.8
1976	100.8	2.4	100.1	-2.7	99.5	-2.4	101.3	7.4	100.4	1.3
1977	101.3	-	103.2	7.7	104.8	6.3	108.1	13.2	104.3	3.9
1978	108.3	0.7	111.1	10.7	112.0	3.3	114.1	7.7	111.4	6.8
1979	113.7	-1.4	113.1	-2.1	112.6	-1.8	111.3	-4.5	112.7	1.2
1980	115.8	17.2	124.9	35.3	118.8	-18.2	116.6	-7.2	119.0	5.6
1981	119.8	11.4	122.9	10.8	120.0	-9.1	118.8	-3.9	120.4	1.2
1982	115.7	-10.0	111.0	-15.3	111.5	1.8	115.0	13.2	113.3	-5.9
1983	118.3	12.0	119.8	5.2	130.4	40.4	105.5	-57.2	118.5	4.6
1984	108.1	10.2	118.9	46.4	118.2	-2.3	118.5	1.0	115.9	-2.2
1985	120.8	8.0	122.0	4.0	123.3	4.3	121.2	-6.6	121.8	5.1
1986	121.2	-	122.9	5.7	126.8	13.3	129.8	9.8	125.2	2.8
1987	127.4	-7.2	125.4	-6.1	119.5	-17.5	128.9	35.4	125.3	0.1
1988	118.4	-28.8	116.7	-5.6	116.8	0.3	124.5	29.1	119.1	-4.9
1989	127.1	8.6	129.7	8.4	130.5	2.5	133.0	7.9	130.1	9.2
1990	138.9	19.0	140.4	4.4	142.2	5.2	140.5	-4.7	140.5	8.0
1991	139.0	-4.2	142.2	9.5	141.4	-2.2	145.3	11.5	142.0	1.1
1992	150.8	16.0	150.0	-2.1	150.9	2.4	157.1	17.5	152.2	7.2
1993	154.5	-6.5	152.7	-4.6	154.2	4.0	153.7	-1.3	153.8	1.1
1994	154.8	2.9	147.7	-17.1	150.5	7.8	157.5	19.9	152.6	-0.8
1995	155.6	-4.7	153.6	-5.0	153.1	-1.3	-	-	-	-

Source: "National Income and Product Account Tables: Selected NIPA Tables," *Survey of Current Business*, November 1995, U.S. Department of Commerce, Bureau of Economic Analysis, National Income and Wealth Division. - indicates that no data are available.

Gross Domestic Product

Government consumption expenditures and gross investment
State and local - Actual Dollars

In billions of actual dollars and percent. Quarterly data are seasonally adjusted and annualized. Growth rates for quarters are compound annual growth rates; changes from year to year are percentage changes.

Year	1st Quarter	% Change	2nd Quarter	% Change	3rd Quarter	% Change	4th Quarter	% Change	TOTAL	% Change
1959	44.7	-	44.9	1.8	44.9	-	44.8	-0.9	44.8	-
1960	46.0	11.2	47.3	11.8	48.2	7.8	49.0	6.8	47.6	6.3
1961	50.8	15.5	50.9	0.8	51.7	6.4	53.6	15.5	51.8	8.8
1962	53.9	2.3	54.5	4.5	55.3	6.0	56.2	6.7	55.0	6.2
1963	57.8	11.9	58.7	6.4	60.4	12.1	61.7	8.9	59.6	8.4
1964	62.9	8.0	64.6	11.3	65.7	7.0	66.7	6.2	65.0	9.1
1965	67.9	7.4	70.1	13.6	72.7	15.7	74.3	9.1	71.2	9.5
1966	76.3	11.2	78.2	10.3	80.2	10.6	83.3	16.4	79.5	11.7
1967	85.6	11.5	87.0	6.7	88.6	7.6	91.2	12.3	88.1	10.8
1968	94.2	13.8	97.3	13.8	99.5	9.4	102.3	11.7	98.3	11.6
1969	104.3	8.1	107.2	11.6	109.2	7.7	111.1	7.1	108.0	9.9
1970	114.7	13.6	117.9	11.6	122.5	16.5	125.5	10.2	120.2	11.3
1971	128.8	10.9	131.9	10.0	133.8	5.9	136.8	9.3	132.8	10.5
1972	140.0	9.7	141.3	3.8	144.7	10.0	149.4	13.6	143.8	8.3
1973	153.5	11.4	157.0	9.4	161.1	10.9	166.1	13.0	159.4	10.8
1974	172.9	17.4	181.0	20.1	187.1	14.2	192.3	11.6	183.3	15.0
1975	201.8	21.3	204.6	5.7	210.2	11.4	215.9	11.3	208.1	13.5
1976	222.3	12.4	222.2	-0.2	222.9	1.3	225.0	3.8	223.1	7.2
1977	231.2	11.5	236.8	10.0	240.7	6.8	245.2	7.7	238.5	6.9
1978	249.5	7.2	261.4	20.5	268.3	11.0	274.6	9.7	263.4	10.4
1979	276.8	3.2	287.3	16.1	297.4	14.8	306.6	13.0	292.0	10.9
1980	317.1	14.4	321.7	5.9	325.9	5.3	332.8	8.7	324.4	11.1
1981	345.6	16.3	345.7	0.1	348.9	3.8	356.8	9.4	349.2	7.6
1982	361.9	5.8	368.7	7.7	374.3	6.2	381.4	7.8	371.6	6.4
1983	384.8	3.6	387.7	3.0	394.5	7.2	397.9	3.5	391.2	5.3
1984	409.3	12.0	418.8	9.6	429.8	10.9	438.2	8.0	424.0	8.4
1985	448.0	9.3	460.4	11.5	471.4	9.9	479.9	7.4	464.9	9.6
1986	491.1	9.7	498.0	5.7	507.3	7.7	516.7	7.6	503.3	8.3
1987	525.3	6.8	532.6	5.7	540.4	6.0	550.4	7.6	537.2	6.7
1988	559.1	6.5	571.6	9.2	578.1	4.6	589.9	8.4	574.7	7.0
1989	599.9	7.0	612.1	8.4	622.1	6.7	637.4	10.2	617.9	7.5
1990	656.6	12.6	664.2	4.7	675.7	7.1	693.7	11.1	672.6	8.9
1991	695.0	0.8	699.2	2.4	705.5	3.7	713.6	4.7	703.4	4.6
1992	726.1	7.2	733.2	4.0	738.7	3.0	745.1	3.5	735.8	4.6
1993	753.8	4.8	765.0	6.1	772.7	4.1	779.7	3.7	767.8	4.3
1994	785.0	2.7	791.4	3.3	804.4	6.7	812.6	4.1	798.4	4.0
1995	826.1	6.8	837.3	5.5	848.2	5.3	-	-	-	-

Source: "National Income and Product Account Tables: Selected NIPA Tables," *Survey of Current Business*, November 1995, U.S. Department of Commerce, Bureau of Economic Analysis, National Income and Wealth Division. - indicates that no data are available.

Gross Domestic Product

Government consumption expenditures and gross investment
State and local - Chained (1992) Dollars

In billions of chained (1992) dollars and percent. Quarterly data are seasonally adjusted and annualized. Growth rates for quarters are compound annual growth rates; changes from year to year are percentage changes.

Year	1st Quarter	% Change	2nd Quarter	% Change	3rd Quarter	% Change	4th Quarter	% Change	TOTAL	% Change
1959	-	-	-	-	257.3	-	255.9	-2.2	256.8	-
1960	259.9	6.4	266.0	9.7	270.0	6.2	273.0	4.5	267.2	4.0
1961	281.8	13.5	280.1	-2.4	282.6	3.6	290.5	11.7	283.8	6.2
1962	288.0	-3.4	290.0	2.8	293.6	5.1	296.7	4.3	292.1	2.9
1963	302.3	7.8	305.3	4.0	313.4	11.0	317.9	5.9	309.7	6.0
1964	322.9	6.4	329.9	9.0	333.6	4.6	337.3	4.5	330.9	6.8
1965	340.4	3.7	349.0	10.5	359.1	12.1	364.2	5.8	353.2	6.7
1966	369.4	5.8	372.3	3.2	376.3	4.4	385.8	10.5	375.9	6.4
1967	390.2	4.6	392.2	2.1	393.9	1.7	400.6	7.0	394.2	4.9
1968	407.1	6.6	414.9	7.9	420.4	5.4	423.6	3.1	416.5	5.7
1969	425.7	2.0	428.8	2.9	429.3	0.5	428.2	-1.0	428.0	2.8
1970	432.5	4.1	435.0	2.3	445.0	9.5	447.5	2.3	440.0	2.8
1971	450.0	2.3	453.1	2.8	454.3	1.1	460.0	5.1	454.4	3.3
1972	462.2	1.9	460.5	-1.5	464.3	3.3	470.8	5.7	464.5	2.2
1973	473.8	2.6	474.7	0.8	479.9	4.5	485.5	4.7	478.5	3.0
1974	491.3	4.9	497.6	5.2	496.7	-0.7	496.6	-0.1	495.6	3.6
1975	508.8	10.2	504.9	-3.0	510.5	4.5	515.9	4.3	510.0	2.9
1976	522.8	5.5	514.1	-6.5	511.0	-2.4	509.4	-1.2	514.3	0.8
1977	513.9	3.6	517.0	2.4	516.9	-0.1	517.7	0.6	516.4	0.4
1978	518.5	0.6	534.2	12.7	540.5	4.8	545.7	3.9	534.7	3.5
1979	536.8	-6.4	541.9	3.9	544.5	1.9	550.9	4.8	543.5	1.6
1980	553.2	1.7	546.1	-5.0	538.6	-5.4	536.6	-1.5	543.6	0.0
1981	540.7	3.1	530.3	-7.5	528.2	-1.6	532.0	2.9	532.8	-2.0
1982	529.6	-1.8	531.2	1.2	530.8	-0.3	533.8	2.3	531.4	-0.3
1983	534.1	0.2	532.7	-1.0	536.6	3.0	536.0	-0.4	534.9	0.7
1984	543.8	5.9	550.9	5.3	559.9	6.7	565.6	4.1	555.0	3.8
1985	571.1	3.9	581.5	7.5	590.5	6.3	595.6	3.5	584.7	5.4
1986	608.7	9.1	615.1	4.3	620.8	3.8	623.2	1.6	616.9	5.5
1987	626.8	2.3	628.8	1.3	632.0	2.1	639.6	4.9	631.8	2.4
1988	645.1	3.5	655.0	6.3	658.4	2.1	667.8	5.8	656.6	3.9
1989	672.3	2.7	679.4	4.3	685.1	3.4	693.7	5.1	682.6	4.0
1990	703.8	6.0	705.4	0.9	708.7	1.9	716.5	4.5	708.6	3.8
1991	715.5	-0.6	716.8	0.7	718.8	1.1	723.8	2.8	718.7	1.4
1992	733.5	5.5	734.2	0.4	736.9	1.5	738.5	0.9	735.8	2.4
1993	741.6	1.7	748.8	3.9	755.7	3.7	761.3	3.0	751.8	2.2
1994	762.7	0.7	766.8	2.2	774.7	4.2	777.7	1.6	770.5	2.5
1995	782.2	2.3	786.3	2.1	791.7	2.8	-		-	

Source: "National Income and Product Account Tables: Selected NIPA Tables," *Survey of Current Business*, November 1995, U.S. Department of Commerce, Bureau of Economic Analysis, National Income and Wealth Division. - indicates that no data are available.

CHAPTER 3

BUSINESS CYCLE INDICATORS

BUSINESS CYCLE INDICATORS

The indexes of economic indicators, also called business cycle indicators, are used by government, industry, and other institutions to forecast tendencies in the national economy. They are composites of several statistical series which tend to signal *changes* in the economy's general direction. They are "business cycle indicators" because they can predict the beginnings and ends of periods of sustained growth; each such period is a single business cycle; each ends when economic growth stops, as measured by Gross Domestic Product (GDP), or shows negative growth.

Arthur F. Burns and Wesley C. Mitchell have described business cycles as follows:

> Business cycles are a type of fluctuation found in the aggregate economic activity of nations that organize their work mainly in business enterprises; a cycle consists of expansions occurring at about the same time in many economic activities, followed by similarly general recessions, contractions, and revivals which merge into the expansion phase of the next cycle; this sequence of changes is recurrent but not periodic; in duration business cycles vary from more than one year to ten or twelve years; they are not divisible into shorter cycles of similar character with amplitudes approximating their own. (Reference 2.)

History

Business cycle indicators were developed by the National Bureau of Economic Research, Inc. (NBER). The first list of cyclic indicators was published by Burns and Mitchell in 1938. Publication of the NBER's indicators by the U.S. Department of Commerce began in 1961. Commerce began to publish composite indexes of leading, coincident, and lagging indicators in 1968. The series are available from 1948 to the present time. The series have been revised from time to time. Significant changes were made in 1983, 1987, and in 1989. After changes are made, the indexes are restated in the new format for past years.

Characteristics of the Indexes

Three composite indexes are used to predict the peaks and troughs of business cycles—the highest points of growth and the bottoms of periods of decline. The composite index of *Leading Indicators* tends to signal a change (downturn or upturn) before the economy actually turns down or resumes growth. The composite index of *Coincident Indicators* tends to turn up or down at the same time as the economy. And the composite index of *Lagging Indicators* shows changes after they have already become visible.

A graphic presentation following this introductory text illustrates the relationships between the indicator series and Gross Domestic Product (GDP) for the period 1959-1995. The vertical rectangular areas indicate periods of recession as commonly defined.

Each composite index combines several component indexes which behave in the appropriate manner. For example, the composite index of leading indicators is formed of several other leading indicators. A composite of selected leading, coincident, or lagging indicators is used because, over time, it has been found that the composite index predicts more accurately than any one of the components taken alone. Revisions of the business cycle indicators have typically taken the form of removing and adding components and changing the relative weight assigned to each component in calculating the composite index. Components will be discussed in separate sections.

Presentation

Data for each of the composite indexes are presented in sequence. Each section begins with a discussion of the composite index and its components. Tables with the indexes follow. The composite indexes are shown in two formats: the actual index and change from previous month.

Format and Calculation

Data are presented, in most cases, for the years 1948 to 1995 and for each month of the year.

The composite indexes relate to a base year. The base year at present (1996) is 1987, with the value of 100. It is expected that this basing will change in a reflection of the 1995 revisions of the national income accounts. When and in what manner remains to be seen. All other data points are calibrated to 1987. The 1987 base value, in turn, is produced by averaging the 1987 monthly values; for this reason, monthly values in 1987 will be very near 100. The significance of the composite indexes lies in month-to-month changes rather than in absolute value. A change is signalled when the index increases or decreases over a period of three or more months.

Values for the component indexes are shown in various formats (hours, weeks, dollars, percentages, index values). The formats are noted at the top of each component table.

Month-to-month percentage changes in the component series are used to construct the composite index. Calculation of each component's contribution is made by applying mathematical methods to minimize the tendency of volatile series to dominate the average and to standardize each series. These technical methods are described in References 1 and 2. At present, each component contributes equally to the composite index; that is to say, the weighting factor for each is 1. Before the 1989 revisions, different weights were assigned to each component to reflect its perceived relative importance; for example, in the composite index of leading indicators, the weighting for Stock Prices was 1.149 but that for Manufacturers' New Orders was .973. A change in Stock Prices of .10 would contribute .1149 to the index; a change of .10 in Manufacturers' New Orders would contribute .0973.

Bibliography

1. Hertzberg, Marie P. and Barry A. Beckman, "Business Cycle Indicators: Revised Composite Indexes." U.S. Department of Commerce, Bureau of Economic Analysis. *Survey of Current Business*. January 1989, Superintendent of Documents, U.S. Government Printing Office, Washington, DC 20302.

2. *Measuring Business Cycles*. National Bureau of Economic Research, Inc., 1946.

3. U.S. Department of Commerce, Bureau of Economic Analysis. "Composite Indexes of Leading, Coincident, and Lagging Indicators," *Survey of Current Business*. November 1987, Superintendent of Documents, U.S. Government Printing Office, Washington, DC 20302.

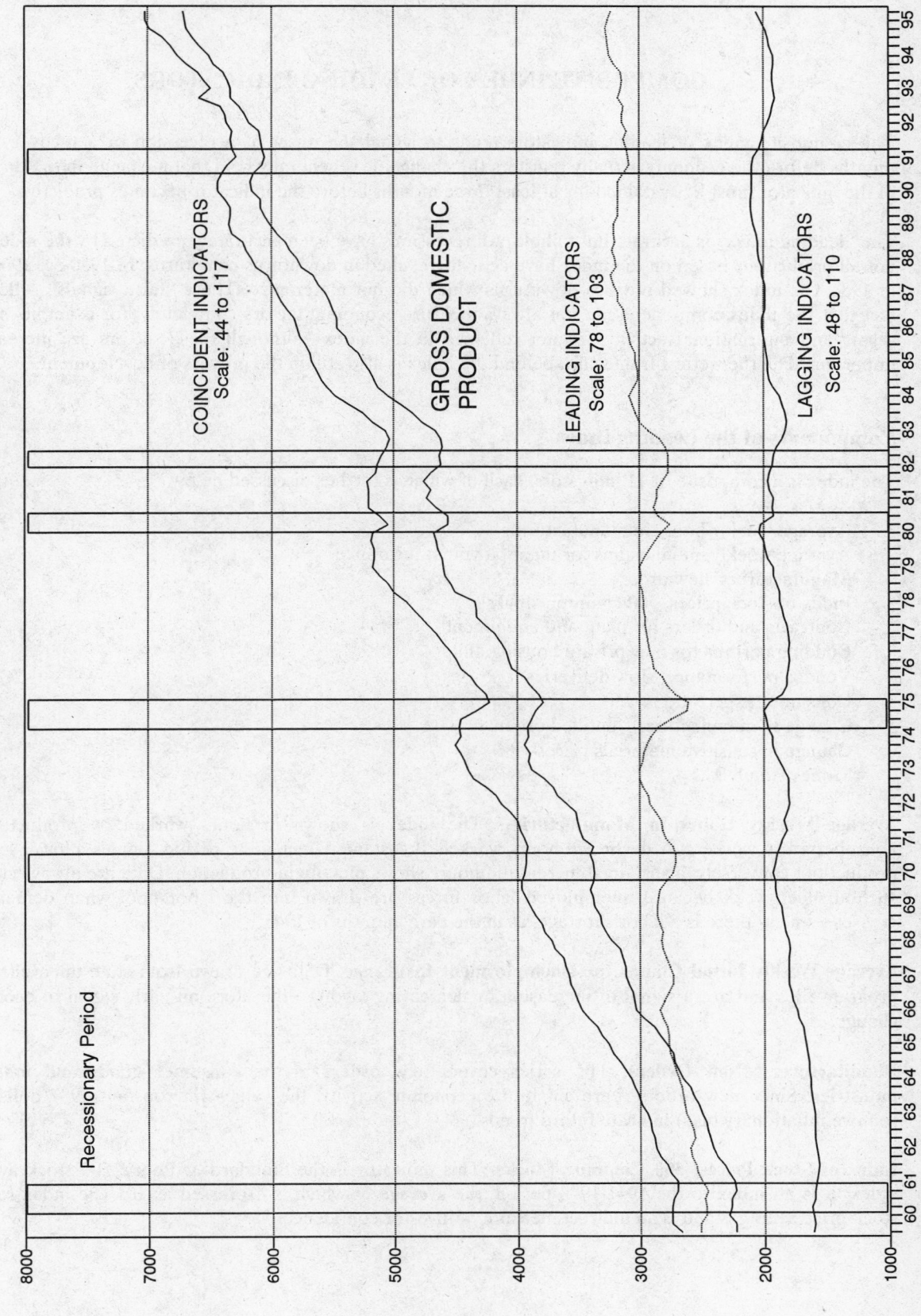

GDP and Economic Indicators: 1959-1995
[In billions of chained (1992) dollars]

COINCIDENT INDICATORS
Scale: 44 to 117

GROSS DOMESTIC
PRODUCT

LEADING INDICATORS
Scale: 78 to 103

LAGGING INDICATORS
Scale: 48 to 110

Recessionary Period

COMPOSITE INDEX OF LEADING INDICATORS

The composite index of leading indicators tends to signal the onset of a recession or a recovery some months before the economy actually registers the change. It is generally held that a change in the direction of the indicator must be sustained for at least three months before the indicator becomes predictive.

The "leading index" is accurate but fallible. All recessions have been accurately predicted by the index. But not all predictions based on the index have actually resulted in downturns or upturns. In 1950-51, 1966, and in 1984, the index showed obvious downturns which did not materialize. These "false signals" reflect the fact that the index components do not always measure economic factors completely; for example, service sector and international activity are not reflected in the index—although these sectors are increasingly important. The theoretical framework behind the index is also still in the process of development.

Components of the Leading Index

The index is a composite of 11 indicators, each of which is further discussed below:

    Average weekly hours in manufacturing
    Average weekly initial claims for unemployment insurance
    Manufacturers' new orders
    Index of stock prices, 500 common stocks
    Contracts and orders for plant and equipment
    Building permits for new private housing units
    Vendor performance, slow deliveries
    Consumer expectations
    Change in manufacturers' unfilled orders
    Change in sensitive materials prices
    Money supply M2

Average Weekly Hours in Manufacturing. The index is shown in hours worked by production or nonsupervisory workers. A decline in hours worked, if sustained over some period, signals a lower level of production; conversely, a sustained increase in hours shows pick-up in production. Data are always close to 40 hours per week because unemployed labor forces are drawn into the labor pool when demand increases—unless there is a labor shortage, as in the early months of 1945.

Average Weekly Initial Claims for Unemployment Insurance. Data are drawn from state unemployment program files and are a signal of increasing or decreasing layoffs—therefore an early signal of economic change.

Manufacturers' New Orders. The series covers new orders in the consumer goods and materials industries. Since new orders represent future economic activity, the values (in constant 1987 dollars, to remove inflationary bias) indicate future trends.

Index of Stock Prices, 500 Common Stocks. This indicator is the Standard & Poor's 500 stock average index; it is an index to the 1941-1943 period, the average of which is expressed as 10. The index reflects stock price averages and is an indirect measure of investor confidence.

Contracts and Orders for Plant and Equipment. The indicator, in constant 1987 dollars, shows future spending on capital goods. It is both an indicator of confidence and a direct commitment to spend money in the future; hence it is predictive of future economic activity.

Building Permits for New Private Housing Units. The data are based on local building permits issued. The indicator is an index with a base of 100 for the year 1967. Since permits must be obtained before building begins, this series predicts future housing starts and is thus a leading indicator. Increases in this index imply confidence that the economy will be strong, that money will be available for construction financing and house purchases.

Vendor Performance. The index charts the percent of companies reporting late deliveries by vendors. Late deliveries are common when vendors are overbooked and have difficulty obtaining raw materials—a situation typically encountered in a strong economy. If late delivery percentages begin to rise in a recessionary economy, it signals the onset of an upturn—again only if the trend is sustained.

Consumer Expectations. The index, based on surveys conducted by the University of Michigan, Survey Research Center, was added to the leading index in 1989. It is based on a monthly telephone survey of approximately 500 people in 48 states and the District of Columbia and combines the respondents' answers to questions about their expectations for the economy. The index is pegged to the year 1966, which is expressed as 100. The indicator, of course, measures consumer confidence. The index values, in themselves—while showing how attitudes have changed since 1966—are less valuable than changes month to month indicating a trend in consumer attitudes.

Change in Manufacturers' Unfilled Orders. The indicator is for durable goods industries and is shown in billions of 1987 dollars. The data shown are *changes* from the previous month rather than total unfilled orders. Positive values mean an increase since the month before, negative values mean a decrease. The series gives an indication of durable goods "backlogs." Increasing backlogs signal increasing demand—before it is actually met; declining backlogs indicate that production in the future will be lower.

Change in Sensitive Materials Prices. "Sensitive materials" are those most vital to a modern economy: metals, fibers, and minerals. Being raw materials (rather than finished components), they are purchased early in the production cycle and therefore can predict future economic behavior. The prices of sensitive materials will reflect their scarcity. When the economy is beginning to slow, purchases of materials will be cut back; these cutbacks will reflect in a drop in commodity prices. In a sluggish economy which is on the brink of turning around, sensitive materials prices will tend to signal the turn-around by increasing in price. The index shows a percent *change* from the previous month. Negative values indicate a decline in price.

Money Supply M2. M2 is one of four monetary aggregates used by the Federal Reserve System to measure money supply. M1 is all currency, checking accounts, and other types of checkable deposits that can be turned into cash easily. M2 includes M1 and adds other liquid assets in the economy, including money market funds, money market deposit accounts, savings accounts, and small time deposits. M3 includes M2 plus large time deposits, institutional money market funds, and other less liquid assets. The fourth measure, labeled L (because it is *L*east under Federal Reserve control and *L*east liquid) includes M3 plus short-term Treasury securities, commercial paper, savings bonds, and bankers' acceptances. M2 is thus a measure of the money supply which includes some funds that are typically held for investment but not assets that are difficult to "liquefy."

M2 is used as a leading indicator because it tends to reach low points in its cycle approximately 12 months before Gross Domestic Product (GDP) reaches the bottom of its cycle. M2 thus serves as an early indicator of future GNP behavior.

Money supply, generally, affects the economy by influencing interest rates; these, in turn, can stimulate housing purchases and investments in capital goods. An increase in money supply usually results in low interest rates: there is more money to lend; a decline in money supply pushes interest rates up. In periods of high inflation, however, interest rates may not respond as just stated because lenders anticipate an inflationary devaluation of their funds and hence compensate by keeping interest rates high.

Sources and Revisions

Sources for the component series are largely drawn from federal sources, including the U.S. Department of Commerce, Bureau of Economic Analysis and Bureau of the Census; and U.S. Department of Labor, Bureau of Labor Statistics and Employment and Training Administration. Other sources are Standard & Poor's Corporation (Stock Index), McGraw-Hill Information Systems Company (contributor to Contracts and Orders for Plant and Equipment), National Association of Purchasing Management and Purchasing Management Association of Chicago (Vendor Performance), University of Michigan (Consumer Expectations), and Commodity Research Bureau, Inc. (contributor to Change in Sensitive Materials Prices).

The composite index itself is constructed by the Bureau of Economic Analysis. In the process, mathematical operations are performed on the component data series to ensure that volatile series do not dominate the index. A volatile series may be one that fluctuates wildly month to month but shows less volatility when averaged over several months. Other smoothing and standardization methods are used as well.

The index was last revised in 1993 to reflect comprehensive revisions of the National Income and Product Accounts which were made in 1991 and to incorporate improvements in methodology.

Bibliography

1. Frumkin, Norman. *Guide to Economic Indicators*. M.E. Sharpe, Inc., 1990.

2. Green, George R. and Barry A. Beckman. "Business Cycle Indicators: Upcoming Revision of the Composite Indexes." U.S. Department of Commerce, Bureau of Economic Analysis. *Survey of Current Business*, October 1993. Superintendent of Documents, U.S. Government Printing Office, Washington, DC 20302.

3. Hertzberg, Marie P. and Barry A. Beckman. "Business Cycle Indicators: Revised Composite Indexes." U.S. Department of Commerce, Bureau of Economic Analysis. *Survey of Current Business*, January 1989. Superintendent of Documents, U.S. Government Printing Office, Washington, DC 20302.

4. U.S. Department of Commerce, Bureau of Economic Analysis. "Composite Indexes of Leading, Coincident, and Lagging Indicators." In *Survey of Current Business*, November 1987. Superintendent of Documents, U.S. Government Printing Office, Washington, DC 20302.

5. U.S. Department of Commerce, Bureau of Economic Analysis. *Survey of Current Business*. Superintendent of Documents, U.S. Government Printing Office, Washington, DC 20302.

Composite Index of 11 Leading Indicators
(1987 = 100)

Year	Jan	Feb	Mar	Apr	May	Jun	Jul	Aug	Sep	Oct	Nov	Dec
1948	72.1	71.4	71.7	72.3	71.5	72.2	71.9	71.5	70.9	70.9	70.6	69.9
1949	69.3	68.9	68.6	68.2	68.2	68.0	68.8	69.6	70.7	70.8	71.4	71.9
1950	72.7	73.0	73.3	73.7	74.5	74.8	76.0	77.4	76.9	77.0	76.8	76.9
1951	77.8	77.2	76.9	76.0	75.6	74.5	73.7	73.0	73.0	72.9	72.7	72.8
1952	72.9	73.1	72.9	72.9	72.9	73.7	73.7	74.4	75.5	75.0	74.9	75.0
1953	75.3	75.3	75.1	74.9	74.5	73.9	73.7	72.7	71.8	71.6	71.2	71.2
1954	71.2	71.6	71.7	72.0	72.5	73.0	73.4	73.6	74.1	74.8	75.5	76.0
1955	76.7	77.3	77.7	77.9	78.1	78.2	78.5	78.3	78.5	78.3	78.6	78.6
1956	78.4	78.1	78.2	78.3	77.6	77.3	77.5	77.5	77.3	77.3	77.4	77.2
1957	76.8	76.6	76.3	75.9	75.8	75.6	75.3	75.1	74.5	74.1	73.6	73.2
1958	73.1	72.7	73.0	73.2	73.9	74.6	75.5	76.2	76.8	77.3	77.9	77.8
1959	78.4	78.8	79.4	79.4	79.5	79.4	79.2	78.8	78.6	78.4	78.0	78.8
1960	78.7	78.1	77.3	77.3	77.4	77.3	77.4	77.5	77.5	77.2	77.1	77.0
1961	77.4	77.6	78.2	78.7	79.1	79.5	79.5	80.2	79.7	80.3	80.7	80.9
1962	80.9	81.3	81.3	81.0	80.5	80.0	80.2	80.2	80.5	80.6	81.2	81.4
1963	81.8	82.1	82.4	82.6	82.9	82.8	82.7	82.7	83.1	83.2	83.3	83.3
1964	83.6	83.9	84.0	84.4	84.6	84.7	85.1	85.3	85.6	85.7	86.0	86.2
1965	86.5	86.4	86.6	86.5	86.8	86.7	86.9	86.8	87.0	87.6	88.0	88.2
1966	88.3	88.3	88.7	88.5	88.0	87.6	87.3	86.7	86.5	86.0	85.8	85.7
1967	86.0	85.7	85.4	85.5	85.8	86.3	86.8	87.4	87.5	87.6	87.7	88.2
1968	88.0	88.4	88.5	88.0	88.2	88.2	88.4	88.2	88.7	89.4	89.5	89.7
1969	90.1	90.0	89.7	89.8	89.6	89.1	88.7	88.6	88.7	88.2	87.7	87.4
1970	86.7	86.0	85.4	84.8	84.8	84.9	84.8	84.9	84.7	84.6	84.7	85.7
1971	86.3	86.9	87.5	87.9	88.0	88.0	88.0	88.1	88.3	88.5	88.8	89.8
1972	90.4	90.9	91.3	91.4	91.5	91.8	92.3	93.0	93.3	93.3	93.7	93.9
1973	93.9	94.1	93.9	93.6	93.5	93.3	93.2	92.7	92.8	92.8	92.8	91.9
1974	91.5	90.7	91.1	90.4	90.3	89.3	88.6	87.4	85.9	84.8	83.3	82.0
1975	81.2	81.0	81.6	83.3	84.4	85.0	85.7	86.4	87.0	87.5	87.9	88.2
1976	89.5	90.0	90.2	90.1	90.4	90.7	91.3	91.4	91.5	91.3	91.4	91.8
1977	91.5	91.8	92.1	92.2	92.4	92.5	92.3	92.5	92.6	92.4	92.5	92.9
1978	92.2	92.6	92.8	93.2	93.2	93.3	93.2	93.4	93.8	94.3	93.9	93.6
1979	93.5	93.4	93.8	92.9	93.0	92.7	91.9	91.5	91.5	90.8	90.3	90.0
1980	90.1	90.4	88.6	87.0	85.6	86.3	87.2	88.2	89.1	89.9	90.4	90.1
1981	89.9	89.4	89.6	90.2	90.1	89.5	89.1	89.0	88.0	87.2	86.7	86.6
1982	86.1	86.9	86.5	86.7	86.8	86.6	87.0	86.6	87.3	87.7	88.2	89.0
1983	90.1	91.0	91.7	92.3	93.0	93.8	94.3	94.4	94.9	95.7	96.0	95.8
1984	96.4	96.4	96.3	96.1	96.0	95.4	95.1	94.8	94.4	93.9	94.1	94.2
1985	94.7	94.6	94.8	94.5	94.7	95.1	95.2	95.6	95.9	95.9	95.8	96.4
1986	96.6	96.8	97.1	97.5	97.4	97.6	97.7	97.7	97.7	98.2	98.5	99.2
1987	99.0	99.3	99.4	99.5	99.7	100.2	100.9	101.0	101.0	100.6	99.8	99.6
1988	99.4	100.0	100.0	100.0	99.9	100.6	100.0	100.2	100.1	100.1	100.0	100.5
1989	100.9	100.7	100.2	100.4	99.6	99.4	99.2	99.2	99.2	98.9	99.1	99.4
1990	99.5	98.9	99.4	99.3	99.5	99.4	99.2	98.4	97.9	97.3	96.5	96.5
1991	96.0	96.5	96.8	96.9	97.1	97.1	97.9	97.8	97.7	97.7	97.5	97.2
1992	97.5	97.9	98.2	98.2	98.4	98.3	98.3	98.0	97.9	98.1	98.3	99.2
1993	98.9	99.3	98.5	98.6	98.2	98.3	98.1	98.5	98.7	99.2	99.6	100.3
1994	100.5	100.7	101.3	101.4	101.5	101.7	101.7	102.3	102.3	102.2	102.3	102.5
1995	102.5	102.2	101.8	101.2	101.0	101.2	101.0	-	-	-	-	-

Source: U.S. Department of Commerce, Bureau of Economic Analysis. - indicates data not available or zero.

Composite Index of 11 Leading Indicators
Change in Index from Previous Month

Year	Jan	Feb	Mar	Apr	May	Jun	Jul	Aug	Sep	Oct	Nov	Dec
1948	-	-0.7	+0.3	+0.6	-0.8	+0.7	-0.3	-0.4	-0.6	-	-0.3	-0.7
1949	-0.6	-0.4	-0.3	-0.4	-	-0.2	+0.8	+0.8	+1.1	+0.1	+0.6	+0.5
1950	+0.8	+0.3	+0.3	+0.4	+0.8	+0.3	+1.2	+1.4	-0.5	+0.1	-0.2	+0.1
1951	+0.9	-0.6	-0.3	-0.9	-0.4	-1.1	-0.8	-0.7	-	-0.1	-0.2	+0.1
1952	+0.1	+0.2	-0.2	-	-	+0.8	-	+0.7	+1.1	-0.5	-0.1	+0.1
1953	+0.3	-	-0.2	-0.2	-0.4	-0.6	-0.2	-1.0	-0.9	-0.2	-0.4	-
1954	-	+0.4	+0.1	+0.3	+0.5	+0.5	+0.4	+0.2	+0.5	+0.7	+0.7	+0.5
1955	+0.7	+0.6	+0.4	+0.2	+0.2	+0.1	+0.3	-0.2	+0.2	-0.2	+0.3	-
1956	-0.2	-0.3	+0.1	+0.1	-0.7	-0.3	+0.2	-	-0.2	-	+0.1	-0.2
1957	-0.4	-0.2	-0.3	-0.4	-0.1	-0.2	-0.3	-0.2	-0.6	-0.4	-0.5	-0.4
1958	-0.1	-0.4	+0.3	+0.2	+0.7	+0.7	+0.9	+0.7	+0.6	+0.5	+0.6	-0.1
1959	+0.6	+0.4	+0.6	-	+0.1	-0.1	-0.2	-0.4	-0.2	-0.2	-0.4	+0.8
1960	-0.1	-0.6	-0.8	-	+0.1	-0.1	+0.1	+0.1	-	-0.3	-0.1	-0.1
1961	+0.4	+0.2	+0.6	+0.5	+0.4	+0.4	-	+0.7	-0.5	+0.6	+0.4	+0.2
1962	-	+0.4	-	-0.3	-0.5	-0.5	+0.2	-	+0.3	+0.1	+0.6	+0.2
1963	+0.4	+0.3	+0.3	+0.2	+0.3	-0.1	-0.1	-	+0.4	+0.1	+0.1	-
1964	+0.3	+0.3	+0.1	+0.4	+0.2	+0.1	+0.4	+0.2	+0.3	+0.1	+0.3	+0.2
1965	+0.3	-0.1	+0.2	-0.1	+0.3	-0.1	+0.2	-0.1	+0.2	+0.6	+0.4	+0.2
1966	+0.1	-	+0.4	-0.2	-0.5	-0.4	-0.3	-0.6	-0.2	-0.5	-0.2	-0.1
1967	+0.3	-0.3	-0.3	+0.1	+0.3	+0.5	+0.5	+0.6	+0.1	+0.1	+0.1	+0.5
1968	-0.2	+0.4	+0.1	-0.5	+0.2	-	+0.2	-0.2	+0.5	+0.7	+0.1	+0.2
1969	+0.4	-0.1	-0.3	+0.1	-0.2	-0.5	-0.4	-0.1	+0.1	-0.5	-0.5	-0.3
1970	-0.7	-0.7	-0.6	-0.6	-	+0.1	-0.1	+0.1	-0.2	-0.1	+0.1	+1.0
1971	+0.6	+0.6	+0.6	+0.4	+0.1	-	-	+0.1	+0.2	+0.2	+0.3	+1.0
1972	+0.6	+0.5	+0.4	+0.1	+0.1	+0.3	+0.5	+0.7	+0.3	-	+0.4	+0.2
1973	-	+0.2	-0.2	-0.3	-0.1	-0.2	-0.1	-0.5	+0.1	-	-	-0.9
1974	-0.4	-0.8	+0.4	-0.7	-0.1	-1.0	-0.7	-1.2	-1.5	-1.1	-1.5	-1.3
1975	-0.8	-0.2	+0.6	+1.7	+1.1	+0.6	+0.7	+0.7	+0.6	+0.5	+0.4	+0.3
1976	+1.3	+0.5	+0.2	-0.1	+0.3	+0.3	+0.6	+0.1	+0.1	-0.2	+0.1	+0.4
1977	-0.3	+0.3	+0.3	+0.1	+0.2	+0.1	-0.2	+0.2	+0.1	-0.2	+0.1	+0.4
1978	-0.7	+0.4	+0.2	+0.4	-	+0.1	-0.1	+0.2	+0.4	+0.5	-0.4	-0.3
1979	-0.1	-0.1	+0.4	-0.9	+0.1	-0.3	-0.8	-0.4	-	-0.7	-0.5	-0.3
1980	+0.1	+0.3	-1.8	-1.6	-1.4	+0.7	+0.9	+1.0	+0.9	+0.8	+0.5	-0.3
1981	-0.2	-0.5	+0.2	+0.6	-0.1	-0.6	-0.4	-0.1	-1.0	-0.8	-0.5	-0.1
1982	-0.5	+0.8	-0.4	+0.2	+0.1	-0.2	+0.4	-0.4	+0.7	+0.4	+0.5	+0.8
1983	+1.1	+0.9	+0.7	+0.6	+0.7	+0.8	+0.5	+0.1	+0.5	+0.8	+0.3	-0.2
1984	+0.6	-	-0.1	-0.2	-0.1	-0.6	-0.3	-0.3	-0.4	-0.5	+0.2	+0.1
1985	+0.5	-0.1	+0.2	-0.3	+0.2	+0.4	+0.1	+0.4	+0.3	-	-0.1	+0.6
1986	+0.2	+0.2	+0.3	+0.4	-0.1	+0.2	+0.1	-	-	+0.5	+0.3	+0.7
1987	-0.2	+0.3	+0.1	+0.1	+0.2	+0.5	+0.7	+0.1	-	-0.4	-0.8	-0.2
1988	-0.2	+0.6	-	-	-0.1	+0.7	-0.6	+0.2	-0.1	-	-0.1	+0.5
1989	+0.4	-0.2	-0.5	+0.2	-0.8	-0.2	-0.2	-	-	-0.3	+0.2	+0.3
1990	+0.1	-0.6	+0.5	-0.1	+0.2	-0.1	-0.2	-0.8	-0.5	-0.6	-0.8	-
1991	-0.5	+0.5	+0.3	+0.1	+0.2	-	+0.8	-0.1	-0.1	-	-0.2	-0.3
1992	+0.3	+0.4	+0.3	-	+0.2	-0.1	-	-0.3	-0.1	+0.2	+0.2	+0.9
1993	-0.3	+0.4	-0.8	+0.1	-0.4	+0.1	-0.2	+0.4	+0.2	+0.5	+0.4	+0.7
1994	+0.2	+0.2	+0.6	+0.1	+0.1	+0.2	-	+0.6	-	-0.1	+0.1	+0.2
1995	-	-0.3	-0.4	-0.6	-0.2	+0.2	-0.2	-	-	-	-	-

Source: U.S. Department of Commerce, Bureau of Economic Analysis. - indicates data not available or zero.

Average Weekly Hours, Manufacturing
(Hours)

Year	Jan	Feb	Mar	Apr	May	Jun	Jul	Aug	Sep	Oct	Nov	Dec
1945	45.3	45.4	45.2	45.1	44.3	44.5	44.3	40.8	41.7	41.4	41.1	41.1
1946	40.8	40.4	40.5	40.4	39.9	39.8	39.8	40.5	40.5	40.3	40.2	40.5
1947	40.5	40.5	40.4	40.5	40.5	40.4	40.2	39.8	40.3	40.3	40.4	40.7
1948	40.4	40.2	40.4	40.4	40.2	40.2	40.1	40.0	39.6	39.7	39.7	39.5
1949	39.4	39.4	39.1	38.8	38.9	38.9	39.1	39.0	39.4	39.4	39.0	39.3
1950	39.6	39.7	39.7	40.1	40.2	40.5	40.8	41.1	40.8	40.9	40.9	40.8
1951	40.8	40.8	41.0	41.2	40.9	40.7	40.5	40.2	40.4	40.2	40.3	40.6
1952	40.7	40.7	40.6	40.1	40.4	40.5	40.1	40.5	41.0	41.1	41.0	41.1
1953	41.0	41.0	41.1	41.1	40.9	40.7	40.6	40.4	39.8	40.0	39.8	39.6
1954	39.5	39.7	39.5	39.4	39.5	39.6	39.6	39.7	39.5	39.6	40.1	40.0
1955	40.3	40.5	40.7	40.6	40.9	40.6	40.6	40.6	40.7	40.9	41.0	40.8
1956	40.8	40.6	40.4	40.6	40.2	40.1	40.2	40.2	40.4	40.5	40.4	40.5
1957	40.3	40.4	40.2	40.1	39.8	39.9	39.9	39.8	39.7	39.3	39.2	39.0
1958	38.8	38.6	38.7	38.6	38.8	39.0	39.2	39.4	39.6	39.5	39.8	39.8
1959	40.1	40.2	40.4	40.5	40.6	40.5	40.2	40.3	40.1	40.1	39.8	40.2
1960	40.5	40.1	39.9	39.7	40.0	39.8	39.8	39.7	39.4	39.6	39.2	38.4
1961	39.2	39.3	39.4	39.6	39.6	39.9	40.0	40.1	39.5	40.2	40.5	40.3
1962	40.0	40.3	40.5	40.7	40.5	40.4	40.4	40.3	40.5	40.2	40.3	40.2
1963	40.4	40.3	40.4	40.2	40.5	40.6	40.5	40.4	40.6	40.6	40.5	40.6
1964	40.1	40.6	40.6	40.8	40.7	40.7	40.8	40.9	40.5	40.6	40.8	41.1
1965	41.2	41.2	41.4	41.0	41.2	41.1	41.1	41.0	40.8	41.2	41.3	41.4
1966	41.4	41.6	41.5	41.5	41.4	41.4	41.2	41.4	41.3	41.3	41.2	40.9
1967	41.0	40.4	40.4	40.5	40.4	40.4	40.5	40.6	40.7	40.6	40.6	40.7
1968	40.3	40.9	40.7	40.0	40.9	40.9	40.8	40.7	40.9	40.9	40.8	40.7
1969	40.7	40.4	40.8	40.7	40.7	40.7	40.6	40.6	40.7	40.6	40.4	40.5
1970	40.4	40.2	40.1	39.9	39.8	39.9	40.0	39.8	39.3	39.5	39.5	39.5
1971	39.9	39.7	39.8	39.7	39.9	40.0	39.9	39.8	39.4	39.9	40.0	40.2
1972	40.2	40.4	40.4	40.7	40.5	40.6	40.5	40.6	40.6	40.7	40.8	40.5
1973	40.4	40.9	40.8	40.9	40.7	40.6	40.7	40.5	40.7	40.6	40.7	40.6
1974	40.5	40.4	40.4	39.3	40.3	40.2	40.2	40.2	40.0	40.0	39.5	39.3
1975	39.2	38.9	38.8	39.2	39.0	39.2	39.4	39.7	39.9	39.8	39.9	40.2
1976	40.5	40.3	40.2	39.6	40.3	40.2	40.3	40.1	39.8	40.0	40.1	40.0
1977	39.7	40.3	40.2	40.4	40.4	40.5	40.3	40.4	40.4	40.5	40.4	40.4
1978	39.6	39.9	40.5	40.8	40.4	40.5	40.6	40.5	40.6	40.5	40.6	40.6
1979	40.5	40.5	40.6	39.2	40.2	40.2	40.2	40.1	40.2	40.2	40.1	40.2
1980	40.0	40.1	39.8	39.5	39.3	39.2	39.1	39.4	39.6	39.8	40.0	40.3
1981	40.1	40.0	40.0	40.1	40.1	39.9	39.9	39.9	39.7	39.7	39.5	39.4
1982	38.0	39.6	39.1	38.9	39.0	39.1	39.2	39.0	39.0	38.9	39.1	39.1
1983	39.4	39.3	39.6	39.8	40.0	40.1	40.3	40.3	40.6	40.7	40.7	40.6
1984	40.7	41.1	40.7	40.9	40.7	40.7	40.6	40.5	40.5	40.5	40.5	40.6
1985	40.4	40.1	40.5	40.3	40.4	40.5	40.4	40.6	40.6	40.7	40.7	41.0
1986	40.8	40.6	40.8	40.6	40.7	40.6	40.6	40.8	40.7	40.6	40.8	40.9
1987	40.9	41.2	41.0	40.9	41.0	41.0	41.0	41.0	40.9	41.1	41.1	41.1
1988	41.1	41.0	41.0	41.1	41.1	41.1	41.1	40.9	41.1	41.1	41.2	41.0
1989	41.2	41.2	41.1	41.2	41.0	41.0	41.0	40.9	40.9	40.7	40.7	40.6
1990	40.8	40.8	40.9	40.9	41.0	40.9	40.9	40.9	41.0	40.7	40.5	40.6
1991	40.4	40.4	40.3	40.3	40.4	40.8	40.8	40.9	41.0	40.9	41.0	41.0
1992	40.8	41.1	41.1	41.0	41.2	41.1	41.1	41.1	41.0	41.1	41.2	41.2
1993	41.4	41.5	41.2	41.3	41.3	41.3	41.4	41.5	41.5	41.6	41.7	41.7
1994	41.7	41.3	42.2	42.1	42.0	42.0	42.0	42.0	42.1	42.1	42.1	42.1
1995	42.2	42.1	42.0	41.5	41.4	41.5	41.3	-	-	-	-	-

Source: U.S. Department of Labor, Bureau of Labor Statistics. - indicates data not available or zero.

Average Weekly Initial Claims, for Unemployment Insurance
(Thousands)

Year	Jan	Feb	Mar	Apr	May	Jun	Jul	Aug	Sep	Oct	Nov	Dec
1945	16	26	28	34	43	70	72	360	375	248	220	185
1946	134	225	192	205	220	206	171	163	191	181	178	211
1947	121	174	185	207	235	219	229	193	179	163	172	172
1948	166	206	201	210	239	219	194	202	218	203	211	234
1949	285	305	333	379	377	359	340	385	320	386	344	298
1950	294	288	276	263	250	252	223	170	182	194	200	197
1951	174	181	166	199	199	209	236	254	242	234	210	213
1952	221	201	209	219	213	242	315	207	168	175	169	190
1953	175	177	188	179	198	195	207	229	238	251	298	280
1954	303	318	320	313	313	314	294	319	322	315	276	253
1955	256	240	228	228	222	222	223	233	204	224	215	214
1956	218	226	221	223	236	227	245	224	236	214	223	230
1957	242	225	219	239	244	246	267	235	305	302	320	355
1958	354	407	436	438	400	410	350	363	338	314	311	320
1959	292	284	258	244	246	258	264	291	271	311	351	275
1960	281	271	303	294	316	322	335	363	351	373	385	381
1961	393	429	379	381	358	334	348	316	329	304	305	296
1962	301	295	287	283	301	304	303	305	300	304	299	310
1963	310	301	288	293	288	284	282	290	285	282	276	301
1964	283	270	277	265	262	257	260	244	245	249	262	251
1965	243	248	237	237	224	224	231	248	218	209	212	206
1966	222	219	182	179	192	194	199	195	197	203	208	219
1967	196	231	256	259	236	231	231	212	217	220	209	204
1968	206	196	194	193	195	194	192	199	194	188	190	190
1969	179	186	185	181	182	197	195	196	195	202	211	210
1970	240	256	262	326	302	291	273	287	319	329	322	299
1971	292	286	294	281	290	289	285	325	307	294	283	265
1972	264	262	258	260	262	286	272	246	245	250	241	236
1973	226	223	227	238	234	233	232	247	241	244	251	284
1974	294	315	302	289	294	314	294	350	374	419	473	494
1975	522	532	536	521	496	491	442	449	447	420	393	364
1976	360	340	358	371	392	394	393	389	410	409	390	361
1977	394	427	346	371	378	358	370	368	363	357	347	342
1978	343	381	335	322	324	331	347	339	321	326	340	347
1979	353	352	346	411	341	358	377	383	378	400	420	428
1980	416	397	438	532	616	581	510	495	488	447	422	420
1981	424	410	413	395	401	405	395	421	483	517	539	551
1982	563	514	566	566	585	551	533	605	653	651	616	531
1983	507	478	479	470	453	406	380	408	387	386	381	378
1984	364	345	348	360	348	350	365	358	368	405	397	386
1985	378	402	389	387	383	392	381	375	381	367	371	391
1986	375	373	395	371	370	374	363	376	380	361	351	350
1987	355	348	326	318	321	320	286	299	294	289	303	308
1988	345	310	302	299	304	295	323	299	290	291	298	304
1989	291	299	317	304	320	334	340	329	337	359	338	351
1990	360	346	345	356	354	362	377	384	397	423	447	442
1991	441	474	494	467	443	432	415	425	429	422	439	441
1992	426	430	424	413	415	426	416	429	445	393	375	340
1993	366	354	377	374	385	375	389	365	368	352	341	327
1994	361	344	328	344	368	339	335	323	321	329	327	325
1995	329	330	330	352	380	369	367	-	-	-	-	-

Source: U.S. Department of Labor, Employment and Training Administration; seasonal adjustment by Bureau of Economic Analysis. - indicates data not available or zero.

Manufacturers' New Orders, Consumer Goods and Materials
(Billions of 1987 $)

Year	Jan	Feb	Mar	Apr	May	Jun	Jul	Aug	Sep	Oct	Nov	Dec
1948	31.29	31.00	32.66	31.76	32.72	35.21	34.63	34.15	32.24	31.20	30.22	28.92
1949	27.93	27.05	26.49	25.31	25.43	24.27	25.98	30.08	30.34	28.33	29.58	29.05
1950	31.31	31.44	31.22	32.68	36.45	36.76	45.79	51.27	40.49	40.87	37.25	39.44
1951	51.43	46.00	47.23	43.00	41.29	39.98	39.76	36.30	34.83	38.59	37.19	36.00
1952	36.60	36.82	41.15	42.46	37.39	43.43	40.81	39.86	42.05	39.88	40.03	43.26
1953	47.00	45.03	45.66	47.23	46.00	45.16	44.70	39.04	34.93	33.79	34.40	34.71
1954	34.67	36.50	36.62	36.78	36.78	38.66	36.97	38.06	40.03	40.51	42.93	46.02
1955	48.27	47.89	51.27	49.90	49.52	50.51	51.45	49.90	49.10	48.54	50.36	49.37
1956	47.89	46.50	46.20	46.88	45.41	44.35	44.63	45.26	44.09	45.54	45.72	46.14
1957	45.11	46.98	46.02	44.55	44.35	44.73	42.95	43.46	43.61	41.75	40.11	37.83
1958	39.82	36.70	37.78	37.66	39.25	41.00	41.93	44.08	43.38	44.40	46.63	46.10
1959	47.87	51.40	51.67	50.73	49.37	49.32	47.79	45.65	45.26	45.25	44.81	48.35
1960	47.08	45.98	44.93	45.15	45.18	45.94	45.54	46.86	46.80	45.18	44.78	44.52
1961	42.54	42.46	45.38	47.02	48.61	49.55	47.71	50.08	49.56	49.51	52.17	53.91
1962	52.50	51.35	51.24	48.94	50.11	49.55	50.94	51.80	52.29	53.03	52.87	51.56
1963	52.97	54.70	55.14	56.84	55.36	53.71	55.93	53.19	54.38	56.40	56.21	55.75
1964	58.36	56.98	56.57	59.54	58.41	59.09	61.09	58.59	62.52	58.95	60.45	62.56
1965	64.00	64.04	64.24	64.43	63.98	64.61	66.59	66.38	62.19	65.16	67.60	69.12
1966	68.48	69.43	72.07	70.43	69.35	70.12	68.43	68.60	70.14	70.26	68.38	67.87
1967	66.96	66.71	66.32	67.01	68.17	68.57	67.98	71.23	69.01	67.80	69.99	75.37
1968	71.80	72.47	72.47	71.90	73.37	73.36	72.62	69.11	76.47	76.97	77.60	75.53
1969	76.42	76.24	76.37	76.27	76.16	75.76	76.34	76.22	77.46	77.31	74.31	74.60
1970	70.74	70.12	69.72	69.39	70.53	71.82	70.12	69.92	69.59	65.26	64.87	71.68
1971	73.05	73.07	73.49	71.80	71.16	70.56	71.44	73.36	72.98	72.61	74.22	75.79
1972	76.70	78.74	78.28	78.56	79.42	81.02	79.11	83.05	86.12	85.31	86.87	89.14
1973	91.46	92.91	93.18	89.94	92.00	90.75	90.85	90.49	89.54	90.82	91.64	88.32
1974	89.58	88.91	86.72	87.67	90.09	88.41	85.72	85.37	82.01	79.42	77.04	69.96
1975	69.06	69.00	66.03	69.00	69.70	70.60	74.27	76.12	76.17	76.01	75.44	76.42
1976	78.80	80.65	82.32	81.65	82.91	83.47	82.73	83.19	82.89	80.91	84.48	87.87
1977	88.15	88.61	92.42	89.44	90.44	91.49	91.59	92.52	91.95	91.89	93.96	94.66
1978	90.17	92.62	94.22	98.30	97.90	98.50	96.80	98.14	96.84	98.70	97.86	101.98
1979	99.35	97.20	99.68	95.79	97.17	97.42	94.47	92.06	92.81	90.96	90.17	89.47
1980	89.76	92.05	86.46	79.57	76.19	77.17	79.25	81.48	86.32	89.44	88.79	89.04
1981	83.77	87.76	87.20	88.68	89.59	89.55	88.14	85.10	83.32	80.65	79.07	78.28
1982	76.99	77.91	80.53	79.18	80.53	79.83	80.29	77.76	78.85	75.53	75.88	75.95
1983	80.51	81.72	81.98	83.34	85.68	88.32	89.35	90.73	90.59	94.07	94.76	96.17
1984	97.67	97.48	95.25	95.41	94.79	92.95	95.95	95.49	91.38	93.63	93.89	94.40
1985	96.95	93.70	94.03	93.80	95.63	94.87	95.01	96.03	96.73	95.94	95.73	95.58
1986	99.96	97.22	94.73	97.05	94.88	97.36	96.09	96.46	99.01	98.14	95.43	100.61
1987	97.25	102.50	102.65	101.18	100.63	102.65	103.59	100.64	102.98	104.07	103.33	104.11
1988	102.46	103.99	104.54	104.22	105.56	106.17	104.75	104.04	105.85	105.53	106.34	111.00
1989	109.85	107.66	104.55	106.40	103.82	103.49	98.21	104.04	104.08	101.43	103.75	103.00
1990	99.13	103.58	106.08	103.09	106.12	104.70	102.82	105.00	101.86	102.55	98.23	94.23
1991	95.69	95.36	92.48	98.00	99.85	96.76	102.46	101.26	102.50	101.70	102.09	97.94
1992	98.64	100.23	100.66	102.21	101.14	102.92	102.35	101.84	101.65	104.29	105.54	110.00
1993	109.26	109.78	107.29	106.76	105.60	106.60	105.36	106.61	108.97	111.33	112.47	114.60
1994	116.08	115.62	118.25	117.64	118.72	117.72	115.36	122.00	120.15	120.80	123.24	124.93
1995	125.28	122.58	121.31	118.98	119.27	119.31	119.43	-	-	-	-	-

Source: U.S. Department of Commerce, Bureau of Economic Analysis, U.S. Department of Commerce, Bureau of the Census. -
indicates data not available or zero.

Index of Stock Prices, 500 Common Stocks
Not seasonally adjusted
(1941-43 = 10)

Year	Jan	Feb	Mar	Apr	May	Jun	Jul	Aug	Sep	Oct	Nov	Dec
1945	13.49	13.94	13.93	14.28	14.82	15.09	14.78	14.83	15.84	16.50	17.04	17.33
1946	18.02	18.07	17.53	18.66	18.70	18.58	18.05	17.70	15.09	14.75	14.69	15.13
1947	15.21	15.80	15.16	14.60	14.34	14.84	15.77	15.46	15.06	15.45	15.27	15.03
1948	14.83	14.10	14.30	15.40	16.15	16.82	16.42	15.94	15.76	16.19	15.29	15.19
1949	15.36	14.77	14.91	14.89	14.78	13.97	14.76	15.29	15.49	15.89	16.11	16.54
1950	16.88	17.21	17.35	17.84	18.44	18.74	17.38	18.43	19.08	19.87	19.83	19.75
1951	21.21	22.00	21.63	21.92	21.93	21.55	21.93	22.89	23.48	23.36	22.71	23.41
1952	24.19	23.75	23.81	23.74	23.73	24.38	25.08	25.18	24.78	24.26	25.03	26.04
1953	26.18	25.86	25.99	24.71	24.84	23.95	24.29	24.39	23.27	23.97	24.50	24.83
1954	25.46	26.02	26.57	27.63	28.73	28.96	30.13	30.73	31.45	32.18	33.44	34.97
1955	35.60	36.79	36.50	37.76	37.60	39.78	42.69	42.43	44.34	42.11	44.95	45.37
1956	44.15	44.43	47.49	48.05	46.54	46.27	48.78	48.49	46.84	46.24	45.76	46.44
1957	45.43	43.47	44.03	45.05	46.78	47.55	48.51	45.84	43.98	41.24	40.35	40.33
1958	41.12	41.26	42.11	42.34	43.70	44.75	45.98	47.70	48.96	50.95	52.50	53.49
1959	55.62	54.77	56.15	57.10	57.96	57.46	59.74	59.40	57.05	57.00	57.23	59.06
1960	58.03	55.78	55.02	55.73	55.22	57.26	55.84	56.51	54.81	53.73	55.47	56.80
1961	59.72	62.17	64.12	65.83	66.50	65.62	65.44	67.79	67.26	68.00	71.08	71.74
1962	69.07	70.22	70.29	68.05	62.99	55.63	56.97	58.52	58.00	56.17	60.04	62.64
1963	65.06	65.92	65.67	68.76	70.14	70.11	69.07	70.98	72.85	73.03	72.62	74.17
1964	76.45	77.39	78.80	79.94	80.72	80.24	83.22	82.00	83.41	84.85	85.44	83.96
1965	86.12	86.75	86.83	87.97	89.28	85.04	84.91	86.49	89.38	91.39	92.15	91.73
1966	93.32	92.69	88.88	91.60	86.78	86.06	85.84	80.65	77.81	77.13	80.99	81.33
1967	84.45	87.36	89.42	90.96	92.59	91.43	93.01	94.49	95.81	95.66	92.66	95.30
1968	95.04	90.75	89.09	95.67	97.87	100.53	100.30	98.11	101.34	103.76	105.40	106.48
1969	102.04	101.46	99.30	101.26	104.62	99.14	94.71	94.18	94.51	95.52	96.21	91.11
1970	90.31	87.16	88.65	85.95	76.06	75.59	75.72	77.92	82.58	84.37	84.28	90.05
1971	93.49	97.11	99.60	103.04	101.64	99.72	99.00	97.24	99.40	97.29	92.78	99.17
1972	103.30	105.24	107.69	108.81	107.65	108.01	107.21	111.01	109.39	109.56	115.05	117.50
1973	118.42	114.16	112.42	110.27	107.22	104.75	105.83	103.80	105.61	109.84	102.03	94.78
1974	96.11	93.45	97.44	92.46	89.67	89.79	82.82	76.03	68.12	69.44	71.74	67.07
1975	72.56	80.10	83.78	84.72	90.10	92.40	92.49	85.71	84.67	88.57	90.07	88.70
1976	96.86	100.64	101.08	101.93	101.16	101.77	104.20	103.29	105.45	101.89	101.19	104.66
1977	103.81	100.96	100.57	99.05	98.76	99.29	100.18	97.75	96.23	93.74	94.28	93.82
1978	90.25	88.98	88.82	92.71	97.41	97.66	97.19	103.92	103.86	100.58	94.71	96.11
1979	99.71	98.23	100.11	102.07	99.73	101.73	102.71	107.36	108.60	104.47	103.66	107.78
1980	110.87	115.34	104.69	102.97	107.69	114.55	119.83	123.50	126.51	130.22	135.65	133.48
1981	132.97	128.40	133.19	134.43	131.73	132.28	129.13	129.63	118.27	119.80	122.92	123.79
1982	117.28	114.50	110.84	116.31	116.35	109.70	109.38	109.65	122.43	132.66	138.10	139.37
1983	144.27	146.80	151.88	157.71	164.10	166.39	166.96	162.42	167.16	167.65	165.23	164.36
1984	166.39	157.25	157.44	157.60	156.55	153.12	151.08	164.42	166.11	164.82	166.27	164.48
1985	171.61	180.88	179.42	180.62	184.90	188.89	192.54	188.31	184.06	186.18	197.45	207.26
1986	208.19	219.37	232.33	237.98	238.46	245.30	240.18	245.00	238.27	237.36	245.09	248.61
1987	264.51	280.93	292.47	289.32	289.12	301.38	310.09	329.36	318.66	280.16	245.01	240.96
1988	250.48	258.13	265.74	262.61	256.12	270.68	269.05	263.73	267.97	277.40	271.02	276.51
1989	285.41	294.01	292.71	302.25	313.93	323.73	331.93	346.61	347.33	347.40	340.22	348.57
1990	339.97	330.45	338.47	338.18	350.25	360.39	360.03	330.75	315.41	307.12	315.29	328.75
1991	325.49	362.26	372.28	379.68	377.99	378.29	380.23	389.40	387.20	386.88	385.92	388.51
1992	416.08	412.56	407.36	407.41	414.81	408.27	415.05	417.93	418.48	412.50	422.84	435.64
1993	435.23	441.70	450.16	443.08	445.25	448.06	447.29	454.13	459.24	463.90	462.89	465.95
1994	472.99	471.58	463.81	447.23	450.90	454.83	451.40	464.24	466.96	463.81	461.01	455.19
1995	465.25	481.92	493.15	507.91	523.81	539.35	557.37	558.89	-	-	-	-

Source: Standard & Poor's Corporation. - indicates data not available or zero.

Contracts and Orders for Plant and Equipment
(Billions of 1987 $)

Year	Jan	Feb	Mar	Apr	May	Jun	Jul	Aug	Sep	Oct	Nov	Dec
1948	8.04	9.26	8.78	9.72	8.40	9.65	8.71	8.12	7.93	8.06	7.88	7.81
1949	6.46	7.01	6.94	6.00	6.18	6.83	6.25	6.79	7.46	7.21	8.17	7.38
1950	8.05	7.95	8.72	8.67	10.65	10.28	12.31	15.18	14.07	12.48	12.43	13.19
1951	14.82	15.15	13.62	13.71	19.62	12.76	12.17	11.72	10.05	11.14	11.18	12.15
1952	10.70	10.85	11.00	10.92	10.19	11.56	11.81	10.66	14.84	10.71	10.16	12.30
1953	12.09	12.39	11.22	12.24	11.69	8.98	11.22	9.29	10.85	11.67	9.87	8.90
1954	9.20	9.32	7.96	8.12	8.37	8.60	8.97	9.01	9.63	10.24	9.44	10.02
1955	10.37	11.23	12.98	12.20	11.54	12.20	12.09	12.72	13.42	12.67	13.66	13.48
1956	13.06	12.71	12.62	12.95	13.42	13.55	12.95	12.72	12.16	12.09	13.63	12.81
1957	13.16	12.67	12.59	11.16	11.70	11.09	10.78	11.00	9.80	10.11	10.10	9.63
1958	9.55	9.22	9.16	9.23	9.32	9.84	9.43	10.86	10.82	10.47	10.20	9.89
1959	10.50	10.81	12.73	11.40	11.69	11.90	12.13	10.74	12.22	11.79	11.09	11.70
1960	10.97	11.22	10.90	11.85	11.86	11.45	11.56	11.53	11.69	11.34	10.87	11.81
1961	11.90	11.53	10.86	11.04	10.90	11.51	11.70	12.34	11.51	11.79	12.59	11.53
1962	12.16	13.28	12.39	12.91	12.39	12.15	12.30	12.34	12.20	12.47	13.40	13.87
1963	12.68	13.08	12.94	13.30	14.72	13.34	13.17	13.53	13.95	14.25	15.20	15.31
1964	15.67	14.16	14.69	14.84	15.93	16.37	15.39	15.55	15.78	15.87	17.02	17.25
1965	16.09	16.28	17.16	17.29	17.07	16.59	17.18	16.52	18.01	17.94	17.57	18.75
1966	18.89	20.30	19.75	20.53	20.09	19.57	20.97	19.62	21.55	19.29	19.11	18.99
1967	16.42	17.64	18.07	17.58	18.13	18.84	18.53	19.18	18.72	19.00	18.95	19.30
1968	23.13	22.38	26.82	21.58	19.24	19.36	23.25	24.29	20.71	25.52	21.00	22.93
1969	26.48	26.02	22.99	26.39	24.59	23.06	23.49	23.72	26.01	23.26	22.49	22.45
1970	25.50	23.47	20.77	20.27	19.76	19.24	20.64	19.87	19.50	17.38	19.71	21.51
1971	20.88	22.59	22.30	21.89	20.48	23.50	18.87	22.11	22.40	19.89	21.45	21.94
1972	20.69	21.25	22.79	22.36	24.69	21.08	24.46	23.35	25.97	24.84	25.30	25.90
1973	26.08	28.04	27.73	28.11	28.74	28.66	29.67	30.70	29.11	32.48	32.07	30.39
1974	30.53	31.17	31.60	30.17	31.23	28.36	33.62	30.09	29.46	27.87	24.15	26.89
1975	23.55	21.77	20.10	23.93	23.94	23.63	22.45	25.32	20.76	20.62	20.13	19.27
1976	23.80	22.89	24.43	23.94	21.14	25.28	27.59	24.47	26.47	26.90	24.47	25.37
1977	25.13	25.22	24.06	26.41	28.69	28.63	25.05	27.57	30.61	26.43	26.61	30.41
1978	29.72	32.56	29.09	28.59	31.84	29.35	31.44	32.91	34.26	39.78	33.25	29.32
1979	34.68	36.79	37.98	36.40	32.35	33.52	34.50	32.64	33.79	34.44	33.36	33.80
1980	34.83	31.08	31.78	31.74	26.25	27.79	28.95	29.54	29.22	30.46	28.13	29.48
1981	32.30	27.61	30.64	32.43	29.05	29.31	29.48	28.00	26.73	27.89	25.43	24.10
1982	28.20	29.45	26.94	24.83	22.46	22.56	23.41	22.23	23.09	23.51	22.07	22.78
1983	22.46	21.55	21.33	22.93	24.24	23.99	22.21	24.43	25.30	26.91	24.91	23.65
1984	27.23	27.32	27.84	26.70	30.31	28.12	29.39	27.51	27.03	28.23	27.55	26.96
1985	27.44	29.81	29.77	27.58	27.82	29.13	28.82	28.87	31.04	30.99	27.55	31.24
1986	28.80	30.42	28.58	27.84	27.29	27.99	27.52	27.11	28.33	29.03	28.51	30.28
1987	29.06	28.83	28.53	29.85	30.92	32.46	33.62	30.77	30.68	32.15	31.72	34.44
1988	35.37	35.84	32.99	34.32	31.74	34.89	36.03	39.05	35.34	33.84	34.62	37.84
1989	39.04	35.97	35.82	37.55	34.96	37.34	38.64	33.60	34.13	33.53	35.55	41.57
1990	36.59	33.79	37.62	34.12	34.14	33.52	36.58	31.88	34.60	37.57	32.46	37.65
1991	33.98	33.87	32.41	30.20	29.40	28.59	36.55	31.35	30.28	31.31	34.18	29.08
1992	32.33	32.29	34.43	34.38	32.92	33.56	32.87	31.93	33.73	34.01	31.91	37.12
1993	33.71	36.64	34.70	35.33	34.98	38.86	36.10	37.56	36.82	39.17	42.04	41.27
1994	42.70	42.71	43.45	42.39	42.61	44.82	43.63	44.54	46.57	45.73	47.67	44.65
1995	48.85	49.83	50.80	47.63	51.13	52.11	48.52	-	-	-	-	-

Source: U.S. Department of Commerce, Bureau of Economic Analysis, U.S. Department of Commerce, Bureau of the Census, McGraw-Hill Information Systems Company. - indicates data not available or zero.

Building Permits for New Private Housing Units
(1967 = 100)

Year	Jan	Feb	Mar	Apr	May	Jun	Jul	Aug	Sep	Oct	Nov	Dec
1946	70.4	74.3	93.3	67.3	67.0	64.8	63.1	63.2	63.7	60.4	62.7	59.3
1947	65.2	69.8	68.2	63.0	65.5	74.5	78.6	88.0	90.5	96.2	95.6	95.5
1948	89.0	81.7	84.6	94.8	86.8	83.9	83.1	77.2	69.0	72.7	70.1	67.4
1949	65.4	66.6	70.6	78.6	84.7	86.6	89.7	91.4	110.8	110.3	115.4	119.3
1950	128.1	129.5	129.5	131.7	131.3	130.7	148.7	128.7	108.8	102.6	100.6	129.0
1951	119.0	93.4	85.0	78.8	80.8	78.8	75.6	77.1	99.4	75.9	74.0	76.6
1952	81.1	93.8	85.9	84.2	82.4	82.6	87.8	87.6	94.0	95.0	95.4	88.1
1953	85.4	90.1	90.8	86.4	86.6	84.2	81.3	80.0	77.0	81.0	81.4	83.3
1954	82.9	81.7	86.1	87.0	88.5	95.1	97.5	96.7	99.2	102.6	110.6	107.4
1955	111.0	122.8	105.2	108.1	108.7	102.6	103.0	99.5	97.9	95.9	87.5	87.1
1956	89.4	86.8	89.4	89.1	82.9	81.4	80.8	79.0	76.9	75.8	76.2	75.5
1957	70.4	74.0	74.6	70.5	73.7	75.2	70.1	74.9	75.2	74.2	72.0	72.6
1958	74.5	64.1	71.0	74.8	78.3	83.6	91.0	90.9	93.2	96.1	109.1	94.3
1959	93.3	97.3	101.7	97.1	95.5	94.0	91.6	92.5	89.1	85.7	81.9	88.0
1960	83.6	83.2	73.1	77.8	80.5	73.3	76.4	76.0	75.4	74.4	74.9	72.6
1961	74.2	73.6	76.5	76.6	78.6	81.9	82.9	88.7	84.0	85.9	88.1	88.9
1962	85.8	91.3	86.8	94.5	87.3	88.2	91.0	91.8	93.5	90.4	94.6	94.6
1963	92.0	89.3	92.6	94.9	99.5	99.1	97.3	96.5	104.1	104.3	100.0	104.8
1964	95.5	106.3	96.7	93.1	95.7	94.3	96.1	96.2	93.2	90.7	92.3	85.7
1965	93.1	87.3	89.2	85.6	88.9	91.4	91.1	92.0	90.4	94.2	96.2	96.9
1966	97.6	85.4	90.9	84.4	79.5	70.4	68.7	64.6	57.1	54.4	54.2	54.7
1967	71.0	64.7	68.0	73.9	76.7	83.4	83.9	87.7	91.2	91.3	92.5	93.8
1968	84.1	95.7	97.6	91.8	92.5	92.7	95.9	96.7	104.4	101.4	102.4	99.1
1969	104.1	106.6	102.5	102.7	94.8	96.2	91.1	94.0	90.1	86.7	84.9	82.4
1970	75.7	79.7	80.7	87.3	94.8	94.3	94.5	99.5	101.7	111.6	107.1	126.0
1971	117.2	113.2	125.5	124.5	140.7	135.8	147.6	142.9	142.3	144.5	148.2	152.1
1972	157.0	152.1	147.6	150.0	145.0	153.0	153.9	158.7	167.8	165.1	156.7	169.6
1973	159.2	156.1	144.6	133.8	135.4	143.8	127.5	126.9	119.5	99.0	98.3	90.3
1974	93.3	95.4	101.0	87.9	79.8	76.2	70.2	64.3	58.9	57.7	54.9	60.9
1975	50.9	51.1	49.7	60.7	64.1	66.3	71.5	69.7	74.6	76.8	77.8	76.5
1976	83.8	83.5	81.6	79.4	83.7	83.3	87.3	91.8	103.9	99.9	107.4	106.0
1977	101.4	109.4	116.4	116.4	116.9	122.8	118.3	124.8	117.4	123.3	124.3	123.0
1978	114.4	114.1	118.2	128.0	116.1	130.3	117.4	111.1	115.1	117.1	118.0	119.5
1979	96.0	98.0	113.0	105.0	110.7	107.8	100.9	104.6	107.6	97.3	83.9	82.4
1980	84.1	78.8	64.9	53.1	56.5	73.5	82.7	89.9	97.5	89.8	90.9	82.0
1981	80.3	78.8	77.8	78.2	77.1	64.2	61.5	58.4	55.7	48.1	49.2	52.3
1982	52.2	53.1	58.6	58.4	62.6	60.0	68.7	60.8	68.5	75.5	80.8	88.8
1983	93.7	96.7	96.9	102.9	109.7	116.3	118.0	112.6	104.2	112.8	109.6	106.9
1984	117.8	128.9	111.9	115.2	113.0	117.7	104.1	99.3	98.8	96.7	106.6	105.5
1985	107.7	107.9	112.0	108.0	110.9	111.3	110.1	117.3	124.3	113.1	109.8	116.4
1986	119.8	114.6	115.5	120.5	116.6	116.1	115.5	112.0	109.4	108.7	106.7	123.4
1987	109.6	109.6	110.6	103.9	97.3	98.8	98.3	98.0	98.2	93.9	94.5	87.3
1988	80.7	93.3	99.0	92.7	93.7	96.4	93.3	94.7	93.2	98.3	97.8	97.4
1989	95.1	89.7	78.8	89.3	89.6	85.8	83.2	86.5	85.3	88.5	87.2	92.3
1990	113.4	86.2	80.8	73.7	69.2	71.9	69.9	69.4	63.3	60.0	61.0	55.9
1991	51.0	55.3	59.1	59.5	64.3	62.5	63.1	61.2	63.2	64.3	63.9	68.9
1992	69.9	74.3	70.2	68.4	68.5	68.6	70.6	69.7	72.3	73.5	72.5	76.3
1993	76.4	74.5	68.5	71.6	72.1	73.3	76.2	79.8	81.2	83.5	88.0	94.8
1994	87.5	80.2	84.3	86.8	86.9	85.2	85.0	87.5	90.0	88.4	85.7	89.6
1995	81.6	80.9	77.9	78.4	78.4	80.5	85.5	-	-	-	-	-

Source: U.S. Department of Commerce, Bureau of the Census. - indicates data not available or zero.

Vendor Performance, Slower Deliveries Diffusion Index
(Percent)

Year	Jan	Feb	Mar	Apr	May	Jun	Jul	Aug	Sep	Oct	Nov	Dec
1948	36.3	37.1	32.7	41.6	40.4	38.4	36.8	31.2	28.3	28.7	28.0	17.7
1949	16.6	13.1	12.4	16.2	15.5	15.0	22.4	33.0	39.9	46.1	51.5	52.2
1950	56.3	68.0	72.0	68.8	82.9	76.5	89.4	81.7	73.7	70.3	79.1	87.5
1951	88.7	93.3	85.1	65.7	45.0	36.7	32.2	32.0	46.4	47.2	34.9	33.6
1952	31.3	24.9	18.8	19.4	22.4	33.0	47.4	41.2	42.7	43.3	45.0	43.5
1953	41.5	41.8	41.8	38.6	35.1	33.3	28.5	26.5	23.2	20.7	20.2	21.8
1954	23.6	26.9	28.0	30.3	34.3	35.8	38.1	36.4	43.6	49.5	51.9	54.5
1955	60.6	67.2	68.5	71.9	68.7	65.7	67.0	64.3	66.3	66.5	64.9	61.4
1956	53.5	51.3	51.0	51.0	38.6	41.0	53.9	46.8	42.8	40.1	44.6	39.5
1957	36.3	31.2	26.3	28.9	30.0	30.0	36.8	30.8	28.8	32.6	27.8	27.3
1958	30.3	31.0	34.0	35.5	38.5	39.2	43.0	44.7	51.1	52.4	55.8	56.4
1959	61.8	67.3	66.3	64.8	63.0	63.7	59.1	57.4	57.5	58.5	54.6	53.7
1960	46.2	31.7	28.8	28.9	32.3	34.8	35.8	38.0	37.3	36.2	37.6	40.4
1961	39.2	41.1	42.1	47.5	47.9	49.3	49.4	50.6	50.7	52.4	51.1	55.8
1962	57.1	56.2	57.0	47.4	45.2	43.3	45.1	43.7	45.1	46.7	48.7	50.1
1963	50.4	51.0	54.9	58.2	56.4	56.3	43.6	48.5	49.7	47.4	48.7	47.6
1964	55.3	51.9	60.3	57.7	61.4	57.6	61.8	66.2	71.9	71.2	70.3	67.8
1965	68.5	68.1	65.9	69.4	68.9	69.3	65.1	65.4	61.2	59.1	65.1	73.5
1966	74.9	80.1	86.4	79.3	74.6	71.6	73.1	74.3	72.4	68.7	62.6	57.9
1967	48.2	49.9	38.0	36.9	34.4	36.5	40.9	44.8	46.5	51.1	51.4	49.9
1968	50.6	53.9	54.0	49.0	49.4	49.9	55.9	47.8	48.4	53.3	61.0	58.3
1969	63.6	60.1	60.5	63.9	64.9	67.0	65.7	70.3	68.9	66.8	64.1	66.8
1970	57.9	57.7	49.3	48.7	67.2	66.1	49.8	46.1	46.5	39.0	37.8	37.5
1971	39.8	44.2	45.0	48.9	49.4	47.9	47.4	49.7	48.9	50.9	50.9	53.3
1972	55.2	52.6	57.1	55.0	56.1	57.7	61.7	62.9	65.5	73.0	74.5	80.7
1973	83.7	85.2	87.5	86.7	86.6	85.6	85.2	86.7	90.1	88.7	96.8	92.8
1974	91.8	88.8	88.9	82.1	74.5	73.1	69.2	66.3	51.8	45.3	34.0	23.2
1975	19.5	15.9	17.3	21.7	22.7	24.9	28.7	35.1	43.8	44.8	46.8	41.2
1976	54.0	56.1	56.7	57.3	58.3	58.6	54.0	55.2	52.6	49.0	47.2	53.3
1977	55.3	65.1	49.6	54.6	55.4	53.3	58.3	53.5	56.7	53.6	56.3	57.1
1978	55.6	63.4	58.9	57.1	57.4	61.1	59.4	60.6	60.0	64.7	64.5	63.5
1979	66.4	64.0	66.7	75.6	63.7	61.4	57.4	52.9	50.7	46.9	46.8	42.2
1980	42.1	46.0	39.1	36.9	29.8	32.4	36.3	40.1	41.2	46.5	46.8	50.1
1981	49.7	48.5	48.7	51.2	50.2	47.9	44.9	49.6	45.9	37.7	40.5	41.2
1982	40.1	40.8	36.4	38.2	42.1	45.2	45.8	45.3	45.9	46.5	46.9	48.6
1983	46.7	49.9	50.8	52.7	51.9	56.8	58.9	60.2	60.7	62.8	67.5	62.1
1984	64.4	61.5	65.5	64.6	62.5	56.2	59.1	55.2	52.8	49.3	48.1	48.8
1985	50.4	48.6	46.7	46.1	48.0	47.1	45.7	46.6	49.5	50.0	48.5	49.3
1986	50.1	49.8	50.5	50.7	50.2	49.9	49.9	50.8	49.6	51.3	52.0	52.8
1987	51.5	51.2	51.9	52.8	54.0	56.8	58.9	60.3	61.5	62.2	64.9	62.7
1988	62.0	61.2	57.3	58.6	56.9	65.6	58.4	57.4	55.2	54.8	52.1	53.0
1989	53.9	54.0	52.5	52.2	49.1	46.5	46.1	44.0	43.9	43.3	42.5	43.5
1990	48.2	44.4	47.2	47.2	48.2	49.8	46.4	50.1	48.9	48.1	48.6	47.2
1991	44.4	44.7	43.9	45.0	46.0	47.1	49.6	48.3	48.8	50.2	50.1	49.4
1992	49.0	49.5	50.3	47.4	49.8	50.6	51.5	50.1	51.2	48.8	51.6	52.2
1993	52.5	52.7	52.5	52.8	51.1	50.1	50.0	51.6	51.3	50.7	51.1	52.3
1994	54.5	58.3	55.1	57.2	59.8	59.7	57.2	61.4	62.1	64.7	65.2	65.7
1995	62.6	62.5	56.7	56.1	52.9	51.2	50.4	-	-	-	-	-

Source: National Association of Purchasing Management and Purchasing Management Association of Chicago. - indicates data not available or zero.

Consumer Expectations

Not seasonally adjusted
(1966:I = 100)

Year	Jan	Feb	Mar	Apr	May	Jun	Jul	Aug	Sep	Oct	Nov	Dec
1952	-	-	-	-	-	-	-	-	-	-	92.4	93.4
1953	94.5	95.5	94.2	92.9	91.6	90.3	89.1	87.8	86.5	85.2	83.9	84.4
1954	84.8	85.3	85.6	85.8	86.1	86.7	87.3	87.9	88.5	89.1	89.7	91.4
1955	93.1	94.8	96.5	98.2	99.9	100.6	101.2	101.9	102.5	103.2	103.8	103.7
1956	103.6	103.6	103.5	103.4	103.3	103.9	104.6	105.2	105.2	105.2	105.2	103.7
1957	102.2	100.7	99.2	97.7	96.2	94.6	92.9	91.3	89.6	88.0	86.3	85.7
1958	85.2	84.6	84.0	83.5	82.9	84.8	86.6	88.5	90.4	92.2	94.1	94.7
1959	95.2	95.8	96.4	96.9	97.5	97.2	96.9	96.7	96.4	96.1	95.8	98.7
1960	101.7	104.6	102.6	100.6	98.6	98.2	97.9	97.5	96.1	94.8	93.4	93.9
1961	94.4	94.9	96.0	97.0	98.1	98.2	98.4	98.5	97.9	97.4	96.8	99.0
1962	101.2	103.4	101.1	98.8	96.5	95.5	94.4	93.4	95.3	97.3	99.2	99.4
1963	99.7	99.9	98.0	96.0	94.1	95.1	96.0	97.0	97.0	97.0	97.0	97.8
1964	98.6	99.4	98.7	97.9	97.2	97.8	98.5	99.1	99.8	100.4	101.1	101.7
1965	102.4	103.0	103.2	103.4	103.7	103.9	104.1	104.3	105.3	106.3	107.3	104.9
1966	102.4	100.0	98.7	97.3	96.0	94.2	92.5	90.7	90.5	90.4	90.2	92.3
1967	94.3	96.4	95.7	95.0	94.3	94.7	95.1	95.5	94.0	92.6	91.1	92.2
1968	93.2	94.3	92.8	91.4	89.9	89.8	89.7	89.6	90.3	90.9	91.6	93.7
1969	95.9	98.0	95.7	93.4	91.1	89.6	88.1	86.6	84.3	81.9	79.6	78.3
1970	77.1	75.8	74.3	72.7	71.2	72.7	74.2	75.7	74.2	72.8	71.3	72.8
1971	74.4	75.9	75.9	75.9	75.9	76.7	77.6	78.4	78.0	77.6	77.2	81.8
1972	86.3	90.9	88.0	85.1	82.2	85.2	88.3	91.3	90.1	89.0	87.8	83.0
1973	78.1	73.3	71.3	69.3	67.3	65.9	64.4	63.0	64.4	65.7	67.1	61.2
1974	55.3	49.4	54.2	59.1	63.9	61.8	59.7	57.6	55.5	53.3	51.2	50.8
1975	50.4	50.0	56.6	63.2	69.8	70.1	70.4	70.7	70.4	70.2	69.9	73.7
1976	77.4	81.2	80.6	80.1	79.5	81.5	83.5	85.5	85.6	85.8	85.9	85.3
1977	84.8	84.2	84.0	83.8	83.6	82.9	82.2	81.5	79.6	77.8	75.9	75.8
1978	75.7	77.2	69.5	71.1	73.0	68.1	72.0	67.0	69.8	71.7	62.8	53.8
1979	58.4	62.2	53.7	53.3	54.9	51.4	44.2	49.3	53.6	49.5	52.0	51.5
1980	54.1	54.9	44.3	44.4	45.3	53.0	53.4	59.6	67.2	68.9	76.2	59.7
1981	67.2	61.4	61.4	68.1	72.9	70.5	66.4	70.1	68.3	61.5	55.6	56.8
1982	62.9	58.7	53.1	61.1	62.0	60.1	57.6	60.9	66.9	70.4	71.0	67.9
1983	65.2	71.2	80.9	86.9	93.4	89.2	91.1	88.2	85.8	86.1	87.9	91.0
1984	97.0	93.2	97.7	91.4	90.6	89.8	91.9	93.7	96.4	91.6	91.5	87.9
1985	90.3	86.5	87.3	87.0	84.2	91.1	87.4	86.3	84.2	80.8	84.5	88.1
1986	85.3	87.8	86.9	88.5	87.5	90.3	88.5	85.9	81.3	87.1	81.6	78.3
1987	80.9	81.6	83.3	84.7	80.6	80.8	83.3	85.8	84.2	80.4	72.7	76.7
1988	80.9	81.9	85.2	82.4	87.3	85.7	82.3	88.8	89.5	87.0	86.3	85.5
1989	89.9	88.8	87.6	83.2	80.1	82.0	85.5	80.3	88.6	87.2	84.3	85.5
1990	83.4	81.3	81.3	83.9	79.3	76.6	77.3	62.9	58.8	50.9	52.8	53.7
1991	55.2	62.0	84.5	74.7	71.5	75.9	74.4	75.3	76.4	70.5	61.9	61.5
1992	59.1	61.8	70.3	70.5	71.2	70.7	67.6	69.5	67.4	67.5	78.2	89.5
1993	83.4	80.6	75.8	76.4	68.5	70.4	64.7	65.8	66.8	72.5	70.3	78.8
1994	86.4	83.5	85.1	82.6	84.2	82.7	78.5	80.8	83.5	85.1	84.8	88.8
1995	88.4	85.9	79.8	83.8	80.1	84.1	87.4	-	-	-	-	-

Source: University of Michigan, Survey Research Center. Used by permission. - indicates data not available or zero.

Change in Manufacturers' Unfilled Orders, Durables
(Billions of 1987 $)

Year	Jan	Feb	Mar	Apr	May	Jun	Jul	Aug	Sep	Oct	Nov	Dec
1947	-	-	-	-	-	-	-5.59	-2.58	-0.81	-4.04	-0.93	-0.45
1948	-2.36	-2.20	-2.10	-0.61	-2.33	1.59	1.08	-0.94	-2.54	-6.27	-3.32	-4.44
1949	-4.99	-3.82	-4.30	-5.82	-4.95	-5.14	-3.58	-1.45	-0.96	1.93	2.38	1.63
1950	2.69	1.23	1.88	1.65	1.50	3.06	9.58	16.46	8.52	6.80	2.95	3.61
1951	20.82	11.02	13.60	12.54	8.89	9.52	8.99	3.86	3.21	7.30	3.27	0.78
1952	2.38	-0.02	7.92	8.75	-0.26	10.89	7.21	2.61	2.21	-3.41	-1.41	-0.74
1953	6.91	1.71	-4.41	-3.21	-1.51	-3.22	-9.71	-10.91	-15.53	-8.85	-6.27	-7.56
1954	-9.55	-6.57	-9.71	-7.10	-6.98	-7.21	-4.60	-4.52	1.14	5.06	-3.15	-0.24
1955	2.32	1.70	4.56	0.66	1.32	0.68	2.36	2.48	2.26	4.00	2.07	5.37
1956	4.00	0.84	0.71	2.87	0.43	-0.58	4.46	5.92	1.18	-2.11	-1.45	-1.27
1957	-1.62	-0.06	-3.70	-3.67	-2.88	-4.24	-6.52	-5.74	-5.40	-6.43	-4.88	-4.85
1958	-15.37	-5.03	-0.91	-2.37	-0.33	1.19	-0.34	-0.48	-1.87	-0.39	1.96	-0.54
1959	2.42	3.16	3.81	2.04	-0.48	0.68	-1.76	-0.05	2.34	2.05	-0.33	-1.40
1960	-4.36	-3.52	-3.82	-2.70	-1.58	-0.64	-1.61	1.08	0.37	-2.56	-0.60	-1.51
1961	-0.27	0.33	-0.80	1.20	0.85	0.36	0.57	1.40	0.30	-0.20	0.88	2.16
1962	1.73	1.85	-1.26	-1.70	-1.19	-0.64	-0.09	-1.48	1.23	2.08	-	4.67
1963	3.80	3.02	4.88	2.59	2.77	-0.70	-0.21	-0.27	0.80	0.56	0.30	-1.64
1964	3.89	1.70	2.24	2.82	3.27	2.84	4.93	1.65	2.94	4.49	1.33	1.69
1965	4.31	3.24	2.79	2.71	3.04	2.77	2.06	2.47	3.26	5.09	3.86	4.49
1966	6.06	5.50	6.84	5.72	3.95	5.60	4.17	3.44	5.89	2.55	1.04	1.08
1967	-0.16	-0.23	-1.16	0.32	3.36	4.08	1.44	0.02	-0.39	2.71	0.19	4.16
1968	-2.34	0.28	3.24	0.02	-2.83	-1.19	-3.80	2.40	2.14	4.14	-0.15	0.16
1969	0.36	1.20	0.67	4.85	0.74	0.20	0.43	0.45	1.74	-1.25	-2.32	-2.88
1970	-3.64	-3.92	-2.99	-3.73	-4.71	-2.63	-4.07	-4.34	-2.00	-4.59	-2.00	-1.06
1971	2.67	2.85	-1.16	-3.12	-5.17	-4.72	-3.46	0.77	0.07	-1.47	0.98	0.75
1972	0.39	0.74	0.53	-0.44	2.18	2.26	2.05	2.10	5.32	2.28	1.61	6.05
1973	4.64	6.80	9.40	6.70	3.24	4.85	2.72	7.24	6.45	6.98	6.12	4.55
1974	6.56	4.38	1.54	4.23	3.70	0.68	-1.28	4.42	-3.10	-9.01	-6.76	-8.67
1975	-7.75	-6.61	-8.48	-7.28	-5.59	-5.45	0.68	-1.70	-2.42	-3.31	-3.35	-4.28
1976	-3.78	-2.34	1.66	0.33	-1.81	-0.18	1.67	-2.91	-0.20	1.67	-0.65	1.36
1977	-0.11	-1.71	0.27	1.75	0.30	2.99	1.00	2.56	1.62	2.98	1.31	4.52
1978	1.28	2.18	5.76	3.64	5.19	4.30	2.98	4.18	6.72	7.68	7.59	3.64
1979	2.37	8.21	6.28	3.10	0.12	2.41	-0.76	-1.14	1.91	1.16	-2.14	-1.69
1980	3.34	0.64	-5.85	-4.02	-4.62	-1.83	3.79	-1.42	1.64	1.27	-0.68	0.62
1981	-0.35	-3.09	-0.19	-0.05	0.11	-2.99	-0.11	-2.90	-1.26	-4.29	-3.69	-5.24
1982	-1.28	-1.92	0.09	-0.51	-5.07	-4.63	-3.82	-4.97	-2.37	-0.06	-2.97	3.19
1983	3.38	-2.09	0.75	-0.55	0.99	3.51	1.58	1.12	3.15	7.22	4.99	2.26
1984	3.74	4.79	9.45	0.78	2.40	-1.16	3.42	-0.10	-0.04	-2.92	1.36	-0.72
1985	3.47	0.48	-1.75	-2.13	-0.73	3.91	-0.08	1.42	3.11	0.23	-2.88	1.89
1986	3.67	1.64	4.64	-2.54	-2.60	-2.63	-0.53	-2.26	1.71	-1.02	0.81	-0.46
1987	-1.90	-1.24	1.17	4.03	3.96	4.71	5.53	2.49	0.02	1.59	1.22	0.99
1988	4.33	3.38	-1.40	0.88	0.93	1.16	1.43	2.97	0.05	1.84	-0.47	7.69
1989	3.96	0.80	2.63	2.93	-1.72	2.60	2.74	-3.51	1.53	-0.65	2.85	7.33
1990	3.00	-1.19	5.26	1.07	-0.01	-2.19	1.46	-1.44	-0.12	1.92	-6.16	2.64
1991	-0.37	0.67	-2.92	-3.28	-2.41	-4.89	6.72	-0.02	-4.29	-2.26	-2.81	-2.76
1992	-1.43	-4.38	-3.23	-1.29	-3.04	-2.51	-5.00	-4.11	-5.00	-1.39	-5.65	-0.24
1993	0.06	-0.35	-5.96	-3.57	-5.48	-3.41	-1.29	-2.07	-4.73	-1.97	-2.90	-3.19
1994	2.05	-0.95	-1.96	0.35	0.46	0.72	-2.27	-2.02	0.31	0.41	0.80	1.92
1995	1.35	0.87	-1.20	-2.90	-0.39	-1.76	-0.62	-	-	-	-	-

Source: U.S. Department of Commerce, Bureau of Economic Analysis, U.S. Department of Commerce, Bureau of the Census, U.S. Department of Labor, Bureau of Labor Statistics. - indicates data not available or zero.

Change in Sensitive Materials Prices
(Percent)

Year	Jan	Feb	Mar	Apr	May	Jun	Jul	Aug	Sep	Oct	Nov	Dec
1948	-	1.28	-1.18	-0.06	1.51	0.42	-0.20	-0.17	-0.79	-0.40	0.54	-0.31
1949	-0.51	-1.54	-1.65	-3.65	-1.59	-1.68	0.47	1.16	1.27	-1.53	1.18	0.12
1950	-	-0.15	0.74	0.21	2.17	2.48	4.66	5.87	4.57	2.24	2.66	2.11
1951	4.34	1.30	-0.11	-1.42	-0.74	-2.18	-3.95	-4.23	-2.62	1.06	-1.08	-0.70
1952	-0.91	-1.45	-2.62	-0.66	-1.13	-1.23	0.17	1.13	1.17	-0.83	-1.09	0.62
1953	-0.76	0.08	0.42	-0.64	0.56	-0.03	-0.51	-0.42	-0.74	-0.37	-0.83	-0.66
1954	-0.79	-0.09	0.62	0.87	0.20	0.81	0.57	-0.60	0.46	0.37	-0.37	-0.37
1955	0.63	0.82	0.14	0.48	0.45	0.42	1.00	-0.36	0.08	-0.25	0.72	1.15
1956	0.38	0.51	0.19	-0.43	-0.49	-0.98	-0.36	0.14	0.38	0.05	0.44	0.35
1957	-0.30	-0.90	-0.22	-0.55	-0.55	-0.86	-0.31	-0.17	-0.53	-1.13	-0.57	-0.63
1958	-0.49	0.09	-1.05	-1.12	0.39	0.15	1.15	0.53	0.67	1.59	0.74	-0.76
1959	0.37	-0.09	0.77	0.76	0.70	0.39	-0.06	0.17	0.36	0.55	0.22	0.66
1960	0.14	-0.68	-0.57	0.14	-0.14	-0.69	-0.25	0.06	-0.22	-0.53	-0.11	-0.73
1961	-0.59	0.96	-0.17	-0.17	0.39	-0.45	0.82	0.28	0.06	0.86	-1.38	1.06
1962	0.22	-0.36	0.03	-0.91	0.42	-0.61	-0.25	-0.31	0.03	0.17	0.25	-0.42
1963	0.14	-0.03	0.08	-0.37	0.11	0.28	0.76	0.25	-0.25	0.50	0.61	0.94
1964	-0.05	-	0.19	0.68	-0.38	0.30	0.22	0.89	0.78	1.36	0.37	0.34
1965	-0.89	-0.37	0.37	0.74	1.07	-0.10	0.18	0.80	0.18	0.61	0.18	-0.08
1966	0.48	0.33	0.63	0.25	-0.42	-0.20	-0.10	-2.36	-0.77	-0.70	-0.71	-0.45
1967	-0.82	-0.72	-1.05	-1.00	-0.19	0.71	-0.08	-0.05	0.35	0.24	0.49	1.11
1968	-0.53	0.56	0.83	0.40	-0.74	0.74	0.76	0.71	0.55	1.11	1.18	0.73
1969	0.98	0.77	0.07	0.25	0.07	0.20	0.34	0.66	1.09	0.12	0.70	0.38
1970	-0.31	-0.64	-0.53	-0.10	-0.34	-0.97	-0.90	-0.17	-0.76	0.32	0.35	-1.01
1971	-0.40	0.05	0.65	1.19	-0.91	0.55	0.62	0.64	0.63	0.39	0.39	1.23
1972	0.47	0.78	2.41	1.21	3.12	0.81	0.61	0.22	0.11	1.08	2.43	1.37
1973	1.48	2.65	1.81	1.70	1.03	2.20	1.57	2.47	2.73	2.03	2.30	4.76
1974	1.70	2.47	1.89	0.10	-1.94	-0.12	1.33	-1.17	-0.56	-3.95	-2.91	-4.55
1975	-1.16	-0.16	-0.52	0.56	0.61	-2.79	-0.39	1.95	3.09	0.88	0.65	0.97
1976	0.56	0.93	0.39	2.10	1.57	1.14	3.46	0.25	0.21	-0.70	-0.40	0.60
1977	0.25	0.98	2.02	-0.55	-0.16	-0.87	0.26	0.82	-0.04	0.77	0.84	1.46
1978	0.99	0.66	-0.39	-0.74	0.36	1.82	0.44	1.65	1.18	2.14	1.63	-0.38
1979	0.92	1.76	1.94	1.93	1.50	1.09	0.70	-0.05	0.02	3.30	1.86	1.06
1980	1.45	1.52	1.27	-1.99	-3.05	-1.50	0.36	1.92	1.17	1.05	0.64	-0.38
1981	-0.95	-1.22	1.24	0.82	-0.05	-0.20	0.16	0.35	-0.90	-1.11	-1.59	-1.31
1982	-0.69	-0.33	-1.03	-2.16	-0.25	-1.67	0.54	-0.52	0.51	-0.10	-0.64	-0.23
1983	0.50	1.56	-0.11	-0.04	0.89	1.00	2.57	2.78	1.67	2.35	1.58	0.63
1984	0.07	0.95	0.81	0.43	-0.23	-0.32	-0.50	-1.18	-0.24	-1.56	0.03	-0.59
1985	-0.87	-0.72	-0.38	-0.81	-0.77	-0.96	-0.39	-0.49	-1.45	0.10	-0.03	0.07
1986	0.24	-0.47	-1.11	-0.27	0.78	1.33	1.57	-2.42	1.73	3.13	2.03	-0.12
1987	0.81	-0.48	0.55	2.06	2.19	0.93	1.38	1.21	0.60	0.45	-0.67	0.47
1988	0.52	0.06	0.87	0.84	0.44	1.21	-0.01	0.32	-0.31	-0.11	2.13	0.82
1989	1.06	0.98	0.31	-0.55	-0.84	-0.78	-0.77	-0.37	0.26	0.20	-1.42	-2.07
1990	-0.81	-1.18	1.10	1.25	0.02	-0.11	0.22	0.38	-0.22	-0.64	-1.67	-0.45
1991	-0.51	-0.62	-0.78	-0.24	-0.16	-0.76	-0.21	-1.15	-1.21	-0.37	0.22	0.04
1992	-0.42	0.18	1.70	1.36	0.69	0.04	-0.16	-0.01	1.22	-1.26	-1.36	0.54
1993	0.54	-0.15	-0.48	-0.89	-0.58	-0.18	-0.28	-0.62	-0.50	0.90	0.84	1.00
1994	1.01	1.72	1.04	1.30	2.17	3.51	3.90	1.14	0.95	1.32	3.18	1.91
1995	1.96	-0.44	1.69	1.19	1.24	-0.02	-1.55	-	-	-	-	-

Source: U.S. Department of Commerce, Bureau of Economic Analysis, U.S. Department of Labor, Bureau of Labor Statistics, Commodity Research Bureau, Inc. - indicates data not available or zero.

Money Supply M2
(Billions of 1987 $)

Year	Jan	Feb	Mar	Apr	May	Jun	Jul	Aug	Sep	Oct	Nov	Dec
1947	1,039.2	1,030.9	1,025.4	1,031.6	1,036.8	1,040.4	1,030.8	1,025.9	1,015.5	1,011.9	1,010.9	991.3
1948	984.1	984.1	985.0	973.7	963.0	958.5	946.5	947.9	947.0	950.9	958.5	956.6
1949	959.7	964.3	964.3	965.7	967.6	967.1	976.0	974.5	968.9	973.6	974.5	976.0
1950	982.6	983.2	985.6	990.9	990.9	993.3	982.1	979.3	975.2	973.5	970.8	955.5
1951	945.7	930.8	929.8	931.6	930.6	937.7	942.5	951.1	949.3	949.6	952.4	949.4
1952	953.2	962.1	964.2	963.1	970.7	970.8	965.5	973.5	979.5	982.5	987.2	986.0
1953	991.5	993.2	994.0	997.0	1,000.0	997.0	1,003.4	1,001.7	1,002.5	1,001.3	1,007.2	1,005.5
1954	1,008.4	1,011.4	1,014.3	1,013.5	1,022.4	1,025.3	1,034.7	1,039.8	1,041.9	1,051.1	1,050.4	1,056.6
1955	1,062.1	1,064.0	1,062.7	1,065.7	1,074.5	1,074.5	1,077.0	1,077.0	1,070.9	1,077.1	1,072.2	1,079.2
1956	1,080.1	1,075.5	1,078.1	1,081.0	1,080.2	1,074.1	1,070.8	1,070.8	1,071.0	1,067.8	1,070.7	1,068.3
1957	1,072.4	1,070.1	1,069.8	1,071.4	1,070.3	1,067.2	1,066.1	1,064.7	1,065.1	1,066.3	1,063.2	1,063.2
1958	1,053.6	1,066.3	1,070.8	1,074.4	1,081.5	1,091.3	1,095.7	1,102.8	1,105.9	1,109.8	1,111.4	1,117.7
1959	1,124.3	1,128.6	1,138.2	1,137.6	1,146.3	1,148.0	1,153.5	1,153.3	1,149.2	1,145.2	1,147.5	1,149.8
1960	1,156.2	1,152.5	1,155.2	1,158.7	1,162.2	1,162.3	1,174.5	1,180.0	1,185.4	1,181.7	1,187.0	1,192.0
1961	1,199.2	1,208.4	1,214.1	1,221.0	1,230.2	1,237.0	1,238.4	1,245.6	1,247.3	1,254.5	1,263.3	1,270.8
1962	1,278.8	1,283.8	1,294.0	1,299.2	1,306.4	1,312.4	1,319.2	1,326.3	1,328.1	1,338.2	1,347.9	1,358.4
1963	1,368.5	1,378.3	1,382.5	1,392.9	1,403.4	1,405.9	1,417.1	1,420.7	1,428.5	1,433.2	1,445.0	1,445.6
1964	1,454.0	1,462.1	1,469.1	1,477.2	1,486.4	1,490.1	1,502.6	1,514.3	1,526.0	1,535.5	1,540.9	1,550.4
1965	1,561.3	1,570.8	1,574.5	1,577.9	1,583.7	1,582.0	1,598.9	1,603.2	1,615.8	1,622.9	1,634.4	1,640.4
1966	1,651.4	1,653.0	1,655.7	1,652.8	1,654.9	1,652.3	1,652.3	1,641.0	1,650.3	1,647.1	1,652.2	1,660.9
1967	1,667.5	1,672.1	1,687.2	1,691.4	1,702.4	1,713.0	1,728.7	1,732.2	1,744.7	1,751.7	1,754.5	1,759.4
1968	1,757.7	1,755.3	1,763.9	1,768.3	1,778.5	1,778.7	1,778.2	1,785.1	1,791.9	1,800.0	1,807.7	1,815.1
1969	1,818.8	1,808.9	1,810.4	1,805.6	1,801.9	1,796.3	1,789.5	1,786.2	1,786.2	1,779.9	1,778.5	1,775.6
1970	1,775.4	1,757.0	1,753.9	1,741.6	1,751.0	1,756.2	1,755.6	1,767.1	1,775.1	1,785.0	1,788.2	1,794.6
1971	1,806.6	1,825.6	1,850.3	1,871.1	1,889.3	1,895.5	1,903.1	1,915.0	1,934.3	1,945.6	1,963.6	1,974.2
1972	1,987.8	2,000.3	2,021.4	2,031.0	2,038.3	2,051.0	2,071.5	2,091.9	2,110.8	2,122.6	2,135.9	2,152.9
1973	2,169.3	2,163.5	2,149.1	2,149.6	2,151.0	2,152.2	2,162.2	2,130.6	2,127.5	2,116.0	2,115.1	2,120.7
1974	2,105.8	2,092.1	2,086.9	2,083.4	2,063.7	2,057.2	2,046.3	2,029.8	2,016.2	2,004.9	1,998.9	1,988.0
1975	1,983.3	1,987.3	2,007.3	2,024.7	2,038.9	2,062.3	2,060.9	2,074.8	2,080.2	2,080.1	2,088.1	2,092.4
1976	2,105.9	2,129.7	2,148.4	2,167.1	2,181.0	2,176.8	2,186.0	2,200.4	2,210.8	2,231.8	2,247.9	2,264.0
1977	2,281.2	2,280.8	2,288.9	2,293.8	2,308.9	2,312.2	2,314.9	2,328.3	2,338.4	2,343.2	2,345.3	2,347.6
1978	2,352.5	2,348.9	2,345.0	2,343.2	2,342.4	2,330.8	2,329.5	2,327.6	2,334.6	2,326.6	2,322.6	2,326.0
1979	2,321.5	2,301.8	2,296.1	2,296.8	2,279.5	2,280.9	2,275.5	2,270.2	2,264.1	2,252.0	2,231.6	2,217.6
1980	2,197.8	2,191.4	2,166.1	2,140.2	2,134.3	2,138.3	2,167.5	2,172.8	2,174.7	2,167.8	2,163.6	2,143.8
1981	2,138.1	2,134.4	2,144.5	2,157.3	2,150.3	2,142.5	2,134.9	2,139.5	2,134.7	2,147.6	2,154.3	2,168.4
1982	2,183.6	2,180.0	2,194.8	2,206.1	2,201.8	2,186.5	2,190.2	2,209.7	2,224.9	2,232.4	2,250.2	2,273.8
1983	2,333.0	2,374.5	2,393.9	2,398.7	2,407.3	2,415.4	2,418.7	2,423.1	2,429.0	2,444.6	2,449.6	2,455.6
1984	2,452.8	2,462.7	2,471.7	2,480.8	2,491.4	2,499.3	2,503.1	2,505.9	2,515.4	2,520.6	2,542.1	2,563.0
1985	2,585.2	2,596.7	2,597.9	2,596.1	2,604.6	2,627.0	2,637.9	2,651.3	2,664.7	2,664.8	2,667.8	2,675.1
1986	2,671.8	2,685.3	2,723.6	2,759.5	2,778.6	2,791.5	2,816.8	2,837.0	2,848.7	2,867.5	2,878.3	2,895.6
1987	2,893.4	2,884.3	2,877.5	2,880.3	2,876.5	2,866.7	2,864.6	2,867.1	2,871.1	2,881.1	2,872.2	2,873.5
1988	2,888.8	2,901.6	2,910.3	2,915.3	2,926.4	2,924.3	2,918.0	2,910.4	2,896.7	2,897.2	2,904.2	2,903.6
1989	2,894.7	2,886.5	2,879.8	2,862.0	2,848.4	2,859.4	2,870.9	2,887.5	2,898.5	2,900.9	2,910.9	2,916.5
1990	2,901.8	2,904.4	2,902.9	2,905.8	2,903.3	2,895.1	2,890.9	2,878.8	2,871.0	2,853.4	2,844.6	2,841.6
1991	2,840.8	2,852.3	2,867.6	2,867.1	2,868.1	2,868.4	2,860.4	2,854.6	2,845.4	2,846.8	2,843.0	2,843.7
1992	2,848.8	2,858.3	2,850.4	2,840.5	2,833.8	2,823.4	2,818.1	2,819.4	2,819.0	2,817.4	2,813.3	2,807.7
1993	2,796.0	2,783.1	2,776.6	2,770.8	2,782.2	2,787.6	2,785.8	2,785.9	2,791.5	2,782.5	2,785.6	2,784.5
1994	2,788.7	2,777.8	2,780.1	2,781.9	2,780.0	2,769.0	2,785.8	2,757.4	2,750.4	2,743.1	2,742.1	2,739.5
1995	2,740.1	2,728.5	2,728.0	2,727.4	2,733.4	2,755.9	2,763.8	-	-	-	-	-

Source: U.S. Department of Commerce, Bureau of Economic Analysis, Board of Governors of the Federal Reserve System. - indicates data not available or zero.

COMPOSITE INDEX OF COINCIDENT INDICATORS

The composite index of coincident indicators tends to *confirm* what the composite index of leading indicators has foreshadowed. In other words, the "coincident index" tends to decline just as the economy does (rather than before) and turns up as the economy turns up. As with the other composite indicators, a tendency signaled by this index must be sustained for at least three months before the indicator "confirms" a change in the economy's direction of growth or decline.

The coincident index is a fairly reliable indicator. In the 1948 to 1988 period, for instance, more than half of the turning points in the economy were marked exactly by the coincident index. With the exception of the 1957 peak, which the index showed six months too early, the rest of the turning points were indicated within three months of the actual turn.

Components of the Coincident Index

The index is a composite of 4 indicators, each of which is further discussed below:

> Employees on nonagricultural payrolls
> Index of industrial production
> Personal income less transfer payments
> Manufacturing and trade sales

Employees on Nonagricultural Payrolls. The index is shown in thousands of employees. Employment tends to drop during recessionary periods and increase with expansions. Before a recession or upturn takes place, producers tend to decrease or increase hours worked (hence Average Weekly Hours is part of the leading index). As the trend is confirmed, layoffs or hirings are reflected in actual employment totals. Total employment, of course, tends to grow over time. The significance of the index lies in month-to-month changes that show a pattern.

Index of Industrial Production. This indicator, expressed as an index with 1987 as its base (1987 = 100), measures changes in the physical goods and power (rather than dollar sales) produced in mining, manufacturing, and utilities. Other sectors of the economy (construction, services, communications, trade, government, etc.) are, of course, indirectly reflected in this measure. Components of this index are measured and indexed; next, these indexes are weighted by their relative importance to the economy as measured by value added—the amount of value added to raw materials purchased by an industry through its own efforts. Industrial production reflects actual output; it does not signal future intent; therefore it serves well as a coincident indicator.

Personal Income Less Transfer Payments. Expressed in billions of 1987 dollars, this index measures all income except that derived from such sources as welfare, unemployment benefits, social security, medicaid, and the like, which are transfer payments. It includes dividends, rents, interest, and wages (the bulk). It is thus a good indicator of money now available to individuals from economic activities—which tends to shrink in recessions (while transfer payments may increase) and grow in periods of economic expansion.

Manufacturing and Trade Sales. The index is reported in millions of 1987 dollars. It represents sales at all levels—production, wholesale, and retail. New orders signal future sales and are therefore indicators of future activity. The actual sales, as they are made, are an indicator of current activity; they drop or increase in cycle with the economy.

Sources and Revisions

The component series are drawn from federal sources, including the U.S. Department of Commerce, Bureau of Economic Analysis and Bureau of the Census; the U.S. Department of Labor, Bureau of Labor Statistics; and the Federal Reserve System.

The composite index itself is constructed by the Bureau of Economic Analysis. In the process, mathematical operations are performed on the component data series to ensure that volatile series do not dominate the index. A volatile series may be one that fluctuates wildly month to month but shows less volatility when averaged over several months. Other smoothing and standardization methods are used as well.

The coincident index was last revised late in 1993. The 1993 revisions transcended the usual annual revisions but were smaller in scope than the comprehensive revisions of 1989 (see reference 2).

Bibliography

1. Frumkin, Norman. *Guide to Economic Indicators*. M.E. Sharpe, Inc., 1990.

2. Green, George R. and Barry A. Beckman. "Business Cycle Indicators: Upcoming Revision of the Composite Indexes." U.S. Department of Commerce, Bureau of Economic Analysis. *Survey of Current Business*, October 1993. Superintendent of Documents, U.S. Government Printing Office, Washington, DC 20302.

3. Hertzberg, Marie P. and Barry A. Beckman. "Business Cycle Indicators: Revised Composite Indexes." U.S. Department of Commerce, Bureau of Economic Analysis. *Survey of Current Business*, January 1989. Superintendent of Documents, U.S. Government Printing Office, Washington, DC 20302.

4. U.S. Department of Commerce, Bureau of Economic Analysis. "Composite Indexes of Leading, Coincident, and Lagging Indicators." In *Survey of Current Business*, November 1987. Superintendent of Documents, U.S. Government Printing Office, Washington, DC 20302.

5. U.S. Department of Commerce, Bureau of Economic Analysis. *Survey of Current Business*. Superintendent of Documents, U.S. Government Printing Office, Washington, DC 20302.

Composite Index of 4 Coincident Indicators
(1987 = 100)

Year	Jan	Feb	Mar	Apr	May	Jun	Jul	Aug	Sep	Oct	Nov	Dec
1948	32.8	32.7	32.8	32.8	33.0	33.3	33.4	33.5	33.5	33.5	33.4	33.3
1949	32.9	32.7	32.6	32.5	32.3	32.2	31.9	32.2	32.5	31.7	32.1	32.3
1950	32.6	32.6	33.2	33.6	34.1	34.6	35.4	36.0	35.8	35.9	35.9	36.4
1951	36.6	36.6	36.8	36.9	36.9	37.0	36.7	36.9	36.9	37.0	37.1	37.2
1952	37.2	37.6	37.6	37.6	37.7	37.5	37.2	38.2	38.8	39.1	39.2	39.5
1953	39.6	39.9	40.1	40.1	40.2	40.1	40.3	40.1	39.9	39.8	39.4	39.0
1954	38.9	38.9	38.7	38.6	38.6	38.7	38.6	38.7	38.8	39.0	39.4	39.7
1955	40.0	40.2	40.6	40.9	41.3	41.4	41.7	41.7	41.9	42.2	42.4	42.6
1956	42.6	42.6	42.7	43.0	42.9	43.0	42.1	42.9	43.2	43.5	43.5	43.7
1957	43.6	43.8	43.8	43.6	43.6	43.7	43.7	43.7	43.5	43.3	43.0	42.6
1958	42.3	41.8	41.6	41.2	41.3	41.7	42.1	42.4	42.7	42.8	43.4	43.4
1959	43.8	44.2	44.6	45.0	45.3	45.4	45.3	44.6	44.5	44.5	44.8	45.8
1960	46.2	46.1	45.9	46.0	45.9	45.8	45.7	45.7	45.6	45.5	45.3	45.0
1961	45.0	44.9	45.1	45.3	45.6	46.0	46.1	46.4	46.5	46.8	47.2	47.4
1962	47.3	47.6	47.9	48.1	48.1	48.2	48.4	48.5	48.5	48.6	48.8	48.8
1963	48.8	49.1	49.2	49.5	49.6	49.8	49.9	50.0	50.2	50.5	50.5	50.8
1964	50.9	51.2	51.2	51.6	51.9	52.0	52.3	52.5	52.8	52.5	53.2	53.7
1965	53.8	54.0	54.4	54.6	54.9	55.2	55.5	55.7	55.8	56.2	56.7	57.0
1966	57.3	57.5	57.9	58.0	58.3	58.6	58.8	58.9	59.0	59.3	59.4	59.5
1967	59.8	59.7	59.7	59.8	59.9	60.0	60.1	60.5	60.5	60.6	61.2	61.7
1968	61.6	61.9	62.1	62.3	62.6	62.9	63.1	63.1	63.4	63.7	64.0	64.2
1969	64.3	64.6	64.9	65.0	65.1	65.4	65.7	65.9	66.0	66.2	66.0	66.1
1970	65.7	65.7	65.7	65.7	65.6	65.5	65.6	65.5	65.5	64.9	64.6	65.3
1971	65.6	65.6	65.7	65.9	66.1	66.3	66.2	66.2	66.6	66.8	67.2	67.6
1972	68.2	68.3	68.8	69.2	69.4	69.5	69.8	70.4	70.8	71.5	72.1	72.6
1973	72.9	73.2	73.3	73.3	73.5	73.8	74.0	74.1	74.3	75.0	75.4	75.1
1974	74.7	74.5	74.4	74.2	74.5	74.5	74.6	74.4	74.3	74.2	73.4	72.2
1975	71.5	71.0	70.4	70.6	70.7	70.9	71.2	71.8	72.2	72.5	72.6	72.9
1976	73.6	74.1	74.3	74.7	74.9	75.0	75.2	75.4	75.6	75.5	76.2	76.7
1977	76.8	77.2	77.6	78.0	78.4	78.8	79.2	79.4	79.8	80.0	80.3	80.6
1978	80.4	80.9	81.6	82.7	82.9	83.4	83.5	83.9	84.2	84.6	85.0	85.3
1979	85.3	85.5	86.2	85.5	86.1	86.1	86.1	86.1	86.1	86.4	86.4	86.4
1980	86.8	86.7	86.3	85.5	84.6	84.2	84.2	84.7	85.3	86.0	86.5	86.8
1981	86.8	86.8	86.9	86.8	86.7	86.9	87.3	87.3	87.1	86.7	86.3	85.9
1982	85.3	85.8	85.7	85.7	85.7	85.2	84.9	84.6	84.4	84.0	84.0	83.9
1983	84.4	84.3	84.6	85.0	85.6	86.2	86.8	86.7	87.7	88.4	88.9	89.5
1984	90.2	90.7	91.2	91.5	91.8	92.4	92.6	92.8	93.2	93.1	93.5	93.8
1985	93.8	94.1	94.5	94.8	94.9	94.8	94.8	95.2	95.4	95.4	95.6	96.1
1986	96.2	96.3	96.4	97.1	96.9	96.8	97.1	97.2	97.8	97.7	97.9	98.5
1987	98.1	99.0	99.1	99.3	99.5	99.7	100.1	100.3	100.5	101.3	101.2	102.0
1988	101.8	102.3	102.7	102.9	103.0	103.4	103.5	103.7	103.8	104.5	104.6	105.3
1989	105.6	105.6	105.8	106.0	105.7	105.6	105.4	105.8	105.6	105.6	106.1	106.3
1990	106.2	106.8	107.2	107.0	107.2	107.3	107.1	107.0	106.7	106.3	105.9	105.9
1991	105.2	104.9	104.8	104.9	105.1	105.3	105.4	105.4	105.6	105.6	105.4	105.4
1992	105.3	105.8	106.0	106.2	106.2	106.3	106.6	106.5	106.9	107.4	107.7	109.8
1993	107.9	108.2	108.3	108.9	109.0	109.2	109.1	109.8	109.9	110.3	110.9	111.5
1994	111.4	112.1	112.7	112.9	113.2	113.6	113.7	114.4	114.7	115.3	115.8	116.4
1995	116.6	116.9	117.0	116.7	116.7	117.1	117.3	-	-	-	-	-

Source: U.S. Department of Commerce, Bureau of Economic Analysis. - indicates data not available or zero.

Composite Index of 4 Coincident Indicators
Change in Index from Previous Month

Year	Jan	Feb	Mar	Apr	May	Jun	Jul	Aug	Sep	Oct	Nov	Dec
1948	-	-0.1	+0.1	-	+0.2	+0.3	+0.1	+0.1	-	-	-0.1	-0.1
1949	-0.4	-0.2	-0.1	-0.1	-0.2	-0.1	-0.3	+0.3	+0.3	-0.8	+0.4	+0.2
1950	+0.3	-	+0.6	+0.4	+0.5	+0.5	+0.8	+0.6	-0.2	+0.1	-	+0.5
1951	+0.2	-	+0.2	+0.1	-	+0.1	-0.3	+0.2	-	+0.1	+0.1	+0.1
1952	-	+0.4	-	-	+0.1	-0.2	-0.3	+1.0	+0.6	+0.3	+0.1	+0.3
1953	+0.1	+0.3	+0.2	-	+0.1	-0.1	+0.2	-0.2	-0.2	-0.1	-0.4	-0.4
1954	-0.1	-	-0.2	-0.1	-	+0.1	-0.1	+0.1	+0.1	+0.2	+0.4	+0.3
1955	+0.3	+0.2	+0.4	+0.3	+0.4	+0.1	+0.3	-	+0.2	+0.3	+0.2	+0.2
1956	-	-	+0.1	+0.3	-0.1	+0.1	-0.9	+0.8	+0.3	+0.3	-	+0.2
1957	-0.1	+0.2	-	-0.2	-	+0.1	-	-	-0.2	-0.2	-0.3	-0.4
1958	-0.3	-0.5	-0.2	-0.4	+0.1	+0.4	+0.4	+0.3	+0.3	+0.1	+0.6	-
1959	+0.4	+0.4	+0.4	+0.4	+0.3	+0.1	-0.1	-0.7	-0.1	-	+0.3	+1.0
1960	+0.4	-0.1	-0.2	+0.1	-0.1	-0.1	-0.1	-	-0.1	-0.1	-0.2	-0.3
1961	-	-0.1	+0.2	+0.2	+0.3	+0.4	+0.1	+0.3	+0.1	+0.3	+0.4	+0.2
1962	-0.1	+0.3	+0.3	+0.2	-	+0.1	+0.2	+0.1	-	+0.1	+0.2	-
1963	-	+0.3	+0.1	+0.3	+0.1	+0.2	+0.1	+0.1	+0.2	+0.3	-	+0.3
1964	+0.1	+0.3	-	+0.4	+0.3	+0.1	+0.3	+0.2	+0.3	-0.3	+0.7	+0.5
1965	+0.1	+0.2	+0.4	+0.2	+0.3	+0.3	+0.3	+0.2	+0.1	+0.4	+0.5	+0.3
1966	+0.3	+0.2	+0.4	+0.1	+0.3	+0.3	+0.2	+0.1	+0.1	+0.3	+0.1	+0.1
1967	+0.3	-0.1	-	+0.1	+0.1	+0.1	+0.1	+0.4	-	+0.1	+0.6	+0.5
1968	-0.1	+0.3	+0.2	+0.2	+0.3	+0.3	+0.2	-	+0.3	+0.3	+0.3	+0.2
1969	+0.1	+0.3	+0.3	+0.1	+0.1	+0.3	+0.3	+0.2	+0.1	+0.2	-0.2	+0.1
1970	-0.4	-	-	-	-0.1	-0.1	+0.1	-0.1	-	-0.6	-0.3	+0.7
1971	+0.3	-	+0.1	+0.2	+0.2	+0.2	-0.1	-	+0.4	+0.2	+0.4	+0.4
1972	+0.6	+0.1	+0.5	+0.4	+0.2	+0.1	+0.3	+0.6	+0.4	+0.7	+0.6	+0.5
1973	+0.3	+0.3	+0.1	-	+0.2	+0.3	+0.2	+0.1	+0.2	+0.7	+0.4	-0.3
1974	-0.4	-0.2	-0.1	-0.2	+0.3	-	+0.1	-0.2	-0.1	-0.1	-0.8	-1.2
1975	-0.7	-0.5	-0.6	+0.2	+0.1	+0.2	+0.3	+0.6	+0.4	+0.3	+0.1	+0.3
1976	+0.7	+0.5	+0.2	+0.4	+0.2	+0.1	+0.2	+0.2	+0.2	-0.1	+0.7	+0.5
1977	+0.1	+0.4	+0.4	+0.4	+0.4	+0.4	+0.4	+0.2	+0.4	+0.2	+0.3	+0.3
1978	-0.2	+0.5	+0.7	+1.1	+0.2	+0.5	+0.1	+0.4	+0.3	+0.4	+0.4	+0.3
1979	-	+0.2	+0.7	-0.7	+0.6	-	-	-	-	+0.3	-	-
1980	+0.4	-0.1	-0.4	-0.8	-0.9	-0.4	-	+0.5	+0.6	+0.7	+0.5	+0.3
1981	-	-	+0.1	-0.1	-0.1	+0.2	+0.4	-	-0.2	-0.4	-0.4	-0.4
1982	-0.6	+0.5	-0.1	-	-	-0.5	-0.3	-0.3	-0.2	-0.4	-	-0.1
1983	+0.5	-0.1	+0.3	+0.4	+0.6	+0.6	+0.6	-0.1	+1.0	+0.7	+0.5	+0.6
1984	+0.7	+0.5	+0.5	+0.3	+0.3	+0.6	+0.2	+0.2	+0.4	-0.1	+0.4	+0.3
1985	-	+0.3	+0.4	+0.3	+0.1	-0.1	-	+0.4	+0.2	-	+0.2	+0.5
1986	+0.1	+0.1	+0.1	+0.7	-0.2	-0.1	+0.3	+0.1	+0.6	-0.1	+0.2	+0.6
1987	-0.4	+0.9	+0.1	+0.2	+0.2	+0.2	+0.4	+0.2	+0.2	+0.8	-0.1	+0.8
1988	-0.2	+0.5	+0.4	+0.2	+0.1	+0.4	+0.1	+0.2	+0.1	+0.7	+0.1	+0.7
1989	+0.3	-	+0.2	+0.2	-0.3	-0.1	-0.2	+0.4	-0.2	-	+0.5	+0.2
1990	-0.1	+0.6	+0.4	-0.2	+0.2	+0.1	-0.2	-0.1	-0.3	-0.4	-0.4	-
1991	-0.7	-0.3	-0.1	+0.1	+0.2	+0.2	+0.1	-	+0.2	-	-0.2	-
1992	-0.1	+0.5	+0.2	+0.2	-	+0.1	+0.3	-0.1	+0.4	+0.5	+0.3	+2.1
1993	-1.9	+0.3	+0.1	+0.6	+0.1	+0.2	-0.1	+0.7	+0.1	+0.4	+0.6	+0.6
1994	-0.1	+0.7	+0.6	+0.2	+0.3	+0.4	+0.1	+0.7	+0.3	+0.6	+0.5	+0.6
1995	+0.2	+0.3	+0.1	-0.3	-	+0.4	+0.2	-	-	-	-	-

Source: U.S. Department of Commerce, Bureau of Economic Analysis. - indicates data not available or zero.

Employees On Nonagricultural Payrolls
(Thousands)

Year	Jan	Feb	Mar	Apr	May	Jun	Jul	Aug	Sep	Oct	Nov	Dec
1945	41,767	41,770	41,715	41,276	41,120	40,899	40,609	40,298	38,356	38,436	38,799	39,009
1946	39,721	39,193	40,183	40,858	41,248	41,551	41,955	42,466	42,749	42,959	43,229	43,314
1947	43,497	43,578	43,621	43,501	43,544	43,685	43,682	43,784	44,001	44,176	44,313	44,519
1948	44,667	44,501	44,624	44,293	44,647	44,879	45,062	45,039	45,162	45,065	45,069	45,022
1949	44,624	44,417	44,136	44,112	43,814	43,592	43,418	43,479	43,699	42,805	43,142	43,491
1950	43,469	43,192	43,824	44,260	44,574	44,952	45,360	46,024	46,301	46,528	46,653	46,752
1951	47,230	47,531	47,794	47,760	47,805	47,913	47,925	47,794	47,748	47,825	48,027	48,122
1952	48,227	48,493	48,416	48,509	48,474	48,125	47,999	48,686	49,085	49,434	49,719	49,937
1953	50,045	50,273	50,382	50,314	50,358	50,389	50,382	50,271	50,226	50,108	49,825	49,625
1954	49,341	49,276	49,046	49,039	48,852	48,791	48,689	48,643	48,765	48,828	49,103	49,234
1955	49,354	49,523	49,851	50,104	50,404	50,693	50,811	50,929	51,103	51,323	51,507	51,714
1956	51,863	52,093	52,228	52,232	52,365	52,433	51,746	52,382	52,439	52,674	52,752	52,908
1957	52,808	53,003	53,062	53,053	52,996	52,941	52,972	52,913	52,816	52,663	52,482	52,307
1958	52,003	51,441	51,142	50,807	50,770	50,801	50,911	51,113	51,355	51,378	51,814	51,986
1959	52,408	52,568	52,883	53,132	53,422	53,584	53,663	53,220	53,257	53,196	53,509	54,040
1960	54,185	54,414	54,287	54,634	54,362	54,276	54,214	54,198	54,063	53,982	53,845	53,577
1961	53,534	53,380	53,510	53,462	53,677	53,916	54,027	54,222	54,285	54,376	54,622	54,744
1962	54,709	55,018	55,107	55,459	55,514	55,561	55,643	55,778	55,849	55,912	55,936	55,918
1963	55,935	56,055	56,153	56,454	56,513	56,563	56,688	56,823	56,962	57,152	57,126	57,252
1964	57,269	57,603	57,732	57,784	57,975	58,121	58,311	58,510	58,798	58,691	59,114	59,335
1965	59,398	59,683	59,864	60,124	60,363	60,595	60,860	61,085	61,367	61,578	61,882	62,230
1966	62,386	62,720	63,087	63,317	63,560	63,978	64,185	64,344	64,433	64,655	64,854	65,076
1967	65,215	65,208	65,338	65,323	65,478	65,654	65,831	65,964	66,089	66,111	66,591	66,776
1968	66,606	67,029	67,132	67,417	67,495	67,783	68,003	68,219	68,365	68,603	68,855	69,161
1969	69,272	69,542	69,791	69,948	70,180	70,498	70,668	70,799	70,833	70,993	70,941	71,127
1970	71,018	71,165	71,347	71,251	70,993	70,905	70,969	70,789	70,857	70,416	70,296	70,666
1971	70,718	70,657	70,746	70,936	71,129	71,163	71,219	71,220	71,527	71,532	71,734	71,996
1972	72,303	72,525	72,808	73,061	73,341	73,643	73,636	73,929	74,115	74,527	74,881	75,235
1973	75,474	75,908	76,137	76,312	76,516	76,738	76,758	77,018	77,164	77,502	77,833	77,992
1974	77,953	78,177	78,177	78,261	78,407	78,434	78,517	78,478	78,498	78,569	78,238	77,565
1975	77,145	76,742	76,419	76,298	76,459	76,388	76,626	76,980	77,188	77,499	77,619	77,915
1976	78,326	78,606	78,819	79,134	79,192	79,258	79,485	79,581	79,842	79,842	80,141	80,338
1977	80,517	80,794	81,221	81,610	81,977	82,381	82,760	82,974	83,431	83,661	84,031	84,271
1978	84,464	84,808	85,338	86,083	86,404	86,811	87,037	87,324	87,434	87,797	88,249	88,559
1979	88,728	88,985	89,426	89,363	89,681	89,955	90,019	90,159	90,149	90,360	90,466	90,617
1980	90,729	90,876	90,995	90,780	90,316	89,974	89,676	89,964	90,046	90,334	90,550	90,774
1981	91,003	91,095	91,206	91,219	91,142	91,285	91,410	91,320	91,191	91,216	91,014	90,831
1982	90,448	90,474	90,337	90,031	89,965	89,703	89,380	89,177	88,995	88,787	88,649	88,675
1983	88,826	88,758	88,946	89,211	89,497	89,886	90,313	89,973	91,088	91,408	91,727	92,110
1984	92,524	93,043	93,312	93,650	93,952	94,325	94,647	94,885	95,186	95,499	95,829	95,997
1985	96,249	96,397	96,734	96,896	97,163	97,280	97,465	97,696	97,878	98,098	98,286	98,500
1986	98,599	98,718	98,796	98,974	99,096	98,973	99,276	99,435	99,747	99,980	100,145	100,394
1987	100,543	100,772	101,005	101,367	101,564	101,713	102,047	102,266	102,430	102,980	103,200	103,544
1988	103,593	104,063	104,349	104,611	104,794	105,156	105,397	105,549	105,789	106,070	106,400	106,703
1989	107,046	107,276	107,466	107,636	107,725	107,871	107,939	108,026	108,200	108,266	108,588	108,695
1990	108,977	109,297	109,487	109,492	109,777	109,911	109,698	109,558	109,484	109,294	109,109	108,976
1991	108,793	108,525	108,346	108,131	108,160	108,176	108,102	108,214	108,231	108,214	108,128	108,120
1992	108,062	108,059	108,153	108,344	108,487	108,517	108,651	108,720	108,795	109,003	109,098	109,274
1993	109,477	109,839	109,820	110,131	110,401	110,529	110,836	110,991	111,237	111,559	111,795	112,094
1994	112,301	112,576	113,087	113,363	113,638	113,943	114,171	114,510	114,762	114,935	115,427	115,624
1995	115,810	116,123	116,302	116,310	116,248	116,498	116,553	-	-	-	-	-

Source: U.S. Department of Labor, Bureau of Labor Statistics. - indicates data not available or zero.

Index of Industrial Production
(1987 = 100)

Year	Jan	Feb	Mar	Apr	May	Jun	Jul	Aug	Sep	Oct	Nov	Dec
1945	26.8	26.7	26.5	26.0	25.3	24.8	24.2	21.7	19.7	18.9	19.6	19.7
1946	18.6	17.7	19.6	19.2	18.5	19.6	20.3	21.1	21.5	21.8	22.0	22.1
1947	22.4	22.5	22.6	22.5	22.6	22.6	22.4	22.6	22.7	22.9	23.3	23.3
1948	23.5	23.5	23.3	23.3	23.7	24.0	24.0	23.9	23.7	23.9	23.6	23.4
1949	23.2	22.9	22.5	22.4	22.1	22.0	22.0	22.2	22.4	21.6	22.2	22.6
1950	22.9	23.0	23.8	24.6	25.2	25.9	26.7	27.6	27.4	27.6	27.5	28.0
1951	28.1	28.3	28.4	28.5	28.4	28.2	27.8	27.5	27.7	27.7	27.9	28.1
1952	28.4	28.5	28.6	28.4	28.1	27.8	27.4	29.2	30.2	30.5	31.1	31.3
1953	31.4	31.6	31.8	32.0	32.2	32.0	32.4	32.2	31.6	31.3	30.6	29.8
1954	29.6	29.7	29.5	29.3	29.5	29.6	29.6	29.6	29.6	30.0	30.5	30.9
1955	31.6	32.0	32.7	33.1	33.7	33.7	34.0	33.9	34.1	34.7	34.8	34.9
1956	35.1	34.8	34.8	35.1	34.8	34.5	33.4	34.8	35.6	35.9	35.6	36.1
1957	36.0	36.3	36.3	35.8	35.7	35.8	36.0	36.0	35.7	35.1	34.3	33.7
1958	33.0	32.3	31.9	31.4	31.7	32.6	33.0	33.7	34.0	34.4	35.4	35.5
1959	36.0	36.7	37.2	38.0	38.6	38.6	37.7	36.4	36.4	36.1	36.3	38.6
1960	39.6	39.2	38.9	38.6	38.5	38.1	37.9	37.9	37.5	37.4	36.9	36.2
1961	36.3	36.2	36.4	37.2	37.7	38.3	38.7	39.1	39.0	39.8	40.4	40.7
1962	40.4	41.1	41.3	41.4	41.3	41.2	41.6	41.7	41.9	42.0	42.2	42.2
1963	42.5	42.9	43.2	43.6	44.1	44.3	44.1	44.2	44.6	44.9	45.1	45.1
1964	45.5	45.8	45.8	46.5	46.8	46.9	47.2	47.5	47.7	47.0	48.5	49.1
1965	49.6	49.9	50.6	50.8	51.2	51.6	52.1	52.3	52.4	52.9	53.2	53.8
1966	54.4	54.7	55.5	55.5	56.1	56.3	56.6	56.7	57.2	57.6	57.2	57.3
1967	57.6	57.0	56.6	57.2	56.7	56.7	56.5	57.6	57.5	58.0	58.8	59.5
1968	59.4	59.6	59.8	59.9	60.6	60.8	60.7	60.9	61.1	61.2	62.0	62.2
1969	62.6	63.0	63.5	63.2	63.0	63.6	63.9	64.1	64.1	64.1	63.5	63.3
1970	62.1	62.1	62.0	61.9	61.8	61.6	61.7	61.6	61.2	60.0	59.6	61.0
1971	61.5	61.3	61.3	61.6	61.9	62.2	62.0	61.7	62.7	63.1	63.4	64.1
1972	65.6	66.0	66.5	67.6	67.5	67.7	67.6	68.5	69.2	70.2	71.1	71.7
1973	71.8	72.8	72.8	73.0	73.4	73.9	74.4	74.3	74.9	75.2	75.2	74.0
1974	73.0	72.7	73.0	72.9	73.8	74.0	73.6	73.4	73.7	73.2	71.1	68.1
1975	66.3	65.3	64.1	64.7	64.5	65.3	65.7	66.9	67.6	67.9	68.6	69.1
1976	69.9	71.1	70.9	71.2	72.0	72.1	72.5	72.9	73.1	73.4	74.6	75.2
1977	75.5	75.9	76.6	77.7	78.3	78.9	78.9	79.0	79.4	79.4	79.5	79.1
1978	78.8	79.0	80.0	82.0	82.3	83.1	83.3	83.6	84.1	84.5	85.2	85.4
1979	85.1	85.8	86.1	85.2	86.2	86.1	85.6	85.3	85.5	86.0	85.7	85.6
1980	85.9	86.2	86.2	84.5	82.5	81.5	81.2	82.4	83.5	84.0	85.5	85.9
1981	85.2	85.4	85.7	85.0	85.6	86.1	87.1	86.9	86.5	85.8	84.8	84.1
1982	82.4	84.2	83.7	83.2	82.7	82.4	82.0	81.6	81.0	80.3	80.0	79.3
1983	80.8	80.7	81.3	82.3	83.2	83.7	85.3	86.5	87.9	88.6	88.8	89.2
1984	91.0	90.9	91.9	92.4	93.0	93.5	93.9	94.0	93.9	93.2	93.3	92.8
1985	93.1	93.8	94.1	94.5	94.7	94.4	94.1	94.5	95.0	94.2	94.6	95.6
1986	96.1	95.5	94.6	94.8	94.7	94.3	94.8	94.9	95.0	95.6	96.3	96.8
1987	96.5	97.9	98.2	98.8	99.4	100.3	100.6	100.9	100.7	102.1	102.2	102.8
1988	103.2	103.4	103.4	104.3	104.0	104.0	104.6	105.2	104.7	105.0	105.6	106.3
1989	106.6	106.2	107.1	107.1	106.7	106.4	105.3	105.8	105.4	105.0	105.4	106.1
1990	105.5	106.1	106.4	105.7	106.5	106.7	106.5	106.8	106.8	106.3	105.0	104.5
1991	104.0	103.1	102.1	102.6	103.5	104.4	104.7	104.8	105.7	105.6	105.6	105.2
1992	104.9	105.8	106.4	106.9	107.5	107.2	108.1	108.0	108.2	108.8	109.9	110.4
1993	110.6	111.3	111.4	111.4	111.1	111.5	112.0	112.2	112.5	112.7	113.7	114.7
1994	114.7	115.6	116.6	116.7	117.4	118.0	118.2	119.1	119.0	119.5	120.3	121.7
1995	122.0	122.1	122.0	121.2	121.2	121.1	121.3	-	-	-	-	-

Source: Board of Governors of the Federal Reserve System. - indicates data not available or zero.

Personal Income Less Transfer Payments
(Annual Rate, Billions of 1987 $)

Year	Jan	Feb	Mar	Apr	May	Jun	Jul	Aug	Sep	Oct	Nov	Dec
1947	888.9	886.4	880.5	865.5	864.7	873.8	867.5	867.3	878.3	876.1	875.8	880.7
1948	897.6	891.1	902.3	903.7	911.2	925.5	923.5	930.3	932.6	937.2	931.2	921.7
1949	906.0	904.6	905.1	906.0	903.7	895.3	887.0	894.0	907.9	887.5	898.1	902.8
1950	919.9	915.7	931.9	937.8	954.4	953.4	969.7	981.6	993.3	1,000.0	1,011.6	1,023.3
1951	1,014.3	1,014.2	1,026.2	1,042.2	1,046.1	1,053.0	1,047.2	1,060.5	1,058.1	1,065.1	1,065.7	1,072.0
1952	1,058.2	1,075.5	1,077.6	1,075.5	1,086.1	1,087.8	1,082.4	1,105.4	1,118.4	1,114.9	1,107.9	1,115.7
1953	1,115.6	1,124.7	1,135.4	1,132.4	1,138.5	1,141.4	1,139.8	1,136.1	1,136.1	1,140.2	1,136.1	1,131.1
1954	1,131.1	1,129.0	1,123.3	1,113.0	1,115.9	1,121.2	1,121.2	1,132.4	1,138.5	1,143.9	1,156.6	1,155.9
1955	1,159.3	1,161.9	1,170.0	1,177.8	1,187.9	1,191.1	1,206.0	1,206.8	1,215.7	1,220.9	1,230.5	1,238.6
1956	1,236.0	1,243.6	1,248.8	1,262.4	1,259.8	1,263.5	1,254.2	1,265.4	1,269.8	1,283.1	1,278.5	1,280.2
1957	1,278.2	1,284.5	1,283.8	1,284.6	1,283.1	1,293.5	1,294.3	1,295.0	1,291.2	1,282.9	1,283.7	1,273.9
1958	1,270.5	1,264.5	1,268.3	1,261.9	1,265.3	1,274.3	1,297.4	1,295.5	1,303.0	1,301.1	1,320.3	1,322.1
1959	1,318.7	1,326.1	1,338.1	1,349.3	1,354.6	1,359.3	1,360.7	1,346.1	1,344.1	1,346.7	1,366.1	1,381.6
1960	1,387.1	1,379.9	1,378.0	1,380.7	1,390.9	1,390.5	1,388.0	1,388.4	1,385.1	1,385.6	1,383.0	1,377.9
1961	1,389.5	1,390.9	1,391.3	1,400.4	1,408.7	1,415.9	1,417.6	1,425.5	1,425.8	1,439.8	1,454.8	1,462.4
1962	1,459.1	1,464.3	1,475.7	1,481.9	1,480.9	1,491.1	1,497.5	1,495.7	1,494.4	1,500.7	1,505.3	1,512.3
1963	1,505.6	1,515.5	1,515.1	1,520.7	1,529.1	1,530.7	1,533.4	1,541.5	1,552.3	1,564.1	1,564.9	1,573.7
1964	1,576.5	1,586.2	1,593.8	1,604.5	1,609.6	1,618.2	1,628.2	1,636.3	1,646.2	1,649.7	1,663.7	1,677.1
1965	1,676.5	1,678.3	1,686.4	1,691.9	1,708.8	1,722.0	1,726.3	1,735.0	1,738.8	1,759.5	1,775.6	1,784.3
1966	1,783.1	1,786.1	1,791.1	1,798.7	1,806.6	1,817.4	1,822.9	1,830.0	1,829.1	1,841.4	1,846.5	1,848.4
1967	1,863.9	1,863.2	1,865.3	1,864.4	1,872.1	1,880.5	1,889.2	1,897.1	1,893.7	1,897.8	1,909.1	1,923.2
1968	1,922.1	1,937.9	1,941.0	1,948.3	1,961.7	1,971.6	1,982.3	1,984.5	2,000.3	2,002.1	2,011.4	2,022.2
1969	2,020.1	2,025.1	2,037.2	2,040.2	2,051.0	2,056.0	2,074.2	2,079.9	2,086.9	2,093.0	2,098.3	2,097.4
1970	2,092.0	2,087.2	2,090.6	2,098.3	2,093.0	2,087.6	2,096.6	2,101.7	2,101.1	2,091.7	2,091.7	2,093.1
1971	2,104.6	2,103.8	2,105.4	2,107.0	2,116.7	2,114.4	2,117.3	2,130.3	2,130.2	2,134.9	2,147.2	2,166.6
1972	2,177.2	2,188.3	2,195.1	2,208.1	2,215.8	2,199.2	2,232.7	2,256.6	2,267.8	2,289.8	2,314.0	2,327.8
1973	2,331.1	2,331.6	2,330.8	2,324.0	2,346.6	2,355.5	2,355.0	2,368.6	2,379.6	2,409.3	2,428.2	2,421.8
1974	2,390.7	2,364.1	2,334.9	2,322.9	2,324.4	2,330.2	2,334.8	2,327.5	2,330.3	2,337.2	2,314.7	2,305.3
1975	2,276.6	2,255.9	2,259.0	2,256.5	2,264.0	2,271.2	2,273.5	2,294.9	2,309.9	2,326.6	2,328.9	2,328.0
1976	2,349.0	2,362.5	2,370.7	2,380.6	2,391.0	2,388.2	2,392.3	2,398.1	2,402.1	2,401.9	2,424.9	2,432.3
1977	2,432.8	2,439.8	2,447.1	2,452.7	2,469.9	2,473.8	2,496.8	2,510.8	2,524.5	2,527.7	2,534.5	2,546.8
1978	2,550.0	2,562.3	2,590.8	2,620.4	2,623.4	2,640.0	2,642.0	2,654.8	2,668.7	2,685.4	2,692.5	2,702.8
1979	2,701.6	2,714.6	2,726.6	2,712.6	2,711.3	2,717.9	2,725.7	2,727.0	2,728.8	2,737.0	2,744.2	2,749.7
1980	2,753.7	2,744.1	2,731.4	2,706.4	2,686.5	2,684.0	2,676.4	2,692.2	2,706.6	2,741.9	2,760.9	2,781.2
1981	2,776.2	2,772.6	2,775.7	2,775.9	2,772.4	2,781.5	2,799.9	2,814.3	2,813.5	2,805.3	2,793.9	2,781.9
1982	2,768.6	2,776.1	2,781.7	2,800.5	2,806.1	2,788.1	2,776.4	2,771.7	2,762.0	2,758.7	2,756.5	2,767.6
1983	2,767.8	2,760.2	2,764.4	2,778.0	2,791.7	2,800.3	2,814.1	2,804.3	2,826.3	2,862.2	2,879.3	2,900.7
1984	2,922.4	2,963.6	2,982.9	2,987.2	2,986.8	3,007.7	3,023.7	3,038.6	3,064.3	3,046.0	3,060.1	3,098.8
1985	3,081.3	3,092.9	3,103.6	3,118.7	3,098.2	3,109.9	3,104.1	3,104.5	3,105.1	3,123.6	3,118.7	3,154.3
1986	3,139.7	3,158.7	3,187.4	3,227.7	3,212.3	3,199.5	3,198.3	3,211.0	3,216.3	3,206.7	3,209.9	3,233.1
1987	3,220.2	3,240.1	3,240.6	3,242.8	3,233.5	3,232.3	3,242.1	3,255.8	3,258.5	3,309.4	3,292.7	3,345.5
1988	3,307.9	3,322.3	3,335.3	3,342.1	3,341.6	3,350.7	3,355.2	3,357.6	3,362.6	3,410.6	3,386.5	3,411.5
1989	3,427.6	3,445.5	3,455.2	3,448.3	3,429.0	3,422.5	3,429.0	3,424.8	3,414.2	3,432.1	3,447.5	3,457.2
1990	3,457.4	3,476.7	3,487.8	3,495.0	3,481.5	3,482.6	3,485.1	3,464.3	3,461.2	3,429.0	3,439.3	3,467.5
1991	3,419.2	3,414.3	3,426.2	3,418.3	3,415.8	3,425.4	3,410.4	3,404.6	3,410.5	3,412.8	3,401.1	3,431.7
1992	3,412.1	3,440.8	3,445.8	3,447.5	3,446.9	3,446.3	3,449.4	3,455.9	3,473.1	3,496.7	3,501.1	3,706.5
1993	3,461.0	3,465.2	3,475.1	3,523.8	3,533.0	3,514.8	3,506.0	3,543.1	3,539.6	3,556.1	3,571.8	3,589.3
1994	3,566.9	3,618.9	3,629.0	3,641.9	3,652.7	3,649.3	3,654.2	3,665.0	3,683.6	3,735.7	3,727.3	3,751.4
1995	3,763.3	3,776.8	3,789.2	3,784.1	3,766.4	3,786.0	3,806.4	-	-	-	-	-

Source: U.S. Department of Commerce, Bureau of Economic Analysis. - indicates data not available or zero.

Manufacturing and Trade Sales
(Million 1987 $)

Year	Jan	Feb	Mar	Apr	May	Jun	Jul	Aug	Sep	Oct	Nov	Dec
1948	124,835	124,910	125,800	126,345	124,888	126,436	127,564	127,824	127,782	127,893	127,342	128,259
1949	127,027	126,820	126,345	125,777	123,840	126,928	123,456	126,132	128,607	123,746	125,394	124,324
1950	126,685	129,318	131,057	132,663	135,960	141,587	152,196	154,455	144,882	141,946	137,578	145,307
1951	149,265	145,359	143,047	140,585	141,818	140,754	137,926	141,418	141,361	142,330	141,980	140,607
1952	142,908	144,424	143,663	145,420	146,916	147,175	144,070	147,275	152,374	157,262	156,711	159,538
1953	160,423	162,734	164,495	164,552	163,828	161,834	164,136	160,742	159,321	158,526	154,589	151,918
1954	152,719	154,444	153,588	154,895	152,195	154,137	153,682	152,696	153,460	154,055	158,685	162,435
1955	164,854	166,234	169,611	171,379	172,115	172,131	172,682	171,979	174,807	174,073	175,542	175,829
1956	174,810	173,428	174,077	174,579	173,984	174,808	167,114	172,717	174,330	175,829	176,662	178,391
1957	178,898	179,508	178,270	175,438	174,779	175,789	175,082	176,271	173,898	173,046	170,731	166,862
1958	166,580	163,715	161,262	160,504	161,136	164,147	165,833	168,752	169,723	172,518	175,180	170,372
1959	177,579	180,295	182,424	185,177	187,213	187,464	186,905	180,702	180,205	180,599	181,001	186,020
1960	189,271	188,409	187,454	187,916	185,445	185,299	184,402	183,416	185,475	184,494	182,100	182,475
1961	178,627	179,133	182,209	181,214	183,946	187,282	185,026	189,399	190,051	192,566	194,393	195,194
1962	195,352	195,537	198,194	198,356	198,124	197,286	198,071	199,471	198,952	200,913	203,713	200,284
1963	201,169	204,347	204,465	206,370	204,950	206,727	209,795	208,574	208,791	211,015	208,723	213,334
1964	214,560	214,575	214,008	217,537	219,879	219,279	222,959	222,257	224,339	220,983	223,310	230,443
1965	229,885	230,640	235,579	236,142	233,649	234,691	238,911	237,557	237,547	239,786	243,138	243,988
1966	246,684	246,953	250,964	249,027	248,149	250,815	249,321	250,896	250,438	251,112	250,109	251,214
1967	252,621	252,020	253,265	253,761	253,796	254,250	254,249	257,298	256,699	254,730	261,763	267,141
1968	265,864	264,932	267,361	267,119	268,528	271,129	274,384	270,066	271,294	275,450	277,670	275,368
1969	275,855	276,373	277,968	279,301	278,781	278,746	280,072	281,564	283,152	285,865	282,135	281,792
1970	279,400	279,282	276,126	274,134	277,364	278,207	278,441	277,112	276,793	272,273	267,731	276,499
1971	279,715	281,661	282,908	284,258	286,259	289,727	288,174	286,277	289,563	290,422	295,093	297,156
1972	300,201	297,396	302,716	305,077	306,605	307,938	308,992	314,304	317,743	321,720	326,386	331,125
1973	335,572	336,568	334,362	332,728	331,496	330,711	335,267	330,662	330,325	337,743	342,034	337,065
1974	338,234	337,134	340,708	339,270	340,309	338,974	340,112	335,795	332,271	327,459	323,059	312,343
1975	314,166	312,571	303,419	308,306	307,936	310,588	313,554	315,628	316,972	317,251	315,777	319,167
1976	327,307	329,157	331,645	334,615	333,800	337,423	338,535	337,677	338,062	334,574	340,175	350,306
1977	348,170	352,455	356,339	357,357	356,424	359,677	360,474	360,774	361,351	362,999	365,148	369,826
1978	361,385	368,449	371,288	381,447	380,766	381,737	379,394	385,200	383,969	388,325	390,207	391,501
1979	390,311	386,651	397,051	384,979	395,454	389,307	389,666	389,991	388,185	388,053	387,094	385,697
1980	392,835	387,465	378,012	370,276	363,974	362,525	368,215	369,349	377,120	384,277	383,965	384,437
1981	386,997	385,511	383,406	384,070	380,834	380,509	380,508	378,832	376,090	370,117	367,217	362,912
1982	360,956	367,357	366,724	366,034	368,412	363,473	363,756	360,466	360,457	357,085	358,425	355,895
1983	364,244	362,022	367,358	367,559	373,644	383,026	383,113	382,368	388,192	392,992	397,711	404,330
1984	406,597	406,454	406,443	409,273	412,897	416,925	414,612	413,394	413,473	415,489	419,077	419,995
1985	419,796	420,338	423,347	423,752	428,318	422,405	423,369	430,477	431,734	426,741	430,444	428,476
1986	434,221	432,399	432,011	440,859	436,751	440,049	443,290	442,924	453,686	447,725	447,543	455,846
1987	442,515	457,546	457,077	455,965	456,567	457,796	461,888	459,794	464,413	463,428	462,360	465,492
1988	464,547	470,126	476,501	474,210	475,560	479,893	476,922	478,295	479,596	483,231	484,494	491,754
1989	491,361	484,434	481,752	486,518	484,551	482,811	478,270	491,174	487,014	481,808	485,802	486,619
1990	482,128	489,452	493,604	488,049	490,649	492,459	488,061	493,015	484,521	482,954	476,887	472,486
1991	467,502	470,922	469,071	478,060	480,621	479,321	484,246	484,883	485,639	486,130	484,716	477,881
1992	484,727	486,571	488,381	489,532	486,602	491,755	495,231	491,825	496,145	498,844	501,508	510,863
1993	512,323	512,635	511,548	511,941	513,911	519,971	515,918	524,224	527,070	529,760	534,944	541,026
1994	539,396	545,346	551,928	549,683	550,130	554,024	549,987	565,578	564,681	566,945	572,659	578,177
1995	577,427	577,835	576,415	571,204	575,322	579,894	-	-	-	-	-	-

Source: U.S. Department of Commerce, Bureau of Economic Analysis, U.S. Department of Commerce, Bureau of the Census. - indicates data not available or zero.

COMPOSITE INDEX OF LAGGING INDICATORS

The composite index of lagging indicators turns down about 10 months after the economy turns down and turns up about six months after the economy has turned up. Thus it lags behind the economy. It is made up of components that have inertial tendencies—they change more slowly than the economy. The "lagging index," of course, also confirms the cyclical behaviour of the economy by moving in tandem with the leading and coincident indicators—at a lag in time.

The lagging index is also a somewhat uncertain indicator. At business cycle peaks, the lags range from 2 to 13 months; at business cycle troughs, the range is 4 to 15 months.

Components of the Lagging Index

The index is a composite of 7 indicators, each of which is further discussed below:

> Index of labor cost per unit of output in manufacturing
> Ratio, manufacturing and trade inventories to sales
> Average duration of unemployment in weeks
> Ratio, consumer installment credit outstanding to personal income
> Commercial and industrial loans outstanding
> Average prime rate charged by banks
> Change in consumer price index for services

Index of Labor Cost per Unit of Output in Manufacturing. The indicator is an index with a 1987 base (1987 = 100). Labor cost in manufacturing is in part a reflection of longer-term contractual arrangements between manufacturers and labor unions which are not subject to rapid adjustment as the economy changes. Even the compensation of non-union labor forces tends to lag behind economic events: managements avoid downward adjustments in wages to maintain morale and productivity and resist demands for increased pay in periods of growth. For these reasons, the index lags economic events. Recessionary forces cause the cost of labor to decline—slowly. In periods of upturn, labor cost rises slowly as well. Thus it is normal to have high wages at the start and during recessions and relatively low wages as the economy begins climbing to a new peak.

Ratio, Manufacturing and Trade Inventories to Sales. The indicator is expressed as a ratio based on inventory and sales measures expressed in 1987 constant dollars. A ratio of 1.0 means that inventories and sales are identical. A high ratio indicates high inventories relative to sales. A low indicator tends to mean that inventories are depleted. A dropping ratio means that inventories are "selling out" while a climbing ratio means that sales are slowing. Manufacturers and merchants caught at the beginning of a recession with high inventories will be unable to sell them; therefore, the ratio will increase as the economy slumps. Conversely, in an expansionary period, the ratio will be dropping because producers cannot keep up with demand. In both cases, the indicator tends to move in the opposite direction of the economy—or in the same direction, but with a lag in time.

Average Duration of Unemployment. The indicator is shown as number of weeks of unemployment. A recession is a sustained downturn in production after a sustained period of growth. The average duration of unemployment, therefore, will tend to be low at the start of a recession. The shrinking of the economy will cause this average to grow. As the economy turns up again, the average will be high; time has to pass until laid-off people are employed again and the average duration of unemployment drops. In this case, also, the indicator grows as the economy shrinks and declines as the economy grows.

Ratio, Consumer Installment Credit Outstanding to Personal Income. The indicator is expressed as a percent. A high percentage indicates that consumer debt relative to income is high. A decline in personal income or an increase in consumer debt will cause the indicator to rise and, of course, an increase in personal income or decrease in debt will cause the ratio to decline. At the start of a recession, personal income tends to drop more rapidly than debt outstanding; this indicator, therefore, will increase as the economy decreases. Later, as debt is paid off and less is borrowed (because times are uncertain), the ratio will decrease just as the economy begins to expand again—the signature of a lagging indicator.

Commercial and Industrial Loans Outstanding. The indicator is shown in millions of constant 1987 dollars. Business and industry assume debt in periods of growth and minimize debt in periods of decline. The total debt outstanding, however, reflects the business cycle at a lag in time; borrowers pay off debt over time and may be late in paying during economic turn-downs; they also contract new obligations later than the economy's upturn because both lenders and borrowers are more cautious after a recessionary period.

Average Prime Rate Charged by Banks. The indicator is shown as a percent of interest charged by major banks to their largest customers. Historically, the prime rate has tended to increase during recessions and to decrease during periods of expansion. At the onset of an economic downturn, the rate reflects the conditions of the previous expansion; as the recession deepens and demand for money slackens, the prime rate drops. The prime rate is strongly influenced by actions of the Federal Reserve System. The Federal Reserve's discount rate (interest charged to member banks for short-term borrowings) has an immediate effect on the prime rate; therefore, the behavior of this indicator is indirectly subject to alteration by government action.

Change in Consumer Price Index for Services. The index is expressed as a percent; the data are "smoothed," meaning that data are arithmetically transformed to remove irregular short-term movements. Prices for services are less volatile than prices for food, fuel, and products. Hence this series is a good lagging indicator: it changes more slowly than the economy. More detailed presentations of the Consumer Price Index are provided later in this book.

Sources and Revisions

The component series are drawn from federal sources, including the U.S. Department of Commerce, Bureau of Economic Analysis and Bureau of the Census; the U.S. Department of Labor, Bureau of Labor Statistics; the Federal Reserve System; and the Federal Reserve Bank of New York.

The composite index itself is constructed by the Bureau of Economic Analysis. In the process, mathematical operations are performed on the component data series to ensure that volatile series do not dominate the index. A volatile series may be one that fluctuates wildly month to month but shows less volatility when averaged over several months. Other smoothing and standardization methods are used as well.

The lagging index was last revised in 1993 to reflect comprehensive revisions of the National Income and Product Accounts which were made in 1991 and to incorporate improvements in methodology.

Bibliography

1. Frumkin, Norman. *Guide to Economic Indicators*. M.E. Sharpe, Inc., 1990.

2. Green, George R. and Barry A. Beckman. "Business Cycle Indicators: Upcoming Revision of the

Composite Indexes." U.S. Department of Commerce, Bureau of Economic Analysis. *Survey of Current Business*, October 1993. Superintendent of Documents, U.S. Government Printing Office, Washington, DC 20302.

3. Hertzberg, Marie P. and Barry A. Beckman. "Business Cycle Indicators: Revised Composite Indexes." U.S. Department of Commerce, Bureau of Economic Analysis. *Survey of Current Business*, January 1989. Superintendent of Documents, U.S. Government Printing Office, Washington, DC 20302.

4. U.S. Department of Commerce, Bureau of Economic Analysis. "Composite Indexes of Leading, Coincident, and Lagging Indicators." In *Survey of Current Business*, November 1987. Superintendent of Documents, U.S. Government Printing Office, Washington, DC 20302.

5. U.S. Department of Commerce, Bureau of Economic Analysis. *Survey of Current Business*. Superintendent of Documents, U.S. Government Printing Office, Washington, DC 20302.

Composite Index of 7 Lagging Indicators
(1987 = 100)

Year	Jan	Feb	Mar	Apr	May	Jun	Jul	Aug	Sep	Oct	Nov	Dec
1948	49.4	49.9	50.2	50.4	50.5	50.5	51.0	52.6	53.0	52.9	53.3	53.4
1949	53.8	54.0	53.8	53.7	54.0	53.9	53.8	53.5	53.2	54.1	53.9	54.0
1950	54.0	54.0	53.9	54.2	54.3	54.2	53.8	54.1	55.7	57.2	58.5	58.1
1951	59.2	60.0	60.6	61.0	61.3	62.0	62.1	62.0	62.1	62.5	62.8	63.5
1952	64.3	64.3	64.5	64.4	65.0	65.9	66.3	65.8	65.8	65.8	66.3	66.9
1953	67.2	67.6	67.8	68.8	69.8	70.0	70.0	70.3	70.7	70.8	71.2	71.3
1954	70.9	70.6	69.6	68.6	68.2	67.7	67.4	66.7	66.6	66.5	66.5	66.7
1955	66.5	66.4	66.7	66.5	66.9	67.7	68.1	70.0	70.4	71.5	72.5	72.6
1956	73.0	73.1	73.8	74.7	75.7	76.0	77.0	76.8	77.2	77.1	77.3	77.2
1957	77.4	77.1	77.4	77.7	77.9	78.0	77.9	78.7	79.2	79.1	79.5	79.6
1958	79.1	78.3	78.1	77.4	76.1	75.3	74.9	74.4	75.1	75.2	74.9	75.2
1959	75.0	75.2	75.4	75.6	76.4	77.2	77.7	78.7	80.1	80.5	80.4	80.0
1960	79.5	79.8	80.1	80.3	80.7	80.9	80.9	80.6	79.9	79.7	79.9	80.0
1961	80.0	79.8	79.4	79.2	78.8	78.4	78.1	78.0	78.2	78.3	78.2	78.5
1962	78.8	78.7	78.9	79.2	79.4	79.6	79.7	79.7	79.7	79.6	79.7	79.9
1963	80.0	80.1	79.9	80.0	80.1	80.3	80.4	80.8	80.9	80.9	81.3	81.6
1964	81.4	81.6	81.7	81.8	81.7	81.9	81.7	82.0	82.1	82.4	82.3	82.4
1965	82.8	83.1	83.3	83.6	83.8	83.7	83.7	84.0	84.2	84.5	84.9	85.9
1966	86.0	86.5	86.7	87.3	88.0	88.3	88.8	89.1	89.1	89.2	89.8	89.9
1967	89.9	89.9	90.1	90.0	89.8	90.1	90.1	89.7	89.9	89.9	89.6	89.8
1968	89.6	90.1	90.4	90.8	91.1	91.4	91.3	91.8	91.8	91.7	91.9	92.2
1969	92.7	93.0	93.1	93.7	94.2	94.8	94.8	95.0	95.2	95.4	95.4	95.6
1970	96.0	96.1	96.4	95.9	95.6	95.5	95.2	95.2	94.8	94.6	94.2	93.4
1971	93.0	92.7	92.2	91.5	91.4	90.8	91.4	92.0	91.9	91.4	90.9	90.9
1972	89.6	89.2	89.5	89.7	90.0	90.3	90.3	90.1	90.1	90.1	90.0	89.9
1973	90.8	91.5	91.9	92.8	93.0	93.5	94.2	94.3	95.1	95.2	95.5	96.3
1974	96.6	96.8	96.5	97.2	97.7	98.0	98.0	98.2	98.9	98.8	99.1	99.8
1975	99.2	98.3	97.6	96.0	94.7	92.5	91.9	91.3	90.8	90.8	90.7	90.6
1976	90.5	90.4	90.3	90.1	90.0	89.6	89.7	89.7	89.9	90.1	89.8	89.5
1977	89.6	89.9	90.0	90.2	90.3	90.8	91.0	91.4	91.7	92.1	92.3	92.4
1978	93.0	93.1	93.4	93.0	93.4	93.8	94.2	94.4	94.8	94.9	95.7	96.2
1979	96.4	96.6	96.1	97.4	97.3	98.0	98.3	98.8	99.5	99.8	100.1	100.1
1980	100.4	100.6	101.7	102.5	102.2	101.4	99.2	97.2	95.8	95.1	95.3	96.3
1981	96.2	95.9	95.7	95.8	96.9	97.4	97.5	97.6	98.4	98.4	98.3	97.9
1982	98.0	96.9	96.3	96.1	95.9	96.1	95.9	95.5	95.0	94.4	93.5	92.6
1983	91.7	91.6	91.2	91.2	90.6	90.5	90.7	91.3	91.2	91.2	91.8	92.3
1984	92.4	93.1	93.6	94.4	95.2	95.7	96.4	97.0	97.5	98.0	97.9	98.0
1985	98.2	98.1	98.5	98.2	98.6	98.7	98.9	99.0	99.2	99.8	99.8	100.0
1986	100.1	100.3	100.8	100.4	100.4	100.4	100.2	100.1	99.6	100.1	100.0	99.4
1987	100.1	99.4	99.3	99.5	99.5	99.6	99.7	99.9	100.6	100.8	100.9	100.7
1988	101.2	101.2	101.5	101.8	101.8	102.2	102.3	102.4	102.4	102.6	103.0	102.8
1989	102.9	103.5	103.9	103.6	104.3	104.8	105.2	105.3	105.3	105.5	105.5	105.4
1990	104.6	104.5	104.5	104.9	104.9	104.8	105.2	104.8	104.8	104.6	104.5	104.5
1991	104.7	104.3	104.2	103.3	102.7	101.9	101.6	101.1	100.7	100.5	100.2	100.0
1992	99.0	98.4	98.0	97.7	97.5	97.2	96.9	97.1	96.7	96.5	96.7	95.4
1993	96.3	96.3	96.1	96.0	96.2	96.3	96.8	96.4	96.7	96.5	96.3	96.2
1994	96.4	96.0	95.8	96.4	96.8	97.4	97.6	97.8	98.4	98.8	99.4	99.5
1995	100.0	100.7	101.1	101.8	102.1	102.6	102.3	-	-	-	-	-

Source: U.S. Department of Commerce, Bureau of Economic Analysis. - indicates data not available or zero.

Composite Index of 7 Lagging Indicators
Change in Index from Previous Month

Year	Jan	Feb	Mar	Apr	May	Jun	Jul	Aug	Sep	Oct	Nov	Dec
1948	-	+0.5	+0.3	+0.2	+0.1	-	+0.5	+1.6	+0.4	-0.1	+0.4	+0.1
1949	+0.4	+0.2	-0.2	-0.1	+0.3	-0.1	-0.1	-0.3	-0.3	+0.9	-0.2	+0.1
1950	-	-	-0.1	+0.3	+0.1	-0.1	-0.4	+0.3	+1.6	+1.5	+1.3	-0.4
1951	+1.1	+0.8	+0.6	+0.4	+0.3	+0.7	+0.1	-0.1	+0.1	+0.4	+0.3	+0.7
1952	+0.8	-	+0.2	-0.1	+0.6	+0.9	+0.4	-0.5	-	-	+0.5	+0.6
1953	+0.3	+0.4	+0.2	+1.0	+1.0	+0.2	-	+0.3	+0.4	+0.1	+0.4	+0.1
1954	-0.4	-0.3	-1.0	-1.0	-0.4	-0.5	-0.3	-0.7	-0.1	-0.1	-	+0.2
1955	-0.2	-0.1	+0.3	-0.2	+0.4	+0.8	+0.4	+1.9	+0.4	+1.1	+1.0	+0.1
1956	+0.4	+0.1	+0.7	+0.9	+1.0	+0.3	+1.0	-0.2	+0.4	-0.1	+0.2	-0.1
1957	+0.2	-0.3	+0.3	+0.3	+0.2	+0.1	-0.1	+0.8	+0.5	-0.1	+0.4	+0.1
1958	-0.5	-0.8	-0.2	-0.7	-1.3	-0.8	-0.4	-0.5	+0.7	+0.1	-0.3	+0.3
1959	-0.2	+0.2	+0.2	+0.2	+0.8	+0.8	+0.5	+1.0	+1.4	+0.4	-0.1	-0.4
1960	-0.5	+0.3	+0.3	+0.2	+0.4	+0.2	-	-0.3	-0.7	-0.2	+0.2	+0.1
1961	-	-0.2	-0.4	-0.2	-0.4	-0.4	-0.3	-0.1	+0.2	+0.1	-0.1	+0.3
1962	+0.3	-0.1	+0.2	+0.3	+0.2	+0.2	+0.1	-	-	-0.1	+0.1	+0.2
1963	+0.1	+0.1	-0.2	+0.1	+0.1	+0.2	+0.1	+0.4	+0.1	-	+0.4	+0.3
1964	-0.2	+0.2	+0.1	+0.i	-0.1	+0.2	-0.2	+0.3	+0.1	+0.3	-0.1	+0.1
1965	+0.4	+0.3	+0.2	+0.3	+0.2	-0.1	-	+0.3	+0.2	+0.3	+0.4	+1.0
1966	+0.1	+0.5	+0.2	+0.6	+0.7	+0.3	+0.5	+0.3	-	+0.1	+0.6	+0.1
1967	-	-	+0.2	-0.1	-0.2	+0.3	-	-0.4	+0.2	-	-0.3	+0.2
1968	-0.2	+0.5	+0.3	+0.4	+0.3	+0.3	-0.1	+0.5	-	-0.1	+0.2	+0.3
1969	+0.5	+0.3	+0.1	+0.6	+0.5	+0.6	-	+0.2	+0.2	+0.2	-	+0.2
1970	+0.4	+0.1	+0.3	-0.5	-0.3	-0.1	-0.3	-	-0.4	-0.2	-0.4	-0.8
1971	-0.4	-0.3	-0.5	-0.7	-0.1	-0.6	+0.6	+0.6	-0.1	-0.5	-0.5	-
1972	-1.3	-0.4	+0.3	+0.2	+0.3	+0.3	-	-0.2	-	-	-0.1	-0.1
1973	+0.9	+0.7	+0.4	+0.9	+0.2	+0.5	+0.7	+0.1	+0.8	+0.1	+0.3	+0.8
1974	+0.3	+0.2	-0.3	+0.7	+0.5	+0.3	-	+0.2	+0.7	-0.1	+0.3	+0.7
1975	-0.6	-0.9	-0.7	-1.6	-1.3	-2.2	-0.6	-0.6	-0.5	-	-0.1	-0.1
1976	-0.1	-0.1	-0.1	-0.2	-0.1	-0.4	+0.1	-	+0.2	+0.2	-0.3	-0.3
1977	+0.1	+0.3	+0.1	+0.2	+0.1	+0.5	+0.2	+0.4	+0.3	+0.4	+0.2	+0.1
1978	+0.6	+0.1	+0.3	-0.4	+0.4	+0.4	+0.4	+0.2	+0.4	+0.1	+0.8	+0.5
1979	+0.2	+0.2	-0.5	+1.3	-0.1	+0.7	+0.3	+0.5	+0.7	+0.3	+0.3	-
1980	+0.3	+0.2	+1.1	+0.8	-0.3	-0.8	-2.2	-2.0	-1.4	-0.7	+0.2	+1.0
1981	-0.1	-0.3	-0.2	+0.1	+1.1	+0.5	+0.1	+0.1	+0.8	-	-0.1	-0.4
1982	+0.1	-1.1	-0.6	-0.2	-0.2	+0.2	-0.2	-0.4	-0.5	-0.6	-0.9	-0.9
1983	-0.9	-0.1	-0.4	-	-0.6	-0.1	+0.2	+0.6	-0.1	-	+0.6	+0.5
1984	+0.1	+0.7	+0.5	+0.8	+0.8	+0.5	+0.7	+0.6	+0.5	+0.5	-0.1	+0.1
1985	+0.2	-0.1	+0.4	-0.3	+0.4	+0.1	+0.2	+0.1	+0.2	+0.6	-	+0.2
1986	+0.1	+0.2	+0.5	-0.4	-	-	-0.2	-0.1	-0.5	+0.5	-0.1	-0.6
1987	+0.7	-0.7	-0.1	+0.2	-	+0.1	+0.1	+0.2	+0.7	+0.2	+0.1	-0.2
1988	+0.5	-	+0.3	+0.3	-	+0.4	+0.1	+0.1	-	+0.2	+0.4	-0.2
1989	+0.1	+0.6	+0.4	-0.3	+0.7	+0.5	+0.4	+0.1	-	+0.2	-	-0.1
1990	-0.8	-0.1	-	+0.4	-	-0.1	+0.4	-0.4	-	-0.2	-0.1	-
1991	+0.2	-0.4	-0.1	-0.9	-0.6	-0.8	-0.3	-0.5	-0.4	-0.2	-0.3	-0.2
1992	-1.0	-0.6	-0.4	-0.3	-0.2	-0.3	-0.3	+0.2	-0.4	-0.2	+0.2	-1.3
1993	+0.9	-	-0.2	-0.1	+0.2	+0.1	+0.5	-0.4	+0.3	-0.2	-0.2	-0.1
1994	+0.2	-0.4	-0.2	+0.6	+0.4	+0.6	+0.2	+0.2	+0.6	+0.4	+0.6	+0.1
1995	+0.5	+0.7	+0.4	+0.7	+0.3	+0.5	-0.3	-	-	-	-	-

Source: U.S. Department of Commerce, Bureau of Economic Analysis. - indicates data not available or zero.

Index of Labor Cost per Unit of Output, Manufacturing
(1987 = 100)

Year	Jan	Feb	Mar	Apr	May	Jun	Jul	Aug	Sep	Oct	Nov	Dec
1947	34.3	34.8	34.6	34.9	35.2	35.2	35.4	35.2	36.0	36.0	35.9	36.9
1948	37.0	37.0	37.6	37.2	36.8	36.9	37.7	38.3	38.2	38.5	38.8	38.7
1949	38.8	38.7	38.1	38.3	38.7	38.2	38.0	37.7	37.4	37.4	37.1	37.1
1950	37.2	37.3	37.3	36.7	37.0	36.4	36.4	36.3	36.6	37.5	38.4	38.5
1951	38.6	39.2	39.5	40.2	40.4	41.1	41.3	41.8	42.0	41.8	41.7	42.1
1952	42.2	42.3	42.1	42.2	42.6	43.1	42.1	42.3	42.6	42.7	42.1	42.9
1953	42.7	43.0	43.0	43.2	42.9	43.3	43.0	42.7	42.9	43.3	43.9	44.6
1954	44.6	44.7	44.5	44.5	44.2	44.0	43.8	44.0	43.6	43.9	44.2	43.9
1955	42.9	43.1	42.8	42.5	42.5	42.7	42.9	42.9	42.9	43.0	43.8	43.3
1956	43.5	43.7	44.1	44.0	44.3	44.7	46.3	45.0	45.0	45.5	45.6	45.5
1957	45.3	45.4	45.2	45.9	45.9	45.8	45.8	46.1	45.9	46.4	47.5	47.4
1958	47.9	48.3	48.5	48.6	47.9	47.3	47.2	47.2	47.1	46.5	46.6	46.8
1959	46.4	46.2	46.2	45.9	45.8	46.1	46.9	47.3	47.8	47.9	48.1	46.5
1960	46.0	46.7	47.2	47.3	47.6	47.9	47.7	47.6	47.8	48.0	48.2	48.2
1961	48.6	48.6	48.6	47.8	47.7	47.4	47.2	46.8	46.6	46.7	46.8	46.4
1962	47.0	46.8	47.0	47.4	47.5	47.6	47.4	47.0	47.2	47.0	46.9	46.9
1963	46.8	46.7	46.4	45.8	45.8	46.0	46.4	46.2	46.1	45.9	46.0	46.5
1964	45.8	46.1	46.6	46.2	46.1	46.2	46.2	46.4	46.4	46.4	46.0	45.8
1965	45.5	45.4	45.3	45.0	44.9	45.0	44.6	44.8	44.8	45.0	45.3	45.2
1966	45.2	45.6	45.5	45.8	45.8	46.0	45.9	46.4	46.3	46.2	46.8	46.6
1967	46.7	46.8	47.3	47.0	47.3	47.5	47.9	47.8	47.6	47.2	47.3	47.3
1968	47.8	48.3	48.4	48.7	48.7	48.9	49.2	49.2	49.5	49.9	49.6	49.8
1969	49.7	49.7	49.8	50.3	50.8	50.9	50.9	51.3	51.6	51.7	52.0	52.6
1970	53.5	53.3	53.8	53.7	53.6	53.8	54.0	54.0	53.8	54.0	53.9	54.0
1971	54.1	54.3	54.4	54.2	54.4	54.3	54.2	54.9	53.7	53.5	53.5	54.0
1972	53.2	53.8	54.1	53.6	54.1	54.2	54.1	54.1	54.2	54.0	54.0	54.2
1973	54.8	55.1	55.3	55.7	55.8	55.7	56.0	56.1	56.2	56.6	57.1	58.5
1974	59.3	59.9	59.9	60.4	60.8	61.1	61.9	62.3	62.5	63.5	64.6	66.7
1975	67.5	68.2	69.7	69.1	69.8	69.2	69.0	69.4	69.3	69.6	69.7	70.0
1976	70.7	69.9	70.8	71.1	71.0	71.3	71.3	71.9	72.0	71.8	72.0	72.0
1977	72.0	72.8	72.9	72.9	73.2	73.8	74.4	74.4	75.0	75.8	76.1	76.5
1978	77.0	77.9	78.7	77.7	78.0	77.9	78.5	78.5	79.0	79.5	79.4	80.8
1979	81.6	81.8	82.3	83.5	83.2	84.0	85.1	85.7	86.5	86.3	86.9	88.1
1980	88.1	88.4	89.3	90.8	92.7	94.1	94.3	94.4	94.4	94.7	94.6	95.6
1981	96.9	96.1	97.1	98.4	98.5	99.1	98.7	99.8	100.1	101.5	102.0	102.8
1982	104.7	102.4	102.8	103.4	103.8	103.9	104.0	104.2	104.3	104.5	104.7	105.5
1983	103.8	103.8	103.0	102.8	102.3	102.2	101.8	101.0	100.4	100.6	101.2	101.8
1984	100.7	101.1	100.9	101.4	101.1	101.1	101.3	101.7	102.0	102.4	102.9	103.9
1985	104.1	103.1	104.4	102.5	102.2	103.2	103.5	103.0	102.8	104.8	103.3	103.8
1986	102.4	102.6	104.7	102.9	103.1	103.3	102.9	102.9	102.6	103.0	101.9	101.2
1987	102.3	100.8	101.0	100.1	99.3	98.5	98.6	99.3	100.5	99.5	99.9	99.9
1988	100.4	101.0	102.4	101.4	102.1	102.8	102.9	102.5	103.2	104.8	103.6	103.0
1989	102.6	103.7	104.3	102.9	103.2	103.7	105.2	104.9	105.2	106.9	106.1	106.1
1990	106.0	106.5	106.8	108.2	107.4	107.8	108.1	107.4	107.8	108.4	108.8	110.5
1991	110.9	111.1	112.0	111.7	111.4	110.9	110.7	111.1	110.2	111.7	111.0	112.1
1992	110.9	110.7	110.3	110.5	110.8	111.1	110.6	110.8	111.0	111.7	110.2	111.6
1993	109.8	109.6	109.5	110.2	110.6	110.5	110.2	110.6	110.8	110.8	110.2	109.6
1994	110.0	109.9	109.0	108.6	108.2	108.3	108.0	107.5	107.9	109.0	107.4	106.7
1995	106.8	108.6	108.2	107.8	107.3	107.6	108.0	-	-	-	-	-

Source: U.S. Department of Commerce, Bureau of Economic Analysis, Board of Governors of the Federal Reserve System. - indicates data not available or zero.

Ratio, Manufacturing and Trade Inventories to Sales in 1987 $
(Ratio)

Year	Jan	Feb	Mar	Apr	May	Jun	Jul	Aug	Sep	Oct	Nov	Dec
1948	1.41	1.42	1.42	1.42	1.44	1.44	1.45	1.44	1.45	1.45	1.45	1.44
1949	1.48	1.48	1.49	1.49	1.51	1.48	1.52	1.49	1.47	1.51	1.48	1.47
1950	1.45	1.42	1.41	1.40	1.38	1.33	1.22	1.23	1.33	1.37	1.44	1.37
1951	1.37	1.41	1.45	1.50	1.51	1.55	1.59	1.57	1.58	1.58	1.59	1.61
1952	1.60	1.58	1.59	1.57	1.55	1.56	1.59	1.56	1.53	1.49	1.51	1.49
1953	1.51	1.49	1.48	1.50	1.51	1.53	1.52	1.55	1.57	1.57	1.60	1.62
1954	1.60	1.58	1.58	1.56	1.58	1.55	1.55	1.55	1.54	1.53	1.49	1.46
1955	1.44	1.43	1.41	1.39	1.39	1.41	1.41	1.42	1.40	1.41	1.40	1.40
1956	1.42	1.45	1.44	1.45	1.47	1.47	1.54	1.50	1.49	1.48	1.48	1.46
1957	1.46	1.45	1.46	1.49	1.50	1.49	1.50	1.50	1.52	1.52	1.53	1.57
1958	1.55	1.57	1.59	1.59	1.58	1.54	1.53	1.50	1.50	1.48	1.46	1.51
1959	1.45	1.43	1.42	1.42	1.41	1.42	1.43	1.48	1.48	1.48	1.47	1.45
1960	1.44	1.46	1.47	1.47	1.49	1.50	1.51	1.52	1.51	1.51	1.53	1.51
1961	1.54	1.53	1.50	1.51	1.48	1.46	1.48	1.45	1.45	1.44	1.43	1.43
1962	1.44	1.44	1.43	1.43	1.44	1.45	1.45	1.45	1.46	1.45	1.43	1.46
1963	1.46	1.44	1.44	1.43	1.44	1.44	1.42	1.44	1.44	1.43	1.45	1.42
1964	1.42	1.43	1.44	1.42	1.41	1.42	1.39	1.41	1.40	1.42	1.42	1.38
1965	1.40	1.40	1.38	1.38	1.40	1.40	1.39	1.41	1.41	1.40	1.39	1.39
1966	1.38	1.40	1.38	1.40	1.42	1.42	1.44	1.45	1.45	1.46	1.48	1.49
1967	1.50	1.51	1.51	1.51	1.51	1.51	1.51	1.51	1.52	1.53	1.50	1.48
1968	1.49	1.50	1.49	1.50	1.50	1.49	1.48	1.51	1.51	1.49	1.49	1.50
1969	1.50	1.51	1.50	1.50	1.51	1.51	1.51	1.52	1.51	1.51	1.53	1.54
1970	1.55	1.55	1.57	1.59	1.57	1.57	1.58	1.59	1.59	1.62	1.64	1.59
1971	1.58	1.57	1.57	1.57	1.57	1.55	1.56	1.58	1.56	1.56	1.53	1.53
1972	1.52	1.53	1.50	1.50	1.50	1.49	1.49	1.47	1.47	1.45	1.44	1.42
1973	1.41	1.41	1.43	1.44	1.45	1.46	1.45	1.47	1.48	1.45	1.44	1.48
1974	1.47	1.48	1.48	1.49	1.50	1.52	1.51	1.53	1.56	1.59	1.62	1.69
1975	1.68	1.67	1.71	1.69	1.68	1.65	1.63	1.62	1.61	1.61	1.62	1.60
1976	1.56	1.56	1.55	1.55	1.56	1.55	1.55	1.56	1.57	1.59	1.57	1.53
1977	1.54	1.53	1.52	1.52	1.53	1.52	1.52	1.53	1.54	1.53	1.53	1.52
1978	1.56	1.54	1.54	1.51	1.52	1.52	1.53	1.51	1.52	1.51	1.51	1.52
1979	1.53	1.55	1.51	1.57	1.53	1.56	1.57	1.56	1.56	1.57	1.57	1.57
1980	1.55	1.57	1.61	1.66	1.68	1.68	1.65	1.64	1.60	1.57	1.57	1.57
1981	1.57	1.58	1.59	1.58	1.60	1.61	1.61	1.62	1.64	1.66	1.69	1.70
1982	1.70	1.66	1.66	1.67	1.65	1.68	1.68	1.69	1.69	1.70	1.68	1.69
1983	1.64	1.65	1.61	1.61	1.59	1.55	1.56	1.57	1.55	1.54	1.53	1.51
1984	1.51	1.53	1.54	1.55	1.55	1.54	1.57	1.59	1.60	1.60	1.60	1.60
1985	1.60	1.60	1.59	1.59	1.58	1.61	1.60	1.58	1.58	1.60	1.59	1.60
1986	1.58	1.60	1.61	1.59	1.60	1.59	1.58	1.58	1.54	1.56	1.56	1.52
1987	1.58	1.53	1.53	1.54	1.55	1.55	1.53	1.54	1.53	1.55	1.56	1.56
1988	1.56	1.55	1.53	1.54	1.54	1.53	1.55	1.55	1.55	1.54	1.54	1.53
1989	1.54	1.57	1.58	1.57	1.58	1.59	1.62	1.58	1.59	1.62	1.61	1.61
1990	1.62	1.60	1.59	1.61	1.61	1.60	1.63	1.61	1.64	1.64	1.67	1.67
1991	1.70	1.69	1.68	1.65	1.63	1.63	1.62	1.61	1.62	1.62	1.62	1.65
1992	1.62	1.61	1.61	1.61	1.61	1.60	1.59	1.60	1.59	1.58	1.57	1.54
1993	1.54	1.55	1.55	1.55	1.55	1.53	1.55	1.52	1.52	1.51	1.50	1.48
1994	1.49	1.48	1.46	1.47	1.48	1.47	1.49	1.45	1.46	1.46	1.45	1.44
1995	1.45	1.45	1.46	1.48	1.47	1.47	-	-	-	-	-	-

Source: U.S. Department of Commerce, Bureau of Economic Analysis, U.S. Department of Commerce, Bureau of the Census. - indicates data not available or zero.

Average Duration of Unemployment in Weeks

Year	Jan	Feb	Mar	Apr	May	Jun	Jul	Aug	Sep	Oct	Nov	Dec
1948	8.9	8.4	8.7	8.5	9.1	8.8	8.6	8.8	8.5	9.5	7.8	8.1
1949	8.2	8.3	8.3	8.8	9.1	10.0	10.8	11.0	11.7	10.9	11.6	11.8
1950	11.3	11.8	12.4	12.6	12.7	13.1	12.5	12.2	12.2	12.3	10.7	10.7
1951	10.6	10.8	10.1	10.6	9.9	8.7	9.2	9.1	9.1	8.9	9.7	9.3
1952	9.3	8.8	8.4	9.0	7.8	7.3	7.5	7.6	8.1	9.1	9.5	8.8
1953	9.3	8.4	8.5	7.8	7.9	8.2	7.9	8.0	7.1	7.2	7.9	8.0
1954	8.7	9.5	10.6	10.9	11.6	12.3	12.5	12.8	12.9	13.3	13.2	13.4
1955	13.4	14.2	13.4	14.3	14.4	13.4	13.8	12.3	11.7	11.5	11.3	12.0
1956	11.7	12.5	11.6	11.0	10.4	10.1	10.5	12.0	11.8	11.6	10.9	11.4
1957	10.4	10.7	10.8	10.6	10.4	10.2	10.1	10.5	9.8	11.1	10.4	10.4
1958	10.5	11.0	11.2	12.1	13.1	14.4	14.6	15.7	16.5	16.5	16.4	15.7
1959	16.3	15.5	15.3	14.9	14.7	14.9	14.3	13.7	13.7	12.9	13.1	13.1
1960	13.5	13.1	13.0	12.6	11.9	11.9	12.6	12.2	12.9	13.5	13.9	12.4
1961	13.7	13.6	14.1	15.5	15.6	16.2	17.3	17.0	16.1	15.9	17.0	15.8
1962	15.3	16.0	15.0	14.9	15.5	15.1	14.6	14.5	14.1	14.1	13.3	13.6
1963	13.8	14.1	14.5	14.5	14.5	14.0	14.0	13.9	14.2	13.9	13.3	13.3
1964	13.5	13.2	13.5	12.4	13.6	13.6	14.7	13.0	12.7	12.6	14.0	12.7
1965	12.2	12.6	12.0	11.4	11.1	11.6	11.6	11.9	11.9	12.1	11.7	11.4
1966	11.9	11.2	11.1	10.8	10.2	9.7	9.7	9.8	10.1	10.3	9.7	9.5
1967	9.3	9.2	8.9	8.8	8.7	8.3	8.3	8.9	8.4	8.7	8.9	8.6
1968	9.4	8.7	8.5	8.7	8.2	7.9	8.4	8.3	8.2	8.4	8.1	8.2
1969	8.1	7.9	7.9	7.9	7.9	7.7	7.8	7.9	8.0	7.6	8.0	8.0
1970	7.9	8.0	8.3	8.2	8.6	8.6	8.9	8.8	8.9	8.7	9.3	9.8
1971	10.5	10.4	10.6	10.9	11.2	11.6	11.5	11.5	11.9	12.6	12.0	11.5
1972	12.1	12.4	12.3	12.4	12.3	12.4	11.8	11.8	12.1	11.7	11.4	11.4
1973	11.0	10.5	10.6	10.0	10.1	9.6	9.6	9.8	9.4	10.2	9.9	9.5
1974	9.5	9.6	9.7	9.8	9.6	9.7	9.9	9.8	9.6	9.9	9.6	10.1
1975	10.7	11.7	11.8	12.9	13.4	15.3	15.0	15.6	16.1	15.4	16.6	16.5
1976	16.6	16.3	16.5	15.9	15.0	16.9	15.7	15.6	15.2	15.2	15.3	15.1
1977	15.2	14.7	14.5	14.4	14.9	14.4	14.3	13.9	14.0	13.7	13.6	13.6
1978	12.9	12.5	12.4	12.3	12.1	12.1	12.0	11.4	11.4	11.7	11.1	10.6
1979	11.1	11.2	11.7	11.0	11.1	10.4	10.3	10.6	10.5	10.5	10.6	10.8
1980	10.4	10.6	11.0	11.4	10.9	11.3	11.8	12.4	12.9	13.1	13.6	13.7
1981	14.3	14.1	14.0	13.9	13.6	13.7	13.8	14.4	13.6	13.5	13.1	13.1
1982	13.4	14.1	14.1	14.5	14.9	15.7	15.4	16.2	16.6	17.2	17.1	18.1
1983	19.4	19.2	19.4	19.5	20.5	20.8	21.2	20.0	20.2	20.2	19.7	19.2
1984	20.4	19.0	19.1	18.9	18.8	18.1	18.0	17.3	17.0	16.7	17.0	16.8
1985	15.9	15.9	16.1	16.4	15.3	15.5	15.5	15.3	15.3	15.3	15.7	15.1
1986	14.8	15.2	14.6	14.7	14.7	15.2	15.2	15.5	15.4	15.2	15.0	15.0
1987	14.9	14.7	14.9	14.8	14.9	14.9	14.2	14.4	14.2	14.0	14.0	14.2
1988	14.2	14.4	13.7	13.3	13.8	13.1	13.4	13.6	13.6	13.4	12.6	12.9
1989	12.6	12.4	12.3	12.5	12.0	11.1	11.8	11.4	11.5	11.9	11.7	11.6
1990	11.9	11.7	11.9	12.0	11.7	11.8	12.0	12.3	12.5	12.1	12.5	12.5
1991	12.4	12.8	13.1	13.7	13.0	13.8	13.9	14.1	14.2	14.4	14.9	15.4
1992	16.2	16.8	17.2	17.5	18.1	18.4	18.3	18.2	18.3	19.1	18.1	19.0
1993	18.5	18.2	17.7	17.7	17.8	17.8	17.9	18.3	18.4	18.4	18.9	18.2
1994	18.4	18.8	19.2	19.1	19.4	18.4	19.0	18.9	18.8	19.3	18.2	17.8
1995	16.7	16.9	17.5	17.7	16.9	15.6	16.5	-	-	-	-	-

Source: U.S. Department of Labor, Bureau of Labor Statistics. - indicates data not available or zero.

Ratio, Consumer Installment Credit to Personal Income
(Percent)

Year	Jan	Feb	Mar	Apr	May	Jun	Jul	Aug	Sep	Oct	Nov	Dec
1946	1.53	1.60	1.63	1.71	1.77	1.83	1.86	1.95	2.08	2.13	2.23	2.31
1947	2.42	2.54	2.66	2.82	2.93	3.00	3.09	3.16	3.02	3.25	3.39	3.49
1948	3.56	3.65	3.78	3.89	3.96	3.97	4.06	4.11	4.22	4.22	4.29	4.40
1949	4.52	4.61	4.65	4.77	4.91	5.07	5.21	5.28	5.31	5.57	5.65	5.74
1950	5.65	5.71	5.69	5.91	6.04	6.20	6.32	6.35	6.46	6.43	6.35	6.21
1951	6.27	6.25	6.19	6.08	6.03	5.98	5.93	5.90	5.94	5.91	5.95	5.98
1952	6.06	6.01	6.04	6.12	6.25	6.45	6.63	6.56	6.63	6.80	6.96	7.09
1953	7.22	7.31	7.45	7.56	7.66	7.73	7.86	7.97	8.04	8.07	8.19	8.21
1954	8.19	8.16	8.16	8.20	8.17	8.18	8.19	8.16	8.15	8.14	8.10	8.15
1955	8.21	8.28	8.40	8.48	8.59	8.74	8.74	8.90	9.01	9.06	9.09	9.14
1956	9.20	9.24	9.32	9.30	9.35	9.34	9.40	9.35	9.33	9.30	9.38	9.38
1957	9.42	9.41	9.42	9.44	9.47	9.45	9.48	9.50	9.58	9.63	9.66	9.71
1958	9.72	9.70	9.61	9.58	9.52	9.43	9.27	9.26	9.24	9.21	9.13	9.17
1959	9.25	9.29	9.32	9.35	9.41	9.48	9.61	9.84	9.96	10.08	10.08	10.02
1960	10.10	10.21	10.35	10.38	10.43	10.51	10.56	10.60	10.64	10.64	10.70	10.79
1961	10.76	10.72	10.65	10.59	10.50	10.40	10.35	10.36	10.38	10.33	10.28	10.30
1962	10.35	10.37	10.33	10.37	10.45	10.51	10.56	10.63	10.66	10.72	10.79	10.85
1963	10.87	11.06	11.10	11.19	11.24	11.26	11.38	11.44	11.48	11.53	11.60	11.60
1964	11.68	11.67	11.84	11.87	11.94	12.00	12.05	12.07	12.14	12.23	12.21	12.20
1965	12.25	12.42	12.44	12.53	12.56	12.58	12.63	12.70	12.48	12.61	12.60	12.60
1966	12.67	12.69	12.68	12.69	12.69	12.65	12.66	12.61	12.55	12.52	12.48	12.53
1967	12.48	12.53	12.45	12.43	12.39	12.35	12.28	12.24	12.26	12.25	12.22	12.20
1968	12.12	12.01	12.08	12.08	12.06	12.07	12.07	12.06	12.06	12.10	12.12	12.18
1969	12.26	12.38	12.33	12.36	12.39	12.40	12.39	12.36	12.38	12.39	12.41	12.37
1970	12.43	12.43	12.38	12.10	12.19	12.25	12.26	12.25	12.23	12.23	12.18	12.17
1971	12.38	12.41	12.39	12.38	12.36	12.15	12.38	12.39	12.46	12.52	12.54	12.55
1972	12.48	12.34	12.50	12.57	12.63	12.88	12.75	12.73	12.75	12.63	12.56	12.61
1973	12.91	13.00	13.05	13.15	13.18	13.21	13.33	13.28	13.28	13.21	13.13	13.12
1974	13.22	13.32	13.34	13.35	13.30	13.29	13.20	13.19	13.15	13.03	13.03	12.97
1975	12.79	12.83	12.74	12.65	12.52	12.21	12.36	12.24	12.18	12.14	12.13	12.16
1976	12.11	12.09	12.15	12.20	12.22	12.27	12.26	12.27	12.32	12.36	12.31	12.41
1977	12.51	12.53	12.64	12.73	12.79	12.89	12.84	12.90	12.96	13.04	13.07	13.15
1978	13.22	13.23	13.24	13.21	13.32	13.44	13.49	13.54	13.58	13.54	13.63	13.69
1979	13.75	13.78	13.77	13.89	13.96	13.98	13.87	13.88	13.91	13.91	13.90	13.80
1980	13.83	13.75	13.76	13.67	13.54	13.36	13.13	12.98	12.77	12.59	12.44	12.35
1981	12.25	12.13	12.16	12.16	12.18	12.13	11.98	11.85	11.93	11.94	11.91	11.93
1982	12.01	11.87	11.91	11.84	11.79	11.81	11.75	11.76	11.78	11.73	11.72	11.80
1983	11.80	11.76	11.88	11.83	11.77	11.87	11.95	12.11	12.10	12.14	12.21	12.32
1984	12.34	12.39	12.51	12.61	12.88	13.01	13.08	13.15	13.17	13.38	13.45	13.53
1985	13.62	13.63	13.89	14.01	14.22	14.28	14.39	14.48	14.69	14.74	14.87	14.82
1986	14.99	15.05	15.03	15.04	15.19	15.27	15.37	15.42	15.52	15.71	15.72	15.57
1987	15.47	15.34	15.33	15.40	15.41	15.53	15.65	15.62	15.63	15.41	15.49	15.39
1988	15.61	15.62	15.60	15.61	15.65	15.70	15.67	15.74	15.72	15.56	15.75	15.71
1989	15.90	15.84	15.80	15.86	15.97	16.02	16.01	16.10	16.12	16.05	15.99	15.95
1990	15.80	15.73	15.62	15.60	15.67	15.62	15.71	15.78	15.77	15.76	15.62	15.31
1991	15.21	15.11	15.05	15.08	15.09	15.04	15.09	15.06	14.98	14.94	14.85	14.63
1992	14.63	14.46	14.38	14.29	14.25	14.22	14.16	14.23	14.05	13.91	13.91	13.25
1993	14.05	14.10	14.03	13.95	13.87	13.99	14.13	14.05	14.18	14.23	14.26	14.33
1994	14.51	14.35	14.46	14.56	14.69	14.84	14.90	15.07	15.14	15.09	15.33	15.35
1995	15.42	15.41	15.58	15.74	16.00	16.08	-	-	-	-	-	-

Source: U.S. Department of Commerce, Bureau of Economic Analysis, Board of Governors of the Federal Reserve System. - indicates data not available or zero.

Commercial and Industrial Loans Outstanding
(Million 1987 $)

Year	Jan	Feb	Mar	Apr	May	Jun	Jul	Aug	Sep	Oct	Nov	Dec
1945	34,369	33,720	33,166	32,899	32,652	33,456	33,685	33,771	34,243	34,107	34,852	37,094
1946	38,221	38,349	38,690	39,492	40,193	40,361	38,291	39,028	42,178	40,726	40,235	40,390
1947	40,890	41,471	42,105	43,810	44,319	44,498	44,451	44,844	44,806	45,361	46,109	46,130
1948	46,338	46,831	46,877	46,880	48,137	48,576	49,133	49,188	49,212	49,397	48,847	48,833
1949	49,089	49,759	49,339	48,991	48,662	48,336	47,124	46,489	46,237	46,526	46,283	46,353
1950	46,736	46,686	46,683	46,997	46,763	47,499	47,566	48,190	49,468	50,218	50,939	51,390
1951	51,623	52,829	54,258	55,987	57,337	58,326	59,071	59,817	60,143	60,597	60,861	61,548
1952	62,462	62,922	63,306	63,685	63,901	64,641	64,972	64,681	65,746	66,846	68,557	69,376
1953	69,685	69,849	70,104	71,408	71,618	71,645	70,744	71,500	70,877	70,790	70,421	68,887
1954	68,217	68,665	68,574	68,109	67,603	67,552	67,318	64,557	64,618	64,731	65,278	66,924
1955	67,156	67,452	68,422	68,615	70,305	71,050	72,511	73,622	74,120	75,553	76,949	78,046
1956	78,808	79,084	81,136	82,225	83,292	84,398	85,779	86,055	86,601	86,850	87,619	87,934
1957	88,275	88,351	89,772	90,461	91,213	92,086	92,430	92,249	92,824	91,890	90,377	89,910
1958	88,566	87,546	86,655	86,410	84,966	84,973	84,851	84,555	85,103	85,663	85,768	86,235
1959	86,169	86,217	86,931	87,468	88,915	90,618	90,570	92,166	92,440	93,555	94,350	94,993
1960	95,123	96,445	96,491	97,092	98,307	99,574	99,519	99,381	99,732	99,528	99,896	99,594
1961	99,215	99,116	99,552	100,103	100,251	100,713	100,227	100,588	100,840	100,844	101,041	101,163
1962	101,295	101,688	102,276	103,257	104,044	104,773	105,131	106,032	105,845	107,488	108,405	108,901
1963	109,061	109,682	110,061	111,052	111,200	111,182	111,219	112,111	113,001	114,453	116,368	118,158
1964	117,050	118,612	118,630	119,698	121,085	121,860	122,343	123,587	124,932	125,556	126,892	128,910
1965	130,974	133,716	136,548	138,021	140,574	140,737	141,781	144,928	147,883	149,387	151,373	152,317
1966	154,439	155,524	157,635	159,281	161,472	164,097	165,925	168,648	170,324	173,168	175,035	175,864
1967	176,879	178,387	180,934	183,494	183,509	184,332	185,475	185,414	186,252	187,650	189,127	189,967
1968	189,914	189,219	189,536	192,740	192,691	194,173	195,527	199,086	200,557	202,872	205,645	207,174
1969	211,778	212,704	214,850	219,752	221,562	223,565	224,009	227,953	230,669	232,548	233,108	234,390
1970	231,662	234,272	237,448	237,017	238,395	239,232	237,879	240,857	240,458	235,941	234,402	234,369
1971	232,757	231,944	232,018	228,839	229,536	226,531	224,043	227,608	232,726	230,305	229,897	227,400
1972	224,080	223,780	226,234	228,644	228,922	228,674	227,324	227,692	226,581	232,056	233,184	230,278
1973	232,788	237,947	237,261	240,019	238,046	237,395	243,892	234,859	238,894	243,698	245,303	242,438
1974	238,925	239,346	239,305	247,696	248,236	250,073	248,964	245,044	252,627	250,184	250,419	251,118
1975	252,065	251,088	249,823	244,301	237,567	232,973	228,919	225,747	221,706	218,211	217,843	217,289
1976	215,007	215,708	211,455	205,075	204,854	205,072	202,551	202,819	200,849	202,276	204,506	204,317
1977	203,682	203,599	202,535	201,149	201,483	204,098	203,570	206,035	206,060	207,169	208,238	208,652
1978	207,935	206,481	209,269	209,568	211,581	213,725	214,507	215,755	215,295	215,617	217,526	216,223
1979	217,235	217,203	217,551	221,648	223,115	226,117	227,688	231,288	233,532	230,787	228,386	229,893
1980	232,893	233,477	235,495	234,875	231,381	234,593	228,827	226,665	228,046	226,719	230,709	231,375
1981	230,039	228,226	224,233	226,213	231,463	235,402	238,488	243,836	248,540	250,912	254,760	257,912
1982	262,570	267,697	269,688	275,220	279,116	280,472	279,591	280,266	282,513	281,904	276,880	270,653
1983	275,439	274,624	275,793	271,857	266,801	266,903	265,688	265,530	264,866	263,409	265,042	268,712
1984	274,494	278,251	284,243	290,731	296,668	306,360	310,035	314,251	319,520	323,706	325,684	327,169
1985	327,702	330,758	333,669	333,491	335,758	335,200	338,026	341,081	341,993	343,513	344,958	346,090
1986	349,702	353,278	356,443	353,604	354,627	355,944	359,322	364,318	362,987	363,679	363,805	369,877
1987	374,734	371,625	369,357	366,515	363,445	363,040	360,147	356,425	360,018	361,306	359,781	362,348
1988	363,268	368,729	370,408	374,105	372,939	373,760	374,905	377,703	376,936	380,374	382,199	384,668
1989	381,975	388,092	388,340	388,817	395,101	398,480	402,652	411,717	409,979	409,431	412,464	412,959
1990	404,326	409,836	418,266	418,945	417,141	419,656	420,878	416,332	414,049	405,374	403,382	408,541
1991	406,610	407,562	412,826	408,147	403,441	401,525	401,809	393,275	389,607	385,259	385,190	382,780
1992	378,821	379,020	378,836	376,895	372,351	367,414	367,878	369,362	366,605	370,405	375,444	374,449
1993	369,455	369,523	364,698	366,099	368,979	370,173	374,608	376,318	375,862	372,881	373,223	375,919
1994	376,453	373,009	371,492	373,950	376,838	378,803	382,721	385,007	391,859	398,455	398,638	402,981
1995	407,523	412,295	416,565	425,224	424,948	427,934	431,089	-	-	-	-	-

Source: U.S. Department of Commerce, Bureau of Economic Analysis, Board of Governors of the Federal Reserve System, The Federal Reserve Bank of New York. - indicates data not available or zero.

Average Prime Rate Charged By Banks
Not seasonally adjusted
(Percent)

Year	Jan	Feb	Mar	Apr	May	Jun	Jul	Aug	Sep	Oct	Nov	Dec
1945	1.50	1.50	1.50	1.50	1.50	1.50	1.50	1.50	1.50	1.50	1.50	1.50
1946	1.50	1.50	1.50	1.50	1.50	1.50	1.50	1.50	1.50	1.50	1.50	1.50
1947	1.50	1.50	1.50	1.50	1.50	1.50	1.50	1.50	1.50	1.50	1.50	1.75
1948	1.75	1.75	1.75	1.75	1.75	1.75	1.75	2.00	2.00	2.00	2.00	2.00
1949	2.00	2.00	2.00	2.00	2.00	2.00	2.00	2.00	2.00	2.00	2.00	2.00
1950	2.00	2.00	2.00	2.00	2.00	2.00	2.00	2.00	2.08	2.25	2.25	2.25
1951	2.44	2.50	2.50	2.50	2.50	2.50	2.50	2.50	2.50	2.62	2.75	2.85
1952	3.00	3.00	3.00	3.00	3.00	3.00	3.00	3.00	3.00	3.00	3.00	3.00
1953	3.00	3.00	3.00	3.03	3.25	3.25	3.25	3.25	3.25	3.25	3.25	3.25
1954	3.25	3.25	3.13	3.00	3.00	3.00	3.00	3.00	3.00	3.00	3.00	3.00
1955	3.00	3.00	3.00	3.00	3.00	3.00	3.00	3.23	3.25	3.40	3.50	3.50
1956	3.50	3.50	3.50	3.65	3.75	3.75	3.75	3.84	4.00	4.00	4.00	4.00
1957	4.00	4.00	4.00	4.00	4.00	4.00	4.00	4.42	4.50	4.50	4.50	4.50
1958	4.34	4.00	4.00	3.83	3.50	3.50	3.50	3.50	3.83	4.00	4.00	4.00
1959	4.00	4.00	4.00	4.00	4.23	4.50	4.50	4.50	5.00	5.00	5.00	5.00
1960	5.00	5.00	5.00	5.00	5.00	5.00	5.00	4.85	4.50	4.50	4.50	4.50
1961	4.50	4.50	4.50	4.50	4.50	4.50	4.50	4.50	4.50	4.50	4.50	4.50
1962	4.50	4.50	4.50	4.50	4.50	4.50	4.50	4.50	4.50	4.50	4.50	4.50
1963	4.50	4.50	4.50	4.50	4.50	4.50	4.50	4.50	4.50	4.50	4.50	4.50
1964	4.50	4.50	4.50	4.50	4.50	4.50	4.50	4.50	4.50	4.50	4.50	4.50
1965	4.50	4.50	4.50	4.50	4.50	4.50	4.50	4.50	4.50	4.50	4.50	4.92
1966	5.00	5.00	5.35	5.50	5.50	5.52	5.75	5.88	6.00	6.00	6.00	6.00
1967	5.96	5.75	5.71	5.50	5.50	5.50	5.50	5.50	5.50	5.50	5.68	6.00
1968	6.00	6.00	6.00	6.20	6.50	6.50	6.50	6.50	6.40	6.00	6.20	6.60
1969	6.95	7.00	7.24	7.50	7.50	8.23	8.50	8.50	8.50	8.50	8.50	8.50
1970	8.50	8.50	8.39	8.00	8.00	8.00	8.00	8.00	7.83	7.50	7.28	6.92
1971	6.29	5.88	5.48	5.25	5.42	5.50	5.90	6.00	6.00	5.91	5.47	5.25
1972	5.18	4.75	4.75	4.98	5.00	5.04	5.25	5.27	5.50	5.73	5.75	5.79
1973	6.00	6.02	6.30	6.60	7.01	7.49	8.30	9.23	9.86	9.94	9.75	9.75
1974	9.73	9.21	8.83	10.02	11.25	11.54	11.98	12.00	12.00	11.68	10.83	10.50
1975	10.05	8.96	7.93	7.50	7.40	7.07	7.15	7.66	7.88	7.96	7.53	7.26
1976	7.00	6.75	6.75	6.75	6.75	7.20	7.25	7.01	7.00	6.78	6.50	6.35
1977	6.25	6.25	6.25	6.25	6.41	6.75	6.75	6.83	7.13	7.52	7.75	7.75
1978	7.93	8.00	8.00	8.00	8.27	8.63	9.00	9.01	9.41	9.94	10.94	11.55
1979	11.75	11.75	11.75	11.75	11.75	11.65	11.54	11.91	12.90	14.39	15.55	15.30
1980	15.25	15.63	18.31	19.77	16.57	12.63	11.48	11.12	12.23	13.79	16.06	20.35
1981	20.16	19.43	18.05	17.15	19.61	20.03	20.39	20.50	20.08	18.45	16.84	15.75
1982	15.75	16.56	16.50	16.50	16.50	16.50	16.26	14.39	13.50	12.52	11.85	11.50
1983	11.16	10.98	10.50	10.50	10.50	10.50	10.50	10.89	11.00	11.00	11.00	11.00
1984	11.00	11.00	11.21	11.93	12.39	12.60	13.00	13.00	12.97	12.58	11.77	11.06
1985	10.61	10.50	10.50	10.50	10.31	9.78	9.50	9.50	9.50	9.50	9.50	9.50
1986	9.50	9.50	9.10	8.83	8.50	8.50	8.16	7.90	7.50	7.50	7.50	7.50
1987	7.50	7.50	7.50	7.75	8.14	8.25	8.25	8.25	8.70	9.07	8.78	8.75
1988	8.75	8.51	8.50	8.50	8.84	9.00	9.29	9.84	10.00	10.00	10.05	10.50
1989	10.50	10.93	11.50	11.50	11.50	11.07	10.98	10.50	10.50	10.50	10.50	10.50
1990	10.11	10.00	10.00	10.00	10.00	10.00	10.00	10.00	10.00	10.00	10.00	10.00
1991	9.52	9.05	9.00	9.00	8.50	8.50	8.50	8.50	8.20	8.00	7.58	7.21
1992	6.50	6.50	6.50	6.50	6.50	6.50	6.02	6.00	6.00	6.00	6.00	6.00
1993	6.00	6.00	6.00	6.00	6.00	6.00	6.00	6.00	6.00	6.00	6.00	6.00
1994	6.00	6.00	6.06	6.45	6.99	7.25	7.25	7.51	7.75	7.75	8.15	8.50
1995	8.50	9.00	9.00	9.00	9.00	9.00	8.80	8.75	-	-	-	-

Source: Board of Governors of the Federal Reserve System. - indicates data not available or zero.

Smoothed Change in CPI for Services
(Annual Rate, Percent)

Year	Jan	Feb	Mar	Apr	May	Jun	Jul	Aug	Sep	Oct	Nov	Dec
1956	-	-	-	-	-	2.3	3.0	3.4	3.9	3.7	3.9	4.3
1957	4.7	4.3	5.1	4.8	4.8	4.9	4.3	4.2	4.2	4.5	4.8	4.3
1958	4.2	4.3	3.8	3.7	3.9	3.5	3.5	3.1	3.1	2.7	2.1	1.5
1959	1.6	2.2	2.3	2.7	3.3	3.2	3.4	3.8	4.2	4.6	4.2	4.1
1960	3.5	3.4	3.5	3.2	3.2	2.8	2.9	2.5	2.7	2.4	2.6	2.4
1961	2.6	2.4	1.9	2.1	1.9	1.5	1.1	1.4	1.4	1.8	1.9	2.3
1962	2.3	1.9	2.1	2.0	2.3	2.1	2.4	2.3	1.9	1.4	1.6	1.5
1963	1.9	1.9	1.6	1.9	1.8	2.1	2.1	2.4	2.2	1.9	2.0	2.5
1964	2.5	2.1	1.6	1.7	1.6	1.9	1.9	1.6	1.2	1.4	2.0	2.1
1965	2.5	3.0	2.9	3.1	2.8	2.2	2.2	1.9	2.1	2.5	3.1	3.0
1966	3.1	2.8	2.8	3.7	4.3	4.7	5.5	5.3	5.6	5.7	6.1	5.6
1967	5.1	4.7	4.4	4.2	3.5	3.8	3.5	3.4	3.4	4.2	4.0	4.5
1968	4.8	4.9	5.4	5.5	5.4	5.7	6.2	6.8	6.8	6.9	6.6	6.6
1969	6.8	6.5	7.1	7.5	7.8	7.4	7.3	7.2	7.8	7.5	7.4	7.3
1970	7.8	8.0	9.1	9.5	9.4	9.0	8.6	8.1	7.6	7.3	7.1	6.9
1971	6.8	6.2	5.1	4.2	3.5	4.1	4.3	4.7	4.8	4.6	4.3	4.0
1972	4.2	4.1	4.0	3.8	3.6	3.4	3.3	3.2	3.2	3.1	3.1	3.1
1973	3.1	3.1	3.5	3.7	3.7	4.1	4.2	4.9	5.9	7.9	9.2	9.5
1974	9.6	9.2	9.3	8.9	9.5	10.1	11.1	12.2	13.0	13.3	13.2	12.8
1975	12.0	11.3	9.7	8.6	7.5	6.8	6.2	6.1	6.6	7.0	8.4	9.1
1976	10.4	10.7	10.5	9.5	8.0	7.1	6.8	6.7	7.1	7.2	7.3	7.3
1977	7.6	7.7	7.9	8.2	7.9	7.8	8.3	8.3	8.1	7.7	7.7	7.5
1978	7.5	7.7	7.9	8.4	8.6	9.1	9.5	9.9	10.4	10.7	10.8	9.9
1979	9.4	9.4	9.5	9.8	10.5	11.0	11.9	13.2	13.9	14.7	15.7	16.3
1980	17.2	17.8	18.9	19.8	19.9	20.5	17.1	12.8	9.7	8.7	9.4	10.8
1981	11.9	12.3	12.4	12.5	13.2	14.0	15.4	16.1	16.9	16.0	14.8	13.0
1982	11.1	9.2	7.0	6.4	6.6	7.3	7.5	7.7	6.8	5.8	4.2	1.4
1983	0.6	0.7	1.0	2.1	2.8	3.3	3.8	3.9	4.1	4.5	5.1	5.3
1984	5.5	5.7	5.7	5.7	5.6	5.2	5.5	5.6	5.8	5.7	5.5	5.3
1985	4.9	4.8	4.8	4.7	5.0	5.2	5.3	5.3	5.0	4.9	5.1	5.1
1986	5.3	5.3	5.5	5.5	5.1	5.2	4.9	4.5	4.3	4.2	3.9	3.7
1987	3.6	3.6	3.6	3.9	4.1	4.2	4.1	4.4	4.6	4.6	4.6	4.5
1988	4.5	4.4	4.3	4.5	4.5	4.7	4.6	4.7	4.9	5.0	5.0	5.0
1989	4.9	4.8	4.8	4.8	5.0	5.0	5.2	5.3	5.0	5.0	5.0	5.0
1990	5.1	5.1	5.5	5.7	5.5	5.9	6.2	6.7	6.8	6.5	6.1	5.6
1991	5.8	5.9	5.6	4.9	4.4	3.9	3.8	3.8	4.1	4.1	4.2	4.3
1992	4.3	4.1	4.0	3.9	3.7	3.6	3.6	3.4	3.2	3.6	3.9	4.0
1993	4.1	4.1	3.9	3.9	4.0	4.1	4.0	3.9	3.8	3.6	3.5	3.5
1994	3.2	3.4	3.5	3.4	3.2	3.0	2.8	3.0	3.1	3.1	3.1	2.9
1995	3.1	3.4	3.6	3.9	4.0	4.0	3.9	-	-	-	-	-

Source: U.S. Department of Commerce, Bureau of Economic Analysis, U.S. Department of Commerce, Bureau of the Census. - indicates data not available or zero.

RATIO, COINCIDENT TO LAGGING INDEX

The composite indexes of coincident and the lagging indicators are used to create what is sometimes referred to as the "second" or the "best" leading indicator—the ratio of the coincident to the lagging index. The "coincident to lagging ratio" tends to signal changes in the economy's turning points (especially downturns) *sooner* than the leading index.

For example, in the 1970 recession the leading index signaled the downturn 8 months ahead of time, the ratio 13 months earlier. In other recessionary periods, similar results were noted: 1974-75, leading was 8, the ratio 11 months in advance of actual events; in 1980, leading was 15, the ratio 21; in 1982, leading was 2, the ratio was 9.

The ratio has been less predictive of turn-arounds. In 1970 it turned up as the economy turned up (acting as a coincident indicator), whereas the leading index gave a one-month warning; in 1974-1975, this pattern repeated; in 1980 and 1982, both the leading index and the ratio turned up 10 months ahead of the economy's actual turn-around.

The coincident to lagging ratio tends to work because of the manner in which its components—the coincident and the lagging indexes—behave. The lagging index tends to reflect the *past* of a business cycle, the coincident index its *present*. As the coincident index reaches a turning point, its rate of change tends to be smaller than that of the lagging indicator. If, for example, the economy is approaching a peak, monthly growth reflected in the coincident indicator will be small; meanwhile, the lagging indicator, which reflects events a few months back, will still be growing rapidly. The ratio between the two will, therefore, turn down, signaling a future decline in the economy as the peak is reached and passed. The process works in the same manner as a trough is reached: the composite index will decline less than the lagging index (which is still mirroring the earlier period of the recession); the consequence is an upturn in the ratio promising the start of an expansion soon.

Components of the Ratio

The ratio is expressed as an index with a 1987 base (1987 = 100) and is constructed by dividing the composite index value for a month by the lagging index value for the same month.

Bibliography

1. Carnes, W. Stansbury and Stephen D. Slifer. *The Atlas of Economic Indicators*. HarperCollins, 1991.

2. Frumkin, Norman. *Guide to Economic Indicators*. M.E. Sharpe, Inc., 1990.

Ratio, Coincident Index to Lagging Index
(1987 = 100)

Year	Jan	Feb	Mar	Apr	May	Jun	Jul	Aug	Sep	Oct	Nov	Dec
1948	66.4	65.5	65.3	65.1	65.3	65.9	65.5	63.7	63.2	63.3	62.7	62.4
1949	61.2	60.6	60.6	60.5	59.8	59.7	59.3	60.2	61.1	58.6	59.6	59.8
1950	60.4	60.4	61.6	62.0	62.8	63.8	65.8	66.5	64.3	62.8	61.4	62.7
1951	61.8	61.0	60.7	60.5	60.2	59.7	59.1	59.5	59.4	59.2	59.1	58.6
1952	57.9	58.5	58.3	58.4	58.0	56.9	56.1	58.1	59.0	59.4	59.1	59.0
1953	58.9	59.0	59.1	58.3	57.6	57.3	57.6	57.0	56.4	56.2	55.3	54.7
1954	54.9	55.1	55.6	56.3	56.6	57.2	57.3	58.0	58.3	58.6	59.2	59.5
1955	60.2	60.5	60.9	61.5	61.7	61.2	61.2	59.6	59.5	59.0	58.5	58.7
1956	58.4	58.3	57.9	57.6	56.7	56.6	54.7	55.9	56.0	56.4	56.3	56.6
1957	56.3	56.8	56.6	56.1	56.0	56.0	56.1	55.5	54.9	54.7	54.1	53.5
1958	53.5	53.4	53.3	53.2	54.3	55.4	56.2	57.0	56.9	56.9	57.9	57.7
1959	58.4	58.8	59.2	59.5	59.3	58.8	58.3	56.7	55.6	55.3	55.7	57.2
1960	58.1	57.8	57.3	57.3	56.9	56.6	56.5	56.7	57.1	57.1	56.7	56.2
1961	56.2	56.3	56.8	57.2	57.9	58.7	59.0	59.5	59.5	59.8	60.4	60.4
1962	60.0	60.5	60.7	60.7	60.6	60.6	60.7	60.9	60.9	61.1	61.2	61.1
1963	61.0	61.3	61.6	61.9	61.9	62.0	62.1	61.9	62.1	62.4	62.1	62.3
1964	62.5	62.7	62.7	63.1	63.5	63.5	64.0	64.0	64.3	63.7	64.6	65.2
1965	65.0	65.0	65.3	65.3	65.5	65.9	66.3	66.3	66.3	66.5	66.8	66.4
1966	66.6	66.5	66.8	66.4	66.2	66.4	66.2	66.1	66.2	66.5	66.1	66.2
1967	66.5	66.4	66.3	66.4	66.7	66.6	66.7	67.4	67.3	67.4	68.3	68.7
1968	68.8	68.7	68.7	68.6	68.7	68.8	69.1	68.7	69.1	69.5	69.6	69.6
1969	69.4	69.5	69.7	69.4	69.1	69.0	69.3	69.4	69.3	69.4	69.2	69.1
1970	68.4	68.4	68.2	68.5	68.6	68.6	68.9	68.8	69.1	68.6	68.6	69.9
1971	70.5	70.8	71.3	72.0	72.3	73.0	72.4	72.0	72.5	73.1	73.9	74.4
1972	76.1	76.6	76.9	77.1	77.1	77.0	77.3	78.1	78.6	79.4	80.1	80.8
1973	80.3	80.0	79.8	79.0	79.0	78.9	78.6	78.6	78.1	78.8	79.0	78.0
1974	77.3	77.0	77.1	76.3	76.3	76.0	76.1	75.8	75.1	75.1	74.1	72.3
1975	72.1	72.2	72.1	73.5	74.7	76.6	77.5	78.6	79.5	79.8	80.0	80.5
1976	81.3	82.0	82.3	82.9	83.2	83.7	83.8	84.1	84.1	83.8	84.9	85.7
1977	85.7	85.9	86.2	86.5	86.8	86.8	87.0	86.9	87.0	86.9	87.0	87.2
1978	86.5	86.9	87.4	88.9	88.8	88.9	88.6	88.9	88.8	89.1	88.8	88.7
1979	88.5	88.5	89.7	87.8	88.5	87.9	87.6	87.1	86.5	86.6	86.3	86.3
1980	86.5	86.2	84.9	83.4	82.8	83.0	84.9	87.1	89.0	90.4	90.8	90.1
1981	90.2	90.5	90.8	90.6	89.5	89.2	89.5	89.4	88.5	88.1	87.8	87.7
1982	87.0	88.5	89.0	89.2	89.4	88.7	88.5	88.6	88.8	89.0	89.8	90.6
1983	92.0	92.0	92.8	93.2	94.5	95.2	95.7	95.0	96.2	96.9	96.8	97.0
1984	97.6	97.4	97.4	96.9	96.4	96.6	96.1	95.7	95.6	95.0	95.5	95.7
1985	95.5	95.9	95.9	96.5	96.2	96.0	95.9	96.2	96.2	95.6	95.8	96.1
1986	96.1	96.0	95.6	96.7	96.5	96.4	96.9	97.1	98.2	97.6	97.9	99.1
1987	98.0	99.6	99.8	99.8	100.0	100.1	100.4	100.4	99.9	100.5	100.3	101.3
1988	100.6	101.1	101.2	101.1	101.2	101.2	101.2	101.3	101.4	101.9	101.6	102.4
1989	102.6	102.0	101.8	102.3	101.3	100.8	100.2	100.5	100.3	100.1	100.6	100.9
1990	101.5	102.2	102.6	102.0	102.2	102.4	101.8	102.1	101.8	101.6	101.3	101.3
1991	100.5	100.6	100.6	101.5	102.3	103.3	103.7	104.3	104.9	105.1	105.2	105.4
1992	106.4	107.5	108.2	108.7	108.9	109.4	110.0	109.7	110.5	111.3	111.4	115.1
1993	112.0	112.4	112.7	113.4	113.3	113.4	112.7	113.9	113.7	114.3	115.2	115.9
1994	115.6	116.8	117.6	117.1	116.9	116.6	116.5	117.0	116.6	116.7	116.5	117.0
1995	116.6	116.1	115.7	114.6	114.3	114.1	114.7	-	-	-	-	-

Source: U.S. Department of Commerce, Bureau of Economic Analysis. - indicates data not available or zero.

CHAPTER 4

CYCLIC INDICATORS

CYCLIC INDICATORS

The Business Cycle Indicators include, all told, 22 economic series which have been found, over time, to work well as indicators of cyclic change in the economy. In this section are presented 49 other economic series which are also considered cyclic indicators but are not part of the composite indexes of leading, coincident, and lagging indicators. They are grouped under seven headings:

Employment
Production and Income
Consumption, Trade, Orders, and Deliveries
Fixed Capital Investment
Inventories and Inventory Investment
Prices, Costs, and Profits
Money and Credit

A brief introduction to each of these sections provides a description of each series covered, the principal analytical uses of each series, and a listing of related series which are included under the Business Cycle Indicators heading.

Bibliography

1. Fischer, Stanley, Rudiger Dornbusch, and Richard Schmalensee. *Introduction to Macroeconomics*. McGraw-Hill Book Company, New York, 1988.

2. Fitch, Thomas P. *Dictionary of Banking Terms*. Barron's, New York, 1990.

3. Siegel, Barry N. *Money, Banking, and the Economy*. Academic Press, New York, 1982.

3. U.S. Department of Commerce, Bureau of Economic Analysis. *Survey of Current Business*. Superintendent of Documents, U.S. Government Printing Office, Washington, DC 20302.

INDICATORS OF EMPLOYMENT

In modern industrial economies, employment is the single most important indicator of economic well-being—and decline in employment a signal of economic woes. This section presents two series:

    Unemployment rate
    Number of persons unemployed

Related series, reported under Business Cycle Indicators, are:

    Average weekly hours in manufacturing (Leading Index)
    Average weekly initial claims for unemployment insurance (Leading Index)
    Employment on nonagricultural payrolls (Coincident Index)
    Average duration of unemployment in weeks (Lagging Index)

Unemployment Rate. Data are presented for persons unemployed 15 weeks and over as a percent of the work force. Data are shown from 1948 to 1995. The series behaves as a lagging indicator but is not part of the composite index of lagging indicators.

Number of Persons Unemployed. Data show total number of people unemployed in thousands from 1948 to 1995. The series is classified as a leading indicator at business cycle peaks, as a lagging indicator of business cycle troughs, and is unclassified overall.

Unemployment Rate, 15 Weeks and Over
(Percent)

Year	Jan	Feb	Mar	Apr	May	Jun	Jul	Aug	Sep	Oct	Nov	Dec
1948	0.5	0.5	0.5	0.5	0.5	0.5	0.5	0.5	0.5	0.5	0.5	0.5
1949	0.5	0.6	0.7	0.8	1.0	1.2	1.4	1.5	1.6	1.6	1.7	1.6
1950	1.5	1.5	1.5	1.5	1.4	1.4	1.2	1.0	1.0	0.9	0.8	0.8
1951	0.7	0.6	0.6	0.5	0.4	0.4	0.4	0.4	0.4	0.4	0.5	0.4
1952	0.5	0.4	0.4	0.4	0.4	0.3	0.3	0.3	0.4	0.4	0.3	0.4
1953	0.4	0.3	0.3	0.3	0.3	0.3	0.3	0.3	0.3	0.3	0.4	0.5
1954	0.6	0.8	1.2	1.2	1.4	1.4	1.5	1.6	1.6	1.6	1.5	1.3
1955	1.4	1.3	1.3	1.3	1.1	1.0	1.0	0.8	0.9	0.9	0.9	0.9
1956	0.8	0.8	0.8	0.7	0.8	0.8	0.8	0.8	0.9	0.8	0.9	0.9
1957	0.8	0.8	0.8	0.8	0.8	0.8	0.8	0.8	0.8	1.0	1.0	1.1
1958	1.3	1.5	1.7	2.1	2.2	2.5	2.6	2.8	2.6	2.5	2.3	2.2
1959	2.1	1.9	1.8	1.5	1.4	1.4	1.3	1.3	1.3	1.3	1.4	1.3
1960	1.3	1.2	1.4	1.3	1.1	1.2	1.3	1.3	1.4	1.7	1.7	1.6
1961	1.9	2.0	2.1	2.3	2.4	2.3	2.6	2.3	2.2	2.1	2.0	1.9
1962	1.8	1.8	1.7	1.6	1.6	1.5	1.5	1.5	1.5	1.4	1.5	1.5
1963	1.6	1.6	1.5	1.5	1.6	1.5	1.5	1.6	1.5	1.5	1.5	1.4
1964	1.5	1.4	1.4	1.3	1.3	1.4	1.4	1.3	1.3	1.2	1.3	1.2
1965	1.1	1.2	1.1	1.1	1.0	1.1	0.9	1.0	1.0	0.9	0.9	0.9
1966	0.8	0.8	0.8	0.8	0.7	0.6	0.6	0.6	0.6	0.6	0.6	0.6
1967	0.6	0.6	0.6	0.6	0.5	0.5	0.5	0.6	0.6	0.6	0.6	0.6
1968	0.6	0.6	0.6	0.5	0.5	0.5	0.5	0.5	0.5	0.5	0.5	0.4
1969	0.4	0.4	0.4	0.5	0.5	0.5	0.5	0.5	0.5	0.5	0.5	0.5
1970	0.5	0.6	0.6	0.7	0.7	0.8	0.8	0.9	0.9	0.9	1.0	1.3
1971	1.3	1.3	1.3	1.4	1.4	1.4	1.5	1.5	1.5	1.5	1.5	1.5
1972	1.5	1.5	1.4	1.4	1.3	1.3	1.3	1.3	1.3	1.3	1.2	1.1
1973	1.1	1.0	1.0	0.9	0.9	0.9	0.8	0.9	0.9	0.9	0.9	0.8
1974	0.9	0.9	0.9	1.0	1.0	1.0	1.0	1.0	1.1	1.2	1.2	1.4
1975	1.7	2.0	2.2	2.6	2.8	3.0	3.1	3.0	3.1	2.9	3.0	3.0
1976	2.9	2.7	2.6	2.3	2.2	2.4	2.4	2.5	2.4	2.4	2.4	2.4
1977	2.3	2.2	2.1	2.0	2.0	1.9	1.9	1.8	1.9	1.8	1.8	1.7
1978	1.6	1.6	1.5	1.5	1.4	1.3	1.3	1.2	1.3	1.3	1.2	1.2
1979	1.2	1.2	1.3	1.2	1.2	1.1	1.1	1.1	1.1	1.2	1.2	1.2
1980	1.3	1.3	1.4	1.6	1.6	1.6	1.9	2.0	2.2	2.1	2.2	2.2
1981	2.2	2.2	2.1	2.0	2.0	2.1	2.0	2.1	2.1	2.1	2.1	2.2
1982	2.2	2.5	2.7	2.8	3.0	3.1	3.2	3.3	3.5	3.8	4.0	4.2
1983	4.2	4.2	4.2	3.9	4.1	4.0	3.9	3.6	3.4	3.3	3.1	3.0
1984	2.9	2.7	2.6	2.5	2.5	2.3	2.3	2.3	2.2	2.2	2.1	2.1
1985	2.0	2.1	2.1	2.1	2.0	2.0	2.0	2.0	1.9	2.0	1.9	1.9
1986	1.8	2.0	1.9	1.8	1.9	2.0	1.9	1.9	2.0	1.8	1.9	1.8
1987	1.8	1.8	1.7	1.8	1.8	1.7	1.6	1.6	1.6	1.5	1.5	1.5
1988	1.4	1.4	1.4	1.3	1.4	1.3	1.3	1.3	1.3	1.3	1.2	1.2
1989	1.2	1.1	1.1	1.1	1.1	1.0	1.2	1.0	1.1	1.1	1.1	1.1
1990	1.1	1.1	1.1	1.1	1.1	1.1	1.2	1.2	1.3	1.3	1.4	1.4
1991	1.5	1.6	1.7	1.8	1.8	2.0	1.9	1.9	1.9	2.0	2.1	2.3
1992	2.4	2.5	2.5	2.4	2.7	2.9	2.8	2.8	2.7	2.7	2.6	2.8
1993	2.6	2.5	2.4	2.3	2.4	2.4	2.3	2.3	2.4	2.4	2.3	2.2
1994	2.3	2.3	2.3	2.3	2.2	2.1	2.2	2.1	2.1	2.2	2.0	1.9
1995	1.8	1.7	1.7	1.9	2.0	1.7	1.8	-	-	-	-	-

Source: U.S. Department of Labor, Bureau of Labor Statistics. - indicates data not available or zero.

Number of Persons Unemployed
(Thousands)

Year	Jan	Feb	Mar	Apr	May	Jun	Jul	Aug	Sep	Oct	Nov	Dec
1948	2,034	2,328	2,399	2,386	2,118	2,214	2,213	2,350	2,302	2,259	2,285	2,429
1949	2,596	2,849	3,030	3,260	3,707	3,776	4,111	4,193	4,049	4,916	3,996	4,063
1950	4,026	3,936	3,876	3,575	3,434	3,367	3,120	2,799	2,774	2,625	2,589	2,639
1951	2,305	2,117	2,125	1,919	1,856	1,995	1,950	1,933	2,067	2,194	2,178	1,960
1952	1,972	1,957	1,813	1,811	1,863	1,884	1,991	2,087	1,936	1,839	1,743	1,667
1953	1,839	1,636	1,647	1,723	1,596	1,607	1,660	1,665	1,821	1,974	2,211	2,818
1954	3,077	3,331	3,607	3,749	3,767	3,551	3,659	3,854	3,927	3,666	3,402	3,196
1955	3,157	2,969	2,918	3,049	2,747	2,701	2,632	2,784	2,678	2,830	2,780	2,761
1956	2,666	2,606	2,764	2,650	2,861	2,882	2,952	2,701	2,635	2,571	2,861	2,790
1957	2,796	2,622	2,509	2,600	2,710	2,856	2,796	2,747	2,943	3,020	3,454	3,476
1958	3,875	4,303	4,492	5,016	5,021	4,944	5,079	5,025	4,821	4,570	4,188	4,191
1959	4,068	3,965	3,801	3,571	3,479	3,429	3,528	3,588	3,775	3,910	4,003	3,653
1960	3,615	3,329	3,726	3,620	3,569	3,766	3,836	3,946	3,884	4,252	4,330	4,617
1961	4,671	4,832	4,853	4,893	5,003	4,885	4,928	4,682	4,676	4,573	4,295	4,177
1962	4,081	3,871	3,921	3,906	3,863	3,844	3,819	4,013	3,961	3,803	4,024	3,907
1963	4,074	4,238	4,072	4,055	4,217	3,977	4,051	3,878	3,957	3,987	4,151	3,975
1964	4,029	3,932	3,950	3,918	3,764	3,814	3,608	3,655	3,712	3,726	3,551	3,651
1965	3,572	3,730	3,510	3,595	3,432	3,387	3,301	3,254	3,216	3,143	3,073	3,031
1966	2,988	2,820	2,887	2,828	2,950	2,872	2,876	2,900	2,798	2,798	2,770	2,912
1967	2,968	2,915	2,889	2,895	2,929	2,992	2,944	2,945	2,958	3,143	3,066	3,018
1968	2,878	3,001	2,877	2,709	2,740	2,938	2,883	2,768	2,686	2,689	2,715	2,685
1969	2,718	2,692	2,712	2,758	2,713	2,816	2,868	2,856	3,040	3,049	2,856	2,884
1970	3,201	3,453	3,635	3,797	3,919	4,071	4,175	4,256	4,456	4,591	4,898	5,076
1971	4,986	4,903	4,987	4,959	4,996	4,949	5,035	5,134	5,042	4,954	5,161	5,154
1972	5,019	4,928	5,038	4,959	4,922	4,923	4,913	4,939	4,849	4,875	4,602	4,543
1973	4,326	4,452	4,394	4,459	4,329	4,363	4,305	4,305	4,350	4,144	4,396	4,489
1974	4,644	4,731	4,634	4,618	4,705	4,927	5,063	5,022	5,437	5,523	6,140	6,636
1975	7,501	7,520	7,978	8,210	8,433	8,220	8,127	7,928	7,923	7,897	7,794	7,744
1976	7,534	7,326	7,230	7,330	7,053	7,322	7,490	7,518	7,380	7,430	7,620	7,545
1977	7,280	7,443	7,307	7,059	6,911	7,134	6,829	6,925	6,751	6,763	6,815	6,386
1978	6,489	6,318	6,337	6,180	6,127	6,028	6,309	6,080	6,125	5,947	6,077	6,228
1979	6,109	6,173	6,109	6,069	5,840	5,959	5,996	6,320	6,190	6,296	6,238	6,325
1980	6,683	6,702	6,729	7,358	7,984	8,098	8,363	8,281	8,021	8,088	8,023	7,718
1981	8,071	8,051	7,982	7,869	8,174	8,098	7,863	8,036	8,230	8,646	9,029	9,267
1982	9,397	9,705	9,895	10,244	10,335	10,538	10,849	10,881	11,217	11,529	11,938	12,051
1983	11,534	11,545	11,408	11,268	11,154	11,246	10,548	10,623	10,282	9,887	9,499	9,331
1984	9,008	8,791	8,746	8,762	8,456	8,226	8,537	8,519	8,367	8,381	8,198	8,358
1985	8,423	8,321	8,339	8,395	8,302	8,460	8,513	8,196	8,248	8,298	8,128	8,138
1986	7,795	8,402	8,383	8,364	8,439	8,508	8,319	8,135	8,310	8,243	8,159	7,883
1987	7,892	7,865	7,862	7,542	7,574	7,398	7,268	7,261	7,102	7,227	7,035	6,936
1988	6,953	6,929	6,876	6,601	6,779	6,546	6,605	6,843	6,604	6,568	6,537	6,518
1989	6,682	6,359	6,205	6,468	6,375	6,577	6,495	6,511	6,590	6,630	6,725	6,667
1990	6,611	6,585	6,490	6,708	6,599	6,414	6,708	7,011	7,115	7,192	7,503	7,733
1991	7,820	8,158	8,465	8,310	8,539	8,489	8,364	8,444	8,465	8,581	8,671	9,005
1992	9,019	9,290	9,290	9,247	9,502	9,771	9,595	9,590	9,534	9,210	9,313	9,314
1993	9,046	8,958	8,878	8,954	8,895	8,869	8,732	8,642	8,540	8,639	8,330	8,237
1994	8,740	8,576	8,546	8,385	7,996	7,903	7,993	7,889	7,647	7,505	7,315	7,155
1995	7,498	7,183	7,237	7,665	7,492	7,384	7,559	-	-	-	-	-

Source: U.S. Department of Labor, Bureau of Labor Statistics. - indicates data not available or zero.

INDICATORS OF PRODUCTION AND INCOME

Production and personal income are indicators of overall economic performance. They are cyclic indicators which tend to be coincident: they turn up or down as the economy does. This section presents four series:

> Personal income
> Wages and salaries
> Capacity utilization rate, all industry
> Capacity utilization rate, manufacturing

Related series, reported under Business Cycle Indicators, are:

> Index of industrial production (Coincident Index)
> Personal income less transfer payments (Coincident Index)

Personal Income. Data are reported for 1947 to 1993 in billions of constant 1987 dollars. Monthly data are annualized, meaning that monthly survey results are multiplied by 12 months. Although not part of any composite index of economic indicators, personal income is viewed as a coincident cyclic indicator. The category includes all income received by individuals from any source, including dividends, rents, and transfer payments (welfare, social security, unemployment benefits, medicaid, etc.).

Wages and Salaries. Data are for wages and salaries in mining, manufacturing, and construction and are reported in billions of constant 1987 dollars. Monthly data are annualized, showing what would be annual results if the month's results were applied to the year as a whole. The series behaves as a coincident indicator overall but is not a component of a composite index.

Capacity Utilization Rate, All Industry. Data, for 1967 through 1993, are shown as percent of total capacity. The series can be used as a cyclic indicator (it is leading at the peak of the business cycle and coincident at the trough) and as an indicator of inflation. High rates of capacity utilization signal high rates of production and hence upward pressure on prices.

Capacity Utilization Rate, Manufacturing. Data are shown for 1948 through 1993 in percent. The series is a leading indicator at the peak and a coincident indicator at the trough of a cycle.

Personal Income

(Annual Rate, Billions of 1987 $)

Year	Jan	Feb	Mar	Apr	May	Jun	Jul	Aug	Sep	Oct	Nov	Dec
1947	942.4	938.2	933.0	918.0	915.4	924.8	921.7	918.5	980.7	933.5	927.5	932.5
1948	950.0	943.7	958.7	958.4	962.3	976.4	974.7	981.2	982.1	985.8	979.4	971.4
1949	956.2	956.5	961.6	961.9	959.5	951.6	944.2	952.1	967.4	945.8	957.4	963.4
1950	1,002.8	1,017.1	1,041.2	1,015.7	1,018.4	1,014.2	1,024.4	1,034.1	1,043.9	1,054.5	1,064.7	1,075.3
1951	1,067.4	1,065.2	1,076.8	1,093.5	1,099.6	1,107.3	1,100.9	1,114.2	1,111.5	1,119.6	1,118.6	1,123.3
1952	1,111.0	1,127.4	1,129.5	1,127.4	1,139.7	1,141.2	1,136.6	1,163.2	1,175.3	1,171.0	1,163.6	1,172.7
1953	1,172.0	1,180.7	1,192.2	1,188.9	1,194.7	1,198.0	1,196.3	1,193.9	1,194.7	1,200.8	1,193.9	1,191.0
1954	1,191.4	1,191.0	1,187.3	1,177.2	1,180.5	1,186.1	1,187.8	1,198.8	1,205.7	1,213.9	1,225.4	1,224.9
1955	1,227.2	1,230.0	1,240.1	1,247.2	1,257.3	1,261.3	1,275.9	1,277.1	1,285.9	1,291.6	1,300.8	1,309.6
1956	1,308.0	1,315.6	1,321.6	1,334.8	1,332.7	1,336.5	1,327.3	1,339.8	1,343.9	1,357.6	1,352.7	1,354.9
1957	1,354.9	1,362.0	1,362.2	1,364.5	1,366.2	1,376.5	1,377.0	1,377.5	1,373.7	1,368.8	1,370.3	1,362.1
1958	1,361.7	1,355.1	1,362.3	1,360.0	1,365.3	1,372.8	1,397.0	1,396.2	1,403.8	1,401.1	1,418.0	1,419.5
1959	1,416.8	1,425.7	1,437.3	1,448.5	1,453.2	1,458.1	1,460.4	1,445.0	1,444.1	1,447.4	1,469.0	1,483.8
1960	1,487.5	1,480.6	1,480.6	1,482.9	1,493.8	1,495.3	1,492.4	1,494.2	1,492.4	1,492.4	1,492.1	1,489.1
1961	1,501.8	1,509.4	1,508.7	1,516.7	1,528.3	1,538.6	1,541.4	1,543.9	1,543.0	1,557.0	1,572.8	1,581.7
1962	1,579.2	1,583.9	1,596.8	1,601.4	1,600.0	1,611.0	1,618.5	1,617.4	1,614.4	1,624.7	1,627.8	1,634.5
1963	1,641.8	1,639.1	1,638.9	1,644.9	1,654.0	1,655.7	1,658.2	1,666.9	1,678.0	1,690.9	1,691.3	1,702.4
1964	1,711.8	1,713.8	1,722.1	1,733.8	1,738.5	1,747.4	1,758.1	1,766.1	1,776.7	1,780.1	1,793.8	1,808.9
1965	1,816.7	1,809.5	1,818.6	1,825.0	1,841.6	1,855.4	1,860.3	1,867.7	1,906.0	1,898.7	1,916.7	1,926.3
1966	1,926.2	1,930.0	1,935.5	1,942.8	1,951.3	1,961.0	1,966.3	1,978.8	1,984.5	1,997.7	2,007.7	2,011.9
1967	2,029.7	2,031.9	2,038.9	2,035.6	2,044.6	2,053.7	2,064.3	2,073.7	2,068.1	2,075.1	2,087.4	2,101.9
1968	2,102.5	2,118.6	2,129.9	2,141.2	2,154.3	2,164.8	2,176.5	2,181.2	2,197.6	2,200.0	2,209.9	2,221.9
1969	2,221.9	2,229.0	2,241.7	2,245.3	2,256.6	2,260.4	2,280.9	2,286.6	2,294.2	2,302.0	2,307.8	2,308.9
1970	2,304.9	2,302.0	2,306.5	2,352.1	2,327.6	2,323.0	2,334.7	2,342.5	2,346.9	2,342.4	2,341.7	2,345.6
1971	2,356.0	2,358.0	2,360.7	2,362.8	2,373.4	2,416.8	2,386.7	2,399.7	2,404.8	2,407.1	2,423.0	2,441.8
1972	2,451.8	2,471.0	2,478.9	2,487.5	2,496.6	2,481.1	2,514.9	2,541.4	2,550.9	2,593.1	2,626.7	2,635.4
1973	2,640.7	2,640.9	2,641.5	2,632.8	2,658.9	2,665.0	2,663.5	2,681.6	2,693.5	2,724.9	2,743.4	2,735.0
1974	2,710.9	2,685.0	2,654.7	2,653.2	2,655.0	2,660.4	2,674.4	2,666.0	2,670.6	2,681.3	2,661.8	2,660.9
1975	2,635.8	2,625.7	2,632.2	2,635.6	2,646.2	2,697.1	2,669.0	2,690.9	2,706.9	2,727.2	2,723.4	2,725.6
1976	2,751.2	2,765.1	2,771.7	2,780.0	2,786.5	2,786.0	2,799.4	2,803.6	2,806.5	2,802.5	2,830.6	2,838.6
1977	2,835.6	2,843.1	2,852.1	2,857.6	2,869.4	2,869.1	2,898.7	2,917.7	2,929.8	2,928.4	2,941.9	2,953.7
1978	2,957.2	2,968.2	2,997.9	3,022.6	3,027.5	3,039.3	3,051.4	3,065.7	3,076.9	3,093.6	3,102.6	3,112.0
1979	3,114.7	3,123.4	3,136.8	3,126.5	3,122.1	3,123.1	3,151.6	3,152.5	3,153.2	3,163.5	3,171.5	3,178.0
1980	3,189.5	3,176.4	3,158.2	3,135.9	3,119.1	3,118.8	3,145.4	3,157.6	3,178.2	3,210.6	3,224.0	3,248.6
1981	3,239.8	3,235.5	3,240.8	3,238.6	3,235.3	3,244.0	3,281.5	3,293.1	3,290.1	3,280.5	3,271.1	3,257.9
1982	3,243.6	3,254.3	3,262.5	3,289.5	3,294.1	3,277.0	3,276.4	3,272.7	3,267.3	3,267.0	3,275.3	3,287.1
1983	3,278.9	3,274.3	3,281.1	3,291.9	3,309.5	3,314.8	3,322.0	3,309.8	3,327.8	3,360.6	3,385.3	3,407.1
1984	3,427.9	3,468.2	3,487.7	3,493.7	3,491.7	3,513.6	3,529.6	3,545.8	3,568.9	3,553.6	3,568.2	3,599.1
1985	3,601.5	3,614.7	3,626.3	3,641.0	3,619.1	3,630.7	3,631.8	3,625.6	3,627.6	3,645.4	3,640.5	3,676.0
1986	3,669.0	3,689.3	3,723.0	3,765.2	3,751.5	3,739.5	3,745.2	3,752.6	3,758.3	3,749.2	3,752.3	3,776.4
1987	3,762.8	3,783.1	3,782.7	3,785.4	3,781.8	3,775.6	3,785.7	3,797.3	3,798.7	3,849.6	3,831.2	3,885.7
1988	3,861.8	3,877.5	3,895.9	3,898.4	3,895.4	3,902.9	3,907.4	3,909.8	3,912.7	3,961.4	3,937.6	3,963.1
1989	3,990.3	4,008.9	4,026.3	4,014.0	3,995.0	3,991.2	3,999.7	3,999.3	3,989.8	4,010.2	4,030.3	4,038.8
1990	4,053.6	4,071.3	4,081.5	4,088.5	4,075.7	4,079.6	4,082.3	4,060.3	4,059.8	4,031.4	4,043.6	4,079.3
1991	4,045.4	4,042.0	4,060.9	4,056.4	4,055.4	4,067.3	4,053.8	4,051.0	4,057.8	4,068.8	4,052.6	4,095.3
1992	4,096.0	4,129.5	4,135.6	4,140.8	4,141.2	4,141.5	4,146.0	4,160.2	4,175.5	4,201.9	4,200.2	4,412.0
1993	4,175.7	4,177.9	4,192.7	4,242.2	4,251.9	4,238.0	4,230.7	4,270.8	4,268.2	4,284.7	4,300.2	4,323.4
1994	4,307.9	4,359.7	4,370.6	4,385.2	4,395.2	4,392.3	4,398.1	4,411.5	4,430.4	4,485.6	4,476.5	4,505.0
1995	4,527.2	4,541.3	4,557.2	4,551.6	4,538.3	4,559.8	4,582.6	-	-	-	-	-

Source: U.S. Department of Commerce, Bureau of Economic Analysis. - indicates data not available or zero.

Wages & Salaries in Mining, Manufacturing, Construction
(Annual Rate, Billions of 1987 $)

Year	Jan	Feb	Mar	Apr	May	Jun	Jul	Aug	Sep	Oct	Nov	Dec
1947	260.3	259.2	259.1	259.1	262.7	264.2	260.5	260.9	262.5	264.7	267.3	267.5
1948	271.6	270.2	275.4	267.9	271.1	274.1	274.0	278.1	276.7	278.5	281.6	278.3
1949	276.8	275.7	269.0	265.2	263.3	258.6	262.0	259.6	262.2	252.4	255.3	260.1
1950	266.2	263.0	273.6	280.8	287.1	291.9	296.7	304.7	304.7	313.5	317.1	315.0
1951	314.3	313.7	317.5	323.2	321.4	325.0	325.0	325.6	323.6	321.3	323.4	325.8
1952	328.3	332.3	334.5	329.2	333.2	328.8	314.9	340.2	352.6	356.4	361.5	365.5
1953	367.9	371.4	373.6	374.0	374.9	372.5	375.7	372.5	366.1	365.8	362.3	357.0
1954	352.7	354.0	351.5	348.9	350.2	348.9	347.9	348.3	347.0	354.0	360.2	363.4
1955	365.5	368.2	373.3	377.1	384.7	386.0	389.4	388.9	388.6	394.9	399.2	401.7
1956	403.0	402.5	404.6	411.8	409.3	408.8	400.8	411.2	414.9	418.6	417.8	422.6
1957	419.3	421.3	418.8	417.1	413.4	414.6	412.1	412.0	408.4	405.2	402.0	396.4
1958	388.9	380.6	378.7	371.3	371.3	375.6	379.5	385.4	389.8	387.8	400.4	403.9
1959	405.9	408.6	416.9	420.8	426.3	427.7	426.6	413.6	412.0	408.9	413.5	426.3
1960	433.7	433.2	430.9	430.9	432.4	427.7	427.4	423.5	420.4	418.3	414.1	406.5
1961	410.3	409.2	411.1	414.1	418.3	424.0	424.0	427.0	421.2	429.2	435.6	438.3
1962	436.4	439.6	444.2	448.5	447.4	447.7	449.6	449.6	451.3	449.8	452.1	452.4
1963	454.3	454.3	453.7	456.0	460.4	461.7	463.2	461.9	465.2	465.7	467.2	469.9
1964	466.9	475.4	478.7	482.0	483.8	484.2	487.5	491.9	496.0	489.4	496.0	504.7
1965	505.8	510.6	510.5	507.2	513.0	512.9	516.2	517.3	519.8	524.4	530.1	534.6
1966	537.5	543.8	547.2	549.6	552.1	556.8	558.2	558.0	560.8	561.9	563.3	563.0
1967	567.5	560.7	562.1	560.5	558.2	560.1	563.8	566.8	564.7	562.8	571.4	575.5
1968	574.0	580.5	583.1	585.1	591.7	590.2	589.6	589.6	593.9	597.7	601.6	603.2
1969	604.5	600.6	607.6	607.2	609.7	610.9	611.4	614.2	615.3	614.0	608.8	608.7
1970	603.9	601.2	603.0	593.2	588.2	589.4	589.2	586.3	575.7	565.6	560.9	569.7
1971	572.6	571.0	573.0	575.1	579.9	577.0	574.0	572.7	574.7	575.3	577.8	586.4
1972	591.7	596.4	602.7	604.9	606.3	606.5	603.8	610.6	615.4	620.7	625.5	628.9
1973	636.5	642.1	639.9	642.6	642.0	642.7	649.6	639.1	644.1	644.1	647.3	648.5
1974	641.1	638.0	633.1	632.2	633.5	633.7	629.3	628.2	624.5	620.3	600.4	591.7
1975	584.3	570.0	567.2	564.9	566.5	567.4	562.8	572.5	576.0	578.3	579.8	585.1
1976	594.3	597.2	601.2	604.3	605.2	602.6	606.4	608.7	607.5	606.7	614.9	615.8
1977	612.0	616.9	622.9	627.3	634.6	640.6	640.1	641.9	647.7	650.0	651.2	647.8
1978	644.3	649.3	658.4	672.4	672.3	674.1	676.2	675.9	679.1	680.5	686.0	690.3
1979	689.5	686.9	690.7	682.6	684.6	684.6	681.9	676.9	676.9	673.7	669.5	671.9
1980	662.8	660.1	652.9	642.1	633.4	625.9	622.3	630.3	633.5	636.6	641.3	643.6
1981	642.1	633.9	637.2	636.7	636.1	637.3	635.2	635.5	629.0	630.1	624.4	619.0
1982	616.6	616.7	614.5	608.6	605.6	595.8	590.1	586.2	581.6	574.7	572.9	576.4
1983	580.0	577.3	578.1	579.4	581.2	585.1	588.8	591.1	598.6	603.3	607.1	610.3
1984	612.8	617.3	618.2	623.1	624.4	629.4	630.4	632.4	631.3	630.6	633.3	636.2
1985	638.0	633.7	643.7	635.0	635.6	636.8	635.5	637.9	638.9	642.5	639.2	641.2
1986	639.3	637.6	647.9	645.4	643.9	641.0	641.5	644.6	642.3	648.2	644.2	645.1
1987	642.3	641.5	644.3	639.0	639.0	637.4	638.2	641.3	646.2	647.4	650.5	652.4
1988	653.1	657.0	666.0	662.6	663.1	664.7	665.9	663.0	663.8	671.8	665.9	664.3
1989	664.8	662.8	666.9	657.1	651.7	651.1	650.2	652.4	651.0	655.3	651.9	648.7
1990	642.8	650.3	651.5	649.7	647.7	646.2	642.9	636.1	633.7	626.4	619.6	623.5
1991	617.1	612.7	608.3	606.2	606.0	607.3	605.9	605.9	605.8	609.3	600.2	604.2
1992	596.1	596.7	598.0	599.4	601.7	601.1	600.6	600.5	599.4	604.1	600.8	664.2
1993	583.4	586.1	583.2	604.0	604.0	602.2	603.4	604.0	606.5	605.6	606.9	608.5
1994	610.4	612.4	613.1	615.0	615.1	616.4	616.8	616.6	619.6	627.2	624.5	625.8
1995	625.4	632.5	630.5	622.2	616.4	619.4	618.5	-	-	-	-	-

Source: U.S. Department of Commerce, Bureau of Economic Analysis. - indicates data not available or zero.

Capacity Utilization Rate
Total industry
(Percent)

Year	Jan	Feb	Mar	Apr	May	Jun	Jul	Aug	Sep	Oct	Nov	Dec
1967	88.7	87.3	86.4	86.8	85.7	85.3	84.8	86.0	85.5	85.8	86.7	87.3
1968	86.8	86.8	86.7	86.5	87.1	87.1	86.6	86.5	86.5	86.4	87.2	87.1
1969	87.3	87.6	87.9	87.3	86.7	87.2	87.4	87.3	86.9	86.7	85.6	85.0
1970	83.2	82.9	82.5	82.1	81.7	81.2	81.1	80.8	80.0	78.1	77.4	79.0
1971	79.3	79.0	78.7	79.0	79.2	79.3	78.9	78.2	79.3	79.7	79.8	80.6
1972	82.1	82.5	83.0	84.1	83.7	83.7	83.4	84.3	85.0	86.0	86.8	87.4
1973	87.3	88.2	88.0	88.0	88.2	88.6	88.9	88.6	89.1	89.2	89.0	87.3
1974	85.9	85.3	85.4	85.0	85.8	85.8	85.2	84.6	84.7	83.9	81.2	77.6
1975	75.4	74.1	72.6	73.1	72.7	73.5	73.8	75.0	75.6	75.8	76.4	76.8
1976	77.5	78.7	78.3	78.4	79.2	79.0	79.3	79.6	79.7	79.8	80.9	81.4
1977	81.5	81.7	82.3	83.3	83.8	84.2	84.0	83.9	84.2	83.9	83.8	83.2
1978	82.7	82.6	83.5	85.4	85.5	86.1	86.1	86.2	86.5	86.7	87.1	87.1
1979	86.6	87.2	87.3	86.2	87.0	86.7	86.0	85.4	85.5	85.8	85.3	85.0
1980	85.1	85.1	84.9	83.0	80.8	79.6	79.1	80.0	80.9	81.2	82.4	82.5
1981	81.6	81.7	81.7	80.7	81.1	81.3	82.1	81.7	81.1	80.2	79.1	78.2
1982	76.4	77.9	77.3	76.7	76.0	75.6	75.0	74.5	73.8	73.0	72.6	71.8
1983	73.0	72.8	73.2	73.9	74.6	74.9	76.1	77.1	78.2	78.7	78.7	78.9
1984	80.4	80.1	80.8	81.1	81.5	81.8	81.9	81.8	81.6	80.9	80.8	80.2
1985	80.3	80.7	80.7	80.9	80.9	80.5	80.0	80.2	80.4	79.6	79.7	80.4
1986	80.6	79.9	79.1	79.1	78.9	78.4	78.7	78.7	78.7	79.1	79.4	79.8
1987	79.3	80.3	80.5	80.8	81.2	81.8	81.9	82.0	81.8	82.7	82.7	83.1
1988	83.2	83.3	83.2	83.8	83.5	83.4	83.8	84.2	83.7	83.8	84.2	84.6
1989	84.8	84.3	84.9	84.8	84.3	83.9	83.0	83.3	82.8	82.3	82.5	82.9
1990	82.4	82.7	82.8	82.1	82.6	82.6	82.4	82.5	82.4	81.8	80.7	80.2
1991	79.7	78.9	78.0	78.3	78.8	79.4	79.5	79.4	80.0	79.8	79.6	79.2
1992	78.8	79.4	79.7	80.0	80.3	79.9	80.4	80.2	80.2	80.6	81.2	81.5
1993	81.5	81.8	81.7	81.6	81.2	81.4	81.6	81.6	81.7	81.7	82.3	82.9
1994	82.7	83.2	83.7	83.6	83.8	84.1	84.1	84.5	84.2	84.4	84.8	85.5
1995	85.5	85.3	84.9	84.1	83.9	83.6	83.4	-	-	-	-	-

Source: Board of Governors of the Federal Reserve System. - indicates data not available or zero.

Capacity Utilization Rate
Manufacturing
(Percent)

Year	Jan	Feb	Mar	Apr	May	Jun	Jul	Aug	Sep	Oct	Nov	Dec
1948	84.4	84.0	83.4	82.8	83.3	83.6	83.4	82.7	81.5	81.7	80.2	79.3
1949	77.9	76.9	75.9	74.2	73.2	73.1	73.1	73.6	74.8	71.7	72.0	73.6
1950	74.9	75.4	76.4	79.2	81.0	83.1	85.5	88.4	87.2	87.5	87.0	88.1
1951	88.3	88.3	88.4	88.2	87.4	86.6	84.9	83.6	83.7	83.1	83.6	83.9
1952	84.4	84.6	84.7	83.6	83.1	81.9	79.8	85.1	87.7	88.8	90.2	90.5
1953	90.5	91.1	91.4	91.5	91.7	90.7	91.0	90.6	88.3	87.2	84.7	82.3
1954	81.3	80.8	80.2	79.4	79.8	79.9	79.4	78.8	79.2	79.7	80.9	81.8
1955	83.5	84.1	85.8	86.7	87.9	87.6	87.7	87.3	87.5	88.4	88.3	89.0
1956	88.2	87.4	87.0	87.8	86.3	85.3	81.5	84.9	86.0	86.5	85.8	86.8
1957	86.2	87.0	86.4	85.0	84.2	84.6	84.3	84.2	83.2	81.4	79.4	77.5
1958	75.7	73.8	72.7	71.3	71.9	73.9	74.3	75.7	76.2	76.4	79.1	79.0
1959	80.2	81.4	82.5	84.0	84.9	84.8	83.0	79.5	79.0	78.2	78.5	83.6
1960	85.6	84.6	83.2	82.3	81.5	80.2	79.7	79.1	77.9	77.5	75.8	74.3
1961	74.1	73.5	73.9	75.4	76.4	77.3	78.1	79.0	78.2	79.6	80.8	81.6
1962	80.2	81.4	81.9	81.7	81.3	80.9	81.5	81.4	81.8	81.4	81.8	81.7
1963	81.9	82.4	82.6	83.5	84.0	83.9	83.3	83.5	83.8	84.3	84.3	84.0
1964	84.5	84.7	84.4	85.6	85.6	85.4	85.9	86.1	86.2	84.6	86.8	88.0
1965	88.6	88.7	89.3	89.3	89.4	89.5	90.3	89.9	89.6	89.8	89.6	90.5
1966	90.9	90.9	91.6	91.5	91.6	91.5	91.4	91.1	91.2	91.6	90.1	90.0
1967	89.8	88.4	87.5	87.7	86.6	86.1	85.3	86.5	86.1	86.4	87.6	88.1
1968	87.5	87.5	87.2	87.0	87.7	87.5	86.8	86.9	86.6	86.8	87.6	87.3
1969	87.4	87.8	88.2	87.5	86.8	87.0	87.3	87.1	86.6	86.4	85.2	84.4
1970	82.3	82.1	81.6	81.1	80.7	80.2	80.2	79.4	78.5	76.5	75.8	77.5
1971	78.0	77.8	77.5	77.7	78.0	78.0	78.0	76.8	78.2	79.2	79.3	79.8
1972	81.5	81.8	82.3	83.4	83.0	83.1	82.9	83.7	84.3	85.4	86.3	87.0
1973	87.0	87.9	87.9	87.9	87.9	88.3	88.5	88.4	88.6	88.9	88.8	86.9
1974	85.7	85.1	85.1	84.6	85.3	85.4	84.7	84.4	84.3	83.3	80.7	76.6
1975	74.2	72.5	70.8	71.4	71.1	72.0	72.6	73.6	74.4	74.8	75.2	75.8
1976	76.4	78.0	77.5	77.5	78.4	78.1	78.6	78.8	78.8	79.0	79.9	80.5
1977	80.9	81.1	81.8	82.5	83.3	83.4	83.3	83.6	83.6	83.3	83.3	83.6
1978	82.9	82.8	83.1	84.9	84.8	85.4	85.4	85.6	85.9	86.1	87.3	86.9
1979	86.5	86.9	86.9	85.2	86.4	86.0	85.4	84.5	84.4	84.7	84.1	83.9
1980	84.0	84.0	83.5	81.3	78.9	77.4	76.9	77.9	78.7	79.4	80.5	80.5
1981	79.8	80.0	79.9	79.6	79.8	79.5	79.9	79.1	78.5	77.4	76.4	75.1
1982	73.7	75.6	74.9	74.0	73.7	73.5	72.9	72.3	71.7	70.9	70.5	70.0
1983	71.4	71.5	72.4	73.0	73.8	74.2	75.2	76.0	77.5	77.9	78.1	78.0
1984	79.6	79.9	80.3	80.4	80.6	80.9	81.0	80.9	80.7	80.5	80.3	79.7
1985	79.5	79.7	80.0	80.0	80.3	79.6	79.2	79.5	79.5	78.6	79.4	79.2
1986	80.0	79.4	78.5	79.0	78.8	78.4	78.7	78.9	78.9	79.3	79.5	80.0
1987	79.3	80.5	80.7	80.9	81.3	81.9	82.1	81.9	81.9	82.6	82.8	83.1
1988	83.2	83.1	83.2	83.6	83.4	83.3	83.6	83.8	83.7	83.7	84.3	84.6
1989	85.2	84.2	84.6	84.6	84.0	83.7	82.5	82.7	82.2	81.7	81.8	81.8
1990	81.6	82.2	82.4	81.5	81.8	81.7	81.3	81.6	81.4	80.8	79.7	79.2
1991	78.4	77.6	76.6	76.9	77.3	78.0	78.2	78.2	78.9	78.7	78.4	78.2
1992	77.9	78.5	78.9	79.0	79.3	79.0	79.5	79.4	79.3	79.6	80.3	80.4
1993	80.7	80.9	80.8	80.8	80.5	80.5	80.7	80.6	80.8	80.7	81.4	82.2
1994	81.8	82.2	82.9	83.0	83.2	83.2	83.3	83.8	83.6	83.8	84.4	85.2
1995	85.2	84.7	84.4	83.5	83.1	82.8	82.3	-	-	-	-	-

Source: Board of Governors of the Federal Reserve System. - indicates data not available or zero.

INDICATORS OF CONSUMPTION, TRADE, ORDERS, AND DELIVERIES

Consumption, trade, orders, and deliveries are indicators of the economy's general performance. They tend, on the whole, to be leading indicators. Included are two series:

    Manufacturers' new orders, durable goods
    Sales of retail stores

Related series, reported under Business Cycle Indicators, are:

    Manufacturers' new orders, consumer goods and materials (Leading Index)
    Vendor performance (Leading Index)
    Consumer expectations (Leading Index)
    Change in manufacturers unfilled orders, durables (Leading Index)
    Manufacturing and trade sales (Coincident Index)

Manufacturers' New Orders, Durable Goods. Orders are reported in billions of constant 1987 dollars from 1947 to 1995. New orders for consumer goods and materials are part of the leading index. This series is also considered to be a leading indicator overall but is not part of the composite index of leading indicators—most likely because orders for durable goods are less predictive than those for consumer goods and materials.

Sales of Retail Stores. The series shows data from 1948 to 1995 in millions of constant 1987 dollars. Retail sales are classified as leading indicators of the trough of business cycles but produce uncertain results at the peak of cycles. In other words, retail sales tend to grow somewhat earlier than the economy as a whole.

Manufacturers' New Orders

Durable goods industries

(Billions of 1987 $)

Year	Jan	Feb	Mar	Apr	May	Jun	Jul	Aug	Sep	Oct	Nov	Dec
1947	-	-	-	29.76	31.04	29.56	29.57	30.47	33.46	34.05	35.69	37.23
1948	35.62	35.62	36.98	37.28	37.38	40.44	40.08	39.12	36.57	36.24	34.36	33.38
1949	30.87	30.62	28.84	26.77	26.28	25.21	26.11	30.32	30.75	30.25	31.77	31.10
1950	33.60	33.69	34.60	36.60	40.10	40.44	49.18	59.86	49.02	49.26	44.37	46.93
1951	60.35	54.77	56.69	53.37	51.12	49.68	48.65	44.38	41.82	46.41	44.72	43.30
1952	42.83	42.84	49.42	49.92	41.88	50.14	46.26	45.01	48.64	45.72	46.09	49.72
1953	55.51	54.38	50.85	51.99	51.38	49.55	45.98	40.72	36.43	37.49	37.31	37.39
1954	37.50	38.68	36.49	38.00	36.45	38.32	39.11	38.92	43.52	47.07	41.34	46.57
1955	49.80	51.25	55.06	52.02	52.81	54.02	53.91	53.74	55.60	55.21	54.99	57.38
1956	54.74	50.50	51.62	53.48	51.46	50.94	50.08	59.78	49.33	49.16	52.10	51.95
1957	49.91	51.31	49.51	46.12	47.50	46.35	43.62	45.57	44.29	42.09	43.94	40.44
1958	43.29	40.22	42.24	39.59	41.40	44.81	43.72	45.94	44.27	47.12	50.95	48.43
1959	51.47	53.69	54.89	55.31	52.81	55.28	51.06	48.65	49.97	50.92	48.06	52.52
1960	50.35	50.18	49.62	49.09	49.85	50.80	49.07	52.06	52.03	48.05	48.30	48.93
1961	46.20	47.35	47.46	50.28	50.73	51.90	51.24	54.09	53.25	53.87	55.71	57.50
1962	57.28	57.61	55.92	55.17	55.40	55.07	55.84	55.50	58.02	59.17	57.68	60.61
1963	60.37	61.04	62.12	61.58	62.30	59.69	61.69	59.80	61.47	62.36	61.23	60.08
1964	66.77	64.34	63.90	66.24	66.25	66.72	69.81	64.16	67.96	66.72	66.33	69.89
1965	72.31	71.40	73.16	74.17	71.94	72.96	75.06	75.73	73.57	77.36	77.93	79.71
1966	81.88	81.53	84.79	82.90	81.39	83.55	81.32	79.23	85.13	82.44	79.43	78.95
1967	77.16	76.70	75.55	76.10	80.15	81.31	78.23	79.64	77.97	79.43	80.04	87.21
1968	81.18	82.35	85.77	82.10	80.32	81.15	80.52	80.10	84.51	88.01	84.53	83.67
1969	85.52	87.32	85.50	90.07	84.77	83.33	83.49	85.10	87.90	85.19	82.83	81.46
1970	78.25	77.75	75.46	73.64	75.56	76.57	75.69	75.01	75.11	68.64	69.75	77.55
1971	79.73	80.79	78.79	76.41	75.09	77.06	75.53	79.16	79.32	77.65	79.82	81.40
1972	82.90	84.44	84.60	85.27	86.87	87.09	85.10	89.31	94.16	92.52	94.05	98.01
1973	100.28	102.47	104.06	102.06	102.29	102.43	103.04	102.82	101.13	104.68	106.71	100.27
1974	103.93	103.14	100.26	100.02	102.38	100.12	100.80	102.84	95.60	88.95	86.84	79.21
1975	78.06	76.42	71.81	75.82	74.52	74.53	81.37	81.65	80.87	79.07	79.29	79.42
1976	82.40	86.07	89.15	88.60	88.44	89.35	91.67	90.53	90.29	89.85	92.15	96.71
1977	94.03	94.57	99.17	97.90	97.91	101.03	99.27	99.85	101.39	103.02	101.75	105.15
1978	98.10	101.21	105.50	108.39	108.58	109.20	106.64	109.21	111.23	114.83	113.60	111.94
1979	111.24	113.77	117.64	108.30	109.84	109.80	106.74	103.74	106.24	104.13	101.54	101.86
1980	104.87	104.23	100.45	93.69	85.80	87.97	94.47	92.19	100.07	102.01	98.32	101.43
1981	96.80	96.55	98.62	100.30	99.77	99.20	98.73	95.79	94.35	89.80	87.79	84.32
1982	88.13	88.08	90.93	88.60	85.23	84.90	85.91	81.86	84.01	82.74	79.94	85.88
1983	89.88	83.52	86.83	89.55	89.06	95.00	93.93	94.16	98.35	103.27	102.90	103.27
1984	105.31	106.35	110.71	102.19	105.03	101.60	105.75	104.59	100.92	101.77	106.27	103.11
1985	108.41	103.36	103.00	101.40	103.74	107.53	104.95	107.30	107.77	105.94	101.83	107.23
1986	110.90	107.57	106.77	104.26	102.49	103.61	105.37	101.77	107.17	104.41	104.10	108.42
1987	103.86	107.15	109.73	110.91	111.10	112.39	114.46	108.74	110.63	112.79	112.36	113.82
1988	115.12	115.19	114.28	114.00	114.61	117.11	115.67	117.08	116.18	117.32	115.38	126.95
1989	123.29	117.82	118.12	118.66	112.03	114.48	112.04	111.76	113.04	109.77	116.49	119.56
1990	109.92	111.70	119.34	111.94	115.12	112.71	114.22	112.23	111.47	114.81	102.92	107.68
1991	104.95	104.72	99.08	102.67	104.69	101.25	114.51	109.26	104.99	107.75	108.06	102.11
1992	105.59	104.94	107.86	108.95	106.47	109.22	105.68	105.64	105.98	110.32	107.98	117.64
1993	114.64	117.19	112.96	112.61	109.77	114.60	111.08	113.68	114.81	117.77	120.00	122.20
1994	126.86	124.58	125.35	125.61	126.94	128.04	122.78	130.42	130.73	129.43	133.21	135.37
1995	136.29	134.99	134.63	128.34	131.39	130.93	128.53	-	-	-	-	-

Source: U.S. Department of Commerce, Bureau of Economic Analysis. - indicates data not available or zero.

127

Sales of Retail Stores
(Million 1987 $)

Year	Jan	Feb	Mar	Apr	May	Jun	Jul	Aug	Sep	Oct	Nov	Dec
1948	37,985	37,879	38,518	38,785	37,312	38,034	38,179	38,288	37,946	38,168	38,129	39,113
1949	37,788	38,398	38,963	39,406	39,223	41,521	38,715	39,264	39,971	39,759	40,134	39,632
1950	40,660	41,504	41,862	41,849	42,290	43,643	46,661	46,535	43,973	42,226	40,785	43,154
1951	45,685	44,438	41,648	40,828	41,166	41,060	40,561	41,472	41,214	41,691	41,491	40,629
1952	41,105	42,019	40,897	41,907	43,494	44,056	42,822	41,821	42,513	44,466	44,022	45,213
1953	45,536	45,502	45,851	45,215	45,000	44,933	44,755	44,474	44,440	44,662	44,111	43,679
1954	43,656	44,750	44,637	44,597	44,539	45,597	44,856	44,976	45,435	45,517	46,564	47,421
1955	47,669	48,091	48,444	49,310	49,443	49,123	50,026	50,013	50,794	50,917	50,771	50,320
1956	50,320	49,974	50,869	50,273	50,857	50,704	50,185	50,503	50,641	50,437	50,984	51,142
1957	51,452	52,119	51,549	51,557	51,626	52,342	52,100	52,382	52,053	51,928	51,499	51,223
1958	50,919	49,633	49,102	49,538	49,584	49,821	50,586	50,977	50,514	50,331	51,223	52,757
1959	53,444	53,673	54,121	53,991	54,414	54,580	54,726	54,910	54,192	54,425	53,310	53,063
1960	54,330	54,368	54,636	55,567	55,066	54,826	54,438	54,461	54,574	54,889	54,105	53,710
1961	53,751	53,560	54,126	53,327	53,967	54,368	54,003	54,761	54,531	55,679	56,071	56,092
1962	56,574	56,412	57,192	57,333	57,723	56,982	58,228	58,417	58,076	58,988	59,471	59,459
1963	59,534	59,259	59,557	59,640	59,437	59,531	60,047	59,971	59,997	60,687	60,177	61,322
1964	60,827	60,756	61,372	61,879	62,715	62,764	63,075	63,963	64,379	62,429	62,832	65,189
1965	65,668	66,083	65,427	65,789	66,618	66,219	67,299	67,706	67,692	69,439	70,276	70,127
1966	70,592	70,403	71,433	70,263	69,056	70,453	70,749	71,153	71,100	70,599	70,430	69,928
1967	66,545	65,873	66,354	66,522	66,038	67,646	67,177	66,829	68,541	67,315	68,528	70,496
1968	68,856	69,484	70,971	70,622	70,700	71,858	72,380	73,138	71,210	72,829	74,438	73,369
1969	73,779	74,125	73,155	73,203	73,904	73,068	72,927	73,596	74,422	75,050	74,615	74,928
1970	74,973	74,953	74,252	74,766	75,650	76,131	76,583	76,373	76,241	76,501	74,629	76,450
1971	77,910	78,520	78,259	79,526	78,874	79,793	80,224	80,297	81,872	82,668	83,433	82,995
1972	82,554	83,051	85,000	85,406	85,938	86,499	86,565	87,191	88,235	89,479	89,878	91,703
1973	92,652	93,168	93,053	91,567	91,171	91,415	91,247	90,165	91,376	91,113	90,698	87,436
1974	87,457	86,922	87,128	87,600	87,742	87,446	88,172	89,820	86,522	85,074	84,006	82,268
1975	85,132	86,055	83,650	84,654	88,090	87,363	87,941	88,264	88,281	88,555	88,458	89,218
1976	91,443	90,799	91,244	92,876	91,809	93,390	93,605	92,784	92,167	92,925	93,312	95,649
1977	94,656	96,036	96,353	97,368	96,468	96,666	97,302	97,061	97,330	98,789	98,938	98,919
1978	96,661	98,477	100,433	102,143	101,851	102,823	101,541	102,262	102,276	103,321	104,129	104,888
1979	103,634	103,451	104,479	103,059	103,105	102,541	101,257	104,287	104,602	103,152	103,829	103,159
1980	104,102	102,166	99,341	97,276	96,720	97,558	98,975	98,970	98,317	100,118	100,206	99,605
1981	101,344	101,571	101,589	100,345	99,260	99,822	100,020	101,256	100,261	98,681	98,077	98,274
1982	96,663	99,217	98,314	98,880	99,518	97,057	98,340	97,967	99,192	100,124	101,677	101,582
1983	101,240	101,520	103,994	103,709	104,986	107,173	107,450	105,392	107,288	108,716	110,013	110,348
1984	112,489	112,116	110,972	112,792	113,528	115,030	113,102	112,118	113,350	113,659	115,707	115,098
1985	115,603	116,355	116,462	117,723	118,583	117,800	117,884	119,451	122,818	118,765	118,971	119,844
1986	120,759	120,369	120,896	122,556	123,948	123,693	124,244	125,385	132,340	126,933	126,083	131,236
1987	121,639	127,053	127,527	128,053	127,773	128,891	129,482	131,506	129,387	128,563	128,795	130,273
1988	130,456	131,466	133,336	132,085	132,872	133,121	132,852	133,357	132,156	134,552	135,544	135,994
1989	136,470	134,134	134,648	135,884	136,281	136,069	136,495	139,018	138,624	136,458	137,398	137,499
1990	139,995	138,382	138,379	137,868	137,069	138,071	138,174	137,974	137,300	136,154	136,417	133,819
1991	131,264	133,562	135,269	134,687	135,392	135,494	135,432	134,691	135,242	133,871	133,771	133,915
1992	137,011	137,543	136,474	136,462	137,338	137,329	137,836	138,479	139,561	141,743	141,595	142,736
1993	144,009	142,481	141,056	143,675	144,601	145,272	146,436	146,899	147,160	148,986	149,970	151,631
1994	149,918	152,702	154,263	153,878	153,269	154,561	153,885	156,031	156,971	159,047	159,568	159,661
1995	160,016	158,700	159,499	158,997	160,582	162,057	162,009	-	-	-	-	-

Source: U.S. Department of Commerce, Bureau of Economic Analysis, U.S. Department of Commerce, Bureau of the Census. - indicates data not available or zero.

INDICATORS OF FIXED CAPITAL INVESTMENT

Indicators of fixed capital investment cover business formations as well as expenditures on tooling and equipment and on buildings and housing. In the context of business cycles, the series reflect relative confidence in the future and hence tend to be leading indicators. Five series are presented:

> New business incorporations
> Contracts and orders for plant and equipment, current dollars
> Manufacturers' new orders, capital goods, nondefense
> Fixed investment in producers durable equipment
> New private housing units started

Related series, reported under Business Cycle Indicators, are:

> Contracts and orders for plant and equipment, Constant Dollars (Leading Index)
> Index of new private housing units (Leading Index)

New Business Incorporations. Data show total incorporations from 1947 to 1995. New businesses are formed when entrepreneurs anticipate a strong economy and can obtain financing. The series, therefore, is classified as a leading indicator—although not included in the composite index of leading indicators.

Contracts and Orders for Plant and Equipment, Current Dollars. Data are shown in billions of current dollars from 1947 to 1995. The same series, in constant 1987 dollars, is included as one of the components of the composite index of leading indicators. The series shows commitments to spend money on capital goods in the future—because payment will be made at a later date. The series, therefore, tends to predict future economic activity.

Manufacturers' New Orders, Capital Goods, Nondefense. Data are reported in billions of constant 1987 dollars. The defense category is excluded because government procurement is less responsive to short-term changes in the economy than is private sector procurement; defense procurement, also, tends to be staged over multiples of budget cycles; for these reasons, inclusion of defense would make the series less predictive of economic activity in the future. The series is classified as a leading indicator but is not part of the composite index.

Fixed Investment in Producers Durable Equipment. This table replaces a table on "New Plant and Equipment Expenditures by Business" which is no longer available. These data are in billions of 1987 constant dollars and are available from 1946 through 1995 by quarter. Quarterly data are annualized. The series is coincident at the peak of business cycles, lags in the trough, and lags overall. Spending grows as the economy reaches for a peak; as the economy begins to move out of a slump, however, businesses tend to hold back on new expenditures on capital goods out of caution; therefore the indicator lags in a trough.

New Private Housing Units Started. Data are in thousands of units, by month, for 1946 through 1995. The composite index of leading indicators measures building permits issued—the first step in a cycle of construction. This series measures actual starts. Both series are leading indicators. Since the construction sector tends to be the first to slump and the first to revive, "housing starts" is a closely watched indicator series.

Number of New Business Incorporations
(Number)

Year	Jan	Feb	Mar	Apr	May	Jun	Jul	Aug	Sep	Oct	Nov	Dec
1947	9,922	9,800	9,743	9,057	8,699	8,748	9,308	9,244	9,316	9,806	9,453	9,690
1948	9,380	8,329	8,349	8,396	8,064	8,210	8,168	7,439	7,483	7,349	7,241	7,054
1949	7,012	6,826	6,791	6,879	7,006	6,879	7,057	7,330	7,403	7,532	7,659	7,788
1950	7,830	8,275	8,078	8,132	8,403	8,394	7,898	7,684	7,092	7,176	7,059	7,007
1951	7,214	7,016	6,937	7,082	6,848	6,759	6,796	6,880	6,952	6,995	7,119	7,181
1952	7,080	7,214	7,348	7,499	7,441	7,700	7,683	8,065	8,259	8,341	8,265	8,096
1953	8,304	8,351	8,634	8,534	8,785	8,605	8,757	8,515	8,185	8,698	8,556	8,696
1954	8,638	8,937	9,155	9,276	9,158	9,436	9,772	9,882	10,085	10,730	11,212	11,604
1955	11,902	11,843	11,679	11,215	11,521	12,072	11,655	11,572	11,968	11,668	11,761	11,560
1956	11,620	12,449	11,591	11,888	12,245	11,999	11,851	11,707	11,193	11,925	11,186	11,139
1957	11,250	11,359	11,367	11,507	11,109	11,739	11,686	11,593	11,318	11,251	10,788	10,791
1958	11,042	11,049	11,042	10,636	11,752	12,032	12,504	13,644	13,933	13,669	14,599	15,577
1959	16,346	16,255	16,548	16,604	16,296	15,204	15,658	15,813	15,728	15,383	15,695	15,959
1960	16,561	15,274	15,233	15,280	15,176	15,630	15,828	15,114	15,112	15,035	14,264	14,097
1961	13,607	14,570	14,658	15,327	15,298	15,431	15,492	15,277	15,402	16,035	16,149	15,881
1962	15,599	15,758	15,670	15,372	15,245	14,947	15,171	15,056	15,249	14,892	14,951	14,985
1963	14,924	15,390	15,563	15,305	15,682	15,536	15,431	16,093	15,689	16,275	15,759	15,867
1964	15,993	16,326	15,917	16,132	16,473	16,282	16,550	15,692	16,948	16,728	16,804	17,021
1965	16,784	16,854	17,131	16,664	16,580	17,017	16,844	16,901	17,136	16,994	17,606	17,625
1966	18,087	17,451	17,266	17,057	16,644	16,577	16,074	16,343	15,764	16,233	16,206	16,583
1967	16,703	15,987	16,244	16,760	17,627	17,799	16,300	17,674	17,818	17,654	17,958	18,238
1968	18,061	18,041	18,538	18,663	18,723	18,839	19,407	19,947	20,582	21,093	20,890	20,619
1969	21,364	22,105	22,083	23,262	23,118	23,439	23,366	22,871	22,594	24,263	23,125	22,404
1970	22,196	22,968	21,346	21,829	21,874	21,796	21,614	21,796	22,181	21,712	22,217	22,272
1971	22,563	21,034	22,883	22,814	23,960	24,481	24,677	25,012	23,623	25,356	25,510	25,634
1972	25,270	25,084	26,231	26,630	26,270	26,175	26,789	26,365	27,168	27,529	26,234	27,699
1973	27,796	28,752	28,964	28,522	28,286	27,999	27,477	26,689	26,240	26,809	26,718	24,881
1974	26,511	27,056	26,458	29,071	27,562	25,785	27,790	26,495	26,313	25,404	25,555	25,003
1975	24,809	24,931	25,076	26,708	26,632	26,307	28,655	27,810	28,359	29,079	28,634	29,282
1976	29,613	29,772	31,000	30,808	28,784	31,420	31,037	31,301	31,921	32,160	33,183	33,124
1977	34,311	33,844	35,018	34,529	35,256	36,694	36,874	38,180	37,271	38,213	38,308	38,900
1978	36,414	39,434	37,847	39,585	39,059	39,860	40,152	41,007	41,553	41,437	41,423	42,179
1979	42,043	42,014	43,299	43,401	44,317	43,504	44,513	43,634	44,173	45,295	44,540	43,563
1980	44,230	44,175	43,359	42,240	42,710	40,648	43,621	44,255	45,746	45,945	46,750	47,840
1981	46,039	48,588	47,972	49,413	48,866	49,172	49,038	48,631	48,450	47,947	49,413	47,556
1982	43,330	47,234	46,899	46,876	46,995	45,936	44,525	46,981	45,552	45,530	48,474	57,507
1983	49,999	48,296	48,032	48,903	50,211	50,992	48,601	52,828	50,445	50,441	51,642	51,557
1984	52,674	53,535	53,075	53,298	50,736	53,884	53,211	52,025	52,646	52,587	53,838	53,558
1985	53,674	53,479	55,335	55,133	55,545	55,339	54,507	56,159	56,662	58,307	57,308	58,074
1986	57,636	59,114	58,870	59,156	57,747	57,446	57,717	56,299	57,942	57,120	56,652	65,691
1987	55,348	58,495	60,248	57,537	56,178	57,612	57,330	57,650	57,568	55,504	56,681	55,226
1988	56,108	56,475	60,655	54,670	58,046	55,620	56,915	59,730	55,915	56,529	54,553	58,592
1989	58,253	58,560	57,383	57,631	57,326	56,950	54,948	55,500	55,390	54,651	55,116	56,945
1990	59,141	56,325	56,172	55,000	53,616	53,784	52,142	52,958	52,176	51,899	51,429	52,060
1991	51,991	50,384	51,536	52,235	52,327	52,071	52,767	53,313	52,284	53,892	54,163	52,923
1992	58,141	55,092	57,449	54,474	48,688	58,730	56,942	51,245	59,179	52,492	55,392	61,695
1993	55,625	59,691	61,002	59,648	51,765	60,422	58,387	58,209	63,758	55,291	61,739	61,873
1994	61,978	60,680	64,119	58,992	58,528	63,097	56,380	64,844	64,564	60,488	64,542	62,908
1995	66,291	64,755	-	-	-	-	-	-	-	-	-	-

Source: Dun & Bradstreet, Inc; seasonal adjustment by Bureau of Economic Analysis. - indicates data not available or zero.

Contracts and Orders for Plant and Equipment
(Billions of $)

Year	Jan	Feb	Mar	Apr	May	Jun	Jul	Aug	Sep	Oct	Nov	Dec
1948	1.50	1.72	1.66	1.84	1.59	1.84	1.68	1.60	1.59	1.62	1.60	1.59
1949	1.31	1.42	1.41	1.21	1.25	1.37	1.26	1.36	1.49	1.43	1.61	1.46
1950	1.60	1.60	1.74	1.74	2.16	2.09	2.53	3.20	3.01	2.71	2.72	3.00
1951	3.43	3.51	3.19	3.21	4.36	2.98	2.84	2.73	2.36	2.63	2.63	2.83
1952	2.51	2.55	2.59	2.56	2.39	2.69	2.76	2.48	3.34	2.50	2.36	2.83
1953	2.84	2.88	2.64	2.88	2.76	2.16	2.66	2.23	2.57	2.72	2.34	2.14
1954	2.20	2.24	1.91	1.96	2.00	2.05	2.15	2.15	2.31	2.43	2.25	2.40
1955	2.50	2.72	3.15	2.93	2.80	2.99	2.97	3.15	3.33	3.20	3.45	3.45
1956	3.35	3.26	3.28	3.40	3.56	3.60	3.43	3.41	3.33	3.34	3.79	3.58
1957	3.65	3.55	3.52	3.15	3.29	3.13	3.06	3.13	2.83	2.89	2.89	2.74
1958	2.77	2.67	2.66	2.69	2.72	2.85	2.75	3.13	3.14	3.04	3.00	2.91
1959	3.09	3.19	3.73	3.35	3.46	3.54	3.61	3.22	3.63	3.50	3.30	3.49
1960	3.27	3.35	3.27	3.52	3.51	3.41	3.41	3.41	3.44	3.34	3.20	3.49
1961	3.48	3.40	3.25	3.27	3.22	3.41	3.49	3.67	3.43	3.51	3.72	3.43
1962	3.62	3.94	3.65	3.85	3.68	3.61	3.65	3.66	3.64	3.73	4.00	4.08
1963	3.80	3.91	3.88	3.98	4.36	3.99	3.96	4.07	4.20	4.28	4.50	4.56
1964	4.70	4.24	4.43	4.46	4.82	4.95	4.64	4.69	4.75	4.79	5.10	5.17
1965	4.89	4.93	5.22	5.25	5.18	5.10	5.27	5.08	5.49	5.51	5.45	5.82
1966	5.81	6.28	6.14	6.41	6.34	6.21	6.64	6.22	6.79	6.20	6.14	6.14
1967	5.30	5.69	5.81	5.70	5.88	6.11	6.05	6.26	6.09	6.19	6.22	6.40
1968	7.74	7.48	9.02	7.35	6.43	6.47	7.85	8.14	6.99	8.66	7.19	7.84
1969	8.99	9.00	7.96	9.24	8.51	8.05	8.24	8.36	9.24	8.24	8.06	8.01
1970	9.08	8.40	7.57	7.35	7.20	7.04	7.53	7.36	7.16	6.45	7.30	8.01
1971	7.80	8.41	8.28	8.19	7.77	8.88	7.24	8.46	8.56	7.66	8.25	8.46
1972	8.09	8.43	9.06	8.88	9.72	8.43	9.68	9.15	10.19	9.78	9.97	10.17
1973	10.35	11.06	11.00	11.14	11.53	11.69	12.06	12.53	11.96	13.29	13.28	12.58
1974	12.82	13.19	13.39	12.95	13.88	12.92	15.66	14.45	14.49	14.00	12.39	13.71
1975	12.42	11.57	10.89	12.82	12.91	12.83	12.21	13.74	11.46	11.40	11.26	10.84
1976	13.38	13.14	13.65	13.71	12.09	14.42	15.84	14.08	15.37	15.80	14.40	15.06
1977	14.98	15.12	14.57	15.87	17.44	17.41	15.55	17.50	18.96	16.75	16.73	19.10
1978	18.53	20.73	18.87	18.79	21.19	19.61	21.16	22.26	23.00	26.76	22.60	20.30
1979	23.78	25.42	27.94	25.41	22.73	23.97	24.62	23.31	24.15	25.20	25.15	24.95
1980	26.66	23.94	24.37	23.95	20.92	22.87	24.64	24.14	24.30	25.54	24.03	25.70
1981	27.48	24.30	26.67	28.22	25.74	26.39	26.43	25.67	24.82	25.74	24.42	23.04
1982	26.34	27.87	25.48	24.24	21.56	21.46	22.42	21.32	22.26	22.89	21.46	22.75
1983	21.94	21.06	21.46	22.90	23.84	24.01	22.32	24.12	25.45	26.79	24.75	23.87
1984	27.28	27.37	27.87	26.82	30.36	28.24	29.40	27.69	27.22	28.39	28.09	27.03
1985	27.49	30.78	30.11	27.57	28.06	29.35	28.95	29.09	31.14	31.14	27.64	31.29
1986	28.73	30.53	28.64	27.87	27.43	28.18	27.68	27.32	28.50	29.18	28.75	30.46
1987	29.18	28.95	28.60	29.88	30.93	32.41	33.52	30.65	30.55	32.07	31.70	34.47
1988	35.51	36.06	33.27	34.66	32.06	35.34	36.56	39.74	36.16	34.66	35.52	39.08
1989	40.49	37.40	37.21	39.11	36.39	39.02	40.63	35.13	35.69	35.21	37.34	43.94
1990	38.60	35.39	39.70	35.78	35.86	35.37	38.65	33.81	36.42	40.16	34.40	40.40
1991	36.05	36.07	34.39	31.88	30.63	29.78	39.01	32.95	31.75	32.68	36.08	30.26
1992	33.49	33.48	35.72	35.52	33.74	34.01	33.07	31.81	33.82	34.44	31.27	37.24
1993	33.18	36.24	33.74	34.69	33.77	38.61	34.67	36.26	35.32	37.35	39.59	39.36
1994	41.64	41.33	41.06	39.85	40.28	42.77	41.07	42.21	43.80	42.08	45.30	41.83
1995	46.85	47.03	47.40	44.42	48.32	47.85	44.85	-	-	-	-	-

Source: U.S. Department of Commerce, Bureau of Economic Analysis, U.S. Department of Commerce, Bureau of the Census, McGraw-Hill Information Systems Company. - indicates data not available or zero.

Manufacturers' New Orders
Nondefense capital goods
(Billions of 1987 $)

Year	Jan	Feb	Mar	Apr	May	Jun	Jul	Aug	Sep	Oct	Nov	Dec
1948	6.75	7.56	7.59	8.43	6.82	8.08	7.03	6.77	6.76	6.74	6.78	6.87
1949	5.42	5.88	5.80	4.88	5.19	5.47	5.10	5.47	6.13	5.80	6.10	5.87
1950	6.44	6.94	6.93	7.20	9.08	8.70	10.54	13.02	12.05	10.75	10.51	11.46
1951	12.88	12.99	12.24	12.04	11.44	10.68	10.25	9.83	8.81	10.01	9.92	9.86
1952	9.10	9.39	9.56	9.25	8.47	9.31	9.87	8.65	9.20	9.18	8.24	9.16
1953	10.75	10.14	9.53	9.95	9.43	7.70	8.46	7.43	7.59	7.24	7.16	7.06
1954	7.16	7.48	6.25	6.60	6.46	6.61	7.03	7.00	7.81	7.78	7.34	7.82
1955	8.36	9.14	10.39	9.11	9.14	9.72	9.51	10.04	9.80	10.04	10.47	10.79
1956	10.20	9.48	9.96	10.34	10.85	10.92	10.02	10.18	10.02	10.09	11.13	10.60
1957	10.16	10.11	9.62	8.86	8.91	8.55	8.50	8.57	8.05	7.82	7.70	7.15
1958	7.54	7.14	7.31	7.40	7.45	7.49	7.55	8.10	8.46	8.18	8.48	8.08
1959	8.58	8.82	9.98	9.07	9.46	9.66	9.71	8.94	9.73	9.39	8.78	9.48
1960	8.74	9.03	8.89	9.24	9.25	9.20	8.89	8.91	8.81	8.63	8.36	9.18
1961	8.77	8.81	8.81	8.76	8.53	9.01	9.43	9.89	9.34	9.43	9.75	9.25
1962	9.82	10.49	9.34	10.22	9.65	9.52	9.59	9.58	9.81	9.94	10.70	10.09
1963	10.27	10.56	10.74	10.76	11.19	10.63	10.73	11.09	11.26	11.29	10.99	11.47
1964	12.56	11.19	11.99	11.78	13.06	13.43	12.36	12.48	12.42	12.72	12.84	13.14
1965	13.04	12.81	13.87	13.68	13.30	13.73	13.99	13.60	14.08	14.49	14.75	15.76
1966	14.92	16.26	15.97	16.39	16.44	16.19	16.94	15.76	16.50	16.11	15.40	15.48
1967	13.17	13.90	14.01	14.15	14.42	14.85	15.12	15.42	14.68	14.78	14.96	15.70
1968	19.53	18.46	22.59	19.13	14.79	14.74	18.62	18.21	15.83	19.91	16.75	17.95
1969	19.31	21.52	18.82	22.91	19.00	18.66	18.91	19.61	21.56	18.34	18.84	16.94
1970	19.15	17.89	15.81	15.02	15.84	14.95	16.25	15.82	15.59	14.90	15.82	17.36
1971	16.79	18.06	17.66	17.17	16.43	19.17	15.20	17.28	18.64	16.55	17.41	18.18
1972	16.77	18.08	18.60	18.06	20.25	17.22	20.30	19.70	21.44	20.61	21.14	21.72
1973	21.62	23.23	23.70	24.74	24.07	23.25	24.68	25.00	24.64	26.88	26.83	26.20
1974	26.78	27.18	27.90	27.23	25.21	24.66	28.83	26.52	24.97	21.87	20.82	20.66
1975	20.71	18.55	16.67	18.79	17.09	16.72	18.83	18.40	17.51	17.83	17.63	16.77
1976	17.70	18.10	18.36	19.37	18.92	18.85	21.93	19.93	20.60	21.33	19.16	21.05
1977	20.67	20.18	20.40	21.24	21.10	23.46	21.43	21.09	23.61	23.29	22.52	24.00
1978	23.60	24.74	23.98	25.24	25.50	25.35	25.26	26.74	28.38	31.15	28.53	25.11
1979	28.40	31.68	31.95	28.46	29.16	29.22	28.73	29.05	29.60	29.94	27.70	28.92
1980	30.76	27.70	27.98	28.48	23.24	23.79	25.39	24.06	25.26	26.19	23.32	25.21
1981	27.90	22.91	26.15	27.01	24.24	24.18	24.83	24.02	22.50	22.75	21.36	18.88
1982	22.57	21.47	22.09	20.89	18.28	18.64	19.47	17.62	18.51	19.77	17.92	17.57
1983	19.36	16.05	17.17	18.63	18.58	19.75	18.22	19.52	20.92	22.58	20.20	19.93
1984	23.08	22.94	23.26	22.38	24.86	23.37	24.17	22.77	22.40	23.15	22.60	22.03
1985	22.70	25.08	24.40	22.44	22.42	24.26	23.27	23.95	25.50	25.18	22.45	26.45
1986	24.11	25.06	24.12	22.90	22.72	23.18	22.82	22.50	23.52	24.48	23.70	25.06
1987	24.43	24.08	23.37	24.92	26.62	26.74	28.43	25.63	25.57	26.81	27.00	29.26
1988	31.02	30.25	28.22	29.26	27.12	29.84	31.24	33.68	30.58	29.34	30.19	33.14
1989	33.49	31.21	31.08	32.46	30.29	32.51	33.93	28.79	28.34	28.17	30.92	35.81
1990	31.46	29.18	33.18	29.83	28.89	28.96	32.44	28.25	30.95	33.18	27.41	34.33
1991	30.46	30.01	28.64	25.97	25.54	25.82	32.96	27.73	26.99	27.82	31.01	25.74
1992	28.69	28.18	30.78	29.13	29.37	30.12	29.00	28.07	30.15	30.19	27.96	32.74
1993	29.70	33.57	30.68	31.67	31.63	34.68	32.10	33.87	33.09	35.28	37.99	37.60
1994	38.43	38.50	39.27	38.98	38.58	40.85	39.64	40.70	42.63	42.59	43.94	41.31
1995	44.71	45.76	46.91	44.09	46.89	48.14	45.04	-	-	-	-	-

Source: U.S. Department of Commerce, Bureau of Economic Analysis, U.S. Department of Commerce, Bureau of the Census. - indicates data not available or zero.

Fixed Investment in Producers Durable Equipment
(Annual Rate, Billions of 1987 $)

Year	1st Quarter	2nd Quarter	3rd Quarter	4th Quarter
1947	83.90	81.80	79.80	82.40
1948	88.00	83.00	81.20	84.10
1949	78.30	72.20	67.90	66.80
1950	68.00	76.60	84.60	84.10
1951	79.60	81.40	84.50	84.20
1952	84.50	85.10	72.50	79.70
1953	85.60	84.70	87.20	85.40
1954	81.10	79.60	82.10	80.70
1955	81.10	88.80	94.30	98.80
1956	94.20	93.50	95.50	93.80
1957	95.00	94.00	97.30	93.80
1958	84.50	80.60	79.00	82.70
1959	87.10	89.80	92.80	93.20
1960	94.70	96.10	91.40	87.80
1961	85.50	88.90	89.80	95.20
1962	97.00	99.90	99.60	98.90
1963	100.40	102.50	107.30	111.30
1964	113.40	115.50	119.60	123.80
1965	132.30	134.50	142.40	147.20
1966	154.40	158.60	158.40	159.00
1967	153.10	155.30	153.20	157.60
1968	162.90	158.30	161.70	168.00
1969	173.00	172.70	174.00	171.90
1970	170.20	169.40	172.20	163.00
1971	163.30	165.00	164.70	169.50
1972	176.00	181.60	186.80	202.60
1973	213.60	223.00	225.40	227.80
1974	228.00	227.80	225.30	215.70
1975	199.50	195.90	198.40	201.40
1976	203.10	205.10	210.00	214.60
1977	229.50	234.60	239.00	249.90
1978	252.50	269.90	273.50	279.30
1979	288.40	283.30	288.50	281.70
1980	284.30	261.40	260.80	264.10
1981	270.20	271.10	276.50	270.30
1982	263.20	254.50	248.90	244.00
1983	240.10	251.50	263.50	287.00
1984	291.60	305.20	312.80	320.10
1985	320.70	326.60	323.30	327.20
1986	321.40	325.00	323.40	325.00
1987	315.70	323.40	333.90	332.70
1988	346.10	356.90	361.00	363.10
1989	362.40	367.50	363.00	356.90
1990	367.30	363.00	370.30	367.40
1991	352.50	353.00	358.60	355.50
1992	354.30	372.90	382.80	394.60
1993	413.00	433.70	450.30	478.50
1994	499.40	506.90	528.40	552.60
1995	583.70	600.90	-	-

Source: U.S. Department of Commerce, Bureau of the Census. - indicates data not available or zero.

New Private Housing Units Started
(Annual Rate, Thousands)

Year	Jan	Feb	Mar	Apr	May	Jun	Jul	Aug	Sep	Oct	Nov	Dec
1946	1,040	1,085	1,167	1,057	1,028	985	972	1,007	958	974	957	991
1947	1,052	1,074	1,032	1,039	1,090	1,174	1,252	1,355	1,532	1,571	1,557	1,447
1948	1,385	1,200	1,379	1,501	1,450	1,441	1,419	1,329	1,303	1,190	1,196	1,218
1949	1,196	1,137	1,171	1,292	1,319	1,341	1,384	1,500	1,603	1,662	1,785	1,824
1950	1,883	1,834	1,976	1,945	2,052	2,042	2,051	2,121	1,821	1,605	1,561	1,900
1951	1,928	1,638	1,481	1,352	1,359	1,419	1,257	1,334	1,456	1,386	1,324	1,330
1952	1,388	1,516	1,483	1,412	1,408	1,353	1,438	1,443	1,483	1,513	1,475	1,476
1953	1,484	1,460	1,506	1,498	1,425	1,380	1,346	1,324	1,348	1,342	1,383	1,343
1954	1,358	1,417	1,411	1,433	1,412	1,498	1,559	1,563	1,618	1,610	1,730	1,807
1955	1,757	1,664	1,684	1,708	1,730	1,704	1,632	1,625	1,580	1,490	1,434	1,431
1956	1,441	1,444	1,401	1,408	1,375	1,325	1,289	1,313	1,234	1,266	1,212	1,184
1957	1,151	1,168	1,173	1,147	1,174	1,175	1,191	1,193	1,191	1,204	1,162	1,146
1958	1,170	1,107	1,108	1,154	1,191	1,236	1,337	1,374	1,451	1,472	1,593	1,598
1959	1,657	1,667	1,620	1,590	1,498	1,503	1,547	1,430	1,540	1,355	1,416	1,601
1960	1,460	1,503	1,109	1,289	1,271	1,247	1,197	1,344	1,097	1,246	1,246	1,063
1961	1,183	1,226	1,312	1,166	1,228	1,382	1,335	1,312	1,429	1,415	1,385	1,365
1962	1,361	1,278	1,443	1,524	1,483	1,404	1,450	1,517	1,324	1,533	1,622	1,564
1963	1,244	1,456	1,534	1,689	1,641	1,588	1,614	1,639	1,763	1,779	1,622	1,491
1964	1,603	1,820	1,517	1,448	1,467	1,550	1,562	1,569	1,455	1,524	1,486	1,484
1965	1,361	1,433	1,423	1,438	1,478	1,488	1,529	1,432	1,482	1,452	1,460	1,656
1966	1,370	1,378	1,394	1,352	1,265	1,194	1,086	1,119	1,046	843	961	990
1967	1,067	1,123	1,056	1,091	1,304	1,248	1,364	1,407	1,421	1,491	1,538	1,308
1968	1,380	1,520	1,466	1,554	1,408	1,405	1,512	1,495	1,556	1,569	1,630	1,548
1969	1,769	1,705	1,561	1,524	1,583	1,528	1,368	1,358	1,507	1,381	1,229	1,327
1970	1,085	1,305	1,319	1,264	1,290	1,385	1,517	1,399	1,534	1,580	1,647	1,893
1971	1,828	1,741	1,910	1,986	2,049	2,026	2,083	2,158	2,041	2,128	2,182	2,295
1972	2,494	2,390	2,334	2,249	2,221	2,254	2,252	2,382	2,481	2,485	2,421	2,366
1973	2,481	2,289	2,365	2,084	2,266	2,067	2,123	2,051	1,874	1,677	1,724	1,526
1974	1,451	1,752	1,555	1,607	1,426	1,513	1,316	1,142	1,150	1,070	1,026	975
1975	1,032	904	993	1,005	1,121	1,087	1,226	1,260	1,264	1,344	1,360	1,321
1976	1,367	1,538	1,421	1,395	1,459	1,495	1,401	1,550	1,720	1,629	1,641	1,804
1977	1,527	1,943	2,063	1,892	1,971	1,893	2,058	2,020	1,949	2,042	2,042	2,142
1978	1,718	1,738	2,032	2,197	2,075	2,070	2,092	1,996	1,970	1,981	2,094	2,044
1979	1,630	1,520	1,847	1,748	1,876	1,913	1,760	1,778	1,832	1,681	1,524	1,498
1980	1,341	1,350	1,047	1,051	927	1,196	1,269	1,436	1,471	1,523	1,510	1,482
1981	1,547	1,246	1,306	1,360	1,140	1,045	1,041	940	911	873	837	910
1982	843	866	931	917	1,025	902	1,166	1,046	1,144	1,173	1,372	1,303
1983	1,586	1,699	1,606	1,472	1,776	1,733	1,785	1,910	1,710	1,715	1,785	1,688
1984	1,897	2,260	1,663	1,851	1,774	1,843	1,732	1,586	1,698	1,590	1,689	1,612
1985	1,711	1,632	1,800	1,821	1,680	1,676	1,684	1,743	1,676	1,834	1,698	1,942
1986	1,972	1,848	1,876	1,933	1,854	1,847	1,782	1,807	1,687	1,681	1,623	1,833
1987	1,774	1,784	1,726	1,614	1,628	1,594	1,575	1,605	1,695	1,515	1,656	1,400
1988	1,271	1,473	1,532	1,573	1,421	1,478	1,467	1,493	1,492	1,522	1,569	1,563
1989	1,621	1,425	1,422	1,339	1,331	1,397	1,427	1,332	1,279	1,410	1,351	1,251
1990	1,551	1,437	1,289	1,248	1,212	1,177	1,171	1,115	1,110	1,014	1,145	969
1991	798	965	921	1,001	996	1,036	1,063	1,049	1,015	1,079	1,103	1,079
1992	1,176	1,250	1,297	1,099	1,214	1,145	1,139	1,226	1,186	1,244	1,214	1,227
1993	1,213	1,198	1,068	1,232	1,245	1,257	1,253	1,318	1,352	1,417	1,401	1,602
1994	1,266	1,318	1,499	1,463	1,489	1,370	1,440	1,463	1,511	1,451	1,536	1,545
1995	1,366	1,319	1,238	1,269	1,282	1,293	1,380	-	-	-	-	-

Source: U.S. Department of Commerce, Bureau of the Census. - indicates data not available or zero.

INDICATORS OF INVENTORIES AND INVENTORY INVESTMENT

Inventory levels tend to be leading indicators of economic activity. Inventories are built up in anticipation of sales; they stay high when sales do not materialize; are are depleted when the economy is growing rapidly, signaling overheating and the potential for inflation; they are "worked down" in anticipation of recession and built up in expectation of turn-arounds. One series is shown:

    Change in business inventories

One related series, reported under Business Cycle Indicators, is:

    Ratio, manufacturing and trade inventories to sales

Change in Business Inventories. The changes are reported quarterly for the 1947-1995 period in billions of constant 1987 dollars. The series is considered a leading indicator but is excluded from the composite index. See also the same category, stated in chained (1992) dollars as a component of GDP.

Change in Business Inventories

(Annual Rate, Billions of 1987 $)

Year	1st Quarter	2nd Quarter	3rd Quarter	4th Quarter
1947	-0.5	-0.4	-5.2	7.1
1948	9.7	14.2	17.2	13.5
1949	-0.3	-16.5	-4.7	-14.8
1950	10.8	13.9	15.9	49.4
1951	30.5	45.1	30.3	14.3
1952	14.7	-5.9	14.5	14.9
1953	11.6	10.7	5.7	-7.8
1954	-5.2	-9.3	-6.6	-1.4
1955	11.3	16.8	15.7	20.6
1956	16.5	12.9	10.2	8.9
1957	4.9	5.3	7.8	-9.6
1958	-13.3	-11.8	3.1	12.8
1959	15.5	24.4	0.5	13.9
1960	29.6	7.2	11.6	-15.9
1961	-8.5	2.6	18.5	16.3
1962	23.3	14.2	17.5	7.4
1963	21.3	14.9	16.7	11.2
1964	16.9	15.4	13.9	16.4
1965	34.0	23.4	24.6	18.6
1966	36.1	32.1	32.9	45.7
1967	34.3	17.8	31.6	26.8
1968	20.0	36.0	26.5	12.1
1969	28.9	23.7	28.2	18.5
1970	5.1	8.4	14.4	-4.0
1971	31.9	23.8	21.9	5.4
1972	18.4	24.2	33.1	14.4
1973	31.3	38.1	24.8	56.7
1974	31.9	29.8	17.6	44.4
1975	-28.0	-30.6	-2.0	4.9
1976	26.9	33.3	27.2	14.7
1977	24.9	34.3	54.0	23.8
1978	36.0	36.9	35.3	40.6
1979	21.7	29.7	5.0	-2.0
1980	7.1	-3.6	-37.2	0.8
1981	32.6	15.8	35.7	14.1
1982	-24.4	-1.5	0.7	-44.9
1983	-33.5	9.9	12.1	29.3
1984	79.9	71.0	73.0	47.9
1985	14.8	23.7	19.8	30.2
1986	48.1	18.2	-12.0	-20.1
1987	22.5	17.3	5.4	59.9
1988	19.2	16.1	23.5	20.9
1989	41.2	36.9	16.0	24.9
1990	4.7	28.1	10.9	-20.9
1991	-16.4	-11.9	10.4	13.5
1992	-6.3	4.2	5.2	6.6
1993	18.5	18.9	13.0	10.8
1994	25.4	59.2	57.1	49.4
1995	51.1	32.7	-	-

Source: U.S. Department of Commerce, Bureau of Economic Analysis. - indicates data not available or zero.

INDICATORS OF PRICES, COSTS, AND PROFITS

Prices, profits, and certain kinds of costs tend to react rapidly to changes in the economy—or anticipated changes. They tend, therefore, to be leading indicators. Some costs, however, most notably wages, are lagging indicators because institutional factors work against rapid response to changing circumstances. Four series are presented:

> Index of sensitive materials prices
> Index of producer prices, sensitive crude and intermediate materials
> Corporate profits after tax
> Index of unit labor costs, all persons, business

Three related series, reported under Business Cycle Indicators, are:

> Index of stock prices (Leading Index)
> Change in sensitive materials (Leading Index)
> Index of labor cost per unit of output, manufacturing (Lagging Index)
> Change in consumer price index for services (Lagging Index)

Index of Sensitive Materials Prices. The index is based on 1987 (1987 = 100) and is available for 1948 through 1995. "Sensitive materials" are those most vital to a modern economy: metals, fibers, and minerals. Being raw materials (rather than finished components), they are purchased early in the production cycle and therefore can predict future economic behavior. A series showing *changes* in these prices is included in the composite index of leading indicators.

Index of Producer Prices, Sensitive Crude and Intermediate Materials. This index, based on 1982 (1982 = 100), is available from 1947 to 1995. Subcomponents of the index include cattle hides, lumber and wood products, waste paper, ferrous and non-ferrous metal scrap, sand, gravel, and crushed stone, raw cotton, and domestic apparel wool. These openly traded commodities are early indicators of slacking demand (as an economy slows) or of the pick-up of the economy's pace (in a turn-around). The series is considered to be a leading indicator but is not part of the composite index of leading indicators.

Corporate Profits after Tax. Data are available from 1947 to 1995 in billions of 1987 constant dollars, on a quarterly, annualized basis. The series is classified as a leading indicator. The leading character of this series is explained by the fact that corporate profits tend to decline even as the economy is still reaching for a peak; the *rate* of economic growth slows before the economy turns around. Similarly, the rate of decline slows before a turn-around, with the consequence that profits improve before the economy as a whole reflects the shift.

Index of Unit Labor Costs, All Persons, Business. This lagging indicator is available in quarterly increments from 1947 to 1995; it is based on 1987 (1987 = 100). A similar index, for manufacturing only, is included in the composite index of lagging indicators. The lagging character of the index is explained by the fact that wage costs respond more slowly to economic cycles than do prices.

Index of Sensitive Materials Prices
(1987 = 100)

Year	Jan	Feb	Mar	Apr	May	Jun	Jul	Aug	Sep	Oct	Nov	Dec
1948	35.05	35.50	35.08	35.06	35.59	35.74	35.67	35.61	35.33	35.19	35.38	35.27
1949	35.09	34.55	33.98	32.74	32.22	31.68	31.83	32.20	32.61	32.11	32.49	32.53
1950	32.53	32.48	32.72	32.79	33.50	34.33	35.93	38.04	39.78	40.67	41.75	42.63
1951	44.48	45.06	45.01	44.37	44.04	43.08	41.38	39.63	38.59	39.00	38.58	38.31
1952	37.96	37.41	36.43	36.19	35.78	35.34	35.40	35.80	36.22	35.92	35.53	35.75
1953	35.48	35.51	35.66	35.43	35.63	35.62	35.44	35.29	35.03	34.90	34.61	34.38
1954	34.11	34.08	34.29	34.59	34.66	34.94	35.14	34.93	35.09	35.22	35.09	34.96
1955	35.18	35.47	35.52	35.69	35.85	36.00	36.36	36.23	36.26	36.17	36.43	36.85
1956	36.99	37.18	37.25	37.09	36.91	36.55	36.42	36.47	36.61	36.63	36.79	36.92
1957	36.81	36.48	36.40	36.20	36.00	35.69	35.58	35.52	35.33	34.93	34.73	34.51
1958	34.34	34.37	34.01	33.63	33.76	33.81	34.20	34.38	34.61	35.16	35.42	35.15
1959	35.28	35.25	35.52	35.79	36.04	36.18	36.16	36.22	36.35	36.55	36.63	36.87
1960	36.92	36.67	36.46	36.51	36.46	36.21	36.12	36.14	36.06	35.87	35.83	35.57
1961	35.36	35.70	35.64	35.58	35.72	35.56	35.85	35.95	35.97	36.28	35.78	36.16
1962	36.24	36.11	36.12	35.79	35.94	35.72	35.63	35.52	35.53	35.59	35.68	35.53
1963	35.58	35.57	35.60	35.47	35.51	35.61	35.88	35.97	35.88	36.06	36.28	36.62
1964	36.60	36.60	36.67	36.92	36.78	36.89	36.97	37.30	37.59	38.10	38.24	38.37
1965	38.03	37.89	38.03	38.31	38.72	38.68	38.75	39.06	39.13	39.37	39.44	39.41
1966	39.60	39.73	39.98	40.08	39.91	39.83	39.79	38.85	38.55	38.28	38.01	37.84
1967	37.53	37.26	36.87	36.50	36.43	36.69	36.66	36.64	36.77	36.86	37.04	37.45
1968	37.25	37.46	37.77	37.92	37.64	37.92	38.21	38.48	38.69	39.12	39.58	39.87
1969	40.26	40.57	40.60	40.70	40.73	40.81	40.95	41.22	41.67	41.72	42.01	42.17
1970	42.04	41.77	41.55	41.51	41.37	40.97	40.60	40.53	40.22	40.35	40.49	40.08
1971	39.92	39.94	40.20	40.68	40.31	40.53	40.78	41.04	41.30	41.46	41.62	42.13
1972	42.33	42.66	43.69	44.22	45.60	45.97	46.25	46.35	46.40	46.90	48.04	48.70
1973	49.42	50.73	51.65	52.53	53.07	54.24	55.09	56.45	57.99	59.17	60.53	63.41
1974	64.49	66.08	67.33	67.40	66.09	66.01	66.89	66.11	65.74	63.14	61.30	58.51
1975	57.83	57.74	57.44	57.76	58.11	56.49	56.27	57.37	59.14	59.66	60.05	60.63
1976	60.97	61.54	61.78	63.08	64.07	64.80	67.04	67.21	67.35	66.88	66.61	67.01
1977	67.18	67.84	69.21	68.83	68.72	68.12	68.30	68.86	68.83	69.36	69.94	70.96
1978	71.66	72.13	71.85	71.32	71.58	72.88	73.20	74.41	75.29	76.90	78.15	77.85
1979	78.57	79.95	81.50	83.07	84.32	85.24	85.84	85.80	85.82	88.65	90.30	91.26
1980	92.58	93.99	95.18	93.29	90.44	89.08	89.40	91.12	92.19	93.16	93.76	93.40
1981	92.51	91.38	92.51	93.27	93.22	93.03	93.18	93.51	92.67	91.64	90.18	89.00
1982	88.39	88.10	87.19	85.31	85.10	83.68	84.13	83.69	84.12	84.04	83.50	83.31
1983	83.73	85.04	84.95	84.92	85.68	86.54	88.76	91.23	92.75	94.93	96.43	97.04
1984	97.11	98.03	98.82	99.24	99.01	98.69	98.20	97.04	96.81	95.30	95.33	94.77
1985	93.95	93.27	92.92	92.17	91.46	90.58	90.23	89.79	88.49	88.58	88.55	88.61
1986	88.82	88.40	87.42	87.18	87.86	89.03	90.43	88.24	89.77	92.58	94.46	94.35
1987	95.11	94.65	95.17	97.13	99.26	100.18	101.56	102.79	103.41	103.88	103.18	103.67
1988	104.21	104.27	105.18	106.06	106.53	107.82	107.81	108.15	107.82	107.70	109.99	110.89
1989	112.07	113.17	113.52	112.89	111.94	111.07	110.22	109.81	110.10	110.32	108.75	106.50
1990	105.64	104.39	105.54	106.86	106.88	106.76	106.99	107.40	107.16	106.47	104.69	104.22
1991	103.69	103.05	102.25	102.00	101.84	101.07	100.86	99.70	98.49	98.13	98.35	98.39
1992	97.98	98.16	99.83	101.19	101.89	101.93	101.77	101.76	103.00	101.70	100.32	100.86
1993	101.40	101.25	100.76	99.86	99.28	99.10	98.82	98.21	97.72	98.60	99.43	100.42
1994	101.43	103.17	104.24	105.60	107.89	111.68	116.03	117.35	118.46	120.02	123.84	126.21
1995	128.68	128.12	130.28	131.83	133.46	133.43	131.36	-	-	-	-	-

Source: U.S. Department of Commerce, Bureau of Economic Analysis, U.S. Department of Labor, Bureau of Labor Statistics, Commodity Research Bureau, Inc. - indicates data not available or zero.

Index of Producer Prices
Sensitive crude and intermediate materials
(1982 = 100)

Year	Jan	Feb	Mar	Apr	May	Jun	Jul	Aug	Sep	Oct	Nov	Dec
1947	38.50	39.90	42.10	43.40	42.20	42.10	42.60	42.60	42.30	43.40	42.80	42.80
1948	43.90	45.20	44.80	46.10	47.50	47.20	46.60	45.10	44.80	44.10	43.70	43.00
1949	42.40	40.80	40.10	37.70	36.20	35.80	35.10	35.30	37.30	37.30	38.10	38.40
1950	38.40	39.20	39.90	41.00	43.20	45.80	46.90	49.60	51.20	51.60	52.90	54.80
1951	57.40	57.80	58.10	56.60	57.30	58.50	57.40	50.50	49.40	48.20	47.20	46.80
1952	46.30	46.30	45.90	45.90	45.50	45.40	45.00	45.60	46.30	45.70	45.20	45.80
1953	45.30	45.90	46.50	46.60	46.50	46.30	46.60	46.10	45.10	44.30	43.50	42.40
1954	41.60	41.50	41.30	41.40	42.10	42.10	42.50	41.90	42.30	43.40	44.20	43.60
1955	44.40	44.90	45.30	45.30	45.70	46.40	47.70	48.00	48.20	48.10	48.80	50.00
1956	50.60	50.50	51.00	51.90	51.60	49.60	48.30	48.90	49.20	48.50	49.10	49.80
1957	46.90	45.20	44.70	43.00	43.80	45.70	44.70	44.30	43.60	42.20	41.20	41.20
1958	40.70	41.40	41.00	40.40	40.70	41.10	41.50	42.40	43.20	44.10	44.40	43.50
1959	44.00	44.80	45.40	45.20	44.90	45.60	45.20	44.80	45.00	45.70	45.70	45.30
1960	42.80	41.60	40.50	40.50	40.20	39.20	38.90	38.10	37.90	37.30	37.20	37.30
1961	37.20	37.50	37.90	38.70	38.80	39.20	39.30	39.30	39.50	39.80	38.80	39.10
1962	39.50	39.40	39.00	38.50	38.20	37.80	37.70	37.80	37.70	37.60	37.40	37.60
1963	37.60	37.80	37.90	37.70	37.90	37.90	38.50	38.70	38.30	38.50	38.60	38.70
1964	38.80	38.70	39.00	39.60	39.60	39.90	40.20	40.70	40.50	41.00	41.20	41.60
1965	41.10	40.70	40.80	40.80	41.30	41.00	41.10	41.60	41.40	41.70	42.00	42.10
1966	42.70	43.00	43.90	44.10	44.20	44.30	44.30	42.20	41.80	41.60	41.10	40.40
1967	39.90	39.20	38.80	38.50	38.80	39.50	39.80	40.00	40.60	40.50	41.10	41.60
1968	41.50	41.60	42.10	42.00	41.80	42.60	43.30	43.60	44.10	45.10	45.60	46.70
1969	47.70	48.30	49.40	48.70	48.30	47.50	47.00	47.50	47.80	47.80	48.60	48.60
1970	48.40	47.80	47.50	47.30	47.60	47.50	46.90	46.60	46.40	46.50	45.10	44.70
1971	45.00	45.40	45.70	46.30	46.10	46.60	47.80	48.60	48.70	48.90	49.10	49.80
1972	50.50	50.70	51.20	51.40	51.80	52.70	53.60	54.20	54.10	55.60	56.60	57.30
1973	58.30	60.50	62.10	64.80	67.20	68.60	68.10	70.50	74.00	77.30	82.50	84.90
1974	83.70	85.70	88.90	92.40	84.90	85.40	86.60	85.20	83.60	79.90	77.60	70.80
1975	68.10	67.90	66.50	66.90	68.90	67.10	65.50	67.60	71.30	71.10	71.40	73.00
1976	75.50	76.50	78.30	80.30	81.10	82.40	86.20	86.00	86.30	84.80	85.00	86.30
1977	85.80	85.70	87.90	87.30	86.70	85.60	86.80	89.00	90.40	89.50	88.90	92.00
1978	94.30	95.30	95.30	95.70	97.30	100.60	101.60	103.20	104.10	106.40	109.70	109.40
1979	110.30	112.50	118.20	118.10	118.50	121.80	119.60	118.50	118.50	120.40	120.00	118.20
1980	119.20	121.20	120.30	113.20	108.50	107.00	109.80	113.80	115.20	117.20	119.70	120.20
1981	116.50	112.90	113.60	114.90	114.90	114.40	113.30	113.10	110.50	109.10	106.20	105.30
1982	105.20	103.50	102.40	101.20	100.80	99.30	99.50	97.90	97.80	97.60	97.10	97.70
1983	99.90	103.00	105.20	104.70	106.80	109.90	113.80	116.70	116.60	117.80	119.40	120.70
1984	120.40	122.10	122.50	121.90	121.30	119.70	117.10	115.00	115.20	113.80	113.20	112.70
1985	112.90	111.40	110.60	109.90	109.60	109.20	109.10	108.70	107.70	108.20	107.80	107.80
1986	108.09	107.39	108.25	110.07	110.56	111.04	112.15	109.90	111.12	112.51	113.67	113.48
1987	113.72	114.31	115.14	115.61	117.60	119.89	122.07	123.90	127.87	131.45	133.29	133.79
1988	134.05	135.73	137.22	136.27	135.47	135.74	137.69	137.32	137.08	137.02	138.04	138.91
1989	140.27	141.09	141.75	141.36	141.70	141.06	140.59	139.77	140.40	142.39	140.94	139.27
1990	138.00	137.20	138.03	140.50	141.46	141.43	141.82	142.80	142.43	141.97	140.53	139.73
1991	138.60	136.88	135.53	135.36	135.79	136.53	137.14	135.52	135.44	136.19	136.16	135.97
1992	135.79	138.07	139.61	140.82	141.17	141.59	142.00	142.69	144.42	144.55	145.02	148.66
1993	153.22	156.74	159.61	161.09	160.31	160.28	161.10	160.76	162.15	166.42	169.14	171.01
1994	173.23	171.45	171.32	169.53	168.41	172.22	176.50	180.52	180.63	182.40	187.06	188.51
1995	190.32	188.88	189.61	190.22	191.09	191.90	191.10	-	-	-	-	-

Source: U.S. Department of Commerce, Bureau of Economic Analysis, U.S. Department of Labor, Bureau of Labor Statistics. - indicates data not available or zero.

Corporate Profits After Tax
(Annual Rate, Billions of 1987 $)

Year	1st Quarter	2nd Quarter	3rd Quarter	4th Quarter
1947	119.2	109.2	105.3	111.8
1948	116.5	120.9	115.4	110.4
1949	101.7	88.7	92.0	90.3
1950	92.6	110.6	130.7	141.3
1951	112.5	95.3	86.8	93.4
1952	90.1	85.7	86.4	93.9
1953	96.5	95.3	92.5	72.5
1954	83.4	86.2	91.9	98.3
1955	111.2	112.3	112.9	116.5
1956	111.4	112.9	106.1	110.5
1957	110.0	104.5	101.3	92.6
1958	79.8	81.3	90.0	101.7
1959	107.7	116.5	104.0	102.4
1960	111.0	102.7	98.2	95.0
1961	92.9	97.7	102.9	110.5
1962	112.1	112.1	115.1	116.8
1963	114.4	120.9	123.8	126.7
1964	137.1	136.0	138.9	137.1
1965	154.6	160.5	162.0	170.0
1966	172.0	171.1	168.2	162.3
1967	154.8	153.5	155.6	161.3
1968	154.8	156.6	155.2	157.8
1969	153.5	146.4	139.6	134.8
1970	127.2	123.5	124.0	115.0
1971	131.3	135.0	142.7	145.2
1972	151.7	152.4	157.5	170.0
1973	195.0	197.2	194.6	199.8
1974	204.7	203.3	207.2	178.8
1975	151.7	158.8	188.2	195.8
1976	202.3	200.9	198.8	196.0
1977	211.0	220.5	225.6	221.1
1978	222.0	242.2	243.7	253.4
1979	248.6	251.7	250.6	239.0
1980	234.3	190.8	193.3	192.8
1981	194.7	172.9	174.6	162.4
1982	133.2	131.8	131.3	125.8
1983	129.4	149.2	161.7	156.4
1984	169.6	166.0	153.5	146.8
1985	134.6	133.5	137.6	140.9
1986	114.5	111.2	115.2	122.8
1987	142.2	158.6	168.7	173.7
1988	191.5	201.1	205.4	215.1
1989	201.8	188.0	175.4	182.6
1990	195.9	205.5	204.1	203.0
1991	203.3	199.3	199.5	206.6
1992	221.6	229.4	197.8	223.8
1993	230.2	240.6	244.8	264.9
1994	253.1	271.5	276.6	283.7
1995	295.0	300.0	-	-

Source: U.S. Department of Commerce, Bureau of Economic Analysis. - indicates data not available or zero.

Unit Labor Cost, All Persons, Business Sector
(1982 = 100)

Year	1st Quarter	2nd Quarter	3rd Quarter	4th Quarter
1947	23.3	23.7	24.0	24.8
1948	24.5	24.3	25.4	25.5
1949	25.1	24.8	24.7	25.1
1950	24.9	24.6	24.6	24.8
1951	26.0	26.5	26.2	26.2
1952	26.5	26.6	26.9	27.4
1953	27.5	27.7	28.1	28.0
1954	28.1	28.2	27.8	28.0
1955	27.5	27.7	27.9	28.2
1956	28.9	29.3	29.5	29.6
1957	30.1	30.3	30.4	30.6
1958	30.9	30.7	30.9	30.7
1959	30.9	31.0	31.6	31.7
1960	31.9	32.2	32.3	32.3
1961	32.4	32.2	32.2	32.1
1962	32.5	32.7	32.6	32.5
1963	32.6	32.3	32.4	32.6
1964	32.5	32.7	32.8	33.0
1965	33.0	33.2	33.2	33.1
1966	33.6	34.4	34.8	35.2
1967	35.4	35.4	35.6	35.8
1968	36.6	37.0	37.5	38.1
1969	38.6	39.5	40.2	40.9
1970	41.8	42.2	42.2	42.7
1971	42.8	43.4	43.8	43.9
1972	44.7	44.7	44.9	45.0
1973	45.9	47.1	48.2	48.8
1974	50.5	52.5	54.3	55.3
1975	57.0	56.8	56.8	57.9
1976	58.7	59.9	61.2	62.3
1977	62.8	63.9	64.4	66.2
1978	67.8	68.5	70.1	71.9
1979	74.2	76.2	78.4	80.2
1980	82.4	86.1	87.7	88.4
1981	90.2	92.0	93.5	96.6
1982	98.8	99.6	100.7	101.0
1983	101.6	100.7	101.5	102.1
1984	102.5	102.7	104.1	104.3
1985	105.6	105.9	106.4	108.0
1986	107.6	108.6	110.1	111.6
1987	112.0	111.4	111.9	113.7
1988	113.6	115.7	117.0	117.9
1989	119.4	120.1	121.5	123.0
1990	124.6	125.8	127.9	129.8
1991	130.3	130.9	131.9	132.9
1992	133.0	133.9	134.7	135.1
1993	136.6	137.5	137.3	136.2
1994	137.3	138.1	138.0	137.8
1995	138.4	138.7	-	-

Source: U.S. Department of Labor, Bureau of Labor Statistics. - indicates data not available or zero.

INDICATORS OF MONEY AND CREDIT

This section presents 10 series commonly used to measure the relationships between the economy and money, expressed in measures of money supply, interest and other yields on investments, and credit. These indicators are leading, coincident, or lagging depending on the nature of the series. The series presented are:

> Ratio, gross domestic product to money supply M1
> Free reserves
> Member bank borrowings from the Federal Reserve
> Federal funds rate
> Discount rate on new issues of 91-day Treasury bills
> Yield on new issues of high-grade corporate bonds
> Yield on long-term Treasury bonds
> Yield on municipal bonds, 20-bond average
> Secondary market yields on FHA mortgages
> Commercial and industrial loans outstanding, current dollars

Three related series, reported under Business Cycle Indicators, are:

> Money supply M2 (Leading Index)
> Commercial and industrial loans outstanding, 1987 dollars (Lagging Index)
> Average prime rate charged by banks (Lagging Index)
> Change in consumer price index for services (Lagging Index)

Ratio, Gross Domestic Product to Money Supply M1. This indicator is a ratio calculated by dividing the GDP by M1. The ratio is calculated in current dollars and is also referred to as the ratio of "nominal GDP" to "nominal" money supply. GDP is the sum of all productive economic activities; M1 is that portion of the money supply which is most liquid (cash, checking accounts). The ratio of GDP to M1 is a measure of the "velocity of money." If GDP is $5,557.7 billion and M1 is $835.0 billion (in current dollars) then the ratio will be 6.66—meaning that the money supply turned over nearly 7 times to finance the nation's economic activities in one year.

The velocity of money is a coincident indicator, but not part of the composite index of coincident indicators. The velocity of money is used in many kinds of analysis. Velocity tends to increase in inflationary times because holding money (in savings accounts, for instance) decreases the value of the money; people prefer to spend. In periods of low inflation, money is held more and velocity drops. The use of alternatives to money, such as credit cards, decreases the need for money and increase velocity; and the velocity of money has tended to rise, historically, with higher levels of income. In countries with very high rates of inflation, velocities 20 to 50 are not uncommon.

Free Reserves. Data are for 1945 to 1995 in millions of dollars; data are not seasonally adjusted. Free reserves are funds held by banks that may be loaned out. Banks are required by the Federal Reserve System to hold reserves in a fixed ratio to their total deposits (the "reserve ratio"). Deposits in excess of the required reserve less borrowings from the Federal Reserve System, are "free" to be lent.

The series is a leading indicator at business cycle peaks. It is an "inverted" indicator: for cyclical analysis, changes from period to period are inverted; a growth is depicted as negative growth, a decline as a growth.

A pattern of decreasing free reserves signals an increasing demand for money for purchases, that is, increasing economic activity; a pattern of increasing free reserves indicates the opposite—no demand for money. Thus by "inverting the sign" of this indicator, the right message is obtained. The series is undefined at cycle troughs and overall.

Member Bank Borrowings from the Federal Reserve. To some extent this series is the inverse of the previous series. Both are shown in millions of current dollars. Members of the Federal Reserve System may borrow from the Fed for short-term purposes paying the prevailing "discount rate" charged by each Federal Reserve bank. Banks borrow to satisfy immediate needs for cash, to maintain required reserve ratios, and to meet contingencies (such as, for instance, sudden withdrawals which exceed the bank's cash reserves). Member borrowings and free reserves move in tandem. With high free reserves on hand, banks borrow less.

The series is classified as a leading indicator of cycle peaks and as a lagging indicator of troughs. Before a business cycle peaks, growth will tend to slow and member borrowings therefore fall before the economy stops growing. On a resumption of growth, member borrowings will tend to lag because members have high levels of free reserves.

Federal Funds Rate. Shown for 1954 through 1995 as a percent. This is the interest rate charged in the interbank market for bank purchases of excess reserve balances. Excess reserves are bank money holdings that exceed minimum deposit requirements; excess reserves minus loans outstanding to the Fed are "free reserves" (see above). Therefore excess reserves are free reserves plus obligations outstanding to the Fed. These assets may be bought and sold in the federal funds market at an interest rate called the federal funds rate. Unlike the discount rate, the funds rate changes with each transaction.

The series is a leading indicator of cycle peaks and a lagging indicator of troughs; slowing demand for reserves as a business cycle draws to its close causes a drop in the funds rate; as the economy turns around, some time passes before bank demand for reserves causes the funds rate to rise again.

Discount Rate on New Issues of 91-Day Treasury Bills. Data are shown for 1945 through 1995 as a percent. Treasury bills are short-term securities issued by the Treasury; 91-day Treasury bills have the shortest maturities. The bills are purchased at prices below the face value (minimum $10,0000); the difference between face value and purchase price is the discount rate. The bills are sold at auction; hence the discount rate is set by market forces. The Federal Reserve usually buys or sells treasury bills to carry out its open market operations; purchases act to decrease money supply; sales act to increase money supply. The series acts as a coincident indicator of the peak of business cycles and as a lagging indicator of troughs.

Yield on New Issues of High-Grade Corporate Bonds. Data for 1946 through 1995 are shown as percent. Bonds are long-term debt instruments issued by corporations; high-grade "corporates" are bonds with high ratings for security based on the financial strength of the issuer. The yield percentage will tend to decline *after* a recessionary trend is well established and turn up *after* a recovery is clearly under way; hence the series is regarded as a lagging indicator of the business cycle.

Yield on Long-Term Treasury Bonds. Data for 1945 through 1995 are shown in percent. Long-term Treasury bonds are debt instruments sold by the U.S. Treasury with maturities of 10 years or more in denominations of $1,000. The series is a coincident indicator of business cycle peaks and a lagging indictor of troughs.

Yield on Municipal Bonds, 20-Bond Average. These instruments are governmental debt instruments sold by municipalities. Data are shown in percent from 1948 through 1995. The series is classified as a lagging indicator of the trough of business cycles; it is unclassified at the peak, indicating behavior that does not follow any discernible pattern. Since most municipal bond yields ("public purpose bonds") are tax exempt, yields will tend to rise in an expanding economy where tax shelters are more valuable than in a declining economy.

Secondary Market Yields on FHA Mortgages. Data are shown in percent from 1949 to 1995. The primary market for Federal Housing Administration (FHA) or other mortgages is that defined by the home buyer and the original mortgage lender. The lender can then sell the loan—at a discount, of course—to investors. This second transaction is the secondary market for mortgages. The original lender receives cash for lending (increases his/her liquidity); the investor obtains an asset. Government agencies buy the original mortgages, assemble them into mortgage pools, and sell them as collateralized mortgage obligations.

The series is a lagging indicator. Before mortgages can be resold, people have to buy homes and take out mortgages. The secondary market, therefore, will tend to "soften" after a downturn in the economy; although housing starts tend to lead an expansion, housing purchases come later and secondary mortgage operations even later than that—explaining the lagging character of this series.

Commercial and Industrial Loans Outstanding, Current Dollars. This series is shown for 1945 through 1995 in millions of current dollars. The same series, in constant 1987 dollars, is a lagging indicator—as is this series. Business and industry assume debt in periods of growth and minimize debt in periods of decline. The total debt outstanding, however, reflects the business cycle at a lag in time; borrowers pay off debt over time and may be late in paying during economic turn-downs; they also contract new obligations later than the economy's upturn because both lenders and borrowers are more cautious after a recessionary period.

Ratio, Gross Domestic Product to Money Supply M1
(Ratio)

Year	1st Quarter	2nd Quarter	3rd Quarter	4th Quarter
1947	2.113	2.116	2.135	2.217
1948	2.272	2.359	2.421	2.441
1949	2.409	2.372	2.398	2.377
1950	2.452	2.501	2.632	2.709
1951	2.811	2.849	2.873	2.855
1952	2.846	2.826	2.845	2.919
1953	2.961	2.970	2.960	2.918
1954	2.905	2.900	2.909	2.943
1955	3.008	3.053	3.102	3.145
1956	3.152	3.188	3.221	3.272
1957	3.328	3.340	3.392	3.376
1958	3.323	3.317	3.381	3.437
1959	3.471	3.532	3.508	3.567
1960	3.674	3.674	3.661	3.628
1961	3.640	3.688	3.742	3.798
1962	3.859	3.884	3.933	3.930
1963	3.952	3.973	4.017	4.036
1964	4.117	4.147	4.145	4.128
1965	4.222	4.271	4.322	4.378
1966	4.438	4.442	4.534	4.598
1967	4.606	4.577	4.571	4.577
1968	4.654	4.701	4.696	4.666
1969	4.703	4.734	4.810	4.810
1970	4.811	4.847	4.873	4.803
1971	4.925	4.906	4.911	4.927
1972	5.000	5.053	5.055	5.090
1973	5.182	5.237	5.271	5.371
1974	5.318	5.394	5.458	5.502
1975	5.504	5.559	5.675	5.802
1976	5.911	5.912	5.963	6.014
1977	6.043	6.163	6.254	6.219
1978	6.226	6.451	6.499	6.607
1979	6.657	6.640	6.665	6.753
1980	6.827	6.867	6.773	6.904
1981	7.117	7.041	7.210	7.159
1982	6.991	7.043	6.999	6.789
1983	6.728	6.752	6.761	6.830
1984	6.946	6.994	7.045	7.063
1985	7.011	6.940	6.834	6.750
1986	6.728	6.498	6.317	6.120
1987	6.026	6.039	6.136	6.217
1988	6.263	6.284	6.318	6.423
1989	6.566	6.738	6.769	6.767
1990	6.841	6.865	6.842	6.805
1991	6.765	6.712	6.647	6.529
1992	6.379	6.284	6.194	6.080
1993	6.026	5.923	5.807	5.776
1994	5.783	5.846	5.899	6.009
1995	6.077	6.133	-	-

Source: U.S. Department of Commerce, Bureau of Economic Analysis, Board of Governors of the Federal Reserve System. - indicates data not available or zero.

Free Reserves
Not seasonally adjusted
(Million $)

Year	Jan	Feb	Mar	Apr	May	Jun	Jul	Aug	Sep	Oct	Nov	Dec
1945	996	720	766	571	373	749	1,056	701	675	699	575	1,157
1946	1,126	807	505	631	806	816	807	765	736	756	643	743
1947	744	602	698	707	677	650	689	673	798	783	576	762
1948	938	560	552	700	599	752	722	750	756	706	655	663
1949	669	600	546	608	601	658	910	861	847	816	677	685
1950	900	614	655	593	624	700	623	483	669	775	586	885
1951	613	298	471	672	152	664	562	412	383	821	389	169
1952	723	330	578	283	65	130	-468	-383	95	-400	-875	-870
1953	-640	-672	-614	-631	-353	365	366	-7	250	390	198	252
1954	836	339	503	626	561	711	770	725	708	638	650	457
1955	369	270	122	95	212	168	92	-189	-286	-359	-492	-245
1956	-255	-267	-409	-533	-504	-195	-139	-339	-214	-195	-154	-36
1957	116	-126	-316	-504	-444	-508	-383	-471	-466	-344	-293	-133
1958	122	324	495	492	547	484	547	382	95	96	20	-41
1959	-54	-51	-139	-261	-320	-523	-545	-542	-484	-466	-415	-435
1960	-373	-356	-218	-180	-51	46	122	246	412	495	610	669
1961	706	516	476	559	461	527	562	514	542	461	493	451
1962	536	434	383	420	456	371	442	405	409	414	437	312
1963	359	295	286	327	220	158	156	116	109	77	92	158
1964	166	111	108	141	94	107	113	106	86	77	8	142
1965	115	7	-45	-130	-161	-175	-175	-151	-144	-130	-80	-21
1966	-41	-135	-218	-282	-346	-351	-363	-368	-398	-401	-222	-193
1967	-7	5	214	204	276	246	303	284	253	206	226	147
1968	141	13	-322	-350	-381	-366	-176	-236	-142	-198	-237	-320
1969	-490	-581	-683	-836	-1,119	-1,081	-1,027	-982	-805	-987	-974	-833
1970	-785	-872	-735	-693	-811	-691	-1,194	-663	-356	-258	-181	-83
1971	-130	-78	-124	15	-65	-291	-639	-613	-306	-194	-147	56
1972	185	119	92	39	28	103	-45	-200	-329	-344	-254	-766
1973	-902	-1,396	-1,615	-1,488	-1,704	-1,626	-1,638	-1,968	-1,595	-1,208	-1,168	-994
1974	-886	-1,007	-1,180	-1,554	-1,772	-1,582	-1,709	-1,611	-1,472	-1,208	-887	-322
1975	-115	100	131	59	93	-10	-93	-4	-192	28	228	148
1976	173	147	172	111	95	88	101	107	139	125	185	221
1977	198	127	112	119	2	-115	-48	-861	-417	-1,096	-611	-379
1978	-217	-165	-129	-409	-993	-916	-1,120	-972	-867	-1,115	-481	-636
1979	-789	-764	-833	-742	-1,624	-1,197	-960	-863	-1,149	-1,750	-1,661	-1,031
1980	-990	-1,444	-2,538	-1,706	-97	131	142	-115	-964	-1,104	-1,538	-1,173
1981	-951	-932	-705	-1,161	-1,960	-1,692	-1,336	-1,048	-741	-465	-154	-169
1982	-902	-1,253	-886	-1,050	-582	-793	-327	-109	-430	68	-31	52
1983	176	132	-42	-128	10	-198	-368	-609	-428	-83	-370	-211
1984	-98	356	-246	-701	-2,381	-659	-287	-289	-153	-365	-73	273
1985	364	378	139	296	-48	376	222	320	30	176	-295	218
1986	848	688	635	497	557	642	507	319	252	366	596	846
1987	728	925	652	124	327	712	328	527	257	622	719	752
1988	592	957	642	496	583	367	116	382	220	545	610	575
1989	533	700	427	217	513	333	378	250	266	486	617	678
1990	603	76	687	672	503	238	385	68	291	455	741	1,361
1991	1,662	1,590	991	886	815	676	345	622	586	834	785	788
1992	771	990	939	1,049	845	684	681	684	707	931	939	1,032
1993	1,096	1,059	1,122	1,023	875	730	845	600	662	804	1,012	981
1994	1,375	1,070	912	1,027	715	772	649	535	573	424	759	959
1995	1,207	887	725	642	730	692	720	-	-	-	-	-

Source: Board of Governors of the Federal Reserve System. - indicates data not available or zero.

Member Bank Borrowings From Federal Reserve
Not seasonally adjusted
(Million $)

Year	Jan	Feb	Mar	Apr	May	Jun	Jul	Aug	Sep	Oct	Nov	Dec
1947	106	203	173	126	107	135	92	127	133	171	274	224
1948	143	244	270	111	144	100	95	87	128	111	118	134
1949	169	110	148	98	176	100	109	94	75	46	134	118
1950	35	123	128	101	80	68	123	164	96	67	145	142
1951	212	330	242	161	438	170	194	292	338	95	340	657
1952	210	365	307	367	563	579	1,077	1,032	683	1,048	1,532	1,593
1953	1,347	1,310	1,202	1,166	944	423	418	651	468	362	486	441
1954	100	293	189	139	155	146	65	115	67	82	164	246
1955	313	354	463	495	368	401	527	765	849	884	1,016	839
1956	807	799	993	1,060	971	769	738	898	792	715	744	688
1957	406	640	834	1,011	909	1,005	917	1,005	988	811	804	710
1958	451	242	138	130	119	142	109	252	476	425	486	557
1959	552	505	599	692	741	930	961	990	927	907	859	941
1960	887	810	641	606	496	434	379	296	215	167	133	74
1961	66	133	70	57	95	63	54	65	38	71	98	133
1962	87	68	89	72	61	102	92	125	81	63	120	260
1963	146	166	148	130	210	259	298	329	319	320	349	332
1964	274	286	278	211	260	268	263	315	345	321	400	264
1965	300	405	411	471	495	537	528	547	554	488	432	444
1966	420	482	560	637	687	707	741	735	769	734	607	532
1967	410	364	200	146	89	106	115	81	89	129	132	228
1968	246	373	659	685	741	694	527	565	503	443	545	746
1969	736	835	902	1,003	1,374	1,385	1,252	1,219	1,079	1,150	1,203	1,119
1970	959	1,080	898	845	968	881	1,360	837	600	463	415	332
1971	364	332	319	153	284	492	823	809	495	357	384	126
1972	21	33	98	117	111	100	238	388	541	555	608	1,050
1973	1,160	1,593	1,824	1,711	1,843	1,851	1,953	2,165	1,852	1,476	1,393	1,298
1974	1,051	1,191	1,314	1,736	2,590	3,006	3,301	3,336	3,282	1,813	1,252	727
1975	398	147	106	110	66	227	301	211	397	190	60	130
1976	78	81	54	44	115	126	133	100	62	94	72	53
1977	68	71	103	73	206	262	323	1,061	626	1,306	862	569
1978	484	406	328	557	1,212	1,094	1,317	1,140	1,060	1,277	703	868
1979	1,003	973	991	918	1,765	1,418	1,171	1,085	1,340	2,022	1,906	1,473
1980	1,241	1,655	2,823	2,455	1,018	379	395	658	1,311	1,310	2,059	1,690
1981	1,395	1,303	1,000	1,338	2,223	2,037	1,679	1,420	1,456	1,181	663	636
1982	1,517	1,789	1,555	1,568	1,117	1,205	691	515	933	477	621	634
1983	529	582	792	1,009	952	1,636	1,453	1,546	1,441	844	905	774
1984	715	567	952	1,234	2,988	3,300	5,924	8,017	7,242	6,017	4,617	3,186
1985	1,395	1,289	1,593	1,323	1,334	1,205	1,107	1,073	1,289	1,187	1,741	1,318
1986	770	884	761	893	876	803	741	872	1,008	841	752	827
1987	580	556	527	993	1,035	776	672	647	940	943	625	777
1988	1,082	396	1,752	2,993	2,578	3,083	3,440	3,241	2,839	2,299	2,861	1,716
1989	1,662	1,487	1,813	2,289	1,720	1,490	694	675	693	555	349	265
1990	440	1,448	2,124	1,628	1,335	881	757	927	624	410	230	326
1991	534	252	241	231	303	340	607	764	645	261	108	192
1992	233	77	91	90	155	229	284	251	287	143	104	124
1993	165	45	91	73	121	181	244	352	428	285	89	82
1994	73	70	55	124	200	333	458	469	487	380	249	209
1995	136	59	69	111	150	272	371	-	-	-	-	-

Source: Board of Governors of the Federal Reserve System. - indicates data not available or zero.

Federal Funds Rate
Not seasonally adjusted
(Percent)

Year	Jan	Feb	Mar	Apr	May	Jun	Jul	Aug	Sep	Oct	Nov	Dec
1954	-	-	-	-	-	-	-	1.21	1.07	0.90	0.91	1.26
1955	1.37	1.29	1.35	1.43	1.43	1.62	1.68	1.90	2.18	2.24	2.35	2.48
1956	2.44	2.50	2.50	2.62	2.75	2.71	2.74	2.74	2.95	2.96	2.88	2.94
1957	2.93	3.00	2.96	3.00	3.00	3.00	2.99	3.24	3.50	3.50	3.22	2.98
1958	2.72	1.67	1.20	1.26	0.63	0.93	0.68	1.53	1.76	1.80	2.27	2.42
1959	2.48	2.40	2.80	2.96	2.90	3.39	3.44	3.50	3.76	3.98	4.00	3.99
1960	3.99	3.97	3.84	3.92	3.85	3.32	3.23	2.98	2.60	2.47	2.44	1.98
1961	1.45	2.54	2.02	1.50	1.98	1.73	1.16	2.00	1.88	2.26	2.62	2.33
1962	2.14	2.37	2.70	2.69	2.29	2.68	2.71	2.93	2.90	2.90	2.94	2.93
1963	2.91	3.00	2.98	2.90	3.00	2.99	3.02	3.49	3.48	3.50	3.48	3.38
1964	3.48	3.48	3.43	3.47	3.50	3.50	3.42	3.50	3.45	3.36	3.52	3.85
1965	3.90	3.98	4.04	4.09	4.10	4.04	4.09	4.12	4.01	4.08	4.10	4.32
1966	4.42	4.60	4.65	4.67	4.90	5.17	5.30	5.53	5.40	5.53	5.77	5.40
1967	4.94	5.00	4.53	4.05	3.94	3.98	3.79	3.89	4.00	3.88	4.12	4.51
1968	4.60	4.72	5.05	5.76	6.12	6.07	6.02	6.03	5.78	5.92	5.81	6.02
1969	6.30	6.64	6.79	7.41	8.67	8.90	8.61	9.19	9.15	9.00	8.85	8.97
1970	8.98	8.98	7.76	8.10	7.94	7.60	7.21	6.61	6.29	6.20	5.60	4.90
1971	4.14	3.72	3.71	4.15	4.63	4.91	5.31	5.57	5.55	5.20	4.91	4.14
1972	3.50	3.29	3.83	4.17	4.27	4.46	4.55	4.80	4.87	5.04	5.06	5.33
1973	5.94	6.58	7.09	7.12	7.84	8.49	10.40	10.50	10.78	10.01	10.03	9.95
1974	9.65	8.97	9.35	10.51	11.31	11.93	12.92	12.01	11.34	10.06	9.45	8.53
1975	7.13	6.24	5.54	5.49	5.22	5.55	6.10	6.14	6.24	5.82	5.22	5.20
1976	4.87	4.77	4.84	4.82	5.29	5.48	5.31	5.29	5.25	5.03	4.95	4.65
1977	4.61	4.68	4.69	4.73	5.35	5.39	5.42	5.90	6.14	6.47	6.51	6.56
1978	6.70	6.78	6.79	6.89	7.36	7.60	7.81	8.04	8.45	8.96	9.76	10.03
1979	10.07	10.06	10.09	10.01	10.24	10.29	10.47	10.94	11.43	13.77	13.18	13.78
1980	13.82	14.13	17.19	17.61	10.98	9.47	9.03	9.61	10.87	12.81	15.85	18.90
1981	19.08	15.93	14.70	15.72	18.52	19.10	19.04	17.82	15.87	15.08	13.31	12.37
1982	13.22	14.78	14.68	14.94	14.45	14.15	12.59	10.12	10.31	9.71	9.20	8.95
1983	8.68	8.51	8.77	8.80	8.63	8.98	9.37	9.56	9.45	9.48	9.34	9.47
1984	9.56	9.59	9.91	10.29	10.32	11.06	11.23	11.64	11.30	9.99	9.43	8.38
1985	8.35	8.50	8.58	8.27	7.97	7.53	7.88	7.90	7.92	7.99	8.05	8.27
1986	8.14	7.86	7.48	6.99	6.85	6.92	6.56	6.17	5.89	5.85	6.04	6.91
1987	6.43	6.10	6.13	6.37	6.85	6.73	6.58	6.73	7.22	7.29	6.69	6.77
1988	6.83	6.58	6.58	6.87	7.09	7.51	7.75	8.01	8.19	8.30	8.35	8.76
1989	9.12	9.36	9.85	9.84	9.81	9.53	9.24	8.99	9.02	8.84	8.55	8.45
1990	8.23	8.24	8.28	8.26	8.18	8.29	8.15	8.13	8.20	8.11	7.81	7.31
1991	6.91	6.25	6.12	5.91	5.78	5.90	5.82	5.66	5.45	5.21	4.81	4.43
1992	4.03	4.06	3.98	3.73	3.82	3.76	3.25	3.30	3.22	3.10	3.09	2.92
1993	3.02	3.03	3.07	2.96	3.00	3.04	3.06	3.03	3.09	2.99	3.02	2.96
1994	3.05	3.25	3.34	3.56	4.01	4.25	4.26	4.47	4.73	4.76	5.29	5.45
1995	5.53	5.92	5.98	6.05	6.01	6.00	5.85	5.75	-	-	-	-

Source: Board of Governors of the Federal Reserve System. - indicates data not available or zero.

Discount Rate On New 91-Day Treasury Bills
Not seasonally adjusted
(Percent)

Year	Jan	Feb	Mar	Apr	May	Jun	Jul	Aug	Sep	Oct	Nov	Dec
1945	0.38	0.38	0.38	0.38	0.38	0.38	0.38	0.38	0.38	0.38	0.38	0.38
1946	0.38	0.38	0.38	0.38	0.38	0.38	0.38	0.38	0.38	0.38	0.38	0.38
1947	0.38	0.38	0.38	0.38	0.38	0.38	0.64	0.74	0.79	0.84	0.92	0.95
1948	0.97	0.99	1.00	1.00	1.00	1.00	1.00	1.03	1.09	1.12	1.14	1.15
1949	1.16	1.16	1.16	1.16	1.15	1.16	0.98	1.02	1.06	1.04	1.06	1.10
1950	1.09	1.12	1.14	1.16	1.17	1.17	1.17	1.21	1.32	1.33	1.36	1.37
1951	1.39	1.39	1.42	1.52	1.58	1.50	1.59	1.64	1.65	1.61	1.61	1.73
1952	1.69	1.57	1.66	1.62	1.71	1.70	1.82	1.88	1.79	1.78	1.86	2.13
1953	2.04	2.02	2.08	2.18	2.20	2.23	2.10	2.09	1.88	1.40	1.43	1.63
1954	1.21	0.98	1.05	1.01	0.78	0.65	0.71	0.89	1.01	0.99	0.95	1.17
1955	1.26	1.18	1.34	1.62	1.49	1.43	1.62	1.88	2.09	2.26	2.22	2.56
1956	2.46	2.37	2.31	2.61	2.65	2.53	2.33	2.61	2.85	2.96	3.00	3.23
1957	3.21	3.16	3.14	3.11	3.04	3.32	3.16	3.40	3.58	3.59	3.34	3.10
1958	2.60	1.56	1.35	1.13	1.05	0.88	0.96	1.69	2.48	2.79	2.76	2.81
1959	2.84	2.71	2.85	2.96	2.85	3.25	3.24	3.36	4.00	4.12	4.21	4.57
1960	4.44	3.95	3.44	3.24	3.39	2.64	2.40	2.29	2.49	2.43	2.38	2.27
1961	2.30	2.41	2.42	2.33	2.29	2.36	2.27	2.40	2.30	2.35	2.46	2.62
1962	2.75	2.75	2.72	2.74	2.69	2.72	2.94	2.84	2.79	2.75	2.80	2.86
1963	2.91	2.92	2.90	2.91	2.92	3.00	3.14	3.32	3.38	3.45	3.52	3.52
1964	3.53	3.53	3.55	3.48	3.48	3.48	3.48	3.51	3.53	3.58	3.62	3.86
1965	3.83	3.93	3.94	3.93	3.90	3.81	3.83	3.84	3.91	4.03	4.08	4.36
1966	4.60	4.67	4.63	4.61	4.64	4.54	4.86	4.93	5.36	5.39	5.34	5.01
1967	4.76	4.55	4.29	3.85	3.64	3.48	4.31	4.28	4.45	4.59	4.76	5.01
1968	5.08	4.97	5.14	5.36	5.62	5.54	5.38	5.10	5.20	5.33	5.49	5.92
1969	6.18	6.16	6.08	6.15	6.08	6.49	7.00	7.01	7.13	7.04	7.19	7.72
1970	7.91	7.16	6.71	6.48	7.04	6.74	6.50	6.41	6.24	5.93	5.29	4.86
1971	4.49	3.77	3.32	3.78	4.14	4.70	5.40	5.08	4.67	4.49	4.19	4.02
1972	3.40	3.18	3.72	3.72	3.65	3.87	4.06	4.01	4.65	4.72	4.77	5.06
1973	5.31	5.56	6.05	6.29	6.35	7.19	8.02	8.67	8.48	7.16	7.87	7.36
1974	7.76	7.06	7.99	8.23	8.43	8.14	7.75	8.74	8.36	7.24	7.58	7.18
1975	6.49	5.58	5.54	5.69	5.32	5.19	6.16	6.46	6.38	6.08	5.47	5.50
1976	4.96	4.85	5.05	4.88	5.18	5.44	5.28	5.15	5.08	4.93	4.81	4.35
1977	4.60	4.66	4.61	4.54	4.94	5.00	5.15	5.50	5.77	6.19	6.16	6.06
1978	6.45	6.46	6.32	6.31	6.43	6.71	7.07	7.04	7.84	8.13	8.79	9.12
1979	9.35	9.27	9.46	9.49	9.58	9.05	9.26	9.45	10.18	11.47	11.87	12.07
1980	12.04	12.81	15.53	14.00	9.15	7.00	8.13	9.26	10.32	11.58	13.89	15.66
1981	14.72	14.90	13.48	13.63	16.30	14.56	14.70	15.61	14.95	13.87	11.27	10.93
1982	12.41	13.78	12.49	12.82	12.15	12.11	11.91	9.01	8.20	7.75	8.04	8.01
1983	7.81	8.13	8.30	8.25	8.19	8.82	9.12	9.39	9.05	8.71	8.71	8.96
1984	8.93	9.03	9.44	9.69	9.90	9.94	10.13	10.49	10.41	9.97	8.79	8.16
1985	7.76	8.22	8.57	8.00	7.56	7.01	7.05	7.18	7.08	7.17	7.20	7.07
1986	7.04	7.03	6.59	6.06	6.12	6.21	5.84	5.57	5.19	5.18	5.35	5.49
1987	5.45	5.59	5.56	5.76	5.75	5.69	5.78	6.00	6.32	6.40	5.81	5.80
1988	5.90	5.69	5.69	5.92	6.27	6.50	6.73	7.02	7.23	7.34	7.68	8.09
1989	8.29	8.48	8.83	8.70	8.40	8.22	7.92	7.91	7.72	7.63	7.65	7.64
1990	7.64	7.76	7.87	7.78	7.78	7.74	7.66	7.44	7.38	7.19	7.07	6.81
1991	6.30	5.95	5.91	5.67	5.51	5.60	5.58	5.39	5.25	5.03	4.60	4.12
1992	3.84	3.84	4.05	3.81	3.66	3.70	3.28	3.14	2.97	2.84	3.14	3.25
1993	3.06	2.95	2.97	2.89	2.96	3.10	3.05	3.05	2.96	3.04	3.12	3.08
1994	3.02	3.21	3.52	3.74	4.19	4.18	4.39	4.50	4.64	4.96	5.25	5.64
1995	5.81	5.80	5.73	5.67	5.70	5.50	5.47	5.42	-	-	-	-

Source: Board of Governors of the Federal Reserve System. - indicates data not available or zero.

Yield On New High-Grade Corporate Bonds
Not seasonally adjusted
(Percent)

Year	Jan	Feb	Mar	Apr	May	Jun	Jul	Aug	Sep	Oct	Nov	Dec
1946	2.56	2.38	2.46	2.27	2.47	2.45	2.48	2.06	2.75	2.70	2.49	2.70
1947	2.46	2.53	2.60	2.43	2.47	2.60	2.57	2.62	2.66	2.91	2.69	2.88
1948	2.97	2.85	2.99	2.81	2.86	2.93	2.80	2.83	2.86	2.99	2.96	3.15
1949	2.66	2.77	2.75	2.74	2.69	2.77	2.68	2.60	2.40	2.50	2.54	2.53
1950	2.60	2.58	2.57	2.40	2.58	2.63	2.55	2.61	2.70	2.64	2.63	2.75
1951	2.74	2.78	2.90	3.06	2.98	3.24	3.20	3.01	2.91	3.09	3.36	3.22
1952	3.08	2.94	3.14	3.09	3.25	3.09	3.11	3.08	3.14	3.16	3.07	3.04
1953	3.17	3.26	3.41	3.53	3.80	3.82	3.59	3.46	3.60	3.09	3.13	3.23
1954	3.00	2.88	2.74	2.88	2.90	2.91	2.94	2.94	3.01	2.84	2.94	2.87
1955	2.99	3.09	3.14	3.11	3.15	3.11	3.14	3.41	3.27	3.15	3.17	3.27
1956	3.20	3.07	3.25	3.55	3.48	3.56	3.56	4.02	3.96	3.94	4.29	4.26
1957	4.28	4.13	4.18	4.23	4.41	4.81	4.59	4.78	4.68	4.71	4.56	4.04
1958	3.62	3.73	3.88	3.67	3.66	3.61	3.85	4.39	4.56	4.48	4.35	4.44
1959	4.58	4.60	4.53	4.60	4.92	5.00	4.95	4.90	5.28	5.37	5.14	5.27
1960	5.34	5.24	4.98	4.97	4.95	4.91	4.79	4.65	4.64	4.75	4.82	4.94
1961	4.63	4.43	4.37	4.57	4.67	4.82	4.81	4.79	4.72	4.60	4.52	4.58
1962	4.56	4.53	4.41	4.37	4.32	4.30	4.41	4.39	4.28	4.26	4.23	4.28
1963	4.22	4.25	4.28	4.35	4.36	4.32	4.34	4.34	4.40	4.37	4.42	4.49
1964	4.50	4.39	4.45	4.48	4.48	4.50	4.44	4.44	4.49	4.49	4.48	4.49
1965	4.45	4.45	4.49	4.48	4.52	4.57	4.57	4.66	4.71	4.70	4.75	4.92
1966	4.93	5.09	5.33	5.38	5.55	5.67	5.81	6.04	6.14	6.04	6.11	5.98
1967	5.53	5.35	5.55	5.59	5.90	6.06	6.06	6.30	6.33	6.53	6.87	6.93
1968	6.57	6.57	6.80	6.79	7.00	7.02	6.91	6.54	6.69	6.88	7.00	7.28
1969	7.29	7.33	7.76	7.54	7.62	8.04	8.06	8.05	8.36	8.46	8.94	9.22
1970	9.00	8.84	9.00	9.09	9.53	9.70	9.09	9.08	9.00	9.14	8.97	8.13
1971	7.63	7.54	7.62	7.76	8.25	8.15	8.24	8.14	7.90	7.72	7.67	7.54
1972	7.36	7.57	7.53	7.77	7.61	7.63	7.72	7.59	7.72	7.66	7.46	7.50
1973	7.61	7.67	7.75	7.70	7.69	7.73	7.97	8.45	8.10	7.97	7.95	8.09
1974	8.32	8.21	8.60	9.04	9.39	9.59	10.18	10.30	10.44	10.29	9.22	9.47
1975	9.17	8.84	9.48	9.81	9.76	9.27	9.56	9.71	9.89	9.54	9.48	9.59
1976	8.97	8.71	8.73	8.68	9.00	8.90	8.76	8.59	8.37	8.25	8.17	7.90
1977	7.96	8.18	8.33	8.30	8.38	8.08	8.12	8.06	8.11	8.21	8.26	8.39
1978	8.70	8.70	8.70	8.88	9.00	9.15	9.27	8.83	8.78	9.14	9.30	9.30
1979	9.47	9.52	9.65	9.69	9.82	9.51	9.47	9.57	9.87	11.17	11.52	11.30
1980	11.65	13.23	14.08	13.36	11.61	11.12	11.48	12.31	12.74	13.17	14.10	14.38
1981	14.01	14.60	14.49	15.00	15.68	14.97	15.67	16.34	16.97	16.96	15.53	15.55
1982	16.34	16.35	15.72	15.62	15.37	15.96	15.75	14.64	13.78	12.63	11.89	12.15
1983	12.04	12.11	11.81	11.58	11.24	11.90	12.46	12.89	12.68	12.54	12.86	12.87
1984	12.65	12.80	13.36	13.64	14.41	14.49	14.25	13.54	13.37	13.02	12.40	12.47
1985	12.46	12.39	12.85	12.45	11.85	11.33	11.28	11.61	11.66	11.51	11.19	10.42
1986	10.33	9.76	8.95	8.71	9.09	9.39	9.11	9.03	9.28	9.29	8.99	8.87
1987	8.59	8.58	8.68	9.36	9.95	9.64	9.70	10.09	10.63	10.80	10.09	10.22
1988	9.81	9.43	9.68	9.92	10.25	10.08	10.12	10.27	10.03	9.86	9.98	10.05
1989	9.92	10.11	10.33	10.11	9.82	9.24	9.20	9.09	9.29	9.04	9.20	9.23
1990	9.56	9.68	9.79	10.02	9.97	9.69	9.72	10.05	10.17	10.09	9.79	9.55
1991	9.60	9.14	9.14	9.07	9.13	9.37	9.38	8.88	8.79	8.81	8.72	8.55
1992	8.36	8.63	8.62	8.59	8.57	8.45	8.19	7.96	7.99	8.17	8.25	8.12
1993	7.91	7.73	7.39	7.48	7.52	7.48	7.35	7.04	6.88	6.88	7.17	7.22
1994	7.16	7.27	7.64	7.95	8.17	8.16	8.30	8.25	8.48	8.76	8.89	8.66
1995	8.59	8.39	8.23	8.10	7.68	7.42	7.54	7.75	-	-	-	-

Source: Citibank and U.S. Department of the Treasury. - indicates data not available or zero.

Yield On Long-Term Treasury Bonds
Not seasonally adjusted
(Percent)

Year	Jan	Feb	Mar	Apr	May	Jun	Jul	Aug	Sep	Oct	Nov	Dec
1945	2.44	2.38	2.40	2.39	2.39	2.35	2.34	2.36	2.37	2.35	2.33	2.33
1946	2.21	2.12	2.09	2.08	2.19	2.16	2.18	2.23	2.28	2.26	2.25	2.24
1947	2.21	2.21	2.19	2.19	2.19	2.22	2.25	2.24	2.24	2.27	2.36	2.39
1948	2.45	2.45	2.44	2.44	2.42	2.41	2.44	2.45	2.45	2.45	2.44	2.44
1949	2.42	2.39	2.38	2.38	2.38	2.38	2.27	2.24	2.22	2.22	2.20	2.19
1950	2.20	2.24	2.27	2.30	2.31	2.33	2.34	2.33	2.36	2.38	2.38	2.39
1951	2.39	2.40	2.47	2.56	2.63	2.65	2.63	2.57	2.56	2.61	2.66	2.70
1952	2.74	2.71	2.70	2.64	2.57	2.61	2.61	2.70	2.71	2.74	2.71	2.75
1953	2.80	2.83	2.89	2.97	3.11	3.13	3.02	3.02	2.98	2.83	2.86	2.79
1954	2.69	2.62	2.53	2.48	2.54	2.55	2.47	2.48	2.52	2.54	2.57	2.59
1955	2.68	2.78	2.78	2.82	2.81	2.82	2.91	2.95	2.92	2.87	2.89	2.91
1956	2.88	2.85	2.93	3.07	2.97	2.93	3.00	3.17	3.21	3.20	3.30	3.40
1957	3.34	3.22	3.26	3.32	3.40	3.58	3.60	3.63	3.66	3.73	3.57	3.30
1958	3.24	3.28	3.25	3.12	3.14	3.20	3.36	3.60	3.75	3.76	3.70	3.80
1959	3.91	3.92	3.92	4.01	4.08	4.09	4.11	4.10	4.26	4.11	4.12	4.27
1960	4.37	4.22	4.08	4.18	4.16	3.98	3.86	3.79	3.84	3.91	3.93	3.88
1961	3.89	3.81	3.78	3.80	3.73	3.88	3.90	4.00	4.02	3.98	3.98	4.06
1962	4.08	4.09	4.01	3.89	3.88	3.90	4.02	3.98	3.94	3.89	3.87	3.87
1963	3.89	3.92	3.93	3.97	3.97	4.00	4.01	3.99	4.04	4.07	4.11	4.14
1964	4.15	4.14	4.18	4.20	4.16	4.13	4.13	4.14	4.16	4.16	4.12	4.14
1965	4.14	4.16	4.15	4.15	4.14	4.14	4.15	4.19	4.25	4.28	4.34	4.43
1966	4.43	4.61	4.63	4.55	4.57	4.63	4.75	4.80	4.79	4.70	4.74	4.65
1967	4.40	4.47	4.45	4.51	4.76	4.86	4.86	4.95	4.99	5.19	5.44	5.36
1968	5.18	5.16	5.39	5.28	5.40	5.23	5.09	5.04	5.09	5.24	5.36	5.66
1969	5.74	5.86	6.05	5.84	5.85	6.05	6.07	6.02	6.32	6.27	6.52	6.81
1970	6.86	6.44	6.39	6.53	6.94	6.99	6.57	6.75	6.63	6.59	6.24	5.97
1971	5.92	5.84	5.71	5.75	5.96	5.94	5.91	5.78	5.56	5.46	5.48	5.62
1972	5.62	5.67	5.66	5.74	5.64	5.59	5.59	5.59	5.70	5.69	5.51	5.63
1973	5.96	6.14	6.20	6.11	6.25	6.32	6.53	6.85	6.41	6.25	6.30	6.35
1974	6.56	6.54	6.81	7.04	7.09	7.02	7.18	7.33	7.30	7.22	6.93	6.77
1975	6.68	6.66	6.77	7.05	7.01	6.86	6.89	7.11	7.28	7.29	7.21	7.17
1976	6.93	6.92	6.88	6.73	7.01	6.92	6.85	6.82	6.70	6.65	6.62	6.38
1977	6.68	7.16	7.20	7.13	7.17	6.99	6.98	7.01	6.94	7.08	7.16	7.24
1978	7.51	7.60	7.63	7.74	7.87	7.94	8.10	7.88	7.82	8.07	8.16	8.36
1979	8.43	8.43	8.45	8.44	8.55	8.32	8.35	8.42	8.68	9.44	9.80	9.58
1980	10.03	11.55	11.87	10.83	9.82	9.40	9.83	10.53	10.94	11.20	11.83	11.89
1981	11.65	12.23	12.15	12.62	12.96	12.39	13.05	13.61	14.14	14.13	12.68	12.88
1982	13.73	13.63	12.98	12.84	12.67	13.32	12.97	12.15	11.48	10.51	10.18	10.33
1983	10.37	10.60	10.34	10.19	10.21	10.64	11.10	11.42	11.26	11.21	11.32	11.44
1984	11.29	11.44	11.90	12.17	12.89	13.00	12.82	12.23	11.97	11.66	11.25	11.21
1985	11.15	11.35	11.78	11.42	10.96	10.36	10.51	10.59	10.67	10.56	10.08	9.60
1986	9.51	9.07	8.13	7.59	8.02	8.23	7.86	7.72	8.08	8.04	7.81	7.67
1987	7.60	7.69	7.62	8.31	8.79	8.63	8.70	8.97	9.58	9.61	8.99	9.12
1988	8.82	8.41	8.61	8.91	9.24	9.04	9.20	9.33	9.06	8.89	9.07	9.13
1989	9.07	9.16	9.33	9.18	8.95	8.40	8.19	8.26	8.31	8.15	8.03	8.02
1990	8.39	8.66	8.74	8.92	8.90	8.62	8.64	8.97	9.11	8.93	8.60	8.31
1991	8.33	8.12	8.38	8.29	8.33	8.54	8.50	8.17	7.96	7.88	7.83	7.58
1992	7.48	7.78	7.93	7.88	7.80	7.72	7.40	7.19	7.08	7.26	7.43	7.30
1993	7.17	6.89	6.65	6.64	6.68	6.55	6.34	6.18	5.94	5.90	6.25	6.27
1994	6.24	6.44	6.90	7.32	7.47	7.43	7.61	7.55	7.81	8.02	8.16	7.97
1995	7.93	7.69	7.52	7.41	6.99	6.59	6.71	6.93	-	-	-	-

Source: U.S. Department of the Treasury. - indicates data not available or zero.

Yield On Municipal Bonds, 20-Bond Average
Not seasonally adjusted
(Percent)

Year	Jan	Feb	Mar	Apr	May	Jun	Jul	Aug	Sep	Oct	Nov	Dec
1948	-	2.47	2.45	2.37	2.31	2.24	2.27	2.37	2.41	2.42	2.38	2.26
1949	2.16	2.20	2.18	2.14	2.14	2.20	2.16	2.12	2.14	2.16	2.12	2.09
1950	2.06	2.03	2.01	2.03	2.00	1.99	2.01	1.83	1.84	1.79	1.74	1.72
1951	1.61	1.58	1.74	1.94	2.00	2.19	2.15	2.02	2.01	2.06	2.05	2.09
1952	2.09	2.07	2.08	2.04	2.06	2.13	2.15	2.24	2.30	2.38	2.38	2.38
1953	2.43	2.55	2.65	2.65	2.78	2.99	2.98	2.90	2.90	2.75	2.62	2.60
1954	2.50	2.42	2.40	2.47	2.50	2.48	2.32	2.26	2.31	2.34	2.32	2.36
1955	2.40	2.44	2.44	2.41	2.38	2.41	2.54	2.60	2.58	2.51	2.46	2.57
1956	2.50	2.44	2.57	2.70	2.68	2.54	2.65	2.80	2.94	2.95	3.16	3.22
1957	3.18	3.00	3.10	3.13	3.27	3.41	3.40	3.54	3.54	3.42	3.37	3.04
1958	2.91	3.02	3.06	2.96	2.92	2.97	3.09	3.36	3.54	3.45	3.32	3.34
1959	3.42	3.36	3.30	3.39	3.58	3.72	3.71	3.58	3.78	3.62	3.55	3.68
1960	3.72	3.60	3.56	3.56	3.60	3.55	3.50	3.34	3.42	3.53	3.40	3.40
1961	3.40	3.31	3.45	3.50	3.43	3.52	3.52	3.52	3.53	3.42	3.41	3.47
1962	3.34	3.21	3.14	3.06	3.11	3.26	3.28	3.23	3.11	3.02	3.04	3.07
1963	3.10	3.15	3.05	3.10	3.11	3.21	3.22	3.13	3.20	3.20	3.30	3.27
1964	3.22	3.14	3.28	3.28	3.20	3.20	3.18	3.19	3.23	3.25	3.18	3.13
1965	3.06	3.09	3.18	3.15	3.17	3.24	3.27	3.24	3.35	3.40	3.46	3.54
1966	3.52	3.64	3.72	3.56	3.65	3.77	3.95	4.12	4.12	3.94	3.86	3.86
1967	3.54	3.52	3.55	3.60	3.89	3.96	4.02	3.99	4.12	4.30	4.34	4.43
1968	4.29	4.31	4.54	4.34	4.54	4.50	4.33	4.21	4.38	4.49	4.60	4.82
1969	4.85	4.98	5.26	5.19	5.33	5.76	5.75	6.00	6.26	6.09	6.30	6.82
1970	6.65	6.36	6.03	6.49	7.00	6.96	6.53	6.20	6.25	6.39	5.93	5.46
1971	5.36	5.23	5.17	5.37	5.90	5.95	6.06	5.82	5.37	5.06	5.20	5.21
1972	5.12	5.28	5.31	5.43	5.30	5.34	5.41	5.30	5.36	5.18	5.02	5.05
1973	5.05	5.13	5.29	5.15	5.14	5.18	5.40	5.48	5.10	5.05	5.18	5.12
1974	5.22	5.20	5.40	5.73	6.02	6.13	6.68	6.71	6.76	6.57	6.61	7.05
1975	6.82	6.39	6.74	6.95	6.97	6.95	7.07	7.17	7.44	7.39	7.43	7.31
1976	7.07	6.94	6.92	6.60	6.87	6.87	6.87	6.79	6.61	6.51	6.30	6.29	5.94
1977	5.87	5.89	5.89	5.73	5.75	5.62	5.63	5.62	5.51	5.64	5.49	5.57
1978	5.71	5.62	5.61	5.80	6.03	6.22	6.28	6.12	6.09	6.13	6.19	6.50
1979	6.47	6.31	6.33	6.29	6.25	6.13	6.13	6.20	6.52	7.08	7.30	7.22
1980	7.35	8.16	9.17	8.63	7.59	7.63	8.13	8.67	8.94	9.11	9.56	10.20
1981	9.68	10.10	10.16	10.62	10.78	10.67	11.14	12.26	12.92	12.83	11.89	12.91
1982	13.28	12.97	12.82	12.59	11.95	12.45	12.28	11.23	10.66	9.69	10.06	9.96
1983	9.50	9.58	9.20	9.05	9.11	9.52	9.53	9.72	9.58	9.66	9.75	9.89
1984	9.63	9.64	9.93	9.96	10.49	10.67	10.42	9.99	10.10	10.25	10.17	9.95
1985	9.51	9.65	9.77	9.42	9.01	8.69	8.81	9.08	9.27	9.08	8.54	8.43
1986	8.08	7.44	7.08	7.20	7.54	7.87	7.51	7.21	7.11	7.08	6.85	6.86
1987	6.61	6.61	6.66	7.55	8.00	7.79	7.72	7.82	8.26	8.70	7.95	7.96
1988	7.69	7.49	7.74	7.81	7.91	7.78	7.76	7.79	7.66	7.47	7.46	7.61
1989	7.35	7.44	7.59	7.49	7.25	7.02	6.96	7.06	7.26	7.22	7.14	6.98
1990	7.10	7.22	7.29	7.39	7.35	7.24	7.19	7.32	7.43	7.49	7.18	7.09
1991	7.08	6.91	7.10	7.02	6.95	7.13	7.05	6.90	6.80	6.68	6.73	6.69
1992	6.54	6.74	6.76	6.67	6.57	6.49	6.13	6.16	6.25	6.41	6.36	6.22
1993	6.16	5.87	5.64	5.76	5.73	5.63	5.57	5.45	5.29	5.25	5.47	5.35
1994	5.31	5.40	5.91	6.23	6.19	6.11	6.23	6.21	6.28	6.52	6.97	6.80
1995	6.53	6.22	6.10	6.02	5.95	5.84	5.92	6.08	-	-	-	-

Source: The Bond Buyer. - indicates data not available or zero.

Secondary Market Yields On FHA Mortgages
Not seasonally adjusted
(Percent)

Year	Jan	Feb	Mar	Apr	May	Jun	Jul	Aug	Sep	Oct	Nov	Dec
1949	4.35	4.35	4.35	4.35	4.34	4.35	4.34	4.34	4.32	4.32	4.32	4.32
1950	4.31	4.31	4.30	-	-	4.09	4.07	4.07	4.07	4.07	4.07	4.07
1951	4.07	4.07	4.12	4.19	4.27	4.29	4.31	4.31	4.30	4.27	4.27	4.26
1952	4.26	4.27	4.29	4.29	4.29	4.30	4.30	4.30	4.30	4.31	4.32	4.32
1953	4.34	4.34	4.34	-	-	4.67	4.74	4.82	4.86	4.82	4.81	4.78
1954	4.75	4.69	4.64	4.62	4.59	4.57	4.56	4.56	4.56	4.56	4.56	4.56
1955	4.56	4.56	4.59	4.60	4.63	4.63	4.64	4.67	4.70	4.73	4.75	4.73
1956	4.73	4.70	4.68	4.71	4.78	4.81	4.81	4.87	4.92	4.95	-	-
1957	5.36	5.35	5.35	5.32	5.35	5.38	-	-	5.63	5.63	5.62
1958	5.59	5.57	5.51	5.44	5.39	5.37	5.35	5.37	5.50	5.58	5.60	5.60
1959	5.60	5.59	5.58	5.59	5.64	5.71	5.75	5.81	-	-	6.23	6.23
1960	6.25	6.23	6.22	6.21	6.20	6.19	6.17	6.14	6.11	6.09	6.07	6.04
1961	6.02	5.86	5.80	5.77	-	5.68	5.68	5.69	5.70	5.70	5.69
1962	5.69	5.68	5.65	5.64	5.60	5.59	5.58	5.57	5.56	5.55	5.54	5.53
1963	5.52	5.48	5.47	5.46	5.45	5.45	5.45	5.45	5.45	5.45	5.45	5.45
1964	5.45	5.45	5.45	5.45	5.45	5.45	5.46	5.46	5.46	5.45	5.45	5.45
1965	5.45	5.45	5.45	5.45	5.45	5.44	5.44	5.45	5.46	5.49	5.51	5.62
1966	5.70	-	6.00	-	6.32	6.45	6.51	6.58	6.63	-	6.81	6.77
1967	6.62	6.46	6.35	6.29	6.44	6.51	6.53	6.60	6.63	6.65	6.77	6.81
1968	6.81	6.78	6.83	6.94	-	7.52	7.42	7.35	7.28	7.29	7.36	7.50
1969	-	7.99	8.05	8.06	8.06	8.35	8.36	8.36	8.40	8.48	8.48	8.62
1970	-	9.29	9.20	9.10	9.11	9.16	9.11	9.07	9.01	8.97	8.90	8.40
1971	-	-	7.32	7.37	7.75	7.89	7.97	7.92	7.84	7.75	7.62	7.59
1972	7.49	7.46	7.45	7.50	7.53	7.54	7.54	7.55	7.56	7.57	7.57	7.56
1973	7.55	7.56	7.63	7.73	7.79	7.89	8.19	-	9.18	8.97	8.86	8.78
1974	-	8.54	8.66	9.17	9.46	9.46	9.85	10.30	10.38	10.13	-	9.51
1975	8.99	8.84	8.69	-	9.16	9.06	9.13	9.32	9.74	9.53	9.41	9.32
1976	9.06	9.04	-	8.82	9.03	9.05	8.99	8.93	8.82	8.55	8.45	8.28
1977	8.45	8.55	8.65	8.64	-	8.77	8.77	8.77	8.74	8.81	8.81	8.96
1978	9.18	-	9.35	9.44	9.74	-	9.96	9.81	9.81	9.98	10.04	10.23
1979	10.24	10.24	10.26	-	10.61	10.49	10.46	10.58	11.37	-	12.41	12.24
1980	12.60	-	14.63	13.45	11.99	11.85	12.39	13.54	14.26	14.38	14.47	14.08
1981	14.23	14.79	15.04	15.91	16.33	16.31	16.76	17.96	18.55	17.43	15.98	16.43
1982	17.38	17.10	16.41	16.31	16.19	16.73	16.29	14.61	14.03	12.99	12.82	12.80
1983	12.87	12.65	12.68	12.50	12.41	12.96	14.23	13.78	13.55	13.23	13.23	13.25
1984	13.08	13.20	13.68	13.80	15.01	14.91	14.58	14.21	13.99	13.43	12.90	12.99
1985	13.01	13.27	13.43	12.97	12.28	11.89	12.12	11.99	12.04	11.87	11.28	10.70
1986	10.78	10.59	9.77	9.80	10.07	9.98	10.01	9.80	9.90	9.80	9.26	9.21
1987	8.79	8.81	8.94	10.02	10.61	10.33	10.38	10.55	11.22	10.90	10.76	10.63
1988	10.17	9.86	10.28	10.46	10.84	10.65	10.66	10.74	10.58	10.23	10.63	10.81
1989	10.69	10.88	11.16	10.88	10.55	10.08	9.61	9.95	9.94	9.73	9.69	9.72
1990	10.01	10.22	10.30	10.75	10.23	10.18	10.11	10.28	10.24	10.23	9.81	9.66
1991	9.58	9.57	9.61	9.61	9.62	9.71	9.59	9.14	9.06	8.71	8.69	8.10
1992	8.72	8.74	8.85	8.79	8.66	8.56	8.12	8.08	8.06	8.29	8.54	8.12
1993	8.04	7.55	7.57	7.56	7.59	7.52	7.51	7.02	7.03	7.08	7.51	7.52
1994	7.05	7.59	8.57	8.63	8.63	9.03	8.65	8.66	9.10	9.23	9.53	9.54
1995	9.10	9.05	8.60	8.56	8.03	8.00	8.09	-	-	-	-	-

Source: U.S. Department of Housing and Urban Development, Federal Housing Administration. - indicates data not available or zero.

Commercial and Industrial Loans Outstanding
(Million $)

Year	Jan	Feb	Mar	Apr	May	Jun	Jul	Aug	Sep	Oct	Nov	Dec
1945	6,511	6,388	6,283	6,268	6,256	6,410	6,454	6,434	6,487	6,498	6,715	7,147
1946	7,364	7,430	7,621	7,864	8,047	8,211	8,614	9,074	9,443	9,863	10,134	10,260
1947	10,475	10,713	11,149	11,506	11,592	11,639	11,770	12,019	12,250	12,548	12,904	13,158
1948	13,417	13,358	13,371	13,473	13,834	14,065	14,385	14,507	14,461	14,356	14,196	14,087
1949	14,055	13,979	13,861	13,605	13,409	13,163	12,833	12,660	12,641	12,670	12,604	12,573
1950	12,677	12,764	12,763	12,849	12,936	13,242	13,619	14,057	14,696	15,027	15,462	15,986
1951	16,503	17,116	17,579	18,079	18,453	18,646	18,757	18,865	18,968	19,111	19,194	19,411
1952	19,632	19,641	19,761	19,742	19,809	19,969	20,141	20,190	20,381	20,650	21,031	21,133
1953	21,227	21,277	21,430	21,675	21,816	21,747	21,778	21,934	21,819	21,640	21,451	21,058
1954	21,000	21,064	21,036	20,967	20,811	20,650	20,651	19,804	19,753	19,718	19,955	20,314
1955	20,529	20,692	20,916	21,049	21,416	21,796	22,244	22,664	22,977	23,421	23,771	24,110
1956	24,515	24,686	25,414	25,932	26,448	26,799	27,145	27,418	27,778	27,858	28,199	28,395
1957	28,695	28,720	29,182	29,503	29,650	30,033	30,245	30,285	30,374	29,969	29,573	29,517
1958	29,171	28,835	28,728	28,554	28,168	28,079	28,039	27,941	28,122	28,215	28,342	28,496
1959	28,567	28,583	28,820	29,092	29,573	30,042	30,026	30,456	30,646	30,915	31,076	31,288
1960	31,433	31,870	32,093	32,293	32,591	33,011	32,993	32,840	32,956	32,996	33,118	33,018
1961	32,999	32,966	33,111	33,079	33,020	32,955	33,012	33,131	33,214	33,215	33,280	33,429
1962	33,582	33,712	33,907	34,121	34,269	34,509	34,740	35,038	35,318	35,635	35,939	35,986
1963	36,039	36,126	36,251	36,458	36,626	36,740	36,872	37,047	37,341	37,821	38,579	39,045
1964	38,931	39,195	39,201	39,554	39,882	40,137	40,428	40,839	41,418	41,625	42,068	42,737
1965	43,562	44,618	45,563	46,203	47,209	47,718	48,072	49,139	50,141	50,812	51,650	52,300
1966	53,195	54,071	54,805	55,377	56,139	57,228	58,223	59,360	59,950	60,578	61,043	61,332
1967	61,876	62,404	63,100	63,598	63,998	64,682	65,083	64,862	65,155	65,644	66,161	67,068
1968	67,254	67,415	67,732	68,877	69,067	69,598	70,294	71,359	72,318	73,153	74,374	75,150
1969	77,048	77,843	79,091	81,132	82,277	83,502	83,909	85,141	86,404	87,358	88,070	89,059
1970	88,521	90,023	91,243	91,333	91,864	92,444	92,433	93,072	93,435	91,680	91,082	91,069
1971	90,944	91,625	91,904	90,891	91,662	90,706	89,951	91,627	93,437	92,465	92,301	91,788
1972	84,478	85,260	86,195	87,342	87,906	88,268	88,429	88,800	88,593	90,502	91,408	92,111
1973	94,279	98,034	100,124	101,768	103,074	105,166	106,581	108,505	108,458	109,664	110,877	111,764
1974	113,967	116,322	117,738	122,857	125,111	126,537	130,706	133,304	137,429	138,352	139,734	139,873
1975	140,652	139,605	138,152	136,564	133,750	131,397	130,713	129,579	128,146	126,999	126,131	126,245
1976	125,349	125,758	123,490	120,789	121,069	122,018	121,328	121,083	120,710	121,770	123,317	124,225
1977	124,450	125,824	126,179	126,925	127,740	128,990	128,860	130,214	130,848	132,174	133,272	134,372
1978	135,158	135,658	138,536	140,620	143,029	145,547	146,937	147,792	148,769	150,501	152,486	152,870
1979	155,975	158,341	160,335	165,793	168,229	171,623	175,320	179,017	183,790	184,399	183,394	186,443
1980	193,068	197,288	200,406	200,583	198,756	202,454	200,910	201,732	203,417	204,727	209,253	211,014
1981	213,016	213,391	211,676	215,581	221,279	225,515	229,664	234,814	238,847	241,377	244,824	247,853
1982	254,693	259,934	261,328	266,688	271,022	272,899	273,160	273,540	274,885	274,856	270,235	264,699
1983	268,553	268,582	269,450	265,604	261,465	262,099	261,703	262,875	262,747	261,829	263,187	267,368
1984	274,768	279,364	287,370	294,220	300,525	310,036	314,375	317,394	321,437	325,648	328,615	329,459
1985	329,668	332,412	334,670	335,158	338,108	336,876	339,378	340,740	339,599	343,857	347,028	348,859
1986	351,101	349,392	347,888	342,642	345,052	345,978	347,464	351,931	351,008	352,769	353,255	358,781
1987	366,490	364,936	363,447	363,216	362,718	363,766	362,668	359,989	363,258	366,003	364,818	367,421
1988	369,444	375,735	377,816	384,954	386,365	389,832	393,650	396,588	396,160	400,153	402,456	407,748
1989	410,623	418,363	421,349	424,588	435,006	437,531	441,709	448,360	448,107	449,146	452,060	453,842
1990	452,036	456,148	464,694	465,029	465,112	466,658	468,858	471,704	476,985	476,314	471,150	471,865
1991	470,448	464,621	466,493	460,390	457,099	454,526	453,642	444,401	439,866	436,113	436,035	431,393
1992	425,795	427,535	427,706	426,268	424,480	421,791	421,956	422,919	420,862	425,595	430,259	428,370
1993	424,134	425,691	421,226	424,675	429,492	430,141	434,171	434,647	434,121	431,796	431,819	433,810
1994	435,933	432,691	432,417	435,278	439,393	443,957	449,314	453,923	461,218	468,583	471,190	477,936
1995	486,990	495,166	501,961	515,372	516,737	521,652	525,498	-	-	-	-	-

Source: U.S. Department of Commerce, Bureau of Economic Analysis, Board of Governors of the Federal Reserve System, Citibank and U.S. Department of the Treasury. - indicates data not available or zero.

CHAPTER 5

ECONOMIC SERIES

Capacity Utilization Rate
Total Industry
Percent

Year	Jan	Feb	Mar	Apr	May	Jun	Jul	Aug	Sep	Oct	Nov	Dec

Source: Board of Governors of the Federal Reserve System. — indicates data not available.

ECONOMIC SERIES

The 21 series in this chapter are classified as "important economic measures" by the Department of Commerce. They are not cyclic indicators but measure other aspects of the economy. The series are grouped under four headings:

Savings
Producer Prices, Wages, and Productivity
Implicit Price Deflators for Gross Domestic Product Sectors
Labor and Employment
International Transactions

The section on implicit price deflators for GDP is a new feature of this edition aimed at providing better data to the user for calculating inflationary pressures on personal or institutional income.

A brief introduction to each of these sections provides a description of each series covered and some discussion of the analytical uses of each series.

Bibliography

1. Fischer, Stanley, Rudiger Dornbusch, and Richard Schmalensee. *Introduction to Macroeconomics*. McGraw-Hill Book Company, New York, 1988.

2. Fitch, Thomas P. *Dictionary of Banking Terms*. Barron's, New York, 1990.

3. Siegel, Barry N. *Money, Banking, and the Economy*. Academic Press, New York, 1982.

3. U.S. Department of Commerce, Bureau of Economic Analysis. *Survey of Current Business*. Superintendent of Documents, U.S. Government Printing Office, Washington, DC 20302.

INDICATORS OF SAVINGS

This section presents 5 series used to measure the nation's savings rate. The series presented are:

Gross saving
Business saving
Personal saving
Personal saving rate
Government surplus or deficit

In the aggregate, savings taken as a total are an indirect indicator of the nation's capacity to invest in future productive facilities. Business and personal savings create the pool of capital available for new housing, infrastructure, tooling, factories, etc.—investment. These private sources of savings are diminished by government deficits and increased by foreign investment in the United States.

Gross Saving. Data for 1946 through 1995 are shown on a quarterly, annualized basis in billions of current dollars. The series is made up of personal savings plus business savings less (currently) government deficits at the federal, state, and local levels.

Business Saving. Presented as billions of current dollars for 1946 through 1995 in quarterly, annualized values, business savings is a complex category made up of the following components:

Undistributed corporate profits
Corporate capital consumption allowances
Noncorporate capital consumption allowances
Wage accruals less disbursements

Corporate profits are adjusted for inventory valuation changes and capital consumption adjustments. Noncorporate capital consumption allowances are also adjusted. The sum of these values combines into savings carried by the business sector from one period into another.

Personal Saving and **Personal Saving Rate**. Data for Personal saving are presented in the same format as Gross and Business saving; Personal saving rate is shown in percent. Personal saving is derived by deducting taxes from personal income, yielding disposable personal income (DPI); personal expenditures are deducted from DPI to obtain personal saving. Personal saving as a percent of DPI is the Personal saving rate. In the first quarter of 1993, this value was 3.9 percent; the highest rate shown in the data was the 2nd quarter of 1975 (10.5%—after a recession) and, before that, in the first quarter of 1946 (11.0%). The saving rate rarely reaches double digits in the United States; in Japan and some European countries, a high double-digit saving rate is the rule rather than the exception.

Government Surplus or Deficit. Data show quarterly values, in billions of current dollars, for 1946 through 1995. In recent years, the government has run large deficits; since deficits are financed from savings, deficits reduce total resources available for investment; the government competes with private users of capital for funds. However, if government deficits were erased by higher taxes, the net result would be largely the same: personal and business savings are income *net* of taxes; therefore higher taxes would also reduce gross savings.

Gross Saving

(Annual Rate, Billions of $)

Year	1st Quarter	2nd Quarter	3rd Quarter	4th Quarter
1946	27.3	36.0	38.6	40.0
1947	42.9	40.3	40.8	46.0
1948	50.4	53.2	52.0	51.3
1949	43.2	35.2	36.2	31.8
1950	40.1	47.7	53.4	64.5
1951	58.7	61.8	57.4	55.2
1952	56.3	49.7	51.6	53.7
1953	54.0	53.9	53.7	47.1
1954	48.7	49.1	51.7	57.1
1955	62.2	67.1	69.5	74.0
1956	75.5	76.7	78.9	79.7
1957	79.3	79.9	79.5	70.4
1958	65.3	60.7	66.0	73.9
1959	77.5	84.2	75.8	80.1
1960	92.6	85.3	84.1	78.5
1961	78.2	81.5	87.3	90.5
1962	92.6	92.3	93.3	93.1
1963	96.3	101.0	99.5	104.7
1964	106.5	106.4	110.2	116.8
1965	124.5	125.9	124.4	125.1
1966	130.6	131.4	129.7	134.5
1967	127.4	125.0	131.9	138.7
1968	136.1	140.8	141.5	148.5
1969	154.2	157.0	163.7	163.1
1970	155.4	157.7	156.2	151.5
1971	167.2	170.8	176.0	180.9
1972	187.3	194.0	203.7	221.7
1973	234.9	241.9	253.5	278.9
1974	255.5	246.5	246.0	249.9
1975	224.1	225.6	252.4	263.6
1976	279.7	287.6	284.9	286.9
1977	299.7	332.3	364.2	356.6
1978	370.3	413.7	426.6	452.3
1979	463.9	470.7	470.8	468.4
1980	465.1	443.0	453.4	500.3
1981	541.1	539.9	579.3	566.2
1982	519.6	542.0	513.4	458.5
1983	476.1	493.3	494.4	542.4
1984	611.0	635.4	652.3	637.0
1985	625.7	619.9	592.1	603.8
1986	625.8	584.4	538.2	550.1
1987	588.2	600.1	619.7	667.9
1988	678.0	701.5	716.5	720.1
1989	760.6	749.4	728.9	728.4
1990	735.5	765.9	705.5	683.8
1991	798.8	744.5	722.1	740.1
1992	719.1	722.3	731.9	718.5
1993	760.1	775.0	788.9	825.8
1994	886.2	923.3	922.6	950.3
1995	1,006.0	992.0	-	-

Source: U.S. Department of Commerce, Bureau of Economic Analysis. - indicates data not available or zero.

Business Saving

(Annual Rate, Billions of $)

Year	1st Quarter	2nd Quarter	3rd Quarter	4th Quarter
1946	15.6	17.1	16.3	17.9
1947	19.0	23.6	24.2	25.7
1948	29.4	31.4	31.5	33.7
1949	33.7	33.1	34.1	30.9
1950	30.1	31.4	32.5	34.3
1951	31.1	35.5	38.8	39.2
1952	39.3	38.1	38.3	40.9
1953	41.2	40.1	40.1	38.1
1954	40.4	42.1	42.9	45.4
1955	48.2	49.5	49.6	50.4
1956	50.1	50.4	51.9	51.8
1957	53.7	54.0	54.5	53.3
1958	50.6	51.4	53.9	57.5
1959	59.4	62.2	59.6	60.6
1960	62.3	60.7	60.9	59.9
1961	59.4	62.4	63.3	64.9
1962	69.2	68.7	69.6	72.0
1963	72.1	73.8	74.9	75.7
1964	79.5	79.5	80.5	80.4
1965	87.2	88.4	89.4	91.7
1966	94.6	95.5	95.3	99.1
1967	97.3	96.8	98.6	102.1
1968	98.8	102.4	103.3	105.5
1969	106.8	106.4	107.2	104.5
1970	103.5	110.0	110.3	109.2
1971	120.5	123.6	128.2	133.3
1972	137.7	146.7	146.0	151.3
1973	156.3	157.5	160.5	163.1
1974	160.2	161.8	158.8	169.4
1975	186.0	200.5	214.5	223.2
1976	228.9	227.5	230.2	233.7
1977	244.0	265.4	280.1	278.9
1978	282.3	302.0	311.9	323.9
1979	321.7	331.6	340.5	344.3
1980	338.0	337.1	346.3	361.7
1981	374.9	383.6	404.4	413.4
1982	400.8	413.7	423.6	431.7
1983	447.8	463.9	476.7	502.4
1984	501.0	514.9	524.9	542.1
1985	528.5	542.4	559.2	555.5
1986	551.5	531.0	527.9	525.3
1987	557.7	582.4	600.7	613.9
1988	638.4	645.1	644.6	658.4
1989	644.7	662.5	682.1	679.8
1990	690.9	712.9	673.9	686.9
1991	720.3	725.4	721.0	736.2
1992	744.3	737.4	779.5	750.1
1993	757.4	772.7	807.6	821.9
1994	861.8	840.4	849.4	850.0
1995	862.7	887.5	-	-

Source: U.S. Department of Commerce, Bureau of Economic Analysis. - indicates data not available or zero.

Personal Saving
(Annual Rate, Billions of $)

Year	1st Quarter	2nd Quarter	3rd Quarter	4th Quarter
1946	16.8	15.2	11.7	10.6
1947	8.0	2.0	6.0	4.1
1948	6.6	10.3	13.8	12.7
1949	8.7	6.4	6.9	6.0
1950	16.5	12.2	5.8	14.5
1951	9.9	19.4	18.8	18.2
1952	17.4	15.7	19.4	16.4
1953	16.7	18.8	18.1	18.6
1954	18.6	15.3	15.0	16.0
1955	14.2	15.3	17.1	17.0
1956	18.8	21.2	22.1	23.1
1957	21.8	23.6	23.3	21.9
1958	22.7	22.4	25.0	26.1
1959	22.8	24.0	19.6	21.7
1960	22.2	19.5	20.9	19.8
1961	22.6	23.2	26.6	27.3
1962	27.1	26.6	26.0	23.7
1963	24.1	24.1	23.1	27.3
1964	27.8	32.1	30.7	35.5
1965	31.2	32.4	38.4	36.4
1966	34.0	34.2	36.0	41.2
1967	45.3	43.0	46.4	48.6
1968	46.1	48.2	39.1	42.0
1969	35.5	38.5	49.0	50.3
1970	48.9	57.4	60.9	62.9
1971	63.8	68.4	67.1	62.3
1972	56.7	51.0	58.7	72.6
1973	72.1	79.7	85.3	107.3
1974	98.3	84.2	88.7	102.4
1975	84.5	121.3	95.0	100.3
1976	97.4	95.7	92.6	86.4
1977	73.4	83.9	100.7	93.7
1978	102.6	102.3	109.4	116.7
1979	119.7	122.5	123.9	127.2
1980	141.8	145.8	152.8	175.0
1981	179.7	176.1	199.1	212.3
1982	191.3	213.5	209.3	183.8
1983	179.2	159.2	160.0	176.3
1984	217.4	213.1	234.8	222.6
1985	190.5	228.8	158.6	179.2
1986	199.3	225.1	174.4	151.1
1987	184.5	98.5	115.2	169.8
1988	162.0	151.8	152.4	156.4
1989	182.0	148.5	129.0	148.8
1990	176.5	175.7	151.6	176.2
1991	212.8	211.9	196.9	224.6
1992	234.7	243.8	225.8	287.4
1993	184.6	214.0	182.3	189.4
1994	175.5	201.1	203.3	232.6
1995	263.7	206.1	-	-

Source: U.S. Department of Commerce, Bureau of Economic Analysis. - indicates data not available or zero.

Personal Saving Rate

(Percent)

Year	1st Quarter	2nd Quarter	3rd Quarter	4th Quarter
1946	11.0	9.7	7.2	6.4
1947	4.8	1.2	3.5	2.4
1948	3.7	5.5	7.1	6.6
1949	4.6	3.4	3.7	3.2
1950	8.2	6.0	2.8	6.7
1951	4.4	8.5	8.2	7.8
1952	7.5	6.7	8.0	6.6
1953	6.6	7.3	7.1	7.2
1954	7.2	5.9	5.8	6.0
1955	5.3	5.5	6.0	5.9
1956	6.4	7.1	7.3	7.5
1957	7.0	7.5	7.3	6.9
1958	7.1	7.0	7.6	7.8
1959	6.7	6.9	5.6	6.2
1960	6.2	5.4	5.8	5.5
1961	6.2	6.2	7.0	7.0
1962	6.9	6.7	6.5	5.9
1963	5.9	5.8	5.5	6.4
1964	6.3	7.1	6.7	7.6
1965	6.6	6.7	7.7	7.1
1966	6.6	6.5	6.7	7.6
1967	8.2	7.6	8.1	8.3
1968	7.7	7.8	6.3	6.6
1969	5.6	5.9	7.3	7.3
1970	7.0	8.0	8.3	8.5
1971	8.4	8.8	8.5	7.7
1972	6.9	6.1	6.9	8.1
1973	7.9	8.5	8.8	10.7
1974	9.7	8.2	8.4	9.5
1975	7.8	10.5	8.2	8.4
1976	7.9	7.7	7.3	6.6
1977	5.5	6.1	7.1	6.5
1978	6.9	6.6	6.9	7.1
1979	7.1	7.1	7.0	7.0
1980	7.5	7.7	7.8	8.5
1981	8.5	8.2	9.0	9.5
1982	8.5	9.3	8.9	7.7
1983	7.4	6.5	6.4	6.8
1984	8.1	7.8	8.4	7.9
1985	6.7	7.8	5.4	6.0
1986	6.5	7.2	5.5	4.8
1987	5.7	3.1	3.5	5.0
1988	4.7	4.3	4.3	4.3
1989	4.9	4.0	3.4	3.9
1990	4.4	4.4	3.7	4.3
1991	5.1	5.0	4.6	5.2
1992	5.3	5.5	5.0	6.2
1993	4.0	4.6	3.9	4.0
1994	3.6	4.1	4.1	4.6
1995	5.1	4.0	-	-

Source: U.S. Department of Commerce, Bureau of Economic Analysis. - indicates data not available or zero.

Government Surplus or Deficit

(Annual Rate, Billions of $)

Year	1st Quarter	2nd Quarter	3rd Quarter	4th Quarter
1946	-5.8	4.6	10.6	11.5
1947	16.0	14.7	10.6	16.2
1948	14.3	11.3	7.0	4.9
1949	0.7	-3.9	-4.8	-5.1
1950	-6.5	4.0	15.0	15.7
1951	17.6	7.0	-0.2	-2.2
1952	-0.5	-4.2	-5.7	-3.5
1953	-3.8	-5.0	-4.5	-9.6
1954	-10.3	-8.3	-6.2	-4.2
1955	-0.1	2.3	2.8	6.6
1956	6.6	5.1	5.0	4.8
1957	3.9	2.4	1.8	-4.9
1958	-8.0	-13.2	-12.8	-9.7
1959	-4.8	-2.0	-3.3	-2.2
1960	8.1	5.1	2.3	-1.2
1961	-3.8	-4.0	-2.6	-1.7
1962	-3.7	-3.0	-2.3	-2.7
1963	0.2	3.0	1.5	1.7
1964	-0.9	-5.3	-1.0	0.9
1965	6.1	5.1	-3.3	-2.9
1966	2.0	1.9	-1.7	-5.9
1967	-15.2	-14.8	-13.0	-12.0
1968	-8.9	-9.7	-0.8	1.0
1969	12.0	12.1	7.5	8.4
1970	2.1	-10.6	-15.8	-21.5
1971	-17.9	-22.2	-20.4	-16.4
1972	-7.0	-4.2	-1.4	-2.9
1973	6.5	4.8	7.7	8.5
1974	5.0	0.6	-1.5	-21.9
1975	-46.3	-96.2	-57.0	-59.8
1976	-46.6	-35.5	-37.9	-33.2
1977	-17.7	-16.9	-16.5	-16.0
1978	-14.5	9.4	5.3	11.6
1979	21.3	15.5	5.3	-4.3
1980	-15.9	-41.1	-47.3	-36.9
1981	-14.6	-20.9	-25.1	-60.7
1982	-72.6	-85.2	-119.6	-156.9
1983	-150.8	-129.8	-142.3	-136.3
1984	-107.5	-92.6	-107.4	-127.8
1985	-93.4	-151.2	-125.7	-130.9
1986	-125.0	-171.7	-164.2	-126.2
1987	-154.0	-80.7	-96.2	-115.8
1988	-122.4	-95.5	-80.5	-94.7
1989	-66.1	-61.5	-82.3	-100.2
1990	-131.9	-122.7	-119.9	-179.3
1991	-134.4	-192.8	-195.8	-220.7
1992	-260.0	-258.9	-273.5	-239.1
1993	-261.9	-211.6	-201.0	-185.6
1994	-151.1	-118.1	-130.1	-132.3
1995	-120.4	-101.7	-	-

Source: U.S. Department of Commerce, Bureau of Economic Analysis. - indicates data not available or zero.

INDICATORS OF PRODUCER PRICES, WAGES, AND PRODUCTIVITY

This section presents 8 series used to measure the nation's inflation rate, prices, and output. The series presented are:

Producer Price Index, crude materials for further processing
Producer Price Index, intermediate materials, supplies, and components
Producer Price Index, capital equipment
Producer Price Index, finished consumer goods
Producer Price Index, finished goods
Producer Price Index, finished goods less food and energy
Index of output per hour, all persons, business sector

Conspicuous by absence, perhaps, is the *Consumer Price Index*. It is presented in the next chapter in considerable detail. Similarly, much more detailed statistics are presented on the *Producer Price Index*, a summary of which is presented later in this section.

Producer Price Index Series. All six tables are indexes based on 1987 (1987 = 100). Detailed PPI tables are presented in the next chapter. The tables included in this section are summary series showing broad categories. Production processes refine crude raw materials (ores, logs, crude oil) into intermediate products (steel, pulp, engine blocks); intermediate products are transformed into finished products (autos, writing paper, gasoline). The tables included follow price trends at each of these levels. The data are used in a variety of ways in macroeconomic analysis and in business planning. For example, note that the inflation rate shown by the PPI for crude and intermediate materials is substantially less than it is for finished goods; at lower levels of refinement and product differentiation, competitive forces are greater (the "stuff" handled is more of a commodity); as raw materials are formed into products, differentiation increases and opportunities for aggressive pricing are greater.

Index of Output Per Hour, All Persons, Business Sector. Data are shown from 1947 to 1995 in quarterly increments as an index based on 1987 (1987 = 100). This is an indicator of national productivity. Output per hour reflects all inputs to the production process, including tooling, fuels, improved raw materials, degree of capacity utilization . . . *and* human effort, measured in time. The indicator, therefore, is influenced by the personal productivity of employees but also, more importantly in today's environment, by technology and therefore by the level of investment. Rising productivity means that more is produced, in absolute terms, by one hour of labor. It does not mean that employment is increasing; it may be decreasing as better machines take over human tasks. Rising productivity may also mean that the capital required per workplace is on the increase. The series, therefore, yields best results when viewed in concert with other series on wages, employment, capacity utilization, and investment.

Producer Price Index
Crude materials
(1982 = 100)

Year	Jan	Feb	Mar	Apr	May	Jun	Jul	Aug	Sep	Oct	Nov	Dec
1947	-	-	-	30.7	30.5	30.6	31.1	31.6	32.4	33.6	33.8	35.3
1948	36.3	34.4	33.5	34.2	35.3	36.2	36.0	35.5	34.8	33.8	33.5	33.0
1949	32.0	31.0	30.7	30.2	30.1	29.7	29.2	29.2	29.5	29.5	29.7	29.7
1950	29.6	30.5	30.3	30.5	31.6	32.1	33.3	34.0	34.5	34.5	35.4	36.7
1951	38.1	39.6	39.1	39.1	38.5	38.1	36.7	36.2	35.9	36.7	36.4	36.5
1952	35.8	35.5	35.0	34.9	34.8	34.7	34.6	34.7	33.9	33.7	33.7	32.9
1953	32.6	32.4	32.5	31.6	31.9	31.4	32.4	31.7	32.0	31.4	31.2	31.7
1954	32.1	32.0	32.1	32.2	32.1	31.5	31.4	31.3	31.0	31.2	31.4	30.9
1955	31.1	31.0	30.7	30.9	30.1	30.7	30.4	30.1	31.0	31.2	31.4	30.9
1956	29.5	29.9	29.8	30.3	30.7	30.5	30.5	31.0	30.5	30.4	29.4	29.5
1957	31.3	31.0	30.8	30.8	30.7	31.5	32.0	32.1	31.0	31.0	31.1	31.6
1958	31.4	31.9	32.3	31.9	32.4	32.0	32.1	31.9	31.2	31.0	31.1	31.5
1959	31.6	31.4	31.5	31.7	31.5	31.3	31.0	30.7	31.7	31.9	32.1	31.6
1960	30.4	30.4	30.7	30.7	30.8	30.5	30.4	29.8	30.9	30.7	30.5	30.4
1961	30.4	30.5	30.3	30.2	29.9	29.4	29.7	30.5	30.2	30.3	30.2	30.3
1962	30.6	30.6	30.5	30.1	30.1	30.0	30.2	30.5	30.2	30.3	30.2	30.6
1963	30.3	30.0	29.5	29.7	29.6	29.9	30.0	30.5	31.2	30.8	31.0	30.7
1964	29.8	29.4	29.5	29.5	29.4	29.1	29.2	29.9	29.8	30.0	30.2	29.4
1965	29.5	29.9	30.0	30.4	30.8	31.6	31.2	31.5	31.4	31.7	32.1	32.7
1966	33.0	33.7	33.5	33.3	33.1	33.0	33.4	33.6	33.4	32.9	32.3	32.0
1967	32.2	31.5	31.1	30.7	31.1	31.4	31.3	31.3	31.2	31.3	31.1	31.5
1968	31.4	31.5	31.6	31.7	31.5	31.3	31.6	31.7	31.9	32.1	32.8	32.4
1969	32.6	32.3	32.7	33.1	34.0	34.5	34.1	34.4	34.4	34.8	35.2	35.1
1970	35.1	35.2	35.6	35.5	35.0	35.0	35.1	34.7	35.5	35.5	35.1	34.5
1971	34.8	35.9	35.4	36.0	36.0	36.2	35.9	35.8	35.7	36.4	37.0	37.2
1972	37.8	38.1	38.1	38.7	39.3	39.4	40.0	40.3	40.5	40.9	42.0	43.8
1973	45.0	47.1	49.3	50.1	52.5	55.0	52.5	64.1	60.9	58.5	59.0	59.1
1974	63.3	64.3	62.3	60.6	58.3	55.4	59.8	62.9	60.9	63.2	64.2	61.5
1975	59.6	57.9	57.1	59.5	61.2	61.5	62.4	63.0	64.5	65.1	64.4	64.0
1976	63.0	62.1	61.5	63.9	63.6	65.2	64.8	63.6	63.4	63.0	63.4	64.5
1977	64.3	65.7	66.6	68.3	67.6	65.5	64.7	63.9	63.7	64.0	65.4	66.4
1978	67.3	68.4	69.8	72.1	72.8	74.6	74.2	73.7	75.1	77.0	77.4	78.0
1979	80.1	82.1	83.8	84.4	84.7	85.6	86.5	85.5	87.9	88.8	90.0	91.2
1980	90.9	92.6	90.8	88.3	89.5	90.1	94.6	99.0	100.4	102.2	103.5	102.7
1981	103.4	104.2	103.8	104.2	103.8	104.9	105.0	104.0	102.7	101.2	99.7	98.8
1982	99.7	100.0	99.7	100.2	101.9	101.8	100.7	99.8	99.2	98.7	99.2	98.8
1983	98.8	100.0	100.5	101.2	100.9	100.5	99.5	102.2	103.3	103.2	102.3	103.5
1984	104.6	103.8	105.7	105.2	104.5	103.3	104.0	103.3	102.8	101.5	101.9	101.4
1985	99.9	99.4	97.6	96.7	95.8	95.2	94.9	92.9	91.8	94.1	95.7	95.5
1986	94.2	90.5	88.2	85.6	86.5	86.2	86.4	86.7	86.6	87.4	87.6	86.9
1987	89.3	90.2	90.5	92.5	93.8	94.5	95.6	96.5	96.0	95.8	95.1	94.9
1988	94.2	95.2	94.1	95.4	95.8	97.0	96.7	97.0	97.0	96.6	95.2	98.1
1989	102.0	101.7	102.9	104.1	104.5	103.2	103.5	101.2	102.5	102.7	103.5	105.1
1990	106.7	106.8	105.1	102.7	103.1	100.6	101.0	110.5	115.8	125.8	117.8	110.8
1991	112.3	103.9	100.5	100.6	100.8	99.5	99.6	99.8	98.5	101.1	100.5	97.4
1992	96.4	98.6	97.0	98.3	100.0	101.7	101.9	101.3	103.0	103.3	102.7	100.8
1993	100.7	101.3	101.5	103.3	105.4	104.1	102.0	101.4	101.5	104.3	103.3	101.0
1994	102.3	101.7	102.9	103.5	101.9	103.0	102.6	102.6	100.1	99.5	100.1	100.6
1995	100.9	102.5	101.2	103.3	102.5	103.2	102.4	-	-	-	-	-

Source: U.S. Department of Labor, Bureau of Labor Statistics. - indicates data not available or zero.

Producer Price Index
Intermediate materials
(1982 = 100)

Year	Jan	Feb	Mar	Apr	May	Jun	Jul	Aug	Sep	Oct	Nov	Dec
1947	-	-	-	23.1	23.0	23.1	23.2	23.3	23.7	23.9	24.2	24.5
1948	25.0	24.7	24.8	25.0	25.2	25.4	25.4	25.5	25.5	25.4	25.4	25.2
1949	25.1	24.9	24.7	24.4	24.3	24.1	24.1	23.9	23.8	23.8	23.7	23.7
1950	23.8	24.0	24.1	24.2	24.6	24.7	25.2	25.6	26.2	26.6	26.9	27.7
1951	28.5	28.7	28.8	28.8	28.8	28.7	28.4	28.0	27.9	27.9	27.9	27.8
1952	27.8	27.7	27.5	27.5	27.4	27.5	27.5	27.5	27.6	27.5	27.4	27.3
1953	27.4	27.4	27.5	27.5	27.7	27.8	28.0	27.9	27.8	27.8	27.8	27.8
1954	27.9	27.8	27.8	27.9	27.9	27.8	27.9	27.8	27.8	27.8	27.9	27.8
1955	27.9	28.0	28.0	28.0	28.1	28.2	28.4	28.5	28.7	28.9	28.9	29.0
1956	29.1	29.1	29.4	29.5	29.6	29.7	29.4	29.7	29.8	30.0	30.0	30.1
1957	30.2	30.3	30.3	30.3	30.2	30.3	30.3	30.4	30.4	30.3	30.4	30.4
1958	30.4	30.3	30.3	30.3	30.3	30.3	30.3	30.4	30.4	30.4	30.5	30.6
1959	30.6	30.7	30.7	30.8	30.9	30.9	30.9	30.8	30.8	30.8	30.9	30.8
1960	30.9	30.9	30.9	30.9	30.8	30.9	30.8	30.8	30.8	30.8	30.7	30.6
1961	30.7	30.7	30.7	30.7	30.6	30.5	30.5	30.5	30.5	30.4	30.5	30.6
1962	30.5	30.5	30.6	30.6	30.6	30.6	30.6	30.6	30.6	30.6	30.5	30.5
1963	30.5	30.5	30.5	30.4	30.7	30.7	30.7	30.7	30.7	30.8	30.8	30.8
1964	30.8	30.8	30.7	30.7	30.7	30.6	30.7	30.7	30.7	30.9	30.9	30.9
1965	30.9	30.9	31.0	31.0	31.1	31.2	31.2	31.3	31.3	31.3	31.4	31.4
1966	31.5	31.6	31.7	31.8	32.0	32.0	32.2	32.3	32.3	32.2	32.2	32.2
1967	32.2	32.1	32.1	32.1	32.1	32.2	32.2	32.2	32.3	32.3	32.4	32.6
1968	32.6	32.7	32.8	32.8	32.8	32.9	33.0	33.0	33.1	33.2	33.2	33.4
1969	33.6	33.7	33.9	33.8	33.9	34.0	34.0	34.2	34.2	34.4	34.6	34.7
1970	35.0	35.0	34.9	35.1	35.2	35.3	35.5	35.5	35.6	35.8	35.9	35.9
1971	36.0	36.1	36.3	36.3	36.5	36.7	36.9	37.2	37.2	37.1	37.2	37.4
1972	37.5	37.7	37.8	37.9	38.0	38.0	38.1	38.2	38.5	38.7	39.0	39.6
1973	39.8	40.4	41.1	41.3	42.2	43.0	42.3	43.5	43.0	43.4	43.8	44.8
1974	45.9	46.8	48.1	49.0	50.6	51.5	53.4	55.8	55.9	57.2	57.8	57.8
1975	58.0	57.8	57.4	57.5	57.3	57.3	57.5	58.0	58.2	58.8	59.0	59.2
1976	59.4	59.6	59.8	60.0	60.3	60.8	61.1	61.3	61.9	62.0	62.4	62.8
1977	63.0	63.3	63.9	64.4	64.9	64.9	65.1	65.4	65.7	65.8	66.3	66.6
1978	66.9	67.4	67.8	68.1	68.7	69.2	69.4	69.9	70.5	71.3	71.9	72.4
1979	73.1	73.7	74.6	75.7	76.6	77.5	78.7	79.8	81.1	82.4	83.2	84.0
1980	86.0	87.6	88.2	88.5	89.0	89.8	90.5	91.5	91.9	92.8	93.5	94.4
1981	95.6	96.1	97.1	98.3	98.7	99.0	99.2	99.7	99.7	99.8	99.9	100.0
1982	100.4	100.3	99.9	99.7	99.7	99.8	100.0	99.9	100.0	99.9	100.1	100.1
1983	99.8	100.0	99.7	99.5	99.8	100.2	100.5	100.9	101.6	101.7	101.8	101.9
1984	102.1	102.5	103.0	103.2	103.4	103.6	103.4	103.2	103.1	103.2	103.3	103.2
1985	103.1	102.8	102.7	102.9	103.2	102.6	102.3	102.3	102.2	102.3	102.5	102.9
1986	102.4	101.2	99.9	98.9	98.7	98.6	98.0	98.0	98.5	98.3	98.3	98.5
1987	99.0	99.8	99.9	100.3	100.8	101.4	101.9	102.4	102.6	103.1	103.5	103.8
1988	104.1	104.4	104.8	105.5	106.2	107.4	108.3	108.5	108.7	108.6	108.8	109.4
1989	110.8	111.3	111.9	112.5	112.6	112.5	112.2	111.8	112.1	112.2	112.0	112.2
1990	113.7	112.8	112.9	113.1	113.1	112.9	112.8	114.0	115.8	117.4	117.7	116.9
1991	116.8	115.9	114.7	114.3	114.1	114.0	113.6	113.8	114.0	113.9	114.0	113.9
1992	113.6	113.9	114.0	114.2	114.6	115.1	115.0	115.0	115.2	115.1	115.0	115.1
1993	115.6	116.1	116.4	116.7	116.4	116.3	116.1	116.1	116.2	116.3	116.5	116.3
1994	116.7	117.1	117.2	117.2	117.4	117.8	118.2	119.0	119.5	119.9	120.9	121.4
1995	123.0	123.9	124.4	125.1	125.4	125.5	125.5	-	-	-	-	-

Source: U.S. Department of Labor, Bureau of Labor Statistics. - indicates data not available or zero.

Producer Price Index

Capital equipment

(1982 = 100)

Year	Jan	Feb	Mar	Apr	May	Jun	Jul	Aug	Sep	Oct	Nov	Dec
1947	-	-	-	19.5	19.8	19.9	19.9	20.0	20.1	20.3	20.4	20.5
1948	20.6	20.7	20.8	20.9	21.0	21.3	21.7	22.1	22.3	22.5	22.5	22.6
1949	22.6	22.8	22.8	22.9	22.8	22.8	22.8	22.7	22.5	22.5	22.5	22.5
1950	22.5	22.5	22.5	22.7	22.8	22.8	23.0	23.4	23.7	23.9	24.1	24.8
1951	25.1	25.2	25.4	25.5	25.6	25.6	25.6	25.5	25.6	25.7	25.7	25.7
1952	25.7	25.9	25.9	25.9	26.0	26.0	26.1	25.9	25.9	25.9	25.9	25.9
1953	25.9	25.9	26.0	26.1	26.2	26.4	26.6	26.5	26.6	26.6	26.4	26.5
1954	26.6	26.6	26.6	26.7	26.7	26.7	26.7	26.7	26.7	26.7	26.7	26.8
1955	26.8	26.9	26.9	27.0	27.1	27.2	27.3	27.6	27.9	28.2	28.1	28.3
1956	28.4	28.6	28.8	29.1	29.2	29.3	29.4	29.6	30.1	30.3	30.6	30.6
1957	30.7	30.9	31.0	31.1	31.1	31.2	31.4	31.5	31.6	31.7	31.9	32.0
1958	32.0	32.0	32.0	32.1	32.1	32.1	32.1	32.1	32.1	32.1	32.3	32.4
1959	32.5	32.5	32.6	32.7	32.8	32.9	32.9	32.9	32.9	32.9	32.7	32.7
1960	32.8	32.8	32.9	32.8	32.8	32.8	32.9	32.9	32.6	32.8	32.8	32.8
1961	32.9	32.8	32.9	32.9	32.9	32.9	32.9	32.9	32.9	32.9	32.9	32.9
1962	32.9	32.9	33.0	33.0	33.0	33.0	33.0	33.0	33.0	33.0	33.0	33.0
1963	33.0	33.0	33.0	33.0	33.0	33.0	33.0	33.0	33.1	33.1	33.1	33.2
1964	33.1	33.2	33.3	33.3	33.4	33.4	33.5	33.5	33.5	33.5	33.5	33.5
1965	33.6	33.6	33.7	33.8	33.7	33.8	33.8	33.9	33.9	33.9	33.9	34.0
1966	34.0	34.1	34.2	34.3	34.5	34.6	34.7	34.8	34.9	35.0	35.2	35.3
1967	35.4	35.5	35.5	35.6	35.7	35.7	35.8	35.9	35.9	36.1	36.2	36.4
1968	36.5	36.6	36.6	36.8	37.0	37.0	37.1	37.2	37.3	37.4	37.5	37.5
1969	37.6	37.7	37.8	37.9	38.0	38.1	38.3	38.4	38.5	38.7	39.0	39.2
1970	39.3	39.4	39.6	39.7	39.8	39.9	40.0	40.2	40.3	40.8	41.0	41.1
1971	41.3	41.4	41.5	41.6	41.7	41.7	41.9	42.0	41.9	41.8	41.8	42.1
1972	42.3	42.5	42.6	42.7	42.8	42.8	42.9	42.9	43.0	42.8	42.9	43.0
1973	43.0	43.3	43.6	43.8	44.1	44.2	44.3	44.4	44.6	44.7	44.9	45.3
1974	45.8	46.2	46.8	47.4	48.7	49.7	50.7	52.1	53.1	54.2	55.0	55.5
1975	56.2	56.7	57.2	57.5	57.8	58.0	58.4	58.5	58.9	59.3	59.7	60.0
1976	60.4	60.7	61.1	61.3	61.5	61.8	62.1	62.5	62.9	63.1	63.4	64.0
1977	64.0	64.3	64.7	65.0	65.3	65.7	66.0	66.6	67.0	67.6	68.1	68.6
1978	68.8	69.1	69.6	69.9	70.5	71.0	71.5	72.0	72.6	72.8	73.5	74.0
1979	74.5	75.2	75.7	76.4	76.8	77.3	77.8	77.8	78.7	79.2	79.8	80.6
1980	81.7	82.3	83.1	84.4	84.6	85.1	86.2	87.0	87.5	88.8	89.3	89.7
1981	90.8	91.7	92.4	93.1	93.8	94.4	95.0	95.4	96.1	96.9	97.5	98.1
1982	98.6	98.2	98.7	99.0	99.5	100.0	100.3	100.7	101.0	101.1	101.3	101.9
1983	101.8	102.1	102.2	102.3	102.5	102.6	102.8	103.1	103.3	103.4	103.5	103.8
1984	104.1	104.5	104.6	105.3	105.1	105.2	105.5	105.6	105.9	105.6	105.8	105.6
1985	106.3	106.9	107.1	107.1	107.4	107.6	107.7	107.9	107.2	108.3	108.5	108.6
1986	108.6	108.7	108.9	109.2	109.3	109.6	109.7	109.8	109.7	110.6	110.8	110.9
1987	111.3	111.1	111.1	111.6	111.6	111.5	111.7	112.0	112.0	112.0	112.1	112.2
1988	112.8	113.0	113.2	113.5	113.8	114.0	114.4	114.9	115.2	115.5	115.7	116.1
1989	116.9	117.3	117.5	117.6	118.3	118.9	118.9	119.3	119.7	120.0	120.4	120.6
1990	121.0	121.4	121.8	122.1	122.1	122.5	122.9	123.3	123.8	124.1	124.5	124.8
1991	125.7	125.9	126.0	126.0	126.4	126.6	126.7	126.8	127.1	127.6	127.8	128.0
1992	128.3	128.4	128.6	128.9	129.0	129.0	129.1	129.4	129.4	129.7	129.9	130.1
1993	130.5	130.8	130.9	131.1	131.1	131.1	131.5	131.7	131.8	131.7	132.2	132.4
1994	132.9	133.1	133.3	133.7	134.1	134.3	134.4	134.7	135.0	134.3	134.5	134.9
1995	135.5	135.7	135.9	136.1	136.4	136.7	136.9	-	-	-	-	-

Source: U.S. Department of Labor, Bureau of Labor Statistics. - indicates data not available or zero.

Producer Price Index
Finished consumer goods
(1982 = 100)

Year	Jan	Feb	Mar	Apr	May	Jun	Jul	Aug	Sep	Oct	Nov	Dec
1947	-	-	-	28.4	28.3	28.3	28.3	28.5	28.9	29.2	29.6	30.1
1948	30.7	30.5	30.5	30.7	30.9	31.0	31.1	31.2	31.0	30.9	30.6	30.4
1949	30.2	29.9	29.8	29.6	29.5	29.5	29.2	29.1	29.0	29.0	28.9	28.8
1950	28.8	28.9	28.9	28.9	29.1	29.2	29.8	30.4	30.7	30.8	31.1	31.7
1951	32.3	32.8	32.8	32.9	33.0	32.8	32.5	32.5	32.4	32.6	32.6	32.7
1952	32.5	32.5	32.5	32.4	32.3	32.2	32.4	32.4	32.2	32.1	32.0	31.7
1953	31.8	31.7	31.7	31.6	31.6	31.7	31.7	31.7	31.9	31.8	31.6	31.7
1954	31.9	31.7	31.7	31.9	31.9	31.7	31.8	31.7	31.5	31.5	31.6	31.5
1955	31.6	31.7	31.5	31.6	31.4	31.6	31.3	31.4	31.5	31.4	31.5	31.5
1956	31.5	31.5	31.7	31.7	32.0	32.1	32.0	32.0	32.2	32.2	32.4	32.5
1957	32.5	32.6	32.6	32.7	32.7	32.8	33.0	33.0	33.0	33.1	33.2	33.4
1958	33.5	33.5	33.9	33.7	33.8	33.7	33.6	33.6	33.6	33.5	33.5	33.5
1959	33.4	33.4	33.3	33.4	33.3	33.3	33.2	33.1	33.5	33.2	33.1	33.2
1960	33.2	33.2	33.5	33.6	33.6	33.6	33.7	33.7	33.7	33.9	34.0	33.9
1961	33.8	34.0	33.8	33.6	33.4	33.4	33.5	33.6	33.5	33.4	33.5	33.6
1962	33.7	33.8	33.7	33.6	33.6	33.5	33.5	33.7	34.0	33.7	33.7	33.6
1963	33.6	33.5	33.3	33.3	33.5	33.6	33.6	33.5	33.5	33.5	33.6	33.5
1964	33.7	33.5	33.5	33.5	33.5	33.5	33.6	33.6	33.6	33.6	33.6	33.6
1965	33.6	33.6	33.8	34.0	34.1	34.3	34.2	34.3	34.3	34.5	34.6	34.9
1966	34.9	35.2	35.3	35.4	35.2	35.1	35.2	35.7	35.8	35.7	35.6	35.5
1967	35.4	35.3	35.2	35.3	35.4	35.7	35.6	35.7	35.8	35.8	35.9	35.9
1968	35.9	36.1	36.2	36.4	36.4	36.5	36.6	36.7	36.9	37.0	37.0	37.0
1969	37.2	37.1	37.3	37.5	37.8	38.0	38.0	38.1	38.2	38.5	38.8	38.8
1970	39.0	38.9	39.0	39.0	38.9	39.0	39.0	39.0	39.4	39.3	39.5	39.4
1971	39.5	39.7	39.8	40.0	40.1	40.3	40.1	40.4	40.3	40.4	40.6	40.9
1972	40.7	40.9	40.9	40.9	41.1	41.4	41.6	41.7	42.0	41.9	42.1	42.6
1973	43.0	43.5	44.7	45.0	45.3	45.9	45.7	47.7	47.5	47.4	47.9	48.3
1974	49.6	50.7	51.1	51.5	52.0	51.8	53.2	54.1	54.6	55.6	56.7	56.6
1975	56.8	56.6	56.4	56.9	57.3	57.8	58.4	59.0	59.4	59.9	60.1	60.1
1976	59.9	59.6	59.6	60.0	60.0	60.1	60.3	60.4	60.5	60.9	61.4	61.9
1977	62.1	62.8	63.4	63.7	64.2	64.2	64.5	64.8	65.0	65.3	65.8	66.1
1978	66.4	66.9	67.3	68.2	68.6	69.3	69.9	69.9	70.6	71.0	71.5	72.5
1979	73.3	74.2	74.8	75.6	75.9	76.4	77.3	78.3	79.8	80.6	81.8	82.6
1980	83.9	85.2	86.1	86.7	87.1	87.9	89.4	90.5	90.8	91.3	92.0	92.4
1981	93.3	94.1	95.3	96.4	96.6	97.0	97.1	97.1	97.5	97.8	98.0	98.4
1982	99.0	99.0	98.8	98.9	98.8	99.8	100.1	100.5	100.7	101.0	101.4	101.7
1983	100.8	100.8	100.7	100.7	101.0	101.3	101.3	101.6	101.8	101.9	101.5	101.9
1984	102.7	103.1	103.6	103.5	103.5	103.4	103.6	103.3	103.2	103.1	103.4	103.5
1985	103.4	103.4	103.3	103.9	104.2	103.8	103.8	103.6	102.9	103.9	104.6	105.3
1986	104.6	102.8	101.0	100.3	101.0	101.2	100.2	100.7	100.9	101.5	101.4	101.5
1987	102.1	102.5	102.6	103.3	103.4	103.8	104.0	104.2	104.5	104.4	104.3	104.1
1988	104.6	104.4	104.7	105.2	105.4	105.7	106.6	107.1	107.3	107.5	107.9	108.3
1989	109.5	110.5	110.9	111.9	112.9	112.7	112.4	111.7	112.5	113.1	113.2	114.1
1990	116.9	116.7	116.3	116.1	116.3	116.3	116.6	118.2	120.0	121.5	122.3	121.4
1991	122.0	120.9	120.3	120.3	120.5	120.1	119.6	119.9	120.0	120.4	120.9	120.6
1992	120.5	120.9	121.0	121.1	121.6	122.0	121.7	121.8	122.1	122.5	122.5	122.5
1993	123.1	123.4	123.6	124.4	124.3	123.6	123.2	121.9	122.0	122.1	122.4	122.2
1994	122.7	123.1	123.1	123.0	122.8	122.8	123.2	123.9	123.4	122.9	123.9	124.3
1995	124.8	125.1	125.3	125.7	125.7	125.5	125.4	-	-	-	-	-

Source: U.S. Department of Labor, Bureau of Labor Statistics. - indicates data not available or zero.

Producer Price Index

Finished goods

(1982 = 100)

Year	Jan	Feb	Mar	Apr	May	Jun	Jul	Aug	Sep	Oct	Nov	Dec
1947	-	-	-	26.0	26.1	26.2	26.2	26.3	26.7	26.8	27.1	27.7
1948	28.1	27.9	28.0	28.1	28.4	28.6	28.8	28.9	28.8	28.7	28.5	28.5
1949	28.3	28.0	28.0	27.9	27.8	27.7	27.5	27.4	27.4	27.3	27.2	27.2
1950	27.2	27.2	27.3	27.3	27.5	27.6	28.0	28.6	28.9	29.0	29.4	30.0
1951	30.5	30.8	30.9	30.9	31.1	31.0	30.8	30.7	30.6	30.8	30.9	30.9
1952	30.8	30.7	30.9	30.7	30.7	30.7	30.8	30.7	30.6	30.5	30.4	30.2
1953	30.3	30.2	30.3	30.2	30.3	30.4	30.5	30.4	30.4	30.4	30.3	30.4
1954	30.5	30.4	30.4	30.6	30.6	30.4	30.5	30.4	30.4	30.4	30.3	30.4
1955	30.4	30.5	30.3	30.4	30.4	30.5	30.4	30.4	30.3	30.2	30.3	30.3
1956	30.7	30.8	30.9	31.0	31.2	31.4	31.3	31.4	31.6	31.8	31.9	31.9
1957	32.1	32.2	32.1	32.3	32.3	32.5	32.6	32.6	32.6	32.7	32.9	33.0
1958	33.2	33.2	33.4	33.2	33.2	33.3	33.2	33.2	33.2	33.2	33.2	33.1
1959	33.1	33.2	33.2	33.2	33.3	33.2	33.1	33.0	33.4	33.1	33.0	33.0
1960	33.1	33.1	33.4	33.4	33.4	33.4	33.5	33.4	33.4	33.7	33.7	33.6
1961	33.6	33.7	33.6	33.4	33.3	33.3	33.3	33.4	33.3	33.3	33.4	33.4
1962	33.5	33.6	33.5	33.5	33.4	33.4	33.4	33.5	33.8	33.6	33.6	33.5
1963	33.4	33.4	33.3	33.3	33.4	33.5	33.4	33.4	33.4	33.5	33.5	33.4
1964	33.5	33.5	33.4	33.5	33.5	33.5	33.5	33.6	33.6	33.6	33.6	33.6
1965	33.6	33.7	33.7	34.0	34.1	34.2	34.1	34.2	34.3	34.4	34.5	34.7
1966	34.7	35.0	35.0	35.1	35.1	34.9	35.1	35.4	35.6	35.5	35.5	35.4
1967	35.4	35.3	35.3	35.3	35.4	35.7	35.7	35.8	35.8	35.9	35.9	36.0
1968	36.1	36.2	36.3	36.5	36.5	36.6	36.7	36.8	37.0	37.0	37.1	37.1
1969	37.2	37.2	37.4	37.6	37.8	38.0	38.1	38.2	38.3	38.5	38.8	38.9
1970	39.1	39.0	39.1	39.1	39.1	39.2	39.2	39.2	39.6	39.6	39.8	39.8
1971	39.9	40.1	40.2	40.3	40.5	40.6	40.4	40.7	40.7	40.7	40.8	41.1
1972	41.0	41.3	41.3	41.3	41.5	41.7	41.8	42.0	42.2	42.0	42.3	42.7
1973	43.0	43.5	44.4	44.7	45.0	45.5	45.4	47.0	46.9	46.8	47.2	47.6
1974	48.8	49.7	50.2	50.7	51.3	51.3	52.7	53.7	54.3	55.3	56.4	56.4
1975	56.7	56.6	56.6	57.1	57.4	57.9	58.4	58.9	59.3	59.8	60.0	60.1
1976	60.0	59.9	60.0	60.3	60.4	60.5	60.7	60.9	61.1	61.4	61.9	62.4
1977	62.5	63.2	63.7	64.0	64.4	64.6	64.8	65.2	65.5	65.9	66.4	66.7
1978	67.0	67.5	67.8	68.6	69.1	69.7	70.3	70.4	71.1	71.4	72.0	72.8
1979	73.7	74.4	75.0	75.8	76.2	76.6	77.4	78.2	79.5	80.4	81.4	82.2
1980	83.4	84.6	85.5	86.2	86.6	87.3	88.7	89.7	90.1	90.8	91.4	91.8
1981	92.8	93.6	94.7	95.7	96.0	96.5	96.7	96.8	97.2	97.6	97.9	98.3
1982	98.9	98.8	98.8	99.0	99.0	99.8	100.2	100.6	100.7	101.0	101.4	101.8
1983	101.0	101.1	101.0	101.1	101.4	101.6	101.6	101.9	102.2	102.2	102.0	102.3
1984	103.0	103.4	103.8	103.9	103.8	103.8	104.0	103.8	103.8	103.6	104.0	104.0
1985	104.0	104.1	104.1	104.6	104.9	104.6	104.7	104.5	103.8	104.9	105.5	106.0
1986	105.5	104.1	102.8	102.3	102.8	103.1	102.3	102.7	102.9	103.5	103.4	103.6
1987	104.1	104.4	104.5	105.1	105.2	105.5	105.7	105.9	106.2	106.0	106.0	105.8
1988	106.4	106.3	106.6	107.0	107.2	107.5	108.4	108.8	109.0	109.2	109.6	110.0
1989	111.1	111.9	112.3	113.1	114.0	114.0	113.8	113.4	114.0	114.6	114.8	115.5
1990	117.7	117.6	117.5	117.4	117.5	117.6	117.9	119.2	120.7	121.9	122.6	122.0
1991	122.7	121.9	121.4	121.4	121.7	121.4	121.1	121.3	121.5	121.9	122.3	122.1
1992	122.1	122.4	122.6	122.7	123.1	123.4	123.2	123.3	123.6	124.0	124.0	124.0
1993	124.6	124.9	125.1	125.7	125.7	125.1	124.9	123.9	124.1	124.0	124.4	124.3
1994	124.9	125.2	125.2	125.2	125.1	125.2	125.5	126.2	125.8	125.3	126.1	126.5
1995	127.1	127.3	127.5	127.9	127.9	127.8	127.8	-	-	-	-	-

Source: U.S. Department of Labor, Bureau of Labor Statistics. - indicates data not available or zero.

Producer Price Index
Finished goods less foods and energy
(1982 = 100)

Year	Jan	Feb	Mar	Apr	May	Jun	Jul	Aug	Sep	Oct	Nov	Dec
1974	49.7	50.0	50.5	51.1	52.2	53.1	54.0	55.0	55.7	56.7	57.4	57.9
1975	58.3	58.7	59.0	59.2	59.3	59.5	59.8	59.9	60.2	60.6	61.0	61.4
1976	61.7	61.9	62.2	62.3	62.4	62.8	63.1	63.5	63.9	64.1	64.6	64.9
1977	65.1	65.4	65.7	65.9	66.1	66.5	66.8	67.3	67.8	68.2	68.8	69.0
1978	69.2	69.5	69.9	70.6	71.1	71.7	72.3	72.8	73.5	73.4	74.1	74.7
1979	75.3	75.9	76.4	77.0	77.4	78.0	78.5	78.8	79.7	80.4	81.0	81.7
1980	83.3	84.2	84.7	85.5	85.7	86.6	87.7	88.4	88.8	89.6	90.1	90.4
1981	91.4	92.0	92.6	93.5	94.0	94.6	94.8	95.3	95.9	96.5	97.0	97.6
1982	98.1	98.1	98.7	99.0	99.4	99.9	100.1	100.6	100.8	101.3	101.6	102.2
1983	101.8	102.2	102.5	102.4	102.6	102.8	103.1	103.5	103.5	103.6	103.8	104.1
1984	104.5	104.7	105.2	105.3	105.3	105.5	105.7	105.9	106.2	105.9	106.2	106.3
1985	106.9	107.3	107.6	107.6	107.8	108.2	108.4	108.5	107.9	108.9	109.1	109.1
1986	109.3	109.5	109.6	110.1	110.2	110.5	110.7	110.8	110.7	111.8	112.0	112.1
1987	112.5	112.3	112.4	112.9	113.0	113.1	113.3	113.6	113.9	114.0	114.2	114.3
1988	115.0	115.3	115.6	115.9	116.2	116.6	117.2	117.7	118.1	118.4	118.7	119.2
1989	119.9	120.5	120.7	120.8	121.6	122.2	122.1	122.7	123.1	123.5	123.9	124.2
1990	124.5	124.9	125.3	125.5	126.0	126.4	126.6	127.1	127.7	128.0	128.4	128.6
1991	129.6	129.9	130.1	130.4	130.6	130.7	131.0	131.4	131.8	132.3	132.5	132.6
1992	133.0	133.1	133.5	133.8	134.3	134.1	134.3	134.3	134.6	134.9	135.1	135.2
1993	135.6	135.9	136.0	136.5	136.6	136.4	136.6	135.0	135.0	134.9	135.4	135.7
1994	136.2	136.3	136.4	136.6	137.0	137.2	137.3	137.6	137.8	137.3	137.6	137.9
1995	138.4	138.6	138.9	139.2	139.6	139.9	140.2	-	-	-	-	-

Source: U.S. Department of Labor, Bureau of Labor Statistics. - indicates data not available or zero.

Output per Hour, Business Sector
(1982 = 100)

Year	1st Quarter	2nd Quarter	3rd Quarter	4th Quarter
1947	43.2	43.5	43.3	43.4
1948	44.7	45.8	45.0	45.7
1949	45.5	45.5	46.5	46.5
1950	48.4	49.5	50.5	51.0
1951	50.4	51.0	52.4	52.9
1952	52.7	53.7	53.9	54.0
1953	54.8	55.3	55.5	55.5
1954	55.6	56.3	57.2	57.7
1955	58.6	58.9	58.5	58.4
1956	58.6	59.1	59.3	60.4
1957	60.5	60.9	61.1	61.7
1958	61.8	62.6	63.3	64.1
1959	64.6	64.6	64.2	64.8
1960	66.2	65.3	65.1	65.7
1961	66.2	68.1	68.5	69.5
1962	69.5	69.8	70.8	71.7
1963	72.1	73.0	73.8	74.4
1964	76.1	76.0	77.0	77.0
1965	77.7	77.8	79.0	79.9
1966	80.7	80.5	80.7	81.1
1967	81.4	82.8	83.2	83.7
1968	84.6	85.2	85.5	85.9
1969	85.3	85.6	85.7	86.2
1970	85.9	86.2	88.0	88.0
1971	89.5	89.3	90.3	90.5
1972	91.1	92.1	93.0	94.7
1973	95.8	94.8	94.5	95.3
1974	93.8	93.2	92.9	93.2
1975	93.3	95.3	96.7	96.9
1976	98.2	98.2	98.3	98.6
1977	99.6	99.5	100.9	100.0
1978	100.0	100.9	100.7	100.6
1979	100.0	99.7	99.0	99.1
1980	99.2	97.6	98.2	99.6
1981	100.1	100.0	100.7	98.9
1982	98.7	99.8	100.5	101.1
1983	101.1	102.9	102.5	103.1
1984	104.1	104.9	104.8	105.4
1985	105.1	106.0	107.0	107.0
1986	108.7	108.8	108.4	108.3
1987	108.4	109.5	110.1	110.6
1988	110.9	110.4	110.8	110.8
1989	110.2	110.1	109.7	109.7
1990	110.2	111.1	110.8	110.5
1991	111.4	112.0	112.3	113.0
1992	114.4	114.9	115.8	116.8
1993	116.2	116.3	117.0	118.4
1994	118.9	118.5	119.5	120.7
1995	121.3	122.2	-	-

Source: U.S. Department of Labor, Bureau of Labor Statistics. - indicates data not available or zero.

PRICE INDEXES FOR GROSS DOMESTIC PRODUCT

The 12 series in this section show the functioning of inflation in the U.S. economy from 1947 through 1993.

Price indexes are presented for:

Gross domestic product as a whole
Busines sector
Nonfarm business sector
    Nonfarm less housing
    Housing sector only
Farms
Households and institutions
    Private households
    Nonprofit institutions
General government
    Federal government
    State and local government

Price Index versus Implicit Price Deflator

Before the 1995 revisions of the national income accounts, a special price index, known as the implicit price deflator (IPD), was used to derive GDP (or its components) in real dollars. The IPD reflects *both* changes in pricing and changes in the composition of GDP from one period to another. For this reason, the IPD was a superior tool for measuring inflation. That is now changing.

With the shift from constant dollar indexes to the chain-type price indexes, IPDs and chain-type price indexes are identical except for the most recent estimates (see Introduction for a full discussion). Both measures use the same weights to aggregate the detailed prices.

For these reasons, chain-type price indexes replace the IPDs in this edition of *EIH*.

Using the Indexes

The simplest explanation for these indexes is that they shows how inflation or deflation influence Gross Domestic Product and its major sectors. Using artificially simple numbers, if GDP in actual, current dollars was $1,000 in 1992 and $2,000 in 1994 and *no inflation in prices* had taken place in the 1992-1994 period, the chained price index for GDP in 1994 would be 100.0, i.e. the *same* as in the reference year. Therefore, the change between 1992 and 1994 was *real growth*.

Assume, however, that cumulative inflation in the period was 30%; this would mean that, in 1994, a person would have to spend $1.30 to have the same purchasing power as in 1992. The chained (1992) dollar value of the $2,000 GDP in 1994 would therefore be $1,538.46 (2000 / 1.30). The price index would be calculated as follows:

(2000 / 1538.46) x 100

This would produce an index of 130.0. The index, in other words, can be read as an indicator of inflation relative to the reference year—in this case 1992. The difference between any two years is the increase or decrease in prices between those years. In the example above, the *real growth* between 1992 and 1994 is only $538.46 rather than the apparent $1,000.

The price index for GDP is an indicator of *overall* inflation or deflation. Indexes are also provided for major sectors of GDP. Thus the user who wishes to calculate how she or he is doing relative to inflation would consult the table for private households; the business owner would consult the table for busines or for nonfarm business less housing.

An example showing the use of the Private Household table is presented below.

An Example. A person who got a job in January of 1989 paying $39,500 a year would like to calculate how he is doing in January 1993. The person now makes $42,300 a year, an increase of $2,800. Has this person gained or lost purchasing power?

The price index for the Private Households sector of GDP was 88.4 in the first quarter of 1989; it was 101.8 in the first quarter of 1993. The following formula provides the percent increase in prices between 1989 and 1993 in the index:

((Current Index / Previous Index) - 1) x 100.

The result is 15.2 percent. Multiplying the 1989 salary by 1.151584 produces $45,488. Therefore the person has not kept up with inflation. On the contrary, he has lost real purchasing power since 1989 despite a 7 percent increase in pay.

Price Indexes for Gross Domestic Product
Based on Chained (1992) Dollars

Year	1st Quarter	2nd Quarter	3rd Quarter	4th Quarter
1959	-	-	23.0	23.1
1960	23.2	23.3	23.4	23.5
1961	23.6	23.6	23.6	23.7
1962	23.8	23.9	23.9	24.1
1963	24.1	24.2	24.2	24.3
1964	24.4	24.5	24.6	24.7
1965	24.8	25.0	25.1	25.2
1966	25.4	25.6	25.9	26.1
1967	26.2	26.4	26.7	27.0
1968	27.3	27.6	27.8	28.2
1969	28.5	28.8	29.2	29.6
1970	30.0	30.4	30.7	31.1
1971	31.6	32.0	32.3	32.6
1972	33.1	33.3	33.6	34.0
1973	34.5	35.0	35.7	36.3
1974	37.0	37.9	39.0	40.2
1975	41.1	41.7	42.5	43.3
1976	43.8	44.2	44.9	45.6
1977	46.4	47.1	47.8	48.6
1978	49.4	50.5	51.4	52.4
1979	53.5	54.7	55.9	57.0
1980	58.3	59.6	61.0	62.6
1981	64.2	65.4	66.7	67.9
1982	68.9	69.7	70.7	71.5
1983	72.1	72.9	73.5	74.2
1984	75.0	75.6	76.3	76.8
1985	77.7	78.3	78.8	79.5
1986	79.8	80.3	80.8	81.5
1987	82.1	82.7	83.4	84.1
1988	84.7	85.6	86.7	87.5
1989	88.4	89.4	90.1	90.9
1990	92.0	93.2	94.2	95.1
1991	96.3	97.0	97.7	98.3
1992	99.1	99.8	100.2	100.9
1993	101.8	102.4	102.8	103.4
1994	104.1	104.6	105.2	105.8
1995	-	-	-	-

Source: U.S. Department of Commerce, Bureau of Economic Analysis. - indicates data not available or zero.

Price Indexes for GDP

Business Sector
Based on Chained (1992) Dollars

Year	1st Quarter	2nd Quarter	3rd Quarter	4th Quarter
1959	-	-	25.5	25.6
1960	25.6	25.7	25.8	25.9
1961	26.0	26.0	26.0	26.0
1962	26.1	26.2	26.3	26.3
1963	26.4	26.4	26.4	26.5
1964	26.6	26.6	26.7	26.9
1965	27.0	27.1	27.2	27.3
1966	27.4	27.6	28.0	28.2
1967	28.3	28.4	28.7	28.9
1968	29.2	29.6	29.8	30.1
1969	30.4	30.8	31.1	31.5
1970	31.8	32.2	32.4	32.8
1971	33.2	33.6	33.9	34.2
1972	34.5	34.7	35.0	35.3
1973	35.7	36.3	37.0	37.6
1974	38.4	39.2	40.5	41.7
1975	42.6	43.2	44.1	44.8
1976	45.2	45.6	46.3	47.0
1977	47.8	48.6	49.2	49.9
1978	50.8	52.0	52.9	54.0
1979	55.1	56.4	57.5	58.6
1980	60.0	61.4	62.8	64.3
1981	66.0	67.2	68.7	69.8
1982	70.7	71.6	72.5	73.2
1983	73.8	74.5	75.1	75.8
1984	76.3	76.9	77.4	78.0
1985	78.7	79.3	79.8	80.4
1986	80.8	81.2	81.7	82.2
1987	82.8	83.3	84.0	84.7
1988	85.2	86.1	87.3	88.2
1989	89.1	90.1	90.8	91.6
1990	92.6	93.7	94.7	95.6
1991	96.7	97.4	98.0	98.5
1992	99.2	99.8	100.1	100.9
1993	101.7	102.4	102.7	103.4
1994	104.0	104.5	105.2	105.7
1995	-	-	-	-

Source: U.S. Department of Commerce, Bureau of Economic Analysis. - indicates data not available or zero.

Price Indexes for GDP
Business Sector - Nonfarm
Based on Chained (1992) Dollars

Year	1st Quarter	2nd Quarter	3rd Quarter	4th Quarter
1959	-	-	24.9	25.0
1960	25.1	25.2	25.3	25.4
1961	25.4	25.4	25.4	25.5
1962	25.5	25.6	25.7	25.7
1963	25.8	25.8	25.9	26.0
1964	26.0	26.1	26.2	26.3
1965	26.5	26.5	26.6	26.7
1966	26.8	27.0	27.3	27.6
1967	27.7	27.9	28.1	28.4
1968	28.7	29.0	29.2	29.5
1969	29.8	30.1	30.5	30.8
1970	31.1	31.6	31.7	32.2
1971	32.6	33.0	33.3	33.5
1972	33.8	34.0	34.2	34.4
1973	34.6	35.0	35.4	36.2
1974	36.9	38.2	39.3	40.4
1975	41.7	42.4	43.1	43.7
1976	44.2	44.7	45.4	46.2
1977	46.9	47.7	48.4	49.3
1978	49.9	50.9	51.9	52.9
1979	53.9	55.3	56.5	57.6
1980	59.1	60.8	61.8	63.1
1981	65.0	66.4	67.9	69.2
1982	70.2	71.1	72.0	72.8
1983	73.2	73.8	74.4	75.0
1984	75.5	76.2	76.9	77.4
1985	78.2	79.0	79.6	80.2
1986	80.6	80.9	81.4	81.9
1987	82.5	83.0	83.7	84.5
1988	85.0	85.9	86.9	87.8
1989	88.7	89.8	90.5	91.2
1990	92.2	93.4	94.4	95.5
1991	96.6	97.3	98.0	98.5
1992	99.2	99.8	100.1	100.9
1993	101.8	102.4	102.7	103.4
1994	104.0	104.6	105.3	105.9
1995	-	-	-	-

Source: U.S. Department of Commerce, Bureau of Economic Analysis. - indicates data not available or zero.

Price Indexes for GDP
Business Sector - Nonfarm Less Housing
Based on Chained (1992) Dollars

Year	1st Quarter	2nd Quarter	3rd Quarter	4th Quarter
1959	-	-	25.1	25.2
1960	25.2	25.3	25.4	25.5
1961	25.6	25.6	25.6	25.6
1962	25.7	25.8	25.8	25.9
1963	25.9	26.0	26.0	26.1
1964	26.2	26.3	26.4	26.5
1965	26.6	26.7	26.8	26.9
1966	26.9	27.2	27.5	27.8
1967	27.9	28.1	28.4	28.6
1968	28.9	29.3	29.4	29.8
1969	30.1	30.4	30.8	31.1
1970	31.4	31.9	32.1	32.6
1971	32.9	33.3	33.7	33.8
1972	34.2	34.3	34.5	34.7
1973	35.0	35.3	35.8	36.6
1974	37.4	38.7	39.9	41.1
1975	42.4	43.1	43.8	44.5
1976	45.0	45.5	46.1	47.0
1977	47.7	48.5	49.2	50.0
1978	50.7	51.7	52.7	53.8
1979	54.8	56.2	57.5	58.6
1980	60.2	62.0	62.9	64.2
1981	66.2	67.6	69.1	70.4
1982	71.3	72.2	73.1	73.9
1983	74.2	74.7	75.3	75.9
1984	76.4	77.0	77.7	78.2
1985	79.0	79.7	80.3	80.7
1986	81.1	81.3	81.7	82.2
1987	82.8	83.2	83.9	84.6
1988	85.1	86.0	87.0	87.9
1989	88.8	89.9	90.6	91.3
1990	92.3	93.5	94.4	95.5
1991	96.8	97.4	98.1	98.6
1992	99.3	99.8	100.1	100.9
1993	101.8	102.4	102.7	103.3
1994	104.0	104.5	105.3	105.8
1995	-	-	-	-

Source: U.S. Department of Commerce, Bureau of Economic Analysis. - indicates data not available or zero.

Price Indexes for GDP
Business Sector - Nonfarm Housing
Based on Chained (1992) Dollars

Year	1st Quarter	2nd Quarter	3rd Quarter	4th Quarter
1959	-	-	23.8	23.9
1960	24.0	24.1	24.2	24.3
1961	24.4	24.4	24.5	24.5
1962	24.6	24.7	24.8	24.8
1963	24.9	24.9	25.0	25.1
1964	25.1	25.2	25.3	25.4
1965	25.4	25.5	25.5	25.6
1966	25.7	25.8	25.9	26.0
1967	26.1	26.3	26.4	26.5
1968	26.7	26.9	27.0	27.2
1969	27.4	27.7	28.0	28.2
1970	28.5	28.8	29.1	29.5
1971	29.8	30.2	30.5	30.7
1972	31.0	31.2	31.5	31.8
1973	32.2	32.6	32.9	33.3
1974	33.4	33.7	34.1	34.6
1975	35.4	35.9	36.5	37.2
1976	37.8	38.3	38.9	39.6
1977	40.6	41.4	42.2	42.9
1978	43.4	44.0	44.5	45.4
1979	46.0	46.8	47.9	49.3
1980	50.1	51.0	52.3	54.0
1981	55.1	56.4	57.8	59.4
1982	60.6	61.2	62.5	63.7
1983	64.6	65.3	66.1	66.8
1984	67.6	68.6	69.7	70.6
1985	71.5	72.7	74.1	75.5
1986	76.4	77.6	78.5	79.5
1987	80.1	80.9	81.8	83.2
1988	84.1	84.8	85.8	86.7
1989	87.6	88.5	89.5	90.7
1990	91.8	93.1	94.7	95.1
1991	95.7	96.4	97.1	98.1
1992	99.0	99.7	100.2	101.1
1993	101.8	102.5	103.0	103.7
1994	104.7	105.3	105.9	106.8
1995	-	-	-	-

Source: U.S. Department of Commerce, Bureau of Economic Analysis. - indicates data not available or zero.

Price Indexes for GDP
Business Sector - Farms
Based on Chained (1992) Dollars

Year	1st Quarter	2nd Quarter	3rd Quarter	4th Quarter
1959	-	-	61.8	61.7
1960	60.8	62.7	61.7	63.3
1961	62.6	60.6	62.0	64.5
1962	64.8	63.0	63.9	65.0
1963	63.5	62.7	63.0	61.7
1964	61.7	61.1	60.4	61.7
1965	61.6	66.6	65.1	67.6
1966	72.3	69.9	72.3	67.5
1967	65.3	63.3	63.9	63.4
1968	65.1	66.9	67.8	68.6
1969	66.9	71.9	73.0	77.3
1970	74.7	72.2	73.8	71.1
1971	72.8	74.1	73.4	78.3
1972	80.8	82.4	88.1	96.1
1973	111.1	127.5	150.3	135.7
1974	142.1	108.9	122.4	131.5
1975	107.4	103.8	112.7	116.9
1976	112.8	109.8	109.1	102.8
1977	106.5	105.2	104.1	95.8
1978	115.7	128.0	125.0	130.7
1979	142.1	137.5	133.1	129.2
1980	119.7	95.2	126.2	146.0
1981	131.3	121.4	115.3	104.5
1982	105.3	106.5	111.7	100.0
1983	113.9	122.9	123.9	129.7
1984	131.2	123.5	115.7	114.1
1985	110.7	102.3	93.5	99.1
1986	94.1	97.3	102.7	104.9
1987	102.7	103.3	100.7	99.5
1988	101.4	103.0	119.1	116.7
1989	119.7	114.9	112.4	115.2
1990	115.9	115.5	113.1	105.7
1991	100.2	105.0	101.0	101.6
1992	99.6	98.5	101.8	100.1
1993	95.1	102.0	106.3	104.4
1994	104.3	98.1	94.5	96.5
1995	-	-	-	-

Source: U.S. Department of Commerce, Bureau of Economic Analysis. - indicates data not available or zero.

Price Indexes for GDP

Households and Institutions
Based on Chained (1992) Dollars

Year	1st Quarter	2nd Quarter	3rd Quarter	4th Quarter
1959	-	-	11.9	12.2
1960	12.2	12.3	12.5	12.6
1961	12.6	12.8	12.8	12.9
1962	13.2	13.3	13.3	13.5
1963	13.7	13.9	13.9	14.0
1964	14.3	14.3	14.6	14.7
1965	14.6	14.9	15.2	15.6
1966	15.5	15.9	16.2	16.5
1967	16.7	16.9	17.2	17.5
1968	18.1	18.3	18.6	19.0
1969	19.5	19.9	20.4	21.2
1970	21.6	22.2	22.9	23.2
1971	23.7	24.1	24.3	24.8
1972	25.3	25.6	25.7	26.4
1973	27.0	27.5	28.0	28.7
1974	29.2	29.9	30.5	31.3
1975	31.7	31.9	32.3	33.2
1976	34.2	34.8	35.2	36.0
1977	36.0	36.8	37.7	38.7
1978	39.7	40.4	41.6	42.2
1979	43.2	43.9	45.0	46.0
1980	47.0	48.3	49.2	50.5
1981	51.7	52.9	54.1	55.0
1982	56.1	56.9	58.1	59.3
1983	60.2	61.2	62.6	63.9
1984	64.9	66.1	67.3	67.8
1985	68.4	68.9	69.7	70.2
1986	70.9	71.3	72.4	73.3
1987	74.7	76.5	78.1	80.0
1988	80.3	80.8	81.3	82.1
1989	83.2	84.0	85.2	86.4
1990	88.1	89.7	91.2	91.4
1991	92.6	94.2	95.2	96.5
1992	97.4	100.4	100.7	101.5
1993	102.5	101.3	103.2	102.7
1994	104.3	104.6	105.2	104.9
1995	-	-	-	-

Source: U.S. Department of Commerce, Bureau of Economic Analysis. - indicates data not available or zero.

Price Indexes for GDP

Private Households
Based on Chained (1992) Dollars

Year	1st Quarter	2nd Quarter	3rd Quarter	4th Quarter
1959	-	-	19.6	20.0
1960	20.2	20.4	20.5	20.5
1961	20.6	20.7	20.6	20.8
1962	21.0	21.1	21.3	21.5
1963	21.6	21.7	21.6	21.7
1964	21.9	22.3	22.5	22.7
1965	22.9	23.2	23.6	23.9
1966	24.2	24.4	24.8	25.3
1967	25.3	25.4	25.6	26.2
1968	27.3	28.1	28.3	29.0
1969	29.6	29.9	30.3	31.1
1970	31.8	32.4	32.9	33.7
1971	34.1	34.5	34.9	35.2
1972	35.9	36.3	36.5	37.0
1973	38.1	38.9	39.1	39.9
1974	39.9	42.1	45.0	45.3
1975	45.4	45.3	46.0	47.6
1976	50.1	51.8	52.7	54.4
1977	55.9	56.3	56.7	56.7
1978	57.9	59.8	61.8	64.0
1979	65.8	67.3	68.7	70.1
1980	71.3	72.7	74.0	75.4
1981	76.8	78.2	79.8	81.2
1982	82.0	82.3	82.3	82.3
1983	82.2	82.5	82.5	82.7
1984	83.2	83.3	83.6	83.8
1985	84.1	84.4	84.4	84.7
1986	85.0	85.2	85.6	86.0
1987	86.2	86.1	86.6	86.6
1988	86.7	87.4	87.7	88.0
1989	88.4	88.8	88.8	89.0
1990	89.8	90.9	92.1	93.8
1991	95.0	95.9	96.7	97.9
1992	98.4	99.4	100.7	101.5
1993	101.8	102.5	103.7	104.8
1994	105.3	105.9	106.9	107.6
1995	-	-	-	-

Source: U.S. Department of Commerce, Bureau of Economic Analysis. - indicates data not available or zero.

Price Indexes for GDP
Nonprofit Institutions
Based on Chained (1992) Dollars

Year	1st Quarter	2nd Quarter	3rd Quarter	4th Quarter
1959	-	-	11.3	11.6
1960	11.4	11.6	11.9	12.0
1961	12.1	12.3	12.4	12.6
1962	12.8	13.0	13.0	13.2
1963	13.4	13.5	13.6	13.7
1964	14.0	14.0	14.3	14.4
1965	14.1	14.5	14.8	15.3
1966	15.1	15.5	15.9	16.1
1967	16.4	16.6	16.8	17.1
1968	17.7	17.8	18.0	18.5
1969	19.0	19.5	20.0	20.8
1970	21.2	21.8	22.5	22.7
1971	23.2	23.6	23.8	24.3
1972	24.8	25.2	25.3	26.0
1973	26.6	27.1	27.6	28.3
1974	28.8	29.5	29.9	30.8
1975	31.1	31.4	31.8	32.7
1976	33.5	34.1	34.5	35.2
1977	35.2	36.0	36.8	37.9
1978	39.0	39.6	40.7	41.3
1979	42.2	42.9	43.9	45.0
1980	46.0	47.2	48.2	49.4
1981	50.6	51.8	53.0	53.9
1982	55.0	55.8	57.1	58.3
1983	59.3	60.3	61.7	63.1
1984	64.1	65.4	66.6	67.1
1985	67.7	68.2	69.1	69.6
1986	70.3	70.8	71.9	72.8
1987	74.3	76.1	77.7	79.8
1988	80.0	80.5	81.0	81.8
1989	83.0	83.8	85.1	86.4
1990	88.1	89.6	91.1	91.3
1991	92.6	94.1	95.2	96.4
1992	97.4	100.4	100.7	101.5
1993	102.5	101.3	103.1	102.7
1994	104.3	104.6	105.1	104.8
1995	-	-	-	-

Source: U.S. Department of Commerce, Bureau of Economic Analysis. - indicates data not available or zero.

Price Indexes for GDP
General Government
Based on Chained (1992) Dollars

Year	1st Quarter	2nd Quarter	3rd Quarter	4th Quarter
1959	-	-	14.0	14.0
1960	14.2	14.2	14.4	14.5
1961	14.6	14.7	14.7	14.9
1962	15.0	15.1	15.2	15.4
1963	15.6	15.6	15.7	16.0
1964	16.2	16.2	16.4	16.5
1965	16.6	16.7	16.9	17.2
1966	17.4	17.6	17.9	18.0
1967	18.2	18.5	18.7	19.2
1968	19.5	19.7	20.2	20.5
1969	20.7	20.9	21.7	21.9
1970	22.9	23.3	23.6	23.9
1971	24.9	25.3	25.7	26.1
1972	27.1	27.5	27.9	28.6
1973	29.2	29.8	30.3	30.9
1974	31.4	32.1	32.8	33.9
1975	34.8	35.6	36.3	37.3
1976	37.8	38.4	38.9	39.8
1977	40.6	41.4	41.9	43.1
1978	43.7	44.3	44.8	45.7
1979	46.7	47.7	48.8	50.0
1980	51.1	52.2	53.4	55.7
1981	57.0	57.8	58.4	60.1
1982	61.4	62.4	63.3	64.6
1983	65.4	66.3	67.0	67.7
1984	70.0	70.9	71.7	72.4
1985	74.0	74.6	75.1	76.1
1986	76.6	77.2	78.0	79.1
1987	80.1	80.8	81.2	81.6
1988	82.8	83.5	84.1	84.7
1989	86.0	86.7	87.5	88.3
1990	89.9	90.9	91.9	93.4
1991	94.7	95.7	96.6	97.4
1992	99.0	100.0	100.3	100.7
1993	102.2	102.6	103.3	103.9
1994	104.8	105.5	105.7	106.8
1995	-	-	-	-

Source: U.S. Department of Commerce, Bureau of Economic Analysis. - indicates data not available or zero.

Price Indexes for GDP
Federal Government
Based on Chained (1992) Dollars

Year	1st Quarter	2nd Quarter	3rd Quarter	4th Quarter
1959	-	-	13.7	13.7
1960	13.8	13.7	14.1	14.1
1961	14.1	14.1	14.1	14.2
1962	14.3	14.3	14.4	14.7
1963	14.9	14.9	14.9	15.3
1964	15.6	15.6	15.8	15.9
1965	16.0	16.1	16.3	16.8
1966	16.9	16.9	17.1	17.1
1967	17.1	17.3	17.4	18.1
1968	18.3	18.4	19.1	19.3
1969	19.3	19.4	20.4	20.5
1970	21.8	22.1	22.3	22.6
1971	23.9	24.5	24.7	25.5
1972	27.1	27.4	27.7	28.7
1973	29.3	29.8	30.4	31.4
1974	31.8	32.4	33.2	34.8
1975	35.7	36.3	36.9	38.3
1976	38.5	39.0	39.6	41.0
1977	42.0	42.6	42.9	44.7
1978	45.0	45.4	46.0	47.7
1979	48.5	49.1	49.8	52.2
1980	53.0	53.9	54.6	58.4
1981	59.5	60.0	60.5	63.3
1982	64.4	65.1	65.5	67.0
1983	67.4	68.3	68.5	68.9
1984	73.1	73.7	74.2	74.5
1985	76.7	76.8	76.9	78.1
1986	78.4	78.8	79.3	79.9
1987	81.3	81.3	81.2	81.3
1988	82.8	83.9	84.5	84.5
1989	86.7	87.1	87.4	87.0
1990	88.9	89.4	90.1	92.2
1991	94.1	95.1	95.9	96.5
1992	99.5	100.3	100.4	99.8
1993	102.7	102.6	103.9	104.8
1994	106.1	107.4	107.1	108.8
1995	-	-	-	-

Source: U.S. Department of Commerce, Bureau of Economic Analysis. - indicates data not available or zero.

Price Indexes for GDP
State and Local Government
Based on Chained (1992) Dollars

Year	1st Quarter	2nd Quarter	3rd Quarter	4th Quarter
1959	-	-	14.0	14.1
1960	14.4	14.5	14.6	14.7
1961	14.8	15.1	15.2	15.4
1962	15.7	15.8	15.8	16.0
1963	16.2	16.3	16.3	16.5
1964	16.6	16.7	16.8	16.9
1965	17.1	17.2	17.4	17.5
1966	17.8	18.1	18.4	18.7
1967	19.2	19.5	19.8	20.1
1968	20.5	20.8	21.1	21.5
1969	21.8	22.3	22.8	23.2
1970	23.8	24.3	24.7	25.1
1971	25.6	26.1	26.4	26.6
1972	27.2	27.6	28.2	28.6
1973	29.2	29.8	30.3	30.7
1974	31.2	31.9	32.6	33.3
1975	34.2	35.2	36.0	36.6
1976	37.4	38.1	38.6	39.0
1977	39.8	40.6	41.4	42.2
1978	42.9	43.6	44.1	44.5
1979	45.7	46.9	48.1	48.7
1980	49.9	51.2	52.6	54.0
1981	55.5	56.5	57.2	58.2
1982	59.5	60.7	61.9	63.1
1983	64.2	65.2	66.0	67.0
1984	68.2	69.1	70.1	71.2
1985	72.4	73.3	74.1	74.9
1986	75.5	76.3	77.3	78.7
1987	79.4	80.4	81.1	81.8
1988	82.7	83.3	83.9	84.8
1989	85.5	86.4	87.6	89.0
1990	90.4	91.7	92.9	94.1
1991	95.1	96.1	97.0	97.8
1992	98.8	99.8	100.2	101.2
1993	102.0	102.6	103.0	103.4
1994	104.1	104.5	105.1	105.8
1995	-	-	-	-

Source: U.S. Department of Commerce, Bureau of Economic Analysis. - indicates data not available or zero.

INDICATORS OF LABOR AND EMPLOYMENT

This section presents 3 indicators of employment and labor:

Civilian labor force
Civilian employment
Civilian labor force participation
  Males, 20 years and over
  Females, 20 years and over
  Both sexes, 16 to 19 years of age

Civilian Labor Force and **Civilian Employment**. The series are available from 1948 through 1995 and are shown in thousands. The two series are the source of unemployment data (number and rate) shown in the section on Other Cyclic Indicators. The labor force is defined as individuals working or actively seeking work. Civilian employment is that portion of the labor force which is now employed. The unemployment rate is calculated by the following formula:

(1-(Civilian Employment / Civilian Labor Force)) x 100

For January 1991, the labor force was 124,638,000 and employment was 116,922,000, indicating unemployment of 7,716,000. This number represents 6.19 percent of the labor force.

A certain level of unemployment is a "natural" phenomenon in a healthy economy. Some economists equate 3-4 percent unemployment with "full employment," on the basis that a certain small fraction of the labor force is, of necessity, in transition between jobs. At the peak of the 1961-1969 expansion (12/69), unemployment was at 3.5 percent; at the peak of the 1971-1973 expansion (10/73), unemployment stood at 4.6 percent. By contrast, at the trough of the 1970 recession, unemployment stood at 6.1 percent; at the trough of the 1974-1975 recession, unemployment stood at 8.6 percent.

Civilian Labor Force Participation. The three tables showing labor force participation extend from 1948 to 1995 and show participation in percent. In January 1991, for instance, 77.3 percent of males 20 years or older participated in the labor force. Base data—the number of people of the gender and age group overall—are derived from the censuses of population and estimates based on them. The participation values are based on estimates of the total labor force.

The values show interesting general patterns. Labor force participation for males has declined gradually from nearly 90 percent in the late 1940s to under 80 percent in recent times. Female labor force participation, however, which was just over 30 percent in the 1940s and 1950s, has reached nearly 60 percent in the 1990s. The participation of young people (16 to 19 years of age) has remained virtually unchanged since the 1940s—although it dipped somewhat in the 1950s and 1960s.

Underlying the labor participation numbers are complex economic and demographic forces, including efforts to maintain family income levels, the rise in the skill level demanded in the work place, the reduced role of manufacturing and the corresponding rise in the services sectors of the economy, and others.

Civilian Labor Force
(Thousands)

Year	Jan	Feb	Mar	Apr	May	Jun	Jul	Aug	Sep	Oct	Nov	Dec
1948	60,095	60,524	60,070	60,677	59,972	60,957	61,181	60,806	60,815	60,646	60,702	61,169
1949	60,771	61,057	61,073	61,007	61,259	60,948	61,301	61,590	61,633	62,185	62,005	61,908
1950	61,661	61,687	61,604	62,158	62,083	62,419	62,121	62,596	62,349	62,428	62,286	62,068
1951	61,941	61,778	62,526	61,808	62,044	61,615	62,106	61,927	61,780	62,204	62,014	62,457
1952	62,432	62,419	61,721	61,720	62,058	62,103	61,962	61,877	62,457	61,971	62,491	62,621
1953	63,439	63,520	63,657	63,167	62,615	63,063	63,057	62,816	62,727	62,867	62,949	62,795
1954	63,101	63,994	63,793	63,934	63,675	63,343	63,302	63,707	64,209	63,936	63,759	63,312
1955	63,910	63,696	63,882	64,564	64,381	64,482	65,145	65,581	65,628	65,821	66,037	66,445
1956	66,419	66,124	66,175	66,264	66,722	66,702	66,752	66,673	66,714	66,546	66,657	66,700
1957	66,428	66,879	66,913	66,647	66,695	67,052	67,336	66,706	67,064	67,066	67,123	67,398
1958	67,095	67,201	67,223	67,647	67,895	67,674	67,824	68,037	68,002	68,045	67,658	67,740
1959	67,936	67,649	68,068	68,339	68,178	68,278	68,539	68,432	68,545	68,821	68,533	68,994
1960	68,962	68,949	68,399	69,579	69,626	69,934	69,745	69,841	70,151	69,884	70,439	70,395
1961	70,447	70,420	70,703	70,267	70,452	70,878	70,536	70,534	70,217	70,492	70,376	70,077
1962	70,189	70,409	70,414	70,278	70,551	70,514	70,302	70,981	71,153	70,917	70,871	70,854
1963	71,146	71,262	71,423	71,697	71,832	71,626	71,956	71,786	72,131	72,281	72,418	72,188
1964	72,356	72,683	72,713	73,274	73,395	73,032	73,007	73,118	73,290	73,308	73,286	73,465
1965	73,569	73,857	73,949	74,228	74,466	74,412	74,761	74,616	74,502	74,838	74,797	75,093
1966	75,186	74,954	75,075	75,338	75,447	75,647	75,736	76,046	76,056	76,199	76,610	76,641
1967	76,639	76,521	76,328	76,777	76,773	77,270	77,464	77,712	77,812	78,194	78,191	78,491
1968	77,578	78,230	78,256	78,270	78,847	79,120	78,970	78,811	78,858	78,913	79,209	79,463
1969	79,523	80,019	80,079	80,281	80,125	80,696	80,827	81,106	81,290	81,494	81,397	81,624
1970	81,981	82,151	82,498	82,727	82,483	82,484	82,901	82,880	82,954	83,276	83,548	83,670
1971	83,850	83,603	83,575	83,946	84,135	83,706	84,340	84,673	84,731	84,872	85,458	85,625
1972	85,978	86,036	86,611	86,614	86,809	87,006	87,143	87,517	87,392	87,491	87,592	87,943
1973	87,487	88,364	88,846	89,018	88,977	89,548	89,604	89,509	89,838	90,131	90,716	90,890
1974	91,199	91,485	91,453	91,287	91,596	91,868	92,212	92,059	92,488	92,518	92,766	92,780
1975	93,128	92,776	93,165	93,399	93,884	93,575	94,021	94,162	94,202	94,267	94,250	94,409
1976	94,934	94,998	95,215	95,746	95,847	95,885	96,583	96,741	96,553	96,704	97,254	97,348
1977	97,208	97,785	98,115	98,330	98,665	99,093	98,913	99,366	99,453	99,815	100,576	100,491
1978	100,873	100,837	101,092	101,574	101,896	102,371	102,399	102,511	102,795	103,080	103,562	103,809
1979	104,057	104,502	104,589	104,172	104,171	104,638	105,002	105,096	105,530	105,700	105,812	106,258
1980	106,562	106,697	106,442	106,591	106,929	106,780	107,159	107,105	107,098	107,405	107,568	107,352
1981	108,026	108,242	108,553	108,925	109,222	108,396	108,556	108,725	108,294	109,024	109,236	108,912
1982	109,089	109,467	109,567	109,820	110,451	110,081	110,342	110,514	110,721	110,744	111,050	111,083
1983	110,695	110,634	110,587	110,828	110,796	111,879	111,756	112,231	112,298	111,926	112,228	112,327
1984	112,209	112,615	112,713	113,098	113,649	113,817	113,972	113,682	113,857	114,019	114,170	114,581
1985	114,725	114,876	115,328	115,331	115,234	114,965	115,320	115,291	115,905	116,145	116,135	116,354
1986	116,682	116,882	117,220	117,316	117,528	118,084	118,129	118,150	118,395	118,516	118,634	118,611
1987	118,845	119,122	119,270	119,336	120,008	119,644	119,902	120,318	120,011	120,509	120,540	120,729
1988	120,969	121,156	120,913	121,251	121,071	121,473	121,665	122,125	121,960	122,206	122,637	122,622
1989	123,390	123,135	123,227	123,565	123,474	123,995	123,967	124,166	123,944	124,211	124,637	124,497
1990	124,601	124,621	124,763	124,813	124,915	124,652	124,657	124,817	124,903	124,910	124,862	125,149
1991	124,787	125,027	125,256	125,721	125,185	125,367	125,102	124,949	125,607	125,578	125,519	125,641
1992	126,149	126,209	126,545	126,917	127,036	127,269	127,358	127,339	127,306	126,933	127,287	127,469
1993	127,224	127,400	127,440	127,539	128,075	128,056	128,102	128,334	128,108	128,580	128,662	128,898
1994	130,643	130,784	130,706	130,787	130,699	130,538	130,774	131,086	131,291	131,646	131,718	131,725
1995	132,136	132,308	132,511	132,737	131,811	131,869	132,519	-	-	-	-	-

Source: U.S. Department of Labor, Bureau of Labor Statistics. - indicates data not available or zero.

Civilian Employment
(Thousands)

Year	Jan	Feb	Mar	Apr	May	Jun	Jul	Aug	Sep	Oct	Nov	Dec
1948	58,061	58,196	57,671	58,291	57,854	58,743	58,968	58,456	58,513	58,387	58,417	58,740
1949	58,175	58,208	58,043	57,747	57,552	57,172	57,190	57,397	57,584	57,269	58,009	57,845
1950	57,635	57,751	57,728	58,583	58,649	59,052	59,001	59,797	59,575	59,803	59,697	59,429
1951	59,636	59,661	60,401	59,889	60,188	59,620	60,156	59,994	59,713	60,010	59,836	60,497
1952	60,460	60,462	59,908	59,909	60,195	60,219	59,971	59,790	60,521	60,132	60,748	60,954
1953	61,600	61,884	62,010	61,444	61,019	61,456	61,397	61,151	60,906	60,893	60,738	59,977
1954	60,024	60,663	60,186	60,185	59,908	59,792	59,643	59,853	60,282	60,270	60,357	60,116
1955	60,753	60,727	60,964	61,515	61,634	61,781	62,513	62,797	62,950	62,991	63,257	63,684
1956	63,753	63,518	63,411	63,614	63,861	63,820	63,800	63,972	64,079	63,975	63,796	63,910
1957	63,632	64,257	64,404	64,047	63,985	64,196	64,540	63,959	64,121	64,046	63,669	63,922
1958	63,220	62,898	62,731	62,631	62,874	62,730	62,745	63,012	63,181	63,475	63,470	63,549
1959	63,868	63,684	64,267	64,768	64,699	64,849	65,011	64,844	64,770	64,911	64,530	65,341
1960	65,347	65,620	64,673	65,959	66,057	66,168	65,909	65,895	66,267	65,632	66,109	65,778
1961	65,776	65,588	65,850	65,374	65,449	65,993	65,608	65,852	65,541	65,919	66,081	65,900
1962	66,108	66,538	66,493	66,372	66,688	66,670	66,483	66,968	67,192	67,114	66,847	66,947
1963	67,072	67,024	67,351	67,642	67,615	67,649	67,905	67,908	68,174	68,294	68,267	68,213
1964	68,327	68,751	68,763	69,356	69,631	69,218	69,399	69,463	69,578	69,582	69,735	69,814
1965	69,997	70,127	70,439	70,633	71,034	71,025	71,460	71,362	71,286	71,695	71,724	72,062
1966	72,198	72,134	72,188	72,510	72,497	72,775	72,860	73,146	73,258	73,401	73,840	73,729
1967	73,671	73,606	73,439	73,882	73,844	74,278	74,520	74,767	74,854	75,051	75,125	75,473
1968	74,700	75,229	75,379	75,561	76,107	76,182	76,087	76,043	76,172	76,224	76,494	76,778
1969	76,805	77,327	77,367	77,523	77,412	77,880	77,959	78,250	78,250	78,445	78,541	78,740
1970	78,780	78,698	78,863	78,930	78,564	78,413	78,726	78,624	78,498	78,685	78,650	78,594
1971	78,864	78,700	78,588	78,987	79,139	78,757	79,305	79,539	79,689	79,918	80,297	80,471
1972	80,959	81,108	81,573	81,655	81,887	82,083	82,230	82,578	82,543	82,616	82,990	83,400
1973	83,161	83,912	84,452	84,559	84,648	85,185	85,299	85,204	85,488	85,987	86,320	86,401
1974	86,555	86,754	86,819	86,669	86,891	86,941	87,149	87,037	87,051	86,995	86,626	86,144
1975	85,627	85,256	85,187	85,189	85,451	85,355	85,894	86,234	86,279	86,370	86,456	86,665
1976	87,400	87,672	87,985	88,416	88,794	88,563	89,093	89,223	89,173	89,274	89,634	89,803
1977	89,928	90,342	90,808	91,271	91,754	91,959	92,084	92,441	92,702	93,052	93,761	94,105
1978	94,384	94,519	94,755	95,394	95,769	96,343	96,090	96,431	96,670	97,133	97,485	97,581
1979	97,948	98,329	98,480	98,103	98,331	98,679	99,006	98,776	99,340	99,404	99,574	99,933
1980	99,879	99,995	99,713	99,233	98,945	98,682	98,796	98,824	99,077	99,317	99,545	99,634
1981	99,955	100,191	100,571	101,056	101,048	100,298	100,693	100,689	100,064	100,378	100,207	99,645
1982	99,692	99,762	99,672	99,576	100,116	99,543	99,493	99,633	99,504	99,215	99,112	99,032
1983	99,161	99,089	99,179	99,560	99,642	100,633	101,208	101,608	102,016	102,039	102,729	102,996
1984	103,201	103,824	103,967	104,336	105,193	105,591	105,435	105,163	105,490	105,638	105,972	106,223
1985	106,302	106,555	106,989	106,936	106,932	106,505	106,807	107,095	107,657	107,847	108,007	108,216
1986	108,887	108,480	108,837	108,952	109,089	109,576	109,810	110,015	110,085	110,273	110,475	110,728
1987	110,953	111,257	111,408	111,794	112,434	112,246	112,634	113,057	112,909	113,282	113,505	113,793
1988	114,016	114,227	114,037	114,650	114,292	114,927	115,060	115,282	115,356	115,638	116,100	116,104
1989	116,708	116,776	117,022	117,097	117,099	117,418	117,472	117,655	117,354	117,581	117,912	117,830
1990	117,990	118,036	118,273	118,105	118,316	118,238	117,949	117,806	117,788	117,718	117,359	117,416
1991	116,967	116,869	116,791	117,411	116,646	116,878	116,738	116,505	117,142	116,997	116,848	116,636
1992	117,130	116,919	117,255	117,670	117,534	117,498	117,763	117,749	117,772	117,723	117,974	118,155
1993	118,178	118,442	118,562	118,585	119,180	119,187	119,370	119,692	119,568	119,941	120,332	120,661
1994	121,903	122,208	122,160	122,402	122,703	122,635	122,781	123,197	123,644	124,141	124,403	124,570
1995	124,639	125,125	125,274	125,072	124,319	124,485	124,959	-	-	-	-	-

Source: U.S. Department of Labor, Bureau of Labor Statistics. - indicates data not available or zero.

Labor Force Participation Rate
Males 20 and over
(Percent)

Year	Jan	Feb	Mar	Apr	May	Jun	Jul	Aug	Sep	Oct	Nov	Dec
1948	88.7	89.0	88.2	88.3	88.1	88.5	88.7	88.8	88.5	88.8	88.7	89.0
1949	88.5	88.5	88.5	88.4	88.4	88.4	88.2	88.7	88.6	89.5	88.7	88.7
1950	88.1	88.0	88.0	88.2	88.4	88.3	88.1	88.5	88.4	88.2	88.2	88.2
1951	88.0	88.4	88.8	88.3	88.4	88.4	88.2	88.4	88.2	88.6	88.4	88.7
1952	88.8	89.0	88.6	88.5	88.4	88.4	88.3	88.0	88.0	87.6	87.6	88.5
1953	88.3	88.6	88.7	88.2	88.0	88.0	88.1	87.9	87.6	87.6	88.0	87.8
1954	87.8	88.1	87.7	88.2	87.9	87.8	87.7	88.2	88.4	88.0	87.6	87.3
1955	87.4	87.2	87.4	87.5	87.4	87.2	87.6	87.6	87.6	87.6	87.7	87.8
1956	88.1	87.9	87.9	87.8	87.6	87.6	87.5	87.5	87.3	87.2	87.3	87.3
1957	87.0	87.2	87.2	87.1	87.0	87.3	87.1	86.7	86.9	86.6	86.5	86.6
1958	86.4	86.2	86.2	86.6	86.9	86.8	87.0	87.1	87.1	87.0	86.5	86.3
1959	86.2	86.0	86.3	86.4	86.2	86.1	86.6	86.3	86.5	86.4	86.3	86.5
1960	86.2	86.0	85.6	86.1	86.0	85.9	85.9	86.0	86.2	86.1	86.3	86.3
1961	86.1	85.8	85.9	85.8	85.9	85.8	85.6	85.6	85.5	85.5	85.5	85.3
1962	85.1	85.3	85.3	84.7	85.0	84.8	84.4	84.9	84.8	84.6	84.6	84.4
1963	84.3	84.3	84.4	84.4	84.3	84.3	84.5	84.3	84.3	84.2	84.3	84.2
1964	84.2	84.1	84.0	84.5	84.5	84.0	84.3	84.1	84.2	84.2	84.0	83.9
1965	84.1	84.1	84.1	84.1	84.3	83.8	83.9	83.8	83.6	83.6	83.5	83.6
1966	83.6	83.5	83.6	83.7	83.6	83.6	83.4	83.5	83.5	83.4	83.5	83.6
1967	83.7	83.5	83.3	83.5	83.4	83.5	83.5	83.4	83.2	83.4	83.3	83.4
1968	83.1	83.1	83.0	83.1	83.2	83.4	83.3	83.2	83.0	82.9	82.9	83.1
1969	82.9	83.1	83.0	82.8	82.7	82.7	82.7	82.9	82.9	82.8	82.5	82.6
1970	82.8	82.8	82.9	83.0	82.9	82.6	82.6	82.5	82.5	82.4	82.5	82.5
1971	82.3	82.0	81.9	82.2	82.3	82.0	82.1	82.1	82.0	81.7	81.9	81.9
1972	81.6	81.5	81.8	81.7	81.6	81.7	81.7	81.6	81.6	81.4	81.4	81.5
1973	81.2	81.4	81.6	81.4	81.2	81.2	81.3	81.1	81.0	81.1	81.3	81.4
1974	81.8	81.7	81.3	81.0	81.1	80.9	80.7	80.9	80.8	80.8	80.9	80.7
1975	80.6	80.4	80.4	80.5	80.7	80.2	80.4	80.4	80.2	80.0	79.9	79.6
1976	79.7	79.6	79.6	79.9	79.8	79.7	79.9	79.9	79.9	79.8	80.0	79.8
1977	79.6	79.8	79.7	79.6	79.6	79.8	79.6	79.7	79.4	79.8	79.9	80.0
1978	79.9	79.8	79.7	79.8	79.8	79.8	79.7	79.6	79.5	79.6	80.0	80.0
1979	80.1	80.3	79.9	79.8	79.5	79.7	79.8	79.7	79.8	79.7	79.5	79.5
1980	79.7	79.9	79.4	79.5	79.6	79.3	79.4	79.4	79.3	79.2	79.2	79.0
1981	79.1	79.1	79.3	79.3	79.5	78.9	78.9	78.9	78.7	78.7	78.7	78.6
1982	78.6	78.7	78.7	78.8	78.9	78.8	78.8	78.7	78.9	78.8	78.8	78.7
1983	78.2	78.2	78.2	78.3	78.3	78.7	78.7	78.7	78.6	78.4	78.5	78.3
1984	78.3	78.3	78.2	78.3	78.3	78.4	78.4	78.3	78.4	78.3	78.3	78.3
1985	78.1	78.0	78.1	78.2	78.1	78.0	77.9	78.0	78.2	78.3	78.1	78.0
1986	78.3	78.1	78.1	78.0	78.0	78.1	78.1	78.0	78.1	78.0	78.2	78.4
1987	78.2	78.1	78.1	78.0	78.2	78.0	78.0	78.0	77.9	78.0	78.0	77.8
1988	77.9	78.0	77.8	78.1	78.0	77.8	77.9	78.1	77.8	77.9	77.9	77.8
1989	78.1	78.1	78.1	78.2	77.9	78.2	78.1	78.0	77.8	78.0	78.0	78.0
1990	78.0	78.0	77.9	77.9	77.9	77.8	77.7	77.7	77.7	77.8	77.9	77.9
1991	77.4	77.5	77.6	77.8	77.4	77.4	77.3	77.2	77.4	77.2	77.1	77.1
1992	77.1	77.1	77.4	77.6	77.7	77.5	77.4	77.4	77.3	77.2	77.1	77.0
1993	76.8	76.9	76.9	76.9	77.1	77.0	77.0	77.0	76.7	77.0	76.8	76.8
1994	77.0	76.9	76.8	76.8	76.6	76.5	76.6	76.6	76.6	76.8	76.9	77.0
1995	77.2	77.1	77.2	77.1	76.7	76.6	76.6	-	-	-	-	-

Source: U.S. Department of Labor, Bureau of Labor Statistics. - indicates data not available or zero.

Labor Force Participation Rate
Females 20 and over
(Percent)

Year	Jan	Feb	Mar	Apr	May	Jun	Jul	Aug	Sep	Oct	Nov	Dec
1948	31.0	31.4	31.1	32.1	31.3	32.5	32.7	32.0	32.3	31.7	31.8	32.1
1949	31.7	32.1	31.9	31.9	32.3	32.2	32.9	32.7	32.5	32.7	32.9	32.7
1950	32.7	32.8	32.7	33.4	33.0	33.8	33.2	33.6	33.1	33.6	33.7	33.5
1951	33.7	33.6	34.3	33.8	34.1	33.6	34.5	33.9	33.8	34.2	34.1	34.5
1952	34.4	34.3	33.5	33.6	34.0	33.8	33.7	33.9	34.9	34.2	34.8	34.2
1953	34.6	34.2	34.5	34.0	33.4	34.1	34.1	33.7	33.7	34.0	33.6	33.2
1954	33.4	34.5	34.5	34.4	34.3	34.1	33.8	33.9	34.5	34.4	34.4	34.0
1955	34.5	34.4	34.3	35.1	34.7	35.0	35.5	36.0	35.9	36.0	36.0	36.4
1956	36.3	36.0	36.0	36.2	36.7	36.4	36.6	36.6	36.8	36.6	36.4	36.4
1957	36.2	36.7	36.5	36.2	36.3	36.4	36.9	36.4	36.5	36.6	36.6	36.9
1958	36.7	36.8	36.8	37.1	37.0	37.0	37.0	37.2	36.8	36.8	36.6	36.7
1959	37.0	36.7	37.0	37.1	37.1	37.2	37.1	36.9	36.9	37.3	37.0	37.2
1960	36.9	36.9	36.3	37.6	37.7	37.9	37.9	37.9	38.1	37.6	38.2	38.2
1961	38.1	38.4	38.5	37.9	38.1	38.4	38.0	37.7	37.5	37.9	37.6	37.5
1962	37.9	38.0	37.7	37.6	37.6	37.5	37.6	38.1	38.3	37.9	37.8	37.8
1963	38.0	38.2	38.2	38.4	38.4	38.2	38.3	38.1	38.4	38.6	38.7	38.5
1964	38.5	38.8	38.8	39.5	39.3	39.0	38.7	38.9	38.6	38.8	38.7	38.9
1965	39.0	39.2	39.2	39.2	39.2	39.7	39.7	39.6	39.3	39.4	39.5	39.6
1966	39.8	39.6	39.6	39.8	40.0	39.9	40.0	40.3	40.6	40.6	40.9	40.8
1967	40.7	40.5	40.4	40.8	40.8	40.9	41.0	41.1	41.4	41.7	41.6	41.8
1968	40.9	41.3	41.4	41.4	42.0	41.9	41.7	41.3	41.6	41.6	41.9	41.9
1969	42.0	42.4	42.4	42.6	42.5	42.8	42.7	42.8	42.8	42.9	42.8	42.9
1970	43.1	43.1	43.4	43.5	43.0	43.2	43.5	43.3	43.0	43.4	43.4	43.4
1971	43.6	43.3	43.2	43.2	43.2	43.0	43.0	43.2	43.4	43.5	43.8	43.8
1972	43.6	43.4	43.7	43.6	43.8	43.6	43.7	43.8	43.7	43.7	43.6	43.7
1973	43.6	44.0	44.1	44.3	44.3	44.5	44.5	44.5	44.6	44.6	44.9	44.8
1974	44.7	45.0	45.1	45.1	45.1	45.3	45.8	45.5	45.5	45.3	45.5	45.6
1975	45.9	45.6	45.9	46.0	46.0	46.0	46.1	46.2	46.1	46.3	46.2	46.3
1976	46.6	46.6	46.7	46.8	46.8	47.0	47.3	47.3	47.1	47.1	47.5	47.6
1977	47.4	47.6	47.9	48.0	48.2	48.1	48.0	48.1	48.5	48.3	48.8	48.7
1978	48.9	48.9	49.1	49.4	49.4	49.6	49.6	49.5	49.9	50.0	50.1	50.2
1979	50.1	50.3	50.5	50.2	50.2	50.3	50.6	50.8	50.8	50.9	51.0	51.2
1980	51.3	51.3	51.2	51.4	51.3	51.2	51.3	51.4	51.2	51.4	51.6	51.4
1981	51.8	51.9	52.1	52.2	52.4	52.2	52.2	52.1	51.7	52.3	52.4	52.2
1982	52.2	52.4	52.5	52.5	52.8	52.9	52.9	52.9	52.9	52.7	52.9	53.1
1983	53.0	53.0	52.9	52.8	52.8	53.1	53.0	53.3	53.5	53.2	53.3	53.3
1984	53.0	53.3	53.4	53.6	54.1	53.8	54.0	53.8	53.6	53.9	53.9	54.1
1985	54.3	54.5	54.8	54.7	54.5	54.5	54.4	54.5	54.8	54.8	54.9	55.1
1986	54.9	55.0	55.1	55.2	55.4	55.7	55.7	55.8	55.8	55.8	55.8	55.6
1987	55.7	55.8	56.0	56.0	56.2	56.2	56.3	56.4	56.3	56.5	56.5	56.6
1988	56.6	56.7	56.7	56.7	56.4	56.5	56.6	56.8	56.8	57.1	57.5	57.4
1989	57.7	57.5	57.5	57.6	57.6	57.5	57.7	57.6	57.7	57.6	58.0	57.8
1990	57.9	58.0	57.9	58.0	58.1	57.9	57.9	58.1	58.0	57.9	57.7	57.8
1991	57.7	57.8	57.8	58.1	57.9	57.9	57.8	57.8	57.9	57.9	57.8	57.9
1992	58.2	58.2	58.4	58.5	58.3	58.5	58.7	58.5	58.3	58.2	58.3	58.4
1993	58.3	58.2	58.2	58.2	58.4	58.5	58.4	58.5	58.4	58.6	58.7	58.9
1994	59.3	59.5	59.3	59.3	59.3	59.1	59.2	59.4	59.6	59.5	59.5	59.2
1995	59.3	59.5	59.4	59.7	59.1	59.0	59.7	-	-	-	-	-

Source: U.S. Department of Labor, Bureau of Labor Statistics. - indicates data not available or zero.

Labor Force Participation Rate
16-19 years of age
(Percent)

Year	Jan	Feb	Mar	Apr	May	Jun	Jul	Aug	Sep	Oct	Nov	Dec
1948	53.2	53.7	54.1	54.2	50.9	53.8	52.6	51.5	51.5	50.6	51.0	53.1
1949	52.8	53.7	54.5	53.0	53.4	49.8	50.3	51.7	53.1	52.5	52.9	52.6
1950	51.9	51.7	50.2	50.8	50.9	50.4	50.8	52.0	52.5	53.5	52.6	52.5
1951	51.4	51.0	53.3	50.9	52.6	51.3	52.6	53.0	52.7	52.4	51.9	52.9
1952	52.2	51.8	50.9	50.7	52.3	52.8	51.2	50.0	50.5	50.2	51.4	51.1
1953	52.4	54.0	53.1	51.8	49.5	50.9	49.5	49.6	49.1	48.2	48.9	49.2
1954	50.9	51.4	51.7	50.1	48.6	46.3	47.1	48.0	48.5	47.3	46.3	44.6
1955	46.8	45.4	46.3	47.3	47.6	46.7	48.4	49.6	50.5	51.1	52.7	53.4
1956	51.4	50.5	50.0	49.4	52.1	52.5	51.7	50.6	50.3	49.7	50.4	50.3
1957	49.5	49.8	50.6	49.5	49.4	50.2	50.2	48.4	49.3	49.3	49.4	49.3
1958	47.4	48.0	47.5	48.1	48.9	46.5	46.8	47.1	47.9	47.9	46.8	47.1
1959	47.5	46.7	46.7	47.7	46.2	46.0	46.3	46.6	46.9	46.6	46.3	47.4
1960	47.2	47.4	46.7	48.5	48.1	49.7	47.3	46.9	47.4	47.3	47.4	46.5
1961	47.4	46.7	47.6	46.0	45.8	47.8	47.1	48.0	46.4	46.4	47.4	45.6
1962	45.6	45.9	46.8	46.5	47.4	47.8	46.5	46.4	45.8	45.3	44.9	44.8
1963	45.4	45.1	44.8	45.3	46.2	44.6	45.0	44.8	45.7	45.8	44.8	43.9
1964	44.4	45.3	45.0	44.0	44.8	44.4	44.0	44.2	45.5	44.1	44.1	44.3
1965	43.0	43.7	44.1	45.3	45.6	44.0	46.3	45.5	46.5	47.8	47.1	48.1
1966	48.0	46.7	46.9	47.4	46.9	48.5	49.1	49.3	47.5	48.2	49.1	49.3
1967	48.3	48.2	47.5	47.6	47.2	48.8	49.0	49.5	48.3	48.7	48.3	48.3
1968	46.6	48.5	48.2	47.9	48.2	49.3	49.1	49.0	47.9	48.0	47.7	47.8
1969	47.7	47.8	48.3	48.7	47.5	49.6	50.0	50.0	50.5	50.9	50.9	50.4
1970	50.4	50.3	50.4	49.9	49.7	49.0	49.4	49.7	50.4	50.1	50.1	49.8
1971	50.0	49.9	49.3	49.7	49.4	47.5	50.5	50.5	49.3	49.7	50.5	50.6
1972	51.1	51.4	51.9	51.8	51.5	51.9	51.6	52.9	51.6	51.9	52.4	52.8
1973	50.8	52.9	53.5	53.7	53.2	54.5	53.3	53.2	54.3	54.8	55.1	55.1
1974	55.1	55.2	55.0	53.8	54.3	55.3	54.9	53.8	55.7	55.5	55.1	54.4
1975	54.9	54.1	54.1	53.6	54.7	53.8	54.1	53.8	54.1	53.5	53.2	53.8
1976	54.2	54.2	54.4	55.2	55.1	53.8	55.3	55.1	53.9	54.4	54.4	54.1
1977	54.2	55.2	55.5	55.7	55.6	57.0	56.1	57.2	55.9	56.5	57.2	56.3
1978	56.7	56.6	56.5	57.0	57.9	58.5	58.4	59.3	58.1	58.3	58.2	58.2
1979	58.5	58.6	58.4	57.9	57.3	58.0	57.7	56.8	57.8	57.5	57.7	58.3
1980	57.7	57.2	57.2	55.9	57.0	57.0	57.3	55.9	56.3	56.6	56.2	55.9
1981	56.7	56.6	56.4	57.0	56.3	54.0	54.5	55.2	54.8	55.0	55.2	53.8
1982	54.4	54.7	53.8	54.3	55.3	52.5	53.2	54.2	54.0	54.4	54.7	53.9
1983	53.7	52.7	52.5	52.6	52.2	55.2	53.8	55.1	53.8	53.0	53.6	53.8
1984	53.2	53.3	53.3	53.9	53.8	55.2	54.8	53.3	54.4	53.9	53.8	54.5
1985	55.0	54.9	55.3	54.7	55.0	53.0	55.5	53.4	54.1	54.5	54.3	54.1
1986	53.3	54.6	55.1	55.6	55.2	55.4	54.7	54.6	54.8	54.9	54.2	53.4
1987	54.0	54.8	54.4	54.4	55.3	53.7	54.1	56.2	54.3	55.1	54.6	55.4
1988	55.6	55.0	53.8	54.4	54.2	56.4	56.4	56.6	56.1	55.1	54.8	55.1
1989	55.6	54.8	54.5	55.5	55.5	57.0	56.1	57.4	55.6	56.3	56.5	55.8
1990	55.3	54.6	55.6	55.2	54.4	53.6	53.1	52.3	52.9	52.9	52.2	52.7
1991	53.1	52.6	53.0	52.6	51.9	51.7	50.6	49.7	51.0	51.6	51.2	51.1
1992	51.7	51.5	50.6	50.4	51.1	51.9	51.2	51.4	52.2	50.4	51.4	51.7
1993	51.4	51.9	51.5	51.8	52.5	51.5	51.8	51.6	51.2	51.1	51.2	50.9
1994	53.1	52.7	52.9	53.6	52.9	53.2	52.5	52.8	51.5	52.7	51.8	52.9
1995	53.6	53.6	54.5	54.3	53.6	54.2	53.6	-	-	-	-	-

Source: U.S. Department of Labor, Bureau of Labor Statistics. - indicates data not available or zero.

INDICATORS OF INTERNATIONAL TRANSACTIONS

International trade has been a subject of concern and debate since the mid-1970s, when the U.S. trade balance turned negative and has continued negative since. As a percent of GDP, foreign trade has also grown. And with the rise of new industrial economies on the Asian rim of the Pacific, a world-wide competition for trade has intensified concerns. Negative trade balances have a direct impact on GDP; they are also, indirectly, a measure of U.S. competitiveness in world markets. The three tables included in this section present the basic facts about this phenomenon as seen from the U.S. vantage point. The tables are:

> Merchandise exports, adjusted, excluding military
> Merchandise imports, adjusted, excluding military
> Balance on merchandise trade

Merchandise Exports, Excluding Military. Data from 1960 to 1995 are shown in millions of current dollars. Data exclude Department of Defense sales contracts (exports) and military grants. Military aid shipments and exports are excluded because, arising from government policy, such shipments would distort the market-based nature of the overall export business.

Merchandise Imports, Excluding Military. Data are also for 1960 to 1995 in millions of current dollars. Data exclude Department of Defense purchases (imports).

Balance on Merchandise Trade. Data are in millions of current dollars for 1960 to 1995. The values shown are merchandise exports less merchandise imports from the earlier tables, indicating to what extent the U.S. enjoyed a trade surplus (positive numbers) or a deficit (negative values).

Surplus or deficit in foreign trade has always played an important role in international relations. In pre-modern times, when gold was the standard of exchange, a trade deficit meant that a country lost some of its gold stock to another country; a surplus meant a gain in gold; for this reason, countries tried to maintain surpluses or, failing that, a balance between imports and exports. International trade has become much more complex since, but underlying concepts remain in force. Thus the purchasing power of the dollar has a direct influence on the trade deficit. A strong dollar (meaning a dollar expensive relative to other currencies) acts to diminish exports—because dollar-denominated goods are expensive elsewhere; importers are aided because their goods are relatively cheap in the U.S. market. Conversely, a weak dollar helps exports and impedes imports. The strong and weak dollar have other consequences as well: a strong dollar tends to reduce production but curbs inflation; a weak dollar is associated with high production but also with inflation.

A strong dollar in the 1980-1985 period was one of the causes of a dramatically increasing trade deficit in that period. A weaker dollar since has reduced the deficit. The value of the dollar, in turn, reflects the strength of an economy relative to other economies and *perceptions* of this strength; perceptions are translated into policy and trading actions by others—which cause the value of the dollar to rise or fall. Public policy can influence—but cannot set—the value of the dollar.

The trade deficit has a negative impact on GDP growth because trade balance is part of GDP. The change from period to period is more important, in this context, than the absolute magnitude of the trade balance or its arithmetic sign. A shrinking deficit or a growing surplus will both translate into a positive signal for GDP.

Exports, imports, and the trade balance are subject to trade policies followed in the U.S. and in foreign countries. Therefore, ultimately, foreign trade data reflect pure market forces only indirectly.

Merchandise Exports
Adjusted, excluding military
(Million $)

Year	1st Quarter	2nd Quarter	3rd Quarter	4th Quarter
1960	4,685	4,916	5,031	5,018
1961	5,095	4,806	5,038	5,169
1962	5,077	5,336	5,331	5,037
1963	5,063	5,599	5,671	5,939
1964	6,242	6,199	6,423	6,637
1965	5,768	6,876	6,643	7,174
1966	7,242	7,169	7,290	7,609
1967	7,751	7,693	7,530	7,692
1968	7,998	8,324	8,745	8,559
1969	7,468	9,536	9,400	10,010
1970	10,258	10,744	10,665	10,802
1971	10,920	10,878	11,548	9,973
1972	11,833	11,618	12,351	13,579
1973	15,474	17,112	18,271	20,553
1974	22,614	24,500	24,629	26,563
1975	27,480	25,866	26,109	27,633
1976	27,575	28,256	29,056	29,858
1977	29,668	30,852	30,752	29,544
1978	30,470	35,674	36,523	39,408
1979	41,475	43,885	47,104	51,975
1980	54,237	55,967	55,830	58,216
1981	60,317	60,141	58,031	58,555
1982	55,163	55,344	52,089	48,561
1983	49,198	49,340	50,324	52,937
1984	52,991	54,626	55,893	56,416
1985	54,866	54,154	52,836	54,059
1986	53,536	56,828	55,645	57,335
1987	56,696	60,202	64,217	69,093
1988	75,655	79,542	80,941	84,092
1989	87,426	92,208	90,163	92,323
1990	95,301	97,573	96,339	100,094
1991	101,345	104,529	103,732	107,307
1992	108,344	109,025	109,593	113,390
1993	111,862	114,131	111,576	119,254
1994	118,445	122,730	127,384	133,926
1995	138,059	-	-	-

Source: U.S. Department of Commerce, Bureau of the Census. - indicates data not available or zero.

Merchandise Imports
Adjusted, excluding military
(Million $)

Year	1st Quarter	2nd Quarter	3rd Quarter	4th Quarter
1960	3,812	3,858	3,648	3,440
1961	3,394	3,438	3,809	3,896
1962	3,966	4,080	4,116	4,098
1963	4,064	4,226	4,372	4,386
1964	4,416	4,598	4,756	4,930
1965	4,711	5,428	5,516	5,855
1966	6,012	6,195	6,576	6,710
1967	6,708	6,475	6,526	7,157
1968	7,796	8,051	8,612	8,532
1969	7,444	9,527	9,380	9,456
1970	9,587	9,766	10,049	10,464
1971	10,600	11,614	12,171	11,194
1972	13,501	13,254	14,022	15,020
1973	16,285	17,168	17,683	19,363
1974	21,952	26,346	27,368	28,145
1975	24,980	22,832	24,487	25,886
1976	28,176	30,182	32,213	33,657
1977	36,585	38,063	38,005	39,254
1978	42,487	43,419	44,422	45,674
1979	47,582	50,778	54,002	59,645
1980	65,815	62,274	59,010	62,651
1981	67,004	67,181	64,407	66,475
1982	63,502	60,580	63,696	59,864
1983	59,757	64,783	70,370	73,991
1984	79,740	83,798	83,918	84,962
1985	80,319	84,565	83,909	89,295
1986	89,220	91,743	92,801	94,661
1987	96,023	100,648	104,412	108,682
1988	109,963	110,836	110,901	115,489
1989	116,477	120,907	118,873	121,108
1990	122,447	122,169	125,389	128,332
1991	120,141	120,705	123,479	126,656
1992	126,284	133,277	136,887	140,010
1993	140,821	147,718	148,181	152,721
1994	154,935	164,224	172,011	177,414
1995	183,111	-	-	-

Source: U.S. Department of Commerce, Bureau of the Census. - indicates data not available or zero.

Balance On Merchandise Trade
(Million $)

Year	1st Quarter	2nd Quarter	3rd Quarter	4th Quarter
1960	873	1,058	1,383	1,578
1961	1,701	1,368	1,229	1,273
1962	1,111	1,256	1,215	939
1963	999	1,373	1,299	1,553
1964	1,826	1,601	1,667	1,707
1965	1,057	1,448	1,127	1,319
1966	1,230	974	714	899
1967	1,043	1,218	1,004	535
1968	202	273	133	27
1969	24	9	20	554
1970	671	978	616	338
1971	320	-736	-623	-1,221
1972	-1,668	-1,636	-1,671	-1,441
1973	-811	-56	588	1,190
1974	662	-1,846	-2,739	-1,582
1975	2,500	3,034	1,622	1,747
1976	-601	-1,926	-3,157	-3,799
1977	-6,917	-7,211	-7,253	-9,710
1978	-12,017	-7,745	-7,899	-6,266
1979	-6,107	-6,893	-6,898	-7,670
1980	-11,578	-6,307	-3,180	-4,435
1981	-6,687	-7,040	-6,376	-7,920
1982	-8,339	-5,236	-11,607	-11,303
1983	-10,559	-15,443	-20,046	-21,054
1984	-26,749	-29,172	-28,025	-28,546
1985	-25,453	-30,411	-31,073	-35,236
1986	-35,684	-34,915	-37,156	-37,326
1987	-39,327	-40,446	-40,195	-39,589
1988	-34,308	-31,294	-29,960	-31,397
1989	-29,051	-28,699	-28,710	-28,785
1990	-27,146	-24,596	-29,050	-28,238
1991	-18,796	-16,176	-19,747	-19,349
1992	-17,940	-24,252	-27,294	-26,620
1993	-28,959	-33,587	-36,605	-33,467
1994	-36,490	-41,494	-44,627	-43,488
1995	-45,052	-	-	-

Source: U.S. Department of Commerce, Bureau of Economic Analysis. - indicates data not available or zero.

CHAPTER 6

CONSUMER PRICE INDEX

CONSUMER PRICE INDEX

The Consumer Price Index (CPI) is the primary system for measuring price change in the United States in a consistent manner. The CPI, therefore, is the chief measure of inflation and the source of data for converting "current dollar" measurements and estimates into "constant" or "real dollar" values used in National Income and Product Accounts and in cyclic indicators of the economy. It is produced by the U.S. Department of Labor, Bureau of Labor Statistics (BLS), Division of Consumer Prices and Price Indexes.

General Concept

The CPI is based on obtaining the price of an *identical* "basket" of goods at two different points in time and measuring the difference. By way of illustration, consider the following simple case:

> A basket of goods is purchased in January 1975 containing a loaf of bread, a quart of milk, a pound of potatoes, a package of bacon, five pounds of flour and of sugar. The price is noted. It is $15.00.
>
> A year later, exactly the same items are purchased. This time the price is $18.00.

In this situation, inflation has been $3.00. Only the price has changed. It has increased by 20%.

Rather than dealing with actual dollar figures, we can express these relationships as an index. If 1975 is chosen as the base year and set to a value of 100, the 1976 value would be 120—showing a 20% inflation rate.

The system works in the same way if prices decrease. Assume that in 1977 the same basket of goods cost $12.00. This price is 20% lower than the price in the base year. The new 1977 index, therefore, would be 80. The change between 1976 and 1977 would be a 33.3% decrease:

$$((80 / 120) - 1) \times 100 = -33.3$$

These concepts underlie the CPI. The index measures the price of a "fixed market basket of goods and services" at monthly intervals. This is a hypothetical basket because it includes not only items one ordinarily buys in a store but also the costs of fuel, housing, transportation, and other services. A base period is selected; currently (1994) it is the average of 1982-1984. The price index is shown with reference to the base period, which is defined as 100.

Implementation of the Concept

In order to implement this concept in a useful manner, it is necessary, first, to determine the make-up of the "fixed market basket": what proportion of a family's budget is devoted to food, clothing, housing, etc. Since consumption patterns differ somewhat from region to region, it is also necessary to know how the market basket's contents change from place to place; fuel costs, typically, will be a lesser proportion of budgets in mild climates, for instance. BLS conducts surveys at regular intervals in selected urban areas to answer these questions. Consumer surveys are then used to change how the index is constructed and what weight or importance to give to each major component in the basket. From the beginning of the CPI, surveys of spending patterns have been followed by comprehensive revisions of the index.

The modern index is built by pricing goods and services in 94 primary sampling units in 91 geographical areas. Sampling units and geographical areas are selected using population census data to arrive at a representative sampling.

Raw data collected from sampling units are processed into geographical indexes and into a U.S. City average. Major components (food, apparel, housing, etc.) are combined by applying appropriate weights to produce a final consumer price index.

History and Revisions

The CPI was initiated during World War I as a tool for calculating cost-of-living adjustments in wages. The first surveys of consumption patterns were carried out by the Department of Labor from 1917-1919; periodic collection of prices began in 1919 by the Department's Bureau of Labor Statistics. Regular publication began in 1921, with indexes estimated back to 1913. The cycle of surveys and revisions began in 1934-36 (survey) and 1940 (index revision). Thereafter, major changes were introduced as follows:

> 1951 - adjustments to reflect immediate postwar changes
> 1953 - comprehensive postwar revisions, statistical overhaul
> 1964 - new expenditure weights reflecting single persons as well as families
> 1978 - changes in sample, data collection, inclusion of all urban consumers
> 1983 - changes in home ownership cost calculations for all urban consumers
> 1985 - changes in home ownership cost calculations for urban wage earners
> 1987 - improvements of sampling, data collection, processing, and estimation

The CPI was originally designed to measure the cost of living of urban wage earners and clerical workers (usually called CPI-W). A more encompassing category including all urban families (CPI-U) was introduced in 1978; CPI-U includes, in addition to CPI-W, professional and salaried workers, part-time workers, the self-employed, the unemployed, and retired people.

Sampling, Components, and Methods

Sampling Universe. CPI pricing data are collected in 91 urban areas; 21,000 retail and service establishments are sampled; these include supermarkets, department stores, filling stations, hospitals, and other establishments. Housing costs are collected from 40,000 tenants and on 20,000 owner-occupied housing units.

Product/Service Categories. Items/services to be priced are subdivided into 7 major product groups: food and beverages, fuels and utilities, household services and furnishings, apparel and upkeep, transportation, medical care, entertainment, and other commodities and services. These major groupings are made up of 69 expenditure classes (e.g. furniture and bedding) which, in turn, are divided into 207 item strata (bedroom furniture) and finally into 364 "entry level items" (mattresses and springs). Pricing on approximately 100,000 entry level items is conducted for the CPI on a regular basis.

Sampling Frequency. Food, fuel, and selected other items are priced monthly in all of the sample geographies. Most other goods and services are surveyed monthly in the five largest urban areas and bimonthly in all the others.

Basing Years. BLS provides data calculated with a base of 1967 and 1982-1984—in which data are expressed with 1967 values as 100 and the 1982-1984 averages as 100. The annual average index for 1982 is 95.6, for 1983 99.6 and for 1984 103.9. The sum of these index values is 300; divided by 3, we get the basing value of 100.

Measurement of Changes. Index movements from one month to the next are expressed as percent changes rather than as changes in index points. The following formula is used in the tables to show change from period to period:

((Current Index / Previous Index) - 1) x 100.

This formula can be used to calculate, for example, how the cost of living has changed between January 1990 and January 1991 without reference to the base year of the series. The U.S. average data for base 1982-1984 were as follows:

January 1990 - 127.4
January 1991 - 134.6

By applying the formula to these values, we get a percent change of 5.7.

The data for the same series but with a 1967 base are:

January 1990 - 381.5
January 1991 - 403.1

These values *also* produce a 5.7% change.

The meaning of the change for a person with a fixed income of $30,000 a year would be that his or her income in 1991 was 5.7% less than in 1990 due to inflation. The purchasing power of the income would be $28,290 in 1991.

Uses of the CPI

The CPI is the most widely used measure of inflation; consequently, it plays a role in economic measurement and in the setting of monetary and fiscal policy and is used widely as an indicator in all manner of institutions, public and private, for a range of activities, including wage settlements.

The CPI is used as a deflator of other economic series. Throughout *Economic Indicators Handbook*, references are made to current dollar and constant dollar presentations of data; the latter are also referred to as "real" dollars, meaning that inflation has been removed by use of a deflator. In the example above, the person with a fixed income of $30,000 had an income in 1991 of $30,000 in *current* dollars but only an income of $28,290 in *constant* or "real" dollars (in this case 1990 dollars).

The CPI is used for income adjustments. More than 3 million union workers are covered by contracts tied to CPI. The income of more than 60 million other people is affected by changes in CPI, including 38 million Social Security recipients, 3 million military and federal retirees and survivors, and about 19 million people receiving food stamps. Federal income tax indexing uses the CPI. There are also many uses of the CPI by the private sector.

Presentation and Limitations of Data

In the following tables, data are presented as follows:

U.S. City Average Data. These data are the overall CPI, calculated for all cities. *EIH* presents the following subsets of the data:

> Annual Averages for all items and 7 subcategories, 1982-1984 basis
> For all urban consumers
> For urban wage earners and clerical workers

> U.S. City Average for all items, monthly, 1982-1984 basis
> All urban consumers
> Urban wage earners and clerical workers

> U.S. City Average for each of 7 subcategories of expenditure, 1982-1984 basis
> Monthly for all urban consumers
> Monthly for urban wage earners and clerical workers

Index values are shown from 1913 to 1993 as available. Percent change from one period to the next is precalculated and shown. In tables of annual averages, the comparison is between two rows in the same column; in monthly tables, the comparison is between two columns of the same row.

Limitations of the U.S. City Average Data. The CPI measures cost changes in urban areas and should not be applied to situations in other contexts. The index is based on a sample of consumer purchases rather than all consumer purchases; hence sampling errors are inherent in the series. The CPI cannot be used for demographic subgroups of the population, such as the elderly.

City/Urban Area Data. Following the U.S. City Average tables, data are presented for 27 cities/urban areas. The cities are ordered alphabetically. For each city, the following tables are presented:

> Annual averages for all items and 7 subcategories, 1982-1984 basis
> For all urban consumers
> For urban wage earners and clerical workers

> All items, monthly, 1982-1984 basis
> All urban consumers
> Urban wage earners and clerical workers

> Seven tables of subcategories, 1982-1984 basis
> Monthly for all urban consumers
> Monthly for urban wage earners and clerical workers

Years and months of coverage for cities varies. For some, categories data are available back to 1913. In other cases, data start at a later date and are shown for the months in which data were collected. The tables, in fact, show how the frequency and timing of collections have changed over time.

Limitations of City/Urban Area Data. Is it more expensive to live in New York than in Los Angeles? *The CPI cannot be used to answer this question*. Cost of living comparisons *between* cities are not a legitimate use of the index. The CPI, in other words, cannot be used to determine "relative" cost of living. The index measures only changes in the cost of living *in* one urban area. The CPI is suitable for determining whether or not prices are rising faster in one city than in another; they do not measure absolute price levels between cities.

Bibliography

1. U.S. Department of Labor, Bureau of Labor Statistics. *BLS Handbook of Methods*, Bulletin 2285, 1987. Washington, DC.

U.S. CITY AVERAGE
Consumer Price Index - All Urban Consumers
Base 1982-1984 = 100
Annual Averages

For 1913-1995. Columns headed % show percentile change in the index from the previous period for which an index is available.

Year	All Items		Food & Beverage		Housing		Apparel & Upkeep		Trans- portation		Medical Care		Entertain- ment		Other Goods & Services	
	Index	%	Index	%	Index	%	Index	%	Index	%	Index	%	Index	%	Index	%
1913	9.9	-	-	-	-	-	14.9	-	-	-	-	-	-	-	-	-
1914	10.0	1.0	-	-	-	-	15.0	0.7	-	-	-	-	-	-	-	-
1915	10.1	1.0	-	-	-	-	15.3	2.0	-	-	-	-	-	-	-	-
1916	10.9	7.9	-	-	-	-	16.8	9.8	-	-	-	-	-	-	-	-
1917	12.8	17.4	-	-	-	-	20.2	20.2	-	-	-	-	-	-	-	-
1918	15.1	18.0	-	-	-	-	27.3	35.1	-	-	-	-	-	-	-	-
1919	17.3	14.6	-	-	-	-	36.2	32.6	-	-	-	-	-	-	-	-
1920	20.0	15.6	-	-	-	-	43.1	19.1	-	-	-	-	-	-	-	-
1921	17.9	-10.5	-	-	-	-	33.2	-23.0	-	-	-	-	-	-	-	-
1922	16.8	-6.1	-	-	-	-	27.0	-18.7	-	-	-	-	-	-	-	-
1923	17.1	1.8	-	-	-	-	27.1	0.4	-	-	-	-	-	-	-	-
1924	17.1	0.0	-	-	-	-	26.8	-1.1	-	-	-	-	-	-	-	-
1925	17.5	2.3	-	-	-	-	26.3	-1.9	-	-	-	-	-	-	-	-
1926	17.7	1.1	-	-	-	-	25.9	-1.5	-	-	-	-	-	-	-	-
1927	17.4	-1.7	-	-	-	-	25.3	-2.3	-	-	-	-	-	-	-	-
1928	17.1	-1.7	-	-	-	-	25.0	-1.2	-	-	-	-	-	-	-	-
1929	17.1	0.0	-	-	-	-	24.7	-1.2	-	-	-	-	-	-	-	-
1930	16.7	-2.3	-	-	-	-	24.2	-2.0	-	-	-	-	-	-	-	-
1931	15.2	-9.0	-	-	-	-	22.0	-9.1	-	-	-	-	-	-	-	-
1932	13.7	-9.9	-	-	-	-	19.5	-11.4	-	-	-	-	-	-	-	-
1933	13.0	-5.1	-	-	-	-	18.8	-3.6	-	-	-	-	-	-	-	-
1934	13.4	3.1	-	-	-	-	20.6	9.6	-	-	-	-	-	-	-	-
1935	13.7	2.2	-	-	-	-	20.8	1.0	14.2	-	10.2	-	-	-	-	-
1936	13.9	1.5	-	-	-	-	21.0	1.0	14.3	0.7	10.2	0.0	-	-	-	-
1937	14.4	3.6	-	-	-	-	22.0	4.8	14.5	1.4	10.3	1.0	-	-	-	-
1938	14.1	-2.1	-	-	-	-	21.9	-0.5	14.6	0.7	10.3	0.0	-	-	-	-
1939	13.9	-1.4	-	-	-	-	21.6	-1.4	14.3	-2.1	10.3	0.0	-	-	-	-
1940	14.0	0.7	-	-	-	-	21.8	0.9	14.2	-0.7	10.4	1.0	-	-	-	-
1941	14.7	5.0	-	-	-	-	22.8	4.6	14.7	3.5	10.4	0.0	-	-	-	-
1942	16.3	10.9	-	-	-	-	26.7	17.1	16.0	8.8	10.7	2.9	-	-	-	-
1943	17.3	6.1	-	-	-	-	27.8	4.1	15.9	-0.6	11.2	4.7	-	-	-	-
1944	17.6	1.7	-	-	-	-	29.8	7.2	15.9	0.0	11.6	3.6	-	-	-	-
1945	18.0	2.3	-	-	-	-	31.4	5.4	15.9	0.0	11.9	2.6	-	-	-	-
1946	19.5	8.3	-	-	-	-	34.4	9.6	16.7	5.0	12.5	5.0	-	-	-	-
1947	22.3	14.4	-	-	-	-	39.9	16.0	18.5	10.8	13.5	8.0	-	-	-	-
1948	24.1	8.1	-	-	-	-	42.5	6.5	20.6	11.4	14.4	6.7	-	-	-	-
1949	23.8	-1.2	-	-	-	-	40.8	-4.0	22.1	7.3	14.8	2.8	-	-	-	-
1950	24.1	1.3	-	-	-	-	40.3	-1.2	22.7	2.7	15.1	2.0	-	-	-	-
1951	26.0	7.9	-	-	-	-	43.9	8.9	24.1	6.2	15.9	5.3	-	-	-	-
1952	26.5	1.9	-	-	-	-	43.5	-0.9	25.7	6.6	16.7	5.0	-	-	-	-
1953	26.7	0.8	-	-	-	-	43.1	-0.9	26.5	3.1	17.3	3.6	-	-	-	-
1954	26.9	0.7	-	-	-	-	43.1	0.0	26.1	-1.5	17.8	2.9	-	-	-	-
1955	26.8	-0.4	-	-	-	-	42.9	-0.5	25.8	-1.1	18.2	2.2	-	-	-	-
1956	27.2	1.5	-	-	-	-	43.7	1.9	26.2	1.6	18.9	3.8	-	-	-	-
1957	28.1	3.3	-	-	-	-	44.5	1.8	27.7	5.7	19.7	4.2	-	-	-	-

[Continued]

U.S. City Average
Consumer Price Index - All Urban Consumers
Base 1982-1984 = 100
Annual Averages
[Continued]

For 1913-1995. Columns headed % show percentile change in the index from the previous period for which an index is available.

Year	All Items Index	%	Food & Beverage Index	%	Housing Index	%	Apparel & Upkeep Index	%	Trans-portation Index	%	Medical Care Index	%	Entertain-ment Index	%	Other Goods & Services Index	%
1958	28.9	2.8	-	-	-	-	44.6	0.2	28.6	3.2	20.6	4.6	-	-	-	-
1959	29.1	0.7	-	-	-	-	45.0	0.9	29.8	4.2	21.5	4.4	-	-	-	-
1960	29.6	1.7	-	-	-	-	45.7	1.6	29.8	0.0	22.3	3.7	-	-	-	-
1961	29.9	1.0	-	-	-	-	46.1	0.9	30.1	1.0	22.9	2.7		-	-	-
1962	30.2	1.0	-	-	-	-	46.3	0.4	30.8	2.3	23.5	2.6		-	-	-
1963	30.6	1.3	-	-	-	-	46.9	1.3	30.9	0.3	24.1	2.6		-	-	-
1964	31.0	1.3	-	-	-	-	47.3	0.9	31.4	1.6	24.6	2.1		-	-	-
1965	31.5	1.6	-	-	-	-	47.8	1.1	31.9	1.6	25.2	2.4		-	-	-
1966	32.4	2.9	-	-	-	-	49.0	2.5	32.3	1.3	26.3	4.4	-	-	-	-
1967	33.4	3.1	35.0	-	30.8	-	51.0	4.1	33.3	3.1	28.2	7.2	40.7	-	35.1	-
1968	34.8	4.2	36.2	3.4	32.0	3.9	53.7	5.3	34.3	3.0	29.9	6.0	43.0	5.7	36.9	5.1
1969	36.7	5.5	38.1	5.2	34.0	6.3	56.8	5.8	35.7	4.1	31.9	6.7	45.2	5.1	38.7	4.9
1970	38.8	5.7	40.1	5.2	36.4	7.1	59.2	4.2	37.5	5.0	34.0	6.6	47.5	5.1	40.9	5.7
1971	40.5	4.4	41.4	3.2	38.0	4.4	61.1	3.2	39.5	5.3	36.1	6.2	50.0	5.3	42.9	4.9
1972	41.8	3.2	43.1	4.1	39.4	3.7	62.3	2.0	39.9	1.0	37.3	3.3	51.5	3.0	44.7	4.2
1973	44.4	6.2	48.8	13.2	41.2	4.6	64.6	3.7	41.2	3.3	38.8	4.0	52.9	2.7	46.4	3.8
1974	49.3	11.0	55.5	13.7	45.8	11.2	69.4	7.4	45.8	11.2	42.4	9.3	56.9	7.6	49.8	7.3
1975	53.8	9.1	60.2	8.5	50.7	10.7	72.5	4.5	50.1	9.4	47.5	12.0	62.0	9.0	53.9	8.2
1976	56.9	5.8	62.1	3.2	53.8	6.1	75.2	3.7	55.1	10.0	52.0	9.5	65.1	5.0	57.0	5.8
1977	60.6	6.5	65.8	6.0	57.4	6.7	78.6	4.5	59.0	7.1	57.0	9.6	68.3	4.9	60.4	6.0
1978	65.2	7.6	72.2	9.7	62.4	8.7	81.4	3.6	61.7	4.6	61.8	8.4	71.9	5.3	64.3	6.5
1979	72.6	11.3	79.9	10.7	70.1	12.3	84.9	4.3	70.5	14.3	67.5	9.2	76.7	6.7	68.9	7.2
1980	82.4	13.5	86.7	8.5	81.1	15.7	90.9	7.1	83.1	17.9	74.9	11.0	83.6	9.0	75.2	9.1
1981	90.9	10.3	93.5	7.8	90.4	11.5	95.3	4.8	93.2	12.2	82.9	10.7	90.1	7.8	82.6	9.8
1982	96.5	6.2	97.3	4.1	96.9	7.2	97.8	2.6	97.0	4.1	92.5	11.6	96.0	6.5	91.1	10.3
1983	99.6	3.2	99.5	2.3	99.5	2.7	100.2	2.5	99.3	2.4	100.6	8.8	100.1	4.3	101.1	11.0
1984	103.9	4.3	103.2	3.7	103.6	4.1	102.1	1.9	103.7	4.4	106.8	6.2	103.8	3.7	107.9	6.7
1985	107.6	3.6	105.6	2.3	107.7	4.0	105.0	2.8	106.4	2.6	113.5	6.3	107.9	3.9	114.5	6.1
1986	109.6	1.9	109.1	3.3	110.9	3.0	105.9	0.9	102.3	-3.9	122.0	7.5	111.6	3.4	121.4	6.0
1987	113.6	3.6	113.5	4.0	114.2	3.0	110.6	4.4	105.4	3.0	130.1	6.6	115.3	3.3	128.5	5.8
1988	118.3	4.1	118.2	4.1	118.5	3.8	115.4	4.3	108.7	3.1	138.6	6.5	120.3	4.3	137.0	6.6
1989	124.0	4.8	124.9	5.7	123.0	3.8	118.6	2.8	114.1	5.0	149.3	7.7	126.5	5.2	147.7	7.8
1990	130.7	5.4	132.1	5.8	128.5	4.5	124.1	4.6	120.5	5.6	162.8	9.0	132.4	4.7	159.0	7.7
1991	136.2	4.2	136.8	3.6	133.6	4.0	128.7	3.7	123.8	2.7	177.0	8.7	138.4	4.5	171.6	7.9
1992	140.3	3.0	138.7	1.4	137.5	2.9	131.9	2.5	126.5	2.2	190.1	7.4	142.3	2.8	183.3	6.8
1993	144.5	3.0	141.6	2.1	141.2	2.7	133.7	1.4	130.4	3.1	201.4	5.9	145.8	2.5	192.9	5.2
1994	148.2	2.6	144.9	2.3	144.8	2.5	133.4	-0.2	134.3	3.0	211.0	4.8	150.1	2.9	198.5	2.9
1995	152.4	2.8	148.9	2.8	148.5	2.6	132.0	-1.0	139.1	3.6	220.5	4.5	153.9	2.5	206.9	4.2

Source: U.S. Department of Labor, Bureau of Labor Statistics, Division of Consumer Prices and Price Indexes.

U.S. CITY AVERAGE
Consumer Price Index - Urban Wage Earners
Base 1982-1984 = 100
Annual Averages

For 1913-1995. Columns headed % show percentile change in the index from the previous period for which an index is available.

Year	All Items		Food & Beverage		Housing		Apparel & Upkeep		Trans-portation		Medical Care		Entertain-ment		Other Goods & Services	
	Index	%	Index	%	Index	%	Index	%	Index	%	Index	%	Index	%	Index	%
1913	10.0	-	-	-	-	-	15.0	-	-	-	-	-	-	-	-	-
1914	10.1	1.0	-	-	-	-	15.1	0.7	-	-	-	-	-	-	-	-
1915	10.2	1.0	-	-	-	-	15.4	2.0	-	-	-	-	-	-	-	-
1916	11.0	7.8	-	-	-	-	16.9	9.7	-	-	-	-	-	-	-	-
1917	12.9	17.3	-	-	-	-	20.3	20.1	-	-	-	-	-	-	-	-
1918	15.1	17.1	-	-	-	-	27.5	35.5	-	-	-	-	-	-	-	-
1919	17.4	15.2	-	-	-	-	36.4	32.4	-	-	-	-	-	-	-	-
1920	20.1	15.5	-	-	-	-	43.3	19.0	-	-	-	-	-	-	-	-
1921	18.0	-10.4	-	-	-	-	33.4	-22.9	-	-	-	-	-	-	-	-
1922	16.9	-6.1	-	-	-	-	27.2	-18.6	-	-	-	-	-	-	-	-
1923	17.2	1.8	-	-	-	-	27.2	0.0	-	-	-	-	-	-	-	-
1924	17.2	0.0	-	-	-	-	26.9	-1.1	-	-	-	-	-	-	-	-
1925	17.6	2.3	-	-	-	-	26.4	-1.9	-	-	-	-	-	-	-	-
1926	17.8	1.1	-	-	-	-	26.0	-1.5	-	-	-	-	-	-	-	-
1927	17.5	-1.7	-	-	-	-	25.5	-1.9	-	-	-	-	-	-	-	-
1928	17.2	-1.7	-	-	-	-	25.1	-1.6	-	-	-	-	-	-	-	-
1929	17.2	0.0	-	-	-	-	24.8	-1.2	-	-	-	-	-	-	-	-
1930	16.8	-2.3	-	-	-	-	24.3	-2.0	-	-	-	-	-	-	-	-
1931	15.3	-8.9	-	-	-	-	22.1	-9.1	-	-	-	-	-	-	-	-
1932	13.7	-10.5	-	-	-	-	19.6	-11.3	-	-	-	-	-	-	-	-
1933	13.0	-5.1	-	-	-	-	18.9	-3.6	-	-	-	-	-	-	-	-
1934	13.5	3.8	-	-	-	-	20.7	9.5	-	-	-	-	-	-	-	-
1935	13.8	2.2	-	-	-	-	20.9	1.0	14.1	-	10.2	-	-	-	-	-
1936	13.9	0.7	-	-	-	-	21.1	1.0	14.2	0.7	10.3	1.0	-	-	-	-
1937	14.4	3.6	-	-	-	-	22.1	4.7	14.5	2.1	10.4	1.0	-	-	-	-
1938	14.2	-1.4	-	-	-	-	22.0	-0.5	14.6	0.7	10.4	0.0	-	-	-	-
1939	14.0	-1.4	-	-	-	-	21.7	-1.4	14.2	-2.7	10.4	0.0	-	-	-	-
1940	14.1	0.7	-	-	-	-	21.9	0.9	14.1	-0.7	10.4	0.0	-	-	-	-
1941	14.8	5.0	-	-	-	-	23.0	5.0	14.6	3.5	10.5	1.0	-	-	-	-
1942	16.4	10.8	-	-	-	-	26.8	16.5	15.9	8.9	10.8	2.9	-	-	-	-
1943	17.4	6.1	-	-	-	-	28.0	4.5	15.8	-0.6	11.3	4.6	-	-	-	-
1944	17.7	1.7	-	-	-	-	30.0	7.1	15.8	0.0	11.6	2.7	-	-	-	-
1945	18.1	2.3	-	-	-	-	31.5	5.0	15.8	0.0	11.9	2.6	-	-	-	-
1946	19.6	8.3	-	-	-	-	34.6	9.8	16.6	5.1	12.6	5.9	-	-	-	-
1947	22.5	14.8	-	-	-	-	40.1	15.9	18.4	10.8	13.6	7.9	-	-	-	-
1948	24.2	7.6	-	-	-	-	42.7	6.5	20.4	10.9	14.5	6.6	-	-	-	-
1949	24.0	-0.8	-	-	-	-	41.0	-4.0	22.0	7.8	14.9	2.8	-	-	-	-
1950	24.2	0.8	-	-	-	-	40.5	-1.2	22.6	2.7	15.2	2.0	-	-	-	-
1951	26.1	7.9	-	-	-	-	44.1	8.9	24.0	6.2	15.9	4.6	-	-	-	-
1952	26.7	2.3	-	-	-	-	43.7	-0.9	25.6	6.7	16.8	5.7	-	-	-	-
1953	26.9	0.7	-	-	-	-	43.3	-0.9	26.3	2.7	17.4	3.6	-	-	-	-
1954	27.0	0.4	-	-	-	-	43.3	0.0	25.9	-1.5	17.9	2.9	-	-	-	-
1955	26.9	-0.4	-	-	-	-	43.1	-0.5	25.6	-1.2	18.3	2.2	-	-	-	-
1956	27.3	1.5	-	-	-	-	44.0	2.1	26.1	2.0	19.0	3.8	-	-	-	-
1957	28.3	3.7	-	-	-	-	44.7	1.6	27.6	5.7	19.8	4.2	-	-	-	-

[Continued]

U.S. City Average
Consumer Price Index - Urban Wage Earners
Base 1982-1984 = 100
Annual Averages
[Continued]

For 1913-1995. Columns headed % show percentile change in the index from the previous period for which an index is available.

Year	All Items		Food & Beverage		Housing		Apparel & Upkeep		Trans-portation		Medical Care		Entertain-ment		Other Goods & Services	
	Index	%	Index	%	Index	%	Index	%	Index	%	Index	%	Index	%	Index	%
1958	29.1	2.8	-	-	-	-	44.8	0.2	28.4	2.9	20.7	4.5	-	-	-	-
1959	29.3	0.7	-	-	-	-	45.2	0.9	29.6	4.2	21.6	4.3	-	-	-	-
1960	29.8	1.7	-	-	-	-	45.9	1.5	29.6	0.0	22.4	3.7	-	-	-	-
1961	30.1	1.0	-	-	-	-	46.3	0.9	30.0	1.4	23.0	2.7	-	-	-	-
1962	30.4	1.0	-	-	-	-	46.6	0.6	30.6	2.0	23.6	2.6	-	-	-	-
1963	30.8	1.3	-	-	-	-	47.1	1.1	30.8	0.7	24.2	2.5	-	-	-	-
1964	31.2	1.3		-	-	-	47.5	0.8	31.2	1.3	24.7	2.1	-	-	-	-
1965	31.7	1.6	-	-	-	-	48.0	1.1	31.7	1.6	25.3	2.4	-	-	-	-
1966	32.6	2.8	-	-	-	-	49.2	2.5	32.2	1.6	26.4	4.3	-	-	-	-
1967	33.6	3.1	35.0	-	31.1	-	51.2	4.1	33.1	2.8	28.3	7.2	41.3	-	35.4	-
1968	35.0	4.2	36.2	3.4	32.3	3.9	54.0	5.5	34.1	3.0	30.0	6.0	43.7	5.8	37.2	5.1
1969	36.9	5.4	38.0	5.0	34.3	6.2	57.1	5.7	35.5	4.1	32.1	7.0	45.9	5.0	39.1	5.1
1970	39.0	5.7	40.1	5.5	36.7	7.0	59.5	4.2	37.3	5.1	34.1	6.2	48.2	5.0	41.3	5.6
1971	40.7	4.4	41.3	3.0	38.3	4.4	61.4	3.2	39.2	5.1	36.3	6.5	50.8	5.4	43.3	4.8
1972	42.1	3.4	43.1	4.4	39.8	3.9	62.7	2.1	39.7	1.3	37.5	3.3	52.3	3.0	45.1	4.2
1973	44.7	6.2	48.8	13.2	41.5	4.3	65.0	3.7	41.0	3.3	39.0	4.0	53.7	2.7	46.9	4.0
1974	49.6	11.0	55.5	13.7	46.2	11.3	69.8	7.4	45.5	11.0	42.6	9.2	57.8	7.6	50.2	7.0
1975	54.1	9.1	60.2	8.5	51.1	10.6	72.9	4.4	49.8	9.5	47.7	12.0	62.9	8.8	54.4	8.4
1976	57.2	5.7	62.0	3.0	54.2	6.1	75.6	3.7	54.7	9.8	52.3	9.6	66.0	4.9	57.6	5.9
1977	60.9	6.5	65.7	6.0	57.9	6.8	79.0	4.5	58.6	7.1	57.3	9.6	69.3	5.0	60.9	5.7
1978	65.6	7.7	72.1	9.7	62.9	8.6	81.7	3.4	61.5	4.9	62.1	8.4	72.8	5.1	64.8	6.4
1979	73.1	11.4	79.9	10.8	70.7	12.4	85.2	4.3	70.4	14.5	68.0	9.5	77.6	6.6	69.4	7.1
1980	82.9	13.4	86.9	8.8	81.7	15.6	90.9	6.7	82.9	17.8	75.6	11.2	84.2	8.5	75.6	8.9
1981	91.4	10.3	93.6	7.7	91.1	11.5	95.6	5.2	93.0	12.2	83.5	10.4	90.5	7.5	82.5	9.1
1982	96.9	6.0	97.3	4.0	97.7	7.2	97.8	2.3	97.0	4.3	92.5	10.8	96.0	6.1	90.9	10.2
1983	99.8	3.0	99.5	2.3	100.0	2.4	100.2	2.5	99.2	2.3	100.5	8.6	100.2	4.4	101.3	11.4
1984	103.3	3.5	103.2	3.7	102.2	2.2	102.0	1.8	103.8	4.6	106.9	6.4	103.8	3.6	107.9	6.5
1985	106.9	3.5	105.5	2.2	106.6	4.3	105.0	2.9	106.4	2.5	113.6	6.3	107.5	3.6	114.2	5.8
1986	108.6	1.6	108.9	3.2	109.7	2.9	105.8	0.8	101.7	-4.4	122.0	7.4	111.0	3.3	120.9	5.9
1987	112.5	3.6	113.3	4.0	112.8	2.8	110.4	4.3	105.1	3.3	130.2	6.7	114.8	3.4	127.8	5.7
1988	117.0	4.0	117.9	4.1	116.8	3.5	114.9	4.1	108.3	3.0	139.0	6.8	119.7	4.3	136.5	6.8
1989	122.6	4.8	124.6	5.7	121.2	3.8	117.9	2.6	113.9	5.2	149.6	7.6	125.8	5.1	147.4	8.0
1990	129.0	5.2	131.8	5.8	126.4	4.3	123.1	4.4	120.1	5.4	162.7	8.8	131.4	4.5	158.9	7.8
1991	134.3	4.1	136.5	3.6	131.2	3.8	127.4	3.5	123.1	2.5	176.5	8.5	136.9	4.2	171.7	8.1
1992	138.2	2.9	138.3	1.3	135.0	2.9	130.7	2.6	125.8	2.2	189.6	7.4	140.8	2.8	183.3	6.8
1993	142.1	2.8	141.2	2.1	138.5	2.6	132.4	1.3	129.4	2.9	200.9	6.0	144.1	2.3	192.2	4.9
1994	145.6	2.5	144.4	2.3	142.0	2.5	132.2	-0.2	133.4	3.1	210.4	4.7	148.2	2.8	196.4	2.2
1995	149.8	2.9	148.3	2.7	145.4	2.4	130.9	-1.0	138.8	4.0	219.8	4.5	151.8	2.4	204.2	4.0

Source: U.S. Department of Labor, Bureau of Labor Statistics, Division of Consumer Prices and Price Indexes.

U.S. CITY AVERAGE
Consumer Price Index - All Urban Consumers
Base 1982-1984 = 100
All Items

For 1913-1995. Columns headed % show percentile change in the index from the previous period for which an index is available.

Year	Jan Index	%	Feb Index	%	Mar Index	%	Apr Index	%	May Index	%	Jun Index	%	Jul Index	%	Aug Index	%	Sep Index	%	Oct Index	%	Nov Index	%	Dec Index	%
1913	9.8	-	9.8	0.0	9.8	0.0	9.8	0.0	9.7	-1.0	9.8	1.0	9.9	1.0	9.9	0.0	10.0	1.0	10.0	0.0	10.1	1.0	10.0	-1.0
1914	10.0	0.0	9.9	-1.0	9.9	0.0	9.8	-1.0	9.9	1.0	9.9	0.0	10.0	1.0	10.2	2.0	10.2	0.0	10.1	-1.0	10.2	1.0	10.1	-1.0
1915	10.1	0.0	10.0	-1.0	9.9	-1.0	10.0	1.0	10.1	1.0	10.1	0.0	10.1	0.0	10.1	0.0	10.1	0.0	10.2	1.0	10.3	1.0	10.3	0.0
1916	10.4	1.0	10.4	0.0	10.5	1.0	10.6	1.0	10.7	0.9	10.8	0.9	10.8	0.0	10.9	0.9	11.1	1.8	11.3	1.8	11.5	1.8	11.6	0.9
1917	11.7	0.9	12.0	2.6	12.0	0.0	12.6	5.0	12.8	1.6	13.0	1.6	12.8	-1.5	13.0	1.6	13.3	2.3	13.5	1.5	13.5	0.0	13.7	1.5
1918	14.0	2.2	14.1	0.7	14.0	-0.7	14.2	1.4	14.5	2.1	14.7	1.4	15.1	2.7	15.4	2.0	15.7	1.9	16.0	1.9	16.3	1.9	16.5	1.2
1919	16.5	0.0	16.2	-1.8	16.4	1.2	16.7	1.8	16.9	1.2	16.9	0.0	17.4	3.0	17.7	1.7	17.8	0.6	18.1	1.7	18.5	2.2	18.9	2.2
1920	19.3	2.1	19.5	1.0	19.7	1.0	20.3	3.0	20.6	1.5	20.9	1.5	20.8	-0.5	20.3	-2.4	20.0	-1.5	19.9	-0.5	19.8	-0.5	19.4	-2.0
1921	19.0	-2.1	18.4	-3.2	18.3	-0.5	18.1	-1.1	17.7	-2.2	17.6	-0.6	17.7	0.6	17.7	0.0	17.5	-1.1	17.5	0.0	17.4	-0.6	17.3	-0.6
1922	16.9	-2.3	16.9	0.0	16.7	-1.2	16.7	0.0	16.7	0.0	16.7	0.0	16.8	0.6	16.6	-1.2	16.6	0.0	16.7	0.6	16.8	0.6	16.9	0.6
1923	16.8	-0.6	16.8	0.0	16.8	0.0	16.9	0.6	16.9	0.0	17.0	0.6	17.2	1.2	17.1	-0.6	17.2	0.6	17.3	0.6	17.3	0.0	17.3	0.0
1924	17.3	0.0	17.2	-0.6	17.1	-0.6	17.0	-0.6	17.0	0.0	17.0	0.0	17.1	0.6	17.0	-0.6	17.1	0.6	17.2	0.6	17.2	0.0	17.3	0.6
1925	17.3	0.0	17.2	-0.6	17.3	0.6	17.2	-0.6	17.3	0.6	17.5	1.2	17.7	1.1	17.7	0.0	17.7	0.0	17.7	0.0	18.0	1.7	17.9	-0.6
1926	17.9	0.0	17.9	0.0	17.8	-0.6	17.9	0.6	17.8	-0.6	17.7	-0.6	17.5	-1.1	17.4	-0.6	17.5	0.6	17.6	0.6	17.7	0.6	17.7	0.0
1927	17.5	-1.1	17.4	-0.6	17.3	-0.6	17.3	0.0	17.4	0.6	17.6	1.1	17.3	-1.7	17.2	-0.6	17.3	0.6	17.4	0.6	17.3	-0.6	17.3	0.0
1928	17.3	0.0	17.1	-1.2	17.1	0.0	17.1	0.0	17.2	0.6	17.1	-0.6	17.1	0.0	17.1	0.0	17.3	1.2	17.2	-0.6	17.2	0.0	17.1	-0.6
1929	17.1	0.0	17.1	0.0	17.0	-0.6	16.9	-0.6	17.0	0.6	17.1	0.6	17.3	1.2	17.3	0.0	17.3	0.0	17.3	0.0	17.3	0.0	17.2	-0.6
1930	17.1	-0.6	17.0	-0.6	16.9	-0.6	17.0	0.6	16.9	-0.6	16.8	-0.6	16.6	-1.2	16.5	-0.6	16.6	0.6	16.5	-0.6	16.4	-0.6	16.1	-1.8
1931	15.9	-1.2	15.7	-1.3	15.6	-0.6	15.5	-0.6	15.3	-1.3	15.1	-1.3	15.1	0.0	15.1	0.0	15.0	-0.7	14.9	-0.7	14.7	-1.3	14.6	-0.7
1932	14.3	-2.1	14.1	-1.4	14.0	-0.7	13.9	-0.7	13.7	-1.4	13.6	-0.7	13.6	0.0	13.5	-0.7	13.4	-0.7	13.3	-0.7	13.2	-0.8	13.1	-0.8
1933	12.9	-1.5	12.7	-1.6	12.6	-0.8	12.6	0.0	12.6	0.0	12.7	0.8	13.1	3.1	13.2	0.8	13.2	0.0	13.2	0.0	13.2	0.0	13.2	0.0
1934	13.2	0.0	13.3	0.8	13.3	0.0	13.3	0.0	13.3	0.0	13.4	0.8	13.4	0.0	13.4	0.0	13.6	1.5	13.5	-0.7	13.5	0.0	13.4	-0.7
1935	13.6	1.5	13.7	0.7	13.7	0.0	13.8	0.7	13.8	0.0	13.7	-0.7	13.7	0.0	13.7	0.0	13.7	0.0	13.7	0.0	13.8	0.7	13.8	0.0
1936	13.8	0.0	13.8	0.0	13.7	-0.7	13.7	0.0	13.7	0.0	13.8	0.7	13.9	0.7	14.0	0.7	14.0	0.0	14.0	0.0	14.0	0.0	14.0	0.0
1937	14.1	0.7	14.1	0.0	14.2	0.7	14.3	0.7	14.4	0.7	14.4	0.0	14.5	0.7	14.5	0.0	14.6	0.7	14.6	0.0	14.5	-0.7	14.4	-0.7
1938	14.2	-1.4	14.1	-0.7	14.1	0.0	14.2	0.7	14.1	-0.7	14.1	0.0	14.1	0.0	14.1	0.0	14.1	0.0	14.0	-0.7	14.0	0.0	14.0	0.0
1939	14.0	0.0	13.9	-0.7	13.9	0.0	13.8	-0.7	13.8	0.0	13.8	0.0	13.8	0.0	13.8	0.0	14.1	2.2	14.0	-0.7	14.0	0.0	14.0	0.0
1940	13.9	-0.7	14.0	0.7	14.0	0.0	14.0	0.0	14.0	0.0	14.1	0.7	14.0	-0.7	14.0	0.0	14.0	0.0	14.0	0.0	14.0	0.0	14.1	0.7
1941	14.1	0.0	14.1	0.0	14.2	0.7	14.3	0.7	14.4	0.7	14.7	2.1	14.7	0.0	14.9	1.4	15.1	1.3	15.3	1.3	15.4	0.7	15.5	0.6
1942	15.7	1.3	15.8	0.6	16.0	1.3	16.1	0.6	16.3	1.2	16.3	0.0	16.4	0.6	16.5	0.6	16.5	0.0	16.7	1.2	16.8	0.6	16.9	0.6
1943	16.9	0.0	16.9	0.0	17.2	1.8	17.4	1.2	17.5	0.6	17.5	0.0	17.4	-0.6	17.3	-0.6	17.4	0.6	17.4	0.0	17.4	0.0	17.4	0.0
1944	17.4	0.0	17.4	0.0	17.4	0.0	17.5	0.6	17.5	0.0	17.6	0.6	17.7	0.6	17.7	0.0	17.7	0.0	17.7	0.0	17.7	0.0	17.8	0.6
1945	17.8	0.0	17.8	0.0	17.8	0.0	17.8	0.0	17.9	0.6	18.1	1.1	18.1	0.0	18.1	0.0	18.1	0.0	18.1	0.0	18.1	0.0	18.2	0.6
1946	18.2	0.0	18.1	-0.5	18.3	1.1	18.4	0.5	18.5	0.5	18.7	1.1	19.8	5.9	20.2	2.0	20.4	1.0	20.8	2.0	21.3	2.4	21.5	0.9
1947	21.5	0.0	21.5	0.0	21.9	1.9	21.9	0.0	21.9	0.0	22.0	0.5	22.2	0.9	22.5	1.4	23.0	2.2	23.0	0.0	23.1	0.4	23.4	1.3
1948	23.7	1.3	23.5	-0.8	23.4	-0.4	23.8	1.7	23.9	0.4	24.1	0.8	24.4	1.2	24.5	0.4	24.5	0.0	24.4	-0.4	24.2	-0.8	24.1	-0.4
1949	24.0	-0.4	23.8	-0.8	23.8	0.0	23.9	0.4	23.8	-0.4	23.9	0.4	23.7	-0.8	23.8	0.4	23.9	0.4	23.7	-0.8	23.8	0.4	23.6	-0.8
1950	23.5	-0.4	23.5	0.0	23.6	0.4	23.6	0.0	23.7	0.4	23.8	0.4	24.1	1.3	24.3	0.8	24.4	0.4	24.6	0.8	24.7	0.4	25.0	1.2
1951	25.4	1.6	25.7	1.2	25.8	0.4	25.8	0.0	25.9	0.4	25.9	0.0	25.9	0.0	25.9	0.0	26.1	0.8	26.2	0.4	26.4	0.8	26.5	0.4
1952	26.5	0.0	26.3	-0.8	26.3	0.0	26.4	0.4	26.4	0.0	26.5	0.4	26.7	0.8	26.7	0.0	26.7	0.0	26.7	0.0	26.7	0.0	26.7	0.0
1953	26.6	-0.4	26.5	-0.4	26.6	0.4	26.6	0.0	26.7	0.4	26.8	0.4	26.8	0.0	26.9	0.4	26.9	0.0	27.0	0.4	26.9	-0.4	26.9	0.0
1954	26.9	0.0	26.9	0.0	26.9	0.0	26.8	-0.4	26.9	0.4	26.9	0.0	26.9	0.0	26.9	0.0	26.8	-0.4	26.8	0.0	26.8	0.0	26.7	-0.4
1955	26.7	0.0	26.7	0.0	26.7	0.0	26.7	0.0	26.7	0.0	26.7	0.0	26.8	0.4	26.8	0.0	26.9	0.4	26.9	0.0	26.9	0.0	26.8	-0.4
1956	26.8	0.0	26.8	0.0	26.8	0.0	26.9	0.4	27.0	0.4	27.2	0.7	27.4	0.7	27.3	-0.4	27.4	0.4	27.5	0.4	27.5	0.0	27.6	0.4
1957	27.6	0.0	27.7	0.4	27.8	0.4	27.9	0.4	28.0	0.4	28.1	0.4	28.3	0.7	28.3	0.0	28.3	0.0	28.3	0.0	28.4	0.4	28.4	0.0

[Continued]

U.S. City Average
Consumer Price Index - All Urban Consumers
Base 1982-1984 = 100
All Items
[Continued]

For 1913-1995. Columns headed % show percentile change in the index from the previous period for which an index is available.

Year	Jan Index	%	Feb Index	%	Mar Index	%	Apr Index	%	May Index	%	Jun Index	%	Jul Index	%	Aug Index	%	Sep Index	%	Oct Index	%	Nov Index	%	Dec Index	%
1958	28.6	0.7	28.6	0.0	28.8	0.7	28.9	0.3	28.9	0.0	28.9	0.0	29.0	0.3	28.9	-0.3	28.9	0.0	28.9	0.0	29.0	0.3	28.9	-0.3
1959	29.0	0.3	28.9	-0.3	28.9	0.0	29.0	0.3	29.0	0.0	29.1	0.3	29.2	0.3	29.2	0.0	29.3	0.3	29.4	0.3	29.4	0.0	29.4	0.0
1960	29.3	-0.3	29.4	0.3	29.4	0.0	29.5	0.3	29.5	0.0	29.6	0.3	29.6	0.0	29.6	0.0	29.6	0.0	29.8	0.7	29.8	0.0	29.8	0.0
1961	29.8	0.0	29.8	0.0	29.8	0.0	29.8	0.0	29.8	0.0	29.8	0.0	30.0	0.7	29.9	-0.3	30.0	0.3	30.0	0.0	30.0	0.0	30.0	0.0
1962	30.0	0.0	30.1	0.3	30.1	0.0	30.2	0.3	30.2	0.0	30.2	0.0	30.3	0.3	30.3	0.0	30.4	0.3	30.4	0.0	30.4	0.0	30.4	0.0
1963	30.4	0.0	30.4	0.0	30.5	0.3	30.5	0.0	30.5	0.0	30.6	0.3	30.7	0.3	30.7	0.0	30.7	0.0	30.8	0.3	30.8	0.0	30.9	0.3
1964	30.9	0.0	30.9	0.0	30.9	0.0	30.9	0.0	30.9	0.0	31.0	0.3	31.1	0.3	31.0	-0.3	31.1	0.3	31.1	0.0	31.2	0.3	31.2	0.0
1965	31.2	0.0	31.2	0.0	31.3	0.3	31.4	0.3	31.4	0.0	31.6	0.6	31.6	0.0	31.6	0.0	31.6	0.0	31.7	0.3	31.7	0.0	31.8	0.3
1966	31.8	0.0	32.0	0.6	32.1	0.3	32.3	0.6	32.3	0.0	32.4	0.3	32.5	0.3	32.7	0.6	32.7	0.0	32.9	0.6	32.9	0.0	32.9	0.0
1967	32.9	0.0	32.9	0.0	33.0	0.3	33.1	0.3	33.2	0.3	33.3	0.3	33.4	0.3	33.5	0.3	33.6	0.3	33.7	0.3	33.8	0.3	33.9	0.3
1968	34.1	0.6	34.2	0.3	34.3	0.3	34.4	0.3	34.5	0.3	34.7	0.6	34.9	0.6	35.0	0.3	35.1	0.3	35.3	0.6	35.4	0.3	35.5	0.3
1969	35.6	0.3	35.8	0.6	36.1	0.8	36.3	0.6	36.4	0.3	36.6	0.5	36.8	0.5	37.0	0.5	37.1	0.3	37.3	0.5	37.5	0.5	37.7	0.5
1970	37.8	0.3	38.0	0.5	38.2	0.5	38.5	0.8	38.6	0.3	38.8	0.5	39.0	0.5	39.0	0.0	39.2	0.5	39.4	0.5	39.6	0.5	39.8	0.5
1971	39.8	0.0	39.9	0.3	40.0	0.3	40.1	0.2	40.3	0.5	40.6	0.7	40.7	0.2	40.8	0.2	40.8	0.0	40.9	0.2	40.9	0.0	41.1	0.5
1972	41.1	0.0	41.3	0.5	41.4	0.2	41.5	0.2	41.6	0.2	41.7	0.2	41.9	0.5	42.0	0.2	42.1	0.2	42.3	0.5	42.4	0.2	42.5	0.2
1973	42.6	0.2	42.9	0.7	43.3	0.9	43.6	0.7	43.9	0.7	44.2	0.7	44.3	0.2	45.1	1.8	45.2	0.2	45.6	0.9	45.9	0.7	46.2	0.7
1974	46.6	0.9	47.2	1.3	47.8	1.3	48.0	0.4	48.6	1.2	49.0	0.8	49.4	0.8	50.0	1.2	50.6	1.2	51.1	1.0	51.5	0.8	51.9	0.8
1975	52.1	0.4	52.5	0.8	52.7	0.4	52.9	0.4	53.2	0.6	53.6	0.8	54.2	1.1	54.3	0.2	54.6	0.6	54.9	0.5	55.3	0.7	55.5	0.4
1976	55.6	0.2	55.8	0.4	55.9	0.2	56.1	0.4	56.5	0.7	56.8	0.5	57.1	0.5	57.4	0.5	57.6	0.3	57.9	0.5	58.0	0.2	58.2	0.3
1977	58.5	0.5	59.1	1.0	59.5	0.7	60.0	0.8	60.3	0.5	60.7	0.7	61.0	0.5	61.2	0.3	61.4	0.3	61.6	0.3	61.9	0.5	62.1	0.3
1978	62.5	0.6	62.9	0.6	63.4	0.8	63.9	0.8	64.5	0.9	65.2	1.1	65.7	0.8	66.0	0.5	66.5	0.8	67.1	0.9	67.4	0.4	67.7	0.4
1979	68.3	0.9	69.1	1.2	69.8	1.0	70.6	1.1	71.5	1.3	72.3	1.1	73.1	1.1	73.8	1.0	74.6	1.1	75.2	0.8	75.9	0.9	76.7	1.1
1980	77.8	1.4	78.9	1.4	80.1	1.5	81.0	1.1	81.8	1.0	82.7	1.1	82.7	0.0	83.3	0.7	84.0	0.8	84.8	1.0	85.5	0.8	86.3	0.9
1981	87.0	0.8	87.9	1.0	88.5	0.7	89.1	0.7	89.8	0.8	90.6	0.9	91.6	1.1	92.3	0.8	93.2	1.0	93.4	0.2	93.7	0.3	94.0	0.3
1982	94.3	0.3	94.6	0.3	94.5	-0.1	94.9	0.4	95.8	0.9	97.0	1.3	97.5	0.5	97.7	0.2	97.9	0.2	98.2	0.3	98.0	-0.2	97.6	-0.4
1983	97.8	0.2	97.9	0.1	97.9	0.0	98.6	0.7	99.2	0.6	99.5	0.3	99.9	0.4	100.2	0.3	100.7	0.5	101.0	0.3	101.2	0.2	101.3	0.1
1984	101.9	0.6	102.4	0.5	102.6	0.2	103.1	0.5	103.4	0.3	103.7	0.3	104.1	0.4	104.5	0.4	105.0	0.5	105.3	0.3	105.3	0.0	105.3	0.0
1985	105.5	0.2	106.0	0.5	106.4	0.4	106.9	0.5	107.3	0.4	107.6	0.3	107.8	0.2	108.0	0.2	108.3	0.3	108.7	0.4	109.0	0.3	109.3	0.3
1986	109.6	0.3	109.3	-0.3	108.8	-0.5	108.6	-0.2	108.9	0.3	109.5	0.6	109.5	0.0	109.7	0.2	110.2	0.5	110.3	0.1	110.4	0.1	110.5	0.1
1987	111.2	0.6	111.6	0.4	112.1	0.4	112.7	0.5	113.1	0.4	113.5	0.4	113.8	0.3	114.4	0.5	115.0	0.5	115.3	0.3	115.4	0.1	115.4	0.0
1988	115.7	0.3	116.0	0.3	116.5	0.4	117.1	0.5	117.5	0.3	118.0	0.4	118.5	0.4	119.0	0.4	119.8	0.7	120.2	0.3	120.3	0.1	120.5	0.2
1989	121.1	0.5	121.6	0.4	122.3	0.6	123.1	0.7	123.8	0.6	124.1	0.2	124.4	0.2	124.6	0.2	125.0	0.3	125.6	0.5	125.9	0.2	126.1	0.2
1990	127.4	1.0	128.0	0.5	128.7	0.5	128.9	0.2	129.2	0.2	129.9	0.5	130.4	0.4	131.6	0.9	132.7	0.8	133.5	0.6	133.8	0.2	133.8	0.0
1991	134.6	0.6	134.8	0.1	135.0	0.1	135.2	0.1	135.6	0.3	136.0	0.3	136.2	0.1	136.6	0.3	137.2	0.4	137.4	0.1	137.8	0.3	137.9	0.1
1992	138.1	0.1	138.6	0.4	139.3	0.5	139.5	0.1	139.7	0.1	140.2	0.4	140.5	0.2	140.9	0.3	141.3	0.3	141.8	0.4	142.0	0.1	141.9	-0.1
1993	142.6	0.5	143.1	0.4	143.6	0.3	144.0	0.3	144.2	0.1	144.4	0.1	144.4	0.0	144.8	0.3	145.1	0.2	145.7	0.4	145.8	0.1	145.8	0.0
1994	146.2	0.3	146.7	0.3	147.2	0.3	147.4	0.1	147.5	0.1	148.0	0.3	148.4	0.3	149.0	0.4	149.4	0.3	149.5	0.1	149.7	0.1	149.7	0.0
1995	150.3	0.4	150.9	0.4	151.4	0.3	151.9	0.3	152.2	0.2	152.5	0.2	152.5	0.0	152.9	0.3	153.2	0.2	153.7	0.3	153.6	-0.1	153.5	-0.1

Source: U.S. Department of Labor, Bureau of Labor Statistics, Division of Consumer Prices and Price Indexes.

U.S. CITY AVERAGE
Consumer Price Index - Urban Wage Earners
Base 1982-1984 = 100
All Items

For 1913-1995. Columns headed % show percentile change in the index from the previous period for which an index is available.

Year	Jan Index	%	Feb Index	%	Mar Index	%	Apr Index	%	May Index	%	Jun Index	%	Jul Index	%	Aug Index	%	Sep Index	%	Oct Index	%	Nov Index	%	Dec Index	%
1913	9.9	-	9.8	-1.0	9.8	0.0	9.9	1.0	9.8	-1.0	9.8	0.0	9.9	1.0	10.0	1.0	10.0	0.0	10.1	1.0	10.1	0.0	10.1	0.0
1914	10.1	0.0	10.0	-1.0	10.0	0.0	9.9	-1.0	9.9	0.0	10.0	1.0	10.1	1.0	10.2	1.0	10.3	1.0	10.2	-1.0	10.2	0.0	10.2	0.0
1915	10.2	0.0	10.1	-1.0	10.0	-1.0	10.1	1.0	10.1	0.0	10.2	1.0	10.2	0.0	10.2	0.0	10.2	0.0	10.3	1.0	10.4	1.0	10.4	0.0
1916	10.5	1.0	10.5	0.0	10.6	1.0	10.7	0.9	10.7	0.0	10.9	1.9	10.9	0.0	11.0	0.9	11.2	1.8	11.3	0.9	11.5	1.8	11.6	0.9
1917	11.8	1.7	12.0	1.7	12.1	0.8	12.6	4.1	12.9	2.4	13.0	0.8	12.9	-0.8	13.1	1.6	13.3	1.5	13.6	2.3	13.6	0.0	13.8	1.5
1918	14.0	1.4	14.2	1.4	14.1	-0.7	14.3	1.4	14.5	1.4	14.8	2.1	15.2	2.7	15.4	1.3	15.8	2.6	16.1	1.9	16.3	1.2	16.6	1.8
1919	16.6	0.0	16.2	-2.4	16.5	1.9	16.8	1.8	17.0	1.2	17.0	0.0	17.5	2.9	17.8	1.7	17.9	0.6	18.2	1.7	18.6	2.2	19.0	2.2
1920	19.4	2.1	19.6	1.0	19.8	1.0	20.4	3.0	20.7	1.5	21.0	1.4	20.9	-0.5	20.4	-2.4	20.1	-1.5	20.0	-0.5	19.9	-0.5	19.5	-2.0
1921	19.1	-2.1	18.5	-3.1	18.4	-0.5	18.2	-1.1	17.8	-2.2	17.7	-0.6	17.8	0.6	17.8	0.0	17.6	-1.1	17.6	0.0	17.5	-0.6	17.4	-0.6
1922	17.0	-2.3	17.0	0.0	16.8	-1.2	16.8	0.0	16.8	0.0	16.8	0.0	16.9	0.6	16.7	-1.2	16.7	0.0	16.8	0.6	16.9	0.6	17.0	0.6
1923	16.9	-0.6	16.9	0.0	16.9	0.0	17.0	0.6	17.0	0.0	17.1	0.6	17.3	1.2	17.2	-0.6	17.3	0.6	17.4	0.6	17.4	0.0	17.4	0.0
1924	17.4	0.0	17.3	-0.6	17.2	-0.6	17.1	-0.6	17.1	0.0	17.1	0.0	17.2	0.6	17.1	-0.6	17.2	0.6	17.3	0.6	17.3	0.0	17.4	0.6
1925	17.4	0.0	17.3	-0.6	17.4	0.6	17.3	-0.6	17.4	0.6	17.6	1.1	17.8	1.1	17.8	0.0	17.8	0.0	17.8	0.0	18.1	1.7	18.0	-0.6
1926	18.0	0.0	18.0	0.0	17.9	-0.6	18.0	0.6	17.9	-0.6	17.8	-0.6	17.6	-1.1	17.5	-0.6	17.6	0.6	17.7	0.6	17.8	0.6	17.8	0.0
1927	17.6	-1.1	17.5	-0.6	17.4	-0.6	17.4	0.0	17.5	0.6	17.7	1.1	17.4	-1.7	17.3	-0.6	17.4	0.6	17.5	0.6	17.4	-0.6	17.4	0.0
1928	17.4	0.0	17.2	-1.1	17.2	0.0	17.2	0.0	17.3	0.6	17.2	-0.6	17.2	0.0	17.2	0.0	17.4	1.2	17.3	-0.6	17.3	0.0	17.2	-0.6
1929	17.2	0.0	17.2	0.0	17.1	-0.6	17.0	-0.6	17.1	0.6	17.2	0.6	17.4	1.2	17.4	0.0	17.4	0.0	17.4	0.0	17.4	0.0	17.3	-0.6
1930	17.2	-0.6	17.1	-0.6	17.0	-0.6	17.1	0.6	17.0	-0.6	16.9	-0.6	16.7	-1.2	16.6	-0.6	16.7	0.6	16.6	-0.6	16.5	-0.6	16.2	-1.8
1931	16.0	-1.2	15.7	-1.9	15.6	-0.6	15.5	-0.6	15.4	-0.6	15.2	-1.3	15.2	0.0	15.1	-0.7	15.1	0.0	15.0	-0.7	14.8	-1.3	14.7	-0.7
1932	14.4	-2.0	14.2	-1.4	14.1	-0.7	14.0	-0.7	13.8	-1.4	13.7	-0.7	13.7	0.0	13.5	-1.5	13.5	0.0	13.4	-0.7	13.3	-0.7	13.2	-0.8
1933	13.0	-1.5	12.8	-1.5	12.7	-0.8	12.6	-0.8	12.7	0.8	12.8	0.8	13.2	3.1	13.3	0.8	13.3	0.0	13.3	0.0	13.3	0.0	13.2	-0.8
1934	13.3	0.8	13.4	0.8	13.4	0.0	13.4	0.0	13.4	0.0	13.4	0.0	13.4	0.0	13.5	0.7	13.7	1.5	13.6	-0.7	13.5	-0.7	13.5	0.0
1935	13.7	1.5	13.8	0.7	13.8	0.0	13.9	0.7	13.8	-0.7	13.8	0.0	13.7	-0.7	13.7	0.0	13.8	0.7	13.8	0.0	13.9	0.7	13.9	0.0
1936	13.9	0.0	13.8	-0.7	13.8	0.0	13.8	0.0	13.8	0.0	13.9	0.7	14.0	0.7	14.1	0.7	14.1	0.0	14.1	0.0	14.1	0.0	14.1	0.0
1937	14.2	0.7	14.2	0.0	14.3	0.7	14.4	0.7	14.4	0.0	14.5	0.7	14.5	0.0	14.6	0.7	14.7	0.7	14.6	-0.7	14.5	-0.7	14.5	0.0
1938	14.3	-1.4	14.2	-0.7	14.2	0.0	14.2	0.0	14.2	0.0	14.2	0.0	14.2	0.0	14.2	0.0	14.2	0.0	14.1	-0.7	14.1	0.0	14.1	0.0
1939	14.0	-0.7	14.0	0.0	13.9	-0.7	13.9	0.0	13.9	0.0	13.9	0.0	13.9	0.0	13.9	0.0	14.2	2.2	14.1	-0.7	14.1	0.0	14.0	-0.7
1940	14.0	0.0	14.1	0.7	14.1	0.0	14.1	0.0	14.1	0.0	14.1	0.0	14.1	0.0	14.1	0.0	14.1	0.0	14.1	0.0	14.1	0.0	14.2	0.7
1941	14.2	0.0	14.2	0.0	14.2	0.0	14.4	1.4	14.5	0.7	14.7	1.4	14.8	0.7	14.9	0.7	15.2	2.0	15.4	1.3	15.5	0.6	15.5	0.0
1942	15.7	1.3	15.9	1.3	16.1	1.3	16.2	0.6	16.3	0.6	16.4	0.6	16.5	0.6	16.6	0.6	16.6	0.0	16.8	1.2	16.9	0.6	17.0	0.6
1943	17.0	0.0	17.0	0.0	17.3	1.8	17.5	1.2	17.6	0.6	17.6	0.0	17.5	-0.6	17.4	-0.6	17.5	0.6	17.5	0.0	17.5	0.0	17.5	0.0
1944	17.5	0.0	17.5	0.0	17.5	0.0	17.6	0.6	17.6	0.0	17.7	0.6	17.8	0.6	17.8	0.0	17.8	0.0	17.8	0.0	17.8	0.0	17.9	0.6
1945	17.9	0.0	17.9	0.0	17.9	0.0	17.9	0.0	18.0	0.6	18.2	1.1	18.2	0.0	18.2	0.0	18.2	0.0	18.2	0.0	18.2	0.0	18.3	0.5
1946	18.3	0.0	18.2	-0.5	18.4	1.1	18.5	0.5	18.6	0.5	18.8	1.1	19.9	5.9	20.3	2.0	20.5	1.0	20.9	2.0	21.5	2.9	21.6	0.5
1947	21.6	0.0	21.6	0.0	22.1	2.3	22.1	0.0	22.0	-0.5	22.2	0.9	22.4	0.9	22.6	0.9	23.1	2.2	23.1	0.0	23.3	0.9	23.6	1.3
1948	23.8	0.8	23.6	-0.8	23.6	0.0	23.9	1.3	24.1	0.8	24.2	0.4	24.5	1.2	24.6	0.4	24.6	0.0	24.5	-0.4	24.4	-0.4	24.2	-0.8
1949	24.2	0.0	23.9	-1.2	24.0	0.4	24.0	0.0	24.0	0.0	24.0	0.0	23.8	-0.8	23.9	0.4	24.0	0.4	23.9	-0.4	23.9	0.0	23.8	-0.4
1950	23.7	-0.4	23.6	-0.4	23.7	0.4	23.7	0.0	23.8	0.4	24.0	0.8	24.2	0.8	24.4	0.8	24.6	0.8	24.7	0.4	24.8	0.4	25.1	1.2
1951	25.5	1.6	25.9	1.6	26.0	0.4	26.0	0.0	26.1	0.4	26.1	0.0	26.1	0.0	26.1	0.0	26.3	0.8	26.4	0.4	26.5	0.4	26.6	0.4
1952	26.6	0.0	26.5	-0.4	26.5	0.0	26.6	0.4	26.6	0.0	26.7	0.4	26.9	0.7	26.9	0.0	26.9	0.0	26.9	0.0	26.9	0.0	26.9	0.0
1953	26.8	-0.4	26.7	-0.4	26.7	0.0	26.8	0.4	26.8	0.0	26.9	0.4	27.0	0.4	27.1	0.4	27.1	0.0	27.2	0.4	27.1	-0.4	27.0	-0.4
1954	27.1	0.4	27.1	0.0	27.0	-0.4	27.0	0.0	27.1	0.4	27.1	0.0	27.1	0.0	27.1	0.0	27.0	-0.4	26.9	-0.4	27.0	0.4	26.9	-0.4
1955	26.9	0.0	26.9	0.0	26.9	0.0	26.9	0.0	26.9	0.0	26.9	0.0	27.0	0.4	26.9	-0.4	27.0	0.4	27.0	0.0	27.1	0.4	27.0	-0.4
1956	27.0	0.0	27.0	0.0	27.0	0.0	27.0	0.0	27.2	0.7	27.3	0.4	27.5	0.7	27.5	0.0	27.5	0.0	27.7	0.7	27.7	0.0	27.8	0.4
1957	27.8	0.0	27.9	0.4	28.0	0.4	28.1	0.4	28.1	0.0	28.3	0.7	28.4	0.4	28.5	0.4	28.5	0.0	28.5	0.0	28.6	0.4	28.6	0.0

[Continued]

U.S. City Average
Consumer Price Index - Urban Wage Earners
Base 1982-1984 = 100
All Items
[Continued]

For 1913-1995. Columns headed % show percentile change in the index from the previous period for which an index is available.

Year	Jan Index	%	Feb Index	%	Mar Index	%	Apr Index	%	May Index	%	Jun Index	%	Jul Index	%	Aug Index	%	Sep Index	%	Oct Index	%	Nov Index	%	Dec Index	%
1958	28.8	0.7	28.8	0.0	29.0	0.7	29.1	0.3	29.1	0.0	29.1	0.0	29.1	0.0	29.1	0.0	29.1	0.0	29.1	0.0	29.1	0.0	29.1	0.0
1959	29.1	0.0	29.1	0.0	29.1	0.0	29.1	0.0	29.2	0.3	29.3	0.3	29.4	0.3	29.3	-0.3	29.4	0.3	29.5	0.3	29.5	0.0	29.5	0.0
1960	29.5	0.0	29.5	0.0	29.5	0.0	29.7	0.7	29.7	0.0	29.8	0.3	29.8	0.0	29.8	0.0	29.8	0.0	29.9	0.3	30.0	0.3	30.0	0.0
1961	30.0	0.0	30.0	0.0	30.0	0.0	30.0	0.0	30.0	0.0	30.0	0.0	30.1	0.3	30.1	0.0	30.2	0.3	30.2	0.0	30.2	0.0	30.2	0.0
1962	30.2	0.0	30.2	0.0	30.3	0.3	30.4	0.3	30.4	0.0	30.4	0.0	30.4	0.0	30.4	0.0	30.6	0.7	30.6	0.0	30.6	0.0	30.6	0.0
1963	30.6	0.0	30.6	0.0	30.7	0.3	30.7	0.0	30.7	0.0	30.8	0.3	30.9	0.3	30.9	0.0	30.9	0.0	31.0	0.3	31.0	0.0	31.1	0.3
1964	31.1	0.0	31.1	0.0	31.1	0.0	31.1	0.0	31.1	0.0	31.2	0.3	31.3	0.3	31.2	-0.3	31.3	0.3	31.3	0.0	31.4	0.3	31.4	0.0
1965	31.4	0.0	31.4	0.0	31.5	0.3	31.6	0.3	31.6	0.0	31.8	0.6	31.8	0.0	31.8	0.0	31.8	0.0	31.9	0.3	31.9	0.0	32.0	0.3
1966	32.0	0.0	32.2	0.6	32.3	0.3	32.5	0.6	32.5	0.0	32.6	0.3	32.7	0.3	32.9	0.6	32.9	0.0	33.1	0.6	33.1	0.0	33.1	0.0
1967	33.1	0.0	33.1	0.0	33.2	0.3	33.3	0.3	33.4	0.3	33.5	0.3	33.6	0.3	33.7	0.3	33.8	0.3	33.9	0.3	34.0	0.3	34.1	0.3
1968	34.2	0.3	34.3	0.3	34.5	0.6	34.6	0.3	34.7	0.3	34.9	0.6	35.1	0.6	35.2	0.3	35.3	0.3	35.5	0.6	35.6	0.3	35.7	0.3
1969	35.8	0.3	36.0	0.6	36.3	0.8	36.5	0.6	36.6	0.3	36.8	0.5	37.0	0.5	37.2	0.5	37.3	0.3	37.5	0.5	37.7	0.5	37.9	0.5
1970	38.0	0.3	38.2	0.5	38.4	0.5	38.7	0.8	38.8	0.3	39.0	0.5	39.2	0.5	39.2	0.0	39.4	0.5	39.6	0.5	39.8	0.5	40.0	0.5
1971	40.0	0.0	40.1	0.2	40.2	0.2	40.4	0.5	40.6	0.5	40.8	0.5	40.9	0.2	41.0	0.2	41.0	0.0	41.1	0.2	41.2	0.2	41.3	0.2
1972	41.4	0.2	41.6	0.5	41.6	0.0	41.7	0.2	41.9	0.5	42.0	0.2	42.1	0.2	42.2	0.2	42.4	0.5	42.5	0.2	42.6	0.2	42.7	0.2
1973	42.9	0.5	43.2	0.7	43.6	0.9	43.9	0.7	44.1	0.5	44.4	0.7	44.5	0.2	45.4	2.0	45.5	0.2	45.9	0.9	46.2	0.7	46.5	0.6
1974	46.9	0.9	47.5	1.3	48.0	1.1	48.3	0.6	48.8	1.0	49.3	1.0	49.7	0.8	50.3	1.2	50.9	1.2	51.4	1.0	51.8	0.8	52.2	0.8
1975	52.4	0.4	52.8	0.8	53.0	0.4	53.2	0.4	53.5	0.6	53.9	0.7	54.5	1.1	54.7	0.4	54.9	0.4	55.3	0.7	55.6	0.5	55.8	0.4
1976	56.0	0.4	56.1	0.2	56.2	0.2	56.5	0.5	56.8	0.5	57.1	0.5	57.4	0.5	57.7	0.5	57.9	0.3	58.2	0.5	58.3	0.2	58.5	0.3
1977	58.9	0.7	59.5	1.0	59.8	0.5	60.3	0.8	60.6	0.5	61.0	0.7	61.3	0.5	61.5	0.3	61.8	0.5	61.9	0.2	62.2	0.5	62.5	0.5
1978	62.8	0.5	63.2	0.6	63.7	0.8	64.3	0.9	64.9	0.9	65.6	1.1	66.0	0.6	66.4	0.6	66.8	0.6	67.4	0.9	67.7	0.4	68.1	0.6
1979	68.7	0.9	69.5	1.2	70.3	1.2	71.1	1.1	71.9	1.1	72.8	1.3	73.7	1.2	74.4	0.9	75.1	0.9	75.7	0.8	76.4	0.9	77.2	1.0
1980	78.3	1.4	79.4	1.4	80.5	1.4	81.4	1.1	82.3	1.1	83.2	1.1	83.3	0.1	83.8	0.6	84.6	1.0	85.3	0.8	86.1	0.9	86.9	0.9
1981	87.5	0.7	88.5	1.1	89.0	0.6	89.6	0.7	90.3	0.8	91.1	0.9	92.2	1.2	92.8	0.7	93.7	1.0	93.9	0.2	94.1	0.2	94.4	0.3
1982	94.7	0.3	95.0	0.3	94.8	-0.2	95.2	0.4	96.2	1.1	97.4	1.2	98.0	0.6	98.2	0.2	98.3	0.1	98.6	0.3	98.4	-0.2	98.0	-0.4
1983	98.1	0.1	98.1	0.0	98.4	0.3	99.0	0.6	99.5	0.5	99.8	0.3	100.1	0.3	100.5	0.4	101.0	0.5	101.2	0.2	101.2	0.0	101.2	0.0
1984	101.6	0.4	101.8	0.2	101.8	0.0	102.1	0.3	102.5	0.4	102.8	0.3	103.2	0.4	104.2	1.0	104.8	0.6	104.8	0.0	104.7	-0.1	104.8	0.1
1985	104.9	0.1	105.4	0.5	105.9	0.5	106.3	0.4	106.7	0.4	107.0	0.3	107.1	0.1	107.3	0.2	107.6	0.3	107.9	0.3	108.3	0.4	108.6	0.3
1986	108.9	0.3	108.5	-0.4	107.9	-0.6	107.6	-0.3	107.9	0.3	108.4	0.5	108.4	0.0	108.6	0.2	109.1	0.5	109.1	0.0	109.2	0.1	109.3	0.1
1987	110.0	0.6	110.5	0.5	111.0	0.5	111.6	0.5	111.9	0.3	112.4	0.4	112.7	0.3	113.3	0.5	113.8	0.4	114.1	0.3	114.3	0.2	114.2	-0.1
1988	114.5	0.3	114.7	0.2	115.1	0.3	115.7	0.5	116.2	0.4	116.7	0.4	117.2	0.4	117.7	0.4	118.5	0.7	118.9	0.3	119.0	0.1	119.2	0.2
1989	119.7	0.4	120.2	0.4	120.8	0.5	121.8	0.8	122.5	0.6	122.8	0.2	123.2	0.3	123.2	0.0	123.6	0.3	124.2	0.5	124.4	0.2	124.6	0.2
1990	125.9	1.0	126.4	0.4	127.1	0.6	127.3	0.2	127.5	0.2	128.3	0.6	128.7	0.3	129.9	0.9	131.1	0.9	131.9	0.6	132.2	0.2	132.2	0.0
1991	132.8	0.5	132.8	0.0	133.0	0.2	133.3	0.2	133.8	0.4	134.1	0.2	134.3	0.1	134.6	0.2	135.2	0.4	135.4	0.1	135.8	0.3	135.9	0.1
1992	136.0	0.1	136.4	0.3	137.0	0.4	137.3	0.2	137.6	0.2	138.1	0.4	138.4	0.2	138.8	0.3	139.1	0.2	139.6	0.4	139.8	0.1	139.8	0.0
1993	140.3	0.4	140.7	0.3	141.1	0.3	141.6	0.4	141.9	0.2	142.0	0.1	142.1	0.1	142.4	0.2	142.6	0.1	143.3	0.5	143.4	0.1	143.3	-0.1
1994	143.6	0.2	144.0	0.3	144.4	0.3	144.7	0.2	144.9	0.1	145.4	0.3	145.8	0.3	146.5	0.5	146.9	0.3	147.0	0.1	147.3	0.2	147.2	-0.1
1995	147.8	0.4	148.3	0.3	148.7	0.3	149.3	0.4	149.6	0.2	149.9	0.2	149.9	0.0	150.2	0.2	150.6	0.3	151.0	0.3	150.9	-0.1	150.9	0.0

Source: U.S. Department of Labor, Bureau of Labor Statistics, Division of Consumer Prices and Price Indexes.

U.S. City Average
Consumer Price Index - All Urban Consumers
Base 1982-1984 = 100
Food and Beverages

For 1967-1995. Columns headed % show percentile change in the index from the previous period for which an index is available.

Year	Jan Index	%	Feb Index	%	Mar Index	%	Apr Index	%	May Index	%	Jun Index	%	Jul Index	%	Aug Index	%	Sep Index	%	Oct Index	%	Nov Index	%	Dec Index	%
1967	34.8	-	34.7	-0.3	34.7	0.0	34.6	-0.3	34.6	0.0	34.9	0.9	35.2	0.9	35.4	0.6	35.2	-0.6	35.2	0.0	35.2	0.0	35.3	0.3
1968	35.6	0.8	35.7	0.3	35.8	0.3	36.0	0.6	36.1	0.3	36.2	0.3	36.4	0.6	36.6	0.5	36.6	0.0	36.7	0.3	36.6	-0.3	36.8	0.5
1969	37.0	0.5	37.0	0.0	37.2	0.5	37.4	0.5	37.5	0.3	38.0	1.3	38.4	1.1	38.6	0.5	38.7	0.3	38.6	-0.3	38.9	0.8	39.4	1.3
1970	39.6	0.5	39.8	0.5	39.8	0.0	40.0	0.5	40.1	0.2	40.2	0.2	40.4	0.5	40.4	0.0	40.4	0.0	40.4	0.0	40.2	-0.5	40.3	0.2
1971	40.4	0.2	40.5	0.2	40.9	1.0	41.2	0.7	41.3	0.2	41.6	0.7	41.8	0.5	41.9	0.2	41.6	-0.7	41.6	0.0	41.6	0.0	42.0	1.0
1972	42.0	0.0	42.6	1.4	42.7	0.2	42.7	0.0	42.7	0.0	42.9	0.5	43.3	0.9	43.4	0.2	43.5	0.2	43.5	0.0	43.7	0.5	43.9	0.5
1973	44.7	1.8	45.5	1.8	46.6	2.4	47.2	1.3	47.7	1.1	48.3	1.3	48.7	0.8	51.3	5.3	51.0	-0.6	51.0	0.0	51.6	1.2	52.0	0.8
1974	52.8	1.5	54.0	2.3	54.5	0.9	54.4	-0.2	54.8	0.7	55.0	0.4	55.1	0.2	55.9	1.5	56.7	1.4	57.1	0.7	57.6	0.9	58.3	1.2
1975	58.7	0.7	58.9	0.3	58.9	0.0	58.8	-0.2	59.0	0.3	59.9	1.5	61.2	2.2	61.1	-0.2	61.0	-0.2	61.4	0.7	61.6	0.3	61.9	0.5
1976	61.9	0.0	61.7	-0.3	61.3	-0.6	61.5	0.3	61.8	0.5	62.1	0.5	62.5	0.6	62.6	0.2	62.3	-0.5	62.4	0.2	62.2	-0.3	62.4	0.3
1977	62.9	0.8	64.3	2.2	64.6	0.5	65.3	1.1	65.6	0.5	66.2	0.9	66.5	0.5	66.7	0.3	66.5	-0.3	66.5	0.0	66.9	0.6	67.1	0.3
1978	68.1	1.5	69.0	1.3	69.8	1.2	70.9	1.6	71.8	1.3	72.9	1.5	73.4	0.7	73.5	0.1	73.6	0.1	74.0	0.5	74.3	0.4	74.9	0.8
1979	76.4	2.0	77.8	1.8	78.5	0.9	79.2	0.9	79.8	0.8	80.2	0.5	80.7	0.6	80.5	-0.2	80.8	0.4	81.2	0.5	81.5	0.4	82.4	1.1
1980	83.1	0.8	83.5	0.5	84.3	1.0	84.9	0.7	85.4	0.6	85.9	0.6	86.9	1.2	88.1	1.4	88.9	0.9	89.4	0.6	90.0	0.7	90.7	0.8
1981	91.4	0.8	92.2	0.9	92.7	0.5	92.9	0.2	92.8	-0.1	93.2	0.4	94.1	1.0	94.5	0.4	94.7	0.2	94.5	-0.2	94.4	-0.1	94.6	0.2
1982	95.7	1.2	96.5	0.8	96.4	-0.1	96.7	0.3	97.3	0.6	98.0	0.7	98.2	0.2	97.9	-0.3	98.0	0.1	97.8	-0.2	97.6	-0.2	97.6	0.0
1983	98.2	0.6	98.5	0.3	99.1	0.6	99.6	0.5	99.7	0.1	99.6	-0.1	99.6	0.0	99.7	0.1	99.8	0.1	99.9	0.1	99.8	-0.1	100.2	0.4
1984	102.0	1.8	102.9	0.9	102.9	0.0	103.0	0.1	102.7	-0.3	102.9	0.2	103.3	0.4	103.9	0.6	103.7	-0.2	103.7	0.0	103.6	-0.1	104.0	0.4
1985	104.7	0.7	105.4	0.7	105.5	0.1	105.5	0.0	105.3	-0.2	105.4	0.1	105.5	0.1	105.6	0.1	105.7	0.1	105.8	0.1	106.2	0.4	106.9	0.7
1986	107.7	0.7	107.6	-0.1	107.7	0.1	107.9	0.2	108.2	0.3	108.3	0.1	109.2	0.8	110.0	0.7	110.2	0.2	110.4	0.2	110.7	0.3	110.9	0.2
1987	112.1	1.1	112.5	0.4	112.5	0.0	112.8	0.3	113.3	0.4	113.8	0.4	113.7	-0.1	113.8	0.1	114.2	0.4	114.3	0.1	114.3	0.0	114.8	0.4
1988	115.7	0.8	115.8	0.1	116.0	0.2	116.7	0.6	117.1	0.3	117.6	0.4	118.8	1.0	119.4	0.5	120.1	0.6	120.3	0.2	120.2	-0.1	120.6	0.3
1989	122.0	1.2	122.7	0.6	123.3	0.5	124.0	0.6	124.7	0.6	124.9	0.2	125.4	0.4	125.6	0.2	125.9	0.2	126.3	0.3	126.7	0.3	127.2	0.4
1990	130.0	2.2	130.9	0.7	131.2	0.2	131.0	-0.2	131.1	0.1	131.7	0.5	132.4	0.5	132.7	0.2	133.0	0.2	133.4	0.3	133.7	0.2	133.9	0.1
1991	135.9	1.5	136.0	0.1	136.3	0.2	137.2	0.7	137.3	0.1	137.7	0.3	137.1	-0.4	136.6	-0.4	136.7	0.1	136.5	-0.1	136.9	0.3	137.3	0.3
1992	137.9	0.4	138.1	0.1	138.8	0.5	138.8	0.0	138.3	-0.4	138.3	0.0	138.1	-0.1	138.8	0.5	139.3	0.4	139.2	-0.1	139.1	-0.1	139.5	0.3
1993	140.5	0.7	140.7	0.1	140.9	0.1	141.4	0.4	141.8	0.3	141.1	-0.5	141.1	0.0	141.5	0.3	141.8	0.2	142.3	0.4	142.6	0.2	143.3	0.5
1994	144.3	0.7	143.6	-0.5	143.9	0.2	144.0	0.1	144.1	0.1	144.2	0.1	144.8	0.4	145.3	0.3	145.6	0.2	145.6	0.0	145.9	0.2	147.2	0.9
1995	147.9	0.5	147.8	-0.1	147.9	0.1	148.9	0.7	148.7	-0.1	148.4	-0.2	148.6	0.1	148.9	0.2	149.4	0.3	149.8	0.3	149.8	0.0	150.3	0.3

Source: U.S. Department of Labor, Bureau of Labor Statistics, Division of Consumer Prices and Price Indexes.

U.S. City Average
Consumer Price Index - Urban Wage Earners
Base 1982-1984 = 100
Food and Beverages

For 1967-1995. Columns headed % show percentile change in the index from the previous period for which an index is available.

Year	Jan Index	%	Feb Index	%	Mar Index	%	Apr Index	%	May Index	%	Jun Index	%	Jul Index	%	Aug Index	%	Sep Index	%	Oct Index	%	Nov Index	%	Dec Index	%
1967	34.8	-	34.6	-0.6	34.6	0.0	34.5	-0.3	34.6	0.3	34.9	0.9	35.2	0.9	35.4	0.6	35.2	-0.6	35.1	-0.3	35.1	0.0	35.3	0.6
1968	35.5	0.6	35.7	0.6	35.8	0.3	35.9	0.3	36.0	0.3	36.1	0.3	36.4	0.8	36.6	0.5	36.5	-0.3	36.7	0.5	36.6	-0.3	36.8	0.5
1969	37.0	0.5	37.0	0.0	37.2	0.5	37.4	0.5	37.5	0.3	38.0	1.3	38.3	0.8	38.6	0.8	38.6	0.0	38.6	0.0	38.8	0.5	39.3	1.3
1970	39.6	0.8	39.8	0.5	39.8	0.0	39.9	0.3	40.1	0.5	40.2	0.2	40.4	0.5	40.4	0.0	40.4	0.0	40.3	-0.2	40.2	-0.2	40.3	0.2
1971	40.4	0.2	40.5	0.2	40.9	1.0	41.1	0.5	41.3	0.5	41.6	0.7	41.8	0.5	41.9	0.2	41.6	-0.7	41.5	-0.2	41.6	0.2	42.0	1.0
1972	42.0	0.0	42.6	1.4	42.7	0.2	42.7	0.0	42.7	0.0	42.9	0.5	43.3	0.9	43.4	0.2	43.5	0.2	43.5	0.0	43.7	0.5	43.9	0.5
1973	44.7	1.8	45.5	1.8	46.6	2.4	47.2	1.3	47.6	0.8	48.3	1.5	48.6	0.6	51.3	5.6	51.0	-0.6	51.0	0.0	51.5	1.0	52.0	1.0
1974	52.7	1.3	54.0	2.5	54.5	0.9	54.4	-0.2	54.7	0.6	55.0	0.5	55.1	0.2	55.9	1.5	56.7	1.4	57.0	0.5	57.6	1.1	58.2	1.0
1975	58.6	0.7	58.9	0.5	58.8	-0.2	58.8	0.0	59.0	0.3	59.8	1.4	61.1	2.2	61.0	-0.2	60.9	-0.2	61.3	0.7	61.5	0.3	61.9	0.7
1976	61.9	0.0	61.7	-0.3	61.3	-0.6	61.5	0.3	61.7	0.3	62.0	0.5	62.4	0.6	62.5	0.2	62.3	-0.3	62.3	0.0	62.1	-0.3	62.4	0.5
1977	62.9	0.8	64.2	2.1	64.5	0.5	65.3	1.2	65.5	0.3	66.2	1.1	66.5	0.5	66.7	0.3	66.5	-0.3	66.4	-0.2	66.8	0.6	67.1	0.4
1978	68.0	1.3	68.9	1.3	69.6	1.0	70.7	1.6	71.7	1.4	72.8	1.5	73.2	0.5	73.4	0.3	73.4	0.0	73.9	0.7	74.2	0.4	74.8	0.8
1979	76.3	2.0	77.8	2.0	78.7	1.2	79.2	0.6	79.8	0.8	80.1	0.4	80.7	0.7	80.5	-0.2	80.8	0.4	81.2	0.5	81.5	0.4	82.4	1.1
1980	83.1	0.8	83.5	0.5	84.3	1.0	85.0	0.8	85.5	0.6	86.1	0.7	87.1	1.2	88.3	1.4	89.2	1.0	89.7	0.6	90.4	0.8	91.0	0.7
1981	91.6	0.7	92.4	0.9	92.8	0.4	93.0	0.2	92.9	-0.1	93.3	0.4	94.2	1.0	94.6	0.4	94.7	0.1	94.6	-0.1	94.5	-0.1	94.6	0.1
1982	95.7	1.2	96.5	0.8	96.4	-0.1	96.7	0.3	97.3	0.6	98.0	0.7	98.3	0.3	97.9	-0.4	98.0	0.1	97.8	-0.2	97.7	-0.1	97.7	0.0
1983	98.2	0.5	98.6	0.4	99.1	0.5	99.6	0.5	99.8	0.2	99.6	-0.2	99.6	0.0	99.6	0.0	99.8	0.2	99.9	0.1	99.8	-0.1	100.2	0.4
1984	102.0	1.8	102.9	0.9	102.9	0.0	103.0	0.1	102.7	-0.3	102.9	0.2	103.2	0.3	103.8	0.6	103.6	-0.2	103.6	0.0	103.5	-0.1	103.8	0.3
1985	104.5	0.7	105.3	0.8	105.4	0.1	105.3	-0.1	105.1	-0.2	105.3	0.2	105.3	0.0	105.4	0.1	105.5	0.1	105.6	0.1	106.0	0.4	106.7	0.7
1986	107.5	0.7	107.5	0.0	107.5	0.0	107.8	0.3	108.0	0.2	108.1	0.1	109.0	0.8	109.9	0.8	110.1	0.2	110.2	0.1	110.5	0.3	110.7	0.2
1987	111.9	1.1	112.3	0.4	112.3	0.0	112.6	0.3	113.1	0.4	113.6	0.4	113.5	-0.1	113.6	0.1	114.0	0.4	114.1	0.1	114.1	0.0	114.5	0.4
1988	115.4	0.8	115.5	0.1	115.7	0.2	116.3	0.5	116.8	0.4	117.4	0.5	118.5	0.9	119.1	0.5	119.8	0.6	120.0	0.2	119.9	-0.1	120.3	0.3
1989	121.7	1.2	122.4	0.6	123.1	0.6	123.7	0.5	124.4	0.6	124.6	0.2	125.1	0.4	125.3	0.2	125.6	0.2	126.0	0.3	126.4	0.3	126.9	0.4
1990	129.7	2.2	130.6	0.7	130.9	0.2	130.7	-0.2	130.7	0.0	131.5	0.6	132.1	0.5	132.4	0.2	132.7	0.2	133.1	0.3	133.5	0.3	133.6	0.1
1991	135.6	1.5	135.7	0.1	136.1	0.3	136.9	0.6	137.0	0.1	137.4	0.3	136.8	-0.4	136.4	-0.3	136.5	0.1	136.2	-0.2	136.5	0.2	136.9	0.3
1992	137.4	0.4	137.8	0.3	138.4	0.4	138.5	0.1	137.9	-0.4	137.9	0.0	137.8	-0.1	138.5	0.5	138.9	0.3	138.8	-0.1	138.8	0.0	139.1	0.2
1993	140.1	0.7	140.2	0.1	140.5	0.2	140.9	0.3	141.4	0.4	140.8	-0.4	140.8	0.0	141.2	0.3	141.5	0.2	142.0	0.4	142.2	0.1	142.9	0.5
1994	143.8	0.6	143.2	-0.4	143.4	0.1	143.6	0.1	143.7	0.1	143.8	0.1	144.4	0.4	144.9	0.3	145.1	0.1	145.1	0.0	145.3	0.1	146.6	0.9
1995	147.2	0.4	147.3	0.1	147.3	0.0	148.3	0.7	148.1	-0.1	147.8	-0.2	148.0	0.1	148.3	0.2	148.9	0.4	149.3	0.3	149.3	0.0	149.8	0.3

Source: U.S. Department of Labor, Bureau of Labor Statistics, Division of Consumer Prices and Price Indexes.

U.S. City Average
Consumer Price Index - All Urban Consumers
Base 1982-1984 = 100
Housing

For 1967-1995. Columns headed % show percentile change in the index from the previous period for which an index is available.

Year	Jan Index	%	Feb Index	%	Mar Index	%	Apr Index	%	May Index	%	Jun Index	%	Jul Index	%	Aug Index	%	Sep Index	%	Oct Index	%	Nov Index	%	Dec Index	%
1967	30.5	-	30.5	0.0	30.5	0.0	30.6	0.3	30.7	0.3	30.7	0.0	30.8	0.3	30.9	0.3	30.9	0.0	31.0	0.3	31.1	0.3	31.2	0.3
1968	31.3	0.3	31.5	0.6	31.5	0.0	31.6	0.3	31.7	0.3	31.9	0.6	32.1	0.6	32.3	0.6	32.4	0.3	32.5	0.3	32.7	0.6	32.9	0.6
1969	32.9	0.0	33.1	0.6	33.4	0.9	33.6	0.6	33.8	0.6	33.9	0.3	34.1	0.6	34.3	0.6	34.5	0.6	34.6	0.3	34.8	0.6	35.0	0.6
1970	35.1	0.3	35.4	0.9	35.8	1.1	36.0	0.6	36.2	0.6	36.3	0.3	36.5	0.6	36.7	0.5	36.9	0.5	37.1	0.5	37.3	0.5	37.5	0.5
1971	37.5	0.0	37.5	0.0	37.4	-0.3	37.4	0.0	37.7	0.8	37.9	0.5	38.1	0.5	38.2	0.3	38.3	0.3	38.5	0.5	38.6	0.3	38.7	0.3
1972	38.9	0.5	39.0	0.3	39.1	0.3	39.2	0.3	39.3	0.3	39.4	0.3	39.5	0.3	39.7	0.5	39.8	0.3	39.8	0.0	39.9	0.3	40.1	0.5
1973	40.1	0.0	40.3	0.5	40.4	0.2	40.5	0.2	40.7	0.5	40.8	0.2	40.9	0.2	41.2	0.7	41.6	1.0	42.1	1.2	42.5	1.0	42.8	0.7
1974	43.3	1.2	43.7	0.9	44.1	0.9	44.5	0.9	44.9	0.9	45.4	1.1	45.9	1.1	46.5	1.3	47.1	1.3	47.6	1.1	48.1	1.1	48.6	1.0
1975	49.0	0.8	49.5	1.0	49.7	0.4	50.0	0.6	50.2	0.4	50.5	0.6	50.7	0.4	50.9	0.4	51.3	0.8	51.5	0.4	52.0	1.0	52.3	0.6
1976	52.6	0.6	52.7	0.2	53.0	0.6	53.1	0.2	53.3	0.4	53.5	0.4	53.9	0.7	54.1	0.4	54.4	0.6	54.6	0.4	54.8	0.4	55.1	0.5
1977	55.5	0.7	55.9	0.7	56.2	0.5	56.6	0.7	56.8	0.4	57.3	0.9	57.7	0.7	58.0	0.5	58.4	0.7	58.6	0.3	58.9	0.5	59.2	0.5
1978	59.7	0.8	60.0	0.5	60.6	1.0	61.1	0.8	61.6	0.8	62.2	1.0	62.8	1.0	63.2	0.6	63.9	1.1	64.5	0.9	64.9	0.6	65.1	0.3
1979	65.6	0.8	66.4	1.2	67.0	0.9	67.7	1.0	68.5	1.2	69.4	1.3	70.3	1.3	71.3	1.4	72.2	1.3	73.2	1.4	74.1	1.2	75.0	1.2
1980	76.2	1.6	77.1	1.2	78.4	1.7	79.4	1.3	80.6	1.5	82.1	1.9	81.6	-0.6	81.8	0.2	82.4	0.7	83.5	1.3	84.3	1.0	85.3	1.2
1981	85.9	0.7	86.5	0.7	87.0	0.6	87.7	0.8	88.8	1.3	90.0	1.4	91.5	1.7	92.3	0.9	93.5	1.3	93.5	0.0	93.7	0.2	94.0	0.3
1982	94.3	0.3	94.6	0.3	94.4	-0.2	95.3	1.0	96.6	1.4	97.8	1.2	98.3	0.5	98.6	0.3	98.4	-0.2	98.8	0.4	98.2	-0.6	97.4	-0.8
1983	97.9	0.5	98.1	0.2	98.1	0.0	98.6	0.5	99.1	0.5	99.5	0.4	99.9	0.4	100.0	0.1	100.5	0.5	100.6	0.1	100.7	0.1	100.8	0.1
1984	101.4	0.6	101.9	0.5	102.1	0.2	102.6	0.5	103.0	0.4	103.5	0.5	104.1	0.6	104.5	0.4	105.1	0.6	105.1	0.0	105.0	-0.1	105.1	0.1
1985	105.3	0.2	105.8	0.5	106.1	0.3	106.5	0.4	107.3	0.8	107.9	0.6	108.3	0.4	108.7	0.4	108.9	0.2	109.1	0.2	109.3	0.2	109.6	0.3
1986	109.9	0.3	109.8	-0.1	109.9	0.1	110.2	0.3	110.4	0.2	111.2	0.7	111.3	0.1	111.6	0.3	112.0	0.4	111.8	-0.2	111.4	-0.4	111.5	0.1
1987	112.0	0.4	112.4	0.4	112.8	0.4	113.2	0.4	113.6	0.4	114.3	0.6	114.7	0.3	115.4	0.6	115.6	0.2	115.5	-0.1	115.5	0.0	115.6	0.1
1988	116.2	0.5	116.6	0.3	117.0	0.3	117.3	0.3	117.7	0.3	118.6	0.8	119.1	0.4	119.5	0.3	119.9	0.3	119.9	0.0	119.9	0.0	120.2	0.3
1989	120.7	0.4	121.1	0.3	121.5	0.3	121.6	0.1	122.1	0.4	122.9	0.7	123.9	0.8	124.2	0.2	124.3	0.1	124.4	0.1	124.5	0.1	124.9	0.3
1990	125.9	0.8	126.1	0.2	126.8	0.6	126.8	0.0	127.1	0.2	128.3	0.9	129.2	0.7	130.2	0.8	130.5	0.2	130.6	0.1	130.4	-0.2	130.5	0.1
1991	131.8	1.0	132.4	0.5	132.6	0.2	132.5	-0.1	132.8	0.2	133.4	0.5	134.2	0.6	134.5	0.2	134.7	0.1	134.7	0.0	134.7	0.0	135.0	0.2
1992	135.7	0.5	136.1	0.3	136.6	0.4	136.5	-0.1	136.7	0.1	137.7	0.7	138.3	0.4	138.6	0.2	138.4	-0.1	138.5	0.1	138.5	0.0	138.5	0.0
1993	139.3	0.6	139.7	0.3	140.2	0.4	140.4	0.1	140.5	0.1	141.5	0.7	141.9	0.3	142.3	0.3	142.3	0.0	142.2	-0.1	142.0	-0.1	142.3	0.2
1994	142.9	0.4	143.7	0.6	144.1	0.3	143.9	-0.1	144.1	0.1	144.9	0.6	145.4	0.3	145.9	0.3	145.8	-0.1	145.7	-0.1	145.5	-0.1	145.4	-0.1
1995	146.4	0.7	147.0	0.4	147.4	0.3	147.4	0.0	147.6	0.1	148.5	0.6	149.2	0.5	149.6	0.3	149.5	-0.1	149.7	0.1	149.4	-0.2	149.7	0.2

Source: U.S. Department of Labor, Bureau of Labor Statistics, Division of Consumer Prices and Price Indexes.

U.S. City Average
Consumer Price Index - Urban Wage Earners
Base 1982-1984 = 100
Housing

For 1967-1995. Columns headed % show percentile change in the index from the previous period for which an index is available.

Year	Jan Index	%	Feb Index	%	Mar Index	%	Apr Index	%	May Index	%	Jun Index	%	Jul Index	%	Aug Index	%	Sep Index	%	Oct Index	%	Nov Index	%	Dec Index	%
1967	30.7	-	30.8	0.3	30.8	0.0	30.9	0.3	31.0	0.3	31.0	0.0	31.1	0.3	31.1	0.0	31.2	0.3	31.3	0.3	31.3	0.0	31.5	0.6
1968	31.6	0.3	31.7	0.3	31.8	0.3	31.9	0.3	32.0	0.3	32.2	0.6	32.4	0.6	32.6	0.6	32.6	0.0	32.8	0.6	33.0	0.6	33.1	0.3
1969	33.2	0.3	33.4	0.6	33.7	0.9	33.9	0.6	34.1	0.6	34.2	0.3	34.4	0.6	34.6	0.6	34.8	0.6	34.9	0.3	35.1	0.6	35.3	0.6
1970	35.4	0.3	35.7	0.8	36.1	1.1	36.3	0.6	36.5	0.6	36.6	0.3	36.8	0.5	37.0	0.5	37.2	0.5	37.4	0.5	37.6	0.5	37.8	0.5
1971	37.8	0.0	37.8	0.0	37.7	-0.3	37.8	0.3	38.0	0.5	38.2	0.5	38.4	0.5	38.5	0.3	38.7	0.5	38.8	0.3	38.9	0.3	39.1	0.5
1972	39.2	0.3	39.3	0.3	39.4	0.3	39.5	0.3	39.6	0.3	39.7	0.3	39.9	0.5	40.0	0.3	40.1	0.2	40.2	0.2	40.3	0.2	40.4	0.2
1973	40.5	0.2	40.6	0.2	40.7	0.2	40.9	0.5	41.0	0.2	41.2	0.5	41.3	0.2	41.6	0.7	42.0	1.0	42.5	1.2	42.8	0.7	43.2	0.9
1974	43.7	1.2	44.1	0.9	44.5	0.9	44.8	0.7	45.3	1.1	45.8	1.1	46.3	1.1	46.9	1.3	47.5	1.3	48.0	1.1	48.5	1.0	49.0	1.0
1975	49.4	0.8	49.9	1.0	50.1	0.4	50.5	0.8	50.7	0.4	51.0	0.6	51.2	0.4	51.4	0.4	51.7	0.6	52.0	0.6	52.5	1.0	52.7	0.4
1976	53.0	0.6	53.2	0.4	53.4	0.4	53.5	0.2	53.7	0.4	54.0	0.6	54.3	0.6	54.6	0.6	54.9	0.5	55.1	0.4	55.3	0.4	55.5	0.4
1977	56.0	0.9	56.3	0.5	56.7	0.7	57.1	0.7	57.3	0.4	57.8	0.9	58.2	0.7	58.5	0.5	58.9	0.7	59.1	0.3	59.4	0.5	59.8	0.7
1978	60.2	0.7	60.6	0.7	61.1	0.8	61.5	0.7	62.1	1.0	62.7	1.0	63.2	0.8	63.6	0.6	64.3	1.1	64.9	0.9	65.3	0.6	65.6	0.5
1979	66.1	0.8	66.9	1.2	67.6	1.0	68.2	0.9	69.0	1.2	70.0	1.4	70.9	1.3	71.9	1.4	72.8	1.3	73.8	1.4	74.8	1.4	75.7	1.2
1980	76.8	1.5	77.8	1.3	79.0	1.5	80.1	1.4	81.3	1.5	82.9	2.0	82.3	-0.7	82.6	0.4	83.1	0.6	84.2	1.3	85.0	1.0	86.1	1.3
1981	86.7	0.7	87.2	0.6	87.6	0.5	88.3	0.8	89.5	1.4	90.7	1.3	92.2	1.7	93.1	1.0	94.3	1.3	94.2	-0.1	94.4	0.2	94.6	0.2
1982	94.9	0.3	95.3	0.4	95.1	-0.2	96.0	0.9	97.4	1.5	98.6	1.2	99.2	0.6	99.5	0.3	99.4	-0.1	99.8	0.4	99.3	-0.5	98.4	-0.9
1983	98.5	0.1	98.6	0.1	99.1	0.5	99.5	0.4	99.8	0.3	100.1	0.3	100.3	0.2	100.7	0.4	101.0	0.3	101.0	0.0	100.8	-0.2	100.7	-0.1
1984	100.8	0.1	100.7	-0.1	100.3	-0.4	100.2	-0.1	101.0	0.8	101.3	0.3	102.1	0.8	103.8	1.7	104.6	0.8	104.2	-0.4	103.9	-0.3	104.0	0.1
1985	104.3	0.3	104.7	0.4	105.0	0.3	105.4	0.4	106.3	0.9	106.8	0.5	107.2	0.4	107.5	0.3	107.8	0.3	107.9	0.1	108.2	0.3	108.4	0.2
1986	108.7	0.3	108.6	-0.1	108.7	0.1	109.0	0.3	109.2	0.2	110.0	0.7	110.1	0.1	110.4	0.3	110.8	0.4	110.4	-0.4	110.0	-0.4	110.2	0.2
1987	110.7	0.5	111.0	0.3	111.4	0.4	111.8	0.4	112.2	0.4	112.9	0.6	113.2	0.3	114.0	0.7	114.1	0.1	114.0	-0.1	113.9	-0.1	114.1	0.2
1988	114.6	0.4	115.0	0.3	115.4	0.3	115.6	0.2	116.0	0.3	116.9	0.8	117.4	0.4	117.8	0.3	118.2	0.3	118.2	0.0	118.3	0.1	118.5	0.2
1989	119.0	0.4	119.3	0.3	119.6	0.3	119.8	0.2	120.3	0.4	121.1	0.7	122.1	0.8	122.4	0.2	122.5	0.1	122.5	0.0	122.7	0.2	123.1	0.3
1990	123.9	0.6	124.1	0.2	124.7	0.5	124.7	0.0	125.1	0.3	126.2	0.9	127.0	0.6	127.9	0.7	128.3	0.3	128.3	0.0	128.2	-0.1	128.3	0.1
1991	129.4	0.9	130.0	0.5	130.2	0.2	130.1	-0.1	130.5	0.3	131.1	0.5	131.8	0.5	132.0	0.2	132.4	0.3	132.3	-0.1	132.4	0.1	132.7	0.2
1992	133.3	0.5	133.6	0.2	134.0	0.3	133.9	-0.1	134.1	0.1	135.1	0.7	135.7	0.4	135.9	0.1	135.8	-0.1	135.9	0.1	136.0	0.1	136.1	0.1
1993	136.7	0.4	137.0	0.2	137.4	0.3	137.7	0.2	137.9	0.1	138.8	0.7	139.1	0.2	139.5	0.3	139.7	0.1	139.6	-0.1	139.4	-0.1	139.7	0.2
1994	140.2	0.4	140.9	0.5	141.3	0.3	141.1	-0.1	141.3	0.1	142.1	0.6	142.5	0.3	143.0	0.4	143.0	0.0	142.8	-0.1	142.7	-0.1	142.7	0.0
1995	143.5	0.6	144.0	0.3	144.3	0.2	144.4	0.1	144.6	0.1	145.5	0.6	146.1	0.4	146.5	0.3	146.5	0.0	146.6	0.1	146.4	-0.1	146.7	0.2

Source: U.S. Department of Labor, Bureau of Labor Statistics, Division of Consumer Prices and Price Indexes.

U.S. City Average
Consumer Price Index - All Urban Consumers
Base 1982-1984 = 100
Apparel and Upkeep

For 1913-1995. Columns headed % show percentile change in the index from the previous period for which an index is available.

Year	Jan Index	%	Feb Index	%	Mar Index	%	Apr Index	%	May Index	%	Jun Index	%	Jul Index	%	Aug Index	%	Sep Index	%	Oct Index	%	Nov Index	%	Dec Index	%
1913	-	-	-	-	-	-	-	-	-	-	-	-	-	-	-	-	-	-	-	-	-	-	-	-
1914	-	-	-	-	-	-	-	-	-	-	-	-	-	-	-	-	-	-	-	-	-	-	15.0	-
1915	-	-	-	-	-	-	-	-	-	-	-	-	-	-	-	-	-	-	-	-	-	-	15.6	4.0
1916	-	-	-	-	-	-	-	-	-	-	-	-	-	-	-	-	-	-	-	-	-	-	17.9	14.7
1917	-	-	-	-	-	-	-	-	-	-	-	-	-	-	-	-	-	-	-	-	-	-	22.2	24.0
1918	-	-	-	-	-	-	-	-	-	-	-	-	-	-	-	-	-	-	-	-	-	-	31.8	43.2
1919	-	-	-	-	-	-	-	-	-	-	34.4	8.2	-	-	-	-	-	-	-	-	-	-	42.6	23.8
1920	-	-	-	-	-	-	-	-	-	-	45.0	5.6	-	-	-	-	-	-	-	-	-	-	40.3	-10.4
1921	-	-	-	-	-	-	-	-	34.7	-13.9	-	-	-	-	-	-	30.0	-13.5	-	-	-	-	28.6	-4.7
1922	-	-	-	-	27.3	-4.5	-	-	-	-	26.8	-1.8	-	-	-	-	26.6	-0.7	-	-	-	-	26.6	0.0
1923	-	-	-	-	27.0	1.5	-	-	-	-	27.0	0.0	-	-	-	-	27.2	0.7	-	-	-	-	27.2	0.0
1924	-	-	-	-	27.1	-0.4	-	-	-	-	26.9	-0.7	-	-	-	-	26.6	-1.1	-	-	-	-	26.4	-0.8
1925	-	-	-	-	-	-	-	-	-	-	26.4	0.0	-	-	-	-	-	-	-	-	-	-	26.2	-0.8
1926	-	-	-	-	-	-	-	-	-	-	25.9	-1.1	-	-	-	-	-	-	-	-	-	-	25.7	-0.8
1927	-	-	-	-	-	-	-	-	-	-	25.4	-1.2	-	-	-	-	-	-	-	-	-	-	25.1	-1.2
1928	-	-	-	-	-	-	-	-	-	-	25.0	-0.4	-	-	-	-	-	-	-	-	-	-	24.9	-0.4
1929	-	-	-	-	-	-	-	-	-	-	24.7	-0.8	-	-	-	-	-	-	-	-	-	-	24.6	-0.4
1930	-	-	-	-	-	-	-	-	-	-	24.5	-0.4	-	-	-	-	-	-	-	-	-	-	23.5	-4.1
1931	-	-	-	-	-	-	-	-	-	-	22.2	-5.5	-	-	-	-	-	-	-	-	-	-	20.6	-7.2
1932	-	-	-	-	-	-	-	-	-	-	19.5	-5.3	-	-	-	-	-	-	-	-	-	-	18.6	-4.6
1933	-	-	-	-	-	-	-	-	-	-	18.2	-2.2	-	-	-	-	-	-	-	-	-	-	20.2	11.0
1934	-	-	-	-	-	-	-	-	-	-	20.7	2.5	-	-	-	-	-	-	-	-	20.7	0.0	-	-
1935	-	-	-	-	20.8	0.5	-	-	-	-	-	-	20.7	-0.5	-	-	-	-	20.9	1.0	-	-	-	-
1936	21.0	0.5	-	-	-	-	21.0	0.0	-	-	-	-	20.9	-0.5	-	-	21.0	0.5	-	-	-	-	21.3	1.4
1937	-	-	-	-	21.7	1.9	-	-	-	-	22.0	1.4	-	-	-	-	22.5	2.3	-	-	-	-	22.5	0.0
1938	-	-	-	-	22.1	-1.8	-	-	-	-	21.9	-0.9	-	-	-	-	21.7	-0.9	-	-	-	-	21.7	0.0
1939	-	-	-	-	21.6	-0.5	-	-	-	-	21.6	0.0	-	-	-	-	21.6	0.0	-	-	-	-	21.7	0.5
1940	-	-	-	-	21.9	0.9	-	-	-	-	21.8	-0.5	-	-	-	-	21.8	0.0	21.8	0.0	21.8	0.0	21.8	0.0
1941	21.6	-0.9	21.6	0.0	21.9	1.4	22.0	0.5	22.0	0.0	22.2	0.9	22.5	1.4	22.9	1.8	23.8	3.9	24.2	1.7	24.5	1.2	24.6	0.4
1942	24.9	1.2	25.5	2.4	26.6	4.3	27.2	2.3	27.1	-0.4	26.9	-0.7	26.9	0.0	26.9	0.0	27.1	0.7	27.1	0.0	27.1	0.0	27.1	0.0
1943	27.1	0.0	27.1	0.0	27.4	1.1	27.5	0.4	27.5	0.0	27.5	0.0	27.7	0.7	27.8	0.4	28.4	2.2	28.6	0.7	28.7	0.3	29.0	1.0
1944	29.0	0.0	29.1	0.3	29.4	1.0	29.5	0.3	29.5	0.0	29.7	0.7	29.7	0.0	30.0	1.0	30.3	1.0	30.4	0.3	30.5	0.3	30.6	0.3
1945	30.7	0.3	30.8	0.3	30.8	0.0	30.9	0.3	31.0	0.3	31.2	0.6	31.4	0.6	31.5	0.3	31.9	1.3	31.9	0.0	31.9	0.0	32.1	0.6
1946	32.2	0.3	32.3	0.3	32.9	1.9	33.2	0.9	33.4	0.6	33.7	0.9	34.1	1.2	34.6	1.5	35.6	2.9	36.1	1.4	36.7	1.7	37.9	3.3
1947	38.4	1.3	38.9	1.3	39.5	1.5	39.7	0.5	39.7	0.0	39.9	0.5	39.6	-0.8	39.9	0.8	40.3	1.0	40.6	0.7	40.8	0.5	41.0	0.5
1948	41.3	0.7	41.9	1.5	42.1	0.5	42.2	0.2	42.4	0.5	42.3	-0.2	42.3	0.0	42.9	1.4	43.1	0.5	43.3	0.5	43.2	-0.2	43.1	-0.2
1949	42.2	-2.1	41.9	-0.7	41.7	-0.5	41.3	-1.0	41.1	-0.5	40.9	-0.5	40.5	-1.0	40.2	-0.7	40.2	0.0	40.1	-0.2	40.0	-0.2	39.9	-0.2
1950	39.7	-0.5	39.7	0.0	39.8	0.3	39.7	-0.3	39.6	-0.3	39.6	0.0	39.6	0.0	39.9	0.8	40.7	2.0	41.4	1.7	41.7	0.7	42.0	0.7
1951	42.6	1.4	43.4	1.9	43.6	0.5	43.7	0.2	43.8	0.2	43.8	0.0	43.7	-0.2	43.7	0.0	44.9	2.7	44.9	0.0	44.6	-0.7	44.4	-0.4
1952	43.9	-1.1	43.9	0.0	43.7	-0.5	43.5	-0.5	43.5	0.0	43.4	-0.2	43.2	-0.5	43.1	-0.2	43.5	0.9	43.4	-0.2	43.2	-0.5	43.1	-0.2
1953	43.0	-0.2	43.0	0.0	43.0	0.0	43.0	0.0	43.1	0.2	43.1	0.0	43.1	0.0	43.0	-0.2	43.4	0.9	43.5	0.2	43.5	0.0	43.4	-0.2
1954	43.2	-0.5	43.1	-0.2	43.0	-0.2	42.9	-0.2	43.0	0.2	43.0	0.0	42.9	-0.2	42.8	-0.2	43.0	0.5	43.1	0.2	43.1	0.0	43.1	0.0
1955	42.7	-0.9	42.7	0.0	42.7	0.0	42.6	-0.2	42.7	0.2	42.7	0.0	42.7	0.0	42.8	0.2	43.2	0.9	43.2	0.0	43.3	0.2	43.3	0.0
1956	43.2	-0.2	43.4	0.5	43.4	0.0	43.5	0.2	43.5	0.0	43.5	0.0	43.6	0.2	43.7	0.2	44.1	0.9	44.3	0.5	44.4	0.2	44.4	0.0
1957	44.2	-0.5	44.1	-0.2	44.4	0.7	44.3	-0.2	44.4	0.2	44.4	0.0	44.4	0.0	44.4	0.0	44.7	0.7	44.9	0.4	45.0	0.2	44.8	-0.4

[Continued]

U.S. City Average
Consumer Price Index - All Urban Consumers
Base 1982-1984 = 100
Apparel and Upkeep
[Continued]

For 1913-1995. Columns headed % show percentile change in the index from the previous period for which an index is available.

Year	Jan Index	%	Feb Index	%	Mar Index	%	Apr Index	%	May Index	%	Jun Index	%	Jul Index	%	Aug Index	%	Sep Index	%	Oct Index	%	Nov Index	%	Dec Index	%
1958	44.6	-0.4	44.6	0.0	44.6	0.0	44.6	0.0	44.6	0.0	44.6	0.0	44.6	0.0	44.5	-0.2	44.7	0.4	44.8	0.2	45.0	0.4	44.9	-0.2
1959	44.6	-0.7	44.6	0.0	44.6	0.0	44.7	0.2	44.8	0.2	44.8	0.0	44.9	0.2	45.1	0.4	45.5	0.9	45.6	0.2	45.6	0.0	45.5	-0.2
1960	45.1	-0.9	45.3	0.4	45.4	0.2	45.5	0.2	45.5	0.0	45.5	0.0	45.6	0.2	45.7	0.2	46.1	0.9	46.3	0.4	46.2	-0.2	46.2	0.0
1961	45.8	-0.9	45.8	0.0	45.9	0.2	45.8	-0.2	45.9	0.2	45.8	-0.2	46.0	0.4	46.0	0.0	46.4	0.9	46.5	0.2	46.4	-0.2	46.4	0.0
1962	45.7	-1.5	45.9	0.4	46.1	0.4	46.1	0.0	46.1	0.0	46.2	0.2	46.2	0.0	46.1	-0.2	46.9	1.7	47.0	0.2	46.8	-0.4	46.7	-0.2
1963	46.4	-0.6	46.5	0.2	46.6	0.2	46.7	0.2	46.6	-0.2	46.7	0.2	46.7	0.0	46.8	0.2	47.2	0.9	47.4	0.4	47.5	0.2	47.5	0.0
1964	47.0	-1.1	47.0	0.0	47.1	0.2	47.2	0.2	47.3	0.2	47.3	0.0	47.2	-0.2	47.1	-0.2	47.4	0.6	47.5	0.2	47.6	0.2	47.7	0.2
1965	47.2	-1.0	47.3	0.2	47.4	0.2	47.5	0.2	47.8	0.6	47.8	0.0	47.5	-0.6	47.6	0.2	47.9	0.6	48.2	0.6	48.3	0.2	48.3	0.0
1966	48.0	-0.6	48.1	0.2	48.4	0.6	48.6	0.4	48.9	0.6	48.9	0.0	48.8	-0.2	48.8	0.0	49.5	1.4	49.9	0.8	50.1	0.4	50.2	0.2
1967	49.8	-0.8	50.1	0.6	50.4	0.6	50.5	0.2	50.9	0.8	50.9	0.0	50.8	-0.2	50.9	0.2	51.5	1.2	51.9	0.8	52.2	0.6	52.3	0.2
1968	51.8	-1.0	52.2	0.8	52.6	0.8	53.0	0.8	53.4	0.8	53.6	0.4	53.5	-0.2	53.8	0.6	54.7	1.7	55.2	0.9	55.5	0.5	55.6	0.2
1969	55.2	-0.7	55.4	0.4	55.9	0.9	56.2	0.5	56.6	0.7	56.8	0.4	56.7	-0.2	56.6	-0.2	57.6	1.8	58.1	0.9	58.4	0.5	58.5	0.2
1970	57.8	-1.2	58.1	0.5	58.4	0.5	58.6	0.3	59.0	0.7	59.1	0.2	58.8	-0.5	58.8	0.0	59.7	1.5	60.3	1.0	60.7	0.7	60.8	0.2
1971	60.0	-1.3	60.2	0.3	60.5	0.5	60.7	0.3	61.3	1.0	61.2	-0.2	60.8	-0.7	60.7	-0.2	61.5	1.3	62.0	0.8	62.1	0.2	62.1	0.0
1972	61.3	-1.3	61.5	0.3	61.8	0.5	62.1	0.5	62.5	0.6	62.2	-0.5	61.7	-0.8	61.6	-0.2	62.8	1.9	63.4	1.0	63.7	0.5	63.7	0.0
1973	62.7	-1.6	63.0	0.5	63.6	1.0	64.1	0.8	64.6	0.8	64.6	0.0	64.1	-0.8	64.5	0.6	65.4	1.4	66.1	1.1	66.5	0.6	66.5	0.0
1974	65.7	-1.2	66.5	1.2	67.4	1.4	68.1	1.0	68.8	1.0	69.2	0.6	69.0	-0.3	70.4	2.0	71.3	1.3	71.9	0.8	72.6	1.0	72.3	-0.4
1975	71.1	-1.7	71.5	0.6	71.8	0.4	72.0	0.3	72.3	0.4	72.1	-0.3	71.9	-0.3	72.5	0.8	73.2	1.0	73.7	0.7	74.2	0.7	74.0	-0.3
1976	73.1	-1.2	73.4	0.4	73.9	0.7	74.3	0.5	74.8	0.7	74.9	0.1	74.7	-0.3	75.5	1.1	76.6	1.5	76.9	0.4	77.4	0.7	77.4	0.0
1977	76.5	-1.2	76.9	0.5	77.3	0.5	77.6	0.4	78.2	0.8	78.5	0.4	78.2	-0.4	78.9	0.9	79.6	0.9	80.1	0.6	80.8	0.9	80.7	-0.1
1978	79.4	-1.6	78.8	-0.8	79.8	1.3	80.8	1.3	81.5	0.9	81.5	0.0	80.5	-1.2	81.4	1.1	82.5	1.4	83.3	1.0	83.7	0.5	83.2	-0.6
1979	81.9	-1.6	82.3	0.5	83.8	1.8	84.3	0.6	84.7	0.5	84.5	-0.2	83.8	-0.8	84.8	1.2	86.6	2.1	87.2	0.7	87.5	0.3	87.8	0.3
1980	87.2	-0.7	87.6	0.5	89.7	2.4	90.4	0.8	90.5	0.1	90.3	-0.2	89.8	-0.6	91.1	1.4	92.9	2.0	93.8	1.0	94.2	0.4	93.8	-0.4
1981	92.3	-1.6	92.8	0.5	94.4	1.7	95.0	0.6	95.0	0.0	94.7	-0.3	94.2	-0.5	95.5	1.4	97.2	1.8	97.6	0.4	97.5	-0.1	97.1	-0.4
1982	95.5	-1.6	95.8	0.3	97.4	1.7	97.8	0.4	97.6	-0.2	97.3	-0.3	96.7	-0.6	97.8	1.1	99.4	1.6	99.7	0.3	99.6	-0.1	98.7	-0.9
1983	97.4	-1.3	97.9	0.5	99.2	1.3	99.7	0.5	100.0	0.3	99.7	-0.3	99.4	-0.3	100.6	1.2	102.2	1.6	102.3	0.1	102.3	0.0	101.6	-0.7
1984	100.1	-1.5	100.0	-0.1	101.3	1.3	101.6	0.3	101.4	-0.2	100.6	-0.8	100.2	-0.4	102.0	1.8	104.1	2.1	104.9	0.8	104.6	-0.3	103.6	-1.0
1985	101.9	-1.6	102.9	1.0	104.7	1.7	105.0	0.3	104.7	-0.3	104.3	-0.4	103.4	-0.9	104.7	1.3	106.9	2.1	107.6	0.7	107.7	0.1	106.5	-1.1
1986	104.5	-1.9	104.1	-0.4	105.2	1.1	105.7	0.5	105.2	-0.5	104.3	-0.9	103.6	-0.7	105.5	1.8	108.1	2.5	108.7	0.6	108.6	-0.1	107.5	-1.0
1987	105.6	-1.8	106.2	0.6	109.7	3.3	111.5	1.6	111.1	-0.4	109.3	-1.6	107.3	-1.8	109.4	2.0	113.3	3.6	115.4	1.9	115.4	0.0	112.7	-2.3
1988	110.4	-2.0	110.2	-0.2	114.3	3.7	117.0	2.4	116.3	-0.6	114.6	-1.5	112.7	-1.7	112.6	-0.1	117.8	4.6	120.7	2.5	119.9	-0.7	118.0	-1.6
1989	115.3	-2.3	115.3	0.0	119.3	3.5	120.9	1.3	120.4	-0.4	117.8	-2.2	115.0	-2.4	115.0	0.0	120.0	4.3	122.7	2.2	122.1	-0.5	119.2	-2.4
1990	116.7	-2.1	120.4	3.2	125.4	4.2	126.7	1.0	125.5	-0.9	123.3	-1.8	120.8	-2.0	122.2	1.2	126.8	3.8	128.4	1.3	127.5	-0.7	125.3	-1.7
1991	123.8	-1.2	126.2	1.9	128.8	2.1	130.1	1.0	129.4	-0.5	126.9	-1.9	125.2	-1.3	127.6	1.9	131.3	2.9	132.7	1.1	132.9	0.2	129.6	-2.5
1992	127.9	-1.3	130.2	1.8	133.4	2.5	133.3	-0.1	133.1	-0.2	131.0	-1.6	129.2	-1.4	130.2	0.8	133.3	2.4	135.0	1.3	134.5	-0.4	131.4	-2.3
1993	129.7	-1.3	133.4	2.9	136.2	2.1	136.9	0.5	135.0	-1.4	131.9	-2.3	129.4	-1.9	131.9	1.9	134.6	2.0	136.1	1.1	136.2	0.1	132.6	-2.6
1994	130.4	-1.7	132.4	1.5	136.1	2.8	136.4	0.2	135.6	-0.6	133.8	-1.3	130.9	-2.2	131.1	0.2	134.2	2.4	135.2	0.7	134.2	-0.7	130.5	-2.8
1995	129.4	-0.8	131.1	1.3	134.4	2.5	134.8	0.3	133.4	-1.0	130.5	-2.2	128.3	-1.7	130.1	1.4	132.7	2.0	134.5	1.4	133.7	-0.6	130.6	-2.3

Source: U.S. Department of Labor, Bureau of Labor Statistics, Division of Consumer Prices and Price Indexes.

U.S. City Average
Consumer Price Index - Urban Wage Earners
Base 1982-1984 = 100
Apparel and Upkeep

For 1913-1995. Columns headed % show percentile change in the index from the previous period for which an index is available.

Year	Jan Index	%	Feb Index	%	Mar Index	%	Apr Index	%	May Index	%	Jun Index	%	Jul Index	%	Aug Index	%	Sep Index	%	Oct Index	%	Nov Index	%	Dec Index	%
1913	-	-	-	-	-	-	-	-	-	-	-	-	-	-	-	-	-	-	-	-	-	-	-	-
1914	-	-	-	-	-	-	-	-	-	-	-	-	-	-	-	-	-	-	-	-	-	-	15.1	-
1915	-	-	-	-	-	-	-	-	-	-	-	-	-	-	-	-	-	-	-	-	-	-	15.7	4.0
1916	-	-	-	-	-	-	-	-	-	-	-	-	-	-	-	-	-	-	-	-	-	-	18.0	14.6
1917	-	-	-	-	-	-	-	-	-	-	-	-	-	-	-	-	-	-	-	-	-	-	22.3	23.9
1918	-	-	-	-	-	-	-	-	-	-	-	-	-	-	-	-	-	-	-	-	-	-	31.9	43.0
1919	-	-	-	-	-	-	-	-	-	-	34.6	8.5	-	-	-	-	-	-	-	-	-	-	42.8	23.7
1920	-	-	-	-	-	-	-	-	-	-	45.2	5.6	-	-	-	-	-	-	-	-	-	-	40.5	-10.4
1921	-	-	-	-	-	-	-	-	34.8	-14.1	-	-	-	-	-	-	30.1	-13.5	-	-	-	-	28.7	-4.7
1922	-	-	-	-	27.5	-4.2	-	-	-	-	26.9	-2.2	-	-	-	-	26.7	-0.7	-	-	-	-	26.7	0.0
1923	-	-	-	-	27.1	1.5	-	-	-	-	27.2	0.4	-	-	-	-	27.4	0.7	-	-	-	-	27.4	0.0
1924	-	-	-	-	27.3	-0.4	-	-	-	-	27.0	-1.1	-	-	-	-	26.7	-1.1	-	-	-	-	26.5	-0.7
1925	-	-	-	-	-	-	-	-	-	-	26.5	0.0	-	-	-	-	-	-	-	-	-	-	26.3	-0.8
1926	-	-	-	-	-	-	-	-	-	-	26.1	-0.8	-	-	-	-	-	-	-	-	-	-	25.8	-1.1
1927	-	-	-	-	-	-	-	-	-	-	25.5	-1.2	-	-	-	-	-	-	-	-	-	-	25.2	-1.2
1928	-	-	-	-	-	-	-	-	-	-	25.2	0.0	-	-	-	-	-	-	-	-	-	-	25.0	-0.8
1929	-	-	-	-	-	-	-	-	-	-	24.8	-0.8	-	-	-	-	-	-	-	-	-	-	24.7	-0.4
1930	-	-	-	-	-	-	-	-	-	-	24.6	-0.4	-	-	-	-	-	-	-	-	-	-	23.6	-4.1
1931	-	-	-	-	-	-	-	-	-	-	22.3	-5.5	-	-	-	-	-	-	-	-	-	-	20.7	-7.2
1932	-	-	-	-	-	-	-	-	-	-	19.6	-5.3	-	-	-	-	-	-	-	-	-	-	18.6	-5.1
1933	-	-	-	-	-	-	-	-	-	-	18.3	-1.6	-	-	-	-	-	-	-	-	-	-	20.3	10.9
1934	-	-	-	-	-	-	-	-	-	-	20.8	2.5	-	-	-	-	-	-	-	-	20.8	0.0	-	-
1935	-	-	-	-	20.9	0.5	-	-	-	-	-	-	20.8	-0.5	-	-	-	-	21.0	1.0	-	-	-	-
1936	21.1	0.5	-	-	-	-	21.1	0.0	-	-	-	-	21.0	-0.5	-	-	21.1	0.5	-	-	-	-	21.4	1.4
1937	-	-	-	-	21.8	1.9	-	-	-	-	22.1	1.4	-	-	-	-	22.6	2.3	-	-	-	-	22.6	0.0
1938	-	-	-	-	22.2	-1.8	-	-	-	-	22.0	-0.9	-	-	-	-	21.8	-0.9	-	-	-	-	21.8	0.0
1939	-	-	-	-	21.7	-0.5	-	-	-	-	21.7	0.0	-	-	-	-	21.7	0.0	-	-	-	-	21.8	0.5
1940	-	-	-	-	22.0	0.9	-	-	-	-	21.9	-0.5	-	-	-	-	21.9	0.0	21.9	0.0	21.9	0.0	21.9	0.0
1941	21.7	-0.9	21.7	0.0	22.0	1.4	22.1	0.5	22.1	0.0	22.3	0.9	22.6	1.3	23.1	2.2	23.9	3.5	24.3	1.7	24.6	1.2	24.7	0.4
1942	25.1	1.6	25.7	2.4	26.7	3.9	27.3	2.2	27.3	0.0	27.0	-1.1	27.0	0.0	27.0	0.0	27.2	0.7	27.2	0.0	27.2	0.0	27.2	0.0
1943	27.3	0.4	27.3	0.0	27.5	0.7	27.6	0.4	27.6	0.0	27.6	0.0	27.9	1.1	28.0	0.4	28.6	2.1	28.7	0.3	28.8	0.3	29.1	1.0
1944	29.1	0.0	29.2	0.3	29.5	1.0	29.6	0.3	29.7	0.3	29.8	0.3	29.8	0.0	30.1	1.0	30.5	1.3	30.6	0.3	30.6	0.0	30.8	0.7
1945	30.9	0.3	30.9	0.0	31.0	0.3	31.0	0.0	31.2	0.6	31.4	0.6	31.5	0.3	31.6	0.3	32.0	1.3	32.0	0.0	32.1	0.3	32.3	0.6
1946	32.3	0.0	32.5	0.6	33.0	1.5	33.3	0.9	33.6	0.9	33.9	0.9	34.2	0.9	34.8	1.8	35.8	2.9	36.3	1.4	36.9	1.7	38.1	3.3
1947	38.6	1.3	39.1	1.3	39.7	1.5	39.9	0.5	39.9	0.0	40.1	0.5	39.8	-0.7	40.1	0.8	40.5	1.0	40.8	0.7	41.0	0.5	41.2	0.5
1948	41.5	0.7	42.1	1.4	42.3	0.5	42.4	0.2	42.6	0.5	42.5	-0.2	42.5	0.0	43.1	1.4	43.3	0.5	43.5	0.5	43.4	-0.2	43.3	-0.2
1949	42.4	-2.1	42.1	-0.7	41.9	-0.5	41.5	-1.0	41.3	-0.5	41.1	-0.5	40.7	-1.0	40.4	-0.7	40.4	0.0	40.3	-0.2	40.2	-0.2	40.1	-0.2
1950	39.9	-0.5	39.9	0.0	40.0	0.3	39.9	-0.2	39.8	-0.3	39.8	0.0	39.8	0.0	40.1	0.8	40.9	2.0	41.6	1.7	41.9	0.7	42.2	0.7
1951	42.8	1.4	43.6	1.9	43.9	0.7	44.0	0.2	44.0	0.0	44.0	0.0	43.9	-0.2	44.0	0.2	45.1	2.5	45.1	0.0	44.8	-0.7	44.6	-0.4
1952	44.2	-0.9	44.1	-0.2	44.0	-0.2	43.7	-0.7	43.7	0.0	43.6	-0.2	43.4	-0.5	43.3	-0.2	43.7	0.9	43.6	-0.2	43.4	-0.5	43.3	-0.2
1953	43.2	-0.2	43.2	0.0	43.2	0.0	43.2	0.0	43.3	0.2	43.3	0.0	43.3	0.0	43.2	-0.2	43.6	0.9	43.7	0.2	43.7	0.0	43.6	-0.2
1954	43.4	-0.5	43.3	-0.2	43.2	-0.2	43.1	-0.2	43.2	0.2	43.2	0.0	43.1	-0.2	43.0	-0.2	43.2	0.5	43.3	0.2	43.3	0.0	43.3	0.0
1955	42.9	-0.9	42.9	0.0	42.9	0.0	42.8	-0.2	42.9	0.2	42.9	0.0	42.9	0.0	43.0	0.2	43.4	0.9	43.4	0.0	43.5	0.2	43.5	0.0
1956	43.4	-0.2	43.6	0.5	43.6	0.0	43.7	0.2	43.7	0.0	43.7	0.0	43.9	0.5	44.0	0.2	44.4	0.9	44.5	0.2	44.6	0.2	44.6	0.0
1957	44.4	-0.4	44.4	0.0	44.6	0.5	44.5	-0.2	44.6	0.2	44.6	0.0	44.6	0.0	44.6	0.0	44.9	0.7	45.1	0.4	45.2	0.2	45.0	-0.4

[Continued]

U.S. City Average
Consumer Price Index - Urban Wage Earners
Base 1982-1984 = 100
Apparel and Upkeep
[Continued]

For 1913-1995. Columns headed % show percentile change in the index from the previous period for which an index is available.

Year	Jan Index	%	Feb Index	%	Mar Index	%	Apr Index	%	May Index	%	Jun Index	%	Jul Index	%	Aug Index	%	Sep Index	%	Oct Index	%	Nov Index	%	Dec Index	%
1958	44.8	-0.4	44.8	0.0	44.8	0.0	44.8	0.0	44.8	0.0	44.8	0.0	44.8	0.0	44.7	-0.2	44.9	0.4	45.0	0.2	45.2	0.4	45.1	-0.2
1959	44.8	-0.7	44.8	0.0	44.8	0.0	44.9	0.2	45.0	0.2	45.0	0.0	45.1	0.2	45.3	0.4	45.7	0.9	45.8	0.2	45.8	0.0	45.7	-0.2
1960	45.3	-0.9	45.5	0.4	45.6	0.2	45.7	0.2	45.7	0.0	45.7	0.0	45.8	0.2	45.9	0.2	46.4	1.1	46.6	0.4	46.5	-0.2	46.4	-0.2
1961	46.0	-0.9	46.1	0.2	46.1	0.0	46.1	0.0	46.1	0.0	46.1	0.0	46.2	0.2	46.2	0.0	46.7	1.1	46.7	0.0	46.7	0.0	46.6	-0.2
1962	46.0	-1.3	46.1	0.2	46.4	0.7	46.4	0.0	46.4	0.0	46.5	0.2	46.5	0.0	46.3	-0.4	47.1	1.7	47.2	0.2	47.0	-0.4	46.9	-0.2
1963	46.6	-0.6	46.7	0.2	46.8	0.2	46.9	0.2	46.9	0.0	47.0	0.2	47.0	0.0	47.0	0.0	47.4	0.9	47.6	0.4	47.7	0.2	47.7	0.0
1964	47.2	-1.0	47.2	0.0	47.3	0.2	47.4	0.2	47.5	0.2	47.5	0.0	47.4	-0.2	47.3	-0.2	47.6	0.6	47.7	0.2	47.8	0.2	47.9	0.2
1965	47.4	-1.0	47.5	0.2	47.6	0.2	47.7	0.2	48.0	0.6	48.1	0.2	47.7	-0.8	47.8	0.2	48.2	0.8	48.5	0.6	48.6	0.2	48.6	0.0
1966	48.2	-0.8	48.4	0.4	48.6	0.4	48.9	0.6	49.1	0.4	49.2	0.2	49.1	-0.2	49.1	0.0	49.7	1.2	50.1	0.8	50.3	0.4	50.5	0.4
1967	50.0	-1.0	50.3	0.6	50.6	0.6	50.8	0.4	51.1	0.6	51.2	0.2	51.1	-0.2	51.1	0.0	51.7	1.2	52.2	1.0	52.4	0.4	52.5	0.2
1968	52.1	-0.8	52.4	0.6	52.9	1.0	53.2	0.6	53.7	0.9	53.9	0.4	53.8	-0.2	54.0	0.4	54.9	1.7	55.4	0.9	55.7	0.5	55.8	0.2
1969	55.4	-0.7	55.7	0.5	56.1	0.7	56.5	0.7	56.9	0.7	57.1	0.4	57.0	-0.2	56.9	-0.2	57.8	1.6	58.3	0.9	58.7	0.7	58.8	0.2
1970	58.1	-1.2	58.4	0.5	58.7	0.5	58.9	0.3	59.3	0.7	59.4	0.2	59.1	-0.5	59.1	0.0	60.0	1.5	60.6	1.0	61.0	0.7	61.1	0.2
1971	60.2	-1.5	60.5	0.5	60.8	0.5	61.0	0.3	61.6	1.0	61.5	-0.2	61.1	-0.7	61.0	-0.2	61.8	1.3	62.3	0.8	62.4	0.2	62.4	0.0
1972	61.6	-1.3	61.8	0.3	62.1	0.5	62.4	0.5	62.8	0.6	62.5	-0.5	62.0	-0.8	61.9	-0.2	63.1	1.9	63.7	1.0	64.0	0.5	64.0	0.0
1973	63.0	-1.6	63.3	0.5	63.9	0.9	64.4	0.8	64.9	0.8	65.0	0.2	64.4	-0.9	64.8	0.6	65.7	1.4	66.4	1.1	66.9	0.8	66.9	0.0
1974	66.0	-1.3	66.8	1.2	67.7	1.3	68.4	1.0	69.2	1.2	69.5	0.4	69.3	-0.3	70.7	2.0	71.7	1.4	72.3	0.8	72.9	0.8	72.7	-0.3
1975	71.4	-1.8	71.8	0.6	72.2	0.6	72.4	0.3	72.6	0.3	72.4	-0.3	72.3	-0.1	72.9	0.8	73.5	0.8	74.1	0.8	74.5	0.5	74.4	-0.1
1976	73.4	-1.3	73.8	0.5	74.3	0.7	74.6	0.4	75.2	0.8	75.3	0.1	75.0	-0.4	75.9	1.2	76.9	1.3	77.3	0.5	77.8	0.6	77.8	0.0
1977	76.8	-1.3	77.3	0.7	77.7	0.5	78.0	0.4	78.6	0.8	78.8	0.3	78.6	-0.3	79.3	0.9	80.0	0.9	80.5	0.6	81.2	0.9	81.0	-0.2
1978	79.6	-1.7	79.1	-0.6	79.9	1.0	81.0	1.4	81.8	1.0	81.9	0.1	81.0	-1.1	81.8	1.0	82.9	1.3	83.8	1.1	84.0	0.2	83.7	-0.4
1979	82.5	-1.4	82.8	0.4	84.1	1.6	84.7	0.7	84.9	0.2	84.7	-0.2	84.3	-0.5	85.1	0.9	86.7	1.9	87.5	0.9	87.8	0.3	87.8	0.0
1980	87.0	-0.9	87.9	1.0	89.7	2.0	90.2	0.6	90.6	0.4	90.2	-0.4	89.9	-0.3	91.1	1.3	92.9	2.0	93.6	0.8	93.9	0.3	93.7	-0.2
1981	92.6	-1.2	93.1	0.5	94.4	1.4	95.3	1.0	95.4	0.1	95.2	-0.2	95.0	-0.2	96.3	1.4	97.6	1.3	97.6	0.0	97.6	0.0	97.0	-0.6
1982	95.5	-1.5	96.0	0.5	97.6	1.7	97.9	0.3	97.6	-0.3	97.1	-0.5	96.7	-0.4	97.7	1.0	99.4	1.7	99.7	0.3	99.6	-0.1	98.8	-0.8
1983	97.3	-1.5	97.8	0.5	99.4	1.6	99.8	0.4	100.0	0.2	99.7	-0.3	99.4	-0.3	100.6	1.2	102.1	1.5	102.4	0.3	102.3	-0.1	101.5	-0.8
1984	100.0	-1.5	100.1	0.1	101.4	1.3	101.5	0.1	101.3	-0.2	100.5	-0.8	100.0	-0.5	101.9	1.9	104.1	2.2	104.9	0.8	104.6	-0.3	103.5	-1.1
1985	101.7	-1.7	102.8	1.1	104.6	1.8	105.0	0.4	104.6	-0.4	104.4	-0.2	103.4	-1.0	104.7	1.3	106.9	2.1	107.7	0.7	107.7	0.0	106.6	-1.0
1986	104.6	-1.9	104.0	-0.6	105.1	1.1	105.6	0.5	105.1	-0.5	104.0	-1.0	103.4	-0.6	105.5	2.0	108.1	2.5	108.6	0.5	108.3	-0.3	107.4	-0.8
1987	105.4	-1.9	106.0	0.6	109.5	3.3	111.4	1.7	110.9	-0.4	109.1	-1.6	107.1	-1.8	109.1	1.9	112.9	3.5	115.2	2.0	115.2	0.0	112.6	-2.3
1988	110.3	-2.0	110.0	-0.3	113.9	3.5	116.3	2.1	115.7	-0.5	114.1	-1.4	112.4	-1.5	112.2	-0.2	117.2	4.5	120.1	2.5	119.5	-0.5	117.6	-1.6
1989	114.8	-2.4	114.7	-0.1	118.4	3.2	120.0	1.4	119.4	-0.5	116.9	-2.1	114.4	-2.1	114.5	0.1	119.3	4.2	122.0	2.3	121.4	-0.5	118.5	-2.4
1990	116.1	-2.0	119.3	2.8	124.4	4.3	125.8	1.1	124.7	-0.9	122.4	-1.8	119.8	-2.1	121.3	1.3	125.7	3.6	127.1	1.1	126.5	-0.5	124.5	-1.6
1991	122.9	-1.3	124.8	1.5	127.5	2.2	128.8	1.0	127.9	-0.7	125.7	-1.7	124.1	-1.3	126.4	1.9	129.7	2.6	131.1	1.1	131.4	0.2	128.4	-2.3
1992	126.8	-1.2	128.8	1.6	132.1	2.6	132.1	0.0	131.8	-0.2	129.8	-1.5	128.1	-1.3	129.5	1.1	132.1	2.0	133.8	1.3	133.4	-0.3	130.4	-2.2
1993	128.4	-1.5	132.0	2.8	134.8	2.1	135.2	0.3	133.6	-1.2	130.7	-2.2	128.4	-1.8	130.5	1.6	133.3	2.1	135.1	1.4	135.0	-0.1	131.3	-2.7
1994	129.4	-1.4	131.4	1.5	134.7	2.5	135.0	0.2	134.3	-0.5	132.4	-1.4	129.8	-2.0	130.2	0.3	133.1	2.2	133.9	0.6	133.0	-0.7	129.3	-2.8
1995	128.3	-0.8	130.0	1.3	133.2	2.5	133.6	0.3	132.1	-1.1	129.6	-1.9	127.4	-1.7	129.1	1.3	131.6	1.9	133.4	1.4	132.5	-0.7	129.5	-2.3

Source: U.S. Department of Labor, Bureau of Labor Statistics, Division of Consumer Prices and Price Indexes.

U.S. City Average

Consumer Price Index - All Urban Consumers
Base 1982-1984 = 100
Transportation

For 1935-1995. Columns headed % show percentile change in the index from the previous period for which an index is available.

Year	Jan Index	%	Feb Index	%	Mar Index	%	Apr Index	%	May Index	%	Jun Index	%	Jul Index	%	Aug Index	%	Sep Index	%	Oct Index	%	Nov Index	%	Dec Index	%
1935	-	-	-	-	14.2	-	-	-	-	-	-	-	14.3	0.7	-	-	-	-	14.1	-1.4	-	-	-	-
1936	14.1	0.0	-	-	-	-	14.3	1.4	-	-	-	-	14.3	0.0	-	-	14.3	0.0	-	-	-	-	14.3	0.0
1937	-	-	-	-	14.5	1.4	-	-	-	-	14.5	0.0	-	-	-	-	14.6	0.7	-	-	-	-	14.7	0.7
1938	-	-	-	-	14.7	0.0	-	-	-	-	14.7	0.0	-	-	-	-	14.7	0.0	-	-	-	-	14.4	-2.0
1939	-	-	-	-	14.3	-0.7	-	-	-	-	14.3	0.0	-	-	-	-	14.3	0.0	-	-	-	-	14.3	0.0
1940	-	-	-	-	14.3	0.0	-	-	-	-	14.1	-1.4	-	-	-	-	14.2	0.7	-	-	-	-	14.3	0.7
1941	-	-	-	-	14.3	0.0	-	-	-	-	14.6	2.1	-	-	-	-	14.8	1.4	-	-	-	-	15.4	4.1
1942	-	-	-	-	16.0	3.9	-	-	-	-	16.1	0.6	-	-	-	-	16.0	-0.6	-	-	-	-	16.0	0.0
1943	-	-	-	-	16.0	0.0	-	-	-	-	15.9	-0.6	-	-	-	-	15.9	0.0	-	-	-	-	15.9	0.0
1944	-	-	-	-	15.9	0.0	-	-	-	-	15.9	0.0	-	-	-	-	15.9	0.0	-	-	-	-	15.9	0.0
1945	-	-	-	-	15.9	0.0	-	-	-	-	15.9	0.0	-	-	-	-	15.9	0.0	-	-	-	-	15.9	0.0
1946	-	-	-	-	16.0	0.6	-	-	-	-	16.2	1.3	-	-	-	-	17.5	8.0	-	-	-	-	17.9	2.3
1947	17.9	0.0	17.9	0.0	18.1	1.1	18.2	0.6	18.3	0.5	18.3	0.0	18.4	0.5	18.5	0.5	18.7	1.1	18.9	1.1	19.0	0.5	19.2	1.1
1948	19.5	1.6	19.6	0.5	19.6	0.0	19.8	1.0	19.8	0.0	19.9	0.5	21.0	5.5	21.4	1.9	21.5	0.5	21.6	0.5	21.6	0.0	21.6	0.0
1949	21.6	0.0	21.8	0.9	21.9	0.5	22.0	0.5	22.1	0.5	22.0	-0.5	22.1	0.5	22.3	0.9	22.3	0.0	22.4	0.4	22.4	0.0	22.5	0.4
1950	22.5	0.0	22.4	-0.4	22.4	0.0	22.3	-0.4	22.4	0.4	22.4	0.0	22.7	1.3	22.9	0.9	23.0	0.4	22.9	-0.4	23.0	0.4	23.3	1.3
1951	23.4	0.4	23.6	0.9	23.8	0.8	23.9	0.4	24.0	0.4	24.0	0.0	24.0	0.0	24.2	0.8	24.4	0.8	24.6	0.8	24.9	1.2	24.9	0.0
1952	25.0	0.4	25.2	0.8	25.4	0.8	25.4	0.0	25.5	0.4	25.7	0.8	25.9	0.8	25.9	0.0	26.0	0.4	26.2	0.8	26.3	0.4	26.3	0.0
1953	26.4	0.4	26.3	-0.4	26.4	0.4	26.4	0.0	26.4	0.0	26.4	0.0	26.5	0.4	26.6	0.4	26.7	0.4	26.7	0.0	26.5	-0.7	26.3	-0.8
1954	26.6	1.1	26.4	-0.8	26.3	-0.4	26.3	0.0	26.3	0.0	26.3	0.0	25.8	-1.9	25.8	0.0	25.8	0.0	25.5	-1.2	26.0	2.0	25.9	-0.4
1955	26.0	0.4	26.0	0.0	25.9	-0.4	25.5	-1.5	25.6	0.4	25.6	0.0	25.6	0.0	25.6	0.0	25.5	-0.4	25.8	1.2	26.2	1.6	25.9	-1.1
1956	25.9	0.0	25.9	0.0	25.8	-0.4	25.8	0.0	25.9	0.4	25.9	0.0	26.0	0.4	26.2	0.8	26.2	0.0	27.0	3.1	27.1	0.4	27.1	0.0
1957	27.2	0.4	27.4	0.7	27.5	0.4	27.6	0.4	27.5	-0.4	27.5	0.0	27.7	0.7	27.7	0.0	27.7	0.0	27.7	0.0	28.5	2.9	28.3	-0.7
1958	28.2	-0.4	28.2	0.0	28.2	0.0	28.2	0.0	28.2	0.0	28.3	0.4	28.6	1.1	28.7	0.3	28.8	0.3	29.1	1.0	29.4	1.0	29.4	0.0
1959	29.4	0.0	29.4	0.0	29.5	0.3	29.6	0.3	29.6	0.0	29.7	0.3	29.8	0.3	29.9	0.3	29.8	-0.3	30.2	1.3	30.3	0.3	30.3	0.0
1960	30.1	-0.7	30.0	-0.3	29.8	-0.7	29.8	0.0	29.6	-0.7	29.7	0.3	29.7	0.0	29.8	0.3	29.5	-1.0	29.8	1.0	29.8	0.0	29.8	0.0
1961	29.8	0.0	29.8	0.0	29.7	-0.3	29.7	0.0	29.8	0.3	30.1	1.0	30.2	0.3	30.4	0.7	30.4	0.0	30.6	0.7	30.6	0.0	30.4	-0.7
1962	30.4	0.0	30.4	0.0	30.4	0.0	30.8	1.3	30.8	0.0	30.8	0.0	30.6	-0.6	30.8	0.7	30.9	0.3	31.0	0.3	31.1	0.3	31.0	-0.3
1963	30.6	-1.3	30.6	0.0	30.7	0.3	30.7	0.0	30.8	0.3	30.8	0.0	30.9	0.3	31.1	0.6	31.0	-0.3	31.3	1.0	31.3	0.0	31.3	0.0
1964	31.4	0.3	31.2	-0.6	31.3	0.3	31.3	0.0	31.3	0.0	31.3	0.0	31.4	0.3	31.4	0.0	31.3	-0.3	31.4	0.3	31.6	0.6	31.7	0.3
1965	31.9	0.6	31.7	-0.6	31.7	0.0	31.9	0.6	32.0	0.3	31.9	-0.3	32.0	0.3	31.9	-0.3	31.9	0.0	31.9	0.0	32.0	0.3	32.0	0.0
1966	31.9	-0.3	31.9	0.0	32.0	0.3	32.1	0.3	32.1	0.0	32.2	0.3	32.6	1.2	32.6	0.0	32.5	-0.3	32.8	0.9	32.9	0.3	32.7	-0.6
1967	32.5	-0.6	32.7	0.6	32.8	0.3	33.0	0.6	33.2	0.6	33.2	0.0	33.4	0.6	33.4	0.0	33.5	0.3	33.8	0.9	34.0	0.6	33.8	-0.6
1968	34.1	0.9	34.0	-0.3	34.2	0.6	34.2	0.0	34.2	0.0	34.4	0.6	34.4	0.0	34.4	0.0	34.3	-0.3	34.6	0.9	34.8	0.6	34.5	-0.9
1969	34.6	0.3	35.0	1.2	35.7	2.0	35.8	0.3	35.6	-0.6	35.8	0.6	35.7	-0.3	35.7	0.0	35.5	-0.6	36.1	1.7	36.1	0.0	36.3	0.6
1970	36.5	0.6	36.5	0.0	36.5	0.0	37.0	1.4	37.3	0.8	37.5	0.5	37.7	0.5	37.5	-0.5	37.6	0.3	38.3	1.9	38.6	0.8	38.9	0.8
1971	39.1	0.5	39.1	0.0	39.2	0.3	39.3	0.3	39.5	0.5	39.8	0.8	39.7	-0.3	39.7	0.0	39.5	-0.5	39.7	0.5	39.5	-0.5	39.4	-0.3
1972	39.6	0.5	39.4	-0.5	39.4	0.0	39.5	0.3	39.8	0.8	39.9	0.3	40.0	0.3	40.1	0.2	40.3	0.5	40.3	0.0	40.4	0.2	40.4	0.0
1973	40.3	-0.2	40.3	0.0	40.4	0.2	40.8	1.0	41.1	0.7	41.5	1.0	41.5	0.0	41.4	-0.2	41.2	-0.5	41.6	1.0	41.9	0.7	42.2	0.7
1974	42.6	0.9	43.0	0.9	43.9	2.1	44.5	1.4	45.4	2.0	46.2	1.8	46.8	1.3	47.0	0.4	47.3	0.6	47.5	0.4	47.7	0.4	47.7	0.0
1975	47.6	-0.2	47.7	0.2	48.2	1.0	48.6	0.8	49.0	0.8	49.8	1.6	50.8	2.0	51.1	0.6	51.7	1.2	51.9	0.4	52.4	1.0	52.4	0.0
1976	52.6	0.4	52.7	0.2	53.2	0.9	53.7	0.9	54.4	1.3	55.2	1.5	55.8	1.1	56.1	0.5	56.4	0.5	56.9	0.9	57.0	0.2	57.0	0.0
1977	57.3	0.5	57.6	0.5	58.1	0.9	58.8	1.2	59.3	0.9	59.6	0.5	59.6	0.0	59.5	-0.2	59.4	-0.2	59.4	0.0	59.5	0.2	59.5	0.0
1978	59.6	0.2	59.7	0.2	59.9	0.3	60.3	0.7	61.0	1.2	61.7	1.1	62.3	1.0	62.6	0.5	62.8	0.3	63.1	0.5	63.7	1.0	64.1	0.6
1979	64.5	0.6	65.1	0.9	65.9	1.2	67.5	2.4	69.1	2.4	70.7	2.3	72.1	2.0	73.1	1.4	73.7	0.8	74.1	0.5	74.8	0.9	75.8	1.3

[Continued]

U.S. City Average
Consumer Price Index - All Urban Consumers
Base 1982-1984 = 100
Transportation

[Continued]

For 1935-1995. Columns headed % show percentile change in the index from the previous period for which an index is available.

Year	Jan Index	%	Feb Index	%	Mar Index	%	Apr Index	%	May Index	%	Jun Index	%	Jul Index	%	Aug Index	%	Sep Index	%	Oct Index	%	Nov Index	%	Dec Index	%
1980	77.7	2.5	79.7	2.6	81.1	1.8	82.1	1.2	82.8	0.9	83.1	0.4	83.5	0.5	84.1	0.7	84.7	0.7	85.2	0.6	86.2	1.2	86.9	0.8
1981	88.1	1.4	90.1	2.3	91.0	1.0	91.6	0.7	92.4	0.9	93.1	0.8	94.0	1.0	94.4	0.4	94.9	0.5	95.6	0.7	96.2	0.6	96.4	0.2
1982	96.5	0.1	95.8	-0.7	94.9	-0.9	94.1	-0.8	95.0	1.0	97.4	2.5	98.5	1.1	98.6	0.1	98.3	-0.3	98.3	0.0	98.4	0.1	98.1	-0.3
1983	97.5	-0.6	96.5	-1.0	95.6	-0.9	97.3	1.8	98.6	1.3	99.3	0.7	100.0	0.7	100.6	0.6	101.0	0.4	101.5	0.5	101.9	0.4	101.9	0.0
1984	101.8	-0.1	101.7	-0.1	102.1	0.4	103.0	0.9	103.9	0.9	104.2	0.3	104.1	-0.1	104.1	0.0	104.4	0.3	105.0	0.6	105.2	0.2	105.1	-0.1
1985	104.7	-0.4	104.6	-0.1	105.4	0.8	106.5	1.0	106.9	0.4	107.1	0.2	107.1	0.0	106.7	-0.4	106.4	-0.3	106.8	0.4	107.5	0.7	107.8	0.3
1986	107.8	0.0	106.2	-1.5	103.0	-3.0	100.9	-2.0	101.7	0.8	102.7	1.0	101.4	-1.3	100.3	-1.1	100.5	0.2	100.7	0.2	101.2	0.5	101.4	0.2
1987	102.6	1.2	103.1	0.5	103.3	0.2	104.2	0.9	104.7	0.5	105.4	0.7	106.0	0.6	106.5	0.5	106.6	0.1	107.1	0.5	107.8	0.7	107.6	-0.2
1988	107.1	-0.5	106.8	-0.3	106.5	-0.3	107.2	0.7	108.1	0.8	108.5	0.4	108.9	0.4	109.6	0.6	109.7	0.1	110.0	0.3	110.7	0.6	110.8	0.1
1989	111.1	0.3	111.6	0.5	111.9	0.3	114.6	2.4	116.0	1.2	115.9	-0.1	115.4	-0.4	114.3	-1.0	113.7	-0.5	114.5	0.7	115.0	0.4	115.2	0.2
1990	117.2	1.7	117.1	-0.1	116.8	-0.3	117.3	0.4	117.7	0.3	118.2	0.4	118.4	0.2	120.6	1.9	123.0	2.0	125.8	2.3	126.9	0.9	127.2	0.2
1991	125.5	-1.3	123.7	-1.4	122.3	-1.1	122.2	-0.1	123.3	0.9	123.7	0.3	123.4	-0.2	123.8	0.3	123.8	0.0	124.0	0.2	125.0	0.8	125.3	0.2
1992	124.5	-0.6	124.1	-0.3	124.4	0.2	125.2	0.6	126.3	0.9	126.9	0.5	127.2	0.2	126.9	-0.2	126.8	-0.1	128.0	0.9	129.2	0.9	129.0	-0.2
1993	129.1	0.1	129.2	0.1	129.0	-0.2	129.4	0.3	130.2	0.6	130.3	0.1	130.3	0.0	130.2	-0.1	130.1	-0.1	131.8	1.3	132.6	0.6	132.1	-0.4
1994	131.6	-0.4	131.9	0.2	132.2	0.2	132.6	0.3	132.8	0.2	133.8	0.8	134.6	0.6	135.9	1.0	135.9	0.0	136.1	0.1	137.1	0.7	137.1	0.0
1995	137.3	0.1	137.5	0.1	138.0	0.4	139.1	0.8	140.3	0.9	141.1	0.6	140.1	-0.7	139.2	-0.6	138.8	-0.3	139.4	0.4	139.4	0.0	139.1	-0.2

Source: U.S. Department of Labor, Bureau of Labor Statistics, Division of Consumer Prices and Price Indexes.

U.S. City Average
Consumer Price Index - Urban Wage Earners
Base 1982-1984 = 100
Transportation

For 1935-1995. Columns headed % show percentile change in the index from the previous period for which an index is available.

Year	Jan Index	%	Feb Index	%	Mar Index	%	Apr Index	%	May Index	%	Jun Index	%	Jul Index	%	Aug Index	%	Sep Index	%	Oct Index	%	Nov Index	%	Dec Index	%
1935	-	-	-	-	14.1	-	-	-	-	-	-	-	14.2	0.7	-	-	-	-	14.0	-1.4	-	-	-	-
1936	14.1	0.7	-	-	-	-	14.2	0.7	-	-	-	-	14.3	0.7	-	-	14.3	0.0	-	-	-	-	14.3	0.0
1937	-	-	-	-	14.4	0.7	-	-	-	-	14.4	0.0	-	-	-	-	14.5	0.7	-	-	-	-	14.6	0.7
1938	-	-	-	-	14.6	0.0	-	-	-	-	14.6	0.0	-	-	-	-	14.6	0.0	-	-	-	-	14.3	-2.1
1939	-	-	-	-	14.2	-0.7	-	-	-	-	14.2	0.0	-	-	-	-	14.3	0.7	-	-	-	-	14.2	-0.7
1940	-	-	-	-	14.2	0.0	-	-	-	-	14.1	-0.7	-	-	-	-	14.1	0.0	-	-	-	-	14.2	0.7
1941	-	-	-	-	14.3	0.7	-	-	-	-	14.6	2.1	-	-	-	-	14.7	0.7	-	-	-	-	15.3	4.1
1942	-	-	-	-	15.9	3.9	-	-	-	-	16.0	0.6	-	-	-	-	15.9	-0.6	-	-	-	-	15.9	0.0
1943	-	-	-	-	15.9	0.0	-	-	-	-	15.8	-0.6	-	-	-	-	15.8	0.0	-	-	-	-	15.8	0.0
1944	-	-	-	-	15.8	0.0	-	-	-	-	15.8	0.0	-	-	-	-	15.8	0.0	-	-	-	-	15.8	0.0
1945	-	-	-	-	15.8	0.0	-	-	-	-	15.8	0.0	-	-	-	-	15.8	0.0	-	-	-	-	15.8	0.0
1946	-	-	-	-	15.9	0.6	-	-	-	-	16.1	1.3	-	-	-	-	17.4	8.1	-	-	-	-	17.8	2.3
1947	17.8	0.0	17.8	0.0	18.0	1.1	18.1	0.6	18.2	0.6	18.2	0.0	18.3	0.5	18.4	0.5	18.6	1.1	18.8	1.1	18.9	0.5	19.1	1.1
1948	19.4	1.6	19.4	0.0	19.4	0.0	19.7	1.5	19.7	0.0	19.8	0.5	20.8	5.1	21.2	1.9	21.3	0.5	21.5	0.9	21.5	0.0	21.5	0.0
1949	21.5	0.0	21.7	0.9	21.8	0.5	21.9	0.5	22.0	0.5	21.9	-0.5	22.0	0.5	22.2	0.9	22.2	0.0	22.3	0.5	22.2	-0.4	22.4	0.9
1950	22.3	-0.4	22.3	0.0	22.2	-0.4	22.2	0.0	22.3	0.5	22.3	0.0	22.5	0.9	22.8	1.3	22.8	0.0	22.8	0.0	22.9	0.4	23.1	0.9
1951	23.2	0.4	23.5	1.3	23.7	0.9	23.7	0.0	23.8	0.4	23.8	0.0	23.8	0.0	24.0	0.8	24.2	0.8	24.4	0.8	24.7	1.2	24.7	0.0
1952	24.9	0.8	25.1	0.8	25.2	0.4	25.3	0.4	25.3	0.0	25.6	1.2	25.7	0.4	25.7	0.0	25.9	0.8	26.0	0.4	26.1	0.4	26.1	0.0
1953	26.2	0.4	26.1	-0.4	26.2	0.4	26.2	0.0	26.2	0.0	26.2	0.0	26.3	0.4	26.5	0.8	26.5	0.0	26.5	0.0	26.3	-0.8	26.1	-0.8
1954	26.4	1.1	26.2	-0.8	26.1	-0.4	26.1	0.0	26.1	0.0	26.1	0.0	25.7	-1.5	25.7	0.0	25.6	-0.4	25.3	-1.2	25.9	2.4	25.8	-0.4
1955	25.9	0.4	25.8	-0.4	25.8	0.0	25.4	-1.6	25.4	0.0	25.5	0.4	25.4	-0.4	25.4	0.0	25.4	0.0	25.7	1.2	26.0	1.2	25.8	-0.8
1956	25.7	-0.4	25.7	0.0	25.7	0.0	25.6	-0.4	25.7	0.4	25.7	0.0	25.9	0.8	26.0	0.4	26.1	0.4	26.9	3.1	27.0	0.4	27.0	0.0
1957	27.1	0.4	27.2	0.4	27.4	0.7	27.5	0.4	27.4	-0.4	27.4	0.0	27.5	0.4	27.6	0.4	27.6	0.0	27.5	-0.4	28.4	3.3	28.1	-1.1
1958	28.1	0.0	28.1	0.0	28.1	0.0	28.0	-0.4	28.1	0.4	28.1	0.0	28.4	1.1	28.6	0.7	28.6	0.0	28.9	1.0	29.3	1.4	29.2	-0.3
1959	29.2	0.0	29.2	0.0	29.3	0.3	29.4	0.3	29.4	0.0	29.5	0.3	29.6	0.3	29.7	0.3	29.6	-0.3	30.1	1.7	30.2	0.3	30.1	-0.3
1960	29.9	-0.7	29.9	0.0	29.7	-0.7	29.6	-0.3	29.5	-0.3	29.5	0.0	29.5	0.0	29.6	0.3	29.3	-1.0	29.6	1.0	29.7	0.3	29.7	0.0
1961	29.6	-0.3	29.6	0.0	29.5	-0.3	29.5	0.0	29.7	0.7	29.9	0.7	30.1	0.7	30.3	0.7	30.3	0.0	30.5	0.7	30.5	0.0	30.3	-0.7
1962	30.3	0.0	30.3	0.0	30.2	-0.3	30.6	1.3	30.6	0.0	30.6	0.0	30.5	-0.3	30.7	0.7	30.8	0.3	30.9	0.3	30.9	0.0	30.8	-0.3
1963	30.4	-1.3	30.5	0.3	30.5	0.0	30.5	0.0	30.7	0.7	30.7	0.0	30.8	0.3	30.9	0.3	30.8	-0.3	31.1	1.0	31.1	0.0	31.1	0.0
1964	31.2	0.3	31.0	-0.6	31.1	0.3	31.1	0.0	31.1	0.0	31.2	0.3	31.2	0.0	31.2	0.0	31.1	-0.3	31.2	0.3	31.4	0.6	31.5	0.3
1965	31.7	0.6	31.6	-0.3	31.6	0.0	31.7	0.3	31.8	0.3	31.7	-0.3	31.8	0.3	31.7	-0.3	31.7	0.0	31.7	0.0	31.8	0.3	31.9	0.3
1966	31.7	-0.6	31.7	0.0	31.8	0.3	32.0	0.6	32.0	0.0	32.0	0.0	32.4	1.3	32.4	0.0	32.4	0.0	32.6	0.6	32.7	0.3	32.5	-0.6
1967	32.4	-0.3	32.5	0.3	32.6	0.3	32.8	0.6	33.0	0.6	33.0	0.0	33.2	0.6	33.2	0.0	33.3	0.3	33.6	0.9	33.8	0.6	33.6	-0.6
1968	33.9	0.9	33.8	-0.3	34.0	0.6	34.0	0.0	34.0	0.0	34.2	0.6	34.2	0.0	34.2	0.0	34.1	-0.3	34.4	0.9	34.6	0.6	34.3	-0.9
1969	34.4	0.3	34.8	1.2	35.5	2.0	35.6	0.3	35.4	-0.6	35.6	0.6	35.5	-0.3	35.5	0.0	35.3	-0.6	35.9	1.7	35.9	0.0	36.1	0.6
1970	36.3	0.6	36.3	0.0	36.3	0.0	36.8	1.4	37.1	0.8	37.3	0.5	37.5	0.5	37.3	-0.5	37.4	0.3	38.1	1.9	38.4	0.8	38.7	0.8
1971	38.9	0.5	38.9	0.0	39.0	0.3	39.1	0.3	39.3	0.5	39.6	0.8	39.5	-0.3	39.5	0.0	39.2	-0.8	39.5	0.8	39.3	-0.5	39.2	-0.3
1972	39.3	0.3	39.1	-0.5	39.2	0.3	39.2	0.0	39.5	0.8	39.6	0.3	39.8	0.5	39.9	0.3	40.0	0.3	40.1	0.2	40.2	0.2	40.1	-0.2
1973	40.0	-0.2	40.1	0.2	40.2	0.2	40.6	1.0	40.9	0.7	41.2	0.7	41.3	0.2	41.2	-0.2	41.0	-0.5	41.3	0.7	41.6	0.7	41.9	0.7
1974	42.4	1.2	42.8	0.9	43.7	2.1	44.2	1.1	45.1	2.0	45.9	1.8	46.5	1.3	46.7	0.4	47.0	0.6	47.3	0.6	47.4	0.2	47.5	0.2
1975	47.4	-0.2	47.5	0.2	47.9	0.8	48.4	1.0	48.8	0.8	49.6	1.6	50.5	1.8	50.8	0.6	51.4	1.2	51.6	0.4	52.1	1.0	52.1	0.0
1976	52.3	0.4	52.4	0.2	52.9	1.0	53.4	0.9	54.1	1.3	54.9	1.5	55.4	0.9	55.7	0.5	56.1	0.7	56.5	0.7	56.7	0.4	56.7	0.0
1977	57.0	0.5	57.3	0.5	57.8	0.9	58.4	1.0	58.9	0.9	59.2	0.5	59.3	0.2	59.1	-0.3	59.0	-0.2	59.1	0.2	59.1	0.0	59.1	0.0
1978	59.2	0.2	59.4	0.3	59.5	0.2	60.0	0.8	60.7	1.2	61.5	1.3	62.1	1.0	62.4	0.5	62.6	0.3	62.9	0.5	63.5	1.0	63.9	0.6
1979	64.3	0.6	64.9	0.9	65.7	1.2	67.4	2.6	69.0	2.4	70.7	2.5	72.0	1.8	73.0	1.4	73.6	0.8	73.9	0.4	74.7	1.1	75.5	1.1

[Continued]

U.S. City Average
Consumer Price Index - Urban Wage Earners
Base 1982-1984 = 100
Transportation
[Continued]

For 1935-1995. Columns headed % show percentile change in the index from the previous period for which an index is available.

Year	Jan Index	%	Feb Index	%	Mar Index	%	Apr Index	%	May Index	%	Jun Index	%	Jul Index	%	Aug Index	%	Sep Index	%	Oct Index	%	Nov Index	%	Dec Index	%
1980	77.4	2.5	79.5	2.7	80.8	1.6	81.9	1.4	82.7	1.0	82.9	0.2	83.3	0.5	83.9	0.7	84.4	0.6	84.9	0.6	85.9	1.2	86.6	0.8
1981	87.9	1.5	90.0	2.4	90.8	0.9	91.4	0.7	92.3	1.0	92.9	0.7	93.9	1.1	94.3	0.4	94.8	0.5	95.6	0.8	96.2	0.6	96.4	0.2
1982	96.5	0.1	95.8	-0.7	94.8	-1.0	94.0	-0.8	95.0	1.1	97.4	2.5	98.5	1.1	98.6	0.1	98.2	-0.4	98.2	0.0	98.3	0.1	98.0	-0.3
1983	97.3	-0.7	96.3	-1.0	95.5	-0.8	97.1	1.7	98.4	1.3	99.1	0.7	99.9	0.8	100.6	0.7	101.1	0.5	101.5	0.4	101.9	0.4	101.9	0.0
1984	101.8	-0.1	101.8	0.0	102.2	0.4	103.2	1.0	104.1	0.9	104.4	0.3	104.3	-0.1	104.3	0.0	104.5	0.2	105.1	0.6	105.3	0.2	105.2	-0.1
1985	104.8	-0.4	104.6	-0.2	105.4	0.8	106.5	1.0	106.9	0.4	107.0	0.1	107.0	0.0	106.6	-0.4	106.2	-0.4	106.6	0.4	107.4	0.8	107.6	0.2
1986	107.5	-0.1	105.9	-1.5	102.6	-3.1	100.4	-2.1	101.2	0.8	102.1	0.9	100.8	-1.3	99.5	-1.3	99.8	0.3	100.0	0.2	100.6	0.6	100.6	0.0
1987	101.9	1.3	102.5	0.6	102.8	0.3	103.8	1.0	104.4	0.6	105.1	0.7	105.8	0.7	106.3	0.5	106.4	0.1	106.9	0.5	107.6	0.7	107.3	-0.3
1988	106.8	-0.5	106.4	-0.4	106.2	-0.2	106.8	0.6	107.8	0.9	108.2	0.4	108.6	0.4	109.4	0.7	109.4	0.0	109.8	0.4	110.3	0.5	110.4	0.1
1989	110.7	0.3	111.2	0.5	111.6	0.4	114.5	2.6	116.0	1.3	116.0	0.0	115.4	-0.5	114.2	-1.0	113.5	-0.6	114.3	0.7	114.6	0.3	114.8	0.2
1990	116.8	1.7	116.6	-0.2	116.2	-0.3	116.6	0.3	117.1	0.4	117.7	0.5	117.8	0.1	120.3	2.1	122.9	2.2	125.7	2.3	126.6	0.7	126.7	0.1
1991	124.7	-1.6	122.6	-1.7	121.2	-1.1	121.3	0.1	122.7	1.2	123.1	0.3	122.9	-0.2	123.2	0.2	123.3	0.1	123.4	0.1	124.5	0.9	124.5	0.0
1992	123.5	-0.8	122.9	-0.5	123.2	0.2	124.1	0.7	125.5	1.1	126.5	0.8	126.7	0.2	126.5	-0.2	126.5	0.0	127.5	0.8	128.5	0.8	128.2	-0.2
1993	128.0	-0.2	128.0	0.0	127.8	-0.2	128.4	0.5	129.2	0.6	129.5	0.2	129.4	-0.1	129.4	0.0	129.2	-0.2	131.0	1.4	131.6	0.5	130.8	-0.6
1994	130.2	-0.5	130.4	0.2	130.5	0.1	131.2	0.5	131.8	0.5	132.9	0.8	133.9	0.8	135.2	1.0	135.3	0.1	135.6	0.2	136.7	0.8	136.7	0.0
1995	136.9	0.1	137.1	0.1	137.6	0.4	138.7	0.8	140.1	1.0	140.8	0.5	139.8	-0.7	138.9	-0.6	138.5	-0.3	139.0	0.4	139.0	0.0	138.9	-0.1

Source: U.S. Department of Labor, Bureau of Labor Statistics, Division of Consumer Prices and Price Indexes.

U.S. City Average
Consumer Price Index - All Urban Consumers
Base 1982-1984 = 100
Medical Care

For 1935-1995. Columns headed % show percentile change in the index from the previous period for which an index is available.

Year	Jan Index	%	Feb Index	%	Mar Index	%	Apr Index	%	May Index	%	Jun Index	%	Jul Index	%	Aug Index	%	Sep Index	%	Oct Index	%	Nov Index	%	Dec Index	%
1935	-		-		10.2	-	-		-		-		10.2	0.0	-		-		10.2	0.0	-		-	
1936	10.2	0.0	-		-		10.2	0.0	-		-		10.2	0.0	-		10.2	0.0	-		-		10.2	0.0
1937	-		-		10.3	1.0	-		-		10.3	0.0	-		-		10.3	0.0	-		-		10.3	0.0
1938	-		-		10.3	0.0	-		-		10.3	0.0	-		-		10.3	0.0	-		-		10.3	0.0
1939	-		-		10.3	0.0	-		-		10.4	1.0	-		-		10.4	0.0	-		-		10.4	0.0
1940	-		-		10.4	0.0	-		-		10.3	-1.0	-		-		10.3	0.0	-		-		10.4	1.0
1941	-		-		10.4	0.0	-		-		10.4	0.0	-		-		10.4	0.0	-		-		10.5	1.0
1942	-		-		10.6	1.0	-		-		10.7	0.9	-		-		10.8	0.9	-		-		10.9	0.9
1943	-		-		11.1	1.8	-		-		11.2	0.9	-		-		11.4	1.8	-		-		11.4	0.0
1944	-		-		11.5	0.9	-		-		11.5	0.0	-		-		11.6	0.9	-		-		11.7	0.9
1945	-		-		11.8	0.9	-		-		11.9	0.8	-		-		11.9	0.0	-		-		12.0	0.8
1946	-		-		12.2	1.7	-		-		12.4	1.6	-		-		12.7	2.4	-		-		13.0	2.4
1947	13.2	1.5	13.3	0.8	13.3	0.0	13.4	0.8	13.5	0.7	13.5	0.0	13.5	0.0	13.6	0.7	13.7	0.7	13.8	0.7	13.8	0.0	13.9	0.7
1948	14.0	0.7	14.0	0.0	14.1	0.7	14.3	1.4	14.3	0.0	14.3	0.0	14.5	1.4	14.5	0.0	14.5	0.0	14.6	0.7	14.7	0.7	14.7	0.0
1949	14.8	0.7	14.8	0.0	14.8	0.0	14.8	0.0	14.8	0.0	14.8	0.0	14.8	0.0	14.9	0.7	14.9	0.0	14.9	0.0	14.9	0.0	14.9	0.0
1950	15.0	0.7	15.0	0.0	15.0	0.0	15.0	0.0	15.0	0.0	15.0	0.0	15.1	0.7	15.1	0.0	15.2	0.7	15.3	0.7	15.3	0.0	15.4	0.7
1951	15.5	0.6	15.5	0.0	15.7	1.3	15.7	0.0	15.8	0.6	15.8	0.0	15.8	0.0	15.9	0.6	15.9	0.0	16.0	0.6	16.1	0.6	16.3	1.2
1952	16.4	0.6	16.4	0.0	16.5	0.6	16.5	0.0	16.5	0.0	16.8	1.8	16.8	0.0	16.8	0.0	16.9	0.6	16.9	0.0	16.9	0.0	17.0	0.6
1953	17.0	0.0	17.0	0.0	17.0	0.0	17.1	0.6	17.2	0.6	17.3	0.6	17.3	0.0	17.4	0.6	17.5	0.6	17.5	0.0	17.6	0.6	17.6	0.0
1954	17.6	0.0	17.7	0.6	17.7	0.0	17.8	0.6	17.8	0.0	17.8	0.0	17.8	0.0	17.9	0.6	17.9	0.0	17.9	0.0	18.0	0.6	18.0	0.0
1955	18.0	0.0	18.1	0.6	18.1	0.0	18.1	0.0	18.2	0.6	18.2	0.0	18.2	0.0	18.2	0.0	18.3	0.5	18.4	0.5	18.5	0.5	18.6	0.5
1956	18.6	0.0	18.7	0.5	18.7	0.0	18.8	0.5	18.8	0.0	18.8	0.0	18.9	0.5	19.0	0.5	19.1	0.5	19.1	0.0	19.2	0.5	19.2	0.0
1957	19.3	0.5	19.3	0.0	19.5	1.0	19.5	0.0	19.6	0.5	19.7	0.5	19.7	0.0	19.8	0.5	19.8	0.0	19.9	0.5	20.0	0.5	20.1	0.5
1958	20.2	0.5	20.2	0.0	20.3	0.5	20.4	0.5	20.5	0.5	20.6	0.5	20.7	0.5	20.7	0.0	20.9	1.0	21.0	0.5	21.0	0.0	21.0	0.0
1959	21.1	0.5	21.2	0.5	21.3	0.5	21.3	0.0	21.4	0.5	21.5	0.5	21.5	0.0	21.6	0.5	21.7	0.5	21.7	0.0	21.8	0.5	21.8	0.0
1960	21.9	0.5	22.0	0.5	22.1	0.5	22.2	0.5	22.2	0.0	22.2	0.0	22.3	0.5	22.3	0.0	22.4	0.4	22.4	0.0	22.5	0.4	22.5	0.0
1961	22.6	0.4	22.7	0.4	22.7	0.0	22.8	0.4	22.9	0.4	22.9	0.0	23.0	0.4	23.0	0.0	23.1	0.4	23.1	0.0	23.1	0.0	23.2	0.4
1962	23.2	0.0	23.3	0.4	23.4	0.4	23.5	0.4	23.5	0.0	23.6	0.4	23.6	0.0	23.6	0.0	23.6	0.0	23.7	0.4	23.7	0.0	23.7	0.0
1963	23.8	0.4	23.9	0.4	23.9	0.0	24.0	0.4	24.0	0.0	24.1	0.4	24.2	0.4	24.2	0.0	24.2	0.0	24.2	0.0	24.3	0.4	24.3	0.0
1964	24.4	0.4	24.4	0.0	24.4	0.0	24.5	0.4	24.5	0.0	24.6	0.4	24.6	0.0	24.7	0.4	24.7	0.0	24.7	0.0	24.7	0.0	24.8	0.4
1965	24.8	0.0	24.9	0.4	25.0	0.4	25.1	0.4	25.1	0.0	25.2	0.4	25.3	0.4	25.3	0.0	25.3	0.0	25.3	0.0	25.4	0.4	25.5	0.4
1966	25.6	0.4	25.6	0.0	25.8	0.8	25.9	0.4	26.0	0.4	26.2	0.8	26.3	0.4	26.4	0.4	26.7	1.1	26.9	0.7	27.0	0.4	27.2	0.7
1967	27.4	0.7	27.5	0.4	27.7	0.7	27.8	0.4	28.0	0.7	28.1	0.4	28.2	0.4	28.3	0.4	28.5	0.7	28.6	0.4	28.8	0.7	28.9	0.3
1968	29.1	0.7	29.2	0.3	29.4	0.7	29.6	0.7	29.6	0.0	29.7	0.3	29.9	0.7	30.0	0.3	30.2	0.7	30.4	0.7	30.5	0.3	30.7	0.7
1969	30.9	0.7	31.2	1.0	31.4	0.6	31.6	0.6	31.8	0.6	32.0	0.6	32.1	0.3	32.3	0.6	32.5	0.6	32.3	-0.6	32.4	0.3	32.6	0.6
1970	32.7	0.3	33.0	0.9	33.3	0.9	33.5	0.6	33.7	0.6	33.9	0.6	34.2	0.9	34.3	0.3	34.5	0.6	34.6	0.3	34.7	0.3	35.0	0.9
1971	35.2	0.6	35.4	0.6	35.7	0.8	35.9	0.6	36.1	0.6	36.2	0.3	36.4	0.6	36.6	0.5	36.7	0.3	36.5	-0.5	36.5	0.0	36.6	0.3
1972	36.7	0.3	36.9	0.5	37.0	0.3	37.1	0.3	37.2	0.3	37.3	0.3	37.4	0.3	37.4	0.0	37.5	0.3	37.7	0.5	37.8	0.3	37.8	0.0
1973	38.0	0.5	38.1	0.3	38.2	0.3	38.3	0.3	38.5	0.5	38.6	0.3	38.7	0.3	38.7	0.0	38.9	0.5	39.6	1.8	39.7	0.3	39.8	0.3
1974	40.0	0.5	40.4	1.0	40.8	1.0	41.0	0.5	41.4	1.0	42.1	1.7	42.6	1.2	43.3	1.6	43.7	0.9	44.0	0.7	44.3	0.7	44.8	1.1
1975	45.3	1.1	45.9	1.3	46.3	0.9	46.7	0.9	47.0	0.6	47.3	0.6	47.8	1.1	48.1	0.6	48.5	0.8	48.8	0.6	48.8	0.0	49.2	0.8
1976	49.7	1.0	50.3	1.2	50.8	1.0	51.1	0.6	51.4	0.6	51.7	0.6	52.2	1.0	52.6	0.8	52.9	0.6	53.2	0.6	53.9	1.3	54.1	0.4
1977	54.6	0.9	55.1	0.9	55.6	0.9	56.1	0.9	56.4	0.5	56.8	0.7	57.3	0.9	57.7	0.7	58.1	0.7	58.3	0.3	58.6	0.5	58.9	0.5
1978	59.5	1.0	60.1	1.0	60.4	0.5	60.7	0.5	61.1	0.7	61.3	0.3	61.8	0.8	62.3	0.8	62.7	0.6	63.3	1.0	63.9	0.9	64.1	0.3
1979	65.0	1.4	65.5	0.8	65.9	0.6	66.2	0.5	66.5	0.5	66.9	0.6	67.5	0.9	68.1	0.9	68.6	0.7	69.2	0.9	69.8	0.9	70.6	1.1

[Continued]

U.S. City Average
Consumer Price Index - All Urban Consumers
Base 1982-1984 = 100
Medical Care
[Continued]

For 1935-1995. Columns headed % show percentile change in the index from the previous period for which an index is available.

Year	Jan Index	%	Feb Index	%	Mar Index	%	Apr Index	%	May Index	%	Jun Index	%	Jul Index	%	Aug Index	%	Sep Index	%	Oct Index	%	Nov Index	%	Dec Index	%
1980	71.5	1.3	72.6	1.5	73.3	1.0	73.8	0.7	74.2	0.5	74.5	0.4	75.1	0.8	75.6	0.7	76.2	0.8	76.8	0.8	77.3	0.7	77.6	0.4
1981	78.7	1.4	79.6	1.1	80.2	0.8	80.8	0.7	81.4	0.7	82.1	0.9	83.2	1.3	84.3	1.3	84.9	0.7	85.8	1.1	86.8	1.2	87.3	0.6
1982	88.2	1.0	89.0	0.9	89.8	0.9	90.6	0.9	91.2	0.7	91.9	0.8	92.9	1.1	93.8	1.0	94.6	0.9	95.4	0.8	96.3	0.9	96.9	0.6
1983	97.9	1.0	98.9	1.0	99.2	0.3	99.5	0.3	99.7	0.2	100.1	0.4	100.7	0.6	101.4	0.7	101.7	0.3	102.2	0.5	102.7	0.5	103.1	0.4
1984	104.0	0.9	105.1	1.1	105.4	0.3	105.8	0.4	106.1	0.3	106.4	0.3	107.1	0.7	107.5	0.4	107.9	0.4	108.5	0.6	109.1	0.6	109.4	0.3
1985	110.1	0.6	110.9	0.7	111.6	0.6	112.1	0.4	112.5	0.4	113.1	0.5	113.7	0.5	114.5	0.7	115.0	0.4	115.6	0.5	116.3	0.6	116.8	0.4
1986	117.7	0.8	118.9	1.0	119.9	0.8	120.5	0.5	121.0	0.4	121.6	0.5	122.4	0.7	123.2	0.7	123.8	0.5	124.5	0.6	125.2	0.6	125.8	0.5
1987	126.6	0.6	127.4	0.6	128.1	0.5	128.7	0.5	129.2	0.4	129.9	0.5	130.7	0.6	131.2	0.4	131.7	0.4	132.3	0.5	132.8	0.4	133.1	0.2
1988	134.4	1.0	135.5	0.8	136.3	0.6	136.9	0.4	137.5	0.4	138.2	0.5	139.3	0.8	139.9	0.4	140.4	0.4	141.2	0.6	141.8	0.4	142.3	0.4
1989	143.8	1.1	145.2	1.0	146.1	0.6	146.8	0.5	147.5	0.5	148.5	0.7	149.7	0.8	150.7	0.7	151.7	0.7	152.7	0.7	153.9	0.8	154.4	0.3
1990	155.9	1.0	157.5	1.0	158.7	0.8	159.8	0.7	160.8	0.6	161.9	0.7	163.5	1.0	165.0	0.9	165.8	0.5	167.1	0.8	168.4	0.8	169.2	0.5
1991	171.0	1.1	172.5	0.9	173.7	0.7	174.4	0.4	175.2	0.5	176.2	0.6	177.5	0.7	178.9	0.8	179.7	0.4	180.7	0.6	181.8	0.6	182.6	0.4
1992	184.3	0.9	186.2	1.0	187.3	0.6	188.1	0.4	188.7	0.3	189.4	0.4	190.7	0.7	191.5	0.4	192.3	0.4	193.3	0.5	194.3	0.5	194.7	0.2
1993	196.4	0.9	198.0	0.8	198.6	0.3	199.4	0.4	200.5	0.6	201.1	0.3	202.2	0.5	202.9	0.3	203.3	0.2	204.4	0.5	204.9	0.2	205.2	0.1
1994	206.4	0.6	207.7	0.6	208.3	0.3	209.2	0.4	209.7	0.2	210.4	0.3	211.5	0.5	212.2	0.3	212.8	0.3	214.0	0.6	214.7	0.3	215.3	0.3
1995	216.6	0.6	217.9	0.6	218.4	0.2	218.9	0.2	219.3	0.2	219.8	0.2	220.8	0.5	221.6	0.4	222.1	0.2	222.9	0.4	223.5	0.3	223.8	0.1

Source: U.S. Department of Labor, Bureau of Labor Statistics, Division of Consumer Prices and Price Indexes.

U.S. City Average
Consumer Price Index - Urban Wage Earners
Base 1982-1984 = 100
Medical Care

For 1935-1995. Columns headed % show percentile change in the index from the previous period for which an index is available.

Year	Jan Index	%	Feb Index	%	Mar Index	%	Apr Index	%	May Index	%	Jun Index	%	Jul Index	%	Aug Index	%	Sep Index	%	Oct Index	%	Nov Index	%	Dec Index	%
1935	-	-	-	-	10.2	-	-	-	-	-	-	-	10.2	0.0	-	-	-	-	10.2	0.0	-	-	-	-
1936	10.2	0.0	-	-	-	-	10.2	0.0	-	-	-	-	10.2	0.0	-	-	10.3	1.0	-	-	-	-	10.3	0.0
1937	-	-	-	-	10.4	1.0	-	-	-	-	10.4	0.0	-	-	-	-	10.4	0.0	-	-	-	-	10.4	0.0
1938	-	-	-	-	10.4	0.0	-	-	-	-	10.4	0.0	-	-	-	-	10.4	0.0	-	-	-	-	10.4	0.0
1939	-	-	-	-	10.4	0.0	-	L	-	-	10.4	0.0	-	-	-	-	10.4	0.0	-	-	-	-	10.4	0.0
1940	-	-	-	-	10.4	0.0	-	-	-	-	10.4	0.0	-	-	-	-	10.4	0.0	-	-	-	-	10.4	0.0
1941	-	-	-	-	10.4	0.0	-	-	-	-	10.4	0.0	-	-	-	-	10.5	1.0	-	-	-	-	10.6	1.0
1942	-	-	-	-	10.6	0.0	-	-	-	-	10.8	1.9	-	-	-	-	10.9	0.9	-	-	-	-	11.0	0.9
1943	-	-	-	-	11.2	1.8	-	-	-	-	11.3	0.9	-	-	-	-	11.4	0.9	-	-	-	-	11.5	0.9
1944	-	-	-	-	11.5	0.0	-	-	-	-	11.6	0.9	-	-	-	-	11.7	0.9	-	-	-	-	11.8	0.9
1945	-	-	-	-	11.8	0.0	-	-	-	-	11.9	0.8	-	-	-	-	11.9	0.0	-	-	-	-	12.1	1.7
1946	-	-	-	-	12.3	1.7	-	-	-	-	12.5	1.6	-	-	-	-	12.8	2.4	-	-	-	-	13.1	2.3
1947	13.3	1.5	13.3	0.0	13.4	0.8	13.5	0.7	13.5	0.0	13.6	0.7	13.6	0.0	13.6	0.0	13.8	1.5	13.8	0.0	13.9	0.7	13.9	0.0
1948	14.1	1.4	14.1	0.0	14.2	0.7	14.4	1.4	14.4	0.0	14.4	0.0	14.6	1.4	14.6	0.0	14.6	0.0	14.7	0.7	14.7	0.0	14.7	0.0
1949	14.8	0.7	14.8	0.0	14.9	0.7	14.9	0.0	14.9	0.0	14.9	0.0	14.9	0.0	14.9	0.0	15.0	0.7	14.9	-0.7	14.9	0.0	15.0	0.7
1950	15.1	0.7	15.1	0.0	15.1	0.0	15.1	0.0	15.1	0.0	15.1	0.0	15.1	0.0	15.2	0.7	15.3	0.7	15.3	0.0	15.4	0.7	15.5	0.6
1951	15.5	0.0	15.6	0.6	15.8	1.3	15.8	0.0	15.9	0.6	15.9	0.0	15.9	0.0	15.9	0.0	16.0	0.6	16.1	0.6	16.2	0.6	16.4	1.2
1952	16.4	0.0	16.4	0.0	16.6	1.2	16.6	0.0	16.6	0.0	16.9	1.8	16.9	0.0	16.9	0.0	17.0	0.6	17.0	0.0	17.0	0.0	17.1	0.6
1953	17.1	0.0	17.1	0.0	17.1	0.0	17.2	0.6	17.3	0.6	17.4	0.6	17.4	0.0	17.5	0.6	17.6	0.6	17.6	0.0	17.7	0.6	17.7	0.0
1954	17.7	0.0	17.8	0.6	17.8	0.0	17.9	0.6	17.9	0.0	17.9	0.0	17.9	0.0	18.0	0.6	18.0	0.0	18.0	0.0	18.1	0.6	18.1	0.0
1955	18.1	0.0	18.2	0.6	18.2	0.0	18.2	0.0	18.3	0.5	18.3	0.0	18.3	0.0	18.3	0.0	18.4	0.5	18.5	0.5	18.6	0.5	18.7	0.5
1956	18.7	0.0	18.8	0.5	18.8	0.0	18.9	0.5	18.9	0.0	18.9	0.0	19.0	0.5	19.1	0.5	19.2	0.5	19.2	0.0	19.3	0.5	19.3	0.0
1957	19.4	0.5	19.4	0.0	19.6	1.0	19.6	0.0	19.7	0.5	19.8	0.5	19.8	0.0	19.9	0.5	19.9	0.0	20.0	0.5	20.1	0.5	20.2	0.5
1958	20.3	0.5	20.3	0.0	20.4	0.5	20.5	0.5	20.6	0.5	20.7	0.5	20.8	0.5	20.8	0.0	21.0	1.0	21.1	0.5	21.1	0.0	21.1	0.0
1959	21.2	0.5	21.3	0.5	21.4	0.5	21.4	0.0	21.5	0.5	21.6	0.5	21.6	0.0	21.7	0.5	21.8	0.5	21.9	0.5	21.9	0.0	21.9	0.0
1960	22.0	0.5	22.2	0.9	22.2	0.0	22.3	0.5	22.3	0.0	22.4	0.4	22.4	0.0	22.4	0.0	22.5	0.4	22.6	0.4	22.6	0.0	22.6	0.0
1961	22.7	0.4	22.8	0.4	22.9	0.4	22.9	0.0	23.0	0.4	23.0	0.0	23.1	0.4	23.1	0.0	23.2	0.4	23.3	0.4	23.3	0.0	23.3	0.0
1962	23.3	0.0	23.4	0.4	23.5	0.4	23.6	0.4	23.6	0.0	23.7	0.4	23.7	0.0	23.7	0.0	23.8	0.4	23.8	0.0	23.8	0.0	23.9	0.4
1963	24.0	0.4	24.0	0.0	24.0	0.0	24.1	0.4	24.2	0.4	24.3	0.4	24.3	0.0	24.3	0.0	24.3	0.0	24.4	0.4	24.4	0.0	24.4	0.0
1964	24.5	0.4	24.5	0.0	24.6	0.4	24.7	0.4	24.7	0.0	24.7	0.0	24.7	0.0	24.8	0.4	24.8	0.0	24.8	0.0	24.9	0.4	24.9	0.0
1965	25.0	0.4	25.1	0.4	25.1	0.0	25.2	0.4	25.2	0.0	25.3	0.4	25.4	0.4	25.4	0.0	25.4	0.0	25.5	0.4	25.6	0.4	25.6	0.0
1966	25.7	0.4	25.8	0.4	26.0	0.8	26.0	0.0	26.2	0.8	26.3	0.4	26.4	0.4	26.6	0.8	26.8	0.8	27.0	0.7	27.2	0.7	27.3	0.4
1967	27.5	0.7	27.7	0.7	27.9	0.7	28.0	0.4	28.1	0.4	28.2	0.4	28.3	0.4	28.5	0.7	28.7	0.7	28.8	0.3	28.9	0.3	29.1	0.7
1968	29.2	0.3	29.4	0.7	29.6	0.7	29.7	0.3	29.8	0.3	29.9	0.3	30.0	0.3	30.1	0.3	30.3	0.7	30.5	0.7	30.7	0.7	30.9	0.7
1969	31.1	0.6	31.3	0.6	31.6	1.0	31.8	0.6	32.0	0.6	32.1	0.3	32.3	0.6	32.5	0.6	32.6	0.3	32.5	-0.3	32.6	0.3	32.8	0.6
1970	32.9	0.3	33.1	0.6	33.5	1.2	33.7	0.6	33.9	0.6	34.1	0.6	34.3	0.6	34.5	0.6	34.7	0.6	34.8	0.3	34.9	0.3	35.2	0.9
1971	35.4	0.6	35.6	0.6	35.9	0.8	36.1	0.6	36.3	0.6	36.4	0.3	36.6	0.5	36.8	0.5	36.9	0.3	36.7	-0.5	36.7	0.0	36.8	0.3
1972	36.9	0.3	37.1	0.5	37.2	0.3	37.3	0.3	37.4	0.3	37.5	0.3	37.6	0.3	37.6	0.0	37.7	0.3	37.9	0.5	38.0	0.3	38.0	0.0
1973	38.2	0.5	38.3	0.3	38.4	0.3	38.6	0.5	38.7	0.3	38.8	0.3	38.9	0.3	39.0	0.3	39.2	0.5	39.8	1.5	39.9	0.3	40.0	0.3
1974	40.3	0.7	40.6	0.7	41.0	1.0	41.2	0.5	41.7	1.2	42.3	1.4	42.9	1.4	43.5	1.4	43.9	0.9	44.2	0.7	44.6	0.9	45.0	0.9
1975	45.6	1.3	46.1	1.1	46.6	1.1	46.9	0.6	47.2	0.6	47.6	0.8	48.1	1.1	48.4	0.6	48.7	0.6	49.1	0.8	49.1	0.0	49.5	0.8
1976	50.0	1.0	50.6	1.2	51.1	1.0	51.4	0.6	51.7	0.6	52.0	0.6	52.5	1.0	52.9	0.8	53.2	0.6	53.5	0.6	54.2	1.3	54.4	0.4
1977	54.9	0.9	55.4	0.9	55.9	0.9	56.4	0.9	56.8	0.7	57.1	0.5	57.6	0.9	58.0	0.7	58.4	0.7	58.7	0.5	58.9	0.3	59.2	0.5
1978	59.8	1.0	60.4	1.0	60.7	0.5	61.0	0.5	61.4	0.7	61.7	0.5	62.1	0.6	62.6	0.8	63.1	0.8	63.7	1.0	64.2	0.8	64.5	0.5
1979	65.2	1.1	65.7	0.8	66.2	0.8	66.6	0.6	66.9	0.5	67.4	0.7	68.1	1.0	68.7	0.9	69.3	0.9	70.0	1.0	70.5	0.7	71.3	1.1

[Continued]

U.S. City Average
Consumer Price Index - Urban Wage Earners
Base 1982-1984 = 100
Medical Care

[Continued]

For 1935-1995. Columns headed % show percentile change in the index from the previous period for which an index is available.

Year	Jan Index	%	Feb Index	%	Mar Index	%	Apr Index	%	May Index	%	Jun Index	%	Jul Index	%	Aug Index	%	Sep Index	%	Oct Index	%	Nov Index	%	Dec Index	%
1980	72.2	1.3	73.2	1.4	73.9	1.0	74.5	0.8	75.0	0.7	75.3	0.4	75.8	0.7	76.4	0.8	77.1	0.9	77.7	0.8	78.2	0.6	78.6	0.5
1981	79.7	1.4	80.5	1.0	81.2	0.9	81.8	0.7	82.3	0.6	82.9	0.7	83.6	0.8	84.5	1.1	85.2	0.8	86.1	1.1	86.9	0.9	87.5	0.7
1982	88.3	0.9	89.1	0.9	89.9	0.9	90.6	0.8	91.2	0.7	91.9	0.8	92.9	1.1	93.8	1.0	94.5	0.7	95.3	0.8	96.2	0.9	96.8	0.6
1983	97.7	0.9	98.8	1.1	99.1	0.3	99.4	0.3	99.7	0.3	100.0	0.3	100.7	0.7	101.3	0.6	101.7	0.4	102.2	0.5	102.7	0.5	103.1	0.4
1984	104.0	0.9	105.1	1.1	105.5	0.4	105.8	0.3	106.2	0.4	106.5	0.3	107.1	0.6	107.6	0.5	107.9	0.3	108.6	0.6	109.2	0.6	109.5	0.3
1985	110.2	0.6	111.0	0.7	111.7	0.6	112.1	0.4	112.6	0.4	113.2	0.5	113.8	0.5	114.5	0.6	115.0	0.4	115.6	0.5	116.3	0.6	116.8	0.4
1986	117.8	0.9	118.9	0.9	119.9	0.8	120.5	0.5	121.0	0.4	121.6	0.5	122.4	0.7	123.1	0.6	123.7	0.5	124.5	0.6	125.0	0.4	125.7	0.6
1987	126.5	0.6	127.3	0.6	128.1	0.6	128.8	0.5	129.3	0.4	130.0	0.5	130.8	0.6	131.4	0.5	132.0	0.5	132.6	0.5	133.0	0.3	133.4	0.3
1988	134.6	0.9	135.8	0.9	136.5	0.5	137.1	0.4	137.8	0.5	138.5	0.5	139.6	0.8	140.3	0.5	140.8	0.4	141.7	0.6	142.2	0.4	142.8	0.4
1989	144.2	1.0	145.6	1.0	146.5	0.6	147.2	0.5	147.9	0.5	148.8	0.6	150.1	0.9	151.1	0.7	152.1	0.7	153.0	0.6	154.2	0.8	154.7	0.3
1990	156.1	0.9	157.6	1.0	158.8	0.8	159.8	0.6	160.8	0.6	161.8	0.6	163.3	0.9	164.7	0.9	165.5	0.5	166.8	0.8	168.1	0.8	168.8	0.4
1991	170.5	1.0	172.1	0.9	173.2	0.6	173.9	0.4	174.6	0.4	175.6	0.6	176.9	0.7	178.3	0.8	179.2	0.5	180.2	0.6	181.2	0.6	182.0	0.4
1992	183.7	0.9	185.7	1.1	186.8	0.6	187.6	0.4	188.2	0.3	188.9	0.4	190.2	0.7	191.2	0.5	191.9	0.4	193.0	0.6	193.8	0.4	194.3	0.3
1993	196.0	0.9	197.6	0.8	198.2	0.3	199.0	0.4	200.1	0.6	200.7	0.3	201.7	0.5	202.4	0.3	202.8	0.2	203.8	0.5	204.2	0.2	204.5	0.1
1994	205.8	0.6	207.0	0.6	207.7	0.3	208.6	0.4	209.1	0.2	209.7	0.3	210.8	0.5	211.5	0.3	212.0	0.2	213.4	0.7	214.0	0.3	214.6	0.3
1995	215.9	0.6	217.3	0.6	217.7	0.2	218.2	0.2	218.7	0.2	219.2	0.2	220.2	0.5	221.1	0.4	221.5	0.2	222.3	0.4	222.8	0.2	223.1	0.1

Source: U.S. Department of Labor, Bureau of Labor Statistics, Division of Consumer Prices and Price Indexes.

U.S. City Average
Consumer Price Index - All Urban Consumers
Base 1982-1984 = 100
Entertainment

For 1967-1995. Columns headed % show percentile change in the index from the previous period for which an index is available.

Year	Jan Index	%	Feb Index	%	Mar Index	%	Apr Index	%	May Index	%	Jun Index	%	Jul Index	%	Aug Index	%	Sep Index	%	Oct Index	%	Nov Index	%	Dec Index	%
1967	39.9	-	40.0	0.3	40.1	0.2	40.4	0.7	40.5	0.2	40.6	0.2	40.7	0.2	40.7	0.0	41.0	0.7	41.3	0.7	41.6	0.7	41.6	0.0
1968	41.9	0.7	42.1	0.5	42.3	0.5	42.7	0.9	42.8	0.2	43.0	0.5	43.1	0.2	43.3	0.5	43.5	0.5	43.7	0.5	43.9	0.5	44.0	0.2
1969	44.2	0.5	44.2	0.0	44.3	0.2	44.7	0.9	45.0	0.7	45.1	0.2	45.3	0.4	45.5	0.4	45.7	0.4	45.8	0.2	46.0	0.4	46.2	0.4
1970	46.4	0.4	46.5	0.2	46.7	0.4	46.9	0.4	47.1	0.4	47.3	0.4	47.6	0.6	47.9	0.6	48.1	0.4	48.4	0.6	48.6	0.4	48.8	0.4
1971	49.1	0.6	49.2	0.2	49.3	0.2	49.7	0.8	50.0	0.6	50.2	0.4	50.4	0.4	50.4	0.0	50.5	0.2	50.5	0.0	50.6	0.2	50.6	0.0
1972	50.8	0.4	50.9	0.2	51.0	0.2	51.3	0.6	51.4	0.2	51.6	0.4	51.7	0.2	51.7	0.0	51.8	0.2	51.9	0.2	51.9	0.0	51.9	0.0
1973	52.0	0.2	52.1	0.2	52.2	0.2	52.6	0.8	52.8	0.4	53.0	0.4	53.2	0.4	53.2	0.0	53.2	0.0	53.4	0.4	53.6	0.4	53.7	0.2
1974	54.1	0.7	54.4	0.6	54.7	0.6	55.2	0.9	56.1	1.6	57.0	1.6	57.5	0.9	57.8	0.5	58.5	1.2	58.7	0.3	59.2	0.9	59.7	0.8
1975	60.3	1.0	60.8	0.8	60.9	0.2	61.7	1.3	61.8	0.2	62.0	0.3	62.2	0.3	62.3	0.2	62.7	0.6	62.7	0.0	62.9	0.3	63.2	0.5
1976	63.6	0.6	63.7	0.2	64.0	0.5	64.3	0.5	64.8	0.8	65.1	0.5	65.3	0.3	65.4	0.2	65.7	0.5	66.0	0.5	66.3	0.5	66.5	0.3
1977	66.8	0.5	67.1	0.4	67.3	0.3	67.4	0.1	67.8	0.6	68.3	0.7	68.4	0.1	68.6	0.3	69.1	0.7	69.3	0.3	69.4	0.1	69.6	0.3
1978	70.0	0.6	70.4	0.6	70.9	0.7	71.5	0.8	71.7	0.3	71.7	0.0	72.1	0.6	72.2	0.1	72.6	0.6	73.0	0.6	73.1	0.1	73.6	0.7
1979	74.2	0.8	74.6	0.5	75.2	0.8	75.9	0.9	76.5	0.8	76.6	0.1	77.0	0.5	77.4	0.5	77.8	0.5	78.2	0.5	78.5	0.4	78.7	0.3
1980	79.5	1.0	80.5	1.3	81.7	1.5	82.4	0.9	83.0	0.7	83.6	0.7	84.1	0.6	84.7	0.7	85.4	0.8	85.9	0.6	86.0	0.1	86.3	0.3
1981	87.3	1.2	88.2	1.0	88.8	0.7	89.2	0.5	89.7	0.6	89.9	0.2	90.0	0.1	90.5	0.6	91.2	0.8	91.8	0.7	92.3	0.5	92.5	0.2
1982	93.3	0.9	94.1	0.9	94.8	0.7	95.2	0.4	95.4	0.2	95.9	0.5	96.3	0.4	96.6	0.3	97.0	0.4	97.8	0.8	97.7	-0.1	97.7	0.0
1983	98.3	0.6	99.0	0.7	99.6	0.6	99.6	0.0	99.7	0.1	99.9	0.2	100.1	0.2	100.4	0.3	100.8	0.4	101.4	0.6	101.6	0.2	101.6	0.0
1984	101.7	0.1	102.4	0.7	102.5	0.1	103.3	0.8	103.2	-0.1	103.6	0.4	103.9	0.3	104.4	0.5	104.7	0.3	105.2	0.5	105.4	0.2	105.9	0.5
1985	106.3	0.4	106.4	0.1	106.7	0.3	107.2	0.5	107.3	0.1	107.8	0.5	108.2	0.4	108.2	0.0	108.6	0.4	109.3	0.6	109.5	0.2	109.2	-0.3
1986	110.2	0.9	110.7	0.5	110.7	0.0	110.9	0.2	111.1	0.2	111.5	0.4	111.7	0.2	111.8	0.1	112.1	0.3	112.6	0.4	112.9	0.3	112.9	0.0
1987	113.3	0.4	113.5	0.2	113.9	0.4	114.5	0.5	114.8	0.3	114.9	0.1	115.4	0.4	115.6	0.2	116.1	0.4	116.9	0.7	117.3	0.3	117.4	0.1
1988	118.1	0.6	118.3	0.2	119.0	0.6	119.6	0.5	119.7	0.1	120.1	0.3	120.5	0.3	120.7	0.2	121.3	0.5	121.8	0.4	122.2	0.3	122.8	0.5
1989	123.8	0.8	124.3	0.4	124.7	0.3	125.4	0.6	125.5	0.1	126.2	0.6	126.9	0.6	127.3	0.3	127.8	0.4	128.4	0.5	128.6	0.2	129.1	0.4
1990	129.9	0.6	130.4	0.4	130.9	0.4	131.4	0.4	131.7	0.2	131.9	0.2	132.7	0.6	133.0	0.2	134.1	0.8	134.3	0.1	134.4	0.1	134.6	0.1
1991	135.5	0.7	136.2	0.5	136.7	0.4	137.7	0.7	137.8	0.1	138.1	0.2	138.6	0.4	139.2	0.4	140.2	0.7	140.5	0.2	140.4	-0.1	139.9	-0.4
1992	140.1	0.1	140.7	0.4	141.2	0.4	142.0	0.6	142.0	0.0	142.0	0.0	142.4	0.3	142.6	0.1	143.2	0.4	143.5	0.2	143.7	0.1	143.8	0.1
1993	144.3	0.3	144.5	0.1	144.8	0.2	145.3	0.3	145.0	-0.2	145.5	0.3	145.3	-0.1	145.8	0.3	146.6	0.5	147.3	0.5	147.7	0.3	147.8	0.1
1994	148.5	0.5	149.1	0.4	149.6	0.3	149.7	0.1	149.9	0.1	149.8	-0.1	150.2	0.3	150.2	0.0	150.7	0.3	151.0	0.2	151.6	0.4	151.2	-0.3
1995	152.1	0.6	152.5	0.3	152.6	0.1	153.3	0.5	153.6	0.2	153.2	-0.3	153.6	0.3	154.1	0.3	154.9	0.5	155.2	0.2	156.0	0.5	156.2	0.1

Source: U.S. Department of Labor, Bureau of Labor Statistics, Division of Consumer Prices and Price Indexes.

U.S. City Average
Consumer Price Index - Urban Wage Earners
Base 1982-1984 = 100
Entertainment

For 1967-1995. Columns headed % show percentile change in the index from the previous period for which an index is available.

Year	Jan Index	%	Feb Index	%	Mar Index	%	Apr Index	%	May Index	%	Jun Index	%	Jul Index	%	Aug Index	%	Sep Index	%	Oct Index	%	Nov Index	%	Dec Index	%
1967	40.5	-	40.6	0.2	40.7	0.2	41.0	0.7	41.1	0.2	41.2	0.2	41.3	0.2	41.3	0.0	41.6	0.7	41.9	0.7	42.2	0.7	42.3	0.2
1968	42.6	0.7	42.7	0.2	42.9	0.5	43.3	0.9	43.4	0.2	43.6	0.5	43.7	0.2	44.0	0.7	44.1	0.2	44.4	0.7	44.6	0.5	44.7	0.2
1969	44.8	0.2	44.8	0.0	45.0	0.4	45.4	0.9	45.7	0.7	45.8	0.2	46.0	0.4	46.2	0.4	46.4	0.4	46.5	0.2	46.7	0.4	46.9	0.4
1970	47.1	0.4	47.2	0.2	47.4	0.4	47.6	0.4	47.8	0.4	48.1	0.6	48.3	0.4	48.6	0.6	48.8	0.4	49.1	0.6	49.4	0.6	49.5	0.2
1971	49.8	0.6	49.9	0.2	50.0	0.2	50.5	1.0	50.7	0.4	51.0	0.6	51.1	0.2	51.2	0.2	51.3	0.2	51.3	0.0	51.4	0.2	51.4	0.0
1972	51.6	0.4	51.7	0.2	51.7	0.0	52.1	0.8	52.2	0.2	52.4	0.4	52.5	0.2	52.4	-0.2	52.6	0.4	52.7	0.2	52.7	0.0	52.7	0.0
1973	52.8	0.2	52.9	0.2	53.0	0.2	53.4	0.8	53.6	0.4	53.8	0.4	54.0	0.4	54.0	0.0	54.1	0.2	54.2	0.2	54.4	0.4	54.5	0.2
1974	54.9	0.7	55.2	0.5	55.5	0.5	56.0	0.9	56.9	1.6	57.8	1.6	58.4	1.0	58.7	0.5	59.4	1.2	59.6	0.3	60.1	0.8	60.6	0.8
1975	61.2	1.0	61.7	0.8	61.8	0.2	62.6	1.3	62.8	0.3	63.0	0.3	63.1	0.2	63.3	0.3	63.6	0.5	63.7	0.2	63.9	0.3	64.2	0.5
1976	64.5	0.5	64.7	0.3	65.0	0.5	65.2	0.3	65.7	0.8	66.1	0.6	66.3	0.3	66.4	0.2	66.7	0.5	67.0	0.4	67.3	0.4	67.5	0.3
1977	67.8	0.4	68.1	0.4	68.3	0.3	68.4	0.1	68.8	0.6	69.3	0.7	69.4	0.1	69.7	0.4	70.1	0.4	70.4	0.4	70.4	0.0	70.7	0.4
1978	71.0	0.4	71.8	1.1	71.9	0.1	72.4	0.7	72.6	0.3	72.5	-0.1	72.8	0.4	72.9	0.1	73.3	0.5	73.7	0.5	73.9	0.3	74.8	1.2
1979	75.2	0.5	75.4	0.3	76.0	0.8	76.7	0.9	77.3	0.8	77.5	0.3	77.9	0.5	78.1	0.3	78.6	0.6	79.1	0.6	79.3	0.3	79.5	0.3
1980	80.1	0.8	81.1	1.2	82.4	1.6	83.2	1.0	83.6	0.5	84.3	0.8	84.5	0.2	85.0	0.6	86.0	1.2	86.4	0.5	86.7	0.3	86.8	0.1
1981	87.7	1.0	88.8	1.3	89.3	0.6	89.7	0.4	90.0	0.3	90.2	0.2	90.4	0.2	90.9	0.6	91.5	0.7	92.3	0.9	92.7	0.4	92.7	0.0
1982	93.4	0.8	94.3	1.0	94.8	0.5	95.2	0.4	95.5	0.3	96.0	0.5	96.5	0.5	96.7	0.2	97.0	0.3	97.7	0.7	97.6	-0.1	97.7	0.1
1983	98.2	0.5	99.0	0.8	99.5	0.5	99.6	0.1	99.7	0.1	100.0	0.3	100.2	0.2	100.5	0.3	100.9	0.4	101.4	0.5	101.5	0.1	101.6	0.1
1984	101.7	0.1	102.4	0.7	102.5	0.1	103.2	0.7	103.1	-0.1	103.6	0.5	103.9	0.3	104.3	0.4	104.7	0.4	105.0	0.3	105.3	0.3	105.7	0.4
1985	106.0	0.3	106.2	0.2	106.3	0.1	106.9	0.6	107.0	0.1	107.5	0.5	107.8	0.3	107.8	0.0	108.1	0.3	108.7	0.6	109.0	0.3	108.7	-0.3
1986	109.7	0.9	110.1	0.4	110.1	0.0	110.3	0.2	110.5	0.2	110.9	0.4	111.2	0.3	111.2	0.0	111.6	0.4	112.0	0.4	112.4	0.4	112.5	0.1
1987	112.8	0.3	113.0	0.2	113.4	0.4	114.0	0.5	114.4	0.4	114.5	0.1	115.0	0.4	115.1	0.1	115.6	0.4	116.3	0.6	116.7	0.3	116.9	0.2
1988	117.4	0.4	117.6	0.2	118.2	0.5	118.9	0.6	119.0	0.1	119.4	0.3	119.8	0.3	120.1	0.3	120.6	0.4	121.2	0.5	121.7	0.4	122.2	0.4
1989	123.1	0.7	123.6	0.4	124.1	0.4	124.8	0.6	124.9	0.1	125.5	0.5	126.1	0.5	126.5	0.3	127.0	0.4	127.7	0.6	127.9	0.2	128.4	0.4
1990	129.1	0.5	129.5	0.3	130.0	0.4	130.6	0.5	130.8	0.2	131.0	0.2	131.7	0.5	132.1	0.3	132.9	0.6	133.1	0.2	133.2	0.1	133.3	0.1
1991	134.2	0.7	134.9	0.5	135.4	0.4	136.4	0.7	136.4	0.0	136.7	0.2	137.1	0.3	137.6	0.4	138.7	0.8	138.8	0.1	138.7	-0.1	138.4	-0.2
1992	138.6	0.1	139.1	0.4	139.7	0.4	140.5	0.6	140.5	0.0	140.5	0.0	141.0	0.4	141.2	0.1	141.6	0.3	141.9	0.2	142.2	0.2	142.2	0.0
1993	142.7	0.4	142.8	0.1	143.1	0.2	143.5	0.3	143.3	-0.1	143.8	0.3	143.7	-0.1	144.1	0.3	144.8	0.5	145.5	0.5	145.8	0.2	146.1	0.2
1994	146.7	0.4	147.1	0.3	147.7	0.4	147.8	0.1	148.1	0.2	148.0	-0.1	148.4	0.3	148.3	-0.1	148.6	0.2	149.0	0.3	149.6	0.4	149.2	-0.3
1995	150.1	0.6	150.4	0.2	150.6	0.1	151.3	0.5	151.5	0.1	151.2	-0.2	151.5	0.2	152.0	0.3	152.7	0.5	152.9	0.1	153.6	0.5	153.8	0.1

Source: U.S. Department of Labor, Bureau of Labor Statistics, Division of Consumer Prices and Price Indexes.

U.S. City Average
Consumer Price Index - All Urban Consumers
Base 1982-1984 = 100
Other Goods and Services

For 1967-1995. Columns headed % show percentile change in the index from the previous period for which an index is available.

Year	Jan Index	%	Feb Index	%	Mar Index	%	Apr Index	%	May Index	%	Jun Index	%	Jul Index	%	Aug Index	%	Sep Index	%	Oct Index	%	Nov Index	%	Dec Index	%
1967	34.4	-	34.5	0.3	34.5	0.0	34.6	0.3	34.7	0.3	34.8	0.3	35.0	0.6	35.3	0.9	35.5	0.6	35.6	0.3	35.8	0.6	35.9	0.3
1968	36.1	0.6	36.1	0.0	36.5	1.1	36.5	0.0	36.6	0.3	36.9	0.8	36.9	0.0	37.1	0.5	37.2	0.3	37.4	0.5	37.6	0.5	37.7	0.3
1969	37.8	0.3	37.8	0.0	38.0	0.5	38.1	0.3	38.2	0.3	38.5	0.8	38.8	0.8	39.0	0.5	39.3	0.8	39.4	0.3	39.7	0.8	39.8	0.3
1970	39.9	0.3	40.0	0.3	40.2	0.5	40.5	0.7	40.6	0.2	40.9	0.7	41.2	0.7	41.3	0.2	41.5	0.5	41.6	0.2	41.8	0.5	41.9	0.2
1971	42.2	0.7	42.2	0.0	42.3	0.2	42.4	0.2	42.5	0.2	42.6	0.2	42.9	0.7	43.1	0.5	43.5	0.9	43.6	0.2	43.6	0.0	43.7	0.2
1972	43.9	0.5	44.2	0.7	44.3	0.2	44.4	0.2	44.6	0.5	44.8	0.4	44.8	0.0	44.8	0.0	45.0	0.4	45.2	0.4	45.2	0.0	45.3	0.2
1973	45.4	0.2	45.5	0.2	45.8	0.7	46.0	0.4	46.2	0.4	46.4	0.4	46.5	0.2	46.6	0.2	46.9	0.6	47.1	0.4	47.4	0.6	47.5	0.2
1974	47.7	0.4	47.9	0.4	48.2	0.6	48.4	0.4	48.9	1.0	49.4	1.0	50.0	1.2	50.3	0.6	50.9	1.2	51.4	1.0	51.9	1.0	52.4	1.0
1975	52.7	0.6	53.1	0.8	53.3	0.4	53.5	0.4	53.6	0.2	53.7	0.2	53.9	0.4	54.0	0.2	54.4	0.7	54.7	0.6	54.9	0.4	55.3	0.7
1976	55.7	0.7	56.1	0.7	56.2	0.2	56.4	0.4	56.6	0.4	56.8	0.4	56.9	0.2	57.1	0.4	57.6	0.9	58.0	0.7	58.4	0.7	58.6	0.3
1977	59.0	0.7	59.2	0.3	59.3	0.2	59.5	0.3	59.7	0.3	60.0	0.5	60.2	0.3	60.4	0.3	61.1	1.2	61.7	1.0	62.1	0.6	62.3	0.3
1978	62.6	0.5	62.7	0.2	62.9	0.3	63.0	0.2	63.2	0.3	63.4	0.3	64.2	1.3	64.5	0.5	65.8	2.0	66.0	0.3	66.2	0.3	66.3	0.2
1979	66.8	0.8	67.3	0.7	67.6	0.4	67.7	0.1	68.0	0.4	68.2	0.3	68.4	0.3	69.1	1.0	70.7	2.3	70.9	0.3	71.1	0.3	71.5	0.6
1980	72.3	1.1	72.9	0.8	73.2	0.4	73.5	0.4	74.0	0.7	74.5	0.7	74.8	0.4	75.2	0.5	77.3	2.8	77.6	0.4	78.1	0.6	78.7	0.8
1981	79.3	0.8	79.7	0.5	80.2	0.6	80.6	0.5	81.4	1.0	81.8	0.5	82.2	0.5	82.6	0.5	85.2	3.1	86.0	0.9	86.2	0.2	86.5	0.3
1982	87.1	0.7	87.7	0.7	88.4	0.8	89.0	0.7	89.4	0.4	89.7	0.3	90.2	0.6	90.5	0.3	93.5	3.3	95.1	1.7	96.0	0.9	97.0	1.0
1983	98.1	1.1	98.7	0.6	98.8	0.1	99.3	0.5	99.4	0.1	99.7	0.3	100.8	1.1	101.3	0.5	103.2	1.9	104.0	0.8	104.5	0.5	104.7	0.2
1984	105.3	0.6	105.7	0.4	105.9	0.2	106.1	0.2	106.3	0.2	106.7	0.4	107.4	0.7	107.7	0.3	110.3	2.4	110.7	0.4	110.9	0.2	111.0	0.1
1985	111.9	0.8	112.3	0.4	112.6	0.3	112.8	0.2	113.0	0.2	113.2	0.2	113.9	0.6	114.3	0.4	116.8	2.2	117.4	0.5	117.5	0.1	118.0	0.4
1986	118.9	0.8	119.3	0.3	119.6	0.3	119.8	0.2	119.9	0.1	120.1	0.2	120.9	0.7	121.4	0.4	123.8	2.0	124.3	0.4	124.4	0.1	124.5	0.1
1987	125.5	0.8	126.1	0.5	126.3	0.2	126.6	0.2	126.9	0.2	127.2	0.2	128.0	0.6	128.5	0.4	131.1	2.0	131.6	0.4	131.8	0.2	132.1	0.2
1988	133.4	1.0	134.2	0.6	134.6	0.3	134.8	0.1	135.1	0.2	135.5	0.3	136.5	0.7	137.5	0.7	140.0	1.8	140.6	0.4	141.0	0.3	141.3	0.2
1989	143.4	1.5	144.1	0.5	144.4	0.2	144.7	0.2	145.4	0.5	146.3	0.6	147.3	0.7	148.7	1.0	151.2	1.7	151.8	0.4	151.9	0.1	152.9	0.7
1990	154.0	0.7	154.7	0.5	155.2	0.3	155.8	0.4	156.6	0.5	157.8	0.8	159.2	0.9	160.4	0.8	162.6	1.4	163.2	0.4	163.6	0.2	164.5	0.6
1991	166.5	1.2	167.4	0.5	167.9	0.3	168.8	0.5	169.1	0.2	170.0	0.5	170.8	0.5	172.2	0.8	175.8	2.1	176.2	0.2	176.9	0.4	177.6	0.4
1992	178.6	0.6	179.4	0.4	179.8	0.2	180.3	0.3	181.3	0.6	181.5	0.1	182.3	0.4	183.9	0.9	187.0	1.7	187.9	0.5	188.0	0.1	189.1	0.6
1993	191.0	1.0	191.5	0.3	192.0	0.3	192.4	0.2	193.2	0.4	193.1	-0.1	193.7	0.3	193.4	-0.2	193.1	-0.2	193.4	0.2	193.8	0.2	194.2	0.2
1994	195.1	0.5	195.2	0.1	195.5	0.2	196.4	0.5	197.1	0.4	197.6	0.3	198.0	0.2	199.4	0.7	201.4	1.0	201.9	0.2	202.3	0.2	202.4	0.0
1995	203.0	0.3	204.1	0.5	204.0	-0.0	204.3	0.1	204.9	0.3	205.3	0.2	205.7	0.2	207.7	1.0	210.2	1.2	210.7	0.2	211.2	0.2	211.1	-0.0

Source: U.S. Department of Labor, Bureau of Labor Statistics, Division of Consumer Prices and Price Indexes.

U.S. City Average
Consumer Price Index - Urban Wage Earners
Base 1982-1984 = 100
Other Goods and Services

For 1967-1995. Columns headed % show percentile change in the index from the previous period for which an index is available.

Year	Jan Index	%	Feb Index	%	Mar Index	%	Apr Index	%	May Index	%	Jun Index	%	Jul Index	%	Aug Index	%	Sep Index	%	Oct Index	%	Nov Index	%	Dec Index	%
1967	34.7	-	34.8	0.3	34.8	0.0	34.9	0.3	35.0	0.3	35.1	0.3	35.3	0.6	35.6	0.8	35.8	0.6	36.0	0.6	36.1	0.3	36.3	0.6
1968	36.4	0.3	36.4	0.0	36.8	1.1	36.8	0.0	36.9	0.3	37.2	0.8	37.3	0.3	37.4	0.3	37.6	0.5	37.8	0.5	37.9	0.3	38.1	0.5
1969	38.1	0.0	38.2	0.3	38.3	0.3	38.5	0.5	38.6	0.3	38.8	0.5	39.1	0.8	39.4	0.8	39.6	0.5	39.8	0.5	40.0	0.5	40.1	0.2
1970	40.3	0.5	40.4	0.2	40.5	0.2	40.8	0.7	41.0	0.5	41.3	0.7	41.5	0.5	41.7	0.5	41.8	0.2	42.0	0.5	42.2	0.5	42.3	0.2
1971	42.6	0.7	42.6	0.0	42.7	0.2	42.8	0.2	42.9	0.2	43.0	0.2	43.3	0.7	43.5	0.5	43.9	0.9	44.0	0.2	44.0	0.0	44.1	0.2
1972	44.3	0.5	44.6	0.7	44.7	0.2	44.8	0.2	45.0	0.4	45.2	0.4	45.2	0.0	45.2	0.0	45.5	0.7	45.6	0.2	45.6	0.0	45.7	0.2
1973	45.8	0.2	46.0	0.4	46.2	0.4	46.4	0.4	46.6	0.4	46.8	0.4	46.9	0.2	47.0	0.2	47.3	0.6	47.6	0.6	47.8	0.4	48.0	0.4
1974	48.1	0.2	48.4	0.6	48.6	0.4	48.9	0.6	49.3	0.8	49.9	1.2	50.4	1.0	50.8	0.8	51.4	1.2	51.9	1.0	52.4	1.0	52.8	0.8
1975	53.2	0.8	53.6	0.8	53.8	0.4	53.9	0.2	54.1	0.4	54.2	0.2	54.4	0.4	54.5	0.2	54.9	0.7	55.2	0.5	55.4	0.4	55.9	0.9
1976	56.2	0.5	56.6	0.7	56.7	0.2	57.0	0.5	57.1	0.2	57.3	0.4	57.4	0.2	57.7	0.5	58.2	0.9	58.5	0.5	58.9	0.7	59.1	0.3
1977	59.5	0.7	59.7	0.3	59.9	0.3	60.1	0.3	60.3	0.3	60.5	0.3	60.7	0.3	60.9	0.3	61.7	1.3	62.3	1.0	62.7	0.6	62.9	0.3
1978	63.1	0.3	63.4	0.5	63.5	0.2	63.7	0.3	63.9	0.3	64.2	0.5	65.0	1.2	65.2	0.3	66.2	1.5	66.4	0.3	66.6	0.3	66.6	0.0
1979	67.3	1.1	67.9	0.9	68.1	0.3	68.3	0.3	68.6	0.4	68.7	0.1	69.0	0.4	69.8	1.2	71.0	1.7	71.2	0.3	71.5	0.4	71.8	0.4
1980	72.9	1.5	73.5	0.8	73.7	0.3	74.0	0.4	74.5	0.7	75.0	0.7	75.3	0.4	75.7	0.5	77.5	2.4	77.8	0.4	78.2	0.5	78.9	0.9
1981	79.4	0.6	79.8	0.5	80.2	0.5	80.6	0.5	81.5	1.1	81.9	0.5	82.2	0.4	82.6	0.5	84.6	2.4	85.4	0.9	85.8	0.5	86.1	0.3
1982	86.7	0.7	87.4	0.8	88.2	0.9	88.8	0.7	89.3	0.6	89.5	0.2	90.0	0.6	90.5	0.6	93.0	2.8	94.7	1.8	95.8	1.2	96.9	1.1
1983	98.3	1.4	98.9	0.6	99.0	0.1	99.5	0.5	99.7	0.2	100.0	0.3	101.3	1.3	101.9	0.6	103.3	1.4	104.0	0.7	104.5	0.5	104.7	0.2
1984	105.4	0.7	105.8	0.4	106.0	0.2	106.3	0.3	106.4	0.1	106.9	0.5	107.7	0.7	108.0	0.3	110.0	1.9	110.3	0.3	110.6	0.3	110.6	0.0
1985	111.6	0.9	112.2	0.5	112.3	0.1	112.6	0.3	112.8	0.2	113.0	0.2	113.8	0.7	114.2	0.4	116.3	1.8	116.8	0.4	116.9	0.1	117.4	0.4
1986	118.5	0.9	118.9	0.3	119.2	0.3	119.4	0.2	119.6	0.2	119.7	0.1	120.7	0.8	121.2	0.4	122.9	1.4	123.4	0.4	123.5	0.1	123.6	0.1
1987	124.8	1.0	125.4	0.5	125.6	0.2	125.9	0.2	126.2	0.2	126.6	0.3	127.5	0.7	128.0	0.4	130.3	1.8	130.8	0.4	131.0	0.2	131.3	0.2
1988	132.7	1.1	133.6	0.7	134.0	0.3	134.2	0.1	134.5	0.2	135.0	0.4	136.3	1.0	137.2	0.7	139.3	1.5	139.9	0.4	140.3	0.3	140.6	0.2
1989	143.0	1.7	143.7	0.5	144.0	0.2	144.4	0.3	145.2	0.6	146.3	0.8	147.5	0.8	148.8	0.9	150.8	1.3	151.4	0.4	151.5	0.1	152.7	0.8
1990	153.9	0.8	154.6	0.5	155.1	0.3	155.7	0.4	156.3	0.4	157.8	1.0	159.4	1.0	160.5	0.7	162.4	1.2	162.8	0.2	163.4	0.4	164.4	0.6
1991	166.6	1.3	167.5	0.5	168.1	0.4	169.1	0.6	169.4	0.2	170.5	0.6	171.2	0.4	172.6	0.8	175.5	1.7	175.9	0.2	176.8	0.5	177.7	0.5
1992	178.6	0.5	179.4	0.4	179.7	0.2	180.3	0.3	181.6	0.7	181.8	0.1	182.7	0.5	184.2	0.8	186.7	1.4	187.7	0.5	187.7	0.0	189.0	0.7
1993	191.2	1.2	191.6	0.2	192.2	0.3	192.8	0.3	193.6	0.4	193.3	-0.2	193.8	0.3	192.7	-0.6	190.9	-0.9	191.1	0.1	191.6	0.3	192.0	0.2
1994	193.1	0.6	193.2	0.1	193.4	0.1	194.4	0.5	195.3	0.5	195.8	0.3	196.3	0.3	197.5	0.6	198.9	0.7	199.1	0.1	191.6	0.3	192.0	0.2
1995	200.5	0.3	201.5	0.5	201.4	-0.0	201.7	0.1	202.5	0.4	203.0	0.2	203.3	0.1	205.0	0.8	207.2	1.1	207.8	0.3	208.3	0.2	208.1	-0.1

Source: U.S. Department of Labor, Bureau of Labor Statistics, Division of Consumer Prices and Price Indexes.

Anchorage, AK
Consumer Price Index - All Urban Consumers
Base 1982-1984 = 100
Annual Averages

For 1960-1995. Columns headed % show percentile change in the index from the previous period for which an index is available.

Year	All Items		Food & Beverage		Housing		Apparel & Upkeep		Transportation		Medical Care		Entertainment		Other Goods & Services	
	Index	%	Index	%	Index	%	Index	%	Index	%	Index	%	Index	%	Index	%
1960	-	-	-	-	-	-	-	-	-	-	-	-	-	-	-	-
1961	34.5	-	-	-	-	-	-	-	-	-	-	-	-	-	-	-
1962	34.7	0.6	-	-	-	-	-	-	-	-	-	-	-	-	-	-
1963	34.8	0.3	-	-	-	-	-	-	-	-	-	-	-	-	-	-
1964	35.0	0.6	-	-	-	-	-	-	-	-	-	-	-	-	-	-
1965	35.3	0.9	-	-	-	-	-	-	-	-	-	-	-	-	-	-
1966	36.3	2.8	-	-	-	-	-	-	-	-	-	-	-	-	-	-
1967	37.2	2.5	-	-	-	-	-	-	-	-	-	-	-	-	-	-
1968	38.1	2.4	-	-	-	-	-	-	-	-	-	-	-	-	-	-
1969	39.6	3.9	-	-	-	-	-	-	-	-	-	-	-	-	-	-
1970	41.1	3.8	-	-	-	-	-	-	-	-	-	-	-	-	-	-
1971	42.3	2.9	-	-	-	-	56.5	-	40.8	-	35.2	-	-	-	-	-
1972	43.4	2.6	-	-	-	-	58.3	3.2	40.9	0.2	35.8	1.7	-	-	-	-
1973	45.3	4.4	-	-	-	-	60.7	4.1	41.4	1.2	37.3	4.2	-	-	-	-
1974	50.2	10.8	-	-	-	-	64.7	6.6	44.9	8.5	41.5	11.3	-	-	-	-
1975	57.1	13.7	-	-	-	-	69.8	7.9	49.3	9.8	46.9	13.0	-	-	-	-
1976	61.5	7.7	64.2	-	62.6	-	74.1	6.2	54.9	11.4	52.6	12.2	64.4	-	63.8	-
1977	65.6	6.7	68.9	7.3	65.5	4.6	79.2	6.9	60.2	9.7	57.9	10.1	69.4	7.8	68.1	6.7
1978	70.2	7.0	75.9	10.2	69.7	6.4	79.7	0.6	64.5	7.1	63.4	9.5	72.6	4.6	71.7	5.3
1979	77.6	10.5	84.0	10.7	78.0	11.9	81.7	2.5	71.3	10.5	69.1	9.0	74.5	2.6	76.9	7.3
1980	85.5	10.2	89.7	6.8	85.9	10.1	89.7	9.8	82.2	15.3	78.8	14.0	79.0	6.0	83.1	8.1
1981	92.4	8.1	94.3	5.1	92.5	7.7	94.1	4.9	92.7	12.8	86.9	10.3	85.9	8.7	88.1	6.0
1982	97.4	5.4	97.2	3.1	98.2	6.2	96.6	2.7	96.8	4.4	94.8	9.1	94.7	10.2	93.2	5.8
1983	99.2	1.8	99.7	2.6	99.0	0.8	101.6	5.2	98.5	1.8	99.7	5.2	100.6	6.2	101.5	8.9
1984	103.3	4.1	103.2	3.5	102.7	3.7	101.7	0.1	104.6	6.2	105.5	5.8	104.6	4.0	105.3	3.7
1985	105.8	2.4	106.2	2.9	103.0	0.3	105.8	4.0	108.2	3.4	110.9	5.1	108.9	4.1	114.2	8.5
1986	107.8	1.9	110.8	4.3	102.6	-0.4	109.0	3.0	107.8	-0.4	127.8	15.2	112.4	3.2	123.2	7.9
1987	118.0	9.5	118.6	7.0	118.0	15.0	109.9	0.8	108.7	0.8	136.1	6.5	119.2	6.0	130.8	6.2
1988	123.7	4.8	124.8	5.2	125.1	6.0	107.4	-2.3	112.8	3.8	144.8	6.4	122.8	3.0	139.5	6.7
1989	130.6	5.6	132.1	5.8	131.8	5.4	114.0	6.1	116.5	3.3	155.8	7.6	129.5	5.5	151.9	8.9
1990	138.5	6.0	139.6	5.7	139.3	5.7	121.8	6.8	123.1	5.7	172.4	10.7	135.6	4.7	164.0	8.0
1991	144.8	4.5	144.3	3.4	145.7	4.6	124.5	2.2	127.9	3.9	186.6	8.2	140.8	3.8	177.2	8.0
1992	150.0	3.6	146.0	1.2	151.4	3.9	128.5	3.2	131.5	2.8	200.0	7.2	146.4	4.0	191.0	7.8
1993	154.5	3.0	149.0	2.1	155.5	2.7	129.3	0.6	137.7	4.7	209.1	4.6	149.8	2.3	200.1	4.8
1994	158.2	2.4	151.9	1.9	159.9	2.8	126.2	-2.4	141.8	3.0	217.6	4.1	154.0	2.8	204.9	2.4
1995	162.2	2.5	155.9	2.6	163.4	2.2	126.0	-0.2	145.9	2.9	226.8	4.2	158.8	3.1	213.5	4.2

Source: U.S. Department of Labor, Bureau of Labor Statistics, Division of Consumer Prices and Price Indexes. - indicates no data collected for period.

Anchorage, AK
Consumer Price Index - Urban Wage Earners
Base 1982-1984 = 100
Annual Averages

For 1960-1995. Columns headed % show percentile change in the index from the previous period for which an index is available.

Year	All Items		Food & Beverage		Housing		Apparel & Upkeep		Trans-portation		Medical Care		Entertain-ment		Other Goods & Services	
	Index	%	Index	%	Index	%	Index	%	Index	%	Index	%	Index	%	Index	%
1960	-	-	-	-	-	-	-	-	-	-	-	-	-	-	-	-
1961	35.4	-	-	-	-	-	-	-	-	-	-	-	-	-	-	-
1962	35.5	0.3	-	-	-	-	-	-	-	-	-	-	-	-	-	-
1963	35.7	0.6	-	-	-	-	-	-	-	-	-	-	-	-	-	-
1964	35.9	0.6	-	-	-	-	-	-	-	-	-	-	-	-	-	-
1965	36.2	0.8	-	-	-	-	-	-	-	-	-	-	-	-	-	-
1966	37.2	2.8	-	-	-	-	-	-	-	-	-	-	-	-	-	-
1967	38.2	2.7	-	-	-	-	-	-	-	-	-	-	-	-	-	-
1968	39.1	2.4	-	-	-	-	-	-	-	-	-	-	-	-	-	-
1969	40.7	4.1	-	-	-	-	-	-	-	-	-	-	-	-	-	-
1970	42.1	3.4	-	-	-	-	-	-	-	-	-	-	-	-	-	-
1971	43.4	3.1	-	-	-	-	57.1	-	40.4	-	36.2	-	-	-	-	-
1972	44.5	2.5	-	-	-	-	58.9	3.2	40.5	0.2	36.9	1.9	-	-	-	-
1973	46.4	4.3	-	-	-	-	61.4	4.2	41.0	1.2	38.4	4.1	-	-	-	-
1974	51.4	10.8	-	-	-	-	65.4	6.5	44.4	8.3	42.7	11.2	-	-	-	-
1975	58.5	13.8	-	-	-	-	70.5	7.8	48.8	9.9	48.3	13.1	-	-	-	-
1976	63.1	7.9	64.5	-	65.7	-	74.9	6.2	54.3	11.3	54.1	12.0	70.5	-	62.6	-
1977	67.2	6.5	69.3	7.4	68.8	4.7	80.0	6.8	59.6	9.8	59.7	10.4	76.0	7.8	66.9	6.9
1978	72.0	7.1	76.9	11.0	73.0	6.1	80.3	0.4	64.1	7.6	67.1	12.4	76.0	0.0	70.1	4.8
1979	79.0	9.7	86.1	12.0	80.5	10.3	81.6	1.6	71.2	11.1	72.8	8.5	77.0	1.3	75.0	7.0
1980	86.3	9.2	90.3	4.9	87.6	8.8	86.5	6.0	82.9	16.4	79.3	8.9	79.9	3.8	81.9	9.2
1981	92.9	7.6	94.2	4.3	93.9	7.2	92.6	7.1	93.4	12.7	86.8	9.5	86.2	7.9	86.4	5.5
1982	98.2	5.7	97.2	3.2	100.1	6.6	96.3	4.0	97.3	4.2	94.9	9.3	94.6	9.7	92.4	6.9
1983	98.9	0.7	99.7	2.6	98.2	-1.9	101.6	5.5	98.4	1.1	99.8	5.2	100.5	6.2	101.9	10.3
1984	102.9	4.0	103.2	3.5	101.6	3.5	102.1	0.5	104.3	6.0	105.3	5.5	105.0	4.5	105.7	3.7
1985	105.8	2.8	106.2	2.9	103.4	1.8	105.5	3.3	107.6	3.2	110.5	4.9	108.7	3.5	114.1	7.9
1986	107.7	1.8	110.9	4.4	103.1	-0.3	108.1	2.5	106.5	-1.0	125.3	13.4	112.5	3.5	123.2	8.0
1987	116.6	8.3	118.2	6.6	116.0	12.5	110.2	1.9	108.4	1.8	136.8	9.2	120.3	6.9	129.5	5.1
1988	121.8	4.5	124.3	5.2	122.5	5.6	106.3	-3.5	112.4	3.7	145.8	6.6	123.9	3.0	137.9	6.5
1989	128.6	5.6	131.7	6.0	129.0	5.3	112.5	5.8	116.1	3.3	157.0	7.7	130.3	5.2	150.7	9.3
1990	136.3	6.0	139.4	5.8	135.9	5.3	120.1	6.8	123.1	6.0	172.0	9.6	136.2	4.5	163.6	8.6
1991	142.1	4.3	144.0	3.3	141.6	4.2	122.1	1.7	127.8	3.8	186.2	8.3	141.3	3.7	177.5	8.5
1992	146.9	3.4	145.6	1.1	146.7	3.6	125.8	3.0	131.6	3.0	200.3	7.6	146.6	3.8	191.0	7.6
1993	151.1	2.9	148.6	2.1	150.6	2.7	126.2	0.3	137.4	4.4	209.0	4.3	149.5	2.0	200.4	4.9
1994	154.5	2.3	151.5	2.0	154.6	2.7	122.7	-2.8	141.6	3.1	217.9	4.3	153.5	2.7	204.8	2.2
1995	158.3	2.5	155.3	2.5	158.0	2.2	121.8	-0.7	146.0	3.1	227.6	4.5	158.1	3.0	213.1	4.1

Source: U.S. Department of Labor, Bureau of Labor Statistics, Division of Consumer Prices and Price Indexes. - indicates no data collected for period.

Anchorage, AK
Consumer Price Index - All Urban Consumers
Base 1982-1984 = 100
All Items

For 1960-1995. Columns headed % show percentile change in the index from the previous period for which an index is available.

Year	Jan Index	%	Feb Index	%	Mar Index	%	Apr Index	%	May Index	%	Jun Index	%	Jul Index	%	Aug Index	%	Sep Index	%	Oct Index	%	Nov Index	%	Dec Index	%
1960	-	-	-	-	-	-	-	-	34.2	-	-	-	-	-	-	-	-	-	34.4	0.6	-	-	-	-
1961	-	-	-	-	-	-	-	-	34.4	0.0	-	-	-	-	-	-	-	-	34.8	1.2	-	-	-	-
1962	-	-	-	-	-	-	-	-	34.6	-0.6	-	-	-	-	-	-	-	-	34.7	0.3	-	-	-	-
1963	-	-	-	-	-	-	34.8	0.3	-	-	-	-	-	-	-	-	-	-	34.9	0.3	-	-	-	-
1964	-	-	-	-	-	-	34.8	-0.3	-	-	-	-	-	-	-	-	-	-	35.2	1.1	-	-	-	-
1965	-	-	-	-	-	-	35.3	0.3	-	-	-	-	-	-	-	-	-	-	35.3	0.0	-	-	-	-
1966	-	-	-	-	-	-	-	-	-	-	-	-	-	-	-	-	-	-	36.7	4.0	-	-	-	-
1967	-	-	-	-	-	-	-	-	-	-	-	-	-	-	-	-	-	-	37.5	2.2	-	-	-	-
1968	-	-	-	-	-	-	-	-	-	-	-	-	-	-	-	-	-	-	38.4	2.4	-	-	-	-
1969	38.9	1.3	-	-	-	-	39.5	1.5	-	-	-	-	39.6	0.3	-	-	-	-	40.2	1.5	-	-	-	-
1970	40.4	0.5	-	-	-	-	40.5	0.2	-	-	-	-	41.1	1.5	-	-	-	-	41.8	1.7	-	-	-	-
1971	41.8	0.0	-	-	-	-	41.8	0.0	-	-	-	-	42.3	1.2	-	-	-	-	42.8	1.2	-	-	-	-
1972	42.8	0.0	-	-	-	-	43.4	1.4	-	-	-	-	43.4	0.0	-	-	-	-	43.8	0.9	-	-	-	-
1973	43.6	-0.5	-	-	-	-	44.7	2.5	-	-	-	-	45.1	0.9	-	-	-	-	46.4	2.9	-	-	-	-
1974	47.1	1.5	-	-	-	-	48.7	3.4	-	-	-	-	50.3	3.3	-	-	-	-	52.5	4.4	-	-	-	-
1975	53.5	1.9	-	-	-	-	56.2	5.0	-	-	-	-	57.6	2.5	-	-	-	-	59.0	2.4	-	-	-	-
1976	59.5	0.8	-	-	-	-	60.6	1.8	-	-	-	-	61.8	2.0	-	-	-	-	62.8	1.6	-	-	-	-
1977	63.5	1.1	-	-	-	-	64.7	1.9	-	-	-	-	66.5	2.8	-	-	-	-	66.4	-0.2	-	-	-	-
1978	67.1	1.1	-	-	67.7	0.9	-	-	69.0	1.9	-	-	70.6	2.3	-	-	72.4	2.5	-	-	72.9	0.7	-	-
1979	74.2	1.8	-	-	75.3	1.5	-	-	76.2	1.2	-	-	77.7	2.0	-	-	79.9	2.8	-	-	80.1	0.3	-	-
1980	81.7	2.0	-	-	83.7	2.4	-	-	84.9	1.4	-	-	85.6	0.8	-	-	86.5	1.1	-	-	88.6	2.4	-	-
1981	90.0	1.6	-	-	90.3	0.3	-	-	91.6	1.4	-	-	92.2	0.7	-	-	93.9	1.8	-	-	95.0	1.2	-	-
1982	94.8	-0.2	-	-	97.4	2.7	-	-	98.8	1.4	-	-	98.8	0.0	-	-	98.7	-0.1	-	-	96.4	-2.3	-	-
1983	96.5	0.1	-	-	97.8	1.3	-	-	98.3	0.5	-	-	99.6	1.3	-	-	100.4	0.8	-	-	101.3	0.9	-	-
1984	101.7	0.4	-	-	102.8	1.1	-	-	103.1	0.3	-	-	103.2	0.1	-	-	104.1	0.9	-	-	104.0	-0.1	-	-
1985	104.3	0.3	-	-	104.9	0.6	-	-	104.5	-0.4	-	-	106.1	1.5	-	-	106.6	0.5	-	-	107.5	0.8	-	-
1986	107.6	0.1	-	-	109.1	1.4	-	-	108.2	-0.8	-	-	107.3	-0.8	-	-	107.2	-0.1	-	-	107.8	0.6	107.4	-0.4
1987	-	-	-	-	-	-	-	-	-	-	116.2	8.2	-	-	-	-	-	-	-	-	-	-	119.7	3.0
1988	-	-	-	-	-	-	-	-	-	-	122.1	2.0	-	-	-	-	-	-	-	-	-	-	125.3	2.6
1989	-	-	-	-	-	-	-	-	-	-	129.0	3.0	-	-	-	-	-	-	-	-	-	-	132.2	2.5
1990	-	-	-	-	-	-	-	-	-	-	136.4	3.2	-	-	-	-	-	-	-	-	-	-	140.7	3.2
1991	-	-	-	-	-	-	-	-	-	-	143.7	2.1	-	-	-	-	-	-	-	-	-	-	145.9	1.5
1992	-	-	-	-	-	-	-	-	-	-	148.7	1.9	-	-	-	-	-	-	-	-	-	-	151.4	1.8
1993	-	-	-	-	-	-	-	-	-	-	153.8	1.6	-	-	-	-	-	-	-	-	-	-	155.2	0.9
1994	-	-	-	-	-	-	-	-	-	-	157.4	1.4	-	-	-	-	-	-	-	-	-	-	159.0	1.0
1995	-	-	-	-	-	-	-	-	-	-	161.1	1.3	-	-	-	-	-	-	-	-	-	-	-	-

Source: U.S. Department of Labor, Bureau of Labor Statistics, Division of Consumer Prices and Price Indexes. - indicates no data collected for period.

Anchorage, AK
Consumer Price Index - Urban Wage Earners
Base 1982-1984 = 100
All Items

For 1960-1995. Columns headed % show percentile change in the index from the previous period for which an index is available.

Year	Jan Index	%	Feb Index	%	Mar Index	%	Apr Index	%	May Index	%	Jun Index	%	Jul Index	%	Aug Index	%	Sep Index	%	Oct Index	%	Nov Index	%	Dec Index	%
1960	-	-	-	-	-	-	-	-	35.1	-	-	-	-	-	-	-	-	-	35.3	0.6	-	-	-	-
1961	-	-	-	-	-	-	-	-	35.2	-0.3	-	-	-	-	-	-	-	-	35.7	1.4	-	-	-	-
1962	-	-	-	-	-	-	-	-	35.5	-0.6	-	-	-	-	-	-	-	-	35.5	0.0	-	-	-	-
1963	-	-	-	-	-	-	35.7	0.6	-	-	-	-	-	-	-	-	-	-	35.8	0.3	-	-	-	-
1964	-	-	-	-	-	-	35.7	-0.3	-	-	-	-	-	-	-	-	-	-	36.1	1.1	-	-	-	-
1965	-	-	-	-	-	-	36.2	0.3	-	-	-	-	-	-	-	-	-	-	36.2	0.0	-	-	-	-
1966	-	-	-	-	-	-	-	-	-	-	-	-	-	-	-	-	-	-	37.6	3.9	-	-	-	-
1967	-	-	-	-	-	-	-	-	-	-	-	-	-	-	-	-	-	-	38.4	2.1	-	-	-	-
1968	-	-	-	-	-	-	-	-	-	-	-	-	-	-	-	-	-	-	39.4	2.6	-	-	-	-
1969	39.8	1.0	-	-	-	-	40.5	1.8	-	-	-	-	40.6	0.2	-	-	-	-	41.2	1.5	-	-	-	-
1970	41.4	0.5	-	-	-	-	41.6	0.5	-	-	-	-	42.1	1.2	-	-	-	-	42.8	1.7	-	-	-	-
1971	42.8	0.0	-	-	-	-	42.9	0.2	-	-	-	-	43.4	1.2	-	-	-	-	43.9	1.2	-	-	-	-
1972	43.9	0.0	-	-	-	-	44.5	1.4	-	-	-	-	44.5	0.0	-	-	-	-	44.9	0.9	-	-	-	-
1973	44.7	-0.4	-	-	-	-	45.9	2.7	-	-	-	-	46.3	0.9	-	-	-	-	47.6	2.8	-	-	-	-
1974	48.3	1.5	-	-	-	-	49.9	3.3	-	-	-	-	51.6	3.4	-	-	-	-	53.9	4.5	-	-	-	-
1975	54.9	1.9	-	-	-	-	57.6	4.9	-	-	-	-	59.1	2.6	-	-	-	-	60.5	2.4	-	-	-	-
1976	61.0	0.8	-	-	-	-	62.1	1.8	-	-	-	-	63.4	2.1	-	-	-	-	64.4	1.6	-	-	-	-
1977	65.1	1.1	-	-	-	-	66.3	1.8	-	-	-	-	68.2	2.9	-	-	-	-	68.1	-0.1	-	-	-	-
1978	68.9	1.2	-	-	69.5	0.9	-	-	70.7	1.7	-	-	72.5	2.5	-	-	74.1	2.2	-	-	74.8	0.9	-	-
1979	75.8	1.3	-	-	77.0	1.6	-	-	77.8	1.0	-	-	79.3	1.9	-	-	81.0	2.1	-	-	81.4	0.5	-	-
1980	83.0	2.0	-	-	84.6	1.9	-	-	85.7	1.3	-	-	86.4	0.8	-	-	87.1	0.8	-	-	89.1	2.3	-	-
1981	90.3	1.3	-	-	90.8	0.6	-	-	92.3	1.7	-	-	92.9	0.7	-	-	94.5	1.7	-	-	95.8	1.4	-	-
1982	95.5	-0.3	-	-	97.8	2.4	-	-	99.1	1.3	-	-	99.6	0.5	-	-	99.5	-0.1	-	-	97.7	-1.8	-	-
1983	96.3	-1.4	-	-	97.6	1.3	-	-	97.9	0.3	-	-	98.9	1.0	-	-	100.2	1.3	-	-	101.4	1.2	-	-
1984	101.4	0.0	-	-	102.2	0.8	-	-	102.1	-0.1	-	-	102.5	0.4	-	-	104.1	1.6	-	-	104.1	0.0	-	-
1985	104.4	0.3	-	-	104.9	0.5	-	-	104.5	-0.4	-	-	106.0	1.4	-	-	106.5	0.5	-	-	107.6	1.0	-	-
1986	107.7	0.1	-	-	109.3	1.5	-	-	108.3	-0.9	-	-	107.0	-1.2	-	-	106.8	-0.2	-	-	107.5	0.7	107.2	-0.3
1987	-	-	-	-	-	-	-	-	-	-	114.8	7.1	-	-	-	-	-	-	-	-	-	-	118.2	3.0
1988	-	-	-	-	-	-	-	-	-	-	120.2	1.7	-	-	-	-	-	-	-	-	-	-	123.4	2.7
1989	-	-	-	-	-	-	-	-	-	-	127.0	2.9	-	-	-	-	-	-	-	-	-	-	130.2	2.5
1990	-	-	-	-	-	-	-	-	-	-	134.3	3.1	-	-	-	-	-	-	-	-	-	-	138.4	3.1
1991	-	-	-	-	-	-	-	-	-	-	141.0	1.9	-	-	-	-	-	-	-	-	-	-	143.2	1.6
1992	-	-	-	-	-	-	-	-	-	-	145.5	1.6	-	-	-	-	-	-	-	-	-	-	148.3	1.9
1993	-	-	-	-	-	-	-	-	-	-	150.5	1.5	-	-	-	-	-	-	-	-	-	-	151.7	0.8
1994	-	-	-	-	-	-	-	-	-	-	153.6	1.3	-	-	-	-	-	-	-	-	-	-	155.4	1.2
1995	-	-	-	-	-	-	-	-	-	-	157.3	1.2	-	-	-	-	-	-	-	-	-	-	-	-

Source: U.S. Department of Labor, Bureau of Labor Statistics, Division of Consumer Prices and Price Indexes. - indicates no data collected for period.

Anchorage, AK
Consumer Price Index - All Urban Consumers
Base 1982-1984 = 100
Food and Beverages

For 1976-1995. Columns headed % show percentile change in the index from the previous period for which an index is available.

Year	Jan Index	%	Feb Index	%	Mar Index	%	Apr Index	%	May Index	%	Jun Index	%	Jul Index	%	Aug Index	%	Sep Index	%	Oct Index	%	Nov Index	%	Dec Index	%
1976	63.2	-	-	-	-	-	63.4	0.3	-	-	-	-	64.4	1.6	-	-	-	-	64.8	0.6	-	-	-	-
1977	65.4	0.9	-	-	-	-	67.3	2.9	-	-	-	-	70.9	5.3	-	-	-	-	69.8	-1.6	-	-	-	-
1978	71.6	2.6	-	-	73.2	2.2	-	-	76.2	4.1	-	-	76.2	0.0	-	-	77.7	2.0	-	-	78.2	0.6	-	-
1979	80.6	3.1	-	-	82.7	2.6	-	-	82.7	0.0	-	-	84.5	2.2	-	-	85.7	1.4	-	-	86.2	0.6	-	-
1980	86.8	0.7	-	-	87.3	0.6	-	-	88.6	1.5	-	-	89.9	1.5	-	-	91.0	1.2	-	-	93.0	2.2	-	-
1981	92.9	-0.1	-	-	92.6	-0.3	-	-	93.1	0.5	-	-	94.6	1.6	-	-	95.7	1.2	-	-	96.0	0.3	-	-
1982	96.5	0.5	-	-	95.6	-0.9	-	-	96.7	1.2	-	-	98.2	1.6	-	-	97.8	-0.4	-	-	97.9	0.1	-	-
1983	97.8	-0.1	-	-	98.4	0.6	-	-	99.2	0.8	-	-	100.2	1.0	-	-	100.3	0.1	-	-	101.0	0.7	-	-
1984	102.2	1.2	-	-	102.9	0.7	-	-	103.3	0.4	-	-	103.2	-0.1	-	-	103.2	0.0	-	-	103.7	0.5	-	-
1985	103.8	0.1	-	-	104.5	0.7	-	-	105.1	0.6	-	-	106.5	1.3	-	-	107.1	0.6	-	-	108.6	1.4	-	-
1986	109.7	1.0	-	-	109.8	0.1	-	-	110.5	0.6	-	-	111.1	0.5	-	-	111.5	0.4	-	-	111.6	0.1	111.9	0.3
1987	-	-	-	-	-	-	-	-	-	-	117.3	4.8	-	-	-	-	-	-	-	-	-	-	119.9	2.2
1988	-	-	-	-	-	-	-	-	-	-	123.3	2.8	-	-	-	-	-	-	-	-	-	-	126.4	2.5
1989	-	-	-	-	-	-	-	-	-	-	131.0	3.6	-	-	-	-	-	-	-	-	-	-	133.2	1.7
1990	-	-	-	-	-	-	-	-	-	-	138.4	3.9	-	-	-	-	-	-	-	-	-	-	140.8	1.7
1991	-	-	-	-	-	-	-	-	-	-	144.7	2.8	-	-	-	-	-	-	-	-	-	-	143.9	-0.6
1992	-	-	-	-	-	-	-	-	-	-	145.7	1.3	-	-	-	-	-	-	-	-	-	-	146.2	0.3
1993	-	-	-	-	-	-	-	-	-	-	148.8	1.8	-	-	-	-	-	-	-	-	-	-	149.3	0.3
1994	-	-	-	-	-	-	-	-	-	-	151.2	1.3	-	-	-	-	-	-	-	-	-	-	152.7	1.0
1995	-	-	-	-	-	-	-	-	-	-	155.1	1.6	-	-	-	-	-	-	-	-	-	-	-	-

Source: U.S. Department of Labor, Bureau of Labor Statistics, Division of Consumer Prices and Price Indexes. - indicates no data collected for period.

Anchorage, AK
Consumer Price Index - Urban Wage Earners
Base 1982-1984 = 100
Food and Beverages

For 1976-1995. Columns headed % show percentile change in the index from the previous period for which an index is available.

Year	Jan Index	%	Feb Index	%	Mar Index	%	Apr Index	%	May Index	%	Jun Index	%	Jul Index	%	Aug Index	%	Sep Index	%	Oct Index	%	Nov Index	%	Dec Index	%
1976	63.6	-	-	-	-	-	63.7	0.2	-	-	-	-	64.8	1.7	-	-	-	-	65.2	0.6	-	-	-	-
1977	65.8	0.9	-	-	-	-	67.7	2.9	-	-	-	-	71.3	5.3	-	-	-	-	70.2	-1.5	-	-	-	-
1978	72.0	2.6	-	-	73.3	1.8	-	-	76.0	3.7	-	-	78.0	2.6	-	-	79.5	1.9	-	-	80.4	1.1	-	-
1979	81.6	1.5	-	-	84.9	4.0	-	-	85.5	0.7	-	-	86.8	1.5	-	-	88.0	1.4	-	-	88.3	0.3	-	-
1980	88.8	0.6	-	-	88.1	-0.8	-	-	89.2	1.2	-	-	90.6	1.6	-	-	91.3	0.8	-	-	93.0	1.9	-	-
1981	92.4	-0.6	-	-	92.2	-0.2	-	-	93.2	1.1	-	-	94.2	1.1	-	-	95.9	1.8	-	-	96.0	0.1	-	-
1982	96.4	0.4	-	-	95.6	-0.8	-	-	96.6	1.0	-	-	98.1	1.6	-	-	97.8	-0.3	-	-	97.9	0.1	-	-
1983	98.1	0.2	-	-	98.5	0.4	-	-	99.1	0.6	-	-	100.2	1.1	-	-	100.4	0.2	-	-	100.9	0.5	-	-
1984	102.1	1.2	-	-	102.9	0.8	-	-	103.3	0.4	-	-	103.3	0.0	-	-	103.3	0.0	-	-	103.8	0.5	-	-
1985	103.8	0.0	-	-	104.6	0.8	-	-	105.2	0.6	-	-	106.6	1.3	-	-	107.0	0.4	-	-	108.5	1.4	-	-
1986	109.6	1.0	-	-	110.0	0.4	-	-	110.5	0.5	-	-	111.1	0.5	-	-	111.6	0.5	-	-	111.8	0.2	111.9	0.1
1987	-	-	-	-	-	-	-	-	-	-	116.9	4.5	-	-	-	-	-	-	-	-	-	-	119.4	2.1
1988	-	-	-	-	-	-	-	-	-	-	122.7	2.8	-	-	-	-	-	-	-	-	-	-	125.9	2.6
1989	-	-	-	-	-	-	-	-	-	-	130.6	3.7	-	-	-	-	-	-	-	-	-	-	132.8	1.7
1990	-	-	-	-	-	-	-	-	-	-	138.1	4.0	-	-	-	-	-	-	-	-	-	-	140.6	1.8
1991	-	-	-	-	-	-	-	-	-	-	144.5	2.8	-	-	-	-	-	-	-	-	-	-	143.6	-0.6
1992	-	-	-	-	-	-	-	-	-	-	145.4	1.3	-	-	-	-	-	-	-	-	-	-	145.8	0.3
1993	-	-	-	-	-	-	-	-	-	-	148.3	1.7	-	-	-	-	-	-	-	-	-	-	148.8	0.3
1994	-	-	-	-	-	-	-	-	-	-	150.8	1.3	-	-	-	-	-	-	-	-	-	-	152.3	1.0
1995	-	-	-	-	-	-	-	-	-	-	154.5	1.4	-	-	-	-	-	-	-	-	-	-	-	-

Source: U.S. Department of Labor, Bureau of Labor Statistics, Division of Consumer Prices and Price Indexes. - indicates no data collected for period.

Anchorage, AK
Consumer Price Index - All Urban Consumers
Base 1982-1984 = 100
Housing

For 1976-1995. Columns headed % show percentile change in the index from the previous period for which an index is available.

Year	Jan Index	%	Feb Index	%	Mar Index	%	Apr Index	%	May Index	%	Jun Index	%	Jul Index	%	Aug Index	%	Sep Index	%	Oct Index	%	Nov Index	%	Dec Index	%
1976	61.0	-	-	-	-	-	61.7	1.1	-	-	-	-	62.8	1.8	-	-	-	-	63.7	1.4	-	-	-	-
1977	64.3	0.9	-	-	-	-	64.6	0.5	-	-	-	-	66.0	2.2	-	-	72.5	3.4	66.4	0.6	-	-	-	-
1978	66.6	0.3	-	-	66.9	0.5	-	-	67.5	0.9	-	-	70.1	3.9	-	-	72.5	3.4	-	-	73.0	0.7	-	-
1979	74.4	1.9	-	-	75.7	1.7	-	-	76.7	1.3	-	-	78.3	2.1	-	-	80.5	2.8	-	-	80.4	-0.1	-	-
1980	82.4	2.5	-	-	84.6	2.7	-	-	85.4	0.9	-	-	85.9	0.6	-	-	86.4	0.6	-	-	88.8	2.8	-	-
1981	90.8	2.3	-	-	90.7	-0.1	-	-	91.6	1.0	-	-	91.9	0.3	-	-	93.7	2.0	-	-	95.2	1.6	-	-
1982	94.4	-0.8	-	-	99.4	5.3	-	-	101.4	2.0	-	-	100.1	-1.3	-	-	99.6	-0.5	-	-	94.8	-4.8	-	-
1983	95.2	0.4	-	-	97.8	2.7	-	-	98.1	0.3	-	-	99.7	1.6	-	-	100.7	1.0	-	-	100.9	0.2	-	-
1984	101.7	0.8	-	-	102.9	1.2	-	-	103.0	0.1	-	-	102.2	-0.8	-	-	103.2	1.0	-	-	102.7	-0.5	-	-
1985	103.0	0.3	-	-	102.7	-0.3	-	-	101.4	-1.3	-	-	104.2	2.8	-	-	103.8	-0.4	-	-	103.2	-0.6	-	-
1986	103.3	0.1	-	-	105.8	2.4	-	-	105.5	-0.3	-	-	101.1	-4.2	-	-	100.2	-0.9	-	-	100.1	-0.1	100.1	0.0
1987	-	-	-	-	-	-	-	-	-	-	116.2	16.1	-	-	-	-	-	-	-	-	-	-	119.9	3.2
1988	-	-	-	-	-	-	-	-	-	-	123.7	3.2	-	-	-	-	-	-	-	-	-	-	126.6	2.3
1989	-	-	-	-	-	-	-	-	-	-	130.0	2.7	-	-	-	-	-	-	-	-	-	-	133.7	2.8
1990	-	-	-	-	-	-	-	-	-	-	137.4	2.8	-	-	-	-	-	-	-	-	-	-	141.2	2.8
1991	-	-	-	-	-	-	-	-	-	-	144.5	2.3	-	-	-	-	-	-	-	-	-	-	146.9	1.7
1992	-	-	-	-	-	-	-	-	-	-	150.2	2.2	-	-	-	-	-	-	-	-	-	-	152.6	1.6
1993	-	-	-	-	-	-	-	-	-	-	154.6	1.3	-	-	-	-	-	-	-	-	-	-	156.4	1.2
1994	-	-	-	-	-	-	-	-	-	-	159.1	1.7	-	-	-	-	-	-	-	-	-	-	160.6	0.9
1995	-	-	-	-	-	-	-	-	-	-	162.3	1.1	-	-	-	-	-	-	-	-	-	-	-	-

Source: U.S. Department of Labor, Bureau of Labor Statistics, Division of Consumer Prices and Price Indexes. - indicates no data collected for period.

Anchorage, AK
Consumer Price Index - Urban Wage Earners
Base 1982-1984 = 100
Housing

For 1976-1995. Columns headed % show percentile change in the index from the previous period for which an index is available.

Year	Jan Index	Jan %	Feb Index	Feb %	Mar Index	Mar %	Apr Index	Apr %	May Index	May %	Jun Index	Jun %	Jul Index	Jul %	Aug Index	Aug %	Sep Index	Sep %	Oct Index	Oct %	Nov Index	Nov %	Dec Index	Dec %
1976	64.1	-	-	-	-	-	64.8	1.1	-	-	-	-	66.0	1.9	-	-	-	-	-	-	66.9	1.4	-	-
1977	67.5	0.9	-	-	-	-	67.8	0.4	-	-	-	-	69.3	2.2	-	-	-	-	69.7	0.6	-	-	-	-
1978	69.9	0.3	-	-	70.3	0.6	-	-	70.9	0.9	-	-	73.3	3.4	-	-	75.6	3.1	-	-	76.2	0.8	-	-
1979	77.4	1.6	-	-	78.7	1.7	-	-	79.2	0.6	-	-	80.7	1.9	-	-	82.6	2.4	-	-	82.6	0.0	-	-
1980	84.3	2.1	-	-	86.3	2.4	-	-	87.3	1.2	-	-	87.6	0.3	-	-	87.9	0.3	-	-	90.3	2.7	-	-
1981	92.1	2.0	-	-	92.0	-0.1	-	-	93.1	1.2	-	-	93.3	0.2	-	-	95.0	1.8	-	-	96.8	1.9	-	-
1982	96.0	-0.8	-	-	100.8	5.0	-	-	103.0	2.2	-	-	102.3	-0.7	-	-	101.7	-0.6	-	-	97.6	-4.0	-	-
1983	94.5	-3.2	-	-	97.1	2.8	-	-	97.0	-0.1	-	-	98.1	1.1	-	-	99.9	1.8	-	-	101.1	1.2	-	-
1984	100.8	-0.3	-	-	101.4	0.6	-	-	100.4	-1.0	-	-	100.6	0.2	-	-	103.0	2.4	-	-	102.9	-0.1	-	-
1985	103.3	0.4	-	-	102.9	-0.4	-	-	101.5	-1.4	-	-	104.4	2.9	-	-	104.2	-0.2	-	-	102.9	-0.1	-	-
1986	103.6	-0.2	-	-	106.6	2.9	-	-	106.3	-0.3	-	-	101.7	-4.3	-	-	100.9	-0.8	-	-	100.4	-0.5	-	-
1987	-	-	-	-	-	-	-	-	-	-	-	-	-	-	-	-	-	-	-	-	100.4	-0.5	100.6	0.2
1988	-	-	-	-	-	-	-	-	-	-	114.2	13.5	-	-	-	-	-	-	-	-	-	-	117.8	3.2
1989	-	-	-	-	-	-	-	-	-	-	121.0	2.7	-	-	-	-	-	-	-	-	-	-	123.9	2.4
1990	-	-	-	-	-	-	-	-	-	-	127.1	2.6	-	-	-	-	-	-	-	-	-	-	131.0	3.1
1991	-	-	-	-	-	-	-	-	-	-	134.3	2.5	-	-	-	-	-	-	-	-	-	-	137.6	2.5
1992	-	-	-	-	-	-	-	-	-	-	140.3	2.0	-	-	-	-	-	-	-	-	-	-	142.9	1.9
1993	-	-	-	-	-	-	-	-	-	-	145.6	1.9	-	-	-	-	-	-	-	-	-	-	147.9	1.6
1994	-	-	-	-	-	-	-	-	-	-	149.9	1.4	-	-	-	-	-	-	-	-	-	-	151.4	1.0
1995	-	-	-	-	-	-	-	-	-	-	153.8	1.6	-	-	-	-	-	-	-	-	-	-	155.5	1.1

Source: U.S. Department of Labor, Bureau of Labor Statistics, Division of Consumer Prices and Price Indexes. - indicates no data collected for period.

Anchorage, AK
Consumer Price Index - All Urban Consumers
Base 1982-1984 = 100
Apparel and Upkeep

For 1971-1995. Columns headed % show percentile change in the index from the previous period for which an index is available.

Year	Jan Index	%	Feb Index	%	Mar Index	%	Apr Index	%	May Index	%	Jun Index	%	Jul Index	%	Aug Index	%	Sep Index	%	Oct Index	%	Nov Index	%	Dec Index	%
1971	55.3	-	-	-	-	-	56.1	1.4	-	-	-	-	56.8	1.2	-	-	-	-	57.0	0.4	-	-	-	-
1972	56.7	-0.5	-	-	-	-	58.5	3.2	-	-	-	-	58.3	-0.3	-	-	-	-	59.0	1.2	-	-	-	-
1973	58.9	-0.2	-	-	-	-	59.9	1.7	-	-	-	-	61.1	2.0	-	-	-	-	62.1	1.6	-	-	-	-
1974	61.7	-0.6	-	-	-	-	62.8	1.8	-	-	-	-	64.9	3.3	-	-	-	-	67.4	3.9	-	-	-	-
1975	67.6	0.3	-	-	-	-	70.1	3.7	-	-	-	-	69.6	-0.7	-	-	-	-	71.2	2.3	-	-	-	-
1976	70.3	-1.3	-	-	-	-	72.3	2.8	-	-	-	-	73.5	1.7	-	-	-	-	77.4	5.3	-	-	-	-
1977	78.7	1.7	-	-	-	-	79.1	0.5	-	-	-	-	79.0	-0.1	-	-	-	-	80.3	1.6	-	-	-	-
1978	77.5	-3.5	-	-	78.2	0.9	-	-	80.1	2.4	-	-	79.1	-1.2	-	-	81.4	2.9	-	-	81.5	0.1	-	-
1979	79.6	-2.3	-	-	79.3	-0.4	-	-	79.7	0.5	-	-	78.9	-1.0	-	-	86.5	9.6	-	-	85.0	-1.7	-	-
1980	83.8	-1.4	-	-	86.4	3.1	-	-	88.4	2.3	-	-	91.7	3.7	-	-	92.1	0.4	-	-	93.5	1.5	-	-
1981	92.7	-0.9	-	-	94.3	1.7	-	-	95.0	0.7	-	-	91.5	-3.7	-	-	95.7	4.6	-	-	95.0	-0.7	-	-
1982	93.9	-1.2	-	-	93.9	0.0	-	-	96.3	2.6	-	-	96.7	0.4	-	-	99.0	2.4	-	-	99.4	0.4	-	-
1983	95.7	-3.7	-	-	101.5	6.1	-	-	101.9	0.4	-	-	102.4	0.5	-	-	102.3	-0.1	-	-	104.8	2.4	-	-
1984	100.8	-3.8	-	-	102.3	1.5	-	-	99.9	-2.3	-	-	101.5	1.6	-	-	104.7	3.2	-	-	101.6	-3.0	-	-
1985	100.4	-1.2	-	-	107.3	6.9	-	-	106.1	-1.1	-	-	103.2	-2.7	-	-	108.7	5.3	-	-	107.6	-1.0	-	-
1986	105.5	-2.0	-	-	110.2	4.5	-	-	107.7	-2.3	-	-	109.0	1.2	-	-	110.3	1.2	-	-	110.7	0.4	108.9	-1.6
1987	-	-	-	-	-	-	-	-	-	-	108.6	-0.3	-	-	-	-	-	-	-	-	-	-	111.2	2.4
1988	-	-	-	-	-	-	-	-	-	-	104.4	-6.1	-	-	-	-	-	-	-	-	-	-	110.4	5.7
1989	-	-	-	-	-	-	-	-	-	-	112.5	1.9	-	-	-	-	-	-	-	-	-	-	115.4	2.6
1990	-	-	-	-	-	-	-	-	-	-	120.3	4.2	-	-	-	-	-	-	-	-	-	-	123.4	2.6
1991	-	-	-	-	-	-	-	-	-	-	122.8	-0.5	-	-	-	-	-	-	-	-	-	-	126.3	2.9
1992	-	-	-	-	-	-	-	-	-	-	125.5	-0.6	-	-	-	-	-	-	-	-	-	-	131.5	4.8
1993	-	-	-	-	-	-	-	-	-	-	129.7	-1.4	-	-	-	-	-	-	-	-	-	-	129.0	-0.5
1994	-	-	-	-	-	-	-	-	-	-	127.6	-1.1	-	-	-	-	-	-	-	-	-	-	124.9	-2.1
1995	-	-	-	-	-	-	-	-	-	-	125.5	0.5	-	-	-	-	-	-	-	-	-	-	-	-

Source: U.S. Department of Labor, Bureau of Labor Statistics, Division of Consumer Prices and Price Indexes. - indicates no data collected for period.

Anchorage, AK
Consumer Price Index - Urban Wage Earners
Base 1982-1984 = 100
Apparel and Upkeep

For 1971-1995. Columns headed % show percentile change in the index from the previous period for which an index is available.

Year	Jan Index	%	Feb Index	%	Mar Index	%	Apr Index	%	May Index	%	Jun Index	%	Jul Index	%	Aug Index	%	Sep Index	%	Oct Index	%	Nov Index	%	Dec Index	%
1971	55.9	-	-	-	-	-	56.7	1.4	-	-	-	-	57.4	1.2	-	-	-	-	57.6	0.3	-	-	-	-
1972	57.3	-0.5	-	-	-	-	59.1	3.1	-	-	-	-	58.9	-0.3	-	-	-	-	59.7	1.4	-	-	-	-
1973	59.6	-0.2	-	-	-	-	60.5	1.5	-	-	-	-	61.8	2.1	-	-	-	-	62.8	1.6	-	-	-	-
1974	62.4	-0.6	-	-	-	-	63.5	1.8	-	-	-	-	65.6	3.3	-	-	-	-	68.2	4.0	-	-	-	-
1975	68.4	0.3	-	-	-	-	70.8	3.5	-	-	-	-	70.3	-0.7	-	-	-	-	71.9	2.3	-	-	-	-
1976	71.1	-1.1	-	-	-	-	73.0	2.7	-	-	-	-	74.3	1.8	-	-	-	-	78.2	5.2	-	-	-	-
1977	79.6	1.8	-	-	-	-	80.0	0.5	-	-	-	-	79.8	-0.2	-	-	-	-	81.2	1.8	-	-	-	-
1978	78.3	-3.6	-	-	78.9	0.8	-	-	80.5	2.0	-	-	80.0	-0.6	-	-	81.6	2.0	-	-	82.0	0.5	-	-
1979	81.1	-1.1	-	-	80.0	-1.4	-	-	80.0	0.0	-	-	80.7	0.9	-	-	84.0	4.1	-	-	83.5	-0.6	-	-
1980	83.1	-0.5	-	-	84.1	1.2	-	-	84.6	0.6	-	-	87.2	3.1	-	-	88.4	1.4	-	-	89.6	1.4	-	-
1981	91.6	2.2	-	-	92.3	0.8	-	-	92.3	0.0	-	-	90.9	-1.5	-	-	93.9	3.3	-	-	94.3	0.4	-	-
1982	92.7	-1.7	-	-	93.5	0.9	-	-	95.0	1.6	-	-	96.9	2.0	-	-	99.3	2.5	-	-	99.8	0.5	-	-
1983	95.7	-4.1	-	-	101.7	6.3	-	-	102.2	0.5	-	-	102.1	-0.1	-	-	102.6	0.5	-	-	104.2	1.6	-	-
1984	100.6	-3.5	-	-	101.8	1.2	-	-	100.2	-1.6	-	-	102.1	1.9	-	-	105.4	3.2	-	-	102.4	-2.8	-	-
1985	101.2	-1.2	-	-	106.5	5.2	-	-	105.8	-0.7	-	-	103.3	-2.4	-	-	108.4	4.9	-	-	106.9	-1.4	-	-
1986	105.0	-1.8	-	-	109.6	4.4	-	-	107.0	-2.4	-	-	108.2	1.1	-	-	108.9	0.6	-	-	109.4	0.5	108.2	-1.1
1987	-	-	-	-	-	-	-	-	-	-	109.4	1.1	-	-	-	-	-	-	-	-	-	-	111.1	1.6
1988	-	-	-	-	-	-	-	-	-	-	103.5	-6.8	-	-	-	-	-	-	-	-	-	-	109.1	5.4
1989	-	-	-	-	-	-	-	-	-	-	111.0	1.7	-	-	-	-	-	-	-	-	-	-	114.0	2.7
1990	-	-	-	-	-	-	-	-	-	-	118.5	3.9	-	-	-	-	-	-	-	-	-	-	121.7	2.7
1991	-	-	-	-	-	-	-	-	-	-	120.4	-1.1	-	-	-	-	-	-	-	-	-	-	123.8	2.8
1992	-	-	-	-	-	-	-	-	-	-	122.2	-1.3	-	-	-	-	-	-	-	-	-	-	129.4	5.9
1993	-	-	-	-	-	-	-	-	-	-	126.6	-2.2	-	-	-	-	-	-	-	-	-	-	125.7	-0.7
1994	-	-	-	-	-	-	-	-	-	-	124.4	-1.0	-	-	-	-	-	-	-	-	-	-	121.0	-2.7
1995	-	-	-	-	-	-	-	-	-	-	121.5	0.4	-	-	-	-	-	-	-	-	-	-	-	-

Source: U.S. Department of Labor, Bureau of Labor Statistics, Division of Consumer Prices and Price Indexes. - indicates no data collected for period.

Anchorage, AK
Consumer Price Index - All Urban Consumers
Base 1982-1984 = 100
Transportation

For 1971-1995. Columns headed % show percentile change in the index from the previous period for which an index is available.

Year	Jan Index	%	Feb Index	%	Mar Index	%	Apr Index	%	May Index	%	Jun Index	%	Jul Index	%	Aug Index	%	Sep Index	%	Oct Index	%	Nov Index	%	Dec Index	%
1971	40.3	-	-	-	-	-	40.6	0.7	-	-	-	-	41.2	1.5	-	-	-	-	40.8	-1.0	-	-	-	-
1972	40.7	-0.2	-	-	-	-	40.6	-0.2	-	-	-	-	41.0	1.0	-	-	-	-	41.2	0.5	-	-	-	-
1973	41.0	-0.5	-	-	-	-	41.1	0.2	-	-	-	-	41.6	1.2	-	-	-	-	41.5	-0.2	-	-	-	-
1974	42.0	1.2	-	-	-	-	43.3	3.1	-	-	-	-	45.6	5.3	-	-	-	-	46.9	2.9	-	-	-	-
1975	46.8	-0.2	-	-	-	-	48.0	2.6	-	-	-	-	50.1	4.4	-	-	-	-	50.7	1.2	-	-	-	-
1976	51.5	1.6	-	-	-	-	53.8	4.5	-	-	-	-	55.4	3.0	-	-	-	-	57.0	2.9	-	-	-	-
1977	57.1	0.2	-	-	-	-	59.8	4.7	-	-	-	-	61.6	3.0	-	-	-	-	60.9	-1.1	-	-	-	-
1978	61.6	1.1	-	-	61.9	0.5	-	-	64.2	3.7	-	-	65.5	2.0	-	-	65.7	0.3	-	-	66.8	1.7	-	-
1979	67.3	0.7	-	-	67.7	0.6	-	-	69.7	3.0	-	-	72.1	3.4	-	-	73.9	2.5	-	-	74.9	1.4	-	-
1980	77.1	2.9	-	-	79.6	3.2	-	-	80.8	1.5	-	-	82.3	1.9	-	-	84.0	2.1	-	-	86.7	3.2	-	-
1981	87.7	1.2	-	-	89.7	2.3	-	-	92.1	2.7	-	-	93.6	1.6	-	-	95.0	1.5	-	-	96.0	1.1	-	-
1982	95.7	-0.3	-	-	95.8	0.1	-	-	95.8	0.0	-	-	97.3	1.6	-	-	97.8	0.5	-	-	98.1	0.3	-	-
1983	97.6	-0.5	-	-	95.8	-1.8	-	-	97.1	1.4	-	-	98.3	1.2	-	-	99.4	1.1	-	-	101.9	2.5	-	-
1984	101.6	-0.3	-	-	102.6	1.0	-	-	104.3	1.7	-	-	105.0	0.7	-	-	106.0	1.0	-	-	107.0	0.9	-	-
1985	107.2	0.2	-	-	107.4	0.2	-	-	107.6	0.2	-	-	107.5	-0.1	-	-	107.9	0.4	-	-	110.6	2.5	-	-
1986	111.1	0.5	-	-	110.8	-0.3	-	-	107.1	-3.3	-	-	105.5	-1.5	-	-	105.0	-0.5	-	-	108.1	3.0	107.9	-0.2
1987	-	-	-	-	-	-	-	-	-	-	106.9	-0.9	-	-	-	-	-	-	-	-	-	-	110.6	3.5
1988	-	-	-	-	-	-	-	-	-	-	111.5	0.8	-	-	-	-	-	-	-	-	-	-	114.0	2.2
1989	-	-	-	-	-	-	-	-	-	-	116.1	1.8	-	-	-	-	-	-	-	-	-	-	116.8	0.6
1990	-	-	-	-	-	-	-	-	-	-	119.6	2.4	-	-	-	-	-	-	-	-	-	-	126.5	5.8
1991	-	-	-	-	-	-	-	-	-	-	127.4	0.7	-	-	-	-	-	-	-	-	-	-	128.4	0.8
1992	-	-	-	-	-	-	-	-	-	-	129.8	1.1	-	-	-	-	-	-	-	-	-	-	133.1	2.5
1993	-	-	-	-	-	-	-	-	-	-	136.8	2.8	-	-	-	-	-	-	-	-	-	-	138.6	1.3
1994	-	-	-	-	-	-	-	-	-	-	140.5	1.4	-	-	-	-	-	-	-	-	-	-	143.2	1.9
1995	-	-	-	-	-	-	-	-	-	-	145.2	1.4	-	-	-	-	-	-	-	-	-	-	-	-

Source: U.S. Department of Labor, Bureau of Labor Statistics, Division of Consumer Prices and Price Indexes. - indicates no data collected for period.

Anchorage, AK
Consumer Price Index - Urban Wage Earners
Base 1982-1984 = 100
Transportation

For 1971-1995. Columns headed % show percentile change in the index from the previous period for which an index is available.

Year	Jan Index	%	Feb Index	%	Mar Index	%	Apr Index	%	May Index	%	Jun Index	%	Jul Index	%	Aug Index	%	Sep Index	%	Oct Index	%	Nov Index	%	Dec Index	%
1971	39.9	-	-	-	-	-	40.2	0.8	-	-	-	-	40.8	1.5	-	-	-	-	40.4	-1.0	-	-	-	-
1972	40.3	-0.2	-	-	-	-	40.2	-0.2	-	-	-	-	40.6	1.0	-	-	-	-	40.8	0.5	-	-	-	-
1973	40.6	-0.5	-	-	-	-	40.7	0.2	-	-	-	-	41.2	1.2	-	-	-	-	41.1	-0.2	-	-	-	-
1974	41.6	1.2	-	-	-	-	42.9	3.1	-	-	-	-	45.1	5.1	-	-	-	-	46.4	2.9	-	-	-	-
1975	46.3	-0.2	-	-	-	-	47.5	2.6	-	-	-	-	49.6	4.4	-	-	-	-	50.1	1.0	-	-	-	-
1976	51.0	1.8	-	-	-	-	53.2	4.3	-	-	-	-	54.8	3.0	-	-	-	-	56.4	2.9	-	-	-	-
1977	56.5	0.2	-	-	-	-	59.2	4.8	-	-	-	-	60.9	2.9	-	-	-	-	60.2	-1.1	-	-	-	-
1978	61.0	1.3	-	-	61.3	0.5	-	-	63.8	4.1	-	-	65.2	2.2	-	-	65.3	0.2	-	-	66.5	1.8	-	-
1979	66.9	0.6	-	-	67.4	0.7	-	-	69.5	3.1	-	-	72.0	3.6	-	-	73.8	2.5	-	-	74.7	1.2	-	-
1980	77.4	3.6	-	-	80.2	3.6	-	-	81.7	1.9	-	-	83.2	1.8	-	-	84.8	1.9	-	-	87.4	3.1	-	-
1981	88.3	1.0	-	-	90.3	2.3	-	-	92.9	2.9	-	-	94.5	1.7	-	-	95.8	1.4	-	-	96.8	1.0	-	-
1982	96.5	-0.3	-	-	96.5	0.0	-	-	96.2	-0.3	-	-	97.9	1.8	-	-	98.1	0.2	-	-	98.5	0.4	-	-
1983	97.7	-0.8	-	-	95.7	-2.0	-	-	96.8	1.1	-	-	98.2	1.4	-	-	99.3	1.1	-	-	101.7	2.4	-	-
1984	101.6	-0.1	-	-	102.3	0.7	-	-	104.0	1.7	-	-	104.7	0.7	-	-	105.5	0.8	-	-	106.5	0.9	-	-
1985	106.6	0.1	-	-	106.7	0.1	-	-	107.0	0.3	-	-	106.8	-0.2	-	-	107.2	0.4	-	-	110.1	2.7	-	-
1986	110.5	0.4	-	-	109.8	-0.6	-	-	105.7	-3.7	-	-	104.0	-1.6	-	-	103.5	-0.5	-	-	106.8	3.2	106.6	-0.2
1987	-	-	-	-	-	-	-	-	-	-	106.4	-0.2	-	-	-	-	-	-	-	-	-	-	110.5	3.9
1988	-	-	-	-	-	-	-	-	-	-	111.2	0.6	-	-	-	-	-	-	-	-	-	-	113.6	2.2
1989	-	-	-	-	-	-	-	-	-	-	115.7	1.8	-	-	-	-	-	-	-	-	-	-	116.6	0.8
1990	-	-	-	-	-	-	-	-	-	-	119.3	2.3	-	-	-	-	-	-	-	-	-	-	127.0	6.5
1991	-	-	-	-	-	-	-	-	-	-	127.2	0.2	-	-	-	-	-	-	-	-	-	-	128.4	0.9
1992	-	-	-	-	-	-	-	-	-	-	129.8	1.1	-	-	-	-	-	-	-	-	-	-	133.5	2.9
1993	-	-	-	-	-	-	-	-	-	-	136.4	2.2	-	-	-	-	-	-	-	-	-	-	138.4	1.5
1994	-	-	-	-	-	-	-	-	-	-	139.8	1.0	-	-	-	-	-	-	-	-	-	-	143.4	2.6
1995	-	-	-	-	-	-	-	-	-	-	145.3	1.3	-	-	-	-	-	-	-	-	-	-	-	-

Source: U.S. Department of Labor, Bureau of Labor Statistics, Division of Consumer Prices and Price Indexes. - indicates no data collected for period.

Anchorage, AK
Consumer Price Index - All Urban Consumers
Base 1982-1984 = 100
Medical Care

For 1971-1995. Columns headed % show percentile change in the index from the previous period for which an index is available.

Year	Jan Index	%	Feb Index	%	Mar Index	%	Apr Index	%	May Index	%	Jun Index	%	Jul Index	%	Aug Index	%	Sep Index	%	Oct Index	%	Nov Index	%	Dec Index	%
1971	34.4	-	-	-	-	-	35.0	1.7	-	-	-	-	35.1	0.3	-	-	-	-	35.5	1.1	-	-	-	-
1972	35.7	0.6	-	-	-	-	35.7	0.0	-	-	-	-	35.7	0.0	-	-	-	-	36.1	1.1	-	-	-	-
1973	36.2	0.3	-	-	-	-	36.5	0.8	-	-	-	-	37.3	2.2	-	-	-	-	38.3	2.7	-	-	-	-
1974	38.7	1.0	-	-	-	-	39.7	2.6	-	-	-	-	41.9	5.5	-	-	-	-	43.6	4.1	-	-	-	-
1975	44.7	2.5	-	-	-	-	45.6	2.0	-	-	-	-	47.0	3.1	-	-	-	-	48.3	2.8	-	-	-	-
1976	49.9	3.3	-	-	-	-	51.1	2.4	-	-	-	-	53.3	4.3	-	-	-	-	54.1	1.5	-	-	-	-
1977	55.4	2.4	-	-	-	-	57.0	2.9	-	-	-	-	58.1	1.9	-	-	-	-	59.0	1.5	-	-	-	-
1978	62.0	5.1	-	-	62.1	0.2	-	-	62.2	0.2	-	-	63.5	2.1	-	-	64.7	1.9	-	-	64.8	0.2	-	-
1979	67.9	4.8	-	-	67.6	-0.4	-	-	69.4	2.7	-	-	69.2	-0.3	-	-	69.4	0.3	-	-	69.8	0.6	-	-
1980	73.4	5.2	-	-	77.4	5.4	-	-	79.0	2.1	-	-	79.8	1.0	-	-	80.2	0.5	-	-	80.9	0.9	-	-
1981	82.7	2.2	-	-	84.7	2.4	-	-	87.2	3.0	-	-	87.7	0.6	-	-	87.5	-0.2	-	-	89.0	1.7	-	-
1982	92.9	4.4	-	-	92.9	0.0	-	-	93.6	0.8	-	-	95.2	1.7	-	-	96.1	0.9	-	-	96.7	0.6	-	-
1983	99.0	2.4	-	-	99.2	0.2	-	-	99.0	-0.2	-	-	99.6	0.6	-	-	100.0	0.4	-	-	100.0	0.0	-	-
1984	103.7	3.7	-	-	104.7	1.0	-	-	104.8	0.1	-	-	105.6	0.8	-	-	106.7	1.0	-	-	106.7	0.0	-	-
1985	107.2	0.5	-	-	108.5	1.2	-	-	108.8	0.3	-	-	112.8	3.7	-	-	112.9	0.1	-	-	113.5	0.5	-	-
1986	115.0	1.3	-	-	118.2	2.8	-	-	119.1	0.8	-	-	137.2	15.2	-	-	137.3	0.1	-	-	137.7	0.3	131.5	-4.5
1987	-	-	-	-	-	-	-	-	-	-	134.6	2.4	-	-	-	-	-	-	-	-	-	-	137.5	2.2
1988	-	-	-	-	-	-	-	-	-	-	142.6	3.7	-	-	-	-	-	-	-	-	-	-	146.9	3.0
1989	-	-	-	-	-	-	-	-	-	-	152.8	4.0	-	-	-	-	-	-	-	-	-	-	158.8	3.9
1990	-	-	-	-	-	-	-	-	-	-	168.6	6.2	-	-	-	-	-	-	-	-	-	-	176.2	4.5
1991	-	-	-	-	-	-	-	-	-	-	183.5	4.1	-	-	-	-	-	-	-	-	-	-	189.6	3.3
1992	-	-	-	-	-	-	-	-	-	-	197.8	4.3	-	-	-	-	-	-	-	-	-	-	202.2	2.2
1993	-	-	-	-	-	-	-	-	-	-	207.2	2.5	-	-	-	-	-	-	-	-	-	-	211.0	1.8
1994	-	-	-	-	-	-	-	-	-	-	215.5	2.1	-	-	-	-	-	-	-	-	-	-	219.7	1.9
1995	-	-	-	-	-	-	-	-	-	-	225.2	2.5	-	-	-	-	-	-	-	-	-	-	-	-

Source: U.S. Department of Labor, Bureau of Labor Statistics, Division of Consumer Prices and Price Indexes. - indicates no data collected for period.

Anchorage, AK
Consumer Price Index - Urban Wage Earners
Base 1982-1984 = 100
Medical Care

For 1971-1995. Columns headed % show percentile change in the index from the previous period for which an index is available.

Year	Jan Index	%	Feb Index	%	Mar Index	%	Apr Index	%	May Index	%	Jun Index	%	Jul Index	%	Aug Index	%	Sep Index	%	Oct Index	%	Nov Index	%	Dec Index	%
1971	35.4	-	-	-	-	-	36.1	2.0	-	-	-	-	36.1	0.0	-	-	-	-	36.6	1.4	-	-	-	-
1972	36.8	0.5	-	-	-	-	36.8	0.0	-	-	-	-	36.8	0.0	-	-	-	-	37.2	1.1	-	-	-	-
1973	37.3	0.3	-	-	-	-	37.6	0.8	-	-	-	-	38.4	2.1	-	-	-	-	39.5	2.9	-	-	-	-
1974	39.8	0.8	-	-	-	-	40.9	2.8	-	-	-	-	43.2	5.6	-	-	-	-	44.9	3.9	-	-	-	-
1975	46.1	2.7	-	-	-	-	47.0	2.0	-	-	-	-	48.4	3.0	-	-	-	-	49.8	2.9	-	-	-	-
1976	51.4	3.2	-	-	-	-	52.6	2.3	-	-	-	-	54.9	4.4	-	-	-	-	55.7	1.5	-	-	-	-
1977	57.0	2.3	-	-	-	-	58.8	3.2	-	-	-	-	59.9	1.9	-	-	-	-	60.7	1.3	-	-	-	-
1978	63.9	5.3	-	-	66.0	3.3	-	-	66.1	0.2	-	-	66.4	0.5	-	-	67.6	1.8	-	-	70.5	4.3	-	-
1979	72.7	3.1	-	-	72.3	-0.6	-	-	72.4	0.1	-	-	72.8	0.6	-	-	72.9	0.1	-	-	73.3	0.5	-	-
1980	75.0	2.3	-	-	77.5	3.3	-	-	79.0	1.9	-	-	80.4	1.8	-	-	80.9	0.6	-	-	80.9	0.0	-	-
1981	82.9	2.5	-	-	84.6	2.1	-	-	86.6	2.4	-	-	87.4	0.9	-	-	87.6	0.2	-	-	89.3	1.9	-	-
1982	92.7	3.8	-	-	92.8	0.1	-	-	93.7	1.0	-	-	95.3	1.7	-	-	96.4	1.2	-	-	97.0	0.6	-	-
1983	99.1	2.2	-	-	99.3	0.2	-	-	99.0	-0.3	-	-	99.8	0.8	-	-	100.3	0.5	-	-	100.3	0.0	-	-
1984	103.3	3.0	-	-	104.5	1.2	-	-	104.6	0.1	-	-	105.4	0.8	-	-	106.6	1.1	-	-	106.4	-0.2	-	-
1985	106.8	0.4	-	-	108.2	1.3	-	-	108.5	0.3	-	-	112.3	3.5	-	-	112.4	0.1	-	-	113.1	0.6	-	-
1986	114.4	1.1	-	-	117.8	3.0	-	-	118.7	0.8	-	-	132.8	11.9	-	-	132.8	0.0	-	-	133.3	0.4	128.4	-3.7
1987	-	-	-	-	-	-	-	-	-	-	135.0	5.1	-	-	-	-	-	-	-	-	-	-	138.6	2.7
1988	-	-	-	-	-	-	-	-	-	-	143.7	3.7	-	-	-	-	-	-	-	-	-	-	148.0	3.0
1989	-	-	-	-	-	-	-	-	-	-	154.0	4.1	-	-	-	-	-	-	-	-	-	-	160.0	3.9
1990	-	-	-	-	-	-	-	-	-	-	168.8	5.5	-	-	-	-	-	-	-	-	-	-	175.2	3.8
1991	-	-	-	-	-	-	-	-	-	-	182.8	4.3	-	-	-	-	-	-	-	-	-	-	189.7	3.8
1992	-	-	-	-	-	-	-	-	-	-	197.8	4.3	-	-	-	-	-	-	-	-	-	-	202.7	2.5
1993	-	-	-	-	-	-	-	-	-	-	207.3	2.3	-	-	-	-	-	-	-	-	-	-	210.8	1.7
1994	-	-	-	-	-	-	-	-	-	-	215.6	2.3	-	-	-	-	-	-	-	-	-	-	220.2	2.1
1995	-	-	-	-	-	-	-	-	-	-	226.0	2.6	-	-	-	-	-	-	-	-	-	-	-	-

Source: U.S. Department of Labor, Bureau of Labor Statistics, Division of Consumer Prices and Price Indexes. - indicates no data collected for period.

Anchorage, AK
Consumer Price Index - All Urban Consumers
Base 1982-1984 = 100
Entertainment

For 1976-1995. Columns headed % show percentile change in the index from the previous period for which an index is available.

Year	Jan Index	%	Feb Index	%	Mar Index	%	Apr Index	%	May Index	%	Jun Index	%	Jul Index	%	Aug Index	%	Sep Index	%	Oct Index	%	Nov Index	%	Dec Index	%
1976	60.6	-	-	-	-	-	64.3	6.1	-	-	-	-	64.6	0.5	-	-	-	-	66.0	2.2	-	-	-	-
1977	66.5	0.8	-	-	-	-	69.0	3.8	-	-	-	-	70.0	1.4	-	-	-	-	70.6	0.9	-	-	-	-
1978	70.2	-0.6	-	-	72.2	2.8	-	-	72.9	1.0	-	-	71.9	-1.4	-	-	74.1	3.1	-	-	73.6	-0.7	-	-
1979	73.7	0.1	-	-	73.8	0.1	-	-	73.3	-0.7	-	-	73.5	0.3	-	-	75.8	3.1	-	-	76.3	0.7	-	-
1980	77.5	1.6	-	-	78.8	1.7	-	-	81.7	3.7	-	-	76.4	-6.5	-	-	79.6	4.2	-	-	79.3	-0.4	-	-
1981	80.5	1.5	-	-	82.0	1.9	-	-	85.2	3.9	-	-	85.6	0.5	-	-	87.2	1.9	-	-	91.6	5.0	-	-
1982	92.8	1.3	-	-	92.6	-0.2	-	-	94.1	1.6	-	-	94.9	0.9	-	-	94.5	-0.4	-	-	97.8	3.5	-	-
1983	99.1	1.3	-	-	101.0	1.9	-	-	99.3	-1.7	-	-	99.7	0.4	-	-	101.4	1.7	-	-	102.6	1.2	-	-
1984	102.0	-0.6	-	-	103.4	1.4	-	-	103.4	0.0	-	-	105.5	2.0	-	-	106.5	0.9	-	-	106.0	-0.5	-	-
1985	106.4	0.4	-	-	108.6	2.1	-	-	106.9	-1.6	-	-	109.5	2.4	-	-	109.1	-0.4	-	-	112.2	2.8	-	-
1986	109.5	-2.4	-	-	111.4	1.7	-	-	110.2	-1.1	-	-	113.4	2.9	-	-	114.5	1.0	-	-	114.8	0.3	113.1	-1.5
1987	-	-	-	-	-	-	-	-	-	-	117.5	3.9	-	-	-	-	-	-	-	-	-	-	120.9	2.9
1988	-	-	-	-	-	-	-	-	-	-	121.6	0.6	-	-	-	-	-	-	-	-	-	-	124.1	2.1
1989	-	-	-	-	-	-	-	-	-	-	127.8	3.0	-	-	-	-	-	-	-	-	-	-	131.3	2.7
1990	-	-	-	-	-	-	-	-	-	-	134.4	2.4	-	-	-	-	-	-	-	-	-	-	136.8	1.8
1991	-	-	-	-	-	-	-	-	-	-	139.6	2.0	-	-	-	-	-	-	-	-	-	-	142.1	1.8
1992	-	-	-	-	-	-	-	-	-	-	145.4	2.3	-	-	-	-	-	-	-	-	-	-	147.5	1.4
1993	-	-	-	-	-	-	-	-	-	-	149.3	1.2	-	-	-	-	-	-	-	-	-	-	150.3	0.7
1994	-	-	-	-	-	-	-	-	-	-	152.9	1.7	-	-	-	-	-	-	-	-	-	-	155.1	1.4
1995	-	-	-	-	-	-	-	-	-	-	157.7	1.7	-	-	-	-	-	-	-	-	-	-	-	-

Source: U.S. Department of Labor, Bureau of Labor Statistics, Division of Consumer Prices and Price Indexes. - indicates no data collected for period.

Anchorage, AK
Consumer Price Index - Urban Wage Earners
Base 1982-1984 = 100
Entertainment

For 1976-1995. Columns headed % show percentile change in the index from the previous period for which an index is available.

Year	Jan Index	%	Feb Index	%	Mar Index	%	Apr Index	%	May Index	%	Jun Index	%	Jul Index	%	Aug Index	%	Sep Index	%	Oct Index	%	Nov Index	%	Dec Index	%
1976	66.4	-	-	-	--	-	70.4	6.0	-	-	-	-	70.7	0.4	-	-	-	-	72.3	2.3	-	-	-	-
1977	72.8	0.7	-	-	-	-	75.6	3.8	-	-	-	-	76.7	1.5	-	-	-	-	77.3	0.8	-	-	-	-
1978	76.9	-0.5	-	-	77.2	0.4	-	-	74.7	-3.2	-	-	74.9	0.3	-	-	76.2	1.7	-	-	76.1	-0.1	-	-
1979	76.6	0.7	-	-	76.6	0.0	-	-	76.1	-0.7	-	-	75.8	-0.4	-	-	77.6	2.4	-	-	78.6	1.3	-	-
1980	80.0	1.8	-	-	81.5	1.9	-	-	82.7	1.5	-	-	76.9	-7.0	-	-	78.9	2.6	-	-	79.6	0.9	-	-
1981	79.7	0.1	-	-	82.0	2.9	-	-	85.6	4.4	-	-	86.7	1.3	-	-	88.6	2.2	-	-	91.4	3.2	-	-
1982	92.8	1.5	-	-	92.4	-0.4	-	-	94.0	1.7	-	-	95.0	1.1	-	-	94.3	-0.7	-	-	97.5	3.4	-	-
1983	99.1	1.6	-	-	100.7	1.6	-	-	99.2	-1.5	-	-	99.7	0.5	-	-	101.1	1.4	-	-	102.3	1.2	-	-
1984	102.2	-0.1	-	-	103.4	1.2	-	-	103.6	0.2	-	-	106.2	2.5	-	-	107.0	0.8	-	-	106.3	-0.7	-	-
1985	106.4	0.1	-	-	108.3	1.8	-	-	106.9	-1.3	-	-	109.2	2.2	-	-	108.7	-0.5	-	-	111.9	2.9	-	-
1986	109.7	-2.0	-	-	110.8	1.0	-	-	110.1	-0.6	-	-	113.9	3.5	-	-	114.8	0.8	-	-	115.2	0.3	113.7	-1.3
1987	-	-	-	-	-	-	-	-	-	-	118.6	4.3	-	-	-	-	-	-	-	-	-	-	122.1	3.0
1988	-	-	-	-	-	-	-	-	-	-	122.5	0.3	-	-	-	-	-	-	-	-	-	-	125.2	2.2
1989	-	-	-	-	-	-	-	-	-	-	128.9	3.0	-	-	-	-	-	-	-	-	-	-	131.8	2.2
1990	-	-	-	-	-	-	-	-	-	-	134.9	2.4	-	-	-	-	-	-	-	-	-	-	137.4	1.9
1991	-	-	-	-	-	-	-	-	-	-	140.1	2.0	-	-	-	-	-	-	-	-	-	-	142.4	1.6
1992	-	-	-	-	-	-	-	-	-	-	145.8	2.4	-	-	-	-	-	-	-	-	-	-	147.3	1.0
1993	-	-	-	-	-	-	-	-	-	-	149.4	1.4	-	-	-	-	-	-	-	-	-	-	149.7	0.2
1994	-	-	-	-	-	-	-	-	-	-	152.1	1.6	-	-	-	-	-	-	-	-	-	-	154.9	1.8
1995	-	-	-	-	-	-	-	-	-	-	157.3	1.5	-	-	-	-	-	-	-	-	-	-	-	-

Source: U.S. Department of Labor, Bureau of Labor Statistics, Division of Consumer Prices and Price Indexes. - indicates no data collected for period.

Anchorage, AK
Consumer Price Index - All Urban Consumers
Base 1982-1984 = 100
Other Goods and Services

For 1976-1995. Columns headed % show percentile change in the index from the previous period for which an index is available.

Year	Jan Index	%	Feb Index	%	Mar Index	%	Apr Index	%	May Index	%	Jun Index	%	Jul Index	%	Aug Index	%	Sep Index	%	Oct Index	%	Nov Index	%	Dec Index	%
1976	60.9	-	-	-	-	-	63.2	3.8	-	-	-	-	63.8	0.9	-	-	-	-	65.0	1.9	-	-	-	-
1977	67.3	3.5	-	-	-	-	67.5	0.3	-	-	-	-	68.2	1.0	-	-	-	-	68.8	0.9	-	-	-	-
1978	69.5	1.0	-	-	70.0	0.7	-	-	71.1	1.6	-	-	71.5	0.6	-	-	73.3	2.5	-	-	73.5	0.3	-	-
1979	74.1	0.8	-	-	75.4	1.8	-	-	76.2	1.1	-	-	76.1	-0.1	-	-	78.8	3.5	-	-	78.9	0.1	-	-
1980	80.5	2.0	-	-	80.9	0.5	-	-	82.7	2.2	-	-	83.3	0.7	-	-	84.7	1.7	-	-	85.0	0.4	-	-
1981	86.3	1.5	-	-	85.9	-0.5	-	-	87.7	2.1	-	-	88.0	0.3	-	-	89.5	1.7	-	-	90.4	1.0	-	-
1982	89.9	-0.6	-	-	92.1	2.4	-	-	92.5	0.4	-	-	92.9	0.4	-	-	94.6	1.8	-	-	95.3	0.7	-	-
1983	98.1	2.9	-	-	99.3	1.2	-	-	100.9	1.6	-	-	102.5	1.6	-	-	103.2	0.7	-	-	103.8	0.6	-	-
1984	103.2	-0.6	-	-	104.6	1.4	-	-	105.1	0.5	-	-	105.5	0.4	-	-	106.7	1.1	-	-	105.4	-1.2	-	-
1985	108.4	2.8	-	-	110.9	2.3	-	-	111.3	0.4	-	-	112.0	0.6	-	-	118.0	5.4	-	-	121.8	3.2	126.9	0.2
1986	119.6	-1.8	-	-	121.0	1.2	-	-	121.7	0.6	-	-	121.9	0.2	-	-	126.5	3.8	-	-	126.6	0.1	126.9	0.2
1987	-	-	-	-	-	-	-	-	-	-	128.6	1.3	-	-	-	-	-	-	-	-	-	-	133.1	3.5
1988	-	-	-	-	-	-	-	-	-	-	137.3	3.2	-	-	-	-	-	-	-	-	-	-	141.7	3.2
1989	-	-	-	-	-	-	-	-	-	-	147.8	4.3	-	-	-	-	-	-	-	-	-	-	155.9	5.5
1990	-	-	-	-	-	-	-	-	-	-	160.6	3.0	-	-	-	-	-	-	-	-	-	-	167.3	4.2
1991	-	-	-	-	-	-	-	-	-	-	172.9	3.3	-	-	-	-	-	-	-	-	-	-	181.5	5.0
1992	-	-	-	-	-	-	-	-	-	-	188.0	3.6	-	-	-	-	-	-	-	-	-	-	194.0	3.2
1993	-	-	-	-	-	-	-	-	-	-	198.8	2.5	-	-	-	-	-	-	-	-	-	-	201.4	1.3
1994	-	-	-	-	-	-	-	-	-	-	202.6	0.6	-	-	-	-	-	-	-	-	-	-	207.2	2.3
1995	-	-	-	-	-	-	-	-	-	-	210.3	1.5	-	-	-	-	-	-	-	-	-	-	-	-

Source: U.S. Department of Labor, Bureau of Labor Statistics, Division of Consumer Prices and Price Indexes. - indicates no data collected for period.

Anchorage, AK
Consumer Price Index - Urban Wage Earners
Base 1982-1984 = 100
Other Goods and Services

For 1976-1995. Columns headed % show percentile change in the index from the previous period for which an index is available.

Year	Jan Index	%	Feb Index	%	Mar Index	%	Apr Index	%	May Index	%	Jun Index	%	Jul Index	%	Aug Index	%	Sep Index	%	Oct Index	%	Nov Index	%	Dec Index	%
1976	59.8	-	-	-	-	-	62.1	3.8	-	-	-	-	62.6	0.8	-	-	-	-	63.8	1.9	-	-	-	-
1977	66.0	3.4	-	-	-	-	66.3	0.5	-	-	-	-	67.0	1.1	-	-	-	-	67.5	0.7	-	-	-	-
1978	68.2	1.0	-	-	68.7	0.7	-	-	69.5	1.2	-	-	70.4	1.3	-	-	71.5	1.6	-	-	71.4	-0.1	-	-
1979	72.1	1.0	-	-	73.5	1.9	-	-	73.6	0.1	-	-	75.0	1.9	-	-	76.5	2.0	-	-	77.7	1.6	-	-
1980	78.8	1.4	-	-	80.3	1.9	-	-	82.1	2.2	-	-	82.6	0.6	-	-	82.5	-0.1	-	-	83.4	1.1	-	-
1981	84.8	1.7	-	-	83.9	-1.1	-	-	85.5	1.9	-	-	85.8	0.4	-	-	88.0	2.6	-	-	89.2	1.4	-	-
1982	88.7	-0.6	-	-	91.4	3.0	-	-	91.5	0.1	-	-	92.0	0.5	-	-	93.8	2.0	-	-	94.7	1.0	-	-
1983	98.0	3.5	-	-	99.2	1.2	-	-	101.2	2.0	-	-	103.1	1.9	-	-	104.0	0.9	-	-	104.5	0.5	-	-
1984	104.0	-0.5	-	-	105.4	1.3	-	-	106.0	0.6	-	-	106.5	0.5	-	-	106.4	-0.1	-	-	104.9	-1.4	-	-
1985	108.4	3.3	-	-	111.4	2.8	-	-	111.8	0.4	-	-	112.7	0.8	-	-	116.4	3.3	-	-	120.9	3.9	-	-
1986	120.0	-0.7	-	-	121.8	1.5	-	-	122.5	0.6	-	-	122.6	0.1	-	-	125.2	2.1	-	-	125.4	0.2	125.8	0.3
1987	-	-	-	-	-	-	-	-	-	-	127.3	1.2	-	-	-	-	-	-	-	-	-	-	131.7	3.5
1988	-	-	-	-	-	-	-	-	-	-	135.7	3.0	-	-	-	-	-	-	-	-	-	-	140.1	3.2
1989	-	-	-	-	-	-	-	-	-	-	146.6	4.6	-	-	-	-	-	-	-	-	-	-	154.7	5.5
1990	-	-	-	-	-	-	-	-	-	-	159.4	3.0	-	-	-	-	-	-	-	-	-	-	167.7	5.2
1991	-	-	-	-	-	-	-	-	-	-	173.2	3.3	-	-	-	-	-	-	-	-	-	-	181.8	5.0
1992	-	-	-	-	-	-	-	-	-	-	188.0	3.4	-	-	-	-	-	-	-	-	-	-	193.9	3.1
1993	-	-	-	-	-	-	-	-	-	-	199.0	2.6	-	-	-	-	-	-	-	-	-	-	201.8	1.4
1994	-	-	-	-	-	-	-	-	-	-	202.6	0.4	-	-	-	-	-	-	-	-	-	-	207.0	2.2
1995	-	-	-	-	-	-	-	-	-	-	209.8	1.4	-	-	-	-	-	-	-	-	-	-	-	-

Source: U.S. Department of Labor, Bureau of Labor Statistics, Division of Consumer Prices and Price Indexes. - indicates no data collected for period.

Atlanta, GA
Consumer Price Index - All Urban Consumers
Base 1982-1984 = 100
Annual Averages

For 1917-1995. Columns headed % show percentile change in the index from the previous period for which an index is available.

Year	All Items		Food & Beverage		Housing		Apparel & Upkeep		Trans- portation		Medical Care		Entertain- ment		Other Goods & Services	
	Index	%	Index	%	Index	%	Index	%	Index	%	Index	%	Index	%	Index	%
1917	-	-	-	-	-	-	-	-	-	-	-	-	-	-	-	-
1918	16.6	-	-	-	-	-	-	-	-	-	-	-	-	-	-	-
1919	19.3	16.3	-	-	-	-	-	-	-	-	-	-	-	-	-	-
1920	21.9	13.5	-	-	-	-	-	-	-	-	-	-	-	-	-	-
1921	19.0	-13.2	-	-	-	-	-	-	-	-	-	-	-	-	-	-
1922	17.5	-7.9	-	-	-	-	-	-	-	-	-	-	-	-	-	-
1923	17.6	0.6	-	-	-	-	-	-	-	-	-	-	-	-	-	-
1924	17.3	-1.7	-	-	-	-	-	-	-	-	-	-	-	-	-	-
1925	17.9	3.5	-	-	-	-	-	-	-	-	-	-	-	-	-	-
1926	18.1	1.1	-	-	-	-	-	-	-	-	-	-	-	-	-	-
1927	17.5	-3.3	-	-	-	-	-	-	-	-	-	-	-	-	-	-
1928	17.3	-1.1	-	-	-	-	-	-	-	-	-	-	-	-	-	-
1929	17.2	-0.6	-	-	-	-	-	-	-	-	-	-	-	-	-	-
1930	16.5	-4.1	-	-	-	-	-	-	-	-	-	-	-	-	-	-
1931	14.9	-9.7	-	-	-	-	-	-	-	-	-	-	-	-	-	-
1932	13.3	-10.7	-	-	-	-	-	-	-	-	-	-	-	-	-	-
1933	12.6	-5.3	-	-	-	-	-	-	-	-	-	-	-	-	-	-
1934	13.2	4.8	-	-	-	-	-	-	-	-	-	-	-	-	-	-
1935	13.5	2.3	-	-	-	-	-	-	-	-	-	-	-	-	-	-
1936	13.7	1.5	-	-	-	-	-	-	-	-	-	-	-	-	-	-
1937	14.1	2.9	-	-	-	-	-	-	-	-	-	-	-	-	-	-
1938	13.7	-2.8	-	-	-	-	-	-	-	-	-	-	-	-	-	-
1939	13.6	-0.7	-	-	-	-	-	-	-	-	-	-	-	-	-	-
1940	13.6	0.0	-	-	-	-	-	-	-	-	-	-	-	-	-	-
1941	14.4	5.9	-	-	-	-	-	-	-	-	-	-	-	-	-	-
1942	15.9	10.4	-	-	-	-	-	-	-	-	-	-	-	-	-	-
1943	17.0	6.9	-	-	-	-	-	-	-	-	-	-	-	-	-	-
1944	17.3	1.8	-	-	-	-	-	-	-	-	-	-	-	-	-	-
1945	17.9	3.5	-	-	-	-	-	-	-	-	-	-	-	-	-	-
1946	19.3	7.8	-	-	-	-	-	-	-	-	-	-	-	-	-	-
1947	22.3	15.5	-	-	-	-	-	-	20.4	-	15.2	-	-	-	-	-
1948	23.8	6.7	-	-	-	-	-	-	22.4	9.8	15.7	3.3	-	-	-	-
1949	23.8	0.0	-	-	-	-	-	-	24.1	7.6	16.1	2.5	-	-	-	-
1950	24.1	1.3	-	-	-	-	-	-	24.6	2.1	16.1	0.0	-	-	-	-
1951	26.4	9.5	-	-	-	-	-	-	26.4	7.3	16.9	5.0	-	-	-	-
1952	27.0	2.3	-	-	-	-	-	-	28.1	6.4	18.1	7.1	-	-	-	-
1953	27.3	1.1	-	-	-	-	42.2	-	28.9	2.8	18.5	2.2	-	-	-	-
1954	27.2	-0.4	-	-	-	-	42.4	0.5	28.0	-3.1	18.9	2.2	-	-	-	-
1955	27.1	-0.4	-	-	-	-	42.1	-0.7	27.5	-1.8	19.6	3.7	-	-	-	-
1956	27.5	1.5	-	-	-	-	42.9	1.9	28.2	2.5	20.2	3.1	-	-	-	-
1957	28.3	2.9	-	-	-	-	43.7	1.9	30.0	6.4	20.7	2.5	-	-	-	-
1958	29.0	2.5	-	-	-	-	44.3	1.4	31.3	4.3	21.4	3.4	-	-	-	-
1959	29.2	0.7	-	-	-	-	44.3	0.0	32.4	3.5	22.3	4.2	-	-	-	-
1960	29.6	1.4	-	-	-	-	45.0	1.6	32.0	-1.2	23.0	3.1	-	-	-	-
1961	29.7	0.3	-	-	-	-	45.1	0.2	32.4	1.3	23.2	0.9	-	-	-	-

[Continued]

250

Atlanta, GA
Consumer Price Index - All Urban Consumers
Base 1982-1984 = 100
Annual Averages
[Continued]

For 1917-1995. Columns headed % show percentile change in the index from the previous period for which an index is available.

Year	All Items		Food & Beverage		Housing		Apparel & Upkeep		Trans- portation		Medical Care		Entertain- ment		Other Goods & Services	
	Index	%	Index	%	Index	%	Index	%	Index	%	Index	%	Index	%	Index	%
1962	30.0	1.0	-	-	-	-	45.1	0.0	33.1	2.2	23.9	3.0	-	-	-	-
1963	30.3	1.0	-	-	-	-	46.1	2.2	33.8	2.1	24.2	1.3	-	-	-	-
1964	30.8	1.7	-	-	-	-	46.2	0.2	34.7	2.7	24.8	2.5	-	-	-	-
1965	31.2	1.3	-	-	-	-	46.7	1.1	34.6	-0.3	25.4	2.4	-	-	-	-
1966	32.2	3.2	-	-	-	-	48.9	4.7	34.6	0.0	26.7	5.1	-	-	-	-
1967	33.2	3.1	-	-	-	-	51.6	5.5	35.2	1.7	28.4	6.4	-	-	-	-
1968	34.5	3.9	-	-	-	-	53.8	4.3	36.1	2.6	30.3	6.7	-	-	-	-
1969	36.5	5.8	-	-	-	-	56.0	4.1	37.3	3.3	33.3	9.9	-	-	-	-
1970	38.6	5.8	-	-	-	-	58.4	4.3	38.2	2.4	35.8	7.5	-	-	-	-
1971	40.4	4.7	-	-	-	-	59.9	2.6	40.6	6.3	38.6	7.8	-	-	-	-
1972	41.6	3.0	-	-	-	-	61.3	2.3	39.8	-2.0	39.6	2.6	-	-	-	-
1973	44.3	6.5	-	-	-	-	63.8	4.1	41.1	3.3	41.5	4.8	-	-	-	-
1974	49.2	11.1	-	-	-	-	69.1	8.3	46.5	13.1	46.1	11.1	-	-	-	-
1975	53.6	8.9	-	-	-	-	71.6	3.6	50.4	8.4	52.1	13.0	-	-	-	-
1976	56.1	4.7	62.5	-	51.9	-	74.3	3.8	54.2	7.5	56.0	7.5	77.2	-	55.4	-
1977	59.6	6.2	65.9	5.4	55.2	6.4	79.5	7.0	57.3	5.7	60.7	8.4	80.3	4.0	58.5	5.6
1978	63.9	7.2	72.2	9.6	59.8	8.3	84.0	5.7	59.6	4.0	63.8	5.1	83.8	4.4	62.7	7.2
1979	70.5	10.3	79.5	10.1	65.9	10.2	87.6	4.3	69.5	16.6	68.1	6.7	85.6	2.1	68.9	9.9
1980	80.3	13.9	85.8	7.9	76.1	15.5	93.1	6.3	84.8	22.0	74.7	9.7	88.7	3.6	75.6	9.7
1981	90.2	12.3	93.1	8.5	87.7	15.2	96.2	3.3	94.9	11.9	82.3	10.2	94.6	6.7	84.1	11.2
1982	96.0	6.4	97.1	4.3	95.4	8.8	96.8	0.6	97.5	2.7	92.6	12.5	97.8	3.4	91.7	9.0
1983	99.9	4.1	99.8	2.8	100.0	4.8	100.5	3.8	99.4	1.9	101.2	9.3	98.0	0.2	100.5	9.6
1984	104.1	4.2	103.1	3.3	104.6	4.6	102.7	2.2	103.0	3.6	106.2	4.9	104.1	6.2	107.9	7.4
1985	108.9	4.6	106.1	2.9	109.9	5.1	111.7	8.8	106.7	3.6	112.9	6.3	111.4	7.0	113.0	4.7
1986	112.2	3.0	111.2	4.8	115.2	4.8	110.4	-1.2	102.9	-3.6	123.7	9.6	118.7	6.6	119.8	6.0
1987	116.8	4.1	112.1	0.8	118.4	2.8	107.7	-2.4	111.5	8.4	133.0	7.5	112.2	-5.5	135.9	13.4
1988	122.4	4.8	116.0	3.5	124.8	5.4	109.9	2.0	115.6	3.7	142.2	6.9	120.8	7.7	145.1	6.8
1989	128.3	4.8	124.2	7.1	130.8	4.8	99.4	-9.6	121.5	5.1	155.3	9.2	128.6	6.5	155.4	7.1
1990	135.8	5.8	131.2	5.6	138.7	6.0	101.4	2.0	127.7	5.1	167.4	7.8	133.5	3.8	171.9	10.6
1991	142.2	4.7	135.4	3.2	145.6	5.0	103.7	2.3	132.3	3.6	183.5	9.6	138.0	3.4	185.5	7.9
1992	146.6	3.1	137.6	1.6	149.6	2.7	106.5	2.7	136.1	2.9	196.6	7.1	144.4	4.6	195.8	5.6
1993	150.2	2.5	139.7	1.5	151.9	1.5	106.0	-0.5	139.5	2.5	211.6	7.6	147.5	2.1	210.7	7.6
1994	154.6	2.9	142.7	2.1	155.1	2.1	105.8	-0.2	144.0	3.2	223.9	5.8	160.3	8.7	222.2	5.5
1995	158.7	2.7	148.8	4.3	158.4	2.1	102.1	-3.5	148.7	3.3	232.5	3.8	166.7	4.0	227.1	2.2

Source: U.S. Department of Labor, Bureau of Labor Statistics, Division of Consumer Prices and Price Indexes. - indicates no data collected for period.

Atlanta, GA
Consumer Price Index - Urban Wage Earners
Base 1982-1984 = 100
Annual Averages

For 1917-1995. Columns headed % show percentile change in the index from the previous period for which an index is available.

Year	All Items		Food & Beverage		Housing		Apparel & Upkeep		Trans- portation		Medical Care		Entertain- ment		Other Goods & Services	
	Index	%	Index	%	Index	%	Index	%	Index	%	Index	%	Index	%	Index	%
1917	-	-	-	-	-	-	-	-	-	-	-	-	-	-	-	-
1918	16.6	-	-	-	-	-	-	-	-	-	-	-	-	-	-	-
1919	19.3	16.3	-	-	-	-	-	-	-	-	-	-	-	-	-	-
1920	21.8	13.0	-	-	-	-	-	-	-	-	-	-	-	-	-	-
1921	18.9	-13.3	-	-	-	-	-	-	-	-	-	-	-	-	-	-
1922	17.5	-7.4	-	-	-	-	-	-	-	-	-	-	-	-	-	-
1923	17.5	0.0	-	-	-	-	-	-	-	-	-	-	-	-	-	-
1924	17.3	-1.1	-	-	-	-	-	-	-	-	-	-	-	-	-	-
1925	17.8	2.9	-	-	-	-	-	-	-	-	-	-	-	-	-	-
1926	18.0	1.1	-	-	-	-	-	-	-	-	-	-	-	-	-	-
1927	17.5	-2.8	-	-	-	-	-	-	-	-	-	-	-	-	-	-
1928	17.3	-1.1	-	-	-	-	-	-	-	-	-	-	-	-	-	-
1929	17.2	-0.6	-	-	-	-	-	-	-	-	-	-	-	-	-	-
1930	16.5	-4.1	-	-	-	-	-	-	-	-	-	-	-	-	-	-
1931	14.8	-10.3	-	-	-	-	-	-	-	-	-	-	-	-	-	-
1932	13.2	-10.8	-	-	-	-	-	-	-	-	-	-	-	-	-	-
1933	12.6	-4.5	-	-	-	-	-	-	-	-	-	-	-	-	-	-
1934	13.2	4.8	-	-	-	-	-	-	-	-	-	-	-	-	-	-
1935	13.5	2.3	-	-	-	-	-	-	-	-	-	-	-	-	-	-
1936	13.7	1.5	-	-	-	-	-	-	-	-	-	-	-	-	-	-
1937	14.1	2.9	-	-	-	-	-	-	-	-	-	-	-	-	-	-
1938	13.7	-2.8	-	-	-	-	-	-	-	-	-	-	-	-	-	-
1939	13.6	-0.7	-	-	-	-	-	-	-	-	-	-	-	-	-	-
1940	13.6	0.0	-	-	-	-	-	-	-	-	-	-	-	-	-	-
1941	14.3	5.1	-	-	-	-	-	-	-	-	-	-	-	-	-	-
1942	15.9	11.2	-	-	-	-	-	-	-	-	-	-	-	-	-	-
1943	17.0	6.9	-	-	-	-	-	-	-	-	-	-	-	-	-	-
1944	17.3	1.8	-	-	-	-	-	-	-	-	-	-	-	-	-	-
1945	17.9	3.5	-	-	-	-	-	-	-	-	-	-	-	-	-	-
1946	19.2	7.3	-	-	-	-	-	-	-	-	-	-	-	-	-	-
1947	22.3	16.1	-	-	-	-	-	-	19.8	-	14.6	-	-	-	-	-
1948	23.7	6.3	-	-	-	-	-	-	21.8	10.1	15.1	3.4	-	-	-	-
1949	23.7	0.0	-	-	-	-	-	-	23.5	7.8	15.5	2.6	-	-	-	-
1950	24.0	1.3	-	-	-	-	-	-	24.0	2.1	15.5	0.0	-	-	-	-
1951	26.3	9.6	-	-	-	-	-	-	25.7	7.1	16.3	5.2	-	-	-	-
1952	27.0	2.7	-	-	-	-	-	-	27.4	6.6	17.4	6.7	-	-	-	-
1953	27.2	0.7	-	-	-	-	40.0	-	28.1	2.6	17.8	2.3	-	-	-	-
1954	27.1	-0.4	-	-	-	-	40.1	0.2	27.2	-3.2	18.2	2.2	-	-	-	-
1955	27.0	-0.4	-	-	-	-	39.9	-0.5	26.8	-1.5	18.8	3.3	-	-	-	-
1956	27.5	1.9	-	-	-	-	40.7	2.0	27.5	2.6	19.5	3.7	-	-	-	-
1957	28.2	2.5	-	-	-	-	41.5	2.0	29.2	6.2	19.9	2.1	-	-	-	-
1958	28.9	2.5	-	-	-	-	42.0	1.2	30.5	4.5	20.6	3.5	-	-	-	-
1959	29.1	0.7	-	-	-	-	42.0	0.0	31.5	3.3	21.5	4.4	-	-	-	-
1960	29.5	1.4	-	-	-	-	42.7	1.7	31.2	-1.0	22.1	2.8	-	-	-	-
1961	29.7	0.7	-	-	-	-	42.7	0.0	31.6	1.3	22.3	0.9	-	-	-	-

[Continued]

Atlanta, GA
Consumer Price Index - Urban Wage Earners
Base 1982-1984 = 100
Annual Averages

[Continued]

For 1917-1995. Columns headed % show percentile change in the index from the previous period for which an index is available.

Year	All Items		Food & Beverage		Housing		Apparel & Upkeep		Trans-portation		Medical Care		Entertain-ment		Other Goods & Services	
	Index	%	Index	%	Index	%	Index	%	Index	%	Index	%	Index	%	Index	%
1962	29.9	0.7	-	-	-	-	42.7	0.0	32.2	1.9	23.0	3.1	-	-	-	-
1963	30.2	1.0	-	-	-	-	43.7	2.3	32.9	2.2	23.3	1.3	-	-	-	-
1964	30.7	1.7	-	-	-	-	43.8	0.2	33.8	2.7	23.9	2.6	-	-	-	-
1965	31.1	1.3	-	-	-	-	44.3	1.1	33.7	-0.3	24.4	2.1	-	-	-	-
1966	32.1	3.2	-	-	-	-	46.4	4.7	33.7	0.0	25.7	5.3	-	-	-	-
1967	33.1	3.1	-	-	-	-	49.0	5.6	34.3	1.8	27.3	6.2	-	-	-	-
1968	34.4	3.9	-	-	-	-	51.0	4.1	35.1	2.3	29.1	6.6	-	-	-	-
1969	36.4	5.8	-	-	-	-	53.1	4.1	36.3	3.4	32.1	10.3	-	-	-	-
1970	38.5	5.8	-	-	-	-	55.3	4.1	37.2	2.5	34.5	7.5	-	-	-	-
1971	40.2	4.4	-	-	-	-	56.8	2.7	39.5	6.2	37.2	7.8	-	-	-	-
1972	41.5	3.2	-	-	-	-	58.1	2.3	38.8	-1.8	38.1	2.4	-	-	-	-
1973	44.2	6.5	-	-	-	-	60.5	4.1	40.0	3.1	40.0	5.0	-	-	-	-
1974	49.1	11.1	-	-	-	-	65.5	8.3	45.3	13.2	44.3	10.8	-	-	-	-
1975	53.5	9.0	-	-	-	-	67.9	3.7	49.0	8.2	50.2	13.3	-	-	-	-
1976	56.0	4.7	61.8	-	52.6	-	70.4	3.7	52.8	7.8	53.9	7.4	69.9	-	58.1	-
1977	59.4	6.1	65.2	5.5	56.0	6.5	75.3	7.0	55.8	5.7	58.4	8.3	72.6	3.9	61.3	5.5
1978	63.8	7.4	71.9	10.3	60.6	8.2	78.2	3.9	58.3	4.5	62.4	6.8	74.6	2.8	65.2	6.4
1979	71.0	11.3	79.4	10.4	67.0	10.6	84.4	7.9	69.0	18.4	68.1	9.1	75.6	1.3	70.2	7.7
1980	81.1	14.2	85.7	7.9	76.7	14.5	89.9	6.5	86.1	24.8	73.0	7.2	89.1	17.9	75.7	7.8
1981	90.8	12.0	93.2	8.8	87.9	14.6	95.9	6.7	96.0	11.5	81.8	12.1	98.9	11.0	83.6	10.4
1982	96.4	6.2	97.1	4.2	95.8	9.0	97.9	2.1	98.2	2.3	92.5	13.1	99.6	0.7	91.4	9.3
1983	100.1	3.8	99.9	2.9	100.7	5.1	100.0	2.1	99.5	1.3	101.3	9.5	94.9	-4.7	100.7	10.2
1984	103.5	3.4	103.0	3.1	103.6	2.9	102.1	2.1	102.3	2.8	106.3	4.9	105.5	11.2	107.9	7.1
1985	107.9	4.3	105.9	2.8	108.4	4.6	109.4	7.1	106.0	3.6	113.0	6.3	110.3	4.5	112.8	4.5
1986	110.8	2.7	111.0	4.8	113.1	4.3	108.2	-1.1	101.9	-3.9	124.0	9.7	118.2	7.2	119.7	6.1
1987	116.7	5.3	112.4	1.3	120.0	6.1	104.4	-3.5	110.8	8.7	132.7	7.0	110.6	-6.4	134.7	12.5
1988	122.2	4.7	116.5	3.6	126.3	5.2	106.0	1.5	115.1	3.9	141.5	6.6	118.8	7.4	144.3	7.1
1989	128.3	5.0	125.1	7.4	133.0	5.3	94.5	-10.8	121.6	5.6	154.0	8.8	126.1	6.1	153.8	6.6
1990	136.1	6.1	132.3	5.8	140.7	5.8	97.6	3.3	128.4	5.6	165.9	7.7	130.2	3.3	170.7	11.0
1991	142.2	4.5	136.5	3.2	147.5	4.8	99.0	1.4	132.8	3.4	180.9	9.0	134.7	3.5	184.3	8.0
1992	146.4	3.0	138.7	1.6	151.3	2.6	103.3	4.3	136.1	2.5	193.9	7.2	140.2	4.1	194.3	5.4
1993	150.1	2.5	140.9	1.6	153.8	1.7	104.7	1.4	139.2	2.3	208.8	7.7	142.6	1.7	208.5	7.3
1994	154.2	2.7	143.9	2.1	156.9	2.0	101.9	-2.7	144.0	3.4	220.5	5.6	155.7	9.2	218.2	4.7
1995	158.3	2.7	150.0	4.2	160.3	2.2	98.1	-3.7	149.5	3.8	228.5	3.6	162.2	4.2	222.2	1.8

Source: U.S. Department of Labor, Bureau of Labor Statistics, Division of Consumer Prices and Price Indexes. - indicates no data collected for period.

Atlanta, GA
Consumer Price Index - All Urban Consumers
Base 1982-1984 = 100
All Items

For 1917-1995. Columns headed % show percentile change in the index from the previous period for which an index is available.

Year	Jan Index	%	Feb Index	%	Mar Index	%	Apr Index	%	May Index	%	Jun Index	%	Jul Index	%	Aug Index	%	Sep Index	%	Oct Index	%	Nov Index	%	Dec Index	%
1917	-	-	-	-	-	-	-	-	-	-	-	-	-	-	-	-	-	-	-	-	-	-	15.2	-
1918	-	-	-	-	-	-	-	-	-	-	-	-	-	-	-	-	-	-	-	-	-	-	18.2	19.7
1919	-	-	-	-	-	-	-	-	-	-	18.9	3.8	-	-	-	-	-	-	-	-	-	-	20.8	10.1
1920	-	-	-	-	-	-	-	-	-	-	23.0	10.6	-	-	-	-	-	-	-	-	-	-	20.8	-9.6
1921	-	-	-	-	-	-	-	-	19.0	-8.7	-	-	-	-	-	-	18.5	-2.6	-	-	-	-	18.0	-2.7
1922	-	-	-	-	17.4	-3.3	-	-	-	-	17.5	0.6	-	-	-	-	17.4	-0.6	-	-	-	-	17.3	-0.6
1923	-	-	-	-	17.4	0.6	-	-	-	-	17.6	1.1	-	-	-	-	17.8	1.1	-	-	-	-	17.5	-1.7
1924	-	-	-	-	17.3	-1.1	-	-	-	-	17.3	0.0	-	-	-	-	17.3	0.0	-	-	-	-	17.3	0.0
1925	-	-	-	-	-	-	-	-	-	-	17.9	3.5	-	-	-	-	-	-	-	-	-	-	18.3	2.2
1926	-	-	-	-	-	-	-	-	-	-	18.0	-1.6	-	-	-	-	-	-	-	-	-	-	17.8	-1.1
1927	-	-	-	-	-	-	-	-	-	-	18.1	1.7	-	-	-	-	-	-	-	-	-	-	17.2	-5.0
1928	-	-	-	-	-	-	-	-	-	-	17.4	1.2	-	-	-	-	-	-	-	-	-	-	17.3	-0.6
1929	-	-	-	-	-	-	-	-	-	-	17.1	-1.2	-	-	-	-	-	-	-	-	-	-	17.1	0.0
1930	-	-	-	-	-	-	-	-	-	-	16.5	-3.5	-	-	-	-	-	-	-	-	-	-	15.8	-4.2
1931	-	-	-	-	-	-	-	-	-	-	14.8	-6.3	-	-	-	-	-	-	-	-	-	-	14.0	-5.4
1932	-	-	-	-	-	-	-	-	-	-	13.4	-4.3	-	-	-	-	-	-	-	-	-	-	12.6	-6.0
1933	-	-	-	-	-	-	-	-	-	-	12.5	-0.8	-	-	-	-	-	-	-	-	-	-	12.9	3.2
1934	-	-	-	-	-	-	-	-	-	-	13.1	1.6	-	-	-	-	-	-	-	-	13.4	2.3	-	-
1935	-	-	-	-	13.4	0.0	-	-	-	-	-	-	13.4	0.0	-	-	-	-	13.7	2.2	-	-	-	-
1936	13.8	0.7	-	-	-	-	13.5	-2.2	-	-	-	-	13.7	1.5	-	-	13.9	1.5	-	-	-	-	13.9	0.0
1937	-	-	-	-	14.0	0.7	-	-	-	-	14.1	0.7	-	-	-	-	14.3	1.4	-	-	-	-	14.1	-1.4
1938	-	-	-	-	13.8	-2.1	-	-	-	-	13.6	-1.4	-	-	-	-	13.8	1.5	-	-	-	-	13.8	0.0
1939	-	-	-	-	13.6	-1.4	-	-	-	-	13.5	-0.7	-	-	-	-	13.8	2.2	-	-	-	-	13.6	-1.4
1940	-	-	-	-	13.7	0.7	-	-	-	-	13.5	-1.5	-	-	-	-	13.6	0.7	-	-	-	-	13.8	1.5
1941	-	-	-	-	13.8	0.0	-	-	-	-	14.2	2.9	-	-	-	-	14.8	4.2	-	-	-	-	15.2	2.7
1942	-	-	-	-	15.7	3.3	-	-	-	-	15.9	1.3	-	-	-	-	16.1	1.3	-	-	-	-	16.4	1.9
1943	-	-	-	-	16.9	3.0	-	-	-	-	17.2	1.8	-	-	-	-	17.1	-0.6	-	-	-	-	17.1	0.0
1944	-	-	-	-	17.0	-0.6	-	-	-	-	17.3	1.8	-	-	-	-	17.5	1.2	-	-	-	-	17.7	1.1
1945	-	-	-	-	17.7	0.0	-	-	-	-	17.9	1.1	-	-	-	-	18.1	1.1	-	-	-	-	18.1	0.0
1946	-	-	-	-	18.1	0.0	-	-	-	-	18.4	1.7	-	-	-	-	20.2	9.8	-	-	-	-	21.4	5.9
1947	-	-	-	-	22.2	3.7	-	-	-	-	21.9	-1.4	-	-	22.3	1.8	-	-	-	-	23.1	3.6	-	-
1948	-	-	23.3	0.9	-	-	-	-	23.6	1.3	-	-	-	-	24.4	3.4	-	-	-	-	24.0	-1.6	-	-
1949	-	-	23.6	-1.7	-	-	-	-	23.7	0.4	-	-	-	-	24.0	1.3	-	-	-	-	23.8	-0.8	-	-
1950	-	-	23.4	-1.7	-	-	-	-	23.6	0.9	-	-	-	-	24.4	3.4	-	-	-	-	24.8	1.6	-	-
1951	-	-	25.8	4.0	-	-	-	-	26.5	2.7	-	-	-	-	26.5	0.0	-	-	-	-	26.9	1.5	-	-
1952	-	-	26.8	-0.4	-	-	-	-	26.7	-0.4	-	-	-	-	27.3	2.2	-	-	-	-	27.3	0.0	27.2	-0.4
1953	-	-	-	-	27.2	0.0	-	-	-	-	27.3	0.4	-	-	-	-	27.4	0.4	-	-	-	-	27.3	-0.4
1954	-	-	-	-	27.3	0.0	-	-	-	-	27.4	0.4	-	-	-	-	27.1	-1.1	-	-	-	-	27.0	-0.4
1955	-	-	-	-	26.9	-0.4	-	-	-	-	27.0	0.4	-	-	-	-	27.3	1.1	-	-	-	-	27.3	0.0
1956	-	-	-	-	27.2	-0.4	-	-	-	-	27.5	1.1	-	-	-	-	27.7	0.7	-	-	-	-	27.8	0.4
1957	-	-	-	-	28.1	1.1	-	-	-	-	28.2	0.4	-	-	-	-	28.5	1.1	-	-	-	-	28.5	0.0
1958	-	-	-	-	29.1	2.1	-	-	-	-	29.1	0.0	-	-	-	-	29.0	-0.3	-	-	-	-	29.0	0.0
1959	-	-	-	-	28.9	-0.3	-	-	-	-	29.2	1.0	-	-	-	-	29.3	0.3	-	-	-	-	29.4	0.3
1960	-	-	-	-	29.5	0.3	-	-	-	-	29.6	0.3	-	-	-	-	29.8	0.7	-	-	-	-	29.7	-0.3
1961	-	-	-	-	29.7	0.0	-	-	-	-	29.7	0.0	-	-	-	-	29.9	0.7	-	-	-	-	29.8	-0.3

[Continued]

Atlanta, GA
Consumer Price Index - All Urban Consumers
Base 1982-1984 = 100
All Items
[Continued]

For 1917-1995. Columns headed % show percentile change in the index from the previous period for which an index is available.

Year	Jan Index	%	Feb Index	%	Mar Index	%	Apr Index	%	May Index	%	Jun Index	%	Jul Index	%	Aug Index	%	Sep Index	%	Oct Index	%	Nov Index	%	Dec Index	%
1962	-	-	-	-	29.9	0.3	-	-	-	-	30.0	0.3	-	-	-	-	30.2	0.7	-	-	-	-	30.1	-0.3
1963	-	-	-	-	30.2	0.3	-	-	-	-	30.2	0.0	-	-	-	-	30.3	0.3	-	-	-	-	30.5	0.7
1964	-	-	-	-	30.7	0.7	-	-	-	-	30.6	-0.3	-	-	-	-	30.9	1.0	-	-	-	-	31.0	0.3
1965	-	-	-	-	31.0	0.0	-	-	-	-	31.1	0.3	-	-	-	-	31.2	0.3	-	-	-	-	31.5	1.0
1966	-	-	-	-	31.8	1.0	-	-	-	-	32.0	0.6	-	-	-	-	32.5	1.6	-	-	-	-	32.7	0.6
1967	-	-	-	-	32.9	0.6	-	-	-	-	33.1	0.6	-	-	-	-	33.3	0.6	-	-	-	-	33.7	1.2
1968	-	-	-	-	34.0	0.9	-	-	-	-	34.3	0.9	-	-	-	-	35.0	2.0	-	-	-	-	35.2	0.6
1969	-	-	-	-	36.0	2.3	-	-	-	-	36.4	1.1	-	-	-	-	37.1	1.9	-	-	-	-	37.5	1.1
1970	-	-	-	-	38.0	1.3	-	-	-	-	38.6	1.6	-	-	-	-	39.0	1.0	-	-	-	-	39.6	1.5
1971	-	-	-	-	39.9	0.8	-	-	-	-	40.6	1.8	-	-	-	-	40.5	-0.2	-	-	-	-	41.0	1.2
1972	-	-	-	-	41.1	0.2	-	-	-	-	41.4	0.7	-	-	-	-	42.1	1.7	-	-	-	-	42.3	0.5
1973	-	-	-	-	43.1	1.9	-	-	-	-	44.0	2.1	-	-	-	-	45.4	3.2	-	-	-	-	46.1	1.5
1974	-	-	-	-	47.8	3.7	-	-	-	-	48.8	2.1	-	-	-	-	50.6	3.7	-	-	-	-	51.7	2.2
1975	-	-	-	-	52.6	1.7	-	-	-	-	53.4	1.5	-	-	-	-	54.6	2.2	-	-	-	-	55.1	0.9
1976	-	-	-	-	55.2	0.2	-	-	-	-	55.9	1.3	-	-	-	-	56.9	1.8	-	-	-	-	57.0	0.2
1977	-	-	-	-	58.4	2.5	-	-	-	-	59.4	1.7	-	-	-	-	60.7	2.2	-	-	-	-	61.2	0.8
1978	-	-	61.7	0.8	-	-	62.5	1.3	-	-	63.6	1.8	-	-	64.7	1.7	-	-	65.9	1.9	-	-	65.9	0.0
1979	-	-	66.9	1.5	-	-	68.5	2.4	-	-	70.5	2.9	-	-	71.9	2.0	-	-	73.2	1.8	-	-	74.0	1.1
1980	-	-	76.4	3.2	-	-	78.0	2.1	-	-	80.3	2.9	-	-	81.7	1.7	-	-	83.0	1.6	-	-	85.7	3.3
1981	-	-	87.2	1.8	-	-	88.2	1.1	-	-	89.3	1.2	-	-	91.6	2.6	-	-	93.3	1.9	-	-	93.6	0.3
1982	-	-	92.8	-0.9	-	-	92.9	0.1	-	-	96.5	3.9	-	-	98.0	1.6	-	-	98.8	0.8	-	-	98.2	-0.6
1983	-	-	97.9	-0.3	-	-	98.7	0.8	-	-	100.2	1.5	-	-	100.8	0.6	-	-	100.9	0.1	-	-	101.9	1.0
1984	-	-	102.6	0.7	-	-	103.2	0.6	-	-	104.1	0.9	-	-	104.8	0.7	-	-	105.4	0.6	-	-	105.5	0.1
1985	-	-	107.0	1.4	-	-	107.6	0.6	-	-	108.8	1.1	-	-	109.9	1.0	-	-	110.4	0.5	-	-	111.2	0.7
1986	-	-	111.7	0.4	-	-	111.1	-0.5	-	-	112.2	1.0	-	-	112.4	0.2	-	-	112.7	0.3	-	-	113.5	0.7
1987	-	-	-	-	-	-	-	-	-	-	115.1	1.4	-	-	-	-	-	-	-	-	-	-	118.5	3.0
1988	-	-	-	-	-	-	-	-	-	-	120.2	1.4	-	-	-	-	-	-	-	-	-	-	124.6	3.7
1989	-	-	-	-	-	-	-	-	-	-	126.8	1.8	-	-	-	-	-	-	-	-	-	-	129.9	2.4
1990	-	-	-	-	-	-	-	-	-	-	133.5	2.8	-	-	-	-	-	-	-	-	-	-	138.2	3.5
1991	-	-	-	-	-	-	-	-	-	-	141.0	2.0	-	-	-	-	-	-	-	-	-	-	143.4	1.7
1992	-	-	-	-	-	-	-	-	-	-	145.4	1.4	-	-	-	-	-	-	-	-	-	-	147.7	1.6
1993	-	-	-	-	-	-	-	-	-	-	149.1	0.9	-	-	-	-	-	-	-	-	-	-	151.3	1.5
1994	-	-	-	-	-	-	-	-	-	-	153.3	1.3	-	-	-	-	-	-	-	-	-	-	156.0	1.8
1995	-	-	-	-	-	-	-	-	-	-	157.7	1.1	-	-	-	-	-	-	-	-	-	-	-	-

Source: U.S. Department of Labor, Bureau of Labor Statistics, Division of Consumer Prices and Price Indexes. - indicates no data collected for period.

Atlanta, GA
Consumer Price Index - Urban Wage Earners
Base 1982-1984 = 100
All Items

For 1917-1995. Columns headed % show percentile change in the index from the previous period for which an index is available.

Year	Jan Index	%	Feb Index	%	Mar Index	%	Apr Index	%	May Index	%	Jun Index	%	Jul Index	%	Aug Index	%	Sep Index	%	Oct Index	%	Nov Index	%	Dec Index	%
1917	-	-	-	-	-	-	-	-	-	-	-	-	-	-	-	-	-	-	-	-	-	-	15.1	-
1918	-	-	-	-	-	-	-	-	-	-	-	-	-	-	-	-	-	-	-	-	-	-	18.1	19.9
1919	-	-	-	-	-	-	-	-	-	-	18.9	4.4	-	-	-	-	-	-	-	-	-	-	20.7	9.5
1920	-	-	-	-	-	-	-	-	-	-	23.0	11.1	-	-	-	-	-	-	-	-	-	-	20.8	-9.6
1921	-	-	-	-	-	-	-	-	18.9	-9.1	-	-	-	-	-	-	18.4	-2.6	-	-	-	-	17.9	-2.7
1922	-	-	-	-	17.4	-2.8	-	-	-	-	17.5	0.6	-	-	-	-	17.3	-1.1	-	-	-	-	17.3	0.0
1923	-	-	-	-	17.3	0.0	-	-	-	-	17.5	1.2	-	-	-	-	17.8	1.7	-	-	-	-	17.5	-1.7
1924	-	-	-	-	17.2	-1.7	-	-	-	-	17.3	0.6	-	-	-	-	17.3	0.0	-	-	-	-	17.3	0.0
1925	-	-	-	-	-	-	-	-	-	-	17.8	2.9	-	-	-	-	-	-	-	-	-	-	18.2	2.2
1926	-	-	-	-	-	-	-	-	-	-	18.0	-1.1	-	-	-	-	-	-	-	-	-	-	17.7	-1.7
1927	-	-	-	-	-	-	-	-	-	-	18.1	2.3	-	-	-	-	-	-	-	-	-	-	17.2	-5.0
1928	-	-	-	-	-	-	-	-	-	-	17.3	0.6	-	-	-	-	-	-	-	-	-	-	17.3	0.0
1929	-	-	-	-	-	-	-	-	-	-	17.1	-1.2	-	-	-	-	-	-	-	-	-	-	17.1	0.0
1930	-	-	-	-	-	-	-	-	-	-	16.4	-4.1	-	-	-	-	-	-	-	-	-	-	15.7	-4.3
1931	-	-	-	-	-	-	-	-	-	-	14.8	-5.7	-	-	-	-	-	-	-	-	-	-	14.0	-5.4
1932	-	-	-	-	-	-	-	-	-	-	13.3	-5.0	-	-	-	-	-	-	-	-	-	-	12.6	-5.3
1933	-	-	-	-	-	-	-	-	-	-	12.5	-0.8	-	-	-	-	-	-	-	-	-	-	12.9	3.2
1934	-	-	-	-	-	-	-	-	-	-	13.1	1.6	-	-	-	-	-	-	-	-	13.3	1.5	-	-
1935	-	-	-	-	13.3	0.0	-	-	-	-	-	-	13.3	0.0	-	-	-	-	13.7	3.0	-	-	-	-
1936	13.7	0.0	-	-	-	-	13.5	-1.5	-	-	-	-	13.7	1.5	-	-	13.8	0.7	-	-	-	-	13.8	0.0
1937	-	-	-	-	14.0	1.4	-	-	-	-	14.1	0.7	-	-	-	-	14.3	1.4	-	-	-	-	14.1	-1.4
1938	-	-	-	-	13.7	-2.8	-	-	-	-	13.6	-0.7	-	-	-	-	13.7	0.7	-	-	-	-	13.7	0.0
1939	-	-	-	-	13.6	-0.7	-	-	-	-	13.4	-1.5	-	-	-	-	13.7	2.2	-	-	-	-	13.5	-1.5
1940	-	-	-	-	13.6	0.7	-	-	-	-	13.5	-0.7	-	-	-	-	13.6	0.7	-	-	-	-	13.7	0.7
1941	-	-	-	-	13.8	0.7	-	-	-	-	14.2	2.9	-	-	-	-	14.7	3.5	-	-	-	-	15.1	2.7
1942	-	-	-	-	15.6	3.3	-	-	-	-	15.8	1.3	-	-	-	-	16.1	1.9	-	-	-	-	16.3	1.2
1943	-	-	-	-	16.9	3.7	-	-	-	-	17.2	1.8	-	-	-	-	17.1	-0.6	-	-	-	-	17.0	-0.6
1944	-	-	-	-	16.9	-0.6	-	-	-	-	17.2	1.8	-	-	-	-	17.5	1.7	-	-	-	-	17.7	1.1
1945	-	-	-	-	17.7	0.0	-	-	-	-	17.8	0.6	-	-	-	-	18.1	1.7	-	-	-	-	18.0	-0.6
1946	-	-	-	-	18.1	0.6	-	-	-	-	18.4	1.7	-	-	-	-	20.1	9.2	-	-	-	-	21.4	6.5
1947	-	-	-	-	22.1	3.3	-	-	-	-	21.8	-1.4	-	-	22.3	2.3	-	-	-	-	23.0	3.1	-	-
1948	-	-	23.3	1.3	-	-	-	-	23.5	0.9	-	-	-	-	24.3	3.4	-	-	-	-	24.0	-1.2	-	-
1949	-	-	23.5	-2.1	-	-	-	-	23.6	0.4	-	-	-	-	23.9	1.3	-	-	-	-	23.7	-0.8	-	-
1950	-	-	23.4	-1.3	-	-	-	-	23.5	0.4	-	-	-	-	24.4	3.8	-	-	-	-	24.7	1.2	-	-
1951	-	-	25.7	4.0	-	-	-	-	26.4	2.7	-	-	-	-	26.5	0.4	-	-	-	-	26.9	1.5	-	-
1952	-	-	26.8	-0.4	-	-	-	-	26.6	-0.7	-	-	-	-	27.2	2.3	-	-	-	-	27.2	0.0	27.1	-0.4
1953	-	-	-	-	27.1	0.0	-	-	-	-	27.2	0.4	-	-	-	-	27.3	0.4	-	-	-	-	27.2	-0.4
1954	-	-	-	-	27.2	0.0	-	-	-	-	27.3	0.4	-	-	-	-	27.0	-1.1	-	-	-	-	26.9	-0.4
1955	-	-	-	-	26.8	-0.4	-	-	-	-	27.0	0.7	-	-	-	-	27.2	0.7	-	-	-	-	27.2	0.0
1956	-	-	-	-	27.1	-0.4	-	-	-	-	27.4	1.1	-	-	-	-	27.6	0.7	-	-	-	-	27.7	0.4
1957	-	-	-	-	28.0	1.1	-	-	-	-	28.1	0.4	-	-	-	-	28.4	1.1	-	-	-	-	28.4	0.0
1958	-	-	-	-	29.0	2.1	-	-	-	-	29.0	0.0	-	-	-	-	28.9	-0.3	-	-	-	-	28.9	0.0
1959	-	-	-	-	28.9	0.0	-	-	-	-	29.2	1.0	-	-	-	-	29.3	0.3	-	-	-	-	29.4	0.3
1960	-	-	-	-	29.4	0.0	-	-	-	-	29.5	0.3	-	-	-	-	29.7	0.7	-	-	-	-	29.7	0.0
1961	-	-	-	-	29.7	0.0	-	-	-	-	29.6	-0.3	-	-	-	-	29.8	0.7	-	-	-	-	29.7	-0.3

[Continued]

Atlanta, GA
Consumer Price Index - Urban Wage Earners
Base 1982-1984 = 100
All Items
[Continued]

For 1917-1995. Columns headed % show percentile change in the index from the previous period for which an index is available.

Year	Jan Index	%	Feb Index	%	Mar Index	%	Apr Index	%	May Index	%	Jun Index	%	Jul Index	%	Aug Index	%	Sep Index	%	Oct Index	%	Nov Index	%	Dec Index	%
1962	-	-	-	-	29.8	0.3	-	-	-	-	29.9	0.3	-	-	-	-	30.1	0.7	-	-	-	-	30.1	0.0
1963	-	-	-	-	30.2	0.3	-	-	-	-	30.2	0.0	-	-	-	-	30.3	0.3	-	-	-	-	30.4	0.3
1964	-	-	-	-	30.7	1.0	-	-	-	-	30.6	-0.3	-	-	-	-	30.8	0.7	-	-	-	-	30.9	0.3
1965	-	-	-	-	31.0	0.3	-	-	-	-	31.0	0.0	-	-	-	-	31.1	0.3	-	-	-	-	31.4	1.0
1966	-	-	-	-	31.7	1.0	-	-	-	-	31.9	0.6	-	-	-	-	32.4	1.6	-	-	-	-	32.6	0.6
1967	-	-	-	-	32.8	0.6	-	-	-	-	33.0	0.6	-	-	-	-	33.2	0.6	-	-	-	-	33.6	1.2
1968	-	-	-	-	33.9	0.9	-	-	-	-	34.2	0.9	-	-	-	-	34.9	2.0	-	-	-	-	35.1	0.6
1969	-	-	-	-	35.9	2.3	-	-	-	-	36.3	1.1	-	-	-	-	37.0	1.9	-	-	-	-	37.4	1.1
1970	-	-	-	-	37.9	1.3	-	-	-	-	38.5	1.6	-	-	-	-	38.9	1.0	-	-	-	-	39.5	1.5
1971	-	-	-	-	39.8	0.8	-	-	-	-	40.4	1.5	-	-	-	-	40.3	-0.2	-	-	-	-	40.8	1.2
1972	-	-	-	-	40.9	0.2	-	-	-	-	41.3	1.0	-	-	-	-	42.0	1.7	-	-	-	-	42.2	0.5
1973	-	-	-	-	43.0	1.9	-	-	-	-	43.9	2.1	-	-	-	-	45.3	3.2	-	-	-	-	45.9	1.3
1974	-	-	-	-	47.7	3.9	-	-	-	-	48.7	2.1	-	-	-	-	50.5	3.7	-	-	-	-	51.6	2.2
1975	-	-	-	-	52.4	1.6	-	-	-	-	53.2	1.5	-	-	-	-	54.5	2.4	-	-	-	-	55.0	0.9
1976	-	-	-	-	55.1	0.2	-	-	-	-	55.7	1.1	-	-	-	-	56.8	2.0	-	-	-	-	56.9	0.2
1977	-	-	-	-	58.2	2.3	-	-	-	-	59.2	1.7	-	-	-	-	60.5	2.2	-	-	-	-	61.0	0.8
1978	-	-	61.7	1.1	-	-	62.5	1.3	-	-	63.7	1.9	-	-	64.6	1.4	-	-	65.6	1.5	-	-	65.9	0.5
1979	-	-	67.0	1.7	-	-	68.9	2.8	-	-	70.9	2.9	-	-	72.4	2.1	-	-	73.9	2.1	-	-	75.1	1.6
1980	-	-	77.2	2.8	-	-	79.1	2.5	-	-	80.9	2.3	-	-	82.6	2.1	-	-	83.5	1.1	-	-	86.1	3.1
1981	-	-	88.1	2.3	-	-	88.9	0.9	-	-	90.2	1.5	-	-	92.0	2.0	-	-	93.6	1.7	-	-	94.0	0.4
1982	-	-	93.5	-0.5	-	-	93.6	0.1	-	-	96.9	3.5	-	-	98.3	1.4	-	-	98.8	0.5	-	-	98.5	-0.3
1983	-	-	98.2	-0.3	-	-	99.3	1.1	-	-	99.9	0.6	-	-	100.6	0.7	-	-	101.3	0.7	-	-	102.4	1.1
1984	-	-	102.4	0.0	-	-	102.3	-0.1	-	-	102.8	0.5	-	-	104.2	1.4	-	-	105.2	1.0	-	-	104.5	-0.7
1985	-	-	105.9	1.3	-	-	106.6	0.7	-	-	107.8	1.1	-	-	108.9	1.0	-	-	109.1	0.2	-	-	110.0	0.8
1986	-	-	110.6	0.5	-	-	109.7	-0.8	-	-	111.0	1.2	-	-	110.9	-0.1	-	-	111.1	0.2	-	-	111.7	0.5
1987	-	-	-	-	-	-	-	-	-	-	114.9	2.9	-	-	-	-	-	-	-	-	-	-	118.5	3.1
1988	-	-	-	-	-	-	-	-	-	-	120.0	1.3	-	-	-	-	-	-	-	-	-	-	124.4	3.7
1989	-	-	-	-	-	-	-	-	-	-	126.7	1.8	-	-	-	-	-	-	-	-	-	-	130.0	2.6
1990	-	-	-	-	-	-	-	-	-	-	133.6	2.8	-	-	-	-	-	-	-	-	-	-	138.5	3.7
1991	-	-	-	-	-	-	-	-	-	-	141.0	1.8	-	-	-	-	-	-	-	-	-	-	143.4	1.7
1992	-	-	-	-	-	-	-	-	-	-	145.2	1.3	-	-	-	-	-	-	-	-	-	-	147.6	1.7
1993	-	-	-	-	-	-	-	-	-	-	149.0	0.9	-	-	-	-	-	-	-	-	-	-	151.2	1.5
1994	-	-	-	-	-	-	-	-	-	-	152.8	1.1	-	-	-	-	-	-	-	-	-	-	155.6	1.8
1995	-	-	-	-	-	-	-	-	-	-	157.4	1.2	-	-	-	-	-	-	-	-	-	-	-	-

Source: U.S. Department of Labor, Bureau of Labor Statistics, Division of Consumer Prices and Price Indexes. - indicates no data collected for period.

Atlanta, GA
Consumer Price Index - All Urban Consumers
Base 1982-1984 = 100
Food and Beverages

For 1975-1995. Columns headed % show percentile change in the index from the previous period for which an index is available.

Year	Jan Index	%	Feb Index	%	Mar Index	%	Apr Index	%	May Index	%	Jun Index	%	Jul Index	%	Aug Index	%	Sep Index	%	Oct Index	%	Nov Index	%	Dec Index	%
1975	-	-	-	-	-	-	-	-	-	-	-	-	-	-	-	-	-	-	-	-	-	-	63.2	-
1976	-	-	-	-	62.1	-1.7	-	-	-	-	62.2	0.2	-	-	-	-	-	-	63.0	1.3	-	-	62.4	-1.0
1977	-	-	-	-	64.9	4.0	-	-	-	-	65.9	1.5	-	-	-	-	-	-	67.2	2.0	-	-	67.6	0.6
1978	-	-	69.0	2.1	-	-	70.2	1.7	-	-	73.1	4.1	-	-	73.8	1.0	-	-	74.0	0.3	-	-	74.9	1.2
1979	-	-	77.7	3.7	-	-	78.8	1.4	-	-	79.1	0.4	-	-	80.8	2.1	-	-	80.7	-0.1	-	-	81.6	1.1
1980	-	-	82.4	1.0	-	-	82.9	0.6	-	-	84.4	1.8	-	-	87.6	3.8	-	-	88.6	1.1	-	-	91.4	3.2
1981	-	-	92.2	0.9	-	-	92.2	0.0	-	-	92.5	0.3	-	-	93.5	1.1	-	-	94.1	0.6	-	-	95.0	1.0
1982	-	-	96.1	1.2	-	-	96.3	0.2	-	-	97.5	1.2	-	-	97.4	-0.1	-	-	97.7	0.3	-	-	98.2	0.5
1983	-	-	98.8	0.6	-	-	100.2	1.4	-	-	100.0	-0.2	-	-	99.9	-0.1	-	-	100.1	0.2	-	-	100.4	0.3
1984	-	-	103.4	3.0	-	-	102.7	-0.7	-	-	102.2	-0.5	-	-	103.8	1.6	-	-	103.5	-0.3	-	-	104.3	0.8
1985	-	-	106.2	1.8	-	-	105.5	-0.7	-	-	105.5	0.0	-	-	105.3	-0.2	-	-	106.3	0.9	-	-	108.6	2.2
1986	-	-	109.4	0.7	-	-	110.5	1.0	-	-	110.6	0.1	-	-	113.0	2.2	-	-	112.5	-0.4	-	-	112.1	-0.4
1987	-	-	-	-	-	-	-	-	-	-	111.2	-0.8	-	-	-	-	-	-	-	-	-	-	112.9	1.5
1988	-	-	-	-	-	-	-	-	-	-	114.4	1.3	-	-	-	-	-	-	-	-	-	-	117.6	2.8
1989	-	-	-	-	-	-	-	-	-	-	121.9	3.7	-	-	-	-	-	-	-	-	-	-	126.5	3.8
1990	-	-	-	-	-	-	-	-	-	-	130.1	2.8	-	-	-	-	-	-	-	-	-	-	132.4	1.8
1991	-	-	-	-	-	-	-	-	-	-	135.6	2.4	-	-	-	-	-	-	-	-	-	-	135.2	-0.3
1992	-	-	-	-	-	-	-	-	-	-	137.2	1.5	-	-	-	-	-	-	-	-	-	-	138.0	0.6
1993	-	-	-	-	-	-	-	-	-	-	139.6	1.2	-	-	-	-	-	-	-	-	-	-	139.7	0.1
1994	-	-	-	-	-	-	-	-	-	-	141.4	1.2	-	-	-	-	-	-	-	-	-	-	144.1	1.9
1995	-	-	-	-	-	-	-	-	-	-	148.3	2.9	-	-	-	-	-	-	-	-	-	-	-	-

Source: U.S. Department of Labor, Bureau of Labor Statistics, Division of Consumer Prices and Price Indexes. - indicates no data collected for period.

Atlanta, GA
Consumer Price Index - Urban Wage Earners
Base 1982-1984 = 100
Food and Beverages

For 1975-1995. Columns headed % show percentile change in the index from the previous period for which an index is available.

Year	Jan Index	%	Feb Index	%	Mar Index	%	Apr Index	%	May Index	%	Jun Index	%	Jul Index	%	Aug Index	%	Sep Index	%	Oct Index	%	Nov Index	%	Dec Index	%
1975	-	-	-	-	-	-	-	-	-	-	-	-	-	-	-	-	-	-	-	-	-	-	62.5	-
1976	-	-	-	-	61.4	-1.8	-	-	-	-	61.5	0.2	-	-	-	-	62.3	1.3	-	-	-	-	61.7	-1.0
1977	-	-	-	-	64.1	3.9	-	-	-	-	65.1	1.6	-	-	-	-	66.5	2.2	-	-	-	-	66.8	0.5
1978	-	-	68.3	2.2	-	-	70.1	2.6	-	-	72.8	3.9	-	-	73.8	1.4	-	-	73.7	-0.1	-	-	74.4	0.9
1979	-	-	77.4	4.0	-	-	78.7	1.7	-	-	79.1	0.5	-	-	80.5	1.8	-	-	80.7	0.2	-	-	81.6	1.1
1980	-	-	82.4	1.0	-	-	83.6	1.5	-	-	84.3	0.8	-	-	87.1	3.3	-	-	88.4	1.5	-	-	90.8	2.7
1981	-	-	91.9	1.2	-	-	92.6	0.8	-	-	93.1	0.5	-	-	93.7	0.6	-	-	94.2	0.5	-	-	94.8	0.6
1982	-	-	95.9	1.2	-	-	96.3	0.4	-	-	97.5	1.2	-	-	97.5	0.0	-	-	97.9	0.4	-	-	98.4	0.5
1983	-	-	98.9	0.5	-	-	100.3	1.4	-	-	100.1	-0.2	-	-	99.9	-0.2	-	-	100.1	0.2	-	-	100.4	0.3
1984	-	-	103.1	2.7	-	-	102.5	-0.6	-	-	102.3	-0.2	-	-	103.6	1.3	-	-	103.4	-0.2	-	-	104.2	0.8
1985	-	-	106.0	1.7	-	-	105.3	-0.7	-	-	105.4	0.1	-	-	105.2	-0.2	-	-	106.1	0.9	-	-	108.4	2.2
1986	-	-	109.2	0.7	-	-	110.3	1.0	-	-	110.3	0.0	-	-	112.9	2.4	-	-	112.5	-0.4	-	-	111.8	-0.6
1987	-	-	-	-	-	-	-	-	-	-	111.4	-0.4	-	-	-	-	-	-	-	-	-	-	113.3	1.7
1988	-	-	-	-	-	-	-	-	-	-	114.7	1.2	-	-	-	-	-	-	-	-	-	-	118.2	3.1
1989	-	-	-	-	-	-	-	-	-	-	122.8	3.9	-	-	-	-	-	-	-	-	-	-	127.4	3.7
1990	-	-	-	-	-	-	-	-	-	-	131.1	2.9	-	-	-	-	-	-	-	-	-	-	133.6	1.9
1991	-	-	-	-	-	-	-	-	-	-	136.7	2.3	-	-	-	-	-	-	-	-	-	-	136.4	-0.2
1992	-	-	-	-	-	-	-	-	-	-	138.2	1.3	-	-	-	-	-	-	-	-	-	-	139.3	0.8
1993	-	-	-	-	-	-	-	-	-	-	140.8	1.1	-	-	-	-	-	-	-	-	-	-	141.0	0.1
1994	-	-	-	-	-	-	-	-	-	-	142.6	1.1	-	-	-	-	-	-	-	-	-	-	145.3	1.9
1995	-	-	-	-	-	-	-	-	-	-	149.4	2.8	-	-	-	-	-	-	-	-	-	-	-	-

Source: U.S. Department of Labor, Bureau of Labor Statistics, Division of Consumer Prices and Price Indexes. - indicates no data collected for period.

Atlanta, GA
Consumer Price Index - All Urban Consumers
Base 1982-1984 = 100
Housing

For 1975-1995. Columns headed % show percentile change in the index from the previous period for which an index is available.

Year	Jan Index	%	Feb Index	%	Mar Index	%	Apr Index	%	May Index	%	Jun Index	%	Jul Index	%	Aug Index	%	Sep Index	%	Oct Index	%	Nov Index	%	Dec Index	%
1975	-	-	-	-	-	-	-	-	-	-	-	-	-	-	-	-	-	-	-	-	-	-	50.7	-
1976	-	-	-	-	51.2	1.0	-	-	-	-	51.8	1.2	-	-	-	-	52.5	1.4	-	-	-	-	52.8	0.6
1977	-	-	-	-	53.7	1.7	-	-	-	-	55.1	2.6	-	-	-	-	56.4	2.4	-	-	-	-	57.2	1.4
1978	-	-	57.6	0.7	-	-	58.5	1.6	-	-	59.2	1.2	-	-	60.4	2.0	-	-	62.2	3.0	-	-	62.0	-0.3
1979	-	-	62.3	0.5	-	-	63.5	1.9	-	-	66.0	3.9	-	-	66.9	1.4	-	-	68.9	3.0	-	-	69.6	1.0
1980	-	-	71.5	2.7	-	-	73.6	2.9	-	-	77.0	4.6	-	-	76.8	-0.3	-	-	78.4	2.1	-	-	82.4	5.1
1981	-	-	83.6	1.5	-	-	84.3	0.8	-	-	86.4	2.5	-	-	90.0	4.2	-	-	92.3	2.6	-	-	92.4	0.1
1982	-	-	90.7	-1.8	-	-	91.7	1.1	-	-	96.4	5.1	-	-	98.5	2.2	-	-	98.7	0.2	-	-	97.7	-1.0
1983	-	-	98.0	0.3	-	-	98.9	0.9	-	-	101.1	2.2	-	-	100.5	-0.6	-	-	100.2	-0.3	-	-	102.5	2.3
1984	-	-	102.7	0.2	-	-	103.4	0.7	-	-	105.3	1.8	-	-	106.0	0.7	-	-	105.4	-0.6	-	-	105.7	0.3
1985	-	-	107.4	1.6	-	-	108.4	0.9	-	-	110.2	1.7	-	-	111.6	1.3	-	-	111.2	-0.4	-	-	112.3	1.0
1986	-	-	112.7	0.4	-	-	114.1	1.2	-	-	116.1	1.8	-	-	116.3	0.2	-	-	115.9	-0.3	-	-	117.4	1.3
1987	-	-	-	-	-	-	-	-	-	-	116.4	-0.9	-	-	-	-	-	-	-	-	-	-	120.4	3.4
1988	-	-	-	-	-	-	-	-	-	-	121.8	1.2	-	-	-	-	-	-	-	-	-	-	127.8	4.9
1989	-	-	-	-	-	-	-	-	-	-	128.8	0.8	-	-	-	-	-	-	-	-	-	-	132.8	3.1
1990	-	-	-	-	-	-	-	-	-	-	136.2	2.6	-	-	-	-	-	-	-	-	-	-	141.1	3.6
1991	-	-	-	-	-	-	-	-	-	-	144.2	2.2	-	-	-	-	-	-	-	-	-	-	147.0	1.9
1992	-	-	-	-	-	-	-	-	-	-	148.5	1.0	-	-	-	-	-	-	-	-	-	-	150.7	1.5
1993	-	-	-	-	-	-	-	-	-	-	151.3	0.4	-	-	-	-	-	-	-	-	-	-	152.5	0.8
1994	-	-	-	-	-	-	-	-	-	-	153.7	0.8	-	-	-	-	-	-	-	-	-	-	156.5	1.8
1995	-	-	-	-	-	-	-	-	-	-	157.0	0.3	-	-	-	-	-	-	-	-	-	-	-	-

Source: U.S. Department of Labor, Bureau of Labor Statistics, Division of Consumer Prices and Price Indexes. - indicates no data collected for period.

Atlanta, GA
Consumer Price Index - Urban Wage Earners
Base 1982-1984 = 100
Housing

For 1975-1995. Columns headed % show percentile change in the index from the previous period for which an index is available.

Year	Jan Index	%	Feb Index	%	Mar Index	%	Apr Index	%	May Index	%	Jun Index	%	Jul Index	%	Aug Index	%	Sep Index	%	Oct Index	%	Nov Index	%	Dec Index	%
1975	-	-	-	-	-	-	-	-	-	-	-	-	-	-	-	-	-	-	-	-	-	-	51.3	-
1976	-	-	-	-	51.9	1.2	-	-	-	-	52.5	1.2	-	-	-	-	53.2	1.3	-	-	-	-	53.5	0.6
1977	-	-	-	-	54.5	1.9	-	-	-	-	55.8	2.4	-	-	-	-	57.2	2.5	-	-	-	-	58.0	1.4
1978	-	-	58.6	1.0	-	-	59.3	1.2	-	-	60.1	1.3	-	-	61.1	1.7	-	-	62.6	2.5	-	-	62.9	0.5
1979	-	-	63.3	0.6	-	-	64.6	2.1	-	-	67.3	4.2	-	-	68.0	1.0	-	-	69.8	2.6	-	-	70.7	1.3
1980	-	-	72.4	2.4	-	-	74.6	3.0	-	-	77.8	4.3	-	-	77.6	-0.3	-	-	78.4	1.0	-	-	82.4	5.1
1981	-	-	83.6	1.5	-	-	84.4	1.0	-	-	86.8	2.8	-	-	90.2	3.9	-	-	92.3	2.3	-	-	92.6	0.3
1982	-	-	91.2	-1.5	-	-	92.4	1.3	-	-	96.8	4.8	-	-	98.8	2.1	-	-	98.7	-0.1	-	-	98.0	-0.7
1983	-	-	99.0	1.0	-	-	100.2	1.2	-	-	100.3	0.1	-	-	100.7	0.4	-	-	101.7	1.0	-	-	103.8	2.1
1984	-	-	102.5	-1.3	-	-	101.7	-0.8	-	-	102.4	0.7	-	-	104.8	2.3	-	-	105.7	0.9	-	-	104.4	-1.2
1985	-	-	106.1	1.6	-	-	107.0	0.8	-	-	108.8	1.7	-	-	110.2	1.3	-	-	109.4	-0.7	-	-	110.4	0.9
1986	-	-	110.7	0.3	-	-	111.9	1.1	-	-	114.2	2.1	-	-	114.2	0.0	-	-	113.7	-0.4	-	-	115.3	1.4
1987	-	-	-	-	-	-	-	-	-	-	117.9	2.3	-	-	-	-	-	-	-	-	-	-	122.0	3.5
1988	-	-	-	-	-	-	-	-	-	-	123.3	1.1	-	-	-	-	-	-	-	-	-	-	129.4	4.9
1989	-	-	-	-	-	-	-	-	-	-	130.9	1.2	-	-	-	-	-	-	-	-	-	-	135.1	3.2
1990	-	-	-	-	-	-	-	-	-	-	138.3	2.4	-	-	-	-	-	-	-	-	-	-	143.1	3.5
1991	-	-	-	-	-	-	-	-	-	-	145.9	2.0	-	-	-	-	-	-	-	-	-	-	149.0	2.1
1992	-	-	-	-	-	-	-	-	-	-	150.2	0.8	-	-	-	-	-	-	-	-	-	-	152.4	1.5
1993	-	-	-	-	-	-	-	-	-	-	153.1	0.5	-	-	-	-	-	-	-	-	-	-	154.5	0.9
1994	-	-	-	-	-	-	-	-	-	-	155.5	0.6	-	-	-	-	-	-	-	-	-	-	158.3	1.8
1995	-	-	-	-	-	-	-	-	-	-	158.9	0.4	-	-	-	-	-	-	-	-	-	-	-	-

Source: U.S. Department of Labor, Bureau of Labor Statistics, Division of Consumer Prices and Price Indexes. - indicates no data collected for period.

Atlanta, GA
Consumer Price Index - All Urban Consumers
Base 1982-1984 = 100
Apparel and Upkeep

For 1952-1995. Columns headed % show percentile change in the index from the previous period for which an index is available.

Year	Jan Index	%	Feb Index	%	Mar Index	%	Apr Index	%	May Index	%	Jun Index	%	Jul Index	%	Aug Index	%	Sep Index	%	Oct Index	%	Nov Index	%	Dec Index	%
1952	-	-	-	-	-	-	-	-	-	-	-	-	-	-	-	-	-	-	-	-	42.1	-	-	-
1953	-	-	-	-	42.2	0.2	-	-	-	-	42.1	-0.2	-	-	-	-	42.5	1.0	-	-	-	-	42.2	-0.7
1954	-	-	-	-	42.5	0.7	-	-	-	-	42.6	0.2	-	-	-	-	42.2	-0.9	-	-	-	-	42.1	-0.2
1955	-	-	-	-	41.5	-1.4	-	-	-	-	42.1	1.4	-	-	-	-	42.5	1.0	-	-	-	-	42.5	0.0
1956	-	-	-	-	42.6	0.2	-	-	-	-	42.8	0.5	-	-	-	-	43.4	1.4	-	-	-	-	43.2	-0.5
1957	-	-	-	-	43.7	1.2	-	-	-	-	43.6	-0.2	-	-	-	-	44.1	1.1	-	-	-	-	44.1	0.0
1958	-	-	-	-	44.3	0.5	-	-	-	-	44.1	-0.5	-	-	-	-	44.3	0.5	-	-	-	-	44.3	0.0
1959	-	-	-	-	44.0	-0.7	-	-	-	-	44.0	0.0	-	-	-	-	44.4	0.9	-	-	-	-	44.7	0.7
1960	-	-	-	-	44.7	0.0	-	-	-	-	44.7	0.0	-	-	-	-	45.5	1.8	-	-	-	-	45.3	-0.4
1961	-	-	-	-	45.1	-0.4	-	-	-	-	45.1	0.0	-	-	-	-	45.0	-0.2	-	-	-	-	44.9	-0.2
1962	-	-	-	-	45.0	0.2	-	-	-	-	44.9	-0.2	-	-	-	-	45.2	0.7	-	-	-	-	45.5	0.7
1963	-	-	-	-	45.9	0.9	-	-	-	-	46.0	0.2	-	-	-	-	46.5	1.1	-	-	-	-	46.2	-0.6
1964	-	-	-	-	46.2	0.0	-	-	-	-	46.0	-0.4	-	-	-	-	46.2	0.4	-	-	-	-	46.3	0.2
1965	-	-	-	-	46.4	0.2	-	-	-	-	46.4	0.0	-	-	-	-	47.0	1.3	-	-	-	-	47.1	0.2
1966	-	-	-	-	47.8	1.5	-	-	-	-	48.4	1.3	-	-	-	-	50.0	3.3	-	-	-	-	50.8	1.6
1967	-	-	-	-	51.3	1.0	-	-	-	-	51.4	0.2	-	-	-	-	52.0	1.2	-	-	-	-	52.3	0.6
1968	-	-	-	-	53.3	1.9	-	-	-	-	53.4	0.2	-	-	-	-	54.3	1.7	-	-	-	-	55.0	1.3
1969	-	-	-	-	55.0	0.0	-	-	-	-	55.8	1.5	-	-	-	-	56.7	1.6	-	-	-	-	57.1	0.7
1970	-	-	-	-	57.8	1.2	-	-	-	-	57.9	0.2	-	-	-	-	59.0	1.9	-	-	-	-	59.4	0.7
1971	-	-	-	-	60.1	1.2	-	-	-	-	59.3	-1.3	-	-	-	-	60.2	1.5	-	-	-	-	60.2	0.0
1972	-	-	-	-	60.4	0.3	-	-	-	-	60.3	-0.2	-	-	-	-	62.6	3.8	-	-	-	-	62.6	0.0
1973	-	-	-	-	63.0	0.6	-	-	-	-	62.7	-0.5	-	-	-	-	65.0	3.7	-	-	-	-	65.4	0.6
1974	-	-	-	-	67.3	2.9	-	-	-	-	69.1	2.7	-	-	-	-	71.1	2.9	-	-	-	-	70.3	-1.1
1975	-	-	-	-	71.6	1.8	-	-	-	-	70.5	-1.5	-	-	-	-	72.7	3.1	-	-	-	-	72.4	-0.4
1976	-	-	-	-	73.1	1.0	-	-	-	-	72.8	-0.4	-	-	-	-	76.3	4.8	-	-	-	-	76.4	0.1
1977	-	-	-	-	78.7	3.0	-	-	-	-	77.0	-2.2	-	-	-	-	82.2	6.8	-	-	-	-	82.0	-0.2
1978	-	-	81.7	-0.4	-	-	83.8	2.6	-	-	83.6	-0.2	-	-	85.9	2.8	-	-	85.1	-0.9	-	-	84.4	-0.8
1979	-	-	85.0	0.7	-	-	86.8	2.1	-	-	88.0	1.4	-	-	88.8	0.9	-	-	89.0	0.2	-	-	89.4	0.4
1980	-	-	92.1	3.0	-	-	90.8	-1.4	-	-	92.1	1.4	-	-	94.1	2.2	-	-	96.0	2.0	-	-	95.0	-1.0
1981	-	-	94.1	-0.9	-	-	96.9	3.0	-	-	94.1	-2.9	-	-	99.6	5.8	-	-	96.5	-3.1	-	-	96.4	-0.1
1982	-	-	94.9	-1.6	-	-	93.9	-1.1	-	-	93.9	0.0	-	-	96.9	3.2	-	-	102.5	5.8	-	-	99.3	-3.1
1983	-	-	97.7	-1.6	-	-	93.8	-4.0	-	-	99.1	5.7	-	-	107.0	8.0	-	-	105.1	-1.8	-	-	101.0	-3.9
1984	-	-	98.4	-2.6	-	-	101.0	2.6	-	-	101.0	0.0	-	-	101.1	0.1	-	-	109.4	8.2	-	-	106.7	-2.5
1985	-	-	113.3	6.2	-	-	107.9	-4.8	-	-	109.1	1.1	-	-	114.0	4.5	-	-	116.9	2.5	-	-	109.5	-6.3
1986	-	-	108.0	-1.4	-	-	110.4	2.2	-	-	107.0	-3.1	-	-	107.9	0.8	-	-	115.8	7.3	-	-	114.4	-1.2
1987	-	-	-	-	-	-	-	-	-	-	105.5	-7.8	-	-	-	-	-	-	-	-	-	-	109.9	4.2
1988	-	-	-	-	-	-	-	-	-	-	108.4	-1.4	-	-	-	-	-	-	-	-	-	-	111.4	2.8
1989	-	-	-	-	-	-	-	-	-	-	104.2	-6.5	-	-	-	-	-	-	-	-	-	-	94.5	-9.3
1990	-	-	-	-	-	-	-	-	-	-	100.4	6.2	-	-	-	-	-	-	-	-	-	-	102.4	2.0
1991	-	-	-	-	-	-	-	-	-	-	103.9	1.5	-	-	-	-	-	-	-	-	-	-	103.6	-0.3
1992	-	-	-	-	-	-	-	-	-	-	106.6	2.9	-	-	-	-	-	-	-	-	-	-	106.3	-0.3
1993	-	-	-	-	-	-	-	-	-	-	105.3	-0.9	-	-	-	-	-	-	-	-	-	-	106.8	1.4
1994	-	-	-	-	-	-	-	-	-	-	106.2	-0.6	-	-	-	-	-	-	-	-	-	-	105.4	-0.8
1995	-	-	-	-	-	-	-	-	-	-	102.9	-2.4	-	-	-	-	-	-	-	-	-	-	-	-

Source: U.S. Department of Labor, Bureau of Labor Statistics, Division of Consumer Prices and Price Indexes. - indicates no data collected for period.

Atlanta, GA
Consumer Price Index - Urban Wage Earners
Base 1982-1984 = 100
Apparel and Upkeep

For 1952-1995. Columns headed % show percentile change in the index from the previous period for which an index is available.

Year	Jan Index	%	Feb Index	%	Mar Index	%	Apr Index	%	May Index	%	Jun Index	%	Jul Index	%	Aug Index	%	Sep Index	%	Oct Index	%	Nov Index	%	Dec Index	%
1952	-	-	-	-	-	-	-	-	-	-	-	-	-	-	-	-	-	-	-	-	39.9		-	-
1953	-	-	-	-	40.0	0.3	-	-	-	-	39.9	-0.2	-	-	-	-	40.2	0.8	-	-	-	-	40.0	-0.5
1954	-	-	-	-	40.3	0.7	-	-	-	-	40.3	0.0	-	-	-	-	40.0	-0.7	-	-	-	-	39.9	-0.2
1955	-	-	-	-	39.3	-1.5	-	-	-	-	39.9	1.5	-	-	-	-	40.3	1.0	-	-	-	-	40.2	-0.2
1956	-	-	-	-	40.4	0.5	-	-	-	-	40.5	0.2	-	-	-	-	41.1	1.5	-	-	-	-	41.0	-0.2
1957	-	-	-	-	41.4	1.0	-	-	-	-	41.3	-0.2	-	-	-	-	41.8	1.2	-	-	-	-	41.8	0.0
1958	-	-	-	-	42.0	0.5	-	-	-	-	41.8	-0.5	-	-	-	-	42.0	0.5	-	-	-	-	42.0	0.0
1959	-	-	-	-	41.7	-0.7	-	-	-	-	41.7	0.0	-	-	-	-	42.1	1.0	-	-	-	-	42.4	0.7
1960	-	-	-	-	42.3	-0.2	-	-	-	-	42.4	0.2	-	-	-	-	43.1	1.7	-	-	-	-	43.0	-0.2
1961	-	-	-	-	42.8	-0.5	-	-	-	-	42.8	0.0	-	-	-	-	42.6	-0.5	-	-	-	-	42.5	-0.2
1962	-	-	-	-	42.6	0.2	-	-	-	-	42.5	-0.2	-	-	-	-	42.8	0.7	-	-	-	-	43.1	0.7
1963	-	-	-	-	43.5	0.9	-	-	-	-	43.6	0.2	-	-	-	-	44.1	1.1	-	-	-	-	43.8	-0.7
1964	-	-	-	-	43.8	0.0	-	-	-	-	43.6	-0.5	-	-	-	-	43.8	0.5	-	-	-	-	43.9	0.2
1965	-	-	-	-	44.0	0.2	-	-	-	-	44.0	0.0	-	-	-	-	44.5	1.1	-	-	-	-	44.6	0.2
1966	-	-	-	-	45.3	1.6	-	-	-	-	45.9	1.3	-	-	-	-	47.4	3.3	-	-	-	-	48.1	1.5
1967	-	-	-	-	48.7	1.2	-	-	-	-	48.8	0.2	-	-	-	-	49.3	1.0	-	-	-	-	49.6	0.6
1968	-	-	-	-	50.5	1.8	-	-	-	-	50.6	0.2	-	-	-	-	51.5	1.8	-	-	-	-	52.1	1.2
1969	-	-	-	-	52.1	0.0	-	-	-	-	52.9	1.5	-	-	-	-	53.8	1.7	-	-	-	-	54.1	0.6
1970	-	-	-	-	54.8	1.3	-	-	-	-	54.9	0.2	-	-	-	-	56.0	2.0	-	-	-	-	56.3	0.5
1971	-	-	-	-	57.0	1.2	-	-	-	-	56.2	-1.4	-	-	-	-	57.0	1.4	-	-	-	-	57.1	0.2
1972	-	-	-	-	57.3	0.4	-	-	-	-	57.2	-0.2	-	-	-	-	59.3	3.7	-	-	-	-	59.3	0.0
1973	-	-	-	-	59.7	0.7	-	-	-	-	59.4	-0.5	-	-	-	-	61.6	3.7	-	-	-	-	62.0	0.6
1974	-	-	-	-	63.8	2.9	-	-	-	-	65.5	2.7	-	-	-	-	67.4	2.9	-	-	-	-	66.7	-1.0
1975	-	-	-	-	67.9	1.8	-	-	-	-	66.8	-1.6	-	-	-	-	68.9	3.1	-	-	-	-	68.6	-0.4
1976	-	-	-	-	69.3	1.0	-	-	-	-	69.0	-0.4	-	-	-	-	72.4	4.9	-	-	-	-	72.5	0.1
1977	-	-	-	-	74.6	2.9	-	-	-	-	72.9	-2.3	-	-	-	-	77.9	6.9	-	-	-	-	77.7	-0.3
1978	-	-	77.3	-0.5	-	-	77.5	0.3	-	-	77.5	0.0	-	-	78.1	0.8	-	-	79.7	2.0	-	-	79.7	0.0
1979	-	-	79.3	-0.5	-	-	82.5	4.0	-	-	84.1	1.9	-	-	86.7	3.1	-	-	87.1	0.5	-	-	88.6	1.7
1980	-	-	86.5	-2.4	-	-	86.5	0.0	-	-	87.9	1.6	-	-	92.3	5.0	-	-	92.9	0.7	-	-	95.1	2.4
1981	-	-	93.4	-1.8	-	-	94.6	1.3	-	-	94.7	0.1	-	-	95.9	1.3	-	-	99.5	3.8	-	-	97.7	-1.8
1982	-	-	96.8	-0.9	-	-	95.5	-1.3	-	-	95.2	-0.3	-	-	98.4	3.4	-	-	102.6	4.3	-	-	99.8	-2.7
1983	-	-	97.5	-2.3	-	-	94.4	-3.2	-	-	98.5	4.3	-	-	105.3	6.9	-	-	104.4	-0.9	-	-	100.1	-4.1
1984	-	-	97.6	-2.5	-	-	100.6	3.1	-	-	101.2	0.6	-	-	101.4	0.2	-	-	108.6	7.1	-	-	104.1	-4.1
1985	-	-	110.8	6.4	-	-	106.0	-4.3	-	-	108.2	2.1	-	-	111.9	3.4	-	-	113.1	1.1	-	-	107.5	-5.0
1986	-	-	106.1	-1.3	-	-	108.9	2.6	-	-	105.6	-3.0	-	-	105.5	-0.1	-	-	112.7	6.8	-	-	111.2	-1.3
1987	-	-	-	-	-	-	-	-	-	-	102.0	-8.3	-	-	-	-	-	-	-	-	-	-	106.9	4.8
1988	-	-	-	-	-	-	-	-	-	-	105.4	-1.4	-	-	-	-	-	-	-	-	-	-	106.6	1.1
1989	-	-	-	-	-	-	-	-	-	-	99.1	-7.0	-	-	-	-	-	-	-	-	-	-	90.0	-9.2
1990	-	-	-	-	-	-	-	-	-	-	96.7	7.4	-	-	-	-	-	-	-	-	-	-	98.6	2.0
1991	-	-	-	-	-	-	-	-	-	-	99.1	0.5	-	-	-	-	-	-	-	-	-	-	98.9	-0.2
1992	-	-	-	-	-	-	-	-	-	-	103.3	4.4	-	-	-	-	-	-	-	-	-	-	103.4	0.1
1993	-	-	-	-	-	-	-	-	-	-	103.8	0.4	-	-	-	-	-	-	-	-	-	-	105.6	1.7
1994	-	-	-	-	-	-	-	-	-	-	102.4	-3.0	-	-	-	-	-	-	-	-	-	-	101.3	-1.1
1995	-	-	-	-	-	-	-	-	-	-	99.0	-2.3	-	-	-	-	-	-	-	-	-	-	-	-

Source: U.S. Department of Labor, Bureau of Labor Statistics, Division of Consumer Prices and Price Indexes. - indicates no data collected for period.

Atlanta, GA
Consumer Price Index - All Urban Consumers
Base 1982-1984 = 100
Transportation

For 1947-1995. Columns headed % show percentile change in the index from the previous period for which an index is available.

Year	Jan Index	%	Feb Index	%	Mar Index	%	Apr Index	%	May Index	%	Jun Index	%	Jul Index	%	Aug Index	%	Sep Index	%	Oct Index	%	Nov Index	%	Dec Index	%
1947	-		-		20.0	-	-	-	-	-	20.2	1.0	-	-	20.4	1.0	-	-	-	-	21.0	2.9	-	-
1948	-		21.5	2.4	-	-	-	-	22.0	2.3	-	-	-	-	23.1	5.0	-	-	-	-	23.1	0.0	-	-
1949	-		23.5	1.7	-	-	-	-	24.1	2.6	-	-	-	-	24.4	1.2	-	-	-.	-	24.4	0.0	-	-
1950	-		24.4	0.0	-	-	-	-	24.4	0.0	-	-	-	-	24.8	1.6	-	-	-	-	25.0	0.8	-	-
1951	-		24.9	-0.4	-	-	-	-	26.6	6.8	-	-	-	-	26.6	0.0	-	-	-	-	27.2	2.3	-	-
1952	-		27.7	1.8	-	-	-	-	27.7	0.0	-	-	-	-	28.0	1.1	-	-	-	-	29.2	4.3	-	-
1953	-		-	-	29.1	-0.3	-	-	-	-	28.8	-1.0	-	-	-	-	28.8	0.0	-	-	-	-	28.8	0.0
1954	-		-	-	28.4	-1.4	-	-	-	-	28.4	0.0	-	-	-	-	26.8	-5.6	-	-	-	-	28.0	4.5
1955	-		-	-	27.5	-1.8	-	-	-	-	27.7	0.7	-	-	-	-	27.2	-1.8	-	-	-	-	27.7	1.8
1956	-		-	-	27.7	0.0	-	-	-	-	27.7	0.0	-	-	-	-	28.7	3.6	-	-	-	-	29.1	1.4
1957	-		-	-	30.2	3.8	-	-	-	-	29.8	-1.3	-	-	-	-	29.5	-1.0	-	-	-	-	31.0	5.1
1958	-		-	-	31.2	0.6	-	-	-	-	31.1	-0.3	-	-	-	-	31.2	0.3	-	-	-	-	32.2	3.2
1959	-		-	-	32.3	0.3	-	-	-	-	31.9	-1.2	-	-	-	-	32.5	1.9	-	-	-	-	33.1	1.8
1960	-		-	-	32.2	-2.7	-	-	-	-	32.0	-0.6	-	-	-	-	31.8	-0.6	-	-	-	-	31.4	-1.3
1961	-		-	-	32.1	2.2	-	-	-	-	32.6	1.6	-	-	-	-	32.5	-0.3	-	-	-	-	32.9	1.2
1962	-		-	-	32.4	-1.5	-	-	-	-	33.0	1.9	-	-	-	-	33.4	1.2	-	-	-	-	33.8	1.2
1963	-		-	-	33.5	-0.9	-	-	-	-	33.8	0.9	-	-	-	-	33.4	-1.2	-	-	-	-	34.8	4.2
1964	-		-	-	34.6	-0.6	-	-	-	-	34.5	-0.3	-	-	-	-	34.7	0.6	-	-	-	-	35.0	0.9
1965	-		-	-	35.0	0.0	-	-	-	-	34.0	-2.9	-	-	-	-	34.5	1.5	-	-	-	-	34.8	0.9
1966	-		-	-	34.4	-1.1	-	-	-	-	34.5	0.3	-	-	-	-	34.6	0.3	-	-	-	-	34.7	0.3
1967	-		-	-	34.7	0.0	-	-	-	-	35.2	1.4	-	-	-	-	35.5	0.9	-	-	-	-	35.9	1.1
1968	-		-	-	35.9	0.0	-	-	-	-	36.1	0.6	-	-	-	-	36.0	-0.3	-	-	-	-	36.5	1.4
1969	-		-	-	37.3	2.2	-	-	-	-	37.3	0.0	-	-	-	-	37.1	-0.5	-	-	-	-	37.6	1.3
1970	-		-	-	37.2	-1.1	-	-	-	-	38.1	2.4	-	-	-	-	38.4	0.8	-	-	-	-	40.1	4.4
1971	-		-	-	40.3	0.5	-	-	-	-	41.2	2.2	-	-	-	-	40.4	-1.9	-	-	-	-	40.7	0.7
1972	-		-	-	39.2	-3.7	-	-	-	-	39.5	0.8	-	-	-	-	40.1	1.5	-	-	-	-	40.4	0.7
1973	-		-	-	40.4	0.0	-	-	-	-	41.3	2.2	-	-	-	-	41.1	-0.5	-	-	-	-	42.2	2.7
1974	-		-	-	44.2	4.7	-	-	-	-	47.0	6.3	-	-	-	-	48.5	3.2	-	-	-	-	48.5	0.0
1975	-		-	-	48.6	0.2	-	-	-	-	50.4	3.7	-	-	-	-	51.5	2.2	-	-	-	-	52.2	1.4
1976	-		-	-	52.4	0.4	-	-	-	-	54.4	3.8	-	-	-	-	55.5	2.0	-	-	-	-	56.0	0.9
1977	-		-	-	56.5	0.9	-	-	-	-	57.9	2.5	-	-	-	-	57.5	-0.7	-	-	-	-	58.0	0.9
1978	-		57.9	-0.2	-	-	58.1	0.3	-	-	59.5	2.4	-	-	60.3	1.3	-	-	61.3	1.7	-	-	61.8	0.8
1979	-		63.0	1.9	-	-	66.3	5.2	-	-	69.4	4.7	-	-	72.3	4.2	-	-	73.8	2.1	-	-	75.6	2.4
1980	-		80.4	6.3	-	-	83.4	3.7	-	-	84.0	0.7	-	-	87.3	3.9	-	-	88.2	1.0	-	-	89.3	1.2
1981	-		92.5	3.6	-	-	94.4	2.1	-	-	95.2	0.8	-	-	95.1	-0.1	-	-	97.0	2.0	-	-	97.5	0.5
1982	-		96.4	-1.1	-	-	94.4	-2.1	-	-	98.3	4.1	-	-	99.2	0.9	-	-	98.7	-0.5	-	-	98.6	-0.1
1983	-		96.4	-2.2	-	-	97.9	1.6	-	-	99.5	1.6	-	-	100.6	1.1	-	-	101.3	0.7	-	-	101.8	0.5
1984	-		101.6	-0.2	-	-	102.7	1.1	-	-	103.3	0.6	-	-	103.1	-0.2	-	-	103.9	0.8	-	-	104.0	0.1
1985	-		103.3	-0.7	-	-	106.1	2.7	-	-	106.6	0.5	-	-	107.5	0.8	-	-	108.2	0.7	-	-	109.7	1.4
1986	-		108.4	-1.2	-	-	101.5	-6.4	-	-	103.3	1.8	-	-	100.6	-2.6	-	-	100.1	-0.5	-	-	101.0	0.9
1987	-		-	-	-	-	-	-	-	-	109.7	8.6	-	-	-	-	-	-	-	-	-	-	113.2	3.2
1988	-		-	-	-	-	-	-	-	-	114.6	1.2	-	-	-	-	-	-	-	-	-	-	116.6	1.7
1989	-		-	-	-	-	-	-	-	-	120.2	3.1	-	-	-	-	-	-	-	-	-	-	122.9	2.2
1990	-		-	-	-	-	-	-	-	-	125.4	2.0	-	-	-	-	-	-	-	-	-	-	130.0	3.7
1991	-		-	-	-	-	-	-	-	-	131.0	0.8	-	-	-	-	-	-	-	-	-	-	133.7	2.1

[Continued]

Atlanta, GA
Consumer Price Index - All Urban Consumers
Base 1982-1984 = 100
Transportation

[Continued]

For 1947-1995. Columns headed % show percentile change in the index from the previous period for which an index is available.

Year	Jan		Feb		Mar		Apr		May		Jun		Jul		Aug		Sep		Oct		Nov		Dec	
	Index	%	Index	%	Index	%	Index	%	Index	%	Index	%	Index	%	Index	%	Index	%	Index	%	Index	%	Index	%
1992	-	-	-	-	-	-	-	-	-	-	135.0	1.0	-	-	-	-	-	-	-	-	-	-	137.2	1.6
1993	-	-	-	-	-	-	-	-	-	-	138.5	0.9	-	-	-	-	-	-	-	-	-	-	140.5	1.4
1994	-	-	-	-	-	-	-	-	-	-	142.4	1.4	-	-	-	-	-	-	-	-	-	-	145.6	2.2
1995	-	-	-	-	-	-	-	-	-	-	148.5	2.0	-	-	-	-	-	-	-	-	-	-	-	-

Source: U.S. Department of Labor, Bureau of Labor Statistics, Division of Consumer Prices and Price Indexes. - indicates no data collected for period.

Atlanta, GA
Consumer Price Index - Urban Wage Earners
Base 1982-1984 = 100
Transportation

For 1947-1995. Columns headed % show percentile change in the index from the previous period for which an index is available.

Year	Jan Index	%	Feb Index	%	Mar Index	%	Apr Index	%	May Index	%	Jun Index	%	Jul Index	%	Aug Index	%	Sep Index	%	Oct Index	%	Nov Index	%	Dec Index	%
1947	-	-	-	-	19.5	-	-	-	-	-	19.6	0.5	-	-	19.9	1.5	-	-	-	-	20.4	2.5	-	-
1948	-	-	20.9	2.5	-	-	-	-	21.4	2.4	-	-	-	-	22.5	5.1	-	-	-	-	22.5	0.0	-	-
1949	-	-	22.9	1.8	-	-	-	-	23.5	2.6	-	-	-	-	23.8	1.3	-	-	-	-	23.8	0.0	-	-
1950	-	-	23.8	0.0	-	-	-	-	23.8	0.0	-	-	-	-	24.1	1.3	-	-	-	-	24.3	0.8	-	-
1951	-	-	24.3	0.0	-	-	-	-	25.9	6.6	-	-	-	-	25.9	0.0	-	-	-	-	26.5	2.3	-	-
1952	-	-	27.0	1.9	-	-	-	-	27.0	0.0	-	-	-	-	27.3	1.1	-	-	-	-	28.4	4.0	-	-
1953	-	-	-	-	28.3	-0.4	-	-	-	-	28.0	-1.1	-	-	-	-	28.0	0.0	-	-	-	-	28.0	0.0
1954	-	-	-	-	27.6	-1.4	-	-	-	-	27.6	0.0	-	-	-	-	26.0	-5.8	-	-	-	-	27.3	5.0
1955	-	-	-	-	26.8	-1.8	-	-	-	-	26.9	0.4	-	-	-	-	26.5	-1.5	-	-	-	-	27.0	1.9
1956	-	-	-	-	27.0	0.0	-	-	-	-	27.0	0.0	-	-	-	-	28.0	3.7	-	-	-	-	28.3	1.1
1957	-	-	-	-	29.4	3.9	-	-	-	-	29.0	-1.4	-	-	-	-	28.7	-1.0	-	-	-	-	30.2	5.2
1958	-	-	-	-	30.3	0.3	-	-	-	-	30.2	-0.3	-	-	-	-	30.4	0.7	-	-	-	-	31.3	3.0
1959	-	-	-	-	31.4	0.3	-	-	-	-	31.1	-1.0	-	-	-	-	31.6	1.6	-	-	-	-	32.2	1.9
1960	-	-	-	-	31.4	-2.5	-	-	-	-	31.2	-0.6	-	-	-	-	31.0	-0.6	-	-	-	-	30.6	-1.3
1961	-	-	-	-	31.3	2.3	-	-	-	-	31.7	1.3	-	-	-	-	31.7	0.0	-	-	-	-	32.0	0.9
1962	-	-	-	-	31.6	-1.2	-	-	-	-	32.1	1.6	-	-	-	-	32.5	1.2	-	-	-	-	32.9	1.2
1963	-	-	-	-	32.6	-0.9	-	-	-	-	32.9	0.9	-	-	-	-	32.5	-1.2	-	-	-	-	33.9	4.3
1964	-	-	-	-	33.7	-0.6	-	-	-	-	33.6	-0.3	-	-	-	-	33.8	0.6	-	-	-	-	34.1	0.9
1965	-	-	-	-	34.1	0.0	-	-	-	-	33.1	-2.9	-	-	-	-	33.6	1.5	-	-	-	-	33.9	0.9
1966	-	-	-	-	33.5	-1.2	-	-	-	-	33.6	0.3	-	-	-	-	33.7	0.3	-	-	-	-	33.8	0.3
1967	-	-	-	-	33.8	0.0	-	-	-	-	34.3	1.5	-	-	-	-	34.6	0.9	-	-	-	-	35.0	1.2
1968	-	-	-	-	34.9	-0.3	-	-	-	-	35.2	0.9	-	-	-	-	35.1	-0.3	-	-	-	-	35.5	1.1
1969	-	-	-	-	36.3	2.3	-	-	-	-	36.3	0.0	-	-	-	-	36.1	-0.6	-	-	-	-	36.6	1.4
1970	-	-	-	-	36.2	-1.1	-	-	-	-	37.1	2.5	-	-	-	-	37.4	0.8	-	-	-	-	39.0	4.3
1971	-	-	-	-	39.2	0.5	-	-	-	-	40.1	2.3	-	-	-	-	39.4	-1.7	-	-	-	-	39.7	0.8
1972	-	-	-	-	38.2	-3.8	-	-	-	-	38.5	0.8	-	-	-	-	39.0	1.3	-	-	-	-	39.3	0.8
1973	-	-	-	-	39.3	0.0	-	-	-	-	40.2	2.3	-	-	-	-	40.0	-0.5	-	-	-	-	41.1	2.8
1974	-	-	-	-	43.1	4.9	-	-	-	-	45.7	6.0	-	-	-	-	47.2	3.3	-	-	-	-	47.2	0.0
1975	-	-	-	-	47.3	0.2	-	-	-	-	49.1	3.8	-	-	-	-	50.1	2.0	-	-	-	-	50.8	1.4
1976	-	-	-	-	51.0	0.4	-	-	-	-	53.0	3.9	-	-	-	-	54.0	1.9	-	-	-	-	54.5	0.9
1977	-	-	-	-	55.0	0.9	-	-	-	-	56.3	2.4	-	-	-	-	56.0	-0.5	-	-	-	-	56.5	0.9
1978	-	-	56.6	0.2	-	-	56.8	0.4	-	-	58.0	2.1	-	-	58.9	1.6	-	-	59.9	1.7	-	-	60.5	1.0
1979	-	-	61.8	2.1	-	-	65.5	6.0	-	-	68.5	4.6	-	-	71.6	4.5	-	-	74.3	3.8	-	-	76.5	3.0
1980	-	-	81.0	5.9	-	-	84.5	4.3	-	-	84.7	0.2	-	-	89.3	5.4	-	-	89.9	0.7	-	-	90.8	1.0
1981	-	-	94.5	4.1	-	-	95.7	1.3	-	-	96.0	0.3	-	-	95.9	-0.1	-	-	97.5	1.7	-	-	98.5	1.0
1982	-	-	97.5	-1.0	-	-	95.1	-2.5	-	-	99.0	4.1	-	-	99.8	0.8	-	-	99.1	-0.7	-	-	98.9	-0.2
1983	-	-	96.5	-2.4	-	-	98.1	1.7	-	-	99.7	1.6	-	-	100.6	0.9	-	-	101.1	0.5	-	-	101.4	0.3
1984	-	-	101.2	-0.2	-	-	102.2	1.0	-	-	102.6	0.4	-	-	102.3	-0.3	-	-	103.0	0.7	-	-	103.1	0.1
1985	-	-	102.3	-0.8	-	-	105.2	2.8	-	-	105.9	0.7	-	-	107.1	1.1	-	-	107.7	0.6	-	-	109.4	1.6
1986	-	-	108.1	-1.2	-	-	100.6	-6.9	-	-	102.5	1.9	-	-	99.6	-2.8	-	-	98.7	-0.9	-	-	99.6	0.9
1987	-	-	-	-	-	-	-	-	-	-	108.8	9.2	-	-	-	-	-	-	-	-	-	-	112.7	3.6
1988	-	-	-	-	-	-	-	-	-	-	114.1	1.2	-	-	-	-	-	-	-	-	-	-	116.2	1.8
1989	-	-	-	-	-	-	-	-	-	-	120.1	3.4	-	-	-	-	-	-	-	-	-	-	123.2	2.6
1990	-	-	-	-	-	-	-	-	-	-	125.6	1.9	-	-	-	-	-	-	-	-	-	-	131.2	4.5
1991	-	-	-	-	-	-	-	-	-	-	131.3	0.1	-	-	-	-	-	-	-	-	-	-	134.3	2.3

[Continued]

Atlanta, GA
Consumer Price Index - Urban Wage Earners
Base 1982-1984 = 100
Transportation
[Continued]

For 1947-1995. Columns headed % show percentile change in the index from the previous period for which an index is available.

Year	Jan Index	%	Feb Index	%	Mar Index	%	Apr Index	%	May Index	%	Jun Index	%	Jul Index	%	Aug Index	%	Sep Index	%	Oct Index	%	Nov Index	%	Dec Index	%
1992	-	-	-	-	-	-	-	-	-	-	134.7	0.3	-	-	-	-	-	-	-	-	-	-	137.4	2.0
1993	-	-	-	-	-	-	-	-	-	-	138.2	0.6	-	-	-	-	-	-	-	-	-	-	140.3	1.5
1994	-	-	-	-	-	-	-	-	-	-	141.8	1.1	-	-	-	-	-	-	-	-	-	-	146.3	3.2
1995	-	-	-	-	-	-	-	-	-	-	149.3	2.1	-	-	-	-	-	-	-	-	-	-	-	-

Source: U.S. Department of Labor, Bureau of Labor Statistics, Division of Consumer Prices and Price Indexes. - indicates no data collected for period.

Atlanta, GA
Consumer Price Index - All Urban Consumers
Base 1982-1984 = 100
Medical Care

For 1947-1995. Columns headed % show percentile change in the index from the previous period for which an index is available.

Year	Jan Index	%	Feb Index	%	Mar Index	%	Apr Index	%	May Index	%	Jun Index	%	Jul Index	%	Aug Index	%	Sep Index	%	Oct Index	%	Nov Index	%	Dec Index	%
1947	-	-	-	-	15.1	-	-	-	-	-	15.1	0.0	-	-	15.3	1.3	-	-	-	-	15.3	0.0	-	-
1948	-	-	15.5	1.3	-	-	-	-	15.6	0.6	-	-	-	-	15.8	1.3	-	-	-	-	16.0	1.3	-	-
1949	-	-	16.1	0.6	-	-	-	-	16.1	0.0	-	-	-	-	16.1	0.0	-	-	-	-	16.1	0.0	-	-
1950	-	-	16.1	0.0	-	-	-	-	16.1	0.0	-	-	-	-	16.1	0.0	-	-	-	-	16.3	1.2	-	-
1951	-	-	16.6	1.8	-	-	-	-	17.0	2.4	-	-	-	-	17.0	0.0	-	-	-	-	17.1	0.6	-	-
1952	-	-	17.5	2.3	-	-	-	-	18.2	4.0	-	-	-	-	18.2	0.0	-	-	-	-	18.5	1.6	-	-
1953	-	-	-	-	18.5	0.0	-	-	-	-	18.6	0.5	-	-	-	-	18.4	-1.1	-	-	-	-	18.7	1.6
1954	-	-	-	-	18.9	1.1	-	-	-	-	18.9	0.0	-	-	-	-	19.0	0.5	-	-	-	-	19.0	0.0
1955	-	-	-	-	19.2	1.1	-	-	-	-	19.2	0.0	-	-	-	-	20.0	4.2	-	-	-	-	20.1	0.5
1956	-	-	-	-	20.1	0.0	-	-	-	-	20.3	1.0	-	-	-	-	20.2	-0.5	-	-	-	-	20.3	0.5
1957	-	-	-	-	20.7	2.0	-	-	-	-	20.7	0.0	-	-	-	-	20.8	0.5	-	-	-	-	20.9	0.5
1958	-	-	-	-	21.3	1.9	-	-	-	-	21.4	0.5	-	-	-	-	21.4	0.0	-	-	-	-	21.6	0.9
1959	-	-	-	-	21.6	0.0	-	-	-	-	22.6	4.6	-	-	-	-	22.6	0.0	-	-	-	-	22.8	0.9
1960	-	-	-	-	23.0	0.9	-	-	-	-	23.0	0.0	-	-	-	-	23.0	0.0	-	-	-	-	22.8	-0.9
1961	-	-	-	-	22.8	0.0	-	-	-	-	23.0	0.9	-	-	-	-	23.4	1.7	-	-	-	-	23.6	0.9
1962	-	-	-	-	23.8	0.8	-	-	-	-	23.9	0.4	-	-	-	-	23.9	0.0	-	-	-	-	23.9	0.0
1963	-	-	-	-	23.9	0.0	-	-	-	-	24.4	2.1	-	-	-	-	24.4	0.0	-	-	-	-	24.4	0.0
1964	-	-	-	-	24.6	0.8	-	-	-	-	24.7	0.4	-	-	-	-	25.0	1.2	-	-	-	-	25.1	0.4
1965	-	-	-	-	25.3	0.8	-	-	-	-	25.3	0.0	-	-	-	-	25.5	0.8	-	-	-	-	25.6	0.4
1966	-	-	-	-	26.1	2.0	-	-	-	-	26.6	1.9	-	-	-	-	27.3	2.6	-	-	-	-	27.4	0.4
1967	-	-	-	-	28.1	2.6	-	-	-	-	28.3	0.7	-	-	-	-	28.8	1.8	-	-	-	-	28.9	0.3
1968	-	-	-	-	29.7	2.8	-	-	-	-	30.0	1.0	-	-	-	-	30.8	2.7	-	-	-	-	31.4	1.9
1969	-	-	-	-	32.7	4.1	-	-	-	-	33.3	1.8	-	-	-	-	34.0	2.1	-	-	-	-	34.2	0.6
1970	-	-	-	-	35.1	2.6	-	-	-	-	35.9	2.3	-	-	-	-	36.2	0.8	-	-	-	-	36.9	1.9
1971	-	-	-	-	38.3	3.8	-	-	-	-	38.8	1.3	-	-	-	-	39.1	0.8	-	-	-	-	38.9	-0.5
1972	-	-	-	-	39.2	0.8	-	-	-	-	39.8	1.5	-	-	-	-	39.8	0.0	-	-	-	-	40.1	0.8
1973	-	-	-	-	40.4	0.7	-	-	-	-	41.5	2.7	-	-	-	-	42.3	1.9	-	-	-	-	42.9	1.4
1974	-	-	-	-	43.9	2.3	-	-	-	-	46.4	5.7	-	-	-	-	47.6	2.6	-	-	-	-	48.3	1.5
1975	-	-	-	-	51.3	6.2	-	-	-	-	51.8	1.0	-	-	-	-	53.5	3.3	-	-	-	-	53.7	0.4
1976	-	-	-	-	55.0	2.4	-	-	-	-	55.3	0.5	-	-	-	-	57.0	3.1	-	-	-	-	58.0	1.8
1977	-	-	-	-	59.9	3.3	-	-	-	-	60.9	1.7	-	-	-	-	61.7	1.3	-	-	-	-	61.7	0.0
1978	-	-	62.9	1.9	-	-	63.3	0.6	-	-	63.8	0.8	-	-	64.3	0.8	-	-	64.7	0.6	-	-	64.6	-0.2
1979	-	-	65.9	2.0	-	-	67.2	2.0	-	-	68.0	1.2	-	-	68.8	1.2	-	-	69.4	0.9	-	-	70.5	1.6
1980	-	-	71.5	1.4	-	-	72.1	0.8	-	-	75.0	4.0	-	-	76.4	1.9	-	-	77.0	0.8	-	-	78.3	1.7
1981	-	-	80.6	2.9	-	-	80.9	0.4	-	-	81.6	0.9	-	-	82.9	1.6	-	-	84.9	2.4	-	-	84.5	-0.5
1982	-	-	85.2	0.8	-	-	87.0	2.1	-	-	92.7	6.6	-	-	95.7	3.2	-	-	99.2	3.7	-	-	100.0	0.8
1983	-	-	100.9	0.9	-	-	101.1	0.2	-	-	101.2	0.1	-	-	101.1	-0.1	-	-	101.5	0.4	-	-	101.8	0.3
1984	-	-	103.5	1.7	-	-	104.6	1.1	-	-	106.0	1.3	-	-	107.3	1.2	-	-	108.8	1.4	-	-	109.0	0.2
1985	-	-	110.9	1.7	-	-	111.6	0.6	-	-	113.1	1.3	-	-	113.5	0.4	-	-	115.0	1.3	-	-	114.7	-0.3
1986	-	-	120.4	5.0	-	-	120.9	0.4	-	-	123.2	1.9	-	-	125.3	1.7	-	-	127.2	1.5	-	-	128.6	1.1
1987	-	-	-	-	-	-	-	-	-	-	131.0	1.9	-	-	-	-	-	-	-	-	-	-	135.1	3.1
1988	-	-	-	-	-	-	-	-	-	-	139.3	3.1	-	-	-	-	-	-	-	-	-	-	145.0	4.1
1989	-	-	-	-	-	-	-	-	-	-	150.3	3.7	-	-	-	-	-	-	-	-	-	-	160.3	6.7
1990	-	-	-	-	-	-	-	-	-	-	163.0	1.7	-	-	-	-	-	-	-	-	-	-	171.8	5.4
1991	-	-	-	-	-	-	-	-	-	-	179.5	4.5	-	-	-	-	-	-	-	-	-	-	187.4	4.4

[Continued]

Atlanta, GA
Consumer Price Index - All Urban Consumers
Base 1982-1984 = 100
Medical Care

[Continued]

For 1947-1995. Columns headed % show percentile change in the index from the previous period for which an index is available.

Year	Jan Index	%	Feb Index	%	Mar Index	%	Apr Index	%	May Index	%	Jun Index	%	Jul Index	%	Aug Index	%	Sep Index	%	Oct Index	%	Nov Index	%	Dec Index	%
1992	-	-	-	-	-	-	-	-	-	-	192.3	2.6	-	-	-	-	-	-	-	-	-	-	200.9	4.5
1993	-	-	-	-	-	-	-	-	-	-	206.9	3.0	-	-	-	-	-	-	-	-	-	-	216.2	4.5
1994	-	-	-	-	-	-	-	-	-	-	221.6	2.5	-	-	-	-	-	-	-	-	-	-	226.2	2.1
1995	-	-	-	-	-	-	-	-	-	-	229.6	1.5	-	-	-	-	-	-	-	-	-	-	-	-

Source: U.S. Department of Labor, Bureau of Labor Statistics, Division of Consumer Prices and Price Indexes. - indicates no data collected for period.

Atlanta, GA
Consumer Price Index - Urban Wage Earners
Base 1982-1984 = 100
Medical Care

For 1947-1995. Columns headed % show percentile change in the index from the previous period for which an index is available.

Year	Jan Index	%	Feb Index	%	Mar Index	%	Apr Index	%	May Index	%	Jun Index	%	Jul Index	%	Aug Index	%	Sep Index	%	Oct Index	%	Nov Index	%	Dec Index	%
1947	-	-	-	-	14.6	-	-	-	-	-	14.6	0.0	-	-	14.7	0.7	-	-	-	-	14.7	0.0	-	-
1948	-	-	14.9	1.4	-	-	-	-	15.0	0.7	-	-	-	-	15.2	1.3	-	-	-	-	15.4	1.3	-	-
1949	-	-	15.5	0.6	-	-	-	-	15.5	0.0	-	-	-	-	15.5	0.0	-	-	-	-	15.5	0.0	-	-
1950	-	-	15.5	0.0	-	-	-	-	15.5	0.0	-	-	-	-	15.5	0.0	-	-	-	-	15.6	0.6	-	-
1951	-	-	16.0	2.6	-	-	-	-	16.4	2.5	-	-	-	-	16.3	-0.6	-	-	-	-	16.4	0.6	-	-
1952	-	-	16.8	2.4	-	-	-	-	17.6	4.8	-	-	-	-	17.5	-0.6	-	-	-	-	17.8	1.7	-	-
1953	-	-	-	-	17.8	0.0	-	-	-	-	17.9	0.6	-	-	-	-	17.7	-1.1	-	-	-	-	18.0	1.7
1954	-	-	-	-	18.2	1.1	-	-	-	-	18.2	0.0	-	-	-	-	18.2	0.0	-	-	-	-	18.3	0.5
1955	-	-	-	-	18.5	1.1	-	-	-	-	18.5	0.0	-	-	-	-	19.2	3.8	-	-	-	-	19.4	1.0
1956	-	-	-	-	19.4	0.0	-	-	-	-	19.6	1.0	-	-	-	-	19.5	-0.5	-	-	-	-	19.6	0.5
1957	-	-	-	-	19.9	1.5	-	-	-	-	19.9	0.0	-	-	-	-	20.0	0.5	-	-	-	-	20.1	0.5
1958	-	-	-	-	20.5	2.0	-	-	-	-	20.6	0.5	-	-	-	-	20.6	0.0	-	-	-	-	20.8	1.0
1959	-	-	-	-	20.8	0.0	-	-	-	-	21.8	4.8	-	-	-	-	21.8	0.0	-	-	-	-	22.0	0.9
1960	-	-	-	-	22.1	0.5	-	-	-	-	22.1	0.0	-	-	-	-	22.2	0.5	-	-	-	-	21.9	-1.4
1961	-	-	-	-	21.9	0.0	-	-	-	-	22.2	1.4	-	-	-	-	22.6	1.8	-	-	-	-	22.7	0.4
1962	-	-	-	-	22.9	0.9	-	-	-	-	23.0	0.4	-	-	-	-	23.0	0.0	-	-	-	-	23.0	0.0
1963	-	-	-	-	23.0	0.0	-	-	-	-	23.5	2.2	-	-	-	-	23.5	0.0	-	-	-	-	23.5	0.0
1964	-	-	-	-	23.7	0.9	-	-	-	-	23.7	0.0	-	-	-	-	24.1	1.7	-	-	-	-	24.1	0.0
1965	-	-	-	-	24.3	0.8	-	-	-	-	24.4	0.4	-	-	-	-	24.5	0.4	-	-	-	-	24.6	0.4
1966	-	-	-	-	25.2	2.4	-	-	-	-	25.6	1.6	-	-	-	-	26.2	2.3	-	-	-	-	26.3	0.4
1967	-	-	-	-	27.0	2.7	-	-	-	-	27.2	0.7	-	-	-	-	27.7	1.8	-	-	-	-	27.9	0.7
1968	-	-	-	-	28.6	2.5	-	-	-	-	28.8	0.7	-	-	-	-	29.6	2.8	-	-	-	-	30.2	2.0
1969	-	-	-	-	31.5	4.3	-	-	-	-	32.0	1.6	-	-	-	-	32.7	2.2	-	-	-	-	32.9	0.6
1970	-	-	-	-	33.8	2.7	-	-	-	-	34.5	2.1	-	-	-	-	34.8	0.9	-	-	-	-	35.6	2.3
1971	-	-	-	-	36.9	3.7	-	-	-	-	37.3	1.1	-	-	-	-	37.6	0.8	-	-	-	-	37.5	-0.3
1972	-	-	-	-	37.7	0.5	-	-	-	-	38.3	1.6	-	-	-	-	38.3	0.0	-	-	-	-	38.6	0.8
1973	-	-	-	-	38.8	0.5	-	-	-	-	40.0	3.1	-	-	-	-	40.7	1.7	-	-	-	-	41.3	1.5
1974	-	-	-	-	42.2	2.2	-	-	-	-	44.6	5.7	-	-	-	-	45.8	2.7	-	-	-	-	46.5	1.5
1975	-	-	-	-	49.4	6.2	-	-	-	-	49.8	0.8	-	-	-	-	51.5	3.4	-	-	-	-	51.7	0.4
1976	-	-	-	-	52.9	2.3	-	-	-	-	53.2	0.6	-	-	-	-	54.8	3.0	-	-	-	-	55.8	1.8
1977	-	-	-	-	57.7	3.4	-	-	-	-	58.6	1.6	-	-	-	-	59.3	1.2	-	-	-	-	59.3	0.0
1978	-	-	60.4	1.9	-	-	61.8	2.3	-	-	62.3	0.8	-	-	63.1	1.3	-	-	63.6	0.8	-	-	64.4	1.3
1979	-	-	66.0	2.5	-	-	67.1	1.7	-	-	68.2	1.6	-	-	69.3	1.6	-	-	69.6	0.4	-	-	70.0	0.6
1980	-	-	70.7	1.0	-	-	70.8	0.1	-	-	72.3	2.1	-	-	74.1	2.5	-	-	75.0	1.2	-	-	76.5	2.0
1981	-	-	80.6	5.4	-	-	80.8	0.2	-	-	81.0	0.2	-	-	82.2	1.5	-	-	83.9	2.1	-	-	84.1	0.2
1982	-	-	84.8	0.8	-	-	86.6	2.1	-	-	92.7	7.0	-	-	95.5	3.0	-	-	99.2	3.9	-	-	100.0	0.8
1983	-	-	101.0	1.0	-	-	101.2	0.2	-	-	101.2	0.0	-	-	101.3	0.1	-	-	101.7	0.4	-	-	102.0	0.3
1984	-	-	103.6	1.6	-	-	104.7	1.1	-	-	106.0	1.2	-	-	107.3	1.2	-	-	108.7	1.3	-	-	109.0	0.3
1985	-	-	111.0	1.8	-	-	111.6	0.5	-	-	113.2	1.4	-	-	113.7	0.4	-	-	115.1	1.2	-	-	114.6	-0.4
1986	-	-	120.6	5.2	-	-	121.1	0.4	-	-	123.6	2.1	-	-	125.8	1.8	-	-	127.6	1.4	-	-	128.8	0.9
1987	-	-	-	-	-	-	-	-	-	-	130.7	1.5	-	-	-	-	-	-	-	-	-	-	134.6	3.0
1988	-	-	-	-	-	-	-	-	-	-	138.8	3.1	-	-	-	-	-	-	-	-	-	-	144.2	3.9
1989	-	-	-	-	-	-	-	-	-	-	149.4	3.6	-	-	-	-	-	-	-	-	-	-	158.6	6.2
1990	-	-	-	-	-	-	-	-	-	-	161.8	2.0	-	-	-	-	-	-	-	-	-	-	170.0	5.1
1991	-	-	-	-	-	-	-	-	-	-	177.2	4.2	-	-	-	-	-	-	-	-	-	-	184.7	4.2

[Continued]

Atlanta, GA
Consumer Price Index - Urban Wage Earners
Base 1982-1984 = 100
Medical Care

[Continued]

For 1947-1995. Columns headed % show percentile change in the index from the previous period for which an index is available.

Year	Jan Index	%	Feb Index	%	Mar Index	%	Apr Index	%	May Index	%	Jun Index	%	Jul Index	%	Aug Index	%	Sep Index	%	Oct Index	%	Nov Index	%	Dec Index	%
1992	-	-	-	-	-	-	-	-	-	-	189.5	2.6	-	-	-	-	-	-	-	-	-	-	198.3	4.6
1993	-	-	-	-	-	-	-	-	-	-	204.3	3.0	-	-	-	-	-	-	-	-	-	-	213.3	4.4
1994	-	-	-	-	-	-	-	-	-	-	218.3	2.3	-	-	-	-	-	-	-	-	-	-	222.7	2.0
1995	-	-	-	-	-	-	-	-	-	-	225.8	1.4	-	-	-	-	-	-	-	-	-	-	-	-

Source: U.S. Department of Labor, Bureau of Labor Statistics, Division of Consumer Prices and Price Indexes. - indicates no data collected for period.

Atlanta, GA
Consumer Price Index - All Urban Consumers
Base 1982-1984 = 100
Entertainment

For 1975-1995. Columns headed % show percentile change in the index from the previous period for which an index is available.

Year	Jan Index	%	Feb Index	%	Mar Index	%	Apr Index	%	May Index	%	Jun Index	%	Jul Index	%	Aug Index	%	Sep Index	%	Oct Index	%	Nov Index	%	Dec Index	%
1975	-	-	-	-	-	-	-	-	-	-	-	-	-	-	-	-	-	-	-	-	-	-	76.6	-
1976	-	-	-	-	76.2	-0.5	-	-	-	-	77.7	2.0	-	-	-	-	77.6	-0.1	-	-	-	-	77.8	0.3
1977	-	-	-	-	78.8	1.3	-	-	-	-	80.7	2.4	-	-	-	-	81.4	0.9	-	-	-	-	81.3	-0.1
1978	-	-	83.2	2.3	-	-	83.7	0.6	-	-	84.4	0.8	-	-	83.9	-0.6	-	-	85.2	1.5	-	-	82.5	-3.2
1979	-	-	84.7	2.7	-	-	87.2	3.0	-	-	86.3	-1.0	-	-	87.3	1.2	-	-	85.7	-1.8	-	-	82.0	-4.3
1980	-	-	85.1	3.8	-	-	85.5	0.5	-	-	86.1	0.7	-	-	94.3	9.5	-	-	92.3	-2.1	-	-	91.0	-1.4
1981	-	-	93.7	3.0	-	-	94.1	0.4	-	-	92.7	-1.5	-	-	94.8	2.3	-	-	97.8	3.2	-	-	95.8	-2.0
1982	-	-	101.0	5.4	-	-	94.3	-6.6	-	-	96.6	2.4	-	-	96.2	-0.4	-	-	101.3	5.3	-	-	98.1	-3.2
1983	-	-	95.4	-2.8	-	-	96.5	1.2	-	-	98.3	1.9	-	-	98.7	0.4	-	-	98.6	-0.1	-	-	101.9	3.3
1984	-	-	102.8	0.9	-	-	103.4	0.6	-	-	103.6	0.2	-	-	104.6	1.0	-	-	106.1	1.4	-	-	105.2	-0.8
1985	-	-	106.1	0.9	-	-	109.1	2.8	-	-	113.5	4.0	-	-	114.7	1.1	-	-	114.4	-0.3	-	-	113.0	-1.2
1986	-	-	116.8	3.4	-	-	117.7	0.8	-	-	120.0	2.0	-	-	119.5	-0.4	-	-	120.0	0.4	-	-	120.1	0.1
1987	-	-	-	-	-	-	-	-	-	-	111.0	-7.6	-	-	-	-	-	-	-	-	-	-	113.3	2.1
1988	-	-	-	-	-	-	-	-	-	-	117.5	3.7	-	-	-	-	-	-	-	-	-	-	124.1	5.6
1989	-	-	-	-	-	-	-	-	-	-	127.7	2.9	-	-	-	-	-	-	-	-	-	-	129.6	1.5
1990	-	-	-	-	-	-	-	-	-	-	132.8	2.5	-	-	-	-	-	-	-	-	-	-	134.1	1.0
1991	-	-	-	-	-	-	-	-	-	-	136.4	1.7	-	-	-	-	-	-	-	-	-	-	139.7	2.4
1992	-	-	-	-	-	-	-	-	-	-	142.9	2.3	-	-	-	-	-	-	-	-	-	-	145.8	2.0
1993	-	-	-	-	-	-	-	-	-	-	144.6	-0.8	-	-	-	-	-	-	-	-	-	-	150.4	4.0
1994	-	-	-	-	-	-	-	-	-	-	159.6	6.1	-	-	-	-	-	-	-	-	-	-	161.0	0.9
1995	-	-	-	-	-	-	-	-	-	-	164.2	2.0	-	-	-	-	-	-	-	-	-	-	-	-

Source: U.S. Department of Labor, Bureau of Labor Statistics, Division of Consumer Prices and Price Indexes. - indicates no data collected for period.

Atlanta, GA
Consumer Price Index - Urban Wage Earners
Base 1982-1984 = 100
Entertainment

For 1975-1995. Columns headed % show percentile change in the index from the previous period for which an index is available.

Year	Jan Index	%	Feb Index	%	Mar Index	%	Apr Index	%	May Index	%	Jun Index	%	Jul Index	%	Aug Index	%	Sep Index	%	Oct Index	%	Nov Index	%	Dec Index	%
1975	-	-	-	-	-	-	-	-	-	-	-	-	-	-	-	-	-	-	-	-	-	-	-	-
1976	-	-	-	-	69.0	-0.4	-	-	-	-	70.3	1.9	-	-	-	-	70.2	-0.1	-	-	-	-	69.3	-
1977	-	-	-	-	71.3	1.3	-	-	-	-	73.0	2.4	-	-	-	-	73.6	0.8	-	-	-	-	70.4	0.3
1978	-	-	74.7	1.5	-	-	74.3	-0.5	-	-	75.0	0.9	-	-	74.9	-0.1	-	-	75.1	0.3	-	-	73.6	0.0
1979	-	-	72.7	-1.1	-	-	75.3	3.6	-	-	75.4	0.1	-	-	76.7	1.7	-	-	76.8	0.1	-	-	73.5	-2.1
1980	-	-	89.6	15.3	-	-	89.8	0.2	-	-	90.9	1.2	-	-	90.0	-1.0	-	-	88.8	-1.3	-	-	77.7	1.2
1981	-	-	99.9	12.9	-	-	99.5	-0.4	-	-	100.5	1.0	-	-	100.5	0.0	-	-	97.8	-2.7	-	-	88.5	-0.3
1982	-	-	102.1	4.8	-	-	96.9	-5.1	-	-	99.0	2.2	-	-	98.3	-0.7	-	-	101.0	2.7	-	-	97.4	-0.4
1983	-	-	89.5	-11.8	-	-	90.8	1.5	-	-	95.1	4.7	-	-	95.6	0.5	-	-	101.5	0.5	-	-	101.5	0.5
1984	-	-	104.9	0.9	-	-	104.9	0.0	-	-	105.0	0.1	-	-	105.7	0.7	-	-	95.1	-0.5	-	-	104.0	9.4
1985	-	-	105.4	0.6	-	-	109.0	3.4	-	-	112.5	3.2	-	-	113.5	0.9	-	-	108.0	2.2	-	-	104.8	-3.0
1986	-	-	116.9	6.7	-	-	117.3	0.3	-	-	120.9	3.1	-	-	118.0	-2.4	-	-	113.4	-0.1	-	-	109.6	-3.4
1987	-	-	-	-	-	-	-	-	-	-	109.2	-8.5	-	-	-	-	-	-	119.3	1.1	-	-	119.3	0.0
1988	-	-	-	-	-	-	-	-	-	-	115.7	3.4	-	-	-	-	-	-	-	-	-	-	111.9	2.5
1989	-	-	-	-	-	-	-	-	-	-	125.2	2.8	-	-	-	-	-	-	-	-	-	-	121.8	5.3
1990	-	-	-	-	-	-	-	-	-	-	129.9	2.3	-	-	-	-	-	-	-	-	-	-	127.0	1.4
1991	-	-	-	-	-	-	-	-	-	-	133.1	1.9	-	-	-	-	-	-	-	-	-	-	130.6	0.5
1992	-	-	-	-	-	-	-	-	-	-	139.0	2.1	-	-	-	-	-	-	-	-	-	-	136.2	2.3
1993	-	-	-	-	-	-	-	-	-	-	140.0	-0.9	-	-	-	-	-	-	-	-	-	-	141.3	1.7
1994	-	-	-	-	-	-	-	-	-	-	155.1	6.9	-	-	-	-	-	-	-	-	-	-	145.1	3.6
1995	-	-	-	-	-	-	-	-	-	-	159.7	2.2	-	-	-	-	-	-	-	-	-	-	156.3	0.8

Source: U.S. Department of Labor, Bureau of Labor Statistics, Division of Consumer Prices and Price Indexes. - indicates no data collected for period.

Atlanta, GA
Consumer Price Index - All Urban Consumers
Base 1982-1984 = 100
Other Goods and Services

For 1975-1995. Columns headed % show percentile change in the index from the previous period for which an index is available.

Year	Jan Index	%	Feb Index	%	Mar Index	%	Apr Index	%	May Index	%	Jun Index	%	Jul Index	%	Aug Index	%	Sep Index	%	Oct Index	%	Nov Index	%	Dec Index	%
1975	-	-	-	-	-	-	-	-	-	-	-	-	-	-	-	-	-	-	-	-	-	-	54.7	-
1976	-	-	-	-	54.8	0.2	-	-	-	-	55.4	1.1	-	-	-	-	55.7	0.5	-	-	-	-	56.5	1.4
1977	-	-	-	-	57.1	1.1	-	-	-	-	58.1	1.8	-	-	-	-	59.5	2.4	-	-	-	-	60.5	1.7
1978	-	-	60.4	-0.2	-	-	61.1	1.2	-	-	61.8	1.1	-	-	63.8	3.2	-	-	65.2	2.2	-	-	65.3	0.2
1979	-	-	67.3	3.1	-	-	67.8	0.7	-	-	67.9	0.1	-	-	69.1	1.8	-	-	71.1	2.9	-	-	72.0	1.3
1980	-	-	73.8	2.5	-	-	74.1	0.4	-	-	75.3	1.6	-	-	75.6	0.4	-	-	77.8	2.9	-	-	79.2	1.8
1981	-	-	81.5	2.9	-	-	83.3	2.2	-	-	83.9	0.7	-	-	84.1	0.2	-	-	86.6	3.0	-	-	87.6	1.2
1982	-	-	87.9	0.3	-	-	90.0	2.4	-	-	91.0	1.1	-	-	91.9	1.0	-	-	95.2	3.6	-	-	96.6	1.5
1983	-	-	98.5	2.0	-	-	98.9	0.4	-	-	98.9	0.0	-	-	100.6	1.7	-	-	103.4	2.8	-	-	104.2	0.8
1984	-	-	106.2	1.9	-	-	106.0	-0.2	-	-	107.7	1.6	-	-	108.3	0.6	-	-	110.2	1.8	-	-	110.3	0.1
1985	-	-	111.7	1.3	-	-	111.3	-0.4	-	-	112.0	0.6	-	-	113.2	1.1	-	-	115.1	1.7	-	-	116.2	1.0
1986	-	-	118.3	1.8	-	-	119.0	0.6	-	-	118.5	-0.4	-	-	120.0	1.3	-	-	121.6	1.3	-	-	122.9	1.1
1987	-	-	-	-	-	-	-	-	-	-	134.0	9.0	-	-	-	-	-	-	-	-	-	-	137.8	2.8
1988	-	-	-	-	-	-	-	-	-	-	142.6	3.5	-	-	-	-	-	-	-	-	-	-	147.5	3.4
1989	-	-	-	-	-	-	-	-	-	-	153.0	3.7	-	-	-	-	-	-	-	-	-	-	157.8	3.1
1990	-	-	-	-	-	-	-	-	-	-	165.2	4.7	-	-	-	-	-	-	-	-	-	-	178.7	8.2
1991	-	-	-	-	-	-	-	-	-	-	182.9	2.4	-	-	-	-	-	-	-	-	-	-	188.1	2.8
1992	-	-	-	-	-	-	-	-	-	-	192.6	2.4	-	-	-	-	-	-	-	-	-	-	199.1	3.4
1993	-	-	-	-	-	-	-	-	-	-	205.9	3.4	-	-	-	-	-	-	-	-	-	-	215.5	4.7
1994	-	-	-	-	-	-	-	-	-	-	220.3	2.2	-	-	-	-	-	-	-	-	-	-	224.2	1.8
1995	-	-	-	-	-	-	-	-	-	-	225.5	0.6	-	-	-	-	-	-	-	-	-	-	-	-

Source: U.S. Department of Labor, Bureau of Labor Statistics, Division of Consumer Prices and Price Indexes. - indicates no data collected for period.

Atlanta, GA
Consumer Price Index - Urban Wage Earners
Base 1982-1984 = 100
Other Goods and Services

For 1975-1995. Columns headed % show percentile change in the index from the previous period for which an index is available.

Year	Jan Index	%	Feb Index	%	Mar Index	%	Apr Index	%	May Index	%	Jun Index	%	Jul Index	%	Aug Index	%	Sep Index	%	Oct Index	%	Nov Index	%	Dec Index	%
1975	-	-	-	-	-	-	-	-	-	-	-	-	-	-	-	-	-	-	-	-	-	-	57.3	-
1976	-	-	-	-	57.4	0.2	-	-	-	-	58.1	1.2	-	-	-	-	58.4	0.5	-	-	-	-	59.2	1.4
1977	-	-	-	-	59.8	1.0	-	-	-	-	60.9	1.8	-	-	-	-	62.4	2.5	-	-	-	-	63.3	1.4
1978	-	-	64.0	1.1	-	-	64.4	0.6	-	-	65.2	1.2	-	-	65.3	0.2	-	-	66.7	2.1	-	-	66.4	-0.4
1979	-	-	68.5	3.2	-	-	68.9	0.6	-	-	69.9	1.5	-	-	70.5	0.9	-	-	72.2	2.4	-	-	72.6	0.6
1980	-	-	74.1	2.1	-	-	74.4	0.4	-	-	75.1	0.9	-	-	75.5	0.5	-	-	77.7	2.9	-	-	79.0	1.7
1981	-	-	81.1	2.7	-	-	81.6	0.6	-	-	83.4	2.2	-	-	84.2	1.0	-	-	86.1	2.3	-	-	87.1	1.2
1982	-	-	87.4	0.3	-	-	89.6	2.5	-	-	90.9	1.5	-	-	91.7	0.9	-	-	94.9	3.5	-	-	96.5	1.7
1983	-	-	98.7	2.3	-	-	99.2	0.5	-	-	99.3	0.1	-	-	101.1	1.8	-	-	103.5	2.4	-	-	104.3	0.8
1984	-	-	106.7	2.3	-	-	106.3	-0.4	-	-	107.9	1.5	-	-	108.5	0.6	-	-	109.7	1.1	-	-	109.8	0.1
1985	-	-	111.4	1.5	-	-	111.3	-0.1	-	-	111.9	0.5	-	-	113.3	1.3	-	-	114.6	1.1	-	-	115.9	1.1
1986	-	-	118.5	2.2	-	-	119.5	0.8	-	-	118.6	-0.8	-	-	119.8	1.0	-	-	121.2	1.2	-	-	122.5	1.1
1987	-	-	-	-	-	-	-	-	-	-	132.8	8.4	-	-	-	-	-	-	-	-	-	-	136.6	2.9
1988	-	-	-	-	-	-	-	-	-	-	141.8	3.8	-	-	-	-	-	-	-	-	-	-	146.9	3.6
1989	-	-	-	-	-	-	-	-	-	-	151.6	3.2	-	-	-	-	-	-	-	-	-	-	156.1	3.0
1990	-	-	-	-	-	-	-	-	-	-	163.5	4.7	-	-	-	-	-	-	-	-	-	-	177.9	8.8
1991	-	-	-	-	-	-	-	-	-	-	182.2	2.4	-	-	-	-	-	-	-	-	-	-	186.5	2.4
1992	-	-	-	-	-	-	-	-	-	-	191.0	2.4	-	-	-	-	-	-	-	-	-	-	197.5	3.4
1993	-	-	-	-	-	-	-	-	-	-	204.6	3.6	-	-	-	-	-	-	-	-	-	-	212.4	3.8
1994	-	-	-	-	-	-	-	-	-	-	216.6	2.0	-	-	-	-	-	-	-	-	-	-	219.8	1.5
1995	-	-	-	-	-	-	-	-	-	-	221.0	0.5	-	-	-	-	-	-	-	-	-	-	-	-

Source: U.S. Department of Labor, Bureau of Labor Statistics, Division of Consumer Prices and Price Indexes. - indicates no data collected for period.

Baltimore, MD
Consumer Price Index - All Urban Consumers
Base 1982-1984 = 100
Annual Averages

For 1914-1995. Columns headed % show percentile change in the index from the previous period for which an index is available.

Year	All Items		Food & Beverage		Housing		Apparel & Upkeep		Trans-portation		Medical Care		Entertain-ment		Other Goods & Services	
	Index	%	Index	%	Index	%	Index	%	Index	%	Index	%	Index	%	Index	%
1914	-	-	-	-	-	-	-	-	-	-	-	-	-	-	-	-
1915	8.9	-	-	-	-	-	-	-	-	-	-	-	-	-	-	-
1916	9.7	9.0	-	-	-	-	-	-	-	-	-	-	-	-	-	-
1917	11.9	22.7	-	-	-	-	-	-	-	-	-	-	-	-	-	-
1918	14.3	20.2	-	-	-	-	-	-	-	-	-	-	-	-	-	-
1919	16.3	14.0	-	-	-	-	-	-	-	-	-	-	-	-	-	-
1920	18.3	12.3	-	-	-	-	-	-	-	-	-	-	-	-	-	-
1921	16.2	-11.5	-	-	-	-	-	-	-	-	-	-	-	-	-	-
1922	15.4	-4.9	-	-	-	-	-	-	-	-	-	-	-	-	-	-
1923	15.7	1.9	-	-	-	-	-	-	-	-	-	-	-	-	-	-
1924	15.7	0.0	-	-	-	-	-	-	-	-	-	-	-	-	-	-
1925	16.2	3.2	-	-	-	-	-	-	-	-	-	-	-	-	-	-
1926	16.4	1.2	-	-	-	-	-	-	-	-	-	-	-	-	-	-
1927	16.0	-2.4	-	-	-	-	-	-	-	-	-	-	-	-	-	-
1928	15.9	-0.6	-	-	-	-	-	-	-	-	-	-	-	-	-	-
1929	15.9	0.0	-	-	-	-	-	-	-	-	-	-	-	-	-	-
1930	15.6	-1.9	-	-	-	-	-	-	-	-	-	-	-	-	-	-
1931	14.4	-7.7	-	-	-	-	-	-	-	-	-	-	-	-	-	-
1932	13.1	-9.0	-	-	-	-	-	-	-	-	-	-	-	-	-	-
1933	12.5	-4.6	-	-	-	-	-	-	-	-	-	-	-	-	-	-
1934	13.0	4.0	-	-	-	-	-	-	-	-	-	-	-	-	-	-
1935	13.3	2.3	-	-	-	-	-	-	-	-	-	-	-	-	-	-
1936	13.4	0.8	-	-	-	-	-	-	-	-	-	-	-	-	-	-
1937	13.8	3.0	-	-	-	-	-	-	-	-	-	-	-	-	-	-
1938	13.5	-2.2	-	-	-	-	-	-	-	-	-	-	-	-	-	-
1939	13.4	-0.7	-	-	-	-	-	-	-	-	-	-	-	-	-	-
1940	13.5	0.7	-	-	-	-	-	-	-	-	-	-	-	-	-	-
1941	14.3	5.9	-	-	-	-	-	-	-	-	-	-	-	-	-	-
1942	16.0	11.9	-	-	-	-	-	-	-	-	-	-	-	-	-	-
1943	17.0	6.3	-	-	-	-	-	-	-	-	-	-	-	-	-	-
1944	17.3	1.8	-	-	-	-	-	-	-	-	-	-	-	-	-	-
1945	17.8	2.9	-	-	-	-	-	-	-	-	-	-	-	-	-	-
1946	19.2	7.9	-	-	-	-	-	-	-	-	-	-	-	-	-	-
1947	22.1	15.1	-	-	-	-	-	-	17.3	-	12.8	-	-	-	-	-
1948	23.8	7.7	-	-	-	-	-	-	18.8	8.7	13.3	3.9	-	-	-	-
1949	23.7	-0.4	-	-	-	-	-	-	21.8	16.0	13.4	0.8	-	-	-	-
1950	23.9	0.8	-	-	-	-	-	-	22.7	4.1	13.6	1.5	-	-	-	-
1951	25.6	7.1	-	-	-	-	-	-	24.2	6.6	14.8	8.8	-	-	-	-
1952	26.3	2.7	-	-	-	-	-	-	25.6	5.8	16.4	10.8	-	-	-	-
1953	26.6	1.1	-	-	-	-	38.1	-	26.9	5.1	17.4	6.1	-	-	-	-
1954	26.7	0.4	-	-	-	-	38.0	-0.3	26.6	-1.1	17.6	1.1	-	-	-	-
1955	26.7	0.0	-	-	-	-	37.9	-0.3	26.4	-0.8	17.8	1.1	-	-	-	-
1956	27.1	1.5	-	-	-	-	39.3	3.7	26.9	1.9	18.6	4.5	-	-	-	-
1957	28.1	3.7	-	-	-	-	40.1	2.0	28.5	5.9	19.1	2.7	-	-	-	-
1958	28.9	2.8	-	-	-	-	40.7	1.5	29.3	2.8	19.7	3.1	-	-	-	-

[Continued]

Baltimore, MD
Consumer Price Index - All Urban Consumers
Base 1982-1984 = 100
Annual Averages
[Continued]

For 1914-1995. Columns headed % show percentile change in the index from the previous period for which an index is available.

Year	All Items		Food & Beverage		Housing		Apparel & Upkeep		Trans-portation		Medical Care		Entertain-ment		Other Goods & Services	
	Index	%	Index	%	Index	%	Index	%	Index	%	Index	%	Index	%	Index	%
1959	29.4	1.7	-	-	-	-	41.6	2.2	31.1	6.1	21.0	6.6	-	-	-	-
1960	29.8	1.4	-	-	-	-	42.2	1.4	30.9	-0.6	22.2	5.7	-	-	-	-
1961	30.1	1.0	-	-	-	-	42.9	1.7	31.4	1.6	23.2	4.5	-	-	-	-
1962	30.3	0.7	-	-	-	-	43.2	0.7	31.4	0.0	23.7	2.2	-	-	-	-
1963	30.8	1.7	-	-	-	-	43.6	0.9	32.0	1.9	25.2	6.3	-	-	-	-
1964	31.1	1.0	-	-	-	-	43.5	-0.2	32.8	2.5	25.8	2.4	-	-	-	-
1965	31.6	1.6	-	-	-	-	44.1	1.4	33.3	1.5	26.4	2.3	-	-	-	-
1966	32.7	3.5	-	-	-	-	45.4	2.9	33.6	0.9	27.5	4.2	-	-	-	-
1967	33.4	2.1	-	-	-	-	47.5	4.6	34.3	2.1	29.8	8.4	-	-	-	-
1968	34.8	4.2	-	-	-	-	49.7	4.6	35.5	3.5	31.5	5.7	-	-	-	-
1969	36.9	6.0	-	-	-	-	53.7	8.0	37.4	5.4	33.6	6.7	-	-	-	-
1970	39.1	6.0	-	-	-	-	56.6	5.4	38.5	2.9	36.7	9.2	-	-	-	-
1971	41.3	5.6	-	-	-	-	58.6	3.5	40.3	4.7	40.5	10.4	-	-	-	-
1972	42.2	2.2	-	-	-	-	58.8	0.3	40.0	-0.7	42.5	4.9	-	-	-	-
1973	45.1	6.9	-	-	-	-	62.0	5.4	41.3	3.2	44.4	4.5	-	-	-	-
1974	51.0	13.1	-	-	-	-	67.1	8.2	46.1	11.6	49.2	10.8	-	-	-	-
1975	55.2	8.2	-	-	-	-	70.1	4.5	50.2	8.9	53.8	9.3	-	-	-	-
1976	58.1	5.3	63.9	-	55.1	-	73.2	4.4	54.5	8.6	57.5	6.9	66.9	-	57.2	-
1977	62.2	7.1	67.9	6.3	59.8	8.5	77.2	5.5	57.7	5.9	61.9	7.7	69.7	4.2	60.3	5.4
1978	66.7	7.2	74.3	9.4	64.9	8.5	80.6	4.4	60.1	4.2	65.7	6.1	72.5	4.0	64.4	6.8
1979	73.0	9.4	81.2	9.3	70.4	8.5	83.2	3.2	68.9	14.6	72.2	9.9	76.6	5.7	69.5	7.9
1980	83.7	14.7	87.9	8.3	82.8	17.6	93.3	12.1	82.3	19.4	79.2	9.7	83.5	9.0	75.8	9.1
1981	91.5	9.3	94.0	6.9	91.2	10.1	96.7	3.6	92.0	11.8	85.0	7.3	90.0	7.8	82.5	8.8
1982	95.6	4.5	96.5	2.7	95.5	4.7	98.2	1.6	96.0	4.3	94.0	10.6	94.4	4.9	89.6	8.6
1983	99.9	4.5	99.5	3.1	99.6	4.3	100.5	2.3	99.8	4.0	100.6	7.0	101.5	7.5	101.2	12.9
1984	104.5	4.6	104.0	4.5	104.8	5.2	101.3	0.8	104.3	4.5	105.4	4.8	104.2	2.7	109.2	7.9
1985	108.2	3.5	107.1	3.0	108.3	3.3	106.3	4.9	107.3	2.9	111.9	6.2	109.3	4.9	114.1	4.5
1986	110.9	2.5	112.0	4.6	111.1	2.6	110.8	4.2	104.5	-2.6	121.8	8.8	113.9	4.2	120.3	5.4
1987	114.2	3.0	116.8	4.3	112.6	1.4	119.7	8.0	106.9	2.3	127.9	5.0	118.9	4.4	127.1	5.7
1988	119.3	4.5	121.8	4.3	116.2	3.2	130.1	8.7	111.5	4.3	134.7	5.3	122.8	3.3	138.9	9.3
1989	124.5	4.4	129.2	6.1	120.0	3.3	127.8	-1.8	116.9	4.8	145.6	8.1	128.7	4.8	149.2	7.4
1990	130.8	5.1	136.9	6.0	125.2	4.3	128.1	0.2	122.8	5.0	158.4	8.8	138.3	7.5	158.5	6.2
1991	136.4	4.3	140.6	2.7	131.0	4.6	132.9	3.7	125.5	2.2	171.9	8.5	143.8	4.0	172.8	9.0
1992	140.1	2.7	142.4	1.3	133.3	1.8	135.2	1.7	128.5	2.4	184.4	7.3	149.3	3.8	188.2	8.9
1993	143.1	2.1	144.3	1.3	135.6	1.7	135.9	0.5	129.7	0.9	198.7	7.8	152.6	2.2	198.1	5.3
1994	146.9	2.7	149.7	3.7	138.4	2.1	135.3	-0.4	132.8	2.4	218.1	9.8	154.7	1.4	199.7	0.8
1995	-	-	-	-	-	-	-	-	-	-	-	-	-	-	-	-

Source: U.S. Department of Labor, Bureau of Labor Statistics, Division of Consumer Prices and Price Indexes. - indicates no data collected for period.

Baltimore, MD
Consumer Price Index - Urban Wage Earners
Base 1982-1984 = 100
Annual Averages

For 1914-1995. Columns headed % show percentile change in the index from the previous period for which an index is available.

Year	All Items		Food & Beverage		Housing		Apparel & Upkeep		Trans- portation		Medical Care		Entertain- ment		Other Goods & Services	
	Index	%	Index	%	Index	%	Index	%	Index	%	Index	%	Index	%	Index	%
1914	-	-	-	-	-	-	-	-	-	-	-	-	-	-	-	-
1915	8.9	-	-	-	-	-	-	-	-	-	-	-	-	-	-	-
1916	9.7	9.0	-	-	-	-	-	-	-	-	-	-	-	-	-	-
1917	11.9	22.7	-	-	-	-	-	-	-	-	-	-	-	-	-	-
1918	14.4	21.0	-	-	-	-	-	-	-	-	-	-	-	-	-	-
1919	16.3	13.2	-	-	-	-	-	-	-	-	-	-	-	-	-	-
1920	18.3	12.3	-	-	-	-	-	-	-	-	-	-	-	-	-	-
1921	16.3	-10.9	-	-	-	-	-	-	-	-	-	-	-	-	-	-
1922	15.4	-5.5	-	-	-	-	-	-	-	-	-	-	-	-	-	-
1923	15.8	2.6	-	-	-	-	-	-	-	-	-	-	-	-	-	-
1924	15.8	0.0	-	-	-	-	-	-	-	-	-	-	-	-	-	-
1925	16.2	2.5	-	-	-	-	-	-	-	-	-	-	-	-	-	-
1926	16.4	1.2	-	-	-	-	-	-	-	-	-	-	-	-	-	-
1927	16.0	-2.4	-	-	-	-	-	-	-	-	-	-	-	-	-	-
1928	15.9	-0.6	-	-	-	-	-	-	-	-	-	-	-	-	-	-
1929	15.9	0.0	-	-	-	-	-	-	-	-	-	-	-	-	-	-
1930	15.7	-1.3	-	-	-	-	-	-	-	-	-	-	-	-	-	-
1931	14.5	-7.6	-	-	-	-	-	-	-	-	-	-	-	-	-	-
1932	13.1	-9.7	-	-	-	-	-	-	-	-	-	-	-	-	-	-
1933	12.5	-4.6	-	-	-	-	-	-	-	-	-	-	-	-	-	-
1934	13.0	4.0	-	-	-	-	-	-	-	-	-	-	-	-	-	-
1935	13.4	3.1	-	-	-	-	-	-	-	-	-	-	-	-	-	-
1936	13.5	0.7	-	-	-	-	-	-	-	-	-	-	-	-	-	-
1937	13.8	2.2	-	-	-	-	-	-	-	-	-	-	-	-	-	-
1938	13.6	-1.4	-	-	-	-	-	-	-	-	-	-	-	-	-	-
1939	13.5	-0.7	-	-	-	-	-	-	-	-	-	-	-	-	-	-
1940	13.5	0.0	-	-	-	-	-	-	-	-	-	-	-	-	-	-
1941	14.4	6.7	-	-	-	-	-	-	-	-	-	-	-	-	-	-
1942	16.0	11.1	-	-	-	-	-	-	-	-	-	-	-	-	-	-
1943	17.1	6.9	-	-	-	-	-	-	-	-	-	-	-	-	-	-
1944	17.3	1.2	-	-	-	-	-	-	-	-	-	-	-	-	-	-
1945	17.9	3.5	-	-	-	-	-	-	-	-	-	-	-	-	-	-
1946	19.3	7.8	-	-	-	-	-	-	-	-	-	-	-	-	-	-
1947	22.2	15.0	-	-	-	-	-	-	17.2	-	13.7	-	-	-	-	-
1948	23.9	7.7	-	-	-	-	-	-	18.7	8.7	14.2	3.6	-	-	-	-
1949	23.8	-0.4	-	-	-	-	-	-	21.7	16.0	14.3	0.7	-	-	-	-
1950	24.0	0.8	-	-	-	-	-	-	22.5	3.7	14.5	1.4	-	-	-	-
1951	25.7	7.1	-	-	-	-	-	-	24.0	6.7	15.7	8.3	-	-	-	-
1952	26.4	2.7	-	-	-	-	-	-	25.5	6.3	17.5	11.5	-	-	-	-
1953	26.7	1.1	-	-	-	-	39.0	-	26.7	4.7	18.5	5.7	-	-	-	-
1954	26.8	0.4	-	-	-	-	38.9	-0.3	26.5	-0.7	18.7	1.1	-	-	-	-
1955	26.8	0.0	-	-	-	-	38.8	-0.3	26.2	-1.1	18.9	1.1	-	-	-	-
1956	27.2	1.5	-	-	-	-	40.2	3.6	26.7	1.9	19.7	4.2	-	-	-	-
1957	28.2	3.7	-	-	-	-	41.1	2.2	28.4	6.4	20.3	3.0	-	-	-	-
1958	29.0	2.8	-	-	-	-	41.6	1.2	29.1	2.5	20.9	3.0	-	-	-	-

[Continued]

Baltimore, MD
Consumer Price Index - Urban Wage Earners
Base 1982-1984 = 100
Annual Averages
[Continued]

For 1914-1995. Columns headed % show percentile change in the index from the previous period for which an index is available.

Year	All Items		Food & Beverage		Housing		Apparel & Upkeep		Trans-portation		Medical Care		Entertain-ment		Other Goods & Services	
	Index	%	Index	%	Index	%	Index	%	Index	%	Index	%	Index	%	Index	%
1959	29.5	1.7	-	-	-	-	42.5	2.2	30.9	6.2	22.3	6.7	-	-	-	-
1960	29.9	1.4	-	-	-	-	43.2	1.6	30.7	-0.6	23.6	5.8	-	-	-	-
1961	30.2	1.0	-	-	-	-	43.9	1.6	31.2	1.6	24.7	4.7	-	-	-	-
1962	30.4	0.7	-	-	-	-	44.2	0.7	31.2	0.0	25.2	2.0	-	-	-	-
1963	30.9	1.6	-	-	-	-	44.6	0.9	31.8	1.9	26.7	6.0	-	-	-	-
1964	31.2	1.0	-	-	-	-	44.6	0.0	32.6	2.5	27.4	2.6	-	-	-	-
1965	31.7	1.6	-	-	-	-	45.1	1.1	33.1	1.5	28.1	2.6	-	-	-	-
1966	32.8	3.5	-	-	-	-	46.5	3.1	33.4	0.9	29.3	4.3	-	-	-	-
1967	33.5	2.1	-	-	-	-	48.6	4.5	34.1	2.1	31.7	8.2	-	-	-	-
1968	34.9	4.2	-	-	-	-	50.8	4.5	35.2	3.2	33.4	5.4	-	-	-	-
1969	37.1	6.3	-	-	-	-	54.9	8.1	37.1	5.4	35.7	6.9	-	-	-	-
1970	39.2	5.7	-	-	-	-	57.9	5.5	38.3	3.2	39.0	9.2	-	-	-	-
1971	41.4	5.6	-	-	-	-	60.0	3.6	40.0	4.4	43.0	10.3	-	-	-	-
1972	42.4	2.4	-	-	-	-	60.2	0.3	39.7	-0.7	45.1	4.9	-	-	-	-
1973	45.3	6.8	-	-	-	-	63.4	5.3	41.1	3.5	47.2	4.7	-	-	-	-
1974	51.1	12.8	-	-	-	-	68.7	8.4	45.8	11.4	52.3	10.8	-	-	-	-
1975	55.4	8.4	-	-	-	-	71.7	4.4	49.9	9.0	57.1	9.2	-	-	-	-
1976	58.3	5.2	63.8	-	55.5	-	74.9	4.5	54.1	8.4	61.1	7.0	66.5	-	58.7	-
1977	62.4	7.0	67.8	6.3	60.2	8.5	79.0	5.5	57.3	5.9	65.8	7.7	69.3	4.2	61.9	5.5
1978	67.0	7.4	73.9	9.0	65.5	8.8	82.4	4.3	59.8	4.4	70.0	6.4	72.0	3.9	65.2	5.3
1979	73.4	9.6	80.4	8.8	71.9	9.8	83.9	1.8	68.0	13.7	76.0	8.6	76.6	6.4	69.2	6.1
1980	83.6	13.9	87.7	9.1	83.5	16.1	91.3	8.8	80.6	18.5	81.1	6.7	83.1	8.5	75.8	9.5
1981	91.8	9.8	93.7	6.8	92.6	10.9	95.9	5.0	91.0	12.9	85.7	5.7	89.1	7.2	83.0	9.5
1982	95.9	4.5	96.5	3.0	96.5	4.2	97.6	1.8	95.5	4.9	94.0	9.7	95.7	7.4	89.5	7.8
1983	99.8	4.1	99.5	3.1	99.4	3.0	100.7	3.2	99.7	4.4	100.6	7.0	101.2	5.7	101.3	13.2
1984	104.3	4.5	104.0	4.5	104.0	4.6	101.7	1.0	104.8	5.1	105.4	4.8	103.1	1.9	109.2	7.8
1985	108.3	3.8	107.1	3.0	108.7	4.5	106.6	4.8	107.6	2.7	111.9	6.2	108.2	4.9	114.1	4.5
1986	110.5	2.0	111.9	4.5	111.3	2.4	110.1	3.3	104.2	-3.2	122.0	9.0	112.8	4.3	120.2	5.3
1987	113.8	3.0	116.6	4.2	112.5	1.1	119.1	8.2	107.2	2.9	127.6	4.6	118.1	4.7	126.7	5.4
1988	118.9	4.5	121.7	4.4	116.0	3.1	128.9	8.2	112.3	4.8	134.1	5.1	123.0	4.1	138.1	9.0
1989	124.1	4.4	128.8	5.8	120.0	3.4	126.0	-2.2	117.7	4.8	143.9	7.3	129.2	5.0	148.2	7.3
1990	130.1	4.8	136.4	5.9	124.9	4.1	125.5	-0.4	123.6	5.0	156.1	8.5	139.0	7.6	157.2	6.1
1991	135.6	4.2	140.2	2.8	130.5	4.5	130.9	4.3	125.9	1.9	169.4	8.5	145.9	5.0	172.1	9.5
1992	139.5	2.9	142.1	1.4	132.6	1.6	135.5	3.5	129.1	2.5	181.3	7.0	151.6	3.9	189.7	10.2
1993	142.3	2.0	143.8	1.2	134.7	1.6	135.9	0.3	130.0	0.7	196.0	8.1	155.0	2.2	199.4	5.1
1994	145.9	2.5	149.1	3.7	137.7	2.2	133.5	-1.8	133.4	2.6	214.1	9.2	158.1	2.0	199.5	0.1
1995	-	-	-	-	-	-	-	-	-	-	-	-	-	-	-	-

Source: U.S. Department of Labor, Bureau of Labor Statistics, Division of Consumer Prices and Price Indexes. - indicates no data collected for period.

Baltimore, MD
Consumer Price Index - All Urban Consumers
Base 1982-1984 = 100
All Items

For 1914-1995. Columns headed % show percentile change in the index from the previous period for which an index is available.

Year	Jan Index	%	Feb Index	%	Mar Index	%	Apr Index	%	May Index	%	Jun Index	%	Jul Index	%	Aug Index	%	Sep Index	%	Oct Index	%	Nov Index	%	Dec Index	%
1914	-	-	-	-	-	-	-	-	-	-	-	-	-	-	-	-	-	-	-	-	-	-	9.0	-
1915	-	-	-	-	-	-	-	-	-	-	-	-	-	-	-	-	-	-	-	-	-	-	9.0	0.0
1916	-	-	-	-	-	-	-	-	-	-	-	-	-	-	-	-	-	-	-	-	-	-	10.4	15.6
1917	-	-	-	-	-	-	-	-	-	-	-	-	-	-	-	-	-	-	-	-	-	-	12.9	24.0
1918	-	-	-	-	-	-	-	-	-	-	-	-	-	-	-	-	-	-	-	-	-	-	15.7	21.7
1919	-	-	-	-	-	-	-	-	-	-	15.9	1.3	-	-	-	-	-	-	-	-	-	-	17.3	8.8
1920	-	-	-	-	-	-	-	-	-	-	19.2	11.0	-	-	-	-	-	-	-	-	-	-	17.5	-8.9
1921	-	-	-	-	-	-	-	-	16.1	-8.0	-	-	-	-	-	-	16.1	0.0	-	-	-	-	15.7	-2.5
1922	-	-	-	-	15.4	-1.9	-	-	-	-	15.4	0.0	-	-	-	-	15.2	-1.3	-	-	-	-	15.5	2.0
1923	-	-	-	-	15.5	0.0	-	-	-	-	15.8	1.9	-	-	-	-	16.0	1.3	-	-	-	-	15.9	-0.6
1924	-	-	-	-	15.7	-1.3	-	-	-	-	15.8	0.6	-	-	-	-	15.7	-0.6	-	-	-	-	15.8	0.6
1925	-	-	-	-	-	-	-	-	-	-	16.2	2.5	-	-	-	-	-	-	-	-	-	-	16.6	2.5
1926	-	-	-	-	-	-	-	-	-	-	16.4	-1.2	-	-	-	-	-	-	-	-	-	-	16.3	-0.6
1927	-	-	-	-	-	-	-	-	-	-	16.2	-0.6	-	-	-	-	-	-	-	-	-	-	15.9	-1.9
1928	-	-	-	-	-	-	-	-	-	-	15.9	0.0	-	-	-	-	-	-	-	-	-	-	15.7	-1.3
1929	-	-	-	-	-	-	-	-	-	-	15.8	0.6	-	-	-	-	-	-	-	-	-	-	15.9	0.6
1930	-	-	-	-	-	-	-	-	-	-	15.8	-0.6	-	-	-	-	-	-	-	-	-	-	15.2	-3.8
1931	-	-	-	-	-	-	-	-	-	-	14.3	-5.9	-	-	-	-	-	-	-	-	-	-	13.9	-2.8
1932	-	-	-	-	-	-	-	-	-	-	13.0	-6.5	-	-	-	-	-	-	-	-	-	-	12.6	-3.1
1933	-	-	-	-	-	-	-	-	-	-	12.2	-3.2	-	-	-	-	-	-	-	-	-	-	12.8	4.9
1934	-	-	-	-	-	-	-	-	-	-	12.9	0.8	-	-	-	-	-	-	-	-	13.1	1.6	-	-
1935	-	-	-	-	13.2	0.8	-	-	-	-	-	-	13.3	0.8	-	-	-	-	13.3	0.0	-	-	-	-
1936	13.5	1.5	-	-	-	-	13.4	-0.7	-	-	-	-	13.4	0.0	-	-	13.6	1.5	-	-	-	-	13.4	-1.5
1937	-	-	-	-	13.7	2.2	-	-	-	-	13.7	0.0	-	-	-	-	13.9	1.5	-	-	-	-	13.8	-0.7
1938	-	-	-	-	13.5	-2.2	-	-	-	-	13.5	0.0	-	-	-	-	13.5	0.0	-	-	-	-	13.5	0.0
1939	-	-	-	-	13.4	-0.7	-	-	-	-	13.4	0.0	-	-	-	-	13.6	1.5	-	-	-	-	13.3	-2.2
1940	-	-	-	-	13.4	0.8	-	-	-	-	13.6	1.5	-	-	-	-	13.5	-0.7	13.5	0.0	13.5	0.0	13.6	0.7
1941	13.6	0.0	13.6	0.0	13.7	0.7	13.8	0.7	14.0	1.4	14.3	2.1	14.4	0.7	14.5	0.7	14.8	2.1	14.9	0.7	15.0	0.7	15.2	1.3
1942	15.4	1.3	15.5	0.6	15.7	1.3	15.8	0.6	15.9	0.6	16.1	1.3	16.0	-0.6	16.1	0.6	16.2	0.6	16.3	0.6	16.3	0.0	16.5	1.2
1943	16.6	0.6	16.6	0.0	16.9	1.8	17.1	1.2	17.4	1.8	17.4	0.0	17.1	-1.7	17.0	-0.6	17.1	0.6	17.2	0.6	17.0	-1.2	17.1	0.6
1944	17.1	0.0	17.0	-0.6	17.1	0.6	17.1	0.0	17.2	0.6	17.3	0.6	17.4	0.6	17.4	0.0	17.3	-0.6	17.4	0.6	17.5	0.6	17.5	0.0
1945	17.6	0.6	17.6	0.0	17.6	0.0	17.6	0.0	17.8	1.1	18.0	1.1	18.0	0.0	18.0	0.0	18.0	0.0	17.9	-0.6	17.9	0.0	18.0	0.6
1946	18.0	0.0	17.8	-1.1	17.9	0.6	18.1	1.1	18.1	0.0	18.4	1.7	19.4	5.4	19.9	2.6	20.1	1.0	20.5	2.0	21.0	2.4	21.1	0.5
1947	21.2	0.5	21.1	-0.5	21.7	2.8	21.7	0.0	21.6	-0.5	21.8	0.9	-	-	-	-	22.8	4.6	-	-	-	-	23.3	2.2
1948	-	-	-	-	23.2	-0.4	-	-	-	-	23.9	3.0	-	-	-	-	24.4	2.1	-	-	-	-	23.7	-2.9
1949	-	-	-	-	23.7	0.0	-	-	-	-	23.8	0.4	-	-	-	-	23.8	0.0	-	-	-	-	23.4	-1.7
1950	-	-	-	-	23.4	0.0	-	-	-	-	23.6	0.9	-	-	-	-	24.4	3.4	-	-	-	-	24.7	1.2
1951	-	-	-	-	25.4	2.8	-	-	-	-	25.6	0.8	-	-	-	-	25.7	0.4	-	-	-	-	26.1	1.6
1952	-	-	-	-	26.1	0.0	-	-	-	-	26.2	0.4	-	-	-	-	26.7	1.9	-	-	-	-	26.5	-0.7
1953	-	-	-	-	26.5	0.0	-	-	-	-	26.7	0.8	-	-	-	-	26.7	0.0	-	-	-	-	26.6	-0.4
1954	-	-	-	-	26.6	0.0	-	-	-	-	26.8	0.8	-	-	-	-	26.7	-0.4	-	-	-	-	26.6	-0.4
1955	-	-	-	-	26.7	0.4	-	-	-	-	26.7	0.0	-	-	-	-	26.8	0.4	-	-	-	-	26.9	0.4
1956	-	-	-	-	26.7	-0.7	-	-	-	-	27.1	1.5	-	-	-	-	27.3	0.7	-	-	-	-	27.7	1.5
1957	-	-	-	-	27.8	0.4	-	-	-	-	28.2	1.4	-	-	-	-	28.3	0.4	-	-	-	-	28.4	0.4
1958	-	-	-	-	28.8	1.4	-	-	-	-	29.0	0.7	-	-	-	-	29.0	0.0	-	-	-	-	29.1	0.3

[Continued]

Baltimore, MD
Consumer Price Index - All Urban Consumers
Base 1982-1984 = 100
All Items
[Continued]

For 1914-1995. Columns headed % show percentile change in the index from the previous period for which an index is available.

Year	Jan Index	%	Feb Index	%	Mar Index	%	Apr Index	%	May Index	%	Jun Index	%	Jul Index	%	Aug Index	%	Sep Index	%	Oct Index	%	Nov Index	%	Dec Index	%
1959	-	-	-	-	29.4	1.0	-	-	-	-	29.4	0.0	-	-	-	-	29.6	0.7	-	-	-	-	29.5	-0.3
1960	-	-	-	-	29.6	0.3	-	-	-	-	29.8	0.7	-	-	-	-	29.9	0.3	-	-	-	-	30.0	0.3
1961	-	-	-	-	30.1	0.3	-	-	-	-	30.1	0.0	-	-	-	-	30.1	0.0	-	-	-	-	30.1	0.0
1962	-	-	-	-	30.1	0.0	-	-	-	-	30.2	0.3	-	-	-	-	30.5	1.0	-	-	-	-	30.4	-0.3
1963	-	-	-	-	30.6	0.7	-	-	-	-	30.8	0.7	-	-	-	-	30.8	0.0	-	-	-	-	31.0	0.6
1964	-	-	-	-	31.0	0.0	-	-	-	-	31.1	0.3	-	-	-	-	31.1	0.0	-	-	-	-	31.3	0.6
1965	-	-	-	-	31.2	-0.3	-	-	-	-	31.7	1.6	-	-	-	-	31.7	0.0	-	-	-	-	31.9	0.6
1966	-	-	-	-	32.4	1.6	-	-	-	-	32.7	0.9	-	-	-	-	32.9	0.6	-	-	-	-	33.0	0.3
1967	-	-	-	-	33.1	0.3	-	-	-	-	33.3	0.6	-	-	-	-	33.9	1.8	-	-	-	-	33.8	-0.3
1968	-	-	-	-	34.2	1.2	-	-	-	-	34.7	1.5	-	-	-	-	35.2	1.4	-	-	-	-	35.7	1.4
1969	-	-	-	-	36.2	1.4	-	-	-	-	36.8	1.7	-	-	-	-	37.5	1.9	-	-	-	-	38.0	1.3
1970	-	-	-	-	38.4	1.1	-	-	-	-	39.0	1.6	-	-	-	-	39.5	1.3	-	-	-	-	40.4	2.3
1971	-	-	-	-	40.8	1.0	-	-	-	-	41.3	1.2	-	-	-	-	41.6	0.7	-	-	-	-	41.8	0.5
1972	-	-	-	-	41.8	0.0	-	-	-	-	42.0	0.5	-	-	-	-	42.7	1.7	-	-	-	-	42.8	0.2
1973	-	-	-	-	44.1	3.0	-	-	-	-	44.7	1.4	-	-	-	-	46.0	2.9	-	-	-	-	47.0	2.2
1974	-	-	-	-	49.2	4.7	-	-	-	-	50.6	2.8	-	-	-	-	52.6	4.0	-	-	-	-	53.5	1.7
1975	-	-	-	-	54.5	1.9	-	-	-	-	55.1	1.1	-	-	-	-	56.0	1.6	-	-	-	-	56.3	0.5
1976	-	-	-	-	57.0	1.2	-	-	-	-	58.1	1.9	-	-	-	-	59.0	1.5	-	-	-	-	59.6	1.0
1977	-	-	-	-	60.9	2.2	-	-	-	-	62.1	2.0	-	-	-	-	63.1	1.6	-	-	-	-	63.8	1.1
1978	-	-	-	-	65.4	2.5	-	-	66.2	1.2	-	-	67.5	2.0	-	-	68.0	0.7	-	-	67.9	-0.1	-	-
1979	68.3	0.6	-	-	69.9	2.3	-	-	72.0	3.0	-	-	73.9	2.6	-	-	75.2	1.8	-	-	76.0	1.1	-	-
1980	78.4	3.2	-	-	81.9	4.5	-	-	83.3	1.7	-	-	84.4	1.3	-	-	85.3	1.1	-	-	86.4	1.3	-	-
1981	88.4	2.3	-	-	90.4	2.3	-	-	90.0	-0.4	-	-	91.1	1.2	-	-	93.6	2.7	-	-	93.9	0.3	-	-
1982	94.3	0.4	-	-	94.3	0.0	-	-	94.8	0.5	-	-	95.7	0.9	-	-	96.7	1.0	-	-	97.0	0.3	-	-
1983	97.4	0.4	-	-	97.9	0.5	-	-	99.1	1.2	-	-	100.4	1.3	-	-	101.3	0.9	-	-	101.9	0.6	-	-
1984	102.8	0.9	-	-	103.8	1.0	-	-	104.1	0.3	-	-	104.7	0.6	-	-	105.8	1.1	-	-	105.4	-0.4	-	-
1985	105.4	0.0	-	-	107.2	1.7	-	-	108.0	0.7	-	-	108.3	0.3	-	-	109.5	1.1	-	-	109.4	-0.1	-	-
1986	111.0	1.5	-	-	110.7	-0.3	-	-	110.0	-0.6	-	-	110.4	0.4	-	-	111.7	1.2	-	-	111.5	-0.2	-	-
1987	111.7	0.2	-	-	112.3	0.5	-	-	113.7	1.2	-	-	115.0	1.1	-	-	115.7	0.6	-	-	115.7	0.0	-	-
1988	116.8	1.0	-	-	117.7	0.8	-	-	117.8	0.1	-	-	119.9	1.8	-	-	121.3	1.2	-	-	121.2	-0.1	-	-
1989	121.3	0.1	-	-	122.8	1.2	-	-	124.1	1.1	-	-	124.9	0.6	-	-	125.9	0.8	-	-	126.6	0.6	-	-
1990	127.9	1.0	-	-	129.3	1.1	-	-	129.0	-0.2	-	-	130.2	0.9	-	-	132.9	2.1	-	-	133.9	0.8	-	-
1991	134.3	0.3	-	-	135.1	0.6	-	-	135.4	0.2	-	-	136.5	0.8	-	-	138.2	1.2	-	-	137.8	-0.3	-	-
1992	138.0	0.1	-	-	138.7	0.5	-	-	139.5	0.6	-	-	140.6	0.8	-	-	141.9	0.9	-	-	141.1	-0.6	-	-
1993	142.0	0.6	-	-	142.6	0.4	-	-	142.8	0.1	-	-	143.7	0.6	-	-	143.6	-0.1	-	-	143.4	-0.1	-	-
1994	143.8	0.3	-	-	145.0	0.8	-	-	145.8	0.6	-	-	148.2	1.6	-	-	148.6	0.3	-	-	148.6	0.0	-	-
1995	148.7	0.1	-	-	150.3	1.1	-	-	150.4	0.1	-	-	151.5	0.7	-	-	151.8	0.2	-	-	151.1	-0.5	-	-

Source: U.S. Department of Labor, Bureau of Labor Statistics, Division of Consumer Prices and Price Indexes. - indicates no data collected for period.

Baltimore, MD
Consumer Price Index - Urban Wage Earners
Base 1982-1984 = 100
All Items

For 1914-1995. Columns headed % show percentile change in the index from the previous period for which an index is available.

Year	Jan Index	%	Feb Index	%	Mar Index	%	Apr Index	%	May Index	%	Jun Index	%	Jul Index	%	Aug Index	%	Sep Index	%	Oct Index	%	Nov Index	%	Dec Index	%
1914	-	-	-	-	-	-	-	-	-	-	-	-	-	-	-	-	-	-	-	-	-	-	9.0	-
1915	-	-	-	-	-	-	-	-	-	-	-	-	-	-	-	-	-	-	-	-	-	-	9.0	0.0
1916	-	-	-	-	-	-	-	-	-	-	-	-	-	-	-	-	-	-	-	-	-	-	10.4	15.6
1917	-	-	-	-	-	-	-	-	-	-	-	-	-	-	-	-	-	-	-	-	-	-	12.9	24.0
1918	-	-	-	-	-	-	-	-	-	-	-	-	-	-	-	-	-	-	-	-	-	-	15.8	22.5
1919	-	-	-	-	-	-	-	-	-	-	16.0	1.3	-	-	-	-	-	-	-	-	-	-	17.3	8.1
1920	-	-	-	-	-	-	-	-	-	-	19.3	11.6	-	-	-	-	-	-	-	-	-	-	17.5	-9.3
1921	-	-	-	-	-	-	-	-	16.1	-8.0	-	-	-	-	-	-	16.1	0.0	-	-	-	-	15.8	-1.9
1922	-	-	-	-	15.4	-2.5	-	-	-	-	15.4	0.0	-	-	-	-	15.3	-0.6	-	-	-	-	15.5	1.3
1923	-	-	-	-	15.5	0.0	-	-	-	-	15.9	2.6	-	-	-	-	16.0	0.6	-	-	-	-	15.9	-0.6
1924	-	-	-	-	15.8	-0.6	-	-	-	-	15.8	0.0	-	-	-	-	15.8	0.0	-	-	-	-	15.9	0.6
1925	-	-	-	-	-	-	-	-	-	-	16.2	1.9	-	-	-	-	-	-	-	-	-	-	16.6	2.5
1926	-	-	-	-	-	-	-	-	-	-	16.5	-0.6	-	-	-	-	-	-	-	-	-	-	16.4	-0.6
1927	-	-	-	-	-	-	-	-	-	-	16.3	-0.6	-	-	-	-	-	-	-	-	-	-	15.9	-2.5
1928	-	-	-	-	-	-	-	-	-	-	15.9	0.0	-	-	-	-	-	-	-	-	-	-	15.8	-0.6
1929	-	-	-	-	-	-	-	-	-	-	15.9	0.6	-	-	-	-	-	-	-	-	-	-	16.0	0.6
1930	-	-	-	-	-	-	-	-	-	-	15.8	-1.2	-	-	-	-	-	-	-	-	-	-	15.2	-3.8
1931	-	-	-	-	-	-	-	-	-	-	14.4	-5.3	-	-	-	-	-	-	-	-	-	-	14.0	-2.8
1932	-	-	-	-	-	-	-	-	-	-	13.0	-7.1	-	-	-	-	-	-	-	-	-	-	12.6	-3.1
1933	-	-	-	-	-	-	-	-	-	-	12.3	-2.4	-	-	-	-	-	-	-	-	-	-	12.9	4.9
1934	-	-	-	-	-	-	-	-	-	-	13.0	0.8	-	-	-	-	-	-	-	-	13.1	0.8	-	-
1935	-	-	-	-	13.3	1.5	-	-	-	-	-	-	13.3	0.0	-	-	-	-	13.4	0.8	-	-	-	-
1936	13.5	0.7	-	-	-	-	13.4	-0.7	-	-	-	-	13.5	0.7	-	-	13.6	0.7	-	-	-	-	13.5	-0.7
1937	-	-	-	-	13.7	1.5	-	-	-	-	13.8	0.7	-	-	-	-	14.0	1.4	-	-	-	-	13.8	-1.4
1938	-	-	-	-	13.6	-1.4	-	-	-	-	13.6	0.0	-	-	-	-	13.6	0.0	-	-	-	-	13.6	0.0
1939	-	-	-	-	13.5	-0.7	-	-	-	-	13.5	0.0	-	-	-	-	13.6	0.7	-	-	-	-	13.4	-1.5
1940	-	-	-	-	13.5	0.7	-	-	-	-	13.6	0.7	-	-	-	-	13.6	0.0	13.5	-0.7	13.5	0.0	13.6	0.7
1941	13.7	0.7	13.7	0.0	13.7	0.0	13.9	1.5	14.1	1.4	14.3	1.4	14.5	1.4	14.6	0.7	14.9	2.1	15.0	0.7	15.1	0.7	15.2	0.7
1942	15.4	1.3	15.6	1.3	15.8	1.3	15.9	0.6	16.0	0.6	16.1	0.6	16.1	0.0	16.1	0.0	16.2	0.6	16.4	1.2	16.4	0.0	16.5	0.6
1943	16.6	0.6	16.6	0.0	17.0	2.4	17.2	1.2	17.4	1.2	17.4	0.0	17.1	-1.7	17.0	-0.6	17.1	0.6	17.2	0.6	17.0	-1.2	17.1	0.6
1944	17.1	0.0	17.0	-0.6	17.1	0.6	17.2	0.6	17.2	0.0	17.3	0.6	17.4	0.6	17.5	0.6	17.4	-0.6	17.4	0.0	17.6	1.1	17.6	0.0
1945	17.6	0.0	17.7	0.6	17.6	-0.6	17.7	0.6	17.8	0.6	18.0	1.1	18.1	0.6	18.0	-0.6	18.0	0.0	18.0	0.0	17.9	-0.6	18.0	0.6
1946	18.0	0.0	17.9	-0.6	18.0	0.6	18.2	1.1	18.2	0.0	18.5	1.6	19.5	5.4	20.0	2.6	20.1	0.5	20.5	2.0	21.1	2.9	21.1	0.0
1947	21.2	0.5	21.2	0.0	21.7	2.4	21.8	0.5	21.7	-0.5	21.9	0.9	-	-	-	-	22.8	4.1	-	-	-	-	23.3	2.2
1948	-	-	-	-	23.3	0.0	-	-	-	-	24.0	3.0	-	-	-	-	24.5	2.1	-	-	-	-	23.8	-2.9
1949	-	-	-	-	23.8	0.0	-	-	-	-	23.9	0.4	-	-	-	-	23.9	0.0	-	-	-	-	23.5	-1.7
1950	-	-	-	-	23.4	-0.4	-	-	-	-	23.6	0.9	-	-	-	-	24.5	3.8	-	-	-	-	24.8	1.2
1951	-	-	-	-	25.5	2.8	-	-	-	-	25.7	0.8	-	-	-	-	25.8	0.4	-	-	-	-	26.2	1.6
1952	-	-	-	-	26.2	0.0	-	-	-	-	26.3	0.4	-	-	-	-	26.8	1.9	-	-	-	-	26.6	-0.7
1953	-	-	-	-	26.6	0.0	-	-	-	-	26.8	0.8	-	-	-	-	26.8	0.0	-	-	-	-	26.7	-0.4
1954	-	-	-	-	26.7	0.0	-	-	-	-	26.9	0.7	-	-	-	-	26.8	-0.4	-	-	-	-	26.7	-0.4
1955	-	-	-	-	26.8	0.4	-	-	-	-	26.8	0.0	-	-	-	-	26.9	0.4	-	-	-	-	27.0	0.4
1956	-	-	-	-	26.8	-0.7	-	-	-	-	27.2	1.5	-	-	-	-	27.4	0.7	-	-	-	-	27.8	1.5
1957	-	-	-	-	27.9	0.4	-	-	-	-	28.2	1.1	-	-	-	-	28.3	0.4	-	-	-	-	28.4	0.4
1958	-	-	-	-	28.9	1.8	-	-	-	-	29.1	0.7	-	-	-	-	29.1	0.0	-	-	-	-	29.2	0.3

[Continued]

Baltimore, MD
Consumer Price Index - Urban Wage Earners
Base 1982-1984 = 100
All Items
[Continued]

For 1914-1995. Columns headed % show percentile change in the index from the previous period for which an index is available.

Year	Jan Index	%	Feb Index	%	Mar Index	%	Apr Index	%	May Index	%	Jun Index	%	Jul Index	%	Aug Index	%	Sep Index	%	Oct Index	%	Nov Index	%	Dec Index	%
1959	-	-	-	-	29.5	1.0	-	-	-	-	29.5	0.0	-	-	-	-	29.7	0.7	-	-	-	-	29.6	-0.3
1960	-	-	-	-	29.7	0.3	-	-	-	-	29.9	0.7	-	-	-	-	30.0	0.3	-	-	-	-	30.1	0.3
1961	-	-	-	-	30.2	0.3	-	-	-	-	30.2	0.0	-	-	-	-	30.2	0.0	-	-	-	-	30.2	0.0
1962	-	-	-	-	30.2	0.0	-	-	-	-	30.3	0.3	-	-	-	-	30.6	1.0	-	-	-	-	30.5	-0.3
1963	-	-	-	-	30.7	0.7	-	-	-	-	30.9	0.7	-	-	-	-	30.9	0.0	-	-	-	-	31.1	0.6
1964	-	-	-	-	31.1	0.0	-	-	-	-	31.2	0.3	-	-	-	-	31.2	0.0	-	-	-	-	31.4	0.6
1965	-	-	-	-	31.3	-0.3	-	-	-	-	31.8	1.6	-	-	-	-	31.8	0.0	-	-	-	-	32.0	0.6
1966	-	-	-	-	32.5	1.6	-	-	-	-	32.8	0.9	-	-	-	-	33.0	0.6	-	-	-	-	33.1	0.3
1967	-	-	-	-	33.2	0.3	-	-	-	-	33.4	0.6	-	-	-	-	34.0	1.8	-	-	-	-	33.9	-0.3
1968	-	-	-	-	34.3	1.2	-	-	-	-	34.9	1.7	-	-	-	-	35.4	1.4	-	-	-	-	35.8	1.1
1969	-	-	-	-	36.3	1.4	-	-	-	-	37.0	1.9	-	-	-	-	37.7	1.9	-	-	-	-	35.8	1.1
1970	-	-	-	-	38.6	1.3	-	-	-	-	39.1	1.3	-	-	-	-	39.7	1.5	-	-	-	-	40.5	2.0
1971	-	-	-	-	41.0	1.2	-	-	-	-	41.4	1.0	-	-	-	-	41.7	0.7	-	-	-	-	42.0	0.7
1972	-	-	-	-	41.9	-0.2	-	-	-	-	42.1	0.5	-	-	-	-	42.8	1.7	-	-	-	-	42.9	0.2
1973	-	-	-	-	44.2	3.0	-	-	-	-	44.8	1.4	-	-	-	-	46.1	2.9	-	-	-	-	42.9	0.2
1974	-	-	-	-	49.4	4.7	-	-	-	-	50.8	2.8	-	-	-	-	52.8	3.9	-	-	-	-	47.2	2.4
1975	-	-	-	-	54.6	1.7	-	-	-	-	55.2	1.1	-	-	-	-	56.2	1.8	-	-	-	-	53.7	1.7
1976	-	-	-	-	57.2	1.2	-	-	-	-	58.3	1.9	-	-	-	-	59.2	1.5	-	-	-	-	56.5	0.5
1977	-	-	-	-	61.1	2.2	-	-	-	-	62.3	2.0	-	-	-	-	63.3	1.6	-	-	-	-	59.8	1.0
1978	-	-	-	-	65.6	2.5	-	-	66.6	1.5	-	-	67.7	1.7	-	-	68.2	0.7	-	-	68.1	-0.1	64.0	1.1
1979	68.8	1.0	-	-	70.6	2.6	-	-	72.5	2.7	-	-	74.3	2.5	-	-	75.4	1.5	-	-	76.5	1.5	-	-
1980	78.7	2.9	-	-	81.8	3.9	-	-	83.1	1.6	-	-	84.1	1.2	-	-	84.9	1.0	-	-	86.3	1.6	-	-
1981	88.1	2.1	-	-	90.3	2.5	-	-	90.1	-0.2	-	-	91.8	1.9	-	-	94.5	2.9	-	-	94.2	-0.3	-	-
1982	94.7	0.5	-	-	94.7	0.0	-	-	95.2	0.5	-	-	96.3	1.2	-	-	96.9	0.6	-	-	97.2	0.3	-	-
1983	97.2	0.0	-	-	99.0	1.9	-	-	99.5	0.5	-	-	99.8	0.3	-	-	100.5	0.7	-	-	101.4	0.9	-	-
1984	101.9	0.5	-	-	103.1	1.2	-	-	103.8	0.7	-	-	104.5	0.7	-	-	106.1	1.5	-	-	105.7	-0.4	-	-
1985	105.7	0.0	-	-	107.4	1.6	-	-	108.1	0.7	-	-	108.5	0.4	-	-	109.5	0.9	-	-	109.5	0.0	-	-
1986	111.1	1.5	-	-	110.5	-0.5	-	-	109.6	-0.8	-	-	110.0	0.4	-	-	111.0	0.9	-	-	110.8	-0.2	-	-
1987	111.1	0.3	-	-	111.8	0.6	-	-	113.2	1.3	-	-	114.7	1.3	-	-	115.5	0.7	-	-	115.3	-0.2	-	-
1988	116.2	0.8	-	-	117.3	0.9	-	-	117.4	0.1	-	-	119.7	2.0	-	-	121.0	1.1	-	-	120.8	-0.2	-	-
1989	120.9	0.1	-	-	122.3	1.2	-	-	123.7	1.1	-	-	124.6	0.7	-	-	125.4	0.6	-	-	126.0	0.5	-	-
1990	127.2	1.0	-	-	128.6	1.1	-	-	128.3	-0.2	-	-	129.5	0.9	-	-	132.3	2.2	-	-	133.2	0.7	-	-
1991	133.7	0.4	-	-	134.1	0.3	-	-	134.4	0.2	-	-	135.8	1.0	-	-	137.5	1.3	-	-	137.0	-0.4	-	-
1992	137.3	0.2	-	-	137.9	0.4	-	-	138.9	0.7	-	-	140.2	0.9	-	-	137.5	1.3	-	-	137.0	-0.4	-	-
1993	141.3	0.5	-	-	141.8	0.4	-	-	142.1	0.2	-	-	140.2	0.9	-	-	141.4	0.9	-	-	140.6	-0.6	-	-
1994	142.7	0.1	-	-	144.2	1.1	-	-	144.9	0.5	-	-	143.0	0.6	-	-	142.8	-0.1	-	-	142.5	-0.2	-	-
1995	147.7	0.1	-	-	149.1	0.9	-	-	149.4	0.2	-	-	150.5	0.7	-	-	150.8	0.2	-	-	149.9	-0.6	-	-

Source: U.S. Department of Labor, Bureau of Labor Statistics, Division of Consumer Prices and Price Indexes. - indicates no data collected for period.

Baltimore, MD
Consumer Price Index - All Urban Consumers
Base 1982-1984 = 100
Food and Beverages

For 1975-1995. Columns headed % show percentile change in the index from the previous period for which an index is available.

Year	Jan Index	%	Feb Index	%	Mar Index	%	Apr Index	%	May Index	%	Jun Index	%	Jul Index	%	Aug Index	%	Sep Index	%	Oct Index	%	Nov Index	%	Dec Index	%
1975	-	-	-	-	-	-	-	-	-	-	-	-	-	-	-	-	-	-	-	-	-	-	63.2	-
1976	-	-	-	-	63.0	-0.3	-	-	-	-	64.1	1.7	-	-	-	-	64.6	0.8	-	-	-	-	64.3	-0.5
1977	-	-	-	-	66.6	3.6	-	-	-	-	68.4	2.7	-	-	-	-	69.1	1.0	-	-	-	-	69.2	0.1
1978	-	-	-	-	72.0	4.0	-	-	74.0	2.8	-	-	76.6	3.5	-	-	75.5	-1.4	-	-	75.8	0.4	-	-
1979	78.4	3.4	-	-	80.1	2.2	-	-	80.7	0.7	-	-	81.9	1.5	-	-	82.4	0.6	-	-	82.3	-0.1	-	-
1980	84.3	2.4	-	-	85.2	1.1	-	-	86.2	1.2	-	-	87.8	1.9	-	-	90.1	2.6	-	-	91.3	1.3	-	-
1981	93.1	2.0	-	-	94.8	1.8	-	-	93.2	-1.7	-	-	93.5	0.3	-	-	94.2	0.7	-	-	94.3	0.1	-	-
1982	95.2	1.0	-	-	95.3	0.1	-	-	96.5	1.3	-	-	97.6	1.1	-	-	97.5	-0.1	-	-	96.3	-1.2	-	-
1983	96.9	0.6	-	-	98.3	1.4	-	-	100.3	2.0	-	-	99.9	-0.4	-	-	99.7	-0.2	-	-	100.6	0.9	-	-
1984	102.9	2.3	-	-	103.6	0.7	-	-	104.2	0.6	-	-	104.2	0.0	-	-	104.3	0.1	-	-	104.2	-0.1	-	-
1985	105.2	1.0	-	-	107.3	2.0	-	-	106.7	-0.6	-	-	107.5	0.7	-	-	106.9	-0.6	-	-	107.8	0.8	-	-
1986	110.5	2.5	-	-	110.2	-0.3	-	-	110.1	-0.1	-	-	112.1	1.8	-	-	113.9	1.6	-	-	114.1	0.2	-	-
1987	115.6	1.3	-	-	115.1	-0.4	-	-	116.2	1.0	-	-	117.0	0.7	-	-	118.0	0.9	-	-	118.0	0.0	-	-
1988	118.8	0.7	-	-	119.7	0.8	-	-	121.1	1.2	-	-	123.1	1.7	-	-	123.2	0.1	-	-	123.5	0.2	-	-
1989	125.5	1.6	-	-	127.4	1.5	-	-	129.0	1.3	-	-	129.7	0.5	-	-	129.3	-0.3	-	-	131.5	1.7	-	-
1990	135.7	3.2	-	-	135.8	0.1	-	-	134.9	-0.7	-	-	137.3	1.8	-	-	137.6	0.2	-	-	138.9	0.9	-	-
1991	140.2	0.9	-	-	140.9	0.5	-	-	140.5	-0.3	-	-	141.3	0.6	-	-	140.3	-0.7	-	-	139.8	-0.4	-	-
1992	141.6	1.3	-	-	142.5	0.6	-	-	141.9	-0.4	-	-	141.8	-0.1	-	-	143.5	1.2	-	-	142.8	-0.5	-	-
1993	143.6	0.6	-	-	144.3	0.5	-	-	143.9	-0.3	-	-	144.0	0.1	-	-	143.8	-0.1	-	-	145.2	1.0	-	-
1994	148.4	2.2	-	-	148.5	0.1	-	-	149.3	0.5	-	-	151.3	1.3	-	-	148.6	-1.8	-	-	151.1	1.7	-	-
1995	151.6	0.3	-	-	153.2	1.1	-	-	154.2	0.7	-	-	153.3	-0.6	-	-	157.8	2.9	-	-	155.8	-1.3	-	-

Source: U.S. Department of Labor, Bureau of Labor Statistics, Division of Consumer Prices and Price Indexes. - indicates no data collected for period.

Baltimore, MD
Consumer Price Index - Urban Wage Earners
Base 1982-1984 = 100
Food and Beverages

For 1975-1995. Columns headed % show percentile change in the index from the previous period for which an index is available.

Year	Jan Index	%	Feb Index	%	Mar Index	%	Apr Index	%	May Index	%	Jun Index	%	Jul Index	%	Aug Index	%	Sep Index	%	Oct Index	%	Nov Index	%	Dec Index	%
1975	-	-	-	-	-	-	-	-	-	-	-	-	-	-	-	-	-	-	-	-	-	-	63.1	-
1976	-	-	-	-	63.0	-0.2	-	-	-	-	64.0	1.6	-	-	-	-	64.5	0.8	-	-	-	-	64.2	-0.5
1977	-	-	-	-	66.5	3.6	-	-	-	-	68.3	2.7	-	-	-	-	69.0	1.0	-	-	-	-	69.1	0.1
1978	-	-	-	-	71.9	4.1	-	-	73.9	2.8	-	-	75.5	2.2	-	-	74.9	-0.8	-	-	75.3	0.5	-	-
1979	77.7	3.2	-	-	79.8	2.7	-	-	80.0	0.3	-	-	80.8	1.0	-	-	80.9	0.1	-	-	82.0	1.4	-	-
1980	83.8	2.2	-	-	85.3	1.8	-	-	85.9	0.7	-	-	87.0	1.3	-	-	90.4	3.9	-	-	91.5	1.2	-	-
1981	92.7	1.3	-	-	94.3	1.7	-	-	92.9	-1.5	-	-	92.9	0.0	-	-	94.5	1.7	-	-	94.5	0.0	-	-
1982	95.1	0.6	-	-	95.3	0.2	-	-	96.5	1.3	-	-	97.7	1.2	-	-	97.4	-0.3	-	-	96.4	-1.0	-	-
1983	97.0	0.6	-	-	98.3	1.3	-	-	100.4	2.1	-	-	99.9	-0.5	-	-	99.7	-0.2	-	-	100.5	0.8	-	-
1984	102.9	2.4	-	-	103.6	0.7	-	-	104.3	0.7	-	-	104.3	0.0	-	-	104.4	0.1	-	-	104.2	-0.2	-	-
1985	105.3	1.1	-	-	107.3	1.9	-	-	106.8	-0.5	-	-	107.4	0.6	-	-	106.9	-0.5	-	-	107.7	0.7	-	-
1986	110.5	2.6	-	-	110.3	-0.2	-	-	110.1	-0.2	-	-	111.8	1.5	-	-	113.7	1.7	-	-	113.9	0.2	-	-
1987	115.5	1.4	-	-	114.8	-0.6	-	-	115.9	1.0	-	-	116.7	0.7	-	-	118.0	1.1	-	-	118.0	0.0	-	-
1988	118.8	0.7	-	-	119.7	0.8	-	-	121.1	1.2	-	-	122.9	1.5	-	-	123.0	0.1	-	-	123.2	0.2	-	-
1989	125.2	1.6	-	-	127.0	1.4	-	-	128.6	1.3	-	-	129.4	0.6	-	-	128.9	-0.4	-	-	131.0	1.6	-	-
1990	135.2	3.2	-	-	135.3	0.1	-	-	134.6	-0.5	-	-	136.9	1.7	-	-	137.2	0.2	-	-	138.4	0.9	-	-
1991	139.9	1.1	-	-	140.5	0.4	-	-	139.9	-0.4	-	-	141.0	0.8	-	-	140.1	-0.6	-	-	139.5	-0.4	-	-
1992	141.2	1.2	-	-	142.3	0.8	-	-	141.5	-0.6	-	-	141.5	0.0	-	-	143.0	1.1	-	-	142.5	-0.3	-	-
1993	143.2	0.5	-	-	143.8	0.4	-	-	143.4	-0.3	-	-	143.5	0.1	-	-	143.4	-0.1	-	-	144.6	0.8	-	-
1994	147.9	2.3	-	-	148.1	0.1	-	-	148.7	0.4	-	-	150.7	1.3	-	-	148.1	-1.7	-	-	150.3	1.5	-	-
1995	150.8	0.3	-	-	152.3	1.0	-	-	153.4	0.7	-	-	152.8	-0.4	-	-	156.9	2.7	-	-	155.1	-1.1	-	-

Source: U.S. Department of Labor, Bureau of Labor Statistics, Division of Consumer Prices and Price Indexes. - indicates no data collected for period.

Baltimore, MD
Consumer Price Index - All Urban Consumers
Base 1982-1984 = 100
Housing

For 1975-1995. Columns headed % show percentile change in the index from the previous period for which an index is available.

Year	Jan Index	%	Feb Index	%	Mar Index	%	Apr Index	%	May Index	%	Jun Index	%	Jul Index	%	Aug Index	%	Sep Index	%	Oct Index	%	Nov Index	%	Dec Index	%
1975	-	-	-	-	-	-	-	-	-	-	-	-	-	-	-	-	-	-	-	-	-	-	52.8	-
1976	-	-	-	-	53.7	1.7	-	-	-	-	54.6	1.7	-	-	-	-	56.1	2.7	-	-	-	-	57.3	2.1
1977	-	-	-	-	58.2	1.6	-	-	-	-	59.0	1.4	-	-	-	-	61.0	3.4	-	-	-	-	62.4	2.3
1978	-	-	-	-	64.1	2.7	-	-	64.0	-0.2	-	-	65.9	3.0	-	-	66.5	0.9	-	-	65.2	-2.0	-	-
1979	65.2	0.0	-	-	66.3	1.7	-	-	69.3	4.5	-	-	72.1	4.0	-	-	73.3	1.7	-	-	73.7	0.5	-	-
1980	76.5	3.8	-	-	81.2	6.1	-	-	82.8	2.0	-	-	84.0	1.4	-	-	83.9	-0.1	-	-	85.3	1.7	-	-
1981	87.9	3.0	-	-	89.6	1.9	-	-	88.5	-1.2	-	-	90.1	1.8	-	-	94.9	5.3	-	-	94.6	-0.3	-	-
1982	95.2	0.6	-	-	94.2	-1.1	-	-	95.2	1.1	-	-	95.4	0.2	-	-	95.9	0.5	-	-	96.9	1.0	-	-
1983	97.4	0.5	-	-	97.7	0.3	-	-	98.3	0.6	-	-	100.6	2.3	-	-	101.4	0.8	-	-	100.9	-0.5	-	-
1984	103.3	2.4	-	-	104.0	0.7	-	-	104.1	0.1	-	-	105.2	1.1	-	-	106.7	1.4	-	-	105.1	-1.5	-	-
1985	105.5	0.4	-	-	107.1	1.5	-	-	108.0	0.8	-	-	108.6	0.6	-	-	110.3	1.6	-	-	109.0	-1.2	-	-
1986	110.7	1.6	-	-	110.8	0.1	-	-	110.3	-0.5	-	-	111.0	0.6	-	-	112.6	1.4	-	-	111.5	-1.0	-	-
1987	111.4	-0.1	-	-	110.9	-0.4	-	-	113.1	2.0	-	-	113.5	0.4	-	-	113.0	-0.4	-	-	112.8	-0.2	-	-
1988	114.9	1.9	-	-	115.1	0.2	-	-	115.0	-0.1	-	-	117.1	1.8	-	-	117.5	0.3	-	-	116.8	-0.6	-	-
1989	117.4	0.5	-	-	117.8	0.3	-	-	118.9	0.9	-	-	121.3	2.0	-	-	122.1	0.7	-	-	121.4	-0.6	-	-
1990	123.1	1.4	-	-	123.6	0.4	-	-	123.8	0.2	-	-	126.1	1.9	-	-	127.1	0.8	-	-	126.7	-0.3	-	-
1991	127.6	0.7	-	-	130.2	2.0	-	-	129.6	-0.5	-	-	131.9	1.8	-	-	134.0	1.6	-	-	131.9	-1.6	-	-
1992	131.9	0.0	-	-	131.7	-0.2	-	-	132.4	0.5	-	-	135.3	2.2	-	-	135.1	-0.1	-	-	132.8	-1.7	-	-
1993	134.1	1.0	-	-	134.5	0.3	-	-	134.2	-0.2	-	-	137.1	2.2	-	-	137.3	0.1	-	-	135.6	-1.2	-	-
1994	136.5	0.7	-	-	137.8	1.0	-	-	137.0	-0.6	-	-	141.0	2.9	-	-	139.9	-0.8	-	-	138.0	-1.4	-	-
1995	137.7	-0.2	-	-	139.4	1.2	-	-	138.9	-0.4	-	-	143.4	3.2	-	-	143.0	-0.3	-	-	140.6	-1.7	-	-

Source: U.S. Department of Labor, Bureau of Labor Statistics, Division of Consumer Prices and Price Indexes. - indicates no data collected for period.

Baltimore, MD
Consumer Price Index - Urban Wage Earners
Base 1982-1984 = 100
Housing

For 1975-1995. Columns headed % show percentile change in the index from the previous period for which an index is available.

Year	Jan Index	%	Feb Index	%	Mar Index	%	Apr Index	%	May Index	%	Jun Index	%	Jul Index	%	Aug Index	%	Sep Index	%	Oct Index	%	Nov Index	%	Dec Index	%
1975	-	-	-	-	-	-	-	-	-	-	-	-	-	-	-	-	-	-	-	-	-	-	53.2	-
1976	-	-	-	-	54.2	1.9	-	-	-	-	55.0	1.5	-	-	-	-	56.6	2.9	-	-	-	-	57.7	1.9
1977	-	-	-	-	58.7	1.7	-	-	-	-	59.5	1.4	-	-	-	-	61.5	3.4	-	-	-	-	62.9	2.3
1978	-	-	-	-	64.6	2.7	-	-	64.9	0.5	-	-	66.4	2.3	-	-	67.1	1.1	-	-	66.0	-1.6	-	-
1979	66.3	0.5	-	-	68.1	2.7	-	-	70.8	4.0	-	-	73.5	3.8	-	-	74.7	1.6	-	-	75.3	0.8	-	-
1980	78.0	3.6	-	-	81.9	5.0	-	-	83.7	2.2	-	-	84.9	1.4	-	-	84.1	-0.9	-	-	85.6	1.8	-	-
1981	88.1	2.9	-	-	90.4	2.6	-	-	89.4	-1.1	-	-	92.4	3.4	-	-	97.4	5.4	-	-	95.7	-1.7	-	-
1982	96.2	0.5	-	-	95.4	-0.8	-	-	96.3	0.9	-	-	96.7	0.4	-	-	96.7	0.0	-	-	97.7	1.0	-	-
1983	97.0	-0.7	-	-	100.5	3.6	-	-	99.5	-1.0	-	-	99.1	-0.4	-	-	99.5	0.4	-	-	99.9	0.4	-	-
1984	100.8	0.9	-	-	102.2	1.4	-	-	103.0	0.8	-	-	104.4	1.4	-	-	107.1	2.6	-	-	105.6	-1.4	-	-
1985	105.9	0.3	-	-	107.5	1.5	-	-	108.2	0.7	-	-	108.9	0.6	-	-	110.8	1.7	-	-	109.6	-1.1	-	-
1986	111.3	1.6	-	-	111.1	-0.2	-	-	110.5	-0.5	-	-	111.2	0.6	-	-	112.7	1.3	-	-	111.4	-1.2	-	-
1987	111.3	-0.1	-	-	110.7	-0.5	-	-	113.0	2.1	-	-	113.5	0.4	-	-	113.1	-0.4	-	-	112.6	-0.4	-	-
1988	114.5	1.7	-	-	114.8	0.3	-	-	114.7	-0.1	-	-	117.0	2.0	-	-	117.4	0.3	-	-	116.7	-0.6	-	-
1989	117.3	0.5	-	-	117.6	0.3	-	-	118.8	1.0	-	-	121.5	2.3	-	-	122.1	0.5	-	-	121.3	-0.7	-	-
1990	122.8	1.2	-	-	123.3	0.4	-	-	123.5	0.2	-	-	126.0	2.0	-	-	126.8	0.6	-	-	126.2	-0.5	-	-
1991	127.2	0.8	-	-	129.5	1.8	-	-	128.8	-0.5	-	-	131.4	2.0	-	-	133.6	1.7	-	-	131.2	-1.8	-	-
1992	131.4	0.2	-	-	131.2	-0.2	-	-	131.6	0.3	-	-	134.8	2.4	-	-	134.3	-0.4	-	-	131.8	-1.9	-	-
1993	133.0	0.9	-	-	133.2	0.2	-	-	133.2	0.0	-	-	136.5	2.5	-	-	136.8	0.2	-	-	134.8	-1.5	-	-
1994	135.7	0.7	-	-	137.1	1.0	-	-	136.3	-0.6	-	-	140.4	3.0	-	-	139.6	-0.6	-	-	137.1	-1.8	-	-
1995	136.8	-0.2	-	-	138.2	1.0	-	-	137.7	-0.4	-	-	142.5	3.5	-	-	142.3	-0.1	-	-	139.5	-2.0	-	-

Source: U.S. Department of Labor, Bureau of Labor Statistics, Division of Consumer Prices and Price Indexes. - indicates no data collected for period.

Baltimore, MD
Consumer Price Index - All Urban Consumers
Base 1982-1984 = 100
Apparel and Upkeep

For 1952-1995. Columns headed % show percentile change in the index from the previous period for which an index is available.

Year	Jan Index	%	Feb Index	%	Mar Index	%	Apr Index	%	May Index	%	Jun Index	%	Jul Index	%	Aug Index	%	Sep Index	%	Oct Index	%	Nov Index	%	Dec Index	%
1952	-	-	-	-	-	-	-	-	-	-	-	-	-	-	-	-	-	-	-	-	-	-	37.9	-
1953	-	-	-	-	38.0	0.3	-	-	-	-	38.4	1.1	-	-	-	-	38.2	-0.5	-	-	-	-	37.8	-1.0
1954	-	-	-	-	37.8	0.0	-	-	-	-	37.8	0.0	-	-	-	-	38.2	1.1	-	-	-	-	38.0	-0.5
1955	-	-	-	-	37.8	-0.5	-	-	-	-	37.9	0.3	-	-	-	-	37.8	-0.3	-	-	-	-	38.3	1.3
1956	-	-	-	-	38.8	1.3	-	-	-	-	39.3	1.3	-	-	-	-	39.8	1.3	-	-	-	-	39.7	-0.3
1957	-	-	-	-	39.6	-0.3	-	-	-	-	40.0	1.0	-	-	-	-	40.8	2.0	-	-	-	-	40.5	-0.7
1958	-	-	-	-	40.7	0.5	-	-	-	-	40.7	0.0	-	-	-	-	40.8	0.2	-	-	-	-	40.3	-1.2
1959	-	-	-	-	41.3	2.5	-	-	-	-	41.4	0.2	-	-	-	-	42.1	1.7	-	-	-	-	41.9	-0.5
1960	-	-	-	-	42.1	0.5	-	-	-	-	41.9	-0.5	-	-	-	-	42.6	1.7	-	-	-	-	42.4	-0.5
1961	-	-	-	-	43.0	1.4	-	-	-	-	42.9	-0.2	-	-	-	-	43.0	0.2	-	-	-	-	42.8	-0.5
1962	-	-	-	-	42.9	0.2	-	-	-	-	42.9	0.0	-	-	-	-	43.5	1.4	-	-	-	-	43.5	0.0
1963	-	-	-	-	43.5	0.0	-	-	-	-	43.6	0.2	-	-	-	-	43.6	0.0	-	-	-	-	43.6	0.0
1964	-	-	-	-	43.3	-0.7	-	-	-	-	43.5	0.5	-	-	-	-	43.6	0.2	-	-	-	-	43.8	0.5
1965	-	-	-	-	43.6	-0.5	-	-	-	-	44.1	1.1	-	-	-	-	44.4	0.7	-	-	-	-	44.5	0.2
1966	-	-	-	-	45.1	1.3	-	-	-	-	45.4	0.7	-	-	-	-	45.6	0.4	-	-	-	-	46.0	0.9
1967	-	-	-	-	46.9	2.0	-	-	-	-	47.4	1.1	-	-	-	-	48.2	1.7	-	-	-	-	48.0	-0.4
1968	-	-	-	-	48.6	1.2	-	-	-	-	49.5	1.9	-	-	-	-	50.5	2.0	-	-	-	-	51.0	1.0
1969	-	-	-	-	52.3	2.5	-	-	-	-	53.5	2.3	-	-	-	-	54.9	2.6	-	-	-	-	55.3	0.7
1970	-	-	-	-	55.7	0.7	-	-	-	-	56.3	1.1	-	-	-	-	57.1	1.4	-	-	-	-	58.3	2.1
1971	-	-	-	-	58.6	0.5	-	-	-	-	57.8	-1.4	-	-	-	-	59.2	2.4	-	-	-	-	59.0	-0.3
1972	-	-	-	-	59.0	0.0	-	-	-	-	58.1	-1.5	-	-	-	-	59.1	1.7	-	-	-	-	58.9	-0.3
1973	-	-	-	-	60.5	2.7	-	-	-	-	61.4	1.5	-	-	-	-	63.4	3.3	-	-	-	-	64.3	1.4
1974	-	-	-	-	65.6	2.0	-	-	-	-	66.7	1.7	-	-	-	-	68.4	2.5	-	-	-	-	69.3	1.3
1975	-	-	-	-	70.0	1.0	-	-	-	-	69.7	-0.4	-	-	-	-	70.7	1.4	-	-	-	-	70.4	-0.4
1976	-	-	-	-	72.0	2.3	-	-	-	-	73.0	1.4	-	-	-	-	74.3	1.8	-	-	-	-	75.0	0.9
1977	-	-	-	-	75.9	1.2	-	-	-	-	77.3	1.8	-	-	-	-	78.3	1.3	-	-	-	-	78.3	0.0
1978	-	-	-	-	81.0	3.4	-	-	83.4	3.0	-	-	76.5	-8.3	-	-	82.1	7.3	-	-	81.9	-0.2	-	-
1979	77.5	-5.4	-	-	83.2	7.4	-	-	84.2	1.2	-	-	80.4	-4.5	-	-	85.1	5.8	-	-	86.9	2.1	-	-
1980	85.0	-2.2	-	-	92.5	8.8	-	-	94.2	1.8	-	-	93.3	-1.0	-	-	95.3	2.1	-	-	97.2	2.0	-	-
1981	94.6	-2.7	-	-	98.5	4.1	-	-	98.2	-0.3	-	-	96.2	-2.0	-	-	96.5	0.3	-	-	96.5	0.0	-	-
1982	92.4	-4.2	-	-	98.7	6.8	-	-	99.1	0.4	-	-	95.5	-3.6	-	-	100.9	5.7	-	-	101.2	0.3	-	-
1983	98.4	-2.8	-	-	99.0	0.6	-	-	101.6	2.6	-	-	101.4	-0.2	-	-	99.3	-2.1	-	-	103.2	3.9	-	-
1984	99.4	-3.7	-	-	101.7	2.3	-	-	101.5	-0.2	-	-	98.5	-3.0	-	-	103.6	5.2	-	-	103.2	-0.4	-	-
1985	98.2	-4.8	-	-	106.5	8.5	-	-	106.6	0.1	-	-	103.9	-2.5	-	-	111.2	7.0	-	-	109.3	-1.7	-	-
1986	106.9	-2.2	-	-	111.5	4.3	-	-	112.3	0.7	-	-	108.5	-3.4	-	-	112.6	3.8	-	-	112.9	0.3	-	-
1987	106.2	-5.9	-	-	120.4	13.4	-	-	120.2	-0.2	-	-	123.0	2.3	-	-	124.4	1.1	-	-	121.2	-2.6	-	-
1988	118.0	-2.6	-	-	129.2	9.5	-	-	123.0	-4.8	-	-	133.1	8.2	-	-	140.1	5.3	-	-	136.0	-2.9	-	-
1989	124.2	-8.7	-	-	136.1	9.6	-	-	130.1	-4.4	-	-	123.1	-5.4	-	-	129.4	5.1	-	-	127.2	-1.7	-	-
1990	112.2	-11.8	-	-	136.6	21.7	-	-	130.9	-4.2	-	-	118.1	-9.8	-	-	137.3	16.3	-	-	130.0	-5.3	-	-
1991	129.2	-0.6	-	-	135.6	5.0	-	-	134.4	-0.9	-	-	129.7	-3.5	-	-	134.4	3.6	-	-	133.8	-0.4	-	-
1992	129.9	-2.9	-	-	142.4	9.6	-	-	140.3	-1.5	-	-	128.4	-8.5	-	-	136.7	6.5	-	-	133.7	-2.2	-	-
1993	130.7	-2.2	-	-	140.3	7.3	-	-	141.9	1.1	-	-	133.6	-5.8	-	-	137.4	2.8	-	-	133.1	-3.1	-	-
1994	124.7	-6.3	-	-	134.7	8.0	-	-	140.6	4.4	-	-	132.9	-5.5	-	-	139.9	5.3	-	-	137.1	-2.0	-	-
1995	132.8	-3.1	-	-	140.1	5.5	-	-	136.1	-2.9	-	-	127.4	-6.4	-	-	124.1	-2.6	-	-	126.3	1.8	-	-

Source: U.S. Department of Labor, Bureau of Labor Statistics, Division of Consumer Prices and Price Indexes. - indicates no data collected for period.

Baltimore, MD
Consumer Price Index - Urban Wage Earners
Base 1982-1984 = 100
Apparel and Upkeep

For 1952-1995. Columns headed % show percentile change in the index from the previous period for which an index is available.

Year	Jan Index	%	Feb Index	%	Mar Index	%	Apr Index	%	May Index	%	Jun Index	%	Jul Index	%	Aug Index	%	Sep Index	%	Oct Index	%	Nov Index	%	Dec Index	%
1952	-	-	-	-	-	-	-	-	-	-	-	-	-	-	-	-	-	-	-	-	-	-	38.8	-
1953	-	-	-	-	38.9	0.3	-	-	-	-	39.3	1.0	-	-	-	-	39.1	-0.5	-	-	-	-	38.7	-1.0
1954	-	-	-	-	38.7	0.0	-	-	-	-	38.7	0.0	-	-	-	-	39.1	1.0	-	-	-	-	38.9	-0.5
1955	-	-	-	-	38.7	-0.5	-	-	-	-	38.8	0.3	-	-	-	-	38.7	-0.3	-	-	-	-	39.2	1.3
1956	-	-	-	-	39.6	1.0	-	-	-	-	40.2	1.5	-	-	-	-	40.8	1.5	-	-	-	-	40.7	-0.2
1957	-	-	-	-	40.5	-0.5	-	-	-	-	40.9	1.0	-	-	-	-	41.8	2.2	-	-	-	-	41.4	-1.0
1958	-	-	-	-	41.6	0.5	-	-	-	-	41.6	0.0	-	-	-	-	41.8	0.5	-	-	-	-	41.3	-1.2
1959	-	-	-	-	42.2	2.2	-	-	-	-	42.3	0.2	-	-	-	-	43.0	1.7	-	-	-	-	42.9	-0.2
1960	-	-	-	-	43.0	0.2	-	-	-	-	42.9	-0.2	-	-	-	-	43.6	1.6	-	-	-	-	43.4	-0.5
1961	-	-	-	-	44.0	1.4	-	-	-	-	43.9	-0.2	-	-	-	-	44.0	0.2	-	-	-	-	43.8	-0.5
1962	-	-	-	-	43.9	0.2	-	-	-	-	43.9	0.0	-	-	-	-	44.6	1.6	-	-	-	-	44.5	-0.2
1963	-	-	-	-	44.6	0.2	-	-	-	-	44.6	0.0	-	-	-	-	44.6	0.0	-	-	-	-	44.6	0.0
1964	-	-	-	-	44.3	-0.7	-	-	-	-	44.5	0.5	-	-	-	-	44.7	0.4	-	-	-	-	44.8	0.2
1965	-	-	-	-	44.7	-0.2	-	-	-	-	45.1	0.9	-	-	-	-	45.4	0.7	-	-	-	-	45.5	0.2
1966	-	-	-	-	46.1	1.3	-	-	-	-	46.5	0.9	-	-	-	-	46.7	0.4	-	-	-	-	47.0	0.6
1967	-	-	-	-	48.0	2.1	-	-	-	-	48.5	1.0	-	-	-	-	49.3	1.6	-	-	-	-	49.1	-0.4
1968	-	-	-	-	49.8	1.4	-	-	-	-	50.7	1.8	-	-	-	-	51.7	2.0	-	-	-	-	52.2	1.0
1969	-	-	-	-	53.5	2.5	-	-	-	-	54.8	2.4	-	-	-	-	56.1	2.4	-	-	-	-	56.6	0.9
1970	-	-	-	-	57.0	0.7	-	-	-	-	57.6	1.1	-	-	-	-	58.5	1.6	-	-	-	-	59.7	2.1
1971	-	-	-	-	60.0	0.5	-	-	-	-	59.2	-1.3	-	-	-	-	60.5	2.2	-	-	-	-	60.3	-0.3
1972	-	-	-	-	60.4	0.2	-	-	-	-	59.5	-1.5	-	-	-	-	60.4	1.5	-	-	-	-	60.3	-0.2
1973	-	-	-	-	62.0	2.8	-	-	-	-	62.8	1.3	-	-	-	-	64.9	3.3	-	-	-	-	65.7	1.2
1974	-	-	-	-	67.1	2.1	-	-	-	-	68.3	1.8	-	-	-	-	70.0	2.5	-	-	-	-	70.9	1.3
1975	-	-	-	-	71.6	1.0	-	-	-	-	71.3	-0.4	-	-	-	-	72.3	1.4	-	-	-	-	72.1	-0.3
1976	-	-	-	-	73.7	2.2	-	-	-	-	74.7	1.4	-	-	-	-	76.0	1.7	-	-	-	-	76.8	1.1
1977	-	-	-	-	77.6	1.0	-	-	-	-	79.1	1.9	-	-	-	-	80.1	1.3	-	-	-	-	80.1	0.0
1978	-	-	-	-	82.9	3.5	-	-	83.8	1.1	-	-	80.5	-3.9	-	-	82.9	3.0	-	-	83.2	0.4	-	-
1979	80.2	-3.6	-	-	83.9	4.6	-	-	85.6	2.0	-	-	81.9	-4.3	-	-	85.2	4.0	-	-	85.5	0.4	-	-
1980	85.4	-0.1	-	-	90.9	6.4	-	-	91.3	0.4	-	-	90.4	-1.0	-	-	92.9	2.8	-	-	94.4	1.6	-	-
1981	95.0	0.6	-	-	96.7	1.8	-	-	97.0	0.3	-	-	94.9	-2.2	-	-	96.4	1.6	-	-	95.9	-0.5	-	-
1982	92.5	-3.5	-	-	98.4	6.4	-	-	98.9	0.5	-	-	95.5	-3.4	-	-	99.4	4.1	-	-	99.7	0.3	-	-
1983	98.0	-1.7	-	-	99.5	1.5	-	-	102.0	2.5	-	-	101.1	-0.9	-	-	99.1	-2.0	-	-	103.5	4.4	-	-
1984	100.8	-2.6	-	-	101.7	0.9	-	-	102.1	0.4	-	-	99.0	-3.0	-	-	103.7	4.7	-	-	103.5	-0.2	-	-
1985	99.0	-4.3	-	-	107.1	8.2	-	-	106.9	-0.2	-	-	105.2	-1.6	-	-	110.5	5.0	-	-	109.0	-1.4	-	-
1986	106.8	-2.0	-	-	111.0	3.9	-	-	111.6	0.5	-	-	107.8	-3.4	-	-	110.8	2.8	-	-	112.0	1.1	-	-
1987	105.9	-5.4	-	-	120.2	13.5	-	-	119.5	-0.6	-	-	122.7	2.7	-	-	124.3	1.3	-	-	119.5	-3.9	-	-
1988	116.0	-2.9	-	-	128.2	10.5	-	-	120.6	-5.9	-	-	133.0	10.3	-	-	139.0	4.5	-	-	135.4	-2.6	-	-
1989	122.0	-9.9	-	-	135.1	10.7	-	-	127.8	-5.4	-	-	120.5	-5.7	-	-	127.7	6.0	-	-	126.0	-1.3	-	-
1990	110.6	-12.2	-	-	133.6	20.8	-	-	128.3	-4.0	-	-	115.8	-9.7	-	-	134.6	16.2	-	-	126.7	-5.9	-	-
1991	126.1	-0.5	-	-	133.3	5.7	-	-	131.6	-1.3	-	-	127.0	-3.5	-	-	133.8	5.4	-	-	132.6	-0.9	-	-
1992	129.0	-2.7	-	-	141.9	10.0	-	-	140.2	-1.2	-	-	128.3	-8.5	-	-	137.4	7.1	-	-	135.8	-1.2	-	-
1993	131.6	-3.1	-	-	141.0	7.1	-	-	142.3	0.9	-	-	133.2	-6.4	-	-	138.3	3.8	-	-	131.7	-4.8	-	-
1994	121.2	-8.0	-	-	134.1	10.6	-	-	139.0	3.7	-	-	131.6	-5.3	-	-	138.2	5.0	-	-	134.6	-2.6	-	-
1995	130.4	-3.1	-	-	137.4	5.4	-	-	133.6	-2.8	-	-	123.9	-7.3	-	-	120.9	-2.4	-	-	122.7	1.5	-	-

Source: U.S. Department of Labor, Bureau of Labor Statistics, Division of Consumer Prices and Price Indexes. - indicates no data collected for period.

Baltimore, MD
Consumer Price Index - All Urban Consumers
Base 1982-1984 = 100
Transportation

For 1947-1995. Columns headed % show percentile change in the index from the previous period for which an index is available.

Year	Jan Index	%	Feb Index	%	Mar Index	%	Apr Index	%	May Index	%	Jun Index	%	Jul Index	%	Aug Index	%	Sep Index	%	Oct Index	%	Nov Index	%	Dec Index	%
1947	16.9	-	16.8	-0.6	16.8	0.0	17.0	1.2	17.0	0.0	17.0	0.0	-	-	-	-	17.8	4.7	-	-	-	-	17.9	0.6
1948	-	-	-	-	18.4	2.8	-	-	-	-	18.4	0.0	-	-	-	-	19.5	6.0	-	-	-	-	19.6	0.5
1949	-	-	-	-	22.0	12.2	-	-	-	-	22.1	0.5	-	-	-	-	22.1	0.0	-	-	-	-	22.0	-0.5
1950	-	-	-	-	22.0	0.0	-	-	-	-	21.9	-0.5	-	-	-	-	23.7	8.2	-	-	-	-	23.7	0.0
1951	-	-	-	-	23.9	0.8	-	-	-	-	23.9	0.0	-	-	-	-	24.5	2.5	-	-	-	-	24.7	0.8
1952	-	-	-	-	24.9	0.8	-	-	-	-	24.9	0.0	-	-	-	-	26.7	7.2	-	-	-	-	26.7	0.0
1953	-	-	-	-	26.7	0.0	-	-	-	-	26.8	0.4	-	-	-	-	27.1	1.1	-	-	-	-	27.0	-0.4
1954	-	-	-	-	26.7	-1.1	-	-	-	-	26.7	0.0	-	-	-	-	26.2	-1.9	-	-	-	-	26.9	2.7
1955	-	-	-	-	26.4	-1.9	-	-	-	-	26.5	0.4	-	-	-	-	26.2	-1.1	-	-	-	-	26.2	0.0
1956	-	-	-	-	26.4	0.8	-	-	-	-	26.5	0.4	-	-	-	-	27.1	2.3	-	-	-	-	28.1	3.7
1957	-	-	-	-	28.5	1.4	-	-	-	-	28.4	-0.4	-	-	-	-	28.6	0.7	-	-	-	-	29.1	1.7
1958	-	-	-	-	28.9	-0.7	-	-	-	-	28.6	-1.0	-	-	-	-	29.4	2.8	-	-	-	-	30.8	4.8
1959	-	-	-	-	30.8	0.0	-	-	-	-	30.9	0.3	-	-	-	-	31.2	1.0	-	-	-	-	31.5	1.0
1960	-	-	-	-	31.3	-0.6	-	-	-	-	30.9	-1.3	-	-	-	-	30.5	-1.3	-	-	-	-	30.8	1.0
1961	-	-	-	-	31.0	0.6	-	-	-	-	31.4	1.3	-	-	-	-	31.8	1.3	-	-	-	-	31.7	-0.3
1962	-	-	-	-	31.5	-0.6	-	-	-	-	30.9	-1.9	-	-	-	-	31.5	1.9	-	-	-	-	31.6	0.3
1963	-	-	-	-	31.7	0.3	-	-	-	-	32.0	0.9	-	-	-	-	32.2	0.6	-	-	-	-	32.6	1.2
1964	-	-	-	-	32.5	-0.3	-	-	-	-	32.9	1.2	-	-	-	-	32.8	-0.3	-	-	-	-	33.2	1.2
1965	-	-	-	-	33.3	0.3	-	-	-	-	33.2	-0.3	-	-	-	-	33.3	0.3	-	-	-	-	33.6	0.9
1966	-	-	-	-	33.5	-0.3	-	-	-	-	33.7	0.6	-	-	-	-	33.7	0.0	-	-	-	-	33.7	0.0
1967	-	-	-	-	33.9	0.6	-	-	-	-	34.2	0.9	-	-	-	-	34.4	0.6	-	-	-	-	34.9	1.5
1968	-	-	-	-	34.9	0.0	-	-	-	-	35.4	1.4	-	-	-	-	35.5	0.3	-	-	-	-	36.4	2.5
1969	-	-	-	-	37.2	2.2	-	-	-	-	37.6	1.1	-	-	-	-	37.3	-0.8	-	-	-	-	37.8	1.3
1970	-	-	-	-	37.7	-0.3	-	-	-	-	38.6	2.4	-	-	-	-	38.5	-0.3	-	-	-	-	39.8	3.4
1971	-	-	-	-	39.8	0.0	-	-	-	-	40.7	2.3	-	-	-	-	40.4	-0.7	-	-	-	-	40.3	-0.2
1972	-	-	-	-	39.5	-2.0	-	-	-	-	39.8	0.8	-	-	-	-	40.3	1.3	-	-	-	-	40.4	0.2
1973	-	-	-	-	40.7	0.7	-	-	-	-	41.5	2.0	-	-	-	-	41.4	-0.2	-	-	-	-	42.3	2.2
1974	-	-	-	-	44.3	4.7	-	-	-	-	46.3	4.5	-	-	-	-	47.7	3.0	-	-	-	-	48.2	1.0
1975	-	-	-	-	48.7	1.0	-	-	-	-	50.1	2.9	-	-	-	-	51.2	2.2	-	-	-	-	51.6	0.8
1976	-	-	-	-	52.8	2.3	-	-	-	-	54.9	4.0	-	-	-	-	55.6	1.3	-	-	-	-	56.0	0.7
1977	-	-	-	-	56.9	1.6	-	-	-	-	58.5	2.8	-	-	-	-	58.1	-0.7	-	-	-	-	58.0	-0.2
1978	-	-	-	-	58.2	0.3	-	-	59.4	2.1	-	-	60.5	1.9	-	-	60.9	0.7	-	-	62.3	2.3	-	-
1979	63.0	1.1	-	-	64.3	2.1	-	-	66.9	4.0	-	-	70.2	4.9	-	-	71.6	2.0	-	-	73.8	3.1	-	-
1980	76.8	4.1	-	-	80.6	4.9	-	-	81.7	1.4	-	-	83.1	1.7	-	-	84.0	1.1	-	-	85.0	1.2	-	-
1981	87.1	2.5	-	-	90.1	3.4	-	-	91.6	1.7	-	-	93.1	1.6	-	-	93.3	0.2	-	-	94.6	1.4	-	-
1982	95.5	1.0	-	-	94.4	-1.2	-	-	94.1	-0.3	-	-	97.3	3.4	-	-	97.3	0.0	-	-	96.9	-0.4	-	-
1983	97.4	0.5	-	-	96.4	-1.0	-	-	98.1	1.8	-	-	99.8	1.7	-	-	102.4	2.6	-	-	103.2	0.8	-	-
1984	102.7	-0.5	-	-	103.2	0.5	-	-	103.8	0.6	-	-	104.8	1.0	-	-	105.1	0.3	-	-	105.5	0.4	-	-
1985	105.2	-0.3	-	-	105.9	0.7	-	-	107.7	1.7	-	-	107.7	0.0	-	-	107.5	-0.2	-	-	108.7	1.1	-	-
1986	110.0	1.2	-	-	106.8	-2.9	-	-	103.5	-3.1	-	-	103.0	-0.5	-	-	102.5	-0.5	-	-	102.8	0.3	-	-
1987	104.1	1.3	-	-	104.5	0.4	-	-	105.3	0.8	-	-	108.2	2.8	-	-	108.5	0.3	-	-	109.3	0.7	-	-
1988	110.1	0.7	-	-	109.5	-0.5	-	-	110.6	1.0	-	-	111.3	0.6	-	-	112.4	1.0	-	-	113.9	1.3	-	-
1989	114.1	0.2	-	-	114.8	0.6	-	-	117.9	2.7	-	-	117.5	-0.3	-	-	117.0	-0.4	-	-	118.6	1.4	-	-
1990	121.2	2.2	-	-	119.9	-1.1	-	-	119.5	-0.3	-	-	120.4	0.8	-	-	124.6	3.5	-	-	129.8	4.2	-	-
1991	128.0	-1.4	-	-	123.1	-3.8	-	-	124.4	1.1	-	-	124.5	0.1	-	-	125.7	1.0	-	-	127.4	1.4	-	-

[Continued]

Baltimore, MD
Consumer Price Index - All Urban Consumers
Base 1982-1984 = 100
Transportation
[Continued]

For 1947-1995. Columns headed % show percentile change in the index from the previous period for which an index is available.

Year	Jan Index	%	Feb Index	%	Mar Index	%	Apr Index	%	May Index	%	Jun Index	%	Jul Index	%	Aug Index	%	Sep Index	%	Oct Index	%	Nov Index	%	Dec Index	%
1992	127.1	-0.2	-	-	126.7	-0.3	-	-	127.7	0.8	-	-	129.0	1.0	-	-	129.0	0.0	-	-	130.8	1.4	-	-
1993	130.2	-0.5	-	-	129.0	-0.9	-	-	129.8	0.6	-	-	129.5	-0.2	-	-	128.6	-0.7	-	-	131.0	1.9	-	-
1994	129.7	-1.0	-	-	129.4	-0.2	-	-	130.4	0.8	-	-	132.7	1.8	-	-	128.6	-0.7	-	-	131.0	1.9	-	-
1995	138.3	0.7	-	-	138.6	0.2	-	-	139.1	0.4	-	-	138.7	-0.3	-	-	136.7	-1.4	-	-	139.1	1.8	-	-

Source: U.S. Department of Labor, Bureau of Labor Statistics, Division of Consumer Prices and Price Indexes. - indicates no data collected for period.

Baltimore, MD
Consumer Price Index - Urban Wage Earners
Base 1982-1984 = 100
Transportation

For 1947-1995. Columns headed % show percentile change in the index from the previous period for which an index is available.

Year	Jan Index	%	Feb Index	%	Mar Index	%	Apr Index	%	May Index	%	Jun Index	%	Jul Index	%	Aug Index	%	Sep Index	%	Oct Index	%	Nov Index	%	Dec Index	%
1947	16.8	-	16.7	-0.6	16.7	0.0	16.9	1.2	16.9	0.0	16.9	0.0	-	-	-	-	17.7	4.7	-	-	-	-	17.8	0.6
1948	-	-	-	-	18.3	2.8	-	-	-	-	18.3	0.0	-	-	-	-	19.4	6.0	-	-	-	-	19.5	0.5
1949	-	-	-	-	21.9	12.3	-	-	-	-	21.9	0.0	-	-	-	-	21.9	0.0	-	-	-	-	21.9	0.0
1950	-	-	-	-	21.9	0.0	-	-	-	-	21.7	-0.9	-	-	-	-	23.5	8.3	-	-	-	-	23.6	0.4
1951	-	-	-	-	23.7	0.4	-	-	-	-	23.8	0.4	-	-	-	-	24.3	2.1	-	-	-	-	24.6	1.2
1952	-	-	-	-	24.8	0.8	-	-	-	-	24.8	0.0	-	-	-	-	26.6	7.3	-	-	-	-	26.6	0.0
1953	-	-	-	-	26.5	-0.4	-	-	-	-	26.7	0.8	-	-	-	-	26.9	0.7	-	-	-	-	26.8	-0.4
1954	-	-	-	-	26.6	-0.7	-	-	-	-	26.5	-0.4	-	-	-	-	26.0	-1.9	-	-	-	-	26.7	2.7
1955	-	-	-	-	26.3	-1.5	-	-	-	-	26.3	0.0	-	-	-	-	26.1	-0.8	-	-	-	-	26.0	-0.4
1956	-	-	-	-	26.3	1.2	-	-	-	-	26.4	0.4	-	-	-	-	26.9	1.9	-	-	-	-	27.9	3.7
1957	-	-	-	-	28.3	1.4	-	-	-	-	28.2	-0.4	-	-	-	-	28.4	0.7	-	-	-	-	28.9	1.8
1958	-	-	-	-	28.8	-0.3	-	-	-	-	28.5	-1.0	-	-	-	-	29.3	2.8	-	-	-	-	30.6	4.4
1959	-	-	-	-	30.6	0.0	-	-	-	-	30.7	0.3	-	-	-	-	31.0	1.0	-	-	-	-	31.3	1.0
1960	-	-	-	-	31.1	-0.6	-	-	-	-	30.7	-1.3	-	-	-	-	30.3	-1.3	-	-	-	-	30.6	1.0
1961	-	-	-	-	30.8	0.7	-	-	-	-	31.2	1.3	-	-	-	-	31.6	1.3	-	-	-	-	31.5	-0.3
1962	-	-	-	-	31.3	-0.6	-	-	-	-	30.7	-1.9	-	-	-	-	31.3	2.0	-	-	-	-	31.4	0.3
1963	-	-	-	-	31.5	0.3	-	-	-	-	31.8	1.0	-	-	-	-	32.0	0.6	-	-	-	-	32.4	1.3
1964	-	-	-	-	32.3	-0.3	-	-	-	-	32.7	1.2	-	-	-	-	32.6	-0.3	-	-	-	-	33.0	1.2
1965	-	-	-	-	33.1	0.3	-	-	-	-	33.0	-0.3	-	-	-	-	33.1	0.3	-	-	-	-	33.4	0.9
1966	-	-	-	-	33.3	-0.3	-	-	-	-	33.5	0.6	-	-	-	-	33.5	0.0	-	-	-	-	33.5	0.0
1967	-	-	-	-	33.7	0.6	-	-	-	-	34.0	0.9	-	-	-	-	34.2	0.6	-	-	-	-	34.7	1.5
1968	-	-	-	-	34.7	0.0	-	-	-	-	35.2	1.4	-	-	-	-	35.3	0.3	-	-	-	-	36.2	2.5
1969	-	-	-	-	37.0	2.2	-	-	-	-	37.4	1.1	-	-	-	-	37.1	-0.8	-	-	-	-	37.5	1.1
1970	-	-	-	-	37.5	0.0	-	-	-	-	38.4	2.4	-	-	-	-	38.3	-0.3	-	-	-	-	39.6	3.4
1971	-	-	-	-	39.6	0.0	-	-	-	-	40.4	2.0	-	-	-	-	40.1	-0.7	-	-	-	-	40.0	-0.2
1972	-	-	-	-	39.3	-1.7	-	-	-	-	39.5	0.5	-	-	-	-	40.0	1.3	-	-	-	-	40.1	0.2
1973	-	-	-	-	40.5	1.0	-	-	-	-	41.3	2.0	-	-	-	-	41.2	-0.2	-	-	-	-	42.1	2.2
1974	-	-	-	-	44.0	4.5	-	-	-	-	46.0	4.5	-	-	-	-	47.4	3.0	-	-	-	-	47.9	1.1
1975	-	-	-	-	48.5	1.3	-	-	-	-	49.8	2.7	-	-	-	-	50.9	2.2	-	-	-	-	51.3	0.8
1976	-	-	-	-	52.5	2.3	-	-	-	-	54.6	4.0	-	-	-	-	55.2	1.1	-	-	-	-	55.6	0.7
1977	-	-	-	-	56.6	1.8	-	-	-	-	58.2	2.8	-	-	-	-	57.8	-0.7	-	-	-	-	57.6	-0.3
1978	-	-	-	-	57.9	0.5	-	-	59.1	2.1	-	-	60.4	2.2	-	-	60.8	0.7	-	-	61.5	1.2	-	-
1979	62.2	1.1	-	-	63.5	2.1	-	-	66.2	4.3	-	-	69.2	4.5	-	-	70.7	2.2	-	-	72.7	2.8	-	-
1980	75.2	3.4	-	-	78.7	4.7	-	-	79.8	1.4	-	-	81.2	1.8	-	-	82.1	1.1	-	-	84.1	2.4	-	-
1981	86.0	2.3	-	-	89.0	3.5	-	-	90.1	1.2	-	-	92.1	2.2	-	-	92.6	0.5	-	-	94.0	1.5	-	-
1982	94.7	0.7	-	-	93.7	-1.1	-	-	93.4	-0.3	-	-	96.9	3.7	-	-	97.0	0.1	-	-	96.7	-0.3	-	-
1983	97.1	0.4	-	-	96.1	-1.0	-	-	97.9	1.9	-	-	99.9	2.0	-	-	102.4	2.5	-	-	103.4	1.0	-	-
1984	102.9	-0.5	-	-	103.4	0.5	-	-	104.5	1.1	-	-	105.4	0.9	-	-	105.7	0.3	-	-	106.0	0.3	-	-
1985	105.8	-0.2	-	-	106.3	0.5	-	-	107.9	1.5	-	-	107.9	0.0	-	-	107.7	-0.2	-	-	108.7	0.9	-	-
1986	109.8	1.0	-	-	106.8	-2.7	-	-	103.2	-3.4	-	-	102.8	-0.4	-	-	102.2	-0.6	-	-	102.4	0.2	-	-
1987	103.7	1.3	-	-	104.4	0.7	-	-	105.5	1.1	-	-	108.9	3.2	-	-	109.4	0.5	-	-	109.9	0.5	-	-
1988	110.8	0.8	-	-	110.5	-0.3	-	-	111.3	0.7	-	-	112.3	0.9	-	-	113.4	1.0	-	-	114.5	1.0	-	-
1989	114.7	0.2	-	-	115.3	0.5	-	-	118.9	3.1	-	-	118.5	-0.3	-	-	117.8	-0.6	-	-	119.4	1.4	-	-
1990	122.0	2.2	-	-	120.5	-1.2	-	-	120.2	-0.2	-	-	120.9	0.6	-	-	125.6	3.9	-	-	131.0	4.3	-	-
1991	128.6	-1.8	-	-	123.2	-4.2	-	-	124.7	1.2	-	-	125.0	0.2	-	-	126.4	1.1	-	-	127.9	1.2	-	-

[Continued]

Baltimore, MD
Consumer Price Index - Urban Wage Earners
Base 1982-1984 = 100
Transportation
[Continued]

For 1947-1995. Columns headed % show percentile change in the index from the previous period for which an index is available.

Year	Jan Index	%	Feb Index	%	Mar Index	%	Apr Index	%	May Index	%	Jun Index	%	Jul Index	%	Aug Index	%	Sep Index	%	Oct Index	%	Nov Index	%	Dec Index	%
1992	127.3	-0.5	-	-	126.6	-0.5	-	-	128.2	1.3	-	-	130.1	1.5	-	-	130.1	0.0	-	-	131.7	1.2	-	-
1993	130.9	-0.6	-	-	129.3	-1.2	-	-	130.2	0.7	-	-	129.8	-0.3	-	-	128.8	-0.8	-	-	131.4	2.0	-	-
1994	130.1	-1.0	-	-	129.6	-0.4	-	-	131.0	1.1	-	-	133.2	1.7	-	-	136.0	2.1	-	-	138.2	1.6	-	-
1995	139.0	0.6	-	-	139.5	0.4	-	-	140.5	0.7	-	-	140.2	-0.2	-	-	138.1	-1.5	-	-	139.7	1.2	-	-

Source: U.S. Department of Labor, Bureau of Labor Statistics, Division of Consumer Prices and Price Indexes. - indicates no data collected for period.

Baltimore, MD
Consumer Price Index - All Urban Consumers
Base 1982-1984 = 100
Medical Care

For 1947-1995. Columns headed % show percentile change in the index from the previous period for which an index is available.

Year	Jan Index	%	Feb Index	%	Mar Index	%	Apr Index	%	May Index	%	Jun Index	%	Jul Index	%	Aug Index	%	Sep Index	%	Oct Index	%	Nov Index	%	Dec Index	%
1947	12.5	-	12.6	0.8	12.6	0.0	12.6	0.0	12.7	0.8	12.8	0.8	-	-	-	-	13.1	2.3	-	-	-	-	13.2	0.8
1948	-	-	-	-	13.2	0.0	-	-	-	-	13.4	1.5	-	-	-	-	13.4	0.0	-	-	-	-	13.4	0.0
1949	-	-	-	-	13.4	0.0	-	-	-	-	13.4	0.0	-	-	-	-	13.4	0.0	-	-	-	-	13.5	0.7
1950	-	-	-	-	13.6	0.7	-	-	-	-	13.6	0.0	-	-	-	-	13.7	0.7	-	-	-	-	13.8	0.7
1951	-	-	-	-	14.3	3.6	-	-	-	-	14.9	4.2	-	-	-	-	14.9	0.0	-	-	-	-	15.9	6.7
1952	-	-	-	-	16.4	3.1	-	-	-	-	16.5	0.6	-	-	-	-	16.5	0.0	-	-	-	-	16.5	0.0
1953	-	-	-	-	17.4	5.5	-	-	-	-	17.4	0.0	-	-	-	-	17.5	0.6	-	-	-	-	17.5	0.0
1954	-	-	-	-	17.6	0.6	-	-	-	-	17.6	0.0	-	-	-	-	17.6	0.0	-	-	-	-	17.6	0.0
1955	-	-	-	-	17.7	0.6	-	-	-	-	17.7	0.0	-	-	-	-	17.8	0.6	-	-	-	-	18.0	1.1
1956	-	-	-	-	18.0	0.0	-	-	-	-	18.8	4.4	-	-	-	-	18.9	0.5	-	-	-	-	19.0	0.5
1957	-	-	-	-	19.1	0.5	-	-	-	-	19.1	0.0	-	-	-	-	19.1	0.0	-	-	-	-	19.1	0.0
1958	-	-	-	-	19.3	1.0	-	-	-	-	19.6	1.6	-	-	-	-	19.7	0.5	-	-	-	-	20.6	4.6
1959	-	-	-	-	20.7	0.5	-	-	-	-	20.9	1.0	-	-	-	-	21.0	0.5	-	-	-	-	21.8	3.8
1960	-	-	-	-	22.0	0.9	-	-	-	-	22.1	0.5	-	-	-	-	22.3	0.9	-	-	-	-	23.0	3.1
1961	-	-	-	-	23.2	0.9	-	-	-	-	23.2	0.0	-	-	-	-	23.3	0.4	-	-	-	-	23.4	0.4
1962	-	-	-	-	23.6	0.9	-	-	-	-	23.7	0.4	-	-	-	-	23.9	0.8	-	-	-	-	23.9	0.0
1963	-	-	-	-	25.0	4.6	-	-	-	-	25.3	1.2	-	-	-	-	25.4	0.4	-	-	-	-	25.5	0.4
1964	-	-	-	-	25.6	0.4	-	-	-	-	25.8	0.8	-	-	-	-	25.9	0.4	-	-	-	-	26.1	0.8
1965	-	-	-	-	26.2	0.4	-	-	-	-	26.3	0.4	-	-	-	-	26.6	1.1	-	-	-	-	26.8	0.8
1966	-	-	-	-	27.0	0.7	-	-	-	-	27.5	1.9	-	-	-	-	27.9	1.5	-	-	-	-	28.2	1.1
1967	-	-	-	-	29.5	4.6	-	-	-	-	29.7	0.7	-	-	-	-	30.3	2.0	-	-	-	-	30.5	0.7
1968	-	-	-	-	31.3	2.6	-	-	-	-	31.4	0.3	-	-	-	-	31.9	1.6	-	-	-	-	32.0	0.3
1969	-	-	-	-	33.0	3.1	-	-	-	-	33.2	0.6	-	-	-	-	34.5	3.9	-	-	-	-	34.5	0.0
1970	-	-	-	-	35.8	3.8	-	-	-	-	36.4	1.7	-	-	-	-	37.3	2.5	-	-	-	-	38.5	3.2
1971	-	-	-	-	39.5	2.6	-	-	-	-	40.3	2.0	-	-	-	-	41.7	3.5	-	-	-	-	41.6	-0.2
1972	-	-	-	-	41.8	0.5	-	-	-	-	42.4	1.4	-	-	-	-	43.1	1.7	-	-	-	-	43.4	0.7
1973	-	-	-	-	43.7	0.7	-	-	-	-	43.9	0.5	-	-	-	-	44.6	1.6	-	-	-	-	46.3	3.8
1974	-	-	-	-	46.9	1.3	-	-	-	-	49.5	5.5	-	-	-	-	50.7	2.4	-	-	-	-	51.4	1.4
1975	-	-	-	-	53.1	3.3	-	-	-	-	53.8	1.3	-	-	-	-	54.6	1.5	-	-	-	-	54.7	0.2
1976	-	-	-	-	56.0	2.4	-	-	-	-	58.0	3.6	-	-	-	-	58.1	0.2	-	-	-	-	59.4	2.2
1977	-	-	-	-	61.3	3.2	-	-	-	-	61.9	1.0	-	-	-	-	62.5	1.0	-	-	-	-	63.1	1.0
1978	-	-	-	-	64.3	1.9	-	-	65.0	1.1	-	-	66.1	1.7	-	-	66.7	0.9	-	-	67.6	1.3	-	-
1979	68.5	1.3	-	-	70.4	2.8	-	-	70.8	0.6	-	-	72.0	1.7	-	-	74.3	3.2	-	-	75.3	1.3	-	-
1980	76.1	1.1	-	-	77.5	1.8	-	-	79.6	2.7	-	-	79.0	-0.8	-	-	80.3	1.6	-	-	81.0	0.9	-	-
1981	81.4	0.5	-	-	83.2	2.2	-	-	84.3	1.3	-	-	85.1	0.9	-	-	87.1	2.4	-	-	86.8	-0.3	-	-
1982	89.3	2.9	-	-	91.4	2.4	-	-	92.7	1.4	-	-	94.0	1.4	-	-	96.8	3.0	-	-	97.5	0.7	-	-
1983	98.7	1.2	-	-	99.2	0.5	-	-	99.5	0.3	-	-	101.2	1.7	-	-	101.6	0.4	-	-	102.9	1.3	-	-
1984	102.7	-0.2	-	-	103.5	0.8	-	-	104.2	0.7	-	-	106.8	2.5	-	-	106.3	-0.5	-	-	107.3	0.9	-	-
1985	108.1	0.7	-	-	109.0	0.8	-	-	110.5	1.4	-	-	111.6	1.0	-	-	113.7	1.9	-	-	115.6	1.7	-	-
1986	118.2	2.2	-	-	119.7	1.3	-	-	121.3	1.3	-	-	122.6	1.1	-	-	123.7	0.9	-	-	123.5	-0.2	-	-
1987	125.4	1.5	-	-	124.5	-0.7	-	-	126.0	1.2	-	-	127.9	1.5	-	-	130.6	2.1	-	-	131.7	0.8	-	-
1988	130.8	-0.7	-	-	133.3	1.9	-	-	134.2	0.7	-	-	133.9	-0.2	-	-	136.8	2.2	-	-	137.1	0.2	-	-
1989	139.8	2.0	-	-	140.9	0.8	-	-	142.3	1.0	-	-	143.4	0.8	-	-	151.0	5.3	-	-	153.5	1.7	-	-
1990	150.3	-2.1	-	-	152.3	1.3	-	-	157.1	3.2	-	-	159.8	1.7	-	-	161.2	0.9	-	-	165.2	2.5	-	-
1991	167.4	1.3	-	-	167.2	-0.1	-	-	170.7	2.1	-	-	172.7	1.2	-	-	172.7	0.0	-	-	177.5	2.8	-	-

[Continued]

Baltimore, MD
Consumer Price Index - All Urban Consumers
Base 1982-1984 = 100
Medical Care
[Continued]

For 1947-1995. Columns headed % show percentile change in the index from the previous period for which an index is available.

Year	Jan		Feb		Mar		Apr		May		Jun		Jul		Aug		Sep		Oct		Nov		Dec	
	Index	%	Index	%	Index	%	Index	%	Index	%	Index	%	Index	%	Index	%	Index	%	Index	%	Index	%	Index	%
1992	181.2	2.1	-	-	179.9	-0.7	-	-	178.8	-0.6	-	-	185.2	3.6	-	-	187.4	1.2	-	-	190.6	1.7	-	-
1993	193.8	1.7	-	-	194.3	0.3	-	-	196.0	0.9	-	-	197.7	0.9	-	-	203.0	2.7	-	-	204.5	0.7	-	-
1994	206.0	0.7	-	-	209.3	1.6	-	-	216.0	3.2	-	-	222.0	2.8	-	-	222.1	0.0	-	-	227.6	2.5	-	-
1995	227.6	0.0	-	-	229.0	0.6	-	-	231.0	0.9	-	-	229.8	-0.5	-	-	230.1	0.1	-	-	231.0	0.4	-	-

Source: U.S. Department of Labor, Bureau of Labor Statistics, Division of Consumer Prices and Price Indexes. - indicates no data collected for period.

Baltimore, MD
Consumer Price Index - Urban Wage Earners
Base 1982-1984 = 100
Medical Care

For 1947-1995. Columns headed % show percentile change in the index from the previous period for which an index is available.

Year	Jan Index	%	Feb Index	%	Mar Index	%	Apr Index	%	May Index	%	Jun Index	%	Jul Index	%	Aug Index	%	Sep Index	%	Oct Index	%	Nov Index	%	Dec Index	%
1947	13.3	-	13.3	0.0	13.4	0.8	13.4	0.0	13.5	0.7	13.6	0.7	-	-	-	-	13.9	2.2	-	-	-	-	14.0	0.7
1948	-	-	-	-	14.1	0.7	-	-	-	-	14.2	0.7	-	-	-	-	14.2	0.0	-	-	-	-	14.2	0.0
1949	-	-	-	-	14.3	0.7	-	-	-	-	14.3	0.0	-	-	-	-	14.3	0.0	-	-	-	-	14.3	0.0
1950	-	-	-	-	14.4	0.7	-	-	-	-	14.5	0.7	-	-	-	-	14.5	0.0	-	-	-	-	14.6	0.7
1951	-	-	-	-	15.1	3.4	-	-	-	-	15.8	4.6	-	-	-	-	15.8	0.0	-	-	-	-	16.9	7.0
1952	-	-	-	-	17.4	3.0	-	-	-	-	17.5	0.6	-	-	-	-	17.5	0.0	-	-	-	-	17.6	0.6
1953	-	-	-	-	18.5	5.1	-	-	-	-	18.5	0.0	-	-	-	-	18.6	0.5	-	-	-	-	18.6	0.0
1954	-	-	-	-	18.7	0.5	-	-	-	-	18.7	0.0	-	-	-	-	18.7	0.0	-	-	-	-	18.7	0.0
1955	-	-	-	-	18.8	0.5	-	-	-	-	18.8	0.0	-	-	-	-	18.9	0.5	-	-	-	-	19.1	1.1
1956	-	-	-	-	19.1	0.0	-	-	-	-	20.0	4.7	-	-	-	-	20.1	0.5	-	-	-	-	20.2	0.5
1957	-	-	-	-	20.3	0.5	-	-	-	-	20.3	0.0	-	-	-	-	20.3	0.0	-	-	-	-	20.3	0.0
1958	-	-	-	-	20.5	1.0	-	-	-	-	20.8	1.5	-	-	-	-	20.9	0.5	-	-	-	-	21.9	4.8
1959	-	-	-	-	22.0	0.5	-	-	-	-	22.2	0.9	-	-	-	-	22.3	0.5	-	-	-	-	23.2	4.0
1960	-	-	-	-	23.3	0.4	-	-	-	-	23.4	0.4	-	-	-	-	23.7	1.3	-	-	-	-	24.5	3.4
1961	-	-	-	-	24.6	0.4	-	-	-	-	24.7	0.4	-	-	-	-	24.7	0.0	-	-	-	-	24.9	0.8
1962	-	-	-	-	25.1	0.8	-	-	-	-	25.2	0.4	-	-	-	-	25.4	0.8	-	-	-	-	25.4	0.0
1963	-	-	-	-	26.5	4.3	-	-	-	-	26.9	1.5	-	-	-	-	27.0	0.4	-	-	-	-	27.1	0.4
1964	-	-	-	-	27.2	0.4	-	-	-	-	27.4	0.7	-	-	-	-	27.5	0.4	-	-	-	-	27.7	0.7
1965	-	-	-	-	27.9	0.7	-	-	-	-	27.9	0.0	-	-	-	-	28.3	1.4	-	-	-	-	28.5	0.7
1966	-	-	-	-	28.7	0.7	-	-	-	-	29.2	1.7	-	-	-	-	29.6	1.4	-	-	-	-	29.9	1.0
1967	-	-	-	-	31.3	4.7	-	-	-	-	31.6	1.0	-	-	-	-	32.2	1.9	-	-	-	-	32.4	0.6
1968	-	-	-	-	33.2	2.5	-	-	-	-	33.4	0.6	-	-	-	-	33.9	1.5	-	-	-	-	34.0	0.3
1969	-	-	-	-	35.0	2.9	-	-	-	-	35.3	0.9	-	-	-	-	36.6	3.7	-	-	-	-	36.7	0.3
1970	-	-	-	-	38.0	3.5	-	-	-	-	38.7	1.8	-	-	-	-	39.6	2.3	-	-	-	-	40.9	3.3
1971	-	-	-	-	42.0	2.7	-	-	-	-	42.8	1.9	-	-	-	-	44.3	3.5	-	-	-	-	44.2	-0.2
1972	-	-	-	-	44.4	0.5	-	-	-	-	45.0	1.4	-	-	-	-	45.7	1.6	-	-	-	-	46.1	0.9
1973	-	-	-	-	46.5	0.9	-	-	-	-	46.6	0.2	-	-	-	-	47.4	1.7	-	-	-	-	49.2	3.8
1974	-	-	-	-	49.8	1.2	-	-	-	-	52.6	5.6	-	-	-	-	53.9	2.5	-	-	-	-	54.6	1.3
1975	-	-	-	-	56.4	3.3	-	-	-	-	57.2	1.4	-	-	-	-	58.0	1.4	-	-	-	-	58.1	0.2
1976	-	-	-	-	59.5	2.4	-	-	-	-	61.6	3.5	-	-	-	-	61.7	0.2	-	-	-	-	63.1	2.3
1977	-	-	-	-	65.2	3.3	-	-	-	-	65.8	0.9	-	-	-	-	66.4	0.9	-	-	-	-	67.0	0.9
1978	-	-	-	-	68.4	2.1	-	-	69.6	1.8	-	-	70.1	0.7	-	-	71.3	1.7	-	-	71.9	0.8	-	-
1979	72.4	0.7	-	-	74.7	3.2	-	-	74.3	-0.5	-	-	75.9	2.2	-	-	78.2	3.0	-	-	78.7	0.6	-	-
1980	79.3	0.8	-	-	80.5	1.5	-	-	82.2	2.1	-	-	81.0	-1.5	-	-	81.4	0.5	-	-	81.6	0.2	-	-
1981	81.8	0.2	-	-	84.4	3.2	-	-	85.3	1.1	-	-	85.6	0.4	-	-	87.4	2.1	-	-	87.8	0.5	-	-
1982	89.6	2.1	-	-	91.5	2.1	-	-	92.6	1.2	-	-	93.9	1.4	-	-	96.8	3.1	-	-	97.5	0.7	-	-
1983	98.7	1.2	-	-	99.2	0.5	-	-	99.3	0.1	-	-	101.1	1.8	-	-	101.6	0.5	-	-	102.8	1.2	-	-
1984	102.6	-0.2	-	-	103.5	0.9	-	-	104.2	0.7	-	-	106.9	2.6	-	-	106.4	-0.5	-	-	107.4	0.9	-	-
1985	108.2	0.7	-	-	109.0	0.7	-	-	110.7	1.6	-	-	111.7	0.9	-	-	113.9	2.0	-	-	115.6	1.5	-	-
1986	118.5	2.5	-	-	120.0	1.3	-	-	121.6	1.3	-	-	122.7	0.9	-	-	123.7	0.8	-	-	123.5	-0.2	-	-
1987	124.7	1.0	-	-	124.4	-0.2	-	-	125.8	1.1	-	-	127.5	1.4	-	-	130.3	2.2	-	-	131.4	0.8	-	-
1988	130.6	-0.6	-	-	132.5	1.5	-	-	133.6	0.8	-	-	133.4	-0.1	-	-	135.9	1.9	-	-	136.5	0.4	-	-
1989	139.1	1.9	-	-	140.0	0.6	-	-	141.1	0.8	-	-	142.4	0.9	-	-	148.2	4.1	-	-	150.4	1.5	-	-
1990	148.1	-1.5	-	-	150.3	1.5	-	-	155.2	3.3	-	-	157.5	1.5	-	-	158.7	0.8	-	-	162.9	2.6	-	-
1991	164.8	1.2	-	-	165.3	0.3	-	-	168.0	1.6	-	-	170.1	1.3	-	-	170.1	0.0	-	-	174.9	2.8	-	-

[Continued]

Baltimore, MD
Consumer Price Index - Urban Wage Earners
Base 1982-1984 = 100
Medical Care

[Continued]

For 1947-1995. Columns headed % show percentile change in the index from the previous period for which an index is available.

Year	Jan Index	%	Feb Index	%	Mar Index	%	Apr Index	%	May Index	%	Jun Index	%	Jul Index	%	Aug Index	%	Sep Index	%	Oct Index	%	Nov Index	%	Dec Index	%
1992	178.2	1.9	-	-	176.3	-1.1	-	-	175.8	-0.3	-	-	182.2	3.6	-	-	184.3	1.2	-	-	187.8	1.9	-	-
1993	191.0	1.7	-	-	191.6	0.3	-	-	193.0	0.7	-	-	195.0	1.0	-	-	200.3	2.7	-	-	201.8	0.7	-	-
1994	203.4	0.8	-	-	206.5	1.5	-	-	212.0	2.7	-	-	217.2	2.5	-	-	217.8	0.3	-	-	223.0	2.4	-	-
1995	223.0	0.0	-	-	224.4	0.6	-	-	226.4	0.9	-	-	225.3	-0.5	-	-	225.4	0.0	-	-	226.5	0.5	-	-

Source: U.S. Department of Labor, Bureau of Labor Statistics, Division of Consumer Prices and Price Indexes. - indicates no data collected for period.

Baltimore, MD
Consumer Price Index - All Urban Consumers
Base 1982-1984 = 100
Entertainment

For 1975-1995. Columns headed % show percentile change in the index from the previous period for which an index is available.

Year	Jan Index	%	Feb Index	%	Mar Index	%	Apr Index	%	May Index	%	Jun Index	%	Jul Index	%	Aug Index	%	Sep Index	%	Oct Index	%	Nov Index	%	Dec Index	%
1975	-	-	-	-	-	-	-	-	-	-	-	-	-	-	-	-	-	-	-	-	-	-	65.5	-
1976	-	-	-	-	65.7	0.3	-	-	-	-	66.8	1.7	-	-	-	-	67.6	1.2	-	-	-	-	68.0	0.6
1977	-	-	-	-	68.8	1.2	-	-	-	-	69.6	1.2	-	-	-	-	70.5	1.3	-	-	-	-	70.9	0.6
1978	-	-	-	-	71.5	0.8	-	-	72.6	1.5	-	-	72.5	-0.1	-	-	73.0	0.7	-	-	73.8	1.1	-	-
1979	74.5	0.9	-	-	76.5	2.7	-	-	77.0	0.7	-	-	75.9	-1.4	-	-	76.2	0.4	-	-	77.8	2.1	-	-
1980	81.4	4.6	-	-	82.2	1.0	-	-	82.4	0.2	-	-	83.5	1.3	-	-	85.1	1.9	-	-	84.7	-0.5	-	-
1981	87.7	3.5	-	-	89.4	1.9	-	-	89.8	0.4	-	-	89.9	0.1	-	-	90.5	0.7	-	-	91.8	1.4	-	-
1982	91.5	-0.3	-	-	94.3	3.1	-	-	91.8	-2.7	-	-	92.6	0.9	-	-	97.1	4.9	-	-	97.2	0.1	-	-
1983	98.5	1.3	-	-	101.8	3.4	-	-	102.2	0.4	-	-	101.1	-1.1	-	-	102.5	1.4	-	-	102.5	0.0	-	-
1984	99.2	-3.2	-	-	103.4	4.2	-	-	104.3	0.9	-	-	104.5	0.2	-	-	105.1	0.6	-	-	106.8	1.6	-	-
1985	106.1	-0.7	-	-	107.6	1.4	-	-	109.8	2.0	-	-	109.6	-0.2	-	-	110.8	1.1	-	-	110.4	-0.4	-	-
1986	111.9	1.4	-	-	112.4	0.4	-	-	114.1	1.5	-	-	113.1	-0.9	-	-	114.8	1.5	-	-	115.8	0.9	-	-
1987	117.1	1.1	-	-	118.4	1.1	-	-	118.9	0.4	-	-	118.8	-0.1	-	-	119.0	0.2	-	-	119.9	0.8	-	-
1988	121.7	1.5	-	-	120.0	-1.4	-	-	121.1	0.9	-	-	122.8	1.4	-	-	125.5	2.2	-	-	124.7	-0.6	-	-
1989	125.3	0.5	-	-	126.7	1.1	-	-	128.4	1.3	-	-	129.0	0.5	-	-	126.5	-1.9	-	-	133.1	5.2	-	-
1990	137.9	3.6	-	-	138.1	0.1	-	-	137.2	-0.7	-	-	137.6	0.3	-	-	138.0	0.3	-	-	140.5	1.8	-	-
1991	140.2	-0.2	-	-	142.3	1.5	-	-	142.6	0.2	-	-	142.3	-0.2	-	-	145.9	2.5	-	-	147.6	1.2	-	-
1992	147.7	0.1	-	-	148.6	0.6	-	-	149.4	0.5	-	-	150.3	0.6	-	-	150.4	0.1	-	-	148.3	-1.4	-	-
1993	152.1	2.6	-	-	152.5	0.3	-	-	151.9	-0.4	-	-	152.7	0.5	-	-	154.4	1.1	-	-	152.1	-1.5	-	-
1994	153.0	0.6	-	-	152.2	-0.5	-	-	153.0	0.5	-	-	154.7	1.1	-	-	158.1	2.2	-	-	156.1	-1.3	-	-
1995	158.6	1.6	-	-	157.4	-0.8	-	-	159.7	1.5	-	-	159.1	-0.4	-	-	163.6	2.8	-	-	163.7	0.1	-	-

Source: U.S. Department of Labor, Bureau of Labor Statistics, Division of Consumer Prices and Price Indexes. - indicates no data collected for period.

Baltimore, MD
Consumer Price Index - Urban Wage Earners
Base 1982-1984 = 100
Entertainment

For 1975-1995. Columns headed % show percentile change in the index from the previous period for which an index is available.

Year	Jan Index	%	Feb Index	%	Mar Index	%	Apr Index	%	May Index	%	Jun Index	%	Jul Index	%	Aug Index	%	Sep Index	%	Oct Index	%	Nov Index	%	Dec Index	%
1975	-	-	-	-	-	-	-	-	-	-	-	-	-	-	-	-	-	-	-	-	-	-	-	-
1976	-	-	-	-	65.3	0.3	-	-	-	-	66.4	1.7	-	-	-	-	-	-	-	-	-	-	65.1	-
1977	-	-	-	-	68.4	1.2	-	-	-	-	69.2	1.2	-	-	-	-	67.2	1.2	-	-	-	-	67.6	0.6
1978	-	-	-	-	71.1	1.0	-	-	72.7	2.3	-	-	71.4	-1.8	-	-	70.1	1.3	-	-	-	-	70.4	0.4
1979	75.4	4.0	-	-	76.3	1.2	-	-	76.4	0.1	-	-	76.8	0.5	-	-	72.8	2.0	-	-	72.5	-0.4	-	-
1980	79.8	2.8	-	-	81.9	2.6	-	-	83.0	1.3	-	-	83.4	0.5	-	-	76.3	-0.7	-	-	77.6	1.7	-	-
1981	85.0	0.7	-	-	87.2	2.6	-	-	87.3	0.1	-	-	89.2	2.2	-	-	85.0	1.9	-	-	84.4	-0.7	-	-
1982	93.3	-0.3	-	-	96.3	3.2	-	-	93.6	-2.8	-	-	94.2	0.6	-	-	90.2	1.1	-	-	93.6	3.8	-	-
1983	98.6	0.9	-	-	101.8	3.2	-	-	102.5	0.7	-	-	100.7	-1.8	-	-	97.8	3.8	-	-	97.7	-0.1	-	-
1984	98.2	-3.6	-	-	102.5	4.4	-	-	103.0	0.5	-	-	103.1	0.1	-	-	101.8	1.1	-	-	101.9	0.1	-	-
1985	105.6	-0.5	-	-	106.8	1.1	-	-	108.8	1.9	-	-	108.4	-0.4	-	-	104.2	1.1	-	-	106.1	1.8	-	-
1986	110.9	1.7	-	-	110.9	0.0	-	-	113.1	2.0	-	-	112.6	-0.4	-	-	109.5	1.0	-	-	109.0	-0.5	-	-
1987	115.5	0.8	-	-	117.0	1.3	-	-	118.1	0.9	-	-	118.2	0.1	-	-	113.4	0.7	-	-	114.6	1.1	-	-
1988	121.3	1.4	-	-	120.4	-0.7	-	-	121.7	1.1	-	-	122.4	0.6	-	-	118.6	0.3	-	-	119.6	0.8	-	-
1989	126.0	0.5	-	-	127.3	1.0	-	-	129.0	1.3	-	-	129.9	0.7	-	-	125.4	2.5	-	-	125.4	0.0	-	-
1990	138.1	3.2	-	-	138.6	0.4	-	-	137.6	-0.7	-	-	138.0	0.3	-	-	126.5	-2.6	-	-	133.8	5.8	-	-
1991	142.0	-0.1	-	-	144.1	1.5	-	-	144.6	0.3	-	-	144.7	0.1	-	-	138.7	0.5	-	-	142.1	2.5	-	-
1992	150.1	-0.1	-	-	151.1	0.7	-	-	151.9	0.5	-	-	152.5	0.4	-	-	147.8	2.1	-	-	150.3	1.7	-	-
1993	153.9	2.2	-	-	154.6	0.5	-	-	154.1	-0.3	-	-	154.9	0.5	-	-	152.7	0.1	-	-	150.6	-1.4	-	-
1994	156.0	0.7	-	-	155.6	-0.3	-	-	156.4	0.5	-	-	158.7	1.5	-	-	156.9	1.3	-	-	154.9	-1.3	-	-
1995	161.8	1.6	-	-	160.6	-0.7	-	-	163.2	1.6	-	-	162.6	-0.4	-	-	161.5	1.8	-	-	159.2	-1.4	-	-
													167.5	3.0			167.5	0.0					-	-

Source: U.S. Department of Labor, Bureau of Labor Statistics, Division of Consumer Prices and Price Indexes. - indicates no data collected for period.

Baltimore, MD
Consumer Price Index - All Urban Consumers
Base 1982-1984 = 100
Other Goods and Services

For 1975-1995. Columns headed % show percentile change in the index from the previous period for which an index is available.

Year	Jan Index	%	Feb Index	%	Mar Index	%	Apr Index	%	May Index	%	Jun Index	%	Jul Index	%	Aug Index	%	Sep Index	%	Oct Index	%	Nov Index	%	Dec Index	%
1975	-	-	-	-	-	-	-	-	-	-	-	-	-	-	-	-	-	-	-	-	-	-	56.2	-
1976	-	-	-	-	56.7	0.9	-	-	-	-	57.0	0.5	-	-	-	-	57.4	0.7	-	-	-	-	58.7	2.3
1977	-	-	-	-	59.1	0.7	-	-	-	-	60.4	2.2	-	-	-	-	61.2	1.3	-	-	-	-	61.8	1.0
1978	-	-	-	-	62.2	0.6	-	-	62.8	1.0	-	-	65.0	3.5	-	-	66.2	1.8	-	-	67.2	1.5	-	-
1979	66.7	-0.7	-	-	69.2	3.7	-	-	69.3	0.1	-	-	68.9	-0.6	-	-	70.5	2.3	-	-	70.7	0.3	-	-
1980	72.1	2.0	-	-	73.2	1.5	-	-	75.0	2.5	-	-	75.6	0.8	-	-	78.2	3.4	-	-	78.5	0.4	-	-
1981	79.3	1.0	-	-	79.7	0.5	-	-	82.1	3.0	-	-	83.2	1.3	-	-	83.1	-0.1	-	-	85.9	3.4	-	-
1982	86.3	0.5	-	-	86.8	0.6	-	-	87.1	0.3	-	-	87.2	0.1	-	-	92.7	6.3	-	-	94.9	2.4	-	-
1983	96.8	2.0	-	-	98.5	1.8	-	-	99.4	0.9	-	-	101.9	2.5	-	-	102.7	0.8	-	-	105.6	2.8	-	-
1984	107.3	1.6	-	-	108.6	1.2	-	-	107.7	-0.8	-	-	107.7	0.0	-	-	110.6	2.7	-	-	112.0	1.3	-	-
1985	112.0	0.0	-	-	112.7	0.6	-	-	112.9	0.2	-	-	113.9	0.9	-	-	115.6	1.5	-	-	116.2	0.5	-	-
1986	117.0	0.7	-	-	118.2	1.0	-	-	119.8	1.4	-	-	120.6	0.7	-	-	121.7	0.9	-	-	122.8	0.9	-	-
1987	122.7	-0.1	-	-	122.5	-0.2	-	-	122.7	0.2	-	-	125.2	2.0	-	-	132.4	5.8	-	-	134.0	1.2	-	-
1988	134.4	0.3	-	-	136.0	1.2	-	-	136.0	0.0	-	-	137.3	1.0	-	-	142.7	3.9	-	-	144.2	1.1	-	-
1989	144.7	0.3	-	-	144.9	0.1	-	-	147.6	1.9	-	-	148.8	0.8	-	-	153.3	3.0	-	-	153.2	-0.1	-	-
1990	155.7	1.6	-	-	155.7	0.0	-	-	154.8	-0.6	-	-	158.7	2.5	-	-	161.8	2.0	-	-	161.8	0.0	-	-
1991	165.3	2.2	-	-	166.2	0.5	-	-	170.5	2.6	-	-	174.2	2.2	-	-	178.5	2.5	-	-	178.5	0.0	-	-
1992	178.9	0.2	-	-	179.0	0.1	-	-	187.5	4.7	-	-	187.8	0.2	-	-	195.0	3.8	-	-	196.3	0.7	-	-
1993	199.2	1.5	-	-	199.0	-0.1	-	-	199.9	0.5	-	-	201.6	0.9	-	-	194.2	-3.7	-	-	195.3	0.6	-	-
1994	196.9	0.8	-	-	197.2	0.2	-	-	198.2	0.5	-	-	199.0	0.4	-	-	202.7	1.9	-	-	202.7	0.0	-	-
1995	204.2	0.7	-	-	205.3	0.5	-	-	206.8	0.7	-	-	207.5	0.3	-	-	209.2	0.8	-	-	209.5	0.1	-	-

Source: U.S. Department of Labor, Bureau of Labor Statistics, Division of Consumer Prices and Price Indexes. - indicates no data collected for period.

Baltimore, MD
Consumer Price Index - Urban Wage Earners
Base 1982-1984 = 100
Other Goods and Services

For 1975-1995. Columns headed % show percentile change in the index from the previous period for which an index is available.

Year	Jan Index	%	Feb Index	%	Mar Index	%	Apr Index	%	May Index	%	Jun Index	%	Jul Index	%	Aug Index	%	Sep Index	%	Oct Index	%	Nov Index	%	Dec Index	%
1975	-	-	-	-	-	-	-	-	-	-	-	-	-	-	-	-	-	-	-	-	-	-	57.7	-
1976	-	-	-	-	58.1	0.7	-	-	-	-	58.5	0.7	-	-	-	-	58.9	0.7	-	-	-	-	60.3	2.4
1977	-	-	-	-	60.6	0.5	-	-	-	-	61.9	2.1	-	-	-	-	62.8	1.5	-	-	-	-	63.4	1.0
1978	-	-	-	-	63.8	0.6	-	-	63.6	-0.3	-	-	65.6	3.1	-	-	66.5	1.4	-	-	67.4	1.4	-	-
1979	67.2	-0.3	-	-	69.2	3.0	-	-	69.1	-0.1	-	-	68.3	-1.2	-	-	69.9	2.3	-	-	70.4	0.7	-	-
1980	72.0	2.3	-	-	73.1	1.5	-	-	74.1	1.4	-	-	76.5	3.2	-	-	78.2	2.2	-	-	79.2	1.3	-	-
1981	79.0	-0.3	-	-	80.7	2.2	-	-	83.4	3.3	-	-	84.0	0.7	-	-	83.7	-0.4	-	-	85.1	1.7	-	-
1982	86.2	1.3	-	-	87.0	0.9	-	-	87.3	0.3	-	-	87.3	0.0	-	-	92.1	5.5	-	-	94.5	2.6	-	-
1983	97.0	2.6	-	-	98.5	1.5	-	-	99.4	0.9	-	-	102.0	2.6	-	-	102.7	0.7	-	-	105.6	2.8	-	-
1984	107.4	1.7	-	-	108.6	1.1	-	-	107.8	-0.7	-	-	108.0	0.2	-	-	110.6	2.4	-	-	111.7	1.0	-	-
1985	111.8	0.1	-	-	112.8	0.9	-	-	112.9	0.1	-	-	114.1	1.1	-	-	115.7	1.4	-	-	116.0	0.3	-	-
1986	117.1	0.9	-	-	118.2	0.9	-	-	119.6	1.2	-	-	120.7	0.9	-	-	121.5	0.7	-	-	122.4	0.7	-	-
1987	122.4	0.0	-	-	122.4	0.0	-	-	122.8	0.3	-	-	125.5	2.2	-	-	131.8	5.0	-	-	132.8	0.8	-	-
1988	133.5	0.5	-	-	135.2	1.3	-	-	135.2	0.0	-	-	137.0	1.3	-	-	142.2	3.8	-	-	143.1	0.6	-	-
1989	143.9	0.6	-	-	144.3	0.3	-	-	146.7	1.7	-	-	148.2	1.0	-	-	151.8	2.4	-	-	151.6	-0.1	-	-
1990	154.3	1.8	-	-	154.3	0.0	-	-	153.5	-0.5	-	-	157.7	2.7	-	-	160.5	1.8	-	-	160.5	0.0	-	-
1991	164.6	2.6	-	-	165.5	0.5	-	-	169.6	2.5	-	-	174.0	2.6	-	-	177.8	2.2	-	-	177.8	0.0	-	-
1992	178.9	0.6	-	-	179.0	0.1	-	-	189.8	6.0	-	-	190.2	0.2	-	-	196.9	3.5	-	-	197.7	0.4	-	-
1993	201.8	2.1	-	-	201.5	-0.1	-	-	202.6	0.5	-	-	203.9	0.6	-	-	193.5	-5.1	-	-	194.5	0.5	-	-
1994	196.6	1.1	-	-	197.1	0.3	-	-	198.4	0.7	-	-	199.1	0.4	-	-	202.1	1.5	-	-	202.0	-0.0	-	-
1995	204.1	1.0	-	-	204.7	0.3	-	-	206.7	1.0	-	-	207.3	0.3	-	-	208.7	0.7	-	-	209.0	0.1	-	-

Source: U.S. Department of Labor, Bureau of Labor Statistics, Division of Consumer Prices and Price Indexes. - indicates no data collected for period.

Boston, MA
Consumer Price Index - All Urban Consumers
Base 1982-1984 = 100
Annual Averages

For 1914-1995. Columns headed % show percentile change in the index from the previous period for which an index is available.

Year	All Items		Food & Beverage		Housing		Apparel & Upkeep		Trans- portation		Medical Care		Entertain- ment		Other Goods & Services	
	Index	%	Index	%	Index	%	Index	%	Index	%	Index	%	Index	%	Index	%
1914	-	-	-	-	-	-	-	-	-	-	-	-	-	-	-	-
1915	10.5	-	-	-	-	-	-	-	-	-	-	-	-	-	-	-
1916	11.3	7.6	-	-	-	-	-	-	-	-	-	-	-	-	-	-
1917	13.3	17.7	-	-	-	-	-	-	-	-	-	-	-	-	-	-
1918	15.7	18.0	-	-	-	-	-	-	-	-	-	-	-	-	-	-
1919	18.0	14.6	-	-	-	-	-	-	-	-	-	-	-	-	-	-
1920	20.6	14.4	-	-	-	-	-	-	-	-	-	-	-	-	-	-
1921	18.3	-11.2	-	-	-	-	-	-	-	-	-	-	-	-	-	-
1922	17.0	-7.1	-	-	-	-	-	-	-	-	-	-	-	-	-	-
1923	17.4	2.4	-	-	-	-	-	-	-	-	-	-	-	-	-	-
1924	17.4	0.0	-	-	-	-	-	-	-	-	-	-	-	-	-	-
1925	17.9	2.9	-	-	-	-	-	-	-	-	-	-	-	-	-	-
1926	18.2	1.7	-	-	-	-	-	-	-	-	-	-	-	-	-	-
1927	17.9	-1.6	-	-	-	-	-	-	-	-	-	-	-	-	-	-
1928	17.7	-1.1	-	-	-	-	-	-	-	-	-	-	-	-	-	-
1929	17.8	0.6	-	-	-	-	-	-	-	-	-	-	-	-	-	-
1930	17.3	-2.8	-	-	-	-	-	-	-	-	-	-	-	-	-	-
1931	15.8	-8.7	-	-	-	-	-	-	-	-	-	-	-	-	-	-
1932	14.2	-10.1	-	-	-	-	-	-	-	-	-	-	-	-	-	-
1933	13.6	-4.2	-	-	-	-	-	-	-	-	-	-	-	-	-	-
1934	14.1	3.7	-	-	-	-	-	-	-	-	-	-	-	-	-	-
1935	14.3	1.4	-	-	-	-	-	-	-	-	-	-	-	-	-	-
1936	14.3	0.0	-	-	-	-	-	-	-	-	-	-	-	-	-	-
1937	14.8	3.5	-	-	-	-	-	-	-	-	-	-	-	-	-	-
1938	14.3	-3.4	-	-	-	-	-	-	-	-	-	-	-	-	-	-
1939	14.1	-1.4	-	-	-	-	-	-	-	-	-	-	-	-	-	-
1940	14.3	1.4	-	-	-	-	-	-	-	-	-	-	-	-	-	-
1941	14.9	4.2	-	-	-	-	-	-	-	-	-	-	-	-	-	-
1942	16.5	10.7	-	-	-	-	-	-	-	-	-	-	-	-	-	-
1943	17.4	5.5	-	-	-	-	-	-	-	-	-	-	-	-	-	-
1944	17.6	1.1	-	-	-	-	-	-	-	-	-	-	-	-	-	-
1945	17.9	1.7	-	-	-	-	-	-	-	-	-	-	-	-	-	-
1946	19.4	8.4	-	-	-	-	-	-	-	-	-	-	-	-	-	-
1947	22.1	13.9	-	-	-	-	-	-	16.4	-	13.4	-	-	-	-	-
1948	23.9	8.1	-	-	-	-	-	-	16.9	3.0	14.3	6.7	-	-	-	-
1949	23.6	-1.3	-	-	-	-	-	-	18.6	10.1	15.1	5.6	-	-	-	-
1950	23.9	1.3	-	-	-	-	-	-	20.6	10.8	15.7	4.0	-	-	-	-
1951	25.5	6.7	-	-	-	-	-	-	21.2	2.9	16.3	3.8	-	-	-	-
1952	26.0	2.0	-	-	-	-	-	-	22.6	6.6	17.2	5.5	-	-	-	-
1953	26.1	0.4	-	-	-	-	39.4	-	23.5	4.0	17.6	2.3	-	-	-	-
1954	26.3	0.8	-	-	-	-	39.1	-0.8	23.6	0.4	17.7	0.6	-	-	-	-
1955	26.4	0.4	-	-	-	-	39.2	0.3	23.2	-1.7	17.9	1.1	-	-	-	-
1956	27.1	2.7	-	-	-	-	39.8	1.5	24.0	3.4	19.0	6.1	-	-	-	-
1957	28.1	3.7	-	-	-	-	40.5	1.8	25.0	4.2	20.8	9.5	-	-	-	-
1958	28.9	2.8	-	-	-	-	41.1	1.5	25.8	3.2	22.2	6.7	-	-	-	-

[Continued]

Boston, MA

Consumer Price Index - All Urban Consumers
Base 1982-1984 = 100
Annual Averages

[Continued]

For 1914-1995. Columns headed % show percentile change in the index from the previous period for which an index is available.

Year	All Items		Food & Beverage		Housing		Apparel & Upkeep		Trans- portation		Medical Care		Entertain- ment		Other Goods & Services	
	Index	%	Index	%	Index	%	Index	%	Index	%	Index	%	Index	%	Index	%
1959	29.1	0.7	-	-	-	-	40.8	-0.7	26.4	2.3	22.8	2.7	-	-	-	-
1960	29.8	2.4	-	-	-	-	42.0	2.9	25.8	-2.3	23.2	1.8				
1961	30.2	1.3	-	-	-	-	42.4	1.0	26.2	1.6	23.9	3.0				
1962	30.8	2.0	-	-	-	-	43.0	1.4	28.2	7.6	24.8	3.8				
1963	31.4	1.9	-	-	-	-	43.3	0.7	28.3	0.4	25.3	2.0				
1964	31.9	1.6	-	-	-	-	43.6	0.7	28.5	0.7	26.1	3.2				
1965	32.5	1.9	-	-	-	-	43.9	0.7	29.2	2.5	27.1	3.8				
1966	33.6	3.4	-	-	-	-	45.0	2.5	29.9	2.4	28.2	4.1				
1967	34.4	2.4	-	-	-	-	46.5	3.3	30.6	2.3	30.1	6.7				
1968	35.8	4.1	-	-	-	-	49.3	6.0	31.6	3.3	32.5	8.0				
1969	37.8	5.6	-	-	-	-	52.1	5.7	33.5	6.0	35.1	8.0				
1970	40.2	6.3	-	-	-	-	54.6	4.8	34.9	4.2	37.4	6.6	-	-	-	-
1971	42.2	5.0	-	-	-	-	56.6	3.7	36.6	4.9	39.2	4.8	-	-	-	-
1972	43.7	3.6					57.8	2.1	36.6	0.0	40.5	3.3				
1973	46.3	5.9	-	-	-	-	59.8	3.5	37.6	2.7	41.8	3.2	-	-	-	-
1974	51.2	10.6					64.1	7.2	41.0	9.0	44.8	7.2				
1975	55.8	9.0	-	-	-	-	68.3	6.6	47.0	14.6	50.1	11.8	-	-	-	-
1976	60.0	7.5	67.0	-	56.3	-	71.5	4.7	59.3	26.2	53.4	6.6	64.6	-	56.4	-
1977	63.1	5.2	69.7	4.0	59.5	5.7	73.2	2.4	63.4	6.9	57.8	8.2	66.2	2.5	59.4	5.3
1978	66.4	5.2	75.3	8.0	63.1	6.1	78.7	7.5	63.0	-0.6	62.0	7.3	69.2	4.5	62.5	5.2
1979	73.2	10.2	83.2	10.5	69.9	10.8	84.9	7.9	69.4	10.2	69.5	12.1	75.6	9.2	67.4	7.8
1980	82.6	12.8	89.1	7.1	80.5	15.2	89.5	5.4	82.7	19.2	76.9	10.6	83.3	10.2	73.6	9.2
1981	91.8	11.1	94.3	5.8	92.0	14.3	93.8	4.8	94.1	13.8	83.7	8.8	89.9	7.9	81.0	10.1
1982	95.5	4.0	96.6	2.4	94.6	2.8	97.4	3.8	98.3	4.5	92.6	10.6	96.3	7.1	90.5	11.7
1983	99.8	4.5	99.1	2.6	100.3	6.0	99.8	2.5	99.2	0.9	98.8	6.7	100.2	4.0	100.1	10.6
1984	104.7	4.9	104.2	5.1	105.0	4.7	102.7	2.9	102.5	3.3	108.6	9.9	103.5	3.3	109.4	9.3
1985	109.4	4.5	108.6	4.2	109.1	3.9	106.1	3.3	105.3	2.7	120.5	11.0	109.8	6.1	118.9	8.7
1986	112.2	2.6	113.7	4.7	111.6	2.3	108.3	2.1	101.6	-3.5	131.8	9.4	114.6	4.4	128.8	8.3
1987	117.1	4.4	119.4	5.0	116.8	4.7	115.8	6.9	103.3	1.7	139.2	5.6	119.4	4.2	136.0	5.6
1988	124.2	6.1	124.4	4.2	123.7	5.9	125.8	8.6	108.3	4.8	152.1	9.3	127.0	6.4	147.1	8.2
1989	131.3	5.7	132.2	6.3	131.3	6.1	125.1	-0.6	113.7	5.0	165.3	8.7	133.6	5.2	157.9	7.3
1990	138.9	5.8	138.6	4.8	137.0	4.3	138.2	10.5	119.7	5.3	181.6	9.9	144.2	7.9	173.4	9.8
1991	145.0	4.4	142.5	2.8	140.9	2.8	144.6	4.6	125.5	4.8	202.7	11.6	152.2	5.5	188.4	8.7
1992	148.6	2.5	143.3	0.6	143.5	1.8	145.1	0.3	129.1	2.9	224.2	10.6	155.0	1.8	197.9	5.0
1993	152.9	2.9	146.3	2.1	146.4	2.0	157.6	8.6	132.5	2.6	239.0	6.6	160.1	3.3	202.6	2.4
1994	154.9	1.3	150.0	2.5	147.9	1.0	146.8	-6.9	135.0	1.9	251.1	5.1	163.9	2.4	206.6	2.0
1995	-	-	-	-	-	-	-	-	-	-	-	-				

Source: U.S. Department of Labor, Bureau of Labor Statistics, Division of Consumer Prices and Price Indexes. - indicates no data collected for period.

Boston, MA
Consumer Price Index - Urban Wage Earners
Base 1982-1984 = 100
Annual Averages

For 1914-1995. Columns headed % show percentile change in the index from the previous period for which an index is available.

Year	All Items		Food & Beverage		Housing		Apparel & Upkeep		Trans- portation		Medical Care		Entertain- ment		Other Goods & Services	
	Index	%	Index	%	Index	%	Index	%	Index	%	Index	%	Index	%	Index	%
1914	-	-	-	-	-	-	-	-	-	-	-	-	-	-	-	-
1915	10.5	-	-	-	-	-	-	-	-	-	-	-	-	-	-	-
1916	11.3	7.6	-	-	-	-	-	-	-	-	-	-	-	-	-	-
1917	13.4	18.6	-	-	-	-	-	-	-	-	-	-	-	-	-	-
1918	15.8	17.9	-	-	-	-	-	-	-	-	-	-	-	-	-	-
1919	18.1	14.6	-	-	-	-	-	-	-	-	-	-	-	-	-	-
1920	20.8	14.9	-	-	-	-	-	-	-	-	-	-	-	-	-	-
1921	18.4	-11.5	-	-	-	-	-	-	-	-	-	-	-	-	-	-
1922	17.1	-7.1	-	-	-	-	-	-	-	-	-	-	-	-	-	-
1923	17.5	2.3	-	-	-	-	-	-	-	-	-	-	-	-	-	-
1924	17.5	0.0	-	-	-	-	-	-	-	-	-	-	-	-	-	-
1925	18.0	2.9	-	-	-	-	-	-	-	-	-	-	-	-	-	-
1926	18.3	1.7	-	-	-	-	-	-	-	-	-	-	-	-	-	-
1927	18.0	-1.6	-	-	-	-	-	-	-	-	-	-	-	-	-	-
1928	17.8	-1.1	-	-	-	-	-	-	-	-	-	-	-	-	-	-
1929	17.9	0.6	-	-	-	-	-	-	-	-	-	-	-	-	-	-
1930	17.4	-2.8	-	-	-	-	-	-	-	-	-	-	-	-	-	-
1931	15.9	-8.6	-	-	-	-	-	-	-	-	-	-	-	-	-	-
1932	14.3	-10.1	-	-	-	-	-	-	-	-	-	-	-	-	-	-
1933	13.7	-4.2	-	-	-	-	-	-	-	-	-	-	-	-	-	-
1934	14.2	3.6	-	-	-	-	-	-	-	-	-	-	-	-	-	-
1935	14.4	1.4	-	-	-	-	-	-	-	-	-	-	-	-	-	-
1936	14.4	0.0	-	-	-	-	-	-	-	-	-	-	-	-	-	-
1937	14.8	2.8	-	-	-	-	-	-	-	-	-	-	-	-	-	-
1938	14.4	-2.7	-	-	-	-	-	-	-	-	-	-	-	-	-	-
1939	14.2	-1.4	-	-	-	-	-	-	-	-	-	-	-	-	-	-
1940	14.4	1.4	-	-	-	-	-	-	-	-	-	-	-	-	-	-
1941	15.0	4.2	-	-	-	-	-	-	-	-	-	-	-	-	-	-
1942	16.6	10.7	-	-	-	-	-	-	-	-	-	-	-	-	-	-
1943	17.5	5.4	-	-	-	-	-	-	-	-	-	-	-	-	-	-
1944	17.7	1.1	-	-	-	-	-	-	-	-	-	-	-	-	-	-
1945	18.0	1.7	-	-	-	-	-	-	-	-	-	-	-	-	-	-
1946	19.5	8.3	-	-	-	-	-	-	-	-	-	-	-	-	-	-
1947	22.2	13.8	-	-	-	-	-	-	16.4	-	13.6	-	-	-	-	-
1948	24.0	8.1	-	-	-	-	-	-	16.9	3.0	14.5	6.6	-	-	-	-
1949	23.7	-1.2	-	-	-	-	-	-	18.5	9.5	15.3	5.5	-	-	-	-
1950	24.0	1.3	-	-	-	-	-	-	20.5	10.8	16.0	4.6	-	-	-	-
1951	25.6	6.7	-	-	-	-	-	-	21.2	3.4	16.5	3.1	-	-	-	-
1952	26.2	2.3	-	-	-	-	-	-	22.6	6.6	17.4	5.5	-	-	-	-
1953	26.3	0.4	-	-	-	-	39.7	-	23.4	3.5	17.9	2.9	-	-	-	-
1954	26.4	0.4	-	-	-	-	39.4	-0.8	23.6	0.9	18.0	0.6	-	-	-	-
1955	26.5	0.4	-	-	-	-	39.5	0.3	23.1	-2.1	18.1	0.6	-	-	-	-
1956	27.3	3.0	-	-	-	-	40.1	1.5	24.0	3.9	19.3	6.6	-	-	-	-
1957	28.2	3.3	-	-	-	-	40.8	1.7	24.9	3.8	21.1	9.3	-	-	-	-
1958	29.1	3.2	-	-	-	-	41.4	1.5	25.7	3.2	22.6	7.1	-	-	-	-

[Continued]

304

Boston, MA
Consumer Price Index - Urban Wage Earners
Base 1982-1984 = 100
Annual Averages
[Continued]

For 1914-1995. Columns headed % show percentile change in the index from the previous period for which an index is available.

Year	All Items		Food & Beverage		Housing		Apparel & Upkeep		Trans-portation		Medical Care		Entertain-ment		Other Goods & Services	
	Index	%	Index	%	Index	%	Index	%	Index	%	Index	%	Index	%	Index	%
1959	29.3	0.7	-	-	-	-	41.1	-0.7	26.3	2.3	23.1	2.2	-	-	-	-
1960	29.9	2.0	-	-	-	-	42.4	3.2	25.7	-2.3	23.5	1.7	-	-	-	-
1961	30.3	1.3	-	-	-	-	42.7	0.7	26.2	1.9	24.3	3.4	-	-	-	-
1962	31.0	2.3	-	-	-	-	43.3	1.4	28.1	7.3	25.1	3.3	-	-	-	-
1963	31.6	1.9	-	-	-	-	43.7	0.9	28.2	0.4	25.7	2.4	-	-	-	-
1964	32.1	1.6	-	-	-	-	43.9	0.5	28.4	0.7	26.5	3.1	-	-	-	-
1965	32.7	1.9	-	-	-	-	44.3	0.9	29.1	2.5	27.5	3.8	-	-	-	-
1966	33.8	3.4	-	-	-	-	45.3	2.3	29.8	2.4	28.6	4.0	-	-	-	-
1967	34.6	2.4	-	-	-	-	46.8	3.3	30.6	2.7	30.5	6.6	-	-	-	-
1968	36.0	4.0	-	-	-	-	49.7	6.2	31.5	2.9	33.0	8.2	-	-	-	-
1969	38.1	5.8	-	-	-	-	52.5	5.6	33.4	6.0	35.6	7.9	-	-	-	-
1970	40.4	6.0	-	-	-	-	55.0	4.8	34.8	4.2	38.0	6.7	-	-	-	-
1971	42.5	5.2	-	-	-	-	57.1	3.8	36.5	4.9	39.8	4.7	-	-	-	-
1972	44.0	3.5	-	-	-	-	58.2	1.9	36.5	0.0	41.1	3.3	-	-	-	-
1973	46.6	5.9	-	-	-	-	60.2	3.4	37.5	2.7	42.4	3.2	-	-	-	-
1974	51.4	10.3	-	-	-	-	64.6	7.3	40.9	9.1	45.4	7.1	-	-	-	-
1975	56.1	9.1	-	-	-	-	68.8	6.5	46.9	14.7	50.8	11.9	-	-	-	-
1976	60.4	7.7	67.6	-	56.2	-	72.0	4.7	59.2	26.2	54.2	6.7	67.0	-	57.1	-
1977	63.5	5.1	70.3	4.0	59.4	5.7	73.7	2.4	63.2	6.8	58.7	8.3	68.5	2.2	60.2	5.4
1978	66.7	5.0	75.8	7.8	63.0	6.1	78.2	6.1	62.9	-0.5	62.8	7.0	70.7	3.2	63.3	5.1
1979	73.5	10.2	83.3	9.9	70.1	11.3	82.6	5.6	70.0	11.3	69.4	10.5	77.0	8.9	68.1	7.6
1980	83.0	12.9	89.6	7.6	81.3	16.0	86.8	5.1	83.4	19.1	76.4	10.1	83.4	8.3	73.7	8.2
1981	92.2	11.1	94.6	5.6	93.2	14.6	92.9	7.0	94.0	12.7	83.8	9.7	89.6	7.4	81.1	10.0
1982	95.9	4.0	96.5	2.0	95.4	2.4	98.0	5.5	98.4	4.7	92.3	10.1	96.2	7.4	90.3	11.3
1983	99.7	4.0	99.1	2.7	100.2	5.0	100.2	2.2	99.1	0.7	98.8	7.0	100.3	4.3	100.1	10.9
1984	104.3	4.6	104.4	5.3	104.2	4.0	101.8	1.6	102.5	3.4	108.9	10.2	103.6	3.3	109.6	9.5
1985	109.3	4.8	108.4	3.8	109.6	5.2	104.8	2.9	105.1	2.5	119.3	9.6	109.2	5.4	119.1	8.7
1986	111.8	2.3	113.1	4.3	111.9	2.1	107.0	2.1	101.1	-3.8	130.6	9.5	114.1	4.5	128.8	8.1
1987	117.1	4.7	118.9	5.1	116.8	4.4	121.3	13.4	103.7	2.6	138.8	6.3	117.8	3.2	136.0	5.6
1988	124.1	6.0	123.8	4.1	123.5	5.7	132.6	9.3	109.2	5.3	151.4	9.1	125.3	6.4	147.0	8.1
1989	131.5	6.0	131.5	6.2	131.0	6.1	134.0	1.1	115.6	5.9	163.9	8.3	133.0	6.1	158.6	7.9
1990	138.8	5.6	137.9	4.9	136.0	3.8	146.9	9.6	122.0	5.5	179.7	9.6	144.5	8.6	174.3	9.9
1991	144.6	4.2	141.6	2.7	139.6	2.6	153.1	4.2	128.3	5.2	199.7	11.1	152.8	5.7	189.6	8.8
1992	148.0	2.4	142.4	0.6	142.0	1.7	153.2	0.1	131.9	2.8	219.9	10.1	155.5	1.8	200.0	5.5
1993	152.1	2.8	145.4	2.1	144.9	2.0	165.9	8.3	134.9	2.3	234.6	6.7	161.2	3.7	203.8	1.9
1994	153.8	1.1	148.7	2.3	146.4	1.0	152.2	-8.3	137.7	2.1	245.7	4.7	165.1	2.4	204.9	0.5
1995	-	-	-	-	-	-	-	-	-	-	-	-	-	-	-	-

Source: U.S. Department of Labor, Bureau of Labor Statistics, Division of Consumer Prices and Price Indexes. - indicates no data collected for period.

Boston, MA
Consumer Price Index - All Urban Consumers
Base 1982-1984 = 100
All Items

For 1914-1995. Columns headed % show percentile change in the index from the previous period for which an index is available.

Year	Jan Index	%	Feb Index	%	Mar Index	%	Apr Index	%	May Index	%	Jun Index	%	Jul Index	%	Aug Index	%	Sep Index	%	Oct Index	%	Nov Index	%	Dec Index	%
1914	-	-	-	-	-	-	-	-	-	-	-	-	-	-	-	-	-	-	-	-	-	-	10.5	-
1915	-	-	-	-	-	-	-	-	-	-	-	-	-	-	-	-	-	-	-	-	-	-	10.7	1.9
1916	-	-	-	-	-	-	-	-	-	-	-	-	-	-	-	-	-	-	-	-	-	-	12.1	13.1
1917	-	-	-	-	-	-	-	-	-	-	-	-	-	-	-	-	-	-	-	-	-	-	14.2	17.4
1918	-	-	-	-	-	-	-	-	-	-	-	-	-	-	-	-	-	-	-	-	-	-	17.3	21.8
1919	-	-	-	-	-	-	-	-	-	-	17.4	0.6	-	-	-	-	-	-	-	-	-	-	19.5	12.1
1920	-	-	-	-	-	-	-	-	-	-	21.5	10.3	-	-	-	-	-	-	-	-	-	-	20.2	-6.0
1921	-	-	-	-	-	-	-	-	18.0	-10.9	-	-	-	-	-	-	18.0	0.0	-	-	-	-	17.8	-1.1
1922	-	-	-	-	16.9	-5.1	-	-	-	-	16.8	-0.6	-	-	-	-	16.9	0.6	-	-	-	-	17.3	2.4
1923	-	-	-	-	17.1	-1.2	-	-	-	-	17.1	0.0	-	-	-	-	17.6	2.9	-	-	-	-	17.8	1.1
1924	-	-	-	-	17.3	-2.8	-	-	-	-	17.2	-0.6	-	-	-	-	17.5	1.7	-	-	-	-	17.6	0.6
1925	-	-	-	-	-	-	-	-	-	-	17.5	-0.6	-	-	-	-	-	-	-	-	-	-	18.5	5.7
1926	-	-	-	-	-	-	-	-	-	-	18.1	-2.2	-	-	-	-	-	-	-	-	-	-	18.2	0.6
1927	-	-	-	-	-	-	-	-	-	-	18.0	-1.1	-	-	-	-	-	-	-	-	-	-	18.0	0.0
1928	-	-	-	-	-	-	-	-	-	-	17.5	-2.8	-	-	-	-	-	-	-	-	-	-	17.8	1.7
1929	-	-	-	-	-	-	-	-	-	-	17.5	-1.7	-	-	-	-	-	-	-	-	-	-	17.8	1.7
1930	-	-	-	-	-	-	-	-	-	-	17.4	-2.2	-	-	-	-	-	-	-	-	-	-	16.9	-2.9
1931	-	-	-	-	-	-	-	-	-	-	15.7	-7.1	-	-	-	-	-	-	-	-	-	-	15.3	-2.5
1932	-	-	-	-	-	-	-	-	-	-	14.1	-7.8	-	-	-	-	-	-	-	-	-	-	13.8	-2.1
1933	-	-	-	-	-	-	-	-	-	-	13.4	-2.9	-	-	-	-	-	-	-	-	-	-	13.9	3.7
1934	-	-	-	-	-	-	-	-	-	-	14.1	1.4	-	-	-	-	-	-	-	-	14.2	0.7	-	-
1935	-	-	-	-	14.5	2.1	-	-	-	-	-	-	14.2	-2.1	-	-	-	-	14.3	0.7	-	-	-	-
1936	14.4	0.7	-	-	-	-	14.3	-0.7	-	-	-	-	14.5	1.4	-	-	14.5	0.0	-	-	-	-	14.3	-1.4
1937	-	-	-	-	14.6	2.1	-	-	-	-	14.8	1.4	-	-	-	-	15.1	2.0	-	-	-	-	14.7	-2.6
1938	-	-	-	-	14.3	-2.7	-	-	-	-	14.3	0.0	-	-	-	-	14.3	0.0	-	-	-	-	14.2	-0.7
1939	-	-	-	-	14.1	-0.7	-	-	-	-	14.0	-0.7	-	-	-	-	14.3	2.1	-	-	-	-	14.1	-1.4
1940	-	-	-	-	14.3	1.4	-	-	-	-	14.4	0.7	-	-	-	-	14.3	-0.7	14.2	-0.7	14.2	0.0	14.3	0.7
1941	14.3	0.0	14.3	0.0	14.3	0.0	14.5	1.4	14.6	0.7	14.8	1.4	15.0	1.4	15.1	0.7	15.3	1.3	15.4	0.7	15.7	1.9	15.6	-0.6
1942	15.8	1.3	16.0	1.3	16.1	0.6	16.1	0.0	16.3	1.2	16.4	0.6	16.7	1.8	16.6	-0.6	16.8	1.2	17.0	1.2	17.1	0.6	17.1	0.0
1943	17.1	0.0	17.1	0.0	17.4	1.8	17.5	0.6	17.6	0.6	17.5	-0.6	17.3	-1.1	17.3	0.0	17.3	0.0	17.5	1.2	17.4	-0.6	17.4	0.0
1944	17.4	0.0	17.3	-0.6	17.3	0.0	17.5	1.2	17.5	0.0	17.5	0.0	17.6	0.6	17.7	0.6	17.8	0.6	17.6	-1.1	17.7	0.6	17.8	0.6
1945	17.8	0.0	17.8	0.0	17.7	-0.6	17.7	0.0	17.8	0.6	18.1	1.7	18.1	0.0	18.1	0.0	18.0	-0.6	17.9	-0.6	18.0	0.6	18.0	0.0
1946	18.1	0.6	18.0	-0.6	18.1	0.6	18.2	0.6	18.2	0.0	18.4	1.1	19.8	7.6	20.2	2.0	20.4	1.0	20.8	2.0	21.1	1.4	21.3	0.9
1947	21.4	0.5	21.3	-0.5	21.7	1.9	21.5	-0.9	21.4	-0.5	21.7	1.4	21.9	0.9	22.3	1.8	22.9	2.7	22.7	-0.9	22.8	0.4	23.2	1.8
1948	23.5	1.3	23.3	-0.9	23.2	-0.4	23.6	1.7	23.7	0.4	24.0	1.3	24.3	1.2	24.4	0.4	24.4	0.0	24.3	-0.4	24.1	-0.8	23.8	-1.2
1949	23.7	-0.4	23.3	-1.7	23.5	0.9	23.5	0.0	23.5	0.0	23.6	0.4	23.5	-0.4	23.7	0.9	23.9	0.8	23.7	-0.8	23.7	0.0	23.5	-0.8
1950	23.4	-0.4	23.3	-0.4	23.5	0.9	23.5	0.0	23.5	0.0	23.8	1.3	24.0	0.8	24.2	0.8	24.2	0.0	24.4	0.8	24.4	0.0	24.6	0.8
1951	25.0	1.6	25.3	1.2	25.3	0.0	25.3	0.0	25.4	0.4	25.4	0.0	25.5	0.4	25.5	0.0	25.6	0.4	25.8	0.8	25.9	0.4	26.0	0.4
1952	25.9	-0.4	25.8	-0.4	25.8	0.0	25.8	0.0	25.9	0.4	26.0	0.4	26.4	1.5	26.4	0.0	26.3	-0.4	26.3	0.0	26.1	-0.8	26.0	-0.4
1953	26.0	0.0	-	-	-	-	25.9	-0.4	-	-	-	-	26.2	1.2	-	-	-	-	26.4	0.8	-	-	-	-
1954	26.1	-1.1	-	-	-	-	26.1	0.0	-	-	-	-	26.4	1.1	-	-	-	-	26.3	-0.4	-	-	-	-
1955	26.2	-0.4	-	-	-	-	26.3	0.4	-	-	-	-	26.4	0.4	-	-	-	-	26.5	0.4	-	-	-	-
1956	26.6	0.4	-	-	-	-	26.7	0.4	-	-	-	-	27.3	2.2	-	-	-	-	27.7	1.5	-	-	-	-
1957	27.6	-0.4	-	-	-	-	27.9	1.1	-	-	-	-	28.3	1.4	-	-	-	-	28.3	0.0	-	-	-	-
1958	28.6	1.1	-	-	-	-	28.9	1.0	-	-	-	-	29.1	0.7	-	-	-	-	29.1	0.0	-	-	-	-

[Continued]

Boston, MA
Consumer Price Index - All Urban Consumers
Base 1982-1984 = 100
All Items
[Continued]

For 1914-1995. Columns headed % show percentile change in the index from the previous period for which an index is available.

Year	Jan Index	%	Feb Index	%	Mar Index	%	Apr Index	%	May Index	%	Jun Index	%	Jul Index	%	Aug Index	%	Sep Index	%	Oct Index	%	Nov Index	%	Dec Index	%
1959	29.1	0.0	-	-	-	-	29.0	-0.3	-	-	-	-	29.1	0.3	-	-	-	-	29.4	1.0	-	-	-	-
1960	29.3	-0.3	-	-	-	-	29.8	1.7	-	-	-	-	29.8	0.0	-	-	-	-	29.9	0.3	-	-	-	-
1961	30.0	0.3	-	-	-	-	30.1	0.3	-	-	-	-	30.2	0.3	-	-	-	-	30.3	0.3	-	-	-	-
1962	30.5	0.7	-	-	-	-	30.8	1.0	-	-	-	-	30.8	0.0	-	-	-	-	31.1	1.0	-	-	-	-
1963	31.2	0.3	-	-	-	-	31.4	0.6	-	-	-	-	31.5	0.3	-	-	-	-	31.6	0.3	-	-	-	-
1964	31.6	0.0	-	-	-	-	31.8	0.6	-	-	-	-	31.9	0.3	-	-	-	-	32.1	0.6	-	-	-	-
1965	32.2	0.3	-	-	-	-	32.4	0.6	-	-	-	-	32.6	0.6	-	-	-	-	32.6	0.0	-	-	-	-
1966	32.7	0.3	-	-	-	-	33.5	2.4	-	-	-	-	33.6	0.3	-	-	-	-	34.0	1.2	-	-	-	-
1967	34.1	0.3	-	-	-	-	34.1	0.0	-	-	-	-	34.4	0.9	-	-	-	-	34.7	0.9	-	-	-	-
1968	35.0	0.9	-	-	-	-	35.5	1.4	-	-	-	-	35.8	0.8	-	-	-	-	36.4	1.7	-	-	-	-
1969	36.7	0.8	-	-	-	-	37.3	1.6	-	-	-	-	37.9	1.6	-	-	-	-	38.7	2.1	-	-	-	-
1970	39.1	1.0	-	-	-	-	39.6	1.3	-	-	-	-	40.0	1.0	-	-	-	-	41.1	2.8	-	-	-	-
1971	41.5	1.0	-	-	-	-	41.8	0.7	-	-	-	-	42.2	1.0	-	-	-	-	42.8	1.4	-	-	-	-
1972	42.9	0.2	-	-	-	-	43.4	1.2	-	-	-	-	43.7	0.7	-	-	-	-	44.3	1.4	-	-	-	-
1973	44.6	0.7	-	-	-	-	45.6	2.2	-	-	-	-	46.1	1.1	-	-	-	-	47.7	3.5	-	-	-	-
1974	48.9	2.5	-	-	-	-	50.0	2.2	-	-	-	-	51.5	3.0	-	-	-	-	52.6	2.1	-	-	-	-
1975	53.8	2.3	-	-	-	-	54.7	1.7	-	-	-	-	56.1	2.6	-	-	-	-	56.7	1.1	-	-	-	-
1976	59.1	4.2	-	-	-	-	59.3	0.3	-	-	-	-	60.3	1.7	-	-	-	-	60.6	0.5	-	-	-	-
1977	61.6	1.7	-	-	-	-	62.5	1.5	-	-	-	-	63.5	1.6	-	-	-	-	63.9	0.6	-	-	-	-
1978	64.5	0.9	-	-	64.8	0.5	-	-	65.6	1.2	-	-	66.4	1.2	-	-	67.4	1.5	-	-	68.7	1.9	-	-
1979	69.4	1.0	-	-	70.6	1.7	-	-	72.1	2.1	-	-	73.7	2.2	-	-	75.0	1.8	-	-	76.6	2.1	-	-
1980	78.2	2.1	-	-	80.6	3.1	-	-	81.5	1.1	-	-	82.9	1.7	-	-	84.1	1.4	-	-	85.6	1.8	-	-
1981	88.2	3.0	-	-	90.2	2.3	-	-	90.7	0.6	-	-	91.6	1.0	-	-	93.9	2.5	-	-	94.3	0.4	-	-
1982	94.3	0.0	-	-	92.8	-1.6	-	-	93.8	1.1	-	-	96.1	2.5	-	-	97.3	1.2	-	-	98.1	0.8	-	-
1983	98.7	0.6	-	-	98.6	-0.1	-	-	99.1	0.5	-	-	99.7	0.6	-	-	100.2	0.5	-	-	101.4	1.2	-	-
1984	102.3	0.9	-	-	103.9	1.6	-	-	104.3	0.4	-	-	104.9	0.6	-	-	105.8	0.9	-	-	105.9	0.1	-	-
1985	106.5	0.6	-	-	108.2	1.6	-	-	108.4	0.2	-	-	109.3	0.8	-	-	110.5	1.1	-	-	112.0	1.4	-	-
1986	112.5	0.4	-	-	111.8	-0.6	-	-	111.0	-0.7	-	-	111.3	0.3	-	-	112.9	1.4	-	-	113.3	0.4	-	-
1987	114.6	1.1	-	-	115.9	1.1	-	-	115.3	-0.5	-	-	116.3	0.9	-	-	119.5	2.8	-	-	119.9	0.3	-	-
1988	120.1	0.2	-	-	122.1	1.7	-	-	123.1	0.8	-	-	123.8	0.6	-	-	126.2	1.9	-	-	127.4	1.0	-	-
1989	129.0	1.3	-	-	129.7	0.5	-	-	130.5	0.6	-	-	130.3	-0.2	-	-	132.2	1.5	-	-	134.3	1.6	-	-
1990	136.0	1.3	-	-	136.3	0.2	-	-	136.6	0.2	-	-	137.6	0.7	-	-	141.3	2.7	-	-	143.7	1.7	-	-
1991	143.8	0.1	-	-	143.9	0.1	-	-	143.5	-0.3	-	-	145.1	1.1	-	-	146.3	0.8	-	-	146.6	0.2	-	-
1992	146.3	-0.2	-	-	147.9	1.1	-	-	147.5	-0.3	-	-	148.9	0.9	-	-	149.4	0.3	-	-	150.4	0.7	-	-
1993	151.9	1.0	-	-	154.1	1.4	-	-	151.9	-1.4	-	-	152.5	0.4	-	-	152.0	-0.3	-	-	154.5	1.6	-	-
1994	153.6	-0.6	-	-	155.0	0.9	-	-	153.6	-0.9	-	-	153.9	0.2	-	-	155.7	1.2	-	-	156.7	0.6	-	-
1995	158.0	0.8	-	-	158.4	0.3	-	-	157.7	-0.4	-	-	157.8	0.1	-	-	158.6	0.5	-	-	160.3	1.1	-	-

Source: U.S. Department of Labor, Bureau of Labor Statistics, Division of Consumer Prices and Price Indexes. - indicates no data collected for period.

Boston, MA
Consumer Price Index - Urban Wage Earners
Base 1982-1984 = 100
All Items

For 1914-1995. Columns headed % show percentile change in the index from the previous period for which an index is available.

Year	Jan Index	%	Feb Index	%	Mar Index	%	Apr Index	%	May Index	%	Jun Index	%	Jul Index	%	Aug Index	%	Sep Index	%	Oct Index	%	Nov Index	%	Dec Index	%
1914	-	-	-	-	-	-	-	-	-	-	-	-	-	-	-	-	-	-	-	-	-	-	10.6	-
1915	-	-	-	-	-	-	-	-	-	-	-	-	-	-	-	-	-	-	-	-	-	-	10.7	0.9
1916	-	-	-	-	-	-	-	-	-	-	-	-	-	-	-	-	-	-	-	-	-	-	12.1	13.1
1917	-	-	-	-	-	-	-	-	-	-	-	-	-	-	-	-	-	-	-	-	-	-	14.3	18.2
1918	-	-	-	-	-	-	-	-	-	-	-	-	-	-	-	-	-	-	-	-	-	-	17.4	21.7
1919	-	-	-	-	-	-	-	-	-	-	17.5	0.6	-	-	-	-	-	-	-	-	-	-	19.6	12.0
1920	-	-	-	-	-	-	-	-	-	-	21.6	10.2	-	-	-	-	-	-	-	-	-	-	20.3	-6.0
1921	-	-	-	-	-	-	-	-	18.1	-10.8	-	-	-	-	-	-	18.1	0.0	-	-	-	-	17.9	-1.1
1922	-	-	-	-	17.0	-5.0	-	-	-	-	16.8	-1.2	-	-	-	-	17.0	1.2	-	-	-	-	17.4	2.4
1923	-	-	-	-	17.2	-1.1	-	-	-	-	17.2	0.0	-	-	-	-	17.7	2.9	-	-	-	-	17.9	1.1
1924	-	-	-	-	17.4	-2.8	-	-	-	-	17.3	-0.6	-	-	-	-	17.6	1.7	-	-	-	-	17.7	0.6
1925	-	-	-	-	-	-	-	-	-	-	17.6	-0.6	-	-	-	-	-	-	-	-	-	-	18.6	5.7
1926	-	-	-	-	-	-	-	-	-	-	18.2	-2.2	-	-	-	-	-	-	-	-	-	-	18.3	0.5
1927	-	-	-	-	-	-	-	-	-	-	18.1	-1.1	-	-	-	-	-	-	-	-	-	-	18.1	0.0
1928	-	-	-	-	-	-	-	-	-	-	17.6	-2.8	-	-	-	-	-	-	-	-	-	-	17.9	1.7
1929	-	-	-	-	-	-	-	-	-	-	17.6	-1.7	-	-	-	-	-	-	-	-	-	-	17.9	1.7
1930	-	-	-	-	-	-	-	-	-	-	17.5	-2.2	-	-	-	-	-	-	-	-	-	-	17.0	-2.9
1931	-	-	-	-	-	-	-	-	-	-	15.8	-7.1	-	-	-	-	-	-	-	-	-	-	15.4	-2.5
1932	-	-	-	-	-	-	-	-	-	-	14.2	-7.8	-	-	-	-	-	-	-	-	-	-	13.9	-2.1
1933	-	-	-	-	-	-	-	-	-	-	13.5	-2.9	-	-	-	-	-	-	-	-	-	-	13.9	3.0
1934	-	-	-	-	-	-	-	-	-	-	14.2	2.2	-	-	-	-	-	-	-	-	14.3	0.7	-	-
1935	-	-	-	-	14.5	1.4	-	-	-	-	-	-	14.3	-1.4	-	-	-	-	14.4	0.7	-	-	-	-
1936	14.5	0.7	-	-	-	-	14.4	-0.7	-	-	-	-	14.6	1.4	-	-	14.5	-0.7	-	-	-	-	14.4	-0.7
1937	-	-	-	-	14.7	2.1	-	-	-	-	14.8	0.7	-	-	-	-	15.2	2.7	-	-	-	-	14.8	-2.6
1938	-	-	-	-	14.4	-2.7	-	-	-	-	14.4	0.0	-	-	-	-	14.4	0.0	-	-	-	-	14.3	-0.7
1939	-	-	-	-	14.2	-0.7	-	-	-	-	14.1	-0.7	-	-	-	-	14.4	2.1	-	-	-	-	14.2	-1.4
1940	-	-	-	-	14.4	1.4	-	-	-	-	14.5	0.7	-	-	-	-	14.4	-0.7	14.3	-0.7	14.3	0.0	14.4	0.7
1941	14.4	0.0	14.4	0.0	14.4	0.0	14.6	1.4	14.7	0.7	14.8	0.7	15.1	2.0	15.2	0.7	15.4	1.3	15.5	0.6	15.7	1.3	15.6	-0.6
1942	15.8	1.3	16.1	1.9	16.2	0.6	16.2	0.0	16.4	1.2	16.5	0.6	16.7	1.2	16.7	0.0	16.8	0.6	17.1	1.8	17.2	0.6	17.2	0.0
1943	17.2	0.0	17.2	0.0	17.5	1.7	17.6	0.6	17.7	0.6	17.6	-0.6	17.4	-1.1	17.4	0.0	17.4	0.0	17.6	1.1	17.5	-0.6	17.5	0.0
1944	17.5	0.0	17.4	-0.6	17.4	0.0	17.6	1.1	17.6	0.0	17.6	0.0	17.7	0.6	17.8	0.6	17.9	0.6	17.7	-1.1	17.8	0.6	17.9	0.6
1945	17.9	0.0	17.9	0.0	17.8	-0.6	17.8	0.0	17.9	0.6	18.2	1.7	18.2	0.0	18.2	0.0	18.1	-0.5	18.0	-0.6	18.1	0.6	18.1	0.0
1946	18.2	0.6	18.1	-0.5	18.2	0.6	18.3	0.5	18.3	0.0	18.5	1.1	19.9	7.6	20.3	2.0	20.5	1.0	21.0	2.4	21.2	1.0	21.5	1.4
1947	21.6	0.5	21.4	-0.9	21.8	1.9	21.7	-0.5	21.6	-0.5	21.8	0.9	22.0	0.9	22.4	1.8	23.0	2.7	22.8	-0.9	23.0	0.9	23.3	1.3
1948	23.7	1.7	23.4	-1.3	23.4	0.0	23.7	1.3	23.8	0.4	24.1	1.3	24.5	1.7	24.5	0.0	24.6	0.4	24.4	-0.8	24.2	-0.8	23.9	-1.2
1949	23.8	-0.4	23.5	-1.3	23.6	0.4	23.6	0.0	23.6	0.0	23.7	0.4	23.7	0.0	23.8	0.4	24.0	0.8	23.8	-0.8	23.8	0.0	23.7	-0.4
1950	23.5	-0.8	23.5	0.0	23.6	0.4	23.6	0.0	23.7	0.4	24.0	1.3	24.2	0.8	24.4	0.8	24.4	0.0	24.6	0.8	24.6	0.0	24.8	0.8
1951	25.1	1.2	25.4	1.2	25.4	0.0	25.4	0.0	25.5	0.4	25.6	0.4	25.6	0.0	25.7	0.4	25.7	0.0	25.9	0.8	26.1	0.8	26.2	0.4
1952	26.1	-0.4	25.9	-0.8	25.9	0.0	25.9	0.0	26.1	0.8	26.1	0.0	26.5	1.5	26.5	0.0	26.4	-0.4	26.4	0.0	26.3	-0.4	26.2	-0.4
1953	26.1	-0.4	-	-	-	-	26.1	0.0	-	-	-	-	26.4	1.1	-	-	-	-	26.5	0.4	-	-	-	-
1954	26.3	-0.8	-	-	-	-	26.3	0.0	-	-	-	-	26.5	0.8	-	-	-	-	26.5	0.0	-	-	-	-
1955	26.3	-0.8	-	-	-	-	26.4	0.4	-	-	-	-	26.5	0.4	-	-	-	-	26.7	0.8	-	-	-	-
1956	26.7	0.0	-	-	-	-	26.8	0.4	-	-	-	-	27.5	2.6	-	-	-	-	27.8	1.1	-	-	-	-
1957	27.7	-0.4	-	-	-	-	28.0	1.1	-	-	-	-	28.4	1.4	-	-	-	-	28.4	0.0	-	-	-	-
1958	28.8	1.4	-	-	-	-	29.0	0.7	-	-	-	-	29.2	0.7	-	-	-	-	29.2	0.0	-	-	-	-

[Continued]

Boston, MA
Consumer Price Index - Urban Wage Earners
Base 1982-1984 = 100
All Items
[Continued]

For 1914-1995. Columns headed % show percentile change in the index from the previous period for which an index is available.

Year	Jan Index	%	Feb Index	%	Mar Index	%	Apr Index	%	May Index	%	Jun Index	%	Jul Index	%	Aug Index	%	Sep Index	%	Oct Index	%	Nov Index	%	Dec Index	%
1959	29.2	0.0	-	-	-	-	29.2	0.0	-	-	-	-	29.3	0.3	-	-	-	-	29.5	0.7	-	-	-	-
1960	29.4	-0.3	-	-	-	-	29.9	1.7	-	-	-	-	30.0	0.3	-	-	-	-	30.1	0.3	-	-	-	-
1961	30.1	0.0	-	-	-	-	30.3	0.7	-	-	-	-	30.4	0.3	-	-	-	-	30.4	0.0	-	-	-	-
1962	30.7	1.0	-	-	-	-	30.9	0.7	-	-	-	-	31.0	0.3	-	-	-	-	31.2	0.6	-	-	-	-
1963	31.4	0.6	-	-	-	-	31.6	0.6	-	-	-	-	31.7	0.3	-	-	-	-	31.8	0.3	-	-	-	-
1964	31.8	0.0	-	-	-	-	31.9	0.3	-	-	-	-	32.1	0.6	-	-	-	-	32.2	0.3	-	-	-	-
1965	32.4	0.6	-	-	-	-	32.6	0.6	-	-	-	-	32.8	0.6	-	-	-	-	32.8	0.0	-	-	-	-
1966	32.9	0.3	-	-	-	-	33.7	2.4	-	-	-	-	33.8	0.3	-	-	-	-	34.2	1.2	-	-	-	-
1967	34.3	0.3	-	-	-	-	34.3	0.0	-	-	-	-	34.6	0.9	-	-	-	-	34.9	0.9	-	-	-	-
1968	35.2	0.9	-	-	-	-	35.7	1.4	-	-	-	-	36.0	0.8	-	-	-	-	36.6	1.7	-	-	-	-
1969	37.0	1.1	-	-	-	-	37.5	1.4	-	-	-	-	38.2	1.9	-	-	-	-	38.9	1.8	-	-	-	-
1970	39.3	1.0	-	-	-	-	39.8	1.3	-	-	-	-	40.3	1.3	-	-	-	-	41.3	2.5	-	-	-	-
1971	41.8	1.2	-	-	-	-	42.1	0.7	-	-	-	-	42.5	1.0	-	-	-	-	43.0	1.2	-	-	-	-
1972	43.2	0.5	-	-	-	-	43.7	1.2	-	-	-	-	43.9	0.5	-	-	-	-	44.6	1.6	-	-	-	-
1973	44.9	0.7	-	-	-	-	45.8	2.0	-	-	-	-	46.4	1.3	-	-	-	-	48.0	3.4	-	-	-	-
1974	49.1	2.3	-	-	-	-	50.2	2.2	-	-	-	-	51.8	3.2	-	-	-	-	52.9	2.1	-	-	-	-
1975	54.1	2.3	-	-	-	-	55.0	1.7	-	-	-	-	56.4	2.5	-	-	-	-	57.0	1.1	-	-	-	-
1976	59.5	4.4	-	-	-	-	59.7	0.3	-	-	-	-	60.6	1.5	-	-	-	-	60.9	0.5	-	-	-	-
1977	61.9	1.6	-	-	-	-	62.8	1.5	-	-	-	-	63.8	1.6	-	-	-	-	64.2	0.6	-	-	-	-
1978	64.9	1.1	-	-	65.0	0.2	-	-	65.8	1.2	-	-	66.7	1.4	-	-	67.6	1.3	-	-	68.9	1.9	-	-
1979	69.4	0.7	-	-	70.7	1.9	-	-	72.2	2.1	-	-	73.9	2.4	-	-	75.4	2.0	-	-	77.0	2.1	-	-
1980	78.5	1.9	-	-	81.0	3.2	-	-	81.9	1.1	-	-	83.3	1.7	-	-	84.6	1.6	-	-	86.2	1.9	-	-
1981	88.5	2.7	-	-	90.6	2.4	-	-	91.2	0.7	-	-	92.2	1.1	-	-	94.7	2.7	-	-	94.9	0.2	-	-
1982	94.6	-0.3	-	-	93.3	-1.4	-	-	94.1	0.9	-	-	96.4	2.4	-	-	97.8	1.5	-	-	98.4	0.6	-	-
1983	98.4	0.0	-	-	98.6	0.2	-	-	98.9	0.3	-	-	99.9	1.0	-	-	100.1	0.2	-	-	101.4	1.3	-	-
1984	102.1	0.7	-	-	103.2	1.1	-	-	104.1	0.9	-	-	104.1	0.0	-	-	105.6	1.4	-	-	106.0	0.4	-	-
1985	106.5	0.5	-	-	108.0	1.4	-	-	108.4	0.4	-	-	109.2	0.7	-	-	110.5	1.2	-	-	111.8	1.2	-	-
1986	112.3	0.4	-	-	111.5	-0.7	-	-	110.5	-0.9	-	-	111.0	0.5	-	-	112.5	1.4	-	-	112.8	0.3	-	-
1987	114.5	1.5	-	-	115.8	1.1	-	-	115.2	-0.5	-	-	116.4	1.0	-	-	119.5	2.7	-	-	119.9	0.3	-	-
1988	120.2	0.3	-	-	121.8	1.3	-	-	123.1	1.1	-	-	123.7	0.5	-	-	126.1	1.9	-	-	127.4	1.0	-	-
1989	128.9	1.2	-	-	129.7	0.6	-	-	130.6	0.7	-	-	130.8	0.2	-	-	132.6	1.4	-	-	134.7	1.6	-	-
1990	136.0	1.0	-	-	136.5	0.4	-	-	136.8	0.2	-	-	137.4	0.4	-	-	140.9	2.5	-	-	143.5	1.8	-	-
1991	143.3	-0.1	-	-	143.3	0.0	-	-	143.4	0.1	-	-	144.7	0.9	-	-	145.8	0.8	-	-	146.2	0.3	-	-
1992	146.1	-0.1	-	-	147.2	0.8	-	-	146.8	-0.3	-	-	148.2	1.0	-	-	148.7	0.3	-	-	150.0	0.9	-	-
1993	151.1	0.7	-	-	154.0	1.9	-	-	151.4	-1.7	-	-	151.6	0.1	-	-	151.0	-0.4	-	-	153.4	1.6	-	-
1994	152.5	-0.6	-	-	153.5	0.7	-	-	152.2	-0.8	-	-	152.9	0.5	-	-	154.7	1.2	-	-	155.8	0.7	-	-
1995	157.0	0.8	-	-	156.9	-0.1	-	-	156.5	-0.3	-	-	156.6	0.1	-	-	157.4	0.5	-	-	159.3	1.2	-	-

Source: U.S. Department of Labor, Bureau of Labor Statistics, Division of Consumer Prices and Price Indexes. - indicates no data collected for period.

Boston, MA
Consumer Price Index - All Urban Consumers
Base 1982-1984 = 100
Food and Beverages

For 1976-1995. Columns headed % show percentile change in the index from the previous period for which an index is available.

Year	Jan Index	%	Feb Index	%	Mar Index	%	Apr Index	%	May Index	%	Jun Index	%	Jul Index	%	Aug Index	%	Sep Index	%	Oct Index	%	Nov Index	%	Dec Index	%
1976	66.9	-	-	-	-	-	66.6	-0.4	-	-	-	-	67.6	1.5	-	-	-	-	67.0	-0.9	-	-	-	-
1977	66.8	-0.3	-	-	-	-	69.0	3.3	-	-	-	-	70.8	2.6	-	-	-	-	70.6	-0.3	-	-	-	-
1978	71.5	1.3	-	-	72.7	1.7	-	-	74.6	2.6	-	-	76.5	2.5	-	-	77.1	0.8	-	-	77.4	0.4	-	-
1979	78.7	1.7	-	-	81.0	2.9	-	-	83.7	3.3	-	-	85.7	2.4	-	-	84.1	-1.9	-	-	84.1	0.0	-	-
1980	86.2	2.5	-	-	87.4	1.4	-	-	87.6	0.2	-	-	89.6	2.3	-	-	90.2	0.7	-	-	91.6	1.6	-	-
1981	94.4	3.1	-	-	94.6	0.2	-	-	94.2	-0.4	-	-	94.4	0.2	-	-	93.8	-0.6	-	-	94.1	0.3	-	-
1982	95.9	1.9	-	-	95.9	0.0	-	-	96.5	0.6	-	-	97.2	0.7	-	-	97.1	-0.1	-	-	96.8	-0.3	-	-
1983	97.4	0.6	-	-	99.1	1.7	-	-	98.6	-0.5	-	-	99.5	0.9	-	-	99.2	-0.3	-	-	100.0	0.8	-	-
1984	102.2	2.2	-	-	103.8	1.6	-	-	104.0	0.2	-	-	104.4	0.4	-	-	105.0	0.6	-	-	104.9	-0.1	-	-
1985	106.6	1.6	-	-	107.7	1.0	-	-	107.8	0.1	-	-	109.2	1.3	-	-	109.0	-0.2	-	-	110.1	1.0	-	-
1986	111.9	1.6	-	-	110.8	-1.0	-	-	112.2	1.3	-	-	114.1	1.7	-	-	116.2	1.8	-	-	115.4	-0.7	-	-
1987	119.3	3.4	-	-	118.4	-0.8	-	-	119.0	0.5	-	-	119.4	0.3	-	-	120.2	0.7	-	-	119.7	-0.4	-	-
1988	122.0	1.9	-	-	120.8	-1.0	-	-	123.5	2.2	-	-	124.8	1.1	-	-	127.3	2.0	-	-	126.4	-0.7	-	-
1989	128.1	1.3	-	-	130.2	1.6	-	-	131.5	1.0	-	-	133.5	1.5	-	-	133.8	0.2	-	-	133.9	0.1	-	-
1990	137.1	2.4	-	-	138.3	0.9	-	-	138.0	-0.2	-	-	138.3	0.2	-	-	139.4	0.8	-	-	139.5	0.1	-	-
1991	142.2	1.9	-	-	141.3	-0.6	-	-	143.2	1.3	-	-	143.0	-0.1	-	-	141.9	-0.8	-	-	142.9	0.7	-	-
1992	143.5	0.4	-	-	143.7	0.1	-	-	142.4	-0.9	-	-	143.1	0.5	-	-	143.3	0.1	-	-	143.5	0.1	-	-
1993	145.4	1.3	-	-	145.2	-0.1	-	-	146.3	0.8	-	-	146.7	0.3	-	-	146.6	-0.1	-	-	146.9	0.2	-	-
1994	148.0	0.7	-	-	149.4	0.9	-	-	148.6	-0.5	-	-	149.8	0.8	-	-	151.4	1.1	-	-	150.8	-0.4	-	-
1995	155.0	2.8	-	-	153.1	-1.2	-	-	154.0	0.6	-	-	152.5	-1.0	-	-	153.4	0.6	-	-	153.7	0.2	-	-

Source: U.S. Department of Labor, Bureau of Labor Statistics, Division of Consumer Prices and Price Indexes. - indicates no data collected for period.

Boston, MA
Consumer Price Index - Urban Wage Earners
Base 1982-1984 = 100
Food and Beverages

For 1976-1995. Columns headed % show percentile change in the index from the previous period for which an index is available.

Year	Jan Index	%	Feb Index	%	Mar Index	%	Apr Index	%	May Index	%	Jun Index	%	Jul Index	%	Aug Index	%	Sep Index	%	Oct Index	%	Nov Index	%	Dec Index	%
1976	67.5	-	-	-	-	-	67.2	-0.4	-	-	-	-	68.1	1.3	-	-	-	-	67.5	-0.9	-	-	-	-
1977	67.4	-0.1	-	-	-	-	69.7	3.4	-	-	-	-	71.4	2.4	-	-	-	-	71.2	-0.3	-	-	-	-
1978	72.1	1.3	-	-	73.3	1.7	-	-	74.9	2.2	-	-	77.6	3.6	-	-	77.5	-0.1	-	-	78.0	0.6	-	-
1979	78.6	0.8	-	-	81.3	3.4	-	-	83.5	2.7	-	-	85.8	2.8	-	-	84.0	-2.1	-	-	84.6	0.7	-	-
1980	86.1	1.8	-	-	87.7	1.9	-	-	88.6	1.0	-	-	90.1	1.7	-	-	90.9	0.9	-	-	92.2	1.4	-	-
1981	94.3	2.3	-	-	95.2	1.0	-	-	94.7	-0.5	-	-	94.7	0.0	-	-	94.4	-0.3	-	-	94.2	-0.2	-	-
1982	95.6	1.5	-	-	95.7	0.1	-	-	96.3	0.6	-	-	97.3	1.0	-	-	97.2	-0.1	-	-	96.7	-0.5	-	-
1983	97.2	0.5	-	-	99.0	1.9	-	-	98.6	-0.4	-	-	99.6	1.0	-	-	99.2	-0.4	-	-	99.9	0.7	-	-
1984	102.3	2.4	-	-	104.1	1.8	-	-	104.2	0.1	-	-	104.8	0.6	-	-	104.9	0.1	-	-	104.7	-0.2	-	-
1985	106.5	1.7	-	-	107.7	1.1	-	-	107.6	-0.1	-	-	109.1	1.4	-	-	108.7	-0.4	-	-	109.4	0.6	-	-
1986	111.3	1.7	-	-	110.3	-0.9	-	-	111.4	1.0	-	-	113.8	2.2	-	-	115.9	1.8	-	-	114.7	-1.0	-	-
1987	119.1	3.8	-	-	117.9	-1.0	-	-	118.2	0.3	-	-	118.8	0.5	-	-	119.6	0.7	-	-	119.0	-0.5	-	-
1988	121.3	1.9	-	-	120.1	-1.0	-	-	123.0	2.4	-	-	124.4	1.1	-	-	126.9	2.0	-	-	125.7	-0.9	-	-
1989	127.5	1.4	-	-	129.5	1.6	-	-	130.8	1.0	-	-	133.0	1.7	-	-	133.1	0.1	-	-	132.9	-0.2	-	-
1990	136.2	2.5	-	-	137.4	0.9	-	-	137.2	-0.1	-	-	137.7	0.4	-	-	138.9	0.9	-	-	138.8	-0.1	-	-
1991	141.3	1.8	-	-	140.4	-0.6	-	-	142.5	1.5	-	-	142.1	-0.3	-	-	141.2	-0.6	-	-	142.1	0.6	-	-
1992	142.6	0.4	-	-	142.8	0.1	-	-	141.6	-0.8	-	-	142.0	0.3	-	-	142.4	0.3	-	-	142.5	0.1	-	-
1993	144.6	1.5	-	-	144.4	-0.1	-	-	145.3	0.6	-	-	145.9	0.4	-	-	145.7	-0.1	-	-	145.9	0.1	-	-
1994	147.0	0.8	-	-	148.3	0.9	-	-	147.4	-0.6	-	-	148.6	0.8	-	-	150.1	1.0	-	-	149.2	-0.6	-	-
1995	153.6	2.9	-	-	151.6	-1.3	-	-	152.4	0.5	-	-	150.8	-1.0	-	-	152.0	0.8	-	-	152.1	0.1	-	-

Source: U.S. Department of Labor, Bureau of Labor Statistics, Division of Consumer Prices and Price Indexes. - indicates no data collected for period.

Boston, MA
Consumer Price Index - All Urban Consumers
Base 1982-1984 = 100
Housing

For 1976-1995. Columns headed % show percentile change in the index from the previous period for which an index is available.

Year	Jan Index	%	Feb Index	%	Mar Index	%	Apr Index	%	May Index	%	Jun Index	%	Jul Index	%	Aug Index	%	Sep Index	%	Oct Index	%	Nov Index	%	Dec Index	%
1976	55.2	-	-	-	-	-	55.6	0.7	-	-	-	-	56.4	1.4	-	-	-	-	56.7	0.5	-	-	-	-
1977	58.7	3.5	-	-	-	-	58.9	0.3	-	-	-	-	59.8	1.5	-	-	-	-	60.0	0.3	-	-	-	-
1978	61.2	2.0	-	-	61.9	1.1	-	-	62.1	0.3	-	-	62.9	1.3	-	-	63.6	1.1	-	-	65.4	2.8	-	-
1979	67.1	2.6	-	-	67.4	0.4	-	-	67.9	0.7	-	-	69.2	1.9	-	-	71.7	3.6	-	-	74.1	3.3	-	-
1980	75.6	2.0	-	-	78.4	3.7	-	-	79.3	1.1	-	-	81.0	2.1	-	-	82.0	1.2	-	-	83.4	1.7	-	-
1981	87.8	5.3	-	-	90.0	2.5	-	-	90.1	0.1	-	-	91.7	1.8	-	-	95.5	4.1	-	-	95.2	-0.3	-	-
1982	94.1	-1.2	-	-	89.6	-4.8	-	-	91.7	2.3	-	-	95.2	3.8	-	-	97.1	2.0	-	-	98.6	1.5	-	-
1983	100.1	1.5	-	-	98.8	-1.3	-	-	99.3	0.5	-	-	99.7	0.4	-	-	100.8	1.1	-	-	102.5	1.7	-	-
1984	103.1	0.6	-	-	104.0	0.9	-	-	104.3	0.3	-	-	105.5	1.2	-	-	106.1	0.6	-	-	106.4	0.3	-	-
1985	106.9	0.5	-	-	107.6	0.7	-	-	107.6	0.0	-	-	109.4	1.7	-	-	110.1	0.6	-	-	112.2	1.9	-	-
1986	111.8	-0.4	-	-	111.4	-0.4	-	-	110.1	-1.2	-	-	110.2	0.1	-	-	112.4	2.0	-	-	113.5	1.0	-	-
1987	114.2	0.6	-	-	115.3	1.0	-	-	114.7	-0.5	-	-	116.1	1.2	-	-	119.1	2.6	-	-	119.9	0.7	-	-
1988	119.8	-0.1	-	-	121.0	1.0	-	-	122.9	1.6	-	-	123.9	0.8	-	-	125.5	1.3	-	-	126.6	0.9	-	-
1989	130.0	2.7	-	-	130.5	0.4	-	-	129.2	-1.0	-	-	129.7	0.4	-	-	132.8	2.4	-	-	134.1	1.0	-	-
1990	136.0	1.4	-	-	135.4	-0.4	-	-	134.4	-0.7	-	-	136.4	1.5	-	-	137.4	0.7	-	-	140.9	2.5	-	-
1991	142.3	1.0	-	-	142.3	0.0	-	-	139.4	-2.0	-	-	140.6	0.9	-	-	140.7	0.1	-	-	140.7	0.0	-	-
1992	140.9	0.1	-	-	143.9	2.1	-	-	142.0	-1.3	-	-	144.1	1.5	-	-	143.7	-0.3	-	-	145.5	1.3	-	-
1993	146.7	0.8	-	-	147.1	0.3	-	-	144.8	-1.6	-	-	146.0	0.8	-	-	145.4	-0.4	-	-	148.1	1.9	-	-
1994	147.0	-0.7	-	-	148.1	0.7	-	-	145.8	-1.6	-	-	147.1	0.9	-	-	148.1	0.7	-	-	150.2	1.4	-	-
1995	151.7	1.0	-	-	153.1	0.9	-	-	149.4	-2.4	-	-	149.9	0.3	-	-	151.0	0.7	-	-	153.4	1.6	-	-

Source: U.S. Department of Labor, Bureau of Labor Statistics, Division of Consumer Prices and Price Indexes. - indicates no data collected for period.

Boston, MA
Consumer Price Index - Urban Wage Earners
Base 1982-1984 = 100
Housing

For 1976-1995. Columns headed % show percentile change in the index from the previous period for which an index is available.

Year	Jan Index	%	Feb Index	%	Mar Index	%	Apr Index	%	May Index	%	Jun Index	%	Jul Index	%	Aug Index	%	Sep Index	%	Oct Index	%	Nov Index	%	Dec Index	%
1976	55.1	-	-	-	-	-	55.5	0.7	-	-	-	-	56.3	1.4	-	-	-	-	56.6	0.5	-	-	-	-
1977	58.6	3.5	-	-	-	-	58.8	0.3	-	-	-	-	59.7	1.5	-	-	-	-	59.9	0.3	-	-	-	-
1978	61.1	2.0	-	-	61.8	1.1	-	-	61.9	0.2	-	-	62.8	1.5	-	-	63.7	1.4	-	-	65.5	2.8	-	-
1979	67.1	2.4	-	-	67.4	0.4	-	-	68.1	1.0	-	-	69.5	2.1	-	-	71.9	3.5	-	-	74.4	3.5	-	-
1980	76.2	2.4	-	-	79.2	3.9	-	-	80.1	1.1	-	-	81.7	2.0	-	-	82.7	1.2	-	-	84.6	2.3	-	-
1981	88.9	5.1	-	-	91.0	2.4	-	-	91.3	0.3	-	-	93.5	2.4	-	-	97.1	3.9	-	-	96.2	-0.9	-	-
1982	95.1	-1.1	-	-	90.2	-5.2	-	-	92.5	2.5	-	-	96.1	3.9	-	-	98.0	2.0	-	-	99.6	1.6	-	-
1983	99.8	0.2	-	-	98.7	-1.1	-	-	98.8	0.1	-	-	100.3	1.5	-	-	100.5	0.2	-	-	99.6	1.6	-	-
1984	102.6	0.0	-	-	102.3	-0.3	-	-	103.8	1.5	-	-	103.3	-0.5	-	-	105.9	2.5	-	-	102.6	2.1	-	-
1985	107.4	0.5	-	-	108.0	0.6	-	-	108.1	0.1	-	-	109.9	1.7	-	-	110.5	0.5	-	-	106.9	0.9	-	-
1986	112.4	-0.2	-	-	111.8	-0.5	-	-	110.3	-1.3	-	-	110.4	0.1	-	-	112.5	1.9	-	-	112.6	1.9	-	-
1987	114.0	0.4	-	-	115.4	1.2	-	-	114.8	-0.5	-	-	116.1	1.1	-	-	119.1	2.6	-	-	113.6	1.0	-	-
1988	119.7	-0.3	-	-	120.8	0.9	-	-	122.8	1.7	-	-	123.6	0.7	-	-	125.2	1.3	-	-	120.1	0.8	-	-
1989	129.6	2.4	-	-	130.1	0.4	-	-	128.7	-1.1	-	-	129.5	0.6	-	-	132.5	2.3	-	-	126.6	1.1	-	-
1990	135.3	0.9	-	-	134.8	-0.4	-	-	133.6	-0.9	-	-	135.2	1.2	-	-	136.1	0.7	-	-	134.1	1.2	-	-
1991	140.6	0.4	-	-	140.5	-0.1	-	-	138.1	-1.7	-	-	139.1	0.7	-	-	139.5	0.3	-	-	140.0	2.9	-	-
1992	139.6	-0.2	-	-	142.2	1.9	-	-	140.4	-1.3	-	-	142.5	1.5	-	-	142.1	-0.3	-	-	139.9	0.3	-	-
1993	145.4	0.6	-	-	145.5	0.1	-	-	143.5	-1.4	-	-	144.2	0.5	-	-	143.9	-0.2	-	-	144.5	1.7	-	-
1994	145.7	-1.0	-	-	146.4	0.5	-	-	144.5	-1.3	-	-	145.4	0.6	-	-	146.5	0.8	-	-	147.2	2.3	-	-
1995	150.2	0.8	-	-	151.1	0.6	-	-	147.8	-2.2	-	-	148.1	0.2	-	-	149.3	0.8	-	-	149.0	1.7	-	-

Source: U.S. Department of Labor, Bureau of Labor Statistics, Division of Consumer Prices and Price Indexes. - indicates no data collected for period.

Boston, MA
Consumer Price Index - All Urban Consumers
Base 1982-1984 = 100
Apparel and Upkeep

For 1952-1995. Columns headed % show percentile change in the index from the previous period for which an index is available.

Year	Jan Index	%	Feb Index	%	Mar Index	%	Apr Index	%	May Index	%	Jun Index	%	Jul Index	%	Aug Index	%	Sep Index	%	Oct Index	%	Nov Index	%	Dec Index	%
1952	-	-	-	-	-	-	-	-	-	-	-	-	-	-	-	-	-	-	39.6		-	-	-	-
1953	39.2	-1.0	-	-	-	-	39.5	0.8	-	-	-	-	39.5	0.0	-	-	-	-	39.6	0.3	-	-	-	-
1954	38.6	-2.5	-	-	-	-	38.8	0.5	-	-	-	-	39.1	0.8	-	-	-	-	39.9	2.0	-	-	-	-
1955	39.0	-2.3	-	-	-	-	39.3	0.8	-	-	-	-	39.1	-0.5	-	-	-	-	39.5	1.0	-	-	-	-
1956	39.0	-1.3	-	-	-	-	39.6	1.5	-	-	-	-	39.7	0.3	-	-	-	-	40.6	2.3	-	-	-	-
1957	39.7	-2.2	-	-	-	-	40.5	2.0	-	-	-	-	40.3	-0.5	-	-	-	-	41.1	2.0	-	-	-	-
1958	40.8	-0.7	-	-	-	-	40.9	0.2	-	-	-	-	41.2	0.7	-	-	-	-	41.8	1.5	-	-	-	-
1959	40.3	-3.6	-	-	-	-	40.3	0.0	-	-	-	-	40.7	1.0	-	-	-	-	41.7	2.5	-	-	-	-
1960	41.3	-1.0	-	-	-	-	41.9	1.5	-	-	-	-	42.3	1.0	-	-	-	-	42.6	0.7	-	-	-	-
1961	42.1	-1.2	-	-	-	-	42.0	-0.2	-	-	-	-	42.3	0.7	-	-	-	-	43.0	1.7	-	-	-	-
1962	41.9	-2.6	-	-	-	-	43.0	2.6	-	-	-	-	43.1	0.2	-	-	-	-	43.7	1.4	-	-	-	-
1963	43.0	-1.6	-	-	-	-	43.3	0.7	-	-	-	-	43.0	-0.7	-	-	-	-	44.1	2.6	-	-	-	-
1964	43.0	-2.5	-	-	-	-	43.8	1.9	-	-	-	-	43.5	-0.7	-	-	-	-	44.1	1.4	-	-	-	-
1965	43.2	-2.0	-	-	-	-	43.7	1.2	-	-	-	-	44.0	0.7	-	-	-	-	44.5	1.1	-	-	-	-
1966	44.4	-0.2	-	-	-	-	44.9	1.1	-	-	-	-	44.6	-0.7	-	-	-	-	45.9	2.9	-	-	-	-
1967	45.3	-1.3	-	-	-	-	46.3	2.2	-	-	-	-	46.3	0.0	-	-	-	-	47.5	2.6	-	-	-	-
1968	46.9	-1.3	-	-	-	-	49.3	5.1	-	-	-	-	48.8	-1.0	-	-	-	-	51.0	4.5	-	-	-	-
1969	50.4	-1.2	-	-	-	-	51.4	2.0	-	-	-	-	51.4	0.0	-	-	-	-	54.4	5.8	-	-	-	-
1970	52.6	-3.3	-	-	-	-	54.9	4.4	-	-	-	-	53.7	-2.2	-	-	-	-	56.5	5.2	-	-	-	-
1971	55.4	-1.9	-	-	-	-	56.6	2.2	-	-	-	-	56.2	-0.7	-	-	-	-	57.9	3.0	-	-	-	-
1972	56.7	-2.1	-	-	-	-	57.2	0.9	-	-	-	-	57.3	0.2	-	-	-	-	59.5	3.8	-	-	-	-
1973	58.1	-2.4	-	-	-	-	59.6	2.6	-	-	-	-	59.2	-0.7	-	-	-	-	61.3	3.5	-	-	-	-
1974	60.7	-1.0	-	-	-	-	63.4	4.4	-	-	-	-	63.8	0.6	-	-	-	-	66.6	4.4	-	-	-	-
1975	66.0	-0.9	-	-	-	-	67.5	2.3	-	-	-	-	67.6	0.1	-	-	-	-	70.4	4.1	-	-	-	-
1976	70.6	0.3	-	-	-	-	71.2	0.8	-	-	-	-	71.1	-0.1	-	-	-	-	72.7	2.3	-	-	-	-
1977	71.4	-1.8	-	-	-	-	72.5	1.5	-	-	-	-	72.0	-0.7	-	-	-	-	75.6	5.0	-	-	-	-
1978	74.8	-1.1	-	-	76.9	2.8	-	-	79.4	3.3	-	-	76.2	-4.0	-	-	81.2	6.6	-	-	83.0	2.2	-	-
1979	78.7	-5.2	-	-	84.6	7.5	-	-	84.6	0.0	-	-	83.7	-1.1	-	-	88.0	5.1	-	-	88.1	0.1	-	-
1980	85.7	-2.7	-	-	88.4	3.2	-	-	88.8	0.5	-	-	87.2	-1.8	-	-	92.5	6.1	-	-	93.2	0.8	-	-
1981	90.6	-2.8	-	-	95.3	5.2	-	-	93.4	-2.0	-	-	92.3	-1.2	-	-	95.6	3.6	-	-	95.6	0.0	-	-
1982	92.5	-3.2	-	-	97.0	4.9	-	-	95.8	-1.2	-	-	95.9	0.1	-	-	101.0	5.3	-	-	100.6	-0.4	-	-
1983	99.3	-1.3	-	-	101.3	2.0	-	-	100.8	-0.5	-	-	99.8	-1.0	-	-	98.4	-1.4	-	-	99.8	1.4	-	-
1984	98.7	-1.1	-	-	103.3	4.7	-	-	102.9	-0.4	-	-	101.0	-1.8	-	-	106.2	5.1	-	-	103.8	-2.3	-	-
1985	100.7	-3.0	-	-	106.8	6.1	-	-	107.1	0.3	-	-	101.7	-5.0	-	-	110.4	8.6	-	-	108.8	-1.4	-	-
1986	106.2	-2.4	-	-	108.4	2.1	-	-	107.8	-0.6	-	-	106.6	-1.1	-	-	111.2	4.3	-	-	108.5	-2.4	-	-
1987	107.4	-1.0	-	-	122.6	14.2	-	-	112.4	-8.3	-	-	110.3	-1.9	-	-	123.4	11.9	-	-	117.8	-4.5	-	-
1988	112.6	-4.4	-	-	134.7	19.6	-	-	128.4	-4.7	-	-	118.9	-7.4	-	-	126.7	6.6	-	-	130.8	3.2	-	-
1989	124.6	-4.7	-	-	121.4	-2.6	-	-	126.3	4.0	-	-	117.6	-6.9	-	-	121.5	3.3	-	-	137.5	13.2	-	-
1990	132.0	-4.0	-	-	129.7	-1.7	-	-	135.2	4.2	-	-	124.7	-7.8	-	-	154.6	24.0	-	-	152.5	-1.4	-	-
1991	135.6	-11.1	-	-	139.3	2.7	-	-	140.8	1.1	-	-	138.1	-1.9	-	-	157.9	14.3	-	-	154.1	-2.4	-	-
1992	144.5	-6.2	-	-	142.5	-1.4	-	-	142.7	0.1	-	-	141.4	-0.9	-	-	152.7	8.0	-	-	145.8	-4.5	-	-
1993	148.6	1.9	-	-	182.1	22.5	-	-	155.8	-14.4	-	-	150.1	-3.7	-	-	151.4	0.9	-	-	158.0	4.4	-	-
1994	149.9	-5.1	-	-	156.2	4.2	-	-	153.3	-1.9	-	-	140.1	-8.6	-	-	144.7	3.3	-	-	139.6	-3.5	-	-
1995	139.0	-0.4	-	-	142.3	2.4	-	-	145.5	2.2	-	-	145.5	0.0	-	-	145.8	0.2	-	-	144.3	-1.0	-	-

Source: U.S. Department of Labor, Bureau of Labor Statistics, Division of Consumer Prices and Price Indexes. - indicates no data collected for period.

Boston, MA
Consumer Price Index - Urban Wage Earners
Base 1982-1984 = 100
Apparel and Upkeep

For 1952-1995. Columns headed % show percentile change in the index from the previous period for which an index is available.

Year	Jan Index	%	Feb Index	%	Mar Index	%	Apr Index	%	May Index	%	Jun Index	%	Jul Index	%	Aug Index	%	Sep Index	%	Oct Index	%	Nov Index	%	Dec Index	%
1952	-	-	-	-	-	-	-	-	-	-	-	-	-	-	-	-	-	-	39.9	-	-	-	-	-
1953	39.4	-1.3	-	-	-	-	39.8	1.0	-	-	-	-	39.8	0.0	-	-	-	-	39.9	0.3	-	-	-	-
1954	38.9	-2.5	-	-	-	-	39.1	0.5	-	-	-	-	39.4	0.8	-	-	-	-	40.1	1.8	-	-	-	-
1955	39.3	-2.0	-	-	-	-	39.6	0.8	-	-	-	-	39.4	-0.5	-	-	-	-	39.8	1.0	-	-	-	-
1956	39.3	-1.3	-	-	-	-	39.9	1.5	-	-	-	-	40.0	0.3	-	-	-	-	40.9	2.3	-	-	-	-
1957	40.0	-2.2	-	-	-	-	40.8	2.0	-	-	-	-	40.6	-0.5	-	-	-	-	41.4	2.0	-	-	-	-
1958	41.1	-0.7	-	-	-	-	41.2	0.2	-	-	-	-	41.5	0.7	-	-	-	-	42.1	1.4	-	-	-	-
1959	40.6	-3.6	-	-	-	-	40.6	0.0	-	-	-	-	41.0	1.0	-	-	-	-	42.0	2.4	-	-	-	-
1960	41.6	-1.0	-	-	-	-	42.2	1.4	-	-	-	-	42.6	0.9	-	-	-	-	42.9	0.7	-	-	-	-
1961	42.4	-1.2	-	-	-	-	42.4	0.0	-	-	-	-	42.6	0.5	-	-	-	-	43.3	1.6	-	-	-	-
1962	42.3	-2.3	-	-	-	-	43.3	2.4	-	-	-	-	43.4	0.2	-	-	-	-	44.0	1.4	-	-	-	-
1963	43.3	-1.6	-	-	-	-	43.6	0.7	-	-	-	-	43.3	-0.7	-	-	-	-	44.4	2.5	-	-	-	-
1964	43.3	-2.5	-	-	-	-	44.1	1.8	-	-	-	-	43.8	-0.7	-	-	-	-	44.4	1.4	-	-	-	-
1965	43.6	-1.8	-	-	-	-	44.0	0.9	-	-	-	-	44.3	0.7	-	-	-	-	44.8	1.1	-	-	-	-
1966	44.7	-0.2	-	-	-	-	45.3	1.3	-	-	-	-	44.9	-0.9	-	-	-	-	46.2	2.9	-	-	-	-
1967	45.7	-1.1	-	-	-	-	46.7	2.2	-	-	-	-	46.7	0.0	-	-	-	-	47.9	2.6	-	-	-	-
1968	47.2	-1.5	-	-	-	-	49.7	5.3	-	-	-	-	49.1	-1.2	-	-	-	-	51.3	4.5	-	-	-	-
1969	50.7	-1.2	-	-	-	-	51.8	2.2	-	-	-	-	51.8	0.0	-	-	-	-	54.8	5.8	-	-	-	-
1970	53.0	-3.3	-	-	-	-	55.3	4.3	-	-	-	-	54.1	-2.2	-	-	-	-	57.0	5.4	-	-	-	-
1971	55.8	-2.1	-	-	-	-	57.0	2.2	-	-	-	-	56.6	-0.7	-	-	-	-	58.4	3.2	-	-	-	-
1972	57.2	-2.1	-	-	-	-	57.7	0.9	-	-	-	-	57.7	0.0	-	-	-	-	59.9	3.8	-	-	-	-
1973	58.5	-2.3	-	-	-	-	60.0	2.6	-	-	-	-	59.6	-0.7	-	-	-	-	61.8	3.7	-	-	-	-
1974	61.1	-1.1	-	-	-	-	63.9	4.6	-	-	-	-	64.3	0.6	-	-	-	-	67.1	4.4	-	-	-	-
1975	66.5	-0.9	-	-	-	-	68.0	2.3	-	-	-	-	68.1	0.1	-	-	-	-	70.9	4.1	-	-	-	-
1976	71.2	0.4	-	-	-	-	71.7	0.7	-	-	-	-	71.6	-0.1	-	-	-	-	73.3	2.4	-	-	-	-
1977	72.0	-1.8	-	-	-	-	73.0	1.4	-	-	-	-	72.5	-0.7	-	-	-	-	76.1	5.0	-	-	-	-
1978	75.4	-0.9	-	-	76.3	1.2	-	-	79.2	3.8	-	-	75.9	-4.2	-	-	81.4	7.2	-	-	80.9	-0.6	-	-
1979	77.2	-4.6	-	-	80.8	4.7	-	-	82.0	1.5	-	-	79.7	-2.8	-	-	87.7	10.0	-	-	86.8	-1.0	-	-
1980	83.0	-4.4	-	-	85.5	3.0	-	-	85.2	-0.4	-	-	84.4	-0.9	-	-	90.3	7.0	-	-	91.4	1.2	-	-
1981	87.6	-4.2	-	-	93.9	7.2	-	-	93.1	-0.9	-	-	89.6	-3.8	-	-	95.9	7.0	-	-	96.3	0.4	-	-
1982	92.2	-4.3	-	-	99.4	7.8	-	-	95.8	-3.6	-	-	95.9	0.1	-	-	102.3	6.7	-	-	101.0	-1.3	-	-
1983	98.5	-2.5	-	-	103.9	5.5	-	-	102.2	-1.6	-	-	99.2	-2.9	-	-	98.4	-0.8	-	-	99.0	0.6	-	-
1984	97.7	-1.3	-	-	101.9	4.3	-	-	101.6	-0.3	-	-	100.3	-1.3	-	-	105.8	5.5	-	-	103.4	-2.3	-	-
1985	99.6	-3.7	-	-	105.4	5.8	-	-	104.8	-0.6	-	-	100.0	-4.6	-	-	110.0	10.0	-	-	107.9	-1.9	-	-
1986	104.4	-3.2	-	-	107.8	3.3	-	-	106.2	-1.5	-	-	105.2	-0.9	-	-	110.1	4.7	-	-	107.2	-2.6	-	-
1987	112.2	4.7	-	-	127.6	13.7	-	-	115.9	-9.2	-	-	115.7	-0.2	-	-	130.1	12.4	-	-	124.3	-4.5	-	-
1988	120.9	-2.7	-	-	139.3	15.2	-	-	134.6	-3.4	-	-	125.9	-6.5	-	-	134.1	6.5	-	-	138.4	3.2	-	-
1989	130.5	-5.7	-	-	128.6	-1.5	-	-	134.9	4.9	-	-	126.8	-6.0	-	-	132.6	4.6	-	-	148.3	11.8	-	-
1990	141.4	-4.7	-	-	139.5	-1.3	-	-	147.3	5.6	-	-	134.5	-8.7	-	-	158.8	18.1	-	-	159.7	0.6	-	-
1991	143.7	-10.0	-	-	151.4	5.4	-	-	151.5	0.1	-	-	149.4	-1.4	-	-	162.6	8.8	-	-	157.7	-3.0	-	-
1992	154.2	-2.2	-	-	149.8	-2.9	-	-	150.1	0.2	-	-	149.1	-0.7	-	-	161.3	8.2	-	-	155.1	-3.8	-	-
1993	153.9	-0.8	-	-	202.4	31.5	-	-	164.3	-18.8	-	-	155.2	-5.5	-	-	157.8	1.7	-	-	163.1	3.4	-	-
1994	154.4	-5.3	-	-	157.5	2.0	-	-	156.5	-0.6	-	-	148.3	-5.2	-	-	152.1	2.6	-	-	163.1	3.4	-	-
1995	146.5	-0.1	-	-	148.5	1.4	-	-	151.8	2.2	-	-	152.8	0.7	-	-	152.5	-0.2	-	-	151.9	-0.4	-	-

Source: U.S. Department of Labor, Bureau of Labor Statistics, Division of Consumer Prices and Price Indexes. - indicates no data collected for period.

Boston, MA
Consumer Price Index - All Urban Consumers
Base 1982-1984 = 100
Transportation

For 1947-1995. Columns headed % show percentile change in the index from the previous period for which an index is available.

Year	Jan Index	%	Feb Index	%	Mar Index	%	Apr Index	%	May Index	%	Jun Index	%	Jul Index	%	Aug Index	%	Sep Index	%	Oct Index	%	Nov Index	%	Dec Index	%
1947	16.2	-	16.2	0.0	16.3	0.6	16.3	0.0	16.3	0.0	16.4	0.6	16.4	0.0	16.5	0.6	16.6	0.6	16.6	0.0	16.6	0.0	16.6	0.0
1948	16.7	0.6	16.8	0.6	16.8	0.0	16.8	0.0	16.8	0.0	16.8	0.0	16.9	0.6	17.1	1.2	17.1	0.0	17.1	0.0	17.1	0.0	17.1	0.0
1949	17.1	0.0	17.2	0.6	17.2	0.0	17.3	0.6	17.3	0.0	17.3	0.0	17.3	0.0	20.4	17.9	20.4	0.0	20.4	0.0	20.4	0.0	20.5	0.5
1950	20.5	0.0	20.4	-0.5	20.4	0.0	20.4	0.0	20.5	0.5	20.5	0.0	20.6	0.5	20.6	0.0	20.7	0.5	20.7	0.0	20.7	0.0	20.8	0.5
1951	20.8	0.0	20.8	0.0	20.8	0.0	20.8	0.0	20.8	0.0	20.8	0.0	20.8	0.0	21.6	3.8	21.6	0.0	21.8	0.9	21.9	0.5	21.9	0.0
1952	22.0	0.5	22.3	1.4	22.3	0.0	22.3	0.0	22.3	0.0	22.3	0.0	23.0	3.1	23.0	0.0	23.1	0.4	23.1	0.0	23.1	0.0	23.1	0.0
1953	23.2	0.4	-		-		23.5	1.3	-		-		23.7	0.9	-		-		23.7	0.0	-		-	
1954	23.4	-1.3	-		-		24.4	4.3	-		-		23.7	-2.9	-		-		23.0	-3.0	-		-	
1955	23.2	0.9	-		-		23.2	0.0	-		-		22.9	-1.3	-		-		23.5	2.6	-		-	
1956	23.5	0.0	-		-		23.6	0.4	-		-		23.5	-0.4	-		-		25.1	6.8	-		-	
1957	24.7	-1.6	-		-		24.9	0.8	-		-		25.0	0.4	-		-		25.2	0.8	-		-	
1958	25.4	0.8	-		-		25.9	2.0	-		-		25.8	-0.4	-		-		25.7	-0.4	-		-	
1959	26.5	3.1	-		-		26.4	-0.4	-		-		26.4	0.0	-		-		26.4	0.0	-		-	
1960	25.7	-2.7	-		-		25.7	0.0	-		-		25.9	0.8	-		-		25.9	0.0	-		-	
1961	25.6	-1.2	-		-		26.0	1.6	-		-		26.4	1.5	-		-		26.2	-0.8	-		-	
1962	28.1	7.3	-		-		28.3	0.7	-		-		28.0	-1.1	-		-		28.3	1.1	-		-	
1963	28.0	-1.1	-		-		28.3	1.1	-		-		28.5	0.7	-		-		28.3	-0.7	-		-	
1964	28.4	0.4	-		-		28.3	-0.4	-		-		28.6	1.1	-		-		28.3	-1.0	-		-	
1965	28.9	2.1	-		-		29.0	0.3	-		-		29.2	0.7	-		-		29.5	1.0	-		-	
1966	29.3	-0.7	-		-		29.9	2.0	-		-		30.1	0.7	-		-		30.1	0.0	-		-	
1967	30.1	0.0	-		-		30.4	1.0	-		-		30.7	1.0	-		-		30.9	0.7	-		-	
1968	31.2	1.0	-		-		31.5	1.0	-		-		31.5	0.0	-		-		31.7	0.6	-		-	
1969	32.9	3.8	-		-		33.6	2.1	-		-		33.6	0.0	-		-		33.6	0.0	-		-	
1970	33.7	0.3	-		-		34.0	0.9	-		-		34.5	1.5	-		-		36.3	5.2	-		-	
1971	36.6	0.8	-		-		36.2	-1.1	-		-		36.9	1.9	-		-		36.7	-0.5	-		-	
1972	36.5	-0.5	-		-		36.3	-0.5	-		-		36.5	0.6	-		-		37.0	1.4	-		-	
1973	37.0	0.0	-		-		37.1	0.3	-		-		37.8	1.9	-		-		37.8	0.0	-		-	
1974	38.6	2.1	-		-		39.8	3.1	-		-		42.0	5.5	-		-		42.3	0.7	-		-	
1975	42.8	1.2	-		-		45.1	5.4	-		-		47.0	4.2	-		-		47.6	1.3	-		-	
1976	57.8	21.4	-		-		58.1	0.5	-		-		59.8	2.9	-		-		60.2	0.7	-		-	
1977	62.2	3.3	-		-		63.3	1.8	-		-		63.9	0.9	-		-		63.6	-0.5	-		-	
1978	63.7	0.2	-		61.2	-3.9	-		62.2	1.6	-		63.3	1.8	-		63.6	0.5	-		64.2	0.9	-	
1979	63.6	-0.9	-		64.8	1.9	-		68.0	4.9	-		70.9	4.3	-		72.1	1.7	-		74.0	2.6	-	
1980	76.6	3.5	-		80.5	5.1	-		81.8	1.6	-		83.5	2.1	-		84.7	1.4	-		86.3	1.9	-	
1981	87.6	1.5	-		91.3	4.2	-		94.0	3.0	-		94.5	0.5	-		96.6	2.2	-		98.0	1.4	-	
1982	97.6	-0.4	-		97.0	-0.6	-		96.1	-0.9	-		99.3	3.3	-		99.8	0.5	-		99.7	-0.1	-	
1983	98.7	-1.0	-		97.2	-1.5	-		98.5	1.3	-		99.6	1.1	-		100.1	0.5	-		100.5	0.4	-	
1984	100.7	0.2	-		101.8	1.1	-		102.9	1.1	-		103.0	0.1	-		103.0	0.0	-		103.1	0.1	-	
1985	102.9	-0.2	-		104.3	1.4	-		105.4	1.1	-		105.7	0.3	-		105.7	0.0	-		106.8	1.0	-	
1986	106.9	0.1	-		103.8	-2.9	-		100.5	-3.2	-		100.5	0.0	-		99.4	-1.1	-		100.1	0.7	-	
1987	101.4	1.3	-		100.6	-0.8	-		101.8	1.2	-		103.4	1.6	-		104.9	1.5	-		106.8	1.8	-	
1988	106.1	-0.7	-		105.5	-0.6	-		106.2	0.7	-		107.9	1.6	-		109.6	1.6	-		112.8	2.9	-	
1989	112.5	-0.3	-		113.5	0.9	-		115.8	2.0	-		112.6	-2.8	-		112.6	0.0	-		114.6	1.8	-	
1990	115.7	1.0	-		116.1	0.3	-		117.1	0.9	-		117.3	0.2	-		122.3	4.3	⌐		127.4	4.2	-	
1991	125.3	-1.6	-		123.0	-1.8	-		124.3	1.1	-		125.7	1.1	-		126.2	0.4	-		127.8	1.3	-	

[Continued]

316

Boston, MA
Consumer Price Index - All Urban Consumers
Base 1982-1984 = 100
Transportation
[Continued]

For 1947-1995. Columns headed % show percentile change in the index from the previous period for which an index is available.

Year	Jan Index	%	Feb Index	%	Mar Index	%	Apr Index	%	May Index	%	Jun Index	%	Jul Index	%	Aug Index	%	Sep Index	%	Oct Index	%	Nov Index	%	Dec Index	%
1992	127.2	-0.5	-	-	128.6	1.1	-	-	129.1	0.4	-	-	129.9	0.6	-	-	128.9	-0.8	-	-	129.8	0.7	-	-
1993	131.9	1.6	-	-	132.4	0.4	-	-	132.1	-0.2	-	-	132.2	0.1	-	-	131.4	-0.6	-	-	134.4	2.3	-	-
1994	133.4	-0.7	-	-	134.1	0.5	-	-	132.5	-1.2	-	-	134.6	1.6	-	-	136.8	1.6	-	-	137.9	0.8	-	-
1995	137.1	-0.6	-	-	135.9	-0.9	-	-	137.5	1.2	-	-	137.4	-0.1	-	-	136.4	-0.7	-	-	137.7	1.0	-	-

Source: U.S. Department of Labor, Bureau of Labor Statistics, Division of Consumer Prices and Price Indexes. - indicates no data collected for period.

Boston, MA
Consumer Price Index - Urban Wage Earners
Base 1982-1984 = 100
Transportation

For 1947-1995. Columns headed % show percentile change in the index from the previous period for which an index is available.

Year	Jan Index	%	Feb Index	%	Mar Index	%	Apr Index	%	May Index	%	Jun Index	%	Jul Index	%	Aug Index	%	Sep Index	%	Oct Index	%	Nov Index	%	Dec Index	%
1947	16.2	-	16.2	0.0	16.2	0.0	16.3	0.6	16.3	0.0	16.3	0.0	16.4	0.6	16.4	0.0	16.5	0.6	16.5	0.0	16.5	0.0	16.6	0.6
1948	16.7	0.6	16.7	0.0	16.8	0.6	16.7	-0.6	16.8	0.6	16.8	0.0	16.9	0.6	17.0	0.6	17.1	0.6	17.1	0.0	17.1	0.0	17.1	0.0
1949	17.1	0.0	17.2	0.6	17.2	0.0	17.2	0.0	17.2	0.0	17.2	0.0	17.2	0.0	20.4	18.6	20.4	0.0	20.4	0.0	20.4	0.0	20.4	0.0
1950	20.4	0.0	20.4	0.0	20.4	0.0	20.4	0.0	20.4	0.0	20.5	0.5	20.5	0.0	20.6	0.5	20.6	0.0	20.6	0.0	20.6	0.0	20.7	0.5
1951	20.7	0.0	20.7	0.0	20.8	0.5	20.8	0.0	20.8	0.0	20.8	0.0	20.7	-0.5	21.5	3.9	21.5	0.0	21.8	1.4	21.9	0.5	21.9	0.0
1952	21.9	0.0	22.2	1.4	22.3	0.5	22.3	0.0	22.3	0.0	22.2	-0.4	23.0	3.6	23.0	0.0	23.0	0.0	23.0	0.0	23.0	0.0	23.0	0.0
1953	23.1	0.4	-	-	-	-	23.4	1.3	-	-	-	-	23.6	0.9	-	-	-	-	23.6	0.0	-	-	-	-
1954	23.4	-0.8	-	-	-	-	24.3	3.8	-	-	-	-	23.7	-2.5	-	-	-	-	22.9	-3.4	-	-	-	-
1955	23.1	0.9	-	-	-	-	23.1	0.0	-	-	-	-	22.9	-0.9	-	-	-	-	23.4	2.2	-	-	-	-
1956	23.4	0.0	-	-	-	-	23.5	0.4	-	-	-	-	23.4	-0.4	-	-	-	-	25.1	7.3	-	-	-	-
1957	24.7	-1.6	-	-	-	-	24.8	0.4	-	-	-	-	24.9	0.4	-	-	-	-	25.2	1.2	-	-	-	-
1958	25.4	0.8	-	-	-	-	25.8	1.6	-	-	-	-	25.7	-0.4	-	-	-	-	25.6	-0.4	-	-	-	-
1959	26.4	3.1	-	-	-	-	26.4	0.0	-	-	-	-	26.4	0.0	-	-	-	-	26.3	-0.4	-	-	-	-
1960	25.6	-2.7	-	-	-	-	25.7	0.4	-	-	-	-	25.8	0.4	-	-	-	-	25.8	0.0	-	-	-	-
1961	25.5	-1.2	-	-	-	-	25.9	1.6	-	-	-	-	26.3	1.5	-	-	-	-	26.1	-0.8	-	-	-	-
1962	28.0	7.3	-	-	-	-	28.3	1.1	-	-	-	-	27.9	-1.4	-	-	-	-	28.2	1.1	-	-	-	-
1963	27.9	-1.1	-	-	-	-	28.2	1.1	-	-	-	-	28.4	0.7	-	-	-	-	28.2	-0.7	-	-	-	-
1964	28.3	0.4	-	-	-	-	28.2	-0.4	-	-	-	-	28.6	1.4	-	-	-	-	28.2	-1.4	-	-	-	-
1965	28.9	2.5	-	-	-	-	28.9	0.0	-	-	-	-	29.1	0.7	-	-	-	-	29.4	1.0	-	-	-	-
1966	29.2	-0.7	-	-	-	-	29.9	2.4	-	-	-	-	30.0	0.3	-	-	-	-	30.0	0.0	-	-	-	-
1967	30.1	0.3	-	-	-	-	30.3	0.7	-	-	-	-	30.7	1.3	-	-	-	-	30.9	0.7	-	-	-	-
1968	31.2	1.0	-	-	-	-	31.4	0.6	-	-	-	-	31.4	0.0	-	-	-	-	31.6	0.6	-	-	-	-
1969	32.8	3.8	-	-	-	-	33.6	2.4	-	-	-	-	33.5	-0.3	-	-	-	-	33.5	0.0	-	-	-	-
1970	33.6	0.3	-	-	-	-	33.9	0.9	-	-	-	-	34.5	1.8	-	-	-	-	36.2	4.9	-	-	-	-
1971	36.6	1.1	-	-	-	-	36.1	-1.4	-	-	-	-	36.8	1.9	-	-	-	-	36.6	-0.5	-	-	-	-
1972	36.4	-0.5	-	-	-	-	36.2	-0.5	-	-	-	-	36.4	0.6	-	-	-	-	36.9	1.4	-	-	-	-
1973	36.9	0.0	-	-	-	-	37.1	0.5	-	-	-	-	37.7	1.6	-	-	-	-	37.8	0.3	-	-	-	-
1974	38.5	1.9	-	-	-	-	39.7	3.1	-	-	-	-	41.9	5.5	-	-	-	-	42.2	0.7	-	-	-	-
1975	42.7	1.2	-	-	-	-	45.0	5.4	-	-	-	-	46.9	4.2	-	-	-	-	47.5	1.3	-	-	-	-
1976	57.6	21.3	-	-	-	-	57.9	0.5	-	-	-	-	59.7	3.1	-	-	-	-	60.1	0.7	-	-	-	-
1977	62.1	3.3	-	-	-	-	63.2	1.8	-	-	-	-	63.7	0.8	-	-	-	-	63.4	-0.5	-	-	-	-
1978	63.6	0.3	-	-	60.9	-4.2	-	-	62.1	2.0	-	-	63.0	1.4	-	-	63.4	0.6	-	-	64.3	1.4	-	-
1979	63.8	-0.8	-	-	65.2	2.2	-	-	68.4	4.9	-	-	71.6	4.7	-	-	72.9	1.8	-	-	74.6	2.3	-	-
1980	77.3	3.6	-	-	81.1	4.9	-	-	82.3	1.5	-	-	84.6	2.8	-	-	85.4	0.9	-	-	86.7	1.5	-	-
1981	88.0	1.5	-	-	90.8	3.2	-	-	93.0	2.4	-	-	94.3	1.4	-	-	96.9	2.8	-	-	98.4	1.5	-	-
1982	97.9	-0.5	-	-	97.3	-0.6	-	-	96.2	-1.1	-	-	99.3	3.2	-	-	99.8	0.5	-	-	99.6	-0.2	-	-
1983	98.6	-1.0	-	-	97.1	-1.5	-	-	98.4	1.3	-	-	99.5	1.1	-	-	100.1	0.6	-	-	100.6	0.5	-	-
1984	100.6	0.0	-	-	101.8	1.2	-	-	103.0	1.2	-	-	102.9	-0.1	-	-	102.9	0.0	-	-	103.2	0.3	-	-
1985	103.0	-0.2	-	-	104.2	1.2	-	-	105.3	1.1	-	-	105.5	0.2	-	-	105.3	-0.2	-	-	106.4	1.0	-	-
1986	106.6	0.2	-	-	103.3	-3.1	-	-	100.0	-3.2	-	-	100.0	0.0	-	-	98.9	-1.1	-	-	99.5	0.6	-	-
1987	100.8	1.3	-	-	100.4	-0.4	-	-	101.9	1.5	-	-	103.8	1.9	-	-	105.9	2.0	-	-	107.7	1.7	-	-
1988	107.3	-0.4	-	-	106.4	-0.8	-	-	107.0	0.6	-	-	108.7	1.6	-	-	110.6	1.7	-	-	113.9	3.0	-	-
1989	113.6	-0.3	-	-	115.3	1.5	-	-	117.9	2.3	-	-	114.8	-2.6	-	-	114.6	-0.2	-	-	116.5	1.7	-	-
1990	117.4	0.8	-	-	117.8	0.3	-	-	118.7	0.8	-	-	119.1	0.3	-	-	125.6	5.5	-	-	131.0	4.3	-	-
1991	127.9	-2.4	-	-	124.9	-2.3	-	-	127.4	2.0	-	-	128.7	1.0	-	-	129.6	0.7	-	-	130.7	0.8	-	-

[Continued]

Boston, MA
Consumer Price Index - Urban Wage Earners
Base 1982-1984 = 100
Transportation

[Continued]

For 1947-1995. Columns headed % show percentile change in the index from the previous period for which an index is available.

Year	Jan		Feb		Mar		Apr		May		Jun		Jul		Aug		Sep		Oct		Nov		Dec	
	Index	%	Index	%	Index	%	Index	%	Index	%	Index	%	Index	%	Index	%	Index	%	Index	%	Index	%	Index	%
1992	130.5	-0.2	-	-	130.8	0.2	-	-	131.5	0.5	-	-	133.0	1.1	-	-	132.2	-0.6	-	-	132.7	0.4	-	-
1993	134.6	1.4	-	-	134.9	0.2	-	-	134.6	-0.2	-	-	134.7	0.1	-	-	133.7	-0.7	-	-	136.5	2.1	-	-
1994	135.6	-0.7	-	-	136.2	0.4	-	-	134.9	-1.0	-	-	137.2	1.7	-	-	140.0	2.0	-	-	141.2	0.9	-	-
1995	140.0	-0.8	-	-	138.4	-1.1	-	-	140.2	1.3	-	-	140.8	0.4	-	-	139.8	-0.7	-	-	141.1	0.9	-	-

Source: U.S. Department of Labor, Bureau of Labor Statistics, Division of Consumer Prices and Price Indexes. - indicates no data collected for period.

Boston, MA
Consumer Price Index - All Urban Consumers
Base 1982-1984 = 100
Medical Care

For 1947-1995. Columns headed % show percentile change in the index from the previous period for which an index is available.

Year	Jan Index	%	Feb Index	%	Mar Index	%	Apr Index	%	May Index	%	Jun Index	%	Jul Index	%	Aug Index	%	Sep Index	%	Oct Index	%	Nov Index	%	Dec Index	%
1947	13.3	-	13.3	0.0	13.4	0.8	13.4	0.0	13.4	0.0	13.4	0.0	13.3	-0.7	13.3	0.0	13.4	0.8	13.4	0.0	13.4	0.0	13.4	0.0
1948	13.8	3.0	13.8	0.0	14.3	3.6	14.4	0.7	14.5	0.7	14.3	-1.4	14.3	0.0	14.4	0.7	14.4	0.0	14.4	0.0	14.4	0.0	14.4	0.0
1949	14.8	2.8	14.8	0.0	14.9	0.7	14.9	0.0	14.9	0.0	15.0	0.7	15.3	2.0	15.3	0.0	15.4	0.7	15.4	0.0	15.4	0.0	15.4	0.0
1950	15.6	1.3	15.6	0.0	15.7	0.6	15.7	0.0	15.7	0.0	15.7	0.0	15.7	0.0	15.7	0.0	15.7	0.0	15.7	0.0	15.8	0.6	16.0	1.3
1951	16.1	0.6	16.1	0.0	16.2	0.6	16.2	0.0	16.2	0.0	16.3	0.6	16.3	0.0	16.3	0.0	16.2	-0.6	16.3	0.6	16.3	0.0	16.7	2.5
1952	16.8	0.6	16.8	0.0	16.8	0.0	16.9	0.6	16.9	0.0	17.1	1.2	17.2	0.6	17.2	0.0	17.5	1.7	17.5	0.0	17.5	0.0	17.5	0.0
1953	17.6	0.6	-	-	-	-	17.6	0.0	-	-	-	-	17.6	0.0	-	-	-	-	17.7	0.6	-	-	-	-
1954	17.7	0.0	-	-	-	-	17.7	0.0	-	-	-	-	17.7	0.0	-	-	-	-	17.7	0.0	-	-	-	-
1955	17.7	0.0	-	-	-	-	17.7	0.0	-	-	-	-	17.8	0.6	-	-	-	-	18.0	1.1	-	-	-	-
1956	18.3	1.7	-	-	-	-	18.3	0.0	-	-	-	-	19.5	6.6	-	-	-	-	19.6	0.5	-	-	-	-
1957	19.7	0.5	-	-	-	-	20.1	2.0	-	-	-	-	21.2	5.5	-	-	-	-	21.2	0.0	-	-	-	-
1958	22.0	3.8	-	-	-	-	22.1	0.5	-	-	-	-	22.3	0.9	-	-	-	-	22.4	0.4	-	-	-	-
1959	22.6	0.9	-	-	-	-	22.7	0.4	-	-	-	-	22.7	0.0	-	-	-	-	22.9	0.9	-	-	-	-
1960	23.0	0.4	-	-	-	-	23.1	0.4	-	-	-	-	23.2	0.4	-	-	-	-	23.3	0.4	-	-	-	-
1961	23.7	1.7	-	-	-	-	23.8	0.4	-	-	-	-	23.9	0.4	-	-	-	-	24.1	0.8	-	-	-	-
1962	24.5	1.7	-	-	-	-	24.8	1.2	-	-	-	-	24.8	0.0	-	-	-	-	24.9	0.4	-	-	-	-
1963	24.9	0.0	-	-	-	-	25.3	1.6	-	-	-	-	25.3	0.0	-	-	-	-	25.5	0.8	-	-	-	-
1964	25.6	0.4	-	-	-	-	25.9	1.2	-	-	-	-	25.9	0.0	-	-	-	-	26.5	2.3	-	-	-	-
1965	26.8	1.1	-	-	-	-	26.8	0.0	-	-	-	-	27.1	1.1	-	-	-	-	27.3	0.7	-	-	-	-
1966	27.4	0.4	-	-	-	-	27.9	1.8	-	-	-	-	28.0	0.4	-	-	-	-	28.8	2.9	-	-	-	-
1967	29.3	1.7	-	-	-	-	29.3	0.0	-	-	-	-	29.9	2.0	-	-	-	-	31.0	3.7	-	-	-	-
1968	31.7	2.3	-	-	-	-	31.8	0.3	-	-	-	-	32.2	1.3	-	-	-	-	33.6	4.3	-	-	-	-
1969	34.2	1.8	-	-	-	-	34.5	0.9	-	-	-	-	34.9	1.2	-	-	-	-	36.0	3.2	-	-	-	-
1970	36.5	1.4	-	-	-	-	36.8	0.8	-	-	-	-	37.2	1.1	-	-	-	-	38.5	3.5	-	-	-	-
1971	38.8	0.8	-	-	-	-	39.2	1.0	-	-	-	-	39.4	0.5	-	-	-	-	39.2	-0.5	-	-	-	-
1972	40.0	2.0	-	-	-	-	40.4	1.0	-	-	-	-	40.5	0.2	-	-	-	-	40.9	1.0	-	-	-	-
1973	41.2	0.7	-	-	-	-	41.4	0.5	-	-	-	-	41.6	0.5	-	-	-	-	42.5	2.2	-	-	-	-
1974	42.8	0.7	-	-	-	-	43.3	1.2	-	-	-	-	44.7	3.2	-	-	-	-	46.6	4.3	-	-	-	-
1975	47.9	2.8	-	-	-	-	49.2	2.7	-	-	-	-	50.2	2.0	-	-	-	-	51.9	3.4	-	-	-	-
1976	51.6	-0.6	-	-	-	-	51.8	0.4	-	-	-	-	53.9	4.1	-	-	-	-	54.9	1.9	-	-	-	-
1977	56.2	2.4	-	-	-	-	56.9	1.2	-	-	-	-	57.9	1.8	-	-	-	-	59.2	2.2	-	-	-	-
1978	59.4	0.3	-	-	59.8	0.7	-	-	60.6	1.3	-	-	61.5	1.5	-	-	62.8	2.1	-	-	66.1	5.3	-	-
1979	66.9	1.2	-	-	67.7	1.2	-	-	68.2	0.7	-	-	69.8	2.3	-	-	70.2	0.6	-	-	72.1	2.7	-	-
1980	74.3	3.1	-	-	74.9	0.8	-	-	76.6	2.3	-	-	76.4	-0.3	-	-	76.5	0.1	-	-	80.9	5.8	-	-
1981	81.6	0.9	-	-	82.0	0.5	-	-	82.3	0.4	-	-	82.7	0.5	-	-	83.4	0.8	-	-	88.0	5.5	-	-
1982	90.3	2.6	-	-	90.6	0.3	-	-	91.4	0.9	-	-	93.2	2.0	-	-	93.4	0.2	-	-	95.1	1.8	-	-
1983	96.9	1.9	-	-	96.6	-0.3	-	-	96.9	0.3	-	-	98.3	1.4	-	-	100.3	2.0	-	-	102.1	1.8	-	-
1984	104.2	2.1	-	-	106.7	2.4	-	-	107.8	1.0	-	-	109.4	1.5	-	-	109.1	-0.3	-	-	112.2	2.8	-	-
1985	112.2	0.0	-	-	119.7	6.7	-	-	121.5	1.5	-	-	121.6	0.1	-	-	120.9	-0.6	-	-	123.5	2.2	-	-
1986	126.5	2.4	-	-	130.2	2.9	-	-	131.9	1.3	-	-	132.9	0.8	-	-	133.8	0.7	-	-	133.5	-0.2	-	-
1987	135.0	1.1	-	-	137.7	2.0	-	-	138.5	0.6	-	-	138.7	0.1	-	-	139.4	0.5	-	-	143.3	2.8	-	-
1988	146.2	2.0	-	-	149.3	2.1	-	-	150.7	0.9	-	-	153.4	1.8	-	-	155.0	1.0	-	-	154.9	-0.1	-	-
1989	157.7	1.8	-	-	160.3	1.6	-	-	164.3	2.5	-	-	166.4	1.3	-	-	169.3	1.7	-	-	170.1	0.5	-	-
1990	173.2	1.8	-	-	177.9	2.7	-	-	181.7	2.1	-	-	182.3	0.3	-	-	182.7	0.2	-	-	187.5	2.6	-	-
1991	189.7	1.2	-	-	198.4	4.6	-	-	201.8	1.7	-	-	205.4	1.8	-	-	204.6	-0.4	-	-	210.4	2.8	-	-

[Continued]

Boston, MA
Consumer Price Index - All Urban Consumers
Base 1982-1984 = 100
Medical Care
[Continued]

For 1947-1995. Columns headed % show percentile change in the index from the previous period for which an index is available.

Year	Jan Index	%	Feb Index	%	Mar Index	%	Apr Index	%	May Index	%	Jun Index	%	Jul Index	%	Aug Index	%	Sep Index	%	Oct Index	%	Nov Index	%	Dec Index	%
1992	213.8	1.6	-	-	218.6	2.2	-	-	223.9	2.4	-	-	223.9	0.0	-	-	227.4	1.6	-	-	232.5	2.2	-	-
1993	233.9	0.6	-	-	232.7	-0.5	-	-	237.7	2.1	-	-	240.1	1.0	-	-	240.2	0.0	-	-	246.1	2.5	-	-
1994	247.3	0.5	-	-	249.3	0.8	-	-	250.4	0.4	-	-	250.2	-0.1	-	-	251.8	0.6	-	-	255.0	1.3	-	-
1995	257.9	1.1	-	-	262.7	1.9	-	-	265.1	0.9	-	-	266.7	0.6	-	-	265.9	-0.3	-	-	273.9	3.0	-	-

Source: U.S. Department of Labor, Bureau of Labor Statistics, Division of Consumer Prices and Price Indexes. - indicates no data collected for period.

Boston, MA
Consumer Price Index - Urban Wage Earners
Base 1982-1984 = 100
Medical Care

For 1947-1995. Columns headed % show percentile change in the index from the previous period for which an index is available.

Year	Jan Index	%	Feb Index	%	Mar Index	%	Apr Index	%	May Index	%	Jun Index	%	Jul Index	%	Aug Index	%	Sep Index	%	Oct Index	%	Nov Index	%	Dec Index	%
1947	13.5	-	13.5	0.0	13.6	0.7	13.6	0.0	13.6	0.0	13.6	0.0	13.5	-0.7	13.5	0.0	13.6	0.7	13.6	0.0	13.6	0.0	13.6	0.0
1948	14.0	2.9	14.0	0.0	14.5	3.6	14.7	1.4	14.7	0.0	14.5	-1.4	14.5	0.0	14.6	0.7	14.6	0.0	14.6	0.0	14.6	0.0	14.6	0.0
1949	15.0	2.7	15.0	0.0	15.1	0.7	15.1	0.0	15.1	0.0	15.2	0.7	15.5	2.0	15.6	0.6	15.6	0.0	15.6	0.0	15.6	0.0	15.6	0.0
1950	15.8	1.3	15.8	0.0	15.9	0.6	15.9	0.0	15.9	0.0	16.0	0.6	16.0	0.0	16.0	0.0	16.0	0.0	16.0	0.0	16.0	0.0	16.2	1.3
1951	16.3	0.6	16.3	0.0	16.5	1.2	16.5	0.0	16.5	0.0	16.5	0.0	16.5	0.0	16.5	0.0	16.5	0.0	16.5	0.0	16.6	0.6	17.0	2.4
1952	17.1	0.6	17.1	0.0	17.1	0.0	17.1	0.0	17.1	0.0	17.3	1.2	17.4	0.6	17.4	0.0	17.7	1.7	17.7	0.0	17.7	0.0	17.8	0.6
1953	17.8	0.0	-	-	-	-	17.8	0.0	-	-	-	-	17.9	0.6	-	-	-	-	18.0	0.6	-	-	-	-
1954	18.0	0.0	-	-	-	-	18.0	0.0	-	-	-	-	18.0	0.0	-	-	-	-	18.0	0.0	-	-	-	-
1955	18.0	0.0	-	-	-	-	18.0	0.0	-	-	-	-	18.1	0.6	-	-	-	-	18.3	1.1	-	-	-	-
1956	18.6	1.6	-	-	-	-	18.6	0.0	-	-	-	-	19.8	6.5	-	-	-	-	19.9	0.5	-	-	-	-
1957	20.0	0.5	-	-	-	-	20.4	2.0	-	-	-	-	21.5	5.4	-	-	-	-	21.6	0.5	-	-	-	-
1958	22.3	3.2	-	-	-	-	22.4	0.4	-	-	-	-	22.6	0.9	-	-	-	-	22.7	0.4	-	-	-	-
1959	23.0	1.3	-	-	-	-	23.0	0.0	-	-	-	-	23.1	0.4	-	-	-	-	23.2	0.4	-	-	-	-
1960	23.3	0.4	-	-	-	-	23.4	0.4	-	-	-	-	23.5	0.4	-	-	-	-	23.6	0.4	-	-	-	-
1961	24.1	2.1	-	-	-	-	24.1	0.0	-	-	-	-	24.3	0.8	-	-	-	-	24.4	0.4	-	-	-	-
1962	24.9	2.0	-	-	-	-	25.1	0.8	-	-	-	-	25.1	0.0	-	-	-	-	25.2	0.4	-	-	-	-
1963	25.3	0.4	-	-	-	-	25.7	1.6	-	-	-	-	25.7	0.0	-	-	-	-	25.9	0.8	-	-	-	-
1964	26.0	0.4	-	-	-	-	26.3	1.2	-	-	-	-	26.3	0.0	-	-	-	-	26.9	2.3	-	-	-	-
1965	27.2	1.1	-	-	-	-	27.2	0.0	-	-	-	-	27.5	1.1	-	-	-	-	27.7	0.7	-	-	-	-
1966	27.8	0.4	-	-	-	-	28.3	1.8	-	-	-	-	28.4	0.4	-	-	-	-	29.2	2.8	-	-	-	-
1967	29.8	2.1	-	-	-	-	29.8	0.0	-	-	-	-	30.4	2.0	-	-	-	-	31.4	3.3	-	-	-	-
1968	32.1	2.2	-	-	-	-	32.3	0.6	-	-	-	-	32.7	1.2	-	-	-	-	34.1	4.3	-	-	-	-
1969	34.7	1.8	-	-	-	-	35.0	0.9	-	-	-	-	35.4	1.1	-	-	-	-	36.5	3.1	-	-	-	-
1970	37.0	1.4	-	-	-	-	37.4	1.1	-	-	-	-	37.8	1.1	-	-	-	-	39.0	3.2	-	-	-	-
1971	39.4	1.0	-	-	-	-	39.7	0.8	-	-	-	-	40.0	0.8	-	-	-	-	39.8	-0.5	-	-	-	-
1972	40.6	2.0	-	-	-	-	41.0	1.0	-	-	-	-	41.1	0.2	-	-	-	-	41.5	1.0	-	-	-	-
1973	41.8	0.7	-	-	-	-	42.0	0.5	-	-	-	-	42.2	0.5	-	-	-	-	43.2	2.4	-	-	-	-
1974	43.4	0.5	-	-	-	-	44.0	1.4	-	-	-	-	45.3	3.0	-	-	-	-	47.3	4.4	-	-	-	-
1975	48.6	2.7	-	-	-	-	49.9	2.7	-	-	-	-	50.9	2.0	-	-	-	-	52.7	3.5	-	-	-	-
1976	52.4	-0.6	-	-	-	-	52.6	0.4	-	-	-	-	54.7	4.0	-	-	-	-	55.7	1.8	-	-	-	-
1977	57.0	2.3	-	-	-	-	57.8	1.4	-	-	-	-	58.7	1.6	-	-	-	-	60.1	2.4	-	-	-	-
1978	60.3	0.3	-	-	61.2	1.5	-	-	61.9	1.1	-	-	62.0	0.2	-	-	63.9	3.1	-	-	65.8	3.0	-	-
1979	66.7	1.4	-	-	67.3	0.9	-	-	68.2	1.3	-	-	69.8	2.3	-	-	69.9	0.1	-	-	72.5	3.7	-	-
1980	73.6	1.5	-	-	74.4	1.1	-	-	77.0	3.5	-	-	75.6	-1.8	-	-	76.1	0.7	-	-	79.7	4.7	-	-
1981	80.5	1.0	-	-	81.9	1.7	-	-	83.9	2.4	-	-	82.8	-1.3	-	-	83.5	0.8	-	-	87.7	5.0	-	-
1982	89.8	2.4	-	-	90.3	0.6	-	-	91.2	1.0	-	-	93.0	2.0	-	-	93.1	0.1	-	-	94.6	1.6	-	-
1983	96.6	2.1	-	-	96.4	-0.2	-	-	96.7	0.3	-	-	98.4	1.8	-	-	100.5	2.1	-	-	102.3	1.8	-	-
1984	104.9	2.5	-	-	107.2	2.2	-	-	108.3	1.0	-	-	109.8	1.4	-	-	109.5	-0.3	-	-	112.0	2.3	-	-
1985	111.8	-0.2	-	-	118.1	5.6	-	-	119.9	1.5	-	-	120.5	0.5	-	-	120.0	-0.4	-	-	122.4	2.0	-	-
1986	125.1	2.2	-	-	128.8	3.0	-	-	130.6	1.4	-	-	131.7	0.8	-	-	132.8	0.8	-	-	132.7	-0.1	-	-
1987	134.6	1.4	-	-	137.1	1.9	-	-	138.2	0.8	-	-	138.2	0.0	-	-	139.3	0.8	-	-	142.8	2.5	-	-
1988	145.7	2.0	-	-	148.5	1.9	-	-	150.2	1.1	-	-	152.6	1.6	-	-	154.0	0.9	-	-	154.5	0.3	-	-
1989	157.1	1.7	-	-	159.5	1.5	-	-	162.7	2.0	-	-	164.5	1.1	-	-	167.7	1.9	-	-	168.4	0.4	-	-
1990	171.3	1.7	-	-	175.8	2.6	-	-	180.0	2.4	-	-	180.7	0.4	-	-	181.1	0.2	-	-	185.3	2.3	-	-
1991	187.4	1.1	-	-	194.9	4.0	-	-	198.9	2.1	-	-	202.5	1.8	-	-	201.9	-0.3	-	-	207.1	2.6	-	-

[Continued]

Boston, MA
Consumer Price Index - Urban Wage Earners
Base 1982-1984 = 100
Medical Care

[Continued]

For 1947-1995. Columns headed % show percentile change in the index from the previous period for which an index is available.

Year	Jan		Feb		Mar		Apr		May		Jun		Jul		Aug		Sep		Oct		Nov		Dec	
	Index	%	Index	%	Index	%	Index	%	Index	%	Index	%	Index	%	Index	%	Index	%	Index	%	Index	%	Index	%
1992	210.2	1.5	-	-	214.4	2.0	-	-	219.1	2.2	-	-	219.1	0.0	-	-	223.7	2.1	-	-	228.4	2.1	-	-
1993	229.5	0.5	-	-	228.7	-0.3	-	-	233.8	2.2	-	-	236.1	1.0	-	-	236.1	0.0	-	-	240.4	1.8	-	-
1994	241.7	0.5	-	-	243.8	0.9	-	-	245.1	0.5	-	-	245.1	0.0	-	-	246.5	0.6	-	-	249.3	1.1	-	-
1995	252.1	1.1	-	-	256.7	1.8	-	-	258.9	0.9	-	-	260.8	0.7	-	-	260.1	-0.3	-	-	267.0	2.7	-	-

Source: U.S. Department of Labor, Bureau of Labor Statistics, Division of Consumer Prices and Price Indexes. - indicates no data collected for period.

Boston, MA
Consumer Price Index - All Urban Consumers
Base 1982-1984 = 100
Entertainment

For 1976-1995. Columns headed % show percentile change in the index from the previous period for which an index is available.

Year	Jan Index	%	Feb Index	%	Mar Index	%	Apr Index	%	May Index	%	Jun Index	%	Jul Index	%	Aug Index	%	Sep Index	%	Oct Index	%	Nov Index	%	Dec Index	%
1976	63.7	-	-	-	-	-	64.0	0.5	-	-	-	-	64.8	1.3	-	-	-	-	65.4	0.9	-	-	-	-
1977	65.5	0.2	-	-	-	-	65.4	-0.2	-	-	-	-	66.6	1.8	-	-	-	-	66.7	0.2	-	-	-	-
1978	67.1	0.6	-	-	68.3	1.8	-	-	69.0	1.0	-	-	68.4	-0.9	-	-	68.7	0.4	-	-	72.6	5.7	-	-
1979	72.4	-0.3	-	-	73.5	1.5	-	-	75.6	2.9	-	-	76.0	0.5	-	-	76.5	0.7	-	-	78.1	2.1	-	-
1980	79.9	2.3	-	-	80.7	1.0	-	-	83.3	3.2	-	-	83.7	0.5	-	-	84.4	0.8	-	-	85.7	1.5	-	-
1981	87.0	1.5	-	-	88.7	2.0	-	-	88.8	0.1	-	-	90.1	1.5	-	-	91.1	1.1	-	-	91.9	0.9	-	-
1982	92.9	1.1	-	-	93.8	1.0	-	-	96.4	2.8	-	-	96.6	0.2	-	-	97.9	1.3	-	-	98.4	0.5	-	-
1983	99.0	0.6	-	-	99.3	0.3	-	-	100.8	1.5	-	-	101.3	0.5	-	-	100.5	-0.8	-	-	100.0	-0.5	-	-
1984	101.8	1.8	-	-	103.8	2.0	-	-	103.2	-0.6	-	-	103.6	0.4	-	-	104.1	0.5	-	-	103.0	-1.1	-	-
1985	107.4	4.3	-	-	110.1	2.5	-	-	107.4	-2.5	-	-	109.4	1.9	-	-	111.0	1.5	-	-	111.0	0.0	-	-
1986	117.0	5.4	-	-	114.0	-2.6	-	-	114.7	0.6	-	-	112.9	-1.6	-	-	113.4	0.4	-	-	115.2	1.6	-	-
1987	118.5	2.9	-	-	118.1	-0.3	-	-	116.9	-1.0	-	-	119.4	2.1	-	-	121.5	1.8	-	-	120.7	-0.7	-	-
1988	122.9	1.8	-	-	127.9	4.1	-	-	125.9	-1.6	-	-	127.5	1.3	-	-	127.9	0.3	-	-	128.2	0.2	-	-
1989	128.9	0.5	-	-	128.9	0.0	-	-	132.5	2.8	-	-	135.4	2.2	-	-	137.0	1.2	-	-	136.7	-0.2	-	-
1990	137.7	0.7	-	-	141.2	2.5	-	-	143.7	1.8	-	-	145.4	1.2	-	-	148.4	2.1	-	-	146.3	-1.4	-	-
1991	147.5	0.8	-	-	148.5	0.7	-	-	150.7	1.5	-	-	156.3	3.7	-	-	156.7	0.3	-	-	152.3	-2.8	-	-
1992	152.8	0.3	-	-	152.8	0.0	-	-	154.0	0.8	-	-	155.9	1.2	-	-	156.3	0.3	-	-	156.9	0.4	-	-
1993	156.9	0.0	-	-	157.7	0.5	-	-	159.5	1.1	-	-	159.5	0.0	-	-	161.9	1.5	-	-	163.5	1.0	-	-
1994	162.3	-0.7	-	-	161.7	-0.4	-	-	163.6	1.2	-	-	164.2	0.4	-	-	165.1	0.5	-	-	165.7	0.4	-	-
1995	166.3	0.4	-	-	166.0	-0.2	-	-	167.1	0.7	-	-	168.4	0.8	-	-	167.0	-0.8	-	-	169.3	1.4	-	-

Source: U.S. Department of Labor, Bureau of Labor Statistics, Division of Consumer Prices and Price Indexes. - indicates no data collected for period.

Boston, MA
Consumer Price Index - Urban Wage Earners
Base 1982-1984 = 100
Entertainment

For 1976-1995. Columns headed % show percentile change in the index from the previous period for which an index is available.

Year	Jan Index	%	Feb Index	%	Mar Index	%	Apr Index	%	May Index	%	Jun Index	%	Jul Index	%	Aug Index	%	Sep Index	%	Oct Index	%	Nov Index	%	Dec Index	%
1976	66.0	-	-	-	-	-	66.3	0.5	-	-	-	-	67.1	1.2	-	-	-	-	67.8	1.0	-	-	-	-
1977	67.8	0.0	-	-	-	-	67.7	-0.1	-	-	-	-	69.0	1.9	-	-	-	-	69.1	0.1	-	-	-	-
1978	69.5	0.6	-	-	70.2	1.0	-	-	70.8	0.9	-	-	68.8	-2.8	-	-	69.0	0.3	-	-	74.6	8.1	-	-
1979	74.9	0.4	-	-	75.6	0.9	-	-	76.4	1.1	-	-	77.3	1.2	-	-	77.8	0.6	-	-	79.1	1.7	-	-
1980	79.6	0.6	-	-	81.8	2.8	-	-	83.2	1.7	-	-	83.5	0.4	-	-	84.4	1.1	-	-	86.1	2.0	-	-
1981	86.6	0.6	-	-	88.3	2.0	-	-	89.0	0.8	-	-	89.4	0.4	-	-	90.7	1.5	-	-	92.2	1.7	-	-
1982	93.0	0.9	-	-	93.7	0.8	-	-	96.5	3.0	-	-	96.1	-0.4	-	-	97.8	1.8	-	-	98.5	0.7	-	-
1983	98.9	0.4	-	-	99.2	0.3	-	-	100.8	1.6	-	-	101.2	0.4	-	-	100.4	-0.8	-	-	100.3	-0.1	-	-
1984	102.1	1.8	-	-	103.2	1.1	-	-	103.4	0.2	-	-	103.9	0.5	-	-	104.1	0.2	-	-	103.4	-0.7	-	-
1985	107.3	3.8	-	-	109.0	1.6	-	-	107.5	-1.4	-	-	109.0	1.4	-	-	109.9	0.8	-	-	110.6	0.6	-	-
1986	116.0	4.9	-	-	113.7	-2.0	-	-	114.4	0.6	-	-	112.4	-1.7	-	-	112.9	0.4	-	-	114.4	1.3	-	-
1987	117.2	2.4	-	-	116.8	-0.3	-	-	115.1	-1.5	-	-	118.3	2.8	-	-	120.0	1.4	-	-	118.9	-0.9	-	-
1988	120.5	1.3	-	-	125.2	3.9	-	-	124.8	-0.3	-	-	126.2	1.1	-	-	125.8	-0.3	-	-	127.4	1.3	-	-
1989	127.8	0.3	-	-	127.7	-0.1	-	-	131.6	3.1	-	-	135.1	2.7	-	-	136.7	1.2	-	-	136.5	-0.1	-	-
1990	137.6	0.8	-	-	140.8	2.3	-	-	144.1	2.3	-	-	146.6	1.7	-	-	149.0	1.6	-	-	146.2	-1.9	-	-
1991	148.1	1.3	-	-	150.0	1.3	-	-	152.2	1.5	-	-	155.7	2.3	-	-	156.1	0.3	-	-	153.4	-1.7	-	-
1992	153.3	-0.1	-	-	153.3	0.0	-	-	154.9	1.0	-	-	156.7	1.2	-	-	156.6	-0.1	-	-	157.1	0.3	-	-
1993	157.1	0.0	-	-	158.4	0.8	-	-	160.3	1.2	-	-	161.9	1.0	-	-	164.0	1.3	-	-	164.3	0.2	-	-
1994	163.0	-0.8	-	-	162.1	-0.6	-	-	164.1	1.2	-	-	166.3	1.3	-	-	166.6	0.2	-	-	167.3	0.4	-	-
1995	169.1	1.1	-	-	168.4	-0.4	-	-	169.8	0.8	-	-	171.3	0.9	-	-	168.8	-1.5	-	-	171.5	1.6	-	-

Source: U.S. Department of Labor, Bureau of Labor Statistics, Division of Consumer Prices and Price Indexes. - indicates no data collected for period.

Boston, MA
Consumer Price Index - All Urban Consumers
Base 1982-1984 = 100
Other Goods and Services

For 1976-1995. Columns headed % show percentile change in the index from the previous period for which an index is available.

Year	Jan Index	%	Feb Index	%	Mar Index	%	Apr Index	%	May Index	%	Jun Index	%	Jul Index	%	Aug Index	%	Sep Index	%	Oct Index	%	Nov Index	%	Dec Index	%
1976	55.1	-	-	-	-	-	55.6	0.9	-	-	-	-	56.3	1.3	-	-	-	-	57.2	1.6	-	-	-	-
1977	58.3	1.9	-	-	-	-	58.6	0.5	-	-	-	-	59.1	0.9	-	-	-	-	60.7	2.7	-	-	-	-
1978	60.8	0.2	-	-	60.9	0.2	-	-	61.1	0.3	-	-	62.1	1.6	-	-	64.3	3.5	-	-	64.6	0.5	-	-
1979	64.6	0.0	-	-	65.3	1.1	-	-	65.9	0.9	-	-	66.7	1.2	-	-	69.8	4.6	-	-	70.4	0.9	-	-
1980	71.0	0.9	-	-	71.5	0.7	-	-	72.1	0.8	-	-	72.9	1.1	-	-	75.9	4.1	-	-	76.5	0.8	-	-
1981	77.4	1.2	-	-	78.4	1.3	-	-	79.3	1.1	-	-	81.0	2.1	-	-	83.5	3.1	-	-	84.7	1.4	-	-
1982	85.4	0.8	-	-	89.5	4.8	-	-	89.9	0.4	-	-	89.9	0.0	-	-	92.2	2.6	-	-	93.7	1.6	-	-
1983	94.7	1.1	-	-	99.0	4.5	-	-	99.5	0.5	-	-	100.4	0.9	-	-	101.4	1.0	-	-	103.4	2.0	-	-
1984	104.3	0.9	-	-	107.7	3.3	-	-	108.0	0.3	-	-	108.4	0.4	-	-	112.7	4.0	-	-	113.1	0.4	-	-
1985	113.2	0.1	-	-	114.7	1.3	-	-	115.7	0.9	-	-	116.0	0.3	-	-	124.4	7.2	-	-	126.1	1.4	-	-
1986	126.7	0.5	-	-	127.4	0.6	-	-	126.8	-0.5	-	-	127.3	0.4	-	-	131.0	2.9	-	-	132.1	0.8	-	-
1987	132.3	0.2	-	-	132.7	0.3	-	-	132.7	0.0	-	-	133.2	0.4	-	-	141.3	6.1	-	-	141.6	0.2	-	-
1988	142.3	0.5	-	-	144.0	1.2	-	-	144.2	0.1	-	-	145.1	0.6	-	-	152.0	4.8	-	-	152.3	0.2	-	-
1989	153.9	1.1	-	-	154.8	0.6	-	-	156.2	0.9	-	-	159.2	1.9	-	-	159.2	0.0	-	-	161.1	1.2	-	-
1990	166.3	3.2	-	-	167.8	0.9	-	-	168.4	0.4	-	-	175.4	4.2	-	-	180.1	2.7	-	-	178.0	-1.2	-	-
1991	183.1	2.9	-	-	182.3	-0.4	-	-	182.7	0.2	-	-	191.9	5.0	-	-	194.0	1.1	-	-	193.5	-0.3	-	-
1992	194.5	0.5	-	-	192.9	-0.8	-	-	196.1	1.7	-	-	200.4	2.2	-	-	199.8	-0.3	-	-	201.5	0.9	-	-
1993	202.7	0.6	-	-	202.2	-0.2	-	-	202.1	-0.0	-	-	205.5	1.7	-	-	202.2	-1.6	-	-	200.6	-0.8	-	-
1994	203.0	1.2	-	-	205.3	1.1	-	-	204.7	-0.3	-	-	204.8	0.0	-	-	209.3	2.2	-	-	210.7	0.7	-	-
1995	209.5	-0.6	-	-	209.0	-0.2	-	-	211.4	1.1	-	-	212.0	0.3	-	-	217.7	2.7	-	-	218.2	0.2	-	-

Source: U.S. Department of Labor, Bureau of Labor Statistics, Division of Consumer Prices and Price Indexes. - indicates no data collected for period.

Boston, MA
Consumer Price Index - Urban Wage Earners
Base 1982-1984 = 100
Other Goods and Services

For 1976-1995. Columns headed % show percentile change in the index from the previous period for which an index is available.

Year	Jan Index	%	Feb Index	%	Mar Index	%	Apr Index	%	May Index	%	Jun Index	%	Jul Index	%	Aug Index	%	Sep Index	%	Oct Index	%	Nov Index	%	Dec Index	%
1976	55.9	-	-	-	-	-	56.4	0.9	-	-	-	-	57.1	1.2	-	-	-	-	58.0	1.6	-	-	-	-
1977	59.1	1.9	-	-	-	-	59.4	0.5	-	-	-	-	59.9	0.8	-	-	-	-	61.5	2.7	-	-	-	-
1978	61.6	0.2	-	-	61.7	0.2	-	-	61.9	0.3	-	-	62.9	1.6	-	-	65.0	3.3	-	-	65.5	0.8	-	-
1979	65.3	-0.3	-	-	66.3	1.5	-	-	66.6	0.5	-	-	67.6	1.5	-	-	70.3	4.0	-	-	70.8	0.7	-	-
1980	71.6	1.1	-	-	72.0	0.6	-	-	71.9	-0.1	-	-	73.1	1.7	-	-	75.8	3.7	-	-	76.5	0.9	-	-
1981	77.1	0.8	-	-	78.8	2.2	-	-	79.5	0.9	-	-	81.2	2.1	-	-	83.4	2.7	-	-	84.7	1.6	-	-
1982	85.1	0.5	-	-	89.4	5.1	-	-	89.7	0.3	-	-	89.7	0.0	-	-	92.0	2.6	-	-	93.6	1.7	-	-
1983	94.6	1.1	-	-	99.0	4.7	-	-	99.5	0.5	-	-	100.4	0.9	-	-	101.3	0.9	-	-	103.5	2.2	-	-
1984	104.4	0.9	-	-	107.9	3.4	-	-	108.2	0.3	-	-	108.7	0.5	-	-	112.8	3.8	-	-	113.2	0.4	-	-
1985	113.3	0.1	-	-	114.9	1.4	-	-	116.0	1.0	-	-	116.3	0.3	-	-	124.6	7.1	-	-	126.2	1.3	-	-
1986	126.8	0.5	-	-	127.5	0.6	-	-	126.9	-0.5	-	-	127.4	0.4	-	-	130.9	2.7	-	-	132.1	0.9	-	-
1987	132.5	0.3	-	-	133.0	0.4	-	-	133.0	0.0	-	-	133.9	0.7	-	-	140.5	4.9	-	-	140.7	0.1	-	-
1988	141.6	0.6	-	-	143.6	1.4	-	-	144.1	0.3	-	-	145.2	0.8	-	-	151.9	4.6	-	-	152.3	0.3	-	-
1989	154.1	1.2	-	-	154.7	0.4	-	-	156.4	1.1	-	-	160.6	2.7	-	-	160.3	-0.2	-	-	162.3	1.2	-	-
1990	167.5	3.2	-	-	170.1	1.6	-	-	170.2	0.1	-	-	176.9	3.9	-	-	180.3	1.9	-	-	176.7	-2.0	-	-
1991	183.7	4.0	-	-	182.4	-0.7	-	-	183.0	0.3	-	-	193.0	5.5	-	-	195.4	1.2	-	-	196.4	0.5	-	-
1992	197.7	0.7	-	-	195.0	-1.4	-	-	199.1	2.1	-	-	203.2	2.1	-	-	200.3	-1.4	-	-	203.2	1.4	-	-
1993	205.0	0.9	-	-	205.8	0.4	-	-	205.6	-0.1	-	-	208.3	1.3	-	-	200.6	-3.7	-	-	198.5	-1.0	-	-
1994	201.5	1.5	-	-	204.3	1.4	-	-	203.2	-0.5	-	-	203.2	0.0	-	-	207.0	1.9	-	-	209.0	1.0	-	-
1995	207.5	-0.7	-	-	205.8	-0.8	-	-	209.4	1.7	-	-	209.7	0.1	-	-	215.8	2.9	-	-	216.4	0.3	-	-

Source: U.S. Department of Labor, Bureau of Labor Statistics, Division of Consumer Prices and Price Indexes. - indicates no data collected for period.

Buffalo, NY
Consumer Price Index - All Urban Consumers
Base 1982-1984 = 100
Annual Averages

For 1963-1995. Columns headed % show percentile change in the index from the previous period for which an index is available.

Year	All Items		Food & Beverage		Housing		Apparel & Upkeep		Trans-portation		Medical Care		Entertain-ment		Other Goods & Services	
	Index	%	Index	%	Index	%	Index	%	Index	%	Index	%	Index	%	Index	%
1963	-	-	-	-	-	-	-	-	-	-	-	-	-	-	-	-
1964	32.6	-	-	-	-	-	40.4	-	32.8	-	29.9	-	-	-	-	-
1965	33.4	2.5	-	-	-	-	41.8	3.5	34.1	4.0	30.7	2.7	-	-	-	-
1966	34.5	3.3	-	-	-	-	43.2	3.3	34.9	2.3	32.4	5.5	-	-	-	-
1967	35.5	2.9	-	-	-	-	45.3	4.9	35.8	2.6	34.4	6.2	-	-	-	-
1968	37.1	4.5	-	-	-	-	48.3	6.6	36.7	2.5	35.7	3.8	-	-	-	-
1969	38.9	4.9	-	-	-	-	51.6	6.8	38.1	3.8	37.5	5.0	-	-	-	-
1970	41.2	5.9	-	-	-	-	53.3	3.3	40.0	5.0	39.7	5.9	-	-	-	-
1971	43.2	4.9	-	-	-	-	55.8	4.7	41.8	4.5	42.1	6.0	-	-	-	-
1972	44.9	3.9	-	-	-	-	57.1	2.3	42.2	1.0	43.4	3.1	-	-	-	-
1973	47.8	6.5	-	-	-	-	61.0	6.8	43.9	4.0	44.8	3.2	-	-	-	-
1974	53.0	10.9	-	-	-	-	66.0	8.2	48.7	10.9	48.9	9.2	-	-	-	-
1975	57.4	8.3	-	-	-	-	69.8	5.8	52.7	8.2	53.4	9.2	-	-	-	-
1976	60.5	5.4	63.4	-	59.5	-	73.2	4.9	57.7	9.5	57.9	8.4	62.9	-	58.1	-
1977	64.4	6.4	66.9	5.5	63.5	6.7	79.0	7.9	61.3	6.2	62.6	8.1	66.3	5.4	60.7	4.5
1978	68.4	6.2	72.8	8.8	67.0	5.5	82.2	4.1	64.3	4.9	68.2	8.9	70.5	6.3	63.4	4.4
1979	74.9	9.5	80.0	9.9	73.0	9.0	86.1	4.7	73.8	14.8	73.1	7.2	72.1	2.3	66.9	5.5
1980	83.5	11.5	86.8	8.5	81.7	11.9	91.1	5.8	86.5	17.2	78.4	7.3	78.8	9.3	72.6	8.5
1981	91.3	9.3	94.2	8.5	89.5	9.5	93.8	3.0	95.6	10.5	85.7	9.3	88.1	11.8	81.7	12.5
1982	94.7	3.7	97.5	3.5	92.5	3.4	97.7	4.2	97.5	2.0	91.5	6.8	94.0	6.7	90.7	11.0
1983	100.9	6.5	99.8	2.4	102.2	10.5	100.4	2.8	99.5	2.1	100.9	10.3	100.6	7.0	101.0	11.4
1984	104.4	3.5	102.6	2.8	105.3	3.0	101.9	1.5	103.0	3.5	107.6	6.6	105.5	4.9	108.3	7.2
1985	108.6	4.0	105.8	3.1	110.2	4.7	108.3	6.3	105.2	2.1	113.0	5.0	111.5	5.7	116.6	7.7
1986	109.6	0.9	108.5	2.6	112.4	2.0	111.4	2.9	98.4	-6.5	119.8	6.0	114.6	2.8	125.5	7.6
1987	113.0	3.1	112.1	3.3	114.8	2.1	117.9	5.8	99.8	1.4	127.6	6.5	122.7	7.1	132.3	5.4
1988	117.4	3.9	116.7	4.1	120.1	4.6	125.8	6.7	101.0	1.2	131.9	3.4	125.1	2.0	139.5	5.4
1989	121.6	3.6	125.8	7.8	125.0	4.1	109.4	-13.0	103.2	2.2	141.9	7.6	132.2	5.7	147.7	5.9
1990	127.7	5.0	131.5	4.5	132.0	5.6	107.6	-1.6	109.1	5.7	151.7	6.9	142.8	8.0	155.0	4.9
1991	133.4	4.5	136.0	3.4	139.4	5.6	112.0	4.1	112.2	2.8	159.0	4.8	148.2	3.8	164.6	6.2
1992	137.9	3.4	137.1	0.8	146.2	4.9	111.3	-0.6	114.0	1.6	166.5	4.7	155.7	5.1	180.0	9.4
1993	142.7	3.5	139.3	1.6	152.1	4.0	112.6	1.2	117.5	3.1	172.4	3.5	167.4	7.5	190.9	6.1
1994	146.8	2.9	143.1	2.7	155.9	2.5	118.7	5.4	120.9	2.9	174.5	1.2	177.7	6.2	194.5	1.9
1995	151.5	3.2	147.1	2.8	159.6	2.4	116.9	-1.5	127.8	5.7	181.8	4.2	187.9	5.7	203.7	4.7

Source: U.S. Department of Labor, Bureau of Labor Statistics, Division of Consumer Prices and Price Indexes. - indicates no data collected for period.

Buffalo, NY
Consumer Price Index - Urban Wage Earners
Base 1982-1984 = 100
Annual Averages

For 1963-1995. Columns headed % show percentile change in the index from the previous period for which an index is available.

Year	All Items		Food & Beverage		Housing		Apparel & Upkeep		Transportation		Medical Care		Entertainment		Other Goods & Services	
	Index	%	Index	%	Index	%	Index	%	Index	%	Index	%	Index	%	Index	%
1963	-	-	-	-	-	-	-	-	-	-	-	-	-	-	-	-
1964	33.0	-	-	-	-	-	41.8	-	32.6	-	29.4	-	-	-	-	-
1965	33.8	2.4	-	-	-	-	43.2	3.3	33.8	3.7	30.2	2.7	-	-	-	-
1966	35.0	3.6	-	-	-	-	44.7	3.5	34.7	2.7	31.8	5.3	-	-	-	-
1967	35.9	2.6	-	-	-	-	46.9	4.9	35.5	2.3	33.8	6.3	-	-	-	-
1968	37.5	4.5	-	-	-	-	50.0	6.6	36.5	2.8	35.1	3.8	-	-	-	-
1969	39.4	5.1	-	-	-	-	53.4	6.8	37.8	3.6	36.8	4.8	-	-	-	-
1970	41.7	5.8	-	-	-	-	55.2	3.4	39.7	5.0	39.0	6.0	-	-	-	-
1971	43.7	4.8	-	-	-	-	57.8	4.7	41.5	4.5	41.3	5.9	-	-	-	-
1972	45.5	4.1	-	-	-	-	59.1	2.2	41.9	1.0	42.6	3.1	-	-	-	-
1973	48.4	6.4	-	-	-	-	63.2	6.9	43.6	4.1	44.0	3.3	-	-	-	-
1974	53.7	11.0	-	-	-	-	68.3	8.1	48.4	11.0	48.0	9.1	-	-	-	-
1975	58.1	8.2	-	-	-	-	72.3	5.9	52.3	8.1	52.5	9.4	-	-	-	-
1976	61.3	5.5	64.3	-	60.3	-	75.7	4.7	57.3	9.6	56.9	8.4	67.2	-	61.0	-
1977	65.3	6.5	68.0	5.8	64.4	6.8	81.7	7.9	60.8	6.1	61.5	8.1	70.9	5.5	63.7	4.4
1978	69.3	6.1	73.9	8.7	68.1	5.7	84.8	3.8	64.0	5.3	67.0	8.9	72.3	2.0	66.7	4.7
1979	76.0	9.7	81.3	10.0	73.9	8.5	87.3	2.9	73.8	15.3	72.2	7.8	72.6	0.4	70.9	6.3
1980	84.3	10.9	87.8	8.0	82.4	11.5	90.0	3.1	86.0	16.5	79.0	9.4	79.3	9.2	76.7	8.2
1981	92.0	9.1	94.5	7.6	90.3	9.6	93.4	3.8	95.5	11.0	85.6	8.4	87.4	10.2	83.8	9.3
1982	95.2	3.5	97.6	3.3	93.0	3.0	97.6	4.5	97.4	2.0	91.7	7.1	94.3	7.9	90.7	8.2
1983	101.3	6.4	99.7	2.2	103.8	11.6	100.3	2.8	99.4	2.1	100.7	9.8	100.6	6.7	101.3	11.7
1984	103.5	2.2	102.7	3.0	103.2	-0.6	102.0	1.7	103.1	3.7	107.6	6.9	105.2	4.6	107.9	6.5
1985	105.1	1.5	106.0	3.2	101.4	-1.7	107.9	5.8	105.0	1.8	112.9	4.9	110.3	4.8	115.2	6.8
1986	105.7	0.6	108.7	2.5	103.5	2.1	111.0	2.9	97.3	-7.3	119.3	5.7	113.8	3.2	123.7	7.4
1987	109.0	3.1	112.1	3.1	105.8	2.2	118.1	6.4	99.3	2.1	126.8	6.3	122.0	7.2	130.4	5.4
1988	113.2	3.9	116.7	4.1	110.5	4.4	126.3	6.9	100.5	1.2	131.0	3.3	124.6	2.1	137.8	5.7
1989	117.3	3.6	125.7	7.7	115.1	4.2	109.9	-13.0	103.0	2.5	141.3	7.9	131.1	5.2	146.3	6.2
1990	123.2	5.0	131.4	4.5	121.6	5.6	107.7	-2.0	109.2	6.0	150.4	6.4	141.7	8.1	154.1	5.3
1991	128.8	4.5	135.7	3.3	128.7	5.8	112.0	4.0	112.3	2.8	158.1	5.1	146.8	3.6	164.5	6.7
1992	133.1	3.3	137.0	1.0	135.1	5.0	111.5	-0.4	113.9	1.4	165.9	4.9	154.3	5.1	180.4	9.7
1993	137.6	3.4	139.1	1.5	140.4	3.9	112.0	0.4	116.9	2.6	172.6	4.0	165.8	7.5	192.4	6.7
1994	141.5	2.8	142.9	2.7	143.7	2.4	118.4	5.7	120.6	3.2	174.8	1.3	176.1	6.2	195.9	1.8
1995	146.3	3.4	146.8	2.7	146.8	2.2	115.9	-2.1	129.2	7.1	181.9	4.1	186.4	5.8	205.3	4.8

Source: U.S. Department of Labor, Bureau of Labor Statistics, Division of Consumer Prices and Price Indexes. - indicates no data collected for period.

Buffalo, NY
Consumer Price Index - All Urban Consumers
Base 1982-1984 = 100
All Items

For 1963-1995. Columns headed % show percentile change in the index from the previous period for which an index is available.

Year	Jan Index	%	Feb Index	%	Mar Index	%	Apr Index	%	May Index	%	Jun Index	%	Jul Index	%	Aug Index	%	Sep Index	%	Oct Index	%	Nov Index	%	Dec Index	%
1963	-	-	-	-	-	-	-	-	-	-	-	-	-	-	-	-	-	-	-	-	32.3	-	-	-
1964	-	-	32.3	0.0	-	-	-	-	32.5	0.6	-	-	-	-	32.7	0.6	-	-	-	-	32.9	0.6	-	-
1965	-	-	33.0	0.3	-	-	-	-	33.2	0.6	-	-	-	-	33.5	0.9	-	-	-	-	33.8	0.9	-	-
1966	-	-	34.1	0.9	-	-	-	-	34.4	0.9	-	-	-	-	34.7	0.9	-	-	-	-	34.9	0.6	-	-
1967	-	-	35.0	0.3	-	-	-	-	35.3	0.9	-	-	-	-	35.6	0.8	-	-	-	-	35.9	0.8	-	-
1968	-	-	36.2	0.8	-	-	-	-	36.9	1.9	-	-	-	-	37.3	1.1	-	-	-	-	37.7	1.1	-	-
1969	-	-	37.8	0.3	-	-	-	-	38.8	2.6	-	-	-	-	39.1	0.8	-	-	-	-	39.7	1.5	-	-
1970	-	-	40.4	1.8	-	-	-	-	41.0	1.5	-	-	-	-	41.3	0.7	-	-	-	-	42.1	1.9	-	-
1971	-	-	42.4	0.7	-	-	-	-	43.0	1.4	-	-	-	-	43.5	1.2	-	-	-	-	43.6	0.2	-	-
1972	-	-	44.3	1.6	-	-	-	-	44.7	0.9	-	-	-	-	45.0	0.7	-	-	-	-	45.6	1.3	-	-
1973	-	-	46.2	1.3	-	-	-	-	47.2	2.2	-	-	-	-	48.4	2.5	-	-	-	-	49.1	1.4	-	-
1974	-	-	51.1	4.1	-	-	-	-	52.3	2.3	-	-	-	-	53.7	2.7	-	-	-	-	55.0	2.4	-	-
1975	-	-	55.9	1.6	-	-	-	-	56.9	1.8	-	-	-	-	58.0	1.9	-	-	-	-	58.8	1.4	-	-
1976	-	-	59.3	0.9	-	-	-	-	60.0	1.2	-	-	-	-	61.0	1.7	-	-	-	-	61.6	1.0	-	-
1977	-	-	62.9	2.1	-	-	-	-	64.3	2.2	-	-	-	-	64.8	0.8	-	-	-	-	65.7	1.4	-	-
1978	-	-	66.5	1.2	-	-	67.0	0.8	-	-	68.3	1.9	-	-	69.0	1.0	-	-	70.2	1.7	-	-	70.8	0.9
1979	-	-	72.0	1.7	-	-	73.3	1.8	-	-	74.2	1.2	-	-	76.1	2.6	-	-	77.5	1.8	-	-	78.4	1.2
1980	-	-	80.8	3.1	-	-	82.9	2.6	-	-	83.5	0.7	-	-	84.0	0.6	-	-	85.0	1.2	-	-	87.4	2.8
1981	-	-	89.1	1.9	-	-	90.3	1.3	-	-	91.2	1.0	-	-	92.3	1.2	-	-	93.1	0.9	-	-	93.7	0.6
1982	-	-	92.2	-1.6	-	-	91.6	-0.7	-	-	94.2	2.8	-	-	94.9	0.7	-	-	98.3	3.6	-	-	98.5	0.2
1983	-	-	99.4	0.9	-	-	100.2	0.8	-	-	100.8	0.6	-	-	101.4	0.6	-	-	102.3	0.9	-	-	102.2	-0.1
1984	-	-	103.0	0.8	-	-	103.9	0.9	-	-	103.7	-0.2	-	-	104.4	0.7	-	-	105.0	0.6	-	-	107.6	2.5
1985	-	-	106.8	-0.7	-	-	108.3	1.4	-	-	109.0	0.6	-	-	108.7	-0.3	-	-	109.7	0.9	-	-	109.9	0.2
1986	-	-	110.0	0.1	-	-	109.2	-0.7	-	-	109.5	0.3	-	-	109.0	-0.5	-	-	109.7	0.6	-	-	110.4	0.6
1987	-	-	-	-	-	-	-	-	-	-	111.8	1.3	-	-	-	-	-	-	-	-	-	-	114.2	2.1
1988	-	-	-	-	-	-	-	-	-	-	115.9	1.5	-	-	-	-	-	-	-	-	-	-	118.9	2.6
1989	-	-	-	-	-	-	-	-	-	-	120.7	1.5	-	-	-	-	-	-	-	-	-	-	122.4	1.4
1990	-	-	-	-	-	-	-	-	-	-	125.8	2.8	-	-	-	-	-	-	-	-	-	-	129.7	3.1
1991	-	-	-	-	-	-	-	-	-	-	132.7	2.3	-	-	-	-	-	-	-	-	-	-	134.1	1.1
1992	-	-	-	-	-	-	-	-	-	-	136.0	1.4	-	-	-	-	-	-	-	-	-	-	139.8	2.8
1993	-	-	-	-	-	-	-	-	-	-	141.2	1.0	-	-	-	-	-	-	-	-	-	-	144.2	2.1
1994	-	-	-	-	-	-	-	-	-	-	145.7	1.0	-	-	-	-	-	-	-	-	-	-	147.8	1.4
1995	-	-	-	-	-	-	-	-	-	-	150.3	1.7	-	-	-	-	-	-	-	-	-	-	-	-

Source: U.S. Department of Labor, Bureau of Labor Statistics, Division of Consumer Prices and Price Indexes. - indicates no data collected for period.

Buffalo, NY
Consumer Price Index - Urban Wage Earners
Base 1982-1984 = 100
All Items

For 1963-1995. Columns headed % show percentile change in the index from the previous period for which an index is available.

Year	Jan Index	Jan %	Feb Index	Feb %	Mar Index	Mar %	Apr Index	Apr %	May Index	May %	Jun Index	Jun %	Jul Index	Jul %	Aug Index	Aug %	Sep Index	Sep %	Oct Index	Oct %	Nov Index	Nov %	Dec Index	Dec %
1963	-	-	-	-	-	-	-	-	-	-	-	-	-	-	-	-	-	-	-	-	-	-	-	-
1964	-	-	32.7	0.0	-	-	-	-	32.9	0.6	-	-	-	-	33.1	0.6	-	-	-	-	32.7	-	-	-
1965	-	-	33.5	0.3	-	-	-	-	33.7	0.6	-	-	-	-	34.0	0.9	-	-	-	-	33.4	0.9	-	-
1966	-	-	34.6	1.2	-	-	-	-	34.8	0.6	-	-	-	-	35.2	1.1	-	-	-	-	34.2	0.6	-	-
1967	-	-	35.4	0.3	-	-	-	-	35.8	1.1	-	-	-	-	36.1	0.8	-	-	-	-	35.3	0.3	-	-
1968	-	-	36.7	1.1	-	-	-	-	37.3	1.6	-	-	-	-	37.8	1.3	-	-	-	-	36.3	0.6	-	-
1969	-	-	38.3	0.3	-	-	-	-	39.3	2.6	-	-	-	-	39.6	0.8	-	-	-	-	38.2	1.1	-	-
1970	-	-	40.9	1.5	-	-	-	-	41.5	1.5	-	-	-	-	41.8	0.7	-	-	-	-	40.3	1.8	-	-
1971	-	-	43.0	0.9	-	-	-	-	43.6	1.4	-	-	-	-	44.1	1.1	-	-	-	-	42.6	1.9	-	-
1972	-	-	44.9	1.6	-	-	-	-	45.3	0.9	-	-	-	-	45.5	0.4	-	-	-	-	44.2	0.2	-	-
1973	-	-	46.8	1.3	-	-	-	-	47.8	2.1	-	-	-	-	49.1	2.7	-	-	-	-	46.2	1.5	-	-
1974	-	-	51.8	4.0	-	-	-	-	53.0	2.3	-	-	-	-	54.4	2.6	-	-	-	-	49.8	1.4	-	-
1975	-	-	56.6	1.6	-	-	-	-	57.6	1.8	-	-	-	-	58.7	1.9	-	-	-	-	55.7	2.4	-	-
1976	-	-	60.0	0.8	-	-	-	-	60.7	1.2	-	-	-	-	61.8	1.8	-	-	-	-	59.5	1.4	-	-
1977	-	-	63.7	2.1	-	-	-	-	65.1	2.2	-	-	-	-	65.6	0.8	-	-	-	-	62.4	1.0	-	-
1978	-	-	67.3	1.2	-	-	67.9	0.9	-	-	69.3	2.1	-	-	69.9	0.9	-	-	-	-	66.5	1.4	-	-
1979	-	-	72.9	1.8	-	-	74.4	2.1	-	-	75.3	1.2	-	-	77.3	2.7	-	-	71.0	1.6	-	-	71.6	0.8
1980	-	-	81.8	3.2	-	-	83.8	2.4	-	-	84.3	0.6	-	-	84.6	0.4	-	-	78.5	1.6	-	-	79.3	1.0
1981	-	-	89.7	1.8	-	-	90.8	1.2	-	-	92.0	1.3	-	-	93.2	1.3	-	-	85.5	1.1	-	-	88.1	3.0
1982	-	-	92.7	-1.7	-	-	92.1	-0.6	-	-	94.8	2.9	-	-	95.3	0.5	-	-	93.8	0.6	-	-	94.3	0.5
1983	-	-	99.3	0.5	-	-	100.0	0.7	-	-	101.7	1.7	-	-	102.4	0.7	-	-	98.5	3.4	-	-	98.8	0.3
1984	-	-	102.7	0.1	-	-	102.9	0.2	-	-	103.2	0.3	-	-	103.6	0.7	-	-	103.0	0.6	-	-	102.6	-0.4
1985	-	-	103.5	-0.6	-	-	104.8	1.3	-	-	105.5	0.7	-	-	103.6	0.4	-	-	104.9	1.3	-	-	104.1	-0.8
1986	-	-	106.2	-0.1	-	-	105.1	-1.0	-	-	105.6	0.5	-	-	105.2	-0.3	-	-	106.1	0.9	-	-	106.3	0.2
1987	-	-	-	-	-	-	-	-	-	-	107.8	1.4	-	-	105.0	-0.6	-	-	105.7	0.7	-	-	106.3	0.6
1988	-	-	-	-	-	-	-	-	-	-	111.7	1.4	-	-	-	-	-	-	-	-	-	-	110.2	2.2
1989	-	-	-	-	-	-	-	-	-	-	116.5	1.7	-	-	-	-	-	-	-	-	-	-	114.6	2.6
1990	-	-	-	-	-	-	-	-	-	-	121.2	2.5	-	-	-	-	-	-	-	-	-	-	118.2	1.5
1991	-	-	-	-	-	-	-	-	128.0	2.2	-	-	-	-	-	-	-	-	-	-	-	-	125.2	3.3
1992	-	-	-	-	-	-	-	-	131.2	1.2	-	-	-	-	-	-	-	-	-	-	-	-	129.6	1.3
1993	-	-	-	-	-	-	-	-	136.1	0.8	-	-	-	-	-	-	-	-	-	-	-	-	135.0	2.9
1994	-	-	-	-	-	-	-	-	140.4	0.9	-	-	-	-	-	-	-	-	-	-	-	-	139.1	2.2
1995	-	-	-	-	-	-	-	-	145.0	1.6	-	-	-	-	-	-	-	-	-	-	-	-	142.7	1.6

Source: U.S. Department of Labor, Bureau of Labor Statistics, Division of Consumer Prices and Price Indexes. - indicates no data collected for period.

Buffalo, NY
Consumer Price Index - All Urban Consumers
Base 1982-1984 = 100
Food and Beverages

For 1975-1995. Columns headed % show percentile change in the index from the previous period for which an index is available.

Year	Jan Index	%	Feb Index	%	Mar Index	%	Apr Index	%	May Index	%	Jun Index	%	Jul Index	%	Aug Index	%	Sep Index	%	Oct Index	%	Nov Index	%	Dec Index	%
1975	-	-	-	-	-	-	-	-	-	-	-	-	-	-	-	-	-	-	-	-	62.5	-	-	-
1976	-	-	63.3	1.3	-	-	-	-	62.7	-0.9	-	-	-	-	63.7	1.6	-	-	-	-	63.4	-0.5	-	-
1977	-	-	66.0	4.1	-	-	-	-	66.7	1.1	-	-	-	-	67.4	1.0	-	-	-	-	67.8	0.6	-	-
1978	-	-	69.8	2.9	-	-	71.3	2.1	-	-	74.3	4.2	-	-	73.8	-0.7	-	-	74.2	0.5	-	-	75.1	1.2
1979	-	-	77.6	3.3	-	-	79.8	2.8	-	-	80.7	1.1	-	-	80.1	-0.7	-	-	81.1	1.2	-	-	82.5	1.7
1980	-	-	83.7	1.5	-	-	84.3	0.7	-	-	86.2	2.3	-	-	87.6	1.6	-	-	89.8	2.5	-	-	91.6	2.0
1981	-	-	93.4	2.0	-	-	94.1	0.7	-	-	94.1	0.0	-	-	94.9	0.9	-	-	94.4	-0.5	-	-	94.9	0.5
1982	-	-	96.5	1.7	-	-	96.6	0.1	-	-	99.0	2.5	-	-	98.0	-1.0	-	-	97.9	-0.1	-	-	97.8	-0.1
1983	-	-	99.2	1.4	-	-	99.6	0.4	-	-	100.5	0.9	-	-	100.0	-0.5	-	-	99.7	-0.3	-	-	100.9	1.2
1984	-	-	103.2	2.3	-	-	103.3	0.1	-	-	102.4	-0.9	-	-	102.7	0.3	-	-	102.4	-0.3	-	-	102.2	-0.2
1985	-	-	104.9	2.6	-	-	106.9	1.9	-	-	106.2	-0.7	-	-	105.5	-0.7	-	-	105.8	0.3	-	-	106.7	0.9
1986	-	-	107.3	0.6	-	-	106.9	-0.4	-	-	107.6	0.7	-	-	109.9	2.1	-	-	110.1	0.2	-	-	110.2	0.1
1987	-	-	-	-	-	-	-	-	-	-	111.7	1.4	-	-	-	-	-	-	-	-	-	-	112.6	0.8
1988	-	-	-	-	-	-	-	-	-	-	114.7	1.9	-	-	-	-	-	-	-	-	-	-	118.8	3.6
1989	-	-	-	-	-	-	-	-	-	-	123.7	4.1	-	-	-	-	-	-	-	-	-	-	127.9	3.4
1990	-	-	-	-	-	-	-	-	-	-	130.9	2.3	-	-	-	-	-	-	-	-	-	-	132.2	1.0
1991	-	-	-	-	-	-	-	-	-	-	136.2	3.0	-	-	-	-	-	-	-	-	-	-	135.9	-0.2
1992	-	-	-	-	-	-	-	-	-	-	136.3	0.3	-	-	-	-	-	-	-	-	-	-	138.0	1.2
1993	-	-	-	-	-	-	-	-	-	-	137.6	-0.3	-	-	-	-	-	-	-	-	-	-	140.9	2.4
1994	-	-	-	-	-	-	-	-	-	-	143.3	1.7	-	-	-	-	-	-	-	-	-	-	142.9	-0.3
1995	-	-	-	-	-	-	-	-	-	-	146.6	2.6	-	-	-	-	-	-	-	-	-	-	-	-

Source: U.S. Department of Labor, Bureau of Labor Statistics, Division of Consumer Prices and Price Indexes. - indicates no data collected for period.

Buffalo, NY
Consumer Price Index - Urban Wage Earners
Base 1982-1984 = 100
Food and Beverages

For 1975-1995. Columns headed % show percentile change in the index from the previous period for which an index is available.

Year	Jan		Feb		Mar		Apr		May		Jun		Jul		Aug		Sep		Oct		Nov		Dec	
	Index	%	Index	%	Index	%	Index	%	Index	%	Index	%	Index	%	Index	%	Index	%	Index	%	Index	%	Index	%
1975	-	-	-	-	-	-	-	-	-	-	-	-	-	-	-	-	-	-	-	-	63.5	-	-	-
1976	-	-	64.3	1.3	-	-	-	-	63.7	-0.9	-	-	-	-	64.7	1.6	-	-	-	-	64.4	-0.5	-	-
1977	-	-	67.0	4.0	-	-	-	-	67.7	1.0	-	-	-	-	68.5	1.2	-	-	-	-	68.8	0.4	-	-
1978	-	-	70.9	3.1	-	-	72.4	2.1	-	-	75.2	3.9	-	-	75.1	-0.1	-	-	75.4	0.4	-	-	76.1	0.9
1979	-	-	78.5	3.2	-	-	81.5	3.8	-	-	82.2	0.9	-	-	82.1	-0.1	-	-	82.4	0.4	-	-	83.0	0.7
1980	-	-	84.5	1.8	-	-	85.5	1.2	-	-	87.2	2.0	-	-	88.6	1.6	-	-	90.8	2.5	-	-	92.6	2.0
1981	-	-	94.0	1.5	-	-	94.0	0.0	-	-	94.5	0.5	-	-	95.4	1.0	-	-	94.6	-0.8	-	-	95.2	0.6
1982	-	-	96.5	1.4	-	-	96.8	0.3	-	-	99.3	2.6	-	-	98.0	-1.3	-	-	97.9	-0.1	-	-	97.9	0.0
1983	-	-	99.2	1.3	-	-	99.3	0.1	-	-	100.5	1.2	-	-	99.9	-0.6	-	-	99.6	-0.3	-	-	100.7	1.1
1984	-	-	103.3	2.6	-	-	103.5	0.2	-	-	102.3	-1.2	-	-	102.6	0.3	-	-	102.4	-0.2	-	-	100.7	1.1
1985	-	-	105.0	2.6	-	-	107.1	2.0	-	-	106.4	-0.7	-	-	105.6	-0.8	-	-	102.4	-0.2	-	-	102.3	-0.1
1986	-	-	107.5	0.6	-	-	107.0	-0.5	-	-	107.6	0.6	-	-	110.5	2.7	-	-	106.1	0.5	-	-	106.9	0.8
1987	-	-	-	-	-	-	-	-	-	-	111.7	1.5	-	-	-	-	-	-	110.3	-0.2	-	-	110.0	-0.3
1988	-	-	-	-	-	-	-	-	-	-	114.7	1.9	-	-	-	-	-	-	-	-	-	-	112.6	0.8
1989	-	-	-	-	-	-	-	-	-	-	123.6	4.1	-	-	-	-	-	-	-	-	-	-	118.7	3.5
1990	-	-	-	-	-	-	-	-	-	-	130.7	2.3	-	-	-	-	-	-	-	-	-	-	127.7	3.3
1991	-	-	-	-	-	-	-	-	-	-	135.7	2.7	-	-	-	-	-	-	-	-	-	-	132.1	1.1
1992	-	-	-	-	-	-	-	-	-	-	136.1	0.4	-	-	-	-	-	-	-	-	-	-	135.6	-0.1
1993	-	-	-	-	-	-	-	-	-	-	137.4	-0.3	-	-	-	-	-	-	-	-	-	-	137.8	1.2
1994	-	-	-	-	-	-	-	-	-	-	143.2	1.8	-	-	-	-	-	-	-	-	-	-	140.7	2.4
1995	-	-	-	-	-	-	-	-	-	-	146.3	2.5	-	-	-	-	-	-	-	-	-	-	142.7	-0.3
	-	-	-	-	-	-	-	-	-	-	-	-	-	-	-	-	-	-	-	-	-	-	-	-

Source: U.S. Department of Labor, Bureau of Labor Statistics, Division of Consumer Prices and Price Indexes. - indicates no data collected for period.

333

Buffalo, NY
Consumer Price Index - All Urban Consumers
Base 1982-1984 = 100
Housing

For 1975-1995. Columns headed % show percentile change in the index from the previous period for which an index is available.

Year	Jan Index	%	Feb Index	%	Mar Index	%	Apr Index	%	May Index	%	Jun Index	%	Jul Index	%	Aug Index	%	Sep Index	%	Oct Index	%	Nov Index	%	Dec Index	%
1975	-	-	-	-	-	-	-	-	-	-	-	-	-	-	-	-	-	-	-	-	57.8	-	-	-
1976	-	-	58.1	0.5	-	-	-	-	58.7	1.0	-	-	-	-	60.1	2.4	-	-	-	-	60.7	1.0	-	-
1977	-	-	62.0	2.1	-	-	-	-	63.5	2.4	-	-	-	-	63.8	0.5	-	-	-	-	65.0	1.9	-	-
1978	-	-	65.4	0.6	-	-	65.7	0.5	-	-	66.2	0.8	-	-	67.3	1.7	-	-	69.1	2.7	-	-	69.7	0.9
1979	-	-	70.9	1.7	-	-	71.2	0.4	-	-	71.4	0.3	-	-	73.8	3.4	-	-	75.7	2.6	-	-	76.6	1.2
1980	-	-	79.0	3.1	-	-	82.2	4.1	-	-	82.3	0.1	-	-	81.4	-1.1	-	-	81.7	0.4	-	-	86.0	5.3
1981	-	-	86.9	1.0	-	-	87.4	0.6	-	-	89.4	2.3	-	-	91.1	1.9	-	-	91.7	0.7	-	-	92.5	0.9
1982	-	-	87.9	-5.0	-	-	87.0	-1.0	-	-	91.0	4.6	-	-	92.5	1.6	-	-	99.1	7.1	-	-	99.4	0.3
1983	-	-	101.5	2.1	-	-	102.0	0.5	-	-	102.0	0.0	-	-	102.7	0.7	-	-	103.5	0.8	-	-	102.5	-1.0
1984	-	-	102.7	0.2	-	-	104.0	1.3	-	-	104.1	0.1	-	-	105.3	1.2	-	-	105.5	0.2	-	-	112.6	6.7
1985	-	-	108.7	-3.5	-	-	109.3	0.6	-	-	110.4	1.0	-	-	110.1	-0.3	-	-	111.3	1.1	-	-	110.9	-0.4
1986	-	-	111.9	0.9	-	-	113.3	1.3	-	-	113.2	-0.1	-	-	111.7	-1.3	-	-	112.0	0.3	-	-	112.7	0.6
1987	-	-	-	-	-	-	-	-	-	-	113.1	0.4	-	-	-	-	-	-	-	-	-	-	116.5	3.0
1988	-	-	-	-	-	-	-	-	-	-	118.4	1.6	-	-	-	-	-	-	-	-	-	-	121.8	2.9
1989	-	-	-	-	-	-	-	-	-	-	123.6	1.5	-	-	-	-	-	-	-	-	-	-	126.4	2.3
1990	-	-	-	-	-	-	-	-	-	-	130.2	3.0	-	-	-	-	-	-	-	-	-	-	133.8	2.8
1991	-	-	-	-	-	-	-	-	-	-	138.2	3.3	-	-	-	-	-	-	-	-	-	-	140.7	1.8
1992	-	-	-	-	-	-	-	-	-	-	144.2	2.5	-	-	-	-	-	-	-	-	-	-	148.1	2.7
1993	-	-	-	-	-	-	-	-	-	-	150.6	1.7	-	-	-	-	-	-	-	-	-	-	153.7	2.1
1994	-	-	-	-	-	-	-	-	-	-	155.1	0.9	-	-	-	-	-	-	-	-	-	-	156.7	1.0
1995	-	-	-	-	-	-	-	-	-	-	158.5	1.1	-	-	-	-	-	-	-	-	-	-	-	-

Source: U.S. Department of Labor, Bureau of Labor Statistics, Division of Consumer Prices and Price Indexes. - indicates no data collected for period.

Buffalo, NY
Consumer Price Index - Urban Wage Earners
Base 1982-1984 = 100
Housing

For 1975-1995. Columns headed % show percentile change in the index from the previous period for which an index is available.

Year	Jan Index	%	Feb Index	%	Mar Index	%	Apr Index	%	May Index	%	Jun Index	%	Jul Index	%	Aug Index	%	Sep Index	%	Oct Index	%	Nov Index	%	Dec Index	%
1975	-	-	-	-	-	-	-	-	-	-	-	-	-	-	-	-	-	-	-	-	58.6	-	-	-
1976	-	-	58.9	0.5	-	-	-	-	59.5	1.0	-	-	-	-	61.0	2.5	-	-	-	-	61.6	1.0	-	-
1977	-	-	62.8	1.9	-	-	-	-	64.3	2.4	-	-	-	-	64.7	0.6	-	-	-	-	65.9	1.9	-	-
1978	-	-	66.3	0.6	-	-	66.5	0.3	-	-	67.2	1.1	-	-	68.4	1.8	-	-	70.3	2.8	-	-	71.0	1.0
1979	-	-	72.1	1.5	-	-	72.1	0.0	-	-	72.0	-0.1	-	-	74.6	3.6	-	-	76.6	2.7	-	-	77.6	1.3
1980	-	-	80.2	3.4	-	-	83.0	3.5	-	-	82.7	-0.4	-	-	81.9	-1.0	-	-	82.1	0.2	-	-	86.7	5.6
1981	-	-	87.4	0.8	-	-	88.0	0.7	-	-	90.1	2.4	-	-	92.2	2.3	-	-	92.6	0.4	-	-	93.5	1.0
1982	-	-	88.2	-5.7	-	-	87.2	-1.1	-	-	91.5	4.9	-	-	92.9	1.5	-	-	99.9	7.5	-	-	100.2	0.3
1983	-	-	101.7	1.5	-	-	102.0	0.3	-	-	104.8	2.7	-	-	105.5	0.7	-	-	105.6	0.1	-	-	103.7	-1.8
1984	-	-	102.2	-1.4	-	-	101.5	-0.7	-	-	103.0	1.5	-	-	103.6	0.6	-	-	105.7	2.0	-	-	103.6	-2.0
1985	-	-	100.1	-3.4	-	-	100.7	0.6	-	-	101.6	0.9	-	-	101.4	-0.2	-	-	102.4	1.0	-	-	102.2	-0.2
1986	-	-	103.0	0.8	-	-	104.3	1.3	-	-	104.2	-0.1	-	-	102.8	-1.3	-	-	103.1	0.3	-	-	104.0	0.9
1987	-	-	-	-	-	-	-	-	-	-	104.4	0.4	-	-	-	-	-	-	-	-	-	-	107.4	2.9
1988	-	-	-	-	-	-	-	-	-	-	108.9	1.4	-	-	-	-	-	-	-	-	-	-	112.1	2.9
1989	-	-	-	-	-	-	-	-	-	-	113.9	1.6	-	-	-	-	-	-	-	-	-	-	116.4	2.2
1990	-	-	-	-	-	-	-	-	-	-	120.0	3.1	-	-	-	-	-	-	-	-	-	-	123.2	2.7
1991	-	-	-	-	-	-	-	-	-	-	127.5	3.5	-	-	-	-	-	-	-	-	-	-	129.9	1.9
1992	-	-	-	-	-	-	-	-	-	-	133.4	2.7	-	-	-	-	-	-	-	-	-	-	136.9	2.6
1993	-	-	-	-	-	-	-	-	-	-	139.0	1.5	-	-	-	-	-	-	-	-	-	-	141.9	2.1
1994	-	-	-	-	-	-	-	-	-	-	143.0	0.8	-	-	-	-	-	-	-	-	-	-	144.4	1.0
1995	-	-	-	-	-	-	-	-	-	-	145.9	1.0	-	-	-	-	-	-	-	-	-	-	-	-

Source: U.S. Department of Labor, Bureau of Labor Statistics, Division of Consumer Prices and Price Indexes. - indicates no data collected for period.

Buffalo, NY
Consumer Price Index - All Urban Consumers
Base 1982-1984 = 100
Apparel and Upkeep

For 1963-1995. Columns headed % show percentile change in the index from the previous period for which an index is available.

Year	Jan Index	%	Feb Index	%	Mar Index	%	Apr Index	%	May Index	%	Jun Index	%	Jul Index	%	Aug Index	%	Sep Index	%	Oct Index	%	Nov Index	%	Dec Index	%
1963	-	-	-	-	-	-	-	-	-		-		-		-		-		-		40.0	-	-	-
1964	-	-	40.1	0.2	-	-	-	-	40.0	-0.2	-		-		40.4	1.0	-		-		40.9	1.2	-	-
1965	-	-	41.2	0.7	-	-	-	-	41.6	1.0	-		-		41.9	0.7	-		-		42.4	1.2	-	-
1966	-	-	42.8	0.9	-	-	-	-	43.3	1.2	-		-		43.1	-0.5	-		-		43.8	1.6	-	-
1967	-	-	44.4	1.4	-	-	-	-	45.4	2.3	-		-		45.2	-0.4	-		-		46.1	2.0	-	-
1968	-	-	46.8	1.5	-	-	-	-	48.2	3.0	-		-		48.9	1.5	-		-		49.5	1.2	-	-
1969	-	-	48.9	-1.2	-	-	-	-	51.9	6.1	-		-		52.0	0.2	-		-		53.9	3.7	-	-
1970	-	-	52.5	-2.6	-	-	-	-	53.1	1.1	-		-		52.5	-1.1	-		-		55.1	5.0	-	-
1971	-	-	54.7	-0.7	-	-	-	-	56.6	3.5	-		-		55.5	-1.9	-		-		56.5	1.8	-	-
1972	-	-	55.4	-1.9	-	-	-	-	57.8	4.3	-		-		56.2	-2.8	-		-		58.9	4.8	-	-
1973	-	-	60.1	2.0	-	-	-	-	60.5	0.7	-		-		61.6	1.8	-		-		61.9	0.5	-	-
1974	-	-	63.1	1.9	-	-	-	-	65.0	3.0	-		-		67.0	3.1	-		-		68.9	2.8	-	-
1975	-	-	68.5	-0.6	-	-	-	-	68.9	0.6	-		-		70.1	1.7	-		-		71.8	2.4	-	-
1976	-	-	70.6	-1.7	-	-	-	-	73.8	4.5	-		-		73.0	-1.1	-		-		75.1	2.9	-	-
1977	-	-	75.1	0.0	-	-	-	-	79.2	5.5	-		-		80.0	1.0	-		-		81.8	2.3	-	-
1978	-	-	80.3	-1.8	-	-	81.1	1.0	-	-	81.0	-0.1	-		83.2	2.7	-		84.4	1.4	-	-	84.0	-0.5
1979	-	-	82.2	-2.1	-	-	84.8	3.2	-	-	83.8	-1.2	-		88.6	5.7	-		90.3	1.9	-	-	88.0	-2.5
1980	-	-	88.1	0.1	-	-	89.1	1.1	-	-	90.0	1.0	-		94.2	4.7	-		94.4	0.2	-	-	91.7	-2.9
1981	-	-	91.1	-0.7	-	-	93.7	2.9	-	-	93.6	-0.1	-		93.9	0.3	-		95.5	1.7	-	-	96.0	0.5
1982	-	-	95.8	-0.2	-	-	97.3	1.6	-	-	97.3	0.0	-		98.2	0.9	-		99.7	1.5	-	-	98.2	-1.5
1983	-	-	96.3	-1.9	-	-	100.9	4.8	-	-	100.4	-0.5	-	-	100.5	0.1	-	-	103.4	2.9	-	-	102.1	-1.3
1984	-	-	101.5	-0.6	-	-	101.1	-0.4	-	-	99.9	-1.2	-	-	101.1	1.2	-	-	103.9	2.8	-	-	104.8	0.9
1985	-	-	103.5	-1.2	-	-	110.0	6.3	-	-	109.6	-0.4	-	-	107.1	-2.3	-	-	111.1	3.7	-	-	109.3	-1.6
1986	-	-	108.2	-1.0	-	-	113.6	5.0	-	-	109.2	-3.9	-	-	112.6	3.1	-	-	111.5	-1.0	-	-	115.0	3.1
1987	-	-	-	-	-	-	-	-	-	-	116.7	1.5	-	-	-	-	-	-	-	-	-	-	119.1	2.1
1988	-	-	-	-	-	-	-	-	-	-	123.5	3.7	-	-	-	-	-	-	-	-	-	-	128.1	3.7
1989	-	-	-	-	-	-	-	-	-	-	113.8	-11.2	-	-	-	-	-	-	-	-	-	-	105.1	-7.6
1990	-	-	-	-	-	-	-	-	-	-	106.1	1.0	-	-	-	-	-	-	-	-	-	-	109.1	2.8
1991	-	-	-	-	-	-	-	-	-	-	109.5	0.4	-	-	-	-	-	-	-	-	-	-	114.5	4.6
1992	-	-	-	-	-	-	-	-	-	-	106.0	-7.4	-	-	-	-	-	-	-	-	-	-	116.7	10.1
1993	-	-	-	-	-	-	-	-	-	-	111.3	-4.6	-	-	-	-	-	-	-	-	-	-	113.9	2.3
1994	-	-	-	-	-	-	-	-	-	-	116.3	2.1	-	-	-	-	-	-	-	-	-	-	121.2	4.2
1995	-	-	-	-	-	-	-	-	-	-	115.9	-4.4	-	-	-	-	-	-	-	-	-	-	-	-

Source: U.S. Department of Labor, Bureau of Labor Statistics, Division of Consumer Prices and Price Indexes. - indicates no data collected for period.

Buffalo, NY
Consumer Price Index - Urban Wage Earners
Base 1982-1984 = 100
Apparel and Upkeep

For 1963-1995. Columns headed % show percentile change in the index from the previous period for which an index is available.

Year	Jan Index	Jan %	Feb Index	Feb %	Mar Index	Mar %	Apr Index	Apr %	May Index	May %	Jun Index	Jun %	Jul Index	Jul %	Aug Index	Aug %	Sep Index	Sep %	Oct Index	Oct %	Nov Index	Nov %	Dec Index	Dec %
1963	-	-	-	-	-	-	-	-	-	-	-	-	-	-	-	-	-	-	-	-	-	-	-	-
1964	-	-	41.5	0.2	-	-	-	-	41.4	-0.2	-	-	-	-	41.8	1.0	-	-	-	-	41.4	-	-	-
1965	-	-	42.6	0.5	-	-	-	-	43.0	0.9	-	-	-	-	43.4	0.9	-	-	-	-	42.4	1.4	-	-
1966	-	-	44.3	0.9	-	-	-	-	44.8	1.1	-	-	-	-	44.6	-0.4	-	-	-	-	43.9	1.2	-	-
1967	-	-	46.0	1.5	-	-	-	-	47.0	2.2	-	-	-	-	46.8	-0.4	-	-	-	-	45.3	1.6	-	-
1968	-	-	48.5	1.7	-	-	-	-	49.9	2.9	-	-	-	-	50.6	1.4	-	-	-	-	47.7	1.9	-	-
1969	-	-	50.6	-1.2	-	-	-	-	53.7	6.1	-	-	-	-	53.8	0.2	-	-	-	-	51.2	1.2	-	-
1970	-	-	54.3	-2.7	-	-	-	-	55.0	1.3	-	-	-	-	54.3	-1.3	-	-	-	-	55.8	3.7	-	-
1971	-	-	56.6	-0.9	-	-	-	-	58.6	3.5	-	-	-	-	57.4	-2.0	-	-	-	-	57.1	5.2	-	-
1972	-	-	57.4	-1.9	-	-	-	-	59.8	4.2	-	-	-	-	58.1	-2.8	-	-	-	-	58.5	1.9	-	-
1973	-	-	62.2	2.0	-	-	-	-	62.6	0.6	-	-	-	-	63.7	1.8	-	-	-	-	61.0	5.0	-	-
1974	-	-	65.4	2.0	-	-	-	-	67.3	2.9	-	-	-	-	69.4	3.1	-	-	-	-	64.1	0.6	-	-
1975	-	-	70.9	-0.6	-	-	-	-	71.4	0.7	-	-	-	-	72.5	1.5	-	-	-	-	71.3	2.7	-	-
1976	-	-	73.1	-1.7	-	-	-	-	76.4	4.5	-	-	-	-	75.6	-1.0	-	-	-	-	74.4	2.6	-	-
1977	-	-	77.7	-0.1	-	-	-	-	82.0	5.5	-	-	-	-	82.8	1.0	-	-	-	-	77.8	2.9	-	-
1978	-	-	83.1	-1.8	-	-	85.6	3.0	-	-	85.4	-0.2	-	-	84.5	-1.1	-	-	-	-	84.6	2.2	-	-
1979	-	-	84.4	-1.1	-	-	86.9	3.0	-	-	85.1	-2.1	-	-	89.1	4.7	-	-	85.2	0.8	-	-	85.3	0.1
1980	-	-	88.6	-0.3	-	-	89.4	0.9	-	-	90.5	1.2	-	-	90.7	0.2	-	-	90.5	-0.2	-	-	88.9	-1.8
1981	-	-	88.1	-3.0	-	-	92.8	5.3	-	-	93.8	1.1	-	-	95.0	1.3	-	-	96.4	1.5	-	-	90.8	0.3
1982	-	-	95.6	0.2	-	-	97.3	1.8	-	-	96.9	-0.4	-	-	98.1	1.2	-	-	100.0	1.9	-	-	95.4	-1.0
1983	-	-	96.8	-2.0	-	-	100.2	3.5	-	-	100.1	-0.1	-	-	99.6	-0.5	-	-	104.0	4.4	-	-	98.8	-1.2
1984	-	-	101.5	-0.7	-	-	101.7	0.2	-	-	99.5	-2.2	-	-	100.7	1.2	-	-	104.6	3.9	-	-	102.2	-1.7
1985	-	-	104.6	-0.5	-	-	108.4	3.6	-	-	108.7	0.3	-	-	107.5	-1.1	-	-	110.2	2.5	-	-	105.1	0.5
1986	-	-	107.9	-1.0	-	-	112.6	4.4	-	-	109.0	-3.2	-	-	111.9	2.7	-	-	110.9	-0.9	-	-	109.0	-1.1
1987	-	-	-	-	-	-	-	-	-	-	117.0	1.2	-	-	-	-	-	-	-	-	115.6	4.2	-	-
1988	-	-	-	-	-	-	-	-	-	-	124.4	4.3	-	-	-	-	-	-	-	-	119.3	2.0	-	-
1989	-	-	-	-	-	-	-	-	-	-	114.4	-10.7	-	-	-	-	-	-	-	-	128.1	3.0	-	-
1990	-	-	-	-	-	-	-	-	-	-	105.9	0.4	-	-	-	-	-	-	-	-	105.5	-7.8	-	-
1991	-	-	-	-	-	-	-	-	-	-	109.2	-0.3	-	-	-	-	-	-	-	-	109.5	3.4	-	-
1992	-	-	-	-	-	-	-	-	-	-	106.2	-7.5	-	-	-	-	-	-	-	-	-	-	114.8	5.1
1993	-	-	-	-	-	-	-	-	-	-	110.0	-5.8	-	-	-	-	-	-	-	-	-	-	116.8	10.0
1994	-	-	-	-	-	-	-	-	-	-	115.8	1.7	-	-	-	-	-	-	-	-	-	-	113.9	3.5
1995	-	-	-	-	-	-	-	-	-	-	114.6	-5.3	-	-	-	-	-	-	-	-	-	-	121.0	4.5

Source: U.S. Department of Labor, Bureau of Labor Statistics, Division of Consumer Prices and Price Indexes. - indicates no data collected for period.

Buffalo, NY
Consumer Price Index - All Urban Consumers
Base 1982-1984 = 100
Transportation

For 1963-1995. Columns headed % show percentile change in the index from the previous period for which an index is available.

Year	Jan Index	%	Feb Index	%	Mar Index	%	Apr Index	%	May Index	%	Jun Index	%	Jul Index	%	Aug Index	%	Sep Index	%	Oct Index	%	Nov Index	%	Dec Index	%
1963	-	-	-	-	-	-	-	-	-	-	-	-	-	-	-	-	-	-	-	-	32.9	-	-	-
1964	-	-	32.5	-1.2	-	-	-	-	33.0	1.5	-	-	-	-	32.6	-1.2	-	-	-	-	33.1	1.5	-	-
1965	-	-	33.6	1.5	-	-	-	-	34.1	1.5	-	-	-	-	34.3	0.6	-	-	-	-	34.3	0.0	-	-
1966	-	-	34.5	0.6	-	-	-	-	34.8	0.9	-	-	-	-	35.1	0.9	-	-	-	-	35.2	0.3	-	-
1967	-	-	35.4	0.6	-	-	-	-	35.7	0.8	-	-	-	-	35.7	0.0	-	-	-	-	36.3	1.7	-	-
1968	-	-	36.4	0.3	-	-	-	-	36.6	0.5	-	-	-	-	36.8	0.5	-	-	-	-	37.1	0.8	-	-
1969	-	-	37.4	0.8	-	-	-	-	38.0	1.6	-	-	-	-	38.1	0.3	-	-	-	-	38.8	1.8	-	-
1970	-	-	39.3	1.3	-	-	-	-	39.8	1.3	-	-	-	-	39.8	0.0	-	-	-	-	40.9	2.8	-	-
1971	-	-	41.8	2.2	-	-	-	-	41.8	0.0	-	-	-	-	42.3	1.2	-	-	-	-	41.3	-2.4	-	-
1972	-	-	41.2	-0.2	-	-	-	-	42.3	2.7	-	-	-	-	42.3	0.0	-	-	-	-	42.8	1.2	-	-
1973	-	-	43.1	0.7	-	-	-	-	43.7	1.4	-	-	-	-	44.2	1.1	-	-	-	-	44.7	1.1	-	-
1974	-	-	46.1	3.1	-	-	-	-	48.6	5.4	-	-	-	-	50.0	2.9	-	-	-	-	50.3	0.6	-	-
1975	-	-	50.7	0.8	-	-	-	-	51.8	2.2	-	-	-	-	53.5	3.3	-	-	-	-	54.7	2.2	-	-
1976	-	-	55.2	0.9	-	-	-	-	57.2	3.6	-	-	-	-	58.7	2.6	-	-	-	-	59.7	1.7	-	-
1977	-	-	59.9	0.3	-	-	-	-	61.3	2.3	-	-	-	-	61.6	0.5	-	-	-	-	62.1	0.8	-	-
1978	-	-	62.1	0.0	-	-	62.5	0.6	-	-	64.3	2.9	-	-	65.2	1.4	-	-	66.0	1.2	-	-	66.4	0.6
1979	-	-	67.4	1.5	-	-	69.9	3.7	-	-	73.7	5.4	-	-	77.2	4.7	-	-	78.3	1.4	-	-	79.6	1.7
1980	-	-	84.3	5.9	-	-	86.1	2.1	-	-	86.4	0.3	-	-	87.4	1.2	-	-	88.4	1.1	-	-	89.1	0.8
1981	-	-	93.0	4.4	-	-	95.4	2.6	-	-	95.7	0.3	-	-	96.3	0.6	-	-	97.5	1.2	-	-	97.9	0.4
1982	-	-	96.9	-1.0	-	-	94.8	-2.2	-	-	97.5	2.8	-	-	98.2	0.7	-	-	99.0	0.8	-	-	99.0	0.0
1983	-	-	96.6	-2.4	-	-	97.2	0.6	-	-	99.1	2.0	-	-	100.8	1.7	-	-	101.9	1.1	-	-	102.0	0.1
1984	-	-	101.6	-0.4	-	-	102.6	1.0	-	-	103.5	0.9	-	-	103.1	-0.4	-	-	103.8	0.7	-	-	103.9	0.1
1985	-	-	103.1	-0.8	-	-	104.6	1.5	-	-	105.9	1.2	-	-	105.6	-0.3	-	-	105.9	0.3	-	-	106.5	0.6
1986	-	-	104.4	-2.0	-	-	97.4	-6.7	-	-	99.2	1.8	-	-	95.0	-4.2	-	-	95.9	0.9	-	-	96.5	0.6
1987	-	-	-	-	-	-	-	-	-	-	98.4	2.0	-	-	-	-	-	-	-	-	-	-	101.1	2.7
1988	-	-	-	-	-	-	-	-	-	-	100.9	-0.2	-	-	-	-	-	-	-	-	-	-	101.2	0.3
1989	-	-	-	-	-	-	-	-	-	-	103.1	1.9	-	-	-	-	-	-	-	-	-	-	103.4	0.3
1990	-	-	-	-	-	-	-	-	-	-	105.8	2.3	-	-	-	-	-	-	-	-	-	-	112.4	6.2
1991	-	-	-	-	-	-	-	-	-	-	112.6	0.2	-	-	-	-	-	-	-	-	-	-	111.9	-0.6
1992	-	-	-	-	-	-	-	-	-	-	112.7	0.7	-	-	-	-	-	-	-	-	-	-	115.2	2.2
1993	-	-	-	-	-	-	-	-	-	-	116.7	1.3	-	-	-	-	-	-	-	-	-	-	118.3	1.4
1994	-	-	-	-	-	-	-	-	-	-	118.9	0.5	-	-	-	-	-	-	-	-	-	-	123.0	3.4
1995	-	-	-	-	-	-	-	-	-	-	126.4	2.8	-	-	-	-	-	-	-	-	-	-	-	-

Source: U.S. Department of Labor, Bureau of Labor Statistics, Division of Consumer Prices and Price Indexes. - indicates no data collected for period.

Buffalo, NY
Consumer Price Index - Urban Wage Earners
Base 1982-1984 = 100
Transportation

For 1963-1995. Columns headed % show percentile change in the index from the previous period for which an index is available.

Year	Jan Index	%	Feb Index	%	Mar Index	%	Apr Index	%	May Index	%	Jun Index	%	Jul Index	%	Aug Index	%	Sep Index	%	Oct Index	%	Nov Index	%	Dec Index	%
1963	-	-	-	-	-	-	-	-	-	-	-	-	-	-	-	-	-	-	-	-	32.7	-	-	-
1964	-	-	32.3	-1.2	-	-	-	-	32.8	1.5	-	-	-	-	32.4	-1.2	-	-	-	-	32.8	1.2	-	-
1965	-	-	33.4	1.8	-	-	-	-	33.8	1.2	-	-	-	-	34.0	0.6	-	-	-	-	34.1	0.3	-	-
1966	-	-	34.3	0.6	-	-	-	-	34.5	0.6	-	-	-	-	34.9	1.2	-	-	-	-	34.9	0.0	-	-
1967	-	-	35.2	0.9	-	-	-	-	35.5	0.9	-	-	-	-	35.4	-0.3	-	-	-	-	36.0	1.7	-	-
1968	-	-	36.1	0.3	-	-	-	-	36.3	0.6	-	-	-	-	36.5	0.6	-	-	-	-	36.8	0.8	-	-
1969	-	-	37.2	1.1	-	-	-	-	37.7	1.3	-	-	-	-	37.8	0.3	-	-	-	-	38.5	1.9	-	-
1970	-	-	39.0	1.3	-	-	-	-	39.5	1.3	-	-	-	-	39.5	0.0	-	-	-	-	40.6	2.8	-	-
1971	-	-	41.5	2.2	-	-	-	-	41.5	0.0	-	-	-	-	42.0	1.2	-	-	-	-	41.0	-2.4	-	-
1972	-	-	40.9	-0.2	-	-	-	-	42.0	2.7	-	-	-	-	42.0	0.0	-	-	-	-	42.5	1.2	-	-
1973	-	-	42.8	0.7	-	-	-	-	43.4	1.4	-	-	-	-	43.9	1.2	-	-	-	-	44.3	0.9	-	-
1974	-	-	45.8	3.4	-	-	-	-	48.2	5.2	-	-	-	-	49.7	3.1	-	-	-	-	50.0	0.6	-	-
1975	-	-	50.3	0.6	-	-	-	-	51.5	2.4	-	-	-	-	53.1	3.1	-	-	-	-	54.3	2.3	-	-
1976	-	-	54.8	0.9	-	-	-	-	56.8	3.6	-	-	-	-	58.3	2.6	-	-	-	-	59.2	1.5	-	-
1977	-	-	59.5	0.5	-	-	-	-	60.9	2.4	-	-	-	-	61.2	0.5	-	-	-	-	61.7	0.8	-	-
1978	-	-	61.7	0.0	-	-	62.1	0.6	-	-	64.1	3.2	-	-	65.2	1.7	-	-	65.7	0.8	-	-	66.0	0.5
1979	-	-	67.3	2.0	-	-	69.9	3.9	-	-	73.9	5.7	-	-	77.5	4.9	-	-	78.1	0.8	-	-	79.3	1.5
1980	-	-	83.7	5.5	-	-	86.1	2.9	-	-	85.8	-0.3	-	-	86.8	1.2	-	-	87.8	1.2	-	-	88.6	0.9
1981	-	-	92.9	4.9	-	-	95.1	2.4	-	-	95.8	0.7	-	-	96.0	0.2	-	-	97.6	1.7	-	-	98.0	0.4
1982	-	-	96.8	-1.2	-	-	94.6	-2.3	-	-	97.4	3.0	-	-	98.2	0.8	-	-	98.9	0.7	-	-	98.9	0.0
1983	-	-	96.4	-2.5	-	-	96.9	0.5	-	-	99.1	2.3	-	-	100.9	1.8	-	-	102.0	1.1	-	-	102.2	0.2
1984	-	-	101.7	-0.5	-	-	102.8	1.1	-	-	103.7	0.9	-	-	103.3	-0.4	-	-	103.8	0.5	-	-	103.9	0.1
1985	-	-	103.0	-0.9	-	-	104.4	1.4	-	-	105.8	1.3	-	-	105.4	-0.4	-	-	105.7	0.3	-	-	106.3	0.6
1986	-	-	103.9	-2.3	-	-	96.3	-7.3	-	-	98.1	1.9	-	-	93.4	-4.8	-	-	94.4	1.1	-	-	94.9	0.5
1987	-	-	-	-	-	-	-	-	-	-	97.8	3.1	-	-	-	-	-	-	-	-	-	-	100.9	3.2
1988	-	-	-	-	-	-	-	-	-	-	100.4	-0.5	-	-	-	-	-	-	-	-	-	-	100.7	0.3
1989	-	-	-	-	-	-	-	-	-	-	102.7	2.0	-	-	-	-	-	-	-	-	-	-	103.3	0.6
1990	-	-	-	-	-	-	-	-	-	-	105.4	2.0	-	-	-	-	-	-	-	-	-	-	113.0	7.2
1991	-	-	-	-	-	-	-	-	-	-	112.6	-0.4	-	-	-	-	-	-	-	-	-	-	112.0	-0.5
1992	-	-	-	-	-	-	-	-	-	-	112.5	0.4	-	-	-	-	-	-	-	-	-	-	115.2	2.4
1993	-	-	-	-	-	-	-	-	-	-	115.9	0.6	-	-	-	-	-	-	-	-	-	-	117.9	1.7
1994	-	-	-	-	-	-	-	-	-	-	117.9	0.0	-	-	-	-	-	-	-	-	-	-	123.2	4.5
1995	-	-	-	-	-	-	-	-	-	-	127.4	3.4	-	-	-	-	-	-	-	-	-	-	-	-

Source: U.S. Department of Labor, Bureau of Labor Statistics, Division of Consumer Prices and Price Indexes. - indicates no data collected for period.

Buffalo, NY
Consumer Price Index - All Urban Consumers
Base 1982-1984 = 100
Medical Care

For 1963-1995. Columns headed % show percentile change in the index from the previous period for which an index is available.

Year	Jan Index	%	Feb Index	%	Mar Index	%	Apr Index	%	May Index	%	Jun Index	%	Jul Index	%	Aug Index	%	Sep Index	%	Oct Index	%	Nov Index	%	Dec Index	%
1963	-	-	-	-	-	-	-	-	-	-	-	-	-	-	-	-	-	-	-	-	29.5	-	-	-
1964	-	-	29.6	0.3	-	-	-	-	29.7	0.3	-	-	-	-	29.9	0.7	-	-	-	-	30.5	2.0	-	-
1965	-	-	30.5	0.0	-	-	-	-	30.5	0.0	-	-	-	-	30.7	0.7	-	-	-	-	31.0	1.0	-	-
1966	-	-	31.4	1.3	-	-	-	-	32.0	1.9	-	-	-	-	32.8	2.5	-	-	-	-	33.3	1.5	-	-
1967	-	-	33.8	1.5	-	-	-	-	34.1	0.9	-	-	-	-	34.6	1.5	-	-	-	-	35.1	1.4	-	-
1968	-	-	35.4	0.9	-	-	-	-	35.4	0.0	-	-	-	-	35.9	1.4	-	-	-	-	36.3	1.1	-	-
1969	-	-	36.8	1.4	-	-	-	-	37.4	1.6	-	-	-	-	37.7	0.8	-	-	-	-	38.0	0.8	-	-
1970	-	-	38.8	2.1	-	-	-	-	39.6	2.1	-	-	-	-	40.0	1.0	-	-	-	-	40.6	1.5	-	-
1971	-	-	41.2	1.5	-	-	-	-	41.8	1.5	-	-	-	-	42.6	1.9	-	-	-	-	42.6	0.0	-	-
1972	-	-	43.1	1.2	-	-	-	-	43.3	0.5	-	-	-	-	43.4	0.2	-	-	-	-	43.6	0.5	-	-
1973	-	-	44.2	1.4	-	-	-	-	44.6	0.9	-	-	-	-	44.8	0.4	-	-	-	-	45.5	1.6	-	-
1974	-	-	47.3	4.0	-	-	-	-	48.1	1.7	-	-	-	-	49.6	3.1	-	-	-	-	50.5	1.8	-	-
1975	-	-	52.1	3.2	-	-	-	-	53.0	1.7	-	-	-	-	53.9	1.7	-	-	-	-	54.6	1.3	-	-
1976	-	-	56.6	3.7	-	-	-	-	57.3	1.2	-	-	-	-	58.5	2.1	-	-	-	-	59.0	0.9	-	-
1977	-	-	61.9	4.9	-	-	-	-	62.2	0.5	-	-	-	-	63.1	1.4	-	-	-	-	64.0	1.4	-	-
1978	-	-	67.2	5.0	-	-	67.5	0.4	-	-	68.2	1.0	-	-	68.4	0.3	-	-	69.0	0.9	-	-	70.1	1.6
1979	-	-	71.9	2.6	-	-	72.0	0.1	-	-	73.2	1.7	-	-	73.9	1.0	-	-	74.3	0.5	-	-	74.8	0.7
1980	-	-	76.7	2.5	-	-	77.5	1.0	-	-	77.8	0.4	-	-	78.8	1.3	-	-	79.7	1.1	-	-	81.3	2.0
1981	-	-	83.5	2.7	-	-	84.7	1.4	-	-	85.6	1.1	-	-	86.5	1.1	-	-	87.5	1.2	-	-	87.8	0.3
1982	-	-	89.9	2.4	-	-	90.8	1.0	-	-	91.3	0.6	-	-	91.5	0.2	-	-	92.2	0.8	-	-	94.9	2.9
1983	-	-	99.2	4.5	-	-	100.3	1.1	-	-	100.5	0.2	-	-	101.7	1.2	-	-	102.6	0.9	-	-	103.0	0.4
1984	-	-	106.4	3.3	-	-	107.6	1.1	-	-	107.8	0.2	-	-	107.9	0.1	-	-	108.5	0.6	-	-	109.2	0.6
1985	-	-	111.1	1.7	-	-	111.6	0.5	-	-	112.7	1.0	-	-	114.2	1.3	-	-	114.9	0.6	-	-	115.2	0.3
1986	-	-	116.6	1.2	-	-	117.3	0.6	-	-	119.2	1.6	-	-	121.5	1.9	-	-	122.6	0.9	-	-	123.4	0.7
1987	-	-	-	-	-	-	-	-	-	-	126.7	2.7	-	-	-	-	-	-	-	-	-	-	128.6	1.5
1988	-	-	-	-	-	-	-	-	-	-	129.9	1.0	-	-	-	-	-	-	-	-	-	-	134.0	3.2
1989	-	-	-	-	-	-	-	-	-	-	140.4	4.8	-	-	-	-	-	-	-	-	-	-	143.4	2.1
1990	-	-	-	-	-	-	-	-	-	-	150.0	4.6	-	-	-	-	-	-	-	-	-	-	153.4	2.3
1991	-	-	-	-	-	-	-	-	-	-	157.7	2.8	-	-	-	-	-	-	-	-	-	-	160.4	1.7
1992	-	-	-	-	-	-	-	-	-	-	165.5	3.2	-	-	-	-	-	-	-	-	-	-	167.4	1.1
1993	-	-	-	-	-	-	-	-	-	-	171.8	2.6	-	-	-	-	-	-	-	-	-	-	173.0	0.7
1994	-	-	-	-	-	-	-	-	-	-	172.9	-0.1	-	-	-	-	-	-	-	-	-	-	176.1	1.9
1995	-	-	-	-	-	-	-	-	-	-	180.1	2.3	-	-	-	-	-	-	-	-	-	-	-	-

Source: U.S. Department of Labor, Bureau of Labor Statistics, Division of Consumer Prices and Price Indexes. - indicates no data collected for period.

Buffalo, NY
Consumer Price Index - Urban Wage Earners
Base 1982-1984 = 100
Medical Care

For 1963-1995. Columns headed % show percentile change in the index from the previous period for which an index is available.

Year	Jan Index	%	Feb Index	%	Mar Index	%	Apr Index	%	May Index	%	Jun Index	%	Jul Index	%	Aug Index	%	Sep Index	%	Oct Index	%	Nov Index	%	Dec Index	%
1963	-		-		-		-		-		-	-	-	-	-		-		-		29.0	-	-	-
1964	-	-	29.1	0.3	-	-	-	-	29.2	0.3	-	-	-	-	29.4	0.7	-		-		30.0	2.0	-	-
1965	-	-	30.0	0.0	-	-	-		30.0	0.0	-	-	-	-	30.1	0.3	-		-		30.5	1.3	-	-
1966	-	-	30.8	1.0	-	-	-		31.5	2.3	-	-	-	-	32.2	2.2	-		-		32.7	1.6	-	-
1967	-	-	33.2	1.5	-	-	-		33.5	0.9	-	-	-	-	34.0	1.5	-		-		34.5	1.5	-	-
1968	-	-	34.8	0.9	-	-	-		34.8	0.0	-	-	-	-	35.2	1.1	-		-		35.7	1.4	-	-
1969	-	-	36.1	1.1	-	-	-		36.8	1.9	-	-	-	-	37.1	0.8	-		-		37.3	0.5	-	-
1970	-	-	38.1	2.1	-	-	-		38.9	2.1	-	-	-	-	39.3	1.0	-		-		39.9	1.5	-	-
1971	-	-	40.4	1.3	-	-	-	-	41.1	1.7	-		-	-	41.9	1.9	-		-	-	41.8	-0.2	-	-
1972	-	-	42.4	1.4	-	-	-	-	42.5	0.2	-		-		42.6	0.2	-		-	-	42.8	0.5	-	-
1973	-	-	43.4	1.4	-	-	-	-	43.8	0.9	-		-		44.0	0.5	-		-	-	44.7	1.6	-	-
1974	-	-	46.4	3.8	-	-	-	-	47.3	1.9	-		-		48.7	3.0	-		-	-	49.6	1.8	-	-
1975	-	-	51.2	3.2	-	-	-	-	52.1	1.8	-		-		52.9	1.5	-		-	-	53.6	1.3	-	-
1976	-	-	55.6	3.7	-	-	-	-	56.3	1.3	-		-		57.5	2.1	-		-	-	58.0	0.9	-	-
1977	-	-	60.8	4.8	-	-	-	-	61.1	0.5	-	-	-		62.0	1.5	-		-	-	62.9	1.5	-	-
1978	-	-	66.0	4.9	-	-	66.2	0.3	-	-	67.1	1.4	-		67.4	0.4	-		67.5	0.1	-	-	69.2	2.5
1979	-	-	71.1	2.7	-	-	71.1	0.0	-	-	72.2	1.5	-		72.9	1.0	-		73.2	0.4	-	-	73.6	0.5
1980	-	-	76.8	4.3	-	-	77.9	1.4	-	-	79.0	1.4	-	-	79.4	0.5	-		81.2	2.3	-	-	81.8	0.7
1981	-	-	83.1	1.6	-	-	84.6	1.8	-	-	85.2	0.7	-	-	86.2	1.2	-		87.7	1.7	-	-	88.3	0.7
1982	-	-	90.3	2.3	-	-	91.1	0.9	-	-	91.6	0.5	-	-	91.8	0.2	-		92.5	0.8	-	-	94.8	2.5
1983	-	-	99.0	4.4	-	-	100.1	1.1	-	-	100.4	0.3	-	-	101.6	1.2	-		102.5	0.9	-	-	103.0	0.5
1984	-	-	106.3	3.2	-	-	107.5	1.1	-	-	107.7	0.2	-	-	107.8	0.1	-		108.4	0.6	-	-	109.1	0.6
1985	-	-	111.1	1.8	-	-	111.5	0.4	-	-	112.5	0.9	-	-	114.1	1.4	-		114.8	0.6	-	-	115.0	0.2
1986	-	-	116.2	1.0	-	-	116.9	0.6	-	-	118.8	1.6	-	-	120.9	1.8	-		121.9	0.8	-	-	122.7	0.7
1987	-	-	-		-		-		-		125.9	2.6	-	-	-		-		-		-	-	127.8	1.5
1988	-	-	-		-		-		-		128.6	0.6	-	-	-		-		-		-	-	133.4	3.7
1989	-	-	-		-		-		-		140.0	4.9	-	-	-		-		-		-	-	142.6	1.9
1990	-	-	-		-		-		-		148.8	4.3	-	-	-		-		-		-	-	152.0	2.2
1991	-	-	-		-		-		-		156.7	3.1	-	-	-		-		-		-	-	159.6	1.9
1992	-	-	-		-		-		-		164.9	3.3	-	-	-		-		-		-	-	167.0	1.3
1993	-	-	-		-		-		-		171.7	2.8	-	-	-		-		-		-	-	173.5	1.0
1994	-	-	-		-		-		-		173.2	-0.2	-	-	-		-		-		-	-	176.3	1.0
1995	-	-	-		-		-		-		180.4	2.3	-	-	-		-		-		-	-	-	-

Source: U.S. Department of Labor, Bureau of Labor Statistics, Division of Consumer Prices and Price Indexes. - indicates no data collected for period.

Buffalo, NY
Consumer Price Index - All Urban Consumers
Base 1982-1984 = 100
Entertainment

For 1975-1995. Columns headed % show percentile change in the index from the previous period for which an index is available.

Year	Jan Index	%	Feb Index	%	Mar Index	%	Apr Index	%	May Index	%	Jun Index	%	Jul Index	%	Aug Index	%	Sep Index	%	Oct Index	%	Nov Index	%	Dec Index	%
1975	-	-	-	-	-	-	-	-			-	-			-	-	-	-	-	-	62.4	-	-	-
1976	-	-	62.3	-0.2	-	-	-	-	62.6	0.5	-	-			62.5	-0.2	-	-	-	-	64.2	2.7	-	-
1977	-	-	64.8	0.9	-	-	-	-	66.5	2.6	-	-			66.3	-0.3	-	-	-	-	67.7	2.1	-	-
1978	-	-	68.9	1.8	-	-	68.7	-0.3	-	-	70.6	2.8			69.8	-1.1	-	-	72.8	4.3	-	-	73.8	1.4
1979	-	-	72.8	-1.4	-	-	73.3	0.7	-	-	70.0	-4.5			70.2	0.3	-	-	72.8	3.7	-	-	73.1	0.4
1980	-	-	73.7	0.8	-	-	77.6	5.3	-	-	77.5	-0.1			78.9	1.8	-	-	82.6	4.7	-	-	85.5	3.5
1981	-	-	87.7	2.6	-	-	88.5	0.9	-	-	86.5	-2.3			86.6	0.1	-	-	90.0	3.9	-	-	90.6	0.7
1982	-	-	92.5	2.1	-	-	93.1	0.6	-	-	91.4	-1.8			93.5	2.3	-	-	97.7	4.5	-	-	97.5	-0.2
1983	-	-	99.6	2.2	-	-	100.0	0.4	-	-	100.6	0.6			99.4	-1.2	-	-	102.4	3.0	-	-	102.6	0.2
1984	-	-	103.7	1.1	-	-	105.8	2.0	-	-	101.9	-3.7			105.0	3.0	-	-	109.2	4.0	-	-	108.8	-0.4
1985	-	-	109.7	0.8	-	-	111.1	1.3	-	-	111.7	0.5			112.6	0.8	-	-	112.3	-0.3	-	-	112.8	0.4
1986	-	-	113.2	0.4	-	-	114.1	0.8	-	-	111.6	-2.2			112.4	0.7	-	-	118.6	5.5	-	-	119.2	0.5
1987	-	-	-	-	-	-	-	-	-	-	121.9	2.3			-	-	-	-	-	-	-	-	123.5	1.3
1988	-	-	-	-	-	-	-	-	-	-	123.5	0.0			-	-	-	-	-	-	-	-	126.7	2.6
1989	-	-	-	-	-	-	-	-	-	-	130.8	3.2			-	-	-	-	-	-	-	-	133.7	2.2
1990	-	-	-	-	-	-	-	-	-	-	140.5	5.1			-	-	-	-	-	-	-	-	145.1	3.3
1991	-	-	-	-	-	-	-	-	-	-	146.8	1.2			-	-	-	-	-	-	-	-	149.5	1.8
1992	-	-	-	-	-	-	-	-	-	-	152.9	2.3			-	-	-	-	-	-	-	-	158.5	3.7
1993	-	-	-	-	-	-	-	-	-	-	162.9	2.8			-	-	-	-	-	-	-	-	172.0	5.6
1994	-	-	-	-	-	-	-	-	-	-	176.0	2.3			-	-	-	-	-	-	-	-	179.4	1.9
1995	-	-	-	-	-	-	-	-	-	-	186.3	3.8			-	-	-	-	-	-	-	-	-	-

Source: U.S. Department of Labor, Bureau of Labor Statistics, Division of Consumer Prices and Price Indexes. - indicates no data collected for period.

Buffalo, NY
Consumer Price Index - Urban Wage Earners
Base 1982-1984 = 100
Entertainment

For 1975-1995. Columns headed % show percentile change in the index from the previous period for which an index is available.

Year	Jan Index	%	Feb Index	%	Mar Index	%	Apr Index	%	May Index	%	Jun Index	%	Jul Index	%	Aug Index	%	Sep Index	%	Oct Index	%	Nov Index	%	Dec Index	%
1975	-	-	-	-	-	-	-	-	-	-	-	-	-	-	-	-	-	-	-	-	66.7	-	-	-
1976	-	-	66.6	-0.1	-	-	-	-	66.9	0.5	-	-	-	-	66.8	-0.1	-	-	-	-	-	-	-	-
1977	-	-	69.2	0.9	-	-	-	-	71.0	2.6	-	-	-	-	70.9	-0.1	-	-	-	-	68.6	2.7	-	-
1978	-	-	73.6	1.8	-	-	72.6	-1.4	-	-	70.7	-2.6	-	-	69.5	-1.7	-	-	73.7	6.0	72.3	2.0	74.3	0.8
1979	-	-	73.2	-1.5	-	-	73.8	0.8	-	-	70.3	-4.7	-	-	70.3	0.0	-	-	73.5	4.6	-	-	74.4	1.2
1980	-	-	75.8	1.9	-	-	78.2	3.2	-	-	78.9	0.9	-	-	79.4	0.6	-	-	82.0	3.3	-	-	83.6	2.0
1981	-	-	85.2	1.9	-	-	86.6	1.6	-	-	86.8	0.2	-	-	87.4	0.7	-	-	89.9	2.9	-	-	90.4	0.6
1982	-	-	92.4	2.2	-	-	93.1	0.8	-	-	92.1	-1.1	-	-	94.5	2.6	-	-	97.6	3.3	-	-	97.4	-0.2
1983	-	-	99.6	2.3	-	-	100.1	0.5	-	-	100.3	0.2	-	-	100.5	0.2	-	-	101.9	1.4	-	-	102.4	0.5
1984	-	-	103.6	1.2	-	-	105.5	1.8	-	-	101.9	-3.4	-	-	105.3	3.3	-	-	108.4	2.9	-	-	107.7	-0.6
1985	-	-	108.5	0.7	-	-	109.9	1.3	-	-	110.6	0.6	-	-	111.4	0.7	-	-	110.9	-0.4	-	-	111.3	0.4
1986	-	-	111.8	0.4	-	-	112.7	0.8	-	-	110.9	-1.6	-	-	111.9	0.9	-	-	118.4	5.8	-	-	118.9	0.4
1987	-	-	-	-	-	-	-	-	-	-	121.2	1.9	-	-	-	-	-	-	-	-	-	-	122.9	1.4
1988	-	-	-	-	-	-	-	-	-	-	123.0	0.1	-	-	-	-	-	-	-	-	-	-	126.1	2.5
1989	-	-	-	-	-	-	-	-	-	-	129.8	2.9	-	-	-	-	-	-	-	-	-	-	132.4	2.0
1990	-	-	-	-	-	-	-	-	-	-	139.4	5.3	-	-	-	-	-	-	-	-	-	-	144.0	3.3
1991	-	-	-	-	-	-	-	-	-	-	145.5	1.0	-	-	-	-	-	-	-	-	-	-	148.0	1.7
1992	-	-	-	-	-	-	-	-	-	-	151.6	2.4	-	-	-	-	-	-	-	-	-	-	157.1	3.6
1993	-	-	-	-	-	-	-	-	-	-	161.5	2.8	-	-	-	-	-	-	-	-	-	-	170.1	5.3
1994	-	-	-	-	-	-	-	-	-	-	174.2	2.4	-	-	-	-	-	-	-	-	-	-	177.9	2.1
1995	-	-	-	-	-	-	-	-	-	-	184.7	3.8	-	-	-	-	-	-	-	-	-	-	-	-

Source: U.S. Department of Labor, Bureau of Labor Statistics, Division of Consumer Prices and Price Indexes. - indicates no data collected for period.

Buffalo, NY
Consumer Price Index - All Urban Consumers
Base 1982-1984 = 100
Other Goods and Services

For 1975-1995. Columns headed % show percentile change in the index from the previous period for which an index is available.

Year	Jan Index	%	Feb Index	%	Mar Index	%	Apr Index	%	May Index	%	Jun Index	%	Jul Index	%	Aug Index	%	Sep Index	%	Oct Index	%	Nov Index	%	Dec Index	%
1975	-	-	-	-	-	-	-	-	-	-	-	-	-	-	-	-	-	-	-	-	55.9	-	-	-
1976	-	-	56.9	1.8	-	-	-	-	57.6	1.2	-	-	-	-	58.3	1.2	-	-	-	-	59.6	2.2	-	-
1977	-	-	60.1	0.8	-	-	-	-	60.1	0.0	-	-	-	-	60.4	0.5	-	-	-	-	62.1	2.8	-	-
1978	-	-	62.3	0.3	-	-	62.5	0.3	-	-	62.8	0.5	-	-	63.9	1.8	-	-	64.7	1.3	-	-	64.8	0.2
1979	-	-	65.5	1.1	-	-	65.9	0.6	-	-	66.3	0.6	-	-	67.5	1.8	-	-	68.3	1.2	-	-	69.0	1.0
1980	-	-	70.4	2.0	-	-	70.7	0.4	-	-	72.3	2.3	-	-	73.2	1.2	-	-	74.7	2.0	-	-	76.3	2.1
1981	-	-	77.6	1.7	-	-	79.4	2.3	-	-	81.6	2.8	-	-	82.1	0.6	-	-	86.1	4.9	-	-	86.2	0.1
1982	-	-	88.7	2.9	-	-	90.2	1.7	-	-	90.0	-0.2	-	-	89.0	-1.1	-	-	93.1	4.6	-	-	95.9	3.0
1983	-	-	97.7	1.9	-	-	100.2	2.6	-	-	100.5	0.3	-	-	101.7	1.2	-	-	103.8	2.1	-	-	104.3	0.5
1984	-	-	105.9	1.5	-	-	107.8	1.8	-	-	107.5	-0.3	-	-	109.8	2.1	-	-	110.3	0.5	-	-	109.7	-0.5
1985	-	-	113.0	3.0	-	-	114.2	1.1	-	-	116.0	1.6	-	-	116.7	0.6	-	-	121.0	3.7	-	-	121.6	0.5
1986	-	-	122.6	0.8	-	-	123.3	0.6	-	-	124.7	1.1	-	-	126.7	1.6	-	-	128.7	1.6	-	-	129.1	0.3
1987	-	-	-	-	-	-	-	-	-	-	130.7	1.2	-	-	-	-	-	-	-	-	-	-	134.0	2.5
1988	-	-	-	-	-	-	-	-	-	-	137.5	2.6	-	-	-	-	-	-	-	-	-	-	141.5	2.9
1989	-	-	-	-	-	-	-	-	-	-	144.8	2.3	-	-	-	-	-	-	-	-	-	-	150.7	4.1
1990	-	-	-	-	-	-	-	-	-	-	151.8	0.7	-	-	-	-	-	-	-	-	-	-	158.2	4.2
1991	-	-	-	-	-	-	-	-	-	-	163.5	3.4	-	-	-	-	-	-	-	-	-	-	165.7	1.3
1992	-	-	-	-	-	-	-	-	-	-	175.6	6.0	-	-	-	-	-	-	-	-	-	-	184.5	5.1
1993	-	-	-	-	-	-	-	-	-	-	189.1	2.5	-	-	-	-	-	-	-	-	-	-	192.7	1.9
1994	-	-	-	-	-	-	-	-	-	-	193.4	0.4	-	-	-	-	-	-	-	-	-	-	195.7	1.2
1995	-	-	-	-	-	-	-	-	-	-	199.6	2.0	-	-	-	-	-	-	-	-	-	-	-	-

Source: U.S. Department of Labor, Bureau of Labor Statistics, Division of Consumer Prices and Price Indexes. - indicates no data collected for period.

Buffalo, NY
Consumer Price Index - Urban Wage Earners
Base 1982-1984 = 100
Other Goods and Services

For 1975-1995. Columns headed % show percentile change in the index from the previous period for which an index is available.

Year	Jan Index	%	Feb Index	%	Mar Index	%	Apr Index	%	May Index	%	Jun Index	%	Jul Index	%	Aug Index	%	Sep Index	%	Oct Index	%	Nov Index	%	Dec Index	%
1975	-	-	-		-		-		-		-	-	-		-		-		-		58.7	-	-	-
1976	-	-	59.8	1.9	-		-		60.5	1.2	-		-		61.2	1.2	-		-		62.5	2.1	-	-
1977	-	-	63.0	0.8	-		-		63.1	0.2	-		-		63.4	0.5	-		-		65.2	2.8	-	-
1978	-	-	65.4	0.3	-		66.2	1.2	-		65.9	-0.5	-		67.3	2.1	-		67.7	0.6	-		68.2	0.7
1979	-	-	69.1	1.3	-		70.2	1.6	-		70.4	0.3	-		71.4	1.4	-		72.2	1.1	-		73.0	1.1
1980	-	-	74.9	2.6	-		74.5	-0.5	-		76.8	3.1	-		77.8	1.3	-		77.6	-0.3	-		80.0	3.1
1981	-	-	81.1	1.4	-		81.9	1.0	-		83.5	2.0	-		84.0	0.6	-		87.5	4.2	-		86.5	-1.1
1982	-	-	88.7	2.5	-		90.2	1.7	-		90.1	-0.1	-		89.2	-1.0	-		92.8	4.0	-		95.9	3.3
1983	-	-	97.8	2.0	-		100.7	3.0	-		100.8	0.1	-		102.3	1.5	-		103.9	1.6	-		104.4	0.5
1984	-	-	106.0	1.5	-		107.3	1.2	-		107.1	-0.2	-		109.2	2.0	-		110.1	0.8	-		109.3	-0.7
1985	-	-	112.3	2.7	-		113.0	0.6	-		114.6	1.4	-		115.2	0.5	-		119.3	3.6	-		119.6	0.3
1986	-	-	120.7	0.9	-		121.5	0.7	-		123.0	1.2	-		125.1	1.7	-		126.9	1.4	-		127.2	0.2
1987	-	-	-		-		-		-		128.7	1.2	-		-		-		-		-		132.2	2.7
1988	-	-	-		-		-		-		135.7	2.6	-		-		-		-		-		139.9	3.1
1989	-	-	-		-		-		-		142.9	2.1	-		-		-		-		-		149.6	4.7
1990	-	-	-		-		-		-		151.1	1.0	-		-		-		-		-		157.0	3.9
1991	-	-	-		-		-		-		163.0	3.8	-		-		-		-		-		166.0	1.8
1992	-	-	-		-		-		-		175.3	5.6	-		-		-		-		-		185.5	5.8
1993	-	-	-		-		-		-		190.7	2.8	-		-		-		-		-		194.0	1.7
1994	-	-	-		-		-		-		194.8	0.4	-		-		-		-		-		197.1	1.2
1995	-	-	-		-		-		-		201.0	2.0	-		-		-		-		-		-	-

Source: U.S. Department of Labor, Bureau of Labor Statistics, Division of Consumer Prices and Price Indexes. - indicates no data collected for period.

Chicago, IL-NW IN
Consumer Price Index - All Urban Consumers
Base 1982-1984 = 100
Annual Averages

For 1914-1995. Columns headed % show percentile change in the index from the previous period for which an index is available.

Year	All Items		Food & Beverage		Housing		Apparel & Upkeep		Trans- portation		Medical Care		Entertain- ment		Other Goods & Services	
	Index	%	Index	%	Index	%	Index	%	Index	%	Index	%	Index	%	Index	%
1914	-	-	-	-	-	-	-	-	-	-	-	-	-	-	-	-
1915	10.1	-	-	-	-	-	-	-	-	-	-	-	-	-	-	-
1916	10.9	7.9	-	-	-	-	-	-	-	-	-	-	-	-	-	-
1917	12.9	18.3	-	-	-	-	-	-	-	-	-	-	-	-	-	-
1918	14.9	15.5	-	-	-	-	-	-	-	-	-	-	-	-	-	-
1919	17.3	16.1	-	-	-	-	-	-	-	-	-	-	-	-	-	-
1920	19.8	14.5	-	-	-	-	-	-	-	-	-	-	-	-	-	-
1921	18.0	-9.1	-	-	-	-	-	-	-	-	-	-	-	-	-	-
1922	17.0	-5.6	-	-	-	-	-	-	-	-	-	-	-	-	-	-
1923	17.4	2.4	-	-	-	-	-	-	-	-	-	-	-	-	-	-
1924	17.7	1.7	-	-	-	-	-	-	-	-	-	-	-	-	-	-
1925	18.2	2.8	-	-	-	-	-	-	-	-	-	-	-	-	-	-
1926	18.3	0.5	-	-	-	-	-	-	-	-	-	-	-	-	-	-
1927	17.9	-2.2	-	-	-	-	-	-	-	-	-	-	-	-	-	-
1928	17.7	-1.1	-	-	-	-	-	-	-	-	-	-	-	-	-	-
1929	17.6	-0.6	-	-	-	-	-	-	-	-	-	-	-	-	-	-
1930	17.2	-2.3	-	-	-	-	-	-	-	-	-	-	-	-	-	-
1931	15.6	-9.3	-	-	-	-	-	-	-	-	-	-	-	-	-	-
1932	13.7	-12.2	-	-	-	-	-	-	-	-	-	-	-	-	-	-
1933	12.6	-8.0	-	-	-	-	-	-	-	-	-	-	-	-	-	-
1934	12.8	1.6	-	-	-	-	-	-	-	-	-	-	-	-	-	-
1935	13.4	4.7	-	-	-	-	-	-	-	-	-	-	-	-	-	-
1936	13.5	0.7	-	-	-	-	-	-	-	-	-	-	-	-	-	-
1937	14.2	5.2	-	-	-	-	-	-	-	-	-	-	-	-	-	-
1938	13.9	-2.1	-	-	-	-	-	-	-	-	-	-	-	-	-	-
1939	13.7	-1.4	-	-	-	-	-	-	-	-	-	-	-	-	-	-
1940	13.8	0.7	-	-	-	-	-	-	-	-	-	-	-	-	-	-
1941	14.5	5.1	-	-	-	-	-	-	-	-	-	-	-	-	-	-
1942	16.0	10.3	-	-	-	-	-	-	-	-	-	-	-	-	-	-
1943	16.9	5.6	-	-	-	-	-	-	-	-	-	-	-	-	-	-
1944	17.1	1.2	-	-	-	-	-	-	-	-	-	-	-	-	-	-
1945	17.5	2.3	-	-	-	-	-	-	-	-	-	-	-	-	-	-
1946	19.0	8.6	-	-	-	-	-	-	-	-	-	-	-	-	-	-
1947	22.1	16.3	-	-	-	-	-	-	17.5	-	12.1	-	-	-	-	-
1948	24.0	8.6	-	-	-	-	-	-	20.2	15.4	12.9	6.6	-	-	-	-
1949	24.0	0.0	-	-	-	-	-	-	22.0	8.9	13.5	4.7	-	-	-	-
1950	24.2	0.8	-	-	-	-	-	-	22.6	2.7	13.7	1.5	-	-	-	-
1951	26.1	7.9	-	-	-	-	-	-	23.9	5.8	14.5	5.8	-	-	-	-
1952	26.7	2.3	-	-	-	-	-	-	26.0	8.8	14.9	2.8	-	-	-	-
1953	26.9	0.7	-	-	-	-	52.4	-	26.6	2.3	15.5	4.0	-	-	-	-
1954	27.4	1.9	-	-	-	-	52.7	0.6	26.4	-0.8	15.9	2.6	-	-	-	-
1955	27.5	0.4	-	-	-	-	52.3	-0.8	26.2	-0.8	16.6	4.4	-	-	-	-
1956	27.9	1.5	-	-	-	-	54.0	3.3	26.7	1.9	17.6	6.0	-	-	-	-
1957	28.8	3.2	-	-	-	-	54.8	1.5	28.4	6.4	18.3	4.0	-	-	-	-
1958	29.7	3.1	-	-	-	-	55.0	0.4	30.0	5.6	19.4	6.0	-	-	-	-

[Continued]

346

Chicago, IL-NW IN
Consumer Price Index - All Urban Consumers
Base 1982-1984 = 100
Annual Averages
[Continued]

For 1914-1995. Columns headed % show percentile change in the index from the previous period for which an index is available.

Year	All Items		Food & Beverage		Housing		Apparel & Upkeep		Trans- portation		Medical Care		Entertain- ment		Other Goods & Services	
	Index	%	Index	%	Index	%	Index	%	Index	%	Index	%	Index	%	Index	%
1959	29.9	0.7	-	-	-	-	55.5	0.9	31.0	3.3	20.3	4.6	-	-	-	-
1960	30.4	1.7	-	-	-	-	56.4	1.6	31.1	0.3	21.5	5.9	-	-	-	-
1961	30.5	0.3	-	-	-	-	56.0	-0.7	30.9	-0.6	22.0	2.3	-	-	-	-
1962	30.8	1.0	-	-	-	-	55.8	-0.4	31.5	1.9	22.7	3.2	-	-	-	-
1963	31.1	1.0	-	-	-	-	56.0	0.4	31.7	0.6	24.3	7.0	-	-	-	-
1964	31.3	0.6	-	-	-	-	56.2	0.4	31.8	0.3	24.7	1.6	-	-	-	-
1965	31.7	1.3	-	-	-	-	56.8	1.1	32.6	2.5	25.1	1.6	-	-	-	-
1966	32.6	2.8	-	-	-	-	58.3	2.6	32.6	0.0	25.9	3.2	-	-	-	-
1967	33.5	2.8	-	-	-	-	60.6	3.9	33.5	2.8	28.0	8.1	-	-	-	-
1968	34.9	4.2	-	-	-	-	63.8	5.3	35.0	4.5	29.6	5.7	-	-	-	-
1969	36.8	5.4	-	-	-	-	66.9	4.9	37.2	6.3	31.4	6.1	-	-	-	-
1970	38.9	5.7	-	-	-	-	68.6	2.5	39.7	6.7	33.5	6.7	-	-	-	-
1971	40.4	3.9	-	-	-	-	71.1	3.6	42.1	6.0	35.9	7.2	-	-	-	-
1972	41.6	3.0	-	-	-	-	72.5	2.0	41.7	-1.0	36.8	2.5	-	-	-	-
1973	44.2	6.3	-	-	-	-	76.0	4.8	42.9	2.9	38.3	4.1	-	-	-	-
1974	48.9	10.6	-	-	-	-	80.4	5.8	47.2	10.0	42.0	9.7	-	-	-	-
1975	52.8	8.0	-	-	-	-	82.7	2.9	50.9	7.8	47.3	12.6	-	-	-	-
1976	55.3	4.7	64.2	-	48.5	-	83.7	1.2	56.1	10.2	52.8	11.6	61.7	-	58.0	-
1977	58.8	6.3	67.9	5.8	51.5	6.2	86.2	3.0	60.8	8.4	58.0	9.8	64.6	4.7	62.2	7.2
1978	63.8	8.5	75.8	11.6	57.3	11.3	88.0	2.1	63.1	3.8	62.1	7.1	68.0	5.3	65.8	5.8
1979	71.8	12.5	83.8	10.6	66.1	15.4	90.5	2.8	71.7	13.6	67.6	8.9	75.7	11.3	69.7	5.9
1980	82.2	14.5	91.2	8.8	77.4	17.1	95.6	5.6	85.0	18.5	76.3	12.9	84.9	12.2	76.1	9.2
1981	90.0	9.5	96.4	5.7	85.6	10.6	96.4	0.8	95.6	12.5	84.3	10.5	92.4	8.8	84.5	11.0
1982	96.2	6.9	98.7	2.4	94.7	10.6	97.7	1.3	98.3	2.8	92.1	9.3	98.4	6.5	91.9	8.8
1983	100.0	4.0	99.4	0.7	100.6	6.2	100.2	2.6	99.0	0.7	101.1	9.8	99.6	1.2	100.5	9.4
1984	103.8	3.8	102.0	2.6	104.7	4.1	102.1	1.9	102.7	3.7	106.8	5.6	102.1	2.5	107.6	7.1
1985	107.7	3.8	104.2	2.2	109.6	4.7	106.0	3.8	105.3	2.5	112.8	5.6	105.1	2.9	115.1	7.0
1986	110.0	2.1	108.9	4.5	112.9	3.0	103.9	-2.0	101.2	-3.9	120.1	6.5	109.9	4.6	124.2	7.9
1987	114.5	4.1	113.2	3.9	116.3	3.0	109.2	5.1	106.1	4.8	129.2	7.6	116.0	5.6	129.6	4.3
1988	119.0	3.9	117.1	3.4	120.7	3.8	116.6	6.8	107.6	1.4	138.0	6.8	122.3	5.4	138.0	6.5
1989	125.0	5.0	122.5	4.6	126.4	4.7	118.1	1.3	112.1	4.2	149.2	8.1	131.6	7.6	153.1	10.9
1990	131.7	5.4	130.3	6.4	131.4	4.0	124.3	5.2	118.7	5.9	163.0	9.2	139.2	5.8	164.3	7.3
1991	137.0	4.0	135.5	4.0	136.4	3.8	125.3	0.8	121.2	2.1	177.9	9.1	145.9	4.8	179.0	8.9
1992	141.1	3.0	139.2	2.7	139.9	2.6	126.2	0.7	123.2	1.7	190.7	7.2	149.4	2.4	192.0	7.3
1993	145.4	3.0	143.1	2.8	143.3	2.4	131.1	3.9	126.2	2.4	203.1	6.5	153.9	3.0	202.5	5.5
1994	148.6	2.2	147.0	2.7	144.8	1.0	131.0	-0.1	130.3	3.2	213.2	5.0	160.0	4.0	208.8	3.1
1995	153.3	3.2	151.3	2.9	150.6	4.0	126.3	-3.6	135.1	3.7	223.3	4.7	160.9	0.6	216.8	3.8

Source: U.S. Department of Labor, Bureau of Labor Statistics, Division of Consumer Prices and Price Indexes. - indicates no data collected for period.

Chicago, IL-NW IN
Consumer Price Index - Urban Wage Earners
Base 1982-1984 = 100
Annual Averages

For 1914-1995. Columns headed % show percentile change in the index from the previous period for which an index is available.

Year	All Items		Food & Beverage		Housing		Apparel & Upkeep		Trans- portation		Medical Care		Entertain- ment		Other Goods & Services	
	Index	%	Index	%	Index	%	Index	%	Index	%	Index	%	Index	%	Index	%
1914	-	-	-	-	-	-	-	-	-	-	-	-	-	-	-	-
1915	10.2	-	-	-	-	-	-	-	-	-	-	-	-	-	-	-
1916	11.1	8.8	-	-	-	-	-	-	-	-	-	-	-	-	-	-
1917	13.1	18.0	-	-	-	-	-	-	-	-	-	-	-	-	-	-
1918	15.2	16.0	-	-	-	-	-	-	-	-	-	-	-	-	-	-
1919	17.6	15.8	-	-	-	-	-	-	-	-	-	-	-	-	-	-
1920	20.2	14.8	-	-	-	-	-	-	-	-	-	-	-	-	-	-
1921	18.3	-9.4	-	-	-	-	-	-	-	-	-	-	-	-	-	-
1922	17.3	-5.5	-	-	-	-	-	-	-	-	-	-	-	-	-	-
1923	17.7	2.3	-	-	-	-	-	-	-	-	-	-	-	-	-	-
1924	18.0	1.7	-	-	-	-	-	-	-	-	-	-	-	-	-	-
1925	18.5	2.8	-	-	-	-	-	-	-	-	-	-	-	-	-	-
1926	18.6	0.5	-	-	-	-	-	-	-	-	-	-	-	-	-	-
1927	18.2	-2.2	-	-	-	-	-	-	-	-	-	-	-	-	-	-
1928	18.0	-1.1	-	-	-	-	-	-	-	-	-	-	-	-	-	-
1929	17.9	-0.6	-	-	-	-	-	-	-	-	-	-	-	-	-	-
1930	17.5	-2.2	-	-	-	-	-	-	-	-	-	-	-	-	-	-
1931	15.9	-9.1	-	-	-	-	-	-	-	-	-	-	-	-	-	-
1932	13.9	-12.6	-	-	-	-	-	-	-	-	-	-	-	-	-	-
1933	12.8	-7.9	-	-	-	-	-	-	-	-	-	-	-	-	-	-
1934	13.0	1.6	-	-	-	-	-	-	-	-	-	-	-	-	-	-
1935	13.6	4.6	-	-	-	-	-	-	-	-	-	-	-	-	-	-
1936	13.7	0.7	-	-	-	-	-	-	-	-	-	-	-	-	-	-
1937	14.4	5.1	-	-	-	-	-	-	-	-	-	-	-	-	-	-
1938	14.2	-1.4	-	-	-	-	-	-	-	-	-	-	-	-	-	-
1939	13.9	-2.1	-	-	-	-	-	-	-	-	-	-	-	-	-	-
1940	14.1	1.4	-	-	-	-	-	-	-	-	-	-	-	-	-	-
1941	14.7	4.3	-	-	-	-	-	-	-	-	-	-	-	-	-	-
1942	16.2	10.2	-	-	-	-	-	-	-	-	-	-	-	-	-	-
1943	17.2	6.2	-	-	-	-	-	-	-	-	-	-	-	-	-	-
1944	17.4	1.2	-	-	-	-	-	-	-	-	-	-	-	-	-	-
1945	17.8	2.3	-	-	-	-	-	-	-	-	-	-	-	-	-	-
1946	19.4	9.0	-	-	-	-	-	-	-	-	-	-	-	-	-	-
1947	22.4	15.5	-	-	-	-	-	-	17.2	-	11.9	-	-	-	-	-
1948	24.4	8.9	-	-	-	-	-	-	19.9	15.7	12.7	6.7	-	-	-	-
1949	24.4	0.0	-	-	-	-	-	-	21.6	8.5	13.3	4.7	-	-	-	-
1950	24.7	1.2	-	-	-	-	-	-	22.3	3.2	13.5	1.5	-	-	-	-
1951	26.6	7.7	-	-	-	-	-	-	23.5	5.4	14.3	5.9	-	-	-	-
1952	27.2	2.3	-	-	-	-	-	-	25.6	8.9	14.7	2.8	-	-	-	-
1953	27.4	0.7	-	-	-	-	50.8	-	26.2	2.3	15.2	3.4	-	-	-	-
1954	27.9	1.8	-	-	-	-	51.1	0.6	26.0	-0.8	15.6	2.6	-	-	-	-
1955	28.0	0.4	-	-	-	-	50.7	-0.8	25.7	-1.2	16.3	4.5	-	-	-	-
1956	28.4	1.4	-	-	-	-	52.3	3.2	26.2	1.9	17.3	6.1	-	-	-	-
1957	29.3	3.2	-	-	-	-	53.1	1.5	27.9	6.5	18.0	4.0	-	-	-	-
1958	30.2	3.1	-	-	-	-	53.3	0.4	29.5	5.7	19.1	6.1	-	-	-	-

[Continued]

348

Chicago, IL-NW IN
Consumer Price Index - Urban Wage Earners
Base 1982-1984 = 100
Annual Averages
[Continued]

For 1914-1995. Columns headed % show percentile change in the index from the previous period for which an index is available.

Year	All Items		Food & Beverage		Housing		Apparel & Upkeep		Trans- portation		Medical Care		Entertain- ment		Other Goods & Services	
	Index	%	Index	%	Index	%	Index	%	Index	%	Index	%	Index	%	Index	%
1959	30.4	0.7	-	-	-	-	53.8	0.9	30.5	3.4	20.0	4.7	-	-	-	-
1960	30.9	1.6	-	-	-	-	54.7	1.7	30.6	0.3	21.1	5.5	-	-	-	-
1961	31.1	0.6	-	-	-	-	54.3	-0.7	30.4	-0.7	21.6	2.4	-	-	-	-
1962	31.4	1.0	-	-	-	-	54.1	-0.4	31.0	2.0	22.4	3.7	-	-	-	-
1963	31.7	1.0	-	-	-	-	54.3	0.4	31.2	0.6	23.9	6.7	-	-	-	-
1964	31.8	0.3	-	-	-	-	54.5	0.4	31.3	0.3	24.3	1.7	-	-	-	-
1965	32.2	1.3	-	-	-	-	55.1	1.1	32.0	2.2	24.7	1.6	-	-	-	-
1966	33.2	3.1	-	-	-	-	56.5	2.5	32.1	0.3	25.5	3.2	-	-	-	-
1967	34.0	2.4	-	-	-	-	58.7	3.9	33.0	2.8	27.5	7.8	-	-	-	-
1968	35.5	4.4	-	-	-	-	61.8	5.3	34.5	4.5	29.1	5.8	-	-	-	-
1969	37.4	5.4	-	-	-	-	64.8	4.9	36.6	6.1	30.9	6.2	-	-	-	-
1970	39.6	5.9	-	-	-	-	66.5	2.6	39.1	6.8	33.0	6.8	-	-	-	-
1971	41.1	3.8	-	-	-	-	68.9	3.6	41.4	5.9	35.3	7.0	-	-	-	-
1972	42.3	2.9	-	-	-	-	70.3	2.0	41.0	-1.0	36.2	2.5	-	-	-	-
1973	44.9	6.1	-	-	-	-	73.7	4.8	42.2	2.9	37.7	4.1	-	-	-	-
1974	49.7	10.7	-	-	-	-	77.9	5.7	46.4	10.0	41.3	9.5	-	-	-	-
1975	53.7	8.0	-	-	-	-	80.2	3.0	50.1	8.0	46.5	12.6	-	-	-	-
1976	56.2	4.7	65.2	-	50.7	-	81.1	1.1	55.2	10.2	51.9	11.6	54.6	-	59.6	-
1977	59.8	6.4	69.0	5.8	53.8	6.1	83.5	3.0	59.8	8.3	57.1	10.0	57.2	4.8	63.9	7.2
1978	64.8	8.4	76.3	10.6	59.6	10.8	86.8	4.0	62.1	3.8	61.3	7.4	59.7	4.4	68.1	6.6
1979	72.9	12.5	84.5	10.7	68.4	14.8	89.7	3.3	71.1	14.5	67.5	10.1	67.1	12.4	71.8	5.4
1980	83.5	14.5	92.3	9.2	79.8	16.7	94.9	5.8	84.5	18.8	76.9	13.9	77.4	15.4	78.1	8.8
1981	91.4	9.5	96.3	4.3	88.3	10.7	95.9	1.1	95.5	13.0	84.4	9.8	88.1	13.8	84.9	8.7
1982	97.7	6.9	98.7	2.5	97.9	10.9	97.9	2.1	98.7	3.4	92.1	9.1	97.4	10.6	91.9	8.2
1983	100.4	2.8	99.4	0.7	101.6	3.8	100.0	2.1	98.8	0.1	101.0	9.7	99.9	2.6	100.6	9.5
1984	101.9	1.5	102.0	2.6	100.6	-1.0	102.2	2.2	102.4	3.6	106.8	5.7	102.8	2.9	107.5	6.9
1985	105.1	3.1	104.2	2.2	103.9	3.3	105.6	3.3	104.8	2.3	112.7	5.5	105.8	2.9	115.2	7.2
1986	106.8	1.6	109.0	4.6	106.9	2.9	104.1	-1.4	99.8	-4.8	119.9	6.4	110.9	4.8	124.8	8.3
1987	111.1	4.0	113.3	3.9	109.7	2.6	109.4	5.1	104.3	4.5	128.9	7.5	118.0	6.4	130.3	4.4
1988	115.3	3.8	117.2	3.4	113.6	3.6	116.1	6.1	106.3	1.9	138.4	7.4	124.2	5.3	138.5	6.3
1989	121.2	5.1	122.6	4.6	118.9	4.7	117.6	1.3	111.0	4.4	150.4	8.7	132.9	7.0	153.6	10.9
1990	127.8	5.4	130.4	6.4	123.8	4.1	124.5	5.9	117.2	5.6	164.3	9.2	140.0	5.3	166.2	8.2
1991	132.9	4.0	135.7	4.1	128.4	3.7	125.6	0.9	119.3	1.8	179.4	9.2	146.0	4.3	182.4	9.7
1992	136.7	2.9	139.2	2.6	131.7	2.6	125.9	0.2	121.2	1.6	192.4	7.2	149.5	2.4	195.9	7.4
1993	140.9	3.1	143.3	2.9	135.0	2.5	130.5	3.7	124.0	2.3	205.6	6.9	153.7	2.8	207.0	5.7
1994	144.0	2.2	147.2	2.7	136.3	1.0	130.0	-0.4	128.4	3.5	215.9	5.0	159.4	3.7	211.3	2.1
1995	148.4	3.1	151.6	3.0	141.4	3.7	125.1	-3.8	133.5	4.0	227.0	5.1	160.1	0.4	217.3	2.8

Source: U.S. Department of Labor, Bureau of Labor Statistics, Division of Consumer Prices and Price Indexes. - indicates no data collected for period.

Chicago, IL-NW IN
Consumer Price Index - All Urban Consumers
Base 1982-1984 = 100
All Items

For 1914-1995. Columns headed % show percentile change in the index from the previous period for which an index is available.

Year	Jan Index	%	Feb Index	%	Mar Index	%	Apr Index	%	May Index	%	Jun Index	%	Jul Index	%	Aug Index	%	Sep Index	%	Oct Index	%	Nov Index	%	Dec Index	%
1914	-	-	-	-	-	-	-	-	-	-	-	-	-	-	-	-	-	-	-	-	-	-	10.0	-
1915	-	-	-	-	-	-	-	-	-	-	-	-	-	-	-	-	-	-	-	-	-	-	10.2	2.0
1916	-	-	-	-	-	-	-	-	-	-	-	-	-	-	-	-	-	-	-	-	-	-	11.6	13.7
1917	-	-	-	-	-	-	-	-	-	-	-	-	-	-	-	-	-	-	-	-	-	-	13.5	16.4
1918	-	-	-	-	-	-	-	-	-	-	-	-	-	-	-	-	-	-	-	-	-	-	16.3	20.7
1919	-	-	-	-	-	-	-	-	-	-	16.6	1.8	-	-	-	-	-	-	-	-	-	-	18.9	13.9
1920	-	-	-	-	-	-	-	-	-	-	20.8	10.1	-	-	-	-	-	-	-	-	-	-	18.9	-9.1
1921	-	-	-	-	-	-	-	-	17.9	-5.3	-	-	-	-	-	-	17.8	-0.6	-	-	-	-	17.5	-1.7
1922	-	-	-	-	-	-	-	-	16.9	-3.4	17.0	0.6	-	-	-	-	17.0	0.0	-	-	-	-	17.1	0.6
1923	-	-	-	-	17.2	0.6	-	-	-	-	17.3	0.6	-	-	-	-	17.7	2.3	-	-	-	-	17.7	0.0
1924	-	-	-	-	17.6	-0.6	-	-	-	-	17.7	0.6	-	-	-	-	17.8	0.6	-	-	-	-	17.9	0.6
1925	-	-	-	-	-	-	-	-	-	-	18.2	1.7	-	-	-	-	-	-	-	-	-	-	18.6	2.2
1926	-	-	-	-	-	-	-	-	-	-	18.3	-1.6	-	-	-	-	-	-	-	-	-	-	18.3	0.0
1927	-	-	-	-	-	-	-	-	-	-	18.3	0.0	-	-	-	-	-	-	-	-	-	-	17.8	-2.7
1928	-	-	-	-	-	-	-	-	-	-	17.6	-1.1	-	-	-	-	-	-	-	-	-	-	17.7	0.6
1929	-	-	-	-	-	-	-	-	-	-	17.6	-0.6	-	-	-	-	-	-	-	-	-	-	17.7	0.6
1930	-	-	-	-	-	-	-	-	-	-	17.4	-1.7	-	-	-	-	-	-	-	-	-	-	16.6	-4.6
1931	-	-	-	-	-	-	-	-	-	-	15.6	-6.0	-	-	-	-	-	-	-	-	-	-	14.9	-4.5
1932	-	-	-	-	-	-	-	-	-	-	13.6	-8.7	-	-	-	-	-	-	-	-	-	-	12.9	-5.1
1933	-	-	-	-	-	-	-	-	-	-	12.4	-3.9	-	-	-	-	-	-	-	-	-	-	12.7	2.4
1934	-	-	-	-	-	-	-	-	-	-	12.7	0.0	-	-	-	-	-	-	-	-	12.8	0.8	-	-
1935	-	-	-	-	13.3	3.9	-	-	-	-	-	-	13.4	0.8	-	-	-	-	13.4	0.0	-	-	-	-
1936	13.4	0.0	-	-	-	-	13.3	-0.7	-	-	-	-	13.6	2.3	-	-	13.8	1.5	-	-	-	-	13.7	-0.7
1937	-	-	-	-	13.9	1.5	-	-	-	-	14.2	2.2	-	-	-	-	14.4	1.4	-	-	-	-	14.2	-1.4
1938	-	-	-	-	13.9	-2.1	-	-	-	-	14.0	0.7	-	-	-	-	14.0	0.0	-	-	-	-	13.8	-1.4
1939	-	-	-	-	13.7	-0.7	-	-	-	-	13.6	-0.7	-	-	-	-	13.8	1.5	-	-	-	-	13.7	-0.7
1940	-	-	-	-	13.7	0.0	-	-	-	-	13.9	1.5	-	-	-	-	13.8	-0.7	13.8	0.0	13.8	0.0	13.9	0.7
1941	13.9	0.0	13.9	0.0	13.9	0.0	14.1	1.4	14.2	0.7	14.4	1.4	14.6	1.4	14.7	0.7	15.0	2.0	15.1	0.7	15.2	0.7	15.2	0.0
1942	15.4	1.3	15.4	0.0	15.6	1.3	15.8	1.3	16.0	1.3	16.0	0.0	16.0	0.0	16.1	0.6	16.1	0.0	16.3	1.2	16.4	0.6	16.4	0.0
1943	16.4	0.0	16.5	0.6	16.8	1.8	16.9	0.6	17.1	1.2	17.0	-0.6	16.8	-1.2	16.9	0.6	17.0	0.6	17.0	0.0	16.9	-0.6	16.9	0.0
1944	16.8	-0.6	16.8	0.0	16.8	0.0	17.0	1.2	17.0	0.0	17.1	0.6	17.3	1.2	17.3	0.0	17.5	-0.6	17.5	0.0	17.3	0.0	17.3	0.0
1945	17.3	0.0	17.3	0.0	17.3	0.0	17.3	0.0	17.6	1.7	17.6	0.0	17.6	0.0	17.6	0.0	17.5	-0.6	17.5	0.0	17.5	0.0	17.6	0.6
1946	17.6	0.0	17.6	0.0	17.6	0.0	17.8	1.1	17.9	0.6	18.0	0.6	19.4	7.8	19.8	2.1	20.0	1.0	20.6	3.0	21.0	1.9	21.1	0.5
1947	21.1	0.0	21.0	-0.5	21.5	2.4	21.4	-0.5	21.5	0.5	21.8	1.4	22.0	0.9	22.4	1.8	23.1	3.1	23.0	-0.4	23.1	0.4	23.4	1.3
1948	23.5	0.4	23.2	-1.3	23.2	0.0	23.7	2.2	24.0	1.3	24.2	0.8	24.5	1.2	24.6	0.4	24.7	0.4	24.5	-0.8	24.2	-1.2	24.1	-0.4
1949	24.0	-0.4	23.8	-0.8	24.0	0.8	24.1	0.4	24.0	-0.4	24.2	0.8	23.9	-1.2	24.0	0.4	24.2	0.8	24.0	-0.8	24.1	0.4	23.8	-1.2
1950	23.7	-0.4	23.7	0.0	23.8	0.4	23.7	-0.4	24.0	1.3	24.0	0.0	24.3	1.2	24.5	0.8	24.6	0.4	24.7	0.4	24.8	0.4	25.2	1.6
1951	25.5	1.2	25.9	1.6	25.9	0.0	26.0	0.4	26.0	0.0	26.1	0.4	26.2	0.4	26.2	0.0	26.3	0.4	26.5	0.8	26.7	0.8	26.6	-0.4
1952	26.6	0.0	26.3	-1.1	26.4	0.4	26.5	0.4	26.7	0.8	26.8	0.4	26.9	0.4	27.0	0.4	26.9	-0.4	26.9	0.0	26.9	0.0	26.8	-0.4
1953	26.7	-0.4	26.6	-0.4	26.6	0.0	26.7	0.4	26.8	0.4	26.9	0.4	27.0	0.4	27.2	0.7	27.2	0.0	27.4	0.7	27.2	-0.7	27.2	0.0
1954	27.2	0.0	27.2	0.0	27.2	0.0	27.2	0.0	27.4	0.7	27.4	0.0	27.6	0.7	27.5	-0.4	27.4	-0.4	27.4	0.0	27.5	0.4	27.3	-0.7
1955	27.3	0.0	27.4	0.4	27.3	-0.4	27.3	0.0	27.4	0.4	27.4	0.0	27.6	0.7	27.7	0.4	27.8	0.4	27.8	0.0	27.8	0.0	27.7	-0.4
1956	27.6	-0.4	27.6	0.0	27.5	-0.4	27.6	0.4	27.7	0.4	27.9	0.7	28.2	1.1	28.0	-0.7	28.1	0.4	28.3	0.7	28.3	0.0	28.3	0.0
1957	28.3	0.0	28.4	0.4	28.4	0.0	28.5	0.4	28.6	0.4	28.7	0.3	29.0	1.0	29.0	0.0	29.1	0.3	29.2	0.3	29.4	0.7	29.4	0.0
1958	29.5	0.3	29.5	0.0	29.7	0.7	29.7	0.0	29.7	0.0	29.8	0.3	29.8	0.0	29.7	-0.3	29.8	0.3	29.8	0.0	29.8	0.0	29.7	-0.3

[Continued]

Chicago, IL-NW IN
Consumer Price Index - All Urban Consumers
Base 1982-1984 = 100
All Items
[Continued]

For 1914-1995. Columns headed % show percentile change in the index from the previous period for which an index is available.

Year	Jan Index	%	Feb Index	%	Mar Index	%	Apr Index	%	May Index	%	Jun Index	%	Jul Index	%	Aug Index	%	Sep Index	%	Oct Index	%	Nov Index	%	Dec Index	%
1959	29.7	0.0	29.7	0.0	29.7	0.0	29.8	0.3	29.8	0.0	29.9	0.3	30.0	0.3	30.0	0.0	30.2	0.7	30.2	0.0	30.2	0.0	30.2	0.0
1960	30.1	-0.3	30.2	0.3	30.2	0.0	30.3	0.3	30.3	0.0	30.4	0.3	30.5	0.3	30.4	-0.3	30.5	0.3	30.5	0.0	30.5	0.0	30.5	0.0
1961	30.5	0.0	30.5	0.0	30.4	-0.3	30.4	0.0	30.4	0.0	30.3	-0.3	30.6	1.0	30.6	0.0	30.6	0.0	30.7	0.3	30.6	-0.3	30.6	0.0
1962	30.6	0.0	30.8	0.7	30.8	0.0	30.9	0.3	30.8	-0.3	30.8	0.0	30.8	0.0	30.8	0.0	31.0	0.6	30.9	-0.3	30.9	0.0	30.9	0.0
1963	31.0	0.3	31.0	0.0	31.1	0.3	31.1	0.0	31.0	-0.3	31.1	0.3	31.3	0.6	31.2	-0.3	31.2	0.0	31.2	0.0	31.2	0.0	31.3	0.3
1964	31.2	-0.3	31.1	-0.3	31.1	0.0	31.1	0.0	31.2	0.3	31.3	0.3	31.4	0.3	31.3	-0.3	31.3	0.0	31.4	0.3	31.4	0.0	31.4	0.0
1965	31.4	0.0	31.4	0.0	31.4	0.0	31.5	0.3	31.6	0.3	31.8	0.6	31.7	-0.3	31.7	0.0	31.8	0.3	31.9	0.3	31.9	0.0	32.1	0.6
1966	32.0	-0.3	32.2	0.6	32.4	0.6	32.4	0.0	32.5	0.3	32.6	0.3	32.6	0.0	32.8	0.6	33.0	0.6	33.0	0.0	33.0	0.0	33.1	0.3
1967	32.9	-0.6	33.1	0.6	33.1	0.0	33.1	0.0	33.2	0.3	33.3	0.3	33.5	0.6	33.7	0.6	33.9	0.6	33.9	0.0	34.0	0.3	34.1	0.3
1968	34.1	0.0	34.3	0.6	34.5	0.6	34.6	0.3	34.7	0.3	34.8	0.3	35.0	0.6	35.1	0.3	35.3	0.6	35.4	0.3	35.4	0.0	35.6	0.6
1969	35.8	0.6	35.9	0.3	36.2	0.8	36.3	0.3	36.4	0.3	36.7	0.8	36.9	0.5	37.2	0.8	37.5	0.8	37.4	-0.3	37.6	0.5	37.8	0.5
1970	38.0	0.5	38.1	0.3	38.3	0.5	38.4	0.3	38.6	0.5	38.8	0.5	39.0	0.5	39.2	0.5	39.4	0.5	39.6	0.5	39.7	0.3	39.9	0.5
1971	39.9	0.0	40.0	0.3	40.1	0.2	40.2	0.2	40.4	0.5	40.5	0.2	40.5	0.0	40.7	0.5	40.7	0.0	40.7	0.0	40.8	0.2	40.9	0.2
1972	40.9	0.0	41.2	0.7	41.2	0.0	41.3	0.2	41.4	0.2	41.6	0.5	41.6	0.0	41.8	0.5	41.9	0.2	42.0	0.2	42.1	0.2	42.2	0.2
1973	42.3	0.2	42.7	0.9	43.2	1.2	43.5	0.7	43.8	0.7	44.1	0.7	44.0	-0.2	45.0	2.3	45.1	0.2	45.4	0.7	45.6	0.4	45.8	0.4
1974	46.4	1.3	47.1	1.5	47.6	1.1	47.8	0.4	48.2	0.8	48.7	1.0	48.9	0.4	49.5	1.2	49.9	0.8	50.4	1.0	50.8	0.8	51.3	1.0
1975	51.3	0.0	51.7	0.8	52.1	0.8	52.2	0.2	52.0	-0.4	52.4	0.8	53.0	1.1	53.3	0.6	53.4	0.2	53.7	0.6	53.8	0.2	54.0	0.4
1976	53.7	-0.6	54.1	0.7	54.2	0.2	54.5	0.6	54.8	0.6	55.2	0.7	55.5	0.5	55.8	0.5	56.1	0.5	56.3	0.4	56.4	0.2	56.6	0.4
1977	56.7	0.2	57.3	1.1	57.7	0.7	58.2	0.9	58.4	0.3	58.6	0.3	59.0	0.7	59.3	0.5	59.7	0.7	59.8	0.2	60.0	0.3	60.2	0.3
1978	61.1	1.5	61.7	1.0	62.4	1.1	62.7	0.5	63.3	1.0	63.7	0.6	64.1	0.6	64.1	0.0	64.9	1.2	65.4	0.8	66.3	1.4	66.5	0.3
1979	66.8	0.5	67.8	1.5	69.2	2.1	69.9	1.0	70.3	0.6	71.5	1.7	72.8	1.8	73.2	0.5	74.1	1.2	74.2	0.1	75.6	1.9	76.4	1.1
1980	77.1	0.9	77.9	1.0	78.8	1.2	80.4	2.0	81.4	1.2	83.1	2.1	82.6	-0.6	82.1	-0.6	83.7	1.9	84.9	1.4	87.0	2.5	87.1	0.1
1981	86.7	-0.5	86.9	0.2	86.9	0.0	88.3	1.6	88.5	0.2	90.1	1.8	91.3	1.3	92.3	1.1	92.7	0.4	92.4	-0.3	92.7	0.3	91.7	-1.1
1982	92.2	0.5	92.0	-0.2	92.5	0.5	93.8	1.4	96.3	2.7	97.7	1.5	98.1	0.4	98.1	0.0	98.4	0.3	98.5	0.1	98.5	0.0	98.1	-0.4
1983	98.4	0.3	98.3	-0.1	98.3	0.0	98.8	0.5	99.2	0.4	99.9	0.7	100.3	0.4	101.0	0.7	101.4	0.4	101.2	-0.2	101.7	0.5	101.7	0.0
1984	102.2	0.5	102.1	-0.1	102.3	0.2	102.7	0.4	102.8	0.1	103.7	0.9	104.0	0.3	104.9	0.9	105.5	0.6	105.1	-0.4	105.1	0.0	105.1	0.0
1985	105.5	0.4	106.0	0.5	106.2	0.2	106.8	0.6	107.0	0.2	108.5	1.4	108.6	0.1	109.1	0.5	109.2	0.1	108.0	-1.1	108.5	0.5	109.1	0.6
1986	109.2	0.1	109.3	0.1	108.4	-0.8	108.3	-0.1	108.5	0.2	110.6	1.9	110.8	0.2	110.9	0.1	111.8	0.8	110.0	-1.6	110.9	0.8	110.8	-0.1
1987	111.9	1.0	111.9	0.0	112.3	0.4	112.8	0.4	113.3	0.4	115.5	1.9	115.9	0.3	116.7	0.7	117.1	0.3	115.1	-1.7	115.7	0.5	115.7	0.0
1988	115.3	-0.3	116.6	1.1	116.9	0.3	117.1	0.2	117.0	-0.1	118.9	1.6	119.8	0.8	120.1	0.3	122.0	1.6	121.6	-0.3	121.0	-0.5	121.3	0.2
1989	121.5	0.2	122.2	0.6	123.0	0.7	123.6	0.5	123.9	0.2	125.7	1.5	126.4	0.6	126.4	0.0	127.1	0.6	126.8	-0.2	126.7	-0.1	126.5	-0.2
1990	128.1	1.3	129.2	0.9	129.5	0.2	130.4	0.7	130.4	0.0	131.7	1.0	132.0	0.2	133.2	0.9	133.8	0.5	133.3	-0.4	134.2	0.7	134.6	0.3
1991	135.1	0.4	135.5	0.3	136.2	0.5	136.1	-0.1	136.8	0.5	137.3	0.4	137.3	0.0	137.6	0.2	138.3	0.5	138.0	-0.2	138.0	0.0	138.3	0.2
1992	138.9	0.4	139.2	0.2	139.7	0.4	139.8	0.1	140.5	0.5	141.2	0.5	141.4	0.1	141.9	0.4	142.7	0.6	142.1	-0.4	142.4	0.2	142.9	0.4
1993	143.2	0.2	143.6	0.3	144.1	0.3	144.7	0.4	145.7	0.7	145.6	-0.1	145.5	-0.1	146.1	0.4	146.7	0.4	147.2	0.3	146.4	-0.5	146.1	-0.2
1994	146.5	0.3	146.8	0.2	147.6	0.5	147.9	0.2	147.6	-0.2	148.1	0.3	148.3	0.1	149.8	1.0	150.2	0.3	149.4	-0.5	150.4	0.7	150.5	0.1
1995	151.8	0.9	152.3	0.3	152.6	0.2	153.1	0.3	153.0	-0.1	153.5	0.3	153.6	0.1	153.8	0.1	154.0	0.1	154.3	0.2	154.0	-0.2	153.8	-0.1

Source: U.S. Department of Labor, Bureau of Labor Statistics, Division of Consumer Prices and Price Indexes. - indicates no data collected for period.

Chicago, IL-NW IN
Consumer Price Index - Urban Wage Earners
Base 1982-1984 = 100
All Items

For 1914-1995. Columns headed % show percentile change in the index from the previous period for which an index is available.

Year	Jan Index	%	Feb Index	%	Mar Index	%	Apr Index	%	May Index	%	Jun Index	%	Jul Index	%	Aug Index	%	Sep Index	%	Oct Index	%	Nov Index	%	Dec Index	%
1914	-	-	-	-	-	-	-	-	-	-	-	-	-	-	-	-	-	-	-	-	-	-	10.1	-
1915	-	-	-	-	-	-	-	-	-	-	-	-	-	-	-	-	-	-	-	-	-	-	10.4	3.0
1916	-	-	-	-	-	-	-	-	-	-	-	-	-	-	-	-	-	-	-	-	-	-	11.8	13.5
1917	-	-	-	-	-	-	-	-	-	-	-	-	-	-	-	-	-	-	-	-	-	-	13.7	16.1
1918	-	-	-	-	-	-	-	-	-	-	-	-	-	-	-	-	-	-	-	-	-	-	16.6	21.2
1919	-	-	-	-	-	-	-	-	-	-	16.9	1.8	-	-	-	-	-	-	-	-	-	-	19.2	13.6
1920	-	-	-	-	-	-	-	-	-	-	21.2	10.4	-	-	-	-	-	-	-	-	-	-	19.2	-9.4
1921	-	-	-	-	-	-	-	-	18.2	-5.2	-	-	-	-	-	-	18.1	-0.5	-	-	-	-	17.8	-1.7
1922	-	-	-	-	-	-	-	-	17.2	-3.4	17.3	0.6	-	-	-	-	17.3	0.0	-	-	-	-	17.4	0.6
1923	-	-	-	-	17.5	0.6	-	-	-	-	17.6	0.6	-	-	-	-	18.0	2.3	-	-	-	-	18.0	0.0
1924	-	-	-	-	17.9	-0.6	-	-	-	-	18.0	0.6	-	-	-	-	18.1	0.6	-	-	-	-	18.2	0.6
1925	-	-	-	-	-	-	-	-	-	-	18.5	1.6	-	-	-	-	-	-	-	-	-	-	18.9	2.2
1926	-	-	-	-	-	-	-	-	-	-	18.7	-1.1	-	-	-	-	-	-	-	-	-	-	18.6	-0.5
1927	-	-	-	-	-	-	-	-	-	-	18.6	0.0	-	-	-	-	-	-	-	-	-	-	18.1	-2.7
1928	-	-	-	-	-	-	-	-	-	-	17.9	-1.1	-	-	-	-	-	-	-	-	-	-	18.0	0.6
1929	-	-	-	-	-	-	-	-	-	-	17.9	-0.6	-	-	-	-	-	-	-	-	-	-	18.0	0.6
1930	-	-	-	-	-	-	-	-	-	-	17.7	-1.7	-	-	-	-	-	-	-	-	-	-	16.9	-4.5
1931	-	-	-	-	-	-	-	-	-	-	15.8	-6.5	-	-	-	-	-	-	-	-	-	-	15.2	-3.8
1932	-	-	-	-	-	-	-	-	-	-	13.8	-9.2	-	-	-	-	-	-	-	-	-	-	13.1	-5.1
1933	-	-	-	-	-	-	-	-	-	-	12.6	-3.8	-	-	-	-	-	-	-	-	-	-	12.9	2.4
1934	-	-	-	-	-	-	-	-	-	-	12.9	0.0	-	-	-	-	-	-	-	-	13.0	0.8	-	-
1935	-	-	-	-	13.6	4.6	-	-	-	-	-	-	13.6	0.0	-	-	-	-	13.6	0.0	-	-	-	-
1936	13.7	0.7	-	-	-	-	13.5	-1.5	-	-	-	-	13.8	2.2	-	-	14.0	1.4	-	-	-	-	13.9	-0.7
1937	-	-	-	-	14.1	1.4	-	-	-	-	14.4	2.1	-	-	-	-	14.6	1.4	-	-	-	-	14.4	-1.4
1938	-	-	-	-	14.1	-2.1	-	-	-	-	14.3	1.4	-	-	-	-	14.3	0.0	-	-	-	-	14.1	-1.4
1939	-	-	-	-	13.9	-1.4	-	-	-	-	13.8	-0.7	-	-	-	-	14.1	2.2	-	-	-	-	13.9	-1.4
1940	-	-	-	-	13.9	0.0	-	-	-	-	14.1	1.4	-	-	-	-	14.1	0.0	14.1	0.0	14.0	-0.7	14.1	0.7
1941	14.1	0.0	14.1	0.0	14.2	0.7	14.3	0.7	14.4	0.7	14.6	1.4	14.8	1.4	14.9	0.7	15.3	2.7	15.4	0.7	15.5	0.6	15.4	-0.6
1942	15.7	1.9	15.7	0.0	15.9	1.3	16.1	1.3	16.2	0.6	16.2	0.0	16.2	0.0	16.4	1.2	16.4	0.0	16.6	1.2	16.7	0.6	16.7	0.0
1943	16.7	0.0	16.8	0.6	17.1	1.8	17.2	0.6	17.4	1.2	17.3	-0.6	17.1	-1.2	17.2	0.6	17.3	0.6	17.3	0.0	17.2	-0.6	17.2	0.0
1944	17.1	-0.6	17.1	0.0	17.1	0.0	17.3	1.2	17.3	0.0	17.4	0.6	17.6	1.1	17.6	0.0	17.6	0.0	17.6	0.0	17.6	0.0	17.6	0.0
1945	17.6	0.0	17.6	0.0	17.6	0.0	17.6	0.0	17.9	1.7	17.9	0.0	17.9	0.0	17.9	0.0	17.8	-0.6	17.8	0.0	17.8	0.0	17.9	0.6
1946	17.9	0.0	17.9	0.0	17.9	0.0	18.1	1.1	18.2	0.6	18.3	0.5	19.7	7.7	20.2	2.5	20.4	1.0	20.9	2.5	21.3	1.9	21.4	0.5
1947	21.4	0.0	21.3	-0.5	21.8	2.3	21.8	0.0	21.9	0.5	22.1	0.9	22.4	1.4	22.7	1.3	23.5	3.5	23.4	-0.4	23.5	0.4	23.8	1.3
1948	23.9	0.4	23.6	-1.3	23.6	0.0	24.1	2.1	24.4	1.2	24.7	1.2	25.0	1.2	25.0	0.0	25.1	0.4	24.9	-0.8	24.6	-1.2	24.5	-0.4
1949	24.4	-0.4	24.2	-0.8	24.4	0.8	24.5	0.4	24.4	-0.4	24.6	0.8	24.3	-1.2	24.4	0.4	24.6	0.8	24.4	-0.8	24.5	0.4	24.2	-1.2
1950	24.1	-0.4	24.1	0.0	24.2	0.4	24.1	-0.4	24.4	1.2	24.4	0.0	24.8	1.6	25.0	0.8	25.1	0.4	25.2	0.4	25.2	0.0	25.6	1.6
1951	25.9	1.2	26.3	1.5	26.4	0.4	26.4	0.0	26.5	0.4	26.5	0.0	26.7	0.8	26.7	0.0	26.8	0.4	27.0	0.7	27.1	0.4	27.1	0.0
1952	27.1	0.0	26.8	-1.1	26.9	0.4	26.9	0.0	27.2	1.1	27.3	0.4	27.3	0.0	27.4	0.4	27.3	-0.4	27.3	0.0	27.4	0.4	27.2	-0.7
1953	27.2	0.0	27.1	-0.4	27.0	-0.4	27.2	0.7	27.2	0.0	27.4	0.7	27.5	0.4	27.6	0.4	27.7	0.4	27.9	0.7	27.7	-0.7	27.7	0.0
1954	27.7	0.0	27.7	0.0	27.7	0.0	27.7	0.0	27.9	0.7	27.9	0.0	28.1	0.7	28.0	-0.4	27.9	-0.4	27.9	0.0	28.0	0.4	27.8	-0.7
1955	27.8	0.0	27.9	0.4	27.8	-0.4	27.8	0.0	27.9	0.4	27.9	0.0	28.1	0.7	28.2	0.4	28.3	0.4	28.3	0.0	28.3	0.0	28.2	-0.4
1956	28.1	-0.4	28.1	0.0	28.0	-0.4	28.1	0.4	28.2	0.4	28.4	0.7	28.7	1.1	28.5	-0.7	28.6	0.4	28.8	0.7	28.8	0.0	28.8	0.0
1957	28.8	0.0	28.9	0.3	28.9	0.0	29.0	0.3	29.0	0.0	29.2	0.7	29.5	1.0	29.5	0.0	29.6	0.3	29.7	0.3	29.9	0.7	29.9	0.0
1958	30.0	0.3	30.0	0.0	30.2	0.7	30.2	0.0	30.2	0.0	30.3	0.3	30.3	0.0	30.2	-0.3	30.3	0.3	30.3	0.0	30.3	0.0	30.2	-0.3

[Continued]

Chicago, IL-NW IN
Consumer Price Index - Urban Wage Earners
Base 1982-1984 = 100
All Items
[Continued]

For 1914-1995. Columns headed % show percentile change in the index from the previous period for which an index is available.

Year	Jan Index	%	Feb Index	%	Mar Index	%	Apr Index	%	May Index	%	Jun Index	%	Jul Index	%	Aug Index	%	Sep Index	%	Oct Index	%	Nov Index	%	Dec Index	%
1959	30.2	0.0	30.2	0.0	30.2	0.0	30.3	0.3	30.3	0.0	30.4	0.3	30.5	0.3	30.5	0.0	30.7	0.7	30.7	0.0	30.7	0.0	30.7	0.0
1960	30.6	-0.3	30.7	0.3	30.7	0.0	30.8	0.3	30.8	0.0	30.9	0.3	31.0	0.3	31.0	0.0	31.0	0.0	31.1	0.3	31.0	-0.3	31.1	0.3
1961	31.0	-0.3	31.0	0.0	31.0	0.0	30.9	-0.3	30.9	0.0	30.8	-0.3	31.1	1.0	31.1	0.0	31.2	0.3	31.2	0.0	31.1	-0.3	31.1	0.0
1962	31.2	0.3	31.3	0.3	31.3	0.0	31.4	0.3	31.4	0.0	31.3	-0.3	31.3	0.0	31.3	0.0	31.5	0.6	31.5	0.0	31.5	0.0	31.4	-0.3
1963	31.5	0.3	31.5	0.0	31.6	0.3	31.6	0.0	31.6	0.0	31.6	0.0	31.9	0.9	31.8	-0.3	31.8	0.0	31.8	0.0	31.7	-0.3	31.8	0.3
1964	31.7	-0.3	31.7	0.0	31.7	0.0	31.7	0.0	31.7	0.0	31.8	0.3	31.9	0.3	31.9	0.0	31.9	0.0	31.9	0.0	31.9	0.0	31.9	0.0
1965	31.9	0.0	31.9	0.0	32.0	0.3	32.0	0.0	32.1	0.3	32.3	0.6	32.3	0.0	32.3	0.0	32.4	0.3	32.4	0.0	32.5	0.3	32.6	0.3
1966	32.6	0.0	32.8	0.6	32.9	0.3	32.9	0.0	33.0	0.3	33.2	0.6	33.1	-0.3	33.4	0.9	33.5	0.3	33.6	0.3	33.5	-0.3	33.6	0.3
1967	33.5	-0.3	33.6	0.3	33.7	0.3	33.6	-0.3	33.7	0.3	33.8	0.3	34.1	0.9	34.3	0.6	34.5	0.6	34.5	0.0	34.6	0.3	34.7	0.3
1968	34.7	0.0	34.9	0.6	35.1	0.6	35.2	0.3	35.3	0.3	35.4	0.3	35.7	0.8	35.8	0.3	35.9	0.3	36.0	0.3	36.1	0.3	36.3	0.6
1969	36.4	0.3	36.5	0.3	36.8	0.8	36.9	0.3	37.0	0.3	37.4	1.1	37.6	0.5	37.8	0.5	38.1	0.8	38.0	-0.3	38.3	0.8	38.4	0.3
1970	38.7	0.8	38.7	0.0	38.9	0.5	39.0	0.3	39.3	0.8	39.4	0.3	39.7	0.8	39.9	0.5	40.1	0.5	40.3	0.5	40.4	0.2	40.6	0.5
1971	40.6	0.0	40.7	0.2	40.8	0.2	40.9	0.2	41.1	0.5	41.2	0.2	41.2	0.0	41.4	0.5	41.4	0.0	41.4	0.0	41.5	0.2	41.6	0.2
1972	41.6	0.0	41.9	0.7	41.9	0.0	42.0	0.2	42.1	0.2	42.3	0.5	42.4	0.2	42.6	0.5	42.7	0.2	42.7	0.0	42.8	0.2	42.9	0.2
1973	43.0	0.2	43.4	0.9	43.9	1.2	44.2	0.7	44.5	0.7	44.8	0.7	44.7	-0.2	45.8	2.5	45.8	0.0	46.2	0.9	46.3	0.2	46.6	0.6
1974	47.2	1.3	47.9	1.5	48.4	1.0	48.7	0.6	49.0	0.6	49.6	1.2	49.8	0.4	50.4	1.2	50.7	0.6	51.3	1.2	51.7	0.8	52.2	1.0
1975	52.2	0.0	52.6	0.8	53.0	0.8	53.1	0.2	52.9	-0.4	53.3	0.8	53.9	1.1	54.2	0.6	54.3	0.2	54.7	0.7	54.7	0.0	54.9	0.4
1976	54.7	-0.4	55.0	0.5	55.2	0.4	55.5	0.5	55.7	0.4	56.1	0.7	56.4	0.5	56.8	0.7	57.0	0.4	57.3	0.5	57.4	0.2	57.6	0.3
1977	57.7	0.2	58.3	1.0	58.7	0.7	59.2	0.9	59.4	0.3	59.6	0.3	60.1	0.8	60.4	0.5	60.8	0.7	60.9	0.2	61.1	0.3	61.3	0.3
1978	62.1	1.3	62.6	0.8	63.2	1.0	63.5	0.5	64.1	0.9	64.7	0.9	65.2	0.8	65.0	-0.3	65.7	1.1	66.5	1.2	67.3	1.2	67.6	0.4
1979	68.0	0.6	68.9	1.3	70.2	1.9	70.9	1.0	71.4	0.7	72.6	1.7	73.8	1.7	74.3	0.7	75.1	1.1	75.5	0.5	76.8	1.7	77.6	1.0
1980	78.3	0.9	79.2	1.1	80.1	1.1	81.7	2.0	82.7	1.2	84.4	2.1	84.1	-0.4	83.6	-0.6	85.0	1.7	86.1	1.3	88.2	2.4	88.2	0.0
1981	87.9	-0.3	88.1	0.2	88.2	0.1	89.6	1.6	89.9	0.3	91.2	1.4	92.5	1.4	93.5	1.1	93.9	0.4	94.1	0.2	94.4	0.3	93.4	-1.1
1982	93.9	0.5	93.8	-0.1	94.1	0.3	95.3	1.3	97.7	2.5	99.3	1.6	99.7	0.4	99.6	-0.1	99.7	0.1	99.8	0.1	99.8	0.0	99.4	-0.4
1983	99.7	0.3	99.2	-0.5	99.2	0.0	100.0	0.8	100.4	0.4	100.7	0.3	100.9	0.2	101.3	0.4	101.8	0.5	100.3	-1.5	100.7	0.4	100.2	-0.5
1984	101.6	1.4	101.1	-0.5	100.9	-0.2	100.9	0.0	101.0	0.1	101.5	0.5	101.8	0.3	102.6	0.8	103.6	1.0	102.8	-0.8	103.0	0.2	102.7	-0.3
1985	103.0	0.3	103.5	0.5	103.8	0.3	104.3	0.5	104.5	0.2	105.9	1.3	105.9	0.0	106.3	0.4	106.3	0.0	105.2	-1.0	105.9	0.7	106.4	0.5
1986	106.5	0.1	106.5	0.0	105.5	-0.9	105.2	-0.3	105.4	0.2	107.5	2.0	107.6	0.1	107.7	0.1	108.4	0.6	106.7	-1.6	107.6	0.8	107.5	-0.1
1987	108.7	1.1	108.6	-0.1	109.0	0.4	109.5	0.5	109.9	0.4	112.0	1.9	112.4	0.4	113.2	0.7	113.6	0.4	111.7	-1.7	112.2	0.4	112.2	0.0
1988	111.9	-0.3	112.9	0.9	113.2	0.3	113.3	0.1	113.3	0.0	115.2	1.7	116.2	0.9	116.4	0.2	118.2	1.5	117.8	-0.3	117.4	-0.3	117.7	0.3
1989	117.9	0.2	118.4	0.4	119.1	0.6	119.8	0.6	120.1	0.3	121.8	1.4	122.6	0.7	122.5	-0.1	123.1	0.5	122.9	-0.2	122.9	0.0	122.8	-0.1
1990	124.4	1.3	125.4	0.8	125.6	0.2	126.5	0.7	126.5	0.0	127.9	1.1	128.0	0.1	129.3	1.0	129.9	0.5	129.4	-0.4	130.3	0.7	130.7	0.3
1991	131.1	0.3	131.5	0.3	132.0	0.4	132.1	0.1	132.7	0.5	133.1	0.3	133.2	0.1	133.4	0.2	133.9	0.4	133.6	-0.2	133.8	0.1	134.1	0.2
1992	134.4	0.2	134.7	0.2	135.2	0.4	135.4	0.1	136.2	0.6	136.9	0.5	137.0	0.1	137.5	0.4	138.3	0.6	137.7	-0.4	138.2	0.4	138.5	0.2
1993	138.9	0.3	139.1	0.1	139.5	0.3	140.3	0.6	141.4	0.8	141.2	-0.1	141.1	-0.1	141.6	0.4	142.1	0.4	142.6	0.4	141.8	-0.6	141.7	-0.1
1994	142.0	0.2	142.3	0.2	143.0	0.5	143.3	0.2	143.1	-0.1	143.6	0.3	143.7	0.1	145.1	1.0	145.4	0.2	144.6	-0.6	145.7	0.8	145.8	0.1
1995	147.1	0.9	147.5	0.3	147.8	0.2	148.3	0.3	148.2	-0.1	148.5	0.2	148.7	0.1	148.8	0.1	149.0	0.1	149.2	0.1	149.0	-0.1	149.0	0.0

Source: U.S. Department of Labor, Bureau of Labor Statistics, Division of Consumer Prices and Price Indexes. - indicates no data collected for period.

Chicago, IL-NW IN
Consumer Price Index - All Urban Consumers
Base 1982-1984 = 100
Food and Beverages

For 1976-1995. Columns headed % show percentile change in the index from the previous period for which an index is available.

Year	Jan Index	%	Feb Index	%	Mar Index	%	Apr Index	%	May Index	%	Jun Index	%	Jul Index	%	Aug Index	%	Sep Index	%	Oct Index	%	Nov Index	%	Dec Index	%
1976	63.6	-	63.7	0.2	63.3	-0.6	64.0	1.1	63.7	-0.5	64.4	1.1	64.9	0.8	65.0	0.2	64.7	-0.5	64.9	0.3	64.5	-0.6	64.4	-0.2
1977	64.7	0.5	65.9	1.9	66.5	0.9	67.3	1.2	67.3	0.0	67.9	0.9	68.6	1.0	69.0	0.6	69.4	0.6	69.5	0.1	69.4	-0.1	70.0	0.9
1978	71.8	2.6	72.8	1.4	73.5	1.0	74.4	1.2	75.1	0.9	76.0	1.2	76.4	0.5	77.0	0.8	77.4	0.5	77.5	0.1	78.4	1.2	78.6	0.3
1979	80.0	1.8	81.2	1.5	82.3	1.4	82.9	0.7	83.7	1.0	83.9	0.2	84.7	1.0	84.1	-0.7	84.3	0.2	85.0	0.8	86.1	1.3	87.0	1.0
1980	86.8	-0.2	87.6	0.9	88.8	1.4	89.5	0.8	90.1	0.7	90.2	0.1	91.4	1.3	92.7	1.4	93.5	0.9	94.1	0.6	94.5	0.4	95.0	0.5
1981	95.6	0.6	96.2	0.6	96.3	0.1	95.9	-0.4	95.4	-0.5	96.2	0.8	96.5	0.3	97.1	0.6	96.9	-0.2	97.1	0.2	96.7	-0.4	96.7	0.0
1982	97.5	0.8	97.6	0.1	97.4	-0.2	98.5	1.1	99.4	0.9	99.9	0.5	99.5	-0.4	99.1	-0.4	98.9	-0.2	98.9	0.0	98.7	-0.2	98.8	0.1
1983	99.7	0.9	99.7	0.0	99.6	-0.1	99.8	0.2	99.4	-0.4	99.3	-0.1	98.5	-0.8	98.4	-0.1	99.3	0.9	99.3	0.0	99.8	0.5	99.5	-0.3
1984	101.8	2.3	102.7	0.9	102.2	-0.5	102.0	-0.2	101.7	-0.3	101.4	-0.3	102.0	0.6	102.5	0.5	102.1	-0.4	102.0	-0.1	101.2	-0.8	101.9	0.7
1985	102.6	0.7	104.0	1.4	104.1	0.1	103.5	-0.6	103.2	-0.3	104.1	0.9	103.8	-0.3	104.0	0.2	104.3	0.3	104.4	0.1	105.6	1.1	107.0	1.3
1986	106.9	-0.1	107.9	0.9	107.7	-0.2	107.8	0.1	107.4	-0.4	108.5	1.0	109.3	0.7	110.4	1.0	110.1	-0.3	109.1	-0.9	111.1	1.8	110.9	-0.2
1987	113.1	2.0	112.7	-0.4	112.0	-0.6	112.9	0.8	112.7	-0.2	113.6	0.8	113.2	-0.4	113.5	0.3	113.7	0.2	113.5	-0.2	113.7	0.2	113.7	0.0
1988	114.4	0.6	114.9	0.4	115.0	0.1	115.2	0.2	115.8	0.5	116.1	0.3	117.9	1.6	118.8	0.8	119.3	0.4	119.2	-0.1	118.9	-0.3	119.3	0.3
1989	120.7	1.2	121.5	0.7	121.5	0.0	122.7	1.0	122.3	-0.3	122.3	0.0	122.7	0.3	122.4	-0.2	122.9	0.4	123.2	0.2	123.6	0.3	124.2	0.5
1990	128.0	3.1	128.7	0.5	129.0	0.2	128.9	-0.1	129.1	0.2	129.8	0.5	131.3	1.2	131.0	-0.2	131.3	0.2	131.1	-0.2	132.2	0.8	132.9	0.5
1991	134.7	1.4	134.8	0.1	135.3	0.4	136.0	0.5	136.5	0.4	136.2	-0.2	136.0	-0.1	134.8	-0.9	135.5	0.5	134.6	-0.7	135.6	0.7	135.9	0.2
1992	136.6	0.5	137.7	0.8	138.8	0.8	139.1	0.2	139.8	0.5	138.9	-0.6	138.8	-0.1	139.2	0.3	140.4	0.9	139.6	-0.6	140.2	0.4	140.8	0.4
1993	142.5	1.2	140.8	-1.2	142.2	1.0	141.9	-0.2	143.3	1.0	142.7	-0.4	142.9	0.1	143.1	0.1	143.3	0.1	144.3	0.7	144.4	0.1	145.6	0.8
1994	147.2	1.1	146.4	-0.5	147.0	0.4	147.4	0.3	146.8	-0.4	145.9	-0.6	146.2	0.2	147.2	0.7	147.2	0.0	147.5	0.2	147.3	-0.1	147.6	0.2
1995	150.2	1.8	151.4	0.8	151.3	-0.1	151.7	0.3	150.9	-0.5	150.8	-0.1	151.2	0.3	150.9	-0.2	150.6	-0.2	151.4	0.5	152.3	0.6	152.9	0.4

Source: U.S. Department of Labor, Bureau of Labor Statistics, Division of Consumer Prices and Price Indexes. - indicates no data collected for period.

Chicago, IL-NW IN

Consumer Price Index - Urban Wage Earners
Base 1982-1984 = 100
Food and Beverages

For 1976-1995. Columns headed % show percentile change in the index from the previous period for which an index is available.

Year	Jan Index	%	Feb Index	%	Mar Index	%	Apr Index	%	May Index	%	Jun Index	%	Jul Index	%	Aug Index	%	Sep Index	%	Oct Index	%	Nov Index	%	Dec Index	%
1976	64.6	-	64.6	0.0	64.2	-0.6	64.9	1.1	64.7	-0.3	65.3	0.9	65.9	0.9	66.0	0.2	65.6	-0.6	65.9	0.5	65.5	-0.6	65.4	-0.2
1977	65.7	0.5	66.9	1.8	67.5	0.9	68.3	1.2	68.3	0.0	68.9	0.9	69.6	1.0	70.1	0.7	70.4	0.4	70.6	0.3	70.5	-0.1	71.1	0.9
1978	72.6	2.1	73.1	0.7	73.6	0.7	74.7	1.5	75.5	1.1	76.5	1.3	77.1	0.8	77.5	0.5	78.0	0.6	78.4	0.5	79.1	0.9	79.3	0.3
1979	81.1	2.3	81.9	1.0	83.3	1.7	83.7	0.5	84.4	0.8	84.6	0.2	85.2	0.7	84.4	-0.9	84.7	0.4	85.9	1.4	86.8	1.0	87.6	0.9
1980	87.9	0.3	88.4	0.6	89.7	1.5	90.5	0.9	91.5	1.1	91.7	0.2	93.0	1.4	93.6	0.6	94.8	1.3	95.0	0.2	95.8	0.8	95.4	-0.4
1981	95.5	0.1	95.9	0.4	95.9	0.0	96.0	0.1	95.4	-0.6	96.2	0.8	96.5	0.3	96.9	0.4	96.8	-0.1	97.1	0.3	96.6	-0.5	96.7	0.1
1982	97.5	0.8	97.6	0.1	97.3	-0.3	98.5	1.2	99.4	0.9	99.8	0.4	99.5	-0.3	99.1	-0.4	98.8	-0.3	98.7	-0.1	98.7	0.0	98.8	0.1
1983	99.6	0.8	99.7	0.1	99.6	-0.1	99.7	0.1	99.4	-0.3	99.3	-0.1	98.5	-0.8	98.4	-0.1	99.3	0.9	99.5	0.2	99.8	0.3	99.7	-0.1
1984	101.9	2.2	102.7	0.8	102.2	-0.5	102.1	-0.1	101.8	-0.3	101.5	-0.3	101.9	0.4	102.5	0.6	102.0	-0.5	101.9	-0.1	101.3	-0.6	102.0	0.7
1985	102.6	0.6	104.0	1.4	104.1	0.1	103.6	-0.5	103.2	-0.4	104.1	0.9	103.7	-0.4	103.9	0.2	104.3	0.4	104.5	0.2	105.7	1.1	106.9	1.1
1986	107.0	0.1	107.9	0.8	107.8	-0.1	107.9	0.1	107.5	-0.4	108.6	1.0	109.4	0.7	110.5	1.0	110.2	-0.3	109.2	-0.9	111.3	1.9	110.9	-0.4
1987	113.2	2.1	112.8	-0.4	112.1	-0.6	113.0	0.8	112.8	-0.2	113.7	0.8	113.3	-0.4	113.6	0.3	113.8	0.2	113.6	-0.2	113.8	0.2	113.8	0.0
1988	114.5	0.6	114.9	0.3	115.1	0.2	115.3	0.2	115.9	0.5	116.1	0.2	118.0	1.6	118.9	0.8	119.4	0.4	119.3	-0.1	119.0	-0.3	119.4	0.3
1989	120.8	1.2	121.5	0.6	121.5	0.0	122.7	1.0	122.3	-0.3	122.4	0.1	122.8	0.3	122.5	-0.2	123.1	0.5	123.3	0.2	123.7	0.3	124.3	0.5
1990	128.3	3.2	128.8	0.4	129.1	0.2	129.1	0.0	129.2	0.1	130.0	0.6	131.4	1.1	131.2	-0.2	131.5	0.2	131.2	-0.2	132.4	0.9	133.0	0.5
1991	134.8	1.4	134.9	0.1	135.5	0.4	136.2	0.5	136.7	0.4	136.4	-0.2	136.2	-0.1	135.0	-0.9	135.7	0.5	134.7	-0.7	135.8	0.8	135.9	0.1
1992	136.6	0.5	137.7	0.8	138.9	0.9	139.2	0.2	139.8	0.4	139.0	-0.6	138.8	-0.1	139.2	0.3	140.4	0.9	139.7	-0.5	140.3	0.4	140.9	0.4
1993	142.6	1.2	140.9	-1.2	142.3	1.0	142.1	-0.1	143.4	0.9	142.8	-0.4	143.1	0.2	143.3	0.1	143.5	0.1	144.5	0.7	144.7	0.1	145.9	0.8
1994	147.4	1.0	146.5	-0.6	147.3	0.5	147.6	0.2	147.0	-0.4	146.1	-0.6	146.4	0.2	147.4	0.7	147.4	0.0	147.7	0.2	147.4	-0.2	147.8	0.3
1995	150.5	1.8	151.7	0.8	151.6	-0.1	151.9	0.2	151.1	-0.5	151.0	-0.1	151.4	0.3	151.1	-0.2	150.9	-0.1	151.7	0.5	152.6	0.6	153.2	0.4

Source: U.S. Department of Labor, Bureau of Labor Statistics, Division of Consumer Prices and Price Indexes. - indicates no data collected for period.

Chicago, IL-NW IN
Consumer Price Index - All Urban Consumers
Base 1982-1984 = 100
Housing

For 1976-1995. Columns headed % show percentile change in the index from the previous period for which an index is available.

Year	Jan Index	%	Feb Index	%	Mar Index	%	Apr Index	%	May Index	%	Jun Index	%	Jul Index	%	Aug Index	%	Sep Index	%	Oct Index	%	Nov Index	%	Dec Index	%
1976	47.5	-	47.6	0.2	47.8	0.4	47.9	0.2	48.1	0.4	48.3	0.4	48.6	0.6	48.8	0.4	49.1	0.6	49.3	0.4	49.3	0.0	49.9	1.2
1977	50.0	0.2	50.4	0.8	50.5	0.2	50.9	0.8	51.0	0.2	51.0	0.0	51.6	1.2	51.9	0.6	52.4	1.0	52.6	0.4	52.9	0.6	53.0	0.2
1978	54.2	2.3	55.0	1.5	56.1	2.0	56.2	0.2	56.6	0.7	57.0	0.7	57.5	0.9	57.0	-0.9	58.2	2.1	58.9	1.2	60.1	2.0	60.3	0.3
1979	60.3	0.0	61.5	2.0	63.3	2.9	64.1	1.3	63.8	-0.5	65.6	2.8	67.2	2.4	68.0	1.2	68.9	1.3	68.6	-0.4	70.6	2.9	71.1	0.7
1980	71.5	0.6	72.0	0.7	72.3	0.4	74.6	3.2	76.2	2.1	79.6	4.5	78.1	-1.9	76.2	-2.4	78.7	3.3	80.7	2.5	84.3	4.5	84.1	-0.2
1981	81.8	-2.7	81.4	-0.5	81.0	-0.5	83.3	2.8	83.6	0.4	86.3	3.2	88.0	2.0	89.3	1.5	89.4	0.1	88.5	-1.0	88.8	0.3	86.3	-2.8
1982	87.5	1.4	87.2	-0.3	88.8	1.8	91.0	2.5	95.6	5.1	97.1	1.6	98.0	0.9	97.9	-0.1	98.5	0.6	98.5	0.0	98.5	0.0	97.8	-0.7
1983	98.2	0.4	98.6	0.4	98.8	0.2	99.1	0.3	99.4	0.3	101.5	2.1	102.1	0.6	102.4	0.3	102.2	-0.2	100.8	-1.4	101.8	1.0	102.3	0.5
1984	102.5	0.2	102.1	-0.4	102.5	0.4	103.0	0.5	103.0	0.0	105.1	2.0	105.0	-0.1	106.7	1.6	107.8	1.0	106.1	-1.6	106.2	0.1	106.3	0.1
1985	107.1	0.8	107.2	0.1	106.8	-0.4	107.6	0.7	108.1	0.5	111.6	3.2	111.7	0.1	113.2	1.3	113.3	0.1	109.4	-3.4	109.2	-0.2	109.6	0.4
1986	110.3	0.6	110.5	0.2	110.4	-0.1	111.3	0.8	111.0	-0.3	115.5	4.1	116.0	0.4	116.1	0.1	117.1	0.9	112.1	-4.3	112.7	0.5	112.1	-0.5
1987	113.1	0.9	113.3	0.2	113.3	0.0	113.9	0.5	114.1	0.2	118.7	4.0	119.6	0.8	120.3	0.6	120.6	0.2	115.4	-4.3	116.6	1.0	117.0	0.3
1988	115.7	-1.1	118.0	2.0	118.0	0.0	118.1	0.1	118.1	0.0	121.9	3.2	122.7	0.7	122.1	-0.5	124.6	2.0	123.7	-0.7	122.3	-1.1	123.1	0.7
1989	123.1	0.0	123.8	0.6	124.2	0.3	124.2	0.0	124.5	0.2	128.2	3.0	128.9	0.5	128.8	-0.1	129.9	0.9	126.9	-2.3	126.9	0.0	127.2	0.2
1990	128.0	0.6	129.2	0.9	129.3	0.1	130.2	0.7	129.6	-0.5	133.2	2.8	133.4	0.2	134.3	0.7	134.2	-0.1	130.8	-2.5	131.7	0.7	132.5	0.6
1991	134.2	1.3	134.3	0.1	135.8	1.1	134.9	-0.7	136.1	0.9	137.6	1.1	138.3	0.5	137.9	-0.3	137.7	-0.1	137.0	-0.5	135.6	-1.0	137.4	1.3
1992	138.9	1.1	138.3	-0.4	138.2	-0.1	138.2	0.0	139.1	0.7	141.4	1.7	140.7	-0.5	140.6	-0.1	141.6	0.7	139.5	-1.5	140.5	0.7	141.8	0.9
1993	141.8	0.0	141.3	-0.4	141.0	-0.2	142.5	1.1	142.9	0.3	144.3	1.0	143.3	-0.7	144.3	0.7	145.2	0.6	145.6	0.3	143.4	-1.5	143.4	0.0
1994	143.2	-0.1	143.2	0.0	143.6	0.3	144.2	0.4	144.1	-0.1	145.3	0.8	144.7	-0.4	145.4	0.5	145.9	0.3	144.2	-1.2	146.4	1.5	147.9	1.0
1995	149.2	0.9	149.1	-0.1	149.1	0.0	149.7	0.4	149.9	0.1	150.7	0.5	151.7	0.7	151.9	0.1	151.3	-0.4	151.3	0.0	151.4	0.1	152.1	0.5

Source: U.S. Department of Labor, Bureau of Labor Statistics, Division of Consumer Prices and Price Indexes. - indicates no data collected for period.

Chicago, IL-NW IN
Consumer Price Index - Urban Wage Earners
Base 1982-1984 = 100
Housing

For 1976-1995. Columns headed % show percentile change in the index from the previous period for which an index is available.

Year	Jan Index	%	Feb Index	%	Mar Index	%	Apr Index	%	May Index	%	Jun Index	%	Jul Index	%	Aug Index	%	Sep Index	%	Oct Index	%	Nov Index	%	Dec Index	%
1976	49.6	-	49.7	0.2	50.0	0.6	50.1	0.2	50.3	0.4	50.5	0.4	50.7	0.4	51.0	0.6	51.3	0.6	51.5	0.4	51.5	0.0	52.1	1.2
1977	52.3	0.4	52.7	0.8	52.8	0.2	53.2	0.8	53.3	0.2	53.3	0.0	53.9	1.1	54.2	0.6	54.7	0.9	54.9	0.4	55.3	0.7	55.4	0.2
1978	56.6	2.2	57.4	1.4	58.5	1.9	58.5	0.0	59.0	0.9	59.4	0.7	60.0	1.0	59.1	-1.5	60.3	2.0	61.3	1.7	62.4	1.8	62.9	0.8
1979	62.8	-0.2	63.9	1.8	65.7	2.8	66.3	0.9	66.1	-0.3	67.9	2.7	69.5	2.4	70.3	1.2	71.2	1.3	71.0	-0.3	73.0	2.8	73.4	0.5
1980	73.8	0.5	74.3	0.7	74.9	0.8	77.0	2.8	78.6	2.1	82.1	4.5	80.6	-1.8	78.7	-2.4	81.1	3.0	82.9	2.2	86.4	4.2	86.5	0.1
1981	84.3	-2.5	83.8	-0.6	83.4	-0.5	85.8	2.9	86.2	0.5	88.9	3.1	90.7	2.0	92.1	1.5	92.3	0.2	91.4	-1.0	91.8	0.4	89.2	-2.8
1982	90.4	1.3	90.2	-0.2	91.8	1.8	94.0	2.4	98.8	5.1	100.5	1.7	101.4	0.9	101.2	-0.2	101.8	0.6	101.8	0.0	101.7	-0.1	101.0	-0.7
1983	101.6	0.6	101.1	-0.5	101.3	0.2	102.1	0.8	102.5	0.4	103.2	0.7	103.4	0.2	103.0	-0.4	103.3	0.3	99.1	-4.1	99.6	0.5	98.8	-0.8
1984	101.4	2.6	100.1	-1.3	99.4	-0.7	99.0	-0.4	98.9	-0.1	99.9	1.0	100.0	0.1	101.3	1.3	103.3	2.0	100.7	-2.5	101.6	0.9	100.9	-0.7
1985	101.5	0.6	101.7	0.2	101.3	-0.4	102.0	0.7	102.4	0.4	106.0	3.5	106.1	0.1	107.4	1.2	107.5	0.1	103.6	-3.6	103.5	-0.1	103.9	0.4
1986	104.5	0.6	104.7	0.2	104.4	-0.3	105.3	0.9	105.0	-0.3	109.4	4.2	110.1	0.6	110.3	0.2	111.0	0.6	105.9	-4.6	106.5	0.6	105.9	-0.6
1987	106.8	0.8	107.0	0.2	106.9	-0.1	107.3	0.4	107.5	0.2	112.0	4.2	112.8	0.7	113.6	0.7	113.8	0.2	108.7	-4.5	109.8	1.0	110.3	0.5
1988	109.1	-1.1	111.2	1.9	110.9	-0.3	111.0	0.1	111.0	0.0	114.7	3.3	115.6	0.8	114.8	-0.7	117.2	2.1	116.4	-0.7	115.3	-0.9	116.1	0.7
1989	116.0	-0.1	116.6	0.5	116.7	0.1	116.7	0.0	117.0	0.3	120.7	3.2	121.3	0.5	121.3	0.0	122.3	0.8	119.3	-2.5	119.6	0.3	119.8	0.2
1990	120.6	0.7	121.7	0.9	121.7	0.0	122.7	0.8	122.1	-0.5	125.5	2.8	125.7	0.2	126.6	0.7	126.7	0.1	123.2	-2.8	124.1	0.7	125.0	0.7
1991	126.4	1.1	126.5	0.1	127.8	1.0	127.0	-0.6	128.0	0.8	129.4	1.1	130.2	0.6	129.7	-0.4	129.6	-0.1	128.8	-0.6	127.6	-0.9	129.5	1.5
1992	130.7	0.9	130.1	-0.5	129.9	-0.2	130.0	0.1	130.9	0.7	133.0	1.6	132.4	-0.5	132.2	-0.2	133.3	0.8	131.4	-1.4	132.5	0.8	133.7	0.9
1993	133.8	0.1	133.3	-0.4	132.8	-0.4	134.3	1.1	134.7	0.3	135.9	0.9	135.0	-0.7	135.9	0.7	136.7	0.6	137.2	0.4	135.1	-1.5	135.3	0.1
1994	135.1	-0.1	134.9	-0.1	135.3	0.3	135.8	0.4	135.5	-0.2	136.8	1.0	136.0	-0.6	136.7	0.5	137.2	0.4	135.6	-1.2	137.7	1.5	139.3	1.2
1995	140.4	0.8	140.3	-0.1	140.2	-0.1	140.7	0.4	140.8	0.1	141.4	0.4	142.2	0.6	142.4	0.1	142.0	-0.3	142.0	0.0	142.2	0.1	142.7	0.4

Source: U.S. Department of Labor, Bureau of Labor Statistics, Division of Consumer Prices and Price Indexes. - indicates no data collected for period.

Chicago, IL-NW IN
Consumer Price Index - All Urban Consumers
Base 1982-1984 = 100
Apparel and Upkeep

For 1952-1995. Columns headed % show percentile change in the index from the previous period for which an index is available.

Year	Jan Index	%	Feb Index	%	Mar Index	%	Apr Index	%	May Index	%	Jun Index	%	Jul Index	%	Aug Index	%	Sep Index	%	Oct Index	%	Nov Index	%	Dec Index	%
1952	-	-	-	-	-	-	-	-	-	-	-	-	-	-	-	-	-	-	-	-	-	-	52.2	-
1953	51.8	-0.8	51.9	0.2	52.0	0.2	52.1	0.2	52.3	0.4	52.4	0.2	52.4	0.0	52.6	0.4	53.1	1.0	53.1	0.0	53.1	0.0	52.9	-0.4
1954	52.9	0.0	52.9	0.0	53.0	0.2	52.9	-0.2	52.9	0.0	52.9	0.0	52.9	0.0	52.4	-0.9	52.5	0.2	52.4	-0.2	52.3	-0.2	52.2	-0.2
1955	51.4	-1.5	51.6	0.4	51.7	0.2	51.3	-0.8	51.4	0.2	51.5	0.2	52.1	1.2	52.3	0.4	53.3	1.9	53.4	0.2	53.7	0.6	53.4	-0.6
1956	53.4	0.0	53.4	0.0	53.5	0.2	53.6	0.2	53.5	-0.2	53.5	0.0	53.8	0.6	54.1	0.6	54.5	0.7	54.8	0.6	54.6	-0.4	54.8	0.4
1957	53.9	-1.6	54.1	0.4	54.7	1.1	54.6	-0.2	54.6	0.0	54.8	0.4	54.7	-0.2	54.8	0.2	55.7	1.6	55.6	-0.2	55.4	-0.4	55.4	0.0
1958	54.9	-0.9	54.8	-0.2	54.8	0.0	54.7	-0.2	54.7	0.0	54.9	0.4	55.2	0.5	54.8	-0.7	55.4	1.1	55.3	-0.2	55.4	0.2	55.1	-0.5
1959	54.8	-0.5	54.6	-0.4	54.5	-0.2	54.9	0.7	55.1	0.4	54.9	-0.4	55.4	0.9	55.6	0.4	56.6	1.8	56.6	0.0	56.6	0.0	56.6	0.0
1960	56.0	-1.1	56.1	0.2	56.2	0.2	55.7	-0.9	56.0	0.5	56.0	0.0	56.4	0.7	56.6	0.4	56.7	0.2	56.8	0.2	56.7	-0.2	56.9	0.4
1961	56.0	-1.6	56.0	0.0	56.0	0.0	56.0	0.0	55.8	-0.4	55.5	-0.5	55.8	0.5	55.5	-0.5	56.7	2.2	56.6	-0.2	56.4	-0.4	56.4	0.0
1962	55.4	-1.8	55.3	-0.2	55.6	0.5	55.5	-0.2	55.6	0.2	55.5	-0.2	55.7	0.4	55.4	-0.5	56.3	1.6	56.3	0.0	56.3	0.0	56.4	0.2
1963	55.6	-1.4	55.7	0.2	55.8	0.2	55.9	0.2	55.8	-0.2	55.4	-0.7	55.7	0.5	55.5	-0.4	56.9	2.5	57.0	0.2	56.6	-0.7	56.8	0.4
1964	55.4	-2.5	55.8	0.7	56.4	1.1	56.4	0.0	56.4	0.0	56.3	-0.2	56.1	-0.4	55.7	-0.7	56.7	1.8	56.6	-0.2	56.4	-0.4	56.5	0.2
1965	56.0	-0.9	55.8	-0.4	56.3	0.9	56.4	0.2	56.9	0.9	57.0	0.2	56.1	-1.6	56.4	0.5	57.5	2.0	57.7	0.3	57.7	0.0	57.9	0.3
1966	56.8	-1.9	56.7	-0.2	58.0	2.3	57.8	-0.3	58.1	0.5	58.3	0.3	57.4	-1.5	57.9	0.9	59.7	3.1	59.7	0.0	59.4	-0.5	59.7	0.5
1967	59.1	-1.0	59.2	0.2	59.7	0.8	59.8	0.2	60.3	0.8	60.4	0.2	59.8	-1.0	60.3	0.8	61.7	2.3	61.9	0.3	62.1	0.3	62.3	0.3
1968	60.5	-2.9	61.2	1.2	62.8	2.6	63.2	0.6	63.9	1.1	64.0	0.2	63.2	-1.2	63.4	0.3	65.2	2.8	65.7	0.8	65.8	0.2	65.9	0.2
1969	64.1	-2.7	65.7	2.5	66.3	0.9	66.0	-0.5	66.6	0.9	67.0	0.6	66.6	-0.6	65.2	-2.1	68.6	5.2	68.5	-0.1	68.9	0.6	68.8	-0.1
1970	66.2	-3.8	66.8	0.9	68.2	2.1	67.6	-0.9	68.7	1.6	68.3	-0.6	67.1	-1.8	67.9	1.2	71.0	4.6	70.7	-0.4	70.7	0.0	70.4	-0.4
1971	68.1	-3.3	69.8	2.5	70.7	1.3	70.5	-0.3	71.1	0.9	71.3	0.3	69.7	-2.2	70.3	0.9	72.9	3.7	72.8	-0.1	73.0	0.3	73.0	0.0
1972	70.4	-3.6	72.0	2.3	72.4	0.6	72.1	-0.4	72.2	0.1	72.1	-0.1	70.2	-2.6	70.4	0.3	74.3	5.5	74.3	0.0	74.7	0.5	74.7	0.0
1973	73.0	-2.3	74.1	1.5	76.1	2.7	76.1	0.0	76.5	0.5	76.2	-0.4	74.7	-2.0	75.5	1.1	77.5	2.6	77.3	-0.3	77.8	0.6	77.5	-0.4
1974	75.5	-2.6	77.2	2.3	78.4	1.6	79.3	1.1	79.6	0.4	80.1	0.6	79.0	-1.4	82.3	4.2	82.6	0.4	82.9	0.4	83.7	1.0	83.7	0.0
1975	81.0	-3.2	81.5	0.6	82.7	1.5	82.9	0.2	82.6	-0.4	82.1	-0.6	81.6	-0.6	82.7	1.3	84.3	1.9	84.1	-0.2	84.1	0.0	83.5	-0.7
1976	80.9	-3.1	82.0	1.4	82.6	0.7	82.2	-0.5	83.0	1.0	83.6	0.7	82.7	-1.1	84.2	1.8	86.0	2.1	85.6	-0.5	85.9	0.4	85.7	-0.2
1977	83.0	-3.2	84.1	1.3	85.4	1.5	85.3	-0.1	85.3	0.0	86.4	1.3	85.9	-0.6	87.0	1.3	88.7	2.0	87.3	-1.6	88.0	0.8	87.8	-0.2
1978	85.2	-3.0	85.0	-0.2	86.4	1.6	87.9	1.7	88.6	0.8	88.4	-0.2	87.7	-0.8	88.8	1.3	89.5	0.8	89.5	0.0	90.2	0.8	88.8	-1.6
1979	87.5	-1.5	88.2	0.8	90.4	2.5	89.6	-0.9	90.2	0.7	89.4	-0.9	89.9	0.6	89.3	-0.7	91.9	2.9	91.9	0.0	93.5	1.7	93.8	0.3
1980	93.7	-0.1	93.0	-0.7	95.1	2.3	94.8	-0.3	94.2	-0.6	95.2	1.1	95.5	0.3	96.2	0.7	97.4	1.2	97.9	0.5	98.3	0.4	95.8	-2.5
1981	93.1	-2.8	93.0	-0.1	94.4	1.5	94.9	0.5	95.1	0.2	94.0	-1.2	94.1	0.1	99.0	5.2	100.8	1.8	99.9	-0.9	100.8	0.9	98.1	-2.7
1982	95.6	-2.5	96.9	1.4	95.7	-1.2	97.2	1.6	98.7	1.5	97.8	-0.9	94.3	-3.6	99.3	5.3	100.5	1.2	99.8	-0.7	99.2	-0.6	97.4	-1.8
1983	96.4	-1.0	95.6	-0.8	98.6	3.1	97.9	-0.7	99.0	1.1	96.8	-2.2	97.4	0.6	102.2	4.9	104.7	2.4	104.7	0.0	106.0	1.2	103.5	-2.4
1984	99.0	-4.3	96.5	-2.5	98.7	2.3	99.7	1.0	100.4	0.7	98.8	-1.6	102.4	3.6	104.9	2.4	106.1	1.1	106.1	0.0	107.8	1.6	104.7	-2.9
1985	100.7	-3.8	103.8	3.1	105.7	1.8	106.7	0.9	105.7	-0.9	104.9	-0.8	105.6	0.7	106.4	0.8	108.4	1.9	108.3	-0.1	108.6	0.3	106.9	-1.6
1986	102.5	-4.1	102.4	-0.1	101.1	-1.3	100.2	-0.9	100.3	0.1	99.3	-1.0	101.1	1.8	105.0	3.9	109.4	4.2	109.4	0.0	108.6	-0.7	107.0	-1.5
1987	104.4	-2.4	102.7	-1.6	108.0	5.2	107.6	-0.4	108.6	0.9	106.7	-1.7	105.1	-1.5	112.7	7.2	114.3	1.4	114.2	-0.1	114.5	0.3	112.0	-2.2
1988	111.1	-0.8	112.2	1.0	115.8	3.2	115.3	-0.4	113.6	-1.5	115.6	1.8	114.7	-0.8	116.8	1.8	122.8	5.1	121.1	-1.4	120.4	-0.6	119.8	-0.5
1989	114.1	-4.8	112.3	-1.6	119.3	6.2	117.8	-1.3	116.0	-1.5	113.5	-2.2	118.1	4.1	119.6	1.3	120.5	0.8	124.8	3.6	123.2	-1.3	117.5	-4.6
1990	114.5	-2.6	121.4	6.0	126.1	3.9	129.4	2.6	129.4	0.0	123.0	-4.9	119.8	-2.6	123.5	3.1	126.7	2.6	126.6	-0.1	127.9	1.0	122.8	-4.0
1991	116.5	-5.1	124.1	6.5	127.1	2.4	128.9	1.4	125.2	-2.9	122.3	-2.3	119.6	-2.2	127.1	6.3	128.8	1.3	129.5	0.5	130.0	0.4	124.0	-4.6
1992	120.8	-2.6	126.5	4.7	129.3	2.2	124.7	-3.6	124.5	-0.2	123.5	-0.8	124.7	1.0	132.3	6.1	130.8	-1.1	129.4	-1.1	125.2	-3.2	123.1	-1.7
1993	121.2	-1.5	133.3	10.0	137.0	2.8	133.4	-2.6	133.9	0.4	126.6	-5.5	128.2	1.3	134.0	4.5	134.3	0.2	133.9	-0.3	131.9	-1.5	125.8	-4.6
1994	126.6	0.6	132.4	4.6	136.5	3.1	133.1	-2.5	129.0	-3.1	128.6	-0.3	126.5	-1.6	135.1	6.8	134.2	-0.7	131.8	-1.8	132.0	0.2	126.0	-4.5
1995	125.3	-0.6	128.2	2.3	130.1	1.5	130.0	-0.1	126.6	-2.6	123.8	-2.2	121.6	-1.8	124.2	2.1	131.0	5.5	131.4	0.3	125.4	-4.6	118.5	-5.5

Source: U.S. Department of Labor, Bureau of Labor Statistics, Division of Consumer Prices and Price Indexes. - indicates no data collected for period.

Chicago, IL-NW IN
Consumer Price Index - Urban Wage Earners
Base 1982-1984 = 100
Apparel and Upkeep

For 1952-1995. Columns headed % show percentile change in the index from the previous period for which an index is available.

Year	Jan Index	%	Feb Index	%	Mar Index	%	Apr Index	%	May Index	%	Jun Index	%	Jul Index	%	Aug Index	%	Sep Index	%	Oct Index	%	Nov Index	%	Dec Index	%
1952	-	-	-	-	-	-	-	-	-	-	-	-	-	-	-	-	-	-	-	-	-	-	50.6	-
1953	50.2	-0.8	50.3	0.2	50.4	0.2	50.5	0.2	50.7	0.4	50.8	0.2	50.8	0.0	51.0	0.4	51.4	0.8	51.4	0.0	51.5	0.2	51.3	-0.4
1954	51.2	-0.2	51.3	0.2	51.4	0.2	51.3	-0.2	51.3	0.0	51.3	0.0	51.3	0.0	50.8	-1.0	50.9	0.2	50.8	-0.2	50.7	-0.2	50.6	-0.2
1955	49.8	-1.6	50.0	0.4	50.1	0.2	49.7	-0.8	49.8	0.2	50.0	0.4	50.5	1.0	50.7	0.4	51.7	2.0	51.7	0.0	52.0	0.6	51.8	-0.4
1956	51.8	0.0	51.7	-0.2	51.9	0.4	52.0	0.2	51.8	-0.4	51.8	0.0	52.2	0.8	52.4	0.4	52.8	0.8	53.1	0.6	52.9	-0.4	53.1	0.4
1957	52.2	-1.7	52.4	0.4	53.0	1.1	52.9	-0.2	52.9	0.0	53.1	0.4	53.0	-0.2	53.1	0.2	54.0	1.7	53.9	-0.2	53.7	-0.4	53.7	0.0
1958	53.2	-0.9	53.1	-0.2	53.1	0.0	53.0	-0.2	53.0	0.0	53.2	0.4	53.5	0.6	53.1	-0.7	53.7	1.1	53.6	-0.2	53.7	0.2	53.4	-0.6
1959	53.1	-0.6	52.9	-0.4	52.8	-0.2	53.2	0.8	53.4	0.4	53.2	-0.4	53.7	0.9	53.9	0.4	54.8	1.7	54.8	0.0	54.8	0.0	54.8	0.0
1960	54.2	-1.1	54.4	0.4	54.5	0.2	54.0	-0.9	54.3	0.6	54.2	-0.2	54.7	0.9	54.8	0.2	55.0	0.4	55.1	0.2	55.0	-0.2	55.1	0.2
1961	54.3	-1.5	54.2	-0.2	54.2	0.0	54.2	0.0	54.1	-0.2	53.8	-0.6	54.1	0.6	53.8	-0.6	54.9	2.0	54.8	-0.2	54.7	-0.2	54.7	0.0
1962	53.7	-1.8	53.6	-0.2	53.9	0.6	53.8	-0.2	53.9	0.2	53.8	-0.2	53.9	0.2	53.7	-0.4	54.6	1.7	54.6	0.0	54.5	-0.2	54.7	0.4
1963	53.9	-1.5	53.9	0.0	54.1	0.4	54.2	0.2	54.1	-0.2	53.7	-0.7	54.0	0.6	53.8	-0.4	55.1	2.4	55.2	0.2	54.9	-0.5	55.1	0.4
1964	53.7	-2.5	54.1	0.7	54.7	1.1	54.7	0.0	54.7	0.0	54.5	-0.4	54.4	-0.2	54.0	-0.7	54.9	1.7	54.9	0.0	54.7	-0.4	54.8	0.2
1965	54.2	-1.1	54.1	-0.2	54.5	0.7	54.7	0.4	55.1	0.7	55.2	0.2	54.4	-1.4	54.7	0.6	55.7	1.8	55.9	0.4	55.9	0.0	56.1	0.4
1966	55.1	-1.8	55.0	-0.2	56.2	2.2	56.1	-0.2	56.3	0.4	56.5	0.4	55.6	-1.6	56.1	0.9	57.8	3.0	57.8	0.0	57.6	-0.3	57.9	0.5
1967	57.2	-1.2	57.4	0.3	57.8	0.7	57.9	0.2	58.4	0.9	58.6	0.3	58.0	-1.0	58.5	0.9	59.8	2.2	60.0	0.3	60.2	0.3	60.3	0.2
1968	58.6	-2.8	59.3	1.2	60.9	2.7	61.3	0.7	61.9	1.0	62.0	0.2	61.2	-1.3	61.5	0.5	63.2	2.8	63.7	0.8	63.8	0.2	63.9	0.2
1969	62.2	-2.7	63.6	2.3	64.2	0.9	64.0	-0.3	64.5	0.8	65.0	0.8	64.6	-0.6	63.2	-2.2	66.5	5.2	66.4	-0.2	66.7	0.5	66.7	0.0
1970	64.2	-3.7	64.7	0.8	66.1	2.2	65.5	-0.9	66.6	1.7	66.2	-0.6	65.0	-1.8	65.8	1.2	68.8	4.6	68.6	-0.3	68.5	-0.1	68.3	-0.3
1971	66.0	-3.4	67.6	2.4	68.5	1.3	68.3	-0.3	68.9	0.9	69.1	0.3	67.5	-2.3	68.1	0.9	70.7	3.8	70.6	-0.1	70.8	0.3	70.7	-0.1
1972	68.3	-3.4	69.7	2.0	70.2	0.7	69.9	-0.4	70.0	0.1	69.9	-0.1	68.0	-2.7	68.2	0.3	72.0	5.6	72.0	0.0	72.4	0.6	72.4	0.0
1973	70.8	-2.2	71.9	1.6	73.7	2.5	73.8	0.1	74.1	0.4	73.8	-0.4	72.4	-1.9	73.2	1.1	75.1	2.6	74.9	-0.3	75.4	0.7	75.1	-0.4
1974	73.1	-2.7	74.8	2.3	76.0	1.6	76.9	1.2	77.1	0.3	77.7	0.8	76.5	-1.5	79.8	4.3	80.1	0.4	80.3	0.2	81.1	1.0	81.1	0.0
1975	78.5	-3.2	79.0	0.6	80.2	1.5	80.4	0.2	80.1	-0.4	79.6	-0.6	79.1	-0.6	80.2	1.4	81.7	1.9	81.5	-0.2	81.5	0.0	80.9	-0.7
1976	78.4	-3.1	79.5	1.4	80.1	0.8	79.7	-0.5	80.4	0.9	81.0	0.7	80.1	-1.1	81.6	1.9	83.4	2.2	82.9	-0.6	83.2	0.4	83.1	-0.1
1977	80.5	-3.1	81.5	1.2	82.8	1.6	82.7	-0.1	82.7	0.0	83.8	1.3	83.3	-0.6	84.3	1.2	85.9	1.9	84.6	-1.5	85.3	0.8	85.1	-0.2
1978	84.4	-0.8	84.6	0.2	84.5	-0.1	86.4	2.2	86.2	-0.2	86.9	0.8	86.9	0.0	86.6	-0.3	87.9	1.5	89.3	1.6	89.6	0.3	88.2	-1.6
1979	85.7	-2.8	87.9	2.6	89.4	1.7	88.8	-0.7	88.9	0.1	88.2	-0.8	88.5	0.3	88.6	0.1	91.8	3.6	91.9	0.1	93.6	1.8	93.3	-0.3
1980	91.5	-1.9	93.0	1.6	93.6	0.6	93.3	-0.3	94.4	1.2	95.7	1.4	95.5	-0.2	96.1	0.6	95.9	-0.2	97.6	1.8	97.0	-0.6	95.1	-2.0
1981	92.2	-3.0	90.8	-1.5	91.8	1.1	93.2	1.5	94.0	0.9	93.2	-0.9	94.9	1.8	99.0	4.3	101.4	2.4	100.7	-0.7	100.7	0.0	98.5	-2.2
1982	96.0	-2.5	97.2	1.2	95.4	-1.9	97.2	1.9	99.1	2.0	98.1	-1.0	95.0	-3.2	98.7	3.9	100.4	1.7	100.0	-0.4	99.3	-0.7	97.6	-1.7
1983	96.2	-1.4	94.9	-1.4	98.1	3.4	97.5	-0.6	98.7	1.2	96.6	-2.1	97.2	0.6	101.8	4.7	104.6	2.8	104.6	0.0	106.0	1.3	103.6	-2.3
1984	98.6	-4.8	96.4	-2.2	99.0	2.7	99.5	0.5	100.4	0.9	99.4	-1.0	101.9	2.5	105.0	3.0	106.5	1.4	106.3	-0.2	108.2	1.8	105.0	-3.0
1985	100.5	-4.3	103.3	2.8	105.4	2.0	106.2	0.8	105.6	-0.6	104.5	-1.0	104.5	0.0	105.3	0.8	108.5	3.0	108.1	-0.4	108.2	0.1	107.0	-1.1
1986	102.9	-3.8	103.1	0.2	101.4	-1.6	100.6	-0.8	100.8	0.2	99.9	-0.9	101.2	1.3	104.7	3.5	109.4	4.5	109.4	0.0	108.7	-0.6	107.3	-1.3
1987	104.5	-2.6	102.9	-1.5	108.4	5.3	108.8	0.4	109.1	0.3	107.2	-1.7	105.5	-1.6	112.3	6.4	113.9	1.4	114.8	0.8	114.0	-0.7	111.9	-1.8
1988	110.5	-1.3	110.8	0.3	115.0	3.8	114.7	-0.3	112.1	-2.3	115.2	2.8	114.6	-0.5	115.8	1.0	122.9	6.1	121.2	-1.4	120.3	-0.7	119.8	-0.4
1989	114.0	-4.8	112.0	-1.8	118.8	6.1	117.9	-0.8	115.1	-2.4	113.2	-1.7	117.4	3.7	118.2	0.7	119.3	0.9	124.5	4.4	122.8	-1.4	117.7	-4.2
1990	114.3	-2.9	121.4	6.2	126.4	4.1	130.4	3.2	130.0	-0.3	123.8	-4.8	120.1	-3.0	123.6	2.9	126.9	2.7	126.6	-0.2	127.8	0.9	123.1	-3.7
1991	117.1	-4.9	125.6	7.3	128.0	1.9	130.2	1.7	126.0	-3.2	122.7	-2.6	120.3	-2.0	126.8	5.4	128.1	1.0	129.1	0.8	130.2	0.9	123.6	-5.1
1992	120.0	-2.9	125.6	4.7	129.2	2.9	125.8	-2.6	125.2	-0.5	123.9	-1.0	124.4	0.4	132.3	6.4	130.2	-1.6	128.7	-1.2	124.1	-3.6	121.3	-2.3
1993	119.3	-1.6	131.1	9.9	135.4	3.3	133.0	-1.8	134.1	0.8	126.9	-5.4	128.5	1.3	133.2	3.7	134.2	0.8	133.7	-0.4	131.6	-1.6	125.5	-4.6
1994	125.9	0.3	132.9	5.6	136.4	2.6	132.6	-2.8	128.8	-2.9	128.4	-0.3	126.5	-1.5	133.0	5.1	132.2	-0.6	129.5	-2.0	129.9	0.3	124.3	-4.3
1995	124.3	0.0	126.6	1.9	128.9	1.8	128.6	-0.2	125.3	-2.6	122.0	-2.6	120.7	-1.1	124.0	2.7	129.6	4.5	129.7	0.1	123.8	-4.5	117.5	-5.1

Source: U.S. Department of Labor, Bureau of Labor Statistics, Division of Consumer Prices and Price Indexes. - indicates no data collected for period.

Chicago, IL-NW IN
Consumer Price Index - All Urban Consumers
Base 1982-1984 = 100
Transportation

For 1947-1995. Columns headed % show percentile change in the index from the previous period for which an index is available.

Year	Jan Index	%	Feb Index	%	Mar Index	%	Apr Index	%	May Index	%	Jun Index	%	Jul Index	%	Aug Index	%	Sep Index	%	Oct Index	%	Nov Index	%	Dec Index	%
1947	16.8	-	16.8	0.0	16.8	0.0	17.1	1.8	17.4	1.8	17.4	0.0	17.4	0.0	17.5	0.6	17.7	1.1	18.1	2.3	18.2	0.6	18.3	0.5
1948	18.6	1.6	18.6	0.0	18.6	0.0	18.6	0.0	19.3	3.8	19.3	0.0	21.2	9.8	21.5	1.4	21.6	0.5	21.6	0.0	21.6	0.0	21.6	0.0
1949	21.6	0.0	21.7	0.5	21.7	0.0	21.7	0.0	21.7	0.0	21.7	0.0	21.7	0.0	21.7	0.0	21.7	0.0	22.9	5.5	22.9	0.0	22.8	-0.4
1950	22.8	0.0	22.7	-0.4	22.6	-0.4	22.4	-0.9	22.4	0.0	22.4	0.0	22.5	0.4	22.8	1.3	22.6	-0.9	22.6	0.0	22.7	0.4	22.9	0.9
1951	22.9	0.0	23.0	0.4	23.3	1.3	23.3	0.0	23.3	0.0	23.3	0.0	23.8	2.1	24.6	3.4	24.8	0.8	24.9	0.4	25.1	0.8	24.4	-2.8
1952	25.2	3.3	25.3	0.4	25.3	0.0	25.3	0.0	25.4	0.4	26.5	4.3	26.5	0.0	26.6	0.4	26.6	0.0	26.6	0.0	26.6	0.0	26.6	0.0
1953	26.8	0.8	26.7	-0.4	26.7	0.0	26.6	-0.4	26.5	-0.4	26.6	0.4	26.7	0.4	26.7	0.0	26.6	-0.4	26.5	-0.4	26.4	-0.4	26.4	0.0
1954	26.6	0.8	26.4	-0.8	26.4	0.0	26.3	-0.4	26.6	1.1	26.7	0.4	26.6	-0.4	26.5	-0.4	26.5	0.0	25.4	-4.2	26.7	5.1	26.5	-0.7
1955	26.6	0.4	26.4	-0.8	26.5	0.4	25.8	-2.6	25.9	0.4	25.9	0.0	25.9	0.0	26.0	0.4	26.0	0.0	26.3	1.2	26.5	0.8	26.1	-1.5
1956	26.0	-0.4	26.1	0.4	26.0	-0.4	26.1	0.4	26.2	0.4	26.2	0.0	26.6	1.5	26.6	0.0	26.6	0.0	27.8	4.5	27.8	0.0	27.7	-0.4
1957	28.0	1.1	27.7	-1.1	27.8	0.4	27.8	0.0	27.7	-0.4	27.7	0.0	28.7	3.6	28.9	0.7	28.6	-1.0	28.5	-0.3	29.6	3.9	30.0	1.4
1958	30.1	0.3	29.7	-1.3	29.5	-0.7	29.4	-0.3	29.5	0.3	29.7	0.7	29.6	-0.3	29.8	0.7	29.8	0.0	30.4	2.0	30.6	0.7	30.9	1.0
1959	30.8	-0.3	30.7	-0.3	30.8	0.3	30.8	0.0	30.7	-0.3	30.6	-0.3	30.9	1.0	30.9	0.0	30.9	0.0	31.5	1.9	31.7	0.6	31.9	0.6
1960	31.5	-1.3	31.4	-0.3	31.2	-0.6	31.0	-0.6	30.8	-0.6	30.9	0.3	31.0	0.3	31.1	0.3	31.0	-0.3	31.4	1.3	31.2	-0.6	31.0	-0.6
1961	30.8	-0.6	30.7	-0.3	30.3	-1.3	30.5	0.7	30.5	0.0	30.2	-1.0	31.2	3.3	31.4	0.6	31.3	-0.3	31.8	1.6	31.3	-1.6	31.1	-0.6
1962	31.2	0.3	31.4	0.6	31.4	0.0	31.8	1.3	31.8	0.0	31.3	-1.6	31.0	-1.0	30.8	-0.6	31.8	3.2	31.8	0.0	31.8	0.0	31.7	-0.3
1963	31.4	-0.9	31.5	0.3	31.8	1.0	31.7	-0.3	32.0		31.9	-0.3	31.9	0.0	31.8	-0.3	31.5	-0.9	31.9	1.3	31.6	-0.9	31.9	0.9
1964	31.5	-1.3	31.4	-0.3	31.3	-0.3	31.3	0.0	31.8	1.6	31.9	0.3	32.1	0.6	32.0	-0.3	31.7	-0.9	31.9	0.6	32.2	0.9	32.2	0.0
1965	32.4	0.6	32.3	-0.3	32.4	0.3	32.7	0.9	32.8	0.3	32.7	-0.3	32.7	0.0	32.5	-0.6	32.3	-0.6	32.6	0.9	32.6	0.0	32.7	0.3
1966	32.4	-0.9	32.4	0.0	32.4	0.0	32.5	0.3	32.5	0.0	32.6	0.3	32.6	0.0	32.8	0.6	32.8	0.0	32.9	0.3	32.9	0.0	32.7	-0.6
1967	32.6	-0.3	33.0	1.2	33.0	0.0	33.1	0.3	33.3	0.6	33.3	0.0	33.5	0.6	33.5	0.0	33.8	0.9	33.9	0.3	34.8	2.7	34.6	-0.6
1968	34.7	0.3	34.7	0.0	34.9	0.6	35.0	0.3	34.9	-0.3	35.0	0.3	35.0	0.0	35.0	0.0	34.9	-0.3	35.2	0.9	35.3	0.3	36.0	2.0
1969	36.2	0.6	36.5	0.8	37.2	1.9	37.4	0.5	37.1	-0.8	37.3	0.5	37.3	0.0	37.3	0.0	37.2	-0.3	37.7	1.3	37.8	0.3	38.0	0.5
1970	38.4	1.1	38.1	-0.8	38.1	0.0	38.7	1.6	38.9	0.5	39.1	0.5	40.3	3.1	40.3	0.0	40.0	-0.7	41.2	3.0	41.7	1.2	42.0	0.7
1971	41.9	-0.2	42.2	0.7	42.0	-0.5	42.0	0.0	42.5	1.2	42.0	-1.2	42.3	0.7	42.5	0.5	42.2	-0.7	41.9	-0.7	41.8	-0.2	42.0	0.5
1972	41.5	-1.2	40.9	-1.4	40.9	0.0	41.2	0.7	41.6	1.0	41.5	-0.2	41.9	1.0	42.1	0.5	42.1	0.0	42.0	-0.2	42.1	0.2	42.1	0.0
1973	41.8	-0.7	41.8	0.0	42.0	0.5	42.4	1.0	42.9	1.2	43.2	0.7	43.2	0.0	43.0	-0.5	42.9	-0.2	43.5	1.4	43.6	0.2	44.0	0.9
1974	44.5	1.1	44.6	0.2	45.3	1.6	45.7	0.9	46.7	2.2	47.4	1.5	48.1	1.5	48.4	0.6	48.6	0.4	48.8	0.4	49.0	0.4	49.0	0.0
1975	48.5	-1.0	48.5	0.0	49.0	1.0	49.4	0.8	49.8	0.8	50.5	1.4	51.6	2.2	52.4	1.6	52.6	0.4	52.7	0.2	52.9	0.4	52.8	-0.2
1976	52.6	-0.4	53.4	1.5	53.8	0.7	54.3	0.9	55.4	2.0	56.2	1.4	56.7	0.9	57.2	0.9	57.8	1.0	58.3	0.9	58.9	1.0	58.8	-0.2
1977	59.0	0.3	59.6	1.0	60.0	0.7	60.9	1.5	61.4	0.8	61.6	0.3	61.5	-0.2	61.4	-0.2	61.0	-0.7	61.1	0.2	61.0	-0.2	61.2	0.3
1978	61.3	0.2	61.3	0.0	61.3	0.0	61.5	0.3	62.4	1.5	63.2	1.3	63.5	0.5	63.9	0.6	63.9	0.0	64.6	1.1	65.0	0.6	65.4	0.6
1979	66.0	0.9	66.5	0.8	67.2	1.1	68.6	2.1	69.9	1.9	71.5	2.3	72.7	1.7	73.8	1.5	74.7	1.2	75.7	1.3	76.3	0.8	77.4	1.4
1980	79.8	3.1	81.2	1.8	83.1	2.3	84.7	1.9	85.5	0.9	85.4	-0.1	85.2	-0.2	85.7	0.6	86.2	0.6	86.6	0.5	88.1	1.7	88.8	0.8
1981	91.1	2.6	92.5	1.5	93.4	1.0	93.6	0.2	94.4	0.9	95.0	0.6	96.6	1.7	96.7	0.1	97.3	0.6	98.3	1.0	98.9	0.6	99.2	0.3
1982	98.7	-0.5	97.7	-1.0	96.7	-1.0	96.3	-0.4	96.9	0.6	99.6	2.8	100.1	0.5	99.8	-0.3	98.6	-1.2	98.9	0.3	98.8	-0.1	98.0	-0.8
1983	97.4	-0.6	96.4	-1.0	95.4	-1.0	97.0	1.7	98.2	1.2	98.4	0.2	99.3	0.9	100.7	1.4	100.6	-0.1	101.6	1.0	101.8	0.2	101.3	-0.5
1984	101.3	0.0	100.9	-0.4	101.5	0.6	102.2	0.7	102.6	0.4	103.0	0.4	103.2	0.2	103.0	-0.2	103.0	0.0	103.8	0.8	103.8	0.0	103.6	-0.2
1985	103.6	0.0	103.3	-0.3	104.2	0.9	105.3	1.1	106.1	0.8	106.0	-0.1	106.3	0.3	105.7	-0.6	104.7	-0.9	105.3	0.6	106.6	1.2	106.6	0.0
1986	106.1	-0.5	104.8	-1.2	101.3	-3.3	99.2	-2.1	100.8	1.6	101.9	1.1	99.9	-2.0	98.9	-1.0	99.0	0.1	99.7	0.7	100.7	1.0	101.9	1.2
1987	103.4	1.5	103.3	-0.1	104.0	0.7	104.6	0.6	105.9	1.2	106.5	0.6	107.2	0.7	107.2	0.0	107.1	-0.1	108.1	0.9	108.1	0.0	107.7	-0.4
1988	107.0	-0.6	107.1	0.1	107.0	-0.1	107.5	0.5	106.6	-0.8	107.1	0.5	107.1	0.0	108.1	0.9	108.3	0.2	108.1	-0.2	109.0	0.8	108.6	-0.4
1989	109.3	0.6	109.5	0.2	109.9	0.4	112.1	2.0	113.7	1.4	114.0	0.3	112.8	-1.1	111.9	-0.8	111.6	-0.3	113.9	2.1	113.1	-0.7	113.1	0.0
1990	116.6	3.1	115.4	-1.0	114.3	-1.0	115.5	1.0	115.9	0.3	116.6	0.6	116.1	-0.4	118.9	2.4	119.8	0.8	124.5	3.9	125.3	0.6	125.5	0.2
1991	123.5	-1.6	121.7	-1.5	120.0	-1.4	119.3	-0.6	121.1	1.5	121.1	0.0	120.4	-0.6	120.4	0.0	120.6	0.2	121.1	0.4	122.5	1.2	122.1	-0.3

[Continued]

Chicago, IL-NW IN
Consumer Price Index - All Urban Consumers
Base 1982-1984 = 100
Transportation
[Continued]

For 1947-1995. Columns headed % show percentile change in the index from the previous period for which an index is available.

Year	Jan Index	%	Feb Index	%	Mar Index	%	Apr Index	%	May Index	%	Jun Index	%	Jul Index	%	Aug Index	%	Sep Index	%	Oct Index	%	Nov Index	%	Dec Index	%
1992	121.9	-0.2	120.7	-1.0	120.6	-0.1	121.9	1.1	123.1	1.0	123.2	0.1	123.6	0.3	122.6	-0.8	122.8	0.2	125.6	2.3	126.3	0.6	125.6	-0.6
1993	124.9	-0.6	125.0	0.1	124.8	-0.2	126.2	1.1	127.4	1.0	126.8	-0.5	126.6	-0.2	125.4	-0.9	125.6	0.2	127.0	1.1	127.7	0.6	126.6	-0.9
1994	125.7	-0.7	126.7	0.8	126.9	0.2	128.1	0.9	128.5	0.3	129.9	1.1	131.9	1.5	133.3	1.1	133.4	0.1	132.7	-0.5	133.7	0.8	133.0	-0.5
1995	133.2	0.2	133.0	-0.2	134.6	1.2	135.2	0.4	136.1	0.7	138.0	1.4	136.3	-1.2	135.2	-0.8	134.8	-0.3	135.9	0.8	134.8	-0.8	134.3	-0.4

Source: U.S. Department of Labor, Bureau of Labor Statistics, Division of Consumer Prices and Price Indexes. - indicates no data collected for period.

Chicago, IL-NW IN
Consumer Price Index - Urban Wage Earners
Base 1982-1984 = 100
Transportation

For 1947-1995. Columns headed % show percentile change in the index from the previous period for which an index is available.

Year	Jan Index	%	Feb Index	%	Mar Index	%	Apr Index	%	May Index	%	Jun Index	%	Jul Index	%	Aug Index	%	Sep Index	%	Oct Index	%	Nov Index	%	Dec Index	%
1947	16.5	-	16.5	0.0	16.6	0.6	16.8	1.2	17.2	2.4	17.2	0.0	17.2	0.0	17.3	0.6	17.5	1.2	17.8	1.7	17.9	0.6	18.0	0.6
1948	18.3	1.7	18.3	0.0	18.3	0.0	18.3	0.0	19.0	3.8	19.0	0.0	20.9	10.0	21.1	1.0	21.2	0.5	21.2	0.0	21.2	0.0	21.2	0.0
1949	21.2	0.0	21.3	0.5	21.3	0.0	21.4	0.5	21.4	0.0	21.3	-0.5	21.3	0.0	21.3	0.0	21.3	0.0	22.5	5.6	22.5	0.0	22.4	-0.4
1950	22.4	0.0	22.4	0.0	22.3	-0.4	22.0	-1.3	22.0	0.0	22.1	0.5	22.1	0.0	22.4	1.4	22.3	-0.4	22.3	0.0	22.3	0.0	22.5	0.9
1951	22.5	0.0	22.6	0.4	23.0	1.8	23.0	0.0	23.0	0.0	23.0	0.0	23.4	1.7	24.2	3.4	24.4	0.8	24.5	0.4	24.7	0.8	24.0	-2.8
1952	24.7	2.9	24.9	0.8	24.9	0.0	24.9	0.0	24.9	0.0	26.1	4.8	26.1	0.0	26.1	0.0	26.1	0.0	26.1	0.0	26.1	0.0	26.1	0.0
1953	26.3	0.8	26.3	0.0	26.2	-0.4	26.2	0.0	26.1	-0.4	26.2	0.4	26.3	0.4	26.3	0.0	26.2	-0.4	26.1	-0.4	26.0	-0.4	26.0	0.0
1954	26.2	0.8	26.0	-0.8	26.0	0.0	25.9	-0.4	26.2	1.2	26.3	0.4	26.2	-0.4	26.1	-0.4	26.1	0.0	25.0	-4.2	26.2	4.8	26.1	-0.4
1955	26.2	0.4	26.0	-0.8	26.0	0.0	25.3	-2.7	25.5	0.8	25.5	0.0	25.4	-0.4	25.5	0.4	25.5	0.0	25.9	1.6	26.1	0.8	25.7	-1.5
1956	25.6	-0.4	25.6	0.0	25.5	-0.4	25.6	0.4	25.8	0.8	25.8	0.0	26.1	1.2	26.2	0.4	26.2	0.0	27.3	4.2	27.3	0.0	27.3	0.0
1957	27.5	0.7	27.3	-0.7	27.4	0.4	27.3	-0.4	27.2	-0.4	27.2	0.0	28.3	4.0	28.4	0.4	28.1	-1.1	28.0	-0.4	29.2	4.3	29.5	1.0
1958	29.6	0.3	29.2	-1.4	29.0	-0.7	29.0	0.0	29.0	0.0	29.2	0.7	29.1	-0.3	29.3	0.7	29.4	0.3	29.9	1.7	30.1	0.7	30.4	1.0
1959	30.3	-0.3	30.2	-0.3	30.3	0.3	30.3	0.0	30.2	-0.3	30.1	-0.3	30.4	1.0	30.4	0.0	30.4	0.0	31.0	2.0	31.2	0.6	31.3	0.3
1960	30.9	-1.3	30.9	0.0	30.7	-0.6	30.5	-0.7	30.3	-0.7	30.4	0.3	30.5	0.3	30.6	0.3	30.5	-0.3	30.8	1.0	30.7	-0.3	30.5	-0.7
1961	30.3	-0.7	30.2	-0.3	29.8	-1.3	30.0	0.7	30.0	0.0	29.7	-1.0	30.7	3.4	30.8	0.3	30.8	0.0	31.3	1.6	30.8	-1.6	30.5	-1.0
1962	30.7	0.7	30.8	0.3	30.9	0.3	31.3	1.3	31.3	0.0	30.8	-1.6	30.5	-1.0	30.3	-0.7	31.2	3.0	31.3	0.3	31.2	-0.3	31.2	0.0
1963	30.8	-1.3	30.9	0.3	31.3	1.3	31.2	-0.3	31.5	1.0	31.4	-0.3	31.4	0.0	31.3	-0.3	31.0	-1.0	31.4	1.3	31.0	-1.3	31.3	1.0
1964	31.0	-1.0	30.8	-0.6	30.8	0.0	30.7	-0.3	31.3	2.0	31.4	0.3	31.6	0.6	31.4	-0.6	31.2	-0.6	31.4	0.6	31.6	0.6	31.6	0.0
1965	31.9	0.9	31.8	-0.3	31.8	0.0	32.2	1.3	32.2	0.0	32.2	0.0	32.2	0.0	32.0	0.0	31.8	-0.6	32.1	0.9	32.1	0.0	32.2	0.3
1966	31.9	-0.9	31.9	0.0	31.8	-0.3	31.9	0.3	32.0	0.3	32.1	0.3	32.1	0.0	32.3	0.6	32.2	-0.3	32.3	0.3	32.3	0.0	32.2	-0.3
1967	32.1	-0.3	32.4	0.9	32.5	0.3	32.6	0.3	32.7	0.3	32.8	0.3	32.9	0.3	33.0	0.3	33.3	0.9	33.3	0.0	34.2	2.7	34.1	-0.3
1968	34.2	0.3	34.2	0.0	34.3	0.3	34.4	0.3	34.3	-0.3	34.4	0.3	34.5	0.3	34.4	-0.3	34.4	0.0	34.6	0.6	34.7	0.3	35.4	2.0
1969	35.6	0.6	35.9	0.8	36.6	1.9	36.8	0.5	36.5	-0.8	36.7	0.5	36.7	0.0	36.7	0.0	36.6	-0.3	37.1	1.4	37.1	0.0	37.4	0.8
1970	37.8	1.1	37.5	-0.8	37.4	-0.3	38.0	1.6	38.2	0.5	38.4	0.5	39.6	3.1	39.6	0.0	39.4	-0.5	40.5	2.8	41.0	1.2	41.3	0.7
1971	41.2	-0.2	41.5	0.7	41.3	-0.5	41.3	0.0	41.8	1.2	41.3	-1.2	41.6	0.7	41.8	0.5	41.5	-0.7	41.2	-0.7	41.1	-0.2	41.3	0.5
1972	40.8	-1.2	40.2	-1.5	40.2	0.0	40.5	0.7	40.9	1.0	40.8	-0.2	41.2	1.0	41.4	0.5	41.4	0.0	41.3	-0.2	41.4	0.2	41.4	0.0
1973	41.1	-0.7	41.1	0.0	41.3	0.5	41.7	1.0	42.2	1.2	42.5	0.7	42.5	0.0	42.3	-0.5	42.2	-0.2	42.8	1.4	42.9	0.2	43.3	0.9
1974	43.8	1.2	43.8	0.0	44.6	1.8	45.0	0.9	45.9	2.0	46.6	1.5	47.3	1.5	47.6	0.6	47.8	0.4	48.0	0.4	48.2	0.4	48.2	0.0
1975	47.7	-1.0	47.7	0.0	48.2	1.0	48.6	0.8	49.0	0.8	49.7	1.4	50.8	2.2	51.6	1.6	51.8	0.4	51.8	0.0	52.1	0.6	52.0	-0.2
1976	51.7	-0.6	52.6	1.7	52.9	0.6	53.4	0.9	54.5	2.1	55.3	1.5	55.8	0.9	56.2	0.7	56.9	1.2	57.3	0.7	57.9	1.0	57.8	-0.2
1977	58.1	0.5	58.6	0.9	59.0	0.7	59.9	1.5	60.4	0.8	60.6	0.3	60.5	-0.2	60.4	-0.2	60.0	-0.7	60.1	0.2	60.0	-0.2	60.2	0.3
1978	60.3	0.2	60.3	0.0	60.4	0.2	60.5	0.2	61.2	1.2	62.0	1.3	62.4	0.6	62.7	0.5	62.8	0.2	63.6	1.3	63.9	0.5	64.4	0.8
1979	65.0	0.9	65.6	0.9	66.4	1.2	67.8	2.1	69.3	2.2	71.0	2.5	72.4	2.0	73.6	1.7	74.4	1.1	75.1	0.9	76.0	1.2	77.0	1.3
1980	79.1	2.7	80.6	1.9	82.3	2.1	84.2	2.3	84.8	0.7	84.9	0.1	85.0	0.1	85.3	0.4	85.5	0.2	85.8	0.4	87.6	2.1	88.0	0.5
1981	90.7	3.1	92.2	1.7	93.0	0.9	93.9	1.0	94.5	0.6	94.9	0.4	96.4	1.6	96.6	0.2	97.2	0.6	98.4	1.2	98.9	0.5	99.7	0.8
1982	99.3	-0.4	98.1	-1.2	97.2	-0.9	96.5	-0.7	97.3	0.8	100.1	2.9	100.6	0.5	100.3	-0.3	98.9	-1.4	99.2	0.3	99.0	-0.2	98.0	-1.0
1983	97.3	-0.7	96.1	-1.2	95.2	-0.9	96.8	1.7	98.0	1.2	98.2	0.2	99.1	0.9	100.7	1.6	100.5	-0.2	101.5	1.0	101.7	0.2	101.2	-0.5
1984	101.1	-0.1	100.8	-0.3	101.2	0.4	102.1	0.9	102.4	0.3	102.8	0.4	103.0	0.2	102.7	-0.3	102.8	0.1	103.6	0.8	103.6	0.0	103.3	-0.3
1985	103.2	-0.1	102.9	-0.3	103.9	1.0	104.8	0.9	105.6	0.8	105.5	-0.1	105.7	0.2	105.1	-0.6	103.9	-1.1	104.6	0.7	106.0	1.3	106.0	0.0
1986	105.3	-0.7	103.9	-1.3	100.0	-3.8	97.8	-2.2	99.4	1.6	100.5	1.1	98.3	-2.2	97.3	-1.0	97.3	0.0	98.1	0.8	99.2	1.1	100.1	0.9
1987	101.9	1.8	101.7	-0.2	102.4	0.7	102.9	0.5	104.0	1.1	104.7	0.7	105.3	0.6	105.3	0.0	105.3	0.0	106.3	0.9	106.0	-0.3	105.7	-0.3
1988	105.2	-0.5	105.3	0.1	105.1	-0.2	105.3	0.2	105.4	0.1	105.9	0.5	106.1	0.2	107.2	1.0	107.4	0.2	107.2	-0.2	107.9	0.7	107.6	-0.3
1989	108.1	0.5	108.3	0.2	108.6	0.3	111.0	2.2	112.7	1.5	113.1	0.4	111.9	-1.1	110.9	-0.9	110.4	-0.5	112.8	2.2	112.0	-0.7	112.0	0.0
1990	115.4	3.0	114.4	-0.9	112.9	-1.3	114.0	1.0	114.4	0.4	115.1	0.6	114.5	-0.5	117.5	2.6	118.3	0.7	122.8	3.8	123.4	0.5	123.5	0.1
1991	121.4	-1.7	119.6	-1.5	117.8	-1.5	117.5	-0.3	119.3	1.5	119.4	0.1	118.6	-0.7	118.8	0.2	118.8	0.0	119.4	0.5	120.6	1.0	120.1	-0.4

[Continued]

Chicago, IL-NW IN
Consumer Price Index - Urban Wage Earners
Base 1982-1984 = 100
Transportation
[Continued]

For 1947-1995. Columns headed % show percentile change in the index from the previous period for which an index is available.

Year	Jan Index	%	Feb Index	%	Mar Index	%	Apr Index	%	May Index	%	Jun Index	%	Jul Index	%	Aug Index	%	Sep Index	%	Oct Index	%	Nov Index	%	Dec Index	%
1992	119.6	-0.4	118.5	-0.9	118.3	-0.2	119.5	1.0	121.2	1.4	121.8	0.5	121.8	0.0	121.0	-0.7	121.4	0.3	123.6	1.8	124.3	0.6	123.6	-0.6
1993	122.8	-0.6	122.9	0.1	122.6	-0.2	123.9	1.1	125.3	1.1	124.9	-0.3	124.4	-0.4	123.4	-0.8	123.4	0.0	124.9	1.2	125.4	0.4	124.4	-0.8
1994	123.5	-0.7	124.4	0.7	124.5	0.1	125.7	1.0	126.7	0.8	128.2	1.2	129.9	1.3	131.4	1.2	131.5	0.1	131.0	-0.4	132.0	0.8	131.5	-0.4
1995	131.5	0.0	131.5	0.0	132.6	0.8	133.5	0.7	134.7	0.9	136.1	1.0	134.6	-1.1	133.6	-0.7	133.2	-0.3	134.0	0.6	133.1	-0.7	133.3	0.2

Source: U.S. Department of Labor, Bureau of Labor Statistics, Division of Consumer Prices and Price Indexes. - indicates no data collected for period.

Chicago, IL-NW IN
Consumer Price Index - All Urban Consumers
Base 1982-1984 = 100
Medical Care

For 1947-1995. Columns headed % show percentile change in the index from the previous period for which an index is available.

Year	Jan Index	%	Feb Index	%	Mar Index	%	Apr Index	%	May Index	%	Jun Index	%	Jul Index	%	Aug Index	%	Sep Index	%	Oct Index	%	Nov Index	%	Dec Index	%
1947	11.7	-	11.7	0.0	11.9	1.7	12.0	0.8	12.1	0.8	12.2	0.8	12.2	0.0	12.4	1.6	12.4	0.0	12.4	0.0	12.4	0.0	12.5	0.8
1948	12.7	1.6	12.7	0.0	12.7	0.0	12.8	0.8	12.9	0.8	12.9	0.0	12.9	0.0	13.0	0.8	13.0	0.0	13.0	0.0	13.3	2.3	13.3	0.0
1949	13.4	0.8	13.4	0.0	13.6	1.5	13.6	0.0	13.6	0.0	13.6	0.0	13.6	0.0	13.6	0.0	13.5	-0.7	13.5	0.0	13.5	0.0	13.5	0.0
1950	13.5	0.0	13.5	0.0	13.5	0.0	13.5	0.0	13.5	0.0	13.5	0.0	13.5	0.0	13.6	0.7	14.2	4.4	14.2	0.0	14.2	0.0	14.3	0.7
1951	14.3	0.0	14.3	0.0	14.4	0.7	14.5	0.7	14.5	0.0	14.5	0.0	14.5	0.0	14.5	0.0	14.7	1.4	14.7	0.0	14.8	0.7	14.8	0.0
1952	14.8	0.0	14.8	0.0	14.9	0.7	14.9	0.0	14.9	0.0	14.9	0.0	14.9	0.0	14.9	0.0	14.9	0.0	14.9	0.0	14.9	0.0	15.0	0.7
1953	15.0	0.0	15.0	0.0	15.0	0.0	15.4	2.7	15.4	0.0	15.4	0.0	15.6	1.3	15.6	0.0	15.6	0.0	15.7	0.6	15.8	0.6	15.8	0.0
1954	15.8	0.0	15.8	0.0	15.8	0.0	15.8	0.0	15.8	0.0	15.8	0.0	15.8	0.0	15.8	0.0	15.8	0.0	16.2	2.5	16.2	0.0	16.2	0.0
1955	16.4	1.2	16.4	0.0	16.4	0.0	16.5	0.6	16.5	0.0	16.5	0.0	16.5	0.0	16.5	0.0	16.5	0.0	16.6	0.6	17.2	3.6	17.2	0.0
1956	17.4	1.2	17.4	0.0	17.4	0.0	17.6	1.1	17.6	0.0	17.5	-0.6	17.6	0.6	17.6	0.0	17.6	0.0	17.7	0.6	17.8	0.6	17.8	0.0
1957	17.9	0.6	17.9	0.0	18.0	0.6	18.2	1.1	18.2	0.0	18.2	0.0	18.2	0.0	18.2	0.0	18.2	0.0	18.8	3.3	18.9	0.5	18.9	0.0
1958	19.3	2.1	19.3	0.0	19.3	0.0	19.4	0.5	19.4	0.0	19.4	0.0	19.4	0.0	19.4	0.0	19.4	0.0	19.5	0.5	19.5	0.0	19.5	0.0
1959	19.5	0.0	20.1	3.1	20.1	0.0	20.4	1.5	20.4	0.0	20.4	0.0	20.4	0.0	20.4	0.0	20.4	0.0	20.5	0.5	20.5	0.0	20.6	0.5
1960	20.7	0.5	21.5	3.9	21.5	0.0	21.6	0.5	21.6	0.0	21.6	0.0	21.4	-0.9	21.4	0.0	21.4	0.0	21.7	1.4	21.7	0.0	21.7	0.0
1961	21.9	0.9	21.9	0.0	21.9	0.0	21.9	0.0	21.9	0.0	21.9	0.0	21.9	0.0	21.9	0.0	21.9	0.0	22.3	1.8	22.3	0.0	22.3	0.0
1962	22.6	1.3	22.6	0.0	22.6	0.0	22.7	0.4	22.7	0.0	22.7	0.0	22.7	0.0	22.7	0.0	22.7	0.0	22.9	0.9	22.9	0.0	22.9	0.0
1963	24.1	5.2	24.1	0.0	24.1	0.0	24.2	0.4	24.3	0.4	24.3	0.0	24.4	0.4	24.4	0.0	24.4	0.0	24.5	0.4	24.5	0.0	24.5	0.0
1964	24.6	0.4	24.6	0.0	24.6	0.0	24.6	0.0	24.6	0.0	24.6	0.0	24.8	0.8	24.8	0.0	24.7	-0.4	24.8	0.4	24.9	0.4	24.9	0.0
1965	24.9	0.0	25.0	0.4	25.0	0.0	25.0	0.0	25.0	0.0	25.1	0.4	25.2	0.4	25.2	0.0	25.2	0.0	25.3	0.4	25.3	0.0	25.4	0.4
1966	25.5	0.4	25.6	0.4	25.6	0.0	25.6	0.0	25.7	0.4	25.8	0.4	25.9	0.4	26.0	0.4	26.3	1.2	26.4	0.4	26.5	0.4	26.7	0.8
1967	26.9	0.7	27.0	0.4	27.5	1.9	27.5	0.0	27.7	0.7	27.8	0.4	28.1	1.1	28.3	0.7	28.6	1.1	28.6	0.0	28.7	0.3	28.8	0.3
1968	29.0	0.7	29.3	1.0	29.4	0.3	29.6	0.7	29.5	-0.3	29.5	0.0	29.5	0.0	29.6	0.3	29.7	0.3	29.8	0.3	30.1	1.0	30.3	0.7
1969	30.4	0.3	30.6	0.7	30.7	0.3	31.3	2.0	31.4	0.3	31.5	0.3	31.5	0.0	31.6	0.3	32.0	1.3	31.9	-0.3	32.1	0.6	32.1	0.0
1970	32.3	0.6	32.5	0.6	33.0	1.5	33.1	0.3	33.2	0.3	33.2	0.0	33.3	0.3	33.8	1.5	34.2	1.2	34.5	0.9	34.6	0.3	34.8	0.6
1971	35.2	1.1	35.6	1.1	35.7	0.3	35.7	0.0	35.9	0.6	36.0	0.3	36.1	0.3	36.3	0.6	36.3	0.0	36.0	-0.8	36.0	0.0	36.1	0.3
1972	36.2	0.3	36.4	0.6	36.4	0.0	36.5	0.3	36.7	0.5	36.7	0.0	36.8	0.3	36.9	0.3	36.9	0.0	37.2	0.8	37.4	0.5	37.4	0.0
1973	37.6	0.5	37.6	0.0	37.8	0.5	37.8	0.0	38.0	0.5	38.0	0.0	38.2	0.5	38.2	0.0	38.6	1.0	39.2	1.6	39.3	0.3	39.3	0.0
1974	39.7	1.0	40.1	1.0	40.4	0.7	40.4	0.0	41.0	1.5	42.1	2.7	42.3	0.5	42.7	0.9	43.2	1.2	43.5	0.7	43.9	0.9	44.4	1.1
1975	45.0	1.4	45.3	0.7	45.8	1.1	45.9	0.2	46.2	0.7	47.0	1.7	47.7	1.5	48.3	1.3	48.7	0.8	49.2	1.0	48.8	-0.8	49.3	1.0
1976	49.7	0.8	50.6	1.8	51.5	1.8	51.8	0.6	52.2	0.8	52.5	0.6	53.2	1.3	53.5	0.6	54.0	0.9	54.3	0.6	54.8	0.9	55.1	0.5
1977	55.7	1.1	56.5	1.4	56.7	0.4	57.1	0.7	57.4	0.5	57.9	0.9	58.3	0.7	58.6	0.5	59.1	0.9	59.5	0.7	59.6	0.2	59.7	0.2
1978	60.4	1.2	60.7	0.5	60.9	0.3	61.3	0.7	61.5	0.3	61.6	0.2	62.2	1.0	62.1	-0.2	62.3	0.3	63.6	2.1	64.4	1.3	64.5	0.2
1979	65.4	1.4	65.4	0.0	65.5	0.2	65.9	0.6	67.1	1.8	67.1	0.0	68.4	1.9	68.5	0.1	68.6	0.1	68.7	0.1	69.0	0.4	71.5	3.6
1980	72.8	1.8	73.8	1.4	74.3	0.7	75.8	2.0	76.3	0.7	76.5	0.3	77.2	0.9	77.5	0.4	77.6	0.1	77.8	0.3	77.8	0.0	78.6	1.0
1981	80.1	1.9	80.7	0.7	81.2	0.6	82.8	2.0	83.1	0.4	84.6	1.8	84.9	0.4	86.1	1.4	86.2	0.1	86.6	0.5	87.0	0.5	88.0	1.1
1982	87.9	-0.1	88.8	1.0	89.3	0.6	90.2	1.0	90.6	0.4	91.8	1.3	93.0	1.3	93.3	0.3	93.5	0.2	94.3	0.9	95.7	1.5	97.2	1.6
1983	98.7	1.5	99.4	0.7	99.8	0.4	100.2	0.4	100.3	0.1	100.8	0.5	101.4	0.6	101.4	0.0	102.4	1.0	102.6	0.2	102.7	0.1	103.1	0.4
1984	104.6	1.5	105.1	0.5	105.1	0.0	105.1	0.0	105.0	-0.1	106.8	1.7	107.8	0.9	107.6	-0.2	107.7	0.1	108.8	1.0	108.9	0.1	109.3	0.4
1985	109.9	0.5	110.0	0.1	111.4	1.3	111.7	0.3	112.3	0.5	112.6	0.3	112.7	0.1	113.3	0.5	114.6	1.1	114.7	0.1	115.1	0.3	115.2	0.1
1986	116.3	1.0	117.1	0.7	118.0	0.8	118.7	0.6	119.2	0.4	119.5	0.3	121.0	1.3	121.1	0.1	122.0	0.7	122.6	0.5	122.7	0.1	123.1	0.3
1987	124.4	1.1	125.7	1.0	125.9	0.2	126.3	0.3	127.6	1.0	129.4	1.4	130.6	0.9	130.9	0.2	132.0	0.8	132.3	0.2	132.7	0.3	132.9	0.2
1988	134.2	1.0	134.8	0.4	135.6	0.6	135.9	0.2	136.4	0.4	137.4	0.7	139.9	1.8	139.5	-0.3	140.4	0.6	140.9	0.4	140.5	-0.3	140.8	0.2
1989	142.1	0.9	143.7	1.1	144.7	0.7	144.9	0.1	146.0	0.8	147.2	0.8	150.2	2.0	152.1	1.3	153.9	1.2	155.2	0.8	155.3	0.1	155.6	0.2
1990	156.2	0.4	157.6	0.9	158.9	0.8	160.2	0.8	161.5	0.8	162.0	0.3	164.3	1.4	165.3	0.6	166.8	0.9	167.4	0.4	168.0	0.4	168.2	0.1
1991	170.2	1.2	172.9	1.6	175.0	1.2	175.7	0.4	176.4	0.4	176.9	0.3	179.2	1.3	179.7	0.3	181.3	0.9	181.3	0.0	183.0	0.9	183.7	0.4

[Continued]

Chicago, IL-NW IN
Consumer Price Index - All Urban Consumers
Base 1982-1984 = 100
Medical Care

[Continued]

For 1947-1995. Columns headed % show percentile change in the index from the previous period for which an index is available.

Year	Jan Index	%	Feb Index	%	Mar Index	%	Apr Index	%	May Index	%	Jun Index	%	Jul Index	%	Aug Index	%	Sep Index	%	Oct Index	%	Nov Index	%	Dec Index	%
1992	185.1	0.8	186.9	1.0	189.4	1.3	189.5	0.1	189.9	0.2	190.2	0.2	191.3	0.6	191.7	0.2	193.1	0.7	192.9	-0.1	194.0	0.6	194.7	0.4
1993	198.4	1.9	199.3	0.5	200.5	0.6	201.0	0.2	202.1	0.5	203.1	0.5	204.8	0.8	205.3	0.2	205.3	0.0	205.4	0.0	205.7	0.1	206.2	0.2
1994	209.6	1.6	210.8	0.6	211.1	0.1	211.1	0.0	211.6	0.2	212.9	0.6	214.5	0.8	214.2	-0.1	215.0	0.4	215.2	0.1	215.5	0.1	217.0	0.7
1995	220.8	1.8	221.7	0.4	221.9	0.1	222.3	0.2	223.2	0.4	222.6	-0.3	223.7	0.5	224.5	0.4	224.5	0.0	225.2	0.3	225.4	0.1	224.2	-0.5

Source: U.S. Department of Labor, Bureau of Labor Statistics, Division of Consumer Prices and Price Indexes. - indicates no data collected for period.

Chicago, IL-NW IN
Consumer Price Index - Urban Wage Earners
Base 1982-1984 = 100
Medical Care

For 1947-1995. Columns headed % show percentile change in the index from the previous period for which an index is available.

Year	Jan Index	%	Feb Index	%	Mar Index	%	Apr Index	%	May Index	%	Jun Index	%	Jul Index	%	Aug Index	%	Sep Index	%	Oct Index	%	Nov Index	%	Dec Index	%
1947	11.5	-	11.5	0.0	11.7	1.7	11.8	0.9	11.9	0.8	12.0	0.8	12.0	0.0	12.2	1.7	12.2	0.0	12.2	0.0	12.2	0.0	12.3	0.8
1948	12.5	1.6	12.5	0.0	12.5	0.0	12.6	0.8	12.7	0.8	12.7	0.0	12.7	0.0	12.8	0.8	12.8	0.0	12.8	0.0	13.1	2.3	13.1	0.0
1949	13.2	0.8	13.2	0.0	13.4	1.5	13.4	0.0	13.4	0.0	13.3	-0.7	13.3	0.0	13.3	0.0	13.3	0.0	13.3	0.0	13.2	-0.8	13.2	0.0
1950	13.2	0.0	13.2	0.0	13.3	0.8	13.3	0.0	13.3	0.0	13.3	0.0	13.3	0.0	13.3	0.0	14.0	5.3	14.0	0.0	14.0	0.0	14.1	0.7
1951	14.1	0.0	14.1	0.0	14.2	0.7	14.3	0.7	14.3	0.0	14.3	0.0	14.3	0.0	14.3	0.0	14.4	0.7	14.4	0.0	14.6	1.4	14.6	0.0
1952	14.6	0.0	14.6	0.0	14.6	0.0	14.7	0.7	14.7	0.0	14.7	0.0	14.7	0.0	14.7	0.0	14.7	0.0	14.7	0.0	14.7	0.0	14.8	0.7
1953	14.8	0.0	14.8	0.0	14.8	0.0	15.1	2.0	15.2	0.7	15.2	0.0	15.3	0.7	15.3	0.0	15.3	0.0	15.5	1.3	15.5	0.0	15.5	0.0
1954	15.5	0.0	15.5	0.0	15.5	0.0	15.5	0.0	15.5	0.0	15.5	0.0	15.5	0.0	15.5	0.0	15.5	0.0	16.0	3.2	16.0	0.0	16.0	0.0
1955	16.1	0.6	16.1	0.0	16.1	0.0	16.2	0.6	16.2	0.0	16.3	0.6	16.3	0.0	16.3	0.0	16.3	0.0	16.3	0.0	16.9	3.7	16.9	0.0
1956	17.1	1.2	17.1	0.0	17.1	0.0	17.3	1.2	17.3	0.0	17.3	0.0	17.3	0.0	17.3	0.0	17.3	0.0	17.4	0.6	17.5	0.6	17.5	0.0
1957	17.6	0.6	17.6	0.0	17.7	0.6	17.9	1.1	17.9	0.0	17.9	0.0	17.9	0.0	17.9	0.0	17.9	0.0	18.5	3.4	18.6	0.5	18.6	0.0
1958	19.0	2.2	19.0	0.0	19.0	0.0	19.0	0.0	19.0	0.0	19.0	0.0	19.0	0.0	19.0	0.0	19.1	0.5	19.2	0.5	19.2	0.0	19.2	0.0
1959	19.2	0.0	19.7	2.6	19.7	0.0	20.1	2.0	20.1	0.0	20.1	0.0	20.1	0.0	20.1	0.0	20.1	0.0	20.1	0.0	20.1	0.0	20.2	0.5
1960	20.3	0.5	21.2	4.4	21.2	0.0	21.3	0.5	21.3	0.0	21.3	0.0	21.1	-0.9	21.1	0.0	21.1	0.0	21.3	0.9	21.3	0.0	21.3	0.0
1961	21.5	0.9	21.5	0.0	21.5	0.0	21.5	0.0	21.6	0.5	21.6	0.0	21.5	-0.5	21.5	0.0	21.5	0.0	21.9	1.9	21.9	0.0	21.9	0.0
1962	22.2	1.4	22.2	0.0	22.2	0.0	22.3	0.5	22.3	0.0	22.3	0.0	22.4	0.4	22.4	0.0	22.4	0.0	22.6	0.9	22.6	0.0	22.6	0.0
1963	23.7	4.9	23.7	0.0	23.7	0.0	23.9	0.8	23.9	0.0	23.9	0.0	24.0	0.4	24.0	0.0	24.0	0.0	24.1	0.4	24.1	0.0	24.1	0.0
1964	24.2	0.4	24.2	0.0	24.2	0.0	24.2	0.0	24.2	0.0	24.2	0.0	24.4	0.8	24.4	0.0	24.3	-0.4	24.4	0.4	24.5	0.4	24.5	0.0
1965	24.5	0.0	24.6	0.4	24.6	0.0	24.6	0.0	24.6	0.0	24.7	0.4	24.8	0.4	24.8	0.0	24.8	0.0	24.9	0.4	24.9	0.0	25.0	0.4
1966	25.1	0.4	25.1	0.0	25.1	0.0	25.2	0.4	25.3	0.4	25.3	0.0	25.5	0.8	25.5	0.0	25.8	1.2	25.9	0.4	26.1	0.8	26.3	0.8
1967	26.4	0.4	26.6	0.8	27.0	1.5	27.1	0.4	27.2	0.4	27.4	0.7	27.6	0.7	27.8	0.7	28.1	1.1	28.1	0.0	28.2	0.4	28.4	0.7
1968	28.5	0.4	28.8	1.1	29.0	0.7	29.1	0.3	29.0	-0.3	29.0	0.0	29.1	0.3	29.1	0.0	29.2	0.3	29.3	0.3	29.6	1.0	29.9	1.0
1969	29.9	0.0	30.1	0.7	30.2	0.3	30.8	2.0	30.9	0.3	31.0	0.3	31.0	0.0	31.1	0.3	31.5	1.3	31.4	-0.3	31.6	0.6	31.6	0.0
1970	31.8	0.6	32.0	0.6	32.5	1.6	32.6	0.3	32.7	0.3	32.7	0.0	32.8	0.3	33.2	1.2	33.7	1.5	33.9	0.6	34.0	0.3	34.3	0.9
1971	34.6	0.9	35.0	1.2	35.2	0.6	35.2	0.0	35.4	0.6	35.4	0.0	35.6	0.6	35.7	0.3	35.7	0.0	35.4	-0.8	35.4	0.0	35.5	0.3
1972	35.7	0.6	35.8	0.3	35.9	0.3	35.9	0.0	36.1	0.6	36.1	0.0	36.2	0.3	36.3	0.3	36.3	0.0	36.6	0.8	36.8	0.5	36.8	0.0
1973	37.0	0.5	37.0	0.0	37.2	0.5	37.2	0.0	37.4	0.5	37.4	0.0	37.6	0.5	37.6	0.0	37.9	0.8	38.6	1.8	38.7	0.3	38.7	0.0
1974	39.0	0.8	39.4	1.0	39.8	1.0	39.8	0.0	40.3	1.3	41.5	3.0	41.6	0.2	42.0	1.0	42.5	1.2	42.8	0.7	43.2	0.9	43.7	1.2
1975	44.3	1.4	44.6	0.7	45.1	1.1	45.2	0.2	45.5	0.7	46.3	1.8	46.9	1.3	47.5	1.3	47.9	0.8	48.4	1.0	48.0	-0.8	48.5	1.0
1976	48.9	0.8	49.8	1.8	50.7	1.8	51.0	0.6	51.4	0.8	51.7	0.6	52.4	1.4	52.6	0.4	53.2	1.1	53.4	0.4	53.9	0.9	54.2	0.6
1977	54.8	1.1	55.6	1.5	55.7	0.2	56.2	0.9	56.5	0.5	57.0	0.9	57.4	0.7	57.7	0.5	58.1	0.7	58.5	0.7	58.6	0.2	58.8	0.3
1978	59.2	0.7	59.5	0.5	59.8	0.5	60.3	0.8	60.6	0.5	60.8	0.3	61.5	1.2	61.5	0.0	61.6	0.2	62.9	2.1	63.9	1.6	64.2	0.5
1979	65.3	1.7	65.4	0.2	65.7	0.5	66.0	0.5	66.7	1.1	66.7	0.0	67.7	1.5	67.9	0.3	68.4	0.7	69.2	1.2	69.4	0.3	72.1	3.9
1980	73.9	2.5	74.6	0.9	74.7	0.1	76.1	1.9	76.7	0.8	76.5	-0.3	77.7	1.6	77.9	0.3	78.3	0.5	78.6	0.4	78.8	0.3	79.2	0.5
1981	80.6	1.8	81.5	1.1	81.9	0.5	82.9	1.2	83.6	0.8	84.4	1.0	84.8	0.5	84.8	0.0	85.8	1.2	86.3	0.6	87.6	1.5	88.1	0.6
1982	87.9	-0.2	88.8	1.0	89.3	0.6	90.1	0.9	90.6	0.6	91.8	1.3	93.0	1.3	93.3	0.3	93.4	0.1	94.3	1.0	95.6	1.4	97.1	1.6
1983	98.6	1.5	99.3	0.7	99.8	0.5	100.1	0.3	100.3	0.2	100.8	0.5	101.4	0.6	101.4	0.0	102.4	1.0	102.6	0.2	102.7	0.1	103.2	0.5
1984	104.7	1.5	105.2	0.5	105.2	0.0	105.2	0.0	105.1	-0.1	106.8	1.6	107.8	0.9	107.5	-0.3	107.7	0.2	108.7	0.9	108.9	0.2	109.2	0.3
1985	109.8	0.5	109.9	0.1	111.3	1.3	111.5	0.2	112.2	0.6	112.5	0.3	112.6	0.1	113.2	0.5	114.5	1.1	114.6	0.1	115.0	0.3	115.2	0.2
1986	116.2	0.9	117.0	0.7	117.8	0.7	118.5	0.6	119.1	0.5	119.3	0.2	120.8	1.3	120.8	0.0	121.8	0.8	122.3	0.4	122.4	0.1	122.8	0.3
1987	124.0	1.0	125.3	1.0	125.5	0.2	125.9	0.3	127.2	1.0	128.8	1.3	130.3	1.2	130.6	0.2	131.8	0.9	132.1	0.2	132.4	0.2	132.7	0.2
1988	134.1	1.1	134.9	0.6	135.5	0.4	136.1	0.4	136.6	0.4	137.4	0.6	140.4	2.2	140.1	-0.2	141.0	0.6	141.5	0.4	141.2	-0.2	141.5	0.2
1989	142.9	1.0	144.8	1.3	145.7	0.6	145.8	0.1	147.1	0.9	148.2	0.7	151.6	2.3	153.2	1.1	155.5	1.5	156.7	0.8	156.7	0.0	157.0	0.2
1990	157.5	0.3	158.8	0.8	159.8	0.6	161.4	1.0	162.7	0.8	163.1	0.2	165.8	1.7	166.6	0.5	168.2	1.0	168.6	0.2	169.2	0.4	169.3	0.1
1991	171.6	1.4	174.6	1.7	176.5	1.1	176.8	0.2	177.7	0.5	178.1	0.2	180.6	1.4	181.2	0.3	182.9	0.9	182.8	-0.1	184.8	1.1	185.5	0.4

[Continued]

Chicago, IL-NW IN
Consumer Price Index - Urban Wage Earners
Base 1982-1984 = 100
Medical Care
[Continued]

For 1947-1995. Columns headed % show percentile change in the index from the previous period for which an index is available.

Year	Jan Index	%	Feb Index	%	Mar Index	%	Apr Index	%	May Index	%	Jun Index	%	Jul Index	%	Aug Index	%	Sep Index	%	Oct Index	%	Nov Index	%	Dec Index	%
1992	186.9	0.8	188.6	0.9	190.7	1.1	190.8	0.1	191.2	0.2	191.7	0.3	193.0	0.7	193.5	0.3	195.2	0.9	194.9	-0.2	195.8	0.5	196.7	0.5
1993	200.7	2.0	201.7	0.5	202.9	0.6	203.4	0.2	204.4	0.5	205.3	0.4	207.4	1.0	207.9	0.2	207.9	0.0	208.0	0.0	208.3	0.1	208.7	0.2
1994	212.4	1.8	213.4	0.5	213.6	0.1	213.6	0.0	214.1	0.2	215.5	0.7	217.3	0.8	217.1	-0.1	217.8	0.3	217.9	0.0	218.3	0.2	219.9	0.7
1995	223.9	1.8	225.1	0.5	225.2	0.0	225.7	0.2	226.6	0.4	226.1	-0.2	227.4	0.6	228.4	0.4	228.4	0.0	229.1	0.3	229.3	0.1	228.3	-0.4

Source: U.S. Department of Labor, Bureau of Labor Statistics, Division of Consumer Prices and Price Indexes. - indicates no data collected for period.

Chicago, IL-NW IN
Consumer Price Index - All Urban Consumers
Base 1982-1984 = 100
Entertainment

For 1976-1995. Columns headed % show percentile change in the index from the previous period for which an index is available.

Year	Jan Index	%	Feb Index	%	Mar Index	%	Apr Index	%	May Index	%	Jun Index	%	Jul Index	%	Aug Index	%	Sep Index	%	Oct Index	%	Nov Index	%	Dec Index	%
1976	60.3	-	60.5	0.3	61.3	1.3	61.6	0.5	61.8	0.3	61.6	-0.3	61.8	0.3	61.9	0.2	62.0	0.2	62.5	0.8	62.8	0.5	62.8	0.0
1977	63.8	1.6	63.8	0.0	64.5	1.1	63.9	-0.9	64.3	0.6	64.3	0.0	64.2	-0.2	64.6	0.6	64.6	0.0	65.2	0.9	65.7	0.8	66.0	0.5
1978	66.7	1.1	67.0	0.4	67.2	0.3	67.4	0.3	67.4	0.0	67.2	-0.3	67.7	0.7	67.9	0.3	68.7	1.2	69.2	0.7	69.6	0.6	69.7	0.1
1979	70.4	1.0	71.8	2.0	73.1	1.8	72.9	-0.3	75.7	3.8	75.7	0.0	77.0	1.7	77.2	0.3	77.6	0.5	78.3	0.9	79.0	0.9	80.3	1.6
1980	80.2	-0.1	82.8	3.2	83.8	1.2	84.0	0.2	84.0	0.0	84.3	0.4	84.9	0.7	85.6	0.8	87.1	1.8	87.5	0.5	87.2	-0.3	87.6	0.5
1981	90.3	3.1	90.4	0.1	89.6	-0.9	91.6	2.2	91.7	0.1	92.1	0.4	92.2	0.1	93.1	1.0	94.4	1.4	93.2	-1.3	94.2	1.1	96.0	1.9
1982	97.1	1.1	97.5	0.4	97.0	-0.5	98.2	1.2	97.3	-0.9	98.0	0.7	98.8	0.8	98.7	-0.1	99.8	1.1	100.6	0.8	97.9	-2.7	99.6	1.7
1983	100.0	0.4	98.8	-1.2	98.6	-0.2	99.3	0.7	99.0	-0.3	99.3	0.3	99.7	0.4	99.2	-0.5	100.4	1.2	100.0	-0.4	100.2	0.2	100.2	0.0
1984	100.5	0.3	100.7	0.2	100.7	0.0	100.7	0.0	100.8	0.1	101.8	1.0	101.3	-0.5	102.0	0.7	104.3	2.3	104.4	0.1	103.1	-1.2	104.3	1.2
1985	104.5	0.2	105.7	1.1	105.2	-0.5	106.7	1.4	106.3	-0.4	105.5	-0.8	105.8	0.3	105.5	-0.3	103.2	-2.2	103.5	0.3	104.5	1.0	104.9	0.4
1986	107.6	2.6	108.2	0.6	108.5	0.3	108.6	0.1	108.2	-0.4	108.2	0.0	109.7	1.4	107.9	-1.6	111.4	3.2	112.8	1.3	113.8	0.9	113.3	-0.4
1987	114.1	0.7	113.9	-0.2	115.6	1.5	116.0	0.3	115.6	-0.3	115.6	0.0	116.3	0.6	115.3	-0.9	116.6	1.1	117.4	0.7	117.5	0.1	118.1	0.5
1988	118.9	0.7	119.0	0.1	120.3	1.1	121.1	0.7	120.3	-0.7	121.3	0.8	122.0	0.6	123.1	0.9	124.0	0.7	125.5	1.2	126.2	0.6	125.8	-0.3
1989	126.9	0.9	128.7	1.4	130.3	1.2	130.5	0.2	130.3	-0.2	132.4	1.6	133.3	0.7	131.3	-1.5	132.7	1.1	134.3	1.2	135.2	0.7	133.2	-1.5
1990	136.0	2.1	136.8	0.6	137.7	0.7	137.8	0.1	139.2	1.0	138.3	-0.6	139.0	0.5	139.9	0.6	140.3	0.3	141.2	0.6	141.3	0.1	142.5	0.8
1991	144.8	1.6	144.6	-0.1	144.4	-0.1	144.7	0.2	145.8	0.8	147.0	0.8	144.4	-1.8	146.5	1.5	148.4	1.3	147.1	-0.9	147.0	-0.1	146.2	-0.5
1992	147.3	0.8	146.9	-0.3	148.0	0.7	148.7	0.5	148.3	-0.3	148.1	-0.1	151.5	2.3	150.7	-0.5	151.3	0.4	151.2	-0.1	150.7	-0.3	150.3	-0.3
1993	151.0	0.5	152.7	1.1	152.9	0.1	153.9	0.7	152.4	-1.0	155.2	1.8	153.9	-0.8	153.4	-0.3	155.2	1.2	154.7	-0.3	154.8	0.1	156.6	1.2
1994	158.4	1.1	157.2	-0.8	159.0	1.1	159.6	0.4	160.3	0.4	158.9	-0.9	159.8	0.6	161.4	1.0	162.7	0.8	163.1	0.2	162.1	-0.6	157.9	-2.6
1995	159.1	0.8	160.2	0.7	160.0	-0.1	160.6	0.4	160.4	-0.1	160.0	-0.2	160.4	0.2	162.7	1.4	162.6	-0.1	160.4	-1.4	162.0	1.0	162.4	0.2

Source: U.S. Department of Labor, Bureau of Labor Statistics, Division of Consumer Prices and Price Indexes. - indicates no data collected for period.

Chicago, IL-NW IN
Consumer Price Index - Urban Wage Earners
Base 1982-1984 = 100
Entertainment

For 1976-1995. Columns headed % show percentile change in the index from the previous period for which an index is available.

Year	Jan Index	%	Feb Index	%	Mar Index	%	Apr Index	%	May Index	%	Jun Index	%	Jul Index	%	Aug Index	%	Sep Index	%	Oct Index	%	Nov Index	%	Dec Index	%
1976	53.4	-	53.5	0.2	54.3	1.5	54.6	0.6	54.7	0.2	54.5	-0.4	54.7	0.4	54.8	0.2	54.9	0.2	55.3	0.7	55.6	0.5	55.6	0.0
1977	56.5	1.6	56.5	0.0	57.1	1.1	56.6	-0.9	56.9	0.5	56.9	0.0	56.9	0.0	57.2	0.5	57.2	0.0	57.8	1.0	58.2	0.7	58.4	0.3
1978	58.8	0.7	59.4	1.0	59.4	0.0	59.3	-0.2	59.4	0.2	59.0	-0.7	59.6	1.0	59.7	0.2	60.1	0.7	60.4	0.5	60.9	0.8	60.8	-0.2
1979	60.9	0.2	61.8	1.5	63.3	2.4	63.3	0.0	66.5	5.1	68.3	2.7	69.3	1.5	69.5	0.3	69.5	0.0	70.3	1.2	71.0	1.0	72.3	1.8
1980	71.8	-0.7	74.1	3.2	74.7	0.8	75.0	0.4	75.3	0.4	76.9	2.1	76.8	-0.1	77.4	0.8	78.3	1.2	82.2	5.0	82.8	0.7	83.1	0.4
1981	84.9	2.2	85.4	0.6	84.6	-0.9	86.1	1.8	86.6	0.6	85.9	-0.8	86.4	0.6	87.5	1.3	86.8	-0.8	93.2	7.4	94.8	1.7	95.0	0.2
1982	96.4	1.5	96.4	0.0	96.0	-0.4	97.0	1.0	95.9	-1.1	96.8	0.9	97.7	0.9	97.6	-0.1	98.9	1.3	99.5	0.6	97.4	-2.1	98.9	1.5
1983	99.3	0.4	99.0	-0.3	98.9	-0.1	99.7	0.8	99.3	-0.4	99.8	0.5	100.0	0.2	99.5	-0.5	100.9	1.4	100.5	-0.4	100.7	0.2	100.8	0.1
1984	101.1	0.3	101.2	0.1	101.0	-0.2	101.4	0.4	101.5	0.1	102.4	0.9	101.8	-0.6	102.6	0.8	105.4	2.7	105.4	0.0	104.0	-1.3	105.3	1.3
1985	106.2	0.9	106.7	0.5	105.9	-0.7	107.5	1.5	107.2	-0.3	106.1	-1.0	106.4	0.3	106.1	-0.3	103.0	-2.9	103.5	0.5	105.0	1.4	105.5	0.5
1986	108.9	3.2	109.2	0.3	109.5	0.3	109.7	0.2	109.0	-0.6	109.0	0.0	110.5	1.4	108.4	-1.9	112.6	3.9	114.4	1.6	115.4	0.9	114.7	-0.6
1987	115.6	0.8	115.4	-0.2	117.5	1.8	118.0	0.4	117.9	-0.1	117.6	-0.3	118.3	0.6	117.4	-0.8	118.7	1.1	119.5	0.7	119.6	0.1	120.3	0.6
1988	120.9	0.5	121.1	0.2	122.4	1.1	123.2	0.7	122.6	-0.5	123.6	0.8	123.9	0.2	124.9	0.8	125.4	0.4	127.0	1.3	127.9	0.7	127.5	-0.3
1989	128.5	0.8	130.4	1.5	132.0	1.2	132.2	0.2	132.2	0.0	133.3	0.8	134.1	0.6	132.5	-1.2	134.0	1.1	135.3	1.0	136.2	0.7	134.3	-1.4
1990	137.0	2.0	137.6	0.4	138.6	0.7	139.0	0.3	140.1	0.8	139.1	-0.7	139.6	0.4	140.8	0.9	141.1	0.2	142.1	0.7	142.1	0.0	143.3	0.8
1991	145.1	1.3	144.9	-0.1	144.5	-0.3	145.2	0.5	146.0	0.6	147.0	0.7	143.8	-2.2	146.4	1.8	148.5	1.4	147.0	-1.0	147.0	0.0	146.2	-0.5
1992	147.3	0.8	146.9	-0.3	147.9	0.7	148.9	0.7	148.4	-0.3	148.2	-0.1	151.8	2.4	151.0	-0.5	151.6	0.4	151.1	-0.3	150.4	-0.5	150.0	-0.3
1993	150.9	0.6	152.4	1.0	152.6	0.1	153.7	0.7	152.2	-1.0	155.2	2.0	153.9	-0.8	153.3	-0.4	155.0	1.1	154.3	-0.5	154.4	0.1	156.2	1.2
1994	157.8	1.0	156.3	-1.0	158.1	1.2	158.7	0.4	159.6	0.6	158.3	-0.8	159.3	0.6	160.7	0.9	162.3	1.0	162.6	0.2	161.7	-0.6	157.0	-2.9
1995	158.7	1.1	159.6	0.6	159.5	-0.1	160.1	0.4	159.4	-0.4	158.8	-0.4	159.4	0.4	161.9	1.6	161.7	-0.1	159.5	-1.4	161.1	1.0	161.5	0.2

Source: U.S. Department of Labor, Bureau of Labor Statistics, Division of Consumer Prices and Price Indexes. - indicates no data collected for period.

Chicago, IL-NW IN
Consumer Price Index - All Urban Consumers
Base 1982-1984 = 100
Other Goods and Services

For 1976-1995. Columns headed % show percentile change in the index from the previous period for which an index is available.

Year	Jan Index	%	Feb Index	%	Mar Index	%	Apr Index	%	May Index	%	Jun Index	%	Jul Index	%	Aug Index	%	Sep Index	%	Oct Index	%	Nov Index	%	Dec Index	%
1976	56.7	-	56.9	0.4	57.2	0.5	57.3	0.2	57.4	0.2	57.8	0.7	57.8	0.0	57.9	0.2	58.6	1.2	59.0	0.7	59.8	1.4	59.9	0.2
1977	60.5	1.0	60.2	-0.5	60.8	1.0	61.0	0.3	61.2	0.3	61.4	0.3	62.0	1.0	62.2	0.3	63.5	2.1	64.3	1.3	64.3	0.0	64.4	0.2
1978	64.7	0.5	64.6	-0.2	64.3	-0.5	64.4	0.2	65.3	1.4	65.1	-0.3	65.7	0.9	65.4	-0.5	67.8	3.7	67.5	-0.4	67.4	-0.1	67.1	-0.4
1979	68.1	1.5	68.2	0.1	69.1	1.3	68.2	-1.3	69.0	1.2	68.5	-0.7	69.2	1.0	68.5	-1.0	71.5	4.4	71.3	-0.3	72.0	1.0	72.8	1.1
1980	72.8	0.0	73.6	1.1	74.1	0.7	74.4	0.4	74.7	0.4	75.8	1.5	75.6	-0.3	75.8	0.3	78.0	2.9	78.6	0.8	79.7	1.4	80.1	0.5
1981	80.5	0.5	81.1	0.7	81.5	0.5	82.8	1.6	84.0	1.4	84.2	0.2	84.4	0.2	84.9	0.6	87.2	2.7	87.7	0.6	87.8	0.1	88.4	0.7
1982	88.5	0.1	89.2	0.8	89.6	0.4	90.0	0.4	89.9	-0.1	90.4	0.6	90.6	0.2	90.7	0.1	94.7	4.4	95.3	0.6	96.5	1.3	97.0	0.5
1983	98.3	1.3	98.6	0.3	98.8	0.2	98.8	0.0	98.8	0.0	99.3	0.5	99.5	0.2	100.0	0.5	102.9	2.9	103.6	0.7	103.6	0.0	104.1	0.5
1984	104.9	0.8	105.8	0.9	105.8	0.0	105.6	-0.2	105.9	0.3	106.8	0.8	107.3	0.5	107.8	0.5	109.6	1.7	110.5	0.8	110.6	0.1	110.6	0.0
1985	112.2	1.4	113.3	1.0	113.1	-0.2	113.1	0.0	113.5	0.4	113.7	0.2	113.9	0.2	113.5	-0.4	117.5	3.5	117.8	0.3	118.1	0.3	121.4	2.8
1986	122.2	0.7	122.8	0.5	123.1	0.2	123.2	0.1	122.8	-0.3	123.1	0.2	124.5	1.1	124.0	-0.4	125.7	1.4	126.5	0.6	126.3	-0.2	126.4	0.1
1987	127.7	1.0	128.2	0.4	128.2	0.0	128.4	0.2	129.2	0.6	129.4	0.2	129.9	0.4	130.5	0.5	130.7	0.2	131.0	0.2	131.2	0.2	131.2	0.0
1988	132.6	1.1	134.9	1.7	135.4	0.4	135.6	0.1	135.6	0.0	135.8	0.1	136.8	0.7	137.7	0.7	142.7	3.6	143.1	0.3	143.2	0.1	143.0	-0.1
1989	144.7	1.2	147.2	1.7	147.9	0.5	148.0	0.1	148.6	0.4	152.5	2.6	155.1	1.7	156.8	1.1	157.9	0.7	158.7	0.5	159.0	0.2	160.3	0.8
1990	159.7	-0.4	160.7	0.6	161.1	0.2	161.5	0.2	162.2	0.4	162.8	0.4	163.1	0.2	164.3	0.7	167.0	1.6	167.8	0.5	170.2	1.4	171.3	0.6
1991	172.8	0.9	174.1	0.8	174.6	0.3	175.9	0.7	175.4	-0.3	175.5	0.1	177.3	1.0	178.3	0.6	184.9	3.7	185.5	0.3	187.0	0.8	186.8	-0.1
1992	186.7	-0.1	188.0	0.7	187.7	-0.2	188.7	0.5	189.9	0.6	189.4	-0.3	191.3	1.0	194.4	1.6	196.2	0.9	196.7	0.3	196.8	0.1	197.6	0.4
1993	198.2	0.3	196.4	-0.9	198.5	1.1	198.5	0.0	204.0	2.8	201.8	-1.1	204.5	1.3	204.8	0.1	206.6	0.9	204.9	-0.8	205.7	0.4	206.1	0.2
1994	206.6	0.2	205.4	-0.6	206.0	0.3	206.3	0.1	206.6	0.1	205.9	-0.3	207.3	0.7	209.0	0.8	211.9	1.4	213.4	0.7	213.5	0.0	214.0	0.2
1995	214.4	0.2	215.2	0.4	214.6	-0.3	214.7	0.0	214.9	0.1	216.1	0.6	216.6	0.2	217.1	0.2	219.3	1.0	219.4	0.0	219.5	0.0	219.6	0.0

Source: U.S. Department of Labor, Bureau of Labor Statistics, Division of Consumer Prices and Price Indexes. - indicates no data collected for period.

Chicago, IL-NW IN
Consumer Price Index - Urban Wage Earners
Base 1982-1984 = 100
Other Goods and Services

For 1976-1995. Columns headed % show percentile change in the index from the previous period for which an index is available.

Year	Jan Index	%	Feb Index	%	Mar Index	%	Apr Index	%	May Index	%	Jun Index	%	Jul Index	%	Aug Index	%	Sep Index	%	Oct Index	%	Nov Index	%	Dec Index	%
1976	58.2	-	58.5	0.5	58.8	0.5	58.9	0.2	59.0	0.2	59.4	0.7	59.3	-0.2	59.5	0.3	60.2	1.2	60.6	0.7	61.5	1.5	61.6	0.2
1977	62.2	1.0	61.9	-0.5	62.4	0.8	62.7	0.5	62.9	0.3	63.1	0.3	63.7	1.0	63.9	0.3	65.2	2.0	66.0	1.2	66.1	0.2	66.2	0.2
1978	66.3	0.2	66.5	0.3	66.5	0.0	67.2	1.1	67.2	0.0	67.7	0.7	68.5	1.2	68.7	0.3	69.6	1.3	69.8	0.3	69.9	0.1	70.0	0.1
1979	70.6	0.9	71.1	0.7	71.3	0.3	71.2	-0.1	71.2	0.0	70.9	-0.4	71.0	0.1	71.1	0.1	72.5	2.0	72.6	0.1	73.3	1.0	74.0	1.0
1980	74.9	1.2	75.7	1.1	76.0	0.4	76.4	0.5	77.0	0.8	78.2	1.6	78.3	0.1	78.4	0.1	80.0	2.0	80.2	0.2	80.9	0.9	81.2	0.4
1981	81.7	0.6	82.1	0.5	82.4	0.4	82.8	0.5	83.7	1.1	83.3	-0.5	84.1	1.0	85.4	1.5	87.7	2.7	88.2	0.6	88.3	0.1	88.4	0.1
1982	88.5	0.1	89.3	0.9	89.8	0.6	90.3	0.6	90.1	-0.2	90.6	0.6	90.8	0.2	90.9	0.1	94.1	3.5	94.9	0.9	96.3	1.5	96.9	0.6
1983	98.6	1.8	99.0	0.4	99.2	0.2	99.2	0.0	99.2	0.0	99.8	0.6	100.0	0.2	100.6	0.6	102.2	1.6	103.1	0.9	103.0	-0.1	103.6	0.6
1984	104.6	1.0	105.6	1.0	105.6	0.0	105.5	-0.1	105.9	0.4	106.7	0.8	107.4	0.7	108.0	0.6	109.4	1.3	110.4	0.9	110.5	0.1	110.5	0.0
1985	112.5	1.8	113.7	1.1	113.4	-0.3	113.5	0.1	113.8	0.3	114.1	0.3	114.3	0.2	114.0	-0.3	116.8	2.5	117.1	0.3	117.5	0.3	121.5	3.4
1986	122.7	1.0	123.3	0.5	123.8	0.4	123.9	0.1	123.4	-0.4	123.8	0.3	125.6	1.5	125.1	-0.4	126.0	0.7	126.8	0.6	126.6	-0.2	126.7	0.1
1987	128.1	1.1	128.6	0.4	128.5	-0.1	128.8	0.2	129.7	0.7	129.9	0.2	130.6	0.5	131.3	0.5	131.7	0.3	132.0	0.2	132.3	0.2	132.4	0.1
1988	134.5	1.6	135.6	0.8	136.1	0.4	136.4	0.2	136.5	0.1	136.7	0.1	138.2	1.1	138.9	0.5	141.9	2.2	142.4	0.4	142.6	0.1	142.5	-0.1
1989	144.8	1.6	146.6	1.2	147.5	0.6	147.6	0.1	148.1	0.3	152.3	2.8	156.2	2.6	158.6	1.5	158.7	0.1	159.9	0.8	160.2	0.2	162.2	1.2
1990	161.0	-0.7	162.5	0.9	163.0	0.3	163.3	0.2	164.3	0.6	165.3	0.6	165.6	0.2	166.7	0.7	168.5	1.1	169.3	0.5	171.9	1.5	173.5	0.9
1991	175.5	1.2	177.2	1.0	177.8	0.3	179.6	1.0	179.0	-0.3	179.8	0.4	181.7	1.1	182.6	0.5	187.4	2.6	187.7	0.2	190.1	1.3	189.9	-0.1
1992	189.8	-0.1	191.1	0.7	190.7	-0.2	192.6	1.0	194.0	0.7	193.4	-0.3	196.1	1.4	199.4	1.7	200.2	0.4	200.7	0.2	201.0	0.1	202.1	0.5
1993	203.1	0.5	200.5	-1.3	202.4	0.9	202.8	0.2	210.6	3.8	207.6	-1.4	210.8	1.5	210.7	-0.0	209.9	-0.4	207.6	-1.1	208.7	0.5	209.2	0.2
1994	209.7	0.2	208.4	-0.6	209.1	0.3	209.4	0.1	209.6	0.1	208.9	-0.3	210.1	0.6	211.6	0.7	213.5	0.9	214.7	0.6	214.9	0.1	215.5	0.3
1995	215.3	-0.1	216.2	0.4	215.2	-0.5	215.3	0.0	215.9	0.3	217.5	0.7	217.8	0.1	217.8	0.0	218.9	0.5	219.0	0.0	219.2	0.1	219.2	0.0

Source: U.S. Department of Labor, Bureau of Labor Statistics, Division of Consumer Prices and Price Indexes. - indicates no data collected for period.

Cincinnati, OH-KY-IN
Consumer Price Index - All Urban Consumers
Base 1982-1984 = 100
Annual Averages

For 1917-1995. Columns headed % show percentile change in the index from the previous period for which an index is available.

Year	All Items		Food & Beverage		Housing		Apparel & Upkeep		Trans- portation		Medical Care		Entertain- ment		Other Goods & Services	
	Index	%	Index	%	Index	%	Index	%	Index	%	Index	%	Index	%	Index	%
1917	-	-	-	-	-	-	-	-	-	-	-	-	-	-	-	-
1918	14.5	-	-	-	-	-	-	-	-	-	-	-	-	-	-	-
1919	16.9	16.6	-	-	-	-	-	-	-	-	-	-	-	-	-	-
1920	19.3	14.2	-	-	-	-	-	-	-	-	-	-	-	-	-	-
1921	16.5	-14.5	-	-	-	-	-	-	-	-	-	-	-	-	-	-
1922	15.5	-6.1	-	-	-	-	-	-	-	-	-	-	-	-	-	-
1923	15.9	2.6	-	-	-	-	-	-	-	-	-	-	-	-	-	-
1924	16.0	0.6	-	-	-	-	-	-	-	-	-	-	-	-	-	-
1925	16.8	5.0	-	-	-	-	-	-	-	-	-	-	-	-	-	-
1926	17.1	1.8	-	-	-	-	-	-	-	-	-	-	-	-	-	-
1927	16.8	-1.8	-	-	-	-	-	-	-	-	-	-	-	-	-	-
1928	16.7	-0.6	-	-	-	-	-	-	-	-	-	-	-	-	-	-
1929	16.9	1.2	-	-	-	-	-	-	-	-	-	-	-	-	-	-
1930	16.7	-1.2	-	-	-	-	-	-	-	-	-	-	-	-	-	-
1931	15.1	-9.6	-	-	-	-	-	-	-	-	-	-	-	-	-	-
1932	13.3	-11.9	-	-	-	-	-	-	-	-	-	-	-	-	-	-
1933	12.8	-3.8	-	-	-	-	-	-	-	-	-	-	-	-	-	-
1934	13.3	3.9	-	-	-	-	-	-	-	-	-	-	-	-	-	-
1935	13.7	3.0	-	-	-	-	-	-	-	-	-	-	-	-	-	-
1936	13.9	1.5	-	-	-	-	-	-	-	-	-	-	-	-	-	-
1937	14.3	2.9	-	-	-	-	-	-	-	-	-	-	-	-	-	-
1938	14.0	-2.1	-	-	-	-	-	-	-	-	-	-	-	-	-	-
1939	13.7	-2.1	-	-	-	-	-	-	-	-	-	-	-	-	-	-
1940	13.8	0.7	-	-	-	-	-	-	-	-	-	-	-	-	-	-
1941	14.5	5.1	-	-	-	-	-	-	-	-	-	-	-	-	-	-
1942	16.2	11.7	-	-	-	-	-	-	-	-	-	-	-	-	-	-
1943	17.1	5.6	-	-	-	-	-	-	-	-	-	-	-	-	-	-
1944	17.5	2.3	-	-	-	-	-	-	-	-	-	-	-	-	-	-
1945	17.8	1.7	-	-	-	-	-	-	-	-	-	-	-	-	-	-
1946	19.3	8.4	-	-	-	-	-	-	-	-	-	-	-	-	-	-
1947	22.4	16.1	-	-	-	-	-	-	20.6	-	11.8	-	-	-	-	-
1948	24.1	7.6	-	-	-	-	-	-	23.3	13.1	13.1	11.0	-	-	-	-
1949	23.7	-1.7	-	-	-	-	-	-	25.1	7.7	13.4	2.3	-	-	-	-
1950	23.9	0.8	-	-	-	-	-	-	25.6	2.0	13.5	0.7	-	-	-	-
1951	25.8	7.9	-	-	-	-	-	-	27.5	7.4	13.8	2.2	-	-	-	-
1952	26.3	1.9	-	-	-	-	-	-	29.2	6.2	14.9	8.0	-	-	-	-
1953	26.7	1.5	-	-	-	-	37.5	-	30.0	2.7	15.6	4.7	-	-	-	-
1954	26.7	0.0	-	-	-	-	37.2	-0.8	29.2	-2.7	16.0	2.6	-	-	-	-
1955	26.6	-0.4	-	-	-	-	37.6	1.1	28.2	-3.4	16.5	3.1	-	-	-	-
1956	27.1	1.9	-	-	-	-	38.5	2.4	28.4	0.7	17.5	6.1	-	-	-	-
1957	28.0	3.3	-	-	-	-	38.8	0.8	30.1	6.0	18.0	2.9	-	-	-	-
1958	28.6	2.1	-	-	-	-	39.1	0.8	30.8	2.3	19.1	6.1	-	-	-	-
1959	28.8	0.7	-	-	-	-	39.5	1.0	32.8	6.5	19.6	2.6	-	-	-	-
1960	29.1	1.0	-	-	-	-	40.1	1.5	33.1	0.9	20.0	2.0	-	-	-	-
1961	29.2	0.3	-	-	-	-	40.3	0.5	33.1	0.0	20.6	3.0	-	-	-	-

[Continued]

Cincinnati, OH-KY-IN
Consumer Price Index - All Urban Consumers
Base 1982-1984 = 100
Annual Averages
[Continued]

For 1917-1995. Columns headed % show percentile change in the index from the previous period for which an index is available.

Year	All Items		Food & Beverage		Housing		Apparel & Upkeep		Trans-portation		Medical Care		Entertain-ment		Other Goods & Services	
	Index	%	Index	%	Index	%	Index	%	Index	%	Index	%	Index	%	Index	%
1962	29.5	1.0	-	-	-	-	40.6	0.7	33.8	2.1	21.1	2.4	-	-	-	-
1963	29.8	1.0	-	-	-	-	41.0	1.0	34.0	0.6	21.8	3.3	-	-	-	-
1964	30.3	1.7	-	-	-	-	41.5	1.2	34.5	1.5	22.4	2.8	-	-	-	-
1965	30.5	0.7	-	-	-	-	41.8	0.7	34.5	0.0	23.9	6.7	-	-	-	-
1966	31.4	3.0	-	-	-	-	43.3	3.6	35.1	1.7	24.9	4.2	-	-	-	-
1967	32.3	2.9	-	-	-	-	45.0	3.9	35.9	2.3	26.7	7.2	-	-	-	-
1968	33.9	5.0	-	-	-	-	48.1	6.9	37.7	5.0	28.7	7.5	-	-	-	-
1969	35.5	4.7	-	-	-	-	51.2	6.4	38.8	2.9	31.1	8.4	-	-	-	-
1970	37.4	5.4	-	-	-	-	53.5	4.5	40.7	4.9	32.7	5.1	-	-	-	-
1971	39.0	4.3	-	-	-	-	55.0	2.8	43.0	5.7	35.2	7.6	-	-	-	-
1972	40.3	3.3	-	-	-	-	55.3	0.5	44.4	3.3	36.4	3.4	-	-	-	-
1973	42.7	6.0	-	-	-	-	57.6	4.2	44.3	-0.2	38.4	5.5	-	-	-	-
1974	47.3	10.8	-	-	-	-	61.6	6.9	47.7	7.7	42.4	10.4	-	-	-	-
1975	51.8	9.5	-	-	-	-	64.6	4.9	51.7	8.4	47.2	11.3	-	-	-	-
1976	55.0	6.2	60.1	-	50.8	-	68.8	6.5	56.0	8.3	52.6	11.4	67.1	-	55.8	-
1977	58.9	7.1	64.3	7.0	54.5	7.3	72.3	5.1	60.0	7.1	58.9	12.0	68.9	2.7	59.2	6.1
1978	64.3	9.2	71.1	10.6	60.4	10.8	77.7	7.5	62.5	4.2	65.5	11.2	72.5	5.2	62.7	5.9
1979	72.3	12.4	79.1	11.3	69.1	14.4	82.1	5.7	71.5	14.4	72.6	10.8	77.1	6.3	67.6	7.8
1980	82.1	13.6	85.9	8.6	80.1	15.9	89.1	8.5	84.1	17.6	79.2	9.1	83.7	8.6	74.2	9.8
1981	87.9	7.1	93.2	8.5	84.2	5.1	93.4	4.8	93.8	11.5	85.9	8.5	87.5	4.5	81.6	10.0
1982	94.9	8.0	97.0	4.1	93.6	11.2	97.6	4.5	97.3	3.7	93.6	9.0	94.8	8.3	90.1	10.4
1983	100.8	6.2	99.2	2.3	102.1	9.1	100.6	3.1	99.7	2.5	100.2	7.1	100.7	6.2	101.5	12.7
1984	104.3	3.5	103.8	4.6	104.2	2.1	101.7	1.1	103.0	3.3	106.3	6.1	104.5	3.8	108.4	6.8
1985	106.6	2.2	104.6	0.8	106.8	2.5	103.4	1.7	106.0	2.9	112.0	5.4	99.8	-4.5	115.5	6.5
1986	107.6	0.9	107.2	2.5	108.6	1.7	105.5	2.0	99.7	-5.9	117.7	5.1	103.8	4.0	120.9	4.7
1987	114.5	6.4	113.2	5.6	116.3	7.1	109.2	3.5	106.1	6.4	129.2	9.8	116.0	11.8	129.6	7.2
1988	119.0	3.9	117.1	3.4	120.7	3.8	116.6	6.8	107.6	1.4	138.0	6.8	122.3	5.4	138.0	6.5
1989	125.0	5.0	122.5	4.6	126.4	4.7	118.1	1.3	112.1	4.2	149.2	8.1	131.6	7.6	153.1	10.9
1990	131.7	5.4	130.3	6.4	131.4	4.0	124.3	5.2	118.7	5.9	163.0	9.2	139.2	5.8	164.3	7.3
1991	137.0	4.0	135.5	4.0	136.4	3.8	125.3	0.8	121.2	2.1	177.9	9.1	145.9	4.8	179.0	8.9
1992	141.1	3.0	139.2	2.7	139.9	2.6	126.2	0.7	123.2	1.7	190.7	7.2	149.4	2.4	192.0	7.3
1993	145.4	3.0	143.1	2.8	143.3	2.4	131.1	3.9	126.2	2.4	203.1	6.5	153.9	3.0	202.5	5.5
1994	148.6	2.2	147.0	2.7	144.8	1.0	131.0	-0.1	130.3	3.2	213.2	5.0	160.0	4.0	208.8	3.1
1995	153.3	3.2	151.3	2.9	150.6	4.0	126.3	-3.6	135.1	3.7	223.3	4.7	160.9	0.6	216.8	3.8

Source: U.S. Department of Labor, Bureau of Labor Statistics, Division of Consumer Prices and Price Indexes. - indicates no data collected for period.

Cincinnati, OH-KY-IN
Consumer Price Index - Urban Wage Earners
Base 1982-1984 = 100
Annual Averages

For 1917-1995. Columns headed % show percentile change in the index from the previous period for which an index is available.

Year	All Items		Food & Beverage		Housing		Apparel & Upkeep		Trans- portation		Medical Care		Entertain- ment		Other Goods & Services	
	Index	%	Index	%	Index	%	Index	%	Index	%	Index	%	Index	%	Index	%
1917	-	-	-	-	-	-	-	-	-	-	-	-	-	-	-	-
1918	14.6	-	-	-	-	-	-	-	-	-	-	-	-	-	-	-
1919	17.0	16.4	-	-	-	-	-	-	-	-	-	-	-	-	-	-
1920	19.5	14.7	-	-	-	-	-	-	-	-	-	-	-	-	-	-
1921	16.7	-14.4	-	-	-	-	-	-	-	-	-	-	-	-	-	-
1922	15.7	-6.0	-	-	-	-	-	-	-	-	-	-	-	-	-	-
1923	16.0	1.9	-	-	-	-	-	-	-	-	-	-	-	-	-	-
1924	16.1	0.6	-	-	-	-	-	-	-	-	-	-	-	-	-	-
1925	17.0	5.6	-	-	-	-	-	-	-	-	-	-	-	-	-	-
1926	17.2	1.2	-	-	-	-	-	-	-	-	-	-	-	-	-	-
1927	16.9	-1.7	-	-	-	-	-	-	-	-	-	-	-	-	-	-
1928	16.8	-0.6	-	-	-	-	-	-	-	-	-	-	-	-	-	-
1929	17.0	1.2	-	-	-	-	-	-	-	-	-	-	-	-	-	-
1930	16.8	-1.2	-	-	-	-	-	-	-	-	-	-	-	-	-	-
1931	15.2	-9.5	-	-	-	-	-	-	-	-	-	-	-	-	-	-
1932	13.4	-11.8	-	-	-	-	-	-	-	-	-	-	-	-	-	-
1933	12.9	-3.7	-	-	-	-	-	-	-	-	-	-	-	-	-	-
1934	13.4	3.9	-	-	-	-	-	-	-	-	-	-	-	-	-	-
1935	13.8	3.0	-	-	-	-	-	-	-	-	-	-	-	-	-	-
1936	14.0	1.4	-	-	-	-	-	-	-	-	-	-	-	-	-	-
1937	14.4	2.9	-	-	-	-	-	-	-	-	-	-	-	-	-	-
1938	14.1	-2.1	-	-	-	-	-	-	-	-	-	-	-	-	-	-
1939	13.8	-2.1	-	-	-	-	-	-	-	-	-	-	-	-	-	-
1940	13.9	0.7	-	-	-	-	-	-	-	-	-	-	-	-	-	-
1941	14.6	5.0	-	-	-	-	-	-	-	-	-	-	-	-	-	-
1942	16.3	11.6	-	-	-	-	-	-	-	-	-	-	-	-	-	-
1943	17.2	5.5	-	-	-	-	-	-	-	-	-	-	-	-	-	-
1944	17.6	2.3	-	-	-	-	-	-	-	-	-	-	-	-	-	-
1945	18.0	2.3	-	-	-	-	-	-	-	-	-	-	-	-	-	-
1946	19.4	7.8	-	-	-	-	-	-	-	-	11.3	-	-	-	-	-
1947	22.6	16.5	-	-	-	-	-	-	20.8	-	12.4	9.7	-	-	-	-
1948	24.3	7.5	-	-	-	-	-	-	23.5	13.0	12.8	3.2	-	-	-	-
1949	23.9	-1.6	-	-	-	-	-	-	25.4	8.1	12.8	0.0	-	-	-	-
1950	24.1	0.8	-	-	-	-	-	-	25.9	2.0	13.2	3.1	-	-	-	-
1951	25.9	7.5	-	-	-	-	-	-	27.7	6.9	14.2	7.6	-	-	-	-
1952	26.5	2.3	-	-	-	-	-	-	29.5	6.5	14.9	4.9	-	-	-	-
1953	26.9	1.5	-	-	-	-	36.4	-	30.3	2.7	15.2	2.0	-	-	-	-
1954	26.9	0.0	-	-	-	-	36.2	-0.5	29.5	-2.6	15.7	3.3	-	-	-	-
1955	26.8	-0.4	-	-	-	-	36.5	0.8	28.5	-3.4	16.7	6.4	-	-	-	-
1956	27.3	1.9	-	-	-	-	37.4	2.5	28.7	0.7	17.2	3.0	-	-	-	-
1957	28.2	3.3	-	-	-	-	37.7	0.8	30.4	5.9	18.2	5.8	-	-	-	-
1958	28.8	2.1	-	-	-	-	37.9	0.5	31.1	2.3	18.7	2.7	-	-	-	-
1959	29.0	0.7	-	-	-	-	38.3	1.1	33.2	6.8	19.0	1.6	-	-	-	-
1960	29.3	1.0	-	-	-	-	38.9	1.6	33.4	0.6	19.6	3.2	-	-	-	-
1961	29.4	0.3	-	-	-	-	39.1	0.5	33.5	0.3						

[Continued]

Cincinnati, OH-KY-IN
Consumer Price Index - Urban Wage Earners
Base 1982-1984 = 100
Annual Averages
[Continued]

For 1917-1995. Columns headed % show percentile change in the index from the previous period for which an index is available.

Year	All Items		Food & Beverage		Housing		Apparel & Upkeep		Trans- portation		Medical Care		Entertain- ment		Other Goods & Services	
	Index	%	Index	%	Index	%	Index	%	Index	%	Index	%	Index	%	Index	%
1962	29.7	1.0	-	-	-	-	39.4	0.8	34.1	1.8	20.1	2.6	-	-	-	-
1963	30.0	1.0	-	-	-	-	39.8	1.0	34.3	0.6	20.8	3.5	-	-	-	-
1964	30.5	1.7	-	-	-	-	40.3	1.3	34.8	1.5	21.4	2.9	-	-	-	-
1965	30.7	0.7	-	-	-	-	40.6	0.7	34.9	0.3	22.7	6.1	-	-	-	-
1966	31.6	2.9	-	-	-	-	42.0	3.4	35.5	1.7	23.8	4.8	-	-	-	-
1967	32.5	2.8	-	-	-	-	43.7	4.0	36.2	2.0	25.4	6.7	-	-	-	-
1968	34.1	4.9	-	-	-	-	46.7	6.9	38.1	5.2	27.4	7.9	-	-	-	-
1969	35.7	4.7	-	-	-	-	49.7	6.4	39.2	2.9	29.7	8.4	-	-	-	-
1970	37.6	5.3	-	-	-	-	52.0	4.6	41.1	4.8	31.2	5.1	-	-	-	-
1971	39.3	4.5	-	-	-	-	53.4	2.7	43.5	5.8	33.5	7.4	-	-	-	-
1972	40.6	3.3	-	-	-	-	53.7	0.6	44.8	3.0	34.7	3.6	-	-	-	-
1973	43.0	5.9	-	-	-	-	55.9	4.1	44.7	-0.2	36.6	5.5	-	-	-	-
1974	47.6	10.7	-	-	-	-	59.8	7.0	48.2	7.8	40.4	10.4	-	-	-	-
1975	52.2	9.7	-	-	-	-	62.7	4.8	52.2	8.3	45.0	11.4	-	-	-	-
1976	55.4	6.1	59.8	-	51.7	-	66.8	6.5	56.5	8.2	50.1	11.3	69.7	-	55.6	-
1977	59.3	7.0	64.1	7.2	55.5	7.4	70.2	5.1	60.6	7.3	56.1	12.0	71.6	2.7	59.0	6.1
1978	64.9	9.4	71.1	10.9	61.7	11.2	75.8	8.0	63.0	4.0	62.0	10.5	75.5	5.4	63.1	6.9
1979	73.3	12.9	79.7	12.1	70.8	14.7	81.0	6.9	72.0	14.3	70.2	13.2	78.3	3.7	68.3	8.2
1980	83.2	13.5	86.3	8.3	82.4	16.4	86.6	6.9	84.5	17.4	78.2	11.4	83.9	7.2	74.6	9.2
1981	89.2	7.2	92.9	7.6	86.3	4.7	93.1	7.5	94.0	11.2	85.6	9.5	88.5	5.5	82.3	10.3
1982	96.4	8.1	97.2	4.6	96.5	11.8	97.5	4.7	97.4	3.6	93.5	9.2	95.2	7.6	90.2	9.6
1983	100.8	4.6	99.2	2.1	102.0	5.7	100.9	3.5	99.7	2.4	100.2	7.2	100.7	5.8	101.7	12.7
1984	102.8	2.0	103.6	4.4	101.5	-0.5	101.6	0.7	102.9	3.2	106.3	6.1	104.0	3.3	108.2	6.4
1985	105.2	2.3	104.3	0.7	104.6	3.1	102.5	0.9	105.7	2.7	112.0	5.4	96.8	-6.9	114.7	6.0
1986	105.8	0.6	106.8	2.4	106.3	1.6	104.5	2.0	99.7	-5.7	117.4	4.8	100.3	3.6	119.9	4.5
1987	111.1	5.0	113.3	6.1	109.7	3.2	109.4	4.7	104.3	4.6	128.9	9.8	118.0	17.6	130.3	8.7
1988	115.3	3.8	117.2	3.4	113.6	3.6	116.1	6.1	106.3	1.9	138.4	7.4	124.2	5.3	138.5	6.3
1989	121.2	5.1	122.6	4.6	118.9	4.7	117.6	1.3	111.0	4.4	150.4	8.7	132.9	7.0	153.6	10.9
1990	127.8	5.4	130.4	6.4	123.8	4.1	124.5	5.9	117.2	5.6	164.3	9.2	140.0	5.3	166.2	8.2
1991	132.9	4.0	135.7	4.1	128.4	3.7	125.6	0.9	119.3	1.8	179.4	9.2	146.0	4.3	182.4	9.7
1992	136.7	2.9	139.2	2.6	131.7	2.6	125.9	0.2	121.2	1.6	192.4	7.2	149.5	2.4	195.9	7.4
1993	140.9	3.1	143.3	2.9	135.0	2.5	130.5	3.7	124.0	2.3	205.6	6.9	153.7	2.8	207.0	5.7
1994	144.0	2.2	147.2	2.7	136.3	1.0	130.0	-0.4	128.4	3.5	215.9	5.0	159.4	3.7	211.3	2.1
1995	148.4	3.1	151.6	3.0	141.4	3.7	125.1	-3.8	133.5	4.0	227.0	5.1	160.1	0.4	217.3	2.8

Source: U.S. Department of Labor, Bureau of Labor Statistics, Division of Consumer Prices and Price Indexes. - indicates no data collected for period.

Cincinnati, OH-KY-IN
Consumer Price Index - All Urban Consumers
Base 1982-1984 = 100
All Items

For 1917-1995. Columns headed % show percentile change in the index from the previous period for which an index is available.

Year	Jan Index	%	Feb Index	%	Mar Index	%	Apr Index	%	May Index	%	Jun Index	%	Jul Index	%	Aug Index	%	Sep Index	%	Oct Index	%	Nov Index	%	Dec Index	%
1917	-	-	-	-	-	-	-	-	-	-	-	-	-	-	-	-	-	-	-	-	-	-	13.5	-
1918	-	-	-	-	-	-	-	-	-	-	-	-	-	-	-	-	-	-	-	-	-	-	15.7	16.3
1919	-	-	-	-	-	-	-	-	-	-	16.5	5.1	-	-	-	-	-	-	-	-	-	-	18.2	10.3
1920	-	-	-	-	-	-	-	-	-	-	20.4	12.1	-	-	-	-	-	-	-	-	-	-	18.3	-10.3
1921	-	-	-	-	-	-	-	-	16.6	-9.3	-	-	-	-	-	-	16.4	-1.2	-	-	-	-	15.8	-3.7
1922	-	-	-	-	15.4	-2.5	-	-	-	-	15.7	1.9	-	-	-	-	15.4	-1.9	-	-	-	-	15.5	0.6
1923	-	-	-	-	15.7	1.3	-	-	-	-	16.0	1.9	-	-	-	-	16.1	0.6	-	-	-	-	16.0	-0.6
1924	-	-	-	-	16.1	0.6	-	-	-	-	16.1	0.0	-	-	-	-	16.1	0.0	-	-	-	-	16.1	0.0
1925	-	-	-	-	-	-	-	-	-	-	17.0	5.6	-	-	-	-	-	-	-	-	-	-	17.1	0.6
1926	-	-	-	-	-	-	-	-	-	-	17.1	0.0	-	-	-	-	-	-	-	-	-	-	17.0	-0.6
1927	-	-	-	-	-	-	-	-	-	-	17.4	2.4	-	-	-	-	-	-	-	-	-	-	16.6	-4.6
1928	-	-	-	-	-	-	-	-	-	-	16.7	0.6	-	-	-	-	-	-	-	-	-	-	16.6	-0.6
1929	-	-	-	-	-	-	-	-	-	-	16.8	1.2	-	-	-	-	-	-	-	-	-	-	17.0	1.2
1930	-	-	-	-	-	-	-	-	-	-	16.7	-1.8	-	-	-	-	-	-	-	-	-	-	16.0	-4.2
1931	-	-	-	-	-	-	-	-	-	-	15.0	-6.3	-	-	-	-	-	-	-	-	-	-	14.4	-4.0
1932	-	-	-	-	-	-	-	-	-	-	13.3	-7.6	-	-	-	-	-	-	-	-	-	-	12.8	-3.8
1933	-	-	-	-	-	-	-	-	-	-	12.6	-1.6	-	-	-	-	-	-	-	-	-	-	12.9	2.4
1934	-	-	-	-	-	-	-	-	-	-	13.2	2.3	-	-	-	-	-	-	-	-	13.3	0.8	-	-
1935	-	-	-	-	13.7	3.0	-	-	-	-	-	-	13.7	0.0	-	-	-	-	13.8	0.7	-	-	-	-
1936	13.8	0.0	-	-	-	-	13.6	-1.4	-	-	-	-	14.0	2.9	-	-	14.1	0.7	-	-	-	-	13.9	-1.4
1937	-	-	-	-	14.3	2.9	-	-	-	-	14.3	0.0	-	-	-	-	14.5	1.4	-	-	-	-	14.3	-1.4
1938	-	-	-	-	14.0	-2.1	-	-	-	-	14.0	0.0	-	-	-	-	14.0	0.0	-	-	-	-	13.8	-1.4
1939	-	-	-	-	13.6	-1.4	-	-	-	-	13.5	-0.7	-	-	-	-	13.8	2.2	-	-	-	-	13.6	-1.4
1940	-	-	-	-	13.7	0.7	-	-	-	-	13.7	0.0	-	-	-	-	13.9	1.5	13.8	-0.7	13.8	0.0	13.8	0.0
1941	13.8	0.0	13.8	0.0	14.0	1.4	14.1	0.7	14.2	0.7	14.4	1.4	14.5	0.7	14.8	2.1	15.0	1.4	15.3	2.0	15.4	0.7	15.3	-0.6
1942	15.5	1.3	15.7	1.3	15.9	1.3	16.0	0.6	16.1	0.6	16.2	0.6	16.2	0.0	16.3	0.6	16.4	0.6	16.6	1.2	16.6	0.0	16.7	0.6
1943	16.6	-0.6	16.7	0.6	16.9	1.2	17.1	1.2	17.2	0.6	17.3	0.6	17.3	0.0	17.3	0.0	17.2	-0.6	17.3	0.6	17.2	-0.6	17.3	0.6
1944	17.2	-0.6	17.1	-0.6	17.1	0.0	17.4	1.8	17.3	-0.6	17.6	1.7	17.6	0.0	17.6	0.0	17.6	0.0	17.5	-0.6	17.6	0.6	17.6	0.0
1945	17.6	0.0	17.6	0.0	17.6	0.0	17.6	0.0	17.8	1.1	18.0	1.1	18.0	0.0	18.0	0.0	17.9	-0.6	18.0	0.6	-	-	18.0	0.0
1946	18.0	0.0	17.9	-0.6	18.0	0.6	18.1	0.6	18.2	0.6	18.4	1.1	19.5	6.0	20.0	2.6	20.2	1.0	20.4	1.0	21.3	4.4	21.2	-0.5
1947	21.2	0.0	21.3	0.5	21.8	2.3	21.9	0.5	21.8	-0.5	22.1	1.4	22.4	1.4	22.6	0.9	23.1	2.2	23.3	0.9	23.3	0.0	23.7	1.7
1948	23.9	0.8	23.7	-0.8	23.6	-0.4	23.8	0.8	24.0	0.8	24.2	0.8	24.5	1.2	24.5	0.0	24.6	0.4	24.5	-0.4	24.2	-1.2	24.0	-0.8
1949	24.0	0.0	23.7	-1.2	23.8	0.4	23.8	0.0	23.6	-0.8	23.8	0.8	23.6	-0.8	23.6	0.0	23.8	0.8	23.6	-0.8	23.5	-0.4	23.4	-0.4
1950	23.4	0.0	23.3	-0.4	23.4	0.4	23.3	-0.4	23.6	1.3	23.7	0.4	23.9	0.8	24.2	1.3	24.4	0.8	24.5	0.4	24.5	0.0	24.8	1.2
1951	25.3	2.0	25.5	0.8	25.6	0.4	25.7	0.4	25.7	0.0	25.7	0.0	25.8	0.4	25.7	-0.4	26.0	1.2	26.0	0.0	26.1	0.4	26.1	0.0
1952	26.2	0.4	26.0	-0.8	26.0	0.0	26.2	0.8	26.3	0.4	26.4	0.4	26.5	0.4	26.5	0.0	26.5	0.0	26.5	0.0	26.3	-0.8	26.3	0.0
1953	-	-	-	-	26.3	0.0	-	-	-	-	26.8	1.9	-	-	-	-	27.0	0.7	-	-	-	-	26.8	-0.7
1954	-	-	-	-	26.7	-0.4	-	-	-	-	26.7	0.0	-	-	-	-	26.7	0.0	-	-	-	-	26.5	-0.7
1955	-	-	-	-	26.5	0.0	-	-	-	-	26.6	0.4	-	-	-	-	26.6	0.0	-	-	-	-	26.7	0.4
1956	-	-	-	-	26.7	0.0	-	-	-	-	27.2	1.9	-	-	-	-	27.4	0.7	-	-	-	-	27.5	0.4
1957	-	-	-	-	27.6	0.4	-	-	-	-	28.0	1.4	-	-	-	-	28.3	1.1	-	-	-	-	28.3	0.0
1958	-	-	-	-	28.6	1.1	-	-	-	-	28.7	0.3	-	-	-	-	28.7	0.0	-	-	-	-	28.6	-0.3
1959	-	-	-	-	28.6	0.0	-	-	-	-	28.8	0.7	-	-	-	-	28.9	0.3	-	-	-	-	29.0	0.3
1960	-	-	-	-	28.9	-0.3	-	-	-	-	29.2	1.0	-	-	-	-	29.2	0.0	-	-	-	-	29.2	0.0
1961	-	-	-	-	29.2	0.0	-	-	-	-	29.2	0.0	-	-	-	-	29.3	0.3	-	-	-	-	29.2	-0.3

[Continued]

Cincinnati, OH-KY-IN
Consumer Price Index - All Urban Consumers
Base 1982-1984 = 100
All Items
[Continued]

For 1917-1995. Columns headed % show percentile change in the index from the previous period for which an index is available.

Year	Jan Index	%	Feb Index	%	Mar Index	%	Apr Index	%	May Index	%	Jun Index	%	Jul Index	%	Aug Index	%	Sep Index	%	Oct Index	%	Nov Index	%	Dec Index	%
1962	-	-	-	-	29.4	0.7	-	-	-	-	29.4	0.0	-	-	-	-	29.7	1.0	-	-	-	-	29.6	-0.3
1963	-	-	-	-	29.8	0.7	-	-	-	-	29.8	0.0	-	-	-	-	29.9	0.3	-	-	-	-	29.9	0.0
1964	-	-	-	-	30.1	0.7	-	-	-	-	30.2	0.3	-	-	-	-	30.5	1.0	-	-	-	-	30.4	-0.3
1965	-	-	-	-	30.4	0.0	-	-	-	-	30.6	0.7	-	-	-	-	30.5	-0.3	-	-	-	-	30.7	0.7
1966	-	-	-	-	31.1	1.3	-	-	-	-	31.4	1.0	-	-	-	-	31.8	1.3	-	-	-	-	31.7	-0.3
1967	-	-	-	-	31.8	0.3	-	-	-	-	32.2	1.3	-	-	-	-	32.7	1.6	-	-	-	-	33.0	0.9
1968	-	-	-	-	33.4	1.2	-	-	-	-	33.8	1.2	-	-	-	-	34.3	1.5	-	-	-	-	34.5	0.6
1969	-	-	-	-	34.9	1.2	-	-	-	-	35.5	1.7	-	-	-	-	35.7	0.6	-	-	-	-	36.4	2.0
1970	-	-	-	-	36.8	1.1	-	-	-	-	37.4	1.6	-	-	-	-	37.7	0.8	-	-	-	-	38.3	1.6
1971	-	-	-	-	38.7	1.0	-	-	-	-	39.0	0.8	-	-	-	-	39.2	0.5	-	-	-	-	39.4	0.5
1972	-	-	-	-	39.8	1.0	-	-	-	-	40.3	1.3	-	-	-	-	40.8	1.2	-	-	-	-	40.9	0.2
1973	-	-	-	-	41.9	2.4	-	-	-	-	42.3	1.0	-	-	-	-	43.4	2.6	-	-	-	-	44.1	1.6
1974	-	-	-	-	45.7	3.6	-	-	-	-	47.1	3.1	-	-	-	-	48.6	3.2	-	-	-	-	49.7	2.3
1975	-	-	-	-	50.4	1.4	-	-	-	-	51.9	3.0	-	-	-	-	53.0	2.1	-	-	-	-	53.2	0.4
1976	-	-	-	-	54.0	1.5	-	-	-	-	54.9	1.7	-	-	-	-	55.6	1.3	-	-	-	-	56.4	1.4
1977	-	-	-	-	57.8	2.5	-	-	-	-	58.8	1.7	-	-	-	-	59.9	1.9	-	-	-	-	60.3	0.7
1978	-	-	-	-	62.1	3.0	-	-	63.8	2.7	-	-	64.7	1.4	-	-	65.8	1.7	-	-	66.9	1.7	-	-
1979	68.3	2.1	-	-	69.7	2.0	-	-	71.6	2.7	-	-	72.7	1.5	-	-	74.0	1.8	-	-	75.4	1.9	-	-
1980	77.4	2.7	-	-	80.1	3.5	-	-	81.3	1.5	-	-	83.0	2.1	-	-	84.0	1.2	-	-	84.7	0.8	-	-
1981	85.5	0.9	-	-	86.0	0.6	-	-	87.8	2.1	-	-	88.3	0.6	-	-	88.9	0.7	-	-	89.4	0.6	-	-
1982	92.3	3.2	-	-	92.1	-0.2	-	-	93.3	1.3	-	-	94.8	1.6	-	-	97.0	2.3	-	-	98.3	1.3	-	-
1983	98.9	0.6	-	-	99.4	0.5	-	-	100.6	1.2	-	-	101.0	0.4	-	-	101.7	0.7	-	-	102.4	0.7	-	-
1984	102.9	0.5	-	-	103.4	0.5	-	-	104.0	0.6	-	-	104.5	0.5	-	-	105.1	0.6	-	-	105.2	0.1	-	-
1985	105.1	-0.1	-	-	106.1	1.0	-	-	106.8	0.7	-	-	106.7	-0.1	-	-	106.6	-0.1	-	-	107.7	1.0	-	-
1986	107.7	0.0	-	-	106.5	-1.1	-	-	107.3	0.8	-	-	107.4	0.1	-	-	107.6	0.2	-	-	108.4	0.7	-	-
1987	-	-	-	-	-	-	-	-	-	-	112.9	4.2	-	-	-	-	-	-	-	-	-	-	116.0	2.7
1988	-	-	-	-	-	-	-	-	-	-	117.0	0.9	-	-	-	-	-	-	-	-	-	-	121.0	3.4
1989	-	-	-	-	-	-	-	-	-	-	123.3	1.9	-	-	-	-	-	-	-	-	-	-	126.7	2.8
1990	-	-	-	-	-	-	-	-	-	-	129.9	2.5	-	-	-	-	-	-	-	-	-	-	133.5	2.8
1991	-	-	-	-	-	-	-	-	-	-	136.2	2.0	-	-	-	-	-	-	-	-	-	-	137.9	1.2
1992	-	-	-	-	-	-	-	-	-	-	139.9	1.5	-	-	-	-	-	-	-	-	-	-	142.2	1.6
1993	-	-	-	-	-	-	-	-	-	-	144.5	1.6	-	-	-	-	-	-	-	-	-	-	146.3	1.2
1994	-	-	-	-	-	-	-	-	-	-	147.4	0.8	-	-	-	-	-	-	-	-	-	-	149.8	1.6
1995	-	-	-	-	-	-	-	-	-	-	152.7	1.9	-	-	-	-	-	-	-	-	-	-	-	-

Source: U.S. Department of Labor, Bureau of Labor Statistics, Division of Consumer Prices and Price Indexes. - indicates no data collected for period.

Cincinnati, OH-KY-IN
Consumer Price Index - Urban Wage Earners
Base 1982-1984 = 100
All Items

For 1917-1995. Columns headed % show percentile change in the index from the previous period for which an index is available.

Year	Jan		Feb		Mar		Apr		May		Jun		Jul		Aug		Sep		Oct		Nov		Dec	
	Index	%	Index	%	Index	%	Index	%	Index	%	Index	%	Index	%	Index	%	Index	%	Index	%	Index	%	Index	%
1917	-		-		-		-		-		-		-		-		-		-		-		13.6	-
1918	-		-		-		-		-		-		-		-		-		-		-		15.8	16.2
1919	-		-		-		-		-		16.6	5.1	-		-		-		-		-		18.4	10.8
1920	-		-		-		-		-		20.6	12.0	-		-		-		-		-		18.4	-10.7
1921	-		-		-		-		16.8	-8.7	-		-		-		16.5	-1.8	-		-		15.9	-3.6
1922	-		-		15.6	-1.9	-		-		15.8	1.3	-		-		15.6	-1.3	-		-		15.6	0.0
1923	-		-		15.8	1.3	-		-		16.1	1.9	-		-		16.2	0.6	-		-		16.1	-0.6
1924	-		-		16.2	0.6	-		-		16.2	0.0	-		-		16.2	0.0	-		-		16.2	0.0
1925	-		-		-		-		-		17.1	5.6	-		-		-		-		-		17.2	0.6
1926	-		-		-		-		-		17.2	0.0	-		-		-		-		-		17.1	-0.6
1927	-		-		-		-		-		17.5	2.3	-		-		-		-		-		16.7	-4.6
1928	-		-		-		-		-		16.8	0.6	-		-		-		-		-		16.7	-0.6
1929	-		-		-		-		-		17.0	1.8	-		-		-		-		-		17.1	0.6
1930	-		-		-		-		-		16.9	-1.2	-		-		-		-		-		16.1	-4.7
1931	-		-		-		-		-		15.1	-6.2	-		-		-		-		-		14.5	-4.0
1932	-		-		-		-		-		13.4	-7.6	-		-		-		-		-		12.9	-3.7
1933	-		-		-		-		-		12.7	-1.6	-		-		-		-		13.4	0.8	13.0	2.4
1934	-		-		-		-		-		13.3	2.3	-		-		-		13.9	0.7	-		-	
1935	-		-		13.8	3.0	-		-		-		13.8	0.0	-		14.2	0.7	-		-		14.0	-1.4
1936	13.9	0.0	-		-		-		13.7	-1.4	-		14.1	2.9	-		14.6	1.4	-		-		14.4	-1.4
1937	-		-		14.4	2.9	-		-		14.4	0.0	-		-		14.1	0.0	-		-		13.9	-1.4
1938	-		-		14.1	-2.1	-		-		14.1	0.0	-		-		13.9	2.2	-		-		13.7	-1.4
1939	-		-		13.7	-1.4	-		-		13.6	-0.7	-		-		14.0	1.4	13.9	-0.7	13.9	0.0	13.9	0.0
1940	-		-		13.8	0.7	-		-		13.8	0.0	-		-		-		-		-		-	
1941	13.9	0.0	13.9	0.0	14.1	1.4	14.2	0.7	14.3	0.7	14.5	1.4	14.6	0.7	14.9	2.1	15.1	1.3	15.4	2.0	15.5	0.6	15.4	-0.6
1942	15.7	1.9	15.8	0.6	16.0	1.3	16.1	0.6	16.2	0.6	16.3	0.6	16.3	0.0	16.4	0.6	16.5	0.6	16.7	1.2	16.7	0.0	16.8	0.6
1943	16.8	0.0	16.8	0.0	17.1	1.8	17.2	0.6	17.3	0.6	17.4	0.6	17.4	0.0	17.4	0.0	17.3	-0.6	17.4	0.6	17.3	-0.6	17.4	0.6
1944	17.3	-0.6	17.2	-0.6	17.2	0.0	17.5	1.7	17.4	-0.6	17.7	1.7	17.8	0.6	17.7	-0.6	17.7	0.0	17.6	-0.6	17.7	0.6	17.7	0.0
1945	17.8	0.6	17.7	-0.6	17.7	0.0	17.8	0.6	17.9	0.6	18.1	1.1	18.2	0.6	18.1	-0.5	18.0	-0.6	18.1	0.6	-		18.2	0.6
1946	18.2	0.0	18.1	-0.5	18.1	0.0	18.2	0.6	18.4	1.1	18.5	0.5	19.7	6.5	20.1	2.0	20.4	1.5	20.5	0.5	21.4	4.4	21.4	0.0
1947	21.3	-0.5	21.5	0.9	22.0	2.3	22.0	0.0	22.0	0.0	22.2	0.9	22.5	1.4	22.8	1.3	23.3	2.2	23.5	0.9	23.5	0.0	23.9	1.7
1948	24.0	0.4	23.9	-0.4	23.8	-0.4	24.0	0.8	24.2	0.8	24.4	0.8	24.7	1.2	24.7	0.0	24.8	0.4	24.6	-0.8	24.4	-0.8	24.2	-0.8
1949	24.2	0.0	23.9	-1.2	24.0	0.4	24.0	0.4	23.8	-0.8	24.0	0.8	24.0	0.4	24.3	1.2	24.5	0.8	24.6	0.4	24.6	0.0	25.0	1.6
1950	23.6	0.0	23.5	-0.4	23.6	0.4	23.5	-0.4	23.8	1.3	23.9	0.4												
1951	25.5	2.0	25.7	0.8	25.8	0.4	25.8	0.0	25.8	0.0	25.9	0.4	26.0	0.4	25.9	-0.4	26.1	0.8	26.2	0.4	26.3	0.4	26.3	0.0
1952	26.4	0.4	26.2	-0.8	26.2	0.0	26.4	0.8	26.5	0.4	26.6	0.4	26.7	0.4	26.7	0.0	27.1	0.4	-		-		27.0	-0.4
1953	-		-		26.5	0.0	-		-		27.0	1.9	-		-		26.9	0.0	-		-		26.7	-0.7
1954	-		-		26.9	-0.4	-		-		26.9	0.0	-		-		26.8	0.0	-		-		26.9	0.4
1955	-		-		26.7	0.0	-		-		26.8	0.4	-		-		27.6	0.7	-		-		27.7	0.4
1956	-		-		26.9	0.0	-		-		27.4	1.9	-		-		28.5	1.1	-		-		28.5	0.0
1957	-		-		27.8	0.4	-		-		28.2	1.4	-		-		28.9	0.0	-		-		28.8	-0.3
1958	-		-		28.8	1.1	-		-		28.9	0.3	-		-		29.1	0.3	-		-		29.2	0.3
1959	-		-		28.8	0.0	-		-		29.0	0.7	-		-		29.4	0.0	-		-		29.4	0.0
1960	-		-		29.1	-0.3	-		-		29.4	1.0	-		-		29.4	0.0	-		-		29.4	-0.3
1961	-		-		29.4	0.0	-		-		29.4	0.0	-		-		29.5	0.3	-		-		29.4	-0.3

[Continued]

Cincinnati, OH-KY-IN
Consumer Price Index - Urban Wage Earners
Base 1982-1984 = 100
All Items
[Continued]

For 1917-1995. Columns headed % show percentile change in the index from the previous period for which an index is available.

Year	Jan Index	%	Feb Index	%	Mar Index	%	Apr Index	%	May Index	%	Jun Index	%	Jul Index	%	Aug Index	%	Sep Index	%	Oct Index	%	Nov Index	%	Dec Index	%
1962	-	-	-	-	29.6	0.7	-	-	-	-	29.6	0.0	-	-	-	-	29.9	1.0	-	-	-	-	29.8	-0.3
1963	-	-	-	-	30.0	0.7	-	-	-	-	30.0	0.0	-	-	-	-	30.1	0.3	-	-	-	-	30.1	0.0
1964	-	-	-	-	30.3	0.7	-	-	-	-	30.4	0.3	-	-	-	-	30.7	1.0	-	-	-	-	30.7	0.0
1965	-	-	-	-	30.6	-0.3	-	-	-	-	30.8	0.7	-	-	-	-	30.7	-0.3	-	-	-	-	30.9	0.7
1966	-	-	-	-	31.3	1.3	-	-	-	-	31.6	1.0	-	-	-	-	32.0	1.3	-	-	-	-	31.9	-0.3
1967	-	-	-	-	32.0	0.3	-	-	-	-	32.4	1.3	-	-	-	-	32.9	1.5	-	-	-	-	33.3	1.2
1968	-	-	-	-	33.6	0.9	-	-	-	-	34.0	1.2	-	-	-	-	34.5	1.5	-	-	-	-	34.7	0.6
1969	-	-	-	-	35.2	1.4	-	-	-	-	35.7	1.4	-	-	-	-	36.0	0.8	-	-	-	-	36.6	1.7
1970	-	-	-	-	37.0	1.1	-	-	-	-	37.6	1.6	-	-	-	-	38.0	1.1	-	-	-	-	38.6	1.6
1971	-	-	-	-	39.0	1.0	-	-	-	-	39.3	0.8	-	-	-	-	39.5	0.5	-	-	-	-	39.7	0.5
1972	-	-	-	-	40.0	0.8	-	-	-	-	40.5	1.3	-	-	-	-	41.1	1.5	-	-	-	-	41.2	0.2
1973	-	-	-	-	42.2	2.4	-	-	-	-	42.6	0.9	-	-	-	-	43.7	2.6	-	-	-	-	44.5	1.8
1974	-	-	-	-	46.0	3.4	-	-	-	-	47.4	3.0	-	-	-	-	48.9	3.2	-	-	-	-	50.0	2.2
1975	-	-	-	-	50.7	1.4	-	-	-	-	52.3	3.2	-	-	-	-	53.3	1.9	-	-	-	-	53.6	0.6
1976	-	-	-	-	54.4	1.5	-	-	-	-	55.3	1.7	-	-	-	-	56.0	1.3	-	-	-	-	56.8	1.4
1977	-	-	-	-	58.2	2.5	-	-	-	-	59.2	1.7	-	-	-	-	60.3	1.9	-	-	-	-	60.8	0.8
1978	-	-	-	-	62.6	3.0	-	-	64.3	2.7	-	-	65.4	1.7	-	-	66.3	1.4	-	-	67.5	1.8	-	-
1979	69.1	2.4	-	-	70.5	2.0	-	-	72.6	3.0	-	-	73.7	1.5	-	-	75.1	1.9	-	-	76.7	2.1	-	-
1980	78.4	2.2	-	-	81.3	3.7	-	-	82.3	1.2	-	-	84.3	2.4	-	-	85.2	1.1	-	-	85.7	0.6	-	-
1981	86.7	1.2	-	-	87.1	0.5	-	-	88.9	2.1	-	-	89.9	1.1	-	-	90.2	0.3	-	-	90.8	0.7	-	-
1982	93.8	3.3	-	-	93.5	-0.3	-	-	94.8	1.4	-	-	96.3	1.6	-	-	98.5	2.3	-	-	99.9	1.4	-	-
1983	99.3	-0.6	-	-	100.1	0.8	-	-	100.7	0.6	-	-	100.2	-0.5	-	-	101.3	1.1	-	-	102.8	1.5	-	-
1984	102.0	-0.8	-	-	102.1	0.1	-	-	101.6	-0.5	-	-	102.3	0.7	-	-	104.4	2.1	-	-	103.9	-0.5	-	-
1985	103.8	-0.1	-	-	104.8	1.0	-	-	105.4	0.6	-	-	105.2	-0.2	-	-	105.0	-0.2	-	-	106.1	1.0	-	-
1986	106.1	0.0	-	-	104.7	-1.3	-	-	105.7	1.0	-	-	105.7	0.0	-	-	105.7	0.0	-	-	106.6	0.9	-	-
1987	-	-	-	-	-	-	-	-	-	-	109.6	2.8	-	-	-	-	-	-	-	-	-	-	112.6	2.7
1988	-	-	-	-	-	-	-	-	-	-	113.3	0.6	-	-	-	-	-	-	-	-	-	-	117.3	3.5
1989	-	-	-	-	-	-	-	-	-	-	119.5	1.9	-	-	-	-	-	-	-	-	-	-	122.8	2.8
1990	-	-	-	-	-	-	-	-	-	-	126.1	2.7	-	-	-	-	-	-	-	-	-	-	129.6	2.8
1991	-	-	-	-	-	-	-	-	-	-	132.1	1.9	-	-	-	-	-	-	-	-	-	-	133.7	1.2
1992	-	-	-	-	-	-	-	-	-	-	135.5	1.3	-	-	-	-	-	-	-	-	-	-	137.9	1.8
1993	-	-	-	-	-	-	-	-	-	-	140.1	1.6	-	-	-	-	-	-	-	-	-	-	141.8	1.2
1994	-	-	-	-	-	-	-	-	-	-	142.9	0.8	-	-	-	-	-	-	-	-	-	-	145.1	1.5
1995	-	-	-	-	-	-	-	-	-	-	147.9	1.9	-	-	-	-	-	-	-	-	-	-	-	-

Source: U.S. Department of Labor, Bureau of Labor Statistics, Division of Consumer Prices and Price Indexes. - indicates no data collected for period.

Cincinnati, OH-KY-IN
Consumer Price Index - All Urban Consumers
Base 1982-1984 = 100
Food and Beverages

For 1975-1995. Columns headed % show percentile change in the index from the previous period for which an index is available.

Year	Jan Index	%	Feb Index	%	Mar Index	%	Apr Index	%	May Index	%	Jun Index	%	Jul Index	%	Aug Index	%	Sep Index	%	Oct Index	%	Nov Index	%	Dec Index	%
1975	-	-	-	-	-	-	-	-	-	-	-	-	-	-	-	-	-	-	-	-	-	-	59.1	-
1976	-	-	-	-	59.2	0.2	-	-	-	-	60.2	1.7	-	-	-	-	60.7	0.8	-	-	-	-	60.7	0.0
1977	-	-	-	-	63.0	3.8	-	-	-	-	64.5	2.4	-	-	-	-	65.5	1.6	-	-	-	-	66.0	0.8
1978	-	-	-	-	68.5	3.8	-	-	70.4	2.8	-	-	72.7	3.3	-	-	72.4	-0.4	-	-	73.5	1.5	-	-
1979	75.6	2.9	-	-	77.5	2.5	-	-	79.5	2.6	-	-	79.7	0.3	-	-	79.9	0.3	-	-	80.8	1.1	-	-
1980	82.2	1.7	-	-	83.5	1.6	-	-	84.7	1.4	-	-	85.8	1.3	-	-	87.9	2.4	-	-	89.1	1.4	-	-
1981	91.4	2.6	-	-	92.5	1.2	-	-	93.1	0.6	-	-	93.2	0.1	-	-	94.0	0.9	-	-	93.8	-0.2	-	-
1982	95.2	1.5	-	-	95.3	0.1	-	-	96.6	1.4	-	-	98.4	1.9	-	-	98.1	-0.3	-	-	97.7	-0.4	-	-
1983	97.7	0.0	-	-	99.0	1.3	-	-	99.5	0.5	-	-	99.2	-0.3	-	-	98.8	-0.4	-	-	99.7	0.9	-	-
1984	102.4	2.7	-	-	103.5	1.1	-	-	103.9	0.4	-	-	103.7	-0.2	-	-	104.7	1.0	-	-	104.5	-0.2	-	-
1985	104.1	-0.4	-	-	105.4	1.2	-	-	105.1	-0.3	-	-	104.4	-0.7	-	-	104.1	-0.3	-	-	104.4	0.3	-	-
1986	105.0	0.6	-	-	105.2	0.2	-	-	106.0	0.8	-	-	107.8	1.7	-	-	109.0	1.1	-	-	109.2	0.2	-	-
1987	-	-	-	-	-	-	-	-	-	-	112.8	3.3	-	-	-	-	-	-	-	-	-	-	113.6	0.7
1988	-	-	-	-	-	-	-	-	-	-	115.2	1.4	-	-	-	-	-	-	-	-	-	-	118.9	3.2
1989	-	-	-	-	-	-	-	-	-	-	121.8	2.4	-	-	-	-	-	-	-	-	-	-	123.2	1.1
1990	-	-	-	-	-	-	-	-	-	-	128.9	4.6	-	-	-	-	-	-	-	-	-	-	131.6	2.1
1991	-	-	-	-	-	-	-	-	-	-	135.6	3.0	-	-	-	-	-	-	-	-	-	-	135.4	-0.1
1992	-	-	-	-	-	-	-	-	-	-	138.5	2.3	-	-	-	-	-	-	-	-	-	-	139.8	0.9
1993	-	-	-	-	-	-	-	-	-	-	142.2	1.7	-	-	-	-	-	-	-	-	-	-	143.9	1.2
1994	-	-	-	-	-	-	-	-	-	-	146.8	2.0	-	-	-	-	-	-	-	-	-	-	147.2	0.3
1995	-	-	-	-	-	-	-	-	-	-	151.1	2.6	-	-	-	-	-	-	-	-	-	-	-	-

Source: U.S. Department of Labor, Bureau of Labor Statistics, Division of Consumer Prices and Price Indexes. - indicates no data collected for period.

Cincinnati, OH-KY-IN
Consumer Price Index - Urban Wage Earners
Base 1982-1984 = 100
Food and Beverages

For 1975-1995. Columns headed % show percentile change in the index from the previous period for which an index is available.

Year	Jan Index	%	Feb Index	%	Mar Index	%	Apr Index	%	May Index	%	Jun Index	%	Jul Index	%	Aug Index	%	Sep Index	%	Oct Index	%	Nov Index	%	Dec Index	%
1975	-	-	-	-	-	-	-	-	-	-	-	-	-	-	-	-	-	-	-	-	-	-	58.9	-
1976	-	-	-	-	59.0	0.2	-	-	-	-	60.0	1.7	-	-	-	-	60.4	0.7	-	-	-	-	60.4	0.0
1977	-	-	-	-	62.7	3.8	-	-	-	-	64.3	2.6	-	-	-	-	65.3	1.6	-	-	-	-	65.8	0.8
1978	-	-	-	-	68.3	3.8	-	-	70.6	3.4	-	-	72.6	2.8	-	-	72.3	-0.4	-	-	73.7	1.9	-	-
1979	76.1	3.3	-	-	77.8	2.2	-	-	80.3	3.2	-	-	80.5	0.2	-	-	80.8	0.4	-	-	81.5	0.9	-	-
1980	82.2	0.9	-	-	83.8	1.9	-	-	85.0	1.4	-	-	86.4	1.6	-	-	88.6	2.5	-	-	89.3	0.8	-	-
1981	91.5	2.5	-	-	92.2	0.8	-	-	92.6	0.4	-	-	92.9	0.3	-	-	93.7	0.9	-	-	93.8	0.1	-	-
1982	95.6	1.9	-	-	95.7	0.1	-	-	96.9	1.3	-	-	98.4	1.5	-	-	98.2	-0.2	-	-	97.8	-0.4	-	-
1983	97.8	0.0	-	-	99.2	1.4	-	-	99.7	0.5	-	-	99.2	-0.5	-	-	98.8	-0.4	-	-	99.7	0.9	-	-
1984	102.3	2.6	-	-	103.3	1.0	-	-	103.7	0.4	-	-	103.3	-0.4	-	-	104.4	1.1	-	-	104.1	-0.3	-	-
1985	104.0	-0.1	-	-	105.3	1.3	-	-	104.8	-0.5	-	-	104.0	-0.8	-	-	103.8	-0.2	-	-	104.1	0.3	-	-
1986	104.7	0.6	-	-	105.0	0.3	-	-	105.7	0.7	-	-	107.4	1.6	-	-	108.4	0.9	-	-	108.8	0.4	-	-
1987	-	-	-	-	-	-	-	-	-	-	113.0	3.9	-	-	-	-	-	-	-	-	-	-	113.7	0.6
1988	-	-	-	-	-	-	-	-	-	-	115.3	1.4	-	-	-	-	-	-	-	-	-	-	119.0	3.2
1989	-	-	-	-	-	-	-	-	-	-	121.9	2.4	-	-	-	-	-	-	-	-	-	-	123.3	1.1
1990	-	-	-	-	-	-	-	-	-	-	129.1	4.7	-	-	-	-	-	-	-	-	-	-	131.8	2.1
1991	-	-	-	-	-	-	-	-	-	-	135.8	3.0	-	-	-	-	-	-	-	-	-	-	135.6	-0.1
1992	-	-	-	-	-	-	-	-	-	-	138.5	2.1	-	-	-	-	-	-	-	-	-	-	139.9	1.0
1993	-	-	-	-	-	-	-	-	-	-	142.4	1.8	-	-	-	-	-	-	-	-	-	-	144.2	1.3
1994	-	-	-	-	-	-	-	-	-	-	147.0	1.9	-	-	-	-	-	-	-	-	-	-	147.4	0.3
1995	-	-	-	-	-	-	-	-	-	-	151.3	2.6	-	-	-	-	-	-	-	-	-	-	-	-

Source: U.S. Department of Labor, Bureau of Labor Statistics, Division of Consumer Prices and Price Indexes. - indicates no data collected for period.

Cincinnati, OH-KY-IN
Consumer Price Index - All Urban Consumers
Base 1982-1984 = 100
Housing

For 1975-1995. Columns headed % show percentile change in the index from the previous period for which an index is available.

Year	Jan Index	%	Feb Index	%	Mar Index	%	Apr Index	%	May Index	%	Jun Index	%	Jul Index	%	Aug Index	%	Sep Index	%	Oct Index	%	Nov Index	%	Dec Index	%
1975	-	-	-	-	-	-	-	-	-	-	-	-	-	-	-	-	-	-	-	-	-	-	49.3	-
1976	-	-	-	-	50.2	1.8	-	-	-	-	50.6	0.8	-	-	-	-	51.0	0.8	-	-	-	-	52.5	2.9
1977	-	-	-	-	53.3	1.5	-	-	-	-	54.2	1.7	-	-	-	-	55.4	2.2	-	-	-	-	56.2	1.4
1978	-	-	-	-	58.0	3.2	-	-	59.9	3.3	-	-	60.4	0.8	-	-	62.2	3.0	-	-	63.5	2.1	-	-
1979	64.7	1.9	-	-	66.6	2.9	-	-	68.1	2.3	-	-	69.2	1.6	-	-	70.5	1.9	-	-	72.7	3.1	-	-
1980	74.7	2.8	-	-	78.1	4.6	-	-	79.3	1.5	-	-	82.2	3.7	-	-	82.1	-0.1	-	-	82.5	0.5	-	-
1981	82.2	-0.4	-	-	81.2	-1.2	-	-	84.7	4.3	-	-	85.4	0.8	-	-	84.6	-0.9	-	-	85.2	0.7	-	-
1982	90.0	5.6	-	-	89.4	-0.7	-	-	91.6	2.5	-	-	92.7	1.2	-	-	96.6	4.2	-	-	99.3	2.8	-	-
1983	99.6	0.3	-	-	101.1	1.5	-	-	102.4	1.3	-	-	102.6	0.2	-	-	103.1	0.5	-	-	103.0	-0.1	-	-
1984	103.3	0.3	-	-	103.6	0.3	-	-	104.0	0.4	-	-	104.6	0.6	-	-	104.6	0.0	-	-	104.7	0.1	-	-
1985	105.7	1.0	-	-	106.2	0.5	-	-	106.7	0.5	-	-	107.4	0.7	-	-	106.7	-0.7	-	-	107.4	0.7	-	-
1986	107.8	0.4	-	-	108.5	0.6	-	-	109.1	0.6	-	-	109.3	0.2	-	-	107.3	-1.8	-	-	109.1	1.7	-	-
1987	-	-	-	-	-	-	-	-	-	-	114.4	4.9	-	-	-	-	-	-	-	-	-	-	118.3	3.4
1988	-	-	-	-	-	-	-	-	-	-	118.3	0.0	-	-	-	-	-	-	-	-	-	-	123.1	4.1
1989	-	-	-	-	-	-	-	-	-	-	124.7	1.3	-	-	-	-	-	-	-	-	-	-	128.1	2.7
1990	-	-	-	-	-	-	-	-	-	-	129.9	1.4	-	-	-	-	-	-	-	-	-	-	132.8	2.2
1991	-	-	-	-	-	-	-	-	-	-	135.5	2.0	-	-	-	-	-	-	-	-	-	-	137.3	1.3
1992	-	-	-	-	-	-	-	-	-	-	139.0	1.2	-	-	-	-	-	-	-	-	-	-	140.8	1.3
1993	-	-	-	-	-	-	-	-	-	-	142.3	1.1	-	-	-	-	-	-	-	-	-	-	144.2	1.3
1994	-	-	-	-	-	-	-	-	-	-	143.9	-0.2	-	-	-	-	-	-	-	-	-	-	145.8	1.3
1995	-	-	-	-	-	-	-	-	-	-	149.6	2.6	-	-	-	-	-	-	-	-	-	-	-	-

Source: U.S. Department of Labor, Bureau of Labor Statistics, Division of Consumer Prices and Price Indexes. - indicates no data collected for period.

Cincinnati, OH-KY-IN
Consumer Price Index - Urban Wage Earners
Base 1982-1984 = 100
Housing

For 1975-1995. Columns headed % show percentile change in the index from the previous period for which an index is available.

Year	Jan Index	%	Feb Index	%	Mar Index	%	Apr Index	%	May Index	%	Jun Index	%	Jul Index	%	Aug Index	%	Sep Index	%	Oct Index	%	Nov Index	%	Dec Index	%
1975	-	-	-	-	-	-	-	-	-	-	51.5	-	-	-	-	-	-	-	-	-	-	-	50.2	-
1976	-	-	-	-	51.1	1.8	-	-	-	-	51.5	0.8	-	-	-	-	51.9	0.8	-	-	-	-	53.5	3.1
1977	-	-	-	-	54.3	1.5	-	-	-	-	55.2	1.7	-	-	-	-	56.5	2.4	-	-	-	-	57.2	1.2
1978	-	-	-	-	59.1	3.3	-	-	61.0	3.2	-	-	61.7	1.1	-	-	63.3	2.6	-	-	65.0	2.7	-	-
1979	66.2	1.8	-	-	68.3	3.2	-	-	69.9	2.3	-	-	71.0	1.6	-	-	72.3	1.8	-	-	74.8	3.5	-	-
1980	76.9	2.8	-	-	80.5	4.7	-	-	81.5	1.2	-	-	84.5	3.7	-	-	84.3	-0.2	-	-	84.7	0.5	-	-
1981	84.4	-0.4	-	-	83.2	-1.4	-	-	86.6	4.1	-	-	87.7	1.3	-	-	86.7	-1.1	-	-	87.5	0.9	-	-
1982	92.7	5.9	-	-	91.9	-0.9	-	-	94.3	2.6	-	-	95.5	1.3	-	-	99.7	4.4	-	-	102.7	3.0	-	-
1983	100.5	-2.1	-	-	102.3	1.8	-	-	102.3	0.0	-	-	100.7	-1.6	-	-	102.0	1.3	-	-	104.1	2.1	-	-
1984	101.4	-2.6	-	-	101.0	-0.4	-	-	99.1	-1.9	-	-	100.4	1.3	-	-	103.9	3.5	-	-	102.7	-1.2	-	-
1985	103.7	1.0	-	-	104.2	0.5	-	-	104.5	0.3	-	-	105.2	0.7	-	-	104.4	-0.8	-	-	105.2	0.8	-	-
1986	105.6	0.4	-	-	106.3	0.7	-	-	107.0	0.7	-	-	107.0	0.0	-	-	104.8	-2.1	-	-	106.8	1.9	-	-
1987	-	-	-	-	-	-	-	-	-	-	107.9	1.0	-	-	-	-	-	-	-	-	-	-	111.5	3.3
1988	-	-	-	-	-	-	-	-	-	-	111.3	-0.2	-	-	-	-	-	-	-	-	-	-	115.9	4.1
1989	-	-	-	-	-	-	-	-	-	-	117.3	1.2	-	-	-	-	-	-	-	-	-	-	120.6	2.8
1990	-	-	-	-	-	-	-	-	-	-	122.4	1.5	-	-	-	-	-	-	-	-	-	-	125.2	2.3
1991	-	-	-	-	-	-	-	-	-	-	127.5	1.8	-	-	-	-	-	-	-	-	-	-	129.2	1.3
1992	-	-	-	-	-	-	-	-	-	-	130.8	1.2	-	-	-	-	-	-	-	-	-	-	132.6	1.4
1993	-	-	-	-	-	-	-	-	-	-	134.1	1.1	-	-	-	-	-	-	-	-	-	-	135.9	1.3
1994	-	-	-	-	-	-	-	-	-	-	135.6	-0.2	-	-	-	-	-	-	-	-	-	-	137.1	1.1
1995	-	-	-	-	-	-	-	-	-	-	140.6	2.6	-	-	-	-	-	-	-	-	-	-	-	-

Source: U.S. Department of Labor, Bureau of Labor Statistics, Division of Consumer Prices and Price Indexes. - indicates no data collected for period.

Cincinnati, OH-KY-IN
Consumer Price Index - All Urban Consumers
Base 1982-1984 = 100
Apparel and Upkeep

For 1952-1995. Columns headed % show percentile change in the index from the previous period for which an index is available.

Year	Jan Index	%	Feb Index	%	Mar Index	%	Apr Index	%	May Index	%	Jun Index	%	Jul Index	%	Aug Index	%	Sep Index	%	Oct Index	%	Nov Index	%	Dec Index	%
1952	-	-	-	-	-	-	-	-	-	-	-	-	-	-	-	-	-	-	-	-	-	-	36.9	-
1953	-	-	-	-	37.1	0.5	-	-	-	-	37.7	1.6	-	-	-	-	37.8	0.3	-	-	-	-	37.4	-1.1
1954	-	-	-	-	37.1	-0.8	-	-	-	-	37.0	-0.3	-	-	-	-	37.5	1.4	-	-	-	-	37.2	-0.8
1955	-	-	-	-	37.3	0.3	-	-	-	-	37.2	-0.3	-	-	-	-	38.0	2.2	-	-	-	-	38.1	0.3
1956	-	-	-	-	38.6	1.3	-	-	-	-	38.4	-0.5	-	-	-	-	38.8	1.0	-	-	-	-	38.7	-0.3
1957	-	-	-	-	38.6	-0.3	-	-	-	-	38.6	0.0	-	-	-	-	39.4	2.1	-	-	-	-	38.9	-1.3
1958	-	-	-	-	39.0	0.3	-	-	-	-	38.7	-0.8	-	-	-	-	39.3	1.6	-	-	-	-	39.3	0.0
1959	-	-	-	-	39.3	0.0	-	-	-	-	39.3	0.0	-	-	-	-	39.7	1.0	-	-	-	-	39.7	0.0
1960	-	-	-	-	39.8	0.3	-	-	-	-	40.1	0.8	-	-	-	-	40.6	1.2	-	-	-	-	40.2	-1.0
1961	-	-	-	-	40.2	0.0	-	-	-	-	39.9	-0.7	-	-	-	-	40.6	1.8	-	-	-	-	40.5	-0.2
1962	-	-	-	-	40.5	0.0	-	-	-	-	40.5	0.0	-	-	-	-	40.9	1.0	-	-	-	-	40.8	-0.2
1963	-	-	-	-	40.9	0.2	-	-	-	-	40.7	-0.5	-	-	-	-	41.3	1.5	-	-	-	-	41.2	-0.2
1964	-	-	-	-	41.3	0.2	-	-	-	-	41.4	0.2	-	-	-	-	41.9	1.2	-	-	-	-	41.4	-1.2
1965	-	-	-	-	41.5	0.2	-	-	-	-	41.5	0.0	-	-	-	-	42.1	1.4	-	-	-	-	42.1	0.0
1966	-	-	-	-	42.7	1.4	-	-	-	-	43.3	1.4	-	-	-	-	44.0	1.6	-	-	-	-	44.0	0.0
1967	-	-	-	-	44.4	0.9	-	-	-	-	44.3	-0.2	-	-	-	-	45.7	3.2	-	-	-	-	46.0	0.7
1968	-	-	-	-	46.9	2.0	-	-	-	-	47.3	0.9	-	-	-	-	49.8	5.3	-	-	-	-	49.9	0.2
1969	-	-	-	-	50.3	0.8	-	-	-	-	50.9	1.2	-	-	-	-	52.3	2.8	-	-	-	-	52.3	0.0
1970	-	-	-	-	52.8	1.0	-	-	-	-	53.1	0.6	-	-	-	-	54.1	1.9	-	-	-	-	54.9	1.5
1971	-	-	-	-	55.2	0.5	-	-	-	-	54.7	-0.9	-	-	-	-	55.2	0.9	-	-	-	-	54.9	-0.5
1972	-	-	-	-	54.6	-0.5	-	-	-	-	54.7	0.2	-	-	-	-	55.9	2.2	-	-	-	-	56.2	0.5
1973	-	-	-	-	56.7	0.9	-	-	-	-	56.8	0.2	-	-	-	-	58.5	3.0	-	-	-	-	59.1	1.0
1974	-	-	-	-	59.8	1.2	-	-	-	-	60.8	1.7	-	-	-	-	63.5	4.4	-	-	-	-	63.7	0.3
1975	-	-	-	-	64.0	0.5	-	-	-	-	63.3	-1.1	-	-	-	-	65.6	3.6	-	-	-	-	66.1	0.8
1976	-	-	-	-	68.0	2.9	-	-	-	-	67.9	-0.1	-	-	-	-	70.6	4.0	-	-	-	-	70.0	-0.8
1977	-	-	-	-	71.1	1.6	-	-	-	-	71.1	0.0	-	-	-	-	73.9	3.9	-	-	-	-	74.7	1.1
1978	-	-	-	-	75.8	1.5	-	-	78.7	3.8	-	-	76.7	-2.5	-	-	78.9	2.9	-	-	80.0	1.4	-	-
1979	80.3	0.4	-	-	78.0	-2.9	-	-	83.1	6.5	-	-	81.5	-1.9	-	-	84.4	3.6	-	-	83.5	-1.1	-	-
1980	86.2	3.2	-	-	88.8	3.0	-	-	88.5	-0.3	-	-	85.2	-3.7	-	-	92.9	9.0	-	-	92.4	-0.5	-	-
1981	89.5	-3.1	-	-	94.7	5.8	-	-	91.5	-3.4	-	-	88.8	-3.0	-	-	97.7	10.0	-	-	96.9	-0.8	-	-
1982	94.3	-2.7	-	-	98.4	4.3	-	-	96.7	-1.7	-	-	95.5	-1.2	-	-	100.4	5.1	-	-	98.9	-1.5	-	-
1983	101.1	2.2	-	-	100.9	-0.2	-	-	98.6	-2.3	-	-	99.5	0.9	-	-	102.6	3.1	-	-	102.1	-0.5	-	-
1984	97.3	-4.7	-	-	101.5	4.3	-	-	102.7	1.2	-	-	101.8	-0.9	-	-	104.4	2.6	-	-	101.6	-2.7	-	-
1985	101.7	0.1	-	-	103.6	1.9	-	-	102.7	-0.9	-	-	98.0	-4.6	-	-	105.4	7.6	-	-	108.6	3.0	-	-
1986	103.3	-4.9	-	-	103.8	0.5	-	-	102.7	-1.1	-	-	101.7	-1.0	-	-	111.3	9.4	-	-	109.3	-1.8	-	-
1987	-	-	-	-	-	-	-	-	-	-	106.4	-2.7	-	-	-	-	-	-	-	-	-	-	112.1	5.4
1988	-	-	-	-	-	-	-	-	-	-	113.9	1.6	-	-	-	-	-	-	-	-	-	-	119.3	4.7
1989	-	-	-	-	-	-	-	-	-	-	115.5	-3.2	-	-	-	-	-	-	-	-	-	-	120.6	4.4
1990	-	-	-	-	-	-	-	-	-	-	124.0	2.8	-	-	-	-	-	-	-	-	-	-	124.6	0.5
1991	-	-	-	-	-	-	-	-	-	-	124.0	-0.5	-	-	-	-	-	-	-	-	-	-	126.5	2.0
1992	-	-	-	-	-	-	-	-	-	-	124.9	-1.3	-	-	-	-	-	-	-	-	-	-	127.6	2.2
1993	-	-	-	-	-	-	-	-	-	-	130.9	2.6	-	-	-	-	-	-	-	-	-	-	131.4	0.4
1994	-	-	-	-	-	-	-	-	-	-	131.0	-0.3	-	-	-	-	-	-	-	-	-	-	130.9	-0.1
1995	-	-	-	-	-	-	-	-	-	-	127.3	-2.8	-	-	-	-	-	-	-	-	-	-	-	-

Source: U.S. Department of Labor, Bureau of Labor Statistics, Division of Consumer Prices and Price Indexes. - indicates no data collected for period.

Cincinnati, OH-KY-IN
Consumer Price Index - Urban Wage Earners
Base 1982-1984 = 100
Apparel and Upkeep

For 1952-1995. Columns headed % show percentile change in the index from the previous period for which an index is available.

Year	Jan Index	%	Feb Index	%	Mar Index	%	Apr Index	%	May Index	%	Jun Index	%	Jul Index	%	Aug Index	%	Sep Index	%	Oct Index	%	Nov Index	%	Dec Index	%
1952	-	-	-	-	-	-	-	-	-	-	-	-	-	-	-	-	-	-	-	-	-	-	35.8	-
1953	-	-	-	-	36.1	0.8	-	-	-	-	36.6	1.4	-	-	-	-	36.7	0.3	-	-	-	-	36.3	-1.1
1954	-	-	-	-	36.1	-0.6	-	-	-	-	35.9	-0.6	-	-	-	-	36.4	1.4	-	-	-	-	36.1	-0.8
1955	-	-	-	-	36.2	0.3	-	-	-	-	36.1	-0.3	-	-	-	-	36.9	2.2	-	-	-	-	37.0	0.3
1956	-	-	-	-	37.5	1.4	-	-	-	-	37.2	-0.8	-	-	-	-	37.6	1.1	-	-	-	-	37.6	0.0
1957	-	-	-	-	37.5	-0.3	-	-	-	-	37.5	0.0	-	-	-	-	38.2	1.9	-	-	-	-	37.8	-1.0
1958	-	-	-	-	37.9	0.3	-	-	-	-	37.5	-1.1	-	-	-	-	38.2	1.9	-	-	-	-	38.2	0.0
1959	-	-	-	-	38.2	0.0	-	-	-	-	38.2	0.0	-	-	-	-	38.6	1.0	-	-	-	-	38.5	-0.3
1960	-	-	-	-	38.7	0.5	-	-	-	-	38.9	0.5	-	-	-	-	39.4	1.3	-	-	-	-	39.0	-1.0
1961	-	-	-	-	39.0	0.0	-	-	-	-	38.8	-0.5	-	-	-	-	39.4	1.5	-	-	-	-	39.3	-0.3
1962	-	-	-	-	39.3	0.0	-	-	-	-	39.3	0.0	-	-	-	-	39.7	1.0	-	-	-	-	39.6	-0.3
1963	-	-	-	-	39.7	0.3	-	-	-	-	39.6	-0.3	-	-	-	-	40.1	1.3	-	-	-	-	40.0	-0.2
1964	-	-	-	-	40.1	0.2	-	-	-	-	40.2	0.2	-	-	-	-	40.6	1.0	-	-	-	-	40.2	-1.0
1965	-	-	-	-	40.3	0.2	-	-	-	-	40.3	0.0	-	-	-	-	40.9	1.5	-	-	-	-	40.9	0.0
1966	-	-	-	-	41.4	1.2	-	-	-	-	42.0	1.4	-	-	-	-	42.7	1.7	-	-	-	-	42.7	0.0
1967	-	-	-	-	43.1	0.9	-	-	-	-	43.1	0.0	-	-	-	-	44.4	3.0	-	-	-	-	44.7	0.7
1968	-	-	-	-	45.5	1.8	-	-	-	-	46.0	1.1	-	-	-	-	48.4	5.2	-	-	-	-	48.4	0.0
1969	-	-	-	-	48.9	1.0	-	-	-	-	49.4	1.0	-	-	-	-	50.8	2.8	-	-	-	-	50.8	0.0
1970	-	-	-	-	51.3	1.0	-	-	-	-	51.5	0.4	-	-	-	-	52.6	2.1	-	-	-	-	53.3	1.3
1971	-	-	-	-	53.6	0.6	-	-	-	-	53.1	-0.9	-	-	-	-	53.6	0.9	-	-	-	-	53.3	-0.6
1972	-	-	-	-	53.0	-0.6	-	-	-	-	53.1	0.2	-	-	-	-	54.3	2.3	-	-	-	-	54.6	0.6
1973	-	-	-	-	55.1	0.9	-	-	-	-	55.1	0.0	-	-	-	-	56.8	3.1	-	-	-	-	57.4	1.1
1974	-	-	-	-	58.0	1.0	-	-	-	-	59.1	1.9	-	-	-	-	61.7	4.4	-	-	-	-	61.9	0.3
1975	-	-	-	-	62.1	0.3	-	-	-	-	61.5	-1.0	-	-	-	-	63.7	3.6	-	-	-	-	64.2	0.8
1976	-	-	-	-	66.0	2.8	-	-	-	-	66.0	0.0	-	-	-	-	68.5	3.8	-	-	-	-	67.9	-0.9
1977	-	-	-	-	69.1	1.8	-	-	-	-	69.1	0.0	-	-	-	-	71.7	3.8	-	-	-	-	72.5	1.1
1978	-	-	-	-	73.6	1.5	-	-	76.3	3.7	-	-	74.8	-2.0	-	-	77.7	3.9	-	-	77.6	-0.1	-	-
1979	79.5	2.4	-	-	76.6	-3.6	-	-	82.2	7.3	-	-	80.2	-2.4	-	-	83.6	4.2	-	-	83.4	-0.2	-	-
1980	81.9	-1.8	-	-	84.7	3.4	-	-	83.9	-0.9	-	-	85.5	1.9	-	-	90.9	6.3	-	-	91.1	0.2	-	-
1981	88.1	-3.3	-	-	92.7	5.2	-	-	91.2	-1.6	-	-	92.0	0.9	-	-	97.2	5.7	-	-	96.2	-1.0	-	-
1982	93.6	-2.7	-	-	97.7	4.4	-	-	96.8	-0.9	-	-	95.8	-1.0	-	-	100.9	5.3	-	-	99.1	-1.8	-	-
1983	100.2	1.1	-	-	101.7	1.5	-	-	98.6	-3.0	-	-	99.2	0.6	-	-	103.5	4.3	-	-	102.5	-1.0	-	-
1984	98.6	-3.8	-	-	101.7	3.1	-	-	102.3	0.6	-	-	100.8	-1.5	-	-	104.2	3.4	-	-	101.2	-2.9	-	-
1985	101.3	0.1	-	-	103.2	1.9	-	-	101.7	-1.5	-	-	97.2	-4.4	-	-	104.9	7.9	-	-	106.6	1.6	-	-
1986	101.9	-4.4	-	-	102.6	0.7	-	-	101.7	-0.9	-	-	102.6	0.9	-	-	109.5	6.7	-	-	108.2	-1.2	-	-
1987	-	-	-	-	-	-	-	-	-	-	106.8	-1.3	-	-	-	-	-	-	-	-	-	-	112.1	5.0
1988	-	-	-	-	-	-	-	-	-	-	113.1	0.9	-	-	-	-	-	-	-	-	-	-	119.1	5.3
1989	-	-	-	-	-	-	-	-	-	-	115.2	-3.3	-	-	-	-	-	-	-	-	-	-	120.0	4.2
1990	-	-	-	-	-	-	-	-	-	-	124.4	3.7	-	-	-	-	-	-	-	-	-	-	124.7	0.2
1991	-	-	-	-	-	-	-	-	-	-	124.9	0.2	-	-	-	-	-	-	-	-	-	-	126.4	1.2
1992	-	-	-	-	-	-	-	-	-	-	125.0	-1.1	-	-	-	-	-	-	-	-	-	-	126.8	1.4
1993	-	-	-	-	-	-	-	-	-	-	130.0	2.5	-	-	-	-	-	-	-	-	-	-	131.1	0.8
1994	-	-	-	-	-	-	-	-	-	-	130.8	-0.2	-	-	-	-	-	-	-	-	-	-	129.2	-1.2
1995	-	-	-	-	-	-	-	-	-	-	126.0	-2.5	-	-	-	-	-	-	-	-	-	-	-	-

Source: U.S. Department of Labor, Bureau of Labor Statistics, Division of Consumer Prices and Price Indexes. - indicates no data collected for period.

Cincinnati, OH-KY-IN
Consumer Price Index - All Urban Consumers
Base 1982-1984 = 100
Transportation

For 1947-1995. Columns headed % show percentile change in the index from the previous period for which an index is available.

Year	Jan Index	%	Feb Index	%	Mar Index	%	Apr Index	%	May Index	%	Jun Index	%	Jul Index	%	Aug Index	%	Sep Index	%	Oct Index	%	Nov Index	%	Dec Index	%
1947	19.8	-	19.8	0.0	20.2	2.0	20.2	0.0	20.2	0.0	20.2	0.0	20.5	1.5	20.5	0.0	21.0	2.4	21.0	0.0	21.9	4.3	22.1	0.9
1948	22.2	0.5	22.2	0.0	22.2	0.0	22.2	0.0	22.2	0.0	22.7	2.3	23.8	4.8	24.2	1.7	24.3	0.4	24.3	0.0	24.3	0.0	24.3	0.0
1949	24.3	0.0	24.6	1.2	25.2	2.4	25.3	0.4	25.3	0.0	25.2	-0.4	25.2	0.0	25.2	0.0	25.2	0.0	25.2	0.0	25.2	0.0	25.1	-0.4
1950	25.1	0.0	25.1	0.0	25.1	0.0	24.9	-0.8	25.6	2.8	25.6	0.0	25.7	0.4	26.0	1.2	26.0	0.0	26.0	0.0	26.0	0.0	26.1	0.4
1951	26.7	2.3	26.7	0.0	27.0	1.1	27.0	0.0	27.0	0.0	27.0	0.0	27.0	0.0	27.4	1.5	28.1	2.6	28.3	0.7	28.6	1.1	28.6	0.0
1952	28.6	0.0	28.9	1.0	28.9	0.0	28.8	-0.3	29.4	2.1	29.4	0.0	29.4	0.0	29.4	0.0	29.4	0.0	29.4	0.0	29.4	0.0	29.4	0.0
1953	-	-	-	-	30.0	2.0	-	-	-	-	29.9	-0.3	-	-	-	-	30.2	1.0	-	-	-	-	30.0	-0.7
1954	-	-	-	-	29.4	-2.0	-	-	-	-	29.1	-1.0	-	-	-	-	29.2	0.3	-	-	-	-	28.4	-2.7
1955	-	-	-	-	28.5	0.4	-	-	-	-	28.3	-0.7	-	-	-	-	27.7	-2.1	-	-	-	-	28.1	1.4
1956	-	-	-	-	27.8	-1.1	-	-	-	-	28.1	1.1	-	-	-	-	28.5	1.4	-	-	-	-	29.5	3.5
1957	-	-	-	-	29.7	0.7	-	-	-	-	29.9	0.7	-	-	-	-	30.4	1.7	-	-	-	-	30.7	1.0
1958	-	-	-	-	30.4	-1.0	-	-	-	-	30.4	0.0	-	-	-	-	30.6	0.7	-	-	-	-	32.1	4.9
1959	-	-	-	-	32.5	1.2	-	-	-	-	32.8	0.9	-	-	-	-	32.7	-0.3	-	-	-	-	34.1	4.3
1960	-	-	-	-	33.5	-1.8	-	-	-	-	32.9	-1.8	-	-	-	-	32.8	-0.3	-	-	-	-	32.8	0.0
1961	-	-	-	-	32.8	0.0	-	-	-	-	33.3	1.5	-	-	-	-	33.6	0.9	-	-	-	-	32.9	-2.1
1962	-	-	-	-	33.8	2.7	-	-	-	-	33.8	0.0	-	-	-	-	33.9	0.3	-	-	-	-	33.8	-0.3
1963	-	-	-	-	33.9	0.3	-	-	-	-	33.8	-0.3	-	-	-	-	34.0	0.6	-	-	-	-	34.2	0.6
1964	-	-	-	-	34.4	0.6	-	-	-	-	34.4	0.0	-	-	-	-	34.5	0.3	-	-	-	-	34.5	0.0
1965	-	-	-	-	34.3	-0.6	-	-	-	-	34.5	0.6	-	-	-	-	34.6	0.3	-	-	-	-	34.8	0.6
1966	-	-	-	-	34.7	-0.3	-	-	-	-	35.1	1.2	-	-	-	-	35.5	1.1	-	-	-	-	35.3	-0.6
1967	-	-	-	-	35.1	-0.6	-	-	-	-	35.6	1.4	-	-	-	-	36.2	1.7	-	-	-	-	37.2	2.8
1968	-	-	-	-	37.4	0.5	-	-	-	-	37.9	1.3	-	-	-	-	37.9	0.0	-	-	-	-	37.6	-0.8
1969	-	-	-	-	38.9	3.5	-	-	-	-	38.9	0.0	-	-	-	-	38.5	-1.0	-	-	-	-	39.4	2.3
1970	-	-	-	-	39.0	-1.0	-	-	-	-	40.8	4.6	-	-	-	-	41.1	0.7	-	-	-	-	42.9	4.4
1971	-	-	-	-	42.3	-1.4	-	-	-	-	43.3	2.4	-	-	-	-	43.1	-0.5	-	-	-	-	43.6	1.2
1972	-	-	-	-	42.7	-2.1	-	-	-	-	44.5	4.2	-	-	-	-	45.6	2.5	-	-	-	-	45.2	-0.9
1973	-	-	-	-	45.5	0.7	-	-	-	-	43.8	-3.7	-	-	-	-	43.6	-0.5	-	-	-	-	43.8	0.5
1974	-	-	-	-	45.1	3.0	-	-	-	-	48.4	7.3	-	-	-	-	49.6	2.5	-	-	-	-	49.6	0.0
1975	-	-	-	-	49.7	0.2	-	-	-	-	51.7	4.0	-	-	-	-	53.3	3.1	-	-	-	-	53.2	-0.2
1976	-	-	-	-	53.2	0.0	-	-	-	-	56.5	6.2	-	-	-	-	57.5	1.8	-	-	-	-	58.2	1.2
1977	-	-	-	-	59.4	2.1	-	-	-	-	60.9	2.5	-	-	-	-	60.2	-1.1	-	-	-	-	60.1	-0.2
1978	-	-	-	-	60.7	1.0	-	-	61.7	1.6	-	-	62.9	1.9	-	-	63.5	1.0	-	-	64.5	1.6	-	-
1979	65.2	1.1	-	-	66.4	1.8	-	-	69.6	4.8	-	-	72.6	4.3	-	-	75.1	3.4	-	-	76.5	1.9	-	-
1980	79.0	3.3	-	-	81.3	2.9	-	-	83.6	2.8	-	-	85.0	1.7	-	-	86.1	1.3	-	-	87.2	1.3	-	-
1981	89.8	3.0	-	-	92.2	2.7	-	-	93.5	1.4	-	-	94.0	0.5	-	-	95.0	1.1	-	-	96.3	1.4	-	-
1982	97.2	0.9	-	-	95.4	-1.9	-	-	95.2	-0.2	-	-	98.8	3.8	-	-	98.5	-0.3	-	-	98.4	-0.1	-	-
1983	98.0	-0.4	-	-	95.8	-2.2	-	-	99.1	3.4	-	-	100.0	0.9	-	-	101.4	1.4	-	-	102.6	1.2	-	-
1984	101.8	-0.8	-	-	101.7	-0.1	-	-	102.9	1.2	-	-	103.2	0.3	-	-	103.7	0.5	-	-	104.8	1.1	-	-
1985	103.3	-1.4	-	-	104.8	1.5	-	-	107.2	2.3	-	-	107.1	-0.1	-	-	105.4	-1.6	-	-	107.6	2.1	-	-
1986	106.8	-0.7	-	-	98.4	-7.9	-	-	100.4	2.0	-	-	97.8	-2.6	-	-	98.0	0.2	-	-	98.7	0.7	-	-
1987	-	-	-	-	-	-	-	-	-	-	104.6	6.0	-	-	-	-	-	-	-	-	-	-	107.6	2.9
1988	-	-	-	-	-	-	-	-	-	-	107.1	-0.5	-	-	-	-	-	-	-	-	-	-	108.2	1.0
1989	-	-	-	-	-	-	-	-	-	-	111.4	3.0	-	-	-	-	-	-	-	-	-	-	112.7	1.2
1990	-	-	-	-	-	-	-	-	-	-	115.7	2.7	-	-	-	-	-	-	-	-	-	-	121.7	5.2
1991	-	-	-	-	-	-	-	-	-	-	121.1	-0.5	-	-	-	-	-	-	-	-	-	-	121.2	0.1

[Continued]

Cincinnati, OH-KY-IN
Consumer Price Index - All Urban Consumers
Base 1982-1984 = 100
Transportation

[Continued]

For 1947-1995. Columns headed % show percentile change in the index from the previous period for which an index is available.

Year	Jan		Feb		Mar		Apr		May		Jun		Jul		Aug		Sep		Oct		Nov		Dec	
	Index	%	Index	%	Index	%	Index	%	Index	%	Index	%	Index	%	Index	%	Index	%	Index	%	Index	%	Index	%
1992	-	-	-	-	-	-	-	-	-	-	121.9	0.6	-	-	-	-	-	-	-	-	-	-	124.4	2.1
1993	-	-	-	-	-	-	-	-	-	-	125.9	1.2	-	-	-	-	-	-	-	-	-	-	126.5	0.5
1994	-	-	-	-	-	-	-	-	-	-	127.6	0.9	-	-	-	-	-	-	-	-	-	-	133.0	4.2
1995	-	-	-	-	-	-	-	-	-	-	135.0	1.5	-	-	-	-	-	-	-	-	-	-	-	-

Source: U.S. Department of Labor, Bureau of Labor Statistics, Division of Consumer Prices and Price Indexes. - indicates no data collected for period.

387

Cincinnati, OH-KY-IN
Consumer Price Index - Urban Wage Earners
Base 1982-1984 = 100
Transportation

For 1947-1995. Columns headed % show percentile change in the index from the previous period for which an index is available.

Year	Jan Index	%	Feb Index	%	Mar Index	%	Apr Index	%	May Index	%	Jun Index	%	Jul Index	%	Aug Index	%	Sep Index	%	Oct Index	%	Nov Index	%	Dec Index	%
1947	20.0	-	20.0	0.0	20.4	2.0	20.4	0.0	20.4	0.0	20.4	0.0	20.7	1.5	20.8	0.5	21.2	1.9	21.2	0.0	22.1	4.2	22.3	0.9
1948	22.5	0.9	22.5	0.0	22.5	0.0	22.5	0.0	22.5	0.0	22.9	1.8	24.0	4.8	24.4	1.7	24.6	0.8	24.6	0.0	24.6	0.0	24.6	0.0
1949	24.6	0.0	24.8	0.8	25.4	2.4	25.5	0.4	25.5	0.0	25.5	0.0	25.4	-0.4	25.5	0.4	25.5	0.0	25.5	0.0	25.5	0.0	25.4	-0.4
1950	25.3	-0.4	25.3	0.0	25.3	0.0	25.2	-0.4	25.8	2.4	25.9	0.4	26.0	0.4	26.3	1.2	26.3	0.0	26.3	0.0	26.3	0.0	26.3	0.0
1951	26.9	2.3	27.0	0.4	27.3	1.1	27.3	0.0	27.3	0.0	27.3	0.0	27.3	0.0	27.6	1.1	28.4	2.9	28.6	0.7	28.9	1.0	28.9	0.0
1952	28.9	0.0	29.2	1.0	29.2	0.0	29.1	-0.3	29.7	2.1	29.7	0.0	29.7	0.0	29.7	0.0	29.7	0.0	29.7	0.0	29.7	0.0	29.7	0.0
1953	-	-	-	-	30.3	2.0	-	-	-	-	30.2	-0.3	-	-	-	-	30.5	1.0	-	-	-	-	30.3	-0.7
1954	-	-	-	-	29.7	-2.0	-	-	-	-	29.4	-1.0	-	-	-	-	29.5	0.3	-	-	-	-	28.7	-2.7
1955	-	-	-	-	28.8	0.3	-	-	-	-	28.6	-0.7	-	-	-	-	28.0	-2.1	-	-	-	-	28.4	1.4
1956	-	-	-	-	28.1	-1.1	-	-	-	-	28.4	1.1	-	-	-	-	28.8	1.4	-	-	-	-	29.8	3.5
1957	-	-	-	-	30.0	0.7	-	-	-	-	30.2	0.7	-	-	-	-	30.7	1.7	-	-	-	-	31.0	1.0
1958	-	-	-	-	30.7	-1.0	-	-	-	-	30.7	0.0	-	-	-	-	30.9	0.7	-	-	-	-	32.4	4.9
1959	-	-	-	-	32.8	1.2	-	-	-	-	33.2	1.2	-	-	-	-	33.0	-0.6	-	-	-	-	34.4	4.2
1960	-	-	-	-	33.8	-1.7	-	-	-	-	33.3	-1.5	-	-	-	-	33.1	-0.6	-	-	-	-	33.2	0.3
1961	-	-	-	-	33.2	0.0	-	-	-	-	33.6	1.2	-	-	-	-	33.9	0.9	-	-	-	-	33.2	-2.1
1962	-	-	-	-	34.1	2.7	-	-	-	-	34.2	0.3	-	-	-	-	34.2	0.0	-	-	-	-	34.2	0.0
1963	-	-	-	-	34.2	0.0	-	-	-	-	34.2	0.0	-	-	-	-	34.3	0.3	-	-	-	-	34.5	0.6
1964	-	-	-	-	34.7	0.6	-	-	-	-	34.8	0.3	-	-	-	-	34.9	0.3	-	-	-	-	34.8	-0.3
1965	-	-	-	-	34.6	-0.6	-	-	-	-	34.8	0.6	-	-	-	-	35.0	0.6	-	-	-	-	35.1	0.3
1966	-	-	-	-	35.1	0.0	-	-	-	-	35.5	1.1	-	-	-	-	35.8	0.8	-	-	-	-	35.6	-0.6
1967	-	-	-	-	35.4	-0.6	-	-	-	-	36.0	1.7	-	-	-	-	36.6	1.7	-	-	-	-	37.6	2.7
1968	-	-	-	-	37.8	0.5	-	-	-	-	38.3	1.3	-	-	-	-	38.3	0.0	-	-	-	-	38.0	-0.8
1969	-	-	-	-	39.3	3.4	-	-	-	-	39.3	0.0	-	-	-	-	38.9	-1.0	-	-	-	-	39.8	2.3
1970	-	-	-	-	39.4	-1.0	-	-	-	-	41.2	4.6	-	-	-	-	41.5	0.7	-	-	-	-	43.3	4.3
1971	-	-	-	-	42.8	-1.2	-	-	-	-	43.7	2.1	-	-	-	-	43.5	-0.5	-	-	-	-	44.1	1.4
1972	-	-	-	-	43.2	-2.0	-	-	-	-	45.0	4.2	-	-	-	-	46.1	2.4	-	-	-	-	45.6	-1.1
1973	-	-	-	-	46.0	0.9	-	-	-	-	44.3	-3.7	-	-	-	-	44.0	-0.7	-	-	-	-	44.2	0.5
1974	-	-	-	-	45.6	3.2	-	-	-	-	48.9	7.2	-	-	-	-	50.1	2.5	-	-	-	-	50.1	0.0
1975	-	-	-	-	50.2	0.2	-	-	-	-	52.2	4.0	-	-	-	-	53.8	3.1	-	-	-	-	53.8	0.0
1976	-	-	-	-	53.7	-0.2	-	-	-	-	57.1	6.3	-	-	-	-	58.1	1.8	-	-	-	-	58.8	1.2
1977	-	-	-	-	60.0	2.0	-	-	-	-	61.5	2.5	-	-	-	-	60.8	-1.1	-	-	-	-	60.7	-0.2
1978	-	-	-	-	61.3	1.0	-	-	62.3	1.6	-	-	63.7	2.2	-	-	63.9	0.3	-	-	65.1	1.9	-	-
1979	65.8	1.1	-	-	67.0	1.8	-	-	70.2	4.8	-	-	73.1	4.1	-	-	75.5	3.3	-	-	77.0	2.0	-	-
1980	79.6	3.4	-	-	82.2	3.3	-	-	83.9	2.1	-	-	85.6	2.0	-	-	86.0	0.5	-	-	87.0	1.2	-	-
1981	89.7	3.1	-	-	92.6	3.2	-	-	93.6	1.1	-	-	94.6	1.1	-	-	95.3	0.7	-	-	96.4	1.2	-	-
1982	97.3	0.9	-	-	95.6	-1.7	-	-	95.4	-0.2	-	-	98.9	3.7	-	-	98.5	-0.4	-	-	98.5	0.0	-	-
1983	98.2	-0.3	-	-	96.1	-2.1	-	-	99.1	3.1	-	-	99.9	0.8	-	-	101.3	1.4	-	-	102.6	1.3	-	-
1984	101.7	-0.9	-	-	101.6	-0.1	-	-	102.8	1.2	-	-	103.0	0.2	-	-	103.5	0.5	-	-	104.6	1.1	-	-
1985	103.1	-1.4	-	-	104.6	1.5	-	-	106.9	2.2	-	-	106.7	-0.2	-	-	105.0	-1.6	-	-	107.3	2.2	-	-
1986	106.5	-0.7	-	-	98.4	-7.6	-	-	100.4	2.0	-	-	97.7	-2.7	-	-	97.9	0.2	-	-	98.7	0.8	-	-
1987	-	-	-	-	-	-	-	-	-	-	102.9	4.3	-	-	-	-	-	-	-	-	-	-	105.7	2.7
1988	-	-	-	-	-	-	-	-	-	-	105.4	-0.3	-	-	-	-	-	-	-	-	-	-	107.2	1.7
1989	-	-	-	-	-	-	-	-	-	-	110.3	2.9	-	-	-	-	-	-	-	-	-	-	111.7	1.3
1990	-	-	-	-	-	-	-	-	-	-	114.4	2.4	-	-	-	-	-	-	-	-	-	-	120.0	4.9
1991	-	-	-	-	-	-	-	-	-	-	119.2	-0.7	-	-	-	-	-	-	-	-	-	-	119.4	0.2

[Continued]

Cincinnati, OH-KY-IN
Consumer Price Index - Urban Wage Earners
Base 1982-1984 = 100
Transportation
[Continued]

For 1947-1995. Columns headed % show percentile change in the index from the previous period for which an index is available.

Year	Jan		Feb		Mar		Apr		May		Jun		Jul		Aug		Sep		Oct		Nov		Dec	
	Index	%	Index	%	Index	%	Index	%	Index	%	Index	%	Index	%	Index	%	Index	%	Index	%	Index	%	Index	%
1992	-	-	-	-	-	-	-	-	-	-	119.8	0.3	-	-	-	-	-	-	-	-	-	-	122.6	2.3
1993	-	-	-	-	-	-	-	-	-	-	123.7	0.9	-	-	-	-	-	-	-	-	-	-	124.3	0.5
1994	-	-	-	-	-	-	-	-	-	-	125.5	1.0	-	-	-	-	-	-	-	-	-	-	131.2	4.5
1995	-	-	-	-	-	-	-	-	-	-	133.3	1.6	-	-	-	-	-	-	-	-	-	-	-	-

Source: U.S. Department of Labor, Bureau of Labor Statistics, Division of Consumer Prices and Price Indexes. - indicates no data collected for period.

Cincinnati, OH-KY-IN
Consumer Price Index - All Urban Consumers
Base 1982-1984 = 100
Medical Care

For 1947-1995. Columns headed % show percentile change in the index from the previous period for which an index is available.

Year	Jan Index	%	Feb Index	%	Mar Index	%	Apr Index	%	May Index	%	Jun Index	%	Jul Index	%	Aug Index	%	Sep Index	%	Oct Index	%	Nov Index	%	Dec Index	%
1947	11.3	-	11.3	0.0	11.3	0.0	11.4	0.9	11.6	1.8	11.7	0.9	12.1	3.4	12.2	0.8	12.2	0.0	12.3	0.8	12.3	0.0	12.4	0.8
1948	12.8	3.2	12.7	-0.8	12.7	0.0	13.1	3.1	13.1	0.0	13.1	0.0	13.2	0.8	13.2	0.0	13.2	0.0	13.2	0.0	13.2	0.0	13.2	0.0
1949	13.2	0.0	13.2	0.0	13.4	1.5	13.4	0.0	13.4	0.0	13.5	0.7	13.5	0.0	13.5	0.0	13.5	0.0	13.5	0.0	13.5	0.0	13.5	0.0
1950	13.5	0.0	13.5	0.0	13.5	0.0	13.5	0.0	13.5	0.0	13.5	0.0	13.5	0.0	13.5	0.0	13.5	0.0	13.5	0.0	13.5	0.0	13.6	0.7
1951	13.6	0.0	13.6	0.0	13.7	0.7	13.7	0.0	13.7	0.0	13.8	0.7	13.8	0.0	13.8	0.0	13.9	0.7	13.9	0.0	13.9	0.0	14.6	5.0
1952	14.6	0.0	14.7	0.7	14.9	1.4	14.9	0.0	14.9	0.0	14.9	0.0	15.0	0.7	15.0	0.0	15.0	0.0	15.0	0.0	15.0	0.0	15.0	0.0
1953	-		-		15.5	3.3	-		-		15.5	0.0	-		-		15.7	1.3	-		-		15.9	1.3
1954	-		-		15.9	0.0	-		-		15.9	0.0	-		-		15.9	0.0	-		-		16.1	1.3
1955	-		-		16.3	1.2	-		-		16.3	0.0	-		-		16.3	0.0	-		-		17.5	7.4
1956	-		-		17.5	0.0	-		-		17.5	0.0	-		-		17.5	0.0	-		-		17.6	0.6
1957	-		-		17.8	1.1	-		-		17.9	0.6	-		-		17.9	0.0	-		-		19.0	6.1
1958	-		-		19.0	0.0	-		-		19.0	0.0	-		-		19.0	0.0	-		-		19.4	2.1
1959	-		-		19.3	-0.5	-		-		19.7	2.1	-		-		19.7	0.0	-		-		19.7	0.0
1960	-		-		19.8	0.5	-		-		19.8	0.0	-		-		20.0	1.0	-		-		20.4	2.0
1961	-		-		20.5	0.5	-		-		20.6	0.5	-		-		20.7	0.5	-		-		20.7	0.0
1962	-		-		20.7	0.0	-		-		20.8	0.5	-		-		21.5	3.4	-		-		21.5	0.0
1963	-		-		21.7	0.9	-		-		21.9	0.9	-		-		21.9	0.0	-		-		21.9	0.0
1964	-		-		22.2	1.4	-		-		22.3	0.5	-		-		22.3	0.0	-		-		23.5	5.4
1965	-		-		23.6	0.4	-		-		23.9	1.3	-		-		23.9	0.0	-		-		24.2	1.3
1966	-		-		24.6	1.7	-		-		24.9	1.2	-		-		25.1	0.8	-		-		25.6	2.0
1967	-		-		26.5	3.5	-		-		26.6	0.4	-		-		27.0	1.5	-		-		27.4	1.5
1968	-		-		28.5	4.0	-		-		28.7	0.7	-		-		29.0	1.0	-		-		29.4	1.4
1969	-		-		30.8	4.8	-		-		31.2	1.3	-		-		31.7	1.6	-		-		31.7	0.0
1970	-		-		32.3	1.9	-		-		32.6	0.9	-		-		32.9	0.9	-		-		33.6	2.1
1971	-		-		35.0	4.2	-		-		35.4	1.1	-		-		35.6	0.6	-		-		35.4	-0.6
1972	-		-		36.4	2.8	-		-		36.5	0.3	-		-		36.5	0.0	-		-		36.9	1.1
1973	-		-		38.0	3.0	-		-		38.3	0.8	-		-		38.5	0.5	-		-		39.7	3.1
1974	-		-		41.4	4.3	-		-		42.0	1.4	-		-		43.3	3.1	-		-		44.4	2.5
1975	-		-		46.5	4.7	-		-		47.1	1.3	-		-		48.0	1.9	-		-		48.4	0.8
1976	-		-		51.6	6.6	-		-		52.3	1.4	-		-		53.6	2.5	-		-		55.1	2.8
1977	-		-		58.2	5.6	-		-		58.8	1.0	-		-		60.0	2.0	-		-		60.2	0.3
1978	-		-		63.3	5.1	-		64.5	1.9	-		65.4	1.4	-		68.1	4.1	-		68.2	0.1	-	
1979	71.6	5.0	-		72.1	0.7	-		71.8	-0.4	-		72.1	0.4	-		73.0	1.2	-		73.9	1.2	-	
1980	76.6	3.7	-		78.5	2.5	-		78.6	0.1	-		79.6	1.3	-		80.1	0.6	-		80.6	0.6	-	
1981	82.0	1.7	-		83.2	1.5	-		83.9	0.8	-		87.3	4.1	-		88.1	0.9	-		88.7	0.7	-	
1982	91.4	3.0	-		91.8	0.4	-		92.7	1.0	-		93.8	1.2	-		95.0	1.3	-		94.9	-0.1	-	
1983	98.5	3.8	-		98.9	0.4	-		99.4	0.5	-		100.6	1.2	-		100.5	-0.1	-		101.7	1.2	-	
1984	104.2	2.5	-		104.5	0.3	-		105.1	0.6	-		107.1	1.9	-		107.8	0.7	-		107.7	-0.1	-	
1985	109.2	1.4	-		110.4	1.1	-		111.5	1.0	-		112.2	0.6	-		113.2	0.9	-		114.3	1.0	-	
1986	115.1	0.7	-		115.8	0.6	-		116.3	0.4	-		119.0	2.3	-		118.8	-0.2	-		119.1	0.3	-	
1987	-		-		-		-		-		126.5	6.2	-		-		-		-		-		131.9	4.3
1988	-		-		-		-		-		135.7	2.9	-		-		-		-		-		140.3	3.4
1989	-		-		-		-		-		144.8	3.2	-		-		-		-		-		153.7	6.1
1990	-		-		-		-		-		159.4	3.7	-		-		-		-		-		166.7	4.6
1991	-		-		-		-		-		174.5	4.7	-		-		-		-		-		181.4	4.0

[Continued]

Cincinnati, OH-KY-IN
Consumer Price Index - All Urban Consumers
Base 1982-1984 = 100
Medical Care

[Continued]

For 1947-1995. Columns headed % show percentile change in the index from the previous period for which an index is available.

Year	Jan		Feb		Mar		Apr		May		Jun		Jul		Aug		Sep		Oct		Nov		Dec	
	Index	%	Index	%	Index	%	Index	%	Index	%	Index	%	Index	%	Index	%	Index	%	Index	%	Index	%	Index	%
1992	-	-	-	-	-	-	-	-	-	-	188.5	3.9	-	-	-	-	-	-	-	-	-	-	193.0	2.4
1993	-	-	-	-	-	-	-	-	-	-	200.7	4.0	-	-	-	-	-	-	-	-	-	-	205.5	2.4
1994	-	-	-	-	-	-	-	-	-	-	211.2	2.8	-	-	-	-	-	-	-	-	-	-	215.2	1.9
1995	-	-	-	-	-	-	-	-	-	-	222.1	3.2	-	-	-	-	-	-	-	-	-	-	-	-

Source: U.S. Department of Labor, Bureau of Labor Statistics, Division of Consumer Prices and Price Indexes. - indicates no data collected for period.

Cincinnati, OH-KY-IN
Consumer Price Index - Urban Wage Earners
Base 1982-1984 = 100
Medical Care

For 1947-1995. Columns headed % show percentile change in the index from the previous period for which an index is available.

Year	Jan Index	%	Feb Index	%	Mar Index	%	Apr Index	%	May Index	%	Jun Index	%	Jul Index	%	Aug Index	%	Sep Index	%	Oct Index	%	Nov Index	%	Dec Index	%
1947	10.8	-	10.8	0.0	10.8	0.0	10.9	0.9	11.0	0.9	11.2	1.8	11.5	2.7	11.6	0.9	11.7	0.9	11.7	0.0	11.7	0.0	11.8	0.9
1948	12.2	3.4	12.1	-0.8	12.1	0.0	12.4	2.5	12.4	0.0	12.5	0.8	12.5	0.0	12.5	0.0	12.6	0.8	12.6	0.0	12.6	0.0	12.6	0.0
1949	12.6	0.0	12.6	0.0	12.7	0.8	12.8	0.8	12.8	0.0	12.8	0.0	12.8	0.0	12.8	0.0	12.8	0.0	12.8	0.0	12.8	0.0	12.8	0.0
1950	12.8	0.0	12.8	0.0	12.8	0.0	12.8	0.0	12.8	0.0	12.8	0.0	12.8	0.0	12.8	0.0	12.8	0.0	12.8	0.0	12.8	0.0	13.0	1.6
1951	13.0	0.0	13.0	0.0	13.0	0.0	13.1	0.8	13.1	0.0	13.1	0.0	13.1	0.0	13.1	0.0	13.3	1.5	13.3	0.0	13.3	0.0	13.9	4.5
1952	13.9	0.0	14.0	0.7	14.2	1.4	14.2	0.0	14.2	0.0	14.2	0.0	14.3	0.7	14.3	0.0	14.3	0.0	14.3	0.0	14.3	0.0	14.3	0.0
1953	-		-		14.7	2.8	-		-		14.8	0.7	-		-		15.0	1.4	-		-		15.2	1.3
1954	-		-		15.2	0.0	-		-		15.2	0.0	-		-		15.2	0.0	-		-		15.4	1.3
1955	-		-		15.5	0.6	-		-		15.5	0.0	-		-		15.5	0.0	-		-		16.7	7.7
1956	-		-		16.7	0.0	-		-		16.7	0.0	-		-		16.7	0.0	-		-		16.7	0.0
1957	-		-		17.0	1.8	-		-		17.0	0.0	-		-		17.1	0.6	-		-		18.1	5.8
1958	-		-		18.1	0.0	-		-		18.1	0.0	-		-		18.1	0.0	-		-		18.5	2.2
1959	-		-		18.4	-0.5	-		-		18.7	1.6	-		-		18.8	0.5	-		-		18.8	0.0
1960	-		-		18.9	0.5	-		-		18.9	0.0	-		-		19.1	1.1	-		-		19.5	2.1
1961	-		-		19.6	0.5	-		-		19.7	0.5	-		-		19.7	0.0	-		-		19.7	0.0
1962	-		-		19.7	0.0	-		-		19.8	0.5	-		-		20.5	3.5	-		-		20.5	0.0
1963	-		-		20.7	1.0	-		-		20.9	1.0	-		-		20.9	0.0	-		-		20.9	0.0
1964	-		-		21.2	1.4	-		-		21.2	0.0	-		-		21.2	0.0	-		-		22.4	5.7
1965	-		-		22.5	0.4	-		-		22.7	0.9	-		-		22.8	0.4	-		-		23.1	1.3
1966	-		-		23.5	1.7	-		-		23.7	0.9	-		-		23.9	0.8	-		-		24.4	2.1
1967	-		-		25.2	3.3	-		-		25.3	0.4	-		-		25.7	1.6	-		-		26.1	1.6
1968	-		-		27.2	4.2	-		-		27.3	0.4	-		-		27.6	1.1	-		-		28.0	1.4
1969	-		-		29.4	5.0	-		-		29.8	1.4	-		-		30.2	1.3	-		-		30.2	0.0
1970	-		-		30.8	2.0	-		-		31.0	0.6	-		-		31.3	1.0	-		-		32.1	2.6
1971	-		-		33.4	4.0	-		-		33.7	0.9	-		-		33.9	0.6	-		-		33.7	-0.6
1972	-		-		34.7	3.0	-		-		34.8	0.3	-		-		34.8	0.0	-		-		35.1	0.9
1973	-		-		36.2	3.1	-		-		36.5	0.8	-		-		36.7	0.5	-		-		37.8	3.0
1974	-		-		39.5	4.5	-		-		40.0	1.3	-		-		41.3	3.2	-		-		42.3	2.4
1975	-		-		44.3	4.7	-		-		44.8	1.1	-		-		45.8	2.2	-		-		46.1	0.7
1976	-		-		49.2	6.7	-		-		49.9	1.4	-		-		51.1	2.4	-		-		52.5	2.7
1977	-		-		55.4	5.5	-		-		56.1	1.3	-		-		57.2	2.0	-		-		57.4	0.3
1978	-		-		60.3	5.1	-		60.6	0.5	-		63.3	4.5	-		63.4	0.2	-		63.9	0.8	-	
1979	68.2	6.7	-		68.5	0.4	-		69.8	1.9	-		70.5	1.0	-		71.2	1.0	-		71.5	0.4	-	
1980	75.0	4.9	-		77.1	2.8	-		77.6	0.6	-		78.8	1.5	-		79.2	0.5	-		79.7	0.6	-	
1981	82.0	2.9	-		82.6	0.7	-		83.4	1.0	-		86.6	3.8	-		87.8	1.4	-		88.8	1.1	-	
1982	91.4	2.9	-		91.7	0.3	-		92.7	1.1	-		93.8	1.2	-		95.0	1.3	-		94.9	-0.1	-	
1983	98.3	3.6	-		98.8	0.5	-		99.4	0.6	-		100.7	1.3	-		100.5	-0.2	-		101.8	1.3	-	
1984	104.3	2.5	-		104.6	0.3	-		105.2	0.6	-		107.1	1.8	-		107.8	0.7	-		107.6	-0.2	-	
1985	109.2	1.5	-		110.4	1.1	-		111.5	1.0	-		112.2	0.6	-		113.1	0.8	-		114.2	1.0	-	
1986	114.9	0.6	-		115.6	0.6	-		116.0	0.3	-		118.7	2.3	-		118.5	-0.2	-		118.8	0.3	-	
1987	-		-		-		-		-		126.1	6.1	-		-		-		-		-		131.7	4.4
1988	-		-		-		-		-		135.8	3.1	-		-		-		-		-		141.0	3.8
1989	-		-		-		-		-		145.8	3.4	-		-		-		-		-		155.1	6.4
1990	-		-		-		-		-		160.6	3.5	-		-		-		-		-		168.0	4.6
1991	-		-		-		-		-		175.9	4.7	-		-		-		-		-		183.0	4.0

[Continued]

Cincinnati, OH-KY-IN
Consumer Price Index - Urban Wage Earners
Base 1982-1984 = 100
Medical Care
[Continued]

For 1947-1995. Columns headed % show percentile change in the index from the previous period for which an index is available.

Year	Jan		Feb		Mar		Apr		May		Jun		Jul		Aug		Sep		Oct		Nov		Dec	
	Index	%	Index	%	Index	%	Index	%	Index	%	Index	%	Index	%	Index	%	Index	%	Index	%	Index	%	Index	%
1992	-	-	-	-	-	-	-	-	-	-	190.0	3.8	-	-	-	-	-	-	-	-	-	-	-	-
1993	-	-	-	-	-	-	-	-	-	-	203.1	4.2	-	-	-	-	-	-	-	-	-	-	194.9	2.6
1994	-	-	-	-	-	-	-	-	-	-	213.8	2.8	-	-	-	-	-	-	-	-	-	-	208.0	2.4
1995	-	-	-	-	-	-	-	-	-	-	225.4	3.3	-	-	-	-	-	-	-	-	-	-	218.1	2.0
																							-	-

Source: U.S. Department of Labor, Bureau of Labor Statistics, Division of Consumer Prices and Price Indexes. - indicates no data collected for period.

Cincinnati, OH-KY-IN
Consumer Price Index - All Urban Consumers
Base 1982-1984 = 100
Entertainment

For 1975-1995. Columns headed % show percentile change in the index from the previous period for which an index is available.

Year	Jan Index	%	Feb Index	%	Mar Index	%	Apr Index	%	May Index	%	Jun Index	%	Jul Index	%	Aug Index	%	Sep Index	%	Oct Index	%	Nov Index	%	Dec Index	%
1975	-	-	-	-	-	-	-	-	-	-	-	-	-	-	-	-	-	-	-	-	-	-	65.3	-
1976	-	-	-	-	66.5	1.8	-	-	-	-	67.1	0.9	-	-	-	-	67.7	0.9	-	-	-	-	67.6	-0.1
1977	-	-	-	-	68.4	1.2	-	-	-	-	68.6	0.3	-	-	-	-	69.6	1.5	-	-	-	-	69.8	0.3
1978	-	-	-	-	71.7	2.7	-	-	73.1	2.0	-	-	72.7	-0.5	-	-	73.0	0.4	-	-	73.2	0.3	-	-
1979	74.2	1.4	-	-	76.1	2.6	-	-	77.1	1.3	-	-	78.1	1.3	-	-	78.3	0.3	-	-	77.4	-1.1	-	-
1980	78.0	0.8	-	-	83.6	7.2	-	-	84.6	1.2	-	-	83.1	-1.8	-	-	84.8	2.0	-	-	86.1	1.5	-	-
1981	86.6	0.6	-	-	88.1	1.7	-	-	86.1	-2.3	-	-	86.4	0.3	-	-	88.0	1.9	-	-	88.0	0.0	-	-
1982	93.2	5.9	-	-	93.5	0.3	-	-	93.5	0.0	-	-	94.4	1.0	-	-	95.6	1.3	-	-	97.3	1.8	-	-
1983	99.7	2.5	-	-	100.1	0.4	-	-	99.7	-0.4	-	-	99.7	0.0	-	-	101.2	1.5	-	-	102.8	1.6	-	-
1984	103.3	0.5	-	-	102.6	-0.7	-	-	103.4	0.8	-	-	105.5	2.0	-	-	106.2	0.7	-	-	106.7	0.5	-	-
1985	99.8	-6.5	-	-	100.4	0.6	-	-	100.0	-0.4	-	-	98.0	-2.0	-	-	98.7	0.7	-	-	101.6	2.9	-	-
1986	101.7	0.1	-	-	102.1	0.4	-	-	104.3	2.2	-	-	104.2	-0.1	-	-	104.7	0.5	-	-	104.7	0.0	-	-
1987	-	-	-	-	-	-	-	-	-	-	115.1	9.9	-	-	-	-	-	-	-	-	-	-	116.9	1.6
1988	-	-	-	-	-	-	-	-	-	-	120.2	2.8	-	-	-	-	-	-	-	-	-	-	124.4	3.5
1989	-	-	-	-	-	-	-	-	-	-	129.9	4.4	-	-	-	-	-	-	-	-	-	-	133.3	2.6
1990	-	-	-	-	-	-	-	-	-	-	137.6	3.2	-	-	-	-	-	-	-	-	-	-	140.7	2.3
1991	-	-	-	-	-	-	-	-	-	-	145.2	3.2	-	-	-	-	-	-	-	-	-	-	146.6	1.0
1992	-	-	-	-	-	-	-	-	-	-	147.9	0.9	-	-	-	-	-	-	-	-	-	-	151.0	2.1
1993	-	-	-	-	-	-	-	-	-	-	153.0	1.3	-	-	-	-	-	-	-	-	-	-	154.8	1.2
1994	-	-	-	-	-	-	-	-	-	-	158.9	2.6	-	-	-	-	-	-	-	-	-	-	161.2	1.4
1995	-	-	-	-	-	-	-	-	-	-	160.1	-0.7	-	-	-	-	-	-	-	-	-	-	-	-

Source: U.S. Department of Labor, Bureau of Labor Statistics, Division of Consumer Prices and Price Indexes. - indicates no data collected for period.

Cincinnati, OH-KY-IN
Consumer Price Index - Urban Wage Earners
Base 1982-1984 = 100
Entertainment

For 1975-1995. Columns headed % show percentile change in the index from the previous period for which an index is available.

Year	Jan Index	%	Feb Index	%	Mar Index	%	Apr Index	%	May Index	%	Jun Index	%	Jul Index	%	Aug Index	%	Sep Index	%	Oct Index	%	Nov Index	%	Dec Index	%
1975	-	-	-	-	-	-	-	-	-	-	-	-	-	-	-	-	-	-	-	-	-	-	67.8	-
1976	-	-	-	-	69.1	1.9	-	-	-	-	69.8	1.0	-	-	-	-	70.4	0.9	-	-	-	-	70.2	-0.3
1977	-	-	-	-	71.1	1.3	-	-	-	-	71.2	0.1	-	-	-	-	72.3	1.5	-	-	-	-	72.6	0.4
1978	-	-	-	-	74.5	2.6	-	-	75.2	0.9	-	-	76.1	1.2	-	-	76.6	0.7	-	-	76.7	0.1	-	-
1979	77.1	0.5	-	-	77.6	0.6	-	-	78.3	0.9	-	-	78.8	0.6	-	-	79.0	0.3	-	-	78.4	-0.8	-	-
1980	79.4	1.3	-	-	83.5	5.2	-	-	85.1	1.9	-	-	83.3	-2.1	-	-	84.7	1.7	-	-	85.7	1.2	-	-
1981	86.7	1.2	-	-	88.0	1.5	-	-	87.8	-0.2	-	-	88.0	0.2	-	-	89.5	1.7	-	-	89.4	-0.1	-	-
1982	93.8	4.9	-	-	94.0	0.2	-	-	94.0	0.0	-	-	94.6	0.6	-	-	96.0	1.5	-	-	97.6	1.7	-	-
1983	99.7	2.2	-	-	100.0	0.3	-	-	99.9	-0.1	-	-	100.0	0.1	-	-	101.3	1.3	-	-	102.6	1.3	-	-
1984	103.2	0.6	-	-	102.6	-0.6	-	-	103.0	0.4	-	-	105.1	2.0	-	-	105.7	0.6	-	-	106.1	0.4	-	-
1985	97.7	-7.9	-	-	98.2	0.5	-	-	97.9	-0.3	-	-	94.5	-3.5	-	-	95.2	0.7	-	-	97.7	2.6	-	-
1986	97.7	0.0	-	-	97.8	0.1	-	-	101.4	3.7	-	-	101.2	-0.2	-	-	101.2	0.0	-	-	101.3	0.1	-	-
1987	-	-	-	-	-	-	-	-	-	-	117.0	15.5	-	-	-	-	-	-	-	-	-	-	119.0	1.7
1988	-	-	-	-	-	-	-	-	-	-	122.3	2.8	-	-	-	-	-	-	-	-	-	-	126.1	3.1
1989	-	-	-	-	-	-	-	-	-	-	131.4	4.2	-	-	-	-	-	-	-	-	-	-	134.4	2.3
1990	-	-	-	-	-	-	-	-	-	-	138.6	3.1	-	-	-	-	-	-	-	-	-	-	141.5	2.1
1991	-	-	-	-	-	-	-	-	-	-	145.5	2.8	-	-	-	-	-	-	-	-	-	-	146.5	0.7
1992	-	-	-	-	-	-	-	-	-	-	147.9	1.0	-	-	-	-	-	-	-	-	-	-	151.0	2.1
1993	-	-	-	-	-	-	-	-	-	-	152.8	1.2	-	-	-	-	-	-	-	-	-	-	154.5	1.1
1994	-	-	-	-	-	-	-	-	-	-	158.1	2.3	-	-	-	-	-	-	-	-	-	-	160.6	1.6
1995	-	-	-	-	-	-	-	-	-	-	159.4	-0.7	-	-	-	-	-	-	-	-	-	-		

Source: U.S. Department of Labor, Bureau of Labor Statistics, Division of Consumer Prices and Price Indexes. - indicates no data collected for period.

Cincinnati, OH-KY-IN
Consumer Price Index - All Urban Consumers
Base 1982-1984 = 100
Other Goods and Services

For 1975-1995. Columns headed % show percentile change in the index from the previous period for which an index is available.

Year	Jan Index	%	Feb Index	%	Mar Index	%	Apr Index	%	May Index	%	Jun Index	%	Jul Index	%	Aug Index	%	Sep Index	%	Oct Index	%	Nov Index	%	Dec Index	%
1975	-	-	-	-	-	-	-	-	-	-	-	-	-	-	-	-	-	-	-	-	-	-	54.7	-
1976	-	-	-	-	55.4	1.3	-	-	-	-	55.3	-0.2	-	-	-	-	56.0	1.3	-	-	-	-	57.7	3.0
1977	-	-	-	-	57.9	0.3	-	-	-	-	58.6	1.2	-	-	-	-	60.6	3.4	-	-	-	-	60.8	0.3
1978	-	-	-	-	61.7	1.5	-	-	61.8	0.2	-	-	62.8	1.6	-	-	64.2	2.2	-	-	63.6	-0.9	-	-
1979	65.2	2.5	-	-	65.7	0.8	-	-	66.3	0.9	-	-	66.9	0.9	-	-	69.6	4.0	-	-	70.3	1.0	-	-
1980	71.5	1.7	-	-	72.4	1.3	-	-	73.3	1.2	-	-	73.8	0.7	-	-	75.6	2.4	-	-	77.0	1.9	-	-
1981	78.9	2.5	-	-	79.0	0.1	-	-	80.3	1.6	-	-	80.8	0.6	-	-	84.1	4.1	-	-	84.9	1.0	-	-
1982	86.3	1.6	-	-	87.6	1.5	-	-	88.1	0.6	-	-	87.8	-0.3	-	-	92.1	4.9	-	-	96.0	4.2	-	-
1983	98.0	2.1	-	-	99.1	1.1	-	-	100.0	0.9	-	-	101.5	1.5	-	-	102.3	0.8	-	-	105.7	3.3	-	-
1984	107.0	1.2	-	-	107.5	0.5	-	-	106.7	-0.7	-	-	108.5	1.7	-	-	109.5	0.9	-	-	109.8	0.3	-	-
1985	111.3	1.4	-	-	113.6	2.1	-	-	114.5	0.8	-	-	115.9	1.2	-	-	117.6	1.5	-	-	118.1	0.4	-	-
1986	119.0	0.8	-	-	119.2	0.2	-	-	119.7	0.4	-	-	120.4	0.6	-	-	122.7	1.9	-	-	123.0	0.2	-	-
1987	-	-	-	-	-	-	-	-	-	-	128.5	4.5	-	-	-	-	-	-	-	-	-	-	130.8	1.8
1988	-	-	-	-	-	-	-	-	-	-	135.0	3.2	-	-	-	-	-	-	-	-	-	-	141.1	4.5
1989	-	-	-	-	-	-	-	-	-	-	148.2	5.0	-	-	-	-	-	-	-	-	-	-	158.0	6.6
1990	-	-	-	-	-	-	-	-	-	-	161.3	2.1	-	-	-	-	-	-	-	-	-	-	167.3	3.7
1991	-	-	-	-	-	-	-	-	-	-	174.7	4.4	-	-	-	-	-	-	-	-	-	-	183.3	4.9
1992	-	-	-	-	-	-	-	-	-	-	188.4	2.8	-	-	-	-	-	-	-	-	-	-	195.5	3.8
1993	-	-	-	-	-	-	-	-	-	-	199.6	2.1	-	-	-	-	-	-	-	-	-	-	205.4	2.9
1994	-	-	-	-	-	-	-	-	-	-	206.1	0.3	-	-	-	-	-	-	-	-	-	-	211.5	2.6
1995	-	-	-	-	-	-	-	-	-	-	215.0	1.7	-	-	-	-	-	-	-	-	-	-	-	-

Source: U.S. Department of Labor, Bureau of Labor Statistics, Division of Consumer Prices and Price Indexes. - indicates no data collected for period.

Cincinnati, OH-KY-IN
Consumer Price Index - Urban Wage Earners
Base 1982-1984 = 100
Other Goods and Services

For 1975-1995. Columns headed % show percentile change in the index from the previous period for which an index is available.

Year	Jan Index	%	Feb Index	%	Mar Index	%	Apr Index	%	May Index	%	Jun Index	%	Jul Index	%	Aug Index	%	Sep Index	%	Oct Index	%	Nov Index	%	Dec Index	%
1975	-	-	-	-	-	-	-	-	-	-	-	-	-	-	-	-	-	-	-	-	-	-	54.5	-
1976	-	-	-	-	55.2	1.3	-	-	-	-	55.1	-0.2	-	-	-	-	55.8	1.3	-	-	-	-	57.5	3.0
1977	-	-	-	-	57.7	0.3	-	-	-	-	58.4	1.2	-	-	-	-	60.4	3.4	-	-	-	-	60.6	0.3
1978	-	-	-	-	61.5	1.5	-	-	62.5	1.6	-	-	63.4	1.4	-	-	64.4	1.6	-	-	64.4	0.0	-	-
1979	66.4	3.1	-	-	67.3	1.4	-	-	66.4	-1.3	-	-	67.4	1.5	-	-	69.9	3.7	-	-	71.0	1.6	-	-
1980	72.1	1.5	-	-	73.0	1.2	-	-	73.7	1.0	-	-	74.5	1.1	-	-	75.7	1.6	-	-	76.9	1.6	-	-
1981	79.5	3.4	-	-	80.0	0.6	-	-	81.2	1.5	-	-	81.7	0.6	-	-	84.5	3.4	-	-	85.1	0.7	-	-
1982	86.2	1.3	-	-	87.7	1.7	-	-	88.2	0.6	-	-	87.9	-0.3	-	-	92.1	4.8	-	-	95.9	4.1	-	-
1983	98.2	2.4	-	-	99.3	1.1	-	-	100.2	0.9	-	-	102.1	1.9	-	-	102.4	0.3	-	-	105.6	3.1	-	-
1984	107.0	1.3	-	-	107.5	0.5	-	-	106.6	-0.8	-	-	108.6	1.9	-	-	109.1	0.5	-	-	109.2	0.1	-	-
1985	110.9	1.6	-	-	112.7	1.6	-	-	113.7	0.9	-	-	115.3	1.4	-	-	116.8	1.3	-	-	117.2	0.3	-	-
1986	118.2	0.9	-	-	118.3	0.1	-	-	118.9	0.5	-	-	119.6	0.6	-	-	121.5	1.6	-	-	121.6	0.1	-	-
1987	-	-	-	-	-	-	-	-	-	-	128.9	6.0	-	-	-	-	-	-	-	-	-	-	131.7	2.2
1988	-	-	-	-	-	-	-	-	-	-	136.0	3.3	-	-	-	-	-	-	-	-	-	-	141.1	3.8
1989	-	-	-	-	-	-	-	-	-	-	147.8	4.7	-	-	-	-	-	-	-	-	-	-	159.3	7.8
1990	-	-	-	-	-	-	-	-	-	-	163.2	2.4	-	-	-	-	-	-	-	-	-	-	169.3	3.7
1991	-	-	-	-	-	-	-	-	-	-	178.2	5.3	-	-	-	-	-	-	-	-	-	-	186.6	4.7
1992	-	-	-	-	-	-	-	-	-	-	191.9	2.8	-	-	-	-	-	-	-	-	-	-	199.9	4.2
1993	-	-	-	-	-	-	-	-	-	-	204.5	2.3	-	-	-	-	-	-	-	-	-	-	209.5	2.4
1994	-	-	-	-	-	-	-	-	-	-	209.2	-0.1	-	-	-	-	-	-	-	-	-	-	213.4	2.0
1995	-	-	-	-	-	-	-	-	-	-	215.9	1.2	-	-	-	-	-	-	-	-	-	-	-	-

Source: U.S. Department of Labor, Bureau of Labor Statistics, Division of Consumer Prices and Price Indexes. - indicates no data collected for period.

Cleveland, OH
Consumer Price Index - All Urban Consumers
Base 1982-1984 = 100
Annual Averages

For 1914-1995. Columns headed % show percentile change in the index from the previous period for which an index is available.

Year	All Items		Food & Beverage		Housing		Apparel & Upkeep		Trans-portation		Medical Care		Entertain-ment		Other Goods & Services	
	Index	%	Index	%	Index	%	Index	%	Index	%	Index	%	Index	%	Index	%
1914	-	-	-	-	-	-	-	-	-	-	-	-	-	-	-	-
1915	8.7	-	-	-	-	-	-	-	-	-	-	-	-	-	-	-
1916	9.4	8.0	-	-	-	-	-	-	-	-	-	-	-	-	-	-
1917	11.4	21.3	-	-	-	-	-	-	-	-	-	-	-	-	-	-
1918	13.2	15.8	-	-	-	-	-	-	-	-	-	-	-	-	-	-
1919	15.5	17.4	-	-	-	-	-	-	-	-	-	-	-	-	-	-
1920	18.3	18.1	-	-	-	-	-	-	-	-	-	-	-	-	-	-
1921	16.6	-9.3	-	-	-	-	-	-	-	-	-	-	-	-	-	-
1922	15.1	-9.0	-	-	-	-	-	-	-	-	-	-	-	-	-	-
1923	15.7	4.0	-	-	-	-	-	-	-	-	-	-	-	-	-	-
1924	15.7	0.0	-	-	-	-	-	-	-	-	-	-	-	-	-	-
1925	16.0	1.9	-	-	-	-	-	-	-	-	-	-	-	-	-	-
1926	16.1	0.6	-	-	-	-	-	-	-	-	-	-	-	-	-	-
1927	15.8	-1.9	-	-	-	-	-	-	-	-	-	-	-	-	-	-
1928	15.6	-1.3	-	-	-	-	-	-	-	-	-	-	-	-	-	-
1929	15.5	-0.6	-	-	-	-	-	-	-	-	-	-	-	-	-	-
1930	15.2	-1.9	-	-	-	-	-	-	-	-	-	-	-	-	-	-
1931	13.7	-9.9	-	-	-	-	-	-	-	-	-	-	-	-	-	-
1932	12.4	-9.5	-	-	-	-	-	-	-	-	-	-	-	-	-	-
1933	11.8	-4.8	-	-	-	-	-	-	-	-	-	-	-	-	-	-
1934	12.2	3.4	-	-	-	-	-	-	-	-	-	-	-	-	-	-
1935	12.7	4.1	-	-	-	-	-	-	-	-	-	-	-	-	-	-
1936	12.8	0.8	-	-	-	-	-	-	-	-	-	-	-	-	-	-
1937	13.4	4.7	-	-	-	-	-	-	-	-	-	-	-	-	-	-
1938	13.3	-0.7	-	-	-	-	-	-	-	-	-	-	-	-	-	-
1939	13.2	-0.8	-	-	-	-	-	-	-	-	-	-	-	-	-	-
1940	13.2	0.0	-	-	-	-	-	-	-	-	-	-	-	-	-	-
1941	14.0	6.1	-	-	-	-	-	-	-	-	-	-	-	-	-	-
1942	15.5	10.7	-	-	-	-	-	-	-	-	-	-	-	-	-	-
1943	16.6	7.1	-	-	-	-	-	-	-	-	-	-	-	-	-	-
1944	16.9	1.8	-	-	-	-	-	-	-	-	-	-	-	-	-	-
1945	17.2	1.8	-	-	-	-	-	-	-	-	-	-	-	-	-	-
1946	18.5	7.6	-	-	-	-	-	-	-	-	-	-	-	-	-	-
1947	21.2	14.6	-	-	-	-	-	-	18.9	-	10.6	-	-	-	-	-
1948	23.0	8.5	-	-	-	-	-	-	21.8	15.3	11.2	5.7	-	-	-	-
1949	22.6	-1.7	-	-	-	-	-	-	23.1	6.0	11.7	4.5	-	-	-	-
1950	22.8	0.9	-	-	-	-	-	-	23.1	0.0	11.8	0.9	-	-	-	-
1951	24.6	7.9	-	-	-	-	-	-	24.6	6.5	12.6	6.8	-	-	-	-
1952	25.2	2.4	-	-	-	-	-	-	26.0	5.7	13.3	5.6	-	-	-	-
1953	25.4	0.8	-	-	-	-	44.1	-	26.3	1.2	13.8	3.8	-	-	-	-
1954	25.7	1.2	-	-	-	-	44.1	0.0	25.8	-1.9	14.5	5.1	-	-	-	-
1955	25.7	0.0	-	-	-	-	43.8	-0.7	25.6	-0.8	15.1	4.1	-	-	-	-
1956	26.2	1.9	-	-	-	-	44.8	2.3	26.7	4.3	16.1	6.6	-	-	-	-
1957	27.2	3.8	-	-	-	-	45.5	1.6	28.5	6.7	16.7	3.7	-	-	-	-
1958	27.8	2.2	-	-	-	-	45.9	0.9	29.0	1.8	17.1	2.4	-	-	-	-

[Continued]

Cleveland, OH
Consumer Price Index - All Urban Consumers
Base 1982-1984 = 100
Annual Averages

[Continued]

For 1914-1995. Columns headed % show percentile change in the index from the previous period for which an index is available.

Year	All Items		Food & Beverage		Housing		Apparel & Upkeep		Trans- portation		Medical Care		Entertain- ment		Other Goods & Services	
	Index	%	Index	%	Index	%	Index	%	Index	%	Index	%	Index	%	Index	%
1959	27.9	0.4	-	-	-	-	46.2	0.7	30.1	3.8	18.7	9.4	-	-	-	-
1960	28.3	1.4	-	-	-	-	46.4	0.4	30.3	0.7	19.3	3.2	-	-	-	-
1961	28.5	0.7	-	-	-	-	46.8	0.9	31.0	2.3	20.7	7.3	-	-	-	-
1962	28.6	0.4	-	-	-	-	47.0	0.4	31.4	1.3	20.8	0.5	-	-	-	-
1963	28.9	1.0	-	-	-	-	47.7	1.5	31.5	0.3	21.9	5.3	-	-	-	-
1964	29.1	0.7	-	-	-	-	47.9	0.4	32.1	1.9	22.5	2.7	-	-	-	-
1965	29.6	1.7	-	-	-	-	48.3	0.8	32.6	1.6	23.2	3.1	-	-	-	-
1966	30.3	2.4	-	-	-	-	49.8	3.1	32.9	0.9	23.7	2.2	-	-	-	-
1967	31.2	3.0	-	-	-	-	51.3	3.0	33.9	3.0	25.2	6.3	-	-	-	-
1968	33.0	5.8	-	-	-	-	54.4	6.0	35.5	4.7	27.3	8.3	-	-	-	-
1969	34.9	5.8	-	-	-	-	57.6	5.9	37.0	4.2	30.5	11.7	-	-	-	-
1970	37.2	6.6	-	-	-	-	60.4	4.9	39.5	6.8	32.9	7.9	-	-	-	-
1971	38.3	3.0	-	-	-	-	62.4	3.3	42.2	6.8	35.2	7.0	-	-	-	-
1972	39.5	3.1	-	-	-	-	63.5	1.8	42.7	1.2	36.2	2.8	-	-	-	-
1973	41.8	5.8	-	-	-	-	66.5	4.7	44.1	3.3	38.0	5.0	-	-	-	-
1974	46.1	10.3	-	-	-	-	72.6	9.2	49.4	12.0	41.3	8.7	-	-	-	-
1975	50.2	8.9	-	-	-	-	74.4	2.5	52.1	5.5	46.0	11.4	-	-	-	-
1976	52.7	5.0	63.1	-	46.2	-	76.2	2.4	54.4	4.4	50.6	10.0	67.3	-	58.3	-
1977	56.3	6.8	66.4	5.2	49.7	7.6	80.5	5.6	57.8	6.3	56.7	12.1	70.6	4.9	61.8	6.0
1978	60.5	7.5	72.1	8.6	53.6	7.8	82.1	2.0	60.8	5.2	61.9	9.2	74.8	5.9	65.9	6.6
1979	68.5	13.2	79.6	10.4	63.0	17.5	84.5	2.9	69.2	13.8	66.0	6.6	78.7	5.2	71.1	7.9
1980	78.9	15.2	85.6	7.5	75.9	20.5	89.4	5.8	80.9	16.9	72.7	10.2	83.6	6.2	76.7	7.9
1981	87.2	10.5	93.2	8.9	83.8	10.4	95.0	6.3	92.0	13.7	81.2	11.7	88.6	6.0	84.9	10.7
1982	94.0	7.8	96.3	3.3	92.3	10.1	99.5	4.7	96.9	5.3	91.5	12.7	95.7	8.0	92.8	9.3
1983	101.2	7.7	99.8	3.6	102.6	11.2	99.3	-0.2	99.5	2.7	101.2	10.6	100.3	4.8	100.6	8.4
1984	104.8	3.6	103.9	4.1	105.1	2.4	101.3	2.0	103.6	4.1	107.4	6.1	104.1	3.8	106.7	6.1
1985	107.8	2.9	106.2	2.2	108.5	3.2	104.1	2.8	105.6	1.9	111.9	4.2	107.0	2.8	111.5	4.5
1986	109.4	1.5	107.6	1.3	111.8	3.0	102.4	-1.6	101.2	-4.2	122.3	9.3	114.2	6.7	117.0	4.9
1987	112.7	3.0	111.3	3.4	114.0	2.0	108.5	6.0	103.9	2.7	128.5	5.1	115.8	1.4	123.8	5.8
1988	116.7	3.5	116.4	4.6	117.8	3.3	105.8	-2.5	107.3	3.3	134.9	5.0	119.9	3.5	133.1	7.5
1989	122.7	5.1	124.0	6.5	122.7	4.2	111.4	5.3	113.0	5.3	143.5	6.4	127.0	5.9	141.0	5.9
1990	129.0	5.1	130.6	5.3	127.7	4.1	117.8	5.7	119.4	5.7	156.6	9.1	133.6	5.2	149.6	6.1
1991	134.2	4.0	135.4	3.7	132.5	3.8	121.9	3.5	123.1	3.1	171.7	9.6	138.6	3.7	160.1	7.0
1992	136.8	1.9	136.1	0.5	135.8	2.5	122.2	0.2	124.1	0.8	178.6	4.0	139.6	0.7	170.2	6.3
1993	140.3	2.6	139.7	2.6	139.0	2.4	125.1	2.4	125.0	0.7	187.2	4.8	143.2	2.6	180.3	5.9
1994	144.4	2.9	144.4	3.4	142.4	2.4	128.8	3.0	128.6	2.9	195.8	4.6	149.4	4.3	184.3	2.2
1995	-	-	-	-	-	-	-	-	-	-	-	-	-	-	-	-

Source: U.S. Department of Labor, Bureau of Labor Statistics, Division of Consumer Prices and Price Indexes. - indicates no data collected for period.

Cleveland, OH
Consumer Price Index - Urban Wage Earners
Base 1982-1984 = 100
Annual Averages

For 1914-1995. Columns headed % show percentile change in the index from the previous period for which an index is available.

Year	All Items		Food & Beverage		Housing		Apparel & Upkeep		Trans-portation		Medical Care		Entertain-ment		Other Goods & Services	
	Index	%	Index	%	Index	%	Index	%	Index	%	Index	%	Index	%	Index	%
1914	-	-	-	-	-	-	-	-	-	-	-	-	-	-	-	-
1915	8.9	-	-	-	-	-	-	-	-	-	-	-	-	-	-	-
1916	9.7	9.0	-	-	-	-	-	-	-	-	-	-	-	-	-	-
1917	11.6	19.6	-	-	-	-	-	-	-	-	-	-	-	-	-	-
1918	13.6	17.2	-	-	-	-	-	-	-	-	-	-	-	-	-	-
1919	15.9	16.9	-	-	-	-	-	-	-	-	-	-	-	-	-	-
1920	18.8	18.2	-	-	-	-	-	-	-	-	-	-	-	-	-	-
1921	17.0	-9.6	-	-	-	-	-	-	-	-	-	-	-	-	-	-
1922	15.5	-8.8	-	-	-	-	-	-	-	-	-	-	-	-	-	-
1923	16.1	3.9	-	-	-	-	-	-	-	-	-	-	-	-	-	-
1924	16.1	0.0	-	-	-	-	-	-	-	-	-	-	-	-	-	-
1925	16.4	1.9	-	-	-	-	-	-	-	-	-	-	-	-	-	-
1926	16.5	0.6	-	-	-	-	-	-	-	-	-	-	-	-	-	-
1927	16.2	-1.8	-	-	-	-	-	-	-	-	-	-	-	-	-	-
1928	16.0	-1.2	-	-	-	-	-	-	-	-	-	-	-	-	-	-
1929	15.9	-0.6	-	-	-	-	-	-	-	-	-	-	-	-	-	-
1930	15.6	-1.9	-	-	-	-	-	-	-	-	-	-	-	-	-	-
1931	14.0	-10.3	-	-	-	-	-	-	-	-	-	-	-	-	-	-
1932	12.7	-9.3	-	-	-	-	-	-	-	-	-	-	-	-	-	-
1933	12.1	-4.7	-	-	-	-	-	-	-	-	-	-	-	-	-	-
1934	12.5	3.3	-	-	-	-	-	-	-	-	-	-	-	-	-	-
1935	13.0	4.0	-	-	-	-	-	-	-	-	-	-	-	-	-	-
1936	13.2	1.5	-	-	-	-	-	-	-	-	-	-	-	-	-	-
1937	13.7	3.8	-	-	-	-	-	-	-	-	-	-	-	-	-	-
1938	13.6	-0.7	-	-	-	-	-	-	-	-	-	-	-	-	-	-
1939	13.5	-0.7	-	-	-	-	-	-	-	-	-	-	-	-	-	-
1940	13.5	0.0	-	-	-	-	-	-	-	-	-	-	-	-	-	-
1941	14.3	5.9	-	-	-	-	-	-	-	-	-	-	-	-	-	-
1942	15.9	11.2	-	-	-	-	-	-	-	-	-	-	-	-	-	-
1943	17.0	6.9	-	-	-	-	-	-	-	-	-	-	-	-	-	-
1944	17.3	1.8	-	-	-	-	-	-	-	-	-	-	-	-	-	-
1945	17.6	1.7	-	-	-	-	-	-	-	-	-	-	-	-	-	-
1946	19.0	8.0	-	-	-	-	-	-	-	-	-	-	-	-	-	-
1947	21.7	14.2	-	-	-	-	-	-	19.1	-	10.4	-	-	-	-	-
1948	23.6	8.8	-	-	-	-	-	-	22.0	15.2	11.0	5.8	-	-	-	-
1949	23.2	-1.7	-	-	-	-	-	-	23.4	6.4	11.5	4.5	-	-	-	-
1950	23.4	0.9	-	-	-	-	-	-	23.4	0.0	11.6	0.9	-	-	-	-
1951	25.3	8.1	-	-	-	-	-	-	24.9	6.4	12.4	6.9	-	-	-	-
1952	25.9	2.4	-	-	-	-	-	-	26.3	5.6	13.1	5.6	-	-	-	-
1953	26.1	0.8	-	-	-	-	42.7	-	26.6	1.1	13.6	3.8	-	-	-	-
1954	26.3	0.8	-	-	-	-	42.7	0.0	26.1	-1.9	14.3	5.1	-	-	-	-
1955	26.4	0.4	-	-	-	-	42.5	-0.5	25.9	-0.8	14.9	4.2	-	-	-	-
1956	26.9	1.9	-	-	-	-	43.4	2.1	27.0	4.2	15.8	6.0	-	-	-	-
1957	27.9	3.7	-	-	-	-	44.1	1.6	28.9	7.0	16.4	3.8	-	-	-	-
1958	28.5	2.2	-	-	-	-	44.5	0.9	29.4	1.7	16.8	2.4	-	-	-	-

[Continued]

400

Cleveland, OH
Consumer Price Index - Urban Wage Earners
Base 1982-1984 = 100
Annual Averages
[Continued]

For 1914-1995. Columns headed % show percentile change in the index from the previous period for which an index is available.

Year	All Items		Food & Beverage		Housing		Apparel & Upkeep		Trans-portation		Medical Care		Entertain-ment		Other Goods & Services	
	Index	%	Index	%	Index	%	Index	%	Index	%	Index	%	Index	%	Index	%
1959	28.6	0.4	-	-	-	-	44.8	0.7	30.4	3.4	18.4	9.5	-	-	-	-
1960	29.0	1.4	-	-	-	-	45.0	0.4	30.7	1.0	19.0	3.3	-	-	-	-
1961	29.3	1.0	-	-	-	-	45.4	0.9	31.3	2.0	20.3	6.8	-	-	-	-
1962	29.3	0.0	-	-	-	-	45.6	0.4	31.8	1.6	20.4	0.5	-	-	-	-
1963	29.7	1.4	-	-	-	-	46.3	1.5	31.9	0.3	21.5	5.4	-	-	-	-
1964	29.8	0.3	-	-	-	-	46.4	0.2	32.5	1.9	22.2	3.3	-	-	-	-
1965	30.3	1.7	-	-	-	-	46.8	0.9	33.0	1.5	22.8	2.7	-	-	-	-
1966	31.1	2.6	-	-	-	-	48.3	3.2	33.3	0.9	23.3	2.2	-	-	-	-
1967	32.0	2.9	-	-	-	-	49.8	3.1	34.3	3.0	24.7	6.0	-	-	-	-
1968	33.9	5.9	-	-	-	-	52.8	6.0	36.0	5.0	26.8	8.5	-	-	-	-
1969	35.8	5.6	-	-	-	-	55.9	5.9	37.5	4.2	30.0	11.9	-	-	-	-
1970	38.2	6.7	-	-	-	-	58.6	4.8	40.0	6.7	32.4	8.0	-	-	-	-
1971	39.3	2.9	-	-	-	-	60.5	3.2	42.7	6.8	34.6	6.8	-	-	-	-
1972	40.5	3.1	-	-	-	-	61.6	1.8	43.3	1.4	35.6	2.9	-	-	-	-
1973	42.9	5.9	-	-	-	-	64.5	4.7	44.6	3.0	37.3	4.8	-	-	-	-
1974	47.3	10.3	-	-	-	-	70.4	9.1	50.0	12.1	40.7	9.1	-	-	-	-
1975	51.5	8.9	-	-	-	-	72.2	2.6	52.7	5.4	45.3	11.3	-	-	-	-
1976	54.1	5.0	62.3	-	48.1	-	73.9	2.4	55.1	4.6	49.8	9.9	67.2	-	57.2	-
1977	57.8	6.8	65.6	5.3	51.8	7.7	78.1	5.7	58.5	6.2	55.8	12.0	70.6	5.1	60.6	5.9
1978	62.2	7.6	72.1	9.9	55.9	7.9	80.7	3.3	61.7	5.5	61.2	9.7	73.9	4.7	64.6	6.6
1979	70.6	13.5	80.4	11.5	65.3	16.8	83.6	3.6	70.6	14.4	66.5	8.7	78.2	5.8	69.8	8.0
1980	81.1	14.9	86.9	8.1	78.7	20.5	87.0	4.1	82.2	16.4	73.7	10.8	84.2	7.7	76.1	9.0
1981	89.2	10.0	94.0	8.2	86.8	10.3	93.2	7.1	92.4	12.4	81.4	10.4	89.3	6.1	84.3	10.8
1982	95.9	7.5	96.5	2.7	95.9	10.5	99.2	6.4	96.7	4.7	91.7	12.7	95.3	6.7	92.5	9.7
1983	101.1	5.4	99.9	3.5	102.4	6.8	99.3	0.1	99.6	3.0	101.1	10.3	100.1	5.0	100.7	8.9
1984	103.0	1.9	103.6	3.7	101.7	-0.7	101.5	2.2	103.7	4.1	107.1	5.9	104.6	4.5	106.8	6.1
1985	103.8	0.8	105.9	2.2	100.7	-1.0	105.0	3.4	105.6	1.8	111.5	4.1	107.4	2.7	111.2	4.1
1986	105.0	1.2	107.3	1.3	103.8	3.1	103.5	-1.4	100.1	-5.2	121.6	9.1	114.9	7.0	116.9	5.1
1987	108.0	2.9	110.9	3.4	105.7	1.8	109.2	5.5	102.1	2.0	127.9	5.2	116.0	1.0	124.7	6.7
1988	111.8	3.5	115.9	4.5	109.3	3.4	106.2	-2.7	105.4	3.2	134.1	4.8	120.6	4.0	134.8	8.1
1989	117.3	4.9	123.5	6.6	113.5	3.8	110.7	4.2	110.7	5.0	142.1	6.0	126.3	4.7	143.4	6.4
1990	123.0	4.9	130.2	5.4	117.9	3.9	117.0	5.7	116.6	5.3	154.6	8.8	130.6	3.4	150.7	5.1
1991	127.8	3.9	134.9	3.6	122.2	3.6	121.3	3.7	120.0	2.9	168.7	9.1	134.5	3.0	162.2	7.6
1992	130.3	2.0	135.7	0.6	125.4	2.6	122.4	0.9	120.8	0.7	175.6	4.1	136.2	1.3	173.3	6.8
1993	133.3	2.3	139.3	2.7	128.2	2.2	124.2	1.5	121.7	0.7	184.0	4.8	139.5	2.4	183.9	6.1
1994	137.0	2.8	143.9	3.3	131.1	2.3	127.5	2.7	125.3	3.0	192.3	4.5	144.9	3.9	186.3	1.3
1995	-	-	-	-	-	-	-	-	-	-	-	-	-	-	-	-

Source: U.S. Department of Labor, Bureau of Labor Statistics, Division of Consumer Prices and Price Indexes. - indicates no data collected for period.

Cleveland, OH
Consumer Price Index - All Urban Consumers
Base 1982-1984 = 100
All Items

For 1914-1995. Columns headed % show percentile change in the index from the previous period for which an index is available.

Year	Jan Index	%	Feb Index	%	Mar Index	%	Apr Index	%	May Index	%	Jun Index	%	Jul Index	%	Aug Index	%	Sep Index	%	Oct Index	%	Nov Index	%	Dec Index	%
1914	-	-	-	-	-	-	-	-	-	-	-	-	-	-	-	-	-	-	-	-	-	-	8.7	-
1915	-	-	-	-	-	-	-	-	-	-	-	-	-	-	-	-	-	-	-	-	-	-	8.8	1.1
1916	-	-	-	-	-	-	-	-	-	-	-	-	-	-	-	-	-	-	-	-	-	-	10.1	14.8
1917	-	-	-	-	-	-	-	-	-	-	-	-	-	-	-	-	-	-	-	-	-	-	12.0	18.8
1918	-	-	-	-	-	-	-	-	-	-	-	-	-	-	-	-	-	-	-	-	-	-	14.4	20.0
1919	-	-	-	-	-	-	-	-	-	-	15.1	4.9	-	-	-	-	-	-	-	-	-	-	16.9	11.9
1920	-	-	-	-	-	-	-	-	-	-	19.0	12.4	-	-	-	-	-	-	-	-	-	-	18.0	-5.3
1921	-	-	-	-	-	-	-	-	16.6	-7.8	-	-	-	-	-	-	16.2	-2.4	-	-	-	-	15.9	-1.9
1922	-	-	-	-	15.0	-5.7	-	-	-	-	15.1	0.7	-	-	-	-	14.9	-1.3	-	-	-	-	15.3	2.7
1923	-	-	-	-	15.4	0.7	-	-	-	-	15.8	2.6	-	-	-	-	16.0	1.3	-	-	-	-	15.9	-0.6
1924	-	-	-	-	15.7	-1.3	-	-	-	-	15.6	-0.6	-	-	-	-	15.7	0.6	-	-	-	-	15.7	0.0
1925	-	-	-	-	-	-	-	-	-	-	16.1	2.5	-	-	-	-	-	-	-	-	-	-	16.2	0.6
1926	-	-	-	-	-	-	-	-	-	-	16.2	0.0	-	-	-	-	-	-	-	-	-	-	16.1	-0.6
1927	-	-	-	-	-	-	-	-	-	-	16.1	0.0	-	-	-	-	-	-	-	-	-	-	15.7	-2.5
1928	-	-	-	-	-	-	-	-	-	-	15.7	0.0	-	-	-	-	-	-	-	-	-	-	15.5	-1.3
1929	-	-	-	-	-	-	-	-	-	-	15.6	0.6	-	-	-	-	-	-	-	-	-	-	15.4	-1.3
1930	-	-	-	-	-	-	-	-	-	-	15.4	0.0	-	-	-	-	-	-	-	-	-	-	14.6	-5.2
1931	-	-	-	-	-	-	-	-	-	-	13.6	-6.8	-	-	-	-	-	-	-	-	-	-	13.1	-3.7
1932	-	-	-	-	-	-	-	-	-	-	12.5	-4.6	-	-	-	-	-	-	-	-	-	-	11.8	-5.6
1933	-	-	-	-	-	-	-	-	-	-	11.6	-1.7	-	-	-	-	-	-	-	-	-	-	12.0	3.4
1934	-	-	-	-	-	-	-	-	-	-	12.2	1.7	-	-	-	-	-	-	-	-	12.2	0.0	-	-
1935	-	-	-	-	12.7	4.1	-	-	-	-	-	-	12.7	0.0	-	-	-	-	12.7	0.0	-	-	-	-
1936	12.7	0.0	-	-	-	-	12.6	-0.8	-	-	-	-	12.9	2.4	-	-	13.1	1.6	-	-	-	-	12.9	-1.5
1937	-	-	-	-	13.1	1.6	-	-	-	-	13.4	2.3	-	-	-	-	13.6	1.5	-	-	-	-	13.4	-1.5
1938	-	-	-	-	13.2	-1.5	-	-	-	-	13.3	0.8	-	-	-	-	13.3	0.0	-	-	-	-	13.2	-0.8
1939	-	-	-	-	13.2	0.0	-	-	-	-	13.2	0.0	-	-	-	-	13.3	0.8	-	-	-	-	13.2	-0.8
1940	-	-	-	-	13.2	0.0	-	-	-	-	13.3	0.8	-	-	-	-	13.4	0.8	13.3	-0.7	13.2	-0.8	13.3	0.8
1941	13.3	0.0	13.4	0.8	13.4	0.0	13.5	0.7	13.6	0.7	13.9	2.2	14.0	0.7	14.2	1.4	14.5	2.1	14.6	0.7	14.8	1.4	14.8	0.0
1942	15.0	1.4	15.0	0.0	15.3	2.0	15.4	0.7	15.5	0.6	15.6	0.6	15.6	0.0	15.5	-0.6	15.6	0.6	15.9	1.9	15.9	0.0	16.1	1.3
1943	16.1	0.0	16.2	0.6	16.4	1.2	16.5	0.6	16.7	1.2	16.9	1.2	16.7	-1.2	16.7	0.0	16.8	0.6	16.8	0.0	16.8	0.0	16.8	0.0
1944	16.7	-0.6	16.7	0.0	16.7	0.0	16.9	1.2	16.9	0.0	16.9	0.0	17.1	1.2	17.1	0.0	17.1	0.0	17.0	-0.6	17.1	0.6	16.9	-1.2
1945	17.0	0.6	17.0	0.0	17.0	0.0	17.0	0.0	17.3	1.8	17.3	0.0	17.3	0.0	17.3	0.0	17.2	-0.6	17.3	0.6	17.3	0.0	17.3	0.0
1946	17.3	0.0	17.3	0.0	17.3	0.0	17.4	0.6	17.5	0.6	17.8	1.7	18.8	5.6	19.3	2.7	19.3	0.0	19.6	1.6	20.2	3.1	20.5	1.5
1947	20.4	-0.5	20.4	0.0	20.9	2.5	20.9	0.0	20.8	-0.5	21.0	1.0	-	-	21.4	1.9	-	-	-	-	21.9	2.3	-	-
1948	-	-	22.5	2.7	-	-	-	-	22.8	1.3	-	-	-	-	23.6	3.5	-	-	-	-	23.1	-2.1	-	-
1949	-	-	22.7	-1.7	-	-	-	-	22.6	-0.4	-	-	-	-	22.6	0.0	-	-	-	-	22.4	-0.9	-	-
1950	-	-	22.2	-0.9	-	-	-	-	22.3	0.5	-	-	-	-	23.1	3.6	-	-	-	-	23.5	1.7	-	-
1951	-	-	24.3	3.4	-	-	-	-	24.6	1.2	-	-	-	-	24.7	0.4	-	-	-	-	25.1	1.6	-	-
1952	-	-	25.1	0.0	-	-	-	-	25.2	0.4	-	-	-	-	25.4	0.8	-	-	-	-	25.3	-0.4	-	-
1953	-	-	25.0	-1.2	-	-	-	-	25.3	1.2	-	-	-	-	25.6	1.2	-	-	-	-	25.7	0.4	-	-
1954	-	-	25.7	0.0	-	-	-	-	25.7	0.0	-	-	-	-	25.7	0.0	-	-	-	-	25.7	0.0	-	-
1955	-	-	25.6	-0.4	-	-	-	-	25.7	0.4	-	-	-	-	25.8	0.4	-	-	-	-	25.9	0.4	-	-
1956	-	-	25.8	-0.4	-	-	-	-	26.1	1.2	-	-	-	-	26.5	1.5	-	-	-	-	26.7	0.8	-	-
1957	-	-	26.8	0.4	-	-	-	-	27.1	1.1	-	-	-	-	27.3	0.7	-	-	-	-	27.5	0.7	-	-
1958	-	-	27.7	0.7	-	-	-	-	27.8	0.4	-	-	-	-	27.8	0.0	-	-	-	-	27.7	-0.4	-	-

[Continued]

Cleveland, OH
Consumer Price Index - All Urban Consumers
Base 1982-1984 = 100
All Items
[Continued]

For 1914-1995. Columns headed % show percentile change in the index from the previous period for which an index is available.

Year	Jan Index	%	Feb Index	%	Mar Index	%	Apr Index	%	May Index	%	Jun Index	%	Jul Index	%	Aug Index	%	Sep Index	%	Oct Index	%	Nov Index	%	Dec Index	%
1959	-	-	27.8	0.4	-	-	-	-	27.9	0.4	-	-	-	-	28.0	0.4	-	-	-	-	28.1	0.4	-	-
1960	-	-	28.1	0.0	-	-	-	-	28.3	0.7	-	-	-	-	28.4	0.4	-	-	-	-	28.5	0.4	-	-
1961	-	-	28.6	0.4	-	-	-	-	28.5	-0.3	-	-	-	-	28.6	0.4	-	-	-	-	28.5	-0.3	-	-
1962	-	-	28.5	0.0	-	-	-	-	28.6	0.4	-	-	-	-	28.7	0.3	-	-	-	-	28.7	0.0	-	-
1963	-	-	28.8	0.3	-	-	-	-	28.8	0.0	-	-	-	-	29.1	1.0	-	-	-	-	29.0	-0.3	-	-
1964	-	-	29.1	0.3	-	-	-	-	28.9	-0.7	-	-	-	-	29.1	0.7	-	-	-	-	29.3	0.7	-	-
1965	-	-	29.3	0.0	-	-	-	-	29.5	0.7	-	-	-	-	29.6	0.3	-	-	-	-	29.8	0.7	-	-
1966	-	-	29.9	0.3	-	-	-	-	30.3	1.3	-	-	-	-	30.5	0.7	-	-	-	-	30.6	0.3	-	-
1967	-	-	30.8	0.7	-	-	-	-	30.9	0.3	-	-	-	-	31.3	1.3	-	-	-	-	31.7	1.3	-	-
1968	-	-	32.5	2.5	-	-	-	-	32.9	1.2	-	-	-	-	33.2	0.9	-	-	-	-	33.7	1.5	-	-
1969	-	-	34.0	0.9	-	-	-	-	34.6	1.8	-	-	-	-	35.2	1.7	-	-	-	-	35.8	1.7	-	-
1970	-	-	36.6	2.2	-	-	-	-	37.1	1.4	-	-	-	-	37.5	1.1	-	-	-	-	37.9	1.1	-	-
1971	-	-	37.9	0.0	-	-	-	-	38.1	0.5	-	-	-	-	38.4	0.8	-	-	-	-	38.8	1.0	-	-
1972	-	-	39.3	1.3	-	-	-	-	39.4	0.3	-	-	-	-	39.4	0.0	-	-	-	-	39.9	1.3	-	-
1973	-	-	40.5	1.5	-	-	-	-	41.4	2.2	-	-	-	-	42.4	2.4	-	-	-	-	42.9	1.2	-	-
1974	-	-	44.3	3.3	-	-	-	-	45.6	2.9	-	-	-	-	46.8	2.6	-	-	-	-	47.7	1.9	-	-
1975	-	-	49.2	3.1	-	-	-	-	49.8	1.2	-	-	-	-	50.7	1.8	-	-	-	-	51.3	1.2	-	-
1976	-	-	51.5	0.4	-	-	-	-	52.1	1.2	-	-	-	-	53.2	2.1	-	-	-	-	54.0	1.5	-	-
1977	-	-	55.1	2.0	-	-	-	-	56.1	1.8	-	-	-	-	56.5	0.7	-	-	-	-	57.5	1.8	-	-
1978	-	-	58.2	1.2	-	-	59.4	2.1	-	-	59.6	0.3	-	-	60.8	2.0	-	-	62.4	2.6	-	-	64.2	2.9
1979	-	-	65.6	2.2	-	-	67.1	2.3	-	-	68.6	2.2	-	-	69.1	0.7	-	-	70.1	1.4	-	-	72.6	3.6
1980	-	-	76.0	4.7	-	-	77.2	1.6	-	-	78.0	1.0	-	-	79.2	1.5	-	-	82.6	4.3	-	-	83.2	0.7
1981	-	-	85.3	2.5	-	-	84.9	-0.5	-	-	89.0	4.8	-	-	88.8	-0.2	-	-	88.3	-0.6	-	-	87.9	-0.5
1982	-	-	89.2	1.5	-	-	89.4	0.2	-	-	92.9	3.9	-	-	97.4	4.8	-	-	98.8	1.4	-	-	99.1	0.3
1983	-	-	99.5	0.4	-	-	99.7	0.2	-	-	101.2	1.5	-	-	101.8	0.6	-	-	103.2	1.4	-	-	102.6	-0.6
1984	-	-	103.3	0.7	-	-	103.9	0.6	-	-	105.1	1.2	-	-	105.3	0.2	-	-	106.1	0.8	-	-	106.0	-0.1
1985	-	-	106.2	0.2	-	-	106.9	0.7	-	-	108.1	1.1	-	-	108.6	0.5	-	-	108.8	0.2	-	-	108.8	0.0
1986	-	-	109.3	0.5	-	-	108.3	-0.9	-	-	109.4	1.0	-	-	110.1	0.6	-	-	109.9	-0.2	110.1	0.2	109.8	-0.3
1987	110.1	0.3	-	-	111.4	1.2	-	-	111.6	0.2	-	-	112.8	1.1	-	-	114.7	1.7	-	-	114.5	-0.2	-	-
1988	113.9	-0.5	-	-	115.1	1.1	-	-	116.6	1.3	-	-	117.6	0.9	-	-	117.6	0.0	-	-	118.0	0.3	-	-
1989	118.9	0.8	-	-	121.5	2.2	-	-	122.8	1.1	-	-	124.4	1.3	-	-	123.7	-0.6	-	-	123.4	-0.2	-	-
1990	125.0	1.3	-	-	127.4	1.9	-	-	128.1	0.5	-	-	128.8	0.5	-	-	131.1	1.8	-	-	131.7	0.5	-	-
1991	131.9	0.2	-	-	133.2	1.0	-	-	134.3	0.8	-	-	133.9	-0.3	-	-	135.4	1.1	-	-	135.7	0.2	-	-
1992	136.2	0.4	-	-	136.3	0.1	-	-	136.1	-0.1	-	-	137.1	0.7	-	-	137.9	0.6	-	-	137.1	-0.6	-	-
1993	137.5	0.3	-	-	138.8	0.9	-	-	139.6	0.6	-	-	140.9	0.9	-	-	141.7	0.6	-	-	142.1	0.3	-	-
1994	142.4	0.2	-	-	143.3	0.6	-	-	143.7	0.3	-	-	143.7	0.0	-	-	146.3	1.8	-	-	146.0	-0.2	-	-
1995	146.6	0.4	-	-	147.3	0.5	-	-	147.4	0.1	-	-	148.1	0.5	-	-	149.0	0.6	-	-	148.2	-0.5	-	-

Source: U.S. Department of Labor, Bureau of Labor Statistics, Division of Consumer Prices and Price Indexes. - indicates no data collected for period.

Cleveland, OH
Consumer Price Index - Urban Wage Earners
Base 1982-1984 = 100
All Items

For 1914-1995. Columns headed % show percentile change in the index from the previous period for which an index is available.

Year	Jan Index	%	Feb Index	%	Mar Index	%	Apr Index	%	May Index	%	Jun Index	%	Jul Index	%	Aug Index	%	Sep Index	%	Oct Index	%	Nov Index	%	Dec Index	%
1914	-	-	-	-	-	-	-	-	-	-	-	-	-	-	-	-	-	-	-	-	-	-	8.9	-
1915	-	-	-	-	-	-	-	-	-	-	-	-	-	-	-	-	-	-	-	-	-	-	9.1	2.2
1916	-	-	-	-	-	-	-	-	-	-	-	-	-	-	-	-	-	-	-	-	-	-	10.4	14.3
1917	-	-	-	-	-	-	-	-	-	-	-	-	-	-	-	-	-	-	-	-	-	-	12.4	19.2
1918	-	-	-	-	-	-	-	-	-	-	-	-	-	-	-	-	-	-	-	-	-	-	14.8	19.4
1919	-	-	-	-	-	-	-	-	-	-	15.5	4.7	-	-	-	-	-	-	-	-	-	-	17.3	11.6
1920	-	-	-	-	-	-	-	-	-	-	19.5	12.7	-	-	-	-	-	-	-	-	-	-	18.5	-5.1
1921	-	-	-	-	-	-	-	-	17.0	-8.1	-	-	-	-	-	-	16.6	-2.4	-	-	-	-	16.3	-1.8
1922	-	-	-	-	15.4	-5.5	-	-	-	-	15.5	0.6	-	-	-	-	15.3	-1.3	-	-	-	-	15.7	2.6
1923	-	-	-	-	15.7	0.0	-	-	-	-	16.2	3.2	-	-	-	-	16.4	1.2	-	-	-	-	16.3	-0.6
1924	-	-	-	-	16.1	-1.2	-	-	-	-	16.0	-0.6	-	-	-	-	16.1	0.6	-	-	-	-	16.1	0.0
1925	-	-	-	-	-	-	-	-	-	-	16.5	2.5	-	-	-	-	-	-	-	-	-	-	16.6	0.6
1926	-	-	-	-	-	-	-	-	-	-	16.6	0.0	-	-	-	-	-	-	-	-	-	-	16.5	-0.6
1927	-	-	-	-	-	-	-	-	-	-	16.5	0.0	-	-	-	-	-	-	-	-	-	-	16.1	-2.4
1928	-	-	-	-	-	-	-	-	-	-	16.1	0.0	-	-	-	-	-	-	-	-	-	-	15.9	-1.2
1929	-	-	-	-	-	-	-	-	-	-	16.0	0.6	-	-	-	-	-	-	-	-	-	-	15.8	-1.2
1930	-	-	-	-	-	-	-	-	-	-	15.8	0.0	-	-	-	-	-	-	-	-	-	-	15.0	-5.1
1931	-	-	-	-	-	-	-	-	-	-	14.0	-6.7	-	-	-	-	-	-	-	-	-	-	13.4	-4.3
1932	-	-	-	-	-	-	-	-	-	-	12.8	-4.5	-	-	-	-	-	-	-	-	-	-	12.1	-5.5
1933	-	-	-	-	-	-	-	-	-	-	11.9	-1.7	-	-	-	-	-	-	-	-	-	-	12.3	3.4
1934	-	-	-	-	-	-	-	-	-	-	12.5	1.6	-	-	-	-	-	-	-	-	12.5	0.0	-	-
1935	-	-	-	-	13.0	4.0	-	-	-	-	-	-	13.0	0.0	-	-	-	-	13.1	0.8	-	-	-	-
1936	13.0	-0.8	-	-	-	-	13.0	0.0	-	-	-	-	13.2	1.5	-	-	13.4	1.5	-	-	-	-	13.2	-1.5
1937	-	-	-	-	13.5	2.3	-	-	-	-	13.8	2.2	-	-	-	-	14.0	1.4	-	-	-	-	13.8	-1.4
1938	-	-	-	-	13.5	-2.2	-	-	-	-	13.6	0.7	-	-	-	-	13.6	0.0	-	-	-	-	13.6	0.0
1939	-	-	-	-	13.5	-0.7	-	-	-	-	13.5	0.0	-	-	-	-	13.6	0.7	-	-	-	-	13.5	-0.7
1940	-	-	-	-	13.5	0.0	-	-	-	-	13.6	0.7	-	-	-	-	13.7	0.7	13.6	-0.7	13.5	-0.7	13.7	1.5
1941	13.7	0.0	13.7	0.0	13.8	0.7	13.9	0.7	14.0	0.7	14.2	1.4	14.3	0.7	14.6	2.1	14.8	1.4	15.0	1.4	15.1	0.7	15.2	0.7
1942	15.4	1.3	15.4	0.0	15.7	1.9	15.8	0.6	15.9	0.6	16.0	0.6	16.0	0.0	15.9	-0.6	16.0	0.6	16.3	1.9	16.4	0.6	16.5	0.6
1943	16.5	0.0	16.6	0.6	16.8	1.2	16.9	0.6	17.2	1.8	17.3	0.6	17.2	-0.6	17.2	0.0	17.2	0.0	17.2	0.0	17.2	0.0	17.2	0.0
1944	17.2	0.0	17.2	0.0	17.2	0.0	17.3	0.6	17.3	0.0	17.3	0.0	17.5	1.2	17.5	0.0	17.5	0.0	17.5	0.0	17.5	0.0	17.3	-1.1
1945	17.4	0.6	17.4	0.0	17.4	0.0	17.5	0.6	17.7	1.1	17.7	0.0	17.7	0.0	17.7	0.0	17.6	-0.6	17.7	0.6	17.7	0.0	17.8	0.6
1946	17.7	-0.6	17.7	0.0	17.7	0.0	17.8	0.6	18.0	1.1	18.2	1.1	19.3	6.0	19.7	2.1	19.8	0.5	20.1	1.5	20.7	3.0	21.0	1.4
1947	21.0	0.0	21.0	0.0	21.4	1.9	21.4	0.0	21.4	0.0	21.6	0.9	-	-	22.0	1.9	-	-	-	-	22.5	2.3	-	-
1948	-	-	23.1	2.7	-	-	-	-	23.4	1.3	-	-	-	-	24.2	3.4	-	-	-	-	23.7	-2.1	-	-
1949	-	-	23.2	-2.1	-	-	-	-	23.1	-0.4	-	-	-	-	23.2	0.4	-	-	-	-	23.0	-0.9	-	-
1950	-	-	22.8	-0.9	-	-	-	-	22.9	0.4	-	-	-	-	23.7	3.5	-	-	-	-	24.1	1.7	-	-
1951	-	-	24.9	3.3	-	-	-	-	25.2	1.2	-	-	-	-	25.3	0.4	-	-	-	-	25.7	1.6	-	-
1952	-	-	25.7	0.0	-	-	-	-	25.8	0.4	-	-	-	-	26.0	0.8	-	-	-	-	25.9	-0.4	-	-
1953	-	-	25.7	-0.8	-	-	-	-	25.9	0.8	-	-	-	-	26.3	1.5	-	-	-	-	26.4	0.4	-	-
1954	-	-	26.3	-0.4	-	-	-	-	26.3	0.0	-	-	-	-	26.3	0.0	-	-	-	-	26.3	0.0	-	-
1955	-	-	26.2	-0.4	-	-	-	-	26.3	0.4	-	-	-	-	26.5	0.8	-	-	-	-	26.5	0.0	-	-
1956	-	-	26.4	-0.4	-	-	-	-	26.8	1.5	-	-	-	-	27.2	1.5	-	-	-	-	27.4	0.7	-	-
1957	-	-	27.5	0.4	-	-	-	-	27.8	1.1	-	-	-	-	28.0	0.7	-	-	-	-	28.2	0.7	-	-
1958	-	-	28.4	0.7	-	-	-	-	28.5	0.4	-	-	-	-	28.5	0.0	-	-	-	-	28.4	-0.4	-	-

[Continued]

Cleveland, OH
Consumer Price Index - Urban Wage Earners
Base 1982-1984 = 100
All Items
[Continued]

For 1914-1995. Columns headed % show percentile change in the index from the previous period for which an index is available.

Year	Jan Index	%	Feb Index	%	Mar Index	%	Apr Index	%	May Index	%	Jun Index	%	Jul Index	%	Aug Index	%	Sep Index	%	Oct Index	%	Nov Index	%	Dec Index	%
1959	-	-	28.5	0.4	-	-	-	-	28.6	0.4	-	-	-	-	28.7	0.3	-	-	-	-	28.9	0.7	-	-
1960	-	-	28.8	-0.3	-	-	-	-	29.0	0.7	-	-	-	-	29.1	0.3	-	-	-	-	29.2	0.3	-	-
1961	-	-	29.3	0.3	-	-	-	-	29.2	-0.3	-	-	-	-	29.4	0.7	-	-	-	-	29.2	-0.7	-	-
1962	-	-	29.2	0.0	-	-	-	-	29.3	0.3	-	-	-	-	29.4	0.3	-	-	-	-	29.4	0.0	-	-
1963	-	-	29.6	0.7	-	-	-	-	29.6	0.0	-	-	-	-	29.8	0.7	-	-	-	-	29.8	0.0	-	-
1964	-	-	29.8	0.0	-	-	-	-	29.6	-0.7	-	-	-	-	29.8	0.7	-	-	-	-	30.0	0.7	-	-
1965	-	-	30.1	0.3	-	-	-	-	30.3	0.7	-	-	-	-	30.4	0.3	-	-	-	-	30.6	0.7	-	-
1966	-	-	30.6	0.0	-	-	-	-	31.1	1.6	-	-	-	-	31.2	0.3	-	-	-	-	31.4	0.6	-	-
1967	-	-	31.6	0.6	-	-	-	-	31.7	0.3	-	-	-	-	32.1	1.3	-	-	-	-	32.5	1.2	-	-
1968	-	-	33.4	2.8	-	-	-	-	33.8	1.2	-	-	-	-	34.0	0.6	-	-	-	-	34.5	1.5	-	-
1969	-	-	34.9	1.2	-	-	-	-	35.5	1.7	-	-	-	-	36.1	1.7	-	-	-	-	36.7	1.7	-	-
1970	-	-	37.5	2.2	-	-	-	-	38.1	1.6	-	-	-	-	38.4	0.8	-	-	-	-	38.8	1.0	-	-
1971	-	-	38.9	0.3	-	-	-	-	39.0	0.3	-	-	-	-	39.4	1.0	-	-	-	-	39.8	1.0	-	-
1972	-	-	40.3	1.3	-	-	-	-	40.4	0.2	-	-	-	-	40.4	0.0	-	-	-	-	40.9	1.2	-	-
1973	-	-	41.6	1.7	-	-	-	-	42.5	2.2	-	-	-	-	43.5	2.4	-	-	-	-	44.0	1.1	-	-
1974	-	-	45.5	3.4	-	-	-	-	46.8	2.9	-	-	-	-	48.0	2.6	-	-	-	-	49.0	2.1	-	-
1975	-	-	50.5	3.1	-	-	-	-	51.0	1.0	-	-	-	-	52.0	2.0	-	-	-	-	52.6	1.2	-	-
1976	-	-	52.8	0.4	-	-	-	-	53.4	1.1	-	-	-	-	54.6	2.2	-	-	-	-	55.4	1.5	-	-
1977	-	-	56.5	2.0	-	-	-	-	57.6	1.9	-	-	-	-	58.0	0.7	-	-	-	-	59.0	1.7	-	-
1978	-	-	59.7	1.2	-	-	61.0	2.2	-	-	61.5	0.8	-	-	62.7	2.0	-	-	64.2	2.4	-	-	65.9	2.6
1979	-	-	67.5	2.4	-	-	69.2	2.5	-	-	70.8	2.3	-	-	71.2	0.6	-	-	72.2	1.4	-	-	74.6	3.3
1980	-	-	78.1	4.7	-	-	79.5	1.8	-	-	80.2	0.9	-	-	81.4	1.5	-	-	84.6	3.9	-	-	85.4	0.9
1981	-	-	87.7	2.7	-	-	87.1	-0.7	-	-	90.8	4.2	-	-	90.6	-0.2	-	-	90.3	-0.3	-	-	90.0	-0.3
1982	-	-	91.2	1.3	-	-	91.4	0.2	-	-	95.0	3.9	-	-	99.4	4.6	-	-	100.5	1.1	-	-	100.8	0.3
1983	-	-	100.3	-0.5	-	-	100.9	0.6	-	-	101.3	0.4	-	-	101.6	0.3	-	-	101.5	-0.1	-	-	100.7	-0.8
1984	-	-	101.8	1.1	-	-	102.6	0.8	-	-	103.0	0.4	-	-	105.0	1.9	-	-	103.8	-1.1	-	-	102.0	-1.7
1985	-	-	102.3	0.3	-	-	103.0	0.7	-	-	104.1	1.1	-	-	104.7	0.6	-	-	104.7	0.0	-	-	104.8	0.1
1986	-	-	105.1	0.3	-	-	103.8	-1.2	-	-	105.0	1.2	-	-	105.6	0.6	-	-	105.4	-0.2	105.5	0.1	105.3	-0.2
1987	105.6	0.3	-	-	106.7	1.0	-	-	107.0	0.3	-	-	108.1	1.0	-	-	109.9	1.7	-	-	109.9	0.0	-	-
1988	109.3	-0.5	-	-	110.2	0.8	-	-	111.7	1.4	-	-	112.6	0.8	-	-	112.7	0.1	-	-	113.0	0.3	-	-
1989	113.8	0.7	-	-	116.2	2.1	-	-	117.7	1.3	-	-	118.8	0.9	-	-	118.2	-0.5	-	-	118.0	-0.2	-	-
1990	119.5	1.3	-	-	121.5	1.7	-	-	122.1	0.5	-	-	122.7	0.5	-	-	125.0	1.9	-	-	125.8	0.6	-	-
1991	125.8	0.0	-	-	126.8	0.8	-	-	127.8	0.8	-	-	127.4	-0.3	-	-	129.0	1.3	-	-	129.3	0.2	-	-
1992	129.6	0.2	-	-	129.7	0.1	-	-	129.6	-0.1	-	-	130.5	0.7	-	-	131.3	0.6	-	-	130.8	-0.4	-	-
1993	130.8	0.0	-	-	131.8	0.8	-	-	132.7	0.7	-	-	133.9	0.9	-	-	134.6	0.5	-	-	135.1	0.4	-	-
1994	135.1	0.0	-	-	135.7	0.4	-	-	136.1	0.3	-	-	136.3	0.1	-	-	138.9	1.9	-	-	138.8	-0.1	-	-
1995	139.0	0.1	-	-	139.7	0.5	-	-	139.9	0.1	-	-	140.3	0.3	-	-	141.3	0.7	-	-	140.6	-0.5	-	-

Source: U.S. Department of Labor, Bureau of Labor Statistics, Division of Consumer Prices and Price Indexes. - indicates no data collected for period.

Cleveland, OH
Consumer Price Index - All Urban Consumers
Base 1982-1984 = 100
Food and Beverages

For 1975-1995. Columns headed % show percentile change in the index from the previous period for which an index is available.

Year	Jan Index	%	Feb Index	%	Mar Index	%	Apr Index	%	May Index	%	Jun Index	%	Jul Index	%	Aug Index	%	Sep Index	%	Oct Index	%	Nov Index	%	Dec Index	%
1975	-	-	-	-	-	-	-	-	-	-	-	-	-	-	-	-	-	-	-	-	62.1	-	-	-
1976	-	-	62.1	0.0	-	-	-	-	63.0	1.4	-	-	-	-	63.2	0.3	-	-	-	-	63.7	0.8	-	-
1977	-	-	65.4	2.7	-	-	-	-	67.6	3.4	-	-	-	-	65.2	-3.6	-	-	-	-	67.4	3.4	-	-
1978	-	-	69.4	3.0	-	-	70.5	1.6	-	-	72.9	3.4	-	-	73.1	0.3	-	-	73.6	0.7	-	-	74.9	1.8
1979	-	-	77.9	4.0	-	-	79.4	1.9	-	-	79.8	0.5	-	-	80.2	0.5	-	-	80.6	0.5	-	-	81.4	1.0
1980	-	-	83.2	2.2	-	-	83.7	0.6	-	-	83.5	-0.2	-	-	86.6	3.7	-	-	89.0	2.8	-	-	89.5	0.6
1981	-	-	91.8	2.6	-	-	91.9	0.1	-	-	94.2	2.5	-	-	94.0	-0.2	-	-	94.4	0.4	-	-	94.2	-0.2
1982	-	-	95.4	1.3	-	-	95.5	0.1	-	-	96.7	1.3	-	-	96.7	0.0	-	-	97.1	0.4	-	-	97.2	0.1
1983	-	-	98.7	1.5	-	-	99.3	0.6	-	-	99.4	0.1	-	-	100.3	0.9	-	-	100.9	0.6	-	-	101.2	0.3
1984	-	-	103.6	2.4	-	-	103.2	-0.4	-	-	103.3	0.1	-	-	104.2	0.9	-	-	104.7	0.5	-	-	105.3	0.6
1985	-	-	107.0	1.6	-	-	106.2	-0.7	-	-	105.4	-0.8	-	-	106.0	0.6	-	-	106.1	0.1	-	-	106.5	0.4
1986	-	-	107.0	0.5	-	-	106.9	-0.1	-	-	106.3	-0.6	-	-	108.2	1.8	-	-	108.7	0.5	108.9	0.2	109.4	0.5
1987	110.6	1.1	-	-	110.7	0.1	-	-	110.9	0.2	-	-	110.6	-0.3	-	-	111.7	1.0	-	-	112.7	0.9	-	-
1988	113.3	0.5	-	-	114.8	1.3	-	-	114.2	-0.5	-	-	116.4	1.9	-	-	118.8	2.1	-	-	118.9	0.1	-	-
1989	121.0	1.8	-	-	121.8	0.7	-	-	123.3	1.2	-	-	124.9	1.3	-	-	125.4	0.4	-	-	125.6	0.2	-	-
1990	128.9	2.6	-	-	129.9	0.8	-	-	128.8	-0.8	-	-	131.2	1.9	-	-	131.5	0.2	-	-	131.6	0.1	-	-
1991	134.8	2.4	-	-	135.3	0.4	-	-	136.6	1.0	-	-	135.5	-0.8	-	-	134.8	-0.5	-	-	134.8	0.0	-	-
1992	136.4	1.2	-	-	136.4	0.0	-	-	136.4	0.0	-	-	134.9	-1.1	-	-	136.8	1.4	-	-	135.8	-0.7	-	-
1993	137.1	1.0	-	-	138.2	0.8	-	-	139.2	0.7	-	-	139.1	-0.1	-	-	141.5	1.7	-	-	141.9	0.3	-	-
1994	142.9	0.7	-	-	141.9	-0.7	-	-	143.7	1.3	-	-	143.6	-0.1	-	-	146.0	1.7	-	-	146.7	0.5	-	-
1995	149.1	1.6	-	-	146.9	-1.5	-	-	148.4	1.0	-	-	148.7	0.2	-	-	149.5	0.5	-	-	150.7	0.8	-	-

Source: U.S. Department of Labor, Bureau of Labor Statistics, Division of Consumer Prices and Price Indexes. - indicates no data collected for period.

Cleveland, OH
Consumer Price Index - Urban Wage Earners
Base 1982-1984 = 100
Food and Beverages

For 1975-1995. Columns headed % show percentile change in the index from the previous period for which an index is available.

Year	Jan Index	%	Feb Index	%	Mar Index	%	Apr Index	%	May Index	%	Jun Index	%	Jul Index	%	Aug Index	%	Sep Index	%	Oct Index	%	Nov Index	%	Dec Index	%
1975	-	-	-	-	-	-	-	-	-	-	-	-	-	-	-	-	-	-	-	-	61.4	-	-	-
1976	-	-	61.4	0.0	-	-	-	-	62.2	1.3	-	-	-	-	62.5	0.5	-	-	-	-	62.9	0.6	-	-
1977	-	-	64.6	2.7	-	-	-	-	66.8	3.4	-	-	-	-	64.4	-3.6	-	-	-	-	66.6	3.4	-	-
1978	-	-	68.5	2.9	-	-	70.0	2.2	-	-	73.3	4.7	-	-	73.7	0.5	-	-	73.8	0.1	-	-	75.3	2.0
1979	-	-	78.4	4.1	-	-	80.3	2.4	-	-	80.8	0.6	-	-	80.9	0.1	-	-	81.2	0.4	-	-	83.0	2.2
1980	-	-	84.1	1.3	-	-	84.9	1.0	-	-	84.6	-0.4	-	-	88.1	4.1	-	-	90.1	2.3	-	-	91.5	1.6
1981	-	-	93.2	1.9	-	-	93.5	0.3	-	-	94.3	0.9	-	-	94.4	0.1	-	-	94.8	0.4	-	-	94.3	-0.5
1982	-	-	95.4	1.2	-	-	95.7	0.3	-	-	96.9	1.3	-	-	96.8	-0.1	-	-	97.4	0.6	-	-	97.6	0.2
1983	-	-	99.0	1.4	-	-	99.5	0.5	-	-	99.5	0.0	-	-	100.3	0.8	-	-	100.8	0.5	-	-	101.0	0.2
1984	-	-	103.3	2.3	-	-	102.9	-0.4	-	-	103.1	0.2	-	-	104.1	1.0	-	-	104.5	0.4	-	-	105.0	0.5
1985	-	-	106.7	1.6	-	-	106.0	-0.7	-	-	105.1	-0.8	-	-	105.8	0.7	-	-	105.9	0.1	-	-	106.2	0.3
1986	-	-	106.6	0.4	-	-	106.6	0.0	-	-	106.0	-0.6	-	-	107.9	1.8	-	-	108.3	0.4	108.6	0.3	109.0	0.4
1987	110.2	1.1	-	-	110.2	0.0	-	-	110.5	0.3	-	-	110.3	-0.2	-	-	111.4	1.0	-	-	112.3	0.8	-	-
1988	112.8	0.4	-	-	114.3	1.3	-	-	113.7	-0.5	-	-	115.9	1.9	-	-	118.3	2.1	-	-	118.4	0.1	-	-
1989	120.5	1.8	-	-	121.3	0.7	-	-	122.8	1.2	-	-	124.4	1.3	-	-	124.9	0.4	-	-	125.2	0.2	-	-
1990	128.5	2.6	-	-	129.5	0.8	-	-	128.4	-0.8	-	-	130.8	1.9	-	-	131.2	0.3	-	-	131.3	0.1	-	-
1991	134.4	2.4	-	-	134.9	0.4	-	-	136.2	1.0	-	-	135.1	-0.8	-	-	134.3	-0.6	-	-	134.3	0.0	-	-
1992	136.0	1.3	-	-	136.0	0.0	-	-	135.8	-0.1	-	-	134.3	-1.1	-	-	136.3	1.5	-	-	135.4	-0.7	-	-
1993	136.7	1.0	-	-	137.8	0.8	-	-	138.7	0.7	-	-	138.6	-0.1	-	-	141.0	1.7	-	-	141.4	0.3	-	-
1994	142.4	0.7	-	-	141.4	-0.7	-	-	143.3	1.3	-	-	143.1	-0.1	-	-	145.4	1.6	-	-	146.2	0.6	-	-
1995	148.5	1.6	-	-	146.3	-1.5	-	-	147.8	1.0	-	-	148.1	0.2	-	-	148.9	0.5	-	-	150.2	0.9	-	-

Source: U.S. Department of Labor, Bureau of Labor Statistics, Division of Consumer Prices and Price Indexes. - indicates no data collected for period.

Cleveland, OH
Consumer Price Index - All Urban Consumers
Base 1982-1984 = 100
Housing

For 1975-1995. Columns headed % show percentile change in the index from the previous period for which an index is available.

Year	Jan Index	%	Feb Index	%	Mar Index	%	Apr Index	%	May Index	%	Jun Index	%	Jul Index	%	Aug Index	%	Sep Index	%	Oct Index	%	Nov Index	%	Dec Index	%
1975	-	-	-	-	-	-	-	-	-	-	-	-	-	-	-	-	-	-	-	-	45.1	-	-	-
1976	-	-	45.0	-0.2	-	-	-	-	45.2	0.4	-	-	-	-	46.8	3.5	-	-	-	-	47.4	1.3	-	-
1977	-	-	48.5	2.3	-	-	-	-	48.9	0.8	-	-	-	-	50.5	3.3	-	-	-	-	50.9	0.8	-	-
1978	-	-	51.1	0.4	-	-	52.7	3.1	-	-	51.8	-1.7	-	-	53.4	3.1	-	-	55.9	4.7	-	-	58.6	4.8
1979	-	-	59.7	1.9	-	-	61.5	3.0	-	-	63.7	3.6	-	-	63.3	-0.6	-	-	63.9	0.9	-	-	67.7	5.9
1980	-	-	72.5	7.1	-	-	73.8	1.8	-	-	75.2	1.9	-	-	75.6	0.5	-	-	80.7	6.7	-	-	80.6	-0.1
1981	-	-	82.4	2.2	-	-	80.4	-2.4	-	-	87.4	8.7	-	-	86.2	-1.4	-	-	84.1	-2.4	-	-	82.6	-1.8
1982	-	-	84.4	2.2	-	-	84.8	0.5	-	-	90.2	6.4	-	-	97.9	8.5	-	-	100.3	2.5	-	-	100.7	0.4
1983	-	-	101.1	0.4	-	-	101.0	-0.1	-	-	103.7	2.7	-	-	102.9	-0.8	-	-	104.7	1.7	-	-	102.8	-1.8
1984	-	-	102.7	-0.1	-	-	104.1	1.4	-	-	105.9	1.7	-	-	105.8	-0.1	-	-	106.9	1.0	-	-	106.0	-0.8
1985	-	-	106.3	0.3	-	-	106.3	0.0	-	-	110.4	3.9	-	-	110.6	0.2	-	-	109.4	-1.1	-	-	108.9	-0.5
1986	-	-	110.0	1.0	-	-	110.9	0.8	-	-	112.7	1.6	-	-	113.9	1.1	-	-	112.2	-1.5	112.5	0.3	111.7	-0.7
1987	111.3	-0.4	-	-	113.1	1.6	-	-	112.9	-0.2	-	-	115.1	1.9	-	-	115.8	0.6	-	-	114.8	-0.9	-	-
1988	114.5	-0.3	-	-	116.3	1.6	-	-	117.7	1.2	-	-	119.2	1.3	-	-	118.5	-0.6	-	-	119.3	0.7	-	-
1989	120.6	1.1	-	-	121.4	0.7	-	-	121.4	0.0	-	-	125.4	3.3	-	-	124.3	-0.9	-	-	122.5	-1.4	-	-
1990	123.7	1.0	-	-	125.6	1.5	-	-	126.9	1.0	-	-	128.5	1.3	-	-	130.7	1.7	-	-	129.2	-1.1	-	-
1991	129.7	0.4	-	-	131.2	1.2	-	-	132.3	0.8	-	-	132.8	0.4	-	-	133.9	0.8	-	-	133.4	-0.4	-	-
1992	136.0	1.9	-	-	134.1	-1.4	-	-	134.1	0.0	-	-	137.8	2.8	-	-	137.3	-0.4	-	-	135.1	-1.6	-	-
1993	136.7	1.2	-	-	138.5	1.3	-	-	137.3	-0.9	-	-	139.7	1.7	-	-	141.3	1.1	-	-	139.9	-1.0	-	-
1994	140.2	0.2	-	-	142.2	1.4	-	-	142.5	0.2	-	-	143.2	0.5	-	-	143.6	0.3	-	-	142.1	-1.0	-	-
1995	143.8	1.2	-	-	143.8	0.0	-	-	143.2	-0.4	-	-	146.6	2.4	-	-	147.0	0.3	-	-	145.7	-0.9	-	-

Source: U.S. Department of Labor, Bureau of Labor Statistics, Division of Consumer Prices and Price Indexes. - indicates no data collected for period.

Cleveland, OH
Consumer Price Index - Urban Wage Earners
Base 1982-1984 = 100
Housing

For 1975-1995. Columns headed % show percentile change in the index from the previous period for which an index is available.

Year	Jan		Feb		Mar		Apr		May		Jun		Jul		Aug		Sep		Oct		Nov		Dec	
	Index	%	Index	%	Index	%	Index	%	Index	%	Index	%	Index	%	Index	%	Index	%	Index	%	Index	%	Index	%
1975	-	-	-	-	-	-	-	-	-	-	-	-	-	-	-	-	-	-	-	-	-	-	-	-
1976	-	-	46.9	-0.2	-	-	-	-	47.1	0.4	-	-	-	-	48.8	3.6	-	-	-	-	47.0	-	-	-
1977	-	-	50.6	2.4	-	-	-	-	50.9	0.6	-	-	-	-	52.6	3.3	-	-	-	-	49.4	1.2	-	-
1978	-	-	53.2	0.2	-	-	55.0	3.4	-	-	54.0	-1.8	-	-	55.7	3.1	-	-	-	-	53.1	1.0	-	-
1979	-	-	62.1	2.0	-	-	63.8	2.7	-	-	66.2	3.8	-	-	65.8	-0.6	-	-	58.3	4.7	-	-	60.9	4.5
1980	-	-	75.3	7.3	-	-	77.0	2.3	-	-	77.9	1.2	-	-	78.4	0.6	-	-	66.3	0.8	-	-	70.2	5.9
1981	-	-	85.5	2.3	-	-	83.3	-2.6	-	-	90.7	8.9	-	-	89.2	-1.7	-	-	87.2	-2.2	-	-	85.8	-1.6
1982	-	-	87.7	2.2	-	-	88.2	0.6	-	-	94.0	6.6	-	-	102.0	8.5	-	-	104.0	2.0	-	-	104.4	0.4
1983	-	-	102.9	-1.4	-	-	103.6	0.7	-	-	103.5	-0.1	-	-	102.6	-0.9	-	-	101.3	-1.3	-	-	99.3	-2.0
1984	-	-	100.3	1.0	-	-	102.0	1.7	-	-	101.6	-0.4	-	-	105.6	3.9	-	-	102.3	-3.1	-	-	98.1	-4.1
1985	-	-	98.6	0.5	-	-	98.6	0.0	-	-	102.6	4.1	-	-	102.9	0.3	-	-	101.4	-1.5	-	-	101.0	-0.4
1986	-	-	102.1	1.1	-	-	102.8	0.7	-	-	104.7	1.8	-	-	105.8	1.1	-	-	104.2	-1.5	104.3	0.1	103.5	-0.8
1987	103.3	-0.2	-	-	104.9	1.5	-	-	104.8	-0.1	-	-	106.7	1.8	-	-	107.5	0.7	-	-	106.5	-0.9	-	-
1988	106.3	-0.2	-	-	108.0	1.6	-	-	109.2	1.1	-	-	110.5	1.2	-	-	109.9	-0.5	-	-	110.4	0.5	-	-
1989	111.6	1.1	-	-	112.2	0.5	-	-	112.4	0.2	-	-	115.7	2.9	-	-	115.1	-0.5	-	-	110.4	0.5	-	-
1989	111.6	1.1	-	-	112.2	0.5	-	-	112.4	0.2	-	-	115.7	2.9	-	-	115.1	-0.5	-	-	113.3	-1.6	-	-
1990	114.4	1.0	-	-	116.0	1.4	-	-	117.1	0.9	-	-	118.6	1.3	-	-	120.6	1.7	-	-	119.3	-1.1	-	-
1991	119.7	0.3	-	-	120.9	1.0	-	-	121.8	0.7	-	-	122.3	0.4	-	-	123.8	1.2	-	-	123.2	-0.5	-	-
1992	125.6	1.9	-	-	123.8	-1.4	-	-	123.9	0.1	-	-	127.1	2.6	-	-	126.6	-0.4	-	-	125.0	-1.3	-	-
1993	126.2	1.0	-	-	127.7	1.2	-	-	126.7	-0.8	-	-	128.8	1.7	-	-	130.1	1.0	-	-	129.3	-0.6	-	-
1994	129.1	-0.2	-	-	130.6	1.2	-	-	130.9	0.2	-	-	131.7	0.6	-	-	132.3	0.5	-	-	131.0	-1.0	-	-
1995	132.3	1.0	-	-	132.2	-0.1	-	-	131.7	-0.4	-	-	134.6	2.2	-	-	135.1	0.4	-	-	133.8	-1.0	-	-

Source: U.S. Department of Labor, Bureau of Labor Statistics, Division of Consumer Prices and Price Indexes. - indicates no data collected for period.

Cleveland, OH
Consumer Price Index - All Urban Consumers
Base 1982-1984 = 100
Apparel and Upkeep

For 1952-1995. Columns headed % show percentile change in the index from the previous period for which an index is available.

Year	Jan		Feb		Mar		Apr		May		Jun		Jul		Aug		Sep		Oct		Nov		Dec	
	Index	%	Index	%	Index	%	Index	%	Index	%	Index	%	Index	%	Index	%	Index	%	Index	%	Index	%	Index	%
1952	-		-		-		-		-		-		-		-		-		-		43.7	-	-	
1953	-		43.3	-0.9	-		-		44.4	2.5	-		-		44.2	-0.5	-		-		44.2	0.0	-	
1954	-		44.1	-0.2	-		-		44.1	0.0	-		-		44.1	0.0	-		-		44.0	-0.2	-	
1955	-		43.8	-0.5	-		-		43.8	0.0	-		-		43.7	-0.2	-		-		44.1	0.9	-	
1956	-		44.2	0.2	-		-		44.6	0.9	-		-		45.0	0.9	-		-		45.3	0.7	-	
1957	-		45.0	-0.7	-		-		45.4	0.9	-		-		45.5	0.2	-		-		45.8	0.7	-	
1958	-		45.9	0.2	-		-		46.0	0.2	-		-		45.9	-0.2	-		-		45.9	0.0	-	
1959	-		46.0	0.2	-		-		46.2	0.4	-		-		46.3	0.2	-		-		46.4	0.2	-	
1960	-		46.4	0.0	-		-		46.3	-0.2	-		-		46.4	0.2	-		-		46.5	0.2	-	
1961	-		46.5	0.0	-		-		46.7	0.4	-		-		46.9	0.4	-		-		47.0	0.2	-	
1962	-		46.9	-0.2	-		-		47.1	0.4	-		-		46.9	-0.4	-		-		47.1	0.4	-	
1963	-		47.3	0.4	-		-		47.8	1.1	-		-		48.1	0.6	-		-		47.7	-0.8	-	
1964	-		47.8	0.2	-		-		48.0	0.4	-		-		47.7	-0.6	-		-		48.0	0.6	-	
1965	-		47.9	-0.2	-		-		48.6	1.5	-		-		48.0	-1.2	-		-		48.5	1.0	-	
1966	-		48.8	0.6	-		-		49.9	2.3	-		-		49.8	-0.2	-		-		50.4	1.2	-	
1967	-		50.5	0.2	-		-		51.1	1.2	-		-		50.8	-0.6	-		-		52.7	3.7	-	
1968	-		53.5	1.5	-		-		54.0	0.9	-		-		54.6	1.1	-		-		55.7	2.0	-	
1969	-		56.1	0.7	-		-		57.3	2.1	-		-		57.7	0.7	-		-		59.3	2.8	-	
1970	-		59.4	0.2	-		-		60.4	1.7	-		-		60.3	-0.2	-		-		61.4	1.8	-	
1971	-		61.4	0.0	-		-		62.8	2.3	-		-		62.4	-0.6	-		-		63.0	1.0	-	
1972	-		62.9	-0.2	-		-		63.5	1.0	-		-		63.4	-0.2	-		-		64.2	1.3	-	
1973	-		64.2	0.0	-		-		65.7	2.3	-		-		66.6	1.4	-		-		69.3	4.1	-	
1974	-		70.6	1.9	-		-		71.5	1.3	-		-		73.2	2.4	-		-		75.6	3.3	-	
1975	-		74.0	-2.1	-		-		74.4	0.5	-		-		74.2	-0.3	-		-		74.9	0.9	-	
1976	-		74.5	-0.5	-		-		75.3	1.1	-		-		76.3	1.3	-		-		78.6	3.0	-	
1977	-		78.1	-0.6	-		-		79.7	2.0	-		-		81.4	2.1	-		-		82.8	1.7	-	
1978	-		81.0	-2.2	-		80.2	-1.0	-		81.3	1.4	-		83.6	2.8	-		84.0	0.5	-		82.9	-1.3
1979	-		83.5	0.7	-		82.4	-1.3	-		81.4	-1.2	-		85.5	5.0	-		87.6	2.5	-		88.2	0.7
1980	-		87.7	-0.6	-		88.7	1.1	-		87.6	-1.2	-		90.4	3.2	-		91.6	1.3	-		91.4	-0.2
1981	-		93.2	2.0	-		96.1	3.1	-		94.6	-1.6	-		95.2	0.6	-		95.0	-0.2	-		97.3	2.4
1982	-		98.0	0.7	-		97.5	-0.5	-		98.4	0.9	-		102.1	3.8	-		101.6	-0.5	-		99.7	-1.9
1983	-		100.6	0.9	-		97.6	-3.0	-		98.7	1.1	-		99.1	0.4	-		99.9	0.8	-		99.5	-0.4
1984	-		101.2	1.7	-		98.4	-2.8	-		101.2	2.8	-		102.9	1.7	-		102.2	-0.7	-		102.8	0.6
1985	-		101.9	-0.9	-		103.2	1.3	-		101.5	-1.6	-		106.5	4.9	-		107.8	1.2	-		103.8	-3.7
1986	-		104.1	0.3	-		100.9	-3.1	-		99.3	-1.6	-		105.1	5.8	-		104.2	-0.9	103.1	-1.1	98.5	-4.5
1987	97.8	-0.7	-		105.5	7.9	-		104.0	-1.4	-		105.0	1.0	-		121.3	15.5	-		100.1	-0.9	-	
1988	106.7	-7.5	-		111.0	4.0	-		111.8	0.7	-		108.0	-3.4	-		101.0	-6.5	-		108.7	-2.2	-	
1989	91.9	-8.2	-		119.5	30.0	-		120.5	0.8	-		114.6	-4.9	-		111.2	-3.0	-		115.0	-0.4	-	
1990	102.6	-5.6	-		128.8	25.5	-		127.6	-0.9	-		115.4	-9.6	-		115.5	0.1	-		127.4	1.0	-	
1991	112.8	-1.9	-		125.1	10.9	-		122.7	-1.9	-		115.2	-6.1	-		126.1	9.5	-		120.7	-3.4	-	
1992	121.0	-5.0	-		128.2	6.0	-		122.7	-4.3	-		116.8	-4.8	-		124.9	6.9	-		128.6	-0.5	-	
1993	116.4	-3.6	-		119.7	2.8	-		126.7	5.8	-		127.2	0.4	-		129.3	1.7	-		132.9	-6.1	-	
1994	126.9	-1.3	-		128.8	1.5	-		127.3	-1.2	-		116.3	-8.6	-		141.6	21.8	-		123.9	-1.9	-	
1995	124.2	-6.5	-		136.5	9.9	-		129.9	-4.8	-		122.5	-5.7	-		126.3	3.1	-		-		-	

Source: U.S. Department of Labor, Bureau of Labor Statistics, Division of Consumer Prices and Price Indexes. - indicates no data collected for period.

Cleveland, OH
Consumer Price Index - Urban Wage Earners
Base 1982-1984 = 100
Apparel and Upkeep

For 1952-1995. Columns headed % show percentile change in the index from the previous period for which an index is available.

Year	Jan Index	Jan %	Feb Index	Feb %	Mar Index	Mar %	Apr Index	Apr %	May Index	May %	Jun Index	Jun %	Jul Index	Jul %	Aug Index	Aug %	Sep Index	Sep %	Oct Index	Oct %	Nov Index	Nov %	Dec Index	Dec %
1952	-	-	-	-	-	-	-	-	-	-	-	-	-	-	-	-	-	-	-	-	42.4	-	-	-
1953	-	-	42.0	-0.9	-	-	-	-	43.0	2.4	-	-	-	-	42.9	-0.2	-	-	-	-	42.9	0.0	-	-
1954	-	-	42.8	-0.2	-	-	-	-	42.8	0.0	-	-	-	-	42.7	-0.2	-	-	-	-	42.6	-0.2	-	-
1955	-	-	42.4	-0.5	-	-	-	-	42.5	0.2	-	-	-	-	42.4	-0.2	-	-	-	-	42.7	0.7	-	-
1956	-	-	42.9	0.5	-	-	-	-	43.2	0.7	-	-	-	-	43.6	0.9	-	-	-	-	44.0	0.9	-	-
1957	-	-	43.6	-0.9	-	-	-	-	44.0	0.9	-	-	-	-	44.1	0.2	-	-	-	-	44.4	0.7	-	-
1958	-	-	44.5	0.2	-	-	-	-	44.6	0.2	-	-	-	-	44.5	-0.2	-	-	-	-	44.5	0.0	-	-
1959	-	-	44.6	0.2	-	-	-	-	44.8	0.4	-	-	-	-	44.9	0.2	-	-	-	-	45.0	0.2	-	-
1960	-	-	45.0	0.0	-	-	-	-	44.9	-0.2	-	-	-	-	45.0	0.2	-	-	-	-	45.1	0.2	-	-
1961	-	-	45.1	0.0	-	-	-	-	45.3	0.4	-	-	-	-	45.5	0.4	-	-	-	-	45.6	0.2	-	-
1962	-	-	45.5	-0.2	-	-	-	-	45.7	0.4	-	-	-	-	45.5	-0.4	-	-	-	-	45.7	0.4	-	-
1963	-	-	45.9	0.4	-	-	-	-	46.4	1.1	-	-	-	-	46.7	0.6	-	-	-	-	46.2	-1.1	-	-
1964	-	-	46.3	0.2	-	-	-	-	46.6	0.6	-	-	-	-	46.2	-0.9	-	-	-	-	46.5	0.6	-	-
1965	-	-	46.4	-0.2	-	-	-	-	47.2	1.7	-	-	-	-	46.6	-1.3	-	-	-	-	47.1	1.1	-	-
1966	-	-	47.3	0.4	-	-	-	-	48.4	2.3	-	-	-	-	48.3	-0.2	-	-	-	-	48.9	1.2	-	-
1967	-	-	49.0	0.2	-	-	-	-	49.6	1.2	-	-	-	-	49.3	-0.6	-	-	-	-	51.1	3.7	-	-
1968	-	-	51.8	1.4	-	-	-	-	52.3	1.0	-	-	-	-	53.0	1.3	-	-	-	-	54.0	1.9	-	-
1969	-	-	54.4	0.7	-	-	-	-	55.6	2.2	-	-	-	-	56.0	0.7	-	-	-	-	57.5	2.7	-	-
1970	-	-	57.6	0.2	-	-	-	-	58.6	1.7	-	-	-	-	58.5	-0.2	-	-	-	-	59.6	1.9	-	-
1971	-	-	59.6	0.0	-	-	-	-	60.9	2.2	-	-	-	-	60.5	-0.7	-	-	-	-	61.1	1.0	-	-
1972	-	-	61.1	0.0	-	-	-	-	61.6	0.8	-	-	-	-	61.5	-0.2	-	-	-	-	62.3	1.3	-	-
1973	-	-	62.2	-0.2	-	-	-	-	63.7	2.4	-	-	-	-	64.6	1.4	-	-	-	-	67.2	4.0	-	-
1974	-	-	68.5	1.9	-	-	-	-	69.3	1.2	-	-	-	-	71.0	2.5	-	-	-	-	73.3	3.2	-	-
1975	-	-	71.8	-2.0	-	-	-	-	72.2	0.6	-	-	-	-	72.0	-0.3	-	-	-	-	72.7	1.0	-	-
1976	-	-	72.3	-0.6	-	-	-	-	73.0	1.0	-	-	-	-	74.0	1.4	-	-	-	-	76.3	3.1	-	-
1977	-	-	75.8	-0.7	-	-	-	-	77.3	2.0	-	-	-	-	79.0	2.2	-	-	-	-	80.4	1.8	-	-
1978	-	-	78.5	-2.4	-	-	79.5	1.3	-	-	79.9	0.5	-	-	81.2	1.6	-	-	82.9	2.1	-	-	83.1	0.2
1979	-	-	83.6	0.6	-	-	83.2	-0.5	-	-	81.5	-2.0	-	-	83.3	2.2	-	-	85.3	2.4	-	-	85.7	0.5
1980	-	-	85.5	-0.2	-	-	86.9	1.6	-	-	85.3	-1.8	-	-	86.7	1.6	-	-	89.1	2.8	-	-	89.9	0.9
1981	-	-	91.1	1.3	-	-	92.8	1.9	-	-	92.3	-0.5	-	-	92.3	0.0	-	-	95.3	3.3	-	-	97.5	2.3
1982	-	-	97.6	0.1	-	-	97.3	-0.3	-	-	98.3	1.0	-	-	101.8	3.6	-	-	101.3	-0.5	-	-	99.7	-1.6
1983	-	-	101.0	1.3	-	-	97.7	-3.3	-	-	98.6	0.9	-	-	99.2	0.6	-	-	100.0	0.8	-	-	99.3	-0.7
1984	-	-	101.8	2.5	-	-	98.3	-3.4	-	-	101.4	3.2	-	-	103.4	2.0	-	-	102.7	-0.7	-	-	102.1	-0.6
1985	-	-	102.6	0.5	-	-	103.9	1.3	-	-	102.2	-1.6	-	-	107.8	5.5	-	-	109.1	1.2	-	-	105.3	-3.5
1986	-	-	104.9	-0.4	-	-	102.1	-2.7	-	-	100.5	-1.6	-	-	106.4	5.9	-	-	105.8	-0.6	103.8	-1.9	99.7	-3.9
1987	98.2	-1.5	-	-	105.9	7.8	-	-	104.6	-1.2	-	-	105.8	1.1	-	-	121.8	15.1	-	-	116.6	-4.3	-	-
1988	107.3	-8.0	-	-	111.5	3.9	-	-	112.4	0.8	-	-	108.4	-3.6	-	-	101.3	-6.5	-	-	100.0	-1.3	-	-
1989	92.0	-8.0	-	-	118.5	28.8	-	-	119.8	1.1	-	-	114.0	-4.8	-	-	109.9	-3.6	-	-	107.9	-1.8	-	-
1990	102.2	-5.3	-	-	127.3	24.6	-	-	126.3	-0.8	-	-	114.2	-9.6	-	-	115.2	0.9	-	-	114.7	-0.4	-	-
1991	112.2	-2.2	-	-	124.2	10.7	-	-	121.9	-1.9	-	-	114.9	-5.7	-	-	125.7	9.4	-	-	127.1	1.1	-	-
1992	120.9	-4.9	-	-	128.4	6.2	-	-	122.9	-4.3	-	-	116.7	-5.0	-	-	125.7	7.7	-	-	121.2	-3.6	-	-
1993	116.9	-3.5	-	-	119.5	2.2	-	-	125.3	4.9	-	-	126.3	0.8	-	-	128.0	1.3	-	-	127.2	-0.6	-	-
1994	125.9	-1.0	-	-	127.4	1.2	-	-	126.4	-0.8	-	-	115.5	-8.6	-	-	140.0	21.2	-	-	131.2	-6.3	-	-
1995	122.3	-6.8	-	-	134.3	9.8	-	-	127.7	-4.9	-	-	120.6	-5.6	-	-	124.8	3.5	-	-	122.6	-1.8	-	-

Source: U.S. Department of Labor, Bureau of Labor Statistics, Division of Consumer Prices and Price Indexes. - indicates no data collected for period.

Cleveland, OH
Consumer Price Index - All Urban Consumers
Base 1982-1984 = 100
Transportation

For 1947-1995. Columns headed % show percentile change in the index from the previous period for which an index is available.

Year	Jan Index	%	Feb Index	%	Mar Index	%	Apr Index	%	May Index	%	Jun Index	%	Jul Index	%	Aug Index	%	Sep Index	%	Oct Index	%	Nov Index	%	Dec Index	%
1947	18.3	-	18.3	0.0	18.6	1.6	18.7	0.5	18.6	-0.5	18.6	0.0	-	-	18.9	1.6	-	-	-	-	19.5	3.2	-	-
1948	-	-	20.7	6.2	-	-	-	-	20.8	0.5	-	-	-	-	22.8	9.6	-	-	-	-	22.9	0.4	-	-
1949	-	-	23.1	0.9	-	-	-	-	23.2	0.4	-	-	-	-	23.1	-0.4	-	-	-	-	23.1	0.0	-	-
1950	-	-	22.8	-1.3	-	-	-	-	22.7	-0.4	-	-	-	-	23.4	3.1	-	-	-	-	23.5	0.4	-	-
1951	-	-	23.7	0.9	-	-	-	-	23.9	0.8	-	-	-	-	24.9	4.2	-	-	-	-	25.6	2.8	-	-
1952	-	-	26.0	1.6	-	-	-	-	26.0	0.0	-	-	-	-	26.0	0.0	-	-	-	-	26.0	0.0	-	-
1953	-	-	26.1	0.4	-	-	-	-	26.2	0.4	-	-	-	-	26.6	1.5	-	-	-	-	26.4	-0.8	-	-
1954	-	-	26.1	-1.1	-	-	-	-	26.0	-0.4	-	-	-	-	25.0	-3.8	-	-	-	-	25.9	3.6	-	-
1955	-	-	25.4	-1.9	-	-	-	-	25.0	-1.6	-	-	-	-	25.4	1.6	-	-	-	-	26.5	4.3	-	-
1956	-	-	26.0	-1.9	-	-	-	-	26.1	0.4	-	-	-	-	26.7	2.3	-	-	-	-	27.8	4.1	-	-
1957	-	-	28.1	1.1	-	-	-	-	28.1	0.0	-	-	-	-	28.6	1.8	-	-	-	-	29.4	2.8	-	-
1958	-	-	28.7	-2.4	-	-	-	-	28.9	0.7	-	-	-	-	29.0	0.3	-	-	-	-	29.4	1.4	-	-
1959	-	-	29.6	0.7	-	-	-	-	29.7	0.3	-	-	-	-	30.3	2.0	-	-	-	-	30.7	1.3	-	-
1960	-	-	30.4	-1.0	-	-	-	-	30.2	-0.7	-	-	-	-	30.1	-0.3	-	-	-	-	30.5	1.3	-	-
1961	-	-	30.5	0.0	-	-	-	-	30.6	0.3	-	-	-	-	31.3	2.3	-	-	-	-	31.4	0.3	-	-
1962	-	-	31.1	-1.0	-	-	-	-	31.4	1.0	-	-	-	-	31.5	0.3	-	-	-	-	31.5	0.0	-	-
1963	-	-	31.3	-0.6	-	-	-	-	31.3	0.0	-	-	-	-	31.6	1.0	-	-	-	-	31.9	0.9	-	-
1964	-	-	31.9	0.0	-	-	-	-	32.0	0.3	-	-	-	-	32.0	0.0	-	-	-	-	32.4	1.3	-	-
1965	-	-	32.5	0.3	-	-	-	-	32.8	0.9	-	-	-	-	32.5	-0.9	-	-	-	-	32.7	0.6	-	-
1966	-	-	32.5	-0.6	-	-	-	-	33.0	1.5	-	-	-	-	32.9	-0.3	-	-	-	-	33.2	0.9	-	-
1967	-	-	33.2	0.0	-	-	-	-	33.4	0.6	-	-	-	-	34.0	1.8	-	-	-	-	34.9	2.6	-	-
1968	-	-	35.2	0.9	-	-	-	-	35.3	0.3	-	-	-	-	35.6	0.8	-	-	-	-	36.3	2.0	-	-
1969	-	-	35.9	-1.1	-	-	-	-	37.0	3.1	-	-	-	-	37.1	0.3	-	-	-	-	38.0	2.4	-	-
1970	-	-	38.4	1.1	-	-	-	-	38.8	1.0	-	-	-	-	39.2	1.0	-	-	-	-	41.9	6.9	-	-
1971	-	-	42.1	0.5	-	-	-	-	42.3	0.5	-	-	-	-	42.4	0.2	-	-	-	-	42.1	-0.7	-	-
1972	-	-	42.4	0.7	-	-	-	-	42.8	0.9	-	-	-	-	42.9	0.2	-	-	-	-	42.9	0.0	-	-
1973	-	-	43.1	0.5	-	-	-	-	44.0	2.1	-	-	-	-	44.2	0.5	-	-	-	-	44.8	1.4	-	-
1974	-	-	47.2	5.4	-	-	-	-	49.9	5.7	-	-	-	-	50.2	0.6	-	-	-	-	50.7	1.0	-	-
1975	-	-	50.7	0.0	-	-	-	-	51.9	2.4	-	-	-	-	53.5	3.1	-	-	-	-	52.1	-2.6	-	-
1976	-	-	52.2	0.2	-	-	-	-	53.7	2.9	-	-	-	-	55.5	3.4	-	-	-	-	56.2	1.3	-	-
1977	-	-	56.4	0.4	-	-	-	-	57.9	2.7	-	-	-	-	58.0	0.2	-	-	-	-	58.7	1.2	-	-
1978	-	-	58.8	0.2	-	-	59.6	1.4	-	-	60.9	2.2	-	-	61.8	1.5	-	-	62.1	0.5	-	-	62.8	1.1
1979	-	-	64.3	2.4	-	-	66.6	3.6	-	-	68.8	3.3	-	-	71.1	3.3	-	-	72.7	2.3	-	-	74.4	2.3
1980	-	-	77.4	4.0	-	-	79.5	2.7	-	-	80.7	1.5	-	-	82.4	2.1	-	-	82.9	0.6	-	-	85.4	3.0
1981	-	-	88.4	3.5	-	-	90.1	1.9	-	-	91.4	1.4	-	-	93.4	2.2	-	-	95.3	2.0	-	-	96.2	0.9
1982	-	-	95.1	-1.1	-	-	94.2	-0.9	-	-	97.2	3.2	-	-	99.1	2.0	-	-	98.0	-1.1	-	-	98.4	0.4
1983	-	-	96.0	-2.4	-	-	97.1	1.1	-	-	98.9	1.9	-	-	101.3	2.4	-	-	102.5	1.2	-	-	102.5	0.0
1984	-	-	101.8	-0.7	-	-	102.7	0.9	-	-	104.3	1.6	-	-	103.8	-0.5	-	-	104.8	1.0	-	-	104.7	-0.1
1985	-	-	103.5	-1.1	-	-	106.0	2.4	-	-	106.1	0.1	-	-	105.4	-0.7	-	-	106.2	0.8	-	-	107.2	0.9
1986	-	-	105.0	-2.1	-	-	99.5	-5.2	-	-	101.7	2.2	-	-	99.0	-2.7	-	-	99.6	0.6	100.3	0.7	100.9	0.6
1987	102.3	1.4	-	-	101.9	-0.4	-	-	103.0	1.1	-	-	104.5	1.5	-	-	104.7	0.2	-	-	106.4	1.6	-	-
1988	105.5	-0.8	-	-	103.7	-1.7	-	-	107.6	3.8	-	-	107.8	0.2	-	-	109.1	1.2	-	-	109.4	0.3	-	-
1989	109.3	-0.1	-	-	110.5	1.1	-	-	116.1	5.1	-	-	113.8	-2.0	-	-	111.9	-1.7	-	-	114.3	2.1	-	-
1990	117.0	2.4	-	-	114.7	-2.0	-	-	116.1	1.2	-	-	116.5	0.3	-	-	122.5	5.2	-	-	128.1	4.6	-	-
1991	123.9	-3.3	-	-	121.6	-1.9	-	-	122.7	0.9	-	-	123.1	0.3	-	-	123.1	0.0	-	-	124.7	1.3	-	-

[Continued]

Cleveland, OH
Consumer Price Index - All Urban Consumers
Base 1982-1984 = 100
Transportation
[Continued]

For 1947-1995. Columns headed % show percentile change in the index from the previous period for which an index is available.

Year	Jan Index	%	Feb Index	%	Mar Index	%	Apr Index	%	May Index	%	Jun Index	%	Jul Index	%	Aug Index	%	Sep Index	%	Oct Index	%	Nov Index	%	Dec Index	%
1992	122.0	-2.2	-	-	123.1	0.9	-	-	124.4	1.1	-	-	124.9	0.4	-	-	123.7	-1.0	-	-	126.6	2.3	-	-
1993	122.8	-3.0	-	-	123.3	0.4	-	-	125.9	2.1	-	-	126.1	0.2	-	-	124.7	-1.1	-	-	126.5	1.4	-	-
1994	125.5	-0.8	-	-	125.8	0.2	-	-	127.2	1.1	-	-	129.6	1.9	-	-	130.0	0.3	-	-	132.1	1.6	-	-
1995	131.0	-0.8	-	-	132.2	0.9	-	-	135.7	2.6	-	-	133.5	-1.6	-	-	133.7	0.1	-	-	131.5	-1.6	-	-

Source: U.S. Department of Labor, Bureau of Labor Statistics, Division of Consumer Prices and Price Indexes. - indicates no data collected for period.

Cleveland, OH
Consumer Price Index - Urban Wage Earners
Base 1982-1984 = 100
Transportation

For 1947-1995. Columns headed % show percentile change in the index from the previous period for which an index is available.

Year	Jan Index	%	Feb Index	%	Mar Index	%	Apr Index	%	May Index	%	Jun Index	%	Jul Index	%	Aug Index	%	Sep Index	%	Oct Index	%	Nov Index	%	Dec Index	%
1947	18.6	-	18.6	0.0	18.8	1.1	18.9	0.5	18.8	-0.5	18.8	0.0	-	-	19.1	1.6	-	-	-	-	19.7	3.1	-	-
1948	-	-	20.9	6.1	-	-	-	-	21.0	0.5	-	-	-	-	23.1	10.0	-	-	-	-	23.1	0.0	-	-
1949	-	-	23.4	1.3	-	-	-	-	23.4	0.0	-	-	-	-	23.4	0.0	-	-	-	-	23.4	0.0	-	-
1950	-	-	23.1	-1.3	-	-	-	-	23.0	-0.4	-	-	-	-	23.7	3.0	-	-	-	-	23.8	0.4	-	-
1951	-	-	24.0	0.8	-	-	-	-	24.2	0.8	-	-	-	-	25.2	4.1	-	-	-	-	26.0	3.2	-	-
1952	-	-	26.3	1.2	-	-	-	-	26.3	0.0	-	-	-	-	26.3	0.0	-	-	-	-	26.4	0.4	-	-
1953	-	-	26.5	0.4	-	-	-	-	26.5	0.0	-	-	-	-	26.9	1.5	-	-	-	-	26.7	-0.7	-	-
1954	-	-	26.5	-0.7	-	-	-	-	26.4	-0.4	-	-	-	-	25.3	-4.2	-	-	-	-	26.2	3.6	-	-
1955	-	-	25.7	-1.9	-	-	-	-	25.3	-1.6	-	-	-	-	25.7	1.6	-	-	-	-	26.8	4.3	-	-
1956	-	-	26.3	-1.9	-	-	-	-	26.4	0.4	-	-	-	-	27.0	2.3	-	-	-	-	28.1	4.1	-	-
1957	-	-	28.4	1.1	-	-	-	-	28.4	0.0	-	-	-	-	28.9	1.8	-	-	-	-	29.7	2.8	-	-
1958	-	-	29.1	-2.0	-	-	-	-	29.2	0.3	-	-	-	-	29.3	0.3	-	-	-	-	29.8	1.7	-	-
1959	-	-	30.0	0.7	-	-	-	-	30.0	0.0	-	-	-	-	30.7	2.3	-	-	-	-	31.1	1.3	-	-
1960	-	-	30.7	-1.3	-	-	-	-	30.6	-0.3	-	-	-	-	30.5	-0.3	-	-	-	-	30.8	1.0	-	-
1961	-	-	30.9	0.3	-	-	-	-	31.0	0.3	-	-	-	-	31.7	2.3	-	-	-	-	31.8	0.3	-	-
1962	-	-	31.5	-0.9	-	-	-	-	31.8	1.0	-	-	-	-	31.9	0.3	-	-	-	-	31.9	0.0	-	-
1963	-	-	31.7	-0.6	-	-	-	-	31.7	0.0	-	-	-	-	32.0	0.9	-	-	-	-	32.3	0.9	-	-
1964	-	-	32.3	0.0	-	-	-	-	32.4	0.3	-	-	-	-	32.4	0.0	-	-	-	-	32.8	1.2	-	-
1965	-	-	32.9	0.3	-	-	-	-	33.2	0.9	-	-	-	-	32.9	-0.9	-	-	-	-	33.1	0.6	-	-
1966	-	-	32.9	-0.6	-	-	-	-	33.4	1.5	-	-	-	-	33.3	-0.3	-	-	-	-	33.6	0.9	-	-
1967	-	-	33.6	0.0	-	-	-	-	33.8	0.6	-	-	-	-	34.4	1.8	-	-	-	-	35.4	2.9	-	-
1968	-	-	35.6	0.6	-	-	-	-	35.7	0.3	-	-	-	-	36.0	0.8	-	-	-	-	36.7	1.9	-	-
1969	-	-	36.4	-0.8	-	-	-	-	37.5	3.0	-	-	-	-	37.6	0.3	-	-	-	-	38.5	2.4	-	-
1970	-	-	38.9	1.0	-	-	-	-	39.2	0.8	-	-	-	-	39.7	1.3	-	-	-	-	42.4	6.8	-	-
1971	-	-	42.6	0.5	-	-	-	-	42.8	0.5	-	-	-	-	42.9	0.2	-	-	-	-	42.6	-0.7	-	-
1972	-	-	42.9	0.7	-	-	-	-	43.3	0.9	-	-	-	-	43.5	0.5	-	-	-	-	43.4	-0.2	-	-
1973	-	-	43.6	0.5	-	-	-	-	44.5	2.1	-	-	-	-	44.7	0.4	-	-	-	-	45.3	1.3	-	-
1974	-	-	47.8	5.5	-	-	-	-	50.5	5.6	-	-	-	-	50.8	0.6	-	-	-	-	51.4	1.2	-	-
1975	-	-	51.3	-0.2	-	-	-	-	52.6	2.5	-	-	-	-	54.2	3.0	-	-	-	-	52.8	-2.6	-	-
1976	-	-	52.9	0.2	-	-	-	-	54.3	2.6	-	-	-	-	56.2	3.5	-	-	-	-	56.9	1.2	-	-
1977	-	-	57.1	0.4	-	-	-	-	58.6	2.6	-	-	-	-	58.7	0.2	-	-	-	-	59.5	1.4	-	-
1978	-	-	59.5	0.0	-	-	60.3	1.3	-	-	61.9	2.7	-	-	62.9	1.6	-	-	62.9	0.0	-	-	63.5	1.0
1979	-	-	65.5	3.1	-	-	68.1	4.0	-	-	70.5	3.5	-	-	72.7	3.1	-	-	74.4	2.3	-	-	75.5	1.5
1980	-	-	79.0	4.6	-	-	80.6	2.0	-	-	82.3	2.1	-	-	83.7	1.7	-	-	84.1	0.5	-	-	86.0	2.3
1981	-	-	89.6	4.2	-	-	90.9	1.5	-	-	91.6	0.8	-	-	93.7	2.3	-	-	95.3	1.7	-	-	95.9	0.6
1982	-	-	94.7	-1.3	-	-	93.6	-1.2	-	-	97.0	3.6	-	-	99.1	2.2	-	-	98.2	-0.9	-	-	98.5	0.3
1983	-	-	96.0	-2.5	-	-	97.1	1.1	-	-	99.2	2.2	-	-	101.4	2.2	-	-	102.5	1.1	-	-	102.5	0.0
1984	-	-	101.8	-0.7	-	-	102.8	1.0	-	-	104.5	1.7	-	-	104.0	-0.5	-	-	104.8	0.8	-	-	104.6	-0.2
1985	-	-	103.3	-1.2	-	-	106.1	2.7	-	-	106.2	0.1	-	-	105.4	-0.8	-	-	105.9	0.5	-	-	107.1	1.1
1986	-	-	104.4	-2.5	-	-	98.3	-5.8	-	-	100.7	2.4	-	-	97.6	-3.1	-	-	98.1	0.5	98.8	0.7	99.4	0.6
1987	100.6	1.2	-	-	100.2	-0.4	-	-	101.3	1.1	-	-	102.6	1.3	-	-	102.6	0.0	-	-	104.5	1.9	-	-
1988	103.8	-0.7	-	-	101.9	-1.8	-	-	105.5	3.5	-	-	105.6	0.1	-	-	107.0	1.3	-	-	107.5	0.5	-	-
1989	107.4	-0.1	-	-	108.5	1.0	-	-	113.7	4.8	-	-	111.4	-2.0	-	-	109.5	-1.7	-	-	112.1	2.4	-	-
1990	114.6	2.2	-	-	112.2	-2.1	-	-	113.6	1.2	-	-	114.0	0.4	-	-	119.3	4.6	-	-	124.4	4.3	-	-
1991	120.7	-3.0	-	-	118.6	-1.7	-	-	119.7	0.9	-	-	120.1	0.3	-	-	120.0	-0.1	-	-	121.4	1.2	-	-

[Continued]

Cleveland, OH
Consumer Price Index - Urban Wage Earners
Base 1982-1984 = 100
Transportation
[Continued]

For 1947-1995. Columns headed % show percentile change in the index from the previous period for which an index is available.

Year	Jan		Feb		Mar		Apr		May		Jun		Jul		Aug		Sep		Oct		Nov		Dec	
	Index	%	Index	%	Index	%	Index	%	Index	%	Index	%	Index	%	Index	%	Index	%	Index	%	Index	%	Index	%
1992	118.8	-2.1	-	-	119.6	0.7	-	-	121.0	1.2	-	-	121.6	0.5	-	-	120.6	-0.8	-	-	123.1	2.1	-	-
1993	119.6	-2.8	-	-	119.7	0.1	-	-	122.4	2.3	-	-	122.8	0.3	-	-	121.7	-0.9	-	-	123.4	1.4	-	-
1994	122.3	-0.9	-	-	122.4	0.1	-	-	123.9	1.2	-	-	126.3	1.9	-	-	126.7	0.3	-	-	123.4	1.4	-	-
1995	128.0	-0.8	-	-	129.0	0.8	-	-	132.2	2.5	-	-	130.2	-1.5	-	-	130.3	0.1	-	-	128.5	-1.4	-	-

Source: U.S. Department of Labor, Bureau of Labor Statistics, Division of Consumer Prices and Price Indexes. - indicates no data collected for period.

Cleveland, OH

Consumer Price Index - All Urban Consumers
Base 1982-1984 = 100

Medical Care

For 1947-1995. Columns headed % show percentile change in the index from the previous period for which an index is available.

Year	Jan Index	%	Feb Index	%	Mar Index	%	Apr Index	%	May Index	%	Jun Index	%	Jul Index	%	Aug Index	%	Sep Index	%	Oct Index	%	Nov Index	%	Dec Index	%
1947	10.5	-	10.5	0.0	10.5	0.0	10.5	0.0	10.5	0.0	10.5	0.0	-	-	10.5	0.0	-	-	-	-	10.9	3.8	-	-
1948	-	-	11.0	0.9	-	-	-	-	11.2	1.8	-	-	-	-	11.2	0.0	-	-	-	-	11.5	2.7	-	-
1949	-	-	11.6	0.9	-	-	-	-	11.6	0.0	-	-	-	-	11.7	0.9	-	-	-	-	11.8	0.9	-	-
1950	-	-	11.8	0.0	-	-	-	-	11.8	0.0	-	-	-	-	11.7	-0.8	-	-	-	-	11.9	1.7	-	-
1951	-	-	12.2	2.5	-	-	-	-	12.6	3.3	-	-	-	-	12.6	0.0	-	-	-	-	13.2	4.8	-	-
1952	-	-	13.2	0.0	-	-	-	-	13.3	0.8	-	-	-	-	13.4	0.8	-	-	-	-	13.3	-0.7	-	-
1953	-	-	13.4	0.8	-	-	-	-	13.4	0.0	-	-	-	-	14.2	6.0	-	-	-	-	14.2	0.0	-	-
1954	-	-	14.4	1.4	-	-	-	-	14.5	0.7	-	-	-	-	14.5	0.0	-	-	-	-	14.6	0.7	-	-
1955	-	-	14.6	0.0	-	-	-	-	15.3	4.8	-	-	-	-	15.3	0.0	-	-	-	-	15.4	0.7	-	-
1956	-	-	15.4	0.0	-	-	-	-	16.3	5.8	-	-	-	-	16.3	0.0	-	-	-	-	16.3	0.0	-	-
1957	-	-	16.4	0.6	-	-	-	-	16.7	1.8	-	-	-	-	16.8	0.6	-	-	-	-	16.8	0.0	-	-
1958	-	-	17.0	1.2	-	-	-	-	17.1	0.6	-	-	-	-	17.1	0.0	-	-	-	-	17.2	0.6	-	-
1959	-	-	18.6	8.1	-	-	-	-	18.7	0.5	-	-	-	-	18.8	0.5	-	-	-	-	19.0	1.1	-	-
1960	-	-	19.0	0.0	-	-	-	-	19.3	1.6	-	-	-	-	19.4	0.5	-	-	-	-	19.4	0.0	-	-
1961	-	-	20.7	6.7	-	-	-	-	20.8	0.5	-	-	-	-	20.6	-1.0	-	-	-	-	20.7	0.5	-	-
1962	-	-	20.7	0.0	-	-	-	-	20.8	0.5	-	-	-	-	20.8	0.0	-	-	-	-	20.8	0.0	-	-
1963	-	-	20.8	0.0	-	-	-	-	22.1	6.3	-	-	-	-	22.2	0.5	-	-	-	-	22.3	0.5	-	-
1964	-	-	22.4	0.4	-	-	-	-	22.5	0.4	-	-	-	-	22.5	0.0	-	-	-	-	22.7	0.9	-	-
1965	-	-	23.1	1.8	-	-	-	-	23.2	0.4	-	-	-	-	23.2	0.0	-	-	-	-	23.3	0.4	-	-
1966	-	-	23.5	0.9	-	-	-	-	23.6	0.4	-	-	-	-	23.7	0.4	-	-	-	-	24.2	2.1	-	-
1967	-	-	24.4	0.8	-	-	-	-	25.1	2.9	-	-	-	-	25.4	1.2	-	-	-	-	25.7	1.2	-	-
1968	-	-	26.4	2.7	-	-	-	-	26.9	1.9	-	-	-	-	27.2	1.1	-	-	-	-	28.5	4.8	-	-
1969	-	-	29.4	3.2	-	-	-	-	30.3	3.1	-	-	-	-	31.2	3.0	-	-	-	-	31.4	0.6	-	-
1970	-	-	32.3	2.9	-	-	-	-	32.8	1.5	-	-	-	-	33.4	1.8	-	-	-	-	33.3	-0.3	-	-
1971	-	-	34.2	2.7	-	-	-	-	34.9	2.0	-	-	-	-	36.1	3.4	-	-	-	-	35.8	-0.8	-	-
1972	-	-	35.7	-0.3	-	-	-	-	36.0	0.8	-	-	-	-	36.5	1.4	-	-	-	-	36.8	0.8	-	-
1973	-	-	37.4	1.6	-	-	-	-	37.7	0.8	-	-	-	-	37.9	0.5	-	-	-	-	38.6	1.8	-	-
1974	-	-	40.2	4.1	-	-	-	-	40.7	1.2	-	-	-	-	41.9	2.9	-	-	-	-	42.4	1.2	-	-
1975	-	-	45.5	7.3	-	-	-	-	46.1	1.3	-	-	-	-	45.8	-0.7	-	-	-	-	46.9	2.4	-	-
1976	-	-	49.5	5.5	-	-	-	-	50.2	1.4	-	-	-	-	50.9	1.4	-	-	-	-	51.9	2.0	-	-
1977	-	-	55.0	6.0	-	-	-	-	56.4	2.5	-	-	-	-	57.4	1.8	-	-	-	-	58.3	1.6	-	-
1978	-	-	61.0	4.6	-	-	61.2	0.3	-	-	61.9	1.1	-	-	62.4	0.8	-	-	62.7	0.5	-	-	63.2	0.8
1979	-	-	64.7	2.4	-	-	65.0	0.5	-	-	66.0	1.5	-	-	66.3	0.5	-	-	66.8	0.8	-	-	68.6	2.7
1980	-	-	71.9	4.8	-	-	71.6	-0.4	-	-	72.1	0.7	-	-	73.4	1.8	-	-	73.9	0.7	-	-	74.9	1.4
1981	-	-	79.7	6.4	-	-	80.6	1.1	-	-	81.3	0.9	-	-	82.1	1.0	-	-	82.1	0.0	-	-	83.4	1.6
1982	-	-	87.9	5.4	-	-	90.8	3.3	-	-	91.4	0.7	-	-	92.5	1.2	-	-	94.1	1.7	-	-	95.0	1.0
1983	-	-	99.8	5.1	-	-	101.3	1.5	-	-	101.5	0.2	-	-	101.9	0.4	-	-	101.7	-0.2	-	-	102.7	1.0
1984	-	-	106.6	3.8	-	-	107.3	0.7	-	-	108.1	0.7	-	-	107.8	-0.3	-	-	107.8	0.0	-	-	108.1	0.3
1985	-	-	110.4	2.1	-	-	111.1	0.6	-	-	111.5	0.4	-	-	112.0	0.4	-	-	112.5	0.4	-	-	116.0	3.1
1986	-	-	119.0	2.6	-	-	119.9	0.8	-	-	123.5	3.0	-	-	124.1	0.5	-	-	124.4	0.2	124.9	0.4	124.8	-0.1
1987	127.4	2.1	-	-	127.7	0.2	-	-	128.0	0.2	-	-	127.7	-0.2	-	-	129.4	1.3	-	-	129.8	0.3	-	-
1988	132.4	2.0	-	-	132.9	0.4	-	-	133.1	0.2	-	-	133.8	0.5	-	-	137.7	2.9	-	-	137.5	-0.1	-	-
1989	140.1	1.9	-	-	141.1	0.7	-	-	141.7	0.4	-	-	144.3	1.8	-	-	144.6	0.2	-	-	146.6	1.4	-	-
1990	150.2	2.5	-	-	151.7	1.0	-	-	153.4	1.1	-	-	158.5	3.3	-	-	159.4	0.6	-	-	162.8	2.1	-	-
1991	166.0	2.0	-	-	168.8	1.7	-	-	171.4	1.5	-	-	171.9	0.3	-	-	174.2	1.3	-	-	175.1	0.5	-	-

[Continued]

Cleveland, OH
Consumer Price Index - All Urban Consumers
Base 1982-1984 = 100
Medical Care

[Continued]

For 1947-1995. Columns headed % show percentile change in the index from the previous period for which an index is available.

Year	Jan Index	%	Feb Index	%	Mar Index	%	Apr Index	%	May Index	%	Jun Index	%	Jul Index	%	Aug Index	%	Sep Index	%	Oct Index	%	Nov Index	%	Dec Index	%
1992	176.5	0.8	-	-	177.8	0.7	-	-	178.5	0.4	-	-	179.0	0.3	-	-	178.4	-0.3	-	-	179.0	0.3	-	-
1993	185.5	3.6	-	-	185.1	-0.2	-	-	186.0	0.5	-	-	188.0	1.1	-	-	188.2	0.1	-	-	188.9	0.4	-	-
1994	192.6	2.0	-	-	195.3	1.4	-	-	194.5	-0.4	-	-	194.7	0.1	-	-	197.7	1.5	-	-	197.6	-0.1	-	-
1995	201.2	1.8	-	-	202.6	0.7	-	-	201.9	-0.3	-	-	202.4	0.2	-	-	202.4	0.0	-	-	203.3	0.4	-	-

Source: U.S. Department of Labor, Bureau of Labor Statistics, Division of Consumer Prices and Price Indexes. - indicates no data collected for period.

Cleveland, OH
Consumer Price Index - Urban Wage Earners
Base 1982-1984 = 100
Medical Care

For 1947-1995. Columns headed % show percentile change in the index from the previous period for which an index is available.

Year	Jan Index	%	Feb Index	%	Mar Index	%	Apr Index	%	May Index	%	Jun Index	%	Jul Index	%	Aug Index	%	Sep Index	%	Oct Index	%	Nov Index	%	Dec Index	%
1947	10.3	-	10.3	0.0	10.3	0.0	10.3	0.0	10.3	0.0	10.3	0.0	-	-	10.4	1.0	-	-	-	-	10.8	3.8	-	-
1948	-	-	10.8	0.0	-	-	-	-	11.0	1.9	-	-	-	-	11.0	0.0	-	-	-	-	11.4	3.6	-	-
1949	-	-	11.4	0.0	-	-	-	-	11.4	0.0	-	-	-	-	11.5	0.9	-	-	-	-	11.6	0.9	-	-
1950	-	-	11.6	0.0	-	-	-	-	11.6	0.0	-	-	-	-	11.5	-0.9	-	-	-	-	11.7	1.7	-	-
1951	-	-	12.0	2.6	-	-	-	-	12.4	3.3	-	-	-	-	12.4	0.0	-	-	-	-	13.0	4.8	-	-
1952	-	-	13.0	0.0	-	-	-	-	13.0	0.0	-	-	-	-	13.1	0.8	-	-	-	-	13.1	0.0	-	-
1953	-	-	13.1	0.0	-	-	-	-	13.2	0.8	-	-	-	-	13.9	5.3	-	-	-	-	14.0	0.7	-	-
1954	-	-	14.2	1.4	-	-	-	-	14.2	0.0	-	-	-	-	14.2	0.0	-	-	-	-	14.4	1.4	-	-
1955	-	-	14.4	0.0	-	-	-	-	15.0	4.2	-	-	-	-	15.0	0.0	-	-	-	-	15.2	1.3	-	-
1956	-	-	15.2	0.0	-	-	-	-	16.0	5.3	-	-	-	-	16.1	0.6	-	-	-	-	16.1	0.0	-	-
1957	-	-	16.2	0.6	-	-	-	-	16.4	1.2	-	-	-	-	16.6	1.2	-	-	-	-	16.6	0.0	-	-
1958	-	-	16.8	1.2	-	-	-	-	16.8	0.0	-	-	-	-	16.8	0.0	-	-	-	-	16.9	0.6	-	-
1959	-	-	18.3	8.3	-	-	-	-	18.4	0.5	-	-	-	-	18.5	0.5	-	-	-	-	18.7	1.1	-	-
1960	-	-	18.7	0.0	-	-	-	-	19.0	1.6	-	-	-	-	19.1	0.5	-	-	-	-	19.1	0.0	-	-
1961	-	-	20.4	6.8	-	-	-	-	20.4	0.0	-	-	-	-	20.3	-0.5	-	-	-	-	20.3	0.0	-	-
1962	-	-	20.4	0.5	-	-	-	-	20.4	0.0	-	-	-	-	20.4	0.0	-	-	-	-	20.4	0.0	-	-
1963	-	-	20.5	0.5	-	-	-	-	21.8	6.3	-	-	-	-	21.9	0.5	-	-	-	-	21.9	0.0	-	-
1964	-	-	22.0	0.5	-	-	-	-	22.1	0.5	-	-	-	-	22.1	0.0	-	-	-	-	22.3	0.9	-	-
1965	-	-	22.7	1.8	-	-	-	-	22.8	0.4	-	-	-	-	22.8	0.0	-	-	-	-	22.9	0.4	-	-
1966	-	-	23.1	0.9	-	-	-	-	23.2	0.4	-	-	-	-	23.3	0.4	-	-	-	-	23.8	2.1	-	-
1967	-	-	24.0	0.8	-	-	-	-	24.7	2.9	-	-	-	-	25.0	1.2	-	-	-	-	25.2	0.8	-	-
1968	-	-	26.0	3.2	-	-	-	-	26.5	1.9	-	-	-	-	26.7	0.8	-	-	-	-	28.1	5.2	-	-
1969	-	-	28.9	2.8	-	-	-	-	29.8	3.1	-	-	-	-	30.7	3.0	-	-	-	-	30.8	0.3	-	-
1970	-	-	31.8	3.2	-	-	-	-	32.2	1.3	-	-	-	-	32.9	2.2	-	-	-	-	32.7	-0.6	-	-
1971	-	-	33.6	2.8	-	-	-	-	34.3	2.1	-	-	-	-	35.5	3.5	-	-	-	-	35.2	-0.8	-	-
1972	-	-	35.1	-0.3	-	-	-	-	35.4	0.9	-	-	-	-	35.9	1.4	-	-	-	-	36.2	0.8	-	-
1973	-	-	36.8	1.7	-	-	-	-	37.1	0.8	-	-	-	-	37.3	0.5	-	-	-	-	38.0	1.9	-	-
1974	-	-	39.5	3.9	-	-	-	-	40.0	1.3	-	-	-	-	41.2	3.0	-	-	-	-	41.7	1.2	-	-
1975	-	-	44.8	7.4	-	-	-	-	45.4	1.3	-	-	-	-	45.1	-0.7	-	-	-	-	46.1	2.2	-	-
1976	-	-	48.7	5.6	-	-	-	-	49.3	1.2	-	-	-	-	50.0	1.4	-	-	-	-	51.0	2.0	-	-
1977	-	-	54.1	6.1	-	-	-	-	55.4	2.4	-	-	-	-	56.4	1.8	-	-	-	-	57.3	1.6	-	-
1978	-	-	60.0	4.7	-	-	60.1	0.2	-	-	61.0	1.5	-	-	61.4	0.7	-	-	62.4	1.6	-	-	63.4	1.6
1979	-	-	65.0	2.5	-	-	65.2	0.3	-	-	65.9	1.1	-	-	67.1	1.8	-	-	67.8	1.0	-	-	69.5	2.5
1980	-	-	72.6	4.5	-	-	72.7	0.1	-	-	73.6	1.2	-	-	74.5	1.2	-	-	74.5	0.0	-	-	75.6	1.5
1981	-	-	80.6	6.6	-	-	80.8	0.2	-	-	80.9	0.1	-	-	81.8	1.1	-	-	82.7	1.1	-	-	83.9	1.5
1982	-	-	88.2	5.1	-	-	91.0	3.2	-	-	91.6	0.7	-	-	92.7	1.2	-	-	94.3	1.7	-	-	95.2	1.0
1983	-	-	100.0	5.0	-	-	101.3	1.3	-	-	101.5	0.2	-	-	101.7	0.2	-	-	101.6	-0.1	-	-	102.5	0.9
1984	-	-	106.4	3.8	-	-	107.1	0.7	-	-	107.9	0.7	-	-	107.5	-0.4	-	-	107.6	0.1	-	-	107.8	0.2
1985	-	-	110.0	2.0	-	-	110.6	0.5	-	-	111.0	0.4	-	-	111.6	0.5	-	-	112.0	0.4	-	-	115.3	2.9
1986	-	-	118.4	2.7	-	-	119.3	0.8	-	-	122.8	2.9	-	-	123.4	0.5	-	-	123.7	0.2	124.2	0.4	124.1	-0.1
1987	126.7	2.1	-	-	127.0	0.2	-	-	127.4	0.3	-	-	127.1	-0.2	-	-	128.8	1.3	-	-	129.0	0.2	-	-
1988	131.6	2.0	-	-	132.1	0.4	-	-	132.4	0.2	-	-	133.1	0.5	-	-	136.8	2.8	-	-	136.6	-0.1	-	-
1989	139.1	1.8	-	-	140.0	0.6	-	-	140.6	0.4	-	-	142.8	1.6	-	-	143.1	0.2	-	-	144.9	1.3	-	-
1990	148.3	2.3	-	-	149.6	0.9	-	-	151.0	0.9	-	-	156.8	3.8	-	-	157.5	0.4	-	-	160.8	2.1	-	-
1991	163.5	1.7	-	-	165.9	1.5	-	-	168.3	1.4	-	-	168.7	0.2	-	-	171.3	1.5	-	-	172.1	0.5	-	-

[Continued]

Cleveland, OH
Consumer Price Index - Urban Wage Earners
Base 1982-1984 = 100
Medical Care
[Continued]

For 1947-1995. Columns headed % show percentile change in the index from the previous period for which an index is available.

Year	Jan		Feb		Mar		Apr		May		Jun		Jul		Aug		Sep		Oct		Nov		Dec	
	Index	%	Index	%	Index	%	Index	%	Index	%	Index	%	Index	%	Index	%	Index	%	Index	%	Index	%	Index	%
1992	173.5	0.8	-	-	174.6	0.6	-	-	175.6	0.6	-	-	176.2	0.3	-	-	175.6	-0.3	-	-	176.1	0.3	-	-
1993	182.2	3.5	-	-	181.9	-0.2	-	-	182.7	0.4	-	-	185.0	1.3	-	-	185.0	0.0	-	-	185.7	0.4	-	-
1994	189.1	1.8	-	-	191.9	1.5	-	-	191.1	-0.4	-	-	191.3	0.1	-	-	194.4	1.6	-	-	194.1	-0.2	-	-
1995	197.5	1.8	-	-	198.8	0.7	-	-	198.5	-0.2	-	-	199.1	0.3	-	-	199.2	0.1	-	-	200.3	0.6	-	-

Source: U.S. Department of Labor, Bureau of Labor Statistics, Division of Consumer Prices and Price Indexes. - indicates no data collected for period.

Cleveland, OH
Consumer Price Index - All Urban Consumers
Base 1982-1984 = 100
Entertainment

For 1975-1995. Columns headed % show percentile change in the index from the previous period for which an index is available.

Year	Jan Index	%	Feb Index	%	Mar Index	%	Apr Index	%	May Index	%	Jun Index	%	Jul Index	%	Aug Index	%	Sep Index	%	Oct Index	%	Nov Index	%	Dec Index	%
1975	-	-	-	-	-	-	-	-	-	-	-	-	-	-	-	-	-	-	-	-	65.8	-	-	-
1976	-	-	65.9	0.2	-	-	-	-	66.6	1.1	-	-	-	-	67.6	1.5	-	-	-	-	68.9	1.9	-	-
1977	-	-	69.8	1.3	-	-	-	-	70.5	1.0	-	-	-	-	70.3	-0.3	-	-	-	-	71.8	2.1	-	-
1978	-	-	73.2	1.9	-	-	74.0	1.1	-	-	73.6	-0.5	-	-	74.3	1.0	-	-	76.7	3.2	-	-	78.2	2.0
1979	-	-	77.9	-0.4	-	-	78.5	0.8	-	-	76.4	-2.7	-	-	77.8	1.8	-	-	80.8	3.9	-	-	81.5	0.9
1980	-	-	81.9	0.5	-	-	82.5	0.7	-	-	82.2	-0.4	-	-	84.2	2.4	-	-	85.9	2.0	-	-	86.4	0.6
1981	-	-	86.8	0.5	-	-	87.9	1.3	-	-	88.2	0.3	-	-	87.4	-0.9	-	-	90.8	3.9	-	-	91.7	1.0
1982	-	-	95.2	3.8	-	-	94.7	-0.5	-	-	95.1	0.4	-	-	95.8	0.7	-	-	97.3	1.6	-	-	97.2	-0.1
1983	-	-	98.9	1.7	-	-	98.7	-0.2	-	-	98.9	0.2	-	-	99.4	0.5	-	-	103.8	4.4	-	-	103.7	-0.1
1984	-	-	104.0	0.3	-	-	104.4	0.4	-	-	103.8	-0.6	-	-	102.4	-1.3	-	-	104.3	1.9	-	-	105.8	1.4
1985	-	-	104.1	-1.6	-	-	105.8	1.6	-	-	105.0	-0.8	-	-	106.5	1.4	-	-	111.0	4.2	-	-	110.7	-0.3
1986	-	-	113.7	2.7	-	-	113.7	0.0	-	-	113.9	0.2	-	-	114.1	0.2	-	-	116.5	2.1	114.5	-1.7	115.1	0.5
1987	114.5	-0.5	-	-	115.3	0.7	-	-	116.4	1.0	-	-	116.2	-0.2	-	-	116.1	-0.1	-	-	116.0	-0.1	-	-
1988	116.5	0.4	-	-	119.5	2.6	-	-	121.8	1.9	-	-	122.8	0.8	-	-	118.8	-3.3	-	-	117.1	-1.4	-	-
1989	128.0	9.3	-	-	126.8	-0.9	-	-	120.3	-5.1	-	-	129.3	7.5	-	-	128.4	-0.7	-	-	128.6	0.2	-	-
1990	131.7	2.4	-	-	132.9	0.9	-	-	132.7	-0.2	-	-	134.9	1.7	-	-	135.2	0.2	-	-	133.4	-1.3	-	-
1991	135.7	1.7	-	-	136.6	0.7	-	-	139.2	1.9	-	-	136.5	-1.9	-	-	142.5	4.4	-	-	140.1	-1.7	-	-
1992	139.8	-0.2	-	-	142.1	1.6	-	-	137.0	-3.6	-	-	138.5	1.1	-	-	139.7	0.9	-	-	140.4	0.5	-	-
1993	141.1	0.5	-	-	140.9	-0.1	-	-	142.9	1.4	-	-	140.2	-1.9	-	-	140.1	-0.1	-	-	151.2	7.9	-	-
1994	152.1	0.6	-	-	151.3	-0.5	-	-	152.0	0.5	-	-	145.0	-4.6	-	-	144.3	-0.5	-	-	152.2	5.5	-	-
1995	151.4	-0.5	-	-	154.1	1.8	-	-	150.2	-2.5	-	-	150.5	0.2	-	-	155.2	3.1	-	-	156.0	0.5	-	-

Source: U.S. Department of Labor, Bureau of Labor Statistics, Division of Consumer Prices and Price Indexes. - indicates no data collected for period.

Cleveland, OH
Consumer Price Index - Urban Wage Earners
Base 1982-1984 = 100
Entertainment

For 1975-1995. Columns headed % show percentile change in the index from the previous period for which an index is available.

Year	Jan Index	%	Feb Index	%	Mar Index	%	Apr Index	%	May Index	%	Jun Index	%	Jul Index	%	Aug Index	%	Sep Index	%	Oct Index	%	Nov Index	%	Dec Index	%
1975	-		-		-		-		-		-		-		-		-		-		-		-	
1976	-		65.9	0.3	-		-		66.5	0.9	-		-		67.5	1.5	-		-		65.7		-	
1977	-		69.7	1.2	-		-		70.5	1.1	-		-		70.2	-0.4	-		-		68.9	2.1	-	
1978	-		73.2	1.9	-		73.9	1.0	-		73.0	-1.2	-		73.5	0.7	-		-		71.8	2.3	-	
1979	-		76.7	0.7	-		76.8	0.1	-		76.2	-0.8	-		78.0	2.4	-		74.9	1.9	-		76.2	1.7
1980	-		83.1	1.8	-		83.4	0.4	-		83.3	-0.1	-		84.3	1.2	-		80.9	3.7	-		81.6	0.9
1981	-		87.4	1.0	-		88.6	1.4	-		89.3	0.8	-		88.7	-0.7	-		86.0	2.0	-		86.5	0.6
1982	-		94.8	2.7	-		94.4	-0.4	-		94.8	0.4	-		95.5	0.7	-		90.8	2.4	-		92.3	1.7
1983	-		98.6	2.1	-		98.4	-0.2	-		98.6	0.2	-		99.4	0.8	-		96.9	1.5	-		96.6	-0.3
1984	-		104.2	0.4	-		104.9	0.7	-		104.4	-0.5	-		103.4	-1.0	-		103.7	4.3	-		103.8	0.1
1985	-		105.0	-1.0	-		106.4	1.3	-		105.2	-1.1	-		106.8	1.5	-		105.0	1.5	-		106.1	1.0
1986	-		114.4	2.9	-		114.4	0.0	-		114.6	0.2	-		114.7	0.1	-		111.4	4.3	-		111.2	-0.2
1987	114.6	-0.9	-		115.4	0.7	-		116.6	1.0	-		116.0	-0.5	-		116.4	0.3	117.3	2.3	115.1	-1.9	115.6	0.4
1988	117.0	0.3	-		120.1	2.6	-		122.6	2.1	-		123.5	0.7	-		119.7	-3.1	-		116.6	0.2	-	
1989	127.2	7.5	-		126.5	-0.6	-		120.0	-5.1	-		128.4	7.0	-		127.8	-0.5	-		118.3	-1.2	-	
1990	128.6	0.6	-		129.8	0.9	-		130.0	0.2	-		131.9	1.5	-		132.0	0.1	-		127.8	0.0	-	
1991	132.5	1.8	-		132.7	0.2	-		135.0	1.7	-		132.4	-1.9	-		138.1	4.3	-		130.1	-1.4	-	
1992	135.0	-0.5	-		138.2	2.4	-		133.7	-3.3	-		135.1	1.0	-		136.9	1.3	-		135.7	-1.7	-	
1993	137.9	0.4	-		136.7	-0.9	-		137.9	0.9	-		137.2	-0.5	-		137.3	0.1	-		137.3	0.3	-	
1994	147.2	-0.3	-		146.1	-0.7	-		147.2	0.8	-		140.5	-4.6	-		137.3	0.1	-		147.7	7.6	-	
1995	146.8	-1.0	-		149.8	2.0	-		145.3	-3.0	-		145.8	0.3	-		150.3	3.1	-		151.4	0.7	-	

Source: U.S. Department of Labor, Bureau of Labor Statistics, Division of Consumer Prices and Price Indexes. - indicates no data collected for period.

Cleveland, OH
Consumer Price Index - All Urban Consumers
Base 1982-1984 = 100
Other Goods and Services

For 1975-1995. Columns headed % show percentile change in the index from the previous period for which an index is available.

Year	Jan Index	%	Feb Index	%	Mar Index	%	Apr Index	%	May Index	%	Jun Index	%	Jul Index	%	Aug Index	%	Sep Index	%	Oct Index	%	Nov Index	%	Dec Index	%
	-		-		-		-		-		-		-		-		-		-		56.3	-	-	
1975	-		-		-		-		57.4	0.3	-		-		58.5	1.9	-		-		60.2	2.9	-	
1976	-		57.2	1.6	-		-		61.5	1.5	-		-		61.6	0.2	-		-		63.3	2.8	-	
1977	-		60.6	0.7	-		-		-		65.1	0.3	-		65.7	0.9	-		67.4	2.6	-		69.3	2.8
1978	-		64.3	1.6	-		64.9	0.9	-		69.9	0.3	-		70.8	1.3	-		73.9	4.4	-		73.6	-0.4
1979	-		69.7	0.6	-		69.7	0.0	-		75.5	0.1	-		76.1	0.8	-		79.4	4.3	-		80.9	1.9
1980	-		74.9	1.8	-		75.4	0.7	-		84.6	1.6	-		85.3	0.8	-		86.8	1.8	-		88.2	1.6
1981	-		82.7	2.2	-		83.3	0.7	-		90.6	-1.0	-		92.2	1.8	-		96.4	4.6	-		97.8	1.5
1982	-		90.3	2.4	-		91.5	1.3	-		99.6	0.5	-		100.7	1.1	-		102.9	2.2	-		103.5	0.6
1983	-		99.1	1.3	-		99.1	0.0	-		105.3	0.4	-		107.3	1.9	-		109.4	2.0	-		109.8	0.4
1984	-		104.8	1.3	-		104.9	0.1	-		110.1	0.2	-		112.2	1.9	-		114.4	2.0	-		114.3	-0.1
1985	-		109.4	-0.4	-		109.9	0.5	-		116.2	0.3	-		117.1	0.8	-		119.2	1.8	119.1	-0.1	119.5	0.3
1986	-		115.9	1.4	-		115.8	-0.1	-		-		-		-		-		-		-		-	
1987	120.9	1.2	-		120.7	-0.2	-		121.7	0.8	-		122.8	0.9	-		126.7	3.2	-		128.0	1.0	-	
1988	129.4	1.1	-		129.3	-0.1	-		131.5	1.7	-		134.4	2.2	-		135.2	0.6	-		136.7	1.1	-	
1989	137.3	0.4	-		137.4	0.1	-		139.4	1.5	-		140.2	0.6	-		144.9	3.4	-		144.9	0.0	-	
1990	145.7	0.6	-		147.4	1.2	-		148.9	1.0	-		148.6	-0.2	-		152.0	2.3	-		152.5	0.3	-	
1991	154.9	1.6	-		156.5	1.0	-		157.7	0.8	-		159.5	1.1	-		163.8	2.7	-		165.4	1.0	-	
1992	166.1	0.4	-		167.5	0.8	-		168.5	0.6	-		168.6	0.1	-		173.9	3.1	-		174.1	0.1	-	
1993	177.0	1.7	-		178.3	0.7	-		179.3	0.6	-		183.4	2.3	-		180.8	-1.4	-		181.3	0.3	-	
1994	183.3	1.1	-		183.7	0.2	-		179.4	-2.3	-		183.5	2.3	-		187.7	2.3	-		186.9	-0.4	-	
1995	187.9	0.5	-		188.0	0.1	-		188.2	0.1	-		189.0	0.4	-		191.6	1.4	-		192.9	0.7	-	

Source: U.S. Department of Labor, Bureau of Labor Statistics, Division of Consumer Prices and Price Indexes. - indicates no data collected for period.

Cleveland, OH
Consumer Price Index - Urban Wage Earners
Base 1982-1984 = 100
Other Goods and Services

For 1975-1995. Columns headed % show percentile change in the index from the previous period for which an index is available.

Year	Jan Index	%	Feb Index	%	Mar Index	%	Apr Index	%	May Index	%	Jun Index	%	Jul Index	%	Aug Index	%	Sep Index	%	Oct Index	%	Nov Index	%	Dec Index	%
1975	-	-	-	-	-	-	-	-	-	-	-	-	-	-	-	-	-	-	-	-	55.2	-	-	-
1976	-	-	56.1	1.6	-	-	-	-	56.3	0.4	-	-	-	-	57.4	2.0	-	-	-	-	59.1	3.0	-	-
1977	-	-	59.5	0.7	-	-	-	-	60.3	1.3	-	-	-	-	60.4	0.2	-	-	-	-	62.1	2.8	-	-
1978	-	-	63.1	1.6	-	-	63.2	0.2	-	-	63.9	1.1	-	-	64.8	1.4	-	-	66.6	2.8	-	-	67.6	1.5
1979	-	-	68.1	0.7	-	-	68.5	0.6	-	-	68.9	0.6	-	-	69.7	1.2	-	-	72.3	3.7	-	-	72.3	0.0
1980	-	-	74.0	2.4	-	-	74.9	1.2	-	-	75.4	0.7	-	-	76.1	0.9	-	-	78.6	3.3	-	-	79.5	1.1
1981	-	-	82.4	3.6	-	-	83.1	0.8	-	-	84.8	2.0	-	-	84.2	-0.7	-	-	85.7	1.8	-	-	87.9	2.6
1982	-	-	89.8	2.2	-	-	91.4	1.8	-	-	90.6	-0.9	-	-	91.9	1.4	-	-	95.9	4.4	-	-	97.7	1.9
1983	-	-	99.1	1.4	-	-	99.3	0.2	-	-	99.8	0.5	-	-	101.2	1.4	-	-	102.9	1.7	-	-	103.6	0.7
1984	-	-	105.3	1.6	-	-	105.5	0.2	-	-	106.0	0.5	-	-	107.4	1.3	-	-	108.9	1.4	-	-	109.3	0.4
1985	-	-	109.2	-0.1	-	-	109.7	0.5	-	-	109.9	0.2	-	-	112.0	1.9	-	-	113.9	1.7	-	-	113.8	-0.1
1986	-	-	115.6	1.6	-	-	115.5	-0.1	-	-	115.9	0.3	-	-	117.2	1.1	-	-	119.3	1.8	119.4	0.1	119.7	0.3
1987	121.3	1.3	-	-	121.2	-0.1	-	-	122.1	0.7	-	-	123.9	1.5	-	-	127.9	3.2	-	-	129.2	1.0	-	-
1988	130.8	1.2	-	-	130.6	-0.2	-	-	133.1	1.9	-	-	136.1	2.3	-	-	137.1	0.7	-	-	139.0	1.4	-	-
1989	139.7	0.5	-	-	139.7	0.0	-	-	141.9	1.6	-	-	143.0	0.8	-	-	147.2	2.9	-	-	147.3	0.1	-	-
1990	146.7	-0.4	-	-	148.5	1.2	-	-	150.4	1.3	-	-	149.4	-0.7	-	-	153.0	2.4	-	-	153.6	0.4	-	-
1991	156.5	1.9	-	-	158.4	1.2	-	-	159.5	0.7	-	-	161.6	1.3	-	-	166.2	2.8	-	-	168.2	1.2	-	-
1992	168.8	0.4	-	-	170.1	0.8	-	-	171.4	0.8	-	-	171.4	0.0	-	-	177.4	3.5	-	-	177.6	0.1	-	-
1993	181.3	2.1	-	-	181.6	0.2	-	-	182.8	0.7	-	-	187.6	2.6	-	-	184.3	-1.8	-	-	184.5	0.1	-	-
1994	186.5	1.1	-	-	186.9	0.2	-	-	180.2	-3.6	-	-	185.2	2.8	-	-	189.6	2.4	-	-	188.6	-0.5	-	-
1995	189.4	0.4	-	-	189.4	0.0	-	-	189.1	-0.2	-	-	189.9	0.4	-	-	192.7	1.5	-	-	194.3	0.8	-	-

Source: U.S. Department of Labor, Bureau of Labor Statistics, Division of Consumer Prices and Price Indexes. - indicates no data collected for period.

Dallas-Fort Worth, TX
Consumer Price Index - All Urban Consumers
Base 1982-1984 = 100
Annual Averages

For 1963-1995. Columns headed % show percentile change in the index from the previous period for which an index is available.

Year	All Items		Food & Beverage		Housing		Apparel & Upkeep		Trans- portation		Medical Care		Entertain- ment		Other Goods & Services	
	Index	%	Index	%	Index	%	Index	%	Index	%	Index	%	Index	%	Index	%
1963	-	-	-	-	-	-	-	-	-	-	-	-	-	-	-	-
1964	29.5	-	-	-	-	-	45.4	-	31.3	-	24.5	-	-	-	-	-
1965	29.9	1.4	-	-	-	-	45.2	-0.4	31.6	1.0	25.0	2.0	-	-	-	-
1966	31.0	3.7	-	-	-	-	46.7	3.3	32.3	2.2	26.4	5.6	-	-	-	-
1967	31.9	2.9	-	-	-	-	48.7	4.3	33.3	3.1	28.3	7.2	-	-	-	-
1968	33.3	4.4	-	-	-	-	51.4	5.5	34.4	3.3	30.0	6.0	-	-	-	-
1969	35.5	6.6	-	-	-	-	54.8	6.6	35.6	3.5	32.4	8.0	-	-	-	-
1970	37.6	5.9	-	-	-	-	57.4	4.7	36.9	3.7	34.8	7.4	-	-	-	-
1971	38.7	2.9	-	-	-	-	57.6	0.3	39.1	6.0	36.4	4.6	-	-	-	-
1972	39.8	2.8	-	-	-	-	59.2	2.8	39.9	2.0	37.2	2.2	-	-	-	-
1973	42.1	5.8	-	-	-	-	62.6	5.7	41.1	3.0	38.7	4.0	-	-	-	-
1974	46.3	10.0	-	-	-	-	66.6	6.4	47.4	15.3	41.8	8.0	-	-	-	-
1975	50.4	8.9	-	-	-	-	68.8	3.3	52.1	9.9	46.0	10.0	-	-	-	-
1976	53.5	6.2	59.0	-	48.1	-	70.9	3.1	56.7	8.8	50.1	8.9	67.2	-	55.9	-
1977	57.4	7.3	63.7	8.0	51.7	7.5	74.8	5.5	61.0	7.6	55.2	10.2	69.5	3.4	59.5	6.4
1978	61.8	7.7	69.5	9.1	56.8	9.9	78.9	5.5	62.8	3.0	59.6	8.0	69.9	0.6	63.4	6.6
1979	69.7	12.8	78.1	12.4	65.3	15.0	83.6	6.0	71.9	14.5	62.9	5.5	73.6	5.3	68.8	8.5
1980	81.5	16.9	85.4	9.3	79.3	21.4	88.9	6.3	86.3	20.0	69.9	11.1	82.4	12.0	76.1	10.6
1981	90.8	11.4	92.4	8.2	90.1	13.6	95.0	6.9	95.5	10.7	80.3	14.9	87.2	5.8	84.0	10.4
1982	96.0	5.7	96.1	4.0	96.4	7.0	97.2	2.3	97.4	2.0	91.9	14.4	93.1	6.8	91.9	9.4
1983	99.7	3.9	99.6	3.6	99.6	3.3	99.7	2.6	99.2	1.8	101.2	10.1	99.6	7.0	100.9	9.8
1984	104.3	4.6	104.3	4.7	104.0	4.4	103.1	3.4	103.4	4.2	107.0	5.7	107.2	7.6	107.3	6.3
1985	108.2	3.7	107.1	2.7	107.3	3.2	107.7	4.5	107.2	3.7	113.9	6.4	114.0	6.3	112.5	4.8
1986	109.9	1.6	111.2	3.8	109.9	2.4	107.6	-0.1	101.1	-5.7	126.7	11.2	115.8	1.6	119.5	6.2
1987	112.9	2.7	115.9	4.2	109.5	-0.4	114.5	6.4	103.5	2.4	134.2	5.9	122.0	5.4	128.8	7.8
1988	116.1	2.8	120.1	3.6	109.8	0.3	123.1	7.5	108.0	4.3	141.9	5.7	127.3	4.3	135.2	5.0
1989	119.5	2.9	125.4	4.4	111.6	1.6	124.5	1.1	110.8	2.6	150.9	6.3	132.7	4.2	146.1	8.1
1990	125.1	4.7	131.1	4.5	114.3	2.4	137.5	10.4	117.2	5.8	161.9	7.3	137.5	3.6	156.3	7.0
1991	130.8	4.6	136.3	4.0	118.6	3.8	151.7	10.3	120.7	3.0	174.8	8.0	142.4	3.6	163.7	4.7
1992	133.9	2.4	138.3	1.5	121.8	2.7	151.3	-0.3	123.4	2.2	188.3	7.7	142.0	-0.3	170.5	4.2
1993	137.3	2.5	139.0	0.5	125.3	2.9	147.8	-2.3	128.9	4.5	196.8	4.5	144.0	1.4	180.5	5.9
1994	141.2	2.8	142.2	2.3	129.0	3.0	148.2	0.3	134.5	4.3	205.6	4.5	147.1	2.2	181.0	0.3
1995	144.9	2.6	145.6	2.4	132.1	2.4	147.8	-0.3	139.4	3.6	216.9	5.5	150.3	2.2	185.7	2.6

Source: U.S. Department of Labor, Bureau of Labor Statistics, Division of Consumer Prices and Price Indexes. - indicates no data collected for period.

Dallas-Fort Worth, TX
Consumer Price Index - Urban Wage Earners
Base 1982-1984 = 100
Annual Averages

For 1963-1995. Columns headed % show percentile change in the index from the previous period for which an index is available.

Year	All Items		Food & Beverage		Housing		Apparel & Upkeep		Trans-portation		Medical Care		Entertain-ment		Other Goods & Services	
	Index	%	Index	%	Index	%	Index	%	Index	%	Index	%	Index	%	Index	%
1963	-	-	-	-	-	-	-	-	-	-	-	-	-	-	-	-
1964	30.0	-	-	-	-	-	47.9	-	31.3	-	24.9	-	-	-	-	-
1965	30.4	1.3	-	-	-	-	47.7	-0.4	31.6	1.0	25.4	2.0	-	-	-	-
1966	31.5	3.6	-	-	-	-	49.3	3.4	32.3	2.2	26.8	5.5	-	-	-	-
1967	32.4	2.9	-	-	-	-	51.4	4.3	33.3	3.1	28.7	7.1	-	-	-	-
1968	33.9	4.6	-	-	-	-	54.3	5.6	34.5	3.6	30.5	6.3	-	-	-	-
1969	36.1	6.5	-	-	-	-	57.9	6.6	35.6	3.2	32.9	7.9	-	-	-	-
1970	38.2	5.8	-	-	-	-	60.6	4.7	37.0	3.9	35.4	7.6	-	-	-	-
1971	39.3	2.9	-	-	-	-	60.9	0.5	39.1	5.7	37.0	4.5	-	-	-	-
1972	40.5	3.1	-	-	-	-	62.5	2.6	39.9	2.0	37.8	2.2	-	-	-	-
1973	42.8	5.7	-	-	-	-	66.1	5.8	41.1	3.0	39.3	4.0	-	-	-	-
1974	47.1	10.0	-	-	-	-	70.4	6.5	47.4	15.3	42.4	7.9	-	-	-	-
1975	51.3	8.9	-	-	-	-	72.7	3.3	52.1	9.9	46.8	10.4	-	-	-	-
1976	54.4	6.0	58.5	-	48.7	-	74.8	2.9	56.7	8.8	50.9	8.8	71.8	-	58.6	-
1977	58.4	7.4	63.2	8.0	52.4	7.6	78.9	5.5	61.0	7.6	56.1	10.2	74.3	3.5	62.4	6.5
1978	62.9	7.7	69.2	9.5	57.6	9.9	82.5	4.6	63.0	3.3	60.6	8.0	74.5	0.3	66.5	6.6
1979	70.9	12.7	77.9	12.6	66.1	14.8	87.3	5.8	72.3	14.8	65.2	7.6	76.7	3.0	71.7	7.8
1980	82.4	16.2	84.9	9.0	79.8	20.7	94.6	8.4	86.7	19.9	72.1	10.6	82.4	7.4	79.4	10.7
1981	91.5	11.0	92.2	8.6	90.5	13.4	98.9	4.5	96.4	11.2	81.2	12.6	87.6	6.3	84.4	6.3
1982	96.4	5.4	96.2	4.3	97.0	7.2	97.5	-1.4	97.6	1.2	91.7	12.9	93.6	6.8	91.6	8.5
1983	99.4	3.1	99.6	3.5	99.0	2.1	99.4	1.9	99.3	1.7	101.2	10.4	99.6	6.4	101.3	10.6
1984	104.2	4.8	104.2	4.6	104.0	5.1	103.0	3.6	103.2	3.9	107.1	5.8	106.8	7.2	107.1	5.7
1985	108.1	3.7	106.9	2.6	107.8	3.7	109.2	6.0	106.9	3.6	114.3	6.7	112.8	5.6	111.8	4.4
1986	109.4	1.2	110.8	3.6	110.3	2.3	109.3	0.1	100.5	-6.0	127.5	11.5	114.5	1.5	118.7	6.2
1987	112.6	2.9	115.6	4.3	109.8	-0.5	115.1	5.3	104.2	3.7	135.5	6.3	120.6	5.3	126.3	6.4
1988	115.8	2.8	119.7	3.5	110.1	0.3	123.1	7.0	108.5	4.1	143.5	5.9	126.0	4.5	132.6	5.0
1989	119.3	3.0	124.9	4.3	111.8	1.5	122.8	-0.2	111.8	3.0	153.2	6.8	131.6	4.4	143.3	8.1
1990	124.5	4.4	130.6	4.6	114.3	2.2	130.9	6.6	118.1	5.6	164.5	7.4	135.6	3.0	153.7	7.3
1991	129.6	4.1	135.7	3.9	118.7	3.8	138.7	6.0	121.6	3.0	177.7	8.0	140.7	3.8	161.8	5.3
1992	133.1	2.7	137.5	1.3	121.4	2.3	141.5	2.0	126.2	3.8	192.1	8.1	140.1	-0.4	168.7	4.3
1993	137.0	2.9	138.2	0.5	124.6	2.6	143.0	1.1	132.8	5.2	200.8	4.5	141.7	1.1	178.2	5.6
1994	140.5	2.6	141.0	2.0	128.3	3.0	140.3	-1.9	138.1	4.0	209.2	4.2	144.9	2.3	177.7	-0.3
1995	144.6	2.9	144.2	2.3	131.5	2.5	141.7	1.0	144.1	4.3	221.5	5.9	147.3	1.7	182.1	2.5

Source: U.S. Department of Labor, Bureau of Labor Statistics, Division of Consumer Prices and Price Indexes. - indicates no data collected for period.

Dallas-Fort Worth, TX
Consumer Price Index - All Urban Consumers
Base 1982-1984 = 100
All Items

For 1963-1995. Columns headed % show percentile change in the index from the previous period for which an index is available.

Year	Jan Index	%	Feb Index	%	Mar Index	%	Apr Index	%	May Index	%	Jun Index	%	Jul Index	%	Aug Index	%	Sep Index	%	Oct Index	%	Nov Index	%	Dec Index	%
1963	-		-		-		-		-		-		-		-		-		-	-	29.5	-	-	-
1964	-		29.4	-0.3	-		-	-	29.6	0.7	-		-		29.5	-0.3	-		-	-	29.7	0.7	-	-
1965	-		29.5	-0.7	-		-	-	29.8	1.0	-		-		30.0	0.7	-		-	-	30.3	1.0	-	-
1966	-		30.5	0.7	-		-	-	30.9	1.3	-		-		31.1	0.6	-		-	-	31.4	1.0	-	-
1967	-		31.6	0.6	-		-	-	31.7	0.3	-		-		32.1	1.3	-		-	-	32.2	0.3	-	-
1968	-		32.5	0.9	-		-	-	33.2	2.2	-		-		33.5	0.9	-		-	-	34.0	1.5	-	-
1969	-		34.4	1.2	-		-	-	35.2	2.3	-		-		35.7	1.4	-		-	-	36.5	2.2	-	-
1970	-		37.0	1.4	-		-	-	37.5	1.4	-		-		37.8	0.8	-		-	-	37.9	0.3	-	-
1971	-		38.2	0.8	-		-	-	38.4	0.5	-		-		39.1	1.8	-		-	-	39.0	-0.3	-	-
1972	-		39.4	1.0	-		-	-	39.7	0.8	-		-		40.0	0.8	-		-	-	40.1	0.2	-	-
1973	-		40.7	1.5	-		-	-	41.6	2.2	-		-		42.6	2.4	-		-	-	43.2	1.4	-	-
1974	-		44.5	3.0	-		-	-	45.6	2.5	-		-		47.0	3.1	-		-	-	48.2	2.6	-	-
1975	-		49.1	1.9	-		-	-	49.7	1.2	-		-		51.2	3.0	-		-	-	51.8	1.2	-	-
1976	-		52.2	0.8	-		-	-	53.0	1.5	-		-		53.9	1.7	-		-	-	54.7	1.5	-	-
1977	-		55.9	2.2	-		-	-	57.2	2.3	-		-		58.1	1.6	-		-	-	58.6	0.9	-	-
1978	-		59.5	1.5	-		60.3	1.3	-		61.7	2.3	-		62.9	1.9	-		63.7	1.3	-		64.3	0.9
1979	-		65.6	2.0	-		67.3	2.6	-		69.3	3.0	-		71.1	2.6	-		72.7	2.3	-		74.6	2.6
1980	-		77.0	3.2	-		80.1	4.0	-		81.7	2.0	-		82.4	0.9	-		84.4	2.4	-		85.9	1.8
1981	-		87.5	1.9	-		89.1	1.8	-		91.2	2.4	-		91.9	0.8	-		93.2	1.4	-		94.1	1.0
1982	-		93.6	-0.5	-		94.7	1.2	-		97.2	2.6	-		97.0	-0.2	-		97.8	0.8	-		96.7	-1.1
1983	-		97.1	0.4	-		98.4	1.3	-		100.1	1.7	-		100.7	0.6	-		101.5	0.8	-		101.2	-0.3
1984	-		102.9	1.7	-		103.3	0.4	-		103.8	0.5	-		105.1	1.3	-		106.4	1.2	-		105.4	-0.9
1985	-		106.2	0.8	-		107.0	0.8	-		108.3	1.2	-		109.5	1.1	-		109.6	0.1	-		109.8	0.2
1986	-		110.6	0.7	-		108.8	-1.6	-		109.9	1.0	-		110.4	0.5	-		110.3	-0.1	-		109.3	-0.9
1987	-		110.9	1.5	-		112.2	1.2	-		112.9	0.6	-		113.5	0.5	-		114.9	1.2	-		113.9	-0.9
1988	-		114.0	0.1	-		115.4	1.2	-		115.6	0.2	-		117.2	1.4	-		117.9	0.6	-		117.2	-0.6
1989	-		117.5	0.3	-		118.7	1.0	-		120.0	1.1	-		120.0	0.0	-		121.4	1.2	-		120.5	-0.7
1990	-		122.2	1.4	-		122.9	0.6	-		123.8	0.7	-		126.0	1.8	-		129.5	2.8	-		128.4	-0.8
1991	-		129.4	0.8	-		129.5	0.1	-		130.1	0.5	-		131.1	0.8	-		133.6	1.9	-		132.0	-1.2
1992	-		132.4	0.3	-		132.5	0.1	-		134.2	1.3	-		134.4	0.1	-		136.1	1.3	-		134.6	-1.1
1993	-		135.4	0.6	-		137.0	1.2	-		136.2	-0.6	-		138.1	1.4	-		139.6	1.1	-		138.8	-0.6
1994	-		139.2	0.3	-		140.3	0.8	-		141.4	0.8	-		142.2	0.6	-		142.8	0.4	-		141.9	-0.6
1995	-		143.3	1.0	-		145.0	1.2	-		144.4	-0.4	-		145.1	0.5	-		146.8	1.2	-		145.5	-0.9

Source: U.S. Department of Labor, Bureau of Labor Statistics, Division of Consumer Prices and Price Indexes. - indicates no data collected for period.

Dallas-Fort Worth, TX
Consumer Price Index - Urban Wage Earners
Base 1982-1984 = 100
All Items

For 1963-1995. Columns headed % show percentile change in the index from the previous period for which an index is available.

Year	Jan		Feb		Mar		Apr		May		Jun		Jul		Aug		Sep		Oct		Nov		Dec	
	Index	%	Index	%	Index	%	Index	%	Index	%	Index	%	Index	%	Index	%	Index	%	Index	%	Index	%	Index	%
1963	-	-	-	-	-	-	-	-	-	-	-	-	-	-	-	-	-	-	-	-	30.0	-	-	-
1964	-	-	29.9	-0.3	-	-	-	-	30.1	0.7	-	-	-	-	30.0	-0.3	-	-	-	-	30.2	0.7	-	-
1965	-	-	30.0	-0.7	-	-	-	-	30.3	1.0	-	-	-	-	30.5	0.7	-	-	-	-	30.8	1.0	-	-
1966	-	-	31.0	0.6	-	-	-	-	31.4	1.3	-	-	-	-	31.7	1.0	-	-	-	-	31.9	0.6	-	-
1967	-	-	32.1	0.6	-	-	-	-	32.2	0.3	-	-	-	-	32.7	1.6	-	-	-	-	32.7	0.0	-	-
1968	-	-	33.1	1.2	-	-	-	-	33.8	2.1	-	-	-	-	34.1	0.9	-	-	-	-	34.6	1.5	-	-
1969	-	-	35.0	1.2	-	-	-	-	35.8	2.3	-	-	-	-	36.4	1.7	-	-	-	-	37.1	1.9	-	-
1970	-	-	37.7	1.6	-	-	-	-	38.1	1.1	-	-	-	-	38.5	1.0	-	-	-	-	38.6	0.3	-	-
1971	-	-	38.8	0.5	-	-	-	-	39.0	0.5	-	-	-	-	39.8	2.1	-	-	-	-	39.7	-0.3	-	-
1972	-	-	40.1	1.0	-	-	-	-	40.4	0.7	-	-	-	-	40.7	0.7	-	-	-	-	40.8	0.2	-	-
1973	-	-	41.4	1.5	-	-	-	-	42.4	2.4	-	-	-	-	43.4	2.4	-	-	-	-	44.0	1.4	-	-
1974	-	-	45.3	3.0	-	-	-	-	46.4	2.4	-	-	-	-	47.8	3.0	-	-	-	-	49.1	2.7	-	-
1975	-	-	49.9	1.6	-	-	-	-	50.5	1.2	-	-	-	-	52.1	3.2	-	-	-	-	52.7	1.2	-	-
1976	-	-	53.1	0.8	-	-	-	-	53.9	1.5	-	-	-	-	54.8	1.7	-	-	-	-	55.7	1.6	-	-
1977	-	-	56.8	2.0	-	-	-	-	58.2	2.5	-	-	-	-	59.2	1.7	-	-	-	-	59.6	0.7	-	-
1978	-	-	60.5	1.5	-	-	61.5	1.7	-	-	62.7	2.0	-	-	64.0	2.1	-	-	64.9	1.4	-	-	65.2	0.5
1979	-	-	66.9	2.6	-	-	68.6	2.5	-	-	70.7	3.1	-	-	72.3	2.3	-	-	73.9	2.2	-	-	75.7	2.4
1980	-	-	78.1	3.2	-	-	80.9	3.6	-	-	82.5	2.0	-	-	83.5	1.2	-	-	85.3	2.2	-	-	87.0	2.0
1981	-	-	88.5	1.7	-	-	89.8	1.5	-	-	92.1	2.6	-	-	92.5	0.4	-	-	93.7	1.3	-	-	94.4	0.7
1982	-	-	94.0	-0.4	-	-	94.9	1.0	-	-	97.4	2.6	-	-	97.4	0.0	-	-	98.1	0.7	-	-	97.1	-1.0
1983	-	-	96.7	-0.4	-	-	97.8	1.1	-	-	99.3	1.5	-	-	100.2	0.9	-	-	102.1	1.9	-	-	101.7	-0.4
1984	-	-	103.0	1.3	-	-	102.6	-0.4	-	-	103.4	0.8	-	-	105.3	1.8	-	-	106.4	1.0	-	-	105.4	-0.9
1985	-	-	106.0	0.6	-	-	106.9	0.8	-	-	108.2	1.2	-	-	109.3	1.0	-	-	109.4	0.1	-	-	109.7	0.3
1986	-	-	110.4	0.6	-	-	108.3	-1.9	-	-	109.4	1.0	-	-	110.0	0.5	-	-	109.8	-0.2	-	-	108.6	-1.1
1987	-	-	110.6	1.8	-	-	111.7	1.0	-	-	112.6	0.8	-	-	113.3	0.6	-	-	114.7	1.2	-	-	113.8	-0.8
1988	-	-	113.8	0.0	-	-	114.8	0.9	-	-	115.4	0.5	-	-	117.0	1.4	-	-	117.7	0.6	-	-	117.0	-0.6
1989	-	-	117.2	0.2	-	-	118.6	1.2	-	-	120.0	1.2	-	-	119.8	-0.2	-	-	121.1	1.1	-	-	120.1	-0.8
1990	-	-	121.3	1.0	-	-	122.2	0.7	-	-	123.2	0.8	-	-	125.4	1.8	-	-	128.8	2.7	-	-	127.8	-0.8
1991	-	-	128.1	0.2	-	-	128.2	0.1	-	-	129.4	0.9	-	-	129.9	0.4	-	-	131.8	1.5	-	-	130.9	-0.7
1992	-	-	131.2	0.2	-	-	131.5	0.2	-	-	133.5	1.5	-	-	134.0	0.4	-	-	135.4	1.0	-	-	134.1	-1.0
1993	-	-	134.8	0.5	-	-	136.3	1.1	-	-	136.5	0.1	-	-	138.0	1.1	-	-	139.1	0.8	-	-	138.6	-0.4
1994	-	-	138.1	-0.4	-	-	139.3	0.9	-	-	140.6	0.9	-	-	141.6	0.7	-	-	142.4	0.6	-	-	141.7	-0.5
1995	-	-	142.7	0.7	-	-	144.5	1.3	-	-	144.4	-0.1	-	-	144.8	0.3	-	-	146.5	1.2	-	-	145.4	-0.8

Source: U.S. Department of Labor, Bureau of Labor Statistics, Division of Consumer Prices and Price Indexes. - indicates no data collected for period.

Dallas-Fort Worth, TX

Consumer Price Index - All Urban Consumers
Base 1982-1984 = 100

Food and Beverages

For 1975-1995. Columns headed % show percentile change in the index from the previous period for which an index is available.

Year	Jan Index	Jan %	Feb Index	Feb %	Mar Index	Mar %	Apr Index	Apr %	May Index	May %	Jun Index	Jun %	Jul Index	Jul %	Aug Index	Aug %	Sep Index	Sep %	Oct Index	Oct %	Nov Index	Nov %	Dec Index	Dec %
1975	-	-	-	-	-	-	-	-	-	-	-	-	-	-	-	-	-	-	-	-	58.8	-	-	-
1976	-	-	58.7	-0.2	-	-	-	-	58.6	-0.2	-	-	-	-	59.3	1.2	-	-	-	-	59.2	-0.2	-	-
1977	-	-	62.3	5.2	-	-	-	-	63.4	1.8	-	-	-	-	64.5	1.7	-	-	-	-	64.9	0.6	-	-
1978	-	-	66.5	2.5	-	-	67.5	1.5	-	-	69.6	3.1	-	-	70.4	1.1	-	-	71.6	1.7	-	-	73.8	3.1
1979	-	-	75.8	2.7	-	-	77.2	1.8	-	-	78.3	1.4	-	-	78.2	-0.1	-	-	79.6	1.8	-	-	81.4	2.3
1980	-	-	81.9	0.6	-	-	82.9	1.2	-	-	84.5	1.9	-	-	86.3	2.1	-	-	88.8	2.9	-	-	90.0	1.4
1981	-	-	91.0	1.1	-	-	92.3	1.4	-	-	92.3	0.0	-	-	92.9	0.7	-	-	93.3	0.4	-	-	93.2	-0.1
1982	-	-	94.6	1.5	-	-	95.3	0.7	-	-	96.4	1.2	-	-	96.7	0.3	-	-	96.9	0.2	-	-	97.7	0.8
1983	-	-	98.3	0.6	-	-	99.3	1.0	-	-	99.4	0.1	-	-	99.7	0.3	-	-	100.9	1.2	-	-	100.9	0.0
1984	-	-	103.5	2.6	-	-	104.2	0.7	-	-	104.1	-0.1	-	-	105.0	0.9	-	-	104.7	-0.3	-	-	105.4	0.7
1985	-	-	106.3	0.9	-	-	107.0	0.7	-	-	107.5	0.5	-	-	106.9	-0.6	-	-	107.0	0.1	-	-	109.0	1.9
1986	-	-	110.0	0.9	-	-	110.1	0.1	-	-	110.6	0.5	-	-	111.9	1.2	-	-	112.6	0.6	-	-	112.8	0.2
1987	-	-	115.6	2.5	-	-	114.5	-1.0	-	-	116.2	1.5	-	-	116.1	-0.1	-	-	117.3	1.0	-	-	116.9	-0.3
1988	-	-	117.5	0.5	-	-	118.3	0.7	-	-	119.9	1.4	-	-	120.8	0.8	-	-	122.4	1.3	-	-	123.1	0.6
1989	-	-	124.4	1.1	-	-	124.8	0.3	-	-	124.9	0.1	-	-	125.3	0.3	-	-	126.6	1.0	-	-	127.9	1.0
1990	-	-	129.6	1.3	-	-	130.7	0.8	-	-	130.5	-0.2	-	-	131.5	0.8	-	-	132.0	0.4	-	-	134.1	1.6
1991	-	-	134.7	0.4	-	-	135.5	0.6	-	-	138.2	2.0	-	-	136.6	-1.2	-	-	135.6	-0.7	-	-	138.0	1.8
1992	-	-	139.6	1.2	-	-	138.6	-0.7	-	-	137.2	-1.0	-	-	138.1	0.7	-	-	138.6	0.4	-	-	137.9	-0.5
1993	-	-	138.1	0.1	-	-	139.3	0.9	-	-	139.1	-0.1	-	-	138.3	-0.6	-	-	137.6	-0.5	-	-	142.5	3.6
1994	-	-	140.2	-1.6	-	-	141.4	0.9	-	-	142.3	0.6	-	-	143.3	0.7	-	-	142.8	-0.3	-	-	143.9	0.8
1995	-	-	144.1	0.1	-	-	145.7	1.1	-	-	144.1	-1.1	-	-	145.5	1.0	-	-	146.8	0.9	-	-	148.2	1.0

Source: U.S. Department of Labor, Bureau of Labor Statistics, Division of Consumer Prices and Price Indexes. - indicates no data collected for period.

Dallas-Fort Worth, TX
Consumer Price Index - Urban Wage Earners
Base 1982-1984 = 100
Food and Beverages

For 1975-1995. Columns headed % show percentile change in the index from the previous period for which an index is available.

Year	Jan Index	%	Feb Index	%	Mar Index	%	Apr Index	%	May Index	%	Jun Index	%	Jul Index	%	Aug Index	%	Sep Index	%	Oct Index	%	Nov Index	%	Dec Index	%
1975	-	-	-	-	-	-	-	-	-	-	-	-	-	-	-	-	-	-	-	-	58.3	-	-	-
1976	-	-	58.2	-0.2	-	-	-	-	58.1	-0.2	-	-	-	-	58.8	1.2	-	-	-	-	58.7	-0.2	-	-
1977	-	-	61.8	5.3	-	-	-	-	62.9	1.8	-	-	-	-	64.0	1.7	-	-	-	-	64.4	0.6	-	-
1978	-	-	65.9	2.3	-	-	67.8	2.9	-	-	69.0	1.8	-	-	70.0	1.4	-	-	71.9	2.7	-	-	72.5	0.8
1979	-	-	75.9	4.7	-	-	77.2	1.7	-	-	78.3	1.4	-	-	77.9	-0.5	-	-	79.4	1.9	-	-	80.7	1.6
1980	-	-	81.4	0.9	-	-	82.5	1.4	-	-	83.6	1.3	-	-	86.2	3.1	-	-	88.5	2.7	-	-	89.8	1.5
1981	-	-	90.3	0.6	-	-	91.1	0.9	-	-	92.1	1.1	-	-	93.7	1.7	-	-	93.6	-0.1	-	-	93.3	-0.3
1982	-	-	94.7	1.5	-	-	95.3	0.6	-	-	96.5	1.3	-	-	96.8	0.3	-	-	97.0	0.2	-	-	97.9	0.9
1983	-	-	98.3	0.4	-	-	99.2	0.9	-	-	99.5	0.3	-	-	99.7	0.2	-	-	100.9	1.2	-	-	100.8	-0.1
1984	-	-	103.5	2.7	-	-	104.2	0.7	-	-	104.0	-0.2	-	-	104.8	0.8	-	-	104.5	-0.3	-	-	105.3	0.8
1985	-	-	106.1	0.8	-	-	106.8	0.7	-	-	107.2	0.4	-	-	106.6	-0.6	-	-	106.5	-0.1	-	-	108.8	2.2
1986	-	-	109.6	0.7	-	-	109.6	0.0	-	-	110.2	0.5	-	-	111.7	1.4	-	-	112.3	0.5	-	-	112.4	0.1
1987	-	-	115.2	2.5	-	-	114.2	-0.9	-	-	115.8	1.4	-	-	115.8	0.0	-	-	116.9	0.9	-	-	116.6	-0.3
1988	-	-	117.1	0.4	-	-	117.9	0.7	-	-	119.5	1.4	-	-	120.4	0.8	-	-	122.0	1.3	-	-	122.7	0.6
1989	-	-	123.9	1.0	-	-	124.2	0.2	-	-	124.4	0.2	-	-	124.7	0.2	-	-	126.0	1.0	-	-	127.5	1.2
1990	-	-	129.1	1.3	-	-	130.0	0.7	-	-	129.8	-0.2	-	-	131.0	0.9	-	-	131.5	0.4	-	-	133.7	1.7
1991	-	-	134.2	0.4	-	-	135.1	0.7	-	-	137.7	1.9	-	-	136.0	-1.2	-	-	135.0	-0.7	-	-	137.1	1.6
1992	-	-	138.9	1.3	-	-	137.8	-0.8	-	-	136.3	-1.1	-	-	137.1	0.6	-	-	137.8	0.5	-	-	137.1	-0.5
1993	-	-	137.5	0.3	-	-	138.6	0.8	-	-	138.4	-0.1	-	-	137.6	-0.6	-	-	137.0	-0.4	-	-	141.4	3.2
1994	-	-	139.0	-1.7	-	-	140.4	1.0	-	-	141.0	0.4	-	-	141.8	0.6	-	-	141.4	-0.3	-	-	142.6	0.8
1995	-	-	142.6	0.0	-	-	144.5	1.3	-	-	142.7	-1.2	-	-	144.0	0.9	-	-	145.4	1.0	-	-	146.9	1.0

Source: U.S. Department of Labor, Bureau of Labor Statistics, Division of Consumer Prices and Price Indexes. - indicates no data collected for period.

Dallas-Fort Worth, TX
Consumer Price Index - All Urban Consumers
Base 1982-1984 = 100
Housing

For 1975-1995. Columns headed % show percentile change in the index from the previous period for which an index is available.

Year	Jan		Feb		Mar		Apr		May		Jun		Jul		Aug		Sep		Oct		Nov		Dec	
	Index	%	Index	%	Index	%	Index	%	Index	%	Index	%	Index	%	Index	%	Index	%	Index	%	Index	%	Index	%
1975	-		-		-		-		-		-		-		-		-		-		46.0	-	-	-
1976	-		47.0	2.2	-		-		47.7	1.5	-		-		48.4	1.5	-		-		49.4	2.1	-	-
1977	-		50.0	1.2	-		-		51.4	2.8	-		-		52.4	1.9	-		-		53.0	1.1	-	-
1978	-		54.3	2.5	-		55.3	1.8	-		56.7	2.5	-		58.2	2.6	-		59.0	1.4	-		58.9	-0.2
1979	-		60.4	2.5	-		62.0	2.6	-		64.8	4.5	-		66.9	3.2	-		69.3	3.6	-		71.3	2.9
1980	-		73.6	3.2	-		77.7	5.6	-		80.2	3.2	-		80.1	-0.1	-		82.7	3.2	-		85.0	2.8
1981	-		86.1	1.3	-		87.6	1.7	-		90.8	3.7	-		91.0	0.2	-		92.9	2.1	-		94.5	1.7
1982	-		92.5	-2.1	-		95.9	3.7	-		98.5	2.7	-		97.4	-1.1	-		98.4	1.0	-		95.8	-2.6
1983	-		96.7	0.9	-		97.9	1.2	-		101.3	3.5	-		101.0	-0.3	-		101.3	0.3	-		100.7	-0.6
1984	-		103.0	2.3	-		102.8	-0.2	-		104.0	1.2	-		105.3	1.3	-		106.3	0.9	-		103.4	-2.7
1985	-		105.0	1.5	-		105.6	0.6	-		107.9	2.2	-		110.0	1.9	-		109.1	-0.8	-		107.7	-1.3
1986	-		109.7	1.9	-		109.8	0.1	-		111.3	1.4	-		111.6	0.3	-		110.0	-1.4	-		107.1	-2.6
1987	-		108.0	0.8	-		109.1	1.0	-		109.7	0.5	-		110.5	0.7	-		111.4	0.8	-		108.9	-2.2
1988	-		107.9	-0.9	-		109.2	1.2	-		109.4	0.2	-		111.9	2.3	-		111.2	-0.6	-		109.2	-1.8
1989	-		110.3	1.0	-		109.7	-0.5	-		112.4	2.5	-		112.9	0.4	-		113.7	0.7	-		111.2	-2.2
1990	-		111.6	0.4	-		112.2	0.5	-		114.0	1.6	-		116.1	1.8	-		118.3	1.9	-		114.8	-3.0
1991	-		116.8	1.7	-		117.1	0.3	-		117.8	0.6	-		119.1	1.1	-		121.9	2.4	-		120.3	-1.3
1992	-		118.4	-1.6	-		119.0	0.5	-		123.9	4.1	-		124.9	0.8	-		123.2	-1.4	-		121.7	-1.2
1993	-		123.9	1.8	-		123.7	-0.2	-		123.6	-0.1	-		127.6	3.2	-		128.1	0.4	-		126.1	-1.6
1994	-		126.6	0.4	-		128.5	1.5	-		129.5	0.8	-		130.1	0.5	-		131.0	0.7	-		128.9	-1.6
1995	-		131.6	2.1	-		131.5	-0.1	-		131.5	0.0	-		132.6	0.8	-		133.8	0.9	-		132.3	-1.1

Source: U.S. Department of Labor, Bureau of Labor Statistics, Division of Consumer Prices and Price Indexes. - indicates no data collected for period.

Dallas-Fort Worth, TX
Consumer Price Index - Urban Wage Earners
Base 1982-1984 = 100
Housing

For 1975-1995. Columns headed % show percentile change in the index from the previous period for which an index is available.

Year	Jan Index	%	Feb Index	%	Mar Index	%	Apr Index	%	May Index	%	Jun Index	%	Jul Index	%	Aug Index	%	Sep Index	%	Oct Index	%	Nov Index	%	Dec Index	%
1975	-	-	-	-	-	-	-	-	-	-	-	-	-	-	-	-	-	-	-	-	46.6	-	-	-
1976	-	-	47.6	2.1	-	-	-	-	48.3	1.5	-	-	-	-	49.1	1.7	-	-	-	-	50.0	1.8	-	-
1977	-	-	50.6	1.2	-	-	-	-	52.1	3.0	-	-	-	-	53.0	1.7	-	-	-	-	53.7	1.3	-	-
1978	-	-	55.0	2.4	-	-	56.1	2.0	-	-	57.5	2.5	-	-	59.0	2.6	-	-	59.8	1.4	-	-	59.6	-0.3
1979	-	-	61.2	27	-	-	62.8	2.6	-	-	65.6	4.5	-	-	67.7	3.2	-	-	70.1	3.5	-	-	72.0	2.7
1980	-	-	74.1	2.9	-	-	78.3	5.7	-	-	80.8	3.2	-	-	80.6	-0.2	-	-	82.9	2.9	-	-	85.5	3.1
1981	-	-	86.6	1.3	-	-	87.9	1.5	-	-	91.2	3.8	-	-	91.3	0.1	-	-	93.2	2.1	-	-	95.1	2.0
1982	-	-	93.1	-2.1	-	-	96.4	3.5	-	-	99.2	2.9	-	-	98.1	-1.1	-	-	99.2	1.1	-	-	96.5	-2.7
1983	-	-	95.8	-0.7	-	-	96.6	0.8	-	-	99.1	2.6	-	-	99.8	0.7	-	-	102.4	2.6	-	-	101.8	-0.6
1984	-	-	103.3	1.5	-	-	101.5	-1.7	-	-	102.9	1.4	-	-	105.8	2.8	-	-	106.9	1.0	-	-	104.0	-2.7
1985	-	-	105.4	1.3	-	-	105.9	0.5	-	-	108.4	2.4	-	-	110.5	1.9	-	-	109.7	-0.7	-	-	108.1	-1.5
1986	-	-	110.1	1.9	-	-	110.0	-0.1	-	-	111.8	1.6	-	-	112.1	0.3	-	-	110.3	-1.6	-	-	107.1	-2.9
1987	-	-	108.2	1.0	-	-	109.1	0.8	-	-	110.3	1.1	-	-	111.1	0.7	-	-	111.9	0.7	-	-	109.0	-2.6
1988	-	-	108.2	-0.7	-	-	109.4	1.1	-	-	110.0	0.5	-	-	112.2	2.0	-	-	111.6	-0.5	-	-	109.4	-2.0
1989	-	-	110.2	0.7	-	-	109.8	-0.4	-	-	112.7	2.6	-	-	113.2	0.4	-	-	114.0	0.7	-	-	111.3	-2.4
1990	-	-	111.3	0.0	-	-	112.2	0.8	-	-	113.9	1.5	-	-	116.1	1.9	-	-	118.7	2.2	-	-	114.4	-3.6
1991	-	-	117.1	2.4	-	-	117.1	0.0	-	-	118.0	0.8	-	-	119.4	1.2	-	-	122.1	2.3	-	-	120.0	-1.7
1992	-	-	118.6	-1.2	-	-	118.9	0.3	-	-	123.2	3.6	-	-	124.3	0.9	-	-	122.8	-1.2	-	-	121.1	-1.4
1993	-	-	123.1	1.7	-	-	122.6	-0.4	-	-	123.2	0.5	-	-	126.7	2.8	-	-	127.8	0.9	-	-	125.4	-1.9
1994	-	-	125.8	0.3	-	-	127.6	1.4	-	-	128.9	1.0	-	-	129.7	0.6	-	-	130.5	0.6	-	-	128.3	-1.7
1995	-	-	130.8	1.9	-	-	130.8	0.0	-	-	131.4	0.5	-	-	132.2	0.6	-	-	133.3	0.8	-	-	131.6	-1.3

Source: U.S. Department of Labor, Bureau of Labor Statistics, Division of Consumer Prices and Price Indexes. - indicates no data collected for period.

Dallas-Fort Worth, TX
Consumer Price Index - All Urban Consumers
Base 1982-1984 = 100
Apparel and Upkeep

For 1963-1995. Columns headed % show percentile change in the index from the previous period for which an index is available.

Year	Jan Index	%	Feb Index	%	Mar Index	%	Apr Index	%	May Index	%	Jun Index	%	Jul Index	%	Aug Index	%	Sep Index	%	Oct Index	%	Nov Index	%	Dec Index	%
1963	-	-	-	-	-	-	-	-	-	-	-	-	-	-	-	-	-	-	-	-	45.6	-	-	-
1964	-	-	45.6	0.0	-	-	-	-	45.5	-0.2	-	-	-	-	45.1	-0.9	-	-	-	-	45.5	0.9	-	-
1965	-	-	45.0	-1.1	-	-	-	-	45.2	0.4	-	-	-	-	44.8	-0.9	-	-	-	-	45.6	1.8	-	-
1966	-	-	45.7	0.2	-	-	-	-	46.6	2.0	-	-	-	-	46.5	-0.2	-	-	-	-	47.9	3.0	-	-
1967	-	-	48.2	0.6	-	-	-	-	48.6	0.8	-	-	-	-	48.8	0.4	-	-	-	-	49.0	0.4	-	-
1968	-	-	49.6	1.2	-	-	-	-	51.4	3.6	-	-	-	-	51.8	0.8	-	-	-	-	52.9	2.1	-	-
1969	-	-	53.3	0.8	-	-	-	-	54.6	2.4	-	-	-	-	54.8	0.4	-	-	-	-	56.7	3.5	-	-
1970	-	-	57.6	1.6	-	-	-	-	57.3	-0.5	-	-	-	-	57.7	0.7	-	-	-	-	57.1	-1.0	-	-
1971	-	-	56.9	-0.4	-	-	-	-	57.7	1.4	-	-	-	-	58.2	0.9	-	-	-	-	57.6	-1.0	-	-
1972	-	-	58.4	1.4	-	-	-	-	59.1	1.2	-	-	-	-	59.2	0.2	-	-	-	-	60.3	1.9	-	-
1973	-	-	61.1	1.3	-	-	-	-	62.4	2.1	-	-	-	-	63.1	1.1	-	-	-	-	63.9	1.3	-	-
1974	-	-	65.2	2.0	-	-	-	-	66.1	1.4	-	-	-	-	67.0	1.4	-	-	-	-	68.3	1.9	-	-
1975	-	-	68.2	-0.1	-	-	-	-	68.1	-0.1	-	-	-	-	69.3	1.8	-	-	-	-	69.6	0.4	-	-
1976	-	-	69.4	-0.3	-	-	-	-	70.7	1.9	-	-	-	-	71.0	0.4	-	-	-	-	72.2	1.7	-	-
1977	-	-	72.9	1.0	-	-	-	-	73.5	0.8	-	-	-	-	76.0	3.4	-	-	-	-	76.7	0.9	-	-
1978	-	-	77.1	0.5	-	-	78.1	1.3	-	-	78.0	-0.1	-	-	79.8	2.3	-	-	80.3	0.6	-	-	81.6	1.6
1979	-	-	81.5	-0.1	-	-	83.4	2.3	-	-	82.2	-1.4	-	-	84.5	2.8	-	-	85.2	0.8	-	-	85.6	0.5
1980	-	-	86.8	1.4	-	-	88.2	1.6	-	-	87.3	-1.0	-	-	89.7	2.7	-	-	92.6	3.2	-	-	90.1	-2.7
1981	-	-	91.6	1.7	-	-	93.1	1.6	-	-	93.5	0.4	-	-	98.0	4.8	-	-	99.5	1.5	-	-	96.2	-3.3
1982	-	-	98.6	2.5	-	-	97.6	-1.0	-	-	97.6	0.0	-	-	96.2	-1.4	-	-	96.6	0.4	-	-	96.8	0.2
1983	-	-	98.4	1.7	-	-	101.1	2.7	-	-	98.6	-2.5	-	-	99.9	1.3	-	-	100.7	0.8	-	-	100.1	-0.6
1984	-	-	103.3	3.2	-	-	102.8	-0.5	-	-	99.6	-3.1	-	-	101.0	1.4	-	-	107.0	5.9	-	-	106.8	-0.2
1985	-	-	106.2	-0.6	-	-	105.8	-0.4	-	-	106.4	0.6	-	-	108.7	2.2	-	-	110.8	1.9	-	-	108.5	-2.1
1986	-	-	107.0	-1.4	-	-	106.2	-0.7	-	-	106.6	0.4	-	-	109.2	2.4	-	-	109.7	0.5	-	-	106.5	-2.9
1987	-	-	108.2	1.6	-	-	117.5	8.6	-	-	114.9	-2.2	-	-	113.9	-0.9	-	-	118.5	4.0	-	-	116.5	-1.7
1988	-	-	117.4	0.8	-	-	125.1	6.6	-	-	120.0	-4.1	-	-	123.0	2.5	-	-	128.8	4.7	-	-	126.7	-1.6
1989	-	-	118.4	-6.6	-	-	130.0	9.8	-	-	122.8	-5.5	-	-	124.6	1.5	-	-	126.1	1.2	-	-	124.9	-1.0
1990	-	-	133.6	7.0	-	-	136.1	1.9	-	-	133.0	-2.3	-	-	137.7	3.5	-	-	146.2	6.2	-	-	142.7	-2.4
1991	-	-	149.8	5.0	-	-	154.1	2.9	-	-	146.9	-4.7	-	-	150.6	2.5	-	-	166.3	10.4	-	-	142.8	-14.1
1992	-	-	157.5	10.3	-	-	152.4	-3.2	-	-	147.6	-3.1	-	-	144.5	-2.1	-	-	157.9	9.3	-	-	149.9	-5.1
1993	-	-	144.3	-3.7	-	-	161.5	11.9	-	-	142.8	-11.6	-	-	139.7	-2.2	-	-	153.9	10.2	-	-	143.3	-6.9
1994	-	-	148.0	3.3	-	-	147.6	-0.3	-	-	151.2	2.4	-	-	147.8	-2.2	-	-	149.3	1.0	-	-	146.2	-2.1
1995	-	-	145.6	-0.4	-	-	154.6	6.2	-	-	147.8	-4.4	-	-	145.0	-1.9	-	-	149.5	3.1	-	-	143.7	-3.9

Source: U.S. Department of Labor, Bureau of Labor Statistics, Division of Consumer Prices and Price Indexes. - indicates no data collected for period.

Dallas-Fort Worth, TX
Consumer Price Index - Urban Wage Earners
Base 1982-1984 = 100
Apparel and Upkeep

For 1963-1995. Columns headed % show percentile change in the index from the previous period for which an index is available.

Year	Jan Index	%	Feb Index	%	Mar Index	%	Apr Index	%	May Index	%	Jun Index	%	Jul Index	%	Aug Index	%	Sep Index	%	Oct Index	%	Nov Index	%	Dec Index	%
1963	-	-	-	-	-	-	-	-	-	-	-	-	-	-	-	-	-	-	-	-	48.1	-	-	-
1964	-	-	48.1	0.0	-	-	-	-	48.0	-0.2	-	-	-	-	47.6	-0.8	-	-	-	-	48.0	0.8	-	-
1965	-	-	47.5	-1.0	-	-	-	-	47.7	0.4	-	-	-	-	47.3	-0.8	-	-	-	-	48.1	1.7	-	-
1966	-	-	48.3	0.4	-	-	-	-	49.2	1.9	-	-	-	-	49.1	-0.2	-	-	-	-	50.6	3.1	-	-
1967	-	-	50.9	0.6	-	-	-	-	51.3	0.8	-	-	-	-	51.5	0.4	-	-	-	-	51.7	0.4	-	-
1968	-	-	52.4	1.4	-	-	-	-	54.3	3.6	-	-	-	-	54.7	0.7	-	-	-	-	55.8	2.0	-	-
1969	-	-	56.3	0.9	-	-	-	-	57.7	2.5	-	-	-	-	57.9	0.3	-	-	-	-	59.9	3.5	-	-
1970	-	-	60.8	1.5	-	-	-	-	60.5	-0.5	-	-	-	-	60.9	0.7	-	-	-	-	60.3	-1.0	-	-
1971	-	-	60.1	-0.3	-	-	-	-	60.9	1.3	-	-	-	-	61.4	0.8	-	-	-	-	60.8	-1.0	-	-
1972	-	-	61.7	1.5	-	-	-	-	62.4	1.1	-	-	-	-	62.5	0.2	-	-	-	-	63.7	1.9	-	-
1973	-	-	64.6	1.4	-	-	-	-	65.9	2.0	-	-	-	-	66.6	1.1	-	-	-	-	67.5	1.4	-	-
1974	-	-	68.8	1.9	-	-	-	-	69.8	1.5	-	-	-	-	70.7	1.3	-	-	-	-	72.1	2.0	-	-
1975	-	-	72.1	0.0	-	-	-	-	72.0	-0.1	-	-	-	-	73.1	1.5	-	-	-	-	73.5	0.5	-	-
1976	-	-	73.2	-0.4	-	-	-	-	74.7	2.0	-	-	-	-	74.9	0.3	-	-	-	-	76.3	1.9	-	-
1977	-	-	76.9	0.8	-	-	-	-	77.6	0.9	-	-	-	-	80.2	3.4	-	-	-	-	81.0	1.0	-	-
1978	-	-	81.5	0.6	-	-	80.5	-1.2	-	-	80.7	0.2	-	-	84.3	4.5	-	-	84.3	0.0	-	-	85.0	0.8
1979	-	-	85.8	0.9	-	-	86.2	0.5	-	-	85.7	-0.6	-	-	88.6	3.4	-	-	89.2	0.7	-	-	89.2	0.0
1980	-	-	90.9	1.9	-	-	93.1	2.4	-	-	94.1	1.1	-	-	96.2	2.2	-	-	97.5	1.4	-	-	98.1	0.6
1981	-	-	98.6	0.5	-	-	99.9	1.3	-	-	100.9	1.0	-	-	99.5	-1.4	-	-	98.2	-1.3	-	-	95.7	-2.5
1982	-	-	98.4	2.8	-	-	97.4	-1.0	-	-	97.3	-0.1	-	-	97.2	-0.1	-	-	97.6	0.4	-	-	97.3	-0.3
1983	-	-	98.6	1.3	-	-	100.8	2.2	-	-	98.4	-2.4	-	-	98.9	0.5	-	-	101.2	2.3	-	-	99.3	-1.9
1984	-	-	103.9	4.6	-	-	102.3	-1.5	-	-	100.1	-2.2	-	-	100.7	0.6	-	-	106.3	5.6	-	-	106.9	0.6
1985	-	-	106.3	-0.6	-	-	107.8	1.4	-	-	108.7	0.8	-	-	110.1	1.3	-	-	112.9	2.5	-	-	110.1	-2.5
1986	-	-	107.7	-2.2	-	-	107.7	0.0	-	-	107.8	0.1	-	-	111.8	3.7	-	-	111.7	-0.1	-	-	108.5	-2.9
1987	-	-	110.6	1.9	-	-	118.2	6.9	-	-	113.8	-3.7	-	-	113.3	-0.4	-	-	119.1	5.1	-	-	117.9	-1.0
1988	-	-	118.8	0.8	-	-	124.1	4.5	-	-	119.6	-3.6	-	-	122.5	2.4	-	-	129.0	5.3	-	-	127.1	-1.5
1989	-	-	118.3	-6.9	-	-	129.7	9.6	-	-	121.0	-6.7	-	-	121.1	0.1	-	-	123.6	2.1	-	-	121.9	-1.4
1990	-	-	125.9	3.3	-	-	131.1	4.1	-	-	127.4	-2.8	-	-	131.2	3.0	-	-	137.2	4.6	-	-	135.8	-1.0
1991	-	-	138.1	1.7	-	-	142.9	3.5	-	-	138.4	-3.1	-	-	134.8	-2.6	-	-	146.4	8.6	-	-	130.5	-10.9
1992	-	-	143.7	10.1	-	-	142.3	-1.0	-	-	139.2	-2.2	-	-	135.8	-2.4	-	-	148.6	9.4	-	-	142.5	-4.1
1993	-	-	139.4	-2.2	-	-	155.9	11.8	-	-	142.5	-8.6	-	-	134.8	-5.4	-	-	145.3	7.8	-	-	139.6	-3.9
1994	-	-	138.7	-0.6	-	-	140.6	1.4	-	-	142.8	1.6	-	-	139.2	-2.5	-	-	142.2	2.2	-	-	138.2	-2.8
1995	-	-	137.2	-0.7	-	-	147.3	7.4	-	-	142.9	-3.0	-	-	137.8	-3.6	-	-	145.1	5.3	-	-	140.3	-3.3

Source: U.S. Department of Labor, Bureau of Labor Statistics, Division of Consumer Prices and Price Indexes. - indicates no data collected for period.

Dallas-Fort Worth, TX

Consumer Price Index - All Urban Consumers
Base 1982-1984 = 100
Transportation

For 1963-1995. Columns headed % show percentile change in the index from the previous period for which an index is available.

Year	Jan Index	%	Feb Index	%	Mar Index	%	Apr Index	%	May Index	%	Jun Index	%	Jul Index	%	Aug Index	%	Sep Index	%	Oct Index	%	Nov Index	%	Dec Index	%
1963	-	-	-	-	-	-	-	-	-	-	-	-	-	-	-	-	-	-	-	-	31.5	-	-	-
1964	-	-	30.7	-2.5	-	-	-	-	31.9	3.9	-	-	-	-	30.6	-4.1	-	-	-	-	31.9	4.2	-	-
1965	-	-	30.1	-5.6	-	-	-	-	31.9	6.0	-	-	-	-	32.0	0.3	-	-	-	-	32.2	0.6	-	-
1966	-	-	31.7	-1.6	-	-	-	-	32.3	1.9	-	-	-	-	32.4	0.3	-	-	-	-	32.7	0.9	-	-
1967	-	-	32.6	-0.3	-	-	-	-	33.1	1.5	-	-	-	-	33.8	2.1	-	-	-	-	33.6	-0.6	-	-
1968	-	-	33.6	0.0	-	-	-	-	34.5	2.7	-	-	-	-	34.8	0.9	-	-	-	-	34.9	0.3	-	-
1969	-	-	34.8	-0.3	-	-	-	-	35.5	2.0	-	-	-	-	35.6	0.3	-	-	-	-	36.4	2.2	-	-
1970	-	-	35.9	-1.4	-	-	-	-	36.8	2.5	-	-	-	-	37.3	1.4	-	-	-	-	37.4	0.3	-	-
1971	-	-	38.5	2.9	-	-	-	-	38.7	0.5	-	-	-	-	39.9	3.1	-	-	-	-	39.5	-1.0	-	-
1972	-	-	39.2	-0.8	-	-	-	-	40.2	2.6	-	-	-	-	40.4	0.5	-	-	-	-	39.8	-1.5	-	-
1973	-	-	39.6	-0.5	-	-	-	-	41.1	3.8	-	-	-	-	41.4	0.7	-	-	-	-	42.0	1.4	-	-
1974	-	-	43.9	4.5	-	-	-	-	47.0	7.1	-	-	-	-	49.2	4.7	-	-	-	-	49.6	0.8	-	-
1975	-	-	49.6	0.0	-	-	-	-	51.1	3.0	-	-	-	-	53.7	5.1	-	-	-	-	54.0	0.6	-	-
1976	-	-	53.6	-0.7	-	-	-	-	56.1	4.7	-	-	-	-	57.7	2.9	-	-	-	-	59.2	2.6	-	-
1977	-	-	59.4	0.3	-	-	-	-	61.5	3.5	-	-	-	-	61.7	0.3	-	-	-	-	61.3	-0.6	-	-
1978	-	-	61.0	-0.5	-	-	61.4	0.7	-	-	62.6	2.0	-	-	63.4	1.3	-	-	64.4	1.6	-	-	65.0	0.9
1979	-	-	66.1	1.7	-	-	68.9	4.2	-	-	72.3	4.9	-	-	74.4	2.9	-	-	75.4	1.3	-	-	77.8	3.2
1980	-	-	83.3	7.1	-	-	86.2	3.5	-	-	86.6	0.5	-	-	87.6	1.2	-	-	88.1	0.6	-	-	88.6	0.6
1981	-	-	92.3	4.2	-	-	95.1	3.0	-	-	96.5	1.5	-	-	96.5	0.0	-	-	97.2	0.7	-	-	97.6	0.4
1982	-	-	97.2	-0.4	-	-	93.8	-3.5	-	-	98.0	4.5	-	-	99.1	1.1	-	-	98.4	-0.7	-	-	97.9	-0.5
1983	-	-	95.6	-2.3	-	-	97.3	1.8	-	-	99.4	2.2	-	-	100.6	1.2	-	-	102.0	1.4	-	-	101.5	-0.5
1984	-	-	100.7	-0.8	-	-	101.7	1.0	-	-	102.4	0.7	-	-	104.8	2.3	-	-	105.9	1.0	-	-	105.6	-0.3
1985	-	-	104.9	-0.7	-	-	106.5	1.5	-	-	107.6	1.0	-	-	108.0	0.4	-	-	108.6	0.6	-	-	108.7	0.1
1986	-	-	107.9	-0.7	-	-	99.2	-8.1	-	-	100.2	1.0	-	-	98.7	-1.5	-	-	99.2	0.5	-	-	98.7	-0.5
1987	-	-	101.2	2.5	-	-	101.0	-0.2	-	-	103.2	2.2	-	-	104.7	1.5	-	-	105.8	1.1	-	-	107.2	1.3
1988	-	-	107.2	0.0	-	-	106.6	-0.6	-	-	108.2	1.5	-	-	108.4	0.2	-	-	108.8	0.4	-	-	109.0	0.2
1989	-	-	108.9	-0.1	-	-	109.5	0.6	-	-	112.6	2.8	-	-	110.4	-2.0	-	-	111.9	1.4	-	-	112.1	0.2
1990	-	-	113.9	1.6	-	-	113.1	-0.7	-	-	114.1	0.9	-	-	116.6	2.2	-	-	123.6	6.0	-	-	125.3	1.4
1991	-	-	121.0	-3.4	-	-	118.3	-2.2	-	-	119.5	1.0	-	-	120.8	1.1	-	-	121.1	0.2	-	-	123.1	1.7
1992	-	-	121.3	-1.5	-	-	122.4	0.9	-	-	123.0	0.5	-	-	122.9	-0.1	-	-	126.1	2.6	-	-	125.6	-0.4
1993	-	-	125.5	-0.1	-	-	126.1	0.5	-	-	127.9	1.4	-	-	130.4	2.0	-	-	132.1	1.3	-	-	133.1	0.8
1994	-	-	132.8	-0.2	-	-	133.1	0.2	-	-	133.3	0.2	-	-	135.7	1.8	-	-	136.4	0.5	-	-	136.5	0.1
1995	-	-	137.4	0.7	-	-	140.3	2.1	-	-	140.6	0.2	-	-	139.7	-0.6	-	-	140.9	0.9	-	-	138.3	-1.8

Source: U.S. Department of Labor, Bureau of Labor Statistics, Division of Consumer Prices and Price Indexes. - indicates no data collected for period.

Dallas-Fort Worth, TX
Consumer Price Index - Urban Wage Earners
Base 1982-1984 = 100
Transportation

For 1963-1995. Columns headed % show percentile change in the index from the previous period for which an index is available.

Year	Jan Index	%	Feb Index	%	Mar Index	%	Apr Index	%	May Index	%	Jun Index	%	Jul Index	%	Aug Index	%	Sep Index	%	Oct Index	%	Nov Index	%	Dec Index	%
1963	-	-	-	-	-	-	-	-	-	-	-	-	-	-	-	-	-	-	-	-	31.5	-	-	-
1964	-	-	30.8	-2.2	-	-	-	-	31.9	3.6	-	-	-	-	30.7	-3.8	-	-	-	-	32.0	4.2	-	-
1965	-	-	30.2	-5.6	-	-	-	-	31.9	5.6	-	-	-	-	32.1	0.6	-	-	-	-	32.2	0.3	-	-
1966	-	-	31.7	-1.6	-	-	-	-	32.3	1.9	-	-	-	-	32.4	0.3	-	-	-	-	32.8	1.2	-	-
1967	-	-	32.6	-0.6	-	-	-	-	33.1	1.5	-	-	-	-	33.9	2.4	-	-	-	-	33.6	-0.9	-	-
1968	-	-	33.7	0.3	-	-	-	-	34.5	2.4	-	-	-	-	34.8	0.9	-	-	-	-	35.0	0.6	-	-
1969	-	-	34.8	-0.6	-	-	-	-	35.6	2.3	-	-	-	-	35.6	0.0	-	-	-	-	36.4	2.2	-	-
1970	-	-	36.0	-1.1	-	-	-	-	36.9	2.5	-	-	-	-	37.3	1.1	-	-	-	-	37.5	0.5	-	-
1971	-	-	38.5	2.7	-	-	-	-	38.8	0.8	-	-	-	-	39.9	2.8	-	-	-	-	39.5	-1.0	-	-
1972	-	-	39.2	-0.8	-	-	-	-	40.2	2.6	-	-	-	-	40.4	0.5	-	-	-	-	39.9	-1.2	-	-
1973	-	-	39.6	-0.8	-	-	-	-	41.2	4.0	-	-	-	-	41.4	0.5	-	-	-	-	42.0	1.4	-	-
1974	-	-	43.9	4.5	-	-	-	-	47.0	7.1	-	-	-	-	49.3	4.9	-	-	-	-	49.7	0.8	-	-
1975	-	-	49.6	-0.2	-	-	-	-	51.1	3.0	-	-	-	-	53.7	5.1	-	-	-	-	54.0	0.6	-	-
1976	-	-	53.7	-0.6	-	-	-	-	56.1	4.5	-	-	-	-	57.7	2.9	-	-	-	-	59.2	2.6	-	-
1977	-	-	59.5	0.5	-	-	-	-	61.6	3.5	-	-	-	-	61.7	0.2	-	-	-	-	61.3	-0.6	-	-
1978	-	-	61.0	-0.5	-	-	61.5	0.8	-	-	62.7	2.0	-	-	63.7	1.6	-	-	64.6	1.4	-	-	65.3	1.1
1979	-	-	66.4	1.7	-	-	69.3	4.4	-	-	72.7	4.9	-	-	75.0	3.2	-	-	75.7	0.9	-	-	78.1	3.2
1980	-	-	83.8	7.3	-	-	86.5	3.2	-	-	86.7	0.2	-	-	87.8	1.3	-	-	88.7	1.0	-	-	89.4	0.8
1981	-	-	93.3	4.4	-	-	95.6	2.5	-	-	97.7	2.2	-	-	97.5	-0.2	-	-	98.6	1.1	-	-	98.0	-0.6
1982	-	-	97.5	-0.5	-	-	94.0	-3.6	-	-	98.2	4.5	-	-	99.3	1.1	-	-	98.6	-0.7	-	-	98.0	-0.6
1983	-	-	95.6	-2.4	-	-	97.4	1.9	-	-	99.4	2.1	-	-	100.6	1.2	-	-	102.0	1.4	-	-	101.4	-0.6
1984	-	-	100.6	-0.8	-	-	101.5	0.9	-	-	102.3	0.8	-	-	104.6	2.2	-	-	105.7	1.1	-	-	105.3	-0.4
1985	-	-	104.5	-0.8	-	-	106.2	1.6	-	-	107.3	1.0	-	-	107.6	0.3	-	-	108.3	0.7	-	-	108.4	0.1
1986	-	-	107.6	-0.7	-	-	98.7	-8.3	-	-	99.7	1.0	-	-	98.1	-1.6	-	-	98.4	0.3	-	-	97.8	-0.6
1987	-	-	101.1	3.4	-	-	101.8	0.7	-	-	104.3	2.5	-	-	106.0	1.6	-	-	106.8	0.8	-	-	107.8	0.9
1988	-	-	107.7	-0.1	-	-	106.9	-0.7	-	-	108.4	1.4	-	-	109.2	0.7	-	-	109.5	0.3	-	-	109.5	0.0
1989	-	-	109.2	-0.3	-	-	110.8	1.5	-	-	114.3	3.2	-	-	111.9	-2.1	-	-	112.9	0.9	-	-	112.6	-0.3
1990	-	-	114.4	1.6	-	-	113.5	-0.8	-	-	115.0	1.3	-	-	117.7	2.3	-	-	125.0	6.2	-	-	126.2	1.0
1991	-	-	120.9	-4.2	-	-	118.5	-2.0	-	-	120.6	1.8	-	-	122.0	1.2	-	-	122.9	0.7	-	-	124.4	1.2
1992	-	-	121.8	-2.1	-	-	123.4	1.3	-	-	126.5	2.5	-	-	127.5	0.8	-	-	129.8	1.8	-	-	129.5	-0.2
1993	-	-	128.3	-0.9	-	-	129.5	0.9	-	-	132.1	2.0	-	-	135.1	2.3	-	-	136.9	1.3	-	-	136.6	-0.2
1994	-	-	135.0	-1.2	-	-	135.5	0.4	-	-	136.8	1.0	-	-	139.8	2.2	-	-	141.3	1.1	-	-	141.8	0.4
1995	-	-	142.3	0.4	-	-	144.5	1.5	-	-	145.4	0.6	-	-	144.5	-0.6	-	-	145.0	0.3	-	-	143.2	-1.2

Source: U.S. Department of Labor, Bureau of Labor Statistics, Division of Consumer Prices and Price Indexes. - indicates no data collected for period.

Dallas-Fort Worth, TX
Consumer Price Index - All Urban Consumers
Base 1982-1984 = 100
Medical Care

For 1963-1995. Columns headed % show percentile change in the index from the previous period for which an index is available.

Year	Jan Index	%	Feb Index	%	Mar Index	%	Apr Index	%	May Index	%	Jun Index	%	Jul Index	%	Aug Index	%	Sep Index	%	Oct Index	%	Nov Index	%	Dec Index	%
1963	-	-	-	-	-	-	-	-	-	-	-	-	-	-	-	-	-	-	-	-	24.1	-	-	-
1964	-	-	24.4	1.2	-	-	-	-	24.5	0.4	-	-	-	-	24.5	0.0	-	-	-	-	24.5	0.0	-	-
1965	-	-	24.8	1.2	-	-	-	-	25.0	0.8	-	-	-	-	25.0	0.0	-	-	-	-	25.2	0.8	-	-
1966	-	-	25.8	2.4	-	-	-	-	26.3	1.9	-	-	-	-	26.6	1.1	-	-	-	-	26.9	1.1	-	-
1967	-	-	28.0	4.1	-	-	-	-	28.0	0.0	-	-	-	-	28.3	1.1	-	-	-	-	28.8	1.8	-	-
1968	-	-	29.5	2.4	-	-	-	-	30.0	1.7	-	-	-	-	30.0	0.0	-	-	-	-	30.5	1.7	-	-
1969	-	-	31.7	3.9	-	-	-	-	32.2	1.6	-	-	-	-	32.6	1.2	-	-	-	-	32.9	0.9	-	-
1970	-	-	34.2	4.0	-	-	-	-	34.8	1.8	-	-	-	-	35.1	0.9	-	-	-	-	35.1	0.0	-	-
1971	-	-	36.1	2.8	-	-	-	-	36.5	1.1	-	-	-	-	36.7	0.5	-	-	-	-	36.4	-0.8	-	-
1972	-	-	36.9	1.4	-	-	-	-	37.1	0.5	-	-	-	-	37.2	0.3	-	-	-	-	37.5	0.8	-	-
1973	-	-	38.2	1.9	-	-	-	-	38.6	1.0	-	-	-	-	38.5	-0.3	-	-	-	-	39.5	2.6	-	-
1974	-	-	40.2	1.8	-	-	-	-	40.9	1.7	-	-	-	-	42.4	3.7	-	-	-	-	43.4	2.4	-	-
1975	-	-	44.6	2.8	-	-	-	-	45.4	1.8	-	-	-	-	46.8	3.1	-	-	-	-	47.2	0.9	-	-
1976	-	-	48.5	2.8	-	-	-	-	48.8	0.6	-	-	-	-	50.7	3.9	-	-	-	-	52.3	3.2	-	-
1977	-	-	53.3	1.9	-	-	-	-	54.8	2.8	-	-	-	-	55.8	1.8	-	-	-	-	57.0	2.2	-	-
1978	-	-	58.3	2.3	-	-	58.9	1.0	-	-	59.8	1.5	-	-	60.0	0.3	-	-	60.4	0.7	-	-	61.1	1.2
1979	-	-	61.3	0.3	-	-	62.2	1.5	-	-	62.4	0.3	-	-	63.5	1.8	-	-	63.6	0.2	-	-	65.2	2.5
1980	-	-	66.5	2.0	-	-	69.0	3.8	-	-	69.7	1.0	-	-	71.9	3.2	-	-	71.8	-0.1	-	-	72.4	0.8
1981	-	-	74.1	2.3	-	-	75.6	2.0	-	-	79.4	5.0	-	-	83.3	4.9	-	-	85.5	2.6	-	-	87.4	2.2
1982	-	-	89.2	2.1	-	-	90.3	1.2	-	-	91.6	1.4	-	-	92.2	0.7	-	-	94.2	2.2	-	-	96.0	1.9
1983	-	-	98.8	2.9	-	-	100.9	2.1	-	-	100.8	-0.1	-	-	102.3	1.5	-	-	102.3	0.0	-	-	104.1	1.8
1984	-	-	105.4	1.2	-	-	106.0	0.6	-	-	106.5	0.5	-	-	107.4	0.8	-	-	108.5	1.0	-	-	109.3	0.7
1985	-	-	110.5	1.1	-	-	111.3	0.7	-	-	112.1	0.7	-	-	114.7	2.3	-	-	116.1	1.2	-	-	122.1	5.2
1986	-	-	123.7	1.3	-	-	125.3	1.3	-	-	126.0	0.6	-	-	127.5	1.2	-	-	129.2	1.3	-	-	130.6	1.1
1987	-	-	130.3	-0.2	-	-	134.0	2.8	-	-	134.3	0.2	-	-	135.4	0.8	-	-	135.3	-0.1	-	-	137.9	1.9
1988	-	-	141.6	2.7	-	-	140.7	-0.6	-	-	140.9	0.1	-	-	141.6	0.5	-	-	142.9	0.9	-	-	145.7	2.0
1989	-	-	148.2	1.7	-	-	148.7	0.3	-	-	149.8	0.7	-	-	151.9	1.4	-	-	154.4	1.6	-	-	154.4	0.0
1990	-	-	156.4	1.3	-	-	156.9	0.3	-	-	162.1	3.3	-	-	163.7	1.0	-	-	167.3	2.2	-	-	168.2	0.5
1991	-	-	170.4	1.3	-	-	170.9	0.3	-	-	174.3	2.0	-	-	176.3	1.1	-	-	179.0	1.5	-	-	180.8	1.0
1992	-	-	182.7	1.1	-	-	185.7	1.6	-	-	187.7	1.1	-	-	188.9	0.6	-	-	193.8	2.6	-	-	194.1	0.2
1993	-	-	193.5	-0.3	-	-	194.0	0.3	-	-	196.7	1.4	-	-	197.9	0.6	-	-	199.7	0.9	-	-	200.6	0.5
1994	-	-	202.1	0.7	-	-	203.7	0.8	-	-	204.5	0.4	-	-	205.3	0.4	-	-	209.6	2.1	-	-	210.8	0.6
1995	-	-	212.8	0.9	-	-	216.2	1.6	-	-	215.6	-0.3	-	-	218.6	1.4	-	-	220.4	0.8	-	-	220.3	-0.0

Source: U.S. Department of Labor, Bureau of Labor Statistics, Division of Consumer Prices and Price Indexes. - indicates no data collected for period.

Dallas-Fort Worth, TX
Consumer Price Index - Urban Wage Earners
Base 1982-1984 = 100
Medical Care

For 1963-1995. Columns headed % show percentile change in the index from the previous period for which an index is available.

Year	Jan Index	%	Feb Index	%	Mar Index	%	Apr Index	%	May Index	%	Jun Index	%	Jul Index	%	Aug Index	%	Sep Index	%	Oct Index	%	Nov Index	%	Dec Index	%
1963	-	-	-	-	-	-	-	-	-	-	-	-	-	-	-	-	-	-	-	-	-	-	-	-
1964	-	-	24.8	1.2	-	-	-	-	24.9	0.4	-	-	-	-	24.9	0.0	-	-	-	-	24.5	-	-	-
1965	-	-	25.2	1.2	-	-	-	-	25.4	0.8	-	-	-	-	25.4	0.0	-	-	-	-	24.9	0.0	-	-
1966	-	-	26.2	2.3	-	-	-	-	26.8	2.3	-	-	-	-	27.0	0.7	-	-	-	-	25.6	0.8	-	-
1967	-	-	28.4	4.0	-	-	-	-	28.5	0.4	-	-	-	-	28.8	1.1	-	-	-	-	27.3	1.1	-	-
1968	-	-	30.0	2.4	-	-	-	-	30.5	1.7	-	-	-	-	30.5	0.0	-	-	-	-	29.3	1.7	-	-
1969	-	-	32.2	3.9	-	-	-	-	32.8	1.9	-	-	-	-	33.2	1.2	-	-	-	-	31.0	1.6	-	-
1970	-	-	34.8	3.9	-	-	-	-	35.4	1.7	-	-	-	-	35.7	0.8	-	-	-	-	33.5	0.9	-	-
1971	-	-	36.7	3.1	-	-	-	-	37.1	1.1	-	-	-	-	37.3	0.5	-	-	-	-	35.6	-0.3	-	-
1972	-	-	37.6	1.6	-	-	-	-	37.7	0.3	-	-	-	-	37.8	0.3	-	-	-	-	37.0	-0.8	-	-
1973	-	-	38.8	1.6	-	-	-	-	39.2	1.0	-	-	-	-	39.2	0.0	-	-	-	-	38.2	1.1	-	-
1974	-	-	40.9	2.0	-	-	-	-	41.6	1.7	-	-	-	-	43.1	3.6	-	-	-	-	40.1	2.3	-	-
1975	-	-	45.3	2.7	-	-	-	-	46.2	2.0	-	-	-	-	47.6	3.0	-	-	-	-	44.1	2.3	-	-
1976	-	-	49.3	2.7	-	-	-	-	49.6	0.6	-	-	-	-	51.5	3.8	-	-	-	-	48.0	0.8	-	-
1977	-	-	54.1	1.7	-	-	-	-	55.7	3.0	-	-	-	-	56.7	1.8	-	-	-	-	53.2	3.3	-	-
1978	-	-	59.2	2.2	-	-	59.9	1.2	-	-	60.1	0.3	-	-	60.9	1.3	-	-	-	-	57.9	2.1	-	-
1979	-	-	63.1	0.0	-	-	64.5	2.2	-	-	65.1	0.9	-	-	66.1	1.5	-	-	61.7	1.3	-	-	63.1	2.3
1980	-	-	68.2	1.3	-	-	70.2	2.9	-	-	71.1	1.3	-	-	74.6	4.9	-	-	66.0	-0.2	-	-	67.3	2.0
1981	-	-	76.8	1.1	-	-	77.6	1.0	-	-	80.4	3.6	-	-	83.3	3.6	-	-	84.8	1.8	-	-	76.0	2.0
1982	-	-	88.8	2.1	-	-	90.1	1.5	-	-	91.3	1.3	-	-	92.0	0.8	-	-	94.1	2.3	-	-	87.0	2.6
1983	-	-	98.8	3.0	-	-	101.0	2.2	-	-	100.7	-0.3	-	-	102.3	1.6	-	-	102.3	0.0	-	-	95.9	1.9
1984	-	-	105.7	1.4	-	-	106.1	0.4	-	-	106.6	0.5	-	-	107.6	0.9	-	-	108.7	1.0	-	-	104.2	1.9
1985	-	-	110.8	1.1	-	-	111.6	0.7	-	-	112.3	0.6	-	-	115.1	2.5	-	-	116.6	1.3	-	-	109.6	0.8
1986	-	-	124.5	1.3	-	-	126.0	1.2	-	-	126.8	0.6	-	-	128.4	1.3	-	-	130.1	1.3	-	-	122.9	5.4
1987	-	-	131.4	-0.1	-	-	135.1	2.8	-	-	135.5	0.3	-	-	136.8	1.0	-	-	136.8	0.0	-	-	131.5	1.1
1988	-	-	143.1	2.4	-	-	142.0	-0.8	-	-	142.4	0.3	-	-	143.4	0.7	-	-	144.4	0.7	-	-	139.8	2.2
1989	-	-	150.6	1.7	-	-	151.0	0.3	-	-	152.2	0.8	-	-	154.2	1.3	-	-	156.5	1.5	-	-	148.1	2.6
1990	-	-	158.8	1.3	-	-	159.3	0.3	-	-	164.7	3.4	-	-	166.6	1.2	-	-	170.1	2.1	-	-	156.8	0.2
1991	-	-	172.9	1.2	-	-	174.0	0.6	-	-	177.2	1.8	-	-	179.5	1.3	-	-	182.4	1.6	-	-	170.8	0.4
1992	-	-	185.7	1.1	-	-	189.5	2.0	-	-	191.9	1.3	-	-	193.1	0.6	-	-	198.1	2.6	-	-	183.7	0.7
1993	-	-	197.2	-0.4	-	-	197.6	0.2	-	-	200.9	1.7	-	-	202.1	0.6	-	-	203.8	0.8	-	-	198.0	-0.1
1994	-	-	205.9	0.6	-	-	207.4	0.7	-	-	207.9	0.2	-	-	208.8	0.4	-	-	213.3	2.2	-	-	204.7	0.4
1995	-	-	216.5	0.9	-	-	220.9	2.0	-	-	220.3	-0.3	-	-	223.3	1.4	-	-	225.3	0.9	-	-	214.6	0.6

Note: The Nov column values appear shifted in the source for years 1981–1995; the values shown in the Dec column above (76.0, 87.0, 95.9, 104.2, 109.6, 122.9, 131.5, 139.8, 148.1, 156.8, 170.8, 183.7, 198.0, 204.7, 214.6) correspond to the Nov position, and the final Dec values (2.0, 2.6, 1.9, 1.9, 0.8, 5.4, 1.1, 2.2, 2.6, 0.2, 0.4, 0.7, -0.1, 0.4, 0.6) are the Dec percentages. For 1995 the last two entries are 225.1 and -0.1.

Source: U.S. Department of Labor, Bureau of Labor Statistics, Division of Consumer Prices and Price Indexes. - indicates no data collected for period.

Dallas-Fort Worth, TX
Consumer Price Index - All Urban Consumers
Base 1982-1984 = 100
Entertainment

For 1975-1995. Columns headed % show percentile change in the index from the previous period for which an index is available.

Year	Jan Index	%	Feb Index	%	Mar Index	%	Apr Index	%	May Index	%	Jun Index	%	Jul Index	%	Aug Index	%	Sep Index	%	Oct Index	%	Nov Index	%	Dec Index	%
1975	-	-	-	-	-	-	-	-	-	-	-	-	-	-	-	-	-	-	-	-	64.6	-	-	-
1976	-	-	65.3	1.1	-	-	-	-	67.2	2.9	-	-	-	-	67.8	0.9	-	-	-	-	68.5	1.0	-	-
1977	-	-	68.5	0.0	-	-	-	-	69.7	1.8	-	-	-	-	70.8	1.6	-	-	-	-	69.1	-2.4	-	-
1978	-	-	68.8	-0.4	-	-	68.4	-0.6	-	-	70.5	3.1	-	-	70.5	0.0	-	-	70.6	0.1	-	-	70.9	0.4
1979	-	-	71.8	1.3	-	-	72.3	0.7	-	-	72.9	0.8	-	-	74.1	1.6	-	-	75.4	1.8	-	-	76.5	1.5
1980	-	-	77.3	1.0	-	-	81.4	5.3	-	-	83.2	2.2	-	-	84.5	1.6	-	-	84.8	0.4	-	-	85.8	1.2
1981	-	-	86.4	0.7	-	-	86.0	-0.5	-	-	86.9	1.0	-	-	87.6	0.8	-	-	88.6	1.1	-	-	88.5	-0.1
1982	-	-	90.7	2.5	-	-	90.7	0.0	-	-	93.2	2.8	-	-	93.3	0.1	-	-	97.0	4.0	-	-	95.7	-1.3
1983	-	-	98.2	2.6	-	-	97.4	-0.8	-	-	98.2	0.8	-	-	101.2	3.1	-	-	102.4	1.2	-	-	102.1	-0.3
1984	-	-	104.4	2.3	-	-	106.2	1.7	-	-	106.4	0.2	-	-	106.8	0.4	-	-	110.0	3.0	-	-	111.9	1.7
1985	-	-	114.3	2.1	-	-	114.1	-0.2	-	-	112.5	-1.4	-	-	114.7	2.0	-	-	114.5	-0.2	-	-	115.0	0.4
1986	-	-	113.5	-1.3	-	-	114.4	0.8	-	-	115.7	1.1	-	-	115.6	-0.1	-	-	117.6	1.7	-	-	119.3	1.4
1987	-	-	120.8	1.3	-	-	121.8	0.8	-	-	121.8	0.0	-	-	122.2	0.3	-	-	124.8	2.1	-	-	121.4	-2.7
1988	-	-	124.0	2.1	-	-	128.4	3.5	-	-	127.9	-0.4	-	-	128.7	0.6	-	-	129.2	0.4	-	-	127.4	-1.4
1989	-	-	128.5	0.9	-	-	133.8	4.1	-	-	134.7	0.7	-	-	131.8	-2.2	-	-	134.3	1.9	-	-	135.3	0.7
1990	-	-	134.6	-0.5	-	-	138.4	2.8	-	-	137.8	-0.4	-	-	136.6	-0.9	-	-	139.8	2.3	-	-	138.7	-0.8
1991	-	-	142.4	2.7	-	-	142.6	0.1	-	-	142.5	-0.1	-	-	143.7	0.8	-	-	142.0	-1.2	-	-	142.1	0.1
1992	-	-	142.1	0.0	-	-	142.9	0.6	-	-	141.6	-0.9	-	-	140.9	-0.5	-	-	141.7	0.6	-	-	143.4	1.2
1993	-	-	144.1	0.5	-	-	142.6	-1.0	-	-	143.5	0.6	-	-	143.7	0.1	-	-	145.8	1.5	-	-	145.1	-0.5
1994	-	-	147.1	1.4	-	-	145.6	-1.0	-	-	147.1	1.0	-	-	148.6	1.0	-	-	147.6	-0.7	-	-	147.2	-0.3
1995	-	-	145.7	-1.0	-	-	145.6	-0.1	-	-	148.2	1.8	-	-	151.6	2.3	-	-	155.8	2.8	-	-	157.7	1.2

Source: U.S. Department of Labor, Bureau of Labor Statistics, Division of Consumer Prices and Price Indexes. - indicates no data collected for period.

Dallas-Fort Worth, TX
Consumer Price Index - Urban Wage Earners
Base 1982-1984 = 100
Entertainment

For 1975-1995. Columns headed % show percentile change in the index from the previous period for which an index is available.

Year	Jan Index	%	Feb Index	%	Mar Index	%	Apr Index	%	May Index	%	Jun Index	%	Jul Index	%	Aug Index	%	Sep Index	%	Oct Index	%	Nov Index	%	Dec Index	%
1975	-	-	-	-	-	-	-	-	-	-	-	-	-	-	-	-	-	-	-	-	-	-	-	-
1976	-	-	69.8	1.2	-	-	-	-	71.8	2.9	-	-	-	-	72.5	1.0	-	-	-	-	69.0	-	-	-
1977	-	-	73.3	0.0	-	-	-	-	74.5	1.6	-	-	-	-	75.7	1.6	-	-	-	-	73.3	1.1	-	-
1978	-	-	73.6	-0.4	-	-	74.3	1.0	-	-	74.8	0.7	-	-	74.5	-0.4	-	-	74.7	0.3	73.9	-2.4	75.3	0.8
1979	-	-	75.7	0.5	-	-	75.9	0.3	-	-	75.4	-0.7	-	-	76.4	1.3	-	-	79.3	3.8	-	-	78.7	-0.8
1980	-	-	79.8	1.4	-	-	80.3	0.6	-	-	82.8	3.1	-	-	84.0	1.4	-	-	84.3	0.4	-	-	84.9	0.7
1981	-	-	86.4	1.8	-	-	87.1	0.8	-	-	87.4	0.3	-	-	87.9	0.6	-	-	89.0	1.3	-	-	89.1	0.1
1982	-	-	91.4	2.6	-	-	91.4	0.0	-	-	93.7	2.5	-	-	93.8	0.1	-	-	97.0	3.4	-	-	96.3	-0.7
1983	-	-	98.2	2.0	-	-	97.5	-0.7	-	-	98.2	0.7	-	-	101.1	3.0	-	-	102.1	1.0	-	-	101.7	-0.4
1984	-	-	104.2	2.5	-	-	105.9	1.6	-	-	106.5	0.6	-	-	106.5	0.0	-	-	109.4	2.7	-	-	110.5	1.0
1985	-	-	113.3	2.5	-	-	113.1	-0.2	-	-	111.1	-1.8	-	-	113.5	2.2	-	-	113.2	-0.3	-	-	113.7	0.4
1986	-	-	112.5	-1.1	-	-	113.3	0.7	-	-	114.2	0.8	-	-	114.3	0.1	-	-	116.1	1.6	-	-	117.4	1.1
1987	-	-	119.4	1.7	-	-	120.2	0.7	-	-	120.2	0.0	-	-	120.7	0.4	-	-	123.2	2.1	-	-	120.5	-2.2
1988	-	-	122.9	2.0	-	-	126.8	3.2	-	-	126.6	-0.2	-	-	127.5	0.7	-	-	127.5	0.0	-	-	126.1	-1.1
1989	-	-	127.3	1.0	-	-	132.7	4.2	-	-	133.7	0.8	-	-	130.9	-2.1	-	-	133.2	1.8	-	-	134.1	0.7
1990	-	-	133.2	-0.7	-	-	136.3	2.3	-	-	135.6	-0.5	-	-	134.8	-0.6	-	-	137.9	2.3	-	-	136.7	-0.9
1991	-	-	140.6	2.9	-	-	140.9	0.2	-	-	140.8	-0.1	-	-	142.0	0.9	-	-	140.2	-1.3	-	-	140.5	0.2
1992	-	-	140.5	0.0	-	-	141.2	0.5	-	-	139.6	-1.1	-	-	138.6	-0.7	-	-	139.6	0.7	-	-	141.3	1.2
1993	-	-	142.0	0.5	-	-	140.4	-1.1	-	-	140.7	0.2	-	-	141.0	0.2	-	-	143.7	1.9	-	-	143.0	-0.5
1994	-	-	145.2	1.5	-	-	143.4	-1.2	-	-	145.1	1.2	-	-	146.5	1.0	-	-	145.1	-1.0	-	-	144.8	-0.2
1995	-	-	142.6	-1.5	-	-	142.7	0.1	-	-	144.5	1.3	-	-	148.6	2.8	-	-	152.9	2.9	-	-	154.9	1.3

Source: U.S. Department of Labor, Bureau of Labor Statistics, Division of Consumer Prices and Price Indexes. - indicates no data collected for period.

Dallas-Fort Worth, TX
Consumer Price Index - All Urban Consumers
Base 1982-1984 = 100
Other Goods and Services

For 1975-1995. Columns headed % show percentile change in the index from the previous period for which an index is available.

Year	Jan Index	%	Feb Index	%	Mar Index	%	Apr Index	%	May Index	%	Jun Index	%	Jul Index	%	Aug Index	%	Sep Index	%	Oct Index	%	Nov Index	%	Dec Index	%
1975	-	-	-	-	-	-	-	-	-	-	-	-	-	-	-	-	-	-	-	-	54.4	-	-	-
1976	-	-	54.8	0.7	-	-	-	-	55.5	1.3	-	-	-	-	55.8	0.5	-	-	-	-	57.5	3.0	-	-
1977	-	-	58.2	1.2	-	-	-	-	59.2	1.7	-	-	-	-	59.9	1.2	-	-	-	-	60.9	1.7	-	-
1978	-	-	61.6	1.1	-	-	61.9	0.5	-	-	61.9	0.0	-	-	64.6	4.4	-	-	65.5	1.4	-	-	66.1	0.9
1979	-	-	67.7	2.4	-	-	67.7	0.0	-	-	67.4	-0.4	-	-	69.0	2.4	-	-	70.5	2.2	-	-	71.6	1.6
1980	-	-	74.1	3.5	-	-	74.6	0.7	-	-	75.0	0.5	-	-	75.1	0.1	-	-	79.2	5.5	-	-	81.2	2.5
1981	-	-	81.3	0.1	-	-	82.9	2.0	-	-	83.3	0.5	-	-	84.6	1.6	-	-	86.5	2.2	-	-	86.8	0.3
1982	-	-	87.9	1.3	-	-	89.5	1.8	-	-	90.7	1.3	-	-	92.5	2.0	-	-	96.1	3.9	-	-	97.2	1.1
1983	-	-	98.3	1.1	-	-	99.5	1.2	-	-	100.3	0.8	-	-	101.9	1.6	-	-	103.4	1.5	-	-	103.5	0.1
1984	-	-	104.9	1.4	-	-	106.2	1.2	-	-	107.0	0.8	-	-	107.2	0.2	-	-	109.8	2.4	-	-	110.1	0.3
1985	-	-	110.1	0.0	-	-	111.0	0.8	-	-	111.2	0.2	-	-	112.5	1.2	-	-	115.7	2.8	-	-	116.0	0.3
1986	-	-	117.0	0.9	-	-	116.7	-0.3	-	-	116.5	-0.2	-	-	120.7	3.6	-	-	122.6	1.6	-	-	126.3	3.0
1987	-	-	128.2	1.5	-	-	128.6	0.3	-	-	127.4	-0.9	-	-	127.3	-0.1	-	-	130.7	2.7	-	-	131.9	0.9
1988	-	-	131.8	-0.1	-	-	133.2	1.1	-	-	134.5	1.0	-	-	135.1	0.4	-	-	138.6	2.6	-	-	139.8	0.9
1989	-	-	143.2	2.4	-	-	144.9	1.2	-	-	144.8	-0.1	-	-	146.0	0.8	-	-	150.5	3.1	-	-	149.9	-0.4
1990	-	-	153.8	2.6	-	-	153.9	0.1	-	-	155.1	0.8	-	-	158.2	2.0	-	-	159.2	0.6	-	-	160.3	0.7
1991	-	-	160.9	0.4	-	-	162.1	0.7	-	-	164.4	1.4	-	-	164.7	0.2	-	-	164.4	-0.2	-	-	167.9	2.1
1992	-	-	170.2	1.4	-	-	169.5	-0.4	-	-	169.4	-0.1	-	-	168.8	-0.4	-	-	173.5	2.8	-	-	172.9	-0.3
1993	-	-	178.4	3.2	-	-	179.9	0.8	-	-	184.9	2.8	-	-	184.7	-0.1	-	-	177.6	-3.8	-	-	178.8	0.7
1994	-	-	179.3	0.3	-	-	179.8	0.3	-	-	182.8	1.7	-	-	182.8	0.0	-	-	180.1	-1.5	-	-	181.9	1.0
1995	-	-	182.2	0.2	-	-	183.5	0.7	-	-	184.5	0.5	-	-	186.9	1.3	-	-	189.1	1.2	-	-	189.8	0.4

Source: U.S. Department of Labor, Bureau of Labor Statistics, Division of Consumer Prices and Price Indexes. - indicates no data collected for period.

Dallas-Fort Worth, TX
Consumer Price Index - Urban Wage Earners
Base 1982-1984 = 100
Other Goods and Services

For 1975-1995. Columns headed % show percentile change in the index from the previous period for which an index is available.

Year	Jan Index	%	Feb Index	%	Mar Index	%	Apr Index	%	May Index	%	Jun Index	%	Jul Index	%	Aug Index	%	Sep Index	%	Oct Index	%	Nov Index	%	Dec Index	%
1975	-	-	-	-	-	-	-	-	-	-	-	-	-	-	-	-	-	-	-	-	-	-	-	-
1976	-	-	57.4	0.7	-	-	-	-	58.2	1.4	-	-	-	-	58.5	0.5	-	-	-	-	57.0	-	-	-
1977	-	-	61.0	1.3	-	-	-	-	62.1	1.8	-	-	-	-	62.8	1.1	-	-	-	-	60.2	2.9	-	-
1978	-	-	64.5	1.1	-	-	65.4	1.4	-	-	65.6	0.3	-	-	67.8	3.4	-	-	-	-	63.8	1.6	-	-
1979	-	-	70.0	2.0	-	-	70.2	0.3	-	-	70.5	0.4	-	-	71.8	1.8	-	-	68.2	0.6	-	-	68.6	0.6
1980	-	-	77.6	3.1	-	-	78.0	0.5	-	-	78.9	1.2	-	-	79.2	0.4	-	-	73.8	2.8	-	-	75.3	2.0
1981	-	-	84.1	1.3	-	-	83.8	-0.4	-	-	84.1	0.4	-	-	83.7	-0.5	-	-	82.0	3.5	-	-	83.0	1.2
1982	-	-	87.3	1.0	-	-	89.1	2.1	-	-	90.4	1.5	-	-	92.3	2.1	-	-	85.3	1.9	-	-	86.4	1.3
1983	-	-	98.5	1.0	-	-	100.2	1.7	-	-	101.0	0.8	-	-	102.5	1.5	-	-	95.8	3.8	-	-	97.5	1.8
1984	-	-	104.8	1.1	-	-	106.1	1.2	-	-	107.1	0.9	-	-	107.3	0.2	-	-	103.5	1.0	-	-	103.7	0.2
1985	-	-	109.8	0.2	-	-	110.4	0.5	-	-	110.3	-0.1	-	-	112.1	1.6	-	-	109.3	1.9	-	-	109.6	0.3
1986	-	-	116.3	1.2	-	-	115.9	-0.3	-	-	115.5	-0.3	-	-	120.5	4.3	-	-	114.6	2.2	-	-	114.9	0.3
1987	-	-	125.8	1.0	-	-	126.3	0.4	-	-	124.9	-1.1	-	-	124.8	-0.1	-	-	121.9	1.2	-	-	124.5	2.1
1988	-	-	129.0	-0.2	-	-	130.7	1.3	-	-	132.3	1.2	-	-	132.9	0.5	-	-	127.8	2.4	-	-	129.3	1.2
1989	-	-	141.3	3.0	-	-	142.1	0.6	-	-	141.9	-0.1	-	-	143.2	0.9	-	-	135.8	2.2	-	-	137.2	1.0
1990	-	-	150.9	2.9	-	-	151.1	0.1	-	-	152.3	0.8	-	-	155.9	2.4	-	-	147.3	2.9	-	-	146.6	-0.5
1991	-	-	158.9	0.4	-	-	160.4	0.9	-	-	162.2	1.1	-	-	162.6	0.2	-	-	156.8	0.6	-	-	158.2	0.9
1992	-	-	168.6	1.4	-	-	167.8	-0.5	-	-	167.6	-0.1	-	-	166.8	-0.5	-	-	162.2	-0.2	-	-	166.3	2.5
1993	-	-	176.4	3.3	-	-	178.0	0.9	-	-	183.0	2.8	-	-	182.9	-0.1	-	-	171.5	2.8	-	-	170.8	-0.4
1994	-	-	176.4	0.3	-	-	177.0	0.3	-	-	179.5	1.4	-	-	179.4	-0.1	-	-	174.4	-4.6	-	-	175.9	0.9
1995	-	-	178.5	0.2	-	-	180.0	0.8	-	-	181.0	0.6	-	-	183.4	1.3	-	-	185.5	1.1	-	-	186.4	0.5

Source: U.S. Department of Labor, Bureau of Labor Statistics, Division of Consumer Prices and Price Indexes. - indicates no data collected for period.

Denver-Boulder, CO
Consumer Price Index - All Urban Consumers
Base 1982-1984 = 100
Annual Averages

For 1964-1995. Columns headed % show percentile change in the index from the previous period for which an index is available.

Year	All Items		Food & Beverage		Housing		Apparel & Upkeep		Trans- portation		Medical Care		Entertain- ment		Other Goods & Services	
	Index	%	Index	%	Index	%	Index	%	Index	%	Index	%	Index	%	Index	%
1964	28.3	-	-	-	-	-	-	-	-	-	-	-	-	-	-	-
1965	28.8	1.8	-	-	-	-	-	-	-	-	-	-	-	-	-	-
1966	29.7	3.1	-	-	-	-	-	-	-	-	-	-	-	-	-	-
1967	30.0	1.0	-	-	-	-	-	-	-	-	-	-	-	-	-	-
1968	30.7	2.3	-	-	-	-	-	-	-	-	-	-	-	-	-	-
1969	32.0	4.2	-	-	-	-	-	-	-	-	-	-	-	-	-	-
1970	34.5	7.8	-	-	-	-	-	-	-	-	-	-	-	-	-	-
1971	35.9	4.1	-	-	-	-	64.3	-	37.9	-	36.5	-	-	-	-	-
1972	37.0	3.1	-	-	-	-	66.1	2.8	37.8	-0.3	37.6	3.0	-	-	-	-
1973	39.6	7.0	-	-	-	-	68.8	4.1	39.6	4.8	39.0	3.7	-	-	-	-
1974	43.9	10.9	-	-	-	-	74.3	8.0	44.0	11.1	42.6	9.2	-	-	-	-
1975	48.4	10.3	-	-	-	-	78.6	5.8	48.3	9.8	47.4	11.3	-	-	-	-
1976	51.1	5.6	63.8	-	44.4	-	83.1	5.7	52.4	8.5	51.0	7.6	57.8	-	52.2	-
1977	55.4	8.4	68.9	8.0	48.6	9.5	88.0	5.9	56.3	7.4	55.8	9.4	61.5	6.4	56.6	8.4
1978	60.6	9.4	74.9	8.7	54.6	12.3	90.2	2.5	59.8	6.2	60.7	8.8	66.1	7.5	60.8	7.4
1979	70.0	15.5	82.8	10.5	65.6	20.1	92.1	2.1	70.3	17.6	66.2	9.1	72.2	9.2	64.8	6.6
1980	78.4	12.0	86.1	4.0	74.7	13.9	95.6	3.8	82.4	17.2	73.7	11.3	79.7	10.4	72.2	11.4
1981	87.2	11.2	93.2	8.2	84.7	13.4	96.4	0.8	91.7	11.3	81.0	9.9	85.9	7.8	80.9	12.0
1982	95.1	9.1	96.1	3.1	94.8	11.9	101.2	5.0	96.3	5.0	91.1	12.5	94.2	9.7	89.4	10.5
1983	100.5	5.7	99.6	3.6	100.9	6.4	98.8	-2.4	100.1	3.9	100.9	10.8	101.8	8.1	101.5	13.5
1984	104.3	3.8	104.3	4.7	104.1	3.2	100.0	1.2	103.6	3.5	108.0	7.0	104.1	2.3	109.1	7.5
1985	107.1	2.7	106.1	1.7	106.8	2.6	102.6	2.6	105.9	2.2	115.1	6.6	104.4	0.3	115.5	5.9
1986	107.9	0.7	107.2	1.0	108.2	1.3	102.8	0.2	100.9	-4.7	124.0	7.7	106.7	2.2	124.1	7.4
1987	112.7	4.4	111.3	3.8	114.0	5.4	108.5	5.5	103.9	3.0	128.5	3.6	115.8	8.5	123.8	-0.2
1988	116.7	3.5	116.4	4.6	117.8	3.3	105.8	-2.5	107.3	3.3	134.9	5.0	119.9	3.5	133.1	7.5
1989	122.7	5.1	124.0	6.5	122.7	4.2	111.4	5.3	113.0	5.3	143.5	6.4	127.0	5.9	141.0	5.9
1990	129.0	5.1	130.6	5.3	127.7	4.1	117.8	5.7	119.4	5.7	156.6	9.1	133.6	5.2	149.6	6.1
1991	134.2	4.0	135.4	3.7	132.5	3.8	121.9	3.5	123.1	3.1	171.7	9.6	138.6	3.7	160.1	7.0
1992	136.8	1.9	136.1	0.5	135.8	2.5	122.2	0.2	124.1	0.8	178.6	4.0	139.6	0.7	170.2	6.3
1993	140.3	2.6	139.7	2.6	139.0	2.4	125.1	2.4	125.0	0.7	187.2	4.8	143.2	2.6	180.3	5.9
1994	144.4	2.9	144.4	3.4	142.4	2.4	128.8	3.0	128.6	2.9	195.8	4.6	149.4	4.3	184.3	2.2
1995	-	-	-	-	-	-	-	-	-	-	-	-	-	-	-	-

Source: U.S. Department of Labor, Bureau of Labor Statistics, Division of Consumer Prices and Price Indexes. - indicates no data collected for period.

Denver-Boulder, CO
Consumer Price Index - Urban Wage Earners
Base 1982-1984 = 100
Annual Averages

For 1964-1995. Columns headed % show percentile change in the index from the previous period for which an index is available.

Year	All Items		Food & Beverage		Housing		Apparel & Upkeep		Trans-portation		Medical Care		Entertain-ment		Other Goods & Services	
	Index	%	Index	%	Index	%	Index	%	Index	%	Index	%	Index	%	Index	%
1964	28.4	-	-	-	-	-	-	-	-	-	-	-	-	-	-	-
1965	28.8	1.4	-	-	-	-	-	-	-	-	-	-	-	-	-	-
1966	29.7	3.1	-	-	-	-	-	-	-	-	-	-	-	-	-	-
1967	30.0	1.0	-	-	-	-	-	-	-	-	-	-	-	-	-	-
1968	30.8	2.7	-	-	-	-	-	-	-	-	-	-	-	-	-	-
1969	32.1	4.2	-	-	-	-	-	-	-	-	-	-	-	-	-	-
1970	34.5	7.5	-	-	-	-	-	-	-	-	-	-	-	-	-	-
1971	35.9	4.1	-	-	-	-	56.2	-	37.6	-	36.9	-	-	-	-	-
1972	37.1	3.3	-	-	-	-	57.9	3.0	37.5	-0.3	38.0	3.0	-	-	-	-
1973	39.6	6.7	-	-	-	-	60.2	4.0	39.3	4.8	39.4	3.7	-	-	-	-
1974	44.0	11.1	-	-	-	-	65.0	8.0	43.6	10.9	43.1	9.4	-	-	-	-
1975	48.5	10.2	-	-	-	-	68.8	5.8	48.0	10.1	47.8	10.9	-	-	-	-
1976	51.2	5.6	61.7	-	45.2	-	72.7	5.7	51.9	8.1	51.6	7.9	-	-	-	-
1977	55.5	8.4	66.6	7.9	49.5	9.5	77.0	5.9	55.9	7.7	56.4	9.3	60.7	-	52.3	-
1978	61.0	9.9	72.9	9.5	55.7	12.5	81.7	6.1	59.1	5.7	61.9	9.8	64.6	6.4	56.8	8.6
1979	70.9	16.2	80.3	10.2	67.5	21.2	88.3	8.1	69.8	18.1	66.4	7.3	68.4	5.9	60.7	6.9
1980	79.9	12.7	85.1	6.0	77.2	14.4	94.2	6.7	82.4	18.1	73.5	10.7	73.2	7.0	65.6	8.1
1981	88.9	11.3	92.9	9.2	87.5	13.3	95.4	1.3	91.8	11.4	81.6	11.0	81.6	11.5	72.1	9.9
1982	97.1	9.2	96.2	3.6	98.2	12.2	100.4	5.2	96.8	5.4	90.9	11.4	87.3	7.0	80.3	11.4
1983	99.8	2.8	99.6	3.5	99.5	1.3	99.0	-1.4	100.0	3.3	101.1	11.2	94.0	7.7	88.9	10.7
1984	103.2	3.4	104.2	4.6	102.3	2.8	100.6	1.6	103.3	3.3	108.0	6.8	102.0	8.5	101.8	14.5
1985	105.9	2.6	106.1	1.8	105.4	3.0	102.4	1.8	105.9	2.5	115.1	6.6	104.0	2.0	109.3	7.4
1986	106.3	0.4	106.9	0.8	106.6	1.1	101.3	-1.1	100.6	-5.0	124.1	7.8	103.1	-0.9	115.4	5.6
1987	108.0	1.6	110.9	3.7	105.7	-0.8	109.2	7.8	102.1	1.5	127.9	3.1	104.4	1.3	124.1	7.5
1988	111.8	3.5	115.9	4.5	109.3	3.4	106.2	-2.7	105.4	3.2	134.1	4.8	116.0	11.1	124.7	0.5
1989	117.3	4.9	123.5	6.6	113.5	3.8	110.7	4.2	110.7	5.0	142.1	6.0	120.6	4.0	134.8	8.1
1990	123.0	4.9	130.2	5.4	117.9	3.9	117.0	5.7	116.6	5.3	154.6	8.8	126.3	4.7	143.4	6.4
1991	127.8	3.9	134.9	3.6	122.2	3.6	121.3	3.7	120.0	2.9	168.7	9.1	130.6	3.4	150.7	5.1
1992	130.3	2.0	135.7	0.6	125.4	2.6	121.3	0.9	120.8	0.7	175.6	4.1	134.5	3.0	162.2	7.6
1993	133.3	2.3	139.3	2.7	128.2	2.2	122.4	1.5	121.7	0.7	184.0	4.8	136.2	1.3	173.3	6.8
1994	137.0	2.8	143.9	3.3	131.1	2.3	124.2	2.7	125.3	3.0	192.3	4.5	139.5	2.4	183.9	6.1
1995	-	-	-	-	-	-	127.5	-	-	-	-	-	144.9	3.9	186.3	1.3

Source: U.S. Department of Labor, Bureau of Labor Statistics, Division of Consumer Prices and Price Indexes. - indicates no data collected for period.

443

Denver-Boulder, CO
Consumer Price Index - All Urban Consumers
Base 1982-1984 = 100
All Items

For 1964-1995. Columns headed % show percentile change in the index from the previous period for which an index is available.

Year	Jan		Feb		Mar		Apr		May		Jun		Jul		Aug		Sep		Oct		Nov		Dec	
	Index	%	Index	%	Index	%	Index	%	Index	%	Index	%	Index	%	Index	%	Index	%	Index	%	Index	%	Index	%
1964	28.2	-	-	-	-	-	28.0	-0.7	-	-	-	-	28.5	1.8	-	-	-	-	28.5	0.0	-	-	-	-
1965	28.5	0.0	-	-	-	-	28.6	0.4	-	-	-	-	28.9	1.0	-	-	-	-	28.9	0.0	-	-	-	-
1966	29.2	1.0	-	-	-	-	29.6	1.4	-	-	-	-	29.7	0.3	-	-	-	-	29.9	0.7	-	-	-	-
1967	29.7	-0.7	-	-	-	-	29.7	0.0	-	-	-	-	30.1	1.3	-	-	-	-	30.2	0.3	-	-	-	-
1968	30.4	0.7	-	-	-	-	30.7	1.0	-	-	-	-	30.7	0.0	-	-	-	-	30.9	0.7	-	-	-	-
1969	31.1	0.6	-	-	-	-	31.6	1.6	-	-	-	-	32.0	1.3	-	-	-	-	32.7	2.2	-	-	-	-
1970	33.0	0.9	-	-	-	-	33.9	2.7	-	-	-	-	34.9	2.9	-	-	-	-	35.2	0.9	-	-	-	-
1971	35.3	0.3	-	-	-	-	35.5	0.6	-	-	-	-	36.0	1.4	-	-	-	-	36.3	0.8	-	-	-	-
1972	36.3	0.0	-	-	-	-	36.9	1.7	-	-	-	-	37.0	0.3	-	-	-	-	37.4	1.1	-	-	-	-
1973	37.8	1.1	-	-	-	-	39.0	3.2	-	-	-	-	39.6	1.5	-	-	-	-	40.6	2.5	-	-	-	-
1974	41.5	2.2	-	-	-	-	42.7	2.9	-	-	-	-	44.1	3.3	-	-	-	-	45.6	3.4	-	-	-	-
1975	46.9	2.9	-	-	-	-	47.6	1.5	-	-	-	-	48.7	2.3	-	-	-	-	49.3	1.2	-	-	-	-
1976	49.7	0.8	-	-	-	-	50.4	1.4	-	-	-	-	51.4	2.0	-	-	-	-	51.9	1.0	-	-	-	-
1977	52.7	1.5	-	-	-	-	54.8	4.0	-	-	-	-	55.8	1.8	-	-	-	-	56.6	1.4	-	-	-	-
1978	57.7	1.9	-	-	58.5	1.4	-	-	59.5	1.7	-	-	60.7	2.0	-	-	62.1	2.3	-	-	63.4	2.1	-	-
1979	64.8	2.2	-	-	66.9	3.2	-	-	69.3	3.6	-	-	70.9	2.3	-	-	72.2	1.8	-	-	73.7	2.1	-	-
1980	74.2	0.7	-	-	76.5	3.1	-	-	77.4	1.2	-	-	78.5	1.4	-	-	80.2	2.2	-	-	81.5	1.6	-	-
1981	83.2	2.1	-	-	84.4	1.4	-	-	86.4	2.4	-	-	88.2	2.1	-	-	89.6	1.6	-	-	89.3	-0.3	-	-
1982	91.6	2.6	-	-	92.7	1.2	-	-	94.0	1.4	-	-	95.9	2.0	-	-	97.3	1.5	-	-	97.8	0.5	-	-
1983	98.2	0.4	-	-	98.8	0.6	-	-	100.4	1.6	-	-	100.7	0.3	-	-	101.8	1.1	-	-	101.9	0.1	-	-
1984	103.0	1.1	-	-	103.5	0.5	-	-	103.9	0.4	-	-	104.9	1.0	-	-	105.4	0.5	-	-	104.8	-0.6	-	-
1985	105.1	0.3	-	-	106.5	1.3	-	-	106.8	0.3	-	-	108.0	1.1	-	-	107.4	-0.6	-	-	107.8	0.4	-	-
1986	109.3	1.4	-	-	106.7	-2.4	-	-	106.8	0.1	-	-	107.5	0.7	-	-	108.8	1.2	-	-	108.3	-0.5	108.4	0.1
1987	-	-	-	-	-	-	-	-	-	-	111.2	2.6	-	-	-	-	-	-	-	-	-	-	114.1	2.6
1988	-	-	-	-	-	-	-	-	-	-	115.5	1.2	-	-	-	-	-	-	-	-	-	-	117.8	2.0
1989	-	-	-	-	-	-	-	-	-	-	121.5	3.1	-	-	-	-	-	-	-	-	-	-	123.9	2.0
1990	-	-	-	-	-	-	-	-	-	-	127.1	2.6	-	-	-	-	-	-	-	-	-	-	130.8	2.9
1991	-	-	-	-	-	-	-	-	-	-	133.3	1.9	-	-	-	-	-	-	-	-	-	-	135.2	1.4
1992	-	-	-	-	-	-	-	-	-	-	136.3	0.8	-	-	-	-	-	-	-	-	-	-	137.4	0.8
1993	-	-	-	-	-	-	-	-	-	-	138.9	1.1	-	-	-	-	-	-	-	-	-	-	141.7	2.0
1994	-	-	-	-	-	-	-	-	-	-	143.2	1.1	-	-	-	-	-	-	-	-	-	-	145.6	1.7
1995	-	-	-	-	-	-	-	-	-	-	147.2	1.1	-	-	-	-	-	-	-	-	-	-	-	-

Source: U.S. Department of Labor, Bureau of Labor Statistics, Division of Consumer Prices and Price Indexes. - indicates no data collected for period.

Denver-Boulder, CO
Consumer Price Index - Urban Wage Earners
Base 1982-1984 = 100
All Items

For 1964-1995. Columns headed % show percentile change in the index from the previous period for which an index is available.

Year	Jan Index	%	Feb Index	%	Mar Index	%	Apr Index	%	May Index	%	Jun Index	%	Jul Index	%	Aug Index	%	Sep Index	%	Oct Index	%	Nov Index	%	Dec Index	%
1964	28.2	-	-	-	-	-	28.1	-0.4	-	-	-	-	28.5	1.4	-	-	-	-	28.5	0.0	-	-	-	-
1965	28.6	0.4	-	-	-	-	28.6	0.0	-	-	-	-	29.0	1.4	-	-	-	-	29.0	0.0	-	-	-	-
1966	29.2	0.7	-	-	-	-	29.7	1.7	-	-	-	-	29.8	0.3	-	-	-	-	30.0	0.7	-	-	-	-
1967	29.8	-0.7	-	-	-	-	29.8	0.0	-	-	-	-	30.1	1.0	-	-	-	-	30.3	0.7	-	-	-	-
1968	30.5	0.7	-	-	-	-	30.7	0.7	-	-	-	-	30.7	0.0	-	-	-	-	31.0	1.0	-	-	-	-
1969	31.1	0.3	-	-	-	-	31.7	1.9	-	-	-	-	32.1	1.3	-	-	-	-	32.8	2.2	-	-	-	-
1970	33.1	0.9	-	-	-	-	34.0	2.7	-	-	-	-	35.0	2.9	-	-	-	-	35.3	0.9	-	-	-	-
1971	35.4	0.3	-	-	-	-	35.6	0.6	-	-	-	-	36.1	1.4	-	-	-	-	36.4	0.8	-	-	-	-
1972	36.4	0.0	-	-	-	-	36.9	1.4	-	-	-	-	37.0	0.3	-	-	-	-	37.5	1.4	-	-	-	-
1973	37.8	0.8	-	-	-	-	39.1	3.4	-	-	-	-	39.7	1.5	-	-	-	-	40.7	2.5	-	-	-	-
1974	41.6	2.2	-	-	-	-	42.8	2.9	-	-	-	-	44.2	3.3	-	-	-	-	45.6	3.2	-	-	-	-
1975	47.0	3.1	-	-	-	-	47.7	1.5	-	-	-	-	48.8	2.3	-	-	-	-	49.4	1.2	-	-	-	-
1976	49.8	0.8	-	-	-	-	50.4	1.2	-	-	-	-	51.5	2.2	-	-	-	-	52.0	1.0	-	-	-	-
1977	52.8	1.5	-	-	-	-	54.9	4.0	-	-	-	-	55.9	1.8	-	-	-	-	56.7	1.4	-	-	-	-
1978	57.8	1.9	-	-	58.8	1.7	-	-	59.9	1.9	-	-	61.0	1.8	-	-	62.5	2.5	-	-	64.0	2.4	-	-
1979	65.5	2.3	-	-	67.6	3.2	-	-	70.1	3.7	-	-	71.9	2.6	-	-	73.2	1.8	-	-	74.7	2.0	-	-
1980	75.4	0.9	-	-	77.9	3.3	-	-	78.8	1.2	-	-	79.9	1.4	-	-	81.6	2.1	-	-	83.1	1.8	-	-
1981	84.8	2.0	-	-	85.9	1.3	-	-	88.1	2.6	-	-	90.1	2.3	-	-	91.4	1.4	-	-	91.0	-0.4	-	-
1982	93.3	2.5	-	-	94.6	1.4	-	-	96.0	1.5	-	-	98.0	2.1	-	-	99.5	1.5	-	-	99.9	0.4	-	-
1983	97.3	-2.6	-	-	98.2	0.9	-	-	99.7	1.5	-	-	99.7	0.0	-	-	101.3	1.6	-	-	101.7	0.4	-	-
1984	101.0	-0.7	-	-	102.7	1.7	-	-	102.4	-0.3	-	-	104.3	1.9	-	-	104.0	-0.3	-	-	103.7	-0.3	-	-
1985	104.0	0.3	-	-	105.4	1.3	-	-	105.7	0.3	-	-	106.9	1.1	-	-	106.1	-0.7	-	-	106.4	0.3	-	-
1986	107.9	1.4	-	-	105.2	-2.5	-	-	105.2	0.0	-	-	105.9	0.7	-	-	107.3	1.3	-	-	106.7	-0.6	106.7	0.0
1987	-	-	-	-	-	-	-	-	-	-	106.6	-0.1	-	-	-	-	-	-	-	-	-	-	109.4	2.6
1988	-	-	-	-	-	-	-	-	-	-	110.7	1.2	-	-	-	-	-	-	-	-	-	-	112.9	2.0
1989	-	-	-	-	-	-	-	-	-	-	116.3	3.0	-	-	-	-	-	-	-	-	-	-	118.4	1.8
1990	-	-	-	-	-	-	-	-	-	-	121.3	2.4	-	-	-	-	-	-	-	-	-	-	124.8	2.9
1991	-	-	-	-	-	-	-	-	-	-	126.9	1.7	-	-	-	-	-	-	-	-	-	-	128.7	1.4
1992	-	-	-	-	-	-	-	-	-	-	129.7	0.8	-	-	-	-	-	-	-	-	-	-	130.9	0.9
1993	-	-	-	-	-	-	-	-	-	-	132.0	0.8	-	-	-	-	-	-	-	-	-	-	134.6	2.0
1994	-	-	-	-	-	-	-	-	-	-	135.7	0.8	-	-	-	-	-	-	-	-	-	-	138.2	1.8
1995	-	-	-	-	-	-	-	-	-	-	139.6	1.0	-	-	-	-	-	-	-	-	-	-	-	-

Source: U.S. Department of Labor, Bureau of Labor Statistics, Division of Consumer Prices and Price Indexes. - indicates no data collected for period.

Denver-Boulder, CO
Consumer Price Index - All Urban Consumers
Base 1982-1984 = 100
Food and Beverages

For 1976-1995. Columns headed % show percentile change in the index from the previous period for which an index is available.

Year	Jan Index	%	Feb Index	%	Mar Index	%	Apr Index	%	May Index	%	Jun Index	%	Jul Index	%	Aug Index	%	Sep Index	%	Oct Index	%	Nov Index	%	Dec Index	%
1976	63.3	-	-	-	-	-	62.7	-0.9	-	-	-	-	64.1	2.2	-	-	-	-	64.3	0.3	-	-	-	-
1977	65.7	2.2	-	-	-	-	69.2	5.3	-	-	-	-	70.1	1.3	-	-	-	-	68.8	-1.9	-	-	-	-
1978	70.8	2.9	-	-	72.4	2.3	-	-	74.7	3.2	-	-	76.1	1.9	-	-	76.2	0.1	-	-	77.2	1.3	-	-
1979	80.2	3.9	-	-	82.4	2.7	-	-	83.4	1.2	-	-	84.1	0.8	-	-	83.0	-1.3	-	-	83.6	0.7	-	-
1980	81.9	-2.0	-	-	82.6	0.9	-	-	84.3	2.1	-	-	86.1	2.1	-	-	89.3	3.7	-	-	90.1	0.9	-	-
1981	90.8	0.8	-	-	92.0	1.3	-	-	92.9	1.0	-	-	94.2	1.4	-	-	94.6	0.4	-	-	93.9	-0.7	-	-
1982	94.9	1.1	-	-	95.6	0.7	-	-	95.9	0.3	-	-	96.5	0.6	-	-	96.5	0.0	-	-	96.7	0.2	-	-
1983	97.1	0.4	-	-	98.2	1.1	-	-	100.2	2.0	-	-	99.8	-0.4	-	-	100.2	0.4	-	-	100.7	0.5	-	-
1984	102.7	2.0	-	-	104.3	1.6	-	-	104.0	-0.3	-	-	104.8	0.8	-	-	104.9	0.1	-	-	104.5	-0.4	-	-
1985	104.9	0.4	-	-	107.4	2.4	-	-	105.9	-1.4	-	-	106.9	0.9	-	-	105.5	-1.3	-	-	105.5	0.0	-	-
1986	107.8	2.2	-	-	107.3	-0.5	-	-	105.5	-1.7	-	-	106.0	0.5	-	-	108.5	2.4	-	-	108.1	-0.4	108.1	0.0
1987	-	-	-	-	-	-	-	-	-	-	110.7	2.4	-	-	-	-	-	-	-	-	-	-	111.9	1.1
1988	-	-	-	-	-	-	-	-	-	-	114.4	2.2	-	-	-	-	-	-	-	-	-	-	118.4	3.5
1989	-	-	-	-	-	-	-	-	-	-	122.4	3.4	-	-	-	-	-	-	-	-	-	-	125.6	2.6
1990	-	-	-	-	-	-	-	-	-	-	129.4	3.0	-	-	-	-	-	-	-	-	-	-	131.7	1.8
1991	-	-	-	-	-	-	-	-	-	-	135.6	3.0	-	-	-	-	-	-	-	-	-	-	135.1	-0.4
1992	-	-	-	-	-	-	-	-	-	-	136.3	0.9	-	-	-	-	-	-	-	-	-	-	136.0	-0.2
1993	-	-	-	-	-	-	-	-	-	-	138.3	1.7	-	-	-	-	-	-	-	-	-	-	141.2	2.1
1994	-	-	-	-	-	-	-	-	-	-	142.9	1.2	-	-	-	-	-	-	-	-	-	-	145.9	2.1
1995	-	-	-	-	-	-	-	-	-	-	148.1	1.5	-	-	-	-	-	-	-	-	-	-	-	-

Source: U.S. Department of Labor, Bureau of Labor Statistics, Division of Consumer Prices and Price Indexes. - indicates no data collected for period.

Denver-Boulder, CO
Consumer Price Index - Urban Wage Earners
Base 1982-1984 = 100
Food and Beverages

For 1976-1995. Columns headed % show percentile change in the index from the previous period for which an index is available.

Year	Jan Index	%	Feb Index	%	Mar Index	%	Apr Index	%	May Index	%	Jun Index	%	Jul Index	%	Aug Index	%	Sep Index	%	Oct Index	%	Nov Index	%	Dec Index	%
1976	61.2	-	-	-	-	-	60.7	-0.8	-	-	-	-	62.0	2.1	-	-	-	-	62.2	0.3	-	-	-	-
1977	63.5	2.1	-	-	-	-	67.0	5.5	-	-	-	-	67.8	1.2	-	-	-	-	66.6	-1.8	-	-	-	-
1978	68.4	2.7	-	-	70.7	3.4	-	-	72.9	3.1	-	-	73.7	1.1	-	-	74.1	0.5	-	-	75.3	1.6	-	-
1979	78.0	3.6	-	-	79.5	1.9	-	-	80.3	1.0	-	-	81.4	1.4	-	-	80.3	-1.4	-	-	81.6	1.6	-	-
1980	80.8	-1.0	-	-	81.8	1.2	-	-	83.5	2.1	-	-	85.4	2.3	-	-	88.1	3.2	-	-	88.7	0.7	-	-
1981	90.1	1.6	-	-	91.5	1.6	-	-	92.1	0.7	-	-	93.9	2.0	-	-	94.1	0.2	-	-	94.2	0.1	-	-
1982	95.0	0.8	-	-	95.6	0.6	-	-	96.0	0.4	-	-	96.7	0.7	-	-	96.7	0.0	-	-	96.8	0.1	-	-
1983	97.2	0.4	-	-	98.3	1.1	-	-	100.1	1.8	-	-	99.8	-0.3	-	-	100.1	0.3	-	-	100.7	0.6	-	-
1984	102.6	1.9	-	-	104.1	1.5	-	-	103.8	-0.3	-	-	104.7	0.9	-	-	105.0	0.3	-	-	104.6	-0.4	-	-
1985	104.9	0.3	-	-	107.4	2.4	-	-	105.8	-1.5	-	-	106.8	0.9	-	-	105.5	-1.2	-	-	105.4	-0.1	-	-
1986	107.7	2.2	-	-	106.9	-0.7	-	-	105.1	-1.7	-	-	105.6	0.5	-	-	108.2	2.5	-	-	107.9	-0.3	107.8	-0.1
1987	-	-	-	-	-	-	-	-	-	-	110.3	2.3	-	-	-	-	-	-	-	-	-	-	111.5	1.1
1988	-	-	-	-	-	-	-	-	-	-	113.9	2.2	-	-	-	-	-	-	-	-	-	-	117.9	3.5
1989	-	-	-	-	-	-	-	-	-	-	121.9	3.4	-	-	-	-	-	-	-	-	-	-	125.2	2.7
1990	-	-	-	-	-	-	-	-	-	-	129.0	3.0	-	-	-	-	-	-	-	-	-	-	131.4	1.9
1991	-	-	-	-	-	-	-	-	-	-	135.2	2.9	-	-	-	-	-	-	-	-	-	-	134.6	-0.4
1992	-	-	-	-	-	-	-	-	-	-	135.8	0.9	-	-	-	-	-	-	-	-	-	-	135.5	-0.2
1993	-	-	-	-	-	-	-	-	-	-	137.9	1.8	-	-	-	-	-	-	-	-	-	-	140.7	2.0
1994	-	-	-	-	-	-	-	-	-	-	142.4	1.2	-	-	-	-	-	-	-	-	-	-	145.3	2.0
1995	-	-	-	-	-	-	-	-	-	-	147.5	1.5	-	-	-	-	-	-	-	-	-	-	-	-

Source: U.S. Department of Labor, Bureau of Labor Statistics, Division of Consumer Prices and Price Indexes. - indicates no data collected for period.

Denver-Boulder, CO
Consumer Price Index - All Urban Consumers
Base 1982-1984 = 100
Housing

For 1976-1995. Columns headed % show percentile change in the index from the previous period for which an index is available.

Year	Jan Index	%	Feb Index	%	Mar Index	%	Apr Index	%	May Index	%	Jun Index	%	Jul Index	%	Aug Index	%	Sep Index	%	Oct Index	%	Nov Index	%	Dec Index	%
1976	43.1	-	-	-	-	-	43.8	1.6	-	-	-	-	44.8	2.3	-	-	-	-	44.9	0.2	-	-	-	-
1977	45.6	1.6	-	-	-	-	47.9	5.0	-	-	-	-	48.8	1.9	-	-	-	-	50.3	3.1	-	-	-	-
1978	51.4	2.2	-	-	52.5	2.1	-	-	53.1	1.1	-	-	54.3	2.3	-	-	56.2	3.5	-	-	58.1	3.4	-	-
1979	59.7	2.8	-	-	61.7	3.4	-	-	64.6	4.7	-	-	66.7	3.3	-	-	68.1	2.1	-	-	70.1	2.9	-	-
1980	70.4	0.4	-	-	73.0	3.7	-	-	73.6	0.8	-	-	74.8	1.6	-	-	76.3	2.0	-	-	77.9	2.1	-	-
1981	80.1	2.8	-	-	80.7	0.7	-	-	83.7	3.7	-	-	86.2	3.0	-	-	87.9	2.0	-	-	87.0	-1.0	-	-
1982	90.3	3.8	-	-	92.0	1.9	-	-	93.8	2.0	-	-	95.9	2.2	-	-	97.7	1.9	-	-	98.1	0.4	-	-
1983	99.4	1.3	-	-	100.6	1.2	-	-	101.0	0.4	-	-	100.5	-0.5	-	-	101.7	1.2	-	-	101.0	-0.7	-	-
1984	103.2	2.2	-	-	102.7	-0.5	-	-	102.9	0.2	-	-	105.5	2.5	-	-	105.5	0.0	-	-	104.3	-1.1	-	-
1985	105.9	1.5	-	-	106.1	0.2	-	-	106.1	0.0	-	-	107.9	1.7	-	-	106.6	-1.2	-	-	107.4	0.8	-	-
1986	110.6	3.0	-	-	107.3	-3.0	-	-	107.7	0.4	-	-	108.1	0.4	-	-	108.2	0.1	-	-	107.6	-0.6	108.2	0.6
1987	-	-	-	-	-	-	-	-	-	-	112.7	4.2	-	-	-	-	-	-	-	-	-	-	115.2	2.2
1988	-	-	-	-	-	-	-	-	-	-	116.6	1.2	-	-	-	-	-	-	-	-	-	-	119.1	2.1
1989	-	-	-	-	-	-	-	-	-	-	121.5	2.0	-	-	-	-	-	-	-	-	-	-	123.9	2.0
1990	-	-	-	-	-	-	-	-	-	-	125.8	1.5	-	-	-	-	-	-	-	-	-	-	129.6	3.0
1991	-	-	-	-	-	-	-	-	-	-	131.3	1.3	-	-	-	-	-	-	-	-	-	-	133.6	1.8
1992	-	-	-	-	-	-	-	-	-	-	134.9	1.0	-	-	-	-	-	-	-	-	-	-	136.6	1.3
1993	-	-	-	-	-	-	-	-	-	-	137.8	0.9	-	-	-	-	-	-	-	-	-	-	140.3	1.8
1994	-	-	-	-	-	-	-	-	-	-	141.9	1.1	-	-	-	-	-	-	-	-	-	-	143.0	0.8
1995	-	-	-	-	-	-	-	-	-	-	143.8	0.6	-	-	-	-	-	-	-	-	-	-	-	-

Source: U.S. Department of Labor, Bureau of Labor Statistics, Division of Consumer Prices and Price Indexes. - indicates no data collected for period.

Denver-Boulder, CO
Consumer Price Index - Urban Wage Earners
Base 1982-1984 = 100
Housing

For 1976-1995. Columns headed % show percentile change in the index from the previous period for which an index is available.

Year	Jan Index	%	Feb Index	%	Mar Index	%	Apr Index	%	May Index	%	Jun Index	%	Jul Index	%	Aug Index	%	Sep Index	%	Oct Index	%	Nov Index	%	Dec Index	%
1976	43.8	-	-	-	-	-	44.6	1.8	-	-	-	-	45.6	2.2	-	-	-	-	45.8	0.4	-	-	-	-
1977	46.4	1.3	-	-	-	-	48.8	5.2	-	-	-	-	49.7	1.8	-	-	-	-	51.2	3.0	-	-	-	-
1978	52.4	2.3	-	-	53.5	2.1	-	-	54.2	1.3	-	-	55.4	2.2	-	-	57.5	3.8	-	-	59.4	3.3	-	-
1979	61.2	3.0	-	-	63.4	3.6	-	-	66.5	4.9	-	-	68.7	3.3	-	-	70.1	2.0	-	-	72.2	3.0	-	-
1980	72.6	0.6	-	-	75.4	3.9	-	-	76.0	0.8	-	-	77.1	1.4	-	-	78.8	2.2	-	-	80.6	2.3	-	-
1981	82.8	2.7	-	-	83.2	0.5	-	-	86.6	4.1	-	-	89.1	2.9	-	-	90.8	1.9	-	-	89.8	-1.1	-	-
1982	93.3	3.9	-	-	95.3	2.1	-	-	97.2	2.0	-	-	99.5	2.4	-	-	101.4	1.9	-	-	101.6	0.2	-	-
1983	97.3	-4.2	-	-	98.6	1.3	-	-	99.6	1.0	-	-	98.8	-0.8	-	-	101.1	2.3	-	-	101.1	0.0	-	-
1984	99.7	-1.4	-	-	101.8	2.1	-	-	100.9	-0.9	-	-	104.3	3.4	-	-	103.1	-1.2	-	-	102.8	-0.3	-	-
1985	104.5	1.7	-	-	104.6	0.1	-	-	104.7	0.1	-	-	106.3	1.5	-	-	105.1	-1.1	-	-	105.9	0.8	-	-
1986	109.0	2.9	-	-	105.6	-3.1	-	-	106.1	0.5	-	-	106.6	0.5	-	-	106.7	0.1	-	-	106.1	-0.6	106.7	0.6
1987	-	-	-	-	-	-	-	-	-	-	104.6	-2.0	-	-	-	-	-	-	-	-	-	-	106.9	2.2
1988	-	-	-	-	-	-	-	-	-	-	108.2	1.2	-	-	-	-	-	-	-	-	-	-	110.4	2.0
1989	-	-	-	-	-	-	-	-	-	-	112.4	1.8	-	-	-	-	-	-	-	-	-	-	114.6	2.0
1990	-	-	-	-	-	-	-	-	-	-	116.2	1.4	-	-	-	-	-	-	-	-	-	-	119.6	2.9
1991	-	-	-	-	-	-	-	-	-	-	121.0	1.2	-	-	-	-	-	-	-	-	-	-	123.4	2.0
1992	-	-	-	-	-	-	-	-	-	-	124.6	1.0	-	-	-	-	-	-	-	-	-	-	126.2	1.3
1993	-	-	-	-	-	-	-	-	-	-	127.1	0.7	-	-	-	-	-	-	-	-	-	-	129.4	1.8
1994	-	-	-	-	-	-	-	-	-	-	130.4	0.8	-	-	-	-	-	-	-	-	-	-	131.7	1.0
1995	-	-	-	-	-	-	-	-	-	-	132.2	0.4	-	-	-	-	-	-	-	-	-	-	-	-

Source: U.S. Department of Labor, Bureau of Labor Statistics, Division of Consumer Prices and Price Indexes. - indicates no data collected for period.

Denver-Boulder, CO
Consumer Price Index - All Urban Consumers
Base 1982-1984 = 100
Apparel and Upkeep

For 1971-1995. Columns headed % show percentile change in the index from the previous period for which an index is available.

Year	Jan Index	%	Feb Index	%	Mar Index	%	Apr Index	%	May Index	%	Jun Index	%	Jul Index	%	Aug Index	%	Sep Index	%	Oct Index	%	Nov Index	%	Dec Index	%
1971	62.3	-	-	-	-	-	63.5	1.9	-	-	-	-	63.3	-0.3	-	-	-	-	66.9	5.7	-	-	-	-
1972	65.3	-2.4	-	-	-	-	66.2	1.4	-	-	-	-	65.4	-1.2	-	-	-	-	67.6	3.4	-	-	-	-
1973	65.6	-3.0	-	-	-	-	68.4	4.3	-	-	-	-	68.2	-0.3	-	-	-	-	71.2	4.4	-	-	-	-
1974	71.2	0.0	-	-	-	-	73.1	2.7	-	-	-	-	74.3	1.6	-	-	-	-	77.3	4.0	-	-	-	-
1975	75.8	-1.9	-	-	-	-	77.2	1.8	-	-	-	-	78.0	1.0	-	-	-	-	82.1	5.3	-	-	-	-
1976	79.9	-2.7	-	-	-	-	82.5	3.3	-	-	-	-	82.5	0.0	-	-	-	-	86.0	4.2	-	-	-	-
1977	83.8	-2.6	-	-	-	-	87.6	4.5	-	-	-	-	87.8	0.2	-	-	-	-	91.1	3.8	-	-	-	-
1978	89.0	-2.3	-	-	86.7	-2.6	-	-	90.3	4.2	-	-	90.9	0.7	-	-	93.4	2.8	-	-	91.4	-2.1	-	-
1979	86.7	-5.1	-	-	92.2	6.3	-	-	92.3	0.1	-	-	90.2	-2.3	-	-	94.7	5.0	-	-	95.7	1.1	-	-
1980	91.3	-4.6	-	-	96.3	5.5	-	-	95.1	-1.2	-	-	94.6	-0.5	-	-	97.7	3.3	-	-	98.0	0.3	-	-
1981	94.4	-3.7	-	-	97.2	3.0	-	-	96.0	-1.2	-	-	95.0	-1.0	-	-	98.1	3.3	-	-	96.9	-1.2	-	-
1982	97.2	0.3	-	-	102.4	5.3	-	-	102.5	0.1	-	-	99.1	-3.3	-	-	102.8	3.7	-	-	103.1	0.3	-	-
1983	97.8	-5.1	-	-	100.6	2.9	-	-	98.0	-2.6	-	-	96.6	-1.4	-	-	99.6	3.1	-	-	100.6	1.0	-	-
1984	97.4	-3.2	-	-	100.3	3.0	-	-	100.4	0.1	-	-	96.6	-3.8	-	-	102.2	5.8	-	-	102.5	0.3	-	-
1985	99.1	-3.3	-	-	103.8	4.7	-	-	104.5	0.7	-	-	102.1	-2.3	-	-	103.6	1.5	-	-	105.5	-1.5	103.1	-2.3
1986	98.7	-3.7	-	-	101.6	2.9	-	-	102.5	0.9	-	-	100.8	-1.7	-	-	107.1	6.3	-	-	-	-	114.0	10.7
1987	-	-	-	-	-	-	-	-	-	-	103.0	-0.1	-	-	-	-	-	-	-	-	-	-	101.7	-7.5
1988	-	-	-	-	-	-	-	-	-	-	109.9	-3.6	-	-	-	-	-	-	-	-	-	-	110.5	-1.7
1989	-	-	-	-	-	-	-	-	-	-	112.4	10.5	-	-	-	-	-	-	-	-	-	-	115.1	-4.6
1990	-	-	-	-	-	-	-	-	-	-	120.6	9.1	-	-	-	-	-	-	-	-	-	-	123.4	2.5
1991	-	-	-	-	-	-	-	-	-	-	120.4	4.6	-	-	-	-	-	-	-	-	-	-	120.8	-2.3
1992	-	-	-	-	-	-	-	-	-	-	123.6	0.2	-	-	-	-	-	-	-	-	-	-	128.3	5.3
1993	-	-	-	-	-	-	-	-	-	-	121.8	0.8	-	-	-	-	-	-	-	-	-	-	130.8	3.2
1994	-	-	-	-	-	-	-	-	-	-	126.8	-1.2	-	-	-	-	-	-	-	-	-	-	-	-
1995	-	-	-	-	-	-	-	-	-	-	130.0	-0.6	-	-	-	-	-	-	-	-	-	-	-	-

Source: U.S. Department of Labor, Bureau of Labor Statistics, Division of Consumer Prices and Price Indexes. - indicates no data collected for period.

Denver-Boulder, CO
Consumer Price Index - Urban Wage Earners
Base 1982-1984 = 100
Apparel and Upkeep

For 1971-1995. Columns headed % show percentile change in the index from the previous period for which an index is available.

Year	Jan Index	%	Feb Index	%	Mar Index	%	Apr Index	%	May Index	%	Jun Index	%	Jul Index	%	Aug Index	%	Sep Index	%	Oct Index	%	Nov Index	%	Dec Index	%
1971	54.5	-	-	-	-	-	55.5	1.8	-	-	-	-	55.4	-0.2	-	-	-	-	58.6	5.8	-	-	-	-
1972	57.1	-2.6	-	-	-	-	57.9	1.4	-	-	-	-	57.2	-1.2	-	-	-	-	59.2	3.5	-	-	-	-
1973	57.3	-3.2	-	-	-	-	59.8	4.4	-	-	-	-	59.6	-0.3	-	-	-	-	62.3	4.5	-	-	-	-
1974	62.3	0.0	-	-	-	-	63.9	2.6	-	-	-	-	65.0	1.7	-	-	-	-	67.6	4.0	-	-	-	-
1975	66.3	-1.9	-	-	-	-	67.6	2.0	-	-	-	-	68.3	1.0	-	-	-	-	71.8	5.1	-	-	-	-
1976	69.9	-2.6	-	-	-	-	72.2	3.3	-	-	-	-	72.2	0.0	-	-	-	-	75.2	4.2	-	-	-	-
1977	73.3	-2.5	-	-	-	-	76.7	4.6	-	-	-	-	76.8	0.1	-	-	-	-	79.7	3.8	-	-	-	-
1978	77.9	-2.3	-	-	78.1	0.3	-	-	82.0	5.0	-	-	82.1	0.1	-	-	85.7	4.4	-	-	83.6	-2.5	-	-
1979	82.2	-1.7	-	-	86.5	5.2	-	-	87.5	1.2	-	-	87.4	-0.1	-	-	92.8	6.2	-	-	91.6	-1.3	-	-
1980	90.2	-1.5	-	-	96.4	6.9	-	-	93.6	-2.9	-	-	91.9	-1.8	-	-	96.4	4.9	-	-	96.2	-0.2	-	-
1981	92.3	-4.1	-	-	94.4	2.3	-	-	93.6	-0.8	-	-	95.4	1.9	-	-	98.7	3.5	-	-	97.0	-1.7	-	-
1982	96.6	-0.4	-	-	102.2	5.8	-	-	101.2	-1.0	-	-	97.8	-3.4	-	-	102.3	4.6	-	-	102.5	0.2	-	-
1983	97.7	-4.7	-	-	100.1	2.5	-	-	97.7	-2.4	-	-	96.7	-1.0	-	-	100.0	3.4	-	-	101.6	1.6	-	-
1984	97.9	-3.6	-	-	101.3	3.5	-	-	100.8	-0.5	-	-	97.0	-3.8	-	-	102.6	5.8	-	-	103.4	0.8	-	-
1985	100.2	-3.1	-	-	103.6	3.4	-	-	104.1	0.5	-	-	102.3	-1.7	-	-	103.1	0.8	-	-	101.6	-1.5	-	-
1986	98.2	-3.3	-	-	100.4	2.2	-	-	101.0	0.6	-	-	99.1	-1.9	-	-	105.9	6.9	-	-	103.5	-2.3	100.9	-2.5
1987	-	-	-	-	-	-	-	-	-	-	103.5	2.6	-	-	-	-	-	-	-	-	-	-	114.8	10.9
1988	-	-	-	-	-	-	-	-	-	-	110.5	-3.7	-	-	-	-	-	-	-	-	-	-	101.8	-7.9
1989	-	-	-	-	-	-	-	-	-	-	111.8	9.8	-	-	-	-	-	-	-	-	-	-	109.6	-2.0
1990	-	-	-	-	-	-	-	-	-	-	119.5	9.0	-	-	-	-	-	-	-	-	-	-	114.5	-4.2
1991	-	-	-	-	-	-	-	-	-	-	119.6	4.5	-	-	-	-	-	-	-	-	-	-	123.1	2.9
1992	-	-	-	-	-	-	-	-	-	-	123.7	0.5	-	-	-	-	-	-	-	-	-	-	121.2	-2.0
1993	-	-	-	-	-	-	-	-	-	-	121.4	0.2	-	-	-	-	-	-	-	-	-	-	127.1	4.7
1994	-	-	-	-	-	-	-	-	-	-	125.7	-1.1	-	-	-	-	-	-	-	-	-	-	129.4	2.9
1995	-	-	-	-	-	-	-	-	-	-	127.9	-1.2	-	-	-	-	-	-	-	-	-	-	-	-

Source: U.S. Department of Labor, Bureau of Labor Statistics, Division of Consumer Prices and Price Indexes. - indicates no data collected for period.

Denver-Boulder, CO
Consumer Price Index - All Urban Consumers
Base 1982-1984 = 100
Transportation

For 1971-1995. Columns headed % show percentile change in the index from the previous period for which an index is available.

Year	Jan Index	%	Feb Index	%	Mar Index	%	Apr Index	%	May Index	%	Jun Index	%	Jul Index	%	Aug Index	%	Sep Index	%	Oct Index	%	Nov Index	%	Dec Index	%
1971	38.0	-	-	-	-	-	38.0	0.0	-	-	-	-	37.8	-0.5	-	-	-	-	38.1	0.8	-	-	-	-
1972	37.1	-2.6	-	-	-	-	37.6	1.3	-	-	-	-	38.0	1.1	-	-	-	-	38.4	1.1	-	-	-	-
1973	38.0	-1.0	-	-	-	-	39.5	3.9	-	-	-	-	40.4	2.3	-	-	-	-	39.5	-2.2	-	-	-	-
1974	41.3	4.6	-	-	-	-	42.7	3.4	-	-	-	-	45.0	5.4	-	-	-	-	45.4	0.9	-	-	-	-
1975	45.9	1.1	-	-	-	-	47.0	2.4	-	-	-	-	49.3	4.9	-	-	-	-	49.8	1.0	-	-	-	-
1976	49.7	-0.2	-	-	-	-	50.8	2.2	-	-	-	-	53.2	4.7	-	-	-	-	53.9	1.3	-	-	-	-
1977	55.1	2.2	-	-	-	-	55.8	1.3	-	-	-	-	56.9	2.0	-	-	-	-	56.7	-0.4	-	-	-	-
1978	57.6	1.6	-	-	57.9	0.5	-	-	58.5	1.0	-	-	60.4	3.2	-	-	61.3	1.5	-	-	61.9	1.0	-	-
1979	63.3	2.3	-	-	65.2	3.0	-	-	68.9	5.7	-	-	71.6	3.9	-	-	73.7	2.9	-	-	75.1	1.9	-	-
1980	77.6	3.3	-	-	80.5	3.7	-	-	82.1	2.0	-	-	83.0	1.1	-	-	84.0	1.2	-	-	85.0	1.2	-	-
1981	87.0	2.4	-	-	89.7	3.1	-	-	91.1	1.6	-	-	92.7	1.8	-	-	93.5	0.9	-	-	94.7	1.3	-	-
1982	94.6	-0.1	-	-	94.0	-0.6	-	-	94.0	0.0	-	-	97.6	3.8	-	-	98.2	0.6	-	-	98.8	0.6	-	-
1983	97.0	-1.8	-	-	95.1	-2.0	-	-	99.6	4.7	-	-	101.5	1.9	-	-	102.7	1.2	-	-	103.3	0.6	-	-
1984	102.0	-1.3	-	-	102.6	0.6	-	-	104.1	1.5	-	-	103.8	-0.3	-	-	104.5	0.7	-	-	104.7	0.2	-	-
1985	102.5	-2.1	-	-	104.4	1.9	-	-	106.7	2.2	-	-	107.2	0.5	-	-	106.6	-0.6	-	-	107.2	0.6	-	-
1986	106.3	-0.8	-	-	98.8	-7.1	-	-	99.5	0.7	-	-	100.1	0.6	-	-	101.6	1.5	-	-	101.0	-0.6	100.3	-0.7
1987	-	-	-	-	-	-	-	-	-	-	102.6	2.3	-	-	-	-	-	-	-	-	-	-	105.3	2.6
1988	-	-	-	-	-	-	-	-	-	-	105.8	0.5	-	-	-	-	-	-	-	-	-	-	108.9	2.9
1989	-	-	-	-	-	-	-	-	-	-	112.3	3.1	-	-	-	-	-	-	-	-	-	-	113.6	1.2
1990	-	-	-	-	-	-	-	-	-	-	115.9	2.0	-	-	-	-	-	-	-	-	-	-	123.0	6.1
1991	-	-	-	-	-	-	-	-	-	-	122.7	-0.2	-	-	-	-	-	-	-	-	-	-	123.5	0.7
1992	-	-	-	-	-	-	-	-	-	-	123.4	-0.1	-	-	-	-	-	-	-	-	-	-	124.9	1.2
1993	-	-	-	-	-	-	-	-	-	-	124.3	-0.5	-	-	-	-	-	-	-	-	-	-	125.7	1.1
1994	-	-	-	-	-	-	-	-	-	-	126.5	0.6	-	-	-	-	-	-	-	-	-	-	130.7	3.3
1995	-	-	-	-	-	-	-	-	-	-	133.2	1.9	-	-	-	-	-	-	-	-	-	-	-	-

Source: U.S. Department of Labor, Bureau of Labor Statistics, Division of Consumer Prices and Price Indexes. - indicates no data collected for period.

Denver-Boulder, CO
Consumer Price Index - Urban Wage Earners
Base 1982-1984 = 100
Transportation

For 1971-1995. Columns headed % show percentile change in the index from the previous period for which an index is available.

Year	Jan Index	%	Feb Index	%	Mar Index	%	Apr Index	%	May Index	%	Jun Index	%	Jul Index	%	Aug Index	%	Sep Index	%	Oct Index	%	Nov Index	%	Dec Index	%
1971	37.7	-	-	-	-	-	37.7	0.0	-	-	-	-	37.5	-0.5	-	-	-	-	37.8	0.8	-	-	-	-
1972	36.8	-2.6	-	-	-	-	37.3	1.4	-	-	-	-	37.7	1.1	-	-	-	-	38.1	1.1	-	-	-	-
1973	37.7	-1.0	-	-	-	-	39.2	4.0	-	-	-	-	40.1	2.3	-	-	-	-	39.2	-2.2	-	-	-	-
1974	40.9	4.3	-	-	-	-	42.3	3.4	-	-	-	-	44.6	5.4	-	-	-	-	45.0	0.9	-	-	-	-
1975	45.6	1.3	-	-	-	-	46.6	2.2	-	-	-	-	48.9	4.9	-	-	-	-	49.4	1.0	-	-	-	-
1976	49.3	-0.2	-	-	-	-	50.4	2.2	-	-	-	-	52.8	4.8	-	-	-	-	53.5	1.3	-	-	-	-
1977	54.6	2.1	-	-	-	-	55.4	1.5	-	-	-	-	56.5	2.0	-	-	-	-	56.2	-0.5	-	-	-	-
1978	57.1	1.6	-	-	57.2	0.2	-	-	58.1	1.6	-	-	59.4	2.2	-	-	60.2	1.3	-	-	61.3	1.8	-	-
1979	62.4	1.8	-	-	64.6	3.5	-	-	68.5	6.0	-	-	71.3	4.1	-	-	73.5	3.1	-	-	74.8	1.8	-	-
1980	77.4	3.5	-	-	80.3	3.7	-	-	82.2	2.4	-	-	83.1	1.1	-	-	83.8	0.8	-	-	85.1	1.6	-	-
1981	86.8	2.0	-	-	89.6	3.2	-	-	90.9	1.5	-	-	92.7	2.0	-	-	93.8	1.2	-	-	95.1	1.4	-	-
1982	95.0	-0.1	-	-	94.7	-0.3	-	-	94.3	-0.4	-	-	98.1	4.0	-	-	98.8	0.7	-	-	99.3	0.5	-	-
1983	97.1	-2.2	-	-	95.1	-2.1	-	-	99.6	4.7	-	-	101.4	1.8	-	-	102.6	1.2	-	-	103.0	0.4	-	-
1984	101.5	-1.5	-	-	102.3	0.8	-	-	103.7	1.4	-	-	103.5	-0.2	-	-	104.2	0.7	-	-	104.3	0.1	-	-
1985	102.0	-2.2	-	-	104.0	2.0	-	-	106.7	2.6	-	-	107.3	0.6	-	-	106.8	-0.5	-	-	107.3	0.5	-	-
1986	106.3	-0.9	-	-	98.6	-7.2	-	-	99.1	0.5	-	-	99.8	0.7	-	-	101.1	1.3	-	-	100.6	-0.5	99.9	-0.7
1987	-	-	-	-	-	-	-	-	-	-	100.9	1.0	-	-	-	-	-	-	-	-	-	-	103.3	2.4
1988	-	-	-	-	-	-	-	-	-	-	103.9	0.6	-	-	-	-	-	-	-	-	-	-	106.8	2.8
1989	-	-	-	-	-	-	-	-	-	-	110.2	3.2	-	-	-	-	-	-	-	-	-	-	111.3	1.0
1990	-	-	-	-	-	-	-	-	-	-	113.4	1.9	-	-	-	-	-	-	-	-	-	-	119.8	5.6
1991	-	-	-	-	-	-	-	-	-	-	119.6	-0.2	-	-	-	-	-	-	-	-	-	-	120.4	0.7
1992	-	-	-	-	-	-	-	-	-	-	120.0	-0.3	-	-	-	-	-	-	-	-	-	-	121.6	1.3
1993	-	-	-	-	-	-	-	-	-	-	120.8	-0.7	-	-	-	-	-	-	-	-	-	-	122.6	1.5
1994	-	-	-	-	-	-	-	-	-	-	123.2	0.5	-	-	-	-	-	-	-	-	-	-	127.5	3.5
1995	-	-	-	-	-	-	-	-	-	-	129.9	1.9	-	-	-	-	-	-	-	-	-	-	-	-

Source: U.S. Department of Labor, Bureau of Labor Statistics, Division of Consumer Prices and Price Indexes. - indicates no data collected for period.

Denver-Boulder, CO
Consumer Price Index - All Urban Consumers
Base 1982-1984 = 100
Medical Care

For 1971-1995. Columns headed % show percentile change in the index from the previous period for which an index is available.

Year	Jan Index	%	Feb Index	%	Mar Index	%	Apr Index	%	May Index	%	Jun Index	%	Jul Index	%	Aug Index	%	Sep Index	%	Oct Index	%	Nov Index	%	Dec Index	%
1971	35.4	-	-	-	-	-	36.1	2.0	-	-	-	-	37.1	2.8	-	-	-	-	36.9	-0.5	-	-	-	-
1972	37.2	0.8	-	-	-	-	37.3	0.3	-	-	-	-	37.5	0.5	-	-	-	-	38.0	1.3	-	-	-	-
1973	38.1	0.3	-	-	-	-	38.5	1.0	-	-	-	-	38.8	0.8	-	-	-	-	39.7	2.3	-	-	-	-
1974	40.7	2.5	-	-	-	-	41.2	1.2	-	-	-	-	43.2	4.9	-	-	-	-	43.7	1.2	-	-	-	-
1975	45.7	4.6	-	-	-	-	46.7	2.2	-	-	-	-	47.6	1.9	-	-	-	-	48.3	1.5	-	-	-	-
1976	49.1	1.7	-	-	-	-	50.3	2.4	-	-	-	-	51.1	1.6	-	-	-	-	52.2	2.2	-	-	-	-
1977	53.3	2.1	-	-	-	-	54.6	2.4	-	-	-	-	56.2	2.9	-	-	-	-	57.3	2.0	-	-	-	-
1978	58.9	2.8	-	-	59.5	1.0	-	-	60.3	1.3	-	-	60.4	0.2	-	-	61.4	1.7	-	-	62.5	1.8	-	-
1979	63.3	1.3	-	-	64.1	1.3	-	-	65.7	2.5	-	-	66.1	0.6	-	-	67.2	1.7	-	-	68.5	1.9	-	-
1980	71.6	4.5	-	-	72.3	1.0	-	-	73.0	1.0	-	-	73.0	0.0	-	-	74.3	1.8	-	-	76.0	2.3	-	-
1981	78.4	3.2	-	-	78.8	0.5	-	-	79.4	0.8	-	-	80.1	0.9	-	-	82.4	2.9	-	-	84.3	2.3	-	-
1982	87.5	3.8	-	-	88.2	0.8	-	-	88.9	0.8	-	-	91.8	3.3	-	-	93.2	1.5	-	-	94.5	1.4	-	-
1983	97.4	3.1	-	-	99.0	1.6	-	-	99.4	0.4	-	-	102.4	3.0	-	-	102.5	0.1	-	-	102.8	0.3	-	-
1984	106.4	3.5	-	-	107.2	0.8	-	-	107.4	0.2	-	-	108.0	0.6	-	-	108.2	0.2	-	-	109.4	1.1	-	-
1985	110.8	1.3	-	-	112.5	1.5	-	-	113.2	0.6	-	-	115.9	2.4	-	-	117.6	1.5	-	-	118.5	0.8	-	-
1986	119.9	1.2	-	-	121.2	1.1	-	-	123.2	1.7	-	-	125.7	2.0	-	-	126.4	0.6	-	-	125.7	-0.6	126.1	0.3
1987	-	-	-	-	-	-	-	-	-	-	127.7	1.3	-	-	-	-	-	-	-	-	-	-	129.4	1.3
1988	-	-	-	-	-	-	-	-	-	-	132.9	2.7	-	-	-	-	-	-	-	-	-	-	136.9	3.0
1989	-	-	-	-	-	-	-	-	-	-	141.3	3.2	-	-	-	-	-	-	-	-	-	-	145.7	3.1
1990	-	-	-	-	-	-	-	-	-	-	152.4	4.6	-	-	-	-	-	-	-	-	-	-	160.9	5.6
1991	-	-	-	-	-	-	-	-	-	-	169.2	5.2	-	-	-	-	-	-	-	-	-	-	174.1	2.9
1992	-	-	-	-	-	-	-	-	-	-	177.8	2.1	-	-	-	-	-	-	-	-	-	-	179.3	0.8
1993	-	-	-	-	-	-	-	-	-	-	185.7	3.6	-	-	-	-	-	-	-	-	-	-	188.7	1.6
1994	-	-	-	-	-	-	-	-	-	-	194.3	3.0	-	-	-	-	-	-	-	-	-	-	197.2	1.5
1995	-	-	-	-	-	-	-	-	-	-	202.0	2.4	-	-	-	-	-	-	-	-	-	-	-	-

Source: U.S. Department of Labor, Bureau of Labor Statistics, Division of Consumer Prices and Price Indexes. - indicates no data collected for period.

Denver-Boulder, CO
Consumer Price Index - Urban Wage Earners
Base 1982-1984 = 100
Medical Care

For 1971-1995. Columns headed % show percentile change in the index from the previous period for which an index is available.

Year	Jan Index	%	Feb Index	%	Mar Index	%	Apr Index	%	May Index	%	Jun Index	%	Jul Index	%	Aug Index	%	Sep Index	%	Oct Index	%	Nov Index	%	Dec Index	%
1971	35.8	-	-	-	-	-	36.5	2.0	-	-	-	-	37.5	2.7	-	-	-	-	37.3	-0.5	-	-	-	-
1972	37.6	0.8	-	-	-	-	37.7	0.3	-	-	-	-	37.9	0.5	-	-	-	-	38.4	1.3	-	-	-	-
1973	38.5	0.3	-	-	-	-	38.9	1.0	-	-	-	-	39.2	0.8	-	-	-	-	40.1	2.3	-	-	-	-
1974	41.1	2.5	-	-	-	-	41.7	1.5	-	-	-	-	43.7	4.8	-	-	-	-	44.1	0.9	-	-	-	-
1975	46.2	4.8	-	-	-	-	47.2	2.2	-	-	-	-	48.1	1.9	-	-	-	-	48.8	1.5	-	-	-	-
1976	49.6	1.6	-	-	-	-	50.8	2.4	-	-	-	-	51.7	1.8	-	-	-	-	52.7	1.9	-	-	-	-
1977	53.9	2.3	-	-	-	-	55.1	2.2	-	-	-	-	56.8	3.1	-	-	-	-	57.9	1.9	-	-	-	-
1978	59.5	2.8	-	-	60.3	1.3	-	-	61.4	1.8	-	-	62.1	1.1	-	-	62.9	1.3	-	-	64.0	1.7	-	-
1979	64.4	0.6	-	-	65.6	1.9	-	-	65.7	0.2	-	-	65.9	0.3	-	-	67.0	1.7	-	-	68.5	2.2	-	-
1980	70.0	2.2	-	-	71.5	2.1	-	-	72.3	1.1	-	-	73.0	1.0	-	-	75.6	3.6	-	-	76.2	0.8	-	-
1981	79.2	3.9	-	-	79.5	0.4	-	-	81.0	1.9	-	-	81.5	0.6	-	-	82.4	1.1	-	-	83.9	1.8	-	-
1982	86.9	3.6	-	-	87.8	1.0	-	-	88.6	0.9	-	-	91.6	3.4	-	-	93.1	1.6	-	-	94.5	1.5	-	-
1983	97.4	3.1	-	-	99.0	1.6	-	-	99.5	0.5	-	-	102.7	3.2	-	-	102.8	0.1	-	-	103.2	0.4	-	-
1984	106.5	3.2	-	-	107.3	0.8	-	-	107.5	0.2	-	-	108.0	0.5	-	-	108.2	0.2	-	-	109.4	1.1	-	-
1985	110.7	1.2	-	-	112.5	1.6	-	-	113.2	0.6	-	-	115.9	2.4	-	-	117.6	1.5	-	-	118.7	0.9	-	-
1986	120.0	1.1	-	-	121.2	1.0	-	-	123.3	1.7	-	-	125.9	2.1	-	-	126.6	0.6	-	-	126.1	-0.4	126.5	0.3
1987	-	-	-	-	-	-	-	-	-	-	127.1	0.5	-	-	-	-	-	-	-	-	-	-	128.7	1.3
1988	-	-	-	-	-	-	-	-	-	-	132.1	2.6	-	-	-	-	-	-	-	-	-	-	136.0	3.0
1989	-	-	-	-	-	-	-	-	-	-	140.2	3.1	-	-	-	-	-	-	-	-	-	-	144.1	2.8
1990	-	-	-	-	-	-	-	-	-	-	150.3	4.3	-	-	-	-	-	-	-	-	-	-	158.9	5.7
1991	-	-	-	-	-	-	-	-	-	-	166.3	4.7	-	-	-	-	-	-	-	-	-	-	171.1	2.9
1992	-	-	-	-	-	-	-	-	-	-	174.8	2.2	-	-	-	-	-	-	-	-	-	-	176.5	1.0
1993	-	-	-	-	-	-	-	-	-	-	182.5	3.4	-	-	-	-	-	-	-	-	-	-	185.6	1.7
1994	-	-	-	-	-	-	-	-	-	-	190.9	2.9	-	-	-	-	-	-	-	-	-	-	193.8	1.5
1995	-	-	-	-	-	-	-	-	-	-	198.4	2.4	-	-	-	-	-	-	-	-	-	-	-	-

Source: U.S. Department of Labor, Bureau of Labor Statistics, Division of Consumer Prices and Price Indexes. - indicates no data collected for period.

Denver-Boulder, CO
Consumer Price Index - All Urban Consumers
Base 1982-1984 = 100
Entertainment

For 1976-1995. Columns headed % show percentile change in the index from the previous period for which an index is available.

Year	Jan Index	%	Feb Index	%	Mar Index	%	Apr Index	%	May Index	%	Jun Index	%	Jul Index	%	Aug Index	%	Sep Index	%	Oct Index	%	Nov Index	%	Dec Index	%
1976	56.6	-	-	-	-	-	57.6	1.8	-	-	-	-	57.8	0.3	-	-	-	-	58.0	0.3	-	-	-	-
1977	59.4	2.4	-	-	-	-	60.8	2.4	-	-	-	-	61.8	1.6	-	-	-	-	62.6	1.3	-	-	-	-
1978	63.1	0.8	-	-	64.5	2.2	-	-	65.9	2.2	-	-	66.6	1.1	-	-	66.9	0.5	-	-	68.3	2.1	-	-
1979	69.0	1.0	-	-	71.1	3.0	-	-	71.6	0.7	-	-	72.8	1.7	-	-	73.2	0.5	-	-	73.8	0.8	-	-
1980	75.8	2.7	-	-	78.1	3.0	-	-	79.0	1.2	-	-	80.4	1.8	-	-	80.6	0.2	-	-	82.3	2.1	-	-
1981	82.9	0.7	-	-	83.9	1.2	-	-	86.4	3.0	-	-	87.1	0.8	-	-	86.5	-0.7	-	-	87.2	0.8	-	-
1982	89.5	2.6	-	-	88.1	-1.6	-	-	93.8	6.5	-	-	96.6	3.0	-	-	97.8	1.2	-	-	97.1	-0.7	-	-
1983	99.1	2.1	-	-	99.8	0.7	-	-	102.2	2.4	-	-	102.6	0.4	-	-	102.8	0.2	-	-	103.0	0.2	-	-
1984	103.5	0.5	-	-	104.8	1.3	-	-	105.7	0.9	-	-	105.7	0.0	-	-	104.8	-0.9	-	-	100.4	-4.2	-	-
1985	101.7	1.3	-	-	103.0	1.3	-	-	104.6	1.6	-	-	107.2	2.5	-	-	105.6	-1.5	-	-	103.2	-2.3	-	-
1986	105.2	1.9	-	-	105.3	0.1	-	-	105.6	0.3	-	-	107.4	1.7	-	-	108.5	1.0	-	-	107.3	-1.1	107.9	0.6
1987	-	-	-	-	-	-	-	-	-	-	115.6	7.1	-	-	-	-	-	-	-	-	-	-	116.1	0.4
1988	-	-	-	-	-	-	-	-	-	-	119.8	3.2	-	-	-	-	-	-	-	-	-	-	120.0	0.2
1989	-	-	-	-	-	-	-	-	-	-	125.1	4.2	-	-	-	-	-	-	-	-	-	-	129.0	3.1
1990	-	-	-	-	-	-	-	-	-	-	132.7	2.9	-	-	-	-	-	-	-	-	-	-	134.6	1.4
1991	-	-	-	-	-	-	-	-	-	-	137.2	1.9	-	-	-	-	-	-	-	-	-	-	140.0	2.0
1992	-	-	-	-	-	-	-	-	-	-	139.5	-0.4	-	-	-	-	-	-	-	-	-	-	139.7	0.1
1993	-	-	-	-	-	-	-	-	-	-	141.6	1.4	-	-	-	-	-	-	-	-	-	-	144.8	2.3
1994	-	-	-	-	-	-	-	-	-	-	151.2	4.4	-	-	-	-	-	-	-	-	-	-	147.7	-2.3
1995	-	-	-	-	-	-	-	-	-	-	151.8	2.8	-	-	-	-	-	-	-	-	-	-	-	-

Source: U.S. Department of Labor, Bureau of Labor Statistics, Division of Consumer Prices and Price Indexes. - indicates no data collected for period.

Denver-Boulder, CO
Consumer Price Index - Urban Wage Earners
Base 1982-1984 = 100
Entertainment

For 1976-1995. Columns headed % show percentile change in the index from the previous period for which an index is available.

Year	Jan Index	%	Feb Index	%	Mar Index	%	Apr Index	%	May Index	%	Jun Index	%	Jul Index	%	Aug Index	%	Sep Index	%	Oct Index	%	Nov Index	%	Dec Index	%
1976	59.4	-	-	-	-	-	60.5	1.9	-	-	-	-	60.7	0.3	-	-	-	-	60.9	0.3	-	-	-	-
1977	62.4	2.5	-	-	-	-	63.8	2.2	-	-	-	-	64.9	1.7	-	-	-	-	65.8	1.4	-	-	-	-
1978	66.3	0.8	-	-	67.1	1.2	-	-	68.3	1.8	-	-	68.2	-0.1	-	-	68.6	0.6	-	-	-	-	-	-
1979	70.8	0.4	-	-	72.8	2.8	-	-	72.5	-0.4	-	-	73.3	1.1	-	-	73.8	0.7	-	-	70.5	2.8	-	-
1980	77.0	3.1	-	-	79.4	3.1	-	-	81.4	2.5	-	-	82.9	1.8	-	-	82.0	-1.1	-	-	74.7	1.2	-	-
1981	85.2	0.2	-	-	86.9	2.0	-	-	89.3	2.8	-	-	89.2	-0.1	-	-	86.8	-2.7	-	-	85.0	3.7	-	-
1982	88.0	2.7	-	-	85.9	-2.4	-	-	94.5	10.0	-	-	97.3	3.0	-	-	98.4	1.1	-	-	85.7	-1.3	-	-
1983	99.4	2.1	-	-	99.9	0.5	-	-	102.3	2.4	-	-	102.9	0.6	-	-	103.0	0.1	-	-	97.4	-1.0	-	-
1984	103.7	0.5	-	-	105.1	1.4	-	-	106.1	1.0	-	-	106.0	-0.1	-	-	104.9	-1.0	-	-	103.2	0.2	-	-
1985	100.4	1.5	-	-	101.8	1.4	-	-	103.3	1.5	-	-	107.1	3.7	-	-	103.9	-3.0	-	-	98.9	-5.7	-	-
1986	103.1	1.8	-	-	103.6	0.5	-	-	103.7	0.1	-	-	105.7	1.9	-	-	105.6	-0.1	-	-	101.3	-2.5	-	-
1987	-	-	-	-	-	-	-	-	-	-	115.7	10.3	-	-	-	-	-	-	-	-	104.2	-1.3	104.9	0.7
1988	-	-	-	-	-	-	-	-	-	-	120.4	3.4	-	-	-	-	-	-	-	-	-	-	116.4	0.6
1989	-	-	-	-	-	-	-	-	-	-	124.6	3.1	-	-	-	-	-	-	-	-	-	-	120.8	0.3
1990	-	-	-	-	-	-	-	-	-	-	129.7	1.3	-	-	-	-	-	-	-	-	-	-	128.0	2.7
1991	-	-	-	-	-	-	-	-	-	-	133.4	1.5	-	-	-	-	-	-	-	-	-	-	131.4	1.3
1992	-	-	-	-	-	-	-	-	-	-	135.6	0.0	-	-	-	-	-	-	-	-	-	-	135.6	1.6
1993	-	-	-	-	-	-	-	-	-	-	137.4	0.5	-	-	-	-	-	-	-	-	-	-	136.7	0.8
1994	-	-	-	-	-	-	-	-	-	-	146.3	3.4	-	-	-	-	-	-	-	-	-	-	141.5	3.0
1995	-	-	-	-	-	-	-	-	-	-	147.2	2.6	-	-	-	-	-	-	-	-	-	-	143.5	-1.9

Source: U.S. Department of Labor, Bureau of Labor Statistics, Division of Consumer Prices and Price Indexes. - indicates no data collected for period.

Denver-Boulder, CO
Consumer Price Index - All Urban Consumers
Base 1982-1984 = 100
Other Goods and Services

For 1976-1995. Columns headed % show percentile change in the index from the previous period for which an index is available.

Year	Jan Index	%	Feb Index	%	Mar Index	%	Apr Index	%	May Index	%	Jun Index	%	Jul Index	%	Aug Index	%	Sep Index	%	Oct Index	%	Nov Index	%	Dec Index	%
1976	50.6	-	-	-	-	-	51.9	2.6	-	-	-	-	52.3	0.8	-	-	-	-	-	-	52.8	1.0	-	-
1977	54.0	2.3	-	-	-	-	54.7	1.3	-	-	-	-	57.1	4.4	-	-	-	-	-	-	59.0	3.3	-	-
1978	59.8	1.4	-	-	60.5	1.2	-	-	60.2	-0.5	-	-	60.2	0.0	-	-	61.2	1.7	-	-	61.9	1.1	-	-
1979	62.7	1.3	-	-	63.7	1.6	-	-	64.0	0.5	-	-	63.3	-1.1	-	-	66.2	4.6	-	-	67.1	1.4	-	-
1980	69.1	3.0	-	-	70.5	2.0	-	-	71.1	0.9	-	-	71.1	0.0	-	-	73.9	3.9	-	-	75.4	2.0	-	-
1981	76.4	1.3	-	-	79.4	3.9	-	-	81.2	2.3	-	-	80.0	-1.5	-	-	82.4	3.0	-	-	83.6	1.5	-	-
1982	85.7	2.5	-	-	87.0	1.5	-	-	87.0	0.0	-	-	88.9	2.2	-	-	90.6	1.9	-	-	94.4	4.2	-	-
1983	96.8	2.5	-	-	98.9	2.2	-	-	99.4	0.5	-	-	101.2	1.8	-	-	103.5	2.3	-	-	106.5	2.9	-	-
1984	107.7	1.1	-	-	108.0	0.3	-	-	108.4	0.4	-	-	108.7	0.3	-	-	109.4	0.6	-	-	111.2	1.6	-	-
1985	113.2	1.8	-	-	114.1	0.8	-	-	114.7	0.5	-	-	114.1	-0.5	-	-	116.9	2.5	-	-	118.3	1.2	-	-
1986	118.8	0.4	-	-	121.7	2.4	-	-	121.2	-0.4	-	-	123.2	1.7	-	-	127.3	3.3	-	-	129.3	1.6	129.3	0.0
1987	-	-	-	-	-	-	-	-	-	-	121.3	-6.2	-	-	-	-	-	-	-	-	-	-	126.4	4.2
1988	-	-	-	-	-	-	-	-	-	-	130.5	3.2	-	-	-	-	-	-	-	-	-	-	135.7	4.0
1989	-	-	-	-	-	-	-	-	-	-	138.3	1.9	-	-	-	-	-	-	-	-	-	-	143.8	4.0
1990	-	-	-	-	-	-	-	-	-	-	147.6	2.6	-	-	-	-	-	-	-	-	-	-	151.6	2.7
1991	-	-	-	-	-	-	-	-	-	-	156.8	3.4	-	-	-	-	-	-	-	-	-	-	163.4	4.2
1992	-	-	-	-	-	-	-	-	-	-	167.6	2.6	-	-	-	-	-	-	-	-	-	-	172.9	3.2
1993	-	-	-	-	-	-	-	-	-	-	178.7	3.4	-	-	-	-	-	-	-	-	-	-	181.8	1.7
1994	-	-	-	-	-	-	-	-	-	-	182.1	0.2	-	-	-	-	-	-	-	-	-	-	186.4	2.4
1995	-	-	-	-	-	-	-	-	-	-	188.1	0.9	-	-	-	-	-	-	-	-	-	-	-	-

Source: U.S. Department of Labor, Bureau of Labor Statistics, Division of Consumer Prices and Price Indexes. - indicates no data collected for period.

Denver-Boulder, CO
Consumer Price Index - Urban Wage Earners
Base 1982-1984 = 100
Other Goods and Services

For 1976-1995. Columns headed % show percentile change in the index from the previous period for which an index is available.

Year	Jan Index	Jan %	Feb Index	Feb %	Mar Index	Mar %	Apr Index	Apr %	May Index	May %	Jun Index	Jun %	Jul Index	Jul %	Aug Index	Aug %	Sep Index	Sep %	Oct Index	Oct %	Nov Index	Nov %	Dec Index	Dec %
1976	50.8	-	-	-	-	-	52.0	2.4	-	-	-	-	52.4	0.8	-	-	-	-	53.0	1.1	-	-	-	-
1977	54.1	2.1	-	-	-	-	54.9	1.5	-	-	-	-	57.2	4.2	-	-	-	-	59.1	3.3	-	-	-	-
1978	59.9	1.4	-	-	60.2	0.5	-	-	60.3	0.2	-	-	60.7	0.7	-	-	60.6	-0.2	-	-	61.8	2.0	-	-
1979	63.0	1.9	-	-	64.8	2.9	-	-	65.0	0.3	-	-	65.2	0.3	-	-	67.0	2.8	-	-	66.6	-0.6	-	-
1980	69.5	4.4	-	-	70.5	1.4	-	-	70.9	0.6	-	-	70.8	-0.1	-	-	73.0	3.1	-	-	76.1	4.2	-	-
1981	78.0	2.5	-	-	78.8	1.0	-	-	80.5	2.2	-	-	79.2	-1.6	-	-	81.3	2.7	-	-	82.3	1.2	-	-
1982	85.1	3.4	-	-	86.8	2.0	-	-	86.5	-0.3	-	-	88.5	2.3	-	-	89.9	1.6	-	-	93.8	4.3	-	-
1983	96.7	3.1	-	-	99.0	2.4	-	-	99.8	0.8	-	-	102.1	2.3	-	-	103.7	1.6	-	-	106.5	2.7	-	-
1984	108.1	1.5	-	-	108.4	0.3	-	-	108.6	0.2	-	-	109.3	0.6	-	-	109.5	0.2	-	-	110.7	1.1	-	-
1985	113.4	2.4	-	-	114.2	0.7	-	-	114.9	0.6	-	-	113.8	-1.0	-	-	116.7	2.5	-	-	117.9	1.0	-	-
1986	118.7	0.7	-	-	121.7	2.5	-	-	121.1	-0.5	-	-	123.4	1.9	-	-	127.9	3.6	-	-	129.3	1.1	129.3	0.0
1987	-	-	-	-	-	-	-	-	-	-	121.7	-5.9	-	-	-	-	-	-	-	-	-	-	127.6	4.8
1988	-	-	-	-	-	-	-	-	-	-	131.9	3.4	-	-	-	-	-	-	-	-	-	-	137.7	4.4
1989	-	-	-	-	-	-	-	-	-	-	140.7	2.2	-	-	-	-	-	-	-	-	-	-	146.1	3.8
1990	-	-	-	-	-	-	-	-	-	-	148.8	1.8	-	-	-	-	-	-	-	-	-	-	152.6	2.6
1991	-	-	-	-	-	-	-	-	-	-	158.5	3.9	-	-	-	-	-	-	-	-	-	-	165.9	4.7
1992	-	-	-	-	-	-	-	-	-	-	170.3	2.7	-	-	-	-	-	-	-	-	-	-	176.3	3.5
1993	-	-	-	-	-	-	-	-	-	-	182.4	3.5	-	-	-	-	-	-	-	-	-	-	185.4	1.6
1994	-	-	-	-	-	-	-	-	-	-	184.4	-0.5	-	-	-	-	-	-	-	-	-	-	188.2	2.1
1995	-	-	-	-	-	-	-	-	-	-	189.3	0.6	-	-	-	-	-	-	-	-	-	-	-	-

Source: U.S. Department of Labor, Bureau of Labor Statistics, Division of Consumer Prices and Price Indexes. - indicates no data collected for period.

Detroit, MI
Consumer Price Index - All Urban Consumers
Base 1982-1984 = 100
Annual Averages

For 1914-1995. Columns headed % show percentile change in the index from the previous period for which an index is available.

Year	All Items		Food & Beverage		Housing		Apparel & Upkeep		Trans- portation		Medical Care		Entertain- ment		Other Goods & Services	
	Index	%	Index	%	Index	%	Index	%	Index	%	Index	%	Index	%	Index	%
1914	-	-	-	-	-	-	-	-	-	-	-	-	-	-	-	-
1915	9.8	-	-	-	-	-	-	-	-	-	-	-	-	-	-	-
1916	10.8	10.2	-	-	-	-	-	-	-	-	-	-	-	-	-	-
1917	13.3	23.1	-	-	-	-	-	-	-	-	-	-	-	-	-	-
1918	15.7	18.0	-	-	-	-	-	-	-	-	-	-	-	-	-	-
1919	18.2	15.9	-	-	-	-	-	-	-	-	-	-	-	-	-	-
1920	21.8	19.8	-	-	-	-	-	-	-	-	-	-	-	-	-	-
1921	19.0	-12.8	-	-	-	-	-	-	-	-	-	-	-	-	-	-
1922	17.4	-8.4	-	-	-	-	-	-	-	-	-	-	-	-	-	-
1923	18.0	3.4	-	-	-	-	-	-	-	-	-	-	-	-	-	-
1924	18.0	0.0	-	-	-	-	-	-	-	-	-	-	-	-	-	-
1925	18.2	1.1	-	-	-	-	-	-	-	-	-	-	-	-	-	-
1926	18.3	0.5	-	-	-	-	-	-	-	-	-	-	-	-	-	-
1927	17.9	-2.2	-	-	-	-	-	-	-	-	-	-	-	-	-	-
1928	17.5	-2.2	-	-	-	-	-	-	-	-	-	-	-	-	-	-
1929	17.6	0.6	-	-	-	-	-	-	-	-	-	-	-	-	-	-
1930	16.9	-4.0	-	-	-	-	-	-	-	-	-	-	-	-	-	-
1931	14.8	-12.4	-	-	-	-	-	-	-	-	-	-	-	-	-	-
1932	12.8	-13.5	-	-	-	-	-	-	-	-	-	-	-	-	-	-
1933	12.1	-5.5	-	-	-	-	-	-	-	-	-	-	-	-	-	-
1934	12.8	5.8	-	-	-	-	-	-	-	-	-	-	-	-	-	-
1935	13.4	4.7	-	-	-	-	-	-	-	-	-	-	-	-	-	-
1936	13.8	3.0	-	-	-	-	-	-	-	-	-	-	-	-	-	-
1937	14.7	6.5	-	-	-	-	-	-	-	-	-	-	-	-	-	-
1938	14.4	-2.0	-	-	-	-	-	-	-	-	-	-	-	-	-	-
1939	14.0	-2.8	-	-	-	-	-	-	-	-	-	-	-	-	-	-
1940	14.1	0.7	-	-	-	-	-	-	-	-	-	-	-	-	-	-
1941	15.0	6.4	-	-	-	-	-	-	-	-	-	-	-	-	-	-
1942	16.7	11.3	-	-	-	-	-	-	-	-	-	-	-	-	-	-
1943	17.5	4.8	-	-	-	-	-	-	-	-	-	-	-	-	-	-
1944	17.8	1.7	-	-	-	-	-	-	-	-	-	-	-	-	-	-
1945	18.3	2.8	-	-	-	-	-	-	-	-	-	-	-	-	-	-
1946	19.9	8.7	-	-	-	-	-	-	-	-	-	-	-	-	-	-
1947	22.7	14.1	-	-	-	-	-	-	19.7	-	11.8	-	-	-	-	-
1948	24.5	7.9	-	-	-	-	-	-	22.2	12.7	12.3	4.2	-	-	-	-
1949	24.2	-1.2	-	-	-	-	-	-	23.4	5.4	12.6	2.4	-	-	-	-
1950	24.6	1.7	-	-	-	-	-	-	23.7	1.3	12.8	1.6	-	-	-	-
1951	26.5	7.7	-	-	-	-	-	-	24.7	4.2	13.4	4.7	-	-	-	-
1952	27.1	2.3	-	-	-	-	-	-	26.4	6.9	14.1	5.2	-	-	-	-
1953	27.6	1.8	-	-	-	-	52.1	-	27.5	4.2	14.7	4.3	-	-	-	-
1954	27.7	0.4	-	-	-	-	51.9	-0.4	26.3	-4.4	15.3	4.1	-	-	-	-
1955	27.7	0.0	-	-	-	-	51.8	-0.2	26.6	1.1	16.3	6.5	-	-	-	-
1956	28.2	1.8	-	-	-	-	52.6	1.5	27.5	3.4	17.4	6.7	-	-	-	-
1957	29.0	2.8	-	-	-	-	53.2	1.1	28.9	5.1	18.0	3.4	-	-	-	-
1958	29.4	1.4	-	-	-	-	53.0	-0.4	29.0	0.3	18.5	2.8	-	-	-	-

[Continued]

460

Detroit, MI
Consumer Price Index - All Urban Consumers
Base 1982-1984 = 100
Annual Averages
[Continued]

For 1914-1995. Columns headed % show percentile change in the index from the previous period for which an index is available.

Year	All Items		Food & Beverage		Housing		Apparel & Upkeep		Trans- portation		Medical Care		Entertain- ment		Other Goods & Services	
	Index	%	Index	%	Index	%	Index	%	Index	%	Index	%	Index	%	Index	%
1959	29.4	0.0	-	-	-	-	53.9	1.7	30.1	3.8	19.3	4.3	-	-	-	-
1960	29.7	1.0	-	-	-	-	54.4	0.9	30.2	0.3	19.6	1.6	-	-	-	-
1961	29.8	0.3	-	-	-	-	55.2	1.5	29.7	-1.7	20.6	5.1	-	-	-	-
1962	29.9	0.3	-	-	-	-	55.5	0.5	30.3	2.0	21.2	2.9	-	-	-	-
1963	30.2	1.0	-	-	-	-	56.1	1.1	30.4	0.3	22.3	5.2	-	-	-	-
1964	30.4	0.7	-	-	-	-	56.8	1.2	30.7	1.0	23.2	4.0	-	-	-	-
1965	31.2	2.6	-	-	-	-	57.7	1.6	32.0	4.2	23.8	2.6	-	-	-	-
1966	32.5	4.2	-	-	-	-	59.0	2.3	32.8	2.5	25.1	5.5	-	-	-	-
1967	33.6	3.4	-	-	-	-	60.6	2.7	33.5	2.1	26.9	7.2	-	-	-	-
1968	35.1	4.5	-	-	-	-	63.2	4.3	34.9	4.2	28.7	6.7	-	-	-	-
1969	37.2	6.0	-	-	-	-	66.0	4.4	36.0	3.2	30.8	7.3	-	-	-	-
1970	39.5	6.2	-	-	-	-	67.9	2.9	36.9	2.5	33.5	8.8	-	-	-	-
1971	40.9	3.5	-	-	-	-	70.0	3.1	38.4	4.1	36.1	7.8	-	-	-	-
1972	42.5	3.9	-	-	-	-	71.7	2.4	39.1	1.8	38.0	5.3	-	-	-	-
1973	45.2	6.4	-	-	-	-	74.1	3.3	41.5	6.1	40.0	5.3	-	-	-	-
1974	50.1	10.8	-	-	-	-	80.2	8.2	46.5	12.0	43.8	9.5	-	-	-	-
1975	53.9	7.6	-	-	-	-	83.6	4.2	50.0	7.5	50.4	15.1	-	-	-	-
1976	56.8	5.4	63.8	-	52.3	-	86.0	2.9	53.7	7.4	56.3	11.7	73.5	-	57.5	-
1977	60.7	6.9	67.6	6.0	55.8	6.7	88.9	3.4	58.6	9.1	63.2	12.3	75.7	3.0	61.3	6.6
1978	65.3	7.6	74.5	10.2	60.3	8.1	89.7	0.9	62.0	5.8	67.7	7.1	80.0	5.7	65.8	7.3
1979	73.6	12.7	82.2	10.3	70.3	16.6	89.7	0.0	70.4	13.5	73.9	9.2	82.8	3.5	70.2	6.7
1980	85.3	15.9	88.9	8.2	85.5	21.6	94.3	5.1	82.8	17.6	80.1	8.4	87.8	6.0	75.1	7.0
1981	93.2	9.3	95.8	7.8	93.4	9.2	96.4	2.2	93.8	13.3	86.1	7.5	92.3	5.1	81.8	8.9
1982	97.0	4.1	99.3	3.7	96.3	3.1	98.3	2.0	97.9	4.4	93.2	8.2	97.0	5.1	91.8	12.2
1983	99.8	2.9	99.3	0.0	100.4	4.3	101.0	2.7	98.5	0.6	98.3	5.5	101.2	4.3	102.0	11.1
1984	103.2	3.4	101.4	2.1	103.3	2.9	100.8	-0.2	103.6	5.2	108.5	10.4	101.8	0.6	106.2	4.1
1985	106.8	3.5	103.2	1.8	107.5	4.1	102.6	1.8	106.6	2.9	116.4	7.3	106.6	4.7	111.6	5.1
1986	108.3	1.4	107.3	4.0	109.8	2.1	103.3	0.7	103.2	-3.2	125.0	7.4	108.6	1.9	114.6	2.7
1987	111.7	3.1	110.5	3.0	113.0	2.9	108.0	4.5	105.3	2.0	132.9	6.3	112.1	3.2	120.4	5.1
1988	116.1	3.9	114.7	3.8	116.1	2.7	115.2	6.7	109.5	4.0	140.2	5.5	114.7	2.3	130.0	8.0
1989	122.3	5.3	120.8	5.3	121.2	4.4	122.7	6.5	117.0	6.8	147.1	4.9	120.5	5.1	137.9	6.1
1990	128.6	5.2	126.5	4.7	126.4	4.3	127.9	4.2	124.0	6.0	159.8	8.6	128.1	6.3	147.5	7.0
1991	133.1	3.5	131.1	3.6	128.6	1.7	131.8	3.0	129.3	4.3	171.0	7.0	132.7	3.6	160.7	8.9
1992	135.9	2.1	133.4	1.8	131.8	2.5	129.9	-1.4	129.9	0.5	181.6	6.2	130.7	-1.5	173.8	8.2
1993	139.6	2.7	135.2	1.3	134.4	2.0	137.9	6.2	132.5	2.0	190.9	5.1	137.7	5.4	183.5	5.6
1994	144.0	3.2	138.7	2.6	137.6	2.4	136.1	-1.3	138.6	4.6	199.7	4.6	145.7	5.8	197.1	7.4
1995	148.6	3.2	143.6	3.5	140.6	2.2	136.9	0.6	143.6	3.6	209.2	4.8	150.5	3.3	210.8	7.0

Source: U.S. Department of Labor, Bureau of Labor Statistics, Division of Consumer Prices and Price Indexes. - indicates no data collected for period.

Detroit, MI
Consumer Price Index - Urban Wage Earners
Base 1982-1984 = 100
Annual Averages

For 1914-1995. Columns headed % show percentile change in the index from the previous period for which an index is available.

Year	All Items		Food & Beverage		Housing		Apparel & Upkeep		Trans- portation		Medical Care		Entertain- ment		Other Goods & Services	
	Index	%	Index	%	Index	%	Index	%	Index	%	Index	%	Index	%	Index	%
1914	-	-	-	-	-	-	-	-	-	-	-	-	-	-	-	-
1915	9.8	-	-	-	-	-	-	-	-	-	-	-	-	-	-	-
1916	10.9	11.2	-	-	-	-	-	-	-	-	-	-	-	-	-	-
1917	13.4	22.9	-	-	-	-	-	-	-	-	-	-	-	-	-	-
1918	15.8	17.9	-	-	-	-	-	-	-	-	-	-	-	-	-	-
1919	18.4	16.5	-	-	-	-	-	-	-	-	-	-	-	-	-	-
1920	22.0	19.6	-	-	-	-	-	-	-	-	-	-	-	-	-	-
1921	19.2	-12.7	-	-	-	-	-	-	-	-	-	-	-	-	-	-
1922	17.6	-8.3	-	-	-	-	-	-	-	-	-	-	-	-	-	-
1923	18.2	3.4	-	-	-	-	-	-	-	-	-	-	-	-	-	-
1924	18.2	0.0	-	-	-	-	-	-	-	-	-	-	-	-	-	-
1925	18.4	1.1	-	-	-	-	-	-	-	-	-	-	-	-	-	-
1926	18.5	0.5	-	-	-	-	-	-	-	-	-	-	-	-	-	-
1927	18.0	-2.7	-	-	-	-	-	-	-	-	-	-	-	-	-	-
1928	17.7	-1.7	-	-	-	-	-	-	-	-	-	-	-	-	-	-
1929	17.7	0.0	-	-	-	-	-	-	-	-	-	-	-	-	-	-
1930	17.0	-4.0	-	-	-	-	-	-	-	-	-	-	-	-	-	-
1931	14.9	-12.4	-	-	-	-	-	-	-	-	-	-	-	-	-	-
1932	12.9	-13.4	-	-	-	-	-	-	-	-	-	-	-	-	-	-
1933	12.2	-5.4	-	-	-	-	-	-	-	-	-	-	-	-	-	-
1934	12.9	5.7	-	-	-	-	-	-	-	-	-	-	-	-	-	-
1935	13.5	4.7	-	-	-	-	-	-	-	-	-	-	-	-	-	-
1936	14.0	3.7	-	-	-	-	-	-	-	-	-	-	-	-	-	-
1937	14.8	5.7	-	-	-	-	-	-	-	-	-	-	-	-	-	-
1938	14.6	-1.4	-	-	-	-	-	-	-	-	-	-	-	-	-	-
1939	14.2	-2.7	-	-	-	-	-	-	-	-	-	-	-	-	-	-
1940	14.2	0.0	-	-	-	-	-	-	-	-	-	-	-	-	-	-
1941	15.1	6.3	-	-	-	-	-	-	-	-	-	-	-	-	-	-
1942	16.8	11.3	-	-	-	-	-	-	-	-	-	-	-	-	-	-
1943	17.7	5.4	-	-	-	-	-	-	-	-	-	-	-	-	-	-
1944	18.0	1.7	-	-	-	-	-	-	-	-	-	-	-	-	-	-
1945	18.4	2.2	-	-	-	-	-	-	-	-	-	-	-	-	-	-
1946	20.1	9.2	-	-	-	-	-	-	-	-	-	-	-	-	-	-
1947	22.9	13.9	-	-	-	-	-	-	20.5	-	12.0	-	-	-	-	-
1948	24.7	7.9	-	-	-	-	-	-	23.0	12.2	12.5	4.2	-	-	-	-
1949	24.4	-1.2	-	-	-	-	-	-	24.3	5.7	12.8	2.4	-	-	-	-
1950	24.8	1.6	-	-	-	-	-	-	24.6	1.2	13.1	2.3	-	-	-	-
1951	26.8	8.1	-	-	-	-	-	-	25.6	4.1	13.6	3.8	-	-	-	-
1952	27.4	2.2	-	-	-	-	-	-	27.4	7.0	14.3	5.1	-	-	-	-
1953	27.8	1.5	-	-	-	-	53.0	-	28.5	4.0	14.9	4.2	-	-	-	-
1954	27.9	0.4	-	-	-	-	52.9	-0.2	27.3	-4.2	15.5	4.0	-	-	-	-
1955	27.9	0.0	-	-	-	-	52.7	-0.4	27.6	1.1	16.6	7.1	-	-	-	-
1956	28.5	2.2	-	-	-	-	53.5	1.5	28.5	3.3	17.7	6.6	-	-	-	-
1957	29.3	2.8	-	-	-	-	54.2	1.3	30.0	5.3	18.3	3.4	-	-	-	-
1958	29.7	1.4	-	-	-	-	54.0	-0.4	30.1	0.3	18.9	3.3	-	-	-	-

[Continued]

Detroit, MI
Consumer Price Index - Urban Wage Earners
Base 1982-1984 = 100
Annual Averages
[Continued]

For 1914-1995. Columns headed % show percentile change in the index from the previous period for which an index is available.

Year	All Items		Food & Beverage		Housing		Apparel & Upkeep		Trans- portation		Medical Care		Entertain- ment		Other Goods & Services	
	Index	%	Index	%	Index	%	Index	%	Index	%	Index	%	Index	%	Index	%
1959	29.7	0.0	-	-	-	-	54.8	1.5	31.3	4.0	19.6	3.7	-	-	-	-
1960	29.9	0.7	-	-	-	-	55.4	1.1	31.3	0.0	20.0	2.0	-	-	-	-
1961	30.1	0.7	-	-	-	-	56.2	1.4	30.8	-1.6	21.0	5.0	-	-	-	-
1962	30.2	0.3	-	-	-	-	56.5	0.5	31.5	2.3	21.6	2.9	-	-	-	-
1963	30.5	1.0	-	-	-	-	57.1	1.1	31.6	0.3	22.7	5.1	-	-	-	-
1964	30.7	0.7	-	-	-	-	57.9	1.4	31.8	0.6	23.6	4.0	-	-	-	-
1965	31.4	2.3	-	-	-	-	58.8	1.6	33.2	4.4	24.2	2.5	-	-	-	-
1966	32.8	4.5	-	-	-	-	60.1	2.2	34.0	2.4	25.6	5.8	-	-	-	-
1967	34.0	3.7	-	-	-	-	61.7	2.7	34.8	2.4	27.4	7.0	-	-	-	-
1968	35.4	4.1	-	-	-	-	64.3	4.2	36.2	4.0	29.2	6.6	-	-	-	-
1969	37.6	6.2	-	-	-	-	67.2	4.5	37.4	3.3	31.4	7.5	-	-	-	-
1970	39.9	6.1	-	-	-	-	69.1	2.8	38.2	2.1	34.1	8.6	-	-	-	-
1971	41.3	3.5	-	-	-	-	71.3	3.2	39.9	4.5	36.8	7.9	-	-	-	-
1972	42.8	3.6	-	-	-	-	73.0	2.4	40.5	1.5	38.8	5.4	-	-	-	-
1973	45.7	6.8	-	-	-	-	75.4	3.3	43.0	6.2	40.7	4.9	-	-	-	-
1974	50.6	10.7	-	-	-	-	81.7	8.4	48.3	12.3	44.6	9.6	-	-	-	-
1975	54.4	7.5	-	-	-	-	85.1	4.2	51.9	7.5	51.4	15.2	-	-	-	-
1976	57.3	5.3	63.2	-	52.5	-	87.6	2.9	55.8	7.5	57.4	11.7	77.0	-	55.5	-
1977	61.3	7.0	66.9	5.9	56.0	6.7	90.5	3.3	60.8	9.0	64.4	12.2	79.3	3.0	59.1	6.5
1978	65.9	7.5	74.2	10.9	60.3	7.7	93.7	3.5	64.1	5.4	69.1	7.3	83.1	4.8	63.0	6.6
1979	74.3	12.7	82.2	10.8	70.3	16.6	93.6	-0.1	72.7	13.4	75.8	9.7	86.0	3.5	67.3	6.8
1980	85.6	15.2	88.7	7.9	85.2	21.2	97.7	4.4	84.5	16.2	81.3	7.3	90.9	5.7	73.5	9.2
1981	92.7	8.3	95.7	7.9	92.6	8.7	97.3	-0.4	93.1	10.2	86.8	6.8	92.7	2.0	80.5	9.5
1982	96.7	4.3	99.4	3.9	95.7	3.3	98.4	1.1	97.8	5.0	93.5	7.7	97.3	5.0	91.7	13.9
1983	101.1	4.6	99.2	-0.2	103.4	8.0	100.8	2.4	98.5	0.7	98.5	5.3	101.1	3.9	102.1	11.3
1984	102.2	1.1	101.4	2.2	100.9	-2.4	100.8	0.0	103.6	5.2	108.1	9.7	101.6	0.5	106.2	4.0
1985	104.5	2.3	102.9	1.5	102.7	1.8	103.5	2.7	106.7	3.0	115.6	6.9	106.5	4.8	111.5	5.0
1986	105.8	1.2	106.9	3.9	104.9	2.1	105.5	1.9	103.2	-3.3	123.6	6.9	109.3	2.6	114.1	2.3
1987	109.1	3.1	110.2	3.1	108.0	3.0	111.3	5.5	105.5	2.2	131.3	6.2	112.9	3.3	120.0	5.2
1988	113.3	3.8	114.2	3.6	110.9	2.7	119.1	7.0	109.5	3.8	139.6	6.3	115.5	2.3	130.1	8.4
1989	119.4	5.4	120.3	5.3	115.7	4.3	125.9	5.7	117.0	6.8	146.9	5.2	121.4	5.1	137.4	5.6
1990	125.6	5.2	126.1	4.8	120.7	4.3	131.8	4.7	124.1	6.1	159.1	8.3	128.8	6.1	147.3	7.2
1991	129.8	3.3	130.7	3.6	122.8	1.7	134.9	2.4	129.2	4.1	169.7	6.7	133.4	3.6	160.3	8.8
1992	132.1	1.8	133.1	1.8	125.7	2.4	133.3	-1.2	129.7	0.4	180.0	6.1	130.8	-1.9	170.0	6.1
1993	135.4	2.5	134.8	1.3	128.1	1.9	140.6	5.5	132.4	2.1	189.3	5.2	137.9	5.4	175.8	3.4
1994	139.5	3.0	138.4	2.7	131.0	2.3	138.9	-1.2	138.6	4.7	197.4	4.3	146.0	5.9	186.7	6.2
1995	143.9	3.2	143.4	3.6	133.8	2.1	139.0	0.1	143.7	3.7	207.1	4.9	150.8	3.3	201.9	8.1

Source: U.S. Department of Labor, Bureau of Labor Statistics, Division of Consumer Prices and Price Indexes. - indicates no data collected for period.

Detroit, MI
Consumer Price Index - All Urban Consumers
Base 1982-1984 = 100
All Items

For 1914-1995. Columns headed % show percentile change in the index from the previous period for which an index is available.

Year	Jan Index	%	Feb Index	%	Mar Index	%	Apr Index	%	May Index	%	Jun Index	%	Jul Index	%	Aug Index	%	Sep Index	%	Oct Index	%	Nov Index	%	Dec Index	%
1914	-	-	-	-	-	-	-	-	-	-	-	-	-	-	-	-	-	-	-	-	-	-	9.7	-
1915	-	-	-	-	-	-	-	-	-	-	-	-	-	-	-	-	-	-	-	-	-	-	10.1	4.1
1916	-	-	-	-	-	-	-	-	-	-	-	-	-	-	-	-	-	-	-	-	-	-	11.7	15.8
1917	-	-	-	-	-	-	-	-	-	-	-	-	-	-	-	-	-	-	-	-	-	-	14.3	22.2
1918	-	-	-	-	-	-	-	-	-	-	-	-	-	-	-	-	-	-	-	-	-	-	17.0	18.9
1919	-	-	-	-	-	-	-	-	-	-	17.8	4.7	-	-	-	-	-	-	-	-	-	-	19.9	11.8
1920	-	-	-	-	-	-	-	-	-	-	22.9	15.1	-	-	-	-	-	-	-	-	-	-	21.2	-7.4
1921	-	-	-	-	-	-	-	-	19.0	-10.4	-	-	-	-	-	-	18.5	-2.6	-	-	-	-	17.9	-3.2
1922	-	-	-	-	17.3	-3.4	-	-	-	-	17.4	0.6	-	-	-	-	17.3	-0.6	-	-	-	-	17.5	1.2
1923	-	-	-	-	17.7	1.1	-	-	-	-	18.0	1.7	-	-	-	-	18.4	2.2	-	-	-	-	18.2	-1.1
1924	-	-	-	-	18.1	-0.5	-	-	-	-	18.1	0.0	-	-	-	-	17.9	-1.1	-	-	-	-	17.9	0.0
1925	-	-	-	-	-	-	-	-	-	-	18.3	2.2	-	-	-	-	-	-	-	-	-	-	18.6	1.6
1926	-	-	-	-	-	-	-	-	-	-	18.4	-1.1	-	-	-	-	-	-	-	-	-	-	18.2	-1.1
1927	-	-	-	-	-	-	-	-	-	-	18.2	0.0	-	-	-	-	-	-	-	-	-	-	17.7	-2.7
1928	-	-	-	-	-	-	-	-	-	-	17.4	-1.7	-	-	-	-	-	-	-	-	-	-	17.4	0.0
1929	-	-	-	-	-	-	-	-	-	-	17.6	1.1	-	-	-	-	-	-	-	-	-	-	17.5	-0.6
1930	-	-	-	-	-	-	-	-	-	-	17.2	-1.7	-	-	-	-	-	-	-	-	-	-	15.9	-7.6
1931	-	-	-	-	-	-	-	-	-	-	14.8	-6.9	-	-	-	-	-	-	-	-	-	-	13.9	-6.1
1932	-	-	-	-	-	-	-	-	-	-	12.9	-7.2	-	-	-	-	-	-	-	-	-	-	12.1	-6.2
1933	-	-	-	-	-	-	-	-	-	-	11.7	-3.3	-	-	-	-	-	-	-	-	-	-	12.3	5.1
1934	-	-	-	-	-	-	-	-	-	-	12.8	4.1	-	-	-	-	-	-	-	-	12.8	0.0	-	-
1935	-	-	-	-	13.3	3.9	-	-	-	-	-	-	13.4	0.8	-	-	-	-	13.4	0.0	-	-	-	-
1936	13.6	1.5	-	-	-	-	13.6	0.0	-	-	-	-	14.0	2.9	-	-	14.1	0.7	-	-	-	-	14.0	-0.7
1937	-	-	-	-	14.4	2.9	-	-	-	-	14.8	2.8	-	-	-	-	14.9	0.7	-	-	-	-	15.0	0.7
1938	-	-	-	-	14.6	-2.7	-	-	-	-	14.5	-0.7	-	-	-	-	14.3	-1.4	-	-	-	-	14.2	-0.7
1939	-	-	-	-	14.0	-1.4	-	-	-	-	13.9	-0.7	-	-	-	-	14.1	1.4	-	-	-	-	14.0	-0.7
1940	-	-	-	-	14.1	0.7	-	-	-	-	14.2	0.7	-	-	-	-	14.1	-0.7	14.1	0.0	14.1	0.0	14.2	0.7
1941	14.2	0.0	14.3	0.7	14.4	0.7	14.6	1.4	14.6	0.0	15.0	2.7	15.0	0.0	15.1	0.7	15.4	2.0	15.7	1.9	15.8	0.6	15.9	0.6
1942	16.1	1.3	16.2	0.6	16.5	1.9	16.7	1.2	16.7	0.0	16.7	0.0	16.7	0.0	16.6	-0.6	16.7	0.6	16.9	1.2	17.0	0.6	17.1	0.6
1943	17.1	0.0	17.2	0.6	17.5	1.7	17.6	0.6	17.9	1.7	17.9	0.0	17.8	-0.6	17.5	-1.7	17.5	0.0	17.6	0.6	17.5	-0.6	17.7	1.1
1944	17.6	-0.6	17.5	-0.6	17.5	0.0	17.7	1.1	17.7	0.0	17.8	0.6	18.0	1.1	18.0	0.0	18.0	0.0	17.9	-0.6	17.9	0.0	18.0	0.6
1945	18.0	0.0	18.0	0.0	18.0	0.0	18.0	0.0	18.2	1.1	18.4	1.1	18.4	0.0	18.5	0.5	18.4	-0.5	18.4	0.0	18.5	0.5	18.5	0.0
1946	18.6	0.5	18.6	0.0	18.6	0.0	18.8	1.1	19.0	1.1	19.2	1.1	20.4	6.2	20.5	0.5	20.7	1.0	21.0	1.4	21.4	1.9	21.6	0.9
1947	21.6	0.0	21.6	0.0	22.1	2.3	22.1	0.0	22.1	0.0	22.4	1.4	22.6	0.9	23.0	1.8	23.2	0.9	23.6	1.7	23.5	-0.4	23.9	1.7
1948	24.1	0.8	23.9	-0.8	23.8	-0.4	24.3	2.1	24.5	0.8	24.7	0.8	24.9	0.8	24.9	0.0	24.8	-0.4	24.7	-0.4	24.5	-0.8	24.5	0.0
1949	24.3	-0.8	24.2	-0.4	24.2	0.0	24.2	0.0	24.3	0.4	24.3	0.0	24.1	-0.8	24.1	0.0	24.1	0.0	23.9	-0.8	24.1	0.8	24.0	-0.4
1950	23.9	-0.4	23.8	-0.4	24.0	0.8	24.0	0.0	24.2	0.8	24.4	0.8	24.6	0.8	24.7	0.4	25.0	1.2	25.2	0.8	25.3	0.4	25.5	0.8
1951	25.9	1.6	26.2	1.2	26.3	0.4	26.3	0.0	26.3	0.0	26.5	0.8	26.5	0.0	26.5	0.0	26.6	0.4	26.7	0.4	26.9	0.7	27.0	0.4
1952	27.0	0.0	26.8	-0.7	26.8	0.0	27.0	0.7	27.0	0.0	27.0	0.0	27.2	0.7	27.3	0.4	27.2	-0.4	27.4	0.7	27.4	0.0	27.6	0.7
1953	27.5	-0.4	27.3	-0.7	27.4	0.4	27.4	0.0	27.5	0.4	27.7	0.7	27.8	0.4	27.8	0.0	27.8	0.0	27.9	0.4	27.7	-0.7	27.7	0.0
1954	27.8	0.4	27.7	-0.4	27.7	0.0	27.7	0.0	27.8	0.4	27.8	0.0	27.9	0.4	27.7	-0.7	27.6	-0.4	27.6	0.0	27.8	0.7	27.6	-0.7
1955	27.6	0.0	27.6	0.0	27.6	0.0	27.6	0.0	27.7	0.4	27.7	0.0	27.7	0.0	27.7	0.0	27.8	0.4	27.7	-0.4	27.7	0.0	27.7	0.0
1956	27.6	-0.4	27.7	0.4	27.8	0.4	27.9	0.4	28.0	0.4	28.2	0.7	28.6	1.4	28.4	-0.7	28.4	0.0	28.5	0.4	28.6	0.4	28.6	0.0
1957	28.6	0.0	28.7	0.3	28.7	0.0	28.8	0.3	29.0	0.7	29.1	0.3	29.2	0.3	29.2	0.0	29.2	0.0	29.1	-0.3	29.3	0.7	29.3	0.0
1958	29.4	0.3	29.4	0.0	29.5	0.3	29.5	0.0	29.5	0.0	29.5	0.0	29.5	0.0	29.4	-0.3	29.4	0.0	29.3	-0.3	29.3	0.0	29.3	0.0

[Continued]

Detroit, MI
Consumer Price Index - All Urban Consumers
Base 1982-1984 = 100
All Items
[Continued]

For 1914-1995. Columns headed % show percentile change in the index from the previous period for which an index is available.

Year	Jan Index	%	Feb Index	%	Mar Index	%	Apr Index	%	May Index	%	Jun Index	%	Jul Index	%	Aug Index	%	Sep Index	%	Oct Index	%	Nov Index	%	Dec Index	%
1959	29.3	0.0	29.3	0.0	29.2	-0.3	29.3	0.3	29.3	0.0	29.3	0.0	29.5	0.7	29.4	-0.3	29.6	0.7	29.7	0.3	29.5	-0.7	29.5	0.0
1960	29.3	-0.7	29.4	0.3	29.4	0.0	29.5	0.3	29.5	0.0	29.7	0.7	29.9	0.7	29.8	-0.3	29.8	0.0	29.8	0.0	29.8	0.0	29.9	0.3
1961	30.0	0.3	30.0	0.0	29.9	-0.3	29.8	-0.3	29.8	0.0	29.9	0.3	29.8	-0.3	29.9	0.3	29.7	-0.7	29.8	0.3	29.7	-0.3	29.5	-0.7
1962	29.6	0.3	29.9	1.0	29.9	0.0	29.9	0.0	29.9	0.0	29.8	-0.3	29.8	0.0	29.9	0.3	30.1	0.7	30.1	0.0	30.0	-0.3	30.0	0.0
1963	30.0	0.0	30.0	0.0	30.0	0.0	29.9	-0.3	30.0	0.3	30.3	1.0	30.4	0.3	30.6	0.7	30.2	-1.3	30.3	0.3	30.4	0.3	30.3	-0.3
1964	30.4	0.3	30.2	-0.7	30.3	0.3	30.4	0.3	30.2	-0.7	30.3	0.3	30.5	0.7	30.5	0.0	30.6	0.3	30.7	0.3	30.6	-0.3	30.7	0.3
1965	30.7	0.0	30.6	-0.3	30.7	0.3	30.9	0.7	31.1	0.6	31.3	0.6	31.3	0.0	31.3	0.0	31.3	0.0	31.5	0.6	31.5	0.0	31.6	0.3
1966	31.7	0.3	31.9	0.6	32.1	0.6	32.3	0.6	32.4	0.3	32.6	0.6	32.6	0.0	32.8	0.6	32.8	0.0	33.0	0.6	33.0	0.0	33.2	0.6
1967	33.2	0.0	33.2	0.0	33.5	0.9	33.5	0.0	33.5	0.0	33.6	0.3	33.7	0.3	33.7	0.0	33.7	0.0	33.8	0.3	34.0	0.6	34.1	0.3
1968	34.1	0.0	34.3	0.6	34.6	0.9	34.7	0.3	34.8	0.3	35.1	0.9	35.2	0.3	35.3	0.3	35.5	0.6	35.6	0.3	35.8	0.6	35.9	0.3
1969	36.0	0.3	36.1	0.3	36.6	1.4	36.8	0.5	37.0	0.5	37.3	0.8	37.4	0.3	37.6	0.5	37.6	0.0	37.8	0.5	38.0	0.5	38.3	0.8
1970	38.4	0.3	38.7	0.8	39.0	0.8	39.2	0.5	39.5	0.8	39.6	0.3	39.7	0.3	39.6	-0.3	39.8	0.5	40.1	0.8	40.3	0.5	40.2	-0.2
1971	40.5	0.7	40.4	-0.2	40.4	0.0	40.4	0.0	40.7	0.7	41.0	0.7	41.0	0.0	41.3	0.7	41.3	0.0	41.3	0.0	41.5	0.5	41.6	0.2
1972	41.8	0.5	42.0	0.5	42.1	0.2	42.1	0.0	42.2	0.2	42.4	0.5	42.6	0.5	42.7	0.2	42.8	0.2	42.8	0.0	42.9	0.2	43.2	0.7
1973	43.2	0.0	43.6	0.9	44.1	1.1	44.5	0.9	44.9	0.9	45.0	0.2	45.0	0.0	46.0	2.2	46.2	0.4	46.4	0.4	46.8	0.9	47.1	0.6
1974	47.6	1.1	48.4	1.7	48.7	0.6	48.9	0.4	49.3	0.8	49.9	1.2	50.3	0.8	50.8	1.0	51.3	1.0	51.7	0.8	52.2	1.0	52.5	0.6
1975	52.3	-0.4	52.7	0.8	52.8	0.2	53.1	0.6	53.2	0.2	53.7	0.9	54.1	0.7	54.3	0.4	54.8	0.9	54.9	0.2	55.1	0.4	55.4	0.5
1976	55.7	0.5	55.8	0.2	55.7	-0.2	56.0	0.5	56.3	0.5	56.5	0.4	56.9	0.7	57.1	0.4	57.6	0.9	57.7	0.2	58.0	0.5	58.2	0.3
1977	58.5	0.5	58.9	0.7	59.5	1.0	60.2	1.2	60.3	0.2	60.9	1.0	61.4	0.8	61.4	0.0	61.5	0.2	61.6	0.2	62.1	0.8	62.0	-0.2
1978	62.2	0.3	62.4	0.3	63.4	1.6	64.0	0.9	64.7	1.1	65.4	1.1	65.5	0.2	65.9	0.6	66.5	0.9	67.6	1.7	68.0	0.6	68.0	0.0
1979	69.0	1.5	70.2	1.7	71.2	1.4	71.7	0.7	72.0	0.4	72.5	0.7	73.8	1.8	74.8	1.4	75.3	0.7	76.4	1.5	77.8	1.8	78.5	0.9
1980	79.8	1.7	80.9	1.4	81.7	1.0	83.5	2.2	83.6	0.1	86.4	3.3	85.4	-1.2	85.8	0.5	87.3	1.7	88.9	1.8	89.6	0.8	90.7	1.2
1981	90.3	-0.4	90.9	0.7	90.2	-0.8	91.6	1.6	92.6	1.1	94.4	1.9	95.2	0.8	95.4	0.2	95.6	0.2	94.7	-0.9	94.1	-0.6	93.6	-0.5
1982	94.5	1.0	93.5	-1.1	93.6	0.1	95.4	1.9	96.2	0.8	97.3	1.1	98.4	1.1	98.5	0.1	99.2	0.7	99.3	0.1	99.6	0.3	98.4	-1.2
1983	98.4	0.0	98.3	-0.1	98.4	0.1	99.2	0.8	99.2	0.0	99.8	0.6	100.4	0.6	100.5	0.1	100.7	0.2	100.3	-0.4	100.9	0.6	101.0	0.1
1984	101.4	0.4	102.0	0.6	102.3	0.3	102.8	0.5	102.8	0.0	103.0	0.2	103.5	0.5	103.6	0.1	104.8	1.2	104.9	0.1	103.9	-1.0	104.0	0.1
1985	104.6	0.6	105.5	0.9	106.1	0.6	106.2	0.1	106.3	0.1	106.6	0.3	107.0	0.4	107.0	0.0	107.8	0.7	107.6	-0.2	108.7	1.0	108.7	0.0
1986	108.7	0.0	108.6	-0.1	107.7	-0.8	107.3	-0.4	108.2	0.8	108.0	-0.2	107.1	-0.8	108.7	1.5	108.0	-0.6	109.1	1.0	109.4	0.3	109.2	-0.2
1987	-	-	110.2	0.9	-	-	111.2	0.9	-	-	111.1	-0.1	-	-	112.2	1.0	-	-	114.1	1.7	-	-	112.6	-1.3
1988	-	-	113.7	1.0	-	-	114.4	0.6	-	-	115.4	0.9	-	-	117.6	1.9	-	-	118.6	0.9	-	-	118.3	-0.3
1989	-	-	120.1	1.5	-	-	121.7	1.3	-	-	122.1	0.3	-	-	122.2	0.1	-	-	124.6	2.0	-	-	124.4	-0.2
1990	-	-	126.1	1.4	-	-	126.9	0.6	-	-	127.7	0.6	-	-	129.4	1.3	-	-	131.8	1.9	-	-	131.2	-0.5
1991	-	-	132.2	0.8	-	-	131.7	-0.4	-	-	133.5	1.4	-	-	133.2	-0.2	-	-	134.6	1.1	-	-	134.0	-0.4
1992	-	-	134.9	0.7	-	-	135.3	0.3	-	-	135.5	0.1	-	-	135.8	0.2	-	-	137.5	1.3	-	-	137.1	-0.3
1993	-	-	138.3	0.9	-	-	138.7	0.3	-	-	139.1	0.3	-	-	139.9	0.6	-	-	141.9	1.4	-	-	140.2	-1.2
1994	-	-	141.7	1.1	-	-	142.6	0.6	-	-	144.8	1.5	-	-	145.3	0.3	-	-	145.7	0.3	-	-	145.5	-0.1
1995	-	-	147.3	1.2	-	-	148.1	0.5	-	-	148.3	0.1	-	-	148.8	0.3	-	-	149.8	0.7	-	-	150.3	0.3

Source: U.S. Department of Labor, Bureau of Labor Statistics, Division of Consumer Prices and Price Indexes. - indicates no data collected for period.

Detroit, MI
Consumer Price Index - Urban Wage Earners
Base 1982-1984 = 100
All Items

For 1914-1995. Columns headed % show percentile change in the index from the previous period for which an index is available.

Year	Jan Index	%	Feb Index	%	Mar Index	%	Apr Index	%	May Index	%	Jun Index	%	Jul Index	%	Aug Index	%	Sep Index	%	Oct Index	%	Nov Index	%	Dec Index	%
1914	-	-	-	-	-	-	-	-	-	-	-	-	-	-	-	-	-	-	-	-	-	-	9.8	-
1915	-	-	-	-	-	-	-	-	-	-	-	-	-	-	-	-	-	-	-	-	-	-	10.2	4.1
1916	-	-	-	-	-	-	-	-	-	-	-	-	-	-	-	-	-	-	-	-	-	-	11.8	15.7
1917	-	-	-	-	-	-	-	-	-	-	-	-	-	-	-	-	-	-	-	-	-	-	14.4	22.0
1918	-	-	-	-	-	-	-	-	-	-	-	-	-	-	-	-	-	-	-	-	-	-	17.2	19.4
1919	-	-	-	-	-	-	-	-	-	-	17.9	4.1	-	-	-	-	-	-	-	-	-	-	20.1	12.3
1920	-	-	-	-	-	-	-	-	-	-	23.2	15.4	-	-	-	-	-	-	-	-	-	-	21.4	-7.8
1921	-	-	-	-	-	-	-	-	19.2	-10.3	-	-	-	-	-	-	18.6	-3.1	-	-	-	-	18.1	-2.7
1922	-	-	-	-	17.5	-3.3	-	-	-	-	17.6	0.6	-	-	-	-	17.5	-0.6	-	-	-	-	17.7	1.1
1923	-	-	-	-	17.9	1.1	-	-	-	-	18.2	1.7	-	-	-	-	18.5	1.6	-	-	-	-	18.4	-0.5
1924	-	-	-	-	18.3	-0.5	-	-	-	-	18.3	0.0	-	-	-	-	18.1	-1.1	-	-	-	-	18.1	0.0
1925	-	-	-	-	-	-	-	-	-	-	18.4	1.7	-	-	-	-	-	-	-	-	-	-	18.8	2.2
1926	-	-	-	-	-	-	-	-	-	-	18.6	-1.1	-	-	-	-	-	-	-	-	-	-	18.3	-1.6
1927	-	-	-	-	-	-	-	-	-	-	18.4	0.5	-	-	-	-	-	-	-	-	-	-	17.8	-3.3
1928	-	-	-	-	-	-	-	-	-	-	17.6	-1.1	-	-	-	-	-	-	-	-	-	-	17.6	0.0
1929	-	-	-	-	-	-	-	-	-	-	17.8	1.1	-	-	-	-	-	-	-	-	-	-	17.7	-0.6
1930	-	-	-	-	-	-	-	-	-	-	17.3	-2.3	-	-	-	-	-	-	-	-	-	-	16.1	-6.9
1931	-	-	-	-	-	-	-	-	-	-	14.9	-7.5	-	-	-	-	-	-	-	-	-	-	14.0	-6.0
1932	-	-	-	-	-	-	-	-	-	-	13.0	-7.1	-	-	-	-	-	-	-	-	-	-	12.2	-6.2
1933	-	-	-	-	-	-	-	-	-	-	11.8	-3.3	-	-	-	-	-	-	-	-	-	-	12.4	5.1
1934	-	-	-	-	-	-	-	-	-	-	12.9	4.0	-	-	-	-	-	-	-	-	12.9	0.0	-	-
1935	-	-	-	-	13.4	3.9	-	-	-	-	-	-	13.5	0.7	-	-	-	-	13.5	0.0	-	-	-	-
1936	13.7	1.5	-	-	-	-	13.7	0.0	-	-	-	-	14.1	2.9	-	-	14.2	0.7	-	-	-	-	14.1	-0.7
1937	-	-	-	-	14.6	3.5	-	-	-	-	14.9	2.1	-	-	-	-	15.1	1.3	-	-	-	-	15.1	0.0
1938	-	-	-	-	14.8	-2.0	-	-	-	-	14.6	-1.4	-	-	-	-	14.4	-1.4	-	-	-	-	14.3	-0.7
1939	-	-	-	-	14.2	-0.7	-	-	-	-	14.1	-0.7	-	-	-	-	14.2	0.7	-	-	-	-	14.2	0.0
1940	-	-	-	-	14.2	0.0	-	-	-	-	14.3	0.7	-	-	-	-	14.3	0.0	14.3	0.0	14.3	0.0	14.3	0.0
1941	14.4	0.7	14.4	0.0	14.5	0.7	14.7	1.4	14.7	0.0	15.1	2.7	15.2	0.7	15.3	0.7	15.6	2.0	15.9	1.9	16.0	0.6	16.0	0.0
1942	16.3	1.9	16.4	0.6	16.6	1.2	16.8	1.2	16.9	0.6	16.8	-0.6	16.8	0.0	16.8	0.0	16.8	0.0	17.0	1.2	17.1	0.6	17.2	0.6
1943	17.2	0.0	17.4	1.2	17.6	1.1	17.8	1.1	18.1	1.7	18.0	-0.6	17.9	-0.6	17.7	-1.1	17.7	0.0	17.8	0.6	17.7	-0.6	17.8	0.6
1944	17.8	0.0	17.7	-0.6	17.7	0.0	17.8	0.6	17.9	0.6	18.0	0.6	18.2	1.1	18.1	-0.5	18.1	0.0	18.1	0.0	18.1	0.0	18.1	0.0
1945	18.1	0.0	18.1	0.0	18.1	0.0	18.2	0.6	18.4	1.1	18.6	1.1	18.6	0.0	18.7	0.5	18.6	-0.5	18.6	0.0	18.6	0.0	18.7	0.5
1946	18.8	0.5	18.8	0.0	18.8	0.0	19.0	1.1	19.1	0.5	19.4	1.6	20.5	5.7	20.7	1.0	20.8	0.5	21.2	1.9	21.6	1.9	21.8	0.9
1947	21.8	0.0	21.8	0.0	22.3	2.3	22.3	0.0	22.3	0.0	22.6	1.3	22.9	1.3	23.2	1.3	23.4	0.9	23.8	1.7	23.8	0.0	24.1	1.3
1948	24.3	0.8	24.1	-0.8	24.0	-0.4	24.5	2.1	24.7	0.8	24.9	0.8	25.1	0.8	25.1	0.0	25.0	-0.4	24.9	-0.4	24.7	-0.8	24.7	0.0
1949	24.5	-0.8	24.4	-0.4	24.4	0.0	24.4	0.0	24.5	0.4	24.5	0.0	24.3	-0.8	24.3	0.0	24.3	0.0	24.1	-0.8	24.3	0.8	24.2	-0.4
1950	24.1	-0.4	24.0	-0.4	24.2	0.8	24.2	0.0	24.4	0.8	24.7	1.2	24.9	0.8	25.0	0.4	25.2	0.8	25.4	0.8	25.5	0.4	25.7	0.8
1951	26.1	1.6	26.4	1.1	26.6	0.8	26.5	-0.4	26.6	0.4	26.8	0.8	26.8	0.0	26.8	0.0	26.8	0.0	27.0	0.7	27.2	0.7	27.2	0.0
1952	27.2	0.0	27.1	-0.4	27.1	0.0	27.2	0.4	27.2	0.0	27.3	0.4	27.5	0.7	27.6	0.4	27.5	-0.4	27.7	0.7	27.6	-0.4	27.8	0.7
1953	27.7	-0.4	27.6	-0.4	27.6	0.0	27.6	0.0	27.7	0.4	27.9	0.7	28.0	0.4	28.0	0.0	28.0	0.0	28.1	0.4	27.9	-0.7	27.9	0.0
1954	28.0	0.4	27.9	-0.4	27.9	0.0	27.9	0.0	28.0	0.4	28.1	0.4	28.1	0.0	28.0	-0.4	27.8	-0.7	27.8	0.0	28.0	0.7	27.8	-0.7
1955	27.8	0.0	27.9	0.4	27.9	0.0	27.8	-0.4	27.9	0.4	27.9	0.0	28.0	0.4	27.9	-0.4	28.0	0.4	27.9	-0.4	28.0	0.4	27.9	-0.4
1956	27.9	0.0	27.9	0.0	28.0	0.4	28.1	0.4	28.3	0.7	28.5	0.7	28.8	1.1	28.7	-0.3	28.7	0.0	28.8	0.3	28.9	0.3	28.8	-0.3
1957	28.9	0.3	29.0	0.3	29.0	0.0	29.1	0.3	29.2	0.3	29.4	0.7	29.5	0.3	29.5	0.0	29.4	-0.3	29.4	0.0	29.6	0.7	29.5	-0.3
1958	29.6	0.3	29.6	0.0	29.7	0.3	29.8	0.3	29.8	0.0	29.7	-0.3	29.8	0.3	29.6	-0.7	29.7	0.3	29.5	-0.7	29.6	0.3	29.5	-0.3

[Continued]

Detroit, MI

Consumer Price Index - Urban Wage Earners
Base 1982-1984 = 100
All Items
[Continued]

For 1914-1995. Columns headed % show percentile change in the index from the previous period for which an index is available.

Year	Jan Index	%	Feb Index	%	Mar Index	%	Apr Index	%	May Index	%	Jun Index	%	Jul Index	%	Aug Index	%	Sep Index	%	Oct Index	%	Nov Index	%	Dec Index	%
1959	29.5	0.0	29.5	0.0	29.5	0.0	29.6	0.3	29.6	0.0	29.6	0.0	29.8	0.7	29.6	-0.7	29.9	1.0	29.9	0.0	29.7	-0.7	29.7	0.0
1960	29.6	-0.3	29.7	0.3	29.7	0.0	29.7	0.0	29.8	0.3	30.0	0.7	30.2	0.7	30.1	-0.3	30.0	-0.3	30.1	0.3	30.1	0.0	30.2	0.3
1961	30.3	0.3	30.3	0.0	30.2	-0.3	30.1	-0.3	30.1	0.0	30.2	0.3	30.1	-0.3	30.2	0.3	29.9	-1.0	30.0	0.3	30.0	0.0	29.8	-0.7
1962	29.9	0.3	30.2	1.0	30.2	0.0	30.2	0.0	30.2	0.0	30.1	-0.3	30.1	0.0	30.2	0.3	30.4	0.7	30.4	0.0	30.3	-0.3	30.3	0.0
1963	30.3	0.0	30.3	0.0	30.3	0.0	30.2	-0.3	30.3	0.3	30.6	1.0	30.7	0.3	30.9	0.7	30.5	-1.3	30.6	0.3	30.7	0.3	30.6	-0.3
1964	30.7	0.3	30.5	-0.7	30.6	0.3	30.7	0.3	30.5	-0.7	30.6	0.3	30.8	0.7	30.8	0.0	30.9	0.3	31.0	0.3	30.9	-0.3	31.0	0.3
1965	31.0	0.0	30.9	-0.3	31.0	0.3	31.2	0.6	31.3	0.3	31.6	1.0	31.6	0.0	31.6	0.0	31.6	0.0	31.7	0.3	31.8	0.3	31.9	0.3
1966	32.0	0.3	32.2	0.6	32.4	0.6	32.6	0.6	32.7	0.3	32.9	0.6	32.9	0.0	33.1	0.6	33.1	0.0	33.3	0.6	33.3	0.0	33.5	0.6
1967	33.5	0.0	33.5	0.0	33.8	0.9	33.9	0.3	33.9	0.0	33.9	0.0	34.0	0.3	34.1	0.3	34.1	0.0	34.1	0.0	34.3	0.6	34.4	0.3
1968	34.5	0.3	34.7	0.6	34.9	0.6	35.0	0.3	35.1	0.3	35.4	0.9	35.5	0.3	35.7	0.6	35.8	0.3	36.0	0.6	36.1	0.3	36.2	0.3
1969	36.3	0.3	36.5	0.6	37.0	1.4	37.1	0.3	37.3	0.3	37.6	0.8	37.7	0.3	38.0	0.8	38.0	0.0	38.2	0.5	38.4	0.5	38.6	0.5
1970	38.7	0.3	39.1	1.0	39.3	0.5	39.5	0.5	39.9	1.0	40.0	0.3	40.0	0.0	40.0	0.0	40.2	0.5	40.5	0.7	40.7	0.5	40.6	-0.2
1971	40.8	0.5	40.7	-0.2	40.8	0.2	40.8	0.0	41.0	0.5	41.4	1.0	41.4	0.0	41.7	0.7	41.7	0.0	41.7	0.0	41.9	0.5	42.0	0.2
1972	42.2	0.5	42.4	0.5	42.4	0.0	42.4	0.0	42.6	0.5	42.8	0.5	43.0	0.5	43.1	0.2	43.2	0.2	43.2	0.0	43.3	0.2	43.6	0.7
1973	43.6	0.0	44.0	0.9	44.5	1.1	45.0	1.1	45.3	0.7	45.4	0.2	45.4	0.0	46.4	2.2	46.6	0.4	46.8	0.4	47.2	0.9	47.5	0.6
1974	48.0	1.1	48.8	1.7	49.2	0.8	49.4	0.4	49.7	0.6	50.4	1.4	50.7	0.6	51.2	1.0	51.7	1.0	52.2	1.0	52.7	1.0	53.0	0.6
1975	52.8	-0.4	53.1	0.6	53.3	0.4	53.5	0.4	53.7	0.4	54.2	0.9	54.6	0.7	54.8	0.4	55.3	0.9	55.4	0.2	55.6	0.4	55.9	0.5
1976	56.3	0.7	56.3	0.0	56.2	-0.2	56.5	0.5	56.8	0.5	57.0	0.4	57.4	0.7	57.6	0.3	58.2	1.0	58.2	0.0	58.6	0.7	58.8	0.3
1977	59.0	0.3	59.5	0.8	60.0	0.8	60.8	1.3	60.9	0.2	61.5	1.0	62.0	0.8	62.0	0.0	62.1	0.2	62.2	0.2	62.6	0.6	62.6	0.0
1978	62.8	0.3	63.1	0.5	63.8	1.1	64.4	0.9	65.2	1.2	66.1	1.4	66.1	0.0	66.6	0.8	67.3	1.1	68.1	1.2	68.5	0.6	68.6	0.1
1979	69.6	1.5	70.9	1.9	71.8	1.3	72.4	0.8	72.7	0.4	73.2	0.7	74.6	1.9	75.6	1.3	75.9	0.4	77.0	1.4	78.4	1.8	78.8	0.5
1980	80.3	1.9	81.5	1.5	82.3	1.0	84.2	2.3	84.5	0.4	86.9	2.8	85.6	-1.5	86.2	0.7	87.5	1.5	88.8	1.5	89.5	0.8	90.1	0.7
1981	89.8	-0.3	90.1	0.3	89.5	-0.7	91.0	1.7	92.1	1.2	93.7	1.7	94.7	1.1	94.8	0.1	95.1	0.3	94.5	-0.6	93.8	-0.7	93.4	-0.4
1982	94.3	1.0	93.3	-1.1	93.4	0.1	95.2	1.9	96.0	0.8	97.1	1.1	98.2	1.1	98.2	0.0	98.9	0.7	98.9	0.0	99.2	0.3	98.0	-1.2
1983	97.8	-0.2	97.5	-0.3	98.4	0.9	100.2	1.8	101.5	1.3	102.1	0.6	103.2	1.1	103.1	-0.1	103.4	0.3	101.5	-1.8	102.5	1.0	102.3	-0.2
1984	104.5	2.2	103.5	-1.0	102.8	-0.7	101.4	-1.4	101.3	-0.1	100.8	-0.5	101.3	0.5	101.5	0.2	102.3	0.8	102.8	0.5	101.8	-1.0	101.9	0.1
1985	102.3	0.4	103.2	0.9	103.9	0.7	104.0	0.1	104.1	0.1	104.4	0.3	104.7	0.3	104.7	0.0	105.4	0.7	105.2	-0.2	106.3	1.0	106.3	0.0
1986	106.4	0.1	106.0	-0.4	105.0	-0.9	104.6	-0.4	105.6	1.0	105.3	-0.3	104.4	-0.9	106.2	1.7	105.4	-0.8	106.5	1.0	106.9	0.4	106.6	-0.3
1987	-	-	107.5	0.8	-	-	108.6	1.0	-	-	108.6	0.0	-	-	109.6	0.9	-	-	111.3	1.6	-	-	109.8	-1.3
1988	-	-	110.9	1.0	-	-	111.9	0.9	-	-	112.7	0.7	-	-	114.6	1.7	-	-	115.6	0.9	-	-	115.7	0.1
1989	-	-	117.3	1.4	-	-	119.0	1.4	-	-	119.3	0.3	-	-	119.2	-0.1	-	-	121.5	1.9	-	-	121.4	-0.1
1990	-	-	123.2	1.5	-	-	123.9	0.6	-	-	124.7	0.6	-	-	126.5	1.4	-	-	128.7	1.7	-	-	128.1	-0.5
1991	-	-	128.9	0.6	-	-	128.3	-0.5	-	-	130.1	1.4	-	-	130.2	0.1	-	-	131.1	0.7	-	-	130.6	-0.4
1992	-	-	131.3	0.5	-	-	131.7	0.3	-	-	131.8	0.1	-	-	132.0	0.2	-	-	133.5	1.1	-	-	133.1	-0.3
1993	-	-	134.4	1.0	-	-	134.6	0.1	-	-	135.1	0.4	-	-	135.7	0.4	-	-	137.5	1.3	-	-	135.7	-1.3
1994	-	-	137.0	1.0	-	-	137.9	0.7	-	-	140.2	1.7	-	-	141.0	0.6	-	-	141.1	0.1	-	-	141.0	-0.1
1995	-	-	142.7	1.2	-	-	143.6	0.6	-	-	143.7	0.1	-	-	144.0	0.2	-	-	145.0	0.7	-	-	145.5	0.3

Source: U.S. Department of Labor, Bureau of Labor Statistics, Division of Consumer Prices and Price Indexes. - indicates no data collected for period.

Detroit, MI
Consumer Price Index - All Urban Consumers
Base 1982-1984 = 100
Food and Beverages

For 1976-1995. Columns headed % show percentile change in the index from the previous period for which an index is available.

Year	Jan Index	%	Feb Index	%	Mar Index	%	Apr Index	%	May Index	%	Jun Index	%	Jul Index	%	Aug Index	%	Sep Index	%	Oct Index	%	Nov Index	%	Dec Index	%
1976	63.8	-	63.8	0.0	63.1	-1.1	63.5	0.6	63.9	0.6	63.9	0.0	64.3	0.6	64.0	-0.5	63.7	-0.5	63.6	-0.2	64.0	0.6	64.5	0.8
1977	64.8	0.5	65.9	1.7	65.8	-0.2	66.9	1.7	67.2	0.4	68.2	1.5	68.5	0.4	68.6	0.1	68.1	-0.7	68.4	0.4	69.2	1.2	69.2	0.0
1978	70.5	1.9	71.2	1.0	72.0	1.1	73.0	1.4	74.0	1.4	75.3	1.8	76.0	0.9	75.7	-0.4	75.9	0.3	76.2	0.4	76.8	0.8	77.6	1.0
1979	79.5	2.4	80.8	1.6	81.3	0.6	81.9	0.7	82.4	0.6	82.5	0.1	82.9	0.5	81.9	-1.2	82.4	0.6	82.9	0.6	83.3	0.5	84.2	1.1
1980	86.0	2.1	86.1	0.1	86.7	0.7	86.9	0.2	87.8	1.0	88.5	0.8	89.4	1.0	90.4	1.1	90.1	-0.3	90.6	0.6	92.1	1.7	92.8	0.8
1981	93.5	0.8	94.9	1.5	94.8	-0.1	95.1	0.3	95.3	0.2	95.4	0.1	96.1	0.7	96.1	0.0	96.6	0.5	96.7	0.1	97.3	0.6	97.4	0.1
1982	98.2	0.8	99.1	0.9	98.9	-0.2	99.1	0.2	99.3	0.2	100.1	0.8	100.2	0.1	99.5	-0.7	99.7	0.2	99.3	-0.4	99.6	0.3	99.2	-0.4
1983	99.7	0.5	100.1	0.4	100.8	0.7	100.7	-0.1	100.2	-0.5	99.9	-0.3	99.6	-0.3	99.3	-0.3	98.4	-0.9	97.1	-1.3	97.5	0.4	98.0	0.5
1984	100.2	2.2	101.1	0.9	101.1	0.0	102.1	1.0	101.6	-0.5	101.3	-0.3	102.1	0.8	101.9	-0.2	101.6	-0.3	101.0	-0.6	100.8	-0.2	101.8	1.0
1985	102.0	0.2	102.9	0.9	103.4	0.5	103.3	-0.1	103.1	-0.2	102.9	-0.2	103.1	0.2	102.5	-0.6	102.4	-0.1	103.3	0.9	104.3	1.0	104.8	0.5
1986	104.7	-0.1	105.3	0.6	105.8	0.5	105.7	-0.1	106.3	0.6	106.4	0.1	107.5	1.0	108.9	1.3	108.6	-0.3	109.3	0.6	109.5	0.2	109.2	-0.3
1987	-	-	109.7	0.5	-	-	109.4	-0.3	-	-	111.4	1.8	-	-	110.8	-0.5	-	-	111.5	0.6	-	-	110.9	-0.5
1988	-	-	112.3	1.3	-	-	113.0	0.6	-	-	114.4	1.2	-	-	115.5	1.0	-	-	116.9	1.2	-	-	117.8	0.8
1989	-	-	119.4	1.4	-	-	120.5	0.9	-	-	120.3	-0.2	-	-	121.2	0.7	-	-	121.5	0.2	-	-	123.0	1.2
1990	-	-	125.3	1.9	-	-	125.4	0.1	-	-	126.5	0.9	-	-	127.6	0.9	-	-	127.7	0.1	-	-	127.9	0.2
1991	-	-	129.0	0.9	-	-	130.3	1.0	-	-	131.6	1.0	-	-	131.6	0.0	-	-	132.6	0.8	-	-	133.0	0.3
1992	-	-	133.6	0.5	-	-	133.4	-0.1	-	-	132.9	-0.4	-	-	133.5	0.5	-	-	133.5	0.0	-	-	134.0	0.4
1993	-	-	134.1	0.1	-	-	134.2	0.1	-	-	135.1	0.7	-	-	135.8	0.5	-	-	136.8	0.7	-	-	136.1	-0.5
1994	-	-	136.4	0.2	-	-	136.9	0.4	-	-	138.9	1.5	-	-	140.1	0.9	-	-	139.7	-0.3	-	-	141.9	1.6
1995	-	-	142.8	0.6	-	-	143.1	0.2	-	-	143.5	0.3	-	-	143.9	0.3	-	-	144.2	0.2	-	-	144.9	0.5

Source: U.S. Department of Labor, Bureau of Labor Statistics, Division of Consumer Prices and Price Indexes. - indicates no data collected for period.

Detroit, MI
Consumer Price Index - Urban Wage Earners
Base 1982-1984 = 100
Food and Beverages

For 1976-1995. Columns headed % show percentile change in the index from the previous period for which an index is available.

Year	Jan Index	%	Feb Index	%	Mar Index	%	Apr Index	%	May Index	%	Jun Index	%	Jul Index	%	Aug Index	%	Sep Index	%	Oct Index	%	Nov Index	%	Dec Index	%
1976	63.2	-	63.1	-0.2	62.5	-1.0	62.9	0.6	63.2	0.5	63.2	0.0	63.6	0.6	63.4	-0.3	63.0	-0.6	62.9	-0.2	63.3	0.6	63.9	0.9
1977	64.2	0.5	65.2	1.6	65.2	0.0	66.2	1.5	66.6	0.6	67.5	1.4	67.8	0.4	67.9	0.1	67.4	-0.7	67.7	0.4	68.5	1.2	68.5	0.0
1978	70.0	2.2	70.8	1.1	71.4	0.8	72.5	1.5	73.5	1.4	75.2	2.3	76.0	1.1	75.9	-0.1	76.0	0.1	75.7	-0.4	76.5	1.1	77.3	1.0
1979	79.2	2.5	80.5	1.6	81.5	1.2	81.8	0.4	82.2	0.5	82.4	0.2	83.2	1.0	82.0	-1.4	82.4	0.5	83.0	0.7	83.3	0.4	84.3	1.2
1980	85.8	1.8	86.0	0.2	86.6	0.7	86.7	0.1	87.6	1.0	88.3	0.8	89.1	0.9	89.9	0.9	90.0	0.1	90.5	0.6	91.5	1.1	92.2	0.8
1981	92.9	0.8	94.2	1.4	94.3	0.1	95.1	0.8	95.3	0.2	95.6	0.3	96.4	0.8	96.3	-0.1	97.0	0.7	96.9	-0.1	97.4	0.5	97.3	-0.1
1982	98.3	1.0	99.0	0.7	98.9	-0.1	99.2	0.3	99.4	0.2	100.2	0.8	100.4	0.2	99.7	-0.7	99.9	0.2	99.4	-0.5	99.6	0.2	99.1	-0.5
1983	99.7	0.6	100.1	0.4	100.8	0.7	100.7	-0.1	100.2	-0.5	99.8	-0.4	99.5	-0.3	99.2	-0.3	98.3	-0.9	97.1	-1.2	97.4	0.3	97.9	0.5
1984	100.1	2.2	101.2	1.1	101.0	-0.2	102.1	1.1	101.5	-0.6	101.3	-0.2	102.0	0.7	102.1	0.1	101.7	-0.4	100.9	-0.8	100.6	-0.3	101.9	1.3
1985	101.8	-0.1	102.8	1.0	103.2	0.4	103.0	-0.2	102.9	-0.1	102.7	-0.2	102.9	0.2	102.2	-0.7	102.1	-0.1	102.9	0.8	104.0	1.1	104.5	0.5
1986	104.4	-0.1	104.7	0.3	105.5	0.8	105.3	-0.2	106.0	0.7	106.1	0.1	107.0	0.8	108.5	1.4	108.1	-0.4	109.0	0.8	109.1	0.1	109.0	-0.1
1987	-	-	109.5	0.5	-	-	109.1	-0.4	-	-	111.1	1.8	-	-	110.5	-0.5	-	-	111.2	0.6	-	-	110.4	-0.7
1988	-	-	112.0	1.4	-	-	112.5	0.4	-	-	113.9	1.2	-	-	115.0	1.0	-	-	116.4	1.2	-	-	117.3	0.8
1989	-	-	119.0	1.4	-	-	120.1	0.9	-	-	119.9	-0.2	-	-	120.8	0.8	-	-	121.0	0.2	-	-	122.7	1.4
1990	-	-	125.0	1.9	-	-	125.0	0.0	-	-	126.1	0.9	-	-	127.2	0.9	-	-	127.2	0.0	-	-	127.4	0.2
1991	-	-	128.6	0.9	-	-	129.9	1.0	-	-	131.2	1.0	-	-	131.1	-0.1	-	-	132.3	0.9	-	-	132.7	0.3
1992	-	-	133.3	0.5	-	-	133.0	-0.2	-	-	132.6	-0.3	-	-	133.1	0.4	-	-	133.0	-0.1	-	-	133.6	0.5
1993	-	-	133.7	0.1	-	-	133.8	0.1	-	-	134.7	0.7	-	-	135.3	0.4	-	-	136.4	0.8	-	-	135.7	-0.5
1994	-	-	136.0	0.2	-	-	136.5	0.4	-	-	138.6	1.5	-	-	139.9	0.9	-	-	139.5	-0.3	-	-	141.8	1.6
1995	-	-	142.5	0.5	-	-	142.8	0.2	-	-	143.2	0.3	-	-	143.6	0.3	-	-	144.0	0.3	-	-	144.8	0.6

Source: U.S. Department of Labor, Bureau of Labor Statistics, Division of Consumer Prices and Price Indexes. - indicates no data collected for period.

Detroit, MI
Consumer Price Index - All Urban Consumers
Base 1982-1984 = 100
Housing

For 1976-1995. Columns headed % show percentile change in the index from the previous period for which an index is available.

Year	Jan Index	%	Feb Index	%	Mar Index	%	Apr Index	%	May Index	%	Jun Index	%	Jul Index	%	Aug Index	%	Sep Index	%	Oct Index	%	Nov Index	%	Dec Index	%
1976	51.2	-	51.2	0.0	51.2	0.0	51.2	0.0	51.5	0.6	51.8	0.6	52.2	0.8	52.6	0.8	53.7	2.1	53.4	-0.6	53.7	0.6	53.9	0.4
1977	54.1	0.4	54.4	0.6	55.1	1.3	55.6	0.9	55.2	-0.7	55.7	0.9	56.6	1.6	56.2	-0.7	56.4	0.4	56.4	0.0	56.9	0.9	56.9	0.0
1978	57.1	0.4	57.1	0.0	58.4	2.3	58.8	0.7	59.4	1.0	60.3	1.5	60.0	-0.5	60.6	1.0	61.8	2.0	63.2	2.3	63.6	0.6	63.4	-0.3
1979	64.4	1.6	66.3	3.0	67.7	2.1	67.7	0.0	67.6	-0.1	68.1	0.7	70.2	3.1	71.7	2.1	72.2	0.7	74.1	2.6	76.6	3.4	77.3	0.9
1980	78.5	1.6	79.8	1.7	80.5	0.9	83.2	3.4	82.6	-0.7	88.0	6.5	86.1	-2.2	85.9	-0.2	87.7	2.1	90.4	3.1	90.5	0.1	92.8	2.5
1981	91.2	-1.7	91.0	-0.2	88.9	-2.3	91.1	2.5	92.3	1.3	96.2	4.2	96.7	0.5	97.2	0.5	97.0	-0.2	94.3	-2.8	92.7	-1.7	91.8	-1.0
1982	93.2	1.5	90.8	-2.6	91.1	0.3	95.0	4.3	95.5	0.5	96.7	1.3	98.0	1.3	98.2	0.2	99.4	1.2	99.6	0.2	100.0	0.4	98.0	-2.0
1983	98.5	0.5	98.3	-0.2	98.3	0.0	100.3	2.0	99.6	-0.7	101.5	1.9	102.1	0.6	101.5	-0.6	101.3	-0.2	101.1	-0.2	101.5	0.4	101.5	0.0
1984	101.5	0.0	101.8	0.3	102.3	0.5	102.5	0.2	102.6	0.1	103.2	0.6	103.8	0.6	103.9	0.1	105.5	1.5	105.5	0.0	102.8	-2.6	103.5	0.7
1985	105.8	2.2	106.0	0.2	106.7	0.7	106.6	-0.1	106.8	0.2	107.8	0.9	107.8	0.0	107.3	-0.5	109.2	1.8	107.5	-1.6	109.3	1.7	109.1	-0.2
1986	109.6	0.5	110.6	0.9	109.6	-0.9	109.9	0.3	110.6	0.6	109.7	-0.8	107.5	-2.0	110.8	3.1	108.8	-1.8	110.5	1.6	110.2	-0.3	110.0	-0.2
1987	-		112.5	2.3	-		112.8	0.3	-		112.2	-0.5	-		114.1	1.7	-		114.7	0.5	-		112.4	-2.0
1988	-		115.0	2.3	-		114.2	-0.7	-		115.4	1.1	-		118.6	2.8	-		117.9	-0.6	-		116.7	-1.0
1989	-		119.6	2.5	-		119.5	-0.1	-		120.5	0.8	-		121.9	1.2	-		124.0	1.7	-		123.5	-0.4
1990	-		123.8	0.2	-		125.0	1.0	-		126.5	1.2	-		127.9	1.1	-		128.7	0.6	-		127.2	-1.2
1991	-		129.1	1.5	-		125.8	-2.6	-		129.9	3.3	-		128.9	-0.8	-		129.8	0.7	-		128.8	-0.8
1992	-		130.7	1.5	-		130.7	0.0	-		131.9	0.9	-		132.5	0.5	-		133.3	0.6	-		133.0	-0.2
1993	-		133.4	0.3	-		132.1	-1.0	-		133.9	1.4	-		135.0	0.8	-		137.0	1.5	-		135.6	-1.0
1994	-		136.4	0.6	-		136.7	0.2	-		137.6	0.7	-		138.3	0.5	-		138.8	0.4	-		138.5	-0.2
1995	-		139.1	0.4	-		139.3	0.1	-		140.2	0.6	-		141.2	0.7	-		142.1	0.6	-		143.1	0.7

Source: U.S. Department of Labor, Bureau of Labor Statistics, Division of Consumer Prices and Price Indexes. - indicates no data collected for period.

Detroit, MI
Consumer Price Index - Urban Wage Earners
Base 1982-1984 = 100
Housing

For 1976-1995. Columns headed % show percentile change in the index from the previous period for which an index is available.

Year	Jan Index	%	Feb Index	%	Mar Index	%	Apr Index	%	May Index	%	Jun Index	%	Jul Index	%	Aug Index	%	Sep Index	%	Oct Index	%	Nov Index	%	Dec Index	%
1976	51.4	-	51.4	0.0	51.3	-0.2	51.4	0.2	51.7	0.6	52.0	0.6	52.3	0.6	52.7	0.8	53.9	2.3	53.6	-0.6	53.9	0.6	54.0	0.2
1977	54.3	0.6	54.5	0.4	55.2	1.3	55.7	0.9	55.4	-0.5	55.8	0.7	56.8	1.8	56.4	-0.7	56.6	0.4	56.6	0.0	57.0	0.7	57.0	0.0
1978	57.2	0.4	57.4	0.3	58.4	1.7	58.8	0.7	59.6	1.4	60.4	1.3	60.0	-0.7	60.6	1.0	61.8	2.0	63.2	2.3	63.4	0.3	63.1	-0.5
1979	64.2	1.7	66.3	3.3	67.7	2.1	67.9	0.3	67.7	-0.3	68.1	0.6	70.2	3.1	71.8	2.3	72.3	0.7	73.8	2.1	76.4	3.5	77.1	0.9
1980	78.3	1.6	79.6	1.7	80.2	0.8	82.8	3.2	82.3	-0.6	87.7	6.6	85.6	-2.4	85.5	-0.1	87.2	2.0	89.7	2.9	90.2	0.6	92.4	2.4
1981	90.7	-1.8	90.1	-0.7	87.9	-2.4	90.2	2.6	91.6	1.6	95.1	3.8	95.9	0.8	96.3	0.4	96.1	-0.2	93.8	-2.4	92.0	-1.9	91.1	-1.0
1982	92.5	1.5	90.0	-2.7	90.4	0.4	94.4	4.4	94.9	0.5	96.1	1.3	97.5	1.5	97.6	0.1	98.8	1.2	99.0	0.2	99.5	0.5	97.4	-2.1
1983	97.1	-0.3	96.5	-0.6	98.4	2.0	102.2	3.9	104.6	2.3	106.1	1.4	107.8	1.6	107.1	-0.6	107.5	0.4	103.6	-3.6	105.0	1.4	104.7	-0.3
1984	108.9	4.0	105.2	-3.4	103.6	-1.5	99.5	-4.0	99.2	-0.3	98.3	-0.9	99.1	0.8	99.2	0.1	99.8	0.6	100.8	1.0	98.7	-2.1	99.1	0.4
1985	101.2	2.1	101.3	0.1	102.0	0.7	101.9	-0.1	102.0	0.1	102.9	0.9	103.0	0.1	102.5	-0.5	104.3	1.8	102.6	-1.6	104.4	1.8	104.3	-0.1
1986	104.7	0.4	105.5	0.8	104.7	-0.8	105.1	0.4	105.6	0.5	104.7	-0.9	102.7	-1.9	105.9	3.1	103.9	-1.9	105.6	1.6	105.3	-0.3	105.1	-0.2
1987	-	-	107.4	2.2	-	-	107.7	0.3	-	-	107.4	-0.3	-	-	109.0	1.5	-	-	109.6	0.6	-	-	107.4	-2.0
1988	-	-	109.8	2.2	-	-	109.1	-0.6	-	-	110.3	1.1	-	-	112.9	2.4	-	-	112.5	-0.4	-	-	111.7	-0.7
1989	-	-	114.2	2.2	-	-	114.1	-0.1	-	-	114.9	0.7	-	-	116.3	1.2	-	-	118.2	1.6	-	-	118.1	-0.1
1990	-	-	118.3	0.2	-	-	119.4	0.9	-	-	120.9	1.3	-	-	122.1	1.0	-	-	123.0	0.7	-	-	121.5	-1.2
1991	-	-	123.3	1.5	-	-	119.7	-2.9	-	-	123.9	3.5	-	-	123.1	-0.6	-	-	123.9	0.6	-	-	123.0	-0.7
1992	-	-	124.7	1.4	-	-	124.6	-0.1	-	-	125.9	1.0	-	-	126.3	0.3	-	-	127.1	0.6	-	-	126.9	-0.2
1993	-	-	127.2	0.2	-	-	125.9	-1.0	-	-	127.7	1.4	-	-	128.6	0.7	-	-	130.6	1.6	-	-	129.4	-0.9
1994	-	-	129.9	0.4	-	-	130.2	0.2	-	-	131.0	0.6	-	-	131.6	0.5	-	-	132.2	0.5	-	-	131.9	-0.2
1995	-	-	132.4	0.4	-	-	132.6	0.2	-	-	133.5	0.7	-	-	134.3	0.6	-	-	135.1	0.6	-	-	136.1	0.7

Source: U.S. Department of Labor, Bureau of Labor Statistics, Division of Consumer Prices and Price Indexes. - indicates no data collected for period.

Detroit, MI
Consumer Price Index - All Urban Consumers
Base 1982-1984 = 100
Apparel and Upkeep

For 1952-1995. Columns headed % show percentile change in the index from the previous period for which an index is available.

Year	Jan Index	%	Feb Index	%	Mar Index	%	Apr Index	%	May Index	%	Jun Index	%	Jul Index	%	Aug Index	%	Sep Index	%	Oct Index	%	Nov Index	%	Dec Index	%
1952	-	-	-	-	-	-	-	-	-	-	-	-	-	-	-	-	-	-	-	-	-	-	51.7	-
1953	51.7	0.0	51.8	0.2	51.9	0.2	52.0	0.2	52.2	0.4	52.2	0.0	52.2	0.0	52.1	-0.2	52.1	0.0	52.3	0.4	52.2	-0.2	52.1	-0.2
1954	52.0	-0.2	52.1	0.2	51.9	-0.4	51.9	0.0	51.9	0.0	52.1	0.4	52.1	0.0	51.9	-0.4	52.1	0.4	51.9	-0.4	51.9	0.0	51.9	0.0
1955	51.9	0.0	51.9	0.0	51.9	0.0	51.7	-0.4	51.7	0.0	51.8	0.2	51.9	0.2	51.7	-0.4	51.9	0.4	51.6	-0.6	51.7	0.2	51.8	0.2
1956	51.7	-0.2	52.0	0.6	52.1	0.2	52.4	0.6	52.3	-0.2	52.3	0.0	52.5	0.4	52.9	0.8	53.3	0.8	53.3	0.0	53.2	-0.2	52.9	-0.6
1957	53.1	0.4	53.2	0.2	53.2	0.0	53.3	0.2	53.4	0.2	53.2	-0.4	53.0	-0.4	53.1	0.2	53.3	0.4	53.2	-0.2	53.3	0.2	53.2	-0.2
1958	52.7	-0.9	52.7	0.0	52.8	0.2	52.9	0.2	52.8	-0.2	52.8	0.0	52.8	0.0	52.9	0.2	53.3	0.8	53.4	0.2	53.4	0.0	53.6	0.4
1959	53.5	-0.2	53.2	-0.6	53.5	0.6	53.6	0.2	53.6	0.0	53.6	0.0	53.3	-0.6	53.7	0.8	54.6	1.7	55.0	0.7	54.5	-0.9	54.5	0.0
1960	54.1	-0.7	54.0	-0.2	53.8	-0.4	53.8	0.0	54.1	0.6	54.2	0.2	54.3	0.2	54.2	-0.2	55.1	1.7	55.1	0.0	55.1	0.0	55.0	-0.2
1961	55.4	0.7	55.5	0.2	55.3	-0.4	55.3	0.0	55.1	-0.4	55.0	-0.2	54.8	-0.4	54.9	0.2	55.2	0.5	55.5	0.5	55.3	-0.4	55.5	0.4
1962	55.1	-0.7	55.4	0.5	55.4	0.0	55.4	0.0	55.5	0.2	55.6	0.2	55.4	-0.4	55.6	0.4	55.9	0.5	55.9	0.0	55.8	-0.2	55.3	-0.9
1963	55.3	0.0	55.6	0.5	55.4	-0.4	55.7	0.5	55.7	0.0	55.9	0.4	55.8	-0.2	56.2	0.7	56.7	0.9	56.6	-0.2	56.9	0.5	56.8	-0.2
1964	56.1	-1.2	56.4	0.5	56.9	0.9	56.9	0.0	56.8	-0.2	56.8	0.0	56.8	0.0	56.8	0.0	57.2	0.7	57.3	0.2	57.2	-0.2	57.4	0.3
1965	56.8	-1.0	57.2	0.7	57.6	0.7	58.1	0.9	57.9	-0.3	58.1	0.3	57.7	-0.7	57.6	-0.2	58.1	0.9	58.1	0.0	58.1	0.0	58.3	0.3
1966	57.6	-1.2	57.9	0.5	58.4	0.9	58.8	0.7	58.8	0.0	58.8	0.0	58.4	-0.7	58.9	0.9	59.9	1.7	60.0	0.2	60.1	0.2	60.2	0.2
1967	59.9	-0.5	60.1	0.3	60.6	0.8	60.6	0.0	60.7	0.2	60.7	0.0	59.8	-1.5	60.1	0.5	61.0	1.5	61.3	0.5	61.3	0.0	61.3	0.0
1968	60.3	-1.6	61.3	1.7	62.2	1.5	62.2	0.0	63.0	1.3	63.0	0.0	62.5	-0.8	63.4	1.4	64.6	1.9	65.1	0.8	65.6	0.8	65.7	0.2
1969	64.8	-1.4	65.6	1.2	65.8	0.3	65.6	-0.3	65.7	0.2	65.7	0.0	65.0	-1.1	65.2	0.3	67.1	2.9	67.1	0.0	67.1	0.0	67.2	0.1
1970	66.0	-1.8	67.1	1.7	68.9	2.7	67.6	-1.9	67.4	-0.3	67.7	0.4	67.1	-0.9	66.8	-0.4	68.8	3.0	68.9	0.1	69.1	0.3	68.6	-0.7
1971	66.8	-2.6	69.6	4.2	70.0	0.6	69.3	-1.0	70.1	1.2	70.0	-0.1	69.6	-0.6	69.9	0.4	70.5	0.9	71.4	1.3	71.6	0.3	71.0	-0.8
1972	69.4	-2.3	70.9	2.2	70.8	-0.1	71.0	0.3	71.6	0.8	71.1	-0.7	70.8	-0.4	71.3	0.7	72.8	2.1	73.4	0.8	73.6	0.3	73.2	-0.5
1973	71.1	-2.9	72.9	2.5	73.9	1.4	74.4	0.7	74.2	-0.3	73.9	-0.4	72.2	-2.3	73.8	2.2	75.3	2.0	76.0	0.9	75.8	-0.3	75.9	0.1
1974	74.2	-2.2	76.2	2.7	77.5	1.7	78.3	1.0	78.7	0.5	79.6	1.1	79.4	-0.3	83.9	5.7	84.5	0.7	83.4	-1.3	83.7	0.4	83.1	-0.7
1975	82.0	-1.3	81.5	-0.6	83.1	2.0	82.9	-0.2	82.8	-0.1	83.6	1.0	83.6	0.0	83.7	0.1	84.5	1.0	85.1	0.7	85.1	0.0	84.9	-0.2
1976	84.6	-0.4	85.2	0.7	85.4	0.2	86.2	0.9	85.3	-1.0	85.1	-0.2	85.0	-0.1	85.9	1.1	87.1	1.4	87.8	0.8	87.6	-0.2	87.5	-0.1
1977	87.0	-0.6	87.8	0.9	88.1	0.3	88.3	0.2	88.0	-0.3	89.2	1.4	89.0	-0.2	89.4	0.4	89.7	0.3	90.0	0.3	90.4	0.4	89.9	-0.6
1978	87.0	-3.2	86.5	-0.6	87.9	1.6	89.6	1.9	91.1	1.7	91.0	-0.1	88.1	-3.2	91.1	3.4	90.3	-0.9	91.9	1.8	91.6	-0.3	90.5	-1.2
1979	87.7	-3.1	87.3	-0.5	89.5	2.5	89.5	0.0	89.9	0.4	88.1	-2.0	88.2	0.1	91.6	3.9	92.1	0.5	91.9	-0.2	91.6	-0.3	89.7	-2.1
1980	89.1	-0.7	89.7	0.7	93.4	4.1	95.5	2.2	95.0	-0.5	93.3	-1.8	93.6	0.3	94.2	0.6	97.0	3.0	96.8	-0.2	98.1	1.3	96.2	-1.9
1981	95.1	-1.1	95.6	0.5	96.8	1.3	97.6	0.8	98.4	0.8	96.5	-1.9	97.0	0.5	95.4	-1.6	96.7	1.4	97.7	1.0	96.1	-1.6	94.3	-1.9
1982	92.7	-1.7	95.2	2.7	96.2	1.1	96.5	0.3	96.5	0.0	93.4	-3.2	98.3	5.2	100.0	1.7	104.8	4.8	103.7	-1.0	103.1	-0.6	99.2	-3.8
1983	96.2	-3.0	99.2	3.1	99.0	-0.2	99.7	0.7	101.1	1.4	99.4	-1.7	99.9	0.5	103.1	3.2	105.4	2.2	104.3	-1.0	104.3	0.0	100.0	-4.1
1984	96.7	-3.3	101.9	5.4	101.6	-0.3	98.8	-2.8	99.3	0.5	99.9	0.6	100.3	0.4	99.8	-0.5	105.7	5.9	103.4	-2.2	102.3	-1.1	99.1	-3.1
1985	93.1	-6.1	99.1	6.4	100.3	1.2	100.5	0.2	101.3	0.8	100.0	-1.3	101.3	1.3	105.3	3.9	108.6	3.1	107.1	-1.4	108.8	1.6	106.0	-2.6
1986	102.0	-3.8	103.1	1.1	102.9	-0.2	102.3	-0.6	101.9	-0.4	100.2	-1.7	98.4	-1.8	103.4	5.1	106.4	2.9	106.9	0.5	106.5	-0.4	105.2	-1.2
1987	-	-	103.0	-2.1	-	-	109.8	6.6	-	-	104.6	-4.7	-	-	104.0	-0.6	-	-	116.8	12.3	-	-	111.8	-4.3
1988	-	-	108.8	-2.7	-	-	118.5	8.9	-	-	111.3	-6.1	-	-	113.2	1.7	-	-	122.8	8.5	-	-	118.5	-3.5
1989	-	-	119.6	0.9	-	-	126.2	5.5	-	-	121.1	-4.0	-	-	118.8	-1.9	-	-	128.8	8.4	-	-	122.8	-4.7
1990	-	-	126.7	3.2	-	-	131.0	3.4	-	-	122.9	-6.2	-	-	127.8	4.0	-	-	131.4	2.8	-	-	129.0	-1.8
1991	-	-	129.6	0.5	-	-	134.1	3.5	-	-	130.0	-3.1	-	-	131.7	1.3	-	-	137.0	4.0	-	-	128.4	-6.3
1992	-	-	131.7	2.6	-	-	133.4	1.3	-	-	127.4	-4.5	-	-	127.8	0.3	-	-	130.1	1.8	-	-	129.6	-0.4
1993	-	-	134.8	4.0	-	-	144.1	6.9	-	-	134.2	-6.9	-	-	138.3	3.1	-	-	144.0	4.1	-	-	133.0	-7.6
1994	-	-	139.7	5.0	-	-	142.4	1.9	-	-	138.9	-2.5	-	-	130.9	-5.8	-	-	135.3	3.4	-	-	128.2	-5.2
1995	-	-	139.6	8.9	-	-	139.2	-0.3	-	-	132.8	-4.6	-	-	139.0	4.7	-	-	137.3	-1.2	-	-	135.7	-1.2

Source: U.S. Department of Labor, Bureau of Labor Statistics, Division of Consumer Prices and Price Indexes. - indicates no data collected for period.

Detroit, MI
Consumer Price Index - Urban Wage Earners
Base 1982-1984 = 100
Apparel and Upkeep

For 1952-1995. Columns headed % show percentile change in the index from the previous period for which an index is available.

Year	Jan Index	%	Feb Index	%	Mar Index	%	Apr Index	%	May Index	%	Jun Index	%	Jul Index	%	Aug Index	%	Sep Index	%	Oct Index	%	Nov Index	%	Dec Index	%
1952	-	-	-	-	-	-	-	-	-	-	-	-	-	-	-	-	-	-	-	-	-	-	52.6	-
1953	52.7	0.2	52.7	0.0	52.9	0.4	52.9	0.0	53.1	0.4	53.2	0.2	53.1	-0.2	53.1	0.0	53.1	0.0	53.2	0.2	53.1	-0.2	53.0	-0.2
1954	52.9	-0.2	53.0	0.2	52.8	-0.4	52.8	0.0	52.8	0.0	53.0	0.4	53.0	0.0	52.8	-0.4	53.0	0.4	52.9	-0.2	52.8	-0.2	52.8	0.0
1955	52.8	0.0	52.8	0.0	52.9	0.2	52.7	-0.4	52.7	0.0	52.7	0.0	52.8	0.2	52.6	-0.4	52.8	0.4	52.5	-0.6	52.6	0.2	52.7	0.2
1956	52.7	0.0	52.9	0.4	53.1	0.4	53.3	0.4	53.2	-0.2	53.2	0.0	53.4	0.4	53.9	0.9	54.3	0.7	54.2	-0.2	54.2	0.0	53.9	-0.6
1957	54.1	0.4	54.2	0.2	54.2	0.0	54.2	0.0	54.4	0.4	54.2	-0.4	53.9	-0.6	54.0	0.2	54.3	0.6	54.2	-0.2	54.3	0.2	54.2	-0.2
1958	53.7	-0.9	53.7	0.0	53.7	0.0	53.9	0.4	53.7	-0.4	53.7	0.0	53.7	0.0	53.9	0.4	54.2	0.6	54.4	0.4	54.4	0.0	54.5	0.2
1959	54.5	0.0	54.2	-0.6	54.5	0.6	54.5	0.0	54.6	0.2	54.5	-0.2	54.2	-0.6	54.7	0.9	55.6	1.6	56.0	0.7	55.5	-0.9	55.5	0.0
1960	55.0	-0.9	55.0	0.0	54.8	-0.4	54.8	0.0	55.0	0.4	55.2	0.4	55.3	0.2	55.2	-0.2	56.1	1.6	56.1	0.0	56.1	0.0	56.0	-0.2
1961	56.4	0.7	56.5	0.2	56.3	-0.4	56.3	0.0	56.1	-0.4	56.0	-0.2	55.8	-0.4	55.9	0.2	56.2	0.5	56.5	0.5	56.3	-0.4	56.5	0.4
1962	56.1	-0.7	56.4	0.5	56.4	0.0	56.4	0.0	56.5	0.2	56.6	0.2	56.4	-0.4	56.6	0.4	56.9	0.5	56.9	0.0	56.8	-0.2	56.3	-0.9
1963	56.3	0.0	56.6	0.5	56.4	-0.4	56.7	0.5	56.8	0.2	56.9	0.2	56.8	-0.2	57.2	0.7	57.7	0.9	57.6	-0.2	57.9	0.5	57.8	-0.2
1964	57.1	-1.2	57.4	0.5	57.9	0.9	57.9	0.0	57.9	0.0	57.8	-0.2	57.8	0.0	57.8	0.0	58.2	0.7	58.3	0.2	58.2	-0.2	58.4	0.3
1965	57.8	-1.0	58.2	0.7	58.7	0.9	59.1	0.7	58.9	-0.3	59.1	0.3	58.7	-0.7	58.7	0.0	59.2	0.9	59.2	0.0	59.2	0.0	59.3	0.2
1966	58.6	-1.2	58.9	0.5	59.5	1.0	59.8	0.5	59.8	0.0	59.8	0.0	59.5	-0.5	60.0	0.8	61.0	1.7	61.1	0.2	61.2	0.2	61.3	0.2
1967	61.0	-0.5	61.2	0.3	61.7	0.8	61.7	0.0	61.8	0.2	61.8	0.0	60.9	-1.5	61.1	0.3	62.1	1.6	62.4	0.5	62.4	0.0	62.4	0.0
1968	61.4	-1.6	62.4	1.6	63.3	1.4	63.3	0.0	64.1	1.3	64.2	0.2	63.7	-0.8	64.6	1.4	65.8	1.9	66.3	0.8	66.8	0.8	66.9	0.1
1969	65.9	-1.5	66.8	1.4	67.0	0.3	66.8	-0.3	66.9	0.1	66.9	0.0	66.1	-1.2	66.4	0.5	68.3	2.9	68.3	0.0	68.4	0.1	68.4	0.0
1970	67.2	-1.8	68.3	1.6	70.1	2.6	68.8	-1.9	68.7	-0.1	68.9	0.3	68.3	-0.9	68.0	-0.4	70.0	2.9	70.1	0.1	70.4	0.4	69.8	-0.9
1971	68.0	-2.6	70.8	4.1	71.3	0.7	70.6	-1.0	71.4	1.1	71.3	-0.1	70.9	-0.6	71.2	0.4	71.7	0.7	72.7	1.4	72.9	0.3	72.2	-1.0
1972	70.6	-2.2	72.2	2.3	72.1	-0.1	72.3	0.3	72.9	0.8	72.4	-0.7	72.1	-0.4	72.6	0.7	74.1	2.1	74.8	0.9	74.9	0.1	74.5	-0.5
1973	72.4	-2.8	74.2	2.5	75.2	1.3	75.7	0.7	75.6	-0.1	75.3	-0.4	73.5	-2.4	75.1	2.2	76.6	2.0	77.4	1.0	77.2	-0.3	77.2	0.0
1974	75.5	-2.2	77.5	2.6	78.9	1.8	79.7	1.0	80.1	0.5	81.0	1.1	80.9	-0.1	85.4	5.6	86.1	0.8	84.9	-1.4	85.3	0.5	84.6	-0.8
1975	83.5	-1.3	83.0	-0.6	84.6	1.9	84.4	-0.2	84.3	-0.1	85.1	0.9	85.1	0.0	85.2	0.1	86.0	0.9	86.6	0.7	86.6	0.0	86.4	-0.2
1976	86.1	-0.3	86.7	0.7	87.0	0.3	87.8	0.9	86.8	-1.1	86.7	-0.1	86.5	-0.2	87.4	1.0	88.7	1.5	89.4	0.8	89.1	-0.3	89.1	0.0
1977	88.6	-0.6	89.4	0.9	89.7	0.3	89.9	0.2	89.6	-0.3	90.8	1.3	90.6	-0.2	91.0	0.4	91.3	0.3	91.7	0.4	92.0	0.3	91.6	-0.4
1978	87.0	-5.0	87.5	0.6	87.9	0.5	90.5	3.0	93.5	3.3	95.2	1.8	92.5	-2.8	98.4	6.4	98.2	-0.2	98.0	-0.2	98.4	0.4	97.5	-0.9
1979	93.0	-4.6	92.5	-0.5	94.0	1.6	94.0	0.0	93.8	-0.2	90.8	-3.2	89.5	-1.4	95.9	7.2	96.1	0.2	95.9	-0.2	95.6	-0.3	92.0	-3.8
1980	92.4	0.4	96.6	4.5	99.4	2.9	100.4	1.0	102.6	2.2	94.1	-8.3	95.6	1.6	95.3	-0.3	96.7	1.5	100.1	3.5	100.9	0.8	97.9	-3.0
1981	97.2	-0.7	96.8	-0.4	98.6	1.9	99.4	0.8	99.4	0.0	97.7	-1.7	98.9	1.2	95.2	-3.7	97.1	2.0	97.5	0.4	95.7	-1.8	94.1	-1.7
1982	94.2	0.1	96.5	2.4	97.4	0.9	97.8	0.4	97.9	0.1	94.1	-3.9	99.1	5.3	99.5	0.4	104.3	4.8	101.4	-2.8	101.0	-0.4	97.6	-3.4
1983	95.3	-2.4	99.2	4.1	99.7	0.5	100.1	0.4	101.9	1.8	100.6	-1.3	100.4	-0.2	102.7	2.3	104.1	1.4	103.4	-0.7	103.7	0.3	98.4	-5.1
1984	95.1	-3.4	102.7	8.0	103.0	0.3	99.9	-3.0	100.3	0.4	100.5	0.2	98.8	-1.7	100.1	1.3	105.7	5.6	103.7	-1.9	101.3	-2.3	98.8	-2.5
1985	91.9	-7.0	98.6	7.3	101.2	2.6	101.4	0.2	102.2	0.8	102.0	-0.2	102.9	0.9	106.7	3.7	109.6	2.7	108.6	-0.9	110.6	1.8	106.7	-3.5
1986	105.2	-1.4	104.5	-0.7	104.0	-0.5	103.3	-0.7	102.8	-0.5	100.5	-2.2	98.3	-2.2	108.3	10.2	110.1	1.7	110.9	0.7	109.4	-1.4	108.2	-1.1
1987	-	-	105.9	-2.1	-	-	114.8	8.4	-	-	107.8	-6.1	-	-	107.6	-0.2	-	-	118.9	10.5	-	-	114.5	-3.7
1988	-	-	112.9	-1.4	-	-	123.0	8.9	-	-	115.4	-6.2	-	-	117.2	1.6	-	-	125.6	7.2	-	-	122.8	-2.2
1989	-	-	123.4	0.5	-	-	129.8	5.2	-	-	124.8	-3.9	-	-	121.1	-3.0	-	-	131.7	8.8	-	-	125.6	-4.6
1990	-	-	130.1	3.6	-	-	134.3	3.2	-	-	126.8	-5.6	-	-	133.4	5.2	-	-	135.7	1.7	-	-	132.3	-2.5
1991	-	-	132.5	0.2	-	-	135.4	2.2	-	-	131.5	-2.9	-	-	137.1	4.3	-	-	140.6	2.6	-	-	132.5	-5.8
1992	-	-	134.8	1.7	-	-	135.9	0.8	-	-	130.3	-4.1	-	-	131.3	0.8	-	-	134.0	2.1	-	-	134.0	0.0
1993	-	-	139.2	3.9	-	-	146.1	5.0	-	-	136.0	-6.9	-	-	140.4	3.2	-	-	146.9	4.6	-	-	135.7	-7.6
1994	-	-	141.7	4.4	-	-	144.2	1.8	-	-	140.9	-2.3	-	-	135.0	-4.2	-	-	139.2	3.1	-	-	131.8	-5.3
1995	-	-	142.0	7.7	-	-	142.1	0.1	-	-	134.3	-5.5	-	-	140.3	4.5	-	-	139.2	-0.8	-	-	137.9	-0.9

Source: U.S. Department of Labor, Bureau of Labor Statistics, Division of Consumer Prices and Price Indexes. - indicates no data collected for period.

Detroit, MI
Consumer Price Index - All Urban Consumers
Base 1982-1984 = 100
Transportation

For 1947-1995. Columns headed % show percentile change in the index from the previous period for which an index is available.

Year	Jan Index	%	Feb Index	%	Mar Index	%	Apr Index	%	May Index	%	Jun Index	%	Jul Index	%	Aug Index	%	Sep Index	%	Oct Index	%	Nov Index	%	Dec Index	%
1947	19.2	-	19.3	0.5	19.4	0.5	19.5	0.5	19.5	0.0	19.5	0.0	19.5	0.0	19.8	1.5	20.1	1.5	20.1	0.0	20.3	1.0	20.7	2.0
1948	20.7	0.0	20.7	0.0	20.7	0.0	21.8	5.3	21.8	0.0	22.0	0.9	22.6	2.7	23.0	1.8	23.1	0.4	23.1	0.0	23.1	0.0	23.1	0.0
1949	23.1	0.0	23.4	1.3	23.4	0.0	23.5	0.4	23.5	0.0	23.4	-0.4	23.4	0.0	23.4	0.0	23.4	0.0	23.4	0.0	23.4	0.0	23.4	0.0
1950	23.4	0.0	23.4	0.0	23.4	0.0	23.4	0.0	23.8	1.7	23.9	0.4	23.9	0.0	23.7	-0.8	23.8	0.4	23.7	-0.4	23.8	0.4	23.8	0.0
1951	23.8	0.0	23.8	0.0	24.1	1.3	24.1	0.0	24.1	0.0	24.6	2.1	24.8	0.8	24.8	0.0	25.1	1.2	25.5	1.6	25.9	1.6	25.9	0.0
1952	25.9	0.0	25.9	0.0	26.1	0.8	26.1	0.0	26.1	0.0	26.1	0.0	26.1	0.0	26.5	1.5	26.6	0.4	27.4	3.0	27.4	0.0	27.4	0.0
1953	27.4	0.0	27.4	0.0	27.3	-0.4	27.4	0.4	27.4	0.0	27.6	0.7	27.8	0.7	27.8	0.0	27.7	-0.4	27.6	-0.4	27.5	-0.4	26.7	-2.9
1954	27.3	2.2	26.5	-2.9	26.4	-0.4	26.3	-0.4	26.3	0.0	26.0	-1.1	26.1	0.4	25.7	-1.5	25.7	0.0	25.7	0.0	27.3	6.2	26.7	-2.2
1955	26.6	-0.4	26.4	-0.8	26.4	0.0	26.3	-0.4	26.3	0.0	26.7	1.5	26.6	-0.4	26.3	-1.1	26.4	0.4	26.7	1.1	27.2	1.9	27.2	0.0
1956	27.1	-0.4	27.1	0.0	27.0	-0.4	27.2	0.7	27.2	0.0	27.1	-0.4	27.5	1.5	27.6	0.4	27.5	-0.4	28.0	1.8	28.3	1.1	28.3	0.0
1957	28.6	1.1	28.5	-0.3	28.7	0.7	28.6	-0.3	28.8	0.7	28.8	0.0	28.8	0.0	28.9	0.3	28.7	-0.7	28.6	-0.3	30.0	4.9	29.7	-1.0
1958	29.3	-1.3	28.6	-2.4	28.6	0.0	28.5	-0.3	28.3	-0.7	28.7	1.4	28.7	0.0	29.2	1.7	29.3	0.3	29.2	-0.3	29.4	0.7	29.7	1.0
1959	29.8	0.3	29.5	-1.0	29.8	1.0	30.1	1.0	30.0	-0.3	29.1	-3.0	30.4	4.5	30.3	-0.3	30.7	1.3	30.7	0.0	30.5	-0.7	30.6	0.3
1960	29.9	-2.3	30.2	1.0	29.8	-1.3	29.3	-1.7	29.5	0.7	30.6	3.7	30.6	0.0	30.7	0.3	30.3	-1.3	30.4	0.3	30.4	0.0	30.0	-1.3
1961	30.2	0.7	30.1	-0.3	29.5	-2.0	29.1	-1.4	29.5	1.4	29.2	-1.0	28.9	-1.0	30.5	5.5	29.8	-2.3	30.1	1.0	30.2	0.3	28.7	-5.0
1962	29.0	1.0	30.6	5.5	30.6	0.0	31.0	1.3	29.8	-3.9	29.9	0.3	29.3	-2.0	30.3	3.4	30.8	1.7	31.0	0.6	30.4	-1.9	31.1	2.3
1963	30.6	-1.6	30.4	-0.7	30.6	0.7	29.5	-3.6	30.4	3.1	30.2	-0.7	30.3	0.3	31.4	3.6	29.7	-5.4	30.5	2.7	31.0	1.6	30.7	-1.0
1964	30.9	0.7	29.7	-3.9	30.3	2.0	30.3	0.0	29.8	-1.7	30.2	1.3	30.7	1.7	31.0	1.0	31.2	0.6	31.6	1.3	31.1	-1.6	31.3	0.6
1965	31.8	1.6	31.2	-1.9	31.1	-0.3	31.8	2.3	32.3	1.6	32.2	-0.3	32.2	0.0	32.0	-0.6	32.0	0.0	32.2	0.6	32.4	0.6	32.4	0.0
1966	32.5	0.3	32.3	-0.6	32.7	1.2	32.9	0.6	32.9	0.0	32.9	0.0	32.8	-0.3	32.9	0.3	32.6	-0.9	33.0	1.2	33.1	0.3	33.0	-0.3
1967	33.0	0.0	33.2	0.6	33.4	0.6	33.6	0.6	33.6	0.0	33.5	-0.3	33.5	0.0	33.4	-0.3	33.5	0.3	33.6	0.3	34.0	1.2	34.1	0.3
1968	34.4	0.9	34.4	0.0	34.9	1.5	34.9	0.0	35.0	0.3	35.1	0.3	35.0	-0.3	34.9	-0.3	34.8	-0.3	35.1	0.9	35.3	0.6	35.1	-0.6
1969	35.0	-0.3	35.4	1.1	36.6	3.4	36.5	-0.3	36.6	0.3	36.7	0.3	35.7	-2.7	36.7	2.8	35.6	-3.0	36.1	1.4	35.8	-0.8	36.0	0.6
1970	36.1	0.3	36.9	2.2	35.4	-4.1	36.5	3.1	37.2	1.9	36.4	-2.2	36.5	0.3	35.8	-1.9	36.0	0.6	38.7	7.5	38.9	0.5	37.8	-2.8
1971	39.5	4.5	38.1	-3.5	37.8	-0.8	38.1	0.8	38.7	1.6	38.8	0.3	37.8	-2.6	38.9	2.9	38.2	-1.8	38.2	0.0	38.6	1.0	38.4	-0.5
1972	39.1	1.8	39.2	0.3	38.8	-1.0	38.7	-0.3	38.7	0.0	39.2	1.3	39.1	-0.3	39.2	0.3	39.0	-0.5	39.2	0.5	39.2	0.0	39.6	1.0
1973	39.6	0.0	40.4	2.0	40.5	0.2	41.2	1.7	41.5	0.7	41.9	1.0	41.9	0.0	41.8	-0.2	41.5	-0.7	42.0	1.2	42.3	0.7	42.9	1.4
1974	43.4	1.2	43.9	1.2	45.2	3.0	45.9	1.5	46.3	0.9	47.1	1.7	47.5	0.8	47.6	0.2	47.8	0.4	47.9	0.2	47.9	0.0	47.9	0.0
1975	47.9	0.0	47.9	0.0	48.4	1.0	48.7	0.6	49.0	0.6	50.0	2.0	51.1	2.2	51.1	0.0	51.3	0.4	51.6	0.6	51.6	0.0	51.6	0.0
1976	51.8	0.4	51.8	0.0	51.9	0.2	52.3	0.8	53.1	1.5	53.8	1.3	54.2	0.7	54.4	0.4	54.8	0.7	55.1	0.5	55.8	1.3	55.9	0.2
1977	56.0	0.2	56.3	0.5	57.4	2.0	58.4	1.7	59.0	1.0	59.3	0.5	59.4	0.2	59.6	0.3	59.5	-0.2	59.5	0.0	59.5	0.0	59.5	0.0
1978	59.6	0.2	59.7	0.2	60.3	1.0	60.6	0.5	61.6	1.7	62.2	1.0	62.7	0.8	62.8	0.2	62.9	0.2	63.8	1.4	64.1	0.5	64.2	0.2
1979	65.3	1.7	65.8	0.8	66.3	0.8	68.0	2.6	68.9	1.3	70.3	2.0	71.5	1.7	72.5	1.4	73.1	0.8	74.0	1.2	74.4	0.5	75.3	1.2
1980	77.1	2.4	78.5	1.8	79.8	1.7	81.2	1.8	82.1	1.1	82.8	0.9	81.5	-1.6	83.2	2.1	85.2	2.4	86.4	1.4	87.9	1.7	87.7	-0.2
1981	88.9	1.4	90.0	1.2	91.1	1.2	92.0	1.0	93.1	1.2	93.3	0.2	95.4	2.3	95.4	0.0	95.4	0.0	96.8	1.5	97.1	0.3	97.0	-0.1
1982	97.4	0.4	96.2	-1.2	95.7	-0.5	95.4	-0.3	96.7	1.4	99.1	2.5	99.8	0.7	99.9	0.1	98.5	-1.4	98.6	0.1	98.6	0.0	98.4	-0.2
1983	97.3	-1.1	96.4	-0.9	96.1	-0.3	96.4	0.3	97.6	1.2	97.5	-0.1	98.7	1.2	99.6	0.9	100.2	0.6	100.3	0.1	101.2	0.9	101.0	-0.2
1984	101.1	0.1	101.4	0.3	102.0	0.6	103.1	1.1	103.6	0.5	103.5	-0.1	103.4	-0.1	103.4	0.0	104.5	1.1	106.0	1.4	106.1	0.1	105.3	-0.8
1985	104.6	-0.7	105.4	0.8	106.1	0.7	106.5	0.4	106.5	0.0	106.6	0.1	106.7	0.1	107.1	0.4	106.0	-1.0	107.2	1.1	107.9	0.7	108.3	0.4
1986	108.0	-0.3	106.0	-1.9	102.7	-3.1	101.2	-1.5	103.5	2.3	103.9	0.4	102.3	-1.5	101.7	-0.6	100.8	-0.9	102.2	1.4	103.6	1.4	103.1	-0.5
1987	-	-	102.9	-0.2	-	-	104.2	1.3	-	-	104.9	0.7	-	-	106.4	1.4	-	-	107.8	1.3	-	-	106.7	-1.0
1988	-	-	105.5	-1.1	-	-	106.8	1.2	-	-	110.3	3.3	-	-	111.3	0.9	-	-	111.7	0.4	-	-	112.8	1.0
1989	-	-	113.7	0.8	-	-	117.9	3.7	-	-	119.0	0.9	-	-	116.0	-2.5	-	-	118.4	2.1	-	-	118.3	-0.1
1990	-	-	120.5	1.9	-	-	120.2	-0.2	-	-	121.7	1.2	-	-	124.1	2.0	-	-	130.4	5.1	-	-	130.5	0.1
1991	-	-	128.3	-1.7	-	-	129.2	0.7	-	-	129.8	0.5	-	-	128.9	-0.7	-	-	129.1	0.2	-	-	130.9	1.4

[Continued]

Detroit, MI
Consumer Price Index - All Urban Consumers
Base 1982-1984 = 100
Transportation
[Continued]

For 1947-1995. Columns headed % show percentile change in the index from the previous period for which an index is available.

Year	Jan Index	%	Feb Index	%	Mar Index	%	Apr Index	%	May Index	%	Jun Index	%	Jul Index	%	Aug Index	%	Sep Index	%	Oct Index	%	Nov Index	%	Dec Index	%
1992	-	-	128.5	-1.8	-	-	130.0	1.2	-	-	130.1	0.1	-	-	128.6	-1.2	-	-	132.1	2.7	-	-	130.3	-1.4
1993	-	-	131.8	1.2	-	-	131.7	-0.1	-	-	132.7	0.8	-	-	132.7	0.0	-	-	134.4	1.3	-	-	132.6	-1.3
1994	-	-	134.9	1.7	-	-	136.3	1.0	-	-	139.9	2.6	-	-	142.2	1.6	-	-	140.4	-1.3	-	-	132.6	-1.3
1995	-	-	142.0	1.4	-	-	144.9	2.0	-	-	145.5	0.4	-	-	141.8	-2.5	-	-	144.4	1.8	-	-	143.8	-0.4

Source: U.S. Department of Labor, Bureau of Labor Statistics, Division of Consumer Prices and Price Indexes. - indicates no data collected for period.

Detroit, MI
Consumer Price Index - Urban Wage Earners
Base 1982-1984 = 100
Transportation

For 1947-1995. Columns headed % show percentile change in the index from the previous period for which an index is available.

Year	Jan Index	%	Feb Index	%	Mar Index	%	Apr Index	%	May Index	%	Jun Index	%	Jul Index	%	Aug Index	%	Sep Index	%	Oct Index	%	Nov Index	%	Dec Index	%
1947	19.9	-	20.0	0.5	20.1	0.5	20.2	0.5	20.2	0.0	20.2	0.0	20.2	0.0	20.5	1.5	20.9	2.0	20.9	0.0	21.1	1.0	21.5	1.9
1948	21.5	0.0	21.5	0.0	21.5	0.0	22.6	5.1	22.6	0.0	22.8	0.9	23.4	2.6	23.9	2.1	24.0	0.4	24.0	0.0	24.0	0.0	24.0	0.0
1949	24.0	0.0	24.3	1.2	24.3	0.0	24.4	0.4	24.4	0.0	24.3	-0.4	24.3	0.0	24.3	0.0	24.3	0.0	24.3	0.0	24.3	0.0	24.3	0.0
1950	24.3	0.0	24.3	0.0	24.3	0.0	24.3	0.0	24.7	1.6	24.8	0.4	24.8	0.0	24.6	-0.8	24.7	0.4	24.6	-0.4	24.7	0.4	24.7	0.0
1951	24.7	0.0	24.7	0.0	25.0	1.2	25.1	0.4	25.1	0.0	25.5	1.6	25.8	1.2	25.8	0.0	26.1	1.2	26.5	1.5	26.8	1.1	26.8	0.0
1952	26.8	0.0	26.9	0.4	27.0	0.4	27.0	0.0	27.0	0.0	27.0	0.0	27.0	0.0	27.5	1.9	27.6	0.4	28.4	2.9	28.4	0.0	28.4	0.0
1953	28.5	0.4	28.4	-0.4	28.4	0.0	28.4	0.0	28.4	0.0	28.6	0.7	28.8	0.7	28.8	0.0	28.7	-0.3	28.6	-0.3	28.5	-0.3	27.7	-2.8
1954	28.4	2.5	27.5	-3.2	27.4	-0.4	27.3	-0.4	27.3	0.0	27.0	-1.1	27.0	0.0	26.7	-1.1	26.7	0.0	26.7	0.0	28.3	6.0	27.7	-2.1
1955	27.6	-0.4	27.4	-0.7	27.4	0.0	27.3	-0.4	27.3	0.0	27.7	1.5	27.6	-0.4	27.3	-1.1	27.4	0.4	27.7	1.1	28.2	1.8	28.3	0.4
1956	28.2	-0.4	28.1	-0.4	28.1	0.0	28.2	0.4	28.3	0.4	28.2	-0.4	28.5	1.1	28.6	0.4	28.6	0.0	29.0	1.4	29.4	1.4	29.4	0.0
1957	29.7	1.0	29.6	-0.3	29.8	0.7	29.7	-0.3	29.9	0.7	29.9	0.0	29.9	0.0	30.0	0.3	29.8	-0.7	29.7	-0.3	31.1	4.7	30.8	-1.0
1958	30.5	-1.0	29.7	-2.6	29.7	0.0	29.5	-0.7	29.4	-0.3	29.8	1.4	29.8	0.0	30.3	1.7	30.4	0.3	30.3	-0.3	30.5	0.7	30.8	1.0
1959	30.9	0.3	30.6	-1.0	30.9	1.0	31.3	1.3	31.1	-0.6	30.2	-2.9	31.6	4.6	31.4	-0.6	31.8	1.3	31.8	0.0	31.6	-0.6	31.8	0.6
1960	31.0	-2.5	31.4	1.3	30.9	-1.6	30.5	-1.3	30.6	0.3	31.8	3.9	31.8	0.0	31.8	0.0	31.4	-1.3	31.5	0.3	31.5	0.0	31.1	-1.3
1961	31.4	1.0	31.2	-0.6	30.6	-1.9	30.2	-1.3	30.7	1.7	30.3	-1.3	30.0	-1.0	31.6	5.3	30.9	-2.2	31.3	1.3	31.3	0.0	29.8	-4.8
1962	30.1	1.0	31.8	5.6	31.8	0.0	32.2	1.3	30.9	-4.0	31.0	0.3	30.4	-1.9	31.5	3.6	32.0	1.6	32.2	0.6	31.6	-1.9	32.3	2.2
1963	31.8	-1.5	31.5	-0.9	31.8	1.0	30.6	-3.8	31.5	2.9	31.3	-0.6	31.4	0.3	32.5	3.5	30.8	-5.2	31.7	2.9	32.2	1.6	31.9	-0.9
1964	32.0	0.3	30.8	-3.8	31.4	1.9	31.4	0.0	30.9	-1.6	31.3	1.3	31.8	1.6	32.2	1.3	32.3	0.3	32.7	1.2	32.3	-1.2	32.4	0.3
1965	33.0	1.9	32.3	-2.1	32.2	-0.3	33.0	2.5	33.5	1.5	33.4	-0.3	33.4	0.0	33.2	-0.6	33.2	0.0	33.4	0.6	33.6	0.6	33.6	0.0
1966	33.7	0.3	33.5	-0.6	34.0	1.5	34.2	0.6	34.1	-0.3	34.1	0.0	34.0	-0.3	34.1	0.3	33.8	-0.9	34.2	1.2	34.4	0.6	34.2	-0.6
1967	34.2	0.0	34.5	0.9	34.7	0.6	34.9	0.6	34.8	-0.3	34.8	0.0	34.7	-0.3	34.7	0.0	34.7	0.0	34.9	0.6	35.3	1.1	35.4	0.3
1968	35.7	0.8	35.7	0.0	36.2	1.4	36.2	0.0	36.3	0.3	36.4	0.3	36.3	-0.3	36.2	-0.3	36.1	-0.3	36.4	0.8	36.6	0.5	36.4	-0.5
1969	36.3	-0.3	36.8	1.4	38.0	3.3	37.9	-0.3	38.0	0.3	38.1	0.3	37.0	-2.9	38.0	2.7	37.0	-2.6	37.4	1.1	37.1	-0.8	37.3	0.5
1970	37.4	0.3	38.3	2.4	36.7	-4.2	37.9	3.3	38.6	1.8	37.8	-2.1	37.8	0.0	37.2	-1.6	37.3	0.3	40.1	7.5	40.4	0.7	39.2	-3.0
1971	41.0	4.6	39.5	-3.7	39.3	-0.5	39.6	0.8	40.1	1.3	40.3	0.5	39.2	-2.7	40.4	3.1	39.7	-1.7	39.7	0.0	40.1	1.0	39.9	-0.5
1972	40.6	1.8	40.7	0.2	40.2	-1.2	40.1	-0.2	40.2	0.2	40.6	1.0	40.5	-0.2	40.7	0.5	40.5	-0.5	40.6	0.2	40.7	0.2	41.1	1.0
1973	41.1	0.0	41.9	1.9	42.0	0.2	42.7	1.7	43.1	0.9	43.4	0.7	43.5	0.2	43.4	-0.2	43.1	-0.7	43.6	1.2	43.9	0.7	44.5	1.4
1974	45.0	1.1	45.6	1.3	46.9	2.9	47.6	1.5	48.0	0.8	48.8	1.7	49.2	0.8	49.4	0.4	49.6	0.4	49.7	0.2	49.7	0.0	49.7	0.0
1975	49.7	0.0	49.7	0.0	50.3	1.2	50.5	0.4	50.8	0.6	51.9	2.2	53.0	2.1	53.0	0.0	53.2	0.4	53.5	0.6	53.5	0.0	53.5	0.0
1976	53.7	0.4	53.7	0.0	53.8	0.2	54.3	0.9	55.1	1.5	55.9	1.5	56.2	0.5	56.4	0.4	56.8	0.7	57.2	0.7	57.9	1.2	58.0	0.2
1977	58.2	0.3	58.4	0.3	59.5	1.9	60.6	1.8	61.2	1.0	61.5	0.5	61.6	0.2	61.8	0.3	61.7	-0.2	61.7	0.0	61.8	0.2	61.8	0.0
1978	61.8	0.0	62.0	0.3	62.3	0.5	62.7	0.6	63.6	1.4	64.2	0.9	64.6	0.6	64.8	0.3	64.9	0.2	65.8	1.4	66.0	0.3	66.2	0.3
1979	67.5	2.0	68.0	0.7	68.6	0.9	70.1	2.2	71.1	1.4	72.6	2.1	74.2	2.2	75.0	1.1	74.9	-0.1	76.4	2.0	76.6	0.3	77.1	0.7
1980	79.1	2.6	80.4	1.6	81.7	1.6	84.3	3.2	85.3	1.2	85.5	0.2	83.4	-2.5	85.6	2.6	87.4	2.1	86.9	-0.6	88.1	1.4	86.9	-1.4
1981	88.0	1.3	89.3	1.5	90.0	0.8	90.9	1.0	92.4	1.7	92.6	0.2	94.3	1.8	94.5	0.2	95.2	0.7	96.4	1.3	96.9	0.5	97.0	0.1
1982	97.3	0.3	96.2	-1.1	95.7	-0.5	95.3	-0.4	96.6	1.4	99.1	2.6	99.8	0.7	99.8	0.0	98.5	-1.3	98.6	0.1	98.6	0.0	98.5	-0.1
1983	97.3	-1.2	96.4	-0.9	96.1	-0.3	96.4	0.3	97.7	1.3	97.6	-0.1	98.7	1.1	99.6	0.9	100.2	0.6	100.3	0.1	101.2	0.9	101.0	-0.2
1984	101.1	0.1	101.4	0.3	102.0	0.6	103.1	1.1	103.6	0.5	103.5	-0.1	103.4	-0.1	103.4	0.0	104.5	1.1	106.0	1.4	106.0	0.0	105.3	-0.7
1985	104.6	-0.7	105.5	0.9	106.1	0.6	106.6	0.5	106.6	0.0	106.7	0.1	106.9	0.2	107.3	0.4	106.1	-1.1	107.3	1.1	108.1	0.7	108.4	0.3
1986	108.1	-0.3	106.0	-1.9	102.6	-3.2	101.1	-1.5	103.5	2.4	103.9	0.4	102.3	-1.5	101.6	-0.7	100.8	-0.8	102.1	1.3	103.5	1.4	103.0	-0.5
1987	-		102.9	-0.1	-		104.3	1.4	-		105.0	0.7	-		106.6	1.5	-		108.1	1.4	-		106.9	-1.1
1988	-		105.6	-1.2	-		107.0	1.3	-		110.2	3.0	-		111.4	1.1	-		111.7	0.3	-		112.8	1.0
1989	-		113.6	0.7	-		118.0	3.9	-		119.2	1.0	-		116.0	-2.7	-		118.3	2.0	-		118.1	-0.2
1990	-		120.5	2.0	-		120.1	-0.3	-		121.7	1.3	-		124.2	2.1	-		130.7	5.2	-		130.6	-0.1
1991	-		128.1	-1.9	-		129.0	0.7	-		129.7	0.5	-		128.8	-0.7	-		129.0	0.2	-		130.7	1.3

[Continued]

Detroit, MI
Consumer Price Index - Urban Wage Earners
Base 1982-1984 = 100
Transportation

[Continued]

For 1947-1995. Columns headed % show percentile change in the index from the previous period for which an index is available.

Year	Jan Index	%	Feb Index	%	Mar Index	%	Apr Index	%	May Index	%	Jun Index	%	Jul Index	%	Aug Index	%	Sep Index	%	Oct Index	%	Nov Index	%	Dec Index	%
1992	-	-	128.2	-1.9	-	-	129.8	1.2	-	-	129.9	0.1	-	-	128.4	-1.2	-	-	131.9	2.7	-	-	130.1	-1.4
1993	-	-	131.6	1.2	-	-	131.6	0.0	-	-	132.7	0.8	-	-	132.6	-0.1	-	-	134.3	1.3	-	-	132.4	-1.4
1994	-	-	134.7	1.7	-	-	136.1	1.0	-	-	139.7	2.6	-	-	142.3	1.9	-	-	140.4	-1.3	-	-	132.4	-1.4
1995	-	-	142.0	1.4	-	-	145.1	2.2	-	-	145.8	0.5	-	-	141.9	-2.7	-	-	144.5	1.8	-	-	143.8	-0.5

Source: U.S. Department of Labor, Bureau of Labor Statistics, Division of Consumer Prices and Price Indexes. - indicates no data collected for period.

Detroit, MI
Consumer Price Index - All Urban Consumers
Base 1982-1984 = 100
Medical Care

For 1947-1995. Columns headed % show percentile change in the index from the previous period for which an index is available.

Year	Jan Index	%	Feb Index	%	Mar Index	%	Apr Index	%	May Index	%	Jun Index	%	Jul Index	%	Aug Index	%	Sep Index	%	Oct Index	%	Nov Index	%	Dec Index	%
1947	11.5	-	11.6	0.9	11.7	0.9	11.7	0.0	11.8	0.9	11.8	0.0	11.8	0.0	11.8	0.0	12.0	1.7	12.0	0.0	12.0	0.0	12.0	0.0
1948	12.1	0.8	12.1	0.0	12.2	0.8	12.2	0.0	12.2	0.0	12.2	0.0	12.2	0.0	12.3	0.8	12.4	0.8	12.4	0.0	12.4	0.0	12.4	0.0
1949	12.4	0.0	12.5	0.8	12.5	0.0	12.5	0.0	12.5	0.0	12.5	0.0	12.5	0.0	12.6	0.8	12.7	0.8	12.7	0.0	12.7	0.0	12.7	0.0
1950	12.7	0.0	12.8	0.8	12.8	0.0	12.8	0.0	12.8	0.0	12.8	0.0	12.8	0.0	12.8	0.0	12.8	0.0	12.9	0.8	12.9	0.0	12.9	0.0
1951	12.9	0.0	12.9	0.0	13.0	0.8	13.0	0.0	13.0	0.0	13.5	3.8	13.6	0.7	13.6	0.0	13.6	0.0	13.6	0.0	13.6	0.0	13.8	1.5
1952	13.7	-0.7	13.7	0.0	14.0	2.2	14.0	0.0	14.0	0.0	14.1	0.7	14.1	0.0	14.1	0.0	14.2	0.7	14.3	0.7	14.3	0.0	14.3	0.0
1953	14.3	0.0	14.3	0.0	14.3	0.0	14.3	0.0	14.8	3.5	14.8	0.0	14.8	0.0	14.9	0.7	14.8	-0.7	14.9	0.7	14.9	0.0	14.9	0.0
1954	14.9	0.0	15.0	0.7	15.0	0.0	15.0	0.0	15.2	1.3	15.2	0.0	15.2	0.0	15.5	2.0	15.5	0.0	15.5	0.0	15.6	0.6	15.6	0.0
1955	15.6	0.0	16.2	3.8	16.2	0.0	16.2	0.0	16.2	0.0	16.2	0.0	16.2	0.0	16.2	0.0	16.2	0.0	16.2	0.0	16.8	3.7	16.8	0.0
1956	16.8	0.0	16.8	0.0	17.4	3.6	17.4	0.0	17.4	0.0	17.4	0.0	17.4	0.0	17.5	0.6	17.5	0.0	17.5	0.0	17.6	0.6	17.6	0.0
1957	17.7	0.6	17.9	1.1	17.9	0.0	17.9	0.0	17.9	0.0	17.9	0.0	17.9	0.0	17.9	0.0	17.9	0.0	17.9	0.0	18.5	3.4	18.5	0.0
1958	18.5	0.0	18.4	-0.5	18.5	0.5	18.5	0.0	18.5	0.0	18.5	0.0	18.5	0.0	18.6	0.5	18.6	0.0	18.6	0.0	18.7	0.5	18.7	0.0
1959	18.7	0.0	19.3	3.2	19.3	0.0	19.3	0.0	19.3	0.0	19.3	0.0	19.3	0.0	19.3	0.0	19.3	0.0	19.3	0.0	19.3	0.0	19.3	0.0
1960	19.3	0.0	19.4	0.5	19.4	0.0	19.4	0.0	19.5	0.5	19.5	0.0	19.8	1.5	19.9	0.5	19.9	0.0	19.9	0.0	19.9	0.0	19.9	0.0
1961	20.0	0.5	20.0	0.0	20.0	0.0	20.0	0.0	20.0	0.0	20.9	4.5	21.0	0.5	21.0	0.0	21.0	0.0	21.0	0.0	21.0	0.0	21.0	0.0
1962	20.9	-0.5	21.0	0.5	21.1	0.5	21.1	0.0	21.3	0.9	21.3	0.0	21.3	0.0	21.3	0.0	21.3	0.0	21.3	0.0	21.3	0.0	21.3	0.0
1963	21.3	0.0	21.4	0.5	21.4	0.0	21.4	0.0	21.5	0.5	22.9	6.5	22.9	0.0	22.9	0.0	22.9	0.0	22.9	0.0	23.0	0.4	23.0	0.0
1964	23.0	0.0	23.0	0.0	23.2	0.9	23.2	0.0	23.2	0.0	23.2	0.0	23.2	0.0	23.2	0.0	23.2	0.0	23.1	-0.4	23.3	0.9	23.3	0.0
1965	23.4	0.4	23.4	0.0	23.7	1.3	23.7	0.0	23.8	0.4	23.8	0.0	23.8	0.0	24.0	0.8	23.9	-0.4	23.9	0.0	23.9	0.0	23.9	0.0
1966	24.3	1.7	24.4	0.4	24.8	1.6	24.8	0.0	24.9	0.4	25.1	0.8	25.2	0.4	25.3	0.4	25.5	0.8	25.6	0.4	25.9	1.2	26.1	0.8
1967	26.2	0.4	26.3	0.4	26.6	1.1	26.5	-0.4	26.6	0.4	26.7	0.4	26.8	0.4	26.8	0.0	27.3	1.9	27.3	0.0	27.7	1.5	27.8	0.4
1968	28.1	1.1	28.3	0.7	28.6	1.1	28.6	0.0	28.7	0.3	28.5	-0.7	28.5	0.0	28.6	0.4	28.8	0.7	29.0	0.7	29.0	0.0	29.4	1.4
1969	29.8	1.4	30.0	0.7	30.3	1.0	30.5	0.7	30.7	0.7	30.9	0.7	31.0	0.3	31.2	0.6	31.5	1.0	31.0	-1.6	31.2	0.6	31.4	0.6
1970	31.9	1.6	32.3	1.3	32.9	1.9	33.1	0.6	33.2	0.3	33.3	0.3	33.6	0.9	34.0	1.2	34.2	0.6	34.2	0.0	34.4	0.6	34.6	0.6
1971	35.1	1.4	35.4	0.9	35.5	0.3	35.6	0.3	35.7	0.3	36.0	0.8	36.2	0.6	36.4	0.6	36.7	0.8	36.6	-0.3	36.7	0.3	37.0	0.8
1972	37.5	1.4	37.6	0.3	37.7	0.3	37.8	0.3	37.8	0.0	38.0	0.5	38.0	0.0	38.2	0.5	38.2	0.0	38.6	1.0	38.6	0.0	38.6	0.0
1973	38.7	0.3	38.8	0.3	39.4	1.5	39.5	0.3	39.7	0.5	39.8	0.3	39.9	0.3	40.0	0.3	40.4	1.0	40.8	1.0	41.2	1.0	41.2	0.0
1974	41.5	0.7	42.0	1.2	42.2	0.5	42.4	0.5	42.9	1.2	43.3	0.9	43.8	1.2	44.5	1.6	45.3	1.8	45.6	0.7	46.0	0.9	46.1	0.2
1975	47.4	2.8	48.5	2.3	48.6	0.2	49.2	1.2	49.4	0.4	49.8	0.8	50.6	1.6	51.6	2.0	52.1	1.0	52.5	0.8	52.4	-0.2	52.7	0.6
1976	54.1	2.7	54.6	0.9	54.8	0.4	55.0	0.4	55.5	0.9	55.6	0.2	57.1	2.7	57.3	0.4	57.3	0.0	57.6	0.5	58.5	1.6	58.5	0.0
1977	59.0	0.9	59.1	0.2	60.5	2.4	61.6	1.8	62.7	1.8	63.4	1.1	63.8	0.6	65.1	2.0	65.4	0.5	65.5	0.2	65.9	0.6	65.8	-0.2
1978	65.8	0.0	66.3	0.8	66.8	0.8	67.2	0.6	67.4	0.3	67.4	0.0	67.5	0.1	67.6	0.1	67.7	0.1	69.5	2.7	69.5	0.0	70.3	1.2
1979	71.7	2.0	72.1	0.6	72.2	0.1	73.0	1.1	72.6	-0.5	73.4	1.1	74.0	0.8	74.2	0.3	74.4	0.3	74.9	0.7	75.8	1.2	78.0	2.9
1980	78.1	0.1	78.2	0.1	78.6	0.5	79.3	0.9	79.4	0.1	79.7	0.4	80.4	0.9	80.0	-0.5	80.9	1.1	81.7	1.0	82.3	0.7	82.4	0.1
1981	83.2	1.0	84.4	1.4	84.7	0.4	85.2	0.6	85.8	0.7	86.0	0.2	86.3	0.3	86.3	0.0	87.1	0.9	88.0	1.0	88.1	0.1	88.3	0.2
1982	89.2	1.0	90.1	1.0	91.0	1.0	91.6	0.7	92.7	1.2	92.7	0.0	93.8	1.2	94.6	0.9	95.5	1.0	95.8	0.3	95.8	0.0	95.8	0.0
1983	96.2	0.4	96.1	-0.1	96.8	0.7	96.7	-0.1	96.5	-0.2	96.3	-0.2	97.9	1.7	98.9	1.0	98.9	0.0	99.4	0.5	101.2	1.8	105.1	3.9
1984	105.8	0.7	106.5	0.7	106.9	0.4	107.7	0.7	107.7	0.0	107.7	0.0	108.9	1.1	109.4	0.5	109.9	0.5	110.0	0.1	110.5	0.5	110.6	0.1
1985	111.4	0.7	113.1	1.5	114.2	1.0	114.5	0.3	115.2	0.6	115.2	0.0	117.1	1.6	117.7	0.5	118.7	0.8	119.2	0.4	120.1	0.8	120.3	0.2
1986	121.7	1.2	122.0	0.2	122.7	0.6	123.0	0.2	123.6	0.5	124.1	0.4	126.5	1.9	126.6	0.1	126.8	0.2	127.2	0.3	127.4	0.2	128.2	0.6
1987	-		130.2	1.6	-		131.6	1.1	-		132.9	1.0	-		134.3	1.1	-		134.9	0.4	-		135.3	0.3
1988	-		138.6	2.4	-		138.5	-0.1	-		137.5	-0.7	-		142.7	3.8	-		142.1	-0.4	-		143.8	1.2
1989	-		142.9	-0.6	-		145.0	1.5	-		146.2	0.8	-		149.5	2.3	-		149.9	0.3	-		150.8	0.6
1990	-		154.7	2.6	-		156.5	1.2	-		158.9	1.5	-		163.7	3.0	-		163.9	0.1	-		164.6	0.4
1991	-		168.4	2.3	-		167.9	-0.3	-		169.5	1.0	-		173.0	2.1	-		174.4	0.8	-		175.6	0.7

[Continued]

Detroit, MI
Consumer Price Index - All Urban Consumers
Base 1982-1984 = 100
Medical Care

[Continued]

For 1947-1995. Columns headed % show percentile change in the index from the previous period for which an index is available.

Year	Jan		Feb		Mar		Apr		May		Jun		Jul		Aug		Sep		Oct		Nov		Dec	
	Index	%	Index	%	Index	%	Index	%	Index	%	Index	%	Index	%	Index	%	Index	%	Index	%	Index	%	Index	%
1992	-	-	179.2	2.1	-	-	180.9	0.9	-	-	181.0	0.1	-	-	182.1	0.6	-	-	184.2	1.2	-	-	184.6	0.2
1993	-	-	188.6	2.2	-	-	191.3	1.4	-	-	191.0	-0.2	-	-	191.6	0.3	-	-	192.3	0.4	-	-	192.5	0.1
1994	-	-	195.3	1.5	-	-	199.0	1.9	-	-	200.0	0.5	-	-	200.0	0.0	-	-	203.1	1.6	-	-	203.9	0.4
1995	-	-	206.2	1.1	-	-	208.8	1.3	-	-	209.8	0.5	-	-	209.9	0.0	-	-	210.0	0.0	-	-	212.8	1.3

Source: U.S. Department of Labor, Bureau of Labor Statistics, Division of Consumer Prices and Price Indexes. - indicates no data collected for period.

Detroit, MI
Consumer Price Index - Urban Wage Earners
Base 1982-1984 = 100
Medical Care

For 1947-1995. Columns headed % show percentile change in the index from the previous period for which an index is available.

Year	Jan Index	%	Feb Index	%	Mar Index	%	Apr Index	%	May Index	%	Jun Index	%	Jul Index	%	Aug Index	%	Sep Index	%	Oct Index	%	Nov Index	%	Dec Index	%
1947	11.7	-	11.8	0.9	11.9	0.8	12.0	0.8	12.0	0.0	12.1	0.8	12.1	0.0	12.1	0.0	12.2	0.8	12.2	0.0	12.2	0.0	12.2	0.0
1948	12.4	1.6	12.4	0.0	12.4	0.0	12.5	0.8	12.5	0.0	12.5	0.0	12.5	0.0	12.6	0.8	12.6	0.0	12.6	0.0	12.6	0.0	12.6	0.0
1949	12.6	0.0	12.7	0.8	12.8	0.8	12.8	0.0	12.8	0.0	12.8	0.0	12.8	0.0	12.8	0.0	12.9	0.8	12.9	0.0	13.0	0.8	13.0	0.0
1950	13.0	0.0	13.0	0.0	13.0	0.0	13.0	0.0	13.0	0.0	13.1	0.8	13.1	0.0	13.1	0.0	13.1	0.0	13.1	0.0	13.2	0.8	13.2	0.0
1951	13.2	0.0	13.2	0.0	13.3	0.8	13.3	0.0	13.3	0.0	13.8	3.8	13.8	0.0	13.8	0.0	13.8	0.0	13.9	0.7	13.9	0.0	14.1	1.4
1952	14.0	-0.7	14.0	0.0	14.3	2.1	14.3	0.0	14.3	0.0	14.4	0.7	14.4	0.0	14.4	0.0	14.5	0.7	14.6	0.7	14.6	0.0	14.6	0.0
1953	14.5	-0.7	14.6	0.7	14.6	0.0	14.6	0.0	15.1	3.4	15.1	0.0	15.1	0.0	15.1	0.0	15.1	0.0	15.1	0.0	15.2	0.7	15.2	0.0
1954	15.2	0.0	15.2	0.0	15.2	0.0	15.2	0.0	15.5	2.0	15.5	0.0	15.5	0.0	15.8	1.9	15.8	0.0	15.8	0.0	15.9	0.6	15.9	0.0
1955	15.9	0.0	16.5	3.8	16.5	0.0	16.5	0.0	16.5	0.0	16.5	0.0	16.5	0.0	16.5	0.0	16.5	0.0	16.5	0.0	17.1	3.6	17.1	0.0
1956	17.1	0.0	17.1	0.0	17.7	3.5	17.7	0.0	17.7	0.0	17.8	0.6	17.8	0.0	17.9	0.6	17.9	0.0	17.8	-0.6	17.9	0.6	17.9	0.0
1957	18.0	0.6	18.3	1.7	18.3	0.0	18.3	0.0	18.2	-0.5	18.2	0.0	18.2	0.0	18.3	0.5	18.3	0.0	18.3	0.0	18.8	2.7	18.8	0.0
1958	18.8	0.0	18.8	0.0	18.8	0.0	18.8	0.0	18.8	0.0	18.9	0.5	18.9	0.0	19.0	0.5	19.0	0.0	19.0	0.0	19.1	0.5	19.1	0.0
1959	19.1	0.0	19.7	3.1	19.7	0.0	19.7	0.0	19.7	0.0	19.7	0.0	19.7	0.0	19.7	0.0	19.7	0.0	19.7	0.0	19.7	0.0	19.7	0.0
1960	19.7	0.0	19.8	0.5	19.8	0.0	19.8	0.0	19.9	0.5	19.9	0.0	20.2	1.5	20.2	0.0	20.2	0.0	20.3	0.5	20.3	0.0	20.3	0.0
1961	20.3	0.0	20.4	0.5	20.4	0.0	20.3	-0.5	20.4	0.5	21.3	4.4	21.4	0.5	21.4	0.0	21.4	0.0	21.4	0.0	21.4	0.0	21.4	0.0
1962	21.3	-0.5	21.4	0.5	21.5	0.5	21.5	0.0	21.7	0.9	21.7	0.0	21.7	0.0	21.7	0.0	21.7	0.0	21.7	0.0	21.7	0.0	21.7	0.0
1963	21.7	0.0	21.8	0.5	21.9	0.5	21.9	0.0	21.9	0.0	23.3	6.4	23.3	0.0	23.3	0.0	23.3	0.0	23.3	0.0	23.4	0.4	23.4	0.0
1964	23.4	0.0	23.5	0.4	23.6	0.4	23.6	0.0	23.6	0.0	23.6	0.0	23.6	0.0	23.7	0.4	23.6	-0.4	23.6	0.0	23.7	0.4	23.7	0.0
1965	23.9	0.8	23.9	0.0	24.1	0.8	24.2	0.4	24.2	0.0	24.3	0.4	24.3	0.0	24.5	0.8	24.4	-0.4	24.4	0.0	24.4	0.0	24.4	0.0
1966	24.8	1.6	24.9	0.4	25.3	1.6	25.3	0.0	25.4	0.4	25.6	0.8	25.6	0.0	25.7	0.4	26.0	1.2	26.1	0.4	26.4	1.1	26.6	0.8
1967	26.7	0.4	26.8	0.4	27.1	1.1	27.0	-0.4	27.1	0.4	27.3	0.7	27.3	0.0	27.3	0.0	27.8	1.8	27.9	0.4	28.2	1.1	28.4	0.7
1968	28.7	1.1	28.8	0.3	29.1	1.0	29.2	0.3	29.3	0.3	29.1	-0.7	29.1	0.0	29.1	0.0	29.3	0.7	29.6	1.0	29.6	0.0	30.0	1.4
1969	30.3	1.0	30.6	1.0	30.9	1.0	31.1	0.6	31.3	0.6	31.5	0.6	31.6	0.3	31.8	0.6	32.1	0.9	31.6	-1.6	31.8	0.6	32.0	0.6
1970	32.5	1.6	32.9	1.2	33.5	1.8	33.8	0.9	33.9	0.3	34.0	0.3	34.2	0.6	34.6	1.2	34.8	0.6	34.8	0.0	35.1	0.9	35.3	0.6
1971	35.8	1.4	36.1	0.8	36.1	0.0	36.3	0.6	36.4	0.3	36.7	0.8	36.9	0.5	37.1	0.5	37.4	0.8	37.3	-0.3	37.4	0.3	37.7	0.8
1972	38.2	1.3	38.4	0.5	38.5	0.3	38.5	0.0	38.5	0.0	38.7	0.5	38.7	0.0	38.9	0.5	38.9	0.0	39.3	1.0	39.3	0.0	39.3	0.0
1973	39.4	0.3	39.5	0.3	40.1	1.5	40.3	0.5	40.4	0.2	40.6	0.5	40.7	0.2	40.8	0.2	41.2	1.0	41.6	1.0	42.0	1.0	42.0	0.0
1974	42.3	0.7	42.8	1.2	43.0	0.5	43.2	0.5	43.7	1.2	44.1	0.9	44.6	1.1	45.4	1.8	46.1	1.5	46.5	0.9	46.9	0.9	47.0	0.2
1975	48.3	2.8	49.4	2.3	49.6	0.4	50.2	1.2	50.4	0.4	50.8	0.8	51.6	1.6	52.6	1.9	53.1	1.0	53.5	0.8	53.4	-0.2	53.7	0.6
1976	55.2	2.8	55.6	0.7	55.9	0.5	56.0	0.2	56.5	0.9	56.7	0.4	58.2	2.6	58.4	0.3	58.4	0.0	58.7	0.5	59.6	1.5	59.6	0.0
1977	60.1	0.8	60.3	0.3	61.6	2.2	62.8	1.9	63.9	1.8	64.6	1.1	65.1	0.8	66.3	1.8	66.7	0.6	66.7	0.0	67.2	0.7	67.1	-0.1
1978	67.2	0.1	67.4	0.3	67.7	0.4	68.4	1.0	68.4	0.0	68.4	0.0	68.4	0.0	68.5	0.1	69.7	1.8	71.5	2.6	71.7	0.3	71.8	0.1
1979	72.9	1.5	72.8	-0.1	73.3	0.7	75.0	2.3	75.3	0.4	75.8	0.7	76.3	0.7	76.6	0.4	76.8	0.3	77.4	0.8	78.1	0.9	79.1	1.3
1980	79.1	0.0	79.2	0.1	79.4	0.3	80.9	1.9	81.4	0.6	81.6	0.2	81.7	0.1	81.6	-0.1	82.1	0.6	82.6	0.6	82.8	0.2	83.4	0.7
1981	84.5	1.3	85.4	1.1	85.9	0.6	86.0	0.1	86.2	0.2	86.6	0.5	86.8	0.2	87.2	0.5	87.7	0.6	88.2	0.6	88.7	0.6	88.6	-0.1
1982	89.6	1.1	90.4	0.9	91.4	1.1	91.9	0.5	93.0	1.2	93.0	0.0	94.0	1.1	94.7	0.7	95.7	1.1	96.0	0.3	95.9	-0.1	95.9	0.0
1983	96.4	0.5	96.3	-0.1	96.9	0.6	96.9	0.0	96.7	-0.2	96.6	-0.1	98.2	1.7	99.0	0.8	99.0	0.0	99.6	0.6	101.2	1.6	104.8	3.6
1984	105.4	0.6	106.2	0.8	106.6	0.4	107.2	0.6	107.3	0.1	107.4	0.1	108.5	1.0	108.9	0.4	109.5	0.6	109.6	0.1	110.2	0.5	110.3	0.1
1985	111.0	0.6	112.6	1.4	113.6	0.9	113.8	0.2	114.6	0.7	114.5	-0.1	116.2	1.5	116.8	0.5	117.7	0.8	118.2	0.4	119.0	0.7	119.3	0.3
1986	120.4	0.9	120.8	0.3	121.4	0.5	121.8	0.3	122.4	0.5	122.9	0.4	125.0	1.7	125.0	0.0	125.2	0.2	125.8	0.5	125.9	0.1	126.7	0.6
1987	-		128.5	1.4	-		130.1	1.2	-		131.3	0.9	-		132.7	1.1	-		133.1	0.3	-		133.9	0.6
1988	-		137.7	2.8	-		137.7	0.0	-		136.5	-0.9	-		142.5	4.4	-		141.9	-0.4	-		143.4	1.1
1989	-		142.9	-0.3	-		144.7	1.3	-		145.9	0.8	-		149.4	2.4	-		149.7	0.2	-		150.5	0.5
1990	-		154.2	2.5	-		155.9	1.1	-		158.0	1.3	-		163.1	3.2	-		163.2	0.1	-		163.6	0.2
1991	-		167.7	2.5	-		166.8	-0.5	-		168.1	0.8	-		171.4	2.0	-		172.8	0.8	-		174.1	0.8

[Continued]

Detroit, MI
Consumer Price Index - Urban Wage Earners
Base 1982-1984 = 100
Medical Care
[Continued]

For 1947-1995. Columns headed % show percentile change in the index from the previous period for which an index is available.

Year	Jan Index	%	Feb Index	%	Mar Index	%	Apr Index	%	May Index	%	Jun Index	%	Jul Index	%	Aug Index	%	Sep Index	%	Oct Index	%	Nov Index	%	Dec Index	%
1992	-	-	177.6	2.0	-	-	179.3	1.0	-	-	179.5	0.1	-	-	180.4	0.5	-	-	182.7	1.3	-	-	182.9	0.1
1993	-	-	187.1	2.3	-	-	189.8	1.4	-	-	189.5	-0.2	-	-	190.0	0.3	-	-	190.7	0.4	-	-	190.7	0.0
1994	-	-	193.3	1.4	-	-	196.8	1.8	-	-	197.7	0.5	-	-	197.6	-0.1	-	-	200.7	1.6	-	-	201.3	0.3
1995	-	-	204.1	1.4	-	-	206.4	1.1	-	-	207.7	0.6	-	-	207.8	0.0	-	-	208.1	0.1	-	-	210.7	1.2

Source: U.S. Department of Labor, Bureau of Labor Statistics, Division of Consumer Prices and Price Indexes. - indicates no data collected for period.

Detroit, MI
Consumer Price Index - All Urban Consumers
Base 1982-1984 = 100
Entertainment

For 1976-1995. Columns headed % show percentile change in the index from the previous period for which an index is available.

Year	Jan Index	%	Feb Index	%	Mar Index	%	Apr Index	%	May Index	%	Jun Index	%	Jul Index	%	Aug Index	%	Sep Index	%	Oct Index	%	Nov Index	%	Dec Index	%
1976	72.1	-	72.4	0.4	72.9	0.7	73.5	0.8	73.6	0.1	73.0	-0.8	73.2	0.3	73.0	-0.3	74.2	1.6	74.3	0.1	74.5	0.3	74.8	0.4
1977	74.9	0.1	74.9	0.0	75.1	0.3	75.0	-0.1	75.2	0.3	75.2	0.0	75.4	0.3	75.7	0.4	76.5	1.1	76.3	-0.3	76.8	0.7	77.3	0.7
1978	77.5	0.3	77.7	0.3	78.3	0.8	79.9	2.0	79.9	0.0	79.5	-0.5	80.0	0.6	81.0	1.3	81.2	0.2	81.2	0.0	81.4	0.2	82.0	0.7
1979	82.2	0.2	82.7	0.6	81.3	-1.7	83.3	2.5	84.2	1.1	84.6	0.5	83.8	-0.9	83.0	-1.0	81.4	-1.9	82.5	1.4	82.9	0.5	81.7	-1.4
1980	84.2	3.1	85.9	2.0	87.4	1.7	87.8	0.5	88.0	0.2	88.8	0.9	88.1	-0.8	87.8	-0.3	88.9	1.3	89.3	0.4	88.9	-0.4	88.9	0.0
1981	89.3	0.4	89.8	0.6	91.4	1.8	93.2	2.0	93.6	0.4	93.4	-0.2	93.4	0.0	92.5	-1.0	91.8	-0.8	93.0	1.3	92.6	-0.4	93.3	0.8
1982	93.1	-0.2	95.3	2.4	96.2	0.9	94.9	-1.4	95.5	0.6	94.9	-0.6	97.7	3.0	98.1	0.4	98.2	0.1	100.1	1.9	100.0	-0.1	100.0	0.0
1983	101.5	1.5	101.9	0.4	100.9	-1.0	100.6	-0.3	100.2	-0.4	100.9	0.7	101.2	0.3	101.8	0.6	100.8	-1.0	101.7	0.9	101.4	-0.3	101.2	-0.2
1984	101.6	0.4	101.4	-0.2	101.2	-0.2	102.2	1.0	100.2	-2.0	101.1	0.9	101.8	0.7	103.1	1.3	103.3	0.2	102.5	-0.8	101.8	-0.7	101.7	-0.1
1985	104.0	2.3	107.0	2.9	106.7	-0.3	106.3	-0.4	106.1	-0.2	105.6	-0.5	106.9	1.2	105.8	-1.0	108.5	2.6	107.0	-1.4	107.5	0.5	107.4	-0.1
1986	108.1	0.7	108.3	0.2	109.7	1.3	107.5	-2.0	106.9	-0.6	107.4	0.5	107.0	-0.4	108.6	1.5	111.1	2.3	108.1	-2.7	109.7	1.5	110.5	0.7
1987	-	-	110.1	-0.4	-	-	112.3	2.0	-	-	110.0	-2.0	-	-	113.1	2.8	-	-	113.6	0.4	-	-	114.3	0.6
1988	-	-	112.7	-1.4	-	-	113.2	0.4	-	-	114.1	0.8	-	-	115.2	1.0	-	-	115.8	0.5	-	-	118.0	1.9
1989	-	-	118.8	0.7	-	-	119.9	0.9	-	-	119.5	-0.3	-	-	119.8	0.3	-	-	122.5	2.3	-	-	124.1	1.3
1990	-	-	128.2	3.3	-	-	127.7	-0.4	-	-	126.8	-0.7	-	-	126.8	0.0	-	-	129.6	2.2	-	-	131.6	1.5
1991	-	-	133.0	1.1	-	-	135.0	1.5	-	-	134.6	-0.3	-	-	134.3	-0.2	-	-	129.6	-3.5	-	-	129.2	-0.3
1992	-	-	130.5	1.0	-	-	130.3	-0.2	-	-	131.0	0.5	-	-	130.2	-0.6	-	-	131.5	1.0	-	-	131.4	-0.1
1993	-	-	134.0	2.0	-	-	136.2	1.6	-	-	137.5	1.0	-	-	138.6	0.8	-	-	140.4	1.3	-	-	142.0	1.1
1994	-	-	143.8	1.3	-	-	145.5	1.2	-	-	146.7	0.8	-	-	147.3	0.4	-	-	145.9	-1.0	-	-	146.3	0.3
1995	-	-	147.9	1.1	-	-	150.4	1.7	-	-	148.3	-1.4	-	-	151.7	2.3	-	-	152.7	0.7	-	-	154.0	0.9

Source: U.S. Department of Labor, Bureau of Labor Statistics, Division of Consumer Prices and Price Indexes. - indicates no data collected for period.

Detroit, MI
Consumer Price Index - Urban Wage Earners
Base 1982-1984 = 100
Entertainment

For 1976-1995. Columns headed % show percentile change in the index from the previous period for which an index is available.

Year	Jan Index	%	Feb Index	%	Mar Index	%	Apr Index	%	May Index	%	Jun Index	%	Jul Index	%	Aug Index	%	Sep Index	%	Oct Index	%	Nov Index	%	Dec Index	%
1976	75.6	-	75.8	0.3	76.3	0.7	77.0	0.9	77.1	0.1	76.5	-0.8	76.7	0.3	76.5	-0.3	77.8	1.7	77.9	0.1	78.0	0.1	78.4	0.5
1977	78.4	0.0	78.5	0.1	78.6	0.1	78.5	-0.1	78.8	0.4	78.8	0.0	79.0	0.3	79.3	0.4	80.2	1.1	80.0	-0.2	80.4	0.5	81.0	0.7
1978	81.1	0.1	81.6	0.6	82.2	0.7	84.0	2.2	83.4	-0.7	82.3	-1.3	82.8	0.6	83.0	0.2	83.2	0.2	83.3	0.1	84.7	1.7	85.3	0.7
1979	85.7	0.5	86.1	0.5	84.7	-1.6	86.7	2.4	87.6	1.0	88.1	0.6	87.8	-0.3	86.3	-1.7	84.6	-2.0	84.9	0.4	85.6	0.8	84.6	-1.2
1980	86.9	2.7	88.6	2.0	91.0	2.7	91.5	0.5	91.5	0.0	92.4	1.0	92.7	0.3	91.9	-0.9	91.8	-0.1	92.3	0.5	92.0	-0.3	88.6	-3.7
1981	88.9	0.3	89.4	0.6	91.6	2.5	93.7	2.3	94.1	0.4	93.6	-0.5	94.1	0.5	93.3	-0.9	93.1	-0.2	93.4	0.3	93.2	-0.2	93.4	0.2
1982	93.2	-0.2	95.3	2.3	96.2	0.9	95.2	-1.0	95.8	0.6	95.4	-0.4	98.2	2.9	98.5	0.3	98.6	0.1	100.3	1.7	100.3	0.0	100.4	0.1
1983	101.7	1.3	102.1	0.4	100.7	-1.4	100.3	-0.4	100.0	-0.3	100.7	0.7	101.4	0.7	101.8	0.4	100.8	-1.0	101.5	0.7	101.1	-0.4	101.1	0.0
1984	101.5	0.4	101.3	-0.2	101.3	0.0	102.2	0.9	100.1	-2.1	100.7	0.6	101.5	0.8	102.8	1.3	103.0	0.2	102.3	-0.7	101.7	-0.6	101.4	-0.3
1985	103.5	2.1	106.9	3.3	106.8	-0.1	106.3	-0.5	105.7	-0.6	105.0	-0.7	106.4	1.3	105.4	-0.9	108.9	3.3	107.6	-1.2	108.1	0.5	107.9	-0.2
1986	108.7	0.7	108.8	0.1	110.3	1.4	108.0	-2.1	107.5	-0.5	107.9	0.4	107.2	-0.6	109.2	1.9	113.1	3.6	108.9	-3.7	110.3	1.3	111.3	0.9
1987	-	-	110.9	-0.4	-	-	113.3	2.2	-	-	110.6	-2.4	-	-	114.0	3.1	-	-	114.5	0.4	-	-	115.2	0.6
1988	-	-	113.8	-1.2	-	-	114.3	0.4	-	-	114.5	0.2	-	-	115.9	1.2	-	-	116.6	0.6	-	-	119.0	2.1
1989	-	-	119.9	0.8	-	-	121.1	1.0	-	-	120.5	-0.5	-	-	120.8	0.2	-	-	123.3	2.1	-	-	124.4	0.9
1990	-	-	129.0	3.7	-	-	128.3	-0.5	-	-	127.5	-0.6	-	-	127.4	-0.1	-	-	130.5	2.4	-	-	132.2	1.3
1991	-	-	133.8	1.2	-	-	136.1	1.7	-	-	135.5	-0.4	-	-	135.0	-0.4	-	-	129.9	-3.8	-	-	129.4	-0.4
1992	-	-	130.6	0.9	-	-	130.5	-0.1	-	-	131.3	0.6	-	-	130.1	-0.9	-	-	131.5	1.1	-	-	131.4	-0.1
1993	-	-	133.9	1.9	-	-	136.1	1.6	-	-	138.0	1.4	-	-	139.0	0.7	-	-	141.0	1.4	-	-	142.4	1.0
1994	-	-	144.0	1.1	-	-	145.7	1.2	-	-	147.0	0.9	-	-	147.5	0.3	-	-	146.3	-0.8	-	-	146.7	0.3
1995	-	-	148.2	1.0	-	-	150.9	1.8	-	-	148.5	-1.6	-	-	151.9	2.3	-	-	153.1	0.8	-	-	154.4	0.8

Source: U.S. Department of Labor, Bureau of Labor Statistics, Division of Consumer Prices and Price Indexes. - indicates no data collected for period.

Detroit, MI
Consumer Price Index - All Urban Consumers
Base 1982-1984 = 100
Other Goods and Services

For 1976-1995. Columns headed % show percentile change in the index from the previous period for which an index is available.

Year	Jan Index	%	Feb Index	%	Mar Index	%	Apr Index	%	May Index	%	Jun Index	%	Jul Index	%	Aug Index	%	Sep Index	%	Oct Index	%	Nov Index	%	Dec Index	%
1976	56.5	-	56.5	0.0	56.7	0.4	57.1	0.7	57.2	0.2	57.3	0.2	57.3	0.0	57.7	0.7	57.8	0.2	58.4	1.0	58.7	0.5	58.8	0.2
1977	59.2	0.7	59.4	0.3	59.6	0.3	60.8	2.0	60.9	0.2	60.9	0.0	61.4	0.8	61.5	0.2	62.3	1.3	63.2	1.4	63.4	0.3	63.5	0.2
1978	63.5	0.0	64.0	0.8	64.1	0.2	64.4	0.5	64.9	0.8	65.5	0.9	66.3	1.2	66.0	-0.5	67.5	2.3	67.7	0.3	67.7	0.0	67.7	0.0
1979	68.6	1.3	68.8	0.3	69.2	0.6	69.2	0.0	69.2	0.0	69.2	0.0	69.7	0.7	70.5	1.1	71.8	1.8	71.9	0.1	71.7	-0.3	71.9	0.3
1980	72.7	1.1	73.2	0.7	73.3	0.1	73.5	0.3	74.1	0.8	74.5	0.5	74.7	0.3	75.3	0.8	77.5	2.9	77.1	-0.5	77.5	0.5	77.7	0.3
1981	77.9	0.3	79.4	1.9	80.0	0.8	80.2	0.2	80.7	0.6	80.9	0.2	81.3	0.5	81.3	0.0	84.9	4.4	85.0	0.1	85.0	0.0	85.3	0.4
1982	85.6	0.4	86.6	1.2	87.4	0.9	87.6	0.2	90.9	3.8	91.0	0.1	91.5	0.5	91.4	-0.1	96.0	5.0	97.2	1.2	97.6	0.4	98.7	1.1
1983	100.4	1.7	100.1	-0.3	100.5	0.4	100.9	0.4	101.4	0.5	101.5	0.1	101.9	0.4	101.5	-0.4	103.6	2.1	103.6	0.0	104.1	0.5	104.5	0.4
1984	105.7	1.1	105.1	-0.6	104.9	-0.2	105.1	0.2	105.0	-0.1	105.0	0.0	105.8	0.8	106.0	0.2	108.3	2.2	108.1	-0.2	107.7	-0.4	107.8	0.1
1985	109.3	1.4	109.6	0.3	109.4	-0.2	109.8	0.4	110.5	0.6	110.8	0.3	111.8	0.9	112.0	0.2	114.3	2.1	114.4	0.1	114.0	-0.3	113.7	-0.3
1986	114.2	0.4	112.5	-1.5	112.4	-0.1	112.4	0.0	112.8	0.4	112.7	-0.1	114.4	1.5	115.6	1.0	116.6	0.9	116.6	0.0	117.6	0.9	117.3	-0.3
1987	-	-	117.5	0.2	-	-	118.2	0.6	-	-	119.2	0.8	-	-	119.7	0.4	-	-	124.7	4.2	-	-	125.0	0.2
1988	-	-	128.3	2.6	-	-	127.8	-0.4	-	-	128.3	0.4	-	-	129.8	1.2	-	-	134.1	3.3	-	-	134.4	0.2
1989	-	-	135.4	0.7	-	-	135.5	0.1	-	-	137.4	1.4	-	-	137.6	0.1	-	-	141.6	2.9	-	-	142.0	0.3
1990	-	-	144.0	1.4	-	-	143.9	-0.1	-	-	146.5	1.8	-	-	146.6	0.1	-	-	152.7	4.2	-	-	154.3	1.0
1991	-	-	156.2	1.2	-	-	157.3	0.7	-	-	158.3	0.6	-	-	159.6	0.8	-	-	168.3	5.5	-	-	167.9	-0.2
1992	-	-	168.8	0.5	-	-	168.8	0.0	-	-	170.4	0.9	-	-	175.8	3.2	-	-	181.8	3.4	-	-	180.6	-0.7
1993	-	-	183.7	1.7	-	-	183.7	0.0	-	-	184.1	0.2	-	-	181.8	-1.2	-	-	183.8	1.1	-	-	184.9	0.6
1994	-	-	184.3	-0.3	-	-	185.1	0.4	-	-	201.0	8.6	-	-	202.6	0.8	-	-	207.4	2.4	-	-	208.2	0.4
1995	-	-	208.8	0.3	-	-	207.5	-0.6	-	-	209.1	0.8	-	-	212.0	1.4	-	-	214.2	1.0	-	-	214.9	0.3

Source: U.S. Department of Labor, Bureau of Labor Statistics, Division of Consumer Prices and Price Indexes. - indicates no data collected for period.

Detroit, MI
Consumer Price Index - Urban Wage Earners
Base 1982-1984 = 100
Other Goods and Services

For 1976-1995. Columns headed % show percentile change in the index from the previous period for which an index is available.

Year	Jan Index	%	Feb Index	%	Mar Index	%	Apr Index	%	May Index	%	Jun Index	%	Jul Index	%	Aug Index	%	Sep Index	%	Oct Index	%	Nov Index	%	Dec Index	%
1976	54.5	-	54.5	0.0	54.7	0.4	55.0	0.5	55.1	0.2	55.2	0.2	55.3	0.2	55.6	0.5	55.8	0.4	56.3	0.9	56.6	0.5	56.7	0.2
1977	57.1	0.7	57.3	0.4	57.5	0.3	58.6	1.9	58.7	0.2	58.7	0.0	59.2	0.9	59.3	0.2	60.1	1.3	61.0	1.5	61.2	0.3	61.2	0.0
1978	61.5	0.5	61.8	0.5	61.4	-0.6	61.8	0.7	61.9	0.2	62.4	0.8	63.3	1.4	63.0	-0.5	64.6	2.5	64.5	-0.2	64.8	0.5	65.0	0.3
1979	66.1	1.7	66.4	0.5	66.3	-0.2	66.1	-0.3	66.1	0.0	66.1	0.0	66.5	0.6	67.7	1.8	69.0	1.9	69.2	0.3	69.0	-0.3	69.6	0.9
1980	71.2	2.3	72.0	1.1	71.8	-0.3	72.0	0.3	72.7	1.0	73.5	1.1	73.2	-0.4	73.9	1.0	75.1	1.6	75.0	-0.1	75.7	0.9	75.9	0.3
1981	76.1	0.3	78.0	2.5	77.9	-0.1	78.5	0.8	79.4	1.1	79.5	0.1	80.3	1.0	80.4	0.1	83.3	3.6	83.9	0.7	84.4	0.6	84.8	0.5
1982	85.2	0.5	86.2	1.2	87.0	0.9	87.2	0.2	91.2	4.6	91.2	0.0	91.7	0.5	91.6	-0.1	95.6	4.4	97.0	1.5	97.4	0.4	98.9	1.5
1983	100.6	1.7	100.3	-0.3	100.8	0.5	101.1	0.3	101.5	0.4	101.7	0.2	102.3	0.6	101.8	-0.5	103.5	1.7	103.5	0.0	104.0	0.5	104.4	0.4
1984	105.8	1.3	105.2	-0.6	105.0	-0.2	105.1	0.1	105.1	0.0	105.1	0.0	105.9	0.8	106.2	0.3	108.1	1.8	107.8	-0.3	107.4	-0.4	107.5	0.1
1985	109.3	1.7	109.5	0.2	109.3	-0.2	109.7	0.4	110.5	0.7	110.8	0.3	111.9	1.0	112.1	0.2	113.9	1.6	114.0	0.1	113.6	-0.4	113.2	-0.4
1986	113.8	0.5	111.9	-1.7	111.8	-0.1	111.8	0.0	112.2	0.4	112.2	0.0	114.1	1.7	115.4	1.1	115.9	0.4	115.9	0.0	117.0	0.9	116.7	-0.3
1987	-	-	116.9	0.2	-	-	118.0	0.9	-	-	119.3	1.1	-	-	120.0	0.6	-	-	123.7	3.1	-	-	124.1	0.3
1988	-	-	128.7	3.7	-	-	128.0	-0.5	-	-	128.5	0.4	-	-	130.7	1.7	-	-	133.2	1.9	-	-	133.7	0.4
1989	-	-	134.8	0.8	-	-	135.0	0.1	-	-	137.7	2.0	-	-	138.0	0.2	-	-	140.2	1.6	-	-	140.7	0.4
1990	-	-	143.5	2.0	-	-	143.6	0.1	-	-	147.1	2.4	-	-	147.2	0.1	-	-	151.6	3.0	-	-	154.0	1.6
1991	-	-	156.4	1.6	-	-	158.0	1.0	-	-	159.6	1.0	-	-	161.3	1.1	-	-	164.9	2.2	-	-	164.5	-0.2
1992	-	-	165.7	0.7	-	-	165.7	0.0	-	-	167.9	1.3	-	-	172.6	2.8	-	-	176.0	2.0	-	-	174.3	-1.0
1993	-	-	178.6	2.5	-	-	178.6	0.0	-	-	179.2	0.3	-	-	174.5	-2.6	-	-	171.2	-1.9	-	-	172.6	0.8
1994	-	-	171.2	-0.8	-	-	171.9	0.4	-	-	193.7	12.7	-	-	195.4	0.9	-	-	196.7	0.7	-	-	197.5	0.4
1995	-	-	198.1	0.3	-	-	198.7	0.3	-	-	200.4	0.9	-	-	203.9	1.7	-	-	206.0	1.0	-	-	206.7	0.3

Source: U.S. Department of Labor, Bureau of Labor Statistics, Division of Consumer Prices and Price Indexes. - indicates no data collected for period.

Honolulu, HI
Consumer Price Index - All Urban Consumers
Base 1982-1984 = 100
Annual Averages

For 1963-1995. Columns headed % show percentile change in the index from the previous period for which an index is available.

Year	All Items		Food & Beverage		Housing		Apparel & Upkeep		Trans-portation		Medical Care		Entertain-ment		Other Goods & Services	
	Index	%	Index	%	Index	%	Index	%	Index	%	Index	%	Index	%	Index	%
1963	-	-	-	-	-	-	-	-	-	-	-	-	-	-	-	-
1964	33.7	-	-	-	-	-	46.7	-	37.7	-	25.1	-	-	-	-	-
1965	34.4	2.1	-	-	-	-	47.1	0.9	37.7	0.0	25.8	2.8	-	-	-	-
1966	35.3	2.6	-	-	-	-	47.9	1.7	37.8	0.3	26.6	3.1	-	-	-	-
1967	36.3	2.8	-	-	-	-	48.8	1.9	38.7	2.4	28.3	6.4	-	-	-	-
1968	37.7	3.9	-	-	-	-	50.7	3.9	40.1	3.6	29.9	5.7	-	-	-	-
1969	39.4	4.5	-	-	-	-	53.4	5.3	41.5	3.5	32.0	7.0	-	-	-	-
1970	41.5	5.3	-	-	-	-	56.2	5.2	43.4	4.6	33.5	4.7	-	-	-	-
1971	43.2	4.1	-	-	-	-	57.4	2.1	46.7	7.6	35.2	5.1	-	-	-	-
1972	44.6	3.2	-	-	-	-	58.9	2.6	47.6	1.9	36.0	2.3	-	-	-	-
1973	46.6	4.5	-	-	-	-	60.6	2.9	48.0	0.8	37.7	4.7	-	-	-	-
1974	51.5	10.5	-	-	-	-	65.1	7.4	52.3	9.0	41.5	10.1	-	-	-	-
1975	56.3	9.3	-	-	-	-	69.0	6.0	56.8	8.6	46.6	12.3	-	-	-	-
1976	59.1	5.0	59.7	-	59.2	-	71.6	3.8	59.5	4.8	51.5	10.5	63.6	-	53.8	-
1977	62.1	5.1	62.8	5.2	61.6	4.1	74.3	3.8	61.8	3.9	57.4	11.5	66.3	4.2	57.5	6.9
1978	66.9	7.7	69.0	9.9	66.0	7.1	78.8	6.1	66.0	6.8	62.5	8.9	69.0	4.1	61.4	6.8
1979	74.3	11.1	77.7	12.6	74.0	12.1	83.9	6.5	73.4	11.2	67.5	8.0	72.8	5.5	66.5	8.3
1980	83.0	11.7	84.2	8.4	83.2	12.4	89.8	7.0	86.6	18.0	73.1	8.3	78.2	7.4	73.3	10.2
1981	91.7	10.5	92.6	10.0	92.3	10.9	94.5	5.2	95.7	10.5	81.8	11.9	87.2	11.5	81.5	11.2
1982	97.2	6.0	96.9	4.6	98.0	6.2	98.4	4.1	99.0	3.4	91.6	12.0	95.7	9.7	92.0	12.9
1983	99.3	2.2	99.5	2.7	98.9	0.9	101.4	3.0	98.2	-0.8	101.1	10.4	100.0	4.5	101.4	10.2
1984	103.5	4.2	103.6	4.1	103.1	4.2	100.2	-1.2	102.9	4.8	107.3	6.1	104.3	4.3	106.6	5.1
1985	106.8	3.2	107.8	4.1	106.0	2.8	99.6	-0.6	104.9	1.9	113.2	5.5	111.9	7.3	112.5	5.5
1986	109.4	2.4	110.0	2.0	108.4	2.3	99.8	0.2	105.2	0.3	122.3	8.0	113.2	1.2	119.6	6.3
1987	111.5	1.9	112.0	1.8	114.3	5.4	111.4	11.6	101.5	-3.5	119.3	-2.5	107.7	-4.9	129.0	7.9
1988	115.9	3.9	115.8	3.4	118.4	3.6	121.0	8.6	103.1	1.6	128.4	7.6	111.3	3.3	139.0	7.8
1989	120.8	4.2	121.1	4.6	122.1	3.1	121.2	0.2	110.0	6.7	139.3	8.5	113.7	2.2	146.9	5.7
1990	126.2	4.5	128.1	5.8	126.0	3.2	126.0	4.0	115.2	4.7	150.8	8.3	118.7	4.4	156.6	6.6
1991	132.2	4.8	135.2	5.5	132.2	4.9	125.4	-0.5	119.1	3.4	159.5	5.8	124.0	4.5	169.8	8.4
1992	137.1	3.7	135.4	0.1	137.7	4.2	124.2	-1.0	123.1	3.4	174.3	9.3	130.0	4.8	182.0	7.2
1993	142.1	3.6	138.1	2.0	142.8	3.7	123.2	-0.8	128.5	4.4	185.5	6.4	133.1	2.4	194.9	7.1
1994	147.0	3.4	141.5	2.5	148.0	3.6	122.5	-0.6	134.2	4.4	201.7	8.7	130.2	-2.2	201.1	3.2
1995	151.0	2.7	146.6	3.6	152.2	2.8	121.4	-0.9	137.5	2.5	213.2	5.7	128.7	-1.2	207.1	3.0

Source: U.S. Department of Labor, Bureau of Labor Statistics, Division of Consumer Prices and Price Indexes. - indicates no data collected for period.

Honolulu, HI
Consumer Price Index - Urban Wage Earners
Base 1982-1984 = 100
Annual Averages

For 1963-1995. Columns headed % show percentile change in the index from the previous period for which an index is available.

Year	All Items		Food & Beverage		Housing		Apparel & Upkeep		Trans-portation		Medical Care		Entertain-ment		Other Goods & Services	
	Index	%	Index	%	Index	%	Index	%	Index	%	Index	%	Index	%	Index	%
1963	-	-	-	-	-	-	-	-	-	-	-	-	-	-	-	-
1964	33.3	-	-	-	-	-	45.2	-	37.8	-	24.6	-	-	-	-	-
1965	33.9	1.8	-	-	-	-	45.6	0.9	37.7	-0.3	25.3	2.8	-	-	-	-
1966	34.8	2.7	-	-	-	-	46.3	1.5	37.8	0.3	26.1	3.2	-	-	-	-
1967	35.8	2.9	-	-	-	-	47.2	1.9	38.7	2.4	27.7	6.1	-	-	-	-
1968	37.2	3.9	-	-	-	-	49.0	3.8	40.2	3.9	29.3	5.8	-	-	-	-
1969	38.8	4.3	-	-	-	-	51.7	5.5	41.5	3.2	31.3	6.8	-	-	-	-
1970	40.9	5.4	-	-	-	-	54.4	5.2	43.5	4.8	32.8	4.8	-	-	-	-
1971	42.6	4.2	-	-	-	-	55.6	2.2	46.7	7.4	34.5	5.2	-	-	-	-
1972	44.0	3.3	-	-	-	-	56.9	2.3	47.6	1.9	35.3	2.3	-	-	-	-
1973	45.9	4.3	-	-	-	-	58.6	3.0	48.0	0.8	36.9	4.5	-	-	-	-
1974	50.8	10.7	-	-	-	-	63.0	7.5	52.3	9.0	40.7	10.3	-	-	-	-
1975	55.5	9.3	-	-	-	-	66.7	5.9	56.9	8.8	45.6	12.0	-	-	-	-
1976	58.3	5.0	58.8	-	58.1	-	69.3	3.9	59.5	4.6	50.4	10.5	60.7	-	54.8	-
1977	61.2	5.0	61.9	5.3	60.4	4.0	71.9	3.8	61.9	4.0	56.2	11.5	63.2	4.1	58.5	6.8
1978	65.9	7.7	68.0	9.9	64.6	7.0	75.3	4.7	65.9	6.5	61.8	10.0	67.4	6.6	61.9	5.8
1979	73.2	11.1	76.4	12.4	72.2	11.8	79.9	6.1	73.5	11.5	66.3	7.3	73.5	9.1	66.9	8.1
1980	81.9	11.9	83.5	9.3	80.4	11.4	91.4	14.4	86.6	17.8	72.3	9.0	79.9	8.7	72.8	8.8
1981	90.5	10.5	92.3	10.5	89.0	10.7	95.3	4.3	96.2	11.1	81.9	13.3	87.4	9.4	81.1	11.4
1982	96.0	6.1	96.8	4.9	94.9	6.6	98.3	3.1	99.1	3.0	92.0	12.3	95.4	9.2	91.6	12.9
1983	99.8	4.0	99.5	2.8	100.1	5.5	101.4	3.2	98.1	-1.0	101.1	9.9	100.0	4.8	101.7	11.0
1984	104.3	4.5	103.7	4.2	104.9	4.8	100.3	-1.1	102.8	4.8	106.9	5.7	104.6	4.6	106.6	4.8
1985	107.9	3.5	108.3	4.4	108.6	3.5	99.4	-0.9	104.7	1.8	112.6	5.3	111.9	7.0	112.5	5.5
1986	110.3	2.2	110.8	2.3	111.0	2.2	100.1	0.7	104.7	0.0	121.1	7.5	113.1	1.1	119.1	5.9
1987	114.1	3.4	111.9	1.0	119.0	7.2	113.0	12.9	102.5	-2.1	120.6	-0.4	107.8	-4.7	128.4	7.8
1988	118.6	3.9	115.8	3.5	123.2	3.5	123.2	9.0	104.3	1.8	129.9	7.7	112.0	3.9	139.2	8.4
1989	123.5	4.1	120.9	4.4	126.9	3.0	123.5	0.2	110.9	6.3	141.4	8.9	115.0	2.7	147.6	6.0
1990	128.9	4.4	128.0	5.9	130.9	3.2	127.4	3.2	116.0	4.6	152.3	7.7	119.7	4.1	157.5	6.7
1991	135.0	4.7	135.1	5.5	137.2	4.8	128.1	0.5	119.3	2.8	160.7	5.5	125.4	4.8	171.6	9.0
1992	139.8	3.6	135.3	0.1	143.0	4.2	126.2	-1.5	123.9	3.9	175.3	9.1	130.9	4.4	184.3	7.4
1993	144.8	3.6	138.0	2.0	148.3	3.7	125.9	-0.2	129.5	4.5	186.2	6.2	133.6	2.1	196.6	6.7
1994	149.4	3.2	141.5	2.5	153.6	3.6	125.0	-0.7	134.6	3.9	202.1	8.5	131.2	-1.8	201.2	2.3
1995	153.5	2.7	146.6	3.6	157.9	2.8	125.4	0.3	137.8	2.4	213.3	5.5	129.2	-1.5	206.7	2.7

Source: U.S. Department of Labor, Bureau of Labor Statistics, Division of Consumer Prices and Price Indexes. - indicates no data collected for period.

Honolulu, HI
Consumer Price Index - All Urban Consumers
Base 1982-1984 = 100
All Items

For 1963-1995. Columns headed % show percentile change in the index from the previous period for which an index is available.

Year	Jan Index	%	Feb Index	%	Mar Index	%	Apr Index	%	May Index	%	Jun Index	%	Jul Index	%	Aug Index	%	Sep Index	%	Oct Index	%	Nov Index	%	Dec Index	%
1963	-	-	-	-	-	-	-	-	-	-	-	-	-	-	-	-	-	-	-	-	-	-	33.7	-
1964	-	-	-	-	33.9	0.6	-	-	-	-	33.6	-0.9	-	-	-	-	33.7	0.3	-	-	-	-	34.0	0.9
1965	-	-	-	-	34.2	0.6	-	-	-	-	34.2	0.0	-	-	-	-	34.4	0.6	-	-	-	-	34.9	1.5
1966	-	-	-	-	35.1	0.6	-	-	-	-	35.2	0.3	-	-	-	-	35.6	1.1	-	-	-	-	35.9	0.8
1967	-	-	-	-	35.9	0.0	-	-	-	-	36.2	0.8	-	-	-	-	36.5	0.8	-	-	-	-	37.0	1.4
1968	-	-	-	-	37.3	0.8	-	-	-	-	37.6	0.8	-	-	-	-	38.0	1.1	-	-	-	-	38.4	1.1
1969	-	-	-	-	38.9	1.3	-	-	-	-	39.3	1.0	-	-	-	-	39.8	1.3	-	-	-	-	40.3	1.3
1970	-	-	-	-	41.1	2.0	-	-	-	-	41.6	1.2	-	-	-	-	41.7	0.2	-	-	-	-	42.0	0.7
1971	-	-	-	-	42.4	1.0	-	-	-	-	43.0	1.4	-	-	-	-	44.0	2.3	-	-	-	-	44.0	0.0
1972	-	-	-	-	44.5	1.1	-	-	-	-	44.4	-0.2	-	-	-	-	44.7	0.7	-	-	-	-	45.2	1.1
1973	-	-	-	-	45.8	1.3	-	-	-	-	46.3	1.1	-	-	-	-	47.1	1.7	-	-	-	-	48.2	2.3
1974	-	-	-	-	50.0	3.7	-	-	-	-	51.3	2.6	-	-	-	-	52.9	3.1	-	-	-	-	53.9	1.9
1975	-	-	-	-	55.2	2.4	-	-	-	-	56.0	1.4	-	-	-	-	57.2	2.1	-	-	-	-	58.0	1.4
1976	-	-	-	-	58.5	0.9	-	-	-	-	59.0	0.9	-	-	-	-	59.6	1.0	-	-	-	-	60.1	0.8
1977	-	-	-	-	61.1	1.7	-	-	-	-	61.9	1.3	-	-	-	-	63.0	1.8	-	-	-	-	63.5	0.8
1978	-	-	64.7	1.9	-	-	65.9	1.9	-	-	66.8	1.4	-	-	67.4	0.9	-	-	68.6	1.8	-	-	69.5	1.3
1979	-	-	71.3	2.6	-	-	72.9	2.2	-	-	74.2	1.8	-	-	75.3	1.5	-	-	76.5	1.6	-	-	78.0	2.0
1980	-	-	80.2	2.8	-	-	82.6	3.0	-	-	82.6	0.0	-	-	83.6	1.2	-	-	85.2	1.9	-	-	85.8	0.7
1981	-	-	88.4	3.0	-	-	90.8	2.7	-	-	91.8	1.1	-	-	93.2	1.5	-	-	94.2	1.1	-	-	93.8	-0.4
1982	-	-	95.2	1.5	-	-	95.6	0.4	-	-	97.7	2.2	-	-	97.9	0.2	-	-	100.0	2.1	-	-	98.0	-2.0
1983	-	-	98.2	0.2	-	-	99.1	0.9	-	-	98.6	-0.5	-	-	99.3	0.7	-	-	100.4	1.1	-	-	101.1	0.7
1984	-	-	102.0	0.9	-	-	102.9	0.9	-	-	103.4	0.5	-	-	103.9	0.5	-	-	104.4	0.5	-	-	105.3	0.9
1985	-	-	106.3	0.9	-	-	106.3	0.0	-	-	106.6	0.3	-	-	106.9	0.3	-	-	107.4	0.5	-	-	108.4	0.9
1986	-	-	109.4	0.9	-	-	108.6	-0.7	-	-	108.7	0.1	-	-	109.5	0.7	-	-	109.8	0.3	-	-	110.9	1.0
1987	-	-	-	-	-	-	-	-	-	-	110.1	-0.7	-	-	-	-	-	-	-	-	-	-	113.0	2.6
1988	-	-	-	-	-	-	-	-	-	-	114.5	1.3	-	-	-	-	-	-	-	-	-	-	117.2	2.4
1989	-	-	-	-	-	-	-	-	-	-	120.3	2.6	-	-	-	-	-	-	-	-	-	-	121.2	0.7
1990	-	-	-	-	-	-	-	-	-	-	123.9	2.2	-	-	-	-	-	-	-	-	-	-	128.6	3.8
1991	-	-	-	-	-	-	-	-	-	-	131.0	1.9	-	-	-	-	-	-	-	-	-	-	133.5	1.9
1992	-	-	-	-	-	-	-	-	-	-	135.9	1.8	-	-	-	-	-	-	-	-	-	-	138.2	1.7
1993	-	-	-	-	-	-	-	-	-	-	140.5	1.7	-	-	-	-	-	-	-	-	-	-	143.7	2.3
1994	-	-	-	-	-	-	-	-	-	-	146.0	1.6	-	-	-	-	-	-	-	-	-	-	147.9	1.3
1995	-	-	-	-	-	-	-	-	-	-	150.6	1.8	-	-	-	-	-	-	-	-	-	-	-	-

Source: U.S. Department of Labor, Bureau of Labor Statistics, Division of Consumer Prices and Price Indexes. - indicates no data collected for period.

Honolulu, HI
Consumer Price Index - Urban Wage Earners
Base 1982-1984 = 100
All Items

For 1963-1995. Columns headed % show percentile change in the index from the previous period for which an index is available.

Year	Jan Index	%	Feb Index	%	Mar Index	%	Apr Index	%	May Index	%	Jun Index	%	Jul Index	%	Aug Index	%	Sep Index	%	Oct Index	%	Nov Index	%	Dec Index	%
1963	-	-	-	-	-	-	-	-	-	-	-	-	-	-	-	-	-	-	-	-	-	-	-	-
1964	-	-	-	-	33.4	0.6	-	-	-	-	33.1	-0.9	-	-	-	-	-	-	-	-	-	-	33.2	-
1965	-	-	-	-	33.7	0.6	-	-	-	-	33.7	0.0	-	-	-	-	33.3	0.6	-	-	-	-	33.5	0.6
1966	-	-	-	-	34.6	0.6	-	-	-	-	34.6	0.0	-	-	-	-	33.9	0.6	-	-	-	-	34.4	1.5
1967	-	-	-	-	35.4	0.0	-	-	-	-	35.7	0.8	-	-	-	-	35.0	1.2	-	-	-	-	35.4	1.1
1968	-	-	-	-	36.8	1.1	-	-	-	-	37.0	0.5	-	-	-	-	36.0	0.8	-	-	-	-	36.4	1.1
1969	-	-	-	-	38.4	1.6	-	-	-	-	38.7	0.8	-	-	-	-	37.4	1.1	-	-	-	-	37.8	1.1
1970	-	-	-	-	40.5	2.0	-	-	-	-	40.9	1.0	-	-	-	-	39.2	1.3	-	-	-	-	39.7	1.3
1971	-	-	-	-	41.8	1.0	-	-	-	-	42.4	1.4	-	-	-	-	41.1	0.5	-	-	-	-	41.4	0.7
1972	-	-	-	-	43.8	1.2	-	-	-	-	43.7	-0.2	-	-	-	-	43.4	2.4	-	-	-	-	43.3	-0.2
1973	-	-	-	-	45.1	1.3	-	-	-	-	45.6	1.1	-	-	-	-	44.1	0.9	-	-	-	-	44.5	0.9
1974	-	-	-	-	49.3	3.8	-	-	-	-	50.5	2.4	-	-	-	-	46.4	1.8	-	-	-	-	47.5	2.4
1975	-	-	-	-	54.4	2.3	-	-	-	-	55.2	1.5	-	-	-	-	52.1	3.2	-	-	-	-	53.2	2.1
1976	-	-	-	-	57.7	0.9	-	-	-	-	58.1	0.7	-	-	-	-	56.4	2.2	-	-	-	-	57.2	1.4
1977	-	-	-	-	60.2	1.7	-	-	-	-	61.0	1.3	-	-	-	-	58.7	1.0	-	-	-	-	59.2	0.9
1978	-	-	63.5	1.4	-	-	64.9	2.2	-	-	65.9	1.5	-	-	-	-	62.1	1.8	-	-	-	-	62.6	0.8
1979	-	-	70.2	2.6	-	-	71.6	2.0	-	-	72.9	1.8	-	-	66.6	1.1	-	-	67.5	1.4	-	-	68.4	1.3
1980	-	-	79.2	2.7	-	-	81.8	3.3	-	-	81.6	-0.2	-	-	74.2	1.8	-	-	75.6	1.9	-	-	77.1	2.0
1981	-	-	87.2	2.8	-	-	89.6	2.8	-	-	90.8	1.3	-	-	82.1	0.6	-	-	83.6	1.8	-	-	84.8	1.4
1982	-	-	94.1	1.4	-	-	94.6	0.5	-	-	96.3	1.8	-	-	91.8	1.1	-	-	92.7	1.0	-	-	92.8	0.1
1983	-	-	98.4	1.4	-	-	99.1	0.7	-	-	97.9	-1.2	-	-	96.5	0.2	-	-	98.3	1.9	-	-	97.0	-1.3
1984	-	-	101.8	-1.4	-	-	103.4	1.6	-	-	104.1	0.7	-	-	99.6	1.7	-	-	102.3	2.7	-	-	103.2	0.9
1985	-	-	107.5	0.9	-	-	107.4	-0.1	-	-	107.5	0.1	-	-	105.1	1.0	-	-	105.4	0.3	-	-	106.5	1.0
1986	-	-	110.4	0.8	-	-	109.5	-0.8	-	-	109.7	0.2	-	-	107.8	0.3	-	-	108.4	0.6	-	-	109.5	1.0
1987	-	-	-	-	-	-	-	-	-	-	112.6	0.6	-	-	110.4	0.6	-	-	110.5	0.1	-	-	111.9	1.3
1988	-	-	-	-	-	-	-	-	-	-	117.2	1.4	-	-	-	-	-	-	-	-	-	-	115.6	2.7
1989	-	-	-	-	-	-	-	-	-	-	123.1	2.5	-	-	-	-	-	-	-	-	-	-	120.1	2.5
1990	-	-	-	-	-	-	-	-	-	-	126.3	1.9	-	-	-	-	-	-	-	-	-	-	124.0	0.7
1991	-	-	-	-	-	-	-	-	-	-	133.6	1.5	-	-	-	-	-	-	-	-	-	-	131.6	4.2
1992	-	-	-	-	-	-	-	-	-	-	138.4	1.5	-	-	-	-	-	-	-	-	-	-	136.3	2.0
1993	-	-	-	-	-	-	-	-	-	-	143.3	1.5	-	-	-	-	-	-	-	-	-	-	141.2	2.0
1994	-	-	-	-	-	-	-	-	-	-	148.4	1.4	-	-	-	-	-	-	-	-	-	-	146.4	2.2
1995	-	-	-	-	-	-	-	-	-	-	153.0	1.7	-	-	-	-	-	-	-	-	-	-	150.5	1.4
																							-	-

Source: U.S. Department of Labor, Bureau of Labor Statistics, Division of Consumer Prices and Price Indexes. - indicates no data collected for period.

Honolulu, HI
Consumer Price Index - All Urban Consumers
Base 1982-1984 = 100
Food and Beverages

For 1975-1995. Columns headed % show percentile change in the index from the previous period for which an index is available.

Year	Jan Index	%	Feb Index	%	Mar Index	%	Apr Index	%	May Index	%	Jun Index	%	Jul Index	%	Aug Index	%	Sep Index	%	Oct Index	%	Nov Index	%	Dec Index	%
1975	-	-	-	-	-	-	-	-	-	-	-	-	-	-	-	-	-	-	-	-	-	-	59.4	-
1976	-	-	-	-	59.5	0.2	-	-	-	-	59.6	0.2	-	-	-	-	59.5	-0.2	-	-	-	-	60.5	1.7
1977	-	-	-	-	61.8	2.1	-	-	-	-	62.6	1.3	-	-	-	-	63.8	1.9	-	-	-	-	64.4	0.9
1978	-	-	65.9	2.3	-	-	67.6	2.6	-	-	69.2	2.4	-	-	70.0	1.2	-	-	71.2	1.7	-	-	72.3	1.5
1979	-	-	74.6	3.2	-	-	76.5	2.5	-	-	78.3	2.4	-	-	78.4	0.1	-	-	79.5	1.4	-	-	80.6	1.4
1980	-	-	81.6	1.2	-	-	83.0	1.7	-	-	83.3	0.4	-	-	85.1	2.2	-	-	86.5	1.6	-	-	87.8	1.5
1981	-	-	90.8	3.4	-	-	92.2	1.5	-	-	92.7	0.5	-	-	93.5	0.9	-	-	94.2	0.7	-	-	93.8	-0.4
1982	-	-	96.1	2.5	-	-	96.2	0.1	-	-	96.9	0.7	-	-	97.3	0.4	-	-	97.7	0.4	-	-	98.3	0.6
1983	-	-	98.8	0.5	-	-	99.6	0.8	-	-	99.4	-0.2	-	-	99.8	0.4	-	-	100.0	0.2	-	-	99.6	-0.4
1984	-	-	101.4	1.8	-	-	102.2	0.8	-	-	103.6	1.4	-	-	104.5	0.9	-	-	104.6	0.1	-	-	107.3	2.6
1985	-	-	108.1	0.7	-	-	108.2	0.1	-	-	107.6	-0.6	-	-	107.5	-0.1	-	-	106.9	-0.6	-	-	108.6	1.6
1986	-	-	108.7	0.1	-	-	107.9	-0.7	-	-	110.1	2.0	-	-	109.7	-0.4	-	-	111.7	1.8	-	-	113.0	1.2
1987	-	-	-	-	-	-	-	-	-	-	112.0	-0.9	-	-	-	-	-	-	-	-	-	-	111.9	-0.1
1988	-	-	-	-	-	-	-	-	-	-	114.3	2.1	-	-	-	-	-	-	-	-	-	-	117.3	2.6
1989	-	-	-	-	-	-	-	-	-	-	120.1	2.4	-	-	-	-	-	-	-	-	-	-	122.0	1.6
1990	-	-	-	-	-	-	-	-	-	-	126.2	3.4	-	-	-	-	-	-	-	-	-	-	130.0	3.0
1991	-	-	-	-	-	-	-	-	-	-	134.8	3.7	-	-	-	-	-	-	-	-	-	-	135.7	0.7
1992	-	-	-	-	-	-	-	-	-	-	135.6	-0.1	-	-	-	-	-	-	-	-	-	-	135.3	-0.2
1993	-	-	-	-	-	-	-	-	-	-	137.0	1.3	-	-	-	-	-	-	-	-	-	-	139.2	1.6
1994	-	-	-	-	-	-	-	-	-	-	140.0	0.6	-	-	-	-	-	-	-	-	-	-	143.1	2.2
1995	-	-	-	-	-	-	-	-	-	-	145.7	1.8	-	-	-	-	-	-	-	-	-	-	-	-

Source: U.S. Department of Labor, Bureau of Labor Statistics, Division of Consumer Prices and Price Indexes. - indicates no data collected for period.

Honolulu, HI
Consumer Price Index - Urban Wage Earners
Base 1982-1984 = 100
Food and Beverages

For 1975-1995. Columns headed % show percentile change in the index from the previous period for which an index is available.

Year	Jan Index	Jan %	Feb Index	Feb %	Mar Index	Mar %	Apr Index	Apr %	May Index	May %	Jun Index	Jun %	Jul Index	Jul %	Aug Index	Aug %	Sep Index	Sep %	Oct Index	Oct %	Nov Index	Nov %	Dec Index	Dec %
1975	-	-	-	-	-	-	-	-	-	-	-	-	-	-	-	-	-	-	-	-	-	-	-	-
1976	-	-	-	-	58.7	0.3	-	-	-	-	58.7	0.0	-	-	-	-	58.6	-0.2	-	-	-	-	58.5	-
1977	-	-	-	-	60.8	2.0	-	-	-	-	61.7	1.5	-	-	-	-	62.8	1.8	-	-	-	-	59.6	1.7
1978	-	-	64.6	1.7	-	-	66.7	3.3	-	-	68.7	3.0	-	-	69.3	0.9	-	-	69.8	0.7	-	-	63.5	1.1
1979	-	-	74.0	4.7	-	-	75.5	2.0	-	-	76.2	0.9	-	-	76.9	0.9	-	-	78.3	1.8	-	-	70.7	1.3
1980	-	-	80.8	1.3	-	-	82.3	1.9	-	-	82.6	0.4	-	-	84.0	1.7	-	-	85.6	1.9	-	-	79.8	1.9
1981	-	-	90.5	3.3	-	-	91.9	1.5	-	-	92.2	0.3	-	-	93.0	0.9	-	-	93.6	0.6	-	-	87.6	2.3
1982	-	-	96.5	2.7	-	-	96.3	-0.2	-	-	96.7	0.4	-	-	93.0	0.9	-	-	93.6	0.6	-	-	94.0	0.4
1983	-	-	98.8	0.6	-	-	99.6	0.8	-	-	99.3	-0.3	-	-	96.9	0.2	-	-	97.4	0.5	-	-	98.2	0.8
1984	-	-	101.8	2.0	-	-	102.5	0.7	-	-	103.3	-0.3	-	-	99.8	0.5	-	-	99.8	0.0	-	-	99.8	0.0
1985	-	-	109.1	0.6	-	-	108.6	-0.5	-	-	103.3	0.8	-	-	104.3	1.0	-	-	104.3	0.0	-	-	108.4	3.9
1986	-	-	109.6	0.4	-	-	108.9	-0.6	-	-	107.7	-0.8	-	-	107.9	0.2	-	-	107.3	-0.6	-	-	109.2	1.8
1987	-	-	-	-	-	-	-	-	-	-	111.0	1.9	-	-	110.1	-0.8	-	-	112.5	2.2	-	-	114.1	1.4
1988	-	-	-	-	-	-	-	-	-	-	111.9	-1.9	-	-	-	-	-	-	-	-	-	-	111.8	-0.1
1989	-	-	-	-	-	-	-	-	-	-	114.4	2.3	-	-	-	-	-	-	-	-	-	-	117.1	2.4
1990	-	-	-	-	-	-	-	-	-	-	119.9	2.4	-	-	-	-	-	-	-	-	-	-	121.9	1.7
1991	-	-	-	-	-	-	-	-	-	-	126.0	3.4	-	-	-	-	-	-	-	-	-	-	130.0	3.2
1992	-	-	-	-	-	-	-	-	-	-	134.7	3.6	-	-	-	-	-	-	-	-	-	-	135.5	0.6
1993	-	-	-	-	-	-	-	-	-	-	135.4	-0.1	-	-	-	-	-	-	-	-	-	-	135.3	-0.1
1994	-	-	-	-	-	-	-	-	-	-	136.8	1.1	-	-	-	-	-	-	-	-	-	-	139.1	1.7
1995	-	-	-	-	-	-	-	-	-	-	139.9	0.6	-	-	-	-	-	-	-	-	-	-	143.1	2.3
	-	-	-	-	-	-	-	-	-	-	145.7	1.8	-	-	-	-	-	-	-	-	-	-	-	-

Source: U.S. Department of Labor, Bureau of Labor Statistics, Division of Consumer Prices and Price Indexes. - indicates no data collected for period.

Honolulu, HI
Consumer Price Index - All Urban Consumers
Base 1982-1984 = 100
Housing

For 1975-1995. Columns headed % show percentile change in the index from the previous period for which an index is available.

Year	Jan Index	%	Feb Index	%	Mar Index	%	Apr Index	%	May Index	%	Jun Index	%	Jul Index	%	Aug Index	%	Sep Index	%	Oct Index	%	Nov Index	%	Dec Index	%
1975	-	-	-	-	-	-	-	-	-	-	-	-	-	-	-	-	-	-	-	-	-	-	58.6	-
1976	-	-	-	-	58.6	0.0	-	-	-	-	59.1	0.9	-	-	-	-	59.8	1.2	-	-	-	-	59.7	-0.2
1977	-	-	-	-	60.7	1.7	-	-	-	-	61.3	1.0	-	-	-	-	62.5	2.0	-	-	-	-	62.8	0.5
1978	-	-	63.7	1.4	-	-	65.0	2.0	-	-	65.9	1.4	-	-	66.2	0.5	-	-	67.9	2.6	-	-	68.7	1.2
1979	-	-	70.9	3.2	-	-	72.8	2.7	-	-	73.9	1.5	-	-	75.1	1.6	-	-	76.3	1.6	-	-	77.7	1.8
1980	-	-	80.3	3.3	-	-	83.7	4.2	-	-	83.2	-0.6	-	-	83.2	0.0	-	-	85.3	2.5	-	-	85.7	0.5
1981	-	-	88.3	3.0	-	-	91.8	4.0	-	-	93.0	1.3	-	-	94.4	1.5	-	-	94.8	0.4	-	-	93.8	-1.1
1982	-	-	95.3	1.6	-	-	95.7	0.4	-	-	99.3	3.8	-	-	98.7	-0.6	-	-	102.2	3.5	-	-	97.8	-4.3
1983	-	-	98.0	0.2	-	-	99.1	1.1	-	-	97.8	-1.3	-	-	98.2	0.4	-	-	100.0	1.8	-	-	101.7	1.7
1984	-	-	101.7	0.0	-	-	102.9	1.2	-	-	103.0	0.1	-	-	103.1	0.1	-	-	104.1	1.0	-	-	104.2	0.1
1985	-	-	105.6	1.3	-	-	105.4	-0.2	-	-	106.3	0.9	-	-	105.4	-0.8	-	-	106.1	0.7	-	-	108.1	1.9
1986	-	-	108.4	0.3	-	-	108.1	-0.3	-	-	107.2	-0.8	-	-	109.4	2.1	-	-	108.3	-1.0	-	-	109.6	1.2
1987	-	-	-	-	-	-	-	-	-	-	112.4	2.6	-	-	-	-	-	-	-	-	-	-	116.2	3.4
1988	-	-	-	-	-	-	-	-	-	-	117.3	0.9	-	-	-	-	-	-	-	-	-	-	119.5	1.9
1989	-	-	-	-	-	-	-	-	-	-	121.8	1.9	-	-	-	-	-	-	-	-	-	-	122.5	0.6
1990	-	-	-	-	-	-	-	-	-	-	123.6	0.9	-	-	-	-	-	-	-	-	-	-	128.5	4.0
1991	-	-	-	-	-	-	-	-	-	-	131.0	1.9	-	-	-	-	-	-	-	-	-	-	133.3	1.8
1992	-	-	-	-	-	-	-	-	-	-	136.4	2.3	-	-	-	-	-	-	-	-	-	-	139.1	2.0
1993	-	-	-	-	-	-	-	-	-	-	140.9	1.3	-	-	-	-	-	-	-	-	-	-	144.7	2.7
1994	-	-	-	-	-	-	-	-	-	-	147.5	1.9	-	-	-	-	-	-	-	-	-	-	148.4	0.6
1995	-	-	-	-	-	-	-	-	-	-	152.1	2.5	-	-	-	-	-	-	-	-	-	-	-	-

Source: U.S. Department of Labor, Bureau of Labor Statistics, Division of Consumer Prices and Price Indexes. - indicates no data collected for period.

Honolulu, HI
Consumer Price Index - Urban Wage Earners
Base 1982-1984 = 100
Housing

For 1975-1995. Columns headed % show percentile change in the index from the previous period for which an index is available.

Year	Jan Index	%	Feb Index	%	Mar Index	%	Apr Index	%	May Index	%	Jun Index	%	Jul Index	%	Aug Index	%	Sep Index	%	Oct Index	%	Nov Index	%	Dec Index	%
1975	-	-	-	-	-	-	-	-	-	-	-	-	-	-	-	-	-	-	-	-	-	-	57.4	-
1976	-	-	-	-	57.5	0.2	-	-	-	-	57.9	0.7	-	-	-	-	58.7	1.4	-	-	-	-	58.5	-0.3
1977	-	-	-	-	59.5	1.7	-	-	-	-	60.1	1.0	-	-	-	-	61.3	2.0	-	-	-	-	61.6	0.5
1978	-	-	62.2	1.0	-	-	63.5	2.1	-	-	64.4	1.4	-	-	65.0	0.9	-	-	66.4	2.2	-	-	67.5	1.7
1979	-	-	68.9	2.1	-	-	70.6	2.5	-	-	71.9	1.8	-	-	73.4	2.1	-	-	74.5	1.5	-	-	76.1	2.1
1980	-	-	77.7	2.1	-	-	81.5	4.9	-	-	80.8	-0.9	-	-	79.9	-1.1	-	-	81.4	1.9	-	-	82.6	1.5
1981	-	-	84.8	2.7	-	-	88.4	4.2	-	-	90.0	1.8	-	-	91.0	1.1	-	-	91.4	0.4	-	-	90.8	-0.7
1982	-	-	92.3	1.7	-	-	92.8	0.5	-	-	96.0	3.4	-	-	95.5	-0.5	-	-	98.8	3.5	-	-	95.1	-3.7
1983	-	-	98.2	3.3	-	-	99.2	1.0	-	-	96.3	-2.9	-	-	98.9	2.7	-	-	104.8	6.0	-	-	106.4	1.5
1984	-	-	101.1	-5.0	-	-	104.1	3.0	-	-	105.0	0.9	-	-	106.2	1.1	-	-	106.7	0.5	-	-	106.7	0.0
1985	-	-	108.2	1.4	-	-	108.2	0.0	-	-	108.9	0.6	-	-	107.9	-0.9	-	-	108.7	0.7	-	-	110.7	1.8
1986	-	-	111.0	0.3	-	-	110.7	-0.3	-	-	109.7	-0.9	-	-	112.2	2.3	-	-	110.5	-1.5	-	-	112.1	1.4
1987	-	-	-	-	-	-	-	-	-	-	117.1	4.5	-	-	-	-	-	-	-	-	-	-	120.9	3.2
1988	-	-	-	-	-	-	-	-	-	-	122.1	1.0	-	-	-	-	-	-	-	-	-	-	124.4	1.9
1989	-	-	-	-	-	-	-	-	-	-	126.6	1.8	-	-	-	-	-	-	-	-	-	-	127.3	0.6
1990	-	-	-	-	-	-	-	-	-	-	128.4	0.9	-	-	-	-	-	-	-	-	-	-	133.4	3.9
1991	-	-	-	-	-	-	-	-	-	-	136.1	2.0	-	-	-	-	-	-	-	-	-	-	138.4	1.7
1992	-	-	-	-	-	-	-	-	-	-	141.5	2.2	-	-	-	-	-	-	-	-	-	-	144.4	2.0
1993	-	-	-	-	-	-	-	-	-	-	146.3	1.3	-	-	-	-	-	-	-	-	-	-	150.2	2.7
1994	-	-	-	-	-	-	-	-	-	-	153.1	1.9	-	-	-	-	-	-	-	-	-	-	154.0	0.6
1995	-	-	-	-	-	-	-	-	-	-	157.7	2.4	-	-	-	-	-	-	-	-	-	-	-	-

Source: U.S. Department of Labor, Bureau of Labor Statistics, Division of Consumer Prices and Price Indexes. - indicates no data collected for period.

Honolulu, HI
Consumer Price Index - All Urban Consumers
Base 1982-1984 = 100
Apparel and Upkeep

For 1963-1995. Columns headed % show percentile change in the index from the previous period for which an index is available.

Year	Jan Index	%	Feb Index	%	Mar Index	%	Apr Index	%	May Index	%	Jun Index	%	Jul Index	%	Aug Index	%	Sep Index	%	Oct Index	%	Nov Index	%	Dec Index	%
1963	-	-	-	-	-	-	-	-	-	-	-	-	-	-	-	-	-	-	-	-	-	-	46.2	-
1964	-	-	-	-	46.4	0.4	-	-	-	-	46.4	0.0	-	-	-	-	47.1	1.5	-	-	-	-	47.0	-0.2
1965	-	-	-	-	46.8	-0.4	-	-	-	-	47.3	1.1	-	-	-	-	47.1	-0.4	-	-	-	-	47.4	0.6
1966	-	-	-	-	47.6	0.4	-	-	-	-	48.1	1.1	-	-	-	-	48.1	0.0	-	-	-	-	48.1	0.0
1967	-	-	-	-	48.2	0.2	-	-	-	-	48.8	1.2	-	-	-	-	49.3	1.0	-	-	-	-	49.5	0.4
1968	-	-	-	-	50.0	1.0	-	-	-	-	50.2	0.4	-	-	-	-	51.5	2.6	-	-	-	-	51.8	0.6
1969	-	-	-	-	52.5	1.4	-	-	-	-	53.5	1.9	-	-	-	-	54.0	0.9	-	-	-	-	54.4	0.7
1970	-	-	-	-	54.7	0.6	-	-	-	-	56.0	2.4	-	-	-	-	57.7	3.0	-	-	-	-	57.5	-0.3
1971	-	-	-	-	57.3	-0.3	-	-	-	-	56.9	-0.7	-	-	-	-	57.5	1.1	-	-	-	-	58.2	1.2
1972	-	-	-	-	58.8	1.0	-	-	-	-	58.8	0.0	-	-	-	-	59.1	0.5	-	-	-	-	58.9	-0.3
1973	-	-	-	-	59.9	1.7	-	-	-	-	59.8	-0.2	-	-	-	-	61.5	2.8	-	-	-	-	62.3	1.3
1974	-	-	-	-	63.6	2.1	-	-	-	-	64.7	1.7	-	-	-	-	66.6	2.9	-	-	-	-	67.2	0.9
1975	-	-	-	-	68.5	1.9	-	-	-	-	68.9	0.6	-	-	-	-	69.6	1.0	-	-	-	-	69.7	0.1
1976	-	-	-	-	70.9	1.7	-	-	-	-	71.7	1.1	-	-	-	-	72.6	1.3	-	-	-	-	72.3	-0.4
1977	-	-	-	-	73.9	2.2	-	-	-	-	73.9	0.0	-	-	-	-	74.7	1.1	-	-	-	-	75.9	1.6
1978	-	-	77.1	1.6	-	-	77.8	0.9	-	-	77.5	-0.4	-	-	80.5	3.9	-	-	80.2	-0.4	-	-	80.8	0.7
1979	-	-	83.1	2.8	-	-	82.5	-0.7	-	-	84.3	2.2	-	-	84.5	0.2	-	-	84.6	0.1	-	-	85.4	0.9
1980	-	-	88.2	3.3	-	-	88.5	0.3	-	-	88.6	0.1	-	-	91.6	3.4	-	-	92.0	0.4	-	-	91.6	-0.4
1981	-	-	93.2	1.7	-	-	93.0	-0.2	-	-	92.9	-0.1	-	-	94.6	1.8	-	-	97.5	3.1	-	-	96.8	-0.7
1982	-	-	97.4	0.6	-	-	98.2	0.8	-	-	99.0	0.8	-	-	98.1	-0.9	-	-	99.1	1.0	-	-	99.3	0.2
1983	-	-	100.4	1.1	-	-	101.9	1.5	-	-	100.4	-1.5	-	-	102.1	1.7	-	-	102.6	0.5	-	-	102.0	-0.6
1984	-	-	103.1	1.1	-	-	101.8	-1.3	-	-	101.0	-0.8	-	-	97.5	-3.5	-	-	97.7	0.2	-	-	99.2	1.5
1985	-	-	99.6	0.4	-	-	98.7	-0.9	-	-	98.4	-0.3	-	-	99.7	1.3	-	-	101.4	1.7	-	-	99.9	-1.5
1986	-	-	100.7	0.8	-	-	100.4	-0.3	-	-	96.4	-4.0	-	-	99.3	3.0	-	-	100.9	1.6	-	-	101.8	0.9
1987	-	-	-	-	-	-	-	-	-	-	107.8	5.9	-	-	-	-	-	-	-	-	-	-	115.0	6.7
1988	-	-	-	-	-	-	-	-	-	-	118.1	2.7	-	-	-	-	-	-	-	-	-	-	123.9	4.9
1989	-	-	-	-	-	-	-	-	-	-	123.4	-0.4	-	-	-	-	-	-	-	-	-	-	119.1	-3.5
1990	-	-	-	-	-	-	-	-	-	-	120.7	1.3	-	-	-	-	-	-	-	-	-	-	131.4	8.9
1991	-	-	-	-	-	-	-	-	-	-	124.1	-5.6	-	-	-	-	-	-	-	-	-	-	126.7	2.1
1992	-	-	-	-	-	-	-	-	-	-	123.6	-2.4	-	-	-	-	-	-	-	-	-	-	124.7	0.9
1993	-	-	-	-	-	-	-	-	-	-	120.5	-3.4	-	-	-	-	-	-	-	-	-	-	125.8	4.4
1994	-	-	-	-	-	-	-	-	-	-	121.3	-3.6	-	-	-	-	-	-	-	-	-	-	123.7	2.0
1995	-	-	-	-	-	-	-	-	-	-	119.6	-3.3	-	-	-	-	-	-	-	-	-	-	-	-

Source: U.S. Department of Labor, Bureau of Labor Statistics, Division of Consumer Prices and Price Indexes. - indicates no data collected for period.

Honolulu, HI
Consumer Price Index - Urban Wage Earners
Base 1982-1984 = 100
Apparel and Upkeep

For 1963-1995. Columns headed % show percentile change in the index from the previous period for which an index is available.

Year	Jan		Feb		Mar		Apr		May		Jun		Jul		Aug		Sep		Oct		Nov		Dec	
	Index	%	Index	%	Index	%	Index	%	Index	%	Index	%	Index	%	Index	%	Index	%	Index	%	Index	%	Index	%
1963	-	-	-	-	-	-	-	-	-	-	-	-	-	-	-	-	-	-	-	-	-	-	44.6	-
1964	-	-	-	-	44.9	0.7	-	-	-	-	44.9	0.0	-	-	-	-	45.6	1.6	-	-	-	-	45.5	-0.2
1965	-	-	-	-	45.3	-0.4	-	-	-	-	45.8	1.1	-	-	-	-	45.5	-0.7	-	-	-	-	45.9	0.9
1966	-	-	-	-	46.0	0.2	-	-	-	-	46.5	1.1	-	-	-	-	46.5	0.0	-	-	-	-	46.5	0.0
1967	-	-	-	-	46.6	0.2	-	-	-	-	47.2	1.3	-	-	-	-	47.7	1.1	-	-	-	-	47.9	0.4
1968	-	-	-	-	48.4	1.0	-	-	-	-	48.6	0.4	-	-	-	-	49.8	2.5	-	-	-	-	50.1	0.6
1969	-	-	-	-	50.7	1.2	-	-	-	-	51.8	2.2	-	-	-	-	52.2	0.8	-	-	-	-	52.6	0.8
1970	-	-	-	-	53.0	0.8	-	-	-	-	54.2	2.3	-	-	-	-	55.8	3.0	-	-	-	-	55.6	-0.4
1971	-	-	-	-	55.5	-0.2	-	-	-	-	55.0	-0.9	-	-	-	-	55.6	1.1	-	-	-	-	56.3	1.3
1972	-	-	-	-	56.9	1.1	-	-	-	-	56.8	-0.2	-	-	-	-	57.2	0.7	-	-	-	-	57.0	-0.3
1973	-	-	-	-	58.0	1.8	-	-	-	-	57.9	-0.2	-	-	-	-	59.5	2.8	-	-	-	-	60.2	1.2
1974	-	-	-	-	61.5	2.2	-	-	-	-	62.6	1.8	-	-	-	-	64.4	2.9	-	-	-	-	65.0	0.9
1975	-	-	-	-	66.2	1.8	-	-	-	-	66.7	0.8	-	-	-	-	67.3	0.9	-	-	-	-	67.5	0.3
1976	-	-	-	-	68.5	1.5	-	-	-	-	69.3	1.2	-	-	-	-	70.2	1.3	-	-	-	-	69.9	-0.4
1977	-	-	-	-	71.5	2.3	-	-	-	-	71.5	0.0	-	-	-	-	72.2	1.0	-	-	-	-	73.5	1.8
1978	-	-	73.4	-0.1	-	-	74.4	1.4	-	-	73.9	-0.7	-	-	75.9	2.7	-	-	77.6	2.2	-	-	77.6	0.0
1979	-	-	78.9	1.7	-	-	78.0	-1.1	-	-	79.1	1.4	-	-	79.8	0.9	-	-	82.4	3.3	-	-	82.6	0.2
1980	-	-	90.8	9.9	-	-	92.3	1.7	-	-	90.2	-2.3	-	-	92.0	2.0	-	-	92.6	0.7	-	-	93.5	1.0
1981	-	-	94.8	1.4	-	-	94.7	-0.1	-	-	95.0	0.3	-	-	95.3	0.3	-	-	96.2	0.9	-	-	96.7	0.5
1982	-	-	97.1	0.4	-	-	98.0	0.9	-	-	98.8	0.8	-	-	97.9	-0.9	-	-	99.1	1.2	-	-	99.8	0.7
1983	-	-	100.5	0.7	-	-	101.8	1.3	-	-	100.3	-1.5	-	-	101.8	1.5	-	-	102.4	0.6	-	-	102.0	-0.4
1984	-	-	103.0	1.0	-	-	102.3	-0.7	-	-	100.3	-2.0	-	-	97.5	-2.8	-	-	98.5	1.0	-	-	99.6	1.1
1985	-	-	100.1	0.5	-	-	98.0	-2.1	-	-	97.6	-0.4	-	-	99.3	1.7	-	-	101.9	2.6	-	-	99.9	-2.0
1986	-	-	100.4	0.5	-	-	100.2	-0.2	-	-	97.1	-3.1	-	-	99.6	2.6	-	-	101.4	1.8	-	-	102.8	1.4
1987	-	-	-	-	-	-	-	-	-	-	109.7	6.7	-	-	-	-	-	-	-	-	-	-	116.3	6.0
1988	-	-	-	-	-	-	-	-	-	-	120.5	3.6	-	-	-	-	-	-	-	-	-	-	125.9	4.5
1989	-	-	-	-	-	-	-	-	-	-	125.9	0.0	-	-	-	-	-	-	-	-	-	-	121.1	-3.8
1990	-	-	-	-	-	-	-	-	-	-	120.9	-0.2	-	-	-	-	-	-	-	-	-	-	133.8	10.7
1991	-	-	-	-	-	-	-	-	-	-	126.0	-5.8	-	-	-	-	-	-	-	-	-	-	130.3	3.4
1992	-	-	-	-	-	-	-	-	-	-	125.1	-4.0	-	-	-	-	-	-	-	-	-	-	127.4	1.8
1993	-	-	-	-	-	-	-	-	-	-	123.8	-2.8	-	-	-	-	-	-	-	-	-	-	128.0	3.4
1994	-	-	-	-	-	-	-	-	-	-	123.4	-3.6	-	-	-	-	-	-	-	-	-	-	126.6	2.6
1995	-	-	-	-	-	-	-	-	-	-	122.8	-3.0	-	-	-	-	-	-	-	-	-	-	-	-

Source: U.S. Department of Labor, Bureau of Labor Statistics, Division of Consumer Prices and Price Indexes. - indicates no data collected for period.

Honolulu, HI
Consumer Price Index - All Urban Consumers
Base 1982-1984 = 100
Transportation

For 1963-1995. Columns headed % show percentile change in the index from the previous period for which an index is available.

Year	Jan Index	%	Feb Index	%	Mar Index	%	Apr Index	%	May Index	%	Jun Index	%	Jul Index	%	Aug Index	%	Sep Index	%	Oct Index	%	Nov Index	%	Dec Index	%
1963	-	-	-	-	-	-	-	-	-	-	-	-	-	-	-	-	-	-	-	-	-	-	38.4	-
1964	-	-	-	-	38.0	-1.0	-	-	-	-	37.4	-1.6	-	-	-	-	37.4	0.0	-	-	-	-	38.0	1.6
1965	-	-	-	-	37.9	-0.3	-	-	-	-	37.5	-1.1	-	-	-	-	37.6	0.3	-	-	-	-	37.7	0.3
1966	-	-	-	-	37.5	-0.5	-	-	-	-	37.7	0.5	-	-	-	-	37.8	0.3	-	-	-	-	38.6	2.1
1967	-	-	-	-	38.4	-0.5	-	-	-	-	38.6	0.5	-	-	-	-	38.6	0.0	-	-	-	-	39.6	2.6
1968	-	-	-	-	40.1	1.3	-	-	-	-	40.0	-0.2	-	-	-	-	40.0	0.0	-	-	-	-	40.8	2.0
1969	-	-	-	-	41.7	2.2	-	-	-	-	41.5	-0.5	-	-	-	-	41.2	-0.7	-	-	-	-	42.2	2.4
1970	-	-	-	-	42.8	1.4	-	-	-	-	43.6	1.9	-	-	-	-	43.6	0.0	-	-	-	-	44.6	2.3
1971	-	-	-	-	45.7	2.5	-	-	-	-	47.7	4.4	-	-	-	-	47.2	-1.0	-	-	-	-	47.1	-0.2
1972	-	-	-	-	47.5	0.8	-	-	-	-	47.8	0.6	-	-	-	-	47.7	-0.2	-	-	-	-	47.7	0.0
1973	-	-	-	-	47.9	0.4	-	-	-	-	47.9	0.0	-	-	-	-	47.7	-0.4	-	-	-	-	48.7	2.1
1974	-	-	-	-	50.8	4.3	-	-	-	-	52.6	3.5	-	-	-	-	53.3	1.3	-	-	-	-	54.2	1.7
1975	-	-	-	-	55.2	1.8	-	-	-	-	57.1	3.4	-	-	-	-	58.1	1.8	-	-	-	-	58.0	-0.2
1976	-	-	-	-	58.7	1.2	-	-	-	-	59.3	1.0	-	-	-	-	60.0	1.2	-	-	-	-	60.9	1.5
1977	-	-	-	-	61.2	0.5	-	-	-	-	62.3	1.8	-	-	-	-	61.9	-0.6	-	-	-	-	62.6	1.1
1978	-	-	63.8	1.9	-	-	64.9	1.7	-	-	66.0	1.7	-	-	66.7	1.1	-	-	67.3	0.9	-	-	68.3	1.5
1979	-	-	68.6	0.4	-	-	70.5	2.8	-	-	72.8	3.3	-	-	74.7	2.6	-	-	76.5	2.4	-	-	79.9	4.4
1980	-	-	83.5	4.5	-	-	85.8	2.8	-	-	86.1	0.3	-	-	88.2	2.4	-	-	88.8	0.7	-	-	89.6	0.9
1981	-	-	92.5	3.2	-	-	94.7	2.4	-	-	95.9	1.3	-	-	97.1	1.3	-	-	97.6	0.5	-	-	98.3	0.7
1982	-	-	98.0	-0.3	-	-	97.6	-0.4	-	-	98.6	1.0	-	-	100.2	1.6	-	-	100.2	0.0	-	-	99.2	-1.0
1983	-	-	97.2	-2.0	-	-	96.6	-0.6	-	-	96.8	0.2	-	-	98.4	1.7	-	-	100.0	1.6	-	-	100.7	0.7
1984	-	-	101.2	0.5	-	-	101.8	0.6	-	-	103.2	1.4	-	-	104.0	0.8	-	-	103.9	-0.1	-	-	103.8	-0.1
1985	-	-	104.0	0.2	-	-	104.3	0.3	-	-	104.3	0.0	-	-	105.2	0.9	-	-	105.8	0.6	-	-	106.2	0.4
1986	-	-	108.1	1.8	-	-	104.6	-3.2	-	-	105.2	0.6	-	-	103.8	-1.3	-	-	103.5	-0.3	-	-	106.0	2.4
1987	-	-	-	-	-	-	-	-	-	-	100.1	-5.6	-	-	-	-	-	-	-	-	-	-	103.0	2.9
1988	-	-	-	-	-	-	-	-	-	-	101.7	-1.3	-	-	-	-	-	-	-	-	-	-	104.4	2.7
1989	-	-	-	-	-	-	-	-	-	-	110.0	5.4	-	-	-	-	-	-	-	-	-	-	110.1	0.1
1990	-	-	-	-	-	-	-	-	-	-	112.9	2.5	-	-	-	-	-	-	-	-	-	-	117.4	4.0
1991	-	-	-	-	-	-	-	-	-	-	117.7	0.3	-	-	-	-	-	-	-	-	-	-	120.6	2.5
1992	-	-	-	-	-	-	-	-	-	-	122.1	1.2	-	-	-	-	-	-	-	-	-	-	124.1	1.6
1993	-	-	-	-	-	-	-	-	-	-	127.3	2.6	-	-	-	-	-	-	-	-	-	-	129.7	1.9
1994	-	-	-	-	-	-	-	-	-	-	132.6	2.2	-	-	-	-	-	-	-	-	-	-	135.8	2.4
1995	-	-	-	-	-	-	-	-	-	-	137.8	1.5	-	-	-	-	-	-	-	-	-	-	-	-

Source: U.S. Department of Labor, Bureau of Labor Statistics, Division of Consumer Prices and Price Indexes. - indicates no data collected for period.

Honolulu, HI
Consumer Price Index - Urban Wage Earners
Base 1982-1984 = 100
Transportation

For 1963-1995. Columns headed % show percentile change in the index from the previous period for which an index is available.

Year	Jan Index	%	Feb Index	%	Mar Index	%	Apr Index	%	May Index	%	Jun Index	%	Jul Index	%	Aug Index	%	Sep Index	%	Oct Index	%	Nov Index	%	Dec Index	%
1963	-	-	-	-	-	-	-	-	-	-	-	-	-	-	-	-	-	-	-	-	-	-	38.5	-
1964	-	-	-	-	38.0	-1.3	-	-	-	-	37.4	-1.6	-	-	-	-	37.4	0.0	-	-	-	-	38.0	1.6
1965	-	-	-	-	37.9	-0.3	-	-	-	-	37.5	-1.1	-	-	-	-	37.6	0.3	-	-	-	-	37.7	0.3
1966	-	-	-	-	37.5	-0.5	-	-	-	-	37.8	0.8	-	-	-	-	37.8	0.0	-	-	-	-	38.6	2.1
1967	-	-	-	-	38.5	-0.3	-	-	-	-	38.6	0.3	-	-	-	-	38.7	0.3	-	-	-	-	39.7	2.6
1968	-	-	-	-	40.1	1.0	-	-	-	-	40.1	0.0	-	-	-	-	40.0	-0.2	-	-	-	-	40.9	2.3
1969	-	-	-	-	41.7	2.0	-	-	-	-	41.5	-0.5	-	-	-	-	41.2	-0.7	-	-	-	-	42.2	2.4
1970	-	-	-	-	42.8	1.4	-	-	-	-	43.6	1.9	-	-	-	-	43.6	0.0	-	-	-	-	44.6	2.3
1971	-	-	-	-	45.7	2.5	-	-	-	-	47.7	4.4	-	-	-	-	47.2	-1.0	-	-	-	-	47.1	-0.2
1972	-	-	-	-	47.6	1.1	-	-	-	-	47.8	0.4	-	-	-	-	47.7	-0.2	-	-	-	-	47.7	0.0
1973	-	-	-	-	48.0	0.6	-	-	-	-	47.9	-0.2	-	-	-	-	47.7	-0.4	-	-	-	-	48.7	2.1
1974	-	-	-	-	50.9	4.5	-	-	-	-	52.6	3.3	-	-	-	-	53.4	1.5	-	-	-	-	54.3	1.7
1975	-	-	-	-	55.3	1.8	-	-	-	-	57.2	3.4	-	-	-	-	58.2	1.7	-	-	-	-	58.0	-0.3
1976	-	-	-	-	58.7	1.2	-	-	-	-	59.3	1.0	-	-	-	-	60.1	1.3	-	-	-	-	60.9	1.3
1977	-	-	-	-	61.2	0.5	-	-	-	-	62.3	1.8	-	-	-	-	61.9	-0.6	-	-	-	-	62.6	1.1
1978	-	-	63.8	1.9	-	-	64.9	1.7	-	-	66.0	1.7	-	-	66.6	0.9	-	-	67.2	0.9	-	-	68.1	1.3
1979	-	-	68.6	0.7	-	-	70.5	2.8	-	-	73.0	3.5	-	-	75.0	2.7	-	-	76.7	2.3	-	-	79.8	4.0
1980	-	-	83.4	4.5	-	-	86.0	3.1	-	-	86.2	0.2	-	-	88.0	2.1	-	-	88.9	1.0	-	-	90.0	1.2
1981	-	-	92.9	3.2	-	-	95.3	2.6	-	-	96.5	1.3	-	-	97.7	1.2	-	-	98.4	0.7	-	-	98.9	0.5
1982	-	-	98.4	-0.5	-	-	97.9	-0.5	-	-	98.8	0.9	-	-	100.3	1.5	-	-	100.3	0.0	-	-	99.1	-1.2
1983	-	-	97.1	-2.0	-	-	96.4	-0.7	-	-	96.7	0.3	-	-	98.4	1.8	-	-	99.9	1.5	-	-	100.7	0.8
1984	-	-	101.2	0.5	-	-	101.7	0.5	-	-	103.1	1.4	-	-	103.9	0.8	-	-	103.9	0.0	-	-	103.7	-0.2
1985	-	-	103.9	0.2	-	-	104.1	0.2	-	-	104.1	0.0	-	-	105.0	0.9	-	-	105.6	0.6	-	-	106.0	0.4
1986	-	-	107.9	1.8	-	-	104.1	-3.5	-	-	104.7	0.6	-	-	103.2	-1.4	-	-	102.8	-0.4	-	-	105.1	2.2
1987	-	-	-	-	-	-	-	-	-	-	100.9	-4.0	-	-	-	-	-	-	-	-	-	-	104.1	3.2
1988	-	-	-	-	-	-	-	-	-	-	102.9	-1.2	-	-	-	-	-	-	-	-	-	-	105.7	2.7
1989	-	-	-	-	-	-	-	-	-	-	110.9	4.9	-	-	-	-	-	-	-	-	-	-	110.8	-0.1
1990	-	-	-	-	-	-	-	-	-	-	113.3	2.3	-	-	-	-	-	-	-	-	-	-	118.7	4.8
1991	-	-	-	-	-	-	-	-	-	-	117.7	-0.8	-	-	-	-	-	-	-	-	-	-	120.9	2.7
1992	-	-	-	-	-	-	-	-	-	-	122.2	1.1	-	-	-	-	-	-	-	-	-	-	125.6	2.8
1993	-	-	-	-	-	-	-	-	-	-	128.3	2.1	-	-	-	-	-	-	-	-	-	-	130.6	1.8
1994	-	-	-	-	-	-	-	-	-	-	132.7	1.6	-	-	-	-	-	-	-	-	-	-	136.6	2.9
1995	-	-	-	-	-	-	-	-	-	-	138.3	1.2	-	-	-	-	-	-	-	-	-	-	-	-

Source: U.S. Department of Labor, Bureau of Labor Statistics, Division of Consumer Prices and Price Indexes. - indicates no data collected for period.

Honolulu, HI
Consumer Price Index - All Urban Consumers
Base 1982-1984 = 100
Medical Care

For 1963-1995. Columns headed % show percentile change in the index from the previous period for which an index is available.

Year	Jan Index	%	Feb Index	%	Mar Index	%	Apr Index	%	May Index	%	Jun Index	%	Jul Index	%	Aug Index	%	Sep Index	%	Oct Index	%	Nov Index	%	Dec Index	%
1963	-	-	-	-	-	-	-	-	-	-	-	-	-	-	-	-	-	-	-	-	-	-	24.7	-
1964	-	-	-	-	25.0	1.2	-	-	-	-	25.1	0.4	-	-	-	-	25.2	0.4	-	-	-	-	25.3	0.4
1965	-	-	-	-	25.7	1.6	-	-	-	-	25.8	0.4	-	-	-	-	26.0	0.8	-	-	-	-	26.1	0.4
1966	-	-	-	-	26.3	0.8	-	-	-	-	26.5	0.8	-	-	-	-	26.8	1.1	-	-	-	-	27.4	2.2
1967	-	-	-	-	27.7	1.1	-	-	-	-	28.3	2.2	-	-	-	-	28.6	1.1	-	-	-	-	29.0	1.4
1968	-	-	-	-	29.3	1.0	-	-	-	-	29.8	1.7	-	-	-	-	30.3	1.7	-	-	-	-	30.7	1.3
1969	-	-	-	-	31.3	2.0	-	-	-	-	32.1	2.6	-	-	-	-	32.6	1.6	-	-	-	-	32.5	-0.3
1970	-	-	-	-	32.6	0.3	-	-	-	-	33.5	2.8	-	-	-	-	33.8	0.9	-	-	-	-	34.5	2.1
1971	-	-	-	-	35.0	1.4	-	-	-	-	35.2	0.6	-	-	-	-	35.6	1.1	-	-	-	-	35.6	0.0
1972	-	-	-	-	35.7	0.3	-	-	-	-	35.8	0.3	-	-	-	-	36.2	1.1	-	-	-	-	36.7	1.4
1973	-	-	-	-	37.1	1.1	-	-	-	-	37.5	1.1	-	-	-	-	38.0	1.3	-	-	-	-	38.7	1.8
1974	-	-	-	-	39.4	1.8	-	-	-	-	41.7	5.8	-	-	-	-	43.1	3.4	-	-	-	-	43.6	1.2
1975	-	-	-	-	45.5	4.4	-	-	-	-	46.5	2.2	-	-	-	-	47.6	2.4	-	-	-	-	48.1	1.1
1976	-	-	-	-	50.1	4.2	-	-	-	-	50.8	1.4	-	-	-	-	52.9	4.1	-	-	-	-	54.1	2.3
1977	-	-	-	-	55.6	2.8	-	-	-	-	56.7	2.0	-	-	-	-	59.3	4.6	-	-	-	-	59.7	0.7
1978	-	-	61.5	3.0	-	-	62.2	1.1	-	-	62.4	0.3	-	-	62.6	0.3	-	-	62.6	0.0	-	-	64.8	3.5
1979	-	-	66.1	2.0	-	-	66.9	1.2	-	-	67.1	0.3	-	-	68.2	1.6	-	-	68.4	0.3	-	-	69.2	1.2
1980	-	-	69.9	1.0	-	-	72.7	4.0	-	-	72.6	-0.1	-	-	74.1	2.1	-	-	75.5	1.9	-	-	75.3	-0.3
1981	-	-	76.9	2.1	-	-	79.3	3.1	-	-	81.1	2.3	-	-	84.1	3.7	-	-	85.8	2.0	-	-	86.4	0.7
1982	-	-	86.8	0.5	-	-	90.6	4.4	-	-	91.4	0.9	-	-	92.6	1.3	-	-	95.0	2.6	-	-	95.9	0.9
1983	-	-	98.6	2.8	-	-	100.4	1.8	-	-	100.6	0.2	-	-	103.3	2.7	-	-	102.5	-0.8	-	-	102.6	0.1
1984	-	-	105.2	2.5	-	-	106.9	1.6	-	-	107.0	0.1	-	-	108.5	1.4	-	-	108.6	0.1	-	-	109.3	0.6
1985	-	-	110.4	1.0	-	-	111.1	0.6	-	-	111.5	0.4	-	-	115.4	3.5	-	-	116.0	0.5	-	-	116.7	0.6
1986	-	-	120.0	2.8	-	-	120.4	0.3	-	-	121.2	0.7	-	-	124.6	2.8	-	-	125.2	0.5	-	-	124.5	-0.6
1987	-	-	-	-	-	-	-	-	-	-	117.8	-5.4	-	-	-	-	-	-	-	-	-	-	120.9	2.6
1988	-	-	-	-	-	-	-	-	-	-	127.4	5.4	-	-	-	-	-	-	-	-	-	-	129.4	1.6
1989	-	-	-	-	-	-	-	-	-	-	137.2	6.0	-	-	-	-	-	-	-	-	-	-	141.5	3.1
1990	-	-	-	-	-	-	-	-	-	-	149.5	5.7	-	-	-	-	-	-	-	-	-	-	152.1	1.7
1991	-	-	-	-	-	-	-	-	-	-	157.3	3.4	-	-	-	-	-	-	-	-	-	-	161.8	2.9
1992	-	-	-	-	-	-	-	-	-	-	172.5	6.6	-	-	-	-	-	-	-	-	-	-	176.1	2.1
1993	-	-	-	-	-	-	-	-	-	-	183.0	3.9	-	-	-	-	-	-	-	-	-	-	188.0	2.7
1994	-	-	-	-	-	-	-	-	-	-	196.6	4.6	-	-	-	-	-	-	-	-	-	-	206.8	5.2
1995	-	-	-	-	-	-	-	-	-	-	212.1	2.6	-	-	-	-	-	-	-	-	-	-	-	-

Source: U.S. Department of Labor, Bureau of Labor Statistics, Division of Consumer Prices and Price Indexes. - indicates no data collected for period.

Honolulu, HI
Consumer Price Index - Urban Wage Earners
Base 1982-1984 = 100
Medical Care

For 1963-1995. Columns headed % show percentile change in the index from the previous period for which an index is available.

Year	Jan Index	%	Feb Index	%	Mar Index	%	Apr Index	%	May Index	%	Jun Index	%	Jul Index	%	Aug Index	%	Sep Index	%	Oct Index	%	Nov Index	%	Dec Index	%
1963	-	-	-	-	-	-	-	-	-	-	-	-	-	-	-	-	-	-	-	-	-	-	24.2	-
1964	-	-	-	-	24.5	1.2	-	-	-	-	24.5	0.0	-	-	-	-	24.7	0.8	-	-	-	-	24.8	0.4
1965	-	-	-	-	25.1	1.2	-	-	-	-	25.2	0.4	-	-	-	-	25.4	0.8	-	-	-	-	25.6	0.8
1966	-	-	-	-	25.7	0.4	-	-	-	-	26.0	1.2	-	-	-	-	26.2	0.8	-	-	-	-	26.8	2.3
1967	-	-	-	-	27.1	1.1	-	-	-	-	27.7	2.2	-	-	-	-	28.0	1.1	-	-	-	-	28.4	1.4
1968	-	-	-	-	28.7	1.1	-	-	-	-	29.2	1.7	-	-	-	-	29.7	1.7	-	-	-	-	30.1	1.3
1969	-	-	-	-	30.7	2.0	-	-	-	-	31.4	2.3	-	-	-	-	32.0	1.9	-	-	-	-	31.8	-0.6
1970	-	-	-	-	32.0	0.6	-	-	-	-	32.8	2.5	-	-	-	-	33.1	0.9	-	-	-	-	33.8	2.1
1971	-	-	-	-	34.2	1.2	-	-	-	-	34.5	0.9	-	-	-	-	34.8	0.9	-	-	-	-	34.9	0.3
1972	-	-	-	-	35.0	0.3	-	-	-	-	35.1	0.3	-	-	-	-	35.4	0.9	-	-	-	-	36.0	1.7
1973	-	-	-	-	36.3	0.8	-	-	-	-	36.7	1.1	-	-	-	-	37.3	1.6	-	-	-	-	37.9	1.6
1974	-	-	-	-	38.6	1.8	-	-	-	-	40.9	6.0	-	-	-	-	42.2	3.2	-	-	-	-	42.7	1.2
1975	-	-	-	-	44.6	4.4	-	-	-	-	45.6	2.2	-	-	-	-	46.6	2.2	-	-	-	-	47.1	1.1
1976	-	-	-	-	49.0	4.0	-	-	-	-	49.7	1.4	-	-	-	-	51.8	4.2	-	-	-	-	53.0	2.3
1977	-	-	-	-	54.4	2.6	-	-	-	-	55.5	2.0	-	-	-	-	58.1	4.7	-	-	-	-	58.5	0.7
1978	-	-	60.4	3.2	-	-	61.9	2.5	-	-	62.0	0.2	-	-	62.2	0.3	-	-	62.2	0.0	-	-	63.4	1.9
1979	-	-	64.8	2.2	-	-	65.3	0.8	-	-	66.4	1.7	-	-	66.3	-0.2	-	-	67.7	2.1	-	-	68.5	1.2
1980	-	-	68.9	0.6	-	-	71.0	3.0	-	-	71.3	0.4	-	-	73.7	3.4	-	-	75.5	2.4	-	-	75.2	-0.4
1981	-	-	76.8	2.1	-	-	78.8	2.6	-	-	81.8	3.8	-	-	84.5	3.3	-	-	85.8	1.5	-	-	86.7	1.0
1982	-	-	87.1	0.5	-	-	90.8	4.2	-	-	91.7	1.0	-	-	93.1	1.5	-	-	95.5	2.6	-	-	96.5	1.0
1983	-	-	99.0	2.6	-	-	100.5	1.5	-	-	100.6	0.1	-	-	103.1	2.5	-	-	102.3	-0.8	-	-	102.4	0.1
1984	-	-	105.0	2.5	-	-	106.6	1.5	-	-	106.7	0.1	-	-	108.0	1.2	-	-	108.0	0.0	-	-	108.7	0.6
1985	-	-	109.9	1.1	-	-	110.6	0.6	-	-	111.0	0.4	-	-	114.6	3.2	-	-	115.2	0.5	-	-	116.0	0.7
1986	-	-	119.0	2.6	-	-	119.4	0.3	-	-	120.2	0.7	-	-	123.1	2.4	-	-	123.7	0.5	-	-	123.2	-0.4
1987	-	-	-	-	-	-	-	-	-	-	118.9	-3.5	-	-	-	-	-	-	-	-	-	-	122.3	2.9
1988	-	-	-	-	-	-	-	-	-	-	128.8	5.3	-	-	-	-	-	-	-	-	-	-	131.0	1.7
1989	-	-	-	-	-	-	-	-	-	-	139.3	6.3	-	-	-	-	-	-	-	-	-	-	143.5	3.0
1990	-	-	-	-	-	-	-	-	-	-	151.1	5.3	-	-	-	-	-	-	-	-	-	-	153.5	1.6
1991	-	-	-	-	-	-	-	-	-	-	158.5	3.3	-	-	-	-	-	-	-	-	-	-	163.0	2.8
1992	-	-	-	-	-	-	-	-	-	-	173.6	6.5	-	-	-	-	-	-	-	-	-	-	177.0	2.0
1993	-	-	-	-	-	-	-	-	-	-	183.7	3.8	-	-	-	-	-	-	-	-	-	-	188.6	2.7
1994	-	-	-	-	-	-	-	-	-	-	196.9	4.4	-	-	-	-	-	-	-	-	-	-	207.4	5.3
1995	-	-	-	-	-	-	-	-	-	-	212.3	2.4	-	-	-	-	-	-	-	-	-	-	-	-

Source: U.S. Department of Labor, Bureau of Labor Statistics, Division of Consumer Prices and Price Indexes. - indicates no data collected for period.

Honolulu, HI
Consumer Price Index - All Urban Consumers
Base 1982-1984 = 100
Entertainment

For 1975-1995. Columns headed % show percentile change in the index from the previous period for which an index is available.

Year	Jan Index	%	Feb Index	%	Mar Index	%	Apr Index	%	May Index	%	Jun Index	%	Jul Index	%	Aug Index	%	Sep Index	%	Oct Index	%	Nov Index	%	Dec Index	%
1975	-	-	-	-	-	-	-	-	-	-	-	-	-	-	-	-	-	-	-	-	-	-	61.5	-
1976	-	-	-	-	62.3	1.3	-	-	-	-	63.5	1.9	-	-	-	-	65.0	2.4	-	-	-	-	64.9	-0.2
1977	-	-	-	-	65.7	1.2	-	-	-	-	66.6	1.4	-	-	-	-	66.6	0.0	-	-	-	-	66.9	0.5
1978	-	-	67.9	1.5	-	-	68.6	1.0	-	-	69.2	0.9	-	-	69.9	1.0	-	-	69.1	-1.1	-	-	69.9	1.2
1979	-	-	70.6	1.0	-	-	71.7	1.6	-	-	73.0	1.8	-	-	73.4	0.5	-	-	74.6	1.6	-	-	74.6	0.0
1980	-	-	76.4	2.4	-	-	77.3	1.2	-	-	77.9	0.8	-	-	78.7	1.0	-	-	79.9	1.5	-	-	80.1	0.3
1981	-	-	83.7	4.5	-	-	85.2	1.8	-	-	87.2	2.3	-	-	87.4	0.2	-	-	91.0	4.1	-	-	92.0	1.1
1982	-	-	96.0	4.3	-	-	95.3	-0.7	-	-	95.5	0.2	-	-	97.1	1.7	-	-	95.7	-1.4	-	-	95.8	0.1
1983	-	-	99.5	3.9	-	-	99.6	0.1	-	-	100.5	0.9	-	-	100.7	0.2	-	-	100.5	-0.2	-	-	99.9	-0.6
1984	-	-	101.7	1.8	-	-	103.9	2.2	-	-	103.8	-0.1	-	-	105.1	1.3	-	-	104.8	-0.3	-	-	109.1	4.1
1985	-	-	109.9	0.7	-	-	111.0	1.0	-	-	112.5	1.4	-	-	113.7	1.1	-	-	113.5	-0.2	-	-	111.5	-1.8
1986	-	-	115.7	3.8	-	-	115.9	0.2	-	-	116.1	0.2	-	-	110.7	-4.7	-	-	111.1	0.4	-	-	109.3	-1.6
1987	-	-	-	-	-	-	-	-	-	-	107.9	-1.3	-	-	-	-	-	-	-	-	-	-	107.5	-0.4
1988	-	-	-	-	-	-	-	-	-	-	109.8	2.1	-	-	-	-	-	-	-	-	-	-	112.9	2.8
1989	-	-	-	-	-	-	-	-	-	-	113.1	0.2	-	-	-	-	-	-	-	-	-	-	114.3	1.1
1990	-	-	-	-	-	-	-	-	-	-	117.5	2.8	-	-	-	-	-	-	-	-	-	-	119.9	2.0
1991	-	-	-	-	-	-	-	-	-	-	122.5	2.2	-	-	-	-	-	-	-	-	-	-	125.5	2.4
1992	-	-	-	-	-	-	-	-	-	-	129.5	3.2	-	-	-	-	-	-	-	-	-	-	130.6	0.8
1993	-	-	-	-	-	-	-	-	-	-	131.4	0.6	-	-	-	-	-	-	-	-	-	-	134.8	2.6
1994	-	-	-	-	-	-	-	-	-	-	135.0	0.1	-	-	-	-	-	-	-	-	-	-	125.5	-7.0
1995	-	-	-	-	-	-	-	-	-	-	127.9	1.9	-	-	-	-	-	-	-	-	-	-	-	-

Source: U.S. Department of Labor, Bureau of Labor Statistics, Division of Consumer Prices and Price Indexes. - indicates no data collected for period.

Honolulu, HI
Consumer Price Index - Urban Wage Earners
Base 1982-1984 = 100
Entertainment

For 1975-1995. Columns headed % show percentile change in the index from the previous period for which an index is available.

Year	Jan Index	%	Feb Index	%	Mar Index	%	Apr Index	%	May Index	%	Jun Index	%	Jul Index	%	Aug Index	%	Sep Index	%	Oct Index	%	Nov Index	%	Dec Index	%
1975	-	-	-	-	-	-	-	-	-	-	-	-	-	-	-	-	-	-	-	-	-	-	58.7	-
1976	-	-	-	-	59.4	1.2	-	-	-	-	60.6	2.0	-	-	-	-	62.0	2.3	-	-	-	-	61.9	-0.2
1977	-	-	-	-	62.7	1.3	-	-	-	-	63.5	1.3	-	-	-	-	63.6	0.2	-	-	-	-	63.9	0.5
1978	-	-	66.5	4.1	-	-	66.6	0.2	-	-	67.4	1.2	-	-	68.3	1.3	-	-	68.2	-0.1	-	-	68.6	0.6
1979	-	-	70.9	3.4	-	-	71.5	0.8	-	-	72.8	1.8	-	-	75.6	3.8	-	-	75.9	0.4	-	-	75.9	0.0
1980	-	-	78.4	3.3	-	-	78.6	0.3	-	-	79.9	1.7	-	-	80.2	0.4	-	-	81.4	1.5	-	-	82.4	1.2
1981	-	-	84.1	2.1	-	-	85.8	2.0	-	-	87.3	1.7	-	-	87.3	0.0	-	-	90.7	3.9	-	-	91.5	0.9
1982	-	-	95.8	4.7	-	-	94.9	-0.9	-	-	95.1	0.2	-	-	97.0	2.0	-	-	95.3	-1.8	-	-	95.5	0.2
1983	-	-	99.6	4.3	-	-	99.5	-0.1	-	-	100.4	0.9	-	-	100.8	0.4	-	-	100.6	-0.2	-	-	100.1	-0.5
1984	-	-	102.1	2.0	-	-	104.2	2.1	-	-	104.0	-0.2	-	-	105.3	1.3	-	-	105.2	-0.1	-	-	109.0	3.6
1985	-	-	110.0	0.9	-	-	111.1	1.0	-	-	112.6	1.4	-	-	113.6	0.9	-	-	113.4	-0.2	-	-	111.5	-1.7
1986	-	-	115.2	3.3	-	-	115.5	0.3	-	-	115.8	0.3	-	-	111.0	-4.1	-	-	111.3	0.3	-	-	109.4	-1.7
1987	-	-	-	-	-	-	-	-	-	-	108.0	-1.3	-	-	-	-	-	-	-	-	-	-	107.7	-0.3
1988	-	-	-	-	-	-	-	-	-	-	110.2	2.3	-	-	-	-	-	-	-	-	-	-	113.8	3.3
1989	-	-	-	-	-	-	-	-	-	-	114.6	0.7	-	-	-	-	-	-	-	-	-	-	115.5	0.8
1990	-	-	-	-	-	-	-	-	-	-	118.4	2.5	-	-	-	-	-	-	-	-	-	-	121.0	2.2
1991	-	-	-	-	-	-	-	-	-	-	124.1	2.6	-	-	-	-	-	-	-	-	-	-	126.8	2.2
1992	-	-	-	-	-	-	-	-	-	-	130.2	2.7	-	-	-	-	-	-	-	-	-	-	131.6	1.1
1993	-	-	-	-	-	-	-	-	-	-	131.7	0.1	-	-	-	-	-	-	-	-	-	-	135.4	2.8
1994	-	-	-	-	-	-	-	-	-	-	136.4	0.7	-	-	-	-	-	-	-	-	-	-	126.0	-7.6
1995	-	-	-	-	-	-	-	-	-	-	128.5	2.0	-	-	-	-	-	-	-	-	-	-	-	-

Source: U.S. Department of Labor, Bureau of Labor Statistics, Division of Consumer Prices and Price Indexes. - indicates no data collected for period.

Honolulu, HI
Consumer Price Index - All Urban Consumers
Base 1982-1984 = 100
Other Goods and Services

For 1975-1995. Columns headed % show percentile change in the index from the previous period for which an index is available.

Year	Jan Index	%	Feb Index	%	Mar Index	%	Apr Index	%	May Index	%	Jun Index	%	Jul Index	%	Aug Index	%	Sep Index	%	Oct Index	%	Nov Index	%	Dec Index	%
1975	-	-	-	-	-	-	-	-	-	-	-	-	-	-	-	-	-	-	-	-	-	-	52.6	-
1976	-	-	-	-	53.3	1.3	-	-	-	-	53.5	0.4	-	-	-	-	54.2	1.3	-	-	-	-	55.3	2.0
1977	-	-	-	-	56.1	1.4	-	-	-	-	56.8	1.2	-	-	-	-	58.8	3.5	-	-	-	-	59.6	1.4
1978	-	-	59.9	0.5	-	-	60.3	0.7	-	-	61.1	1.3	-	-	61.9	1.3	-	-	62.9	1.6	-	-	63.1	0.3
1979	-	-	64.6	2.4	-	-	65.1	0.8	-	-	65.6	0.8	-	-	66.2	0.9	-	-	68.7	3.8	-	-	70.6	2.8
1980	-	-	71.3	1.0	-	-	70.4	-1.3	-	-	72.4	2.8	-	-	73.6	1.7	-	-	77.0	4.6	-	-	76.9	-0.1
1981	-	-	78.3	1.8	-	-	78.7	0.5	-	-	79.1	0.5	-	-	82.3	4.0	-	-	86.3	4.9	-	-	87.2	1.0
1982	-	-	87.5	0.3	-	-	90.1	3.0	-	-	91.0	1.0	-	-	91.1	0.1	-	-	96.3	5.7	-	-	99.2	3.0
1983	-	-	98.1	-1.1	-	-	101.4	3.4	-	-	102.0	0.6	-	-	101.8	-0.2	-	-	103.0	1.2	-	-	103.1	0.1
1984	-	-	104.6	1.5	-	-	104.9	0.3	-	-	105.5	0.6	-	-	107.7	2.1	-	-	109.1	1.3	-	-	115.0	0.1
1985	-	-	111.0	1.7	-	-	110.8	-0.2	-	-	111.2	0.4	-	-	113.3	1.9	-	-	114.9	1.4	-	-	124.9	0.5
1986	-	-	115.6	0.5	-	-	117.3	1.5	-	-	117.4	0.1	-	-	120.3	2.5	-	-	124.3	3.3	-	-	131.8	4.4
1987	-	-	-	-	-	-	-	-	-	-	126.3	1.1	-	-	-	-	-	-	-	-	-	-	141.6	3.7
1988	-	-	-	-	-	-	-	-	-	-	136.5	3.6	-	-	-	-	-	-	-	-	-	-	148.8	2.6
1989	-	-	-	-	-	-	-	-	-	-	145.0	2.4	-	-	-	-	-	-	-	-	-	-	159.7	4.0
1990	-	-	-	-	-	-	-	-	-	-	153.6	3.2	-	-	-	-	-	-	-	-	-	-	172.9	3.8
1991	-	-	-	-	-	-	-	-	-	-	166.6	4.3	-	-	-	-	-	-	-	-	-	-	186.4	5.0
1992	-	-	-	-	-	-	-	-	-	-	177.6	2.7	-	-	-	-	-	-	-	-	-	-	195.6	0.7
1993	-	-	-	-	-	-	-	-	-	-	194.2	4.2	-	-	-	-	-	-	-	-	-	-	204.0	2.9
1994	-	-	-	-	-	-	-	-	-	-	198.2	1.3	-	-	-	-	-	-	-	-	-	-	-	-
1995	-	-	-	-	-	-	-	-	-	-	205.0	0.5	-	-	-	-	-	-	-	-	-	-	-	-

Source: U.S. Department of Labor, Bureau of Labor Statistics, Division of Consumer Prices and Price Indexes. - indicates no data collected for period.

Honolulu, HI
Consumer Price Index - Urban Wage Earners
Base 1982-1984 = 100
Other Goods and Services

For 1975-1995. Columns headed % show percentile change in the index from the previous period for which an index is available.

Year	Jan Index	%	Feb Index	%	Mar Index	%	Apr Index	%	May Index	%	Jun Index	%	Jul Index	%	Aug Index	%	Sep Index	%	Oct Index	%	Nov Index	%	Dec Index	%
1975	-	-	-	-	-	-	-	-	-	-	-	-	-	-	-	-	-	-	-	-	-	-	53.5	-
1976	-	-	-	-	54.3	1.5	-	-	-	-	54.4	0.2	-	-	-	-	55.1	1.3	-	-	-	-	56.3	2.2
1977	-	-	-	-	57.1	1.4	-	-	-	-	57.8	1.2	-	-	-	-	59.8	3.5	-	-	-	-	60.6	1.3
1978	-	-	60.4	-0.3	-	-	60.8	0.7	-	-	61.3	0.8	-	-	62.4	1.8	-	-	63.5	1.8	-	-	63.6	0.2
1979	-	-	65.2	2.5	-	-	65.5	0.5	-	-	66.4	1.4	-	-	67.1	1.1	-	-	69.3	3.3	-	-	69.7	0.6
1980	-	-	70.6	1.3	-	-	70.4	-0.3	-	-	72.1	2.4	-	-	73.1	1.4	-	-	75.9	3.8	-	-	76.8	1.2
1981	-	-	77.5	0.9	-	-	78.4	1.2	-	-	79.9	1.9	-	-	80.7	1.0	-	-	86.3	6.9	-	-	86.7	0.5
1982	-	-	87.0	0.3	-	-	89.8	3.2	-	-	90.4	0.7	-	-	90.5	0.1	-	-	96.0	6.1	-	-	99.5	3.6
1983	-	-	98.5	-1.0	-	-	101.9	3.5	-	-	102.3	0.4	-	-	102.3	0.0	-	-	103.1	0.8	-	-	103.2	0.1
1984	-	-	104.7	1.5	-	-	105.1	0.4	-	-	105.5	0.4	-	-	107.8	2.2	-	-	109.1	1.2	-	-	109.0	-0.1
1985	-	-	111.2	2.0	-	-	110.9	-0.3	-	-	111.3	0.4	-	-	113.4	1.9	-	-	114.7	1.1	-	-	114.7	0.0
1986	-	-	115.5	0.7	-	-	117.0	1.3	-	-	117.1	0.1	-	-	120.2	2.6	-	-	123.2	2.5	-	-	123.9	0.6
1987	-	-	-	-	-	-	-	-	-	-	125.5	1.3	-	-	-	-	-	-	-	-	-	-	131.4	4.7
1988	-	-	-	-	-	-	-	-	-	-	136.5	3.9	-	-	-	-	-	-	-	-	-	-	141.9	4.0
1989	-	-	-	-	-	-	-	-	-	-	145.6	2.6	-	-	-	-	-	-	-	-	-	-	149.6	2.7
1990	-	-	-	-	-	-	-	-	-	-	154.3	3.1	-	-	-	-	-	-	-	-	-	-	160.8	4.2
1991	-	-	-	-	-	-	-	-	-	-	168.4	4.7	-	-	-	-	-	-	-	-	-	-	174.9	3.9
1992	-	-	-	-	-	-	-	-	-	-	179.6	2.7	-	-	-	-	-	-	-	-	-	-	189.1	5.3
1993	-	-	-	-	-	-	-	-	-	-	196.7	4.0	-	-	-	-	-	-	-	-	-	-	196.5	-0.1
1994	-	-	-	-	-	-	-	-	-	-	198.5	1.0	-	-	-	-	-	-	-	-	-	-	204.0	2.8
1995	-	-	-	-	-	-	-	-	-	-	204.7	0.3	-	-	-	-	-	-	-	-	-	-	-	-

Source: U.S. Department of Labor, Bureau of Labor Statistics, Division of Consumer Prices and Price Indexes. - indicates no data collected for period.

Houston, TX
Consumer Price Index - All Urban Consumers
Base 1982-1984 = 100
Annual Averages

For 1914-1995. Columns headed % show percentile change in the index from the previous period for which an index is available.

Year	All Items		Food & Beverage		Housing		Apparel & Upkeep		Trans- portation		Medical Care		Entertain- ment		Other Goods & Services	
	Index	%	Index	%	Index	%	Index	%	Index	%	Index	%	Index	%	Index	%
1914	-	-	-	-	-	-	-	-	-	-	-	-	-	-	-	-
1915	9.4	-	-	-	-	-	-	-	-	-	-	-	-	-	-	-
1916	10.1	7.4	-	-	-	-	-	-	-	-	-	-	-	-	-	-
1917	12.4	22.8	-	-	-	-	-	-	-	-	-	-	-	-	-	-
1918	14.5	16.9	-	-	-	-	-	-	-	-	-	-	-	-	-	-
1919	16.9	16.6	-	-	-	-	-	-	-	-	-	-	-	-	-	-
1920	19.2	13.6	-	-	-	-	-	-	-	-	-	-	-	-	-	-
1921	17.0	-11.5	-	-	-	-	-	-	-	-	-	-	-	-	-	-
1922	15.9	-6.5	-	-	-	-	-	-	-	-	-	-	-	-	-	-
1923	15.9	0.0	-	-	-	-	-	-	-	-	-	-	-	-	-	-
1924	15.8	-0.6	-	-	-	-	-	-	-	-	-	-	-	-	-	-
1925	16.2	2.5	-	-	-	-	-	-	-	-	-	-	-	-	-	-
1926	16.0	-1.2	-	-	-	-	-	-	-	-	-	-	-	-	-	-
1927	15.7	-1.9	-	-	-	-	-	-	-	-	-	-	-	-	-	-
1928	15.6	-0.6	-	-	-	-	-	-	-	-	-	-	-	-	-	-
1929	15.7	0.6	-	-	-	-	-	-	-	-	-	-	-	-	-	-
1930	15.3	-2.5	-	-	-	-	-	-	-	-	-	-	-	-	-	-
1931	13.9	-9.2	-	-	-	-	-	-	-	-	-	-	-	-	-	-
1932	12.3	-11.5	-	-	-	-	-	-	-	-	-	-	-	-	-	-
1933	11.8	-4.1	-	-	-	-	-	-	-	-	-	-	-	-	-	-
1934	12.3	4.2	-	-	-	-	-	-	-	-	-	-	-	-	-	-
1935	12.7	3.3	-	-	-	-	-	-	-	-	-	-	-	-	-	-
1936	12.8	0.8	-	-	-	-	-	-	-	-	-	-	-	-	-	-
1937	13.3	3.9	-	-	-	-	-	-	-	-	-	-	-	-	-	-
1938	13.3	0.0	-	-	-	-	-	-	-	-	-	-	-	-	-	-
1939	13.2	-0.8	-	-	-	-	-	-	-	-	-	-	-	-	-	-
1940	13.2	0.0	-	-	-	-	-	-	-	-	-	-	-	-	-	-
1941	13.8	4.5	-	-	-	-	-	-	-	-	-	-	-	-	-	-
1942	15.2	10.1	-	-	-	-	-	-	-	-	-	-	-	-	-	-
1943	16.0	5.3	-	-	-	-	-	-	-	-	-	-	-	-	-	-
1944	16.2	1.3	-	-	-	-	-	-	-	-	-	-	-	-	-	-
1945	16.6	2.5	-	-	-	-	-	-	-	-	-	-	-	-	-	-
1946	17.9	7.8	-	-	-	-	-	-	-	-	-	-	-	-	-	-
1947	21.0	17.3	-	-	-	-	-	-	20.8	-	14.5	-	-	-	-	-
1948	22.7	8.1	-	-	-	-	-	-	23.2	11.5	14.9	2.8	-	-	-	-
1949	22.7	0.0	-	-	-	-	-	-	24.7	6.5	15.2	2.0	-	-	-	-
1950	23.4	3.1	-	-	-	-	-	-	25.7	4.0	15.6	2.6	-	-	-	-
1951	25.2	7.7	-	-	-	-	-	-	28.0	8.9	15.9	1.9	-	-	-	-
1952	25.5	1.2	-	-	-	-	-	-	28.5	1.8	16.8	5.7	-	-	-	-
1953	25.8	1.2	-	-	-	-	36.1	-	29.0	1.8	17.5	4.2	-	-	-	-
1954	25.8	0.0	-	-	-	-	36.0	-0.3	28.6	-1.4	17.7	1.1	-	-	-	-
1955	25.7	-0.4	-	-	-	-	36.0	0.0	28.3	-1.0	18.4	4.0	-	-	-	-
1956	26.1	1.6	-	-	-	-	36.7	1.9	28.9	2.1	18.9	2.7	-	-	-	-
1957	26.9	3.1	-	-	-	-	37.6	2.5	30.9	6.9	19.2	1.6	-	-	-	-
1958	27.3	1.5	-	-	-	-	38.3	1.9	31.5	1.9	19.7	2.6	-	-	-	-

[Continued]

Houston, TX
Consumer Price Index - All Urban Consumers
Base 1982-1984 = 100
Annual Averages
[Continued]

For 1914-1995. Columns headed % show percentile change in the index from the previous period for which an index is available.

Year	All Items		Food & Beverage		Housing		Apparel & Upkeep		Trans-portation		Medical Care		Entertain-ment		Other Goods & Services	
	Index	%	Index	%	Index	%	Index	%	Index	%	Index	%	Index	%	Index	%
1959	27.6	1.1	-	-	-	-	38.7	1.0	33.0	4.8	20.0	1.5	-	-	-	-
1960	27.8	0.7	-	-	-	-	38.7	0.0	32.9	-0.3	20.5	2.5	-	-	-	-
1961	28.0	0.7	-	-	-	-	38.9	0.5	33.1	0.6	20.8	1.5	-	-	-	-
1962	28.5	1.8	-	-	-	-	40.0	2.8	34.2	3.3	21.0	1.0	-	-	-	-
1963	28.8	1.1	-	-	-	-	40.5	1.3	33.5	-2.0	21.6	2.9	-	-	-	-
1964	29.2	1.4	-	-	-	-	40.8	0.7	34.3	2.4	22.2	2.8	-	-	-	-
1965	29.6	1.4	-	-	-	-	40.8	0.0	34.2	-0.3	22.8	2.7	-	-	-	-
1966	30.4	2.7	-	-	-	-	41.5	1.7	34.8	1.8	23.4	2.6	-	-	-	-
1967	31.2	2.6	-	-	-	-	42.2	1.7	36.0	3.4	24.9	6.4	-	-	-	-
1968	32.5	4.2	-	-	-	-	44.6	5.7	37.1	3.1	26.2	5.2	-	-	-	-
1969	34.6	6.5	-	-	-	-	48.1	7.8	38.4	3.5	28.5	8.8	-	-	-	-
1970	36.4	5.2	-	-	-	-	50.6	5.2	39.1	1.8	30.6	7.4	-	-	-	-
1971	37.7	3.6	-	-	-	-	51.5	1.8	40.8	4.3	32.4	5.9	-	-	-	-
1972	39.0	3.4	-	-	-	-	53.1	3.1	41.4	1.5	33.7	4.0	-	-	-	-
1973	41.2	5.6	-	-	-	-	55.1	3.8	42.2	1.9	35.0	3.9	-	-	-	-
1974	46.1	11.9	-	-	-	-	60.3	9.4	47.3	12.1	37.9	8.3	-	-	-	-
1975	51.4	11.5	-	-	-	-	64.2	6.5	51.9	9.7	43.2	14.0	-	-	-	-
1976	55.3	7.6	58.5	-	53.0	-	68.0	5.9	56.3	8.5	48.0	11.1	61.3	-	56.3	-
1977	59.3	7.2	61.6	5.3	57.4	8.3	72.0	5.9	60.5	7.5	54.2	12.9	64.0	4.4	59.8	6.2
1978	64.9	9.4	67.8	10.1	64.4	12.2	76.9	6.8	62.8	3.8	59.4	9.6	65.7	2.7	65.5	9.5
1979	73.5	13.3	76.8	13.3	73.6	14.3	83.1	8.1	72.3	15.1	65.1	9.6	70.1	6.7	71.7	9.5
1980	82.7	12.5	83.8	9.1	82.7	12.4	89.1	7.2	85.6	18.4	72.2	10.9	79.7	13.7	79.3	10.6
1981	91.0	10.0	91.8	9.5	91.2	10.3	95.6	7.3	94.8	10.7	80.0	10.8	86.4	8.4	85.3	7.6
1982	97.3	6.9	96.4	5.0	99.8	9.4	98.4	2.9	97.7	3.1	90.7	13.4	92.8	7.4	91.8	7.6
1983	100.0	2.8	99.3	3.0	100.3	0.5	99.8	1.4	99.1	1.4	101.1	11.5	103.1	11.1	101.0	10.0
1984	102.7	2.7	104.3	5.0	99.9	-0.4	101.9	2.1	103.3	4.2	108.1	6.9	104.1	1.0	107.2	6.1
1985	104.9	2.1	105.0	0.7	100.2	0.3	104.4	2.5	106.2	2.8	116.8	8.0	111.9	7.5	112.5	4.9
1986	103.9	-1.0	107.3	2.2	98.1	-2.1	106.1	1.6	99.2	-6.6	123.5	5.7	114.5	2.3	118.6	5.4
1987	106.5	2.5	111.8	4.2	97.0	-1.1	113.6	7.1	102.5	3.3	130.4	5.6	118.5	3.5	124.8	5.2
1988	109.5	2.8	116.2	3.9	98.0	1.0	121.1	6.6	104.5	2.0	136.7	4.8	124.5	5.1	131.2	5.1
1989	114.1	4.2	121.7	4.7	100.5	2.6	123.9	2.3	109.2	4.5	148.0	8.3	133.8	7.5	138.5	5.6
1990	120.6	5.7	128.7	5.8	104.8	4.3	132.5	6.9	116.0	6.2	161.2	8.9	134.9	0.8	152.1	9.8
1991	125.1	3.7	131.6	2.3	109.5	4.5	134.8	1.7	119.6	3.1	177.7	10.2	139.6	3.5	157.7	3.7
1992	129.1	3.2	130.8	-0.6	113.2	3.4	135.8	0.7	122.9	2.8	193.6	8.9	146.4	4.9	172.1	9.1
1993	133.4	3.3	132.4	1.2	116.8	3.2	142.1	4.6	128.2	4.3	200.8	3.7	153.2	4.6	180.8	5.1
1994	137.9	3.4	137.5	3.9	120.4	3.1	146.7	3.2	132.9	3.7	204.6	1.9	157.4	2.7	187.6	3.8
1995	139.8	1.4	140.2	2.0	121.1	0.6	138.3	-5.7	137.0	3.1	217.7	6.4	157.3	-0.1	193.4	3.1

Source: U.S. Department of Labor, Bureau of Labor Statistics, Division of Consumer Prices and Price Indexes. - indicates no data collected for period.

Houston, TX
Consumer Price Index - Urban Wage Earners
Base 1982-1984 = 100
Annual Averages

For 1914-1995. Columns headed % show percentile change in the index from the previous period for which an index is available.

Year	All Items		Food & Beverage		Housing		Apparel & Upkeep		Trans- portation		Medical Care		Entertain- ment		Other Goods & Services	
	Index	%	Index	%	Index	%	Index	%	Index	%	Index	%	Index	%	Index	%
1914	-	-	-	-	-	-	-	-	-	-	-	-	-	-	-	-
1915	9.5	-	-	-	-	-	-	-	-	-	-	-	-	-	-	-
1916	10.1	6.3	-	-	-	-	-	-	-	-	-	-	-	-	-	-
1917	12.5	23.8	-	-	-	-	-	-	-	-	-	-	-	-	-	-
1918	14.5	16.0	-	-	-	-	-	-	-	-	-	-	-	-	-	-
1919	17.0	17.2	-	-	-	-	-	-	-	-	-	-	-	-	-	-
1920	19.3	13.5	-	-	-	-	-	-	-	-	-	-	-	-	-	-
1921	17.1	-11.4	-	-	-	-	-	-	-	-	-	-	-	-	-	-
1922	16.0	-6.4	-	-	-	-	-	-	-	-	-	-	-	-	-	-
1923	16.0	0.0	-	-	-	-	-	-	-	-	-	-	-	-	-	-
1924	15.9	-0.6	-	-	-	-	-	-	-	-	-	-	-	-	-	-
1925	16.2	1.9	-	-	-	-	-	-	-	-	-	-	-	-	-	-
1926	16.1	-0.6	-	-	-	-	-	-	-	-	-	-	-	-	-	-
1927	15.8	-1.9	-	-	-	-	-	-	-	-	-	-	-	-	-	-
1928	15.6	-1.3	-	-	-	-	-	-	-	-	-	-	-	-	-	-
1929	15.7	0.6	-	-	-	-	-	-	-	-	-	-	-	-	-	-
1930	15.4	-1.9	-	-	-	-	-	-	-	-	-	-	-	-	-	-
1931	13.9	-9.7	-	-	-	-	-	-	-	-	-	-	-	-	-	-
1932	12.4	-10.8	-	-	-	-	-	-	-	-	-	-	-	-	-	-
1933	11.8	-4.8	-	-	-	-	-	-	-	-	-	-	-	-	-	-
1934	12.4	5.1	-	-	-	-	-	-	-	-	-	-	-	-	-	-
1935	12.8	3.2	-	-	-	-	-	-	-	-	-	-	-	-	-	-
1936	12.9	0.8	-	-	-	-	-	-	-	-	-	-	-	-	-	-
1937	13.4	3.9	-	-	-	-	-	-	-	-	-	-	-	-	-	-
1938	13.3	-0.7	-	-	-	-	-	-	-	-	-	-	-	-	-	-
1939	13.2	-0.8	-	-	-	-	-	-	-	-	-	-	-	-	-	-
1940	13.3	0.8	-	-	-	-	-	-	-	-	-	-	-	-	-	-
1941	13.8	3.8	-	-	-	-	-	-	-	-	-	-	-	-	-	-
1942	15.3	10.9	-	-	-	-	-	-	-	-	-	-	-	-	-	-
1943	16.1	5.2	-	-	-	-	-	-	-	-	-	-	-	-	-	-
1944	16.3	1.2	-	-	-	-	-	-	-	-	-	-	-	-	-	-
1945	16.6	1.8	-	-	-	-	-	-	-	-	-	-	-	-	-	-
1946	18.0	8.4	-	-	-	-	-	-	-	-	-	-	-	-	-	-
1947	21.1	17.2	-	-	-	-	-	-	20.7	-	13.9	-	-	-	-	-
1948	22.8	8.1	-	-	-	-	-	-	23.2	12.1	14.2	2.2	-	-	-	-
1949	22.8	0.0	-	-	-	-	-	-	24.6	6.0	14.6	2.8	-	-	-	-
1950	23.5	3.1	-	-	-	-	-	-	25.6	4.1	14.9	2.1	-	-	-	-
1951	25.3	7.7	-	-	-	-	-	-	27.9	9.0	15.3	2.7	-	-	-	-
1952	25.7	1.6	-	-	-	-	-	-	28.4	1.8	16.1	5.2	-	-	-	-
1953	26.0	1.2	-	-	-	-	36.8	-	28.9	1.8	16.8	4.3	-	-	-	-
1954	25.9	-0.4	-	-	-	-	36.7	-0.3	28.5	-1.4	17.0	1.2	-	-	-	-
1955	25.8	-0.4	-	-	-	-	36.7	0.0	28.1	-1.4	17.7	4.1	-	-	-	-
1956	26.2	1.6	-	-	-	-	37.4	1.9	28.8	2.5	18.2	2.8	-	-	-	-
1957	27.0	3.1	-	-	-	-	38.3	2.4	30.8	6.9	18.4	1.1	-	-	-	-
1958	27.5	1.9	-	-	-	-	39.1	2.1	31.3	1.6	18.8	2.2	-	-	-	-

[Continued]

Houston, TX
Consumer Price Index - Urban Wage Earners
Base 1982-1984 = 100
Annual Averages
[Continued]

For 1914-1995. Columns headed % show percentile change in the index from the previous period for which an index is available.

Year	All Items		Food & Beverage		Housing		Apparel & Upkeep		Trans-portation		Medical Care		Entertain-ment		Other Goods & Services	
	Index	%	Index	%	Index	%	Index	%	Index	%	Index	%	Index	%	Index	%
1959	27.7	0.7	-	-	-	-	39.5	1.0	32.8	4.8	19.2	2.1	-	-	-	-
1960	27.9	0.7	-	-	-	-	39.4	-0.3	32.8	0.0	19.6	2.1	-	-	-	-
1961	28.1	0.7	-	-	-	-	39.6	0.5	32.9	0.3	19.9	1.5	-	-	-	-
1962	28.6	1.8	-	-	-	-	40.8	3.0	34.0	3.3	20.2	1.5	-	-	-	-
1963	28.9	1.0	-	-	-	-	41.3	1.2	33.4	-1.8	20.7	2.5	-	-	-	-
1964	29.4	1.7	-	-	-	-	41.6	0.7	34.2	2.4	21.3	2.9	-	-	-	-
1965	29.7	1.0	-	-	-	-	41.6	0.0	34.1	-0.3	21.8	2.3	-	-	-	-
1966	30.5	2.7	-	-	-	-	42.3	1.7	34.7	1.8	22.5	3.2	-	-	-	-
1967	31.3	2.6	-	-	-	-	43.0	1.7	35.9	3.5	23.9	6.2	-	-	-	-
1968	32.7	4.5	-	-	-	-	45.4	5.6	36.9	2.8	25.1	5.0	-	-	-	-
1969	34.8	6.4	-	-	-	-	49.1	8.1	38.3	3.8	27.4	9.2	-	-	-	-
1970	36.6	5.2	-	-	-	-	51.6	5.1	39.0	1.8	29.3	6.9	-	-	-	-
1971	37.9	3.6	-	-	-	-	52.5	1.7	40.6	4.1	31.0	5.8	-	-	-	-
1972	39.2	3.4	-	-	-	-	54.1	3.0	41.2	1.5	32.3	4.2	-	-	-	-
1973	41.5	5.9	-	-	-	-	56.2	3.9	42.0	1.9	33.6	4.0	-	-	-	-
1974	46.3	11.6	-	-	-	-	61.4	9.3	47.1	12.1	36.4	8.3	-	-	-	-
1975	51.7	11.7	-	-	-	-	65.5	6.7	51.7	9.8	41.4	13.7	-	-	-	-
1976	55.6	7.5	59.5	-	53.0	-	69.3	5.8	56.0	8.3	46.0	11.1	63.1	-	56.2	-
1977	59.6	7.2	62.6	5.2	57.4	8.3	73.4	5.9	60.2	7.5	51.9	12.8	65.8	4.3	59.6	6.0
1978	65.1	9.2	68.6	9.6	64.3	12.0	78.5	6.9	62.7	4.2	57.0	9.8	67.9	3.2	64.7	8.6
1979	73.4	12.7	77.0	12.2	72.7	13.1	85.3	8.7	72.1	15.0	64.7	13.5	71.6	5.4	70.6	9.1
1980	82.1	11.9	83.8	8.8	81.4	12.0	90.3	5.9	84.3	16.9	71.7	10.8	79.0	10.3	78.5	11.2
1981	90.3	10.0	91.6	9.3	90.0	10.6	96.4	6.8	93.4	10.8	79.6	11.0	85.2	7.8	84.6	7.8
1982	96.9	7.3	96.4	5.2	98.7	9.7	98.5	2.2	97.1	4.0	90.5	13.7	91.3	7.2	91.7	8.4
1983	100.1	3.3	99.4	3.1	100.4	1.7	99.8	1.3	99.0	2.0	101.2	11.8	104.0	13.9	101.0	10.1
1984	103.1	3.0	104.2	4.8	100.8	0.4	101.8	2.0	103.9	4.9	108.3	7.0	104.8	0.8	107.3	6.2
1985	104.6	1.5	104.8	0.6	100.1	-0.7	104.2	2.4	106.7	2.7	117.0	8.0	112.6	7.4	112.4	4.8
1986	103.6	-1.0	107.3	2.4	98.0	-2.1	105.7	1.4	100.3	-6.0	123.7	5.7	115.7	2.8	117.4	4.4
1987	106.4	2.7	111.7	4.1	96.5	-1.5	112.7	6.6	104.7	4.4	130.9	5.8	120.0	3.7	123.0	4.8
1988	109.7	3.1	116.1	3.9	97.5	1.0	121.1	7.5	107.1	2.3	137.7	5.2	126.3	5.2	130.4	6.0
1989	114.4	4.3	121.7	4.8	100.2	2.8	124.0	2.4	111.9	4.5	149.3	8.4	135.7	7.4	139.1	6.7
1990	120.9	5.7	128.8	5.8	104.5	4.3	132.8	7.1	118.7	6.1	162.3	8.7	136.6	0.7	152.8	9.8
1991	125.3	3.6	131.7	2.3	109.4	4.7	133.9	0.8	122.1	2.9	178.9	10.2	141.2	3.4	157.7	3.2
1992	128.9	2.9	131.0	-0.5	113.3	3.6	134.4	0.4	125.2	2.5	195.3	9.2	148.3	5.0	171.5	8.8
1993	133.0	3.2	132.6	1.2	117.2	3.4	138.9	3.3	129.4	3.4	202.9	3.9	156.2	5.3	179.6	4.7
1994	137.4	3.3	137.7	3.8	120.7	3.0	145.4	4.7	134.0	3.6	206.6	1.8	160.3	2.6	185.1	3.1
1995	139.4	1.5	140.3	1.9	121.2	0.4	137.6	-5.4	138.6	3.4	219.5	6.2	161.3	0.6	190.0	2.6

Source: U.S. Department of Labor, Bureau of Labor Statistics, Division of Consumer Prices and Price Indexes. - indicates no data collected for period.

Houston, TX
Consumer Price Index - All Urban Consumers
Base 1982-1984 = 100
All Items

For 1914-1995. Columns headed % show percentile change in the index from the previous period for which an index is available.

Year	Jan Index	%	Feb Index	%	Mar Index	%	Apr Index	%	May Index	%	Jun Index	%	Jul Index	%	Aug Index	%	Sep Index	%	Oct Index	%	Nov Index	%	Dec Index	%
1914	-	-	-	-	-	-	-	-	-	-	-	-	-	-	-	-	-	-	-	-	-	-	9.5	-
1915	-	-	-	-	-	-	-	-	-	-	-	-	-	-	-	-	-	-	-	-	-	-	9.5	0.0
1916	-	-	-	-	-	-	-	-	-	-	-	-	-	-	-	-	-	-	-	-	-	-	10.9	14.7
1917	-	-	-	-	-	-	-	-	-	-	-	-	-	-	-	-	-	-	-	-	-	-	13.2	21.1
1918	-	-	-	-	-	-	-	-	-	-	-	-	-	-	-	-	-	-	-	-	-	-	15.9	20.5
1919	-	-	-	-	-	-	-	-	-	-	16.4	3.1	-	-	-	-	-	-	-	-	-	-	18.5	12.8
1920	-	-	-	-	-	-	-	-	-	-	19.7	6.5	-	-	-	-	-	-	-	-	-	-	18.9	-4.1
1921	-	-	-	-	-	-	-	-	16.9	-10.6	-	-	-	-	-	-	16.6	-1.8	-	-	-	-	16.4	-1.2
1922	-	-	-	-	15.9	-3.0	-	-	-	-	15.8	-0.6	-	-	-	-	15.7	-0.6	-	-	-	-	15.9	1.3
1923	-	-	-	-	15.7	-1.3	-	-	-	-	15.9	1.3	-	-	-	-	16.0	0.6	-	-	-	-	16.1	0.6
1924	-	-	-	-	15.9	-1.2	-	-	-	-	15.6	-1.9	-	-	-	-	15.8	1.3	-	-	-	-	16.0	1.3
1925	-	-	-	-	-	-	-	-	-	-	16.1	0.6	-	-	-	-	-	-	-	-	-	-	16.4	1.9
1926	-	-	-	-	-	-	-	-	-	-	16.0	-2.4	-	-	-	-	-	-	-	-	-	-	16.0	0.0
1927	-	-	-	-	-	-	-	-	-	-	15.7	-1.9	-	-	-	-	-	-	-	-	-	-	15.8	0.6
1928	-	-	-	-	-	-	-	-	-	-	15.5	-1.9	-	-	-	-	-	-	-	-	-	-	15.6	0.6
1929	-	-	-	-	-	-	-	-	-	-	15.6	0.0	-	-	-	-	-	-	-	-	-	-	15.8	1.3
1930	-	-	-	-	-	-	-	-	-	-	15.4	-2.5	-	-	-	-	-	-	-	-	-	-	14.7	-4.5
1931	-	-	-	-	-	-	-	-	-	-	13.8	-6.1	-	-	-	-	-	-	-	-	-	-	13.4	-2.9
1932	-	-	-	-	-	-	-	-	-	-	12.3	-8.2	-	-	-	-	-	-	-	-	-	-	11.7	-4.9
1933	-	-	-	-	-	-	-	-	-	-	11.6	-0.9	-	-	-	-	-	-	-	-	-	-	12.1	4.3
1934	-	-	-	-	-	-	-	-	-	-	12.2	0.8	-	-	-	-	-	-	-	-	12.6	3.3	-	-
1935	-	-	-	-	12.8	1.6	-	-	-	-	-	-	12.6	-1.6	-	-	-	-	12.7	0.8	-	-	-	-
1936	12.8	0.8	-	-	-	-	12.6	-1.6	-	-	-	-	12.9	2.4	-	-	13.0	0.8	-	-	-	-	13.0	0.0
1937	-	-	-	-	13.3	2.3	-	-	-	-	13.3	0.0	-	-	-	-	13.5	1.5	-	-	-	-	13.5	0.0
1938	-	-	-	-	13.3	-1.5	-	-	-	-	13.2	-0.8	-	-	-	-	13.3	0.8	-	-	-	-	13.3	0.0
1939	-	-	-	-	13.1	-1.5	-	-	-	-	13.1	0.0	-	-	-	-	13.3	1.5	-	-	-	-	13.2	-0.8
1940	-	-	-	-	13.2	0.0	-	-	-	-	13.2	0.0	-	-	-	-	13.2	0.0	13.3	0.8	13.3	0.0	13.3	0.0
1941	13.3	0.0	13.3	0.0	13.3	0.0	13.5	1.5	13.5	0.0	13.6	0.7	13.7	0.7	13.8	0.7	14.1	2.2	14.4	2.1	14.5	0.7	14.6	0.7
1942	14.7	0.7	14.9	1.4	15.1	1.3	15.1	0.0	15.2	0.7	15.1	-0.7	15.3	1.3	15.4	0.7	15.5	0.6	15.5	0.0	15.5	0.0	15.6	0.6
1943	15.7	0.6	15.8	0.6	16.2	2.5	16.2	0.0	16.3	0.6	16.1	-1.2	16.0	-0.6	15.9	-0.6	16.1	1.3	16.1	0.0	16.1	0.0	16.1	0.0
1944	16.1	0.0	16.1	0.0	16.0	-0.6	16.1	0.6	16.2	0.6	16.2	0.0	16.3	0.6	16.3	0.0	16.3	0.0	16.3	0.0	16.2	-0.6	16.3	0.6
1945	16.4	0.6	16.3	-0.6	16.3	0.0	16.4	0.6	16.5	0.6	16.6	0.6	16.7	0.6	16.7	0.0	16.7	0.0	16.6	-0.6	16.6	0.0	16.7	0.6
1946	16.6	-0.6	16.6	0.0	16.7	0.6	16.8	0.6	16.8	0.0	17.1	1.8	17.9	4.7	18.4	2.8	18.7	1.6	18.9	1.1	19.7	4.2	20.0	1.5
1947	20.2	1.0	20.2	0.0	20.6	2.0	20.8	1.0	20.7	-0.5	20.7	0.0	20.8	0.5	21.0	1.0	21.3	1.4	21.5	0.9	21.8	1.4	22.2	1.8
1948	22.4	0.9	22.4	0.0	22.4	0.0	22.5	0.4	22.5	0.0	22.7	0.9	22.9	0.9	23.1	0.9	23.1	0.0	23.0	-0.4	22.9	-0.4	22.9	0.0
1949	22.8	-0.4	22.5	-1.3	22.5	0.0	22.6	0.4	22.5	-0.4	22.5	0.0	22.5	0.0	22.6	0.4	22.7	0.4	22.8	0.4	23.0	0.9	23.0	0.0
1950	22.9	-0.4	22.9	0.0	23.0	0.4	22.9	-0.4	22.9	0.0	23.0	0.4	23.2	0.9	23.6	1.7	23.8	0.8	23.8	0.0	23.9	0.4	24.3	1.7
1951	24.8	2.1	25.0	0.8	25.1	0.4	25.2	0.4	25.2	0.0	25.1	-0.4	25.2	0.4	25.2	0.0	25.3	0.4	25.4	0.4	25.5	0.4	25.6	0.4
1952	25.5	-0.4	25.4	-0.4	25.4	0.0	25.4	0.0	25.4	0.0	25.4	0.0	25.5	0.4	25.6	0.4	25.5	-0.4	25.7	0.8	25.7	0.0	25.8	0.4
1953	-	-	25.7	-0.4	-	-	-	-	25.8	0.4	-	-	-	-	25.8	0.0	-	-	-	-	25.9	0.4	-	-
1954	-	-	25.9	0.0	-	-	-	-	25.8	-0.4	-	-	-	-	25.8	0.0	-	-	-	-	25.8	0.0	-	-
1955	-	-	25.6	-0.8	-	-	-	-	25.5	-0.4	-	-	-	-	25.5	0.0	-	-	-	-	25.8	1.2	-	-
1956	-	-	25.8	0.0	-	-	-	-	25.8	0.0	-	-	-	-	26.1	1.2	-	-	-	-	26.5	1.5	-	-
1957	-	-	26.7	0.8	-	-	-	-	26.8	0.4	-	-	-	-	27.0	0.7	-	-	-	-	27.1	0.4	-	-
1958	-	-	27.1	0.0	-	-	-	-	27.4	1.1	-	-	-	-	27.4	0.0	-	-	-	-	27.5	0.4	-	-

[Continued]

Houston, TX
Consumer Price Index - All Urban Consumers
Base 1982-1984 = 100
All Items
[Continued]

For 1914-1995. Columns headed % show percentile change in the index from the previous period for which an index is available.

Year	Jan Index	%	Feb Index	%	Mar Index	%	Apr Index	%	May Index	%	Jun Index	%	Jul Index	%	Aug Index	%	Sep Index	%	Oct Index	%	Nov Index	%	Dec Index	%
1959	-		27.4	-0.4	-		-		27.4	0.0	-		-		27.6	0.7	-		-		27.7	0.4	-	
1960	-		27.8	0.4	-		-		27.7	-0.4	-		-		27.9	0.7	-		-		28.0	0.4	-	
1961	-		27.7	-1.1	-		-		27.9	0.7	-		-		27.9	0.0	-		-		28.3	1.4	-	
1962	-		28.5	0.7	-		-		28.5	0.0	-		-		28.5	0.0	-		-		28.5	0.0	-	
1963	-		28.6	0.4	-		-		28.5	-0.3	-		-		28.9	1.4	-		-		29.1	0.7	-	
1964	-		29.2	0.3	-		-		29.1	-0.3	-		-		29.2	0.3	-		-		29.2	0.0	-	
1965	-		29.3	0.3	-		29.4	0.3	-		-		29.6	0.7	-		-		29.8	0.7	-		-	
1966	30.0	0.7	-		-		30.2	0.7	-		-		30.4	0.7	-		-		30.6	0.7	-		-	
1967	30.8	0.7	-		-		31.0	0.6	-		-		31.1	0.3	-		-		31.5	1.3	-		-	
1968	31.8	1.0	-		-		32.1	0.9	-		-		32.5	1.2	-		-		33.0	1.5	-		-	
1969	33.6	1.8	-		-		34.2	1.8	-		-		34.6	1.2	-		-		35.4	2.3	-		-	
1970	35.7	0.8	-		-		36.2	1.4	-		-		36.4	0.6	-		-		36.8	1.1	-		-	
1971	37.2	1.1	-		-		37.3	0.3	-		-		37.8	1.3	-		-		38.2	1.1	-		-	
1972	38.4	0.5	-		-		38.9	1.3	-		-		39.0	0.3	-		-		39.4	1.0	-		-	
1973	39.7	0.8	-		-		40.7	2.5	-		-		41.0	0.7	-		-		42.5	3.7	-		-	
1974	43.4	2.1	-		-		44.6	2.8	-		-		46.1	3.4	-		-		48.1	4.3	-		-	
1975	49.7	3.3	-		-		50.3	1.2	-		-		51.8	3.0	-		-		52.6	1.5	-		-	
1976	53.7	2.1	-		-		54.3	1.1	-		-		55.2	1.7	-		-		56.7	2.7	-		-	
1977	57.2	0.9	-		-		58.8	2.8	-		-		59.7	1.5	-		-		60.1	0.7	-		-	
1978	61.3	2.0	-		-		63.3	3.3	-		64.7	2.2	-		65.9	1.9	-		67.0	1.7	-		68.5	2.2
1979	-		69.9	2.0	-		71.1	1.7	-		73.4	3.2	-		75.0	2.2	-		76.1	1.5	-		77.5	1.8
1980	-		79.8	3.0	-		81.3	1.9	-		83.1	2.2	-		83.7	0.7	-		84.9	1.4	-		85.7	0.9
1981	-		87.8	2.5	-		89.3	1.7	-		91.3	2.2	-		91.9	0.7	-		93.5	1.7	-		94.4	1.0
1982	-		94.8	0.4	-		95.1	0.3	-		97.9	2.9	-		99.3	1.4	-		99.0	-0.3	-		99.2	0.2
1983	-		98.9	-0.3	-		98.7	-0.2	-		100.2	1.5	-		101.0	0.8	-		101.1	0.1	-		100.0	-1.1
1984	-		100.9	0.9	-		101.5	0.6	-		103.0	1.5	-		103.5	0.5	-		104.3	0.8	-		103.9	-0.4
1985	-		104.0	0.1	-		104.5	0.5	-		105.3	0.8	-		105.4	0.1	-		105.3	-0.1	-		105.0	-0.3
1986	-		105.1	0.1	-		102.9	-2.1	-		103.9	1.0	-		103.8	-0.1	-		104.1	0.3	-		103.2	-0.9
1987	-		104.4	1.2	-		106.4	1.9	-		106.5	0.1	-		107.3	0.8	-		108.0	0.7	-		107.3	-0.6
1988	-		108.0	0.7	-		108.2	0.2	-		109.4	1.1	-		110.3	0.8	-		111.1	0.7	-		111.3	0.2
1989	-		112.7	1.3	-		113.2	0.4	-		114.1	0.8	-		114.4	0.3	-		115.7	1.1	-		115.5	-0.2
1990	-		118.7	2.8	-		118.3	-0.3	-		119.7	1.2	-		121.5	1.5	-		124.0	2.1	-		123.0	-0.8
1991	-		124.3	1.1	-		123.5	-0.6	-		124.9	1.1	-		124.8	-0.1	-		127.3	2.0	-		127.0	-0.2
1992	-		127.0	0.0	-		128.7	1.3	-		129.4	0.5	-		129.9	0.4	-		130.8	0.7	-		129.3	-1.1
1993	-		131.7	1.9	-		131.8	0.1	-		132.9	0.8	-		133.0	0.1	-		136.6	2.7	-		136.5	-0.1
1994	-		137.0	0.4	-		136.8	-0.1	-		137.4	0.4	-		139.2	1.3	-		139.3	0.1	-		137.8	-1.1
1995	-		139.3	1.1	-		138.0	-0.9	-		139.9	1.4	-		140.1	0.1	-		141.6	1.1	-		140.9	-0.5

Source: U.S. Department of Labor, Bureau of Labor Statistics, Division of Consumer Prices and Price Indexes. - indicates no data collected for period.

Houston, TX
Consumer Price Index - Urban Wage Earners
Base 1982-1984 = 100
All Items

For 1914-1995. Columns headed % show percentile change in the index from the previous period for which an index is available.

Year	Jan Index	%	Feb Index	%	Mar Index	%	Apr Index	%	May Index	%	Jun Index	%	Jul Index	%	Aug Index	%	Sep Index	%	Oct Index	%	Nov Index	%	Dec Index	%
1914	-	-	-	-	-	-	-	-	-	-	-	-	-	-	-	-	-	-	-	-	-	-	9.6	-
1915	-	-	-	-	-	-	-	-	-	-	-	-	-	-	-	-	-	-	-	-	-	-	9.5	-1.0
1916	-	-	-	-	-	-	-	-	-	-	-	-	-	-	-	-	-	-	-	-	-	-	10.9	14.7
1917	-	-	-	-	-	-	-	-	-	-	-	-	-	-	-	-	-	-	-	-	-	-	13.3	22.0
1918	-	-	-	-	-	-	-	-	-	-	-	-	-	-	-	-	-	-	-	-	-	-	16.0	20.3
1919	-	-	-	-	-	-	-	-	-	-	16.4	2.5	-	-	-	-	-	-	-	-	-	-	18.6	13.4
1920	-	-	-	-	-	-	-	-	-	-	19.8	6.5	-	-	-	-	-	-	-	-	-	-	19.0	-4.0
1921	-	-	-	-	-	-	-	-	17.0	-10.5	-	-	-	-	-	-	16.6	-2.4	-	-	-	-	16.4	-1.2
1922	-	-	-	-	16.0	-2.4	-	-	-	-	15.9	-0.6	-	-	-	-	15.8	-0.6	-	-	-	-	16.0	1.3
1923	-	-	-	-	15.8	-1.2	-	-	-	-	15.9	0.6	-	-	-	-	16.0	0.6	-	-	-	-	16.2	1.3
1924	-	-	-	-	16.0	-1.2	-	-	-	-	15.7	-1.9	-	-	-	-	15.9	1.3	-	-	-	-	16.0	0.6
1925	-	-	-	-	-	-	-	-	-	-	16.2	1.3	-	-	-	-	-	-	-	-	-	-	16.4	1.2
1926	-	-	-	-	-	-	-	-	-	-	16.0	-2.4	-	-	-	-	-	-	-	-	-	-	16.1	0.6
1927	-	-	-	-	-	-	-	-	-	-	15.8	-1.9	-	-	-	-	-	-	-	-	-	-	15.9	0.6
1928	-	-	-	-	-	-	-	-	-	-	15.5	-2.5	-	-	-	-	-	-	-	-	-	-	15.7	1.3
1929	-	-	-	-	-	-	-	-	-	-	15.6	-0.6	-	-	-	-	-	-	-	-	-	-	15.9	1.9
1930	-	-	-	-	-	-	-	-	-	-	15.4	-3.1	-	-	-	-	-	-	-	-	-	-	14.7	-4.5
1931	-	-	-	-	-	-	-	-	-	-	13.9	-5.4	-	-	-	-	-	-	-	-	-	-	13.5	-2.9
1932	-	-	-	-	-	-	-	-	-	-	12.3	-8.9	-	-	-	-	-	-	-	-	-	-	11.7	-4.9
1933	-	-	-	-	-	-	-	-	-	-	11.7	0.0	-	-	-	-	-	-	-	-	-	-	12.1	3.4
1934	-	-	-	-	-	-	-	-	-	-	12.2	0.8	-	-	-	-	-	-	-	-	12.6	3.3	-	-
1935	-	-	-	-	12.8	1.6	-	-	-	-	-	-	12.7	-0.8	-	-	-	-	12.7	0.0	-	-	-	-
1936	12.8	0.8	-	-	-	-	12.7	-0.8	-	-	-	-	12.9	1.6	-	-	13.1	1.6	-	-	-	-	13.1	0.0
1937	-	-	-	-	13.3	1.5	-	-	-	-	13.3	0.0	-	-	-	-	13.6	2.3	-	-	-	-	13.5	-0.7
1938	-	-	-	-	13.4	-0.7	-	-	-	-	13.3	-0.7	-	-	-	-	13.3	0.0	-	-	-	-	13.3	0.0
1939	-	-	-	-	13.2	-0.8	-	-	-	-	13.2	0.0	-	-	-	-	13.3	0.8	-	-	-	-	13.3	0.0
1940	-	-	-	-	13.2	-0.8	-	-	-	-	13.2	0.0	-	-	-	-	13.3	0.8	13.4	0.8	13.4	0.0	13.4	0.0
1941	13.4	0.0	13.4	0.0	13.4	0.0	13.6	1.5	13.6	0.0	13.6	0.0	13.8	1.5	13.9	0.7	14.2	2.2	14.5	2.1	14.6	0.7	14.7	0.7
1942	14.8	0.7	15.0	1.4	15.2	1.3	15.2	0.0	15.3	0.7	15.2	-0.7	15.4	1.3	15.4	0.0	15.5	0.6	15.6	0.6	15.6	0.0	15.7	0.6
1943	15.7	0.0	15.9	1.3	16.2	1.9	16.3	0.6	16.4	0.6	16.2	-1.2	16.1	-0.6	16.0	-0.6	16.2	1.3	16.2	0.0	16.2	0.0	16.2	0.0
1944	16.2	0.0	16.2	0.0	16.1	-0.6	16.2	0.6	16.3	0.6	16.2	-0.6	16.4	1.2	16.4	0.0	16.4	0.0	16.4	0.0	16.3	-0.6	16.4	0.6
1945	16.4	0.0	16.4	0.0	16.4	0.0	16.5	0.6	16.6	0.6	16.7	0.6	16.8	0.6	16.8	0.0	16.8	0.0	16.7	-0.6	16.7	0.0	16.8	0.6
1946	16.7	-0.6	16.7	0.0	16.8	0.6	16.9	0.6	16.9	0.0	17.2	1.8	18.0	4.7	18.5	2.8	18.8	1.6	19.0	1.1	19.8	4.2	20.1	1.5
1947	20.3	1.0	20.3	0.0	20.7	2.0	20.9	1.0	20.8	-0.5	20.8	0.0	20.9	0.5	21.1	1.0	21.4	1.4	21.6	0.9	21.9	1.4	22.3	1.8
1948	22.5	0.9	22.5	0.0	22.5	0.0	22.7	0.9	22.7	0.0	22.8	0.4	23.0	0.9	23.2	0.9	23.2	0.0	23.2	0.0	23.0	-0.9	23.0	0.0
1949	22.9	-0.4	22.6	-1.3	22.6	0.0	22.7	0.4	22.7	0.0	22.7	0.0	22.7	0.0	22.7	0.0	22.8	0.4	22.9	0.4	23.1	0.9	23.1	0.0
1950	23.1	0.0	23.0	-0.4	23.1	0.4	23.0	-0.4	23.0	0.0	23.1	0.4	23.3	0.9	23.7	1.7	23.9	0.8	23.9	0.0	24.0	0.4	24.4	1.7
1951	25.0	2.5	25.1	0.4	25.3	0.8	25.3	0.0	25.3	0.0	25.3	0.0	25.3	0.0	25.3	0.0	25.5	0.8	25.5	0.0	25.6	0.4	25.8	0.8
1952	25.7	-0.4	25.5	-0.8	25.5	0.0	25.6	0.4	25.5	-0.4	25.6	0.4	25.6	0.0	25.8	0.8	25.7	-0.4	25.8	0.4	25.8	0.0	25.9	0.4
1953	-	-	25.8	-0.4	-	-	-	-	26.0	0.8	-	-	-	-	26.0	0.0	-	-	-	-	26.1	0.4	-	-
1954	-	-	26.0	-0.4	-	-	-	-	25.9	-0.4	-	-	-	-	25.9	0.0	-	-	-	-	25.9	0.0	-	-
1955	-	-	25.7	-0.8	-	-	-	-	25.7	0.0	-	-	-	-	25.7	0.0	-	-	-	-	25.9	0.8	-	-
1956	-	-	25.9	0.0	-	-	-	-	26.0	0.4	-	-	-	-	26.3	1.2	-	-	-	-	26.6	1.1	-	-
1957	-	-	26.8	0.8	-	-	-	-	26.9	0.4	-	-	-	-	27.1	0.7	-	-	-	-	27.2	0.4	-	-
1958	-	-	27.2	0.0	-	-	-	-	27.5	1.1	-	-	-	-	27.5	0.0	-	-	-	-	27.6	0.4	-	-

[Continued]

Houston, TX
Consumer Price Index - Urban Wage Earners
Base 1982-1984 = 100
All Items
[Continued]

For 1914-1995. Columns headed % show percentile change in the index from the previous period for which an index is available.

Year	Jan Index	%	Feb Index	%	Mar Index	%	Apr Index	%	May Index	%	Jun Index	%	Jul Index	%	Aug Index	%	Sep Index	%	Oct Index	%	Nov Index	%	Dec Index	%
1959	-	-	27.6	0.0	-	-	-	-	27.6	0.0	-	-	-	-	27.7	0.4	-	-	-	-	27.9	0.7	-	-
1960	-	-	27.9	0.0	-	-	-	-	27.8	-0.4	-	-	-	-	28.0	0.7	-	-	-	-	28.1	0.4	-	-
1961	-	-	27.8	-1.1	-	-	-	-	28.0	0.7	-	-	-	-	28.1	0.4	-	-	-	-	28.5	1.4	-	-
1962	-	-	28.6	0.4	-	-	-	-	28.7	0.3	-	-	-	-	28.6	-0.3	-	-	-	-	28.6	0.0	-	-
1963	-	-	28.8	0.7	-	-	-	-	28.6	-0.7	-	-	-	-	29.1	1.7	-	-	-	-	29.2	0.3	-	-
1964	-	-	29.4	0.7	-	-	-	-	29.3	-0.3	-	-	-	-	29.4	0.3	-	-	-	-	29.4	0.0	-	-
1965	-	-	29.4	0.0	-	-	29.5	0.3	-	-	-	-	29.7	0.7	-	-	-	-	29.9	0.7	-	-	-	-
1966	30.1	0.7	-	-	-	-	30.4	1.0	-	-	-	-	30.6	0.7	-	-	-	-	30.8	0.7	-	-	-	-
1967	31.0	0.6	-	-	-	-	31.1	0.3	-	-	-	-	31.3	0.6	-	-	-	-	31.6	1.0	-	-	-	-
1968	32.0	1.3	-	-	-	-	32.3	0.9	-	-	-	-	32.7	1.2	-	-	-	-	33.2	1.5	-	-	-	-
1969	33.7	1.5	-	-	-	-	34.4	2.1	-	-	-	-	34.8	1.2	-	-	-	-	35.6	2.3	-	-	-	-
1970	35.8	0.6	-	-	-	-	36.4	1.7	-	-	-	-	36.6	0.5	-	-	-	-	36.9	0.8	-	-	-	-
1971	37.4	1.4	-	-	-	-	37.4	0.0	-	-	-	-	38.0	1.6	-	-	-	-	38.4	1.1	-	-	-	-
1972	38.6	0.5	-	-	-	-	39.1	1.3	-	-	-	-	39.2	0.3	-	-	-	-	39.6	1.0	-	-	-	-
1973	39.9	0.8	-	-	-	-	40.9	2.5	-	-	-	-	41.2	0.7	-	-	-	-	42.7	3.6	-	-	-	-
1974	43.6	2.1	-	-	-	-	44.8	2.8	-	-	-	-	46.4	3.6	-	-	-	-	48.3	4.1	-	-	-	-
1975	49.9	3.3	-	-	-	-	50.6	1.4	-	-	-	-	52.0	2.8	-	-	-	-	52.9	1.7	-	-	-	-
1976	54.0	2.1	-	-	-	-	54.5	0.9	-	-	-	-	55.5	1.8	-	-	-	-	57.0	2.7	-	-	-	-
1977	57.5	0.9	-	-	-	-	59.1	2.8	-	-	-	-	60.0	1.5	-	-	-	-	60.4	0.7	-	-	-	-
1978	61.6	2.0	-	-	-	-	63.6	3.2	-	-	65.0	2.2	-	-	66.1	1.7	-	-	67.0	1.4	-	-	68.4	2.1
1979	-	-	69.9	2.2	-	-	71.3	2.0	-	-	73.5	3.1	-	-	74.9	1.9	-	-	75.8	1.2	-	-	77.1	1.7
1980	-	-	78.9	2.3	-	-	80.6	2.2	-	-	82.3	2.1	-	-	83.2	1.1	-	-	84.4	1.4	-	-	85.3	1.1
1981	-	-	87.0	2.0	-	-	88.7	2.0	-	-	90.7	2.3	-	-	91.4	0.8	-	-	92.7	1.4	-	-	93.6	1.0
1982	-	-	94.1	0.5	-	-	94.7	0.6	-	-	97.4	2.9	-	-	98.8	1.4	-	-	98.7	-0.1	-	-	99.0	0.3
1983	-	-	99.4	0.4	-	-	99.5	0.1	-	-	100.2	0.7	-	-	100.8	0.6	-	-	101.0	0.2	-	-	99.6	-1.4
1984	-	-	101.4	1.8	-	-	101.8	0.4	-	-	103.2	1.4	-	-	104.5	1.3	-	-	104.8	0.3	-	-	103.7	-1.0
1985	-	-	103.7	0.0	-	-	104.3	0.6	-	-	105.0	0.7	-	-	105.1	0.1	-	-	105.0	-0.1	-	-	104.7	-0.3
1986	-	-	104.7	0.0	-	-	102.7	-1.9	-	-	103.7	1.0	-	-	103.6	-0.1	-	-	103.9	0.3	-	-	102.9	-1.0
1987	-	-	104.3	1.4	-	-	106.1	1.7	-	-	106.4	0.3	-	-	107.1	0.7	-	-	108.1	0.9	-	-	107.4	-0.6
1988	-	-	108.1	0.7	-	-	108.1	0.0	-	-	109.4	1.2	-	-	110.6	1.1	-	-	111.4	0.7	-	-	111.4	0.0
1989	-	-	112.9	1.3	-	-	113.5	0.5	-	-	114.5	0.9	-	-	114.9	0.3	-	-	115.8	0.8	-	-	115.8	0.0
1990	-	-	118.9	2.7	-	-	118.6	-0.3	-	-	120.0	1.2	-	-	121.9	1.6	-	-	124.7	2.3	-	-	123.4	-1.0
1991	-	-	124.4	0.8	-	-	123.6	-0.6	-	-	125.2	1.3	-	-	124.9	-0.2	-	-	127.4	2.0	-	-	127.2	-0.2
1992	-	-	126.9	-0.2	-	-	128.4	1.2	-	-	129.2	0.6	-	-	129.8	0.5	-	-	130.7	0.7	-	-	129.2	-1.1
1993	-	-	131.3	1.6	-	-	131.3	0.0	-	-	132.4	0.8	-	-	132.7	0.2	-	-	136.1	2.6	-	-	136.0	-0.1
1994	-	-	136.3	0.2	-	-	136.2	-0.1	-	-	137.0	0.6	-	-	138.8	1.3	-	-	139.0	0.1	-	-	137.8	-0.9
1995	-	-	138.9	0.8	-	-	137.6	-0.9	-	-	139.5	1.4	-	-	139.8	0.2	-	-	140.9	0.8	-	-	140.5	-0.3

Source: U.S. Department of Labor, Bureau of Labor Statistics, Division of Consumer Prices and Price Indexes. - indicates no data collected for period.

Houston, TX
Consumer Price Index - All Urban Consumers
Base 1982-1984 = 100
Food and Beverages

For 1976-1995. Columns headed % show percentile change in the index from the previous period for which an index is available.

Year	Jan Index	%	Feb Index	%	Mar Index	%	Apr Index	%	May Index	%	Jun Index	%	Jul Index	%	Aug Index	%	Sep Index	%	Oct Index	%	Nov Index	%	Dec Index	%
1976	58.0	-	-	-	-	-	57.7	-0.5	-	-	-	-	58.9	2.1	-	-	-	-	59.0	0.2	-	-	-	-
1977	59.3	0.5	-	-	-	-	61.3	3.4	-	-	-	-	62.3	1.6	-	-	-	-	62.0	-0.5	-	-	-	-
1978	63.5	2.4	-	-	-	-	66.0	3.9	-	-	68.1	3.2	-	-	68.7	0.9	-	-	70.0	1.9	-	-	71.7	2.4
1979	-	-	74.7	4.2	-	-	75.7	1.3	-	-	77.2	2.0	-	-	77.8	0.8	-	-	78.0	0.3	-	-	79.5	1.9
1980	-	-	80.8	1.6	-	-	81.8	1.2	-	-	82.2	0.5	-	-	84.7	3.0	-	-	87.3	3.1	-	-	88.1	0.9
1981	-	-	89.9	2.0	-	-	90.9	1.1	-	-	91.7	0.9	-	-	93.2	1.6	-	-	93.3	0.1	-	-	93.3	0.0
1982	-	-	94.6	1.4	-	-	95.2	0.6	-	-	96.7	1.6	-	-	97.6	0.9	-	-	97.5	-0.1	-	-	97.8	0.3
1983	-	-	98.3	0.5	-	-	99.0	0.7	-	-	99.7	0.7	-	-	100.0	0.3	-	-	99.8	-0.2	-	-	99.7	-0.1
1984	-	-	104.0	4.3	-	-	104.2	0.2	-	-	104.3	0.1	-	-	104.6	0.3	-	-	104.6	0.0	-	-	105.4	0.8
1985	-	-	105.4	0.0	-	-	104.6	-0.8	-	-	104.6	0.0	-	-	105.0	0.4	-	-	104.6	-0.4	-	-	105.8	1.1
1986	-	-	106.4	0.6	-	-	106.3	-0.1	-	-	106.7	0.4	-	-	107.8	1.0	-	-	108.4	0.6	-	-	109.3	0.8
1987	-	-	111.4	1.9	-	-	111.2	-0.2	-	-	111.8	0.5	-	-	111.6	-0.2	-	-	113.1	1.3	-	-	112.5	-0.5
1988	-	-	113.9	1.2	-	-	114.3	0.4	-	-	114.6	0.3	-	-	117.8	2.8	-	-	119.6	1.5	-	-	118.2	-1.2
1989	-	-	121.7	3.0	-	-	121.7	0.0	-	-	121.8	0.1	-	-	121.1	-0.6	-	-	121.8	0.6	-	-	123.5	1.4
1990	-	-	127.9	3.6	-	-	127.1	-0.6	-	-	128.6	1.2	-	-	129.5	0.7	-	-	131.3	1.4	-	-	129.2	-1.6
1991	-	-	132.2	2.3	-	-	132.3	0.1	-	-	130.9	-1.1	-	-	131.4	0.4	-	-	131.7	0.2	-	-	131.5	-0.2
1992	-	-	132.7	0.9	-	-	132.2	-0.4	-	-	129.9	-1.7	-	-	129.6	-0.2	-	-	129.7	0.1	-	-	130.4	0.5
1993	-	-	132.2	1.4	-	-	128.9	-2.5	-	-	130.2	1.0	-	-	133.4	2.5	-	-	134.9	1.1	-	-	136.5	1.2
1994	-	-	135.9	-0.4	-	-	137.3	1.0	-	-	137.1	-0.1	-	-	138.0	0.7	-	-	137.7	-0.2	-	-	139.7	1.5
1995	-	-	139.7	0.0	-	-	140.7	0.7	-	-	139.7	-0.7	-	-	140.1	0.3	-	-	140.5	0.3	-	-	141.0	0.4

Source: U.S. Department of Labor, Bureau of Labor Statistics, Division of Consumer Prices and Price Indexes. - indicates no data collected for period.

Houston, TX
Consumer Price Index - Urban Wage Earners
Base 1982-1984 = 100
Food and Beverages

For 1976-1995. Columns headed % show percentile change in the index from the previous period for which an index is available.

Year	Jan Index	%	Feb Index	%	Mar Index	%	Apr Index	%	May Index	%	Jun Index	%	Jul Index	%	Aug Index	%	Sep Index	%	Oct Index	%	Nov Index	%	Dec Index	%
1976	59.0	-	-	-	-	-	58.7	-0.5	-	-	-	-	59.9	2.0	-	-	-	-	60.0	0.2	-	-	-	-
1977	60.3	0.5	-	-	-	-	62.3	3.3	-	-	-	-	63.3	1.6	-	-	-	-	63.1	-0.3	-	-	-	-
1978	64.6	2.4	-	-	-	-	67.1	3.9	-	-	69.3	3.3	-	-	69.4	0.1	-	-	70.4	1.4	-	-	72.0	2.3
1979	-	-	74.9	4.0	-	-	76.1	1.6	-	-	77.2	1.4	-	-	77.9	0.9	-	-	78.4	0.6	-	-	79.5	1.4
1980	-	-	80.1	0.8	-	-	81.8	2.1	-	-	82.6	1.0	-	-	84.8	2.7	-	-	87.3	2.9	-	-	88.5	1.4
1981	-	-	90.0	1.7	-	-	90.6	0.7	-	-	91.1	0.6	-	-	92.9	2.0	-	-	93.0	0.1	-	-	93.1	0.1
1982	-	-	94.6	1.6	-	-	95.3	0.7	-	-	96.7	1.5	-	-	97.6	0.9	-	-	97.6	0.0	-	-	97.9	0.3
1983	-	-	98.5	0.6	-	-	99.1	0.6	-	-	99.6	0.5	-	-	99.9	0.3	-	-	99.7	-0.2	-	-	99.7	0.0
1984	-	-	104.2	4.5	-	-	104.2	0.0	-	-	104.2	0.0	-	-	104.4	0.2	-	-	104.5	0.1	-	-	105.3	0.8
1985	-	-	105.1	-0.2	-	-	104.5	-0.6	-	-	104.5	0.0	-	-	104.8	0.3	-	-	104.5	-0.3	-	-	105.8	1.2
1986	-	-	106.3	0.5	-	-	106.4	0.1	-	-	106.7	0.3	-	-	107.7	0.9	-	-	108.5	0.7	-	-	109.3	0.7
1987	-	-	111.3	1.8	-	-	111.0	-0.3	-	-	111.6	0.5	-	-	111.4	-0.2	-	-	113.1	1.5	-	-	112.4	-0.6
1988	-	-	113.7	1.2	-	-	114.1	0.4	-	-	114.5	0.4	-	-	117.8	2.9	-	-	119.6	1.5	-	-	118.1	-1.3
1989	-	-	121.7	3.0	-	-	121.7	0.0	-	-	121.7	0.0	-	-	121.0	-0.6	-	-	121.8	0.7	-	-	123.6	1.5
1990	-	-	128.1	3.6	-	-	127.3	-0.6	-	-	128.7	1.1	-	-	129.6	0.7	-	-	131.4	1.4	-	-	129.4	-1.5
1991	-	-	132.2	2.2	-	-	132.4	0.2	-	-	130.9	-1.1	-	-	131.5	0.5	-	-	131.9	0.3	-	-	131.8	-0.1
1992	-	-	133.0	0.9	-	-	132.4	-0.5	-	-	130.0	-1.8	-	-	129.8	-0.2	-	-	129.8	0.0	-	-	130.4	0.5
1993	-	-	132.2	1.4	-	-	129.1	-2.3	-	-	130.3	0.9	-	-	133.6	2.5	-	-	135.2	1.2	-	-	136.9	1.3
1994	-	-	136.3	-0.4	-	-	137.6	1.0	-	-	137.4	-0.1	-	-	138.1	0.5	-	-	137.8	-0.2	-	-	139.8	1.5
1995	-	-	139.7	-0.1	-	-	140.7	0.7	-	-	139.7	-0.7	-	-	140.2	0.4	-	-	140.6	0.3	-	-	141.2	0.4

Source: U.S. Department of Labor, Bureau of Labor Statistics, Division of Consumer Prices and Price Indexes. - indicates no data collected for period.

Houston, TX
Consumer Price Index - All Urban Consumers
Base 1982-1984 = 100
Housing

For 1976-1995. Columns headed % show percentile change in the index from the previous period for which an index is available.

Year	Jan Index	%	Feb Index	%	Mar Index	%	Apr Index	%	May Index	%	Jun Index	%	Jul Index	%	Aug Index	%	Sep Index	%	Oct Index	%	Nov Index	%	Dec Index	%
1976	51.2	-	-	-	-	-	52.0	1.6	-	-	-	-	52.9	1.7	-	-	-	-	54.7	3.4	-	-	-	-
1977	55.3	1.1	-	-	-	-	56.7	2.5	-	-	-	-	57.8	1.9	-	-	-	-	58.2	0.7	-	-	-	-
1978	60.0	3.1	-	-	-	-	62.3	3.8	-	-	64.2	3.0	-	-	66.0	2.8	-	-	66.9	1.4	-	-	69.0	3.1
1979	-	-	70.0	1.4	-	-	70.5	0.7	-	-	73.5	4.3	-	-	75.3	2.4	-	-	76.7	1.9	-	-	78.1	1.8
1980	-	-	79.2	1.4	-	-	80.8	2.0	-	-	84.1	4.1	-	-	84.0	-0.1	-	-	84.8	1.0	-	-	85.4	0.7
1981	-	-	86.7	1.5	-	-	88.7	2.3	-	-	91.8	3.5	-	-	92.4	0.7	-	-	94.6	2.4	-	-	95.8	1.3
1982	-	-	96.4	0.6	-	-	97.6	1.2	-	-	100.8	3.3	-	-	102.8	2.0	-	-	101.5	-1.3	-	-	100.9	-0.6
1983	-	-	99.7	-1.2	-	-	98.3	-1.4	-	-	101.2	3.0	-	-	102.2	1.0	-	-	101.4	-0.8	-	-	98.8	-2.6
1984	-	-	98.4	-0.4	-	-	99.1	0.7	-	-	101.7	2.6	-	-	100.1	-1.6	-	-	101.0	0.9	-	-	99.2	-1.8
1985	-	-	100.0	0.8	-	-	100.0	0.0	-	-	101.1	1.1	-	-	101.0	-0.1	-	-	100.4	-0.6	-	-	98.4	-2.0
1986	-	-	99.2	0.8	-	-	97.6	-1.6	-	-	98.9	1.3	-	-	98.9	0.0	-	-	98.3	-0.6	-	-	95.2	-3.2
1987	-	-	94.8	-0.4	-	-	98.3	3.7	-	-	97.5	-0.8	-	-	97.9	0.4	-	-	97.5	-0.4	-	-	95.9	-1.6
1988	-	-	96.6	0.7	-	-	97.7	1.1	-	-	98.8	1.1	-	-	98.8	0.0	-	-	98.0	-0.8	-	-	99.3	1.3
1989	-	-	100.0	0.7	-	-	99.0	-1.0	-	-	100.6	1.6	-	-	101.7	1.1	-	-	101.8	0.1	-	-	100.4	-1.4
1990	-	-	103.1	2.7	-	-	102.8	-0.3	-	-	104.7	1.8	-	-	106.6	1.8	-	-	107.2	0.6	-	-	105.8	-1.3
1991	-	-	107.6	1.7	-	-	108.0	0.4	-	-	110.2	2.0	-	-	109.8	-0.4	-	-	111.4	1.5	-	-	111.0	-0.4
1992	-	-	109.9	-1.0	-	-	112.7	2.5	-	-	114.6	1.7	-	-	113.9	-0.6	-	-	115.4	1.3	-	-	113.3	-1.8
1993	-	-	114.7	1.2	-	-	114.7	0.0	-	-	117.5	2.4	-	-	117.2	-0.3	-	-	119.0	1.5	-	-	119.3	0.3
1994	-	-	119.9	0.5	-	-	119.0	-0.8	-	-	119.9	0.8	-	-	122.7	2.3	-	-	121.7	-0.8	-	-	119.5	-1.8
1995	-	-	122.3	2.3	-	-	116.5	-4.7	-	-	121.5	4.3	-	-	122.2	0.6	-	-	123.7	1.2	-	-	120.6	-2.5

Source: U.S. Department of Labor, Bureau of Labor Statistics, Division of Consumer Prices and Price Indexes. - indicates no data collected for period.

Houston, TX
Consumer Price Index - Urban Wage Earners
Base 1982-1984 = 100
Housing

For 1976-1995. Columns headed % show percentile change in the index from the previous period for which an index is available.

Year	Jan Index	%	Feb Index	%	Mar Index	%	Apr Index	%	May Index	%	Jun Index	%	Jul Index	%	Aug Index	%	Sep Index	%	Oct Index	%	Nov Index	%	Dec Index	%
1976	51.2	-	-	-	-	-	52.0	1.6	-	-	-	-	52.9	1.7	-	-	-	-	54.8	3.6	-	-	-	-
1977	55.3	0.9	-	-	-	-	56.7	2.5	-	-	-	-	57.9	2.1	-	-	-	-	58.3	0.7	-	-	-	-
1978	60.1	3.1	-	-	-	-	62.3	3.7	-	-	64.1	2.9	-	-	65.8	2.7	-	-	66.4	0.9	-	-	68.4	3.0
1979	-	-	69.3	1.3	-	-	69.9	0.9	-	-	72.7	4.0	-	-	74.3	2.2	-	-	75.4	1.5	-	-	76.8	1.9
1980	-	-	77.7	1.2	-	-	79.4	2.2	-	-	82.5	3.9	-	-	82.7	0.2	-	-	83.5	1.0	-	-	84.2	0.8
1981	-	-	85.2	1.2	-	-	87.5	2.7	-	-	90.7	3.7	-	-	91.3	0.7	-	-	93.3	2.2	-	-	94.2	1.0
1982	-	-	94.9	0.7	-	-	96.6	1.8	-	-	99.8	3.3	-	-	101.6	1.8	-	-	100.6	-1.0	-	-	100.2	-0.4
1983	-	-	100.8	0.6	-	-	100.3	-0.5	-	-	101.0	0.7	-	-	101.3	0.3	-	-	101.0	-0.3	-	-	97.8	-3.2
1984	-	-	99.7	1.9	-	-	99.7	0.0	-	-	101.9	2.2	-	-	102.8	0.9	-	-	102.4	-0.4	-	-	99.0	-3.3
1985	-	-	100.0	1.0	-	-	99.9	-0.1	-	-	101.0	1.1	-	-	100.9	-0.1	-	-	100.3	-0.6	-	-	98.2	-2.1
1986	-	-	98.9	0.7	-	-	97.4	-1.5	-	-	98.8	1.4	-	-	98.7	-0.1	-	-	98.2	-0.5	-	-	94.9	-3.4
1987	-	-	94.5	-0.4	-	-	97.6	3.3	-	-	97.2	-0.4	-	-	97.1	-0.1	-	-	97.2	0.1	-	-	95.8	-1.4
1988	-	-	96.1	0.3	-	-	97.0	0.9	-	-	98.1	1.1	-	-	98.2	0.1	-	-	97.6	-0.6	-	-	98.7	1.1
1989	-	-	99.3	0.6	-	-	98.5	-0.8	-	-	100.3	1.8	-	-	101.6	1.3	-	-	101.4	-0.2	-	-	100.2	-1.2
1990	-	-	102.2	2.0	-	-	102.4	0.2	-	-	104.5	2.1	-	-	106.4	1.8	-	-	107.2	0.8	-	-	105.6	-1.5
1991	-	-	107.4	1.7	-	-	107.9	0.5	-	-	110.5	2.4	-	-	109.8	-0.6	-	-	111.1	1.2	-	-	111.3	0.2
1992	-	-	109.6	-1.5	-	-	112.6	2.7	-	-	114.7	1.9	-	-	114.2	-0.4	-	-	115.7	1.3	-	-	113.6	-1.8
1993	-	-	114.9	1.1	-	-	115.1	0.2	-	-	118.0	2.5	-	-	117.8	-0.2	-	-	119.4	1.4	-	-	119.7	0.3
1994	-	-	119.9	0.2	-	-	118.9	-0.8	-	-	120.1	1.0	-	-	123.0	2.4	-	-	122.2	-0.7	-	-	120.1	-1.7
1995	-	-	122.3	1.8	-	-	116.4	-4.8	-	-	121.6	4.5	-	-	122.5	0.7	-	-	123.6	0.9	-	-	121.0	-2.1

Source: U.S. Department of Labor, Bureau of Labor Statistics, Division of Consumer Prices and Price Indexes. - indicates no data collected for period.

Houston, TX
Consumer Price Index - All Urban Consumers
Base 1982-1984 = 100
Apparel and Upkeep

For 1952-1995. Columns headed % show percentile change in the index from the previous period for which an index is available.

Year	Jan Index	%	Feb Index	%	Mar Index	%	Apr Index	%	May Index	%	Jun Index	%	Jul Index	%	Aug Index	%	Sep Index	%	Oct Index	%	Nov Index	%	Dec Index	%
1952	-	-	-	-	-	-	-	-	-	-	-	-	-	-	-	-	-	-	-	-	-	-	36.1	-
1953	-	-	36.0	-0.3	-	-	-	-	36.0	0.0	-	-	-	-	35.9	-0.3	-	-	-	-	36.4	1.4	-	-
1954	-	-	36.0	-1.1	-	-	-	-	36.0	0.0	-	-	-	-	36.1	0.3	-	-	-	-	36.1	0.0	-	-
1955	-	-	35.9	-0.6	-	-	-	-	36.1	0.6	-	-	-	-	35.8	-0.8	-	-	-	-	36.1	0.8	-	-
1956	-	-	36.4	0.8	-	-	-	-	36.2	-0.5	-	-	-	-	36.7	1.4	-	-	-	-	37.6	2.5	-	-
1957	-	-	37.2	-1.1	-	-	-	-	37.6	1.1	-	-	-	-	37.6	0.0	-	-	-	-	38.2	1.6	-	-
1958	-	-	38.3	0.3	-	-	-	-	38.4	0.3	-	-	-	-	38.3	-0.3	-	-	-	-	38.4	0.3	-	-
1959	-	-	38.7	0.8	-	-	-	-	38.6	-0.3	-	-	-	-	38.8	0.5	-	-	-	-	38.8	0.0	-	-
1960	-	-	38.2	-1.5	-	-	-	-	38.8	1.6	-	-	-	-	38.9	0.3	-	-	-	-	38.8	-0.3	-	-
1961	-	-	38.6	-0.5	-	-	-	-	38.8	0.5	-	-	-	-	38.7	-0.3	-	-	-	-	39.6	2.3	-	-
1962	-	-	39.7	0.3	-	-	-	-	40.0	0.8	-	-	-	-	40.2	0.5	-	-	-	-	40.3	0.2	-	-
1963	-	-	40.4	0.2	-	-	-	-	40.3	-0.2	-	-	-	-	40.8	1.2	-	-	-	-	40.6	-0.5	-	-
1964	-	-	41.0	1.0	-	-	-	-	40.7	-0.7	-	-	-	-	40.7	0.0	-	-	-	-	40.7	0.0	-	-
1965	-	-	40.2	-1.2	-	-	41.0	2.0	-	-	-	-	40.8	-0.5	-	-	-	-	41.3	1.2	-	-	-	-
1966	41.0	-0.7	-	-	-	-	41.4	1.0	-	-	-	-	41.6	0.5	-	-	-	-	42.0	1.0	-	-	-	-
1967	41.2	-1.9	-	-	-	-	41.9	1.7	-	-	-	-	42.0	0.2	-	-	-	-	43.2	2.9	-	-	-	-
1968	43.1	-0.2	-	-	-	-	43.9	1.9	-	-	-	-	44.3	0.9	-	-	-	-	46.0	3.8	-	-	-	-
1969	46.5	1.1	-	-	-	-	47.3	1.7	-	-	-	-	47.7	0.8	-	-	-	-	50.1	5.0	-	-	-	-
1970	49.7	-0.8	-	-	-	-	50.2	1.0	-	-	-	-	50.1	-0.2	-	-	-	-	52.2	4.2	-	-	-	-
1971	50.8	-2.7	-	-	-	-	51.4	1.2	-	-	-	-	50.8	-1.2	-	-	-	-	52.7	3.7	-	-	-	-
1972	52.3	-0.8	-	-	-	-	53.2	1.7	-	-	-	-	52.0	-2.3	-	-	-	-	54.4	4.6	-	-	-	-
1973	53.1	-2.4	-	-	-	-	55.1	3.8	-	-	-	-	53.5	-2.9	-	-	-	-	57.3	7.1	-	-	-	-
1974	57.6	0.5	-	-	-	-	59.3	3.0	-	-	-	-	60.5	2.0	-	-	-	-	62.2	2.8	-	-	-	-
1975	61.8	-0.6	-	-	-	-	63.3	2.4	-	-	-	-	64.3	1.6	-	-	-	-	66.3	3.1	-	-	-	-
1976	65.7	-0.9	-	-	-	-	67.4	2.6	-	-	-	-	66.9	-0.7	-	-	-	-	70.4	5.2	-	-	-	-
1977	70.0	-0.6	-	-	-	-	71.6	2.3	-	-	-	-	71.6	0.0	-	-	-	-	74.0	3.4	-	-	-	-
1978	72.8	-1.6	-	-	-	-	75.7	4.0	-	-	76.6	1.2	-	-	78.0	1.8	-	-	79.9	2.4	-	-	79.7	-0.3
1979	-	-	80.6	1.1	-	-	82.8	2.7	-	-	82.4	-0.5	-	-	83.2	1.0	-	-	85.1	2.3	-	-	86.0	1.1
1980	-	-	88.3	2.7	-	-	88.3	0.0	-	-	87.8	-0.6	-	-	89.4	1.8	-	-	91.6	2.5	-	-	90.7	-1.0
1981	-	-	93.4	3.0	-	-	94.8	1.5	-	-	95.0	0.2	-	-	95.5	0.5	-	-	97.8	2.4	-	-	99.5	1.7
1982	-	-	98.6	-0.9	-	-	98.6	0.0	-	-	97.5	-1.1	-	-	98.0	0.5	-	-	98.7	0.7	-	-	98.7	0.0
1983	-	-	101.5	2.8	-	-	100.0	-1.5	-	-	98.0	-2.0	-	-	98.8	0.8	-	-	100.3	1.5	-	-	100.6	0.3
1984	-	-	100.3	-0.3	-	-	100.8	0.5	-	-	102.1	1.3	-	-	102.1	0.0	-	-	102.6	0.5	-	-	104.0	1.4
1985	-	-	104.2	0.2	-	-	104.4	0.2	-	-	103.8	-0.6	-	-	104.2	0.4	-	-	104.9	0.7	-	-	105.5	0.6
1986	-	-	106.1	0.6	-	-	106.6	0.5	-	-	104.6	-1.9	-	-	107.6	2.9	-	-	105.7	-1.8	-	-	106.1	0.4
1987	-	-	107.9	1.7	-	-	112.8	4.5	-	-	111.6	-1.1	-	-	115.4	3.4	-	-	118.4	2.6	-	-	118.3	-0.1
1988	-	-	121.3	2.5	-	-	117.4	-3.2	-	-	122.0	3.9	-	-	121.1	-0.7	-	-	125.3	3.5	-	-	119.9	-4.3
1989	-	-	122.7	2.3	-	-	126.7	3.3	-	-	121.0	-4.5	-	-	122.0	0.8	-	-	127.5	4.5	-	-	124.9	-2.0
1990	-	-	136.9	9.6	-	-	130.0	-5.0	-	-	133.3	2.5	-	-	132.5	-0.6	-	-	134.9	1.8	-	-	128.6	-4.7
1991	-	-	138.2	7.5	-	-	133.3	-3.5	-	-	135.3	1.5	-	-	129.7	-4.1	-	-	138.8	7.0	-	-	135.0	-2.7
1992	-	-	137.1	1.6	-	-	135.8	-0.9	-	-	134.4	-1.0	-	-	141.4	5.2	-	-	137.8	-2.5	-	-	126.1	-8.5
1993	-	-	140.4	11.3	-	-	142.4	1.4	-	-	137.8	-3.2	-	-	132.2	-4.1	-	-	155.4	17.5	-	-	151.3	-2.6
1994	-	-	153.8	1.7	-	-	149.1	-3.1	-	-	145.3	-2.5	-	-	144.1	-0.8	-	-	147.3	2.2	-	-	136.8	-7.1
1995	-	-	139.1	1.7	-	-	140.9	1.3	-	-	131.5	-6.7	-	-	134.0	1.9	-	-	138.4	3.3	-	-	149.1	7.7

Source: U.S. Department of Labor, Bureau of Labor Statistics, Division of Consumer Prices and Price Indexes. - indicates no data collected for period.

Houston, TX
Consumer Price Index - Urban Wage Earners
Base 1982-1984 = 100
Apparel and Upkeep

For 1952-1995. Columns headed % show percentile change in the index from the previous period for which an index is available.

Year	Jan Index	%	Feb Index	%	Mar Index	%	Apr Index	%	May Index	%	Jun Index	%	Jul Index	%	Aug Index	%	Sep Index	%	Oct Index	%	Nov Index	%	Dec Index	%
1952	-		-		-		-		-		-		-		-		-		-		-		36.8	-
1953	-		36.7	-0.3	-		-		36.7	0.0	-		-		36.6	-0.3	-		-		37.1	1.4	-	
1954	-		36.7	-1.1	-		-		36.7	0.0	-		-		36.8	0.3	-		-		36.8	0.0	-	
1955	-		36.6	-0.5	-		-		36.8	0.5	-		-		36.4	-1.1	-		-		36.8	1.1	-	
1956	-		37.1	0.8	-		-		36.9	-0.5	-		-		37.4	1.4	-		-		38.3	2.4	-	
1957	-		37.9	-1.0	-		-		38.3	1.1	-		-		38.3	0.0	-		-		38.9	1.6	-	
1958	-		39.1	0.5	-		-		39.1	0.0	-		-		39.0	-0.3	-		-		39.2	0.5	-	
1959	-		39.4	0.5	-		-		39.3	-0.3	-		-		39.5	0.5	-		-		39.5	0.0	-	
1960	-		38.9	-1.5	-		-		39.5	1.5	-		-		39.6	0.3	-		-		39.5	-0.3	-	
1961	-		39.4	-0.3	-		-		39.5	0.3	-		-		39.4	-0.3	-		-		40.3	2.3	-	
1962	-		40.4	0.2	-		-		40.8	1.0	-		-		40.9	0.2	-		-		41.1	0.5	-	
1963	-		41.2	0.2	-		-		41.1	-0.2	-		-		41.6	1.2	-		-		41.4	-0.5	-	
1964	-		41.8	1.0	-		-		41.4	-1.0	-		-		41.5	0.2	-		-		41.5	0.0	-	
1965	-		41.0	-1.2	-		41.7	1.7	-		-		41.6	-0.2	-		-		42.0	1.0	-		-	
1966	41.8	-0.5	-		-		42.2	1.0	-		-		42.3	0.2	-		-		42.8	1.2	-		-	
1967	42.0	-1.9	-		-		42.7	1.7	-		-		42.8	0.2	-		-		44.0	2.8	-		-	
1968	43.9	-0.2	-		-		44.8	2.1	-		-		45.1	0.7	-		-		46.9	4.0	-		-	
1969	47.3	0.9	-		-		48.2	1.9	-		-		48.6	0.8	-		-		51.0	4.9	-		-	
1970	50.6	-0.8	-		-		51.2	1.2	-		-		51.0	-0.4	-		-		53.2	4.3	-		-	
1971	51.8	-2.6	-		-		52.4	1.2	-		-		51.7	-1.3	-		-		53.7	3.9	-		-	
1972	53.3	-0.7	-		-		54.3	1.9	-		-		53.0	-2.4	-		-		55.5	4.7	-		-	
1973	54.1	-2.5	-		-		56.1	3.7	-		-		54.5	-2.9	-		-		58.4	7.2	-		-	
1974	58.7	0.5	-		-		60.5	3.1	-		-		61.7	2.0	-		-		63.4	2.8	-		-	
1975	63.0	-0.6	-		-		64.5	2.4	-		-		65.5	1.6	-		-		67.6	3.2	-		-	
1976	67.0	-0.9	-		-		68.6	2.4	-		-		68.2	-0.6	-		-		71.8	5.3	-		-	
1977	71.4	-0.6	-		-		72.9	2.1	-		-		72.9	0.0	-		-		75.4	3.4	-		-	
1978	74.1	-1.7	-		-		77.2	4.2	-		78.4	1.6	-		79.4	1.3	-		81.1	2.1	-		81.9	1.0
1979	-		83.1	1.5	-		85.3	2.6	-		84.4	-1.1	-		85.3	1.1	-		87.0	2.0	-		88.2	1.4
1980	-		89.2	1.1	-		89.7	0.6	-		89.4	-0.3	-		90.8	1.6	-		91.5	0.8	-		92.2	0.8
1981	-		94.6	2.6	-		95.8	1.3	-		95.2	-0.6	-		96.7	1.6	-		98.5	1.9	-		99.0	0.5
1982	-		98.3	-0.7	-		98.5	0.2	-		97.9	-0.6	-		98.2	0.3	-		98.8	0.6	-		99.2	0.4
1983	-		101.3	2.1	-		100.0	-1.3	-		98.0	-2.0	-		98.8	0.8	-		100.3	1.5	-		100.8	0.5
1984	-		100.4	-0.4	-		100.4	0.0	-		102.0	1.6	-		101.9	-0.1	-		102.7	0.8	-		103.8	1.1
1985	-		103.8	0.0	-		104.1	0.3	-		103.8	-0.3	-		104.1	0.3	-		104.7	0.6	-		105.3	0.6
1986	-		105.8	0.5	-		106.3	0.5	-		104.5	-1.7	-		106.9	2.3	-		105.5	-1.3	-		105.3	-0.2
1987	-		107.4	2.0	-		111.7	4.0	-		110.7	-0.9	-		114.7	3.6	-		117.2	2.2	-		117.6	0.3
1988	-		120.9	2.8	-		117.0	-3.2	-		122.1	4.4	-		121.2	-0.7	-		125.6	3.6	-		120.5	-4.1
1989	-		123.1	2.2	-		126.7	2.9	-		121.9	-3.8	-		122.0	0.1	-		126.8	3.9	-		124.8	-1.6
1990	-		137.4	10.1	-		130.7	-4.9	-		133.5	2.1	-		133.2	-0.2	-		134.8	1.2	-		127.8	-5.2
1991	-		137.1	7.3	-		132.7	-3.2	-		134.7	1.5	-		128.2	-4.8	-		137.9	7.6	-		134.2	-2.7
1992	-		136.4	1.6	-		134.7	-1.2	-		133.0	-1.3	-		139.2	4.7	-		136.5	-1.9	-		124.6	-8.7
1993	-		137.3	10.2	-		138.7	1.0	-		134.1	-3.3	-		130.2	-2.9	-		151.7	16.5	-		147.2	-3.0
1994	-		152.2	3.4	-		147.8	-2.9	-		144.3	-2.4	-		143.2	-0.8	-		146.1	2.0	-		136.1	-6.8
1995	-		139.0	2.1	-		139.8	0.6	-		132.2	-5.4	-		133.9	1.3	-		137.8	2.9	-		145.7	5.7

Source: U.S. Department of Labor, Bureau of Labor Statistics, Division of Consumer Prices and Price Indexes. - indicates no data collected for period.

Houston, TX
Consumer Price Index - All Urban Consumers
Base 1982-1984 = 100
Transportation

For 1947-1995. Columns headed % show percentile change in the index from the previous period for which an index is available.

Year	Jan Index	%	Feb Index	%	Mar Index	%	Apr Index	%	May Index	%	Jun Index	%	Jul Index	%	Aug Index	%	Sep Index	%	Oct Index	%	Nov Index	%	Dec Index	%
1947	19.9	-	20.1	1.0	20.2	0.5	20.4	1.0	20.5	0.5	20.5	0.0	20.6	0.5	20.8	1.0	21.0	1.0	21.4	1.9	21.9	2.3	22.0	0.5
1948	22.6	2.7	22.7	0.4	22.7	0.0	22.7	0.0	22.7	0.0	22.8	0.4	23.2	1.8	23.7	2.2	23.8	0.4	23.9	0.4	24.0	0.4	24.0	0.0
1949	24.0	0.0	24.3	1.2	24.3	0.0	24.4	0.4	24.4	0.0	24.3	-0.4	25.0	2.9	25.0	0.0	25.0	0.0	25.1	0.4	25.2	0.4	25.2	0.0
1950	25.3	0.4	25.3	0.0	25.3	0.0	25.3	0.0	25.5	0.8	25.5	0.0	25.6	0.4	25.7	0.4	25.7	0.0	25.7	0.0	25.7	0.0	27.2	5.8
1951	27.3	0.4	27.5	0.7	27.8	1.1	27.7	-0.4	27.7	0.0	27.9	0.7	27.9	0.0	27.9	0.0	28.2	1.1	28.2	0.0	28.6	1.4	28.6	0.0
1952	28.0	-2.1	28.4	1.4	28.4	0.0	28.4	0.0	28.4	0.0	28.4	0.0	28.4	0.0	28.4	0.0	28.4	0.0	29.2	2.8	29.2	0.0	29.2	0.0
1953	-	-	29.0	-0.7	-	-	-	-	29.0	0.0	-	-	-	-	29.1	0.3	-	-	-	-	29.0	-0.3	-	-
1954	-	-	28.7	-1.0	-	-	-	-	28.6	-0.3	-	-	-	-	28.2	-1.4	-	-	-	-	28.8	2.1	-	-
1955	-	-	28.3	-1.7	-	-	-	-	27.9	-1.4	-	-	-	-	27.8	-0.4	-	-	-	-	28.9	4.0	-	-
1956	-	-	28.7	-0.7	-	-	-	-	28.5	-0.7	-	-	-	-	28.9	1.4	-	-	-	-	29.7	2.8	-	-
1957	-	-	30.3	2.0	-	-	-	-	30.8	1.7	-	-	-	-	31.1	1.0	-	-	-	-	31.8	2.3	-	-
1958	-	-	29.0	-8.8	-	-	-	-	31.5	8.6	-	-	-	-	32.4	2.9	-	-	-	-	32.7	0.9	-	-
1959	-	-	32.5	-0.6	-	-	-	-	32.9	1.2	-	-	-	-	33.2	0.9	-	-	-	-	33.4	0.6	-	-
1960	-	-	33.7	0.9	-	-	-	-	31.4	-6.8	-	-	-	-	33.6	7.0	-	-	-	-	33.4	-0.6	-	-
1961	-	-	31.5	-5.7	-	-	-	-	33.4	6.0	-	-	-	-	32.6	-2.4	-	-	-	-	34.7	6.4	-	-
1962	-	-	34.6	-0.3	-	-	-	-	34.6	0.0	-	-	-	-	34.2	-1.2	-	-	-	-	33.2	-2.9	-	-
1963	-	-	33.9	2.1	-	-	-	-	32.4	-4.4	-	-	-	-	33.8	4.3	-	-	-	-	34.3	1.5	-	-
1964	-	-	34.0	-0.9	-	-	-	-	34.5	1.5	-	-	-	-	34.4	-0.3	-	-	-	-	34.6	0.6	-	-
1965	-	-	33.8	-2.3	-	-	34.1	0.9	-	-	-	-	34.0	-0.3	-	-	-	-	34.6	1.8	-	-	-	-
1966	34.6	0.0	-	-	-	-	34.6	0.0	-	-	-	-	35.0	1.2	-	-	-	-	35.0	0.0	-	-	-	-
1967	35.4	1.1	-	-	-	-	35.7	0.8	-	-	-	-	35.9	0.6	-	-	-	-	36.7	2.2	-	-	-	-
1968	36.7	0.0	-	-	-	-	37.0	0.8	-	-	-	-	37.0	0.0	-	-	-	-	37.3	0.8	-	-	-	-
1969	37.7	1.1	-	-	-	-	38.4	1.9	-	-	-	-	38.3	-0.3	-	-	-	-	38.8	1.3	-	-	-	-
1970	38.6	-0.5	-	-	-	-	39.0	1.0	-	-	-	-	38.9	-0.3	-	-	-	-	39.0	0.3	-	-	-	-
1971	41.3	5.9	-	-	-	-	40.8	-1.2	-	-	-	-	40.3	-1.2	-	-	-	-	40.8	1.2	-	-	-	-
1972	41.1	0.7	-	-	-	-	41.7	1.5	-	-	-	-	41.7	0.0	-	-	-	-	41.0	-1.7	-	-	-	-
1973	41.1	0.2	-	-	-	-	41.9	1.9	-	-	-	-	42.3	1.0	-	-	-	-	42.4	0.2	-	-	-	-
1974	43.9	3.5	-	-	-	-	45.9	4.6	-	-	-	-	48.0	4.6	-	-	-	-	49.6	3.3	-	-	-	-
1975	49.1	-1.0	-	-	-	-	50.4	2.6	-	-	-	-	52.9	5.0	-	-	-	-	53.4	0.9	-	-	-	-
1976	54.1	1.3	-	-	-	-	54.6	0.9	-	-	-	-	56.5	3.5	-	-	-	-	58.3	3.2	-	-	-	-
1977	58.6	0.5	-	-	-	-	60.4	3.1	-	-	-	-	61.3	1.5	-	-	-	-	60.7	-1.0	-	-	-	-
1978	61.1	0.7	-	-	-	-	61.6	0.8	-	-	62.5	1.5	-	-	63.3	1.3	-	-	64.1	1.3	-	-	65.1	1.6
1979	-	-	66.1	1.5	-	-	68.9	4.2	-	-	72.5	5.2	-	-	75.3	3.9	-	-	76.0	0.9	-	-	77.9	2.5
1980	-	-	82.8	6.3	-	-	85.4	3.1	-	-	86.1	0.8	-	-	86.6	0.6	-	-	87.0	0.5	-	-	88.2	1.4
1981	-	-	92.0	4.3	-	-	93.7	1.8	-	-	95.3	1.7	-	-	95.1	-0.2	-	-	97.0	2.0	-	-	97.9	0.9
1982	-	-	96.8	-1.1	-	-	93.9	-3.0	-	-	98.3	4.7	-	-	99.2	0.9	-	-	98.8	-0.4	-	-	99.2	0.4
1983	-	-	96.7	-2.5	-	-	97.3	0.6	-	-	98.8	1.5	-	-	99.9	1.1	-	-	101.1	1.2	-	-	100.9	-0.2
1984	-	-	100.2	-0.7	-	-	101.4	1.2	-	-	102.5	1.1	-	-	105.3	2.7	-	-	106.1	0.8	-	-	105.7	-0.4
1985	-	-	104.0	-1.6	-	-	105.7	1.6	-	-	106.9	1.1	-	-	106.8	-0.1	-	-	106.7	-0.1	-	-	107.1	0.4
1986	-	-	105.2	-1.8	-	-	97.2	-7.6	-	-	99.1	2.0	-	-	96.6	-2.5	-	-	97.7	1.1	-	-	97.3	-0.4
1987	-	-	100.3	3.1	-	-	101.3	1.0	-	-	102.8	1.5	-	-	103.9	1.1	-	-	104.3	0.4	-	-	104.2	-0.1
1988	-	-	102.9	-1.2	-	-	102.9	0.0	-	-	104.2	1.3	-	-	105.2	1.0	-	-	106.1	0.9	-	-	106.4	0.3
1989	-	-	106.9	0.5	-	-	108.5	1.5	-	-	110.3	1.7	-	-	109.1	-1.1	-	-	110.0	0.8	-	-	111.4	1.3
1990	-	-	112.8	1.3	-	-	112.5	-0.3	-	-	113.1	0.5	-	-	114.4	1.1	-	-	122.1	6.7	-	-	124.3	1.8
1991	-	-	120.1	-3.4	-	-	115.4	-3.9	-	-	118.4	2.6	-	-	118.3	-0.1	-	-	122.0	3.1	-	-	123.2	1.0

[Continued]

Houston, TX
Consumer Price Index - All Urban Consumers
Base 1982-1984 = 100
Transportation
[Continued]

For 1947-1995. Columns headed % show percentile change in the index from the previous period for which an index is available.

Year	Jan Index	%	Feb Index	%	Mar Index	%	Apr Index	%	May Index	%	Jun Index	%	Jul Index	%	Aug Index	%	Sep Index	%	Oct Index	%	Nov Index	%	Dec Index	%
1992	-	-	121.0	-1.8	-	-	122.0	0.8	-	-	123.0	0.8	-	-	123.1	0.1	-	-	124.3	1.0	-	-	124.3	0.0
1993	-	-	124.8	0.4	-	-	127.2	1.9	-	-	127.8	0.5	-	-	128.8	0.8	-	-	131.2	1.9	-	-	130.9	-0.2
1994	-	-	130.6	-0.2	-	-	131.0	0.3	-	-	132.2	0.9	-	-	134.5	1.7	-	-	134.9	0.3	-	-	135.4	0.4
1995	-	-	135.9	0.4	-	-	136.7	0.6	-	-	139.0	1.7	-	-	136.6	-1.7	-	-	137.8	0.9	-	-	135.9	-1.4

Source: U.S. Department of Labor, Bureau of Labor Statistics, Division of Consumer Prices and Price Indexes. - indicates no data collected for period.

Houston, TX
Consumer Price Index - Urban Wage Earners
Base 1982-1984 = 100
Transportation

For 1947-1995. Columns headed % show percentile change in the index from the previous period for which an index is available.

Year	Jan Index	%	Feb Index	%	Mar Index	%	Apr Index	%	May Index	%	Jun Index	%	Jul Index	%	Aug Index	%	Sep Index	%	Oct Index	%	Nov Index	%	Dec Index	%
1947	19.8	-	20.1	1.5	20.1	0.0	20.3	1.0	20.4	0.5	20.4	0.0	20.5	0.5	20.7	1.0	21.0	1.4	21.3	1.4	21.8	2.3	21.9	0.5
1948	22.5	2.7	22.6	0.4	22.6	0.0	22.6	0.0	22.6	0.0	22.7	0.4	23.2	2.2	23.7	2.2	23.7	0.0	23.8	0.4	23.9	0.4	23.9	0.0
1949	23.9	0.0	24.2	1.3	24.2	0.0	24.3	0.4	24.3	0.0	24.2	-0.4	24.9	2.9	24.9	0.0	24.9	0.0	25.0	0.4	25.1	0.4	25.1	0.0
1950	25.2	0.4	25.2	0.0	25.2	0.0	25.2	0.0	25.4	0.8	25.4	0.0	25.5	0.4	25.6	0.4	25.6	0.0	25.6	0.0	25.6	0.0	27.1	5.9
1951	27.2	0.4	27.4	0.7	27.7	1.1	27.6	-0.4	27.6	0.0	27.8	0.7	27.8	0.0	27.8	0.0	28.1	1.1	28.1	0.0	28.5	1.4	28.5	0.0
1952	27.9	-2.1	28.2	1.1	28.2	0.0	28.2	0.0	28.2	0.0	28.2	0.0	28.2	0.0	28.2	0.0	28.3	0.4	29.0	2.5	29.0	0.0	29.0	0.0
1953	-		28.9	-0.3	-		-		28.9	0.0	-		-		29.0	0.3	-		-		28.9	-0.3	-	
1954	-		28.6	-1.0	-		-		28.5	-0.3	-		-		28.1	-1.4	-		-		28.7	2.1	-	
1955	-		28.2	-1.7	-		-		27.8	-1.4	-		-		27.7	-0.4	-		-		28.8	4.0	-	
1956	-		28.6	-0.7	-		-		28.4	-0.7	-		-		28.8	1.4	-		-		29.6	2.8	-	
1957	-		30.1	1.7	-		-		30.7	2.0	-		-		30.9	0.7	-		-		31.7	2.6	-	
1958	-		28.9	-8.8	-		-		31.4	8.7	-		-		32.2	2.5	-		-		32.6	1.2	-	
1959	-		32.4	-0.6	-		-		32.8	1.2	-		-		33.0	0.6	-		-		33.2	0.6	-	
1960	-		33.6	1.2	-		-		31.3	-6.8	-		-		33.5	7.0	-		-		33.2	-0.9	-	
1961	-		31.4	-5.4	-		-		33.2	5.7	-		-		32.5	-2.1	-		-		34.5	6.2	-	
1962	-		34.4	-0.3	-		-		34.5	0.3	-		-		34.1	-1.2	-		-		33.0	-3.2	-	
1963	-		33.8	2.4	-		-		32.3	-4.4	-		-		33.6	4.0	-		-		34.1	1.5	-	
1964	-		33.9	-0.6	-		-		34.3	1.2	-		-		34.2	-0.3	-		-		34.4	0.6	-	
1965	-		33.6	-2.3	-		34.0	1.2	-		-		33.9	-0.3	-		-		34.5	1.8	-		-	
1966	34.4	-0.3	-		-		34.5	0.3	-		-		34.9	1.2	-		-		34.9	0.0	-		-	
1967	35.2	0.9	-		-		35.6	1.1	-		-		35.7	0.3	-		-		36.6	2.5	-		-	
1968	36.6	0.0	-		-		36.8	0.5	-		-		36.9	0.3	-		-		37.1	0.5	-		-	
1969	37.5	1.1	-		-		38.3	2.1	-		-		38.2	-0.3	-		-		38.7	1.3	-		-	
1970	38.5	-0.5	-		-		38.8	0.8	-		-		38.8	0.0	-		-		38.9	0.3	-		-	
1971	41.1	5.7	-		-		40.6	-1.2	-		-		40.1	-1.2	-		-		40.6	1.2	-		-	
1972	41.0	1.0	-		-		41.5	1.2	-		-		41.5	0.0	-		-		40.8	-1.7	-		-	
1973	41.0	0.5	-		-		41.7	1.7	-		-		42.1	1.0	-		-		42.2	0.2	-		-	
1974	43.8	3.8	-		-		45.7	4.3	-		-		47.8	4.6	-		-		49.4	3.3	-		-	
1975	48.9	-1.0	-		-		50.2	2.7	-		-		52.7	5.0	-		-		53.2	0.9	-		-	
1976	53.9	1.3	-		-		54.4	0.9	-		-		56.2	3.3	-		-		58.1	3.4	-		-	
1977	58.4	0.5	-		-		60.2	3.1	-		-		61.1	1.5	-		-		60.4	-1.1	-		-	
1978	60.8	0.7	-		-		61.3	0.8	-		62.5	2.0	-		63.4	1.4	-		64.1	1.1	-		65.2	1.7
1979	-		66.2	1.5	-		69.2	4.5	-		72.7	5.1	-		75.0	3.2	-		75.4	0.5	-		77.1	2.3
1980	-		81.5	5.7	-		83.9	2.9	-		84.8	1.1	-		85.2	0.5	-		85.8	0.7	-		86.9	1.3
1981	-		90.4	4.0	-		92.2	2.0	-		93.9	1.8	-		94.2	0.3	-		95.4	1.3	-		97.0	1.7
1982	-		95.9	-1.1	-		93.5	-2.5	-		97.8	4.6	-		98.7	0.9	-		98.3	-0.4	-		98.7	0.4
1983	-		96.5	-2.2	-		97.1	0.6	-		98.6	1.5	-		99.8	1.2	-		101.2	1.4	-		101.2	0.0
1984	-		100.6	-0.6	-		102.1	1.5	-		103.3	1.2	-		106.0	2.6	-		106.8	0.8	-		106.4	-0.4
1985	-		104.8	-1.5	-		106.3	1.4	-		107.3	0.9	-		107.2	-0.1	-		107.2	0.0	-		107.5	0.3
1986	-		105.7	-1.7	-		98.5	-6.8	-		100.1	1.6	-		97.9	-2.2	-		98.9	1.0	-		98.5	-0.4
1987	-		102.2	3.8	-		103.4	1.2	-		105.0	1.5	-		106.2	1.1	-		107.0	0.8	-		106.7	-0.3
1988	-		105.5	-1.1	-		105.2	-0.3	-		106.6	1.3	-		108.0	1.3	-		108.7	0.6	-		109.0	0.3
1989	-		109.4	0.4	-		111.4	1.8	-		113.3	1.7	-		112.0	-1.1	-		112.6	0.5	-		113.9	1.2
1990	-		115.3	1.2	-		115.0	-0.3	-		115.6	0.5	-		117.1	1.3	-		125.4	7.1	-		127.5	1.7
1991	-		122.3	-4.1	-		117.6	-3.8	-		121.0	2.9	-		120.8	-0.2	-		124.6	3.1	-		125.6	0.8

[Continued]

Houston, TX
Consumer Price Index - Urban Wage Earners
Base 1982-1984 = 100
Transportation

[Continued]

For 1947-1995. Columns headed % show percentile change in the index from the previous period for which an index is available.

Year	Jan Index	%	Feb Index	%	Mar Index	%	Apr Index	%	May Index	%	Jun Index	%	Jul Index	%	Aug Index	%	Sep Index	%	Oct Index	%	Nov Index	%	Dec Index	%
1992	-	-	123.0	-2.1	-	-	123.9	0.7	-	-	125.6	1.4	-	-	125.8	0.2	-	-	126.5	0.6	-	-	126.5	0.0
1993	-	-	126.1	-0.3	-	-	128.5	1.9	-	-	129.4	0.7	-	-	130.1	0.5	-	-	132.3	1.7	-	-	131.5	-0.6
1994	-	-	130.9	-0.5	-	-	131.6	0.5	-	-	133.4	1.4	-	-	135.9	1.9	-	-	136.6	0.5	-	-	137.4	0.6
1995	-	-	137.7	0.2	-	-	138.3	0.4	-	-	140.5	1.6	-	-	138.5	-1.4	-	-	138.9	0.3	-	-	137.7	-0.9

Source: U.S. Department of Labor, Bureau of Labor Statistics, Division of Consumer Prices and Price Indexes. - indicates no data collected for period.

Houston, TX
Consumer Price Index - All Urban Consumers
Base 1982-1984 = 100
Medical Care

For 1947-1995. Columns headed % show percentile change in the index from the previous period for which an index is available.

Year	Jan Index	%	Feb Index	%	Mar Index	%	Apr Index	%	May Index	%	Jun Index	%	Jul Index	%	Aug Index	%	Sep Index	%	Oct Index	%	Nov Index	%	Dec Index	%
1947	14.1	-	14.2	0.7	14.2	0.0	14.3	0.7	14.5	1.4	14.6	0.7	14.5	-0.7	14.5	0.0	14.6	0.7	14.7	0.7	14.7	0.0	14.7	0.0
1948	14.7	0.0	14.7	0.0	14.9	1.4	14.8	-0.7	14.8	0.0	14.9	0.7	14.9	0.0	14.9	0.0	14.9	0.0	14.9	0.0	14.9	0.0	14.9	0.0
1949	15.1	1.3	15.1	0.0	15.1	0.0	15.1	0.0	15.2	0.7	15.3	0.7	15.3	0.0	15.3	0.0	15.3	0.0	15.3	0.0	15.2	-0.7	15.5	2.0
1950	15.5	0.0	15.5	0.0	15.5	0.0	15.5	0.0	15.5	0.0	15.5	0.0	15.5	0.0	15.8	0.0	15.8	0.0	16.6	5.1	16.6	0.0	16.7	0.6
1951	15.6	0.0	15.6	0.0	15.8	1.3	15.8	0.0	15.8	0.0	15.8	0.0	15.8	0.0	16.7	0.0	16.7	0.0	16.7	0.0	16.7	0.0	17.4	4.2
1952	16.6	-0.6	16.6	0.0	16.6	0.0	16.7	0.6	16.7	0.0	16.7	0.0	16.7	0.0	17.6	0.0	-		-		17.7	0.6	-	
1953	-		17.4	0.0	-		-		17.6	1.1	-		-		17.8	0.6	-		-		17.8	0.0	-	
1954	-		17.7	0.0	-		-		17.7	0.0	-		-		18.5	0.0	-		-		18.9	2.2	-	
1955	-		17.8	0.0	-		-		18.5	3.9	-		-		19.0	1.1	-		-		19.1	0.5	-	
1956	-		18.9	0.0	-		-		18.8	-0.5	-		-		19.1	-0.5	-		-		19.2	0.5	-	
1957	-		19.3	1.0	-		-		19.2	-0.5	-		-		19.6	0.0	-		-		19.8	1.0	-	
1958	-		19.6	2.1	-		-		19.6	0.0	-		-		20.1	0.0	-		-		20.1	0.0	-	
1959	-		19.8	0.0	-		-		20.1	1.5	-		-		20.6	0.0	-		-		20.6	0.0	-	
1960	-		20.3	1.0	-		-		20.6	1.5	-		-		20.8	0.0	-		-		20.9	0.5	-	
1961	-		20.6	0.0	-		-		20.8	1.0	-		-		21.0	0.0	-		-		21.2	1.0	-	
1962	-		20.9	0.0	-		-		21.0	0.5	-		-		21.6	0.0	-		-		21.8	0.9	-	
1963	-		21.5	1.4	-		-		21.6	0.5	-		-		22.2	0.0	-		-		22.2	0.0	-	
1964	-		22.0	0.9	-		-		22.2	0.9	-		-		-		-		22.9	0.4	-		-	
1965	-		22.5	1.4	-		22.7	0.9	-		-		22.8	0.4	-		-		23.9	2.6	-		-	
1966	23.0	0.4	-		-		23.1	0.4	-		-		23.3	0.9	-		-		25.2	1.6	-		-	
1967	24.4	2.1	-		-		24.7	1.2	-		-		24.8	0.4	-		-		26.7	2.3	-		-	
1968	25.7	2.0	-		-		25.8	0.4	-		-		26.1	1.2	-		-		29.1	2.1	-		-	
1969	27.6	3.4	-		-		28.3	2.5	-		-		28.5	0.7	-		-		30.8	0.7	-		-	
1970	29.8	2.4	-		-		30.5	2.3	-		-		30.6	0.3	-		-		32.7	-0.9	-		-	
1971	31.5	2.3	-		-		31.9	1.3	-		-		33.0	3.4	-		-		34.1	1.5	-		-	
1972	32.8	0.3	-		-		33.6	2.4	-		-		33.6	0.0	-		-		35.6	2.3	-		-	
1973	34.4	0.9	-		-		34.7	0.9	-		-		34.8	0.3	-		-		39.2	2.3	-		-	
1974	36.3	2.0	-		-		36.5	0.6	-		-		38.3	4.9	-		-		45.0	3.2	-		-	
1975	40.6	3.6	-		-		42.0	3.4	-		-		43.6	3.8	-		-		49.8	3.8	-		-	
1976	45.5	1.1	-		-		46.7	2.6	-		-		48.0	2.8	-		-		55.5	2.0	-		-	
1977	51.3	3.0	-		-		53.5	4.3	-		-		54.4	1.7	60.0	1.5	-		61.0	1.7	-		61.4	0.7
1978	57.4	3.4	-		-		58.5	1.9	-		59.1	1.0	-		65.3	1.2	-		67.6	3.5	-		67.9	0.4
1979	-		63.0	2.6	-		63.9	1.4	-		64.5	0.9	-		72.2	0.6	-		74.3	2.9	-		76.0	2.3
1980	-		69.7	2.7	-		71.0	1.9	-		71.8	1.1	-		80.9	0.9	-		82.8	2.3	-		84.1	1.6
1981	-		76.7	0.9	-		77.6	1.2	-		80.2	3.4	-		92.2	3.7	-		95.3	3.4	-		98.6	3.5
1982	-		85.6	1.8	-		87.4	2.1	-		88.9	1.7	-		101.7	0.3	-		101.5	-0.2	-		100.9	-0.6
1983	-		100.2	1.6	-		101.7	1.5	-		101.4	-0.3	-		109.7	0.8	-		111.4	1.5	-		112.5	1.0
1984	-		104.2	3.3	-		105.0	0.8	-		108.8	3.6	-		117.7	1.0	-		118.8	0.9	-		119.5	0.6
1985	-		113.9	1.2	-		115.9	1.8	-		116.5	0.5	-		124.5	0.8	-		125.6	0.5	-		126.4	0.6
1986	-		120.8	1.1	-		121.8	0.8	-		123.5	1.4	-		132.2	1.8	-		132.9	0.5	-		133.5	0.5
1987	-		127.3	0.7	-		128.6	1.0	-		129.9	1.0	-		136.0	-0.4	-		138.9	2.1	-		140.6	1.2
1988	-		134.7	0.9	-		135.6	0.7	-		136.5	0.7	-		149.9	1.1	-		151.1	0.8	-		152.2	0.7
1989	-		144.0	2.4	-		145.7	1.2	-		148.3	1.8	-		163.9	3.4	-		168.0	2.5	-		169.1	0.7
1990	-		153.7	1.0	-		158.1	2.9	-		158.5	0.3	-		180.3	3.1	-		185.1	2.7	-		186.0	0.5
1991	-		170.4	0.8	-		173.8	2.0	-		174.9	0.6	-		-		-		-		-		-	

[Continued]

Houston, TX
Consumer Price Index - All Urban Consumers
Base 1982-1984 = 100
Medical Care

[Continued]

For 1947-1995. Columns headed % show percentile change in the index from the previous period for which an index is available.

Year	Jan Index	%	Feb Index	%	Mar Index	%	Apr Index	%	May Index	%	Jun Index	%	Jul Index	%	Aug Index	%	Sep Index	%	Oct Index	%	Nov Index	%	Dec Index	%
1992	-	-	190.7	2.5	-	-	192.2	0.8	-	-	194.5	1.2	-	-	195.1	0.3	-	-	195.7	0.3	-	-	196.1	0.2
1993	-	-	200.4	2.2	-	-	201.3	0.4	-	-	200.8	-0.2	-	-	200.8	0.0	-	-	201.9	0.5	-	-	201.2	-0.3
1994	-	-	200.9	-0.1	-	-	202.1	0.6	-	-	204.7	1.3	-	-	204.6	-0.0	-	-	208.5	1.9	-	-	208.7	0.1
1995	-	-	213.2	2.2	-	-	217.3	1.9	-	-	218.7	0.6	-	-	220.1	0.6	-	-	219.5	-0.3	-	-	220.6	0.5

Source: U.S. Department of Labor, Bureau of Labor Statistics, Division of Consumer Prices and Price Indexes. - indicates no data collected for period.

Houston, TX
Consumer Price Index - Urban Wage Earners
Base 1982-1984 = 100
Medical Care

For 1947-1995. Columns headed % show percentile change in the index from the previous period for which an index is available.

Year	Jan Index	%	Feb Index	%	Mar Index	%	Apr Index	%	May Index	%	Jun Index	%	Jul Index	%	Aug Index	%	Sep Index	%	Oct Index	%	Nov Index	%	Dec Index	%
1947	13.5	-	13.6	0.7	13.6	0.0	13.7	0.7	13.9	1.5	14.0	0.7	13.9	-0.7	13.9	0.0	14.0	0.7	14.1	0.7	14.1	0.0	14.1	0.0
1948	14.1	0.0	14.1	0.0	14.3	1.4	14.2	-0.7	14.2	0.0	14.2	0.0	14.3	0.7	14.3	0.0	14.3	0.0	14.3	0.0	14.3	0.0	14.3	0.0
1949	14.4	0.7	14.4	0.0	14.4	0.0	14.5	0.7	14.6	0.7	14.7	0.7	14.6	-0.7	14.6	0.0	14.6	0.0	14.6	0.0	14.6	0.0	14.9	2.1
1950	14.9	0.0	14.9	0.0	14.9	0.0	14.9	0.0	14.9	0.0	14.9	0.0	14.9	0.0	14.9	0.0	15.0	0.7	15.0	0.0	15.0	0.0	15.0	0.0
1951	15.0	0.0	15.0	0.0	15.1	0.7	15.1	0.0	15.1	0.0	15.1	0.0	15.1	0.0	15.1	0.0	15.1	0.0	15.9	5.3	15.9	0.0	16.0	0.6
1952	15.9	-0.6	15.9	0.0	15.9	0.0	16.0	0.6	16.0	0.0	16.0	0.0	16.0	0.0	16.0	0.0	16.0	0.0	16.0	0.0	16.0	0.0	16.7	4.4
1953	-		16.7	0.0	-		-		16.8	0.6	-		-		16.8	0.0	-		-		17.0	1.2	-	
1954	-		17.0	0.0	-		-		17.0	0.0	-		-		17.1	0.6	-		-		17.1	0.0	-	
1955	-		17.1	0.0	-		-		17.7	3.5	-		-		17.8	0.6	-		-		18.1	1.7	-	
1956	-		18.2	0.6	-		-		18.0	-1.1	-		-		18.2	1.1	-		-		18.3	0.5	-	
1957	-		18.5	1.1	-		-		18.4	-0.5	-		-		18.3	-0.5	-		-		18.4	0.5	-	
1958	-		18.8	2.2	-		-		18.8	0.0	-		-		18.8	0.0	-		-		19.0	1.1	-	
1959	-		19.0	0.0	-		-		19.3	1.6	-		-		19.2	-0.5	-		-		19.2	0.0	-	
1960	-		19.4	1.0	-		-		19.7	1.5	-		-		19.7	0.0	-		-		19.8	0.5	-	
1961	-		19.7	-0.5	-		-		19.9	1.0	-		-		19.9	0.0	-		-		20.0	0.5	-	
1962	-		20.0	0.0	-		-		20.2	1.0	-		-		20.2	0.0	-		-		20.4	1.0	-	
1963	-		20.6	1.0	-		-		20.7	0.5	-		-		20.7	0.0	-		-		20.9	1.0	-	
1964	-		21.1	1.0	-		-		21.3	0.9	-		-		21.3	0.0	-		-		21.3	0.0	-	
1965	-		21.6	1.4	-		21.8	0.9	-		-		21.9	0.5	-		-		22.0	0.5	-		-	
1966	22.1	0.5	-		-		22.1	0.0	-		-		22.3	0.9	-		-		22.9	2.7	-		-	
1967	23.4	2.2	-		-		23.6	0.9	-		-		23.8	0.8	-		-		24.2	1.7	-		-	
1968	24.7	2.1	-		-		24.8	0.4	-		-		25.0	0.8	-		-		25.6	2.4	-		-	
1969	26.4	3.1	-		-		27.1	2.7	-		-		27.3	0.7	-		-		27.9	2.2	-		-	
1970	28.6	2.5	-		-		29.2	2.1	-		-		29.4	0.7	-		-		29.5	0.3	-		-	
1971	30.2	2.4	-		-		30.6	1.3	-		-		31.6	3.3	-		-		31.4	-0.6	-		-	
1972	31.5	0.3	-		-		32.2	2.2	-		-		32.2	0.0	-		-		32.7	1.6	-		-	
1973	33.0	0.9	-		-		33.3	0.9	-		-		33.4	0.3	-		-		34.1	2.1	-		-	
1974	34.8	2.1	-		-		35.0	0.6	-		-		36.7	4.9	-		-		37.6	2.5	-		-	
1975	38.9	3.5	-		-		40.3	3.6	-		-		41.8	3.7	-		-		43.2	3.3	-		-	
1976	43.6	0.9	-		-		44.8	2.8	-		-		46.1	2.9	-		-		47.8	3.7	-		-	
1977	49.2	2.9	-		-		51.3	4.3	-		-		52.2	1.8	-		-		53.2	1.9	-		-	
1978	55.0	3.4	-		-		56.1	2.0	-		56.3	0.4	-		57.8	2.7	-		58.4	1.0	-		59.0	1.0
1979	-		62.2	5.4	-		63.5	2.1	-		64.8	2.0	-		65.4	0.9	-		66.9	2.3	-		67.7	1.2
1980	-		68.6	1.3	-		70.5	2.8	-		70.6	0.1	-		72.9	3.3	-		74.0	1.5	-		75.4	1.9
1981	-		76.4	1.3	-		77.5	1.4	-		79.8	3.0	-		80.5	0.9	-		81.7	1.5	-		83.7	2.4
1982	-		85.3	1.9	-		87.1	2.1	-		88.6	1.7	-		92.1	4.0	-		95.3	3.5	-		98.8	3.7
1983	-		100.4	1.6	-		101.9	1.5	-		101.5	-0.4	-		101.7	0.2	-		101.3	-0.4	-		100.8	-0.5
1984	-		104.2	3.4	-		105.0	0.8	-		109.0	3.8	-		109.9	0.8	-		111.6	1.5	-		112.7	1.0
1985	-		114.2	1.3	-		116.2	1.8	-		116.8	0.5	-		117.9	0.9	-		119.0	0.9	-		119.6	0.5
1986	-		121.0	1.2	-		122.0	0.8	-		123.7	1.4	-		124.7	0.8	-		125.8	0.9	-		126.6	0.6
1987	-		127.6	0.8	-		129.0	1.1	-		130.4	1.1	-		132.7	1.8	-		133.4	0.5	-		134.3	0.7
1988	-		135.5	0.9	-		136.4	0.7	-		137.4	0.7	-		137.1	-0.2	-		140.1	2.2	-		141.8	1.2
1989	-		145.3	2.5	-		147.0	1.2	-		149.6	1.8	-		151.3	1.1	-		152.4	0.7	-		153.5	0.7
1990	-		154.7	0.8	-		159.3	3.0	-		159.5	0.1	-		165.0	3.4	-		169.2	2.5	-		170.3	0.7
1991	-		171.4	0.6	-		174.9	2.0	-		175.9	0.6	-		181.5	3.2	-		186.7	2.9	-		187.6	0.5

[Continued]

Houston, TX
Consumer Price Index - Urban Wage Earners
Base 1982-1984 = 100
Medical Care

[Continued]

For 1947-1995. Columns headed % show percentile change in the index from the previous period for which an index is available.

Year	Jan Index	%	Feb Index	%	Mar Index	%	Apr Index	%	May Index	%	Jun Index	%	Jul Index	%	Aug Index	%	Sep Index	%	Oct Index	%	Nov Index	%	Dec Index	%
1992	-	-	192.4	2.6	-	-	193.8	0.7	-	-	196.1	1.2	-	-	196.7	0.3	-	-	197.5	0.4	-	-	197.9	0.2
1993	-	-	202.3	2.2	-	-	203.3	0.5	-	-	202.9	-0.2	-	-	202.9	0.0	-	-	203.9	0.5	-	-	203.2	-0.3
1994	-	-	202.9	-0.1	-	-	204.0	0.5	-	-	206.7	1.3	-	-	206.5	-0.1	-	-	210.5	1.9	-	-	210.8	0.1
1995	-	-	215.3	2.1	-	-	218.9	1.7	-	-	220.4	0.7	-	-	221.9	0.7	-	-	221.0	-0.4	-	-	222.4	0.6

Source: U.S. Department of Labor, Bureau of Labor Statistics, Division of Consumer Prices and Price Indexes. - indicates no data collected for period.

Houston, TX
Consumer Price Index - All Urban Consumers
Base 1982-1984 = 100
Entertainment

For 1976-1995. Columns headed % show percentile change in the index from the previous period for which an index is available.

Year	Jan Index	%	Feb Index	%	Mar Index	%	Apr Index	%	May Index	%	Jun Index	%	Jul Index	%	Aug Index	%	Sep Index	%	Oct Index	%	Nov Index	%	Dec Index	%
1976	59.9	-	-	-	-	-	60.6	1.2	-	-	-	-	61.7	1.8	-	-	-	-	61.8	0.2	-	-	-	-
1977	63.1	2.1	-	-	-	-	63.3	0.3	-	-	-	-	64.5	1.9	-	-	-	-	64.4	-0.2	-	-	-	-
1978	64.8	0.6	-	-	-	-	65.8	1.5	-	-	64.5	-2.0	-	-	65.2	1.1	-	-	66.7	2.3	-	-	67.7	1.5
1979	-	-	68.9	1.8	-	-	69.6	1.0	-	-	69.8	0.3	-	-	70.2	0.6	-	-	71.5	1.9	-	-	71.7	0.3
1980	-	-	78.4	9.3	-	-	79.2	1.0	-	-	80.2	1.3	-	-	81.2	1.2	-	-	80.8	-0.5	-	-	81.2	0.5
1981	-	-	87.3	7.5	-	-	86.5	-0.9	-	-	86.2	-0.3	-	-	86.2	0.0	-	-	86.8	0.7	-	-	86.9	0.1
1982	-	-	88.5	1.8	-	-	89.9	1.6	-	-	94.7	5.3	-	-	94.2	-0.5	-	-	95.9	1.8	-	-	95.9	0.0
1983	-	-	102.2	6.6	-	-	102.4	0.2	-	-	103.8	1.4	-	-	105.3	1.4	-	-	104.4	-0.9	-	-	102.1	-2.2
1984	-	-	102.6	0.5	-	-	102.8	0.2	-	-	101.9	-0.9	-	-	105.1	3.1	-	-	105.5	0.4	-	-	108.4	2.7
1985	-	-	109.5	1.0	-	-	112.2	2.5	-	-	113.3	1.0	-	-	113.6	0.3	-	-	111.9	-1.5	-	-	111.7	-0.2
1986	-	-	112.2	0.4	-	-	114.6	2.1	-	-	115.3	0.6	-	-	114.8	-0.4	-	-	115.4	0.5	-	-	116.0	0.5
1987	-	-	116.9	0.8	-	-	117.4	0.4	-	-	118.2	0.7	-	-	118.7	0.4	-	-	121.0	1.9	-	-	120.2	-0.7
1988	-	-	124.5	3.6	-	-	123.3	-1.0	-	-	123.6	0.2	-	-	123.4	-0.2	-	-	125.6	1.8	-	-	129.1	2.8
1989	-	-	128.4	-0.5	-	-	132.5	3.2	-	-	137.2	3.5	-	-	136.3	-0.7	-	-	135.8	-0.4	-	-	133.6	-1.6
1990	-	-	134.2	0.4	-	-	134.8	0.4	-	-	132.8	-1.5	-	-	135.8	2.3	-	-	136.1	0.2	-	-	136.2	0.1
1991	-	-	137.4	0.9	-	-	139.4	1.5	-	-	139.8	0.3	-	-	139.7	-0.1	-	-	141.2	1.1	-	-	141.2	0.0
1992	-	-	143.2	1.4	-	-	144.7	1.0	-	-	145.0	0.2	-	-	147.4	1.7	-	-	150.6	2.2	-	-	149.8	-0.5
1993	-	-	152.9	2.1	-	-	152.2	-0.5	-	-	153.4	0.8	-	-	150.8	-1.7	-	-	158.7	5.2	-	-	151.8	-4.3
1994	-	-	156.6	3.2	-	-	155.7	-0.6	-	-	159.0	2.1	-	-	162.4	2.1	-	-	159.3	-1.9	-	-	151.0	-5.2
1995	-	-	150.3	-0.5	-	-	154.6	2.9	-	-	158.2	2.3	-	-	161.0	1.8	-	-	161.8	0.5	-	-	160.5	-0.8

Source: U.S. Department of Labor, Bureau of Labor Statistics, Division of Consumer Prices and Price Indexes. - indicates no data collected for period.

Houston, TX
Consumer Price Index - Urban Wage Earners
Base 1982-1984 = 100
Entertainment

For 1976-1995. Columns headed % show percentile change in the index from the previous period for which an index is available.

Year	Jan Index	%	Feb Index	%	Mar Index	%	Apr Index	%	May Index	%	Jun Index	%	Jul Index	%	Aug Index	%	Sep Index	%	Oct Index	%	Nov Index	%	Dec Index	%
1976	61.7	-	-	-	-	-	62.4	1.1	-	-	-	-	63.5	1.8	-	-	-	-	63.7	0.3	-	-	-	-
1977	64.9	1.9	-	-	-	-	65.2	0.5	-	-	-	-	66.4	1.8	-	-	-	-	66.3	-0.2	-	-	-	-
1978	66.7	0.6	-	-	-	-	67.7	1.5	-	-	67.0	-1.0	-	-	67.7	1.0	-	-	68.9	1.8	-	-	70.2	1.9
1979	-	-	69.9	-0.4	-	-	72.7	4.0	-	-	71.3	-1.9	-	-	71.4	0.1	-	-	72.5	1.5	-	-	72.8	0.4
1980	-	-	76.1	4.5	-	-	76.4	0.4	-	-	77.9	2.0	-	-	81.2	4.2	-	-	82.8	2.0	-	-	82.4	-0.5
1981	-	-	84.9	3.0	-	-	85.9	1.2	-	-	86.4	0.6	-	-	84.5	-2.2	-	-	85.0	0.6	-	-	85.0	0.0
1982	-	-	86.5	1.8	-	-	88.5	2.3	-	-	93.6	5.8	-	-	92.8	-0.9	-	-	94.3	1.6	-	-	94.3	0.0
1983	-	-	103.2	9.4	-	-	103.3	0.1	-	-	104.5	1.2	-	-	106.6	2.0	-	-	105.0	-1.5	-	-	103.3	-1.6
1984	-	-	103.8	0.5	-	-	103.8	0.0	-	-	101.8	-1.9	-	-	105.9	4.0	-	-	106.2	0.3	-	-	108.6	2.3
1985	-	-	109.8	1.1	-	-	112.9	2.8	-	-	113.9	0.9	-	-	114.1	0.2	-	-	113.1	-0.9	-	-	112.9	-0.2
1986	-	-	113.3	0.4	-	-	115.1	1.6	-	-	116.3	1.0	-	-	116.3	0.0	-	-	116.9	0.5	-	-	117.6	0.6
1987	-	-	118.4	0.7	-	-	118.9	0.4	-	-	119.7	0.7	-	-	120.2	0.4	-	-	122.5	1.9	-	-	121.6	-0.7
1988	-	-	126.3	3.9	-	-	124.9	-1.1	-	-	125.3	0.3	-	-	125.1	-0.2	-	-	127.5	1.9	-	-	130.9	2.7
1989	-	-	130.0	-0.7	-	-	134.3	3.3	-	-	139.3	3.7	-	-	138.3	-0.7	-	-	138.1	-0.1	-	-	135.3	-2.0
1990	-	-	135.9	0.4	-	-	136.6	0.5	-	-	134.6	-1.5	-	-	137.5	2.2	-	-	137.9	0.3	-	-	137.9	0.0
1991	-	-	139.2	0.9	-	-	141.0	1.3	-	-	141.4	0.3	-	-	141.4	0.0	-	-	142.8	1.0	-	-	142.7	-0.1
1992	-	-	144.4	1.2	-	-	146.1	1.2	-	-	146.4	0.2	-	-	149.0	1.8	-	-	153.8	3.2	-	-	152.8	-0.7
1993	-	-	155.8	2.0	-	-	155.1	-0.4	-	-	156.3	0.8	-	-	153.7	-1.7	-	-	161.9	5.3	-	-	154.7	-4.4
1994	-	-	159.4	3.0	-	-	158.4	-0.6	-	-	161.6	2.0	-	-	165.3	2.3	-	-	161.9	-2.1	-	-	155.5	-4.0
1995	-	-	153.5	-1.3	-	-	158.3	3.1	-	-	162.0	2.3	-	-	165.4	2.1	-	-	166.0	0.4	-	-	165.2	-0.5

Source: U.S. Department of Labor, Bureau of Labor Statistics, Division of Consumer Prices and Price Indexes. - indicates no data collected for period.

527

Houston, TX
Consumer Price Index - All Urban Consumers
Base 1982-1984 = 100
Other Goods and Services

For 1976-1995. Columns headed % show percentile change in the index from the previous period for which an index is available.

Year	Jan Index	%	Feb Index	%	Mar Index	%	Apr Index	%	May Index	%	Jun Index	%	Jul Index	%	Aug Index	%	Sep Index	%	Oct Index	%	Nov Index	%	Dec Index	%
1976	55.4	-	-	-	-	-	56.1	1.3	-	-	-	-	56.1	0.0	-	-	-	-	56.8	1.2	-	-	-	-
1977	58.5	3.0	-	-	-	-	59.2	1.2	-	-	-	-	59.3	0.2	-	-	-	-	60.8	2.5	-	-	-	-
1978	62.6	3.0	-	-	-	-	64.0	2.2	-	-	64.6	0.9	-	-	66.1	2.3	-	-	68.0	2.9	-	-	68.7	1.0
1979	-	-	69.9	1.7	-	-	71.0	1.6	-	-	71.2	0.3	-	-	71.6	0.6	-	-	73.2	2.2	-	-	74.8	2.2
1980	-	-	76.8	2.7	-	-	78.1	1.7	-	-	78.9	1.0	-	-	79.6	0.9	-	-	81.7	2.6	-	-	82.9	1.5
1981	-	-	83.6	0.8	-	-	84.3	0.8	-	-	85.4	1.3	-	-	85.7	0.4	-	-	87.1	1.6	-	-	86.8	-0.3
1982	-	-	88.0	1.4	-	-	89.6	1.8	-	-	91.3	1.9	-	-	92.6	1.4	-	-	94.6	2.2	-	-	97.6	3.2
1983	-	-	99.8	2.3	-	-	99.6	-0.2	-	-	100.4	0.8	-	-	101.1	0.7	-	-	103.3	2.2	-	-	103.1	-0.2
1984	-	-	105.2	2.0	-	-	105.6	0.4	-	-	106.0	0.4	-	-	108.3	2.2	-	-	109.6	1.2	-	-	110.2	0.5
1985	-	-	111.0	0.7	-	-	111.1	0.1	-	-	111.5	0.4	-	-	112.1	0.5	-	-	115.2	2.8	-	-	115.2	0.0
1986	-	-	116.3	1.0	-	-	117.2	0.8	-	-	117.2	0.0	-	-	119.0	1.5	-	-	122.1	2.6	-	-	121.2	-0.7
1987	-	-	123.4	1.8	-	-	123.2	-0.2	-	-	123.6	0.3	-	-	124.3	0.6	-	-	127.8	2.8	-	-	128.1	0.2
1988	-	-	129.3	0.9	-	-	128.7	-0.5	-	-	130.1	1.1	-	-	133.1	2.3	-	-	133.6	0.4	-	-	133.5	-0.1
1989	-	-	134.5	0.7	-	-	135.0	0.4	-	-	134.4	-0.4	-	-	137.7	2.5	-	-	146.5	6.4	-	-	146.0	-0.3
1990	-	-	147.2	0.8	-	-	150.1	2.0	-	-	151.4	0.9	-	-	156.6	3.4	-	-	156.6	0.0	-	-	152.4	-2.7
1991	-	-	155.3	1.9	-	-	157.5	1.4	-	-	157.2	-0.2	-	-	159.0	1.1	-	-	160.7	1.1	-	-	157.6	-1.9
1992	-	-	161.7	2.6	-	-	168.9	4.5	-	-	172.6	2.2	-	-	176.8	2.4	-	-	178.8	1.1	-	-	179.0	0.1
1993	-	-	180.7	0.9	-	-	181.0	0.2	-	-	179.8	-0.7	-	-	179.3	-0.3	-	-	181.3	1.1	-	-	184.0	1.5
1994	-	-	184.6	0.3	-	-	186.6	1.1	-	-	186.8	0.1	-	-	187.9	0.6	-	-	191.3	1.8	-	-	189.9	-0.7
1995	-	-	188.5	-0.7	-	-	191.9	1.8	-	-	192.6	0.4	-	-	192.5	-0.1	-	-	198.5	3.1	-	-	198.7	0.1

Source: U.S. Department of Labor, Bureau of Labor Statistics, Division of Consumer Prices and Price Indexes. - indicates no data collected for period.

Houston, TX
Consumer Price Index - Urban Wage Earners
Base 1982-1984 = 100
Other Goods and Services

For 1976-1995. Columns headed % show percentile change in the index from the previous period for which an index is available.

Year	Jan Index	%	Feb Index	%	Mar Index	%	Apr Index	%	May Index	%	Jun Index	%	Jul Index	%	Aug Index	%	Sep Index	%	Oct Index	%	Nov Index	%	Dec Index	%
1976	55.3	-	-	-	-	-	55.9	1.1	-	-	-	-	56.0	0.2	-	-	-	-	56.6	1.1	-	-	-	-
1977	58.3	3.0	-	-	-	-	59.0	1.2	-	-	-	-	59.1	0.2	-	-	-	-	60.7	2.7	-	-	-	-
1978	62.4	2.8	-	-	-	-	63.8	2.2	-	-	64.5	1.1	-	-	64.8	0.5	-	-	67.0	3.4	-	-	66.2	-1.2
1979	-	-	69.2	4.5	-	-	70.5	1.9	-	-	69.8	-1.0	-	-	71.1	1.9	-	-	71.6	0.7	-	-	73.1	2.1
1980	-	-	76.3	4.4	-	-	77.1	1.0	-	-	79.1	2.6	-	-	78.4	-0.9	-	-	80.8	3.1	-	-	81.1	0.4
1981	-	-	81.3	0.2	-	-	82.5	1.5	-	-	85.7	3.9	-	-	85.9	0.2	-	-	86.7	0.9	-	-	87.0	0.3
1982	-	-	88.2	1.4	-	-	89.9	1.9	-	-	90.8	1.0	-	-	92.1	1.4	-	-	94.2	2.3	-	-	97.7	3.7
1983	-	-	100.1	2.5	-	-	99.9	-0.2	-	-	100.3	0.4	-	-	101.1	0.8	-	-	103.1	2.0	-	-	102.9	-0.2
1984	-	-	105.0	2.0	-	-	105.5	0.5	-	-	106.2	0.7	-	-	108.6	2.3	-	-	109.9	1.2	-	-	110.5	0.5
1985	-	-	111.4	0.8	-	-	111.5	0.1	-	-	111.6	0.1	-	-	112.2	0.5	-	-	114.5	2.0	-	-	114.1	-0.3
1986	-	-	115.2	1.0	-	-	116.3	1.0	-	-	116.3	0.0	-	-	118.3	1.7	-	-	120.4	1.8	-	-	119.5	-0.7
1987	-	-	121.4	1.6	-	-	121.2	-0.2	-	-	121.8	0.5	-	-	122.6	0.7	-	-	126.3	3.0	-	-	126.4	0.1
1988	-	-	127.9	1.2	-	-	127.1	-0.6	-	-	128.9	1.4	-	-	133.2	3.3	-	-	133.7	0.4	-	-	133.7	0.0
1989	-	-	135.1	1.0	-	-	135.7	0.4	-	-	134.7	-0.7	-	-	139.6	3.6	-	-	146.8	5.2	-	-	146.0	-0.5
1990	-	-	147.4	1.0	-	-	150.4	2.0	-	-	151.7	0.9	-	-	158.3	4.4	-	-	158.1	-0.1	-	-	152.2	-3.7
1991	-	-	155.5	2.2	-	-	157.6	1.4	-	-	157.4	-0.1	-	-	158.6	0.8	-	-	161.3	1.7	-	-	157.0	-2.7
1992	-	-	162.3	3.4	-	-	166.7	2.7	-	-	171.7	3.0	-	-	176.3	2.7	-	-	178.8	1.4	-	-	179.0	0.1
1993	-	-	181.2	1.2	-	-	181.5	0.2	-	-	179.3	-1.2	-	-	176.4	-1.6	-	-	178.4	1.1	-	-	181.6	1.8
1994	-	-	182.3	0.4	-	-	184.7	1.3	-	-	184.8	0.1	-	-	185.4	0.3	-	-	188.2	1.5	-	-	186.2	-1.1
1995	-	-	185.1	-0.6	-	-	188.5	1.8	-	-	189.6	0.6	-	-	189.3	-0.2	-	-	194.9	3.0	-	-	194.9	0.0

Source: U.S. Department of Labor, Bureau of Labor Statistics, Division of Consumer Prices and Price Indexes. - indicates no data collected for period.

Kansas City, MO-KS
Consumer Price Index - All Urban Consumers
Base 1982-1984 = 100
Annual Averages

For 1917-1995. Columns headed % show percentile change in the index from the previous period for which an index is available.

Year	All Items		Food & Beverage		Housing		Apparel & Upkeep		Trans-portation		Medical Care		Entertain-ment		Other Goods & Services	
	Index	%	Index	%	Index	%	Index	%	Index	%	Index	%	Index	%	Index	%
1917	-	-	-	-	-	-	-	-	-	-	-	-	-	-	-	-
1918	16.1	-	-	-	-	-	-	-	-	-	-	-	-	-	-	-
1919	18.5	14.9	-	-	-	-	-	-	-	-	-	-	-	-	-	-
1920	21.7	17.3	-	-	-	-	-	-	-	-	-	-	-	-	-	-
1921	19.2	-11.5	-	-	-	-	-	-	-	-	-	-	-	-	-	-
1922	17.5	-8.9	-	-	-	-	-	-	-	-	-	-	-	-	-	-
1923	17.4	-0.6	-	-	-	-	-	-	-	-	-	-	-	-	-	-
1924	17.3	-0.6	-	-	-	-	-	-	-	-	-	-	-	-	-	-
1925	17.5	1.2	-	-	-	-	-	-	-	-	-	-	-	-	-	-
1926	17.5	0.0	-	-	-	-	-	-	-	-	-	-	-	-	-	-
1927	17.0	-2.9	-	-	-	-	-	-	-	-	-	-	-	-	-	-
1928	16.7	-1.8	-	-	-	-	-	-	-	-	-	-	-	-	-	-
1929	16.8	0.6	-	-	-	-	-	-	-	-	-	-	-	-	-	-
1930	16.5	-1.8	-	-	-	-	-	-	-	-	-	-	-	-	-	-
1931	15.5	-6.1	-	-	-	-	-	-	-	-	-	-	-	-	-	-
1932	13.9	-10.3	-	-	-	-	-	-	-	-	-	-	-	-	-	-
1933	13.3	-4.3	-	-	-	-	-	-	-	-	-	-	-	-	-	-
1934	13.7	3.0	-	-	-	-	-	-	-	-	-	-	-	-	-	-
1935	14.0	2.2	-	-	-	-	-	-	-	-	-	-	-	-	-	-
1936	14.1	0.7	-	-	-	-	-	-	-	-	-	-	-	-	-	-
1937	14.6	3.5	-	-	-	-	-	-	-	-	-	-	-	-	-	-
1938	14.3	-2.1	-	-	-	-	-	-	-	-	-	-	-	-	-	-
1939	14.1	-1.4	-	-	-	-	-	-	-	-	-	-	-	-	-	-
1940	14.0	-0.7	-	-	-	-	-	-	-	-	-	-	-	-	-	-
1941	14.7	5.0	-	-	-	-	-	-	-	-	-	-	-	-	-	-
1942	16.3	10.9	-	-	-	-	-	-	-	-	-	-	-	-	-	-
1943	17.3	6.1	-	-	-	-	-	-	-	-	-	-	-	-	-	-
1944	17.6	1.7	-	-	-	-	-	-	-	-	-	-	-	-	-	-
1945	18.1	2.8	-	-	-	-	-	-	-	-	-	-	-	-	-	-
1946	19.3	6.6	-	-	-	-	-	-	-	-	-	-	-	-	-	-
1947	21.9	13.5	-	-	-	-	-	-	18.2	-	11.0	-	-	-	-	-
1948	23.6	7.8	-	-	-	-	-	-	20.2	11.0	11.9	8.2	-	-	-	-
1949	23.3	-1.3	-	-	-	-	-	-	21.5	6.4	12.2	2.5	-	-	-	-
1950	23.7	1.7	-	-	-	-	-	-	21.9	1.9	12.4	1.6	-	-	-	-
1951	25.5	7.6	-	-	-	-	-	-	23.2	5.9	13.0	4.8	-	-	-	-
1952	26.3	3.1	-	-	-	-	-	-	25.4	9.5	13.7	5.4	-	-	-	-
1953	26.4	0.4	-	-	-	-	39.2	-	26.0	2.4	14.0	2.2	-	-	-	-
1954	26.5	0.4	-	-	-	-	38.9	-0.8	25.2	-3.1	15.6	11.4	-	-	-	-
1955	26.5	0.0	-	-	-	-	38.9	0.0	25.0	-0.8	15.9	1.9	-	-	-	-
1956	26.9	1.5	-	-	-	-	39.4	1.3	25.4	1.6	16.6	4.4	-	-	-	-
1957	27.8	3.3	-	-	-	-	40.3	2.3	27.6	8.7	17.7	6.6	-	-	-	-
1958	28.5	2.5	-	-	-	-	40.4	0.2	29.1	5.4	19.0	7.3	-	-	-	-
1959	28.9	1.4	-	-	-	-	40.7	0.7	30.6	5.2	20.0	5.3	-	-	-	-
1960	29.3	1.4	-	-	-	-	41.7	2.5	30.6	0.0	20.3	1.5	-	-	-	-
1961	29.6	1.0	-	-	-	-	42.0	0.7	30.6	0.0	21.1	3.9	-	-	-	-

[Continued]

Kansas City, MO-KS
Consumer Price Index - All Urban Consumers
Base 1982-1984 = 100
Annual Averages
[Continued]

For 1917-1995. Columns headed % show percentile change in the index from the previous period for which an index is available.

Year	All Items		Food & Beverage		Housing		Apparel & Upkeep		Trans-portation		Medical Care		Entertain-ment		Other Goods & Services	
	Index	%	Index	%	Index	%	Index	%	Index	%	Index	%	Index	%	Index	%
1962	30.1	1.7	-	-	-	-	42.0	0.0	31.3	2.3	21.5	1.9	-	-	-	-
1963	30.4	1.0	-	-	-	-	42.6	1.4	31.3	0.0	21.7	0.9	-	-	-	-
1964	31.2	2.6	-	-	-	-	43.6	2.3	31.6	1.0	22.8	5.1	-	-	-	-
1965	32.2	3.2	-	-	-	-	44.5	2.1	33.8	7.0	24.0	5.3	-	-	-	-
1966	33.0	2.5	-	-	-	-	45.7	2.7	34.5	2.1	25.3	5.4	-	-	-	-
1967	33.7	2.1	-	-	-	-	47.3	3.5	34.7	0.6	27.2	7.5	-	-	-	-
1968	35.0	3.9	-	-	-	-	50.8	7.4	35.5	2.3	28.9	6.3	-	-	-	-
1969	36.9	5.4	-	-	-	-	54.4	7.1	37.2	4.8	30.4	5.2	-	-	-	-
1970	39.0	5.7	-	-	-	-	57.4	5.5	38.2	2.7	31.8	4.6	-	-	-	-
1971	40.6	4.1	-	-	-	-	58.9	2.6	41.0	7.3	33.8	6.3	-	-	-	-
1972	41.8	3.0	-	-	-	-	60.3	2.4	41.0	0.0	35.1	3.8	-	-	-	-
1973	43.9	5.0	-	-	-	-	61.8	2.5	42.6	3.9	36.7	4.6	-	-	-	-
1974	48.6	10.7	-	-	-	-	65.7	6.3	47.3	11.0	40.1	9.3	-	-	-	-
1975	53.2	9.5	-	-	-	-	69.0	5.0	51.5	8.9	43.6	8.7	-	-	-	-
1976	56.1	5.5	62.9	-	52.7	-	70.7	2.5	55.5	7.8	47.3	8.5	65.3	-	57.7	-
1977	60.0	7.0	67.0	6.5	56.6	7.4	77.0	8.9	59.2	6.7	51.8	9.5	68.3	4.6	61.4	6.4
1978	64.6	7.7	74.6	11.3	61.5	8.7	79.0	2.6	62.1	4.9	56.7	9.5	70.9	3.8	64.7	5.4
1979	73.8	14.2	82.6	10.7	72.1	17.2	84.3	6.7	72.3	16.4	63.7	12.3	74.2	4.7	69.9	8.0
1980	83.6	13.3	89.6	8.5	82.7	14.7	87.6	3.9	85.0	17.6	70.9	11.3	83.1	12.0	76.7	9.7
1981	90.5	8.3	95.0	6.0	89.5	8.2	92.3	5.4	93.2	9.6	79.7	12.4	90.4	8.8	84.5	10.2
1982	95.0	5.0	97.5	2.6	93.8	4.8	95.7	3.7	97.5	4.6	91.0	14.2	95.8	6.0	91.3	8.0
1983	100.5	5.8	99.2	1.7	101.2	7.9	101.8	6.4	99.5	2.1	101.1	11.1	99.9	4.3	100.6	10.2
1984	104.5	4.0	103.3	4.1	105.0	3.8	102.5	0.7	103.0	3.5	107.8	6.6	104.3	4.4	108.1	7.5
1985	107.7	3.1	106.0	2.6	107.6	2.5	105.0	2.4	106.5	3.4	111.7	3.6	107.0	2.6	115.7	7.0
1986	108.7	0.9	109.5	3.3	109.4	1.7	107.0	1.9	100.0	-6.1	117.7	5.4	111.0	3.7	125.5	8.5
1987	113.1	4.0	112.8	3.0	113.6	3.8	109.7	2.5	102.9	2.9	123.4	4.8	123.6	11.4	134.9	7.5
1988	117.4	3.8	115.8	2.7	118.3	4.1	113.1	3.1	107.2	4.2	130.8	6.0	124.2	0.5	141.6	5.0
1989	121.6	3.6	119.9	3.5	119.6	1.1	119.7	5.8	112.2	4.7	142.0	8.6	132.0	6.3	152.3	7.6
1990	126.0	3.6	127.5	6.3	121.8	1.8	116.5	-2.7	116.2	3.6	156.8	10.4	142.0	7.6	159.6	4.8
1991	131.2	4.1	130.9	2.7	125.4	3.0	124.7	7.0	119.2	2.6	173.5	10.7	149.3	5.1	175.7	10.1
1992	134.3	2.4	132.9	1.5	127.2	1.4	124.8	0.1	121.8	2.2	183.8	5.9	154.0	3.1	189.4	7.8
1993	138.1	2.8	137.7	3.6	130.4	2.5	125.3	0.4	124.7	2.4	195.6	6.4	152.5	-1.0	196.7	3.9
1994	141.3	2.3	140.2	1.8	133.1	2.1	123.3	-1.6	128.1	2.7	202.9	3.7	160.5	5.2	203.5	3.5
1995	145.3	2.8	144.6	3.1	136.7	2.7	125.8	2.0	133.4	4.1	208.5	2.8	160.4	-0.1	208.4	2.4

Source: U.S. Department of Labor, Bureau of Labor Statistics, Division of Consumer Prices and Price Indexes. - indicates no data collected for period.

Kansas City, MO-KS
Consumer Price Index - Urban Wage Earners
Base 1982-1984 = 100
Annual Averages

For 1917-1995. Columns headed % show percentile change in the index from the previous period for which an index is available.

Year	All Items		Food & Beverage		Housing		Apparel & Upkeep		Trans- portation		Medical Care		Entertain- ment		Other Goods & Services	
	Index	%	Index	%	Index	%	Index	%	Index	%	Index	%	Index	%	Index	%
1917	-	-	-	-	-	-	-	-	-	-	-	-	-	-	-	-
1918	16.3	-	-	-	-	-	-	-	-	-	-	-	-	-	-	-
1919	18.7	14.7	-	-	-	-	-	-	-	-	-	-	-	-	-	-
1920	22.0	17.6	-	-	-	-	-	-	-	-	-	-	-	-	-	-
1921	19.4	-11.8	-	-	-	-	-	-	-	-	-	-	-	-	-	-
1922	17.7	-8.8	-	-	-	-	-	-	-	-	-	-	-	-	-	-
1923	17.7	0.0	-	-	-	-	-	-	-	-	-	-	-	-	-	-
1924	17.5	-1.1	-	-	-	-	-	-	-	-	-	-	-	-	-	-
1925	17.8	1.7	-	-	-	-	-	-	-	-	-	-	-	-	-	-
1926	17.8	0.0	-	-	-	-	-	-	-	-	-	-	-	-	-	-
1927	17.2	-3.4	-	-	-	-	-	-	-	-	-	-	-	-	-	-
1928	16.9	-1.7	-	-	-	-	-	-	-	-	-	-	-	-	-	-
1929	17.0	0.6	-	-	-	-	-	-	-	-	-	-	-	-	-	-
1930	16.7	-1.8	-	-	-	-	-	-	-	-	-	-	-	-	-	-
1931	15.7	-6.0	-	-	-	-	-	-	-	-	-	-	-	-	-	-
1932	14.1	-10.2	-	-	-	-	-	-	-	-	-	-	-	-	-	-
1933	13.4	-5.0	-	-	-	-	-	-	-	-	-	-	-	-	-	-
1934	13.9	3.7	-	-	-	-	-	-	-	-	-	-	-	-	-	-
1935	14.2	2.2	-	-	-	-	-	-	-	-	-	-	-	-	-	-
1936	14.3	0.7	-	-	-	-	-	-	-	-	-	-	-	-	-	-
1937	14.8	3.5	-	-	-	-	-	-	-	-	-	-	-	-	-	-
1938	14.5	-2.0	-	-	-	-	-	-	-	-	-	-	-	-	-	-
1939	14.3	-1.4	-	-	-	-	-	-	-	-	-	-	-	-	-	-
1940	14.2	-0.7	-	-	-	-	-	-	-	-	-	-	-	-	-	-
1941	14.9	4.9	-	-	-	-	-	-	-	-	-	-	-	-	-	-
1942	16.5	10.7	-	-	-	-	-	-	-	-	-	-	-	-	-	-
1943	17.5	6.1	-	-	-	-	-	-	-	-	-	-	-	-	-	-
1944	17.8	1.7	-	-	-	-	-	-	-	-	-	-	-	-	-	-
1945	18.3	2.8	-	-	-	-	-	-	-	-	-	-	-	-	-	-
1946	19.6	7.1	-	-	-	-	-	-	-	-	-	-	-	-	-	-
1947	22.2	13.3	-	-	-	-	-	-	18.1	-	11.0	-	-	-	-	-
1948	23.9	7.7	-	-	-	-	-	-	20.1	11.0	11.9	8.2	-	-	-	-
1949	23.7	-0.8	-	-	-	-	-	-	21.3	6.0	12.2	2.5	-	-	-	-
1950	24.0	1.3	-	-	-	-	-	-	21.8	2.3	12.4	1.6	-	-	-	-
1951	25.8	7.5	-	-	-	-	-	-	23.0	5.5	13.0	4.8	-	-	-	-
1952	26.6	3.1	-	-	-	-	-	-	25.2	9.6	13.7	5.4	-	-	-	-
1953	26.7	0.4	-	-	-	-	40.5	-	25.8	2.4	14.0	2.2	-	-	-	-
1954	26.9	0.7	-	-	-	-	40.1	-1.0	25.1	-2.7	15.6	11.4	-	-	-	-
1955	26.9	0.0	-	-	-	-	40.1	0.0	24.9	-0.8	15.9	1.9	-	-	-	-
1956	27.3	1.5	-	-	-	-	40.6	1.2	25.3	1.6	16.6	4.4	-	-	-	-
1957	28.2	3.3	-	-	-	-	41.5	2.2	27.4	8.3	17.7	6.6	-	-	-	-
1958	28.8	2.1	-	-	-	-	41.6	0.2	28.9	5.5	19.0	7.3	-	-	-	-
1959	29.3	1.7	-	-	-	-	42.0	1.0	30.4	5.2	20.0	5.3	-	-	-	-
1960	29.7	1.4	-	-	-	-	43.0	2.4	30.4	0.0	20.3	1.5	-	-	-	-
1961	30.0	1.0	-	-	-	-	43.3	0.7	30.4	0.0	21.1	3.9	-	-	-	-

[Continued]

532

Kansas City, MO-KS
Consumer Price Index - Urban Wage Earners
Base 1982-1984 = 100
Annual Averages
[Continued]

For 1917-1995. Columns headed % show percentile change in the index from the previous period for which an index is available.

Year	All Items		Food & Beverage		Housing		Apparel & Upkeep		Trans-portation		Medical Care		Entertain-ment		Other Goods & Services	
	Index	%	Index	%	Index	%	Index	%	Index	%	Index	%	Index	%	Index	%
1962	30.5	1.7	-	-	-	-	43.3	0.0	31.1	2.3	21.5	1.9	-	-	-	-
1963	30.8	1.0	-	-	-	-	43.9	1.4	31.1	0.0	21.7	0.9	-	-	-	-
1964	31.6	2.6	-	-	-	-	45.0	2.5	31.4	1.0	22.8	5.1	-	-	-	-
1965	32.6	3.2	-	-	-	-	45.9	2.0	33.6	7.0	24.0	5.3	-	-	-	-
1966	33.4	2.5	-	-	-	-	47.1	2.6	34.3	2.1	25.3	5.4	-	-	-	-
1967	34.1	2.1	-	-	-	-	48.8	3.6	34.5	0.6	27.2	7.5	-	-	-	-
1968	35.5	4.1	-	-	-	-	52.4	7.4	35.3	2.3	28.9	6.3	-	-	-	-
1969	37.4	5.4	-	-	-	-	56.1	7.1	36.9	4.5	30.4	5.2	-	-	-	-
1970	39.5	5.6	-	-	-	-	59.2	5.5	38.0	3.0	31.8	4.6	-	-	-	-
1971	41.1	4.1	-	-	-	-	60.7	2.5	40.8	7.4	33.8	6.3	-	-	-	-
1972	42.3	2.9	-	-	-	-	62.2	2.5	40.8	0.0	35.1	3.8	-	-	-	-
1973	44.5	5.2	-	-	-	-	63.7	2.4	42.4	3.9	36.7	4.6	-	-	-	-
1974	49.2	10.6	-	-	-	-	67.8	6.4	47.0	10.8	40.1	9.3	-	-	-	-
1975	53.9	9.6	-	-	-	-	71.1	4.9	51.2	8.9	43.6	8.7	-	-	-	-
1976	56.8	5.4	63.7	-	53.8	-	72.9	2.5	55.2	7.8	47.3	8.5	61.9	-	57.9	-
1977	60.9	7.2	67.8	6.4	57.8	7.4	79.4	8.9	58.8	6.5	51.8	9.5	64.7	4.5	61.6	6.4
1978	65.5	7.6	75.0	10.6	62.9	8.8	82.1	3.4	61.7	4.9	56.4	8.9	66.8	3.2	65.1	5.7
1979	74.4	13.6	82.0	9.3	73.2	16.4	84.4	2.8	72.2	17.0	63.9	13.3	71.1	6.4	71.4	9.7
1980	84.1	13.0	89.1	8.7	83.4	13.9	87.0	3.1	85.0	17.7	71.3	11.6	82.4	15.9	78.6	10.1
1981	91.2	8.4	94.7	6.3	90.3	8.3	92.3	6.1	93.7	10.2	79.2	11.1	90.4	9.7	84.9	8.0
1982	95.7	4.9	97.5	3.0	94.9	5.1	95.8	3.8	97.5	4.1	91.0	14.9	95.6	5.8	91.2	7.4
1983	101.3	5.9	99.3	1.8	103.2	8.7	102.2	6.7	99.5	2.1	101.1	11.1	100.0	4.6	100.7	10.4
1984	103.0	1.7	103.2	3.9	102.0	-1.2	102.1	-0.1	103.1	3.6	107.9	6.7	104.4	4.4	108.0	7.2
1985	105.7	2.6	105.8	2.5	103.5	1.5	105.7	3.5	106.5	3.3	111.8	3.6	107.0	2.5	115.5	6.9
1986	106.1	0.4	109.4	3.4	105.2	1.6	106.7	0.9	99.2	-6.9	117.6	5.2	110.6	3.4	125.3	8.5
1987	110.2	3.9	112.7	3.0	109.0	3.6	110.4	3.5	101.2	2.0	123.8	5.3	122.8	11.0	134.6	7.4
1988	114.4	3.8	115.8	2.8	113.4	4.0	114.2	3.4	105.5	4.2	131.6	6.3	123.1	0.2	141.4	5.1
1989	118.5	3.6	119.8	3.5	114.8	1.2	120.3	5.3	109.9	4.2	143.0	8.7	130.5	6.0	153.1	8.3
1990	122.4	3.3	127.4	6.3	117.0	1.9	116.8	-2.9	112.6	2.5	157.6	10.2	140.4	7.6	160.1	4.6
1991	127.4	4.1	131.0	2.8	120.2	2.7	125.6	7.5	115.9	2.9	173.7	10.2	147.6	5.1	176.8	10.4
1992	130.4	2.4	132.7	1.3	121.9	1.4	125.1	-0.4	119.1	2.8	184.2	6.0	152.7	3.5	191.3	8.2
1993	134.3	3.0	137.8	3.8	125.1	2.6	126.1	0.8	122.2	2.6	196.7	6.8	152.1	-0.4	198.5	3.8
1994	137.5	2.4	140.2	1.7	127.7	2.1	124.2	-1.5	126.1	3.2	203.9	3.7	160.4	5.5	205.5	3.5
1995	141.7	3.1	144.6	3.1	131.0	2.6	126.8	2.1	131.8	4.5	209.0	2.5	160.0	-0.2	210.9	2.6

Source: U.S. Department of Labor, Bureau of Labor Statistics, Division of Consumer Prices and Price Indexes. - indicates no data collected for period.

Kansas City, MO-KS
Consumer Price Index - All Urban Consumers
Base 1982-1984 = 100
All Items

For 1917-1995. Columns headed % show percentile change in the index from the previous period for which an index is available.

Year	Jan Index	%	Feb Index	%	Mar Index	%	Apr Index	%	May Index	%	Jun Index	%	Jul Index	%	Aug Index	%	Sep Index	%	Oct Index	%	Nov Index	%	Dec Index	%
1917	-	-	-	-	-	-	-	-	-	-	-	-	-	-	-	-	-	-	-	-	-	-	14.8	-
1918	-	-	-	-	-	-	-	-	-	-	-	-	-	-	-	-	-	-	-	-	-	-	17.6	18.9
1919	-	-	-	-	-	-	-	-	-	-	17.7	0.6	-	-	-	-	-	-	-	-	-	-	20.4	15.3
1920	-	-	-	-	-	-	-	-	-	-	22.8	11.8	-	-	-	-	-	-	-	-	-	-	20.7	-9.2
1921	-	-	-	-	-	-	-	-	19.1	-7.7	-	-	-	-	-	-	18.7	-2.1	-	-	-	-	18.5	-1.1
1922	-	-	-	-	17.4	-5.9	-	-	-	-	17.4	0.0	-	-	-	-	17.3	-0.6	-	-	-	-	17.4	0.6
1923	-	-	-	-	17.4	0.0	-	-	-	-	17.4	0.0	-	-	-	-	17.5	0.6	-	-	-	-	17.5	0.0
1924	-	-	-	-	17.4	-0.6	-	-	-	-	17.2	-1.1	-	-	-	-	17.1	-0.6	-	-	-	-	17.3	1.2
1925	-	-	-	-	-	-	-	-	-	-	17.5	1.2	-	-	-	-	-	-	-	-	-	-	17.8	1.7
1926	-	-	-	-	-	-	-	-	-	-	17.7	-0.6	-	-	-	-	-	-	-	-	-	-	17.4	-1.7
1927	-	-	-	-	-	-	-	-	-	-	17.3	-0.6	-	-	-	-	-	-	-	-	-	-	16.7	-3.5
1928	-	-	-	-	-	-	-	-	-	-	16.7	0.0	-	-	-	-	-	-	-	-	-	-	16.7	0.0
1929	-	-	-	-	-	-	-	-	-	-	16.6	-0.6	-	-	-	-	-	-	-	-	-	-	16.8	1.2
1930	-	-	-	-	-	-	-	-	-	-	16.6	-1.2	-	-	-	-	-	-	-	-	-	-	16.1	-3.0
1931	-	-	-	-	-	-	-	-	-	-	15.5	-3.7	-	-	-	-	-	-	-	-	-	-	14.9	-3.9
1932	-	-	-	-	-	-	-	-	-	-	13.8	-7.4	-	-	-	-	-	-	-	-	-	-	13.5	-2.2
1933	-	-	-	-	-	-	-	-	-	-	13.2	-2.2	-	-	-	-	-	-	-	-	-	-	13.4	1.5
1934	-	-	-	-	-	-	-	-	-	-	13.6	1.5	-	-	-	-	-	-	-	-	13.8	1.5	-	-
1935	-	-	-	-	13.9	0.7	-	-	-	-	-	-	13.8	-0.7	-	-	-	-	13.9	0.7	-	-	-	-
1936	14.1	1.4	-	-	-	-	13.9	-1.4	-	-	-	-	14.1	1.4	-	-	14.3	1.4	-	-	-	-	14.2	-0.7
1937	-	-	-	-	14.5	2.1	-	-	-	-	14.7	1.4	-	-	-	-	14.8	0.7	-	-	-	-	14.6	-1.4
1938	-	-	-	-	14.4	-1.4	-	-	-	-	14.3	-0.7	-	-	-	-	14.3	0.0	-	-	-	-	14.2	-0.7
1939	-	-	-	-	14.1	-0.7	-	-	-	-	14.1	0.0	-	-	-	-	14.3	1.4	-	-	-	-	14.1	-1.4
1940	-	-	-	-	14.0	-0.7	-	-	-	-	14.0	0.0	-	-	-	-	13.9	-0.7	13.9	0.0	14.0	0.7	14.0	0.0
1941	14.0	0.0	14.0	0.0	14.1	0.7	14.3	1.4	14.3	0.0	14.5	1.4	14.5	0.0	14.7	1.4	15.1	2.7	15.3	1.3	15.4	0.7	15.5	0.6
1942	15.6	0.6	15.8	1.3	16.1	1.9	16.2	0.6	16.3	0.6	16.3	0.0	16.2	-0.6	16.4	1.2	16.3	-0.6	16.6	1.8	16.7	0.6	16.8	0.6
1943	16.8	0.0	16.9	0.6	17.2	1.8	17.4	1.2	17.4	0.0	17.4	0.0	17.2	-1.1	17.2	0.0	17.3	0.6	17.4	0.6	17.4	0.0	17.4	0.0
1944	17.4	0.0	17.4	0.0	17.4	0.0	17.5	0.6	17.6	0.6	17.6	0.0	17.7	0.6	17.6	-0.6	17.7	0.6	17.7	0.0	17.7	0.0	17.8	0.6
1945	17.8	0.0	17.8	0.0	17.8	0.0	17.9	0.6	18.0	0.6	18.1	0.6	18.2	0.6	18.2	0.0	18.1	-0.5	18.1	0.0	18.2	0.6	18.3	0.5
1946	18.3	0.0	18.2	-0.5	18.2	0.0	18.3	0.5	18.4	0.5	18.5	0.5	19.5	5.4	20.1	3.1	20.1	0.0	20.3	1.0	21.0	3.4	21.0	0.0
1947	21.1	0.5	21.2	0.5	21.5	1.4	21.6	0.5	21.5	-0.5	21.4	-0.5	21.5	0.5	-	-	-	-	22.6	5.1	-	-	-	-
1948	23.2	2.7	-	-	-	-	23.3	0.4	-	-	-	-	23.8	2.1	-	-	-	-	24.0	0.8	-	-	-	-
1949	23.6	-1.7	-	-	-	-	23.4	-0.8	-	-	-	-	23.3	-0.4	-	-	-	-	23.2	-0.4	-	-	-	-
1950	23.1	-0.4	-	-	-	-	23.3	0.9	-	-	-	-	23.8	2.1	-	-	-	-	24.1	1.3	-	-	-	-
1951	25.0	3.7	-	-	-	-	25.5	2.0	-	-	-	-	25.6	0.4	-	-	-	-	25.7	0.4	-	-	-	-
1952	26.0	1.2	-	-	-	-	26.1	0.4	-	-	-	-	26.4	1.1	-	-	-	-	26.4	0.0	-	-	-	-
1953	26.2	-0.8	-	-	-	-	26.2	0.0	-	-	-	-	26.4	0.8	-	-	-	-	26.5	0.4	-	-	-	-
1954	26.4	-0.4	-	-	-	-	26.5	0.4	-	-	-	-	26.5	0.0	-	-	-	-	26.5	0.0	-	-	-	-
1955	26.4	-0.4	-	-	-	-	26.4	0.0	-	-	-	-	26.6	0.8	-	-	-	-	26.6	0.0	-	-	-	-
1956	26.5	-0.4	-	-	-	-	26.7	0.8	-	-	-	-	27.0	1.1	-	-	-	-	27.3	1.1	-	-	-	-
1957	27.5	0.7	-	-	-	-	27.6	0.4	-	-	-	-	27.9	1.1	-	-	-	-	28.0	0.4	-	-	-	-
1958	28.1	0.4	-	-	-	-	28.4	1.1	-	-	-	-	28.6	0.7	-	-	-	-	28.7	0.3	-	-	-	-
1959	28.6	-0.3	-	-	-	-	28.8	0.7	-	-	-	-	28.9	0.3	-	-	-	-	29.1	0.7	-	-	-	-
1960	29.1	0.0	-	-	-	-	29.0	-0.3	-	-	-	-	29.3	1.0	-	-	-	-	29.4	0.3	-	-	-	-
1961	29.3	-0.3	-	-	-	-	29.7	1.4	-	-	-	-	29.8	0.3	-	-	-	-	29.7	-0.3	-	-	-	-

[Continued]

Kansas City, MO-KS
Consumer Price Index - All Urban Consumers
Base 1982-1984 = 100
All Items
[Continued]

For 1917-1995. Columns headed % show percentile change in the index from the previous period for which an index is available.

Year	Jan Index	%	Feb Index	%	Mar Index	%	Apr Index	%	May Index	%	Jun Index	%	Jul Index	%	Aug Index	%	Sep Index	%	Oct Index	%	Nov Index	%	Dec Index	%
1962	29.8	0.3	-	-	-	-	30.0	0.7	-	-	-	-	30.1	0.3	-	-	-	-	30.4	1.0	-	-	-	-
1963	30.0	-1.3	-	-	-	-	30.2	0.7	-	-	-	-	30.4	0.7	-	-	-	-	30.8	1.3	-	-	-	-
1964	30.8	0.0	-	-	-	-	30.9	0.3	-	-	-	-	31.3	1.3	-	-	-	-	31.4	0.3	-	-	-	-
1965	31.6	0.6	-	-	-	-	31.8	0.6	-	-	32.3	1.6	-	-	-	-	32.4	0.3	-	-	-	-	32.5	0.3
1966	-	-	-	-	32.7	0.6	-	-	-	-	33.0	0.9	-	-	-	-	33.2	0.6	-	-	-	-	33.3	0.3
1967	-	-	-	-	33.4	0.3	-	-	-	-	33.3	-0.3	-	-	-	-	34.1	2.4	-	-	-	-	34.1	0.0
1968	-	-	-	-	34.5	1.2	-	-	-	-	35.2	2.0	-	-	-	-	35.3	0.3	-	-	-	-	35.6	0.8
1969	-	-	-	-	36.3	2.0	-	-	-	-	37.0	1.9	-	-	-	-	37.3	0.8	-	-	-	-	37.8	1.3
1970	-	-	-	-	38.2	1.1	-	-	-	-	39.1	2.4	-	-	-	-	39.3	0.5	-	-	-	-	40.1	2.0
1971	-	-	-	-	40.1	0.0	-	-	-	-	40.6	1.2	-	-	-	-	40.9	0.7	-	-	-	-	40.9	0.0
1972	-	-	-	-	41.2	0.7	-	-	-	-	41.7	1.2	-	-	-	-	42.3	1.4	-	-	-	-	42.3	0.0
1973	-	-	-	-	42.9	1.4	-	-	-	-	43.7	1.9	-	-	-	-	44.6	2.1	-	-	-	-	45.3	1.6
1974	-	-	-	-	46.7	3.1	-	-	-	-	48.3	3.4	-	-	-	-	49.9	3.3	-	-	-	-	51.4	3.0
1975	-	-	-	-	52.1	1.4	-	-	-	-	52.9	1.5	-	-	-	-	54.0	2.1	-	-	-	-	54.9	1.7
1976	-	-	-	-	55.0	0.2	-	-	-	-	55.9	1.6	-	-	-	-	56.8	1.6	-	-	-	-	57.5	1.2
1977	-	-	-	-	58.9	2.4	-	-	-	-	60.3	2.4	-	-	-	-	60.8	0.8	-	-	-	-	61.5	1.2
1978	-	-	61.9	0.7	-	-	63.6	2.7	-	-	64.7	1.7	-	-	65.4	1.1	-	-	66.3	1.4	-	-	67.0	1.1
1979	-	-	68.9	2.8	-	-	71.2	3.3	-	-	73.9	3.8	-	-	75.6	2.3	-	-	77.4	2.4	-	-	78.7	1.7
1980	-	-	80.4	2.2	-	-	82.1	2.1	-	-	83.5	1.7	-	-	84.5	1.2	-	-	85.8	1.5	-	-	87.3	1.7
1981	-	-	88.2	1.0	-	-	89.4	1.4	-	-	91.1	1.9	-	-	91.4	0.3	-	-	91.8	0.4	-	-	92.1	0.3
1982	-	-	92.9	0.9	-	-	92.3	-0.6	-	-	94.8	2.7	-	-	96.0	1.3	-	-	97.4	1.5	-	-	97.9	0.5
1983	-	-	98.4	0.5	-	-	99.7	1.3	-	-	100.2	0.5	-	-	101.5	1.3	-	-	102.1	0.6	-	-	102.0	-0.1
1984	-	-	103.2	1.2	-	-	104.1	0.9	-	-	104.7	0.6	-	-	104.8	0.1	-	-	105.8	1.0	-	-	105.6	-0.2
1985	-	-	105.9	0.3	-	-	107.7	1.7	-	-	107.8	0.1	-	-	108.1	0.3	-	-	108.8	0.6	-	-	108.4	-0.4
1986	-	-	108.1	-0.3	-	-	108.0	-0.1	-	-	108.7	0.6	-	-	109.1	0.4	-	-	109.0	-0.1	-	-	109.3	0.3
1987	-	-	-	-	-	-	-	-	-	-	111.5	2.0	-	-	-	-	-	-	-	-	-	-	114.6	2.8
1988	-	-	-	-	-	-	-	-	-	-	116.3	1.5	-	-	-	-	-	-	-	-	-	-	118.4	1.8
1989	-	-	-	-	-	-	-	-	-	-	120.6	1.9	-	-	-	-	-	-	-	-	-	-	122.6	1.7
1990	-	-	-	-	-	-	-	-	-	-	124.3	1.4	-	-	-	-	-	-	-	-	-	-	127.7	2.7
1991	-	-	-	-	-	-	-	-	-	-	130.2	2.0	-	-	-	-	-	-	-	-	-	-	132.3	1.6
1992	-	-	-	-	-	-	-	-	-	-	133.4	0.8	-	-	-	-	-	-	-	-	-	-	135.2	1.3
1993	-	-	-	-	-	-	-	-	-	-	137.5	1.7	-	-	-	-	-	-	-	-	-	-	138.7	0.9
1994	-	-	-	-	-	-	-	-	-	-	140.6	1.4	-	-	-	-	-	-	-	-	-	-	141.9	0.9
1995	-	-	-	-	-	-	-	-	-	-	144.3	1.7	-	-	-	-	-	-	-	-	-	-	-	-

Source: U.S. Department of Labor, Bureau of Labor Statistics, Division of Consumer Prices and Price Indexes. - indicates no data collected for period.

Kansas City, MO-KS
Consumer Price Index - Urban Wage Earners
Base 1982-1984 = 100
All Items

For 1917-1995. Columns headed % show percentile change in the index from the previous period for which an index is available.

Year	Jan Index	%	Feb Index	%	Mar Index	%	Apr Index	%	May Index	%	Jun Index	%	Jul Index	%	Aug Index	%	Sep Index	%	Oct Index	%	Nov Index	%	Dec Index	%
1917	-	-	-	-	-	-	-	-	-	-	-	-	-	-	-	-	-	-	-	-	-	-	15.0	-
1918	-	-	-	-	-	-	-	-	-	-	-	-	-	-	-	-	-	-	-	-	-	-	17.8	18.7
1919	-	-	-	-	-	-	-	-	-	-	18.0	1.1	-	-	-	-	-	-	-	-	-	-	20.7	15.0
1920	-	-	-	-	-	-	-	-	-	-	23.1	11.6	-	-	-	-	-	-	-	-	-	-	21.0	-9.1
1921	-	-	-	-	-	-	-	-	19.4	-7.6	-	-	-	-	-	-	19.0	-2.1	-	-	-	-	18.7	-1.6
1922	-	-	-	-	17.7	-5.3	-	-	-	-	17.7	0.0	-	-	-	-	17.5	-1.1	-	-	-	-	17.6	0.6
1923	-	-	-	-	17.6	0.0	-	-	-	-	17.6	0.0	-	-	-	-	17.8	1.1	-	-	-	-	17.8	0.0
1924	-	-	-	-	17.6	-1.1	-	-	-	-	17.4	-1.1	-	-	-	-	17.4	0.0	-	-	-	-	17.5	0.6
1925	-	-	-	-	-	-	-	-	-	-	17.8	1.7	-	-	-	-	-	-	-	-	-	-	18.0	1.1
1926	-	-	-	-	-	-	-	-	-	-	17.9	-0.6	-	-	-	-	-	-	-	-	-	-	17.6	-1.7
1927	-	-	-	-	-	-	-	-	-	-	17.6	0.0	-	-	-	-	-	-	-	-	-	-	17.0	-3.4
1928	-	-	-	-	-	-	-	-	-	-	17.0	0.0	-	-	-	-	-	-	-	-	-	-	16.9	-0.6
1929	-	-	-	-	-	-	-	-	-	-	16.9	0.0	-	-	-	-	-	-	-	-	-	-	17.0	0.6
1930	-	-	-	-	-	-	-	-	-	-	16.8	-1.2	-	-	-	-	-	-	-	-	-	-	16.3	-3.0
1931	-	-	-	-	-	-	-	-	-	-	15.7	-3.7	-	-	-	-	-	-	-	-	-	-	15.1	-3.8
1932	-	-	-	-	-	-	-	-	-	-	14.0	-7.3	-	-	-	-	-	-	-	-	-	-	13.7	-2.1
1933	-	-	-	-	-	-	-	-	-	-	13.4	-2.2	-	-	-	-	-	-	-	-	-	-	13.5	0.7
1934	-	-	-	-	-	-	-	-	-	-	13.8	2.2	-	-	-	-	-	-	-	-	14.0	1.4	-	-
1935	-	-	-	-	14.1	0.7	-	-	-	-	-	-	14.0	-0.7	-	-	-	-	14.1	0.7	-	-	-	-
1936	14.3	1.4	-	-	-	-	14.1	-1.4	-	-	-	-	14.3	1.4	-	-	14.5	1.4	-	-	-	-	14.4	-0.7
1937	-	-	-	-	14.7	2.1	-	-	-	-	14.9	1.4	-	-	-	-	15.0	0.7	-	-	-	-	14.8	-1.3
1938	-	-	-	-	14.6	-1.4	-	-	-	-	14.5	-0.7	-	-	-	-	14.5	0.0	-	-	-	-	14.4	-0.7
1939	-	-	-	-	14.3	-0.7	-	-	-	-	14.3	0.0	-	-	-	-	14.5	1.4	-	-	-	-	14.3	-1.4
1940	-	-	-	-	14.2	-0.7	-	-	-	-	14.2	0.0	-	-	-	-	14.1	-0.7	14.1	0.0	14.2	0.7	14.2	0.0
1941	14.2	0.0	14.2	0.0	14.3	0.7	14.5	1.4	14.5	0.0	14.7	1.4	14.7	0.0	14.9	1.4	15.3	2.7	15.5	1.3	15.6	0.6	15.7	0.6
1942	15.8	0.6	16.0	1.3	16.3	1.9	16.4	0.6	16.5	0.6	16.5	0.0	16.5	0.0	16.6	0.6	16.6	0.0	16.8	1.2	16.9	0.6	17.0	0.6
1943	17.0	0.0	17.2	1.2	17.4	1.2	17.6	1.1	17.7	0.6	17.6	-0.6	17.4	-1.1	17.4	0.0	17.5	0.6	17.6	0.6	17.6	0.0	17.7	0.6
1944	17.6	-0.6	17.6	0.0	17.6	0.0	17.8	1.1	17.8	0.0	17.8	0.0	18.0	1.1	17.9	-0.6	18.0	0.6	17.9	-0.6	18.0	0.6	18.0	0.0
1945	18.1	0.6	18.1	0.0	18.1	0.0	18.2	0.6	18.3	0.5	18.4	0.5	18.4	0.0	18.5	0.5	18.4	-0.5	18.4	0.0	18.4	0.0	18.5	0.5
1946	18.5	0.0	18.4	-0.5	18.5	0.5	18.6	0.5	18.6	0.0	18.7	0.5	19.7	5.3	20.3	3.0	20.4	0.5	20.5	0.5	21.3	3.9	21.3	0.0
1947	21.4	0.5	21.5	0.5	21.8	1.4	21.8	0.0	21.8	0.0	21.6	-0.9	21.8	0.9	-	-	-	-	22.9	5.0	-	-	-	-
1948	23.5	2.6	-	-	-	-	23.7	0.9	-	-	-	-	24.1	1.7	-	-	-	-	24.3	0.8	-	-	-	-
1949	24.0	-1.2	-	-	-	-	23.8	-0.8	-	-	-	-	23.6	-0.8	-	-	-	-	23.5	-0.4	-	-	-	-
1950	23.4	-0.4	-	-	-	-	23.6	0.9	-	-	-	-	24.1	2.1	-	-	-	-	24.4	1.2	-	-	-	-
1951	25.4	4.1	-	-	-	-	25.8	1.6	-	-	-	-	25.9	0.4	-	-	-	-	26.0	0.4	-	-	-	-
1952	26.3	1.2	-	-	-	-	26.5	0.8	-	-	-	-	26.8	1.1	-	-	-	-	26.8	0.0	-	-	-	-
1953	26.6	-0.7	-	-	-	-	26.6	0.0	-	-	-	-	26.8	0.8	-	-	-	-	26.9	0.4	-	-	-	-
1954	26.7	-0.7	-	-	-	-	26.9	0.7	-	-	-	-	26.9	0.0	-	-	-	-	26.9	0.0	-	-	-	-
1955	26.8	-0.4	-	-	-	-	26.8	0.0	-	-	-	-	26.9	0.4	-	-	-	-	27.0	0.4	-	-	-	-
1956	26.9	-0.4	-	-	-	-	27.1	0.7	-	-	-	-	27.3	0.7	-	-	-	-	27.6	1.1	-	-	-	-
1957	27.8	0.7	-	-	-	-	28.0	0.7	-	-	-	-	28.3	1.1	-	-	-	-	28.3	0.0	-	-	-	-
1958	28.4	0.4	-	-	-	-	28.7	1.1	-	-	-	-	29.0	1.0	-	-	-	-	29.0	0.0	-	-	-	-
1959	28.9	-0.3	-	-	-	-	29.2	1.0	-	-	-	-	29.3	0.3	-	-	-	-	29.5	0.7	-	-	-	-
1960	29.5	0.0	-	-	-	-	29.4	-0.3	-	-	-	-	29.7	1.0	-	-	-	-	29.8	0.3	-	-	-	-
1961	29.7	-0.3	-	-	-	-	30.1	1.3	-	-	-	-	30.2	0.3	-	-	-	-	30.1	-0.3	-	-	-	-

[Continued]

Kansas City, MO-KS

Consumer Price Index - Urban Wage Earners
Base 1982-1984 = 100

All Items

[Continued]

For 1917-1995. Columns headed % show percentile change in the index from the previous period for which an index is available.

Year	Jan Index	%	Feb Index	%	Mar Index	%	Apr Index	%	May Index	%	Jun Index	%	Jul Index	%	Aug Index	%	Sep Index	%	Oct Index	%	Nov Index	%	Dec Index	%
1962	30.2	0.3	-	-	-	-	30.4	0.7	-	-	-	-	30.5	0.3	-	-	-	-	30.8	1.0	-	-	-	-
1963	30.4	-1.3	-	-	-	-	30.6	0.7	-	-	-	-	30.8	0.7	-	-	-	-	31.3	1.6	-	-	-	-
1964	31.2	-0.3	-	-	-	-	31.3	0.3	-	-	-	-	31.7	1.3	-	-	-	-	31.8	0.3	-	-	-	-
1965	32.0	0.6	-	-	-	-	32.2	0.6	-	-	32.8	1.9	-	-	-	-	32.9	0.3	-	-	-	-	32.9	0.0
1966	-	-	-	-	33.1	0.6	-	-	-	-	33.5	1.2	-	-	-	-	33.7	0.6	-	-	-	-	33.7	0.0
1967	-	-	-	-	33.9	0.6	-	-	-	-	33.8	-0.3	-	-	-	-	34.5	2.1	-	-	-	-	34.6	0.3
1968	-	-	-	-	35.0	1.2	-	-	-	-	35.7	2.0	-	-	-	-	35.8	0.3	-	-	-	-	36.1	0.8
1969	-	-	-	-	36.8	1.9	-	-	-	-	37.5	1.9	-	-	-	-	37.8	0.8	-	-	-	-	38.3	1.3
1970	-	-	-	-	38.7	1.0	-	-	-	-	39.7	2.6	-	-	-	-	39.8	0.3	-	-	-	-	40.6	2.0
1971	-	-	-	-	40.7	0.2	-	-	-	-	41.2	1.2	-	-	-	-	41.5	0.7	-	-	-	-	41.4	-0.2
1972	-	-	-	-	41.8	1.0	-	-	-	-	42.3	1.2	-	-	-	-	42.8	1.2	-	-	-	-	42.8	0.0
1973	-	-	-	-	43.5	1.6	-	-	-	-	44.3	1.8	-	-	-	-	45.2	2.0	-	-	-	-	45.9	1.5
1974	-	-	-	-	47.3	3.1	-	-	-	-	48.9	3.4	-	-	-	-	50.5	3.3	-	-	-	-	52.1	3.2
1975	-	-	-	-	52.8	1.3	-	-	-	-	53.7	1.7	-	-	-	-	54.7	1.9	-	-	-	-	55.6	1.6
1976	-	-	-	-	55.8	0.4	-	-	-	-	56.6	1.4	-	-	-	-	57.6	1.8	-	-	-	-	58.3	1.2
1977	-	-	-	-	59.7	2.4	-	-	-	-	61.1	2.3	-	-	-	-	61.6	0.8	-	-	-	-	62.4	1.3
1978	-	-	62.9	0.8	-	-	64.4	2.4	-	-	65.6	1.9	-	-	66.3	1.1	-	-	67.3	1.5	-	-	67.9	0.9
1979	-	-	69.7	2.7	-	-	72.0	3.3	-	-	74.5	3.5	-	-	76.1	2.1	-	-	77.8	2.2	-	-	79.3	1.9
1980	-	-	80.8	1.9	-	-	82.7	2.4	-	-	84.1	1.7	-	-	85.1	1.2	-	-	86.3	1.4	-	-	87.8	1.7
1981	-	-	88.8	1.1	-	-	90.2	1.6	-	-	91.8	1.8	-	-	92.2	0.4	-	-	92.6	0.4	-	-	92.8	0.2
1982	-	-	93.5	0.8	-	-	92.9	-0.6	-	-	95.6	2.9	-	-	96.8	1.3	-	-	98.1	1.3	-	-	98.5	0.4
1983	-	-	98.6	0.1	-	-	100.2	1.6	-	-	101.8	1.6	-	-	102.2	0.4	-	-	103.7	1.5	-	-	102.4	-1.3
1984	-	-	101.2	-1.2	-	-	102.3	1.1	-	-	102.4	0.1	-	-	103.9	1.5	-	-	105.0	1.1	-	-	103.8	-1.1
1985	-	-	103.9	0.1	-	-	105.7	1.7	-	-	106.0	0.3	-	-	106.2	0.2	-	-	106.8	0.6	-	-	106.4	-0.4
1986	-	-	105.8	-0.6	-	-	105.4	-0.4	-	-	106.3	0.9	-	-	106.5	0.2	-	-	106.2	-0.3	-	-	106.6	0.4
1987	-	-	-	-	-	-	-	-	-	-	108.6	1.9	-	-	-	-	-	-	-	-	-	-	111.7	2.9
1988	-	-	-	-	-	-	-	-	-	-	113.3	1.4	-	-	-	-	-	-	-	-	-	-	115.5	1.9
1989	-	-	-	-	-	-	-	-	-	-	117.6	1.8	-	-	-	-	-	-	-	-	-	-	119.4	1.5
1990	-	-	-	-	-	-	-	-	-	-	120.8	1.2	-	-	-	-	-	-	-	-	-	-	124.0	2.6
1991	-	-	-	-	-	-	-	-	-	-	126.2	1.8	-	-	-	-	-	-	-	-	-	-	128.5	1.8
1992	-	-	-	-	-	-	-	-	-	-	129.4	0.7	-	-	-	-	-	-	-	-	-	-	131.4	1.5
1993	-	-	-	-	-	-	-	-	-	-	133.5	1.6	-	-	-	-	-	-	-	-	-	-	135.0	1.1
1994	-	-	-	-	-	-	-	-	-	-	136.9	1.4	-	-	-	-	-	-	-	-	-	-	138.1	0.9
1995	-	-	-	-	-	-	-	-	-	-	140.9	2.0	-	-	-	-	-	-	-	-	-	-	-	-

Source: U.S. Department of Labor, Bureau of Labor Statistics, Division of Consumer Prices and Price Indexes. - indicates no data collected for period.

Kansas City, MO-KS
Consumer Price Index - All Urban Consumers
Base 1982-1984 = 100
Food and Beverages

For 1975-1995. Columns headed % show percentile change in the index from the previous period for which an index is available.

Year	Jan Index	%	Feb Index	%	Mar Index	%	Apr Index	%	May Index	%	Jun Index	%	Jul Index	%	Aug Index	%	Sep Index	%	Oct Index	%	Nov Index	%	Dec Index	%
1975	-	-	-	-	-	-	-	-	-	-	-	-	-	-	-	-	-	-	-	-	-	-	63.9	-
1976	-	-	-	-	62.7	-1.9	-	-	-	-	62.2	-0.8	-	-	-	-	63.4	1.9	-	-	-	-	63.2	-0.3
1977	-	-	-	-	65.6	3.8	-	-	-	-	67.7	3.2	-	-	-	-	68.0	0.4	-	-	-	-	68.5	0.7
1978	-	-	70.5	2.9	-	-	72.7	3.1	-	-	75.6	4.0	-	-	76.1	0.7	-	-	76.9	1.1	-	-	78.1	1.6
1979	-	-	81.3	4.1	-	-	82.3	1.2	-	-	82.6	0.4	-	-	83.1	0.6	-	-	83.3	0.2	-	-	84.9	1.9
1980	-	-	86.5	1.9	-	-	88.3	2.1	-	-	89.2	1.0	-	-	90.4	1.3	-	-	91.8	1.5	-	-	93.4	1.7
1981	-	-	95.0	1.7	-	-	95.5	0.5	-	-	93.5	-2.1	-	-	95.0	1.6	-	-	95.5	0.5	-	-	95.9	0.4
1982	-	-	96.9	1.0	-	-	96.2	-0.7	-	-	98.4	2.3	-	-	98.3	-0.1	-	-	98.1	-0.2	-	-	97.9	-0.2
1983	-	-	98.6	0.7	-	-	98.8	0.2	-	-	99.6	0.8	-	-	99.1	-0.5	-	-	99.8	0.7	-	-	99.6	-0.1
1984	-	-	102.6	3.0	-	-	103.2	0.6	-	-	102.6	-0.6	-	-	103.5	0.9	-	-	104.6	1.1	-	-	104.5	-0.1
1985	-	-	105.8	1.2	-	-	106.5	0.7	-	-	106.1	-0.4	-	-	105.7	-0.4	-	-	105.8	0.1	-	-	106.7	0.9
1986	-	-	107.9	1.1	-	-	108.6	0.6	-	-	109.0	0.4	-	-	110.8	1.7	-	-	110.7	-0.1	-	-	111.1	0.4
1987	-	-	-	-	-	-	-	-	-	-	112.7	1.4	-	-	-	-	-	-	-	-	-	-	112.9	0.2
1988	-	-	-	-	-	-	-	-	-	-	114.7	1.6	-	-	-	-	-	-	-	-	-	-	116.9	1.9
1989	-	-	-	-	-	-	-	-	-	-	118.8	1.6	-	-	-	-	-	-	-	-	-	-	120.9	1.8
1990	-	-	-	-	-	-	-	-	-	-	127.0	5.0	-	-	-	-	-	-	-	-	-	-	127.9	0.7
1991	-	-	-	-	-	-	-	-	-	-	131.1	2.5	-	-	-	-	-	-	-	-	-	-	130.8	-0.2
1992	-	-	-	-	-	-	-	-	-	-	130.7	-0.1	-	-	-	-	-	-	-	-	-	-	135.1	3.4
1993	-	-	-	-	-	-	-	-	-	-	137.4	1.7	-	-	-	-	-	-	-	-	-	-	138.1	0.5
1994	-	-	-	-	-	-	-	-	-	-	138.8	0.5	-	-	-	-	-	-	-	-	-	-	141.6	2.0
1995	-	-	-	-	-	-	-	-	-	-	142.8	0.8	-	-	-	-	-	-	-	-	-	-	-	-

Source: U.S. Department of Labor, Bureau of Labor Statistics, Division of Consumer Prices and Price Indexes. - indicates no data collected for period.

Kansas City, MO-KS
Consumer Price Index - Urban Wage Earners
Base 1982-1984 = 100
Food and Beverages

For 1975-1995. Columns headed % show percentile change in the index from the previous period for which an index is available.

Year	Jan Index	%	Feb Index	%	Mar Index	%	Apr Index	%	May Index	%	Jun Index	%	Jul Index	%	Aug Index	%	Sep Index	%	Oct Index	%	Nov Index	%	Dec Index	%
1975	-	-	-	-	-	-	-	-	-	-	-	-	-	-	-	-	-	-	-	-	-	-	64.7	-
1976	-	-	-	-	63.4	-2.0	-	-	-	-	63.0	-0.6	-	-	-	-	64.2	1.9	-	-	-	-	63.9	-0.5
1977	-	-	-	-	66.4	3.9	-	-	-	-	68.6	3.3	-	-	-	-	68.8	0.3	-	-	-	-	69.3	0.7
1978	-	-	71.0	2.5	-	-	73.0	2.8	-	-	76.1	4.2	-	-	76.5	0.5	-	-	77.2	0.9	-	-	78.6	1.8
1979	-	-	81.0	3.1	-	-	81.8	1.0	-	-	81.9	0.1	-	-	82.2	0.4	-	-	82.4	0.2	-	-	83.9	1.8
1980	-	-	85.7	2.1	-	-	87.4	2.0	-	-	88.3	1.0	-	-	90.0	1.9	-	-	91.9	2.1	-	-	93.3	1.5
1981	-	-	94.2	1.0	-	-	94.8	0.6	-	-	93.6	-1.3	-	-	94.9	1.4	-	-	95.9	1.1	-	-	95.9	0.0
1982	-	-	96.8	0.9	-	-	96.1	-0.7	-	-	98.4	2.4	-	-	98.5	0.1	-	-	98.1	-0.4	-	-	97.9	-0.2
1983	-	-	98.8	0.9	-	-	99.0	0.2	-	-	99.6	0.6	-	-	99.3	-0.3	-	-	99.8	0.5	-	-	99.6	-0.2
1984	-	-	102.5	2.9	-	-	103.1	0.6	-	-	102.5	-0.6	-	-	103.4	0.9	-	-	104.5	1.1	-	-	104.3	-0.2
1985	-	-	105.4	1.1	-	-	106.2	0.8	-	-	105.9	-0.3	-	-	105.6	-0.3	-	-	105.6	0.0	-	-	106.6	0.9
1986	-	-	107.9	1.2	-	-	108.5	0.6	-	-	108.7	0.2	-	-	110.7	1.8	-	-	110.7	0.0	-	-	111.1	0.4
1987	-	-	-	-	-	-	-	-	-	-	112.5	1.3	-	-	-	-	-	-	-	-	-	-	112.9	0.4
1988	-	-	-	-	-	-	-	-	-	-	114.7	1.6	-	-	-	-	-	-	-	-	-	-	116.9	1.9
1989	-	-	-	-	-	-	-	-	-	-	118.8	1.6	-	-	-	-	-	-	-	-	-	-	120.9	1.8
1990	-	-	-	-	-	-	-	-	-	-	126.9	5.0	-	-	-	-	-	-	-	-	-	-	127.9	0.8
1991	-	-	-	-	-	-	-	-	-	-	131.0	2.4	-	-	-	-	-	-	-	-	-	-	131.0	0.0
1992	-	-	-	-	-	-	-	-	-	-	130.4	-0.5	-	-	-	-	-	-	-	-	-	-	135.1	3.6
1993	-	-	-	-	-	-	-	-	-	-	137.3	1.6	-	-	-	-	-	-	-	-	-	-	138.2	0.7
1994	-	-	-	-	-	-	-	-	-	-	138.7	0.4	-	-	-	-	-	-	-	-	-	-	141.6	2.1
1995	-	-	-	-	-	-	-	-	-	-	142.7	0.8	-	-	-	-	-	-	-	-	-	-	-	-

Source: U.S. Department of Labor, Bureau of Labor Statistics, Division of Consumer Prices and Price Indexes. - indicates no data collected for period.

Kansas City, MO-KS
Consumer Price Index - All Urban Consumers
Base 1982-1984 = 100
Housing

For 1975-1995. Columns headed % show percentile change in the index from the previous period for which an index is available.

Year	Jan Index	%	Feb Index	%	Mar Index	%	Apr Index	%	May Index	%	Jun Index	%	Jul Index	%	Aug Index	%	Sep Index	%	Oct Index	%	Nov Index	%	Dec Index	%
1975	-	-	-	-	-	-	-	-	-	-	-	-	-	-	-	-	-	-	-	-	-	-	51.2	-
1976	-	-	-	-	51.6	0.8	-	-	-	-	52.5	1.7	-	-	-	-	53.4	1.7	-	-	-	-	54.4	1.9
1977	-	-	-	-	55.3	1.7	-	-	-	-	56.6	2.4	-	-	-	-	57.5	1.6	-	-	-	-	58.4	1.6
1978	-	-	58.8	0.7	-	-	60.9	3.6	-	-	61.7	1.3	-	-	62.2	0.8	-	-	63.0	1.3	-	-	63.2	0.3
1979	-	-	65.3	3.3	-	-	68.5	4.9	-	-	72.2	5.4	-	-	74.4	3.0	-	-	77.3	3.9	-	-	78.6	1.7
1980	-	-	79.3	0.9	-	-	80.6	1.6	-	-	83.0	3.0	-	-	83.8	1.0	-	-	85.2	1.7	-	-	86.6	1.6
1981	-	-	86.3	-0.3	-	-	88.0	2.0	-	-	91.5	4.0	-	-	91.0	-0.5	-	-	90.5	-0.5	-	-	90.5	0.0
1982	-	-	91.6	1.2	-	-	89.9	-1.9	-	-	93.1	3.6	-	-	94.5	1.5	-	-	97.1	2.8	-	-	98.4	1.3
1983	-	-	99.6	1.2	-	-	100.7	1.1	-	-	100.7	0.0	-	-	102.9	2.2	-	-	101.9	-1.0	-	-	102.2	0.3
1984	-	-	103.3	1.1	-	-	104.3	1.0	-	-	106.0	1.6	-	-	106.1	0.1	-	-	105.7	-0.4	-	-	105.8	0.1
1985	-	-	106.1	0.3	-	-	107.3	1.1	-	-	108.1	0.7	-	-	108.6	0.5	-	-	108.7	0.1	-	-	107.1	-1.5
1986	-	-	108.0	0.8	-	-	109.3	1.2	-	-	109.2	-0.1	-	-	111.3	1.9	-	-	109.5	-1.6	-	-	110.3	0.7
1987	-	-	-	-	-	-	-	-	-	-	112.2	1.7	-	-	-	-	-	-	-	-	-	-	114.9	2.4
1988	-	-	-	-	-	-	-	-	-	-	117.9	2.6	-	-	-	-	-	-	-	-	-	-	118.7	0.7
1989	-	-	-	-	-	-	-	-	-	-	119.6	0.8	-	-	-	-	-	-	-	-	-	-	119.7	0.1
1990	-	-	-	-	-	-	-	-	-	-	121.3	1.3	-	-	-	-	-	-	-	-	-	-	122.4	0.9
1991	-	-	-	-	-	-	-	-	-	-	124.5	1.7	-	-	-	-	-	-	-	-	-	-	126.3	1.4
1992	-	-	-	-	-	-	-	-	-	-	126.8	0.4	-	-	-	-	-	-	-	-	-	-	127.6	0.6
1993	-	-	-	-	-	-	-	-	-	-	129.3	1.3	-	-	-	-	-	-	-	-	-	-	131.6	1.8
1994	-	-	-	-	-	-	-	-	-	-	132.4	0.6	-	-	-	-	-	-	-	-	-	-	133.8	1.1
1995	-	-	-	-	-	-	-	-	-	-	135.0	0.9	-	-	-	-	-	-	-	-	-	-	-	-

Source: U.S. Department of Labor, Bureau of Labor Statistics, Division of Consumer Prices and Price Indexes. - indicates no data collected for period.

Kansas City, MO-KS
Consumer Price Index - Urban Wage Earners
Base 1982-1984 = 100
Housing

For 1975-1995. Columns headed % show percentile change in the index from the previous period for which an index is available.

Year	Jan Index	%	Feb Index	%	Mar Index	%	Apr Index	%	May Index	%	Jun Index	%	Jul Index	%	Aug Index	%	Sep Index	%	Oct Index	%	Nov Index	%	Dec Index	%
1975	-	-	-	-	-	-	-	-	-	-	-	-	-	-	-	-	-	-	-	-	-	-	52.2	-
1976	-	-	-	-	52.7	1.0	-	-	-	-	53.6	1.7	-	-	-	-	54.5	1.7	-	-	-	-	55.5	1.8
1977	-	-	-	-	56.4	1.6	-	-	-	-	57.8	2.5	-	-	-	-	58.7	1.6	-	-	-	-	59.6	1.5
1978	-	-	60.2	1.0	-	-	62.3	3.5	-	-	63.1	1.3	-	-	63.6	0.8	-	-	64.5	1.4	-	-	64.7	0.3
1979	-	-	66.8	3.2	-	-	69.8	4.5	-	-	73.4	5.2	-	-	75.4	2.7	-	-	78.1	3.6	-	-	79.6	1.9
1980	-	-	79.5	-0.1	-	-	81.1	2.0	-	-	83.8	3.3	-	-	84.6	1.0	-	-	85.8	1.4	-	-	87.3	1.7
1981	-	-	87.0	-0.3	-	-	88.8	2.1	-	-	92.2	3.8	-	-	91.9	-0.3	-	-	91.4	-0.5	-	-	91.4	0.0
1982	-	-	92.5	1.2	-	-	90.8	-1.8	-	-	94.2	3.7	-	-	95.7	1.6	-	-	98.2	2.6	-	-	99.8	1.6
1983	-	-	100.0	0.2	-	-	101.9	1.9	-	-	104.5	2.6	-	-	104.2	-0.3	-	-	106.0	1.7	-	-	103.4	-2.5
1984	-	-	99.3	-4.0	-	-	100.7	1.4	-	-	100.9	0.2	-	-	104.3	3.4	-	-	104.4	0.1	-	-	101.9	-2.4
1985	-	-	102.1	0.2	-	-	103.2	1.1	-	-	104.1	0.9	-	-	104.6	0.5	-	-	104.6	0.0	-	-	103.0	-1.5
1986	-	-	104.0	1.0	-	-	105.0	1.0	-	-	104.9	-0.1	-	-	107.1	2.1	-	-	105.1	-1.9	-	-	106.0	0.9
1987	-	-	-	-	-	-	-	-	-	-	107.8	1.7	-	-	-	-	-	-	-	-	-	-	110.3	2.3
1988	-	-	-	-	-	-	-	-	-	-	113.0	2.4	-	-	-	-	-	-	-	-	-	-	113.8	0.7
1989	-	-	-	-	-	-	-	-	-	-	114.8	0.9	-	-	-	-	-	-	-	-	-	-	114.8	0.0
1990	-	-	-	-	-	-	-	-	-	-	116.5	1.5	-	-	-	-	-	-	-	-	-	-	117.5	0.9
1991	-	-	-	-	-	-	-	-	-	-	119.4	1.6	-	-	-	-	-	-	-	-	-	-	121.0	1.3
1992	-	-	-	-	-	-	-	-	-	-	121.5	0.4	-	-	-	-	-	-	-	-	-	-	122.3	0.7
1993	-	-	-	-	-	-	-	-	-	-	123.9	1.3	-	-	-	-	-	-	-	-	-	-	126.3	1.9
1994	-	-	-	-	-	-	-	-	-	-	127.1	0.6	-	-	-	-	-	-	-	-	-	-	128.3	0.9
1995	-	-	-	-	-	-	-	-	-	-	129.5	0.9	-	-	-	-	-	-	-	-	-	-	-	-

Source: U.S. Department of Labor, Bureau of Labor Statistics, Division of Consumer Prices and Price Indexes. - indicates no data collected for period.

Kansas City, MO-KS
Consumer Price Index - All Urban Consumers
Base 1982-1984 = 100
Apparel and Upkeep

For 1952-1995. Columns headed % show percentile change in the index from the previous period for which an index is available.

Year	Jan Index	%	Feb Index	%	Mar Index	%	Apr Index	%	May Index	%	Jun Index	%	Jul Index	%	Aug Index	%	Sep Index	%	Oct Index	%	Nov Index	%	Dec Index	%
	-	-	-	-	-	-	-	-	-	-	-	-	-	-	-	-	-	-	39.3	-	-	-	-	-
1952	-	-	-	-	-	-	-	-	-	-	-	-	39.4	0.5	-	-	-	-	39.3	-0.3	-	-	-	-
1953	39.2	-0.3	-	-	-	-	39.2	0.0	-	-	-	-	38.8	0.0	-	-	-	-	39.1	0.8	-	-	-	-
1954	39.0	-0.8	-	-	-	-	38.8	-0.5	-	-	-	-	38.6	0.0	-	-	-	-	39.4	2.1	-	-	-	-
1955	38.5	-1.5	-	-	-	-	38.6	0.3	-	-	-	-	39.2	0.3	-	-	-	-	39.7	1.3	-	-	-	-
1956	39.1	-0.8	-	-	-	-	39.1	0.0	-	-	-	-	39.9	-0.7	-	-	-	-	40.6	1.8	-	-	-	-
1957	40.5	2.0	-	-	-	-	40.2	-0.7	-	-	-	-	40.2	-0.5	-	-	-	-	40.8	1.5	-	-	-	-
1958	40.0	-1.5	-	-	-	-	40.4	1.0	-	-	-	-	40.5	0.0	-	-	-	-	41.4	2.2	-	-	-	-
1959	40.3	-1.2	-	-	-	-	40.5	0.5	-	-	-	-	42.0	1.0	-	-	-	-	42.2	0.5	-	-	-	-
1960	40.8	-1.4	-	-	-	-	41.6	2.0	-	-	-	-	42.1	0.5	-	-	-	-	42.5	1.0	-	-	-	-
1961	41.6	-1.4	-	-	-	-	41.9	0.7	-	-	-	-	41.4	-1.0	-	-	-	-	43.0	3.9	-	-	-	-
1962	41.9	-1.4	-	-	-	-	41.8	-0.2	-	-	-	-	42.1	-0.2	-	-	-	-	43.8	4.0	-	-	-	-
1963	41.8	-2.8	-	-	-	-	42.2	1.0	-	-	-	-	43.3	0.0	-	-	-	-	44.4	2.5	-	-	-	-
1964	43.1	-1.6	-	-	-	-	43.3	0.5	-	-	-	-	-	-	-	-	45.3	2.0	-	-	-	-	45.4	0.2
1965	43.6	-1.8	-	-	-	-	43.6	0.0	-	-	44.4	1.8	-	-	-	-	46.0	0.4	-	-	-	-	46.0	0.0
1966	-	-	-	-	45.0	-0.9	-	-	-	-	45.8	1.8	-	-	-	-	48.6	4.1	-	-	-	-	48.6	0.0
1967	-	-	-	-	46.3	0.7	-	-	-	-	46.7	0.9	-	-	-	-	52.4	4.0	-	-	-	-	52.6	0.4
1968	-	-	-	-	49.3	1.4	-	-	-	-	50.4	2.2	-	-	-	-	55.6	2.6	-	-	-	-	55.8	0.4
1969	-	-	-	-	53.1	1.0	-	-	-	-	54.2	2.1	-	-	-	-	58.3	2.3	-	-	-	-	58.7	0.7
1970	-	-	-	-	56.4	1.1	-	-	-	-	57.0	1.1	-	-	-	-	59.8	2.6	-	-	-	-	58.9	-1.5
1971	-	-	-	-	58.6	-0.2	-	-	-	-	58.3	-0.5	-	-	-	-	61.5	2.7	-	-	-	-	61.1	-0.7
1972	-	-	-	-	59.7	1.4	-	-	-	-	59.9	0.3	-	-	-	-	62.6	1.6	-	-	-	-	62.3	-0.5
1973	-	-	-	-	61.2	0.2	-	-	-	-	61.6	0.7	-	-	-	-	68.2	5.1	-	-	-	-	68.3	0.1
1974	-	-	-	-	63.6	2.1	-	-	-	-	64.9	2.0	-	-	-	-	69.5	1.5	-	-	-	-	68.3	-1.7
1975	-	-	-	-	69.5	1.8	-	-	-	-	68.5	-1.4	-	-	-	-	73.2	3.1	-	-	-	-	73.0	-0.3
1976	-	-	-	-	69.5	1.8	-	-	-	-	71.0	2.2	-	-	-	-	78.8	3.3	-	-	-	-	79.0	0.3
1977	-	-	-	-	75.9	4.0	-	-	-	-	76.3	0.5	-	-	80.3	2.8	-	-	80.2	-0.1	-	-	81.0	1.0
1978	-	-	75.6	-4.3	-	-	79.2	4.8	-	-	78.1	-1.4	-	-	86.4	4.0	-	-	86.6	0.2	-	-	83.1	-4.0
1979	-	-	84.0	3.7	-	-	83.2	-1.0	-	-	83.1	-0.1	-	-	87.9	2.6	-	-	91.1	3.6	-	-	91.1	0.0
1980	-	-	84.5	1.7	-	-	87.5	3.6	-	-	85.7	-2.1	-	-	93.5	2.6	-	-	95.3	1.9	-	-	90.2	-5.4
1981	-	-	91.8	0.8	-	-	91.7	-0.1	-	-	91.1	-0.7	-	-	97.8	2.6	-	-	96.1	-1.7	-	-	97.6	1.6
1982	-	-	92.6	2.7	-	-	96.3	4.0	-	-	95.3	-1.0	-	-	101.4	0.1	-	-	105.6	4.1	-	-	102.6	-2.8
1983	-	-	98.6	1.0	-	-	102.6	4.1	-	-	101.3	-1.3	-	-	101.9	1.7	-	-	104.0	2.1	-	-	102.0	-1.9
1984	-	-	102.8	0.2	-	-	104.2	1.4	-	-	100.2	-3.8	-	-	104.1	1.3	-	-	106.5	2.3	-	-	104.0	-2.3
1985	-	-	104.8	2.7	-	-	108.1	3.1	-	-	102.8	-4.9	-	-	106.2	-1.6	-	-	106.0	-0.2	-	-	101.4	-4.3
1986	-	-	108.7	4.5	-	-	111.0	2.1	-	-	107.9	-2.8	-	-	-	-	-	-	-	-	-	-	114.6	9.4
1987	-	-	-	-	-	-	-	-	-	-	104.8	3.4	-	-	-	-	-	-	-	-	-	-	115.0	3.3
1988	-	-	-	-	-	-	-	-	-	-	111.3	-2.9	-	-	-	-	-	-	-	-	-	-	125.1	9.5
1989	-	-	-	-	-	-	-	-	-	-	114.2	-0.7	-	-	-	-	-	-	-	-	-	-	119.3	4.8
1990	-	-	-	-	-	-	-	-	-	-	113.8	-9.0	-	-	-	-	-	-	-	-	-	-	128.4	6.1
1991	-	-	-	-	-	-	-	-	-	-	121.0	1.4	-	-	-	-	-	-	-	-	-	-	124.2	-0.9
1992	-	-	-	-	-	-	-	-	-	-	125.3	-2.4	-	-	-	-	-	-	-	-	-	-	124.5	-1.3
1993	-	-	-	-	-	-	-	-	-	-	126.2	1.6	-	-	-	-	-	-	-	-	-	-	117.1	-9.5
1994	-	-	-	-	-	-	-	-	-	-	129.4	3.9	-	-	-	-	-	-	-	-	-	-	-	-
1995	-	-	-	-	-	-	-	-	-	-	128.1	9.4	-	-	-	-	-	-	-	-	-	-	-	-

Source: U.S. Department of Labor, Bureau of Labor Statistics, Division of Consumer Prices and Price Indexes. - indicates no data collected for period.

Kansas City, MO-KS
Consumer Price Index - Urban Wage Earners
Base 1982-1984 = 100
Apparel and Upkeep

For 1952-1995. Columns headed % show percentile change in the index from the previous period for which an index is available.

Year	Jan Index	%	Feb Index	%	Mar Index	%	Apr Index	%	May Index	%	Jun Index	%	Jul Index	%	Aug Index	%	Sep Index	%	Oct Index	%	Nov Index	%	Dec Index	%
1952	-		-		-		-		-		-		-		-		-		40.6	-	-		-	-
1953	40.5	-0.2	-		-		40.4	-0.2	-		-		40.6	0.5	-		-		40.5	-0.2	-		-	-
1954	40.3	-0.5	-		-		40.0	-0.7	-		-		40.0	0.0	-		-		40.3	0.7	-		-	-
1955	39.7	-1.5	-		-		39.8	0.3	-		-		39.8	0.0	-		-		40.6	2.0	-		-	-
1956	40.3	-0.7	-		-		40.3	0.0	-		-		40.5	0.5	-		-		41.0	1.2	-		-	-
1957	41.8	2.0	-		-		41.5	-0.7	-		-		41.1	-1.0	-		-		41.9	1.9	-		-	-
1958	41.3	-1.4	-		-		41.6	0.7	-		-		41.5	-0.2	-		-		42.1	1.4	-		-	-
1959	41.5	-1.4	-		-		41.8	0.7	-		-		41.7	-0.2	-		-		42.7	2.4	-		-	-
1960	42.1	-1.4	-		-		42.9	1.9	-		-		43.3	0.9	-		-		43.5	0.5	-		-	-
1961	42.9	-1.4	-		-		43.2	0.7	-		-		43.4	0.5	-		-		43.8	0.9	-		-	-
1962	43.2	-1.4	-		-		43.1	-0.2	-		-		42.7	-0.9	-		-		44.3	3.7	-		-	-
1963	43.1	-2.7	-		-		43.5	0.9	-		-		43.4	-0.2	-		-		45.2	4.1	-		-	-
1964	44.4	-1.8	-		-		44.7	0.7	-		-		44.7	0.0	-		-		45.8	2.5	-		-	-
1965	45.0	-1.7	-		-		45.0	0.0	-		45.7	1.6	-		-		46.8	2.4	-		-		46.9	0.2
1966	-		-		46.4	-1.1	-		-		47.2	1.7	-		-		47.4	0.4	-		-		47.4	0.0
1967	-		-		47.7	0.6	-		-		48.1	0.8	-		-		50.1	4.2	-		-		50.1	0.0
1968	-		-		50.8	1.4	-		-		52.0	2.4	-		-		54 0	3.8	-		-		54.3	0.6
1969	-		-		54.7	0.7	-		-		55.9	2.2	-		-		57.3	2.5	-		-		57.5	0.3
1970	-		-		58.1	1.0	-		-		58.8	1.2	-		-		60.1	2.2	-		-		60.5	0.7
1971	-		-		60.4	-0.2	-		-		60.1	-0.5	-		-		61.6	2.5	-		-		60.7	-1.5
1972	-		-		61.6	1.5	-		-		61.7	0.2	-		-		63.4	2.8	-		-		63.0	-0.6
1973	-		-		63.1	0.2	-		-		63.6	0.8	-		-		64.5	1.4	-		-		64.2	-0.5
1974	-		-		65.6	2.2	-		-		66.9	2.0	-		-		70.3	5.1	-		-		70.5	0.3
1975	-		-		71.7	1.7	-		-		70.6	-1.5	-		-		71.7	1.6	-		-		70.5	-1.7
1976	-		-		71.7	1.7	-		-		73.2	2.1	-		-		75.5	3.1	-		-		75.3	-0.3
1977	-		-		78.3	4.0	-		-		78.7	0.5	-		-		81.3	3.3	-		-		81.5	0.2
1978	-		81.1	-0.5	-		82.2	1.4	-		79.9	-2.8	-		82.2	2.9	-		83.8	1.9	-		84.0	0.2
1979	-		84.3	0.4	-		84.9	0.7	-		82.7	-2.6	-		85.1	2.9	-		85.1	0.0	-		84.6	-0.6
1980	-		85.6	1.2	-		87.0	1.6	-		85.4	-1.8	-		86.5	1.3	-		89.7	3.7	-		88.8	-1.0
1981	-		91.6	3.2	-		92.8	1.3	-		91.7	-1.2	-		93.8	2.3	-		94.4	0.6	-		89.8	-4.9
1982	-		91.9	2.3	-		96.7	5.2	-		95.0	-1.8	-		98.4	3.6	-		96.6	-1.8	-		98.2	1.7
1983	-		98.8	0.6	-		102.8	4.0	-		101.6	-1.2	-		102.6	1.0	-		105.7	3.0	-		102.6	-2.9
1984	-		102.9	0.3	-		103.6	0.7	-		98.4	-5.0	-		101.2	2.8	-		104.2	3.0	-		102.1	-2.0
1985	-		104.5	2.4	-		108.5	3.8	-		104.1	-4.1	-		104.9	0.8	-		107.7	2.7	-		105.5	-2.0
1986	-		107.4	1.8	-		110.5	2.9	-		108.2	-2.1	-		106.4	-1.7	-		105.2	-1.1	-		101.8	-3.2
1987	-		-		-		-		-		105.6	3.7	-		-		-		-		-		115.3	9.2
1988	-		-		-		-		-		112.3	-2.6	-		-		-		-		-		116.2	3.5
1989	-		-		-		-		-		115.0	-1.0	-		-		-		-		-		125.6	9.2
1990	-		-		-		-		-		114.0	-9.2	-		-		-		-		-		119.6	4.9
1991	-		-		-		-		-		121.5	1.6	-		-		-		-		-		129.7	6.7
1992	-		-		-		-		-		125.1	-3.5	-		-		-		-		-		125.0	-0.1
1993	-		-		-		-		-		126.1	0.9	-		-		-		-		-		126.2	0.1
1994	-		-		-		-		-		131.4	4.1	-		-		-		-		-		117.1	-10.9
1995	-		-		-		-		-		129.3	10.4	-		-		-		-		-		-	-

Source: U.S. Department of Labor, Bureau of Labor Statistics, Division of Consumer Prices and Price Indexes. - indicates no data collected for period.

Kansas City, MO-KS
Consumer Price Index - All Urban Consumers
Base 1982-1984 = 100
Transportation

For 1947-1995. Columns headed % show percentile change in the index from the previous period for which an index is available.

Year	Jan Index	%	Feb Index	%	Mar Index	%	Apr Index	%	May Index	%	Jun Index	%	Jul Index	%	Aug Index	%	Sep Index	%	Oct Index	%	Nov Index	%	Dec Index	%
1947	17.7	-	17.7	0.0	17.7	0.0	18.0	1.7	18.0	0.0	18.0	0.0	18.1	0.6	-	-	-	-	18.7	3.3	-	-	-	-
1948	19.5	4.3	-	-	-	-	19.6	0.5	-	-	-	-	20.1	2.6	-	-	-	-	21.1	5.0	-	-	-	-
1949	21.1	0.0	-	-	-	-	21.5	1.9	-	-	-	-	21.3	-0.9	-	-	-	-	21.6	1.4	-	-	-	-
1950	21.7	0.5	-	-	-	-	21.7	0.0	-	-	-	-	22.3	2.8	-	-	-	-	21.9	-1.8	-	-	-	-
1951	22.5	2.7	-	-	-	-	22.9	1.8	-	-	-	-	23.1	0.9	-	-	-	-	23.6	2.2	-	-	-	-
1952	23.9	1.3	-	-	-	-	25.3	5.9	-	-	-	-	25.7	1.6	-	-	-	-	26.0	1.2	-	-	-	-
1953	26.1	0.4	-	-	-	-	26.0	-0.4	-	-	-	-	26.0	0.0	-	-	-	-	26.1	0.4	-	-	-	-
1954	25.1	-3.8	-	-	-	-	25.9	3.2	-	-	-	-	25.0	-3.5	-	-	-	-	24.8	-0.8	-	-	-	-
1955	25.1	1.2	-	-	-	-	24.6	-2.0	-	-	-	-	25.1	2.0	-	-	-	-	25.4	1.2	-	-	-	-
1956	25.0	-1.6	-	-	-	-	25.5	2.0	-	-	-	-	24.5	-3.9	-	-	-	-	26.1	6.5	-	-	-	-
1957	27.1	3.8	-	-	-	-	27.4	1.1	-	-	-	-	27.6	0.7	-	-	-	-	27.7	0.4	-	-	-	-
1958	28.1	1.4	-	-	-	-	28.4	1.1	-	-	-	-	29.7	4.6	-	-	-	-	30.1	1.3	-	-	-	-
1959	29.4	-2.3	-	-	-	-	30.6	4.1	-	-	-	-	30.7	0.3	-	-	-	-	31.2	1.6	-	-	-	-
1960	30.9	-1.0	-	-	-	-	29.8	-3.6	-	-	-	-	30.9	3.7	-	-	-	-	31.0	0.3	-	-	-	-
1961	30.0	-3.2	-	-	-	-	30.8	2.7	-	-	-	-	31.0	0.6	-	-	-	-	30.3	-2.3	-	-	-	-
1962	31.0	2.3	-	-	-	-	31.7	2.3	-	-	-	-	30.6	-3.5	-	-	-	-	31.9	4.2	-	-	-	-
1963	30.6	-4.1	-	-	-	-	31.3	2.3	-	-	-	-	30.9	-1.3	-	-	-	-	32.2	4.2	-	-	-	-
1964	31.5	-2.2	-	-	-	-	31.4	-0.3	-	-	-	-	31.7	1.0	-	-	-	-	31.4	-0.9	-	-	-	-
1965	32.8	4.5	-	-	-	-	33.0	0.6	-	-	34.5	4.5	-	-	-	-	34.3	-0.6	-	-	-	-	34.1	-0.6
1966	-	-	-	-	34.1	0.0	-	-	-	-	34.7	1.8	-	-	-	-	34.6	-0.3	-	-	-	-	34.8	0.6
1967	-	-	-	-	34.9	0.3	-	-	-	-	33.6	-3.7	-	-	-	-	35.5	5.7	-	-	-	-	34.8	-2.0
1968	-	-	-	-	35.0	0.6	-	-	-	-	36.7	4.9	-	-	-	-	35.0	-4.6	-	-	-	-	35.8	2.3
1969	-	-	-	-	37.6	5.0	-	-	-	-	37.5	-0.3	-	-	-	-	36.6	-2.4	-	-	-	-	37.7	3.0
1970	-	-	-	-	36.7	-2.7	-	-	-	-	38.5	4.9	-	-	-	-	37.9	-1.6	-	-	-	-	41.1	8.4
1971	-	-	-	-	41.0	-0.2	-	-	-	-	41.7	1.7	-	-	-	-	40.9	-1.9	-	-	-	-	40.2	-1.7
1972	-	-	-	-	40.0	-0.5	-	-	-	-	41.3	3.2	-	-	-	-	41.7	1.0	-	-	-	-	41.8	0.2
1973	-	-	-	-	42.1	0.7	-	-	-	-	42.9	1.9	-	-	-	-	42.6	-0.7	-	-	-	-	43.4	1.9
1974	-	-	-	-	45.4	4.6	-	-	-	-	47.7	5.1	-	-	-	-	48.8	2.3	-	-	-	-	49.3	1.0
1975	-	-	-	-	49.5	0.4	-	-	-	-	51.1	3.2	-	-	-	-	53.1	3.9	-	-	-	-	53.7	1.1
1976	-	-	-	-	53.7	0.0	-	-	-	-	55.8	3.9	-	-	-	-	56.4	1.1	-	-	-	-	57.5	2.0
1977	-	-	-	-	58.6	1.9	-	-	-	-	59.9	2.2	-	-	-	-	59.2	-1.2	-	-	-	-	59.9	1.2
1978	-	-	59.9	0.0	-	-	60.2	0.5	-	-	62.0	3.0	-	-	62.8	1.3	-	-	64.0	1.9	-	-	65.1	1.7
1979	-	-	65.9	1.2	-	-	69.3	5.2	-	-	73.0	5.3	-	-	75.1	2.9	-	-	75.8	0.9	-	-	78.1	3.0
1980	-	-	82.0	5.0	-	-	85.0	3.7	-	-	85.1	0.1	-	-	85.7	0.7	-	-	86.3	0.7	-	-	88.2	2.2
1981	-	-	90.9	3.1	-	-	92.2	1.4	-	-	93.4	1.3	-	-	93.6	0.2	-	-	94.6	1.1	-	-	96.5	2.0
1982	-	-	95.6	-0.9	-	-	95.0	-0.6	-	-	98.7	3.9	-	-	99.3	0.6	-	-	98.9	-0.4	-	-	97.8	-1.1
1983	-	-	96.1	-1.7	-	-	97.8	1.8	-	-	99.6	1.8	-	-	100.6	1.0	-	-	102.3	1.7	-	-	101.7	-0.6
1984	-	-	101.4	-0.3	-	-	102.4	1.0	-	-	103.6	1.2	-	-	102.5	-1.1	-	-	104.6	2.0	-	-	104.3	-0.3
1985	-	-	102.9	-1.3	-	-	106.9	3.9	-	-	107.6	0.7	-	-	106.9	-0.7	-	-	107.7	0.7	-	-	107.6	-0.1
1986	-	-	102.5	-4.7	-	-	98.5	-3.9	-	-	101.7	3.2	-	-	97.7	-3.9	-	-	98.7	1.0	-	-	98.9	0.2
1987	-	-	-	-	-	-	-	-	-	-	101.0	2.1	-	-	-	-	-	-	-	-	-	-	104.7	3.7
1988	-	-	-	-	-	-	-	-	-	-	105.5	0.8	-	-	-	-	-	-	-	-	-	-	108.8	3.1
1989	-	-	-	-	-	-	-	-	-	-	112.0	2.9	-	-	-	-	-	-	-	-	-	-	112.4	0.4
1990	-	-	-	-	-	-	-	-	-	-	112.8	0.4	-	-	-	-	-	-	-	-	-	-	119.5	5.9
1991	-	-	-	-	-	-	-	-	-	-	118.5	-0.8	-	-	-	-	-	-	-	-	-	-	119.9	1.2

[Continued]

Kansas City, MO-KS
Consumer Price Index - All Urban Consumers
Base 1982-1984 = 100
Transportation
[Continued]

For 1947-1995. Columns headed % show percentile change in the index from the previous period for which an index is available.

Year	Jan Index	%	Feb Index	%	Mar Index	%	Apr Index	%	May Index	%	Jun Index	%	Jul Index	%	Aug Index	%	Sep Index	%	Oct Index	%	Nov Index	%	Dec Index	%
1992	-	-	-	-	-	-	-	-	-	-	120.9	0.8	-	-	-	-	-	-	-	-	-	-	122.8	1.6
1993	-	-	-	-	-	-	-	-	-	-	124.6	1.5	-	-	-	-	-	-	-	-	-	-	124.7	0.1
1994	-	-	-	-	-	-	-	-	-	-	126.6	1.5	-	-	-	-	-	-	-	-	-	-	129.6	2.4
1995	-	-	-	-	-	-	-	-	-	-	133.3	2.9	-	-	-	-	-	-	-	-	-	-	-	-

Source: U.S. Department of Labor, Bureau of Labor Statistics, Division of Consumer Prices and Price Indexes. - indicates no data collected for period.

Kansas City, MO-KS
Consumer Price Index - Urban Wage Earners
Base 1982-1984 = 100
Transportation

For 1947-1995. Columns headed % show percentile change in the index from the previous period for which an index is available.

Year	Jan Index	%	Feb Index	%	Mar Index	%	Apr Index	%	May Index	%	Jun Index	%	Jul Index	%	Aug Index	%	Sep Index	%	Oct Index	%	Nov Index	%	Dec Index	%
1947	17.6	-	17.6	0.0	17.6	0.0	17.9	1.7	17.9	0.0	17.9	0.0	18.0	0.6	-	-	-	-	18.5	2.8	-	-	-	-
1948	19.4	4.9	-	-	-	-	19.5	0.5	-	-	-	-	20.0	2.6	-	-	-	-	21.0	5.0	-	-	-	-
1949	21.0	0.0	-	-	-	-	21.4	1.9	-	-	-	-	21.2	-0.9	-	-	-	-	21.5	1.4	-	-	-	-
1950	21.6	0.5	-	-	-	-	21.6	0.0	-	-	-	-	22.1	2.3	-	-	-	-	21.7	-1.8	-	-	-	-
1951	22.3	2.8	-	-	-	-	22.8	2.2	-	-	-	-	23.0	0.9	-	-	-	-	23.5	2.2	-	-	-	-
1952	23.7	0.9	-	-	-	-	25.2	6.3	-	-	-	-	25.5	1.2	-	-	-	-	25.8	1.2	-	-	-	-
1953	25.9	0.4	-	-	-	-	25.8	-0.4	-	-	-	-	25.9	0.4	-	-	-	-	25.9	0.0	-	-	-	-
1954	25.0	-3.5	-	-	-	-	25.7	2.8	-	-	-	-	24.9	-3.1	-	-	-	-	24.6	-1.2	-	-	-	-
1955	25.0	1.6	-	-	-	-	24.5	-2.0	-	-	-	-	24.9	1.6	-	-	-	-	25.2	1.2	-	-	-	-
1956	24.8	-1.6	-	-	-	-	25.3	2.0	-	-	-	-	24.3	-4.0	-	-	-	-	26.0	7.0	-	-	-	-
1957	27.0	3.8	-	-	-	-	27.3	1.1	-	-	-	-	27.4	0.4	-	-	-	-	27.5	0.4	-	-	-	-
1958	27.9	1.5	-	-	-	-	28.2	1.1	-	-	-	-	29.5	4.6	-	-	-	-	29.9	1.4	-	-	-	-
1959	29.2	-2.3	-	-	-	-	30.4	4.1	-	-	-	-	30.6	0.7	-	-	-	-	31.0	1.3	-	-	-	-
1960	30.7	-1.0	-	-	-	-	29.6	-3.6	-	-	-	-	30.7	3.7	-	-	-	-	30.8	0.3	-	-	-	-
1961	29.8	-3.2	-	-	-	-	30.6	2.7	-	-	-	-	30.8	0.7	-	-	-	-	30.2	-1.9	-	-	-	-
1962	30.8	2.0	-	-	-	-	31.5	2.3	-	-	-	-	30.5	-3.2	-	-	-	-	31.7	3.9	-	-	-	-
1963	30.4	-4.1	-	-	-	-	31.2	2.6	-	-	-	-	30.7	-1.6	-	-	-	-	32.0	4.2	-	-	-	-
1964	31.3	-2.2	-	-	-	-	31.3	0.0	-	-	-	-	31.5	0.6	-	-	-	-	31.2	-1.0	-	-	-	-
1965	32.6	4.5	-	-	-	-	32.8	0.6	-	-	34.3	4.6	-	-	-	-	34.1	-0.6	-	-	-	-	33.9	-0.6
1966	-	-	-	-	33.9	0.0	-	-	-	-	34.5	1.8	-	-	-	-	34.4	-0.3	-	-	-	-	34.6	0.6
1967	-	-	-	-	34.7	0.3	-	-	-	-	33.4	-3.7	-	-	-	-	35.3	5.7	-	-	-	-	34.6	-2.0
1968	-	-	-	-	34.8	0.6	-	-	-	-	36.5	4.9	-	-	-	-	34.8	-4.7	-	-	-	-	35.6	2.3
1969	-	-	-	-	37.4	5.1	-	-	-	-	37.3	-0.3	-	-	-	-	36.4	-2.4	-	-	-	-	37.5	3.0
1970	-	-	-	-	36.5	-2.7	-	-	-	-	38.3	4.9	-	-	-	-	37.6	-1.8	-	-	-	-	40.9	8.8
1971	-	-	-	-	40.8	-0.2	-	-	-	-	41.5	1.7	-	-	-	-	40.7	-1.9	-	-	-	-	39.9	-2.0
1972	-	-	-	-	39.8	-0.3	-	-	-	-	41.0	3.0	-	-	-	-	41.4	1.0	-	-	-	-	41.5	0.2
1973	-	-	-	-	41.8	0.7	-	-	-	-	42.7	2.2	-	-	-	-	42.4	-0.7	-	-	-	-	43.1	1.7
1974	-	-	-	-	45.1	4.6	-	-	-	-	47.5	5.3	-	-	-	-	48.6	2.3	-	-	-	-	49.0	0.8
1975	-	-	-	-	49.2	0.4	-	-	-	-	50.8	3.3	-	-	-	-	52.8	3.9	-	-	-	-	53.3	0.9
1976	-	-	-	-	53.4	0.2	-	-	-	-	55.5	3.9	-	-	-	-	56.1	1.1	-	-	-	-	57.2	2.0
1977	-	-	-	-	58.2	1.7	-	-	-	-	59.6	2.4	-	-	-	-	58.8	-1.3	-	-	-	-	59.5	1.2
1978	-	-	59.4	-0.2	-	-	59.6	0.3	-	-	61.5	3.2	-	-	62.4	1.5	-	-	63.7	2.1	-	-	64.8	1.7
1979	-	-	65.6	1.2	-	-	69.2	5.5	-	-	72.9	5.3	-	-	75.1	3.0	-	-	75.8	0.9	-	-	78.2	3.2
1980	-	-	82.1	5.0	-	-	85.2	3.8	-	-	85.3	0.1	-	-	85.6	0.4	-	-	86.2	0.7	-	-	88.1	2.2
1981	-	-	91.2	3.5	-	-	92.9	1.9	-	-	94.1	1.3	-	-	94.3	0.2	-	-	95.3	1.1	-	-	96.6	1.4
1982	-	-	95.6	-1.0	-	-	94.7	-0.9	-	-	98.7	4.2	-	-	99.4	0.7	-	-	98.9	-0.5	-	-	97.8	-1.1
1983	-	-	95.9	-1.9	-	-	97.7	1.9	-	-	99.6	1.9	100.7	1.1	-	-	-	-	102.3	1.6	-	-	101.6	-0.7
1984	-	-	101.3	-0.3	-	-	102.5	1.2	-	-	103.7	1.2	-	-	102.5	-1.2	-	-	104.7	2.1	-	-	104.4	-0.3
1985	-	-	102.8	-1.5	-	-	107.0	4.1	-	-	107.8	0.7	-	-	107.0	-0.7	-	-	107.6	0.6	-	-	107.5	-0.1
1986	-	-	102.1	-5.0	-	-	97.5	-4.5	-	-	101.0	3.6	-	-	96.6	-4.4	-	-	97.7	1.1	-	-	97.8	0.1
1987	-	-	-	-	-	-	-	-	-	-	99.4	1.6	-	-	-	-	-	-	-	-	-	-	103.0	3.6
1988	-	-	-	-	-	-	-	-	-	-	104.0	1.0	-	-	-	-	-	-	-	-	-	-	107.1	3.0
1989	-	-	-	-	-	-	-	-	-	-	109.8	2.5	-	-	-	-	-	-	-	-	-	-	110.1	0.3
1990	-	-	-	-	-	-	-	-	-	-	110.0	-0.1	-	-	-	-	-	-	-	-	-	-	115.2	4.7
1991	-	-	-	-	-	-	-	-	-	-	114.9	-0.3	-	-	-	-	-	-	-	-	-	-	116.8	1.7

[Continued]

Kansas City, MO-KS
Consumer Price Index - Urban Wage Earners
Base 1982-1984 = 100
Transportation
[Continued]

For 1947-1995. Columns headed % show percentile change in the index from the previous period for which an index is available.

Year	Jan		Feb		Mar		Apr		May		Jun		Jul		Aug		Sep		Oct		Nov		Dec	
	Index	%	Index	%	Index	%	Index	%	Index	%	Index	%	Index	%	Index	%	Index	%	Index	%	Index	%	Index	%
1992	-	-	-	-	-	-	-	-	-	-	117.9	0.9	-	-	-	-	-	-	-	-	-	-		
1993	-	-	-	-	-	-	-	-	-	-	121.8	1.3	-	-	-	-	-	-	-	-	-	-	120.2	2.0
1994	-	-	-	-	-	-	-	-	-	-	124.5	1.5	-	-	-	-	-	-	-	-	-	-	122.6	0.7
1995	-	-	-	-	-	-	-	-	-	-	131.8	3.2	-	-	-	-	-	-	-	-	-	-	127.7	2.6
																							-	-

Source: U.S. Department of Labor, Bureau of Labor Statistics, Division of Consumer Prices and Price Indexes. - indicates no data collected for period.

Kansas City, MO-KS
Consumer Price Index - All Urban Consumers
Base 1982-1984 = 100
Medical Care

For 1947-1995. Columns headed % show percentile change in the index from the previous period for which an index is available.

Year	Jan Index	%	Feb Index	%	Mar Index	%	Apr Index	%	May Index	%	Jun Index	%	Jul Index	%	Aug Index	%	Sep Index	%	Oct Index	%	Nov Index	%	Dec Index	%
1947	10.8	-	10.9	0.9	10.9	0.0	11.0	0.9	11.0	0.0	11.0	0.0	11.0	0.0	-	-	-	-	11.1	0.9	-	-	-	-
1948	11.5	3.6	-	-	-	-	11.9	3.5	-	-	-	-	11.9	0.0	-	-	-	-	12.1	1.7	-	-	-	-
1949	12.1	0.0	-	-	-	-	12.1	0.0	-	-	-	-	12.2	0.8	-	-	-	-	12.2	0.0	-	-	-	-
1950	12.2	0.0	-	-	-	-	12.3	0.8	-	-	-	-	12.3	0.0	-	-	-	-	12.7	3.3	-	-	-	-
1951	12.8	0.8	-	-	-	-	12.9	0.8	-	-	-	-	13.0	0.8	-	-	-	-	13.1	0.8	-	-	-	-
1952	13.3	1.5	-	-	-	-	13.4	0.8	-	-	-	-	13.9	3.7	-	-	-	-	13.9	0.0	-	-	-	-
1953	13.9	0.0	-	-	-	-	14.0	0.7	-	-	-	-	14.0	0.0	-	-	-	-	14.0	0.0	-	-	-	-
1954	14.0	0.0	-	-	-	-	15.8	12.9	-	-	-	-	15.9	0.6	-	-	-	-	15.9	0.0	-	-	-	-
1955	15.9	0.0	-	-	-	-	15.9	0.0	-	-	-	-	16.0	0.6	-	-	-	-	16.0	0.0	-	-	-	-
1956	16.0	0.0	-	-	-	-	16.2	1.3	-	-	-	-	16.2	0.0	-	-	-	-	17.5	8.0	-	-	-	-
1957	17.5	0.0	-	-	-	-	17.6	0.6	-	-	-	-	17.6	0.0	-	-	-	-	17.8	1.1	-	-	-	-
1958	17.9	0.6	-	-	-	-	17.9	0.0	-	-	-	-	19.9	11.2	-	-	-	-	19.9	0.0	-	-	-	-
1959	19.9	0.0	-	-	-	-	19.9	0.0	-	-	-	-	20.0	0.5	-	-	-	-	20.0	0.0	-	-	-	-
1960	20.1	0.5	-	-	-	-	20.2	0.5	-	-	-	-	20.5	1.5	-	-	-	-	20.4	-0.5	-	-	-	-
1961	20.4	0.0	-	-	-	-	21.2	3.9	-	-	-	-	21.1	-0.5	-	-	-	-	21.3	0.9	-	-	-	-
1962	21.4	0.5	-	-	-	-	21.4	0.0	-	-	-	-	21.5	0.5	-	-	-	-	21.6	0.5	-	-	-	-
1963	21.6	0.0	-	-	-	-	21.6	0.0	-	-	-	-	21.7	0.5	-	-	-	-	21.8	0.5	-	-	-	-
1964	21.8	0.0	-	-	-	-	22.0	0.9	-	-	-	-	23.5	6.8	-	-	-	-	23.5	0.0	-	-	-	-
1965	23.5	0.0	-	-	-	-	23.7	0.9	-	-	23.8	0.4	-	-	-	-	24.2	1.7	-	-	-	-	24.4	0.8
1966	-	-	-	-	25.2	3.3	-	-	-	-	25.4	0.8	-	-	-	-	25.5	0.4	-	-	-	-	25.7	0.8
1967	-	-	-	-	26.9	4.7	-	-	-	-	27.1	0.7	-	-	-	-	27.6	1.8	-	-	-	-	27.6	0.0
1968	-	-	-	-	28.7	4.0	-	-	-	-	29.0	1.0	-	-	-	-	29.1	0.3	-	-	-	-	29.6	1.7
1969	-	-	-	-	30.0	1.4	-	-	-	-	30.5	1.7	-	-	-	-	30.8	1.0	-	-	-	-	30.9	0.3
1970	-	-	-	-	31.2	1.0	-	-	-	-	31.7	1.6	-	-	-	-	32.1	1.3	-	-	-	-	32.7	1.9
1971	-	-	-	-	33.2	1.5	-	-	-	-	33.7	1.5	-	-	-	-	34.5	2.4	-	-	-	-	34.4	-0.3
1972	-	-	-	-	34.7	0.9	-	-	-	-	35.0	0.9	-	-	-	-	35.2	0.6	-	-	-	-	35.8	1.7
1973	-	-	-	-	36.4	1.7	-	-	-	-	36.5	0.3	-	-	-	-	36.7	0.5	-	-	-	-	37.7	2.7
1974	-	-	-	-	39.1	3.7	-	-	-	-	39.9	2.0	-	-	-	-	41.1	3.0	-	-	-	-	41.6	1.2
1975	-	-	-	-	43.3	4.1	-	-	-	-	43.3	0.0	-	-	-	-	44.0	1.6	-	-	-	-	44.9	2.0
1976	-	-	-	-	46.3	3.1	-	-	-	-	47.3	2.2	-	-	-	-	47.6	0.6	-	-	-	-	49.5	4.0
1977	-	-	-	-	51.1	3.2	-	-	-	-	51.7	1.2	-	-	-	-	52.5	1.5	-	-	-	-	53.3	1.5
1978	-	-	54.2	1.7	-	-	55.2	1.8	-	-	56.4	2.2	-	-	56.9	0.9	-	-	59.3	4.2	-	-	59.7	0.7
1979	-	-	61.8	3.5	-	-	62.8	1.6	-	-	63.4	1.0	-	-	63.9	0.8	-	-	65.3	2.2	-	-	66.6	2.0
1980	-	-	68.7	3.2	-	-	69.9	1.7	-	-	70.6	1.0	-	-	71.5	1.3	-	-	73.1	2.2	-	-	73.5	0.5
1981	-	-	77.7	5.7	-	-	78.2	0.6	-	-	79.0	1.0	-	-	80.2	1.5	-	-	82.5	2.9	-	-	83.2	0.8
1982	-	-	85.7	3.0	-	-	89.4	4.3	-	-	89.8	0.4	-	-	93.1	3.7	-	-	96.1	3.2	-	-	95.2	-0.9
1983	-	-	98.6	3.6	-	-	99.6	1.0	-	-	100.0	0.4	-	-	102.3	2.3	-	-	103.8	1.5	-	-	104.9	1.1
1984	-	-	107.0	2.0	-	-	108.0	0.9	-	-	107.5	-0.5	-	-	107.6	0.1	-	-	108.9	1.2	-	-	109.0	0.1
1985	-	-	109.4	0.4	-	-	109.9	0.5	-	-	111.0	1.0	-	-	113.2	2.0	-	-	113.5	0.3	-	-	114.5	0.9
1986	-	-	115.6	1.0	-	-	116.5	0.8	-	-	116.9	0.3	-	-	119.1	1.9	-	-	118.9	-0.2	-	-	120.9	1.7
1987	-	-	-	-	-	-	-	-	-	-	123.1	1.8	-	-	-	-	-	-	-	-	-	-	123.6	0.4
1988	-	-	-	-	-	-	-	-	-	-	128.8	4.2	-	-	-	-	-	-	-	-	-	-	132.9	3.2
1989	-	-	-	-	-	-	-	-	-	-	138.3	4.1	-	-	-	-	-	-	-	-	-	-	145.6	5.3
1990	-	-	-	-	-	-	-	-	-	-	152.8	4.9	-	-	-	-	-	-	-	-	-	-	160.8	5.2
1991	-	-	-	-	-	-	-	-	-	-	172.4	7.2	-	-	-	-	-	-	-	-	-	-	174.5	1.2

[Continued]

Kansas City, MO-KS

Consumer Price Index - All Urban Consumers
Base 1982-1984 = 100
Medical Care

[Continued]

For 1947-1995. Columns headed % show percentile change in the index from the previous period for which an index is available.

Year	Jan Index	%	Feb Index	%	Mar Index	%	Apr Index	%	May Index	%	Jun Index	%	Jul Index	%	Aug Index	%	Sep Index	%	Oct Index	%	Nov Index	%	Dec Index	%
1992	-	-	-	-	-	-	-	-	-	-	181.7	4.1	-	-	-	-	-	-	-	-	-	-	185.9	2.3
1993	-	-	-	-	-	-	-	-	-	-	195.5	5.2	-	-	-	-	-	-	-	-	-	-	195.8	0.2
1994	-	-	-	-	-	-	-	-	-	-	200.7	2.5	-	-	-	-	-	-	-	-	-	-	205.2	2.2
1995	-	-	-	-	-	-	-	-	-	-	207.8	1.3	-	-	-	-	-	-	-	-	-	-	-	-

Source: U.S. Department of Labor, Bureau of Labor Statistics, Division of Consumer Prices and Price Indexes. - indicates no data collected for period.

Kansas City, MO-KS
Consumer Price Index - Urban Wage Earners
Base 1982-1984 = 100
Medical Care

For 1947-1995. Columns headed % show percentile change in the index from the previous period for which an index is available.

Year	Jan Index	%	Feb Index	%	Mar Index	%	Apr Index	%	May Index	%	Jun Index	%	Jul Index	%	Aug Index	%	Sep Index	%	Oct Index	%	Nov Index	%	Dec Index	%
1947	10.8	-	10.9	0.9	10.9	0.0	11.0	0.9	11.0	0.0	11.0	0.0	11.0	0.0	-	-	-	-	11.1	0.9	-	-	-	-
1948	11.5	3.6	-	-	-	-	11.9	3.5	-	-	-	-	11.9	0.0	-	-	-	-	12.1	1.7	-	-	-	-
1949	12.1	0.0	-	-	-	-	12.1	0.0	-	-	-	-	12.2	0.8	-	-	-	-	12.2	0.0	-	-	-	-
1950	12.2	0.0	-	-	-	-	12.3	0.8	-	-	-	-	12.3	0.0	-	-	-	-	12.7	3.3	-	-	-	-
1951	12.8	0.8	-	-	-	-	12.9	0.8	-	-	-	-	13.0	0.8	-	-	-	-	13.1	0.8	-	-	-	-
1952	13.3	1.5	-	-	-	-	13.4	0.8	-	-	-	-	13.9	3.7	-	-	-	-	13.9	0.0	-	-	-	-
1953	13.9	0.0	-	-	-	-	14.0	0.7	-	-	-	-	14.0	0.0	-	-	-	-	14.0	0.0	-	-	-	-
1954	14.0	0.0	-	-	-	-	15.8	12.9	-	-	-	-	15.9	0.6	-	-	-	-	15.9	0.0	-	-	-	-
1955	15.9	0.0	-	-	-	-	15.9	0.0	-	-	-	-	16.0	0.6	-	-	-	-	16.0	0.0	-	-	-	-
1956	16.0	0.0	-	-	-	-	16.2	1.3	-	-	-	-	16.2	0.0	-	-	-	-	17.5	8.0	-	-	-	-
1957	17.5	0.0	-	-	-	-	17.6	0.6	-	-	-	-	17.6	0.0	-	-	-	-	17.8	1.1	-	-	-	-
1958	17.9	0.6	-	-	-	-	17.9	0.0	-	-	-	-	19.9	11.2	-	-	-	-	19.9	0.0	-	-	-	-
1959	19.9	0.0	-	-	-	-	19.9	0.0	-	-	-	-	20.0	0.5	-	-	-	-	20.0	0.0	-	-	-	-
1960	20.1	0.5	-	-	-	-	20.2	0.5	-	-	-	-	20.5	1.5	-	-	-	-	20.4	-0.5	-	-	-	-
1961	20.4	0.0	-	-	-	-	21.2	3.9	-	-	-	-	21.1	-0.5	-	-	-	-	21.3	0.9	-	-	-	-
1962	21.4	0.5	-	-	-	-	21.4	0.0	-	-	-	-	21.5	0.5	-	-	-	-	21.6	0.5	-	-	-	-
1963	21.6	0.0	-	-	-	-	21.6	0.0	-	-	-	-	21.7	0.5	-	-	-	-	21.8	0.5	-	-	-	-
1964	21.8	0.0	-	-	-	-	22.0	0.9	-	-	-	-	23.5	6.8	-	-	-	-	23.5	0.0	-	-	-	-
1965	23.5	0.0	-	-	-	-	23.7	0.9	-	-	23.8	0.4	-	-	-	-	24.2	1.7	-	-	-	-	24.4	0.8
1966	-	-	-	-	25.1	2.9	-	-	-	-	25.4	1.2	-	-	-	-	25.5	0.4	-	-	-	-	25.7	0.8
1967	-	-	-	-	26.9	4.7	-	-	-	-	27.1	0.7	-	-	-	-	27.6	1.8	-	-	-	-	27.6	0.0
1968	-	-	-	-	28.7	4.0	-	-	-	-	29.0	1.0	-	-	-	-	29.1	0.3	-	-	-	-	29.6	1.7
1969	-	-	-	-	30.0	1.4	-	-	-	-	30.5	1.7	-	-	-	-	30.8	1.0	-	-	-	-	30.9	0.3
1970	-	-	-	-	31.2	1.0	-	-	-	-	31.7	1.6	-	-	-	-	32.1	1.3	-	-	-	-	32.7	1.9
1971	-	-	-	-	33.2	1.5	-	-	-	-	33.6	1.2	-	-	-	-	34.5	2.7	-	-	-	-	34.4	-0.3
1972	-	-	-	-	34.7	0.9	-	-	-	-	35.0	0.9	-	-	-	-	35.2	0.6	-	-	-	-	35.8	1.7
1973	-	-	-	-	36.4	1.7	-	-	-	-	36.5	0.3	-	-	-	-	36.7	0.5	-	-	-	-	37.7	2.7
1974	-	-	-	-	39.1	3.7	-	-	-	-	39.9	2.0	-	-	-	-	41.1	3.0	-	-	-	-	41.6	1.2
1975	-	-	-	-	43.3	4.1	-	-	-	-	43.3	0.0	-	-	-	-	44.0	1.6	-	-	-	-	44.9	2.0
1976	-	-	-	-	46.3	3.1	-	-	-	-	47.3	2.2	-	-	-	-	47.6	0.6	-	-	-	-	49.5	4.0
1977	-	-	-	-	51.1	3.2	-	-	-	-	51.7	1.2	-	-	-	-	52.5	1.5	-	-	-	-	53.3	1.5
1978	-	-	54.2	1.7	-	-	55.0	1.5	-	-	56.3	2.4	-	-	56.8	0.9	-	-	58.4	2.8	-	-	59.3	1.5
1979	-	-	61.8	4.2	-	-	62.8	1.6	-	-	63.7	1.4	-	-	64.1	0.6	-	-	65.7	2.5	-	-	67.1	2.1
1980	-	-	67.8	1.0	-	-	69.9	3.1	-	-	70.2	0.4	-	-	72.8	3.7	-	-	74.2	1.9	-	-	74.7	0.7
1981	-	-	77.0	3.1	-	-	77.3	0.4	-	-	78.1	1.0	-	-	79.8	2.2	-	-	81.9	2.6	-	-	83.3	1.7
1982	-	-	85.9	3.1	-	-	89.5	4.2	-	-	89.9	0.4	-	-	93.0	3.4	-	-	95.9	3.1	-	-	95.0	-0.9
1983	-	-	98.4	3.6	-	-	99.5	1.1	-	-	100.1	0.6	-	-	102.3	2.2	-	-	103.7	1.4	-	-	104.9	1.2
1984	-	-	107.0	2.0	-	-	108.0	0.9	-	-	107.6	-0.4	-	-	107.7	0.1	-	-	109.1	1.3	-	-	109.2	0.1
1985	-	-	109.6	0.4	-	-	110.0	0.4	-	-	111.1	1.0	-	-	113.2	1.9	-	-	113.5	0.3	-	-	114.5	0.9
1986	-	-	115.6	1.0	-	-	116.4	0.7	-	-	116.8	0.3	-	-	119.0	1.9	-	-	118.8	-0.2	-	-	120.7	1.6
1987	-	-	-	-	-	-	-	-	-	-	123.4	2.2	-	-	-	-	-	-	-	-	-	-	124.2	0.6
1988	-	-	-	-	-	-	-	-	-	-	129.3	4.1	-	-	-	-	-	-	-	-	-	-	133.9	3.6
1989	-	-	-	-	-	-	-	-	-	-	139.4	4.1	-	-	-	-	-	-	-	-	-	-	146.5	5.1
1990	-	-	-	-	-	-	-	-	-	-	153.8	5.0	-	-	-	-	-	-	-	-	-	-	161.3	4.9
1991	-	-	-	-	-	-	-	-	-	-	172.7	7.1	-	-	-	-	-	-	-	-	-	-	174.7	1.2

[Continued]

Kansas City, MO-KS
Consumer Price Index - Urban Wage Earners
Base 1982-1984 = 100
Medical Care
[Continued]

For 1947-1995. Columns headed % show percentile change in the index from the previous period for which an index is available.

Year	Jan		Feb		Mar		Apr		May		Jun		Jul		Aug		Sep		Oct		Nov		Dec	
	Index	%	Index	%	Index	%	Index	%	Index	%	Index	%	Index	%	Index	%	Index	%	Index	%	Index	%	Index	%
1992	-	-	-	-	-	-	-	-	-	-	182.1	4.2	-	-	-	-	-	-	-	-	-	-	186.4	2.4
1993	-	-	-	-	-	-	-	-	-	-	196.7	5.5	-	-	-	-	-	-	-	-	-	-	196.7	0.0
1994	-	-	-	-	-	-	-	-	-	-	201.7	2.5	-	-	-	-	-	-	-	-	-	-	206.1	2.2
1995	-	-	-	-	-	-	-	-	-	-	208.4	1.1	-	-	-	-	-	-	-	-	-	-	-	-

Source: U.S. Department of Labor, Bureau of Labor Statistics, Division of Consumer Prices and Price Indexes. - indicates no data collected for period.

Kansas City, MO-KS
Consumer Price Index - All Urban Consumers
Base 1982-1984 = 100
Entertainment

For 1975-1995. Columns headed % show percentile change in the index from the previous period for which an index is available.

Year	Jan Index	%	Feb Index	%	Mar Index	%	Apr Index	%	May Index	%	Jun Index	%	Jul Index	%	Aug Index	%	Sep Index	%	Oct Index	%	Nov Index	%	Dec Index	%
1975	-	-	-	-	-	-	-	-	-	-	-	-	-	-	-	-	-	-	-	-	-	-	63.6	-
1976	-	-	-	-	64.0	0.6	-	-	-	-	65.2	1.9	-	-	-	-	66.4	1.8	-	-	-	-	66.4	0.0
1977	-	-	-	-	66.9	0.8	-	-	-	-	68.0	1.6	-	-	-	-	69.6	2.4	-	-	-	-	69.5	-0.1
1978	-	-	69.9	0.6	-	-	70.9	1.4	-	-	70.0	-1.3	-	-	71.0	1.4	-	-	72.0	1.4	-	-	72.2	0.3
1979	-	-	73.3	1.5	-	-	73.0	-0.4	-	-	73.6	0.8	-	-	74.2	0.8	-	-	76.2	2.7	-	-	76.4	0.3
1980	-	-	79.7	4.3	-	-	80.7	1.3	-	-	81.1	0.5	-	-	85.8	5.8	-	-	86.0	0.2	-	-	88.4	2.8
1981	-	-	88.9	0.6	-	-	89.1	0.2	-	-	90.2	1.2	-	-	90.4	0.2	-	-	92.0	1.8	-	-	92.7	0.8
1982	-	-	94.6	2.0	-	-	94.7	0.1	-	-	95.4	0.7	-	-	96.6	1.3	-	-	97.2	0.6	-	-	97.4	0.2
1983	-	-	99.2	1.8	-	-	98.9	-0.3	-	-	98.7	-0.2	-	-	100.9	2.2	-	-	101.3	0.4	-	-	101.7	0.4
1984	-	-	102.8	1.1	-	-	103.5	0.7	-	-	104.0	0.5	-	-	105.0	1.0	-	-	105.8	0.8	-	-	105.7	-0.1
1985	-	-	106.8	1.0	-	-	107.0	0.2	-	-	106.9	-0.1	-	-	106.9	0.0	-	-	107.6	0.7	-	-	107.0	-0.6
1986	-	-	108.1	1.0	-	-	109.3	1.1	-	-	110.4	1.0	-	-	110.6	0.2	-	-	114.4	3.4	-	-	114.8	0.3
1987	-	-	-	-	-	-	-	-	-	-	120.8	5.2	-	-	-	-	-	-	-	-	-	-	126.4	4.6
1988	-	-	-	-	-	-	-	-	-	-	123.3	-2.5	-	-	-	-	-	-	-	-	-	-	125.2	1.5
1989	-	-	-	-	-	-	-	-	-	-	129.9	3.8	-	-	-	-	-	-	-	-	-	-	134.1	3.2
1990	-	-	-	-	-	-	-	-	-	-	136.6	1.9	-	-	-	-	-	-	-	-	-	-	147.4	7.9
1991	-	-	-	-	-	-	-	-	-	-	147.3	-0.1	-	-	-	-	-	-	-	-	-	-	151.4	2.8
1992	-	-	-	-	-	-	-	-	-	-	154.5	2.0	-	-	-	-	-	-	-	-	-	-	153.5	-0.6
1993	-	-	-	-	-	-	-	-	-	-	152.4	-0.7	-	-	-	-	-	-	-	-	-	-	152.5	0.1
1994	-	-	-	-	-	-	-	-	-	-	159.6	4.7	-	-	-	-	-	-	-	-	-	-	161.5	1.2
1995	-	-	-	-	-	-	-	-	-	-	161.9	0.2	-	-	-	-	-	-	-	-	-	-	-	-

Source: U.S. Department of Labor, Bureau of Labor Statistics, Division of Consumer Prices and Price Indexes. - indicates no data collected for period.

Kansas City, MO-KS
Consumer Price Index - Urban Wage Earners
Base 1982-1984 = 100
Entertainment

For 1975-1995. Columns headed % show percentile change in the index from the previous period for which an index is available.

Year	Jan Index	%	Feb Index	%	Mar Index	%	Apr Index	%	May Index	%	Jun Index	%	Jul Index	%	Aug Index	%	Sep Index	%	Oct Index	%	Nov Index	%	Dec Index	%
1975	-	-	-	-	-	-	-	-	-	-	-	-	-	-	-	-	-	-	-	-	-	-	-	-
1976	-	-	-	-	60.7	0.7	-	-	-	-	61.8	1.8	-	-	-	-	-	-	-	-	-	-	60.3	-
1977	-	-	-	-	63.4	0.8	-	-	-	-	64.5	1.7	-	-	-	-	62.9	1.8	-	-	-	-	62.9	0.0
1978	-	-	66.3	0.6	-	-	66.8	0.8	-	-	66.6	-0.3	-	-	67.3	1.1	65.9	2.2	-	-	-	-	65.9	0.0
1979	-	-	68.6	2.7	-	-	68.7	0.1	-	-	70.0	1.9	-	-	70.9	1.3	-	-	67.4	0.1	-	-	66.8	-0.9
1980	-	-	78.7	4.5	-	-	80.8	2.7	-	-	81.8	1.2	-	-	85.0	3.9	-	-	75.3	6.2	-	-	75.3	0.0
1981	-	-	87.5	0.8	-	-	90.1	3.0	-	-	90.8	0.8	-	-	91.4	0.7	-	-	84.3	-0.8	-	-	86.8	3.0
1982	-	-	94.5	2.2	-	-	94.4	-0.1	-	-	95.2	0.8	-	-	96.5	1.4	-	-	91.8	0.4	-	-	92.5	0.8
1983	-	-	99.2	2.0	-	-	98.9	-0.3	-	-	98.9	0.0	-	-	100.9	2.0	-	-	97.1	0.6	-	-	97.3	0.2
1984	-	-	103.1	1.4	-	-	103.7	0.6	-	-	104.1	0.4	-	-	105.0	0.9	-	-	101.3	0.4	-	-	101.7	0.4
1985	-	-	106.9	0.8	-	-	106.9	0.0	-	-	106.9	0.0	-	-	106.8	-0.1	-	-	105.7	0.7	-	-	106.0	0.3
1986	-	-	108.4	1.1	-	-	109.4	0.9	-	-	110.5	1.0	-	-	110.7	0.2	-	-	107.5	0.7	-	-	107.2	-0.3
1987	-	-	-	-	-	-	-	-	-	-	119.9	5.5	-	-	-	-	-	-	112.8	1.9	-	-	113.6	0.7
1988	-	-	-	-	-	-	-	-	-	-	122.1	-2.9	-	-	-	-	-	-	-	-	-	-	125.7	4.8
1989	-	-	-	-	-	-	-	-	-	-	128.7	3.7	-	-	-	-	-	-	-	-	-	-	124.1	1.6
1990	-	-	-	-	-	-	-	-	-	-	134.9	1.9	-	-	-	-	-	-	-	-	-	-	132.4	2.9
1991	-	-	-	-	-	-	-	-	-	-	145.2	-0.5	-	-	-	-	-	-	-	-	-	-	145.9	8.2
1992	-	-	-	-	-	-	-	-	-	-	152.9	1.9	-	-	-	-	-	-	-	-	-	-	150.0	3.3
1993	-	-	-	-	-	-	-	-	-	-	151.9	-0.4	-	-	-	-	-	-	-	-	-	-	152.5	-0.3
1994	-	-	-	-	-	-	-	-	-	-	159.5	4.8	-	-	-	-	-	-	-	-	-	-	152.2	0.2
1995	-	-	-	-	-	-	-	-	-	-	161.7	0.2	-	-	-	-	-	-	-	-	-	-	161.4	1.2

Source: U.S. Department of Labor, Bureau of Labor Statistics, Division of Consumer Prices and Price Indexes. - indicates no data collected for period.

Kansas City, MO-KS
Consumer Price Index - All Urban Consumers
Base 1982-1984 = 100
Other Goods and Services

For 1975-1995. Columns headed % show percentile change in the index from the previous period for which an index is available.

Year	Jan Index	%	Feb Index	%	Mar Index	%	Apr Index	%	May Index	%	Jun Index	%	Jul Index	%	Aug Index	%	Sep Index	%	Oct Index	%	Nov Index	%	Dec Index	%
1975	-	-	-	-	-	-	-	-	-	-	-	-	-	-	-	-	-	-	-	-	-	-	56.2	-
1976	-	-	-	-	56.9	1.2	-	-	-	-	57.3	0.7	-	-	-	-	58.1	1.4	-	-	-	-	59.4	2.2
1977	-	-	-	-	60.1	1.2	-	-	-	-	61.0	1.5	-	-	-	-	62.6	2.6	-	-	-	-	63.0	0.6
1978	-	-	62.7	-0.5	-	-	64.2	2.4	-	-	63.9	-0.5	-	-	65.2	2.0	-	-	66.4	1.8	-	-	66.7	0.5
1979	-	-	67.7	1.5	-	-	67.9	0.3	-	-	69.9	2.9	-	-	70.4	0.7	-	-	71.9	2.1	-	-	73.2	1.8
1980	-	-	74.7	2.0	-	-	75.0	0.4	-	-	76.0	1.3	-	-	77.0	1.3	-	-	79.0	2.6	-	-	80.4	1.8
1981	-	-	81.6	1.5	-	-	81.7	0.1	-	-	84.2	3.1	-	-	85.1	1.1	-	-	87.9	3.3	-	-	88.5	0.7
1982	-	-	89.1	0.7	-	-	89.8	0.8	-	-	88.9	-1.0	-	-	90.5	1.8	-	-	95.5	5.5	-	-	95.9	0.4
1983	-	-	97.6	1.8	-	-	99.0	1.4	-	-	99.1	0.1	-	-	100.9	1.8	-	-	104.5	3.6	-	-	104.9	0.4
1984	-	-	105.7	0.8	-	-	106.4	0.7	-	-	107.3	0.8	-	-	107.7	0.4	-	-	111.4	3.4	-	-	111.9	0.4
1985	-	-	113.2	1.2	-	-	112.9	-0.3	-	-	112.5	-0.4	-	-	115.5	2.7	-	-	121.0	4.8	-	-	121.7	0.6
1986	-	-	122.4	0.6	-	-	123.0	0.5	-	-	123.8	0.7	-	-	125.5	1.4	-	-	129.8	3.4	-	-	130.3	0.4
1987	-	-	-	-	-	-	-	-	-	-	132.5	1.7	-	-	-	-	-	-	-	-	-	-	137.4	3.7
1988	-	-	-	-	-	-	-	-	-	-	139.5	1.5	-	-	-	-	-	-	-	-	-	-	143.7	3.0
1989	-	-	-	-	-	-	-	-	-	-	150.2	4.5	-	-	-	-	-	-	-	-	-	-	154.5	2.9
1990	-	-	-	-	-	-	-	-	-	-	157.5	1.9	-	-	-	-	-	-	-	-	-	-	161.8	2.7
1991	-	-	-	-	-	-	-	-	-	-	171.5	6.0	-	-	-	-	-	-	-	-	-	-	180.0	5.0
1992	-	-	-	-	-	-	-	-	-	-	187.8	4.3	-	-	-	-	-	-	-	-	-	-	191.1	1.8
1993	-	-	-	-	-	-	-	-	-	-	194.7	1.9	-	-	-	-	-	-	-	-	-	-	198.8	2.1
1994	-	-	-	-	-	-	-	-	-	-	202.3	1.8	-	-	-	-	-	-	-	-	-	-	204.6	1.1
1995	-	-	-	-	-	-	-	-	-	-	205.9	0.6	-	-	-	-	-	-	-	-	-	-	-	-

Source: U.S. Department of Labor, Bureau of Labor Statistics, Division of Consumer Prices and Price Indexes. - indicates no data collected for period.

Kansas City, MO-KS
Consumer Price Index - Urban Wage Earners
Base 1982-1984 = 100
Other Goods and Services

For 1975-1995. Columns headed % show percentile change in the index from the previous period for which an index is available.

Year	Jan Index	%	Feb Index	%	Mar Index	%	Apr Index	%	May Index	%	Jun Index	%	Jul Index	%	Aug Index	%	Sep Index	%	Oct Index	%	Nov Index	%	Dec Index	%
1975	-	-	-	-	-	-	-	-	-	-	-	-	-	-	-	-	-	-	-	-	-	-	56.4	-
1976	-	-	-	-	57.1	1.2	-	-	-	-	57.5	0.7	-	-	-	-	58.3	1.4	-	-	-	-	59.6	2.2
1977	-	-	-	-	60.3	1.2	-	-	-	-	61.3	1.7	-	-	-	-	62.8	2.4	-	-	-	-	63.3	0.8
1978	-	-	64.1	1.3	-	-	64.3	0.3	-	-	64.4	0.2	-	-	65.4	1.6	-	-	66.7	2.0	-	-	66.6	-0.1
1979	-	-	68.4	2.7	-	-	69.7	1.9	-	-	72.0	3.3	-	-	72.3	0.4	-	-	73.6	1.8	-	-	74.3	1.0
1980	-	-	76.5	3.0	-	-	76.4	-0.1	-	-	78.0	2.1	-	-	79.4	1.8	-	-	81.0	2.0	-	-	82.2	1.5
1981	-	-	83.2	1.2	-	-	81.5	-2.0	-	-	84.7	3.9	-	-	85.7	1.2	-	-	87.7	2.3	-	-	88.2	0.6
1982	-	-	88.8	0.7	-	-	89.8	1.1	-	-	88.7	-1.2	-	-	90.6	2.1	-	-	95.6	5.5	-	-	95.9	0.3
1983	-	-	97.5	1.7	-	-	99.3	1.8	-	-	99.3	0.0	-	-	101.5	2.2	-	-	104.3	2.8	-	-	104.7	0.4
1984	-	-	105.7	1.0	-	-	106.5	0.8	-	-	107.5	0.9	-	-	108.0	0.5	-	-	110.9	2.7	-	-	111.4	0.5
1985	-	-	113.0	1.4	-	-	112.6	-0.4	-	-	112.1	-0.4	-	-	115.8	3.3	-	-	120.6	4.1	-	-	121.3	0.6
1986	-	-	122.2	0.7	-	-	122.8	0.5	-	-	123.8	0.8	-	-	125.9	1.7	-	-	129.3	2.7	-	-	129.8	0.4
1987	-	-	-	-	-	-	-	-	-	-	132.1	1.8	-	-	-	-	-	-	-	-	-	-	137.1	3.8
1988	-	-	-	-	-	-	-	-	-	-	139.4	1.7	-	-	-	-	-	-	-	-	-	-	143.4	2.9
1989	-	-	-	-	-	-	-	-	-	-	150.9	5.2	-	-	-	-	-	-	-	-	-	-	155.4	3.0
1990	-	-	-	-	-	-	-	-	-	-	158.3	1.9	-	-	-	-	-	-	-	-	-	-	162.0	2.3
1991	-	-	-	-	-	-	-	-	-	-	172.7	6.6	-	-	-	-	-	-	-	-	-	-	180.8	4.7
1992	-	-	-	-	-	-	-	-	-	-	189.9	5.0	-	-	-	-	-	-	-	-	-	-	192.8	1.5
1993	-	-	-	-	-	-	-	-	-	-	196.8	2.1	-	-	-	-	-	-	-	-	-	-	200.3	1.8
1994	-	-	-	-	-	-	-	-	-	-	204.6	2.1	-	-	-	-	-	-	-	-	-	-	206.5	0.9
1995	-	-	-	-	-	-	-	-	-	-	208.4	0.9	-	-	-	-	-	-	-	-	-	-	-	-

Source: U.S. Department of Labor, Bureau of Labor Statistics, Division of Consumer Prices and Price Indexes. - indicates no data collected for period.

Los Angeles, CA
Consumer Price Index - All Urban Consumers
Base 1982-1984 = 100
Annual Averages

For 1914-1995. Columns headed % show percentile change in the index from the previous period for which an index is available.

Year	All Items		Food & Beverage		Housing		Apparel & Upkeep		Trans- portation		Medical Care		Entertain- ment		Other Goods & Services	
	Index	%	Index	%	Index	%	Index	%	Index	%	Index	%	Index	%	Index	%
1914	-	-	-	-	-	-	-	-	-	-	-	-	-	-	-	-
1915	10.0	-	-	-	-	-	-	-	-	-	-	-	-	-	-	-
1916	10.5	5.0	-	-	-	-	-	-	-	-	-	-	-	-	-	-
1917	12.1	15.2	-	-	-	-	-	-	-	-	-	-	-	-	-	-
1918	14.4	19.0	-	-	-	-	-	-	-	-	-	-	-	-	-	-
1919	17.0	18.1	-	-	-	-	-	-	-	-	-	-	-	-	-	-
1920	19.9	17.1	-	-	-	-	-	-	-	-	-	-	-	-	-	-
1921	18.6	-6.5	-	-	-	-	-	-	-	-	-	-	-	-	-	-
1922	18.1	-2.7	-	-	-	-	-	-	-	-	-	-	-	-	-	-
1923	18.3	1.1	-	-	-	-	-	-	-	-	-	-	-	-	-	-
1924	18.4	0.5	-	-	-	-	-	-	-	-	-	-	-	-	-	-
1925	18.4	0.0	-	-	-	-	-	-	-	-	-	-	-	-	-	-
1926	17.9	-2.7	-	-	-	-	-	-	-	-	-	-	-	-	-	-
1927	17.6	-1.7	-	-	-	-	-	-	-	-	-	-	-	-	-	-
1928	17.3	-1.7	-	-	-	-	-	-	-	-	-	-	-	-	-	-
1929	17.3	0.0	-	-	-	-	-	-	-	-	-	-	-	-	-	-
1930	16.7	-3.5	-	-	-	-	-	-	-	-	-	-	-	-	-	-
1931	15.1	-9.6	-	-	-	-	-	-	-	-	-	-	-	-	-	-
1932	13.6	-9.9	-	-	-	-	-	-	-	-	-	-	-	-	-	-
1933	12.8	-5.9	-	-	-	-	-	-	-	-	-	-	-	-	-	-
1934	12.9	0.8	-	-	-	-	-	-	-	-	-	-	-	-	-	-
1935	13.3	3.1	-	-	-	-	-	-	-	-	-	-	-	-	-	-
1936	13.5	1.5	-	-	-	-	-	-	-	-	-	-	-	-	-	-
1937	14.2	5.2	-	-	-	-	-	-	-	-	-	-	-	-	-	-
1938	14.0	-1.4	-	-	-	-	-	-	-	-	-	-	-	-	-	-
1939	13.9	-0.7	-	-	-	-	-	-	-	-	-	-	-	-	-	-
1940	13.9	0.0	-	-	-	-	-	-	-	-	-	-	-	-	-	-
1941	14.7	5.8	-	-	-	-	-	-	-	-	-	-	-	-	-	-
1942	16.5	12.2	-	-	-	-	-	-	-	-	-	-	-	-	-	-
1943	17.3	4.8	-	-	-	-	-	-	-	-	-	-	-	-	-	-
1944	17.6	1.7	-	-	-	-	-	-	-	-	-	-	-	-	-	-
1945	18.1	2.8	-	-	-	-	-	-	-	-	-	-	-	-	-	-
1946	19.5	7.7	-	-	-	-	-	-	-	-	-	-	-	-	-	-
1947	22.0	12.8	-	-	-	-	-	-	17.9	-	13.4	-	-	-	-	-
1948	23.6	7.3	-	-	-	-	-	-	19.8	10.6	14.2	6.0	-	-	-	-
1949	23.6	0.0	-	-	-	-	-	-	21.0	6.1	14.7	3.5	-	-	-	-
1950	23.7	0.4	-	-	-	-	-	-	20.7	-1.4	15.0	2.0	-	-	-	-
1951	25.7	8.4	-	-	-	-	-	-	21.6	4.3	15.9	6.0	-	-	-	-
1952	26.5	3.1	-	-	-	-	-	-	23.8	10.2	16.5	3.8	-	-	-	-
1953	26.7	0.8	-	-	-	-	48.7	-	24.8	4.2	16.9	2.4	-	-	-	-
1954	26.7	0.0	-	-	-	-	48.9	0.4	24.6	-0.8	17.3	2.4	-	-	-	-
1955	26.7	0.0	-	-	-	-	48.9	0.0	24.4	-0.8	17.4	0.6	-	-	-	-
1956	27.1	1.5	-	-	-	-	49.8	1.8	24.8	1.6	17.9	2.9	-	-	-	-
1957	28.0	3.3	-	-	-	-	50.9	2.2	25.8	4.0	18.4	2.8	-	-	-	-
1958	28.9	3.2	-	-	-	-	51.0	0.2	26.5	2.7	19.9	8.2	-	-	-	-

[Continued]

Los Angeles, CA
Consumer Price Index - All Urban Consumers
Base 1982-1984 = 100
Annual Averages

[Continued]

For 1914-1995. Columns headed % show percentile change in the index from the previous period for which an index is available.

Year	All Items		Food & Beverage		Housing		Apparel & Upkeep		Trans-portation		Medical Care		Entertain-ment		Other Goods & Services	
	Index	%	Index	%	Index	%	Index	%	Index	%	Index	%	Index	%	Index	%
1959	29.4	1.7	-	-	-	-	51.6	1.2	27.8	4.9	20.8	4.5	-	-	-	-
1960	30.0	2.0	-	-	-	-	52.8	2.3	28.0	0.7	21.4	2.9	-	-	-	-
1961	30.3	1.0	-	-	-	-	52.9	0.2	28.9	3.2	21.6	0.9	-	-	-	-
1962	30.7	1.3	-	-	-	-	53.0	0.2	29.9	3.5	22.3	3.2	-	-	-	-
1963	31.1	1.3	-	-	-	-	53.7	1.3	29.9	0.0	22.7	1.8	-	-	-	-
1964	31.7	1.9	-	-	-	-	54.5	1.5	31.1	4.0	23.2	2.2	-	-	-	-
1965	32.4	2.2	-	-	-	-	55.0	0.9	31.7	1.9	23.7	2.2	-	-	-	-
1966	33.0	1.9	-	-	-	-	55.9	1.6	31.9	0.6	24.6	3.8	-	-	-	-
1967	33.8	2.4	-	-	-	-	58.1	3.9	32.3	1.3	26.4	7.3	-	-	-	-
1968	35.2	4.1	-	-	-	-	61.2	5.3	33.3	3.1	27.8	5.3	-	-	-	-
1969	36.8	4.5	-	-	-	-	63.6	3.9	34.3	3.0	29.5	6.1	-	-	-	-
1970	38.7	5.2	-	-	-	-	66.5	4.6	35.4	3.2	31.6	7.1	-	-	-	-
1971	40.1	3.6	-	-	-	-	68.5	3.0	37.1	4.8	33.2	5.1	-	-	-	-
1972	41.4	3.2	-	-	-	-	69.7	1.8	38.0	2.4	33.9	2.1	-	-	-	-
1973	43.7	5.6	-	-	-	-	71.5	2.6	39.8	4.7	35.6	5.0	-	-	-	-
1974	48.2	10.3	-	-	-	-	76.7	7.3	44.5	11.8	39.0	9.6	-	-	-	-
1975	53.3	10.6	-	-	-	-	79.2	3.3	49.3	10.8	43.7	12.1	-	-	-	-
1976	56.9	6.8	60.5	-	54.4	-	80.9	2.1	54.2	9.9	49.3	12.8	70.5	-	57.3	-
1977	60.8	6.9	64.7	6.9	58.4	7.4	84.1	4.0	58.1	7.2	53.9	9.3	73.2	3.8	60.6	5.8
1978	65.3	7.4	71.6	10.7	63.2	8.2	85.8	2.0	60.6	4.3	58.6	8.7	74.4	1.6	65.1	7.4
1979	72.3	10.7	79.2	10.6	69.9	10.6	89.0	3.7	70.3	16.0	64.6	10.2	78.6	5.6	69.2	6.3
1980	83.7	15.8	85.7	8.2	83.7	19.7	98.3	10.4	82.5	17.4	72.7	12.5	85.7	9.0	76.4	10.4
1981	91.9	9.8	92.5	7.9	92.4	10.4	101.5	3.3	91.3	10.7	82.0	12.8	93.1	8.6	83.9	9.8
1982	97.3	5.9	96.8	4.6	97.8	5.8	98.9	-2.6	97.5	6.8	94.1	14.8	97.6	4.8	92.0	9.7
1983	99.1	1.8	100.1	3.4	98.3	0.5	99.7	0.8	98.8	1.3	100.7	7.0	99.8	2.3	101.2	10.0
1984	103.6	4.5	103.1	3.0	103.9	5.7	101.3	1.6	103.7	5.0	105.2	4.5	102.6	2.8	106.8	5.5
1985	108.4	4.6	105.5	2.3	109.7	5.6	105.1	3.8	107.5	3.7	112.9	7.3	106.9	4.2	115.3	8.0
1986	111.9	3.2	108.7	3.0	116.1	5.8	106.9	1.7	105.2	-2.1	120.9	7.1	109.0	2.0	122.3	6.1
1987	116.7	4.3	113.2	4.1	121.0	4.2	112.5	5.2	108.9	3.5	129.5	7.1	111.2	2.0	127.9	4.6
1988	122.1	4.6	117.2	3.5	126.6	4.6	114.3	1.6	113.8	4.5	139.6	7.8	115.4	3.8	139.9	9.4
1989	128.3	5.1	124.0	5.8	131.7	4.0	118.8	3.9	119.6	5.1	149.8	7.3	120.9	4.8	155.3	11.0
1990	135.9	5.9	130.9	5.6	139.3	5.8	126.4	6.4	126.5	5.8	163.3	9.0	125.4	3.7	166.3	7.1
1991	141.4	4.0	136.6	4.4	144.9	4.0	130.9	3.6	126.6	0.1	178.2	9.1	135.4	8.0	179.9	8.2
1992	146.5	3.6	140.9	3.1	148.6	2.6	133.2	1.8	133.0	5.1	192.4	8.0	134.1	-1.0	197.1	9.6
1993	150.3	2.6	145.1	3.0	150.4	1.2	131.6	-1.2	137.5	3.4	206.6	7.4	135.8	1.3	211.9	7.5
1994	152.3	1.3	148.5	2.3	151.0	0.4	129.6	-1.5	140.5	2.2	215.2	4.2	137.2	1.0	218.0	2.9
1995	154.6	1.5	153.4	3.3	152.2	0.8	126.7	-2.2	142.3	1.3	221.8	3.1	141.3	3.0	225.6	3.5

Source: U.S. Department of Labor, Bureau of Labor Statistics, Division of Consumer Prices and Price Indexes. - indicates no data collected for period.

Los Angeles, CA
Consumer Price Index - Urban Wage Earners
Base 1982-1984 = 100
Annual Averages

For 1914-1995. Columns headed % show percentile change in the index from the previous period for which an index is available.

Year	All Items		Food & Beverage		Housing		Apparel & Upkeep		Trans- portation		Medical Care		Entertain- ment		Other Goods & Services	
	Index	%	Index	%	Index	%	Index	%	Index	%	Index	%	Index	%	Index	%
1914	-	-	-	-	-	-	-	-	-	-	-	-	-	-	-	-
1915	9.9	-	-	-	-	-	-	-	-	-	-	-	-	-	-	-
1916	10.5	6.1	-	-	-	-	-	-	-	-	-	-	-	-	-	-
1917	12.1	15.2	-	-	-	-	-	-	-	-	-	-	-	-	-	-
1918	14.4	19.0	-	-	-	-	-	-	-	-	-	-	-	-	-	-
1919	17.0	18.1	-	-	-	-	-	-	-	-	-	-	-	-	-	-
1920	19.9	17.1	-	-	-	-	-	-	-	-	-	-	-	-	-	-
1921	18.6	-6.5	-	-	-	-	-	-	-	-	-	-	-	-	-	-
1922	18.1	-2.7	-	-	-	-	-	-	-	-	-	-	-	-	-	-
1923	18.3	1.1	-	-	-	-	-	-	-	-	-	-	-	-	-	-
1924	18.4	0.5	-	-	-	-	-	-	-	-	-	-	-	-	-	-
1925	18.4	0.0	-	-	-	-	-	-	-	-	-	-	-	-	-	-
1926	17.9	-2.7	-	-	-	-	-	-	-	-	-	-	-	-	-	-
1927	17.6	-1.7	-	-	-	-	-	-	-	-	-	-	-	-	-	-
1928	17.3	-1.7	-	-	-	-	-	-	-	-	-	-	-	-	-	-
1929	17.3	0.0	-	-	-	-	-	-	-	-	-	-	-	-	-	-
1930	16.7	-3.5	-	-	-	-	-	-	-	-	-	-	-	-	-	-
1931	15.1	-9.6	-	-	-	-	-	-	-	-	-	-	-	-	-	-
1932	13.6	-9.9	-	-	-	-	-	-	-	-	-	-	-	-	-	-
1933	12.8	-5.9	-	-	-	-	-	-	-	-	-	-	-	-	-	-
1934	12.9	0.8	-	-	-	-	-	-	-	-	-	-	-	-	-	-
1935	13.3	3.1	-	-	-	-	-	-	-	-	-	-	-	-	-	-
1936	13.5	1.5	-	-	-	-	-	-	-	-	-	-	-	-	-	-
1937	14.2	5.2	-	-	-	-	-	-	-	-	-	-	-	-	-	-
1938	14.0	-1.4	-	-	-	-	-	-	-	-	-	-	-	-	-	-
1939	13.9	-0.7	-	-	-	-	-	-	-	-	-	-	-	-	-	-
1940	13.9	0.0	-	-	-	-	-	-	-	-	-	-	-	-	-	-
1941	14.7	5.8	-	-	-	-	-	-	-	-	-	-	-	-	-	-
1942	16.5	12.2	-	-	-	-	-	-	-	-	-	-	-	-	-	-
1943	17.3	4.8	-	-	-	-	-	-	-	-	-	-	-	-	-	-
1944	17.6	1.7	-	-	-	-	-	-	-	-	-	-	-	-	-	-
1945	18.1	2.8	-	-	-	-	-	-	-	-	-	-	-	-	-	-
1946	19.5	7.7	-	-	-	-	-	-	-	-	-	-	-	-	-	-
1947	22.0	12.8	-	-	-	-	-	-	17.8	-	13.6	-	-	-	-	-
1948	23.6	7.3	-	-	-	-	-	-	19.7	10.7	14.4	5.9	-	-	-	-
1949	23.6	0.0	-	-	-	-	-	-	20.9	6.1	14.9	3.5	-	-	-	-
1950	23.7	0.4	-	-	-	-	-	-	20.6	-1.4	15.2	2.0	-	-	-	-
1951	25.7	8.4	-	-	-	-	-	-	21.5	4.4	16.1	5.9	-	-	-	-
1952	26.5	3.1	-	-	-	-	-	-	23.7	10.2	16.7	3.7	-	-	-	-
1953	26.7	0.8	-	-	-	-	48.9	-	24.6	3.8	17.2	3.0	-	-	-	-
1954	26.7	0.0	-	-	-	-	49.1	0.4	24.4	-0.8	17.5	1.7	-	-	-	-
1955	26.7	0.0	-	-	-	-	49.1	0.0	24.3	-0.4	17.6	0.6	-	-	-	-
1956	27.1	1.5	-	-	-	-	50.0	1.8	24.6	1.2	18.2	3.4	-	-	-	-
1957	28.0	3.3	-	-	-	-	51.1	2.2	25.6	4.1	18.7	2.7	-	-	-	-
1958	28.9	3.2	-	-	-	-	51.2	0.2	26.3	2.7	20.2	8.0	-	-	-	-

[Continued]

Los Angeles, CA
Consumer Price Index - Urban Wage Earners
Base 1982-1984 = 100
Annual Averages

[Continued]

For 1914-1995. Columns headed % show percentile change in the index from the previous period for which an index is available.

Year	All Items Index	%	Food & Beverage Index	%	Housing Index	%	Apparel & Upkeep Index	%	Transportation Index	%	Medical Care Index	%	Entertainment Index	%	Other Goods & Services Index	%
1959	29.4	1.7	-	-	-	-	51.8	1.2	27.7	5.3	21.1	4.5	-	-	-	-
1960	29.9	1.7	-	-	-	-	53.0	2.3	27.8	0.4	21.7	2.8	-	-	-	-
1961	30.3	1.3	-	-	-	-	53.1	0.2	28.7	3.2	22.0	1.4	-	-	-	-
1962	30.7	1.3	-	-	-	-	53.2	0.2	29.7	3.5	22.7	3.2	-	-	-	-
1963	31.1	1.3	-	-	-	-	53.9	1.3	29.8	0.3	23.0	1.3	-	-	-	-
1964	31.7	1.9	-	-	-	-	54.7	1.5	30.9	3.7	23.6	2.6	-	-	-	-
1965	32.4	2.2	-	-	-	-	55.2	0.9	31.6	2.3	24.0	1.7	-	-	-	-
1966	33.0	1.9	-	-	-	-	56.1	1.6	31.7	0.3	24.9	3.8	-	-	-	-
1967	33.8	2.4	-	-	-	-	58.3	3.9	32.1	1.3	26.8	7.6	-	-	-	-
1968	35.2	4.1	-	-	-	-	61.4	5.3	33.1	3.1	28.2	5.2	-	-	-	-
1969	36.8	4.5	-	-	-	-	63.9	4.1	34.1	3.0	29.9	6.0	-	-	-	-
1970	38.7	5.2	-	-	-	-	66.7	4.4	35.2	3.2	32.1	7.4	-	-	-	-
1971	40.1	3.6	-	-	-	-	68.8	3.1	36.9	4.8	33.7	5.0	-	-	-	-
1972	41.4	3.2	-	-	-	-	69.9	1.6	37.8	2.4	34.5	2.4	-	-	-	-
1973	43.7	5.6	-	-	-	-	71.8	2.7	39.6	4.8	36.1	4.6	-	-	-	-
1974	48.2	10.3	-	-	-	-	76.9	7.1	44.2	11.6	39.5	9.4	-	-	-	-
1975	53.3	10.6	-	-	-	-	79.5	3.4	49.1	11.1	44.4	12.4	-	-	-	-
1976	56.8	6.6	59.4	-	54.5	-	81.2	2.1	53.9	9.8	50.1	12.8	77.4	-	57.0	-
1977	60.8	7.0	63.5	6.9	58.5	7.3	84.4	3.9	57.8	7.2	54.7	9.2	80.3	3.7	60.2	5.6
1978	65.1	7.1	70.0	10.2	63.3	8.2	87.1	3.2	60.3	4.3	59.0	7.9	80.2	-0.1	64.3	6.8
1979	72.8	11.8	78.0	11.4	70.6	11.5	91.5	5.1	70.5	16.9	65.3	10.7	83.4	4.0	68.6	6.7
1980	84.7	16.3	85.2	9.2	85.3	20.8	97.3	6.3	83.2	18.0	74.0	13.3	90.8	8.9	75.3	9.8
1981	93.1	9.9	92.2	8.2	94.8	11.1	100.7	3.5	92.0	10.6	83.5	12.8	94.4	4.0	82.9	10.1
1982	98.5	5.8	96.8	5.0	100.4	5.9	99.0	-1.7	97.8	6.3	94.1	12.7	97.6	3.4	91.7	10.6
1983	99.3	0.8	100.2	3.5	99.0	-1.4	99.6	0.6	98.6	0.8	100.7	7.0	99.8	2.3	101.7	10.9
1984	102.2	2.9	103.1	2.9	100.6	1.6	101.4	1.8	103.5	5.0	105.2	4.5	102.6	2.8	106.7	4.9
1985	106.5	4.2	105.4	2.2	106.2	5.6	105.0	3.6	107.0	3.4	112.9	7.3	106.6	3.9	113.7	6.6
1986	109.5	2.8	108.5	2.9	112.3	5.7	107.2	2.1	103.9	-2.9	120.7	6.9	108.4	1.7	120.7	6.2
1987	114.0	4.1	113.0	4.1	117.0	4.2	111.9	4.4	107.0	3.0	129.0	6.9	110.5	1.9	126.4	4.7
1988	119.0	4.4	117.1	3.6	122.3	4.5	114.0	1.9	111.4	4.1	139.1	7.8	114.6	3.7	137.6	8.9
1989	124.9	5.0	123.9	5.8	127.1	3.9	118.8	4.2	116.6	4.7	148.7	6.9	120.0	4.7	154.9	12.6
1990	131.9	5.6	131.0	5.7	134.1	5.5	126.1	6.1	122.2	4.8	161.5	8.6	124.4	3.7	166.1	7.2
1991	137.1	3.9	136.8	4.4	139.6	4.1	130.8	3.7	122.5	0.2	175.7	8.8	134.1	7.8	179.1	7.8
1992	142.0	3.6	141.4	3.4	143.0	2.4	133.6	2.1	128.6	5.0	190.0	8.1	134.4	0.2	194.2	8.4
1993	145.2	2.3	145.6	3.0	144.8	1.3	132.4	-0.9	132.5	3.0	203.9	7.3	136.4	1.5	204.6	5.4
1994	147.0	1.2	148.8	2.2	145.4	0.4	130.0	-1.8	135.7	2.4	211.7	3.8	137.5	0.8	207.4	1.4
1995	149.4	1.6	153.5	3.2	146.4	0.7	126.8	-2.5	138.4	2.0	218.8	3.4	142.1	3.3	213.9	3.1

Source: U.S. Department of Labor, Bureau of Labor Statistics, Division of Consumer Prices and Price Indexes. - indicates no data collected for period.

Los Angeles, CA
Consumer Price Index - All Urban Consumers
Base 1982-1984 = 100
All Items

For 1914-1995. Columns headed % show percentile change in the index from the previous period for which an index is available.

Year	Jan Index	%	Feb Index	%	Mar Index	%	Apr Index	%	May Index	%	Jun Index	%	Jul Index	%	Aug Index	%	Sep Index	%	Oct Index	%	Nov Index	%	Dec Index	%
1914	-	-	-	-	-	-	-	-	-	-	-	-	-	-	-	-	-	-	-	-	-	-	10.2	-
1915	-	-	-	-	-	-	-	-	-	-	-	-	-	-	-	-	-	-	-	-	-	-	10.1	-1.0
1916	-	-	-	-	-	-	-	-	-	-	-	-	-	-	-	-	-	-	-	-	-	-	11.0	8.9
1917	-	-	-	-	-	-	-	-	-	-	-	-	-	-	-	-	-	-	-	-	-	-	13.0	18.2
1918	-	-	-	-	-	-	-	-	-	-	-	-	-	-	-	-	-	-	-	-	-	-	15.8	21.5
1919	-	-	-	-	-	-	-	-	-	-	16.4	3.8	-	-	-	-	-	-	-	-	-	-	18.6	13.4
1920	-	-	-	-	-	-	-	-	-	-	20.4	9.7	-	-	-	-	-	-	-	-	-	-	19.9	-2.5
1921	-	-	-	-	-	-	-	-	18.5	-7.0	-	-	-	-	-	-	18.3	-1.1	-	-	-	-	18.4	0.5
1922	-	-	-	-	18.2	-1.1	-	-	-	-	18.1	-0.5	-	-	-	-	18.0	-0.6	-	-	-	-	18.1	0.6
1923	-	-	-	-	18.0	-0.6	-	-	-	-	18.3	1.7	-	-	-	-	18.5	1.1	-	-	-	-	18.6	0.5
1924	-	-	-	-	18.5	-0.5	-	-	-	-	18.3	-1.1	-	-	-	-	18.4	0.5	-	-	-	-	18.2	-1.1
1925	-	-	-	-	-	-	-	-	-	-	18.5	1.6	-	-	-	-	-	-	-	-	-	-	18.5	0.0
1926	-	-	-	-	-	-	-	-	-	-	17.8	-3.8	-	-	-	-	-	-	-	-	-	-	17.8	0.0
1927	-	-	-	-	-	-	-	-	-	-	17.8	0.0	-	-	-	-	-	-	-	-	-	-	17.5	-1.7
1928	-	-	-	-	-	-	-	-	-	-	17.2	-1.7	-	-	-	-	-	-	-	-	-	-	17.4	1.2
1929	-	-	-	-	-	-	-	-	-	-	17.2	-1.1	-	-	-	-	-	-	-	-	-	-	17.2	0.0
1930	-	-	-	-	-	-	-	-	-	-	16.7	-2.9	-	-	-	-	-	-	-	-	-	-	16.0	-4.2
1931	-	-	-	-	-	-	-	-	-	-	14.9	-6.9	-	-	-	-	-	-	-	-	-	-	14.6	-2.0
1932	-	-	-	-	-	-	-	-	-	-	13.6	-6.8	-	-	-	-	-	-	-	-	-	-	13.1	-3.7
1933	-	-	-	-	-	-	-	-	-	-	12.5	-4.6	-	-	-	-	-	-	-	-	-	-	13.0	4.0
1934	-	-	-	-	-	-	-	-	-	-	12.9	-0.8	-	-	-	-	-	-	-	-	13.3	3.1	-	-
1935	-	-	-	-	13.6	2.3	-	-	-	-	-	-	13.2	-2.9	-	-	-	-	13.1	-0.8	-	-	13.7	0.0
1936	13.4	2.3	-	-	-	-	13.2	-1.5	-	-	-	-	13.4	1.5	-	-	13.7	2.2	-	-	-	-	13.7	0.0
1937	-	-	-	-	14.3	4.4	-	-	-	-	14.2	-0.7	-	-	-	-	14.4	1.4	-	-	-	-	14.3	-0.7
1938	-	-	-	-	14.0	-2.1	-	-	-	-	14.0	0.0	-	-	-	-	14.0	0.0	-	-	-	-	14.1	0.7
1939	-	-	-	-	14.0	-0.7	-	-	-	-	13.8	-1.4	-	-	-	-	14.1	2.2	-	-	-	-	13.9	-1.4
1940	-	-	-	-	13.9	0.0	-	-	-	-	13.9	0.0	-	-	-	-	14.0	0.7	14.0	0.0	14.1	0.7	14.1	0.0
1941	14.2	0.7	14.0	-1.4	14.1	0.7	14.3	1.4	14.4	0.7	14.6	1.4	14.6	0.0	14.7	0.7	15.0	2.0	15.2	1.3	15.3	0.7	15.5	1.3
1942	15.7	1.3	15.8	0.6	16.1	1.9	16.2	0.6	16.3	0.6	16.4	0.6	16.6	1.2	16.8	1.2	16.8	0.0	17.0	1.2	17.1	0.6	17.1	0.0
1943	17.1	0.0	17.0	-0.6	17.2	1.2	17.4	1.2	17.4	0.0	17.4	0.0	17.3	-0.6	17.2	-0.6	17.3	0.6	17.4	0.6	17.5	0.6	17.5	0.0
1944	17.4	-0.6	17.4	0.0	17.4	0.0	17.4	0.0	17.6	1.1	17.5	-0.6	17.5	0.0	17.6	0.6	17.7	0.6	17.8	0.6	17.8	0.0	17.9	0.6
1945	17.9	0.0	17.8	-0.6	17.9	0.6	18.0	0.6	18.0	0.0	18.0	0.0	18.0	0.0	18.1	0.6	18.1	0.0	18.3	1.1	18.3	0.0	18.4	0.5	18.5	0.5
1946	18.4	-0.5	18.4	0.0	18.4	0.0	18.5	0.5	18.6	0.5	18.8	1.1	19.7	4.8	20.0	1.5	20.1	0.5	20.5	2.0	21.4	4.4	21.4	0.0
1947	21.5	0.5	21.6	0.5	21.7	0.5	21.8	0.5	21.8	0.0	21.7	-0.5	21.8	0.5	21.9	0.5	22.4	2.3	22.4	0.0	22.8	1.8	23.0	0.9
1948	23.3	1.3	23.4	0.4	23.3	-0.4	23.5	0.9	23.5	0.0	23.5	0.0	23.7	0.9	23.8	0.4	23.8	0.0	23.9	0.4	24.0	0.4	24.1	0.4
1949	24.1	0.0	23.9	-0.8	23.9	0.0	23.9	0.0	23.7	-0.8	23.6	-0.4	23.4	-0.8	23.4	0.0	23.4	0.0	23.3	-0.4	23.4	0.4	23.2	-0.9
1950	23.4	0.9	23.3	-0.4	23.4	0.4	23.4	0.0	23.4	0.0	23.4	0.0	23.5	0.4	23.8	1.3	23.9	0.4	24.1	0.8	24.3	0.8	24.6	1.2
1951	25.0	1.6	25.5	2.0	25.7	0.8	25.7	0.0	25.7	0.0	25.7	0.0	25.8	0.4	25.8	0.0	25.9	0.4	25.9	0.0	26.2	1.2	26.3	0.4
1952	26.3	0.0	26.3	0.0	26.4	0.4	26.4	0.0	26.4	0.0	26.5	0.4	26.5	0.0	26.5	0.0	26.5	0.0	26.5	0.0	26.6	0.4	26.6	0.0
1953	26.6	0.0	26.5	-0.4	26.6	0.4	26.7	0.4	26.6	-0.4	26.6	0.0	26.7	0.4	26.7	0.0	26.8	0.4	26.8	0.0	26.8	0.0	26.7	-0.4
1954	27.0	1.1	26.9	-0.4	26.8	-0.4	26.7	-0.4	26.7	0.0	26.7	0.0	26.5	-0.7	26.6	0.4	26.6	0.0	26.5	-0.4	26.5	0.0	26.6	0.4
1955	26.6	0.0	26.5	-0.4	26.6	0.4	26.4	-0.8	26.6	0.8	26.6	0.0	26.7	0.4	26.6	-0.4	26.8	0.8	26.8	0.0	26.8	0.0	26.8	0.0
1956	26.8	0.0	26.7	-0.4	26.8	0.4	26.8	0.0	27.0	0.7	27.1	0.4	27.2	0.4	27.1	-0.4	27.2	0.4	27.3	0.4	27.5	0.7	27.6	0.4
1957	27.6	0.0	27.8	0.7	27.8	0.0	27.8	0.0	27.9	0.4	27.9	0.0	28.0	0.4	28.0	0.0	28.2	0.7	28.2	0.0	28.4	0.7	28.4	0.0
1958	28.6	0.7	28.6	0.0	28.8	0.7	29.0	0.7	28.9	-0.3	28.9	0.0	29.0	0.3	28.9	-0.3	29.1	0.7	29.1	0.0	29.2	0.3	29.2	0.0

[Continued]

Los Angeles, CA
Consumer Price Index - All Urban Consumers
Base 1982-1984 = 100
All Items
[Continued]

For 1914-1995. Columns headed % show percentile change in the index from the previous period for which an index is available.

Year	Jan Index	%	Feb Index	%	Mar Index	%	Apr Index	%	May Index	%	Jun Index	%	Jul Index	%	Aug Index	%	Sep Index	%	Oct Index	%	Nov Index	%	Dec Index	%
1959	29.2	0.0	29.2	0.0	29.2	0.0	29.2	0.0	29.3	0.3	29.3	0.0	29.4	0.3	29.4	0.0	29.5	0.3	29.7	0.7	29.7	0.0	29.8	0.3
1960	29.8	0.0	29.7	-0.3	29.9	0.7	30.0	0.3	30.0	0.0	29.9	-0.3	29.9	0.0	29.8	-0.3	30.0	0.7	30.1	0.3	30.1	0.0	30.3	0.7
1961	30.3	0.0	30.3	0.0	30.2	-0.3	30.3	0.3	30.3	0.0	30.3	0.0	30.3	0.0	30.3	0.0	30.3	0.0	30.4	0.3	30.5	0.3	30.5	0.0
1962	30.4	-0.3	30.4	0.0	30.5	0.3	30.6	0.3	30.8	0.7	30.8	0.0	30.7	-0.3	30.7	0.0	30.9	0.7	30.9	0.0	30.8	-0.3	30.9	0.3
1963	30.9	0.0	31.0	0.3	31.0	0.0	31.1	0.3	31.0	-0.3	30.9	-0.3	31.1	0.6	31.2	0.3	31.2	0.0	31.4	0.6	31.4	0.0	31.3	-0.3
1964	31.5	0.6	31.4	-0.3	31.6	0.6	31.6	0.0	31.6	0.0	31.6	0.0	31.6	0.0	31.7	0.3	31.6	-0.3	32.0	1.3	32.0	0.0	32.1	0.3
1965	32.1	0.0	32.2	0.3	32.3	0.3	32.4	0.3	32.4	0.0	32.5	0.3	32.4	-0.3	32.1	-0.9	32.5	1.2	32.4	-0.3	32.5	0.3	32.6	0.3
1966	32.5	-0.3	32.6	0.3	32.7	0.3	32.9	0.6	32.9	0.0	33.0	0.3	33.1	0.3	33.0	-0.3	33.3	0.9	33.4	0.3	33.5	0.3	33.5	0.0
1967	33.3	-0.6	33.3	0.0	33.2	-0.3	33.5	0.9	33.6	0.3	33.7	0.3	33.8	0.3	34.1	0.9	34.3	0.6	34.2	-0.3	34.5	0.9	34.5	0.0
1968	34.7	0.6	34.7	0.0	34.9	0.6	34.9	0.0	34.8	-0.3	35.1	0.9	35.2	0.3	35.3	0.3	35.3	0.0	35.6	0.8	35.7	0.3	35.7	0.0
1969	35.9	0.6	36.0	0.3	36.5	1.4	36.5	0.0	36.5	0.0	36.8	0.8	37.0	0.5	37.1	0.3	37.3	0.5	37.4	0.3	37.4	0.0	37.7	0.8
1970	37.8	0.3	37.9	0.3	38.0	0.3	38.4	1.1	38.5	0.3	38.6	0.3	38.9	0.8	38.7	-0.5	39.2	1.3	39.3	0.3	39.3	0.0	39.5	0.5
1971	39.5	0.0	39.3	-0.5	39.6	0.8	39.5	-0.3	40.0	1.3	40.2	0.5	40.3	0.2	40.4	0.2	40.6	0.5	40.7	0.2	40.6	-0.2	40.6	0.0
1972	40.6	0.0	40.7	0.2	41.0	0.7	41.0	0.0	41.1	0.2	41.2	0.2	41.5	0.7	41.6	0.2	41.9	0.7	41.9	0.0	42.1	0.5	42.1	0.0
1973	42.2	0.2	42.5	0.7	42.8	0.7	43.0	0.5	43.1	0.2	43.5	0.9	43.7	0.5	44.3	1.4	44.4	0.2	44.8	0.9	45.2	0.9	45.4	0.4
1974	45.8	0.9	46.1	0.7	46.6	1.1	47.0	0.9	47.5	1.1	47.9	0.8	48.4	1.0	49.0	1.2	49.8	1.6	49.8	0.0	50.3	1.0	50.8	1.0
1975	51.0	0.4	51.5	1.0	52.2	1.4	52.7	1.0	53.1	0.8	53.0	-0.2	53.5	0.9	53.7	0.4	54.3	1.1	54.7	0.7	55.0	0.5	55.4	0.7
1976	55.7	0.5	55.4	-0.5	55.5	0.2	55.5	0.0	56.3	1.4	56.5	0.4	57.1	1.1	57.4	0.5	57.8	0.7	58.0	0.3	58.3	0.5	58.5	0.3
1977	59.2	1.2	59.7	0.8	59.8	0.2	60.2	0.7	60.4	0.3	60.8	0.7	61.1	0.5	61.1	0.0	61.5	0.7	61.5	0.0	61.9	0.7	62.4	0.8
1978	62.8	0.6	63.1	0.5	63.4	0.5	64.2	1.3	64.8	0.9	65.5	1.1	65.8	0.5	66.0	0.3	66.8	1.2	66.9	0.1	67.1	0.3	66.7	-0.6
1979	67.6	1.3	68.3	1.0	69.0	1.0	70.3	1.9	71.4	1.6	72.1	1.0	72.7	0.8	73.6	1.2	74.7	1.5	75.1	0.5	75.9	1.1	77.2	1.7
1980	78.7	1.9	80.4	2.2	81.7	1.6	82.8	1.3	84.3	1.8	84.7	0.5	84.2	-0.6	83.7	-0.6	84.5	1.0	85.5	1.2	86.5	1.2	87.6	1.3
1981	87.8	0.2	88.5	0.8	89.1	0.7	89.9	0.9	90.5	0.7	90.7	0.2	92.1	1.5	93.0	1.0	94.5	1.6	95.2	0.7	95.3	0.1	95.5	0.2
1982	96.7	1.3	96.6	-0.1	96.9	0.3	97.0	0.1	97.2	0.2	98.2	1.0	97.9	-0.3	97.9	0.0	97.5	-0.4	98.0	0.5	97.6	-0.4	96.6	-1.0
1983	96.7	0.1	97.1	0.4	97.2	0.1	98.0	0.8	98.8	0.8	99.4	0.6	99.7	0.3	99.9	0.2	100.3	0.4	100.5	0.2	100.4	-0.1	100.8	0.4
1984	101.2	0.4	101.6	0.4	101.8	0.2	102.5	0.7	103.4	0.9	103.4	0.0	103.5	0.1	104.5	1.0	105.0	0.5	105.5	0.5	105.5	0.0	105.3	-0.2
1985	105.9	0.6	106.3	0.4	106.5	0.2	106.9	0.4	108.0	1.0	108.1	0.1	108.8	0.6	109.6	0.7	109.6	0.0	110.4	0.7	110.0	-0.4	110.4	0.4
1986	110.6	0.2	110.5	-0.1	111.1	0.5	110.6	-0.5	111.5	0.8	112.1	0.5	112.0	-0.1	112.0	0.0	113.3	1.2	113.8	0.4	113.0	-0.7	112.7	-0.3
1987	113.4	0.6	114.7	1.1	115.5	0.7	116.0	0.4	116.8	0.7	116.5	-0.3	116.5	0.0	117.3	0.7	118.0	0.6	118.6	0.5	118.2	-0.3	118.5	0.3
1988	118.9	0.3	119.7	0.7	120.6	0.8	121.1	0.4	122.0	0.7	122.0	0.0	122.1	0.1	122.6	0.4	123.4	0.7	124.0	0.5	124.1	0.1	124.2	0.1
1989	124.6	0.3	125.5	0.7	126.2	0.6	127.2	0.8	128.3	0.9	128.7	0.3	129.0	0.2	128.9	-0.1	130.1	0.9	130.0	-0.1	130.0	0.0	130.6	0.5
1990	132.1	1.1	133.6	1.1	134.5	0.7	134.2	-0.2	134.6	0.3	135.0	0.3	135.6	0.4	136.3	0.5	137.7	1.0	138.7	0.7	138.9	0.1	139.2	0.2
1991	140.0	0.6	139.9	-0.1	139.7	-0.1	140.7	0.7	140.8	0.1	140.8	0.0	141.5	0.5	141.7	0.1	142.6	0.6	142.9	0.2	143.5	0.4	143.1	-0.3
1992	144.3	0.8	144.9	0.4	145.5	0.4	145.8	0.2	146.0	0.1	146.2	0.1	146.7	0.3	146.9	0.1	147.4	0.3	148.4	0.7	148.2	-0.1	148.2	0.0
1993	149.2	0.7	150.0	0.5	149.8	-0.1	149.9	0.1	150.1	0.1	149.7	-0.3	149.8	0.1	149.9	0.1	150.2	0.2	150.9	0.5	151.6	0.5	151.9	0.2
1994	152.2	0.2	152.2	0.0	152.5	0.2	152.0	-0.3	151.4	-0.4	151.3	-0.1	151.7	0.3	152.0	0.2	152.7	0.5	153.4	0.5	152.9	-0.3	153.4	0.3
1995	154.3	0.6	154.5	0.1	154.6	0.1	154.7	0.1	155.1	0.3	154.8	-0.2	154.5	-0.2	154.4	-0.1	154.6	0.1	155.2	0.4	154.4	-0.5	154.6	0.1

Source: U.S. Department of Labor, Bureau of Labor Statistics, Division of Consumer Prices and Price Indexes. - indicates no data collected for period.

Los Angeles, CA
Consumer Price Index - Urban Wage Earners
Base 1982-1984 = 100
All Items

For 1914-1995. Columns headed % show percentile change in the index from the previous period for which an index is available.

Year	Jan Index	%	Feb Index	%	Mar Index	%	Apr Index	%	May Index	%	Jun Index	%	Jul Index	%	Aug Index	%	Sep Index	%	Oct Index	%	Nov Index	%	Dec Index	%
1914	-	-	-	-	-	-	-	-	-	-	-	-	-	-	-	-	-	-	-	-	-	-	10.2	-
1915	-	-	-	-	-	-	-	-	-	-	-	-	-	-	-	-	-	-	-	-	-	-	10.0	-2.0
1916	-	-	-	-	-	-	-	-	-	-	-	-	-	-	-	-	-	-	-	-	-	-	11.0	10.0
1917	-	-	-	-	-	-	-	-	-	-	-	-	-	-	-	-	-	-	-	-	-	-	13.0	18.2
1918	-	-	-	-	-	-	-	-	-	-	-	-	-	-	-	-	-	-	-	-	-	-	15.8	21.5
1919	-	-	-	-	-	-	-	-	-	-	16.4	3.8	-	-	-	-	-	-	-	-	-	-	18.6	13.4
1920	-	-	-	-	-	-	-	-	-	-	20.4	9.7	-	-	-	-	-	-	-	-	-	-	19.9	-2.5
1921	-	-	-	-	-	-	-	-	18.5	-7.0	-	-	-	-	-	-	18.3	-1.1	-	-	-	-	18.4	0.5
1922	-	-	-	-	18.2	-1.1	-	-	-	-	18.1	-0.5	-	-	-	-	18.0	-0.6	-	-	-	-	18.1	0.6
1923	-	-	-	-	18.0	-0.6	-	-	-	-	18.3	1.7	-	-	-	-	18.5	1.1	-	-	-	-	18.6	0.5
1924	-	-	-	-	18.5	-0.5	-	-	-	-	18.3	-1.1	-	-	-	-	18.4	0.5	-	-	-	-	18.2	-1.1
1925	-	-	-	-	-	-	-	-	-	-	18.5	1.6	-	-	-	-	-	-	-	-	-	-	18.5	0.0
1926	-	-	-	-	-	-	-	-	-	-	17.8	-3.8	-	-	-	-	-	-	-	-	-	-	17.8	0.0
1927	-	-	-	-	-	-	-	-	-	-	17.8	0.0	-	-	-	-	-	-	-	-	-	-	17.5	-1.7
1928	-	-	-	-	-	-	-	-	-	-	17.2	-1.7	-	-	-	-	-	-	-	-	-	-	17.4	1.2
1929	-	-	-	-	-	-	-	-	-	-	17.2	-1.1	-	-	-	-	-	-	-	-	-	-	17.2	0.0
1930	-	-	-	-	-	-	-	-	-	-	16.7	-2.9	-	-	-	-	-	-	-	-	-	-	16.0	-4.2
1931	-	-	-	-	-	-	-	-	-	-	14.9	-6.9	-	-	-	-	-	-	-	-	-	-	14.6	-2.0
1932	-	-	-	-	-	-	-	-	-	-	13.6	-6.8	-	-	-	-	-	-	-	-	-	-	13.1	-3.7
1933	-	-	-	-	-	-	-	-	-	-	12.5	-4.6	-	-	-	-	-	-	-	-	-	-	13.0	4.0
1934	-	-	-	-	-	-	-	-	-	-	12.9	-0.8	-	-	-	-	-	-	-	-	13.3	3.1	-	-
1935	-	-	-	-	13.6	2.3	-	-	-	-	-	-	13.2	-2.9	-	-	-	-	13.1	-0.8	-	-	-	-
1936	13.4	2.3	-	-	-	-	13.2	-1.5	-	-	-	-	13.4	1.5	-	-	13.7	2.2	-	-	-	-	13.7	0.0
1937	-	-	-	-	14.3	4.4	-	-	-	-	14.2	-0.7	-	-	-	-	14.4	1.4	-	-	-	-	14.3	-0.7
1938	-	-	-	-	14.0	-2.1	-	-	-	-	14.0	0.0	-	-	-	-	14.0	0.0	-	-	-	-	14.1	0.7
1939	-	-	-	-	14.0	-0.7	-	-	-	-	13.8	-1.4	-	-	-	-	14.1	2.2	-	-	-	-	13.9	-1.4
1940	-	-	-	-	13.9	0.0	-	-	-	-	13.9	0.0	-	-	-	-	14.0	0.7	14.0	0.0	14.1	0.7	14.1	0.0
1941	14.2	0.7	14.0	-1.4	14.1	0.7	14.3	1.4	14.4	0.7	14.6	1.4	14.6	0.0	14.7	0.7	15.0	2.0	15.2	1.3	15.3	0.7	15.5	1.3
1942	15.7	1.3	15.8	0.6	16.1	1.9	16.2	0.6	16.3	0.6	16.4	0.6	16.6	1.2	16.7	0.6	16.8	0.6	17.0	1.2	17.1	0.6	17.1	0.0
1943	17.1	0.0	17.0	-0.6	17.2	1.2	17.4	1.2	17.4	0.0	17.4	0.0	17.3	-0.6	17.2	-0.6	17.3	0.6	17.4	0.6	17.5	0.6	17.5	0.0
1944	17.4	-0.6	17.4	0.0	17.4	0.0	17.4	0.0	17.6	1.1	17.5	-0.6	17.5	0.0	17.6	0.6	17.7	0.6	17.8	0.6	17.8	0.0	17.9	0.6
1945	17.9	0.0	17.8	-0.6	17.9	0.6	18.0	0.6	18.0	0.0	18.0	0.0	18.1	0.6	18.1	0.0	18.3	1.1	18.3	0.0	18.4	0.5	18.5	0.5
1946	18.4	-0.5	18.4	0.0	18.4	0.0	18.5	0.5	18.6	0.5	18.8	1.1	19.7	4.8	20.0	1.5	20.1	0.5	20.5	2.0	21.4	4.4	21.4	0.0
1947	21.5	0.5	21.6	0.5	21.7	0.5	21.8	0.5	21.8	0.0	21.7	-0.5	21.8	0.5	21.9	0.5	22.4	2.3	22.4	0.0	22.8	1.8	23.0	0.9
1948	23.2	0.9	23.3	0.4	23.2	-0.4	23.5	1.3	23.5	0.0	23.5	0.0	23.7	0.9	23.8	0.4	23.8	0.0	23.9	0.4	24.0	0.4	24.1	0.4
1949	24.1	0.0	23.9	-0.8	23.9	0.0	23.9	0.0	23.7	-0.8	23.6	-0.4	23.3	-1.3	23.3	0.0	23.3	0.0	23.3	0.0	23.3	0.0	23.2	-0.4
1950	23.4	0.9	23.3	-0.4	23.3	0.0	23.4	0.4	23.4	0.0	23.3	-0.4	23.5	0.9	23.8	1.3	23.9	0.4	24.1	0.8	24.3	0.8	24.6	1.2
1951	25.0	1.6	25.4	1.6	25.6	0.8	25.6	0.0	25.7	0.4	25.7	0.0	25.8	0.4	25.8	0.0	25.9	0.4	25.9	0.0	26.2	1.2	26.3	0.4
1952	26.3	0.0	26.3	0.0	26.4	0.4	26.4	0.0	26.4	0.0	26.5	0.4	26.5	0.0	26.5	0.0	26.5	0.0	26.5	0.0	26.6	0.4	26.6	0.0
1953	26.6	0.0	26.5	-0.4	26.6	0.4	26.7	0.4	26.6	-0.4	26.6	0.0	26.7	0.4	26.7	0.0	26.8	0.4	26.8	0.0	26.8	0.0	26.7	-0.4
1954	27.0	1.1	26.9	-0.4	26.8	-0.4	26.7	-0.4	26.7	0.0	26.7	0.0	26.5	-0.7	26.6	0.4	26.6	0.0	26.5	-0.4	26.5	0.0	26.6	0.4
1955	26.6	0.0	26.5	-0.4	26.6	0.4	26.4	-0.8	26.6	0.8	26.6	0.0	26.7	0.4	26.6	-0.4	26.8	0.8	26.8	0.0	26.8	0.0	26.8	0.0
1956	26.8	0.0	26.7	-0.4	26.8	0.4	26.8	0.0	27.0	0.7	27.1	0.4	27.2	0.4	27.1	-0.4	27.2	0.4	27.3	0.4	27.5	0.7	27.5	0.0
1957	27.6	0.4	27.8	0.7	27.8	0.0	27.8	0.0	27.9	0.4	27.9	0.0	27.9	0.0	28.0	0.4	28.2	0.7	28.2	0.0	28.4	0.7	28.4	0.0
1958	28.6	0.7	28.6	0.0	28.8	0.7	29.0	0.7	28.9	-0.3	28.9	0.0	29.0	0.3	28.9	-0.3	29.1	0.7	29.1	0.0	29.2	0.3	29.2	0.0

[Continued]

Los Angeles, CA
Consumer Price Index - Urban Wage Earners
Base 1982-1984 = 100
All Items
[Continued]

For 1914-1995. Columns headed % show percentile change in the index from the previous period for which an index is available.

Year	Jan Index	%	Feb Index	%	Mar Index	%	Apr Index	%	May Index	%	Jun Index	%	Jul Index	%	Aug Index	%	Sep Index	%	Oct Index	%	Nov Index	%	Dec Index	%
1959	29.2	0.0	29.2	0.0	29.2	0.0	29.2	0.0	29.3	0.3	29.3	0.0	29.4	0.3	29.4	0.0	29.5	0.3	29.6	0.3	29.7	0.3	29.7	0.0
1960	29.8	0.3	29.7	-0.3	29.8	0.3	30.0	0.7	29.9	-0.3	29.9	0.0	29.9	0.0	29.8	-0.3	29.9	0.3	30.1	0.7	30.1	0.0	30.3	0.7
1961	30.3	0.0	30.3	0.0	30.2	-0.3	30.3	0.3	30.3	0.0	30.3	0.0	30.3	0.0	30.3	0.0	30.3	0.0	30.4	0.3	30.5	0.3	30.5	0.0
1962	30.4	-0.3	30.4	0.0	30.5	0.3	30.6	0.3	30.8	0.7	30.8	0.0	30.7	-0.3	30.7	0.0	30.9	0.7	30.9	0.0	30.8	-0.3	30.9	0.3
1963	30.9	0.0	31.0	0.3	31.0	0.0	31.1	0.3	31.0	-0.3	30.9	-0.3	31.1	0.6	31.2	0.3	31.2	0.0	31.4	0.6	31.4	0.0	31.3	-0.3
1964	31.5	0.6	31.4	-0.3	31.6	0.6	31.6	0.0	31.6	0.0	31.6	0.0	31.6	0.0	31.7	0.3	31.6	-0.3	31.9	0.9	32.0	0.3	32.0	0.0
1965	32.1	0.3	32.2	0.3	32.3	0.3	32.4	0.3	32.4	0.0	32.5	0.3	32.4	-0.3	32.1	-0.9	32.5	1.2	32.4	-0.3	32.5	0.3	32.6	0.3
1966	32.5	-0.3	32.6	0.3	32.7	0.3	32.9	0.6	32.9	0.0	33.0	0.3	33.1	0.3	33.0	-0.3	33.3	0.9	33.4	0.3	33.5	0.3	33.5	0.0
1967	33.3	-0.6	33.3	0.0	33.2	-0.3	33.5	0.9	33.6	0.3	33.7	0.3	33.8	0.3	34.0	0.6	34.3	0.9	34.2	-0.3	34.5	0.9	34.5	0.0
1968	34.7	0.6	34.7	0.0	34.9	0.6	34.9	0.0	34.8	-0.3	35.1	0.9	35.2	0.3	35.3	0.3	35.3	0.0	35.6	0.8	35.7	0.3	35.7	0.0
1969	35.9	0.6	36.0	0.3	36.4	1.1	36.5	0.3	36.5	0.0	36.8	0.8	37.0	0.5	37.1	0.3	37.3	0.5	37.4	0.3	37.4	0.0	37.7	0.8
1970	37.8	0.3	37.9	0.3	38.0	0.3	38.4	1.1	38.5	0.3	38.5	0.0	38.9	1.0	38.6	-0.8	39.2	1.6	39.3	0.3	39.3	0.0	39.5	0.5
1971	39.5	0.0	39.3	-0.5	39.6	0.8	39.5	-0.3	40.0	1.3	40.2	0.5	40.3	0.2	40.4	0.2	40.6	0.5	40.7	0.2	40.6	-0.2	40.6	0.0
1972	40.6	0.0	40.7	0.2	41.0	0.7	41.0	0.0	41.0	0.0	41.1	0.2	41.5	1.0	41.6	0.2	41.9	0.7	41.9	0.0	42.1	0.5	42.1	0.0
1973	42.2	0.2	42.5	0.7	42.8	0.7	42.9	0.2	43.1	0.5	43.5	0.9	43.7	0.5	44.3	1.4	44.4	0.2	44.8	0.9	45.2	0.9	45.4	0.4
1974	45.7	0.7	46.1	0.9	46.6	1.1	47.0	0.9	47.5	1.1	47.8	0.6	48.4	1.3	49.0	1.2	49.7	1.4	49.8	0.2	50.3	1.0	50.8	1.0
1975	51.0	0.4	51.5	1.0	52.2	1.4	52.7	1.0	53.1	0.8	53.0	-0.2	53.5	0.9	53.7	0.4	54.3	1.1	54.6	0.6	55.0	0.7	55.4	0.7
1976	55.7	0.5	55.4	-0.5	55.5	0.2	55.5	0.0	56.3	1.4	56.5	0.4	57.1	1.1	57.4	0.5	57.8	0.7	58.0	0.3	58.2	0.3	58.5	0.5
1977	59.1	1.0	59.7	1.0	59.8	0.2	60.2	0.7	60.4	0.3	60.7	0.5	61.0	0.5	61.1	0.2	61.4	0.5	61.4	0.0	61.9	0.8	62.4	0.8
1978	62.8	0.6	63.2	0.6	63.3	0.2	63.9	0.9	64.7	1.3	65.3	0.9	65.7	0.6	65.9	0.3	66.6	1.1	66.7	0.2	66.8	0.1	66.7	-0.1
1979	67.6	1.3	68.5	1.3	69.2	1.0	70.7	2.2	71.9	1.7	72.6	1.0	73.4	1.1	74.3	1.2	75.5	1.6	75.8	0.4	76.4	0.8	77.8	1.8
1980	79.5	2.2	81.2	2.1	82.5	1.6	83.8	1.6	85.5	2.0	85.7	0.2	85.1	-0.7	84.6	-0.6	85.3	0.8	86.3	1.2	87.4	1.3	88.7	1.5
1981	88.9	0.2	89.7	0.9	90.2	0.6	91.1	1.0	91.6	0.5	91.9	0.3	93.5	1.7	94.3	0.9	95.7	1.5	96.4	0.7	96.5	0.1	96.7	0.2
1982	98.0	1.3	97.9	-0.1	98.2	0.3	98.2	0.0	98.3	0.1	99.4	1.1	99.1	-0.3	99.1	0.0	98.7	-0.4	99.1	0.4	98.7	-0.4	97.5	-1.2
1983	97.5	0.0	98.2	0.7	98.0	-0.2	98.2	0.2	98.8	0.6	98.8	0.0	99.2	0.4	99.4	0.2	100.4	1.0	101.2	0.8	100.8	-0.4	101.5	0.7
1984	100.8	-0.7	101.2	0.4	100.8	-0.4	101.1	0.3	102.6	1.5	102.7	0.1	101.6	-1.1	103.2	1.6	102.9	-0.3	102.4	-0.5	102.9	0.5	103.7	0.8
1985	104.3	0.6	104.6	0.3	104.8	0.2	105.3	0.5	106.3	0.9	106.3	0.0	106.9	0.6	107.6	0.7	107.5	-0.1	108.3	0.7	108.0	-0.3	108.3	0.3
1986	108.6	0.3	108.4	-0.2	108.8	0.4	108.3	-0.5	109.2	0.8	109.8	0.5	109.6	-0.2	109.5	-0.1	110.6	1.0	111.1	0.5	110.4	-0.6	110.1	-0.3
1987	110.8	0.6	112.1	1.2	112.8	0.6	113.3	0.4	114.1	0.7	113.8	-0.3	113.8	0.0	114.6	0.7	115.2	0.5	115.8	0.5	115.4	-0.3	115.7	0.3
1988	115.9	0.2	116.6	0.6	117.5	0.8	118.0	0.4	118.9	0.8	118.9	0.0	119.0	0.1	119.5	0.4	120.3	0.7	121.0	0.6	120.9	-0.1	121.1	0.2
1989	121.4	0.2	122.3	0.7	122.9	0.5	124.0	0.9	125.0	0.8	125.3	0.2	125.7	0.3	125.5	-0.2	126.5	0.8	126.5	0.0	126.4	-0.1	127.0	0.5
1990	128.5	1.2	129.8	1.0	130.5	0.5	130.2	-0.2	130.7	0.4	131.1	0.3	131.6	0.4	132.3	0.5	133.5	0.9	134.5	0.7	134.8	0.2	135.2	0.3
1991	135.8	0.4	135.5	-0.2	135.3	-0.1	136.3	0.7	136.5	0.1	136.4	-0.1	137.3	0.7	137.4	0.1	138.2	0.6	138.5	0.2	139.0	0.4	138.6	-0.3
1992	139.6	0.7	140.3	0.5	141.0	0.5	141.3	0.2	141.4	0.1	141.8	0.3	142.2	0.3	142.4	0.1	142.8	0.3	143.6	0.6	143.5	-0.1	143.5	0.0
1993	144.4	0.6	145.0	0.4	144.8	-0.1	144.9	0.1	145.1	0.1	144.8	-0.2	144.8	0.0	144.9	0.1	145.0	0.1	145.7	0.5	146.4	0.5	146.7	0.2
1994	146.8	0.1	146.9	0.1	147.0	0.1	146.6	-0.3	146.2	-0.3	146.1	-0.1	146.5	0.3	146.8	0.2	147.3	0.3	148.0	0.5	147.7	-0.2	148.1	0.3
1995	149.0	0.6	149.2	0.1	149.3	0.1	149.5	0.1	149.8	0.2	149.7	-0.1	149.3	-0.3	149.2	-0.1	149.3	0.1	149.9	0.4	149.2	-0.5	149.4	0.1

Source: U.S. Department of Labor, Bureau of Labor Statistics, Division of Consumer Prices and Price Indexes. - indicates no data collected for period.

Los Angeles, CA
Consumer Price Index - All Urban Consumers
Base 1982-1984 = 100
Food and Beverages

For 1976-1995. Columns headed % show percentile change in the index from the previous period for which an index is available.

Year	Jan Index	%	Feb Index	%	Mar Index	%	Apr Index	%	May Index	%	Jun Index	%	Jul Index	%	Aug Index	%	Sep Index	%	Oct Index	%	Nov Index	%	Dec Index	%
1976	60.6	-	59.8	-1.3	59.5	-0.5	59.5	0.0	60.2	1.2	60.4	0.3	61.0	1.0	61.0	0.0	60.6	-0.7	60.7	0.2	61.0	0.5	61.5	0.8
1977	62.3	1.3	62.9	1.0	63.3	0.6	63.9	0.9	64.3	0.6	64.9	0.9	65.2	0.5	65.4	0.3	65.5	0.2	65.7	0.3	66.1	0.6	66.6	0.8
1978	67.6	1.5	68.4	1.2	69.2	1.2	70.7	2.2	71.1	0.6	72.2	1.5	72.3	0.1	72.6	0.4	73.1	0.7	73.7	0.8	73.8	0.1	74.6	1.1
1979	75.9	1.7	77.2	1.7	77.9	0.9	79.0	1.4	79.9	1.1	79.6	-0.4	79.2	-0.5	79.1	-0.1	79.7	0.8	80.3	0.8	80.9	0.7	82.0	1.4
1980	82.5	0.6	82.4	-0.1	83.4	1.2	84.1	0.8	84.5	0.5	84.9	0.5	85.6	0.8	86.9	1.5	88.3	1.6	88.3	0.0	88.7	0.5	89.2	0.6
1981	89.7	0.6	91.3	1.8	91.9	0.7	92.2	0.3	92.3	0.1	92.4	0.1	92.7	0.3	93.4	0.8	93.4	0.0	93.5	0.1	93.1	-0.4	93.9	0.9
1982	95.0	1.2	95.4	0.4	95.7	0.3	95.8	0.1	96.5	0.7	96.7	0.2	97.6	0.9	97.5	-0.1	97.5	0.0	98.2	0.7	98.4	0.2	97.8	-0.6
1983	98.9	1.1	99.2	0.3	100.1	0.9	100.5	0.4	101.1	0.6	100.2	-0.9	100.0	-0.2	99.9	-0.1	99.9	0.0	100.4	0.5	100.1	-0.3	100.8	0.7
1984	102.3	1.5	102.6	0.3	102.9	0.3	102.6	-0.3	102.3	-0.3	102.0	-0.3	102.9	0.9	103.6	0.7	103.6	0.0	103.7	0.1	104.1	0.4	104.2	0.1
1985	105.0	0.8	105.2	0.2	104.8	-0.4	104.9	0.1	105.4	0.5	105.4	0.0	104.8	-0.6	105.2	0.4	105.5	0.3	105.9	0.4	106.8	0.8	107.9	1.0
1986	108.3	0.4	107.8	-0.5	107.8	0.0	107.7	-0.1	108.1	0.4	108.4	0.3	108.4	0.0	108.9	0.5	108.8	-0.1	109.3	0.5	110.3	0.9	110.5	0.2
1987	112.3	1.6	113.7	1.2	112.8	-0.8	112.9	0.1	113.6	0.6	113.0	-0.5	112.8	-0.2	113.2	0.4	113.4	0.2	113.6	0.2	113.3	-0.3	114.0	0.6
1988	114.6	0.5	114.8	0.2	115.4	0.5	116.0	0.5	116.2	0.2	116.2	0.0	117.8	1.4	118.8	0.8	118.8	0.0	119.1	0.3	119.1	0.0	120.0	0.8
1989	121.5	1.3	122.2	0.6	122.8	0.5	123.6	0.7	124.1	0.4	123.5	-0.5	123.6	0.1	124.1	0.4	124.6	0.4	125.2	0.5	126.1	0.7	126.8	0.6
1990	129.6	2.2	130.9	1.0	130.6	-0.2	130.1	-0.4	130.4	0.2	130.5	0.1	130.6	0.1	130.7	0.1	131.0	0.2	131.5	0.4	132.5	0.8	132.7	0.2
1991	135.9	2.4	135.6	-0.2	135.7	0.1	137.4	1.3	137.0	-0.3	137.3	0.2	136.9	-0.3	135.8	-0.8	135.6	-0.1	136.3	0.5	137.3	0.7	138.0	0.5
1992	139.4	1.0	139.5	0.1	141.1	1.1	140.9	-0.1	139.6	-0.9	140.3	0.5	140.1	-0.1	141.0	0.6	142.2	0.9	142.7	0.4	142.3	-0.3	142.2	-0.1
1993	144.2	1.4	143.4	-0.6	143.9	0.3	144.6	0.5	145.4	0.6	144.9	-0.3	144.3	-0.4	144.3	0.0	145.1	0.6	146.2	0.8	146.4	0.1	148.6	1.5
1994	149.0	0.3	147.7	-0.9	147.8	0.1	147.1	-0.5	146.7	-0.3	147.0	0.2	147.6	0.4	147.7	0.1	148.7	0.7	149.9	0.8	150.1	0.1	153.1	2.0
1995	153.4	0.2	152.7	-0.5	152.7	0.0	153.8	0.7	152.8	-0.7	152.8	0.0	152.2	-0.4	152.7	0.3	153.2	0.3	154.7	1.0	154.5	-0.1	154.8	0.2

Source: U.S. Department of Labor, Bureau of Labor Statistics, Division of Consumer Prices and Price Indexes. - indicates no data collected for period.

Los Angeles, CA
Consumer Price Index - Urban Wage Earners
Base 1982-1984 = 100
Food and Beverages

For 1976-1995. Columns headed % show percentile change in the index from the previous period for which an index is available.

Year	Jan Index	%	Feb Index	%	Mar Index	%	Apr Index	%	May Index	%	Jun Index	%	Jul Index	%	Aug Index	%	Sep Index	%	Oct Index	%	Nov Index	%	Dec Index	%
1976	59.5	-	58.7	-1.3	58.4	-0.5	58.5	0.2	59.1	1.0	59.3	0.3	59.9	1.0	59.9	0.0	59.5	-0.7	59.7	0.3	59.9	0.3	60.4	0.8
1977	61.2	1.3	61.8	1.0	62.1	0.5	62.8	1.1	63.1	0.5	63.8	1.1	64.1	0.5	64.3	0.3	64.3	0.0	64.5	0.3	64.9	0.6	65.4	0.8
1978	66.5	1.7	67.4	1.4	67.7	0.4	68.9	1.8	69.6	1.0	70.4	1.1	70.7	0.4	70.9	0.3	71.4	0.7	71.8	0.6	71.7	-0.1	72.6	1.3
1979	73.9	1.8	75.3	1.9	76.6	1.7	77.5	1.2	78.1	0.8	78.4	0.4	78.3	-0.1	78.3	0.0	79.0	0.9	79.5	0.6	79.7	0.3	80.9	1.5
1980	81.3	0.5	81.4	0.1	82.3	1.1	83.5	1.5	83.9	0.5	84.3	0.5	85.1	0.9	86.4	1.5	88.0	1.9	87.9	-0.1	88.7	0.9	89.1	0.5
1981	89.6	0.6	90.8	1.3	91.5	0.8	91.8	0.3	91.5	-0.3	92.2	0.8	92.5	0.3	93.3	0.9	93.1	-0.2	92.9	-0.2	92.8	-0.1	93.7	1.0
1982	94.9	1.3	95.4	0.5	95.7	0.3	95.9	0.2	96.4	0.5	96.6	0.2	97.4	0.8	97.4	0.0	97.3	-0.1	98.1	0.8	98.3	0.2	97.8	-0.5
1983	98.9	1.1	99.3	0.4	100.2	0.9	100.6	0.4	101.2	0.6	100.3	-0.9	100.0	-0.3	100.0	0.0	99.9	-0.1	100.5	0.6	100.2	-0.3	100.9	0.7
1984	102.4	1.5	102.8	0.4	103.1	0.3	102.7	-0.4	102.3	-0.4	102.0	-0.3	102.9	0.9	103.5	0.6	103.5	0.0	103.6	0.1	103.9	0.3	104.1	0.2
1985	104.8	0.7	105.0	0.2	104.7	-0.3	104.8	0.1	105.2	0.4	105.2	0.0	104.6	-0.6	105.0	0.4	105.3	0.3	105.7	0.4	106.6	0.9	107.6	0.9
1986	108.1	0.5	107.6	-0.5	107.6	0.0	107.6	0.0	107.8	0.2	108.1	0.3	108.1	0.0	108.5	0.4	108.5	0.0	109.1	0.6	110.1	0.9	110.3	0.2
1987	112.0	1.5	113.4	1.3	112.5	-0.8	112.7	0.2	113.4	0.6	112.7	-0.6	112.6	-0.1	113.1	0.4	113.2	0.1	113.5	0.3	113.2	-0.3	113.9	0.6
1988	114.3	0.4	114.6	0.3	115.2	0.5	115.9	0.6	116.1	0.2	116.1	0.0	117.7	1.4	118.7	0.8	118.6	-0.1	119.0	0.3	119.0	0.0	119.9	0.8
1989	121.3	1.2	122.0	0.6	122.6	0.5	123.4	0.7	123.9	0.4	123.3	-0.5	123.5	0.2	124.1	0.5	124.6	0.4	125.1	0.4	126.1	0.8	126.9	0.6
1990	129.6	2.1	130.9	1.0	130.7	-0.2	130.2	-0.4	130.4	0.2	130.6	0.2	130.8	0.2	130.9	0.1	131.1	0.2	131.6	0.4	132.6	0.8	132.8	0.2
1991	136.0	2.4	135.7	-0.2	136.0	0.2	137.6	1.2	137.2	-0.3	137.5	0.2	137.2	-0.2	136.2	-0.7	135.9	-0.2	136.7	0.6	137.5	0.6	138.2	0.5
1992	139.6	1.0	139.8	0.1	141.6	1.3	141.4	-0.1	140.0	-1.0	140.7	0.5	140.6	-0.1	141.4	0.6	142.5	0.8	143.1	0.4	142.8	-0.2	142.7	-0.1
1993	144.6	1.3	143.8	-0.6	144.3	0.3	145.0	0.5	145.9	0.6	145.5	-0.3	144.8	-0.5	144.9	0.1	145.7	0.6	146.8	0.8	146.9	0.1	149.0	1.4
1994	149.4	0.3	148.2	-0.8	148.1	-0.1	147.4	-0.5	147.0	-0.3	147.4	0.3	147.9	0.3	148.0	0.1	148.9	0.6	149.9	0.7	150.0	0.1	153.1	2.1
1995	153.4	0.2	152.8	-0.4	152.9	0.1	153.8	0.6	152.9	-0.6	153.0	0.1	152.3	-0.5	152.9	0.4	153.3	0.3	154.8	1.0	154.7	-0.1	155.0	0.2

Source: U.S. Department of Labor, Bureau of Labor Statistics, Division of Consumer Prices and Price Indexes. - indicates no data collected for period.

Los Angeles, CA
Consumer Price Index - All Urban Consumers
Base 1982-1984 = 100
Housing

For 1976-1995. Columns headed % show percentile change in the index from the previous period for which an index is available.

Year	Jan Index	%	Feb Index	%	Mar Index	%	Apr Index	%	May Index	%	Jun Index	%	Jul Index	%	Aug Index	%	Sep Index	%	Oct Index	%	Nov Index	%	Dec Index	%
1976	53.9	-	53.2	-1.3	53.1	-0.2	52.9	-0.4	53.9	1.9	53.8	-0.2	54.4	1.1	54.7	0.6	55.4	1.3	55.7	0.5	55.7	0.0	56.0	0.5
1977	57.1	2.0	57.5	0.7	57.5	0.0	57.8	0.5	58.0	0.3	58.1	0.2	58.6	0.9	58.5	-0.2	59.1	1.0	58.8	-0.5	59.6	1.4	60.5	1.5
1978	60.9	0.7	61.2	0.5	61.4	0.3	62.2	1.3	62.9	1.1	63.5	1.0	63.8	0.5	64.0	0.3	65.1	1.7	65.0	-0.2	64.9	-0.2	63.7	-1.8
1979	64.7	1.6	65.6	1.4	66.1	0.8	67.4	2.0	68.6	1.8	69.4	1.2	70.1	1.0	71.3	1.7	72.6	1.8	73.0	0.6	74.1	1.5	75.9	2.4
1980	77.7	2.4	79.6	2.4	81.2	2.0	82.7	1.8	85.6	3.5	86.2	0.7	84.7	-1.7	83.0	-2.0	83.4	0.5	85.2	2.2	86.6	1.6	88.4	2.1
1981	88.4	0.0	88.6	0.2	88.8	0.2	89.6	0.9	90.4	0.9	90.3	-0.1	92.3	2.2	93.4	1.2	96.2	3.0	97.0	0.8	96.7	-0.3	96.7	0.0
1982	97.9	1.2	97.5	-0.4	98.3	0.8	98.4	0.1	98.3	-0.1	99.4	1.1	98.1	-1.3	98.0	-0.1	97.5	-0.5	97.8	0.3	97.0	-0.8	95.3	-1.8
1983	95.4	0.1	96.6	1.3	96.5	-0.1	97.0	0.5	97.8	0.8	98.4	0.6	98.7	0.3	99.1	0.4	100.2	1.1	100.4	0.2	100.0	-0.4	99.9	-0.1
1984	99.9	0.0	101.2	1.3	101.5	0.3	102.2	0.7	103.7	1.5	104.3	0.6	104.7	0.4	105.8	1.1	106.3	0.5	106.1	-0.2	105.6	-0.5	105.3	-0.3
1985	106.6	1.2	107.0	0.4	106.4	-0.6	106.6	0.2	109.1	2.3	108.4	-0.6	110.6	2.0	112.7	1.9	112.3	-0.4	113.5	1.1	111.7	-1.6	111.6	-0.1
1986	111.6	0.0	112.6	0.9	114.9	2.0	114.0	-0.8	115.4	1.2	115.9	0.4	116.9	0.9	117.2	0.3	120.0	2.4	120.4	0.3	117.5	-2.4	116.8	-0.6
1987	116.7	-0.1	118.3	1.4	119.5	1.0	120.4	0.8	121.6	1.0	120.7	-0.7	121.1	0.3	122.2	0.9	122.8	0.5	123.6	0.7	122.7	-0.7	122.9	0.2
1988	123.0	0.1	124.5	1.2	125.2	0.6	125.4	0.2	126.8	1.1	126.6	-0.2	126.4	-0.2	127.1	0.6	128.2	0.9	128.7	0.4	128.9	0.2	128.9	0.0
1989	128.7	-0.2	129.2	0.4	128.8	-0.3	128.6	-0.2	130.4	1.4	131.7	1.0	133.0	1.0	133.0	0.0	134.6	1.2	134.5	-0.1	134.0	-0.4	134.3	0.2
1990	135.8	1.1	136.7	0.7	138.1	1.0	137.1	-0.7	137.8	0.5	138.5	0.5	139.9	1.0	140.8	0.6	141.5	0.5	142.0	0.4	141.3	-0.5	141.5	0.1
1991	142.8	0.9	143.4	0.4	143.9	0.3	144.7	0.6	144.5	-0.1	144.4	-0.1	145.4	0.7	145.6	0.1	146.0	0.3	145.9	-0.1	146.3	0.3	146.1	-0.1
1992	147.0	0.6	147.7	0.5	147.9	0.1	147.9	0.0	148.1	0.1	148.8	0.5	149.0	0.1	149.3	0.2	149.2	-0.1	149.5	0.2	149.4	-0.1	148.9	-0.3
1993	149.9	0.7	150.8	0.6	150.0	-0.5	150.4	0.3	150.6	0.1	150.6	0.0	150.7	0.1	150.7	0.0	149.8	-0.6	150.2	0.3	150.4	0.1	151.0	0.4
1994	151.5	0.3	151.9	0.3	151.6	-0.2	150.8	-0.5	150.7	-0.1	150.6	-0.1	151.2	0.4	151.4	0.1	151.2	-0.1	151.2	0.0	149.9	-0.9	150.4	0.3
1995	151.3	0.6	152.0	0.5	152.0	0.0	151.6	-0.3	152.5	0.6	153.0	0.3	152.4	-0.4	152.5	0.1	152.7	0.1	152.7	0.0	150.9	-1.2	152.4	1.0

Source: U.S. Department of Labor, Bureau of Labor Statistics, Division of Consumer Prices and Price Indexes. - indicates no data collected for period.

Los Angeles, CA
Consumer Price Index - Urban Wage Earners
Base 1982-1984 = 100
Housing

For 1976-1995. Columns headed % show percentile change in the index from the previous period for which an index is available.

Year	Jan Index	%	Feb Index	%	Mar Index	%	Apr Index	%	May Index	%	Jun Index	%	Jul Index	%	Aug Index	%	Sep Index	%	Oct Index	%	Nov Index	%	Dec Index	%
1976	54.0	-	53.3	-1.3	53.1	-0.4	53.0	-0.2	54.0	1.9	53.9	-0.2	54.5	1.1	54.8	0.6	55.4	1.1	55.8	0.7	55.8	0.0	56.0	0.4
1977	57.2	2.1	57.6	0.7	57.5	-0.2	57.9	0.7	58.0	0.2	58.2	0.3	58.6	0.7	58.6	0.0	59.1	0.9	58.9	-0.3	59.7	1.4	60.6	1.5
1978	61.0	0.7	61.3	0.5	61.6	0.5	62.3	1.1	62.9	1.0	63.5	1.0	63.9	0.6	64.1	0.3	65.1	1.6	64.9	-0.3	64.8	-0.2	63.8	-1.5
1979	64.9	1.7	65.9	1.5	66.5	0.9	68.0	2.3	69.4	2.1	70.1	1.0	70.8	1.0	72.3	2.1	73.7	1.9	74.0	0.4	75.1	1.5	76.9	2.4
1980	79.2	3.0	81.2	2.5	82.9	2.1	84.4	1.8	87.6	3.8	88.1	0.6	86.4	-1.9	84.6	-2.1	84.7	0.1	86.6	2.2	88.2	1.8	90.3	2.4
1981	90.3	0.0	90.4	0.1	90.7	0.3	91.7	1.1	92.5	0.9	92.4	-0.1	95.1	2.9	96.2	1.2	99.1	3.0	99.9	0.8	99.5	-0.4	99.6	0.1
1982	100.9	1.3	100.3	-0.6	101.1	0.8	101.2	0.1	101.0	-0.2	102.2	1.2	100.7	-1.5	100.6	-0.1	100.0	-0.6	100.3	0.3	99.3	-1.0	97.4	-1.9
1983	97.3	-0.1	98.9	1.6	98.4	-0.5	97.6	-0.8	97.9	0.3	97.3	-0.6	97.7	0.4	98.0	0.3	100.3	2.3	101.7	1.4	100.9	-0.8	101.4	0.5
1984	99.1	-2.3	100.2	1.1	99.2	-1.0	99.1	-0.1	101.6	2.5	102.3	0.7	100.2	-2.1	102.8	2.6	101.6	-1.2	99.2	-2.4	100.2	1.0	102.0	1.8
1985	103.2	1.2	103.6	0.4	103.0	-0.6	103.2	0.2	105.8	2.5	104.9	-0.9	107.0	2.0	109.1	2.0	108.7	-0.4	109.8	1.0	108.1	-1.5	107.9	-0.2
1986	107.9	0.0	108.9	0.9	111.2	2.1	110.3	-0.8	111.7	1.3	112.2	0.4	113.1	0.8	113.4	0.3	116.1	2.4	116.5	0.3	113.6	-2.5	113.0	-0.5
1987	112.9	-0.1	114.4	1.3	115.4	0.9	116.3	0.8	117.6	1.1	116.7	-0.8	117.1	0.3	118.2	0.9	118.7	0.4	119.4	0.6	118.6	-0.7	118.9	0.3
1988	118.9	0.0	120.1	1.0	121.0	0.7	121.1	0.1	122.5	1.2	122.3	-0.2	122.1	-0.2	122.6	0.4	123.9	1.1	124.5	0.5	124.5	0.0	124.5	0.0
1989	124.2	-0.2	124.7	0.4	124.2	-0.4	124.1	-0.1	125.8	1.4	127.0	1.0	128.4	1.1	128.3	-0.1	129.7	1.1	129.7	0.0	129.1	-0.5	129.4	0.2
1990	130.9	1.2	131.7	0.6	133.0	1.0	132.0	-0.8	132.8	0.6	133.4	0.5	134.8	1.0	135.5	0.5	136.2	0.5	136.8	0.4	136.1	-0.5	136.3	0.1
1991	137.5	0.9	138.1	0.4	138.5	0.3	139.4	0.6	139.2	-0.1	139.1	-0.1	140.1	0.7	140.2	0.1	140.7	0.4	140.7	0.0	141.0	0.2	140.7	-0.2
1992	141.4	0.5	142.2	0.6	142.4	0.1	142.4	0.0	142.5	0.1	143.2	0.5	143.3	0.1	143.6	0.2	143.5	-0.1	143.9	0.3	143.8	-0.1	143.4	-0.3
1993	144.4	0.7	145.1	0.5	144.3	-0.6	144.7	0.3	144.9	0.1	144.9	0.0	144.9	0.0	145.0	0.1	144.1	-0.6	144.5	0.3	144.9	0.3	145.4	0.3
1994	145.8	0.3	146.3	0.3	145.9	-0.3	145.1	-0.5	145.1	0.0	144.9	-0.1	145.6	0.5	145.8	0.1	145.5	-0.2	145.4	-0.1	144.3	-0.8	144.7	0.3
1995	145.5	0.6	146.2	0.5	146.1	-0.1	145.9	-0.1	146.7	0.5	147.3	0.4	146.6	-0.5	146.7	0.1	147.0	0.2	146.9	-0.1	145.1	-1.2	146.8	1.2

Source: U.S. Department of Labor, Bureau of Labor Statistics, Division of Consumer Prices and Price Indexes. - indicates no data collected for period.

Los Angeles, CA
Consumer Price Index - All Urban Consumers
Base 1982-1984 = 100
Apparel and Upkeep

For 1952-1995. Columns headed % show percentile change in the index from the previous period for which an index is available.

Year	Jan Index	%	Feb Index	%	Mar Index	%	Apr Index	%	May Index	%	Jun Index	%	Jul Index	%	Aug Index	%	Sep Index	%	Oct Index	%	Nov Index	%	Dec Index	%
1952	-		-		-		-		-		-		-		-		-		-		-		49.2	-
1953	48.9	-0.6	48.9	0.0	48.7	-0.4	48.6	-0.2	48.6	0.0	48.5	-0.2	48.7	0.4	48.4	-0.6	48.9	1.0	48.8	-0.2	48.8	0.0	48.9	0.2
1954	48.7	-0.4	48.9	0.4	49.0	0.2	48.7	-0.6	48.5	-0.4	48.9	0.8	48.8	-0.2	48.7	-0.2	49.3	1.2	49.3	0.0	49.2	-0.2	49.2	0.0
1955	48.8	-0.8	48.9	0.2	48.7	-0.4	48.7	0.0	48.8	0.2	48.7	-0.2	48.8	0.2	48.8	0.0	49.2	0.8	49.2	0.0	49.0	-0.4	49.2	0.4
1956	49.1	-0.2	49.3	0.4	49.4	0.2	49.3	-0.2	49.8	1.0	49.8	0.0	49.9	0.2	49.8	-0.2	50.5	1.4	50.5	0.0	50.5	0.0	50.6	0.2
1957	50.4	-0.4	50.5	0.2	50.7	0.4	50.7	0.0	50.8	0.2	50.8	0.0	50.8	0.0	50.6	-0.4	51.3	1.4	51.2	-0.2	51.3	0.2	51.3	0.0
1958	51.0	-0.6	51.4	0.8	51.1	-0.6	50.9	-0.4	50.9	0.0	50.6	-0.6	50.8	0.4	50.6	-0.4	51.0	0.8	51.0	0.0	51.1	0.2	51.0	-0.2
1959	51.0	0.0	51.0	0.0	51.0	0.0	51.0	0.0	51.3	0.6	51.0	-0.6	51.6	1.2	51.4	-0.4	52.2	1.6	52.4	0.4	52.6	0.4	52.6	0.0
1960	52.5	-0.2	52.7	0.4	52.7	0.0	52.9	0.4	52.9	0.0	52.6	-0.6	52.7	0.2	52.6	-0.2	52.9	0.6	53.0	0.2	53.0	0.0	53.0	0.0
1961	52.7	-0.6	53.1	0.8	53.1	0.0	52.7	-0.8	53.0	0.6	52.7	-0.6	53.1	0.8	52.8	-0.6	53.0	0.4	52.9	-0.2	52.9	0.0	53.0	0.2
1962	52.7	-0.6	52.7	0.0	52.8	0.2	52.6	-0.4	52.7	0.2	52.7	0.0	52.8	0.2	52.5	-0.6	53.7	2.3	53.6	-0.2	53.6	0.0	53.7	0.2
1963	53.5	-0.4	53.5	0.0	53.6	0.2	53.4	-0.4	53.6	0.4	53.4	-0.4	53.5	0.2	53.6	0.2	54.1	0.9	54.1	0.0	54.1	0.0	54.5	0.7
1964	53.8	-1.3	54.3	0.9	54.4	0.2	54.5	0.2	54.5	0.0	54.6	0.2	54.6	0.0	54.4	-0.4	54.6	0.4	54.6	0.0	54.6	0.0	54.8	0.4
1965	54.6	-0.4	55.0	0.7	55.1	0.2	55.1	0.0	55.3	0.4	55.4	0.2	54.7	-1.3	54.5	-0.4	54.9	0.7	55.0	0.2	55.2	0.4	55.0	-0.4
1966	55.1	0.2	55.4	0.5	55.3	-0.2	55.5	0.4	55.9	0.7	55.9	0.0	55.7	-0.4	55.5	-0.4	56.6	2.0	56.4	-0.4	56.7	0.5	57.0	0.5
1967	56.4	-1.1	57.0	1.1	57.0	0.0	57.1	0.2	57.4	0.5	57.6	0.3	57.7	0.2	58.7	1.7	59.5	1.4	59.4	-0.2	59.6	0.3	59.6	0.0
1968	59.2	-0.7	59.8	1.0	60.4	1.0	60.4	0.0	60.6	0.3	60.8	0.3	61.2	0.7	61.2	0.0	62.2	1.6	62.5	0.5	62.5	0.0	63.0	0.8
1969	62.5	-0.8	62.9	0.6	63.1	0.3	62.7	-0.6	63.2	0.8	63.4	0.3	63.5	0.2	63.1	-0.6	64.6	2.4	64.6	0.0	64.9	0.5	65.1	0.3
1970	64.9	-0.3	65.4	0.8	65.7	0.5	66.0	0.5	66.7	1.1	66.8	0.1	66.3	-0.7	66.1	-0.3	67.2	1.7	67.2	0.0	67.7	0.7	67.9	0.3
1971	67.1	-1.2	67.5	0.6	67.7	0.3	67.7	0.0	68.8	1.6	68.9	0.1	68.9	0.0	68.5	-0.6	69.6	1.6	69.3	-0.4	69.3	0.0	69.1	-0.3
1972	68.6	-0.7	68.9	0.4	69.7	1.2	69.8	0.1	69.8	0.0	69.7	-0.1	69.2	-0.7	69.0	-0.3	70.3	1.9	70.3	0.0	70.3	0.0	70.6	0.4
1973	69.3	-1.8	69.7	0.6	71.2	2.2	71.0	-0.3	71.3	0.4	71.4	0.1	71.0	-0.6	71.6	0.8	73.0	2.0	72.6	-0.5	72.7	0.1	72.8	0.1
1974	71.8	-1.4	73.0	1.7	75.0	2.7	75.8	1.1	76.9	1.5	77.1	0.3	76.9	-0.3	78.3	1.8	79.0	0.9	78.6	-0.5	79.2	0.8	78.6	-0.8
1975	77.6	-1.3	78.0	0.5	78.0	0.0	78.5	0.6	79.1	0.8	79.4	0.4	78.6	-1.0	79.7	1.4	80.6	1.1	80.7	0.1	80.2	-0.6	80.1	-0.1
1976	79.0	-1.4	79.1	0.1	80.5	1.8	79.9	-0.7	80.7	1.0	80.5	-0.2	79.8	-0.9	81.4	2.0	82.3	1.1	82.2	-0.1	82.3	0.1	82.8	0.6
1977	82.8	0.0	83.7	1.1	84.0	0.4	83.7	-0.4	83.9	0.2	83.6	-0.4	82.7	-1.1	83.4	0.8	84.3	1.1	85.3	1.2	85.7	0.5	86.1	0.5
1978	86.2	0.1	85.0	-1.4	85.1	0.1	84.7	-0.5	85.5	0.9	85.5	0.0	85.4	-0.1	85.8	0.5	86.2	0.5	86.2	0.0	87.2	1.2	87.3	0.1
1979	85.9	-1.6	86.4	0.6	87.3	1.0	88.6	1.5	88.8	0.2	89.5	0.8	87.6	-2.1	88.0	0.5	90.7	3.1	90.5	-0.2	92.5	2.2	91.9	-0.6
1980	94.6	2.9	97.2	2.7	98.5	1.3	98.3	-0.2	97.8	-0.5	98.3	0.5	98.0	-0.3	98.4	0.4	99.0	0.6	99.7	0.7	100.1	0.4	99.7	-0.4
1981	97.7	-2.0	98.4	0.7	101.0	2.6	102.1	1.1	103.0	0.9	102.7	-0.3	101.6	-1.1	101.9	0.3	102.8	0.9	102.6	-0.2	102.8	0.2	101.5	-1.3
1982	99.9	-1.6	101.7	1.8	100.6	-1.1	99.5	-1.1	99.0	-0.5	98.6	-0.4	97.9	-0.7	97.7	-0.2	97.3	-0.4	97.9	0.6	98.8	0.9	98.1	-0.7
1983	95.3	-2.9	98.0	2.8	98.1	0.1	98.6	0.5	98.4	-0.2	99.9	1.5	99.9	0.0	101.7	1.8	102.0	0.3	101.8	-0.2	101.7	-0.1	101.2	-0.5
1984	101.3	0.1	101.2	-0.1	100.1	-1.1	100.5	0.4	100.3	-0.2	98.0	-2.3	97.7	-0.3	103.0	5.4	104.0	1.0	104.4	0.4	103.5	-0.9	102.3	-1.2
1985	99.8	-2.4	103.7	3.9	104.4	0.7	103.3	-1.1	103.5	0.2	104.3	0.8	103.0	-1.2	105.8	2.7	108.7	2.7	108.0	-0.6	108.0	0.0	108.4	0.4
1986	107.3	-1.0	106.4	-0.8	106.8	0.4	106.6	-0.2	105.9	-0.7	106.4	0.5	106.3	-0.1	105.9	-0.4	108.0	2.0	107.7	-0.3	108.4	0.6	107.3	-1.0
1987	109.6	2.1	108.8	-0.7	114.3	5.1	111.6	-2.4	112.2	0.5	113.5	1.2	110.1	-3.0	113.5	3.1	115.1	1.4	113.9	-1.0	113.1	-0.7	113.8	0.6
1988	113.2	-0.5	114.1	0.8	118.5	3.9	116.7	-1.5	117.6	0.8	115.9	-1.4	113.8	-1.8	109.7	-3.6	110.5	0.7	113.3	2.5	114.1	0.7	113.9	-0.2
1989	111.7	-1.9	114.1	2.1	122.0	6.9	122.1	0.1	122.7	0.5	120.3	-2.0	117.1	-2.7	116.8	-0.3	120.3	3.0	119.4	-0.7	119.3	-0.1	119.4	0.1
1990	119.3	-0.1	128.3	7.5	129.6	1.0	130.4	0.6	129.2	-0.9	126.3	-2.2	123.1	-2.5	122.3	-0.6	125.7	2.8	127.4	1.4	127.7	0.2	127.3	-0.3
1991	127.5	0.2	129.1	1.3	129.2	0.1	132.8	2.8	130.2	-2.0	125.2	-3.8	128.2	2.4	130.2	1.6	136.3	4.7	136.2	-0.1	136.1	-0.1	130.3	-4.3
1992	132.7	1.8	135.2	1.9	136.9	1.3	136.3	-0.4	136.0	-0.2	130.4	-4.1	130.8	0.3	132.0	0.9	131.8	-0.2	134.6	2.1	131.6	-2.2	129.5	-1.6
1993	128.9	-0.5	134.7	4.5	135.7	0.7	133.7	-1.5	129.8	-2.9	127.8	-1.5	127.4	-0.3	130.7	2.6	134.9	3.2	131.9	-2.2	133.9	1.5	130.2	-2.8
1994	129.1	-0.8	131.0	1.5	133.2	1.7	133.8	0.5	131.3	-1.9	125.0	-4.8	122.4	-2.1	123.7	1.1	132.2	6.9	133.3	0.8	132.3	-0.8	128.0	-3.3
1995	129.7	1.3	130.5	0.6	131.0	0.4	129.1	-1.5	128.8	-0.2	123.7	-4.0	128.0	3.5	123.8	-3.3	124.7	0.7	125.9	1.0	125.2	-0.6	120.1	-4.1

Source: U.S. Department of Labor, Bureau of Labor Statistics, Division of Consumer Prices and Price Indexes. - indicates no data collected for period.

Los Angeles, CA
Consumer Price Index - Urban Wage Earners
Base 1982-1984 = 100
Apparel and Upkeep

For 1952-1995. Columns headed % show percentile change in the index from the previous period for which an index is available.

Year	Jan Index	%	Feb Index	%	Mar Index	%	Apr Index	%	May Index	%	Jun Index	%	Jul Index	%	Aug Index	%	Sep Index	%	Oct Index	%	Nov Index	%	Dec Index	%
1952	-	-	-	-	-	-	-	-	-	-	-	-	-	-	-	-	-	-	-	-	-	-	49.4	-
1953	49.1	-0.6	49.1	0.0	48.9	-0.4	48.8	-0.2	48.8	0.0	48.7	-0.2	48.8	0.2	48.6	-0.4	49.1	1.0	49.0	-0.2	49.0	0.0	49.1	0.2
1954	48.9	-0.4	49.1	0.4	49.1	0.0	48.9	-0.4	48.7	-0.4	49.1	0.8	49.0	-0.2	48.8	-0.4	49.5	1.4	49.5	0.0	49.4	-0.2	49.4	0.0
1955	49.0	-0.8	49.1	0.2	48.9	-0.4	48.8	-0.2	49.0	0.4	48.8	-0.4	49.0	0.4	49.0	0.0	49.4	0.8	49.4	0.0	49.2	-0.4	49.4	0.4
1956	49.3	-0.2	49.5	0.4	49.5	0.0	49.5	0.0	50.0	1.0	50.0	0.0	50.1	0.2	50.0	-0.2	50.7	1.4	50.7	0.0	50.7	0.0	50.8	0.2
1957	50.6	-0.4	50.7	0.2	50.9	0.4	50.9	0.0	51.0	0.2	50.9	-0.2	51.0	0.2	50.8	-0.4	51.5	1.4	51.4	-0.2	51.5	0.2	51.5	0.0
1958	51.2	-0.6	51.6	0.8	51.3	-0.6	51.1	-0.4	51.1	0.0	50.8	-0.6	50.9	0.2	50.8	-0.2	51.2	0.8	51.2	0.0	51.3	0.2	51.2	-0.2
1959	51.2	0.0	51.2	0.0	51.2	0.0	51.2	0.0	51.5	0.6	51.2	-0.6	51.8	1.2	51.6	-0.4	52.4	1.6	52.6	0.4	52.8	0.4	52.8	0.0
1960	52.7	-0.2	52.9	0.4	52.9	0.0	53.1	0.4	53.1	0.0	52.8	-0.6	52.9	0.2	52.8	-0.2	53.1	0.6	53.2	0.2	53.2	0.0	53.2	0.0
1961	52.9	-0.6	53.3	0.8	53.3	0.0	52.9	-0.8	53.2	0.6	52.9	-0.6	53.3	0.8	53.0	-0.6	53.2	0.4	53.1	-0.2	53.1	0.0	53.2	0.2
1962	52.9	-0.6	52.9	0.0	53.0	0.2	52.8	-0.4	52.9	0.2	52.9	0.0	53.0	0.2	52.7	-0.6	53.9	2.3	53.8	-0.2	53.8	0.0	53.9	0.2
1963	53.7	-0.4	53.7	0.0	53.8	0.2	53.6	-0.4	53.8	0.4	53.6	-0.4	53.7	0.2	53.8	0.2	54.3	0.9	54.3	0.0	54.3	0.0	54.7	0.7
1964	54.0	-1.3	54.5	0.9	54.6	0.2	54.7	0.2	54.7	0.0	54.8	0.2	54.8	0.0	54.6	-0.4	54.8	0.4	54.8	0.0	54.8	0.0	55.0	0.4
1965	54.8	-0.4	55.2	0.7	55.3	0.2	55.3	0.0	55.5	0.4	55.6	0.2	54.9	-1.3	54.7	-0.4	55.1	0.7	55.2	0.2	55.4	0.4	55.2	-0.4
1966	55.3	0.2	55.6	0.5	55.5	-0.2	55.7	0.4	56.1	0.7	56.1	0.0	55.9	-0.4	55.7	-0.4	56.8	2.0	56.7	-0.2	56.9	0.4	57.2	0.5
1967	56.6	-1.0	57.2	1.1	57.2	0.0	57.4	0.3	57.6	0.3	57.8	0.3	57.9	0.2	58.9	1.7	59.7	1.4	59.6	-0.2	59.8	0.3	59.8	0.0
1968	59.4	-0.7	60.0	1.0	60.6	1.0	60.6	0.0	60.9	0.5	61.0	0.2	61.4	0.7	61.4	0.0	62.4	1.6	62.8	0.6	62.7	-0.2	63.2	0.8
1969	62.8	-0.6	63.1	0.5	63.3	0.3	63.0	-0.5	63.5	0.8	63.7	0.3	63.7	0.0	63.3	-0.6	64.9	2.5	64.9	0.0	65.2	0.5	65.3	0.2
1970	65.2	-0.2	65.6	0.6	65.9	0.5	66.2	0.5	67.0	1.2	67.1	0.1	66.6	-0.7	66.4	-0.3	67.5	1.7	67.5	0.0	67.9	0.6	68.1	0.3
1971	67.4	-1.0	67.8	0.6	68.0	0.3	68.0	0.0	69.0	1.5	69.2	0.3	69.1	-0.1	68.7	-0.6	69.8	1.6	69.6	-0.3	69.5	-0.1	69.4	-0.1
1972	68.9	-0.7	69.2	0.4	69.9	1.0	70.1	0.3	70.1	0.0	69.9	-0.3	69.4	-0.7	69.2	-0.3	70.6	2.0	70.6	0.0	70.6	0.0	70.8	0.3
1973	69.6	-1.7	69.9	0.4	71.5	2.3	71.2	-0.4	71.5	0.4	71.7	0.3	71.3	-0.6	71.9	0.8	73.3	1.9	72.9	-0.5	73.0	0.1	73.0	0.0
1974	72.0	-1.4	73.3	1.8	75.3	2.7	76.1	1.1	77.2	1.4	77.3	0.1	77.2	-0.1	78.6	1.8	79.3	0.9	78.9	-0.5	79.4	0.6	78.9	-0.6
1975	77.9	-1.3	78.3	0.5	78.3	0.0	78.7	0.5	79.4	0.9	79.7	0.4	78.9	-1.0	80.0	1.4	80.9	1.1	81.0	0.1	80.5	-0.6	80.4	-0.1
1976	79.3	-1.4	79.4	0.1	80.8	1.8	80.2	-0.7	81.0	1.0	80.8	-0.2	80.1	-0.9	81.7	2.0	82.6	1.1	82.5	-0.1	82.6	0.1	83.1	0.6
1977	83.1	0.0	84.1	1.2	84.3	0.2	84.1	-0.2	84.2	0.1	83.9	-0.4	83.0	-1.1	83.7	0.8	84.6	1.1	85.6	1.2	86.0	0.5	86.4	0.5
1978	85.5	-1.0	85.2	-0.4	85.6	0.5	85.7	0.1	86.6	1.1	87.7	1.3	86.1	-1.8	87.0	1.0	88.2	1.4	88.1	-0.1	89.7	1.8	89.5	-0.2
1979	89.1	-0.4	90.1	1.1	90.1	0.0	90.8	0.8	90.8	0.0	91.5	0.8	90.2	-1.4	91.2	1.1	93.2	2.2	93.8	0.6	93.8	0.0	93.7	-0.1
1980	95.5	1.9	96.8	1.4	98.2	1.4	97.8	-0.4	96.8	-1.0	96.9	0.1	96.7	-0.2	97.0	0.3	97.3	0.3	97.2	-0.1	98.7	1.5	99.3	0.6
1981	96.9	-2.4	98.7	1.9	99.3	0.6	100.6	1.3	101.1	0.5	100.7	-0.4	100.6	-0.1	101.8	1.2	102.4	0.6	101.9	-0.5	102.7	0.8	101.8	-0.9
1982	99.9	-1.9	101.8	1.9	100.7	-1.1	99.6	-1.1	99.1	-0.5	98.7	-0.4	98.2	-0.5	97.8	-0.4	97.6	-0.2	97.9	0.3	98.9	1.0	98.2	-0.7
1983	95.2	-3.1	97.9	2.8	97.9	0.0	98.5	0.6	98.2	-0.3	99.8	1.6	100.1	0.3	101.7	1.6	101.9	0.2	101.6	-0.3	101.5	-0.1	101.2	-0.3
1984	101.1	-0.1	101.0	-0.1	100.2	-0.8	100.8	0.6	100.3	-0.5	97.9	-2.4	97.7	-0.2	102.8	5.2	103.8	1.0	104.6	0.8	103.6	-1.0	102.2	-1.4
1985	100.0	-2.2	103.5	3.5	104.3	0.8	103.0	-1.2	103.3	0.3	104.0	0.7	102.8	-1.2	105.9	3.0	108.4	2.4	107.9	-0.5	108.0	0.1	108.6	0.6
1986	107.7	-0.8	106.8	-0.8	106.9	0.1	106.9	0.0	106.3	-0.6	106.9	0.6	106.5	-0.4	105.9	-0.6	108.2	2.2	108.1	-0.1	108.6	0.5	107.5	-1.0
1987	109.0	1.4	108.5	-0.5	113.7	4.8	111.0	-2.4	111.3	0.3	113.1	1.6	109.9	-2.8	113.1	2.9	114.4	1.1	113.3	-1.0	112.6	-0.6	113.4	0.7
1988	112.5	-0.8	113.8	1.2	116.6	2.5	115.5	-0.9	116.3	0.7	114.7	-1.4	113.1	-1.4	109.9	-2.8	111.1	1.1	114.2	2.8	115.2	0.9	115.1	-0.1
1989	112.1	-2.6	114.3	2.0	120.7	5.6	121.2	0.4	121.9	0.6	119.8	-1.7	117.2	-2.2	117.2	0.0	120.6	2.9	120.1	-0.4	120.0	-0.1	119.9	-0.1
1990	120.1	0.2	127.4	6.1	128.8	1.1	129.7	0.7	128.6	-0.8	125.7	-2.3	122.7	-2.4	122.2	-0.4	125.2	2.5	127.2	1.6	127.7	0.4	127.5	-0.2
1991	127.3	-0.2	128.6	1.0	128.8	0.2	132.8	3.1	129.9	-2.2	125.1	-3.7	128.5	2.7	130.4	1.5	135.8	4.1	135.9	0.1	136.2	0.2	130.4	-4.3
1992	132.4	1.5	135.7	2.5	137.3	1.2	136.2	-0.8	135.9	-0.2	131.2	-3.5	131.8	0.5	132.4	0.5	132.1	-0.2	135.2	2.3	132.4	-2.1	130.4	-1.5
1993	129.5	-0.7	134.9	4.2	136.2	1.0	134.1	-1.5	130.3	-2.8	128.6	-1.3	128.1	-0.4	131.7	2.8	136.0	3.3	132.8	-2.4	135.0	1.7	131.2	-2.8
1994	130.2	-0.8	132.1	1.5	133.6	1.1	134.1	0.4	131.3	-2.1	125.4	-4.5	123.2	-1.8	124.9	1.4	132.2	5.8	133.2	0.8	132.2	-0.8	127.7	-3.4
1995	129.7	1.6	130.3	0.5	131.3	0.8	129.6	-1.3	129.0	-0.5	124.0	-3.9	127.8	3.1	124.0	-3.0	124.5	0.4	126.3	1.4	125.1	-1.0	120.4	-3.8

Source: U.S. Department of Labor, Bureau of Labor Statistics, Division of Consumer Prices and Price Indexes. - indicates no data collected for period.

Los Angeles, CA
Consumer Price Index - All Urban Consumers
Base 1982-1984 = 100
Transportation

For 1947-1995. Columns headed % show percentile change in the index from the previous period for which an index is available.

Year	Jan Index	%	Feb Index	%	Mar Index	%	Apr Index	%	May Index	%	Jun Index	%	Jul Index	%	Aug Index	%	Sep Index	%	Oct Index	%	Nov Index	%	Dec Index	%
1947	17.3	-	17.5	1.2	17.5	0.0	17.7	1.1	17.6	-0.6	17.6	0.0	18.0	2.3	18.1	0.6	18.3	1.1	18.4	0.5	18.4	0.0	18.4	0.0
1948	19.2	4.3	19.2	0.0	19.2	0.0	19.3	0.5	19.2	-0.5	19.2	0.0	20.1	4.7	20.4	1.5	20.5	0.5	20.5	0.0	20.5	0.0	20.6	0.5
1949	20.6	0.0	21.0	1.9	20.9	-0.5	21.0	0.5	21.0	0.0	21.0	0.0	21.0	0.0	21.0	0.0	21.0	0.0	21.0	0.0	21.0	0.0	21.0	0.0
1950	21.0	0.0	20.9	-0.5	20.7	-1.0	20.5	-1.0	20.5	0.0	20.5	0.0	20.6	0.5	20.7	0.5	20.7	0.0	20.8	0.5	20.9	0.5	21.0	0.5
1951	21.0	0.0	21.3	1.4	21.5	0.9	21.5	0.0	21.5	0.0	21.5	0.0	21.6	0.5	21.6	0.0	21.8	0.9	22.0	0.9	22.3	1.4	22.3	0.0
1952	22.2	-0.4	23.5	5.9	23.5	0.0	23.5	0.0	23.7	0.9	23.7	0.0	24.2	2.1	24.2	0.0	24.2	0.0	24.2	0.0	24.4	0.8	24.4	0.0
1953	24.6	0.8	24.6	0.0	24.9	1.2	24.9	0.0	24.8	-0.4	24.8	0.0	25.0	0.8	25.1	0.4	24.9	-0.8	25.0	0.4	24.9	-0.4	24.1	-3.2
1954	25.2	4.6	25.1	-0.4	25.0	-0.4	24.9	-0.4	24.9	0.0	24.6	-1.2	23.7	-3.7	23.9	0.8	24.1	0.8	23.6	-2.1	24.7	4.7	24.7	0.0
1955	24.7	0.0	24.7	0.0	24.9	0.8	23.9	-4.0	24.2	1.3	24.0	-0.8	24.0	0.0	24.0	0.0	24.1	0.4	24.3	0.8	24.9	2.5	24.7	-0.8
1956	24.5	-0.8	24.4	-0.4	24.5	0.4	24.2	-1.2	24.6	1.7	24.6	0.0	25.0	1.6	24.7	-1.2	24.7	0.0	25.3	2.4	25.5	0.8	25.6	0.4
1957	25.5	-0.4	25.9	1.6	25.9	0.0	25.9	0.0	26.1	0.8	25.9	-0.8	25.9	0.0	25.4	-1.9	25.7	1.2	25.7	0.0	26.0	1.2	25.7	-1.2
1958	25.6	-0.4	26.0	1.6	26.0	0.0	26.2	0.8	26.3	0.4	26.2	-0.4	26.7	1.9	26.8	0.4	26.9	0.4	26.8	-0.4	27.1	1.1	27.1	0.0
1959	27.2	0.4	27.5	1.1	27.5	0.0	27.7	0.7	27.8	0.4	27.7	-0.4	27.6	-0.4	27.9	1.1	27.7	-0.7	28.3	2.2	28.5	0.7	28.5	0.0
1960	28.1	-1.4	27.9	-0.7	28.3	1.4	28.2	-0.4	28.0	-0.7	28.0	0.0	27.9	-0.4	27.8	-0.4	27.6	-0.7	27.9	1.1	27.9	0.0	28.2	1.1
1961	28.6	1.4	28.6	0.0	27.9	-2.4	27.9	0.0	28.1	0.7	29.3	4.3	29.3	0.0	29.5	0.7	29.2	-1.0	29.2	0.0	29.6	1.4	29.6	0.0
1962	29.3	-1.0	29.2	-0.3	29.3	0.3	29.6	1.0	30.0	1.4	30.2	0.7	30.1	-0.3	30.2	0.3	30.1	-0.3	30.3	0.7	30.2	-0.3	30.2	0.0
1963	29.8	-1.3	29.9	0.3	29.7	-0.7	30.0	1.0	29.8	-0.7	29.1	-2.3	29.1	0.0	30.2	3.8	30.1	-0.3	30.7	2.0	30.8	0.3	29.6	-3.9
1964	31.3	5.7	29.8	-4.8	31.0	4.0	31.1	0.3	31.0	-0.3	31.3	1.0	30.5	-2.6	31.1	2.0	30.5	-1.9	31.4	3.0	31.8	1.3	31.8	0.0
1965	31.6	-0.6	31.6	0.0	31.6	0.0	31.9	0.9	31.9	0.0	31.8	-0.3	32.0	0.6	31.1	-2.8	31.8	2.3	31.3	-1.6	32.0	2.2	32.0	0.0
1966	31.0	-3.1	31.3	1.0	31.5	0.6	31.9	1.3	31.6	-0.9	31.8	0.6	32.4	1.9	31.3	-3.4	32.3	3.2	32.5	0.6	32.7	0.6	32.2	-1.5
1967	31.6	-1.9	31.5	-0.3	31.2	-1.0	32.3	3.5	32.4	0.3	32.4	0.0	32.4	0.0	32.5	0.3	33.2	2.2	32.4	-2.4	33.5	3.4	32.3	-3.6
1968	33.3	3.1	33.3	0.0	33.6	0.9	32.9	-2.1	32.8	-0.3	33.7	2.7	33.3	-1.2	33.6	0.9	32.9	-2.1	33.6	2.1	34.0	1.2	32.8	-3.5
1969	33.6	2.4	33.6	0.0	34.6	3.0	34.3	-0.9	33.6	-2.0	34.5	2.7	34.5	0.0	34.3	-0.6	34.2	-0.3	35.0	2.3	33.8	-3.4	34.9	3.3
1970	34.4	-1.4	33.9	-1.5	33.9	0.0	35.5	4.7	35.0	-1.4	34.7	-0.9	36.0	3.7	34.7	-3.6	36.4	4.9	36.8	1.1	36.5	-0.8	37.1	1.6
1971	36.8	-0.8	36.2	-1.6	37.5	3.6	36.5	-2.7	36.8	0.8	37.1	0.8	37.1	0.0	37.5	1.1	37.5	0.0	37.9	1.1	37.3	-1.6	37.1	-0.5
1972	37.0	-0.3	36.3	-1.9	37.5	3.3	37.4	-0.3	37.8	1.1	37.3	-1.3	38.1	2.1	38.2	0.3	38.9	1.8	39.1	0.5	39.2	0.3	39.2	0.0
1973	38.8	-1.0	38.9	0.3	39.0	0.3	39.4	1.0	39.7	0.8	40.0	0.8	40.4	1.0	40.2	-0.5	39.9	-0.7	40.1	0.5	40.5	1.0	40.5	0.0
1974	41.3	2.0	41.8	1.2	42.7	2.2	43.3	1.4	44.0	1.6	44.9	2.0	45.4	1.1	45.6	0.4	45.8	0.4	45.9	0.2	46.3	0.9	46.5	0.4
1975	46.6	0.2	46.8	0.4	47.1	0.6	47.9	1.7	48.5	1.3	49.4	1.9	50.4	2.0	50.8	0.8	50.8	0.0	51.4	1.2	51.4	0.0	51.2	-0.4
1976	51.3	0.2	51.4	0.2	51.7	0.6	52.3	1.2	53.0	1.3	53.8	1.5	55.3	2.8	55.7	0.7	56.2	0.9	56.6	0.7	56.7	0.2	56.6	-0.2
1977	56.7	0.2	57.0	0.5	57.3	0.5	57.9	1.0	58.3	0.7	58.8	0.9	59.2	0.7	58.9	-0.5	58.7	-0.3	58.5	-0.3	58.2	-0.5	58.1	-0.2
1978	58.2	0.2	58.6	0.7	58.7	0.2	58.9	0.3	59.8	1.5	60.5	1.2	61.1	1.0	61.3	0.3	61.7	0.7	62.1	0.6	62.8	1.1	63.0	0.3
1979	63.4	0.6	63.9	0.8	65.0	1.7	67.4	3.7	69.1	2.5	70.3	1.7	71.8	2.1	73.4	2.2	74.3	1.2	74.4	0.1	74.7	0.4	75.8	1.5
1980	77.8	2.6	80.3	3.2	81.3	1.2	82.2	1.1	82.3	0.1	82.0	-0.4	82.3	0.4	82.8	0.6	83.9	1.3	84.2	0.4	85.0	1.0	85.4	0.5
1981	86.1	0.8	87.9	2.1	88.6	0.8	89.7	1.2	90.5	0.9	91.3	0.9	92.3	1.1	92.3	0.0	92.8	0.5	94.2	1.5	94.8	0.6	94.9	0.1
1982	97.1	2.3	96.7	-0.4	95.8	-0.9	95.5	-0.3	96.1	0.6	98.2	2.2	99.1	0.9	99.0	-0.1	98.5	-0.5	98.8	0.3	98.2	-0.6	96.8	-1.4
1983	96.4	-0.4	94.7	-1.8	94.1	-0.6	96.7	2.8	98.5	1.9	100.1	1.6	100.9	0.8	100.9	0.0	100.6	-0.3	100.4	-0.2	100.3	-0.1	102.0	1.7
1984	102.2	0.2	101.0	-1.2	101.1	0.1	103.1	2.0	104.9	1.7	104.6	-0.3	103.1	-1.4	103.4	0.3	103.4	0.0	105.6	2.1	106.1	0.5	106.1	0.0
1985	105.6	-0.5	105.2	-0.4	106.5	1.2	108.4	1.8	108.3	-0.1	108.8	0.5	108.6	-0.2	107.4	-1.1	106.7	-0.7	107.5	0.7	108.0	0.5	108.6	0.6
1986	108.9	0.3	107.2	-1.6	105.3	-1.8	104.6	-0.7	105.6	1.0	106.8	1.1	104.6	-2.1	103.2	-1.3	103.4	0.2	104.3	0.9	104.3	0.0	104.0	-0.3
1987	105.3	1.3	106.9	1.5	107.8	0.8	108.4	0.6	108.9	0.5	109.1	0.2	108.9	-0.2	109.5	0.6	109.6	0.1	110.8	1.1	110.9	0.1	110.7	-0.2
1988	111.0	0.3	110.6	-0.4	110.8	0.2	112.9	1.9	114.1	1.1	114.7	0.5	114.6	-0.1	115.5	0.8	115.4	-0.1	115.5	0.1	115.0	-0.4	115.0	0.0
1989	114.6	-0.3	116.0	1.2	117.5	1.3	121.9	3.7	122.7	0.7	122.8	0.1	121.8	-0.8	120.3	-1.2	119.1	-1.0	119.0	-0.1	119.0	0.0	120.0	0.8
1990	121.4	1.2	122.3	0.7	123.2	0.7	123.5	0.2	123.9	0.3	125.1	1.0	125.3	0.2	127.1	1.4	129.0	1.5	131.5	1.9	132.5	0.8	133.6	0.8
1991	129.9	-2.8	127.1	-2.2	124.2	-2.3	123.8	-0.3	125.8	1.6	126.2	0.3	126.2	0.0	126.4	0.2	126.4	0.0	126.6	0.2	127.4	0.6	128.6	0.9

[Continued]

Los Angeles, CA
Consumer Price Index - All Urban Consumers
Base 1982-1984 = 100
Transportation

[Continued]

For 1947-1995. Columns headed % show percentile change in the index from the previous period for which an index is available.

Year	Jan Index	%	Feb Index	%	Mar Index	%	Apr Index	%	May Index	%	Jun Index	%	Jul Index	%	Aug Index	%	Sep Index	%	Oct Index	%	Nov Index	%	Dec Index	%
1992	129.3	0.5	129.6	0.2	130.1	0.4	130.6	0.4	132.3	1.3	132.7	0.3	134.6	1.4	133.8	-0.6	134.5	0.5	135.5	0.7	136.1	0.4	137.0	0.7
1993	137.5	0.4	137.9	0.3	137.7	-0.1	136.6	-0.8	137.0	0.3	136.4	-0.4	136.9	0.4	135.9	-0.7	136.7	0.6	138.2	1.1	139.6	1.0	139.4	-0.1
1994	139.0	-0.3	139.0	0.0	140.3	0.9	139.2	-0.8	137.9	-0.9	139.5	1.2	140.4	0.6	141.3	0.6	140.9	-0.3	142.5	1.1	142.9	0.3	142.6	-0.2
1995	143.3	0.5	142.3	-0.7	142.8	0.4	143.5	0.5	144.2	0.5	143.4	-0.6	142.2	-0.8	142.0	-0.1	140.9	-0.8	141.6	0.5	141.5	-0.1	140.1	-1.0

Source: U.S. Department of Labor, Bureau of Labor Statistics, Division of Consumer Prices and Price Indexes. - indicates no data collected for period.

Los Angeles, CA
Consumer Price Index - Urban Wage Earners
Base 1982-1984 = 100
Transportation

For 1947-1995. Columns headed % show percentile change in the index from the previous period for which an index is available.

Year	Jan Index	%	Feb Index	%	Mar Index	%	Apr Index	%	May Index	%	Jun Index	%	Jul Index	%	Aug Index	%	Sep Index	%	Oct Index	%	Nov Index	%	Dec Index	%
1947	17.2	-	17.4	1.2	17.4	0.0	17.6	1.1	17.5	-0.6	17.5	0.0	17.9	2.3	18.0	0.6	18.2	1.1	18.3	0.5	18.3	0.0	18.3	0.0
1948	19.1	4.4	19.1	0.0	19.1	0.0	19.2	0.5	19.1	-0.5	19.1	0.0	20.0	4.7	20.3	1.5	20.3	0.0	20.3	0.0	20.3	0.0	20.5	1.0
1949	20.5	0.0	20.9	2.0	20.8	-0.5	20.9	0.5	20.9	0.0	20.9	0.0	20.9	0.0	20.9	0.0	20.9	0.0	20.9	0.0	20.9	0.0	20.9	0.0
1950	20.9	0.0	20.8	-0.5	20.6	-1.0	20.4	-1.0	20.4	0.0	20.4	0.0	20.4	0.0	20.6	1.0	20.6	0.0	20.7	0.5	20.8	0.5	20.9	0.5
1951	20.9	0.0	21.2	1.4	21.4	0.9	21.4	0.0	21.4	0.0	21.4	0.0	21.4	0.0	21.4	0.0	21.7	1.4	21.9	0.9	22.1	0.9	22.1	0.0
1952	22.1	0.0	23.4	5.9	23.4	0.0	23.4	0.0	23.6	0.9	23.6	0.0	24.0	1.7	24.0	0.0	24.1	0.4	24.1	0.0	24.3	0.8	24.3	0.0
1953	24.5	0.8	24.4	-0.4	24.8	1.6	24.7	-0.4	24.6	-0.4	24.6	0.0	24.9	1.2	24.9	0.0	24.8	-0.4	24.8	0.0	24.8	0.0	24.0	-3.2
1954	25.1	4.6	25.0	-0.4	24.8	-0.8	24.7	-0.4	24.8	0.4	24.5	-1.2	23.5	-4.1	23.8	1.3	23.9	0.4	23.5	-1.7	24.6	4.7	24.6	0.0
1955	24.6	0.0	24.6	0.0	24.8	0.8	23.8	-4.0	24.1	1.3	23.8	-1.2	23.9	0.4	23.8	-0.4	23.9	0.4	24.2	1.3	24.7	2.1	24.6	-0.4
1956	24.4	-0.8	24.2	-0.8	24.4	0.8	24.1	-1.2	24.4	1.2	24.4	0.0	24.9	2.0	24.6	-1.2	24.6	0.0	25.2	2.4	25.4	0.8	25.4	0.0
1957	25.4	0.0	25.8	1.6	25.7	-0.4	25.8	0.4	25.9	0.4	25.8	-0.4	25.7	-0.4	25.3	-1.6	25.6	1.2	25.6	0.0	25.9	1.2	25.6	-1.2
1958	25.5	-0.4	25.8	1.2	25.9	0.4	26.0	0.4	26.1	0.4	26.1	0.0	26.5	1.5	26.6	0.4	26.7	0.4	26.7	0.0	26.9	0.7	27.0	0.4
1959	27.1	0.4	27.4	1.1	27.4	0.0	27.5	0.4	27.6	0.4	27.6	0.0	27.5	-0.4	27.8	1.1	27.5	-1.1	28.1	2.2	28.3	0.7	28.3	0.0
1960	27.9	-1.4	27.7	-0.7	28.2	1.8	28.1	-0.4	27.9	-0.7	27.8	-0.4	27.8	0.0	27.7	-0.4	27.5	-0.7	27.7	0.7	27.8	0.4	28.1	1.1
1961	28.4	1.1	28.5	0.4	27.7	-2.8	27.7	0.0	28.0	1.1	29.1	3.9	29.1	0.0	29.3	0.7	29.1	-0.7	29.1	0.0	29.5	1.4	29.4	-0.3
1962	29.2	-0.7	29.0	-0.7	29.1	0.3	29.5	1.4	29.8	1.0	30.0	0.7	30.0	0.0	30.0	0.0	29.9	-0.3	30.1	0.7	30.0	-0.3	30.0	0.0
1963	29.6	-1.3	29.7	0.3	29.5	-0.7	29.9	1.4	29.6	-1.0	29.0	-2.0	29.0	0.0	30.0	3.4	30.0	0.0	30.5	1.7	30.6	0.3	29.4	-3.9
1964	31.2	6.1	29.6	-5.1	30.9	4.4	30.9	0.0	30.9	0.0	31.1	0.6	30.4	-2.3	30.9	1.6	30.3	-1.9	31.2	3.0	31.6	1.3	31.6	0.0
1965	31.5	-0.3	31.5	0.0	31.4	-0.3	31.7	1.0	31.8	0.3	31.6	-0.6	31.8	0.6	30.9	-2.8	31.6	2.3	31.2	-1.3	31.8	1.9	31.8	0.0
1966	30.8	-3.1	31.1	1.0	31.3	0.6	31.8	1.6	31.4	-1.3	31.6	0.6	32.2	1.9	31.1	-3.4	32.1	3.2	32.3	0.6	32.5	0.6	32.0	-1.5
1967	31.4	-1.9	31.3	-0.3	31.0	-1.0	32.1	3.5	32.2	0.3	32.2	0.0	32.2	0.0	32.3	0.3	33.0	2.2	32.2	-2.4	33.4	3.7	32.1	-3.9
1968	33.2	3.4	33.1	-0.3	33.4	0.9	32.7	-2.1	32.6	-0.3	33.5	2.8	33.1	-1.2	33.5	1.2	32.7	-2.4	33.4	2.1	33.8	1.2	32.6	-3.6
1969	33.5	2.8	33.5	0.0	34.5	3.0	34.1	-1.2	33.4	-2.1	34.4	3.0	34.4	0.0	34.1	-0.9	34.0	-0.3	34.8	2.4	33.6	-3.4	34.7	3.3
1970	34.2	-1.4	33.7	-1.5	33.7	0.0	35.3	4.7	34.8	-1.4	34.5	-0.9	35.8	3.8	34.5	-3.6	36.2	4.9	36.6	1.1	36.3	-0.8	36.9	1.7
1971	36.6	-0.8	36.0	-1.6	37.3	3.6	36.3	-2.7	36.6	0.8	36.9	0.8	36.9	0.0	37.2	0.8	37.3	0.3	37.7	1.1	37.1	-1.6	36.9	-0.5
1972	36.8	-0.3	36.1	-1.9	37.2	3.0	37.2	0.0	37.6	1.1	37.1	-1.3	37.9	2.2	38.0	0.3	38.7	1.8	38.9	0.5	39.0	0.3	39.0	0.0
1973	38.6	-1.0	38.7	0.3	38.8	0.3	39.2	1.0	39.5	0.8	39.8	0.8	40.1	0.8	39.9	-0.5	39.7	-0.5	39.9	0.5	40.3	1.0	40.3	0.0
1974	41.1	2.0	41.5	1.0	42.5	2.4	43.1	1.4	43.8	1.6	44.6	1.8	45.1	1.1	45.4	0.7	45.6	0.4	45.7	0.2	46.1	0.9	46.2	0.2
1975	46.3	0.2	46.5	0.4	46.9	0.9	47.7	1.7	48.2	1.0	49.1	1.9	50.1	2.0	50.5	0.8	50.5	0.0	51.1	1.2	51.1	0.0	50.9	-0.4
1976	51.0	0.2	51.2	0.4	51.4	0.4	52.0	1.2	52.7	1.3	53.5	1.5	55.0	2.8	55.4	0.7	55.9	0.9	56.3	0.7	56.4	0.2	56.3	-0.2
1977	56.4	0.2	56.7	0.5	57.0	0.5	57.6	1.1	58.0	0.7	58.5	0.9	58.9	0.7	58.6	-0.5	58.4	-0.3	58.2	-0.3	57.9	-0.5	57.8	-0.2
1978	58.0	0.3	58.0	0.0	58.3	0.5	58.7	0.7	59.5	1.4	60.3	1.3	60.9	1.0	61.2	0.5	61.5	0.5	61.9	0.7	62.7	1.3	63.0	0.5
1979	63.4	0.6	63.9	0.8	65.0	1.7	67.6	4.0	69.4	2.7	70.6	1.7	72.3	2.4	73.8	2.1	74.5	0.9	74.4	-0.1	75.0	0.8	76.1	1.5
1980	77.9	2.4	80.8	3.7	82.0	1.5	83.5	1.8	83.5	0.0	83.3	-0.2	83.3	0.0	83.8	0.6	84.4	0.7	84.6	0.2	85.4	0.9	85.8	0.5
1981	86.6	0.9	88.4	2.1	89.1	0.8	90.6	1.7	91.5	1.0	92.4	1.0	93.3	1.0	93.0	-0.3	93.0	0.0	94.9	2.0	95.5	0.6	95.5	0.0
1982	97.6	2.2	97.0	-0.6	96.2	-0.8	95.7	-0.5	96.3	0.6	98.7	2.5	99.6	0.9	99.6	0.0	99.0	-0.6	99.1	0.1	98.2	-0.9	96.8	-1.4
1983	96.2	-0.6	94.6	-1.7	93.9	-0.7	96.4	2.7	98.3	2.0	100.0	1.7	100.8	0.8	100.8	0.0	100.4	-0.4	100.1	-0.3	100.1	0.0	101.8	1.7
1984	101.9	0.1	100.8	-1.1	101.0	0.2	103.0	2.0	104.9	1.8	104.5	-0.4	102.9	-1.5	103.1	0.2	103.4	0.3	105.5	2.0	105.9	0.4	105.8	-0.1
1985	105.3	-0.5	104.8	-0.5	106.2	1.3	108.1	1.8	107.9	-0.2	108.4	0.5	108.2	-0.2	106.9	-1.2	106.0	-0.8	106.8	0.8	107.4	0.6	107.8	0.4
1986	108.0	0.2	106.2	-1.7	104.3	-1.8	103.5	-0.8	104.4	0.9	105.6	1.1	103.3	-2.2	101.7	-1.5	101.8	0.1	102.5	0.7	102.7	0.2	102.4	-0.3
1987	103.4	1.0	105.1	1.6	105.9	0.8	106.6	0.7	107.1	0.5	107.3	0.2	107.1	-0.2	107.6	0.5	107.6	0.0	108.9	1.2	109.0	0.1	108.8	-0.2
1988	109.0	0.2	108.7	-0.3	108.8	0.1	110.6	1.7	111.8	1.1	112.2	0.4	111.9	-0.3	112.8	0.8	112.9	0.1	113.2	0.3	112.5	-0.6	112.6	0.1
1989	112.1	-0.4	113.5	1.2	114.8	1.1	119.0	3.7	119.7	0.6	119.7	0.0	118.7	-0.8	117.1	-1.3	116.0	-0.9	115.8	-0.2	115.6	-0.2	116.7	1.0
1990	117.9	1.0	118.5	0.5	119.0	0.4	119.3	0.3	119.6	0.3	120.7	0.9	121.1	0.3	122.8	1.4	124.5	1.4	126.6	1.7	127.6	0.8	128.5	0.7
1991	125.1	-2.6	122.4	-2.2	119.8	-2.1	119.6	-0.2	121.7	1.8	122.2	0.4	122.2	0.0	122.5	0.2	122.8	0.2	123.0	0.2	123.6	0.5	124.6	0.8

[Continued]

Los Angeles, CA
Consumer Price Index - Urban Wage Earners
Base 1982-1984 = 100
Transportation
[Continued]

For 1947-1995. Columns headed % show percentile change in the index from the previous period for which an index is available.

Year	Jan Index	%	Feb Index	%	Mar Index	%	Apr Index	%	May Index	%	Jun Index	%	Jul Index	%	Aug Index	%	Sep Index	%	Oct Index	%	Nov Index	%	Dec Index	%
1992	125.1	0.4	125.4	0.2	125.7	0.2	126.3	0.5	128.0	1.3	128.8	0.6	129.9	0.9	129.6	-0.2	130.0	0.3	130.9	0.7	131.7	0.6	132.2	0.4
1993	132.4	0.2	132.7	0.2	132.5	-0.2	131.7	-0.6	131.9	0.2	131.7	-0.2	132.0	0.2	131.4	-0.5	131.9	0.4	133.5	1.2	134.5	0.7	134.0	-0.4
1994	133.7	-0.2	133.4	-0.2	134.4	0.7	134.0	-0.3	133.7	-0.2	135.1	1.0	135.9	0.6	136.6	0.5	136.4	-0.1	137.9	1.1	138.6	0.5	138.4	-0.1
1995	138.7	0.2	138.1	-0.4	138.5	0.3	139.1	0.4	139.8	0.5	139.4	-0.3	138.4	-0.7	138.0	-0.3	137.3	-0.5	138.0	0.5	138.0	0.0	137.1	-0.7

Source: U.S. Department of Labor, Bureau of Labor Statistics, Division of Consumer Prices and Price Indexes. - indicates no data collected for period.

Los Angeles, CA
Consumer Price Index - All Urban Consumers
Base 1982-1984 = 100
Medical Care

For 1947-1995. Columns headed % show percentile change in the index from the previous period for which an index is available.

Year	Jan Index	%	Feb Index	%	Mar Index	%	Apr Index	%	May Index	%	Jun Index	%	Jul Index	%	Aug Index	%	Sep Index	%	Oct Index	%	Nov Index	%	Dec Index	%
1947	13.3	-	13.3	0.0	13.3	0.0	13.4	0.8	13.3	-0.7	13.3	0.0	13.3	0.0	13.3	0.0	13.3	0.0	13.4	0.8	13.6	1.5	13.6	0.0
1948	13.7	0.7	13.7	0.0	13.7	0.0	14.0	2.2	14.0	0.0	14.1	0.7	14.4	2.1	14.4	0.0	14.5	0.7	14.6	0.7	14.6	0.0	14.6	0.0
1949	14.7	0.7	14.7	0.0	14.7	0.0	14.7	0.0	14.7	0.0	14.7	0.0	14.7	0.0	14.7	0.0	14.7	0.0	14.7	0.0	14.7	0.0	14.7	0.0
1950	14.7	0.0	14.8	0.7	14.8	0.0	14.8	0.0	14.8	0.0	14.8	0.0	14.8	0.0	14.8	0.0	15.3	3.4	15.4	0.7	15.4	0.0	15.7	1.9
1951	15.7	0.0	15.7	0.0	15.9	1.3	15.9	0.0	15.9	0.0	15.9	0.0	16.0	0.6	16.0	0.0	16.0	0.0	16.0	0.0	16.0	0.0	16.0	0.0
1952	16.1	0.6	16.1	0.0	16.1	0.0	16.1	0.0	16.1	0.0	16.7	3.7	16.7	0.0	16.7	0.0	16.7	0.0	16.7	0.0	16.7	0.0	16.7	0.0
1953	16.7	0.0	16.7	0.0	16.7	0.0	16.9	1.2	16.9	0.0	16.9	0.0	16.9	0.0	17.0	0.6	17.0	0.0	17.1	0.6	17.1	0.0	17.1	0.0
1954	17.1	0.0	17.1	0.0	17.1	0.0	17.3	1.2	17.3	0.0	17.3	0.0	17.3	0.0	17.3	0.0	17.3	0.0	17.3	0.0	17.3	0.0	17.3	0.0
1955	17.3	0.0	17.3	0.0	17.3	0.0	17.1	-1.2	17.1	0.0	17.1	0.0	17.5	2.3	17.5	0.0	17.5	0.0	17.5	0.0	17.5	0.0	17.6	0.6
1956	17.8	1.1	17.8	0.0	17.8	0.0	17.9	0.6	17.9	0.0	17.9	0.0	17.9	0.0	18.0	0.6	18.0	0.0	18.1	0.6	18.1	0.0	18.0	-0.6
1957	18.3	1.7	18.3	0.0	18.3	0.0	18.3	0.0	18.3	0.0	18.4	0.5	18.4	0.0	18.5	0.5	18.5	0.0	18.5	0.0	18.5	0.0	18.6	0.5
1958	18.9	1.6	18.9	0.0	18.9	0.0	19.3	2.1	19.3	0.0	20.3	5.2	20.3	0.0	20.4	0.5	20.4	0.0	20.5	0.5	20.5	0.0	20.5	0.0
1959	20.6	0.5	20.6	0.0	20.6	0.0	20.6	0.0	20.7	0.5	20.7	0.0	20.7	0.0	20.7	0.0	20.7	0.0	21.1	1.9	21.1	0.0	21.1	0.0
1960	21.1	0.0	21.1	0.0	21.1	0.0	21.3	0.9	21.3	0.0	21.3	0.0	21.5	0.9	21.5	0.0	21.5	0.0	21.6	0.5	21.6	0.0	21.6	0.0
1961	21.6	0.0	21.6	0.0	21.6	0.0	21.6	0.0	21.6	0.0	21.6	0.0	21.6	0.0	21.7	0.5	21.7	0.0	21.7	0.0	21.7	0.0	21.7	0.0
1962	21.7	0.0	21.7	0.0	22.3	2.8	22.4	0.4	22.4	0.0	22.4	0.0	22.5	0.4	22.4	-0.4	22.4	0.0	22.4	0.0	22.4	0.0	22.4	0.0
1963	22.5	0.4	22.5	0.0	22.5	0.0	22.6	0.4	22.7	0.4	22.7	0.0	22.7	0.0	22.7	0.0	22.7	0.0	22.9	0.9	22.9	0.0	22.9	0.0
1964	23.0	0.4	23.1	0.4	23.1	0.0	23.2	0.4	23.2	0.0	23.2	0.0	23.3	0.4	23.3	0.0	23.3	0.0	23.5	0.9	23.5	0.0	23.4	-0.4
1965	23.4	0.0	23.5	0.4	23.5	0.0	23.6	0.4	23.7	0.4	23.7	0.0	23.7	0.0	23.7	0.0	23.7	0.0	23.7	0.0	23.8	0.4	23.8	0.0
1966	23.9	0.4	24.0	0.4	24.0	0.0	24.2	0.8	24.1	-0.4	24.2	0.4	24.3	0.4	24.3	0.0	25.2	3.7	25.4	0.8	25.5	0.4	25.7	0.8
1967	25.7	0.0	25.7	0.0	25.8	0.4	26.0	0.8	26.3	1.2	26.4	0.4	26.6	0.8	26.6	0.0	26.7	0.4	26.8	0.4	26.9	0.4	27.0	0.4
1968	27.2	0.7	27.3	0.4	27.3	0.0	27.5	0.7	27.8	1.1	27.8	0.0	28.0	0.7	28.1	0.4	28.1	0.0	28.2	0.4	28.3	0.4	28.5	0.7
1969	28.6	0.4	28.8	0.7	28.9	0.3	29.3	1.4	29.4	0.3	29.5	0.3	29.6	0.3	29.8	0.7	29.9	0.3	29.8	-0.3	30.0	0.7	30.4	1.3
1970	30.4	0.0	30.7	1.0	31.0	1.0	31.6	1.9	31.8	0.6	31.8	0.0	31.9	0.3	32.0	0.3	32.0	0.0	31.9	-0.3	31.9	0.0	32.1	0.6
1971	32.1	0.0	32.2	0.3	32.4	0.6	33.2	2.5	33.4	0.6	33.5	0.3	33.6	0.3	33.6	0.0	33.7	0.3	33.4	-0.9	33.4	0.0	33.4	0.0
1972	33.5	0.3	33.6	0.3	33.6	0.0	33.7	0.3	33.7	0.0	33.8	0.3	34.1	0.9	34.1	0.0	34.2	0.3	34.4	0.6	34.3	-0.3	34.5	0.6
1973	34.6	0.3	34.7	0.3	35.0	0.9	35.2	0.6	35.3	0.3	35.4	0.3	35.6	0.6	35.8	0.6	35.9	0.3	36.6	1.9	36.6	0.0	36.6	0.0
1974	36.9	0.8	37.2	0.8	37.5	0.8	37.6	0.3	38.4	2.1	38.8	1.0	39.3	1.3	39.8	1.3	40.0	0.5	40.3	0.7	40.9	1.5	41.1	0.5
1975	41.3	0.5	42.1	1.9	42.4	0.7	42.9	1.2	43.3	0.9	43.6	0.7	43.9	0.7	44.3	0.9	44.5	0.5	44.8	0.7	45.5	1.6	46.1	1.3
1976	46.4	0.7	47.7	2.8	47.9	0.4	48.3	0.8	48.9	1.2	49.3	0.8	49.7	0.8	50.1	0.8	50.3	0.4	50.6	0.6	51.3	1.4	51.3	0.0
1977	51.6	0.6	52.4	1.6	52.6	0.4	53.0	0.8	53.2	0.4	53.6	0.8	54.1	0.9	54.5	0.7	54.9	0.7	55.3	0.7	55.5	0.4	55.6	0.2
1978	56.0	0.7	56.3	0.5	56.4	0.2	56.6	0.4	58.2	2.8	58.4	0.3	58.7	0.5	60.0	2.2	60.2	0.3	60.6	0.7	61.1	0.8	61.1	0.0
1979	62.1	1.6	62.3	0.3	62.6	0.5	62.7	0.2	63.6	1.4	64.1	0.8	65.2	1.7	65.1	-0.2	66.2	1.7	66.6	0.6	66.8	0.3	67.7	1.3
1980	68.3	0.9	70.4	3.1	70.8	0.6	72.5	2.4	72.5	0.0	72.5	0.0	73.4	1.2	73.2	-0.3	73.6	0.5	74.7	1.5	75.2	0.7	75.3	0.1
1981	76.2	1.2	77.0	1.0	77.2	0.3	77.9	0.9	78.2	0.4	78.7	0.6	84.5	7.4	85.1	0.7	85.5	0.5	85.5	0.0	88.7	3.7	89.2	0.6
1982	90.0	0.9	90.1	0.1	90.6	0.6	91.6	1.1	92.6	1.1	94.4	1.9	94.8	0.4	95.9	1.2	97.1	1.3	96.9	-0.2	97.5	0.6	97.7	0.2
1983	99.3	1.6	99.6	0.3	99.7	0.1	100.2	0.5	100.2	0.0	101.0	0.8	101.6	0.6	101.2	-0.4	101.2	0.0	101.3	0.1	101.6	0.3	101.6	0.0
1984	103.2	1.6	103.3	0.1	103.6	0.3	104.0	0.4	104.5	0.5	104.5	0.0	105.6	1.1	106.1	0.5	106.0	-0.1	107.0	0.9	107.1	0.1	107.4	0.3
1985	110.1	2.5	110.5	0.4	111.1	0.5	111.2	0.1	111.3	0.1	112.2	0.8	112.8	0.5	113.7	0.8	114.6	0.8	115.1	0.4	115.7	0.5	116.4	0.6
1986	117.0	0.5	118.1	0.9	118.9	0.7	119.4	0.4	119.7	0.3	120.2	0.4	120.7	0.4	121.7	0.8	121.9	0.2	123.0	0.9	124.5	1.2	125.3	0.6
1987	126.6	1.0	127.2	0.5	127.6	0.3	128.1	0.4	128.1	0.0	129.3	0.9	129.6	0.2	130.2	0.5	130.6	0.3	131.7	0.8	132.3	0.5	132.6	0.2
1988	135.5	2.2	136.5	0.7	137.3	0.6	137.4	0.1	137.9	0.4	139.1	0.9	139.6	0.4	140.8	0.9	141.6	0.6	143.1	1.1	143.0	-0.1	143.1	0.1
1989	145.0	1.3	145.2	0.1	146.1	0.6	147.4	0.9	148.0	0.4	149.1	0.7	150.6	1.0	151.5	0.6	152.5	0.7	152.9	0.3	154.2	0.9	154.6	0.3
1990	157.0	1.6	158.2	0.8	159.0	0.5	160.0	0.6	160.8	0.5	161.7	0.6	163.6	1.2	164.0	0.2	165.9	1.2	168.5	1.6	170.1	0.9	170.4	0.2
1991	172.9	1.5	172.9	0.0	174.7	1.0	174.9	0.1	176.1	0.7	177.6	0.9	180.1	1.4	179.9	-0.1	180.4	0.3	181.0	0.3	183.4	1.3	184.2	0.4

[Continued]

Los Angeles, CA
Consumer Price Index - All Urban Consumers
Base 1982-1984 = 100
Medical Care
[Continued]

For 1947-1995. Columns headed % show percentile change in the index from the previous period for which an index is available.

Year	Jan Index	%	Feb Index	%	Mar Index	%	Apr Index	%	May Index	%	Jun Index	%	Jul Index	%	Aug Index	%	Sep Index	%	Oct Index	%	Nov Index	%	Dec Index	%
1992	186.5	1.2	187.8	0.7	188.7	0.5	189.5	0.4	190.8	0.7	191.9	0.6	193.5	0.8	193.9	0.2	194.6	0.4	197.0	1.2	196.7	-0.2	197.9	0.6
1993	199.0	0.6	202.3	1.7	201.9	-0.2	202.6	0.3	207.2	2.3	207.0	-0.1	207.3	0.1	207.8	0.2	208.8	0.5	211.3	1.2	211.4	0.0	212.0	0.3
1994	212.7	0.3	213.3	0.3	213.4	0.0	214.0	0.3	214.2	0.1	214.4	0.1	215.7	0.6	216.0	0.1	216.2	0.1	216.5	0.1	217.6	0.5	217.8	0.1
1995	219.1	0.6	219.6	0.2	220.7	0.5	220.4	-0.1	220.9	0.2	222.1	0.5	221.8	-0.1	222.3	0.2	222.3	0.0	223.5	0.5	224.1	0.3	224.2	0.0

Source: U.S. Department of Labor, Bureau of Labor Statistics, Division of Consumer Prices and Price Indexes. - indicates no data collected for period.

575

Los Angeles, CA
Consumer Price Index - Urban Wage Earners
Base 1982-1984 = 100
Medical Care

For 1947-1995. Columns headed % show percentile change in the index from the previous period for which an index is available.

Year	Jan Index	%	Feb Index	%	Mar Index	%	Apr Index	%	May Index	%	Jun Index	%	Jul Index	%	Aug Index	%	Sep Index	%	Oct Index	%	Nov Index	%	Dec Index	%
1947	13.5	-	13.5	0.0	13.5	0.0	13.6	0.7	13.5	-0.7	13.5	0.0	13.5	0.0	13.5	0.0	13.6	0.7	13.8	1.5	13.8	0.0	13.8	0.0
1948	13.9	0.7	13.9	0.0	13.9	0.0	14.2	2.2	14.2	0.0	14.3	0.7	14.6	2.1	14.6	0.0	14.7	0.7	14.8	0.7	14.8	0.0	14.8	0.0
1949	14.9	0.7	14.9	0.0	14.9	0.0	14.9	0.0	14.9	0.0	14.9	0.0	14.9	0.0	14.9	0.0	15.0	0.7	15.0	0.0	15.0	0.0	15.0	0.0
1950	15.0	0.0	15.0	0.0	15.0	0.0	15.0	0.0	15.0	0.0	15.0	0.0	15.0	0.0	15.0	0.0	15.5	3.3	15.6	0.6	15.7	0.6	16.0	1.9
1951	16.0	0.0	16.0	0.0	16.2	1.3	16.2	0.0	16.2	0.0	16.2	0.0	16.2	0.0	16.2	0.0	16.2	0.0	16.2	0.0	16.2	0.0	16.2	0.0
1952	16.3	0.6	16.3	0.0	16.4	0.6	16.4	0.0	16.4	0.0	16.9	3.0	16.9	0.0	16.9	0.0	16.9	0.0	16.9	0.0	16.9	0.0	16.9	0.0
1953	16.9	0.0	16.9	0.0	16.9	0.0	17.1	1.2	17.2	0.6	17.2	0.0	17.2	0.0	17.2	0.0	17.2	0.0	17.3	0.6	17.3	0.0	17.4	0.6
1954	17.3	-0.6	17.3	0.0	17.4	0.6	17.5	0.6	17.5	0.0	17.5	0.0	17.6	0.6	17.6	0.0	17.6	0.0	17.6	0.0	17.6	0.0	17.6	0.0
1955	17.6	0.0	17.6	0.0	17.6	0.0	17.4	-1.1	17.4	0.0	17.4	0.0	17.8	2.3	17.8	0.0	17.8	0.0	17.8	0.0	17.8	0.0	17.9	0.6
1956	18.1	1.1	18.1	0.0	18.1	0.0	18.1	0.0	18.2	0.6	18.2	0.0	18.2	0.0	18.2	0.0	18.3	0.5	18.3	0.0	18.3	0.0	18.3	0.0
1957	18.5	1.1	18.5	0.0	18.5	0.0	18.6	0.5	18.6	0.0	18.6	0.0	18.7	0.5	18.7	0.0	18.7	0.0	18.7	0.0	18.8	0.5	18.9	0.5
1958	19.2	1.6	19.2	0.0	19.2	0.0	19.6	2.1	19.6	0.0	20.6	5.1	20.6	0.0	20.7	0.5	20.7	0.0	20.9	1.0	20.9	0.0	20.9	0.0
1959	20.9	0.0	20.9	0.0	20.9	0.0	20.9	0.0	21.0	0.5	21.0	0.0	21.0	0.0	21.0	0.0	21.0	0.0	21.4	1.9	21.4	0.0	21.4	0.0
1960	21.4	0.0	21.4	0.0	21.4	0.0	21.6	0.9	21.6	0.0	21.6	0.0	21.8	0.9	21.8	0.0	21.8	0.0	21.9	0.5	21.9	0.0	21.9	0.0
1961	21.9	0.0	21.9	0.0	21.9	0.0	21.9	0.0	21.9	0.0	22.0	0.5	22.0	0.0	22.0	0.0	22.1	0.5	22.1	0.0	22.1	0.0	22.1	0.0
1962	22.0	-0.5	22.0	0.0	22.7	3.2	22.8	0.4	22.8	0.0	22.8	0.0	22.8	0.0	22.8	0.0	22.8	0.0	22.8	0.0	22.8	0.0	22.8	0.0
1963	22.9	0.4	22.9	0.0	22.9	0.0	23.0	0.4	23.0	0.0	23.0	0.0	23.1	0.4	23.1	0.0	23.0	-0.4	23.2	0.9	23.2	0.0	23.2	0.0
1964	23.3	0.4	23.4	0.4	23.4	0.0	23.6	0.9	23.6	0.0	23.6	0.0	23.7	0.4	23.7	0.0	23.6	-0.4	23.8	0.8	23.8	0.0	23.8	0.0
1965	23.8	0.0	23.8	0.0	23.9	0.4	24.0	0.4	24.0	0.0	24.0	0.0	24.1	0.4	24.1	0.0	24.0	-0.4	24.1	0.4	24.1	0.0	24.2	0.4
1966	24.2	0.0	24.3	0.4	24.4	0.4	24.5	0.4	24.5	0.0	24.6	0.4	24.6	0.0	24.7	0.4	25.6	3.6	25.8	0.8	25.9	0.4	26.1	0.8
1967	26.1	0.0	26.1	0.0	26.2	0.4	26.4	0.8	26.7	1.1	26.8	0.4	27.0	0.7	27.0	0.0	27.2	0.7	27.2	0.0	27.3	0.4	27.4	0.4
1968	27.6	0.7	27.7	0.4	27.7	0.0	28.0	1.1	28.2	0.7	28.2	0.0	28.4	0.7	28.5	0.4	28.5	0.0	28.6	0.4	28.7	0.3	28.9	0.7
1969	29.0	0.3	29.2	0.7	29.3	0.3	29.7	1.4	29.9	0.7	30.0	0.3	30.0	0.0	30.2	0.7	30.3	0.3	30.2	-0.3	30.4	0.7	30.8	1.3
1970	30.9	0.3	31.2	1.0	31.5	1.0	32.1	1.9	32.2	0.3	32.3	0.3	32.4	0.3	32.5	0.3	32.5	0.0	32.3	-0.6	32.4	0.3	32.5	0.3
1971	32.6	0.3	32.7	0.3	32.9	0.6	33.7	2.4	33.9	0.6	34.0	0.3	34.1	0.3	34.1	0.0	34.2	0.3	34.0	-0.6	34.0	0.0	34.0	0.0
1972	34.0	0.0	34.1	0.3	34.1	0.0	34.2	0.3	34.2	0.0	34.4	0.6	34.6	0.6	34.6	0.0	34.7	0.3	34.9	0.6	34.9	0.0	35.0	0.3
1973	35.1	0.3	35.3	0.6	35.5	0.6	35.7	0.6	35.8	0.3	35.9	0.3	36.1	0.6	36.3	0.6	36.4	0.3	37.1	1.9	37.1	0.0	37.1	0.0
1974	37.4	0.8	37.7	0.8	38.1	1.1	38.2	0.3	38.9	1.8	39.3	1.0	39.9	1.5	40.4	1.3	40.6	0.5	40.9	0.7	41.5	1.5	41.7	0.5
1975	41.9	0.5	42.7	1.9	43.0	0.7	43.5	1.2	43.9	0.9	44.2	0.7	44.5	0.7	45.0	1.1	45.2	0.4	45.5	0.7	46.2	1.5	46.8	1.3
1976	47.1	0.6	48.4	2.8	48.6	0.4	49.0	0.8	49.7	1.4	50.1	0.8	50.4	0.6	50.9	1.0	51.0	0.2	51.4	0.8	52.1	1.4	52.1	0.0
1977	52.4	0.6	53.2	1.5	53.4	0.4	53.8	0.7	54.0	0.4	54.4	0.7	54.9	0.9	55.3	0.7	55.7	0.7	56.1	0.7	56.4	0.5	56.4	0.0
1978	56.8	0.7	57.1	0.5	57.2	0.2	57.4	0.3	58.7	2.3	58.7	0.0	59.1	0.7	59.8	1.2	60.2	0.7	60.8	1.0	61.4	1.0	61.2	-0.3
1979	62.3	1.8	62.5	0.3	62.7	0.3	62.8	0.2	63.6	1.3	64.1	0.8	66.0	3.0	66.8	1.2	67.7	1.3	67.8	0.1	68.1	0.4	68.6	0.7
1980	69.3	1.0	70.4	1.6	70.6	0.3	72.6	2.8	73.9	1.8	73.7	-0.3	74.5	1.1	74.7	0.3	75.4	0.9	76.4	1.3	77.8	1.8	78.3	0.6
1981	79.0	0.9	80.7	2.2	81.0	0.4	81.5	0.6	81.9	0.5	82.8	1.1	83.7	1.1	84.3	0.7	85.3	1.2	85.2	-0.1	87.7	2.9	89.3	1.8
1982	90.0	0.8	90.2	0.2	90.8	0.7	91.8	1.1	92.8	1.1	94.5	1.8	94.9	0.4	95.9	1.1	97.0	1.1	96.7	-0.3	97.4	0.7	97.5	0.1
1983	99.2	1.7	99.4	0.2	99.7	0.3	100.2	0.5	100.3	0.1	101.1	0.8	101.6	0.5	101.2	-0.4	101.2	0.0	101.3	0.1	101.5	0.2	101.6	0.1
1984	103.1	1.5	103.2	0.1	103.6	0.4	104.1	0.5	104.6	0.5	104.6	0.0	105.5	0.9	106.1	0.6	105.8	-0.3	107.0	1.1	107.1	0.1	107.3	0.2
1985	110.0	2.5	110.5	0.5	111.1	0.5	111.2	0.1	111.4	0.2	112.2	0.7	112.8	0.5	113.7	0.8	114.5	0.7	115.0	0.4	115.7	0.6	116.4	0.6
1986	117.0	0.5	118.1	0.9	118.8	0.6	119.2	0.3	119.6	0.3	120.0	0.3	120.5	0.4	121.5	0.8	121.7	0.2	122.8	0.9	124.1	1.1	124.9	0.6
1987	126.1	1.0	126.7	0.5	127.1	0.3	127.7	0.5	127.6	-0.1	128.9	1.0	129.1	0.2	129.8	0.5	130.3	0.4	131.2	0.7	131.8	0.5	132.1	0.2
1988	135.1	2.3	136.2	0.8	137.0	0.6	136.9	-0.1	137.4	0.4	138.8	1.0	139.3	0.4	140.3	0.7	140.9	0.4	142.5	1.1	142.2	-0.2	142.3	0.1
1989	144.2	1.3	144.4	0.1	145.3	0.6	146.5	0.8	147.2	0.5	148.2	0.7	149.4	0.8	150.1	0.5	151.4	0.9	151.8	0.3	153.0	0.8	153.4	0.3
1990	155.8	1.6	156.9	0.7	157.5	0.4	158.6	0.7	159.3	0.4	160.2	0.6	161.4	0.7	161.7	0.2	163.6	1.2	166.3	1.7	168.5	1.3	168.7	0.1
1991	170.9	1.3	170.6	-0.2	172.2	0.9	172.3	0.1	173.5	0.7	175.3	1.0	177.7	1.4	177.5	-0.1	178.0	0.3	178.2	0.1	180.9	1.5	181.6	0.4

[Continued]

Los Angeles, CA
Consumer Price Index - Urban Wage Earners
Base 1982-1984 = 100
Medical Care
[Continued]

For 1947-1995. Columns headed % show percentile change in the index from the previous period for which an index is available.

Year	Jan		Feb		Mar		Apr		May		Jun		Jul		Aug		Sep		Oct		Nov		Dec	
	Index	%	Index	%	Index	%	Index	%	Index	%	Index	%	Index	%	Index	%	Index	%	Index	%	Index	%	Index	%
1992	183.7	1.2	185.2	0.8	186.2	0.5	186.9	0.4	188.3	0.7	189.4	0.6	191.2	1.0	191.8	0.3	192.6	0.4	194.6	1.0	194.2	-0.2	195.5	0.7
1993	196.6	0.6	199.6	1.5	199.4	-0.1	200.1	0.4	204.8	2.3	204.3	-0.2	204.7	0.2	205.1	0.2	206.0	0.4	208.5	1.2	208.3	-0.1	208.9	0.3
1994	209.6	0.3	210.0	0.2	210.0	0.0	210.8	0.4	210.8	0.0	211.1	0.1	212.1	0.5	212.4	0.1	212.6	0.1	213.0	0.2	214.1	0.5	214.2	0.0
1995	215.6	0.7	216.0	0.2	217.5	0.7	217.1	-0.2	217.6	0.2	219.0	0.6	219.3	0.1	219.7	0.2	219.6	-0.0	220.8	0.5	221.5	0.3	221.6	0.0

Source: U.S. Department of Labor, Bureau of Labor Statistics, Division of Consumer Prices and Price Indexes. - indicates no data collected for period.

Los Angeles, CA
Consumer Price Index - All Urban Consumers
Base 1982-1984 = 100
Entertainment

For 1976-1995. Columns headed % show percentile change in the index from the previous period for which an index is available.

Year	Jan Index	%	Feb Index	%	Mar Index	%	Apr Index	%	May Index	%	Jun Index	%	Jul Index	%	Aug Index	%	Sep Index	%	Oct Index	%	Nov Index	%	Dec Index	%
1976	68.9	-	69.4	0.7	69.6	0.3	70.1	0.7	70.2	0.1	70.2	0.0	71.2	1.4	70.8	-0.6	71.1	0.4	70.7	-0.6	71.8	1.6	72.0	0.3
1977	72.1	0.1	73.1	1.4	73.2	0.1	73.4	0.3	72.7	-1.0	72.8	0.1	72.9	0.1	73.6	1.0	73.5	-0.1	73.3	-0.3	73.4	0.1	73.8	0.5
1978	71.9	-2.6	73.8	2.6	74.6	1.1	76.3	2.3	76.0	-0.4	74.3	-2.2	74.6	0.4	72.6	-2.7	74.4	2.5	75.1	0.9	73.8	-1.7	75.4	2.2
1979	76.2	1.1	75.6	-0.8	77.4	2.4	77.6	0.3	78.1	0.6	78.5	0.5	79.0	0.6	79.3	0.4	79.8	0.6	79.8	0.0	80.9	1.4	81.3	0.5
1980	81.9	0.7	82.9	1.2	84.1	1.4	83.7	-0.5	84.1	0.5	84.8	0.8	85.9	1.3	87.0	1.3	88.7	2.0	88.3	-0.5	88.5	0.2	89.1	0.7
1981	91.2	2.4	91.0	-0.2	92.1	1.2	91.7	-0.4	92.7	1.1	92.1	-0.6	92.0	-0.1	94.7	2.9	95.1	0.4	94.7	-0.4	94.9	0.2	95.5	0.6
1982	96.2	0.7	96.9	0.7	98.3	1.4	99.4	1.1	99.2	-0.2	98.5	-0.7	97.5	-1.0	96.8	-0.7	96.4	-0.4	97.0	0.6	97.1	0.1	98.4	1.3
1983	98.4	0.0	100.0	1.6	101.0	1.0	99.8	-1.2	99.1	-0.7	99.4	0.3	98.7	-0.7	99.2	0.5	99.1	-0.1	100.7	1.6	100.4	-0.3	102.1	1.7
1984	101.7	-0.4	102.7	1.0	102.3	-0.4	102.3	0.0	102.1	-0.2	102.5	0.4	102.0	-0.5	102.3	0.3	103.1	0.8	103.3	0.2	103.6	0.3	103.0	-0.6
1985	104.1	1.1	104.0	-0.1	105.7	1.6	105.7	0.0	105.3	-0.4	107.9	2.5	107.7	-0.2	108.1	0.4	108.1	0.0	108.8	0.6	108.6	-0.2	108.4	-0.2
1986	108.4	0.0	108.5	0.1	108.1	-0.4	108.3	0.2	109.3	0.9	109.8	0.5	109.6	-0.2	109.5	-0.1	108.4	-1.0	108.7	0.3	109.9	1.1	109.8	-0.1
1987	110.1	0.3	110.1	0.0	109.9	-0.2	110.9	0.9	110.3	-0.5	110.8	0.5	111.4	0.5	110.9	-0.4	111.6	0.6	111.9	0.3	112.9	0.9	113.0	0.1
1988	113.1	0.1	114.0	0.8	114.3	0.3	114.9	0.5	114.9	0.0	114.7	-0.2	115.4	0.6	115.9	0.4	116.0	0.1	116.7	0.6	117.4	0.6	117.3	-0.1
1989	118.2	0.8	118.7	0.4	118.5	-0.2	119.8	1.1	120.1	0.3	120.7	0.5	121.0	0.2	121.1	0.1	123.1	1.7	122.9	-0.2	123.1	0.2	123.5	0.3
1990	122.5	-0.8	123.1	0.5	123.8	0.6	124.1	0.2	124.0	-0.1	124.0	0.0	125.5	1.2	123.6	-1.5	128.8	4.2	128.2	-0.5	128.3	0.1	128.6	0.2
1991	130.5	1.5	131.1	0.5	131.1	0.0	133.7	2.0	134.8	0.8	135.4	0.4	137.2	1.3	138.7	1.1	138.5	-0.1	140.9	1.7	139.9	-0.7	133.3	-4.7
1992	133.8	0.4	133.8	0.0	134.1	0.2	134.9	0.6	134.8	-0.1	132.9	-1.4	133.5	0.5	133.2	-0.2	134.0	0.6	134.6	0.4	134.3	-0.2	135.1	0.6
1993	135.9	0.6	135.5	-0.3	135.7	0.1	135.4	-0.2	134.1	-1.0	133.0	-0.8	133.9	0.7	135.0	0.8	136.0	0.7	137.7	1.2	138.9	0.9	138.8	-0.1
1994	139.4	0.4	138.0	-1.0	138.1	0.1	138.5	0.3	138.3	-0.1	136.6	-1.2	136.6	0.0	135.1	-1.1	134.9	-0.1	136.4	1.1	137.1	0.5	137.0	-0.1
1995	140.6	2.6	140.9	0.2	141.2	0.2	141.8	0.4	140.9	-0.6	139.7	-0.9	140.2	0.4	139.6	-0.4	140.2	0.4	142.6	1.7	143.9	0.9	143.6	-0.2

Source: U.S. Department of Labor, Bureau of Labor Statistics, Division of Consumer Prices and Price Indexes. - indicates no data collected for period.

Los Angeles, CA
Consumer Price Index - Urban Wage Earners
Base 1982-1984 = 100
Entertainment

For 1976-1995. Columns headed % show percentile change in the index from the previous period for which an index is available.

Year	Jan Index	%	Feb Index	%	Mar Index	%	Apr Index	%	May Index	%	Jun Index	%	Jul Index	%	Aug Index	%	Sep Index	%	Oct Index	%	Nov Index	%	Dec Index	%
1976	75.6	-	76.2	0.8	76.4	0.3	76.9	0.7	77.0	0.1	77.0	0.0	78.2	1.6	77.8	-0.5	78.1	0.4	77.7	-0.5	78.8	1.4	79.1	0.4
1977	79.2	0.1	80.2	1.3	80.4	0.2	80.6	0.2	79.8	-1.0	80.0	0.3	80.0	0.0	80.8	1.0	80.7	-0.1	80.5	-0.2	80.5	0.0	81.0	0.6
1978	81.5	0.6	83.3	2.2	79.2	-4.9	78.8	-0.5	80.7	2.4	79.4	-1.6	79.9	0.6	78.7	-1.5	79.6	1.1	80.1	0.6	78.9	-1.5	81.4	3.2
1979	82.0	0.7	81.3	-0.9	81.2	-0.1	81.4	0.2	83.4	2.5	84.0	0.7	85.1	1.3	81.6	-4.1	84.7	3.8	84.7	0.0	85.1	0.5	86.7	1.9
1980	87.7	1.2	88.0	0.3	88.8	0.9	89.4	0.7	89.6	0.2	90.5	1.0	90.6	0.1	90.7	0.1	93.0	2.5	93.3	0.3	94.0	0.8	94.3	0.3
1981	94.1	-0.2	94.0	-0.1	94.6	0.6	92.9	-1.8	93.7	0.9	93.6	-0.1	93.8	0.2	94.7	1.0	95.6	1.0	95.3	-0.3	95.6	0.3	95.6	0.0
1982	96.2	0.6	96.9	0.7	98.2	1.3	99.4	1.2	99.1	-0.3	98.4	-0.7	97.7	-0.7	96.9	-0.8	96.3	-0.6	96.7	0.4	96.9	0.2	98.2	1.3
1983	98.2	0.0	99.9	1.7	100.9	1.0	99.7	-1.2	99.1	-0.6	99.5	0.4	98.8	-0.7	99.3	0.5	99.1	-0.2	100.6	1.5	100.4	-0.2	101.9	1.5
1984	101.8	-0.1	102.7	0.9	102.4	-0.3	102.3	-0.1	102.1	-0.2	102.5	0.4	102.1	-0.4	102.4	0.3	103.2	0.8	103.3	0.1	103.6	0.3	103.2	-0.4
1985	104.2	1.0	104.0	-0.2	105.5	1.4	105.6	0.1	105.2	-0.4	107.5	2.2	107.3	-0.2	107.8	0.5	107.7	-0.1	108.3	0.6	108.3	0.0	107.9	-0.4
1986	108.0	0.1	108.0	0.0	107.6	-0.4	107.7	0.1	108.8	1.0	109.2	0.4	109.0	-0.2	108.9	-0.1	107.7	-1.1	108.0	0.3	109.2	1.1	109.1	-0.1
1987	109.3	0.2	109.5	0.2	109.1	-0.4	110.2	1.0	109.5	-0.6	110.2	0.6	110.6	0.4	110.5	-0.1	111.2	0.6	110.8	-0.4	111.9	1.0	112.6	0.6
1988	112.5	-0.1	112.7	0.2	113.1	0.4	113.7	0.5	114.2	0.4	114.0	-0.2	114.8	0.7	115.3	0.4	115.5	0.2	116.2	0.6	116.4	0.2	116.4	0.0
1989	117.3	0.8	118.0	0.6	117.6	-0.3	118.9	1.1	119.3	0.3	119.8	0.4	120.3	0.4	120.4	0.1	122.1	1.4	121.8	-0.2	122.1	0.2	122.6	0.4
1990	121.8	-0.7	122.3	0.4	122.8	0.4	123.3	0.4	123.3	0.0	123.4	0.1	124.5	0.9	123.8	-0.6	127.3	2.8	126.8	-0.4	126.8	0.0	127.1	0.2
1991	129.1	1.6	129.4	0.2	129.4	0.0	132.3	2.2	133.1	0.6	134.1	0.8	136.7	1.9	137.1	0.3	137.6	0.4	139.4	1.3	138.5	-0.6	132.2	-4.5
1992	132.6	0.3	132.6	0.0	133.5	0.7	134.2	0.5	134.2	0.0	134.2	0.0	134.9	0.5	134.4	-0.4	135.0	0.4	135.6	0.4	135.3	-0.2	136.2	0.7
1993	136.5	0.2	135.8	-0.5	136.6	0.6	136.3	-0.2	134.8	-1.1	134.2	-0.4	134.9	0.5	135.6	0.5	136.2	0.4	137.9	1.2	138.9	0.7	138.8	-0.1
1994	139.2	0.3	137.9	-0.9	138.5	0.4	138.8	0.2	139.1	0.2	137.1	-1.4	137.4	0.2	135.8	-1.2	134.2	-1.2	137.2	2.2	137.4	0.1	137.5	0.1
1995	141.7	3.1	141.9	0.1	142.1	0.1	143.2	0.8	142.4	-0.6	141.3	-0.8	140.9	-0.3	140.3	-0.4	141.0	0.5	142.7	1.2	144.3	1.1	143.3	-0.7

Source: U.S. Department of Labor, Bureau of Labor Statistics, Division of Consumer Prices and Price Indexes. - indicates no data collected for period.

Los Angeles, CA
Consumer Price Index - All Urban Consumers
Base 1982-1984 = 100
Other Goods and Services

For 1976-1995. Columns headed % show percentile change in the index from the previous period for which an index is available.

Year	Jan Index	%	Feb Index	%	Mar Index	%	Apr Index	%	May Index	%	Jun Index	%	Jul Index	%	Aug Index	%	Sep Index	%	Oct Index	%	Nov Index	%	Dec Index	%
1976	55.9	-	55.9	0.0	56.5	1.1	56.6	0.2	56.8	0.4	57.3	0.9	57.4	0.2	57.4	0.0	57.8	0.7	58.3	0.9	58.9	1.0	59.2	0.5
1977	59.3	0.2	59.5	0.3	59.7	0.3	59.8	0.2	59.7	-0.2	60.1	0.7	60.3	0.3	60.3	0.0	61.5	2.0	62.1	1.0	62.0	-0.2	62.5	0.8
1978	63.4	1.4	63.6	0.3	63.4	-0.3	63.9	0.8	63.9	0.0	64.9	1.6	65.0	0.2	65.5	0.8	67.0	2.3	66.9	-0.1	66.8	-0.1	66.7	-0.1
1979	67.3	0.9	68.1	1.2	67.8	-0.4	68.5	1.0	68.0	-0.7	68.2	0.3	68.9	1.0	69.9	1.5	71.1	1.7	71.3	0.3	70.5	-1.1	71.3	1.1
1980	72.5	1.7	74.6	2.9	74.5	-0.1	75.6	1.5	76.0	0.5	76.1	0.1	76.1	0.0	76.4	0.4	78.2	2.4	78.5	0.4	78.6	0.1	79.3	0.9
1981	79.4	0.1	80.0	0.8	81.1	1.4	82.4	1.6	82.8	0.5	84.1	1.6	84.5	0.5	85.5	1.2	86.4	1.1	86.6	0.2	87.2	0.7	87.1	-0.1
1982	87.6	0.6	89.1	1.7	90.2	1.2	91.1	1.0	90.0	-1.2	90.3	0.3	91.5	1.3	92.1	0.7	92.9	0.9	94.8	2.0	97.2	2.5	97.8	0.6
1983	98.8	1.0	100.0	1.2	100.4	0.4	100.4	0.0	100.6	0.2	100.7	0.1	101.7	1.0	101.5	-0.2	102.1	0.6	102.6	0.5	102.6	0.0	102.5	-0.1
1984	103.3	0.8	103.9	0.6	103.8	-0.1	104.0	0.2	103.4	-0.6	103.3	-0.1	105.2	1.8	105.2	0.0	112.4	6.8	112.4	0.0	112.4	0.0	112.2	-0.2
1985	112.3	0.1	113.6	1.2	114.2	0.5	114.0	-0.2	113.9	-0.1	115.0	1.0	115.2	0.2	115.8	0.5	116.5	0.6	117.4	0.8	117.2	-0.2	118.1	0.8
1986	120.4	1.9	121.0	0.5	120.6	-0.3	121.4	0.7	121.7	0.2	122.3	0.5	121.2	-0.9	122.8	1.3	123.8	0.8	124.4	0.5	124.0	-0.3	123.3	-0.6
1987	124.1	0.6	124.9	0.6	125.0	0.1	125.4	0.3	126.4	0.8	126.6	0.2	126.7	0.1	127.4	0.6	131.4	3.1	131.5	0.1	132.0	0.4	133.4	1.1
1988	134.0	0.4	136.1	1.6	137.6	1.1	138.3	0.5	137.7	-0.4	138.3	0.4	139.0	0.5	139.9	0.6	143.4	2.5	144.6	0.8	144.8	0.1	145.1	0.2
1989	151.5	4.4	152.9	0.9	152.6	-0.2	152.9	0.2	152.6	-0.2	152.9	0.2	153.6	0.5	155.3	1.1	159.8	2.9	159.5	-0.2	158.8	-0.4	160.9	1.3
1990	161.6	0.4	163.3	1.1	162.5	-0.5	164.4	1.2	165.1	0.4	165.7	0.4	165.2	-0.3	165.9	0.4	169.2	2.0	170.3	0.7	170.7	0.2	171.6	0.5
1991	173.9	1.3	174.2	0.2	175.2	0.6	176.1	0.5	176.3	0.1	176.7	0.2	177.6	0.5	179.0	0.8	186.9	4.4	187.8	0.5	187.3	-0.3	188.2	0.5
1992	189.9	0.9	190.6	0.4	190.3	-0.2	195.7	2.8	195.6	-0.1	195.9	0.2	195.8	-0.1	195.8	0.0	199.3	1.8	204.3	2.5	205.6	0.6	206.4	0.4
1993	209.7	1.6	209.7	0.0	209.7	0.0	210.7	0.5	210.8	0.0	211.0	0.1	212.4	0.7	210.9	-0.7	213.2	1.1	213.3	0.0	215.4	1.0	216.2	0.4
1994	216.1	-0.0	216.7	0.3	216.1	-0.3	217.1	0.5	216.8	-0.1	217.0	0.1	217.2	0.1	217.7	0.2	219.7	0.9	220.9	0.5	220.3	-0.3	220.7	0.2
1995	222.1	0.6	224.3	1.0	222.8	-0.7	223.7	0.4	224.8	0.5	224.8	0.0	225.3	0.2	227.2	0.8	228.1	0.4	227.7	-0.2	228.4	0.3	228.5	0.0

Source: U.S. Department of Labor, Bureau of Labor Statistics, Division of Consumer Prices and Price Indexes. - indicates no data collected for period.

Los Angeles, CA
Consumer Price Index - Urban Wage Earners
Base 1982-1984 = 100
Other Goods and Services

For 1976-1995. Columns headed % show percentile change in the index from the previous period for which an index is available.

Year	Jan Index	Jan %	Feb Index	Feb %	Mar Index	Mar %	Apr Index	Apr %	May Index	May %	Jun Index	Jun %	Jul Index	Jul %	Aug Index	Aug %	Sep Index	Sep %	Oct Index	Oct %	Nov Index	Nov %	Dec Index	Dec %
1976	55.6	-	55.6	0.0	56.2	1.1	56.3	0.2	56.4	0.2	57.0	1.1	57.1	0.2	57.1	0.0	57.4	0.5	57.9	0.9	58.6	1.2	58.8	0.3
1977	59.0	0.3	59.1	0.2	59.3	0.3	59.4	0.2	59.4	0.0	59.7	0.5	59.9	0.3	59.9	0.0	61.1	2.0	61.7	1.0	61.6	-0.2	62.1	0.8
1978	62.7	1.0	63.2	0.8	63.4	0.3	62.9	-0.8	63.3	0.6	64.0	1.1	64.8	1.3	64.9	0.2	65.6	1.1	65.8	0.3	65.6	-0.3	65.3	-0.5
1979	66.7	2.1	67.3	0.9	67.4	0.1	67.8	0.6	68.0	0.3	68.1	0.1	68.7	0.9	69.2	0.7	69.9	1.0	70.1	0.3	69.6	-0.7	70.6	1.4
1980	72.2	2.3	73.5	1.8	73.6	0.1	74.5	1.2	75.3	1.1	74.6	-0.9	74.6	0.0	75.5	1.2	77.2	2.3	77.1	-0.1	77.3	0.3	78.6	1.7
1981	79.4	1.0	79.9	0.6	80.1	0.3	81.8	2.1	81.9	0.1	82.6	0.9	82.9	0.4	83.8	1.1	85.3	1.8	84.9	-0.5	85.7	0.9	86.3	0.7
1982	86.8	0.6	88.4	1.8	89.6	1.4	90.7	1.2	89.5	-1.3	89.9	0.4	91.1	1.3	91.8	0.8	92.5	0.8	94.6	2.3	97.1	2.6	97.8	0.7
1983	99.0	1.2	100.3	1.3	100.8	0.5	100.8	0.0	101.0	0.2	101.2	0.2	102.3	1.1	102.2	-0.1	102.8	0.6	103.2	0.4	103.3	0.1	103.0	-0.3
1984	103.9	0.9	104.6	0.7	104.5	-0.1	104.7	0.2	104.0	-0.7	103.9	-0.1	105.9	1.9	105.9	0.0	110.8	4.6	110.9	0.1	110.9	0.0	110.6	-0.3
1985	110.7	0.1	112.1	1.3	112.8	0.6	112.6	-0.2	112.5	-0.1	113.4	0.8	113.3	-0.1	114.2	0.8	114.8	0.5	115.8	0.9	115.5	-0.3	116.5	0.9
1986	118.9	2.1	119.6	0.6	119.1	-0.4	119.9	0.7	120.2	0.3	120.7	0.4	119.7	-0.8	121.4	1.4	122.1	0.6	122.7	0.5	122.4	-0.2	121.7	-0.6
1987	122.7	0.8	123.6	0.7	123.8	0.2	124.1	0.2	125.0	0.7	125.2	0.2	125.3	0.1	126.0	0.6	129.8	3.0	129.9	0.1	130.4	0.4	131.1	0.5
1988	131.9	0.6	133.6	1.3	135.1	1.1	135.9	0.6	135.1	-0.6	135.8	0.5	136.7	0.7	137.5	0.6	141.1	2.6	142.6	1.1	142.7	0.1	143.1	0.3
1989	151.0	5.5	152.7	1.1	152.4	-0.2	152.7	0.2	152.3	-0.3	152.5	0.1	153.4	0.6	155.3	1.2	159.4	2.6	159.0	-0.3	158.0	-0.6	160.5	1.6
1990	161.1	0.4	163.0	1.2	162.3	-0.4	164.3	1.2	164.9	0.4	165.8	0.5	165.3	-0.3	166.1	0.5	168.9	1.7	169.7	0.5	170.2	0.3	171.2	0.6
1991	173.7	1.5	173.8	0.1	174.8	0.6	175.6	0.5	175.9	0.2	176.5	0.3	177.6	0.6	179.3	1.0	184.8	3.1	185.4	0.3	185.2	-0.1	186.2	0.5
1992	188.1	1.0	189.1	0.5	188.5	-0.3	193.3	2.5	193.3	0.0	193.8	0.3	193.8	0.0	193.4	-0.2	195.8	1.2	199.0	1.6	200.4	0.7	201.5	0.5
1993	203.9	1.2	204.0	0.0	204.0	0.0	205.2	0.6	205.2	0.0	205.8	0.3	207.5	0.8	205.0	-1.2	202.1	-1.4	202.2	0.0	204.8	1.3	205.9	0.5
1994	205.8	-0.0	206.9	0.5	206.0	-0.4	207.3	0.6	206.9	-0.2	206.6	-0.1	206.8	0.1	206.8	0.0	208.0	0.6	209.4	0.7	208.6	-0.4	209.2	0.3
1995	210.6	0.7	212.6	0.9	211.4	-0.6	212.1	0.3	213.1	0.5	213.2	0.0	213.8	0.3	215.3	0.7	216.3	0.5	215.7	-0.3	216.6	0.4	216.6	0.0

Source: U.S. Department of Labor, Bureau of Labor Statistics, Division of Consumer Prices and Price Indexes. - indicates no data collected for period.

Miami, FL
Consumer Price Index - All Urban Consumers
Base 1982-1984 = 100
Annual Averages

For 1977-1995. Columns headed % show percentile change in the index from the previous period for which an index is available.

Year	All Items		Food & Beverage		Housing		Apparel & Upkeep		Trans- portation		Medical Care		Entertain- ment		Other Goods & Services	
	Index	%	Index	%	Index	%	Index	%	Index	%	Index	%	Index	%	Index	%
1977	-	-	-	-	-	-	-	-	-	-	-	-	-	-	-	-
1978	64.8	-	69.8	-	62.9	-	77.6	-	59.6	-	61.4	-	80.2	-	63.7	-
1979	71.2	9.9	78.6	12.6	68.5	8.9	81.2	4.6	67.1	12.6	68.9	12.2	85.0	6.0	69.1	8.5
1980	81.1	13.9	84.7	7.8	80.8	18.0	87.0	7.1	78.5	17.0	75.6	9.7	89.6	5.4	76.2	10.3
1981	90.5	11.6	91.3	7.8	92.0	13.9	91.9	5.6	88.8	13.1	81.9	8.3	95.1	6.1	84.7	11.2
1982	96.7	6.9	96.8	6.0	97.8	6.3	98.2	6.9	94.8	6.8	93.8	14.5	98.4	3.5	93.1	9.9
1983	99.9	3.3	99.5	2.8	99.7	1.9	100.1	1.9	100.2	5.7	101.0	7.7	100.4	2.0	100.0	7.4
1984	103.5	3.6	103.6	4.1	102.6	2.9	101.7	1.6	105.0	4.8	105.1	4.1	101.3	0.9	106.9	6.9
1985	106.5	2.9	104.4	0.8	105.7	3.0	105.7	3.9	108.3	3.1	109.2	3.9	104.5	3.2	113.3	6.0
1986	107.9	1.3	107.1	2.6	107.0	1.2	109.0	3.1	103.7	-4.2	117.4	7.5	107.9	3.3	121.8	7.5
1987	111.8	3.6	113.0	5.5	108.7	1.6	115.6	6.1	106.6	2.8	126.6	7.8	113.7	5.4	128.3	5.3
1988	116.8	4.5	118.7	5.0	113.1	4.0	123.5	6.8	110.7	3.8	134.6	6.3	115.9	1.9	133.6	4.1
1989	121.5	4.0	125.6	5.8	116.2	2.7	131.3	6.3	114.8	3.7	140.5	4.4	117.8	1.6	139.8	4.6
1990	128.0	5.3	134.3	6.9	120.4	3.6	135.6	3.3	121.6	5.9	151.8	8.0	121.0	2.7	153.2	9.6
1991	132.3	3.4	137.7	2.5	123.7	2.7	140.4	3.5	126.0	3.6	162.8	7.2	126.4	4.5	161.5	5.4
1992	134.5	1.7	140.6	2.1	126.2	2.0	138.8	-1.1	127.8	1.4	172.3	5.8	124.6	-1.4	160.5	-0.6
1993	139.1	3.4	146.9	4.5	130.4	3.3	140.1	0.9	131.9	3.2	181.9	5.6	129.5	3.9	162.5	1.2
1994	143.6	3.2	152.7	3.9	135.2	3.7	143.5	2.4	135.3	2.6	188.1	3.4	134.4	3.8	162.8	0.2
1995	-	-	-	-	-	-	-	-	-	-	-	-	-	-	-	-

Source: U.S. Department of Labor, Bureau of Labor Statistics, Division of Consumer Prices and Price Indexes. - indicates no data collected for period.

Miami, FL
Consumer Price Index - Urban Wage Earners
Base 1982-1984 = 100
Annual Averages

For 1977-1995. Columns headed % show percentile change in the index from the previous period for which an index is available.

Year	All Items		Food & Beverage		Housing		Apparel & Upkeep		Trans-portation		Medical Care		Entertain-ment		Other Goods & Services	
	Index	%	Index	%	Index	%	Index	%	Index	%	Index	%	Index	%	Index	%
1977	-	-	-	-	-	-	-	-	-	-	-	-	-	-	-	-
1978	64.5	-	68.6	-	62.9	-	76.0	-	59.4	-	61.9	-	75.7	-	66.0	-
1979	71.3	10.5	78.3	14.1	68.3	8.6	80.2	5.5	67.5	13.6	67.8	9.5	81.4	7.5	71.3	8.0
1980	81.4	14.2	85.4	9.1	80.4	17.7	86.7	8.1	79.5	17.8	74.3	9.6	88.1	8.2	77.3	8.4
1981	90.5	11.2	91.6	7.3	92.1	14.6	91.7	5.8	89.6	12.7	79.8	7.4	94.6	7.4	84.4	9.2
1982	96.8	7.0	96.9	5.8	98.1	6.5	97.8	6.7	94.9	5.9	93.7	17.4	98.5	4.1	93.1	10.3
1983	99.9	3.2	99.5	2.7	99.6	1.5	100.0	2.2	100.3	5.7	101.3	8.1	100.5	2.0	100.1	7.5
1984	103.3	3.4	103.6	4.1	102.2	2.6	102.2	2.2	104.8	4.5	105.0	3.7	101.0	0.5	106.9	6.8
1985	106.4	3.0	104.3	0.7	106.0	3.7	106.0	3.7	107.9	3.0	108.7	3.5	105.2	4.2	112.4	5.1
1986	107.4	0.9	107.5	3.1	107.3	1.2	109.6	3.4	102.3	-5.2	116.6	7.3	108.4	3.0	120.8	7.5
1987	111.1	3.4	113.0	5.1	109.0	1.6	115.7	5.6	105.1	2.7	125.8	7.9	114.3	5.4	126.8	5.0
1988	115.9	4.3	118.5	4.9	113.4	4.0	122.8	6.1	109.0	3.7	133.1	5.8	116.2	1.7	132.6	4.6
1989	120.3	3.8	126.3	6.6	116.2	2.5	129.7	5.6	112.6	3.3	139.0	4.4	118.8	2.2	138.9	4.8
1990	126.2	4.9	134.8	6.7	120.2	3.4	133.3	2.8	118.3	5.1	150.7	8.4	122.1	2.8	151.5	9.1
1991	130.4	3.3	137.8	2.2	123.3	2.6	139.7	4.8	122.6	3.6	161.7	7.3	127.6	4.5	159.7	5.4
1992	132.6	1.7	139.7	1.4	125.7	1.9	138.3	-1.0	125.3	2.2	171.5	6.1	125.5	-1.6	157.7	-1.3
1993	137.3	3.5	145.8	4.4	129.8	3.3	140.8	1.8	130.1	3.8	181.0	5.5	130.2	3.7	159.0	0.8
1994	141.5	3.1	151.3	3.8	134.4	3.5	145.5	3.3	133.5	2.6	185.5	2.5	135.1	3.8	157.2	-1.1
1995	-	-	-	-	-	-	-	-	-	-	-	-	-	-	-	-

Source: U.S. Department of Labor, Bureau of Labor Statistics, Division of Consumer Prices and Price Indexes. - indicates no data collected for period.

583

Miami, FL
Consumer Price Index - All Urban Consumers
Base 1982-1984 = 100
All Items

For 1977-1995. Columns headed % show percentile change in the index from the previous period for which an index is available.

Year	Jan Index	%	Feb Index	%	Mar Index	%	Apr Index	%	May Index	%	Jun Index	%	Jul Index	%	Aug Index	%	Sep Index	%	Oct Index	%	Nov Index	%	Dec Index	%
1977	-	-	-	-	-	-		-	-	-	-	-	-	-	-	-	-	-	-	-	62.0	-	-	-
1978	62.5	0.8	-	-	63.4	1.4	-	-	63.8	0.6	-	-	65.1	2.0	-	-	66.1	1.5	-	-	66.6	0.8	-	-
1979	67.6	1.5	-	-	69.0	2.1	-	-	69.8	1.2	-	-	71.8	2.9	-	-	72.8	1.4	-	-	74.1	1.8	-	-
1980	76.5	3.2	-	-	79.2	3.5	-	-	80.5	1.6	-	-	82.9	3.0	-	-	82.6	-0.4	-	-	83.1	0.6	-	-
1981	85.2	2.5	-	-	86.9	2.0	-	-	88.8	2.2	-	-	90.6	2.0	-	-	93.2	2.9	-	-	95.3	2.3	-	-
1982	96.3	1.0	-	-	96.2	-0.1	-	-	96.6	0.4	-	-	96.2	-0.4	-	-	96.8	0.6	-	-	97.3	0.5	-	-
1983	98.0	0.7	-	-	98.6	0.6	-	-	98.9	0.3	-	-	99.8	0.9	-	-	101.1	1.3	-	-	101.7	0.6	-	-
1984	102.4	0.7	-	-	102.7	0.3	-	-	103.2	0.5	-	-	103.6	0.4	-	-	104.2	0.6	-	-	104.4	0.2	-	-
1985	104.6	0.2	-	-	105.5	0.9	-	-	106.1	0.6	-	-	106.3	0.2	-	-	107.6	1.2	-	-	107.9	0.3	-	-
1986	108.3	0.4	-	-	108.3	0.0	-	-	107.3	-0.9	-	-	106.2	-1.0	-	-	108.1	1.8	-	-	109.1	0.9	-	-
1987	109.9	0.7	-	-	110.7	0.7	-	-	111.1	0.4	-	-	112.0	0.8	-	-	112.5	0.4	-	-	113.8	1.2	-	-
1988	114.5	0.6	-	-	115.1	0.5	-	-	116.2	1.0	-	-	116.8	0.5	-	-	118.8	1.7	-	-	118.3	-0.4	-	-
1989	120.0	1.4	-	-	119.8	-0.2	-	-	120.9	0.9	-	-	121.6	0.6	-	-	122.9	1.1	-	-	123.0	0.1	-	-
1990	124.6	1.3	-	-	125.1	0.4	-	-	126.4	1.0	-	-	128.7	1.8	-	-	130.1	1.1	-	-	131.2	0.8	-	-
1991	131.5	0.2	-	-	132.0	0.4	-	-	132.0	0.0	-	-	132.0	0.0	-	-	132.1	0.1	-	-	133.5	1.1	-	-
1992	133.7	0.1	-	-	134.5	0.6	-	-	133.7	-0.6	-	-	133.8	0.1	-	-	134.6	0.6	-	-	135.9	1.0	-	-
1993	137.8	1.4	-	-	139.2	1.0	-	-	139.0	-0.1	-	-	139.0	0.0	-	-	139.2	0.1	-	-	139.8	0.4	-	-
1994	141.0	0.9	-	-	143.5	1.8	-	-	143.3	-0.1	-	-	143.4	0.1	-	-	144.5	0.8	-	-	144.5	0.0	-	-
1995	147.3	1.9	-	-	148.7	1.0	-	-	148.6	-0.1	-	-	148.3	-0.2	-	-	148.9	0.4	-	-	150.2	0.9	-	-

Source: U.S. Department of Labor, Bureau of Labor Statistics, Division of Consumer Prices and Price Indexes. - indicates no data collected for period.

Miami, FL
Consumer Price Index - Urban Wage Earners
Base 1982-1984 = 100
All Items

For 1977-1995. Columns headed % show percentile change in the index from the previous period for which an index is available.

Year	Jan Index	%	Feb Index	%	Mar Index	%	Apr Index	%	May Index	%	Jun Index	%	Jul Index	%	Aug Index	%	Sep Index	%	Oct Index	%	Nov Index	%	Dec Index	%
1977	-	-	-	-	-	-	-	-	-	-	-	-	-	-	-	-	-	-	-	-	61.6	-	-	-
1978	61.9	0.5	-	-	63.0	1.8	-	-	63.6	1.0	-	-	65.0	2.2	-	-	65.9	1.4	-	-	66.4	0.8	-	-
1979	67.2	1.2	-	-	69.2	3.0	-	-	70.0	1.2	-	-	72.0	2.9	-	-	73.1	1.5	-	-	74.2	1.5	-	-
1980	76.9	3.6	-	-	79.3	3.1	-	-	80.6	1.6	-	-	82.9	2.9	-	-	83.0	0.1	-	-	83.5	0.6	-	-
1981	85.4	2.3	-	-	87.2	2.1	-	-	89.1	2.2	-	-	90.7	1.8	-	-	92.9	2.4	-	-	95.2	2.5	-	-
1982	96.3	1.2	-	-	96.3	0.0	-	-	96.6	0.3	-	-	96.6	0.0	-	-	96.9	0.3	-	-	97.3	0.4	-	-
1983	98.0	0.7	-	-	98.3	0.3	-	-	99.3	1.0	-	-	100.2	0.9	-	-	101.1	0.9	-	-	101.5	0.4	-	-
1984	102.1	0.6	-	-	102.4	0.3	-	-	102.9	0.5	-	-	103.4	0.5	-	-	104.5	1.1	-	-	104.4	-0.1	-	-
1985	104.5	0.1	-	-	105.4	0.9	-	-	106.0	0.6	-	-	106.3	0.3	-	-	107.4	1.0	-	-	107.7	0.3	-	-
1986	108.1	0.4	-	-	107.8	-0.3	-	-	106.7	-1.0	-	-	105.6	-1.0	-	-	107.4	1.7	-	-	108.4	0.9	-	-
1987	109.3	0.8	-	-	109.9	0.5	-	-	110.3	0.4	-	-	111.3	0.9	-	-	111.8	0.4	-	-	113.1	1.2	-	-
1988	113.8	0.6	-	-	114.3	0.4	-	-	115.1	0.7	-	-	116.0	0.8	-	-	117.8	1.6	-	-	117.2	-0.5	-	-
1989	118.8	1.4	-	-	118.7	-0.1	-	-	120.0	1.1	-	-	120.6	0.5	-	-	121.4	0.7	-	-	121.5	0.1	-	-
1990	123.2	1.4	-	-	123.4	0.2	-	-	124.6	1.0	-	-	126.7	1.7	-	-	128.2	1.2	-	-	129.3	0.9	-	-
1991	129.8	0.4	-	-	130.1	0.2	-	-	130.2	0.1	-	-	130.2	0.0	-	-	130.2	0.0	-	-	131.4	0.9	-	-
1992	131.7	0.2	-	-	132.3	0.5	-	-	131.6	-0.5	-	-	132.0	0.3	-	-	132.8	0.6	-	-	134.2	1.1	-	-
1993	135.9	1.3	-	-	137.1	0.9	-	-	137.2	0.1	-	-	137.2	0.0	-	-	137.5	0.2	-	-	138.0	0.4	-	-
1994	138.7	0.5	-	-	141.1	1.7	-	-	141.2	0.1	-	-	141.4	0.1	-	-	142.5	0.8	-	-	142.7	0.1	-	-
1995	145.3	1.8	-	-	146.6	0.9	-	-	146.8	0.1	-	-	146.5	-0.2	-	-	146.9	0.3	-	-	148.2	0.9	-	-

Source: U.S. Department of Labor, Bureau of Labor Statistics, Division of Consumer Prices and Price Indexes. - indicates no data collected for period.

Miami, FL
Consumer Price Index - All Urban Consumers
Base 1982-1984 = 100
Food and Beverages

For 1977-1995. Columns headed % show percentile change in the index from the previous period for which an index is available.

Year	Jan Index	%	Feb Index	%	Mar Index	%	Apr Index	%	May Index	%	Jun Index	%	Jul Index	%	Aug Index	%	Sep Index	%	Oct Index	%	Nov Index	%	Dec Index	%
1977	-	-	-	-	-	-	-	-	-	-	-	-	-	-	-	-	-	-	-	-	65.1	-	-	-
1978	65.9	1.2	-	-	67.5	2.4	-	-	69.2	2.5	-	-	71.0	2.6	-	-	71.1	0.1	-	-	72.1	1.4	-	-
1979	74.9	3.9	-	-	76.9	2.7	-	-	78.3	1.8	-	-	79.9	2.0	-	-	80.2	0.4	-	-	80.1	-0.1	-	-
1980	81.4	1.6	-	-	82.0	0.7	-	-	82.7	0.9	-	-	84.8	2.5	-	-	87.2	2.8	-	-	88.3	1.3	-	-
1981	89.4	1.2	-	-	89.6	0.2	-	-	89.8	0.2	-	-	91.1	1.4	-	-	92.8	1.9	-	-	93.9	1.2	-	-
1982	94.9	1.1	-	-	95.8	0.9	-	-	96.9	1.1	-	-	97.8	0.9	-	-	97.8	0.0	-	-	97.0	-0.8	-	-
1983	97.9	0.9	-	-	98.9	1.0	-	-	99.1	0.2	-	-	99.0	-0.1	-	-	100.2	1.2	-	-	100.8	0.6	-	-
1984	104.0	3.2	-	-	104.2	0.2	-	-	102.6	-1.5	-	-	103.2	0.6	-	-	103.5	0.3	-	-	104.3	0.8	-	-
1985	104.1	-0.2	-	-	105.2	1.1	-	-	103.5	-1.6	-	-	104.4	0.9	-	-	104.1	-0.3	-	-	104.7	0.6	-	-
1986	106.3	1.5	-	-	106.9	0.6	-	-	106.9	0.0	-	-	103.1	-3.6	-	-	108.3	5.0	-	-	110.0	1.6	-	-
1987	110.7	0.6	-	-	112.2	1.4	-	-	113.9	1.5	-	-	113.6	-0.3	-	-	113.4	-0.2	-	-	113.5	0.1	-	-
1988	114.8	1.1	-	-	116.9	1.8	-	-	117.6	0.6	-	-	118.4	0.7	-	-	121.1	2.3	-	-	121.7	0.5	-	-
1989	122.3	0.5	-	-	123.0	0.6	-	-	124.0	0.8	-	-	126.7	2.2	-	-	126.4	-0.2	-	-	128.5	1.7	-	-
1990	134.1	4.4	-	-	134.1	0.0	-	-	132.4	-1.3	-	-	134.2	1.4	-	-	134.4	0.1	-	-	136.1	1.3	-	-
1991	136.0	-0.1	-	-	137.7	1.2	-	-	137.7	0.0	-	-	138.0	0.2	-	-	138.2	0.1	-	-	138.1	-0.1	-	-
1992	138.7	0.4	-	-	140.5	1.3	-	-	138.9	-1.1	-	-	139.9	0.7	-	-	142.0	1.5	-	-	142.2	0.1	-	-
1993	144.9	1.9	-	-	145.7	0.6	-	-	146.1	0.3	-	-	145.9	-0.1	-	-	147.6	1.2	-	-	149.3	1.2	-	-
1994	151.8	1.7	-	-	151.7	-0.1	-	-	152.1	0.3	-	-	152.3	0.1	-	-	152.8	0.3	-	-	154.6	1.2	-	-
1995	156.2	1.0	-	-	156.4	0.1	-	-	157.0	0.4	-	-	156.8	-0.1	-	-	157.6	0.5	-	-	157.9	0.2	-	-

Source: U.S. Department of Labor, Bureau of Labor Statistics, Division of Consumer Prices and Price Indexes. - indicates no data collected for period.

Miami, FL
Consumer Price Index - Urban Wage Earners
Base 1982-1984 = 100
Food and Beverages

For 1977-1995. Columns headed % show percentile change in the index from the previous period for which an index is available.

Year	Jan Index	%	Feb Index	%	Mar Index	%	Apr Index	%	May Index	%	Jun Index	%	Jul Index	%	Aug Index	%	Sep Index	%	Oct Index	%	Nov Index	%	Dec Index	%
1977	-	-	-	-	-	-	-	-	-	-	-	-	-	-	-	-	-	-	-	-	-	-	-	-
1978	63.5	0.8	-	-	66.1	4.1	-	-	68.2	3.2	-	-	69.8	2.3	-	-	70.5	-	-	-	63.0	-	-	-
1979	73.1	2.2	-	-	77.1	5.5	-	-	78.2	1.4	-	-	79.3	1.4	-	-	70.5	1.0	-	-	71.5	1.4	-	-
1980	81.8	2.0	-	-	82.7	1.1	-	-	83.7	1.2	-	-	85.5	2.2	-	-	79.7	0.5	-	-	80.2	0.6	-	-
1981	89.5	1.1	-	-	89.8	0.3	-	-	90.0	0.2	-	-	91.8	2.0	-	-	88.1	3.0	-	-	88.5	0.5	-	-
1982	94.7	1.2	-	-	95.6	1.0	-	-	97.0	1.5	-	-	98.2	1.2	-	-	93.8	2.2	-	-	93.6	-0.2	-	-
1983	97.8	0.8	-	-	99.0	1.2	-	-	99.2	0.2	-	-	99.2	0.0	-	-	98.2	0.0	-	-	97.0	-1.2	-	-
1984	103.8	3.3	-	-	104.0	0.2	-	-	102.6	-1.3	-	-	103.1	0.5	-	-	100.2	1.0	-	-	100.5	0.3	-	-
1985	103.9	-0.4	-	-	105.1	1.2	-	-	103.4	-1.6	-	-	104.3	0.9	-	-	103.6	0.5	-	-	104.3	0.7	-	-
1986	106.3	1.6	-	-	107.0	0.7	-	-	107.2	0.2	-	-	104.2	-2.8	-	-	104.0	-0.3	-	-	104.6	0.6	-	-
1987	111.4	0.9	-	-	112.4	0.9	-	-	113.8	1.2	-	-	113.6	-0.2	-	-	108.7	4.3	-	-	110.4	1.6	-	-
1988	114.2	1.0	-	-	116.5	2.0	-	-	116.9	0.3	-	-	118.2	1.1	-	-	113.1	-0.4	-	-	113.1	0.0	-	-
1989	122.7	0.7	-	-	123.5	0.7	-	-	124.9	1.1	-	-	127.5	2.1	-	-	121.4	2.7	-	-	121.9	0.4	-	-
1990	135.5	5.1	-	-	135.7	0.1	-	-	132.8	-2.1	-	-	134.1	1.0	-	-	126.9	-0.5	-	-	128.9	1.6	-	-
1991	136.3	-0.1	-	-	138.1	1.3	-	-	138.2	0.1	-	-	138.4	0.1	-	-	134.2	0.1	-	-	136.4	1.6	-	-
1992	138.0	0.5	-	-	139.9	1.4	-	-	137.9	-1.4	-	-	138.7	0.6	-	-	138.0	-0.3	-	-	137.3	-0.5	-	-
1993	143.7	1.9	-	-	144.8	0.8	-	-	145.2	0.3	-	-	144.5	-0.5	-	-	141.2	1.8	-	-	141.0	-0.1	-	-
1994	150.1	1.1	-	-	150.5	0.3	-	-	151.1	0.4	-	-	150.8	-0.2	-	-	146.4	1.3	-	-	148.5	1.4	-	-
1995	155.1	1.7	-	-	155.1	0.0	-	-	155.6	0.3	-	-	155.2	-0.3	-	-	151.3	0.3	-	-	152.5	0.8	-	-

Source: U.S. Department of Labor, Bureau of Labor Statistics, Division of Consumer Prices and Price Indexes. - indicates no data collected for period.

Miami, FL
Consumer Price Index - All Urban Consumers
Base 1982-1984 = 100
Housing

For 1977-1995. Columns headed % show percentile change in the index from the previous period for which an index is available.

Year	Jan Index	%	Feb Index	%	Mar Index	%	Apr Index	%	May Index	%	Jun Index	%	Jul Index	%	Aug Index	%	Sep Index	%	Oct Index	%	Nov Index	%	Dec Index	%
1977	-	-	-	-	-	-	-	-	-	-	-	-	-	-	-	-	-	-	-	-	60.6	-	-	-
1978	61.0	0.7	-	-	62.0	1.6	-	-	61.7	-0.5	-	-	63.2	2.4	-	-	64.4	1.9	-	-	64.5	0.2	-	-
1979	65.1	0.9	-	-	66.4	2.0	-	-	66.3	-0.2	-	-	68.8	3.8	-	-	69.8	1.5	-	-	71.8	2.9	-	-
1980	74.7	4.0	-	-	78.8	5.5	-	-	80.6	2.3	-	-	84.4	4.7	-	-	82.1	-2.7	-	-	81.9	-0.2	-	-
1981	84.8	3.5	-	-	86.7	2.2	-	-	89.8	3.6	-	-	92.3	2.8	-	-	95.7	3.7	-	-	99.2	3.7	-	-
1982	99.9	0.7	-	-	99.2	-0.7	-	-	98.7	-0.5	-	-	95.8	-2.9	-	-	96.7	0.9	-	-	96.7	0.0	-	-
1983	98.2	1.6	-	-	99.4	1.2	-	-	98.8	-0.6	-	-	99.7	0.9	-	-	100.6	0.9	-	-	100.8	0.2	-	-
1984	101.1	0.3	-	-	101.2	0.1	-	-	102.5	1.3	-	-	102.9	0.4	-	-	103.9	1.0	-	-	103.2	-0.7	-	-
1985	103.7	0.5	-	-	104.0	0.3	-	-	105.2	1.2	-	-	105.2	0.0	-	-	107.9	2.6	-	-	107.2	-0.6	-	-
1986	106.7	-0.5	-	-	107.6	0.8	-	-	106.8	-0.7	-	-	106.0	-0.7	-	-	107.3	1.2	-	-	107.6	0.3	-	-
1987	108.1	0.5	-	-	108.0	-0.1	-	-	106.9	-1.0	-	-	108.3	1.3	-	-	109.3	0.9	-	-	110.8	1.4	-	-
1988	111.8	0.9	-	-	111.1	-0.6	-	-	112.9	1.6	-	-	113.6	0.6	-	-	114.9	1.1	-	-	113.4	-1.3	-	-
1989	115.2	1.6	-	-	115.0	-0.2	-	-	115.2	0.2	-	-	116.5	1.1	-	-	117.9	1.2	-	-	117.2	-0.6	-	-
1990	116.7	-0.4	-	-	116.1	-0.5	-	-	119.6	3.0	-	-	123.3	3.1	-	-	123.1	-0.2	-	-	122.3	-0.6	-	-
1991	122.3	0.0	-	-	122.5	0.2	-	-	123.0	0.4	-	-	124.2	1.0	-	-	123.7	-0.4	-	-	125.4	1.4	-	-
1992	126.0	0.5	-	-	126.6	0.5	-	-	126.2	-0.3	-	-	125.7	-0.4	-	-	125.1	-0.5	-	-	127.0	1.5	-	-
1993	128.5	1.2	-	-	130.3	1.4	-	-	129.8	-0.4	-	-	130.5	0.5	-	-	131.2	0.5	-	-	131.1	-0.1	-	-
1994	133.0	1.4	-	-	134.3	1.0	-	-	134.9	0.4	-	-	135.3	0.3	-	-	136.1	0.6	-	-	136.0	-0.1	-	-
1995	138.5	1.8	-	-	139.1	0.4	-	-	138.4	-0.5	-	-	139.0	0.4	-	-	140.6	1.2	-	-	142.6	1.4	-	-

Source: U.S. Department of Labor, Bureau of Labor Statistics, Division of Consumer Prices and Price Indexes. - indicates no data collected for period.

Miami, FL
Consumer Price Index - Urban Wage Earners
Base 1982-1984 = 100
Housing

For 1977-1995. Columns headed % show percentile change in the index from the previous period for which an index is available.

Year	Jan Index	%	Feb Index	%	Mar Index	%	Apr Index	%	May Index	%	Jun Index	%	Jul Index	%	Aug Index	%	Sep Index	%	Oct Index	%	Nov Index	%	Dec Index	%
1977	-	-	-	-	-	-	-	-	-	-	-	-	-	-	-	-	-	-	-	-	60.6	-	-	-
1978	60.9	0.5	-	-	62.0	1.8	-	-	61.6	-0.6	-	-	63.2	2.6	-	-	64.2	1.6	-	-	64.4	0.3	-	-
1979	65.1	1.1	-	-	66.3	1.8	-	-	66.3	0.0	-	-	68.7	3.6	-	-	69.7	1.5	-	-	71.5	2.6	-	-
1980	74.4	4.1	-	-	78.3	5.2	-	-	80.0	2.2	-	-	84.1	5.1	-	-	81.7	-2.9	-	-	81.7	0.0	-	-
1981	84.6	3.5	-	-	86.6	2.4	-	-	89.9	3.8	-	-	92.3	2.7	-	-	95.7	3.7	-	-	99.5	4.0	-	-
1982	100.4	0.9	-	-	99.7	-0.7	-	-	99.1	-0.6	-	-	96.0	-3.1	-	-	96.9	0.9	-	-	97.0	0.1	-	-
1983	97.9	0.9	-	-	98.4	0.5	-	-	99.6	1.2	-	-	100.4	0.8	-	-	100.4	0.0	-	-	100.4	0.0	-	-
1984	100.6	0.2	-	-	100.4	-0.2	-	-	101.8	1.4	-	-	102.4	0.6	-	-	104.5	2.1	-	-	103.3	-1.1	-	-
1985	103.9	0.6	-	-	104.4	0.5	-	-	105.6	1.1	-	-	105.6	0.0	-	-	108.2	2.5	-	-	107.5	-0.6	-	-
1986	107.0	-0.5	-	-	107.9	0.8	-	-	107.0	-0.8	-	-	106.1	-0.8	-	-	107.5	1.3	-	-	107.9	0.4	-	-
1987	108.4	0.5	-	-	108.3	-0.1	-	-	107.1	-1.1	-	-	108.6	1.4	-	-	109.5	0.8	-	-	111.1	1.5	-	-
1988	112.2	1.0	-	-	111.4	-0.7	-	-	113.0	1.4	-	-	113.8	0.7	-	-	115.3	1.3	-	-	113.7	-1.4	-	-
1989	115.3	1.4	-	-	114.9	-0.3	-	-	115.4	0.4	-	-	116.7	1.1	-	-	117.7	0.9	-	-	117.1	-0.5	-	-
1990	116.7	-0.3	-	-	116.0	-0.6	-	-	119.3	2.8	-	-	122.9	3.0	-	-	122.8	-0.1	-	-	122.0	-0.7	-	-
1991	122.0	0.0	-	-	122.2	0.2	-	-	122.6	0.3	-	-	123.8	1.0	-	-	123.4	-0.3	-	-	125.0	1.3	-	-
1992	125.6	0.5	-	-	126.2	0.5	-	-	125.6	-0.5	-	-	125.3	-0.2	-	-	124.6	-0.6	-	-	126.5	1.5	-	-
1993	127.9	1.1	-	-	129.6	1.3	-	-	129.3	-0.2	-	-	129.9	0.5	-	-	130.6	0.5	-	-	130.3	-0.2	-	-
1994	132.2	1.5	-	-	133.5	1.0	-	-	134.2	0.5	-	-	134.4	0.1	-	-	135.2	0.6	-	-	135.5	0.2	-	-
1995	137.5	1.5	-	-	138.1	0.4	-	-	137.7	-0.3	-	-	138.3	0.4	-	-	140.0	1.2	-	-	142.0	1.4	-	-

Source: U.S. Department of Labor, Bureau of Labor Statistics, Division of Consumer Prices and Price Indexes. - indicates no data collected for period.

Miami, FL
Consumer Price Index - All Urban Consumers
Base 1982-1984 = 100
Apparel and Upkeep

For 1977-1995. Columns headed % show percentile change in the index from the previous period for which an index is available.

Year	Jan Index	%	Feb Index	%	Mar Index	%	Apr Index	%	May Index	%	Jun Index	%	Jul Index	%	Aug Index	%	Sep Index	%	Oct Index	%	Nov Index	%	Dec Index	%
1977	-	-	-	-	-	-	-	-	-	-	-	-	-	-	-	-	-	-	-	-	74.8	-	-	-
1978	75.6	1.1	-	-	77.2	2.1	-	-	77.1	-0.1	-	-	77.6	0.6	-	-	78.7	1.4	-	-	78.9	0.3	-	-
1979	78.7	-0.3	-	-	79.8	1.4	-	-	80.3	0.6	-	-	81.5	1.5	-	-	82.2	0.9	-	-	83.7	1.8	-	-
1980	82.3	-1.7	-	-	86.0	4.5	-	-	87.2	1.4	-	-	87.8	0.7	-	-	88.0	0.2	-	-	88.8	0.9	-	-
1981	90.9	2.4	-	-	89.8	-1.2	-	-	90.3	0.6	-	-	92.3	2.2	-	-	93.2	1.0	-	-	93.6	0.4	-	-
1982	95.7	2.2	-	-	97.6	2.0	-	-	98.3	0.7	-	-	99.4	1.1	-	-	97.0	-2.4	-	-	100.3	3.4	-	-
1983	99.0	-1.3	-	-	99.8	0.8	-	-	99.2	-0.6	-	-	100.6	1.4	-	-	99.9	-0.7	-	-	102.2	2.3	-	-
1984	99.8	-2.3	-	-	100.6	0.8	-	-	101.8	1.2	-	-	102.0	0.2	-	-	102.7	0.7	-	-	102.7	0.0	-	-
1985	101.5	-1.2	-	-	104.9	3.3	-	-	104.5	-0.4	-	-	104.7	0.2	-	-	107.5	2.7	-	-	108.8	1.2	-	-
1986	109.5	0.6	-	-	108.5	-0.9	-	-	108.6	0.1	-	-	108.5	-0.1	-	-	108.6	0.1	-	-	110.4	1.7	-	-
1987	110.5	0.1	-	-	114.8	3.9	-	-	117.1	2.0	-	-	116.3	-0.7	-	-	115.8	-0.4	-	-	117.3	1.3	-	-
1988	119.0	1.4	-	-	121.7	2.3	-	-	121.4	-0.2	-	-	122.4	0.8	-	-	126.2	3.1	-	-	127.1	0.7	-	-
1989	131.0	3.1	-	-	129.0	-1.5	-	-	129.3	0.2	-	-	125.2	-3.2	-	-	138.0	10.2	-	-	135.8	-1.6	-	-
1990	130.4	-4.0	-	-	136.6	4.8	-	-	132.1	-3.3	-	-	134.9	2.1	-	-	138.6	2.7	-	-	139.5	0.6	-	-
1991	135.6	-2.8	-	-	143.6	5.9	-	-	142.3	-0.9	-	-	137.1	-3.7	-	-	140.6	2.6	-	-	142.2	1.1	-	-
1992	140.4	-1.3	-	-	140.7	0.2	-	-	138.8	-1.4	-	-	134.2	-3.3	-	-	144.2	7.5	-	-	134.8	-6.5	-	-
1993	139.4	3.4	-	-	148.9	6.8	-	-	144.5	-3.0	-	-	139.0	-3.8	-	-	137.5	-1.1	-	-	134.1	-2.5	-	-
1994	127.5	-4.9	-	-	154.9	21.5	-	-	149.1	-3.7	-	-	143.7	-3.6	-	-	144.4	0.5	-	-	136.6	-5.4	-	-
1995	148.2	8.5	-	-	158.9	7.2	-	-	150.2	-5.5	-	-	139.8	-6.9	-	-	142.1	1.6	-	-	142.4	0.2	-	-

Source: U.S. Department of Labor, Bureau of Labor Statistics, Division of Consumer Prices and Price Indexes. - indicates no data collected for period.

Miami, FL
Consumer Price Index - Urban Wage Earners
Base 1982-1984 = 100
Apparel and Upkeep

For 1977-1995. Columns headed % show percentile change in the index from the previous period for which an index is available.

Year	Jan Index	%	Feb Index	%	Mar Index	%	Apr Index	%	May Index	%	Jun Index	%	Jul Index	%	Aug Index	%	Sep Index	%	Oct Index	%	Nov Index	%	Dec Index	%
1977	-	-	-	-	-	-	-	-	-	-	-	-	-	-	-	-	-	-	-	-	74.5	-	-	-
1978	74.8	0.4	-	-	74.9	0.1	-	-	75.3	0.5	-	-	76.3	1.3	-	-	76.7	0.5	-	-	77.3	0.8	-	-
1979	76.9	-0.5	-	-	79.5	3.4	-	-	79.4	-0.1	-	-	80.1	0.9	-	-	81.6	1.9	-	-	82.5	1.1	-	-
1980	82.8	0.4	-	-	84.0	1.4	-	-	85.7	2.0	-	-	86.6	1.1	-	-	89.2	3.0	-	-	90.1	1.0	-	-
1981	90.7	0.7	-	-	91.2	0.6	-	-	91.5	0.3	-	-	91.3	-0.2	-	-	91.5	0.2	-	-	93.0	1.6	-	-
1982	95.1	2.3	-	-	97.1	2.1	-	-	97.9	0.8	-	-	99.2	1.3	-	-	96.5	-2.7	-	-	100.0	3.6	-	-
1983	98.9	-1.1	-	-	99.2	0.3	-	-	99.2	0.0	-	-	100.6	1.4	-	-	99.9	-0.7	-	-	101.9	2.0	-	-
1984	100.0	-1.9	-	-	100.9	0.9	-	-	102.4	1.5	-	-	102.8	0.4	-	-	103.4	0.6	-	-	103.5	0.1	-	-
1985	102.0	-1.4	-	-	105.5	3.4	-	-	104.7	-0.8	-	-	104.7	0.0	-	-	108.0	3.2	-	-	109.1	1.0	-	-
1986	110.0	0.8	-	-	109.0	-0.9	-	-	109.5	0.5	-	-	109.2	-0.3	-	-	109.1	-0.1	-	-	110.6	1.4	-	-
1987	110.8	0.2	-	-	114.9	3.7	-	-	117.1	1.9	-	-	116.1	-0.9	-	-	115.9	-0.2	-	-	117.2	1.1	-	-
1988	118.8	1.4	-	-	121.8	2.5	-	-	121.0	-0.7	-	-	122.5	1.2	-	-	124.5	1.6	-	-	125.6	0.9	-	-
1989	129.2	2.9	-	-	127.5	-1.3	-	-	127.9	0.3	-	-	123.4	-3.5	-	-	136.7	10.8	-	-	133.9	-2.0	-	-
1990	128.6	-4.0	-	-	134.3	4.4	-	-	129.6	-3.5	-	-	132.3	2.1	-	-	137.3	3.8	-	-	136.4	-0.7	-	-
1991	134.5	-1.4	-	-	142.4	5.9	-	-	141.3	-0.8	-	-	137.2	-2.9	-	-	139.9	2.0	-	-	141.8	1.4	-	-
1992	140.5	-0.9	-	-	140.5	0.0	-	-	138.0	-1.8	-	-	132.7	-3.8	-	-	143.5	8.1	-	-	134.9	-6.0	-	-
1993	139.5	3.4	-	-	147.7	5.9	-	-	145.6	-1.4	-	-	140.1	-3.8	-	-	139.5	-0.4	-	-	134.9	-3.3	-	-
1994	129.0	-4.4	-	-	157.0	21.7	-	-	150.6	-4.1	-	-	145.8	-3.2	-	-	146.8	0.7	-	-	139.0	-5.3	-	-
1995	150.5	8.3	-	-	162.5	8.0	-	-	152.5	-6.2	-	-	142.7	-6.4	-	-	145.1	1.7	-	-	142.8	-1.6	-	-

Source: U.S. Department of Labor, Bureau of Labor Statistics, Division of Consumer Prices and Price Indexes. - indicates no data collected for period.

Miami, FL
Consumer Price Index - All Urban Consumers
Base 1982-1984 = 100
Transportation

For 1977-1995. Columns headed % show percentile change in the index from the previous period for which an index is available.

Year	Jan Index	%	Feb Index	%	Mar Index	%	Apr Index	%	May Index	%	Jun Index	%	Jul Index	%	Aug Index	%	Sep Index	%	Oct Index	%	Nov Index	%	Dec Index	%
1977	-	-	-	-	-	-	-	-	-	-	-	-	-	-	-	-	-	-	-	-	58.0	-	-	-
1978	58.0	0.0	-	-	58.2	0.3	-	-	58.5	0.5	-	-	60.0	2.6	-	-	60.6	1.0	-	-	61.6	1.7	-	-
1979	62.2	1.0	-	-	63.4	1.9	-	-	66.0	4.1	-	-	68.5	3.8	-	-	69.5	1.5	-	-	70.0	0.7	-	-
1980	74.0	5.7	-	-	76.8	3.8	-	-	77.9	1.4	-	-	79.2	1.7	-	-	79.7	0.6	-	-	81.3	2.0	-	-
1981	83.0	2.1	-	-	86.8	4.6	-	-	88.4	1.8	-	-	89.8	1.6	-	-	90.5	0.8	-	-	91.8	1.4	-	-
1982	93.0	1.3	-	-	92.6	-0.4	-	-	93.4	0.9	-	-	96.1	2.9	-	-	96.0	-0.1	-	-	96.7	0.7	-	-
1983	96.9	0.2	-	-	96.6	-0.3	-	-	98.8	2.3	-	-	100.4	1.6	-	-	103.2	2.8	-	-	103.8	0.6	-	-
1984	103.1	-0.7	-	-	103.7	0.6	-	-	105.1	1.4	-	-	105.4	0.3	-	-	105.6	0.2	-	-	106.5	0.9	-	-
1985	106.1	-0.4	-	-	106.9	0.8	-	-	108.8	1.8	-	-	109.1	0.3	-	-	108.6	-0.5	-	-	109.3	0.6	-	-
1986	109.5	0.2	-	-	105.5	-3.7	-	-	102.5	-2.8	-	-	102.2	-0.3	-	-	101.4	-0.8	-	-	102.2	0.8	-	-
1987	104.0	1.8	-	-	104.8	0.8	-	-	106.2	1.3	-	-	107.0	0.8	-	-	107.3	0.3	-	-	109.3	1.9	-	-
1988	108.8	-0.5	-	-	109.0	0.2	-	-	109.8	0.7	-	-	110.7	0.8	-	-	112.2	1.4	-	-	112.3	0.1	-	-
1989	113.9	1.4	-	-	113.5	-0.4	-	-	116.3	2.5	-	-	115.9	-0.3	-	-	113.7	-1.9	-	-	114.3	0.5	-	-
1990	118.8	3.9	-	-	118.4	-0.3	-	-	119.8	1.2	-	-	119.0	-0.7	-	-	123.0	3.4	-	-	128.2	4.2	-	-
1991	129.4	0.9	-	-	126.2	-2.5	-	-	126.4	0.2	-	-	124.3	-1.7	-	-	124.4	0.1	-	-	126.3	1.5	-	-
1992	125.6	-0.6	-	-	125.5	-0.1	-	-	126.7	1.0	-	-	128.7	1.6	-	-	127.8	-0.7	-	-	131.3	2.7	-	-
1993	131.7	0.3	-	-	130.9	-0.6	-	-	131.7	0.6	-	-	132.0	0.2	-	-	130.7	-1.0	-	-	134.1	2.6	-	-
1994	133.8	-0.2	-	-	134.6	0.6	-	-	134.3	-0.2	-	-	135.3	0.7	-	-	136.0	0.5	-	-	137.1	0.8	-	-
1995	138.0	0.7	-	-	138.9	0.7	-	-	141.7	2.0	-	-	141.6	-0.1	-	-	138.0	-2.5	-	-	140.1	1.5	-	-

Source: U.S. Department of Labor, Bureau of Labor Statistics, Division of Consumer Prices and Price Indexes. - indicates no data collected for period.

Miami, FL
Consumer Price Index - Urban Wage Earners
Base 1982-1984 = 100
Transportation

For 1977-1995. Columns headed % show percentile change in the index from the previous period for which an index is available.

Year	Jan Index	%	Feb Index	%	Mar Index	%	Apr Index	%	May Index	%	Jun Index	%	Jul Index	%	Aug Index	%	Sep Index	%	Oct Index	%	Nov Index	%	Dec Index	%
1977	-		-	-	-		-	-	-		-	-	-	-	-	-	-	-	-	-	57.6	-	-	-
1978	57.6	0.0	-	-	57.7	0.2	-	-	58.4	1.2	-	-	59.8	2.4	-	-	60.5	1.2	-	-	61.2	1.2	-	-
1979	62.0	1.3	-	-	63.5	2.4	-	-	66.4	4.6	-	-	69.0	3.9	-	-	70.0	1.4	-	-	70.5	0.7	-	-
1980	75.0	6.4	-	-	77.6	3.5	-	-	79.0	1.8	-	-	80.0	1.3	-	-	81.0	1.3	-	-	82.4	1.7	-	-
1981	84.4	2.4	-	-	88.0	4.3	-	-	89.4	1.6	-	-	90.1	0.8	-	-	91.0	1.0	-	-	92.6	1.8	-	-
1982	93.5	1.0	-	-	93.0	-0.5	-	-	93.1	0.1	-	-	96.2	3.3	-	-	96.1	-0.1	-	-	96.8	0.7	-	-
1983	97.4	0.6	-	-	96.6	-0.8	-	-	98.8	2.3	-	-	100.5	1.7	-	-	103.4	2.9	-	-	103.7	0.3	-	-
1984	102.9	-0.8	-	-	103.5	0.6	-	-	104.9	1.4	-	-	105.2	0.3	-	-	105.4	0.2	-	-	106.1	0.7	-	-
1985	105.7	-0.4	-	-	106.5	0.8	-	-	108.4	1.8	-	-	108.7	0.3	-	-	108.2	-0.5	-	-	108.8	0.6	-	-
1986	109.0	0.2	-	-	104.5	-4.1	-	-	101.0	-3.3	-	-	100.6	-0.4	-	-	99.9	-0.7	-	-	100.7	0.8	-	-
1987	102.0	1.3	-	-	103.0	1.0	-	-	104.7	1.7	-	-	105.8	1.1	-	-	105.9	0.1	-	-	107.8	1.8	-	-
1988	107.4	-0.4	-	-	107.5	0.1	-	-	108.1	0.6	-	-	109.0	0.8	-	-	110.3	1.2	-	-	110.4	0.1	-	-
1989	112.0	1.4	-	-	111.6	-0.4	-	-	114.0	2.2	-	-	113.7	-0.3	-	-	111.6	-1.8	-	-	112.0	0.4	-	-
1990	115.9	3.5	-	-	115.3	-0.5	-	-	116.6	1.1	-	-	116.0	-0.5	-	-	119.7	3.2	-	-	124.1	3.7	-	-
1991	125.1	0.8	-	-	122.3	-2.2	-	-	122.9	0.5	-	-	121.3	-1.3	-	-	121.5	0.2	-	-	123.1	1.3	-	-
1992	122.3	-0.6	-	-	121.9	-0.3	-	-	123.8	1.6	-	-	126.5	2.2	-	-	126.3	-0.2	-	-	129.2	2.3	-	-
1993	129.5	0.2	-	-	128.6	-0.7	-	-	129.6	0.8	-	-	130.3	0.5	-	-	129.6	-0.5	-	-	132.3	2.1	-	-
1994	131.5	-0.6	-	-	131.6	0.1	-	-	132.1	0.4	-	-	133.7	1.2	-	-	134.8	0.8	-	-	136.1	1.0	-	-
1995	137.0	0.7	-	-	137.5	0.4	-	-	140.7	2.3	-	-	140.6	-0.1	-	-	137.4	-2.3	-	-	139.4	1.5	-	-

Source: U.S. Department of Labor, Bureau of Labor Statistics, Division of Consumer Prices and Price Indexes. - indicates no data collected for period.

Miami, FL
Consumer Price Index - All Urban Consumers
Base 1982-1984 = 100
Medical Care

For 1977-1995. Columns headed % show percentile change in the index from the previous period for which an index is available.

Year	Jan Index	%	Feb Index	%	Mar Index	%	Apr Index	%	May Index	%	Jun Index	%	Jul Index	%	Aug Index	%	Sep Index	%	Oct Index	%	Nov Index	%	Dec Index	%
1977	-	-	-	-	-	-	-	-	-	-	-	-	-	-	-	-	-	-	-	-	57.9	-	-	-
1978	59.3	2.4	-	-	59.5	0.3	-	-	60.3	1.3	-	-	60.6	0.5	-	-	63.0	4.0	-	-	64.4	2.2	-	-
1979	65.2	1.2	-	-	67.4	3.4	-	-	67.5	0.1	-	-	68.4	1.3	-	-	70.5	3.1	-	-	72.3	2.6	-	-
1980	74.6	3.2	-	-	75.5	1.2	-	-	75.6	0.1	-	-	75.4	-0.3	-	-	75.8	0.5	-	-	75.7	-0.1	-	-
1981	77.8	2.8	-	-	79.1	1.7	-	-	80.2	1.4	-	-	81.6	1.7	-	-	84.6	3.7	-	-	85.6	1.2	-	-
1982	87.8	2.6	-	-	89.1	1.5	-	-	92.0	3.3	-	-	95.1	3.4	-	-	96.5	1.5	-	-	99.8	3.4	-	-
1983	99.7	-0.1	-	-	100.0	0.3	-	-	100.0	0.0	-	-	101.0	1.0	-	-	101.5	0.5	-	-	102.9	1.4	-	-
1984	103.9	1.0	-	-	105.0	1.1	-	-	105.0	0.0	-	-	105.0	0.0	-	-	104.8	-0.2	-	-	106.3	1.4	-	-
1985	107.0	0.7	-	-	108.6	1.5	-	-	108.4	-0.2	-	-	108.7	0.3	-	-	109.7	0.9	-	-	111.2	1.4	-	-
1986	113.4	2.0	-	-	115.4	1.8	-	-	115.6	0.2	-	-	116.0	0.3	-	-	120.1	3.5	-	-	121.1	0.8	-	-
1987	122.9	1.5	-	-	123.7	0.7	-	-	124.8	0.9	-	-	128.4	2.9	-	-	127.7	-0.5	-	-	130.2	2.0	-	-
1988	131.4	0.9	-	-	133.3	1.4	-	-	134.0	0.5	-	-	134.4	0.3	-	-	136.1	1.3	-	-	136.7	0.4	-	-
1989	137.9	0.9	-	-	137.9	0.0	-	-	140.5	1.9	-	-	140.9	0.3	-	-	141.7	0.6	-	-	142.6	0.6	-	-
1990	143.3	0.5	-	-	145.0	1.2	-	-	150.1	3.5	-	-	153.5	2.3	-	-	156.4	1.9	-	-	158.3	1.2	-	-
1991	159.7	0.9	-	-	160.4	0.4	-	-	161.8	0.9	-	-	163.1	0.8	-	-	162.9	-0.1	-	-	166.7	2.3	-	-
1992	169.6	1.7	-	-	171.0	0.8	-	-	171.7	0.4	-	-	171.2	-0.3	-	-	171.3	0.1	-	-	176.4	3.0	-	-
1993	179.2	1.6	-	-	180.1	0.5	-	-	182.0	1.1	-	-	183.1	0.6	-	-	183.1	0.0	-	-	182.7	-0.2	-	-
1994	184.7	1.1	-	-	185.2	0.3	-	-	187.0	1.0	-	-	186.4	-0.3	-	-	190.7	2.3	-	-	191.6	0.5	-	-
1995	196.6	2.6	-	-	200.1	1.8	-	-	201.7	0.8	-	-	204.3	1.3	-	-	204.9	0.3	-	-	206.2	0.6	-	-

Source: U.S. Department of Labor, Bureau of Labor Statistics, Division of Consumer Prices and Price Indexes. - indicates no data collected for period.

Miami, FL
Consumer Price Index - Urban Wage Earners
Base 1982-1984 = 100
Medical Care

For 1977-1995. Columns headed % show percentile change in the index from the previous period for which an index is available.

Year	Jan Index	%	Feb Index	%	Mar Index	%	Apr Index	%	May Index	%	Jun Index	%	Jul Index	%	Aug Index	%	Sep Index	%	Oct Index	%	Nov Index	%	Dec Index	%
1977	-	-	-	-	-	-	-	-	-	-	-	-	-	-	-	-	-	-	-	-	58.2	-	-	-
1978	59.3	1.9	-	-	59.5	0.3	-	-	61.9	4.0	-	-	62.2	0.5	-	-	63.4	1.9	-	-	64.0	0.9	-	-
1979	64.7	1.1	-	-	65.5	1.2	-	-	65.8	0.5	-	-	66.8	1.5	-	-	70.4	5.4	-	-	71.4	1.4	-	-
1980	73.5	2.9	-	-	74.3	1.1	-	-	74.2	-0.1	-	-	74.0	-0.3	-	-	74.4	0.5	-	-	74.8	0.5	-	-
1981	76.0	1.6	-	-	77.1	1.4	-	-	77.5	0.5	-	-	79.5	2.6	-	-	80.7	1.5	-	-	85.4	5.8	-	-
1982	87.6	2.6	-	-	89.1	1.7	-	-	91.9	3.1	-	-	94.7	3.0	-	-	96.1	1.5	-	-	99.9	4.0	-	-
1983	100.0	0.1	-	-	100.4	0.4	-	-	100.4	0.0	-	-	101.3	0.9	-	-	101.8	0.5	-	-	103.0	1.2	-	-
1984	103.9	0.9	-	-	104.9	1.0	-	-	104.9	0.0	-	-	104.9	0.0	-	-	104.6	-0.3	-	-	106.0	1.3	-	-
1985	106.5	0.5	-	-	108.1	1.5	-	-	108.0	-0.1	-	-	108.2	0.2	-	-	109.2	0.9	-	-	110.6	1.3	-	-
1986	112.5	1.7	-	-	114.6	1.9	-	-	114.8	0.2	-	-	115.3	0.4	-	-	119.4	3.6	-	-	120.4	0.8	-	-
1987	122.2	1.5	-	-	123.0	0.7	-	-	124.2	1.0	-	-	127.6	2.7	-	-	126.9	-0.5	-	-	129.0	1.7	-	-
1988	130.4	1.1	-	-	131.8	1.1	-	-	132.6	0.6	-	-	132.8	0.2	-	-	134.5	1.3	-	-	134.8	0.2	-	-
1989	136.2	1.0	-	-	136.4	0.1	-	-	138.9	1.8	-	-	139.3	0.3	-	-	140.5	0.9	-	-	141.5	0.7	-	-
1990	142.1	0.4	-	-	143.7	1.1	-	-	149.0	3.7	-	-	152.2	2.1	-	-	155.6	2.2	-	-	157.3	1.1	-	-
1991	158.7	0.9	-	-	159.4	0.4	-	-	160.8	0.9	-	-	162.0	0.7	-	-	161.8	-0.1	-	-	165.4	2.2	-	-
1992	168.3	1.8	-	-	169.9	1.0	-	-	170.9	0.6	-	-	171.0	0.1	-	-	170.8	-0.1	-	-	175.6	2.8	-	-
1993	178.5	1.7	-	-	179.5	0.6	-	-	181.4	1.1	-	-	182.0	0.3	-	-	181.8	-0.1	-	-	181.6	-0.1	-	-
1994	182.6	0.6	-	-	182.8	0.1	-	-	184.0	0.7	-	-	183.6	-0.2	-	-	188.1	2.5	-	-	189.2	0.6	-	-
1995	193.6	2.3	-	-	196.9	1.7	-	-	198.6	0.9	-	-	201.3	1.4	-	-	202.1	0.4	-	-	203.4	0.6	-	-

Source: U.S. Department of Labor, Bureau of Labor Statistics, Division of Consumer Prices and Price Indexes. - indicates no data collected for period.

Miami, FL

Consumer Price Index - All Urban Consumers
Base 1982-1984 = 100

Entertainment

For 1977-1995. Columns headed % show percentile change in the index from the previous period for which an index is available.

Year	Jan Index	%	Feb Index	%	Mar Index	%	Apr Index	%	May Index	%	Jun Index	%	Jul Index	%	Aug Index	%	Sep Index	%	Oct Index	%	Nov Index	%	Dec Index	%
1977	-	-	-	-	-	-	-	-	-	-	-	-	-	-	-	-	-	-	-	-	77.8	-	-	-
1978	78.2	0.5	-	-	78.0	-0.3	-	-	79.5	1.9	-	-	80.9	1.8	-	-	81.3	0.5	-	-	82.0	0.9	-	-
1979	83.2	1.5	-	-	84.4	1.4	-	-	84.9	0.6	-	-	84.8	-0.1	-	-	85.9	1.3	-	-	86.0	0.1	-	-
1980	87.3	1.5	-	-	88.1	0.9	-	-	88.3	0.2	-	-	88.7	0.5	-	-	91.6	3.3	-	-	92.3	0.8	-	-
1981	92.3	0.0	-	-	93.6	1.4	-	-	96.3	2.9	-	-	94.1	-2.3	-	-	95.6	1.6	-	-	97.8	2.3	-	-
1982	97.2	-0.6	-	-	97.5	0.3	-	-	98.1	0.6	-	-	98.3	0.2	-	-	98.7	0.4	-	-	99.9	1.2	-	-
1983	99.8	-0.1	-	-	100.7	0.9	-	-	101.0	0.3	-	-	99.4	-1.6	-	-	99.8	0.4	-	-	101.3	1.5	-	-
1984	101.2	-0.1	-	-	101.8	0.6	-	-	100.9	-0.9	-	-	101.0	0.1	-	-	100.2	-0.8	-	-	102.0	1.8	-	-
1985	102.7	0.7	-	-	103.1	0.4	-	-	104.8	1.6	-	-	104.1	-0.7	-	-	104.6	0.5	-	-	106.6	1.9	-	-
1986	107.0	0.4	-	-	108.4	1.3	-	-	106.5	-1.8	-	-	106.3	-0.2	-	-	106.8	0.5	-	-	111.2	4.1	-	-
1987	113.2	1.8	-	-	112.6	-0.5	-	-	113.2	0.5	-	-	113.5	0.3	-	-	114.4	0.8	-	-	114.9	0.4	-	-
1988	115.2	0.3	-	-	116.8	1.4	-	-	118.1	1.1	-	-	116.2	-1.6	-	-	116.8	0.5	-	-	112.0	-4.1	-	-
1989	116.0	3.6	-	-	117.0	0.9	-	-	117.6	0.5	-	-	118.0	0.3	-	-	118.5	0.4	-	-	119.0	0.4	-	-
1990	119.6	0.5	-	-	118.9	-0.6	-	-	119.3	0.3	-	-	122.3	2.5	-	-	122.1	-0.2	-	-	122.1	0.0	-	-
1991	127.3	4.3	-	-	128.8	1.2	-	-	123.1	-4.4	-	-	127.0	3.2	-	-	126.4	-0.5	-	-	126.3	-0.1	-	-
1992	126.1	-0.2	-	-	127.8	1.3	-	-	122.1	-4.5	-	-	122.4	0.2	-	-	122.4	0.0	-	-	125.6	2.6	-	-
1993	130.4	3.8	-	-	131.3	0.7	-	-	130.1	-0.9	-	-	128.2	-1.5	-	-	128.4	0.2	-	-	128.5	0.1	-	-
1994	132.1	2.8	-	-	133.9	1.4	-	-	132.9	-0.7	-	-	134.8	1.4	-	-	135.2	0.3	-	-	135.6	0.3	-	-
1995	140.5	3.6	-	-	140.1	-0.3	-	-	140.2	0.1	-	-	139.1	-0.8	-	-	141.1	1.4	-	-	141.1	0.0	-	-

Source: U.S. Department of Labor, Bureau of Labor Statistics, Division of Consumer Prices and Price Indexes. - indicates no data collected for period.

Miami, FL
Consumer Price Index - Urban Wage Earners
Base 1982-1984 = 100
Entertainment

For 1977-1995. Columns headed % show percentile change in the index from the previous period for which an index is available.

Year	Jan Index	%	Feb Index	%	Mar Index	%	Apr Index	%	May Index	%	Jun Index	%	Jul Index	%	Aug Index	%	Sep Index	%	Oct Index	%	Nov Index	%	Dec Index	%
1977	-	-	-	-	-	-	-	-	-	-	-	-	-	-	-	-	-	-	-	-	73.1	-	-	-
1978	73.6	0.7	-	-	73.8	0.3	-	-	75.0	1.6	-	-	76.4	1.9	-	-	76.7	0.4	-	-	77.9	1.6	-	-
1979	77.9	0.0	-	-	80.6	3.5	-	-	81.5	1.1	-	-	81.2	-0.4	-	-	82.3	1.4	-	-	83.1	1.0	-	-
1980	84.9	2.2	-	-	86.9	2.4	-	-	86.4	-0.6	-	-	87.2	0.9	-	-	90.6	3.9	-	-	91.1	0.6	-	-
1981	91.5	0.4	-	-	92.3	0.9	-	-	95.9	3.9	-	-	93.7	-2.3	-	-	94.9	1.3	-	-	98.1	3.4	-	-
1982	97.3	-0.8	-	-	97.7	0.4	-	-	98.4	0.7	-	-	98.5	0.1	-	-	98.7	0.2	-	-	99.9	1.2	-	-
1983	99.7	-0.2	-	-	101.0	1.3	-	-	101.3	0.3	-	-	99.4	-1.9	-	-	100.0	0.6	-	-	100.9	0.9	-	-
1984	100.9	0.0	-	-	101.9	1.0	-	-	100.8	-1.1	-	-	100.5	-0.3	-	-	100.2	-0.3	-	-	101.6	1.4	-	-
1985	102.9	1.3	-	-	103.2	0.3	-	-	105.2	1.9	-	-	104.8	-0.4	-	-	106.1	1.2	-	-	107.6	1.4	-	-
1986	107.7	0.1	-	-	108.8	1.0	-	-	107.2	-1.5	-	-	107.0	-0.2	-	-	106.7	-0.3	-	-	111.8	4.8	-	-
1987	113.8	1.8	-	-	113.2	-0.5	-	-	113.6	0.4	-	-	113.9	0.3	-	-	115.2	1.1	-	-	115.5	0.3	-	-
1988	115.9	0.3	-	-	117.4	1.3	-	-	118.2	0.7	-	-	116.7	-1.3	-	-	117.0	0.3	-	-	111.9	-4.4	-	-
1989	116.9	4.5	-	-	118.0	0.9	-	-	118.5	0.4	-	-	119.0	0.4	-	-	119.5	0.4	-	-	120.0	0.4	-	-
1990	120.6	0.5	-	-	119.8	-0.7	-	-	120.1	0.3	-	-	123.6	2.9	-	-	123.6	0.0	-	-	123.2	-0.3	-	-
1991	128.5	4.3	-	-	129.6	0.9	-	-	123.8	-4.5	-	-	128.6	3.9	-	-	127.9	-0.5	-	-	127.4	-0.4	-	-
1992	127.0	-0.3	-	-	128.7	1.3	-	-	122.9	-4.5	-	-	123.7	0.7	-	-	123.6	-0.1	-	-	126.2	2.1	-	-
1993	131.0	3.8	-	-	132.3	1.0	-	-	131.2	-0.8	-	-	128.9	-1.8	-	-	129.1	0.2	-	-	128.6	-0.4	-	-
1994	132.5	3.0	-	-	134.3	1.4	-	-	133.2	-0.8	-	-	135.8	2.0	-	-	136.1	0.2	-	-	136.6	0.4	-	-
1995	142.0	4.0	-	-	141.3	-0.5	-	-	141.5	0.1	-	-	140.3	-0.8	-	-	143.1	2.0	-	-	142.9	-0.1	-	-

Source: U.S. Department of Labor, Bureau of Labor Statistics, Division of Consumer Prices and Price Indexes. - indicates no data collected for period.

Miami, FL
Consumer Price Index - All Urban Consumers
Base 1982-1984 = 100
Other Goods and Services

For 1977-1995. Columns headed % show percentile change in the index from the previous period for which an index is available.

Year	Jan Index	%	Feb Index	%	Mar Index	%	Apr Index	%	May Index	%	Jun Index	%	Jul Index	%	Aug Index	%	Sep Index	%	Oct Index	%	Nov Index	%	Dec Index	%
1977	-	-	-	-	-	-	-	-	-	-	-	-	-	-	-	-	-	-	-	-	61.5	-	-	-
1978	61.5	0.0	-	-	62.3	1.3	-	-	63.1	1.3	-	-	63.4	0.5	-	-	65.6	3.5	-	-	65.5	-0.2	-	-
1979	65.7	0.3	-	-	66.1	0.6	-	-	67.5	2.1	-	-	68.4	1.3	-	-	72.2	5.6	-	-	72.5	0.4	-	-
1980	74.2	2.3	-	-	74.4	0.3	-	-	74.9	0.7	-	-	75.7	1.1	-	-	78.2	3.3	-	-	78.3	0.1	-	-
1981	79.6	1.7	-	-	81.3	2.1	-	-	82.0	0.9	-	-	84.1	2.6	-	-	89.5	6.4	-	-	89.3	-0.2	-	-
1982	90.0	0.8	-	-	90.3	0.3	-	-	91.4	1.2	-	-	92.0	0.7	-	-	96.1	4.5	-	-	97.0	0.9	-	-
1983	97.5	0.5	-	-	97.1	-0.4	-	-	97.3	0.2	-	-	99.4	2.2	-	-	102.7	3.3	-	-	104.2	1.5	-	-
1984	105.4	1.2	-	-	105.7	0.3	-	-	105.8	0.1	-	-	106.5	0.7	-	-	108.2	1.6	-	-	108.8	0.6	-	-
1985	109.6	0.7	-	-	111.5	1.7	-	-	112.2	0.6	-	-	112.5	0.3	-	-	116.3	3.4	-	-	116.0	-0.3	-	-
1986	117.3	1.1	-	-	119.8	2.1	-	-	120.4	0.5	-	-	120.4	0.0	-	-	125.3	4.1	-	-	125.4	0.1	-	-
1987	125.9	0.4	-	-	126.0	0.1	-	-	126.2	0.2	-	-	128.1	1.5	-	-	131.2	2.4	-	-	131.2	0.0	-	-
1988	131.3	0.1	-	-	131.8	0.4	-	-	132.0	0.2	-	-	132.0	0.0	-	-	136.5	3.4	-	-	136.7	0.1	-	-
1989	137.6	0.7	-	-	137.6	0.0	-	-	138.4	0.6	-	-	138.4	0.0	-	-	143.1	3.4	-	-	142.4	-0.5	-	-
1990	143.7	0.9	-	-	149.9	4.3	-	-	150.2	0.2	-	-	154.1	2.6	-	-	158.8	3.0	-	-	158.2	-0.4	-	-
1991	161.0	1.8	-	-	161.9	0.6	-	-	160.9	-0.6	-	-	160.5	-0.2	-	-	162.2	1.1	-	-	162.3	0.1	-	-
1992	162.1	-0.1	-	-	162.0	-0.1	-	-	158.0	-2.5	-	-	158.0	0.0	-	-	160.4	1.5	-	-	162.4	1.2	-	-
1993	162.8	0.2	-	-	162.8	0.0	-	-	163.0	0.1	-	-	163.3	0.2	-	-	162.8	-0.3	-	-	160.3	-1.5	-	-
1994	163.4	1.9	-	-	162.5	-0.6	-	-	160.0	-1.5	-	-	160.9	0.6	-	-	164.7	2.4	-	-	164.8	0.1	-	-
1995	166.5	1.0	-	-	167.4	0.5	-	-	166.9	-0.3	-	-	169.6	1.6	-	-	173.1	2.1	-	-	173.1	0.0	-	-

Source: U.S. Department of Labor, Bureau of Labor Statistics, Division of Consumer Prices and Price Indexes. - indicates no data collected for period.

Miami, FL
Consumer Price Index - Urban Wage Earners
Base 1982-1984 = 100
Other Goods and Services

For 1977-1995. Columns headed % show percentile change in the index from the previous period for which an index is available.

Year	Jan Index	%	Feb Index	%	Mar Index	%	Apr Index	%	May Index	%	Jun Index	%	Jul Index	%	Aug Index	%	Sep Index	%	Oct Index	%	Nov Index	%	Dec Index	%
1977	-		-	-	-		-	-	-		-	-	-		-	-	-		-	-	64.0	-	-	-
1978	63.9	-0.2	-	-	64.5	0.9	-	-	65.6	1.7	-	-	65.9	0.5	-	-	67.8	2.9	-	-	67.5	-0.4	-	-
1979	67.8	0.4	-	-	68.7	1.3	-	-	69.9	1.7	-	-	70.4	0.7	-	-	74.1	5.3	-	-	74.7	0.8	-	-
1980	76.0	1.7	-	-	75.9	-0.1	-	-	76.8	1.2	-	-	77.2	0.5	-	-	78.5	1.7	-	-	78.6	0.1	-	-
1981	80.2	2.0	-	-	81.3	1.4	-	-	82.1	1.0	-	-	83.1	1.2	-	-	88.4	6.4	-	-	88.9	0.6	-	-
1982	90.0	1.2	-	-	90.4	0.4	-	-	91.9	1.7	-	-	92.8	1.0	-	-	95.3	2.7	-	-	96.4	1.2	-	-
1983	97.1	0.7	-	-	97.1	0.0	-	-	97.4	0.3	-	-	100.3	3.0	-	-	101.8	1.5	-	-	104.5	2.7	-	-
1984	105.5	1.0	-	-	105.9	0.4	-	-	105.9	0.0	-	-	106.9	0.9	-	-	107.6	0.7	-	-	108.3	0.7	-	-
1985	109.4	1.0	-	-	110.4	0.9	-	-	111.3	0.8	-	-	111.6	0.3	-	-	115.2	3.2	-	-	114.9	-0.3	-	-
1986	116.3	1.2	-	-	119.2	2.5	-	-	119.7	0.4	-	-	119.9	0.2	-	-	123.9	3.3	-	-	123.7	-0.2	-	-
1987	124.4	0.6	-	-	124.6	0.2	-	-	124.9	0.2	-	-	126.5	1.3	-	-	129.4	2.3	-	-	129.4	0.0	-	-
1988	130.2	0.6	-	-	130.9	0.5	-	-	131.1	0.2	-	-	131.3	0.2	-	-	135.2	3.0	-	-	135.5	0.2	-	-
1989	136.6	0.8	-	-	136.6	0.0	-	-	137.8	0.9	-	-	137.8	0.0	-	-	142.0	3.0	-	-	141.1	-0.6	-	-
1990	142.6	1.1	-	-	147.9	3.7	-	-	148.3	0.3	-	-	153.8	3.7	-	-	156.5	1.8	-	-	155.7	-0.5	-	-
1991	159.5	2.4	-	-	160.8	0.8	-	-	159.4	-0.9	-	-	158.9	-0.3	-	-	159.7	0.5	-	-	159.8	0.1	-	-
1992	160.8	0.6	-	-	160.7	-0.1	-	-	154.6	-3.8	-	-	154.6	0.0	-	-	156.3	1.1	-	-	159.2	1.9	-	-
1993	160.1	0.6	-	-	160.1	0.0	-	-	160.3	0.1	-	-	160.4	0.1	-	-	158.9	-0.9	-	-	154.8	-2.6	-	-
1994	158.0	2.1	-	-	156.7	-0.8	-	-	154.9	-1.1	-	-	155.6	0.5	-	-	158.7	2.0	-	-	158.8	0.1	-	-
1995	160.3	0.9	-	-	161.3	0.6	-	-	160.8	-0.3	-	-	163.5	1.7	-	-	166.5	1.8	-	-	166.5	0.0	-	-

Source: U.S. Department of Labor, Bureau of Labor Statistics, Division of Consumer Prices and Price Indexes. - indicates no data collected for period.

Milwaukee, WI
Consumer Price Index - All Urban Consumers
Base 1982-1984 = 100
Annual Averages

For 1935-1995. Columns headed % show percentile change in the index from the previous period for which an index is available.

Year	All Items		Food & Beverage		Housing		Apparel & Upkeep		Trans- portation		Medical Care		Entertain- ment		Other Goods & Services	
	Index	%	Index	%	Index	%	Index	%	Index	%	Index	%	Index	%	Index	%
1935	13.4	-	-	-	-	-	-	-	-	-	-	-	-	-	-	-
1936	13.6	1.5	-	-	-	-	-	-	-	-	-	-	-	-	-	-
1937	14.2	4.4	-	-	-	-	-	-	-	-	-	-	-	-	-	-
1938	13.8	-2.8	-	-	-	-	-	-	-	-	-	-	-	-	-	-
1939	13.5	-2.2	-	-	-	-	-	-	-	-	-	-	-	-	-	-
1940	13.5	0.0	-	-	-	-	-	-	-	-	-	-	-	-	-	-
1941	14.2	5.2	-	-	-	-	-	-	-	-	-	-	-	-	-	-
1942	15.7	10.6	-	-	-	-	-	-	-	-	-	-	-	-	-	-
1943	16.6	5.7	-	-	-	-	-	-	-	-	-	-	-	-	-	-
1944	16.9	1.8	-	-	-	-	-	-	-	-	-	-	-	-	-	-
1945	17.3	2.4	-	-	-	-	-	-	-	-	-	-	-	-	-	-
1946	18.6	7.5	-	-	-	-	-	-	-	-	-	-	-	-	-	-
1947	21.7	16.7	-	-	-	-	-	-	20.3	-	12.8	-	-	-	-	-
1948	23.4	7.8	-	-	-	-	-	-	21.9	7.9	13.6	6.3	-	-	-	-
1949	23.1	-1.3	-	-	-	-	-	-	22.8	4.1	14.2	4.4	-	-	-	-
1950	23.9	3.5	-	-	-	-	-	-	23.2	1.8	14.9	4.9	-	-	-	-
1951	26.2	9.6	-	-	-	-	-	-	24.8	6.9	16.5	10.7	-	-	-	-
1952	27.0	3.1	-	-	-	-	-	-	26.2	5.6	17.3	4.8	-	-	-	-
1953	27.1	0.4	-	-	-	-	39.6	-	27.1	3.4	17.9	3.5	-	-	-	-
1954	27.1	0.0	-	-	-	-	39.5	-0.3	26.8	-1.1	19.0	6.1	-	-	-	-
1955	27.1	0.0	-	-	-	-	39.3	-0.5	26.5	-1.1	19.5	2.6	-	-	-	-
1956	27.5	1.5	-	-	-	-	40.3	2.5	27.2	2.6	19.9	2.1	-	-	-	-
1957	28.4	3.3	-	-	-	-	40.9	1.5	28.4	4.4	21.4	7.5	-	-	-	-
1958	28.8	1.4	-	-	-	-	40.9	0.0	28.9	1.8	22.1	3.3	-	-	-	-
1959	28.8	0.0	-	-	-	-	41.3	1.0	29.8	3.1	22.5	1.8	-	-	-	-
1960	29.2	1.4	-	-	-	-	41.8	1.2	29.5	-1.0	23.1	2.7	-	-	-	-
1961	29.4	0.7	-	-	-	-	42.0	0.5	29.8	1.0	23.2	0.4	-	-	-	-
1962	29.8	1.4	-	-	-	-	42.2	0.5	30.8	3.4	23.4	0.9	-	-	-	-
1963	30.1	1.0	-	-	-	-	42.2	0.0	31.0	0.6	23.9	2.1	-	-	-	-
1964	30.4	1.0	-	-	-	-	42.8	1.4	31.1	0.3	24.4	2.1	-	-	-	-
1965	31.0	2.0	-	-	-	-	43.5	1.6	32.2	3.5	25.3	3.7	-	-	-	-
1966	31.7	2.3	-	-	-	-	44.2	1.6	32.4	0.6	26.7	5.5	-	-	-	-
1967	32.4	2.2	-	-	-	-	45.8	3.6	32.9	1.5	28.8	7.9	-	-	-	-
1968	33.5	3.4	-	-	-	-	47.7	4.1	33.2	0.9	30.4	5.6	-	-	-	-
1969	35.5	6.0	-	-	-	-	51.7	8.4	35.0	5.4	32.6	7.2	-	-	-	-
1970	37.5	5.6	-	-	-	-	55.9	8.1	36.4	4.0	34.3	5.2	-	-	-	-
1971	38.9	3.7	-	-	-	-	56.9	1.8	38.5	5.8	36.3	5.8	-	-	-	-
1972	40.1	3.1	-	-	-	-	58.1	2.1	39.2	1.8	36.9	1.7	-	-	-	-
1973	42.6	6.2	-	-	-	-	60.9	4.8	41.4	5.6	38.6	4.6	-	-	-	-
1974	46.7	9.6	-	-	-	-	64.9	6.6	46.0	11.1	42.4	9.8	-	-	-	-
1975	50.8	8.8	-	-	-	-	70.0	7.9	49.9	8.5	47.1	11.1	-	-	-	-
1976	54.1	6.5	63.4	-	47.4	-	74.2	6.0	53.5	7.2	52.6	11.7	61.8	-	59.9	-
1977	57.6	6.5	66.9	5.5	50.9	7.4	77.5	4.4	57.0	6.5	57.3	8.9	68.4	10.7	63.1	5.3
1978	62.3	8.2	73.4	9.7	55.9	9.8	78.3	1.0	60.5	6.1	61.9	8.0	72.2	5.6	66.5	5.4
1979	70.8	13.6	81.6	11.2	65.2	16.6	82.2	5.0	70.5	16.5	69.3	12.0	77.9	7.9	70.5	6.0

[Continued]

Milwaukee, WI
Consumer Price Index - All Urban Consumers
Base 1982-1984 = 100
Annual Averages
[Continued]

For 1935-1995. Columns headed % show percentile change in the index from the previous period for which an index is available.

Year	All Items		Food & Beverage		Housing		Apparel & Upkeep		Trans- portation		Medical Care		Entertain- ment		Other Goods & Services	
	Index	%	Index	%	Index	%	Index	%	Index	%	Index	%	Index	%	Index	%
1980	81.4	15.0	87.2	6.9	78.2	19.9	87.5	6.4	83.2	18.0	77.9	12.4	84.4	8.3	75.7	7.4
1981	90.7	11.4	94.9	8.8	88.3	12.9	92.3	5.5	93.5	12.4	86.7	11.3	92.1	9.1	83.2	9.9
1982	95.9	5.7	98.5	3.8	94.0	6.5	96.9	5.0	98.5	5.3	93.7	8.1	95.8	4.0	92.4	11.1
1983	100.2	4.5	99.6	1.1	100.7	7.1	101.8	5.1	99.0	0.5	100.6	7.4	100.3	4.7	100.8	9.1
1984	103.8	3.6	101.9	2.3	105.1	4.4	101.3	-0.5	102.5	3.5	105.7	5.1	103.9	3.6	106.8	6.0
1985	107.0	3.1	105.7	3.7	108.5	3.2	103.4	2.1	103.9	1.4	109.3	3.4	109.6	5.5	113.1	5.9
1986	107.4	0.4	107.9	2.1	109.5	0.9	105.1	1.6	98.7	-5.0	114.6	4.8	110.3	0.6	121.6	7.5
1987	114.2	6.3	116.8	8.2	112.6	2.8	119.7	13.9	106.9	8.3	127.9	11.6	118.9	7.8	127.1	4.5
1988	119.3	4.5	121.8	4.3	116.2	3.2	130.1	8.7	111.5	4.3	134.7	5.3	122.8	3.3	138.9	9.3
1989	124.5	4.4	129.2	6.1	120.0	3.3	127.8	-1.8	116.9	4.8	145.6	8.1	128.7	4.8	149.2	7.4
1990	130.8	5.1	136.9	6.0	125.2	4.3	128.1	0.2	122.8	5.0	158.4	8.8	138.3	7.5	158.5	6.2
1991	136.4	4.3	140.6	2.7	131.0	4.6	132.9	3.7	125.5	2.2	171.9	8.5	143.8	4.0	172.8	9.0
1992	140.1	2.7	142.4	1.3	133.3	1.8	135.2	1.7	128.5	2.4	184.4	7.3	149.3	3.8	188.2	8.9
1993	143.1	2.1	144.3	1.3	135.6	1.7	135.9	0.5	129.7	0.9	198.7	7.8	152.6	2.2	198.1	5.3
1994	146.9	2.7	149.7	3.7	138.4	2.1	135.3	-0.4	132.8	2.4	218.1	9.8	154.7	1.4	199.7	0.8
1995	-	-	-	-	-	-	-	-	-	-	-	-	-	-	-	-

Source: U.S. Department of Labor, Bureau of Labor Statistics, Division of Consumer Prices and Price Indexes. - indicates no data collected for period.

Milwaukee, WI
Consumer Price Index - Urban Wage Earners
Base 1982-1984 = 100
Annual Averages

For 1935-1995. Columns headed % show percentile change in the index from the previous period for which an index is available.

Year	All Items		Food & Beverage		Housing		Apparel & Upkeep		Trans-portation		Medical Care		Entertain-ment		Other Goods & Services	
	Index	%	Index	%	Index	%	Index	%	Index	%	Index	%	Index	%	Index	%
1935	12.9	-	-	-	-	-	-	-	-	-	-	-	-	-	-	-
1936	13.2	2.3	-	-	-	-	-	-	-	-	-	-	-	-	-	-
1937	13.7	3.8	-	-	-	-	-	-	-	-	-	-	-	-	-	-
1938	13.4	-2.2	-	-	-	-	-	-	-	-	-	-	-	-	-	-
1939	13.0	-3.0	-	-	-	-	-	-	-	-	-	-	-	-	-	-
1940	13.0	0.0	-	-	-	-	-	-	-	-	-	-	-	-	-	-
1941	13.7	5.4	-	-	-	-	-	-	-	-	-	-	-	-	-	-
1942	15.1	10.2	-	-	-	-	-	-	-	-	-	-	-	-	-	-
1943	16.0	6.0	-	-	-	-	-	-	-	-	-	-	-	-	-	-
1944	16.3	1.9	-	-	-	-	-	-	-	-	-	-	-	-	-	-
1945	16.7	2.5	-	-	-	-	-	-	-	-	-	-	-	-	-	-
1946	18.0	7.8	-	-	-	-	-	-	-	-	-	-	-	-	-	-
1947	20.9	16.1	-	-	-	-	-	-	20.5	-	13.0	-	-	-	-	-
1948	22.6	8.1	-	-	-	-	-	-	22.1	7.8	13.8	6.2	-	-	-	-
1949	22.4	-0.9	-	-	-	-	-	-	23.1	4.5	14.4	4.3	-	-	-	-
1950	23.1	3.1	-	-	-	-	-	-	23.5	1.7	15.0	4.2	-	-	-	-
1951	25.3	9.5	-	-	-	-	-	-	25.1	6.8	16.6	10.7	-	-	-	-
1952	26.1	3.2	-	-	-	-	-	-	26.5	5.6	17.5	5.4	-	-	-	-
1953	26.2	0.4	-	-	-	-	40.5	-	27.4	3.4	18.1	3.4	-	-	-	-
1954	26.2	0.0	-	-	-	-	40.4	-0.2	27.1	-1.1	19.2	6.1	-	-	-	-
1955	26.2	0.0	-	-	-	-	40.2	-0.5	26.8	-1.1	19.7	2.6	-	-	-	-
1956	26.6	1.5	-	-	-	-	41.2	2.5	27.5	2.6	20.1	2.0	-	-	-	-
1957	27.5	3.4	-	-	-	-	41.8	1.5	28.7	4.4	21.6	7.5	-	-	-	-
1958	27.8	1.1	-	-	-	-	41.8	0.0	29.2	1.7	22.3	3.2	-	-	-	-
1959	27.8	0.0	-	-	-	-	42.2	1.0	30.1	3.1	22.8	2.2	-	-	-	-
1960	28.2	1.4	-	-	-	-	42.7	1.2	29.9	-0.7	23.3	2.2	-	-	-	-
1961	28.4	0.7	-	-	-	-	43.0	0.7	30.1	0.7	23.5	0.9	-	-	-	-
1962	28.8	1.4	-	-	-	-	43.1	0.2	31.1	3.3	23.7	0.9	-	-	-	-
1963	29.1	1.0	-	-	-	-	43.1	0.0	31.3	0.6	24.2	2.1	-	-	-	-
1964	29.4	1.0	-	-	-	-	43.8	1.6	31.4	0.3	24.6	1.7	-	-	-	-
1965	30.0	2.0	-	-	-	-	44.5	1.6	32.6	3.8	25.6	4.1	-	-	-	-
1966	30.7	2.3	-	-	-	-	45.2	1.6	32.8	0.6	27.0	5.5	-	-	-	-
1967	31.3	2.0	-	-	-	-	46.8	3.5	33.2	1.2	29.1	7.8	-	-	-	-
1968	32.4	3.5	-	-	-	-	48.8	4.3	33.6	1.2	30.8	5.8	-	-	-	-
1969	34.3	5.9	-	-	-	-	52.9	8.4	35.4	5.4	32.9	6.8	-	-	-	-
1970	36.2	5.5	-	-	-	-	57.2	8.1	36.8	4.0	34.7	5.5	-	-	-	-
1971	37.6	3.9	-	-	-	-	58.2	1.7	38.9	5.7	36.7	5.8	-	-	-	-
1972	38.7	2.9	-	-	-	-	59.4	2.1	39.7	2.1	37.3	1.6	-	-	-	-
1973	41.1	6.2	-	-	-	-	62.3	4.9	41.9	5.5	39.0	4.6	-	-	-	-
1974	45.1	9.7	-	-	-	-	66.3	6.4	46.5	11.0	42.9	10.0	-	-	-	-
1975	49.1	8.9	-	-	-	-	71.5	7.8	50.4	8.4	47.6	11.0	-	-	-	-
1976	52.3	6.5	61.9	-	43.7	-	75.9	6.2	54.1	7.3	53.2	11.8	64.1	-	57.4	-
1977	55.6	6.3	65.3	5.5	46.9	7.3	79.2	4.3	57.6	6.5	58.0	9.0	70.9	10.6	60.4	5.2
1978	60.5	8.8	72.0	10.3	51.8	10.4	80.2	1.3	61.3	6.4	63.6	9.7	75.4	6.3	64.9	7.5
1979	69.2	14.4	81.1	12.6	61.3	18.3	84.6	5.5	70.9	15.7	69.9	9.9	80.2	6.4	68.9	6.2

[Continued]

Milwaukee, WI
Consumer Price Index - Urban Wage Earners
Base 1982-1984 = 100
Annual Averages

[Continued]

For 1935-1995. Columns headed % show percentile change in the index from the previous period for which an index is available.

Year	All Items		Food & Beverage		Housing		Apparel & Upkeep		Trans- portation		Medical Care		Entertain- ment		Other Goods & Services	
	Index	%	Index	%	Index	%	Index	%	Index	%	Index	%	Index	%	Index	%
1980	80.2	15.9	87.8	8.3	74.7	21.9	89.8	6.1	83.3	17.5	79.1	13.2	88.5	10.3	75.1	9.0
1981	89.2	11.2	95.1	8.3	84.7	13.4	95.1	5.9	93.5	12.2	87.6	10.7	94.6	6.9	82.3	9.6
1982	93.8	5.2	98.5	3.6	89.7	5.9	97.8	2.8	98.0	4.8	93.9	7.2	95.7	1.2	92.1	11.9
1983	100.0	6.6	99.7	1.2	100.3	11.8	101.6	3.9	99.1	1.1	100.2	6.7	100.0	4.5	101.0	9.7
1984	106.2	6.2	101.9	2.2	110.0	9.7	100.6	-1.0	102.9	3.8	105.9	5.7	104.3	4.3	106.9	5.8
1985	109.4	3.0	105.6	3.6	113.3	3.0	103.0	2.4	104.5	1.6	110.0	3.9	109.9	5.4	112.9	5.6
1986	109.6	0.2	107.9	2.2	114.1	0.7	105.6	2.5	99.0	-5.3	115.5	5.0	109.7	-0.2	121.1	7.3
1987	113.8	3.8	116.6	8.1	112.5	-1.4	119.1	12.8	107.2	8.3	127.6	10.5	118.1	7.7	126.7	4.6
1988	118.9	4.5	121.7	4.4	116.0	3.1	128.9	8.2	112.3	4.8	134.1	5.1	123.0	4.1	138.1	9.0
1989	124.1	4.4	128.8	5.8	120.0	3.4	126.0	-2.2	117.7	4.8	143.9	7.3	129.2	5.0	148.2	7.3
1990	130.1	4.8	136.4	5.9	124.9	4.1	125.5	-0.4	123.6	5.0	156.1	8.5	139.0	7.6	157.2	6.1
1991	135.6	4.2	140.2	2.8	130.5	4.5	130.9	4.3	125.9	1.9	169.4	8.5	145.9	5.0	172.1	9.5
1992	139.5	2.9	142.1	1.4	132.6	1.6	135.5	3.5	129.1	2.5	181.3	7.0	151.6	3.9	189.7	10.2
1993	142.3	2.0	143.8	1.2	134.7	1.6	135.9	0.3	130.0	0.7	196.0	8.1	155.0	2.2	199.4	5.1
1994	145.9	2.5	149.1	3.7	137.7	2.2	133.5	-1.8	133.4	2.6	214.1	9.2	158.1	2.0	199.5	0.1
1995	-	-	-	-	-	-	-	-	-	-	-	-	-	-	-	-

Source: U.S. Department of Labor, Bureau of Labor Statistics, Division of Consumer Prices and Price Indexes. - indicates no data collected for period.

Milwaukee, WI
Consumer Price Index - All Urban Consumers
Base 1982-1984 = 100
All Items

For 1935-1995. Columns headed % show percentile change in the index from the previous period for which an index is available.

Year	Jan Index	%	Feb Index	%	Mar Index	%	Apr Index	%	May Index	%	Jun Index	%	Jul Index	%	Aug Index	%	Sep Index	%	Oct Index	%	Nov Index	%	Dec Index	%
1935	-	-	-	-	13.3	-	-	-	-	-	-	-	13.3	0.0	-	-	-	-	13.4	0.8	-	-	-	-
1936	13.5	0.7	-	-	-	-	13.4	-0.7	-	-	-	-	13.6	1.5	-	-	13.9	2.2	-	-	-	-	13.7	-1.4
1937	-	-	-	-	14.0	2.2	-	-	-	-	14.3	2.1	-	-	-	-	14.4	0.7	-	-	-	-	14.2	-1.4
1938	-	-	-	-	13.9	-2.1	-	-	-	-	13.9	0.0	-	-	-	-	13.7	-1.4	-	-	-	-	13.6	-0.7
1939	-	-	-	-	13.4	-1.5	-	-	-	-	13.4	0.0	-	-	-	-	13.6	1.5	-	-	-	-	13.4	-1.5
1940	-	-	-	-	13.4	0.0	-	-	-	-	13.6	1.5	-	-	-	-	13.5	-0.7	-	-	-	-	13.6	0.7
1941	-	-	-	-	13.6	0.0	-	-	-	-	14.2	4.4	-	-	-	-	14.6	2.8	-	-	-	-	15.0	2.7
1942	-	-	-	-	15.4	2.7	-	-	-	-	15.8	2.6	-	-	-	-	15.8	0.0	-	-	-	-	16.2	2.5
1943	-	-	-	-	16.5	1.9	-	-	-	-	16.8	1.8	-	-	-	-	16.6	-1.2	-	-	-	-	16.6	0.0
1944	-	-	-	-	16.6	0.0	-	-	-	-	16.9	1.8	-	-	-	-	17.0	0.6	-	-	-	-	17.0	0.0
1945	-	-	-	-	17.0	0.0	-	-	-	-	17.4	2.4	-	-	-	-	17.3	-0.6	-	-	-	-	17.4	0.6
1946	-	-	-	-	17.4	0.0	-	-	-	-	17.9	2.9	-	-	-	-	19.6	9.5	-	-	-	-	20.6	5.1
1947	-	-	-	-	21.2	2.9	-	-	-	-	21.5	1.4	-	-	21.8	1.4	-	-	-	-	22.5	3.2	-	-
1948	-	-	22.9	1.8	-	-	-	-	23.5	2.6	-	-	-	-	24.0	2.1	-	-	-	-	23.5	-2.1	-	-
1949	-	-	23.2	-1.3	-	-	-	-	23.2	0.0	-	-	-	-	23.0	-0.9	-	-	-	-	23.2	0.9	-	-
1950	-	-	23.1	-0.4	-	-	-	-	23.5	1.7	-	-	-	-	24.2	3.0	-	-	-	-	24.7	2.1	-	-
1951	-	-	25.7	4.0	-	-	-	-	26.1	1.6	-	-	-	-	26.3	0.8	-	-	-	-	26.7	1.5	-	-
1952	-	-	26.7	0.0	-	-	-	-	27.1	1.5	-	-	-	-	27.3	0.7	-	-	-	-	27.2	-0.4	27.1	-0.4
1953	-	-	26.9	-0.7	-	-	-	-	27.1	0.7	-	-	-	-	27.3	0.7	-	-	-	-	27.1	-0.7	-	-
1954	-	-	27.1	0.0	-	-	-	-	27.2	0.4	-	-	-	-	27.1	-0.4	-	-	-	-	27.1	0.0	-	-
1955	-	-	27.0	-0.4	-	-	-	-	27.0	0.0	-	-	-	-	27.1	0.4	-	-	-	-	27.2	0.4	-	-
1956	-	-	27.1	-0.4	-	-	-	-	27.3	0.7	-	-	-	-	27.7	1.5	-	-	-	-	27.8	0.4	-	-
1957	-	-	28.1	1.1	-	-	-	-	28.4	1.1	-	-	-	-	28.6	0.7	-	-	-	-	28.6	0.0	-	-
1958	-	-	28.8	0.7	-	-	-	-	28.9	0.3	-	-	-	-	28.9	0.0	-	-	-	-	28.8	-0.3	-	-
1959	-	-	28.7	-0.3	-	-	-	-	28.7	0.0	-	-	-	-	28.9	0.7	-	-	-	-	29.0	0.3	-	-
1960	-	-	28.9	-0.3	-	-	-	-	29.2	1.0	-	-	-	-	29.3	0.3	-	-	-	-	29.4	0.3	-	-
1961	-	-	29.4	0.0	-	-	-	-	29.3	-0.3	-	-	-	-	29.4	0.3	-	-	-	-	29.4	0.0	-	-
1962	-	-	29.8	1.4	-	-	-	-	29.8	0.0	-	-	-	-	29.8	0.0	-	-	-	-	29.9	0.3	-	-
1963	-	-	29.9	0.0	-	-	-	-	30.0	0.3	-	-	-	-	30.1	0.3	-	-	-	-	30.2	0.3	-	-
1964	-	-	30.2	0.0	-	-	-	-	30.3	0.3	-	-	-	-	30.5	0.7	-	-	-	-	30.6	0.3	-	-
1965	-	-	30.7	0.3	-	-	-	-	31.0	1.0	-	-	-	-	31.2	0.6	-	-	-	-	31.2	0.0	-	-
1966	-	-	31.4	0.6	-	-	-	-	31.6	0.6	-	-	-	-	32.0	1.3	-	-	-	-	32.0	0.0	-	-
1967	-	-	32.0	0.0	-	-	-	-	32.2	0.6	-	-	-	-	32.6	1.2	-	-	-	-	32.8	0.6	-	-
1968	-	-	33.0	0.6	-	-	-	-	33.3	0.9	-	-	-	-	33.7	1.2	-	-	-	-	34.0	0.9	-	-
1969	-	-	34.6	1.8	-	-	-	-	35.2	1.7	-	-	-	-	35.5	0.9	-	-	-	-	36.4	2.5	-	-
1970	-	-	36.8	1.1	-	-	-	-	37.3	1.4	-	-	-	-	37.6	0.8	-	-	-	-	38.1	1.3	-	-
1971	-	-	38.5	1.0	-	-	-	-	38.6	0.3	-	-	-	-	39.3	1.8	-	-	-	-	39.1	-0.5	-	-
1972	-	-	39.6	1.3	-	-	-	-	39.8	0.5	-	-	-	-	40.3	1.3	-	-	-	-	40.5	0.5	-	-
1973	-	-	41.1	1.5	-	-	-	-	42.1	2.4	-	-	-	-	43.1	2.4	-	-	-	-	43.9	1.9	-	-
1974	-	-	45.0	2.5	-	-	-	-	46.0	2.2	-	-	-	-	47.2	2.6	-	-	-	-	48.6	3.0	-	-
1975	-	-	49.3	1.4	-	-	-	-	50.3	2.0	-	-	-	-	51.5	2.4	-	-	-	-	52.3	1.6	-	-
1976	-	-	52.6	0.6	-	-	-	-	53.7	2.1	-	-	-	-	54.7	1.9	-	-	-	-	55.2	0.9	-	-
1977	-	-	56.2	1.8	-	-	-	-	57.6	2.5	-	-	-	-	57.9	0.5	-	-	-	-	58.8	1.6	-	-
1978	59.4	1.0	-	-	60.3	1.5	-	-	61.1	1.3	-	-	62.7	2.6	-	-	64.2	2.4	-	-	64.4	0.3	-	-
1979	64.9	0.8	-	-	67.2	3.5	-	-	70.3	4.6	-	-	72.1	2.6	-	-	73.2	1.5	-	-	74.4	1.6	-	-

[Continued]

Milwaukee, WI
Consumer Price Index - All Urban Consumers
Base 1982-1984 = 100
All Items
[Continued]

For 1935-1995. Columns headed % show percentile change in the index from the previous period for which an index is available.

Year	Jan Index	%	Feb Index	%	Mar Index	%	Apr Index	%	May Index	%	Jun Index	%	Jul Index	%	Aug Index	%	Sep Index	%	Oct Index	%	Nov Index	%	Dec Index	%
1980	76.5	2.8	-	-	78.6	2.7	-	-	81.0	3.1	-	-	81.5	0.6	-	-	83.7	2.7	-	-	84.9	1.4	-	-
1981	86.2	1.5	-	-	87.4	1.4	-	-	90.2	3.2	-	-	92.5	2.5	-	-	92.9	0.4	-	-	93.1	0.2	-	-
1982	94.3	1.3	-	-	93.7	-0.6	-	-	94.8	1.2	-	-	96.0	1.3	-	-	97.9	2.0	-	-	98.1	0.2	-	-
1983	98.7	0.6	-	-	98.7	0.0	-	-	100.0	1.3	-	-	100.3	0.3	-	-	101.6	1.3	-	-	101.2	-0.4	-	-
1984	101.7	0.5	-	-	102.6	0.9	-	-	103.8	1.2	-	-	104.0	0.2	-	-	104.9	0.9	-	-	105.0	0.1	-	-
1985	105.1	0.1	-	-	106.1	1.0	-	-	107.1	0.9	-	-	107.2	0.1	-	-	107.6	0.4	-	-	108.1	0.5	-	-
1986	108.1	0.0	-	-	106.6	-1.4	-	-	107.5	0.8	-	-	107.3	-0.2	-	-	107.8	0.5	-	-	107.1	-0.6	107.8	0.7
1987	-	-	-	-	-	-	-	-	-	-	112.8	4.6	-	-	-	-	-	-	-	-	-	-	115.6	2.5
1988	-	-	-	-	-	-	-	-	-	-	117.7	1.8	-	-	-	-	-	-	-	-	-	-	120.9	2.7
1989	-	-	-	-	-	-	-	-	-	-	123.0	1.7	-	-	-	-	-	-	-	-	-	-	126.0	2.4
1990	-	-	-	-	-	-	-	-	-	-	128.9	2.3	-	-	-	-	-	-	-	-	-	-	132.7	2.9
1991	-	-	-	-	-	-	-	-	-	-	135.1	1.8	-	-	-	-	-	-	-	-	-	-	137.6	1.9
1992	-	-	-	-	-	-	-	-	-	-	138.9	0.9	-	-	-	-	-	-	-	-	-	-	141.3	1.7
1993	-	-	-	-	-	-	-	-	-	-	142.6	0.9	-	-	-	-	-	-	-	-	-	-	143.6	0.7
1994	-	-	-	-	-	-	-	-	-	-	145.2	1.1	-	-	-	-	-	-	-	-	-	-	148.5	2.3
1995	-	-	-	-	-	-	-	-	-	-	150.0	1.0	-	-	-	-	-	-	-	-	-	-	-	-

Source: U.S. Department of Labor, Bureau of Labor Statistics, Division of Consumer Prices and Price Indexes. - indicates no data collected for period.

Milwaukee, WI
Consumer Price Index - Urban Wage Earners
Base 1982-1984 = 100
All Items

For 1935-1995. Columns headed % show percentile change in the index from the previous period for which an index is available.

Year	Jan Index	%	Feb Index	%	Mar Index	%	Apr Index	%	May Index	%	Jun Index	%	Jul Index	%	Aug Index	%	Sep Index	%	Oct Index	%	Nov Index	%	Dec Index	%
1935	-	-	-	-	12.9	-	-	-	-	-	-	-	12.9	0.0	-	-	-	-	13.0	0.8	-	-	-	-
1936	13.0	0.0	-	-	-	-	13.0	0.0	-	-	-	-	13.2	1.5	-	-	13.4	1.5	-	-	-	-	13.3	-0.7
1937	-	-	-	-	13.5	1.5	-	-	-	-	13.8	2.2	-	-	-	-	13.9	0.7	-	-	-	-	13.7	-1.4
1938	-	-	-	-	13.5	-1.5	-	-	-	-	13.5	0.0	-	-	-	-	13.2	-2.2	-	-	-	-	13.2	0.0
1939	-	-	-	-	13.0	-1.5	-	-	-	-	12.9	-0.8	-	-	-	-	13.1	1.6	-	-	-	-	13.0	-0.8
1940	-	-	-	-	13.0	0.0	-	-	-	-	13.2	1.5	-	-	-	-	13.0	-1.5	-	-	-	-	13.1	0.8
1941	-	-	-	-	13.2	0.8	-	-	-	-	13.7	3.8	-	-	-	-	14.1	2.9	-	-	-	-	14.5	2.8
1942	-	-	-	-	14.9	2.8	-	-	-	-	15.3	2.7	-	-	-	-	15.2	-0.7	-	-	-	-	15.6	2.6
1943	-	-	-	-	16.0	2.6	-	-	-	-	16.2	1.3	-	-	-	-	16.1	-0.6	-	-	-	-	16.1	0.0
1944	-	-	-	-	16.1	0.0	-	-	-	-	16.4	1.9	-	-	-	-	16.4	0.0	-	-	-	-	16.4	0.0
1945	-	-	-	-	16.4	0.0	-	-	-	-	16.8	2.4	-	-	-	-	16.7	-0.6	-	-	-	-	16.8	0.6
1946	-	-	-	-	16.8	0.0	-	-	-	-	17.3	3.0	-	-	-	-	18.9	9.2	-	-	-	-	19.9	5.3
1947	-	-	-	-	20.5	3.0	-	-	-	-	20.7	1.0	-	-	21.1	1.9	-	-	-	-	21.7	2.8	-	-
1948	-	-	22.1	1.8	-	-	-	-	22.7	2.7	-	-	-	-	23.1	1.8	-	-	-	-	22.7	-1.7	-	-
1949	-	-	22.4	-1.3	-	-	-	-	22.5	0.4	-	-	-	-	22.2	-1.3	-	-	-	-	22.4	0.9	-	-
1950	-	-	22.3	-0.4	-	-	-	-	22.7	1.8	-	-	-	-	23.4	3.1	-	-	-	-	23.8	1.7	-	-
1951	-	-	24.8	4.2	-	-	-	-	25.2	1.6	-	-	-	-	25.4	0.8	-	-	-	-	25.8	1.6	-	-
1952	-	-	25.8	0.0	-	-	-	-	26.2	1.6	-	-	-	-	26.3	0.4	-	-	-	-	26.2	-0.4	26.2	0.0
1953	-	-	26.0	-0.8	-	-	-	-	26.2	0.8	-	-	-	-	26.3	0.4	-	-	-	-	26.2	-0.4	-	-
1954	-	-	26.2	0.0	-	-	-	-	26.3	0.4	-	-	-	-	26.2	-0.4	-	-	-	-	26.2	0.0	-	-
1955	-	-	26.1	-0.4	-	-	-	-	26.1	0.0	-	-	-	-	26.2	0.4	-	-	-	-	26.3	0.4	-	-
1956	-	-	26.2	-0.4	-	-	-	-	26.3	0.4	-	-	-	-	26.7	1.5	-	-	-	-	26.9	0.7	-	-
1957	-	-	27.1	0.7	-	-	-	-	27.4	1.1	-	-	-	-	27.7	1.1	-	-	-	-	27.7	0.0	-	-
1958	-	-	27.8	0.4	-	-	-	-	27.9	0.4	-	-	-	-	27.9	0.0	-	-	-	-	27.8	-0.4	-	-
1959	-	-	27.7	-0.4	-	-	-	-	27.7	0.0	-	-	-	-	27.9	0.7	-	-	-	-	28.1	0.7	-	-
1960	-	-	27.9	-0.7	-	-	-	-	28.2	1.1	-	-	-	-	28.3	0.4	-	-	-	-	28.4	0.4	-	-
1961	-	-	28.4	0.0	-	-	-	-	28.3	-0.4	-	-	-	-	28.4	0.4	-	-	-	-	28.4	0.0	-	-
1962	-	-	28.8	1.4	-	-	-	-	28.8	0.0	-	-	-	-	28.7	-0.3	-	-	-	-	28.9	0.7	-	-
1963	-	-	28.9	0.0	-	-	-	-	29.0	0.3	-	-	-	-	29.1	0.3	-	-	-	-	29.2	0.3	-	-
1964	-	-	29.2	0.0	-	-	-	-	29.2	0.0	-	-	-	-	29.5	1.0	-	-	-	-	29.6	0.3	-	-
1965	-	-	29.7	0.3	-	-	-	-	30.0	1.0	-	-	-	-	30.2	0.7	-	-	-	-	30.1	-0.3	-	-
1966	-	-	30.3	0.7	-	-	-	-	30.5	0.7	-	-	-	-	30.9	1.3	-	-	-	-	30.9	0.0	-	-
1967	-	-	30.9	0.0	-	-	-	-	31.1	0.6	-	-	-	-	31.5	1.3	-	-	-	-	31.7	0.6	-	-
1968	-	-	31.9	0.6	-	-	-	-	32.1	0.6	-	-	-	-	32.5	1.2	-	-	-	-	32.9	1.2	-	-
1969	-	-	33.5	1.8	-	-	-	-	34.0	1.5	-	-	-	-	34.3	0.9	-	-	-	-	35.2	2.6	-	-
1970	-	-	35.6	1.1	-	-	-	-	36.0	1.1	-	-	-	-	36.3	0.8	-	-	-	-	36.8	1.4	-	-
1971	-	-	37.2	1.1	-	-	-	-	37.3	0.3	-	-	-	-	38.0	1.9	-	-	-	-	37.8	-0.5	-	-
1972	-	-	38.2	1.1	-	-	-	-	38.4	0.5	-	-	-	-	39.0	1.6	-	-	-	-	39.1	0.3	-	-
1973	-	-	39.7	1.5	-	-	-	-	40.7	2.5	-	-	-	-	41.7	2.5	-	-	-	-	42.4	1.7	-	-
1974	-	-	43.5	2.6	-	-	-	-	44.4	2.1	-	-	-	-	45.6	2.7	-	-	-	-	46.9	2.9	-	-
1975	-	-	47.6	1.5	-	-	-	-	48.6	2.1	-	-	-	-	49.8	2.5	-	-	-	-	50.5	1.4	-	-
1976	-	-	50.8	0.6	-	-	-	-	51.9	2.2	-	-	-	-	52.9	1.9	-	-	-	-	53.3	0.8	-	-
1977	-	-	54.3	1.9	-	-	-	-	55.7	2.6	-	-	-	-	55.9	0.4	-	-	-	-	56.8	1.6	-	-
1978	57.6	1.4	-	-	58.3	1.2	-	-	59.3	1.7	-	-	60.9	2.7	-	-	62.6	2.8	-	-	62.8	0.3	-	-
1979	63.1	0.5	-	-	65.5	3.8	-	-	68.7	4.9	-	-	70.4	2.5	-	-	71.5	1.6	-	-	72.7	1.7	-	-

[Continued]

Milwaukee, WI
Consumer Price Index - Urban Wage Earners
Base 1982-1984 = 100
All Items
[Continued]

For 1935-1995. Columns headed % show percentile change in the index from the previous period for which an index is available.

Year	Jan Index	%	Feb Index	%	Mar Index	%	Apr Index	%	May Index	%	Jun Index	%	Jul Index	%	Aug Index	%	Sep Index	%	Oct Index	%	Nov Index	%	Dec Index	%
1980	75.3	3.6	-	-	77.5	2.9	-	-	79.8	3.0	-	-	80.0	0.3	-	-	82.3	2.9	-	-	83.7	1.7	-	-
1981	85.1	1.7	-	-	85.9	0.9	-	-	88.7	3.3	-	-	91.1	2.7	-	-	91.4	0.3	-	-	91.2	-0.2	-	-
1982	92.4	1.3	-	-	91.5	-1.0	-	-	92.6	1.2	-	-	93.7	1.2	-	-	95.8	2.2	-	-	96.0	0.2	-	-
1983	94.9	-1.1	-	-	97.3	2.5	-	-	98.7	1.4	-	-	101.6	2.9	-	-	102.9	1.3	-	-	102.9	0.0	-	-
1984	102.4	-0.5	-	-	104.9	2.4	-	-	105.8	0.9	-	-	106.9	1.0	-	-	108.8	1.8	-	-	107.2	-1.5	-	-
1985	107.4	0.2	-	-	108.5	1.0	-	-	109.5	0.9	-	-	109.6	0.1	-	-	109.9	0.3	-	-	110.5	0.5	-	-
1986	110.4	-0.1	-	-	108.6	-1.6	-	-	109.7	1.0	-	-	109.5	-0.2	-	-	110.0	0.5	-	-	109.3	-0.6	110.0	0.6
1987	-	-	-	-	-	-	-	-	-	-	112.3	2.1	-	-	-	-	-	-	-	-	-	-	115.3	2.7
1988	-	-	-	-	-	-	-	-	-	-	117.2	1.6	-	-	-	-	-	-	-	-	-	-	120.6	2.9
1989	-	-	-	-	-	-	-	-	-	-	122.6	1.7	-	-	-	-	-	-	-	-	-	-	125.6	2.4
1990	-	-	-	-	-	-	-	-	-	-	128.2	2.1	-	-	-	-	-	-	-	-	-	-	132.0	3.0
1991	-	-	-	-	-	-	-	-	-	-	134.2	1.7	-	-	-	-	-	-	-	-	-	-	136.9	2.0
1992	-	-	-	-	-	-	-	-	-	-	138.3	1.0	-	-	-	-	-	-	-	-	-	-	140.8	1.8
1993	-	-	-	-	-	-	-	-	-	-	141.9	0.8	-	-	-	-	-	-	-	-	-	-	142.7	0.6
1994	-	-	-	-	-	-	-	-	-	-	144.3	1.1	-	-	-	-	-	-	-	-	-	-	147.6	2.3
1995	-	-	-	-	-	-	-	-	-	-	149.0	0.9	-	-	-	-	-	-	-	-	-	-	-	-

Source: U.S. Department of Labor, Bureau of Labor Statistics, Division of Consumer Prices and Price Indexes. - indicates no data collected for period.

Milwaukee, WI
Consumer Price Index - All Urban Consumers
Base 1982-1984 = 100
Food and Beverages

For 1975-1995. Columns headed % show percentile change in the index from the previous period for which an index is available.

Year	Jan Index	%	Feb Index	%	Mar Index	%	Apr Index	%	May Index	%	Jun Index	%	Jul Index	%	Aug Index	%	Sep Index	%	Oct Index	%	Nov Index	%	Dec Index	%
1975	-	-	-	-	-	-	-	-	-	-	-	-	-	-	-	-	-	-	-	-	62.1	-	-	-
1976	-	-	62.6	0.8	-	-	-	-	63.0	0.6	-	-	-	-	64.1	1.7	-	-	-	-	63.9	-0.3	-	-
1977	-	-	65.6	2.7	-	-	-	-	66.9	2.0	-	-	-	-	67.7	1.2	-	-	-	-	67.3	-0.6	-	-
1978	69.5	3.3	-	-	70.9	2.0	-	-	72.7	2.5	-	-	74.3	2.2	-	-	75.2	1.2	-	-	75.5	0.4	-	-
1979	78.0	3.3	-	-	80.3	2.9	-	-	81.7	1.7	-	-	82.1	0.5	-	-	82.3	0.2	-	-	83.7	1.7	-	-
1980	84.0	0.4	-	-	84.9	1.1	-	-	85.5	0.7	-	-	87.3	2.1	-	-	89.2	2.2	-	-	90.4	1.3	-	-
1981	91.9	1.7	-	-	94.3	2.6	-	-	94.7	0.4	-	-	95.7	1.1	-	-	95.9	0.2	-	-	95.8	-0.1	-	-
1982	96.4	0.6	-	-	97.0	0.6	-	-	98.9	2.0	-	-	99.9	1.0	-	-	99.2	-0.7	-	-	98.6	-0.6	-	-
1983	99.2	0.6	-	-	99.8	0.6	-	-	100.0	0.2	-	-	99.7	-0.3	-	-	99.6	-0.1	-	-	98.9	-0.7	-	-
1984	100.7	1.8	-	-	100.8	0.1	-	-	101.6	0.8	-	-	103.0	1.4	-	-	102.2	-0.8	-	-	102.4	0.2	-	-
1985	104.8	2.3	-	-	105.8	1.0	-	-	106.0	0.2	-	-	106.0	0.0	-	-	105.6	-0.4	-	-	105.8	0.2	-	-
1986	105.6	-0.2	-	-	106.1	0.5	-	-	107.0	0.8	-	-	108.0	0.9	-	-	109.4	1.3	-	-	110.5	1.0	110.1	-0.4
1987	-	-	-	-	-	-	-	-	-	-	115.8	5.2	-	-	-	-	-	-	-	-	-	-	117.8	1.7
1988	-	-	-	-	-	-	-	-	-	-	120.2	2.0	-	-	-	-	-	-	-	-	-	-	123.5	2.7
1989	-	-	-	-	-	-	-	-	-	-	127.6	3.3	-	-	-	-	-	-	-	-	-	-	130.7	2.4
1990	-	-	-	-	-	-	-	-	-	-	135.6	3.7	-	-	-	-	-	-	-	-	-	-	138.2	1.9
1991	-	-	-	-	-	-	-	-	-	-	140.6	1.7	-	-	-	-	-	-	-	-	-	-	140.5	-0.1
1992	-	-	-	-	-	-	-	-	-	-	142.0	1.1	-	-	-	-	-	-	-	-	-	-	142.8	0.6
1993	-	-	-	-	-	-	-	-	-	-	144.0	0.8	-	-	-	-	-	-	-	-	-	-	144.7	0.5
1994	-	-	-	-	-	-	-	-	-	-	149.0	3.0	-	-	-	-	-	-	-	-	-	-	150.3	0.9
1995	-	-	-	-	-	-	-	-	-	-	153.1	1.9	-	-	-	-	-	-	-	-	-	-	-	-

Source: U.S. Department of Labor, Bureau of Labor Statistics, Division of Consumer Prices and Price Indexes. - indicates no data collected for period.

Milwaukee, WI
Consumer Price Index - Urban Wage Earners
Base 1982-1984 = 100
Food and Beverages

For 1975-1995. Columns headed % show percentile change in the index from the previous period for which an index is available.

Year	Jan Index	%	Feb Index	%	Mar Index	%	Apr Index	%	May Index	%	Jun Index	%	Jul Index	%	Aug Index	%	Sep Index	%	Oct Index	%	Nov Index	%	Dec Index	%
1975	-	-	-	-	-	-	-	-	-	-	-	-	-	-	-	-	-	-	-	-	60.7	-	-	-
1976	-	-	61.1	0.7	-	-	-	-	61.5	0.7	-	-	-	-	62.6	1.8	-	-	-	-	62.4	-0.3	-	-
1977	-	-	64.1	2.7	-	-	-	-	65.3	1.9	-	-	-	-	66.1	1.2	-	-	-	-	65.7	-0.6	-	-
1978	67.9	3.3	-	-	69.3	2.1	-	-	71.5	3.2	-	-	72.6	1.5	-	-	73.9	1.8	-	-	74.6	0.9	-	-
1979	77.1	3.4	-	-	79.9	3.6	-	-	81.6	2.1	-	-	81.9	0.4	-	-	81.8	-0.1	-	-	82.6	1.0	-	-
1980	83.8	1.5	-	-	85.4	1.9	-	-	86.3	1.1	-	-	87.9	1.9	-	-	90.0	2.4	-	-	91.2	1.3	-	-
1981	93.1	2.1	-	-	94.5	1.5	-	-	94.3	-0.2	-	-	95.8	1.6	-	-	96.1	0.3	-	-	95.9	-0.2	-	-
1982	96.5	0.6	-	-	96.8	0.3	-	-	99.0	2.3	-	-	100.1	1.1	-	-	99.3	-0.8	-	-	98.7	-0.6	-	-
1983	99.2	0.5	-	-	99.9	0.7	-	-	100.1	0.2	-	-	99.8	-0.3	-	-	99.7	-0.1	-	-	98.9	-0.8	-	-
1984	100.6	1.7	-	-	100.6	0.0	-	-	101.5	0.9	-	-	102.9	1.4	-	-	102.2	-0.7	-	-	102.2	0.0	-	-
1985	104.7	2.4	-	-	105.8	1.1	-	-	106.0	0.2	-	-	106.0	0.0	-	-	105.5	-0.5	-	-	105.6	0.1	-	-
1986	105.6	0.0	-	-	105.9	0.3	-	-	106.9	0.9	-	-	107.9	0.9	-	-	109.4	1.4	-	-	110.4	0.9	110.1	-0.3
1987	-	-	-	-	-	-	-	-	-	-	115.5	4.9	-	-	-	-	-	-	-	-	-	-	117.7	1.9
1988	-	-	-	-	-	-	-	-	-	-	120.2	2.1	-	-	-	-	-	-	-	-	-	-	123.2	2.5
1989	-	-	-	-	-	-	-	-	-	-	127.3	3.3	-	-	-	-	-	-	-	-	-	-	130.2	2.3
1990	-	-	-	-	-	-	-	-	-	-	135.2	3.8	-	-	-	-	-	-	-	-	-	-	137.7	1.8
1991	-	-	-	-	-	-	-	-	-	-	140.2	1.8	-	-	-	-	-	-	-	-	-	-	140.2	0.0
1992	-	-	-	-	-	-	-	-	-	-	141.7	1.1	-	-	-	-	-	-	-	-	-	-	142.5	0.6
1993	-	-	-	-	-	-	-	-	-	-	143.5	0.7	-	-	-	-	-	-	-	-	-	-	144.2	0.5
1994	-	-	-	-	-	-	-	-	-	-	148.5	3.0	-	-	-	-	-	-	-	-	-	-	149.7	0.8
1995	-	-	-	-	-	-	-	-	-	-	152.3	1.7	-	-	-	-	-	-	-	-	-	-	-	-

Source: U.S. Department of Labor, Bureau of Labor Statistics, Division of Consumer Prices and Price Indexes. - indicates no data collected for period.

Milwaukee, WI
Consumer Price Index - All Urban Consumers
Base 1982-1984 = 100
Housing

For 1975-1995. Columns headed % show percentile change in the index from the previous period for which an index is available.

Year	Jan Index	%	Feb Index	%	Mar Index	%	Apr Index	%	May Index	%	Jun Index	%	Jul Index	%	Aug Index	%	Sep Index	%	Oct Index	%	Nov Index	%	Dec Index	%
1975	-	-	-	-	-	-	-	-	-	-	-	-	-	-	-	-	-	-	-	-	45.7	-	-	-
1976	-	-	46.0	0.7	-	-	-	-	47.2	2.6	-	-	-	-	47.9	1.5	-	-	-	-	48.5	1.3	-	-
1977	-	-	49.5	2.1	-	-	-	-	50.8	2.6	-	-	-	-	50.8	0.0	-	-	-	-	52.4	3.1	-	-
1978	53.1	1.3	-	-	54.0	1.7	-	-	54.3	0.6	-	-	56.6	4.2	-	-	58.5	3.4	-	-	58.0	-0.9	-	-
1979	57.6	-0.7	-	-	60.6	5.2	-	-	64.9	7.1	-	-	67.0	3.2	-	-	68.1	1.6	-	-	69.2	1.6	-	-
1980	72.5	4.8	-	-	74.5	2.8	-	-	77.9	4.6	-	-	78.3	0.5	-	-	81.0	3.4	-	-	82.3	1.6	-	-
1981	83.0	0.9	-	-	83.0	0.0	-	-	88.1	6.1	-	-	92.2	4.7	-	-	91.3	-1.0	-	-	90.2	-1.2	-	-
1982	92.8	2.9	-	-	91.0	-1.9	-	-	92.4	1.5	-	-	92.8	0.4	-	-	96.9	4.4	-	-	97.5	0.6	-	-
1983	99.2	1.7	-	-	99.4	0.2	-	-	100.6	1.2	-	-	101.7	1.1	-	-	102.1	0.4	-	-	100.8	-1.3	-	-
1984	102.3	1.5	-	-	103.9	1.6	-	-	105.5	1.5	-	-	105.1	-0.4	-	-	106.5	1.3	-	-	106.1	-0.4	-	-
1985	106.5	0.4	-	-	107.2	0.7	-	-	108.8	1.5	-	-	108.7	-0.1	-	-	109.7	0.9	-	-	109.4	-0.3	-	-
1986	110.4	0.9	-	-	109.1	-1.2	-	-	110.2	1.0	-	-	109.8	-0.4	-	-	110.2	0.4	-	-	106.7	-3.2	109.2	2.3
1987	-	-	-	-	-	-	-	-	-	-	112.0	2.6	-	-	-	-	-	-	-	-	-	-	113.2	1.1
1988	-	-	-	-	-	-	-	-	-	-	115.2	1.8	-	-	-	-	-	-	-	-	-	-	117.2	1.7
1989	-	-	-	-	-	-	-	-	-	-	118.4	1.0	-	-	-	-	-	-	-	-	-	-	121.7	2.8
1990	-	-	-	-	-	-	-	-	-	-	123.7	1.6	-	-	-	-	-	-	-	-	-	-	126.8	2.5
1991	-	-	-	-	-	-	-	-	-	-	129.5	2.1	-	-	-	-	-	-	-	-	-	-	132.6	2.4
1992	-	-	-	-	-	-	-	-	-	-	132.3	-0.2	-	-	-	-	-	-	-	-	-	-	134.3	1.5
1993	-	-	-	-	-	-	-	-	-	-	134.5	0.1	-	-	-	-	-	-	-	-	-	-	136.6	1.6
1994	-	-	-	-	-	-	-	-	-	-	137.5	0.7	-	-	-	-	-	-	-	-	-	-	139.3	1.3
1995	-	-	-	-	-	-	-	-	-	-	139.1	-0.1	-	-	-	-	-	-	-	-	-	-	-	-

Source: U.S. Department of Labor, Bureau of Labor Statistics, Division of Consumer Prices and Price Indexes. - indicates no data collected for period.

Milwaukee, WI
Consumer Price Index - Urban Wage Earners
Base 1982-1984 = 100
Housing

For 1975-1995. Columns headed % show percentile change in the index from the previous period for which an index is available.

Year	Jan Index	%	Feb Index	%	Mar Index	%	Apr Index	%	May Index	%	Jun Index	%	Jul Index	%	Aug Index	%	Sep Index	%	Oct Index	%	Nov Index	%	Dec Index	%
1975	-	-	-	-	-	-	-	-	-	-	-	-	-	-	-	-	-	-	-	-	42.1	-	-	-
1976	-	-	42.5	1.0	-	-	-	-	43.5	2.4	-	-	-	-	44.2	1.6	-	-	-	-	44.7	1.1	-	-
1977	-	-	45.7	2.2	-	-	-	-	46.9	2.6	-	-	-	-	46.9	0.0	-	-	-	-	48.4	3.2	-	-
1978	49.2	1.7	-	-	49.9	1.4	-	-	50.1	0.4	-	-	52.4	4.6	-	-	54.5	4.0	-	-	54.0	-0.9	-	-
1979	53.3	-1.3	-	-	56.5	6.0	-	-	61.1	8.1	-	-	63.1	3.3	-	-	64.1	1.6	-	-	65.5	2.2	-	-
1980	69.2	5.6	-	-	71.2	2.9	-	-	74.2	4.2	-	-	74.5	0.4	-	-	77.4	3.9	-	-	79.2	2.3	-	-
1981	79.3	0.1	-	-	78.9	-0.5	-	-	84.4	7.0	-	-	88.8	5.2	-	-	88.1	-0.8	-	-	86.4	-1.9	-	-
1982	88.9	2.9	-	-	86.6	-2.6	-	-	87.9	1.5	-	-	88.1	0.2	-	-	92.6	5.1	-	-	93.2	0.6	-	-
1983	90.9	-2.5	-	-	96.2	5.8	-	-	97.7	1.6	-	-	104.1	6.6	-	-	105.0	0.9	-	-	104.8	-0.2	-	-
1984	104.0	-0.8	-	-	108.6	4.4	-	-	109.4	0.7	-	-	111.0	1.5	-	-	114.6	3.2	-	-	110.8	-3.3	-	-
1985	111.2	0.4	-	-	112.0	0.7	-	-	113.6	1.4	-	-	113.6	0.0	-	-	114.5	0.8	-	-	114.1	-0.3	-	-
1986	115.2	1.0	-	-	113.7	-1.3	-	-	115.0	1.1	-	-	114.5	-0.4	-	-	114.8	0.3	-	-	111.0	-3.3	113.8	2.5
1987	-	-	-	-	-	-	-	-	-	-	111.8	-1.8	-	-	-	-	-	-	-	-	-	-	113.1	1.2
1988	-	-	-	-	-	-	-	-	-	-	114.9	1.6	-	-	-	-	-	-	-	-	-	-	117.1	1.9
1989	-	-	-	-	-	-	-	-	-	-	118.2	0.9	-	-	-	-	-	-	-	-	-	-	121.7	3.0
1990	-	-	-	-	-	-	-	-	-	-	123.5	1.5	-	-	-	-	-	-	-	-	-	-	126.4	2.3
1991	-	-	-	-	-	-	-	-	-	-	128.8	1.9	-	-	-	-	-	-	-	-	-	-	132.1	2.6
1992	-	-	-	-	-	-	-	-	-	-	131.7	-0.3	-	-	-	-	-	-	-	-	-	-	133.5	1.4
1993	-	-	-	-	-	-	-	-	-	-	133.4	-0.1	-	-	-	-	-	-	-	-	-	-	136.0	1.9
1994	-	-	-	-	-	-	-	-	-	-	136.8	0.6	-	-	-	-	-	-	-	-	-	-	138.7	1.4
1995	-	-	-	-	-	-	-	-	-	-	138.0	-0.5	-	-	-	-	-	-	-	-	-	-	-	-

Source: U.S. Department of Labor, Bureau of Labor Statistics, Division of Consumer Prices and Price Indexes. - indicates no data collected for period.

Milwaukee, WI
Consumer Price Index - All Urban Consumers
Base 1982-1984 = 100
Apparel and Upkeep

For 1952-1995. Columns headed % show percentile change in the index from the previous period for which an index is available.

Year	Jan Index	%	Feb Index	%	Mar Index	%	Apr Index	%	May Index	%	Jun Index	%	Jul Index	%	Aug Index	%	Sep Index	%	Oct Index	%	Nov Index	%	Dec Index	%
1952	-	-	-	-	-	-	-	-	-	-	-	-	-	-	-	-	-	-	-	-	39.4	-	-	-
1953	-	-	39.3	-0.3	-	-	-	-	39.5	0.5	-	-	-	-	39.7	0.5	-	-	-	-	39.7	0.0	-	-
1954	-	-	39.9	0.5	-	-	-	-	39.7	-0.5	-	-	-	-	39.4	-0.8	-	-	-	-	39.2	-0.5	-	-
1955	-	-	39.1	-0.3	-	-	-	-	39.2	0.3	-	-	-	-	39.3	0.3	-	-	-	-	39.7	1.0	-	-
1956	-	-	39.9	0.5	-	-	-	-	40.1	0.5	-	-	-	-	40.5	1.0	-	-	-	-	40.6	0.2	-	-
1957	-	-	40.7	0.2	-	-	-	-	40.9	0.5	-	-	-	-	41.1	0.5	-	-	-	-	41.0	-0.2	-	-
1958	-	-	41.1	0.2	-	-	-	-	40.9	-0.5	-	-	-	-	41.0	0.2	-	-	-	-	40.9	-0.2	-	-
1959	-	-	40.7	-0.5	-	-	-	-	41.3	1.5	-	-	-	-	41.4	0.2	-	-	-	-	41.6	0.5	-	-
1960	-	-	41.7	0.2	-	-	-	-	41.9	0.5	-	-	-	-	41.8	-0.2	-	-	-	-	41.8	0.0	-	-
1961	-	-	42.1	0.7	-	-	-	-	42.1	0.0	-	-	-	-	41.7	-1.0	-	-	-	-	42.2	1.2	-	-
1962	-	-	42.1	-0.2	-	-	-	-	42.3	0.5	-	-	-	-	42.2	-0.2	-	-	-	-	42.1	-0.2	-	-
1963	-	-	41.9	-0.5	-	-	-	-	42.0	0.2	-	-	-	-	42.4	1.0	-	-	-	-	42.4	0.0	-	-
1964	-	-	42.3	-0.2	-	-	-	-	42.8	1.2	-	-	-	-	43.1	0.7	-	-	-	-	43.3	0.5	-	-
1965	-	-	43.2	-0.2	-	-	-	-	43.8	1.4	-	-	-	-	43.6	-0.5	-	-	-	-	43.3	-0.7	-	-
1966	-	-	43.6	0.7	-	-	-	-	43.9	0.7	-	-	-	-	44.3	0.9	-	-	-	-	44.8	1.1	-	-
1967	-	-	45.3	1.1	-	-	-	-	46.0	1.5	-	-	-	-	45.7	-0.7	-	-	-	-	46.4	1.5	-	-
1968	-	-	46.5	0.2	-	-	-	-	47.8	2.8	-	-	-	-	48.0	0.4	-	-	-	-	48.7	1.5	-	-
1969	-	-	49.6	1.8	-	-	-	-	51.5	3.8	-	-	-	-	51.5	0.0	-	-	-	-	54.4	5.6	-	-
1970	-	-	54.6	0.4	-	-	-	-	55.5	1.6	-	-	-	-	56.2	1.3	-	-	-	-	57.5	2.3	-	-
1971	-	-	56.7	-1.4	-	-	-	-	56.7	0.0	-	-	-	-	55.8	-1.6	-	-	-	-	58.3	4.5	-	-
1972	-	-	57.2	-1.9	-	-	-	-	58.3	1.9	-	-	-	-	57.2	-1.9	-	-	-	-	59.4	3.8	-	-
1973	-	-	59.8	0.7	-	-	-	-	60.6	1.3	-	-	-	-	60.7	0.2	-	-	-	-	62.7	3.3	-	-
1974	-	-	61.6	-1.8	-	-	-	-	64.2	4.2	-	-	-	-	65.4	1.9	-	-	-	-	68.2	4.3	-	-
1975	-	-	67.7	-0.7	-	-	-	-	69.8	3.1	-	-	-	-	69.6	-0.3	-	-	-	-	72.8	4.6	-	-
1976	-	-	71.7	-1.5	-	-	-	-	74.5	3.9	-	-	-	-	74.8	0.4	-	-	-	-	75.9	1.5	-	-
1977	-	-	75.2	-0.9	-	-	-	-	77.8	3.5	-	-	-	-	77.0	-1.0	-	-	-	-	80.1	4.0	-	-
1978	75.2	-6.1	-	-	77.6	3.2	-	-	80.0	3.1	-	-	76.7	-4.1	-	-	80.1	4.4	-	-	79.6	-0.6	-	-
1979	77.2	-3.0	-	-	81.5	5.6	-	-	80.5	-1.2	-	-	81.4	1.1	-	-	85.4	4.9	-	-	85.7	0.4	-	-
1980	83.5	-2.6	-	-	89.0	6.6	-	-	86.6	-2.7	-	-	83.7	-3.3	-	-	91.3	9.1	-	-	89.3	-2.2	-	-
1981	89.1	-0.2	-	-	91.8	3.0	-	-	89.4	-2.6	-	-	89.2	-0.2	-	-	97.0	8.7	-	-	97.2	0.2	-	-
1982	89.2	-8.2	-	-	94.8	6.3	-	-	96.4	1.7	-	-	96.9	0.5	-	-	102.2	5.5	-	-	100.1	-2.1	-	-
1983	95.6	-4.5	-	-	100.5	5.1	-	-	101.5	1.0	-	-	97.3	-4.1	-	-	108.2	11.2	-	-	107.4	-0.7	-	-
1984	98.8	-8.0	-	-	101.3	2.5	-	-	101.3	0.0	-	-	100.5	-0.8	-	-	102.4	1.9	-	-	103.5	1.1	-	-
1985	98.6	-4.7	-	-	103.6	5.1	-	-	102.5	-1.1	-	-	102.1	-0.4	-	-	106.0	3.8	-	-	106.5	0.5	-	-
1986	102.9	-3.4	-	-	107.3	4.3	-	-	106.3	-0.9	-	-	104.6	-1.6	-	-	105.3	0.7	-	-	105.0	-0.3	103.0	-1.9
1987	-	-	-	-	-	-	-	-	-	-	117.0	13.6	-	-	-	-	-	-	-	-	-	-	122.5	4.7
1988	-	-	-	-	-	-	-	-	-	-	124.6	1.7	-	-	-	-	-	-	-	-	-	-	135.6	8.8
1989	-	-	-	-	-	-	-	-	-	-	130.0	-4.1	-	-	-	-	-	-	-	-	-	-	125.6	-3.4
1990	-	-	-	-	-	-	-	-	-	-	126.9	1.0	-	-	-	-	-	-	-	-	-	-	129.3	1.9
1991	-	-	-	-	-	-	-	-	-	-	133.1	2.9	-	-	-	-	-	-	-	-	-	-	132.6	-0.4
1992	-	-	-	-	-	-	-	-	-	-	137.4	3.6	-	-	-	-	-	-	-	-	-	-	133.1	-3.1
1993	-	-	-	-	-	-	-	-	-	-	137.9	3.6	-	-	-	-	-	-	-	-	-	-	133.9	-2.9
1994	-	-	-	-	-	-	-	-	-	-	134.0	0.1	-	-	-	-	-	-	-	-	-	-	136.6	1.9
1995	-	-	-	-	-	-	-	-	-	-	135.9	-0.5	-	-	-	-	-	-	-	-	-	-	-	-

Source: U.S. Department of Labor, Bureau of Labor Statistics, Division of Consumer Prices and Price Indexes. - indicates no data collected for period.

Milwaukee, WI
Consumer Price Index - Urban Wage Earners
Base 1982-1984 = 100
Apparel and Upkeep

For 1952-1995. Columns headed % show percentile change in the index from the previous period for which an index is available.

Year	Jan Index	%	Feb Index	%	Mar Index	%	Apr Index	%	May Index	%	Jun Index	%	Jul Index	%	Aug Index	%	Sep Index	%	Oct Index	%	Nov Index	%	Dec Index	%
1952	-	-	-	-	-	-	-	-	-	-	-	-	-	-	-	-	-	-	-	-	40.3	-	-	-
1953	-	-	40.2	-0.2	-	-	-	-	40.4	0.5	-	-	-	-	40.6	0.5	-	-	-	-	40.6	0.0	-	-
1954	-	-	40.8	0.5	-	-	-	-	40.6	-0.5	-	-	-	-	40.3	-0.7	-	-	-	-	40.1	-0.5	-	-
1955	-	-	40.0	-0.2	-	-	-	-	40.1	0.2	-	-	-	-	40.1	0.0	-	-	-	-	40.6	1.2	-	-
1956	-	-	40.8	0.5	-	-	-	-	41.0	0.5	-	-	-	-	41.4	1.0	-	-	-	-	41.5	0.2	-	-
1957	-	-	41.6	0.2	-	-	-	-	41.8	0.5	-	-	-	-	42.0	0.5	-	-	-	-	41.9	-0.2	-	-
1958	-	-	42.0	0.2	-	-	-	-	41.8	-0.5	-	-	-	-	41.9	0.2	-	-	-	-	41.8	-0.2	-	-
1959	-	-	41.6	-0.5	-	-	-	-	42.3	1.7	-	-	-	-	42.3	0.0	-	-	-	-	42.5	0.5	-	-
1960	-	-	42.6	0.2	-	-	-	-	42.8	0.5	-	-	-	-	42.7	-0.2	-	-	-	-	42.7	0.0	-	-
1961	-	-	43.0	0.7	-	-	-	-	43.0	0.0	-	-	-	-	42.7	-0.7	-	-	-	-	43.1	0.9	-	-
1962	-	-	43.1	0.0	-	-	-	-	43.2	0.2	-	-	-	-	43.1	-0.2	-	-	-	-	43.0	-0.2	-	-
1963	-	-	42.8	-0.5	-	-	-	-	42.9	0.2	-	-	-	-	43.4	1.2	-	-	-	-	43.4	0.0	-	-
1964	-	-	43.3	-0.2	-	-	-	-	43.8	1.2	-	-	-	-	44.0	0.5	-	-	-	-	44.2	0.5	-	-
1965	-	-	44.2	0.0	-	-	-	-	44.8	1.4	-	-	-	-	44.6	-0.4	-	-	-	-	44.3	-0.7	-	-
1966	-	-	44.6	0.7	-	-	-	-	44.9	0.7	-	-	-	-	45.3	0.9	-	-	-	-	45.8	1.1	-	-
1967	-	-	46.3	1.1	-	-	-	-	47.0	1.5	-	-	-	-	46.7	-0.6	-	-	-	-	47.4	1.5	-	-
1968	-	-	47.5	0.2	-	-	-	-	48.9	2.9	-	-	-	-	49.0	0.2	-	-	-	-	49.8	1.6	-	-
1969	-	-	50.7	1.8	-	-	-	-	52.6	3.7	-	-	-	-	52.7	0.2	-	-	-	-	55.6	5.5	-	-
1970	-	-	55.8	0.4	-	-	-	-	56.7	1.6	-	-	-	-	57.5	1.4	-	-	-	-	58.8	2.3	-	-
1971	-	-	58.0	-1.4	-	-	-	-	58.0	0.0	-	-	-	-	57.1	-1.6	-	-	-	-	59.6	4.4	-	-
1972	-	-	58.5	-1.8	-	-	-	-	59.6	1.9	-	-	-	-	58.5	-1.8	-	-	-	-	60.8	3.9	-	-
1973	-	-	61.1	0.5	-	-	-	-	62.0	1.5	-	-	-	-	62.1	0.2	-	-	-	-	64.1	3.2	-	-
1974	-	-	63.0	-1.7	-	-	-	-	65.6	4.1	-	-	-	-	66.8	1.8	-	-	-	-	69.7	4.3	-	-
1975	-	-	69.2	-0.7	-	-	-	-	71.3	3.0	-	-	-	-	71.2	-0.1	-	-	-	-	74.4	4.5	-	-
1976	-	-	73.4	-1.3	-	-	-	-	76.2	3.8	-	-	-	-	76.5	0.4	-	-	-	-	77.6	1.4	-	-
1977	-	-	76.9	-0.9	-	-	-	-	79.6	3.5	-	-	-	-	78.7	-1.1	-	-	-	-	81.9	4.1	-	-
1978	76.3	-6.8	-	-	78.0	2.2	-	-	80.1	2.7	-	-	78.3	-2.2	-	-	83.6	6.8	-	-	83.7	0.1	-	-
1979	80.2	-4.2	-	-	83.4	4.0	-	-	82.4	-1.2	-	-	82.8	0.5	-	-	88.0	6.3	-	-	89.0	1.1	-	-
1980	87.1	-2.1	-	-	90.2	3.6	-	-	89.6	-0.7	-	-	87.1	-2.8	-	-	93.1	6.9	-	-	90.3	-3.0	-	-
1981	93.4	3.4	-	-	94.9	1.6	-	-	93.4	-1.6	-	-	94.7	1.4	-	-	97.2	2.6	-	-	97.6	0.4	-	-
1982	90.3	-7.5	-	-	96.4	6.8	-	-	97.4	1.0	-	-	97.9	0.5	-	-	102.9	5.1	-	-	100.4	-2.4	-	-
1983	96.3	-4.1	-	-	101.3	5.2	-	-	101.1	-0.2	-	-	96.9	-4.2	-	-	107.2	10.6	-	-	106.4	-0.7	-	-
1984	98.8	-7.1	-	-	101.0	2.2	-	-	101.0	0.0	-	-	99.2	-1.8	-	-	101.4	2.2	-	-	102.2	0.8	-	-
1985	98.8	-3.3	-	-	103.1	4.4	-	-	102.0	-1.1	-	-	101.4	-0.6	-	-	104.8	3.4	-	-	106.7	1.8	-	-
1986	103.2	-3.3	-	-	106.7	3.4	-	-	107.0	0.3	-	-	105.6	-1.3	-	-	105.6	0.0	-	-	105.8	0.2	104.1	-1.6
1987	-	-	-	-	-	-	-	-	-	-	116.6	12.0	-	-	-	-	-	-	-	-	-	-	121.6	4.3
1988	-	-	-	-	-	-	-	-	-	-	122.9	1.1	-	-	-	-	-	-	-	-	-	-	134.9	9.8
1989	-	-	-	-	-	-	-	-	-	-	128.1	-5.0	-	-	-	-	-	-	-	-	-	-	123.8	-3.4
1990	-	-	-	-	-	-	-	-	-	-	124.5	0.6	-	-	-	-	-	-	-	-	-	-	126.5	1.6
1991	-	-	-	-	-	-	-	-	-	-	130.4	3.1	-	-	-	-	-	-	-	-	-	-	131.3	0.7
1992	-	-	-	-	-	-	-	-	-	-	136.9	4.3	-	-	-	-	-	-	-	-	-	-	134.1	-2.0
1993	-	-	-	-	-	-	-	-	-	-	138.4	3.2	-	-	-	-	-	-	-	-	-	-	133.4	-3.6
1994	-	-	-	-	-	-	-	-	-	-	132.3	-0.8	-	-	-	-	-	-	-	-	-	-	134.7	1.8
1995	-	-	-	-	-	-	-	-	-	-	133.3	-1.0	-	-	-	-	-	-	-	-	-	-	-	-

Source: U.S. Department of Labor, Bureau of Labor Statistics, Division of Consumer Prices and Price Indexes. - indicates no data collected for period.

Milwaukee, WI
Consumer Price Index - All Urban Consumers
Base 1982-1984 = 100
Transportation

For 1946-1995. Columns headed % show percentile change in the index from the previous period for which an index is available.

Year	Jan Index	%	Feb Index	%	Mar Index	%	Apr Index	%	May Index	%	Jun Index	%	Jul Index	%	Aug Index	%	Sep Index	%	Oct Index	%	Nov Index	%	Dec Index	%
1946	-	-	-	-	-	-	-	-	-	-	20.0	-	-	-	-	-	-	-	-	-	19.9	-	-	-
1947	-	-	-	-	20.0	0.5	-	-	-	-	20.0	0.0	-	-	20.2	1.0	-	-	-	-	20.8	3.0	-	-
1948	-	-	21.2	1.9	-	-	-	-	21.3	0.5	-	-	-	-	22.6	6.1	-	-	-	-	22.7	0.4	-	-
1949	-	-	23.0	1.3	-	-	-	-	23.1	0.4	-	-	-	-	22.9	-0.9	-	-	-	-	22.3	-2.6	-	-
1950	-	-	22.0	-1.3	-	-	-	-	23.2	5.5	-	-	-	-	23.8	2.6	-	-	-	-	23.8	0.0	-	-
1951	-	-	23.9	0.4	-	-	-	-	24.8	3.8	-	-	-	-	24.8	0.0	-	-	-	-	25.6	3.2	-	-
1952	-	-	26.1	2.0	-	-	-	-	26.2	0.4	-	-	-	-	26.2	0.0	-	-	-	-	27.0	3.1	-	-
1953	-	-	27.0	0.0	-	-	-	-	27.0	0.0	-	-	-	-	27.3	1.1	-	-	-	-	27.1	-0.7	-	-
1954	-	-	26.8	-1.1	-	-	-	-	26.8	0.0	-	-	-	-	26.4	-1.5	-	-	-	-	27.2	3.0	-	-
1955	-	-	26.5	-2.6	-	-	-	-	26.4	-0.4	-	-	-	-	26.3	-0.4	-	-	-	-	26.9	2.3	-	-
1956	-	-	26.7	-0.7	-	-	-	-	26.6	-0.4	-	-	-	-	27.3	2.6	-	-	-	-	28.1	2.9	-	-
1957	-	-	28.2	0.4	-	-	-	-	28.2	0.0	-	-	-	-	28.3	0.4	-	-	-	-	28.8	1.8	-	-
1958	-	-	28.5	-1.0	-	-	-	-	28.4	-0.4	-	-	-	-	29.2	2.8	-	-	-	-	29.3	0.3	-	-
1959	-	-	29.4	0.3	-	-	-	-	29.5	0.3	-	-	-	-	29.9	1.4	-	-	-	-	30.5	2.0	-	-
1960	-	-	29.2	-4.3	-	-	-	-	29.5	1.0	-	-	-	-	29.8	1.0	-	-	-	-	29.5	-1.0	-	-
1961	-	-	29.9	1.4	-	-	-	-	29.0	-3.0	-	-	-	-	30.1	3.8	-	-	-	-	29.9	-0.7	-	-
1962	-	-	30.5	2.0	-	-	-	-	31.0	1.6	-	-	-	-	30.3	-2.3	-	-	-	-	31.2	3.0	-	-
1963	-	-	30.5	-2.2	-	-	-	-	31.1	2.0	-	-	-	-	30.8	-1.0	-	-	-	-	31.5	2.3	-	-
1964	-	-	30.9	-1.9	-	-	-	-	30.5	-1.3	-	-	-	-	31.3	2.6	-	-	-	-	31.7	1.3	-	-
1965	-	-	32.1	1.3	-	-	-	-	32.6	1.6	-	-	-	-	32.1	-1.5	-	-	-	-	32.1	0.0	-	-
1966	-	-	32.3	0.6	-	-	-	-	32.0	-0.9	-	-	-	-	32.8	2.5	-	-	-	-	32.7	-0.3	-	-
1967	-	-	32.5	-0.6	-	-	-	-	32.7	0.6	-	-	-	-	32.8	0.3	-	-	-	-	33.7	2.7	-	-
1968	-	-	33.6	-0.3	-	-	-	-	32.8	-2.4	-	-	-	-	32.9	0.3	-	-	-	-	33.6	2.1	-	-
1969	-	-	35.0	4.2	-	-	-	-	34.8	-0.6	-	-	-	-	34.5	-0.9	-	-	-	-	35.8	3.8	-	-
1970	-	-	34.9	-2.5	-	-	-	-	36.6	4.9	-	-	-	-	36.1	-1.4	-	-	-	-	37.8	4.7	-	-
1971	-	-	38.9	2.9	-	-	-	-	37.8	-2.8	-	-	-	-	39.3	4.0	-	-	-	-	38.1	-3.1	-	-
1972	-	-	37.9	-0.5	-	-	-	-	38.6	1.8	-	-	-	-	40.3	4.4	-	-	-	-	40.0	-0.7	-	-
1973	-	-	40.2	0.5	-	-	-	-	41.6	3.5	-	-	-	-	41.5	-0.2	-	-	-	-	42.2	1.7	-	-
1974	-	-	43.4	2.8	-	-	-	-	45.7	5.3	-	-	-	-	47.4	3.7	-	-	-	-	47.8	0.8	-	-
1975	-	-	48.3	1.0	-	-	-	-	49.2	1.9	-	-	-	-	50.9	3.5	-	-	-	-	51.1	0.4	-	-
1976	-	-	51.1	0.0	-	-	-	-	52.4	2.5	-	-	-	-	55.0	5.0	-	-	-	-	55.4	0.7	-	-
1977	-	-	55.7	0.5	-	-	-	-	57.3	2.9	-	-	-	-	57.5	0.3	-	-	-	-	57.7	0.3	-	-
1978	57.9	0.3	-	-	58.2	0.5	-	-	59.1	1.5	-	-	61.1	3.4	-	-	61.7	1.0	-	-	63.5	2.9	-	-
1979	64.4	1.4	-	-	65.5	1.7	-	-	69.1	5.5	-	-	72.5	4.9	-	-	73.3	1.1	-	-	75.0	2.3	-	-
1980	77.4	3.2	-	-	80.7	4.3	-	-	84.5	4.7	-	-	84.0	-0.6	-	-	83.9	-0.1	-	-	86.1	2.6	-	-
1981	88.9	3.3	-	-	90.6	1.9	-	-	92.5	2.1	-	-	93.7	1.3	-	-	95.0	1.4	-	-	98.1	3.3	-	-
1982	98.2	0.1	-	-	97.2	-1.0	-	-	96.8	-0.4	-	-	100.6	3.9	-	-	99.1	-1.5	-	-	98.9	-0.2	-	-
1983	98.1	-0.8	-	-	95.9	-2.2	-	-	98.3	2.5	-	-	99.0	0.7	-	-	100.8	1.8	-	-	101.3	0.5	-	-
1984	100.8	-0.5	-	-	101.3	0.5	-	-	102.8	1.5	-	-	102.7	-0.1	-	-	103.3	0.6	-	-	103.9	0.6	-	-
1985	102.1	-1.7	-	-	103.0	0.9	-	-	104.7	1.7	-	-	104.6	-0.1	-	-	103.4	-1.1	-	-	105.1	1.6	-	-
1986	104.2	-0.9	-	-	97.5	-6.4	-	-	98.8	1.3	-	-	97.7	-1.1	-	-	97.1	-0.6	-	-	98.7	1.6	98.2	-0.5
1987	-	-	-	-	-	-	-	-	-	-	105.0	6.9	-	-	-	-	-	-	-	-	-	-	108.8	3.6
1988	-	-	-	-	-	-	-	-	-	-	110.2	1.3	-	-	-	-	-	-	-	-	-	-	112.8	2.4
1989	-	-	-	-	-	-	-	-	-	-	115.9	2.7	-	-	-	-	-	-	-	-	-	-	118.0	1.8
1990	-	-	-	-	-	-	-	-	-	-	120.1	1.8	-	-	-	-	-	-	-	-	-	-	125.6	4.6

[Continued]

Milwaukee, WI
Consumer Price Index - All Urban Consumers
Base 1982-1984 = 100
Transportation

[Continued]

For 1946-1995. Columns headed % show percentile change in the index from the previous period for which an index is available.

Year	Jan		Feb		Mar		Apr		May		Jun		Jul		Aug		Sep		Oct		Nov		Dec	
	Index	%	Index	%	Index	%	Index	%	Index	%	Index	%	Index	%	Index	%	Index	%	Index	%	Index	%	Index	%
1991	-	-	-	-	-	-	-	-	-	-	124.9	-0.6	-	-	-	-	-	-	-	-	-	-	126.1	1.0
1992	-	-	-	-	-	-	-	-	-	-	127.3	1.0	-	-	-	-	-	-	-	-	-	-	129.7	1.9
1993	-	-	-	-	-	-	-	-	-	-	129.6	-0.1	-	-	-	-	-	-	-	-	-	-	129.7	0.1
1994	-	-	-	-	-	-	-	-	-	-	130.1	0.3	-	-	-	-	-	-	-	-	-	-	135.5	4.2
1995	-	-	-	-	-	-	-	-	-	-	138.7	2.4	-	-	-	-	-	-	-	-	-	-	-	-

Source: U.S. Department of Labor, Bureau of Labor Statistics, Division of Consumer Prices and Price Indexes. - indicates no data collected for period.

Milwaukee, WI
Consumer Price Index - Urban Wage Earners
Base 1982-1984 = 100
Transportation

For 1946-1995. Columns headed % show percentile change in the index from the previous period for which an index is available.

Year	Jan Index	%	Feb Index	%	Mar Index	%	Apr Index	%	May Index	%	Jun Index	%	Jul Index	%	Aug Index	%	Sep Index	%	Oct Index	%	Nov Index	%	Dec Index	%
1946	-		-		-				-		-		-		-		-		-		20.1		-	
1947	-		-		20.2	0.5	-		-		20.2	0.0	-		20.4	1.0	-		-		21.1	3.4	-	
1948	-		21.5	1.9	-		-		21.5	0.0	-		-		22.8	6.0	-		-		22.9	0.4	-	
1949	-		23.2	1.3	-		-		23.3	0.4	-		-		23.2	-0.4	-		-		22.6	-2.6	-	
1950	-		22.2	-1.8	-		-		23.4	5.4	-		-		24.1	3.0	-		-		24.1	0.0	-	
1951	-		24.1	0.0	-		-		25.0	3.7	-		-		25.1	0.4	-		-		25.9	3.2	-	
1952	-		26.4	1.9	-		-		26.5	0.4	-		-		26.5	0.0	-		-		27.3	3.0	-	
1953	-		27.3	0.0	-		-		27.3	0.0	-		-		27.6	1.1	-		-		27.4	-0.7	-	
1954	-		27.1	-1.1	-		-		27.1	0.0	-		-		26.7	-1.5	-		-		27.5	3.0	-	
1955	-		26.8	-2.5	-		-		26.7	-0.4	-		-		26.6	-0.4	-		-		27.2	2.3	-	
1956	-		27.0	-0.7	-		-		26.9	-0.4	-		-		27.6	2.6	-		-		28.4	2.9	-	
1957	-		28.6	0.7	-		-		28.6	0.0	-		-		28.7	0.3	-		-		29.1	1.4	-	
1958	-		28.9	-0.7	-		-		28.7	-0.7	-		-		29.5	2.8	-		-		29.6	0.3	-	
1959	-		29.7	0.3	-		-		29.8	0.3	-		-		30.3	1.7	-		-		30.8	1.7	-	
1960	-		29.6	-3.9	-		-		29.8	0.7	-		-		30.1	1.0	-		-		29.9	-0.7	-	
1961	-		30.2	1.0	-		-		29.4	-2.6	-		-		30.4	3.4	-		-		30.2	-0.7	-	
1962	-		30.9	2.3	-		-		31.4	1.6	-		-		30.7	-2.2	-		-		31.6	2.9	-	
1963	-		30.8	-2.5	-		-		31.4	1.9	-		-		31.1	-1.0	-		-		31.8	2.3	-	
1964	-		31.3	-1.6	-		-		30.8	-1.6	-		-		31.6	2.6	-		-		32.0	1.3	-	
1965	-		32.4	1.3	-		-		32.9	1.5	-		-		32.5	-1.2	-		-		32.5	0.0	-	
1966	-		32.6	0.3	-		-		32.3	-0.9	-		-		33.1	2.5	-		-		33.1	0.0	-	
1967	-		32.8	-0.9	-		-		33.0	0.6	-		-		33.1	0.3	-		-		34.0	2.7	-	
1968	-		34.0	0.0	-		-		33.2	-2.4	-		-		33.3	0.3	-		-		33.9	1.8	-	
1969	-		35.4	4.4	-		-		35.2	-0.6	-		-		34.9	-0.9	-		-		36.2	3.7	-	
1970	-		35.2	-2.8	-		-		37.0	5.1	-		-		36.5	-1.4	-		-		38.2	4.7	-	
1971	-		39.3	2.9	-		-		38.3	-2.5	-		-		39.8	3.9	-		-		38.5	-3.3	-	
1972	-		38.4	-0.3	-		-		39.0	1.6	-		-		40.7	4.4	-		-		40.4	-0.7	-	
1973	-		40.7	0.7	-		-		42.1	3.4	-		-		42.0	-0.2	-		-		42.7	1.7	-	
1974	-		43.9	2.8	-		-		46.2	5.2	-		-		47.9	3.7	-		-		48.3	0.8	-	
1975	-		48.8	1.0	-		-		49.7	1.8	-		-		51.4	3.4	-		-		51.7	0.6	-	
1976	-		51.6	-0.2	-		-		53.0	2.7	-		-		55.6	4.9	-		-		56.0	0.7	-	
1977	-		56.3	0.5	-		-		57.9	2.8	-		-		58.1	0.3	-		-		58.3	0.3	-	
1978	58.6	0.5	-		58.9	0.5	-		60.2	2.2	-		62.1	3.2	-		62.7	1.0	-		63.7	1.6	-	
1979	64.6	1.4	-		66.2	2.5	-		69.1	4.4	-		72.4	4.8	-		74.1	2.3	-		75.6	2.0	-	
1980	78.1	3.3	-		81.1	3.8	-		84.3	3.9	-		83.6	-0.8	-		84.0	0.5	-		86.3	2.7	-	
1981	88.9	3.0	-		91.1	2.5	-		92.7	1.8	-		93.6	1.0	-		94.9	1.4	-		97.7	3.0	-	
1982	97.6	-0.1	-		96.6	-1.0	-		96.2	-0.4	-		100.2	4.2	-		98.9	-1.3	-		98.8	-0.1	-	
1983	97.9	-0.9	-		95.7	-2.2	-		98.4	2.8	-		99.2	0.8	-		101.0	1.8	-		101.6	0.6	-	
1984	101.0	-0.6	-		101.6	0.6	-		103.2	1.6	-		103.0	-0.2	-		103.7	0.7	-		104.3	0.6	-	
1985	102.5	-1.7	-		103.5	1.0	-		105.3	1.7	-		105.2	-0.1	-		104.0	-1.1	-		105.7	1.6	-	
1986	104.8	-0.9	-		97.7	-6.8	-		99.2	1.5	-		97.9	-1.3	-		97.6	-0.3	-		98.8	1.2	98.4	-0.4
1987	-		-		-		-		-		105.0	6.7	-		-		-		-		-		109.5	4.3
1988	-		-		-		-		-		111.0	1.4	-		-		-		-		-		113.6	2.3
1989	-		-		-		-		-		116.6	2.6	-		-		-		-		-		118.9	2.0
1990	-		-		-		-		-		120.8	1.6	-		-		-		-		-		126.5	4.7

[Continued]

Milwaukee, WI
Consumer Price Index - Urban Wage Earners
Base 1982-1984 = 100
Transportation
[Continued]

For 1946-1995. Columns headed % show percentile change in the index from the previous period for which an index is available.

Year	Jan		Feb		Mar		Apr		May		Jun		Jul		Aug		Sep		Oct		Nov		Dec	
	Index	%	Index	%	Index	%	Index	%	Index	%	Index	%	Index	%	Index	%	Index	%	Index	%	Index	%	Index	%
1991	-	-	-	-	-	-	-	-	-	-	125.2	-1.0	-	-	-	-	-	-	-	-	-	-	126.6	1.1
1992	-	-	-	-	-	-	-	-	-	-	127.6	0.8	-	-	-	-	-	-	-	-	-	-	130.7	2.4
1993	-	-	-	-	-	-	-	-	-	-	130.0	-0.5	-	-	-	-	-	-	-	-	-	-	130.0	0.0
1994	-	-	-	-	-	-	-	-	-	-	130.5	0.4	-	-	-	-	-	-	-	-	-	-	136.3	4.4
1995	-	-	-	-	-	-	-	-	-	-	139.8	2.6	-	-	-	-	-	-	-	-	-	-	-	-

Source: U.S. Department of Labor, Bureau of Labor Statistics, Division of Consumer Prices and Price Indexes. - indicates no data collected for period.

Milwaukee, WI
Consumer Price Index - All Urban Consumers
Base 1982-1984 = 100
Medical Care

For 1946-1995. Columns headed % show percentile change in the index from the previous period for which an index is available.

Year	Jan Index	%	Feb Index	%	Mar Index	%	Apr Index	%	May Index	%	Jun Index	%	Jul Index	%	Aug Index	%	Sep Index	%	Oct Index	%	Nov Index	%	Dec Index	%
1946	-	-	-	-	-	-	-	-	-	-	-	-	-	-	-	-	-	-	-	-	-	-	12.3	-
1947	-	-	-	-	12.7	3.3	-	-	-	-	12.8	0.8	-	-	12.9	0.8	-	-	-	-	13.0	0.8	-	-
1948	-	-	13.3	2.3	-	-	-	-	13.4	0.8	-	-	-	-	13.6	1.5	-	-	-	-	14.1	3.7	-	-
1949	-	-	14.2	0.7	-	-	-	-	14.2	0.0	-	-	-	-	14.3	0.7	-	-	-	-	14.3	0.0	-	-
1950	-	-	14.4	0.7	-	-	-	-	14.5	0.7	-	-	-	-	15.1	4.1	-	-	-	-	15.6	3.3	-	-
1951	-	-	15.7	0.6	-	-	-	-	16.4	4.5	-	-	-	-	16.8	2.4	-	-	-	-	17.0	1.2	-	-
1952	-	-	17.1	0.6	-	-	-	-	17.3	1.2	-	-	-	-	17.5	1.2	-	-	-	-	17.5	0.0	-	-
1953	-	-	17.7	1.1	-	-	-	-	17.8	0.6	-	-	-	-	18.1	1.7	-	-	-	-	18.2	0.6	-	-
1954	-	-	18.3	0.5	-	-	-	-	19.2	4.9	-	-	-	-	19.2	0.0	-	-	-	-	19.3	0.5	-	-
1955	-	-	19.3	0.0	-	-	-	-	19.4	0.5	-	-	-	-	19.8	2.1	-	-	-	-	19.6	-1.0	-	-
1956	-	-	19.7	0.5	-	-	-	-	19.9	1.0	-	-	-	-	19.9	0.0	-	-	-	-	20.0	0.5	-	-
1957	-	-	20.4	2.0	-	-	-	-	21.6	5.9	-	-	-	-	21.6	0.0	-	-	-	-	21.9	1.4	-	-
1958	-	-	22.0	0.5	-	-	-	-	22.1	0.5	-	-	-	-	22.1	0.0	-	-	-	-	22.1	0.0	-	-
1959	-	-	22.2	0.5	-	-	-	-	22.2	0.0	-	-	-	-	22.8	2.7	-	-	-	-	23.0	0.9	-	-
1960	-	-	23.0	0.0	-	-	-	-	23.0	0.0	-	-	-	-	23.1	0.4	-	-	-	-	23.1	0.0	-	-
1961	-	-	23.1	0.0	-	-	-	-	23.2	0.4	-	-	-	-	23.3	0.4	-	-	-	-	23.3	0.0	-	-
1962	-	-	23.4	0.4	-	-	-	-	23.4	0.0	-	-	-	-	23.4	0.0	-	-	-	-	23.4	0.0	-	-
1963	-	-	23.5	0.4	-	-	-	-	24.0	2.1	-	-	-	-	24.0	0.0	-	-	-	-	24.2	0.8	-	-
1964	-	-	24.2	0.0	-	-	-	-	24.3	0.4	-	-	-	-	24.4	0.4	-	-	-	-	24.5	0.4	-	-
1965	-	-	25.1	2.4	-	-	-	-	25.2	0.4	-	-	-	-	25.3	0.4	-	-	-	-	25.6	1.2	-	-
1966	-	-	25.9	1.2	-	-	-	-	26.3	1.5	-	-	-	-	26.9	2.3	-	-	-	-	27.7	3.0	-	-
1967	-	-	28.1	1.4	-	-	-	-	28.3	0.7	-	-	-	-	29.0	2.5	-	-	-	-	29.8	2.8	-	-
1968	-	-	29.9	0.3	-	-	-	-	29.9	0.0	-	-	-	-	30.5	2.0	-	-	-	-	31.4	3.0	-	-
1969	-	-	32.0	1.9	-	-	-	-	32.4	1.3	-	-	-	-	32.8	1.2	-	-	-	-	33.0	0.6	-	-
1970	-	-	33.9	2.7	-	-	-	-	34.2	0.9	-	-	-	-	34.6	1.2	-	-	-	-	34.6	0.0	-	-
1971	-	-	35.9	3.8	-	-	-	-	36.2	0.8	-	-	-	-	36.8	1.7	-	-	-	-	36.5	-0.8	-	-
1972	-	-	36.6	0.3	-	-	-	-	36.7	0.3	-	-	-	-	36.9	0.5	-	-	-	-	37.2	0.8	-	-
1973	-	-	37.6	1.1	-	-	-	-	38.2	1.6	-	-	-	-	38.8	1.6	-	-	-	-	39.6	2.1	-	-
1974	-	-	40.5	2.3	-	-	-	-	41.9	3.5	-	-	-	-	43.4	3.6	-	-	-	-	44.0	1.4	-	-
1975	-	-	45.3	3.0	-	-	-	-	46.4	2.4	-	-	-	-	48.0	3.4	-	-	-	-	48.7	1.5	-	-
1976	-	-	50.7	4.1	-	-	-	-	52.1	2.8	-	-	-	-	53.4	2.5	-	-	-	-	54.3	1.7	-	-
1977	-	-	55.1	1.5	-	-	-	-	57.2	3.8	-	-	-	-	58.0	1.4	-	-	-	-	58.9	1.6	-	-
1978	59.7	1.4	-	-	60.9	2.0	-	-	61.4	0.8	-	-	61.9	0.8	-	-	63.0	1.8	-	-	63.2	0.3	-	-
1979	66.3	4.9	-	-	67.2	1.4	-	-	67.8	0.9	-	-	69.8	2.9	-	-	71.0	1.7	-	-	71.7	1.0	-	-
1980	73.6	2.6	-	-	75.4	2.4	-	-	75.9	0.7	-	-	78.0	2.8	-	-	80.8	3.6	-	-	81.2	0.5	-	-
1981	83.2	2.5	-	-	86.1	3.5	-	-	86.3	0.2	-	-	87.0	0.8	-	-	87.9	1.0	-	-	88.1	0.2	-	-
1982	90.1	2.3	-	-	90.4	0.3	-	-	92.5	2.3	-	-	93.4	1.0	-	-	95.4	2.1	-	-	98.0	2.7	-	-
1983	99.2	1.2	-	-	99.2	0.0	-	-	99.3	0.1	-	-	101.0	1.7	-	-	101.8	0.8	-	-	102.0	0.2	-	-
1984	104.5	2.5	-	-	104.9	0.4	-	-	105.2	0.3	-	-	106.1	0.9	-	-	106.3	0.2	-	-	106.5	0.2	-	-
1985	107.1	0.6	-	-	108.3	1.1	-	-	109.0	0.6	-	-	109.5	0.5	-	-	110.1	0.5	-	-	110.5	0.4	-	-
1986	112.1	1.4	-	-	113.1	0.9	-	-	113.8	0.6	-	-	114.9	1.0	-	-	115.3	0.3	-	-	117.0	1.5	117.0	0.0
1987	-	-	-	-	-	-	-	-	-	-	125.5	7.3	-	-	-	-	-	-	-	-	-	-	130.3	3.8
1988	-	-	-	-	-	-	-	-	-	-	133.0	2.1	-	-	-	-	-	-	-	-	-	-	136.4	2.6
1989	-	-	-	-	-	-	-	-	-	-	141.3	3.6	-	-	-	-	-	-	-	-	-	-	149.9	6.1
1990	-	-	-	-	-	-	-	-	-	-	154.0	2.7	-	-	-	-	-	-	-	-	-	-	162.7	5.6

[Continued]

Milwaukee, WI
Consumer Price Index - All Urban Consumers
Base 1982-1984 = 100
Medical Care

[Continued]

For 1946-1995. Columns headed % show percentile change in the index from the previous period for which an index is available.

Year	Jan		Feb		Mar		Apr		May		Jun		Jul		Aug		Sep		Oct		Nov		Dec	
	Index	%	Index	%	Index	%	Index	%	Index	%	Index	%	Index	%	Index	%	Index	%	Index	%	Index	%	Index	%
1991	-	-	-	-	-	-	-	-	-	-	168.9	3.8	-	-	-	-	-	-	-	-	-	-	-	-
1992	-	-	-	-	-	-	-	-	-	-	180.3	3.0	-	-	-	-	-	-	-	-	-	-	175.0	3.6
1993	-	-	-	-	-	-	-	-	-	-	195.0	3.4	-	-	-	-	-	-	-	-	-	-	188.5	4.5
1994	-	-	-	-	-	-	-	-	-	-	211.8	4.6	-	-	-	-	-	-	-	-	-	-	202.4	3.8
1995	-	-	-	-	-	-	-	-	-	-	229.4	2.2	-	-	-	-	-	-	-	-	-	-	-	-

Source: U.S. Department of Labor, Bureau of Labor Statistics, Division of Consumer Prices and Price Indexes. - indicates no data collected for period.

Milwaukee, WI
Consumer Price Index - Urban Wage Earners
Base 1982-1984 = 100
Medical Care

For 1946-1995. Columns headed % show percentile change in the index from the previous period for which an index is available.

Year	Jan Index	%	Feb Index	%	Mar Index	%	Apr Index	%	May Index	%	Jun Index	%	Jul Index	%	Aug Index	%	Sep Index	%	Oct Index	%	Nov Index	%	Dec Index	%
1946	-	-	-	-	-	-	-	-	-	-	-	-	-	-	-	-	-	-	-	-	-	-	12.4	-
1947	-	-	-	-	12.9	4.0	-	-	-	-	12.9	0.0	-	-	13.0	0.8	-	-	-	-	13.1	0.8	-	-
1948	-	-	13.4	2.3	-	-	-	-	13.5	0.7	-	-	-	-	13.8	2.2	-	-	-	-	14.3	3.6	-	-
1949	-	-	14.3	0.0	-	-	-	-	14.3	0.0	-	-	-	-	14.5	1.4	-	-	-	-	14.5	0.0	-	-
1950	-	-	14.5	0.0	-	-	-	-	14.7	1.4	-	-	-	-	15.3	4.1	-	-	-	-	15.7	2.6	-	-
1951	-	-	15.9	1.3	-	-	-	-	16.6	4.4	-	-	-	-	17.0	2.4	-	-	-	-	17.1	0.6	-	-
1952	-	-	17.3	1.2	-	-	-	-	17.5	1.2	-	-	-	-	17.7	1.1	-	-	-	-	17.7	0.0	-	-
1953	-	-	17.9	1.1	-	-	-	-	18.0	0.6	-	-	-	-	18.3	1.7	-	-	-	-	18.4	0.5	-	-
1954	-	-	18.5	0.5	-	-	-	-	19.4	4.9	-	-	-	-	19.4	0.0	-	-	-	-	19.5	0.5	-	-
1955	-	-	19.5	0.0	-	-	-	-	19.6	0.5	-	-	-	-	20.0	2.0	-	-	-	-	19.8	-1.0	-	-
1956	-	-	20.0	1.0	-	-	-	-	20.1	0.5	-	-	-	-	20.1	0.0	-	-	-	-	20.3	1.0	-	-
1957	-	-	20.6	1.5	-	-	-	-	21.8	5.8	-	-	-	-	21.9	0.5	-	-	-	-	22.1	0.9	-	-
1958	-	-	22.3	0.9	-	-	-	-	22.3	0.0	-	-	-	-	22.3	0.0	-	-	-	-	22.4	0.4	-	-
1959	-	-	22.4	0.0	-	-	-	-	22.5	0.4	-	-	-	-	23.1	2.7	-	-	-	-	23.2	0.4	-	-
1960	-	-	23.3	0.4	-	-	-	-	23.3	0.0	-	-	-	-	23.4	0.4	-	-	-	-	23.4	0.0	-	-
1961	-	-	23.4	0.0	-	-	-	-	23.5	0.4	-	-	-	-	23.6	0.4	-	-	-	-	23.6	0.0	-	-
1962	-	-	23.7	0.4	-	-	-	-	23.7	0.0	-	-	-	-	23.7	0.0	-	-	-	-	23.7	0.0	-	-
1963	-	-	23.8	0.4	-	-	-	-	24.2	1.7	-	-	-	-	24.3	0.4	-	-	-	-	24.5	0.8	-	-
1964	-	-	24.5	0.0	-	-	-	-	24.6	0.4	-	-	-	-	24.7	0.4	-	-	-	-	24.7	0.0	-	-
1965	-	-	25.3	2.4	-	-	-	-	25.5	0.8	-	-	-	-	25.6	0.4	-	-	-	-	25.9	1.2	-	-
1966	-	-	26.2	1.2	-	-	-	-	26.6	1.5	-	-	-	-	27.2	2.3	-	-	-	-	28.0	2.9	-	-
1967	-	-	28.4	1.4	-	-	-	-	28.6	0.7	-	-	-	-	29.3	2.4	-	-	-	-	30.2	3.1	-	-
1968	-	-	30.2	0.0	-	-	-	-	30.3	0.3	-	-	-	-	30.9	2.0	-	-	-	-	31.8	2.9	-	-
1969	-	-	32.4	1.9	-	-	-	-	32.7	0.9	-	-	-	-	33.1	1.2	-	-	-	-	33.4	0.9	-	-
1970	-	-	34.3	2.7	-	-	-	-	34.6	0.9	-	-	-	-	35.0	1.2	-	-	-	-	35.0	0.0	-	-
1971	-	-	36.3	3.7	-	-	-	-	36.6	0.8	-	-	-	-	37.2	1.6	-	-	-	-	36.9	-0.8	-	-
1972	-	-	37.0	0.3	-	-	-	-	37.1	0.3	-	-	-	-	37.3	0.5	-	-	-	-	37.6	0.8	-	-
1973	-	-	38.0	1.1	-	-	-	-	38.7	1.8	-	-	-	-	39.2	1.3	-	-	-	-	40.1	2.3	-	-
1974	-	-	40.9	2.0	-	-	-	-	42.3	3.4	-	-	-	-	43.9	3.8	-	-	-	-	44.4	1.1	-	-
1975	-	-	45.8	3.2	-	-	-	-	46.9	2.4	-	-	-	-	48.5	3.4	-	-	-	-	49.2	1.4	-	-
1976	-	-	51.3	4.3	-	-	-	-	52.7	2.7	-	-	-	-	54.0	2.5	-	-	-	-	54.9	1.7	-	-
1977	-	-	55.7	1.5	-	-	-	-	57.8	3.8	-	-	-	-	58.7	1.6	-	-	-	-	59.5	1.4	-	-
1978	61.4	3.2	-	-	62.0	1.0	-	-	63.3	2.1	-	-	63.9	0.9	-	-	64.8	1.4	-	-	64.9	0.2	-	-
1979	67.3	3.7	-	-	68.0	1.0	-	-	68.1	0.1	-	-	70.5	3.5	-	-	71.8	1.8	-	-	72.1	0.4	-	-
1980	74.5	3.3	-	-	77.2	3.6	-	-	78.1	1.2	-	-	79.4	1.7	-	-	81.3	2.4	-	-	81.9	0.7	-	-
1981	84.0	2.6	-	-	86.9	3.5	-	-	87.1	0.2	-	-	88.1	1.1	-	-	88.7	0.7	-	-	88.9	0.2	-	-
1982	91.0	2.4	-	-	91.2	0.2	-	-	92.9	1.9	-	-	93.6	0.8	-	-	95.3	1.8	-	-	97.3	2.1	-	-
1983	98.5	1.2	-	-	98.7	0.2	-	-	98.9	0.2	-	-	100.7	1.8	-	-	101.4	0.7	-	-	101.6	0.2	-	-
1984	104.4	2.8	-	-	104.9	0.5	-	-	105.3	0.4	-	-	106.6	1.2	-	-	106.7	0.1	-	-	107.0	0.3	-	-
1985	107.8	0.7	-	-	108.9	1.0	-	-	109.7	0.7	-	-	110.2	0.5	-	-	110.8	0.5	-	-	111.3	0.5	118.0	0.1
1986	113.0	1.5	-	-	114.0	0.9	-	-	114.7	0.6	-	-	115.6	0.8	-	-	116.3	0.6	-	-	117.9	1.4	130.0	3.8
1987	-	-	-	-	-	-	-	-	-	-	125.2	6.1	-	-	-	-	-	-	-	-	-	-	135.7	2.4
1988	-	-	-	-	-	-	-	-	-	-	132.5	1.9	-	-	-	-	-	-	-	-	-	-	147.5	5.1
1989	-	-	-	-	-	-	-	-	-	-	140.3	3.4	-	-	-	-	-	-	-	-	-	-	160.3	5.5
1990	-	-	-	-	-	-	-	-	-	-	152.0	3.1	-	-	-	-	-	-	-	-	-	-	-	-

[Continued]

Milwaukee, WI
Consumer Price Index - Urban Wage Earners
Base 1982-1984 = 100
Medical Care

[Continued]

For 1946-1995. Columns headed % show percentile change in the index from the previous period for which an index is available.

Year	Jan		Feb		Mar		Apr		May		Jun		Jul		Aug		Sep		Oct		Nov		Dec	
	Index	%	Index	%	Index	%	Index	%	Index	%	Index	%	Index	%	Index	%	Index	%	Index	%	Index	%	Index	%
1991	-	-	-	-	-	-	-	-	-	-	166.5	3.9	-	-	-	-	-	-	-	-	-	-	172.4	3.5
1992	-	-	-	-	-	-	-	-	-	-	177.1	2.7	-	-	-	-	-	-	-	-	-	-	185.5	4.7
1993	-	-	-	-	-	-	-	-	-	-	192.2	3.6	-	-	-	-	-	-	-	-	-	-	199.7	3.9
1994	-	-	-	-	-	-	-	-	-	-	208.4	4.4	-	-	-	-	-	-	-	-	-	-	219.8	5.5
1995	-	-	-	-	-	-	-	-	-	-	224.8	2.3	-	-	-	-	-	-	-	-	-	-	-	-

Source: U.S. Department of Labor, Bureau of Labor Statistics, Division of Consumer Prices and Price Indexes. - indicates no data collected for period.

Milwaukee, WI
Consumer Price Index - All Urban Consumers
Base 1982-1984 = 100
Entertainment

For 1975-1995. Columns headed % show percentile change in the index from the previous period for which an index is available.

Year	Jan Index	%	Feb Index	%	Mar Index	%	Apr Index	%	May Index	%	Jun Index	%	Jul Index	%	Aug Index	%	Sep Index	%	Oct Index	%	Nov Index	%	Dec Index	%
1975	-	-	-	-	-	-	-	-	-	-	-	-	-	-	-	-	-	-	-	-	59.6	-	-	-
1976	-	-	59.8	0.3	-	-	-	-	61.0	2.0	-	-	-	-	62.8	3.0	-	-	-	-	63.3	0.8	-	-
1977	-	-	67.1	6.0	-	-	-	-	68.5	2.1	-	-	-	-	68.7	0.3	-	-	-	-	69.6	1.3	-	-
1978	70.0	0.6	-	-	71.1	1.6	-	-	71.3	0.3	-	-	71.4	0.1	-	-	73.4	2.8	-	-	74.6	1.6	-	-
1979	75.1	0.7	-	-	75.4	0.4	-	-	77.6	2.9	-	-	78.3	0.9	-	-	79.4	1.4	-	-	79.8	0.5	-	-
1980	81.0	1.5	-	-	80.5	-0.6	-	-	84.2	4.6	-	-	84.8	0.7	-	-	86.9	2.5	-	-	86.9	0.0	-	-
1981	88.4	1.7	-	-	92.2	4.3	-	-	92.6	0.4	-	-	91.6	-1.1	-	-	93.2	1.7	-	-	92.6	-0.6	-	-
1982	96.9	4.6	-	-	96.2	-0.7	-	-	95.5	-0.7	-	-	95.4	-0.1	-	-	94.6	-0.8	-	-	96.0	1.5	-	-
1983	97.3	1.4	-	-	98.2	0.9	-	-	100.1	1.9	-	-	100.1	0.0	-	-	102.3	2.2	-	-	103.0	0.7	-	-
1984	101.0	-1.9	-	-	101.7	0.7	-	-	102.5	0.8	-	-	104.8	2.2	-	-	106.1	1.2	-	-	105.8	-0.3	-	-
1985	107.8	1.9	-	-	108.1	0.3	-	-	108.3	0.2	-	-	110.3	1.8	-	-	111.6	1.2	-	-	111.2	-0.4	-	-
1986	109.1	-1.9	-	-	110.9	1.6	-	-	110.8	-0.1	-	-	111.1	0.3	-	-	110.3	-0.7	-	-	109.5	-0.7	109.6	0.1
1987	-	-	-	-	-	-	-	-	-	-	118.3	7.9	-	-	-	-	-	-	-	-	-	-	119.5	1.0
1988	-	-	-	-	-	-	-	-	-	-	121.0	1.3	-	-	-	-	-	-	-	-	-	-	124.5	2.9
1989	-	-	-	-	-	-	-	-	-	-	127.1	2.1	-	-	-	-	-	-	-	-	-	-	130.3	2.5
1990	-	-	-	-	-	-	-	-	-	-	137.7	5.7	-	-	-	-	-	-	-	-	-	-	138.9	0.9
1991	-	-	-	-	-	-	-	-	-	-	141.9	2.2	-	-	-	-	-	-	-	-	-	-	145.7	2.7
1992	-	-	-	-	-	-	-	-	-	-	148.8	2.1	-	-	-	-	-	-	-	-	-	-	149.8	0.7
1993	-	-	-	-	-	-	-	-	-	-	152.2	1.6	-	-	-	-	-	-	-	-	-	-	153.1	0.6
1994	-	-	-	-	-	-	-	-	-	-	152.9	-0.1	-	-	-	-	-	-	-	-	-	-	156.6	2.4
1995	-	-	-	-	-	-	-	-	-	-	158.6	1.3	-	-	-	-	-	-	-	-	-	-	-	-

Source: U.S. Department of Labor, Bureau of Labor Statistics, Division of Consumer Prices and Price Indexes. - indicates no data collected for period.

Milwaukee, WI
Consumer Price Index - Urban Wage Earners
Base 1982-1984 = 100
Entertainment

For 1975-1995. Columns headed % show percentile change in the index from the previous period for which an index is available.

Year	Jan Index	%	Feb Index	%	Mar Index	%	Apr Index	%	May Index	%	Jun Index	%	Jul Index	%	Aug Index	%	Sep Index	%	Oct Index	%	Nov Index	%	Dec Index	%
1975	-	-	-	-	-	-	-	-	-	-	-	-	-	-	-	-	-	-	-	-	61.8	-	-	-
1976	-	-	62.0	0.3	-	-	-	-	63.3	2.1	-	-	-	-	65.1	2.8	-	-	-	-	65.6	0.8	-	-
1977	-	-	69.5	5.9	-	-	-	-	71.0	2.2	-	-	-	-	71.2	0.3	-	-	-	-	72.1	1.3	-	-
1978	73.3	1.7	-	-	74.4	1.5	-	-	74.6	0.3	-	-	74.7	0.1	-	-	76.3	2.1	-	-	77.6	1.7	-	-
1979	78.2	0.8	-	-	78.0	-0.3	-	-	81.2	4.1	-	-	80.5	-0.9	-	-	81.8	1.6	-	-	80.4	-1.7	-	-
1980	82.9	3.1	-	-	87.5	5.5	-	-	89.3	2.1	-	-	88.5	-0.9	-	-	90.9	2.7	-	-	88.9	-2.2	-	-
1981	94.8	6.6	-	-	98.1	3.5	-	-	96.5	-1.6	-	-	92.7	-3.9	-	-	92.8	0.1	-	-	92.3	-0.5	-	-
1982	96.7	4.8	-	-	96.1	-0.6	-	-	95.8	-0.3	-	-	95.3	-0.5	-	-	94.6	-0.7	-	-	95.7	1.2	-	-
1983	97.0	1.4	-	-	98.0	1.0	-	-	99.8	1.8	-	-	99.9	0.1	-	-	101.9	2.0	-	-	102.6	0.7	-	-
1984	100.8	-1.8	-	-	102.1	1.3	-	-	103.2	1.1	-	-	105.7	2.4	-	-	106.2	0.5	-	-	105.9	-0.3	-	-
1985	107.7	1.7	-	-	108.3	0.6	-	-	108.6	0.3	-	-	110.4	1.7	-	-	112.3	1.7	-	-	112.0	-0.3	-	-
1986	108.4	-3.2	-	-	110.2	1.7	-	-	110.3	0.1	-	-	110.6	0.3	-	-	109.8	-0.7	-	-	109.1	-0.6	109.2	0.1
1987	-	-	-	-	-	-	-	-	-	-	117.1	7.2	-	-	-	-	-	-	-	-	-	-	119.1	1.7
1988	-	-	-	-	-	-	-	-	-	-	121.2	1.8	-	-	-	-	-	-	-	-	-	-	124.7	2.9
1989	-	-	-	-	-	-	-	-	-	-	127.7	2.4	-	-	-	-	-	-	-	-	-	-	130.7	2.3
1990	-	-	-	-	-	-	-	-	-	-	138.1	5.7	-	-	-	-	-	-	-	-	-	-	139.9	1.3
1991	-	-	-	-	-	-	-	-	-	-	143.8	2.8	-	-	-	-	-	-	-	-	-	-	148.0	2.9
1992	-	-	-	-	-	-	-	-	-	-	151.2	2.2	-	-	-	-	-	-	-	-	-	-	152.0	0.5
1993	-	-	-	-	-	-	-	-	-	-	154.3	1.5	-	-	-	-	-	-	-	-	-	-	155.7	0.9
1994	-	-	-	-	-	-	-	-	-	-	156.2	0.3	-	-	-	-	-	-	-	-	-	-	160.1	2.5
1995	-	-	-	-	-	-	-	-	-	-	161.9	1.1	-	-	-	-	-	-	-	-	-	-	-	-

Source: U.S. Department of Labor, Bureau of Labor Statistics, Division of Consumer Prices and Price Indexes. - indicates no data collected for period.

Milwaukee, WI
Consumer Price Index - All Urban Consumers
Base 1982-1984 = 100
Other Goods and Services

For 1975-1995. Columns headed % show percentile change in the index from the previous period for which an index is available.

Year	Jan Index	%	Feb Index	%	Mar Index	%	Apr Index	%	May Index	%	Jun Index	%	Jul Index	%	Aug Index	%	Sep Index	%	Oct Index	%	Nov Index	%	Dec Index	%
1975	-	-	-	-	-	-	-	-	-	-	-	-	-	-	-	-	-	-	-	-	58.2	-	-	-
1976	-	-	59.3	1.9	-	-	-	-	59.7	0.7	-	-	-	-	59.8	0.2	-	-	-	-	61.1	2.2	-	-
1977	-	-	61.9	1.3	-	-	-	-	62.6	1.1	-	-	-	-	63.1	0.8	-	-	-	-	64.8	2.7	-	-
1978	65.6	1.2	-	-	65.1	-0.8	-	-	65.4	0.5	-	-	65.9	0.8	-	-	67.8	2.9	-	-	68.4	0.9	-	-
1979	68.6	0.3	-	-	69.3	1.0	-	-	69.8	0.7	-	-	69.4	-0.6	-	-	71.9	3.6	-	-	72.6	1.0	-	-
1980	73.9	1.8	-	-	74.0	0.1	-	-	74.7	0.9	-	-	74.8	0.1	-	-	77.3	3.3	-	-	77.7	0.5	-	-
1981	80.2	3.2	-	-	81.2	1.2	-	-	81.9	0.9	-	-	81.9	0.0	-	-	84.9	3.7	-	-	86.9	2.4	-	-
1982	87.6	0.8	-	-	89.2	1.8	-	-	91.3	2.4	-	-	91.9	0.7	-	-	95.1	3.5	-	-	96.3	1.3	-	-
1983	99.7	3.5	-	-	100.1	0.4	-	-	100.0	-0.1	-	-	99.7	-0.3	-	-	101.5	1.8	-	-	102.7	1.2	-	-
1984	103.8	1.1	-	-	104.3	0.5	-	-	104.5	0.2	-	-	105.9	1.3	-	-	110.2	4.1	-	-	110.6	0.4	-	-
1985	110.8	0.2	-	-	111.1	0.3	-	-	111.2	0.1	-	-	111.9	0.6	-	-	114.4	2.2	-	-	117.4	2.6	-	-
1986	118.9	1.3	-	-	119.0	0.1	-	-	119.7	0.6	-	-	120.7	0.8	-	-	124.7	3.3	-	-	125.0	0.2	125.2	0.2
1987	-	-	-	-	-	-	-	-	-	-	122.9	-1.8	-	-	-	-	-	-	-	-	-	-	131.3	6.8
1988	-	-	-	-	-	-	-	-	-	-	135.7	3.4	-	-	-	-	-	-	-	-	-	-	142.0	4.6
1989	-	-	-	-	-	-	-	-	-	-	146.1	2.9	-	-	-	-	-	-	-	-	-	-	152.3	4.2
1990	-	-	-	-	-	-	-	-	-	-	155.6	2.2	-	-	-	-	-	-	-	-	-	-	161.3	3.7
1991	-	-	-	-	-	-	-	-	-	-	168.1	4.2	-	-	-	-	-	-	-	-	-	-	177.5	5.6
1992	-	-	-	-	-	-	-	-	-	-	182.5	2.8	-	-	-	-	-	-	-	-	-	-	194.0	6.3
1993	-	-	-	-	-	-	-	-	-	-	199.6	2.9	-	-	-	-	-	-	-	-	-	-	196.6	-1.5
1994	-	-	-	-	-	-	-	-	-	-	197.6	0.5	-	-	-	-	-	-	-	-	-	-	201.9	2.2
1995	-	-	-	-	-	-	-	-	-	-	205.7	1.9	-	-	-	-	-	-	-	-	-	-	-	-

Source: U.S. Department of Labor, Bureau of Labor Statistics, Division of Consumer Prices and Price Indexes. - indicates no data collected for period.

Milwaukee, WI
Consumer Price Index - Urban Wage Earners
Base 1982-1984 = 100
Other Goods and Services

For 1975-1995. Columns headed % show percentile change in the index from the previous period for which an index is available.

Year	Jan Index	%	Feb Index	%	Mar Index	%	Apr Index	%	May Index	%	Jun Index	%	Jul Index	%	Aug Index	%	Sep Index	%	Oct Index	%	Nov Index	%	Dec Index	%
1975	-	-	-	-	-	-	-	-	-	-	-	-	-	-	-	-	-	-	-	-	55.7	-	-	-
1976	-	-	56.7	1.8	-	-	-	-	57.2	0.9	-	-	-	-	57.2	0.0	-	-	-	-	58.5	2.3	-	-
1977	-	-	59.3	1.4	-	-	-	-	59.9	1.0	-	-	-	-	60.4	0.8	-	-	-	-	62.0	2.6	-	-
1978	63.2	1.9	-	-	63.9	1.1	-	-	64.1	0.3	-	-	64.5	0.6	-	-	66.3	2.8	-	-	66.6	0.5	-	-
1979	66.7	0.2	-	-	67.7	1.5	-	-	67.7	0.0	-	-	68.0	0.4	-	-	70.1	3.1	-	-	71.5	2.0	-	-
1980	73.5	2.8	-	-	73.8	0.4	-	-	74.5	0.9	-	-	74.5	0.0	-	-	76.8	3.1	-	-	76.5	-0.4	-	-
1981	78.6	2.7	-	-	79.7	1.4	-	-	80.9	1.5	-	-	81.3	0.5	-	-	84.5	3.9	-	-	86.6	2.5	-	-
1982	87.0	0.5	-	-	88.6	1.8	-	-	91.1	2.8	-	-	91.7	0.7	-	-	94.8	3.4	-	-	96.1	1.4	-	-
1983	100.0	4.1	-	-	100.3	0.3	-	-	100.2	-0.1	-	-	100.0	-0.2	-	-	101.7	1.7	-	-	102.9	1.2	-	-
1984	104.0	1.1	-	-	104.5	0.5	-	-	104.8	0.3	-	-	106.2	1.3	-	-	110.1	3.7	-	-	110.4	0.3	-	-
1985	110.6	0.2	-	-	111.0	0.4	-	-	111.0	0.0	-	-	111.8	0.7	-	-	113.8	1.8	-	-	116.9	2.7	-	-
1986	118.5	1.4	-	-	118.7	0.2	-	-	119.4	0.6	-	-	120.4	0.8	-	-	123.9	2.9	-	-	124.2	0.2	124.5	0.2
1987	-	-	-	-	-	-	-	-	-	-	122.8	-1.4	-	-	-	-	-	-	-	-	-	-	130.7	6.4
1988	-	-	-	-	-	-	-	-	-	-	134.9	3.2	-	-	-	-	-	-	-	-	-	-	141.3	4.7
1989	-	-	-	-	-	-	-	-	-	-	145.3	2.8	-	-	-	-	-	-	-	-	-	-	151.0	3.9
1990	-	-	-	-	-	-	-	-	-	-	154.3	2.2	-	-	-	-	-	-	-	-	-	-	160.1	3.8
1991	-	-	-	-	-	-	-	-	-	-	167.3	4.5	-	-	-	-	-	-	-	-	-	-	176.9	5.7
1992	-	-	-	-	-	-	-	-	-	-	183.5	3.7	-	-	-	-	-	-	-	-	-	-	195.9	6.8
1993	-	-	-	-	-	-	-	-	-	-	202.1	3.2	-	-	-	-	-	-	-	-	-	-	196.7	-2.7
1994	-	-	-	-	-	-	-	-	-	-	197.6	0.5	-	-	-	-	-	-	-	-	-	-	201.5	2.0
1995	-	-	-	-	-	-	-	-	-	-	205.4	1.9	-	-	-	-	-	-	-	-	-	-	-	-

Source: U.S. Department of Labor, Bureau of Labor Statistics, Division of Consumer Prices and Price Indexes. - indicates no data collected for period.

Minneapolis-St. Paul, MN
Consumer Price Index - All Urban Consumers
Base 1982-1984 = 100
Annual Averages

For 1917-1995. Columns headed % show percentile change in the index from the previous period for which an index is available.

Year	All Items Index	%	Food & Beverage Index	%	Housing Index	%	Apparel & Upkeep Index	%	Trans-portation Index	%	Medical Care Index	%	Entertain-ment Index	%	Other Goods & Services Index	%
1917	-	-	-	-	-	-	-	-	-	-	-	-	-	-	-	-
1918	14.1	-	-	-	-	-	-	-	-	-	-	-	-	-	-	-
1919	16.0	13.5	-	-	-	-	-	-	-	-	-	-	-	-	-	-
1920	18.6	16.3	-	-	-	-	-	-	-	-	-	-	-	-	-	-
1921	16.7	-10.2	-	-	-	-	-	-	-	-	-	-	-	-	-	-
1922	15.8	-5.4	-	-	-	-	-	-	-	-	-	-	-	-	-	-
1923	15.9	0.6	-	-	-	-	-	-	-	-	-	-	-	-	-	-
1924	15.8	-0.6	-	-	-	-	-	-	-	-	-	-	-	-	-	-
1925	15.9	0.6	-	-	-	-	-	-	-	-	-	-	-	-	-	-
1926	16.1	1.3	-	-	-	-	-	-	-	-	-	-	-	-	-	-
1927	15.7	-2.5	-	-	-	-	-	-	-	-	-	-	-	-	-	-
1928	15.5	-1.3	-	-	-	-	-	-	-	-	-	-	-	-	-	-
1929	15.6	0.6	-	-	-	-	-	-	-	-	-	-	-	-	-	-
1930	15.3	-1.9	-	-	-	-	-	-	-	-	-	-	-	-	-	-
1931	14.2	-7.2	-	-	-	-	-	-	-	-	-	-	-	-	-	-
1932	12.9	-9.2	-	-	-	-	-	-	-	-	-	-	-	-	-	-
1933	12.2	-5.4	-	-	-	-	-	-	-	-	-	-	-	-	-	-
1934	12.6	3.3	-	-	-	-	-	-	-	-	-	-	-	-	-	-
1935	13.0	3.2	-	-	-	-	-	-	-	-	-	-	-	-	-	-
1936	13.2	1.5	-	-	-	-	-	-	-	-	-	-	-	-	-	-
1937	13.8	4.5	-	-	-	-	-	-	-	-	-	-	-	-	-	-
1938	13.6	-1.4	-	-	-	-	-	-	-	-	-	-	-	-	-	-
1939	13.5	-0.7	-	-	-	-	-	-	-	-	-	-	-	-	-	-
1940	13.5	0.0	-	-	-	-	-	-	-	-	-	-	-	-	-	-
1941	14.2	5.2	-	-	-	-	-	-	-	-	-	-	-	-	-	-
1942	15.5	9.2	-	-	-	-	-	-	-	-	-	-	-	-	-	-
1943	16.2	4.5	-	-	-	-	-	-	-	-	-	-	-	-	-	-
1944	16.4	1.2	-	-	-	-	-	-	-	-	-	-	-	-	-	-
1945	16.7	1.8	-	-	-	-	-	-	-	-	-	-	-	-	-	-
1946	18.2	9.0	-	-	-	-	-	-	-	-	-	-	-	-	-	-
1947	21.0	15.4	-	-	-	-	-	-	21.6	-	10.7	-	-	-	-	-
1948	22.9	9.0	-	-	-	-	-	-	24.7	14.4	11.8	10.3	-	-	-	-
1949	22.7	-0.9	-	-	-	-	-	-	26.4	6.9	12.2	3.4	-	-	-	-
1950	22.9	0.9	-	-	-	-	-	-	26.5	0.4	12.6	3.3	-	-	-	-
1951	24.6	7.4	-	-	-	-	-	-	26.9	1.5	13.6	7.9	-	-	-	-
1952	25.4	3.3	-	-	-	-	-	-	28.7	6.7	14.5	6.6	-	-	-	-
1953	25.7	1.2	-	-	-	-	45.9	-	29.5	2.8	15.6	7.6	-	-	-	-
1954	25.9	0.8	-	-	-	-	45.9	0.0	29.2	-1.0	16.4	5.1	-	-	-	-
1955	25.9	0.0	-	-	-	-	45.2	-1.5	28.3	-3.1	17.0	3.7	-	-	-	-
1956	26.0	0.4	-	-	-	-	46.5	2.9	27.9	-1.4	17.3	1.8	-	-	-	-
1957	26.9	3.5	-	-	-	-	47.1	1.3	29.3	5.0	18.7	8.1	-	-	-	-
1958	27.6	2.6	-	-	-	-	47.3	0.4	30.3	3.4	21.2	13.4	-	-	-	-
1959	27.9	1.1	-	-	-	-	47.0	-0.6	31.6	4.3	22.7	7.1	-	-	-	-
1960	28.3	1.4	-	-	-	-	48.0	2.1	32.0	1.3	24.3	7.0	-	-	-	-
1961	28.6	1.1	-	-	-	-	46.9	-2.3	32.2	0.6	25.8	6.2	-	-	-	-

[Continued]

626

Minneapolis-St. Paul, MN
Consumer Price Index - All Urban Consumers
Base 1982-1984 = 100
Annual Averages
[Continued]

For 1917-1995. Columns headed % show percentile change in the index from the previous period for which an index is available.

Year	All Items		Food & Beverage		Housing		Apparel & Upkeep		Trans- portation		Medical Care		Entertain- ment		Other Goods & Services	
	Index	%	Index	%	Index	%	Index	%	Index	%	Index	%	Index	%	Index	%
1962	29.0	1.4	-	-	-	-	47.9	2.1	32.7	1.6	26.7	3.5	-	-	-	-
1963	29.4	1.4	-	-	-	-	48.8	1.9	33.2	1.5	27.0	1.1	-	-	-	-
1964	29.7	1.0	-	-	-	-	48.8	0.0	33.2	0.0	27.5	1.9	-	-	-	-
1965	30.1	1.3	-	-	-	-	49.9	2.3	33.8	1.8	27.6	0.4	-	-	-	-
1966	30.8	2.3	-	-	-	-	51.2	2.6	34.4	1.8	28.9	4.7				
1967	31.8	3.2	-	-	-	-	53.0	3.5	35.6	3.5	30.4	5.2				
1968	33.3	4.7	-	-	-	-	55.3	4.3	36.7	3.1	32.0	5.3				
1969	35.0	5.1	-	-	-	-	58.3	5.4	37.4	1.9	33.6	5.0	-	-	-	-
1970	37.4	6.9	-	-	-	-	61.2	5.0	39.7	6.1	35.8	6.5	-	-	-	-
1971	38.7	3.5	-	-	-	-	62.6	2.3	41.1	3.5	37.7	5.3	-	-	-	-
1972	39.9	3.1	-	-	-	-	63.4	1.3	41.4	0.7	38.4	1.9	-	-	-	-
1973	42.3	6.0	-	-	-	-	66.3	4.6	43.1	4.1	40.3	4.9	-	-	-	-
1974	47.2	11.6	-	-	-	-	72.6	9.5	47.8	10.9	43.9	8.9	-	-	-	-
1975	51.2	8.5					74.0	1.9	50.9	6.5	48.6	10.7				
1976	54.4	6.3	62.5	-	49.0	-	75.0	1.4	55.4	8.8	52.3	7.6	62.2	-	56.8	-
1977	58.2	7.0	65.8	5.3	53.2	8.6	78.1	4.1	59.6	7.6	56.6	8.2	65.5	5.3	60.0	5.6
1978	63.5	9.1	72.3	9.9	59.3	11.5	81.3	4.1	62.5	4.9	61.2	8.1	71.1	8.5	64.9	8.2
1979	70.8	11.5	80.9	11.9	66.3	11.8	85.5	5.2	71.8	14.9	66.2	8.2	75.1	5.6	69.3	6.8
1980	78.9	11.4	87.6	8.3	74.0	11.6	90.8	6.2	83.7	16.6	73.7	11.3	81.3	8.3	75.3	8.7
1981	88.6	12.3	92.7	5.8	85.9	16.1	94.7	4.3	93.6	11.8	80.3	9.0	93.1	14.5	83.2	10.5
1982	97.4	9.9	96.6	4.2	98.7	14.9	99.7	5.3	97.5	4.2	90.0	12.1	97.2	4.4	91.7	10.2
1983	99.5	2.2	99.5	3.0	99.3	0.6	101.5	1.8	99.3	1.8	100.3	11.4	100.2	3.1	100.7	9.8
1984	103.1	3.6	104.0	4.5	102.0	2.7	98.8	-2.7	103.2	3.9	109.7	9.4	102.6	2.4	107.6	6.9
1985	107.0	3.8	106.5	2.4	105.8	3.7	106.2	7.5	106.1	2.8	116.9	6.6	106.6	3.9	114.5	6.4
1986	108.4	1.3	109.4	2.7	107.8	1.9	107.0	0.8	100.5	-5.3	126.8	8.5	111.8	4.9	120.9	5.6
1987	106.5	-1.8	111.8	2.2	97.0	-10.0	113.6	6.2	102.5	2.0	130.4	2.8	118.5	6.0	124.8	3.2
1988	109.5	2.8	116.2	3.9	98.0	1.0	121.1	6.6	104.5	2.0	136.7	4.8	124.5	5.1	131.2	5.1
1989	114.1	4.2	121.7	4.7	100.5	2.6	123.9	2.3	109.2	4.5	148.0	8.3	133.8	7.5	138.5	5.6
1990	120.6	5.7	128.7	5.8	104.8	4.3	132.5	6.9	116.0	6.2	161.2	8.9	134.9	0.8	152.1	9.8
1991	125.1	3.7	131.6	2.3	109.5	4.5	134.8	1.7	119.6	3.1	177.7	10.2	139.6	3.5	157.7	3.7
1992	129.1	3.2	130.8	-0.6	113.2	3.4	135.8	0.7	122.9	2.8	193.6	8.9	146.4	4.9	172.1	9.1
1993	133.4	3.3	132.4	1.2	116.8	3.2	142.1	4.6	128.2	4.3	200.8	3.7	153.2	4.6	180.8	5.1
1994	137.9	3.4	137.5	3.9	120.4	3.1	146.7	3.2	132.9	3.7	204.6	1.9	157.4	2.7	187.6	3.8
1995	139.8	1.4	140.2	2.0	121.1	0.6	138.3	-5.7	137.0	3.1	217.7	6.4	157.3	-0.1	193.4	3.1

Source: U.S. Department of Labor, Bureau of Labor Statistics, Division of Consumer Prices and Price Indexes. - indicates no data collected for period.

Minneapolis-St. Paul, MN
Consumer Price Index - Urban Wage Earners
Base 1982-1984 = 100
Annual Averages

For 1917-1995. Columns headed % show percentile change in the index from the previous period for which an index is available.

Year	All Items		Food & Beverage		Housing		Apparel & Upkeep		Trans- portation		Medical Care		Entertain- ment		Other Goods & Services	
	Index	%	Index	%	Index	%	Index	%	Index	%	Index	%	Index	%	Index	%
1917	-	-	-	-	-	-	-	-	-	-	-	-	-	-	-	-
1918	14.1	-	-	-	-	-	-	-	-	-	-	-	-	-	-	-
1919	16.1	14.2	-	-	-	-	-	-	-	-	-	-	-	-	-	-
1920	18.6	15.5	-	-	-	-	-	-	-	-	-	-	-	-	-	-
1921	16.8	-9.7	-	-	-	-	-	-	-	-	-	-	-	-	-	-
1922	15.8	-6.0	-	-	-	-	-	-	-	-	-	-	-	-	-	-
1923	15.9	0.6	-	-	-	-	-	-	-	-	-	-	-	-	-	-
1924	15.8	-0.6	-	-	-	-	-	-	-	-	-	-	-	-	-	-
1925	15.9	0.6	-	-	-	-	-	-	-	-	-	-	-	-	-	-
1926	16.1	1.3	-	-	-	-	-	-	-	-	-	-	-	-	-	-
1927	15.7	-2.5	-	-	-	-	-	-	-	-	-	-	-	-	-	-
1928	15.5	-1.3	-	-	-	-	-	-	-	-	-	-	-	-	-	-
1929	15.6	0.6	-	-	-	-	-	-	-	-	-	-	-	-	-	-
1930	15.3	-1.9	-	-	-	-	-	-	-	-	-	-	-	-	-	-
1931	14.2	-7.2	-	-	-	-	-	-	-	-	-	-	-	-	-	-
1932	12.9	-9.2	-	-	-	-	-	-	-	-	-	-	-	-	-	-
1933	12.2	-5.4	-	-	-	-	-	-	-	-	-	-	-	-	-	-
1934	12.6	3.3	-	-	-	-	-	-	-	-	-	-	-	-	-	-
1935	13.0	3.2	-	-	-	-	-	-	-	-	-	-	-	-	-	-
1936	13.2	1.5	-	-	-	-	-	-	-	-	-	-	-	-	-	-
1937	13.8	4.5	-	-	-	-	-	-	-	-	-	-	-	-	-	-
1938	13.6	-1.4	-	-	-	-	-	-	-	-	-	-	-	-	-	-
1939	13.5	-0.7	-	-	-	-	-	-	-	-	-	-	-	-	-	-
1940	13.5	0.0	-	-	-	-	-	-	-	-	-	-	-	-	-	-
1941	14.2	5.2	-	-	-	-	-	-	-	-	-	-	-	-	-	-
1942	15.5	9.2	-	-	-	-	-	-	-	-	-	-	-	-	-	-
1943	16.2	4.5	-	-	-	-	-	-	-	-	-	-	-	-	-	-
1944	16.4	1.2	-	-	-	-	-	-	-	-	-	-	-	-	-	-
1945	16.7	1.8	-	-	-	-	-	-	-	-	-	-	-	-	-	-
1946	18.2	9.0	-	-	-	-	-	-	-	-	-	-	-	-	-	-
1947	21.0	15.4	-	-	-	-	-	-	21.3	-	10.8	-	-	-	-	-
1948	22.9	9.0	-	-	-	-	-	-	24.3	14.1	11.9	10.2	-	-	-	-
1949	22.7	-0.9	-	-	-	-	-	-	26.0	7.0	12.4	4.2	-	-	-	-
1950	22.9	0.9	-	-	-	-	-	-	26.1	0.4	12.8	3.2	-	-	-	-
1951	24.6	7.4	-	-	-	-	-	-	26.5	1.5	13.8	7.8	-	-	-	-
1952	25.4	3.3	-	-	-	-	-	-	28.3	6.8	14.7	6.5	-	-	-	-
1953	25.7	1.2	-	-	-	-	46.9	-	29.0	2.5	15.9	8.2	-	-	-	-
1954	25.9	0.8	-	-	-	-	47.0	0.2	28.8	-0.7	16.6	4.4	-	-	-	-
1955	25.9	0.0	-	-	-	-	46.3	-1.5	27.9	-3.1	17.2	3.6	-	-	-	-
1956	26.0	0.4	-	-	-	-	47.6	2.8	27.5	-1.4	17.5	1.7	-	-	-	-
1957	26.9	3.5	-	-	-	-	48.2	1.3	28.8	4.7	19.0	8.6	-	-	-	-
1958	27.6	2.6	-	-	-	-	48.4	0.4	29.8	3.5	21.5	13.2	-	-	-	-
1959	27.9	1.1	-	-	-	-	48.1	-0.6	31.1	4.4	23.0	7.0	-	-	-	-
1960	28.4	1.8	-	-	-	-	49.1	2.1	31.5	1.3	24.6	7.0	-	-	-	-
1961	28.6	0.7	-	-	-	-	48.0	-2.2	31.7	0.6	26.2	6.5	-	-	-	-

[Continued]

Minneapolis-St. Paul, MN
Consumer Price Index - Urban Wage Earners
Base 1982-1984 = 100
Annual Averages
[Continued]

For 1917-1995. Columns headed % show percentile change in the index from the previous period for which an index is available.

Year	All Items		Food & Beverage		Housing		Apparel & Upkeep		Trans- portation		Medical Care		Entertain- ment		Other Goods & Services	
	Index	%	Index	%	Index	%	Index	%	Index	%	Index	%	Index	%	Index	%
1962	29.0	1.4	-	-	-	-	49.0	2.1	32.2	1.6	27.1	3.4	-	-	-	-
1963	29.4	1.4	-	-	-	-	50.0	2.0	32.7	1.6	27.4	1.1	-	-	-	-
1964	29.7	1.0	-	-	-	-	50.0	0.0	32.7	0.0	27.9	1.8	-	-	-	-
1965	30.1	1.3	-	-	-	-	51.0	2.0	33.3	1.8	28.0	0.4	-	-	-	-
1966	30.8	2.3	-	-	-	-	52.3	2.5	33.9	1.8	29.3	4.6	-	-	-	-
1967	31.9	3.6	-	-	-	-	54.2	3.6	35.0	3.2	30.9	5.5	-	-	-	-
1968	33.3	4.4	-	-	-	-	56.5	4.2	36.2	3.4	32.5	5.2	-	-	-	-
1969	35.0	5.1	-	-	-	-	59.7	5.7	36.8	1.7	34.1	4.9	-	-	-	-
1970	37.4	6.9	-	-	-	-	62.5	4.7	39.1	6.3	36.3	6.5	-	-	-	-
1971	38.8	3.7	-	-	-	-	64.1	2.6	40.5	3.6	38.2	5.2	-	-	-	-
1972	40.0	3.1	-	-	-	-	64.8	1.1	40.8	0.7	38.9	1.8	-	-	-	-
1973	42.4	6.0	-	-	-	-	67.9	4.8	42.4	3.9	40.9	5.1	-	-	-	-
1974	47.3	11.6	-	-	-	-	74.3	9.4	47.1	11.1	44.5	8.8	-	-	-	-
1975	51.3	8.5	-	-	-	-	75.7	1.9	50.1	6.4	49.3	10.8	-	-	-	-
1976	54.5	6.2	63.6	-	48.2	-	76.7	1.3	54.6	9.0	53.1	7.7	63.9	-	58.5	-
1977	58.3	7.0	66.9	5.2	52.4	8.7	79.9	4.2	58.7	7.5	57.4	8.1	67.3	5.3	61.8	5.6
1978	63.7	9.3	73.3	9.6	58.6	11.8	82.9	3.8	61.6	4.9	62.0	8.0	73.1	8.6	66.7	7.9
1979	71.2	11.8	81.6	11.3	65.7	12.1	86.0	3.7	71.5	16.1	66.3	6.9	81.6	11.6	71.1	6.6
1980	79.4	11.5	88.5	8.5	73.2	11.4	91.7	6.6	83.9	17.3	72.9	10.0	88.5	8.5	76.5	7.6
1981	88.9	12.0	92.7	4.7	85.7	17.1	96.3	5.0	93.9	11.9	79.5	9.1	92.6	4.6	83.8	9.5
1982	97.5	9.7	96.5	4.1	98.9	15.4	99.5	3.3	97.7	4.0	89.5	12.6	96.5	4.2	91.8	9.5
1983	99.1	1.6	99.5	3.1	98.2	-0.7	101.4	1.9	99.4	1.7	100.2	12.0	100.6	4.2	101.0	10.0
1984	103.5	4.4	104.1	4.6	102.9	4.8	99.2	-2.2	103.0	3.6	110.4	10.2	102.9	2.3	107.2	6.1
1985	105.7	2.1	106.5	2.3	103.5	0.6	106.6	7.5	105.8	2.7	117.6	6.5	106.7	3.7	114.1	6.4
1986	106.6	0.9	109.5	2.8	105.5	1.9	106.6	0.0	99.5	-6.0	127.4	8.3	112.1	5.1	120.6	5.7
1987	106.4	-0.2	111.7	2.0	96.5	-8.5	112.7	5.7	104.7	5.2	130.9	2.7	120.0	7.0	123.0	2.0
1988	109.7	3.1	116.1	3.9	97.5	1.0	121.1	7.5	107.1	2.3	137.7	5.2	126.3	5.2	130.4	6.0
1989	114.4	4.3	121.7	4.8	100.2	2.8	124.0	2.4	111.9	4.5	149.3	8.4	135.7	7.4	139.1	6.7
1990	120.9	5.7	128.8	5.8	104.5	4.3	132.8	7.1	118.7	6.1	162.3	8.7	136.6	0.7	152.8	9.8
1991	125.3	3.6	131.7	2.3	109.4	4.7	133.9	0.8	122.1	2.9	178.9	10.2	141.2	3.4	157.7	3.2
1992	128.9	2.9	131.0	-0.5	113.3	3.6	134.4	0.4	125.2	2.5	195.3	9.2	148.3	5.0	171.5	8.8
1993	133.0	3.2	132.6	1.2	117.2	3.4	138.9	3.3	129.4	3.4	202.9	3.9	156.2	5.3	179.6	4.7
1994	137.4	3.3	137.7	3.8	120.7	3.0	145.4	4.7	134.0	3.6	206.6	1.8	160.3	2.6	185.1	3.1
1995	139.4	1.5	140.3	1.9	121.2	0.4	137.6	-5.4	138.6	3.4	219.5	6.2	161.3	0.6	190.0	2.6

Source: U.S. Department of Labor, Bureau of Labor Statistics, Division of Consumer Prices and Price Indexes. - indicates no data collected for period.

Minneapolis-St. Paul, MN
Consumer Price Index - All Urban Consumers
Base 1982-1984 = 100
All Items

For 1917-1995. Columns headed % show percentile change in the index from the previous period for which an index is available.

Year	Jan Index	%	Feb Index	%	Mar Index	%	Apr Index	%	May Index	%	Jun Index	%	Jul Index	%	Aug Index	%	Sep Index	%	Oct Index	%	Nov Index	%	Dec Index	%
1917	-	-	-	-	-	-	-	-	-	-	-	-	-	-	-	-	-	-	-	-	-	-	13.1	-
1918	-	-	-	-	-	-	-	-	-	-	-	-	-	-	-	-	-	-	-	-	-	-	15.2	16.0
1919	-	-	-	-	-	-	-	-	-	-	15.6	2.6	-	-	-	-	-	-	-	-	-	-	17.5	12.2
1920	-	-	-	-	-	-	-	-	-	-	19.4	10.9	-	-	-	-	-	-	-	-	-	-	18.1	-6.7
1921	-	-	-	-	-	-	-	-	16.6	-8.3	-	-	-	-	-	-	16.5	-0.6	-	-	-	-	16.3	-1.2
1922	-	-	-	-	15.8	-3.1	-	-	-	-	15.9	0.6	-	-	-	-	15.5	-2.5	-	-	-	-	15.8	1.9
1923	-	-	-	-	15.8	0.0	-	-	-	-	15.8	0.0	-	-	-	-	15.9	0.6	-	-	-	-	16.0	0.6
1924	-	-	-	-	15.9	-0.6	-	-	-	-	15.7	-1.3	-	-	-	-	15.5	-1.3	-	-	-	-	15.7	1.3
1925	-	-	-	-	-	-	-	-	-	-	15.8	0.6	-	-	-	-	-	-	-	-	-	-	16.3	3.2
1926	-	-	-	-	-	-	-	-	-	-	16.3	0.0	-	-	-	-	-	-	-	-	-	-	16.0	-1.8
1927	-	-	-	-	-	-	-	-	-	-	16.0	0.0	-	-	-	-	-	-	-	-	-	-	15.6	-2.5
1928	-	-	-	-	-	-	-	-	-	-	15.6	0.0	-	-	-	-	-	-	-	-	-	-	15.5	-0.6
1929	-	-	-	-	-	-	-	-	-	-	15.5	0.0	-	-	-	-	-	-	-	-	-	-	15.7	1.3
1930	-	-	-	-	-	-	-	-	-	-	15.5	-1.3	-	-	-	-	-	-	-	-	-	-	14.9	-3.9
1931	-	-	-	-	-	-	-	-	-	-	14.2	-4.7	-	-	-	-	-	-	-	-	-	-	13.7	-3.5
1932	-	-	-	-	-	-	-	-	-	-	12.9	-5.8	-	-	-	-	-	-	-	-	-	-	12.4	-3.9
1933	-	-	-	-	-	-	-	-	-	-	11.9	-4.0	-	-	-	-	-	-	-	-	-	-	12.4	4.2
1934	-	-	-	-	-	-	-	-	-	-	12.6	1.6	-	-	-	-	-	-	-	-	12.6	0.0	-	-
1935	-	-	-	-	12.9	2.4	-	-	-	-	-	-	12.9	0.0	-	-	-	-	13.0	0.8	-	-	-	-
1936	13.1	0.8	-	-	-	-	13.0	-0.8	-	-	-	-	13.1	0.8	-	-	13.4	2.3	-	-	-	-	13.4	0.0
1937	-	-	-	-	13.6	1.5	-	-	-	-	13.7	0.7	-	-	-	-	13.9	1.5	-	-	-	-	13.8	-0.7
1938	-	-	-	-	13.6	-1.4	-	-	-	-	13.7	0.7	-	-	-	-	13.6	-0.7	-	-	-	-	13.5	-0.7
1939	-	-	-	-	13.4	-0.7	-	-	-	-	13.4	0.0	-	-	-	-	13.6	1.5	-	-	-	-	13.6	0.0
1940	-	-	-	-	13.5	-0.7	-	-	-	-	13.5	0.0	-	-	-	-	13.5	0.0	13.5	0.0	13.6	0.7	13.7	0.7
1941	13.6	-0.7	13.7	0.7	13.7	0.0	13.7	0.0	13.9	1.5	14.2	2.2	14.3	0.7	14.4	0.7	14.6	1.4	14.8	1.4	14.8	0.0	14.8	0.0
1942	15.0	1.4	15.1	0.7	15.3	1.3	15.4	0.7	15.5	0.6	15.5	0.0	15.6	0.6	15.6	0.0	15.7	0.6	15.8	0.6	15.9	0.6	16.0	0.6
1943	15.9	-0.6	16.0	0.6	16.2	1.3	16.2	0.0	16.3	0.6	16.3	0.0	16.2	-0.6	16.2	0.0	16.2	0.0	16.3	0.6	16.3	0.0	16.4	0.6
1944	16.2	-1.2	16.2	0.0	16.3	0.6	16.3	0.0	16.4	0.6	16.4	0.0	16.5	0.6	16.5	0.0	16.5	0.0	16.5	0.0	16.5	0.0	16.5	0.0
1945	16.5	0.0	16.5	0.0	16.5	0.0	16.5	0.0	16.6	0.6	16.7	0.6	16.7	0.0	16.7	0.0	16.8	0.6	16.8	0.0	16.9	0.6	16.9	0.0
1946	16.9	0.0	16.9	0.0	16.9	0.0	17.0	0.6	17.1	0.6	17.3	1.2	18.5	6.9	18.7	1.1	19.1	2.1	19.6	2.6	20.0	2.0	20.1	0.5
1947	19.9	-1.0	20.0	0.5	20.3	1.5	20.3	0.0	20.3	0.0	20.5	1.0	-	-	-	-	21.8	6.3	-	-	-	-	22.3	2.3
1948	-	-	-	-	22.5	0.9	-	-	-	-	23.0	2.2	-	-	-	-	23.3	1.3	-	-	-	-	22.9	-1.7
1949	-	-	-	-	22.8	-0.4	-	-	-	-	22.7	-0.4	-	-	-	-	22.7	0.0	-	-	-	-	22.5	-0.9
1950	-	-	-	-	22.4	-0.4	-	-	-	-	22.7	1.3	-	-	-	-	23.1	1.8	-	-	-	-	23.8	3.0
1951	-	-	-	-	24.5	2.9	-	-	-	-	24.6	0.4	-	-	-	-	24.5	-0.4	-	-	-	-	25.1	2.4
1952	-	-	-	-	25.2	0.4	-	-	-	-	25.5	1.2	-	-	-	-	25.5	0.0	-	-	-	-	25.4	-0.4
1953	25.4	0.0	-	-	-	-	25.5	0.4	-	-	-	-	25.7	0.8	-	-	-	-	25.9	0.8	-	-	-	-
1954	25.9	0.0	-	-	-	-	25.8	-0.4	-	-	-	-	26.0	0.8	-	-	-	-	25.9	-0.4	-	-	-	-
1955	25.9	0.0	-	-	-	-	26.0	0.4	-	-	-	-	26.1	0.4	-	-	-	-	25.8	-1.1	-	-	-	-
1956	25.8	0.0	-	-	-	-	25.7	-0.4	-	-	-	-	26.1	1.6	-	-	-	-	26.1	0.0	-	-	-	-
1957	26.5	1.5	-	-	-	-	26.6	0.4	-	-	-	-	27.0	1.5	-	-	-	-	27.1	0.4	-	-	-	-
1958	27.3	0.7	-	-	-	-	27.5	0.7	-	-	-	-	27.7	0.7	-	-	-	-	27.6	-0.4	-	-	-	-
1959	27.8	0.7	-	-	-	-	27.7	-0.4	-	-	-	-	27.8	0.4	-	-	-	-	28.1	1.1	-	-	-	-
1960	28.0	-0.4	-	-	-	-	28.2	0.7	-	-	-	-	28.3	0.4	-	-	-	-	28.5	0.7	-	-	-	-
1961	28.4	-0.4	-	-	-	-	28.6	0.7	-	-	-	-	28.7	0.3	-	-	-	-	28.7	0.0	-	-	-	-

[Continued]

Minneapolis-St. Paul, MN

Consumer Price Index - All Urban Consumers
Base 1982-1984 = 100
All Items
[Continued]

For 1917-1995. Columns headed % show percentile change in the index from the previous period for which an index is available.

Year	Jan Index	%	Feb Index	%	Mar Index	%	Apr Index	%	May Index	%	Jun Index	%	Jul Index	%	Aug Index	%	Sep Index	%	Oct Index	%	Nov Index	%	Dec Index	%
1962	28.6	-0.3	-	-	-	-	29.0	1.4	-	-	-	-	29.0	0.0	-	-	-	-	29.1	0.3	-	-	-	-
1963	29.1	0.0	-	-	-	-	29.2	0.3	-	-	-	-	29.6	1.4	-	-	-	-	29.5	-0.3	-	-	-	-
1964	29.5	0.0	-	-	-	-	29.5	0.0	-	-	-	-	29.7	0.7	-	-	-	-	29.8	0.3	-	-	-	-
1965	29.8	0.0	-	-	-	-	29.9	0.3	-	-	-	-	30.1	0.7	-	-	-	-	30.2	0.3	-	-	-	-
1966	30.3	0.3	-	-	-	-	30.7	1.3	-	-	-	-	30.7	0.0	-	-	-	-	31.1	1.3	-	-	-	-
1967	31.1	0.0	-	-	-	-	31.3	0.6	-	-	-	-	31.7	1.3	-	-	-	-	32.5	2.5	-	-	-	-
1968	32.7	0.6	-	-	-	-	33.1	1.2	-	-	-	-	33.4	0.9	-	-	-	-	33.5	0.3	-	-	-	-
1969	33.7	0.6	-	-	-	-	34.3	1.8	-	-	-	-	35.1	2.3	-	-	-	-	35.8	2.0	-	-	-	-
1970	36.5	2.0	-	-	-	-	37.1	1.6	-	-	-	-	37.5	1.1	-	-	-	-	37.9	1.1	-	-	-	-
1971	38.2	0.8	-	-	-	-	38.3	0.3	-	-	-	-	38.8	1.3	-	-	-	-	39.3	1.3	-	-	-	-
1972	39.4	0.3	-	-	-	-	39.5	0.3	-	-	-	-	39.9	1.0	-	-	-	-	40.5	1.5	-	-	-	-
1973	40.7	0.5	-	-	-	-	41.6	2.2	-	-	-	-	42.4	1.9	-	-	-	-	43.4	2.4	-	-	-	-
1974	44.6	2.8	-	-	-	-	46.2	3.6	-	-	-	-	47.3	2.4	-	-	-	-	49.0	3.6	-	-	-	-
1975	49.7	1.4	-	-	-	-	49.9	0.4	-	-	-	-	51.5	3.2	-	-	-	-	52.5	1.9	-	-	-	-
1976	53.2	1.3	-	-	-	-	53.7	0.9	-	-	-	-	54.6	1.7	-	-	-	-	55.2	1.1	-	-	-	-
1977	56.0	1.4	-	-	-	-	57.2	2.1	-	-	-	-	58.7	2.6	-	-	-	-	59.5	1.4	-	-	-	-
1978	60.7	2.0	-	-	-	-	62.0	2.1	-	-	63.2	1.9	-	-	64.5	2.1	-	-	65.6	1.7	-	-	66.4	1.2
1979	-	-	67.4	1.5	-	-	68.7	1.9	-	-	70.7	2.9	-	-	72.2	2.1	-	-	73.6	1.9	-	-	74.5	1.2
1980	-	-	75.7	1.6	-	-	77.7	2.6	-	-	78.4	0.9	-	-	79.6	1.5	-	-	81.3	2.1	-	-	82.4	1.4
1981	-	-	82.9	0.6	-	-	84.8	2.3	-	-	87.9	3.7	-	-	91.2	3.8	-	-	92.8	1.8	-	-	95.1	2.5
1982	-	-	97.4	2.4	-	-	96.0	-1.4	-	-	96.8	0.8	-	-	99.9	3.2	-	-	97.9	-2.0	-	-	97.4	-0.5
1983	-	-	97.3	-0.1	-	-	98.5	1.2	-	-	99.5	1.0	-	-	100.6	1.1	-	-	100.8	0.2	-	-	101.0	0.2
1984	-	-	101.7	0.7	-	-	102.5	0.8	-	-	103.1	0.6	-	-	103.4	0.3	-	-	104.4	1.0	-	-	104.3	-0.1
1985	-	-	105.1	0.8	-	-	106.2	1.0	-	-	107.1	0.8	-	-	107.8	0.7	-	-	108.4	0.6	-	-	108.3	-0.1
1986	-	-	108.2	-0.1	-	-	107.7	-0.5	-	-	108.9	1.1	-	-	108.3	-0.6	-	-	108.5	0.2	108.4	-0.1	109.0	0.6
1987	-	-	-	-	-	-	-	-	-	-	105.5	-3.2	-	-	-	-	-	-	-	-	-	-	107.5	1.9
1988	-	-	-	-	-	-	-	-	-	-	108.4	0.8	-	-	-	-	-	-	-	-	-	-	110.7	2.1
1989	-	-	-	-	-	-	-	-	-	-	113.1	2.2	-	-	-	-	-	-	-	-	-	-	115.1	1.8
1990	-	-	-	-	-	-	-	-	-	-	118.6	3.0	-	-	-	-	-	-	-	-	-	-	122.6	3.4
1991	-	-	-	-	-	-	-	-	-	-	124.1	1.2	-	-	-	-	-	-	-	-	-	-	126.2	1.7
1992	-	-	-	-	-	-	-	-	-	-	128.2	1.6	-	-	-	-	-	-	-	-	-	-	130.0	1.4
1993	-	-	-	-	-	-	-	-	-	-	131.8	1.4	-	-	-	-	-	-	-	-	-	-	135.1	2.5
1994	-	-	-	-	-	-	-	-	-	-	137.0	1.4	-	-	-	-	-	-	-	-	-	-	138.7	1.2
1995	-	-	-	-	-	-	-	-	-	-	138.9	0.1	-	-	-	-	-	-	-	-	-	-	-	-

Source: U.S. Department of Labor, Bureau of Labor Statistics, Division of Consumer Prices and Price Indexes. - indicates no data collected for period.

Minneapolis-St. Paul, MN
Consumer Price Index - Urban Wage Earners
Base 1982-1984 = 100
All Items

For 1917-1995. Columns headed % show percentile change in the index from the previous period for which an index is available.

Year	Jan Index	%	Feb Index	%	Mar Index	%	Apr Index	%	May Index	%	Jun Index	%	Jul Index	%	Aug Index	%	Sep Index	%	Oct Index	%	Nov Index	%	Dec Index	%
1917	-	-	-	-	-	-	-	-	-	-	-	-	-	-	-	-	-	-	-	-	-	-	13.2	-
1918	-	-	-	-	-	-	-	-	-	-	-	-	-	-	-	-	-	-	-	-	-	-	15.2	15.2
1919	-	-	-	-	-	-	-	-	-	-	15.6	2.6	-	-	-	-	-	-	-	-	-	-	17.5	12.2
1920	-	-	-	-	-	-	-	-	-	-	19.4	10.9	-	-	-	-	-	-	-	-	-	-	18.2	-6.2
1921	-	-	-	-	-	-	-	-	16.6	-8.8	-	-	-	-	-	-	16.5	-0.6	-	-	-	-	16.3	-1.2
1922	-	-	-	-	15.8	-3.1	-	-	-	-	15.9	0.6	-	-	-	-	15.5	-2.5	-	-	-	-	15.8	1.9
1923	-	-	-	-	15.9	0.6	-	-	-	-	15.8	-0.6	-	-	-	-	15.9	0.6	-	-	-	-	16.0	0.6
1924	-	-	-	-	15.9	-0.6	-	-	-	-	15.7	-1.3	-	-	-	-	15.5	-1.3	-	-	-	-	15.7	1.3
1925	-	-	-	-	-	-	-	-	-	-	15.8	0.6	-	-	-	-	-	-	-	-	-	-	16.3	3.2
1926	-	-	-	-	-	-	-	-	-	-	16.3	0.0	-	-	-	-	-	-	-	-	-	-	16.0	-1.8
1927	-	-	-	-	-	-	-	-	-	-	16.1	0.6	-	-	-	-	-	-	-	-	-	-	15.6	-3.1
1928	-	-	-	-	-	-	-	-	-	-	15.6	0.0	-	-	-	-	-	-	-	-	-	-	15.5	-0.6
1929	-	-	-	-	-	-	-	-	-	-	15.5	0.0	-	-	-	-	-	-	-	-	-	-	15.7	1.3
1930	-	-	-	-	-	-	-	-	-	-	15.5	-1.3	-	-	-	-	-	-	-	-	-	-	14.9	-3.9
1931	-	-	-	-	-	-	-	-	-	-	14.2	-4.7	-	-	-	-	-	-	-	-	-	-	13.8	-2.8
1932	-	-	-	-	-	-	-	-	-	-	12.9	-6.5	-	-	-	-	-	-	-	-	-	-	12.5	-3.1
1933	-	-	-	-	-	-	-	-	-	-	11.9	-4.8	-	-	-	-	-	-	-	-	-	-	12.5	5.0
1934	-	-	-	-	-	-	-	-	-	-	12.6	0.8	-	-	-	-	-	-	-	-	12.6	0.0	-	-
1935	-	-	-	-	12.9	2.4	-	-	-	-	-	-	12.9	0.0	-	-	-	-	13.0	0.8	-	-	-	-
1936	13.2	1.5	-	-	-	-	13.0	-1.5	-	-	-	-	13.2	1.5	-	-	13.4	1.5	-	-	-	-	13.4	0.0
1937	-	-	-	-	13.6	1.5	-	-	-	-	13.8	1.5	-	-	-	-	14.0	1.4	-	-	-	-	13.9	-0.7
1938	-	-	-	-	13.6	-2.2	-	-	-	-	13.7	0.7	-	-	-	-	13.6	-0.7	-	-	-	-	13.5	-0.7
1939	-	-	-	-	13.4	-0.7	-	-	-	-	13.4	0.0	-	-	-	-	13.6	1.5	-	-	-	-	13.6	0.0
1940	-	-	-	-	13.5	-0.7	-	-	-	-	13.5	0.0	-	-	-	-	13.5	0.0	13.5	0.0	13.6	0.7	13.7	0.7
1941	13.6	-0.7	13.7	0.7	13.7	0.0	13.8	0.7	13.9	0.7	14.2	2.2	14.3	0.7	14.4	0.7	14.6	1.4	14.8	1.4	14.8	0.0	14.8	0.0
1942	15.0	1.4	15.1	0.7	15.3	1.3	15.4	0.7	15.5	0.6	15.5	0.0	15.6	0.6	15.6	0.0	15.7	0.6	15.8	0.6	15.9	0.6	16.0	0.6
1943	16.0	0.0	16.1	0.6	16.2	0.6	16.2	0.0	16.3	0.6	16.3	0.0	16.2	-0.6	16.2	0.0	16.2	0.0	16.3	0.6	16.3	0.0	16.4	0.6
1944	16.2	-1.2	16.2	0.0	16.3	0.6	16.3	0.0	16.4	0.6	16.4	0.0	16.5	0.6	16.5	0.0	16.5	0.0	16.5	0.0	16.5	0.0	16.5	0.0
1945	16.5	0.0	16.5	0.0	16.5	0.0	16.5	0.0	16.6	0.6	16.7	0.6	16.8	0.6	16.8	0.0	16.8	0.0	16.8	0.0	16.9	0.6	16.9	0.0
1946	17.0	0.6	16.9	-0.6	16.9	0.0	17.0	0.6	17.1	0.6	17.4	1.8	18.5	6.3	18.7	1.1	19.1	2.1	19.6	2.6	20.0	2.0	20.1	0.5
1947	19.9	-1.0	20.0	0.5	20.4	2.0	20.3	-0.5	20.4	0.5	20.6	1.0	-	-	-	-	21.8	5.8	-	-	-	-	22.3	2.3
1948	-	-	-	-	22.6	1.3	-	-	-	-	23.0	1.8	-	-	-	-	23.4	1.7	-	-	-	-	23.0	-1.7
1949	-	-	-	-	22.8	-0.9	-	-	-	-	22.7	-0.4	-	-	-	-	22.7	0.0	-	-	-	-	22.6	-0.4
1950	-	-	-	-	22.5	-0.4	-	-	-	-	22.7	0.9	-	-	-	-	23.2	2.2	-	-	-	-	23.8	2.6
1951	-	-	-	-	24.6	3.4	-	-	-	-	24.7	0.4	-	-	-	-	24.6	-0.4	-	-	-	-	25.2	2.4
1952	-	-	-	-	25.2	0.0	-	-	-	-	25.6	1.6	-	-	-	-	25.5	-0.4	-	-	-	-	25.5	0.0
1953	25.4	-0.4	-	-	-	-	25.6	0.8	-	-	-	-	25.7	0.4	-	-	-	-	25.9	0.8	-	-	-	-
1954	25.9	0.0	-	-	-	-	25.8	-0.4	-	-	-	-	26.1	1.2	-	-	-	-	26.0	-0.4	-	-	-	-
1955	25.9	-0.4	-	-	-	-	26.0	0.4	-	-	-	-	26.1	0.4	-	-	-	-	25.9	-0.8	-	-	-	-
1956	25.8	-0.4	-	-	-	-	25.7	-0.4	-	-	-	-	26.2	1.9	-	-	-	-	26.1	-0.4	-	-	-	-
1957	26.5	1.5	-	-	-	-	26.6	0.4	-	-	-	-	27.0	1.5	-	-	-	-	27.1	0.4	-	-	-	-
1958	27.4	1.1	-	-	-	-	27.6	0.7	-	-	-	-	27.8	0.7	-	-	-	-	27.7	-0.4	-	-	-	-
1959	27.8	0.4	-	-	-	-	27.8	0.0	-	-	-	-	27.9	0.4	-	-	-	-	28.1	0.7	-	-	-	-
1960	28.0	-0.4	-	-	-	-	28.2	0.7	-	-	-	-	28.4	0.7	-	-	-	-	28.5	0.4	-	-	-	-
1961	28.4	-0.4	-	-	-	-	28.7	1.1	-	-	-	-	28.7	0.0	-	-	-	-	28.7	0.0	-	-	-	-

[Continued]

Minneapolis-St. Paul, MN
Consumer Price Index - Urban Wage Earners
Base 1982-1984 = 100
All Items
[Continued]

For 1917-1995. Columns headed % show percentile change in the index from the previous period for which an index is available.

Year	Jan Index	%	Feb Index	%	Mar Index	%	Apr Index	%	May Index	%	Jun Index	%	Jul Index	%	Aug Index	%	Sep Index	%	Oct Index	%	Nov Index	%	Dec Index	%
1962	28.7	0.0	-	-	-	-	29.0	1.0	-	-	-	-	29.1	0.3	-	-	-	-	29.1	0.0	-	-	-	-
1963	29.2	0.3	-	-	-	-	29.3	0.3	-	-	-	-	29.6	1.0	-	-	-	-	29.5	-0.3	-	-	-	-
1964	29.6	0.3	-	-	-	-	29.5	-0.3	-	-	-	-	29.7	0.7	-	-	-	-	29.9	0.7	-	-	-	-
1965	29.9	0.0	-	-	-	-	29.9	0.0	-	-	-	-	30.2	1.0	-	-	-	-	30.3	0.3	-	-	-	-
1966	30.4	0.3	-	-	-	-	30.7	1.0	-	-	-	-	30.8	0.3	-	-	-	-	31.2	1.3	-	-	-	-
1967	31.2	0.0	-	-	-	-	31.4	0.6	-	-	-	-	31.8	1.3	-	-	-	-	32.6	2.5	-	-	-	-
1968	32.8	0.6	-	-	-	-	33.1	0.9	-	-	-	-	33.5	1.2	-	-	-	-	33.5	0.0	-	-	-	-
1969	33.8	0.9	-	-	-	-	34.4	1.8	-	-	-	-	35.2	2.3	-	-	-	-	35.8	1.7	-	-	-	-
1970	36.5	2.0	-	-	-	-	37.2	1.9	-	-	-	-	37.6	1.1	-	-	-	-	38.0	1.1	-	-	-	-
1971	38.3	0.8	-	-	-	-	38.3	0.0	-	-	-	-	38.8	1.3	-	-	-	-	39.3	1.3	-	-	-	-
1972	39.4	0.3	-	-	-	-	39.6	0.5	-	-	-	-	40.0	1.0	-	-	-	-	40.5	1.3	-	-	-	-
1973	40.7	0.5	-	-	-	-	41.7	2.5	-	-	-	-	42.4	1.7	-	-	-	-	43.4	2.4	-	-	-	-
1974	44.7	3.0	-	-	-	-	46.2	3.4	-	-	-	-	47.4	2.6	-	-	-	-	49.0	3.4	-	-	-	-
1975	49.8	1.6	-	-	-	-	50.0	0.4	-	-	-	-	51.6	3.2	-	-	-	-	52.6	1.9	-	-	-	-
1976	53.2	1.1	-	-	-	-	53.7	0.9	-	-	-	-	54.7	1.9	-	-	-	-	55.2	0.9	-	-	-	-
1977	56.0	1.4	-	-	-	-	57.2	2.1	-	-	-	-	58.8	2.8	-	-	-	-	59.6	1.4	-	-	-	-
1978	60.8	2.0	-	-	-	-	62.1	2.1	-	-	63.3	1.9	-	-	64.8	2.4	-	-	65.7	1.4	-	-	66.7	1.5
1979	-	-	67.7	1.5	-	-	68.8	1.6	-	-	71.2	3.5	-	-	72.8	2.2	-	-	74.2	1.9	-	-	74.8	0.8
1980	-	-	76.3	2.0	-	-	78.3	2.6	-	-	79.1	1.0	-	-	79.8	0.9	-	-	81.8	2.5	-	-	83.0	1.5
1981	-	-	83.6	0.7	-	-	85.2	1.9	-	-	88.1	3.4	-	-	91.4	3.7	-	-	92.9	1.6	-	-	95.0	2.3
1982	-	-	97.3	2.4	-	-	96.0	-1.3	-	-	96.8	0.8	-	-	99.8	3.1	-	-	98.0	-1.8	-	-	97.5	-0.5
1983	-	-	98.5	1.0	-	-	99.5	1.0	-	-	99.3	-0.2	-	-	98.3	-1.0	-	-	99.6	1.3	-	-	99.6	0.0
1984	-	-	101.5	1.9	-	-	102.3	0.8	-	-	104.8	2.4	-	-	105.9	1.0	-	-	104.2	-1.6	-	-	103.2	-1.0
1985	-	-	103.9	0.7	-	-	104.9	1.0	-	-	105.9	1.0	-	-	106.5	0.6	-	-	107.1	0.6	-	-	107.1	0.0
1986	-	-	106.7	-0.4	-	-	105.9	-0.7	-	-	107.1	1.1	-	-	106.6	-0.5	-	-	106.6	0.0	106.6	0.0	107.0	0.4
1987	-	-	-	-	-	-	-	-	-	-	105.3	-1.6	-	-	-	-	-	-	-	-	-	-	107.4	2.0
1988	-	-	-	-	-	-	-	-	-	-	108.4	0.9	-	-	-	-	-	-	-	-	-	-	111.0	2.4
1989	-	-	-	-	-	-	-	-	-	-	113.4	2.2	-	-	-	-	-	-	-	-	-	-	115.4	1.8
1990	-	-	-	-	-	-	-	-	-	-	118.8	2.9	-	-	-	-	-	-	-	-	-	-	123.0	3.5
1991	-	-	-	-	-	-	-	-	-	-	124.3	1.1	-	-	-	-	-	-	-	-	-	-	126.3	1.6
1992	-	-	-	-	-	-	-	-	-	-	128.0	1.3	-	-	-	-	-	-	-	-	-	-	129.9	1.5
1993	-	-	-	-	-	-	-	-	-	-	131.4	1.2	-	-	-	-	-	-	-	-	-	-	134.6	2.4
1994	-	-	-	-	-	-	-	-	-	-	136.4	1.3	-	-	-	-	-	-	-	-	-	-	138.5	1.5
1995	-	-	-	-	-	-	-	-	-	-	138.5	0.0	-	-	-	-	-	-	-	-	-	-	-	-

Source: U.S. Department of Labor, Bureau of Labor Statistics, Division of Consumer Prices and Price Indexes. - indicates no data collected for period.

Minneapolis-St. Paul, MN
Consumer Price Index - All Urban Consumers
Base 1982-1984 = 100
Food and Beverages

For 1976-1995. Columns headed % show percentile change in the index from the previous period for which an index is available.

Year	Jan Index	%	Feb Index	%	Mar Index	%	Apr Index	%	May Index	%	Jun Index	%	Jul Index	%	Aug Index	%	Sep Index	%	Oct Index	%	Nov Index	%	Dec Index	%
1976	62.4	-	-	-	-	-	62.0	-0.6	-	-	-	-	62.8	1.3	-	-	-	-	62.7	-0.2	-	-	-	-
1977	63.1	0.6	-	-	-	-	65.0	3.0	-	-	-	-	66.7	2.6	-	-	-	-	66.8	0.1	-	-	-	-
1978	67.9	1.6	-	-	-	-	70.6	4.0	-	-	72.9	3.3	-	-	73.6	1.0	-	-	74.3	1.0	-	-	75.5	1.6
1979	-	-	78.2	3.6	-	-	79.4	1.5	-	-	81.7	2.9	-	-	82.3	0.7	-	-	82.6	0.4	-	-	83.6	1.2
1980	-	-	84.4	1.0	-	-	86.0	1.9	-	-	87.6	1.9	-	-	88.6	1.1	-	-	89.9	1.5	-	-	90.7	0.9
1981	-	-	91.3	0.7	-	-	91.7	0.4	-	-	92.2	0.5	-	-	93.8	1.7	-	-	94.1	0.3	-	-	94.1	0.0
1982	-	-	94.9	0.9	-	-	95.4	0.5	-	-	96.8	1.5	-	-	97.5	0.7	-	-	97.9	0.4	-	-	97.9	0.0
1983	-	-	97.9	0.0	-	-	99.4	1.5	-	-	99.2	-0.2	-	-	99.6	0.4	-	-	100.0	0.4	-	-	101.5	1.5
1984	-	-	103.4	1.9	-	-	103.6	0.2	-	-	103.8	0.2	-	-	104.1	0.3	-	-	104.8	0.7	-	-	105.3	0.5
1985	-	-	106.5	1.1	-	-	106.3	-0.2	-	-	106.2	-0.1	-	-	106.3	0.1	-	-	106.9	0.6	-	-	107.7	0.7
1986	-	-	108.4	0.6	-	-	108.7	0.3	-	-	108.6	-0.1	-	-	109.4	0.7	-	-	110.4	0.9	111.1	0.6	112.2	1.0
1987	-	-	-	-	-	-	-	-	-	-	111.3	-0.8	-	-	-	-	-	-	-	-	-	-	112.3	0.9
1988	-	-	-	-	-	-	-	-	-	-	114.1	1.6	-	-	-	-	-	-	-	-	-	-	118.2	3.6
1989	-	-	-	-	-	-	-	-	-	-	121.4	2.7	-	-	-	-	-	-	-	-	-	-	122.0	0.5
1990	-	-	-	-	-	-	-	-	-	-	127.4	4.4	-	-	-	-	-	-	-	-	-	-	129.9	2.0
1991	-	-	-	-	-	-	-	-	-	-	131.7	1.4	-	-	-	-	-	-	-	-	-	-	131.5	-0.2
1992	-	-	-	-	-	-	-	-	-	-	131.7	0.2	-	-	-	-	-	-	-	-	-	-	129.8	-1.4
1993	-	-	-	-	-	-	-	-	-	-	130.4	0.5	-	-	-	-	-	-	-	-	-	-	134.4	3.1
1994	-	-	-	-	-	-	-	-	-	-	136.7	1.7	-	-	-	-	-	-	-	-	-	-	138.2	1.1
1995	-	-	-	-	-	-	-	-	-	-	140.0	1.3	-	-	-	-	-	-	-	-	-	-	-	-

Source: U.S. Department of Labor, Bureau of Labor Statistics, Division of Consumer Prices and Price Indexes. - indicates no data collected for period.

Minneapolis-St. Paul, MN
Consumer Price Index - Urban Wage Earners
Base 1982-1984 = 100
Food and Beverages

For 1976-1995. Columns headed % show percentile change in the index from the previous period for which an index is available.

Year	Jan Index	%	Feb Index	%	Mar Index	%	Apr Index	%	May Index	%	Jun Index	%	Jul Index	%	Aug Index	%	Sep Index	%	Oct Index	%	Nov Index	%	Dec Index	%
1976	63.5	-	-	-	-	-	63.1	-0.6	-	-	-	-	63.9	1.3	-	-	-	-	63.8	-0.2	-	-	-	-
1977	64.2	0.6	-	-	-	-	66.1	3.0	-	-	-	-	67.9	2.7	-	-	-	-	68.0	0.1	-	-	-	-
1978	69.0	1.5	-	-	-	-	71.9	4.2	-	-	73.4	2.1	-	-	75.0	2.2	-	-	75.3	0.4	-	-	76.1	1.1
1979	-	-	79.1	3.9	-	-	79.3	0.3	-	-	82.2	3.7	-	-	83.5	1.6	-	-	83.9	0.5	-	-	83.3	-0.7
1980	-	-	85.3	2.4	-	-	86.9	1.9	-	-	88.3	1.6	-	-	89.3	1.1	-	-	91.3	2.2	-	-	91.8	0.5
1981	-	-	91.3	-0.5	-	-	91.7	0.4	-	-	92.1	0.4	-	-	94.1	2.2	-	-	94.0	-0.1	-	-	93.7	-0.3
1982	-	-	94.5	0.9	-	-	95.2	0.7	-	-	96.6	1.5	-	-	97.4	0.8	-	-	98.0	0.6	-	-	98.0	0.0
1983	-	-	97.9	-0.1	-	-	99.4	1.5	-	-	99.1	-0.3	-	-	99.6	0.5	-	-	100.1	0.5	-	-	101.6	1.5
1984	-	-	103.4	1.8	-	-	103.8	0.4	-	-	103.8	0.0	-	-	104.2	0.4	-	-	105.0	0.8	-	-	105.4	0.4
1985	-	-	106.6	1.1	-	-	106.4	-0.2	-	-	106.1	-0.3	-	-	106.2	0.1	-	-	106.8	0.6	-	-	107.6	0.7
1986	-	-	108.5	0.8	-	-	108.6	0.1	-	-	108.6	0.0	-	-	109.6	0.9	-	-	110.4	0.7	111.1	0.6	112.1	0.9
1987	-	-	-	-	-	-	-	-	-	-	111.1	-0.9	-	-	-	-	-	-	-	-	-	-	112.2	1.0
1988	-	-	-	-	-	-	-	-	-	-	113.9	1.5	-	-	-	-	-	-	-	-	-	-	118.2	3.8
1989	-	-	-	-	-	-	-	-	-	-	121.4	2.7	-	-	-	-	-	-	-	-	-	-	122.0	0.5
1990	-	-	-	-	-	-	-	-	-	-	127.6	4.6	-	-	-	-	-	-	-	-	-	-	130.1	2.0
1991	-	-	-	-	-	-	-	-	-	-	131.7	1.2	-	-	-	-	-	-	-	-	-	-	131.7	0.0
1992	-	-	-	-	-	-	-	-	-	-	132.0	0.2	-	-	-	-	-	-	-	-	-	-	130.0	-1.5
1993	-	-	-	-	-	-	-	-	-	-	130.5	0.4	-	-	-	-	-	-	-	-	-	-	134.7	3.2
1994	-	-	-	-	-	-	-	-	-	-	137.1	1.8	-	-	-	-	-	-	-	-	-	-	138.4	0.9
1995	-	-	-	-	-	-	-	-	-	-	140.0	1.2	-	-	-	-	-	-	-	-	-	-	-	-

Source: U.S. Department of Labor, Bureau of Labor Statistics, Division of Consumer Prices and Price Indexes. - indicates no data collected for period.

Minneapolis-St. Paul, MN
Consumer Price Index - All Urban Consumers
Base 1982-1984 = 100
Housing

For 1976-1995. Columns headed % show percentile change in the index from the previous period for which an index is available.

Year	Jan Index	%	Feb Index	%	Mar Index	%	Apr Index	%	May Index	%	Jun Index	%	Jul Index	%	Aug Index	%	Sep Index	%	Oct Index	%	Nov Index	%	Dec Index	%
1976	47.7	-	-	-	-	-	48.1	0.8	-	-	-	-	49.1	2.1	-	-	-	-	49.8	1.4	-	-	-	-
1977	50.8	2.0	-	-	-	-	51.6	1.6	-	-	-	-	53.7	4.1	-	-	-	-	54.9	2.2	-	-	-	-
1978	56.5	2.9	-	-	-	-	57.5	1.8	-	-	58.7	2.1	-	-	60.3	2.7	-	-	61.6	2.2	-	-	62.2	1.0
1979	-	-	63.0	1.3	-	-	64.1	1.7	-	-	65.8	2.7	-	-	67.2	2.1	-	-	69.6	3.6	-	-	70.0	0.6
1980	-	-	70.7	1.0	-	-	73.0	3.3	-	-	73.4	0.5	-	-	74.4	1.4	-	-	76.7	3.1	-	-	77.8	1.4
1981	-	-	77.5	-0.4	-	-	79.7	2.8	-	-	84.7	6.3	-	-	89.9	6.1	-	-	91.9	2.2	-	-	96.1	4.6
1982	-	-	100.3	4.4	-	-	98.1	-2.2	-	-	97.1	-1.0	-	-	102.2	5.3	-	-	98.2	-3.9	-	-	96.8	-1.4
1983	-	-	97.7	0.9	-	-	98.7	1.0	-	-	99.9	1.2	-	-	100.3	0.4	-	-	100.3	0.0	-	-	99.6	-0.7
1984	-	-	100.0	0.4	-	-	101.5	1.5	-	-	102.3	0.8	-	-	102.5	0.2	-	-	103.3	0.8	-	-	103.0	-0.3
1985	-	-	103.7	0.7	-	-	104.7	1.0	-	-	106.0	1.2	-	-	107.1	1.0	-	-	107.6	0.5	-	-	106.7	-0.8
1986	-	-	106.8	0.1	-	-	107.6	0.7	-	-	109.4	1.7	-	-	109.2	-0.2	-	-	107.2	-1.8	106.4	-0.7	107.5	1.0
1987	-	-	-	-	-	-	-	-	-	-	96.7	-10.0	-	-	-	-	-	-	-	-	-	-	97.2	0.5
1988	-	-	-	-	-	-	-	-	-	-	97.4	0.2	-	-	-	-	-	-	-	-	-	-	98.7	1.3
1989	-	-	-	-	-	-	-	-	-	-	99.8	1.1	-	-	-	-	-	-	-	-	-	-	101.3	1.5
1990	-	-	-	-	-	-	-	-	-	-	103.2	1.9	-	-	-	-	-	-	-	-	-	-	106.4	3.1
1991	-	-	-	-	-	-	-	-	-	-	108.2	1.7	-	-	-	-	-	-	-	-	-	-	110.7	2.3
1992	-	-	-	-	-	-	-	-	-	-	112.1	1.3	-	-	-	-	-	-	-	-	-	-	114.3	2.0
1993	-	-	-	-	-	-	-	-	-	-	115.3	0.9	-	-	-	-	-	-	-	-	-	-	118.3	2.6
1994	-	-	-	-	-	-	-	-	-	-	119.5	1.0	-	-	-	-	-	-	-	-	-	-	121.3	1.5
1995	-	-	-	-	-	-	-	-	-	-	119.9	-1.2	-	-	-	-	-	-	-	-	-	-	-	-

Source: U.S. Department of Labor, Bureau of Labor Statistics, Division of Consumer Prices and Price Indexes. - indicates no data collected for period.

Minneapolis-St. Paul, MN
Consumer Price Index - Urban Wage Earners
Base 1982-1984 = 100
Housing

For 1976-1995. Columns headed % show percentile change in the index from the previous period for which an index is available.

Year	Jan Index	%	Feb Index	%	Mar Index	%	Apr Index	%	May Index	%	Jun Index	%	Jul Index	%	Aug Index	%	Sep Index	%	Oct Index	%	Nov Index	%	Dec Index	%
1976	47.0	-	-	-	-	-	47.4	0.9	-	-	-	-	48.4	2.1	-	-	-	-	49.1	1.4	-	-	-	-
1977	50.1	2.0	-	-	-	-	50.9	1.6	-	-	-	-	52.9	3.9	-	-	-	-	54.0	2.1	-	-	-	-
1978	55.7	3.1	-	-	-	-	56.6	1.6	-	-	58.1	2.7	-	-	59.9	3.1	-	-	61.0	1.8	-	-	61.7	1.1
1979	-	-	62.5	1.3	-	-	63.5	1.6	-	-	65.4	3.0	-	-	66.8	2.1	-	-	68.8	3.0	-	-	69.3	0.7
1980	-	-	70.1	1.2	-	-	72.0	2.7	-	-	72.5	0.7	-	-	73.5	1.4	-	-	76.0	3.4	-	-	77.4	1.8
1981	-	-	77.3	-0.1	-	-	79.5	2.8	-	-	84.5	6.3	-	-	89.8	6.3	-	-	91.7	2.1	-	-	96.2	4.9
1982	-	-	100.5	4.5	-	-	98.3	-2.2	-	-	97.1	-1.2	-	-	102.5	5.6	-	-	98.3	-4.1	-	-	96.8	-1.5
1983	-	-	99.8	3.1	-	-	100.7	0.9	-	-	99.2	-1.5	-	-	95.2	-4.0	-	-	97.6	2.5	-	-	96.6	-1.0
1984	-	-	99.9	3.4	-	-	101.2	1.3	-	-	105.9	4.6	-	-	107.9	1.9	-	-	103.1	-4.4	-	-	100.7	-2.3
1985	-	-	101.5	0.8	-	-	102.3	0.8	-	-	103.6	1.3	-	-	104.7	1.1	-	-	105.3	0.6	-	-	104.4	-0.9
1986	-	-	104.5	0.1	-	-	105.2	0.7	-	-	107.1	1.8	-	-	106.9	-0.2	-	-	104.7	-2.1	103.9	-0.8	104.9	1.0
1987	-	-	-	-	-	-	-	-	-	-	96.2	-8.3	-	-	-	-	-	-	-	-	-	-	96.8	0.6
1988	-	-	-	-	-	-	-	-	-	-	96.9	0.1	-	-	-	-	-	-	-	-	-	-	98.1	1.2
1989	-	-	-	-	-	-	-	-	-	-	99.2	1.1	-	-	-	-	-	-	-	-	-	-	101.1	1.9
1990	-	-	-	-	-	-	-	-	-	-	102.7	1.6	-	-	-	-	-	-	-	-	-	-	106.3	3.5
1991	-	-	-	-	-	-	-	-	-	-	108.2	1.8	-	-	-	-	-	-	-	-	-	-	110.7	2.3
1992	-	-	-	-	-	-	-	-	-	-	112.0	1.2	-	-	-	-	-	-	-	-	-	-	114.6	2.3
1993	-	-	-	-	-	-	-	-	-	-	115.6	0.9	-	-	-	-	-	-	-	-	-	-	118.8	2.8
1994	-	-	-	-	-	-	-	-	-	-	119.6	0.7	-	-	-	-	-	-	-	-	-	-	121.8	1.8
1995	-	-	-	-	-	-	-	-	-	-	120.0	-1.5	-	-	-	-	-	-	-	-	-	-	-	-

Source: U.S. Department of Labor, Bureau of Labor Statistics, Division of Consumer Prices and Price Indexes. - indicates no data collected for period.

Minneapolis-St. Paul, MN
Consumer Price Index - All Urban Consumers
Base 1982-1984 = 100
Apparel and Upkeep

For 1952-1995. Columns headed % show percentile change in the index from the previous period for which an index is available.

Year	Jan Index	%	Feb Index	%	Mar Index	%	Apr Index	%	May Index	%	Jun Index	%	Jul Index	%	Aug Index	%	Sep Index	%	Oct Index	%	Nov Index	%	Dec Index	%
1952	-		-		-		-		-		-		-		-		-		-		-		46.0	-
1953	45.6	-0.9	-		-		45.9	0.7	-		-		45.6	-0.7	-		-		46.4	1.8	-		-	
1954	45.9	-1.1	-		-		45.9	0.0	-		-		46.0	0.2	-		-		46.1	0.2	-		-	
1955	45.2	-2.0	-		-		45.0	-0.4	-		-		44.8	-0.4	-		-		45.7	2.0	-		-	
1956	46.0	0.7	-		-		46.1	0.2	-		-		46.5	0.9	-		-		47.1	1.3	-		-	
1957	46.9	-0.4	-		-		47.2	0.6	-		-		46.9	-0.6	-		-		47.4	1.1	-		-	
1958	47.4	0.0	-		-		47.3	-0.2	-		-		47.3	0.0	-		-		47.5	0.4	-		-	
1959	47.0	-1.1	-		-		46.9	-0.2	-		-		46.9	0.0	-		-		47.1	0.4	-		-	
1960	47.3	0.4	-		-		47.8	1.1	-		-		47.9	0.2	-		-		49.0	2.3	-		-	
1961	46.8	-4.5	-		-		46.6	-0.4	-		-		46.6	0.0	-		-		47.6	2.1	-		-	
1962	47.4	-0.4	-		-		47.7	0.6	-		-		47.6	-0.2	-		-		48.8	2.5	-		-	
1963	48.6	-0.4	-		-		48.8	0.4	-		-		49.0	0.4	-		-		49.3	0.6	-		-	
1964	48.1	-2.4	-		-		48.6	1.0	-		-		48.6	0.0	-		-		49.8	2.5	-		-	
1965	49.2	-1.2	-		-		49.7	1.0	-		-		49.4	-0.6	-		-		50.7	2.6	-		-	
1966	50.3	-0.8	-		-		50.7	0.8	-		-		51.2	1.0	-		-		52.2	2.0	-		-	
1967	51.6	-1.1	-		-		52.9	2.5	-		-		52.6	-0.6	-		-		54.3	3.2	-		-	
1968	53.7	-1.1	-		-		55.2	2.8	-		-		55.1	-0.2	-		-		56.2	2.0	-		-	
1969	56.3	0.2	-		-		57.8	2.7	-		-		58.3	0.9	-		-		60.1	3.1	-		-	
1970	59.3	-1.3	-		-		60.9	2.7	-		-		60.1	-1.3	-		-		63.3	5.3	-		-	
1971	62.1	-1.9	-		-		62.8	1.1	-		-		62.2	-1.0	-		-		63.3	1.8	-		-	
1972	62.4	-1.4	-		-		63.0	1.0	-		-		62.2	-1.3	-		-		65.2	4.8	-		-	
1973	64.5	-1.1	-		-		65.4	1.4	-		-		66.1	1.1	-		-		68.1	3.0	-		-	
1974	68.4	0.4	-		-		71.0	3.8	-		-		71.1	0.1	-		-		77.5	9.0	-		-	
1975	75.8	-2.2	-		-		73.9	-2.5	-		-		73.1	-1.1	-		-		73.8	1.0	-		-	
1976	73.7	-0.1	-		-		74.5	1.1	-		-		74.0	-0.7	-		-		77.0	4.1	-		-	
1977	75.8	-1.6	-		-		77.2	1.8	-		-		78.9	2.2	-		-		79.4	0.6	-		-	
1978	78.8	-0.8	-		-		81.1	2.9	-		80.3	-1.0	-		81.8	1.9	-		82.4	0.7	-		84.2	2.2
1979	-		82.8	-1.7	-		85.5	3.3	-		84.4	-1.3	-		86.8	2.8	-		86.4	-0.5	-		88.1	2.0
1980	-		88.5	0.5	-		91.2	3.1	-		91.5	0.3	-		92.1	0.7	-		90.9	-1.3	-		91.5	0.7
1981	-		91.6	0.1	-		94.2	2.8	-		94.2	0.0	-		95.7	1.6	-		97.0	1.4	-		96.8	-0.2
1982	-		97.9	1.1	-		99.1	1.2	-		97.4	-1.7	-		101.2	3.9	-		100.9	-0.3	-		103.0	2.1
1983	-		99.7	-3.2	-		104.0	4.3	-		101.5	-2.4	-		101.6	0.1	-		100.8	-0.8	-		101.2	0.4
1984	-		98.6	-2.6	-		99.8	1.2	-		98.4	-1.4	-		96.7	-1.7	-		99.9	3.3	-		98.9	-1.0
1985	-		103.3	4.4	-		107.7	4.3	-		108.0	0.3	-		104.7	-3.1	-		107.2	2.4	-		108.7	1.4
1986	-		104.5	-3.9	-		108.9	4.2	-		106.7	-2.0	-		105.9	-0.7	-		108.7	2.6	107.3	-1.3	107.0	-0.3
1987	-		-		-		-		-		110.3	3.1	-		-		-		-		-		116.8	5.9
1988	-		-		-		-		-		119.9	2.7	-		-		-		-		-		122.3	2.0
1989	-		-		-		-		-		123.4	0.9	-		-		-		-		-		124.5	0.9
1990	-		-		-		-		-		132.7	6.6	-		-		-		-		-		132.4	-0.2
1991	-		-		-		-		-		135.0	2.0	-		-		-		-		-		134.5	-0.4
1992	-		-		-		-		-		135.8	1.0	-		-		-		-		-		135.8	0.0
1993	-		-		-		-		-		139.2	2.5	-		-		-		-		-		145.1	4.2
1994	-		-		-		-		-		149.9	3.3	-		-		-		-		-		143.4	-4.3
1995	-		-		-		-		-		137.6	-4.0	-		-		-		-		-			

Source: U.S. Department of Labor, Bureau of Labor Statistics, Division of Consumer Prices and Price Indexes. - indicates no data collected for period.

Minneapolis-St. Paul, MN
Consumer Price Index - Urban Wage Earners
Base 1982-1984 = 100
Apparel and Upkeep

For 1952-1995. Columns headed % show percentile change in the index from the previous period for which an index is available.

Year	Jan Index	%	Feb Index	%	Mar Index	%	Apr Index	%	May Index	%	Jun Index	%	Jul Index	%	Aug Index	%	Sep Index	%	Oct Index	%	Nov Index	%	Dec Index	%
1952	-		-		-		-		-		-		-		-		-		-		-		47.0	-
1953	46.6	-0.9	-	-	-	-	47.0	0.9	-	-	-	-	46.6	-0.9	-	-	-	-	47.5	1.9	-	-	-	-
1954	47.0	-1.1	-	-	-	-	46.9	-0.2	-	-	-	-	47.0	0.2	-	-	-	-	47.1	0.2	-	-	-	-
1955	46.3	-1.7	-	-	-	-	46.0	-0.6	-	-	-	-	45.8	-0.4	-	-	-	-	46.8	2.2	-	-	-	-
1956	47.1	0.6	-	-	-	-	47.2	0.2	-	-	-	-	47.5	0.6	-	-	-	-	48.2	1.5	-	-	-	-
1957	47.9	-0.6	-	-	-	-	48.3	0.8	-	-	-	-	47.9	-0.8	-	-	-	-	48.4	1.0	-	-	-	-
1958	48.5	0.2	-	-	-	-	48.4	-0.2	-	-	-	-	48.3	-0.2	-	-	-	-	48.5	0.4	-	-	-	-
1959	48.1	-0.8	-	-	-	-	47.9	-0.4	-	-	-	-	47.9	0.0	-	-	-	-	48.2	0.6	-	-	-	-
1960	48.4	0.4	-	-	-	-	48.9	1.0	-	-	-	-	49.0	0.2	-	-	-	-	50.1	2.2	-	-	-	-
1961	47.9	-4.4	-	-	-	-	47.7	-0.4	-	-	-	-	47.7	0.0	-	-	-	-	48.7	2.1	-	-	-	-
1962	48.5	-0.4	-	-	-	-	48.8	0.6	-	-	-	-	48.7	-0.2	-	-	-	-	49.9	2.5	-	-	-	-
1963	49.7	-0.4	-	-	-	-	49.9	0.4	-	-	-	-	50.1	0.4	-	-	-	-	50.4	0.6	-	-	-	-
1964	49.2	-2.4	-	-	-	-	49.7	1.0	-	-	-	-	49.7	0.0	-	-	-	-	50.9	2.4	-	-	-	-
1965	50.3	-1.2	-	-	-	-	50.9	1.2	-	-	-	-	50.6	-0.6	-	-	-	-	51.8	2.4	-	-	-	-
1966	51.4	-0.8	-	-	-	-	51.8	0.8	-	-	-	-	52.4	1.2	-	-	-	-	53.4	1.9	-	-	-	-
1967	52.7	-1.3	-	-	-	-	54.1	2.7	-	-	-	-	53.8	-0.6	-	-	-	-	55.5	3.2	-	-	-	-
1968	54.9	-1.1	-	-	-	-	56.5	2.9	-	-	-	-	56.3	-0.4	-	-	-	-	57.4	2.0	-	-	-	-
1969	57.5	0.2	-	-	-	-	59.1	2.8	-	-	-	-	59.7	1.0	-	-	-	-	61.5	3.0	-	-	-	-
1970	60.7	-1.3	-	-	-	-	62.3	2.6	-	-	-	-	61.5	-1.3	-	-	-	-	64.8	5.4	-	-	-	-
1971	63.5	-2.0	-	-	-	-	64.3	1.3	-	-	-	-	63.6	-1.1	-	-	-	-	64.7	1.7	-	-	-	-
1972	63.8	-1.4	-	-	-	-	64.4	0.9	-	-	-	-	63.6	-1.2	-	-	-	-	66.7	4.9	-	-	-	-
1973	66.0	-1.0	-	-	-	-	66.9	1.4	-	-	-	-	67.6	1.0	-	-	-	-	69.6	3.0	-	-	-	-
1974	69.9	0.4	-	-	-	-	72.6	3.9	-	-	-	-	72.7	0.1	-	-	-	-	79.2	8.9	-	-	-	-
1975	77.5	-2.1	-	-	-	-	75.6	-2.5	-	-	-	-	74.8	-1.1	-	-	-	-	75.5	0.9	-	-	-	-
1976	75.4	-0.1	-	-	-	-	76.2	1.1	-	-	-	-	75.7	-0.7	-	-	-	-	78.7	4.0	-	-	-	-
1977	77.6	-1.4	-	-	-	-	79.0	1.8	-	-	-	-	80.7	2.2	-	-	-	-	81.3	0.7	-	-	-	-
1978	80.5	-1.0	-	-	-	-	82.9	3.0	-	-	83.1	0.2	-	-	83.0	-0.1	-	-	83.1	0.1	-	-	85.6	3.0
1979	-	-	83.0	-3.0	-	-	85.8	3.4	-	-	84.3	-1.7	-	-	87.3	3.6	-	-	87.9	0.7	-	-	88.2	0.3
1980	-	-	88.7	0.6	-	-	91.5	3.2	-	-	92.4	1.0	-	-	93.5	1.2	-	-	92.7	-0.9	-	-	92.4	-0.3
1981	-	-	94.1	1.8	-	-	95.8	1.8	-	-	96.7	0.9	-	-	97.8	1.1	-	-	98.1	0.3	-	-	96.7	-1.4
1982	-	-	97.6	0.9	-	-	99.0	1.4	-	-	97.0	-2.0	-	-	101.2	4.3	-	-	100.7	-0.5	-	-	103.3	2.6
1983	-	-	99.8	-3.4	-	-	103.9	4.1	-	-	100.9	-2.9	-	-	101.2	0.3	-	-	100.4	-0.8	-	-	101.6	1.2
1984	-	-	98.9	-2.7	-	-	100.5	1.6	-	-	98.4	-2.1	-	-	97.7	-0.7	-	-	99.8	2.1	-	-	98.8	-1.0
1985	-	-	104.0	5.3	-	-	108.0	3.8	-	-	108.6	0.6	-	-	105.2	-3.1	-	-	107.4	2.1	-	-	109.0	1.5
1986	-	-	104.3	-4.3	-	-	109.4	4.9	-	-	105.4	-3.7	-	-	105.9	0.5	-	-	108.2	2.2	106.9	-1.2	106.0	-0.8
1987	-	-	-	-	-	-	-	-	-	-	109.5	3.3	-	-	-	-	-	-	-	-	-	-	115.9	5.8
1988	-	-	-	-	-	-	-	-	-	-	119.6	3.2	-	-	-	-	-	-	-	-	-	-	122.6	2.5
1989	-	-	-	-	-	-	-	-	-	-	123.8	1.0	-	-	-	-	-	-	-	-	-	-	124.3	0.4
1990	-	-	-	-	-	-	-	-	-	-	133.1	7.1	-	-	-	-	-	-	-	-	-	-	132.4	-0.5
1991	-	-	-	-	-	-	-	-	-	-	134.3	1.4	-	-	-	-	-	-	-	-	-	-	133.5	-0.6
1992	-	-	-	-	-	-	-	-	-	-	134.8	1.0	-	-	-	-	-	-	-	-	-	-	134.1	-0.5
1993	-	-	-	-	-	-	-	-	-	-	135.9	1.3	-	-	-	-	-	-	-	-	-	-	141.9	4.4
1994	-	-	-	-	-	-	-	-	-	-	148.3	4.5	-	-	-	-	-	-	-	-	-	-	142.5	-3.9
1995	-	-	-	-	-	-	-	-	-	-	137.3	-3.6	-	-	-	-	-	-	-	-	-	-	-	-

Source: U.S. Department of Labor, Bureau of Labor Statistics, Division of Consumer Prices and Price Indexes. - indicates no data collected for period.

Minneapolis-St. Paul, MN
Consumer Price Index - All Urban Consumers
Base 1982-1984 = 100
Transportation

For 1947-1995. Columns headed % show percentile change in the index from the previous period for which an index is available.

Year	Jan Index	%	Feb Index	%	Mar Index	%	Apr Index	%	May Index	%	Jun Index	%	Jul Index	%	Aug Index	%	Sep Index	%	Oct Index	%	Nov Index	%	Dec Index	%
1947	20.9	-	21.0	0.5	21.1	0.5	21.1	0.0	21.3	0.9	21.3	0.0	-	-	-	-	21.9	2.8	-	-	-	-	23.3	6.4
1948	-	-	-	-	23.7	1.7	-	-	-	-	23.7	0.0	-	-	-	-	26.1	10.1	-	-	-	-	25.9	-0.8
1949	-	-	-	-	26.2	1.2	-	-	-	-	26.3	0.4	-	-	-	-	26.6	1.1	-	-	-	-	26.8	0.8
1950	-	-	-	-	26.3	-1.9	-	-	-	-	26.1	-0.8	-	-	-	-	26.7	2.3	-	-	-	-	26.8	0.4
1951	-	-	-	-	27.1	1.1	-	-	-	-	27.1	0.0	-	-	-	-	25.8	-4.8	-	-	-	-	27.8	7.8
1952	-	-	-	-	28.3	1.8	-	-	-	-	28.8	1.8	-	-	-	-	29.2	1.4	-	-	-	-	29.2	0.0
1953	29.3	0.3	-	-	-	-	29.5	0.7	-	-	-	-	29.5	0.0	-	-	-	-	29.4	-0.3	-	-	-	-
1954	29.5	0.3	-	-	-	-	29.3	-0.7	-	-	-	-	29.4	0.3	-	-	-	-	28.7	-2.4	-	-	-	-
1955	29.5	2.8	-	-	-	-	28.5	-3.4	-	-	-	-	28.8	1.1	-	-	-	-	27.1	-5.9	-	-	-	-
1956	27.6	1.8	-	-	-	-	27.0	-2.2	-	-	-	-	28.0	3.7	-	-	-	-	28.6	2.1	-	-	-	-
1957	29.3	2.4	-	-	-	-	29.4	0.3	-	-	-	-	29.4	0.0	-	-	-	-	28.8	-2.0	-	-	-	-
1958	30.1	4.5	-	-	-	-	29.6	-1.7	-	-	-	-	30.3	2.4	-	-	-	-	30.5	0.7	-	-	-	-
1959	31.7	3.9	-	-	-	-	31.5	-0.6	-	-	-	-	30.6	-2.9	-	-	-	-	32.2	5.2	-	-	-	-
1960	32.0	-0.6	-	-	-	-	31.4	-1.9	-	-	-	-	32.1	2.2	-	-	-	-	32.2	0.3	-	-	-	-
1961	32.0	-0.6	-	-	-	-	32.5	1.6	-	-	-	-	32.1	-1.2	-	-	-	-	32.2	0.3	-	-	-	-
1962	32.1	-0.3	-	-	-	-	32.9	2.5	-	-	-	-	32.4	-1.5	-	-	-	-	33.4	3.1	-	-	-	-
1963	32.6	-2.4	-	-	-	-	33.1	1.5	-	-	-	-	33.7	1.8	-	-	-	-	33.2	-1.5	-	-	-	-
1964	33.6	1.2	-	-	-	-	32.5	-3.3	-	-	-	-	33.1	1.8	-	-	-	-	33.5	1.2	-	-	-	-
1965	33.5	0.0	-	-	-	-	33.6	0.3	-	-	-	-	33.8	0.6	-	-	-	-	34.0	0.6	-	-	-	-
1966	34.1	0.3	-	-	-	-	34.2	0.3	-	-	-	-	34.4	0.6	-	-	-	-	34.7	0.9	-	-	-	-
1967	34.7	0.0	-	-	-	-	35.1	1.2	-	-	-	-	35.4	0.9	-	-	-	-	36.5	3.1	-	-	-	-
1968	36.7	0.5	-	-	-	-	36.4	-0.8	-	-	-	-	36.7	0.8	-	-	-	-	37.2	1.4	-	-	-	-
1969	36.6	-1.6	-	-	-	-	37.8	3.3	-	-	-	-	37.0	-2.1	-	-	-	-	37.6	1.6	-	-	-	-
1970	38.2	1.6	-	-	-	-	39.2	2.6	-	-	-	-	39.8	1.5	-	-	-	-	40.5	1.8	-	-	-	-
1971	41.9	3.5	-	-	-	-	40.7	-2.9	-	-	-	-	41.0	0.7	-	-	-	-	40.9	-0.2	-	-	-	-
1972	41.7	2.0	-	-	-	-	40.6	-2.6	-	-	-	-	41.4	2.0	-	-	-	-	41.9	1.2	-	-	-	-
1973	42.2	0.7	-	-	-	-	42.8	1.4	-	-	-	-	43.3	1.2	-	-	-	-	43.2	-0.2	-	-	-	-
1974	44.9	3.9	-	-	-	-	47.0	4.7	-	-	-	-	49.2	4.7	-	-	-	-	48.8	-0.8	-	-	-	-
1975	48.6	-0.4	-	-	-	-	49.2	1.2	-	-	-	-	51.6	4.9	-	-	-	-	52.5	1.7	-	-	-	-
1976	53.0	1.0	-	-	-	-	54.2	2.3	-	-	-	-	56.3	3.9	-	-	-	-	56.7	0.7	-	-	-	-
1977	57.9	2.1	-	-	-	-	59.5	2.8	-	-	-	-	60.3	1.3	-	-	-	-	60.0	-0.5	-	-	-	-
1978	60.4	0.7	-	-	-	-	60.9	0.8	-	-	62.4	2.5	-	-	63.3	1.4	-	-	63.9	0.9	-	-	64.6	1.1
1979	-	-	65.6	1.5	-	-	68.2	4.0	-	-	72.3	6.0	-	-	74.7	3.3	-	-	75.6	1.2	-	-	77.4	2.4
1980	-	-	80.4	3.9	-	-	83.2	3.5	-	-	83.9	0.8	-	-	84.2	0.4	-	-	85.9	2.0	-	-	87.3	1.6
1981	-	-	89.8	2.9	-	-	91.7	2.1	-	-	94.1	2.6	-	-	94.7	0.6	-	-	96.8	2.2	-	-	97.2	0.4
1982	-	-	96.0	-1.2	-	-	93.7	-2.4	-	-	99.2	5.9	-	-	99.3	0.1	-	-	98.7	-0.6	-	-	98.6	-0.1
1983	-	-	96.1	-2.5	-	-	96.9	0.8	-	-	99.1	2.3	-	-	101.1	2.0	-	-	101.4	0.3	-	-	101.9	0.5
1984	-	-	101.9	0.0	-	-	102.3	0.4	-	-	103.5	1.2	-	-	103.6	0.1	-	-	104.2	0.6	-	-	104.4	0.2
1985	-	-	103.4	-1.0	-	-	105.4	1.9	-	-	107.1	1.6	-	-	107.5	0.4	-	-	106.8	-0.7	-	-	107.3	0.5
1986	-	-	104.5	-2.6	-	-	98.8	-5.5	-	-	101.2	2.4	-	-	98.3	-2.9	-	-	98.9	0.6	99.3	0.4	99.0	-0.3
1987	-	-	-	-	-	-	-	-	-	-	101.0	2.0	-	-	-	-	-	-	-	-	-	-	104.0	3.0
1988	-	-	-	-	-	-	-	-	-	-	103.3	-0.7	-	-	-	-	-	-	-	-	-	-	105.7	2.3
1989	-	-	-	-	-	-	-	-	-	-	108.2	2.4	-	-	-	-	-	-	-	-	-	-	110.1	1.8
1990	-	-	-	-	-	-	-	-	-	-	112.7	2.4	-	-	-	-	-	-	-	-	-	-	119.3	5.9
1991	-	-	-	-	-	-	-	-	-	-	118.5	-0.7	-	-	-	-	-	-	-	-	-	-	120.8	1.9

[Continued]

Minneapolis-St. Paul, MN
Consumer Price Index - All Urban Consumers
Base 1982-1984 = 100
Transportation
[Continued]

For 1947-1995. Columns headed % show percentile change in the index from the previous period for which an index is available.

Year	Jan		Feb		Mar		Apr		May		Jun		Jul		Aug		Sep		Oct		Nov		Dec	
	Index	%	Index	%	Index	%	Index	%	Index	%	Index	%	Index	%	Index	%	Index	%	Index	%	Index	%	Index	%
1992	-	-	-	-	-	-	-	-	-	-	122.0	1.0	-	-	-	-	-	-	-	-	-	-	-	-
1993	-	-	-	-	-	-	-	-	-	-	126.3	2.0	-	-	-	-	-	-	-	-	-	-	123.8	1.5
1994	-	-	-	-	-	-	-	-	-	-	131.2	0.9	-	-	-	-	-	-	-	-	-	-	130.0	2.9
1995	-	-	-	-	-	-	-	-	-	-	136.9	1.6	-	-	-	-	-	-	-	-	-	-	134.7	2.7

Source: U.S. Department of Labor, Bureau of Labor Statistics, Division of Consumer Prices and Price Indexes. - indicates no data collected for period.

Minneapolis-St. Paul, MN
Consumer Price Index - Urban Wage Earners
Base 1982-1984 = 100
Transportation

For 1947-1995. Columns headed % show percentile change in the index from the previous period for which an index is available.

Year	Jan Index	%	Feb Index	%	Mar Index	%	Apr Index	%	May Index	%	Jun Index	%	Jul Index	%	Aug Index	%	Sep Index	%	Oct Index	%	Nov Index	%	Dec Index	%
1947	20.6	-	20.6	0.0	20.7	0.5	20.8	0.5	21.0	1.0	21.0	0.0	-	-	-	-	21.5	2.4	-	-	-	-	22.9	6.5
1948	-	-	-	-	23.3	1.7	-	-	-	-	23.4	0.4	-	-	-	-	25.7	9.8	-	-	-	-	25.5	-0.8
1949	-	-	-	-	25.8	1.2	-	-	-	-	25.9	0.4	-	-	-	-	26.2	1.2	-	-	-	-	26.4	0.8
1950	-	-	-	-	25.9	-1.9	-	-	-	-	25.7	-0.8	-	-	-	-	26.3	2.3	-	-	-	-	26.4	0.4
1951	-	-	-	-	26.7	1.1	-	-	-	-	26.7	0.0	-	-	-	-	25.4	-4.9	-	-	-	-	27.4	7.9
1952	-	-	-	-	27.8	1.5	-	-	-	-	28.3	1.8	-	-	-	-	28.8	1.8	-	-	-	-	28.8	0.0
1953	28.8	0.0	-	-	-	-	29.1	1.0	-	-	-	-	29.1	0.0	-	-	-	-	28.9	-0.7	-	-	-	-
1954	29.1	0.7	-	-	-	-	28.8	-1.0	-	-	-	-	29.0	0.7	-	-	-	-	28.2	-2.8	-	-	-	-
1955	29.0	2.8	-	-	-	-	28.0	-3.4	-	-	-	-	28.3	1.1	-	-	-	-	26.7	-5.7	-	-	-	-
1956	27.2	1.9	-	-	-	-	26.6	-2.2	-	-	-	-	27.5	3.4	-	-	-	-	28.1	2.2	-	-	-	-
1957	28.8	2.5	-	-	-	-	28.9	0.3	-	-	-	-	29.0	0.3	-	-	-	-	28.3	-2.4	-	-	-	-
1958	29.6	4.6	-	-	-	-	29.2	-1.4	-	-	-	-	29.8	2.1	-	-	-	-	30.1	1.0	-	-	-	-
1959	31.3	4.0	-	-	-	-	31.1	-0.6	-	-	-	-	30.2	-2.9	-	-	-	-	31.7	5.0	-	-	-	-
1960	31.5	-0.6	-	-	-	-	30.9	-1.9	-	-	-	-	31.6	2.3	-	-	-	-	31.7	0.3	-	-	-	-
1961	31.5	-0.6	-	-	-	-	32.0	1.6	-	-	-	-	31.6	-1.2	-	-	-	-	31.7	0.3	-	-	-	-
1962	31.6	-0.3	-	-	-	-	32.4	2.5	-	-	-	-	31.9	-1.5	-	-	-	-	32.9	3.1	-	-	-	-
1963	32.1	-2.4	-	-	-	-	32.6	1.6	-	-	-	-	33.2	1.8	-	-	-	-	32.7	-1.5	-	-	-	-
1964	33.1	1.2	-	-	-	-	32.0	-3.3	-	-	-	-	32.6	1.9	-	-	-	-	32.9	0.9	-	-	-	-
1965	32.9	0.0	-	-	-	-	33.1	0.6	-	-	-	-	33.3	0.6	-	-	-	-	33.5	0.6	-	-	-	-
1966	33.5	0.0	-	-	-	-	33.7	0.6	-	-	-	-	33.9	0.6	-	-	-	-	34.2	0.9	-	-	-	-
1967	34.1	-0.3	-	-	-	-	34.5	1.2	-	-	-	-	34.9	1.2	-	-	-	-	36.0	3.2	-	-	-	-
1968	36.2	0.6	-	-	-	-	35.9	-0.8	-	-	-	-	36.1	0.6	-	-	-	-	36.6	1.4	-	-	-	-
1969	36.0	-1.6	-	-	-	-	37.2	3.3	-	-	-	-	36.5	-1.9	-	-	-	-	37.0	1.4	-	-	-	-
1970	37.6	1.6	-	-	-	-	38.6	2.7	-	-	-	-	39.2	1.6	-	-	-	-	39.8	1.5	-	-	-	-
1971	41.2	3.5	-	-	-	-	40.1	-2.7	-	-	-	-	40.3	0.5	-	-	-	-	40.3	0.0	-	-	-	-
1972	41.0	1.7	-	-	-	-	40.0	-2.4	-	-	-	-	40.7	1.7	-	-	-	-	41.2	1.2	-	-	-	-
1973	41.6	1.0	-	-	-	-	42.2	1.4	-	-	-	-	42.6	0.9	-	-	-	-	42.5	-0.2	-	-	-	-
1974	44.2	4.0	-	-	-	-	46.3	4.8	-	-	-	-	48.5	4.8	-	-	-	-	48.1	-0.8	-	-	-	-
1975	47.9	-0.4	-	-	-	-	48.5	1.3	-	-	-	-	50.8	4.7	-	-	-	-	51.7	1.8	-	-	-	-
1976	52.1	0.8	-	-	-	-	53.4	2.5	-	-	-	-	55.5	3.9	-	-	-	-	55.8	0.5	-	-	-	-
1977	57.0	2.2	-	-	-	-	58.6	2.8	-	-	-	-	59.4	1.4	-	-	-	-	59.1	-0.5	-	-	-	-
1978	59.5	0.7	-	-	-	-	60.0	0.8	-	-	61.6	2.7	-	-	62.5	1.5	-	-	63.3	1.3	-	-	64.1	1.3
1979	-	-	65.0	1.4	-	-	67.8	4.3	-	-	72.2	6.5	-	-	74.5	3.2	-	-	75.5	1.3	-	-	77.4	2.5
1980	-	-	80.5	4.0	-	-	83.3	3.5	-	-	84.2	1.1	-	-	84.2	0.0	-	-	85.9	2.0	-	-	87.6	2.0
1981	-	-	90.5	3.3	-	-	92.2	1.9	-	-	94.1	2.1	-	-	95.0	1.0	-	-	96.9	2.0	-	-	97.4	0.5
1982	-	-	96.3	-1.1	-	-	93.7	-2.7	-	-	99.4	6.1	-	-	99.4	0.0	-	-	98.8	-0.6	-	-	98.8	0.0
1983	-	-	96.1	-2.7	-	-	96.9	0.8	-	-	99.4	2.6	-	-	101.3	1.9	-	-	101.4	0.1	-	-	101.8	0.4
1984	-	-	101.7	-0.1	-	-	102.1	0.4	-	-	103.1	1.0	-	-	103.4	0.3	-	-	104.0	0.6	-	-	104.1	0.1
1985	-	-	102.8	-1.2	-	-	105.1	2.2	-	-	106.9	1.7	-	-	107.3	0.4	-	-	106.4	-0.8	-	-	107.1	0.7
1986	-	-	103.9	-3.0	-	-	97.6	-6.1	-	-	100.3	2.8	-	-	97.1	-3.2	-	-	97.7	0.6	98.1	0.4	97.8	-0.3
1987	-	-	-	-	-	-	-	-	-	-	103.0	5.3	-	-	-	-	-	-	-	-	-	-	106.5	3.4
1988	-	-	-	-	-	-	-	-	-	-	105.8	-0.7	-	-	-	-	-	-	-	-	-	-	108.4	2.5
1989	-	-	-	-	-	-	-	-	-	-	111.0	2.4	-	-	-	-	-	-	-	-	-	-	112.8	1.6
1990	-	-	-	-	-	-	-	-	-	-	115.2	2.1	-	-	-	-	-	-	-	-	-	-	122.3	6.2
1991	-	-	-	-	-	-	-	-	-	-	120.8	-1.2	-	-	-	-	-	-	-	-	-	-	123.3	2.1

[Continued]

Minneapolis-St. Paul, MN
Consumer Price Index - Urban Wage Earners
Base 1982-1984 = 100
Transportation
[Continued]

For 1947-1995. Columns headed % show percentile change in the index from the previous period for which an index is available.

Year	Jan		Feb		Mar		Apr		May		Jun		Jul		Aug		Sep		Oct		Nov		Dec	
	Index	%	Index	%	Index	%	Index	%	Index	%	Index	%	Index	%	Index	%	Index	%	Index	%	Index	%	Index	%
1992	-	-	-	-	-	-	-	-	-	-	124.2	0.7	-	-	-	-	-	-	-	-	-	-	126.2	1.6
1993	-	-	-	-	-	-	-	-	-	-	127.8	1.3	-	-	-	-	-	-	-	-	-	-	131.1	2.6
1994	-	-	-	-	-	-	-	-	-	-	131.8	0.5	-	-	-	-	-	-	-	-	-	-	136.3	3.4
1995	-	-	-	-	-	-	-	-	-	-	138.6	1.7	-	-	-	-	-	-	-	-	-	-	-	-

Source: U.S. Department of Labor, Bureau of Labor Statistics, Division of Consumer Prices and Price Indexes. - indicates no data collected for period.

Minneapolis-St. Paul, MN
Consumer Price Index - All Urban Consumers
Base 1982-1984 = 100
Medical Care

For 1947-1995. Columns headed % show percentile change in the index from the previous period for which an index is available.

Year	Jan Index	%	Feb Index	%	Mar Index	%	Apr Index	%	May Index	%	Jun Index	%	Jul Index	%	Aug Index	%	Sep Index	%	Oct Index	%	Nov Index	%	Dec Index	%
1947	10.2	-	10.2	0.0	10.2	0.0	10.4	2.0	10.5	1.0	10.6	1.0	-	-	-	-	11.0	3.8	-	-	-	-	11.2	1.8
1948	-	-	-	-	11.4	1.8	-	-	-	-	11.8	3.5	-	-	-	-	11.9	0.8	-	-	-	-	12.1	1.7
1949	-	-	-	-	12.1	0.0	-	-	-	-	12.2	0.8	-	-	-	-	12.3	0.8	-	-	-	-	12.4	0.8
1950	-	-	-	-	12.4	0.0	-	-	-	-	12.4	0.0	-	-	-	-	12.8	3.2	-	-	-	-	12.9	0.8
1951	-	-	-	-	13.6	5.4	-	-	-	-	13.6	0.0	-	-	-	-	13.8	1.5	-	-	-	-	13.9	0.7
1952	-	-	-	-	14.5	4.3	-	-	-	-	14.5	0.0	-	-	-	-	14.6	0.7	-	-	-	-	14.5	-0.7
1953	14.5	0.0	-	-	-	-	15.8	9.0	-	-	-	-	15.9	0.6	-	-	-	-	15.9	0.0	-	-	-	-
1954	16.0	0.6	-	-	-	-	16.4	2.5	-	-	-	-	16.5	0.6	-	-	-	-	16.4	-0.6	-	-	-	-
1955	16.6	1.2	-	-	-	-	17.0	2.4	-	-	-	-	17.1	0.6	-	-	-	-	17.1	0.0	-	-	-	-
1956	17.2	0.6	-	-	-	-	17.2	0.0	-	-	-	-	17.3	0.6	-	-	-	-	17.3	0.0	-	-	-	-
1957	17.4	0.6	-	-	-	-	17.6	1.1	-	-	-	-	19.5	10.8	-	-	-	-	19.6	0.5	-	-	-	-
1958	19.8	1.0	-	-	-	-	20.2	2.0	-	-	-	-	21.9	8.4	-	-	-	-	22.0	0.5	-	-	-	-
1959	22.2	0.9	-	-	-	-	22.2	0.0	-	-	-	-	22.4	0.9	-	-	-	-	23.5	4.9	-	-	-	-
1960	23.5	0.0	-	-	-	-	24.1	2.6	-	-	-	-	24.7	2.5	-	-	-	-	24.4	-1.2	-	-	-	-
1961	24.4	0.0	-	-	-	-	25.4	4.1	-	-	-	-	26.4	3.9	-	-	-	-	26.5	0.4	-	-	-	-
1962	26.5	0.0	-	-	-	-	26.5	0.0	-	-	-	-	26.8	1.1	-	-	-	-	26.9	0.4	-	-	-	-
1963	27.0	0.4	-	-	-	-	27.0	0.0	-	-	-	-	27.0	0.0	-	-	-	-	27.1	0.4	-	-	-	-
1964	27.2	0.4	-	-	-	-	27.6	1.5	-	-	-	-	27.5	-0.4	-	-	-	-	27.5	0.0	-	-	-	-
1965	27.5	0.0	-	-	-	-	27.6	0.4	-	-	-	-	27.6	0.0	-	-	-	-	27.7	0.4	-	-	-	-
1966	27.9	0.7	-	-	-	-	28.6	2.5	-	-	-	-	29.0	1.4	-	-	-	-	29.4	1.4	-	-	-	-
1967	30.0	2.0	-	-	-	-	30.1	0.3	-	-	-	-	30.4	1.0	-	-	-	-	30.8	1.3	-	-	-	-
1968	31.4	1.9	-	-	-	-	31.8	1.3	-	-	-	-	32.0	0.6	-	-	-	-	32.4	1.3	-	-	-	-
1969	32.8	1.2	-	-	-	-	33.3	1.5	-	-	-	-	34.0	2.1	-	-	-	-	33.9	-0.3	-	-	-	-
1970	34.2	0.9	-	-	-	-	35.6	4.1	-	-	-	-	36.3	2.0	-	-	-	-	36.3	0.0	-	-	-	-
1971	36.9	1.7	-	-	-	-	37.5	1.6	-	-	-	-	38.1	1.6	-	-	-	-	37.9	-0.5	-	-	-	-
1972	37.9	0.0	-	-	-	-	38.0	0.3	-	-	-	-	38.3	0.8	-	-	-	-	38.8	1.3	-	-	-	-
1973	39.4	1.5	-	-	-	-	39.8	1.0	-	-	-	-	40.0	0.5	-	-	-	-	41.0	2.5	-	-	-	-
1974	42.0	2.4	-	-	-	-	42.6	1.4	-	-	-	-	43.8	2.8	-	-	-	-	45.3	3.4	-	-	-	-
1975	47.4	4.6	-	-	-	-	47.6	0.4	-	-	-	-	48.9	2.7	-	-	-	-	49.4	1.0	-	-	-	-
1976	50.5	2.2	-	-	-	-	51.4	1.8	-	-	-	-	52.4	1.9	-	-	-	-	53.5	2.1	-	-	-	-
1977	54.9	2.6	-	-	-	-	55.7	1.5	-	-	-	-	56.9	2.2	-	-	-	-	57.5	1.1	-	-	-	-
1978	59.1	2.8	-	-	-	-	60.3	2.0	-	-	60.9	1.0	-	-	62.3	2.3	-	-	62.2	-0.2	-	-	63.2	1.6
1979	-	-	65.1	3.0	-	-	64.0	-1.7	-	-	65.2	1.9	-	-	66.7	2.3	-	-	68.1	2.1	-	-	70.2	3.1
1980	-	-	72.7	3.6	-	-	72.9	0.3	-	-	73.0	0.1	-	-	74.6	2.2	-	-	74.6	0.0	-	-	75.5	1.2
1981	-	-	77.2	2.3	-	-	78.4	1.6	-	-	79.3	1.1	-	-	82.2	3.7	-	-	82.8	0.7	-	-	84.2	1.7
1982	-	-	86.5	2.7	-	-	87.7	1.4	-	-	89.0	1.5	-	-	92.0	3.4	-	-	92.9	1.0	-	-	94.3	1.5
1983	-	-	96.4	2.2	-	-	96.4	0.0	-	-	99.7	3.4	-	-	102.3	2.6	-	-	104.7	2.3	-	-	104.8	0.1
1984	-	-	107.3	2.4	-	-	107.5	0.2	-	-	109.5	1.9	-	-	110.8	1.2	-	-	112.7	1.7	-	-	112.6	-0.1
1985	-	-	114.8	2.0	-	-	115.4	0.5	-	-	116.1	0.6	-	-	117.4	1.1	-	-	119.6	1.9	-	-	120.3	0.6
1986	-	-	123.0	2.2	-	-	124.9	1.5	-	-	125.9	0.8	-	-	127.2	1.0	-	-	130.7	2.8	131.4	0.5	131.6	0.2
1987	-	-	-	-	-	-	-	-	-	-	128.3	-2.5	-	-	-	-	-	-	-	-	-	-	132.6	3.4
1988	-	-	-	-	-	-	-	-	-	-	135.3	2.0	-	-	-	-	-	-	-	-	-	-	138.1	2.1
1989	-	-	-	-	-	-	-	-	-	-	145.4	5.3	-	-	-	-	-	-	-	-	-	-	150.7	3.6
1990	-	-	-	-	-	-	-	-	-	-	156.2	3.6	-	-	-	-	-	-	-	-	-	-	166.1	6.3
1991	-	-	-	-	-	-	-	-	-	-	172.5	3.9	-	-	-	-	-	-	-	-	-	-	182.9	6.0

[Continued]

Minneapolis-St. Paul, MN
Consumer Price Index - All Urban Consumers
Base 1982-1984 = 100
Medical Care
[Continued]

For 1947-1995. Columns headed % show percentile change in the index from the previous period for which an index is available.

Year	Jan		Feb		Mar		Apr		May		Jun		Jul		Aug		Sep		Oct		Nov		Dec	
	Index	%	Index	%	Index	%	Index	%	Index	%	Index	%	Index	%	Index	%	Index	%	Index	%	Index	%	Index	%
1992	-	-	-	-	-	-	-	-	-	-	191.7	4.8	-	-	-	-	-	-	-	-	-	-	195.5	2.0
1993	-	-	-	-	-	-	-	-	-	-	200.4	2.5	-	-	-	-	-	-	-	-	-	-	201.3	0.4
1994	-	-	-	-	-	-	-	-	-	-	202.3	0.5	-	-	-	-	-	-	-	-	-	-	206.9	2.3
1995	-	-	-	-	-	-	-	-	-	-	215.6	4.2	-	-	-	-	-	-	-	-	-	-	-	-

Source: U.S. Department of Labor, Bureau of Labor Statistics, Division of Consumer Prices and Price Indexes. - indicates no data collected for period.

Minneapolis-St. Paul, MN
Consumer Price Index - Urban Wage Earners
Base 1982-1984 = 100
Medical Care

For 1947-1995. Columns headed % show percentile change in the index from the previous period for which an index is available.

Year	Jan Index	%	Feb Index	%	Mar Index	%	Apr Index	%	May Index	%	Jun Index	%	Jul Index	%	Aug Index	%	Sep Index	%	Oct Index	%	Nov Index	%	Dec Index	%
1947	10.4	-	10.4	0.0	10.4	0.0	10.5	1.0	10.7	1.9	10.8	0.9	-	-	-	-	11.1	2.8	-	-	-	-	11.4	2.7
1948	-	-	-	-	11.5	0.9	-	-	-	-	12.0	4.3	-	-	-	-	12.1	0.8	-	-	-	-	12.3	1.7
1949	-	-	-	-	12.3	0.0	-	-	-	-	12.4	0.8	-	-	-	-	12.5	0.8	-	-	-	-	12.5	0.0
1950	-	-	-	-	12.6	0.8	-	-	-	-	12.6	0.0	-	-	-	-	12.9	2.4	-	-	-	-	13.1	1.6
1951	-	-	-	-	13.8	5.3	-	-	-	-	13.8	0.0	-	-	-	-	14.0	1.4	-	-	-	-	14.1	0.7
1952	-	-	-	-	14.7	4.3	-	-	-	-	14.7	0.0	-	-	-	-	14.8	0.7	-	-	-	-	14.7	-0.7
1953	14.7	0.0	-	-	-	-	16.0	8.8	-	-	-	-	16.1	0.6	-	-	-	-	16.2	0.6	-	-	-	-
1954	16.3	0.6	-	-	-	-	16.6	1.8	-	-	-	-	16.7	0.6	-	-	-	-	16.6	-0.6	-	-	-	-
1955	16.8	1.2	-	-	-	-	17.2	2.4	-	-	-	-	17.4	1.2	-	-	-	-	17.4	0.0	-	-	-	-
1956	17.4	0.0	-	-	-	-	17.4	0.0	-	-	-	-	17.5	0.6	-	-	-	-	17.5	0.0	-	-	-	-
1957	17.6	0.6	-	-	-	-	17.8	1.1	-	-	-	-	19.8	11.2	-	-	-	-	19.9	0.5	-	-	-	-
1958	20.1	1.0	-	-	-	-	20.4	1.5	-	-	-	-	22.2	8.8	-	-	-	-	22.3	0.5	-	-	-	-
1959	22.5	0.9	-	-	-	-	22.5	0.0	-	-	-	-	22.7	0.9	-	-	-	-	23.8	4.8	-	-	-	-
1960	23.8	0.0	-	-	-	-	24.5	2.9	-	-	-	-	25.0	2.0	-	-	-	-	24.8	-0.8	-	-	-	-
1961	24.7	-0.4	-	-	-	-	25.8	4.5	-	-	-	-	26.8	3.9	-	-	-	-	26.9	0.4	-	-	-	-
1962	26.9	0.0	-	-	-	-	26.9	0.0	-	-	-	-	27.1	0.7	-	-	-	-	27.3	0.7	-	-	-	-
1963	27.4	0.4	-	-	-	-	27.4	0.0	-	-	-	-	27.4	0.0	-	-	-	-	27.5	0.4	-	-	-	-
1964	27.6	0.4	-	-	-	-	27.9	1.1	-	-	-	-	27.9	0.0	-	-	-	-	27.9	0.0	-	-	-	-
1965	27.9	0.0	-	-	-	-	28.0	0.4	-	-	-	-	27.9	-0.4	-	-	-	-	28.1	0.7	-	-	-	-
1966	28.3	0.7	-	-	-	-	29.0	2.5	-	-	-	-	29.4	1.4	-	-	-	-	29.9	1.7	-	-	-	-
1967	30.4	1.7	-	-	-	-	30.6	0.7	-	-	-	-	30.8	0.7	-	-	-	-	31.2	1.3	-	-	-	-
1968	31.8	1.9	-	-	-	-	32.3	1.6	-	-	-	-	32.5	0.6	-	-	-	-	32.9	1.2	-	-	-	-
1969	33.3	1.2	-	-	-	-	33.8	1.5	-	-	-	-	34.5	2.1	-	-	-	-	34.4	-0.3	-	-	-	-
1970	34.7	0.9	-	-	-	-	36.2	4.3	-	-	-	-	36.8	1.7	-	-	-	-	36.9	0.3	-	-	-	-
1971	37.4	1.4	-	-	-	-	38.0	1.6	-	-	-	-	38.7	1.8	-	-	-	-	38.5	-0.5	-	-	-	-
1972	38.4	-0.3	-	-	-	-	38.5	0.3	-	-	-	-	38.9	1.0	-	-	-	-	39.3	1.0	-	-	-	-
1973	39.9	1.5	-	-	-	-	40.4	1.3	-	-	-	-	40.6	0.5	-	-	-	-	41.6	2.5	-	-	-	-
1974	42.6	2.4	-	-	-	-	43.2	1.4	-	-	-	-	44.5	3.0	-	-	-	-	46.0	3.4	-	-	-	-
1975	48.1	4.6	-	-	-	-	48.3	0.4	-	-	-	-	49.6	2.7	-	-	-	-	50.1	1.0	-	-	-	-
1976	51.2	2.2	-	-	-	-	52.2	2.0	-	-	-	-	53.1	1.7	-	-	-	-	54.3	2.3	-	-	-	-
1977	55.7	2.6	-	-	-	-	56.5	1.4	-	-	-	-	57.7	2.1	-	-	-	-	58.3	1.0	-	-	-	-
1978	60.0	2.9	-	-	-	-	61.2	2.0	-	-	61.9	1.1	-	-	62.8	1.5	-	-	63.3	0.8	-	-	63.7	0.6
1979	-	-	64.8	1.7	-	-	64.0	-1.2	-	-	65.1	1.7	-	-	66.1	1.5	-	-	68.6	3.8	-	-	70.7	3.1
1980	-	-	72.4	2.4	-	-	72.1	-0.4	-	-	72.1	0.0	-	-	72.9	1.1	-	-	73.8	1.2	-	-	75.1	1.8
1981	-	-	75.9	1.1	-	-	76.8	1.2	-	-	78.0	1.6	-	-	81.8	4.9	-	-	82.9	1.3	-	-	83.7	1.0
1982	-	-	86.1	2.9	-	-	87.3	1.4	-	-	88.5	1.4	-	-	91.5	3.4	-	-	92.3	0.9	-	-	93.7	1.5
1983	-	-	95.7	2.1	-	-	95.7	0.0	-	-	99.6	4.1	-	-	102.3	2.7	-	-	105.2	2.8	-	-	105.3	0.1
1984	-	-	107.8	2.4	-	-	108.0	0.2	-	-	110.2	2.0	-	-	111.5	1.2	-	-	113.4	1.7	-	-	113.3	-0.1
1985	-	-	115.5	1.9	-	-	116.0	0.4	-	-	116.7	0.6	-	-	118.1	1.2	-	-	120.3	1.9	-	-	121.1	0.7
1986	-	-	123.6	2.1	-	-	125.5	1.5	-	-	126.5	0.8	-	-	127.9	1.1	-	-	131.4	2.7	132.1	0.5	132.4	0.2
1987	-	-	-	-	-	-	-	-	-	-	128.7	-2.8	-	-	-	-	-	-	-	-	-	-	133.1	3.4
1988	-	-	-	-	-	-	-	-	-	-	136.2	2.3	-	-	-	-	-	-	-	-	-	-	139.3	2.3
1989	-	-	-	-	-	-	-	-	-	-	146.6	5.2	-	-	-	-	-	-	-	-	-	-	152.1	3.8
1990	-	-	-	-	-	-	-	-	-	-	157.3	3.4	-	-	-	-	-	-	-	-	-	-	167.3	6.4
1991	-	-	-	-	-	-	-	-	-	-	173.6	3.8	-	-	-	-	-	-	-	-	-	-	184.3	6.2

[Continued]

Minneapolis-St. Paul, MN
Consumer Price Index - Urban Wage Earners
Base 1982-1984 = 100
Medical Care

[Continued]

For 1947-1995. Columns headed % show percentile change in the index from the previous period for which an index is available.

Year	Jan		Feb		Mar		Apr		May		Jun		Jul		Aug		Sep		Oct		Nov		Dec	
	Index	%	Index	%	Index	%	Index	%	Index	%	Index	%	Index	%	Index	%	Index	%	Index	%	Index	%	Index	%
1992	-	-	-	-	-	-	-	-	-	-	193.4	4.9	-	-	-	-	-	-	-	-	-	-	197.2	2.0
1993	-	-	-	-	-	-	-	-	-	-	202.4	2.6	-	-	-	-	-	-	-	-	-	-	203.3	0.4
1994	-	-	-	-	-	-	-	-	-	-	204.2	0.4	-	-	-	-	-	-	-	-	-	-	208.9	2.3
1995	-	-	-	-	-	-	-	-	-	-	217.4	4.1	-	-	-	-	-	-	-	-	-	-	-	-

Source: U.S. Department of Labor, Bureau of Labor Statistics, Division of Consumer Prices and Price Indexes. - indicates no data collected for period.

Minneapolis-St. Paul, MN
Consumer Price Index - All Urban Consumers
Base 1982-1984 = 100
Entertainment

For 1976-1995. Columns headed % show percentile change in the index from the previous period for which an index is available.

Year	Jan Index	%	Feb Index	%	Mar Index	%	Apr Index	%	May Index	%	Jun Index	%	Jul Index	%	Aug Index	%	Sep Index	%	Oct Index	%	Nov Index	%	Dec Index	%
1976	59.5	-	-	-	-	-	62.9	5.7	-	-	-	-	62.7	-0.3	-	-	-	-	62.4	-0.5	-	-	-	-
1977	63.1	1.1	-	-	-	-	64.7	2.5	-	-	-	-	63.7	-1.5	-	-	-	-	68.3	7.2	-	-	-	-
1978	69.4	1.6	-	-	-	-	70.1	1.0	-	-	70.1	0.0	-	-	70.3	0.3	-	-	73.5	4.6	-	-	74.2	1.0
1979	-	-	73.9	-0.4	-	-	74.1	0.3	-	-	76.1	2.7	-	-	78.0	2.5	-	-	74.2	-4.9	-	-	74.4	0.3
1980	-	-	75.9	2.0	-	-	76.9	1.3	-	-	78.1	1.6	-	-	85.7	9.7	-	-	86.3	0.7	-	-	88.4	2.4
1981	-	-	88.9	0.6	-	-	93.2	4.8	-	-	92.6	-0.6	-	-	95.1	2.7	-	-	95.3	0.2	-	-	95.3	0.0
1982	-	-	98.0	2.8	-	-	95.3	-2.8	-	-	98.2	3.0	-	-	99.3	1.1	-	-	96.3	-3.0	-	-	96.4	0.1
1983	-	-	97.0	0.6	-	-	99.4	2.5	-	-	98.8	-0.6	-	-	105.0	6.3	-	-	101.0	-3.8	-	-	101.2	0.2
1984	-	-	101.9	0.7	-	-	102.5	0.6	-	-	102.5	0.0	-	-	102.6	0.1	-	-	103.4	0.8	-	-	103.3	-0.1
1985	-	-	104.6	1.3	-	-	105.3	0.7	-	-	106.4	1.0	-	-	108.3	1.8	-	-	108.6	0.3	-	-	106.9	-1.6
1986	-	-	110.8	3.6	-	-	111.5	0.6	-	-	112.2	0.6	-	-	109.6	-2.3	-	-	114.6	4.6	114.5	-0.1	114.1	-0.3
1987	-	-	-	-	-	-	-	-	-	-	117.3	2.8	-	-	-	-	-	-	-	-	-	-	119.8	2.1
1988	-	-	-	-	-	-	-	-	-	-	123.5	3.1	-	-	-	-	-	-	-	-	-	-	125.6	1.7
1989	-	-	-	-	-	-	-	-	-	-	132.0	5.1	-	-	-	-	-	-	-	-	-	-	135.5	2.7
1990	-	-	-	-	-	-	-	-	-	-	134.0	-1.1	-	-	-	-	-	-	-	-	-	-	135.7	1.3
1991	-	-	-	-	-	-	-	-	-	-	138.6	2.1	-	-	-	-	-	-	-	-	-	-	140.6	1.4
1992	-	-	-	-	-	-	-	-	-	-	144.0	2.4	-	-	-	-	-	-	-	-	-	-	148.9	3.4
1993	-	-	-	-	-	-	-	-	-	-	152.5	2.4	-	-	-	-	-	-	-	-	-	-	153.9	0.9
1994	-	-	-	-	-	-	-	-	-	-	156.5	1.7	-	-	-	-	-	-	-	-	-	-	158.2	1.1
1995	-	-	-	-	-	-	-	-	-	-	153.8	-2.8	-	-	-	-	-	-	-	-	-	-	-	-

Source: U.S. Department of Labor, Bureau of Labor Statistics, Division of Consumer Prices and Price Indexes. - indicates no data collected for period.

Minneapolis-St. Paul, MN
Consumer Price Index - Urban Wage Earners
Base 1982-1984 = 100
Entertainment

For 1976-1995. Columns headed % show percentile change in the index from the previous period for which an index is available.

Year	Jan Index	%	Feb Index	%	Mar Index	%	Apr Index	%	May Index	%	Jun Index	%	Jul Index	%	Aug Index	%	Sep Index	%	Oct Index	%	Nov Index	%	Dec Index	%
1976	61.1	-	-	-	-	-	64.6	5.7	-	-	-	-	64.4	-0.3	-	-	-	-	64.1	-0.5	-	-	-	-
1977	64.8	1.1	-	-	-	-	66.5	2.6	-	-	-	-	65.4	-1.7	-	-	-	-	70.2	7.3	-	-	-	-
1978	71.3	1.6	-	-	-	-	72.1	1.1	-	-	69.9	-3.1	-	-	72.6	3.9	-	-	74.8	3.0	-	-	79.7	6.6
1979	-	-	78.8	-1.1	-	-	78.2	-0.8	-	-	82.2	5.1	-	-	82.8	0.7	-	-	84.4	1.9	-	-	83.9	-0.6
1980	-	-	84.7	1.0	-	-	86.9	2.6	-	-	91.0	4.7	-	-	90.6	-0.4	-	-	89.2	-1.5	-	-	90.6	1.6
1981	-	-	91.6	1.1	-	-	91.6	0.0	-	-	92.0	0.4	-	-	92.9	1.0	-	-	94.2	1.4	-	-	94.0	-0.2
1982	-	-	97.0	3.2	-	-	95.0	-2.1	-	-	97.0	2.1	-	-	97.8	0.8	-	-	96.2	-1.6	-	-	96.5	0.3
1983	-	-	97.3	0.8	-	-	100.3	3.1	-	-	99.7	-0.6	-	-	104.4	4.7	-	-	101.7	-2.6	-	-	101.7	0.0
1984	-	-	102.4	0.7	-	-	103.1	0.7	-	-	102.8	-0.3	-	-	102.8	0.0	-	-	103.5	0.7	-	-	103.3	-0.2
1985	-	-	104.8	1.5	-	-	105.3	0.5	-	-	106.6	1.2	-	-	108.5	1.8	-	-	108.8	0.3	-	-	107.7	-1.0
1986	-	-	111.1	3.2	-	-	111.6	0.5	-	-	112.4	0.7	-	-	110.3	-1.9	-	-	114.3	3.6	114.9	0.5	114.0	-0.8
1987	-	-	-	-	-	-	-	-	-	-	118.8	4.2	-	-	-	-	-	-	-	-	-	-	121.3	2.1
1988	-	-	-	-	-	-	-	-	-	-	125.2	3.2	-	-	-	-	-	-	-	-	-	-	127.4	1.8
1989	-	-	-	-	-	-	-	-	-	-	133.8	5.0	-	-	-	-	-	-	-	-	-	-	137.6	2.8
1990	-	-	-	-	-	-	-	-	-	-	135.8	-1.3	-	-	-	-	-	-	-	-	-	-	137.5	1.3
1991	-	-	-	-	-	-	-	-	-	-	140.2	2.0	-	-	-	-	-	-	-	-	-	-	142.2	1.4
1992	-	-	-	-	-	-	-	-	-	-	145.3	2.2	-	-	-	-	-	-	-	-	-	-	151.3	4.1
1993	-	-	-	-	-	-	-	-	-	-	155.4	2.7	-	-	-	-	-	-	-	-	-	-	156.9	1.0
1994	-	-	-	-	-	-	-	-	-	-	159.2	1.5	-	-	-	-	-	-	-	-	-	-	161.4	1.4
1995	-	-	-	-	-	-	-	-	-	-	157.4	-2.5	-	-	-	-	-	-	-	-	-	-	-	-

Source: U.S. Department of Labor, Bureau of Labor Statistics, Division of Consumer Prices and Price Indexes. - indicates no data collected for period.

Minneapolis-St. Paul, MN
Consumer Price Index - All Urban Consumers
Base 1982-1984 = 100
Other Goods and Services

For 1976-1995. Columns headed % show percentile change in the index from the previous period for which an index is available.

Year	Jan Index	%	Feb Index	%	Mar Index	%	Apr Index	%	May Index	%	Jun Index	%	Jul Index	%	Aug Index	%	Sep Index	%	Oct Index	%	Nov Index	%	Dec Index	%
1976	56.0	-	-	-	-	-	56.5	0.9	-	-	-	-	56.4	-0.2	-	-	-	-	57.5	2.0	-	-	-	-
1977	58.3	1.4	-	-	-	-	59.0	1.2	-	-	-	-	59.7	1.2	-	-	-	-	61.6	3.2	-	-	-	-
1978	62.9	2.1	-	-	-	-	63.9	1.6	-	-	64.1	0.3	-	-	65.4	2.0	-	-	66.9	2.3	-	-	67.3	0.6
1979	-	-	67.8	0.7	-	-	67.8	0.0	-	-	68.4	0.9	-	-	69.4	1.5	-	-	71.7	3.3	-	-	72.2	0.7
1980	-	-	73.5	1.8	-	-	74.0	0.7	-	-	74.4	0.5	-	-	75.4	1.3	-	-	77.6	2.9	-	-	79.0	1.8
1981	-	-	79.6	0.8	-	-	80.7	1.4	-	-	82.6	2.4	-	-	84.0	1.7	-	-	87.2	3.8	-	-	87.4	0.2
1982	-	-	89.1	1.9	-	-	90.1	1.1	-	-	90.1	0.0	-	-	90.7	0.7	-	-	95.8	5.6	-	-	97.0	1.3
1983	-	-	98.6	1.6	-	-	98.5	-0.1	-	-	99.3	0.8	-	-	100.4	1.1	-	-	104.6	4.2	-	-	104.9	0.3
1984	-	-	106.0	1.0	-	-	105.7	-0.3	-	-	106.4	0.7	-	-	107.7	1.2	-	-	110.6	2.7	-	-	110.4	-0.2
1985	-	-	112.0	1.4	-	-	112.2	0.2	-	-	112.7	0.4	-	-	115.2	2.2	-	-	118.6	3.0	-	-	118.1	-0.4
1986	-	-	119.6	1.3	-	-	119.8	0.2	-	-	119.8	0.0	-	-	120.8	0.8	-	-	123.2	2.0	123.4	0.2	123.6	0.2
1987	-	-	-	-	-	-	-	-	-	-	123.2	-0.3	-	-	-	-	-	-	-	-	-	-	126.3	2.5
1988	-	-	-	-	-	-	-	-	-	-	129.2	2.3	-	-	-	-	-	-	-	-	-	-	133.1	3.0
1989	-	-	-	-	-	-	-	-	-	-	134.6	1.1	-	-	-	-	-	-	-	-	-	-	142.4	5.8
1990	-	-	-	-	-	-	-	-	-	-	149.1	4.7	-	-	-	-	-	-	-	-	-	-	155.1	4.0
1991	-	-	-	-	-	-	-	-	-	-	156.3	0.8	-	-	-	-	-	-	-	-	-	-	159.1	1.8
1992	-	-	-	-	-	-	-	-	-	-	166.5	4.7	-	-	-	-	-	-	-	-	-	-	177.7	6.7
1993	-	-	-	-	-	-	-	-	-	-	180.4	1.5	-	-	-	-	-	-	-	-	-	-	181.2	0.4
1994	-	-	-	-	-	-	-	-	-	-	185.8	2.5	-	-	-	-	-	-	-	-	-	-	189.4	1.9
1995	-	-	-	-	-	-	-	-	-	-	190.8	0.7	-	-	-	-	-	-	-	-	-	-	-	-

Source: U.S. Department of Labor, Bureau of Labor Statistics, Division of Consumer Prices and Price Indexes. - indicates no data collected for period.

Minneapolis-St. Paul, MN
Consumer Price Index - Urban Wage Earners
Base 1982-1984 = 100
Other Goods and Services

For 1976-1995. Columns headed % show percentile change in the index from the previous period for which an index is available.

Year	Jan Index	%	Feb Index	%	Mar Index	%	Apr Index	%	May Index	%	Jun Index	%	Jul Index	%	Aug Index	%	Sep Index	%	Oct Index	%	Nov Index	%	Dec Index	%
1976	57.7	-	-	-	-	-	58.1	0.7	-	-	-	-	58.1	0.0	-	-	-	-	59.2	1.9	-	-	-	-
1977	60.0	1.4	-	-	-	-	60.7	1.2	-	-	-	-	61.5	1.3	-	-	-	-	63.4	3.1	-	-	-	-
1978	64.8	2.2	-	-	-	-	65.8	1.5	-	-	66.3	0.8	-	-	66.9	0.9	-	-	68.2	1.9	-	-	68.8	0.9
1979	-	-	69.5	1.0	-	-	69.6	0.1	-	-	70.3	1.0	-	-	71.8	2.1	-	-	73.2	1.9	-	-	73.4	0.3
1980	-	-	74.5	1.5	-	-	75.5	1.3	-	-	76.0	0.7	-	-	76.7	0.9	-	-	78.3	2.1	-	-	80.0	2.2
1981	-	-	81.2	1.5	-	-	82.0	1.0	-	-	83.2	1.5	-	-	83.9	0.8	-	-	87.2	3.9	-	-	87.1	-0.1
1982	-	-	89.2	2.4	-	-	90.2	1.1	-	-	90.3	0.1	-	-	90.8	0.6	-	-	95.9	5.6	-	-	97.2	1.4
1983	-	-	99.1	2.0	-	-	99.0	-0.1	-	-	99.7	0.7	-	-	101.0	1.3	-	-	104.3	3.3	-	-	104.5	0.2
1984	-	-	105.8	1.2	-	-	105.5	-0.3	-	-	106.2	0.7	-	-	107.8	1.5	-	-	109.7	1.8	-	-	109.7	0.0
1985	-	-	111.6	1.7	-	-	111.7	0.1	-	-	112.3	0.5	-	-	115.4	2.8	-	-	118.2	2.4	-	-	117.7	-0.4
1986	-	-	119.4	1.4	-	-	119.5	0.1	-	-	119.6	0.1	-	-	120.8	1.0	-	-	122.7	1.6	122.9	0.2	123.1	0.2
1987	-	-	-	-	-	-	-	-	-	-	121.3	-1.5	-	-	-	-	-	-	-	-	-	-	124.7	2.8
1988	-	-	-	-	-	-	-	-	-	-	127.8	2.5	-	-	-	-	-	-	-	-	-	-	133.1	4.1
1989	-	-	-	-	-	-	-	-	-	-	135.1	1.5	-	-	-	-	-	-	-	-	-	-	143.2	6.0
1990	-	-	-	-	-	-	-	-	-	-	149.4	4.3	-	-	-	-	-	-	-	-	-	-	156.2	4.6
1991	-	-	-	-	-	-	-	-	-	-	156.4	0.1	-	-	-	-	-	-	-	-	-	-	159.0	1.7
1992	-	-	-	-	-	-	-	-	-	-	165.7	4.2	-	-	-	-	-	-	-	-	-	-	177.4	7.1
1993	-	-	-	-	-	-	-	-	-	-	180.6	1.8	-	-	-	-	-	-	-	-	-	-	178.6	-1.1
1994	-	-	-	-	-	-	-	-	-	-	183.7	2.9	-	-	-	-	-	-	-	-	-	-	186.5	1.5
1995	-	-	-	-	-	-	-	-	-	-	187.4	0.5	-	-	-	-	-	-	-	-	-	-	-	-

Source: U.S. Department of Labor, Bureau of Labor Statistics, Division of Consumer Prices and Price Indexes. - indicates no data collected for period.

New York, NY, NE NJ
Consumer Price Index - All Urban Consumers
Base 1982-1984 = 100
Annual Averages

For 1914-1995. Columns headed % show percentile change in the index from the previous period for which an index is available.

Year	All Items		Food & Beverage		Housing		Apparel & Upkeep		Trans- portation		Medical Care		Entertain- ment		Other Goods & Services	
	Index	%	Index	%	Index	%	Index	%	Index	%	Index	%	Index	%	Index	%
1914	-	-	-	-	-	-	-	-	-	-	-	-	-	-	-	-
1915	9.9	-	-	-	-	-	-	-	-	-	-	-	-	-	-	-
1916	10.6	7.1	-	-	-	-	-	-	-	-	-	-	-	-	-	-
1917	12.8	20.8	-	-	-	-	-	-	-	-	-	-	-	-	-	-
1918	15.1	18.0	-	-	-	-	-	-	-	-	-	-	-	-	-	-
1919	17.7	17.2	-	-	-	-	-	-	-	-	-	-	-	-	-	-
1920	20.2	14.1	-	-	-	-	-	-	-	-	-	-	-	-	-	-
1921	18.1	-10.4	-	-	-	-	-	-	-	-	-	-	-	-	-	-
1922	17.2	-5.0	-	-	-	-	-	-	-	-	-	-	-	-	-	-
1923	17.5	1.7	-	-	-	-	-	-	-	-	-	-	-	-	-	-
1924	17.5	0.0	-	-	-	-	-	-	-	-	-	-	-	-	-	-
1925	17.9	2.3	-	-	-	-	-	-	-	-	-	-	-	-	-	-
1926	18.1	1.1	-	-	-	-	-	-	-	-	-	-	-	-	-	-
1927	17.9	-1.1	-	-	-	-	-	-	-	-	-	-	-	-	-	-
1928	17.8	-0.6	-	-	-	-	-	-	-	-	-	-	-	-	-	-
1929	17.9	0.6	-	-	-	-	-	-	-	-	-	-	-	-	-	-
1930	17.4	-2.8	-	-	-	-	-	-	-	-	-	-	-	-	-	-
1931	16.1	-7.5	-	-	-	-	-	-	-	-	-	-	-	-	-	-
1932	14.7	-8.7	-	-	-	-	-	-	-	-	-	-	-	-	-	-
1933	13.9	-5.4	-	-	-	-	-	-	-	-	-	-	-	-	-	-
1934	14.3	2.9	-	-	-	-	-	-	-	-	-	-	-	-	-	-
1935	14.5	1.4	-	-	-	-	-	-	-	-	-	-	-	-	-	-
1936	14.5	0.0	-	-	-	-	-	-	-	-	-	-	-	-	-	-
1937	14.8	2.1	-	-	-	-	-	-	-	-	-	-	-	-	-	-
1938	14.6	-1.4	-	-	-	-	-	-	-	-	-	-	-	-	-	-
1939	14.5	-0.7	-	-	-	-	-	-	-	-	-	-	-	-	-	-
1940	14.7	1.4	-	-	-	-	-	-	-	-	-	-	-	-	-	-
1941	15.3	4.1	-	-	-	-	-	-	-	-	-	-	-	-	-	-
1942	16.7	9.2	-	-	-	-	-	-	-	-	-	-	-	-	-	-
1943	17.9	7.2	-	-	-	-	-	-	-	-	-	-	-	-	-	-
1944	18.4	2.8	-	-	-	-	-	-	-	-	-	-	-	-	-	-
1945	18.9	2.7	-	-	-	-	-	-	-	-	-	-	-	-	-	-
1946	20.7	9.5	-	-	-	-	-	-	-	-	-	-	-	-	-	-
1947	23.2	12.1	-	-	-	-	-	-	16.1	-	14.3	-	-	-	-	-
1948	24.7	6.5	-	-	-	-	-	-	18.8	16.8	15.7	9.8	-	-	-	-
1949	24.5	-0.8	-	-	-	-	-	-	21.5	14.4	16.0	1.9	-	-	-	-
1950	24.6	0.4	-	-	-	-	-	-	22.4	4.2	16.3	1.9	-	-	-	-
1951	26.5	7.7	-	-	-	-	-	-	23.5	4.9	17.0	4.3	-	-	-	-
1952	26.9	1.5	-	-	-	-	-	-	23.9	1.7	18.1	6.5	-	-	-	-
1953	27.1	0.7	-	-	-	-	44.9	-	24.5	2.5	18.6	2.8	-	-	-	-
1954	27.2	0.4	-	-	-	-	44.5	-0.9	24.9	1.6	19.0	2.2	-	-	-	-
1955	27.1	-0.4	-	-	-	-	43.9	-1.3	24.2	-2.8	19.3	1.6	-	-	-	-
1956	27.5	1.5	-	-	-	-	44.9	2.3	25.0	3.3	19.5	1.0	-	-	-	-
1957	28.4	3.3	-	-	-	-	45.7	1.8	25.9	3.6	19.8	1.5	-	-	-	-
1958	29.2	2.8	-	-	-	-	46.0	0.7	26.3	1.5	20.2	2.0	-	-	-	-

[Continued]

652

New York, NY, NE NJ
Consumer Price Index - All Urban Consumers
Base 1982-1984 = 100
Annual Averages
[Continued]

For 1914-1995. Columns headed % show percentile change in the index from the previous period for which an index is available.

Year	All Items		Food & Beverage		Housing		Apparel & Upkeep		Trans- portation		Medical Care		Entertain- ment		Other Goods & Services	
	Index	%	Index	%	Index	%	Index	%	Index	%	Index	%	Index	%	Index	%
1959	29.6	1.4	-	-	-	-	46.4	0.9	27.6	4.9	21.5	6.4	-	-	-	-
1960	30.2	2.0	-	-	-	-	47.3	1.9	27.7	0.4	22.2	3.3	-	-	-	-
1961	30.5	1.0	-	-	-	-	47.8	1.1	27.8	0.4	23.0	3.6	-	-	-	-
1962	30.9	1.3	-	-	-	-	48.3	1.0	28.0	0.7	23.5	2.2	-	-	-	-
1963	31.6	2.3	-	-	-	-	49.2	1.9	28.2	0.7	23.9	1.7	-	-	-	-
1964	32.1	1.6	-	-	-	-	50.0	1.6	28.3	0.4	24.4	2.1	-	-	-	-
1965	32.6	1.6	-	-	-	-	50.7	1.4	28.7	1.4	25.3	3.7	-	-	-	-
1966	33.7	3.4	-	-	-	-	51.9	2.4	29.8	3.8	26.6	5.1	-	-	-	-
1967	34.6	2.7	-	-	-	-	54.5	5.0	31.2	4.7	28.4	6.8	-	-	-	-
1968	36.1	4.3	-	-	-	-	57.6	5.7	32.0	2.6	30.3	6.7	-	-	-	-
1969	38.3	6.1	-	-	-	-	61.4	6.6	33.9	5.9	33.1	9.2	-	-	-	-
1970	41.2	7.6	-	-	-	-	64.1	4.4	38.1	12.4	35.6	7.6	-	-	-	-
1971	43.6	5.8	-	-	-	-	65.6	2.3	40.2	5.5	38.6	8.4	-	-	-	-
1972	45.5	4.4	-	-	-	-	67.0	2.1	41.5	3.2	39.8	3.1	-	-	-	-
1973	48.3	6.2	-	-	-	-	68.8	2.7	42.3	1.9	41.2	3.5	-	-	-	-
1974	53.5	10.8	-	-	-	-	74.2	7.8	45.6	7.8	45.6	10.7	-		-	-
1975	57.6	7.7	-	-	-	-	76.9	3.6	50.3	10.3	51.4	12.7	-	-	-	-
1976	61.0	5.9	62.7	-	59.9	-	78.9	2.6	57.5	14.3	56.8	10.5	64.5	-	58.6	-
1977	64.2	5.2	65.8	4.9	63.0	5.2	81.3	3.0	60.5	5.2	61.6	8.5	68.5	6.2	62.3	6.3
1978	67.8	5.6	71.4	8.5	66.3	5.2	85.1	4.7	62.6	3.5	65.4	6.2	72.3	5.5	65.1	4.5
1979	73.7	8.7	78.0	9.2	72.1	8.7	86.8	2.0	70.6	12.8	70.5	7.8	75.7	4.7	68.7	5.5
1980	82.1	11.4	85.1	9.1	80.8	12.1	92.7	6.8	82.5	16.9	77.3	9.6	81.5	7.7	74.1	7.9
1981	90.1	9.7	92.7	8.9	89.4	10.6	96.3	3.9	92.4	12.0	84.3	9.1	88.3	8.3	80.9	9.2
1982	95.3	5.8	97.3	5.0	95.0	6.3	97.3	1.0	95.9	3.8	91.8	8.9	95.5	8.2	89.7	10.9
1983	99.8	4.7	99.0	1.7	100.2	5.5	100.6	3.4	99.1	3.3	100.1	9.0	100.4	5.1	101.2	12.8
1984	104.8	5.0	103.7	4.7	104.8	4.6	102.0	1.4	105.0	6.0	108.1	8.0	104.0	3.6	109.0	7.7
1985	108.7	3.7	107.3	3.5	108.7	3.7	104.5	2.5	107.1	2.0	115.9	7.2	108.6	4.4	116.1	6.5
1986	112.3	3.3	112.2	4.6	112.8	3.8	104.2	-0.3	104.8	-2.1	125.6	8.4	115.1	6.0	123.6	6.5
1987	118.0	5.1	118.6	5.7	118.0	4.6	109.9	5.5	108.7	3.7	136.1	8.4	119.2	3.6	130.8	5.8
1988	123.7	4.8	124.8	5.2	125.1	6.0	107.4	-2.3	112.8	3.8	144.8	6.4	122.8	3.0	139.5	6.7
1989	130.6	5.6	132.1	5.8	131.8	5.4	114.0	6.1	116.5	3.3	155.8	7.6	129.5	5.5	151.9	8.9
1990	138.5	6.0	139.6	5.7	139.3	5.7	121.8	6.8	123.1	5.7	172.4	10.7	135.6	4.7	164.0	8.0
1991	144.8	4.5	144.3	3.4	145.7	4.6	124.5	2.2	127.9	3.9	186.6	8.2	140.8	3.8	177.2	8.0
1992	150.0	3.6	146.0	1.2	151.4	3.9	128.5	3.2	131.5	2.8	200.0	7.2	146.4	4.0	191.0	7.8
1993	154.5	3.0	149.0	2.1	155.5	2.7	129.3	0.6	137.7	4.7	209.1	4.6	149.8	2.3	200.1	4.8
1994	158.2	2.4	151.9	1.9	159.9	2.8	126.2	-2.4	141.8	3.0	217.6	4.1	154.0	2.8	204.9	2.4
1995	162.2	2.5	155.9	2.6	163.4	2.2	126.0	-0.2	145.9	2.9	226.8	4.2	158.8	3.1	213.5	4.2

Source: U.S. Department of Labor, Bureau of Labor Statistics, Division of Consumer Prices and Price Indexes. - indicates no data collected for period.

New York, NY, NE NJ
Consumer Price Index - Urban Wage Earners
Base 1982-1984 = 100
Annual Averages

For 1914-1995. Columns headed % show percentile change in the index from the previous period for which an index is available.

Year	All Items		Food & Beverage		Housing		Apparel & Upkeep		Trans-portation		Medical Care		Entertain-ment		Other Goods & Services	
	Index	%	Index	%	Index	%	Index	%	Index	%	Index	%	Index	%	Index	%
1914	-	-	-	-	-	-	-	-	-	-	-	-	-	-	-	-
1915	10.0	-	-	-	-	-	-	-	-	-	-	-	-	-	-	-
1916	10.8	8.0	-	-	-	-	-	-	-	-	-	-	-	-	-	-
1917	13.0	20.4	-	-	-	-	-	-	-	-	-	-	-	-	-	-
1918	15.3	17.7	-	-	-	-	-	-	-	-	-	-	-	-	-	-
1919	18.0	17.6	-	-	-	-	-	-	-	-	-	-	-	-	-	-
1920	20.5	13.9	-	-	-	-	-	-	-	-	-	-	-	-	-	-
1921	18.4	-10.2	-	-	-	-	-	-	-	-	-	-	-	-	-	-
1922	17.5	-4.9	-	-	-	-	-	-	-	-	-	-	-	-	-	-
1923	17.7	1.1	-	-	-	-	-	-	-	-	-	-	-	-	-	-
1924	17.7	0.0	-	-	-	-	-	-	-	-	-	-	-	-	-	-
1925	18.2	2.8	-	-	-	-	-	-	-	-	-	-	-	-	-	-
1926	18.4	1.1	-	-	-	-	-	-	-	-	-	-	-	-	-	-
1927	18.2	-1.1	-	-	-	-	-	-	-	-	-	-	-	-	-	-
1928	18.1	-0.5	-	-	-	-	-	-	-	-	-	-	-	-	-	-
1929	18.2	0.6	-	-	-	-	-	-	-	-	-	-	-	-	-	-
1930	17.7	-2.7	-	-	-	-	-	-	-	-	-	-	-	-	-	-
1931	16.4	-7.3	-	-	-	-	-	-	-	-	-	-	-	-	-	-
1932	14.9	-9.1	-	-	-	-	-	-	-	-	-	-	-	-	-	-
1933	14.1	-5.4	-	-	-	-	-	-	-	-	-	-	-	-	-	-
1934	14.5	2.8	-	-	-	-	-	-	-	-	-	-	-	-	-	-
1935	14.7	1.4	-	-	-	-	-	-	-	-	-	-	-	-	-	-
1936	14.7	0.0	-	-	-	-	-	-	-	-	-	-	-	-	-	-
1937	15.1	2.7	-	-	-	-	-	-	-	-	-	-	-	-	-	-
1938	14.8	-2.0	-	-	-	-	-	-	-	-	-	-	-	-	-	-
1939	14.7	-0.7	-	-	-	-	-	-	-	-	-	-	-	-	-	-
1940	14.9	1.4	-	-	-	-	-	-	-	-	-	-	-	-	-	-
1941	15.5	4.0	-	-	-	-	-	-	-	-	-	-	-	-	-	-
1942	17.0	9.7	-	-	-	-	-	-	-	-	-	-	-	-	-	-
1943	18.2	7.1	-	-	-	-	-	-	-	-	-	-	-	-	-	-
1944	18.7	2.7	-	-	-	-	-	-	-	-	-	-	-	-	-	-
1945	19.1	2.1	-	-	-	-	-	-	-	-	-	-	-	-	-	-
1946	21.0	9.9	-	-	-	-	-	-	-	-	-	-	-	-	-	-
1947	23.5	11.9	-	-	-	-	-	-	15.9	-	14.9	-	-	-	-	-
1948	25.1	6.8	-	-	-	-	-	-	18.6	17.0	16.3	9.4	-	-	-	-
1949	24.8	-1.2	-	-	-	-	-	-	21.3	14.5	16.7	2.5	-	-	-	-
1950	25.0	0.8	-	-	-	-	-	-	22.2	4.2	17.0	1.8	-	-	-	-
1951	26.9	7.6	-	-	-	-	-	-	23.3	5.0	17.7	4.1	-	-	-	-
1952	27.3	1.5	-	-	-	-	-	-	23.7	1.7	18.9	6.8	-	-	-	-
1953	27.5	0.7	-	-	-	-	44.8	-	24.2	2.1	19.4	2.6	-	-	-	-
1954	27.6	0.4	-	-	-	-	44.4	-0.9	24.6	1.7	19.8	2.1	-	-	-	-
1955	27.5	-0.4	-	-	-	-	43.8	-1.4	24.0	-2.4	20.1	1.5	-	-	-	-
1956	27.9	1.5	-	-	-	-	44.9	2.5	24.8	3.3	20.3	1.0	-	-	-	-
1957	28.8	3.2	-	-	-	-	45.6	1.6	25.7	3.6	20.6	1.5	-	-	-	-
1958	29.7	3.1	-	-	-	-	46.0	0.9	26.1	1.6	21.1	2.4	-	-	-	-

[Continued]

654

New York, NY, NE NJ
Consumer Price Index - Urban Wage Earners
Base 1982-1984 = 100
Annual Averages
[Continued]

For 1914-1995. Columns headed % show percentile change in the index from the previous period for which an index is available.

Year	All Items		Food & Beverage		Housing		Apparel & Upkeep		Trans-portation		Medical Care		Entertain-ment		Other Goods & Services	
	Index	%	Index	%	Index	%	Index	%	Index	%	Index	%	Index	%	Index	%
1959	30.1	1.3	-	-	-	-	46.3	0.7	27.3	4.6	22.4	6.2	-	-	-	-
1960	30.7	2.0	-	-	-	-	47.2	1.9	27.5	0.7	23.1	3.1	-	-	-	-
1961	30.9	0.7	-	-	-	-	47.7	1.1	27.5	0.0	24.0	3.9	-	-	-	-
1962	31.4	1.6	-	-	-	-	48.2	1.0	27.7	0.7	24.5	2.1	-	-	-	-
1963	32.1	2.2	-	-	-	-	49.2	2.1	27.9	0.7	25.0	2.0	-	-	-	-
1964	32.6	1.6	-	-	-	-	49.9	1.4	28.0	0.4	25.5	2.0	-	-	-	-
1965	33.1	1.5	-	-	-	-	50.6	1.4	28.4	1.4	26.4	3.5	-	-	-	-
1966	34.2	3.3	-	-	-	-	51.8	2.4	29.5	3.9	27.7	4.9	-	-	-	-
1967	35.1	2.6	-	-	-	-	54.4	5.0	30.9	4.7	29.6	6.9	-	-	-	-
1968	36.6	4.3	-	-	-	-	57.5	5.7	31.7	2.6	31.6	6.8	-	-	-	-
1969	38.9	6.3	-	-	-	-	61.3	6.6	33.6	6.0	34.5	9.2	-	-	-	-
1970	41.8	7.5	-	-	-	-	64.0	4.4	37.8	12.5	37.1	7.5	-	-	-	-
1971	44.2	5.7	-	-	-	-	65.5	2.3	39.8	5.3	40.2	8.4	-	-	-	-
1972	46.1	4.3	-	-	-	-	66.9	2.1	41.1	3.3	41.5	3.2	-	-	-	-
1973	49.1	6.5	-	-	-	-	68.7	2.7	41.9	1.9	43.0	3.6	-	-	-	-
1974	54.4	10.8	-	-	-	-	74.1	7.9	45.1	7.6	47.6	10.7	-	-	-	-
1975	58.5	7.5	-	-	-	-	76.7	3.5	49.8	10.4	53.6	12.6	-	-	-	-
1976	61.9	5.8	63.4	-	61.6	-	78.8	2.7	57.0	14.5	59.2	10.4	66.0	-	59.3	-
1977	65.2	5.3	66.5	4.9	64.8	5.2	81.2	3.0	59.9	5.1	64.3	8.6	70.0	6.1	63.0	6.2
1978	68.6	5.2	72.0	8.3	67.7	4.5	84.1	3.6	62.2	3.8	67.8	5.4	73.2	4.6	66.0	4.8
1979	74.7	8.9	78.7	9.3	73.6	8.7	87.3	3.8	70.3	13.0	72.5	6.9	76.7	4.8	69.6	5.5
1980	83.2	11.4	85.9	9.1	82.5	12.1	93.2	6.8	82.2	16.9	78.7	8.6	82.5	7.6	74.8	7.5
1981	91.3	9.7	92.9	8.1	91.4	10.8	96.0	3.0	92.3	12.3	86.2	9.5	89.4	8.4	80.9	8.2
1982	96.3	5.5	97.3	4.7	97.2	6.3	97.2	1.2	95.8	3.8	91.9	6.6	95.5	6.8	89.7	10.9
1983	100.1	3.9	99.1	1.8	100.9	3.8	100.6	3.5	98.9	3.2	99.9	8.7	100.5	5.2	101.6	13.3
1984	103.6	3.5	103.6	4.5	101.9	1.0	102.1	1.5	105.2	6.4	108.3	8.4	104.1	3.6	108.7	7.0
1985	107.9	4.2	107.0	3.3	107.3	5.3	104.4	2.3	107.2	1.9	116.2	7.3	108.3	4.0	115.4	6.2
1986	111.0	2.9	111.9	4.6	111.2	3.6	104.0	-0.4	104.2	-2.8	125.8	8.3	115.0	6.2	122.7	6.3
1987	116.6	5.0	118.2	5.6	116.0	4.3	110.2	6.0	108.4	4.0	136.8	8.7	120.3	4.6	129.5	5.5
1988	121.8	4.5	124.3	5.2	122.5	5.6	106.3	-3.5	112.4	3.7	145.8	6.6	123.9	3.0	137.9	6.5
1989	128.6	5.6	131.7	6.0	129.0	5.3	112.5	5.8	116.1	3.3	157.0	7.7	130.3	5.2	150.7	9.3
1990	136.3	6.0	139.4	5.8	135.9	5.3	120.1	6.8	123.1	6.0	172.0	9.6	136.2	4.5	163.6	8.6
1991	142.1	4.3	144.0	3.3	141.6	4.2	122.1	1.7	127.8	3.8	186.2	8.3	141.3	3.7	177.5	8.5
1992	146.9	3.4	145.6	1.1	146.7	3.6	125.8	3.0	131.6	3.0	200.3	7.6	146.6	3.8	191.0	7.6
1993	151.1	2.9	148.6	2.1	150.6	2.7	126.2	0.3	137.4	4.4	209.0	4.3	149.5	2.0	200.4	4.9
1994	154.5	2.3	151.5	2.0	154.6	2.7	122.7	-2.8	141.6	3.1	217.9	4.3	153.5	2.7	204.8	2.2
1995	158.3	2.5	155.3	2.5	158.0	2.2	121.8	-0.7	146.0	3.1	227.6	4.5	158.1	3.0	213.1	4.1

Source: U.S. Department of Labor, Bureau of Labor Statistics, Division of Consumer Prices and Price Indexes. - indicates no data collected for period.

New York, NY, NE NJ
Consumer Price Index - All Urban Consumers
Base 1982-1984 = 100
All Items

For 1914-1995. Columns headed % show percentile change in the index from the previous period for which an index is available.

Year	Jan Index	Jan %	Feb Index	Feb %	Mar Index	Mar %	Apr Index	Apr %	May Index	May %	Jun Index	Jun %	Jul Index	Jul %	Aug Index	Aug %	Sep Index	Sep %	Oct Index	Oct %	Nov Index	Nov %	Dec Index	Dec %
1914	-	-	-	-	-	-	-	-	-	-	-	-	-	-	-	-	-	-	-	-	-	-	9.9	-
1915	-	-	-	-	-	-	-	-	-	-	-	-	-	-	-	-	-	-	-	-	-	-	10.1	2.0
1916	-	-	-	-	-	-	-	-	-	-	-	-	-	-	-	-	-	-	-	-	-	-	11.3	11.9
1917	-	-	-	-	-	-	-	-	-	-	-	-	-	-	-	-	-	-	-	-	-	-	13.8	22.1
1918	-	-	-	-	-	-	-	-	-	-	-	-	-	-	-	-	-	-	-	-	-	-	16.8	21.7
1919	-	-	-	-	-	-	-	-	-	-	17.1	1.8	-	-	-	-	-	-	-	-	-	-	19.3	12.9
1920	-	-	-	-	-	-	-	-	-	-	20.9	8.3	-	-	-	-	-	-	-	-	-	-	19.5	-6.7
1921	-	-	-	-	-	-	-	-	17.9	-8.2	-	-	-	-	-	-	17.8	-0.6	-	-	-	-	17.9	0.6
1922	-	-	-	-	17.1	-4.5	-	-	-	-	17.2	0.6	-	-	-	-	17.1	-0.6	-	-	-	-	17.4	1.8
1923	-	-	-	-	17.3	-0.6	-	-	-	-	17.4	0.6	-	-	-	-	17.6	1.1	-	-	-	-	17.8	1.1
1924	-	-	-	-	17.4	-2.2	-	-	-	-	17.4	0.0	-	-	-	-	17.4	0.0	-	-	-	-	17.7	1.7
1925	-	-	-	-	-	-	-	-	-	-	17.7	0.0	-	-	-	-	-	-	-	-	-	-	18.5	4.5
1926	-	-	-	-	-	-	-	-	-	-	18.1	-2.2	-	-	-	-	-	-	-	-	-	-	18.1	0.0
1927	-	-	-	-	-	-	-	-	-	-	18.0	-0.6	-	-	-	-	-	-	-	-	-	-	18.1	0.6
1928	-	-	-	-	-	-	-	-	-	-	17.7	-2.2	-	-	-	-	-	-	-	-	-	-	17.8	0.6
1929	-	-	-	-	-	-	-	-	-	-	17.8	0.0	-	-	-	-	-	-	-	-	-	-	17.9	0.6
1930	-	-	-	-	-	-	-	-	-	-	17.4	-2.8	-	-	-	-	-	-	-	-	-	-	17.0	-2.3
1931	-	-	-	-	-	-	-	-	-	-	16.0	-5.9	-	-	-	-	-	-	-	-	-	-	15.4	-3.8
1932	-	-	-	-	-	-	-	-	-	-	14.7	-4.5	-	-	-	-	-	-	-	-	-	-	14.2	-3.4
1933	-	-	-	-	-	-	-	-	-	-	13.7	-3.5	-	-	-	-	-	-	-	-	-	-	14.0	2.2
1934	-	-	-	-	-	-	-	-	-	-	14.3	2.1	-	-	-	-	-	-	-	-	14.4	0.7	-	-
1935	-	-	-	-	14.4	0.0	-	-	-	-	-	-	14.3	-0.7	-	-	-	-	14.4	0.7	-	-	-	-
1936	14.6	1.4	-	-	-	-	14.4	-1.4	-	-	-	-	14.5	0.7	-	-	14.7	1.4	-	-	-	-	14.5	-1.4
1937	-	-	-	-	14.8	2.1	-	-	-	-	14.8	0.0	-	-	-	-	15.2	2.7	-	-	-	-	15.0	-1.3
1938	-	-	-	-	14.5	-3.3	-	-	-	-	14.5	0.0	-	-	-	-	14.6	0.7	-	-	-	-	14.6	0.0
1939	-	-	-	-	14.5	-0.7	-	-	-	-	14.3	-1.4	-	-	-	-	14.8	3.5	-	-	-	-	14.6	-1.4
1940	-	-	-	-	14.7	0.7	-	-	-	-	14.8	0.7	-	-	-	-	14.7	-0.7	14.6	-0.7	14.7	0.7	14.7	0.0
1941	14.7	0.0	14.8	0.7	14.8	0.0	14.9	0.7	15.0	0.7	15.2	1.3	15.3	0.7	15.4	0.7	15.6	1.3	15.7	0.6	15.8	0.6	15.8	0.0
1942	16.1	1.9	16.2	0.6	16.3	0.6	16.4	0.6	16.5	0.6	16.7	1.2	16.8	0.6	16.9	0.6	16.9	0.0	17.1	1.2	17.3	1.2	17.4	0.6
1943	17.5	0.6	17.5	0.0	17.8	1.7	17.9	0.6	18.1	1.1	18.1	0.0	18.1	0.0	17.9	-1.1	18.1	1.1	18.2	0.6	18.2	0.0	18.2	0.0
1944	18.2	0.0	18.1	-0.5	18.2	0.6	18.3	0.5	18.4	0.5	18.4	0.0	18.5	0.5	18.5	0.0	18.5	0.0	18.5	0.0	18.6	0.5	18.6	0.0
1945	18.6	0.0	18.6	0.0	18.5	-0.5	18.6	0.5	18.7	0.5	18.9	1.1	19.1	1.1	19.0	-0.5	18.9	-0.5	18.9	0.0	19.0	0.5	19.1	0.5
1946	19.2	0.5	19.2	0.0	19.3	0.5	19.5	1.0	19.6	0.5	19.8	1.0	21.0	6.1	21.3	1.4	21.8	2.3	22.3	2.3	22.5	0.9	22.7	0.9
1947	22.6	-0.4	22.5	-0.4	23.0	2.2	22.9	-0.4	22.7	-0.9	22.9	0.9	23.0	0.4	23.2	0.9	23.6	1.7	23.6	0.0	23.9	1.3	24.1	0.8
1948	24.4	1.2	24.3	-0.4	24.0	-1.2	24.4	1.7	24.5	0.4	24.7	0.8	25.2	2.0	25.3	0.4	25.3	0.0	25.1	-0.8	25.0	-0.4	24.7	-1.2
1949	24.7	0.0	24.4	-1.2	24.5	0.4	24.6	0.4	24.5	-0.4	24.5	0.0	24.5	0.0	24.5	0.0	24.6	0.4	24.3	-1.2	24.3	0.0	24.2	-0.4
1950	24.0	-0.8	24.1	0.4	24.1	0.0	24.2	0.4	24.2	0.0	24.3	0.4	24.7	1.6	24.7	0.0	25.0	1.2	25.1	0.4	25.3	0.8	25.6	1.2
1951	25.9	1.2	26.3	1.5	26.3	0.0	26.3	0.0	26.5	0.8	26.3	-0.8	26.4	0.4	26.4	0.0	26.6	0.8	26.7	0.4	26.8	0.4	26.8	0.0
1952	26.8	0.0	26.7	-0.4	26.6	-0.4	26.7	0.4	26.7	0.0	26.7	0.0	27.1	1.5	27.1	0.0	27.1	0.0	27.1	0.0	27.2	0.4	27.0	-0.7
1953	26.9	-0.4	26.8	-0.4	26.8	0.0	26.8	0.0	26.8	0.0	27.0	0.7	27.1	0.4	27.2	0.4	27.3	0.4	27.3	0.0	27.2	-0.4	27.3	0.4
1954	27.3	0.0	27.2	-0.4	27.1	-0.4	27.2	0.4	27.2	0.0	27.2	0.0	27.3	0.4	27.3	0.0	27.2	-0.4	27.2	0.0	27.2	0.0	27.1	-0.4
1955	27.1	0.0	27.2	0.4	27.1	-0.4	27.1	0.0	27.0	-0.4	27.0	0.0	27.0	0.0	27.0	0.0	27.2	0.7	27.1	-0.4	27.2	0.4	27.0	-0.7
1956	27.1	0.4	27.1	0.0	27.1	0.0	27.1	0.0	27.3	0.7	27.4	0.4	27.6	0.7	27.6	0.0	27.8	0.7	27.9	0.4	27.9	0.0	27.9	0.0
1957	27.9	0.0	28.0	0.4	28.0	0.0	28.2	0.7	28.3	0.4	28.4	0.4	28.6	0.7	28.6	0.0	28.5	-0.3	28.6	0.4	28.6	0.0	28.6	0.0
1958	29.0	1.4	29.0	0.0	29.2	0.7	29.2	0.0	29.2	0.0	29.2	0.0	29.2	0.0	29.2	0.0	29.3	0.3	29.3	0.0	29.4	0.3	29.3	-0.3

[Continued]

New York, NY, NE NJ
Consumer Price Index - All Urban Consumers
Base 1982-1984 = 100
All Items
[Continued]

For 1914-1995. Columns headed % show percentile change in the index from the previous period for which an index is available.

Year	Jan Index	%	Feb Index	%	Mar Index	%	Apr Index	%	May Index	%	Jun Index	%	Jul Index	%	Aug Index	%	Sep Index	%	Oct Index	%	Nov Index	%	Dec Index	%
1959	29.4	0.3	29.4	0.0	29.4	0.0	29.4	0.0	29.4	0.0	29.6	0.7	29.8	0.7	29.7	-0.3	29.8	0.3	29.9	0.3	30.0	0.3	30.0	0.0
1960	30.0	0.0	30.0	0.0	30.0	0.0	30.1	0.3	30.1	0.0	30.1	0.0	30.1	0.0	30.2	0.3	30.3	0.3	30.4	0.3	30.5	0.3	30.5	0.0
1961	30.4	-0.3	30.4	0.0	30.4	0.0	30.3	-0.3	30.3	0.0	30.3	0.0	30.5	0.7	30.5	0.0	30.6	0.3	30.6	0.0	30.6	0.0	30.6	0.0
1962	30.7	0.3	30.8	0.3	30.8	0.0	30.8	0.0	30.7	-0.3	30.8	0.3	30.9	0.3	31.0	0.3	31.2	0.6	31.2	0.0	31.1	-0.3	31.1	0.0
1963	31.2	0.3	31.3	0.3	31.3	0.0	31.4	0.3	31.3	-0.3	31.6	1.0	31.8	0.6	31.8	0.0	31.8	0.0	31.8	0.0	31.9	0.3	32.0	0.3
1964	31.9	-0.3	32.0	0.3	32.0	0.0	32.0	0.0	32.0	0.0	32.0	0.0	32.1	0.3	32.1	0.0	32.2	0.3	32.2	0.0	32.3	0.3	32.3	0.0
1965	32.2	-0.3	32.3	0.3	32.3	0.0	32.4	0.3	32.5	0.3	32.6	0.3	32.7	0.3	32.7	0.0	32.8	0.3	32.9	0.3	32.9	0.0	33.0	0.3
1966	33.0	0.0	33.2	0.6	33.4	0.6	33.5	0.3	33.5	0.0	33.5	0.0	33.8	0.9	33.9	0.3	34.1	0.6	34.2	0.3	34.2	0.0	34.2	0.0
1967	34.1	-0.3	34.3	0.6	34.3	0.0	34.3	0.0	34.4	0.3	34.5	0.3	34.6	0.3	34.7	0.3	34.8	0.3	34.9	0.3	35.0	0.3	35.1	0.3
1968	35.1	0.0	35.3	0.6	35.5	0.6	35.6	0.3	35.7	0.3	35.9	0.6	36.1	0.6	36.4	0.8	36.6	0.5	36.8	0.5	36.9	0.3	37.0	0.3
1969	37.2	0.5	37.3	0.3	37.7	1.1	37.9	0.5	38.0	0.3	38.3	0.8	38.4	0.3	38.5	0.3	38.8	0.8	39.0	0.5	39.1	0.3	39.5	1.0
1970	39.8	0.8	40.2	1.0	40.4	0.5	40.7	0.7	40.9	0.5	41.2	0.7	41.3	0.2	41.4	0.2	41.7	0.7	41.9	0.5	42.0	0.2	42.3	0.7
1971	42.4	0.2	42.7	0.7	43.0	0.7	43.1	0.2	43.3	0.5	43.6	0.7	43.9	0.7	43.9	0.0	44.0	0.2	44.1	0.2	44.1	0.0	44.3	0.5
1972	44.5	0.5	44.8	0.7	45.0	0.4	45.1	0.2	45.2	0.2	45.3	0.2	45.5	0.4	45.6	0.2	46.0	0.9	46.1	0.2	46.1	0.0	46.2	0.2
1973	46.3	0.2	46.7	0.9	47.2	1.1	47.6	0.8	47.8	0.4	48.1	0.6	48.2	0.2	49.0	1.7	49.2	0.4	49.5	0.6	50.0	1.0	50.5	1.0
1974	50.8	0.6	51.6	1.6	52.2	1.2	52.2	0.0	52.8	1.1	53.2	0.8	53.4	0.4	54.3	1.7	54.9	1.1	55.4	0.9	55.7	0.5	56.0	0.5
1975	56.0	0.0	56.5	0.9	56.5	0.0	56.6	0.2	56.8	0.4	57.1	0.5	57.6	0.9	57.9	0.5	58.6	1.2	58.8	0.3	59.3	0.9	59.6	0.5
1976	59.7	0.2	60.0	0.5	60.2	0.3	60.3	0.2	60.5	0.3	60.9	0.7	61.1	0.3	61.4	0.5	61.8	0.7	61.9	0.2	61.9	0.0	62.2	0.5
1977	62.4	0.3	63.0	1.0	63.3	0.5	63.5	0.3	63.9	0.6	64.4	0.8	64.5	0.2	64.8	0.5	64.8	0.0	64.9	0.2	65.2	0.5	65.3	0.2
1978	65.7	0.6	66.0	0.5	66.5	0.8	66.9	0.6	67.3	0.6	68.0	1.0	68.1	0.1	68.4	0.4	68.8	0.6	69.3	0.7	69.5	0.5	69.7	0.3
1979	70.2	0.7	71.0	1.1	71.4	0.6	72.1	1.0	72.8	1.0	73.5	1.0	74.0	0.7	74.5	0.7	75.4	1.2	76.1	0.9	76.6	0.7	77.1	0.7
1980	78.2	1.4	78.9	0.9	80.0	1.4	80.6	0.7	81.1	0.6	82.1	1.2	82.6	0.6	83.3	0.8	83.6	0.4	84.1	0.6	84.6	0.6	85.5	1.1
1981	86.3	0.9	87.4	1.3	87.8	0.5	88.3	0.6	88.8	0.6	89.5	0.8	90.8	1.5	91.6	0.9	93.0	1.5	92.7	-0.3	92.6	-0.1	92.7	0.1
1982	92.9	0.2	93.1	0.2	92.5	-0.6	92.8	0.3	93.7	1.0	95.7	2.1	95.9	0.2	96.3	0.4	97.1	0.8	98.4	1.3	98.1	-0.3	97.5	-0.6
1983	97.8	0.3	98.0	0.2	98.1	0.1	99.1	1.0	99.4	0.3	99.7	0.3	100.0	0.3	100.1	0.1	101.0	0.9	101.3	0.3	101.7	0.4	101.8	0.1
1984	102.8	1.0	103.4	0.6	103.7	0.3	104.1	0.4	104.1	0.0	104.3	0.2	104.8	0.5	105.5	0.7	106.2	0.7	106.1	-0.1	106.5	0.4	106.5	0.0
1985	106.7	0.2	107.3	0.6	107.5	0.2	107.9	0.4	108.1	0.2	108.3	0.2	108.4	0.1	109.2	0.7	109.6	0.4	109.8	0.2	110.7	0.8	111.0	0.3
1986	111.8	0.7	111.5	-0.3	111.5	0.0	111.2	-0.3	110.9	-0.3	111.7	0.7	112.5	0.7	112.7	0.2	113.0	0.3	113.4	0.4	113.3	-0.1	113.8	0.4
1987	114.7	0.8	115.3	0.5	115.8	0.4	116.6	0.7	117.3	0.6	117.8	0.4	117.9	0.1	118.9	0.8	119.8	0.8	120.2	0.3	120.5	0.2	120.6	0.1
1988	121.3	0.6	121.1	-0.2	121.5	0.3	122.6	0.9	122.7	0.1	123.1	0.3	123.6	0.4	124.2	0.5	126.0	1.4	126.2	0.2	125.9	-0.2	126.0	0.1
1989	127.0	0.8	127.6	0.5	128.9	1.0	129.5	0.5	130.2	0.5	130.5	0.2	130.6	0.1	130.9	0.2	132.2	1.0	132.8	0.5	133.2	0.3	133.3	0.1
1990	135.1	1.4	135.3	0.1	136.6	1.0	137.3	0.5	137.2	-0.1	137.1	-0.1	138.4	0.9	140.0	1.2	140.8	0.6	141.6	0.6	141.5	-0.1	141.6	0.1
1991	143.0	1.0	143.6	0.4	143.4	-0.1	143.7	0.2	144.0	0.2	144.6	0.4	145.2	0.4	145.4	0.1	145.8	0.3	145.7	-0.1	146.6	0.6	146.6	0.0
1992	147.3	0.5	148.0	0.5	149.1	0.7	149.2	0.1	148.9	-0.2	149.5	0.4	149.9	0.3	150.8	0.6	151.4	0.4	152.1	0.5	152.2	0.1	151.9	-0.2
1993	153.0	0.7	153.6	0.4	154.1	0.3	154.0	-0.1	153.8	-0.1	154.2	0.3	154.3	0.1	155.3	0.6	155.3	0.0	155.5	0.1	155.4	-0.1	155.6	0.1
1994	156.0	0.3	157.4	0.9	157.9	0.3	157.7	-0.1	157.3	-0.3	157.8	0.3	158.2	0.3	159.1	0.6	159.0	-0.1	159.5	0.3	159.4	-0.1	158.9	-0.3
1995	159.9	0.6	160.3	0.3	160.9	0.4	161.4	0.3	161.8	0.2	162.2	0.2	162.3	0.1	162.8	0.3	163.2	0.2	163.6	0.2	163.8	0.1	163.7	-0.1

Source: U.S. Department of Labor, Bureau of Labor Statistics, Division of Consumer Prices and Price Indexes. - indicates no data collected for period.

New York, NY, NE NJ
Consumer Price Index - Urban Wage Earners
Base 1982-1984 = 100
All Items

For 1914-1995. Columns headed % show percentile change in the index from the previous period for which an index is available.

Year	Jan Index	%	Feb Index	%	Mar Index	%	Apr Index	%	May Index	%	Jun Index	%	Jul Index	%	Aug Index	%	Sep Index	%	Oct Index	%	Nov Index	%	Dec Index	%
1914	-	-	-	-	-	-	-	-	-	-	-	-	-	-	-	-	-	-	-	-	-	-	10.1	-
1915	-	-	-	-	-	-	-	-	-	-	-	-	-	-	-	-	-	-	-	-	-	-	10.3	2.0
1916	-	-	-	-	-	-	-	-	-	-	-	-	-	-	-	-	-	-	-	-	-	-	11.5	11.7
1917	-	-	-	-	-	-	-	-	-	-	-	-	-	-	-	-	-	-	-	-	-	-	14.0	21.7
1918	-	-	-	-	-	-	-	-	-	-	-	-	-	-	-	-	-	-	-	-	-	-	17.1	22.1
1919	-	-	-	-	-	-	-	-	-	-	17.4	1.8	-	-	-	-	-	-	-	-	-	-	19.6	12.6
1920	-	-	-	-	-	-	-	-	-	-	21.2	8.2	-	-	-	-	-	-	-	-	-	-	19.8	-6.6
1921	-	-	-	-	-	-	-	-	18.2	-8.1	-	-	-	-	-	-	18.1	-0.5	-	-	-	-	18.2	0.6
1922	-	-	-	-	17.4	-4.4	-	-	-	-	17.4	0.0	-	-	-	-	17.4	0.0	-	-	-	-	17.7	1.7
1923	-	-	-	-	17.6	-0.6	-	-	-	-	17.7	0.6	-	-	-	-	17.9	1.1	-	-	-	-	18.1	1.1
1924	-	-	-	-	17.7	-2.2	-	-	-	-	17.7	0.0	-	-	-	-	17.7	0.0	-	-	-	-	18.0	1.7
1925	-	-	-	-	-	-	-	-	-	-	18.0	0.0	-	-	-	-	-	-	-	-	-	-	18.8	4.4
1926	-	-	-	-	-	-	-	-	-	-	18.4	-2.1	-	-	-	-	-	-	-	-	-	-	18.4	0.0
1927	-	-	-	-	-	-	-	-	-	-	18.3	-0.5	-	-	-	-	-	-	-	-	-	-	18.4	0.5
1928	-	-	-	-	-	-	-	-	-	-	18.0	-2.2	-	-	-	-	-	-	-	-	-	-	18.1	0.6
1929	-	-	-	-	-	-	-	-	-	-	18.1	0.0	-	-	-	-	-	-	-	-	-	-	18.2	0.6
1930	-	-	-	-	-	-	-	-	-	-	17.7	-2.7	-	-	-	-	-	-	-	-	-	-	17.2	-2.8
1931	-	-	-	-	-	-	-	-	-	-	16.2	-5.8	-	-	-	-	-	-	-	-	-	-	15.7	-3.1
1932	-	-	-	-	-	-	-	-	-	-	15.0	-4.5	-	-	-	-	-	-	-	-	-	-	14.4	-4.0
1933	-	-	-	-	-	-	-	-	-	-	13.9	-3.5	-	-	-	-	-	-	-	-	-	-	14.3	2.9
1934	-	-	-	-	-	-	-	-	-	-	14.5	1.4	-	-	-	-	-	-	-	-	14.6	0.7	-	-
1935	-	-	-	-	14.6	0.0	-	-	-	-	-	-	14.5	-0.7	-	-	-	-	14.6	0.7	-	-	-	-
1936	14.8	1.4	-	-	-	-	14.6	-1.4	-	-	-	-	14.7	0.7	-	-	14.9	1.4	-	-	-	-	14.7	-1.3
1937	-	-	-	-	15.0	2.0	-	-	-	-	15.0	0.0	-	-	-	-	15.4	2.7	-	-	-	-	15.2	-1.3
1938	-	-	-	-	14.8	-2.6	-	-	-	-	14.8	0.0	-	-	-	-	14.9	0.7	-	-	-	-	14.8	-0.7
1939	-	-	-	-	14.7	-0.7	-	-	-	-	14.5	-1.4	-	-	-	-	15.0	3.4	-	-	-	-	14.8	-1.3
1940	-	-	-	-	15.0	1.4	-	-	-	-	15.1	0.7	-	-	-	-	14.9	-1.3	14.8	-0.7	14.9	0.7	14.9	0.0
1941	15.0	0.7	15.0	0.0	15.0	0.0	15.1	0.7	15.2	0.7	15.5	2.0	15.5	0.0	15.6	0.6	15.8	1.3	16.0	1.3	16.1	0.6	16.1	0.0
1942	16.4	1.9	16.4	0.0	16.6	1.2	16.7	0.6	16.8	0.6	16.9	0.6	17.1	1.2	17.2	0.6	17.2	0.0	17.4	1.2	17.6	1.1	17.7	0.6
1943	17.7	0.0	17.8	0.6	18.1	1.7	18.2	0.6	18.4	1.1	18.4	0.0	18.3	-0.5	18.2	-0.5	18.4	1.1	18.4	0.0	18.5	0.5	18.5	0.0
1944	18.5	0.0	18.4	-0.5	18.5	0.5	18.6	0.5	18.6	0.0	18.6	0.0	18.8	1.1	18.8	0.0	18.8	0.0	18.8	0.0	18.9	0.5	18.9	0.0
1945	18.9	0.0	18.9	0.0	18.8	-0.5	18.9	0.5	19.0	0.5	19.2	1.1	19.4	1.0	19.2	-1.0	19.2	0.0	19.1	-0.5	19.3	1.0	19.4	0.5
1946	19.5	0.5	19.5	0.0	19.6	0.5	19.8	1.0	19.9	0.5	20.1	1.0	21.4	6.5	21.6	0.9	22.1	2.3	22.7	2.7	22.9	0.9	23.0	0.4
1947	22.9	-0.4	22.8	-0.4	23.3	2.2	23.3	0.0	23.0	-1.3	23.3	1.3	23.4	0.4	23.5	0.4	24.0	2.1	24.0	0.0	24.2	0.8	24.4	0.8
1948	24.8	1.6	24.7	-0.4	24.4	-1.2	24.8	1.6	24.9	0.4	25.1	0.8	25.6	2.0	25.7	0.4	25.7	0.0	25.5	-0.8	25.4	-0.4	25.1	-1.2
1949	25.1	0.0	24.8	-1.2	24.9	0.4	25.0	0.4	24.8	-0.8	24.8	0.0	24.9	0.4	24.8	-0.4	24.9	0.4	24.7	-0.8	24.7	0.0	24.6	-0.4
1950	24.4	-0.8	24.4	0.0	24.5	0.4	24.6	0.4	24.6	0.0	24.7	0.4	25.1	1.6	25.1	0.0	25.4	1.2	25.5	0.4	25.6	0.4	26.0	1.6
1951	26.3	1.2	26.7	1.5	26.7	0.0	26.7	0.0	26.9	0.7	26.7	-0.7	26.8	0.4	26.8	0.0	27.0	0.7	27.1	0.4	27.3	0.7	27.3	0.0
1952	27.3	0.0	27.1	-0.7	27.0	-0.4	27.1	0.4	27.1	0.0	27.1	0.0	27.5	1.5	27.5	0.0	27.5	0.0	27.5	0.0	27.6	0.4	27.4	-0.7
1953	27.4	0.0	27.2	-0.7	27.3	0.4	27.2	-0.4	27.3	0.4	27.4	0.4	27.5	0.4	27.6	0.4	27.7	0.4	27.7	0.0	27.6	-0.4	27.7	0.4
1954	27.7	0.0	27.6	-0.4	27.5	-0.4	27.6	0.4	27.6	0.0	27.6	0.0	27.7	0.4	27.7	0.0	27.6	-0.4	27.6	0.0	27.6	0.0	27.5	-0.4
1955	27.5	0.0	27.6	0.4	27.5	-0.4	27.5	0.0	27.4	-0.4	27.4	0.0	27.4	0.0	27.4	0.0	27.6	0.7	27.5	-0.4	27.6	0.4	27.4	-0.7
1956	27.5	0.4	27.5	0.0	27.5	0.0	27.5	0.0	27.7	0.7	27.9	0.7	28.1	0.7	28.0	-0.4	28.2	0.7	28.3	0.4	28.3	0.0	28.3	0.0
1957	28.3	0.0	28.4	0.4	28.4	0.0	28.6	0.7	28.7	0.3	28.9	0.7	29.0	0.3	29.1	0.3	29.0	-0.3	29.0	0.0	29.0	0.0	29.1	0.3
1958	29.4	1.0	29.5	0.3	29.7	0.7	29.7	0.0	29.7	0.0	29.6	-0.3	29.7	0.3	29.7	0.0	29.7	0.0	29.7	0.0	29.8	0.3	29.7	-0.3

[Continued]

New York, NY, NE NJ
Consumer Price Index - Urban Wage Earners
Base 1982-1984 = 100
All Items
[Continued]

For 1914-1995. Columns headed % show percentile change in the index from the previous period for which an index is available.

Year	Jan Index	%	Feb Index	%	Mar Index	%	Apr Index	%	May Index	%	Jun Index	%	Jul Index	%	Aug Index	%	Sep Index	%	Oct Index	%	Nov Index	%	Dec Index	%
1959	29.9	0.7	29.8	-0.3	29.8	0.0	29.9	0.3	29.9	0.0	30.0	0.3	30.2	0.7	30.1	-0.3	30.2	0.3	30.3	0.3	30.4	0.3	30.4	0.0
1960	30.4	0.0	30.5	0.3	30.5	0.0	30.6	0.3	30.6	0.0	30.6	0.0	30.6	0.0	30.7	0.3	30.7	0.0	30.9	0.7	31.0	0.3	30.9	-0.3
1961	30.9	0.0	30.9	0.0	30.9	0.0	30.8	-0.3	30.8	0.0	30.8	0.0	31.0	0.6	31.0	0.0	31.0	0.0	31.1	0.3	31.0	-0.3	31.1	0.3
1962	31.2	0.3	31.3	0.3	31.3	0.0	31.3	0.0	31.2	-0.3	31.2	0.0	31.4	0.6	31.5	0.3	31.7	0.6	31.6	-0.3	31.6	0.0	31.5	-0.3
1963	31.7	0.6	31.7	0.0	31.7	0.0	31.9	0.6	31.8	-0.3	32.1	0.9	32.2	0.3	32.2	0.0	32.2	0.0	32.3	0.3	32.4	0.3	32.5	0.3
1964	32.4	-0.3	32.5	0.3	32.5	0.0	32.5	0.0	32.5	0.0	32.5	0.0	32.6	0.3	32.6	0.0	32.7	0.3	32.7	0.0	32.8	0.3	32.8	0.0
1965	32.7	-0.3	32.8	0.3	32.8	0.0	32.9	0.3	33.0	0.3	33.1	0.3	33.2	0.3	33.2	0.0	33.3	0.3	33.4	0.3	33.4	0.0	33.5	0.3
1966	33.5	0.0	33.7	0.6	33.9	0.6	34.0	0.3	34.0	0.0	34.0	0.0	34.3	0.9	34.5	0.6	34.6	0.3	34.8	0.6	34.7	-0.3	34.7	0.0
1967	34.7	0.0	34.8	0.3	34.9	0.3	34.9	0.0	34.9	0.0	35.0	0.3	35.2	0.6	35.2	0.0	35.3	0.3	35.5	0.6	35.5	0.0	35.6	0.3
1968	35.7	0.3	35.9	0.6	36.0	0.3	36.1	0.3	36.3	0.6	36.5	0.6	36.7	0.5	36.9	0.5	37.2	0.8	37.3	0.3	37.4	0.3	37.5	0.3
1969	37.7	0.5	37.9	0.5	38.2	0.8	38.5	0.8	38.6	0.3	38.8	0.5	39.0	0.5	39.1	0.3	39.4	0.8	39.6	0.5	39.7	0.3	40.1	1.0
1970	40.4	0.7	40.8	1.0	41.1	0.7	41.3	0.5	41.5	0.5	41.8	0.7	41.9	0.2	42.1	0.5	42.3	0.5	42.6	0.7	42.7	0.2	43.0	0.7
1971	43.0	0.0	43.4	0.9	43.7	0.7	43.8	0.2	44.0	0.5	44.3	0.7	44.5	0.5	44.6	0.2	44.7	0.2	44.8	0.2	44.8	0.0	45.0	0.4
1972	45.2	0.4	45.5	0.7	45.7	0.4	45.8	0.2	45.9	0.2	46.0	0.2	46.1	0.2	46.3	0.4	46.7	0.9	46.8	0.2	46.8	0.0	47.0	0.4
1973	47.0	0.0	47.4	0.9	47.9	1.1	48.3	0.8	48.5	0.4	48.9	0.8	48.9	0.0	49.8	1.8	50.0	0.4	50.3	0.6	50.7	0.8	51.2	1.0
1974	51.6	0.8	52.4	1.6	53.0	1.1	53.0	0.0	53.6	1.1	54.0	0.7	54.3	0.6	55.1	1.5	55.8	1.3	56.3	0.9	56.5	0.4	56.8	0.5
1975	56.9	0.2	57.3	0.7	57.4	0.2	57.5	0.2	57.7	0.3	58.0	0.5	58.5	0.9	58.8	0.5	59.5	1.2	59.7	0.3	60.2	0.8	60.5	0.5
1976	60.7	0.3	60.9	0.3	61.1	0.3	61.2	0.2	61.4	0.3	61.8	0.7	62.1	0.5	62.4	0.5	62.7	0.5	62.9	0.3	62.9	0.0	63.1	0.3
1977	63.4	0.5	64.0	0.9	64.2	0.3	64.5	0.5	64.8	0.5	65.4	0.9	65.5	0.2	65.7	0.3	65.8	0.2	65.9	0.2	66.2	0.5	66.3	0.2
1978	66.7	0.6	67.0	0.4	67.4	0.6	67.7	0.4	68.0	0.4	68.7	1.0	68.8	0.1	69.1	0.4	69.4	0.4	70.0	0.9	70.2	0.3	70.6	0.6
1979	71.1	0.7	71.9	1.1	72.5	0.8	73.1	0.8	73.9	1.1	74.5	0.8	75.2	0.9	75.6	0.5	76.5	1.2	77.0	0.7	77.5	0.6	78.1	0.8
1980	79.2	1.4	80.0	1.0	81.1	1.4	81.6	0.6	82.2	0.7	83.1	1.1	83.7	0.7	84.5	1.0	84.8	0.4	85.2	0.5	85.8	0.7	86.8	1.2
1981	87.5	0.8	88.8	1.5	89.1	0.3	89.5	0.4	89.9	0.4	90.6	0.8	92.1	1.7	92.7	0.7	94.1	1.5	93.8	-0.3	93.7	-0.1	93.7	0.0
1982	94.0	0.3	94.1	0.1	93.4	-0.7	93.6	0.2	94.6	1.1	96.7	2.2	97.0	0.3	97.3	0.3	98.0	0.7	99.3	1.3	99.0	-0.3	98.4	-0.6
1983	98.6	0.2	98.2	-0.4	98.4	0.2	99.1	0.7	99.7	0.6	100.4	0.7	100.5	0.1	101.3	0.8	101.2	-0.1	101.4	0.2	100.9	-0.5	101.2	0.3
1984	101.9	0.7	102.0	0.1	101.8	-0.2	102.3	0.5	102.4	0.1	102.9	0.5	103.5	0.6	104.3	0.8	105.3	1.0	105.5	0.2	105.8	0.3	105.9	0.1
1985	106.1	0.2	106.6	0.5	106.8	0.2	107.2	0.4	107.4	0.2	107.6	0.2	107.6	0.0	108.4	0.7	108.6	0.2	108.8	0.2	109.8	0.9	110.1	0.3
1986	110.9	0.7	110.5	-0.4	110.5	0.0	110.0	-0.5	109.7	-0.3	110.4	0.6	111.2	0.7	111.4	0.2	111.5	0.1	111.9	0.4	111.9	0.0	112.4	0.4
1987	113.2	0.7	113.8	0.5	114.4	0.5	115.3	0.8	116.0	0.6	116.5	0.4	116.5	0.0	117.4	0.8	118.5	0.9	118.8	0.3	119.1	0.3	119.1	0.0
1988	119.6	0.4	119.3	-0.3	119.7	0.3	120.6	0.8	120.7	0.1	121.2	0.4	121.7	0.4	122.2	0.4	124.1	1.6	124.3	0.2	124.1	-0.2	124.1	0.0
1989	125.1	0.8	125.5	0.3	126.8	1.0	127.5	0.6	128.2	0.5	128.7	0.4	128.7	0.0	128.9	0.2	130.3	1.1	130.8	0.4	131.3	0.4	131.3	0.0
1990	133.0	1.3	133.1	0.1	134.5	1.1	135.0	0.4	134.9	-0.1	135.0	0.1	136.0	0.7	137.4	1.0	138.7	0.9	139.5	0.6	139.5	0.0	139.5	0.0
1991	140.3	0.6	140.6	0.2	140.5	-0.1	141.0	0.4	141.4	0.3	142.1	0.5	142.3	0.1	142.6	0.2	143.2	0.4	143.0	-0.1	144.0	0.7	143.9	-0.1
1992	144.4	0.3	144.8	0.3	145.8	0.7	145.9	0.1	145.8	-0.1	146.5	0.5	146.6	0.1	147.6	0.7	148.3	0.5	149.1	0.5	149.2	0.1	149.1	-0.1
1993	149.9	0.5	150.3	0.3	150.7	0.3	150.7	0.0	150.4	-0.2	150.7	0.2	150.7	0.0	151.7	0.7	151.8	0.1	152.1	0.2	152.0	-0.1	152.1	0.1
1994	152.4	0.2	153.5	0.7	154.0	0.3	153.9	-0.1	153.6	-0.2	154.2	0.4	154.4	0.1	155.3	0.6	155.5	0.1	156.0	0.3	155.9	-0.1	155.4	-0.3
1995	156.3	0.6	156.6	0.2	157.1	0.3	157.5	0.3	158.0	0.3	158.4	0.3	158.3	-0.1	158.9	0.4	159.5	0.4	159.7	0.1	159.9	0.1	159.9	0.0

Source: U.S. Department of Labor, Bureau of Labor Statistics, Division of Consumer Prices and Price Indexes. - indicates no data collected for period.

New York, NY, NE NJ
Consumer Price Index - All Urban Consumers
Base 1982-1984 = 100
Food and Beverages

For 1976-1995. Columns headed % show percentile change in the index from the previous period for which an index is available.

Year	Jan Index	%	Feb Index	%	Mar Index	%	Apr Index	%	May Index	%	Jun Index	%	Jul Index	%	Aug Index	%	Sep Index	%	Oct Index	%	Nov Index	%	Dec Index	%
1976	62.5	-	62.3	-0.3	62.0	-0.5	62.1	0.2	62.4	0.5	62.8	0.6	63.2	0.6	63.2	0.0	63.0	-0.3	63.1	0.2	62.8	-0.5	63.2	0.6
1977	63.4	0.3	64.7	2.1	64.8	0.2	65.4	0.9	65.8	0.6	66.3	0.8	66.6	0.5	66.7	0.2	66.1	-0.9	66.2	0.2	66.8	0.9	66.8	0.0
1978	68.0	1.8	68.8	1.2	69.3	0.7	70.4	1.6	71.1	1.0	72.4	1.8	72.5	0.1	72.4	-0.1	72.4	0.0	72.8	0.6	73.3	0.7	73.6	0.4
1979	74.8	1.6	76.1	1.7	76.6	0.7	77.1	0.7	77.7	0.8	78.0	0.4	79.0	1.3	78.3	-0.9	78.9	0.8	79.5	0.8	79.6	0.1	80.3	0.9
1980	81.7	1.7	81.6	-0.1	82.6	1.2	83.3	0.8	83.6	0.4	84.2	0.7	85.1	1.1	86.6	1.8	87.3	0.8	87.6	0.3	88.4	0.9	88.7	0.3
1981	89.5	0.9	90.4	1.0	91.1	0.8	91.9	0.9	92.1	0.2	92.6	0.5	93.7	1.2	94.1	0.4	94.7	0.6	94.1	-0.6	93.8	-0.3	94.0	0.2
1982	96.0	2.1	96.8	0.8	96.9	0.1	97.0	0.1	97.3	0.3	98.6	1.3	98.3	-0.3	97.6	-0.7	97.9	0.3	97.9	0.0	96.8	-1.1	97.1	0.3
1983	97.5	0.4	98.1	0.6	98.5	0.4	98.7	0.2	98.8	0.1	98.9	0.1	98.9	0.0	99.0	0.1	99.9	0.9	99.8	-0.1	99.5	-0.3	100.3	0.8
1984	102.3	2.0	103.0	0.7	103.5	0.5	103.3	-0.2	102.9	-0.4	103.4	0.5	103.7	0.3	104.4	0.7	104.3	-0.1	104.4	0.1	104.1	-0.3	104.8	0.7
1985	105.8	1.0	106.5	0.7	106.8	0.3	107.0	0.2	106.8	-0.2	106.9	0.1	107.0	0.1	107.4	0.4	108.0	0.6	108.1	0.1	108.2	0.1	108.9	0.6
1986	110.1	1.1	109.9	-0.2	110.1	0.2	110.9	0.7	111.2	0.3	110.9	-0.3	112.8	1.7	113.6	0.7	113.5	-0.1	114.2	0.6	114.2	0.0	114.7	0.4
1987	116.3	1.4	116.5	0.2	116.8	0.3	117.2	0.3	117.8	0.5	119.2	1.2	118.9	-0.3	119.2	0.3	119.7	0.4	119.9	0.2	120.1	0.2	121.3	1.0
1988	122.5	1.0	122.7	0.2	122.5	-0.2	124.0	1.2	123.5	-0.4	124.5	0.8	125.5	0.8	126.3	0.6	126.8	0.4	126.2	-0.5	126.8	0.5	126.8	0.0
1989	129.2	1.9	130.2	0.8	130.6	0.3	131.2	0.5	132.2	0.8	132.6	0.3	133.0	0.3	133.3	0.2	133.1	-0.2	132.9	-0.2	133.4	0.4	133.7	0.2
1990	136.9	2.4	138.4	1.1	138.5	0.1	138.7	0.1	138.7	0.0	139.2	0.4	140.4	0.9	140.8	0.3	140.4	-0.3	141.1	0.5	141.1	0.0	141.2	0.1
1991	143.3	1.5	143.8	0.3	144.2	0.3	145.6	1.0	145.2	-0.3	146.1	0.6	144.6	-1.0	143.7	-0.6	143.9	0.1	143.5	-0.3	143.4	-0.1	144.1	0.5
1992	145.2	0.8	145.6	0.3	146.2	0.4	146.2	0.0	145.3	-0.6	145.8	0.3	144.9	-0.6	145.9	0.7	146.0	0.1	146.7	0.5	146.4	-0.2	147.2	0.5
1993	148.7	1.0	148.5	-0.1	148.8	0.2	149.3	0.3	149.3	0.0	147.9	-0.9	147.9	0.0	149.0	0.7	148.9	-0.1	149.1	0.1	149.9	0.5	151.0	0.7
1994	151.8	0.5	150.9	-0.6	150.8	-0.1	150.9	0.1	151.3	0.3	151.2	-0.1	152.3	0.7	152.7	0.3	152.7	0.0	152.8	0.1	152.9	0.1	153.0	0.1
1995	154.6	1.0	154.3	-0.2	154.4	0.1	156.0	1.0	155.5	-0.3	155.7	0.1	155.9	0.1	156.4	0.3	156.8	0.3	157.0	0.1	157.2	0.1	157.0	-0.1

Source: U.S. Department of Labor, Bureau of Labor Statistics, Division of Consumer Prices and Price Indexes. - indicates no data collected for period.

New York, NY, NE NJ
Consumer Price Index - Urban Wage Earners
Base 1982-1984 = 100
Food and Beverages

For 1976-1995. Columns headed % show percentile change in the index from the previous period for which an index is available.

Year	Jan Index	%	Feb Index	%	Mar Index	%	Apr Index	%	May Index	%	Jun Index	%	Jul Index	%	Aug Index	%	Sep Index	%	Oct Index	%	Nov Index	%	Dec Index	%
1976	63.2	-	63.0	-0.3	62.7	-0.5	62.8	0.2	63.1	0.5	63.5	0.6	63.9	0.6	63.9	0.0	63.7	-0.3	63.8	0.2	63.5	-0.5	63.9	0.6
1977	64.1	0.3	65.4	2.0	65.5	0.2	66.2	1.1	66.5	0.5	67.1	0.9	67.4	0.4	67.4	0.0	66.9	-0.7	66.9	0.0	67.6	1.0	67.5	-0.1
1978	68.5	1.5	69.3	1.2	70.0	1.0	70.7	1.0	71.7	1.4	73.0	1.8	72.9	-0.1	72.9	0.0	73.0	0.1	73.6	0.8	73.9	0.4	74.4	0.7
1979	75.7	1.7	77.2	2.0	77.8	0.8	78.2	0.5	78.5	0.4	78.7	0.3	79.8	1.4	79.0	-1.0	79.4	0.5	79.7	0.4	80.0	0.4	81.0	1.3
1980	82.5	1.9	82.8	0.4	83.3	0.6	84.0	0.8	84.4	0.5	85.2	0.9	85.9	0.8	87.1	1.4	87.9	0.9	88.6	0.8	89.2	0.7	89.6	0.4
1981	90.1	0.6	91.0	1.0	91.5	0.5	92.1	0.7	92.1	0.0	92.7	0.7	93.9	1.3	94.1	0.2	94.6	0.5	94.2	-0.4	94.0	-0.2	94.1	0.1
1982	96.1	2.1	96.8	0.7	96.9	0.1	96.9	0.0	97.3	0.4	98.4	1.1	98.1	-0.3	97.4	-0.7	97.7	0.3	97.5	-0.2	96.8	-0.7	97.2	0.4
1983	97.6	0.4	98.2	0.6	98.6	0.4	98.9	0.3	99.0	0.1	99.0	0.0	98.9	-0.1	99.0	0.1	100.0	1.0	99.9	-0.1	99.6	-0.3	100.5	0.9
1984	102.5	2.0	103.2	0.7	103.6	0.4	103.4	-0.2	102.9	-0.5	103.3	0.4	103.5	0.2	104.2	0.7	104.0	-0.2	104.2	0.2	104.0	-0.2	104.8	0.8
1985	105.8	1.0	106.3	0.5	106.7	0.4	106.7	0.0	106.6	-0.1	106.7	0.1	106.7	0.0	107.0	0.3	107.5	0.5	107.6	0.1	107.9	0.3	108.8	0.8
1986	110.0	1.1	109.7	-0.3	109.9	0.2	110.7	0.7	110.9	0.2	110.7	-0.2	112.5	1.6	113.2	0.6	113.2	0.0	113.9	0.6	113.9	0.0	114.5	0.5
1987	115.9	1.2	116.1	0.2	116.4	0.3	116.8	0.3	117.4	0.5	118.8	1.2	118.5	-0.3	118.8	0.3	119.2	0.3	119.5	0.3	119.6	0.1	120.8	1.0
1988	121.9	0.9	122.1	0.2	121.9	-0.2	123.4	1.2	123.0	-0.3	124.0	0.8	125.1	0.9	125.9	0.6	126.4	0.4	125.7	-0.6	126.2	0.4	126.3	0.1
1989	128.8	2.0	129.8	0.8	130.2	0.3	130.8	0.5	131.7	0.7	132.2	0.4	132.6	0.3	133.0	0.3	132.6	-0.3	132.5	-0.1	133.0	0.4	133.1	0.1
1990	136.6	2.6	138.2	1.2	138.2	0.0	138.4	0.1	138.4	0.0	139.0	0.4	140.2	0.9	140.6	0.3	140.2	-0.3	140.9	0.5	140.9	0.0	141.0	0.1
1991	143.1	1.5	143.6	0.3	143.9	0.2	145.3	1.0	144.9	-0.3	146.0	0.8	144.4	-1.1	143.5	-0.6	143.6	0.1	143.2	-0.3	143.0	-0.1	143.7	0.5
1992	144.8	0.8	145.3	0.3	145.9	0.4	145.9	0.0	144.8	-0.8	145.4	0.4	144.5	-0.6	145.5	0.7	145.6	0.1	146.3	0.5	146.1	-0.1	146.7	0.4
1993	148.3	1.1	147.9	-0.3	148.4	0.3	148.9	0.3	148.9	0.0	147.4	-1.0	147.4	0.0	148.5	0.7	148.5	0.0	148.6	0.1	149.4	0.5	150.4	0.7
1994	151.4	0.7	150.5	-0.6	150.4	-0.1	150.5	0.1	150.9	0.3	151.0	0.1	151.9	0.6	152.4	0.3	152.2	-0.1	152.4	0.1	152.4	0.0	152.5	0.1
1995	154.1	1.0	153.7	-0.3	153.9	0.1	155.5	1.0	154.8	-0.5	155.1	0.2	155.3	0.1	155.7	0.3	156.3	0.4	156.4	0.1	156.5	0.1	156.3	-0.1

Source: U.S. Department of Labor, Bureau of Labor Statistics, Division of Consumer Prices and Price Indexes. - indicates no data collected for period.

New York, NY, NE NJ
Consumer Price Index - All Urban Consumers
Base 1982-1984 = 100
Housing

For 1976-1995. Columns headed % show percentile change in the index from the previous period for which an index is available.

Year	Jan Index	%	Feb Index	%	Mar Index	%	Apr Index	%	May Index	%	Jun Index	%	Jul Index	%	Aug Index	%	Sep Index	%	Oct Index	%	Nov Index	%	Dec Index	%
1976	58.8	-	59.1	0.5	59.3	0.3	59.4	0.2	59.5	0.2	59.9	0.7	59.9	0.0	60.1	0.3	60.3	0.3	60.6	0.5	60.6	0.0	61.0	0.7
1977	61.6	1.0	61.8	0.3	62.2	0.6	62.4	0.3	62.6	0.3	63.2	1.0	63.2	0.0	63.4	0.3	63.7	0.5	63.8	0.2	63.9	0.2	64.1	0.3
1978	64.4	0.5	64.5	0.2	65.0	0.8	65.2	0.3	65.5	0.5	66.2	1.1	66.4	0.3	66.9	0.8	67.4	0.7	67.9	0.7	67.9	0.0	68.2	0.4
1979	68.7	0.7	69.2	0.7	69.4	0.3	70.1	1.0	70.9	1.1	71.8	1.3	72.2	0.6	73.0	1.1	74.1	1.5	74.7	0.8	75.4	0.9	75.9	0.7
1980	76.9	1.3	77.3	0.5	78.5	1.6	79.0	0.6	79.9	1.1	81.5	2.0	82.0	0.6	82.5	0.6	82.1	-0.5	82.5	0.5	83.1	0.7	84.7	1.9
1981	85.4	0.8	86.4	1.2	86.4	0.0	86.8	0.5	87.5	0.8	88.5	1.1	90.1	1.8	91.3	1.3	93.2	2.1	92.6	-0.6	92.3	-0.3	92.2	-0.1
1982	91.8	-0.4	91.4	-0.4	90.0	-1.5	90.8	0.9	92.7	2.1	95.9	3.5	96.0	0.1	96.7	0.7	97.3	0.6	100.0	2.8	99.7	-0.3	98.1	-1.6
1983	98.4	0.3	98.4	0.0	98.3	-0.1	99.7	1.4	100.0	0.3	100.4	0.4	100.8	0.4	100.4	-0.4	100.9	0.5	101.2	0.3	101.8	0.6	102.0	0.2
1984	102.7	0.7	103.5	0.8	103.3	-0.2	104.0	0.7	103.8	-0.2	104.1	0.3	104.9	0.8	105.5	0.6	106.4	0.9	105.8	-0.6	106.9	1.0	106.6	-0.3
1985	106.5	-0.1	107.1	0.6	106.9	-0.2	107.4	0.5	108.1	0.7	108.4	0.3	108.5	0.1	109.6	1.0	109.6	0.0	109.4	-0.2	111.2	1.6	111.5	0.3
1986	112.0	0.4	111.6	-0.4	112.2	0.5	112.0	-0.2	111.1	-0.8	112.7	1.4	113.7	0.9	113.9	0.2	113.7	-0.2	113.6	-0.1	113.1	-0.4	114.0	0.8
1987	115.2	1.1	115.6	0.3	115.4	-0.2	115.8	0.3	117.1	1.1	118.0	0.8	118.3	0.3	119.5	1.0	119.8	0.3	120.0	0.2	120.3	0.3	121.5	1.0
1988	123.2	1.4	122.8	-0.3	123.0	0.2	123.7	0.6	124.3	0.5	124.9	0.5	125.8	0.7	126.0	0.2	126.9	0.7	126.7	-0.2	126.9	0.2	127.1	0.2
1989	128.2	0.9	128.8	0.5	129.6	0.6	130.2	0.5	131.1	0.7	132.2	0.8	132.7	0.4	132.7	0.0	133.0	0.2	133.7	0.5	134.5	0.6	135.3	0.6
1990	136.3	0.7	135.8	-0.4	137.5	1.3	138.2	0.5	138.3	0.1	138.3	0.0	140.3	1.4	142.1	1.3	141.4	-0.5	141.2	-0.1	140.8	-0.3	141.1	0.2
1991	143.6	1.8	144.8	0.8	144.4	-0.3	144.2	-0.1	144.4	0.1	145.5	0.8	147.4	1.3	147.3	-0.1	146.6	-0.5	145.7	-0.6	147.2	1.0	147.4	0.1
1992	148.3	0.6	149.4	0.7	150.9	1.0	150.8	-0.1	150.2	-0.4	151.6	0.9	152.4	0.5	152.9	0.3	152.6	-0.2	152.6	0.0	152.6	0.0	152.2	-0.3
1993	153.5	0.9	153.8	0.2	154.7	0.6	154.6	-0.1	154.7	0.1	156.5	1.2	156.7	0.1	157.2	0.3	156.4	-0.5	156.2	-0.1	155.6	-0.4	156.3	0.4
1994	157.1	0.5	159.8	1.7	160.3	0.3	159.2	-0.7	158.8	-0.3	159.5	0.4	160.4	0.6	161.8	0.9	160.9	-0.6	160.7	-0.1	160.0	-0.4	159.7	-0.2
1995	160.9	0.8	161.5	0.4	162.0	0.3	162.4	0.2	162.8	0.2	163.9	0.7	165.0	0.7	165.0	0.0	164.1	-0.5	164.2	0.1	164.4	0.1	164.6	0.1

Source: U.S. Department of Labor, Bureau of Labor Statistics, Division of Consumer Prices and Price Indexes. - indicates no data collected for period.

New York, NY, NE NJ
Consumer Price Index - Urban Wage Earners
Base 1982-1984 = 100
Housing

For 1976-1995. Columns headed % show percentile change in the index from the previous period for which an index is available.

Year	Jan Index	%	Feb Index	%	Mar Index	%	Apr Index	%	May Index	%	Jun Index	%	Jul Index	%	Aug Index	%	Sep Index	%	Oct Index	%	Nov Index	%	Dec Index	%
1976	60.6	-	60.9	0.5	61.0	0.2	61.1	0.2	61.2	0.2	61.7	0.8	61.7	0.0	61.8	0.2	62.1	0.5	62.4	0.5	62.4	0.0	62.8	0.6
1977	63.3	0.8	63.6	0.5	64.0	0.6	64.2	0.3	64.4	0.3	65.1	1.1	65.0	-0.2	65.3	0.5	65.5	0.3	65.6	0.2	65.7	0.2	66.0	0.5
1978	66.3	0.5	66.4	0.2	66.7	0.5	66.8	0.1	66.8	0.0	67.5	1.0	67.8	0.4	68.1	0.4	68.5	0.6	69.0	0.7	69.1	0.1	69.5	0.6
1979	70.0	0.7	70.5	0.7	70.8	0.4	71.4	0.8	72.4	1.4	73.3	1.2	73.7	0.5	74.4	0.9	75.6	1.6	76.4	1.1	77.0	0.8	77.5	0.6
1980	78.5	1.3	79.0	0.6	79.9	1.1	80.6	0.9	81.4	1.0	83.2	2.2	83.7	0.6	84.3	0.7	83.6	-0.8	84.0	0.5	84.7	0.8	86.6	2.2
1981	87.2	0.7	88.5	1.5	88.4	-0.1	88.5	0.1	89.2	0.8	90.4	1.3	92.2	2.0	93.3	1.2	95.4	2.3	94.8	-0.6	94.5	-0.3	94.3	-0.2
1982	93.9	-0.4	93.4	-0.5	91.6	-1.9	92.5	1.0	94.6	2.3	98.1	3.7	98.3	0.2	99.0	0.7	99.6	0.6	102.5	2.9	102.3	-0.2	100.5	-1.8
1983	100.6	0.1	99.1	-1.5	99.5	0.4	99.9	0.4	100.7	0.8	102.3	1.6	102.0	-0.3	103.3	1.3	101.5	-1.7	101.6	0.1	100.0	-1.6	100.5	0.5
1984	100.2	-0.3	99.8	-0.4	98.4	-1.4	99.5	1.1	99.6	0.1	100.6	1.0	101.8	1.2	102.8	1.0	104.7	1.8	104.8	0.1	105.4	0.6	105.3	-0.1
1985	105.2	-0.1	105.9	0.7	105.6	-0.3	106.1	0.5	106.7	0.6	107.1	0.4	107.0	-0.1	108.1	1.0	108.0	-0.1	108.0	0.0	109.7	1.6	110.2	0.5
1986	110.6	0.4	110.1	-0.5	110.8	0.6	110.4	-0.4	109.4	-0.9	111.1	1.6	112.0	0.8	112.2	0.2	112.0	-0.2	111.8	-0.2	111.3	-0.4	112.1	0.7
1987	113.1	0.9	113.5	0.4	113.3	-0.2	113.9	0.5	115.2	1.1	116.1	0.8	116.3	0.2	117.4	0.9	117.7	0.3	117.9	0.2	118.2	0.3	119.3	0.9
1988	120.6	1.1	120.2	-0.3	120.4	0.2	120.8	0.3	121.4	0.5	122.5	0.9	123.3	0.7	123.4	0.1	124.2	0.6	123.9	-0.2	124.3	0.3	124.5	0.2
1989	125.5	0.8	125.9	0.3	126.4	0.4	127.4	0.8	128.1	0.5	129.4	1.0	129.9	0.4	129.9	0.0	130.4	0.4	130.9	0.4	131.9	0.8	132.7	0.6
1990	133.3	0.5	132.8	-0.4	134.5	1.3	135.0	0.4	135.1	0.1	135.2	0.1	136.6	1.0	138.0	1.0	137.9	-0.1	137.8	-0.1	137.4	-0.3	137.6	0.1
1991	139.4	1.3	140.2	0.6	139.9	-0.2	140.1	0.1	140.7	0.4	141.7	0.7	143.1	1.0	142.9	-0.1	142.6	-0.2	141.8	-0.6	143.4	1.1	143.5	0.1
1992	144.0	0.3	144.8	0.6	146.0	0.8	146.1	0.1	145.8	-0.2	147.0	0.8	147.5	0.3	147.9	0.3	147.7	-0.1	147.9	0.1	148.1	0.1	148.0	-0.1
1993	149.0	0.7	149.1	0.1	149.8	0.5	149.9	0.1	149.9	0.0	151.6	1.1	151.7	0.1	152.0	0.2	151.4	-0.4	151.1	-0.2	150.6	-0.3	151.4	0.5
1994	151.9	0.3	154.3	1.6	154.9	0.4	154.0	-0.6	153.5	-0.3	154.1	0.4	154.9	0.5	156.2	0.8	156.0	-0.1	155.6	-0.3	155.1	-0.3	154.9	-0.1
1995	155.9	0.6	156.3	0.3	156.7	0.3	157.1	0.3	157.5	0.3	158.4	0.6	159.2	0.5	159.2	0.0	158.8	-0.3	158.7	-0.1	159.1	0.3	159.4	0.2

Source: U.S. Department of Labor, Bureau of Labor Statistics, Division of Consumer Prices and Price Indexes. - indicates no data collected for period.

New York, NY, NE NJ
Consumer Price Index - All Urban Consumers
Base 1982-1984 = 100
Apparel and Upkeep

For 1952-1995. Columns headed % show percentile change in the index from the previous period for which an index is available.

Year	Jan Index	%	Feb Index	%	Mar Index	%	Apr Index	%	May Index	%	Jun Index	%	Jul Index	%	Aug Index	%	Sep Index	%	Oct Index	%	Nov Index	%	Dec Index	%
1952	-	-	-	-	-	-	-	-	-	-	-	-	-	-	-	-	-	-	-	-	-	-	45.1	-
1953	45.0	-0.2	44.9	-0.2	45.0	0.2	44.7	-0.7	44.8	0.2	44.7	-0.2	44.6	-0.2	44.5	-0.2	45.1	1.3	45.1	0.0	45.1	0.0	45.0	-0.2
1954	44.8	-0.4	44.7	-0.2	44.6	-0.2	44.4	-0.4	44.4	0.0	44.4	0.0	44.2	-0.5	44.2	0.0	44.6	0.9	44.5	-0.2	44.6	0.2	44.3	-0.7
1955	43.8	-1.1	43.7	-0.2	43.7	0.0	43.5	-0.5	43.6	0.2	43.5	-0.2	43.3	-0.5	43.5	0.5	44.5	2.3	44.5	0.0	44.6	0.2	44.6	0.0
1956	44.2	-0.9	44.5	0.7	44.5	0.0	44.6	0.2	44.5	-0.2	44.7	0.4	44.8	0.2	44.8	0.0	45.6	1.8	45.8	0.4	45.7	-0.2	45.7	0.0
1957	45.5	-0.4	45.2	-0.7	45.7	1.1	45.4	-0.7	45.6	0.4	45.7	0.2	45.6	-0.2	45.7	0.2	46.0	0.7	46.1	0.2	46.2	0.2	46.1	-0.2
1958	46.2	0.2	46.2	0.0	46.2	0.0	45.9	-0.6	45.8	-0.2	45.8	0.0	45.8	0.0	46.0	0.4	46.3	0.7	46.1	-0.4	46.3	0.4	46.2	-0.2
1959	46.0	-0.4	46.0	0.0	46.1	0.2	46.0	-0.2	46.0	0.0	46.1	0.2	46.3	0.4	46.5	0.4	46.6	0.2	46.7	0.2	46.9	0.4	46.9	0.0
1960	46.6	-0.6	46.8	0.4	47.1	0.6	47.2	0.2	47.1	-0.2	47.1	0.0	47.0	-0.2	47.1	0.2	47.7	1.3	48.0	0.6	47.9	-0.2	48.0	0.2
1961	47.6	-0.8	47.6	0.0	47.5	-0.2	47.4	-0.2	47.3	-0.2	47.3	0.0	47.4	0.2	47.7	0.6	48.2	1.0	48.4	0.4	48.4	0.0	48.3	-0.2
1962	47.8	-1.0	47.8	0.0	48.0	0.4	47.9	-0.2	47.7	-0.4	47.9	0.4	48.0	0.2	47.8	-0.4	48.9	2.3	49.1	0.4	49.0	-0.2	48.9	-0.2
1963	48.8	-0.2	48.7	-0.2	48.7	0.0	48.8	0.2	48.5	-0.6	49.0	1.0	49.2	0.4	49.2	0.0	50.0	1.6	50.1	0.2	50.1	0.0	50.2	0.2
1964	49.2	-2.0	49.6	0.8	49.9	0.6	49.8	-0.2	50.0	0.4	49.9	-0.2	49.8	-0.2	49.6	-0.4	50.6	2.0	50.4	-0.4	50.4	0.0	50.6	0.4
1965	49.4	-2.4	50.1	1.4	50.2	0.2	50.2	0.0	50.4	0.4	50.6	0.4	50.0	-1.2	50.6	1.2	51.7	2.2	51.8	0.2	51.6	-0.4	51.4	-0.4
1966	50.3	-2.1	50.8	1.0	51.3	1.0	51.4	0.2	51.7	0.6	51.5	-0.4	51.4	-0.2	51.0	-0.8	53.0	3.9	53.4	0.8	53.3	-0.2	53.4	0.2
1967	52.4	-1.9	53.3	1.7	54.1	1.5	53.9	-0.4	54.3	0.7	54.3	0.0	54.3	0.0	54.1	-0.4	55.5	2.6	55.8	0.5	55.8	0.0	55.8	0.0
1968	54.7	-2.0	55.6	1.6	56.3	1.3	56.5	0.4	57.0	0.9	57.3	0.5	56.9	-0.7	57.5	1.1	59.4	3.3	59.6	0.3	59.9	0.5	60.0	0.2
1969	58.9	-1.8	59.4	0.8	60.8	2.4	60.8	0.0	61.2	0.7	61.3	0.2	61.1	-0.3	60.8	-0.5	62.9	3.5	63.1	0.3	63.2	0.2	63.0	-0.3
1970	61.6	-2.2	63.0	2.3	63.3	0.5	63.1	-0.3	63.5	0.6	63.8	0.5	63.0	-1.3	63.6	1.0	65.9	3.6	65.9	0.0	65.9	0.0	66.0	0.2
1971	64.2	-2.7	65.0	1.2	65.5	0.8	65.0	-0.8	65.7	1.1	65.5	-0.3	64.8	-1.1	64.8	0.0	67.0	3.4	66.9	-0.1	66.7	-0.3	66.7	0.0
1972	65.0	-2.5	66.5	2.3	67.5	1.5	67.3	-0.3	67.3	0.0	66.2	-1.6	65.5	-1.1	65.4	-0.2	68.5	4.7	68.5	0.0	68.4	-0.1	68.3	-0.1
1973	65.1	-4.7	66.3	1.8	68.4	3.2	68.5	0.1	69.0	0.7	68.6	-0.6	67.5	-1.6	68.6	1.6	70.4	2.6	70.7	0.4	71.1	0.6	71.0	-0.1
1974	68.5	-3.5	70.8	3.4	72.9	3.0	72.2	-1.0	73.3	1.5	73.3	0.0	72.3	-1.4	76.1	5.3	77.6	2.0	77.9	0.4	78.2	0.4	76.9	-1.7
1975	75.1	-2.3	77.0	2.5	77.0	0.0	76.2	-1.0	76.6	0.5	75.3	-1.7	75.1	-0.3	77.4	3.1	78.3	1.2	78.3	0.0	78.4	0.1	77.6	-1.0
1976	76.2	-1.8	77.6	1.8	77.7	0.1	77.8	0.1	77.9	0.1	77.4	-0.6	77.4	0.0	80.1	3.5	81.7	2.0	80.9	-1.0	81.3	0.5	81.3	0.0
1977	79.3	-2.5	79.4	0.1	79.5	0.1	79.4	-0.1	79.9	0.6	81.0	1.4	80.8	-0.2	82.7	2.4	83.3	0.7	83.0	-0.4	83.9	1.1	83.6	-0.4
1978	81.8	-2.2	82.2	0.5	83.7	1.8	85.6	2.3	86.2	0.7	86.5	0.3	84.0	-2.9	84.8	1.0	86.2	1.7	87.0	0.9	86.9	-0.1	86.5	-0.5
1979	83.6	-3.4	85.0	1.7	86.7	2.0	86.6	-0.1	87.5	1.0	85.9	-1.8	84.2	-2.0	86.2	2.4	88.4	2.6	88.9	0.6	88.8	-0.1	89.8	1.1
1980	88.5	-1.4	90.3	2.0	92.1	2.0	92.6	0.5	92.4	-0.2	92.3	-0.1	91.2	-1.2	91.9	0.8	94.1	2.4	95.8	1.8	95.8	0.0	95.3	-0.5
1981	93.3	-2.1	95.7	2.6	96.2	0.5	96.6	0.4	96.4	-0.2	95.9	-0.5	95.5	-0.4	96.9	1.5	98.4	1.5	97.1	-1.3	97.1	0.0	96.3	-0.8
1982	94.0	-2.4	96.5	2.7	97.7	1.2	97.5	-0.2	97.0	-0.5	97.2	0.2	97.1	-0.1	97.9	0.8	99.1	1.2	99.0	-0.1	98.2	-0.8	97.3	-0.9
1983	96.7	-0.6	97.9	1.2	99.6	1.7	100.2	0.6	101.9	1.7	100.9	-1.0	100.0	-0.9	100.9	0.9	102.9	2.0	103.2	0.3	102.3	-0.9	100.6	-1.7
1984	99.4	-1.2	99.0	-0.4	101.2	2.2	101.0	-0.2	101.9	0.9	100.3	-1.6	99.4	-0.9	103.9	4.5	104.9	1.0	105.5	0.6	105.0	-0.5	102.9	-2.0
1985	101.2	-1.7	102.8	1.6	104.5	1.7	104.6	0.1	103.6	-1.0	101.9	-1.6	101.6	-0.3	106.7	5.0	107.0	0.3	107.1	0.1	107.4	0.3	105.3	-2.0
1986	103.4	-1.8	102.7	-0.7	103.8	1.1	104.5	0.7	103.9	-0.6	102.4	-1.4	100.9	-1.5	104.3	3.4	107.2	2.8	106.3	-0.8	105.6	-0.7	105.2	-0.4
1987	102.7	-2.4	105.7	2.9	110.4	4.4	112.9	2.3	112.0	-0.8	108.0	-3.6	105.0	-2.8	108.8	3.6	115.2	5.9	115.6	0.3	115.4	-0.2	106.9	-7.4
1988	102.0	-4.6	100.2	-1.8	105.0	4.8	108.9	3.7	106.9	-1.8	103.6	-3.1	100.3	-3.2	102.4	2.1	116.2	13.5	119.9	3.2	112.7	-6.0	111.0	-1.5
1989	107.3	-3.3	108.1	0.7	117.4	8.6	117.0	-0.3	114.5	-2.1	110.7	-3.3	106.7	-3.6	108.7	1.9	120.8	11.1	121.7	0.7	119.8	-1.6	114.7	-4.3
1990	116.9	1.9	116.2	-0.6	122.6	5.5	126.0	2.8	122.1	-3.1	117.7	-3.6	115.1	-2.2	121.2	5.3	126.9	4.7	128.0	0.9	126.1	-1.5	122.9	-2.5
1991	121.0	-1.5	121.9	0.7	123.4	1.2	123.5	0.1	124.0	0.4	122.8	-1.0	120.6	-1.8	123.7	2.6	127.3	2.9	129.5	1.7	130.6	0.8	125.8	-3.7
1992	123.7	-1.7	123.4	-0.2	127.0	2.9	127.1	0.1	127.3	0.2	124.6	-2.1	124.5	-0.1	128.8	3.5	136.1	5.7	135.6	-0.4	134.1	-1.1	129.7	-3.3
1993	126.8	-2.2	133.8	5.5	134.2	0.3	131.7	-1.9	126.8	-3.7	124.6	-1.7	123.4	-1.0	128.5	4.1	132.4	3.0	133.0	0.5	131.4	-1.2	125.3	-4.6
1994	122.2	-2.5	125.9	3.0	129.5	2.9	131.7	1.7	128.4	-2.5	127.7	-0.5	123.4	-3.4	123.4	0.0	126.4	2.4	127.2	0.6	127.2	0.0	121.7	-4.3
1995	122.9	1.0	123.9	0.8	127.9	3.2	127.5	-0.3	127.3	-0.2	123.5	-3.0	119.0	-3.6	123.1	3.4	129.1	4.9	130.5	1.1	130.2	-0.2	126.7	-2.7

Source: U.S. Department of Labor, Bureau of Labor Statistics, Division of Consumer Prices and Price Indexes. - indicates no data collected for period.

New York, NY, NE NJ
Consumer Price Index - Urban Wage Earners
Base 1982-1984 = 100
Apparel and Upkeep

For 1952-1995. Columns headed % show percentile change in the index from the previous period for which an index is available.

Year	Jan Index	%	Feb Index	%	Mar Index	%	Apr Index	%	May Index	%	Jun Index	%	Jul Index	%	Aug Index	%	Sep Index	%	Oct Index	%	Nov Index	%	Dec Index	%
1952	-		-		-		-		-		-		-		-		-		-		-		45.0	-
1953	45.0	0.0	44.9	-0.2	44.9	0.0	44.7	-0.4	44.7	0.0	44.7	0.0	44.5	-0.4	44.4	-0.2	45.0	1.4	45.0	0.0	45.0	0.0	44.9	-0.2
1954	44.7	-0.4	44.7	0.0	44.5	-0.4	44.4	-0.2	44.4	0.0	44.3	-0.2	44.2	-0.2	44.1	-0.2	44.5	0.9	44.4	-0.2	44.5	0.2	44.3	-0.4
1955	43.7	-1.4	43.6	-0.2	43.7	0.2	43.5	-0.5	43.5	0.0	43.4	-0.2	43.2	-0.5	43.4	0.5	44.4	2.3	44.4	0.0	44.5	0.2	44.5	0.0
1956	44.1	-0.9	44.4	0.7	44.4	0.0	44.5	0.2	44.4	-0.2	44.6	0.5	44.7	0.2	44.7	0.0	45.5	1.8	45.7	0.4	45.6	-0.2	45.6	0.0
1957	45.5	-0.2	45.1	-0.9	45.6	1.1	45.4	-0.4	45.6	0.4	45.6	0.0	45.6	0.0	45.6	0.0	45.9	0.7	46.0	0.2	46.1	0.2	46.0	-0.2
1958	46.1	0.2	46.2	0.2	46.2	0.0	45.8	-0.9	45.7	-0.2	45.7	0.0	45.7	0.0	45.9	0.4	46.2	0.7	46.1	-0.2	46.2	0.2	46.2	0.0
1959	45.9	-0.6	45.9	0.0	46.0	0.2	46.0	0.0	46.0	0.0	46.1	0.2	46.2	0.2	46.4	0.4	46.5	0.2	46.6	0.2	46.8	0.4	46.8	0.0
1960	46.5	-0.6	46.7	0.4	47.0	0.6	47.1	0.2	47.0	-0.2	47.0	0.0	46.9	-0.2	47.0	0.2	47.6	1.3	47.9	0.6	47.9	0.0	47.9	0.0
1961	47.5	-0.8	47.5	0.0	47.4	-0.2	47.3	-0.2	47.2	-0.2	47.3	0.2	47.4	0.2	47.6	0.4	48.1	1.1	48.3	0.4	48.4	0.2	48.2	-0.4
1962	47.7	-1.0	47.8	0.2	47.9	0.2	47.8	-0.2	47.6	-0.4	47.8	0.4	48.0	0.4	47.8	-0.4	48.8	2.1	49.1	0.6	48.9	-0.4	48.8	-0.2
1963	48.7	-0.2	48.6	-0.2	48.6	0.0	48.7	0.2	48.5	-0.4	48.9	0.8	49.1	0.4	49.2	0.2	49.9	1.4	50.0	0.2	50.0	0.0	50.1	0.2
1964	49.2	-1.8	49.5	0.6	49.8	0.6	49.8	0.0	49.9	0.2	49.8	-0.2	49.8	0.0	49.5	-0.6	50.5	2.0	50.4	-0.2	50.3	-0.2	50.5	0.4
1965	49.3	-2.4	50.0	1.4	50.1	0.2	50.1	0.0	50.4	0.6	50.5	0.2	49.9	-1.2	50.5	1.2	51.6	2.2	51.7	0.2	51.6	-0.2	51.3	-0.6
1966	50.3	-1.9	50.7	0.8	51.2	1.0	51.3	0.2	51.7	0.8	51.4	-0.6	51.3	-0.2	51.0	-0.6	52.9	3.7	53.3	0.8	53.2	-0.2	53.3	0.2
1967	52.3	-1.9	53.2	1.7	54.1	1.7	53.8	-0.6	54.2	0.7	54.2	0.0	54.2	0.0	54.1	-0.2	55.4	2.4	55.7	0.5	55.7	0.0	55.7	0.0
1968	54.6	-2.0	55.5	1.6	56.2	1.3	56.5	0.5	56.9	0.7	57.2	0.5	56.8	-0.7	57.4	1.1	59.3	3.3	59.5	0.3	59.8	0.5	59.9	0.2
1969	58.8	-1.8	59.3	0.9	60.8	2.5	60.8	0.0	61.1	0.5	61.2	0.2	61.0	-0.3	60.8	-0.3	62.8	3.3	63.0	0.3	63.1	0.2	62.9	-0.3
1970	61.5	-2.2	62.9	2.3	63.2	0.5	63.0	-0.3	63.4	0.6	63.7	0.5	62.9	-1.3	63.5	1.0	65.8	3.6	65.8	0.0	65.8	0.0	65.9	0.2
1971	64.1	-2.7	64.9	1.2	65.4	0.8	64.9	-0.8	65.6	1.1	65.4	-0.3	64.7	-1.1	64.7	0.0	66.9	3.4	66.8	-0.1	66.6	-0.3	66.6	0.0
1972	64.9	-2.6	66.4	2.3	67.4	1.5	67.2	-0.3	67.2	0.0	66.1	-1.6	65.4	-1.1	65.3	-0.2	68.4	4.7	68.4	0.0	68.3	-0.1	68.1	-0.3
1973	65.0	-4.6	66.2	1.8	68.3	3.2	68.4	0.1	68.9	0.7	68.5	-0.6	67.4	-1.6	68.5	1.6	70.3	2.6	70.6	0.4	71.0	0.6	70.9	-0.1
1974	68.4	-3.5	70.7	3.4	72.8	3.0	72.1	-1.0	73.2	1.5	73.2	0.0	72.2	-1.4	76.0	5.3	77.5	2.0	77.8	0.4	78.1	0.4	76.7	-1.8
1975	75.0	-2.2	76.9	2.5	76.9	0.0	76.0	-1.2	76.5	0.7	75.2	-1.7	75.0	-0.3	77.2	2.9	78.2	1.3	78.2	0.0	78.3	0.1	77.5	-1.0
1976	76.1	-1.8	77.4	1.7	77.6	0.3	77.7	0.1	77.8	0.1	77.2	-0.8	77.2	0.0	80.0	3.6	81.5	1.9	80.8	-0.9	81.2	0.5	81.1	-0.1
1977	79.1	-2.5	79.3	0.3	79.4	0.1	79.2	-0.3	79.7	0.6	80.9	1.5	80.7	-0.2	82.6	2.4	83.2	0.7	82.8	-0.5	83.8	1.2	83.5	-0.4
1978	81.7	-2.2	82.2	0.6	83.2	1.2	84.7	1.8	84.7	0.0	84.6	-0.1	83.1	-1.8	84.1	1.2	84.6	0.6	85.7	1.3	85.4	-0.4	84.8	-0.7
1979	82.9	-2.2	85.0	2.5	86.9	2.2	87.4	0.6	88.1	0.8	86.2	-2.2	85.4	-0.9	87.2	2.1	89.1	2.2	89.7	0.7	89.7	0.0	90.4	0.8
1980	88.1	-2.5	89.2	1.2	92.7	3.9	92.8	0.1	94.1	1.4	92.5	-1.7	91.6	-1.0	93.9	2.5	95.8	2.0	96.1	0.3	95.8	-0.3	95.6	-0.2
1981	94.7	-0.9	95.3	0.6	95.4	0.1	95.4	0.0	96.1	0.7	95.5	-0.6	95.3	-0.2	97.0	1.8	98.0	1.0	96.8	-1.2	96.3	-0.5	95.9	-0.4
1982	94.0	-2.0	96.4	2.6	97.6	1.2	97.6	0.0	97.0	-0.6	97.1	0.1	96.8	-0.3	97.6	0.8	98.8	1.2	98.9	0.1	97.8	-1.1	97.3	-0.5
1983	96.8	-0.5	98.0	1.2	99.5	1.5	100.3	0.8	102.1	1.8	101.0	-1.1	99.9	-1.1	100.8	0.9	102.8	2.0	103.1	0.3	102.2	-0.9	100.7	-1.5
1984	99.5	-1.2	99.3	-0.2	101.3	2.0	101.1	-0.2	101.8	0.7	100.2	-1.6	99.3	-0.9	104.0	4.7	105.2	1.2	105.6	0.4	105.1	-0.5	103.2	-1.8
1985	101.5	-1.6	102.7	1.2	104.5	1.8	104.6	0.1	103.3	-1.2	101.6	-1.6	101.0	-0.6	106.6	5.5	107.2	0.6	107.1	-0.1	107.4	0.3	105.3	-2.0
1986	103.2	-2.0	102.5	-0.7	103.4	0.9	104.2	0.8	103.4	-0.8	101.7	-1.6	100.6	-1.1	104.3	3.7	107.3	2.9	106.1	-1.1	105.8	-0.3	105.5	-0.3
1987	103.2	-2.2	105.9	2.6	111.3	5.1	114.1	2.5	113.0	-1.0	108.5	-4.0	105.1	-3.1	108.0	2.8	115.3	6.8	115.8	0.4	115.8	0.0	106.7	-7.9
1988	101.3	-5.1	98.8	-2.5	104.3	5.6	108.0	3.5	106.0	-1.9	102.3	-3.5	98.8	-3.4	100.5	1.7	115.1	14.5	118.7	3.1	111.6	-6.0	109.9	-1.5
1989	106.2	-3.4	106.4	0.2	116.2	9.2	115.6	-0.5	112.8	-2.4	109.0	-3.4	104.9	-3.8	106.8	1.8	119.6	12.0	120.3	0.6	118.8	-1.2	113.3	-4.6
1990	115.2	1.7	113.9	-1.1	121.1	6.3	124.4	2.7	120.3	-3.3	116.0	-3.6	113.2	-2.4	119.0	5.1	125.8	5.7	126.4	0.5	124.6	-1.4	121.1	-2.8
1991	119.0	-1.7	119.2	0.2	121.1	1.6	121.1	0.0	121.4	0.2	120.4	-0.8	117.7	-2.2	121.8	3.5	124.8	2.5	126.8	1.6	127.9	0.9	123.5	-3.4
1992	120.9	-2.1	119.4	-1.2	123.6	3.5	123.3	-0.2	124.3	0.8	121.7	-2.1	121.8	0.1	126.8	4.1	133.8	5.5	134.0	0.1	132.1	-1.4	127.9	-3.2
1993	124.6	-2.6	131.2	5.3	131.5	0.2	128.3	-2.4	123.1	-4.1	121.0	-1.7	119.5	-1.2	124.7	4.4	129.1	3.5	130.1	0.8	128.6	-1.2	122.1	-5.1
1994	119.5	-2.1	123.4	3.3	126.4	2.4	128.1	1.3	124.6	-2.7	124.2	-0.3	119.6	-3.7	119.9	0.3	122.3	2.0	122.9	0.5	123.5	0.5	117.7	-4.7
1995	119.2	1.3	120.0	0.7	123.6	3.0	123.2	-0.3	123.2	0.0	119.6	-2.9	114.5	-4.3	119.3	4.2	125.5	5.2	126.1	0.5	125.5	-0.5	122.0	-2.8

Source: U.S. Department of Labor, Bureau of Labor Statistics, Division of Consumer Prices and Price Indexes. - indicates no data collected for period.

New York, NY, NE NJ
Consumer Price Index - All Urban Consumers
Base 1982-1984 = 100
Transportation

For 1947-1995. Columns headed % show percentile change in the index from the previous period for which an index is available.

Year	Jan Index	%	Feb Index	%	Mar Index	%	Apr Index	%	May Index	%	Jun Index	%	Jul Index	%	Aug Index	%	Sep Index	%	Oct Index	%	Nov Index	%	Dec Index	%
1947	15.8	-	15.8	0.0	15.8	0.0	15.9	0.6	16.0	0.6	16.0	0.0	16.1	0.6	16.1	0.0	16.2	0.6	16.2	0.0	16.3	0.6	16.5	1.2
1948	16.5	0.0	16.5	0.0	16.5	0.0	16.5	0.0	16.5	0.0	16.5	0.0	20.9	26.7	21.1	1.0	21.2	0.5	21.3	0.5	21.3	0.0	21.3	0.0
1949	21.4	0.5	21.4	0.0	21.4	0.0	21.5	0.5	21.5	0.0	21.5	0.0	21.5	0.0	21.5	0.0	21.5	0.0	21.5	0.0	21.5	0.0	21.6	0.5
1950	21.6	0.0	21.6	0.0	21.6	0.0	21.6	0.0	21.6	0.0	21.6	0.0	23.1	6.9	23.2	0.4	23.2	0.0	23.2	0.0	23.3	0.4	23.3	0.0
1951	23.3	0.0	23.3	0.0	23.4	0.4	23.4	0.0	23.4	0.0	23.4	0.0	23.5	0.4	23.5	0.0	23.6	0.4	23.7	0.4	23.8	0.4	23.8	0.0
1952	23.8	0.0	23.9	0.4	23.9	0.0	23.9	0.0	23.9	0.0	23.9	0.0	23.9	0.0	23.9	0.0	24.0	0.4	24.0	0.0	24.0	0.0	24.0	0.0
1953	24.0	0.0	23.9	-0.4	23.9	0.0	23.9	0.0	23.9	0.0	24.0	0.4	24.2	0.8	25.2	4.1	25.2	0.0	25.2	0.0	25.1	-0.4	25.1	0.0
1954	25.5	1.6	25.4	-0.4	25.3	-0.4	25.2	-0.4	25.2	0.0	25.3	0.4	24.3	-4.0	24.2	-0.4	24.3	0.4	24.4	0.4	24.7	1.2	24.6	-0.4
1955	24.4	-0.8	24.4	0.0	24.4	0.0	24.3	-0.4	24.2	-0.4	24.2	0.0	23.9	-1.2	23.8	-0.4	23.8	0.0	24.0	0.8	24.6	2.5	24.3	-1.2
1956	24.5	0.8	24.7	0.8	24.6	-0.4	24.7	0.4	24.7	0.0	24.7	0.0	24.8	0.4	25.1	1.2	25.0	-0.4	25.9	3.6	25.7	-0.8	25.7	0.0
1957	25.7	0.0	25.9	0.8	25.9	0.0	26.0	0.4	26.0	0.0	26.0	0.0	25.8	-0.8	25.8	0.0	25.8	0.0	25.7	-0.4	26.3	2.3	26.2	-0.4
1958	26.2	0.0	26.1	-0.4	26.1	0.0	26.2	0.4	26.2	0.0	26.1	-0.4	26.2	0.4	26.3	0.4	26.3	0.0	26.5	0.8	27.0	1.9	27.2	0.7
1959	27.1	-0.4	27.1	0.0	27.2	0.4	27.4	0.7	27.4	0.0	27.4	0.0	27.6	0.7	27.6	0.0	27.6	0.0	28.0	1.4	28.1	0.4	28.1	0.0
1960	28.1	0.0	28.1	0.0	27.9	-0.7	27.8	-0.4	27.8	0.0	27.7	-0.4	27.6	-0.4	27.6	0.0	27.4	-0.7	27.6	0.7	27.7	0.4	27.7	0.0
1961	27.6	-0.4	27.5	-0.4	27.6	0.4	27.7	0.4	27.8	0.4	27.9	0.4	27.9	0.0	27.9	0.0	27.9	0.0	28.1	0.7	28.0	-0.4	27.8	-0.7
1962	27.9	0.4	27.8	-0.4	27.8	0.0	27.9	0.4	28.1	0.7	28.1	0.0	28.0	-0.4	28.1	0.4	28.0	-0.4	28.1	0.4	28.1	0.0	28.0	-0.4
1963	28.0	0.0	27.9	-0.4	28.0	0.4	28.1	0.4	28.0	-0.4	28.3	1.1	28.3	0.0	28.3	0.0	28.3	0.0	28.4	0.4	28.6	0.7	28.5	-0.3
1964	28.4	-0.4	28.4	0.0	28.3	-0.4	28.3	0.0	28.3	0.0	28.2	-0.4	28.2	0.0	28.2	0.0	28.1	-0.4	28.2	0.4	28.5	1.1	28.6	0.4
1965	28.7	0.3	28.5	-0.7	28.6	0.4	28.6	0.0	28.5	-0.3	28.4	-0.4	28.6	0.7	28.7	0.3	28.7	0.0	28.9	0.7	28.9	0.0	28.9	0.0
1966	29.0	0.3	29.0	0.0	29.1	0.3	29.2	0.3	29.1	-0.3	29.2	0.3	30.5	4.5	30.5	0.0	30.3	-0.7	30.6	1.0	30.7	0.3	30.6	-0.3
1967	30.5	-0.3	30.7	0.7	30.8	0.3	30.9	0.3	31.0	0.3	31.0	0.0	31.2	0.6	31.4	0.6	31.3	-0.3	31.7	1.3	31.6	-0.3	31.7	0.3
1968	31.7	0.0	31.7	0.0	31.7	0.0	31.7	0.0	31.7	0.0	31.9	0.6	32.1	0.6	32.2	0.3	32.1	-0.3	32.4	0.9	32.5	0.3	32.2	-0.9
1969	33.0	2.5	33.3	0.9	33.8	1.5	33.9	0.3	33.7	-0.6	33.9	0.6	33.9	0.0	33.9	0.0	33.6	-0.9	34.2	1.8	34.2	0.0	35.1	2.6
1970	37.4	6.6	37.5	0.3	37.5	0.0	37.8	0.8	38.0	0.5	38.1	0.3	38.2	0.3	38.1	-0.3	38.1	0.0	38.6	1.3	38.9	0.8	39.1	0.5
1971	39.3	0.5	40.0	1.8	40.1	0.2	40.1	0.0	40.2	0.2	40.6	1.0	40.6	0.0	40.5	-0.2	40.1	-1.0	40.3	0.5	40.3	0.0	40.2	-0.2
1972	41.2	2.5	41.2	0.0	41.1	-0.2	41.1	0.0	41.3	0.5	41.4	0.2	41.5	0.2	41.6	0.2	41.7	0.2	41.7	0.0	41.8	0.2	41.8	0.0
1973	41.7	-0.2	41.8	0.2	41.8	0.0	42.0	0.5	42.1	0.2	42.4	0.7	42.4	0.0	42.4	0.0	42.2	-0.5	42.5	0.7	42.7	0.5	43.1	0.9
1974	43.2	0.2	43.4	0.5	43.9	1.2	44.3	0.9	45.0	1.6	45.8	1.8	46.4	1.3	46.5	0.2	46.8	0.6	47.0	0.4	47.1	0.2	47.4	0.6
1975	47.3	-0.2	47.3	0.0	47.8	1.1	48.1	0.6	48.2	0.2	48.8	1.2	49.5	1.4	49.7	0.4	53.3	7.2	53.6	0.6	54.7	2.1	55.3	1.1
1976	55.3	0.0	55.4	0.2	56.4	1.8	56.5	0.2	56.9	0.7	57.5	1.1	57.9	0.7	58.1	0.3	58.7	1.0	59.1	0.7	59.1	0.0	59.0	-0.2
1977	59.4	0.7	59.7	0.5	60.1	0.7	60.4	0.5	60.6	0.3	60.8	0.3	60.8	0.0	60.8	0.0	60.7	-0.2	60.9	0.3	61.0	0.2	61.1	0.2
1978	61.1	0.0	61.3	0.3	61.3	0.0	61.6	0.5	61.8	0.3	62.2	0.6	62.6	0.6	62.8	0.3	63.3	0.8	64.1	1.3	64.4	0.5	64.8	0.6
1979	65.1	0.5	65.7	0.9	66.4	1.1	67.7	2.0	69.0	1.9	70.6	2.3	72.2	2.3	72.9	1.0	73.6	1.0	74.1	0.7	74.7	0.8	75.4	0.9
1980	77.2	2.4	79.1	2.5	80.5	1.8	81.5	1.2	81.8	0.4	82.1	0.4	83.6	1.8	83.9	0.4	84.4	0.6	84.6	0.2	85.3	0.8	86.0	0.8
1981	87.4	1.6	89.3	2.2	90.1	0.9	90.7	0.7	91.0	0.3	91.5	0.5	93.9	2.6	94.0	0.1	94.4	0.4	94.7	0.3	95.4	0.7	95.6	0.2
1982	95.4	-0.2	95.0	-0.4	94.0	-1.1	93.3	-0.7	93.6	0.3	95.6	2.1	96.6	1.0	96.9	0.3	97.4	0.5	97.9	0.5	97.8	-0.1	97.8	0.0
1983	97.5	-0.3	96.9	-0.6	96.1	-0.8	97.8	1.8	98.1	0.3	98.7	0.6	99.2	0.5	99.9	0.7	100.5	0.6	100.9	0.4	101.6	0.7	101.5	-0.1
1984	103.3	1.8	103.5	0.2	104.1	0.6	104.5	0.4	105.0	0.5	105.1	0.1	105.5	0.4	105.5	0.0	105.5	0.0	105.8	0.3	106.1	0.3	106.1	0.0
1985	106.1	0.0	106.1	0.0	106.6	0.5	106.8	0.2	107.1	0.3	107.4	0.3	107.4	0.0	107.1	-0.3	106.8	-0.3	107.6	0.7	108.1	0.5	108.4	0.3
1986	109.5	1.0	108.5	-0.9	106.1	-2.2	103.4	-2.5	103.4	0.0	104.5	1.1	103.9	-0.6	102.9	-1.0	102.4	-0.5	104.0	1.6	104.5	0.5	104.8	0.3
1987	105.4	0.6	105.7	0.3	106.1	0.4	107.4	1.2	108.0	0.6	108.8	0.7	109.4	0.6	110.2	0.7	110.3	0.1	110.7	0.4	111.5	0.7	111.2	-0.3
1988	111.3	0.1	111.3	0.0	110.7	-0.5	111.2	0.5	111.8	0.5	112.6	0.7	113.0	0.4	113.4	0.4	113.7	0.3	114.4	0.6	114.7	0.3	114.9	0.2
1989	115.2	0.3	115.1	-0.1	115.3	0.2	116.3	0.9	117.5	1.0	117.3	-0.2	116.9	-0.3	116.4	-0.4	115.8	-0.5	116.9	0.9	117.3	0.3	117.5	0.2
1990	119.5	1.7	119.8	0.3	119.5	-0.3	119.2	-0.3	119.3	0.1	120.4	0.9	120.8	0.3	122.1	1.1	125.3	2.6	129.0	3.0	130.6	1.2	131.4	0.6
1991	129.1	-1.8	127.8	-1.0	126.6	-0.9	126.2	-0.3	127.3	0.9	127.6	0.2	127.7	0.1	127.6	-0.1	128.1	0.4	128.6	0.4	129.1	0.4	129.1	0.0

[Continued]

New York, NY, NE NJ
Consumer Price Index - All Urban Consumers
Base 1982-1984 = 100
Transportation

[Continued]

For 1947-1995. Columns headed % show percentile change in the index from the previous period for which an index is available.

Year	Jan Index	%	Feb Index	%	Mar Index	%	Apr Index	%	May Index	%	Jun Index	%	Jul Index	%	Aug Index	%	Sep Index	%	Oct Index	%	Nov Index	%	Dec Index	%
1992	129.5	0.3	129.7	0.2	129.9	0.2	129.6	-0.2	129.8	0.2	130.1	0.2	130.9	0.6	130.6	-0.2	130.9	0.2	134.6	2.8	135.5	0.7	136.3	0.6
1993	137.3	0.7	136.9	-0.3	136.2	-0.5	136.4	0.1	137.1	0.5	136.7	-0.3	137.1	0.3	137.2	0.1	137.1	-0.1	139.1	1.5	140.1	0.7	141.0	0.6
1994	140.4	-0.4	140.6	0.1	139.9	-0.5	140.5	0.4	140.3	-0.1	141.2	0.6	141.5	0.2	142.2	0.5	142.3	0.1	143.9	1.1	144.5	0.4	144.6	0.1
1995	144.4	-0.1	144.5	0.1	144.5	0.0	144.1	-0.3	146.0	1.3	147.4	1.0	146.5	-0.6	145.7	-0.5	145.9	0.1	146.8	0.6	146.9	0.1	147.8	0.6

Source: U.S. Department of Labor, Bureau of Labor Statistics, Division of Consumer Prices and Price Indexes. - indicates no data collected for period.

New York, NY, NE NJ
Consumer Price Index - Urban Wage Earners
Base 1982-1984 = 100
Transportation

For 1947-1995. Columns headed % show percentile change in the index from the previous period for which an index is available.

Year	Jan Index	%	Feb Index	%	Mar Index	%	Apr Index	%	May Index	%	Jun Index	%	Jul Index	%	Aug Index	%	Sep Index	%	Oct Index	%	Nov Index	%	Dec Index	%
1947	15.7	-	15.7	0.0	15.7	0.0	15.8	0.6	15.8	0.0	15.9	0.6	15.9	0.0	16.0	0.6	16.1	0.6	16.1	0.0	16.1	0.0	16.3	1.2
1948	16.3	0.0	16.3	0.0	16.3	0.0	16.3	0.0	16.3	0.0	16.3	0.0	20.7	27.0	20.9	1.0	21.0	0.5	21.1	0.5	21.1	0.0	21.1	0.0
1949	21.1	0.0	21.2	0.5	21.2	0.0	21.3	0.5	21.3	0.0	21.3	0.0	21.3	0.0	21.3	0.0	21.3	0.0	21.3	0.0	21.3	0.0	21.4	0.5
1950	21.4	0.0	21.4	0.0	21.4	0.0	21.4	0.0	21.4	0.0	21.4	0.0	22.9	7.0	23.0	0.4	22.9	-0.4	22.9	0.0	23.0	0.4	23.0	0.0
1951	23.0	0.0	23.1	0.4	23.2	0.4	23.2	0.0	23.2	0.0	23.2	0.0	23.3	0.4	23.3	0.0	23.4	0.4	23.5	0.4	23.6	0.4	23.6	0.0
1952	23.6	0.0	23.7	0.4	23.7	0.0	23.7	0.0	23.7	0.0	23.7	0.0	23.7	0.0	23.7	0.0	23.8	0.4	23.8	0.0	23.8	0.0	23.7	-0.4
1953	23.8	0.4	23.7	-0.4	23.7	0.0	23.7	0.0	23.7	0.0	23.7	0.0	23.9	0.8	25.0	4.6	24.9	-0.4	25.0	0.4	24.8	-0.8	24.9	0.4
1954	25.2	1.2	25.1	-0.4	25.0	-0.4	24.9	-0.4	25.0	0.4	25.0	0.0	24.0	-4.0	24.0	0.0	24.1	0.4	24.1	0.0	24.4	1.2	24.3	-0.4
1955	24.2	-0.4	24.2	0.0	24.2	0.0	24.1	-0.4	24.0	-0.4	23.9	-0.4	23.7	-0.8	23.6	-0.4	23.6	0.0	23.8	0.8	24.4	2.5	24.1	-1.2
1956	24.3	0.8	24.4	0.4	24.4	0.0	24.4	0.0	24.5	0.4	24.4	-0.4	24.6	0.8	24.8	0.8	24.8	0.0	25.6	3.2	25.4	-0.8	25.4	0.0
1957	25.5	0.4	25.6	0.4	25.6	0.0	25.7	0.4	25.7	0.0	25.7	0.0	25.6	-0.4	25.6	0.0	25.5	-0.4	25.5	0.0	26.1	2.4	26.0	-0.4
1958	26.0	0.0	25.9	-0.4	25.8	-0.4	25.9	0.4	25.9	0.0	25.9	0.0	25.9	0.0	26.1	0.8	26.1	0.0	26.2	0.4	26.7	1.9	26.9	0.7
1959	26.9	0.0	26.9	0.0	27.0	0.4	27.2	0.7	27.2	0.0	27.2	0.0	27.3	0.4	27.4	0.4	27.3	-0.4	27.7	1.5	27.8	0.4	27.8	0.0
1960	27.8	0.0	27.8	0.0	27.6	-0.7	27.5	-0.4	27.5	0.0	27.4	-0.4	27.3	-0.4	27.3	0.0	27.2	-0.4	27.3	0.4	27.4	0.4	27.5	0.4
1961	27.3	-0.7	27.2	-0.4	27.3	0.4	27.5	0.7	27.5	0.0	27.6	0.4	27.6	0.0	27.6	0.0	27.6	0.0	27.8	0.7	27.8	0.0	27.5	-1.1
1962	27.6	0.4	27.5	-0.4	27.5	0.0	27.7	0.7	27.8	0.4	27.8	0.0	27.8	0.0	27.8	0.0	27.7	-0.4	27.8	0.4	27.9	0.4	27.7	-0.7
1963	27.7	0.0	27.7	0.0	27.7	0.0	27.8	0.4	27.7	-0.4	28.1	1.4	28.1	0.0	28.1	0.0	28.0	-0.4	28.1	0.4	28.3	0.7	28.2	-0.4
1964	28.1	-0.4	28.1	0.0	28.0	-0.4	28.0	0.0	28.0	0.0	27.9	-0.4	28.0	0.4	27.9	-0.4	27.8	-0.4	27.9	0.4	28.2	1.1	28.3	0.4
1965	28.4	0.4	28.2	-0.7	28.3	0.4	28.3	0.0	28.2	-0.4	28.1	-0.4	28.3	0.7	28.4	0.4	28.4	0.0	28.6	0.7	28.6	0.0	28.6	0.0
1966	28.7	0.3	28.7	0.0	28.8	0.3	29.0	0.7	28.9	-0.3	29.0	0.3	30.3	4.5	30.3	0.0	30.0	-1.0	30.3	1.0	30.4	0.3	30.3	-0.3
1967	30.3	0.0	30.4	0.3	30.5	0.3	30.6	0.3	30.7	0.3	30.7	0.0	30.9	0.7	31.1	0.6	31.0	-0.3	31.4	1.3	31.3	-0.3	31.4	0.3
1968	31.4	0.0	31.4	0.0	31.4	0.0	31.4	0.0	31.4	0.0	31.6	0.6	31.8	0.6	31.9	0.3	31.8	-0.3	32.1	0.9	32.2	0.3	31.9	-0.9
1969	32.7	2.5	33.0	0.9	33.5	1.5	33.6	0.3	33.4	-0.6	33.5	0.3	33.6	0.3	33.6	0.0	33.3	-0.9	33.8	1.5	33.8	0.0	34.7	2.7
1970	37.0	6.6	37.1	0.3	37.2	0.3	37.4	0.5	37.6	0.5	37.7	0.3	37.8	0.3	37.7	-0.3	37.7	0.0	38.2	1.3	38.6	1.0	38.7	0.3
1971	38.9	0.5	39.6	1.8	39.8	0.5	39.7	-0.3	39.8	0.3	40.2	1.0	40.3	0.2	40.1	-0.5	39.7	-1.0	39.9	0.5	39.9	0.0	39.8	-0.3
1972	40.8	2.5	40.8	0.0	40.7	-0.2	40.7	0.0	40.9	0.5	41.0	0.2	41.1	0.2	41.1	0.0	41.3	0.5	41.3	0.0	41.4	0.2	41.4	0.0
1973	41.3	-0.2	41.4	0.2	41.4	0.0	41.6	0.5	41.7	0.2	42.0	0.7	42.0	0.0	42.0	0.0	41.8	-0.5	42.1	0.7	42.3	0.5	42.7	0.9
1974	42.8	0.2	43.0	0.5	43.5	1.2	43.9	0.9	44.6	1.6	45.4	1.8	46.0	1.3	46.1	0.2	46.3	0.4	46.5	0.4	46.7	0.4	47.0	0.6
1975	46.9	-0.2	46.9	0.0	47.4	1.1	47.7	0.6	47.8	0.2	48.3	1.0	49.0	1.4	49.3	0.6	52.8	7.1	53.1	0.6	54.2	2.1	54.8	1.1
1976	54.8	0.0	54.9	0.2	55.8	1.6	56.0	0.4	56.4	0.7	57.0	1.1	57.3	0.5	57.5	0.3	58.1	1.0	58.6	0.9	58.6	0.0	58.5	-0.2
1977	58.8	0.5	59.1	0.5	59.5	0.7	59.8	0.5	60.0	0.3	60.2	0.3	60.2	0.0	60.2	0.0	60.1	-0.2	60.3	0.3	60.4	0.2	60.5	0.2
1978	60.5	0.0	60.7	0.3	60.8	0.2	61.1	0.5	61.4	0.5	61.9	0.8	62.3	0.6	62.6	0.5	63.0	0.6	63.6	1.0	64.0	0.6	64.4	0.6
1979	64.7	0.5	65.3	0.9	66.0	1.1	67.4	2.1	68.7	1.9	70.5	2.6	72.0	2.1	72.8	1.1	73.5	1.0	73.7	-0.3	74.4	0.9	75.1	0.9
1980	77.0	2.5	78.8	2.3	80.2	1.8	81.1	1.1	81.3	0.2	81.6	0.4	83.3	2.1	83.7	0.5	84.1	0.5	84.4	0.4	85.1	0.8	85.9	0.9
1981	87.2	1.5	89.2	2.3	90.0	0.9	90.7	0.8	90.7	0.0	91.3	0.7	93.9	2.8	94.1	0.2	94.6	0.5	94.9	0.3	95.5	0.6	95.7	0.2
1982	95.5	-0.2	95.0	-0.5	94.0	-1.1	93.0	-1.1	93.4	0.4	95.5	2.2	96.7	1.3	97.0	0.3	97.3	0.3	97.8	0.5	97.5	-0.3	97.6	0.1
1983	97.3	-0.3	96.6	-0.7	95.7	-0.9	97.3	1.7	97.8	0.5	98.5	0.7	99.1	0.6	99.9	0.8	100.6	0.7	101.0	0.4	101.7	0.7	101.7	0.0
1984	103.5	1.8	103.6	0.1	104.2	0.6	104.6	0.4	105.2	0.6	105.5	0.3	105.7	0.2	105.7	0.0	105.8	0.1	106.1	0.3	106.3	0.2	106.3	0.0
1985	106.2	-0.1	106.2	0.0	106.7	0.5	107.0	0.3	107.2	0.2	107.5	0.3	107.5	0.0	107.1	-0.4	106.7	-0.4	107.5	0.7	108.1	0.6	108.3	0.2
1986	109.5	1.1	108.4	-1.0	105.8	-2.4	102.9	-2.7	102.8	-0.1	103.8	1.0	103.1	-0.7	102.1	-1.0	101.5	-0.6	103.1	1.6	103.4	0.3	103.6	0.2
1987	104.4	0.8	105.0	0.6	105.5	0.5	107.0	1.4	107.7	0.7	108.7	0.9	109.3	0.6	110.2	0.8	110.4	0.2	110.7	0.3	111.3	0.5	111.1	-0.2
1988	111.2	0.1	111.1	-0.1	110.5	-0.5	110.8	0.3	111.3	0.5	112.0	0.6	112.5	0.4	113.1	0.5	113.3	0.2	113.9	0.5	114.1	0.2	114.4	0.3
1989	114.5	0.1	114.4	-0.1	114.6	0.2	115.8	1.0	117.4	1.4	117.4	0.0	117.1	-0.3	116.5	-0.5	115.7	-0.7	116.5	0.7	116.9	0.3	116.9	0.0
1990	119.3	2.1	119.4	0.1	119.0	-0.3	118.8	-0.2	118.8	0.0	120.2	1.2	120.9	0.6	122.3	1.2	126.1	3.1	129.7	2.9	131.3	1.2	131.8	0.4
1991	129.1	-2.0	127.3	-1.4	126.0	-1.0	125.9	-0.1	127.2	1.0	127.6	0.3	127.8	0.2	127.7	-0.1	128.4	0.5	128.6	0.2	129.1	0.4	129.0	-0.1

[Continued]

New York, NY, NE NJ

Consumer Price Index - Urban Wage Earners
Base 1982-1984 = 100

Transportation

[Continued]

For 1947-1995. Columns headed % show percentile change in the index from the previous period for which an index is available.

Year	Jan Index	%	Feb Index	%	Mar Index	%	Apr Index	%	May Index	%	Jun Index	%	Jul Index	%	Aug Index	%	Sep Index	%	Oct Index	%	Nov Index	%	Dec Index	%
1992	129.5	0.4	129.4	-0.1	129.6	0.2	129.3	-0.2	129.9	0.5	130.8	0.7	131.4	0.5	131.0	-0.3	131.5	0.4	134.9	2.6	135.7	0.6	136.5	0.6
1993	137.0	0.4	136.5	-0.4	135.9	-0.4	135.8	-0.1	136.7	0.7	136.7	0.0	136.9	0.1	137.0	0.1	136.9	-0.1	139.2	1.7	139.9	0.5	140.6	0.5
1994	139.8	-0.6	139.6	-0.1	139.1	-0.4	139.6	0.4	139.8	0.1	140.9	0.8	141.4	0.4	142.2	0.6	142.7	0.4	144.4	1.2	145.0	0.4	144.9	-0.1
1995	144.5	-0.3	144.5	0.0	144.5	0.0	144.3	-0.1	146.2	1.3	147.5	0.9	147.0	-0.3	146.2	-0.5	146.0	-0.1	146.8	0.5	146.8	0.0	148.1	0.9

Source: U.S. Department of Labor, Bureau of Labor Statistics, Division of Consumer Prices and Price Indexes. - indicates no data collected for period.

New York, NY, NE NJ
Consumer Price Index - All Urban Consumers
Base 1982-1984 = 100
Medical Care

For 1947-1995. Columns headed % show percentile change in the index from the previous period for which an index is available.

Year	Jan Index	%	Feb Index	%	Mar Index	%	Apr Index	%	May Index	%	Jun Index	%	Jul Index	%	Aug Index	%	Sep Index	%	Oct Index	%	Nov Index	%	Dec Index	%
1947	14.0	-	14.1	0.7	14.1	0.0	14.1	0.0	14.2	0.7	14.3	0.7	14.3	0.0	14.3	0.0	14.4	0.7	14.5	0.7	14.5	0.0	14.5	0.0
1948	14.8	2.1	14.9	0.7	15.0	0.7	15.6	4.0	15.6	0.0	15.6	0.0	16.0	2.6	16.0	0.0	16.1	0.6	16.1	0.0	16.1	0.0	16.1	0.0
1949	16.2	0.6	16.2	0.0	16.0	-1.2	16.0	0.0	16.0	0.0	16.0	0.0	16.0	0.0	16.0	0.0	16.0	0.0	16.0	0.0	16.0	0.0	16.2	1.3
1950	16.3	0.6	16.3	0.0	16.3	0.0	16.3	0.0	16.3	0.0	16.4	0.6	16.4	0.0	16.4	0.0	16.3	-0.6	16.4	0.6	16.4	0.0	16.4	0.0
1951	16.6	1.2	16.6	0.0	16.9	1.8	17.0	0.6	17.0	0.0	17.0	0.0	17.0	0.0	17.0	0.0	17.2	1.2	17.2	0.0	17.2	0.0	17.4	1.2
1952	17.6	1.1	17.6	0.0	17.6	0.0	17.6	0.0	17.6	0.0	18.3	4.0	18.3	0.0	18.4	0.5	18.6	1.1	18.6	0.0	18.7	0.5	18.6	-0.5
1953	18.6	0.0	18.5	-0.5	18.5	0.0	18.5	0.0	18.5	0.0	18.5	0.0	18.5	0.0	18.6	0.5	18.6	0.0	18.6	0.0	18.9	1.6	18.9	0.0
1954	18.9	0.0	18.9	0.0	18.9	0.0	19.0	0.5	19.0	0.0	19.0	0.0	19.0	0.0	19.0	0.0	19.0	0.0	19.0	0.0	19.1	0.5	19.1	0.0
1955	19.1	0.0	19.2	0.5	19.2	0.0	19.2	0.0	19.3	0.5	19.3	0.0	19.4	0.5	19.4	0.0	19.4	0.0	19.4	0.0	19.4	0.0	19.4	0.0
1956	19.4	0.0	19.4	0.0	19.4	0.0	19.4	0.0	19.4	0.0	19.4	0.0	19.4	0.0	19.6	1.0	19.6	0.0	19.6	0.0	19.6	0.0	19.6	0.0
1957	19.7	0.5	19.7	0.0	19.7	0.0	19.7	0.0	19.8	0.5	19.9	0.5	19.9	0.0	19.8	-0.5	19.8	0.0	19.8	0.0	19.9	0.5	19.9	0.0
1958	19.9	0.0	19.9	0.0	20.0	0.5	20.0	0.0	20.0	0.0	20.0	0.0	20.0	0.0	20.1	0.5	20.7	3.0	20.7	0.0	20.8	0.5	20.8	0.0
1959	20.8	0.0	21.1	1.4	21.1	0.0	21.1	0.0	21.4	1.4	21.5	0.5	21.5	0.0	21.4	-0.5	22.0	2.8	22.0	0.0	22.0	0.0	22.0	0.0
1960	22.0	0.0	22.0	0.0	22.1	0.5	22.1	0.0	22.1	0.0	22.1	0.0	22.1	0.0	22.1	0.0	22.1	0.0	22.1	0.0	22.7	2.7	22.7	0.0
1961	22.7	0.0	22.7	0.0	22.8	0.4	22.8	0.0	23.0	0.9	23.0	0.0	23.0	0.0	23.1	0.4	23.1	0.0	23.1	0.0	23.1	0.0	23.1	0.0
1962	23.1	0.0	23.3	0.9	23.4	0.4	23.4	0.0	23.5	0.4	23.5	0.0	23.5	0.0	23.6	0.4	23.6	0.0	23.5	-0.4	23.6	0.4	23.7	0.4
1963	23.7	0.0	23.9	0.8	23.9	0.0	23.9	0.0	24.0	0.4	23.9	-0.4	23.9	0.0	24.0	0.4	24.0	0.0	24.0	0.0	24.1	0.4	24.1	0.0
1964	24.2	0.4	24.3	0.4	24.3	0.0	24.4	0.4	24.4	0.0	24.4	0.0	24.4	0.0	24.6	0.8	24.4	-0.8	24.5	0.4	24.7	0.8	24.7	0.0
1965	24.9	0.8	25.1	0.8	25.2	0.4	25.2	0.0	25.2	0.0	25.4	0.8	25.4	0.0	25.3	-0.4	25.3	0.0	25.3	0.0	25.4	0.4	25.6	0.8
1966	25.7	0.4	25.8	0.4	26.0	0.8	26.1	0.4	26.3	0.8	26.7	1.5	26.8	0.4	27.0	0.7	27.0	0.0	27.2	0.7	27.3	0.4	27.3	0.0
1967	27.6	1.1	27.8	0.7	27.9	0.4	28.0	0.4	28.1	0.4	28.3	0.7	28.5	0.7	28.7	0.7	28.8	0.3	28.9	0.3	28.9	0.0	29.2	1.0
1968	29.3	0.3	29.4	0.3	29.6	0.7	29.8	0.7	29.8	0.0	30.1	1.0	30.5	1.3	30.5	0.0	30.8	1.0	31.0	0.6	31.1	0.3	31.2	0.3
1969	31.9	2.2	32.0	0.3	32.5	1.6	32.8	0.9	33.0	0.6	33.4	1.2	33.4	0.0	33.6	0.6	33.6	0.0	33.5	-0.3	33.6	0.3	33.8	0.6
1970	34.0	0.6	34.1	0.3	34.6	1.5	34.9	0.9	34.9	0.0	35.6	2.0	35.9	0.8	36.1	0.6	36.4	0.8	36.5	0.3	36.8	0.8	37.3	1.4
1971	37.6	0.8	37.8	0.5	38.2	1.1	38.2	0.0	38.4	0.5	38.5	0.3	38.8	0.8	39.0	0.5	39.0	0.0	38.9	-0.3	39.0	0.3	39.1	0.3
1972	39.4	0.8	39.4	0.0	39.4	0.0	39.5	0.3	39.6	0.3	39.8	0.5	39.8	0.0	39.9	0.3	39.9	0.0	40.1	0.5	40.3	0.5	40.6	0.7
1973	40.7	0.2	40.7	0.0	40.6	-0.2	40.6	0.0	40.9	0.7	41.0	0.2	41.0	0.0	41.1	0.2	41.3	0.5	42.0	1.7	42.1	0.2	42.3	0.5
1974	42.8	1.2	43.2	0.9	43.8	1.4	44.1	0.7	44.7	1.4	45.4	1.6	45.7	0.7	46.9	2.6	47.4	1.1	47.5	0.2	47.8	0.6	48.2	0.8
1975	48.9	1.5	49.6	1.4	50.3	1.4	50.6	0.6	51.0	0.8	51.3	0.6	51.7	0.8	51.9	0.4	52.6	1.3	52.8	0.4	52.6	-0.4	53.4	1.5
1976	54.5	2.1	55.0	0.9	55.5	0.9	55.7	0.4	55.9	0.4	56.5	1.1	57.1	1.1	57.5	0.7	57.9	0.7	57.9	0.0	58.8	1.6	58.9	0.2
1977	59.7	1.4	59.9	0.3	60.7	1.3	61.2	0.8	61.4	0.3	61.7	0.5	62.0	0.5	62.2	0.3	62.3	0.2	62.6	0.5	62.8	0.3	63.3	0.8
1978	64.1	1.3	64.5	0.6	64.6	0.2	64.8	0.3	65.5	1.1	65.5	0.0	65.5	0.0	65.5	0.0	65.7	0.3	65.7	0.0	66.7	1.5	66.3	-0.6
1979	68.1	2.7	69.0	1.3	69.2	0.3	69.7	0.7	69.8	0.1	70.1	0.4	70.2	0.1	70.5	0.4	71.1	0.9	72.2	1.5	73.0	1.1	73.5	0.7
1980	74.5	1.4	75.4	1.2	76.2	1.1	76.9	0.9	76.9	0.0	77.0	0.1	77.2	0.3	77.8	0.8	78.3	0.6	78.7	0.5	79.0	0.4	79.3	0.4
1981	80.2	1.1	80.6	0.5	81.6	1.2	82.5	1.1	82.7	0.2	84.1	1.7	85.0	1.1	85.2	0.2	86.2	1.2	87.2	1.2	87.7	0.6	88.1	0.5
1982	89.1	1.1	89.9	0.9	90.7	0.9	90.9	0.2	91.2	0.3	91.6	0.4	91.5	-0.1	91.9	0.4	92.8	1.0	93.3	0.5	94.1	0.9	94.4	0.3
1983	95.4	1.1	97.3	2.0	98.1	0.8	98.7	0.6	99.4	0.7	99.4	0.0	100.0	0.6	101.2	1.2	101.7	0.5	102.3	0.6	103.2	0.9	103.9	0.7
1984	104.7	0.8	106.1	1.3	106.7	0.6	106.7	0.0	107.3	0.6	107.2	-0.1	107.7	0.5	109.0	1.2	109.8	0.7	110.1	0.3	110.8	0.6	111.4	0.5
1985	112.0	0.5	113.8	1.6	114.3	0.4	114.6	0.3	115.4	0.7	116.2	0.7	116.7	0.4	116.8	0.1	117.2	0.3	117.5	0.3	117.8	0.3	117.7	-0.1
1986	120.0	2.0	122.2	1.8	123.7	1.2	124.2	0.4	124.6	0.3	125.1	0.4	126.0	0.7	126.4	0.3	127.8	1.1	128.7	0.7	128.7	0.0	130.3	1.2
1987	131.1	0.6	132.9	1.4	135.0	1.6	136.1	0.8	136.1	0.0	136.3	0.1	136.8	0.4	137.2	0.3	137.2	0.0	137.5	0.2	137.9	0.3	138.5	0.4
1988	139.7	0.9	141.3	1.1	142.7	1.0	143.2	0.4	144.1	0.6	144.7	0.4	146.1	1.0	145.9	-0.1	146.9	0.7	147.1	0.1	147.6	0.3	147.9	0.2
1989	149.5	1.1	151.1	1.1	152.9	1.2	153.4	0.3	154.3	0.6	155.6	0.8	156.2	0.4	157.1	0.6	157.7	0.4	159.7	1.3	160.5	0.5	161.5	0.6
1990	163.9	1.5	166.7	1.7	169.2	1.5	170.1	0.5	170.5	0.2	171.4	0.5	171.8	0.2	175.1	1.9	175.9	0.5	177.5	0.9	178.0	0.3	178.7	0.4
1991	180.8	1.2	182.8	1.1	183.9	0.6	184.2	0.2	183.9	-0.2	185.3	0.8	187.2	1.0	188.7	0.8	189.3	0.3	189.6	0.2	191.0	0.7	192.0	0.5

[Continued]

New York, NY, NE NJ
Consumer Price Index - All Urban Consumers
Base 1982-1984 = 100
Medical Care
[Continued]

For 1947-1995. Columns headed % show percentile change in the index from the previous period for which an index is available.

Year	Jan Index	%	Feb Index	%	Mar Index	%	Apr Index	%	May Index	%	Jun Index	%	Jul Index	%	Aug Index	%	Sep Index	%	Oct Index	%	Nov Index	%	Dec Index	%
1992	195.1	1.6	196.4	0.7	197.7	0.7	198.4	0.4	199.1	0.4	200.0	0.5	201.2	0.6	200.8	-0.2	201.9	0.5	202.8	0.4	203.1	0.1	203.3	0.1
1993	205.1	0.9	205.5	0.2	206.6	0.5	207.9	0.6	208.9	0.5	208.9	0.0	209.5	0.3	210.7	0.6	211.0	0.1	211.3	0.1	211.4	0.0	212.0	0.3
1994	213.5	0.7	214.2	0.3	215.1	0.4	215.8	0.3	216.5	0.3	217.7	0.6	218.2	0.2	218.7	0.2	218.6	-0.0	220.6	0.9	220.6	0.0	221.7	0.5
1995	223.2	0.7	225.1	0.9	225.3	0.1	225.6	0.1	226.0	0.2	226.0	0.0	226.2	0.1	227.4	0.5	228.0	0.3	229.5	0.7	229.6	0.0	230.0	0.2

Source: U.S. Department of Labor, Bureau of Labor Statistics, Division of Consumer Prices and Price Indexes. - indicates no data collected for period.

New York, NY, NE NJ
Consumer Price Index - Urban Wage Earners
Base 1982-1984 = 100
Medical Care

For 1947-1995. Columns headed % show percentile change in the index from the previous period for which an index is available.

Year	Jan Index	%	Feb Index	%	Mar Index	%	Apr Index	%	May Index	%	Jun Index	%	Jul Index	%	Aug Index	%	Sep Index	%	Oct Index	%	Nov Index	%	Dec Index	%
1947	14.6	-	14.7	0.7	14.7	0.0	14.7	0.0	14.8	0.7	14.9	0.7	14.9	0.0	15.0	0.7	15.0	0.0	15.2	1.3	15.2	0.0	15.2	0.0
1948	15.5	2.0	15.5	0.0	15.6	0.6	16.3	4.5	16.3	0.0	16.3	0.0	16.7	2.5	16.7	0.0	16.8	0.6	16.8	0.0	16.8	0.0	16.8	0.0
1949	16.9	0.6	16.8	-0.6	16.7	-0.6	16.7	0.0	16.7	0.0	16.7	0.0	16.7	0.0	16.6	-0.6	16.6	0.0	16.7	0.6	16.7	0.0	16.9	1.2
1950	17.0	0.6	17.0	0.0	17.0	0.0	17.0	0.0	17.0	0.0	17.1	0.6	17.1	0.0	17.1	0.0	17.0	-0.6	17.1	0.6	17.1	0.0	17.1	0.0
1951	17.3	1.2	17.4	0.6	17.6	1.1	17.7	0.6	17.7	0.0	17.7	0.0	17.7	0.0	17.7	0.0	17.9	1.1	17.9	0.0	17.9	0.0	18.1	1.1
1952	18.3	1.1	18.4	0.5	18.4	0.0	18.4	0.0	18.4	0.0	19.1	3.8	19.1	0.0	19.2	0.5	19.4	1.0	19.4	0.0	19.5	0.5	19.4	-0.5
1953	19.4	0.0	19.3	-0.5	19.3	0.0	19.3	0.0	19.3	0.0	19.3	0.0	19.3	0.0	19.4	0.5	19.4	0.0	19.4	0.0	19.7	1.5	19.7	0.0
1954	19.7	0.0	19.7	0.0	19.7	0.0	19.8	0.5	19.8	0.0	19.8	0.0	19.8	0.0	19.8	0.0	19.8	0.0	19.8	0.0	19.9	0.5	19.9	0.0
1955	20.0	0.5	20.0	0.0	20.0	0.0	20.0	0.0	20.2	1.0	20.2	0.0	20.2	0.0	20.2	0.0	20.2	0.0	20.2	0.0	20.2	0.0	20.2	0.0
1956	20.3	0.5	20.3	0.0	20.3	0.0	20.2	-0.5	20.3	0.5	20.3	0.0	20.3	0.0	20.5	1.0	20.5	0.0	20.5	0.0	20.5	0.0	20.5	0.0
1957	20.5	0.0	20.5	0.0	20.5	0.0	20.5	0.0	20.7	1.0	20.7	0.0	20.7	0.0	20.7	0.0	20.7	0.0	20.7	0.0	20.7	0.0	20.7	0.0
1958	20.8	0.5	20.8	0.0	20.8	0.0	20.8	0.0	20.9	0.5	20.9	0.0	20.9	0.0	21.0	0.5	21.6	2.9	21.6	0.0	21.6	0.0	21.6	0.0
1959	21.7	0.5	22.0	1.4	22.0	0.0	22.0	0.0	22.4	1.8	22.4	0.0	22.4	0.0	22.4	0.0	22.9	2.2	22.9	0.0	22.9	0.0	22.9	0.0
1960	22.9	0.0	23.0	0.4	23.0	0.0	23.0	0.0	23.0	0.0	23.0	0.0	23.0	0.0	23.0	0.0	23.0	0.0	23.0	0.0	23.7	3.0	23.7	0.0
1961	23.7	0.0	23.7	0.0	23.7	0.0	23.8	0.4	24.0	0.8	24.0	0.0	24.0	0.0	24.1	0.4	24.1	0.0	24.1	0.0	24.1	0.0	24.1	0.0
1962	24.1	0.0	24.2	0.4	24.4	0.8	24.4	0.0	24.5	0.4	24.5	0.0	24.5	0.0	24.6	0.4	24.6	0.0	24.5	-0.4	24.6	0.4	24.7	0.4
1963	24.8	0.4	24.9	0.4	25.0	0.4	25.0	0.0	25.0	0.0	24.9	-0.4	24.9	0.0	25.0	0.4	25.0	0.0	25.0	0.0	25.1	0.4	25.1	0.0
1964	25.2	0.4	25.3	0.4	25.4	0.4	25.4	0.0	25.5	0.4	25.4	-0.4	25.4	0.0	25.6	0.8	25.5	-0.4	25.6	0.4	25.7	0.4	25.8	0.4
1965	26.0	0.8	26.1	0.4	26.2	0.4	26.2	0.0	26.3	0.4	26.4	0.4	26.5	0.4	26.4	-0.4	26.4	0.0	26.4	0.0	26.5	0.4	26.7	0.8
1966	26.8	0.4	26.9	0.4	27.1	0.7	27.2	0.4	27.4	0.7	27.8	1.5	28.0	0.7	28.2	0.7	28.2	0.0	28.3	0.4	28.5	0.7	28.5	0.0
1967	28.8	1.1	29.0	0.7	29.1	0.3	29.2	0.3	29.3	0.3	29.5	0.7	29.7	0.7	29.9	0.7	30.0	0.3	30.1	0.3	30.1	0.0	30.4	1.0
1968	30.6	0.7	30.6	0.0	30.9	1.0	31.0	0.3	31.1	0.3	31.4	1.0	31.8	1.3	31.8	0.0	32.1	0.9	32.3	0.6	32.4	0.3	32.5	0.3
1969	33.3	2.5	33.4	0.3	33.9	1.5	34.2	0.9	34.4	0.6	34.8	1.2	34.8	0.0	35.1	0.9	35.1	0.0	35.0	-0.3	35.0	0.0	35.3	0.9
1970	35.4	0.3	35.6	0.6	36.1	1.4	36.4	0.8	36.4	0.0	37.1	1.9	37.4	0.8	37.7	0.8	37.9	0.5	38.1	0.5	38.4	0.8	38.8	1.0
1971	39.2	1.0	39.4	0.5	39.8	1.0	39.8	0.0	40.1	0.8	40.1	0.0	40.5	1.0	40.7	0.5	40.7	0.0	40.5	-0.5	40.7	0.5	40.8	0.2
1972	41.0	0.5	41.0	0.0	41.1	0.2	41.2	0.2	41.2	0.0	41.5	0.7	41.5	0.0	41.6	0.2	41.6	0.0	41.8	0.5	42.0	0.5	42.3	0.7
1973	42.5	0.5	42.4	-0.2	42.3	-0.2	42.4	0.2	42.6	0.5	42.7	0.2	42.8	0.2	42.8	0.0	43.1	0.7	43.8	1.6	43.9	0.2	44.1	0.5
1974	44.6	1.1	45.1	1.1	45.7	1.3	46.0	0.7	46.6	1.3	47.3	1.5	47.7	0.8	48.9	2.5	49.4	1.0	49.5	0.2	49.9	0.8	50.2	0.6
1975	51.0	1.6	51.8	1.6	52.5	1.4	52.8	0.6	53.2	0.8	53.5	0.6	53.9	0.7	54.1	0.4	54.8	1.3	55.0	0.4	54.8	-0.4	55.7	1.6
1976	56.8	2.0	57.4	1.1	57.9	0.9	58.1	0.3	58.3	0.3	59.0	1.2	59.5	0.8	59.9	0.7	60.4	0.8	60.4	0.0	61.3	1.5	61.4	0.2
1977	62.3	1.5	62.4	0.2	63.3	1.4	63.8	0.8	64.0	0.3	64.3	0.5	64.7	0.6	64.8	0.2	65.0	0.3	65.3	0.5	65.5	0.3	66.0	0.8
1978	66.5	0.8	66.9	0.6	67.1	0.3	67.2	0.1	67.8	0.9	67.9	0.1	67.8	-0.1	67.9	0.1	68.0	0.1	68.3	0.4	69.1	1.2	69.5	0.6
1979	70.4	1.3	70.9	0.7	71.3	0.6	71.9	0.8	72.0	0.1	72.3	0.4	72.6	0.4	72.8	0.3	73.2	0.5	73.5	0.4	73.8	0.4	74.4	0.8
1980	75.4	1.3	76.6	1.6	77.5	1.2	78.1	0.8	78.4	0.4	78.3	-0.1	78.6	0.4	79.1	0.6	80.4	1.6	80.4	0.0	80.7	0.4	80.9	0.2
1981	82.3	1.7	82.8	0.6	84.9	2.5	85.9	1.2	86.0	0.1	86.5	0.6	87.2	0.8	87.1	-0.1	87.5	0.5	87.8	0.3	88.1	0.3	88.4	0.3
1982	89.3	1.0	90.2	1.0	91.0	0.9	91.1	0.1	91.5	0.4	91.8	0.3	91.5	-0.3	91.9	0.4	92.8	1.0	93.3	0.5	94.0	0.8	94.2	0.2
1983	95.3	1.2	97.1	1.9	97.8	0.7	98.4	0.6	99.0	0.6	99.2	0.2	99.8	0.6	101.1	1.3	101.6	0.5	102.2	0.6	103.1	0.9	103.8	0.7
1984	104.7	0.9	106.1	1.3	106.7	0.6	106.8	0.1	107.4	0.6	107.4	0.0	107.9	0.5	109.2	1.2	109.9	0.6	110.4	0.5	111.1	0.6	111.6	0.5
1985	112.4	0.7	114.1	1.5	114.6	0.4	115.0	0.3	115.8	0.7	116.5	0.6	117.1	0.5	117.2	0.1	117.6	0.3	117.9	0.3	118.2	0.3	117.8	-0.3
1986	120.3	2.1	122.5	1.8	123.8	1.1	124.4	0.5	124.9	0.4	125.2	0.2	126.2	0.8	126.6	0.3	128.0	1.1	128.8	0.6	128.7	-0.1	130.4	1.3
1987	131.1	0.5	133.1	1.5	135.4	1.7	136.7	1.0	136.7	0.0	137.1	0.3	137.6	0.4	138.1	0.4	138.2	0.1	138.5	0.2	139.3	0.6	140.0	0.5
1988	141.1	0.8	142.5	1.0	143.6	0.8	144.1	0.3	145.0	0.6	145.6	0.4	147.0	1.0	146.9	-0.1	148.1	0.8	148.3	0.1	148.8	0.3	149.1	0.2
1989	150.4	0.9	152.1	1.1	154.1	1.3	154.8	0.5	155.6	0.5	157.0	0.9	157.7	0.4	158.6	0.6	159.2	0.4	160.6	0.9	161.5	0.6	162.5	0.6
1990	164.4	1.2	166.9	1.5	169.3	1.4	170.2	0.5	170.5	0.2	171.4	0.5	172.0	0.4	174.2	1.3	174.9	0.4	176.3	0.8	176.7	0.2	177.3	0.3
1991	180.0	1.5	182.1	1.2	183.3	0.7	183.5	0.1	183.2	-0.2	184.8	0.9	186.9	1.1	188.6	0.9	189.2	0.3	189.7	0.3	191.3	0.8	192.3	0.5

[Continued]

New York, NY, NE NJ
Consumer Price Index - Urban Wage Earners
Base 1982-1984 = 100
Medical Care
[Continued]

For 1947-1995. Columns headed % show percentile change in the index from the previous period for which an index is available.

Year	Jan		Feb		Mar		Apr		May		Jun		Jul		Aug		Sep		Oct		Nov		Dec	
	Index	%	Index	%	Index	%	Index	%	Index	%	Index	%	Index	%	Index	%	Index	%	Index	%	Index	%	Index	%
1992	195.2	1.5	196.5	0.7	197.7	0.6	198.6	0.5	199.0	0.2	200.0	0.5	201.2	0.6	201.2	0.0	202.5	0.6	203.5	0.5	203.7	0.1	204.0	0.1
1993	205.6	0.8	205.7	0.0	206.8	0.5	208.1	0.6	208.9	0.4	208.9	0.0	209.6	0.3	210.4	0.4	210.7	0.1	211.1	0.2	211.1	0.0	211.6	0.2
1994	213.7	1.0	214.3	0.3	215.3	0.5	216.0	0.3	216.5	0.2	217.9	0.6	218.3	0.2	219.0	0.3	219.0	0.0	221.2	1.0	221.2	0.0	222.3	0.5
1995	224.2	0.9	226.0	0.8	226.2	0.1	226.3	0.0	226.6	0.1	226.7	0.0	226.9	0.1	228.1	0.5	228.7	0.3	230.1	0.6	230.3	0.1	230.6	0.1

Source: U.S. Department of Labor, Bureau of Labor Statistics, Division of Consumer Prices and Price Indexes. - indicates no data collected for period.

New York, NY, NE NJ
Consumer Price Index - All Urban Consumers
Base 1982-1984 = 100
Entertainment

For 1976-1995. Columns headed % show percentile change in the index from the previous period for which an index is available.

Year	Jan Index	%	Feb Index	%	Mar Index	%	Apr Index	%	May Index	%	Jun Index	%	Jul Index	%	Aug Index	%	Sep Index	%	Oct Index	%	Nov Index	%	Dec Index	%
1976	62.5	-	62.9	0.6	63.0	0.2	63.3	0.5	63.7	0.6	64.8	1.7	65.0	0.3	65.2	0.3	65.7	0.8	66.1	0.6	65.9	-0.3	66.3	0.6
1977	66.5	0.3	67.1	0.9	66.7	-0.6	66.9	0.3	67.3	0.6	69.1	2.7	69.1	0.0	69.3	0.3	70.4	1.6	70.4	0.0	69.4	-1.4	69.5	0.1
1978	69.9	0.6	71.2	1.9	71.9	1.0	72.5	0.8	72.5	0.0	72.1	-0.6	72.9	1.1	73.2	0.4	73.1	-0.1	72.8	-0.4	72.9	0.1	72.4	-0.7
1979	72.9	0.7	74.5	2.2	75.2	0.9	75.4	0.3	75.3	-0.1	75.7	0.5	75.9	0.3	76.4	0.7	76.6	0.3	76.8	0.3	77.2	0.5	77.1	-0.1
1980	78.0	1.2	79.1	1.4	81.3	2.8	81.5	0.2	81.2	-0.4	81.7	0.6	81.3	-0.5	81.9	0.7	82.4	0.6	83.0	0.7	83.0	0.0	83.4	0.5
1981	84.4	1.2	86.0	1.9	86.9	1.0	87.1	0.2	87.2	0.1	87.8	0.7	87.7	-0.1	89.6	2.2	90.5	1.0	91.3	0.9	90.7	-0.7	90.9	0.2
1982	91.0	0.1	92.3	1.4	94.1	2.0	94.1	0.0	94.2	0.1	95.0	0.8	95.5	0.5	98.0	2.6	97.5	-0.5	98.3	0.8	98.0	-0.3	97.9	-0.1
1983	98.3	0.4	99.0	0.7	100.2	1.2	99.7	-0.5	100.1	0.4	100.3	0.2	100.6	0.3	100.5	-0.1	101.1	0.6	101.8	0.7	102.0	0.2	101.6	-0.4
1984	101.8	0.2	102.2	0.4	102.4	0.2	103.1	0.7	102.9	-0.2	104.4	1.5	104.9	0.5	104.5	-0.4	105.4	0.9	105.6	0.2	105.5	-0.1	106.0	0.5
1985	105.9	-0.1	105.9	0.0	106.9	0.9	107.2	0.3	107.8	0.6	108.2	0.4	108.4	0.2	107.8	-0.6	110.4	2.4	111.2	0.7	111.4	0.2	111.8	0.4
1986	113.8	1.8	114.1	0.3	113.4	-0.6	113.6	0.2	114.1	0.4	115.4	1.1	116.1	0.6	116.3	0.2	115.9	-0.3	115.9	0.0	116.4	0.4	116.1	-0.3
1987	117.3	1.0	116.5	-0.7	117.0	0.4	117.9	0.8	117.8	-0.1	118.5	0.6	120.2	1.4	120.4	0.2	120.7	0.2	121.1	0.3	121.4	0.2	121.6	0.2
1988	122.0	0.3	122.0	0.0	120.4	-1.3	122.1	1.4	120.7	-1.1	122.3	1.3	123.6	1.1	124.1	0.4	123.0	-0.9	124.1	0.9	124.4	0.2	125.3	0.7
1989	127.6	1.8	127.0	-0.5	127.4	0.3	128.8	1.1	128.6	-0.2	127.5	-0.9	129.2	1.3	130.2	0.8	131.8	1.2	131.7	-0.1	132.4	0.5	132.3	-0.1
1990	134.2	1.4	134.5	0.2	133.2	-1.0	134.2	0.8	135.8	1.2	134.5	-1.0	136.8	1.7	134.9	-1.4	136.3	1.0	137.1	0.6	137.8	0.5	137.6	-0.1
1991	140.0	1.7	139.6	-0.3	138.6	-0.7	140.0	1.0	140.4	0.3	138.8	-1.1	140.1	0.9	140.5	0.3	142.3	1.3	142.9	0.4	142.6	-0.2	144.0	1.0
1992	144.0	0.0	145.0	0.7	144.3	-0.5	145.9	1.1	146.3	0.3	147.0	0.5	147.3	0.2	147.3	0.0	146.9	-0.3	146.2	-0.5	148.5	1.6	148.5	0.0
1993	149.4	0.6	149.0	-0.3	149.5	0.3	149.9	0.3	149.1	-0.5	149.1	0.0	148.7	-0.3	150.2	1.0	150.5	0.2	151.4	0.6	151.2	-0.1	149.8	-0.9
1994	151.5	1.1	152.9	0.9	154.1	0.8	152.7	-0.9	153.0	0.2	152.9	-0.1	154.0	0.7	152.4	-1.0	153.2	0.5	156.8	2.3	157.2	0.3	156.9	-0.2
1995	157.7	0.5	157.1	-0.4	157.0	-0.1	158.2	0.8	158.6	0.3	157.7	-0.6	157.8	0.1	158.0	0.1	159.3	0.8	160.5	0.8	162.2	1.1	161.6	-0.4

Source: U.S. Department of Labor, Bureau of Labor Statistics, Division of Consumer Prices and Price Indexes. - indicates no data collected for period.

New York, NY, NE NJ
Consumer Price Index - Urban Wage Earners
Base 1982-1984 = 100
Entertainment

For 1976-1995. Columns headed % show percentile change in the index from the previous period for which an index is available.

Year	Jan Index	%	Feb Index	%	Mar Index	%	Apr Index	%	May Index	%	Jun Index	%	Jul Index	%	Aug Index	%	Sep Index	%	Oct Index	%	Nov Index	%	Dec Index	%
1976	63.9	-	64.3	0.6	64.5	0.3	64.8	0.5	65.2	0.6	66.3	1.7	66.4	0.2	66.7	0.5	67.2	0.7	67.6	0.6	67.5	-0.1	67.8	0.4
1977	68.0	0.3	68.6	0.9	68.3	-0.4	68.5	0.3	68.8	0.4	70.7	2.8	70.7	0.0	70.9	0.3	72.0	1.6	72.0	0.0	71.0	-1.4	71.1	0.1
1978	71.3	0.3	73.1	2.5	73.5	0.5	73.4	-0.1	72.7	-1.0	72.4	-0.4	72.9	0.7	73.2	0.4	73.6	0.5	73.5	-0.1	73.7	0.3	74.2	0.7
1979	74.5	0.4	74.9	0.5	76.1	1.6	76.1	0.0	76.1	0.0	76.4	0.4	76.6	0.3	77.0	0.5	77.8	1.0	78.4	0.8	79.2	1.0	78.0	-1.5
1980	79.0	1.3	80.1	1.4	82.6	3.1	82.1	-0.6	81.6	-0.6	83.0	1.7	81.7	-1.6	83.1	1.7	84.6	1.8	83.5	-1.3	84.0	0.6	84.6	0.7
1981	85.8	1.4	88.3	2.9	88.8	0.6	88.9	0.1	88.9	0.0	88.9	0.0	89.3	0.4	89.9	0.7	90.4	0.6	91.2	0.9	91.0	-0.2	91.1	0.1
1982	91.3	0.2	92.5	1.3	94.1	1.7	94.1	0.0	94.3	0.2	95.0	0.7	95.9	0.9	97.9	2.1	97.5	-0.4	98.0	0.5	97.6	-0.4	97.4	-0.2
1983	98.0	0.6	99.0	1.0	100.1	1.1	99.9	-0.2	100.2	0.3	100.2	0.0	100.8	0.6	100.7	-0.1	101.1	0.4	101.8	0.7	102.0	0.2	101.5	-0.5
1984	101.9	0.4	102.2	0.3	102.5	0.3	103.2	0.7	103.1	-0.1	104.5	1.4	104.9	0.4	104.7	-0.2	105.4	0.7	105.5	0.1	105.2	-0.3	106.0	0.8
1985	105.8	-0.2	105.8	0.0	106.4	0.6	107.0	0.6	107.7	0.7	108.5	0.7	108.7	0.2	108.0	-0.6	109.8	1.7	110.7	0.8	110.9	0.2	111.0	0.1
1986	113.1	1.9	113.3	0.2	112.7	-0.5	113.1	0.4	113.8	0.6	115.4	1.4	116.1	0.6	116.5	0.3	115.8	-0.6	115.9	0.1	117.0	0.9	116.7	-0.3
1987	118.2	1.3	117.8	-0.3	118.1	0.3	119.1	0.8	118.7	-0.3	119.5	0.7	121.3	1.5	121.4	0.1	121.8	0.3	122.3	0.4	122.8	0.4	123.0	0.2
1988	123.0	0.0	123.1	0.1	121.3	-1.5	123.5	1.8	121.3	-1.8	122.9	1.3	124.4	1.2	124.6	0.2	124.0	-0.5	125.5	1.2	125.9	0.3	126.7	0.6
1989	129.1	1.9	127.9	-0.9	128.4	0.4	129.9	1.2	129.7	-0.2	128.2	-1.2	129.6	1.1	130.3	0.5	132.4	1.6	132.3	-0.1	133.1	0.6	133.0	-0.1
1990	134.7	1.3	134.9	0.1	133.5	-1.0	134.7	0.9	136.6	1.4	135.2	-1.0	137.5	1.7	135.0	-1.8	136.9	1.4	137.8	0.7	138.8	0.7	138.6	-0.1
1991	141.0	1.7	140.4	-0.4	139.4	-0.7	140.8	1.0	140.6	-0.1	138.6	-1.4	140.1	1.1	140.5	0.3	142.7	1.6	143.2	0.4	142.8	-0.3	145.0	1.5
1992	144.6	-0.3	145.4	0.6	144.6	-0.6	146.4	1.2	146.5	0.1	147.1	0.4	147.3	0.1	147.3	0.0	146.5	-0.5	145.4	-0.8	148.8	2.3	148.7	-0.1
1993	149.9	0.8	149.3	-0.4	149.8	0.3	149.5	-0.2	148.9	-0.4	148.7	-0.1	148.0	-0.5	149.9	1.3	150.2	0.2	150.8	0.4	150.5	-0.2	149.0	-1.0
1994	150.8	1.2	151.1	0.2	153.0	1.3	152.5	-0.3	152.7	0.1	152.6	-0.1	153.8	0.8	152.2	-1.0	153.1	0.6	156.4	2.2	157.0	0.4	156.6	-0.3
1995	157.6	0.6	156.7	-0.6	156.6	-0.1	157.5	0.6	158.2	0.4	157.2	-0.6	157.3	0.1	157.3	0.0	158.5	0.8	159.5	0.6	160.9	0.9	160.2	-0.4

Source: U.S. Department of Labor, Bureau of Labor Statistics, Division of Consumer Prices and Price Indexes. - indicates no data collected for period.

New York, NY, NE NJ
Consumer Price Index - All Urban Consumers
Base 1982-1984 = 100
Other Goods and Services

For 1976-1995. Columns headed % show percentile change in the index from the previous period for which an index is available.

Year	Jan Index	%	Feb Index	%	Mar Index	%	Apr Index	%	May Index	%	Jun Index	%	Jul Index	%	Aug Index	%	Sep Index	%	Oct Index	%	Nov Index	%	Dec Index	%
1976	56.5	-	57.3	1.4	57.7	0.7	57.9	0.3	57.9	0.0	58.2	0.5	58.4	0.3	59.0	1.0	59.6	1.0	59.8	0.3	60.1	0.5	60.1	0.0
1977	61.1	1.7	61.5	0.7	61.6	0.2	61.5	-0.2	61.7	0.3	61.9	0.3	62.0	0.2	62.1	0.2	62.7	1.0	62.9	0.3	63.9	1.6	64.0	0.2
1978	64.1	0.2	64.2	0.2	64.4	0.3	64.2	-0.3	64.2	0.0	64.4	0.3	64.9	0.8	65.0	0.2	66.4	2.2	66.4	0.0	66.7	0.5	66.7	0.0
1979	67.0	0.4	67.2	0.3	67.5	0.4	67.6	0.1	67.8	0.3	68.0	0.3	68.0	0.0	68.5	0.7	70.2	2.5	70.5	0.4	70.6	0.1	71.1	0.7
1980	71.7	0.8	72.2	0.7	72.1	-0.1	72.3	0.3	72.8	0.7	73.4	0.8	73.7	0.4	73.9	0.3	76.0	2.8	76.6	0.8	76.8	0.3	77.4	0.8
1981	78.1	0.9	78.2	0.1	78.3	0.1	78.5	0.3	79.1	0.8	79.1	0.0	79.7	0.8	79.9	0.3	84.4	5.6	84.9	0.6	85.1	0.2	85.1	0.0
1982	85.6	0.6	86.1	0.6	86.5	0.5	87.0	0.6	87.3	0.3	87.3	0.0	88.1	0.9	89.0	1.0	93.4	4.9	94.5	1.2	95.4	1.0	96.3	0.9
1983	97.1	0.8	97.3	0.2	97.6	0.3	98.9	1.3	98.7	-0.2	99.2	0.5	100.7	1.5	101.2	0.5	105.0	3.8	105.9	0.9	106.6	0.7	106.6	0.0
1984	107.0	0.4	107.1	0.1	107.0	-0.1	107.1	0.1	107.5	0.4	107.6	0.1	107.9	0.3	108.2	0.3	111.7	3.2	112.0	0.3	112.7	0.6	112.8	0.1
1985	113.6	0.7	113.7	0.1	113.9	0.2	114.3	0.4	114.4	0.1	114.6	0.2	115.2	0.5	115.4	0.2	119.0	3.1	119.4	0.3	119.7	0.3	120.3	0.5
1986	121.4	0.9	121.3	-0.1	122.0	0.6	121.9	-0.1	121.8	-0.1	121.4	-0.3	123.0	1.3	122.7	-0.2	125.9	2.6	126.9	0.8	127.3	0.3	126.9	-0.3
1987	127.9	0.8	127.9	0.0	128.6	0.5	128.8	0.2	128.9	0.1	129.4	0.4	130.1	0.5	130.0	-0.1	133.9	3.0	134.7	0.6	134.8	0.1	135.0	0.1
1988	136.6	1.2	136.9	0.2	137.5	0.4	137.6	0.1	137.4	-0.1	137.5	0.1	138.2	0.5	138.9	0.5	142.9	2.9	143.1	0.1	143.5	0.3	143.6	0.1
1989	146.3	1.9	146.6	0.2	147.0	0.3	146.9	-0.1	149.3	1.6	150.9	1.1	151.2	0.2	153.1	1.3	157.7	3.0	157.3	-0.3	157.7	0.3	158.2	0.3
1990	159.4	0.8	159.8	0.3	160.5	0.4	160.6	0.1	161.3	0.4	162.0	0.4	164.4	1.5	165.2	0.5	168.4	1.9	168.3	-0.1	168.5	0.1	169.2	0.4
1991	171.4	1.3	171.9	0.3	172.0	0.1	173.3	0.8	174.3	0.6	174.7	0.2	175.4	0.4	177.4	1.1	183.2	3.3	183.4	0.1	184.7	0.7	185.1	0.2
1992	187.3	1.2	187.6	0.2	187.6	0.0	187.9	0.2	188.6	0.4	189.0	0.2	189.5	0.3	192.5	1.6	195.4	1.5	195.3	-0.1	195.3	0.0	195.8	0.3
1993	197.4	0.8	198.3	0.5	198.8	0.3	199.3	0.3	199.1	-0.1	200.1	0.5	200.8	0.3	201.7	0.4	202.5	0.4	201.1	-0.7	201.0	-0.0	201.2	0.1
1994	202.0	0.4	202.0	0.0	201.9	-0.0	202.5	0.3	202.8	0.1	204.5	0.8	203.9	-0.3	206.6	1.3	207.5	0.4	208.0	0.2	208.5	0.2	208.4	-0.0
1995	208.8	0.2	210.3	0.7	209.9	-0.2	210.2	0.1	211.0	0.4	211.8	0.4	212.5	0.3	215.6	1.5	217.3	0.8	217.9	0.3	218.2	0.1	218.2	0.0

Source: U.S. Department of Labor, Bureau of Labor Statistics, Division of Consumer Prices and Price Indexes. - indicates no data collected for period.

New York, NY, NE NJ
Consumer Price Index - Urban Wage Earners
Base 1982-1984 = 100
Other Goods and Services

For 1976-1995. Columns headed % show percentile change in the index from the previous period for which an index is available.

Year	Jan Index	%	Feb Index	%	Mar Index	%	Apr Index	%	May Index	%	Jun Index	%	Jul Index	%	Aug Index	%	Sep Index	%	Oct Index	%	Nov Index	%	Dec Index	%
1976	57.2	-	58.0	1.4	58.4	0.7	58.6	0.3	58.6	0.0	58.9	0.5	59.1	0.3	59.7	1.0	60.3	1.0	60.5	0.3	60.8	0.5	60.9	0.2
1977	61.8	1.5	62.3	0.8	62.3	0.0	62.2	-0.2	62.4	0.3	62.6	0.3	62.7	0.2	62.9	0.3	63.4	0.8	63.7	0.5	64.7	1.6	64.7	0.0
1978	64.8	0.2	65.1	0.5	65.2	0.2	65.1	-0.2	65.2	0.2	65.7	0.8	66.3	0.9	66.1	-0.3	67.2	1.7	67.1	-0.1	67.5	0.6	67.2	-0.4
1979	67.8	0.9	68.3	0.7	68.6	0.4	68.6	0.0	68.6	0.0	68.7	0.1	69.2	0.7	70.0	1.2	70.9	1.3	71.3	0.6	71.5	0.3	71.9	0.6
1980	72.6	1.0	73.2	0.8	73.0	-0.3	73.3	0.4	73.8	0.7	74.1	0.4	74.4	0.4	74.9	0.7	76.5	2.1	76.9	0.5	76.9	0.0	77.5	0.8
1981	77.6	0.1	78.2	0.8	78.4	0.3	78.9	0.6	79.6	0.9	79.6	0.0	80.3	0.9	80.5	0.2	83.7	4.0	84.2	0.6	84.8	0.7	84.9	0.1
1982	85.4	0.6	86.1	0.8	86.6	0.6	87.1	0.6	87.4	0.3	87.5	0.1	88.5	1.1	89.5	1.1	92.6	3.5	94.1	1.6	95.2	1.2	96.4	1.3
1983	97.4	1.0	97.6	0.2	97.9	0.3	99.6	1.7	99.2	-0.4	99.9	0.7	101.7	1.8	102.4	0.7	104.8	2.3	105.5	0.7	106.4	0.9	106.5	0.1
1984	106.9	0.4	107.1	0.2	106.8	-0.3	107.0	0.2	107.4	0.4	107.6	0.2	108.0	0.4	108.3	0.3	110.8	2.3	111.0	0.2	111.8	0.7	111.9	0.1
1985	112.8	0.8	113.0	0.2	113.2	0.2	113.6	0.4	113.7	0.1	114.0	0.3	114.9	0.8	115.1	0.2	117.9	2.4	118.3	0.3	118.6	0.3	119.4	0.7
1986	120.8	1.2	120.7	-0.1	121.4	0.6	121.4	0.0	121.2	-0.2	120.7	-0.4	122.6	1.6	122.4	-0.2	124.4	1.6	125.4	0.8	126.0	0.5	125.5	-0.4
1987	126.7	1.0	126.8	0.1	127.2	0.3	127.4	0.2	127.5	0.1	127.9	0.3	128.6	0.5	128.7	0.1	132.4	2.9	133.2	0.6	133.4	0.2	133.6	0.1
1988	135.1	1.1	135.3	0.1	135.9	0.4	136.0	0.1	136.0	0.0	136.0	0.0	136.7	0.5	137.4	0.5	141.2	2.8	141.4	0.1	141.8	0.3	141.9	0.1
1989	144.8	2.0	145.2	0.3	145.6	0.3	145.6	0.0	148.4	1.9	150.0	1.1	150.3	0.2	152.0	1.1	156.4	2.9	156.2	-0.1	156.4	0.1	157.1	0.4
1990	158.3	0.8	158.6	0.2	159.3	0.4	159.4	0.1	160.0	0.4	160.9	0.6	164.6	2.3	165.3	0.4	168.8	2.1	168.6	-0.1	169.1	0.3	169.9	0.5
1991	171.6	1.0	171.9	0.2	172.2	0.2	173.5	0.8	174.6	0.6	175.3	0.4	175.8	0.3	178.2	1.4	183.1	2.7	183.7	0.3	184.8	0.6	185.2	0.2
1992	187.3	1.1	187.5	0.1	187.4	-0.1	188.0	0.3	188.7	0.4	189.2	0.3	189.6	0.2	193.1	1.8	195.0	1.0	195.1	0.1	195.2	0.1	195.6	0.2
1993	197.4	0.9	198.3	0.5	198.9	0.3	199.4	0.3	199.3	-0.1	200.6	0.7	201.4	0.4	202.4	0.5	203.4	0.5	201.7	-0.8	201.3	-0.2	200.8	-0.2
1994	201.9	0.5	201.9	0.0	202.0	0.0	202.5	0.2	202.7	0.1	204.7	1.0	203.8	-0.4	206.8	1.5	207.5	0.3	207.9	0.2	208.1	0.1	208.0	-0.0
1995	208.3	0.1	209.8	0.7	209.4	-0.2	209.4	0.0	210.3	0.4	211.4	0.5	211.9	0.2	215.5	1.7	217.3	0.8	217.8	0.2	218.0	0.1	217.7	-0.1

Source: U.S. Department of Labor, Bureau of Labor Statistics, Division of Consumer Prices and Price Indexes. - indicates no data collected for period.

Philadelphia, PA-NJ
Consumer Price Index - All Urban Consumers
Base 1982-1984 = 100
Annual Averages

For 1914-1995. Columns headed % show percentile change in the index from the previous period for which an index is available.

Year	All Items		Food & Beverage		Housing		Apparel & Upkeep		Trans- portation		Medical Care		Entertain- ment		Other Goods & Services	
	Index	%	Index	%	Index	%	Index	%	Index	%	Index	%	Index	%	Index	%
1914	-	-	-	-	-	-	-	-	-	-	-	-	-	-	-	-
1915	10.1	-	-	-	-	-	-	-	-	-	-	-	-	-	-	-
1916	10.8	6.9	-	-	-	-	-	-	-	-	-	-	-	-	-	-
1917	13.1	21.3	-	-	-	-	-	-	-	-	-	-	-	-	-	-
1918	15.5	18.3	-	-	-	-	-	-	-	-	-	-	-	-	-	-
1919	17.9	15.5	-	-	-	-	-	-	-	-	-	-	-	-	-	-
1920	20.5	14.5	-	-	-	-	-	-	-	-	-	-	-	-	-	-
1921	18.2	-11.2	-	-	-	-	-	-	-	-	-	-	-	-	-	-
1922	17.2	-5.5	-	-	-	-	-	-	-	-	-	-	-	-	-	-
1923	17.6	2.3	-	-	-	-	-	-	-	-	-	-	-	-	-	-
1924	17.7	0.6	-	-	-	-	-	-	-	-	-	-	-	-	-	-
1925	18.4	4.0	-	-	-	-	-	-	-	-	-	-	-	-	-	-
1926	18.7	1.6	-	-	-	-	-	-	-	-	-	-	-	-	-	-
1927	18.3	-2.1	-	-	-	-	-	-	-	-	-	-	-	-	-	-
1928	18.0	-1.6	-	-	-	-	-	-	-	-	-	-	-	-	-	-
1929	17.8	-1.1	-	-	-	-	-	-	-	-	-	-	-	-	-	-
1930	17.4	-2.2	-	-	-	-	-	-	-	-	-	-	-	-	-	-
1931	15.9	-8.6	-	-	-	-	-	-	-	-	-	-	-	-	-	-
1932	14.2	-10.7	-	-	-	-	-	-	-	-	-	-	-	-	-	-
1933	13.5	-4.9	-	-	-	-	-	-	-	-	-	-	-	-	-	-
1934	14.2	5.2	-	-	-	-	-	-	-	-	-	-	-	-	-	-
1935	14.3	0.7	-	-	-	-	-	-	-	-	-	-	-	-	-	-
1936	14.5	1.4	-	-	-	-	-	-	-	-	-	-	-	-	-	-
1937	14.9	2.8	-	-	-	-	-	-	-	-	-	-	-	-	-	-
1938	14.5	-2.7	-	-	-	-	-	-	-	-	-	-	-	-	-	-
1939	14.3	-1.4	-	-	-	-	-	-	-	-	-	-	-	-	-	-
1940	14.3	0.0	-	-	-	-	-	-	-	-	-	-	-	-	-	-
1941	15.0	4.9	-	-	-	-	-	-	-	-	-	-	-	-	-	-
1942	16.7	11.3	-	-	-	-	-	-	-	-	-	-	-	-	-	-
1943	17.8	6.6	-	-	-	-	-	-	-	-	-	-	-	-	-	-
1944	18.0	1.1	-	-	-	-	-	-	-	-	-	-	-	-	-	-
1945	18.5	2.8	-	-	-	-	-	-	-	-	-	-	-	-	-	-
1946	20.1	8.6	-	-	-	-	-	-	-	-	-	-	-	-	-	-
1947	23.0	14.4	-	-	-	-	-	-	16.8	-	12.4	-	-	-	-	-
1948	24.8	7.8	-	-	-	-	-	-	18.4	9.5	13.0	4.8	-	-	-	-
1949	24.5	-1.2	-	-	-	-	-	-	19.5	6.0	13.4	3.1	-	-	-	-
1950	24.7	0.8	-	-	-	-	-	-	19.5	0.0	13.6	1.5	-	-	-	-
1951	27.0	9.3	-	-	-	-	-	-	23.2	19.0	14.2	4.4	-	-	-	-
1952	27.5	1.9	-	-	-	-	-	-	24.1	3.9	15.0	5.6	-	-	-	-
1953	27.6	0.4	-	-	-	-	44.3	-	24.5	1.7	15.6	4.0	-	-	-	-
1954	27.9	1.1	-	-	-	-	44.6	0.7	25.1	2.4	16.4	5.1	-	-	-	-
1955	27.9	0.0	-	-	-	-	44.4	-0.4	24.9	-0.8	17.5	6.7	-	-	-	-
1956	28.2	1.1	-	-	-	-	44.8	0.9	24.9	0.0	17.8	1.7	-	-	-	-
1957	29.1	3.2	-	-	-	-	46.0	2.7	25.8	3.6	18.2	2.2	-	-	-	-
1958	29.7	2.1	-	-	-	-	45.6	-0.9	26.6	3.1	18.9	3.8	-	-	-	-

[Continued]

Philadelphia, PA-NJ
Consumer Price Index - All Urban Consumers
Base 1982-1984 = 100
Annual Averages
[Continued]

For 1914-1995. Columns headed % show percentile change in the index from the previous period for which an index is available.

Year	All Items		Food & Beverage		Housing		Apparel & Upkeep		Trans-portation		Medical Care		Entertain-ment		Other Goods & Services	
	Index	%	Index	%	Index	%	Index	%	Index	%	Index	%	Index	%	Index	%
1959	30.0	1.0	-	-	-	-	46.3	1.5	28.0	5.3	20.0	5.8	-	-	-	-
1960	30.6	2.0	-	-	-	-	48.0	3.7	28.3	1.1	20.8	4.0	-	-	-	-
1961	30.9	1.0	-	-	-	-	49.1	2.3	29.0	2.5	21.7	4.3	-	-	-	-
1962	31.2	1.0	-	-	-	-	49.6	1.0	29.2	0.7	22.6	4.1	-	-	-	-
1963	31.8	1.9	-	-	-	-	50.2	1.2	29.9	2.4	23.1	2.2	-	-	-	-
1964	32.3	1.6	-	-	-	-	50.3	0.2	30.5	2.0	23.4	1.3	-	-	-	-
1965	32.8	1.5	-	-	-	-	51.0	1.4	31.3	2.6	24.0	2.6	-	-	-	-
1966	33.7	2.7	-	-	-	-	52.9	3.7	31.8	1.6	25.1	4.6	-	-	-	-
1967	34.6	2.7	-	-	-	-	55.3	4.5	32.6	2.5	26.7	6.4	-	-	-	-
1968	36.3	4.9	-	-	-	-	58.5	5.8	34.3	5.2	28.9	8.2	-	-	-	-
1969	38.2	5.2	-	-	-	-	61.5	5.1	35.9	4.7	31.4	8.7	-	-	-	-
1970	40.8	6.8	-	-	-	-	64.1	4.2	37.9	5.6	34.0	8.3	-	-	-	-
1971	42.7	4.7	-	-	-	-	65.9	2.8	40.2	6.1	36.7	7.9	-	-	-	-
1972	44.0	3.0	-	-	-	-	66.4	0.8	40.8	1.5	38.0	3.5	-	-	-	-
1973	46.9	6.6	-	-	-	-	69.0	3.9	41.6	2.0	39.8	4.7	-	-	-	-
1974	52.5	11.9	-	-	-	-	73.1	5.9	45.9	10.3	43.4	9.0	-	-	-	-
1975	56.8	8.2	-	-	-	-	75.2	2.9	49.8	8.5	49.3	13.6	-	-	-	-
1976	59.7	5.1	62.2	-	59.1	-	77.1	2.5	54.0	8.4	53.7	8.9	68.8	-	56.0	-
1977	63.5	6.4	66.0	6.1	62.7	6.1	79.1	2.6	59.3	9.8	59.0	9.9	71.6	4.1	59.2	5.7
1978	67.3	6.0	72.4	9.7	65.7	4.8	80.9	2.3	62.5	5.4	63.2	7.1	74.0	3.4	62.4	5.4
1979	73.9	9.8	79.5	9.8	71.9	9.4	86.2	6.6	70.9	13.4	68.4	8.2	81.1	9.6	67.0	7.4
1980	83.6	13.1	86.0	8.2	83.5	16.1	94.4	9.5	83.6	17.9	75.4	10.2	84.0	3.6	73.2	9.3
1981	92.1	10.2	92.5	7.6	93.7	12.2	95.9	1.6	93.2	11.5	83.9	11.3	92.1	9.6	79.5	8.6
1982	96.6	4.9	97.7	5.6	97.6	4.2	98.8	3.0	96.1	3.1	91.7	9.3	96.4	4.7	89.5	12.6
1983	99.4	2.9	100.0	2.4	98.4	0.8	100.3	1.5	99.4	3.4	100.6	9.7	100.5	4.3	101.0	12.8
1984	104.1	4.7	102.4	2.4	104.0	5.7	100.9	0.6	104.5	5.1	107.7	7.1	103.1	2.6	109.5	8.4
1985	108.8	4.5	105.0	2.5	109.1	4.9	101.4	0.5	109.4	4.7	119.1	10.6	105.2	2.0	117.1	6.9
1986	111.5	2.5	107.8	2.7	112.9	3.5	101.3	-0.1	107.1	-2.1	126.6	6.3	109.3	3.9	126.5	8.0
1987	116.8	4.8	112.1	4.0	118.4	4.9	107.7	6.3	111.5	4.1	133.0	5.1	112.2	2.7	135.9	7.4
1988	122.4	4.8	116.0	3.5	124.8	5.4	109.9	2.0	115.6	3.7	142.2	6.9	120.8	7.7	145.1	6.8
1989	128.3	4.8	124.2	7.1	130.8	4.8	99.4	-9.6	121.5	5.1	155.3	9.2	128.6	6.5	155.4	7.1
1990	135.8	5.8	131.2	5.6	138.7	6.0	101.4	2.0	127.7	5.1	167.4	7.8	133.5	3.8	171.9	10.6
1991	142.2	4.7	135.4	3.2	145.6	5.0	103.7	2.3	132.3	3.6	183.5	9.6	138.0	3.4	185.5	7.9
1992	146.6	3.1	137.6	1.6	149.6	2.7	106.5	2.7	136.1	2.9	196.6	7.1	144.4	4.6	195.8	5.6
1993	150.2	2.5	139.7	1.5	151.9	1.5	106.0	-0.5	139.5	2.5	211.6	7.6	147.5	2.1	210.7	7.6
1994	154.6	2.9	142.7	2.1	155.1	2.1	105.8	-0.2	144.0	3.2	223.9	5.8	160.3	8.7	222.2	5.5
1995	158.7	2.7	148.8	4.3	158.4	2.1	102.1	-3.5	148.7	3.3	232.5	3.8	166.7	4.0	227.1	2.2

Source: U.S. Department of Labor, Bureau of Labor Statistics, Division of Consumer Prices and Price Indexes. - indicates no data collected for period.

Philadelphia, PA-NJ
Consumer Price Index - Urban Wage Earners
Base 1982-1984 = 100
Annual Averages

For 1914-1995. Columns headed % show percentile change in the index from the previous period for which an index is available.

Year	All Items		Food & Beverage		Housing		Apparel & Upkeep		Trans-portation		Medical Care		Entertain-ment		Other Goods & Services	
	Index	%	Index	%	Index	%	Index	%	Index	%	Index	%	Index	%	Index	%
1914	-	-	-	-	-	-	-	-	-	-	-	-	-	-	-	-
1915	10.0	-	-	-	-	-	-	-	-	-	-	-	-	-	-	-
1916	10.8	8.0	-	-	-	-	-	-	-	-	-	-	-	-	-	-
1917	13.0	20.4	-	-	-	-	-	-	-	-	-	-	-	-	-	-
1918	15.5	19.2	-	-	-	-	-	-	-	-	-	-	-	-	-	-
1919	17.8	14.8	-	-	-	-	-	-	-	-	-	-	-	-	-	-
1920	20.3	14.0	-	-	-	-	-	-	-	-	-	-	-	-	-	-
1921	18.1	-10.8	-	-	-	-	-	-	-	-	-	-	-	-	-	-
1922	17.1	-5.5	-	-	-	-	-	-	-	-	-	-	-	-	-	-
1923	17.5	2.3	-	-	-	-	-	-	-	-	-	-	-	-	-	-
1924	17.6	0.6	-	-	-	-	-	-	-	-	-	-	-	-	-	-
1925	18.3	4.0	-	-	-	-	-	-	-	-	-	-	-	-	-	-
1926	18.6	1.6	-	-	-	-	-	-	-	-	-	-	-	-	-	-
1927	18.2	-2.2	-	-	-	-	-	-	-	-	-	-	-	-	-	-
1928	17.9	-1.6	-	-	-	-	-	-	-	-	-	-	-	-	-	-
1929	17.7	-1.1	-	-	-	-	-	-	-	-	-	-	-	-	-	-
1930	17.3	-2.3	-	-	-	-	-	-	-	-	-	-	-	-	-	-
1931	15.8	-8.7	-	-	-	-	-	-	-	-	-	-	-	-	-	-
1932	14.1	-10.8	-	-	-	-	-	-	-	-	-	-	-	-	-	-
1933	13.4	-5.0	-	-	-	-	-	-	-	-	-	-	-	-	-	-
1934	14.1	5.2	-	-	-	-	-	-	-	-	-	-	-	-	-	-
1935	14.3	1.4	-	-	-	-	-	-	-	-	-	-	-	-	-	-
1936	14.5	1.4	-	-	-	-	-	-	-	-	-	-	-	-	-	-
1937	14.8	2.1	-	-	-	-	-	-	-	-	-	-	-	-	-	-
1938	14.5	-2.0	-	-	-	-	-	-	-	-	-	-	-	-	-	-
1939	14.2	-2.1	-	-	-	-	-	-	-	-	-	-	-	-	-	-
1940	14.3	0.7	-	-	-	-	-	-	-	-	-	-	-	-	-	-
1941	14.9	4.2	-	-	-	-	-	-	-	-	-	-	-	-	-	-
1942	16.6	11.4	-	-	-	-	-	-	-	-	-	-	-	-	-	-
1943	17.7	6.6	-	-	-	-	-	-	-	-	-	-	-	-	-	-
1944	17.9	1.1	-	-	-	-	-	-	-	-	-	-	-	-	-	-
1945	18.4	2.8	-	-	-	-	-	-	-	-	-	-	-	-	-	-
1946	20.0	8.7	-	-	-	-	-	-	-	-	-	-	-	-	-	-
1947	22.9	14.5	-	-	-	-	-	-	16.3	-	11.7	-	-	-	-	-
1948	24.7	7.9	-	-	-	-	-	-	17.9	9.8	12.3	5.1	-	-	-	-
1949	24.4	-1.2	-	-	-	-	-	-	19.0	6.1	12.6	2.4	-	-	-	-
1950	24.5	0.4	-	-	-	-	-	-	19.0	0.0	12.8	1.6	-	-	-	-
1951	26.8	9.4	-	-	-	-	-	-	22.5	18.4	13.4	4.7	-	-	-	-
1952	27.4	2.2	-	-	-	-	-	-	23.4	4.0	14.1	5.2	-	-	-	-
1953	27.5	0.4	-	-	-	-	51.1	-	23.8	1.7	14.7	4.3	-	-	-	-
1954	27.8	1.1	-	-	-	-	51.5	0.8	24.3	2.1	15.5	5.4	-	-	-	-
1955	27.7	-0.4	-	-	-	-	51.2	-0.6	24.1	-0.8	16.5	6.5	-	-	-	-
1956	28.1	1.4	-	-	-	-	51.7	1.0	24.2	0.4	16.8	1.8	-	-	-	-
1957	29.0	3.2	-	-	-	-	53.0	2.5	25.0	3.3	17.1	1.8	-	-	-	-
1958	29.5	1.7	-	-	-	-	52.7	-0.6	25.8	3.2	17.8	4.1	-	-	-	-

[Continued]

Philadelphia, PA-NJ
Consumer Price Index - Urban Wage Earners
Base 1982-1984 = 100
Annual Averages
[Continued]

For 1914-1995. Columns headed % show percentile change in the index from the previous period for which an index is available.

Year	All Items		Food & Beverage		Housing		Apparel & Upkeep		Trans- portation		Medical Care		Entertain- ment		Other Goods & Services	
	Index	%	Index	%	Index	%	Index	%	Index	%	Index	%	Index	%	Index	%
1959	29.9	1.4	-	-	-	-	53.4	1.3	27.2	5.4	18.9	6.2	-	-	-	-
1960	30.4	1.7	-	-	-	-	55.4	3.7	27.4	0.7	19.6	3.7	-	-	-	-
1961	30.8	1.3	-	-	-	-	56.7	2.3	28.2	2.9	20.5	4.6	-	-	-	-
1962	31.0	0.6	-	-	-	-	57.2	0.9	28.4	0.7	21.3	3.9	-	-	-	-
1963	31.6	1.9	-	-	-	-	58.0	1.4	29.0	2.1	21.8	2.3	-	-	-	-
1964	32.1	1.6	-	-	-	-	58.1	0.2	29.6	2.1	22.1	1.4	-	-	-	-
1965	32.6	1.6	-	-	-	-	58.9	1.4	30.4	2.7	22.7	2.7	-	-	-	-
1966	33.5	2.8	-	-	-	-	61.0	3.6	30.9	1.6	23.7	4.4	-	-	-	-
1967	34.4	2.7	-	-	-	-	63.8	4.6	31.7	2.6	25.2	6.3	-	-	-	-
1968	36.1	4.9	-	-	-	-	67.5	5.8	33.3	5.0	27.3	8.3	-	-	-	-
1969	38.0	5.3	-	-	-	-	70.9	5.0	34.9	4.8	29.6	8.4	-	-	-	-
1970	40.6	6.8	-	-	-	-	73.9	4.2	36.8	5.4	32.1	8.4	-	-	-	-
1971	42.5	4.7	-	-	-	-	76.1	3.0	39.0	6.0	34.7	8.1	-	-	-	-
1972	43.7	2.8	-	-	-	-	76.6	0.7	39.6	1.5	35.9	3.5	-	-	-	-
1973	46.6	6.6	-	-	-	-	79.6	3.9	40.4	2.0	37.6	4.7	-	-	-	-
1974	52.2	12.0	-	-	-	-	84.3	5.9	44.6	10.4	41.0	9.0	-	-	-	-
1975	56.5	8.2	-	-	-	-	86.8	3.0	48.4	8.5	46.5	13.4	-	-	-	-
1976	59.4	5.1	60.5	-	58.9	-	89.0	2.5	52.4	8.3	50.7	9.0	70.9	-	58.2	-
1977	63.2	6.4	64.3	6.3	62.6	6.3	91.3	2.6	57.6	9.9	55.7	9.9	73.8	4.1	61.5	5.7
1978	67.1	6.2	70.8	10.1	65.5	4.6	90.5	-0.9	61.3	6.4	60.2	8.1	77.3	4.7	64.7	5.2
1979	73.9	10.1	79.2	11.9	71.5	9.2	89.4	-1.2	70.1	14.4	66.6	10.6	86.3	11.6	68.4	5.7
1980	83.5	13.0	86.8	9.6	82.4	15.2	94.4	5.6	83.2	18.7	76.0	14.1	86.4	0.1	73.9	8.0
1981	91.9	10.1	93.2	7.4	92.1	11.8	96.3	2.0	93.6	12.5	83.9	10.4	94.1	8.9	80.4	8.8
1982	95.8	4.2	97.7	4.8	95.6	3.8	98.8	2.6	96.2	2.8	91.6	9.2	96.5	2.6	89.4	11.2
1983	99.7	4.1	99.9	2.3	99.3	3.9	100.2	1.4	99.4	3.3	100.6	9.8	100.6	4.2	101.2	13.2
1984	104.5	4.8	102.4	2.5	105.2	5.9	100.9	0.7	104.4	5.0	107.9	7.3	102.9	2.3	109.4	8.1
1985	109.2	4.5	105.1	2.6	110.8	5.3	100.5	-0.4	109.2	4.6	119.0	10.3	104.4	1.5	116.8	6.8
1986	111.5	2.1	107.9	2.7	114.5	3.3	99.7	-0.8	106.0	-2.9	126.3	6.1	108.2	3.6	125.9	7.8
1987	116.7	4.7	112.4	4.2	120.0	4.8	104.4	4.7	110.8	4.5	132.7	5.1	110.6	2.2	134.7	7.0
1988	122.2	4.7	116.5	3.6	126.3	5.2	106.0	1.5	115.1	3.9	141.5	6.6	118.8	7.4	144.3	7.1
1989	128.3	5.0	125.1	7.4	133.0	5.3	94.5	-10.8	121.6	5.6	154.0	8.8	126.1	6.1	153.8	6.6
1990	136.1	6.1	132.3	5.8	140.7	5.8	97.6	3.3	128.4	5.6	165.9	7.7	130.2	3.3	170.7	11.0
1991	142.2	4.5	136.5	3.2	147.5	4.8	99.0	1.4	132.8	3.4	180.9	9.0	134.7	3.5	184.3	8.0
1992	146.4	3.0	138.7	1.6	151.3	2.6	103.3	4.3	136.1	2.5	193.9	7.2	140.2	4.1	194.3	5.4
1993	150.1	2.5	140.9	1.6	153.8	1.7	104.7	1.4	139.2	2.3	208.8	7.7	142.6	1.7	208.5	7.3
1994	154.2	2.7	143.9	2.1	156.9	2.0	101.9	-2.7	144.0	3.4	220.5	5.6	155.7	9.2	218.2	4.7
1995	158.3	2.7	150.0	4.2	160.3	2.2	98.1	-3.7	149.5	3.8	228.5	3.6	162.2	4.2	222.2	1.8

Source: U.S. Department of Labor, Bureau of Labor Statistics, Division of Consumer Prices and Price Indexes. - indicates no data collected for period.

Philadelphia, PA-NJ
Consumer Price Index - All Urban Consumers
Base 1982-1984 = 100
All Items

For 1914-1995. Columns headed % show percentile change in the index from the previous period for which an index is available.

Year	Jan Index	%	Feb Index	%	Mar Index	%	Apr Index	%	May Index	%	Jun Index	%	Jul Index	%	Aug Index	%	Sep Index	%	Oct Index	%	Nov Index	%	Dec Index	%
1914	-	-	-	-	-	-	-	-	-	-	-	-	-	-	-	-	-	-	-	-	-	-	10.2	-
1915	-	-	-	-	-	-	-	-	-	-	-	-	-	-	-	-	-	-	-	-	-	-	10.3	1.0
1916	-	-	-	-	-	-	-	-	-	-	-	-	-	-	-	-	-	-	-	-	-	-	11.6	12.6
1917	-	-	-	-	-	-	-	-	-	-	-	-	-	-	-	-	-	-	-	-	-	-	14.1	21.6
1918	-	-	-	-	-	-	-	-	-	-	-	-	-	-	-	-	-	-	-	-	-	-	17.0	20.6
1919	-	-	-	-	-	-	-	-	-	-	17.5	2.9	-	-	-	-	-	-	-	-	-	-	19.2	9.7
1920	-	-	-	-	-	-	-	-	-	-	21.3	10.9	-	-	-	-	-	-	-	-	-	-	19.9	-6.6
1921	-	-	-	-	-	-	-	-	18.1	-9.0	-	-	-	-	-	-	17.9	-1.1	-	-	-	-	17.7	-1.1
1922	-	-	-	-	17.3	-2.3	-	-	-	-	17.3	0.0	-	-	-	-	16.9	-2.3	-	-	-	-	17.3	2.4
1923	-	-	-	-	17.3	0.0	-	-	-	-	17.6	1.7	-	-	-	-	17.8	1.1	-	-	-	-	17.8	0.0
1924	-	-	-	-	17.6	-1.1	-	-	-	-	17.7	0.6	-	-	-	-	17.6	-0.6	-	-	-	-	18.0	2.3
1925	-	-	-	-	-	-	-	-	-	-	18.4	2.2	-	-	-	-	-	-	-	-	-	-	18.9	2.7
1926	-	-	-	-	-	-	-	-	-	-	18.8	-0.5	-	-	-	-	-	-	-	-	-	-	18.7	-0.5
1927	-	-	-	-	-	-	-	-	-	-	18.5	-1.1	-	-	-	-	-	-	-	-	-	-	18.3	-1.1
1928	-	-	-	-	-	-	-	-	-	-	18.1	-1.1	-	-	-	-	-	-	-	-	-	-	17.8	-1.7
1929	-	-	-	-	-	-	-	-	-	-	17.8	0.0	-	-	-	-	-	-	-	-	-	-	17.9	0.6
1930	-	-	-	-	-	-	-	-	-	-	17.5	-2.2	-	-	-	-	-	-	-	-	-	-	16.8	-4.0
1931	-	-	-	-	-	-	-	-	-	-	15.9	-5.4	-	-	-	-	-	-	-	-	-	-	15.3	-3.8
1932	-	-	-	-	-	-	-	-	-	-	14.2	-7.2	-	-	-	-	-	-	-	-	-	-	13.5	-4.9
1933	-	-	-	-	-	-	-	-	-	-	13.2	-2.2	-	-	-	-	-	-	-	-	-	-	13.8	4.5
1934	-	-	-	-	-	-	-	-	-	-	14.2	2.9	-	-	-	-	-	-	-	-	14.1	-0.7	-	-
1935	-	-	-	-	14.2	0.7	-	-	-	-	-	-	14.2	0.0	-	-	-	-	14.4	1.4	-	-	-	-
1936	14.5	0.7	-	-	-	-	14.4	-0.7	-	-	-	-	14.5	0.7	-	-	14.6	0.7	-	-	-	-	14.6	0.0
1937	-	-	-	-	14.8	1.4	-	-	-	-	14.9	0.7	-	-	-	-	15.1	1.3	-	-	-	-	14.7	-2.6
1938	-	-	-	-	14.5	-1.4	-	-	-	-	14.6	0.7	-	-	-	-	14.5	-0.7	-	-	-	-	14.4	-0.7
1939	-	-	-	-	14.2	-1.4	-	-	-	-	14.2	0.0	-	-	-	-	14.5	2.1	-	-	-	-	14.3	-1.4
1940	-	-	-	-	14.3	0.0	-	-	-	-	14.4	0.7	-	-	-	-	14.3	-0.7	14.3	0.0	14.3	0.0	14.4	0.7
1941	14.4	0.0	14.4	0.0	14.5	0.7	14.6	0.7	14.7	0.7	15.0	2.0	15.0	0.0	15.2	1.3	15.5	2.0	15.7	1.3	15.7	0.0	15.8	0.6
1942	16.1	1.9	16.1	0.0	16.3	1.2	16.5	1.2	16.6	0.6	16.7	0.6	16.9	1.2	16.9	0.0	17.0	0.6	17.1	0.6	17.2	0.6	17.4	1.2
1943	17.4	0.0	17.4	0.0	17.6	1.1	18.0	2.3	18.1	0.6	18.0	-0.6	17.8	-1.1	17.8	0.0	17.8	0.0	17.9	0.6	17.9	0.0	17.9	0.0
1944	17.9	0.0	17.9	0.0	17.8	-0.6	17.9	0.6	18.0	0.6	18.1	0.6	18.1	0.0	18.2	0.6	18.2	0.0	18.1	-0.5	18.1	0.0	18.2	0.6
1945	18.3	0.5	18.4	0.5	18.3	-0.5	18.3	0.0	18.5	1.1	18.6	0.5	18.7	0.5	18.7	0.0	18.6	-0.5	18.6	0.0	18.6	0.0	18.7	0.5
1946	18.7	0.0	18.7	0.0	18.8	0.5	18.9	0.5	19.0	0.5	19.2	1.1	20.3	5.7	20.9	3.0	21.2	1.4	21.5	1.4	21.9	1.9	22.2	1.4
1947	22.1	-0.5	22.0	-0.5	22.7	3.2	22.5	-0.9	22.5	0.0	22.8	1.3	23.0	0.9	23.2	0.9	23.7	2.2	23.6	-0.4	23.8	0.8	24.2	1.7
1948	24.4	0.8	24.2	-0.8	24.0	-0.8	24.6	2.5	24.8	0.8	25.0	0.8	25.1	0.4	25.4	1.2	25.4	0.0	25.3	-0.4	25.0	-1.2	24.8	-0.8
1949	24.6	-0.8	24.5	-0.4	24.6	0.4	24.6	0.0	24.7	0.4	24.6	-0.4	24.4	-0.8	24.5	0.4	24.6	0.4	24.6	0.0	24.5	-0.4	24.3	-0.8
1950	24.1	-0.8	24.1	0.0	24.2	0.4	24.2	0.0	24.3	0.4	24.5	0.8	24.7	0.8	24.9	0.8	25.1	0.8	25.2	0.4	25.2	0.0	25.8	2.4
1951	26.3	1.9	26.9	2.3	26.9	0.0	27.0	0.4	27.0	0.0	26.9	-0.4	26.9	0.0	26.9	0.0	27.0	0.4	27.1	0.4	27.4	1.1	27.4	0.0
1952	27.4	0.0	27.1	-1.1	27.2	0.4	27.3	0.4	27.3	0.0	27.4	0.4	27.7	1.1	27.7	0.0	27.7	0.0	27.7	0.0	27.7	0.0	27.7	0.0
1953	27.6	-0.4	27.4	-0.7	27.5	0.4	27.4	-0.4	27.5	0.4	27.7	0.7	27.7	0.0	27.7	0.0	27.8	0.4	27.8	0.0	27.7	-0.4	27.7	0.0
1954	27.8	0.4	27.8	0.0	27.7	-0.4	27.8	0.4	27.8	0.0	28.0	0.7	28.1	0.4	28.0	-0.4	28.0	0.0	28.0	0.0	28.0	0.0	27.9	-0.4
1955	27.9	0.0	27.9	0.0	27.9	0.0	27.9	0.0	27.9	0.0	27.9	0.0	27.9	0.0	27.9	0.0	27.8	-0.4	27.8	0.0	27.7	-0.4	27.7	0.0
1956	27.7	0.0	27.7	0.0	27.9	0.7	28.0	0.4	28.0	0.0	28.2	0.7	28.5	1.1	28.5	0.0	28.6	0.4	28.6	0.0	28.5	-0.3	28.6	0.4
1957	28.7	0.3	28.9	0.7	28.9	0.0	28.9	0.0	28.9	0.0	29.0	0.3	29.2	0.7	29.4	0.7	29.4	0.0	29.4	0.0	29.5	0.3	29.5	0.0
1958	29.5	0.0	29.5	0.0	29.7	0.7	29.7	0.0	29.7	0.0	29.7	0.0	29.8	0.3	29.8	0.0	29.8	0.0	29.8	0.0	29.8	0.0	29.8	0.0

[Continued]

Philadelphia, PA-NJ
Consumer Price Index - All Urban Consumers
Base 1982-1984 = 100
All Items
[Continued]

For 1914-1995. Columns headed % show percentile change in the index from the previous period for which an index is available.

Year	Jan Index	%	Feb Index	%	Mar Index	%	Apr Index	%	May Index	%	Jun Index	%	Jul Index	%	Aug Index	%	Sep Index	%	Oct Index	%	Nov Index	%	Dec Index	%
1959	29.8	0.0	29.8	0.0	29.8	0.0	29.8	0.0	29.7	-0.3	29.9	0.7	30.0	0.3	30.0	0.0	30.4	1.3	30.4	0.0	30.5	0.3	30.5	0.0
1960	30.3	-0.7	30.3	0.0	30.4	0.3	30.5	0.3	30.5	0.0	30.5	0.0	30.6	0.3	30.6	0.0	30.7	0.3	30.8	0.3	30.9	0.3	30.9	0.0
1961	30.8	-0.3	30.9	0.3	30.8	-0.3	30.9	0.3	30.9	0.0	30.8	-0.3	31.0	0.6	30.9	-0.3	31.0	0.3	31.0	0.0	31.1	0.3	31.0	-0.3
1962	31.0	0.0	31.1	0.3	31.1	0.0	31.2	0.3	31.0	-0.6	31.1	0.3	31.2	0.3	31.2	0.0	31.4	0.6	31.4	0.0	31.4	0.0	31.3	-0.3
1963	31.4	0.3	31.5	0.3	31.5	0.0	31.5	0.0	31.5	0.0	31.8	1.0	31.8	0.0	31.8	0.0	31.9	0.3	32.1	0.6	32.1	0.0	32.2	0.3
1964	32.2	0.0	32.2	0.0	32.1	-0.3	32.1	0.0	32.1	0.0	32.2	0.3	32.3	0.3	32.2	-0.3	32.3	0.3	32.4	0.3	32.5	0.3	32.5	0.0
1965	32.5	0.0	32.6	0.3	32.6	0.0	32.5	-0.3	32.6	0.3	32.8	0.6	32.9	0.3	32.8	-0.3	32.8	0.0	32.9	0.3	33.0	0.3	33.1	0.3
1966	33.1	0.0	33.3	0.6	33.4	0.3	33.5	0.3	33.5	0.0	33.6	0.3	33.7	0.3	33.9	0.6	34.0	0.3	34.1	0.3	34.1	0.0	34.2	0.3
1967	34.1	-0.3	34.2	0.3	34.2	0.0	34.3	0.3	34.4	0.3	34.5	0.3	34.6	0.3	34.8	0.6	34.9	0.3	35.1	0.6	35.1	0.0	35.2	0.3
1968	35.4	0.6	35.6	0.6	35.8	0.6	35.9	0.3	36.0	0.3	36.2	0.6	36.3	0.3	36.4	0.3	36.7	0.8	36.9	0.5	37.0	0.3	37.1	0.3
1969	37.1	0.0	37.3	0.5	37.6	0.8	37.8	0.5	37.8	0.0	38.0	0.5	38.3	0.8	38.6	0.8	38.8	0.5	38.9	0.3	39.0	0.3	39.2	0.5
1970	39.4	0.5	39.8	1.0	40.1	0.8	40.2	0.2	40.5	0.7	40.6	0.2	40.7	0.2	40.9	0.5	41.4	1.2	41.7	0.7	41.9	0.5	42.0	0.2
1971	42.0	0.0	42.2	0.5	42.3	0.2	42.4	0.2	42.7	0.7	43.0	0.7	42.8	-0.5	42.8	0.0	43.1	0.7	43.3	0.5	43.2	-0.2	43.3	0.2
1972	43.2	-0.2	43.3	0.2	43.5	0.5	43.6	0.2	43.6	0.0	43.8	0.5	44.0	0.5	44.1	0.2	44.4	0.7	44.5	0.2	44.7	0.4	44.6	-0.2
1973	44.7	0.2	45.2	1.1	45.9	1.5	46.2	0.7	46.4	0.4	46.6	0.4	46.7	0.2	47.5	1.7	47.8	0.6	48.3	1.0	48.6	0.6	48.9	0.6
1974	49.4	1.0	50.2	1.6	50.9	1.4	51.3	0.8	51.7	0.8	52.2	1.0	52.5	0.6	53.1	1.1	53.9	1.5	54.4	0.9	54.9	0.9	55.1	0.4
1975	55.2	0.2	55.5	0.5	55.8	0.5	55.8	0.0	56.1	0.5	56.6	0.9	57.1	0.9	57.3	0.4	57.8	0.9	58.2	0.7	58.3	0.2	58.3	0.0
1976	58.5	0.3	58.7	0.3	58.7	0.0	58.9	0.3	59.2	0.5	59.5	0.5	59.8	0.5	59.9	0.2	60.4	0.8	60.6	0.3	60.8	0.3	60.7	-0.2
1977	61.2	0.8	61.9	1.1	62.4	0.8	63.0	1.0	63.4	0.6	63.6	0.3	64.0	0.6	64.0	0.0	64.6	0.9	64.7	0.2	64.9	0.3	64.7	-0.3
1978	64.9	0.3	65.1	0.3	65.6	0.8	66.0	0.6	66.4	0.6	67.1	1.1	67.9	1.2	68.0	0.1	68.5	0.7	68.7	0.3	69.1	0.6	69.6	0.7
1979	70.0	0.6	70.6	0.9	70.9	0.4	71.9	1.4	72.9	1.4	74.0	1.5	74.8	1.1	75.4	0.8	76.0	0.8	76.2	0.3	77.0	1.0	77.4	0.5
1980	78.6	1.6	80.0	1.8	81.2	1.5	82.2	1.2	82.9	0.9	83.9	1.2	84.5	0.7	85.2	0.8	85.6	0.5	85.8	0.2	86.3	0.6	86.7	0.5
1981	87.6	1.0	88.6	1.1	89.4	0.9	90.3	1.0	90.7	0.4	91.9	1.3	92.7	0.9	93.6	1.0	95.0	1.5	95.1	0.1	94.9	-0.2	95.2	0.3
1982	95.4	0.2	95.4	0.0	95.1	-0.3	95.2	0.1	95.2	0.0	96.8	1.7	97.3	0.5	97.4	0.1	98.0	0.6	97.5	-0.5	97.9	0.4	97.5	-0.4
1983	97.6	0.1	97.6	0.0	98.0	0.4	98.1	0.1	98.4	0.3	99.0	0.6	99.8	0.8	100.3	0.5	100.9	0.6	100.8	-0.1	101.0	0.2	101.0	0.0
1984	101.9	0.9	102.6	0.7	102.7	0.1	103.2	0.5	103.4	0.2	103.8	0.4	104.3	0.5	104.8	0.5	105.2	0.4	105.1	-0.1	105.9	0.8	105.6	-0.3
1985	106.0	0.4	107.0	0.9	107.4	0.4	108.1	0.7	108.8	0.6	108.8	0.0	109.2	0.4	109.3	0.1	109.6	0.3	109.9	0.3	110.4	0.5	110.7	0.3
1986	110.9	0.2	110.8	-0.1	110.5	-0.3	110.0	-0.5	110.4	0.4	111.4	0.9	111.8	0.4	111.8	0.0	112.8	0.9	112.4	-0.4	112.2	-0.2	112.6	0.4
1987	113.4	0.7	113.9	0.4	114.0	0.1	115.5	1.3	116.4	0.8	117.4	0.9	117.4	0.0	118.4	0.9	118.7	0.3	119.1	0.3	118.6	-0.4	118.9	0.3
1988	119.3	0.3	119.3	0.0	119.6	0.3	120.0	0.3	120.9	0.7	121.9	0.8	123.2	1.1	123.9	0.6	125.2	1.0	124.6	-0.5	125.3	0.6	125.6	0.2
1989	125.7	0.1	125.4	-0.2	126.0	0.5	126.7	0.6	127.9	0.9	128.8	0.7	129.3	0.4	129.1	-0.2	130.2	0.9	130.5	0.2	130.1	-0.3	129.9	-0.2
1990	131.2	1.0	132.2	0.8	133.6	1.1	134.3	0.5	134.6	0.2	135.1	0.4	136.3	0.9	137.3	0.7	138.2	0.7	138.8	0.4	139.1	0.2	139.4	0.2
1991	140.4	0.7	140.6	0.1	141.0	0.3	140.8	-0.1	141.3	0.4	141.8	0.4	142.4	0.4	143.3	0.6	143.8	0.3	143.1	-0.5	143.3	0.1	144.4	0.8
1992	144.4	0.0	144.2	-0.1	145.4	0.8	145.4	0.0	145.7	0.2	147.5	1.2	147.3	-0.1	148.0	0.5	148.1	0.1	148.0	-0.1	147.5	-0.3	147.5	0.0
1993	147.5	0.0	148.5	0.7	149.3	0.5	149.6	0.2	149.4	-0.1	150.5	0.7	150.7	0.1	150.6	-0.1	151.1	0.3	152.2	0.7	152.1	-0.1	151.3	-0.5
1994	152.5	0.8	152.9	0.3	153.5	0.4	153.1	-0.3	153.2	0.1	154.6	0.9	155.3	0.5	155.7	0.3	156.2	0.3	156.6	0.3	156.7	0.1	155.4	-0.8
1995	156.6	0.8	157.8	0.8	158.0	0.1	157.8	-0.1	157.8	0.0	158.4	0.4	158.9	0.3	159.6	0.4	160.3	0.4	160.4	0.1	159.6	-0.5	159.1	-0.3

Source: U.S. Department of Labor, Bureau of Labor Statistics, Division of Consumer Prices and Price Indexes. - indicates no data collected for period.

Philadelphia, PA-NJ
Consumer Price Index - Urban Wage Earners
Base 1982-1984 = 100
All Items

For 1914-1995. Columns headed % show percentile change in the index from the previous period for which an index is available.

Year	Jan Index	%	Feb Index	%	Mar Index	%	Apr Index	%	May Index	%	Jun Index	%	Jul Index	%	Aug Index	%	Sep Index	%	Oct Index	%	Nov Index	%	Dec Index	%
1914	-	-	-	-	-	-	-	-	-	-	-	-	-	-	-	-	-	-	-	-	-	-	10.1	-
1915	-	-	-	-	-	-	-	-	-	-	-	-	-	-	-	-	-	-	-	-	-	-	10.3	2.0
1916	-	-	-	-	-	-	-	-	-	-	-	-	-	-	-	-	-	-	-	-	-	-	11.5	11.7
1917	-	-	-	-	-	-	-	-	-	-	-	-	-	-	-	-	-	-	-	-	-	-	14.0	21.7
1918	-	-	-	-	-	-	-	-	-	-	-	-	-	-	-	-	-	-	-	-	-	-	16.9	20.7
1919	-	-	-	-	-	-	-	-	-	-	17.4	3.0	-	-	-	-	-	-	-	-	-	-	19.1	9.8
1920	-	-	-	-	-	-	-	-	-	-	21.2	11.0	-	-	-	-	-	-	-	-	-	-	19.8	-6.6
1921	-	-	-	-	-	-	-	-	18.0	-9.1	-	-	-	-	-	-	17.8	-1.1	-	-	-	-	17.6	-1.1
1922	-	-	-	-	17.2	-2.3	-	-	-	-	17.2	0.0	-	-	-	-	16.8	-2.3	-	-	-	-	17.2	2.4
1923	-	-	-	-	17.2	0.0	-	-	-	-	17.5	1.7	-	-	-	-	17.7	1.1	-	-	-	-	17.7	0.0
1924	-	-	-	-	17.5	-1.1	-	-	-	-	17.6	0.6	-	-	-	-	17.5	-0.6	-	-	-	-	17.9	2.3
1925	-	-	-	-	-	-	-	-	-	-	18.3	2.2	-	-	-	-	-	-	-	-	-	-	18.8	2.7
1926	-	-	-	-	-	-	-	-	-	-	18.7	-0.5	-	-	-	-	-	-	-	-	-	-	18.6	-0.5
1927	-	-	-	-	-	-	-	-	-	-	18.4	-1.1	-	-	-	-	-	-	-	-	-	-	18.2	-1.1
1928	-	-	-	-	-	-	-	-	-	-	18.0	-1.1	-	-	-	-	-	-	-	-	-	-	17.7	-1.7
1929	-	-	-	-	-	-	-	-	-	-	17.7	0.0	-	-	-	-	-	-	-	-	-	-	17.8	0.6
1930	-	-	-	-	-	-	-	-	-	-	17.4	-2.2	-	-	-	-	-	-	-	-	-	-	16.7	-4.0
1931	-	-	-	-	-	-	-	-	-	-	15.8	-5.4	-	-	-	-	-	-	-	-	-	-	15.3	-3.2
1932	-	-	-	-	-	-	-	-	-	-	14.1	-7.8	-	-	-	-	-	-	-	-	-	-	13.5	-4.3
1933	-	-	-	-	-	-	-	-	-	-	13.2	-2.2	-	-	-	-	-	-	-	-	-	-	13.8	4.5
1934	-	-	-	-	-	-	-	-	-	-	14.1	2.2	-	-	-	-	-	-	-	-	14.0	-0.7	-	-
1935	-	-	-	-	14.1	0.7	-	-	-	-	-	-	14.1	0.0	-	-	-	-	14.3	1.4	-	-	-	-
1936	14.5	1.4	-	-	-	-	14.3	-1.4	-	-	-	-	14.5	1.4	-	-	14.6	0.7	-	-	-	-	14.5	-0.7
1937	-	-	-	-	14.7	1.4	-	-	-	-	14.8	0.7	-	-	-	-	15.0	1.4	-	-	-	-	14.7	-2.0
1938	-	-	-	-	14.5	-1.4	-	-	-	-	14.5	0.0	-	-	-	-	14.5	0.0	-	-	-	-	14.3	-1.4
1939	-	-	-	-	14.1	-1.4	-	-	-	-	14.1	0.0	-	-	-	-	14.4	2.1	-	-	-	-	14.3	-0.7
1940	-	-	-	-	14.2	-0.7	-	-	-	-	14.3	0.7	-	-	-	-	14.3	0.0	14.3	0.0	14.3	0.0	14.3	0.0
1941	14.3	0.0	14.3	0.0	14.4	0.7	14.5	0.7	14.7	1.4	14.9	1.4	14.9	0.0	15.1	1.3	15.4	2.0	15.6	1.3	15.6	0.0	15.7	0.6
1942	16.0	1.9	16.0	0.0	16.2	1.3	16.4	1.2	16.5	0.6	16.6	0.6	16.8	1.2	16.8	0.0	16.9	0.6	17.0	0.6	17.1	0.6	17.3	1.2
1943	17.3	0.0	17.3	0.0	17.5	1.2	17.9	2.3	18.0	0.6	17.9	-0.6	17.7	-1.1	17.7	0.0	17.7	0.0	17.8	0.6	17.8	0.0	17.8	0.0
1944	17.8	0.0	17.8	0.0	17.7	-0.6	17.8	0.6	17.9	0.6	18.0	0.6	18.0	0.0	18.1	0.6	18.1	0.0	18.0	-0.6	18.0	0.0	18.1	0.6
1945	18.2	0.6	18.3	0.5	18.2	-0.5	18.2	0.0	18.4	1.1	18.5	0.5	18.6	0.5	18.6	0.0	18.5	-0.5	18.5	0.0	18.5	0.0	18.6	0.5
1946	18.6	0.0	18.6	0.0	18.7	0.5	18.8	0.5	18.9	0.5	19.1	1.1	20.2	5.8	20.8	3.0	21.1	1.4	21.3	0.9	21.8	2.3	22.0	0.9
1947	22.0	0.0	21.9	-0.5	22.5	2.7	22.4	-0.4	22.4	0.0	22.7	1.3	22.9	0.9	23.1	0.9	23.6	2.2	23.4	-0.8	23.7	1.3	24.0	1.3
1948	24.3	1.2	24.1	-0.8	23.9	-0.8	24.5	2.5	24.6	0.4	24.9	1.2	25.0	0.4	25.3	1.2	25.3	0.0	25.2	-0.4	24.8	-1.6	24.7	-0.4
1949	24.5	-0.8	24.4	-0.4	24.4	0.0	24.4	0.0	24.5	0.4	24.5	0.0	24.2	-1.2	24.4	0.8	24.5	0.4	24.4	-0.4	24.4	0.0	24.2	-0.8
1950	24.0	-0.8	23.9	-0.4	24.1	0.8	24.1	0.0	24.1	0.0	24.4	1.2	24.6	0.8	24.8	0.8	25.0	0.8	25.1	0.4	25.1	0.0	25.7	2.4
1951	26.1	1.6	26.8	2.7	26.8	0.0	26.8	0.0	26.9	0.4	26.8	-0.4	26.8	0.0	26.8	0.0	26.8	0.0	27.0	0.7	27.3	1.1	27.3	0.0
1952	27.2	-0.4	27.0	-0.7	27.1	0.4	27.2	0.4	27.2	0.0	27.3	0.4	27.6	1.1	27.6	0.0	27.5	-0.4	27.5	0.0	27.5	0.0	27.5	0.0
1953	27.4	-0.4	27.3	-0.4	27.4	0.4	27.3	-0.4	27.3	0.0	27.5	0.7	27.5	0.0	27.6	0.4	27.6	0.0	27.7	0.4	27.5	-0.7	27.6	0.4
1954	27.7	0.4	27.6	-0.4	27.6	0.0	27.6	0.0	27.7	0.4	27.8	0.4	27.9	0.4	27.9	0.0	27.9	0.0	27.9	0.0	27.8	-0.4	27.7	-0.4
1955	27.7	0.0	27.8	0.4	27.8	0.0	27.8	0.0	27.7	-0.4	27.7	0.0	27.8	0.4	27.8	0.0	27.6	-0.7	27.7	0.4	27.6	-0.4	27.6	0.0
1956	27.5	-0.4	27.5	0.0	27.8	1.1	27.9	0.4	27.9	0.0	28.0	0.4	28.3	1.1	28.3	0.0	28.4	0.4	28.5	0.4	28.4	-0.4	28.5	0.4
1957	28.5	0.0	28.7	0.7	28.8	0.3	28.7	-0.3	28.8	0.3	28.8	0.0	29.1	1.0	29.2	0.3	29.3	0.3	29.3	0.0	29.3	0.0	29.3	0.0
1958	29.3	0.0	29.4	0.3	29.5	0.3	29.5	0.0	29.5	0.0	29.5	0.0	29.6	0.3	29.6	0.0	29.6	0.0	29.6	0.0	29.6	0.0	29.6	0.0

[Continued]

Philadelphia, PA-NJ
Consumer Price Index - Urban Wage Earners
Base 1982-1984 = 100
All Items
[Continued]

For 1914-1995. Columns headed % show percentile change in the index from the previous period for which an index is available.

Year	Jan Index	%	Feb Index	%	Mar Index	%	Apr Index	%	May Index	%	Jun Index	%	Jul Index	%	Aug Index	%	Sep Index	%	Oct Index	%	Nov Index	%	Dec Index	%
1959	29.6	0.0	29.6	0.0	29.6	0.0	29.7	0.3	29.6	-0.3	29.8	0.7	29.8	0.0	29.8	0.0	30.2	1.3	30.2	0.0	30.3	0.3	30.4	0.3
1960	30.1	-1.0	30.1	0.0	30.2	0.3	30.3	0.3	30.3	0.0	30.3	0.0	30.4	0.3	30.4	0.0	30.5	0.3	30.6	0.3	30.7	0.3	30.7	0.0
1961	30.7	0.0	30.7	0.0	30.6	-0.3	30.7	0.3	30.7	0.0	30.7	0.0	30.8	0.3	30.7	-0.3	30.8	0.3	30.9	0.3	30.9	0.0	30.9	0.0
1962	30.8	-0.3	31.0	0.6	31.0	0.0	31.0	0.0	30.8	-0.6	30.9	0.3	31.1	0.6	31.0	-0.3	31.3	1.0	31.2	-0.3	31.2	0.0	31.2	0.0
1963	31.2	0.0	31.3	0.3	31.4	0.3	31.4	0.0	31.3	-0.3	31.6	1.0	31.7	0.3	31.7	0.0	31.7	0.0	31.9	0.6	31.9	0.0	32.0	0.3
1964	32.0	0.0	32.1	0.3	31.9	-0.6	31.9	0.0	31.9	0.0	32.0	0.3	32.1	0.3	32.0	-0.3	32.1	0.3	32.2	0.3	32.3	0.3	32.3	0.0
1965	32.3	0.0	32.4	0.3	32.4	0.0	32.3	-0.3	32.5	0.6	32.6	0.3	32.7	0.3	32.6	-0.3	32.7	0.3	32.7	0.0	32.8	0.3	32.9	0.3
1966	32.9	0.0	33.1	0.6	33.2	0.3	33.4	0.6	33.3	-0.3	33.4	0.3	33.5	0.3	33.7	0.6	33.8	0.3	33.9	0.3	33.9	0.0	34.0	0.3
1967	33.9	-0.3	34.0	0.3	34.0	0.0	34.1	0.3	34.2	0.3	34.4	0.6	34.4	0.0	34.6	0.6	34.7	0.3	34.9	0.6	34.9	0.0	35.0	0.3
1968	35.3	0.9	35.4	0.3	35.6	0.6	35.7	0.3	35.8	0.3	36.0	0.6	36.1	0.3	36.3	0.6	36.5	0.6	36.7	0.5	36.8	0.3	36.9	0.3
1969	36.9	0.0	37.1	0.5	37.4	0.8	37.6	0.5	37.6	0.0	37.8	0.5	38.1	0.8	38.4	0.8	38.6	0.5	38.7	0.3	38.8	0.3	39.0	0.5
1970	39.2	0.5	39.6	1.0	39.9	0.8	40.0	0.3	40.2	0.5	40.4	0.5	40.5	0.2	40.7	0.5	41.2	1.2	41.5	0.7	41.7	0.5	41.8	0.2
1971	41.8	0.0	41.9	0.2	42.1	0.5	42.2	0.2	42.5	0.7	42.7	0.5	42.6	-0.2	42.6	0.0	42.9	0.7	43.0	0.2	42.9	-0.2	43.1	0.5
1972	42.9	-0.5	43.1	0.5	43.3	0.5	43.4	0.2	43.4	0.0	43.6	0.5	43.7	0.2	43.9	0.5	44.2	0.7	44.3	0.2	44.4	0.2	44.4	0.0
1973	44.4	0.0	45.0	1.4	45.6	1.3	45.9	0.7	46.2	0.7	46.4	0.4	46.4	0.0	47.2	1.7	47.5	0.6	48.0	1.1	48.4	0.8	48.7	0.6
1974	49.2	1.0	49.9	1.4	50.6	1.4	51.0	0.8	51.4	0.8	52.0	1.2	52.3	0.6	52.8	1.0	53.6	1.5	54.1	0.9	54.6	0.9	54.8	0.4
1975	54.9	0.2	55.2	0.5	55.5	0.5	55.5	0.0	55.8	0.5	56.3	0.9	56.8	0.9	57.0	0.4	57.5	0.9	57.9	0.7	58.0	0.2	58.0	0.0
1976	58.2	0.3	58.4	0.3	58.4	0.0	58.6	0.3	58.9	0.5	59.2	0.5	59.5	0.5	59.6	0.2	60.1	0.8	60.3	0.3	60.5	0.3	60.4	-0.2
1977	60.8	0.7	61.5	1.2	62.1	1.0	62.6	0.8	63.0	0.6	63.3	0.5	63.6	0.5	63.7	0.2	64.2	0.8	64.4	0.3	64.5	0.2	64.3	-0.3
1978	64.5	0.3	65.0	0.8	65.3	0.5	65.9	0.9	66.3	0.6	67.0	1.1	67.4	0.6	68.0	0.9	68.2	0.3	68.5	0.4	69.1	0.9	69.7	0.9
1979	70.2	0.7	70.9	1.0	71.2	0.4	72.0	1.1	72.8	1.1	73.8	1.4	74.7	1.2	75.1	0.5	75.8	0.9	76.2	0.5	77.0	1.0	77.3	0.4
1980	78.5	1.6	79.7	1.5	80.9	1.5	81.9	1.2	82.6	0.9	83.9	1.6	84.5	0.7	85.1	0.7	85.5	0.5	85.9	0.5	86.4	0.6	86.9	0.6
1981	88.0	1.3	88.9	1.0	89.3	0.4	90.0	0.8	90.5	0.6	91.4	1.0	92.4	1.1	93.5	1.2	94.5	1.1	94.7	0.2	94.5	-0.2	94.4	-0.1
1982	94.7	0.3	94.7	0.0	94.4	-0.3	94.5	0.1	94.6	0.1	96.1	1.6	96.7	0.6	96.6	-0.1	97.1	0.5	96.8	-0.3	97.1	0.3	96.7	-0.4
1983	97.3	0.6	97.5	0.2	98.3	0.8	98.7	0.4	98.6	-0.1	99.4	0.8	100.2	0.8	101.0	0.8	101.3	0.3	101.3	0.0	101.5	0.2	101.3	-0.2
1984	102.1	0.8	102.8	0.7	102.9	0.1	102.9	0.0	103.5	0.6	104.2	0.7	104.8	0.6	105.4	0.6	106.2	0.8	106.3	0.1	106.4	0.1	106.0	-0.4
1985	106.5	0.5	107.6	1.0	107.9	0.3	108.5	0.6	109.2	0.6	109.2	0.0	109.7	0.5	109.7	0.0	109.9	0.2	110.3	0.4	110.7	0.4	111.0	0.3
1986	111.2	0.2	111.1	-0.1	110.6	-0.5	110.1	-0.5	110.4	0.3	111.4	0.9	111.8	0.4	111.7	-0.1	112.5	0.7	112.3	-0.2	112.0	-0.3	112.5	0.4
1987	113.3	0.7	113.6	0.3	113.8	0.2	115.3	1.3	116.2	0.8	117.2	0.9	117.3	0.1	118.4	0.9	118.5	0.1	119.0	0.4	118.6	-0.3	119.0	0.3
1988	119.3	0.3	119.0	-0.3	119.5	0.4	119.8	0.3	120.8	0.8	121.8	0.8	123.1	1.1	123.6	0.4	124.9	1.1	124.4	-0.4	125.0	0.5	125.2	0.2
1989	125.5	0.2	125.4	-0.1	125.8	0.3	126.7	0.7	127.9	0.9	128.9	0.8	129.3	0.3	129.3	0.0	130.4	0.9	130.6	0.2	130.1	-0.4	130.0	-0.1
1990	131.0	0.8	132.2	0.9	133.8	1.2	134.4	0.4	134.9	0.4	135.5	0.4	136.6	0.8	137.5	0.7	138.6	0.8	139.1	0.4	139.4	0.2	139.8	0.3
1991	140.4	0.4	140.5	0.1	141.0	0.4	140.8	-0.1	141.2	0.3	141.8	0.4	142.5	0.5	143.2	0.5	143.7	0.3	142.9	-0.6	143.4	0.3	144.4	0.7
1992	144.2	-0.1	143.9	-0.2	145.0	0.8	145.1	0.1	145.5	0.3	147.4	1.3	147.3	-0.1	147.8	0.3	147.9	0.1	147.8	-0.1	147.6	-0.1	147.4	-0.1
1993	147.4	0.0	148.6	0.8	149.0	0.3	149.4	0.3	149.3	-0.1	150.4	0.7	150.6	0.1	150.4	-0.1	150.9	0.3	151.9	0.7	151.9	0.0	151.2	-0.5
1994	152.1	0.6	152.2	0.1	152.8	0.4	152.6	-0.1	152.7	0.1	154.2	1.0	154.9	0.5	155.3	0.3	155.9	0.4	156.1	0.1	156.1	0.0	155.1	-0.6
1995	156.4	0.8	157.5	0.7	157.5	0.0	157.4	-0.1	157.4	0.0	158.1	0.4	158.5	0.3	159.2	0.4	159.8	0.4	159.7	-0.1	159.2	-0.3	158.7	-0.3

Source: U.S. Department of Labor, Bureau of Labor Statistics, Division of Consumer Prices and Price Indexes. - indicates no data collected for period.

Philadelphia, PA-NJ
Consumer Price Index - All Urban Consumers
Base 1982-1984 = 100
Food and Beverages

For 1976-1995. Columns headed % show percentile change in the index from the previous period for which an index is available.

Year	Jan Index	%	Feb Index	%	Mar Index	%	Apr Index	%	May Index	%	Jun Index	%	Jul Index	%	Aug Index	%	Sep Index	%	Oct Index	%	Nov Index	%	Dec Index	%
1976	62.3	-	62.3	0.0	61.7	-1.0	61.8	0.2	62.0	0.3	62.3	0.5	62.4	0.2	62.5	0.2	62.5	0.0	62.4	-0.2	62.3	-0.2	62.2	-0.2
1977	63.1	1.4	64.7	2.5	65.3	0.9	65.8	0.8	65.9	0.2	66.3	0.6	66.7	0.6	66.3	-0.6	66.5	0.3	66.9	0.6	67.4	0.7	67.5	0.1
1978	68.3	1.2	69.3	1.5	70.1	1.2	70.6	0.7	71.6	1.4	73.5	2.7	74.1	0.8	74.0	-0.1	73.9	-0.1	73.8	-0.1	74.7	1.2	75.0	0.4
1979	76.3	1.7	77.4	1.4	78.2	1.0	78.7	0.6	79.2	0.6	79.3	0.1	80.3	1.3	80.1	-0.2	79.8	-0.4	80.9	1.4	81.3	0.5	82.0	0.9
1980	82.3	0.4	82.1	-0.2	83.0	1.1	83.9	1.1	84.8	1.1	86.2	1.7	86.7	0.6	87.5	0.9	87.9	0.5	88.6	0.8	89.3	0.8	89.6	0.3
1981	90.7	1.2	90.8	0.1	90.9	0.1	91.2	0.3	91.6	0.4	91.9	0.3	93.0	1.2	93.4	0.4	94.5	1.2	94.1	-0.4	93.9	-0.2	94.6	0.7
1982	95.5	1.0	96.7	1.3	96.7	0.0	97.7	1.0	97.4	-0.3	98.2	0.8	98.8	0.6	98.5	-0.3	98.7	0.2	98.1	-0.6	98.0	-0.1	97.8	-0.2
1983	98.3	0.5	98.8	0.5	99.1	0.3	99.7	0.6	99.9	0.2	100.7	0.8	100.4	-0.3	100.8	0.4	100.8	0.0	100.6	-0.2	100.1	-0.5	100.2	0.1
1984	101.6	1.4	102.6	1.0	102.7	0.1	102.3	-0.4	102.2	-0.1	102.4	0.2	103.2	0.8	103.6	0.4	102.2	-1.4	102.2	0.0	101.9	-0.3	101.8	-0.1
1985	103.2	1.4	104.5	1.3	104.9	0.4	104.9	0.0	104.9	0.0	104.6	-0.3	105.6	1.0	104.9	-0.7	105.6	0.7	105.8	0.2	105.3	-0.5	106.0	0.7
1986	106.1	0.1	106.0	-0.1	106.9	0.8	106.9	0.0	107.1	0.2	107.1	0.0	107.8	0.7	108.5	0.6	109.4	0.8	109.5	0.1	108.9	-0.5	109.3	0.4
1987	110.8	1.4	110.8	0.0	110.5	-0.3	111.4	0.8	111.9	0.4	112.0	0.1	112.4	0.4	112.7	0.3	112.7	0.0	113.4	0.6	113.1	-0.3	113.0	-0.1
1988	114.2	1.1	113.7	-0.4	112.7	-0.9	114.4	1.5	115.1	0.6	116.1	0.9	117.3	1.0	117.1	-0.2	117.4	0.3	118.5	0.9	117.3	-1.0	118.2	0.8
1989	119.4	1.0	120.1	0.6	121.7	1.3	122.3	0.5	123.1	0.7	125.0	1.5	125.7	0.6	125.4	-0.2	126.0	0.5	127.0	0.8	127.4	0.3	127.7	0.2
1990	128.4	0.5	130.2	1.4	130.6	0.3	130.1	-0.4	130.4	0.2	130.6	0.2	131.6	0.8	132.3	0.5	131.6	-0.5	132.5	0.7	132.5	0.0	133.6	0.8
1991	134.6	0.7	135.2	0.4	135.5	0.2	135.9	0.3	136.0	0.1	136.1	0.1	135.7	-0.3	135.2	-0.4	135.0	-0.1	135.0	0.0	135.1	0.1	135.1	0.0
1992	136.0	0.7	136.4	0.3	137.1	0.5	137.7	0.4	138.0	0.2	137.7	-0.2	138.1	0.3	137.7	-0.3	138.3	0.4	138.1	-0.1	137.6	-0.4	138.4	0.6
1993	138.6	0.1	139.0	0.3	139.4	0.3	140.4	0.7	140.9	0.4	139.5	-1.0	138.6	-0.6	138.6	0.0	140.2	1.2	139.7	-0.4	141.0	0.9	140.3	-0.5
1994	142.0	1.2	140.6	-1.0	141.0	0.3	141.8	0.6	141.1	-0.5	141.7	0.4	142.5	0.6	142.4	-0.1	144.0	1.1	144.9	0.6	144.7	-0.1	146.2	1.0
1995	147.9	1.2	148.4	0.3	147.8	-0.4	148.5	0.5	149.2	0.5	148.2	-0.7	148.7	0.3	149.1	0.3	149.9	0.5	149.7	-0.1	149.6	-0.1	149.0	-0.4

Source: U.S. Department of Labor, Bureau of Labor Statistics, Division of Consumer Prices and Price Indexes. - indicates no data collected for period.

Philadelphia, PA-NJ
Consumer Price Index - Urban Wage Earners
Base 1982-1984 = 100
Food and Beverages

For 1976-1995. Columns headed % show percentile change in the index from the previous period for which an index is available.

Year	Jan Index	%	Feb Index	%	Mar Index	%	Apr Index	%	May Index	%	Jun Index	%	Jul Index	%	Aug Index	%	Sep Index	%	Oct Index	%	Nov Index	%	Dec Index	%
1976	60.6	-	60.6	0.0	60.0	-1.0	60.1	0.2	60.3	0.3	60.6	0.5	60.7	0.2	60.8	0.2	60.8	0.0	60.7	-0.2	60.6	-0.2	60.5	-0.2
1977	61.4	1.5	63.0	2.6	63.5	0.8	64.1	0.9	64.2	0.2	64.5	0.5	64.9	0.6	64.5	-0.6	64.7	0.3	65.1	0.6	65.6	0.8	65.7	0.2
1978	66.3	0.9	68.2	2.9	68.7	0.7	69.3	0.9	70.3	1.4	71.4	1.6	72.0	0.8	72.7	1.0	72.1	-0.8	72.1	0.0	73.1	1.4	73.3	0.3
1979	75.5	3.0	76.9	1.9	78.2	1.7	78.7	0.6	78.9	0.3	78.7	-0.3	79.6	1.1	79.5	-0.1	79.9	0.5	80.9	1.3	81.3	0.5	81.9	0.7
1980	82.1	0.2	82.1	0.0	83.5	1.7	84.7	1.4	85.6	1.1	87.6	2.3	88.1	0.6	88.9	0.9	88.8	-0.1	89.8	1.1	90.3	0.6	90.4	0.1
1981	91.4	1.1	91.6	0.2	92.1	0.5	91.9	-0.2	92.5	0.7	92.9	0.4	93.9	1.1	94.4	0.5	94.7	0.3	94.3	-0.4	93.8	-0.5	94.5	0.7
1982	95.4	1.0	96.7	1.4	96.8	0.1	97.7	0.9	97.4	-0.3	98.3	0.9	98.8	0.5	98.6	-0.2	98.8	0.2	98.0	-0.8	97.8	-0.2	97.7	-0.1
1983	98.3	0.6	98.7	0.4	99.0	0.3	99.6	0.6	99.9	0.3	100.7	0.8	100.5	-0.2	100.9	0.4	100.8	-0.1	100.6	-0.2	100.0	-0.6	100.2	0.2
1984	101.5	1.3	102.6	1.1	102.7	0.1	102.2	-0.5	102.1	-0.1	102.5	0.4	103.2	0.7	103.7	0.5	102.5	-1.2	102.4	-0.1	101.9	-0.5	101.8	-0.1
1985	103.2	1.4	104.5	1.3	105.0	0.5	104.9	-0.1	105.0	0.1	104.6	-0.4	105.7	1.1	105.0	-0.7	105.6	0.6	105.8	0.2	105.3	-0.5	106.1	0.8
1986	106.1	0.0	106.0	-0.1	106.9	0.8	107.0	0.1	107.2	0.2	107.0	-0.2	107.9	0.8	108.6	0.6	109.5	0.8	109.7	0.2	109.0	-0.6	109.4	0.4
1987	111.2	1.6	110.9	-0.3	110.5	-0.4	111.7	1.1	112.2	0.4	112.3	0.1	112.7	0.4	113.2	0.4	113.1	-0.1	113.6	0.4	113.6	0.0	113.3	-0.3
1988	114.7	1.2	114.0	-0.6	113.0	-0.9	114.6	1.4	115.5	0.8	116.6	1.0	117.8	1.0	117.6	-0.2	117.9	0.3	119.1	1.0	117.9	-1.0	118.7	0.7
1989	120.0	1.1	120.8	0.7	122.7	1.6	123.2	0.4	124.0	0.6	125.8	1.5	126.5	0.6	126.1	-0.3	126.9	0.6	128.0	0.9	128.4	0.3	128.6	0.2
1990	129.2	0.5	131.3	1.6	131.6	0.2	131.0	-0.5	131.5	0.4	131.8	0.2	133.0	0.9	133.5	0.4	132.9	-0.4	133.7	0.6	133.8	0.1	134.8	0.7
1991	135.7	0.7	136.4	0.5	136.7	0.2	136.8	0.1	137.1	0.2	137.2	0.1	137.1	-0.1	136.5	-0.4	136.1	-0.3	135.9	-0.1	136.3	0.3	136.2	-0.1
1992	137.0	0.6	137.4	0.3	138.3	0.7	138.8	0.4	139.0	0.1	138.9	-0.1	139.4	0.4	138.9	-0.4	139.5	0.4	139.4	-0.1	138.9	-0.4	139.4	0.4
1993	139.8	0.3	140.0	0.1	140.5	0.4	141.4	0.6	142.0	0.4	140.8	-0.8	140.0	-0.6	139.9	-0.1	141.7	1.3	140.8	-0.6	142.2	1.0	141.5	-0.5
1994	143.2	1.2	141.6	-1.1	142.4	0.6	143.0	0.4	142.3	-0.5	143.1	0.6	143.9	0.6	143.5	-0.3	145.3	1.3	146.2	0.6	145.7	-0.3	147.0	0.9
1995	149.1	1.4	149.3	0.1	148.8	-0.3	149.6	0.5	150.4	0.5	149.4	-0.7	149.7	0.2	150.3	0.4	150.8	0.3	150.9	0.1	150.9	0.0	150.4	-0.3

Source: U.S. Department of Labor, Bureau of Labor Statistics, Division of Consumer Prices and Price Indexes. - indicates no data collected for period.

Philadelphia, PA-NJ

Consumer Price Index - All Urban Consumers
Base 1982-1984 = 100

Housing

For 1976-1995. Columns headed % show percentile change in the index from the previous period for which an index is available.

Year	Jan Index	%	Feb Index	%	Mar Index	%	Apr Index	%	May Index	%	Jun Index	%	Jul Index	%	Aug Index	%	Sep Index	%	Oct Index	%	Nov Index	%	Dec Index	%
1976	57.8	-	58.1	0.5	58.3	0.3	58.4	0.2	58.7	0.5	58.7	0.0	59.0	0.5	59.0	0.0	59.9	1.5	60.2	0.5	60.5	0.5	60.5	0.0
1977	60.8	0.5	61.0	0.3	61.7	1.1	62.1	0.6	62.6	0.8	62.7	0.2	63.0	0.5	63.4	0.6	64.2	1.3	64.1	-0.2	64.0	-0.2	63.5	-0.8
1978	63.7	0.3	63.8	0.2	64.2	0.6	64.4	0.3	64.5	0.2	64.8	0.5	65.8	1.5	66.3	0.8	67.1	1.2	67.5	0.6	67.8	0.4	68.3	0.7
1979	68.1	-0.3	68.2	0.1	68.1	-0.1	69.3	1.8	70.7	2.0	72.5	2.5	72.8	0.4	73.4	0.8	74.4	1.4	74.5	0.1	75.4	1.2	75.9	0.7
1980	77.6	2.2	79.3	2.2	80.5	1.5	82.1	2.0	82.9	1.0	84.7	2.2	85.3	0.7	85.5	0.2	85.8	0.4	85.7	-0.1	85.9	0.2	86.8	1.0
1981	87.7	1.0	88.8	1.3	90.2	1.6	91.7	1.7	91.8	0.1	94.0	2.4	95.2	1.3	96.5	1.4	97.8	1.3	97.4	-0.4	97.1	-0.3	96.6	-0.5
1982	97.2	0.6	96.9	-0.3	96.4	-0.5	96.0	-0.4	96.2	0.2	98.6	2.5	98.7	0.1	98.5	-0.2	99.2	0.7	97.9	-1.3	98.6	0.7	97.5	-1.1
1983	97.3	-0.2	97.3	0.0	97.4	0.1	97.1	-0.3	97.6	0.5	98.2	0.6	99.4	1.2	99.1	-0.3	99.5	0.4	98.6	-0.9	99.1	0.5	99.7	0.6
1984	100.9	1.2	102.1	1.2	102.2	0.1	102.7	0.5	103.4	0.7	104.3	0.9	104.3	0.0	104.6	0.3	105.4	0.8	105.4	0.0	106.8	1.3	105.8	-0.9
1985	106.0	0.2	107.2	1.1	107.3	0.1	108.2	0.8	109.6	1.3	109.9	0.3	110.2	0.3	110.3	0.1	109.6	-0.6	109.5	-0.1	110.6	1.0	111.5	0.8
1986	111.5	0.0	111.7	0.2	111.2	-0.4	111.5	0.3	111.7	0.2	113.8	1.9	113.7	-0.1	114.1	0.4	114.9	0.7	113.5	-1.2	113.3	-0.2	113.5	0.2
1987	113.5	0.0	114.9	1.2	115.0	0.1	116.2	1.0	118.4	1.9	120.6	1.9	120.1	-0.4	121.4	1.1	120.8	-0.5	120.7	-0.1	119.2	-1.2	120.0	0.7
1988	120.4	0.3	120.5	0.1	120.7	0.2	121.5	0.7	122.3	0.7	125.2	2.4	126.5	1.0	128.0	1.2	129.1	0.9	126.2	-2.2	128.2	1.6	128.6	0.3
1989	127.6	-0.8	127.2	-0.3	128.9	1.3	128.4	-0.4	129.5	0.9	131.3	1.4	132.4	0.8	132.7	0.2	134.2	1.1	132.9	-1.0	131.9	-0.8	132.7	0.6
1990	134.5	1.4	134.6	0.1	136.2	1.2	136.8	0.4	136.9	0.1	138.4	1.1	139.9	1.1	141.4	1.1	141.7	0.2	141.1	-0.4	141.1	0.0	141.3	0.1
1991	143.2	1.3	143.4	0.1	144.5	0.8	143.4	-0.8	144.2	0.6	146.2	1.4	147.8	1.1	148.1	0.2	147.9	-0.1	145.7	-1.5	145.0	-0.5	147.2	1.5
1992	147.9	0.5	148.0	0.1	148.5	0.3	147.3	-0.8	147.4	0.1	151.8	3.0	151.0	-0.5	152.2	0.8	151.8	-0.3	151.0	-0.5	149.1	-1.3	148.9	-0.1
1993	148.9	0.0	151.5	1.7	152.6	0.7	151.7	-0.6	150.3	-0.9	152.8	1.7	152.6	-0.1	153.1	0.3	153.2	0.1	153.1	-0.1	151.6	-1.0	151.6	0.0
1994	152.7	0.7	153.5	0.5	154.2	0.5	152.6	-1.0	153.1	0.3	156.1	2.0	156.6	0.3	157.3	0.4	157.4	0.1	157.0	-0.3	156.4	-0.4	154.0	-1.5
1995	155.5	1.0	156.9	0.9	157.3	0.3	156.8	-0.3	157.0	0.1	158.3	0.8	160.2	1.2	160.1	-0.1	160.3	0.1	160.2	-0.1	158.6	-1.0	159.0	0.3

Source: U.S. Department of Labor, Bureau of Labor Statistics, Division of Consumer Prices and Price Indexes. - indicates no data collected for period.

Philadelphia, PA-NJ
Consumer Price Index - Urban Wage Earners
Base 1982-1984 = 100
Housing

For 1976-1995. Columns headed % show percentile change in the index from the previous period for which an index is available.

Year	Jan Index	%	Feb Index	%	Mar Index	%	Apr Index	%	May Index	%	Jun Index	%	Jul Index	%	Aug Index	%	Sep Index	%	Oct Index	%	Nov Index	%	Dec Index	%
1976	57.6	-	58.0	0.7	58.1	0.2	58.3	0.3	58.5	0.3	58.5	0.0	58.8	0.5	58.9	0.2	59.8	1.5	60.0	0.3	60.3	0.5	60.4	0.2
1977	60.6	0.3	60.9	0.5	61.5	1.0	62.0	0.8	62.4	0.6	62.6	0.3	62.8	0.3	63.2	0.6	64.0	1.3	63.9	-0.2	63.8	-0.2	63.3	-0.8
1978	63.5	0.3	63.5	0.0	63.9	0.6	64.4	0.8	64.4	0.0	64.7	0.5	65.6	1.4	66.1	0.8	66.8	1.1	67.1	0.4	67.5	0.6	68.1	0.9
1979	67.9	-0.3	68.1	0.3	67.9	-0.3	69.0	1.6	70.1	1.6	71.7	2.3	72.3	0.8	72.9	0.8	73.8	1.2	73.9	0.1	75.0	1.5	75.3	0.4
1980	76.9	2.1	78.1	1.6	79.4	1.7	81.0	2.0	81.5	0.6	83.4	2.3	84.1	0.8	84.5	0.5	84.5	0.0	84.4	-0.1	84.9	0.6	85.7	0.9
1981	86.7	1.2	87.5	0.9	88.3	0.9	89.8	1.7	90.4	0.7	92.1	1.9	93.5	1.5	94.7	1.3	96.0	1.4	95.8	-0.2	95.3	-0.5	94.4	-0.9
1982	95.0	0.6	94.8	-0.2	94.2	-0.6	93.9	-0.3	94.1	0.2	96.6	2.7	96.6	0.0	96.4	-0.2	97.1	0.7	95.9	-1.2	96.7	0.8	95.6	-1.1
1983	96.4	0.8	97.3	0.9	98.4	1.1	98.6	0.2	97.8	-0.8	99.0	1.2	100.4	1.4	100.7	0.3	100.7	0.0	100.2	-0.5	100.9	0.7	100.9	0.0
1984	101.8	0.9	102.7	0.9	102.4	-0.3	102.1	-0.3	103.6	1.5	105.2	1.5	105.4	0.2	106.0	0.6	108.2	2.1	108.7	0.5	108.7	0.0	107.5	-1.1
1985	107.7	0.2	109.0	1.2	109.0	0.0	109.9	0.8	111.3	1.3	111.6	0.3	111.8	0.2	111.9	0.1	111.2	-0.6	111.2	0.0	112.3	1.0	113.2	0.8
1986	113.2	0.0	113.4	0.2	112.9	-0.4	113.3	0.4	113.4	0.1	115.5	1.9	115.3	-0.2	115.7	0.3	116.5	0.7	115.1	-1.2	115.0	-0.1	115.2	0.2
1987	115.2	0.0	116.4	1.0	116.5	0.1	117.5	0.9	119.8	2.0	122.2	2.0	121.7	-0.4	123.0	1.1	122.4	-0.5	122.3	-0.1	120.9	-1.1	121.9	0.8
1988	122.2	0.2	122.0	-0.2	122.2	0.2	122.9	0.6	123.8	0.7	126.8	2.4	128.2	1.1	129.5	1.0	130.7	0.9	127.8	-2.2	129.8	1.6	130.2	0.3
1989	129.6	-0.5	129.1	-0.4	130.8	1.3	130.5	-0.2	131.7	0.9	133.5	1.4	134.7	0.9	135.1	0.3	136.6	1.1	135.0	-1.2	134.1	-0.7	134.9	0.6
1990	136.5	1.2	136.7	0.1	138.3	1.2	138.8	0.4	139.0	0.1	140.7	1.2	141.9	0.9	143.2	0.9	143.8	0.4	143.0	-0.6	143.1	0.1	143.3	0.1
1991	144.7	1.0	145.0	0.2	146.1	0.8	145.2	-0.6	146.2	0.7	148.3	1.4	149.8	1.0	150.1	0.2	150.1	0.0	147.8	-1.5	147.0	-0.5	149.2	1.5
1992	149.6	0.3	149.6	0.0	150.1	0.3	149.1	-0.7	149.3	0.1	153.7	2.9	152.8	-0.6	154.0	0.8	153.6	-0.3	152.3	-0.8	150.9	-0.9	150.9	0.0
1993	150.7	-0.1	153.1	1.6	154.2	0.7	153.7	-0.3	152.3	-0.9	154.8	1.6	154.5	-0.2	155.1	0.4	155.3	0.1	154.8	-0.3	153.7	-0.7	153.7	0.0
1994	154.5	0.5	155.2	0.5	155.8	0.4	154.6	-0.8	155.1	0.3	158.0	1.9	158.4	0.3	159.0	0.4	159.3	0.2	158.6	-0.4	158.0	-0.4	156.3	-1.1
1995	157.4	0.7	158.7	0.8	159.1	0.3	158.6	-0.3	158.9	0.2	160.4	0.9	162.1	1.1	162.0	-0.1	162.2	0.1	161.8	-0.2	160.8	-0.6	161.1	0.2

Source: U.S. Department of Labor, Bureau of Labor Statistics, Division of Consumer Prices and Price Indexes. - indicates no data collected for period.

Philadelphia, PA-NJ
Consumer Price Index - All Urban Consumers
Base 1982-1984 = 100
Apparel and Upkeep

For 1952-1995. Columns headed % show percentile change in the index from the previous period for which an index is available.

Year	Jan Index	%	Feb Index	%	Mar Index	%	Apr Index	%	May Index	%	Jun Index	%	Jul Index	%	Aug Index	%	Sep Index	%	Oct Index	%	Nov Index	%	Dec Index	%
1952	-	-	-	-	-	-	-	-	-	-	-	-	-	-	-	-	-	-	-	-	-	-	44.2	-
1953	43.8	-0.9	44.0	0.5	44.1	0.2	43.8	-0.7	44.0	0.5	44.0	0.0	44.0	0.0	44.0	0.0	44.9	2.0	44.9	0.0	45.0	0.2	45.0	0.0
1954	44.7	-0.7	44.6	-0.2	44.5	-0.2	44.5	0.0	44.3	-0.4	44.3	0.0	44.4	0.2	44.5	0.2	44.7	0.4	44.8	0.2	44.9	0.2	44.7	-0.4
1955	44.6	-0.2	44.6	0.0	44.2	-0.9	44.1	-0.2	44.0	-0.2	44.0	0.0	43.8	-0.5	44.0	0.5	44.6	1.4	44.6	0.0	45.0	0.9	44.9	-0.2
1956	43.9	-2.2	44.3	0.9	44.4	0.2	44.4	0.0	44.4	0.0	44.4	0.0	44.5	0.2	44.5	0.0	45.9	3.1	45.6	-0.7	45.8	0.4	45.9	0.2
1957	45.4	-1.1	45.9	1.1	46.1	0.4	45.7	-0.9	45.4	-0.7	45.4	0.0	45.9	1.1	45.9	0.0	46.5	1.3	46.7	0.4	46.6	-0.2	46.2	-0.9
1958	45.2	-2.2	45.2	0.0	45.4	0.4	45.2	-0.4	45.5	0.7	45.4	-0.2	44.9	-1.1	45.1	0.4	46.5	3.1	46.4	-0.2	46.4	0.0	46.4	0.0
1959	45.3	-2.4	45.4	0.2	45.6	0.4	45.6	0.0	45.6	0.0	45.7	0.2	45.9	0.4	46.0	0.2	47.6	3.5	47.7	0.2	47.6	-0.2	47.5	-0.2
1960	46.9	-1.3	47.2	0.6	47.6	0.8	47.6	0.0	47.6	0.0	47.4	-0.4	47.6	0.4	47.6	0.0	48.9	2.7	49.2	0.6	49.2	0.0	49.4	0.4
1961	48.9	-1.0	48.8	-0.2	49.0	0.4	48.8	-0.4	48.6	-0.4	48.6	0.0	48.6	0.0	48.6	0.0	49.7	2.3	50.0	0.6	49.9	-0.2	50.0	0.2
1962	48.8	-2.4	48.9	0.2	49.0	0.2	49.2	0.4	49.2	0.0	49.3	0.2	49.2	-0.2	49.4	0.4	50.4	2.0	50.4	0.0	50.5	0.2	50.3	-0.4
1963	49.9	-0.8	49.9	0.0	50.1	0.4	50.2	0.2	49.8	-0.8	50.0	0.4	50.1	0.2	49.8	-0.6	50.6	1.6	50.8	0.4	50.8	0.0	50.8	0.0
1964	50.1	-1.4	50.2	0.2	50.2	0.0	50.3	0.2	50.1	-0.4	50.0	-0.2	49.7	-0.6	49.8	0.2	50.7	1.8	51.1	0.8	51.2	0.2	51.1	-0.2
1965	50.4	-1.4	50.6	0.4	50.7	0.2	50.6	-0.2	51.1	1.0	51.0	-0.2	50.3	-1.4	50.6	0.6	51.4	1.6	51.7	0.6	51.8	0.2	51.8	0.0
1966	51.0	-1.5	51.6	1.2	52.2	1.2	52.4	0.4	52.5	0.2	52.5	0.0	52.8	0.6	52.4	-0.8	54.1	3.2	54.0	-0.2	54.4	0.7	54.6	0.4
1967	53.5	-2.0	53.9	0.7	54.4	0.9	55.0	1.1	55.3	0.5	55.4	0.2	54.9	-0.9	55.0	0.2	56.3	2.4	56.5	0.4	56.6	0.2	56.6	0.0
1968	56.0	-1.1	56.8	1.4	57.4	1.1	57.9	0.9	58.1	0.3	58.0	-0.2	57.9	-0.2	57.9	0.0	59.8	3.3	60.5	1.2	60.4	-0.2	60.6	0.3
1969	59.6	-1.7	60.3	1.2	61.2	1.5	60.9	-0.5	60.6	-0.5	60.1	-0.8	-	-	60.6	0.8	62.8	3.6	63.1	0.5	63.3	0.3	63.2	-0.2
1970	62.7	-0.8	63.3	1.0	64.0	1.1	63.1	-1.4	63.3	0.3	63.4	0.2	62.2	-1.9	62.8	1.0	65.5	4.3	66.3	1.2	66.2	-0.2	65.5	-1.1
1971	63.9	-2.4	64.7	1.3	65.4	1.1	66.8	2.1	67.0	0.3	66.9	-0.1	65.0	-2.8	64.6	-0.6	66.9	3.6	67.2	0.4	66.7	-0.7	66.4	-0.4
1972	64.7	-2.6	64.2	-0.8	66.3	3.3	66.7	0.6	66.4	-0.4	66.4	0.0	65.1	-2.0	64.9	-0.3	67.8	4.5	68.1	0.4	67.9	-0.3	67.8	-0.1
1973	66.0	-2.7	67.8	2.7	69.2	2.1	69.4	0.3	69.4	0.0	69.3	-0.1	67.6	-2.5	67.5	-0.1	69.6	3.1	70.6	1.4	70.7	0.1	70.7	0.0
1974	68.6	-3.0	70.7	3.1	72.0	1.8	72.0	0.0	72.1	0.1	73.0	1.2	71.7	-1.8	73.3	2.2	75.2	2.6	75.8	0.8	76.6	1.1	76.0	-0.8
1975	74.2	-2.4	74.5	0.4	74.9	0.5	75.0	0.1	74.7	-0.4	74.3	-0.5	73.4	-1.2	75.2	2.5	76.1	1.2	76.1	0.0	76.8	0.9	76.6	-0.3
1976	74.8	-2.3	75.8	1.3	76.3	0.7	76.4	0.1	76.9	0.7	77.1	0.3	76.2	-1.2	76.8	0.8	78.4	2.1	78.9	0.6	79.2	0.4	78.7	-0.6
1977	77.8	-1.1	77.9	0.1	78.7	1.0	78.8	0.1	78.4	-0.5	78.3	-0.1	78.7	0.5	79.6	1.1	79.9	0.4	80.6	0.9	80.6	0.0	80.2	-0.5
1978	77.9	-2.9	76.1	-2.3	78.0	2.5	79.1	1.4	79.9	1.0	81.4	1.9	83.2	2.2	82.1	-1.3	82.4	0.4	83.6	1.5	83.9	0.4	82.7	-1.4
1979	81.9	-1.0	86.1	5.1	85.3	-0.9	85.5	0.2	85.3	-0.2	85.0	-0.4	83.9	-1.3	87.1	3.8	88.6	1.7	86.6	-2.3	89.0	2.8	89.6	0.7
1980	88.2	-1.6	92.6	5.0	96.7	4.4	96.5	-0.2	95.5	-1.0	93.4	-2.2	93.9	0.5	96.0	2.2	95.2	-0.8	96.9	1.8	95.2	-1.8	93.1	-2.2
1981	92.6	-0.5	92.6	0.0	95.4	3.0	95.4	0.0	95.1	-0.3	95.1	0.0	90.2	-5.2	97.7	8.3	100.4	2.8	100.4	0.0	98.2	-2.2	98.0	-0.2
1982	96.4	-1.6	95.7	-0.7	96.6	0.9	98.6	2.1	97.0	-1.6	98.9	2.0	97.5	-1.4	98.8	1.3	102.8	4.0	102.8	0.0	101.2	-1.6	99.3	-1.9
1983	97.6	-1.7	98.2	0.6	100.6	2.4	100.4	-0.2	98.1	-2.3	99.5	1.4	99.3	-0.2	101.8	2.5	102.7	0.9	103.7	1.0	102.4	-1.3	99.5	-2.8
1984	100.0	0.5	99.2	-0.8	99.2	0.0	100.5	1.3	99.0	-1.5	97.6	-1.4	99.0	1.4	102.4	3.4	103.8	1.4	104.3	0.5	103.1	-1.2	102.4	-0.7
1985	99.6	-2.7	100.3	0.7	101.1	0.8	103.3	2.2	102.4	-0.9	100.2	-2.1	100.0	-0.2	102.7	2.7	101.9	-0.8	101.8	-0.1	103.3	1.5	100.6	-2.6
1986	100.2	-0.4	100.0	-0.2	100.4	0.4	99.7	-0.7	100.0	0.3	97.1	-2.9	100.6	3.6	102.1	1.5	104.8	2.6	104.4	-0.4	103.5	-0.9	102.8	-0.7
1987	104.7	1.8	103.5	-1.1	104.3	0.8	110.6	6.0	106.6	-3.6	103.7	-2.7	102.0	-1.6	110.3	8.1	111.3	0.9	112.4	1.0	113.0	0.5	110.3	-2.4
1988	109.1	-1.1	106.9	-2.0	112.7	5.4	107.9	-4.3	109.2	1.2	104.6	-4.2	108.7	3.9	108.9	0.2	112.7	3.5	113.7	0.9	113.8	0.1	110.3	-3.1
1989	111.3	0.9	108.9	-2.2	101.0	-7.3	102.7	1.7	102.8	0.1	98.4	-4.3	96.4	-2.0	91.8	-4.8	93.4	1.7	97.8	4.7	95.8	-2.0	92.0	-4.0
1990	87.8	-4.6	94.4	7.5	101.4	7.4	107.1	5.6	108.7	1.5	102.8	-5.4	100.4	-2.3	100.7	0.3	105.9	5.2	105.1	-0.8	101.9	-3.0	100.6	-1.3
1991	103.0	2.4	103.1	0.1	106.6	3.4	105.5	-1.0	106.0	0.5	98.9	-6.7	92.8	-6.2	100.3	8.1	107.6	7.3	104.1	-3.3	108.4	4.1	108.6	0.2
1992	104.9	-3.4	100.5	-4.2	107.1	6.6	110.4	3.1	110.9	0.5	105.8	-4.6	103.6	-2.1	107.4	3.7	107.0	-0.4	107.0	0.0	108.8	1.7	104.0	-4.4
1993	103.2	-0.8	107.5	4.2	105.7	-1.7	108.8	2.9	101.0	-7.2	105.6	4.6	106.9	1.2	108.4	1.4	105.3	-2.9	111.8	6.2	108.6	-2.9	99.5	-8.4
1994	103.5	4.0	106.1	2.5	107.1	0.9	107.0	-0.1	107.8	0.7	105.4	-2.2	107.8	2.3	105.3	-2.3	105.2	-0.1	108.0	2.7	106.3	-1.6	99.8	-6.1
1995	101.4	1.6	107.7	6.2	107.0	-0.6	103.3	-3.5	99.8	-3.4	98.1	-1.7	95.4	-2.8	102.9	7.9	104.2	1.3	104.4	0.2	104.1	-0.3	96.7	-7.1

Source: U.S. Department of Labor, Bureau of Labor Statistics, Division of Consumer Prices and Price Indexes. - indicates no data collected for period.

Philadelphia, PA-NJ
Consumer Price Index - Urban Wage Earners
Base 1982-1984 = 100
Apparel and Upkeep

For 1952-1995. Columns headed % show percentile change in the index from the previous period for which an index is available.

Year	Jan Index	%	Feb Index	%	Mar Index	%	Apr Index	%	May Index	%	Jun Index	%	Jul Index	%	Aug Index	%	Sep Index	%	Oct Index	%	Nov Index	%	Dec Index	%
1952	-	-	-	-	-	-	-	-	-	-	-	-	-	-	-	-	-	-	-	-	-	-	51.0	-
1953	50.5	-1.0	50.8	0.6	50.9	0.2	50.5	-0.8	50.8	0.6	50.8	0.0	50.8	0.0	50.8	0.0	51.8	2.0	51.8	0.0	51.9	0.2	51.9	0.0
1954	51.6	-0.6	51.5	-0.2	51.4	-0.2	51.4	0.0	51.1	-0.6	51.1	0.0	51.3	0.4	51.4	0.2	51.6	0.4	51.7	0.2	51.8	0.2	51.6	-0.4
1955	51.5	-0.2	51.5	0.0	51.0	-1.0	50.9	-0.2	50.8	-0.2	50.8	0.0	50.5	-0.6	50.8	0.6	51.5	1.4	51.5	0.0	52.0	1.0	51.8	-0.4
1956	50.7	-2.1	51.1	0.8	51.2	0.2	51.3	0.2	51.2	-0.2	51.2	0.0	51.3	0.2	51.4	0.2	52.9	2.9	52.7	-0.4	52.9	0.4	52.9	0.0
1957	52.3	-1.1	52.9	1.1	53.2	0.6	52.8	-0.8	52.3	-0.9	52.3	0.0	53.0	1.3	52.9	-0.2	53.6	1.3	53.9	0.6	53.8	-0.2	53.4	-0.7
1958	52.2	-2.2	52.2	0.0	52.3	0.2	52.2	-0.2	52.5	0.6	52.3	-0.4	51.8	-1.0	52.0	0.4	53.7	3.3	53.5	-0.4	53.6	0.2	53.5	-0.2
1959	52.3	-2.2	52.4	0.2	52.7	0.6	52.7	0.0	52.7	0.0	52.8	0.2	53.0	0.4	53.0	0.0	55.0	3.8	55.0	0.0	55.0	0.0	54.8	-0.4
1960	54.1	-1.3	54.5	0.7	54.9	0.7	54.9	0.0	54.9	0.0	54.7	-0.4	54.9	0.4	55.0	0.2	56.4	2.5	56.8	0.7	56.8	0.0	57.1	0.5
1961	56.4	-1.2	56.3	-0.2	56.6	0.5	56.3	-0.5	56.1	-0.4	56.1	0.0	56.0	-0.2	56.1	0.2	57.3	2.1	57.7	0.7	57.6	-0.2	57.7	0.2
1962	56.3	-2.4	56.4	0.2	56.6	0.4	56.8	0.4	56.8	0.0	56.9	0.2	56.8	-0.2	57.1	0.5	58.2	1.9	58.2	0.0	58.3	0.2	58.0	-0.5
1963	57.6	-0.7	57.6	0.0	57.8	0.3	57.9	0.2	57.5	-0.7	57.7	0.3	57.8	0.2	57.5	-0.5	58.3	1.4	58.7	0.7	58.6	-0.2	58.6	0.0
1964	57.8	-1.4	58.0	0.3	57.9	-0.2	58.0	0.2	57.8	-0.3	57.7	-0.2	57.4	-0.5	57.5	0.2	58.5	1.7	58.9	0.7	59.0	0.2	59.0	0.0
1965	58.2	-1.4	58.3	0.2	58.5	0.3	58.3	-0.3	58.9	1.0	58.9	0.0	58.0	-1.5	58.3	0.5	59.3	1.7	59.6	0.5	59.8	0.3	59.8	0.0
1966	58.9	-1.5	59.6	1.2	60.2	1.0	60.5	0.5	60.6	0.2	60.6	0.0	61.0	0.7	60.5	-0.8	62.4	3.1	62.4	0.0	62.8	0.6	63.1	0.5
1967	61.8	-2.1	62.2	0.6	62.8	1.0	63.5	1.1	63.8	0.5	64.0	0.3	63.3	-1.1	63.5	0.3	64.9	2.2	65.2	0.5	65.3	0.2	65.3	0.0
1968	64.6	-1.1	65.6	1.5	66.2	0.9	66.8	0.9	67.1	0.4	67.0	-0.1	66.8	-0.3	66.8	0.0	69.1	3.4	69.8	1.0	69.7	-0.1	69.9	0.3
1969	68.8	-1.6	69.6	1.2	70.7	1.6	70.6	-0.1	70.3	-0.4	70.0	-0.4	69.3	-1.0	70.0	1.0	72.5	3.6	72.8	0.4	73.1	0.4	73.0	-0.1
1970	72.3	-1.0	73.1	1.1	73.9	1.1	72.8	-1.5	73.1	0.4	73.2	0.1	71.8	-1.9	72.5	1.0	75.6	4.3	76.5	1.2	76.4	-0.1	75.6	-1.0
1971	73.8	-2.4	74.7	1.2	75.5	1.1	77.1	2.1	77.4	0.4	77.2	-0.3	75.0	-2.8	74.5	-0.7	77.2	3.6	77.5	0.4	76.9	-0.8	76.6	-0.4
1972	74.6	-2.6	74.1	-0.7	76.5	3.2	76.9	0.5	76.7	-0.3	76.6	-0.1	75.1	-2.0	74.9	-0.3	78.2	4.4	78.6	0.5	78.4	-0.3	78.2	-0.3
1973	76.2	-2.6	78.2	2.6	79.9	2.2	80.1	0.3	80.1	0.0	79.9	-0.2	78.0	-2.4	77.9	-0.1	80.4	3.2	81.5	1.4	81.6	0.1	81.6	0.0
1974	79.2	-2.9	81.6	3.0	83.1	1.8	83.1	0.0	83.2	0.1	84.2	1.2	82.8	-1.7	84.6	2.2	86.8	2.6	87.5	0.8	88.4	1.0	87.7	-0.8
1975	85.6	-2.4	86.0	0.5	86.4	0.5	86.6	0.2	86.2	-0.5	85.7	-0.6	84.7	-1.2	86.8	2.5	87.8	1.2	87.8	0.0	88.6	0.9	88.4	-0.2
1976	86.3	-2.4	87.5	1.4	88.1	0.7	88.2	0.1	88.8	0.7	88.9	0.1	87.9	-1.1	88.7	0.9	90.5	2.0	91.1	0.7	91.4	0.3	90.8	-0.7
1977	89.8	-1.1	89.9	0.1	90.8	1.0	91.0	0.2	90.5	-0.5	90.3	-0.2	90.8	0.6	91.9	1.2	92.2	0.3	93.0	0.9	93.1	0.1	92.6	-0.5
1978	89.1	-3.8	87.2	-2.1	87.5	0.3	91.4	4.5	92.2	0.9	92.6	0.4	88.2	-4.8	90.2	2.3	90.7	0.6	91.7	1.1	92.8	1.2	91.7	-1.2
1979	90.7	-1.1	90.8	0.1	89.4	-1.5	88.6	-0.9	88.6	0.0	89.2	0.7	87.2	-2.2	87.9	0.8	89.1	1.4	89.1	0.0	90.3	1.3	91.4	1.2
1980	90.5	-1.0	93.8	3.6	94.4	0.6	94.9	0.5	94.2	-0.7	93.1	-1.2	93.0	-0.1	94.6	1.7	96.6	2.1	96.9	0.3	95.9	-1.0	94.5	-1.5
1981	93.6	-1.0	95.1	1.6	94.3	-0.8	94.7	0.4	94.6	-0.1	95.3	0.7	91.4	-4.1	99.3	8.6	100.7	1.4	99.6	-1.1	99.6	0.0	96.6	-3.0
1982	96.4	-0.2	95.8	-0.6	98.1	2.4	99.5	1.4	98.3	-1.2	99.3	1.0	98.2	-1.1	97.9	-0.3	101.8	4.0	102.1	0.3	100.5	-1.6	98.1	-2.4
1983	96.3	-1.8	97.0	0.7	102.5	5.7	101.3	-1.2	99.3	-2.0	100.2	0.9	99.9	-0.3	101.0	1.1	102.3	1.3	103.0	0.7	101.4	-1.6	98.5	-2.9
1984	99.2	0.7	98.3	-0.9	100.4	2.1	100.9	0.5	98.9	-2.0	97.5	-1.4	99.6	2.2	102.7	3.1	104.4	1.7	104.3	-0.1	103.0	-1.2	101.9	-1.1
1985	99.1	-2.7	100.3	1.2	100.3	0.0	102.3	2.0	101.6	-0.7	99.8	-1.8	99.3	-0.5	100.9	1.6	100.2	-0.7	100.5	0.3	101.8	1.3	99.5	-2.3
1986	98.9	-0.6	99.3	0.4	99.7	0.4	98.7	-1.0	98.4	-0.3	96.1	-2.3	98.4	2.4	100.3	1.9	101.2	0.9	102.6	1.4	101.9	-0.7	101.3	-0.6
1987	101.5	0.2	99.5	-2.0	100.6	1.1	106.9	6.3	103.3	-3.4	100.2	-3.0	99.4	-0.8	106.7	7.3	106.9	0.2	109.8	2.7	110.0	0.2	108.3	-1.5
1988	106.1	-2.0	103.1	-2.8	110.3	7.0	104.8	-5.0	106.8	1.9	101.0	-5.4	103.9	2.9	103.4	-0.5	108.3	4.7	109.2	0.8	109.5	0.3	105.0	-4.1
1989	106.3	1.2	104.2	-2.0	95.2	-8.6	98.0	2.9	97.7	-0.3	93.2	-4.6	90.2	-3.2	87.2	-3.3	88.6	1.6	94.0	6.1	91.7	-2.4	88.0	-4.0
1990	82.6	-6.1	88.7	7.4	98.4	10.9	104.1	5.8	106.3	2.1	99.8	-6.1	96.9	-2.9	95.7	-1.2	101.3	5.9	100.2	-1.1	98.0	-2.2	99.2	1.2
1991	99.8	0.6	99.2	-0.6	102.2	3.0	101.5	-0.7	98.9	-2.6	93.1	-5.9	88.5	-4.9	95.0	7.3	101.1	6.4	98.1	-3.0	105.2	7.2	105.7	0.5
1992	101.5	-4.0	97.5	-3.9	104.1	6.8	107.7	3.5	105.9	-1.7	103.1	-2.6	101.0	-2.0	103.2	2.2	102.6	-0.6	104.0	1.4	107.4	3.3	101.9	-5.1
1993	101.4	-0.5	106.9	5.4	103.4	-3.3	107.5	4.0	99.9	-7.1	103.5	3.6	105.5	1.9	105.9	0.4	103.3	-2.5	110.7	7.2	108.4	-2.1	99.6	-8.1
1994	101.4	1.8	103.1	1.7	103.0	-0.1	103.0	0.0	102.4	-0.6	101.7	-0.7	103.9	2.2	102.3	-1.5	101.7	-0.6	103.4	1.7	101.2	-2.1	95.2	-5.9
1995	97.4	2.3	104.4	7.2	103.2	-1.1	99.6	-3.5	95.4	-4.2	94.0	-1.5	91.5	-2.7	98.9	8.1	100.5	1.6	100.0	-0.5	100.1	0.1	92.5	-7.6

Source: U.S. Department of Labor, Bureau of Labor Statistics, Division of Consumer Prices and Price Indexes. - indicates no data collected for period.

Philadelphia, PA-NJ

Consumer Price Index - All Urban Consumers
Base 1982-1984 = 100

Transportation

For 1947-1995. Columns headed % show percentile change in the index from the previous period for which an index is available.

Year	Jan		Feb		Mar		Apr		May		Jun		Jul		Aug		Sep		Oct		Nov		Dec	
	Index	%	Index	%	Index	%	Index	%	Index	%	Index	%	Index	%	Index	%	Index	%	Index	%	Index	%	Index	%
1947	15.6	-	15.6	0.0	16.8	7.7	16.9	0.6	16.9	0.0	16.9	0.0	16.9	0.0	17.1	1.2	17.2	0.6	17.2	0.0	17.2	0.0	17.3	0.6
1948	17.4	0.6	17.5	0.6	17.5	0.0	18.2	4.0	18.2	0.0	18.4	1.1	18.7	1.6	19.0	1.6	19.0	0.0	19.0	0.0	19.0	0.0	19.1	0.5
1949	19.2	0.5	19.3	0.5	19.3	0.0	19.3	0.0	21.1	9.3	19.4	-8.1	19.5	0.5	19.5	0.0	19.5	0.0	19.5	0.0	19.5	0.0	19.5	0.0
1950	19.5	0.0	19.5	0.0	19.5	0.0	19.4	-0.5	19.4	0.0	19.4	0.0	19.4	0.0	19.5	0.5	19.4	-0.5	19.2	-1.0	19.2	0.0	21.0	9.4
1951	21.2	1.0	23.4	10.4	23.5	0.4	23.5	0.0	23.5	0.0	23.1	-1.7	22.8	-1.3	23.0	0.9	23.0	0.0	22.8	-0.9	23.9	4.8	23.9	0.0
1952	23.9	0.0	23.2	-2.9	24.1	3.9	24.1	0.0	24.1	0.0	24.2	0.4	24.2	0.0	24.2	0.0	24.2	0.0	24.2	0.0	24.2	0.0	24.2	0.0
1953	24.3	0.4	24.2	-0.4	24.2	0.0	24.3	0.4	24.4	0.4	24.4	0.0	24.6	0.8	24.6	0.0	24.7	0.4	24.8	0.4	24.7	-0.4	24.7	0.0
1954	24.8	0.4	25.0	0.8	25.1	0.4	25.0	-0.4	25.1	0.4	25.0	-0.4	25.0	0.0	25.0	0.0	25.1	0.4	25.1	0.0	25.3	0.8	25.2	-0.4
1955	25.1	-0.4	25.2	0.4	25.1	-0.4	25.0	-0.4	25.3	1.2	25.4	0.4	25.3	-0.4	25.3	0.0	23.6	-6.7	24.1	2.1	24.7	2.5	24.5	-0.8
1956	24.8	1.2	24.7	-0.4	24.8	0.4	24.6	-0.8	24.5	-0.4	24.4	-0.4	24.7	1.2	25.0	1.2	25.0	0.0	25.1	0.4	25.6	2.0	25.7	0.4
1957	25.8	0.4	25.8	0.0	25.8	0.0	25.8	0.0	25.8	0.0	25.5	-1.2	25.4	-0.4	25.5	0.4	25.5	0.0	25.5	0.0	26.5	3.9	26.3	-0.8
1958	25.9	-1.5	25.8	-0.4	26.4	2.3	26.5	0.4	26.3	-0.8	26.3	0.0	26.5	0.8	26.7	0.8	26.8	0.4	26.7	-0.4	27.3	2.2	27.4	0.4
1959	27.6	0.7	27.4	-0.7	27.5	0.4	27.6	0.4	27.8	0.7	27.9	0.4	28.1	0.7	28.2	0.4	28.2	0.0	28.4	0.7	28.5	0.4	28.5	0.0
1960	28.5	0.0	28.5	0.0	28.4	-0.4	28.3	-0.4	28.2	-0.4	28.1	-0.4	28.0	-0.4	28.0	0.0	27.9	-0.4	28.4	1.8	28.5	0.4	28.5	0.0
1961	28.4	-0.4	28.5	0.4	28.6	0.4	29.0	1.4	29.1	0.3	29.2	0.3	29.2	0.0	29.2	0.0	29.1	-0.3	29.4	1.0	29.3	-0.3	29.0	-1.0
1962	29.0	0.0	29.0	0.0	29.0	0.0	29.3	1.0	29.1	-0.7	29.1	0.0	29.2	0.3	29.2	0.0	29.4	0.7	29.2	-0.7	29.5	1.0	29.4	-0.3
1963	28.9	-1.7	29.7	2.8	29.8	0.3	29.9	0.3	29.9	0.0	29.9	0.0	29.9	0.0	29.9	0.0	29.9	0.0	30.2	1.0	30.3	0.3	30.3	0.0
1964	30.4	0.3	30.4	0.0	30.4	0.0	30.5	0.3	30.5	0.0	30.2	-1.0	30.5	1.0	30.5	0.0	30.3	-0.7	30.5	0.7	30.8	1.0	31.0	0.6
1965	31.1	0.3	31.4	1.0	31.3	-0.3	31.4	0.3	31.6	0.6	31.4	-0.6	31.4	0.0	31.3	-0.3	31.3	0.0	31.4	0.3	31.4	0.0	31.4	0.0
1966	31.4	0.0	31.4	0.0	31.5	0.3	31.6	0.3	31.7	0.3	31.8	0.3	31.9	0.3	32.1	0.6	31.8	-0.9	32.1	0.9	32.1	0.0	31.9	-0.6
1967	31.9	0.0	32.0	0.3	32.4	1.3	32.4	0.0	32.4	0.0	32.5	0.3	32.7	0.6	32.8	0.3	32.7	-0.3	33.0	0.9	33.3	0.9	33.3	0.0
1968	33.9	1.8	33.9	0.0	34.0	0.3	33.9	-0.3	34.1	0.6	34.2	0.3	34.4	0.6	34.5	0.3	34.4	-0.3	34.6	0.6	34.9	0.9	34.7	-0.6
1969	34.7	0.0	35.6	2.6	36.0	1.1	36.1	0.3	35.9	-0.6	36.1	0.6	36.1	0.0	36.1	0.0	35.9	-0.6	35.6	-0.8	36.2	1.7	36.3	0.3
1970	36.2	-0.3	37.1	2.5	37.1	0.0	37.6	1.3	37.9	0.8	37.9	0.0	38.1	0.5	38.1	0.0	38.0	-0.3	37.9	-0.3	38.4	1.3	39.1	1.3
1971	39.4	0.8	39.9	1.3	39.8	-0.3	40.1	0.8	40.2	0.2	40.5	0.7	40.6	0.2	40.3	-0.7	40.0	-0.7	40.2	0.5	40.3	0.2	40.4	0.2
1972	40.5	0.2	40.3	-0.5	40.4	0.2	40.4	0.0	40.9	1.2	41.0	0.2	40.9	-0.2	41.0	0.2	41.0	0.0	40.9	-0.2	41.1	0.5	41.2	0.2
1973	41.1	-0.2	41.1	0.0	41.1	0.0	41.4	0.7	41.6	0.5	41.9	0.7	41.9	0.0	41.7	-0.5	41.4	-0.7	41.9	1.2	42.0	0.2	42.5	1.2
1974	42.9	0.9	43.4	1.2	44.3	2.1	44.6	0.7	45.3	1.6	46.1	1.8	46.7	1.3	46.9	0.4	47.2	0.6	47.4	0.4	47.8	0.8	47.9	0.2
1975	47.7	-0.4	47.9	0.4	48.3	0.8	48.6	0.6	48.9	0.6	49.8	1.8	50.4	1.2	50.6	0.4	50.8	0.4	51.3	1.0	51.8	1.0	51.8	0.0
1976	51.7	-0.2	51.7	0.0	52.3	1.2	52.9	1.1	53.5	1.1	54.2	1.3	54.7	0.9	54.9	0.4	55.1	0.4	55.4	0.5	55.6	0.4	55.6	0.0
1977	56.2	1.1	56.8	1.1	57.2	0.7	58.5	2.3	60.0	2.6	60.3	0.5	60.3	0.0	60.1	-0.3	60.6	0.8	60.6	0.0	60.6	0.0	60.5	-0.2
1978	60.7	0.3	60.7	0.0	61.1	0.7	61.4	0.5	61.9	0.8	62.7	1.3	63.1	0.6	63.2	0.2	63.2	0.0	63.0	-0.3	64.2	1.9	64.4	0.3
1979	65.0	0.9	65.4	0.6	66.2	1.2	67.6	2.1	69.3	2.5	71.5	3.2	73.1	2.2	73.7	0.8	74.1	0.5	74.1	0.0	74.7	0.8	75.8	1.5
1980	77.8	2.6	79.9	2.7	81.5	2.0	82.2	0.9	83.4	1.5	83.7	0.4	83.9	0.2	85.2	1.5	85.4	0.2	85.6	0.2	86.9	1.5	87.4	0.6
1981	88.6	1.4	90.6	2.3	91.0	0.4	91.7	0.8	92.3	0.7	92.7	0.4	93.9	1.3	93.8	-0.1	94.4	0.6	95.8	1.5	96.5	0.7	97.2	0.7
1982	96.6	-0.6	95.5	-1.1	94.8	-0.7	93.9	-0.9	94.1	0.2	95.6	1.6	97.1	1.6	96.9	-0.2	96.4	-0.5	97.0	0.6	97.1	0.1	97.5	0.4
1983	98.0	0.5	96.9	-1.1	96.4	-0.5	97.6	1.2	98.4	0.8	98.5	0.1	99.1	0.6	100.7	1.6	101.3	0.6	102.0	0.7	102.4	0.4	102.1	-0.3
1984	102.8	0.7	102.7	-0.1	103.0	0.3	103.8	0.8	104.0	0.2	104.4	0.4	104.8	0.4	105.4	0.6	105.7	0.3	105.3	-0.4	106.0	0.7	106.3	0.3
1985	106.3	0.0	107.1	0.8	107.8	0.7	108.7	0.8	109.2	0.5	109.7	0.5	109.9	0.2	110.0	0.1	110.4	0.4	111.4	0.9	111.5	0.1	111.7	0.2
1986	112.1	0.4	110.9	-1.1	108.4	-2.3	104.7	-3.4	105.8	1.1	107.1	1.2	106.9	-0.2	104.8	-2.0	105.1	0.3	106.1	1.0	106.2	0.1	107.0	0.8
1987	108.5	1.4	108.4	-0.1	108.9	0.5	110.4	1.4	110.7	0.3	111.5	0.7	112.2	0.6	112.0	-0.2	112.6	0.5	113.5	0.8	114.3	0.7	114.6	0.3
1988	114.5	-0.1	114.2	-0.3	114.5	0.3	114.2	-0.3	115.1	0.8	114.8	-0.3	115.3	0.4	115.1	-0.2	115.9	0.7	117.4	1.3	117.7	0.3	117.9	0.2
1989	118.5	0.5	118.0	-0.4	118.0	0.0	120.2	1.9	122.9	2.2	123.3	0.3	123.1	-0.2	122.3	-0.6	122.5	0.2	123.4	0.7	123.0	-0.3	123.1	0.1
1990	124.9	1.5	125.6	0.6	125.2	-0.3	125.2	0.0	125.4	0.2	125.9	0.4	125.3	-0.5	125.9	0.5	128.3	1.9	132.1	3.0	133.8	1.3	134.6	0.6
1991	132.7	-1.4	131.4	-1.0	130.2	-0.9	130.0	-0.2	130.5	0.4	131.0	0.4	132.2	0.9	132.3	0.1	132.5	0.2	134.0	1.1	135.3	1.0	135.7	0.3

[Continued]

Philadelphia, PA-NJ
Consumer Price Index - All Urban Consumers
Base 1982-1984 = 100
Transportation
[Continued]

For 1947-1995. Columns headed % show percentile change in the index from the previous period for which an index is available.

Year	Jan Index	%	Feb Index	%	Mar Index	%	Apr Index	%	May Index	%	Jun Index	%	Jul Index	%	Aug Index	%	Sep Index	%	Oct Index	%	Nov Index	%	Dec Index	%
1992	135.1	-0.4	134.6	-0.4	134.4	-0.1	134.8	0.3	135.0	0.1	136.0	0.7	136.6	0.4	135.9	-0.5	136.1	0.1	137.0	0.7	138.3	0.9	139.4	0.8
1993	139.2	-0.1	138.4	-0.6	138.5	0.1	137.5	-0.7	139.0	1.1	138.4	-0.4	139.4	0.7	137.4	-1.4	139.2	1.3	140.9	1.2	143.2	1.6	143.0	-0.1
1994	142.6	-0.3	142.3	-0.2	142.6	0.2	141.8	-0.6	141.6	-0.1	143.2	1.1	143.5	0.2	144.9	1.0	145.1	0.1	145.7	0.4	147.5	1.2	146.9	-0.4
1995	147.6	0.5	148.0	0.3	148.5	0.3	148.7	0.1	148.5	-0.1	149.5	0.7	148.6	-0.6	148.4	-0.1	148.9	0.3	150.1	0.8	149.1	-0.7	148.6	-0.3

Source: U.S. Department of Labor, Bureau of Labor Statistics, Division of Consumer Prices and Price Indexes. - indicates no data collected for period.

Philadelphia, PA-NJ
Consumer Price Index - Urban Wage Earners
Base 1982-1984 = 100
Transportation

For 1947-1995. Columns headed % show percentile change in the index from the previous period for which an index is available.

Year	Jan Index	%	Feb Index	%	Mar Index	%	Apr Index	%	May Index	%	Jun Index	%	Jul Index	%	Aug Index	%	Sep Index	%	Oct Index	%	Nov Index	%	Dec Index	%
1947	15.1	-	15.1	0.0	16.3	7.9	16.4	0.6	16.4	0.0	16.4	0.0	16.4	0.0	16.6	1.2	16.7	0.6	16.7	0.0	16.7	0.0	16.8	0.6
1948	16.9	0.6	17.0	0.6	17.0	0.0	17.7	4.1	17.7	0.0	17.9	1.1	18.1	1.1	18.4	1.7	18.5	0.5	18.5	0.0	18.4	-0.5	18.5	0.5
1949	18.6	0.5	18.7	0.5	18.7	0.0	18.8	0.5	20.5	9.0	18.9	-7.8	18.9	0.0	18.9	0.0	18.9	0.0	18.9	0.0	19.0	0.5	19.0	0.0
1950	19.0	0.0	19.0	0.0	19.0	0.0	18.8	-1.1	18.9	0.5	18.9	0.0	18.9	0.0	19.0	0.5	18.8	-1.1	18.6	-1.1	18.7	0.5	20.4	9.1
1951	20.6	1.0	22.8	10.7	22.9	0.4	22.9	0.0	22.9	0.0	22.4	-2.2	22.2	-0.9	22.3	0.5	22.4	0.4	22.2	-0.9	23.2	4.5	23.2	0.0
1952	23.2	0.0	22.5	-3.0	23.4	4.0	23.4	0.0	23.4	0.0	23.5	0.4	23.5	0.0	23.5	0.0	23.5	0.0	23.5	-0.0	23.5	0.0	23.5	0.0
1953	23.6	0.4	23.5	-0.4	23.5	0.0	23.6	0.4	23.7	0.4	23.7	0.0	23.9	0.8	23.9	0.0	24.0	0.4	24.1	0.4	24.0	-0.4	24.0	0.0
1954	24.1	0.4	24.3	0.8	24.4	0.4	24.3	-0.4	24.3	0.0	24.3	0.0	24.2	-0.4	24.3	0.4	24.3	0.0	24.4	0.4	24.6	0.8	24.4	-0.8
1955	24.4	0.0	24.4	0.0	24.3	-0.4	24.3	0.0	24.6	1.2	24.7	0.4	24.6	-0.4	24.5	-0.4	22.9	-6.5	23.4	2.2	24.0	2.6	23.8	-0.8
1956	24.1	1.3	24.0	-0.4	24.1	0.4	23.9	-0.8	23.8	-0.4	23.7	-0.4	24.0	1.3	24.3	1.2	24.2	-0.4	24.4	0.8	24.9	2.0	25.0	0.4
1957	25.1	0.4	25.1	0.0	25.1	0.0	25.0	-0.4	25.1	0.4	24.8	-1.2	24.7	-0.4	24.7	0.0	24.8	0.4	24.7	-0.4	25.7	4.0	25.6	-0.4
1958	25.2	-1.6	25.1	-0.4	25.6	2.0	25.7	0.4	25.5	-0.8	25.6	0.4	25.8	0.8	26.0	0.8	26.0	0.0	25.9	-0.4	26.6	2.7	26.7	0.4
1959	26.8	0.4	26.6	-0.7	26.7	0.4	26.8	0.4	27.0	0.7	27.1	0.4	27.3	0.7	27.4	0.4	27.4	0.0	27.6	0.7	27.7	0.4	27.7	0.0
1960	27.7	0.0	27.7	0.0	27.6	-0.4	27.5	-0.4	27.4	-0.4	27.3	-0.4	27.2	-0.4	27.2	0.0	27.1	-0.4	27.5	1.5	27.6	0.4	27.7	0.4
1961	27.6	-0.4	27.7	0.4	27.7	0.0	28.2	1.8	28.3	0.4	28.4	0.4	28.4	0.0	28.3	-0.4	28.2	-0.4	28.5	1.1	28.5	0.0	28.1	-1.4
1962	28.2	0.4	28.2	0.0	28.1	-0.4	28.4	1.1	28.3	-0.4	28.3	0.0	28.3	0.0	28.3	0.0	28.5	0.7	28.4	-0.4	28.6	0.7	28.5	-0.3
1963	28.1	-1.4	28.9	2.8	28.9	0.0	29.0	0.3	29.0	0.0	29.0	0.0	29.1	0.3	29.0	-0.3	29.1	0.3	29.3	0.7	29.4	0.3	29.4	0.0
1964	29.5	0.3	29.5	0.0	29.5	0.0	29.6	0.3	29.6	0.0	29.3	-1.0	29.6	1.0	29.7	0.3	29.5	-0.7	29.7	0.7	29.9	0.7	30.1	0.7
1965	30.2	0.3	30.5	1.0	30.4	-0.3	30.5	0.3	30.7	0.7	30.5	-0.7	30.5	0.0	30.4	-0.3	30.1	-1.0	30.5	1.3	30.5	0.0	30.5	0.0
1966	30.5	0.0	30.5	0.0	30.6	0.3	30.7	0.3	30.7	0.0	30.9	0.7	31.0	0.3	31.2	0.6	30.9	-1.0	31.2	1.0	31.2	0.0	31.0	-0.6
1967	31.0	0.0	31.1	0.3	31.5	1.3	31.5	0.0	31.5	0.0	31.6	0.3	31.8	0.6	31.9	0.3	31.8	-0.3	32.1	0.9	32.3	0.6	32.4	0.3
1968	32.9	1.5	32.9	0.0	33.0	0.3	33.0	0.0	33.1	0.3	33.2	0.3	33.4	0.6	33.5	0.3	33.4	-0.3	33.6	0.6	33.9	0.9	33.7	-0.6
1969	33.7	0.0	34.5	2.4	35.0	1.4	35.1	0.3	34.9	-0.6	35.1	0.6	35.0	-0.3	34.9	-0.3	34.6	-0.9	35.1	1.4	35.2	0.3	35.2	0.0
1970	35.2	0.0	36.0	2.3	36.1	0.3	36.5	1.1	36.8	0.8	37.0	0.5	37.0	0.0	37.0	0.0	36.8	-0.5	37.3	1.4	37.5	0.5	38.0	1.3
1971	38.2	0.5	38.8	1.6	38.7	-0.3	38.9	0.5	39.1	0.5	39.4	0.8	39.5	0.3	39.2	-0.8	38.8	-1.0	39.1	0.8	39.2	0.3	39.3	0.3
1972	39.3	0.0	39.2	-0.3	39.3	0.3	39.3	0.0	39.7	1.0	39.8	0.3	39.7	-0.3	39.8	0.3	39.8	0.0	39.7	-0.3	40.0	0.8	40.1	0.2
1973	39.9	-0.5	39.9	0.0	39.9	0.0	40.2	0.8	40.4	0.5	40.7	0.7	40.7	0.0	40.5	-0.5	40.2	-0.7	40.7	1.2	40.8	0.2	41.3	1.2
1974	41.7	1.0	42.1	1.0	43.0	2.1	43.3	0.7	44.0	1.6	44.8	1.8	45.4	1.3	45.6	0.4	45.9	0.7	46.1	0.4	46.5	0.9	46.5	0.0
1975	46.4	-0.2	46.5	0.2	46.9	0.9	47.2	0.6	47.5	0.6	48.4	1.9	48.9	1.0	49.2	0.6	49.3	0.2	49.8	1.0	50.3	1.0	50.3	0.0
1976	50.2	-0.2	50.2	0.0	50.8	1.2	51.3	1.0	52.0	1.4	52.7	1.3	53.1	0.8	53.3	0.4	53.6	0.6	53.8	0.4	54.0	0.4	54.0	0.0
1977	54.5	0.9	55.1	1.1	55.6	0.9	56.8	2.2	58.3	2.6	58.6	0.5	58.6	0.0	58.3	-0.5	58.9	1.0	58.8	-0.2	58.8	0.0	58.8	0.0
1978	58.9	0.2	59.1	0.3	59.6	0.8	59.9	0.5	60.6	1.2	61.4	1.3	61.9	0.8	62.2	0.5	62.1	-0.2	62.4	0.5	63.4	1.6	63.6	0.3
1979	64.0	0.6	64.6	0.9	65.4	1.2	66.9	2.3	68.3	2.1	70.5	3.2	72.3	2.6	72.7	0.6	73.6	1.2	73.4	-0.3	74.3	1.2	75.2	1.2
1980	77.6	3.2	79.8	2.8	81.3	1.9	82.0	0.9	82.9	1.1	83.5	0.7	83.6	0.1	84.6	1.2	84.6	0.0	85.3	0.8	86.4	1.3	87.2	0.9
1981	88.7	1.7	91.0	2.6	91.4	0.4	91.9	0.5	92.7	0.9	93.0	0.3	94.2	1.3	94.3	0.1	94.8	0.5	96.8	2.1	97.0	0.2	97.6	0.6
1982	97.0	-0.6	95.8	-1.2	95.0	-0.8	94.1	-0.9	94.2	0.1	95.8	1.7	97.4	1.7	97.1	-0.3	96.6	-0.5	97.2	0.6	97.2	0.0	97.6	0.4
1983	98.0	0.4	96.8	-1.2	96.2	-0.6	97.5	1.4	98.3	0.8	98.5	0.2	99.2	0.7	100.7	1.5	101.3	0.6	102.0	0.7	102.3	0.3	102.0	-0.3
1984	102.6	0.6	102.6	0.0	102.9	0.3	103.7	0.8	104.0	0.3	104.3	0.3	104.6	0.3	105.2	0.6	105.6	0.4	105.1	-0.5	105.7	0.6	105.9	0.2
1985	106.1	0.2	106.8	0.7	107.5	0.7	108.4	0.8	109.0	0.6	109.5	0.5	109.7	0.2	109.8	0.1	110.1	0.3	111.1	0.9	111.2	0.1	111.3	0.1
1986	111.8	0.4	110.4	-1.3	107.6	-2.5	103.5	-3.8	104.7	1.2	106.0	1.2	105.8	-0.2	103.5	-2.2	103.8	0.3	104.6	0.8	104.7	0.1	105.6	0.9
1987	107.2	1.5	107.3	0.1	107.9	0.6	109.6	1.6	110.1	0.5	110.9	0.7	111.7	0.7	111.8	0.1	112.0	0.2	113.0	0.9	113.7	0.6	113.9	0.2
1988	113.8	-0.1	113.5	-0.3	114.0	0.4	113.8	-0.2	114.7	0.8	114.5	-0.2	115.1	0.5	115.0	-0.1	115.7	0.6	116.9	1.0	117.2	0.3	117.4	0.2
1989	118.0	0.5	117.6	-0.3	117.7	0.1	120.2	2.1	123.2	2.5	123.7	0.4	123.4	-0.2	122.9	-0.4	123.1	0.2	123.9	0.6	123.0	-0.7	123.0	0.0
1990	124.6	1.3	125.8	1.0	125.4	-0.3	125.3	-0.1	125.6	0.2	126.6	0.8	125.8	-0.6	126.8	0.8	129.7	2.3	133.9	3.2	135.2	1.0	135.6	0.3
1991	133.2	-1.8	131.4	-1.4	130.3	-0.8	130.4	0.1	130.9	0.4	131.3	0.3	133.0	1.3	133.0	0.0	133.6	0.5	134.8	0.9	135.6	0.6	135.8	0.1

[Continued]

Philadelphia, PA-NJ
Consumer Price Index - Urban Wage Earners
Base 1982-1984 = 100
Transportation
[Continued]

For 1947-1995. Columns headed % show percentile change in the index from the previous period for which an index is available.

Year	Jan Index	%	Feb Index	%	Mar Index	%	Apr Index	%	May Index	%	Jun Index	%	Jul Index	%	Aug Index	%	Sep Index	%	Oct Index	%	Nov Index	%	Dec Index	%
1992	135.1	-0.5	134.3	-0.6	133.7	-0.4	133.9	0.1	135.0	0.8	136.3	1.0	136.7	0.3	136.4	-0.2	136.4	0.0	137.3	0.7	138.5	0.9	139.1	0.4
1993	138.9	-0.1	138.4	-0.4	138.0	-0.3	137.0	-0.7	138.3	0.9	138.3	0.0	138.9	0.4	137.6	-0.9	138.9	0.9	140.9	1.4	142.8	1.3	142.4	-0.3
1994	141.7	-0.5	141.4	-0.2	141.6	0.1	141.1	-0.4	141.6	0.4	143.2	1.1	143.8	0.4	145.5	1.2	145.6	0.1	146.5	0.6	148.3	1.2	147.9	-0.3
1995	148.4	0.3	149.1	0.5	149.0	-0.1	149.3	0.2	149.6	0.2	150.5	0.6	149.7	-0.5	149.3	-0.3	149.6	0.2	150.5	0.6	149.6	-0.6	149.3	-0.2

Source: U.S. Department of Labor, Bureau of Labor Statistics, Division of Consumer Prices and Price Indexes. - indicates no data collected for period.

Philadelphia, PA-NJ
Consumer Price Index - All Urban Consumers
Base 1982-1984 = 100
Medical Care

For 1947-1995. Columns headed % show percentile change in the index from the previous period for which an index is available.

Year	Jan Index	%	Feb Index	%	Mar Index	%	Apr Index	%	May Index	%	Jun Index	%	Jul Index	%	Aug Index	%	Sep Index	%	Oct Index	%	Nov Index	%	Dec Index	%
1947	12.1	-	12.1	0.0	12.2	0.8	12.4	1.6	12.5	0.8	12.5	0.0	12.5	0.0	12.5	0.0	12.5	0.0	12.6	0.8	12.6	0.0	12.7	0.8
1948	12.8	0.8	12.9	0.8	12.8	-0.8	12.9	0.8	12.9	0.0	12.9	0.0	13.0	0.8	13.0	0.0	13.0	0.0	13.0	0.0	13.2	1.5	13.2	0.0
1949	13.2	0.0	13.3	0.8	13.3	0.0	13.3	0.0	13.3	0.0	13.4	0.8	13.4	0.0	13.4	0.0	13.4	0.0	13.4	0.0	13.4	0.0	13.5	0.7
1950	13.5	0.0	13.5	0.0	13.5	0.0	13.5	0.0	13.6	0.7	13.6	0.0	13.6	0.0	13.6	0.0	13.7	0.7	13.7	0.0	13.7	0.0	13.7	0.0
1951	13.9	1.5	14.0	0.7	14.2	1.4	14.2	0.0	14.2	0.0	14.2	0.0	14.2	0.0	14.2	0.0	14.2	0.0	14.3	0.7	14.3	0.0	14.3	0.0
1952	14.3	0.0	14.3	0.0	14.5	1.4	14.5	0.0	14.5	0.0	14.5	0.0	15.2	4.8	15.2	0.0	15.5	2.0	15.5	0.0	15.5	0.0	15.5	0.0
1953	15.5	0.0	15.5	0.0	15.5	0.0	15.5	0.0	15.5	0.0	15.6	0.6	15.6	0.0	15.6	0.0	15.6	0.0	15.6	0.0	15.6	0.0	15.9	1.9
1954	15.9	0.0	16.0	0.6	16.0	0.0	16.0	0.0	16.0	0.0	16.2	1.3	16.2	0.0	16.2	0.0	17.1	5.6	17.1	0.0	17.1	0.0	17.3	1.2
1955	17.3	0.0	17.3	0.0	17.5	1.2	17.5	0.0	17.5	0.0	17.5	0.0	17.5	0.0	17.5	0.0	17.5	0.0	17.5	0.0	17.5	0.0	17.6	0.6
1956	17.6	0.0	17.6	0.0	17.8	1.1	17.8	0.0	17.8	0.0	17.8	0.0	17.8	0.0	17.8	0.0	17.9	0.6	17.9	0.0	17.9	0.0	17.9	0.0
1957	17.9	0.0	17.9	0.0	18.2	1.7	18.2	0.0	18.2	0.0	18.2	0.0	18.2	0.0	18.2	0.0	18.2	0.0	18.2	0.0	18.2	0.0	18.5	1.6
1958	18.5	0.0	18.5	0.0	18.5	0.0	18.6	0.5	18.6	0.0	18.6	0.0	19.2	3.2	19.2	0.0	19.2	0.0	19.2	0.0	19.2	0.0	19.3	0.5
1959	19.3	0.0	19.3	0.0	19.7	2.1	19.7	0.0	19.7	0.0	19.9	1.0	19.9	0.0	20.5	3.0	20.5	0.0	20.5	0.0	20.5	0.0	20.6	0.5
1960	20.6	0.0	20.6	0.0	20.8	1.0	20.8	0.0	20.8	0.0	20.9	0.5	20.9	0.0	20.9	0.0	20.9	0.0	20.9	0.0	20.9	0.0	21.0	0.5
1961	21.0	0.0	21.0	0.0	21.0	0.0	21.4	1.9	22.0	2.8	22.0	0.0	22.0	0.0	22.0	0.0	22.1	0.5	22.1	0.0	22.1	0.0	22.1	0.0
1962	22.1	0.0	22.1	0.0	22.1	0.0	22.1	0.0	22.1	0.0	22.9	3.6	22.9	0.0	22.9	0.0	22.9	0.0	22.9	0.0	22.9	0.0	22.9	0.0
1963	22.9	0.0	23.0	0.4	23.0	0.0	23.0	0.0	23.0	0.0	23.1	0.4	23.1	0.0	23.1	0.0	23.2	0.4	23.2	0.0	23.2	0.0	23.2	0.0
1964	23.3	0.4	23.3	0.0	23.3	0.0	23.3	0.0	23.3	0.0	23.3	0.0	23.5	0.9	23.4	-0.4	23.5	0.4	23.5	0.0	23.6	0.4	23.6	0.0
1965	23.6	0.0	23.6	0.0	23.8	0.8	23.8	0.0	23.9	0.4	24.1	0.8	24.2	0.4	24.2	0.0	24.3	0.4	24.3	0.0	24.3	0.0	24.4	0.4
1966	24.4	0.0	24.5	0.4	24.7	0.8	24.8	0.4	24.8	0.0	24.9	0.4	25.2	1.2	25.3	0.4	25.3	0.0	25.4	0.4	25.6	0.8	25.9	1.2
1967	26.0	0.4	26.1	0.4	26.1	0.0	26.2	0.4	26.3	0.4	26.6	1.1	26.8	0.8	26.8	0.0	27.3	1.9	27.5	0.7	27.5	0.0	27.7	0.7
1968	27.9	0.7	27.9	0.0	28.0	0.4	28.1	0.4	28.5	1.4	28.7	0.7	29.3	2.1	29.4	0.3	29.5	0.3	29.8	1.0	29.8	0.0	30.0	0.7
1969	30.1	0.3	30.2	0.3	30.6	1.3	30.7	0.3	30.9	0.7	31.1	0.6	32.1	3.2	32.2	0.3	32.4	0.6	32.1	-0.9	32.1	0.0	32.2	0.3
1970	32.5	0.9	32.7	0.6	32.9	0.6	33.1	0.6	33.3	0.6	33.4	0.3	34.6	3.6	34.9	0.9	34.9	0.0	34.8	-0.3	35.6	2.3	35.6	0.0
1971	35.8	0.6	36.0	0.6	36.0	0.0	36.1	0.3	36.2	0.3	36.7	1.4	37.4	1.9	37.4	0.0	37.5	0.3	37.2	-0.8	37.3	0.3	37.3	0.0
1972	37.3	0.0	37.5	0.5	37.5	0.0	37.6	0.3	37.6	0.0	37.7	0.3	38.0	0.8	38.3	0.8	38.3	0.0	38.6	0.8	38.6	0.0	38.7	0.3
1973	38.7	0.0	38.7	0.0	39.2	1.3	39.4	0.5	39.4	0.0	39.4	0.0	39.6	0.5	40.1	1.3	40.2	0.2	41.0	2.0	41.1	0.2	41.1	0.0
1974	41.1	0.0	41.5	1.0	41.7	0.5	41.8	0.2	42.5	1.7	43.6	2.6	44.2	1.4	44.2	0.0	44.4	0.5	45.2	1.8	45.3	0.2	45.7	0.9
1975	46.5	1.8	47.2	1.5	47.7	1.1	47.9	0.4	48.0	0.2	48.7	1.5	50.3	3.3	50.3	0.0	50.9	1.2	51.5	1.2	51.0	-1.0	51.3	0.6
1976	51.7	0.8	52.0	0.6	52.1	0.2	52.4	0.6	52.5	0.2	53.2	1.3	54.5	2.4	54.6	0.2	55.0	0.7	55.3	0.5	55.7	0.7	55.6	-0.2
1977	56.1	0.9	56.8	1.2	57.6	1.4	57.7	0.2	58.1	0.7	58.6	0.9	60.2	2.7	60.4	0.3	60.7	0.5	60.6	-0.2	60.6	0.0	60.5	-0.2
1978	61.7	2.0	62.0	0.5	62.2	0.3	63.0	1.3	61.9	-1.7	61.9	0.0	63.0	1.8	63.6	1.0	64.7	1.7	64.7	0.0	65.1	0.6	65.1	0.0
1979	65.7	0.9	66.4	1.1	66.4	0.0	66.6	0.3	66.9	0.5	67.9	1.5	69.4	2.2	69.9	0.7	69.9	0.0	70.1	0.3	70.3	0.3	71.1	1.1
1980	71.7	0.8	73.6	2.6	73.5	-0.1	73.9	0.5	73.7	-0.3	73.9	0.3	76.3	3.2	77.2	1.2	77.5	0.4	77.7	0.3	78.3	0.8	78.4	0.1
1981	80.1	2.2	81.0	1.1	81.2	0.2	81.7	0.6	81.7	0.0	82.4	0.9	85.2	3.4	86.1	1.1	86.6	0.6	86.5	-0.1	86.7	0.2	87.3	0.7
1982	89.1	2.1	89.2	0.1	89.1	-0.1	89.4	0.3	89.5	0.1	89.9	0.4	93.5	4.0	93.9	0.4	93.3	-0.6	93.6	0.3	95.0	1.5	95.3	0.3
1983	96.1	0.8	97.7	1.7	97.9	0.2	98.3	0.4	98.6	0.3	99.5	0.9	102.4	2.9	103.0	0.6	103.1	0.1	103.7	0.6	103.5	-0.2	103.6	0.1
1984	103.9	0.3	104.8	0.9	104.7	-0.1	105.6	0.9	105.6	0.0	105.9	0.3	107.5	1.5	108.4	0.8	109.0	0.6	109.3	0.3	113.4	3.8	114.0	0.5
1985	115.8	1.6	116.1	0.3	117.1	0.9	117.4	0.3	117.7	0.3	118.5	0.7	119.3	0.7	119.8	0.4	121.0	1.0	121.7	0.6	122.6	0.7	122.2	-0.3
1986	122.5	0.2	123.5	0.8	124.3	0.6	125.5	1.0	125.0	-0.4	125.5	0.4	127.6	1.7	128.3	0.5	129.0	0.5	129.2	0.2	129.2	0.0	130.0	0.6
1987	129.9	-0.1	130.3	0.3	130.7	0.3	130.6	-0.1	131.7	0.8	132.9	0.9	134.0	0.8	134.0	0.0	135.3	1.0	135.3	0.0	135.2	-0.1	136.6	1.0
1988	137.7	0.8	138.7	0.7	138.4	-0.2	139.8	1.0	140.7	0.6	140.7	0.0	143.8	2.2	143.5	-0.2	144.7	0.8	145.5	0.6	146.1	0.4	146.2	0.1
1989	146.9	0.5	147.8	0.6	148.8	0.7	151.1	1.5	152.0	0.6	155.1	2.0	156.0	0.6	155.9	-0.1	159.9	2.6	164.1	2.6	166.1	1.2	159.8	-3.8
1990	160.4	0.4	160.1	-0.2	162.1	1.2	164.2	1.3	165.2	0.6	166.2	0.6	169.2	1.8	170.4	0.7	171.0	0.4	171.5	0.3	174.3	1.6	174.6	0.2
1991	176.0	0.8	178.4	1.4	178.8	0.2	180.5	1.0	181.3	0.4	182.0	0.4	184.7	1.5	186.5	1.0	186.7	0.1	188.4	0.9	188.5	0.1	189.6	0.6

[Continued]

Philadelphia, PA-NJ
Consumer Price Index - All Urban Consumers
Base 1982-1984 = 100
Medical Care
[Continued]

For 1947-1995. Columns headed % show percentile change in the index from the previous period for which an index is available.

Year	Jan Index	%	Feb Index	%	Mar Index	%	Apr Index	%	May Index	%	Jun Index	%	Jul Index	%	Aug Index	%	Sep Index	%	Oct Index	%	Nov Index	%	Dec Index	%
1992	188.0	-0.8	188.7	0.4	192.1	1.8	193.0	0.5	195.6	1.3	196.4	0.4	199.4	1.5	199.5	0.1	200.4	0.5	202.0	0.8	202.0	0.0	202.2	0.1
1993	202.0	-0.1	205.0	1.5	206.3	0.6	207.3	0.5	209.7	1.2	211.2	0.7	214.7	1.7	214.2	-0.2	214.1	-0.0	218.1	1.9	217.8	-0.1	218.3	0.2
1994	219.7	0.6	220.8	0.5	220.3	-0.2	223.2	1.3	223.1	-0.0	222.3	-0.4	224.8	1.1	225.5	0.3	225.5	0.0	226.2	0.3	226.9	0.3	228.1	0.5
1995	228.9	0.4	228.9	0.0	229.1	0.1	229.2	0.0	229.8	0.3	231.7	0.8	234.2	1.1	234.7	0.2	234.9	0.1	235.6	0.3	236.1	0.2	236.6	0.2

Source: U.S. Department of Labor, Bureau of Labor Statistics, Division of Consumer Prices and Price Indexes. - indicates no data collected for period.

Philadelphia, PA-NJ
Consumer Price Index - Urban Wage Earners
Base 1982-1984 = 100
Medical Care

For 1947-1995. Columns headed % show percentile change in the index from the previous period for which an index is available.

Year	Jan Index	%	Feb Index	%	Mar Index	%	Apr Index	%	May Index	%	Jun Index	%	Jul Index	%	Aug Index	%	Sep Index	%	Oct Index	%	Nov Index	%	Dec Index	%
1947	11.4	-	11.5	0.9	11.5	0.0	11.7	1.7	11.8	0.9	11.8	0.0	11.8	0.0	11.8	0.0	11.8	0.0	11.9	0.8	11.9	0.0	12.0	0.8
1948	12.1	0.8	12.2	0.8	12.1	-0.8	12.2	0.8	12.2	0.0	12.2	0.0	12.3	0.8	12.3	0.0	12.3	0.0	12.3	0.0	12.5	1.6	12.5	0.0
1949	12.5	0.0	12.5	0.0	12.6	0.8	12.6	0.0	12.6	0.0	12.6	0.0	12.6	0.0	12.6	0.0	12.7	0.8	12.7	0.0	12.7	0.0	12.7	0.0
1950	12.7	0.0	12.7	0.0	12.7	0.0	12.7	0.0	12.8	0.8	12.8	0.0	12.8	0.0	12.8	0.0	12.9	0.8	12.9	0.0	12.9	0.0	13.0	0.8
1951	13.2	1.5	13.2	0.0	13.4	1.5	13.4	0.0	13.4	0.0	13.4	0.0	13.4	0.0	13.4	0.0	13.4	0.0	13.5	0.7	13.5	0.0	13.5	0.0
1952	13.5	0.0	13.5	0.0	13.7	1.5	13.7	0.0	13.7	0.0	14.4	5.1	14.4	0.0	14.4	0.0	14.6	1.4	14.6	0.0	14.6	0.0	14.6	0.0
1953	14.6	0.0	14.6	0.0	14.6	0.0	14.6	0.0	14.6	0.0	14.7	0.7	14.7	0.0	14.7	0.0	14.7	0.0	14.7	0.0	14.7	0.0	15.0	2.0
1954	15.0	0.0	15.1	0.7	15.1	0.0	15.1	0.0	15.1	0.0	15.3	1.3	15.3	0.0	15.3	0.0	16.1	5.2	16.1	0.0	16.2	0.6	16.3	0.6
1955	16.3	0.0	16.3	0.0	16.5	1.2	16.5	0.0	16.5	0.0	16.5	0.0	16.5	0.0	16.5	0.0	16.5	0.0	16.5	0.0	16.5	0.0	16.6	0.6
1956	16.6	0.0	16.6	0.0	16.8	1.2	16.8	0.0	16.8	0.0	16.8	0.0	16.8	0.0	16.8	0.0	16.9	0.6	16.9	0.0	16.9	0.0	16.9	0.0
1957	16.9	0.0	16.9	0.0	17.1	1.2	17.1	0.0	17.1	0.0	17.2	0.6	17.2	0.0	17.2	0.0	17.2	0.0	17.2	0.0	17.2	0.0	17.4	1.2
1958	17.4	0.0	17.4	0.0	17.5	0.6	17.5	0.0	17.5	0.0	17.6	0.6	18.1	2.8	18.1	0.0	18.1	0.0	18.1	0.0	18.1	0.0	18.2	0.6
1959	18.3	0.5	18.3	0.0	18.6	1.6	18.6	0.0	18.6	0.0	18.8	1.1	18.8	0.0	19.3	2.7	19.4	0.5	19.4	0.0	19.4	0.0	19.4	0.0
1960	19.4	0.0	19.4	0.0	19.6	1.0	19.6	0.0	19.6	0.0	19.7	0.5	19.7	0.0	19.7	0.0	19.7	0.0	19.7	0.0	19.7	0.0	19.8	0.5
1961	19.8	0.0	19.8	0.0	19.9	0.5	20.2	1.5	20.8	3.0	20.8	0.0	20.8	0.0	20.8	0.0	20.9	0.5	20.8	-0.5	20.8	0.0	20.8	0.0
1962	20.9	0.5	20.9	0.0	20.9	0.0	20.9	0.0	20.9	0.0	21.6	3.3	21.6	0.0	21.6	0.0	21.7	0.5	21.6	-0.5	21.6	0.0	21.7	0.5
1963	21.7	0.0	21.7	0.0	21.7	0.0	21.7	0.0	21.7	0.0	21.8	0.5	21.8	0.0	21.8	0.0	21.9	0.5	21.9	0.0	21.9	0.0	21.9	0.0
1964	22.0	0.5	22.0	0.0	22.0	0.0	22.0	0.0	22.0	0.0	22.0	0.0	22.2	0.9	22.1	-0.5	22.2	0.5	22.2	0.0	22.3	0.5	22.3	0.0
1965	22.3	0.0	22.3	0.0	22.5	0.9	22.5	0.0	22.6	0.4	22.7	0.4	22.8	0.4	22.8	0.0	22.9	0.4	22.9	0.0	22.9	0.0	23.0	0.4
1966	23.1	0.4	23.1	0.0	23.3	0.9	23.4	0.4	23.4	0.0	23.5	0.4	23.8	1.3	23.9	0.4	23.9	0.0	24.0	0.4	24.2	0.8	24.5	1.2
1967	24.6	0.4	24.6	0.0	24.6	0.0	24.7	0.4	24.9	0.8	25.1	0.8	25.3	0.8	25.3	0.0	25.8	2.0	25.9	0.4	26.0	0.4	26.2	0.8
1968	26.3	0.4	26.4	0.4	26.5	0.4	26.6	0.4	26.9	1.1	27.1	0.7	27.6	1.8	27.7	0.4	27.9	0.7	28.1	0.7	28.2	0.4	28.3	0.4
1969	28.4	0.4	28.5	0.4	28.9	1.4	29.0	0.3	29.2	0.7	29.3	0.3	30.3	3.4	30.4	0.3	30.6	0.7	30.3	-1.0	30.3	0.0	30.4	0.3
1970	30.7	1.0	30.9	0.7	31.0	0.3	31.3	1.0	31.4	0.3	31.6	0.6	32.6	3.2	33.0	1.2	33.0	0.0	32.9	-0.3	33.6	2.1	33.7	0.3
1971	33.8	0.3	34.0	0.6	34.0	0.0	34.1	0.3	34.2	0.3	34.6	1.2	35.3	2.0	35.3	0.0	35.4	0.3	35.2	-0.6	35.2	0.0	35.2	0.0
1972	35.2	0.0	35.4	0.6	35.4	0.0	35.5	0.3	35.5	0.0	35.6	0.3	35.9	0.8	36.2	0.8	36.2	0.0	36.4	0.6	36.5	0.3	36.5	0.0
1973	36.6	0.3	36.6	0.0	37.0	1.1	37.2	0.5	37.2	0.0	37.2	0.0	37.4	0.5	37.8	1.1	38.0	0.5	38.7	1.8	38.8	0.3	38.8	0.0
1974	38.8	0.0	39.2	1.0	39.4	0.5	39.5	0.3	40.1	1.5	41.2	2.7	41.7	1.2	41.7	0.0	41.9	0.5	42.6	1.7	42.7	0.2	43.1	0.9
1975	43.9	1.9	44.6	1.6	45.0	0.9	45.3	0.7	45.4	0.2	46.0	1.3	47.5	3.3	47.5	0.0	48.0	1.1	48.7	1.5	48.2	-1.0	48.4	0.4
1976	48.9	1.0	49.1	0.4	49.2	0.2	49.5	0.6	49.6	0.2	50.3	1.4	51.5	2.4	51.6	0.2	51.9	0.6	52.2	0.6	52.6	0.8	52.5	-0.2
1977	53.0	1.0	53.6	1.1	54.4	1.5	54.5	0.2	54.9	0.7	55.3	0.7	56.9	2.9	57.0	0.2	57.3	0.5	57.2	-0.2	57.3	0.2	57.2	-0.2
1978	58.2	1.7	58.6	0.7	58.6	0.0	58.8	0.3	58.8	0.0	58.8	0.0	59.7	1.5	60.6	1.5	62.2	2.6	62.2	0.0	62.5	0.5	63.3	1.3
1979	63.3	0.0	63.9	0.9	64.0	0.2	64.1	0.2	64.4	0.5	66.8	3.7	67.6	1.2	67.9	0.4	68.3	0.6	69.1	1.2	69.3	0.3	69.8	0.7
1980	70.5	1.0	73.3	4.0	73.2	-0.1	73.8	0.8	74.3	0.7	74.8	0.7	77.3	3.3	78.6	1.7	78.9	0.4	79.2	0.4	79.2	0.0	79.2	0.0
1981	81.0	2.3	80.6	-0.5	80.7	0.1	81.2	0.6	81.2	0.0	81.4	0.2	84.7	4.1	86.2	1.8	87.3	1.3	87.4	0.1	87.7	0.3	87.6	-0.1
1982	89.3	1.9	89.2	-0.1	89.0	-0.2	89.4	0.4	89.6	0.2	89.8	0.2	93.1	3.7	93.7	0.6	93.1	-0.6	93.3	0.2	94.6	1.4	94.8	0.2
1983	95.8	1.1	97.7	2.0	97.8	0.1	98.2	0.4	98.5	0.3	99.7	1.2	102.4	2.7	103.0	0.6	103.1	0.1	103.6	0.5	103.5	-0.1	103.7	0.2
1984	104.0	0.3	105.1	1.1	105.0	-0.1	106.0	1.0	106.0	0.0	106.4	0.4	107.5	1.0	108.5	0.9	109.1	0.6	109.5	0.4	113.3	3.5	113.8	0.4
1985	115.9	1.8	116.2	0.3	117.2	0.9	117.3	0.1	117.7	0.3	118.5	0.7	119.1	0.5	119.6	0.4	120.8	1.0	121.7	0.7	122.6	0.7	122.1	-0.4
1986	122.3	0.2	123.3	0.8	124.1	0.6	125.4	1.0	124.8	-0.5	125.4	0.5	127.0	1.3	127.7	0.6	128.6	0.7	128.8	0.2	128.7	-0.1	129.5	0.6
1987	129.5	0.0	129.9	0.3	130.3	0.3	130.3	0.0	131.5	0.9	132.9	1.1	133.7	0.6	133.6	-0.1	134.5	0.7	134.9	0.3	134.7	-0.1	136.2	1.1
1988	137.3	0.8	138.1	0.6	137.7	-0.3	139.2	1.1	140.2	0.7	140.3	0.1	143.2	2.1	142.8	-0.3	144.1	0.9	144.7	0.4	145.3	0.4	145.3	0.0
1989	146.1	0.6	146.9	0.5	147.9	0.7	150.4	1.7	151.3	0.6	153.8	1.7	154.6	0.5	154.8	0.1	158.2	2.2	161.9	2.3	163.8	1.2	158.4	-3.3
1990	159.1	0.4	158.8	-0.2	160.8	1.3	163.0	1.4	163.9	0.6	164.9	0.6	167.6	1.6	168.7	0.7	169.3	0.4	169.7	0.2	172.3	1.5	172.5	0.1
1991	173.8	0.8	176.2	1.4	176.4	0.1	178.1	1.0	178.8	0.4	179.7	0.5	182.0	1.3	184.0	1.1	184.1	0.1	185.6	0.8	185.7	0.1	186.8	0.6

[Continued]

698

Philadelphia, PA-NJ
Consumer Price Index - Urban Wage Earners
Base 1982-1984 = 100
Medical Care
[Continued]

For 1947-1995. Columns headed % show percentile change in the index from the previous period for which an index is available.

Year	Jan Index	%	Feb Index	%	Mar Index	%	Apr Index	%	May Index	%	Jun Index	%	Jul Index	%	Aug Index	%	Sep Index	%	Oct Index	%	Nov Index	%	Dec Index	%
1992	185.5	-0.7	186.1	0.3	189.1	1.6	189.9	0.4	192.8	1.5	193.6	0.4	196.7	1.6	196.7	0.0	197.7	0.5	199.2	0.8	199.5	0.2	199.7	0.1
1993	199.4	-0.2	202.7	1.7	203.8	0.5	204.8	0.5	206.8	1.0	208.4	0.8	211.9	1.7	211.4	-0.2	211.2	-0.1	215.2	1.9	214.7	-0.2	215.3	0.3
1994	216.4	0.5	217.6	0.6	217.1	-0.2	219.8	1.2	219.9	0.0	218.9	-0.5	221.4	1.1	221.9	0.2	222.0	0.0	222.8	0.4	223.4	0.3	224.6	0.5
1995	225.1	0.2	225.1	0.0	225.3	0.1	225.3	0.0	225.9	0.3	227.9	0.9	230.0	0.9	230.6	0.3	230.7	0.0	231.3	0.3	231.9	0.3	232.3	0.2

Source: U.S. Department of Labor, Bureau of Labor Statistics, Division of Consumer Prices and Price Indexes. - indicates no data collected for period.

Philadelphia, PA-NJ
Consumer Price Index - All Urban Consumers
Base 1982-1984 = 100
Entertainment

For 1976-1995. Columns headed % show percentile change in the index from the previous period for which an index is available.

Year	Jan Index	%	Feb Index	%	Mar Index	%	Apr Index	%	May Index	%	Jun Index	%	Jul Index	%	Aug Index	%	Sep Index	%	Oct Index	%	Nov Index	%	Dec Index	%
1976	68.7	-	68.1	-0.9	67.8	-0.4	68.4	0.9	68.8	0.6	68.9	0.1	69.2	0.4	69.2	0.0	68.6	-0.9	69.0	0.6	69.2	0.3	69.8	0.9
1977	70.4	0.9	70.4	0.0	70.5	0.1	71.1	0.9	71.2	0.1	72.0	1.1	72.0	0.0	71.7	-0.4	71.9	0.3	72.4	0.7	72.8	0.6	73.2	0.5
1978	73.5	0.4	73.7	0.3	73.5	-0.3	74.2	1.0	74.3	0.1	75.6	1.7	75.1	-0.7	73.3	-2.4	73.3	0.0	73.2	-0.1	71.9	-1.8	76.6	6.5
1979	77.8	1.6	78.1	0.4	78.5	0.5	81.5	3.8	81.2	-0.4	80.3	-1.1	81.8	1.9	82.8	1.2	82.8	0.0	83.6	1.0	84.5	1.1	80.8	-4.4
1980	83.0	2.7	83.1	0.1	83.3	0.2	82.9	-0.5	83.5	0.7	83.5	0.0	83.7	0.2	84.0	0.4	84.8	1.0	85.3	0.6	85.2	-0.1	85.2	0.0
1981	87.2	2.3	88.4	1.4	88.8	0.5	90.5	1.9	91.7	1.3	93.7	2.2	93.9	0.2	92.9	-1.1	93.6	0.8	94.5	1.0	94.3	-0.2	95.9	1.7
1982	94.6	-1.4	94.9	0.3	95.7	0.8	96.3	0.6	96.8	0.5	96.3	-0.5	96.0	-0.3	97.9	2.0	96.2	-1.7	97.4	1.2	97.5	0.1	97.0	-0.5
1983	97.4	0.4	97.7	0.3	100.9	3.3	100.6	-0.3	99.0	-1.6	100.6	1.6	100.9	0.3	100.5	-0.4	100.8	0.3	101.6	0.8	103.1	1.5	102.8	-0.3
1984	101.1	-1.7	102.3	1.2	101.7	-0.6	103.4	1.7	103.2	-0.2	103.7	0.5	104.1	0.4	104.0	-0.1	103.4	-0.6	103.1	-0.3	103.3	0.2	104.2	0.9
1985	103.8	-0.4	103.9	0.1	104.9	1.0	105.1	0.2	105.7	0.6	104.5	-1.1	104.5	0.0	104.5	0.0	104.8	0.3	106.7	1.8	108.0	1.2	106.8	-1.1
1986	107.6	0.7	107.1	-0.5	107.1	0.0	108.9	1.7	108.7	-0.2	109.4	0.6	110.6	1.1	110.5	-0.1	111.2	0.6	109.8	-1.3	110.3	0.5	110.6	0.3
1987	110.9	0.3	109.5	-1.3	109.4	-0.1	111.8	2.2	112.2	0.4	112.4	0.2	112.7	0.3	112.2	-0.4	112.8	0.5	113.8	0.9	113.9	0.1	114.2	0.3
1988	114.8	0.5	116.0	1.0	116.4	0.3	116.9	0.4	119.9	2.6	121.1	1.0	121.8	0.6	122.6	0.7	124.0	1.1	125.1	0.9	124.6	-0.4	126.5	1.5
1989	125.9	-0.5	126.8	0.7	127.3	0.4	129.2	1.5	129.3	0.1	127.9	-1.1	128.3	0.3	128.6	0.2	130.3	1.3	130.3	0.0	129.7	-0.5	130.1	0.3
1990	131.9	1.4	133.4	1.1	133.0	-0.3	132.8	-0.2	133.3	0.4	132.3	-0.8	134.1	1.4	134.2	0.1	134.2	0.0	133.7	-0.4	134.5	0.6	134.1	-0.3
1991	133.2	-0.7	133.1	-0.1	135.0	1.4	139.5	3.3	139.4	-0.1	138.2	-0.9	138.9	0.5	139.3	0.3	140.3	0.7	140.9	0.4	140.0	-0.6	138.5	-1.1
1992	139.2	0.5	139.1	-0.1	142.9	2.7	144.9	1.4	145.2	0.2	146.3	0.8	146.4	0.1	145.9	-0.3	146.6	0.5	145.4	-0.8	145.7	0.2	144.6	-0.8
1993	143.2	-1.0	134.2	-6.3	140.7	4.8	150.6	7.0	149.6	-0.7	149.5	-0.1	149.5	0.0	149.7	0.1	150.3	0.4	151.1	0.5	150.6	-0.3	150.9	0.2
1994	155.7	3.2	157.4	1.1	158.3	0.6	163.8	3.5	161.9	-1.2	160.7	-0.7	161.9	0.7	159.7	-1.4	160.1	0.3	159.3	-0.5	163.0	2.3	161.7	-0.8
1995	163.9	1.4	163.4	-0.3	163.9	0.3	164.1	0.1	165.0	0.5	165.0	0.0	164.7	-0.2	167.4	1.6	170.5	1.9	168.4	-1.2	171.5	1.8	172.7	0.7

Source: U.S. Department of Labor, Bureau of Labor Statistics, Division of Consumer Prices and Price Indexes. - indicates no data collected for period.

Philadelphia, PA-NJ
Consumer Price Index - Urban Wage Earners
Base 1982-1984 = 100
Entertainment

For 1976-1995. Columns headed % show percentile change in the index from the previous period for which an index is available.

Year	Jan Index	%	Feb Index	%	Mar Index	%	Apr Index	%	May Index	%	Jun Index	%	Jul Index	%	Aug Index	%	Sep Index	%	Oct Index	%	Nov Index	%	Dec Index	%
1976	70.8	-	70.2	-0.8	69.9	-0.4	70.5	0.9	70.9	0.6	71.0	0.1	71.3	0.4	71.3	0.0	70.7	-0.8	71.1	0.6	71.4	0.4	72.0	0.8
1977	72.6	0.8	72.5	-0.1	72.7	0.3	73.2	0.7	73.4	0.3	74.2	1.1	74.2	0.0	73.9	-0.4	74.1	0.3	74.7	0.8	75.0	0.4	75.5	0.7
1978	75.5	0.0	75.6	0.1	75.2	-0.5	76.4	1.6	75.7	-0.9	77.7	2.6	77.7	0.0	78.1	0.5	77.9	-0.3	77.8	-0.1	75.8	-2.6	84.4	11.3
1979	85.2	0.9	85.5	0.4	85.7	0.2	86.4	0.8	86.5	0.1	84.3	-2.5	86.5	2.6	87.0	0.6	87.2	0.2	88.7	1.7	90.0	1.5	82.8	-8.0
1980	83.3	0.6	84.1	1.0	85.0	1.1	82.7	-2.7	85.1	2.9	85.3	0.2	85.6	0.4	85.3	-0.4	90.0	5.5	89.3	-0.8	90.8	1.7	90.3	-0.6
1981	92.3	2.2	93.1	0.9	93.1	0.0	93.7	0.6	91.1	-2.8	93.9	3.1	94.1	0.2	94.4	0.3	95.8	1.5	95.9	0.1	95.4	-0.5	95.9	0.5
1982	94.5	-1.5	94.8	0.3	95.4	0.6	95.8	0.4	96.3	0.5	96.1	-0.2	97.4	1.4	97.6	0.2	97.1	-0.5	97.6	0.5	97.7	0.1	97.5	-0.2
1983	97.5	0.0	97.5	0.0	100.4	3.0	100.9	0.5	100.3	-0.6	100.8	0.5	101.3	0.5	100.7	-0.6	100.6	-0.1	101.5	0.9	103.0	1.5	102.5	-0.5
1984	100.5	-2.0	101.8	1.3	102.1	0.3	102.9	0.8	102.9	0.0	103.7	0.8	104.0	0.3	104.0	0.0	103.3	-0.7	103.1	-0.2	103.3	0.2	103.6	0.3
1985	103.1	-0.5	103.2	0.1	104.0	0.8	104.2	0.2	104.6	0.4	103.3	-1.2	103.8	0.5	103.7	-0.1	104.0	0.3	105.9	1.8	106.8	0.8	105.6	-1.1
1986	106.4	0.8	106.1	-0.3	106.0	-0.1	107.9	1.8	107.7	-0.2	108.5	0.7	109.4	0.8	109.4	0.0	110.1	0.6	108.7	-1.3	109.3	0.6	109.1	-0.2
1987	109.4	0.3	107.2	-2.0	107.1	-0.1	110.4	3.1	110.6	0.2	110.7	0.1	111.5	0.7	110.7	-0.7	111.3	0.5	112.4	1.0	112.5	0.1	112.8	0.3
1988	113.4	0.5	114.3	0.8	114.7	0.3	115.2	0.4	117.8	2.3	118.9	0.9	119.7	0.7	120.6	0.8	121.7	0.9	122.8	0.9	122.0	-0.7	124.1	1.7
1989	123.6	-0.4	124.5	0.7	125.1	0.5	126.4	1.0	126.5	0.1	125.1	-1.1	125.4	0.2	126.0	0.5	127.8	1.4	127.8	0.0	127.4	-0.3	127.7	0.2
1990	129.2	1.2	130.4	0.9	130.3	-0.1	130.0	-0.2	130.3	0.2	129.0	-1.0	130.5	1.2	130.5	0.0	130.7	0.2	130.4	-0.2	131.1	0.5	130.5	-0.5
1991	129.6	-0.7	130.1	0.4	132.1	1.5	135.7	2.7	135.9	0.1	135.1	-0.6	135.8	0.5	136.0	0.1	136.3	0.2	137.2	0.7	136.6	-0.4	135.5	-0.8
1992	136.2	0.5	135.8	-0.3	139.2	2.5	140.4	0.9	140.8	0.3	141.6	0.6	141.6	0.0	141.4	-0.1	142.3	0.6	140.7	-1.1	141.5	0.6	140.4	-0.8
1993	139.3	-0.8	130.6	-6.2	136.7	4.7	145.3	6.3	144.3	-0.7	143.9	-0.3	143.9	0.0	144.2	0.2	145.0	0.6	146.1	0.8	145.4	-0.5	146.1	0.5
1994	151.7	3.8	152.8	0.7	153.9	0.7	158.4	2.9	157.2	-0.8	156.3	-0.6	156.9	0.4	155.6	-0.8	155.1	-0.3	155.0	-0.1	158.4	2.2	156.9	-0.9
1995	159.5	1.7	158.5	-0.6	159.5	0.6	159.7	0.1	160.4	0.4	160.4	0.0	160.4	0.0	163.4	1.9	165.6	1.3	164.1	-0.9	167.0	1.8	168.4	0.8

Source: U.S. Department of Labor, Bureau of Labor Statistics, Division of Consumer Prices and Price Indexes. - indicates no data collected for period.

Philadelphia, PA-NJ
Consumer Price Index - All Urban Consumers
Base 1982-1984 = 100
Other Goods and Services

For 1976-1995. Columns headed % show percentile change in the index from the previous period for which an index is available.

Year	Jan Index	%	Feb Index	%	Mar Index	%	Apr Index	%	May Index	%	Jun Index	%	Jul Index	%	Aug Index	%	Sep Index	%	Oct Index	%	Nov Index	%	Dec Index	%
1976	54.7	-	55.0	0.5	54.8	-0.4	55.1	0.5	55.2	0.2	55.6	0.7	56.1	0.9	56.1	0.0	56.5	0.7	57.5	1.8	57.6	0.2	57.7	0.2
1977	57.8	0.2	58.0	0.3	58.0	0.0	58.6	1.0	58.5	-0.2	58.7	0.3	58.8	0.2	58.7	-0.2	60.1	2.4	60.7	1.0	60.9	0.3	60.8	-0.2
1978	60.9	0.2	61.1	0.3	61.2	0.2	61.6	0.7	61.4	-0.3	61.8	0.7	62.3	0.8	62.1	-0.3	63.8	2.7	64.0	0.3	63.9	-0.2	64.1	0.3
1979	64.9	1.2	65.4	0.8	65.6	0.3	65.7	0.2	65.7	0.0	65.6	-0.2	66.0	0.6	66.6	0.9	69.1	3.8	69.1	0.0	70.0	1.3	70.0	0.0
1980	71.0	1.4	71.1	0.1	71.1	0.0	71.5	0.6	71.9	0.6	72.2	0.4	72.9	1.0	73.0	0.1	75.7	3.7	75.3	-0.5	76.1	1.1	76.5	0.5
1981	76.6	0.1	76.5	-0.1	76.8	0.4	76.9	0.1	77.9	1.3	78.5	0.8	78.1	-0.5	78.3	0.3	83.3	6.4	83.8	0.6	83.2	-0.7	84.8	1.9
1982	84.7	-0.1	85.2	0.6	85.1	-0.1	86.9	2.1	87.2	0.3	88.2	1.1	87.5	-0.8	88.7	1.4	93.1	5.0	94.9	1.9	95.7	0.8	96.8	1.1
1983	97.8	1.0	97.0	-0.8	98.0	1.0	97.6	-0.4	97.9	0.3	98.1	0.2	99.4	1.3	101.7	2.3	105.1	3.3	106.2	1.0	106.4	0.2	106.5	0.1
1984	107.4	0.8	107.3	-0.1	107.2	-0.1	108.1	0.8	107.7	-0.4	108.2	0.5	109.3	1.0	109.3	0.0	112.3	2.7	112.3	0.0	112.4	0.1	112.5	0.1
1985	113.8	1.2	114.8	0.9	115.0	0.2	116.0	0.9	115.5	-0.4	115.6	0.1	116.5	0.8	116.6	0.1	120.6	3.4	120.5	-0.1	120.4	-0.1	120.2	-0.2
1986	121.6	1.2	123.3	1.4	123.8	0.4	124.5	0.6	125.7	1.0	126.0	0.2	126.6	0.5	126.8	0.2	129.8	2.4	129.8	0.0	129.9	0.1	130.1	0.2
1987	133.2	2.4	133.7	0.4	133.9	0.1	134.1	0.1	134.3	0.1	134.6	0.2	135.2	0.4	135.2	0.0	138.6	2.5	139.3	0.5	139.1	-0.1	139.5	0.3
1988	140.6	0.8	142.7	1.5	142.3	-0.3	143.4	0.8	143.3	-0.1	143.5	0.1	144.1	0.4	144.5	0.3	148.5	2.8	148.8	0.2	148.8	0.0	150.4	1.1
1989	152.0	1.1	152.1	0.1	152.3	0.1	153.8	1.0	153.6	-0.1	153.9	0.2	155.5	1.0	157.7	1.4	158.1	0.3	158.0	-0.1	159.2	0.8	158.4	-0.5
1990	161.9	2.2	162.1	0.1	165.7	2.2	166.1	0.2	166.3	0.1	168.8	1.5	177.4	5.1	179.3	1.1	179.0	-0.2	178.5	-0.3	178.7	0.1	179.0	0.2
1991	182.0	1.7	185.5	1.9	182.0	-1.9	182.7	0.4	182.6	-0.1	182.6	0.0	183.5	0.5	187.5	2.2	188.2	0.4	189.2	0.5	189.7	0.3	190.4	0.4
1992	190.0	-0.2	191.4	0.7	192.5	0.6	192.8	0.2	194.0	0.6	194.9	0.5	195.3	0.2	197.2	1.0	199.5	1.2	200.6	0.6	200.3	-0.1	201.4	0.5
1993	202.6	0.6	202.7	0.0	202.9	0.1	203.1	0.1	211.8	4.3	212.5	0.3	213.3	0.4	212.6	-0.3	212.7	0.0	217.1	2.1	218.1	0.5	218.9	0.4
1994	219.0	0.0	219.1	0.0	220.6	0.7	220.6	0.0	221.2	0.3	221.3	0.0	221.6	0.1	223.0	0.6	225.0	0.9	225.2	0.1	225.1	-0.0	225.1	0.0
1995	224.7	-0.2	224.4	-0.1	224.7	0.1	225.8	0.5	226.2	0.2	227.2	0.4	226.9	-0.1	227.9	0.4	230.0	0.9	229.6	-0.2	228.6	-0.4	229.5	0.4

Source: U.S. Department of Labor, Bureau of Labor Statistics, Division of Consumer Prices and Price Indexes. - indicates no data collected for period.

Philadelphia, PA-NJ
Consumer Price Index - Urban Wage Earners
Base 1982-1984 = 100
Other Goods and Services

For 1976-1995. Columns headed % show percentile change in the index from the previous period for which an index is available.

Year	Jan Index	%	Feb Index	%	Mar Index	%	Apr Index	%	May Index	%	Jun Index	%	Jul Index	%	Aug Index	%	Sep Index	%	Oct Index	%	Nov Index	%	Dec Index	%
1976	56.8	-	57.2	0.7	57.0	-0.3	57.3	0.5	57.3	0.0	57.8	0.9	58.3	0.9	58.3	0.0	58.7	0.7	59.8	1.9	59.9	0.2	59.9	0.0
1977	60.1	0.3	60.3	0.3	60.3	0.0	60.9	1.0	60.8	-0.2	61.0	0.3	61.2	0.3	61.1	-0.2	62.5	2.3	63.1	1.0	63.3	0.3	63.2	-0.2
1978	63.4	0.3	63.6	0.3	63.6	0.0	64.0	0.6	63.8	-0.3	64.3	0.8	65.0	1.1	64.0	-1.5	65.5	2.3	66.2	1.1	66.1	-0.2	66.1	0.0
1979	66.8	1.1	67.3	0.7	67.2	-0.1	67.2	0.0	67.3	0.1	67.0	-0.4	67.5	0.7	68.0	0.7	70.1	3.1	70.0	-0.1	71.3	1.9	71.3	0.0
1980	71.9	0.8	72.0	0.1	72.0	0.0	72.2	0.3	72.8	0.8	73.4	0.8	73.4	0.0	73.8	0.5	75.9	2.8	76.1	0.3	76.6	0.7	77.2	0.8
1981	77.8	0.8	77.7	-0.1	78.1	0.5	78.3	0.3	79.2	1.1	79.0	-0.3	79.2	0.3	79.4	0.3	83.4	5.0	84.0	0.7	84.6	0.7	84.6	0.0
1982	84.5	-0.1	85.1	0.7	85.0	-0.1	86.8	2.1	87.2	0.5	88.2	1.1	87.6	-0.7	88.9	1.5	92.5	4.0	94.6	2.3	95.6	1.1	97.0	1.5
1983	98.0	1.0	97.2	-0.8	98.2	1.0	97.9	-0.3	98.0	0.1	98.3	0.3	99.9	1.6	102.6	2.7	105.3	2.6	106.0	0.7	106.2	0.2	106.3	0.1
1984	107.4	1.0	107.1	-0.3	107.3	0.2	108.2	0.8	107.8	-0.4	108.5	0.6	109.5	0.9	109.6	0.1	111.8	2.0	111.8	0.0	111.9	0.1	112.0	0.1
1985	113.6	1.4	114.5	0.8	114.7	0.2	115.9	1.0	115.5	-0.3	115.6	0.1	116.6	0.9	116.7	0.1	119.8	2.7	119.7	-0.1	119.6	-0.1	119.6	0.0
1986	121.1	1.3	122.8	1.4	123.3	0.4	124.1	0.6	125.5	1.1	125.8	0.2	126.5	0.6	126.5	0.0	128.8	1.8	128.8	0.0	128.9	0.1	129.0	0.1
1987	132.0	2.3	132.4	0.3	132.7	0.2	133.0	0.2	133.1	0.1	133.5	0.3	134.2	0.5	134.1	-0.1	137.3	2.4	138.0	0.5	137.8	-0.1	138.2	0.3
1988	139.4	0.9	141.6	1.6	141.1	-0.4	142.7	1.1	142.7	0.0	143.0	0.2	143.8	0.6	144.1	0.2	147.8	2.6	148.2	0.3	148.1	-0.1	149.5	0.9
1989	150.9	0.9	150.9	0.0	151.0	0.1	152.1	0.7	151.9	-0.1	152.6	0.5	153.9	0.9	156.0	1.4	156.4	0.3	156.3	-0.1	157.5	0.8	156.5	-0.6
1990	160.5	2.6	160.2	-0.2	163.8	2.2	164.2	0.2	164.6	0.2	167.5	1.8	177.0	5.7	178.6	0.9	178.1	-0.3	177.6	-0.3	177.9	0.2	178.2	0.2
1991	181.0	1.6	184.2	1.8	181.5	-1.5	182.2	0.4	182.1	-0.1	182.2	0.1	183.0	0.4	185.5	1.4	186.0	0.3	187.4	0.8	188.1	0.4	188.8	0.4
1992	188.5	-0.2	189.7	0.6	190.7	0.5	190.9	0.1	192.3	0.7	193.9	0.8	194.2	0.2	195.3	0.6	197.7	1.2	199.1	0.7	198.8	-0.2	200.1	0.7
1993	201.4	0.6	201.5	0.0	201.6	0.0	202.0	0.2	210.2	4.1	211.0	0.4	211.8	0.4	210.0	-0.8	209.8	-0.1	213.1	1.6	214.2	0.5	215.2	0.5
1994	215.3	0.0	215.5	0.1	216.8	0.6	216.8	0.0	217.4	0.3	217.5	0.0	217.8	0.1	218.8	0.5	220.5	0.8	220.7	0.1	220.6	-0.0	220.6	0.0
1995	220.1	-0.2	219.8	-0.1	220.1	0.1	221.3	0.5	221.8	0.2	222.6	0.4	221.8	-0.4	222.4	0.3	224.9	1.1	224.2	-0.3	223.4	-0.4	224.2	0.4

Source: U.S. Department of Labor, Bureau of Labor Statistics, Division of Consumer Prices and Price Indexes. - indicates no data collected for period.

Pittsburgh, PA

Consumer Price Index - All Urban Consumers
Base 1982-1984 = 100
Annual Averages

For 1917-1995. Columns headed % show percentile change in the index from the previous period for which an index is available.

Year	All Items		Food & Beverage		Housing		Apparel & Upkeep		Trans- portation		Medical Care		Entertain- ment		Other Goods & Services	
	Index	%	Index	%	Index	%	Index	%	Index	%	Index	%	Index	%	Index	%
1917	-	-	-	-	-	-	-	-	-	-	-	-	-	-	-	-
1918	14.8	-	-	-	-	-	-	-	-	-	-	-	-	-	-	-
1919	17.0	14.9	-	-	-	-	-	-	-	-	-	-	-	-	-	-
1920	19.5	14.7	-	-	-	-	-	-	-	-	-	-	-	-	-	-
1921	17.5	-10.3	-	-	-	-	-	-	-	-	-	-	-	-	-	-
1922	16.3	-6.9	-	-	-	-	-	-	-	-	-	-	-	-	-	-
1923	16.6	1.8	-	-	-	-	-	-	-	-	-	-	-	-	-	-
1924	16.8	1.2	-	-	-	-	-	-	-	-	-	-	-	-	-	-
1925	17.4	3.6	-	-	-	-	-	-	-	-	-	-	-	-	-	-
1926	17.5	0.6	-	-	-	-	-	-	-	-	-	-	-	-	-	-
1927	17.2	-1.7	-	-	-	-	-	-	-	-	-	-	-	-	-	-
1928	17.1	-0.6	-	-	-	-	-	-	-	-	-	-	-	-	-	-
1929	17.1	0.0	-	-	-	-	-	-	-	-	-	-	-	-	-	-
1930	16.5	-3.5	-	-	-	-	-	-	-	-	-	-	-	-	-	-
1931	15.0	-9.1	-	-	-	-	-	-	-	-	-	-	-	-	-	-
1932	13.3	-11.3	-	-	-	-	-	-	-	-	-	-	-	-	-	-
1933	12.5	-6.0	-	-	-	-	-	-	-	-	-	-	-	-	-	-
1934	12.9	3.2	-	-	-	-	-	-	-	-	-	-	-	-	-	-
1935	13.3	3.1	-	-	-	-	-	-	-	-	-	-	-	-	-	-
1936	13.5	1.5	-	-	-	-	-	-	-	-	-	-	-	-	-	-
1937	14.0	3.7	-	-	-	-	-	-	-	-	-	-	-	-	-	-
1938	13.7	-2.1	-	-	-	-	-	-	-	-	-	-	-	-	-	-
1939	13.4	-2.2	-	-	-	-	-	-	-	-	-	-	-	-	-	-
1940	13.6	1.5	-	-	-	-	-	-	-	-	-	-	-	-	-	-
1941	14.4	5.9	-	-	-	-	-	-	-	-	-	-	-	-	-	-
1942	15.8	9.7	-	-	-	-	-	-	-	-	-	-	-	-	-	-
1943	16.8	6.3	-	-	-	-	-	-	-	-	-	-	-	-	-	-
1944	17.2	2.4	-	-	-	-	-	-	-	-	-	-	-	-	-	-
1945	17.6	2.3	-	-	-	-	-	-	-	-	-	-	-	-	-	-
1946	19.1	8.5	-	-	-	-	-	-	-	-	-	-	-	-	-	-
1947	22.2	16.2	-	-	-	-	-	-	16.2	-	11.7	-	-	-	-	-
1948	23.8	7.2	-	-	-	-	-	-	17.9	10.5	12.4	6.0	-	-	-	-
1949	23.5	-1.3	-	-	-	-	-	-	18.9	5.6	12.6	1.6	-	-	-	-
1950	23.7	0.9	-	-	-	-	-	-	21.0	11.1	12.9	2.4	-	-	-	-
1951	25.6	8.0	-	-	-	-	-	-	22.8	8.6	13.5	4.7	-	-	-	-
1952	26.1	2.0	-	-	-	-	-	-	24.4	7.0	14.0	3.7	-	-	-	-
1953	26.3	0.8	-	-	-	-	42.9	-	24.7	1.2	14.7	5.0	-	-	-	-
1954	26.5	0.8	-	-	-	-	42.9	0.0	24.3	-1.6	15.4	4.8	-	-	-	-
1955	26.3	-0.8	-	-	-	-	42.2	-1.6	24.2	-0.4	15.8	2.6	-	-	-	-
1956	27.0	2.7	-	-	-	-	43.2	2.4	24.5	1.2	16.8	6.3	-	-	-	-
1957	27.8	3.0	-	-	-	-	44.4	2.8	25.7	4.9	17.7	5.4	-	-	-	-
1958	28.7	3.2	-	-	-	-	44.5	0.2	26.9	4.7	18.5	4.5	-	-	-	-
1959	29.0	1.0	-	-	-	-	44.6	0.2	28.5	5.9	19.7	6.5	-	-	-	-
1960	29.7	2.4	-	-	-	-	45.3	1.6	29.1	2.1	20.7	5.1	-	-	-	-
1961	29.9	0.7	-	-	-	-	45.6	0.7	29.2	0.3	21.4	3.4	-	-	-	-

[Continued]

Pittsburgh, PA
Consumer Price Index - All Urban Consumers
Base 1982-1984 = 100
Annual Averages

[Continued]

For 1917-1995. Columns headed % show percentile change in the index from the previous period for which an index is available.

Year	All Items		Food & Beverage		Housing		Apparel & Upkeep		Trans-portation		Medical Care		Entertain-ment		Other Goods & Services	
	Index	%	Index	%	Index	%	Index	%	Index	%	Index	%	Index	%	Index	%
1962	30.2	1.0	-	-	-	-	45.9	0.7	29.9	2.4	22.4	4.7	-	-	-	-
1963	30.5	1.0	-	-	-	-	46.9	2.2	29.9	0.0	23.0	2.7	-	-	-	-
1964	30.9	1.3	-	-	-	-	47.7	1.7	30.3	1.3	23.7	3.0	-	-	-	-
1965	31.4	1.6	-	-	-	-	48.6	1.9	30.8	1.7	24.3	2.5	-	-	-	-
1966	32.2	2.5	-	-	-	-	49.9	2.7	31.1	1.0	25.1	3.3	-	-	-	-
1967	32.8	1.9	-	-	-	-	51.2	2.6	31.6	1.6	26.9	7.2	-	-	-	-
1968	34.3	4.6	-	-	-	-	54.2	5.9	32.7	3.5	28.4	5.6	-	-	-	-
1969	36.2	5.5	-	-	-	-	57.8	6.6	34.1	4.3	30.1	6.0	-	-	-	-
1970	38.1	5.2	-	-	-	-	59.1	2.2	36.0	5.6	31.6	5.0	-	-	-	-
1971	39.8	4.5	-	-	-	-	61.2	3.6	37.9	5.3	32.9	4.1	-	-	-	-
1972	41.1	3.3	-	-	-	-	63.3	3.4	38.3	1.1	34.6	5.2	-	-	-	-
1973	43.6	6.1	-	-	-	-	65.4	3.3	39.3	2.6	36.0	4.0	-	-	-	-
1974	48.3	10.8	-	-	-	-	70.5	7.8	43.4	10.4	39.5	9.7	-	-	-	-
1975	52.4	8.5	-	-	-	-	72.5	2.8	47.0	8.3	43.7	10.6	-	-	-	-
1976	55.2	5.3	62.3	-	50.7	-	73.8	1.8	51.6	9.8	48.2	10.3	65.0	-	57.9	-
1977	58.9	6.7	66.4	6.6	54.4	7.3	75.2	1.9	56.3	9.1	53.3	10.6	68.3	5.1	61.8	6.7
1978	64.1	8.8	72.8	9.6	60.5	11.2	77.6	3.2	59.7	6.0	58.0	8.8	71.3	4.4	65.5	6.0
1979	71.2	11.1	80.0	9.9	67.9	12.2	82.6	6.4	68.5	14.7	64.2	10.7	73.7	3.4	70.3	7.3
1980	81.0	13.8	87.2	9.0	78.9	16.2	87.1	5.4	82.1	19.9	71.2	10.9	82.1	11.4	75.2	7.0
1981	89.3	10.2	93.8	7.6	86.7	9.9	93.7	7.6	93.6	14.0	79.7	11.9	90.3	10.0	82.4	9.6
1982	94.4	5.7	98.0	4.5	92.2	6.3	97.7	4.3	96.6	3.2	89.6	12.4	95.5	5.8	90.8	10.2
1983	101.1	7.1	101.1	3.2	101.7	10.3	101.2	3.6	99.8	3.3	100.9	12.6	100.4	5.1	101.0	11.2
1984	104.5	3.4	100.9	-0.2	106.1	4.3	101.2	0.0	103.6	3.8	109.6	8.6	104.1	3.7	108.2	7.1
1985	106.9	2.3	102.3	1.4	108.5	2.3	102.8	1.6	105.4	1.7	113.4	3.5	109.8	5.5	113.0	4.4
1986	108.2	1.2	105.0	2.6	111.3	2.6	100.4	-2.3	99.5	-5.6	121.2	6.9	118.7	8.1	118.0	4.4
1987	111.4	3.0	109.4	4.2	113.4	1.9	107.0	6.6	100.5	1.0	130.2	7.4	121.4	2.3	122.7	4.0
1988	114.9	3.1	111.9	2.3	115.7	2.0	114.2	6.7	102.3	1.8	138.2	6.1	127.1	4.7	132.7	8.1
1989	120.1	4.5	118.0	5.5	119.2	3.0	121.2	6.1	107.2	4.8	146.8	6.2	133.1	4.7	140.7	6.0
1990	126.2	5.1	124.3	5.3	124.8	4.7	125.0	3.1	112.1	4.6	160.6	9.4	138.8	4.3	150.4	6.9
1991	131.3	4.0	129.2	3.9	131.4	5.3	129.5	3.6	112.9	0.7	175.7	9.4	143.0	3.0	155.0	3.1
1992	136.0	3.6	132.9	2.9	135.8	3.3	133.0	2.7	115.6	2.4	185.9	5.8	145.4	1.7	168.1	8.5
1993	139.9	2.9	137.2	3.2	139.1	2.4	134.5	1.1	118.1	2.2	196.8	5.9	149.8	3.0	177.2	5.4
1994	144.6	3.4	140.6	2.5	145.2	4.4	133.2	-1.0	122.3	3.6	207.0	5.2	153.6	2.5	182.9	3.2
1995	149.2	3.2	143.6	2.1	150.1	3.4	135.3	1.6	127.6	4.3	212.6	2.7	156.4	1.8	192.2	5.1

Source: U.S. Department of Labor, Bureau of Labor Statistics, Division of Consumer Prices and Price Indexes. - indicates no data collected for period.

Pittsburgh, PA
Consumer Price Index - Urban Wage Earners
Base 1982-1984 = 100
Annual Averages

For 1917-1995. Columns headed % show percentile change in the index from the previous period for which an index is available.

Year	All Items		Food & Beverage		Housing		Apparel & Upkeep		Trans- portation		Medical Care		Entertain- ment		Other Goods & Services	
	Index	%	Index	%	Index	%	Index	%	Index	%	Index	%	Index	%	Index	%
1917	-	-	-	-	-	-	-	-	-	-	-	-	-	-	-	-
1918	15.2	-	-	-	-	-	-	-	-	-	-	-	-	-	-	-
1919	17.5	15.1	-	-	-	-	-	-	-	-	-	-	-	-	-	-
1920	20.0	14.3	-	-	-	-	-	-	-	-	-	-	-	-	-	-
1921	17.9	-10.5	-	-	-	-	-	-	-	-	-	-	-	-	-	-
1922	16.7	-6.7	-	-	-	-	-	-	-	-	-	-	-	-	-	-
1923	17.1	2.4	-	-	-	-	-	-	-	-	-	-	-	-	-	-
1924	17.2	0.6	-	-	-	-	-	-	-	-	-	-	-	-	-	-
1925	17.8	3.5	-	-	-	-	-	-	-	-	-	-	-	-	-	-
1926	18.0	1.1	-	-	-	-	-	-	-	-	-	-	-	-	-	-
1927	17.7	-1.7	-	-	-	-	-	-	-	-	-	-	-	-	-	-
1928	17.5	-1.1	-	-	-	-	-	-	-	-	-	-	-	-	-	-
1929	17.5	0.0	-	-	-	-	-	-	-	-	-	-	-	-	-	-
1930	16.9	-3.4	-	-	-	-	-	-	-	-	-	-	-	-	-	-
1931	15.4	-8.9	-	-	-	-	-	-	-	-	-	-	-	-	-	-
1932	13.7	-11.0	-	-	-	-	-	-	-	-	-	-	-	-	-	-
1933	12.8	-6.6	-	-	-	-	-	-	-	-	-	-	-	-	-	-
1934	13.3	3.9	-	-	-	-	-	-	-	-	-	-	-	-	-	-
1935	13.7	3.0	-	-	-	-	-	-	-	-	-	-	-	-	-	-
1936	13.9	1.5	-	-	-	-	-	-	-	-	-	-	-	-	-	-
1937	14.4	3.6	-	-	-	-	-	-	-	-	-	-	-	-	-	-
1938	14.1	-2.1	-	-	-	-	-	-	-	-	-	-	-	-	-	-
1939	13.8	-2.1	-	-	-	-	-	-	-	-	-	-	-	-	-	-
1940	14.0	1.4	-	-	-	-	-	-	-	-	-	-	-	-	-	-
1941	14.7	5.0	-	-	-	-	-	-	-	-	-	-	-	-	-	-
1942	16.2	10.2	-	-	-	-	-	-	-	-	-	-	-	-	-	-
1943	17.3	6.8	-	-	-	-	-	-	-	-	-	-	-	-	-	-
1944	17.6	1.7	-	-	-	-	-	-	-	-	-	-	-	-	-	-
1945	18.1	2.8	-	-	-	-	-	-	-	-	-	-	-	-	-	-
1946	19.6	8.3	-	-	-	-	-	-	-	-	-	-	-	-	-	-
1947	22.8	16.3	-	-	-	-			16.0	-	11.8	-	-	-	-	-
1948	24.4	7.0	-	-	-	-			17.7	10.6	12.4	5.1	-	-	-	-
1949	24.1	-1.2	-	-	-	-			18.7	5.6	12.7	2.4	-	-	-	-
1950	24.3	0.8	-	-	-	-			20.7	10.7	13.0	2.4	-	-	-	-
1951	26.3	8.2	-	-	-	-			22.5	8.7	13.6	4.6	-	-	-	-
1952	26.8	1.9	-	-	-	-			24.1	7.1	14.1	3.7	-	-	-	-
1953	27.0	0.7	-	-	-	-	44.4	-	24.4	1.2	14.8	5.0	-	-	-	-
1954	27.2	0.7		-	-	-	44.4	0.0	24.0	-1.6	15.5	4.7	-	-	-	-
1955	27.0	-0.7	-	-	-	-	43.8	-1.4	23.9	-0.4	15.9	2.6	-	-	-	-
1956	27.7	2.6	-	-	-	-	44.8	2.3	24.1	0.8	16.9	6.3	-	-	-	-
1957	28.5	2.9	-	-	-	-	46.0	2.7	25.3	5.0	17.9	5.9	-	-	-	-
1958	29.4	3.2	-	-	-	-	46.1	0.2	26.6	5.1	18.6	3.9	-	-	-	-
1959	29.8	1.4	-	-	-	-	46.3	0.4	28.1	5.6	19.8	6.5	-	-	-	-
1960	30.4	2.0	-	-	-	-	47.0	1.5	28.8	2.5	20.9	5.6	-	-	-	-
1961	30.7	1.0	-	-	-	-	47.3	0.6	28.8	0.0	21.6	3.3	-	-	-	-

[Continued]

Pittsburgh, PA
Consumer Price Index - Urban Wage Earners
Base 1982-1984 = 100
Annual Averages
[Continued]

For 1917-1995. Columns headed % show percentile change in the index from the previous period for which an index is available.

Year	All Items		Food & Beverage		Housing		Apparel & Upkeep		Trans- portation		Medical Care		Entertain- ment		Other Goods & Services	
	Index	%	Index	%	Index	%	Index	%	Index	%	Index	%	Index	%	Index	%
1962	31.0	1.0	-	-	-	-	47.6	0.6	29.5	2.4	22.5	4.2	-	-	-	-
1963	31.3	1.0	-	-	-	-	48.7	2.3	29.5	0.0	23.2	3.1	-	-	-	-
1964	31.7	1.3	-	-	-	-	49.4	1.4	29.9	1.4	23.9	3.0	-	-	-	-
1965	32.2	1.6	-	-	-	-	50.4	2.0	30.4	1.7	24.5	2.5	-	-	-	-
1966	33.1	2.8	-	-	-	-	51.8	2.8	30.7	1.0	25.3	3.3	-	-	-	-
1967	33.6	1.5	-	-	-	-	53.1	2.5	31.2	1.6	27.0	6.7	-	-	-	-
1968	35.2	4.8	-	-	-	-	56.2	5.8	32.3	3.5	28.5	5.6	-	-	-	-
1969	37.1	5.4	-	-	-	-	59.9	6.6	33.7	4.3	30.3	6.3	-	-	-	-
1970	39.1	5.4	-	-	-	-	61.3	2.3	35.5	5.3	31.8	5.0	-	-	-	-
1971	40.9	4.6	-	-	-	-	63.5	3.6	37.4	5.4	33.1	4.1	-	-	-	-
1972	42.1	2.9	-	-	-	-	65.6	3.3	37.8	1.1	34.8	5.1	-	-	-	-
1973	44.7	6.2	-	-	-	-	67.8	3.4	38.8	2.6	36.3	4.3	-	-	-	-
1974	49.5	10.7	-	-	-	-	73.1	7.8	42.8	10.3	39.7	9.4	-	-	-	-
1975	53.8	8.7	-	-	-	-	75.2	2.9	46.4	8.4	44.0	10.8	-	-	-	-
1976	56.6	5.2	62.2	-	53.8	-	76.5	1.7	50.9	9.7	48.5	10.2	67.2	-	57.1	-
1977	60.5	6.9	66.2	6.4	57.7	7.2	77.9	1.8	55.6	9.2	53.7	10.7	70.7	5.2	61.0	6.8
1978	65.6	8.4	72.8	10.0	64.1	11.1	78.5	0.8	59.1	6.3	57.9	7.8	73.2	3.5	64.7	6.1
1979	73.1	11.4	80.5	10.6	72.0	12.3	83.8	6.8	67.9	14.9	64.4	11.2	77.2	5.5	69.2	7.0
1980	83.4	14.1	87.4	8.6	83.9	16.5	89.4	6.7	81.4	19.9	73.3	13.8	83.6	8.3	75.2	8.7
1981	92.0	10.3	94.1	7.7	92.5	10.3	93.3	4.4	93.7	15.1	80.6	10.0	90.0	7.7	82.1	9.2
1982	97.0	5.4	98.0	4.1	98.5	6.5	97.7	4.7	96.9	3.4	89.9	11.5	95.4	6.0	89.9	9.5
1983	101.3	4.4	101.1	3.2	102.8	4.4	100.9	3.3	99.4	2.6	100.6	11.9	100.6	5.5	101.1	12.5
1984	101.6	0.3	100.9	-0.2	98.7	-4.0	101.4	0.5	103.7	4.3	109.5	8.8	104.0	3.4	108.9	7.7
1985	103.7	2.1	102.1	1.2	100.4	1.7	102.8	1.4	105.2	1.4	113.6	3.7	109.9	5.7	113.7	4.4
1986	104.2	0.5	104.7	2.5	102.9	2.5	100.0	-2.7	98.2	-6.7	121.7	7.1	118.7	8.0	118.7	4.4
1987	107.1	2.8	109.1	4.2	104.8	1.8	106.1	6.1	99.3	1.1	130.9	7.6	121.4	2.3	123.1	3.7
1988	110.4	3.1	111.9	2.6	106.9	2.0	112.6	6.1	101.7	2.4	139.4	6.5	126.5	4.2	134.3	9.1
1989	115.4	4.5	118.0	5.5	110.3	3.2	118.6	5.3	106.8	5.0	147.5	5.8	131.6	4.0	142.5	6.1
1990	121.3	5.1	124.5	5.5	115.6	4.8	122.1	3.0	111.5	4.4	161.3	9.4	137.2	4.3	153.4	7.6
1991	125.9	3.8	129.6	4.1	121.6	5.2	124.5	2.0	111.9	0.4	175.4	8.7	140.8	2.6	158.6	3.4
1992	130.1	3.3	133.1	2.7	125.5	3.2	128.0	2.8	114.7	2.5	184.1	5.0	143.0	1.6	172.6	8.8
1993	133.9	2.9	137.4	3.2	128.6	2.5	128.8	0.6	117.5	2.4	194.1	5.4	147.4	3.1	181.6	5.2
1994	138.3	3.3	140.5	2.3	134.1	4.3	128.5	-0.2	121.7	3.6	203.8	5.0	151.5	2.8	186.6	2.8
1995	142.9	3.3	143.4	2.1	138.5	3.3	128.9	0.3	128.5	5.6	208.6	2.4	154.6	2.0	195.2	4.6

Source: U.S. Department of Labor, Bureau of Labor Statistics, Division of Consumer Prices and Price Indexes. - indicates no data collected for period.

Pittsburgh, PA
Consumer Price Index - All Urban Consumers
Base 1982-1984 = 100
All Items

For 1917-1995. Columns headed % show percentile change in the index from the previous period for which an index is available.

Year	Jan Index	%	Feb Index	%	Mar Index	%	Apr Index	%	May Index	%	Jun Index	%	Jul Index	%	Aug Index	%	Sep Index	%	Oct Index	%	Nov Index	%	Dec Index	%
1917	-	-	-	-	-	-	-	-	-	-	-	-	-	-	-	-	-	-	-	-	-	-	13.5	-
1918	-	-	-	-	-	-	-	-	-	-	-	-	-	-	-	-	-	-	-	-	-	-	16.2	20.0
1919	-	-	-	-	-	-	-	-	-	-	16.5	1.9	-	-	-	-	-	-	-	-	-	-	18.4	11.5
1920	-	-	-	-	-	-	-	-	-	-	20.4	10.9	-	-	-	-	-	-	-	-	-	-	18.9	-7.4
1921	-	-	-	-	-	-	-	-	17.5	-7.4	-	-	-	-	-	-	17.1	-2.3	-	-	-	-	16.7	-2.3
1922	-	-	-	-	16.2	-3.0	-	-	-	-	16.3	0.6	-	-	-	-	16.2	-0.6	-	-	-	-	16.4	1.2
1923	-	-	-	-	16.4	0.0	-	-	-	-	16.7	1.8	-	-	-	-	16.8	0.6	-	-	-	-	16.7	-0.6
1924	-	-	-	-	16.5	-1.2	-	-	-	-	16.8	1.8	-	-	-	-	16.9	0.6	-	-	-	-	17.0	0.6
1925	-	-	-	-	-	-	-	-	-	-	17.4	2.4	-	-	-	-	-	-	-	-	-	-	17.7	1.7
1926	-	-	-	-	-	-	-	-	-	-	17.6	-0.6	-	-	-	-	-	-	-	-	-	-	17.5	-0.6
1927	-	-	-	-	-	-	-	-	-	-	17.5	0.0	-	-	-	-	-	-	-	-	-	-	17.1	-2.3
1928	-	-	-	-	-	-	-	-	-	-	16.9	-1.2	-	-	-	-	-	-	-	-	-	-	17.1	1.2
1929	-	-	-	-	-	-	-	-	-	-	17.1	0.0	-	-	-	-	-	-	-	-	-	-	17.0	-0.6
1930	-	-	-	-	-	-	-	-	-	-	16.7	-1.8	-	-	-	-	-	-	-	-	-	-	15.9	-4.8
1931	-	-	-	-	-	-	-	-	-	-	14.9	-6.3	-	-	-	-	-	-	-	-	-	-	14.3	-4.0
1932	-	-	-	-	-	-	-	-	-	-	13.2	-7.7	-	-	-	-	-	-	-	-	-	-	12.8	-3.0
1933	-	-	-	-	-	-	-	-	-	-	12.2	-4.7	-	-	-	-	-	-	-	-	-	-	12.7	4.1
1934	-	-	-	-	-	-	-	-	-	-	13.0	2.4	-	-	-	-	-	-	-	-	13.0	0.0	-	-
1935	-	-	-	-	13.2	1.5	-	-	-	-	-	-	13.2	0.0	-	-	-	-	13.4	1.5	-	-	-	-
1936	13.4	0.0	-	-	-	-	13.3	-0.7	-	-	-	-	13.6	2.3	-	-	13.8	1.5	-	-	-	-	13.6	-1.4
1937	-	-	-	-	13.9	2.2	-	-	-	-	14.1	1.4	-	-	-	-	14.3	1.4	-	-	-	-	13.9	-2.8
1938	-	-	-	-	13.7	-1.4	-	-	-	-	13.8	0.7	-	-	-	-	13.8	0.0	-	-	-	-	13.7	-0.7
1939	-	-	-	-	13.3	-2.9	-	-	-	-	13.4	0.8	-	-	-	-	13.6	1.5	-	-	-	-	13.4	-1.5
1940	-	-	-	-	13.5	0.7	-	-	-	-	13.7	1.5	-	-	-	-	13.7	0.0	13.7	0.0	13.7	0.0	13.8	0.7
1941	13.8	0.0	13.7	-0.7	13.8	0.7	13.9	0.7	14.1	1.4	14.3	1.4	14.5	1.4	14.5	0.0	14.8	2.1	14.9	0.7	15.0	0.7	15.1	0.7
1942	15.2	0.7	15.4	1.3	15.5	0.6	15.5	0.0	15.8	1.9	15.9	0.6	15.9	0.0	15.9	0.0	16.0	0.6	16.2	1.3	16.2	0.0	16.3	0.6
1943	16.4	0.6	16.5	0.6	16.7	1.2	16.8	0.6	17.0	1.2	17.0	0.0	16.9	-0.6	16.8	-0.6	16.9	0.6	17.0	0.6	17.0	0.0	16.9	-0.6
1944	16.9	0.0	16.9	0.0	16.9	0.0	17.1	1.2	17.1	0.0	17.2	0.6	17.3	0.6	17.4	0.6	17.4	0.0	17.4	0.0	17.3	-0.6	17.4	0.6
1945	17.4	0.0	17.4	0.0	17.4	0.0	17.4	0.0	17.5	0.6	17.8	1.7	17.8	0.0	17.7	-0.6	17.7	0.0	17.7	0.0	17.7	0.0	17.8	0.6
1946	17.9	0.6	17.8	-0.6	17.9	0.6	17.9	0.0	18.0	0.6	18.3	1.7	19.4	6.0	19.8	2.1	20.1	1.5	20.3	1.0	20.9	3.0	21.1	1.0
1947	21.2	0.5	21.3	0.5	21.7	1.9	21.6	-0.5	21.7	0.5	21.9	0.9	22.2	1.4	22.4	0.9	22.9	2.2	22.8	-0.4	22.9	0.4	23.2	1.3
1948	23.5	1.3	23.1	-1.7	23.1	0.0	23.4	1.3	23.6	0.9	23.9	1.3	24.2	1.3	24.3	0.4	24.3	0.0	24.1	-0.8	23.9	-0.8	23.8	-0.4
1949	23.8	0.0	23.4	-1.7	23.5	0.4	23.5	0.0	23.5	0.0	23.6	0.4	23.4	-0.8	23.5	0.4	23.5	0.0	23.3	-0.9	23.3	0.0	23.2	-0.4
1950	23.1	-0.4	23.0	-0.4	23.0	0.0	23.1	0.4	23.3	0.9	23.4	0.4	23.5	0.4	23.9	1.7	24.2	1.3	24.3	0.4	24.3	0.0	24.5	0.8
1951	25.0	2.0	25.2	0.8	25.3	0.4	25.4	0.4	25.6	0.8	25.6	0.0	25.8	0.8	25.7	-0.4	25.9	0.8	26.0	0.4	26.1	0.4	26.1	0.0
1952	26.2	0.4	26.0	-0.8	25.9	-0.4	26.0	0.4	26.0	0.0	26.0	0.0	26.1	0.4	26.2	0.4	26.2	0.0	26.2	0.0	26.2	0.0	26.2	0.0
1953	26.1	-0.4	-	-	-	-	26.1	0.0	-	-	-	-	26.3	0.8	-	-	-	-	26.5	0.8	-	-	-	-
1954	26.5	0.0	-	-	-	-	26.5	0.0	-	-	-	-	26.7	0.8	-	-	-	-	26.4	-1.1	-	-	-	-
1955	26.3	-0.4	-	-	-	-	26.3	0.0	-	-	-	-	26.3	0.0	-	-	-	-	26.3	0.0	-	-	-	-
1956	26.3	0.0	-	-	-	-	26.6	1.1	-	-	-	-	27.1	1.9	-	-	-	-	27.3	0.7	-	-	-	-
1957	27.5	0.7	-	-	-	-	27.5	0.0	-	-	-	-	27.9	1.5	-	-	-	-	28.0	0.4	-	-	-	-
1958	28.3	1.1	-	-	-	-	28.6	1.1	-	-	-	-	28.8	0.7	-	-	-	-	28.8	0.0	-	-	-	-
1959	28.8	0.0	-	-	-	-	28.8	0.0	-	-	-	-	29.1	1.0	-	-	-	-	29.3	0.7	-	-	-	-
1960	29.3	0.0	-	-	-	-	29.6	1.0	-	-	-	-	29.8	0.7	-	-	-	-	29.8	0.0	-	-	-	-
1961	29.9	0.3	-	-	-	-	29.9	0.0	-	-	-	-	30.0	0.3	-	-	-	-	29.9	-0.3	-	-	-	-

[Continued]

Pittsburgh, PA
Consumer Price Index - All Urban Consumers
Base 1982-1984 = 100
All Items
[Continued]

For 1917-1995. Columns headed % show percentile change in the index from the previous period for which an index is available.

Year	Jan Index	%	Feb Index	%	Mar Index	%	Apr Index	%	May Index	%	Jun Index	%	Jul Index	%	Aug Index	%	Sep Index	%	Oct Index	%	Nov Index	%	Dec Index	%
1962	30.0	0.3	-	-	-	-	30.1	0.3	-	-	-	-	30.2	0.3	-	-	-	-	30.3	0.3	-	-	-	-
1963	30.3	0.0	-	-	-	-	30.3	0.0	-	-	-	-	30.7	1.3	-	-	-	-	30.6	-0.3	-	-	-	-
1964	30.7	0.3	-	-	-	-	30.8	0.3	-	-	-	-	31.0	0.6	-	-	-	-	31.0	0.0	-	-	-	-
1965	31.1	0.3	-	-	-	-	31.3	0.6	-	-	-	-	31.6	1.0	-	-	-	-	31.6	0.0	-	-	-	-
1966	31.6	0.0	-	-	-	-	32.2	1.9	-	-	-	-	32.1	-0.3	-	-	-	-	32.5	1.2	-	-	-	-
1967	32.5	0.0	-	-	-	-	32.5	0.0	-	-	-	-	32.8	0.9	-	-	-	-	32.9	0.3	-	-	-	-
1968	33.5	1.8	-	-	-	-	34.0	1.5	-	-	-	-	34.2	0.6	-	-	-	-	34.9	2.0	-	-	-	-
1969	35.3	1.1	-	-	-	-	35.9	1.7	-	-	-	-	36.4	1.4	-	-	-	-	36.6	0.5	-	-	-	-
1970	36.9	0.8	-	-	-	-	37.7	2.2	-	-	-	-	38.3	1.6	-	-	-	-	39.0	1.8	-	-	-	-
1971	39.1	0.3	-	-	-	-	39.6	1.3	-	-	-	-	39.9	0.8	-	-	-	-	40.3	1.0	-	-	-	-
1972	40.4	0.2	-	-	-	-	40.9	1.2	-	-	-	-	41.1	0.5	-	-	-	-	41.5	1.0	-	-	-	-
1973	41.7	0.5	-	-	-	-	43.0	3.1	-	-	-	-	43.5	1.2	-	-	-	-	44.8	3.0	-	-	-	-
1974	45.7	2.0	-	-	-	-	47.2	3.3	-	-	-	-	48.6	3.0	-	-	-	-	49.9	2.7	-	-	-	-
1975	50.6	1.4	-	-	-	-	51.7	2.2	-	-	-	-	53.0	2.5	-	-	-	-	53.4	0.8	-	-	-	-
1976	53.8	0.7	-	-	-	-	54.6	1.5	-	-	-	-	55.2	1.1	-	-	-	-	56.0	1.4	-	-	-	-
1977	56.7	1.3	-	-	-	-	58.4	3.0	-	-	-	-	59.2	1.4	-	-	-	-	60.1	1.5	-	-	-	-
1978	60.6	0.8	-	-	-	-	62.3	2.8	-	-	63.5	1.9	-	-	65.5	3.1	-	-	66.4	1.4	-	-	67.2	1.2
1979	-	-	68.6	2.1	-	-	69.5	1.3	-	-	70.3	1.2	-	-	71.8	2.1	-	-	74.1	3.2	-	-	75.1	1.3
1980	-	-	77.2	2.8	-	-	78.9	2.2	-	-	80.6	2.2	-	-	82.2	2.0	-	-	84.0	2.2	-	-	85.9	2.3
1981	-	-	87.0	1.3	-	-	87.1	0.1	-	-	88.9	2.1	-	-	91.0	2.4	-	-	91.0	0.0	-	-	92.3	1.4
1982	-	-	91.3	-1.1	-	-	90.2	-1.2	-	-	93.4	3.5	-	-	95.5	2.2	-	-	98.5	3.1	-	-	99.0	0.5
1983	-	-	99.9	0.9	-	-	100.0	0.1	-	-	100.1	0.1	-	-	101.7	1.6	-	-	102.8	1.1	-	-	103.0	0.2
1984	-	-	103.4	0.4	-	-	104.4	1.0	-	-	104.8	0.4	-	-	104.6	-0.2	-	-	105.2	0.6	-	-	105.6	0.4
1985	-	-	106.1	0.5	-	-	106.3	0.2	-	-	106.8	0.5	-	-	106.8	0.0	-	-	107.6	0.7	-	-	108.6	0.9
1986	-	-	108.2	-0.4	-	-	107.5	-0.6	-	-	107.7	0.2	-	-	108.2	0.5	-	-	108.7	0.5	-	-	109.1	0.4
1987	-	-	109.8	0.6	-	-	110.8	0.9	-	-	111.1	0.3	-	-	112.0	0.8	-	-	112.8	0.7	-	-	113.0	0.2
1988	-	-	113.3	0.3	-	-	114.5	1.1	-	-	114.3	-0.2	-	-	115.3	0.9	-	-	116.3	0.9	-	-	116.7	0.3
1989	-	-	117.9	1.0	-	-	119.2	1.1	-	-	120.4	1.0	-	-	120.8	0.3	-	-	121.7	0.7	-	-	121.8	0.1
1990	-	-	123.4	1.3	-	-	124.9	1.2	-	-	125.0	0.1	-	-	127.1	1.7	-	-	129.6	2.0	-	-	129.1	-0.4
1991	-	-	129.3	0.2	-	-	130.3	0.8	-	-	130.7	0.3	-	-	131.5	0.6	-	-	133.2	1.3	-	-	134.4	0.9
1992	-	-	134.3	-0.1	-	-	135.1	0.6	-	-	135.2	0.1	-	-	136.9	1.3	-	-	137.7	0.6	-	-	137.3	-0.3
1993	-	-	139.2	1.4	-	-	139.6	0.3	-	-	139.5	-0.1	-	-	140.4	0.6	-	-	140.6	0.1	-	-	141.1	0.4
1994	-	-	142.6	1.1	-	-	143.9	0.9	-	-	144.0	0.1	-	-	145.7	1.2	-	-	146.4	0.5	-	-	146.5	0.1
1995	-	-	147.3	0.5	-	-	148.9	1.1	-	-	149.2	0.2	-	-	150.1	0.6	-	-	150.5	0.3	-	-	150.0	-0.3

Source: U.S. Department of Labor, Bureau of Labor Statistics, Division of Consumer Prices and Price Indexes. - indicates no data collected for period.

Pittsburgh, PA
Consumer Price Index - Urban Wage Earners
Base 1982-1984 = 100
All Items

For 1917-1995. Columns headed % show percentile change in the index from the previous period for which an index is available.

Year	Jan Index	Jan %	Feb Index	Feb %	Mar Index	Mar %	Apr Index	Apr %	May Index	May %	Jun Index	Jun %	Jul Index	Jul %	Aug Index	Aug %	Sep Index	Sep %	Oct Index	Oct %	Nov Index	Nov %	Dec Index	Dec %
1917	-	-	-	-	-	-	-	-	-	-	-	-	-	-	-	-	-	-	-	-	-	-	13.9	-
1918	-	-	-	-	-	-	-	-	-	-	-	-	-	-	-	-	-	-	-	-	-	-	16.6	19.4
1919	-	-	-	-	-	-	-	-	-	-	16.9	1.8	-	-	-	-	-	-	-	-	-	-	18.8	11.2
1920	-	-	-	-	-	-	-	-	-	-	20.9	11.2	-	-	-	-	-	-	-	-	-	-	19.4	-7.2
1921	-	-	-	-	-	-	-	-	17.9	-7.7	-	-	-	-	-	-	17.5	-2.2	-	-	-	-	17.2	-1.7
1922	-	-	-	-	16.6	-3.5	-	-	-	-	16.7	0.6	-	-	-	-	16.6	-0.6	-	-	-	-	16.8	1.2
1923	-	-	-	-	16.8	0.0	-	-	-	-	17.2	2.4	-	-	-	-	17.3	0.6	-	-	-	-	17.2	-0.6
1924	-	-	-	-	17.0	-1.2	-	-	-	-	17.3	1.8	-	-	-	-	17.3	0.0	-	-	-	-	17.5	1.2
1925	-	-	-	-	-	-	-	-	-	-	17.8	1.7	-	-	-	-	-	-	-	-	-	-	18.2	2.2
1926	-	-	-	-	-	-	-	-	-	-	18.0	-1.1	-	-	-	-	-	-	-	-	-	-	18.0	0.0
1927	-	-	-	-	-	-	-	-	-	-	17.9	-0.6	-	-	-	-	-	-	-	-	-	-	17.6	-1.7
1928	-	-	-	-	-	-	-	-	-	-	17.4	-1.1	-	-	-	-	-	-	-	-	-	-	17.6	1.1
1929	-	-	-	-	-	-	-	-	-	-	17.5	-0.6	-	-	-	-	-	-	-	-	-	-	17.5	0.0
1930	-	-	-	-	-	-	-	-	-	-	17.1	-2.3	-	-	-	-	-	-	-	-	-	-	16.3	-4.7
1931	-	-	-	-	-	-	-	-	-	-	15.3	-6.1	-	-	-	-	-	-	-	-	-	-	14.7	-3.9
1932	-	-	-	-	-	-	-	-	-	-	13.6	-7.5	-	-	-	-	-	-	-	-	-	-	13.1	-3.7
1933	-	-	-	-	-	-	-	-	-	-	12.5	-4.6	-	-	-	-	-	-	-	-	-	-	13.0	4.0
1934	-	-	-	-	-	-	-	-	-	-	13.3	2.3	-	-	-	-	-	-	-	-	13.3	0.0	-	-
1935	-	-	-	-	13.6	2.3	-	-	-	-	-	-	13.6	0.0	-	-	-	-	13.7	0.7	-	-	-	-
1936	13.8	0.7	-	-	-	-	13.6	-1.4	-	-	-	-	14.0	2.9	-	-	14.1	0.7	-	-	-	-	14.0	-0.7
1937	-	-	-	-	14.2	1.4	-	-	-	-	14.5	2.1	-	-	-	-	14.7	1.4	-	-	-	-	14.3	-2.7
1938	-	-	-	-	14.1	-1.4	-	-	-	-	14.1	0.0	-	-	-	-	14.1	0.0	-	-	-	-	14.0	-0.7
1939	-	-	-	-	13.7	-2.1	-	-	-	-	13.8	0.7	-	-	-	-	14.0	1.4	-	-	-	-	13.8	-1.4
1940	-	-	-	-	13.8	0.0	-	-	-	-	14.1	2.2	-	-	-	-	14.1	0.0	14.0	-0.7	14.1	0.7	14.1	0.0
1941	14.1	0.0	14.1	0.0	14.2	0.7	14.3	0.7	14.5	1.4	14.7	1.4	14.8	0.7	14.9	0.7	15.2	2.0	15.3	0.7	15.4	0.7	15.5	0.6
1942	15.6	0.6	15.8	1.3	15.9	0.6	15.9	0.0	16.2	1.9	16.3	0.6	16.3	0.0	16.3	0.0	16.4	0.6	16.6	1.2	16.6	0.0	16.7	0.6
1943	16.8	0.6	16.9	0.6	17.1	1.2	17.3	1.2	17.5	1.2	17.5	0.0	17.7	1.1	17.7	0.0	17.8	0.6	17.8	0.0	17.7	-0.6	17.9	1.1
1944	17.4	0.0	17.3	-0.6	17.3	0.0	17.5	1.2	17.5	0.0	17.7	1.1	17.7	0.0	17.8	0.6	17.8	0.0	17.8	0.0	17.8	0.0	17.9	0.6
1945	17.9	0.0	17.9	0.0	17.8	-0.6	17.9	0.6	18.0	0.6	18.2	1.1	18.3	0.5	18.2	-0.5	18.1	-0.5	18.2	0.6	18.2	0.0	18.3	0.5
1946	18.3	0.0	18.3	0.0	18.3	0.0	18.4	0.5	18.5	0.5	18.8	1.6	19.9	5.9	20.3	2.0	20.6	1.5	20.8	1.0	21.5	3.4	21.7	0.9
1947	21.8	0.5	21.9	0.5	22.2	1.4	22.2	0.0	22.3	0.5	22.5	0.9	22.7	0.9	23.0	1.3	23.5	2.2	23.4	-0.4	23.5	0.4	23.8	1.3
1948	24.1	1.3	23.7	-1.7	23.7	0.0	24.0	1.3	24.2	0.8	24.5	1.2	24.8	1.2	24.9	0.4	24.9	0.0	24.7	-0.8	24.5	-0.8	24.4	-0.4
1949	24.4	0.0	24.0	-1.6	24.1	0.4	24.1	0.0	24.1	0.0	24.2	0.4	24.0	-0.8	24.1	0.4	24.1	0.0	23.9	-0.8	23.9	0.0	23.8	-0.4
1950	23.7	-0.4	23.6	-0.4	23.6	0.0	23.7	0.4	23.9	0.8	24.0	0.4	24.1	0.4	24.5	1.7	24.8	1.2	25.0	0.8	24.9	-0.4	25.1	0.8
1951	25.6	2.0	25.9	1.2	26.0	0.4	26.1	0.4	26.2	0.4	26.2	0.0	26.4	0.8	26.4	0.0	26.5	0.4	26.7	0.8	26.8	0.4	26.8	0.0
1952	26.8	0.0	26.7	-0.4	26.6	-0.4	26.7	0.4	26.7	0.0	26.6	-0.4	26.8	0.8	26.9	0.4	26.9	0.0	26.9	0.0	26.9	0.0	26.9	0.0
1953	26.7	-0.7	-	-	-	-	26.8	0.4	-	-	-	-	27.0	0.7	-	-	-	-	27.2	0.7	-	-	-	-
1954	27.2	0.0	-	-	-	-	27.2	0.0	-	-	-	-	27.4	0.7	-	-	-	-	27.1	-1.1	-	-	-	-
1955	27.0	-0.4	-	-	-	-	27.0	0.0	-	-	-	-	27.0	0.0	-	-	-	-	27.0	0.0	-	-	-	-
1956	27.0	0.0	-	-	-	-	27.3	1.1	-	-	-	-	27.8	1.8	-	-	-	-	28.0	0.7	-	-	-	-
1957	28.2	0.7	-	-	-	-	28.2	0.0	-	-	-	-	28.6	1.4	-	-	-	-	28.7	0.3	-	-	-	-
1958	29.1	1.4	-	-	-	-	29.4	1.0	-	-	-	-	29.6	0.7	-	-	-	-	29.6	0.0	-	-	-	-
1959	29.5	-0.3	-	-	-	-	29.6	0.3	-	-	-	-	29.8	0.7	-	-	-	-	30.1	1.0	-	-	-	-
1960	30.1	0.0	-	-	-	-	30.4	1.0	-	-	-	-	30.6	0.7	-	-	-	-	30.6	0.0	-	-	-	-
1961	30.7	0.3	-	-	-	-	30.7	0.0	-	-	-	-	30.8	0.3	-	-	-	-	30.7	-0.3	-	-	-	-

[Continued]

Pittsburgh, PA
Consumer Price Index - Urban Wage Earners
Base 1982-1984 = 100
All Items
[Continued]

For 1917-1995. Columns headed % show percentile change in the index from the previous period for which an index is available.

Year	Jan Index	%	Feb Index	%	Mar Index	%	Apr Index	%	May Index	%	Jun Index	%	Jul Index	%	Aug Index	%	Sep Index	%	Oct Index	%	Nov Index	%	Dec Index	%
1962	30.8	0.3	-	-	-	-	30.9	0.3	-	-	-	-	31.0	0.3	-	-	-	-	31.1	0.3	-	-	-	-
1963	31.1	0.0	-	-	-	-	31.1	0.0	-	-	-	-	31.5	1.3	-	-	-	-	31.4	-0.3	-	-	-	-
1964	31.5	0.3	-	-	-	-	31.6	0.3	-	-	-	-	31.8	0.6	-	-	-	-	31.8	0.0	-	-	-	-
1965	31.9	0.3	-	-	-	-	32.1	0.6	-	-	-	-	32.4	0.9	-	-	-	-	32.4	0.0	-	-	-	-
1966	32.4	0.0	-	-	-	-	33.1	2.2	-	-	-	-	33.0	-0.3	-	-	-	-	33.4	1.2	-	-	-	-
1967	33.3	-0.3	-	-	-	-	33.4	0.3	-	-	-	-	33.6	0.6	-	-	-	-	33.8	0.6	-	-	-	-
1968	34.4	1.8	-	-	-	-	34.9	1.5	-	-	-	-	35.1	0.6	-	-	-	-	35.8	2.0	-	-	-	-
1969	36.2	1.1	-	-	-	-	36.9	1.9	-	-	-	-	37.3	1.1	-	-	-	-	37.6	0.8	-	-	-	-
1970	37.8	0.5	-	-	-	-	38.7	2.4	-	-	-	-	39.3	1.6	-	-	-	-	40.0	1.8	-	-	-	-
1971	40.1	0.2	-	-	-	-	40.7	1.5	-	-	-	-	41.0	0.7	-	-	-	-	41.3	0.7	-	-	-	-
1972	41.4	0.2	-	-	-	-	41.9	1.2	-	-	-	-	42.2	0.7	-	-	-	-	42.5	0.7	-	-	-	-
1973	42.8	0.7	-	-	-	-	44.1	3.0	-	-	-	-	44.6	1.1	-	-	-	-	45.9	2.9	-	-	-	-
1974	46.8	2.0	-	-	-	-	48.5	3.6	-	-	-	-	49.9	2.9	-	-	-	-	51.2	2.6	-	-	-	-
1975	51.9	1.4	-	-	-	-	53.0	2.1	-	-	-	-	54.4	2.6	-	-	-	-	54.7	0.6	-	-	-	-
1976	55.2	0.9	-	-	-	-	56.0	1.4	-	-	-	-	56.7	1.3	-	-	-	-	57.5	1.4	-	-	-	-
1977	58.1	1.0	-	-	-	-	59.9	3.1	-	-	-	-	60.7	1.3	-	-	-	-	61.7	1.6	-	-	-	-
1978	62.2	0.8	-	-	-	-	63.9	2.7	-	-	65.1	1.9	-	-	66.9	2.8	-	-	67.8	1.3	-	-	68.7	1.3
1979	-	-	70.1	2.0	-	-	71.4	1.9	-	-	72.3	1.3	-	-	74.0	2.4	-	-	76.0	2.7	-	-	77.2	1.6
1980	-	-	79.3	2.7	-	-	81.4	2.6	-	-	83.0	2.0	-	-	84.5	1.8	-	-	86.6	2.5	-	-	88.4	2.1
1981	-	-	89.6	1.4	-	-	89.9	0.3	-	-	91.8	2.1	-	-	93.5	1.9	-	-	93.6	0.1	-	-	95.0	1.5
1982	-	-	94.1	-0.9	-	-	93.0	-1.2	-	-	96.1	3.3	-	-	98.1	2.1	-	-	101.0	3.0	-	-	101.4	0.4
1983	-	-	99.7	-1.7	-	-	101.1	1.4	-	-	100.7	-0.4	-	-	102.3	1.6	-	-	102.4	0.1	-	-	101.7	-0.7
1984	-	-	100.7	-1.0	-	-	101.4	0.7	-	-	101.3	-0.1	-	-	102.0	0.7	-	-	102.3	0.3	-	-	102.4	0.1
1985	-	-	102.9	0.5	-	-	103.2	0.3	-	-	103.7	0.5	-	-	103.6	-0.1	-	-	104.2	0.6	-	-	105.2	1.0
1986	-	-	104.7	-0.5	-	-	103.5	-1.1	-	-	103.7	0.2	-	-	104.0	0.3	-	-	104.4	0.4	-	-	104.8	0.4
1987	-	-	105.7	0.9	-	-	106.4	0.7	-	-	106.8	0.4	-	-	107.7	0.8	-	-	108.3	0.6	-	-	108.6	0.3
1988	-	-	108.9	0.3	-	-	110.1	1.1	-	-	110.0	-0.1	-	-	110.7	0.6	-	-	111.7	0.9	-	-	112.2	0.4
1989	-	-	113.4	1.1	-	-	114.7	1.1	-	-	115.9	1.0	-	-	116.0	0.1	-	-	116.8	0.7	-	-	117.1	0.3
1990	-	-	118.6	1.3	-	-	120.1	1.3	-	-	120.3	0.2	-	-	122.0	1.4	-	-	124.6	2.1	-	-	124.2	-0.3
1991	-	-	124.1	-0.1	-	-	124.9	0.6	-	-	125.3	0.3	-	-	125.9	0.5	-	-	127.5	1.3	-	-	128.7	0.9
1992	-	-	128.7	0.0	-	-	129.4	0.5	-	-	129.5	0.1	-	-	131.0	1.2	-	-	131.6	0.5	-	-	131.4	-0.2
1993	-	-	133.2	1.4	-	-	133.6	0.3	-	-	133.7	0.1	-	-	134.2	0.4	-	-	134.5	0.2	-	-	135.1	0.4
1994	-	-	136.3	0.9	-	-	137.4	0.8	-	-	137.8	0.3	-	-	139.4	1.2	-	-	140.1	0.5	-	-	140.3	0.1
1995	-	-	141.1	0.6	-	-	142.6	1.1	-	-	143.0	0.3	-	-	143.7	0.5	-	-	144.2	0.3	-	-	143.7	-0.3

Source: U.S. Department of Labor, Bureau of Labor Statistics, Division of Consumer Prices and Price Indexes. - indicates no data collected for period.

Pittsburgh, PA
Consumer Price Index - All Urban Consumers
Base 1982-1984 = 100
Food and Beverages

For 1976-1995. Columns headed % show percentile change in the index from the previous period for which an index is available.

Year	Jan Index	%	Feb Index	%	Mar Index	%	Apr Index	%	May Index	%	Jun Index	%	Jul Index	%	Aug Index	%	Sep Index	%	Oct Index	%	Nov Index	%	Dec Index	%
1976	62.0	-	-	-	-	-	62.0	0.0	-	-	-	-	62.3	0.5	-	-	-	-	62.7	0.6	-	-	-	-
1977	62.9	0.3	-	-	-	-	66.0	4.9	-	-	-	-	67.1	1.7	-	-	-	-	67.6	0.7	-	-	-	-
1978	68.5	1.3	-	-	-	-	71.4	4.2	-	-	73.6	3.1	-	-	74.4	1.1	-	-	75.1	0.9	-	-	75.3	0.3
1979	-	-	78.5	4.2	-	-	78.8	0.4	-	-	80.0	1.5	-	-	80.4	0.5	-	-	81.7	1.6	-	-	82.6	1.1
1980	-	-	83.5	1.1	-	-	84.5	1.2	-	-	86.7	2.6	-	-	89.0	2.7	-	-	90.1	1.2	-	-	91.5	1.6
1981	-	-	92.5	1.1	-	-	93.2	0.8	-	-	93.4	0.2	-	-	94.8	1.5	-	-	95.1	0.3	-	-	94.9	-0.2
1982	-	-	96.4	1.6	-	-	96.5	0.1	-	-	98.9	2.5	-	-	97.8	-1.1	-	-	99.4	1.6	-	-	99.9	0.5
1983	-	-	100.5	0.6	-	-	101.1	0.6	-	-	101.4	0.3	-	-	101.1	-0.3	-	-	101.2	0.1	-	-	101.7	0.5
1984	-	-	100.4	-1.3	-	-	101.1	0.7	-	-	101.1	0.0	-	-	101.4	0.3	-	-	100.7	-0.7	-	-	100.7	0.0
1985	-	-	102.7	2.0	-	-	102.3	-0.4	-	-	102.5	0.2	-	-	102.3	-0.2	-	-	101.9	-0.4	-	-	102.5	0.6
1986	-	-	104.0	1.5	-	-	103.8	-0.2	-	-	104.0	0.2	-	-	106.7	2.6	-	-	105.6	-1.0	-	-	107.2	1.5
1987	-	-	108.4	1.1	-	-	109.4	0.9	-	-	110.6	1.1	-	-	109.4	-1.1	-	-	109.7	0.3	-	-	109.7	0.0
1988	-	-	110.6	0.8	-	-	112.0	1.3	-	-	111.2	-0.7	-	-	113.1	1.7	-	-	112.3	-0.7	-	-	113.4	1.0
1989	-	-	116.5	2.7	-	-	117.5	0.9	-	-	118.2	0.6	-	-	119.0	0.7	-	-	118.9	-0.1	-	-	119.7	0.7
1990	-	-	122.9	2.7	-	-	123.8	0.7	-	-	124.6	0.6	-	-	125.1	0.4	-	-	125.9	0.6	-	-	124.8	-0.9
1991	-	-	128.7	3.1	-	-	129.3	0.5	-	-	129.5	0.2	-	-	128.9	-0.5	-	-	129.1	0.2	-	-	131.4	1.8
1992	-	-	132.3	0.7	-	-	131.7	-0.5	-	-	133.7	1.5	-	-	133.5	-0.1	-	-	133.3	-0.1	-	-	133.2	-0.1
1993	-	-	135.6	1.8	-	-	137.5	1.4	-	-	137.5	0.0	-	-	137.2	-0.2	-	-	137.9	0.5	-	-	139.1	0.9
1994	-	-	138.4	-0.5	-	-	139.8	1.0	-	-	140.8	0.7	-	-	141.5	0.5	-	-	140.2	-0.9	-	-	143.9	2.6
1995	-	-	140.9	-2.1	-	-	143.9	2.1	-	-	141.9	-1.4	-	-	144.5	1.8	-	-	144.9	0.3	-	-	146.1	0.8

Source: U.S. Department of Labor, Bureau of Labor Statistics, Division of Consumer Prices and Price Indexes. - indicates no data collected for period.

Pittsburgh, PA
Consumer Price Index - Urban Wage Earners
Base 1982-1984 = 100
Food and Beverages

For 1976-1995. Columns headed % show percentile change in the index from the previous period for which an index is available.

Year	Jan Index	%	Feb Index	%	Mar Index	%	Apr Index	%	May Index	%	Jun Index	%	Jul Index	%	Aug Index	%	Sep Index	%	Oct Index	%	Nov Index	%	Dec Index	%
1976	61.8	-	-	-	-	-	61.9	0.2	-	-	-	-	62.1	0.3	-	-	-	-	62.6	0.8	-	-	-	-
1977	62.7	0.2	-	-	-	-	65.9	5.1	-	-	-	-	66.9	1.5	-	-	-	-	67.4	0.7	-	-	-	-
1978	68.3	1.3	-	-	-	-	71.2	4.2	-	-	73.3	2.9	-	-	74.9	2.2	-	-	74.8	-0.1	-	-	75.4	0.8
1979	-	-	78.7	4.4	-	-	79.5	1.0	-	-	80.3	1.0	-	-	81.2	1.1	-	-	82.2	1.2	-	-	83.0	1.0
1980	-	-	83.7	0.8	-	-	85.5	2.2	-	-	86.6	1.3	-	-	88.8	2.5	-	-	90.1	1.5	-	-	92.1	2.2
1981	-	-	93.0	1.0	-	-	93.6	0.6	-	-	93.8	0.2	-	-	94.8	1.1	-	-	94.9	0.1	-	-	95.0	0.1
1982	-	-	96.4	1.5	-	-	96.6	0.2	-	-	99.0	2.5	-	-	97.8	-1.2	-	-	99.5	1.7	-	-	99.9	0.4
1983	-	-	100.4	0.5	-	-	101.1	0.7	-	-	101.4	0.3	-	-	101.2	-0.2	-	-	101.3	0.1	-	-	101.7	0.4
1984	-	-	100.3	-1.4	-	-	101.0	0.7	-	-	101.1	0.1	-	-	101.6	0.5	-	-	100.6	-1.0	-	-	100.6	0.0
1985	-	-	102.5	1.9	-	-	102.1	-0.4	-	-	102.4	0.3	-	-	102.1	-0.3	-	-	101.5	-0.6	-	-	102.2	0.7
1986	-	-	103.5	1.3	-	-	103.3	-0.2	-	-	103.6	0.3	-	-	106.5	2.8	-	-	105.3	-1.1	-	-	106.9	1.5
1987	-	-	108.0	1.0	-	-	109.0	0.9	-	-	110.1	1.0	-	-	109.2	-0.8	-	-	109.6	0.4	-	-	109.6	0.0
1988	-	-	110.5	0.8	-	-	111.7	1.1	-	-	111.2	-0.4	-	-	113.0	1.6	-	-	112.5	-0.4	-	-	113.6	1.0
1989	-	-	116.4	2.5	-	-	117.4	0.9	-	-	118.1	0.6	-	-	119.0	0.8	-	-	119.0	0.0	-	-	119.7	0.6
1990	-	-	122.8	2.6	-	-	124.0	1.0	-	-	124.8	0.6	-	-	125.4	0.5	-	-	126.2	0.6	-	-	125.3	-0.7
1991	-	-	129.1	3.0	-	-	129.7	0.5	-	-	129.9	0.2	-	-	129.2	-0.5	-	-	129.6	0.3	-	-	131.8	1.7
1992	-	-	132.6	0.6	-	-	132.1	-0.4	-	-	133.9	1.4	-	-	133.7	-0.1	-	-	133.4	-0.2	-	-	133.4	0.0
1993	-	-	135.7	1.7	-	-	137.7	1.5	-	-	137.7	0.0	-	-	137.6	-0.1	-	-	138.2	0.4	-	-	139.3	0.8
1994	-	-	138.4	-0.6	-	-	139.8	1.0	-	-	140.6	0.6	-	-	141.4	0.6	-	-	140.5	-0.6	-	-	143.6	2.2
1995	-	-	141.0	-1.8	-	-	143.6	1.8	-	-	141.4	-1.5	-	-	144.6	2.3	-	-	144.7	0.1	-	-	145.8	0.8

Source: U.S. Department of Labor, Bureau of Labor Statistics, Division of Consumer Prices and Price Indexes. - indicates no data collected for period.

Pittsburgh, PA
Consumer Price Index - All Urban Consumers
Base 1982-1984 = 100
Housing

For 1976-1995. Columns headed % show percentile change in the index from the previous period for which an index is available.

Year	Jan Index	%	Feb Index	%	Mar Index	%	Apr Index	%	May Index	%	Jun Index	%	Jul Index	%	Aug Index	%	Sep Index	%	Oct Index	%	Nov Index	%	Dec Index	%
1976	49.2	-	-	-	-	-	50.6	2.8	-	-	-	-	50.6	0.0	-	-	-	-	51.3	1.4	-	-	-	-
1977	52.6	2.5	-	-	-	-	53.7	2.1	-	-	-	-	54.2	0.9	-	-	-	-	55.7	2.8	-	-	-	-
1978	56.8	2.0	-	-	-	-	58.2	2.5	-	-	59.3	1.9	-	-	61.9	4.4	-	-	63.4	2.4	-	-	64.9	2.4
1979	-	-	65.8	1.4	-	-	66.4	0.9	-	-	66.7	0.5	-	-	67.5	1.2	-	-	71.1	5.3	-	-	72.1	1.4
1980	-	-	74.3	3.1	-	-	76.9	3.5	-	-	78.6	2.2	-	-	79.9	1.7	-	-	82.0	2.6	-	-	84.7	3.3
1981	-	-	84.5	-0.2	-	-	83.3	-1.4	-	-	86.6	4.0	-	-	89.1	2.9	-	-	87.6	-1.7	-	-	90.8	3.7
1982	-	-	87.3	-3.9	-	-	85.4	-2.2	-	-	90.9	6.4	-	-	94.1	3.5	-	-	98.8	5.0	-	-	99.2	0.4
1983	-	-	100.5	1.3	-	-	101.4	0.9	-	-	100.7	-0.7	-	-	102.3	1.6	-	-	103.0	0.7	-	-	103.2	0.2
1984	-	-	104.9	1.6	-	-	106.4	1.4	-	-	106.9	0.5	-	-	105.7	-1.1	-	-	106.4	0.7	-	-	107.4	0.9
1985	-	-	107.8	0.4	-	-	108.1	0.3	-	-	108.7	0.6	-	-	108.6	-0.1	-	-	108.2	-0.4	-	-	110.4	2.0
1986	-	-	109.9	-0.5	-	-	111.8	1.7	-	-	111.0	-0.7	-	-	111.5	0.5	-	-	112.2	0.6	-	-	111.9	-0.3
1987	-	-	113.0	1.0	-	-	112.8	-0.2	-	-	112.8	0.0	-	-	114.1	1.2	-	-	114.0	-0.1	-	-	114.7	0.6
1988	-	-	114.4	-0.3	-	-	115.8	1.2	-	-	116.7	0.8	-	-	115.6	-0.9	-	-	115.6	0.0	-	-	116.6	0.9
1989	-	-	117.8	1.0	-	-	118.0	0.2	-	-	118.8	0.7	-	-	119.7	0.8	-	-	120.8	0.9	-	-	121.2	0.3
1990	-	-	121.3	0.1	-	-	123.6	1.9	-	-	124.0	0.3	-	-	126.7	2.2	-	-	127.6	0.7	-	-	127.0	-0.5
1991	-	-	128.8	1.4	-	-	130.3	1.2	-	-	131.3	0.8	-	-	131.7	0.3	-	-	133.2	1.1	-	-	134.8	1.2
1992	-	-	134.2	-0.4	-	-	135.5	1.0	-	-	134.9	-0.4	-	-	137.7	2.1	-	-	136.6	-0.8	-	-	136.6	0.0
1993	-	-	138.7	1.5	-	-	138.0	-0.5	-	-	138.7	0.5	-	-	139.6	0.6	-	-	139.8	0.1	-	-	141.0	0.9
1994	-	-	144.1	2.2	-	-	144.2	0.1	-	-	144.2	0.0	-	-	146.1	1.3	-	-	147.5	1.0	-	-	146.9	-0.4
1995	-	-	149.0	1.4	-	-	149.6	0.4	-	-	150.2	0.4	-	-	151.0	0.5	-	-	151.0	0.0	-	-	150.4	-0.4

Source: U.S. Department of Labor, Bureau of Labor Statistics, Division of Consumer Prices and Price Indexes. - indicates no data collected for period.

Pittsburgh, PA
Consumer Price Index - Urban Wage Earners
Base 1982-1984 = 100
Housing

For 1976-1995. Columns headed % show percentile change in the index from the previous period for which an index is available.

Year	Jan Index	%	Feb Index	%	Mar Index	%	Apr Index	%	May Index	%	Jun Index	%	Jul Index	%	Aug Index	%	Sep Index	%	Oct Index	%	Nov Index	%	Dec Index	%
1976	52.2	-	-	-	-	-	53.7	2.9	-	-	-	-	53.7	0.0	-	-	-	-	54.4	1.3	-	-	-	-
1977	55.7	2.4	-	-	-	-	57.0	2.3	-	-	-	-	57.4	0.7	-	-	-	-	59.1	3.0	-	-	-	-
1978	60.2	1.9	-	-	-	-	61.7	2.5	-	-	63.1	2.3	-	-	65.3	3.5	-	-	67.1	2.8	-	-	68.5	2.1
1979	-	-	69.5	1.5	-	-	70.3	1.2	-	-	70.6	0.4	-	-	71.6	1.4	-	-	75.4	5.3	-	-	76.6	1.6
1980	-	-	79.0	3.1	-	-	81.9	3.7	-	-	83.7	2.2	-	-	85.0	1.6	-	-	87.2	2.6	-	-	90.1	3.3
1981	-	-	90.1	0.0	-	-	88.8	-1.4	-	-	92.6	4.3	-	-	94.9	2.5	-	-	93.3	-1.7	-	-	96.9	3.9
1982	-	-	93.3	-3.7	-	-	91.3	-2.1	-	-	97.2	6.5	-	-	100.6	3.5	-	-	105.3	4.7	-	-	105.7	0.4
1983	-	-	100.7	-4.7	-	-	104.9	4.2	-	-	103.0	-1.8	-	-	104.3	1.3	-	-	102.5	-1.7	-	-	100.2	-2.2
1984	-	-	98.1	-2.1	-	-	98.7	0.6	-	-	97.9	-0.8	-	-	98.7	0.8	-	-	99.0	0.3	-	-	99.4	0.4
1985	-	-	99.8	0.4	-	-	100.0	0.2	-	-	100.6	0.6	-	-	100.5	-0.1	-	-	100.2	-0.3	-	-	102.2	2.0
1986	-	-	101.9	-0.3	-	-	103.3	1.4	-	-	102.5	-0.8	-	-	103.0	0.5	-	-	103.7	0.7	-	-	103.4	-0.3
1987	-	-	104.4	1.0	-	-	104.1	-0.3	-	-	104.3	0.2	-	-	105.5	1.2	-	-	105.4	-0.1	-	-	106.0	0.6
1988	-	-	105.7	-0.3	-	-	107.0	1.2	-	-	107.8	0.7	-	-	106.8	-0.9	-	-	106.9	0.1	-	-	107.9	0.9
1989	-	-	108.9	0.9	-	-	109.1	0.2	-	-	110.2	1.0	-	-	110.8	0.5	-	-	111.7	0.8	-	-	112.3	0.5
1990	-	-	112.4	0.1	-	-	114.6	2.0	-	-	114.9	0.3	-	-	117.2	2.0	-	-	118.1	0.8	-	-	117.6	-0.4
1991	-	-	119.2	1.4	-	-	120.6	1.2	-	-	121.5	0.7	-	-	121.9	0.3	-	-	123.3	1.1	-	-	124.7	1.1
1992	-	-	124.1	-0.5	-	-	125.2	0.9	-	-	124.6	-0.5	-	-	127.2	2.1	-	-	126.3	-0.7	-	-	126.3	0.0
1993	-	-	128.2	1.5	-	-	127.6	-0.5	-	-	128.3	0.5	-	-	129.0	0.5	-	-	129.1	0.1	-	-	130.3	0.9
1994	-	-	133.0	2.1	-	-	133.1	0.1	-	-	133.2	0.1	-	-	134.9	1.3	-	-	136.1	0.9	-	-	135.5	-0.4
1995	-	-	137.5	1.5	-	-	138.1	0.4	-	-	138.6	0.4	-	-	139.3	0.5	-	-	139.3	0.0	-	-	138.8	-0.4

Source: U.S. Department of Labor, Bureau of Labor Statistics, Division of Consumer Prices and Price Indexes. - indicates no data collected for period.

Pittsburgh, PA
Consumer Price Index - All Urban Consumers
Base 1982-1984 = 100
Apparel and Upkeep

For 1952-1995. Columns headed % show percentile change in the index from the previous period for which an index is available.

Year	Jan Index	%	Feb Index	%	Mar Index	%	Apr Index	%	May Index	%	Jun Index	%	Jul Index	%	Aug Index	%	Sep Index	%	Oct Index	%	Nov Index	%	Dec Index	%
1952	-		-		-		-		-		-		-		-		-		42.4	-	-		-	
1953	42.5	0.2	-		-		42.9	0.9	-		-		42.5	-0.9	-		-		43.1	1.4	-		-	
1954	43.1	0.0	-		-		42.8	-0.7	-		-		42.9	0.2	-		-		42.9	0.0	-		-	
1955	42.3	-1.4	-		-		42.5	0.5	-		-		41.9	-1.4	-		-		42.2	0.7	-		-	
1956	42.7	1.2	-		-		43.0	0.7	-		-		43.0	0.0	-		-		43.5	1.2	-		-	
1957	43.9	0.9	-		-		44.1	0.5	-		-		43.9	-0.5	-		-		45.3	3.2	-		-	
1958	44.9	-0.9	-		-		44.6	-0.7	-		-		44.2	-0.9	-		-		44.5	0.7	-		-	
1959	44.0	-1.1	-		-		44.5	1.1	-		-		44.7	0.4	-		-		45.2	1.1	-		-	
1960	44.6	-1.3	-		-		45.3	1.6	-		-		45.3	0.0	-		-		45.9	1.3	-		-	
1961	45.0	-2.0	-		-		45.2	0.4	-		-		45.5	0.7	-		-		46.3	1.8	-		-	
1962	45.5	-1.7	-		-		45.7	0.4	-		-		46.0	0.7	-		-		46.2	0.4	-		-	
1963	46.5	0.6	-		-		46.8	0.6	-		-		46.9	0.2	-		-		47.3	0.9	-		-	
1964	47.2	-0.2	-		-		47.6	0.8	-		-		47.7	0.2	-		-		48.2	1.0	-		-	
1965	47.6	-1.2	-		-		49.0	2.9	-		-		48.4	-1.2	-		-		49.3	1.9	-		-	
1966	48.2	-2.2	-		-		49.8	3.3	-		-		49.7	-0.2	-		-		51.0	2.6	-		-	
1967	50.8	-0.4	-		-		51.2	0.8	-		-		50.8	-0.8	-		-		51.8	2.0	-		-	
1968	51.4	-0.8	-		-		54.1	5.3	-		-		53.7	-0.7	-		-		56.1	4.5	-		-	
1969	55.9	-0.4	-		-		57.8	3.4	-		-		57.4	-0.7	-		-		59.5	3.7	-		-	
1970	57.2	-3.9	-		-		58.7	2.6	-		-		58.3	-0.7	-		-		61.4	5.3	-		-	
1971	59.1	-3.7	-		-		60.7	2.7	-		-		60.0	-1.2	-		-		64.0	6.7	-		-	
1972	62.4	-2.5	-		-		63.5	1.8	-		-		62.4	-1.7	-		-		64.7	3.7	-		-	
1973	63.0	-2.6	-		-		64.8	2.9	-		-		64.3	-0.8	-		-		68.1	5.9	-		-	
1974	67.3	-1.2	-		-		70.2	4.3	-		-		71.4	1.7	-		-		72.2	1.1	-		-	
1975	69.9	-3.2	-		-		72.5	3.7	-		-		71.8	-1.0	-		-		74.5	3.8	-		-	
1976	73.5	-1.3	-		-		73.2	-0.4	-		-		72.9	-0.4	-		-		75.2	3.2	-		-	
1977	74.5	-0.9	-		-		74.3	-0.3	-		-		75.4	1.5	-		-		76.9	2.0	-		-	
1978	73.3	-4.7	-		-		75.1	2.5	-		75.3	0.3	-		80.5	6.9	-		81.6	1.4	-		81.0	-0.7
1979	-		81.3	0.4	-		81.5	0.2	-		79.7	-2.2	-		83.2	4.4	-		85.5	2.8	-		85.9	0.5
1980	-		85.8	-0.1	-		86.0	0.2	-		84.0	-2.3	-		86.9	3.5	-		91.1	4.8	-		89.6	-1.6
1981	-		92.1	2.8	-		92.6	0.5	-		92.9	0.3	-		95.9	3.2	-		96.3	0.4	-		94.0	-2.4
1982	-		95.7	1.8	-		96.9	1.3	-		95.4	-1.5	-		99.0	3.8	-		101.3	2.3	-		99.0	-2.3
1983	-		103.4	4.4	-		100.9	-2.4	-		98.2	-2.7	-		101.1	3.0	-		102.8	1.7	-		101.4	-1.4
1984	-		100.4	-1.0	-		103.2	2.8	-		99.3	-3.8	-		100.3	1.0	-		102.7	2.4	-		100.9	-1.8
1985	-		104.4	3.5	-		101.2	-3.1	-		99.5	-1.7	-		100.0	0.5	-		108.8	8.8	-		104.0	-4.4
1986	-		97.7	-6.1	-		98.7	1.0	-		96.5	-2.2	-		101.9	5.6	-		104.8	2.8	-		102.4	-2.3
1987	-		101.1	-1.3	-		107.5	6.3	-		104.3	-3.0	-		108.3	3.8	-		112.4	3.8	-		110.5	-1.7
1988	-		109.7	-0.7	-		114.8	4.6	-		107.7	-6.2	-		114.7	6.5	-		122.7	7.0	-		117.3	-4.4
1989	-		116.5	-0.7	-		119.6	2.7	-		119.9	0.3	-		123.3	2.8	-		127.4	3.3	-		121.4	-4.7
1990	-		124.3	2.4	-		125.7	1.1	-		121.0	-3.7	-		125.5	3.7	-		129.1	2.9	-		125.4	-2.9
1991	-		125.9	0.4	-		131.4	4.4	-		125.0	-4.9	-		129.4	3.5	-		135.5	4.7	-		131.7	-2.8
1992	-		129.3	-1.8	-		133.2	3.0	-		127.9	-4.0	-		130.8	2.3	-		143.2	9.5	-		134.8	-5.9
1993	-		135.9	0.8	-		139.9	2.9	-		130.0	-7.1	-		140.2	7.8	-		131.4	-6.3	-		127.7	-2.8
1994	-		133.5	4.5	-		141.6	6.1	-		131.4	-7.2	-		133.1	1.3	-		133.8	0.5	-		125.1	-6.5
1995	-		133.3	6.6	-		140.4	5.3	-		134.1	-4.5	-		137.3	2.4	-		138.2	0.7	-		129.5	-6.3

Source: U.S. Department of Labor, Bureau of Labor Statistics, Division of Consumer Prices and Price Indexes. - indicates no data collected for period.

Pittsburgh, PA
Consumer Price Index - Urban Wage Earners
Base 1982-1984 = 100
Apparel and Upkeep

For 1952-1995. Columns headed % show percentile change in the index from the previous period for which an index is available.

Year	Jan Index	%	Feb Index	%	Mar Index	%	Apr Index	%	May Index	%	Jun Index	%	Jul Index	%	Aug Index	%	Sep Index	%	Oct Index	%	Nov Index	%	Dec Index	%
1952	-	-	-	-	-	-	-	-	-	-	-	-	-	-	-	-	-	-	44.0	-	-	-	-	-
1953	44.1	0.2	-	-	-	-	44.5	0.9	-	-	-	-	44.1	-0.9	-	-	-	-	44.6	1.1	-	-	-	-
1954	44.7	0.2	-	-	-	-	44.4	-0.7	-	-	-	-	44.4	0.0	-	-	-	-	44.4	0.0	-	-	-	-
1955	43.9	-1.1	-	-	-	-	44.1	0.5	-	-	-	-	43.4	-1.6	-	-	-	-	43.7	0.7	-	-	-	-
1956	44.3	1.4	-	-	-	-	44.5	0.5	-	-	-	-	44.5	0.0	-	-	-	-	45.1	1.3	-	-	-	-
1957	45.6	1.1	-	-	-	-	45.8	0.4	-	-	-	-	45.5	-0.7	-	-	-	-	46.9	3.1	-	-	-	-
1958	46.6	-0.6	-	-	-	-	46.2	-0.9	-	-	-	-	45.8	-0.9	-	-	-	-	46.2	0.9	-	-	-	-
1959	45.7	-1.1	-	-	-	-	46.1	0.9	-	-	-	-	46.3	0.4	-	-	-	-	46.9	1.3	-	-	-	-
1960	46.2	-1.5	-	-	-	-	46.9	1.5	-	-	-	-	46.9	0.0	-	-	-	-	47.6	1.5	-	-	-	-
1961	46.7	-1.9	-	-	-	-	46.9	0.4	-	-	-	-	47.2	0.6	-	-	-	-	48.0	1.7	-	-	-	-
1962	47.1	-1.9	-	-	-	-	47.4	0.6	-	-	-	-	47.7	0.6	-	-	-	-	47.9	0.4	-	-	-	-
1963	48.3	0.8	-	-	-	-	48.6	0.6	-	-	-	-	48.7	0.2	-	-	-	-	49.1	0.8	-	-	-	-
1964	48.9	-0.4	-	-	-	-	49.3	0.8	-	-	-	-	49.5	0.4	-	-	-	-	50.0	1.0	-	-	-	-
1965	49.3	-1.4	-	-	-	-	50.8	3.0	-	-	-	-	50.2	-1.2	-	-	-	-	51.1	1.8	-	-	-	-
1966	50.0	-2.2	-	-	-	-	51.7	3.4	-	-	-	-	51.6	-0.2	-	-	-	-	52.9	2.5	-	-	-	-
1967	52.7	-0.4	-	-	-	-	53.1	0.8	-	-	-	-	52.7	-0.8	-	-	-	-	53.7	1.9	-	-	-	-
1968	53.3	-0.7	-	-	-	-	56.1	5.3	-	-	-	-	55.7	-0.7	-	-	-	-	58.1	4.3	-	-	-	-
1969	58.0	-0.2	-	-	-	-	59.9	3.3	-	-	-	-	59.6	-0.5	-	-	-	-	61.7	3.5	-	-	-	-
1970	59.3	-3.9	-	-	-	-	60.8	2.5	-	-	-	-	60.5	-0.5	-	-	-	-	63.7	5.3	-	-	-	-
1971	61.3	-3.8	-	-	-	-	62.9	2.6	-	-	-	-	62.2	-1.1	-	-	-	-	66.4	6.8	-	-	-	-
1972	64.7	-2.6	-	-	-	-	65.8	1.7	-	-	-	-	64.7	-1.7	-	-	-	-	67.1	3.7	-	-	-	-
1973	65.4	-2.5	-	-	-	-	67.2	2.8	-	-	-	-	66.6	-0.9	-	-	-	-	70.7	6.2	-	-	-	-
1974	69.8	-1.3	-	-	-	-	72.8	4.3	-	-	-	-	74.0	1.6	-	-	-	-	74.9	1.2	-	-	-	-
1975	72.5	-3.2	-	-	-	-	75.2	3.7	-	-	-	-	74.4	-1.1	-	-	-	-	77.3	3.9	-	-	-	-
1976	76.2	-1.4	-	-	-	-	75.9	-0.4	-	-	-	-	75.6	-0.4	-	-	-	-	78.0	3.2	-	-	-	-
1977	77.3	-0.9	-	-	-	-	77.0	-0.4	-	-	-	-	78.2	1.6	-	-	-	-	79.7	1.9	-	-	-	-
1978	76.0	-4.6	-	-	-	-	77.8	2.4	-	-	76.5	-1.7	-	-	80.3	5.0	-	-	80.3	0.0	-	-	81.0	0.9
1979	-	-	81.4	0.5	-	-	82.9	1.8	-	-	81.5	-1.7	-	-	84.1	3.2	-	-	87.5	4.0	-	-	87.2	-0.3
1980	-	-	86.6	-0.7	-	-	86.8	0.2	-	-	85.4	-1.6	-	-	91.5	7.1	-	-	96.3	5.2	-	-	90.5	-6.0
1981	-	-	90.4	-0.1	-	-	93.1	3.0	-	-	93.1	0.0	-	-	95.5	2.6	-	-	94.9	-0.6	-	-	93.9	-1.1
1982	-	-	95.9	2.1	-	-	97.3	1.5	-	-	95.3	-2.1	-	-	98.7	3.6	-	-	101.2	2.5	-	-	99.2	-2.0
1983	-	-	102.9	3.7	-	-	100.3	-2.5	-	-	97.2	-3.1	-	-	101.1	4.0	-	-	102.9	1.8	-	-	101.5	-1.4
1984	-	-	101.5	0.0	-	-	103.2	1.7	-	-	99.1	-4.0	-	-	100.8	1.7	-	-	102.6	1.8	-	-	100.9	-1.7
1985	-	-	103.5	2.6	-	-	101.6	-1.8	-	-	100.0	-1.6	-	-	100.3	0.3	-	-	108.6	8.3	-	-	103.6	-4.6
1986	-	-	97.8	-5.6	-	-	98.6	0.8	-	-	96.4	-2.2	-	-	100.9	4.7	-	-	104.1	3.2	-	-	101.5	-2.5
1987	-	-	101.6	0.1	-	-	106.3	4.6	-	-	104.0	-2.2	-	-	107.9	3.8	-	-	110.0	1.9	-	-	108.5	-1.4
1988	-	-	108.5	0.0	-	-	113.1	4.2	-	-	108.2	-4.3	-	-	112.1	3.6	-	-	120.6	7.6	-	-	114.6	-5.0
1989	-	-	113.7	-0.8	-	-	117.8	3.6	-	-	117.7	-0.1	-	-	120.2	2.1	-	-	124.1	3.2	-	-	119.1	-4.0
1990	-	-	121.5	2.0	-	-	124.5	2.5	-	-	119.0	-4.4	-	-	120.1	0.9	-	-	125.7	4.7	-	-	122.6	-2.5
1991	-	-	122.0	-0.5	-	-	126.7	3.9	-	-	121.3	-4.3	-	-	123.2	1.6	-	-	129.3	5.0	-	-	124.9	-3.4
1992	-	-	126.8	1.5	-	-	130.1	2.6	-	-	124.0	-4.7	-	-	123.7	-0.2	-	-	135.7	9.7	-	-	128.5	-5.3
1993	-	-	130.9	1.9	-	-	135.6	3.6	-	-	125.7	-7.3	-	-	132.1	5.1	-	-	125.0	-5.4	-	-	122.3	-2.2
1994	-	-	129.0	5.5	-	-	137.0	6.2	-	-	127.7	-6.8	-	-	128.2	0.4	-	-	128.7	0.4	-	-	119.6	-7.1
1995	-	-	127.4	6.5	-	-	134.1	5.3	-	-	128.3	-4.3	-	-	127.9	-0.3	-	-	133.0	4.0	-	-	123.8	-6.9

Source: U.S. Department of Labor, Bureau of Labor Statistics, Division of Consumer Prices and Price Indexes. - indicates no data collected for period.

Pittsburgh, PA
Consumer Price Index - All Urban Consumers
Base 1982-1984 = 100
Transportation

For 1947-1995. Columns headed % show percentile change in the index from the previous period for which an index is available.

Year	Jan Index	%	Feb Index	%	Mar Index	%	Apr Index	%	May Index	%	Jun Index	%	Jul Index	%	Aug Index	%	Sep Index	%	Oct Index	%	Nov Index	%	Dec Index	%
1947	15.9	-	15.8	-0.6	15.9	0.6	16.1	1.3	16.1	0.0	16.1	0.0	16.1	0.0	16.3	1.2	16.5	1.2	16.5	0.0	16.5	0.0	16.5	0.0
1948	17.4	5.5	17.6	1.1	17.6	0.0	17.6	0.0	17.6	0.0	17.6	0.0	18.0	2.3	18.3	1.7	18.3	0.0	18.4	0.5	18.4	0.0	18.4	0.0
1949	18.5	0.5	18.7	1.1	18.6	-0.5	18.7	0.5	18.8	0.5	18.9	0.5	18.9	0.0	18.9	0.0	18.9	0.0	18.9	0.0	18.9	0.0	20.2	6.9
1950	20.3	0.5	20.3	0.0	20.2	-0.5	20.1	-0.5	20.3	1.0	20.3	0.0	20.4	0.5	22.0	7.8	22.1	0.5	22.1	0.0	22.1	0.0	22.1	0.0
1951	22.1	0.0	22.1	0.0	22.3	0.9	22.3	0.0	22.3	0.0	22.3	0.0	22.3	0.0	22.3	0.0	23.3	4.5	23.6	1.3	24.0	1.7	24.0	0.0
1952	24.3	1.2	24.4	0.4	24.4	0.0	24.4	0.0	24.4	0.0	24.4	0.0	24.4	0.0	24.4	0.0	24.4	0.0	24.4	0.0	24.4	0.0	24.6	0.8
1953	24.6	0.0	-	-	-	-	24.6	0.0	-	-	-	-	24.9	1.2	-	-	-	-	24.9	0.0	-	-	-	-
1954	24.6	-1.2	-	-	-	-	24.5	-0.4	-	-	-	-	24.3	-0.8	-	-	-	-	23.7	-2.5	-	-	-	-
1955	24.4	3.0	-	-	-	-	24.3	-0.4	-	-	-	-	24.3	0.0	-	-	-	-	24.0	-1.2	-	-	-	-
1956	23.6	-1.7	-	-	-	-	24.0	1.7	-	-	-	-	24.1	0.4	-	-	-	-	25.4	5.4	-	-	-	-
1957	25.7	1.2	-	-	-	-	25.5	-0.8	-	-	-	-	25.4	-0.4	-	-	-	-	25.7	1.2	-	-	-	-
1958	26.4	2.7	-	-	-	-	26.3	-0.4	-	-	-	-	26.9	2.3	-	-	-	-	27.5	2.2	-	-	-	-
1959	27.8	1.1	-	-	-	-	28.0	0.7	-	-	-	-	28.6	2.1	-	-	-	-	29.1	1.7	-	-	-	-
1960	29.1	0.0	-	-	-	-	29.4	1.0	-	-	-	-	29.1	-1.0	-	-	-	-	29.0	-0.3	-	-	-	-
1961	29.0	0.0	-	-	-	-	29.3	1.0	-	-	-	-	28.9	-1.4	-	-	-	-	29.3	1.4	-	-	-	-
1962	29.7	1.4	-	-	-	-	30.0	1.0	-	-	-	-	29.9	-0.3	-	-	-	-	30.0	0.3	-	-	-	-
1963	29.7	-1.0	-	-	-	-	29.8	0.3	-	-	-	-	30.1	1.0	-	-	-	-	29.7	-1.3	-	-	-	-
1964	30.3	2.0	-	-	-	-	30.2	-0.3	-	-	-	-	30.0	-0.7	-	-	-	-	30.3	1.0	-	-	-	-
1965	30.8	1.7	-	-	-	-	30.8	0.0	-	-	-	-	30.8	0.0	-	-	-	-	30.8	0.0	-	-	-	-
1966	30.7	-0.3	-	-	-	-	30.9	0.7	-	-	-	-	31.2	1.0	-	-	-	-	31.3	0.3	-	-	-	-
1967	31.1	-0.6	-	-	-	-	31.5	1.3	-	-	-	-	31.6	0.3	-	-	-	-	31.9	0.9	-	-	-	-
1968	32.4	1.6	-	-	-	-	32.4	0.0	-	-	-	-	32.6	0.6	-	-	-	-	33.1	1.5	-	-	-	-
1969	33.1	0.0	-	-	-	-	34.3	3.6	-	-	-	-	34.2	-0.3	-	-	-	-	34.3	0.3	-	-	-	-
1970	34.3	0.0	-	-	-	-	35.7	4.1	-	-	-	-	36.3	1.7	-	-	-	-	36.5	0.6	-	-	-	-
1971	37.0	1.4	-	-	-	-	37.8	2.2	-	-	-	-	38.6	2.1	-	-	-	-	38.1	-1.3	-	-	-	-
1972	37.8	-0.8	-	-	-	-	38.1	0.8	-	-	-	-	38.5	1.0	-	-	-	-	38.6	0.3	-	-	-	-
1973	38.5	-0.3	-	-	-	-	39.0	1.3	-	-	-	-	39.5	1.3	-	-	-	-	39.6	0.3	-	-	-	-
1974	40.5	2.3	-	-	-	-	42.2	4.2	-	-	-	-	44.3	5.0	-	-	-	-	45.1	1.8	-	-	-	-
1975	44.9	-0.4	-	-	-	-	45.9	2.2	-	-	-	-	47.7	3.9	-	-	-	-	48.3	1.3	-	-	-	-
1976	48.4	0.2	-	-	-	-	50.3	3.9	-	-	-	-	52.5	4.4	-	-	-	-	53.2	1.3	-	-	-	-
1977	53.9	1.3	-	-	-	-	56.5	4.8	-	-	-	-	57.0	0.9	-	-	-	-	56.8	-0.4	-	-	-	-
1978	56.9	0.2	-	-	-	-	58.4	2.6	-	-	60.0	2.7	-	-	61.0	1.7	-	-	61.1	0.2	-	-	61.9	1.3
1979	-	-	63.0	1.8	-	-	65.3	3.7	-	-	68.0	4.1	-	-	71.3	4.9	-	-	72.4	1.5	-	-	74.0	2.2
1980	-	-	78.0	5.4	-	-	80.0	2.6	-	-	82.4	3.0	-	-	83.2	1.0	-	-	85.0	2.2	-	-	87.3	2.7
1981	-	-	90.7	3.9	-	-	92.1	1.5	-	-	93.4	1.4	-	-	94.9	1.6	-	-	96.1	1.3	-	-	96.5	0.4
1982	-	-	95.7	-0.8	-	-	93.6	-2.2	-	-	95.6	2.1	-	-	97.3	1.8	-	-	98.8	1.5	-	-	99.6	0.8
1983	-	-	97.9	-1.7	-	-	97.1	-0.8	-	-	98.4	1.3	-	-	100.7	2.3	-	-	102.4	1.7	-	-	102.8	0.4
1984	-	-	101.9	-0.9	-	-	102.7	0.8	-	-	104.3	1.6	-	-	104.0	-0.3	-	-	104.6	0.6	-	-	104.7	0.1
1985	-	-	104.0	-0.7	-	-	105.0	1.0	-	-	105.8	0.8	-	-	105.3	-0.5	-	-	106.1	0.8	-	-	107.1	0.9
1986	-	-	105.3	-1.7	-	-	98.1	-6.8	-	-	99.9	1.8	-	-	96.4	-3.5	-	-	97.2	0.8	-	-	97.7	0.5
1987	-	-	98.5	0.8	-	-	99.9	1.4	-	-	100.2	0.3	-	-	101.3	1.1	-	-	101.9	0.6	-	-	102.3	0.4
1988	-	-	100.5	-1.8	-	-	100.3	-0.2	-	-	102.2	1.9	-	-	102.3	0.1	-	-	104.4	2.1	-	-	104.7	0.3
1989	-	-	105.3	0.6	-	-	108.2	2.8	-	-	109.6	1.3	-	-	106.6	-2.7	-	-	107.1	0.5	-	-	107.3	0.2
1990	-	-	109.3	1.9	-	-	108.4	-0.8	-	-	109.2	0.7	-	-	111.4	2.0	-	-	118.8	6.6	-	-	118.7	-0.1
1991	-	-	113.0	-4.8	-	-	110.7	-2.0	-	-	111.9	1.1	-	-	112.1	0.2	-	-	113.7	1.4	-	-	114.8	1.0

[Continued]

Pittsburgh, PA
Consumer Price Index - All Urban Consumers
Base 1982-1984 = 100
Transportation
[Continued]

For 1947-1995. Columns headed % show percentile change in the index from the previous period for which an index is available.

Year	Jan Index	%	Feb Index	%	Mar Index	%	Apr Index	%	May Index	%	Jun Index	%	Jul Index	%	Aug Index	%	Sep Index	%	Oct Index	%	Nov Index	%	Dec Index	%
1992	-	-	113.5	-1.1	-	-	114.0	0.4	-	-	115.6	1.4	-	-	116.2	0.5	-	-	117.5	1.1	-	-	117.7	0.2
1993	-	-	117.6	-0.1	-	-	116.9	-0.6	-	-	117.5	0.5	-	-	116.5	-0.9	-	-	120.8	3.7	-	-	119.8	-0.8
1994	-	-	119.5	-0.3	-	-	119.7	0.2	-	-	122.1	2.0	-	-	124.4	1.9	-	-	124.0	-0.3	-	-	125.3	1.0
1995	-	-	126.0	0.6	-	-	126.5	0.4	-	-	130.5	3.2	-	-	127.9	-2.0	-	-	128.2	0.2	-	-	127.3	-0.7

Source: U.S. Department of Labor, Bureau of Labor Statistics, Division of Consumer Prices and Price Indexes. - indicates no data collected for period.

Pittsburgh, PA
Consumer Price Index - Urban Wage Earners
Base 1982-1984 = 100
Transportation

For 1947-1995. Columns headed % show percentile change in the index from the previous period for which an index is available.

Year	Jan Index	%	Feb Index	%	Mar Index	%	Apr Index	%	May Index	%	Jun Index	%	Jul Index	%	Aug Index	%	Sep Index	%	Oct Index	%	Nov Index	%	Dec Index	%
1947	15.7	-	15.6	-0.6	15.7	0.6	15.9	1.3	15.9	0.0	15.9	0.0	15.9	0.0	16.1	1.3	16.3	1.2	16.3	0.0	16.3	0.0	16.3	0.0
1948	17.2	5.5	17.3	0.6	17.3	0.0	17.3	0.0	17.3	0.0	17.4	0.6	17.8	2.3	18.1	1.7	18.1	0.0	18.2	0.6	18.1	-0.5	18.2	0.6
1949	18.3	0.5	18.4	0.5	18.4	0.0	18.5	0.5	18.6	0.5	18.7	0.5	18.7	0.0	18.7	0.0	18.7	0.0	18.7	0.0	18.7	0.0	20.0	7.0
1950	20.0	0.0	20.0	0.0	20.0	0.0	19.9	-0.5	20.0	0.5	20.1	0.5	20.1	0.0	21.7	8.0	21.8	0.5	21.8	0.0	21.8	0.0	21.8	0.0
1951	21.8	0.0	21.8	0.0	22.0	0.9	22.0	0.0	22.0	0.0	22.0	0.0	22.0	0.0	22.0	0.0	23.0	4.5	23.3	1.3	23.7	1.7	23.7	0.0
1952	24.0	1.3	24.1	0.4	24.1	0.0	24.1	0.0	24.1	0.0	24.1	0.0	24.1	0.0	24.1	0.0	24.1	0.0	24.1	0.0	24.1	0.0	24.3	0.8
1953	24.3	0.0	-	-	-	-	24.3	0.0	-	-	-	-	24.6	1.2	-	-	-	-	24.6	0.0	-	-	-	-
1954	24.3	-1.2	-	-	-	-	24.2	-0.4	-	-	-	-	24.0	-0.8	-	-	-	-	23.4	-2.5	-	-	-	-
1955	24.1	3.0	-	-	-	-	24.0	-0.4	-	-	-	-	24.0	0.0	-	-	-	-	23.7	-1.2	-	-	-	-
1956	23.3	-1.7	-	-	-	-	23.7	1.7	-	-	-	-	23.8	0.4	-	-	-	-	25.1	5.5	-	-	-	-
1957	25.4	1.2	-	-	-	-	25.2	-0.8	-	-	-	-	25.1	-0.4	-	-	-	-	25.4	1.2	-	-	-	-
1958	26.1	2.8	-	-	-	-	26.0	-0.4	-	-	-	-	26.6	2.3	-	-	-	-	27.1	1.9	-	-	-	-
1959	27.5	1.5	-	-	-	-	27.6	0.4	-	-	-	-	28.2	2.2	-	-	-	-	28.8	2.1	-	-	-	-
1960	28.8	0.0	-	-	-	-	29.0	0.7	-	-	-	-	28.8	-0.7	-	-	-	-	28.7	-0.3	-	-	-	-
1961	28.6	-0.3	-	-	-	-	28.9	1.0	-	-	-	-	28.5	-1.4	-	-	-	-	28.9	1.4	-	-	-	-
1962	29.3	1.4	-	-	-	-	29.6	1.0	-	-	-	-	29.5	-0.3	-	-	-	-	29.6	0.3	-	-	-	-
1963	29.3	-1.0	-	-	-	-	29.5	0.7	-	-	-	-	29.7	0.7	-	-	-	-	29.3	-1.3	-	-	-	-
1964	29.9	2.0	-	-	-	-	29.9	0.0	-	-	-	-	29.7	-0.7	-	-	-	-	30.0	1.0	-	-	-	-
1965	30.4	1.3	-	-	-	-	30.4	0.0	-	-	-	-	30.5	0.3	-	-	-	-	30.5	0.0	-	-	-	-
1966	30.3	-0.7	-	-	-	-	30.5	0.7	-	-	-	-	30.8	1.0	-	-	-	-	30.9	0.3	-	-	-	-
1967	30.7	-0.6	-	-	-	-	31.1	1.3	-	-	-	-	31.2	0.3	-	-	-	-	31.5	1.0	-	-	-	-
1968	32.0	1.6	-	-	-	-	32.0	0.0	-	-	-	-	32.2	0.6	-	-	-	-	32.7	1.6	-	-	-	-
1969	32.7	0.0	-	-	-	-	33.9	3.7	-	-	-	-	33.8	-0.3	-	-	-	-	33.9	0.3	-	-	-	-
1970	33.9	0.0	-	-	-	-	35.3	4.1	-	-	-	-	35.9	1.7	-	-	-	-	36.1	0.6	-	-	-	-
1971	36.5	1.1	-	-	-	-	37.3	2.2	-	-	-	-	38.1	2.1	-	-	-	-	37.6	-1.3	-	-	-	-
1972	37.3	-0.8	-	-	-	-	37.6	0.8	-	-	-	-	38.0	1.1	-	-	-	-	38.1	0.3	-	-	-	-
1973	38.0	-0.3	-	-	-	-	38.5	1.3	-	-	-	-	39.0	1.3	-	-	-	-	39.1	0.3	-	-	-	-
1974	40.0	2.3	-	-	-	-	41.7	4.2	-	-	-	-	43.7	4.8	-	-	-	-	44.5	1.8	-	-	-	-
1975	44.4	-0.2	-	-	-	-	45.3	2.0	-	-	-	-	47.1	4.0	-	-	-	-	47.7	1.3	-	-	-	-
1976	47.8	0.2	-	-	-	-	49.7	4.0	-	-	-	-	51.8	4.2	-	-	-	-	52.6	1.5	-	-	-	-
1977	53.3	1.3	-	-	-	-	55.8	4.7	-	-	-	-	56.3	0.9	-	-	-	-	56.1	-0.4	-	-	-	-
1978	56.2	0.2	-	-	-	-	57.7	2.7	-	-	59.3	2.8	-	-	60.3	1.7	-	-	60.8	0.8	-	-	61.3	0.8
1979	-	-	62.5	2.0	-	-	64.6	3.4	-	-	67.5	4.5	-	-	70.9	5.0	-	-	71.8	1.3	-	-	73.2	1.9
1980	-	-	77.4	5.7	-	-	79.4	2.6	-	-	81.8	3.0	-	-	82.0	0.2	-	-	84.7	3.3	-	-	86.9	2.6
1981	-	-	90.5	4.1	-	-	92.1	1.8	-	-	93.5	1.5	-	-	95.0	1.6	-	-	96.5	1.6	-	-	96.9	0.4
1982	-	-	96.0	-0.9	-	-	93.7	-2.4	-	-	95.7	2.1	-	-	97.9	2.3	-	-	99.1	1.2	-	-	99.6	0.5
1983	-	-	97.6	-2.0	-	-	96.6	-1.0	-	-	97.9	1.3	-	-	100.5	2.7	-	-	102.2	1.7	-	-	102.6	0.4
1984	-	-	101.7	-0.9	-	-	102.7	1.0	-	-	104.4	1.7	-	-	104.2	-0.2	-	-	104.7	0.5	-	-	104.8	0.1
1985	-	-	104.1	-0.7	-	-	105.0	0.9	-	-	105.7	0.7	-	-	105.1	-0.6	-	-	105.6	0.5	-	-	106.6	0.9
1986	-	-	104.7	-1.8	-	-	97.0	-7.4	-	-	98.5	1.5	-	-	94.8	-3.8	-	-	95.4	0.6	-	-	95.9	0.5
1987	-	-	97.0	1.1	-	-	98.5	1.5	-	-	99.1	0.6	-	-	100.4	1.3	-	-	101.0	0.6	-	-	101.4	0.4
1988	-	-	99.7	-1.7	-	-	99.7	0.0	-	-	101.5	1.8	-	-	101.7	0.2	-	-	103.9	2.2	-	-	104.1	0.2
1989	-	-	104.8	0.7	-	-	107.9	3.0	-	-	109.3	1.3	-	-	106.3	-2.7	-	-	106.7	0.4	-	-	106.8	0.1
1990	-	-	108.7	1.8	-	-	107.9	-0.7	-	-	108.8	0.8	-	-	110.8	1.8	-	-	117.9	6.4	-	-	117.7	-0.2
1991	-	-	111.8	-5.0	-	-	109.6	-2.0	-	-	111.0	1.3	-	-	111.5	0.5	-	-	113.0	1.3	-	-	113.9	0.8

[Continued]

Pittsburgh, PA
Consumer Price Index - Urban Wage Earners
Base 1982-1984 = 100
Transportation
[Continued]

For 1947-1995. Columns headed % show percentile change in the index from the previous period for which an index is available.

Year	Jan Index	%	Feb Index	%	Mar Index	%	Apr Index	%	May Index	%	Jun Index	%	Jul Index	%	Aug Index	%	Sep Index	%	Oct Index	%	Nov Index	%	Dec Index	%
1992	-	-	112.3	-1.4	-	-	112.9	0.5	-	-	114.7	1.6	-	-	115.4	0.6	-	-	116.9	1.3	-	-	116.9	0.0
1993	-	-	116.8	-0.1	-	-	116.2	-0.5	-	-	117.1	0.8	-	-	116.2	-0.8	-	-	120.2	3.4	-	-	119.2	-0.8
1994	-	-	118.4	-0.7	-	-	118.8	0.3	-	-	121.6	2.4	-	-	123.9	1.9	-	-	123.9	0.0	-	-	125.4	1.2
1995	-	-	126.4	0.8	-	-	127.3	0.7	-	-	131.6	3.4	-	-	129.1	-1.9	-	-	129.1	0.0	-	-	128.3	-0.6

Source: U.S. Department of Labor, Bureau of Labor Statistics, Division of Consumer Prices and Price Indexes. - indicates no data collected for period.

721

Pittsburgh, PA
Consumer Price Index - All Urban Consumers
Base 1982-1984 = 100
Medical Care

For 1947-1995. Columns headed % show percentile change in the index from the previous period for which an index is available.

Year	Jan Index	%	Feb Index	%	Mar Index	%	Apr Index	%	May Index	%	Jun Index	%	Jul Index	%	Aug Index	%	Sep Index	%	Oct Index	%	Nov Index	%	Dec Index	%
1947	11.5	-	11.5	0.0	11.6	0.9	11.6	0.0	11.6	0.0	11.6	0.0	11.7	0.9	11.6	-0.9	11.7	0.9	11.7	0.0	11.9	1.7	11.9	0.0
1948	12.2	2.5	12.2	0.0	12.2	0.0	12.2	0.0	12.4	1.6	12.4	0.0	12.4	0.0	12.4	0.0	12.4	0.0	12.4	0.0	12.5	0.8	12.6	0.8
1949	12.6	0.0	12.6	0.0	12.6	0.0	12.6	0.0	12.6	0.0	12.6	0.0	12.6	0.0	12.6	0.0	12.6	0.0	12.6	0.0	12.6	0.0	12.7	0.8
1950	12.7	0.0	12.7	0.0	12.9	1.6	12.9	0.0	12.9	0.0	12.9	0.0	12.9	0.0	12.9	0.0	13.0	0.8	12.9	-0.8	13.0	0.8	13.0	0.0
1951	13.1	0.8	13.1	0.0	13.2	0.8	13.3	0.8	13.3	0.0	13.7	3.0	13.7	0.0	13.7	0.0	13.7	0.0	13.7	0.0	13.7	0.0	13.7	0.0
1952	13.8	0.7	13.8	0.0	13.9	0.7	13.9	0.0	13.9	0.0	13.9	0.0	13.9	0.0	13.9	0.0	14.1	1.4	14.1	0.0	14.1	0.0	14.3	1.4
1953	14.3	0.0	-	-	-	-	14.8	3.5	-	-	-	-	14.8	0.0	-	-	-	-	14.7	-0.7	-	-	-	-
1954	14.8	0.7	-	-	-	-	15.6	5.4	-	-	-	-	15.6	0.0	-	-	-	-	15.4	-1.3	-	-	-	-
1955	15.4	0.0	-	-	-	-	15.5	0.6	-	-	-	-	16.1	3.9	-	-	-	-	16.1	0.0	-	-	-	-
1956	16.1	0.0	-	-	-	-	16.5	2.5	-	-	-	-	16.5	0.0	-	-	-	-	17.5	6.1	-	-	-	-
1957	17.6	0.6	-	-	-	-	17.7	0.6	-	-	-	-	17.7	0.0	-	-	-	-	17.9	1.1	-	-	-	-
1958	18.0	0.6	-	-	-	-	18.0	0.0	-	-	-	-	18.8	4.4	-	-	-	-	18.9	0.5	-	-	-	-
1959	19.1	1.1	-	-	-	-	19.3	1.0	-	-	-	-	19.3	0.0	-	-	-	-	20.5	6.2	-	-	-	-
1960	20.6	0.5	-	-	-	-	20.7	0.5	-	-	-	-	20.7	0.0	-	-	-	-	20.8	0.5	-	-	-	-
1961	20.9	0.5	-	-	-	-	21.5	2.9	-	-	-	-	21.5	0.0	-	-	-	-	21.6	0.5	-	-	-	-
1962	21.7	0.5	-	-	-	-	21.7	0.0	-	-	-	-	22.8	5.1	-	-	-	-	23.0	0.9	-	-	-	-
1963	23.0	0.0	-	-	-	-	23.0	0.0	-	-	-	-	23.0	0.0	-	-	-	-	23.1	0.4	-	-	-	-
1964	23.2	0.4	-	-	-	-	23.6	1.7	-	-	-	-	23.9	1.3	-	-	-	-	23.9	0.0	-	-	-	-
1965	24.0	0.4	-	-	-	-	24.2	0.8	-	-	-	-	24.4	0.8	-	-	-	-	24.5	0.4	-	-	-	-
1966	24.6	0.4	-	-	-	-	24.8	0.8	-	-	-	-	25.1	1.2	-	-	-	-	25.3	0.8	-	-	-	-
1967	26.5	4.7	-	-	-	-	26.7	0.8	-	-	-	-	26.8	0.4	-	-	-	-	27.1	1.1	-	-	-	-
1968	27.5	1.5	-	-	-	-	27.7	0.7	-	-	-	-	28.5	2.9	-	-	-	-	29.1	2.1	-	-	-	-
1969	29.4	1.0	-	-	-	-	29.9	1.7	-	-	-	-	30.2	1.0	-	-	-	-	30.4	0.7	-	-	-	-
1970	30.6	0.7	-	-	-	-	31.3	2.3	-	-	-	-	31.8	1.6	-	-	-	-	32.1	0.9	-	-	-	-
1971	32.5	1.2	-	-	-	-	32.8	0.9	-	-	-	-	32.9	0.3	-	-	-	-	33.2	0.9	-	-	-	-
1972	33.6	1.2	-	-	-	-	34.2	1.8	-	-	-	-	34.9	2.0	-	-	-	-	35.0	0.3	-	-	-	-
1973	35.4	1.1	-	-	-	-	35.6	0.6	-	-	-	-	35.9	0.8	-	-	-	-	36.7	2.2	-	-	-	-
1974	37.3	1.6	-	-	-	-	38.0	1.9	-	-	-	-	40.1	5.5	-	-	-	-	40.9	2.0	-	-	-	-
1975	41.6	1.7	-	-	-	-	42.5	2.2	-	-	-	-	44.2	4.0	-	-	-	-	45.3	2.5	-	-	-	-
1976	45.8	1.1	-	-	-	-	46.4	1.3	-	-	-	-	49.1	5.8	-	-	-	-	49.9	1.6	-	-	-	-
1977	50.7	1.6	-	-	-	-	51.7	2.0	-	-	-	-	54.1	4.6	-	-	-	-	55.1	1.8	-	-	-	-
1978	55.5	0.7	-	-	-	-	56.7	2.2	-	-	57.0	0.5	-	-	59.5	4.4	-	-	59.7	0.3	-	-	60.3	1.0
1979	-	-	61.3	1.7	-	-	62.4	1.8	-	-	63.7	2.1	-	-	65.7	3.1	-	-	66.7	1.5	-	-	66.9	0.3
1980	-	-	67.9	1.5	-	-	69.1	1.8	-	-	70.8	2.5	-	-	73.4	3.7	-	-	73.4	0.0	-	-	74.2	1.1
1981	-	-	75.8	2.2	-	-	77.6	2.4	-	-	78.1	0.6	-	-	81.7	4.6	-	-	83.5	2.2	-	-	84.2	0.8
1982	-	-	85.7	1.8	-	-	86.8	1.3	-	-	87.8	1.2	-	-	92.3	5.1	-	-	93.0	0.8	-	-	94.3	1.4
1983	-	-	97.8	3.7	-	-	97.7	-0.1	-	-	99.4	1.7	-	-	102.1	2.7	-	-	105.6	3.4	-	-	105.6	0.0
1984	-	-	108.5	2.7	-	-	109.0	0.5	-	-	109.4	0.4	-	-	110.1	0.6	-	-	110.8	0.6	-	-	110.9	0.1
1985	-	-	111.4	0.5	-	-	112.1	0.6	-	-	112.3	0.2	-	-	114.0	1.5	-	-	115.0	0.9	-	-	117.0	1.7
1986	-	-	118.6	1.4	-	-	119.2	0.5	-	-	120.9	1.4	-	-	122.0	0.9	-	-	123.9	1.6	-	-	124.5	0.5
1987	-	-	125.5	0.8	-	-	127.8	1.8	-	-	130.7	2.3	-	-	132.4	1.3	-	-	133.2	0.6	-	-	134.1	0.7
1988	-	-	135.5	1.0	-	-	136.0	0.4	-	-	137.8	1.3	-	-	139.2	1.0	-	-	140.8	1.1	-	-	142.2	1.0
1989	-	-	142.3	0.1	-	-	144.0	1.2	-	-	146.3	1.6	-	-	149.2	2.0	-	-	149.9	0.5	-	-	151.3	0.9
1990	-	-	154.4	2.0	-	-	159.1	3.0	-	-	159.6	0.3	-	-	162.4	1.8	-	-	165.1	1.7	-	-	166.7	1.0
1991	-	-	168.9	1.3	-	-	171.2	1.4	-	-	175.3	2.4	-	-	179.6	2.5	-	-	181.3	0.9	-	-	182.1	0.4

[Continued]

Pittsburgh, PA
Consumer Price Index - All Urban Consumers
Base 1982-1984 = 100
Medical Care
[Continued]

For 1947-1995. Columns headed % show percentile change in the index from the previous period for which an index is available.

Year	Jan		Feb		Mar		Apr		May		Jun		Jul		Aug		Sep		Oct		Nov		Dec	
	Index	%	Index	%	Index	%	Index	%	Index	%	Index	%	Index	%	Index	%	Index	%	Index	%	Index	%	Index	%
1992	-	-	184.6	1.4	-	-	184.5	-0.1	-	-	182.8	-0.9	-	-	186.6	2.1	-	-	189.1	1.3	-	-	190.2	0.6
1993	-	-	194.1	2.1	-	-	194.7	0.3	-	-	197.7	1.5	-	-	198.4	0.4	-	-	199.1	0.4	-	-	199.3	0.1
1994	-	-	202.4	1.6	-	-	204.8	1.2	-	-	207.0	1.1	-	-	208.5	0.7	-	-	211.0	1.2	-	-	211.6	0.3
1995	-	-	208.2	-1.6	-	-	210.2	1.0	-	-	210.9	0.3	-	-	215.3	2.1	-	-	214.3	-0.5	-	-	218.5	2.0

Source: U.S. Department of Labor, Bureau of Labor Statistics, Division of Consumer Prices and Price Indexes. - indicates no data collected for period.

Pittsburgh, PA
Consumer Price Index - Urban Wage Earners
Base 1982-1984 = 100
Medical Care

For 1947-1995. Columns headed % show percentile change in the index from the previous period for which an index is available.

Year	Jan Index	%	Feb Index	%	Mar Index	%	Apr Index	%	May Index	%	Jun Index	%	Jul Index	%	Aug Index	%	Sep Index	%	Oct Index	%	Nov Index	%	Dec Index	%
1947	11.6	-	11.6	0.0	11.6	0.0	11.7	0.9	11.7	0.0	11.7	0.0	11.8	0.9	11.7	-0.8	11.7	0.0	11.8	0.9	11.9	0.8	11.9	0.0
1948	12.2	2.5	12.3	0.8	12.3	0.0	12.3	0.0	12.5	1.6	12.5	0.0	12.5	0.0	12.4	-0.8	12.4	0.0	12.4	0.0	12.6	1.6	12.7	0.8
1949	12.7	0.0	12.7	0.0	12.7	0.0	12.7	0.0	12.7	0.0	12.7	0.0	12.7	0.0	12.7	0.0	12.7	0.0	12.7	0.0	12.7	0.0	12.8	0.8
1950	12.8	0.0	12.8	0.0	12.9	0.8	12.9	0.0	12.9	0.0	13.0	0.8	13.0	0.0	13.0	0.0	13.1	0.8	13.0	-0.8	13.1	0.8	13.1	0.0
1951	13.2	0.8	13.2	0.0	13.3	0.8	13.4	0.8	13.4	0.0	13.8	3.0	13.8	0.0	13.8	0.0	13.8	0.0	13.8	0.0	13.8	0.0	13.8	0.0
1952	13.9	0.7	13.9	0.0	14.0	0.7	14.0	0.0	14.0	0.0	14.0	0.0	14.0	0.0	14.0	0.0	14.2	1.4	14.2	0.0	14.2	0.0	14.4	1.4
1953	14.4	0.0	-	-	-	-	14.9	3.5	-	-	-	-	14.9	0.0	-	-	-	-	14.8	-0.7	-	-	-	-
1954	14.9	0.7	-	-	-	-	15.7	5.4	-	-	-	-	15.7	0.0	-	-	-	-	15.5	-1.3	-	-	-	-
1955	15.5	0.0	-	-	-	-	15.6	0.6	-	-	-	-	16.2	3.8	-	-	-	-	16.2	0.0	-	-	-	-
1956	16.2	0.0	-	-	-	-	16.6	2.5	-	-	-	-	16.6	0.0	-	-	-	-	17.6	6.0	-	-	-	-
1957	17.7	0.6	-	-	-	-	17.8	0.6	-	-	-	-	17.8	0.0	-	-	-	-	18.0	1.1	-	-	-	-
1958	18.1	0.6	-	-	-	-	18.1	0.0	-	-	-	-	18.9	4.4	-	-	-	-	19.0	0.5	-	-	-	-
1959	19.2	1.1	-	-	-	-	19.4	1.0	-	-	-	-	19.4	0.0	-	-	-	-	20.7	6.7	-	-	-	-
1960	20.7	0.0	-	-	-	-	20.8	0.5	-	-	-	-	20.9	0.5	-	-	-	-	20.9	0.0	-	-	-	-
1961	21.1	1.0	-	-	-	-	21.6	2.4	-	-	-	-	21.7	0.5	-	-	-	-	21.7	0.0	-	-	-	-
1962	21.8	0.5	-	-	-	-	21.8	0.0	-	-	-	-	22.9	5.0	-	-	-	-	23.1	0.9	-	-	-	-
1963	23.1	0.0	-	-	-	-	23.1	0.0	-	-	-	-	23.2	0.4	-	-	-	-	23.2	0.0	-	-	-	-
1964	23.4	0.9	-	-	-	-	23.8	1.7	-	-	-	-	24.1	1.3	-	-	-	-	24.1	0.0	-	-	-	-
1965	24.2	0.4	-	-	-	-	24.4	0.8	-	-	-	-	24.5	0.4	-	-	-	-	24.7	0.8	-	-	-	-
1966	24.7	0.0	-	-	-	-	24.9	0.8	-	-	-	-	25.2	1.2	-	-	-	-	25.5	1.2	-	-	-	-
1967	26.7	4.7	-	-	-	-	26.9	0.7	-	-	-	-	27.0	0.4	-	-	-	-	27.2	0.7	-	-	-	-
1968	27.7	1.8	-	-	-	-	27.9	0.7	-	-	-	-	28.7	2.9	-	-	-	-	29.3	2.1	-	-	-	-
1969	29.6	1.0	-	-	-	-	30.1	1.7	-	-	-	-	30.4	1.0	-	-	-	-	30.6	0.7	-	-	-	-
1970	30.8	0.7	-	-	-	-	31.5	2.3	-	-	-	-	32.0	1.6	-	-	-	-	32.4	1.3	-	-	-	-
1971	32.7	0.9	-	-	-	-	33.0	0.9	-	-	-	-	33.1	0.3	-	-	-	-	33.4	0.9	-	-	-	-
1972	33.8	1.2	-	-	-	-	34.4	1.8	-	-	-	-	35.1	2.0	-	-	-	-	35.2	0.3	-	-	-	-
1973	35.6	1.1	-	-	-	-	35.8	0.6	-	-	-	-	36.2	1.1	-	-	-	-	36.9	1.9	-	-	-	-
1974	37.5	1.6	-	-	-	-	38.3	2.1	-	-	-	-	40.4	5.5	-	-	-	-	41.2	2.0	-	-	-	-
1975	41.9	1.7	-	-	-	-	42.8	2.1	-	-	-	-	44.5	4.0	-	-	-	-	45.6	2.5	-	-	-	-
1976	46.1	1.1	-	-	-	-	46.7	1.3	-	-	-	-	49.4	5.8	-	-	-	-	50.3	1.8	-	-	-	-
1977	51.0	1.4	-	-	-	-	52.1	2.2	-	-	-	-	54.5	4.6	-	-	-	-	55.4	1.7	-	-	-	-
1978	55.9	0.9	-	-	-	-	57.1	2.1	-	-	56.8	-0.5	-	-	58.6	3.2	-	-	59.1	0.9	-	-	60.5	2.4
1979	-	-	62.0	2.5	-	-	62.7	1.1	-	-	63.4	1.1	-	-	65.5	3.3	-	-	66.6	1.7	-	-	68.4	2.7
1980	-	-	68.8	0.6	-	-	70.7	2.8	-	-	73.4	3.8	-	-	76.2	3.8	-	-	76.2	0.0	-	-	76.4	0.3
1981	-	-	77.3	1.2	-	-	78.2	1.2	-	-	78.4	0.3	-	-	82.9	5.7	-	-	84.3	1.7	-	-	84.8	0.6
1982	-	-	86.3	1.8	-	-	87.5	1.4	-	-	88.4	1.0	-	-	92.4	4.5	-	-	93.1	0.8	-	-	94.3	1.3
1983	-	-	97.6	3.5	-	-	97.5	-0.1	-	-	99.2	1.7	-	-	101.7	2.5	-	-	105.0	3.2	-	-	105.1	0.1
1984	-	-	108.4	3.1	-	-	108.9	0.5	-	-	109.4	0.5	-	-	110.0	0.5	-	-	110.8	0.7	-	-	110.9	0.1
1985	-	-	111.4	0.5	-	-	112.2	0.7	-	-	112.5	0.3	-	-	114.2	1.5	-	-	115.3	1.0	-	-	117.5	1.9
1986	-	-	119.1	1.4	-	-	119.8	0.6	-	-	121.4	1.3	-	-	122.5	0.9	-	-	124.4	1.6	-	-	125.2	0.6
1987	-	-	126.0	0.6	-	-	128.6	2.1	-	-	131.6	2.3	-	-	133.0	1.1	-	-	133.8	0.6	-	-	135.0	0.9
1988	-	-	136.6	1.2	-	-	137.3	0.5	-	-	139.1	1.3	-	-	140.3	0.9	-	-	141.7	1.0	-	-	143.3	1.1
1989	-	-	143.2	-0.1	-	-	145.0	1.3	-	-	147.2	1.5	-	-	149.7	1.7	-	-	150.1	0.3	-	-	152.0	1.3
1990	-	-	155.4	2.2	-	-	160.0	3.0	-	-	160.5	0.3	-	-	163.0	1.6	-	-	165.8	1.7	-	-	167.2	0.8
1991	-	-	169.4	1.3	-	-	171.9	1.5	-	-	174.9	1.7	-	-	178.4	2.0	-	-	180.2	1.0	-	-	181.0	0.4

[Continued]

Pittsburgh, PA
Consumer Price Index - Urban Wage Earners
Base 1982-1984 = 100
Medical Care
[Continued]

For 1947-1995. Columns headed % show percentile change in the index from the previous period for which an index is available.

Year	Jan		Feb		Mar		Apr		May		Jun		Jul		Aug		Sep		Oct		Nov		Dec	
	Index	%	Index	%	Index	%	Index	%	Index	%	Index	%	Index	%	Index	%	Index	%	Index	%	Index	%	Index	%
1992	-	-	183.3	1.3	-	-	183.1	-0.1	-	-	181.1	-1.1	-	-	184.2	1.7	-	-	186.9	1.5	-	-	187.8	0.5
1993	-	-	191.9	2.2	-	-	192.0	0.1	-	-	195.0	1.6	-	-	195.7	0.4	-	-	196.1	0.2	-	-	196.1	0.0
1994	-	-	199.3	1.6	-	-	201.6	1.2	-	-	204.0	1.2	-	-	204.9	0.4	-	-	207.7	1.4	-	-	208.3	0.3
1995	-	-	204.2	-2.0	-	-	206.5	1.1	-	-	207.2	0.3	-	-	211.2	1.9	-	-	209.9	-0.6	-	-	214.5	2.2

Source: U.S. Department of Labor, Bureau of Labor Statistics, Division of Consumer Prices and Price Indexes. - indicates no data collected for period.

Pittsburgh, PA
Consumer Price Index - All Urban Consumers
Base 1982-1984 = 100
Entertainment

For 1976-1995. Columns headed % show percentile change in the index from the previous period for which an index is available.

Year	Jan Index	%	Feb Index	%	Mar Index	%	Apr Index	%	May Index	%	Jun Index	%	Jul Index	%	Aug Index	%	Sep Index	%	Oct Index	%	Nov Index	%	Dec Index	%
1976	64.0	-	-	-	-	-	64.4	0.6	-	-	-	-	64.9	0.8	-	-	-	-	65.7	1.2	-	-	-	-
1977	66.7	1.5	-	-	-	-	67.5	1.2	-	-	-	-	68.6	1.6	-	-	-	-	69.4	1.2	-	-	-	-
1978	70.4	1.4	-	-	-	-	71.1	1.0	-	-	71.4	0.4	-	-	72.3	1.3	-	-	71.3	-1.4	-	-	70.9	-0.6
1979	-	-	71.6	1.0	-	-	72.9	1.8	-	-	72.9	0.0	-	-	74.6	2.3	-	-	74.4	-0.3	-	-	77.7	4.4
1980	-	-	80.0	3.0	-	-	80.4	0.5	-	-	82.0	2.0	-	-	82.7	0.9	-	-	84.9	2.7	-	-	84.5	-0.5
1981	-	-	88.9	5.2	-	-	89.5	0.7	-	-	90.8	1.5	-	-	90.0	-0.9	-	-	92.5	2.8	-	-	91.5	-1.1
1982	-	-	94.5	3.3	-	-	94.5	0.0	-	-	94.5	0.0	-	-	95.1	0.6	-	-	98.5	3.6	-	-	97.8	-0.7
1983	-	-	98.9	1.1	-	-	99.1	0.2	-	-	100.8	1.7	-	-	101.1	0.3	-	-	101.3	0.2	-	-	102.1	0.8
1984	-	-	102.5	0.4	-	-	101.8	-0.7	-	-	102.7	0.9	-	-	105.2	2.4	-	-	106.3	1.0	-	-	107.6	1.2
1985	-	-	105.4	-2.0	-	-	107.3	1.8	-	-	110.5	3.0	-	-	109.6	-0.8	-	-	113.4	3.5	-	-	114.4	0.9
1986	-	-	115.5	1.0	-	-	117.4	1.6	-	-	120.1	2.3	-	-	120.4	0.2	-	-	118.8	-1.3	-	-	122.1	2.8
1987	-	-	119.5	-2.1	-	-	120.1	0.5	-	-	119.9	-0.2	-	-	119.1	-0.7	-	-	125.5	5.4	-	-	124.9	-0.5
1988	-	-	126.6	1.4	-	-	128.0	1.1	-	-	127.8	-0.2	-	-	127.6	-0.2	-	-	125.5	-1.6	-	-	127.9	1.9
1989	-	-	127.5	-0.3	-	-	129.4	1.5	-	-	135.9	5.0	-	-	136.2	0.2	-	-	135.7	-0.4	-	-	135.8	0.1
1990	-	-	136.7	0.7	-	-	138.2	1.1	-	-	139.9	1.2	-	-	139.8	-0.1	-	-	139.1	-0.5	-	-	140.6	1.1
1991	-	-	139.5	-0.8	-	-	143.2	2.7	-	-	143.1	-0.1	-	-	144.6	1.0	-	-	144.0	-0.4	-	-	144.9	0.6
1992	-	-	146.0	0.8	-	-	145.2	-0.5	-	-	144.6	-0.4	-	-	144.9	0.2	-	-	145.6	0.5	-	-	146.9	0.9
1993	-	-	147.4	0.3	-	-	148.4	0.7	-	-	151.0	1.8	-	-	152.0	0.7	-	-	150.7	-0.9	-	-	150.3	-0.3
1994	-	-	150.7	0.3	-	-	152.2	1.0	-	-	155.2	2.0	-	-	155.1	-0.1	-	-	154.9	-0.1	-	-	154.6	-0.2
1995	-	-	154.0	-0.4	-	-	155.6	1.0	-	-	157.0	0.9	-	-	155.9	-0.7	-	-	157.0	0.7	-	-	160.2	2.0

Source: U.S. Department of Labor, Bureau of Labor Statistics, Division of Consumer Prices and Price Indexes. - indicates no data collected for period.

Pittsburgh, PA
Consumer Price Index - Urban Wage Earners
Base 1982-1984 = 100
Entertainment

For 1976-1995. Columns headed % show percentile change in the index from the previous period for which an index is available.

Year	Jan Index	%	Feb Index	%	Mar Index	%	Apr Index	%	May Index	%	Jun Index	%	Jul Index	%	Aug Index	%	Sep Index	%	Oct Index	%	Nov Index	%	Dec Index	%
1976	66.2	-	-	-	-	-	66.7	0.8	-	-	-	-	67.2	0.7	-	-	-	-	68.0	1.2	-	-	-	-
1977	69.0	1.5	-	-	-	-	69.9	1.3	-	-	-	-	71.0	1.6	-	-	-	-	71.8	1.1	-	-	-	-
1978	72.8	1.4	-	-	-	-	73.6	1.1	-	-	72.7	-1.2	-	-	73.5	1.1	-	-	73.6	0.1	-	-	72.8	-1.1
1979	-	-	75.2	3.3	-	-	77.5	3.1	-	-	77.7	0.3	-	-	77.8	0.1	-	-	76.2	-2.1	-	-	80.7	5.9
1980	-	-	81.7	1.2	-	-	82.8	1.3	-	-	83.6	1.0	-	-	83.2	-0.5	-	-	85.5	2.8	-	-	86.3	0.9
1981	-	-	87.9	1.9	-	-	89.3	1.6	-	-	91.8	2.8	-	-	89.4	-2.6	-	-	91.4	2.2	-	-	91.5	0.1
1982	-	-	94.3	3.1	-	-	94.1	-0.2	-	-	94.3	0.2	-	-	95.1	0.8	-	-	98.3	3.4	-	-	98.0	-0.3
1983	-	-	99.2	1.2	-	-	99.4	0.2	-	-	101.1	1.7	-	-	101.3	0.2	-	-	101.5	0.2	-	-	102.4	0.9
1984	-	-	102.4	0.0	-	-	100.9	-1.5	-	-	102.6	1.7	-	-	105.3	2.6	-	-	106.2	0.9	-	-	107.6	1.3
1985	-	-	105.2	-2.2	-	-	107.4	2.1	-	-	110.8	3.2	-	-	109.9	-0.8	-	-	113.6	3.4	-	-	114.5	0.8
1986	-	-	115.6	1.0	-	-	117.4	1.6	-	-	120.2	2.4	-	-	120.5	0.2	-	-	118.7	-1.5	-	-	121.9	2.7
1987	-	-	119.9	-1.6	-	-	120.6	0.6	-	-	119.8	-0.7	-	-	119.2	-0.5	-	-	125.1	4.9	-	-	124.6	-0.4
1988	-	-	126.3	1.4	-	-	127.3	0.8	-	-	126.8	-0.4	-	-	126.6	-0.2	-	-	125.2	-1.1	-	-	127.4	1.8
1989	-	-	126.8	-0.5	-	-	128.1	1.0	-	-	134.1	4.7	-	-	134.3	0.1	-	-	134.1	-0.1	-	-	134.0	-0.1
1990	-	-	135.3	1.0	-	-	136.4	0.8	-	-	138.2	1.3	-	-	138.1	-0.1	-	-	137.5	-0.4	-	-	138.8	0.9
1991	-	-	137.5	-0.9	-	-	141.0	2.5	-	-	140.9	-0.1	-	-	142.4	1.1	-	-	141.4	-0.7	-	-	142.4	0.7
1992	-	-	143.5	0.8	-	-	142.8	-0.5	-	-	142.2	-0.4	-	-	142.4	0.1	-	-	143.0	0.4	-	-	144.4	1.0
1993	-	-	144.9	0.3	-	-	146.0	0.8	-	-	148.6	1.8	-	-	149.5	0.6	-	-	148.3	-0.8	-	-	148.1	-0.1
1994	-	-	148.4	0.2	-	-	150.1	1.1	-	-	152.9	1.9	-	-	152.5	-0.3	-	-	153.4	0.6	-	-	153.1	-0.2
1995	-	-	152.4	-0.5	-	-	154.1	1.1	-	-	155.1	0.6	-	-	154.2	-0.6	-	-	155.0	0.5	-	-	157.8	1.8

Source: U.S. Department of Labor, Bureau of Labor Statistics, Division of Consumer Prices and Price Indexes. - indicates no data collected for period.

Pittsburgh, PA
Consumer Price Index - All Urban Consumers
Base 1982-1984 = 100
Other Goods and Services

For 1976-1995. Columns headed % show percentile change in the index from the previous period for which an index is available.

Year	Jan Index	%	Feb Index	%	Mar Index	%	Apr Index	%	May Index	%	Jun Index	%	Jul Index	%	Aug Index	%	Sep Index	%	Oct Index	%	Nov Index	%	Dec Index	%
1976	56.7	-	-		-		57.2	0.9	-	-	-	-	57.8	1.0	-		-		58.7	1.6	-	-	-	
1977	59.9	2.0	-		-		60.7	1.3	-	-	-	-	61.6	1.5	-		-		63.5	3.1	-	-	-	
1978	64.0	0.8	-		-		64.6	0.9	-	-	64.5	-0.2	-	-	65.8	2.0	-		67.4	2.4	-	-	67.6	0.3
1979	-	-	68.5	1.3	-		68.9	0.6	-	-	69.1	0.3	-	-	70.9	2.6	-		72.5	2.3	-	-	72.9	0.6
1980	-	-	73.5	0.8	-		73.9	0.5	-	-	74.5	0.8	-	-	75.2	0.9	-		77.2	2.7	-	-	78.3	1.4
1981	-	-	78.9	0.8	-		79.5	0.8	-	-	81.0	1.9	-	-	83.1	2.6	-		87.0	4.7	-	-	87.3	0.3
1982	-	-	88.2	1.0	-		88.5	0.3	-	-	88.9	0.5	-	-	90.4	1.7	-		94.3	4.3	-	-	96.8	2.7
1983	-	-	98.7	2.0	-		98.7	0.0	-	-	98.0	-0.7	-	-	101.9	4.0	-		105.2	3.2	-	-	105.3	0.1
1984	-	-	107.3	1.9	-		106.7	-0.6	-	-	106.7	0.0	-	-	107.7	0.9	-		111.4	3.4	-	-	111.3	-0.1
1985	-	-	111.1	-0.2	-		111.3	0.2	-	-	112.1	0.7	-	-	112.9	0.7	-		115.7	2.5	-	-	116.2	0.4
1986	-	-	116.4	0.2	-		117.1	0.6	-	-	116.7	-0.3	-	-	117.7	0.9	-		120.4	2.3	-	-	120.7	0.2
1987	-	-	121.3	0.5	-		121.5	0.2	-	-	122.1	0.5	-	-	123.3	1.0	-		124.5	1.0	-	-	124.1	-0.3
1988	-	-	132.4	6.7	-		132.9	0.4	-	-	126.9	-4.5	-	-	134.0	5.6	-		136.4	1.8	-	-	136.6	0.1
1989	-	-	138.7	1.5	-		139.4	0.5	-	-	139.7	0.2	-	-	140.8	0.8	-		143.1	1.6	-	-	144.9	1.3
1990	-	-	147.1	1.5	-		149.7	1.8	-	-	148.4	-0.9	-	-	150.5	1.4	-		153.8	2.2	-	-	155.3	1.0
1991	-	-	151.2	-2.6	-		152.4	0.8	-	-	152.5	0.1	-	-	154.4	1.2	-		159.5	3.3	-	-	161.9	1.5
1992	-	-	165.4	2.2	-		166.3	0.5	-	-	167.7	0.8	-	-	170.6	1.7	-		169.7	-0.5	-	-	171.5	1.1
1993	-	-	176.5	2.9	-		177.4	0.5	-	-	178.7	0.7	-	-	178.0	-0.4	-		175.1	-1.6	-	-	179.3	2.4
1994	-	-	178.2	-0.6	-		179.7	0.8	-	-	180.3	0.3	-	-	183.7	1.9	-		188.9	2.8	-	-	188.7	-0.1
1995	-	-	189.6	0.5	-		189.4	-0.1	-	-	190.8	0.7	-	-	193.1	1.2	-		196.4	1.7	-	-	195.9	-0.3

Source: U.S. Department of Labor, Bureau of Labor Statistics, Division of Consumer Prices and Price Indexes. - indicates no data collected for period.

Pittsburgh, PA
Consumer Price Index - Urban Wage Earners
Base 1982-1984 = 100
Other Goods and Services

For 1976-1995. Columns headed % show percentile change in the index from the previous period for which an index is available.

Year	Jan Index	Jan %	Feb Index	Feb %	Mar Index	Mar %	Apr Index	Apr %	May Index	May %	Jun Index	Jun %	Jul Index	Jul %	Aug Index	Aug %	Sep Index	Sep %	Oct Index	Oct %	Nov Index	Nov %	Dec Index	Dec %
1976	56.0	-	-	-	-	-	56.5	0.9	-	-	-	-	57.1	1.1	-	-	-	-	58.0	1.6	-	-	-	-
1977	59.2	2.1	-	-	-	-	59.9	1.2	-	-	-	-	60.8	1.5	-	-	-	-	62.7	3.1	-	-	-	-
1978	63.2	0.8	-	-	-	-	63.8	0.9	-	-	63.7	-0.2	-	-	65.2	2.4	-	-	66.4	1.8	-	-	66.4	0.0
1979	-	-	67.2	1.2	-	-	67.7	0.7	-	-	68.5	1.2	-	-	69.7	1.8	-	-	71.2	2.2	-	-	72.3	1.5
1980	-	-	73.4	1.5	-	-	73.8	0.5	-	-	74.6	1.1	-	-	75.3	0.9	-	-	77.1	2.4	-	-	78.6	1.9
1981	-	-	79.1	0.6	-	-	79.9	1.0	-	-	81.2	1.6	-	-	82.2	1.2	-	-	85.8	4.4	-	-	86.3	0.6
1982	-	-	87.3	1.2	-	-	87.7	0.5	-	-	88.1	0.5	-	-	89.4	1.5	-	-	93.3	4.4	-	-	96.5	3.4
1983	-	-	98.5	2.1	-	-	98.6	0.1	-	-	98.0	-0.6	-	-	102.7	4.8	-	-	105.6	2.8	-	-	105.7	0.1
1984	-	-	108.2	2.4	-	-	107.6	-0.6	-	-	107.6	0.0	-	-	108.6	0.9	-	-	111.7	2.9	-	-	111.5	-0.2
1985	-	-	112.0	0.4	-	-	112.1	0.1	-	-	112.8	0.6	-	-	113.9	1.0	-	-	116.2	2.0	-	-	116.7	0.4
1986	-	-	117.0	0.3	-	-	117.8	0.7	-	-	117.5	-0.3	-	-	118.9	1.2	-	-	120.9	1.7	-	-	121.3	0.3
1987	-	-	121.8	0.4	-	-	121.9	0.1	-	-	122.5	0.5	-	-	123.4	0.7	-	-	125.3	1.5	-	-	125.0	-0.2
1988	-	-	134.1	7.3	-	-	134.4	0.2	-	-	127.9	-4.8	-	-	135.6	6.0	-	-	138.5	2.1	-	-	138.7	0.1
1989	-	-	140.6	1.4	-	-	141.1	0.4	-	-	141.4	0.2	-	-	142.2	0.6	-	-	144.9	1.9	-	-	147.2	1.6
1990	-	-	149.6	1.6	-	-	152.3	1.8	-	-	151.5	-0.5	-	-	153.7	1.5	-	-	157.4	2.4	-	-	159.0	1.0
1991	-	-	154.8	-2.6	-	-	155.7	0.6	-	-	155.9	0.1	-	-	157.8	1.2	-	-	163.3	3.5	-	-	165.9	1.6
1992	-	-	169.3	2.0	-	-	170.2	0.5	-	-	171.9	1.0	-	-	175.7	2.2	-	-	174.5	-0.7	-	-	176.5	1.1
1993	-	-	181.3	2.7	-	-	182.3	0.6	-	-	183.5	0.7	-	-	182.3	-0.7	-	-	179.0	-1.8	-	-	182.6	2.0
1994	-	-	181.8	-0.4	-	-	183.8	1.1	-	-	184.4	0.3	-	-	188.4	2.2	-	-	191.7	1.8	-	-	191.6	-0.1
1995	-	-	192.3	0.4	-	-	192.2	-0.1	-	-	193.5	0.7	-	-	196.4	1.5	-	-	199.6	1.6	-	-	199.2	-0.2

Source: U.S. Department of Labor, Bureau of Labor Statistics, Division of Consumer Prices and Price Indexes. - indicates no data collected for period.

Portland, OR-WA
Consumer Price Index - All Urban Consumers
Base 1982-1984 = 100
Annual Averages

For 1914-1995. Columns headed % show percentile change in the index from the previous period for which an index is available.

Year	All Items		Food & Beverage		Housing		Apparel & Upkeep		Trans-portation		Medical Care		Entertain-ment		Other Goods & Services	
	Index	%	Index	%	Index	%	Index	%	Index	%	Index	%	Index	%	Index	%
1914	10.5	-	-	-	-	-	16.5	-	-	-	-	-	-	-	-	-
1915	10.2	-2.9	-	-	-	-	16.8	1.8	-	-	-	-	-	-	-	-
1916	10.5	2.9	-	-	-	-	18.2	8.3	-	-	-	-	-	-	-	-
1917	12.3	17.1	-	-	-	-	21.7	19.2	-	-	-	-	-	-	-	-
1918	15.1	22.8	-	-	-	-	28.6	31.8	-	-	-	-	-	-	-	-
1919	17.7	17.2	-	-	-	-	36.3	26.9	-	-	-	-	-	-	-	-
1920	20.0	13.0	-	-	-	-	40.5	11.6	-	-	-	-	-	-	-	-
1921	17.3	-13.5	-	-	-	-	30.8	-24.0	-	-	-	-	-	-	-	-
1922	16.4	-5.2	-	-	-	-	25.7	-16.6	-	-	-	-	-	-	-	-
1923	16.6	1.2	-	-	-	-	26.6	3.5	-	-	-	-	-	-	-	-
1924	16.5	-0.6	-	-	-	-	26.6	0.0	-	-	-	-	-	-	-	-
1925	16.6	0.6	-	-	-	-	26.1	-1.9	-	-	-	-	-	-	-	-
1926	16.4	-1.2	-	-	-	-	25.9	-0.8	-	-	-	-	-	-	-	-
1927	16.2	-1.2	-	-	-	-	25.2	-2.7	-	-	-	-	-	-	-	-
1928	16.0	-1.2	-	-	-	-	24.9	-1.2	-	-	-	-	-	-	-	-
1929	15.8	-1.2	-	-	-	-	24.5	-1.6	-	-	-	-	-	-	-	-
1930	15.5	-1.9	-	-	-	-	23.8	-2.9	-	-	-	-	-	-	-	-
1931	14.0	-9.7	-	-	-	-	21.7	-8.8	-	-	-	-	-	-	-	-
1932	12.7	-9.3	-	-	-	-	19.2	-11.5	-	-	-	-	-	-	-	-
1933	12.1	-4.7	-	-	-	-	18.8	-2.1	-	-	-	-	-	-	-	-
1934	12.5	3.3	-	-	-	-	20.5	9.0	-	-	-	-	-	-	-	-
1935	12.9	3.2	-	-	-	-	20.5	0.0	-	-	-	-	-	-	-	-
1936	13.2	2.3	-	-	-	-	20.6	0.5	-	-	-	-	-	-	-	-
1937	13.9	5.3	-	-	-	-	21.5	4.4	-	-	-	-	-	-	-	-
1938	13.7	-1.4	-	-	-	-	21.4	-0.5	-	-	-	-	-	-	-	-
1939	13.6	-0.7	-	-	-	-	21.3	-0.5	-	-	-	-	-	-	-	-
1940	13.6	0.0	-	-	-	-	21.7	1.9	-	-	-	-	-	-	-	-
1941	14.4	5.9	-	-	-	-	22.5	3.7	-	-	-	-	-	-	-	-
1942	16.5	14.6	-	-	-	-	26.0	15.6	-	-	-	-	-	-	-	-
1943	17.5	6.1	-	-	-	-	27.6	6.2	-	-	-	-	-	-	-	-
1944	17.7	1.1	-	-	-	-	29.4	6.5	-	-	-	-	-	-	-	-
1945	18.2	2.8	-	-	-	-	30.0	2.0	-	-	-	-	-	-	-	-
1946	19.5	7.1	-	-	-	-	32.1	7.0	-	-	-	-	-	-	-	-
1947	22.1	13.3	-	-	-	-	37.9	18.1	19.8	-	14.2	-	-	-	-	-
1948	24.1	9.0	-	-	-	-	41.2	8.7	21.9	10.6	14.7	3.5	-	-	-	-
1949	23.8	-1.2	-	-	-	-	39.8	-3.4	23.6	7.8	15.0	2.0	-	-	-	-
1950	24.3	2.1	-	-	-	-	39.5	-0.8	24.0	1.7	15.4	2.7	-	-	-	-
1951	26.2	7.8	-	-	-	-	42.3	7.1	25.1	4.6	16.3	5.8	-	-	-	-
1952	26.8	2.3	-	-	-	-	41.9	-0.9	26.8	6.8	17.1	4.9	-	-	-	-
1953	26.9	0.4	-	-	-	-	41.6	-0.7	27.6	3.0	17.5	2.3	-	-	-	-
1954	26.9	0.0	-	-	-	-	41.9	0.7	26.8	-2.9	17.9	2.3	-	-	-	-
1955	26.8	-0.4	-	-	-	-	42.2	0.7	26.9	0.4	18.6	3.9	-	-	-	-
1956	27.5	2.6	-	-	-	-	43.2	2.4	26.9	0.0	19.2	3.2	-	-	-	-
1957	28.4	3.3	-	-	-	-	44.1	2.1	28.2	4.8	20.3	5.7	-	-	-	-
1958	29.0	2.1	-	-	-	-	44.2	0.2	29.8	5.7	20.6	1.5	-	-	-	-

[Continued]

Portland, OR-WA
Consumer Price Index - All Urban Consumers
Base 1982-1984 = 100
Annual Averages
[Continued]

For 1914-1995. Columns headed % show percentile change in the index from the previous period for which an index is available.

Year	All Items		Food & Beverage		Housing		Apparel & Upkeep		Transportation		Medical Care		Entertainment		Other Goods & Services	
	Index	%	Index	%	Index	%	Index	%	Index	%	Index	%	Index	%	Index	%
1959	29.3	1.0	-	-	-	-	44.5	0.7	31.1	4.4	20.8	1.0	-	-	-	-
1960	29.8	1.7	-	-	-	-	45.5	2.2	30.8	-1.0	21.8	4.8	-	-	-	-
1961	30.1	1.0	-	-	-	-	45.8	0.7	30.9	0.3	22.4	2.8	-	-	-	-
1962	30.2	0.3	-	-	-	-	45.5	-0.7	31.2	1.0	22.5	0.4	-	-	-	-
1963	30.8	2.0	-	-	-	-	46.3	1.8	31.5	1.0	23.0	2.2	-	-	-	-
1964	31.5	2.3	-	-	-	-	46.8	1.1	32.0	1.6	24.4	6.1	-	-	-	-
1965	32.3	2.5	-	-	-	-	48.2	3.0	32.4	1.3	25.2	3.3	-	-	-	-
1966	33.3	3.1	-	-	-	-	49.8	3.3	32.7	0.9	26.0	3.2	-	-	-	-
1967	34.2	2.7	-	-	-	-	51.0	2.4	34.1	4.3	27.7	6.5	-	-	-	-
1968	35.4	3.5	-	-	-	-	53.2	4.3	34.9	2.3	29.2	5.4	-	-	-	-
1969	37.1	4.8	-	-	-	-	56.2	5.6	36.1	3.4	30.9	5.8	-	-	-	-
1970	38.7	4.3	-	-	-	-	58.8	4.6	37.1	2.8	32.9	6.5	-	-	-	-
1971	39.7	2.6	-	-	-	-	59.5	1.2	37.3	0.5	34.2	4.0	-	-	-	-
1972	40.8	2.8	-	-	-	-	61.1	2.7	37.6	0.8	35.3	3.2	-	-	-	-
1973	43.5	6.6	-	-	-	-	65.0	6.4	38.6	2.7	37.6	6.5	-	-	-	-
1974	48.8	12.2	-	-	-	-	68.9	6.0	42.4	9.8	41.4	10.1	-	-	-	-
1975	53.5	9.6	-	-	-	-	72.9	5.8	46.8	10.4	46.0	11.1	-	-	-	-
1976	57.0	6.5	60.8	-	56.3	-	76.7	5.2	51.3	9.6	50.1	8.9	68.8	-	52.2	-
1977	61.6	8.1	64.6	6.3	61.2	8.7	82.1	7.0	56.2	9.6	55.2	10.2	71.4	3.8	56.3	7.9
1978	67.8	10.1	71.1	10.1	69.1	12.9	84.5	2.9	60.4	7.5	60.2	9.1	75.9	6.3	60.3	7.1
1979	77.0	13.6	79.8	12.2	79.7	15.3	85.7	1.4	70.6	16.9	65.9	9.5	80.7	6.3	65.5	8.6
1980	87.2	13.2	85.5	7.1	92.4	15.9	87.8	2.5	81.7	15.7	74.3	12.7	86.9	7.7	73.6	12.4
1981	95.0	8.9	92.3	8.0	100.0	8.2	92.6	5.5	91.8	12.4	83.3	12.1	90.4	4.0	82.1	11.5
1982	98.0	3.2	97.2	5.3	100.1	0.1	95.5	3.1	97.8	6.5	93.6	12.4	94.8	4.9	92.5	12.7
1983	99.1	1.1	99.7	2.6	98.6	-1.5	99.6	4.3	98.5	0.7	100.6	7.5	101.4	7.0	101.5	9.7
1984	102.8	3.7	103.2	3.5	101.2	2.6	104.9	5.3	103.6	5.2	105.8	5.2	103.8	2.4	106.0	4.4
1985	106.7	3.8	105.6	2.3	104.8	3.6	107.5	2.5	108.3	4.5	111.2	5.1	109.6	5.6	111.6	5.3
1986	108.2	1.4	108.2	2.5	106.2	1.3	100.5	-6.5	107.4	-0.8	119.1	7.1	111.2	1.5	121.0	8.4
1987	115.4	6.7	113.7	5.1	121.5	14.4	104.6	4.1	102.4	-4.7	128.7	8.1	121.6	9.4	130.9	8.2
1988	120.5	4.4	120.4	5.9	126.9	4.4	102.4	-2.1	105.3	2.8	136.9	6.4	129.1	6.2	140.1	7.0
1989	126.4	4.9	128.2	6.5	132.4	4.3	104.2	1.8	109.6	4.1	147.9	8.0	133.1	3.1	152.2	8.6
1990	132.1	4.5	134.7	5.1	137.3	3.7	107.5	3.2	114.7	4.7	160.5	8.5	140.7	5.7	161.0	5.8
1991	137.9	4.4	140.3	4.2	142.7	3.9	113.1	5.2	117.1	2.1	172.9	7.7	152.4	8.3	174.5	8.4
1992	142.5	3.3	143.3	2.1	146.2	2.5	117.8	4.2	119.8	2.3	187.0	8.2	156.5	2.7	195.9	12.3
1993	146.3	2.7	146.2	2.0	149.2	2.1	118.2	0.3	123.7	3.3	199.1	6.5	162.3	3.7	207.0	5.7
1994	148.7	1.6	148.9	1.8	151.5	1.5	115.5	-2.3	125.7	1.6	204.3	2.6	164.5	1.4	213.2	3.0
1995	151.6	2.0	151.6	1.8	154.5	2.0	114.0	-1.3	129.0	2.6	209.0	2.3	166.2	1.0	220.6	3.5

Source: U.S. Department of Labor, Bureau of Labor Statistics, Division of Consumer Prices and Price Indexes. - indicates no data collected for period.

Portland, OR-WA
Consumer Price Index - Urban Wage Earners
Base 1982-1984 = 100
Annual Averages

For 1914-1995. Columns headed % show percentile change in the index from the previous period for which an index is available.

Year	All Items		Food & Beverage		Housing		Apparel & Upkeep		Trans-portation		Medical Care		Entertain-ment		Other Goods & Services	
	Index	%	Index	%	Index	%	Index	%	Index	%	Index	%	Index	%	Index	%
1914	10.6	-	-	-	-	-	16.6	-	-	-	-	-	-	-	-	-
1915	10.4	-1.9	-	-	-	-	16.9	1.8	-	-	-	-	-	-	-	-
1916	10.7	2.9	-	-	-	-	18.3	8.3	-	-	-	-	-	-	-	-
1917	12.5	16.8	-	-	-	-	21.9	19.7	-	-	-	-	-	-	-	-
1918	15.3	22.4	-	-	-	-	28.8	31.5	-	-	-	-	-	-	-	-
1919	17.9	17.0	-	-	-	-	36.5	26.7	-	-	-	-	-	-	-	-
1920	20.3	13.4	-	-	-	-	40.7	11.5	-	-	-	-	-	-	-	-
1921	17.6	-13.3	-	-	-	-	31.0	-23.8	-	-	-	-	-	-	-	-
1922	16.7	-5.1	-	-	-	-	25.9	-16.5	-	-	-	-	-	-	-	-
1923	16.8	0.6	-	-	-	-	26.8	3.5	-	-	-	-	-	-	-	-
1924	16.8	0.0	-	-	-	-	26.7	-0.4	-	-	-	-	-	-	-	-
1925	16.8	0.0	-	-	-	-	26.3	-1.5	-	-	-	-	-	-	-	-
1926	16.7	-0.6	-	-	-	-	26.0	-1.1	-	-	-	-	-	-	-	-
1927	16.5	-1.2	-	-	-	-	25.4	-2.3	-	-	-	-	-	-	-	-
1928	16.2	-1.8	-	-	-	-	25.0	-1.6	-	-	-	-	-	-	-	-
1929	16.1	-0.6	-	-	-	-	24.7	-1.2	-	-	-	-	-	-	-	-
1930	15.7	-2.5	-	-	-	-	23.9	-3.2	-	-	-	-	-	-	-	-
1931	14.2	-9.6	-	-	-	-	21.9	-8.4	-	-	-	-	-	-	-	-
1932	12.9	-9.2	-	-	-	-	19.3	-11.9	-	-	-	-	-	-	-	-
1933	12.3	-4.7	-	-	-	-	18.9	-2.1	-	-	-	-	-	-	-	-
1934	12.7	3.3	-	-	-	-	20.6	9.0	-	-	-	-	-	-	-	-
1935	13.2	3.9	-	-	-	-	20.6	0.0	-	-	-	-	-	-	-	-
1936	13.4	1.5	-	-	-	-	20.7	0.5	-	-	-	-	-	-	-	-
1937	14.1	5.2	-	-	-	-	21.6	4.3	-	-	-	-	-	-	-	-
1938	13.9	-1.4	-	-	-	-	21.6	0.0	-	-	-	-	-	-	-	-
1939	13.8	-0.7	-	-	-	-	21.4	-0.9	-	-	-	-	-	-	-	-
1940	13.8	0.0	-	-	-	-	21.8	1.9	-	-	-	-	-	-	-	-
1941	14.7	6.5	-	-	-	-	22.6	3.7	-	-	-	-	-	-	-	-
1942	16.7	13.6	-	-	-	-	26.2	15.9	-	-	-	-	-	-	-	-
1943	17.8	6.6	-	-	-	-	27.8	6.1	-	-	-	-	-	-	-	-
1944	18.0	1.1	-	-	-	-	29.6	6.5	-	-	-	-	-	-	-	-
1945	18.5	2.8	-	-	-	-	30.2	2.0	-	-	-	-	-	-	-	-
1946	19.8	7.0	-	-	-	-	32.3	7.0	-	-	-	-	-	-	-	-
1947	22.4	13.1	-	-	-	-	38.2	18.3	19.7	-	15.8	-	-	-	-	-
1948	24.5	9.4	-	-	-	-	41.5	8.6	21.9	11.2	16.4	3.8	-	-	-	-
1949	24.2	-1.2	-	-	-	-	40.1	-3.4	23.6	7.8	16.7	1.8	-	-	-	-
1950	24.6	1.7	-	-	-	-	39.8	-0.7	24.0	1.7	17.2	3.0	-	-	-	-
1951	26.6	8.1	-	-	-	-	42.6	7.0	25.1	4.6	18.2	5.8	-	-	-	-
1952	27.2	2.3	-	-	-	-	42.2	-0.9	26.8	6.8	19.0	4.4	-	-	-	-
1953	27.3	0.4	-	-	-	-	41.8	-0.9	27.6	3.0	19.5	2.6	-	-	-	-
1954	27.3	0.0	-	-	-	-	42.1	0.7	26.8	-2.9	19.9	2.1	-	-	-	-
1955	27.3	0.0	-	-	-	-	42.5	1.0	26.9	0.4	20.7	4.0	-	-	-	-
1956	27.9	2.2	-	-	-	-	43.5	2.4	26.9	0.0	21.4	3.4	-	-	-	-
1957	28.8	3.2	-	-	-	-	44.3	1.8	28.2	4.8	22.6	5.6	-	-	-	-
1958	29.5	2.4	-	-	-	-	44.4	0.2	29.8	5.7	22.9	1.3	-	-	-	-

[Continued]

Portland, OR-WA
Consumer Price Index - Urban Wage Earners
Base 1982-1984 = 100
Annual Averages
[Continued]

For 1914-1995. Columns headed % show percentile change in the index from the previous period for which an index is available.

Year	All Items		Food & Beverage		Housing		Apparel & Upkeep		Trans- portation		Medical Care		Entertain- ment		Other Goods & Services	
	Index	%	Index	%	Index	%	Index	%	Index	%	Index	%	Index	%	Index	%
1959	29.8	1.0	-	-	-	-	44.7	0.7	31.0	4.0	23.2	1.3	-	-	-	-
1960	30.2	1.3	-	-	-	-	45.8	2.5	30.8	-0.6	24.3	4.7	-	-	-	-
1961	30.6	1.3	-	-	-	-	46.1	0.7	30.9	0.3	25.0	2.9	-	-	-	-
1962	30.7	0.3	-	-	-	-	45.8	-0.7	31.1	0.6	25.1	0.4	-	-	-	-
1963	31.3	2.0	-	-	-	-	46.6	1.7	31.5	1.3	25.7	2.4	-	-	-	-
1964	32.0	2.2	-	-	-	-	47.1	1.1	31.9	1.3	27.2	5.8	-	-	-	-
1965	32.8	2.5	-	-	-	-	48.5	3.0	32.4	1.6	28.1	3.3	-	-	-	-
1966	33.8	3.0	-	-	-	-	50.1	3.3	32.7	0.9	29.0	3.2	-	-	-	-
1967	34.7	2.7	-	-	-	-	51.3	2.4	34.1	4.3	30.9	6.6	-	-	-	-
1968	35.9	3.5	-	-	-	-	53.6	4.5	34.9	2.3	32.5	5.2	-	-	-	-
1969	37.7	5.0	-	-	-	-	56.6	5.6	36.0	3.2	34.4	5.8	-	-	-	-
1970	39.3	4.2	-	-	-	-	59.2	4.6	37.0	2.8	36.6	6.4			-	-
1971	40.3	2.5	-	-	-	-	59.9	1.2	37.3	0.8	38.1	4.1	-	-	-	-
1972	41.5	3.0			-	-	61.5	2.7	37.6	0.8	39.4	3.4	-	-	-	-
1973	44.2	6.5			-	-	65.4	6.3	38.5	2.4	41.9	6.3	-	-	-	-
1974	49.5	12.0	-	-	-	-	69.4	6.1	42.3	9.9	46.1	10.0	-	-	-	-
1975	54.3	9.7	-	-	-	-	73.4	5.8	46.8	10.6	51.2	11.1	-	-	-	-
1976	57.9	6.6	60.6	-	57.1	-	77.2	5.2	51.2	9.4	55.8	9.0	75.7	-	55.7	-
1977	62.5	7.9	64.4	6.3	62.1	8.8	82.6	7.0	56.2	9.8	61.5	10.2	78.5	3.7	60.0	7.7
1978	69.0	10.4	71.8	11.5	70.1	12.9	85.3	3.3	61.3	9.1	66.1	7.5	82.5	5.1	63.4	5.7
1979	78.3	13.5	81.0	12.8	81.1	15.7	86.9	1.9	70.7	15.3	71.8	8.6	86.9	5.3	67.6	6.6
1980	88.2	12.6	86.3	6.5	94.2	16.2	88.8	2.2	80.6	14.0	77.6	8.1	94.6	8.9	74.0	9.5
1981	95.8	8.6	92.5	7.2	102.2	8.5	93.2	5.0	91.3	13.3	83.8	8.0	91.8	-3.0	81.3	9.9
1982	98.8	3.1	97.1	5.0	101.9	-0.3	95.3	2.3	97.0	6.2	93.8	11.9	95.1	3.6	92.2	13.4
1983	99.2	0.4	99.7	2.7	98.7	-3.1	98.9	3.8	98.5	1.5	100.8	7.5	101.2	6.4	102.1	10.7
1984	102.1	2.9	103.2	3.5	99.4	0.7	105.8	7.0	104.4	6.0	105.4	4.6	103.7	2.5	105.8	3.6
1985	105.1	2.9	105.6	2.3	101.3	1.9	108.8	2.8	109.0	4.4	111.1	5.4	109.2	5.3	111.2	5.1
1986	106.0	0.9	108.0	2.3	102.6	1.3	100.4	-7.7	107.5	-1.4	118.7	6.8	110.3	1.0	120.2	8.1
1987	114.3	7.8	113.8	5.4	119.4	16.4	105.4	5.0	103.7	-3.5	130.0	9.5	117.3	6.3	130.4	8.5
1988	119.4	4.5	120.4	5.8	124.6	4.4	104.4	-0.9	107.1	3.3	138.1	6.2	124.0	5.7	140.1	7.4
1989	125.5	5.1	128.3	6.6	129.7	4.1	107.0	2.5	111.8	4.4	149.0	7.9	130.1	4.9	154.6	10.3
1990	131.1	4.5	134.7	5.0	134.6	3.8	110.6	3.4	116.7	4.4	160.8	7.9	136.3	4.8	164.5	6.4
1991	136.3	4.0	140.4	4.2	139.7	3.8	116.2	5.1	118.6	1.6	172.1	7.0	143.5	5.3	177.8	8.1
1992	140.6	3.2	143.3	2.1	143.1	2.4	121.5	4.6	121.9	2.8	186.4	8.3	147.5	2.8	195.8	10.1
1993	144.3	2.6	146.4	2.2	146.1	2.1	122.7	1.0	125.7	3.1	197.9	6.2	151.6	2.8	204.8	4.6
1994	146.3	1.4	149.2	1.9	148.3	1.5	120.6	-1.7	127.9	1.8	202.4	2.3	152.9	0.9	208.8	2.0
1995	149.3	2.1	151.8	1.7	151.1	1.9	120.0	-0.5	132.1	3.3	206.8	2.2	154.8	1.2	215.1	3.0

Source: U.S. Department of Labor, Bureau of Labor Statistics, Division of Consumer Prices and Price Indexes. - indicates no data collected for period.

Portland, OR-WA
Consumer Price Index - All Urban Consumers
Base 1982-1984 = 100
All Items

For 1914-1995. Columns headed % show percentile change in the index from the previous period for which an index is available.

Year	Jan Index	%	Feb Index	%	Mar Index	%	Apr Index	%	May Index	%	Jun Index	%	Jul Index	%	Aug Index	%	Sep Index	%	Oct Index	%	Nov Index	%	Dec Index	%
1914	-	-	-	-	-	-	-	-	-	-	-	-	-	-	-	-	-	-	-	-	-	-	10.5	-
1915	-	-	-	-	-	-	-	-	-	-	-	-	-	-	-	-	-	-	-	-	-	-	10.1	-3.8
1916	-	-	-	-	-	-	-	-	-	-	-	-	-	-	-	-	-	-	-	-	-	-	10.9	7.9
1917	-	-	-	-	-	-	-	-	-	-	-	-	-	-	-	-	-	-	-	-	-	-	13.2	21.1
1918	-	-	-	-	-	-	-	-	-	-	-	-	-	-	-	-	-	-	-	-	-	-	16.6	25.8
1919	-	-	-	-	-	-	-	-	-	-	17.3	4.2	-	-	-	-	-	-	-	-	-	-	19.0	9.8
1920	-	-	-	-	-	-	-	-	-	-	21.1	11.1	-	-	-	-	-	-	-	-	-	-	18.8	-10.9
1921	-	-	-	-	17.1	-9.0	-	-	-	-	-	-	-	-	-	-	17.0	-0.6	-	-	-	-	16.8	-1.2
1922	-	-	-	-	16.3	-3.0	-	-	-	-	16.2	-0.6	-	-	-	-	16.4	1.2	-	-	-	-	16.5	0.6
1923	-	-	-	-	16.4	-0.6	-	-	-	-	16.5	0.6	-	-	-	-	16.6	0.6	-	-	-	-	16.7	0.6
1924	-	-	-	-	16.6	-0.6	-	-	-	-	16.4	-1.2	-	-	-	-	16.5	0.6	-	-	-	-	16.5	0.0
1925	-	-	-	-	-	-	-	-	-	-	16.6	0.6	-	-	-	-	-	-	-	-	-	-	16.7	0.6
1926	-	-	-	-	-	-	-	-	-	-	16.5	-1.2	-	-	-	-	-	-	-	-	-	-	16.4	-0.6
1927	-	-	-	-	-	-	-	-	-	-	16.4	0.0	-	-	-	-	-	-	-	-	-	-	16.1	-1.8
1928	-	-	-	-	-	-	-	-	-	-	15.8	-1.9	-	-	-	-	-	-	-	-	-	-	15.9	0.6
1929	-	-	-	-	-	-	-	-	-	-	15.7	-1.3	-	-	-	-	-	-	-	-	-	-	15.8	0.6
1930	-	-	-	-	-	-	-	-	-	-	15.7	-0.6	-	-	-	-	-	-	-	-	-	-	14.8	-5.7
1931	-	-	-	-	-	-	-	-	-	-	14.1	-4.7	-	-	-	-	-	-	-	-	-	-	13.6	-3.5
1932	-	-	-	-	-	-	-	-	-	-	12.7	-6.6	-	-	-	-	-	-	-	-	-	-	12.4	-2.4
1933	-	-	-	-	-	-	-	-	-	-	11.9	-4.0	-	-	-	-	-	-	-	-	-	-	12.2	2.5
1934	-	-	-	-	-	-	-	-	-	-	12.4	1.6	-	-	-	-	-	-	-	-	12.7	2.4	-	-
1935	-	-	-	-	13.0	2.4	-	-	-	-	-	-	12.8	-1.5	-	-	-	-	12.9	0.8	-	-	-	-
1936	13.0	0.8	-	-	-	-	12.9	-0.8	-	-	-	-	13.2	2.3	-	-	13.4	1.5	-	-	-	-	13.4	0.0
1937	-	-	-	-	13.7	2.2	-	-	-	-	13.9	1.5	-	-	-	-	14.1	1.4	-	-	-	-	13.9	-1.4
1938	-	-	-	-	13.8	-0.7	-	-	-	-	13.7	-0.7	-	-	-	-	13.7	0.0	-	-	-	-	13.7	0.0
1939	-	-	-	-	13.6	-0.7	-	-	-	-	13.5	-0.7	-	-	-	-	13.7	1.5	-	-	-	-	13.6	-0.7
1940	-	-	-	-	13.4	-1.5	-	-	-	-	13.6	1.5	-	-	-	-	13.7	0.7	-	-	-	-	13.7	0.0
1941	-	-	-	-	13.8	0.7	-	-	-	-	14.3	3.6	-	-	-	-	14.9	4.2	-	-	-	-	15.3	2.7
1942	-	-	-	-	16.1	5.2	-	-	-	-	16.5	2.5	-	-	-	-	16.8	1.8	-	-	-	-	17.1	1.8
1943	-	-	-	-	17.4	1.8	-	-	-	-	17.7	1.7	-	-	-	-	17.5	-1.1	-	-	-	-	17.5	0.0
1944	-	-	-	-	17.5	0.0	-	-	-	-	17.5	0.0	-	-	-	-	17.8	1.7	-	-	-	-	18.0	1.1
1945	-	-	-	-	18.0	0.0	-	-	-	-	18.3	1.7	-	-	-	-	18.3	0.0	-	-	-	-	18.5	1.1
1946	-	-	-	-	18.4	-0.5	-	-	-	-	19.0	3.3	-	-	-	-	20.4	7.4	-	-	-	-	21.3	4.4
1947	-	-	-	-	21.7	1.9	-	-	-	-	21.8	0.5	21.9	0.5	-	-	-	-	22.5	2.7	-	-	-	-
1948	23.6	4.9	-	-	-	-	23.8	0.8	-	-	-	-	24.4	2.5	-	-	-	-	24.4	0.0	-	-	-	-
1949	24.1	-1.2	-	-	-	-	24.0	-0.4	-	-	-	-	23.7	-1.2	-	-	-	-	23.5	-0.8	-	-	-	-
1950	23.6	0.4	-	-	-	-	23.7	0.4	-	-	-	-	24.1	1.7	-	-	-	-	24.8	2.9	-	-	-	-
1951	25.6	3.2	-	-	-	-	26.2	2.3	-	-	-	-	26.4	0.8	-	-	-	-	26.4	0.0	-	-	-	-
1952	26.8	1.5	-	-	-	-	26.7	-0.4	-	-	-	-	26.7	0.0	-	-	-	-	26.8	0.4	-	-	26.7	-0.4
1953	26.7	0.0	-	-	-	-	26.9	0.7	-	-	-	-	26.9	0.0	-	-	-	-	27.1	0.7	-	-	-	-
1954	26.9	-0.7	-	-	-	-	26.8	-0.4	-	-	-	-	26.9	0.4	-	-	-	-	26.9	0.0	-	-	-	-
1955	26.7	-0.7	-	-	-	-	26.6	-0.4	-	-	-	-	26.7	0.4	-	-	-	-	27.1	1.5	-	-	-	-
1956	27.1	0.0	-	-	-	-	27.1	0.0	-	-	-	-	27.7	2.2	-	-	-	-	27.9	0.7	-	-	-	-
1957	28.0	0.4	-	-	-	-	28.4	1.4	-	-	-	-	28.5	0.4	-	-	-	-	28.4	-0.4	-	-	-	-
1958	28.8	1.4	-	-	-	-	29.2	1.4	-	-	-	-	29.1	-0.3	-	-	-	-	29.0	-0.3	-	-	-	-

[Continued]

Portland, OR-WA
Consumer Price Index - All Urban Consumers
Base 1982-1984 = 100
All Items
[Continued]

For 1914-1995. Columns headed % show percentile change in the index from the previous period for which an index is available.

Year	Jan		Feb		Mar		Apr		May		Jun		Jul		Aug		Sep		Oct		Nov		Dec	
	Index	%	Index	%	Index	%	Index	%	Index	%	Index	%	Index	%	Index	%	Index	%	Index	%	Index	%	Index	%
1959	29.0	0.0	-	-	-	-	29.2	0.7	-	-	-	-	29.4	0.7	-	-	-	-	29.4	0.0	-	-	-	-
1960	29.7	1.0	-	-	-	-	29.8	0.3	-	-	-	-	29.8	0.0	-	-	-	-	29.7	-0.3	-	-	-	-
1961	30.1	1.3	-	-	-	-	29.9	-0.7	-	-	-	-	30.2	1.0	-	-	-	-	30.2	0.0	-	-	-	-
1962	30.0	-0.7	-	-	-	-	30.0	0.0	-	-	-	-	30.3	1.0	-	-	-	-	30.4	0.3	-	-	-	-
1963	30.5	0.3	-	-	-	-	30.7	0.7	-	-	-	-	30.9	0.7	-	-	-	-	30.9	0.0	-	-	-	-
1964	31.1	0.6	-	-	-	-	31.4	1.0	-	-	-	-	31.6	0.6	-	-	-	-	31.7	0.3	-	-	-	-
1965	31.8	0.3	-	-	-	-	32.1	0.9	-	-	-	-	32.5	1.2	-	-	-	-	32.6	0.3	-	-	-	-
1966	32.6	0.0	-	-	-	-	33.1	1.5	-	-	-	-	33.4	0.9	-	-	-	-	33.7	0.9	-	-	-	-
1967	33.9	0.6	-	-	-	-	33.9	0.0	-	-	-	-	34.2	0.9	-	-	-	-	34.5	0.9	-	-	-	-
1968	34.6	0.3	-	-	-	-	35.0	1.2	-	-	-	-	35.4	1.1	-	-	-	-	35.8	1.1	-	-	-	-
1969	36.2	1.1	-	-	-	-	37.0	2.2	-	-	-	-	37.1	0.3	-	-	-	-	37.6	1.3	-	-	-	-
1970	37.8	0.5	-	-	-	-	38.6	2.1	-	-	-	-	38.8	0.5	-	-	-	-	39.1	0.8	-	-	-	-
1971	39.2	0.3	-	-	-	-	39.2	0.0	-	-	-	-	39.7	1.3	-	-	-	-	40.1	1.0	-	-	-	-
1972	40.3	0.5	-	-	-	-	40.4	0.2	-	-	-	-	40.9	1.2	-	-	-	-	41.2	0.7	-	-	-	-
1973	41.6	1.0	-	-	-	-	42.8	2.9	-	-	-	-	43.4	1.4	-	-	-	-	44.7	3.0	-	-	-	-
1974	45.7	2.2	-	-	-	-	47.5	3.9	-	-	-	-	49.1	3.4	-	-	-	-	50.6	3.1	-	-	-	-
1975	52.1	3.0	-	-	-	-	52.7	1.2	-	-	-	-	53.7	1.9	-	-	-	-	54.4	1.3	-	-	-	-
1976	55.4	1.8	-	-	-	-	56.2	1.4	-	-	-	-	57.4	2.1	-	-	-	-	58.0	1.0	-	-	-	-
1977	58.9	1.6	-	-	-	-	60.7	3.1	-	-	-	-	62.0	2.1	-	-	-	-	62.8	1.3	-	-	-	-
1978	64.2	2.2	-	-	65.5	2.0	-	-	66.7	1.8	-	-	68.0	1.9	-	-	69.4	2.1	-	-	70.7	1.9	-	-
1979	72.3	2.3	-	-	73.6	1.8	-	-	75.4	2.4	-	-	77.7	3.1	-	-	79.3	2.1	-	-	80.8	1.9	-	-
1980	83.6	3.5	-	-	86.6	3.6	-	-	87.9	1.5	-	-	86.3	-1.8	-	-	87.8	1.7	-	-	89.5	1.9	-	-
1981	91.0	1.7	-	-	91.6	0.7	-	-	95.1	3.8	-	-	95.9	0.8	-	-	99.4	3.6	-	-	95.2	-4.2	-	-
1982	98.5	3.5	-	-	97.9	-0.6	-	-	96.4	-1.5	-	-	99.9	3.6	-	-	98.4	-1.5	-	-	97.6	-0.8	-	-
1983	97.9	0.3	-	-	97.2	-0.7	-	-	98.5	1.3	-	-	99.6	1.1	-	-	100.2	0.6	-	-	100.4	0.2	-	-
1984	100.8	0.4	-	-	101.8	1.0	-	-	103.1	1.3	-	-	102.8	-0.3	-	-	103.3	0.5	-	-	104.1	0.8	-	-
1985	104.8	0.7	-	-	105.5	0.7	-	-	106.0	0.5	-	-	106.9	0.8	-	-	107.6	0.7	-	-	108.3	0.7	-	-
1986	109.7	1.3	-	-	107.6	-1.9	-	-	107.5	-0.1	-	-	107.5	0.0	-	-	108.6	1.0	-	-	108.6	0.0	-	-
1987	-	-	-	-	-	-	-	-	-	-	114.1	5.1	-	-	-	-	-	-	-	-	-	-	116.7	2.3
1988	-	-	-	-	-	-	-	-	-	-	119.0	2.0	-	-	-	-	-	-	-	-	-	-	122.0	2.5
1989	-	-	-	-	-	-	-	-	-	-	125.3	2.7	-	-	-	-	-	-	-	-	-	-	127.4	1.7
1990	-	-	-	-	-	-	-	-	-	-	130.1	2.1	-	-	-	-	-	-	-	-	-	-	134.0	3.0
1991	-	-	-	-	-	-	-	-	-	-	136.5	1.9	-	-	-	-	-	-	-	-	-	-	139.4	2.1
1992	-	-	-	-	-	-	-	-	-	-	141.4	1.4	-	-	-	-	-	-	-	-	-	-	143.6	1.6
1993	-	-	-	-	-	-	-	-	-	-	146.0	1.7	-	-	-	-	-	-	-	-	-	-	146.7	0.5
1994	-	-	-	-	-	-	-	-	-	-	147.9	0.8	-	-	-	-	-	-	-	-	-	-	149.4	1.0
1995	-	-	-	-	-	-	-	-	-	-	151.1	1.1	-	-	-	-	-	-	-	-	-	-	-	-

Source: U.S. Department of Labor, Bureau of Labor Statistics, Division of Consumer Prices and Price Indexes. - indicates no data collected for period.

Portland, OR-WA
Consumer Price Index - Urban Wage Earners
Base 1982-1984 = 100
All Items

For 1914-1995. Columns headed % show percentile change in the index from the previous period for which an index is available.

Year	Jan Index	%	Feb Index	%	Mar Index	%	Apr Index	%	May Index	%	Jun Index	%	Jul Index	%	Aug Index	%	Sep Index	%	Oct Index	%	Nov Index	%	Dec Index	%
1914	-	-	-	-	-	-	-	-	-	-	-	-	-	-	-	-	-	-	-	-	-	-	10.6	-
1915	-	-	-	-	-	-	-	-	-	-	-	-	-	-	-	-	-	-	-	-	-	-	10.2	-3.8
1916	-	-	-	-	-	-	-	-	-	-	-	-	-	-	-	-	-	-	-	-	-	-	11.0	7.8
1917	-	-	-	-	-	-	-	-	-	-	-	-	-	-	-	-	-	-	-	-	-	-	13.4	21.8
1918	-	-	-	-	-	-	-	-	-	-	-	-	-	-	-	-	-	-	-	-	-	-	16.9	26.1
1919	-	-	-	-	-	-	-	-	-	-	17.6	4.1	-	-	-	-	-	-	-	-	-	-	19.3	9.7
1920	-	-	-	-	-	-	-	-	-	-	21.4	10.9	-	-	-	-	-	-	-	-	-	-	19.1	-10.7
1921	-	-	-	-	17.4	-8.9	-	-	-	-	-	-	-	-	-	-	17.3	-0.6	-	-	-	-	17.1	-1.2
1922	-	-	-	-	16.5	-3.5	-	-	-	-	16.5	0.0	-	-	-	-	16.7	1.2	-	-	-	-	16.8	0.6
1923	-	-	-	-	16.7	-0.6	-	-	-	-	16.7	0.0	-	-	-	-	16.9	1.2	-	-	-	-	17.0	0.6
1924	-	-	-	-	16.8	-1.2	-	-	-	-	16.6	-1.2	-	-	-	-	16.7	0.6	-	-	-	-	16.8	0.6
1925	-	-	-	-	-	-	-	-	-	-	16.9	0.6	-	-	-	-	-	-	-	-	-	-	16.9	0.0
1926	-	-	-	-	-	-	-	-	-	-	16.7	-1.2	-	-	-	-	-	-	-	-	-	-	16.7	0.0
1927	-	-	-	-	-	-	-	-	-	-	16.7	0.0	-	-	-	-	-	-	-	-	-	-	16.4	-1.8
1928	-	-	-	-	-	-	-	-	-	-	16.1	-1.8	-	-	-	-	-	-	-	-	-	-	16.2	0.6
1929	-	-	-	-	-	-	-	-	-	-	16.0	-1.2	-	-	-	-	-	-	-	-	-	-	16.1	0.6
1930	-	-	-	-	-	-	-	-	-	-	16.0	-0.6	-	-	-	-	-	-	-	-	-	-	15.0	-6.3
1931	-	-	-	-	-	-	-	-	-	-	14.3	-4.7	-	-	-	-	-	-	-	-	-	-	13.8	-3.5
1932	-	-	-	-	-	-	-	-	-	-	12.9	-6.5	-	-	-	-	-	-	-	-	-	-	12.6	-2.3
1933	-	-	-	-	-	-	-	-	-	-	12.1	-4.0	-	-	-	-	-	-	-	-	-	-	12.4	2.5
1934	-	-	-	-	-	-	-	-	-	-	12.6	1.6	-	-	-	-	-	-	-	-	12.9	2.4	-	-
1935	-	-	-	-	13.2	2.3	-	-	-	-	-	-	13.0	-1.5	-	-	-	-	13.1	0.8	-	-	-	-
1936	13.3	1.5	-	-	-	-	13.2	-0.8	-	-	-	-	13.4	1.5	-	-	13.6	1.5	-	-	-	-	13.6	0.0
1937	-	-	-	-	13.9	2.2	-	-	-	-	14.1	1.4	-	-	-	-	14.3	1.4	-	-	-	-	14.1	-1.4
1938	-	-	-	-	14.1	0.0	-	-	-	-	13.9	-1.4	-	-	-	-	13.9	0.0	-	-	-	-	13.9	0.0
1939	-	-	-	-	13.8	-0.7	-	-	-	-	13.7	-0.7	-	-	-	-	13.9	1.5	-	-	-	-	13.8	-0.7
1940	-	-	-	-	13.6	-1.4	-	-	-	-	13.8	1.5	-	-	-	-	13.9	0.7	-	-	-	-	13.9	0.0
1941	-	-	-	-	14.1	1.4	-	-	-	-	14.5	2.8	-	-	-	-	15.2	4.8	-	-	-	-	15.5	2.0
1942	-	-	-	-	16.3	5.2	-	-	-	-	16.7	2.5	-	-	-	-	17.1	2.4	-	-	-	-	17.4	1.8
1943	-	-	-	-	17.6	1.1	-	-	-	-	17.9	1.7	-	-	-	-	17.7	-1.1	-	-	-	-	17.8	0.6
1944	-	-	-	-	17.8	0.0	-	-	-	-	17.8	0.0	-	-	-	-	18.1	1.7	-	-	-	-	18.3	1.1
1945	-	-	-	-	18.3	0.0	-	-	-	-	18.6	1.6	-	-	-	-	18.6	0.0	-	-	-	-	18.8	1.1
1946	-	-	-	-	18.7	-0.5	-	-	-	-	19.3	3.2	-	-	-	-	20.7	7.3	-	-	-	-	21.7	4.8
1947	-	-	-	-	22.0	1.4	-	-	-	-	22.2	0.9	22.2	0.0	-	-	-	-	22.9	3.2	-	-	-	-
1948	24.0	4.8	-	-	-	-	24.1	0.4	-	-	-	-	24.8	2.9	-	-	-	-	24.7	-0.4	-	-	-	-
1949	24.5	-0.8	-	-	-	-	24.4	-0.4	-	-	-	-	24.1	-1.2	-	-	-	-	23.9	-0.8	-	-	-	-
1950	23.9	0.0	-	-	-	-	24.0	0.4	-	-	-	-	24.5	2.1	-	-	-	-	25.2	2.9	-	-	-	-
1951	26.0	3.2	-	-	-	-	26.6	2.3	-	-	-	-	26.8	0.8	-	-	-	-	26.8	0.0	-	-	-	-
1952	27.2	1.5	-	-	-	-	27.2	0.0	-	-	-	-	27.2	0.0	-	-	-	-	27.2	0.0	-	-	27.2	0.0
1953	27.2	0.0	-	-	-	-	27.3	0.4	-	-	-	-	27.3	0.0	-	-	-	-	27.5	0.7	-	-	-	-
1954	27.3	-0.7	-	-	-	-	27.2	-0.4	-	-	-	-	27.3	0.4	-	-	-	-	27.3	0.0	-	-	-	-
1955	27.2	-0.4	-	-	-	-	27.1	-0.4	-	-	-	-	27.2	0.4	-	-	-	-	27.6	1.5	-	-	-	-
1956	27.6	0.0	-	-	-	-	27.6	0.0	-	-	-	-	28.1	1.8	-	-	-	-	28.3	0.7	-	-	-	-
1957	28.5	0.7	-	-	-	-	28.8	1.1	-	-	-	-	28.9	0.3	-	-	-	-	28.9	0.0	-	-	-	-
1958	29.2	1.0	-	-	-	-	29.6	1.4	-	-	-	-	29.5	-0.3	-	-	-	-	29.5	0.0	-	-	-	-

[Continued]

Portland, OR-WA
Consumer Price Index - Urban Wage Earners
Base 1982-1984 = 100
All Items
[Continued]

For 1914-1995. Columns headed % show percentile change in the index from the previous period for which an index is available.

Year	Jan Index	%	Feb Index	%	Mar Index	%	Apr Index	%	May Index	%	Jun Index	%	Jul Index	%	Aug Index	%	Sep Index	%	Oct Index	%	Nov Index	%	Dec Index	%
1959	29.4	-0.3	-	-	-	-	29.7	1.0	-	-	-	-	29.9	0.7	-	-	-	-	29.9	0.0	-	-	-	-
1960	30.2	1.0	-	-	-	-	30.2	0.0	-	-	-	-	30.2	0.0	-	-	-	-	30.2	0.0	-	-	-	-
1961	30.5	1.0	-	-	-	-	30.4	-0.3	-	-	-	-	30.6	0.7	-	-	-	-	30.7	0.3	-	-	-	-
1962	30.5	-0.7	-	-	-	-	30.5	0.0	-	-	-	-	30.8	1.0	-	-	-	-	30.9	0.3	-	-	-	-
1963	31.0	0.3	-	-	-	-	31.2	0.6	-	-	-	-	31.4	0.6	-	-	-	-	31.4	0.0	-	-	-	-
1964	31.6	0.6	-	-	-	-	31.9	0.9	-	-	-	-	32.1	0.6	-	-	-	-	32.2	0.3	-	-	-	-
1965	32.3	0.3	-	-	-	-	32.6	0.9	-	-	-	-	33.0	1.2	-	-	-	-	33.1	0.3	-	-	-	-
1966	33.1	0.0	-	-	-	-	33.7	1.8	-	-	-	-	33.9	0.6	-	-	-	-	34.2	0.9	-	-	-	-
1967	34.4	0.6	-	-	-	-	34.5	0.3	-	-	-	-	34.7	0.6	-	-	-	-	35.0	0.9	-	-	-	-
1968	35.2	0.6	-	-	-	-	35.6	1.1	-	-	-	-	35.9	0.8	-	-	-	-	36.4	1.4	-	-	-	-
1969	36.8	1.1	-	-	-	-	37.5	1.9	-	-	-	-	37.7	0.5	-	-	-	-	38.2	1.3	-	-	-	-
1970	38.4	0.5	-	-	-	-	39.2	2.1	-	-	-	-	39.4	0.5	-	-	-	-	39.7	0.8	-	-	-	-
1971	39.9	0.5	-	-	-	-	39.8	-0.3	-	-	-	-	40.3	1.3	-	-	-	-	40.7	1.0	-	-	-	-
1972	41.0	0.7	-	-	-	-	41.1	0.2	-	-	-	-	41.5	1.0	-	-	-	-	41.8	0.7	-	-	-	-
1973	42.3	1.2	-	-	-	-	43.5	2.8	-	-	-	-	44.1	1.4	-	-	-	-	45.4	2.9	-	-	-	-
1974	46.5	2.4	-	-	-	-	48.3	3.9	-	-	-	-	49.9	3.3	-	-	-	-	51.4	3.0	-	-	-	-
1975	52.9	2.9	-	-	-	-	53.5	1.1	-	-	-	-	54.5	1.9	-	-	-	-	55.2	1.3	-	-	-	-
1976	56.2	1.8	-	-	-	-	57.0	1.4	-	-	-	-	58.3	2.3	-	-	-	-	58.9	1.0	-	-	-	-
1977	59.8	1.5	-	-	-	-	61.7	3.2	-	-	-	-	63.0	2.1	-	-	-	-	63.8	1.3	-	-	-	-
1978	65.2	2.2	-	-	66.6	2.1	-	-	68.0	2.1	-	-	69.4	2.1	-	-	70.9	2.2	-	-	72.1	1.7	-	-
1979	73.6	2.1	-	-	74.9	1.8	-	-	77.0	2.8	-	-	79.1	2.7	-	-	80.7	2.0	-	-	82.1	1.7	-	-
1980	84.5	2.9	-	-	87.3	3.3	-	-	88.8	1.7	-	-	87.5	-1.5	-	-	88.6	1.3	-	-	90.5	2.1	-	-
1981	91.9	1.5	-	-	92.6	0.8	-	-	95.8	3.5	-	-	96.9	1.1	-	-	100.2	3.4	-	-	95.9	-4.3	-	-
1982	99.1	3.3	-	-	98.5	-0.6	-	-	97.0	-1.5	-	-	100.8	3.9	-	-	99.2	-1.6	-	-	98.4	-0.8	-	-
1983	97.7	-0.7	-	-	98.2	0.5	-	-	98.5	0.3	-	-	99.4	0.9	-	-	100.0	0.6	-	-	100.5	0.5	-	-
1984	100.5	0.0	-	-	101.4	0.9	-	-	103.2	1.8	-	-	102.2	-1.0	-	-	101.9	-0.3	-	-	102.6	0.7	-	-
1985	103.2	0.6	-	-	104.0	0.8	-	-	104.5	0.5	-	-	105.2	0.7	-	-	106.0	0.8	-	-	106.6	0.6	-	-
1986	107.9	1.2	-	-	105.6	-2.1	-	-	105.2	-0.4	-	-	105.3	0.1	-	-	106.3	0.9	-	-	106.2	-0.1	-	-
1987	-	-	-	-	-	-	-	-	-	-	113.1	6.5	-	-	-	-	-	-	-	-	-	-	115.6	2.2
1988	-	-	-	-	-	-	-	-	-	-	118.0	2.1	-	-	-	-	-	-	-	-	-	-	120.9	2.5
1989	-	-	-	-	-	-	-	-	-	-	124.4	2.9	-	-	-	-	-	-	-	-	-	-	126.5	1.7
1990	-	-	-	-	-	-	-	-	-	-	129.2	2.1	-	-	-	-	-	-	-	-	-	-	132.9	2.9
1991	-	-	-	-	-	-	-	-	-	-	134.9	1.5	-	-	-	-	-	-	-	-	-	-	137.6	2.0
1992	-	-	-	-	-	-	-	-	-	-	139.6	1.5	-	-	-	-	-	-	-	-	-	-	141.7	1.5
1993	-	-	-	-	-	-	-	-	-	-	144.0	1.6	-	-	-	-	-	-	-	-	-	-	144.5	0.3
1994	-	-	-	-	-	-	-	-	-	-	145.6	0.8	-	-	-	-	-	-	-	-	-	-	147.1	1.0
1995	-	-	-	-	-	-	-	-	-	-	148.9	1.2	-	-	-	-	-	-	-	-	-	-	-	-

Source: U.S. Department of Labor, Bureau of Labor Statistics, Division of Consumer Prices and Price Indexes. - indicates no data collected for period.

Portland, OR-WA
Consumer Price Index - All Urban Consumers
Base 1982-1984 = 100
Food and Beverages

For 1976-1995. Columns headed % show percentile change in the index from the previous period for which an index is available.

Year	Jan Index	%	Feb Index	%	Mar Index	%	Apr Index	%	May Index	%	Jun Index	%	Jul Index	%	Aug Index	%	Sep Index	%	Oct Index	%	Nov Index	%	Dec Index	%
1976	60.1	-	-	-	-	-	60.2	0.2	-	-	-	-	61.3	1.8	-	-	-	-	61.0	-0.5	-	-	-	-
1977	61.6	1.0	-	-	-	-	64.1	4.1	-	-	-	-	65.4	2.0	-	-	-	-	65.4	0.0	-	-	-	-
1978	66.7	2.0	-	-	68.3	2.4	-	-	70.6	3.4	-	-	72.5	2.7	-	-	73.0	0.7	-	-	73.3	0.4	-	-
1979	76.1	3.8	-	-	78.2	2.8	-	-	79.6	1.8	-	-	80.4	1.0	-	-	80.7	0.4	-	-	81.8	1.4	-	-
1980	82.7	1.1	-	-	84.0	1.6	-	-	84.7	0.8	-	-	85.8	1.3	-	-	86.4	0.7	-	-	87.9	1.7	-	-
1981	89.4	1.7	-	-	91.0	1.8	-	-	91.9	1.0	-	-	93.1	1.3	-	-	93.6	0.5	-	-	93.4	-0.2	-	-
1982	94.7	1.4	-	-	95.1	0.4	-	-	95.5	0.4	-	-	99.6	4.3	-	-	98.7	-0.9	-	-	98.4	-0.3	-	-
1983	98.7	0.3	-	-	99.0	0.3	-	-	99.6	0.6	-	-	100.0	0.4	-	-	100.0	0.0	-	-	100.2	0.2	-	-
1984	101.2	1.0	-	-	102.6	1.4	-	-	103.3	0.7	-	-	103.6	0.3	-	-	103.4	-0.2	-	-	104.1	0.7	-	-
1985	104.1	0.0	-	-	105.1	1.0	-	-	105.1	0.0	-	-	105.7	0.6	-	-	106.4	0.7	-	-	106.3	-0.1	-	-
1986	108.1	1.7	-	-	107.7	-0.4	-	-	107.2	-0.5	-	-	106.8	-0.4	-	-	108.9	2.0	-	-	109.6	0.6	-	-
1987	-	-	-	-	-	-	-	-	-	-	113.0	3.1	-	-	-	-	-	-	-	-	-	-	114.4	1.2
1988	-	-	-	-	-	-	-	-	-	-	118.3	3.4	-	-	-	-	-	-	-	-	-	-	122.6	3.6
1989	-	-	-	-	-	-	-	-	-	-	127.1	3.7	-	-	-	-	-	-	-	-	-	-	129.4	1.8
1990	-	-	-	-	-	-	-	-	-	-	133.2	2.9	-	-	-	-	-	-	-	-	-	-	136.1	2.2
1991	-	-	-	-	-	-	-	-	-	-	139.9	2.8	-	-	-	-	-	-	-	-	-	-	140.7	0.6
1992	-	-	-	-	-	-	-	-	-	-	142.8	1.5	-	-	-	-	-	-	-	-	-	-	143.9	0.8
1993	-	-	-	-	-	-	-	-	-	-	146.5	1.8	-	-	-	-	-	-	-	-	-	-	146.0	-0.3
1994	-	-	-	-	-	-	-	-	-	-	148.4	1.6	-	-	-	-	-	-	-	-	-	-	149.4	0.7
1995	-	-	-	-	-	-	-	-	-	-	152.1	1.8	-	-	-	-	-	-	-	-	-	-	-	-

Source: U.S. Department of Labor, Bureau of Labor Statistics, Division of Consumer Prices and Price Indexes. - indicates no data collected for period.

Portland, OR-WA
Consumer Price Index - Urban Wage Earners
Base 1982-1984 = 100
Food and Beverages

For 1976-1995. Columns headed % show percentile change in the index from the previous period for which an index is available.

Year	Jan Index	%	Feb Index	%	Mar Index	%	Apr Index	%	May Index	%	Jun Index	%	Jul Index	%	Aug Index	%	Sep Index	%	Oct Index	%	Nov Index	%	Dec Index	%
1976	59.9	-	-	-	-	-	60.1	0.3	-	-	-	-	61.1	1.7	-	-	-	-	60.8	-0.5	-	-	-	-
1977	61.5	1.2	-	-	-	-	63.9	3.9	-	-	-	-	65.2	2.0	-	-	-	-	65.2	0.0	-	-	-	-
1978	66.5	2.0	-	-	69.4	4.4	-	-	71.4	2.9	-	-	73.3	2.7	-	-	73.5	0.3	-	-	74.4	1.2	-	-
1979	77.3	3.9	-	-	79.2	2.5	-	-	81.3	2.7	-	-	81.8	0.6	-	-	82.3	0.6	-	-	82.5	0.2	-	-
1980	83.8	1.6	-	-	84.7	1.1	-	-	85.7	1.2	-	-	86.8	1.3	-	-	86.6	-0.2	-	-	88.3	2.0	-	-
1981	90.4	2.4	-	-	91.2	0.9	-	-	92.2	1.1	-	-	93.2	1.1	-	-	93.3	0.1	-	-	93.6	0.3	-	-
1982	94.8	1.3	-	-	95.0	0.2	-	-	95.7	0.7	-	-	99.4	3.9	-	-	98.5	-0.9	-	-	98.3	-0.2	-	-
1983	98.8	0.5	-	-	99.0	0.2	-	-	99.6	0.6	-	-	100.1	0.5	-	-	99.9	-0.2	-	-	100.3	0.4	-	-
1984	101.2	0.9	-	-	102.5	1.3	-	-	103.3	0.8	-	-	103.7	0.4	-	-	103.4	-0.3	-	-	104.2	0.8	-	-
1985	104.2	0.0	-	-	105.1	0.9	-	-	105.2	0.1	-	-	105.6	0.4	-	-	106.5	0.9	-	-	106.3	-0.2	-	-
1986	108.2	1.8	-	-	107.6	-0.6	-	-	107.1	-0.5	-	-	106.4	-0.7	-	-	108.6	2.1	-	-	109.4	0.7	-	-
1987	-	-	-	-	-	-	-	-	-	-	113.1	3.4	-	-	-	-	-	-	-	-	-	-	114.4	1.1
1988	-	-	-	-	-	-	-	-	-	-	118.3	3.4	-	-	-	-	-	-	-	-	-	-	122.6	3.6
1989	-	-	-	-	-	-	-	-	-	-	127.2	3.8	-	-	-	-	-	-	-	-	-	-	129.5	1.8
1990	-	-	-	-	-	-	-	-	-	-	133.3	2.9	-	-	-	-	-	-	-	-	-	-	136.2	2.2
1991	-	-	-	-	-	-	-	-	-	-	140.0	2.8	-	-	-	-	-	-	-	-	-	-	140.7	0.5
1992	-	-	-	-	-	-	-	-	-	-	142.8	1.5	-	-	-	-	-	-	-	-	-	-	143.9	0.8
1993	-	-	-	-	-	-	-	-	-	-	146.6	1.9	-	-	-	-	-	-	-	-	-	-	146.2	-0.3
1994	-	-	-	-	-	-	-	-	-	-	148.7	1.7	-	-	-	-	-	-	-	-	-	-	149.7	0.7
1995	-	-	-	-	-	-	-	-	-	-	152.1	1.6	-	-	-	-	-	-	-	-	-	-	-	-

Source: U.S. Department of Labor, Bureau of Labor Statistics, Division of Consumer Prices and Price Indexes. - indicates no data collected for period.

Portland, OR-WA
Consumer Price Index - All Urban Consumers
Base 1982-1984 = 100
Housing

For 1976-1995. Columns headed % show percentile change in the index from the previous period for which an index is available.

Year	Jan Index	%	Feb Index	%	Mar Index	%	Apr Index	%	May Index	%	Jun Index	%	Jul Index	%	Aug Index	%	Sep Index	%	Oct Index	%	Nov Index	%	Dec Index	%
1976	54.3	-	-	-	-	-	55.5	2.2	-	-	-	-	56.6	2.0	-	-	-	-	57.4	1.4	-	-	-	-
1977	58.2	1.4	-	-	-	-	60.0	3.1	-	-	-	-	61.7	2.8	-	-	-	-	62.9	1.9	-	-	-	-
1978	64.7	2.9	-	-	66.6	2.9	-	-	67.5	1.4	-	-	69.1	2.4	-	-	70.8	2.5	-	-	73.0	3.1	-	-
1979	74.8	2.5	-	-	75.3	0.7	-	-	77.2	2.5	-	-	80.3	4.0	-	-	82.5	2.7	-	-	84.9	2.9	-	-
1980	88.4	4.1	-	-	92.5	4.6	-	-	94.3	1.9	-	-	90.6	-3.9	-	-	92.2	1.8	-	-	94.4	2.4	-	-
1981	96.0	1.7	-	-	95.1	-0.9	-	-	101.2	6.4	-	-	101.6	0.4	-	-	107.2	5.5	-	-	97.6	-9.0	-	-
1982	102.8	5.3	-	-	101.7	-1.1	-	-	97.9	-3.7	-	-	102.5	4.7	-	-	99.4	-3.0	-	-	97.8	-1.6	-	-
1983	98.2	0.4	-	-	97.3	-0.9	-	-	98.4	1.1	-	-	98.9	0.5	-	-	99.2	0.3	-	-	99.3	0.1	-	-
1984	99.9	0.6	-	-	100.5	0.6	-	-	101.3	0.8	-	-	101.0	-0.3	-	-	101.7	0.7	-	-	102.2	0.5	-	-
1985	103.5	1.3	-	-	103.7	0.2	-	-	103.8	0.1	-	-	105.6	1.7	-	-	105.2	-0.4	-	-	105.8	0.6	-	-
1986	108.1	2.2	-	-	106.0	-1.9	-	-	105.6	-0.4	-	-	104.7	-0.9	-	-	106.5	1.7	-	-	106.7	0.2	-	-
1987	-	-	-	-	-	-	-	-	-	-	120.0	12.5	-	-	-	-	-	-	-	-	-	-	123.0	2.5
1988	-	-	-	-	-	-	-	-	-	-	125.0	1.6	-	-	-	-	-	-	-	-	-	-	128.8	3.0
1989	-	-	-	-	-	-	-	-	-	-	131.1	1.8	-	-	-	-	-	-	-	-	-	-	133.6	1.9
1990	-	-	-	-	-	-	-	-	-	-	135.8	1.6	-	-	-	-	-	-	-	-	-	-	138.7	2.1
1991	-	-	-	-	-	-	-	-	-	-	141.2	1.8	-	-	-	-	-	-	-	-	-	-	144.2	2.1
1992	-	-	-	-	-	-	-	-	-	-	145.5	0.9	-	-	-	-	-	-	-	-	-	-	147.0	1.0
1993	-	-	-	-	-	-	-	-	-	-	148.6	1.1	-	-	-	-	-	-	-	-	-	-	149.8	0.8
1994	-	-	-	-	-	-	-	-	-	-	150.8	0.7	-	-	-	-	-	-	-	-	-	-	152.3	1.0
1995	-	-	-	-	-	-	-	-	-	-	153.7	0.9	-	-	-	-	-	-	-	-	-	-	-	-

Source: U.S. Department of Labor, Bureau of Labor Statistics, Division of Consumer Prices and Price Indexes. - indicates no data collected for period.

Portland, OR-WA
Consumer Price Index - Urban Wage Earners
Base 1982-1984 = 100
Housing

For 1976-1995. Columns headed % show percentile change in the index from the previous period for which an index is available.

Year	Jan Index	%	Feb Index	%	Mar Index	%	Apr Index	%	May Index	%	Jun Index	%	Jul Index	%	Aug Index	%	Sep Index	%	Oct Index	%	Nov Index	%	Dec Index	%
1976	55.1	-	-	-	-	-	56.3	2.2	-	-	-	-	57.4	2.0	-	-	-	-	58.2	1.4	-	-	-	-
1977	59.0	1.4	-	-	-	-	60.9	3.2	-	-	-	-	62.6	2.8	-	-	-	-	63.8	1.9	-	-	-	-
1978	65.7	3.0	-	-	67.5	2.7	-	-	68.5	1.5	-	-	70.0	2.2	-	-	72.0	2.9	-	-	74.1	2.9	-	-
1979	76.0	2.6	-	-	76.6	0.8	-	-	78.6	2.6	-	-	81.6	3.8	-	-	84.0	2.9	-	-	86.6	3.1	-	-
1980	90.4	4.4	-	-	94.4	4.4	-	-	96.4	2.1	-	-	92.2	-4.4	-	-	93.7	1.6	-	-	96.2	2.7	-	-
1981	97.8	1.7	-	-	97.3	-0.5	-	-	103.0	5.9	-	-	104.0	1.0	-	-	110.2	6.0	-	-	99.2	-10.0	-	-
1982	104.6	5.4	-	-	103.7	-0.9	-	-	99.5	-4.1	-	-	104.7	5.2	-	-	101.0	-3.5	-	-	99.4	-1.6	-	-
1983	97.8	-1.6	-	-	99.6	1.8	-	-	98.2	-1.4	-	-	98.3	0.1	-	-	98.8	0.5	-	-	99.4	0.6	-	-
1984	98.9	-0.5	-	-	99.4	0.5	-	-	101.2	1.8	-	-	99.5	-1.7	-	-	98.4	-1.1	-	-	98.8	0.4	-	-
1985	100.0	1.2	-	-	100.2	0.2	-	-	100.3	0.1	-	-	102.2	1.9	-	-	101.8	-0.4	-	-	102.2	0.4	-	-
1986	104.3	2.1	-	-	102.4	-1.8	-	-	102.0	-0.4	-	-	101.3	-0.7	-	-	103.0	1.7	-	-	103.1	0.1	-	-
1987	-	-	-	-	-	-	-	-	-	-	118.0	14.5	-	-	-	-	-	-	-	-	-	-	120.7	2.3
1988	-	-	-	-	-	-	-	-	-	-	122.9	1.8	-	-	-	-	-	-	-	-	-	-	126.3	2.8
1989	-	-	-	-	-	-	-	-	-	-	128.4	1.7	-	-	-	-	-	-	-	-	-	-	130.9	1.9
1990	-	-	-	-	-	-	-	-	-	-	133.3	1.8	-	-	-	-	-	-	-	-	-	-	136.0	2.0
1991	-	-	-	-	-	-	-	-	-	-	138.2	1.6	-	-	-	-	-	-	-	-	-	-	141.2	2.2
1992	-	-	-	-	-	-	-	-	-	-	142.4	0.8	-	-	-	-	-	-	-	-	-	-	143.9	1.1
1993	-	-	-	-	-	-	-	-	-	-	145.6	1.2	-	-	-	-	-	-	-	-	-	-	146.7	0.8
1994	-	-	-	-	-	-	-	-	-	-	147.6	0.6	-	-	-	-	-	-	-	-	-	-	149.0	0.9
1995	-	-	-	-	-	-	-	-	-	-	150.4	0.9	-	-	-	-	-	-	-	-	-	-	-	-

Source: U.S. Department of Labor, Bureau of Labor Statistics, Division of Consumer Prices and Price Indexes. - indicates no data collected for period.

Portland, OR-WA
Consumer Price Index - All Urban Consumers
Base 1982-1984 = 100
Apparel and Upkeep

For 1914-1995. Columns headed % show percentile change in the index from the previous period for which an index is available.

Year	Jan Index	%	Feb Index	%	Mar Index	%	Apr Index	%	May Index	%	Jun Index	%	Jul Index	%	Aug Index	%	Sep Index	%	Oct Index	%	Nov Index	%	Dec Index	%
1914	-	-	-	-	-	-	-	-	-	-	-	-	-	-	-	-	-	-	-	-	-	-	16.5	-
1915	-	-	-	-	-	-	-	-	-	-	-	-	-	-	-	-	-	-	-	-	-	-	17.1	3.6
1916	-	-	-	-	-	-	-	-	-	-	-	-	-	-	-	-	-	-	-	-	-	-	19.2	12.3
1917	-	-	-	-	-	-	-	-	-	-	-	-	-	-	-	-	-	-	-	-	-	-	23.9	24.5
1918	-	-	-	-	-	-	-	-	-	-	-	-	-	-	-	-	-	-	-	-	-	-	32.5	36.0
1919	-	-	-	-	-	-	-	-	-	-	35.6	9.5	-	-	-	-	-	-	-	-	-	-	40.1	12.6
1920	-	-	-	-	-	-	-	-	-	-	42.8	6.7	-	-	-	-	-	-	-	-	-	-	36.8	-14.0
1921	-	-	-	-	31.7	-13.9	-	-	-	-	-	-	-	-	-	-	28.2	-11.0	-	-	-	-	27.4	-2.8
1922	-	-	-	-	25.8	-5.8	-	-	-	-	25.4	-1.6	-	-	-	-	25.4	0.0	-	-	-	-	25.6	0.8
1923	-	-	-	-	26.5	3.5	-	-	-	-	26.7	0.8	-	-	-	-	26.8	0.4	-	-	-	-	26.8	0.0
1924	-	-	-	-	26.8	0.0	-	-	-	-	26.7	-0.4	-	-	-	-	26.3	-1.5	-	-	-	-	26.4	0.4
1925	-	-	-	-	-	-	-	-	-	-	26.1	-1.1	-	-	-	-	-	-	-	-	-	-	26.0	-0.4
1926	-	-	-	-	-	-	-	-	-	-	25.9	-0.4	-	-	-	-	-	-	-	-	-	-	25.5	-1.5
1927	-	-	-	-	-	-	-	-	-	-	25.4	-0.4	-	-	-	-	-	-	-	-	-	-	25.0	-1.6
1928	-	-	-	-	-	-	-	-	-	-	25.0	0.0	-	-	-	-	-	-	-	-	-	-	24.8	-0.8
1929	-	-	-	-	-	-	-	-	-	-	24.5	-1.2	-	-	-	-	-	-	-	-	-	-	24.5	0.0
1930	-	-	-	-	-	-	-	-	-	-	24.0	-2.0	-	-	-	-	-	-	-	-	-	-	22.8	-5.0
1931	-	-	-	-	-	-	-	-	-	-	22.0	-3.5	-	-	-	-	-	-	-	-	-	-	20.4	-7.3
1932	-	-	-	-	-	-	-	-	-	-	19.2	-5.9	-	-	-	-	-	-	-	-	-	-	18.2	-5.2
1933	-	-	-	-	-	-	-	-	-	-	18.3	0.5	-	-	-	-	-	-	-	-	-	-	20.1	9.8
1934	-	-	-	-	-	-	-	-	-	-	20.6	2.5	-	-	-	-	-	-	-	-	20.5	-0.5	-	-
1935	-	-	-	-	20.5	0.0	-	-	-	-	-	-	20.5	0.0	-	-	-	-	20.5	0.0	-	-	-	-
1936	20.6	0.5	-	-	-	-	20.7	0.5	-	-	-	-	20.6	-0.5	-	-	20.6	0.0	-	-	-	-	20.8	1.0
1937	-	-	-	-	21.3	2.4	-	-	-	-	21.5	0.9	-	-	-	-	21.8	1.4	-	-	-	-	21.7	-0.5
1938	-	-	-	-	21.5	-0.9	-	-	-	-	21.4	-0.5	-	-	-	-	21.4	0.0	-	-	-	-	21.3	-0.5
1939	-	-	-	-	21.2	-0.5	-	-	-	-	21.2	0.0	-	-	-	-	21.3	0.5	-	-	-	-	21.4	0.5
1940	-	-	-	-	21.7	1.4	-	-	-	-	21.7	0.0	-	-	-	-	21.7	0.0	-	-	-	-	21.7	0.0
1941	-	-	-	-	21.7	0.0	-	-	-	-	21.8	0.5	-	-	-	-	23.2	6.4	-	-	-	-	23.8	2.6
1942	-	-	-	-	25.8	8.4	-	-	-	-	26.2	1.6	-	-	-	-	26.5	1.1	-	-	-	-	26.5	0.0
1943	-	-	-	-	27.1	2.3	-	-	-	-	27.2	0.4	-	-	-	-	28.2	3.7	-	-	-	-	28.5	1.1
1944	-	-	-	-	29.1	2.1	-	-	-	-	29.5	1.4	-	-	-	-	29.8	1.0	-	-	-	-	29.8	0.0
1945	-	-	-	-	29.9	0.3	-	-	-	-	30.0	0.3	-	-	-	-	30.2	0.7	-	-	-	-	30.0	-0.7
1946	-	-	-	-	30.2	0.7	-	-	-	-	31.5	4.3	-	-	-	-	32.9	4.4	-	-	-	-	35.2	7.0
1947	-	-	-	-	37.5	6.5	-	-	-	-	37.9	1.1	37.5	-1.1	-	-	-	-	38.9	3.7	-	-	-	-
1948	40.0	2.8	-	-	-	-	41.3	3.2	-	-	-	-	41.0	-0.7	-	-	-	-	42.3	3.2	-	-	-	-
1949	41.1	-2.8	-	-	-	-	40.2	-2.2	-	-	-	-	39.7	-1.2	-	-	-	-	39.2	-1.3	-	-	-	-
1950	38.7	-1.3	-	-	-	-	39.0	0.8	-	-	-	-	38.8	-0.5	-	-	-	-	40.7	4.9	-	-	-	-
1951	41.4	1.7	-	-	-	-	42.0	1.4	-	-	-	-	42.5	1.2	-	-	-	-	42.9	0.9	-	-	-	-
1952	42.8	-0.2	-	-	-	-	41.8	-2.3	-	-	-	-	41.6	-0.5	-	-	-	-	42.1	1.2	-	-	-	-
1953	41.4	-1.7	-	-	-	-	41.3	-0.2	-	-	-	-	41.2	-0.2	-	-	-	-	42.4	2.9	-	-	-	-
1954	41.8	-1.4	-	-	-	-	41.5	-0.7	-	-	-	-	41.5	0.0	-	-	-	-	42.6	2.7	-	-	-	-
1955	42.1	-1.2	-	-	-	-	42.1	0.0	-	-	-	-	41.7	-1.0	-	-	-	-	42.8	2.6	-	-	-	-
1956	43.1	0.7	-	-	-	-	43.0	-0.2	-	-	-	-	42.9	-0.2	-	-	-	-	43.7	1.9	-	-	-	-
1957	43.5	-0.5	-	-	-	-	44.0	1.1	-	-	-	-	44.1	0.2	-	-	-	-	44.4	0.7	-	-	-	-
1958	44.2	-0.5	-	-	-	-	44.3	0.2	-	-	-	-	44.2	-0.2	-	-	-	-	44.1	-0.2	-	-	-	-

[Continued]

Portland, OR-WA
Consumer Price Index - All Urban Consumers
Base 1982-1984 = 100
Apparel and Upkeep

[Continued]

For 1914-1995. Columns headed % show percentile change in the index from the previous period for which an index is available.

Year	Jan Index	%	Feb Index	%	Mar Index	%	Apr Index	%	May Index	%	Jun Index	%	Jul Index	%	Aug Index	%	Sep Index	%	Oct Index	%	Nov Index	%	Dec Index	%
1959	44.0	-0.2	-	-	-	-	44.0	0.0	-	-	-	-	44.4	0.9	-	-	-	-	45.2	1.8	-	-	-	-
1960	45.2	0.0	-	-	-	-	45.5	0.7	-	-	-	-	45.5	0.0	-	-	-	-	45.7	0.4	-	-	-	-
1961	45.8	0.2	-	-	-	-	45.8	0.0	-	-	-	-	45.8	0.0	-	-	-	-	45.9	0.2	-	-	-	-
1962	45.3	-1.3	-	-	-	-	45.2	-0.2	-	-	-	-	45.1	-0.2	-	-	-	-	46.2	2.4	-	-	-	-
1963	46.2	0.0	-	-	-	-	46.4	0.4	-	-	-	-	46.2	-0.4	-	-	-	-	46.6	0.9	-	-	-	-
1964	45.9	-1.5	-	-	-	-	46.8	2.0	-	-	-	-	46.5	-0.6	-	-	-	-	47.6	2.4	-	-	-	-
1965	46.7	-1.9	-	-	-	-	47.5	1.7	-	-	-	-	47.9	0.8	-	-	-	-	50.0	4.4	-	-	-	-
1966	49.2	-1.6	-	-	-	-	49.7	1.0	-	-	-	-	49.8	0.2	-	-	-	-	50.3	1.0	-	-	-	-
1967	50.3	0.0	-	-	-	-	50.8	1.0	-	-	-	-	50.8	0.0	-	-	-	-	51.8	2.0	-	-	-	-
1968	51.1	-1.4	-	-	-	-	53.0	3.7	-	-	-	-	53.2	0.4	-	-	-	-	54.5	2.4	-	-	-	-
1969	54.2	-0.6	-	-	-	-	55.7	2.8	-	-	-	-	55.7	0.0	-	-	-	-	58.4	4.8	-	-	-	-
1970	57.2	-2.1	-	-	-	-	58.6	2.4	-	-	-	-	59.1	0.9	-	-	-	-	60.0	1.5	-	-	-	-
1971	58.2	-3.0	-	-	-	-	58.5	0.5	-	-	-	-	58.9	0.7	-	-	-	-	61.7	4.8	-	-	-	-
1972	60.3	-2.3	-	-	-	-	60.4	0.2	-	-	-	-	61.0	1.0	-	-	-	-	62.3	2.1	-	-	-	-
1973	61.9	-0.6	-	-	-	-	64.3	3.9	-	-	-	-	65.0	1.1	-	-	-	-	67.4	3.7	-	-	-	-
1974	66.3	-1.6	-	-	-	-	67.3	1.5	-	-	-	-	69.0	2.5	-	-	-	-	71.4	3.5	-	-	-	-
1975	71.3	-0.1	-	-	-	-	72.7	2.0	-	-	-	-	72.5	-0.3	-	-	-	-	74.6	2.9	-	-	-	-
1976	73.3	-1.7	-	-	-	-	75.5	3.0	-	-	-	-	76.9	1.9	-	-	-	-	79.2	3.0	-	-	-	-
1977	79.2	0.0	-	-	-	-	80.7	1.9	-	-	-	-	81.9	1.5	-	-	-	-	84.8	3.5	-	-	-	-
1978	84.0	-0.9	-	-	84.4	0.5	-	-	84.8	0.5	-	-	81.9	-3.4	-	-	86.0	5.0	-	-	85.6	-0.5	-	-
1979	83.9	-2.0	-	-	86.5	3.1	-	-	85.8	-0.8	-	-	84.5	-1.5	-	-	87.6	3.7	-	-	86.0	-1.8	-	-
1980	84.4	-1.9	-	-	88.3	4.6	-	-	87.3	-1.1	-	-	87.5	0.2	-	-	88.6	1.3	-	-	89.3	0.8	-	-
1981	89.6	0.3	-	-	93.1	3.9	-	-	92.2	-1.0	-	-	90.8	-1.5	-	-	94.6	4.2	-	-	94.4	-0.2	-	-
1982	92.8	-1.7	-	-	95.1	2.5	-	-	95.8	0.7	-	-	93.4	-2.5	-	-	96.6	3.4	-	-	98.2	1.7	-	-
1983	96.6	-1.6	-	-	98.2	1.7	-	-	98.8	0.6	-	-	98.8	0.0	-	-	103.4	4.7	-	-	101.4	-1.9	-	-
1984	100.0	-1.4	-	-	107.7	7.7	-	-	107.0	-0.6	-	-	101.4	-5.2	-	-	107.0	5.5	-	-	106.1	-0.8	-	-
1985	100.5	-5.3	-	-	110.6	10.0	-	-	113.6	2.7	-	-	103.3	-9.1	-	-	108.7	5.2	-	-	108.2	-0.5	-	-
1986	102.3	-5.5	-	-	100.7	-1.6	-	-	100.1	-0.6	-	-	96.1	-4.0	-	-	102.8	7.0	-	-	102.3	-0.5	-	-
1987	-	-	-	-	-	-	-	-	-	-	103.5	1.2	-	-	-	-	-	-	-	-	-	-	105.6	2.0
1988	-	-	-	-	-	-	-	-	-	-	105.0	-0.6	-	-	-	-	-	-	-	-	-	-	99.7	-5.0
1989	-	-	-	-	-	-	-	-	-	-	103.7	4.0	-	-	-	-	-	-	-	-	-	-	104.7	1.0
1990	-	-	-	-	-	-	-	-	-	-	105.5	0.8	-	-	-	-	-	-	-	-	-	-	109.5	3.8
1991	-	-	-	-	-	-	-	-	-	-	111.6	1.9	-	-	-	-	-	-	-	-	-	-	114.6	2.7
1992	-	-	-	-	-	-	-	-	-	-	118.8	3.7	-	-	-	-	-	-	-	-	-	-	116.7	-1.8
1993	-	-	-	-	-	-	-	-	-	-	119.5	2.4	-	-	-	-	-	-	-	-	-	-	116.9	-2.2
1994	-	-	-	-	-	-	-	-	-	-	115.5	-1.2	-	-	-	-	-	-	-	-	-	-	115.5	0.0
1995	-	-	-	-	-	-	-	-	-	-	115.2	-0.3	-	-	-	-	-	-	-	-	-	-	-	-

Source: U.S. Department of Labor, Bureau of Labor Statistics, Division of Consumer Prices and Price Indexes. - indicates no data collected for period.

Portland, OR-WA
Consumer Price Index - Urban Wage Earners
Base 1982-1984 = 100
Apparel and Upkeep

For 1914-1995. Columns headed % show percentile change in the index from the previous period for which an index is available.

Year	Jan Index	Jan %	Feb Index	Feb %	Mar Index	Mar %	Apr Index	Apr %	May Index	May %	Jun Index	Jun %	Jul Index	Jul %	Aug Index	Aug %	Sep Index	Sep %	Oct Index	Oct %	Nov Index	Nov %	Dec Index	Dec %
1914	-	-	-	-	-	-	-	-	-	-	-	-	-	-	-	-	-	-	-	-	-	-	16.6	-
1915	-	-	-	-	-	-	-	-	-	-	-	-	-	-	-	-	-	-	-	-	-	-	17.2	3.6
1916	-	-	-	-	-	-	-	-	-	-	-	-	-	-	-	-	-	-	-	-	-	-	19.3	12.2
1917	-	-	-	-	-	-	-	-	-	-	-	-	-	-	-	-	-	-	-	-	-	-	24.0	24.4
1918	-	-	-	-	-	-	-	-	-	-	-	-	-	-	-	-	-	-	-	-	-	-	32.7	36.3
1919	-	-	-	-	-	-	-	-	-	-	35.9	9.8	-	-	-	-	-	-	-	-	-	-	40.4	12.5
1920	-	-	-	-	-	-	-	-	-	-	43.1	6.7	-	-	-	-	-	-	-	-	-	-	37.0	-14.2
1921	-	-	-	-	31.9	-13.8	-	-	-	-	-	-	-	-	-	-	28.4	-11.0	-	-	-	-	27.6	-2.8
1922	-	-	-	-	25.9	-6.2	-	-	-	-	25.6	-1.2	-	-	-	-	25.6	0.0	-	-	-	-	25.8	0.8
1923	-	-	-	-	26.7	3.5	-	-	-	-	26.9	0.7	-	-	-	-	26.9	0.0	-	-	-	-	26.9	0.0
1924	-	-	-	-	27.0	0.4	-	-	-	-	26.9	-0.4	-	-	-	-	26.4	-1.9	-	-	-	-	26.5	0.4
1925	-	-	-	-	-	-	-	-	-	-	26.3	-0.8	-	-	-	-	-	-	-	-	-	-	26.1	-0.8
1926	-	-	-	-	-	-	-	-	-	-	26.1	0.0	-	-	-	-	-	-	-	-	-	-	25.7	-1.5
1927	-	-	-	-	-	-	-	-	-	-	25.6	-0.4	-	-	-	-	-	-	-	-	-	-	25.2	-1.6
1928	-	-	-	-	-	-	-	-	-	-	25.1	-0.4	-	-	-	-	-	-	-	-	-	-	24.9	-0.8
1929	-	-	-	-	-	-	-	-	-	-	24.7	-0.8	-	-	-	-	-	-	-	-	-	-	24.6	-0.4
1930	-	-	-	-	-	-	-	-	-	-	24.2	-1.6	-	-	-	-	-	-	-	-	-	-	23.0	-5.0
1931	-	-	-	-	-	-	-	-	-	-	22.2	-3.5	-	-	-	-	-	-	-	-	-	-	20.5	-7.7
1932	-	-	-	-	-	-	-	-	-	-	19.3	-5.9	-	-	-	-	-	-	-	-	-	-	18.3	-5.2
1933	-	-	-	-	-	-	-	-	-	-	18.4	0.5	-	-	-	-	-	-	-	-	-	-	20.3	10.3
1934	-	-	-	-	-	-	-	-	-	-	20.7	2.0	-	-	-	-	-	-	-	-	20.6	-0.5	-	-
1935	-	-	-	-	20.6	0.0	-	-	-	-	-	-	20.6	0.0	-	-	-	-	20.6	0.0	-	-	-	-
1936	20.7	0.5	-	-	-	-	20.8	0.5	-	-	-	-	20.7	-0.5	-	-	20.7	0.0	-	-	-	-	20.9	1.0
1937	-	-	-	-	21.4	2.4	-	-	-	-	21.6	0.9	-	-	-	-	21.9	1.4	-	-	-	-	21.9	0.0
1938	-	-	-	-	21.6	-1.4	-	-	-	-	21.5	-0.5	-	-	-	-	21.5	0.0	-	-	-	-	21.5	0.0
1939	-	-	-	-	21.3	-0.9	-	-	-	-	21.3	0.0	-	-	-	-	21.4	0.5	-	-	-	-	21.5	0.5
1940	-	-	-	-	21.9	1.9	-	-	-	-	21.9	0.0	-	-	-	-	21.8	-0.5	-	-	-	-	21.8	0.0
1941	-	-	-	-	21.8	0.0	-	-	-	-	22.0	0.9	-	-	-	-	23.3	5.9	-	-	-	-	24.0	3.0
1942	-	-	-	-	26.0	8.3	-	-	-	-	26.4	1.5	-	-	-	-	26.7	1.1	-	-	-	-	26.7	0.0
1943	-	-	-	-	27.3	2.2	-	-	-	-	27.4	0.4	-	-	-	-	28.4	3.6	-	-	-	-	28.6	0.7
1944	-	-	-	-	29.3	2.4	-	-	-	-	29.7	1.4	-	-	-	-	30.0	1.0	-	-	-	-	30.0	0.0
1945	-	-	-	-	30.1	0.3	-	-	-	-	30.2	0.3	-	-	-	-	30.4	0.7	-	-	-	-	30.2	-0.7
1946	-	-	-	-	30.4	0.7	-	-	-	-	31.7	4.3	-	-	-	-	33.1	4.4	-	-	-	-	35.5	7.3
1947	-	-	-	-	37.8	6.5	-	-	-	-	38.1	0.8	37.8	-0.8	-	-	-	-	39.2	3.7	-	-	-	-
1948	40.2	2.6	-	-	-	-	41.5	3.2	-	-	-	-	41.3	-0.5	-	-	-	-	42.5	2.9	-	-	-	-
1949	41.3	-2.8	-	-	-	-	40.4	-2.2	-	-	-	-	39.9	-1.2	-	-	-	-	39.4	-1.3	-	-	-	-
1950	38.9	-1.3	-	-	-	-	39.2	0.8	-	-	-	-	39.0	-0.5	-	-	-	-	41.0	5.1	-	-	-	-
1951	41.6	1.5	-	-	-	-	42.3	1.7	-	-	-	-	42.8	1.2	-	-	-	-	43.2	0.9	-	-	-	-
1952	43.1	-0.2	-	-	-	-	42.1	-2.3	-	-	-	-	41.8	-0.7	-	-	-	-	42.4	1.4	-	-	-	-
1953	41.6	-1.9	-	-	-	-	41.5	-0.2	-	-	-	-	41.5	0.0	-	-	-	-	42.6	2.7	-	-	-	-
1954	42.1	-1.2	-	-	-	-	41.8	-0.7	-	-	-	-	41.8	0.0	-	-	-	-	42.9	2.6	-	-	-	-
1955	42.3	-1.4	-	-	-	-	42.3	0.0	-	-	-	-	42.0	-0.7	-	-	-	-	43.1	2.6	-	-	-	-
1956	43.4	0.7	-	-	-	-	43.3	-0.2	-	-	-	-	43.2	-0.2	-	-	-	-	43.9	1.6	-	-	-	-
1957	43.8	-0.2	-	-	-	-	44.2	0.9	-	-	-	-	44.3	0.2	-	-	-	-	44.7	0.9	-	-	-	-
1958	44.4	-0.7	-	-	-	-	44.6	0.5	-	-	-	-	44.4	-0.4	-	-	-	-	44.4	0.0	-	-	-	-

[Continued]

Portland, OR-WA
Consumer Price Index - Urban Wage Earners
Base 1982-1984 = 100
Apparel and Upkeep
[Continued]

For 1914-1995. Columns headed % show percentile change in the index from the previous period for which an index is available.

Year	Jan Index	%	Feb Index	%	Mar Index	%	Apr Index	%	May Index	%	Jun Index	%	Jul Index	%	Aug Index	%	Sep Index	%	Oct Index	%	Nov Index	%	Dec Index	%
1959	44.2	-0.5	-	-	-	-	44.2	0.0	-	-	-	-	44.7	1.1	-	-	-	-	45.5	1.8	-	-	-	-
1960	45.5	0.0	-	-	-	-	45.8	0.7	-	-	-	-	45.8	0.0	-	-	-	-	46.0	0.4	-	-	-	-
1961	46.1	0.2	-	-	-	-	46.1	0.0	-	-	-	-	46.1	0.0	-	-	-	-	46.2	0.2	-	-	-	-
1962	45.6	-1.3	-	-	-	-	45.5	-0.2	-	-	-	-	45.4	-0.2	-	-	-	-	46.4	2.2	-	-	-	-
1963	46.4	0.0	-	-	-	-	46.7	0.6	-	-	-	-	46.4	-0.6	-	-	-	-	46.9	1.1	-	-	-	-
1964	46.2	-1.5	-	-	-	-	47.1	1.9	-	-	-	-	46.8	-0.6	-	-	-	-	47.9	2.4	-	-	-	-
1965	47.0	-1.9	-	-	-	-	47.8	1.7	-	-	-	-	48.2	0.8	-	-	-	-	50.3	4.4	-	-	-	-
1966	49.5	-1.6	-	-	-	-	50.0	1.0	-	-	-	-	50.1	0.2	-	-	-	-	50.6	1.0	-	-	-	-
1967	50.6	0.0	-	-	-	-	51.2	1.2	-	-	-	-	51.1	-0.2	-	-	-	-	52.1	2.0	-	-	-	-
1968	51.5	-1.2	-	-	-	-	53.4	3.7	-	-	-	-	53.5	0.2	-	-	-	-	54.9	2.6	-	-	-	-
1969	54.5	-0.7	-	-	-	-	56.1	2.9	-	-	-	-	56.1	0.0	-	-	-	-	58.8	4.8	-	-	-	-
1970	57.5	-2.2	-	-	-	-	59.0	2.6	-	-	-	-	59.5	0.8	-	-	-	-	60.3	1.3	-	-	-	-
1971	58.6	-2.8	-	-	-	-	58.9	0.5	-	-	-	-	59.3	0.7	-	-	-	-	62.1	4.7	-	-	-	-
1972	60.7	-2.3	-	-	-	-	60.8	0.2	-	-	-	-	61.4	1.0	-	-	-	-	62.7	2.1	-	-	-	-
1973	62.2	-0.8	-	-	-	-	64.7	4.0	-	-	-	-	65.4	1.1	-	-	-	-	67.8	3.7	-	-	-	-
1974	66.8	-1.5	-	-	-	-	67.7	1.3	-	-	-	-	69.5	2.7	-	-	-	-	71.9	3.5	-	-	-	-
1975	71.7	-0.3	-	-	-	-	73.1	2.0	-	-	-	-	72.9	-0.3	-	-	-	-	75.0	2.9	-	-	-	-
1976	73.7	-1.7	-	-	-	-	76.0	3.1	-	-	-	-	77.3	1.7	-	-	-	-	79.7	3.1	-	-	-	-
1977	79.7	0.0	-	-	-	-	81.2	1.9	-	-	-	-	82.4	1.5	-	-	-	-	85.3	3.5	-	-	-	-
1978	84.5	-0.9	-	-	84.4	-0.1	-	-	85.9	1.8	-	-	82.8	-3.6	-	-	87.7	5.9	-	-	86.7	-1.1	-	-
1979	85.4	-1.5	-	-	84.8	-0.7	-	-	85.4	0.7	-	-	85.4	0.0	-	-	90.3	5.7	-	-	90.3	0.0	-	-
1980	85.0	-5.9	-	-	87.6	3.1	-	-	86.5	-1.3	-	-	89.0	2.9	-	-	91.1	2.4	-	-	92.1	1.1	-	-
1981	92.0	-0.1	-	-	93.5	1.6	-	-	93.8	0.3	-	-	91.0	-3.0	-	-	94.5	3.8	-	-	94.4	-0.1	-	-
1982	92.5	-2.0	-	-	95.1	2.8	-	-	96.2	1.2	-	-	93.8	-2.5	-	-	96.1	2.5	-	-	97.2	1.1	-	-
1983	95.4	-1.9	-	-	98.1	2.8	-	-	99.0	0.9	-	-	98.0	-1.0	-	-	102.3	4.4	-	-	99.8	-2.4	-	-
1984	99.7	-0.1	-	-	110.1	10.4	-	-	108.8	-1.2	-	-	102.4	-5.9	-	-	107.5	5.0	-	-	106.3	-1.1	-	-
1985	99.6	-6.3	-	-	112.8	13.3	-	-	116.3	3.1	-	-	102.8	-11.6	-	-	110.6	7.6	-	-	110.0	-0.5	-	-
1986	103.6	-5.8	-	-	100.7	-2.8	-	-	99.9	-0.8	-	-	95.6	-4.3	-	-	102.5	7.2	-	-	102.0	-0.5	-	-
1987	-	-	-	-	-	-	-	-	-	-	103.9	1.9	-	-	-	-	-	-	-	-	-	-	106.8	2.8
1988	-	-	-	-	-	-	-	-	-	-	106.8	0.0	-	-	-	-	-	-	-	-	-	-	102.0	-4.5
1989	-	-	-	-	-	-	-	-	-	-	106.5	4.4	-	-	-	-	-	-	-	-	-	-	107.6	1.0
1990	-	-	-	-	-	-	-	-	-	-	108.6	0.9	-	-	-	-	-	-	-	-	-	-	112.7	3.8
1991	-	-	-	-	-	-	-	-	-	-	114.5	1.6	-	-	-	-	-	-	-	-	-	-	117.9	3.0
1992	-	-	-	-	-	-	-	-	-	-	122.1	3.6	-	-	-	-	-	-	-	-	-	-	120.8	-1.1
1993	-	-	-	-	-	-	-	-	-	-	123.5	2.2	-	-	-	-	-	-	-	-	-	-	121.9	-1.3
1994	-	-	-	-	-	-	-	-	-	-	120.6	-1.1	-	-	-	-	-	-	-	-	-	-	120.5	-0.1
1995	-	-	-	-	-	-	-	-	-	-	121.8	1.1	-	-	-	-	-	-	-	-	-	-	-	-

Source: U.S. Department of Labor, Bureau of Labor Statistics, Division of Consumer Prices and Price Indexes. - indicates no data collected for period.

Portland, OR-WA
Consumer Price Index - All Urban Consumers
Base 1982-1984 = 100
Transportation

For 1947-1995. Columns headed % show percentile change in the index from the previous period for which an index is available.

Year	Jan Index	%	Feb Index	%	Mar Index	%	Apr Index	%	May Index	%	Jun Index	%	Jul Index	%	Aug Index	%	Sep Index	%	Oct Index	%	Nov Index	%	Dec Index	%
1947	-	-	-	-	19.5	-	-	-	-	-	19.6	0.5	19.6	0.0	-	-	-	-	20.0	2.0	-	-	-	-
1948	20.9	4.5	-	-	-	-	21.0	0.5	-	-	-	-	22.2	5.7	-	-	-	-	22.6	1.8	-	-	-	-
1949	22.9	1.3	-	-	-	-	23.2	1.3	-	-	-	-	24.0	3.4	-	-	-	-	24.0	0.0	-	-	-	-
1950	24.2	0.8	-	-	-	-	23.7	-2.1	-	-	-	-	23.8	0.4	-	-	-	-	24.2	1.7	-	-	-	-
1951	24.4	0.8	-	-	-	-	24.8	1.6	-	-	-	-	25.0	0.8	-	-	-	-	25.5	2.0	-	-	-	-
1952	26.0	2.0	-	-	-	-	26.7	2.7	-	-	-	-	26.7	0.0	-	-	-	-	27.3	2.2	-	-	-	-
1953	27.5	0.7	-	-	-	-	27.7	0.7	-	-	-	-	27.5	-0.7	-	-	-	-	27.5	0.0	-	-	-	-
1954	27.4	-0.4	-	-	-	-	27.1	-1.1	-	-	-	-	26.6	-1.8	-	-	-	-	26.4	-0.8	-	-	-	-
1955	26.9	1.9	-	-	-	-	26.7	-0.7	-	-	-	-	26.6	-0.4	-	-	-	-	27.4	3.0	-	-	-	-
1956	27.1	-1.1	-	-	-	-	26.1	-3.7	-	-	-	-	26.7	2.3	-	-	-	-	27.6	3.4	-	-	-	-
1957	27.6	0.0	-	-	-	-	28.1	1.8	-	-	-	-	28.6	1.8	-	-	-	-	28.1	-1.7	-	-	-	-
1958	29.0	3.2	-	-	-	-	29.8	2.8	-	-	-	-	30.0	0.7	-	-	-	-	30.3	1.0	-	-	-	-
1959	29.6	-2.3	-	-	-	-	31.4	6.1	-	-	-	-	30.6	-2.5	-	-	-	-	31.8	3.9	-	-	-	-
1960	31.6	-0.6	-	-	-	-	31.1	-1.6	-	-	-	-	30.6	-1.6	-	-	-	-	30.1	-1.6	-	-	-	-
1961	31.1	3.3	-	-	-	-	29.2	-6.1	-	-	-	-	31.5	7.9	-	-	-	-	31.8	1.0	-	-	-	-
1962	31.4	-1.3	-	-	-	-	30.7	-2.2	-	-	-	-	31.5	2.6	-	-	-	-	31.1	-1.3	-	-	-	-
1963	31.0	-0.3	-	-	-	-	31.6	1.9	-	-	-	-	31.5	-0.3	-	-	-	-	31.7	0.6	-	-	-	-
1964	32.0	0.9	-	-	-	-	32.1	0.3	-	-	-	-	32.2	0.3	-	-	-	-	31.5	-2.2	-	-	-	-
1965	32.4	2.9	-	-	-	-	32.5	0.3	-	-	-	-	32.7	0.6	-	-	-	-	32.2	-1.5	-	-	-	-
1966	32.1	-0.3	-	-	-	-	32.6	1.6	-	-	-	-	32.7	0.3	-	-	-	-	33.3	1.8	-	-	-	-
1967	33.1	-0.6	-	-	-	-	33.9	2.4	-	-	-	-	34.4	1.5	-	-	-	-	34.6	0.6	-	-	-	-
1968	34.7	0.3	-	-	-	-	34.7	0.0	-	-	-	-	35.0	0.9	-	-	-	-	35.0	0.0	-	-	-	-
1969	35.6	1.7	-	-	-	-	36.1	1.4	-	-	-	-	35.9	-0.6	-	-	-	-	36.3	1.1	-	-	-	-
1970	36.7	1.1	-	-	-	-	36.9	0.5	-	-	-	-	37.2	0.8	-	-	-	-	37.1	-0.3	-	-	-	-
1971	38.1	2.7	-	-	-	-	36.9	-3.1	-	-	-	-	37.3	1.1	-	-	-	-	37.3	0.0	-	-	-	-
1972	37.5	0.5	-	-	-	-	37.1	-1.1	-	-	-	-	37.4	0.8	-	-	-	-	38.1	1.9	-	-	-	-
1973	37.9	-0.5	-	-	-	-	38.2	0.8	-	-	-	-	38.7	1.3	-	-	-	-	38.8	0.3	-	-	-	-
1974	39.8	2.6	-	-	-	-	41.1	3.3	-	-	-	-	43.2	5.1	-	-	-	-	43.6	0.9	-	-	-	-
1975	45.0	3.2	-	-	-	-	45.3	0.7	-	-	-	-	47.7	5.3	-	-	-	-	48.0	0.6	-	-	-	-
1976	49.0	2.1	-	-	-	-	49.4	0.8	-	-	-	-	52.3	5.9	-	-	-	-	53.0	1.3	-	-	-	-
1977	53.6	1.1	-	-	-	-	56.4	5.2	-	-	-	-	56.6	0.4	-	-	-	-	56.7	0.2	-	-	-	-
1978	58.3	2.8	-	-	57.9	-0.7	-	-	59.5	2.8	-	-	60.9	2.4	-	-	61.9	1.6	-	-	62.8	1.5	-	-
1979	63.3	0.8	-	-	65.9	4.1	-	-	69.2	5.0	-	-	73.0	5.5	-	-	74.1	1.5	-	-	74.5	0.5	-	-
1980	77.6	4.2	-	-	79.9	3.0	-	-	80.8	1.1	-	-	81.6	1.0	-	-	83.1	1.8	-	-	85.0	2.3	-	-
1981	85.9	1.1	-	-	88.7	3.3	-	-	90.5	2.0	-	-	92.3	2.0	-	-	94.1	2.0	-	-	96.2	2.2	-	-
1982	97.9	1.8	-	-	96.1	-1.8	-	-	96.1	0.0	-	-	99.3	3.3	-	-	99.3	0.0	-	-	98.6	-0.7	-	-
1983	97.2	-1.4	-	-	94.4	-2.9	-	-	96.9	2.6	-	-	99.9	3.1	-	-	100.7	0.8	-	-	101.2	0.5	-	-
1984	100.8	-0.4	-	-	100.8	0.0	-	-	104.6	3.8	-	-	104.4	-0.2	-	-	104.2	-0.2	-	-	105.7	1.4	-	-
1985	106.6	0.9	-	-	106.2	-0.4	-	-	107.4	1.1	-	-	108.3	0.8	-	-	109.3	0.9	-	-	110.9	1.5	-	-
1986	112.5	1.4	-	-	107.3	-4.6	-	-	106.0	-1.2	-	-	108.1	2.0	-	-	106.8	-1.2	-	-	105.1	-1.6	-	-
1987	-	-	-	-	-	-	-	-	-	-	101.2	-3.7	-	-	-	-	-	-	-	-	-	-	103.6	2.4
1988	-	-	-	-	-	-	-	-	-	-	104.1	0.5	-	-	-	-	-	-	-	-	-	-	106.4	2.2
1989	-	-	-	-	-	-	-	-	-	-	109.4	2.8	-	-	-	-	-	-	-	-	-	-	109.8	0.4
1990	-	-	-	-	-	-	-	-	-	-	111.7	1.7	-	-	-	-	-	-	-	-	-	-	117.7	5.4
1991	-	-	-	-	-	-	-	-	-	-	116.5	-1.0	-	-	-	-	-	-	-	-	-	-	117.7	1.0

[Continued]

Portland, OR-WA
Consumer Price Index - All Urban Consumers
Base 1982-1984 = 100
Transportation
[Continued]

For 1947-1995. Columns headed % show percentile change in the index from the previous period for which an index is available.

Year	Jan Index	%	Feb Index	%	Mar Index	%	Apr Index	%	May Index	%	Jun Index	%	Jul Index	%	Aug Index	%	Sep Index	%	Oct Index	%	Nov Index	%	Dec Index	%
1992	-	-	-	-	-	-	-	-	-	-	117.7	0.0	-	-	-	-	-	-	-	-	-	-	122.0	3.7
1993	-	-	-	-	-	-	-	-	-	-	123.8	1.5	-	-	-	-	-	-	-	-	-	-	123.6	-0.2
1994	-	-	-	-	-	-	-	-	-	-	124.7	0.9	-	-	-	-	-	-	-	-	-	-	126.7	1.6
1995	-	-	-	-	-	-	-	-	-	-	128.1	1.1	-	-	-	-	-	-	-	-	-	-	-	-

Source: U.S. Department of Labor, Bureau of Labor Statistics, Division of Consumer Prices and Price Indexes. - indicates no data collected for period.

Portland, OR-WA
Consumer Price Index - Urban Wage Earners
Base 1982-1984 = 100
Transportation

For 1947-1995. Columns headed % show percentile change in the index from the previous period for which an index is available.

Year	Jan Index	%	Feb Index	%	Mar Index	%	Apr Index	%	May Index	%	Jun Index	%	Jul Index	%	Aug Index	%	Sep Index	%	Oct Index	%	Nov Index	%	Dec Index	%
1947	-	-	-	-	19.5	-	-	-	-	-	19.6	0.5	19.6	0.0	-	-	-	-	20.0	2.0	-	-	-	-
1948	20.9	4.5	-	-	-	-	21.0	0.5	-	-	-	-	22.2	5.7	-	-	-	-	22.6	1.8	-	-	-	-
1949	22.9	1.3	-	-	-	-	23.2	1.3	-	-	-	-	23.9	3.0	-	-	-	-	24.0	0.4	-	-	-	-
1950	24.1	0.4	-	-	-	-	23.7	-1.7	-	-	-	-	23.8	0.4	-	-	-	-	24.2	1.7	-	-	-	-
1951	24.4	0.8	-	-	-	-	24.8	1.6	-	-	-	-	25.0	0.8	-	-	-	-	25.5	2.0	-	-	-	-
1952	26.0	2.0	-	-	-	-	26.6	2.3	-	-	-	-	26.7	0.4	-	-	-	-	27.3	2.2	-	-	-	-
1953	27.4	0.4	-	-	-	-	27.7	1.1	-	-	-	-	27.5	-0.7	-	-	-	-	27.5	0.0	-	-	-	-
1954	27.3	-0.7	-	-	-	-	27.1	-0.7	-	-	-	-	26.6	-1.8	-	-	-	-	26.4	-0.8	-	-	-	-
1955	26.9	1.9	-	-	-	-	26.7	-0.7	-	-	-	-	26.6	-0.4	-	-	-	-	27.3	2.6	-	-	-	-
1956	27.1	-0.7	-	-	-	-	26.0	-4.1	-	-	-	-	26.7	2.7	-	-	-	-	27.6	3.4	-	-	-	-
1957	27.6	0.0	-	-	-	-	28.1	1.8	-	-	-	-	28.5	1.4	-	-	-	-	28.1	-1.4	-	-	-	-
1958	29.0	3.2	-	-	-	-	29.7	2.4	-	-	-	-	30.0	1.0	-	-	-	-	30.3	1.0	-	-	-	-
1959	29.6	-2.3	-	-	-	-	31.3	5.7	-	-	-	-	30.6	-2.2	-	-	-	-	31.8	3.9	-	-	-	-
1960	31.5	-0.9	-	-	-	-	31.1	-1.3	-	-	-	-	30.6	-1.6	-	-	-	-	30.0	-2.0	-	-	-	-
1961	31.1	3.7	-	-	-	-	29.2	-6.1	-	-	-	-	31.4	7.5	-	-	-	-	31.7	1.0	-	-	-	-
1962	31.4	-0.9	-	-	-	-	30.7	-2.2	-	-	-	-	31.4	2.3	-	-	-	-	31.1	-1.0	-	-	-	-
1963	31.0	-0.3	-	-	-	-	31.6	1.9	-	-	-	-	31.4	-0.6	-	-	-	-	31.6	0.6	-	-	-	-
1964	32.0	1.3	-	-	-	-	32.1	0.3	-	-	-	-	32.2	0.3	-	-	-	-	31.5	-2.2	-	-	-	-
1965	32.4	2.9	-	-	-	-	32.4	0.0	-	-	-	-	32.7	0.9	-	-	-	-	32.2	-1.5	-	-	-	-
1966	32.1	-0.3	-	-	-	-	32.6	1.6	-	-	-	-	32.7	0.9	-	-	-	-	33.2	1.5	-	-	-	-
1967	33.1	-0.3	-	-	-	-	33.8	2.1	-	-	-	-	34.3	1.5	-	-	-	-	34.6	0.9	-	-	-	-
1968	34.7	0.3	-	-	-	-	34.7	0.0	-	-	-	-	35.0	0.9	-	-	-	-	35.0	0.0	-	-	-	-
1969	35.6	1.7	-	-	-	-	36.1	1.4	-	-	-	-	35.8	-0.8	-	-	-	-	36.3	1.4	-	-	-	-
1970	36.7	1.1	-	-	-	-	36.8	0.3	-	-	-	-	37.1	0.8	-	-	-	-	37.1	0.0	-	-	-	-
1971	38.1	2.7	-	-	-	-	36.9	-3.1	-	-	-	-	37.2	0.8	-	-	-	-	37.3	0.3	-	-	-	-
1972	37.5	0.5	-	-	-	-	37.1	-1.1	-	-	-	-	37.4	0.8	-	-	-	-	38.1	1.9	-	-	-	-
1973	37.9	-0.5	-	-	-	-	38.2	0.8	-	-	-	-	38.7	1.3	-	-	-	-	38.7	0.0	-	-	-	-
1974	39.8	2.8	-	-	-	-	41.1	3.3	-	-	-	-	43.2	5.1	-	-	-	-	43.6	0.9	-	-	-	-
1975	45.0	3.2	-	-	-	-	45.2	0.4	-	-	-	-	47.6	5.3	-	-	-	-	48.0	0.8	-	-	-	-
1976	49.0	2.1	-	-	-	-	49.4	0.8	-	-	-	-	52.2	5.7	-	-	-	-	52.9	1.3	-	-	-	-
1977	53.6	1.3	-	-	-	-	56.4	5.2	-	-	-	-	56.6	0.4	-	-	-	-	56.6	0.0	-	-	-	-
1978	58.2	2.8	-	-	58.0	-0.3	-	-	60.7	4.7	-	-	62.3	2.6	-	-	63.3	1.6	-	-	63.8	0.8	-	-
1979	64.2	0.6	-	-	66.8	4.0	-	-	69.8	4.5	-	-	72.8	4.3	-	-	73.5	1.0	-	-	74.2	1.0	-	-
1980	76.3	2.8	-	-	78.5	2.9	-	-	79.8	1.7	-	-	80.8	1.3	-	-	82.1	1.6	-	-	83.9	2.2	-	-
1981	85.8	2.3	-	-	88.5	3.1	-	-	90.3	2.0	-	-	92.1	2.0	-	-	93.6	1.6	-	-	95.2	1.7	-	-
1982	96.8	1.7	-	-	95.1	-1.8	-	-	95.2	0.1	-	-	98.5	3.5	-	-	98.5	0.0	-	-	98.1	-0.4	-	-
1983	96.7	-1.4	-	-	94.0	-2.8	-	-	96.7	2.9	-	-	99.9	3.3	-	-	100.9	1.0	-	-	101.7	0.8	-	-
1984	101.4	-0.3	-	-	101.5	0.1	-	-	105.5	3.9	-	-	105.3	-0.2	-	-	105.1	-0.2	-	-	106.5	1.3	-	-
1985	107.4	0.8	-	-	107.0	-0.4	-	-	108.2	1.1	-	-	108.9	0.6	-	-	109.9	0.9	-	-	111.3	1.3	-	-
1986	112.7	1.3	-	-	107.6	-4.5	-	-	106.1	-1.4	-	-	108.0	1.8	-	-	106.8	-1.1	-	-	105.2	-1.5	-	-
1987	-	-	-	-	-	-	-	-	-	-	102.2	-2.9	-	-	-	-	-	-	-	-	-	-	105.2	2.9
1988	-	-	-	-	-	-	-	-	-	-	106.0	0.8	-	-	-	-	-	-	-	-	-	-	108.1	2.0
1989	-	-	-	-	-	-	-	-	-	-	111.6	3.2	-	-	-	-	-	-	-	-	-	-	112.1	0.4
1990	-	-	-	-	-	-	-	-	-	-	113.4	1.2	-	-	-	-	-	-	-	-	-	-	120.0	5.8
1991	-	-	-	-	-	-	-	-	-	-	117.7	-1.9	-	-	-	-	-	-	-	-	-	-	119.4	1.4

[Continued]

Portland, OR-WA
Consumer Price Index - Urban Wage Earners
Base 1982-1984 = 100
Transportation
[Continued]

For 1947-1995. Columns headed % show percentile change in the index from the previous period for which an index is available.

Year	Jan		Feb		Mar		Apr		May		Jun		Jul		Aug		Sep		Oct		Nov		Dec	
	Index	%	Index	%	Index	%	Index	%	Index	%	Index	%	Index	%	Index	%	Index	%	Index	%	Index	%	Index	%
1992	-	-	-	-	-	-	-	-	-	-	119.6	0.2	-	-	-	-	-	-	-	-	-	-	124.2	3.8
1993	-	-	-	-	-	-	-	-	-	-	125.5	1.0	-	-	-	-	-	-	-	-	-	-	125.9	0.3
1994	-	-	-	-	-	-	-	-	-	-	126.0	0.1	-	-	-	-	-	-	-	-	-	-	129.7	2.9
1995	-	-	-	-	-	-	-	-	-	-	131.3	1.2	-	-	-	-	-	-	-	-	-	-	-	-

Source: U.S. Department of Labor, Bureau of Labor Statistics, Division of Consumer Prices and Price Indexes. - indicates no data collected for period.

Portland, OR-WA
Consumer Price Index - All Urban Consumers
Base 1982-1984 = 100
Medical Care

For 1947-1995. Columns headed % show percentile change in the index from the previous period for which an index is available.

Year	Jan Index	%	Feb Index	%	Mar Index	%	Apr Index	%	May Index	%	Jun Index	%	Jul Index	%	Aug Index	%	Sep Index	%	Oct Index	%	Nov Index	%	Dec Index	%
1947	-		-		14.1		-		-		14.1	0.0	14.1	0.0	-		-		14.5	2.8	-		-	
1948	14.6	0.7	-		-		14.6	0.0	-		-		14.8	1.4	-		-		14.8	0.0	-		-	
1949	14.9	0.7	-		-		15.0	0.7	-		-		15.0	0.0	-		-		15.1	0.7	-		-	
1950	15.1	0.0	-		-		15.1	0.0	-		-		15.6	3.3	-		-		15.8	1.3	-		-	
1951	15.8	0.0	-		-		16.2	2.5	-		-		16.2	0.0	-		-		16.7	3.1	-		-	
1952	16.8	0.6	-		-		17.0	1.2	-		-		17.2	1.2	-		-		17.2	0.0	-		-	
1953	17.2	0.0	-		-		17.3	0.6	-		-		17.5	1.2	-		-		17.7	1.1	-		-	
1954	17.7	0.0	-		-		17.8	0.6	-		-		17.9	0.6	-		-		18.0	0.6	-		-	
1955	18.4	2.2	-		-		18.5	0.5	-		-		18.4	-0.5	-		-		18.9	2.7	-		-	
1956	18.9	0.0	-		-		19.0	0.5	-		-		19.2	1.1	-		-		19.5	1.6	-		-	
1957	20.0	2.6	-		-		20.2	1.0	-		-		20.3	0.5	-		-		20.4	0.5	-		-	
1958	20.5	0.5	-		-		20.6	0.5	-		-		20.6	0.0	-		-		20.7	0.5	-		-	
1959	20.7	0.0	-		-		20.7	0.0	-		-		20.8	0.5	-		-		20.8	0.0	-		-	
1960	20.8	0.0	-		-		21.8	4.8	-		-		21.9	0.5	-		-		22.2	1.4	-		-	
1961	22.2	0.0	-		-		22.4	0.9	-		-		22.6	0.9	-		-		22.5	-0.4	-		-	
1962	22.3	-0.9	-		-		22.4	0.4	-		-		22.5	0.4	-		-		22.6	0.4	-		-	
1963	22.8	0.9	-		-		22.8	0.0	-		-		23.0	0.9	-		-		23.4	1.7	-		-	
1964	23.4	0.0	-		-		24.1	3.0	-		-		24.7	2.5	-		-		24.8	0.4	-		-	
1965	24.9	0.4	-		-		25.0	0.4	-		-		25.3	1.2	-		-		25.3	0.0	-		-	
1966	25.6	1.2	-		-		25.7	0.4	-		-		25.9	0.8	-		-		26.4	1.9	-		-	
1967	27.1	2.7	-		-		27.2	0.4	-		-		27.7	1.8	-		-		28.2	1.8	-		-	
1968	28.8	2.1	-		-		28.8	0.0	-		-		29.0	0.7	-		-		29.6	2.1	-		-	
1969	30.0	1.4	-		-		30.5	1.7	-		-		31.0	1.6	-		-		31.2	0.6	-		-	
1970	32.1	2.9	-		-		32.6	1.6	-		-		33.1	1.5	-		-		33.2	0.3	-		-	
1971	34.1	2.7	-		-		34.2	0.3	-		-		34.2	0.0	-		-		34.1	-0.3	-		-	
1972	34.6	1.5	-		-		34.9	0.9	-		-		35.3	1.1	-		-		36.0	2.0	-		-	
1973	36.3	0.8	-		-		37.3	2.8	-		-		37.3	0.0	-		-		38.6	3.5	-		-	
1974	39.3	1.8	-		-		40.1	2.0	-		-		42.1	5.0	-		-		42.6	1.2	-		-	
1975	44.1	3.5	-		-		45.0	2.0	-		-		46.6	3.6	-		-		46.9	0.6	-		-	
1976	48.7	3.8	-		-		49.0	0.6	-		-		50.3	2.7	-		-		50.9	1.2	-		-	
1977	53.3	4.7	-		-		54.4	2.1	-		-		55.7	2.4	-		-		56.1	0.7	-		-	
1978	57.6	2.7	-		59.2	2.8	-		59.7	0.8	-		60.6	1.5	-		61.0	0.7	-		61.8	1.3	-	
1979	63.5	2.8	-		64.0	0.8	-		64.5	0.8	-		65.6	1.7	-		67.2	2.4	-		68.8	2.4	-	
1980	70.6	2.6	-		73.0	3.4	-		73.7	1.0	-		74.0	0.4	-		76.1	2.8	-		76.6	0.7	-	
1981	78.6	2.6	-		79.3	0.9	-		81.2	2.4	-		84.5	4.1	-		85.3	0.9	-		88.0	3.2	-	
1982	89.4	1.6	-		91.0	1.8	-		92.3	1.4	-		94.3	2.2	-		95.4	1.2	-		96.7	1.4	-	
1983	99.0	2.4	-		99.8	0.8	-		100.3	0.5	-		100.7	0.4	-		100.4	-0.3	-		102.1	1.7	-	
1984	104.7	2.5	-		105.0	0.3	-		104.8	-0.2	-		105.9	1.0	-		106.4	0.5	-		107.1	0.7	-	
1985	108.7	1.5	-		109.0	0.3	-		109.6	0.6	-		112.0	2.2	-		112.3	0.3	-		114.0	1.5	-	
1986	116.0	1.8	-		116.9	0.8	-		119.4	2.1	-		120.1	0.6	-		119.7	-0.3	-		121.1	1.2	-	
1987	-		-		-		-		-		126.1	4.1	-		-		-		-		-		131.4	4.2
1988	-		-		-		-		-		134.2	2.1	-		-		-		-		-		139.5	3.9
1989	-		-		-		-		-		145.1	4.0	-		-		-		-		-		150.6	3.8
1990	-		-		-		-		-		157.5	4.6	-		-		-		-		-		163.5	3.8
1991	-		-		-		-		-		168.4	3.0	-		-		-		-		-		177.4	5.3

[Continued]

Portland, OR-WA
Consumer Price Index - All Urban Consumers
Base 1982-1984 = 100
Medical Care

[Continued]

For 1947-1995. Columns headed % show percentile change in the index from the previous period for which an index is available.

Year	Jan		Feb		Mar		Apr		May		Jun		Jul		Aug		Sep		Oct		Nov		Dec	
	Index	%	Index	%	Index	%	Index	%	Index	%	Index	%	Index	%	Index	%	Index	%	Index	%	Index	%	Index	%
1992	-	-	-	-	-	-	-	-	-	-	183.8	3.6	-	-	-	-	-	-	-	-	-	-	190.2	3.5
1993	-	-	-	-	-	-	-	-	-	-	196.3	3.2	-	-	-	-	-	-	-	-	-	-	201.8	2.8
1994	-	-	-	-	-	-	-	-	-	-	203.2	0.7	-	-	-	-	-	-	-	-	-	-	205.5	1.1
1995	-	-	-	-	-	-	-	-	-	-	208.2	1.3	-	-	-	-	-	-	-	-	-	-	-	-

Source: U.S. Department of Labor, Bureau of Labor Statistics, Division of Consumer Prices and Price Indexes. - indicates no data collected for period.

Portland, OR-WA
Consumer Price Index - Urban Wage Earners
Base 1982-1984 = 100
Medical Care

For 1947-1995. Columns headed % show percentile change in the index from the previous period for which an index is available.

Year	Jan Index	%	Feb Index	%	Mar Index	%	Apr Index	%	May Index	%	Jun Index	%	Jul Index	%	Aug Index	%	Sep Index	%	Oct Index	%	Nov Index	%	Dec Index	%
1947	-	-	-	-	15.7	-	-	-	-	-	15.7	0.0	15.7	0.0	-	-	-	-	16.2	3.2	-	-	-	-
1948	16.2	0.0	-	-	-	-	16.3	0.6	-	-	-	-	16.5	1.2	-	-	-	-	16.5	0.0	-	-	-	-
1949	16.6	0.6	-	-	-	-	16.7	0.6	-	-	-	-	16.7	0.0	-	-	-	-	16.8	0.6	-	-	-	-
1950	16.8	0.0	-	-	-	-	16.8	0.0	-	-	-	-	17.3	3.0	-	-	-	-	17.6	1.7	-	-	-	-
1951	17.6	0.0	-	-	-	-	18.1	2.8	-	-	-	-	18.1	0.0	-	-	-	-	18.6	2.8	-	-	-	-
1952	18.7	0.5	-	-	-	-	18.9	1.1	-	-	-	-	19.1	1.1	-	-	-	-	19.1	0.0	-	-	-	-
1953	19.2	0.5	-	-	-	-	19.2	0.0	-	-	-	-	19.5	1.6	-	-	-	-	19.7	1.0	-	-	-	-
1954	19.7	0.0	-	-	-	-	19.8	0.5	-	-	-	-	19.9	0.5	-	-	-	-	20.0	0.5	-	-	-	-
1955	20.4	2.0	-	-	-	-	20.6	1.0	-	-	-	-	20.5	-0.5	-	-	-	-	21.0	2.4	-	-	-	-
1956	21.0	0.0	-	-	-	-	21.2	1.0	-	-	-	-	21.4	0.9	-	-	-	-	21.7	1.4	-	-	-	-
1957	22.3	2.8	-	-	-	-	22.5	0.9	-	-	-	-	22.7	0.9	-	-	-	-	22.7	0.0	-	-	-	-
1958	22.8	0.4	-	-	-	-	22.9	0.4	-	-	-	-	22.9	0.0	-	-	-	-	23.0	0.4	-	-	-	-
1959	23.0	0.0	-	-	-	-	23.0	0.0	-	-	-	-	23.2	0.9	-	-	-	-	23.2	0.0	-	-	-	-
1960	23.2	0.0	-	-	-	-	24.3	4.7	-	-	-	-	24.4	0.4	-	-	-	-	24.7	1.2	-	-	-	-
1961	24.7	0.0	-	-	-	-	25.0	1.2	-	-	-	-	25.2	0.8	-	-	-	-	25.1	-0.4	-	-	-	-
1962	24.8	-1.2	-	-	-	-	24.9	0.4	-	-	-	-	25.1	0.8	-	-	-	-	25.2	0.4	-	-	-	-
1963	25.4	0.8	-	-	-	-	25.4	0.0	-	-	-	-	25.6	0.8	-	-	-	-	26.0	1.6	-	-	-	-
1964	26.1	0.4	-	-	-	-	26.8	2.7	-	-	-	-	27.5	2.6	-	-	-	-	27.6	0.4	-	-	-	-
1965	27.7	0.4	-	-	-	-	27.8	0.4	-	-	-	-	28.2	1.4	-	-	-	-	28.2	0.0	-	-	-	-
1966	28.5	1.1	-	-	-	-	28.6	0.4	-	-	-	-	28.8	0.7	-	-	-	-	29.4	2.1	-	-	-	-
1967	30.2	2.7	-	-	-	-	30.3	0.3	-	-	-	-	30.9	2.0	-	-	-	-	31.4	1.6	-	-	-	-
1968	32.1	2.2	-	-	-	-	32.1	0.0	-	-	-	-	32.3	0.6	-	-	-	-	33.0	2.2	-	-	-	-
1969	33.4	1.2	-	-	-	-	34.0	1.8	-	-	-	-	34.5	1.5	-	-	-	-	34.8	0.9	-	-	-	-
1970	35.7	2.6	-	-	-	-	36.3	1.7	-	-	-	-	36.9	1.7	-	-	-	-	36.9	0.0	-	-	-	-
1971	37.9	2.7	-	-	-	-	38.1	0.5	-	-	-	-	38.1	0.0	-	-	-	-	37.9	-0.5	-	-	-	-
1972	38.6	1.8	-	-	-	-	38.8	0.5	-	-	-	-	39.4	1.5	-	-	-	-	40.0	1.5	-	-	-	-
1973	40.4	1.0	-	-	-	-	41.5	2.7	-	-	-	-	41.5	0.0	-	-	-	-	42.9	3.4	-	-	-	-
1974	43.8	2.1	-	-	-	-	44.6	1.8	-	-	-	-	46.8	4.9	-	-	-	-	47.4	1.3	-	-	-	-
1975	49.1	3.6	-	-	-	-	50.1	2.0	-	-	-	-	51.9	3.6	-	-	-	-	52.2	0.6	-	-	-	-
1976	54.2	3.8	-	-	-	-	54.5	0.6	-	-	-	-	56.0	2.8	-	-	-	-	56.6	1.1	-	-	-	-
1977	59.4	4.9	-	-	-	-	60.5	1.9	-	-	-	-	62.0	2.5	-	-	-	-	62.4	0.6	-	-	-	-
1978	64.1	2.7	-	-	65.1	1.6	-	-	65.3	0.3	-	-	66.2	1.4	-	-	66.9	1.1	-	-	68.0	1.6	-	-
1979	68.8	1.2	-	-	70.2	2.0	-	-	71.4	1.7	-	-	72.6	1.7	-	-	72.7	0.1	-	-	73.8	1.5	-	-
1980	74.8	1.4	-	-	76.0	1.6	-	-	77.7	2.2	-	-	78.2	0.6	-	-	78.7	0.6	-	-	79.2	0.6	-	-
1981	79.7	0.6	-	-	80.5	1.0	-	-	82.4	2.4	-	-	85.3	3.5	-	-	84.8	-0.6	-	-	87.9	3.7	-	-
1982	89.5	1.8	-	-	91.0	1.7	-	-	92.4	1.5	-	-	94.6	2.4	-	-	95.7	1.2	-	-	97.0	1.4	-	-
1983	99.5	2.6	-	-	100.2	0.7	-	-	100.7	0.5	-	-	100.9	0.2	-	-	100.6	-0.3	-	-	102.0	1.4	-	-
1984	104.4	2.4	-	-	104.6	0.2	-	-	104.3	-0.3	-	-	105.4	1.1	-	-	106.1	0.7	-	-	106.6	0.5	-	-
1985	108.3	1.6	-	-	108.7	0.4	-	-	109.2	0.5	-	-	111.9	2.5	-	-	112.4	0.4	-	-	114.1	1.5	-	-
1986	115.8	1.5	-	-	116.8	0.9	-	-	119.0	1.9	-	-	119.6	0.5	-	-	119.0	-0.5	-	-	120.6	1.3	-	-
1987	-	-	-	-	-	-	-	-	-	-	127.2	5.5	-	-	-	-	-	-	-	-	-	-	132.7	4.3
1988	-	-	-	-	-	-	-	-	-	-	135.5	2.1	-	-	-	-	-	-	-	-	-	-	140.7	3.8
1989	-	-	-	-	-	-	-	-	-	-	146.4	4.1	-	-	-	-	-	-	-	-	-	-	151.6	3.6
1990	-	-	-	-	-	-	-	-	-	-	158.0	4.2	-	-	-	-	-	-	-	-	-	-	163.5	3.5
1991	-	-	-	-	-	-	-	-	-	-	167.9	2.7	-	-	-	-	-	-	-	-	-	-	176.3	5.0

[Continued]

Portland, OR-WA
Consumer Price Index - Urban Wage Earners
Base 1982-1984 = 100
Medical Care
[Continued]

For 1947-1995. Columns headed % show percentile change in the index from the previous period for which an index is available.

Year	Jan		Feb		Mar		Apr		May		Jun		Jul		Aug		Sep		Oct		Nov		Dec	
	Index	%	Index	%	Index	%	Index	%	Index	%	Index	%	Index	%	Index	%	Index	%	Index	%	Index	%	Index	%
1992	-	-	-	-	-	-	-	-	-	-	183.0	3.8	-	-	-	-	-	-	-	-	-	-	189.7	3.7
1993	-	-	-	-	-	-	-	-	-	-	195.4	3.0	-	-	-	-	-	-	-	-	-	-	200.4	2.6
1994	-	-	-	-	-	-	-	-	-	-	201.4	0.5	-	-	-	-	-	-	-	-	-	-	203.4	1.0
1995	-	-	-	-	-	-	-	-	-	-	206.1	1.3	-	-	-	-	-	-	-	-	-	-	-	-

Source: U.S. Department of Labor, Bureau of Labor Statistics, Division of Consumer Prices and Price Indexes. - indicates no data collected for period.

Portland, OR-WA
Consumer Price Index - All Urban Consumers
Base 1982-1984 = 100
Entertainment

For 1976-1995. Columns headed % show percentile change in the index from the previous period for which an index is available.

Year	Jan Index	%	Feb Index	%	Mar Index	%	Apr Index	%	May Index	%	Jun Index	%	Jul Index	%	Aug Index	%	Sep Index	%	Oct Index	%	Nov Index	%	Dec Index	%
1976	68.4	-	-	-	-	-	68.4	0.0	-	-	-	-	68.3	-0.1	-	-	-	-	69.4	1.6	-	-	-	-
1977	70.8	2.0	-	-	-	-	71.2	0.6	-	-	-	-	70.4	-1.1	-	-	-	-	72.3	2.7	-	-	-	-
1978	72.9	0.8	-	-	74.5	2.2	-	-	75.7	1.6	-	-	76.8	1.5	-	-	76.9	0.1	-	-	77.1	0.3	-	-
1979	78.2	1.4	-	-	80.6	3.1	-	-	81.6	1.2	-	-	81.0	-0.7	-	-	80.7	-0.4	-	-	80.7	0.0	-	-
1980	83.7	3.7	-	-	87.6	4.7	-	-	87.9	0.3	-	-	87.0	-1.0	-	-	87.5	0.6	-	-	86.3	-1.4	-	-
1981	91.2	5.7	-	-	92.3	1.2	-	-	90.1	-2.4	-	-	88.9	-1.3	-	-	89.5	0.7	-	-	90.2	0.8	-	-
1982	92.9	3.0	-	-	93.6	0.8	-	-	96.4	3.0	-	-	96.6	0.2	-	-	94.7	-2.0	-	-	93.5	-1.3	-	-
1983	98.1	4.9	-	-	100.2	2.1	-	-	102.5	2.3	-	-	102.1	-0.4	-	-	102.8	0.7	-	-	101.6	-1.2	-	-
1984	102.3	0.7	-	-	103.0	0.7	-	-	104.0	1.0	-	-	103.3	-0.7	-	-	103.1	-0.2	-	-	105.9	2.7	-	-
1985	107.7	1.7	-	-	109.2	1.4	-	-	108.5	-0.6	-	-	111.3	2.6	-	-	110.8	-0.4	-	-	109.7	-1.0	-	-
1986	109.0	-0.6	-	-	107.1	-1.7	-	-	110.7	3.4	-	-	112.4	1.5	-	-	112.2	-0.2	-	-	114.3	1.9	-	-
1987	-	-	-	-	-	-	-	-	-	-	121.0	5.9	-	-	-	-	-	-	-	-	-	-	122.3	1.1
1988	-	-	-	-	-	-	-	-	-	-	127.9	4.6	-	-	-	-	-	-	-	-	-	-	130.3	1.9
1989	-	-	-	-	-	-	-	-	-	-	133.8	2.7	-	-	-	-	-	-	-	-	-	-	132.5	-1.0
1990	-	-	-	-	-	-	-	-	-	-	136.7	3.2	-	-	-	-	-	-	-	-	-	-	144.7	5.9
1991	-	-	-	-	-	-	-	-	-	-	149.8	3.5	-	-	-	-	-	-	-	-	-	-	154.9	3.4
1992	-	-	-	-	-	-	-	-	-	-	156.6	1.1	-	-	-	-	-	-	-	-	-	-	156.5	-0.1
1993	-	-	-	-	-	-	-	-	-	-	161.0	2.9	-	-	-	-	-	-	-	-	-	-	163.6	1.6
1994	-	-	-	-	-	-	-	-	-	-	165.0	0.9	-	-	-	-	-	-	-	-	-	-	164.1	-0.5
1995	-	-	-	-	-	-	-	-	-	-	166.2	1.3	-	-	-	-	-	-	-	-	-	-	-	-

Source: U.S. Department of Labor, Bureau of Labor Statistics, Division of Consumer Prices and Price Indexes. - indicates no data collected for period.

Portland, OR-WA
Consumer Price Index - Urban Wage Earners
Base 1982-1984 = 100
Entertainment

For 1976-1995. Columns headed % show percentile change in the index from the previous period for which an index is available.

Year	Jan Index	%	Feb Index	%	Mar Index	%	Apr Index	%	May Index	%	Jun Index	%	Jul Index	%	Aug Index	%	Sep Index	%	Oct Index	%	Nov Index	%	Dec Index	%
1976	75.2	-	-	-	-	-	75.3	0.1	-	-	-	-	75.2	-0.1	-	-	-	-	76.3	1.5	-	-	-	-
1977	77.9	2.1	-	-	-	-	78.4	0.6	-	-	-	-	77.4	-1.3	-	-	-	-	79.5	2.7	-	-	-	-
1978	80.2	0.9	-	-	81.1	1.1	-	-	81.1	0.0	-	-	83.0	2.3	-	-	83.9	1.1	-	-	84.6	0.8	-	-
1979	84.9	0.4	-	-	85.4	0.6	-	-	88.2	3.3	-	-	86.7	-1.7	-	-	87.4	0.8	-	-	87.6	0.2	-	-
1980	88.2	0.7	-	-	94.8	7.5	-	-	96.1	1.4	-	-	96.2	0.1	-	-	96.2	0.0	-	-	94.8	-1.5	-	-
1981	93.5	-1.4	-	-	94.2	0.7	-	-	90.1	-4.4	-	-	90.5	0.4	-	-	92.0	1.7	-	-	90.8	-1.3	-	-
1982	93.4	2.9	-	-	94.1	0.7	-	-	97.6	3.7	-	-	97.4	-0.2	-	-	95.1	-2.4	-	-	92.4	-2.8	-	-
1983	97.2	5.2	-	-	99.7	2.6	-	-	102.2	2.5	-	-	102.1	-0.1	-	-	103.0	0.9	-	-	101.4	-1.6	-	-
1984	102.8	1.4	-	-	102.9	0.1	-	-	104.1	1.2	-	-	103.2	-0.9	-	-	103.0	-0.2	-	-	105.2	2.1	-	-
1985	107.0	1.7	-	-	108.4	1.3	-	-	107.8	-0.6	-	-	111.6	3.5	-	-	110.9	-0.6	-	-	109.4	-1.4	-	-
1986	108.7	-0.6	-	-	106.5	-2.0	-	-	109.6	2.9	-	-	111.6	1.8	-	-	111.2	-0.4	-	-	113.3	1.9	-	-
1987	-	-	-	-	-	-	-	-	-	-	116.9	3.2	-	-	-	-	-	-	-	-	-	-	117.8	0.8
1988	-	-	-	-	-	-	-	-	-	-	122.8	4.2	-	-	-	-	-	-	-	-	-	-	125.2	2.0
1989	-	-	-	-	-	-	-	-	-	-	129.8	3.7	-	-	-	-	-	-	-	-	-	-	130.3	0.4
1990	-	-	-	-	-	-	-	-	-	-	134.6	3.3	-	-	-	-	-	-	-	-	-	-	138.0	2.5
1991	-	-	-	-	-	-	-	-	-	-	141.6	2.6	-	-	-	-	-	-	-	-	-	-	145.3	2.6
1992	-	-	-	-	-	-	-	-	-	-	147.6	1.6	-	-	-	-	-	-	-	-	-	-	147.3	-0.2
1993	-	-	-	-	-	-	-	-	-	-	150.5	2.2	-	-	-	-	-	-	-	-	-	-	152.7	1.5
1994	-	-	-	-	-	-	-	-	-	-	153.5	0.5	-	-	-	-	-	-	-	-	-	-	152.3	-0.8
1995	-	-	-	-	-	-	-	-	-	-	154.8	1.6	-	-	-	-	-	-	-	-	-	-	-	-

Source: U.S. Department of Labor, Bureau of Labor Statistics, Division of Consumer Prices and Price Indexes. - indicates no data collected for period.

Portland, OR-WA
Consumer Price Index - All Urban Consumers
Base 1982-1984 = 100
Other Goods and Services

For 1976-1995. Columns headed % show percentile change in the index from the previous period for which an index is available.

Year	Jan Index	%	Feb Index	%	Mar Index	%	Apr Index	%	May Index	%	Jun Index	%	Jul Index	%	Aug Index	%	Sep Index	%	Oct Index	%	Nov Index	%	Dec Index	%
1976	50.4	-	-	-	-	-	51.2	1.6	-	-	-	-	52.7	2.9	-	-	-	-	53.1	0.8	-	-	-	-
1977	54.8	3.2	-	-	-	-	55.3	0.9	-	-	-	-	56.2	1.6	-	-	-	-	57.6	2.5	-	-	-	-
1978	58.3	1.2	-	-	58.5	0.3	-	-	59.3	1.4	-	-	60.2	1.5	-	-	62.1	3.2	-	-	62.2	0.2	-	-
1979	63.5	2.1	-	-	64.3	1.3	-	-	64.4	0.2	-	-	64.0	-0.6	-	-	67.0	4.7	-	-	68.1	1.6	-	-
1980	71.0	4.3	-	-	71.3	0.4	-	-	72.7	2.0	-	-	73.4	1.0	-	-	75.4	2.7	-	-	76.1	0.9	-	-
1981	78.5	3.2	-	-	79.7	1.5	-	-	80.5	1.0	-	-	81.5	1.2	-	-	84.2	3.3	-	-	85.9	2.0	-	-
1982	88.6	3.1	-	-	89.8	1.4	-	-	90.8	1.1	-	-	92.5	1.9	-	-	95.0	2.7	-	-	95.8	0.8	-	-
1983	99.3	3.7	-	-	99.0	-0.3	-	-	100.3	1.3	-	-	101.4	1.1	-	-	103.0	1.6	-	-	105.0	1.9	-	-
1984	103.8	-1.1	-	-	105.5	1.6	-	-	105.2	-0.3	-	-	105.7	0.5	-	-	107.4	1.6	-	-	106.9	-0.5	-	-
1985	108.5	1.5	-	-	109.1	0.6	-	-	108.5	-0.5	-	-	110.0	1.4	-	-	113.9	3.5	-	-	116.9	2.6	-	-
1986	118.8	1.6	-	-	119.0	0.2	-	-	120.7	1.4	-	-	121.1	0.3	-	-	121.9	0.7	-	-	122.4	0.4	-	-
1987	-	-	-	-	-	-	-	-	-	-	128.6	5.1	-	-	-	-	-	-	-	-	-	-	133.1	3.5
1988	-	-	-	-	-	-	-	-	-	-	137.9	3.6	-	-	-	-	-	-	-	-	-	-	142.3	3.2
1989	-	-	-	-	-	-	-	-	-	-	149.2	4.8	-	-	-	-	-	-	-	-	-	-	155.1	4.0
1990	-	-	-	-	-	-	-	-	-	-	159.3	2.7	-	-	-	-	-	-	-	-	-	-	162.8	2.2
1991	-	-	-	-	-	-	-	-	-	-	169.8	4.3	-	-	-	-	-	-	-	-	-	-	179.2	5.5
1992	-	-	-	-	-	-	-	-	-	-	191.6	6.9	-	-	-	-	-	-	-	-	-	-	200.2	4.5
1993	-	-	-	-	-	-	-	-	-	-	206.6	3.2	-	-	-	-	-	-	-	-	-	-	207.4	0.4
1994	-	-	-	-	-	-	-	-	-	-	211.1	1.8	-	-	-	-	-	-	-	-	-	-	215.4	2.0
1995	-	-	-	-	-	-	-	-	-	-	218.3	1.3	-	-	-	-	-	-	-	-	-	-	-	-

Source: U.S. Department of Labor, Bureau of Labor Statistics, Division of Consumer Prices and Price Indexes. - indicates no data collected for period.

Portland, OR-WA
Consumer Price Index - Urban Wage Earners
Base 1982-1984 = 100
Other Goods and Services

For 1976-1995. Columns headed % show percentile change in the index from the previous period for which an index is available.

Year	Jan Index	%	Feb Index	%	Mar Index	%	Apr Index	%	May Index	%	Jun Index	%	Jul Index	%	Aug Index	%	Sep Index	%	Oct Index	%	Nov Index	%	Dec Index	%
1976	53.8	-	-	-	-	-	54.6	1.5	-	-	-	-	56.2	2.9	-	-	-	-	56.6	0.7	-	-	-	-
1977	58.5	3.4	-	-	-	-	58.9	0.7	-	-	-	-	60.0	1.9	-	-	-	-	61.4	2.3	-	-	-	-
1978	62.1	1.1	-	-	62.2	0.2	-	-	62.7	0.8	-	-	63.3	1.0	-	-	64.4	1.7	-	-	64.7	0.5	-	-
1979	65.6	1.4	-	-	66.6	1.5	-	-	66.5	-0.2	-	-	66.6	0.2	-	-	68.7	3.2	-	-	69.9	1.7	-	-
1980	72.2	3.3	-	-	72.3	0.1	-	-	72.9	0.8	-	-	73.9	1.4	-	-	75.4	2.0	-	-	76.1	0.9	-	-
1981	78.0	2.5	-	-	78.7	0.9	-	-	80.3	2.0	-	-	80.9	0.7	-	-	82.7	2.2	-	-	84.7	2.4	-	-
1982	87.7	3.5	-	-	89.2	1.7	-	-	90.2	1.1	-	-	92.1	2.1	-	-	94.8	2.9	-	-	95.9	1.2	-	-
1983	100.0	4.3	-	-	99.3	-0.7	-	-	100.9	1.6	-	-	102.3	1.4	-	-	103.5	1.2	-	-	105.5	1.9	-	-
1984	104.0	-1.4	-	-	105.3	1.3	-	-	105.2	-0.1	-	-	105.8	0.6	-	-	107.1	1.2	-	-	106.1	-0.9	-	-
1985	108.1	1.9	-	-	108.8	0.6	-	-	108.1	-0.6	-	-	110.0	1.8	-	-	113.0	2.7	-	-	116.8	3.4	-	-
1986	118.6	1.5	-	-	118.1	-0.4	-	-	119.9	1.5	-	-	120.4	0.4	-	-	120.9	0.4	-	-	121.1	0.2	-	-
1987	-	-	-	-	-	-	-	-	-	-	128.1	5.8	-	-	-	-	-	-	-	-	-	-	132.7	3.6
1988	-	-	-	-	-	-	-	-	-	-	137.6	3.7	-	-	-	-	-	-	-	-	-	-	142.6	3.6
1989	-	-	-	-	-	-	-	-	-	-	151.2	6.0	-	-	-	-	-	-	-	-	-	-	157.9	4.4
1990	-	-	-	-	-	-	-	-	-	-	162.6	3.0	-	-	-	-	-	-	-	-	-	-	166.4	2.3
1991	-	-	-	-	-	-	-	-	-	-	173.7	4.4	-	-	-	-	-	-	-	-	-	-	181.9	4.7
1992	-	-	-	-	-	-	-	-	-	-	192.2	5.7	-	-	-	-	-	-	-	-	-	-	199.4	3.7
1993	-	-	-	-	-	-	-	-	-	-	205.9	3.3	-	-	-	-	-	-	-	-	-	-	203.7	-1.1
1994	-	-	-	-	-	-	-	-	-	-	207.2	1.7	-	-	-	-	-	-	-	-	-	-	210.4	1.5
1995	-	-	-	-	-	-	-	-	-	-	213.2	1.3	-	-	-	-	-	-	-	-	-	-	-	-

Source: U.S. Department of Labor, Bureau of Labor Statistics, Division of Consumer Prices and Price Indexes. - indicates no data collected for period.

San Diego, CA
Consumer Price Index - All Urban Consumers
Base 1982-1984 = 100
Annual Averages

For 1965-1995. Columns headed % show percentile change in the index from the previous period for which an index is available.

Year	All Items		Food & Beverage		Housing		Apparel & Upkeep		Trans- portation		Medical Care		Entertain- ment		Other Goods & Services	
	Index	%	Index	%	Index	%	Index	%	Index	%	Index	%	Index	%	Index	%
1965	28.2	-	-	-	-	-	48.1	-	32.1	-	26.6	-	-	-	-	-
1966	28.7	1.8	-	-	-	-	48.7	1.2	32.1	0.0	28.0	5.3	-	-	-	-
1967	29.6	3.1	-	-	-	-	49.5	1.6	33.3	3.7	30.0	7.1	-	-	-	-
1968	30.8	4.1	-	-	-	-	52.4	5.9	34.1	2.4	30.8	2.7	-	-	-	-
1969	32.4	5.2	-	-	-	-	54.7	4.4	34.9	2.3	32.4	5.2	-	-	-	-
1970	34.1	5.2	-	-	-	-	56.8	3.8	35.9	2.9	34.5	6.5	-		-	-
1971	35.4	3.8					58.3	2.6	37.9	5.6	36.3	5.2	-	-	-	-
1972	36.8	4.0	-	-	-	-	60.4	3.6	39.0	2.9	37.2	2.5	-	-	-	-
1973	39.2	6.5	-	-	-	-	62.7	3.8	40.7	4.4	39.0	4.8	-	-	-	-
1974	43.5	11.0	-	-	-	-	67.9	8.3	46.1	13.3	43.2	10.8	-	-	-	-
1975	47.6	9.4	-	-	-	-	69.5	2.4	51.0	10.6	48.5	12.3	-	-	-	-
1976	50.5	6.1	59.3	-	44.3	-	71.4	2.7	54.6	7.1	53.6	10.5	62.6	-	58.0	-
1977	53.8	6.5	62.9	6.1	47.9	8.1	72.8	2.0	58.1	6.4	58.6	9.3	65.1	4.0	61.1	5.3
1978	59.2	10.0	69.7	10.8	53.8	12.3	76.9	5.6	61.2	5.3	63.6	8.5	69.3	6.5	66.2	8.3
1979	68.9	16.4	77.3	10.9	65.2	21.2	81.5	6.0	69.9	14.2	69.5	9.3	75.0	8.2	71.3	7.7
1980	79.4	15.2	84.4	9.2	76.8	17.8	87.4	7.2	82.2	17.6	76.2	9.6	83.1	10.8	77.2	8.3
1981	90.1	13.5	90.5	7.2	89.6	16.7	92.2	5.5	91.4	11.2	83.0	8.9	89.9	8.2	85.1	10.2
1982	96.2	6.8	94.8	4.8	96.3	7.5	96.5	4.7	95.7	4.7	93.1	12.2	96.1	6.9	91.5	7.5
1983	99.0	2.9	100.4	5.9	98.6	2.4	99.7	3.3	98.8	3.2	100.7	8.2	100.8	4.9	100.2	9.5
1984	104.8	5.9	104.8	4.4	104.9	6.4	103.8	4.1	105.5	6.8	106.2	5.5	103.1	2.3	108.4	8.2
1985	110.4	5.3	107.2	2.3	113.7	8.4	105.9	2.0	109.4	3.7	110.1	3.7	107.4	4.2	115.7	6.7
1986	113.5	2.8	111.2	3.7	119.2	4.8	107.3	1.3	105.6	-3.5	118.2	7.4	111.9	4.2	120.0	3.7
1987	109.2	-3.8	111.9	0.6	108.1	-9.3	109.4	2.0	102.3	-3.1	124.6	5.4	110.9	-0.9	122.5	2.1
1988	112.8	3.3	114.9	2.7	111.9	3.5	115.6	5.7	103.5	1.2	132.9	6.7	115.5	4.1	127.4	4.0
1989	118.1	4.7	123.1	7.1	116.3	3.9	107.4	-7.1	109.2	5.5	141.6	6.5	126.0	9.1	135.4	6.3
1990	126.8	7.4	133.0	8.0	125.4	7.8	112.0	4.3	116.1	6.3	154.6	9.2	129.9	3.1	146.8	8.4
1991	134.1	5.8	140.6	5.7	134.0	6.9	113.4	1.3	119.9	3.3	169.4	9.6	135.9	4.6	156.5	6.6
1992	139.0	3.7	141.1	0.4	139.3	4.0	118.7	4.7	123.9	3.3	184.2	8.7	140.1	3.1	169.1	8.1
1993	142.9	2.8	142.4	0.9	143.5	3.0	115.5	-2.7	128.4	3.6	193.1	4.8	144.2	2.9	179.5	6.2
1994	147.8	3.4	146.9	3.2	147.9	3.1	120.9	4.7	135.0	5.1	199.8	3.5	146.7	1.7	184.9	3.0
1995	152.3	3.0	152.0	3.5	151.5	2.4	121.2	0.2	139.5	3.3	209.4	4.8	147.6	0.6	198.0	7.1

Source: U.S. Department of Labor, Bureau of Labor Statistics, Division of Consumer Prices and Price Indexes. - indicates no data collected for period.

San Diego, CA
Consumer Price Index - Urban Wage Earners
Base 1982-1984 = 100
Annual Averages

For 1965-1995. Columns headed % show percentile change in the index from the previous period for which an index is available.

Year	All Items		Food & Beverage		Housing		Apparel & Upkeep		Trans-portation		Medical Care		Entertain-ment		Other Goods & Services	
	Index	%	Index	%	Index	%	Index	%	Index	%	Index	%	Index	%	Index	%
1965	29.5	-	-	-	-	-	50.2	-	31.9	-	26.0	-	-	-	-	-
1966	30.1	2.0	-	-	-	-	50.8	1.2	31.9	0.0	27.4	5.4	-	-	-	-
1967	31.0	3.0	-	-	-	-	51.6	1.6	33.1	3.8	29.4	7.3	-	-	-	-
1968	32.3	4.2	-	-	-	-	54.7	6.0	33.9	2.4	30.1	2.4	-	-	-	-
1969	34.0	5.3	-	-	-	-	57.1	4.4	34.7	2.4	31.7	5.3	-	-	-	-
1970	35.8	5.3	-	-	-	-	59.3	3.9	35.7	2.9	33.7	6.3	-	-	-	-
1971	37.1	3.6	-	-	-	-	60.8	2.5	37.7	5.6	35.5	5.3	-	-	-	-
1972	38.6	4.0	-	-	-	-	63.1	3.8	38.8	2.9	36.4	2.5	-	-	-	-
1973	41.1	6.5	-	-	-	-	65.5	3.8	40.5	4.4	38.2	4.9	-	-	-	-
1974	45.6	10.9	-	-	-	-	70.9	8.2	45.8	13.1	42.3	10.7	-	-	-	-
1975	49.9	9.4	-	-	-	-	72.6	2.4	50.6	10.5	47.4	12.1	-	-	-	-
1976	52.9	6.0	57.9	-	48.1	-	74.6	2.8	54.2	7.1	52.4	10.5	60.8	-	59.3	-
1977	56.4	6.6	61.4	6.0	52.0	8.1	76.0	1.9	57.7	6.5	57.3	9.4	63.2	3.9	62.5	5.4
1978	61.9	9.8	67.9	10.6	58.4	12.3	77.9	2.5	61.0	5.7	62.0	8.2	67.5	6.8	67.6	8.2
1979	71.4	15.3	75.9	11.8	69.9	19.7	81.0	4.0	69.6	14.1	69.4	11.9	73.4	8.7	72.5	7.2
1980	82.1	15.0	82.9	9.2	82.4	17.9	88.5	9.3	81.2	16.7	76.2	9.8	81.8	11.4	78.5	8.3
1981	92.8	13.0	89.9	8.4	96.2	16.7	92.5	4.5	90.2	11.1	83.5	9.6	88.7	8.4	85.0	8.3
1982	99.4	7.1	94.6	5.2	103.7	7.8	96.5	4.3	95.4	5.8	93.1	11.5	96.1	8.3	91.4	7.5
1983	99.0	-0.4	100.5	6.2	98.2	-5.3	99.8	3.4	98.8	3.6	100.6	8.1	100.9	5.0	100.3	9.7
1984	101.7	2.7	104.9	4.4	98.1	-0.1	103.8	4.0	105.9	7.2	106.3	5.7	103.0	2.1	108.3	8.0
1985	104.5	2.8	107.4	2.4	100.8	2.8	106.3	2.4	109.6	3.5	110.6	4.0	107.7	4.6	115.0	6.2
1986	107.2	2.6	111.2	3.5	105.6	4.8	107.5	1.1	106.2	-3.1	118.9	7.5	113.1	5.0	118.9	3.4
1987	107.4	0.2	111.6	0.4	104.5	-1.0	108.3	0.7	102.7	-3.3	126.2	6.1	109.6	-3.1	123.0	3.4
1988	110.9	3.3	114.6	2.7	108.0	3.3	114.1	5.4	104.6	1.9	134.7	6.7	113.4	3.5	128.0	4.1
1989	116.1	4.7	122.7	7.1	111.9	3.6	105.7	-7.4	110.2	5.4	143.4	6.5	124.2	9.5	136.3	6.5
1990	124.4	7.1	132.7	8.1	120.5	7.7	111.0	5.0	116.7	5.9	156.0	8.8	127.8	2.9	147.7	8.4
1991	131.3	5.5	140.2	5.7	128.4	6.6	112.2	1.1	120.6	3.3	170.0	9.0	132.9	4.0	157.4	6.6
1992	136.0	3.6	140.8	0.4	133.0	3.6	117.7	4.9	125.0	3.6	184.9	8.8	136.4	2.6	170.4	8.3
1993	140.0	2.9	142.5	1.2	137.0	3.0	115.0	-2.3	130.1	4.1	193.9	4.9	140.2	2.8	181.6	6.6
1994	145.1	3.6	146.6	2.9	141.4	3.2	120.5	4.8	137.8	5.9	200.2	3.2	143.0	2.0	186.7	2.8
1995	149.3	2.9	151.0	3.0	144.5	2.2	120.4	-0.1	143.1	3.8	209.1	4.4	142.4	-0.4	200.3	7.3

Source: U.S. Department of Labor, Bureau of Labor Statistics, Division of Consumer Prices and Price Indexes. - indicates no data collected for period.

San Diego, CA
Consumer Price Index - All Urban Consumers
Base 1982-1984 = 100
All Items

For 1965-1995. Columns headed % show percentile change in the index from the previous period for which an index is available.

Year	Jan Index	%	Feb Index	%	Mar Index	%	Apr Index	%	May Index	%	Jun Index	%	Jul Index	%	Aug Index	%	Sep Index	%	Oct Index	%	Nov Index	%	Dec Index	%
1965	-	-	28.1	-	-	-	-	-	28.3	0.7	-	-	-	-	28.0	-1.1	-	-	-	-	28.2	0.7	-	-
1966	-	-	28.5	1.1	-	-	-	-	28.6	0.4	-	-	-	-	28.7	0.3	-	-	-	-	29.1	1.4	-	-
1967	-	-	29.2	0.3	-	-	-	-	29.3	0.3	-	-	-	-	29.8	1.7	-	-	-	-	30.0	0.7	-	-
1968	-	-	30.3	1.0	-	-	-	-	30.6	1.0	-	-	-	-	31.0	1.3	-	-	-	-	31.3	1.0	-	-
1969	-	-	31.7	1.3	-	-	-	-	32.2	1.6	-	-	-	-	32.7	1.6	-	-	-	-	32.9	0.6	-	-
1970	-	-	33.4	1.5	-	-	-	-	34.0	1.8	-	-	-	-	34.3	0.9	-	-	-	-	34.8	1.5	-	-
1971	-	-	35.0	0.6	-	-	-	-	35.3	0.9	-	-	-	-	35.6	0.8	-	-	-	-	35.7	0.3	-	-
1972	-	-	36.1	1.1	-	-	-	-	36.6	1.4	-	-	-	-	37.0	1.1	-	-	-	-	37.5	1.4	-	-
1973	-	-	37.9	1.1	-	-	-	-	38.7	2.1	-	-	-	-	39.7	2.6	-	-	-	-	40.4	1.8	-	-
1974	-	-	41.5	2.7	-	-	-	-	42.9	3.4	-	-	-	-	44.3	3.3	-	-	-	-	45.4	2.5	-	-
1975	-	-	46.5	2.4	-	-	-	-	47.0	1.1	-	-	-	-	48.1	2.3	-	-	-	-	48.8	1.5	-	-
1976	-	-	49.5	1.4	-	-	-	-	50.1	1.2	-	-	-	-	50.9	1.6	-	-	-	-	51.4	1.0	-	-
1977	-	-	52.2	1.6	-	-	-	-	53.4	2.3	-	-	-	-	54.4	1.9	-	-	-	-	55.2	1.5	-	-
1978	55.9	1.3	-	-	56.6	1.3	-	-	57.8	2.1	-	-	59.7	3.3	-	-	61.1	2.3	-	-	62.0	1.5	-	-
1979	63.5	2.4	-	-	65.5	3.1	-	-	67.5	3.1	-	-	69.8	3.4	-	-	71.1	1.9	-	-	73.3	3.1	-	-
1980	75.1	2.5	-	-	76.4	1.7	-	-	79.8	4.5	-	-	79.8	0.0	-	-	80.4	0.8	-	-	82.5	2.6	-	-
1981	85.1	3.2	-	-	86.7	1.9	-	-	88.0	1.5	-	-	90.3	2.6	-	-	92.8	2.8	-	-	95.0	2.4	-	-
1982	95.6	0.6	-	-	94.3	-1.4	-	-	97.4	3.3	-	-	99.0	1.6	-	-	96.3	-2.7	-	-	95.1	-1.2	-	-
1983	96.1	1.1	-	-	96.9	0.8	-	-	98.2	1.3	-	-	99.1	0.9	-	-	100.7	1.6	-	-	101.2	0.5	-	-
1984	102.4	1.2	-	-	103.3	0.9	-	-	104.4	1.1	-	-	103.9	-0.5	-	-	105.6	1.6	-	-	107.6	1.9	-	-
1985	107.7	0.1	-	-	109.2	1.4	-	-	110.0	0.7	-	-	110.3	0.3	-	-	111.6	1.2	-	-	112.1	0.4	-	-
1986	112.9	0.7	-	-	112.1	-0.7	-	-	113.2	1.0	-	-	113.3	0.1	-	-	114.1	0.7	-	-	114.6	0.4	-	-
1987	-	-	-	-	-	-	-	-	-	-	108.2	-5.6	-	-	-	-	-	-	-	-	-	-	110.3	1.9
1988	-	-	-	-	-	-	-	-	-	-	111.9	1.5	-	-	-	-	-	-	-	-	-	-	113.8	1.7
1989	-	-	-	-	-	-	-	-	-	-	116.7	2.5	-	-	-	-	-	-	-	-	-	-	119.6	2.5
1990	-	-	-	-	-	-	-	-	-	-	124.2	3.8	-	-	-	-	-	-	-	-	-	-	129.4	4.2
1991	-	-	-	-	-	-	-	-	-	-	133.0	2.8	-	-	-	-	-	-	-	-	-	-	135.2	1.7
1992	-	-	-	-	-	-	-	-	-	-	137.8	1.9	-	-	-	-	-	-	-	-	-	-	140.2	1.7
1993	-	-	-	-	-	-	-	-	-	-	141.9	1.2	-	-	-	-	-	-	-	-	-	-	143.9	1.4
1994	-	-	-	-	-	-	-	-	-	-	146.4	1.7	-	-	-	-	-	-	-	-	-	-	149.2	1.9
1995	-	-	-	-	-	-	-	-	-	-	151.2	1.3	-	-	-	-	-	-	-	-	-	-	-	-

Source: U.S. Department of Labor, Bureau of Labor Statistics, Division of Consumer Prices and Price Indexes. - indicates no data collected for period.

San Diego, CA
Consumer Price Index - Urban Wage Earners
Base 1982-1984 = 100
All Items

For 1965-1995. Columns headed % show percentile change in the index from the previous period for which an index is available.

Year	Jan Index	%	Feb Index	%	Mar Index	%	Apr Index	%	May Index	%	Jun Index	%	Jul Index	%	Aug Index	%	Sep Index	%	Oct Index	%	Nov Index	%	Dec Index	%
1965	-		29.5	-	-		-		29.6	0.3	-		-		29.4	-0.7	-		-		29.6	0.7	-	-
1966	-		29.9	1.0	-		-		30.0	0.3	-		-		30.1	0.3	-		-		30.5	1.3	-	-
1967	-		30.6	0.3	-		-		30.7	0.3	-		-		31.3	2.0	-		-		31.4	0.3	-	-
1968	-		31.8	1.3	-		-		32.1	0.9	-		-		32.5	1.2	-		-		32.8	0.9	-	-
1969	-		33.3	1.5	-		-		33.7	1.2	-		-		34.2	1.5	-		-		34.5	0.9	-	-
1970	-		35.0	1.4	-		-		35.7	2.0	-		-		35.9	0.6	-		-		36.5	1.7	-	-
1971	-		36.7	0.5	-		-		37.1	1.1	-		-		37.4	0.8	-		-		37.5	0.3		
1972	-		37.9	1.1	-		-		38.3	1.1	-		-		38.8	1.3	-		-		39.3	1.3		
1973	-		39.8	1.3	-		-		40.5	1.8	-		-		41.7	3.0	-		-		42.3	1.4		
1974	-		43.5	2.8	-		-		45.0	3.4	-		-		46.5	3.3	-		-		47.6	2.4		
1975	-		48.7	2.3	-		-		49.2	1.0	-		-		50.4	2.4	-		-		51.1	1.4		
1976	-		51.9	1.6	-		-		52.5	1.2	-		-		53.4	1.7	-		-		53.9	0.9		
1977	-		54.8	1.7	-		-		56.0	2.2	-		-		57.1	2.0	-		-		57.9	1.4		
1978	58.6	1.2	-		59.3	1.2	-		60.6	2.2	-		62.5	3.1	-		63.7	1.9	-		64.7	1.6		
1979	65.9	1.9	-		67.8	2.9	-		70.1	3.4	-		72.3	3.1	-		73.7	1.9	-		75.9	3.0		
1980	77.8	2.5	-		79.3	1.9	-		82.1	3.5	-		82.4	0.4	-		83.0	0.7	-		85.3	2.8		
1981	87.7	2.8	-		89.3	1.8	-		90.7	1.6	-		93.2	2.8	-		95.5	2.5	-		97.7	2.3		
1982	98.4	0.7	-		97.3	-1.1	-		100.3	3.1	-		102.1	1.8	-		99.6	-2.4	-		98.7	-0.9		
1983	97.2	-1.5	-		97.8	0.6	-		97.6	-0.2	-		99.2	1.6	-		100.4	1.2	-		100.4	0.0		
1984	102.1	1.7	-		101.2	-0.9	-		101.6	0.4	-		100.7	-0.9	-		102.5	1.8	-		102.0	-0.5		
1985	102.1	0.1	-		103.5	1.4	-		104.3	0.8	-		104.5	0.2	-		105.5	1.0	-		106.0	0.5		
1986	106.9	0.8	-		106.0	-0.8	-		107.0	0.9	-		107.0	0.0	-		107.7	0.7	-		108.2	0.5	-	
1987	-		-		-		-		-		106.4	-1.7	-		-		-		-		-		108.4	1.9
1988	-		-		-		-		-		109.9	1.4	-		-		-		-		-		112.0	1.9
1989	-		-		-		-		-		114.7	2.4	-		-		-		-		-		117.6	2.5
1990	-		-		-		-		-		122.0	3.7	-		-		-		-		-		126.9	4.0
1991	-		-		-		-		-		130.2	2.6	-		-		-		-		-		132.4	1.7
1992	-		-		-		-		-		134.8	1.8	-		-		-		-		-		137.2	1.8
1993	-		-		-		-		-		138.9	1.2	-		-		-		-		-		141.1	1.6
1994	-		-		-		-		-		143.7	1.8	-		-		-		-		-		146.5	1.9
1995	-		-		-		-		-		148.3	1.2	-		-		-		-		-		-	

Source: U.S. Department of Labor, Bureau of Labor Statistics, Division of Consumer Prices and Price Indexes. - indicates no data collected for period.

San Diego, CA
Consumer Price Index - All Urban Consumers
Base 1982-1984 = 100
Food and Beverages

For 1975-1995. Columns headed % show percentile change in the index from the previous period for which an index is available.

Year	Jan Index	%	Feb Index	%	Mar Index	%	Apr Index	%	May Index	%	Jun Index	%	Jul Index	%	Aug Index	%	Sep Index	%	Oct Index	%	Nov Index	%	Dec Index	%
1975	-	-	-	-	-	-	-	-	-	-	-	-	-	-	-	-	-	-	-	-	58.9	-	-	-
1976	-	-	58.9	0.0	-	-	-	-	59.2	0.5	-	-	-	-	59.7	0.8	-	-	-	-	59.6	-0.2	-	-
1977	-	-	61.0	2.3	-	-	-	-	62.8	3.0	-	-	-	-	63.6	1.3	-	-	-	-	64.3	1.1	-	-
1978	65.8	2.3	-	-	67.3	2.3	-	-	69.8	3.7	-	-	71.0	1.7	-	-	71.3	0.4	-	-	71.0	-0.4	-	-
1979	73.6	3.7	-	-	75.6	2.7	-	-	77.4	2.4	-	-	77.5	0.1	-	-	78.4	1.2	-	-	79.4	1.3	-	-
1980	81.0	2.0	-	-	82.2	1.5	-	-	83.5	1.6	-	-	84.1	0.7	-	-	86.2	2.5	-	-	87.5	1.5	-	-
1981	88.7	1.4	-	-	89.6	1.0	-	-	89.7	0.1	-	-	90.9	1.3	-	-	91.8	1.0	-	-	91.2	-0.7	-	-
1982	93.2	2.2	-	-	93.7	0.5	-	-	94.2	0.5	-	-	95.5	1.4	-	-	95.0	-0.5	-	-	96.7	1.8	-	-
1983	96.1	-0.6	-	-	100.3	4.4	-	-	100.5	0.2	-	-	100.2	-0.3	-	-	101.0	0.8	-	-	102.1	1.1	-	-
1984	104.7	2.5	-	-	105.3	0.6	-	-	103.6	-1.6	-	-	103.9	0.3	-	-	105.1	1.2	-	-	105.6	0.5	-	-
1985	107.4	1.7	-	-	106.9	-0.5	-	-	106.9	0.0	-	-	105.9	-0.9	-	-	106.8	0.8	-	-	108.0	1.1	-	-
1986	111.2	3.0	-	-	108.9	-2.1	-	-	111.0	1.9	-	-	110.1	-0.8	-	-	111.0	0.8	-	-	113.7	2.4	-	-
1987	-	-	-	-	-	-	-	-	-	-	111.7	-1.8	-	-	-	-	-	-	-	-	-	-	112.2	0.4
1988	-	-	-	-	-	-	-	-	-	-	114.0	1.6	-	-	-	-	-	-	-	-	-	-	115.8	1.6
1989	-	-	-	-	-	-	-	-	-	-	121.7	5.1	-	-	-	-	-	-	-	-	-	-	124.4	2.2
1990	-	-	-	-	-	-	-	-	-	-	131.8	5.9	-	-	-	-	-	-	-	-	-	-	134.2	1.8
1991	-	-	-	-	-	-	-	-	-	-	141.1	5.1	-	-	-	-	-	-	-	-	-	-	140.2	-0.6
1992	-	-	-	-	-	-	-	-	-	-	141.1	0.6	-	-	-	-	-	-	-	-	-	-	141.1	0.0
1993	-	-	-	-	-	-	-	-	-	-	142.8	1.2	-	-	-	-	-	-	-	-	-	-	142.1	-0.5
1994	-	-	-	-	-	-	-	-	-	-	145.3	2.3	-	-	-	-	-	-	-	-	-	-	148.5	2.2
1995	-	-	-	-	-	-	-	-	-	-	151.9	2.3	-	-	-	-	-	-	-	-	-	-	-	-

Source: U.S. Department of Labor, Bureau of Labor Statistics, Division of Consumer Prices and Price Indexes. - indicates no data collected for period.

San Diego, CA
Consumer Price Index - Urban Wage Earners
Base 1982-1984 = 100
Food and Beverages

For 1975-1995. Columns headed % show percentile change in the index from the previous period for which an index is available.

Year	Jan Index	%	Feb Index	%	Mar Index	%	Apr Index	%	May Index	%	Jun Index	%	Jul Index	%	Aug Index	%	Sep Index	%	Oct Index	%	Nov Index	%	Dec Index	%
1975	-	-	-	-	-	-	-	-	-	-	-	-	-	-	-	-	-	-	-	-	57.4	-	-	-
1976	-	-	57.5	0.2	-	-	-	-	57.7	0.3	-	-	-	-	58.2	0.9	-	-	-	-	58.1	-0.2	-	-
1977	-	-	59.6	2.6	-	-	-	-	61.3	2.9	-	-	-	-	62.1	1.3	-	-	-	-	62.7	1.0	-	-
1978	63.9	1.9	-	-	65.4	2.3	-	-	67.9	3.8	-	-	69.3	2.1	-	-	69.7	0.6	-	-	69.4	-0.4	-	-
1979	72.0	3.7	-	-	74.2	3.1	-	-	76.0	2.4	-	-	76.5	0.7	-	-	77.1	0.8	-	-	77.9	1.0	-	-
1980	79.5	2.1	-	-	80.9	1.8	-	-	81.5	0.7	-	-	82.1	0.7	-	-	84.6	3.0	-	-	86.8	2.6	-	-
1981	87.6	0.9	-	-	88.8	1.4	-	-	89.1	0.3	-	-	90.2	1.2	-	-	91.3	1.2	-	-	90.8	-0.5	-	-
1982	92.6	2.0	-	-	93.3	0.8	-	-	93.9	0.6	-	-	95.4	1.6	-	-	94.9	-0.5	-	-	96.7	1.9	-	-
1983	96.0	-0.7	-	-	100.5	4.7	-	-	100.6	0.1	-	-	100.2	-0.4	-	-	101.0	0.8	-	-	102.3	1.3	-	-
1984	104.8	2.4	-	-	105.2	0.4	-	-	103.8	-1.3	-	-	104.0	0.2	-	-	105.4	1.3	-	-	105.8	0.4	-	-
1985	107.5	1.6	-	-	107.1	-0.4	-	-	107.2	0.1	-	-	106.2	-0.9	-	-	107.0	0.8	-	-	108.4	1.3	-	-
1986	111.4	2.8	-	-	108.9	-2.2	-	-	110.9	1.8	-	-	110.2	-0.6	-	-	111.0	0.7	-	-	114.0	2.7	-	-
1987	-	-	-	-	-	-	-	-	-	-	111.3	-2.4	-	-	-	-	-	-	-	-	-	-	111.8	0.4
1988	-	-	-	-	-	-	-	-	-	-	113.6	1.6	-	-	-	-	-	-	-	-	-	-	115.6	1.8
1989	-	-	-	-	-	-	-	-	-	-	121.3	4.9	-	-	-	-	-	-	-	-	-	-	124.1	2.3
1990	-	-	-	-	-	-	-	-	-	-	131.5	6.0	-	-	-	-	-	-	-	-	-	-	134.0	1.9
1991	-	-	-	-	-	-	-	-	-	-	140.5	4.9	-	-	-	-	-	-	-	-	-	-	140.0	-0.4
1992	-	-	-	-	-	-	-	-	-	-	140.5	0.4	-	-	-	-	-	-	-	-	-	-	141.0	0.4
1993	-	-	-	-	-	-	-	-	-	-	142.4	1.0	-	-	-	-	-	-	-	-	-	-	142.5	0.1
1994	-	-	-	-	-	-	-	-	-	-	145.2	1.9	-	-	-	-	-	-	-	-	-	-	147.9	1.9
1995	-	-	-	-	-	-	-	-	-	-	150.8	2.0	-	-	-	-	-	-	-	-	-	-	-	-

Source: U.S. Department of Labor, Bureau of Labor Statistics, Division of Consumer Prices and Price Indexes. - indicates no data collected for period.

San Diego, CA
Consumer Price Index - All Urban Consumers
Base 1982-1984 = 100
Housing

For 1975-1995. Columns headed % show percentile change in the index from the previous period for which an index is available.

Year	Jan Index	%	Feb Index	%	Mar Index	%	Apr Index	%	May Index	%	Jun Index	%	Jul Index	%	Aug Index	%	Sep Index	%	Oct Index	%	Nov Index	%	Dec Index	%
1975	-		-		-		-		-		-		-		-		-		-		42.4	-	-	-
1976	-		43.5	2.6	-		-		43.8	0.7	-		-		44.6	1.8	-		-		45.4	1.8	-	-
1977	-		46.2	1.8	-		-		47.0	1.7	-		-		48.7	3.6	-		-		49.6	1.8	-	-
1978	50.3	1.4	-		51.0	1.4	-		51.9	1.8	-		54.1	4.2	-		56.1	3.7	-		57.3	2.1	-	-
1979	58.9	2.8	-		61.3	4.1	-		63.2	3.1	-		66.4	5.1	-		67.5	1.7	-		70.5	4.4	-	-
1980	72.5	2.8	-		72.8	0.4	-		77.7	6.7	-		77.3	-0.5	-		77.3	0.0	-		80.2	3.8	-	-
1981	83.7	4.4	-		85.3	1.9	-		86.8	1.8	-		89.5	3.1	-		92.9	3.8	-		96.2	3.6		
1982	96.7	0.5	-		94.6	-2.2	-		99.3	5.0	-		100.4	1.1	-		95.5	-4.9	-		93.2	-2.4		
1983	95.5	2.5	-		96.5	1.0	-		97.1	0.6	-		98.3	1.2	-		101.1	2.8	-		101.2	0.1		
1984	101.3	0.1	-		103.1	1.8	-		104.1	1.0	-		103.8	-0.3	-		106.1	2.2	-		109.1	2.8		
1985	108.9	-0.2	-		111.8	2.7	-		112.1	0.3	-		113.6	1.3	-		116.7	2.7	-		116.9	0.2		
1986	117.1	0.2	-		117.2	0.1	-		118.3	0.9	-		119.8	1.3	-		120.8	0.8	-		121.1	0.2	-	-
1987	-		-		-		-		-		107.2	-11.5	-		-		-		-		-		109.1	1.8
1988	-		-		-		-		-		111.0	1.7	-		-		-		-		-		112.9	1.7
1989	-		-		-		-		-		114.6	1.5	-		-		-		-		-		118.1	3.1
1990	-		-		-		-		-		122.0	3.3	-		-		-		-		-		128.9	5.7
1991	-		-		-		-		-		132.3	2.6	-		-		-		-		-		135.8	2.6
1992	-		-		-		-		-		138.3	1.8	-		-		-		-		-		140.2	1.4
1993	-		-		-		-		-		142.0	1.3	-		-		-		-		-		144.9	2.0
1994	-		-		-		-		-		147.0	1.4	-		-		-		-		-		148.9	1.3
1995	-		-		-		-		-		150.5	1.1	-		-		-		-		-		-	-

Source: U.S. Department of Labor, Bureau of Labor Statistics, Division of Consumer Prices and Price Indexes. - indicates no data collected for period.

San Diego, CA
Consumer Price Index - Urban Wage Earners
Base 1982-1984 = 100
Housing

For 1975-1995. Columns headed % show percentile change in the index from the previous period for which an index is available.

Year	Jan Index	%	Feb Index	%	Mar Index	%	Apr Index	%	May Index	%	Jun Index	%	Jul Index	%	Aug Index	%	Sep Index	%	Oct Index	%	Nov Index	%	Dec Index	%
1975	-	-	-	-	-	-	-	-	-	-	-	-	-	-	-	-	-	-	-	-	46.0	-	-	-
1976	-	-	47.2	2.6	-	-	-	-	47.6	0.8	-	-	-	-	48.4	1.7	-	-	-	-	49.3	1.9	-	-
1977	-	-	50.2	1.8	-	-	-	-	51.1	1.8	-	-	-	-	52.8	3.3	-	-	-	-	53.9	2.1	-	-
1978	54.7	1.5	-	-	55.3	1.1	-	-	56.4	2.0	-	-	58.8	4.3	-	-	60.8	3.4	-	-	62.1	2.1	-	-
1979	63.3	1.9	-	-	65.8	3.9	-	-	67.8	3.0	-	-	70.9	4.6	-	-	72.3	2.0	-	-	75.8	4.8	-	-
1980	77.9	2.8	-	-	78.2	0.4	-	-	83.1	6.3	-	-	82.9	-0.2	-	-	82.9	0.0	-	-	86.0	3.7	-	-
1981	90.0	4.7	-	-	91.5	1.7	-	-	93.0	1.6	-	-	96.2	3.4	-	-	99.6	3.5	-	-	103.3	3.7	-	-
1982	104.1	0.8	-	-	101.8	-2.2	-	-	107.0	5.1	-	-	108.1	1.0	-	-	102.7	-5.0	-	-	100.4	-2.2	-	-
1983	97.7	-2.7	-	-	97.9	0.2	-	-	95.8	-2.1	-	-	98.3	2.6	-	-	99.9	1.6	-	-	98.8	-1.1	-	-
1984	100.4	1.6	-	-	98.2	-2.2	-	-	98.1	-0.1	-	-	96.6	-1.5	-	-	99.2	2.7	-	-	96.9	-2.3	-	-
1985	96.5	-0.4	-	-	99.1	2.7	-	-	99.5	0.4	-	-	100.9	1.4	-	-	103.5	2.6	-	-	103.6	0.1	-	-
1986	103.7	0.1	-	-	103.8	0.1	-	-	104.8	1.0	-	-	106.1	1.2	-	-	107.1	0.9	-	-	107.3	0.2	-	-
1987	-	-	-	-	-	-	-	-	-	-	103.7	-3.4	-	-	-	-	-	-	-	-	-	-	105.2	1.4
1988	-	-	-	-	-	-	-	-	-	-	107.1	1.8	-	-	-	-	-	-	-	-	-	-	108.9	1.7
1989	-	-	-	-	-	-	-	-	-	-	110.3	1.3	-	-	-	-	-	-	-	-	-	-	113.5	2.9
1990	-	-	-	-	-	-	-	-	-	-	117.4	3.4	-	-	-	-	-	-	-	-	-	-	123.6	5.3
1991	-	-	-	-	-	-	-	-	-	-	126.7	2.5	-	-	-	-	-	-	-	-	-	-	130.1	2.7
1992	-	-	-	-	-	-	-	-	-	-	132.2	1.6	-	-	-	-	-	-	-	-	-	-	133.8	1.2
1993	-	-	-	-	-	-	-	-	-	-	135.7	1.4	-	-	-	-	-	-	-	-	-	-	138.4	2.0
1994	-	-	-	-	-	-	-	-	-	-	140.5	1.5	-	-	-	-	-	-	-	-	-	-	142.3	1.3
1995	-	-	-	-	-	-	-	-	-	-	143.6	0.9	-	-	-	-	-	-	-	-	-	-	-	-

Source: U.S. Department of Labor, Bureau of Labor Statistics, Division of Consumer Prices and Price Indexes. - indicates no data collected for period.

San Diego, CA
Consumer Price Index - All Urban Consumers
Base 1982-1984 = 100
Apparel and Upkeep

For 1965-1995. Columns headed % show percentile change in the index from the previous period for which an index is available.

Year	Jan Index	%	Feb Index	%	Mar Index	%	Apr Index	%	May Index	%	Jun Index	%	Jul Index	%	Aug Index	%	Sep Index	%	Oct Index	%	Nov Index	%	Dec Index	%
1965	-	-	48.5	-	-	-	-	-	48.4	-0.2	-	-	-	-	47.7	-1.4	-	-	-	-	47.8	0.2	-	-
1966	-	-	48.0	0.4	-	-	-	-	48.8	1.7	-	-	-	-	48.9	0.2	-	-	-	-	49.2	0.6	-	-
1967	-	-	48.8	-0.8	-	-	-	-	49.3	1.0	-	-	-	-	49.2	-0.2	-	-	-	-	50.5	2.6	-	-
1968	-	-	50.9	0.8	-	-	-	-	51.9	2.0	-	-	-	-	52.8	1.7	-	-	-	-	54.2	2.7	-	-
1969	-	-	53.9	-0.6	-	-	-	-	54.4	0.9	-	-	-	-	55.0	1.1	-	-	-	-	55.2	0.4	-	-
1970	-	-	55.8	1.1	-	-	-	-	57.2	2.5	-	-	-	-	56.8	-0.7	-	-	-	-	57.5	1.2	-	-
1971	-	-	57.5	0.0	-	-	-	-	58.4	1.6	-	-	-	-	58.5	0.2	-	-	-	-	58.7	0.3	-	-
1972	-	-	59.8	1.9	-	-	-	-	60.7	1.5	-	-	-	-	59.8	-1.5	-	-	-	-	61.4	2.7	-	-
1973	-	-	60.9	-0.8	-	-	-	-	61.7	1.3	-	-	-	-	63.3	2.6	-	-	-	-	64.7	2.2	-	-
1974	-	-	66.2	2.3	-	-	-	-	68.6	3.6	-	-	-	-	67.9	-1.0	-	-	-	-	69.1	1.8	-	-
1975	-	-	68.6	-0.7	-	-	-	-	70.3	2.5	-	-	-	-	69.2	-1.6	-	-	-	-	70.0	1.2	-	-
1976	-	-	71.0	1.4	-	-	-	-	71.5	0.7	-	-	-	-	71.9	0.6	-	-	-	-	71.5	-0.6	-	-
1977	-	-	71.1	-0.6	-	-	-	-	73.0	2.7	-	-	-	-	73.0	0.0	-	-	-	-	73.8	1.1	-	-
1978	74.0	0.3	-	-	73.8	-0.3	-	-	76.9	4.2	-	-	77.3	0.5	-	-	78.5	1.6	-	-	79.5	1.3	-	-
1979	79.2	-0.4	-	-	79.7	0.6	-	-	81.8	2.6	-	-	81.2	-0.7	-	-	82.9	2.1	-	-	82.9	0.0	-	-
1980	83.4	0.6	-	-	88.6	6.2	-	-	87.5	-1.2	-	-	86.7	-0.9	-	-	87.8	1.3	-	-	89.5	1.9	-	-
1981	87.9	-1.8	-	-	90.8	3.3	-	-	90.3	-0.6	-	-	93.5	3.5	-	-	95.0	1.6	-	-	95.0	0.0	-	-
1982	92.2	-2.9	-	-	95.1	3.1	-	-	96.4	1.4	-	-	95.9	-0.5	-	-	99.4	3.6	-	-	98.7	-0.7	-	-
1983	97.8	-0.9	-	-	97.3	-0.5	-	-	98.4	1.1	-	-	101.3	2.9	-	-	101.6	0.3	-	-	100.5	-1.1	-	-
1984	101.8	1.3	-	-	101.6	-0.2	-	-	103.8	2.2	-	-	100.6	-3.1	-	-	106.4	5.8	-	-	108.0	1.5	-	-
1985	105.1	-2.7	-	-	105.5	0.4	-	-	107.5	1.9	-	-	105.1	-2.2	-	-	106.1	1.0	-	-	106.3	0.2	-	-
1986	105.1	-1.1	-	-	108.3	3.0	-	-	108.1	-0.2	-	-	104.5	-3.3	-	-	109.0	4.3	-	-	108.2	-0.7	-	-
1987	-	-	-	-	-	-	-	-	-	-	107.0	-1.1	-	-	-	-	-	-	-	-	-	-	111.9	4.6
1988	-	-	-	-	-	-	-	-	-	-	115.7	3.4	-	-	-	-	-	-	-	-	-	-	115.6	-0.1
1989	-	-	-	-	-	-	-	-	-	-	110.4	-4.5	-	-	-	-	-	-	-	-	-	-	104.4	-5.4
1990	-	-	-	-	-	-	-	-	-	-	110.4	5.7	-	-	-	-	-	-	-	-	-	-	113.6	2.9
1991	-	-	-	-	-	-	-	-	-	-	112.3	-1.1	-	-	-	-	-	-	-	-	-	-	114.4	1.9
1992	-	-	-	-	-	-	-	-	-	-	118.5	3.6	-	-	-	-	-	-	-	-	-	-	118.9	0.3
1993	-	-	-	-	-	-	-	-	-	-	115.5	-2.9	-	-	-	-	-	-	-	-	-	-	115.5	0.0
1994	-	-	-	-	-	-	-	-	-	-	122.5	6.1	-	-	-	-	-	-	-	-	-	-	119.3	-2.6
1995	-	-	-	-	-	-	-	-	-	-	120.3	0.8	-	-	-	-	-	-	-	-	-	-	-	-

Source: U.S. Department of Labor, Bureau of Labor Statistics, Division of Consumer Prices and Price Indexes. - indicates no data collected for period.

San Diego, CA
Consumer Price Index - Urban Wage Earners
Base 1982-1984 = 100
Apparel and Upkeep

For 1965-1995. Columns headed % show percentile change in the index from the previous period for which an index is available.

Year	Jan Index	%	Feb Index	%	Mar Index	%	Apr Index	%	May Index	%	Jun Index	%	Jul Index	%	Aug Index	%	Sep Index	%	Oct Index	%	Nov Index	%	Dec Index	%
1965	-	-	50.6	-	-	-	-	-	50.6	0.0	-	-	-	-	49.8	-1.6	-	-	-	-	49.9	0.2	-	-
1966	-	-	50.1	0.4	-	-	-	-	50.9	1.6	-	-	-	-	51.0	0.2	-	-	-	-	51.3	0.6	-	-
1967	-	-	51.0	-0.6	-	-	-	-	51.5	1.0	-	-	-	-	51.4	-0.2	-	-	-	-	52.7	2.5	-	-
1968	-	-	53.2	0.9	-	-	-	-	54.2	1.9	-	-	-	-	55.1	1.7	-	-	-	-	56.5	2.5	-	-
1969	-	-	56.2	-0.5	-	-	-	-	56.8	1.1	-	-	-	-	57.5	1.2	-	-	-	-	57.7	0.3	-	-
1970	-	-	58.3	1.0	-	-	-	-	59.7	2.4	-	-	-	-	59.3	-0.7	-	-	-	-	60.0	1.2	-	-
1971	-	-	60.0	0.0	-	-	-	-	60.9	1.5	-	-	-	-	61.0	0.2	-	-	-	-	61.2	0.3	-	-
1972	-	-	62.4	2.0	-	-	-	-	63.4	1.6	-	-	-	-	62.5	-1.4	-	-	-	-	64.1	2.6	-	-
1973	-	-	63.6	-0.8	-	-	-	-	64.4	1.3	-	-	-	-	66.0	2.5	-	-	-	-	67.5	2.3	-	-
1974	-	-	69.1	2.4	-	-	-	-	71.6	3.6	-	-	-	-	70.8	-1.1	-	-	-	-	72.2	2.0	-	-
1975	-	-	71.6	-0.8	-	-	-	-	73.4	2.5	-	-	-	-	72.2	-1.6	-	-	-	-	73.1	1.2	-	-
1976	-	-	74.1	1.4	-	-	-	-	74.6	0.7	-	-	-	-	75.0	0.5	-	-	-	-	74.7	-0.4	-	-
1977	-	-	74.2	-0.7	-	-	-	-	76.3	2.8	-	-	-	-	76.2	-0.1	-	-	-	-	77.0	1.0	-	-
1978	75.9	-1.4	-	-	76.7	1.1	-	-	77.8	1.4	-	-	78.2	0.5	-	-	79.0	1.0	-	-	79.6	0.8	-	-
1979	77.5	-2.6	-	-	77.0	-0.6	-	-	80.3	4.3	-	-	81.4	1.4	-	-	83.4	2.5	-	-	84.6	1.4	-	-
1980	84.5	-0.1	-	-	90.0	6.5	-	-	90.1	0.1	-	-	87.6	-2.8	-	-	87.9	0.3	-	-	89.6	1.9	-	-
1981	88.8	-0.9	-	-	91.1	2.6	-	-	92.5	1.5	-	-	93.2	0.8	-	-	93.9	0.8	-	-	94.6	0.7	-	-
1982	92.3	-2.4	-	-	95.0	2.9	-	-	95.9	0.9	-	-	95.8	-0.1	-	-	99.2	3.5	-	-	98.9	-0.3	-	-
1983	98.5	-0.4	-	-	97.9	-0.6	-	-	98.6	0.7	-	-	101.0	2.4	-	-	101.7	0.7	-	-	100.4	-1.3	-	-
1984	101.5	1.1	-	-	101.7	0.2	-	-	103.7	2.0	-	-	100.8	-2.8	-	-	106.2	5.4	-	-	107.8	1.5	-	-
1985	105.0	-2.6	-	-	105.8	0.8	-	-	107.8	1.9	-	-	105.5	-2.1	-	-	106.4	0.9	-	-	106.8	0.4	-	-
1986	106.4	-0.4	-	-	108.8	2.3	-	-	109.0	0.2	-	-	104.3	-4.3	-	-	107.9	3.5	-	-	108.0	0.1	-	-
1987	-	-	-	-	-	-	-	-	-	-	105.3	-2.5	-	-	-	-	-	-	-	-	-	-	111.3	5.7
1988	-	-	-	-	-	-	-	-	-	-	114.2	2.6	-	-	-	-	-	-	-	-	-	-	114.0	-0.2
1989	-	-	-	-	-	-	-	-	-	-	108.5	-4.8	-	-	-	-	-	-	-	-	-	-	103.0	-5.1
1990	-	-	-	-	-	-	-	-	-	-	109.1	5.9	-	-	-	-	-	-	-	-	-	-	112.8	3.4
1991	-	-	-	-	-	-	-	-	-	-	111.1	-1.5	-	-	-	-	-	-	-	-	-	-	113.2	1.9
1992	-	-	-	-	-	-	-	-	-	-	117.0	3.4	-	-	-	-	-	-	-	-	-	-	118.4	1.2
1993	-	-	-	-	-	-	-	-	-	-	114.3	-3.5	-	-	-	-	-	-	-	-	-	-	115.7	1.2
1994	-	-	-	-	-	-	-	-	-	-	122.2	5.6	-	-	-	-	-	-	-	-	-	-	118.8	-2.8
1995	-	-	-	-	-	-	-	-	-	-	119.6	0.7	-	-	-	-	-	-	-	-	-	-	-	-

Source: U.S. Department of Labor, Bureau of Labor Statistics, Division of Consumer Prices and Price Indexes. - indicates no data collected for period.

San Diego, CA
Consumer Price Index - All Urban Consumers
Base 1982-1984 = 100
Transportation

For 1965-1995. Columns headed % show percentile change in the index from the previous period for which an index is available.

Year	Jan Index	%	Feb Index	%	Mar Index	%	Apr Index	%	May Index	%	Jun Index	%	Jul Index	%	Aug Index	%	Sep Index	%	Oct Index	%	Nov Index	%	Dec Index	%
1965	-	-	32.0	-	-	-	-	-	32.7	2.2	-	-	-	-	32.4	-0.9	-	-	-	-	31.4	-3.1	-	-
1966	-	-	31.7	1.0	-	-	-	-	31.8	0.3	-	-	-	-	31.9	0.3	-	-	-	-	33.2	4.1	-	-
1967	-	-	33.0	-0.6	-	-	-	-	33.0	0.0	-	-	-	-	33.7	2.1	-	-	-	-	33.5	-0.6	-	-
1968	-	-	33.8	0.9	-	-	-	-	34.0	0.6	-	-	-	-	34.2	0.6	-	-	-	-	34.4	0.6	-	-
1969	-	-	34.5	0.3	-	-	-	-	35.0	1.4	-	-	-	-	35.1	0.3	-	-	-	-	35.0	-0.3	-	-
1970	-	-	34.8	-0.6	-	-	-	-	35.6	2.3	-	-	-	-	35.7	0.3	-	-	-	-	37.5	5.0	-	-
1971	-	-	36.9	-1.6	-	-	-	-	38.0	3.0	-	-	-	-	38.6	1.6	-	-	-	-	38.2	-1.0	-	-
1972	-	-	37.5	-1.8	-	-	-	-	38.8	3.5	-	-	-	-	39.7	2.3	-	-	-	-	40.2	1.3	-	-
1973	-	-	39.5	-1.7	-	-	-	-	40.6	2.8	-	-	-	-	41.2	1.5	-	-	-	-	41.3	0.2	-	-
1974	-	-	43.4	5.1	-	-	-	-	45.8	5.5	-	-	-	-	47.4	3.5	-	-	-	-	48.1	1.5	-	-
1975	-	-	48.8	1.5	-	-	-	-	50.1	2.7	-	-	-	-	52.5	4.8	-	-	-	-	52.6	0.2	-	-
1976	-	-	52.5	-0.2	-	-	-	-	53.8	2.5	-	-	-	-	55.5	3.2	-	-	-	-	56.4	1.6	-	-
1977	-	-	56.8	0.7	-	-	-	-	58.1	2.3	-	-	-	-	58.6	0.9	-	-	-	-	58.9	0.5	-	-
1978	58.8	-0.2	-	-	58.8	0.0	-	-	60.1	2.2	-	-	62.2	3.5	-	-	62.4	0.3	-	-	63.4	1.6	-	-
1979	64.1	1.1	-	-	65.2	1.7	-	-	68.9	5.7	-	-	71.2	3.3	-	-	72.9	2.4	-	-	74.2	1.8	-	-
1980	77.0	3.8	-	-	80.7	4.8	-	-	82.0	1.6	-	-	82.9	1.1	-	-	84.0	1.3	-	-	84.6	0.7	-	-
1981	86.0	1.7	-	-	88.6	3.0	-	-	90.7	2.4	-	-	92.8	2.3	-	-	93.7	1.0	-	-	94.7	1.1	-	-
1982	94.6	-0.1	-	-	93.2	-1.5	-	-	93.4	0.2	-	-	98.2	5.1	-	-	97.8	-0.4	-	-	96.6	-1.2	-	-
1983	96.2	-0.4	-	-	94.4	-1.9	-	-	98.5	4.3	-	-	100.3	1.8	-	-	100.6	0.3	-	-	101.3	0.7	-	-
1984	103.1	1.8	-	-	103.3	0.2	-	-	106.9	3.5	-	-	105.2	-1.6	-	-	105.9	0.7	-	-	107.6	1.6	-	-
1985	107.5	-0.1	-	-	108.6	1.0	-	-	111.1	2.3	-	-	110.1	-0.9	-	-	108.9	-1.1	-	-	109.3	0.4	-	-
1986	110.0	0.6	-	-	106.3	-3.4	-	-	106.6	0.3	-	-	105.3	-1.2	-	-	104.1	-1.1	-	-	102.9	-1.2	-	-
1987	-	-	-	-	-	-	-	-	-	-	100.9	-1.9	-	-	-	-	-	-	-	-	-	-	103.8	2.9
1988	-	-	-	-	-	-	-	-	-	-	102.5	-1.3	-	-	-	-	-	-	-	-	-	-	104.6	2.0
1989	-	-	-	-	-	-	-	-	-	-	107.5	2.8	-	-	-	-	-	-	-	-	-	-	110.8	3.1
1990	-	-	-	-	-	-	-	-	-	-	113.4	2.3	-	-	-	-	-	-	-	-	-	-	118.9	4.9
1991	-	-	-	-	-	-	-	-	-	-	119.3	0.3	-	-	-	-	-	-	-	-	-	-	120.6	1.1
1992	-	-	-	-	-	-	-	-	-	-	121.8	1.0	-	-	-	-	-	-	-	-	-	-	126.0	3.4
1993	-	-	-	-	-	-	-	-	-	-	126.6	0.5	-	-	-	-	-	-	-	-	-	-	130.1	2.8
1994	-	-	-	-	-	-	-	-	-	-	133.0	2.2	-	-	-	-	-	-	-	-	-	-	137.0	3.0
1995	-	-	-	-	-	-	-	-	-	-	138.2	0.9	-	-	-	-	-	-	-	-	-	-	-	-

Source: U.S. Department of Labor, Bureau of Labor Statistics, Division of Consumer Prices and Price Indexes. - indicates no data collected for period.

San Diego, CA
Consumer Price Index - Urban Wage Earners
Base 1982-1984 = 100
Transportation

For 1965-1995. Columns headed % show percentile change in the index from the previous period for which an index is available.

Year	Jan Index	%	Feb Index	%	Mar Index	%	Apr Index	%	May Index	%	Jun Index	%	Jul Index	%	Aug Index	%	Sep Index	%	Oct Index	%	Nov Index	%	Dec Index	%
1965	-	-	31.8	-	-	-	-	-	32.5	2.2	-	-	-	-	32.1	-1.2	-	-	-	-	31.2	-2.8	-	-
1966	-	-	31.5	1.0	-	-	-	-	31.5	0.0	-	-	-	-	31.6	0.3	-	-	-	-	33.0	4.4	-	-
1967	-	-	32.8	-0.6	-	-	-	-	32.8	0.0	-	-	-	-	33.5	2.1	-	-	-	-	33.3	-0.6	-	-
1968	-	-	33.6	0.9	-	-	-	-	33.8	0.6	-	-	-	-	33.9	0.3	-	-	-	-	34.2	0.9	-	-
1969	-	-	34.3	0.3	-	-	-	-	34.8	1.5	-	-	-	-	34.9	0.3	-	-	-	-	34.7	-0.6	-	-
1970	-	-	34.6	-0.3	-	-	-	-	35.4	2.3	-	-	-	-	35.5	0.3	-	-	-	-	37.2	4.8	-	-
1971	-	-	36.6	-1.6	-	-	-	-	37.8	3.3	-	-	-	-	38.3	1.3	-	-	-	-	38.0	-0.8	-	-
1972	-	-	37.2	-2.1	-	-	-	-	38.6	3.8	-	-	-	-	39.4	2.1	-	-	-	-	39.9	1.3	-	-
1973	-	-	39.2	-1.8	-	-	-	-	40.3	2.8	-	-	-	-	40.9	1.5	-	-	-	-	41.0	0.2	-	-
1974	-	-	43.1	5.1	-	-	-	-	45.5	5.6	-	-	-	-	47.1	3.5	-	-	-	-	47.8	1.5	-	-
1975	-	-	48.4	1.3	-	-	-	-	49.8	2.9	-	-	-	-	52.1	4.6	-	-	-	-	52.2	0.2	-	-
1976	-	-	52.2	0.0	-	-	-	-	53.4	2.3	-	-	-	-	55.1	3.2	-	-	-	-	56.0	1.6	-	-
1977	-	-	56.4	0.7	-	-	-	-	57.7	2.3	-	-	-	-	58.2	0.9	-	-	-	-	58.5	0.5	-	-
1978	58.7	0.3	-	-	58.8	0.2	-	-	60.0	2.0	-	-	61.9	3.2	-	-	62.0	0.2	-	-	63.3	2.1	-	-
1979	64.0	1.1	-	-	65.1	1.7	-	-	68.8	5.7	-	-	70.9	3.1	-	-	72.6	2.4	-	-	73.5	1.2	-	-
1980	76.3	3.8	-	-	79.9	4.7	-	-	80.9	1.3	-	-	81.8	1.1	-	-	82.5	0.9	-	-	83.5	1.2	-	-
1981	84.7	1.4	-	-	87.1	2.8	-	-	89.3	2.5	-	-	91.5	2.5	-	-	92.4	1.0	-	-	93.8	1.5	-	-
1982	93.9	0.1	-	-	92.7	-1.3	-	-	93.0	0.3	-	-	98.0	5.4	-	-	97.6	-0.4	-	-	96.4	-1.2	-	-
1983	95.9	-0.5	-	-	94.4	-1.6	-	-	98.4	4.2	-	-	100.2	1.8	-	-	100.6	0.4	-	-	101.4	0.8	-	-
1984	103.3	1.9	-	-	103.6	0.3	-	-	107.1	3.4	-	-	105.8	-1.2	-	-	106.2	0.4	-	-	107.9	1.6	-	-
1985	107.9	0.0	-	-	108.8	0.8	-	-	111.3	2.3	-	-	110.4	-0.8	-	-	109.1	-1.2	-	-	109.5	0.4	-	-
1986	110.1	0.5	-	-	106.9	-2.9	-	-	107.2	0.3	-	-	105.8	-1.3	-	-	104.7	-1.0	-	-	103.5	-1.1	-	-
1987	-	-	-	-	-	-	-	-	-	-	101.1	-2.3	-	-	-	-	-	-	-	-	-	-	104.2	3.1
1988	-	-	-	-	-	-	-	-	-	-	103.6	-0.6	-	-	-	-	-	-	-	-	-	-	105.7	2.0
1989	-	-	-	-	-	-	-	-	-	-	108.6	2.7	-	-	-	-	-	-	-	-	-	-	111.9	3.0
1990	-	-	-	-	-	-	-	-	-	-	113.8	1.7	-	-	-	-	-	-	-	-	-	-	119.5	5.0
1991	-	-	-	-	-	-	-	-	-	-	119.7	0.2	-	-	-	-	-	-	-	-	-	-	121.5	1.5
1992	-	-	-	-	-	-	-	-	-	-	122.8	1.1	-	-	-	-	-	-	-	-	-	-	127.2	3.6
1993	-	-	-	-	-	-	-	-	-	-	127.9	0.6	-	-	-	-	-	-	-	-	-	-	132.3	3.4
1994	-	-	-	-	-	-	-	-	-	-	135.4	2.3	-	-	-	-	-	-	-	-	-	-	140.2	3.5
1995	-	-	-	-	-	-	-	-	-	-	141.9	1.2	-	-	-	-	-	-	-	-	-	-	-	-

Source: U.S. Department of Labor, Bureau of Labor Statistics, Division of Consumer Prices and Price Indexes. - indicates no data collected for period.

San Diego, CA
Consumer Price Index - All Urban Consumers
Base 1982-1984 = 100
Medical Care

For 1965-1995. Columns headed % show percentile change in the index from the previous period for which an index is available.

Year	Jan Index	%	Feb Index	%	Mar Index	%	Apr Index	%	May Index	%	Jun Index	%	Jul Index	%	Aug Index	%	Sep Index	%	Oct Index	%	Nov Index	%	Dec Index	%
1965	-	-	26.4	-	-	-	-	-	26.5	0.4	-	-	-	-	26.6	0.4	-	-	-	-	26.8	0.8	-	-
1966	-	-	27.2	1.5	-	-	-	-	27.7	1.8	-	-	-	-	27.9	0.7	-	-	-	-	29.2	4.7	-	-
1967	-	-	29.4	0.7	-	-	-	-	29.9	1.7	-	-	-	-	30.2	1.0	-	-	-	-	30.5	1.0	-	-
1968	-	-	30.5	0.0	-	-	-	-	30.5	0.0	-	-	-	-	30.9	1.3	-	-	-	-	31.2	1.0	-	-
1969	-	-	31.9	2.2	-	-	-	-	32.3	1.3	-	-	-	-	32.7	1.2	-	-	-	-	32.7	0.0	-	-
1970	-	-	33.4	2.1	-	-	-	-	34.3	2.7	-	-	-	-	34.9	1.7	-	-	-	-	35.2	0.9	-	-
1971	-	-	35.6	1.1	-	-	-	-	36.3	2.0	-	-	-	-	36.8	1.4	-	-	-	-	36.6	-0.5	-	-
1972	-	-	36.7	0.3	-	-	-	-	36.8	0.3	-	-	-	-	37.2	1.1	-	-	-	-	38.0	2.2	-	-
1973	-	-	38.1	0.3	-	-	-	-	38.5	1.0	-	-	-	-	39.3	2.1	-	-	-	-	40.2	2.3	-	-
1974	-	-	41.1	2.2	-	-	-	-	42.2	2.7	-	-	-	-	44.4	5.2	-	-	-	-	45.0	1.4	-	-
1975	-	-	47.1	4.7	-	-	-	-	47.8	1.5	-	-	-	-	49.0	2.5	-	-	-	-	50.1	2.2	-	-
1976	-	-	52.0	3.8	-	-	-	-	52.8	1.5	-	-	-	-	54.3	2.8	-	-	-	-	55.3	1.8	-	-
1977	-	-	56.7	2.5	-	-	-	-	58.3	2.8	-	-	-	-	59.3	1.7	-	-	-	-	60.0	1.2	-	-
1978	61.2	2.0	-	-	62.5	2.1	-	-	62.7	0.3	-	-	63.8	1.8	-	-	64.0	0.3	-	-	65.7	2.7	-	-
1979	67.2	2.3	-	-	67.6	0.6	-	-	68.4	1.2	-	-	69.2	1.2	-	-	71.1	2.7	-	-	72.3	1.7	-	-
1980	72.7	0.6	-	-	73.8	1.5	-	-	76.2	3.3	-	-	76.5	0.4	-	-	77.1	0.8	-	-	79.1	2.6	-	-
1981	79.4	0.4	-	-	79.5	0.1	-	-	80.4	1.1	-	-	84.1	4.6	-	-	84.9	1.0	-	-	87.4	2.9	-	-
1982	88.7	1.5	-	-	89.2	0.6	-	-	90.1	1.0	-	-	93.7	4.0	-	-	95.4	1.8	-	-	98.8	3.6	-	-
1983	99.9	1.1	-	-	99.9	0.0	-	-	99.9	0.0	-	-	99.7	-0.2	-	-	101.1	1.4	-	-	102.8	1.7	-	-
1984	104.3	1.5	-	-	105.2	0.9	-	-	105.5	0.3	-	-	107.5	1.9	-	-	106.9	-0.6	-	-	107.2	0.3	-	-
1985	106.9	-0.3	-	-	108.8	1.8	-	-	109.9	1.0	-	-	110.6	0.6	-	-	110.9	0.3	-	-	112.1	1.1	-	-
1986	112.8	0.6	-	-	115.0	2.0	-	-	116.4	1.2	-	-	117.8	1.2	-	-	121.4	3.1	-	-	123.0	1.3	-	-
1987	-	-	-	-	-	-	-	-	-	-	122.6	-0.3	-	-	-	-	-	-	-	-	-	-	126.6	3.3
1988	-	-	-	-	-	-	-	-	-	-	131.2	3.6	-	-	-	-	-	-	-	-	-	-	134.6	2.6
1989	-	-	-	-	-	-	-	-	-	-	140.6	4.5	-	-	-	-	-	-	-	-	-	-	142.6	1.4
1990	-	-	-	-	-	-	-	-	-	-	152.6	7.0	-	-	-	-	-	-	-	-	-	-	156.6	2.6
1991	-	-	-	-	-	-	-	-	-	-	166.2	6.1	-	-	-	-	-	-	-	-	-	-	172.6	3.9
1992	-	-	-	-	-	-	-	-	-	-	181.2	5.0	-	-	-	-	-	-	-	-	-	-	187.1	3.3
1993	-	-	-	-	-	-	-	-	-	-	192.4	2.8	-	-	-	-	-	-	-	-	-	-	193.8	0.7
1994	-	-	-	-	-	-	-	-	-	-	197.3	1.8	-	-	-	-	-	-	-	-	-	-	202.4	2.6
1995	-	-	-	-	-	-	-	-	-	-	207.5	2.5	-	-	-	-	-	-	-	-	-	-	-	-

Source: U.S. Department of Labor, Bureau of Labor Statistics, Division of Consumer Prices and Price Indexes. - indicates no data collected for period.

Economic Indicators Handbook, 3rd Edition

Consumer Price Index - San Diego

San Diego, CA
Consumer Price Index - Urban Wage Earners
Base 1982-1984 = 100
Medical Care

For 1965-1995. Columns headed % show percentile change in the index from the previous period for which an index is available.

Year	Jan Index	%	Feb Index	%	Mar Index	%	Apr Index	%	May Index	%	Jun Index	%	Jul Index	%	Aug Index	%	Sep Index	%	Oct Index	%	Nov Index	%	Dec Index	%
1965	-	-	25.8	-	-	-	-	-	26.0	0.8	-	-	-	-	26.1	0.4	-	-	-	-	26.2	0.4	-	-
1966	-	-	26.6	1.5	-	-	-	-	27.1	1.9	-	-	-	-	27.3	0.7	-	-	-	-	28.6	4.8	-	-
1967	-	-	28.8	0.7	-	-	-	-	29.2	1.4	-	-	-	-	29.6	1.4	-	-	-	-	29.9	1.0	-	-
1968	-	-	29.9	0.0	-	-	-	-	29.9	0.0	-	-	-	-	30.2	1.0	-	-	-	-	30.5	1.0	-	-
1969	-	-	31.2	2.3	-	-	-	-	31.6	1.3	-	-	-	-	32.0	1.3	-	-	-	-	32.0	0.0	-	-
1970	-	-	32.7	2.2	-	-	-	-	33.5	2.4	-	-	-	-	34.1	1.8	-	-	-	-	34.4	0.9	-	-
1971	-	-	34.9	1.5	-	-	-	-	35.5	1.7	-	-	-	-	36.0	1.4	-	-	-	-	35.8	-0.6	-	-
1972	-	-	35.9	0.3	-	-	-	-	36.0	0.3	-	-	-	-	36.4	1.1	-	-	-	-	37.1	1.9	-	-
1973	-	-	37.3	0.5	-	-	-	-	37.7	1.1	-	-	-	-	38.4	1.9	-	-	-	-	39.3	2.3	-	-
1974	-	-	40.2	2.3	-	-	-	-	41.3	2.7	-	-	-	-	43.4	5.1	-	-	-	-	44.0	1.4	-	-
1975	-	-	46.0	4.5	-	-	-	-	46.8	1.7	-	-	-	-	47.9	2.4	-	-	-	-	49.0	2.3	-	-
1976	-	-	50.9	3.9	-	-	-	-	51.6	1.4	-	-	-	-	53.1	2.9	-	-	-	-	54.1	1.9	-	-
1977	-	-	55.5	2.6	-	-	-	-	57.1	2.9	-	-	-	-	58.0	1.6	-	-	-	-	58.8	1.4	-	-
1978	60.3	2.6	-	-	60.8	0.8	-	-	61.1	0.5	-	-	62.5	2.3	-	-	62.8	0.5	-	-	63.7	1.4	-	-
1979	65.2	2.4	-	-	66.2	1.5	-	-	68.7	3.8	-	-	69.4	1.0	-	-	72.0	3.7	-	-	73.0	1.4	-	-
1980	73.8	1.1	-	-	74.4	0.8	-	-	75.1	0.9	-	-	77.0	2.5	-	-	77.6	0.8	-	-	77.9	0.4	-	-
1981	79.5	2.1	-	-	79.4	-0.1	-	-	80.1	0.9	-	-	85.4	6.6	-	-	86.5	1.3	-	-	87.9	1.6	-	-
1982	89.1	1.4	-	-	89.5	0.4	-	-	90.3	0.9	-	-	93.5	3.5	-	-	95.0	1.6	-	-	98.6	3.8	-	-
1983	99.5	0.9	-	-	99.6	0.1	-	-	99.6	0.0	-	-	99.4	-0.2	-	-	101.2	1.8	-	-	102.9	1.7	-	-
1984	104.4	1.5	-	-	105.3	0.9	-	-	105.6	0.3	-	-	107.5	1.8	-	-	107.1	-0.4	-	-	107.4	0.3	-	-
1985	107.3	-0.1	-	-	109.3	1.9	-	-	110.5	1.1	-	-	111.1	0.5	-	-	111.5	0.4	-	-	112.6	1.0	-	-
1986	113.3	0.6	-	-	115.6	2.0	-	-	117.1	1.3	-	-	118.5	1.2	-	-	122.4	3.3	-	-	123.8	1.1	-	-
1987	-	-	-	-	-	-	-	-	-	-	124.3	0.4	-	-	-	-	-	-	-	-	-	-	128.2	3.1
1988	-	-	-	-	-	-	-	-	-	-	133.0	3.7	-	-	-	-	-	-	-	-	-	-	136.5	2.6
1989	-	-	-	-	-	-	-	-	-	-	142.5	4.4	-	-	-	-	-	-	-	-	-	-	144.3	1.3
1990	-	-	-	-	-	-	-	-	-	-	154.0	6.7	-	-	-	-	-	-	-	-	-	-	157.9	2.5
1991	-	-	-	-	-	-	-	-	-	-	166.9	5.7	-	-	-	-	-	-	-	-	-	-	173.1	3.7
1992	-	-	-	-	-	-	-	-	-	-	181.9	5.1	-	-	-	-	-	-	-	-	-	-	188.0	3.4
1993	-	-	-	-	-	-	-	-	-	-	193.2	2.8	-	-	-	-	-	-	-	-	-	-	194.5	0.7
1994	-	-	-	-	-	-	-	-	-	-	197.7	1.6	-	-	-	-	-	-	-	-	-	-	202.7	2.5
1995	-	-	-	-	-	-	-	-	-	-	207.4	2.3	-	-	-	-	-	-	-	-	-	-	-	-

Source: U.S. Department of Labor, Bureau of Labor Statistics, Division of Consumer Prices and Price Indexes. - indicates no data collected for period.

San Diego, CA
Consumer Price Index - All Urban Consumers
Base 1982-1984 = 100
Entertainment

For 1975-1995. Columns headed % show percentile change in the index from the previous period for which an index is available.

Year	Jan Index	%	Feb Index	%	Mar Index	%	Apr Index	%	May Index	%	Jun Index	%	Jul Index	%	Aug Index	%	Sep Index	%	Oct Index	%	Nov Index	%	Dec Index	%
1975	-	-	-	-	-	-	-	-	-	-	-	-	-	-	-	-	-	-	-	-	60.3	-	-	-
1976	-	-	61.6	2.2	-	-	-	-	62.6	1.6	-	-	-	-	63.1	0.8	-	-	-	-	63.1	0.0	-	-
1977	-	-	63.4	0.5	-	-	-	-	64.9	2.4	-	-	-	-	65.9	1.5	-	-	-	-	66.1	0.3	-	-
1978	67.1	1.5	-	-	67.8	1.0	-	-	68.7	1.3	-	-	69.5	1.2	-	-	70.7	1.7	-	-	70.7	0.0	-	-
1979	72.6	2.7	-	-	73.3	1.0	-	-	74.3	1.4	-	-	75.5	1.6	-	-	76.0	0.7	-	-	76.5	0.7	-	-
1980	77.8	1.7	-	-	81.5	4.8	-	-	83.4	2.3	-	-	84.4	1.2	-	-	84.3	-0.1	-	-	85.1	0.9	-	-
1981	86.5	1.6	-	-	87.6	1.3	-	-	89.3	1.9	-	-	90.2	1.0	-	-	91.9	1.9	-	-	92.2	0.3	-	-
1982	93.3	1.2	-	-	94.6	1.4	-	-	95.4	0.8	-	-	96.5	1.2	-	-	96.7	0.2	-	-	98.4	1.8	-	-
1983	99.7	1.3	-	-	99.5	-0.2	-	-	101.5	2.0	-	-	101.0	-0.5	-	-	101.2	0.2	-	-	101.4	0.2	-	-
1984	101.9	0.5	-	-	102.4	0.5	-	-	102.7	0.3	-	-	102.4	-0.3	-	-	103.2	0.8	-	-	105.3	2.0	-	-
1985	105.4	0.1	-	-	106.5	1.0	-	-	107.3	0.8	-	-	108.4	1.0	-	-	108.2	-0.2	-	-	108.1	-0.1	-	-
1986	108.7	0.6	-	-	110.5	1.7	-	-	112.0	1.4	-	-	113.2	1.1	-	-	112.9	-0.3	-	-	112.7	-0.2	-	-
1987	-	-	-	-	-	-	-	-	-	-	110.0	-2.4	-	-	-	-	-	-	-	-	-	-	111.8	1.6
1988	-	-	-	-	-	-	-	-	-	-	113.9	1.9	-	-	-	-	-	-	-	-	-	-	117.1	2.8
1989	-	-	-	-	-	-	-	-	-	-	124.1	6.0	-	-	-	-	-	-	-	-	-	-	127.9	3.1
1990	-	-	-	-	-	-	-	-	-	-	129.1	0.9	-	-	-	-	-	-	-	-	-	-	130.8	1.3
1991	-	-	-	-	-	-	-	-	-	-	135.3	3.4	-	-	-	-	-	-	-	-	-	-	136.5	0.9
1992	-	-	-	-	-	-	-	-	-	-	138.0	1.1	-	-	-	-	-	-	-	-	-	-	142.3	3.1
1993	-	-	-	-	-	-	-	-	-	-	143.8	1.1	-	-	-	-	-	-	-	-	-	-	144.7	0.6
1994	-	-	-	-	-	-	-	-	-	-	145.4	0.5	-	-	-	-	-	-	-	-	-	-	148.0	1.8
1995	-	-	-	-	-	-	-	-	-	-	148.2	0.1	-	-	-	-	-	-	-	-	-	-	-	-

Source: U.S. Department of Labor, Bureau of Labor Statistics, Division of Consumer Prices and Price Indexes. - indicates no data collected for period.

San Diego, CA
Consumer Price Index - Urban Wage Earners
Base 1982-1984 = 100
Entertainment

For 1975-1995. Columns headed % show percentile change in the index from the previous period for which an index is available.

Year	Jan Index	%	Feb Index	%	Mar Index	%	Apr Index	%	May Index	%	Jun Index	%	Jul Index	%	Aug Index	%	Sep Index	%	Oct Index	%	Nov Index	%	Dec Index	%
1975	-	-	-	-	-	-	-	-	-	-	-	-	-	-	-	-	-	-	-	-	58.6	-	-	-
1976	-	-	59.9	2.2	-	-	-	-	60.8	1.5	-	-	-	-	61.3	0.8	-	-	-	-	61.3	0.0	-	-
1977	-	-	61.6	0.5	-	-	-	-	63.0	2.3	-	-	-	-	64.0	1.6	-	-	-	-	64.3	0.5	-	-
1978	64.8	0.8	-	-	65.4	0.9	-	-	66.2	1.2	-	-	68.2	3.0	-	-	69.3	1.6	-	-	69.5	0.3	-	-
1979	70.6	1.6	-	-	71.2	0.8	-	-	73.1	2.7	-	-	73.5	0.5	-	-	74.6	1.5	-	-	76.0	1.9	-	-
1980	76.2	0.3	-	-	79.8	4.7	-	-	80.7	1.1	-	-	83.2	3.1	-	-	84.7	1.8	-	-	84.6	-0.1	-	-
1981	84.2	-0.5	-	-	86.7	3.0	-	-	86.9	0.2	-	-	88.9	2.3	-	-	91.4	2.8	-	-	91.8	0.4	-	-
1982	93.2	1.5	-	-	94.4	1.3	-	-	95.4	1.1	-	-	96.8	1.5	-	-	96.6	-0.2	-	-	98.2	1.7	-	-
1983	99.8	1.6	-	-	99.2	-0.6	-	-	101.7	2.5	-	-	101.3	-0.4	-	-	101.4	0.1	-	-	101.6	0.2	-	-
1984	101.9	0.3	-	-	102.4	0.5	-	-	102.6	0.2	-	-	102.2	-0.4	-	-	103.0	0.8	-	-	105.2	2.1	-	-
1985	105.3	0.1	-	-	106.4	1.0	-	-	107.3	0.8	-	-	108.7	1.3	-	-	108.6	-0.1	-	-	108.8	0.2	-	-
1986	109.6	0.7	-	-	111.5	1.7	-	-	113.0	1.3	-	-	114.3	1.2	-	-	114.3	0.0	-	-	114.2	-0.1	-	-
1987	-	-	-	-	-	-	-	-	-	-	109.0	-4.6	-	-	-	-	-	-	-	-	-	-	110.2	1.1
1988	-	-	-	-	-	-	-	-	-	-	111.2	0.9	-	-	-	-	-	-	-	-	-	-	115.5	3.9
1989	-	-	-	-	-	-	-	-	-	-	122.1	5.7	-	-	-	-	-	-	-	-	-	-	126.3	3.4
1990	-	-	-	-	-	-	-	-	-	-	127.2	0.7	-	-	-	-	-	-	-	-	-	-	128.4	0.9
1991	-	-	-	-	-	-	-	-	-	-	133.1	3.7	-	-	-	-	-	-	-	-	-	-	132.8	-0.2
1992	-	-	-	-	-	-	-	-	-	-	135.1	1.7	-	-	-	-	-	-	-	-	-	-	137.7	1.9
1993	-	-	-	-	-	-	-	-	-	-	139.3	1.2	-	-	-	-	-	-	-	-	-	-	141.1	1.3
1994	-	-	-	-	-	-	-	-	-	-	141.9	0.6	-	-	-	-	-	-	-	-	-	-	144.2	1.6
1995	-	-	-	-	-	-	-	-	-	-	143.2	-0.7	-	-	-	-	-	-	-	-	-	-	-	-

Source: U.S. Department of Labor, Bureau of Labor Statistics, Division of Consumer Prices and Price Indexes. - indicates no data collected for period.

San Diego, CA
Consumer Price Index - All Urban Consumers
Base 1982-1984 = 100
Other Goods and Services

For 1975-1995. Columns headed % show percentile change in the index from the previous period for which an index is available.

Year	Jan Index	%	Feb Index	%	Mar Index	%	Apr Index	%	May Index	%	Jun Index	%	Jul Index	%	Aug Index	%	Sep Index	%	Oct Index	%	Nov Index	%	Dec Index	%
1975	-	-	-	-	-	-	-	-	-	-	-	-	-	-	-	-	-	-	-	-	55.4	-	-	-
1976	-	-	56.6	2.2	-	-	-	-	57.8	2.1	-	-	-	-	58.3	0.9	-	-	-	-	59.5	2.1	-	-
1977	-	-	59.7	0.3	-	-	-	-	60.5	1.3	-	-	-	-	61.5	1.7	-	-	-	-	62.7	2.0	-	-
1978	63.8	1.8	-	-	64.7	1.4	-	-	65.1	0.6	-	-	65.7	0.9	-	-	67.8	3.2	-	-	68.8	1.5	-	-
1979	69.4	0.9	-	-	70.0	0.9	-	-	70.2	0.3	-	-	70.7	0.7	-	-	72.8	3.0	-	-	73.4	0.8	-	-
1980	73.9	0.7	-	-	75.1	1.6	-	-	75.2	0.1	-	-	76.7	2.0	-	-	79.3	3.4	-	-	80.7	1.8	-	-
1981	83.0	2.9	-	-	83.1	0.1	-	-	84.4	1.6	-	-	84.3	-0.1	-	-	86.7	2.8	-	-	87.6	1.0	-	-
1982	88.9	1.5	-	-	89.6	0.8	-	-	90.2	0.7	-	-	88.6	-1.8	-	-	94.2	6.3	-	-	95.4	1.3	-	-
1983	98.0	2.7	-	-	97.1	-0.9	-	-	98.8	1.8	-	-	99.2	0.4	-	-	101.7	2.5	-	-	104.5	2.8	-	-
1984	104.9	0.4	-	-	105.0	0.1	-	-	107.6	2.5	-	-	107.1	-0.5	-	-	110.5	3.2	-	-	112.6	1.9	-	-
1985	114.2	1.4	-	-	115.1	0.8	-	-	114.6	-0.4	-	-	114.5	-0.1	-	-	117.6	2.7	-	-	117.2	-0.3	-	-
1986	118.6	1.2	-	-	119.4	0.7	-	-	119.6	0.2	-	-	118.4	-1.0	-	-	120.9	2.1	-	-	121.7	0.7	-	-
1987	-	-	-	-	-	-	-	-	-	-	121.0	-0.6	-	-	-	-	-	-	-	-	-	-	124.0	2.5
1988	-	-	-	-	-	-	-	-	-	-	126.5	2.0	-	-	-	-	-	-	-	-	-	-	128.2	1.3
1989	-	-	-	-	-	-	-	-	-	-	132.9	3.7	-	-	-	-	-	-	-	-	-	-	137.9	3.8
1990	-	-	-	-	-	-	-	-	-	-	144.2	4.6	-	-	-	-	-	-	-	-	-	-	149.5	3.7
1991	-	-	-	-	-	-	-	-	-	-	154.1	3.1	-	-	-	-	-	-	-	-	-	-	158.9	3.1
1992	-	-	-	-	-	-	-	-	-	-	166.0	4.5	-	-	-	-	-	-	-	-	-	-	172.1	3.7
1993	-	-	-	-	-	-	-	-	-	-	178.6	3.8	-	-	-	-	-	-	-	-	-	-	180.4	1.0
1994	-	-	-	-	-	-	-	-	-	-	181.4	0.6	-	-	-	-	-	-	-	-	-	-	188.4	3.9
1995	-	-	-	-	-	-	-	-	-	-	193.3	2.6	-	-	-	-	-	-	-	-	-	-	-	-

Source: U.S. Department of Labor, Bureau of Labor Statistics, Division of Consumer Prices and Price Indexes. - indicates no data collected for period.

San Diego, CA
Consumer Price Index - Urban Wage Earners
Base 1982-1984 = 100
Other Goods and Services

For 1975-1995. Columns headed % show percentile change in the index from the previous period for which an index is available.

Year	Jan Index	%	Feb Index	%	Mar Index	%	Apr Index	%	May Index	%	Jun Index	%	Jul Index	%	Aug Index	%	Sep Index	%	Oct Index	%	Nov Index	%	Dec Index	%
1975	-	-	-	-	-	-	-	-	-	-	-	-	-	-	-	-	-	-	-	-	56.6	-	-	-
1976	-	-	57.8	2.1	-	-	-	-	59.1	2.2	-	-	-	-	59.5	0.7	-	-	-	-	60.8	2.2	-	-
1977	-	-	61.0	0.3	-	-	-	-	61.9	1.5	-	-	-	-	62.9	1.6	-	-	-	-	64.1	1.9	-	-
1978	64.7	0.9	-	-	66.9	3.4	-	-	67.1	0.3	-	-	67.1	0.0	-	-	68.6	2.2	-	-	69.5	1.3	-	-
1979	70.4	1.3	-	-	71.0	0.9	-	-	71.0	0.0	-	-	71.9	1.3	-	-	74.5	3.6	-	-	74.8	0.4	-	-
1980	76.1	1.7	-	-	77.1	1.3	-	-	76.9	-0.3	-	-	78.3	1.8	-	-	80.0	2.2	-	-	81.2	1.5	-	-
1981	82.8	2.0	-	-	82.6	-0.2	-	-	84.6	2.4	-	-	83.8	-0.9	-	-	87.0	3.8	-	-	87.6	0.7	-	-
1982	88.8	1.4	-	-	89.7	1.0	-	-	90.2	0.6	-	-	88.9	-1.4	-	-	93.4	5.1	-	-	94.9	1.6	-	-
1983	98.4	3.7	-	-	97.3	-1.1	-	-	98.9	1.6	-	-	99.6	0.7	-	-	101.5	1.9	-	-	104.5	3.0	-	-
1984	105.3	0.8	-	-	105.5	0.2	-	-	107.7	2.1	-	-	107.9	0.2	-	-	109.7	1.7	-	-	111.8	1.9	-	-
1985	113.5	1.5	-	-	114.5	0.9	-	-	114.3	-0.2	-	-	114.3	0.0	-	-	116.6	2.0	-	-	116.0	-0.5	-	-
1986	117.7	1.5	-	-	118.7	0.8	-	-	118.9	0.2	-	-	117.8	-0.9	-	-	119.0	1.0	-	-	119.9	0.8	-	-
1987	-	-	-	-	-	-	-	-	-	-	121.6	1.4	-	-	-	-	-	-	-	-	-	-	124.3	2.2
1988	-	-	-	-	-	-	-	-	-	-	126.8	2.0	-	-	-	-	-	-	-	-	-	-	129.1	1.8
1989	-	-	-	-	-	-	-	-	-	-	134.0	3.8	-	-	-	-	-	-	-	-	-	-	138.6	3.4
1990	-	-	-	-	-	-	-	-	-	-	145.6	5.1	-	-	-	-	-	-	-	-	-	-	149.8	2.9
1991	-	-	-	-	-	-	-	-	-	-	154.9	3.4	-	-	-	-	-	-	-	-	-	-	159.9	3.2
1992	-	-	-	-	-	-	-	-	-	-	167.2	4.6	-	-	-	-	-	-	-	-	-	-	173.5	3.8
1993	-	-	-	-	-	-	-	-	-	-	181.6	4.7	-	-	-	-	-	-	-	-	-	-	181.5	-0.1
1994	-	-	-	-	-	-	-	-	-	-	182.4	0.5	-	-	-	-	-	-	-	-	-	-	191.0	4.7
1995	-	-	-	-	-	-	-	-	-	-	194.6	1.9	-	-	-	-	-	-	-	-	-	-	-	-

Source: U.S. Department of Labor, Bureau of Labor Statistics, Division of Consumer Prices and Price Indexes. - indicates no data collected for period.

San Francisco-Oakland, CA
Consumer Price Index - All Urban Consumers
Base 1982-1984 = 100
Annual Averages

For 1914-1995. Columns headed % show percentile change in the index from the previous period for which an index is available.

Year	All Items		Food & Beverage		Housing		Apparel & Upkeep		Trans-portation		Medical Care		Entertain-ment		Other Goods & Services	
	Index	%	Index	%	Index	%	Index	%	Index	%	Index	%	Index	%	Index	%
1914	-	-	-	-	-	-	-	-	-	-	-	-	-	-	-	-
1915	9.2	-	-	-	-	-	-	-	-	-	-	-	-	-	-	-
1916	9.5	3.3	-	-	-	-	-	-	-	-	-	-	-	-	-	-
1917	10.9	14.7	-	-	-	-	-	-	-	-	-	-	-	-	-	-
1918	12.9	18.3	-	-	-	-	-	-	-	-	-	-	-	-	-	-
1919	15.0	16.3	-	-	-	-	-	-	-	-	-	-	-	-	-	-
1920	17.0	13.3	-	-	-	-	-	-	-	-	-	-	-	-	-	-
1921	15.3	-10.0	-	-	-	-	-	-	-	-	-	-	-	-	-	-
1922	14.6	-4.6	-	-	-	-	-	-	-	-	-	-	-	-	-	-
1923	14.7	0.7	-	-	-	-	-	-	-	-	-	-	-	-	-	-
1924	14.7	0.0	-	-	-	-	-	-	-	-	-	-	-	-	-	-
1925	15.1	2.7	-	-	-	-	-	-	-	-	-	-	-	-	-	-
1926	15.0	-0.7	-	-	-	-	-	-	-	-	-	-	-	-	-	-
1927	14.9	-0.7	-	-	-	-	-	-	-	-	-	-	-	-	-	-
1928	14.8	-0.7	-	-	-	-	-	-	-	-	-	-	-	-	-	-
1929	14.9	0.7	-	-	-	-	-	-	-	-	-	-	-	-	-	-
1930	14.5	-2.7	-	-	-	-	-	-	-	-	-	-	-	-	-	-
1931	13.3	-8.3	-	-	-	-	-	-	-	-	-	-	-	-	-	-
1932	12.3	-7.5	-	-	-	-	-	-	-	-	-	-	-	-	-	-
1933	11.8	-4.1	-	-	-	-	-	-	-	-	-	-	-	-	-	-
1934	12.1	2.5	-	-	-	-	-	-	-	-	-	-	-	-	-	-
1935	12.4	2.5	-	-	-	-	-	-	-	-	-	-	-	-	-	-
1936	12.4	0.0	-	-	-	-	-	-	-	-	-	-	-	-	-	-
1937	12.8	3.2	-	-	-	-	-	-	-	-	-	-	-	-	-	-
1938	12.8	0.0	-	-	-	-	-	-	-	-	-	-	-	-	-	-
1939	12.6	-1.6	-	-	-	-	-	-	-	-	-	-	-	-	-	-
1940	12.7	0.8	-	-	-	-	-	-	-	-	-	-	-	-	-	-
1941	13.4	5.5	-	-	-	-	-	-	-	-	-	-	-	-	-	-
1942	15.0	11.9	-	-	-	-	-	-	-	-	-	-	-	-	-	-
1943	16.0	6.7	-	-	-	-	-	-	-	-	-	-	-	-	-	-
1944	16.4	2.5	-	-	-	-	-	-	-	-	-	-	-	-	-	-
1945	16.8	2.4	-	-	-	-	-	-	-	-	-	-	-	-	-	-
1946	18.2	8.3	-	-	-	-	-	-	-	-	-	-	-	-	-	-
1947	20.6	13.2	-	-	-	-	-	-	16.4	-	13.6	-	-	-	-	-
1948	22.0	6.8	-	-	-	-	-	-	18.0	9.8	14.3	5.1	-	-	-	-
1949	22.0	0.0	-	-	-	-	-	-	19.4	7.8	14.7	2.8	-	-	-	-
1950	22.0	0.0	-	-	-	-	-	-	19.5	0.5	15.1	2.7	-	-	-	-
1951	23.8	8.2	-	-	-	-	-	-	20.8	6.7	15.8	4.6	-	-	-	-
1952	24.6	3.4	-	-	-	-	-	-	23.7	13.9	16.8	6.3	-	-	-	-
1953	25.0	1.6	-	-	-	-	39.3	-	25.7	8.4	17.2	2.4	-	-	-	-
1954	25.1	0.4	-	-	-	-	38.8	-1.3	25.5	-0.8	17.5	1.7	-	-	-	-
1955	24.9	-0.8	-	-	-	-	39.0	0.5	25.1	-1.6	17.6	0.6	-	-	-	-
1956	25.5	2.4	-	-	-	-	39.8	2.1	25.4	1.2	18.6	5.7	-	-	-	-
1957	26.5	3.9	-	-	-	-	40.7	2.3	27.1	6.7	19.6	5.4	-	-	-	-
1958	27.5	3.8	-	-	-	-	41.0	0.7	28.3	4.4	21.0	7.1	-	-	-	-

[Continued]

San Francisco-Oakland, CA
Consumer Price Index - All Urban Consumers
Base 1982-1984 = 100
Annual Averages
[Continued]

For 1914-1995. Columns headed % show percentile change in the index from the previous period for which an index is available.

Year	All Items		Food & Beverage		Housing		Apparel & Upkeep		Trans-portation		Medical Care		Entertain-ment		Other Goods & Services	
	Index	%	Index	%	Index	%	Index	%	Index	%	Index	%	Index	%	Index	%
1959	28.0	1.8	-	-	-	-	41.4	1.0	29.8	5.3	21.9	4.3	-	-	-	-
1960	28.6	2.1	-	-	-	-	42.5	2.7	29.6	-0.7	22.5	2.7	-	-	-	-
1961	28.9	1.0	-	-	-	-	43.2	1.6	29.8	0.7	23.0	2.2	-	-	-	-
1962	29.4	1.7	-	-	-	-	43.8	1.4	30.4	2.0	24.1	4.8	-	-	-	-
1963	29.8	1.4	-	-	-	-	44.2	0.9	30.7	1.0	24.7	2.5	-	-	-	-
1964	30.2	1.3	-	-	-	-	44.7	1.1	31.5	2.6	25.3	2.4	-	-	-	-
1965	30.8	2.0	-	-	-	-	45.4	1.6	31.7	0.6	25.9	2.4	-	-	-	-
1966	31.6	2.6	-	-	-	-	46.5	2.4	32.0	0.9	27.3	5.4	-	-	-	-
1967	32.5	2.8	-	-	-	-	48.5	4.3	32.9	2.8	28.9	5.9	-	-	-	-
1968	34.0	4.6	-	-	-	-	51.2	5.6	33.8	2.7	30.4	5.2	-	-	-	-
1969	35.8	5.3	-	-	-	-	53.7	4.9	35.3	4.4	31.9	4.9	-	-	-	-
1970	37.7	5.3	-	-	-	-	55.3	3.0	36.7	4.0	33.6	5.3	-	-	-	-
1971	39.1	3.7	-	-	-	-	57.7	4.3	38.8	5.7	35.6	6.0	-	-	-	-
1972	40.4	3.3	-	-	-	-	59.0	2.3	39.6	2.1	36.8	3.4	-	-	-	-
1973	42.8	5.9	-	-	-	-	61.4	4.1	40.5	2.3	38.2	3.8	-	-	-	-
1974	47.0	9.8	-	-	-	-	65.9	7.3	44.8	10.6	41.5	8.6	-	-	-	-
1975	51.8	10.2	-	-	-	-	68.7	4.2	49.9	11.4	47.7	14.9	-	-	-	-
1976	54.6	5.4	59.5	-	50.5	-	70.5	2.6	54.2	8.6	52.5	10.1	64.8	-	54.3	-
1977	58.8	7.7	64.0	7.6	55.0	8.9	73.1	3.7	58.0	7.0	57.8	10.1	67.6	4.3	58.2	7.2
1978	64.3	9.4	70.7	10.5	61.6	12.0	77.2	5.6	61.4	5.9	63.3	9.5	71.8	6.2	63.4	8.9
1979	69.8	8.6	79.3	12.2	65.1	5.7	82.0	6.2	70.4	14.7	69.1	9.2	75.5	5.2	67.6	6.6
1980	80.4	15.2	85.2	7.4	77.2	18.6	88.6	8.0	83.7	18.9	76.6	10.9	84.8	12.3	72.7	7.5
1981	90.8	12.9	91.2	7.0	90.5	17.2	92.6	4.5	92.0	9.9	84.6	10.4	92.4	9.0	79.8	9.8
1982	97.6	7.5	97.1	6.5	97.8	8.1	97.6	5.4	97.2	5.7	94.2	11.3	98.4	6.5	90.7	13.7
1983	98.4	0.8	99.3	2.3	97.7	-0.1	97.8	0.2	99.1	2.0	100.7	6.9	98.7	0.3	101.2	11.6
1984	104.0	5.7	103.7	4.4	104.5	7.0	104.6	7.0	103.7	4.6	105.1	4.4	102.8	4.2	108.2	6.9
1985	108.4	4.2	105.9	2.1	111.2	6.4	103.5	-1.1	105.5	1.7	111.1	5.7	108.6	5.6	116.3	7.5
1986	111.6	3.0	109.5	3.4	117.5	5.7	101.7	-1.7	101.2	-4.1	119.7	7.7	117.4	8.1	123.2	5.9
1987	115.4	3.4	113.7	3.8	121.5	3.4	104.6	2.9	102.4	1.2	128.7	7.5	121.6	3.6	130.9	6.3
1988	120.5	4.4	120.4	5.9	126.9	4.4	102.4	-2.1	105.3	2.8	136.9	6.4	129.1	6.2	140.1	7.0
1989	126.4	4.9	128.2	6.5	132.4	4.3	104.2	1.8	109.6	4.1	147.9	8.0	133.1	3.1	152.2	8.6
1990	132.1	4.5	134.7	5.1	137.3	3.7	107.5	3.2	114.7	4.7	160.5	8.5	140.7	5.7	161.0	5.8
1991	137.9	4.4	140.3	4.2	142.7	3.9	113.1	5.2	117.1	2.1	172.9	7.7	152.4	8.3	174.5	8.4
1992	142.5	3.3	143.3	2.1	146.2	2.5	117.8	4.2	119.8	2.3	187.0	8.2	156.5	2.7	195.9	12.3
1993	146.3	2.7	146.2	2.0	149.2	2.1	118.2	0.3	123.7	3.3	199.1	6.5	162.3	3.7	207.0	5.7
1994	148.7	1.6	148.9	1.8	151.5	1.5	115.5	-2.3	125.7	1.6	204.3	2.6	164.5	1.4	213.2	3.0
1995	151.6	2.0	151.6	1.8	154.5	2.0	114.0	-1.3	129.0	2.6	209.0	2.3	166.2	1.0	220.6	3.5

Source: U.S. Department of Labor, Bureau of Labor Statistics, Division of Consumer Prices and Price Indexes. - indicates no data collected for period.

San Francisco-Oakland, CA
Consumer Price Index - Urban Wage Earners
Base 1982-1984 = 100
Annual Averages

For 1914-1995. Columns headed % show percentile change in the index from the previous period for which an index is available.

Year	All Items		Food & Beverage		Housing		Apparel & Upkeep		Trans- portation		Medical Care		Entertain- ment		Other Goods & Services	
	Index	%	Index	%	Index	%	Index	%	Index	%	Index	%	Index	%	Index	%
1914	-	-	-	-	-	-	-	-	-	-	-	-	-	-	-	-
1915	9.3	-	-	-	-	-	-	-	-	-	-	-	-	-	-	-
1916	9.6	3.2	-	-	-	-	-	-	-	-	-	-	-	-	-	-
1917	11.0	14.6	-	-	-	-	-	-	-	-	-	-	-	-	-	-
1918	13.0	18.2	-	-	-	-	-	-	-	-	-	-	-	-	-	-
1919	15.2	16.9	-	-	-	-	-	-	-	-	-	-	-	-	-	-
1920	17.1	12.5	-	-	-	-	-	-	-	-	-	-	-	-	-	-
1921	15.5	-9.4	-	-	-	-	-	-	-	-	-	-	-	-	-	-
1922	14.8	-4.5	-	-	-	-	-	-	-	-	-	-	-	-	-	-
1923	14.8	0.0	-	-	-	-	-	-	-	-	-	-	-	-	-	-
1924	14.8	0.0	-	-	-	-	-	-	-	-	-	-	-	-	-	-
1925	15.2	2.7	-	-	-	-	-	-	-	-	-	-	-	-	-	-
1926	15.2	0.0	-	-	-	-	-	-	-	-	-	-	-	-	-	-
1927	15.0	-1.3	-	-	-	-	-	-	-	-	-	-	-	-	-	-
1928	15.0	0.0	-	-	-	-	-	-	-	-	-	-	-	-	-	-
1929	15.0	0.0	-	-	-	-	-	-	-	-	-	-	-	-	-	-
1930	14.7	-2.0	-	-	-	-	-	-	-	-	-	-	-	-	-	-
1931	13.4	-8.8	-	-	-	-	-	-	-	-	-	-	-	-	-	-
1932	12.4	-7.5	-	-	-	-	-	-	-	-	-	-	-	-	-	-
1933	11.9	-4.0	-	-	-	-	-	-	-	-	-	-	-	-	-	-
1934	12.2	2.5	-	-	-	-	-	-	-	-	-	-	-	-	-	-
1935	12.5	2.5	-	-	-	-	-	-	-	-	-	-	-	-	-	-
1936	12.5	0.0	-	-	-	-	-	-	-	-	-	-	-	-	-	-
1937	13.0	4.0	-	-	-	-	-	-	-	-	-	-	-	-	-	-
1938	12.9	-0.8	-	-	-	-	-	-	-	-	-	-	-	-	-	-
1939	12.7	-1.6	-	-	-	-	-	-	-	-	-	-	-	-	-	-
1940	12.8	0.8	-	-	-	-	-	-	-	-	-	-	-	-	-	-
1941	13.5	5.5	-	-	-	-	-	-	-	-	-	-	-	-	-	-
1942	15.1	11.9	-	-	-	-	-	-	-	-	-	-	-	-	-	-
1943	16.1	6.6	-	-	-	-	-	-	-	-	-	-	-	-	-	-
1944	16.5	2.5	-	-	-	-	-	-	-	-	-	-	-	-	-	-
1945	17.0	3.0	-	-	-	-	-	-	-	-	-	-	-	-	-	-
1946	18.3	7.6	-	-	-	-	-	-	-	-	-	-	-	-	-	-
1947	20.8	13.7	-	-	-	-	-	-	16.0	-	13.7	-	-	-	-	-
1948	22.2	6.7	-	-	-	-	-	-	17.6	10.0	14.4	5.1	-	-	-	-
1949	22.2	0.0	-	-	-	-	-	-	19.0	8.0	14.8	2.8	-	-	-	-
1950	22.2	0.0	-	-	-	-	-	-	19.0	0.0	15.2	2.7	-	-	-	-
1951	24.0	8.1	-	-	-	-	-	-	20.3	6.8	15.9	4.6	-	-	-	-
1952	24.9	3.8	-	-	-	-	-	-	23.2	14.3	16.9	6.3	-	-	-	-
1953	25.3	1.6	-	-	-	-	40.8	-	25.1	8.2	17.4	3.0	-	-	-	-
1954	25.3	0.0	-	-	-	-	40.3	-1.2	24.9	-0.8	17.6	1.1	-	-	-	-
1955	25.2	-0.4	-	-	-	-	40.4	0.2	24.5	-1.6	17.8	1.1	-	-	-	-
1956	25.7	2.0	-	-	-	-	41.3	2.2	24.8	1.2	18.7	5.1	-	-	-	-
1957	26.8	4.3	-	-	-	-	42.2	2.2	26.4	6.5	19.7	5.3	-	-	-	-
1958	27.7	3.4	-	-	-	-	42.5	0.7	27.6	4.5	21.2	7.6	-	-	-	-

[Continued]

San Francisco-Oakland, CA
Consumer Price Index - Urban Wage Earners
Base 1982-1984 = 100
Annual Averages
[Continued]

For 1914-1995. Columns headed % show percentile change in the index from the previous period for which an index is available.

Year	All Items		Food & Beverage		Housing		Apparel & Upkeep		Trans- portation		Medical Care		Entertain- ment		Other Goods & Services	
	Index	%	Index	%	Index	%	Index	%	Index	%	Index	%	Index	%	Index	%
1959	28.3	2.2	-	-	-	-	43.0	1.2	29.1	5.4	22.0	3.8	-	-	-	-
1960	28.8	1.8	-	-	-	-	44.2	2.8	28.9	-0.7	22.7	3.2	-	-	-	-
1961	29.2	1.4	-	-	-	-	44.8	1.4	29.1	0.7	23.2	2.2	-	-	-	-
1962	29.7	1.7	-	-	-	-	45.4	1.3	29.7	2.1	24.2	4.3	-	-	-	-
1963	30.0	1.0	-	-	-	-	45.9	1.1	30.0	1.0	24.8	2.5	-	-	-	-
1964	30.5	1.7	-	-	-	-	46.4	1.1	30.8	2.7	25.4	2.4	-	-	-	-
1965	31.1	2.0	-	-	-	-	47.1	1.5	31.0	0.6	26.1	2.8	-	-	-	-
1966	31.9	2.6	-	-	-	-	48.3	2.5	31.2	0.6	27.5	5.4	-	-	-	-
1967	32.8	2.8	-	-	-	-	50.3	4.1	32.1	2.9	29.1	5.8	-	-	-	-
1968	34.3	4.6	-	-	-	-	53.2	5.8	33.0	2.8	30.6	5.2	-	-	-	-
1969	36.2	5.5	-	-	-	-	55.7	4.7	34.5	4.5	32.1	4.9	-	-	-	-
1970	38.0	5.0	-	-	-	-	57.4	3.1	35.9	4.1	33.8	5.3	-	-	-	-
1971	39.4	3.7	-	-	-	-	59.8	4.2	37.9	5.6	35.9	6.2	-	-	-	-
1972	40.8	3.6	-	-	-	-	61.2	2.3	38.6	1.8	37.0	3.1	-	-	-	-
1973	43.2	5.9	-	-	-	-	63.7	4.1	39.5	2.3	38.5	4.1	-	-	-	-
1974	47.4	9.7	-	-	-	-	68.4	7.4	43.8	10.9	41.8	8.6	-	-	-	-
1975	52.2	10.1	-	-	-	-	71.3	4.2	48.7	11.2	48.0	14.8	-	-	-	-
1976	55.2	5.7	59.1	-	51.8	-	73.1	2.5	52.9	8.6	52.9	10.2	72.6	-	54.0	-
1977	59.4	7.6	63.6	7.6	56.4	8.9	75.8	3.7	56.6	7.0	58.2	10.0	75.7	4.3	57.9	7.2
1978	64.8	9.1	70.3	10.5	63.0	11.7	78.4	3.4	60.3	6.5	63.5	9.1	81.2	7.3	61.7	6.6
1979	70.5	8.8	78.4	11.5	66.5	5.6	82.9	5.7	69.5	15.3	69.2	9.0	83.8	3.2	66.7	8.1
1980	81.2	15.2	84.9	8.3	78.9	18.6	88.8	7.1	82.3	18.4	76.9	11.1	91.7	9.4	73.1	9.6
1981	91.6	12.8	91.8	8.1	92.3	17.0	95.1	7.1	91.1	10.7	85.1	10.7	98.8	7.7	80.2	9.7
1982	98.2	7.2	97.0	5.7	100.0	8.3	98.1	3.2	96.8	6.3	94.1	10.6	100.0	1.2	91.0	13.5
1983	98.2	0.0	99.3	2.4	96.9	-3.1	97.7	-0.4	99.2	2.5	100.6	6.9	97.7	-2.3	101.1	11.1
1984	103.7	5.6	103.7	4.4	103.2	6.5	104.2	6.7	104.0	4.8	105.4	4.8	102.3	4.7	107.9	6.7
1985	107.8	4.0	105.9	2.1	109.6	6.2	103.9	-0.3	105.7	1.6	111.8	6.1	107.2	4.8	115.9	7.4
1986	110.7	2.7	109.5	3.4	115.9	5.7	102.3	-1.5	101.5	-4.0	120.5	7.8	114.1	6.4	122.5	5.7
1987	114.3	3.3	113.8	3.9	119.4	3.0	105.4	3.0	103.7	2.2	130.0	7.9	117.3	2.8	130.4	6.4
1988	119.4	4.5	120.4	5.8	124.6	4.4	104.4	-0.9	107.1	3.3	138.1	6.2	124.0	5.7	140.1	7.4
1989	125.5	5.1	128.3	6.6	129.7	4.1	107.0	2.5	111.8	4.4	149.0	7.9	130.1	4.9	154.6	10.3
1990	131.1	4.5	134.7	5.0	134.6	3.8	110.6	3.4	116.7	4.4	160.8	7.9	136.3	4.8	164.5	6.4
1991	136.3	4.0	140.4	4.2	139.7	3.8	116.2	5.1	118.6	1.6	172.1	7.0	143.5	5.3	177.8	8.1
1992	140.6	3.2	143.3	2.1	143.1	2.4	121.5	4.6	121.9	2.8	186.4	8.3	147.5	2.8	195.8	10.1
1993	144.3	2.6	146.4	2.2	146.1	2.1	122.7	1.0	125.7	3.1	197.9	6.2	151.6	2.8	204.8	4.6
1994	146.3	1.4	149.2	1.9	148.3	1.5	120.6	-1.7	127.9	1.8	202.4	2.3	152.9	0.9	208.8	2.0
1995	149.3	2.1	151.8	1.7	151.1	1.9	120.0	-0.5	132.1	3.3	206.8	2.2	154.8	1.2	215.1	3.0

Source: U.S. Department of Labor, Bureau of Labor Statistics, Division of Consumer Prices and Price Indexes. - indicates no data collected for period.

San Francisco-Oakland, CA
Consumer Price Index - All Urban Consumers
Base 1982-1984 = 100
All Items

For 1914-1995. Columns headed % show percentile change in the index from the previous period for which an index is available.

Year	Jan Index	%	Feb Index	%	Mar Index	%	Apr Index	%	May Index	%	Jun Index	%	Jul Index	%	Aug Index	%	Sep Index	%	Oct Index	%	Nov Index	%	Dec Index	%
1914	-	-	-	-	-	-	-	-	-	-	-	-	-	-	-	-	-	-	-	-	-	-	9.2	-
1915	-	-	-	-	-	-	-	-	-	-	-	-	-	-	-	-	-	-	-	-	-	-	9.2	0.0
1916	-	-	-	-	-	-	-	-	-	-	-	-	-	-	-	-	-	-	-	-	-	-	10.0	8.7
1917	-	-	-	-	-	-	-	-	-	-	-	-	-	-	-	-	-	-	-	-	-	-	11.6	16.0
1918	-	-	-	-	-	-	-	-	-	-	-	-	-	-	-	-	-	-	-	-	-	-	14.1	21.6
1919	-	-	-	-	-	-	-	-	-	-	14.7	4.3	-	-	-	-	-	-	-	-	-	-	16.3	10.9
1920	-	-	-	-	-	-	-	-	-	-	17.5	7.4	-	-	-	-	-	-	-	-	-	-	16.5	-5.7
1921	-	-	-	-	-	-	-	-	15.2	-7.9	-	-	-	-	-	-	15.0	-1.3	-	-	-	-	15.0	0.0
1922	-	-	-	-	14.7	-2.0	-	-	-	-	14.6	-0.7	-	-	-	-	14.5	-0.7	-	-	-	-	14.6	0.7
1923	-	-	-	-	14.4	-1.4	-	-	-	-	14.6	1.4	-	-	-	-	14.8	1.4	-	-	-	-	15.0	1.4
1924	-	-	-	-	14.6	-2.7	-	-	-	-	14.6	0.0	-	-	-	-	14.7	0.7	-	-	-	-	14.8	0.7
1925	-	-	-	-	-	-	-	-	-	-	15.1	2.0	-	-	-	-	-	-	-	-	-	-	15.3	1.3
1926	-	-	-	-	-	-	-	-	-	-	15.0	-2.0	-	-	-	-	-	-	-	-	-	-	15.0	0.0
1927	-	-	-	-	-	-	-	-	-	-	15.0	0.0	-	-	-	-	-	-	-	-	-	-	14.9	-0.7
1928	-	-	-	-	-	-	-	-	-	-	14.8	-0.7	-	-	-	-	-	-	-	-	-	-	15.0	1.4
1929	-	-	-	-	-	-	-	-	-	-	14.8	-1.3	-	-	-	-	-	-	-	-	-	-	14.9	0.7
1930	-	-	-	-	-	-	-	-	-	-	14.6	-2.0	-	-	-	-	-	-	-	-	-	-	14.1	-3.4
1931	-	-	-	-	-	-	-	-	-	-	13.3	-5.7	-	-	-	-	-	-	-	-	-	-	12.9	-3.0
1932	-	-	-	-	-	-	-	-	-	-	12.2	-5.4	-	-	-	-	-	-	-	-	-	-	12.0	-1.6
1933	-	-	-	-	-	-	-	-	-	-	11.7	-2.5	-	-	-	-	-	-	-	-	-	-	12.1	3.4
1934	-	-	-	-	-	-	-	-	-	-	12.2	0.8	-	-	-	-	-	-	-	-	12.5	2.5	-	-
1935	-	-	-	-	12.6	0.8	-	-	-	-	-	-	12.3	-2.4	-	-	-	-	12.3	0.0	-	-	-	-
1936	12.4	0.8	-	-	-	-	12.2	-1.6	-	-	-	-	12.4	1.6	-	-	12.4	0.0	-	-	-	-	12.4	0.0
1937	-	-	-	-	12.8	3.2	-	-	-	-	12.8	0.0	-	-	-	-	12.9	0.8	-	-	-	-	13.0	0.8
1938	-	-	-	-	12.8	-1.5	-	-	-	-	12.8	0.0	-	-	-	-	12.8	0.0	-	-	-	-	12.8	0.0
1939	-	-	-	-	12.7	-0.8	-	-	-	-	12.5	-1.6	-	-	-	-	12.8	2.4	-	-	-	-	12.6	-1.6
1940	-	-	-	-	12.6	0.0	-	-	-	-	12.6	0.0	-	-	-	-	12.7	0.8	12.8	0.8	12.8	0.0	12.8	0.0
1941	12.8	0.0	12.9	0.8	12.9	0.0	13.1	1.6	13.1	0.0	13.3	1.5	13.3	0.0	13.4	0.8	13.6	1.5	13.8	1.5	14.0	1.4	14.0	0.0
1942	14.3	2.1	14.4	0.7	14.6	1.4	14.8	1.4	14.8	0.0	14.9	0.7	14.9	0.0	15.1	1.3	15.2	0.7	15.3	0.7	15.6	2.0	15.6	0.0
1943	15.7	0.6	15.7	0.0	15.9	1.3	16.2	1.9	16.2	0.0	16.2	0.0	15.8	-2.5	15.7	-0.6	15.8	0.6	16.0	1.3	16.1	0.6	16.1	0.0
1944	16.1	0.0	16.0	-0.6	16.1	0.6	16.2	0.6	16.4	1.2	16.3	-0.6	16.4	0.6	16.4	0.0	16.4	0.0	16.6	1.2	16.6	0.0	16.8	1.2
1945	16.7	-0.6	16.6	-0.6	16.7	0.6	16.8	0.6	16.7	-0.6	16.8	0.6	16.9	0.6	16.8	-0.6	16.8	0.0	16.8	0.0	17.0	1.2	17.2	1.2
1946	17.0	-1.2	16.8	-1.2	16.9	0.6	16.9	0.0	17.0	0.6	17.4	2.4	18.2	4.6	18.7	2.7	19.1	2.1	19.4	1.6	20.1	3.6	20.3	1.0
1947	20.1	-1.0	20.0	-0.5	20.3	1.5	20.4	0.5	20.3	-0.5	20.1	-1.0	-	-	-	-	21.0	4.5	-	-	-	-	21.4	1.9
1948	-	-	-	-	21.7	1.4	-	-	-	-	22.0	1.4	-	-	-	-	22.4	1.8	-	-	-	-	22.4	0.0
1949	-	-	-	-	22.1	-1.3	-	-	-	-	22.0	-0.5	-	-	-	-	21.9	-0.5	-	-	-	-	21.7	-0.9
1950	-	-	-	-	21.8	0.5	-	-	-	-	21.7	-0.5	-	-	-	-	22.1	1.8	-	-	-	-	22.9	3.6
1951	-	-	-	-	23.8	3.9	-	-	-	-	23.7	-0.4	-	-	-	-	23.7	0.0	-	-	-	-	24.3	2.5
1952	-	-	-	-	24.3	0.0	-	-	-	-	24.8	2.1	-	-	-	-	24.7	-0.4	-	-	-	-	24.9	0.8
1953	-	-	-	-	24.9	0.0	-	-	-	-	25.0	0.4	-	-	-	-	25.2	0.8	-	-	-	-	25.2	0.0
1954	-	-	-	-	25.1	-0.4	-	-	-	-	25.1	0.0	-	-	-	-	25.0	-0.4	-	-	-	-	24.9	-0.4
1955	-	-	-	-	24.9	0.0	-	-	-	-	24.9	0.0	-	-	-	-	24.9	0.0	-	-	-	-	24.9	0.0
1956	-	-	-	-	25.1	0.8	-	-	-	-	25.4	1.2	-	-	-	-	25.6	0.8	-	-	-	-	26.2	2.3
1957	-	-	-	-	26.3	0.4	-	-	-	-	26.4	0.4	-	-	-	-	26.6	0.8	-	-	-	-	26.9	1.1
1958	-	-	-	-	27.3	1.5	-	-	-	-	27.6	1.1	-	-	-	-	27.6	0.0	-	-	-	-	27.6	0.0

[Continued]

San Francisco-Oakland, CA
Consumer Price Index - All Urban Consumers
Base 1982-1984 = 100
All Items
[Continued]

For 1914-1995. Columns headed % show percentile change in the index from the previous period for which an index is available.

Year	Jan Index	%	Feb Index	%	Mar Index	%	Apr Index	%	May Index	%	Jun Index	%	Jul Index	%	Aug Index	%	Sep Index	%	Oct Index	%	Nov Index	%	Dec Index	%
1959	-	-	-	-	27.8	0.7	-	-	-	-	27.9	0.4	-	-	-	-	28.2	1.1	-	-	-	-	28.4	0.7
1960	-	-	-	-	28.3	-0.4	-	-	-	-	28.5	0.7	-	-	-	-	28.7	0.7	-	-	-	-	28.9	0.7
1961	-	-	-	-	28.8	-0.3	-	-	-	-	28.8	0.0	-	-	-	-	29.0	0.7	-	-	-	-	29.1	0.3
1962	-	-	-	-	29.3	0.7	-	-	-	-	29.4	0.3	-	-	-	-	29.4	0.0	-	-	-	-	29.5	0.3
1963	-	-	-	-	29.6	0.3	-	-	-	-	29.8	0.7	-	-	-	-	29.9	0.3	-	-	-	-	30.1	0.7
1964	-	-	-	-	30.1	0.0	-	-	-	-	30.2	0.3	-	-	-	-	30.3	0.3	-	-	-	-	30.5	0.7
1965	-	-	-	-	30.7	0.7	-	-	-	-	30.9	0.7	-	-	-	-	30.8	-0.3	-	-	-	-	31.1	1.0
1966	-	-	-	-	31.4	1.0	-	-	-	-	31.5	0.3	-	-	-	-	31.8	1.0	-	-	-	-	32.0	0.6
1967	-	-	-	-	32.0	0.0	-	-	-	-	32.4	1.3	-	-	-	-	32.9	1.5	-	-	-	-	33.1	0.6
1968	-	-	-	-	33.5	1.2	-	-	-	-	34.0	1.5	-	-	-	-	34.3	0.9	-	-	-	-	34.6	0.9
1969	-	-	-	-	35.2	1.7	-	-	-	-	35.7	1.4	-	-	-	-	36.3	1.7	-	-	-	-	36.8	1.4
1970	-	-	-	-	37.2	1.1	-	-	-	-	37.6	1.1	-	-	-	-	38.0	1.1	-	-	-	-	38.5	1.3
1971	-	-	-	-	38.7	0.5	-	-	-	-	39.0	0.8	-	-	-	-	39.3	0.8	-	-	-	-	39.6	0.8
1972	-	-	-	-	39.9	0.8	-	-	-	-	40.4	1.3	-	-	-	-	40.9	1.2	-	-	-	-	41.1	0.5
1973	-	-	-	-	41.9	1.9	-	-	-	-	42.5	1.4	-	-	-	-	43.8	3.1	-	-	-	-	44.0	0.5
1974	-	-	-	-	45.3	3.0	-	-	-	-	46.8	3.3	-	-	-	-	48.2	3.0	-	-	-	-	49.5	2.7
1975	-	-	-	-	50.7	2.4	-	-	-	-	51.6	1.8	-	-	-	-	52.5	1.7	-	-	-	-	53.4	1.7
1976	-	-	-	-	53.8	0.7	-	-	-	-	54.3	0.9	-	-	-	-	55.3	1.8	-	-	-	-	56.0	1.3
1977	-	-	-	-	57.2	2.1	-	-	-	-	58.8	2.8	-	-	-	-	59.9	1.9	-	-	-	-	60.9	1.7
1978	-	-	61.5	1.0	-	-	62.7	2.0	-	-	64.8	3.3	-	-	66.6	2.8	-	-	66.1	-0.8	-	-	65.3	-1.2
1979	-	-	66.3	1.5	-	-	67.9	2.4	-	-	69.1	1.8	-	-	71.0	2.7	-	-	72.0	1.4	-	-	74.9	4.0
1980	-	-	78.3	4.5	-	-	79.2	1.1	-	-	80.7	1.9	-	-	81.6	1.1	-	-	81.9	0.4	-	-	82.9	1.2
1981	-	-	84.7	2.2	-	-	87.9	3.8	-	-	89.1	1.4	-	-	93.6	5.1	-	-	96.6	3.2	-	-	95.6	-1.0
1982	-	-	96.2	0.6	-	-	97.2	1.0	-	-	99.1	2.0	-	-	99.0	-0.1	-	-	98.4	-0.6	-	-	95.6	-2.8
1983	-	-	96.7	1.2	-	-	97.4	0.7	-	-	98.6	1.2	-	-	99.5	0.9	-	-	99.4	-0.1	-	-	100.0	0.6
1984	-	-	101.4	1.4	-	-	102.9	1.5	-	-	103.7	0.8	-	-	105.2	1.4	-	-	106.5	1.2	-	-	106.0	-0.5
1985	-	-	106.9	0.8	-	-	107.5	0.6	-	-	108.4	0.8	-	-	109.2	0.7	-	-	109.5	0.3	-	-	109.4	-0.1
1986	-	-	111.0	1.5	-	-	110.4	-0.5	-	-	111.9	1.4	-	-	112.4	0.4	-	-	113.1	0.6	-	-	111.8	-1.1
1987	112.5	0.6	113.4	0.8	113.7	0.3	114.8	1.0	115.0	0.2	115.0	0.0	115.8	0.7	116.1	0.3	116.6	0.4	117.1	0.4	117.3	0.2	117.4	0.1
1988	118.4	0.9	117.9	-0.4	119.1	1.0	118.7	-0.3	119.7	0.8	120.1	0.3	120.9	0.7	122.0	0.9	122.1	0.1	122.3	0.2	122.2	-0.1	122.6	0.3
1989	124.0	1.1	124.0	0.0	125.9	1.5	125.4	-0.4	126.3	0.7	126.2	-0.1	127.4	1.0	128.1	0.5	126.8	-1.0	127.5	0.6	127.2	-0.2	127.4	0.2
1990	128.5	0.9	129.2	0.5	130.0	0.6	130.7	0.5	130.8	0.1	131.6	0.6	132.3	0.5	133.1	0.6	134.0	0.7	134.6	0.4	134.7	0.1	135.1	0.3
1991	136.7	1.2	136.1	-0.4	136.3	0.1	135.8	-0.4	136.2	0.3	137.6	1.0	138.2	0.4	139.1	0.7	139.7	0.4	139.6	-0.1	139.8	0.1	139.8	0.0
1992	140.3	0.4	141.0	0.5	141.9	0.6	141.6	-0.2	141.9	0.2	141.9	0.0	142.2	0.2	142.7	0.4	143.7	0.7	144.3	0.4	144.2	-0.1	144.3	0.1
1993	145.1	0.6	145.5	0.3	145.7	0.1	146.8	0.8	146.9	0.1	146.1	-0.5	146.1	0.0	146.2	0.1	146.5	0.2	147.0	0.3	147.2	0.1	147.0	-0.1
1994	147.5	0.3	147.4	-0.1	148.2	0.5	148.0	-0.1	148.3	0.2	148.1	-0.1	148.9	0.5	149.4	0.3	149.4	0.0	149.4	0.0	149.8	0.3	149.4	-0.3
1995	150.3	0.6	150.5	0.1	151.1	0.4	151.5	0.3	151.3	-0.1	151.7	0.3	151.5	-0.1	151.5	0.0	152.3	0.5	152.6	0.2	152.4	-0.1	152.1	-0.2

Source: U.S. Department of Labor, Bureau of Labor Statistics, Division of Consumer Prices and Price Indexes. - indicates no data collected for period.

San Francisco-Oakland, CA
Consumer Price Index - Urban Wage Earners
Base 1982-1984 = 100
All Items

For 1914-1995. Columns headed % show percentile change in the index from the previous period for which an index is available.

Year	Jan Index	%	Feb Index	%	Mar Index	%	Apr Index	%	May Index	%	Jun Index	%	Jul Index	%	Aug Index	%	Sep Index	%	Oct Index	%	Nov Index	%	Dec Index	%
1914	-	-	-	-	-	-	-	-	-	-	-	-	-	-	-	-	-	-	-	-	-	-	9.3	-
1915	-	-	-	-	-	-	-	-	-	-	-	-	-	-	-	-	-	-	-	-	-	-	9.3	0.0
1916	-	-	-	-	-	-	-	-	-	-	-	-	-	-	-	-	-	-	-	-	-	-	10.0	7.5
1917	-	-	-	-	-	-	-	-	-	-	-	-	-	-	-	-	-	-	-	-	-	-	11.7	17.0
1918	-	-	-	-	-	-	-	-	-	-	-	-	-	-	-	-	-	-	-	-	-	-	14.3	22.2
1919	-	-	-	-	-	-	-	-	-	-	14.8	3.5	-	-	-	-	-	-	-	-	-	-	16.4	10.8
1920	-	-	-	-	-	-	-	-	-	-	17.7	7.9	-	-	-	-	-	-	-	-	-	-	16.7	-5.6
1921	-	-	-	-	-	-	-	-	15.3	-8.4	-	-	-	-	-	-	15.2	-0.7	-	-	-	-	15.1	-0.7
1922	-	-	-	-	14.8	-2.0	-	-	-	-	14.7	-0.7	-	-	-	-	14.6	-0.7	-	-	-	-	14.8	1.4
1923	-	-	-	-	14.6	-1.4	-	-	-	-	14.7	0.7	-	-	-	-	14.9	1.4	-	-	-	-	15.1	1.3
1924	-	-	-	-	14.7	-2.6	-	-	-	-	14.7	0.0	-	-	-	-	14.8	0.7	-	-	-	-	14.9	0.7
1925	-	-	-	-	-	-	-	-	-	-	15.3	2.7	-	-	-	-	-	-	-	-	-	-	15.4	0.7
1926	-	-	-	-	-	-	-	-	-	-	15.1	-1.9	-	-	-	-	-	-	-	-	-	-	15.1	0.0
1927	-	-	-	-	-	-	-	-	-	-	15.2	0.7	-	-	-	-	-	-	-	-	-	-	15.0	-1.3
1928	-	-	-	-	-	-	-	-	-	-	14.9	-0.7	-	-	-	-	-	-	-	-	-	-	15.1	1.3
1929	-	-	-	-	-	-	-	-	-	-	15.0	-0.7	-	-	-	-	-	-	-	-	-	-	15.0	0.0
1930	-	-	-	-	-	-	-	-	-	-	14.7	-2.0	-	-	-	-	-	-	-	-	-	-	14.2	-3.4
1931	-	-	-	-	-	-	-	-	-	-	13.4	-5.6	-	-	-	-	-	-	-	-	-	-	13.0	-3.0
1932	-	-	-	-	-	-	-	-	-	-	12.3	-5.4	-	-	-	-	-	-	-	-	-	-	12.1	-1.6
1933	-	-	-	-	-	-	-	-	-	-	11.8	-2.5	-	-	-	-	-	-	-	-	-	-	12.2	3.4
1934	-	-	-	-	-	-	-	-	-	-	12.3	0.8	-	-	-	-	-	-	-	-	12.6	2.4	-	-
1935	-	-	-	-	12.7	0.8	-	-	-	-	-	-	12.4	-2.4	-	-	-	-	12.4	0.0	-	-	-	-
1936	12.5	0.8	-	-	-	-	12.3	-1.6	-	-	-	-	12.5	1.6	-	-	12.5	0.0	-	-	-	-	12.5	0.0
1937	-	-	-	-	12.9	3.2	-	-	-	-	12.9	0.0	-	-	-	-	13.1	1.6	-	-	-	-	13.1	0.0
1938	-	-	-	-	12.9	-1.5	-	-	-	-	12.9	0.0	-	-	-	-	12.9	0.0	-	-	-	-	12.9	0.0
1939	-	-	-	-	12.8	-0.8	-	-	-	-	12.6	-1.6	-	-	-	-	12.9	2.4	-	-	-	-	12.7	-1.6
1940	-	-	-	-	12.7	0.0	-	-	-	-	12.7	0.0	-	-	-	-	12.8	0.8	12.9	0.8	12.9	0.0	12.9	0.0
1941	13.0	0.8	13.0	0.0	13.0	0.0	13.2	1.5	13.3	0.8	13.4	0.8	13.4	0.0	13.5	0.7	13.7	1.5	13.9	1.5	14.1	1.4	14.2	0.7
1942	14.5	2.1	14.5	0.0	14.7	1.4	14.9	1.4	14.9	0.0	15.0	0.7	15.0	0.0	15.2	1.3	15.4	1.3	15.5	0.6	15.7	1.3	15.8	0.6
1943	15.8	0.0	15.8	0.0	16.1	1.9	16.4	1.9	16.3	-0.6	16.4	0.6	16.0	-2.4	15.8	-1.2	16.0	1.3	16.2	1.3	16.3	0.6	16.3	0.0
1944	16.3	0.0	16.2	-0.6	16.3	0.6	16.4	0.6	16.5	0.6	16.5	0.0	16.5	0.0	16.5	0.0	16.6	0.6	16.7	0.6	16.8	0.6	16.9	0.6
1945	16.8	-0.6	16.7	-0.6	16.8	0.6	16.9	0.6	16.8	-0.6	16.9	0.6	17.0	0.6	16.9	-0.6	16.9	0.0	17.0	0.6	17.2	1.2	17.3	0.6
1946	17.1	-1.2	17.0	-0.6	17.0	0.0	17.1	0.6	17.2	0.6	17.6	2.3	18.4	4.5	18.9	2.7	19.3	2.1	19.6	1.6	20.3	3.6	20.5	1.0
1947	20.3	-1.0	20.2	-0.5	20.5	1.5	20.6	0.5	20.5	-0.5	20.3	-1.0	-	-	-	-	21.2	4.4	-	-	-	-	21.6	1.9
1948	-	-	-	-	21.9	1.4	-	-	-	-	22.2	1.4	-	-	-	-	22.6	1.8	-	-	-	-	22.6	0.0
1949	-	-	-	-	22.3	-1.3	-	-	-	-	22.2	-0.4	-	-	-	-	22.1	-0.5	-	-	-	-	21.9	-0.9
1950	-	-	-	-	22.0	0.5	-	-	-	-	21.9	-0.5	-	-	-	-	22.3	1.8	-	-	-	-	23.1	3.6
1951	-	-	-	-	24.0	3.9	-	-	-	-	23.9	-0.4	-	-	-	-	23.9	0.0	-	-	-	-	24.6	2.9
1952	-	-	-	-	24.6	0.0	-	-	-	-	25.0	1.6	-	-	-	-	24.9	-0.4	-	-	-	-	25.2	1.2
1953	-	-	-	-	25.1	-0.4	-	-	-	-	25.3	0.8	-	-	-	-	25.4	0.4	-	-	-	-	25.4	0.0
1954	-	-	-	-	25.3	-0.4	-	-	-	-	25.4	0.4	-	-	-	-	25.3	-0.4	-	-	-	-	25.2	-0.4
1955	-	-	-	-	25.2	0.0	-	-	-	-	25.1	-0.4	-	-	-	-	25.2	0.4	-	-	-	-	25.2	0.0
1956	-	-	-	-	25.4	0.8	-	-	-	-	25.6	0.8	-	-	-	-	25.9	1.2	-	-	-	-	26.4	1.9
1957	-	-	-	-	26.6	0.8	-	-	-	-	26.7	0.4	-	-	-	-	26.9	0.7	-	-	-	-	27.1	0.7
1958	-	-	-	-	27.6	1.8	-	-	-	-	27.8	0.7	-	-	-	-	27.9	0.4	-	-	-	-	27.8	-0.4

[Continued]

San Francisco-Oakland, CA
Consumer Price Index - Urban Wage Earners
Base 1982-1984 = 100
All Items
[Continued]

For 1914-1995. Columns headed % show percentile change in the index from the previous period for which an index is available.

Year	Jan Index	%	Feb Index	%	Mar Index	%	Apr Index	%	May Index	%	Jun Index	%	Jul Index	%	Aug Index	%	Sep Index	%	Oct Index	%	Nov Index	%	Dec Index	%
1959	-	-	-	-	28.1	1.1	-	-	-	-	28.2	0.4	-	-	-	-	28.4	0.7	-	-	-	-	28.7	1.1
1960	-	-	-	-	28.6	-0.3	-	-	-	-	28.8	0.7	-	-	-	-	28.9	0.3	-	-	-	-	29.1	0.7
1961	-	-	-	-	29.1	0.0	-	-	-	-	29.1	0.0	-	-	-	-	29.3	0.7	-	-	-	-	29.4	0.3
1962	-	-	-	-	29.6	0.7	-	-	-	-	29.7	0.3	-	-	-	-	29.7	0.0	-	-	-	-	29.8	0.3
1963	-	-	-	-	29.9	0.3	-	-	-	-	30.0	0.3	-	-	-	-	30.1	0.3	-	-	-	-	30.3	0.7
1964	-	-	-	-	30.3	0.0	-	-	-	-	30.5	0.7	-	-	-	-	30.6	0.3	-	-	-	-	30.8	0.7
1965	-	-	-	-	31.0	0.6	-	-	-	-	31.2	0.6	-	-	-	-	31.1	-0.3	-	-	-	-	31.4	1.0
1966	-	-	-	-	31.7	1.0	-	-	-	-	31.8	0.3	-	-	-	-	32.1	0.9	-	-	-	-	32.3	0.6
1967	-	-	-	-	32.3	0.0	-	-	-	-	32.7	1.2	-	-	-	-	33.2	1.5	-	-	-	-	33.5	0.9
1968	-	-	-	-	33.9	1.2	-	-	-	-	34.3	1.2	-	-	-	-	34.6	0.9	-	-	-	-	35.0	1.2
1969	-	-	-	-	35.6	1.7	-	-	-	-	36.1	1.4	-	-	-	-	36.6	1.4	-	-	-	-	37.1	1.4
1970	-	-	-	-	37.6	1.3	-	-	-	-	37.9	0.8	-	-	-	-	38.3	1.1	-	-	-	-	38.9	1.6
1971	-	-	-	-	39.1	0.5	-	-	-	-	39.4	0.8	-	-	-	-	39.6	0.5	-	-	-	-	39.9	0.8
1972	-	-	-	-	40.3	1.0	-	-	-	-	40.8	1.2	-	-	-	-	41.2	1.0	-	-	-	-	41.5	0.7
1973	-	-	-	-	42.3	1.9	-	-	-	-	42.9	1.4	-	-	-	-	44.2	3.0	-	-	-	-	44.4	0.5
1974	-	-	-	-	45.7	2.9	-	-	-	-	47.2	3.3	-	-	-	-	48.6	3.0	-	-	-	-	49.9	2.7
1975	-	-	-	-	51.2	2.6	-	-	-	-	52.1	1.8	-	-	-	-	53.0	1.7	-	-	-	-	53.9	1.7
1976	-	-	-	-	54.3	0.7	-	-	-	-	54.8	0.9	-	-	-	-	55.8	1.8	-	-	-	-	56.6	1.4
1977	-	-	-	-	57.8	2.1	-	-	-	-	59.3	2.6	-	-	-	-	60.4	1.9	-	-	-	-	61.5	1.8
1978	-	-	62.2	1.1	-	-	63.2	1.6	-	-	65.3	3.3	-	-	67.0	2.6	-	-	66.5	-0.7	-	-	65.8	-1.1
1979	-	-	67.1	2.0	-	-	68.7	2.4	-	-	70.2	2.2	-	-	71.8	2.3	-	-	72.5	1.0	-	-	75.2	3.7
1980	-	-	78.8	4.8	-	-	79.7	1.1	-	-	81.3	2.0	-	-	82.6	1.6	-	-	83.0	0.5	-	-	84.0	1.2
1981	-	-	85.9	2.3	-	-	89.0	3.6	-	-	90.1	1.2	-	-	94.3	4.7	-	-	97.1	3.0	-	-	96.1	-1.0
1982	-	-	96.8	0.7	-	-	97.8	1.0	-	-	99.6	1.8	-	-	99.4	-0.2	-	-	98.9	-0.5	-	-	96.4	-2.5
1983	-	-	96.5	0.1	-	-	96.8	0.3	-	-	98.1	1.3	-	-	99.0	0.9	-	-	99.0	0.0	-	-	100.5	1.5
1984	-	-	101.4	0.9	-	-	102.2	0.8	-	-	103.5	1.3	-	-	106.0	2.4	-	-	104.9	-1.0	-	-	105.6	0.7
1985	-	-	106.5	0.9	-	-	107.1	0.6	-	-	107.9	0.7	-	-	108.6	0.6	-	-	108.7	0.1	-	-	108.8	0.1
1986	-	-	110.3	1.4	-	-	109.4	-0.8	-	-	111.0	1.5	-	-	111.3	0.3	-	-	112.0	0.6	-	-	110.7	-1.2
1987	111.3	0.5	112.4	1.0	112.8	0.4	113.9	1.0	113.9	0.0	114.0	0.1	114.7	0.6	114.9	0.2	115.4	0.4	116.0	0.5	116.2	0.2	116.4	0.2
1988	117.5	0.9	117.0	-0.4	117.9	0.8	117.8	-0.1	118.7	0.8	119.0	0.3	119.7	0.6	120.5	0.7	121.1	0.5	121.3	0.2	121.1	-0.2	121.5	0.3
1989	122.8	1.1	122.9	0.1	124.6	1.4	124.8	0.2	125.7	0.7	125.6	-0.1	126.4	0.6	127.0	0.5	126.1	-0.7	126.7	0.5	126.4	-0.2	126.6	0.2
1990	127.6	0.8	128.2	0.5	129.0	0.6	129.8	0.6	129.9	0.1	130.7	0.6	131.3	0.5	132.0	0.5	132.9	0.7	133.6	0.5	133.7	0.1	133.9	0.1
1991	135.3	1.0	134.5	-0.6	134.7	0.1	134.2	-0.4	134.8	0.4	136.0	0.9	136.4	0.3	137.2	0.6	137.9	0.5	137.8	-0.1	138.1	0.2	138.2	0.1
1992	138.5	0.2	139.1	0.4	139.9	0.6	139.6	-0.2	140.1	0.4	140.3	0.1	140.4	0.1	141.0	0.4	141.8	0.6	142.3	0.4	142.3	0.0	142.3	0.0
1993	143.0	0.5	143.5	0.3	143.8	0.2	144.8	0.7	144.8	0.0	144.0	-0.6	144.1	0.1	144.0	-0.1	144.4	0.3	145.0	0.4	145.0	0.0	144.7	-0.2
1994	145.3	0.4	145.0	-0.2	145.6	0.4	145.6	0.0	146.1	0.3	145.7	-0.3	146.6	0.6	147.1	0.3	147.1	0.0	147.0	-0.1	147.6	0.4	147.4	-0.1
1995	148.2	0.5	148.3	0.1	148.9	0.4	149.4	0.3	149.0	-0.3	149.6	0.4	149.3	-0.2	149.3	0.0	150.0	0.5	150.2	0.1	149.9	-0.2	149.6	-0.2

Source: U.S. Department of Labor, Bureau of Labor Statistics, Division of Consumer Prices and Price Indexes. - indicates no data collected for period.

San Francisco-Oakland, CA
Consumer Price Index - All Urban Consumers
Base 1982-1984 = 100
Food and Beverages

For 1975-1995. Columns headed % show percentile change in the index from the previous period for which an index is available.

Year	Jan Index	%	Feb Index	%	Mar Index	%	Apr Index	%	May Index	%	Jun Index	%	Jul Index	%	Aug Index	%	Sep Index	%	Oct Index	%	Nov Index	%	Dec Index	%
1975	-	-	-	-	-	-	-	-	-	-	-	-	-	-	-	-	-	-	-	-	-	-	60.2	-
1976	-	-	-	-	59.1	-1.8	-	-	-	-	59.3	0.3	-	-	-	-	59.7	0.7	-	-	-	-	60.0	0.5
1977	-	-	-	-	62.5	4.2	-	-	-	-	64.6	3.4	-	-	-	-	65.0	0.6	-	-	-	-	65.9	1.4
1978	-	-	67.3	2.1	-	-	69.1	2.7	-	-	71.4	3.3	-	-	72.3	1.3	-	-	72.9	0.8	-	-	73.0	0.1
1979	-	-	76.5	4.8	-	-	78.8	3.0	-	-	79.6	1.0	-	-	79.8	0.3	-	-	81.3	1.9	-	-	81.9	0.7
1980	-	-	82.5	0.7	-	-	83.7	1.5	-	-	84.2	0.6	-	-	85.9	2.0	-	-	87.7	2.1	-	-	89.3	1.8
1981	-	-	90.1	0.9	-	-	91.0	1.0	-	-	90.1	-1.0	-	-	92.7	2.9	-	-	91.9	-0.9	-	-	92.3	0.4
1982	-	-	95.8	3.8	-	-	96.2	0.4	-	-	97.5	1.4	-	-	97.8	0.3	-	-	99.0	1.2	-	-	97.7	-1.3
1983	-	-	98.3	0.6	-	-	100.1	1.8	-	-	98.9	-1.2	-	-	98.9	0.0	-	-	99.4	0.5	-	-	100.7	1.3
1984	-	-	102.7	2.0	-	-	103.2	0.5	-	-	103.4	0.2	-	-	103.9	0.5	-	-	104.6	0.7	-	-	105.3	0.7
1985	-	-	106.1	0.8	-	-	105.8	-0.3	-	-	105.3	-0.5	-	-	106.0	0.7	-	-	105.3	-0.7	-	-	107.2	1.8
1986	-	-	107.9	0.7	-	-	108.8	0.8	-	-	109.1	0.3	-	-	110.5	1.3	-	-	111.0	0.5	-	-	110.7	-0.3
1987	112.5	1.6	111.9	-0.5	112.5	0.5	113.5	0.9	113.5	0.0	114.0	0.4	114.1	0.1	114.2	0.1	114.0	-0.2	114.0	0.0	114.1	0.1	115.8	1.5
1988	117.3	1.3	116.6	-0.6	117.8	1.0	118.5	0.6	119.4	0.8	119.9	0.4	121.2	1.1	121.6	0.3	122.8	1.0	122.8	0.0	122.6	-0.2	124.3	1.4
1989	126.1	1.4	126.8	0.6	126.9	0.1	127.0	0.1	128.2	0.9	127.8	-0.3	127.4	-0.3	128.2	0.6	129.0	0.6	130.0	0.8	130.5	0.4	131.0	0.4
1990	132.8	1.4	133.2	0.3	133.0	-0.2	133.6	0.5	133.0	-0.4	133.7	0.5	135.1	1.0	134.9	-0.1	135.7	0.6	136.5	0.6	137.2	0.5	137.1	-0.1
1991	140.0	2.1	139.1	-0.6	140.0	0.6	140.1	0.1	139.8	-0.2	140.2	0.3	139.3	-0.6	139.1	-0.1	139.8	0.5	140.1	0.2	142.4	1.6	143.6	0.8
1992	142.2	-1.0	142.9	0.5	143.1	0.1	142.8	-0.2	142.8	0.0	142.9	0.1	142.3	-0.4	144.0	1.2	143.9	-0.1	143.9	0.0	144.0	0.1	145.1	0.8
1993	146.6	1.0	146.6	0.0	146.6	0.0	146.9	0.2	146.5	-0.3	145.5	-0.7	145.8	0.2	145.1	-0.5	145.1	0.0	146.6	1.0	146.3	-0.2	147.3	0.7
1994	148.9	1.1	148.2	-0.5	148.4	0.1	149.2	0.5	148.0	-0.8	147.6	-0.3	148.7	0.7	148.2	-0.3	148.2	0.0	148.9	0.5	150.4	1.0	152.2	1.2
1995	152.9	0.5	151.7	-0.8	152.2	0.3	153.1	0.6	151.5	-1.0	150.9	-0.4	151.3	0.3	149.9	-0.9	151.5	1.1	151.8	0.2	150.7	-0.7	151.6	0.6

Source: U.S. Department of Labor, Bureau of Labor Statistics, Division of Consumer Prices and Price Indexes. - indicates no data collected for period.

San Francisco-Oakland, CA
Consumer Price Index - Urban Wage Earners
Base 1982-1984 = 100
Food and Beverages

For 1975-1995. Columns headed % show percentile change in the index from the previous period for which an index is available.

Year	Jan Index	%	Feb Index	%	Mar Index	%	Apr Index	%	May Index	%	Jun Index	%	Jul Index	%	Aug Index	%	Sep Index	%	Oct Index	%	Nov Index	%	Dec Index	%
1975	-	-	-	-	-	-	-	-	-	-	-	-	-	-	-	-	-	-	-	-	-	-	59.8	-
1976	-	-	-	-	58.7	-1.8	-	-	-	-	58.8	0.2	-	-	-	-	59.3	0.9	-	-	-	-	59.6	0.5
1977	-	-	-	-	62.1	4.2	-	-	-	-	64.1	3.2	-	-	-	-	64.6	0.8	-	-	-	-	65.4	1.2
1978	-	-	67.0	2.4	-	-	68.7	2.5	-	-	70.9	3.2	-	-	71.9	1.4	-	-	72.3	0.6	-	-	72.7	0.6
1979	-	-	76.2	4.8	-	-	78.1	2.5	-	-	79.0	1.2	-	-	78.9	-0.1	-	-	79.9	1.3	-	-	80.5	0.8
1980	-	-	82.5	2.5	-	-	83.1	0.7	-	-	83.9	1.0	-	-	85.5	1.9	-	-	87.3	2.1	-	-	89.1	2.1
1981	-	-	90.6	1.7	-	-	92.1	1.7	-	-	91.2	-1.0	-	-	93.0	2.0	-	-	92.4	-0.6	-	-	92.4	0.0
1982	-	-	95.8	3.7	-	-	96.3	0.5	-	-	97.5	1.2	-	-	97.6	0.1	-	-	98.7	1.1	-	-	97.6	-1.1
1983	-	-	98.3	0.7	-	-	100.0	1.7	-	-	98.9	-1.1	-	-	99.0	0.1	-	-	99.5	0.5	-	-	100.9	1.4
1984	-	-	102.8	1.9	-	-	103.4	0.6	-	-	103.4	0.0	-	-	103.9	0.5	-	-	104.5	0.6	-	-	105.2	0.7
1985	-	-	106.1	0.9	-	-	105.9	-0.2	-	-	105.2	-0.7	-	-	106.0	0.8	-	-	105.3	-0.7	-	-	107.2	1.8
1986	-	-	108.0	0.7	-	-	108.8	0.7	-	-	109.0	0.2	-	-	110.5	1.4	-	-	110.8	0.3	-	-	110.7	-0.1
1987	112.6	1.7	111.9	-0.6	112.6	0.6	113.7	1.0	113.7	0.0	114.2	0.4	114.3	0.1	114.4	0.1	114.1	-0.3	114.0	-0.1	114.1	0.1	115.7	1.4
1988	117.2	1.3	116.6	-0.5	117.7	0.9	118.6	0.8	119.5	0.8	120.0	0.4	121.3	1.1	121.7	0.3	122.9	1.0	122.8	-0.1	122.6	-0.2	124.3	1.4
1989	125.9	1.3	126.9	0.8	127.0	0.1	127.2	0.2	128.4	0.9	128.0	-0.3	127.5	-0.4	128.3	0.6	129.1	0.6	130.1	0.8	130.6	0.4	131.1	0.4
1990	132.8	1.3	133.4	0.5	133.1	-0.2	133.7	0.5	133.1	-0.4	133.8	0.5	135.2	1.0	135.0	-0.1	135.8	0.6	136.6	0.6	137.2	0.4	137.2	0.0
1991	140.1	2.1	139.3	-0.6	140.2	0.6	140.3	0.1	139.9	-0.3	140.4	0.4	139.4	-0.7	139.1	-0.2	139.8	0.5	140.0	0.1	142.3	1.6	143.5	0.8
1992	142.2	-0.9	143.0	0.6	143.2	0.1	142.8	-0.3	142.7	-0.1	142.9	0.1	142.4	-0.3	144.0	1.1	143.8	-0.1	143.9	0.1	144.0	0.1	145.2	0.8
1993	146.6	1.0	146.8	0.1	146.8	0.0	147.1	0.2	146.7	-0.3	145.7	-0.7	146.0	0.2	145.3	-0.5	145.4	0.1	146.8	1.0	146.5	-0.2	147.4	0.6
1994	149.1	1.2	148.4	-0.5	148.7	0.2	149.6	0.6	148.4	-0.8	148.0	-0.3	149.1	0.7	148.5	-0.4	148.5	0.0	149.1	0.4	150.5	0.9	152.3	1.2
1995	152.9	0.4	151.8	-0.7	152.3	0.3	153.1	0.5	151.6	-1.0	151.1	-0.3	151.6	0.3	150.2	-0.9	151.9	1.1	152.1	0.1	150.9	-0.8	151.9	0.7

Source: U.S. Department of Labor, Bureau of Labor Statistics, Division of Consumer Prices and Price Indexes. - indicates no data collected for period.

San Francisco-Oakland, CA
Consumer Price Index - All Urban Consumers
Base 1982-1984 = 100
Housing

For 1975-1995. Columns headed % show percentile change in the index from the previous period for which an index is available.

Year	Jan Index	%	Feb Index	%	Mar Index	%	Apr Index	%	May Index	%	Jun Index	%	Jul Index	%	Aug Index	%	Sep Index	%	Oct Index	%	Nov Index	%	Dec Index	%
1975	-	-	-	-	-	-	-	-	-	-	-	-	-	-	-	-	-	-	-	-	-	-	49.3	-
1976	-	-	-	-	50.0	1.4	-	-	-	-	50.4	0.8	-	-	-	-	51.4	2.0	-	-	-	-	50.9	-1.0
1977	-	-	-	-	53.1	4.3	-	-	-	-	54.8	3.2	-	-	-	-	56.5	3.1	-	-	-	-	58.2	3.0
1978	-	-	58.9	1.2	-	-	59.7	1.4	-	-	62.5	4.7	-	-	64.9	3.8	-	-	63.1	-2.8	-	-	61.0	-3.3
1979	-	-	61.7	1.1	-	-	63.0	2.1	-	-	63.9	1.4	-	-	66.4	3.9	-	-	67.0	0.9	-	-	71.4	6.6
1980	-	-	75.8	6.2	-	-	75.2	-0.8	-	-	78.1	3.9	-	-	78.6	0.6	-	-	78.2	-0.5	-	-	79.1	1.2
1981	-	-	81.1	2.5	-	-	86.2	6.3	-	-	87.7	1.7	-	-	95.2	8.6	-	-	100.1	5.1	-	-	97.3	-2.8
1982	-	-	97.4	0.1	-	-	98.5	1.1	-	-	100.2	1.7	-	-	99.5	-0.7	-	-	97.3	-2.2	-	-	92.9	-4.5
1983	-	-	95.7	3.0	-	-	96.2	0.5	-	-	97.4	1.2	-	-	99.3	2.0	-	-	99.6	0.3	-	-	99.4	-0.2
1984	-	-	100.9	1.5	-	-	102.7	1.8	-	-	103.7	1.0	-	-	106.9	3.1	-	-	108.0	1.0	-	-	106.7	-1.2
1985	-	-	108.2	1.4	-	-	109.3	1.0	-	-	111.0	1.6	-	-	113.4	2.2	-	-	114.2	0.7	-	-	112.8	-1.2
1986	-	-	115.7	2.6	-	-	115.5	-0.2	-	-	117.9	2.1	-	-	119.4	1.3	-	-	120.1	0.6	-	-	117.8	-1.9
1987	118.5	0.6	119.5	0.8	119.1	-0.3	120.4	1.1	121.2	0.7	121.2	0.0	122.7	1.2	122.9	0.2	123.3	0.3	123.7	0.3	122.6	-0.9	122.6	0.0
1988	123.7	0.9	123.8	0.1	125.6	1.5	124.2	-1.1	126.1	1.5	126.7	0.5	127.9	0.9	130.0	1.6	128.5	-1.2	128.9	0.3	128.5	-0.3	128.9	0.3
1989	130.4	1.2	130.0	-0.3	133.0	2.3	130.1	-2.2	131.3	0.9	131.6	0.2	134.4	2.1	135.0	0.4	133.0	-1.5	133.4	0.3	132.7	-0.5	133.3	0.5
1990	134.2	0.7	135.1	0.7	135.7	0.4	135.9	0.1	136.5	0.4	137.5	0.7	138.1	0.4	138.5	0.3	138.8	0.2	138.6	-0.1	139.1	0.4	139.2	0.1
1991	141.2	1.4	140.9	-0.2	141.2	0.2	140.2	-0.7	140.8	0.4	142.8	1.4	143.8	0.7	144.5	0.5	145.0	0.3	144.1	-0.6	144.1	0.0	143.7	-0.3
1992	144.7	0.7	145.3	0.4	146.6	0.9	145.5	-0.8	145.6	0.1	145.3	-0.2	146.0	0.5	145.9	-0.1	147.5	1.1	147.9	0.3	147.1	-0.5	147.3	0.1
1993	147.5	0.1	147.6	0.1	147.8	0.1	149.5	1.2	150.0	0.3	149.4	-0.4	149.1	-0.2	149.4	0.2	149.7	0.2	149.8	0.1	150.3	0.3	150.4	0.1
1994	150.4	0.0	150.4	0.0	150.8	0.3	150.2	-0.4	151.2	0.7	151.7	0.3	152.5	0.5	153.0	0.3	152.7	-0.2	152.2	-0.3	151.7	-0.3	151.6	-0.1
1995	152.6	0.7	153.2	0.4	153.5	0.2	153.9	0.3	154.4	0.3	154.8	0.3	154.8	0.0	155.0	0.1	155.7	0.5	155.6	-0.1	155.5	-0.1	155.2	-0.2

Source: U.S. Department of Labor, Bureau of Labor Statistics, Division of Consumer Prices and Price Indexes. - indicates no data collected for period.

San Francisco-Oakland, CA
Consumer Price Index - Urban Wage Earners
Base 1982-1984 = 100
Housing

For 1975-1995. Columns headed % show percentile change in the index from the previous period for which an index is available.

Year	Jan Index	%	Feb Index	%	Mar Index	%	Apr Index	%	May Index	%	Jun Index	%	Jul Index	%	Aug Index	%	Sep Index	%	Oct Index	%	Nov Index	%	Dec Index	%
1975	-	-	-	-	-	-	-	-	-	-	-	-	-	-	-	-	-	-	-	-	-	-	50.6	-
1976	-	-	-	-	51.2	1.2	-	-	-	-	51.7	1.0	-	-	-	-	52.7	1.9	-	-	-	-	52.1	-1.1
1977	-	-	-	-	54.4	4.4	-	-	-	-	56.2	3.3	-	-	-	-	57.9	3.0	-	-	-	-	59.7	3.1
1978	-	-	60.3	1.0	-	-	61.1	1.3	-	-	63.8	4.4	-	-	66.3	3.9	-	-	64.5	-2.7	-	-	62.4	-3.3
1979	-	-	63.2	1.3	-	-	64.4	1.9	-	-	65.4	1.6	-	-	67.7	3.5	-	-	68.3	0.9	-	-	72.8	6.6
1980	-	-	77.4	6.3	-	-	76.9	-0.6	-	-	80.1	4.2	-	-	80.6	0.6	-	-	79.8	-1.0	-	-	81.0	1.5
1981	-	-	83.0	2.5	-	-	87.8	5.8	-	-	89.4	1.8	-	-	96.9	8.4	-	-	101.9	5.2	-	-	99.3	-2.6
1982	-	-	99.6	0.3	-	-	100.7	1.1	-	-	102.4	1.7	-	-	101.5	-0.9	-	-	99.4	-2.1	-	-	95.0	-4.4
1983	-	-	95.5	0.5	-	-	95.2	-0.3	-	-	96.2	1.1	-	-	97.8	1.7	-	-	98.0	0.2	-	-	100.0	2.0
1984	-	-	100.5	0.5	-	-	100.5	0.0	-	-	102.8	2.3	-	-	107.7	4.8	-	-	103.6	-3.8	-	-	105.2	1.5
1985	-	-	106.7	1.4	-	-	107.8	1.0	-	-	109.5	1.6	-	-	111.6	1.9	-	-	112.2	0.5	-	-	111.1	-1.0
1986	-	-	114.1	2.7	-	-	113.9	-0.2	-	-	116.3	2.1	-	-	117.7	1.2	-	-	118.5	0.7	-	-	116.0	-2.1
1987	116.7	0.6	117.7	0.9	117.2	-0.4	118.5	1.1	119.0	0.4	119.0	0.0	120.4	1.2	120.5	0.1	120.9	0.3	121.4	0.4	120.5	-0.7	120.5	0.0
1988	121.7	1.0	121.9	0.2	123.1	1.0	122.2	-0.7	123.9	1.4	124.5	0.5	125.4	0.7	127.0	1.3	126.2	-0.6	126.6	0.3	126.0	-0.5	126.4	0.3
1989	127.6	0.9	127.3	-0.2	129.8	2.0	127.8	-1.5	128.9	0.9	129.1	0.2	131.2	1.6	131.9	0.5	130.4	-1.1	131.0	0.5	130.3	-0.5	130.8	0.4
1990	131.7	0.7	132.6	0.7	133.0	0.3	133.4	0.3	134.1	0.5	135.0	0.7	135.4	0.3	135.8	0.3	136.0	0.1	136.0	0.0	136.4	0.3	136.3	-0.1
1991	138.2	1.4	137.9	-0.2	138.1	0.1	137.1	-0.7	138.1	0.7	140.0	1.4	140.8	0.6	141.3	0.4	141.9	0.4	141.0	-0.6	141.2	0.1	140.7	-0.4
1992	141.6	0.6	142.1	0.4	143.2	0.8	142.2	-0.7	142.5	0.2	142.5	0.0	143.0	0.4	142.8	-0.1	144.3	1.1	144.8	0.3	144.1	-0.5	144.1	0.0
1993	144.3	0.1	144.5	0.1	144.8	0.2	146.6	1.2	146.9	0.2	146.2	-0.5	146.0	-0.1	146.3	0.2	146.5	0.1	146.8	0.2	147.3	0.3	147.2	-0.1
1994	147.2	0.0	147.2	0.0	147.6	0.3	147.1	-0.3	148.0	0.6	148.6	0.4	149.3	0.5	149.6	0.2	149.4	-0.1	148.9	-0.3	148.5	-0.3	148.4	-0.1
1995	149.4	0.7	149.9	0.3	150.1	0.1	150.5	0.3	151.0	0.3	151.4	0.3	151.4	0.0	151.5	0.1	152.2	0.5	152.2	0.0	152.1	-0.1	151.8	-0.2

Source: U.S. Department of Labor, Bureau of Labor Statistics, Division of Consumer Prices and Price Indexes. - indicates no data collected for period.

San Francisco-Oakland, CA
Consumer Price Index - All Urban Consumers
Base 1982-1984 = 100
Apparel and Upkeep

For 1952-1995. Columns headed % show percentile change in the index from the previous period for which an index is available.

Year	Jan Index	%	Feb Index	%	Mar Index	%	Apr Index	%	May Index	%	Jun Index	%	Jul Index	%	Aug Index	%	Sep Index	%	Oct Index	%	Nov Index	%	Dec Index	%
1952	-	-	-	-	-	-	-	-	-	-	-	-	-	-	-	-	-	-	-	-	-	-	39.3	-
1953	-	-	-	-	39.4	0.3	-	-	-	-	38.9	-1.3	-	-	-	-	39.4	1.3	-	-	-	-	39.4	0.0
1954	-	-	-	-	38.9	-1.3	-	-	-	-	38.8	-0.3	-	-	-	-	38.8	0.0	-	-	-	-	38.4	-1.0
1955	-	-	-	-	38.8	1.0	-	-	-	-	38.8	0.0	-	-	-	-	39.3	1.3	-	-	-	-	39.3	0.0
1956	-	-	-	-	39.6	0.8	-	-	-	-	39.7	0.3	-	-	-	-	39.8	0.3	-	-	-	-	40.5	1.8
1957	-	-	-	-	40.7	0.5	-	-	-	-	40.6	-0.2	-	-	-	-	40.8	0.5	-	-	-	-	41.0	0.5
1958	-	-	-	-	41.0	0.0	-	-	-	-	40.9	-0.2	-	-	-	-	40.9	0.0	-	-	-	-	41.0	0.2
1959	-	-	-	-	41.0	0.0	-	-	-	-	41.2	0.5	-	-	-	-	41.9	1.7	-	-	-	-	42.1	0.5
1960	-	-	-	-	42.1	0.0	-	-	-	-	42.4	0.7	-	-	-	-	42.9	1.2	-	-	-	-	43.0	0.2
1961	-	-	-	-	43.0	0.0	-	-	-	-	43.2	0.5	-	-	-	-	43.2	0.0	-	-	-	-	43.4	0.5
1962	-	-	-	-	43.7	0.7	-	-	-	-	43.9	0.5	-	-	-	-	43.8	-0.2	-	-	-	-	44.0	0.5
1963	-	-	-	-	44.0	0.0	-	-	-	-	44.1	0.2	-	-	-	-	44.3	0.5	-	-	-	-	44.5	0.5
1964	-	-	-	-	44.6	0.2	-	-	-	-	44.6	0.0	-	-	-	-	44.6	0.0	-	-	-	-	44.9	0.7
1965	-	-	-	-	45.2	0.7	-	-	-	-	45.5	0.7	-	-	-	-	45.2	-0.7	-	-	-	-	45.6	0.9
1966	-	-	-	-	46.3	1.5	-	-	-	-	46.5	0.4	-	-	-	-	46.8	0.6	-	-	-	-	47.1	0.6
1967	-	-	-	-	47.7	1.3	-	-	-	-	47.8	0.2	-	-	-	-	49.5	3.6	-	-	-	-	49.7	0.4
1968	-	-	-	-	50.5	1.6	-	-	-	-	51.0	1.0	-	-	-	-	51.9	1.8	-	-	-	-	52.3	0.8
1969	-	-	-	-	53.1	1.5	-	-	-	-	53.3	0.4	-	-	-	-	54.5	2.3	-	-	-	-	54.7	0.4
1970	-	-	-	-	54.6	-0.2	-	-	-	-	54.5	-0.2	-	-	-	-	56.1	2.9	-	-	-	-	56.5	0.7
1971	-	-	-	-	57.2	1.2	-	-	-	-	57.5	0.5	-	-	-	-	58.5	1.7	-	-	-	-	58.0	-0.9
1972	-	-	-	-	58.2	0.3	-	-	-	-	58.0	-0.3	-	-	-	-	60.1	3.6	-	-	-	-	60.1	0.0
1973	-	-	-	-	60.4	0.5	-	-	-	-	61.0	1.0	-	-	-	-	62.4	2.3	-	-	-	-	62.7	0.5
1974	-	-	-	-	64.1	2.2	-	-	-	-	65.9	2.8	-	-	-	-	67.4	2.3	-	-	-	-	68.4	1.5
1975	-	-	-	-	68.4	0.0	-	-	-	-	68.1	-0.4	-	-	-	-	68.8	1.0	-	-	-	-	69.8	1.5
1976	-	-	-	-	70.5	1.0	-	-	-	-	69.8	-1.0	-	-	-	-	70.6	1.1	-	-	-	-	71.4	1.1
1977	-	-	-	-	72.6	1.7	-	-	-	-	72.7	0.1	-	-	-	-	73.7	1.4	-	-	-	-	74.1	0.5
1978	-	-	73.6	-0.7	-	-	78.3	6.4	-	-	76.5	-2.3	-	-	77.2	0.9	-	-	79.6	3.1	-	-	79.3	-0.4
1979	-	-	80.1	1.0	-	-	80.1	0.0	-	-	81.3	1.5	-	-	81.4	0.1	-	-	84.3	3.6	-	-	86.7	2.8
1980	-	-	86.9	0.2	-	-	88.3	1.6	-	-	85.4	-3.3	-	-	90.7	6.2	-	-	91.0	0.3	-	-	90.5	-0.5
1981	-	-	89.6	-1.0	-	-	91.0	1.6	-	-	92.2	1.3	-	-	94.3	2.3	-	-	93.8	-0.5	-	-	96.4	2.8
1982	-	-	97.3	0.9	-	-	97.3	0.0	-	-	97.1	-0.2	-	-	98.9	1.9	-	-	98.6	-0.3	-	-	96.4	-2.2
1983	-	-	98.8	2.5	-	-	99.1	0.3	-	-	97.8	-1.3	-	-	98.2	0.4	-	-	95.5	-2.7	-	-	98.0	2.6
1984	-	-	102.1	4.2	-	-	104.4	2.3	-	-	100.6	-3.6	-	-	107.1	6.5	-	-	109.5	2.2	-	-	105.7	-3.5
1985	-	-	108.1	2.3	-	-	105.0	-2.9	-	-	104.7	-0.3	-	-	100.6	-3.9	-	-	102.2	1.6	-	-	99.1	-3.0
1986	-	-	98.1	-1.0	-	-	103.9	5.9	-	-	100.0	-3.8	-	-	102.6	2.6	-	-	105.9	3.2	-	-	99.6	-5.9
1987	96.8	-2.8	103.1	6.5	106.6	3.4	108.6	1.9	103.7	-4.5	102.2	-1.4	100.4	-1.8	100.2	-0.2	105.1	4.9	107.4	2.2	112.2	4.5	108.4	-3.4
1988	108.9	0.5	106.3	-2.4	106.2	-0.1	105.4	-0.8	103.6	-1.7	99.7	-3.8	97.3	-2.4	95.2	-2.2	101.9	7.0	101.7	-0.2	102.7	1.0	99.5	-3.1
1989	100.6	1.1	100.2	-0.4	104.7	4.5	107.5	2.7	105.6	-1.8	103.5	-2.0	101.3	-2.1	103.1	1.8	106.9	3.7	108.2	1.2	105.5	-2.5	103.0	-2.4
1990	99.6	-3.3	104.5	4.9	107.3	2.7	108.4	1.0	106.5	-1.8	106.5	0.0	105.7	-0.8	107.6	1.8	112.2	4.3	113.2	0.9	109.2	-3.5	109.1	-0.1
1991	112.1	2.7	110.9	-1.1	112.0	1.0	114.0	1.8	111.3	-2.4	109.1	-2.0	109.2	0.1	115.6	5.9	115.8	0.2	116.6	0.7	115.8	-0.7	114.8	-0.9
1992	114.2	-0.5	117.7	3.1	121.6	3.3	119.5	-1.7	121.3	1.5	118.4	-2.4	115.4	-2.5	118.0	2.3	117.6	-0.3	117.0	-0.5	117.9	0.8	114.4	-3.0
1993	114.7	0.3	117.2	2.2	121.9	4.0	124.3	2.0	121.6	-2.2	117.1	-3.7	116.2	-0.8	115.2	-0.9	120.0	4.2	119.0	-0.8	117.3	-1.4	113.5	-3.2
1994	115.1	1.4	114.7	-0.3	116.3	1.4	116.1	-0.2	119.0	2.5	111.9	-6.0	114.5	2.3	116.4	1.7	117.8	1.2	113.7	-3.5	118.3	4.0	112.5	-4.9
1995	113.4	0.8	115.0	1.4	117.8	2.4	118.3	0.4	111.9	-5.4	115.0	2.8	110.5	-3.9	114.7	3.8	113.4	-1.1	114.6	1.1	114.1	-0.4	108.7	-4.7

Source: U.S. Department of Labor, Bureau of Labor Statistics, Division of Consumer Prices and Price Indexes. - indicates no data collected for period.

San Francisco-Oakland, CA
Consumer Price Index - Urban Wage Earners
Base 1982-1984 = 100
Apparel and Upkeep

For 1952-1995. Columns headed % show percentile change in the index from the previous period for which an index is available.

Year	Jan Index	%	Feb Index	%	Mar Index	%	Apr Index	%	May Index	%	Jun Index	%	Jul Index	%	Aug Index	%	Sep Index	%	Oct Index	%	Nov Index	%	Dec Index	%
1952	-	-	-	-	-	-	-	-	-	-	-	-	-	-	-	-	-	-	-	-	-	-	40.8	-
1953	-	-	-	-	40.9	0.2	-	-	-	-	40.4	-1.2	-	-	-	-	40.9	1.2	-	-	-	-	40.9	0.0
1954	-	-	-	-	40.4	-1.2	-	-	-	-	40.3	-0.2	-	-	-	-	40.2	-0.2	-	-	-	-	39.8	-1.0
1955	-	-	-	-	40.3	1.3	-	-	-	-	40.3	0.0	-	-	-	-	40.8	1.2	-	-	-	-	40.8	0.0
1956	-	-	-	-	41.1	0.7	-	-	-	-	41.2	0.2	-	-	-	-	41.3	0.2	-	-	-	-	42.0	1.7
1957	-	-	-	-	42.2	0.5	-	-	-	-	42.1	-0.2	-	-	-	-	42.3	0.5	-	-	-	-	42.5	0.5
1958	-	-	-	-	42.5	0.0	-	-	-	-	42.5	0.0	-	-	-	-	42.5	0.0	-	-	-	-	42.5	0.0
1959	-	-	-	-	42.6	0.2	-	-	-	-	42.7	0.2	-	-	-	-	43.5	1.9	-	-	-	-	43.7	0.5
1960	-	-	-	-	43.7	0.0	-	-	-	-	44.0	0.7	-	-	-	-	44.6	1.4	-	-	-	-	44.7	0.2
1961	-	-	-	-	44.6	-0.2	-	-	-	-	44.9	0.7	-	-	-	-	44.9	0.0	-	-	-	-	45.0	0.2
1962	-	-	-	-	45.3	0.7	-	-	-	-	45.5	0.4	-	-	-	-	45.5	0.0	-	-	-	-	45.7	0.4
1963	-	-	-	-	45.7	0.0	-	-	-	-	45.8	0.2	-	-	-	-	46.0	0.4	-	-	-	-	46.2	0.4
1964	-	-	-	-	46.3	0.2	-	-	-	-	46.3	0.0	-	-	-	-	46.3	0.0	-	-	-	-	46.6	0.6
1965	-	-	-	-	46.9	0.6	-	-	-	-	47.2	0.6	-	-	-	-	46.9	-0.6	-	-	-	-	47.4	1.1
1966	-	-	-	-	48.0	1.3	-	-	-	-	48.2	0.4	-	-	-	-	48.5	0.6	-	-	-	-	48.9	0.8
1967	-	-	-	-	49.5	1.2	-	-	-	-	49.6	0.2	-	-	-	-	51.4	3.6	-	-	-	-	51.5	0.2
1968	-	-	-	-	52.4	1.7	-	-	-	-	52.9	1.0	-	-	-	-	53.9	1.9	-	-	-	-	54.3	0.7
1969	-	-	-	-	55.1	1.5	-	-	-	-	55.3	0.4	-	-	-	-	56.6	2.4	-	-	-	-	56.7	0.2
1970	-	-	-	-	56.7	0.0	-	-	-	-	56.5	-0.4	-	-	-	-	58.2	3.0	-	-	-	-	58.7	0.9
1971	-	-	-	-	59.4	1.2	-	-	-	-	59.6	0.3	-	-	-	-	60.8	2.0	-	-	-	-	60.1	-1.2
1972	-	-	-	-	60.4	0.5	-	-	-	-	60.2	-0.3	-	-	-	-	62.4	3.7	-	-	-	-	62.4	0.0
1973	-	-	-	-	62.7	0.5	-	-	-	-	63.3	1.0	-	-	-	-	64.8	2.4	-	-	-	-	65.0	0.3
1974	-	-	-	-	66.5	2.3	-	-	-	-	68.4	2.9	-	-	-	-	69.9	2.2	-	-	-	-	71.0	1.6
1975	-	-	-	-	71.0	0.0	-	-	-	-	70.7	-0.4	-	-	-	-	71.4	1.0	-	-	-	-	72.4	1.4
1976	-	-	-	-	73.2	1.1	-	-	-	-	72.4	-1.1	-	-	-	-	73.3	1.2	-	-	-	-	74.1	1.1
1977	-	-	-	-	75.3	1.6	-	-	-	-	75.4	0.1	-	-	-	-	76.5	1.5	-	-	-	-	76.9	0.5
1978	-	-	75.1	-2.3	-	-	79.0	5.2	-	-	78.1	-1.1	-	-	78.8	0.9	-	-	80.4	2.0	-	-	79.9	-0.6
1979	-	-	81.3	1.8	-	-	81.8	0.6	-	-	83.9	2.6	-	-	82.6	-1.5	-	-	83.6	1.2	-	-	85.9	2.8
1980	-	-	86.2	0.3	-	-	87.2	1.2	-	-	85.9	-1.5	-	-	90.8	5.7	-	-	92.3	1.7	-	-	91.7	-0.7
1981	-	-	92.7	1.1	-	-	94.5	1.9	-	-	95.1	0.6	-	-	96.1	1.1	-	-	97.0	0.9	-	-	96.6	-0.4
1982	-	-	97.7	1.1	-	-	97.8	0.1	-	-	98.3	0.5	-	-	99.1	0.8	-	-	98.9	-0.2	-	-	97.1	-1.8
1983	-	-	98.5	1.4	-	-	98.5	0.0	-	-	97.6	-0.9	-	-	98.2	0.6	-	-	95.8	-2.4	-	-	98.0	2.3
1984	-	-	102.0	4.1	-	-	103.6	1.6	-	-	100.0	-3.5	-	-	106.6	6.6	-	-	109.0	2.3	-	-	105.9	-2.8
1985	-	-	107.7	1.7	-	-	105.3	-2.2	-	-	104.7	-0.6	-	-	101.7	-2.9	-	-	102.7	1.0	-	-	100.2	-2.4
1986	-	-	99.5	-0.7	-	-	104.5	5.0	-	-	100.5	-3.8	-	-	103.0	2.5	-	-	106.1	3.0	-	-	100.4	-5.4
1987	97.5	-2.9	103.1	5.7	106.7	3.5	109.2	2.3	104.0	-4.8	103.0	-1.0	101.2	-1.7	100.8	-0.4	105.6	4.8	109.3	3.5	113.8	4.1	110.0	-3.3
1988	110.8	0.7	108.0	-2.5	108.1	0.1	107.2	-0.8	105.2	-1.9	101.4	-3.6	99.4	-2.0	97.0	-2.4	104.4	7.6	104.1	-0.3	105.2	1.1	101.9	-3.1
1989	103.7	1.8	103.2	-0.5	107.0	3.7	110.1	2.9	108.0	-1.9	106.9	-1.0	104.8	-2.0	106.4	1.5	109.5	2.9	111.3	1.6	108.1	-2.9	105.5	-2.4
1990	103.7	-1.7	106.9	3.1	110.1	3.0	111.3	1.1	109.6	-1.5	109.7	0.1	108.9	-0.7	110.2	1.2	115.4	4.7	116.7	1.1	112.2	-3.9	112.8	0.5
1991	115.8	2.7	113.5	-2.0	114.8	1.1	117.0	1.9	114.2	-2.4	111.7	-2.2	112.1	0.4	118.6	5.8	118.9	0.3	120.2	1.1	119.3	-0.7	118.4	-0.8
1992	117.6	-0.7	120.7	2.6	124.9	3.5	122.7	-1.8	124.8	1.7	122.0	-2.2	119.2	-2.3	121.9	2.3	121.4	-0.4	120.8	-0.5	122.4	1.3	119.1	-2.7
1993	118.8	-0.3	121.4	2.2	125.2	3.1	128.7	2.8	126.0	-2.1	121.1	-3.9	120.7	-0.3	119.2	-1.2	125.6	5.4	124.9	-0.6	122.7	-1.8	118.5	-3.4
1994	120.8	1.9	119.5	-1.1	120.9	1.2	120.9	0.0	125.4	3.7	116.3	-7.3	119.4	2.7	122.0	2.2	122.8	0.7	117.8	-4.1	123.7	5.0	117.4	-5.1
1995	119.8	2.0	121.1	1.1	124.4	2.7	125.2	0.6	116.8	-6.7	123.2	5.5	115.9	-5.9	122.3	5.5	120.0	-1.9	119.4	-0.5	119.1	-0.3	112.7	-5.4

Source: U.S. Department of Labor, Bureau of Labor Statistics, Division of Consumer Prices and Price Indexes. - indicates no data collected for period.

San Francisco-Oakland, CA
Consumer Price Index - All Urban Consumers
Base 1982-1984 = 100
Transportation

For 1947-1995. Columns headed % show percentile change in the index from the previous period for which an index is available.

Year	Jan Index	%	Feb Index	%	Mar Index	%	Apr Index	%	May Index	%	Jun Index	%	Jul Index	%	Aug Index	%	Sep Index	%	Oct Index	%	Nov Index	%	Dec Index	%
1947	16.0	-	16.1	0.6	16.1	0.0	16.3	1.2	16.2	-0.6	16.2	0.0	-	-	-	-	16.7	3.1	-	-	-	-	17.0	1.8
1948	-	-	-	-	17.4	2.4	-	-	-	-	18.0	3.4	-	-	-	-	18.6	3.3	-	-	-	-	18.7	0.5
1949	-	-	-	-	19.3	3.2	-	-	-	-	19.5	1.0	-	-	-	-	19.5	0.0	-	-	-	-	19.6	0.5
1950	-	-	-	-	19.6	0.0	-	-	-	-	19.2	-2.0	-	-	-	-	19.4	1.0	-	-	-	-	19.5	0.5
1951	-	-	-	-	20.6	5.6	-	-	-	-	20.8	1.0	-	-	-	-	21.3	2.4	-	-	-	-	21.4	0.5
1952	-	-	-	-	21.6	0.9	-	-	-	-	24.1	11.6	-	-	-	-	25.2	4.6	-	-	-	-	25.2	0.0
1953	-	-	-	-	25.7	2.0	-	-	-	-	25.5	-0.8	-	-	-	-	25.8	1.2	-	-	-	-	25.9	0.4
1954	-	-	-	-	25.8	-0.4	-	-	-	-	25.7	-0.4	-	-	-	-	25.2	-1.9	-	-	-	-	25.4	0.8
1955	-	-	-	-	25.3	-0.4	-	-	-	-	24.8	-2.0	-	-	-	-	24.8	0.0	-	-	-	-	25.3	2.0
1956	-	-	-	-	25.0	-1.2	-	-	-	-	25.1	0.4	-	-	-	-	25.3	0.8	-	-	-	-	26.7	5.5
1957	-	-	-	-	27.1	1.5	-	-	-	-	26.9	-0.7	-	-	-	-	27.1	0.7	-	-	-	-	27.4	1.1
1958	-	-	-	-	28.0	2.2	-	-	-	-	28.4	1.4	-	-	-	-	28.8	1.4	-	-	-	-	28.4	-1.4
1959	-	-	-	-	29.7	4.6	-	-	-	-	29.6	-0.3	-	-	-	-	30.0	1.4	-	-	-	-	30.5	1.7
1960	-	-	-	-	29.6	-3.0	-	-	-	-	29.5	-0.3	-	-	-	-	29.3	-0.7	-	-	-	-	29.9	2.0
1961	-	-	-	-	29.6	-1.0	-	-	-	-	29.3	-1.0	-	-	-	-	30.1	2.7	-	-	-	-	30.5	1.3
1962	-	-	-	-	30.2	-1.0	-	-	-	-	30.5	1.0	-	-	-	-	30.5	0.0	-	-	-	-	30.4	-0.3
1963	-	-	-	-	30.5	0.3	-	-	-	-	30.6	0.3	-	-	-	-	30.8	0.7	-	-	-	-	31.4	1.9
1964	-	-	-	-	31.4	0.0	-	-	-	-	31.6	0.6	-	-	-	-	31.4	-0.6	-	-	-	-	31.9	1.6
1965	-	-	-	-	31.7	-0.6	-	-	-	-	31.7	0.0	-	-	-	-	31.6	-0.3	-	-	-	-	31.9	0.9
1966	-	-	-	-	31.9	0.0	-	-	-	-	31.6	-0.9	-	-	-	-	32.2	1.9	-	-	-	-	32.4	0.6
1967	-	-	-	-	32.4	0.0	-	-	-	-	32.9	1.5	-	-	-	-	33.2	0.9	-	-	-	-	33.4	0.6
1968	-	-	-	-	33.6	0.6	-	-	-	-	33.8	0.6	-	-	-	-	33.8	0.0	-	-	-	-	34.1	0.9
1969	-	-	-	-	35.0	2.6	-	-	-	-	35.3	0.9	-	-	-	-	35.4	0.3	-	-	-	-	36.1	2.0
1970	-	-	-	-	35.6	-1.4	-	-	-	-	36.5	2.5	-	-	-	-	37.0	1.4	-	-	-	-	38.6	4.3
1971	-	-	-	-	38.8	0.5	-	-	-	-	38.9	0.3	-	-	-	-	38.7	-0.5	-	-	-	-	38.6	-0.3
1972	-	-	-	-	39.0	1.0	-	-	-	-	39.5	1.3	-	-	-	-	40.1	1.5	-	-	-	-	40.2	0.2
1973	-	-	-	-	39.8	-1.0	-	-	-	-	40.7	2.3	-	-	-	-	40.6	-0.2	-	-	-	-	41.1	1.2
1974	-	-	-	-	42.6	3.6	-	-	-	-	45.0	5.6	-	-	-	-	46.5	3.3	-	-	-	-	47.3	1.7
1975	-	-	-	-	48.3	2.1	-	-	-	-	50.0	3.5	-	-	-	-	51.0	2.0	-	-	-	-	51.6	1.2
1976	-	-	-	-	52.5	1.7	-	-	-	-	53.9	2.7	-	-	-	-	55.7	3.3	-	-	-	-	56.3	1.1
1977	-	-	-	-	56.9	1.1	-	-	-	-	58.5	2.8	-	-	-	-	58.4	-0.2	-	-	-	-	59.1	1.2
1978	-	-	59.5	0.7	-	-	59.7	0.3	-	-	61.5	3.0	-	-	62.2	1.1	-	-	62.9	1.1	-	-	64.0	1.7
1979	-	-	64.7	1.1	-	-	67.4	4.2	-	-	70.5	4.6	-	-	72.9	3.4	-	-	74.3	1.9	-	-	76.0	2.3
1980	-	-	80.7	6.2	-	-	83.7	3.7	-	-	83.7	0.0	-	-	84.9	1.4	-	-	85.6	0.8	-	-	86.5	1.1
1981	-	-	88.6	2.4	-	-	90.6	2.3	-	-	92.8	2.4	-	-	93.0	0.2	-	-	94.1	1.2	-	-	94.9	0.9
1982	-	-	94.0	-0.9	-	-	94.5	0.5	-	-	98.1	3.8	-	-	99.6	1.5	-	-	99.8	0.2	-	-	98.2	-1.6
1983	-	-	96.2	-2.0	-	-	96.5	0.3	-	-	100.4	4.0	-	-	101.2	0.8	-	-	100.0	-1.2	-	-	100.8	0.8
1984	-	-	100.6	-0.2	-	-	103.2	2.6	-	-	104.9	1.6	-	-	103.8	-1.0	-	-	105.9	2.0	-	-	105.1	-0.8
1985	-	-	104.6	-0.5	-	-	105.9	1.2	-	-	106.7	0.8	-	-	105.3	-1.3	-	-	105.0	-0.3	-	-	105.5	0.5
1986	-	-	105.3	-0.2	-	-	99.8	-5.2	-	-	102.8	3.0	-	-	99.4	-3.3	-	-	99.7	0.3	-	-	98.5	-1.2
1987	99.4	0.9	100.2	0.8	101.4	1.2	101.8	0.4	102.0	0.2	102.1	0.1	102.6	0.5	103.2	0.6	103.3	0.1	103.5	0.2	104.6	1.1	104.5	-0.1
1988	104.4	-0.1	103.5	-0.9	103.4	-0.1	103.7	0.3	104.4	0.7	105.3	0.9	105.7	0.4	106.5	0.8	106.7	0.2	107.0	0.3	106.1	-0.8	106.4	0.3
1989	106.8	0.4	107.2	0.4	107.6	0.4	110.9	3.1	112.1	1.1	111.6	-0.4	111.5	-0.1	110.7	-0.7	108.7	-1.8	109.0	0.3	109.5	0.5	109.1	-0.4
1990	110.4	1.2	110.4	0.0	111.5	1.0	112.0	0.4	112.7	0.6	113.4	0.6	113.8	0.4	115.4	1.4	116.8	1.2	119.1	2.0	119.6	0.4	121.2	1.3
1991	119.5	-1.4	117.0	-2.1	115.2	-1.5	113.7	-1.3	115.9	1.9	117.6	1.5	117.7	0.1	118.4	0.6	117.5	-0.8	117.9	0.3	117.4	-0.4	117.0	-0.3

[Continued]

San Francisco-Oakland, CA
Consumer Price Index - All Urban Consumers
Base 1982-1984 = 100
Transportation

[Continued]

For 1947-1995. Columns headed % show percentile change in the index from the previous period for which an index is available.

Year	Jan Index	%	Feb Index	%	Mar Index	%	Apr Index	%	May Index	%	Jun Index	%	Jul Index	%	Aug Index	%	Sep Index	%	Oct Index	%	Nov Index	%	Dec Index	%
1992	116.6	-0.3	116.2	-0.3	116.7	0.4	117.6	0.8	119.1	1.3	120.1	0.8	121.4	1.1	121.5	0.1	120.7	-0.7	122.1	1.2	122.7	0.5	123.3	0.5
1993	125.1	1.5	124.3	-0.6	123.5	-0.6	123.1	-0.3	123.4	0.2	123.1	-0.2	123.0	-0.1	123.6	0.5	122.2	-1.1	124.4	1.8	124.7	0.2	123.5	-1.0
1994	123.9	0.3	123.4	-0.4	124.9	1.2	125.3	0.3	125.1	-0.2	125.6	0.4	126.1	0.4	127.2	0.9	126.3	-0.7	127.3	0.8	127.2	-0.1	126.2	-0.8
1995	126.7	0.4	126.6	-0.1	127.4	0.6	128.2	0.6	129.1	0.7	130.4	1.0	130.3	-0.1	129.5	-0.6	129.8	0.2	130.4	0.5	130.0	-0.3	129.9	-0.1

Source: U.S. Department of Labor, Bureau of Labor Statistics, Division of Consumer Prices and Price Indexes. - indicates no data collected for period.

San Francisco-Oakland, CA
Consumer Price Index - Urban Wage Earners
Base 1982-1984 = 100
Transportation

For 1947-1995. Columns headed % show percentile change in the index from the previous period for which an index is available.

Year	Jan Index	Jan %	Feb Index	Feb %	Mar Index	Mar %	Apr Index	Apr %	May Index	May %	Jun Index	Jun %	Jul Index	Jul %	Aug Index	Aug %	Sep Index	Sep %	Oct Index	Oct %	Nov Index	Nov %	Dec Index	Dec %
1947	15.7	-	15.7	0.0	15.8	0.6	15.9	0.6	15.8	-0.6	15.8	0.0	-	-	-	-	16.3	3.2	-	-	-	-	16.6	1.8
1948	-	-	-	-	17.0	2.4	-	-	-	-	17.5	2.9	-	-	-	-	18.2	4.0	-	-	-	-	18.3	0.5
1949	-	-	-	-	18.9	3.3	-	-	-	-	19.0	0.5	-	-	-	-	19.1	0.5	-	-	-	-	19.2	0.5
1950	-	-	-	-	19.2	0.0	-	-	-	-	18.8	-2.1	-	-	-	-	19.0	1.1	-	-	-	-	19.0	0.0
1951	-	-	-	-	20.1	5.8	-	-	-	-	20.3	1.0	-	-	-	-	20.8	2.5	-	-	-	-	20.9	0.5
1952	-	-	-	-	21.1	1.0	-	-	-	-	23.6	11.8	-	-	-	-	24.6	4.2	-	-	-	-	24.6	0.0
1953	-	-	-	-	25.1	2.0	-	-	-	-	24.9	-0.8	-	-	-	-	25.2	1.2	-	-	-	-	25.3	0.4
1954	-	-	-	-	25.2	-0.4	-	-	-	-	25.1	-0.4	-	-	-	-	24.6	-2.0	-	-	-	-	24.8	0.8
1955	-	-	-	-	24.7	-0.4	-	-	-	-	24.2	-2.0	-	-	-	-	24.3	0.4	-	-	-	-	24.7	1.6
1956	-	-	-	-	24.4	-1.2	-	-	-	-	24.5	0.4	-	-	-	-	24.7	0.8	-	-	-	-	26.1	5.7
1957	-	-	-	-	26.5	1.5	-	-	-	-	26.3	-0.8	-	-	-	-	26.4	0.4	-	-	-	-	26.7	1.1
1958	-	-	-	-	27.3	2.2	-	-	-	-	27.7	1.5	-	-	-	-	28.2	1.8	-	-	-	-	27.7	-1.8
1959	-	-	-	-	29.0	4.7	-	-	-	-	28.9	-0.3	-	-	-	-	29.3	1.4	-	-	-	-	29.7	1.4
1960	-	-	-	-	28.9	-2.7	-	-	-	-	28.8	-0.3	-	-	-	-	28.6	-0.7	-	-	-	-	29.2	2.1
1961	-	-	-	-	28.9	-1.0	-	-	-	-	28.6	-1.0	-	-	-	-	29.4	2.8	-	-	-	-	29.8	1.4
1962	-	-	-	-	29.4	-1.3	-	-	-	-	29.7	1.0	-	-	-	-	29.8	0.3	-	-	-	-	29.7	-0.3
1963	-	-	-	-	29.7	0.0	-	-	-	-	29.9	0.7	-	-	-	-	30.0	0.3	-	-	-	-	30.6	2.0
1964	-	-	-	-	30.6	0.0	-	-	-	-	30.9	1.0	-	-	-	-	30.7	-0.6	-	-	-	-	31.1	1.3
1965	-	-	-	-	31.0	-0.3	-	-	-	-	31.0	0.0	-	-	-	-	30.8	-0.6	-	-	-	-	31.2	1.3
1966	-	-	-	-	31.2	0.0	-	-	-	-	30.9	-1.0	-	-	-	-	31.5	1.9	-	-	-	-	31.6	0.3
1967	-	-	-	-	31.6	0.0	-	-	-	-	32.1	1.6	-	-	-	-	32.4	0.9	-	-	-	-	32.6	0.6
1968	-	-	-	-	32.8	0.6	-	-	-	-	33.0	0.6	-	-	-	-	33.0	0.0	-	-	-	-	33.3	0.9
1969	-	-	-	-	34.2	2.7	-	-	-	-	34.4	0.6	-	-	-	-	34.6	0.6	-	-	-	-	35.2	1.7
1970	-	-	-	-	34.8	-1.1	-	-	-	-	35.7	2.6	-	-	-	-	36.2	1.4	-	-	-	-	37.7	4.1
1971	-	-	-	-	37.9	0.5	-	-	-	-	38.0	0.3	-	-	-	-	37.8	-0.5	-	-	-	-	37.7	-0.3
1972	-	-	-	-	38.1	1.1	-	-	-	-	38.5	1.0	-	-	-	-	39.2	1.8	-	-	-	-	39.2	0.0
1973	-	-	-	-	38.8	-1.0	-	-	-	-	39.8	2.6	-	-	-	-	39.7	-0.3	-	-	-	-	40.1	1.0
1974	-	-	-	-	41.6	3.7	-	-	-	-	44.0	5.8	-	-	-	-	45.4	3.2	-	-	-	-	46.2	1.8
1975	-	-	-	-	47.2	2.2	-	-	-	-	48.8	3.4	-	-	-	-	49.8	2.0	-	-	-	-	50.4	1.2
1976	-	-	-	-	51.2	1.6	-	-	-	-	52.6	2.7	-	-	-	-	54.4	3.4	-	-	-	-	55.0	1.1
1977	-	-	-	-	55.6	1.1	-	-	-	-	57.1	2.7	-	-	-	-	57.0	-0.2	-	-	-	-	57.7	1.2
1978	-	-	58.1	0.7	-	-	58.4	0.5	-	-	60.3	3.3	-	-	61.2	1.5	-	-	61.9	1.1	-	-	63.0	1.8
1979	-	-	63.6	1.0	-	-	66.6	4.7	-	-	69.8	4.8	-	-	72.1	3.3	-	-	73.2	1.5	-	-	75.0	2.5
1980	-	-	79.4	5.9	-	-	81.9	3.1	-	-	81.9	0.0	-	-	83.5	2.0	-	-	84.4	1.1	-	-	85.2	0.9
1981	-	-	87.8	3.1	-	-	89.8	2.3	-	-	91.5	1.9	-	-	92.3	0.9	-	-	93.5	1.3	-	-	94.3	0.9
1982	-	-	93.4	-1.0	-	-	94.2	0.9	-	-	97.6	3.6	-	-	99.2	1.6	-	-	99.4	0.2	-	-	98.0	-1.4
1983	-	-	96.0	-2.0	-	-	96.4	0.4	-	-	100.5	4.3	-	-	101.3	0.8	-	-	100.4	-0.9	-	-	101.3	0.9
1984	-	-	101.1	-0.2	-	-	103.6	2.5	-	-	105.1	1.4	-	-	103.9	-1.1	-	-	106.0	2.0	-	-	105.3	-0.7
1985	-	-	104.8	-0.5	-	-	106.1	1.2	-	-	107.0	0.8	-	-	105.6	-1.3	-	-	105.2	-0.4	-	-	105.7	0.5
1986	-	-	105.6	-0.1	-	-	100.0	-5.3	-	-	102.9	2.9	-	-	99.7	-3.1	-	-	100.0	0.3	-	-	98.8	-1.2
1987	99.3	0.5	100.8	1.5	102.3	1.5	103.2	0.9	103.5	0.3	103.8	0.3	104.1	0.3	104.8	0.7	104.8	0.0	105.3	0.5	105.9	0.6	106.1	0.2
1988	106.1	0.0	105.5	-0.6	105.4	-0.1	105.5	0.1	106.2	0.7	107.1	0.8	107.6	0.5	108.1	0.5	108.3	0.2	108.8	0.5	108.0	-0.7	108.0	0.0
1989	108.5	0.5	108.9	0.4	109.6	0.6	113.4	3.5	114.9	1.3	114.4	-0.4	114.1	-0.3	113.3	-0.7	111.3	-1.8	111.1	-0.2	111.5	0.4	111.1	-0.4
1990	111.7	0.5	112.1	0.4	113.2	1.0	113.7	0.4	114.4	0.6	115.4	0.9	115.7	0.3	117.6	1.6	119.2	1.4	122.0	2.3	122.3	0.2	123.2	0.7
1991	121.0	-1.8	118.1	-2.4	116.2	-1.6	114.8	-1.2	117.2	2.1	118.9	1.5	119.2	0.3	119.8	0.5	119.5	-0.3	120.0	0.4	119.1	-0.8	118.9	-0.2

[Continued]

San Francisco-Oakland, CA
Consumer Price Index - Urban Wage Earners
Base 1982-1984 = 100
Transportation
[Continued]

For 1947-1995. Columns headed % show percentile change in the index from the previous period for which an index is available.

Year	Jan Index	%	Feb Index	%	Mar Index	%	Apr Index	%	May Index	%	Jun Index	%	Jul Index	%	Aug Index	%	Sep Index	%	Oct Index	%	Nov Index	%	Dec Index	%
1992	118.3	-0.5	118.0	-0.3	118.3	0.3	119.2	0.8	121.1	1.6	122.5	1.2	123.5	0.8	123.8	0.2	123.4	-0.3	124.3	0.7	125.0	0.6	125.3	0.2
1993	126.4	0.9	125.8	-0.5	125.2	-0.5	125.0	-0.2	125.3	0.2	125.3	0.0	125.3	0.0	125.7	0.3	125.1	-0.5	127.0	1.5	126.9	-0.1	125.6	-1.0
1994	125.5	-0.1	124.7	-0.6	125.6	0.7	126.3	0.6	126.5	0.2	127.4	0.7	128.3	0.7	129.6	1.0	129.3	-0.2	130.5	0.9	130.5	0.0	130.1	-0.3
1995	129.8	-0.2	129.7	-0.1	130.6	0.7	131.6	0.8	132.4	0.6	133.4	0.8	133.2	-0.1	132.6	-0.5	132.4	-0.2	133.5	0.8	133.2	-0.2	133.1	-0.1

Source: U.S. Department of Labor, Bureau of Labor Statistics, Division of Consumer Prices and Price Indexes. - indicates no data collected for period.

San Francisco-Oakland, CA
Consumer Price Index - All Urban Consumers
Base 1982-1984 = 100
Medical Care

For 1947-1995. Columns headed % show percentile change in the index from the previous period for which an index is available.

Year	Jan Index	%	Feb Index	%	Mar Index	%	Apr Index	%	May Index	%	Jun Index	%	Jul Index	%	Aug Index	%	Sep Index	%	Oct Index	%	Nov Index	%	Dec Index	%
1947	13.3	-	13.4	0.8	13.4	0.0	13.4	0.0	13.4	0.0	13.4	0.0	-	-	-	-	13.8	3.0	-	-	-	-	13.9	0.7
1948	-	-	-	-	14.0	0.7	-	-	-	-	14.2	1.4	-	-	-	-	14.4	1.4	-	-	-	-	14.6	1.4
1949	-	-	-	-	14.7	0.7	-	-	-	-	14.7	0.0	-	-	-	-	14.8	0.7	-	-	-	-	14.8	0.0
1950	-	-	-	-	14.8	0.0	-	-	-	-	14.8	0.0	-	-	-	-	15.5	4.7	-	-	-	-	15.7	1.3
1951	-	-	-	-	15.7	0.0	-	-	-	-	15.8	0.6	-	-	-	-	15.8	0.0	-	-	-	-	16.0	1.3
1952	-	-	-	-	16.8	5.0	-	-	-	-	16.9	0.6	-	-	-	-	16.9	0.0	-	-	-	-	17.0	0.6
1953	-	-	-	-	17.0	0.0	-	-	-	-	17.2	1.2	-	-	-	-	17.4	1.2	-	-	-	-	17.4	0.0
1954	-	-	-	-	17.5	0.6	-	-	-	-	17.5	0.0	-	-	-	-	17.5	0.0	-	-	-	-	17.5	0.0
1955	-	-	-	-	17.5	0.0	-	-	-	-	17.6	0.6	-	-	-	-	17.8	1.1	-	-	-	-	17.9	0.6
1956	-	-	-	-	18.2	1.7	-	-	-	-	18.2	0.0	-	-	-	-	19.2	5.5	-	-	-	-	19.3	0.5
1957	-	-	-	-	19.3	0.0	-	-	-	-	19.5	1.0	-	-	-	-	19.6	0.5	-	-	-	-	20.0	2.0
1958	-	-	-	-	20.3	1.5	-	-	-	-	21.4	5.4	-	-	-	-	21.5	0.5	-	-	-	-	21.6	0.5
1959	-	-	-	-	21.7	0.5	-	-	-	-	22.0	1.4	-	-	-	-	22.0	0.0	-	-	-	-	22.0	0.0
1960	-	-	-	-	22.4	1.8	-	-	-	-	22.5	0.4	-	-	-	-	22.7	0.9	-	-	-	-	22.8	0.4
1961	-	-	-	-	22.9	0.4	-	-	-	-	23.0	0.4	-	-	-	-	23.1	0.4	-	-	-	-	23.2	0.4
1962	-	-	-	-	24.0	3.4	-	-	-	-	24.1	0.4	-	-	-	-	24.2	0.4	-	-	-	-	24.4	0.8
1963	-	-	-	-	24.5	0.4	-	-	-	-	24.6	0.4	-	-	-	-	24.7	0.4	-	-	-	-	24.8	0.4
1964	-	-	-	-	25.1	1.2	-	-	-	-	25.3	0.8	-	-	-	-	25.5	0.8	-	-	-	-	25.5	0.0
1965	-	-	-	-	25.8	1.2	-	-	-	-	25.9	0.4	-	-	-	-	25.9	0.0	-	-	-	-	26.3	1.5
1966	-	-	-	-	26.6	1.1	-	-	-	-	27.1	1.9	-	-	-	-	27.8	2.6	-	-	-	-	28.2	1.4
1967	-	-	-	-	28.7	1.8	-	-	-	-	28.9	0.7	-	-	-	-	29.1	0.7	-	-	-	-	29.4	1.0
1968	-	-	-	-	30.1	2.4	-	-	-	-	30.3	0.7	-	-	-	-	30.5	0.7	-	-	-	-	30.9	1.3
1969	-	-	-	-	31.4	1.6	-	-	-	-	31.7	1.0	-	-	-	-	32.2	1.6	-	-	-	-	32.5	0.9
1970	-	-	-	-	33.2	2.2	-	-	-	-	33.5	0.9	-	-	-	-	34.1	1.8	-	-	-	-	34.2	0.3
1971	-	-	-	-	35.3	3.2	-	-	-	-	35.7	1.1	-	-	-	-	36.2	1.4	-	-	-	-	35.9	-0.8
1972	-	-	-	-	36.4	1.4	-	-	-	-	36.7	0.8	-	-	-	-	37.1	1.1	-	-	-	-	37.4	0.8
1973	-	-	-	-	37.9	1.3	-	-	-	-	38.0	0.3	-	-	-	-	38.4	1.1	-	-	-	-	39.0	1.6
1974	-	-	-	-	40.1	2.8	-	-	-	-	41.2	2.7	-	-	-	-	42.7	3.6	-	-	-	-	43.5	1.9
1975	-	-	-	-	45.7	5.1	-	-	-	-	48.3	5.7	-	-	-	-	49.1	1.7	-	-	-	-	49.8	1.4
1976	-	-	-	-	51.7	3.8	-	-	-	-	52.3	1.2	-	-	-	-	53.2	1.7	-	-	-	-	54.6	2.6
1977	-	-	-	-	56.4	3.3	-	-	-	-	57.4	1.8	-	-	-	-	59.3	3.3	-	-	-	-	59.7	0.7
1978	-	-	61.0	2.2	-	-	62.6	2.6	-	-	62.6	0.0	-	-	63.7	1.8	-	-	65.5	2.8	-	-	65.9	0.6
1979	-	-	67.0	1.7	-	-	67.3	0.4	-	-	67.8	0.7	-	-	69.3	2.2	-	-	72.1	4.0	-	-	73.2	1.5
1980	-	-	74.4	1.6	-	-	76.0	2.2	-	-	76.4	0.5	-	-	76.8	0.5	-	-	78.4	2.1	-	-	78.6	0.3
1981	-	-	81.1	3.2	-	-	82.9	2.2	-	-	84.0	1.3	-	-	85.7	2.0	-	-	87.2	1.8	-	-	89.1	2.2
1982	-	-	90.8	1.9	-	-	93.1	2.5	-	-	94.3	1.3	-	-	95.2	1.0	-	-	96.3	1.2	-	-	97.6	1.3
1983	-	-	99.5	1.9	-	-	99.7	0.2	-	-	101.2	1.5	-	-	101.9	0.7	-	-	101.6	-0.3	-	-	101.7	0.1
1984	-	-	103.8	2.1	-	-	104.4	0.6	-	-	104.6	0.2	-	-	105.4	0.8	-	-	106.4	0.9	-	-	107.0	0.6
1985	-	-	107.8	0.7	-	-	108.5	0.6	-	-	110.3	1.7	-	-	113.2	2.6	-	-	113.9	0.6	-	-	115.1	1.1
1986	-	-	115.9	0.7	-	-	117.4	1.3	-	-	118.9	1.3	-	-	121.9	2.5	-	-	122.4	0.4	-	-	124.0	1.3
1987	125.1	0.9	125.2	0.1	125.8	0.5	126.6	0.6	126.4	-0.2	127.3	0.7	130.1	2.2	131.3	0.9	131.1	-0.2	131.4	0.2	132.0	0.5	132.2	0.2
1988	133.2	0.8	133.1	-0.1	133.7	0.5	134.3	0.4	134.7	0.3	136.1	1.0	137.9	1.3	138.1	0.1	139.1	0.7	140.1	0.7	140.5	0.3	141.4	0.6
1989	143.0	1.1	144.6	1.1	145.0	0.3	145.7	0.5	145.8	0.1	146.6	0.5	147.8	0.8	148.4	0.4	149.9	1.0	150.4	0.3	154.1	2.5	152.9	-0.8
1990	155.2	1.5	156.1	0.6	158.3	1.4	158.3	0.0	158.3	0.0	158.7	0.3	161.3	1.6	162.7	0.9	163.1	0.2	164.2	0.7	164.8	0.4	164.9	0.1
1991	166.6	1.0	167.8	0.7	168.7	0.5	168.7	0.0	169.0	0.2	169.7	0.4	173.2	2.1	176.6	2.0	177.9	0.7	178.2	0.2	178.9	0.4	179.4	0.3

[Continued]

San Francisco-Oakland, CA
Consumer Price Index - All Urban Consumers
Base 1982-1984 = 100
Medical Care
[Continued]

For 1947-1995. Columns headed % show percentile change in the index from the previous period for which an index is available.

Year	Jan Index	%	Feb Index	%	Mar Index	%	Apr Index	%	May Index	%	Jun Index	%	Jul Index	%	Aug Index	%	Sep Index	%	Oct Index	%	Nov Index	%	Dec Index	%
1992	180.1	0.4	182.2	1.2	183.1	0.5	185.3	1.2	185.2	-0.1	186.7	0.8	188.5	1.0	188.7	0.1	190.3	0.8	190.9	0.3	191.2	0.2	191.4	0.1
1993	193.1	0.9	194.9	0.9	194.7	-0.1	197.8	1.6	197.8	0.0	199.5	0.9	201.4	1.0	201.6	0.1	201.2	-0.2	202.2	0.5	202.0	-0.1	202.4	0.2
1994	202.4	0.0	202.5	0.0	203.1	0.3	203.9	0.4	203.5	-0.2	203.9	0.2	203.3	-0.3	204.9	0.8	205.7	0.4	205.8	0.0	206.3	0.2	206.8	0.2
1995	209.0	1.1	208.6	-0.2	209.2	0.3	207.7	-0.7	207.7	0.0	207.1	-0.3	208.8	0.8	208.8	0.0	209.9	0.5	210.1	0.1	210.6	0.2	210.6	0.0

Source: U.S. Department of Labor, Bureau of Labor Statistics, Division of Consumer Prices and Price Indexes. - indicates no data collected for period.

San Francisco-Oakland, CA
Consumer Price Index - Urban Wage Earners
Base 1982-1984 = 100
Medical Care

For 1947-1995. Columns headed % show percentile change in the index from the previous period for which an index is available.

Year	Jan Index	%	Feb Index	%	Mar Index	%	Apr Index	%	May Index	%	Jun Index	%	Jul Index	%	Aug Index	%	Sep Index	%	Oct Index	%	Nov Index	%	Dec Index	%
1947	13.4	-	13.5	0.7	13.5	0.0	13.5	0.0	13.5	0.0	13.5	0.0	-	-	-	-	13.9	3.0	-	-	-	-	14.0	0.7
1948	-	-	-	-	14.1	0.7	-	-	-	-	14.3	1.4	-	-	-	-	14.5	1.4	-	-	-	-	14.7	1.4
1949	-	-	-	-	14.8	0.7	-	-	-	-	14.8	0.0	-	-	-	-	14.9	0.7	-	-	-	-	14.9	0.0
1950	-	-	-	-	14.9	0.0	-	-	-	-	14.9	0.0	-	-	-	-	15.6	4.7	-	-	-	-	15.8	1.3
1951	-	-	-	-	15.8	0.0	-	-	-	-	15.9	0.6	-	-	-	-	15.9	0.0	-	-	-	-	16.1	1.3
1952	-	-	-	-	16.9	5.0	-	-	-	-	17.0	0.6	-	-	-	-	17.0	0.0	-	-	-	-	17.1	0.6
1953	-	-	-	-	17.1	0.0	-	-	-	-	17.3	1.2	-	-	-	-	17.5	1.2	-	-	-	-	17.6	0.6
1954	-	-	-	-	17.6	0.0	-	-	-	-	17.6	0.0	-	-	-	-	17.6	0.0	-	-	-	-	17.7	0.6
1955	-	-	-	-	17.7	0.0	-	-	-	-	17.7	0.0	-	-	-	-	17.9	1.1	-	-	-	-	18.0	0.6
1956	-	-	-	-	18.3	1.7	-	-	-	-	18.3	0.0	-	-	-	-	19.4	6.0	-	-	-	-	19.4	0.0
1957	-	-	-	-	19.5	0.5	-	-	-	-	19.6	0.5	-	-	-	-	19.7	0.5	-	-	-	-	20.1	2.0
1958	-	-	-	-	20.4	1.5	-	-	-	-	21.6	5.9	-	-	-	-	21.6	0.0	-	-	-	-	21.7	0.5
1959	-	-	-	-	21.8	0.5	-	-	-	-	22.1	1.4	-	-	-	-	22.1	0.0	-	-	-	-	22.2	0.5
1960	-	-	-	-	22.5	1.4	-	-	-	-	22.7	0.9	-	-	-	-	22.8	0.4	-	-	-	-	22.9	0.4
1961	-	-	-	-	23.0	0.4	-	-	-	-	23.1	0.4	-	-	-	-	23.3	0.9	-	-	-	-	23.4	0.4
1962	-	-	-	-	24.2	3.4	-	-	-	-	24.3	0.4	-	-	-	-	24.4	0.4	-	-	-	-	24.5	0.4
1963	-	-	-	-	24.7	0.8	-	-	-	-	24.8	0.4	-	-	-	-	24.9	0.4	-	-	-	-	25.0	0.4
1964	-	-	-	-	25.2	0.8	-	-	-	-	25.4	0.8	-	-	-	-	25.7	1.2	-	-	-	-	25.7	0.0
1965	-	-	-	-	26.0	1.2	-	-	-	-	26.0	0.0	-	-	-	-	26.1	0.4	-	-	-	-	26.5	1.5
1966	-	-	-	-	26.8	1.1	-	-	-	-	27.3	1.9	-	-	-	-	28.0	2.6	-	-	-	-	28.4	1.4
1967	-	-	-	-	28.9	1.8	-	-	-	-	29.1	0.7	-	-	-	-	29.3	0.7	-	-	-	-	29.6	1.0
1968	-	-	-	-	30.3	2.4	-	-	-	-	30.5	0.7	-	-	-	-	30.7	0.7	-	-	-	-	31.1	1.3
1969	-	-	-	-	31.6	1.6	-	-	-	-	32.0	1.3	-	-	-	-	32.4	1.3	-	-	-	-	32.7	0.9
1970	-	-	-	-	33.4	2.1	-	-	-	-	33.7	0.9	-	-	-	-	34.3	1.8	-	-	-	-	34.5	0.6
1971	-	-	-	-	35.5	2.9	-	-	-	-	35.9	1.1	-	-	-	-	36.4	1.4	-	-	-	-	36.2	-0.5
1972	-	-	-	-	36.6	1.1	-	-	-	-	36.9	0.8	-	-	-	-	37.3	1.1	-	-	-	-	37.7	1.1
1973	-	-	-	-	38.2	1.3	-	-	-	-	38.3	0.3	-	-	-	-	38.6	0.8	-	-	-	-	39.3	1.8
1974	-	-	-	-	40.4	2.8	-	-	-	-	41.5	2.7	-	-	-	-	43.0	3.6	-	-	-	-	43.8	1.9
1975	-	-	-	-	46.0	5.0	-	-	-	-	48.6	5.7	-	-	-	-	49.5	1.9	-	-	-	-	50.1	1.2
1976	-	-	-	-	52.1	4.0	-	-	-	-	52.6	1.0	-	-	-	-	53.6	1.9	-	-	-	-	54.9	2.4
1977	-	-	-	-	56.8	3.5	-	-	-	-	57.8	1.8	-	-	-	-	59.7	3.3	-	-	-	-	60.1	0.7
1978	-	-	62.3	3.7	-	-	62.7	0.6	-	-	62.3	-0.6	-	-	64.4	3.4	-	-	65.0	0.9	-	-	65.8	1.2
1979	-	-	66.4	0.9	-	-	66.9	0.8	-	-	68.2	1.9	-	-	69.9	2.5	-	-	72.2	3.3	-	-	73.4	1.7
1980	-	-	74.7	1.8	-	-	75.8	1.5	-	-	76.0	0.3	-	-	77.4	1.8	-	-	79.1	2.2	-	-	80.0	1.1
1981	-	-	82.2	2.8	-	-	83.2	1.2	-	-	83.8	0.7	-	-	87.0	3.8	-	-	87.5	0.6	-	-	89.2	1.9
1982	-	-	90.9	1.9	-	-	93.1	2.4	-	-	94.3	1.3	-	-	95.0	0.7	-	-	96.0	1.1	-	-	97.1	1.1
1983	-	-	99.1	2.1	-	-	99.5	0.4	-	-	101.0	1.5	-	-	101.7	0.7	-	-	101.5	-0.2	-	-	101.7	0.2
1984	-	-	103.8	2.1	-	-	104.6	0.8	-	-	104.9	0.3	-	-	105.8	0.9	-	-	106.9	1.0	-	-	107.6	0.7
1985	-	-	108.5	0.8	-	-	109.1	0.6	-	-	110.8	1.6	-	-	113.8	2.7	-	-	114.5	0.6	-	-	115.8	1.1
1986	-	-	116.6	0.7	-	-	118.0	1.2	-	-	119.8	1.5	-	-	122.7	2.4	-	-	123.1	0.3	-	-	124.7	1.3
1987	126.0	1.0	126.3	0.2	126.9	0.5	127.7	0.6	127.7	0.0	128.7	0.8	131.5	2.2	132.6	0.8	132.4	-0.2	132.8	0.3	133.4	0.5	133.6	0.1
1988	134.4	0.6	134.4	0.0	135.0	0.4	135.6	0.4	136.0	0.3	137.3	1.0	138.9	1.2	139.3	0.3	140.0	0.5	141.5	1.1	142.0	0.4	142.5	0.4
1989	144.3	1.3	146.0	1.2	145.9	-0.1	147.0	0.8	147.1	0.1	147.9	0.5	149.1	0.8	149.4	0.2	151.0	1.1	151.5	0.3	155.1	2.4	153.6	-1.0
1990	156.1	1.6	156.8	0.4	158.9	1.3	158.8	-0.1	158.5	-0.2	158.9	0.3	161.3	1.5	163.1	1.1	163.4	0.2	164.3	0.6	164.9	0.4	164.1	-0.5
1991	166.3	1.3	167.1	0.5	168.0	0.5	168.3	0.2	168.6	0.2	169.3	0.4	172.3	1.8	175.8	2.0	177.1	0.7	176.6	-0.3	177.6	0.6	178.3	0.4

[Continued]

San Francisco-Oakland, CA
Consumer Price Index - Urban Wage Earners
Base 1982-1984 = 100
Medical Care

[Continued]

For 1947-1995. Columns headed % show percentile change in the index from the previous period for which an index is available.

Year	Jan		Feb		Mar		Apr		May		Jun		Jul		Aug		Sep		Oct		Nov		Dec	
	Index	%	Index	%	Index	%	Index	%	Index	%	Index	%	Index	%	Index	%	Index	%	Index	%	Index	%	Index	%
1992	178.6	0.2	181.4	1.6	182.2	0.4	184.7	1.4	184.4	-0.2	186.8	1.3	188.5	0.9	188.7	0.1	190.0	0.7	190.2	0.1	190.3	0.1	190.6	0.2
1993	192.2	0.8	194.2	1.0	194.0	-0.1	196.8	1.4	196.8	0.0	198.3	0.8	200.1	0.9	200.5	0.2	199.4	-0.5	201.0	0.8	200.6	-0.2	201.0	0.2
1994	200.9	-0.0	200.3	-0.3	201.4	0.5	202.2	0.4	201.5	-0.3	201.9	0.2	201.4	-0.2	203.0	0.8	203.6	0.3	203.6	0.0	204.1	0.2	204.7	0.3
1995	206.7	1.0	206.4	-0.1	207.1	0.3	205.6	-0.7	205.6	0.0	204.9	-0.3	206.6	0.8	206.6	0.0	207.6	0.5	207.8	0.1	208.3	0.2	208.4	0.0

Source: U.S. Department of Labor, Bureau of Labor Statistics, Division of Consumer Prices and Price Indexes. - indicates no data collected for period.

San Francisco-Oakland, CA
Consumer Price Index - All Urban Consumers
Base 1982-1984 = 100
Entertainment

For 1975-1995. Columns headed % show percentile change in the index from the previous period for which an index is available.

Year	Jan Index	%	Feb Index	%	Mar Index	%	Apr Index	%	May Index	%	Jun Index	%	Jul Index	%	Aug Index	%	Sep Index	%	Oct Index	%	Nov Index	%	Dec Index	%
1975	-	-	-	-	-	-	-	-	-	-	-	-	-	-	-	-	-	-	-	-	-	-	62.9	-
1976	-	-	-	-	63.8	1.4	-	-	-	-	64.5	1.1	-	-	-	-	65.6	1.7	-	-	-	-	66.2	0.9
1977	-	-	-	-	66.7	0.8	-	-	-	-	67.4	1.0	-	-	-	-	68.2	1.2	-	-	-	-	68.8	0.9
1978	-	-	66.6	-3.2	-	-	70.2	5.4	-	-	71.2	1.4	-	-	73.9	3.8	-	-	75.2	1.8	-	-	75.5	0.4
1979	-	-	73.6	-2.5	-	-	76.2	3.5	-	-	76.1	-0.1	-	-	76.9	1.1	-	-	74.5	-3.1	-	-	75.7	1.6
1980	-	-	77.9	2.9	-	-	86.7	11.3	-	-	87.7	1.2	-	-	85.9	-2.1	-	-	85.8	-0.1	-	-	87.7	2.2
1981	-	-	91.5	4.3	-	-	89.6	-2.1	-	-	89.7	0.1	-	-	90.8	1.2	-	-	97.3	7.2	-	-	97.7	0.4
1982	-	-	97.0	-0.7	-	-	98.8	1.9	-	-	101.7	2.9	-	-	97.2	-4.4	-	-	98.1	0.9	-	-	98.0	-0.1
1983	-	-	97.5	-0.5	-	-	97.9	0.4	-	-	99.1	1.2	-	-	99.3	0.2	-	-	99.3	0.0	-	-	99.8	0.5
1984	-	-	101.5	1.7	-	-	101.5	0.0	-	-	102.6	1.1	-	-	103.3	0.7	-	-	103.7	0.4	-	-	106.1	2.3
1985	-	-	106.5	0.4	-	-	107.1	0.6	-	-	108.1	0.9	-	-	109.3	1.1	-	-	110.6	1.2	-	-	110.7	0.1
1986	-	-	114.9	3.8	-	-	117.1	1.9	-	-	116.7	-0.3	-	-	118.9	1.9	-	-	119.3	0.3	-	-	119.5	0.2
1987	120.1	0.5	121.2	0.9	119.3	-1.6	120.7	1.2	122.6	1.6	121.9	-0.6	120.7	-1.0	120.9	0.2	119.6	-1.1	121.8	1.8	124.8	2.5	126.0	1.0
1988	127.3	1.0	124.1	-2.5	128.9	3.9	129.1	0.2	128.6	-0.4	129.3	0.5	130.0	0.5	129.3	-0.5	131.2	1.5	128.7	-1.9	130.9	1.7	131.7	0.6
1989	133.8	1.6	133.3	-0.4	132.9	-0.3	134.4	1.1	134.3	-0.1	134.2	-0.1	135.0	0.6	137.4	1.8	130.0	-5.4	131.6	1.2	129.2	-1.8	131.5	1.8
1990	133.5	1.5	130.6	-2.2	134.8	3.2	139.8	3.7	139.9	0.1	141.3	1.0	142.6	0.9	145.4	2.0	146.0	0.4	144.6	-1.0	143.7	-0.6	145.7	1.4
1991	147.9	1.5	148.0	0.1	150.1	1.4	151.1	0.7	149.1	-1.3	152.7	2.4	154.4	1.1	154.3	-0.1	155.1	0.5	155.8	0.5	153.8	-1.3	156.0	1.4
1992	156.6	0.4	156.7	0.1	156.0	-0.4	157.5	1.0	155.4	-1.3	157.1	1.1	154.8	-1.5	155.5	0.5	155.2	-0.2	156.4	0.8	158.7	1.5	158.1	-0.4
1993	155.5	-1.6	160.9	3.5	161.3	0.2	161.7	0.2	163.5	1.1	163.1	-0.2	162.8	-0.2	163.1	0.2	162.9	-0.1	163.6	0.4	164.3	0.4	164.6	0.2
1994	164.0	-0.4	164.9	0.5	166.6	1.0	165.5	-0.7	164.4	-0.7	164.3	-0.1	163.8	-0.3	163.0	-0.5	162.7	-0.2	164.4	1.0	165.7	0.8	164.9	-0.5
1995	165.8	0.5	166.9	0.7	166.6	-0.2	165.9	-0.4	166.4	0.3	165.4	-0.6	164.7	-0.4	163.7	-0.6	166.6	1.8	166.4	-0.1	167.5	0.7	168.6	0.7

Source: U.S. Department of Labor, Bureau of Labor Statistics, Division of Consumer Prices and Price Indexes. - indicates no data collected for period.

San Francisco-Oakland, CA
Consumer Price Index - Urban Wage Earners
Base 1982-1984 = 100
Entertainment

For 1975-1995. Columns headed % show percentile change in the index from the previous period for which an index is available.

Year	Jan Index	%	Feb Index	%	Mar Index	%	Apr Index	%	May Index	%	Jun Index	%	Jul Index	%	Aug Index	%	Sep Index	%	Oct Index	%	Nov Index	%	Dec Index	%
1975	-	-	-	-	-	-	-	-	-	-	-	-	-	-	-	-	-	-	-	-	-	-	70.5	-
1976	-	-	-	-	71.5	1.4	-	-	-	-	72.3	1.1	-	-	-	-	73.6	1.8	-	-	-	-	74.2	0.8
1977	-	-	-	-	74.8	0.8	-	-	-	-	75.6	1.1	-	-	-	-	76.4	1.1	-	-	-	-	77.1	0.9
1978	-	-	78.7	2.1	-	-	79.7	1.3	-	-	80.7	1.3	-	-	83.2	3.1	-	-	83.2	0.0	-	-	83.0	-0.2
1979	-	-	82.9	-0.1	-	-	86.1	3.9	-	-	85.6	-0.6	-	-	86.7	1.3	-	-	80.3	-7.4	-	-	80.4	0.1
1980	-	-	81.7	1.6	-	-	92.6	13.3	-	-	92.9	0.3	-	-	94.8	2.0	-	-	96.9	2.2	-	-	95.1	-1.9
1981	-	-	97.0	2.0	-	-	95.9	-1.1	-	-	98.1	2.3	-	-	99.6	1.5	-	-	102.4	2.8	-	-	101.4	-1.0
1982	-	-	101.4	0.0	-	-	102.6	1.2	-	-	105.0	2.3	-	-	96.0	-8.6	-	-	97.0	1.0	-	-	96.9	-0.1
1983	-	-	96.3	-0.6	-	-	96.5	0.2	-	-	97.9	1.5	-	-	98.5	0.6	-	-	98.6	0.1	-	-	99.2	0.6
1984	-	-	101.1	1.9	-	-	100.8	-0.3	-	-	102.1	1.3	-	-	103.1	1.0	-	-	102.8	-0.3	-	-	105.3	2.4
1985	-	-	105.8	0.5	-	-	106.4	0.6	-	-	107.5	1.0	-	-	107.8	0.3	-	-	108.1	0.3	-	-	108.3	0.2
1986	-	-	112.6	4.0	-	-	113.9	1.2	-	-	113.5	-0.4	-	-	115.3	1.6	-	-	115.6	0.3	-	-	115.8	0.2
1987	115.8	0.0	117.4	1.4	115.6	-1.5	116.4	0.7	118.6	1.9	117.8	-0.7	116.6	-1.0	116.9	0.3	115.5	-1.2	116.7	1.0	120.0	2.8	120.8	0.7
1988	122.0	1.0	119.2	-2.3	123.4	3.5	123.8	0.3	123.6	-0.2	124.5	0.7	124.9	0.3	124.1	-0.6	125.7	1.3	123.7	-1.6	125.9	1.8	126.6	0.6
1989	128.4	1.4	128.4	0.0	129.6	0.9	130.9	1.0	130.5	-0.3	131.2	0.5	131.9	0.5	133.3	1.1	128.2	-3.8	130.1	1.5	127.5	-2.0	130.6	2.4
1990	131.9	1.0	127.7	-3.2	133.1	4.2	138.1	3.8	138.3	0.1	138.4	0.1	138.7	0.2	140.1	1.0	138.4	-1.2	136.9	-1.1	135.8	-0.8	137.9	1.5
1991	139.7	1.3	140.2	0.4	142.0	1.3	143.0	0.7	141.0	-1.4	143.9	2.1	145.1	0.8	144.5	-0.4	145.5	0.7	145.7	0.1	143.5	-1.5	147.4	2.7
1992	148.2	0.5	147.7	-0.3	146.7	-0.7	148.6	1.3	146.4	-1.5	148.1	1.2	146.1	-1.4	146.5	0.3	146.2	-0.2	147.3	0.8	149.1	1.2	148.6	-0.3
1993	146.2	-1.6	150.4	2.9	150.9	0.3	150.8	-0.1	152.5	1.1	152.0	-0.3	152.0	0.0	152.3	0.2	152.1	-0.1	152.7	0.4	152.9	0.1	154.4	1.0
1994	152.8	-1.0	153.6	0.5	155.0	0.9	153.8	-0.8	153.1	-0.5	152.9	-0.1	152.4	-0.3	151.8	-0.4	151.5	-0.2	151.6	0.1	152.8	0.8	153.6	0.5
1995	154.5	0.6	155.6	0.7	155.1	-0.3	154.5	-0.4	155.0	0.3	154.2	-0.5	154.0	-0.1	152.7	-0.8	155.2	1.6	154.4	-0.5	155.8	0.9	157.0	0.8

Source: U.S. Department of Labor, Bureau of Labor Statistics, Division of Consumer Prices and Price Indexes. - indicates no data collected for period.

San Francisco-Oakland, CA
Consumer Price Index - All Urban Consumers
Base 1982-1984 = 100
Other Goods and Services

For 1975-1995. Columns headed % show percentile change in the index from the previous period for which an index is available.

Year	Jan Index	%	Feb Index	%	Mar Index	%	Apr Index	%	May Index	%	Jun Index	%	Jul Index	%	Aug Index	%	Sep Index	%	Oct Index	%	Nov Index	%	Dec Index	%
1975	-	-	-	-	-	-	-	-	-	-	-	-	-	-	-	-	-	-	-	-	-	-	53.0	-
1976	-	-	-	-	53.4	0.8	-	-	-	-	53.9	0.9	-	-	-	-	54.9	1.9	-	-	-	-	56.0	2.0
1977	-	-	-	-	56.8	1.4	-	-	-	-	57.8	1.8	-	-	-	-	59.6	3.1	-	-	-	-	59.9	0.5
1978	-	-	60.4	0.8	-	-	61.6	2.0	-	-	63.4	2.9	-	-	64.7	2.1	-	-	66.0	2.0	-	-	66.2	0.3
1979	-	-	66.5	0.5	-	-	66.9	0.6	-	-	66.8	-0.1	-	-	67.4	0.9	-	-	69.3	2.8	-	-	69.6	0.4
1980	-	-	70.6	1.4	-	-	71.9	1.8	-	-	71.3	-0.8	-	-	73.2	2.7	-	-	74.8	2.2	-	-	76.1	1.7
1981	-	-	77.1	1.3	-	-	77.8	0.9	-	-	79.7	2.4	-	-	79.9	0.3	-	-	82.8	3.6	-	-	83.8	1.2
1982	-	-	86.5	3.2	-	-	88.6	2.4	-	-	88.7	0.1	-	-	89.9	1.4	-	-	96.2	7.0	-	-	97.7	1.6
1983	-	-	100.0	2.4	-	-	100.2	0.2	-	-	101.3	1.1	-	-	100.5	-0.8	-	-	102.7	2.2	-	-	103.9	1.2
1984	-	-	105.6	1.6	-	-	105.9	0.3	-	-	107.6	1.6	-	-	108.0	0.4	-	-	111.6	3.3	-	-	112.4	0.7
1985	-	-	115.0	2.3	-	-	115.5	0.4	-	-	115.7	0.2	-	-	117.0	1.1	-	-	117.4	0.3	-	-	119.0	1.4
1986	-	-	122.2	2.7	-	-	122.3	0.1	-	-	123.2	0.7	-	-	122.6	-0.5	-	-	124.2	1.3	-	-	126.2	1.6
1987	127.5	1.0	128.5	0.8	128.7	0.2	129.0	0.2	128.8	-0.2	129.1	0.2	130.3	0.9	131.5	0.9	133.7	1.7	134.1	0.3	134.6	0.4	134.4	-0.1
1988	137.2	2.1	137.2	0.0	137.2	0.0	138.3	0.8	138.7	0.3	138.5	-0.1	139.1	0.4	140.6	1.1	142.1	1.1	142.6	0.4	144.3	1.2	144.9	0.4
1989	148.0	2.1	146.4	-1.1	149.5	2.1	149.6	0.1	150.4	0.5	151.5	0.7	153.3	1.2	156.2	1.9	155.0	-0.8	155.0	0.0	155.1	0.1	156.0	0.6
1990	159.2	2.1	158.6	-0.4	158.3	-0.2	160.2	1.2	159.3	-0.6	160.3	0.6	160.3	0.0	161.4	0.7	162.8	0.9	163.8	0.6	164.1	0.2	164.2	0.1
1991	165.5	0.8	170.0	2.7	169.3	-0.4	170.2	0.5	171.4	0.7	172.2	0.5	173.2	0.6	175.0	1.0	180.8	3.3	181.6	0.4	182.4	0.4	182.4	0.0
1992	190.4	4.4	191.2	0.4	191.4	0.1	192.5	0.6	192.0	-0.3	192.0	0.0	192.7	0.4	193.7	0.5	202.8	4.7	204.1	0.6	203.9	-0.1	203.7	-0.1
1993	205.9	1.1	207.3	0.7	207.1	-0.1	206.5	-0.3	207.0	0.2	205.7	-0.6	206.8	0.5	206.7	-0.0	209.6	1.4	207.1	-1.2	207.1	0.0	207.2	0.0
1994	210.1	1.4	210.7	0.3	212.3	0.8	211.5	-0.4	211.1	-0.2	210.6	-0.2	211.1	0.2	211.6	0.2	216.9	2.5	217.5	0.3	218.2	0.3	216.9	-0.6
1995	217.2	0.1	217.2	0.0	218.1	0.4	218.5	0.2	219.2	0.3	219.7	0.2	219.7	0.0	220.7	0.5	223.2	1.1	223.9	0.3	224.7	0.4	224.7	0.0

Source: U.S. Department of Labor, Bureau of Labor Statistics, Division of Consumer Prices and Price Indexes. - indicates no data collected for period.

San Francisco-Oakland, CA
Consumer Price Index - Urban Wage Earners
Base 1982-1984 = 100
Other Goods and Services

For 1975-1995. Columns headed % show percentile change in the index from the previous period for which an index is available.

Year	Jan Index	%	Feb Index	%	Mar Index	%	Apr Index	%	May Index	%	Jun Index	%	Jul Index	%	Aug Index	%	Sep Index	%	Oct Index	%	Nov Index	%	Dec Index	%
1975	-	-	-	-	-	-	-	-	-	-	-	-	-	-	-	-	-	-	-	-	-	-	52.7	-
1976	-	-	-	-	53.1	0.8	-	-	-	-	53.6	0.9	-	-	-	-	54.5	1.7	-	-	-	-	55.7	2.2
1977	-	-	-	-	56.5	1.4	-	-	-	-	57.5	1.8	-	-	-	-	59.2	3.0	-	-	-	-	59.5	0.5
1978	-	-	59.5	0.0	-	-	60.4	1.5	-	-	61.3	1.5	-	-	62.5	2.0	-	-	63.9	2.2	-	-	63.4	-0.8
1979	-	-	64.9	2.4	-	-	65.1	0.3	-	-	66.5	2.2	-	-	67.1	0.9	-	-	68.7	2.4	-	-	69.3	0.9
1980	-	-	70.3	1.4	-	-	72.0	2.4	-	-	72.9	1.3	-	-	73.5	0.8	-	-	75.2	2.3	-	-	76.7	2.0
1981	-	-	77.3	0.8	-	-	78.1	1.0	-	-	79.8	2.2	-	-	80.3	0.6	-	-	83.3	3.7	-	-	84.5	1.4
1982	-	-	87.0	3.0	-	-	88.9	2.2	-	-	89.0	0.1	-	-	90.3	1.5	-	-	96.2	6.5	-	-	97.9	1.8
1983	-	-	99.9	2.0	-	-	100.0	0.1	-	-	101.1	1.1	-	-	100.7	-0.4	-	-	102.7	2.0	-	-	103.7	1.0
1984	-	-	105.5	1.7	-	-	105.8	0.3	-	-	107.2	1.3	-	-	107.6	0.4	-	-	111.4	3.5	-	-	112.2	0.7
1985	-	-	114.7	2.2	-	-	115.3	0.5	-	-	115.2	-0.1	-	-	116.7	1.3	-	-	116.8	0.1	-	-	118.3	1.3
1986	-	-	121.5	2.7	-	-	121.5	0.0	-	-	122.5	0.8	-	-	122.1	-0.3	-	-	123.6	1.2	-	-	125.7	1.7
1987	126.7	0.8	128.0	1.0	128.4	0.3	128.6	0.2	128.2	-0.3	128.7	0.4	130.1	1.1	131.1	0.8	133.5	1.8	133.7	0.1	134.0	0.2	133.7	-0.2
1988	137.0	2.5	137.0	0.0	137.0	0.0	138.0	0.7	138.3	0.2	138.1	-0.1	138.9	0.6	140.9	1.4	142.3	1.0	142.8	0.4	144.9	1.5	145.8	0.6
1989	149.8	2.7	147.4	-1.6	151.9	3.1	151.9	0.0	152.2	0.2	153.8	1.1	156.4	1.7	159.1	1.7	157.6	-0.9	157.6	0.0	157.8	0.1	159.1	0.8
1990	162.3	2.0	161.4	-0.6	161.4	0.0	163.6	1.4	162.8	-0.5	164.2	0.9	164.2	0.0	165.2	0.6	165.8	0.4	167.4	1.0	167.8	0.2	168.0	0.1
1991	169.3	0.8	173.7	2.6	173.3	-0.2	174.3	0.6	175.4	0.6	176.0	0.3	177.1	0.6	178.6	0.8	182.4	2.1	183.6	0.7	184.7	0.6	184.7	0.0
1992	191.6	3.7	191.8	0.1	192.0	0.1	193.1	0.6	192.4	-0.4	192.4	0.0	193.5	0.6	194.4	0.5	201.2	3.5	202.6	0.7	202.4	-0.1	202.2	-0.1
1993	205.1	1.4	207.0	0.9	206.7	-0.1	205.8	-0.4	206.3	0.2	204.5	-0.9	206.1	0.8	204.9	-0.6	205.4	0.2	201.8	-1.8	201.9	0.0	202.0	0.0
1994	206.4	2.2	207.0	0.3	208.6	0.8	207.7	-0.4	207.1	-0.3	206.4	-0.3	207.1	0.3	207.5	0.2	211.4	1.9	212.1	0.3	213.0	0.4	211.1	-0.9
1995	211.6	0.2	211.7	0.0	212.9	0.6	213.3	0.2	214.4	0.5	215.0	0.3	214.4	-0.3	215.0	0.3	217.2	1.0	218.3	0.5	218.9	0.3	218.5	-0.2

Source: U.S. Department of Labor, Bureau of Labor Statistics, Division of Consumer Prices and Price Indexes. - indicates no data collected for period.

Seattle-Everett, WA
Consumer Price Index - All Urban Consumers
Base 1982-1984 = 100
Annual Averages

For 1914-1995. Columns headed % show percentile change in the index from the previous period for which an index is available.

Year	All Items		Food & Beverage		Housing		Apparel & Upkeep		Trans- portation		Medical Care		Entertain- ment		Other Goods & Services	
	Index	%	Index	%	Index	%	Index	%	Index	%	Index	%	Index	%	Index	%
1914	-	-	-	-	-	-	-	-	-	-	-	-	-	-	-	-
1915	9.0	-	-	-	-	-	-	-	-	-	-	-	-	-	-	-
1916	9.4	4.4	-	-	-	-	-	-	-	-	-	-	-	-	-	-
1917	11.0	17.0	-	-	-	-	-	-	-	-	-	-	-	-	-	-
1918	13.7	24.5	-	-	-	-	-	-	-	-	-	-	-	-	-	-
1919	16.5	20.4	-	-	-	-	-	-	-	-	-	-	-	-	-	-
1920	18.8	13.9	-	-	-	-	-	-	-	-	-	-	-	-	-	-
1921	16.7	-11.2	-	-	-	-	-	-	-	-	-	-	-	-	-	-
1922	15.6	-6.6	-	-	-	-	-	-	-	-	-	-	-	-	-	-
1923	15.5	-0.6	-	-	-	-	-	-	-	-	-	-	-	-	-	-
1924	15.5	0.0	-	-	-	-	-	-	-	-	-	-	-	-	-	-
1925	15.8	1.9	-	-	-	-	-	-	-	-	-	-	-	-	-	-
1926	15.8	0.0	-	-	-	-	-	-	-	-	-	-	-	-	-	-
1927	15.5	-1.9	-	-	-	-	-	-	-	-	-	-	-	-	-	-
1928	15.4	-0.6	-	-	-	-	-	-	-	-	-	-	-	-	-	-
1929	15.5	0.6	-	-	-	-	-	-	-	-	-	-	-	-	-	-
1930	15.2	-1.9	-	-	-	-	-	-	-	-	-	-	-	-	-	-
1931	13.8	-9.2	-	-	-	-	-	-	-	-	-	-	-	-	-	-
1932	12.6	-8.7	-	-	-	-	-	-	-	-	-	-	-	-	-	-
1933	12.0	-4.8	-	-	-	-	-	-	-	-	-	-	-	-	-	-
1934	12.3	2.5	-	-	-	-	-	-	-	-	-	-	-	-	-	-
1935	12.6	2.4	-	-	-	-	-	-	-	-	-	-	-	-	-	-
1936	12.7	0.8	-	-	-	-	-	-	-	-	-	-	-	-	-	-
1937	13.4	5.5	-	-	-	-	-	-	-	-	-	-	-	-	-	-
1938	13.2	-1.5	-	-	-	-	-	-	-	-	-	-	-	-	-	-
1939	13.2	0.0	-	-	-	-	-	-	-	-	-	-	-	-	-	-
1940	13.2	0.0	-	-	-	-	-	-	-	-	-	-	-	-	-	-
1941	14.0	6.1	-	-	-	-	-	-	-	-	-	-	-	-	-	-
1942	15.8	12.9	-	-	-	-	-	-	-	-	-	-	-	-	-	-
1943	16.7	5.7	-	-	-	-	-	-	-	-	-	-	-	-	-	-
1944	16.9	1.2	-	-	-	-	-	-	-	-	-	-	-	-	-	-
1945	17.3	2.4	-	-	-	-	-	-	-	-	-	-	-	-	-	-
1946	18.6	7.5	-	-	-	-	-	-	19.1	-	14.4	-	-	-	-	-
1947	21.1	13.4	-	-	-	-	-	-	20.8	8.9	15.1	4.9	-	-	-	-
1948	22.8	8.1	-	-	-	-	-	-	22.2	6.7	15.8	4.6	-	-	-	-
1949	22.7	-0.4	-	-	-	-	-	-	22.9	3.2	16.1	1.9	-	-	-	-
1950	23.1	1.8	-	-	-	-	-	-	24.2	5.7	17.1	6.2	-	-	-	-
1951	24.8	7.4	-	-	-	-	-	-	25.6	5.8	18.4	7.6	-	-	-	-
1952	25.5	2.8	-	-	-	-	-	-	27.4	7.0	19.0	3.3	-	-	-	-
1953	25.8	1.2	-	-	-	-	43.9	-	26.9	-1.8	19.7	3.7	-	-	-	-
1954	25.8	0.0	-	-	-	-	43.6	-0.7	26.4	-1.9	20.1	2.0	-	-	-	-
1955	25.9	0.4	-	-	-	-	43.8	0.5	26.6	0.8	20.6	2.5	-	-	-	-
1956	26.2	1.2	-	-	-	-	44.2	0.9	28.6	7.5	21.3	3.4	-	-	-	-
1957	27.3	4.2	-	-	-	-	45.1	2.0	29.7	3.8	22.3	4.7	-	-	-	-
1958	27.9	2.2	-	-	-	-	44.9	-0.4								

[Continued]

Seattle-Everett, WA
Consumer Price Index - All Urban Consumers
Base 1982-1984 = 100
Annual Averages
[Continued]

For 1914-1995. Columns headed % show percentile change in the index from the previous period for which an index is available.

Year	All Items		Food & Beverage		Housing		Apparel & Upkeep		Trans-portation		Medical Care		Entertain-ment		Other Goods & Services	
	Index	%	Index	%	Index	%	Index	%	Index	%	Index	%	Index	%	Index	%
1959	28.5	2.2	-	-	-	-	45.4	1.1	31.1	4.7	22.8	2.2	-	-	-	-
1960	28.8	1.1	-	-	-	-	46.0	1.3	30.8	-1.0	23.9	4.8	-	-	-	-
1961	29.3	1.7	-	-	-	-	46.7	1.5	31.7	2.9	24.0	0.4	-	-	-	-
1962	29.7	1.4	-	-	-	-	47.5	1.7	32.6	2.8	24.3	1.2	-	-	-	-
1963	30.2	1.7	-	-	-	-	48.2	1.5	32.5	-0.3	24.5	0.8	-	-	-	-
1964	30.6	1.3	-	-	-	-	48.7	1.0	32.6	0.3	25.0	2.0	-	-	-	-
1965	31.0	1.3	-	-	-	-	49.0	0.6	33.5	2.8	26.0	4.0	-	-	-	-
1966	31.9	2.9	-	-	-	-	50.4	2.9	34.0	1.5	27.6	6.2	-	-	-	-
1967	32.8	2.8	-	-	-	-	52.2	3.6	35.3	3.8	29.1	5.4	-	-	-	-
1968	34.1	4.0	-	-	-	-	53.7	2.9	35.9	1.7	30.8	5.8	-	-	-	-
1969	35.8	5.0	-	-	-	-	55.8	3.9	36.2	0.8	32.9	6.8	-	-	-	-
1970	37.4	4.5	-	-	-	-	58.3	4.5	37.1	2.5	34.5	4.9	-	-	-	-
1971	38.2	2.1	-	-	-	-	60.6	3.9	37.8	1.9	35.8	3.8	-	-	-	-
1972	39.3	2.9	-	-	-	-	61.4	1.3	38.6	2.1	36.5	2.0	-	-	-	-
1973	41.8	6.4	-	-	-	-	64.2	4.6	39.6	2.6	37.8	3.6	-	-	-	-
1974	46.4	11.0	-	-	-	-	68.2	6.2	44.0	11.1	41.2	9.0	-	-	-	-
1975	51.1	10.1	-	-	-	-	72.7	6.6	48.1	9.3	46.1	11.9	-	-	-	-
1976	54.0	5.7	61.3	-	50.3	-	76.9	5.8	51.8	7.7	50.9	10.4	62.2	-	50.8	-
1977	58.3	8.0	65.6	7.0	54.8	8.9	80.4	4.6	56.9	9.8	56.0	10.0	65.4	5.1	54.2	6.7
1978	63.9	9.6	71.0	8.2	61.7	12.6	82.6	2.7	61.2	7.6	62.2	11.1	68.5	4.7	57.8	6.6
1979	71.0	11.1	78.3	10.3	68.1	10.4	87.9	6.4	71.1	16.2	67.4	8.4	73.3	7.0	64.2	11.1
1980	82.7	16.5	84.5	7.9	82.7	21.4	95.0	8.1	83.1	16.9	75.8	12.5	82.0	11.9	71.5	11.4
1981	91.8	11.0	91.6	8.4	92.2	11.5	99.0	4.2	94.2	13.4	84.9	12.0	88.2	7.6	80.0	11.9
1982	97.7	6.4	98.3	7.3	98.4	6.7	99.6	0.6	98.0	4.0	93.5	10.1	93.8	6.3	91.7	14.6
1983	99.3	1.6	100.1	1.8	98.7	0.3	101.2	1.6	98.9	0.9	100.9	7.9	100.0	6.6	101.1	10.3
1984	103.0	3.7	101.6	1.5	102.8	4.2	99.2	-2.0	103.1	4.2	105.6	4.7	106.2	6.2	107.3	6.1
1985	105.6	2.5	103.2	1.6	105.5	2.6	102.5	3.3	105.0	1.8	112.2	6.3	108.5	2.2	111.9	4.3
1986	106.7	1.0	106.8	3.5	106.8	1.2	104.7	2.1	101.7	-3.1	117.6	4.8	108.6	0.1	117.1	4.6
1987	110.9	3.9	111.3	4.2	108.1	1.2	102.1	-2.5	109.2	7.4	126.8	7.8	116.6	7.4	128.7	9.9
1988	114.7	3.4	112.0	0.6	111.8	3.4	111.9	9.6	110.6	1.3	138.8	9.5	120.9	3.7	136.0	5.7
1989	120.4	5.0	118.7	6.0	116.5	4.2	114.4	2.2	118.3	7.0	145.2	4.6	124.4	2.9	145.1	6.7
1990	127.4	5.8	126.1	6.2	122.6	5.2	120.7	5.5	125.5	6.1	154.4	6.3	128.6	3.4	157.9	8.8
1991	133.9	5.1	130.7	3.6	130.4	6.4	122.3	1.3	130.1	3.7	166.0	7.5	132.6	3.1	172.2	9.1
1992	139.8	4.4	131.7	0.8	138.2	6.0	124.8	2.0	134.0	3.0	176.3	6.2	139.9	5.5	183.6	6.6
1993	144.7	3.5	134.0	1.7	143.7	4.0	122.2	-2.1	136.2	1.6	186.6	5.8	148.7	6.3	201.2	9.6
1994	148.9	2.9	135.9	1.4	149.5	4.0	123.7	1.2	138.6	1.8	192.8	3.3	157.7	6.1	203.1	0.9
1995	-	-	-	-	-	-	-	-	-	-	-	-	-	-	-	-

Source: U.S. Department of Labor, Bureau of Labor Statistics, Division of Consumer Prices and Price Indexes. - indicates no data collected for period.

Seattle-Everett, WA
Consumer Price Index - Urban Wage Earners
Base 1982-1984 = 100
Annual Averages

For 1914-1995. Columns headed % show percentile change in the index from the previous period for which an index is available.

Year	All Items		Food & Beverage		Housing		Apparel & Upkeep		Trans- portation		Medical Care		Entertain- ment		Other Goods & Services	
	Index	%	Index	%	Index	%	Index	%	Index	%	Index	%	Index	%	Index	%
1914	-	-	-	-	-	-	-	-	-	-	-	-	-	-	-	-
1915	9.3	-	-	-	-	-	-	-	-	-	-	-	-	-	-	-
1916	9.6	3.2	-	-	-	-	-	-	-	-	-	-	-	-	-	-
1917	11.3	17.7	-	-	-	-	-	-	-	-	-	-	-	-	-	-
1918	14.1	24.8	-	-	-	-	-	-	-	-	-	-	-	-	-	-
1919	17.0	20.6	-	-	-	-	-	-	-	-	-	-	-	-	-	-
1920	19.4	14.1	-	-	-	-	-	-	-	-	-	-	-	-	-	-
1921	17.1	-11.9	-	-	-	-	-	-	-	-	-	-	-	-	-	-
1922	16.0	-6.4	-	-	-	-	-	-	-	-	-	-	-	-	-	-
1923	15.9	-0.6	-	-	-	-	-	-	-	-	-	-	-	-	-	-
1924	15.9	0.0	-	-	-	-	-	-	-	-	-	-	-	-	-	-
1925	16.3	2.5	-	-	-	-	-	-	-	-	-	-	-	-	-	-
1926	16.3	0.0	-	-	-	-	-	-	-	-	-	-	-	-	-	-
1927	15.9	-2.5	-	-	-	-	-	-	-	-	-	-	-	-	-	-
1928	15.8	-0.6	-	-	-	-	-	-	-	-	-	-	-	-	-	-
1929	15.9	0.6	-	-	-	-	-	-	-	-	-	-	-	-	-	-
1930	15.6	-1.9	-	-	-	-	-	-	-	-	-	-	-	-	-	-
1931	14.2	-9.0	-	-	-	-	-	-	-	-	-	-	-	-	-	-
1932	12.9	-9.2	-	-	-	-	-	-	-	-	-	-	-	-	-	-
1933	12.3	-4.7	-	-	-	-	-	-	-	-	-	-	-	-	-	-
1934	12.6	2.4	-	-	-	-	-	-	-	-	-	-	-	-	-	-
1935	12.9	2.4	-	-	-	-	-	-	-	-	-	-	-	-	-	-
1936	13.1	1.6	-	-	-	-	-	-	-	-	-	-	-	-	-	-
1937	13.7	4.6	-	-	-	-	-	-	-	-	-	-	-	-	-	-
1938	13.6	-0.7	-	-	-	-	-	-	-	-	-	-	-	-	-	-
1939	13.5	-0.7	-	-	-	-	-	-	-	-	-	-	-	-	-	-
1940	13.6	0.7	-	-	-	-	-	-	-	-	-	-	-	-	-	-
1941	14.4	5.9	-	-	-	-	-	-	-	-	-	-	-	-	-	-
1942	16.2	12.5	-	-	-	-	-	-	-	-	-	-	-	-	-	-
1943	17.1	5.6	-	-	-	-	-	-	-	-	-	-	-	-	-	-
1944	17.4	1.8	-	-	-	-	-	-	-	-	-	-	-	-	-	-
1945	17.8	2.3	-	-	-	-	-	-	-	-	-	-	-	-	-	-
1946	19.2	7.9	-	-	-	-	-	-	-	-	-	-	-	-	-	-
1947	21.7	13.0	-	-	-	-	-	-	19.5	-	14.3	-	-	-	-	-
1948	23.5	8.3	-	-	-	-	-	-	21.2	8.7	15.0	4.9	-	-	-	-
1949	23.4	-0.4	-	-	-	-	-	-	22.7	7.1	15.7	4.7	-	-	-	-
1950	23.7	1.3	-	-	-	-	-	-	23.3	2.6	15.9	1.3	-	-	-	-
1951	25.5	7.6	-	-	-	-	-	-	24.7	6.0	16.9	6.3	-	-	-	-
1952	26.2	2.7	-	-	-	-	-	-	26.1	5.7	18.2	7.7	-	-	-	-
1953	26.5	1.1	-	-	-	-	44.4	-	27.9	6.9	18.9	3.8	-	-	-	-
1954	26.5	0.0	-	-	-	-	44.1	-0.7	27.4	-1.8	19.5	3.2	-	-	-	-
1955	26.6	0.4	-	-	-	-	44.3	0.5	27.0	-1.5	19.9	2.1	-	-	-	-
1956	27.0	1.5	-	-	-	-	44.7	0.9	27.1	0.4	20.4	2.5	-	-	-	-
1957	28.1	4.1	-	-	-	-	45.6	2.0	29.2	7.7	21.1	3.4	-	-	-	-
1958	28.7	2.1	-	-	-	-	45.4	-0.4	30.3	3.8	22.1	4.7	-	-	-	-

[Continued]

Seattle-Everett, WA
Consumer Price Index - Urban Wage Earners
Base 1982-1984 = 100
Annual Averages
[Continued]

For 1914-1995. Columns headed % show percentile change in the index from the previous period for which an index is available.

Year	All Items		Food & Beverage		Housing		Apparel & Upkeep		Trans-portation		Medical Care		Entertain-ment		Other Goods & Services	
	Index	%	Index	%	Index	%	Index	%	Index	%	Index	%	Index	%	Index	%
1959	29.3	2.1	-	-	-	-	45.9	1.1	31.7	4.6	22.6	2.3	-	-	-	-
1960	29.6	1.0	-	-	-	-	46.5	1.3	31.4	-0.9	23.7	4.9	-	-	-	-
1961	30.1	1.7	-	-	-	-	47.2	1.5	32.3	2.9	23.8	0.4	-	-	-	-
1962	30.5	1.3	-	-	-	-	48.0	1.7	33.3	3.1	24.1	1.3	-	-	-	-
1963	31.1	2.0	-	-	-	-	48.8	1.7	33.2	-0.3	24.3	0.8	-	-	-	-
1964	31.5	1.3	-	-	-	-	49.3	1.0	33.3	0.3	24.7	1.6	-	-	-	-
1965	31.9	1.3	-	-	-	-	49.6	0.6	34.2	2.7	25.7	4.0	-	-	-	-
1966	32.7	2.5	-	-	-	-	51.0	2.8	34.7	1.5	27.4	6.6	-	-	-	-
1967	33.7	3.1	-	-	-	-	52.8	3.5	36.0	3.7	28.8	5.1	-	-	-	-
1968	35.1	4.2	-	-	-	-	54.3	2.8	36.6	1.7	30.5	5.9	-	-	-	-
1969	36.8	4.8	-	-	-	-	56.5	4.1	36.9	0.8	32.6	6.9	-	-	-	-
1970	38.4	4.3	-	-	-	-	59.0	4.4	37.9	2.7	34.1	4.6	-	-	-	-
1971	39.2	2.1	-	-	-	-	61.3	3.9	38.6	1.8	35.4	3.8	-	-	-	-
1972	40.4	3.1	-	-	-	-	62.1	1.3	39.4	2.1	36.2	2.3	-	-	-	-
1973	43.0	6.4	-	-	-	-	65.0	4.7	40.4	2.5	37.4	3.3	-	-	-	-
1974	47.7	10.9	-	-	-	-	69.1	6.3	44.9	11.1	40.8	9.1	-	-	-	-
1975	52.5	10.1	-	-	-	-	73.5	6.4	49.1	9.4	45.7	12.0	-	-	-	-
1976	55.5	5.7	61.6	-	52.5	-	77.8	5.9	52.8	7.5	50.4	10.3	60.0	-	52.6	-
1977	59.9	7.9	65.9	7.0	57.2	9.0	81.3	4.5	58.1	10.0	55.4	9.9	63.1	5.2	56.1	6.7
1978	65.3	9.0	71.2	8.0	64.4	12.6	83.5	2.7	61.4	5.7	61.1	10.3	66.5	5.4	60.0	7.0
1979	72.4	10.9	78.3	10.0	70.9	10.1	87.9	5.3	70.8	15.3	67.4	10.3	71.4	7.4	65.2	8.7
1980	84.0	16.0	84.8	8.3	85.9	21.2	93.9	6.8	82.3	16.2	75.1	11.4	80.3	12.5	71.6	9.8
1981	93.1	10.8	92.1	8.6	95.5	11.2	97.9	4.3	93.4	13.5	84.1	12.0	87.1	8.5	79.9	11.6
1982	99.1	6.4	98.3	6.7	101.7	6.5	99.7	1.8	97.8	4.7	93.4	11.1	94.2	8.2	91.2	14.1
1983	98.9	-0.2	100.1	1.8	97.6	-4.0	100.9	1.2	98.9	1.1	100.8	7.9	100.1	6.3	101.5	11.3
1984	102.1	3.2	101.6	1.5	100.8	3.3	99.4	-1.5	103.3	4.4	105.8	5.0	105.7	5.6	107.3	5.7
1985	104.2	2.1	103.3	1.7	102.2	1.4	102.5	3.1	105.4	2.0	112.6	6.4	108.0	2.2	111.9	4.3
1986	105.0	0.8	106.6	3.2	103.3	1.1	103.7	1.2	101.8	-3.4	118.4	5.2	107.9	-0.1	117.2	4.7
1987	108.5	3.3	111.1	4.2	104.4	1.1	101.8	-1.8	109.3	7.4	126.4	6.8	115.5	7.0	127.7	9.0
1988	112.0	3.2	111.9	0.7	107.8	3.3	112.0	10.0	110.7	1.3	138.3	9.4	119.6	3.5	135.7	6.3
1989	117.6	5.0	118.6	6.0	112.3	4.2	114.4	2.1	117.9	6.5	144.7	4.6	123.0	2.8	145.6	7.3
1990	124.2	5.6	125.9	6.2	118.1	5.2	120.9	5.7	124.2	5.3	153.2	5.9	127.0	3.3	158.4	8.8
1991	130.8	5.3	130.5	3.7	125.9	6.6	123.6	2.2	129.1	3.9	164.3	7.2	131.1	3.2	171.9	8.5
1992	136.6	4.4	131.7	0.9	133.7	6.2	125.1	1.2	133.1	3.1	174.9	6.5	139.2	6.2	183.0	6.5
1993	141.5	3.6	133.9	1.7	139.1	4.0	123.0	-1.7	136.0	2.2	185.0	5.8	148.8	6.9	200.1	9.3
1994	145.6	2.9	135.5	1.2	144.8	4.1	123.8	0.7	138.8	2.1	191.1	3.3	158.1	6.3	203.1	1.5
1995	-	-	-	-	-	-	-	-	-	-	-	-	-	-	-	-

Source: U.S. Department of Labor, Bureau of Labor Statistics, Division of Consumer Prices and Price Indexes. - indicates no data collected for period.

Seattle-Everett, WA
Consumer Price Index - All Urban Consumers
Base 1982-1984 = 100
All Items

For 1914-1995. Columns headed % show percentile change in the index from the previous period for which an index is available.

Year	Jan Index	%	Feb Index	%	Mar Index	%	Apr Index	%	May Index	%	Jun Index	%	Jul Index	%	Aug Index	%	Sep Index	%	Oct Index	%	Nov Index	%	Dec Index	%
1914	-	-	-	-	-	-	-	-	-	-	-	-	-	-	-	-	-	-	-	-	-	-	9.2	-
1915	-	-	-	-	-	-	-	-	-	-	-	-	-	-	-	-	-	-	-	-	-	-	9.1	-1.1
1916	-	-	-	-	-	-	-	-	-	-	-	-	-	-	-	-	-	-	-	-	-	-	9.7	6.6
1917	-	-	-	-	-	-	-	-	-	-	-	-	-	-	-	-	-	-	-	-	-	-	11.8	21.6
1918	-	-	-	-	-	-	-	-	-	-	-	-	-	-	-	-	-	-	-	-	-	-	15.4	30.5
1919	-	-	-	-	-	-	-	-	-	-	16.0	3.9	-	-	-	-	-	-	-	-	-	-	18.2	13.8
1920	-	-	-	-	-	-	-	-	-	-	19.6	7.7	-	-	-	-	-	-	-	-	-	-	17.9	-8.7
1921	-	-	-	-	-	-	-	-	16.8	-6.1	-	-	-	-	-	-	16.3	-3.0	-	-	-	-	16.0	-1.8
1922	-	-	-	-	15.7	-1.9	-	-	-	-	15.6	-0.6	-	-	-	-	15.5	-0.6	-	-	-	-	15.5	0.0
1923	-	-	-	-	15.1	-2.6	-	-	-	-	15.5	2.6	-	-	-	-	15.6	0.6	-	-	-	-	15.6	0.0
1924	-	-	-	-	15.5	-0.6	-	-	-	-	15.6	0.6	-	-	-	-	15.5	-0.6	-	-	-	-	15.6	0.6
1925	-	-	-	-	-	-	-	-	-	-	16.0	2.6	-	-	-	-	-	-	-	-	-	-	16.0	0.0
1926	-	-	-	-	-	-	-	-	-	-	15.8	-1.2	-	-	-	-	-	-	-	-	-	-	15.7	-0.6
1927	-	-	-	-	-	-	-	-	-	-	15.8	0.6	-	-	-	-	-	-	-	-	-	-	15.4	-2.5
1928	-	-	-	-	-	-	-	-	-	-	15.3	-0.6	-	-	-	-	-	-	-	-	-	-	15.4	0.7
1929	-	-	-	-	-	-	-	-	-	-	15.5	0.6	-	-	-	-	-	-	-	-	-	-	15.5	0.0
1930	-	-	-	-	-	-	-	-	-	-	15.5	0.0	-	-	-	-	-	-	-	-	-	-	14.4	-7.1
1931	-	-	-	-	-	-	-	-	-	-	13.9	-3.5	-	-	-	-	-	-	-	-	-	-	13.4	-3.6
1932	-	-	-	-	-	-	-	-	-	-	12.6	-6.0	-	-	-	-	-	-	-	-	-	-	12.1	-4.0
1933	-	-	-	-	-	-	-	-	-	-	12.0	-0.8	-	-	-	-	-	-	-	-	-	-	12.1	0.8
1934	-	-	-	-	-	-	-	-	-	-	12.2	0.8	-	-	-	-	-	-	-	-	12.4	1.6	-	-
1935	-	-	-	-	12.7	2.4	-	-	-	-	-	-	12.5	-1.6	-	-	-	-	12.5	0.0	-	-	-	-
1936	12.7	1.6	-	-	-	-	12.5	-1.6	-	-	-	-	12.7	1.6	-	-	12.9	1.6	-	-	-	-	12.9	0.0
1937	-	-	-	-	13.3	3.1	-	-	-	-	13.3	0.0	-	-	-	-	13.5	1.5	-	-	-	-	13.4	-0.7
1938	-	-	-	-	13.3	-0.7	-	-	-	-	13.2	-0.8	-	-	-	-	13.2	0.0	-	-	-	-	13.2	0.0
1939	-	-	-	-	13.1	-0.8	-	-	-	-	13.1	0.0	-	-	-	-	13.3	1.5	-	-	-	-	13.1	-1.5
1940	-	-	-	-	13.2	0.8	-	-	-	-	13.2	0.0	-	-	-	-	13.2	0.0	13.2	0.0	13.2	0.0	13.3	0.8
1941	13.3	0.0	13.3	0.0	13.4	0.8	13.5	0.7	13.8	2.2	13.9	0.7	14.0	0.7	14.1	0.7	14.5	2.8	14.7	1.4	14.7	0.0	14.9	1.4
1942	15.2	2.0	15.3	0.7	15.5	1.3	15.6	0.6	15.8	1.3	15.5	-1.9	15.6	0.6	15.8	1.3	16.0	1.3	16.1	0.6	16.2	0.6	16.4	1.2
1943	16.4	0.0	16.4	0.0	16.6	1.2	16.7	0.6	16.9	1.2	16.8	-0.6	16.5	-1.8	16.4	-0.6	16.7	1.8	16.8	0.6	16.8	0.0	16.8	0.0
1944	16.8	0.0	16.7	-0.6	16.8	0.6	16.8	0.0	16.9	0.6	16.9	0.0	17.0	0.6	17.0	0.0	17.0	0.0	17.1	0.6	17.1	0.0	17.2	0.6
1945	17.2	0.0	17.1	-0.6	17.2	0.6	17.2	0.0	17.3	0.6	17.3	0.0	17.4	0.6	17.4	0.0	17.4	0.0	17.3	-0.6	17.4	0.6	17.6	1.1
1946	17.5	-0.6	17.5	0.0	17.6	0.6	17.6	0.0	17.7	0.6	17.9	1.1	18.7	4.5	19.0	1.6	19.4	2.1	19.9	2.6	20.3	2.0	20.6	1.5
1947	20.4	-1.0	20.3	-0.5	20.7	2.0	20.8	0.5	20.8	0.0	20.7	-0.5	-	-	21.2	2.4	-	-	-	-	21.8	2.8	-	-
1948	-	-	22.4	2.8	-	-	-	-	22.9	2.2	-	-	-	-	23.2	1.3	-	-	-	-	22.9	-1.3	-	-
1949	-	-	23.0	0.4	-	-	-	-	22.8	-0.9	-	-	-	-	22.5	-1.3	-	-	-	-	22.7	0.9	-	-
1950	-	-	22.6	-0.4	-	-	-	-	22.6	0.0	-	-	-	-	23.0	1.8	-	-	-	-	23.8	3.5	-	-
1951	-	-	24.5	2.9	-	-	-	-	24.9	1.6	-	-	-	-	24.8	-0.4	-	-	-	-	25.3	2.0	-	-
1952	-	-	25.4	0.4	-	-	-	-	25.5	0.4	-	-	-	-	25.5	0.0	-	-	-	-	25.7	0.8	-	-
1953	-	-	25.5	-0.8	-	-	-	-	25.8	1.2	-	-	-	-	25.9	0.4	-	-	-	-	25.8	-0.4	-	-
1954	-	-	25.8	0.0	-	-	-	-	25.8	0.0	-	-	-	-	25.8	0.0	-	-	-	-	25.7	-0.4	-	-
1955	-	-	25.8	0.4	-	-	-	-	25.9	0.4	-	-	-	-	25.9	0.0	-	-	-	-	26.1	0.8	-	-
1956	-	-	25.8	-1.1	-	-	-	-	26.0	0.8	-	-	-	-	26.4	1.5	-	-	-	-	26.7	1.1	-	-
1957	-	-	27.1	1.5	-	-	-	-	27.3	0.7	-	-	-	-	27.5	0.7	-	-	-	-	27.5	0.0	-	-
1958	-	-	27.8	1.1	-	-	-	-	28.0	0.7	-	-	-	-	28.0	0.0	-	-	-	-	28.0	0.0	-	-

[Continued]

Seattle-Everett, WA
Consumer Price Index - All Urban Consumers
Base 1982-1984 = 100
All Items
[Continued]

For 1914-1995. Columns headed % show percentile change in the index from the previous period for which an index is available.

Year	Jan Index	%	Feb Index	%	Mar Index	%	Apr Index	%	May Index	%	Jun Index	%	Jul Index	%	Aug Index	%	Sep Index	%	Oct Index	%	Nov Index	%	Dec Index	%
1959	-	-	28.2	0.7	-	-	-	-	28.4	0.7	-	-	-	-	28.6	0.7	-	-	-	-	28.7	0.3	-	-
1960	-	-	28.6	-0.3	-	-	-	-	28.8	0.7	-	-	-	-	28.8	0.0	-	-	-	-	29.0	0.7	-	-
1961	-	-	29.1	0.3	-	-	-	-	29.3	0.7	-	-	-	-	29.3	0.0	-	-	-	-	29.5	0.7	-	-
1962	-	-	29.6	0.3	-	-	-	-	29.7	0.3	-	-	-	-	29.8	0.3	-	-	-	-	29.9	0.3	-	-
1963	-	-	29.9	0.0	-	-	-	-	30.0	0.3	-	-	-	-	30.5	1.7	-	-	-	-	30.5	0.0	-	-
1964	-	-	30.5	0.0	-	-	-	-	30.5	0.0	-	-	-	-	30.8	1.0	-	-	-	-	30.7	-0.3	-	-
1965	-	-	30.6	-0.3	-	-	-	-	30.9	1.0	-	-	-	-	31.1	0.6	-	-	-	-	31.2	0.3	-	-
1966	-	-	31.4	0.6	-	-	-	-	31.8	1.3	-	-	-	-	32.0	0.6	-	-	-	-	32.3	0.9	-	-
1967	-	-	32.3	0.0	-	-	-	-	32.6	0.9	-	-	-	-	33.0	1.2	-	-	-	-	33.3	0.9	-	-
1968	-	-	33.6	0.9	-	-	-	-	33.8	0.6	-	-	-	-	34.4	1.8	-	-	-	-	34.8	1.2	-	-
1969	-	-	35.1	0.9	-	-	-	-	35.6	1.4	-	-	-	-	36.2	1.7	-	-	-	-	36.3	0.3	-	-
1970	-	-	36.9	1.7	-	-	-	-	37.4	1.4	-	-	-	-	37.6	0.5	-	-	-	-	37.7	0.3	-	-
1971	-	-	37.6	-0.3	-	-	-	-	37.9	0.8	-	-	-	-	38.6	1.8	-	-	-	-	38.6	0.0	-	-
1972	-	-	39.0	1.0	-	-	-	-	39.0	0.0	-	-	-	-	39.3	0.8	-	-	-	-	39.8	1.3	-	-
1973	-	-	40.4	1.5	-	-	-	-	41.4	2.5	-	-	-	-	42.3	2.2	-	-	-	-	43.1	1.9	-	-
1974	-	-	44.5	3.2	-	-	-	-	45.7	2.7	-	-	-	-	46.9	2.6	-	-	-	-	48.5	3.4	-	-
1975	-	-	49.8	2.7	-	-	-	-	50.7	1.8	-	-	-	-	51.6	1.8	-	-	-	-	52.4	1.6	-	-
1976	-	-	53.0	1.1	-	-	-	-	53.3	0.6	-	-	-	-	54.4	2.1	-	-	-	-	55.1	1.3	-	-
1977	-	-	56.2	2.0	-	-	-	-	57.8	2.8	-	-	-	-	59.1	2.2	-	-	-	-	59.9	1.4	-	-
1978	60.4	0.8	-	-	61.4	1.7	-	-	63.5	3.4	-	-	63.9	0.6	-	-	65.9	3.1	-	-	66.8	1.4	-	-
1979	66.3	-0.7	-	-	67.9	2.4	-	-	69.7	2.7	-	-	71.3	2.3	-	-	73.0	2.4	-	-	74.7	2.3	-	-
1980	77.4	3.6	-	-	80.0	3.4	-	-	81.9	2.4	-	-	83.7	2.2	-	-	84.7	1.2	-	-	86.1	1.7	-	-
1981	86.9	0.9	-	-	88.9	2.3	-	-	90.1	1.3	-	-	92.6	2.8	-	-	94.7	2.3	-	-	94.9	0.2	-	-
1982	97.1	2.3	-	-	96.2	-0.9	-	-	98.8	2.7	-	-	97.3	-1.5	-	-	99.1	1.8	-	-	97.6	-1.5	-	-
1983	97.6	0.0	-	-	97.7	0.1	-	-	98.7	1.0	-	-	99.7	1.0	-	-	100.5	0.8	-	-	100.7	0.2	-	-
1984	101.3	0.6	-	-	101.8	0.5	-	-	102.7	0.9	-	-	103.1	0.4	-	-	103.8	0.7	-	-	104.4	0.6	-	-
1985	104.8	0.4	-	-	105.4	0.6	-	-	105.3	-0.1	-	-	105.6	0.3	-	-	105.6	0.0	-	-	106.3	0.7	-	-
1986	107.3	0.9	-	-	106.6	-0.7	-	-	106.1	-0.5	-	-	106.2	0.1	-	-	107.0	0.8	-	-	106.9	-0.1	106.8	-0.1
1987	-	-	-	-	-	-	-	-	-	-	109.9	2.9	-	-	-	-	-	-	-	-	-	-	111.9	1.8
1988	-	-	-	-	-	-	-	-	-	-	113.6	1.5	-	-	-	-	-	-	-	-	-	-	115.9	2.0
1989	-	-	-	-	-	-	-	-	-	-	119.3	2.9	-	-	-	-	-	-	-	-	-	-	121.6	1.9
1990	-	-	-	-	-	-	-	-	-	-	124.9	2.7	-	-	-	-	-	-	-	-	-	-	129.8	3.9
1991	-	-	-	-	-	-	-	-	-	-	132.8	2.3	-	-	-	-	-	-	-	-	-	-	135.1	1.7
1992	-	-	-	-	-	-	-	-	-	-	138.8	2.7	-	-	-	-	-	-	-	-	-	-	140.9	1.5
1993	-	-	-	-	-	-	-	-	-	-	143.6	1.9	-	-	-	-	-	-	-	-	-	-	145.8	1.5
1994	-	-	-	-	-	-	-	-	-	-	147.7	1.3	-	-	-	-	-	-	-	-	-	-	150.1	1.6
1995	-	-	-	-	-	-	-	-	-	-	152.5	1.6	-	-	-	-	-	-	-	-	-	-	-	-

Source: U.S. Department of Labor, Bureau of Labor Statistics, Division of Consumer Prices and Price Indexes. - indicates no data collected for period.

Seattle-Everett, WA
Consumer Price Index - Urban Wage Earners
Base 1982-1984 = 100
All Items

For 1914-1995. Columns headed % show percentile change in the index from the previous period for which an index is available.

Year	Jan Index	Jan %	Feb Index	Feb %	Mar Index	Mar %	Apr Index	Apr %	May Index	May %	Jun Index	Jun %	Jul Index	Jul %	Aug Index	Aug %	Sep Index	Sep %	Oct Index	Oct %	Nov Index	Nov %	Dec Index	Dec %
1914	-	-	-	-	-	-	-	-	-	-	-	-	-	-	-	-	-	-	-	-	-	-	9.4	-
1915	-	-	-	-	-	-	-	-	-	-	-	-	-	-	-	-	-	-	-	-	-	-	9.3	-1.1
1916	-	-	-	-	-	-	-	-	-	-	-	-	-	-	-	-	-	-	-	-	-	-	10.0	7.5
1917	-	-	-	-	-	-	-	-	-	-	-	-	-	-	-	-	-	-	-	-	-	-	12.1	21.0
1918	-	-	-	-	-	-	-	-	-	-	-	-	-	-	-	-	-	-	-	-	-	-	15.8	30.6
1919	-	-	-	-	-	-	-	-	-	-	16.5	4.4	-	-	-	-	-	-	-	-	-	-	18.7	13.3
1920	-	-	-	-	-	-	-	-	-	-	20.2	8.0	-	-	-	-	-	-	-	-	-	-	18.4	-8.9
1921	-	-	-	-	-	-	-	-	17.2	-6.5	-	-	-	-	-	-	16.7	-2.9	-	-	-	-	16.4	-1.8
1922	-	-	-	-	16.1	-1.8	-	-	-	-	16.0	-0.6	-	-	-	-	15.9	-0.6	-	-	-	-	15.9	0.0
1923	-	-	-	-	15.5	-2.5	-	-	-	-	15.9	2.6	-	-	-	-	16.1	1.3	-	-	-	-	16.0	-0.6
1924	-	-	-	-	15.9	-0.6	-	-	-	-	16.0	0.6	-	-	-	-	15.9	-0.6	-	-	-	-	16.0	0.6
1925	-	-	-	-	-	-	-	-	-	-	16.4	2.5	-	-	-	-	-	-	-	-	-	-	16.5	0.6
1926	-	-	-	-	-	-	-	-	-	-	16.3	-1.2	-	-	-	-	-	-	-	-	-	-	16.1	-1.2
1927	-	-	-	-	-	-	-	-	-	-	16.3	1.2	-	-	-	-	-	-	-	-	-	-	15.8	-3.1
1928	-	-	-	-	-	-	-	-	-	-	15.7	-0.6	-	-	-	-	-	-	-	-	-	-	15.8	0.6
1929	-	-	-	-	-	-	-	-	-	-	15.9	0.6	-	-	-	-	-	-	-	-	-	-	16.0	0.6
1930	-	-	-	-	-	-	-	-	-	-	15.9	-0.6	-	-	-	-	-	-	-	-	-	-	14.8	-6.9
1931	-	-	-	-	-	-	-	-	14.3	-3.4	-	-	-	-	-	-	-	-	-	-	-	-	13.8	-3.5
1932	-	-	-	-	-	-	-	-	13.0	-5.8	-	-	-	-	-	-	-	-	-	-	-	-	12.4	-4.6
1933	-	-	-	-	-	-	-	-	12.3	-0.8	-	-	-	-	-	-	-	-	-	-	-	-	12.4	0.8
1934	-	-	-	-	-	-	-	-	12.5	0.8	-	-	-	-	-	-	-	-	-	-	12.8	2.4	-	-
1935	-	-	-	-	13.0	1.6	-	-	-	-	-	-	12.8	-1.5	-	-	-	-	12.8	0.0	-	-	-	-
1936	13.0	1.6	-	-	-	-	12.9	-0.8	-	-	-	-	13.0	0.8	-	-	13.2	1.5	-	-	-	-	13.3	0.8
1937	-	-	-	-	13.6	2.3	-	-	-	-	13.7	0.7	-	-	-	-	13.9	1.5	-	-	-	-	13.8	-0.7
1938	-	-	-	-	13.7	-0.7	-	-	-	-	13.5	-1.5	-	-	-	-	13.5	0.0	-	-	-	-	13.5	0.0
1939	-	-	-	-	13.5	0.0	-	-	-	-	13.5	0.0	-	-	-	-	13.7	1.5	-	-	-	-	13.5	-1.5
1940	-	-	-	-	13.6	0.7	-	-	-	-	13.6	0.0	-	-	-	-	13.6	0.0	13.6	0.0	13.6	0.0	13.6	0.0
1941	13.7	0.7	13.7	0.0	13.8	0.7	13.9	0.7	14.2	2.2	14.3	0.7	14.4	0.7	14.5	0.7	14.9	2.8	15.1	1.3	15.1	0.0	15.3	1.3
1942	15.6	2.0	15.7	0.6	16.0	1.9	16.1	0.6	16.2	0.6	15.9	-1.9	16.0	0.6	16.3	1.9	16.5	1.2	16.6	0.6	16.7	0.6	16.8	0.6
1943	16.9	0.6	16.9	0.0	17.0	0.6	17.2	1.2	17.4	1.2	17.2	-1.1	17.0	-1.2	16.9	-0.6	17.2	1.8	17.2	0.0	17.3	0.6	17.3	0.0
1944	17.3	0.0	17.2	-0.6	17.2	0.0	17.2	0.0	17.4	1.2	17.3	-0.6	17.4	0.6	17.4	0.0	17.5	0.6	17.6	0.6	17.5	-0.6	17.6	0.6
1945	17.6	0.0	17.6	0.0	17.7	0.6	17.7	0.0	17.8	0.6	17.8	0.0	17.8	0.0	17.9	0.6	17.8	-0.6	17.8	0.0	17.9	0.6	18.1	1.1
1946	18.0	-0.6	18.0	0.0	18.0	0.0	18.1	0.6	18.2	0.6	18.4	1.1	19.3	4.9	19.5	1.0	19.9	2.1	20.4	2.5	20.9	2.5	21.1	1.0
1947	20.9	-0.9	20.9	0.0	21.3	1.9	21.4	0.5	21.3	-0.5	21.3	0.0	21.3	0.0	-	-	21.8	2.3	-	-	22.4	2.8	-	-
1948	-	-	23.0	2.7	-	-	-	-	23.5	2.2	-	-	-	-	23.8	1.3	-	-	-	-	23.6	-0.8	-	-
1949	-	-	23.6	0.0	-	-	-	-	23.4	-0.8	-	-	-	-	23.2	-0.9	-	-	-	-	23.3	0.4	-	-
1950	-	-	23.3	0.0	-	-	-	-	23.3	0.0	-	-	-	-	23.7	1.7	-	-	-	-	24.4	3.0	-	-
1951	-	-	25.2	3.3	-	-	-	-	25.6	1.6	-	-	-	-	25.5	-0.4	-	-	-	-	26.0	2.0	-	-
1952	-	-	26.1	0.4	-	-	-	-	26.2	0.4	-	-	-	-	26.2	0.0	-	-	-	-	26.4	0.8	-	-
1953	-	-	26.2	-0.8	-	-	-	-	26.5	1.1	-	-	-	-	26.7	0.8	-	-	-	-	26.6	-0.4	-	-
1954	-	-	26.5	-0.4	-	-	-	-	26.5	0.0	-	-	-	-	26.5	0.0	-	-	-	-	26.4	-0.4	-	-
1955	-	-	26.5	0.4	-	-	-	-	26.7	0.8	-	-	-	-	26.6	-0.4	-	-	-	-	26.8	0.8	-	-
1956	-	-	26.5	-1.1	-	-	-	-	26.7	0.8	-	-	-	-	27.1	1.5	-	-	-	-	27.4	1.1	-	-
1957	-	-	27.9	1.8	-	-	-	-	28.0	0.4	-	-	-	-	28.2	0.7	-	-	-	-	28.3	0.4	-	-
1958	-	-	28.5	0.7	-	-	-	-	28.8	1.1	-	-	-	-	28.8	0.0	-	-	-	-	28.8	0.0	-	-

[Continued]

Seattle-Everett, WA

Consumer Price Index - Urban Wage Earners
Base 1982-1984 = 100
All Items

[Continued]

For 1914-1995. Columns headed % show percentile change in the index from the previous period for which an index is available.

Year	Jan Index	%	Feb Index	%	Mar Index	%	Apr Index	%	May Index	%	Jun Index	%	Jul Index	%	Aug Index	%	Sep Index	%	Oct Index	%	Nov Index	%	Dec Index	%
1959	-	-	29.0	0.7	-	-	-	-	29.2	0.7	-	-	-	-	29.4	0.7	-	-	-	-	29.5	0.3	-	-
1960	-	-	29.4	-0.3	-	-	-	-	29.6	0.7	-	-	-	-	29.6	0.0	-	-	-	-	29.8	0.7	-	-
1961	-	-	29.9	0.3	-	-	-	-	30.1	0.7	-	-	-	-	30.1	0.0	-	-	-	-	30.3	0.7	-	-
1962	-	-	30.4	0.3	-	-	-	-	30.5	0.3	-	-	-	-	30.6	0.3	-	-	-	-	30.7	0.3	-	-
1963	-	-	30.7	0.0	-	-	-	-	30.8	0.3	-	-	-	-	31.3	1.6	-	-	-	-	31.4	0.3	-	-
1964	-	-	31.4	0.0	-	-	-	-	31.3	-0.3	-	-	-	-	31.7	1.3	-	-	-	-	31.6	-0.3	-	-
1965	-	-	31.5	-0.3	-	-	-	-	31.8	1.0	-	-	-	-	32.0	0.6	-	-	-	-	32.1	0.3	-	-
1966	-	-	32.3	0.6	-	-	-	-	32.6	0.9	-	-	-	-	32.8	0.6	-	-	-	-	33.2	1.2	-	-
1967	-	-	33.2	0.0	-	-	-	-	33.5	0.9	-	-	-	-	33.9	1.2	-	-	-	-	34.2	0.9	-	-
1968	-	-	34.5	0.9	-	-	-	-	34.8	0.9	-	-	-	-	35.4	1.7	-	-	-	-	35.7	0.8	-	-
1969	-	-	36.1	1.1	-	-	-	-	36.6	1.4	-	-	-	-	37.2	1.6	-	-	-	-	37.3	0.3	-	-
1970	-	-	37.9	1.6	-	-	-	-	38.4	1.3	-	-	-	-	38.6	0.5	-	-	-	-	38.7	0.3	-	-
1971	-	-	38.6	-0.3	-	-	-	-	38.9	0.8	-	-	-	-	39.6	1.8	-	-	-	-	39.6	0.0	-	-
1972	-	-	40.1	1.3	-	-	-	-	40.1	0.0	-	-	-	-	40.4	0.7	-	-	-	-	40.9	1.2	-	-
1973	-	-	41.5	1.5	-	-	-	-	42.6	2.7	-	-	-	-	43.4	1.9	-	-	-	-	44.3	2.1	-	-
1974	-	-	45.8	3.4	-	-	-	-	47.0	2.6	-	-	-	-	48.2	2.6	-	-	-	-	49.9	3.5	-	-
1975	-	-	51.2	2.6	-	-	-	-	52.1	1.8	-	-	-	-	53.0	1.7	-	-	-	-	53.8	1.5	-	-
1976	-	-	54.5	1.3	-	-	-	-	54.8	0.6	-	-	-	-	55.9	2.0	-	-	-	-	56.6	1.3	-	-
1977	-	-	57.8	2.1	-	-	-	-	59.4	2.8	-	-	-	-	60.8	2.4	-	-	-	-	61.5	1.2	-	-
1978	62.0	0.8	-	-	63.0	1.6	-	-	64.9	3.0	-	-	65.4	0.8	-	-	67.3	2.9	-	-	68.1	1.2	-	-
1979	67.6	-0.7	-	-	69.4	2.7	-	-	71.1	2.4	-	-	72.8	2.4	-	-	74.5	2.3	-	-	76.0	2.0	-	-
1980	78.8	3.7	-	-	81.4	3.3	-	-	83.2	2.2	-	-	84.8	1.9	-	-	85.8	1.2	-	-	87.5	2.0	-	-
1981	88.4	1.0	-	-	90.3	2.1	-	-	91.5	1.3	-	-	93.7	2.4	-	-	95.9	2.3	-	-	96.3	0.4	-	-
1982	98.4	2.2	-	-	97.6	-0.8	-	-	100.2	2.7	-	-	98.8	-1.4	-	-	100.6	1.8	-	-	99.2	-1.4	-	-
1983	98.2	-1.0	-	-	98.0	-0.2	-	-	97.9	-0.1	-	-	98.5	0.6	-	-	99.7	1.2	-	-	100.1	0.4	-	-
1984	100.2	0.1	-	-	101.1	0.9	-	-	102.1	1.0	-	-	102.2	0.1	-	-	102.9	0.7	-	-	103.0	0.1	-	-
1985	103.4	0.4	-	-	104.2	0.8	-	-	104.0	-0.2	-	-	104.2	0.2	-	-	104.1	-0.1	-	-	104.8	0.7	-	-
1986	105.7	0.9	-	-	105.0	-0.7	-	-	104.3	-0.7	-	-	104.6	0.3	-	-	105.3	0.7	-	-	105.1	-0.2	105.1	0.0
1987	-	-	-	-	-	-	-	-	-	-	107.5	2.3	-	-	-	-	-	-	-	-	-	-	109.5	1.9
1988	-	-	-	-	-	-	-	-	-	-	110.9	1.3	-	-	-	-	-	-	-	-	-	-	113.0	1.9
1989	-	-	-	-	-	-	-	-	-	-	116.4	3.0	-	-	-	-	-	-	-	-	-	-	118.7	2.0
1990	-	-	-	-	-	-	-	-	-	-	121.8	2.6	-	-	-	-	-	-	-	-	-	-	126.6	3.9
1991	-	-	-	-	-	-	-	-	-	-	129.6	2.4	-	-	-	-	-	-	-	-	-	-	132.1	1.9
1992	-	-	-	-	-	-	-	-	-	-	135.5	2.6	-	-	-	-	-	-	-	-	-	-	137.7	1.6
1993	-	-	-	-	-	-	-	-	-	-	140.3	1.9	-	-	-	-	-	-	-	-	-	-	142.6	1.6
1994	-	-	-	-	-	-	-	-	-	-	144.3	1.2	-	-	-	-	-	-	-	-	-	-	146.8	1.7
1995	-	-	-	-	-	-	-	-	-	-	149.1	1.6	-	-	-	-	-	-	-	-	-	-	-	-

Source: U.S. Department of Labor, Bureau of Labor Statistics, Division of Consumer Prices and Price Indexes. - indicates no data collected for period.

Seattle-Everett, WA
Consumer Price Index - All Urban Consumers
Base 1982-1984 = 100
Food and Beverages

For 1975-1995. Columns headed % show percentile change in the index from the previous period for which an index is available.

Year	Jan Index	%	Feb Index	%	Mar Index	%	Apr Index	%	May Index	%	Jun Index	%	Jul Index	%	Aug Index	%	Sep Index	%	Oct Index	%	Nov Index	%	Dec Index	%
1975	-	-	-	-	-	-	-	-	-	-	-	-	-	-	-	-	-	-	-	-	60.8	-	-	-
1976	-	-	60.6	-0.3	-	-	-	-	60.8	0.3	-	-	-	-	61.8	1.6	-	-	-	-	61.8	0.0	-	-
1977	-	-	63.5	2.8	-	-	-	-	65.2	2.7	-	-	-	-	66.8	2.5	-	-	-	-	66.8	0.0	-	-
1978	67.1	0.4	-	-	69.2	3.1	-	-	72.5	4.8	-	-	70.9	-2.2	-	-	71.9	1.4	-	-	72.5	0.8	-	-
1979	74.1	2.2	-	-	77.5	4.6	-	-	78.8	1.7	-	-	78.8	0.0	-	-	78.5	-0.4	-	-	80.1	2.0	-	-
1980	81.4	1.6	-	-	82.5	1.4	-	-	83.6	1.3	-	-	84.4	1.0	-	-	86.4	2.4	-	-	87.2	0.9	-	-
1981	88.7	1.7	-	-	90.4	1.9	-	-	90.7	0.3	-	-	92.0	1.4	-	-	93.1	1.2	-	-	93.1	0.0	-	-
1982	95.1	2.1	-	-	94.6	-0.5	-	-	99.6	5.3	-	-	100.0	0.4	-	-	99.8	-0.2	-	-	99.5	-0.3	-	-
1983	100.0	0.5	-	-	101.5	1.5	-	-	102.4	0.9	-	-	98.9	-3.4	-	-	98.7	-0.2	-	-	99.0	0.3	-	-
1984	100.8	1.8	-	-	101.3	0.5	-	-	101.4	0.1	-	-	101.7	0.3	-	-	102.1	0.4	-	-	102.1	0.0	-	-
1985	101.7	-0.4	-	-	103.3	1.6	-	-	103.3	0.0	-	-	103.6	0.3	-	-	103.5	-0.1	-	-	103.3	-0.2	-	-
1986	104.9	1.5	-	-	105.9	1.0	-	-	107.1	1.1	-	-	106.7	-0.4	-	-	107.5	0.7	-	-	107.9	0.4	108.1	0.2
1987	-	-	-	-	-	-	-	-	-	-	111.7	3.3	-	-	-	-	-	-	-	-	-	-	110.9	-0.7
1988	-	-	-	-	-	-	-	-	-	-	111.0	0.1	-	-	-	-	-	-	-	-	-	-	113.0	1.8
1989	-	-	-	-	-	-	-	-	-	-	118.0	4.4	-	-	-	-	-	-	-	-	-	-	119.5	1.3
1990	-	-	-	-	-	-	-	-	-	-	124.9	4.5	-	-	-	-	-	-	-	-	-	-	127.4	2.0
1991	-	-	-	-	-	-	-	-	-	-	131.4	3.1	-	-	-	-	-	-	-	-	-	-	129.9	-1.1
1992	-	-	-	-	-	-	-	-	-	-	132.1	1.7	-	-	-	-	-	-	-	-	-	-	131.3	-0.6
1993	-	-	-	-	-	-	-	-	-	-	133.8	1.9	-	-	-	-	-	-	-	-	-	-	134.3	0.4
1994	-	-	-	-	-	-	-	-	-	-	135.5	0.9	-	-	-	-	-	-	-	-	-	-	136.2	0.5
1995	-	-	-	-	-	-	-	-	-	-	137.3	0.8	-	-	-	-	-	-	-	-	-	-	-	-

Source: U.S. Department of Labor, Bureau of Labor Statistics, Division of Consumer Prices and Price Indexes. - indicates no data collected for period.

Seattle-Everett, WA
Consumer Price Index - Urban Wage Earners
Base 1982-1984 = 100
Food and Beverages

For 1975-1995. Columns headed % show percentile change in the index from the previous period for which an index is available.

Year	Jan Index	%	Feb Index	%	Mar Index	%	Apr Index	%	May Index	%	Jun Index	%	Jul Index	%	Aug Index	%	Sep Index	%	Oct Index	%	Nov Index	%	Dec Index	%
1975	-	-	-	-	-	-	-	-	-	-	-	-	-	-	-	-	-	-	-	-	61.1	-	-	-
1976	-	-	60.9	-0.3	-	-	-	-	61.1	0.3	-	-	-	-	62.1	1.6	-	-	-	-	62.1	0.0	-	-
1977	-	-	63.8	2.7	-	-	-	-	65.5	2.7	-	-	-	-	67.1	2.4	-	-	-	-	67.1	0.0	-	-
1978	67.7	0.9	-	-	69.8	3.1	-	-	72.1	3.3	-	-	71.0	-1.5	-	-	72.3	1.8	-	-	72.7	0.6	-	-
1979	74.4	2.3	-	-	77.8	4.6	-	-	78.8	1.3	-	-	78.7	-0.1	-	-	79.0	0.4	-	-	79.3	0.4	-	-
1980	81.4	2.6	-	-	82.6	1.5	-	-	83.7	1.3	-	-	84.7	1.2	-	-	86.6	2.2	-	-	87.6	1.2	-	-
1981	89.6	2.3	-	-	91.2	1.8	-	-	91.5	0.3	-	-	92.5	1.1	-	-	93.5	1.1	-	-	93.1	-0.4	-	-
1982	95.1	2.1	-	-	94.7	-0.4	-	-	99.5	5.1	-	-	99.9	0.4	-	-	99.7	-0.2	-	-	99.5	-0.2	-	-
1983	100.0	0.5	-	-	101.6	1.6	-	-	102.5	0.9	-	-	98.9	-3.5	-	-	98.6	-0.3	-	-	99.0	0.4	-	-
1984	100.7	1.7	-	-	101.3	0.6	-	-	101.4	0.1	-	-	101.6	0.2	-	-	102.2	0.6	-	-	102.2	0.0	-	-
1985	101.7	-0.5	-	-	103.4	1.7	-	-	103.3	-0.1	-	-	103.6	0.3	-	-	103.7	0.1	-	-	103.3	-0.4	-	-
1986	104.9	1.5	-	-	105.8	0.9	-	-	106.9	1.0	-	-	106.6	-0.3	-	-	107.2	0.6	-	-	107.6	0.4	107.9	0.3
1987	-	-	-	-	-	-	-	-	-	-	111.4	3.2	-	-	-	-	-	-	-	-	-	-	110.8	-0.5
1988	-	-	-	-	-	-	-	-	-	-	110.8	0.0	-	-	-	-	-	-	-	-	-	-	112.9	1.9
1989	-	-	-	-	-	-	-	-	-	-	117.8	4.3	-	-	-	-	-	-	-	-	-	-	119.4	1.4
1990	-	-	-	-	-	-	-	-	-	-	124.6	4.4	-	-	-	-	-	-	-	-	-	-	127.2	2.1
1991	-	-	-	-	-	-	-	-	-	-	131.1	3.1	-	-	-	-	-	-	-	-	-	-	130.0	-0.8
1992	-	-	-	-	-	-	-	-	-	-	132.1	1.6	-	-	-	-	-	-	-	-	-	-	131.4	-0.5
1993	-	-	-	-	-	-	-	-	-	-	133.8	1.8	-	-	-	-	-	-	-	-	-	-	134.1	0.2
1994	-	-	-	-	-	-	-	-	-	-	135.1	0.7	-	-	-	-	-	-	-	-	-	-	135.8	0.5
1995	-	-	-	-	-	-	-	-	-	-	136.6	0.6	-	-	-	-	-	-	-	-	-	-	-	-

Source: U.S. Department of Labor, Bureau of Labor Statistics, Division of Consumer Prices and Price Indexes. - indicates no data collected for period.

Economic Indicators Handbook, 3rd Edition

Seattle-Everett, WA
Consumer Price Index - All Urban Consumers
Base 1982-1984 = 100
Housing

For 1975-1995. Columns headed % show percentile change in the index from the previous period for which an index is available.

Year	Jan Index	%	Feb Index	%	Mar Index	%	Apr Index	%	May Index	%	Jun Index	%	Jul Index	%	Aug Index	%	Sep Index	%	Oct Index	%	Nov Index	%	Dec Index	%
1975	-	-	-	-	-	-	-	-	-	-	-	-	-	-	-	-	-	-	-	-	48.9	-	-	-
1976	-	-	49.8	1.8	-	-	-	-	49.2	-1.2	-	-	-	-	50.7	3.0	-	-	-	-	51.5	1.6	-	-
1977	-	-	52.2	1.4	-	-	-	-	54.2	3.8	-	-	-	-	55.8	3.0	-	-	-	-	57.0	2.2	-	-
1978	57.5	0.9	-	-	58.7	2.1	-	-	60.9	3.7	-	-	61.6	1.1	-	-	64.5	4.7	-	-	65.5	1.6	-	-
1979	63.6	-2.9	-	-	64.8	1.9	-	-	66.3	2.3	-	-	68.4	3.2	-	-	70.3	2.8	-	-	72.1	2.6	-	-
1980	76.3	5.8	-	-	79.2	3.8	-	-	82.0	3.5	-	-	84.5	3.0	-	-	84.8	0.4	-	-	86.7	2.2	-	-
1981	87.2	0.6	-	-	88.8	1.8	-	-	89.8	1.1	-	-	93.1	3.7	-	-	95.9	3.0	-	-	95.7	-0.2	-	-
1982	99.0	3.4	-	-	97.7	-1.3	-	-	101.1	3.5	-	-	96.6	-4.5	-	-	99.8	3.3	-	-	97.1	-2.7	-	-
1983	97.2	0.1	-	-	97.0	-0.2	-	-	97.7	0.7	-	-	99.2	1.5	-	-	100.0	0.8	-	-	100.2	0.2	-	-
1984	100.9	0.7	-	-	101.9	1.0	-	-	102.1	0.2	-	-	102.6	0.5	-	-	103.8	1.2	-	-	104.6	0.8	-	-
1985	105.2	0.6	-	-	105.4	0.2	-	-	105.3	-0.1	-	-	105.0	-0.3	-	-	104.8	-0.2	-	-	106.5	1.6	-	-
1986	107.7	1.1	-	-	107.0	-0.6	-	-	106.2	-0.7	-	-	105.9	-0.3	-	-	107.3	1.3	-	-	107.1	-0.2	106.6	-0.5
1987	-	-	-	-	-	-	-	-	-	-	107.1	0.5	-	-	-	-	-	-	-	-	-	-	109.2	2.0
1988	-	-	-	-	-	-	-	-	-	-	111.0	1.6	-	-	-	-	-	-	-	-	-	-	112.7	1.5
1989	-	-	-	-	-	-	-	-	-	-	115.1	2.1	-	-	-	-	-	-	-	-	-	-	118.0	2.5
1990	-	-	-	-	-	-	-	-	-	-	120.7	2.3	-	-	-	-	-	-	-	-	-	-	124.6	3.2
1991	-	-	-	-	-	-	-	-	-	-	128.0	2.7	-	-	-	-	-	-	-	-	-	-	132.7	3.7
1992	-	-	-	-	-	-	-	-	-	-	137.4	3.5	-	-	-	-	-	-	-	-	-	-	139.0	1.2
1993	-	-	-	-	-	-	-	-	-	-	141.6	1.9	-	-	-	-	-	-	-	-	-	-	145.8	3.0
1994	-	-	-	-	-	-	-	-	-	-	148.3	1.7	-	-	-	-	-	-	-	-	-	-	150.8	1.7
1995	-	-	-	-	-	-	-	-	-	-	153.8	2.0	-	-	-	-	-	-	-	-	-	-	-	-

Source: U.S. Department of Labor, Bureau of Labor Statistics, Division of Consumer Prices and Price Indexes. - indicates no data collected for period.

Seattle-Everett, WA
Consumer Price Index - Urban Wage Earners
Base 1982-1984 = 100
Housing

For 1975-1995. Columns headed % show percentile change in the index from the previous period for which an index is available.

Year	Jan Index	%	Feb Index	%	Mar Index	%	Apr Index	%	May Index	%	Jun Index	%	Jul Index	%	Aug Index	%	Sep Index	%	Oct Index	%	Nov Index	%	Dec Index	%
1975	-	-	-	-	-	-	-	-	-	-	-		-		-		-		-		51.0	-	-	-
1976	-	-	51.9	1.8	-	-	-	-	51.4	-1.0	-		-		52.9	2.9	-		-		53.7	1.5	-	-
1977	-	-	54.5	1.5	-	-	-	-	56.6	3.9	-		-		58.3	3.0	-		-		59.5	2.1	-	-
1978	60.1	1.0	-	-	61.3	2.0	-	-	63.5	3.6	-		64.2	1.1	-		67.3	4.8	-		68.2	1.3	-	-
1979	66.1	-3.1	-	-	67.6	2.3	-	-	69.1	2.2	-		71.1	2.9	-		73.1	2.8	-		75.1	2.7	-	-
1980	79.5	5.9	-	-	82.3	3.5	-	-	85.4	3.8	-		87.8	2.8	-		88.0	0.2	-		90.0	2.3	-	-
1981	90.4	0.4	-	-	92.4	2.2	-	-	93.2	0.9	-		96.0	3.0	-		99.1	3.2	-		99.0	-0.1	-	-
1982	102.3	3.3	-	-	100.9	-1.4	-	-	104.5	3.6	-		99.7	-4.6	-		103.1	3.4	-		100.5	-2.5	-	-
1983	98.7	-1.8	-	-	97.9	-0.8	-	-	96.1	-1.8	-		96.4	0.3	-		97.9	1.6	-		98.7	0.8	-	-
1984	98.7	0.0	-	-	100.3	1.6	-	-	100.7	0.4	-		100.6	-0.1	-		101.8	1.2	-		101.4	-0.4	-	-
1985	102.1	0.7	-	-	102.4	0.3	-	-	102.0	-0.4	-		101.5	-0.5	-		101.4	-0.1	-		103.0	1.6	-	-
1986	104.1	1.1	-	-	103.5	-0.6	-	-	102.6	-0.9	-		102.5	-0.1	-		103.9	1.4	-		103.6	-0.3	103.2	-0.4
1987	-	-	-	-	-	-	-	-	-	-	103.3	0.1	-		-		-		-		-		105.3	1.9
1988	-	-	-	-	-	-	-	-	-	-	107.0	1.6	-		-		-		-		-		108.6	1.5
1989	-	-	-	-	-	-	-	-	-	-	110.9	2.1	-		-		-		-		-		113.7	2.5
1990	-	-	-	-	-	-	-	-	-	-	116.2	2.2	-		-		-		-		-		120.0	3.3
1991	-	-	-	-	-	-	-	-	-	-	123.5	2.9	-		-		-		-		-		128.2	3.8
1992	-	-	-	-	-	-	-	-	-	-	132.9	3.7	-		-		-		-		-		134.6	1.3
1993	-	-	-	-	-	-	-	-	-	-	137.1	1.9	-		-		-		-		-		141.1	2.9
1994	-	-	-	-	-	-	-	-	-	-	143.6	1.8	-		-		-		-		-		146.1	1.7
1995	-	-	-	-	-	-	-	-	-	-	148.7	1.8	-		-		-		-		-		-	-

Source: U.S. Department of Labor, Bureau of Labor Statistics, Division of Consumer Prices and Price Indexes. - indicates no data collected for period.

Seattle-Everett, WA
Consumer Price Index - All Urban Consumers
Base 1982-1984 = 100
Apparel and Upkeep

For 1952-1995. Columns headed % show percentile change in the index from the previous period for which an index is available.

Year	Jan Index	%	Feb Index	%	Mar Index	%	Apr Index	%	May Index	%	Jun Index	%	Jul Index	%	Aug Index	%	Sep Index	%	Oct Index	%	Nov Index	%	Dec Index	%
1952	-	-	-	-	-	-	-	-	-	-	-	-	-	-	-	-	-	-	-	-	43.9	-	-	-
1953	-	-	43.9	0.0	-	-	-	-	43.8	-0.2	-	-	-	-	44.1	0.7	-	-	-	-	44.0	-0.2	-	-
1954	-	-	43.5	-1.1	-	-	-	-	43.7	0.5	-	-	-	-	43.6	-0.2	-	-	-	-	43.5	-0.2	-	-
1955	-	-	43.7	0.5	-	-	-	-	43.4	-0.7	-	-	-	-	43.9	1.2	-	-	-	-	44.1	0.5	-	-
1956	-	-	43.8	-0.7	-	-	-	-	44.0	0.5	-	-	-	-	44.1	0.2	-	-	-	-	45.0	2.0	-	-
1957	-	-	44.8	-0.4	-	-	-	-	45.0	0.4	-	-	-	-	45.3	0.7	-	-	-	-	45.2	-0.2	-	-
1958	-	-	45.1	-0.2	-	-	-	-	45.1	0.0	-	-	-	-	44.8	-0.7	-	-	-	-	44.7	-0.2	-	-
1959	-	-	44.7	0.0	-	-	-	-	45.1	0.9	-	-	-	-	45.5	0.9	-	-	-	-	46.1	1.3	-	-
1960	-	-	46.0	-0.2	-	-	-	-	45.4	-1.3	-	-	-	-	45.8	0.9	-	-	-	-	46.6	1.7	-	-
1961	-	-	46.5	-0.2	-	-	-	-	46.7	0.4	-	-	-	-	46.2	-1.1	-	-	-	-	47.4	2.6	-	-
1962	-	-	47.2	-0.4	-	-	-	-	47.4	0.4	-	-	-	-	47.5	0.2	-	-	-	-	47.8	0.6	-	-
1963	-	-	48.2	0.8	-	-	-	-	47.7	-1.0	-	-	-	-	48.1	0.8	-	-	-	-	48.8	1.5	-	-
1964	-	-	48.9	0.2	-	-	-	-	49.1	0.4	-	-	-	-	48.1	-2.0	-	-	-	-	48.9	1.7	-	-
1965	-	-	48.8	-0.2	-	-	-	-	49.0	0.4	-	-	-	-	48.7	-0.6	-	-	-	-	49.7	2.1	-	-
1966	-	-	50.1	0.8	-	-	-	-	50.6	1.0	-	-	-	-	50.2	-0.8	-	-	-	-	51.0	1.6	-	-
1967	-	-	51.4	0.8	-	-	-	-	52.2	1.6	-	-	-	-	52.3	0.2	-	-	-	-	53.1	1.5	-	-
1968	-	-	52.9	-0.4	-	-	-	-	53.5	1.1	-	-	-	-	53.6	0.2	-	-	-	-	54.6	1.9	-	-
1969	-	-	54.7	0.2	-	-	-	-	55.7	1.8	-	-	-	-	55.7	0.0	-	-	-	-	57.2	2.7	-	-
1970	-	-	57.1	-0.2	-	-	-	-	58.1	1.8	-	-	-	-	58.0	-0.2	-	-	-	-	60.0	3.4	-	-
1971	-	-	59.5	-0.8	-	-	-	-	61.1	2.7	-	-	-	-	60.3	-1.3	-	-	-	-	61.4	1.8	-	-
1972	-	-	61.0	-0.7	-	-	-	-	61.0	0.0	-	-	-	-	60.8	-0.3	-	-	-	-	62.6	3.0	-	-
1973	-	-	62.9	0.5	-	-	-	-	64.3	2.2	-	-	-	-	64.1	-0.3	-	-	-	-	65.5	2.2	-	-
1974	-	-	65.8	0.5	-	-	-	-	67.5	2.6	-	-	-	-	68.6	1.6	-	-	-	-	71.1	3.6	-	-
1975	-	-	71.8	1.0	-	-	-	-	72.9	1.5	-	-	-	-	72.5	-0.5	-	-	-	-	73.4	1.2	-	-
1976	-	-	75.4	2.7	-	-	-	-	77.4	2.7	-	-	-	-	76.9	-0.6	-	-	-	-	77.9	1.3	-	-
1977	-	-	78.5	0.8	-	-	-	-	79.9	1.8	-	-	-	-	80.6	0.9	-	-	-	-	82.4	2.2	-	-
1978	81.6	-1.0	-	-	81.4	-0.2	-	-	82.8	1.7	-	-	81.5	-1.6	-	-	84.2	3.3	-	-	84.0	-0.2	-	-
1979	82.8	-1.4	-	-	86.1	4.0	-	-	87.6	1.7	-	-	86.9	-0.8	-	-	89.4	2.9	-	-	92.7	3.7	-	-
1980	90.6	-2.3	-	-	93.7	3.4	-	-	92.3	-1.5	-	-	94.5	2.4	-	-	98.8	4.6	-	-	98.5	-0.3	-	-
1981	96.8	-1.7	-	-	98.0	1.2	-	-	98.8	0.8	-	-	99.4	0.6	-	-	100.4	1.0	-	-	100.6	0.2	-	-
1982	97.7	-2.9	-	-	99.9	2.3	-	-	99.3	-0.6	-	-	97.5	-1.8	-	-	102.9	5.5	-	-	100.5	-2.3	-	-
1983	96.9	-3.6	-	-	101.6	4.9	-	-	103.1	1.5	-	-	101.6	-1.5	-	-	103.6	2.0	-	-	100.3	-3.2	-	-
1984	97.3	-3.0	-	-	100.2	3.0	-	-	98.2	-2.0	-	-	97.8	-0.4	-	-	101.6	3.9	-	-	100.4	-1.2	-	-
1985	96.9	-3.5	-	-	104.6	7.9	-	-	100.6	-3.8	-	-	100.8	0.2	-	-	107.8	6.9	-	-	103.7	-3.8	-	-
1986	99.2	-4.3	-	-	104.0	4.8	-	-	103.9	-0.1	-	-	103.9	0.0	-	-	108.3	4.2	-	-	108.6	0.3	105.1	-3.2
1987	-	-	-	-	-	-	-	-	-	-	98.5	-6.3	-	-	-	-	-	-	-	-	-	-	105.7	7.3
1988	-	-	-	-	-	-	-	-	-	-	109.4	3.5	-	-	-	-	-	-	-	-	-	-	114.5	4.7
1989	-	-	-	-	-	-	-	-	-	-	114.5	0.0	-	-	-	-	-	-	-	-	-	-	114.3	-0.2
1990	-	-	-	-	-	-	-	-	-	-	118.4	3.6	-	-	-	-	-	-	-	-	-	-	123.0	3.9
1991	-	-	-	-	-	-	-	-	-	-	123.2	0.2	-	-	-	-	-	-	-	-	-	-	121.4	-1.5
1992	-	-	-	-	-	-	-	-	-	-	124.3	2.4	-	-	-	-	-	-	-	-	-	-	125.3	0.8
1993	-	-	-	-	-	-	-	-	-	-	124.8	-0.4	-	-	-	-	-	-	-	-	-	-	119.6	-4.2
1994	-	-	-	-	-	-	-	-	-	-	124.7	4.3	-	-	-	-	-	-	-	-	-	-	122.8	-1.5
1995	-	-	-	-	-	-	-	-	-	-	127.8	4.1	-	-	-	-	-	-	-	-	-	-	-	-

Source: U.S. Department of Labor, Bureau of Labor Statistics, Division of Consumer Prices and Price Indexes. - indicates no data collected for period.

Seattle-Everett, WA
Consumer Price Index - Urban Wage Earners
Base 1982-1984 = 100
Apparel and Upkeep

For 1952-1995. Columns headed % show percentile change in the index from the previous period for which an index is available.

Year	Jan Index	%	Feb Index	%	Mar Index	%	Apr Index	%	May Index	%	Jun Index	%	Jul Index	%	Aug Index	%	Sep Index	%	Oct Index	%	Nov Index	%	Dec Index	%
1952	-	-	-	-	-	-	-	-	-	-	-	-	-	-	-	-	-	-	-	-	44.4	-	-	-
1953	-	-	44.4	0.0	-	-	-	-	44.3	-0.2	-	-	-	-	44.6	0.7	-	-	-	-	44.5	-0.2	-	-
1954	-	-	44.1	-0.9	-	-	-	-	44.2	0.2	-	-	-	-	44.1	-0.2	-	-	-	-	44.0	-0.2	-	-
1955	-	-	44.2	0.5	-	-	-	-	43.9	-0.7	-	-	-	-	44.4	1.1	-	-	-	-	44.6	0.5	-	-
1956	-	-	44.3	-0.7	-	-	-	-	44.5	0.5	-	-	-	-	44.6	0.2	-	-	-	-	45.5	2.0	-	-
1957	-	-	45.3	-0.4	-	-	-	-	45.5	0.4	-	-	-	-	45.8	0.7	-	-	-	-	45.7	-0.2	-	-
1958	-	-	45.6	-0.2	-	-	-	-	45.6	0.0	-	-	-	-	45.3	-0.7	-	-	-	-	45.2	-0.2	-	-
1959	-	-	45.3	0.2	-	-	-	-	45.6	0.7	-	-	-	-	46.1	1.1	-	-	-	-	46.6	1.1	-	-
1960	-	-	46.5	-0.2	-	-	-	-	46.0	-1.1	-	-	-	-	46.4	0.9	-	-	-	-	47.1	1.5	-	-
1961	-	-	47.0	-0.2	-	-	-	-	47.2	0.4	-	-	-	-	46.7	-1.1	-	-	-	-	47.9	2.6	-	-
1962	-	-	47.8	-0.2	-	-	-	-	48.0	0.4	-	-	-	-	48.0	0.0	-	-	-	-	48.4	0.8	-	-
1963	-	-	48.8	0.8	-	-	-	-	48.3	-1.0	-	-	-	-	48.7	0.8	-	-	-	-	49.4	1.4	-	-
1964	-	-	49.5	0.2	-	-	-	-	49.7	0.4	-	-	-	-	48.7	-2.0	-	-	-	-	49.5	1.6	-	-
1965	-	-	49.4	-0.2	-	-	-	-	49.6	0.4	-	-	-	-	49.2	-0.8	-	-	-	-	50.2	2.0	-	-
1966	-	-	50.7	1.0	-	-	-	-	51.2	1.0	-	-	-	-	50.8	-0.8	-	-	-	-	51.6	1.6	-	-
1967	-	-	52.0	0.8	-	-	-	-	52.8	1.5	-	-	-	-	52.9	0.2	-	-	-	-	53.7	1.5	-	-
1968	-	-	53.5	-0.4	-	-	-	-	54.2	1.3	-	-	-	-	54.3	0.2	-	-	-	-	55.3	1.8	-	-
1969	-	-	55.4	0.2	-	-	-	-	56.4	1.8	-	-	-	-	56.4	0.0	-	-	-	-	57.9	2.7	-	-
1970	-	-	57.8	-0.2	-	-	-	-	58.8	1.7	-	-	-	-	58.7	-0.2	-	-	-	-	60.8	3.6	-	-
1971	-	-	60.2	-1.0	-	-	-	-	61.9	2.8	-	-	-	-	61.0	-1.5	-	-	-	-	62.1	1.8	-	-
1972	-	-	61.8	-0.5	-	-	-	-	61.7	-0.2	-	-	-	-	61.5	-0.3	-	-	-	-	63.3	2.9	-	-
1973	-	-	63.7	0.6	-	-	-	-	65.1	2.2	-	-	-	-	64.9	-0.3	-	-	-	-	66.3	2.2	-	-
1974	-	-	66.6	0.5	-	-	-	-	68.3	2.6	-	-	-	-	69.4	1.6	-	-	-	-	72.0	3.7	-	-
1975	-	-	72.6	0.8	-	-	-	-	73.8	1.7	-	-	-	-	73.4	-0.5	-	-	-	-	74.3	1.2	-	-
1976	-	-	76.3	2.7	-	-	-	-	78.3	2.6	-	-	-	-	77.8	-0.6	-	-	-	-	78.8	1.3	-	-
1977	-	-	79.5	0.9	-	-	-	-	80.9	1.8	-	-	-	-	81.5	0.7	-	-	-	-	83.4	2.3	-	-
1978	82.2	-1.4	-	-	82.7	0.6	-	-	84.3	1.9	-	-	81.9	-2.8	-	-	85.5	4.4	-	-	84.7	-0.9	-	-
1979	82.1	-3.1	-	-	85.6	4.3	-	-	87.6	2.3	-	-	88.1	0.6	-	-	90.1	2.3	-	-	92.0	2.1	-	-
1980	89.8	-2.4	-	-	92.8	3.3	-	-	91.8	-1.1	-	-	94.6	3.1	-	-	96.1	1.6	-	-	97.3	1.2	-	-
1981	95.4	-2.0	-	-	98.4	3.1	-	-	97.3	-1.1	-	-	97.0	-0.3	-	-	99.3	2.4	-	-	99.7	0.4	-	-
1982	97.3	-2.4	-	-	100.1	2.9	-	-	100.1	0.0	-	-	98.1	-2.0	-	-	102.6	4.6	-	-	100.4	-2.1	-	-
1983	96.3	-4.1	-	-	101.0	4.9	-	-	102.5	1.5	-	-	101.9	-0.6	-	-	103.4	1.5	-	-	100.3	-3.0	-	-
1984	97.2	-3.1	-	-	100.5	3.4	-	-	98.2	-2.3	-	-	98.0	-0.2	-	-	101.6	3.7	-	-	100.8	-0.8	-	-
1985	96.6	-4.2	-	-	104.7	8.4	-	-	101.0	-3.5	-	-	101.5	0.5	-	-	107.9	6.3	-	-	103.1	-4.4	-	-
1986	99.0	-4.0	-	-	103.0	4.0	-	-	103.4	0.4	-	-	102.9	-0.5	-	-	106.7	3.7	-	-	107.0	0.3	103.9	-2.9
1987	-	-	-	-	-	-	-	-	-	-	98.5	-5.2	-	-	-	-	-	-	-	-	-	-	105.2	6.8
1988	-	-	-	-	-	-	-	-	-	-	109.3	3.9	-	-	-	-	-	-	-	-	-	-	114.8	5.0
1989	-	-	-	-	-	-	-	-	-	-	114.7	-0.1	-	-	-	-	-	-	-	-	-	-	114.1	-0.5
1990	-	-	-	-	-	-	-	-	-	-	118.7	4.0	-	-	-	-	-	-	-	-	-	-	123.2	3.8
1991	-	-	-	-	-	-	-	-	-	-	124.6	1.1	-	-	-	-	-	-	-	-	-	-	122.6	-1.6
1992	-	-	-	-	-	-	-	-	-	-	124.6	1.6	-	-	-	-	-	-	-	-	-	-	125.6	0.8
1993	-	-	-	-	-	-	-	-	-	-	125.4	-0.2	-	-	-	-	-	-	-	-	-	-	120.6	-3.8
1994	-	-	-	-	-	-	-	-	-	-	124.6	3.3	-	-	-	-	-	-	-	-	-	-	123.1	-1.2
1995	-	-	-	-	-	-	-	-	-	-	128.0	4.0	-	-	-	-	-	-	-	-	-	-	-	-

Source: U.S. Department of Labor, Bureau of Labor Statistics, Division of Consumer Prices and Price Indexes. - indicates no data collected for period.

Seattle-Everett, WA
Consumer Price Index - All Urban Consumers
Base 1982-1984 = 100
Transportation

For 1947-1995. Columns headed % show percentile change in the index from the previous period for which an index is available.

Year	Jan Index	%	Feb Index	%	Mar Index	%	Apr Index	%	May Index	%	Jun Index	%	Jul Index	%	Aug Index	%	Sep Index	%	Oct Index	%	Nov Index	%	Dec Index	%
1947	18.7	-	18.7	0.0	18.8	0.5	18.9	0.5	18.9	0.0	18.9	0.0	-	-	19.1	1.1	-	-	-	-	19.5	2.1	-	-
1948	-		20.4	4.6	-	-	-	-	20.4	0.0	-	-	-	-	21.1	3.4	-	-	-	-	21.4	1.4	-	-
1949	-		21.6	0.9	-	-	-	-	22.0	1.9	-	-	-	-	22.6	2.7	-	-	-	-	22.6	0.0	-	-
1950	-		22.8	0.9	-	-	-	-	22.3	-2.2	-	-	-	-	22.6	1.3	-	-	-	-	23.7	4.9	-	-
1951	-		23.8	0.4	-	-	-	-	24.0	0.8	-	-	-	-	24.2	0.8	-	-	-	-	24.8	2.5		
1952	-		25.0	0.8	-	-	-	-	25.2	0.8	-	-	-	-	25.2	0.0	-	-	-	-	26.8	6.3		
1953	-		26.9	0.4	-	-	-	-	27.6	2.6	-	-	-	-	27.6	0.0	-	-	-	-	27.4	-0.7		
1954	-		27.5	0.4	-	-	-	-	26.9	-2.2	-	-	-	-	26.6	-1.1	-	-	-	-	26.7	0.4		
1955	-		26.6	-0.4	-	-	-	-	26.2	-1.5	-	-	-	-	26.1	-0.4	-	-	-	-	26.9	3.1		
1956	-		25.8	-4.1	-	-	-	-	25.9	0.4	-	-	-	-	26.7	3.1	-	-	-	-	27.6	3.4		
1957	-		28.4	2.9	-	-	-	-	28.6	0.7	-	-	-	-	28.1	-1.7	-	-	-	-	29.2	3.9		
1958	-		29.1	-0.3	-	-	-	-	29.4	1.0	-	-	-	-	30.1	2.4	-	-	-	-	29.9	-0.7		
1959	-		30.7	2.7	-	-	-	-	30.8	0.3	-	-	-	-	32.0	3.9	-	-	-	-	31.0	-3.1		
1960	-		30.3	-2.3	-	-	-	-	31.0	2.3	-	-	-	-	30.7	-1.0	-	-	-	-	31.0	1.0		
1961	-		30.9	-0.3	-	-	-	-	31.4	1.6	-	-	-	-	31.8	1.3	-	-	-	-	32.6	2.5		
1962	-		32.3	-0.9	-	-	-	-	32.5	0.6	-	-	-	-	32.6	0.3	-	-	-	-	33.0	1.2		
1963	-		32.3	-2.1	-	-	-	-	32.2	-0.3	-	-	-	-	32.9	2.2	-	-	-	-	32.4	-1.5		
1964	-		32.4	0.0	-	-	-	-	31.8	-1.9	-	-	-	-	33.5	5.3	-	-	-	-	32.8	-2.1		
1965	-		32.4	-1.2	-	-	-	-	33.9	4.6	-	-	-	-	33.8	-0.3	-	-	-	-	33.8	0.0		
1966	-		33.7	-0.3	-	-	-	-	33.4	-0.9	-	-	-	-	34.1	2.1	-	-	-	-	34.8	2.1		
1967	-		34.6	-0.6	-	-	-	-	35.3	2.0	-	-	-	-	35.6	0.8	-	-	-	-	35.7	0.3		
1968	-		35.7	0.0	-	-	-	-	35.6	-0.3	-	-	-	-	36.2	1.7	-	-	-	-	36.2	0.0		
1969	-		36.3	0.3	-	-	-	-	36.0	-0.8	-	-	-	-	36.5	1.4	-	-	-	-	35.9	-1.6		
1970	-		36.9	2.8	-	-	-	-	37.1	0.5	-	-	-	-	37.5	1.1	-	-	-	-	37.1	-1.1		
1971	-		37.4	0.8	-	-	-	-	37.6	0.5	-	-	-	-	38.5	2.4	-	-	-	-	37.7	-2.1		
1972	-		38.2	1.3	-	-	-	-	38.3	0.3	-	-	-	-	38.7	1.0	-	-	-	-	39.4	1.8		
1973	-		39.0	-1.0	-	-	-	-	39.4	1.0	-	-	-	-	39.7	0.8	-	-	-	-	40.0	0.8		
1974	-		41.3	3.2	-	-	-	-	43.6	5.6	-	-	-	-	45.4	4.1	-	-	-	-	45.8	0.9		
1975	-		46.1	0.7	-	-	-	-	47.5	3.0	-	-	-	-	49.0	3.2	-	-	-	-	49.7	1.4		
1976	-		49.7	0.0	-	-	-	-	51.1	2.8	-	-	-	-	52.8	3.3	-	-	-	-	53.3	0.9		
1977	-		55.2	3.6	-	-	-	-	56.5	2.4	-	-	-	-	58.3	3.2	-	-	-	-	57.8	-0.9		
1978	58.3	0.9	-	-	58.5	0.3	-	-	60.2	2.9	-	-	61.8	2.7	-	-	63.1	2.1	-	-	63.8	1.1		
1979	64.5	1.1	-	-	66.0	2.3	-	-	69.6	5.5	-	-	72.5	4.2	-	-	74.7	3.0	-	-	76.1	1.9		
1980	78.0	2.5	-	-	81.3	4.2	-	-	82.5	1.5	-	-	83.7	1.5	-	-	84.7	1.2	-	-	85.9	1.4		
1981	86.8	1.0	-	-	91.0	4.8	-	-	93.6	2.9	-	-	96.2	2.8	-	-	97.1	0.9	-	-	97.7	0.6		
1982	98.2	0.5	-	-	97.0	-1.2	-	-	96.6	-0.4	-	-	99.7	3.2	-	-	99.1	-0.6	-	-	97.8	-1.3		
1983	96.4	-1.4	-	-	94.0	-2.5	-	-	96.8	3.0	-	-	100.9	4.2	-	-	102.0	1.1	-	-	102.2	0.2		
1984	101.0	-1.2	-	-	99.9	-1.1	-	-	103.8	3.9	-	-	104.5	0.7	-	-	104.0	-0.5	-	-	104.4	0.4		
1985	105.1	0.7	-	-	104.4	-0.7	-	-	105.0	0.6	-	-	105.5	0.5	-	-	104.5	-0.9	-	-	105.1	0.6		
1986	106.5	1.3	-	-	102.9	-3.4	-	-	100.9	-1.9	-	-	100.9	0.0	-	-	100.4	-0.5	-	-	99.7	-0.7	100.4	0.7
1987	-		-		-		-		-		108.1	7.7	-		-		-		-		-		110.2	1.9
1988	-		-		-		-		-		109.7	-0.5	-		-		-		-		-		111.5	1.6
1989	-		-		-		-		-		117.8	5.7	-		-		-		-		-		118.8	0.8
1990	-		-		-		-		-		120.1	1.1	-		-		-		-		-		130.8	8.9
1991	-		-		-		-		-		130.0	-0.6	-		-		-		-		-		130.1	0.1

[Continued]

Seattle-Everett, WA
Consumer Price Index - All Urban Consumers
Base 1982-1984 = 100
Transportation

[Continued]

For 1947-1995. Columns headed % show percentile change in the index from the previous period for which an index is available.

Year	Jan		Feb		Mar		Apr		May		Jun		Jul		Aug		Sep		Oct		Nov		Dec	
	Index	%	Index	%	Index	%	Index	%	Index	%	Index	%	Index	%	Index	%	Index	%	Index	%	Index	%	Index	%
1992	-	-	-	-	-	-	-	-	-	-	131.7	1.2	-	-	-	-	-	-	-	-	-	-	136.4	3.6
1993	-	-	-	-	-	-	-	-	-	-	135.5	-0.7	-	-	-	-	-	-	-	-	-	-	136.9	1.0
1994	-	-	-	-	-	-	-	-	-	-	136.6	-0.2	-	-	-	-	-	-	-	-	-	-	140.6	2.9
1995	-	-	-	-	-	-	-	-	-	-	141.6	0.7	-	-	-	-	-	-	-	-	-	-	-	-

Source: U.S. Department of Labor, Bureau of Labor Statistics, Division of Consumer Prices and Price Indexes. - indicates no data collected for period.

Seattle-Everett, WA
Consumer Price Index - Urban Wage Earners
Base 1982-1984 = 100
Transportation

For 1947-1995. Columns headed % show percentile change in the index from the previous period for which an index is available.

Year	Jan Index	%	Feb Index	%	Mar Index	%	Apr Index	%	May Index	%	Jun Index	%	Jul Index	%	Aug Index	%	Sep Index	%	Oct Index	%	Nov Index	%	Dec Index	%
1947	19.1	-	19.1	0.0	19.2	0.5	19.2	0.0	19.3	0.5	19.3	0.0	-	-	19.5	1.0	-	-	-	-	19.9	2.1	-	-
1948	-	-	20.8	4.5	-	-	-	-	20.8	0.0	-	-	-	-	21.5	3.4	-	-	-	-	21.8	1.4	-	-
1949	-	-	22.0	0.9	-	-	-	-	22.5	2.3	-	-	-	-	23.0	2.2	-	-	-	-	23.1	0.4	-	-
1950	-	-	23.3	0.9	-	-	-	-	22.8	-2.1	-	-	-	-	23.1	1.3	-	-	-	-	24.1	4.3	-	-
1951	-	-	24.3	0.8	-	-	-	-	24.5	0.8	-	-	-	-	24.6	0.4	-	-	-	-	25.3	2.8	-	-
1952	-	-	25.5	0.8	-	-	-	-	25.8	1.2	-	-	-	-	25.8	0.0	-	-	-	-	27.4	6.2	-	-
1953	-	-	27.4	0.0	-	-	-	-	28.2	2.9	-	-	-	-	28.1	-0.4	-	-	-	-	28.0	-0.4	-	-
1954	-	-	28.1	0.4	-	-	-	-	27.4	-2.5	-	-	-	-	27.1	-1.1	-	-	-	-	27.2	0.4	-	-
1955	-	-	27.1	-0.4	-	-	-	-	26.8	-1.1	-	-	-	-	26.6	-0.7	-	-	-	-	27.4	3.0	-	-
1956	-	-	26.3	-4.0	-	-	-	-	26.4	0.4	-	-	-	-	27.2	3.0	-	-	-	-	28.2	3.7	-	-
1957	-	-	29.0	2.8	-	-	-	-	29.2	0.7	-	-	-	-	28.7	-1.7	-	-	-	-	29.8	3.8	-	-
1958	-	-	29.7	-0.3	-	-	-	-	30.0	1.0	-	-	-	-	30.7	2.3	-	-	-	-	30.5	-0.7	-	-
1959	-	-	31.3	2.6	-	-	-	-	31.4	0.3	-	-	-	-	32.7	4.1	-	-	-	-	31.6	-3.4	-	-
1960	-	-	30.9	-2.2	-	-	-	-	31.6	2.3	-	-	-	-	31.3	-0.9	-	-	-	-	31.6	1.0	-	-
1961	-	-	31.5	-0.3	-	-	-	-	32.1	1.9	-	-	-	-	32.4	0.9	-	-	-	-	33.3	2.8	-	-
1962	-	-	33.0	-0.9	-	-	-	-	33.2	0.6	-	-	-	-	33.3	0.3	-	-	-	-	33.7	1.2	-	-
1963	-	-	33.0	-2.1	-	-	-	-	32.8	-0.6	-	-	-	-	33.6	2.4	-	-	-	-	33.0	-1.8	-	-
1964	-	-	33.1	0.3	-	-	-	-	32.5	-1.8	-	-	-	-	34.2	5.2	-	-	-	-	33.5	-2.0	-	-
1965	-	-	33.1	-1.2	-	-	-	-	34.6	4.5	-	-	-	-	34.5	-0.3	-	-	-	-	34.5	0.0	-	-
1966	-	-	34.4	-0.3	-	-	-	-	34.1	-0.9	-	-	-	-	34.8	2.1	-	-	-	-	35.6	2.3	-	-
1967	-	-	35.3	-0.8	-	-	-	-	36.1	2.3	-	-	-	-	36.3	0.6	-	-	-	-	36.4	0.3	-	-
1968	-	-	36.5	0.3	-	-	-	-	36.3	-0.5	-	-	-	-	36.9	1.7	-	-	-	-	37.0	0.3	-	-
1969	-	-	37.0	0.0	-	-	-	-	36.8	-0.5	-	-	-	-	37.3	1.4	-	-	-	-	36.6	-1.9	-	-
1970	-	-	37.7	3.0	-	-	-	-	37.9	0.5	-	-	-	-	38.3	1.1	-	-	-	-	37.8	-1.3	-	-
1971	-	-	38.2	1.1	-	-	-	-	38.3	0.3	-	-	-	-	39.3	2.6	-	-	-	-	38.4	-2.3	-	-
1972	-	-	39.0	1.6	-	-	-	-	39.1	0.3	-	-	-	-	39.5	1.0	-	-	-	-	40.2	1.8	-	-
1973	-	-	39.9	-0.7	-	-	-	-	40.2	0.8	-	-	-	-	40.5	0.7	-	-	-	-	40.9	1.0	-	-
1974	-	-	42.2	3.2	-	-	-	-	44.5	5.5	-	-	-	-	46.3	4.0	-	-	-	-	46.7	0.9	-	-
1975	-	-	47.1	0.9	-	-	-	-	48.5	3.0	-	-	-	-	50.1	3.3	-	-	-	-	50.7	1.2	-	-
1976	-	-	50.7	0.0	-	-	-	-	52.1	2.8	-	-	-	-	53.9	3.5	-	-	-	-	54.4	0.9	-	-
1977	-	-	56.4	3.7	-	-	-	-	57.7	2.3	-	-	-	-	59.5	3.1	-	-	-	-	59.0	-0.8	-	-
1978	59.0	0.0	-	-	59.2	0.3	-	-	60.6	2.4	-	-	62.2	2.6	-	-	62.8	1.0	-	-	63.5	1.1	-	-
1979	64.2	1.1	-	-	65.9	2.6	-	-	69.4	5.3	-	-	72.2	4.0	-	-	74.3	2.9	-	-	75.7	1.9	-	-
1980	77.2	2.0	-	-	80.9	4.8	-	-	81.9	1.2	-	-	82.7	1.0	-	-	83.8	1.3	-	-	85.3	1.8	-	-
1981	86.4	1.3	-	-	89.8	3.9	-	-	92.6	3.1	-	-	95.2	2.8	-	-	95.8	0.6	-	-	97.6	1.9	-	-
1982	98.1	0.5	-	-	96.8	-1.3	-	-	96.4	-0.4	-	-	99.5	3.2	-	-	98.8	-0.7	-	-	97.7	-1.1	-	-
1983	96.2	-1.5	-	-	93.9	-2.4	-	-	96.8	3.1	-	-	101.0	4.3	-	-	102.2	1.2	-	-	102.3	0.1	-	-
1984	101.2	-1.1	-	-	100.2	-1.0	-	-	103.9	3.7	-	-	104.5	0.6	-	-	104.1	-0.4	-	-	104.7	0.6	-	-
1985	105.4	0.7	-	-	104.7	-0.7	-	-	105.5	0.8	-	-	105.9	0.4	-	-	105.0	-0.8	-	-	105.6	0.6	-	-
1986	106.7	1.0	-	-	103.1	-3.4	-	-	101.0	-2.0	-	-	101.0	0.0	-	-	100.5	-0.5	-	-	99.8	-0.7	100.2	0.4
1987	-	-	-	-	-	-	-	-	-	-	108.3	8.1	-	-	-	-	-	-	-	-	-	-	110.2	1.8
1988	-	-	-	-	-	-	-	-	-	-	109.9	-0.3	-	-	-	-	-	-	-	-	-	-	111.5	1.5
1989	-	-	-	-	-	-	-	-	-	-	117.4	5.3	-	-	-	-	-	-	-	-	-	-	118.3	0.8
1990	-	-	-	-	-	-	-	-	-	-	119.3	0.8	-	-	-	-	-	-	-	-	-	-	129.1	8.2
1991	-	-	-	-	-	-	-	-	-	-	128.9	-0.2	-	-	-	-	-	-	-	-	-	-	129.3	0.3

[Continued]

Seattle-Everett, WA
Consumer Price Index - Urban Wage Earners
Base 1982-1984 = 100
Transportation

[Continued]

For 1947-1995. Columns headed % show percentile change in the index from the previous period for which an index is available.

Year	Jan Index	%	Feb Index	%	Mar Index	%	Apr Index	%	May Index	%	Jun Index	%	Jul Index	%	Aug Index	%	Sep Index	%	Oct Index	%	Nov Index	%	Dec Index	%
1992	-	-	-	-	-	-	-	-	-	-	130.8	1.2	-	-	-	-	-	-	-	-	-	-	135.4	3.5
1993	-	-	-	-	-	-	-	-	-	-	135.1	-0.2	-	-	-	-	-	-	-	-	-	-	137.0	1.4
1994	-	-	-	-	-	-	-	-	-	-	136.7	-0.2	-	-	-	-	-	-	-	-	-	-	141.0	3.1
1995	-	-	-	-	-	-	-	-	-	-	142.5	1.1	-	-	-	-	-	-	-	-	-	-	-	-

Source: U.S. Department of Labor, Bureau of Labor Statistics, Division of Consumer Prices and Price Indexes. - indicates no data collected for period.

Seattle-Everett, WA
Consumer Price Index - All Urban Consumers
Base 1982-1984 = 100
Medical Care

For 1947-1995. Columns headed % show percentile change in the index from the previous period for which an index is available.

Year	Jan Index	%	Feb Index	%	Mar Index	%	Apr Index	%	May Index	%	Jun Index	%	Jul Index	%	Aug Index	%	Sep Index	%	Oct Index	%	Nov Index	%	Dec Index	%
1947	14.1	-	14.3	1.4	14.3	0.0	14.4	0.7	14.4	0.0	14.4	0.0	-	-	14.4	0.0	-	-	-	-	14.6	1.4	-	-
1948	-	-	14.7	0.7	-	-	-	-	15.0	2.0	-	-	-	-	15.3	2.0	-	-	-	-	15.6	2.0	-	-
1949	-	-	15.6	0.0	-	-	-	-	15.9	1.9	-	-	-	-	15.9	0.0	-	-	-	-	16.0	0.6	-	-
1950	-	-	16.0	0.0	-	-	-	-	16.0	0.0	-	-	-	-	16.0	0.0	-	-	-	-	16.1	0.6	-	-
1951	-	-	16.6	3.1	-	-	-	-	17.1	3.0	-	-	-	-	17.2	0.6	-	-	-	-	17.4	1.2	-	-
1952	-	-	17.8	2.3	-	-	-	-	18.3	2.8	-	-	-	-	18.7	2.2	-	-	-	-	18.7	0.0	-	-
1953	-	-	18.7	0.0	-	-	-	-	18.9	1.1	-	-	-	-	19.0	0.5	-	-	-	-	19.6	3.2	-	-
1954	-	-	19.6	0.0	-	-	-	-	19.8	1.0	-	-	-	-	19.6	-1.0	-	-	-	-	19.7	0.5	-	-
1955	-	-	19.8	0.5	-	-	-	-	19.8	0.0	-	-	-	-	19.9	0.5	-	-	-	-	21.1	6.0	-	-
1956	-	-	20.4	-3.3	-	-	-	-	20.5	0.5	-	-	-	-	20.8	1.5	-	-	-	-	20.7	-0.5	-	-
1957	-	-	20.9	1.0	-	-	-	-	21.0	0.5	-	-	-	-	21.6	2.9	-	-	-	-	21.7	0.5	-	-
1958	-	-	22.1	1.8	-	-	-	-	22.2	0.5	-	-	-	-	22.4	0.9	-	-	-	-	22.5	0.4	-	-
1959	-	-	22.6	0.4	-	-	-	-	22.6	0.0	-	-	-	-	22.9	1.3	-	-	-	-	23.3	1.7	-	-
1960	-	-	23.9	2.6	-	-	-	-	23.9	0.0	-	-	-	-	24.1	0.8	-	-	-	-	23.9	-0.8	-	-
1961	-	-	23.9	0.0	-	-	-	-	24.0	0.4	-	-	-	-	24.0	0.0	-	-	-	-	24.1	0.4	-	-
1962	-	-	24.2	0.4	-	-	-	-	24.3	0.4	-	-	-	-	24.4	0.4	-	-	-	-	24.4	0.0	-	-
1963	-	-	24.4	0.0	-	-	-	-	24.5	0.4	-	-	-	-	24.6	0.4	-	-	-	-	24.6	0.0	-	-
1964	-	-	24.6	0.0	-	-	-	-	24.9	1.2	-	-	-	-	25.1	0.8	-	-	-	-	25.2	0.4	-	-
1965	-	-	25.4	0.8	-	-	-	-	25.9	2.0	-	-	-	-	26.1	0.8	-	-	-	-	26.6	1.9	-	-
1966	-	-	26.8	0.8	-	-	-	-	27.3	1.9	-	-	-	-	27.8	1.8	-	-	-	-	28.5	2.5	-	-
1967	-	-	28.5	0.0	-	-	-	-	28.8	1.1	-	-	-	-	29.3	1.7	-	-	-	-	29.8	1.7	-	-
1968	-	-	30.1	1.0	-	-	-	-	30.6	1.7	-	-	-	-	31.1	1.6	-	-	-	-	31.5	1.3	-	-
1969	-	-	32.1	1.9	-	-	-	-	32.7	1.9	-	-	-	-	33.3	1.8	-	-	-	-	33.5	0.6	-	-
1970	-	-	34.0	1.5	-	-	-	-	34.3	0.9	-	-	-	-	34.7	1.2	-	-	-	-	34.8	0.3	-	-
1971	-	-	35.4	1.7	-	-	-	-	35.6	0.6	-	-	-	-	36.1	1.4	-	-	-	-	36.0	-0.3	-	-
1972	-	-	36.2	0.6	-	-	-	-	36.4	0.6	-	-	-	-	36.7	0.8	-	-	-	-	36.7	0.0	-	-
1973	-	-	37.2	1.4	-	-	-	-	37.4	0.5	-	-	-	-	37.9	1.3	-	-	-	-	38.6	1.8	-	-
1974	-	-	39.4	2.1	-	-	-	-	40.7	3.3	-	-	-	-	41.7	2.5	-	-	-	-	42.8	2.6	-	-
1975	-	-	44.8	4.7	-	-	-	-	45.7	2.0	-	-	-	-	46.7	2.2	-	-	-	-	47.4	1.5	-	-
1976	-	-	49.4	4.2	-	-	-	-	50.5	2.2	-	-	-	-	51.1	1.2	-	-	-	-	52.8	3.3	-	-
1977	-	-	54.6	3.4	-	-	-	-	55.5	1.6	-	-	-	-	56.4	1.6	-	-	-	-	57.3	1.6	-	-
1978	60.6	5.8	-	-	60.7	0.2	-	-	61.3	1.0	-	-	62.4	1.8	-	-	62.8	0.6	-	-	64.0	1.9	-	-
1979	64.7	1.1	-	-	66.1	2.2	-	-	66.3	0.3	-	-	67.4	1.7	-	-	68.1	1.0	-	-	69.8	2.5	-	-
1980	72.6	4.0	-	-	73.9	1.8	-	-	75.1	1.6	-	-	76.4	1.7	-	-	76.4	0.0	-	-	78.4	2.6	-	-
1981	81.2	3.6	-	-	83.2	2.5	-	-	83.8	0.7	-	-	85.3	1.8	-	-	86.1	0.9	-	-	87.5	1.6	-	-
1982	89.7	2.5	-	-	91.7	2.2	-	-	92.4	0.8	-	-	93.8	1.5	-	-	94.8	1.1	-	-	96.1	1.4	-	-
1983	99.5	3.5	-	-	101.1	1.6	-	-	100.6	-0.5	-	-	101.3	0.7	-	-	101.3	0.0	-	-	100.7	-0.6	-	-
1984	103.2	2.5	-	-	104.6	1.4	-	-	104.7	0.1	-	-	105.7	1.0	-	-	106.5	0.8	-	-	107.4	0.8	-	-
1985	109.7	2.1	-	-	111.9	2.0	-	-	112.3	0.4	-	-	113.1	0.7	-	-	113.2	0.1	-	-	112.1	-1.0	-	-
1986	113.2	1.0	-	-	116.0	2.5	-	-	116.0	0.0	-	-	118.9	2.5	-	-	119.9	0.8	-	-	119.6	-0.3	120.5	0.8
1987	-	-	-	-	-	-	-	-	-	-	123.7	2.7	-	-	-	-	-	-	-	-	-	-	129.8	4.9
1988	-	-	-	-	-	-	-	-	-	-	136.2	4.9	-	-	-	-	-	-	-	-	-	-	141.3	3.7
1989	-	-	-	-	-	-	-	-	-	-	143.9	1.8	-	-	-	-	-	-	-	-	-	-	146.5	1.8
1990	-	-	-	-	-	-	-	-	-	-	152.0	3.8	-	-	-	-	-	-	-	-	-	-	156.7	3.1
1991	-	-	-	-	-	-	-	-	-	-	163.5	4.3	-	-	-	-	-	-	-	-	-	-	168.4	3.0

[Continued]

Seattle-Everett, WA
Consumer Price Index - All Urban Consumers
Base 1982-1984 = 100
Medical Care
[Continued]

For 1947-1995. Columns headed % show percentile change in the index from the previous period for which an index is available.

Year	Jan		Feb		Mar		Apr		May		Jun		Jul		Aug		Sep		Oct		Nov		Dec	
	Index	%	Index	%	Index	%	Index	%	Index	%	Index	%	Index	%	Index	%	Index	%	Index	%	Index	%	Index	%
1992	-	-	-	-	-	-	-	-	-	-	174.5	3.6	-	-	-	-	-	-	-	-	-	-	178.2	2.1
1993	-	-	-	-	-	-	-	-	-	-	184.8	3.7	-	-	-	-	-	-	-	-	-	-	188.4	1.9
1994	-	-	-	-	-	-	-	-	-	-	190.8	1.3	-	-	-	-	-	-	-	-	-	-	194.7	2.0
1995	-	-	-	-	-	-	-	-	-	-	195.9	0.6	-	-	-	-	-	-	-	-	-	-	-	-

Source: U.S. Department of Labor, Bureau of Labor Statistics, Division of Consumer Prices and Price Indexes. - indicates no data collected for period.

Seattle-Everett, WA
Consumer Price Index - Urban Wage Earners
Base 1982-1984 = 100
Medical Care

For 1947-1995. Columns headed % show percentile change in the index from the previous period for which an index is available.

Year	Jan Index	%	Feb Index	%	Mar Index	%	Apr Index	%	May Index	%	Jun Index	%	Jul Index	%	Aug Index	%	Sep Index	%	Oct Index	%	Nov Index	%	Dec Index	%
1947	14.0	-	14.2	1.4	14.2	0.0	14.2	0.0	14.2	0.0	14.3	0.7	-	-	14.3	0.0	-	-	-	-	14.5	1.4	-	-
1948	-	-	14.6	0.7	-	-	-	-	14.8	1.4	-	-	-	-	15.2	2.7	-	-	-	-	15.4	1.3	-	-
1949	-	-	15.4	0.0	-	-	-	-	15.7	1.9	-	-	-	-	15.7	0.0	-	-	-	-	15.9	1.3	-	-
1950	-	-	15.9	0.0	-	-	-	-	15.9	0.0	-	-	-	-	15.9	0.0	-	-	-	-	16.0	0.6	-	-
1951	-	-	16.4	2.5	-	-	-	-	17.0	3.7	-	-	-	-	17.0	0.0	-	-	-	-	17.2	1.2	-	-
1952	-	-	17.7	2.9	-	-	-	-	18.1	2.3	-	-	-	-	18.5	2.2	-	-	-	-	18.5	0.0	-	-
1953	-	-	18.5	0.0	-	-	-	-	18.7	1.1	-	-	-	-	18.8	0.5	-	-	-	-	19.4	3.2	-	-
1954	-	-	19.4	0.0	-	-	-	-	19.6	1.0	-	-	-	-	19.4	-1.0	-	-	-	-	19.5	0.5	-	-
1955	-	-	19.6	0.5	-	-	-	-	19.6	0.0	-	-	-	-	19.7	0.5	-	-	-	-	20.9	6.1	-	-
1956	-	-	20.2	-3.3	-	-	-	-	20.3	0.5	-	-	-	-	20.6	1.5	-	-	-	-	20.5	-0.5	-	-
1957	-	-	20.7	1.0	-	-	-	-	20.8	0.5	-	-	-	-	21.4	2.9	-	-	-	-	21.5	0.5	-	-
1958	-	-	21.9	1.9	-	-	-	-	22.0	0.5	-	-	-	-	22.2	0.9	-	-	-	-	22.3	0.5	-	-
1959	-	-	22.4	0.4	-	-	-	-	22.4	0.0	-	-	-	-	22.7	1.3	-	-	-	-	23.1	1.8	-	-
1960	-	-	23.7	2.6	-	-	-	-	23.7	0.0	-	-	-	-	23.9	0.8	-	-	-	-	23.7	-0.8	-	-
1961	-	-	23.7	0.0	-	-	-	-	23.8	0.4	-	-	-	-	23.8	0.0	-	-	-	-	23.9	0.4	-	-
1962	-	-	24.0	0.4	-	-	-	-	24.1	0.4	-	-	-	-	24.1	0.0	-	-	-	-	24.2	0.4	-	-
1963	-	-	24.2	0.0	-	-	-	-	24.3	0.4	-	-	-	-	24.4	0.4	-	-	-	-	24.4	0.0	-	-
1964	-	-	24.4	0.0	-	-	-	-	24.6	0.8	-	-	-	-	24.8	0.8	-	-	-	-	25.0	0.8	-	-
1965	-	-	25.2	0.8	-	-	-	-	25.6	1.6	-	-	-	-	25.8	0.8	-	-	-	-	26.4	2.3	-	-
1966	-	-	26.6	0.8	-	-	-	-	27.0	1.5	-	-	-	-	27.5	1.9	-	-	-	-	28.3	2.9	-	-
1967	-	-	28.2	-0.4	-	-	-	-	28.5	1.1	-	-	-	-	29.1	2.1	-	-	-	-	29.5	1.4	-	-
1968	-	-	29.9	1.4	-	-	-	-	30.3	1.3	-	-	-	-	30.8	1.7	-	-	-	-	31.2	1.3	-	-
1969	-	-	31.8	1.9	-	-	-	-	32.4	1.9	-	-	-	-	33.0	1.9	-	-	-	-	33.2	0.6	-	-
1970	-	-	33.6	1.2	-	-	-	-	34.0	1.2	-	-	-	-	34.4	1.2	-	-	-	-	34.5	0.3	-	-
1971	-	-	35.0	1.4	-	-	-	-	35.3	0.9	-	-	-	-	35.8	1.4	-	-	-	-	35.7	-0.3	-	-
1972	-	-	35.9	0.6	-	-	-	-	36.1	0.6	-	-	-	-	36.4	0.8	-	-	-	-	36.3	-0.3	-	-
1973	-	-	36.9	1.7	-	-	-	-	37.1	0.5	-	-	-	-	37.6	1.3	-	-	-	-	38.3	1.9	-	-
1974	-	-	39.1	2.1	-	-	-	-	40.3	3.1	-	-	-	-	41.3	2.5	-	-	-	-	42.4	2.7	-	-
1975	-	-	44.3	4.5	-	-	-	-	45.2	2.0	-	-	-	-	46.3	2.4	-	-	-	-	47.0	1.5	-	-
1976	-	-	48.9	4.0	-	-	-	-	50.0	2.2	-	-	-	-	50.6	1.2	-	-	-	-	52.3	3.4	-	-
1977	-	-	54.0	3.3	-	-	-	-	55.0	1.9	-	-	-	-	55.8	1.5	-	-	-	-	56.8	1.8	-	-
1978	59.0	3.9	-	-	59.2	0.3	-	-	60.1	1.5	-	-	61.2	1.8	-	-	61.5	0.5	-	-	63.9	3.9	-	-
1979	64.6	1.1	-	-	65.5	1.4	-	-	66.2	1.1	-	-	67.8	2.4	-	-	68.2	0.6	-	-	69.9	2.5	-	-
1980	72.4	3.6	-	-	73.2	1.1	-	-	74.6	1.9	-	-	74.4	-0.3	-	-	76.0	2.2	-	-	78.0	2.6	-	-
1981	79.9	2.4	-	-	81.4	1.9	-	-	82.9	1.8	-	-	84.1	1.4	-	-	86.2	2.5	-	-	87.9	2.0	-	-
1982	89.8	2.2	-	-	91.7	2.1	-	-	92.4	0.8	-	-	93.8	1.5	-	-	94.5	0.7	-	-	95.9	1.5	-	-
1983	99.2	3.4	-	-	100.7	1.5	-	-	100.5	-0.2	-	-	101.3	0.8	-	-	101.2	-0.1	-	-	100.9	-0.3	-	-
1984	103.2	2.3	-	-	104.7	1.5	-	-	104.9	0.2	-	-	106.0	1.0	-	-	106.9	0.8	-	-	107.5	0.6	-	-
1985	109.9	2.2	-	-	112.2	2.1	-	-	112.5	0.3	-	-	113.3	0.7	-	-	113.6	0.3	-	-	112.8	-0.7	-	-
1986	114.0	1.1	-	-	116.9	2.5	-	-	116.8	-0.1	-	-	119.8	2.6	-	-	120.7	0.8	-	-	120.4	-0.2	121.5	0.9
1987	-	-	-	-	-	-	-	-	-	-	123.3	1.5	-	-	-	-	-	-	-	-	-	-	129.5	5.0
1988	-	-	-	-	-	-	-	-	-	-	135.7	4.8	-	-	-	-	-	-	-	-	-	-	140.9	3.8
1989	-	-	-	-	-	-	-	-	-	-	143.6	1.9	-	-	-	-	-	-	-	-	-	-	145.9	1.6
1990	-	-	-	-	-	-	-	-	-	-	151.0	3.5	-	-	-	-	-	-	-	-	-	-	155.3	2.8
1991	-	-	-	-	-	-	-	-	-	-	161.8	4.2	-	-	-	-	-	-	-	-	-	-	166.8	3.1

[Continued]

Seattle-Everett, WA
Consumer Price Index - Urban Wage Earners
Base 1982-1984 = 100
Medical Care

[Continued]

For 1947-1995. Columns headed % show percentile change in the index from the previous period for which an index is available.

Year	Jan Index	%	Feb Index	%	Mar Index	%	Apr Index	%	May Index	%	Jun Index	%	Jul Index	%	Aug Index	%	Sep Index	%	Oct Index	%	Nov Index	%	Dec Index	%
1992	-	-	-	-	-	-	-	-	-	-	173.0	3.7	-	-	-	-	-	-	-	-	-	-	176.8	2.2
1993	-	-	-	-	-	-	-	-	-	-	183.1	3.6	-	-	-	-	-	-	-	-	-	-	186.8	2.0
1994	-	-	-	-	-	-	-	-	-	-	189.0	1.2	-	-	-	-	-	-	-	-	-	-	193.3	2.3
1995	-	-	-	-	-	-	-	-	-	-	194.7	0.7	-	-	-	-	-	-	-	-	-	-	-	-

Source: U.S. Department of Labor, Bureau of Labor Statistics, Division of Consumer Prices and Price Indexes. - indicates no data collected for period.

Seattle-Everett, WA
Consumer Price Index - All Urban Consumers
Base 1982-1984 = 100
Entertainment

For 1975-1995. Columns headed % show percentile change in the index from the previous period for which an index is available.

Year	Jan Index	%	Feb Index	%	Mar Index	%	Apr Index	%	May Index	%	Jun Index	%	Jul Index	%	Aug Index	%	Sep Index	%	Oct Index	%	Nov Index	%	Dec Index	%
1975	-	-	-	-	-	-	-	-	-	-	-	-	-	-	-	-	-	-	-	-	61.1	-	-	-
1976	-	-	61.2	0.2	-	-	-	-	61.7	0.8	-	-	-	-	62.1	0.6	-	-	-	-	63.4	2.1	-	-
1977	-	-	65.2	2.8	-	-	-	-	65.1	-0.2	-	-	-	-	65.2	0.2	-	-	-	-	66.5	2.0	-	-
1978	66.6	0.2	-	-	67.2	0.9	-	-	68.4	1.8	-	-	68.9	0.7	-	-	69.0	0.1	-	-	69.9	1.3	-	-
1979	70.1	0.3	-	-	70.3	0.3	-	-	72.8	3.6	-	-	73.3	0.7	-	-	75.5	3.0	-	-	76.2	0.9	-	-
1980	77.3	1.4	-	-	79.1	2.3	-	-	80.2	1.4	-	-	81.9	2.1	-	-	84.6	3.3	-	-	86.4	2.1	-	-
1981	87.0	0.7	-	-	86.6	-0.5	-	-	87.8	1.4	-	-	87.4	-0.5	-	-	89.4	2.3	-	-	89.6	0.2	-	-
1982	91.5	2.1	-	-	90.9	-0.7	-	-	93.3	2.6	-	-	94.0	0.8	-	-	96.1	2.2	-	-	95.9	-0.2	-	-
1983	96.9	1.0	-	-	99.4	2.6	-	-	97.6	-1.8	-	-	99.7	2.2	-	-	101.6	1.9	-	-	102.5	0.9	-	-
1984	105.1	2.5	-	-	105.9	0.8	-	-	106.4	0.5	-	-	106.3	-0.1	-	-	105.2	-1.0	-	-	107.6	2.3	-	-
1985	108.0	0.4	-	-	108.1	0.1	-	-	107.6	-0.5	-	-	109.6	1.9	-	-	107.6	-1.8	-	-	109.4	1.7	-	-
1986	110.3	0.8	-	-	109.0	-1.2	-	-	107.4	-1.5	-	-	109.2	1.7	-	-	107.6	-1.5	-	-	108.6	0.9	108.6	0.0
1987	-	-	-	-	-	-	-	-	-	-	115.5	6.4	-	-	-	-	-	-	-	-	-	-	117.7	1.9
1988	-	-	-	-	-	-	-	-	-	-	119.4	1.4	-	-	-	-	-	-	-	-	-	-	122.5	2.6
1989	-	-	-	-	-	-	-	-	-	-	122.8	0.2	-	-	-	-	-	-	-	-	-	-	126.1	2.7
1990	-	-	-	-	-	-	-	-	-	-	127.5	1.1	-	-	-	-	-	-	-	-	-	-	129.8	1.8
1991	-	-	-	-	-	-	-	-	-	-	131.5	1.3	-	-	-	-	-	-	-	-	-	-	133.6	1.6
1992	-	-	-	-	-	-	-	-	-	-	138.5	3.7	-	-	-	-	-	-	-	-	-	-	141.4	2.1
1993	-	-	-	-	-	-	-	-	-	-	146.6	3.7	-	-	-	-	-	-	-	-	-	-	150.8	2.9
1994	-	-	-	-	-	-	-	-	-	-	154.9	2.7	-	-	-	-	-	-	-	-	-	-	160.5	3.6
1995	-	-	-	-	-	-	-	-	-	-	162.9	1.5	-	-	-	-	-	-	-	-	-	-	-	-

Source: U.S. Department of Labor, Bureau of Labor Statistics, Division of Consumer Prices and Price Indexes. - indicates no data collected for period.

Seattle-Everett, WA
Consumer Price Index - Urban Wage Earners
Base 1982-1984 = 100
Entertainment

For 1975-1995. Columns headed % show percentile change in the index from the previous period for which an index is available.

Year	Jan Index	%	Feb Index	%	Mar Index	%	Apr Index	%	May Index	%	Jun Index	%	Jul Index	%	Aug Index	%	Sep Index	%	Oct Index	%	Nov Index	%	Dec Index	%
1975	-	-	-	-	-	-	-	-	-	-	-	-	-	-	-	-	-	-	-	-	58.9	-	-	-
1976	-	-	59.1	0.3	-	-	-	-	59.5	0.7	-	-	-	-	60.0	0.8	-	-	-	-	61.2	2.0	-	-
1977	-	-	62.9	2.8	-	-	-	-	62.8	-0.2	-	-	-	-	62.9	0.2	-	-	-	-	64.2	2.1	-	-
1978	64.4	0.3	-	-	64.5	0.2	-	-	66.7	3.4	-	-	67.3	0.9	-	-	66.6	-1.0	-	-	68.3	2.6	-	-
1979	68.9	0.9	-	-	68.8	-0.1	-	-	69.9	1.6	-	-	70.5	0.9	-	-	73.5	4.3	-	-	74.9	1.9	-	-
1980	76.1	1.6	-	-	77.9	2.4	-	-	78.0	0.1	-	-	79.9	2.4	-	-	82.8	3.6	-	-	84.2	1.7	-	-
1981	87.3	3.7	-	-	83.4	-4.5	-	-	86.0	3.1	-	-	86.4	0.5	-	-	88.6	2.5	-	-	89.4	0.9	-	-
1982	91.1	1.9	-	-	91.3	0.2	-	-	93.6	2.5	-	-	94.3	0.7	-	-	97.1	3.0	-	-	96.6	-0.5	-	-
1983	96.8	0.2	-	-	100.0	3.3	-	-	96.5	-3.5	-	-	99.7	3.3	-	-	102.5	2.8	-	-	103.2	0.7	-	-
1984	104.4	1.2	-	-	105.6	1.1	-	-	106.0	0.4	-	-	105.9	-0.1	-	-	104.7	-1.1	-	-	106.7	1.9	-	-
1985	107.4	0.7	-	-	108.2	0.7	-	-	107.0	-1.1	-	-	109.5	2.3	-	-	106.5	-2.7	-	-	109.2	2.5	-	-
1986	109.7	0.5	-	-	108.7	-0.9	-	-	105.3	-3.1	-	-	108.7	3.2	-	-	107.5	-1.1	-	-	108.0	0.5	108.1	0.1
1987	-	-	-	-	-	-	-	-	-	-	114.5	5.9	-	-	-	-	-	-	-	-	-	-	116.6	1.8
1988	-	-	-	-	-	-	-	-	-	-	118.2	1.4	-	-	-	-	-	-	-	-	-	-	121.1	2.5
1989	-	-	-	-	-	-	-	-	-	-	121.2	0.1	-	-	-	-	-	-	-	-	-	-	124.8	3.0
1990	-	-	-	-	-	-	-	-	-	-	126.1	1.0	-	-	-	-	-	-	-	-	-	-	128.0	1.5
1991	-	-	-	-	-	-	-	-	-	-	129.8	1.4	-	-	-	-	-	-	-	-	-	-	132.4	2.0
1992	-	-	-	-	-	-	-	-	-	-	137.7	4.0	-	-	-	-	-	-	-	-	-	-	140.7	2.2
1993	-	-	-	-	-	-	-	-	-	-	146.8	4.3	-	-	-	-	-	-	-	-	-	-	150.9	2.8
1994	-	-	-	-	-	-	-	-	-	-	155.0	2.7	-	-	-	-	-	-	-	-	-	-	161.2	4.0
1995	-	-	-	-	-	-	-	-	-	-	163.7	1.6	-	-	-	-	-	-	-	-	-	-	-	-

Source: U.S. Department of Labor, Bureau of Labor Statistics, Division of Consumer Prices and Price Indexes. - indicates no data collected for period.

Seattle-Everett, WA
Consumer Price Index - All Urban Consumers
Base 1982-1984 = 100
Other Goods and Services

For 1975-1995. Columns headed % show percentile change in the index from the previous period for which an index is available.

Year	Jan Index	%	Feb Index	%	Mar Index	%	Apr Index	%	May Index	%	Jun Index	%	Jul Index	%	Aug Index	%	Sep Index	%	Oct Index	%	Nov Index	%	Dec Index	%
1975	-	-	-	-	-	-	-	-	-	-	-	-	-	-	-	-	-	-	-	-	48.2	-	-	-
1976	-	-	49.2	2.1	-	-	-	-	50.6	2.8	-	-	-	-	50.9	0.6	-	-	-	-	52.3	2.8	-	-
1977	-	-	53.3	1.9	-	-	-	-	53.6	0.6	-	-	-	-	54.2	1.1	-	-	-	-	55.6	2.6	-	-
1978	55.8	0.4	-	-	55.9	0.2	-	-	56.6	1.3	-	-	57.3	1.2	-	-	58.9	2.8	-	-	60.9	3.4	-	-
1979	60.8	-0.2	-	-	62.5	2.8	-	-	62.4	-0.2	-	-	63.6	1.9	-	-	66.7	4.9	-	-	67.3	0.9	-	-
1980	67.9	0.9	-	-	69.9	2.9	-	-	70.9	1.4	-	-	71.2	0.4	-	-	73.6	3.4	-	-	73.9	0.4	-	-
1981	74.7	1.1	-	-	75.2	0.7	-	-	76.7	2.0	-	-	79.4	3.5	-	-	84.3	6.2	-	-	86.7	2.8	-	-
1982	88.1	1.6	-	-	89.2	1.2	-	-	90.3	1.2	-	-	91.1	0.9	-	-	92.9	2.0	-	-	96.0	3.3	-	-
1983	98.1	2.2	-	-	99.1	1.0	-	-	99.4	0.3	-	-	99.6	0.2	-	-	102.5	2.9	-	-	105.6	3.0	-	-
1984	106.4	0.8	-	-	106.5	0.1	-	-	105.9	-0.6	-	-	106.6	0.7	-	-	108.2	1.5	-	-	108.8	0.6	-	-
1985	110.6	1.7	-	-	110.5	-0.1	-	-	109.8	-0.6	-	-	111.9	1.9	-	-	112.7	0.7	-	-	114.9	2.0	-	-
1986	115.0	0.1	-	-	114.3	-0.6	-	-	117.0	2.4	-	-	117.7	0.6	-	-	118.5	0.7	-	-	118.6	0.1	119.8	1.0
1987	-	-	-	-	-	-	-	-	-	-	127.3	6.3	-	-	-	-	-	-	-	-	-	-	130.1	2.2
1988	-	-	-	-	-	-	-	-	-	-	134.7	3.5	-	-	-	-	-	-	-	-	-	-	137.3	1.9
1989	-	-	-	-	-	-	-	-	-	-	141.6	3.1	-	-	-	-	-	-	-	-	-	-	148.5	4.9
1990	-	-	-	-	-	-	-	-	-	-	155.0	4.4	-	-	-	-	-	-	-	-	-	-	160.8	3.7
1991	-	-	-	-	-	-	-	-	-	-	169.0	5.1	-	-	-	-	-	-	-	-	-	-	175.4	3.8
1992	-	-	-	-	-	-	-	-	-	-	179.8	2.5	-	-	-	-	-	-	-	-	-	-	187.5	4.3
1993	-	-	-	-	-	-	-	-	-	-	201.1	7.3	-	-	-	-	-	-	-	-	-	-	201.3	0.1
1994	-	-	-	-	-	-	-	-	-	-	202.1	0.4	-	-	-	-	-	-	-	-	-	-	204.0	0.9
1995	-	-	-	-	-	-	-	-	-	-	209.1	2.5	-	-	-	-	-	-	-	-	-	-	-	-

Source: U.S. Department of Labor, Bureau of Labor Statistics, Division of Consumer Prices and Price Indexes. - indicates no data collected for period.

Seattle-Everett, WA
Consumer Price Index - Urban Wage Earners
Base 1982-1984 = 100
Other Goods and Services

For 1975-1995. Columns headed % show percentile change in the index from the previous period for which an index is available.

Year	Jan Index	%	Feb Index	%	Mar Index	%	Apr Index	%	May Index	%	Jun Index	%	Jul Index	%	Aug Index	%	Sep Index	%	Oct Index	%	Nov Index	%	Dec Index	%
1975	-	-	-	-	-	-	-	-	-	-	-	-	-	-	-	-	-	-	-	-	49.9	-	-	-
1976	-	-	50.9	2.0	-	-	-	-	52.4	2.9	-	-	-	-	52.7	0.6	-	-	-	-	54.2	2.8	-	-
1977	-	-	55.1	1.7	-	-	-	-	55.5	0.7	-	-	-	-	56.2	1.3	-	-	-	-	57.6	2.5	-	-
1978	58.1	0.9	-	-	58.4	0.5	-	-	59.0	1.0	-	-	59.9	1.5	-	-	61.4	2.5	-	-	62.0	1.0	-	-
1979	62.5	0.8	-	-	64.1	2.6	-	-	63.7	-0.6	-	-	64.6	1.4	-	-	67.0	3.7	-	-	67.9	1.3	-	-
1980	68.6	1.0	-	-	70.1	2.2	-	-	70.5	0.6	-	-	71.1	0.9	-	-	73.4	3.2	-	-	73.9	0.7	-	-
1981	75.5	2.2	-	-	75.8	0.4	-	-	77.5	2.2	-	-	79.0	1.9	-	-	83.5	5.7	-	-	85.4	2.3	-	-
1982	87.3	2.2	-	-	88.7	1.6	-	-	89.6	1.0	-	-	90.6	1.1	-	-	92.5	2.1	-	-	96.0	3.8	-	-
1983	98.6	2.7	-	-	99.6	1.0	-	-	99.8	0.2	-	-	100.2	0.4	-	-	103.1	2.9	-	-	105.5	2.3	-	-
1984	106.5	0.9	-	-	106.5	0.0	-	-	106.1	-0.4	-	-	107.0	0.8	-	-	108.0	0.9	-	-	108.6	0.6	-	-
1985	110.6	1.8	-	-	110.6	0.0	-	-	109.8	-0.7	-	-	112.1	2.1	-	-	112.6	0.4	-	-	114.6	1.8	-	-
1986	114.7	0.1	-	-	113.9	-0.7	-	-	117.3	3.0	-	-	118.2	0.8	-	-	118.9	0.6	-	-	118.5	-0.3	119.9	1.2
1987	-	-	-	-	-	-	-	-	-	-	125.9	5.0	-	-	-	-	-	-	-	-	-	-	129.5	2.9
1988	-	-	-	-	-	-	-	-	-	-	134.2	3.6	-	-	-	-	-	-	-	-	-	-	137.2	2.2
1989	-	-	-	-	-	-	-	-	-	-	141.9	3.4	-	-	-	-	-	-	-	-	-	-	149.2	5.1
1990	-	-	-	-	-	-	-	-	-	-	155.5	4.2	-	-	-	-	-	-	-	-	-	-	161.3	3.7
1991	-	-	-	-	-	-	-	-	-	-	168.4	4.4	-	-	-	-	-	-	-	-	-	-	175.5	4.2
1992	-	-	-	-	-	-	-	-	-	-	179.6	2.3	-	-	-	-	-	-	-	-	-	-	186.4	3.8
1993	-	-	-	-	-	-	-	-	-	-	199.8	7.2	-	-	-	-	-	-	-	-	-	-	200.4	0.3
1994	-	-	-	-	-	-	-	-	-	-	202.1	0.8	-	-	-	-	-	-	-	-	-	-	204.1	1.0
1995	-	-	-	-	-	-	-	-	-	-	208.8	2.3	-	-	-	-	-	-	-	-	-	-	-	-

Source: U.S. Department of Labor, Bureau of Labor Statistics, Division of Consumer Prices and Price Indexes. - indicates no data collected for period.

St. Louis, MO-IL
Consumer Price Index - All Urban Consumers
Base 1982-1984 = 100
Annual Averages

For 1917-1995. Columns headed % show percentile change in the index from the previous period for which an index is available.

Year	All Items Index	%	Food & Beverage Index	%	Housing Index	%	Apparel & Upkeep Index	%	Transportation Index	%	Medical Care Index	%	Entertainment Index	%	Other Goods & Services Index	%
1917	-	-	-	-	-	-	-	-	-	-	-	-	-	-	-	-
1918	14.8	-	-	-	-	-	-	-	-	-	-	-	-	-	-	-
1919	16.8	13.5	-	-	-	-	-	-	-	-	-	-	-	-	-	-
1920	19.9	18.5	-	-	-	-	-	-	-	-	-	-	-	-	-	-
1921	17.4	-12.6	-	-	-	-	-	-	-	-	-	-	-	-	-	-
1922	16.3	-6.3	-	-	-	-	-	-	-	-	-	-	-	-	-	-
1923	16.7	2.5	-	-	-	-	-	-	-	-	-	-	-	-	-	-
1924	16.8	0.6	-	-	-	-	-	-	-	-	-	-	-	-	-	-
1925	17.3	3.0	-	-	-	-	-	-	-	-	-	-	-	-	-	-
1926	17.6	1.7	-	-	-	-	-	-	-	-	-	-	-	-	-	-
1927	17.3	-1.7	-	-	-	-	-	-	-	-	-	-	-	-	-	-
1928	16.9	-2.3	-	-	-	-	-	-	-	-	-	-	-	-	-	-
1929	17.1	1.2	-	-	-	-	-	-	-	-	-	-	-	-	-	-
1930	16.7	-2.3	-	-	-	-	-	-	-	-	-	-	-	-	-	-
1931	15.0	-10.2	-	-	-	-	-	-	-	-	-	-	-	-	-	-
1932	13.4	-10.7	-	-	-	-	-	-	-	-	-	-	-	-	-	-
1933	12.8	-4.5	-	-	-	-	-	-	-	-	-	-	-	-	-	-
1934	13.3	3.9	-	-	-	-	-	-	-	-	-	-	-	-	-	-
1935	13.7	3.0	-	-	-	-	-	-	-	-	-	-	-	-	-	-
1936	13.8	0.7	-	-	-	-	-	-	-	-	-	-	-	-	-	-
1937	14.3	3.6	-	-	-	-	-	-	-	-	-	-	-	-	-	-
1938	13.9	-2.8	-	-	-	-	-	-	-	-	-	-	-	-	-	-
1939	13.8	-0.7	-	-	-	-	-	-	-	-	-	-	-	-	-	-
1940	13.9	0.7	-	-	-	-	-	-	-	-	-	-	-	-	-	-
1941	14.6	5.0	-	-	-	-	-	-	-	-	-	-	-	-	-	-
1942	16.2	11.0	-	-	-	-	-	-	-	-	-	-	-	-	-	-
1943	17.0	4.9	-	-	-	-	-	-	-	-	-	-	-	-	-	-
1944	17.3	1.8	-	-	-	-	-	-	-	-	-	-	-	-	-	-
1945	17.6	1.7	-	-	-	-	-	-	-	-	-	-	-	-	-	-
1946	19.1	8.5	-	-	-	-	-	-	-	-	-	-	-	-	-	-
1947	22.2	16.2	-	-	-	-	-	-	18.2	-	13.2	-	-	-	-	-
1948	23.9	7.7	-	-	-	-	-	-	19.8	8.8	14.0	6.1	-	-	-	-
1949	23.6	-1.3	-	-	-	-	-	-	20.8	5.1	14.4	2.9	-	-	-	-
1950	23.9	1.3	-	-	-	-	-	-	21.3	2.4	14.5	0.7	-	-	-	-
1951	25.9	8.4	-	-	-	-	-	-	23.5	10.3	15.5	6.9	-	-	-	-
1952	26.7	3.1	-	-	-	-	-	-	25.8	9.8	18.0	16.1	-	-	-	-
1953	27.0	1.1	-	-	-	-	44.1	-	26.8	3.9	18.5	2.8	-	-	-	-
1954	27.1	0.4	-	-	-	-	44.0	-0.2	26.0	-3.0	18.9	2.2	-	-	-	-
1955	27.0	-0.4	-	-	-	-	44.0	0.0	26.1	0.4	19.5	3.2	-	-	-	-
1956	27.2	0.7	-	-	-	-	44.4	0.9	26.3	0.8	19.9	2.1	-	-	-	-
1957	28.1	3.3	-	-	-	-	45.0	1.4	28.0	6.5	21.5	8.0	-	-	-	-
1958	29.0	3.2	-	-	-	-	45.8	1.8	29.6	5.7	22.2	3.3	-	-	-	-
1959	29.4	1.4	-	-	-	-	46.2	0.9	31.6	6.8	23.3	5.0	-	-	-	-
1960	29.5	0.3	-	-	-	-	47.1	1.9	31.4	-0.6	23.7	1.7	-	-	-	-
1961	30.0	1.7	-	-	-	-	47.6	1.1	32.0	1.9	24.2	2.1	-	-	-	-

[Continued]

828

St. Louis, MO-IL
Consumer Price Index - All Urban Consumers
Base 1982-1984 = 100
Annual Averages

[Continued]

For 1917-1995. Columns headed % show percentile change in the index from the previous period for which an index is available.

Year	All Items		Food & Beverage		Housing		Apparel & Upkeep		Trans-portation		Medical Care		Entertain-ment		Other Goods & Services	
	Index	%	Index	%	Index	%	Index	%	Index	%	Index	%	Index	%	Index	%
1962	30.3	1.0	-	-	-	-	47.6	0.0	32.4	1.3	25.5	5.4	-	-	-	-
1963	30.6	1.0	-	-	-	-	48.0	0.8	32.3	-0.3	25.7	0.8	-	-	-	-
1964	31.2	2.0	-	-	-	-	48.7	1.5	32.7	1.2	25.9	0.8	-	-	-	-
1965	31.7	1.6	-	-	-	-	49.2	1.0	33.0	0.9	26.8	3.5	-	-	-	-
1966	32.7	3.2	-	-	-	-	50.7	3.0	34.0	3.0	28.2	5.2	-	-	-	-
1967	33.7	3.1	-	-	-	-	52.4	3.4	35.3	3.8	29.7	5.3	-	-	-	-
1968	35.0	3.9	-	-	-	-	55.4	5.7	36.0	2.0	31.1	4.7	-	-	-	-
1969	36.8	5.1	-	-	-	-	58.2	5.1	37.2	3.3	33.0	6.1	-	-	-	-
1970	38.8	5.4	-	-	-	-	60.4	3.8	39.4	5.9	35.2	6.7	-	-	-	-
1971	40.3	3.9	-	-	-	-	62.4	3.3	42.1	6.9	36.7	4.3	-	-	-	-
1972	41.2	2.2	-	-	-	-	63.0	1.0	42.4	0.7	37.4	1.9	-	-	-	-
1973	43.5	5.6	-	-	-	-	64.5	2.4	43.8	3.3	38.6	3.2	-	-	-	-
1974	47.9	10.1	-	-	-	-	68.0	5.4	47.4	8.2	41.8	8.3	-	-	-	-
1975	52.6	9.8	-	-	-	-	70.8	4.1	51.5	8.6	46.3	10.8	-	-	-	-
1976	55.6	5.7	62.5	-	50.5	-	74.3	4.9	56.1	8.9	50.2	8.4	66.4	-	57.2	-
1977	59.5	7.0	66.8	6.9	54.0	6.9	79.2	6.6	59.5	6.1	55.4	10.4	70.2	5.7	60.5	5.8
1978	64.5	8.4	72.7	8.8	59.4	10.0	80.2	1.3	63.5	6.7	59.6	7.6	77.5	10.4	64.6	6.8
1979	72.7	12.7	81.0	11.4	67.9	14.3	85.2	6.2	73.8	16.2	64.8	8.7	81.5	5.2	68.7	6.3
1980	82.5	13.5	87.1	7.5	79.8	17.5	91.7	7.6	85.1	15.3	72.9	12.5	88.2	8.2	74.7	8.7
1981	90.1	9.2	93.5	7.3	87.6	9.8	95.3	3.9	94.4	10.9	81.8	12.2	93.9	6.5	82.0	9.8
1982	96.6	7.2	97.1	3.9	96.6	10.3	97.6	2.4	97.8	3.6	93.4	14.2	96.3	2.6	90.6	10.5
1983	100.1	3.6	99.7	2.7	100.4	3.9	100.8	3.3	99.2	1.4	100.9	8.0	101.3	5.2	101.0	11.5
1984	103.3	3.2	103.2	3.5	102.9	2.5	101.6	0.8	102.9	3.7	105.8	4.9	102.4	1.1	108.5	7.4
1985	107.1	3.7	105.7	2.4	107.8	4.8	104.4	2.8	105.3	2.3	111.0	4.9	106.0	3.5	115.4	6.4
1986	108.6	1.4	109.7	3.8	110.4	2.4	102.7	-1.6	100.3	-4.7	120.3	8.4	110.2	4.0	122.1	5.8
1987	112.2	3.3	114.0	3.9	112.1	1.5	107.6	4.8	103.9	3.6	127.9	6.3	113.9	3.4	128.1	4.9
1988	115.7	3.1	117.7	3.2	114.9	2.5	112.5	4.6	106.0	2.0	135.6	6.0	117.9	3.5	136.8	6.8
1989	121.8	5.3	125.8	6.9	120.3	4.7	118.4	5.2	110.5	4.2	145.6	7.4	122.3	3.7	145.4	6.3
1990	128.1	5.2	134.9	7.2	124.9	3.8	120.9	2.1	117.4	6.2	159.0	9.2	124.4	1.7	153.6	5.6
1991	132.1	3.1	139.6	3.5	127.7	2.2	122.5	1.3	118.5	0.9	171.7	8.0	134.5	8.1	163.4	6.4
1992	134.7	2.0	140.1	0.4	129.7	1.6	121.7	-0.7	121.9	2.9	181.0	5.4	137.8	2.5	172.3	5.4
1993	137.5	2.1	140.1	0.0	133.0	2.5	122.8	0.9	125.1	2.6	191.5	5.8	137.3	-0.4	175.9	2.1
1994	141.3	2.8	144.0	2.8	136.7	2.8	125.1	1.9	129.2	3.3	201.7	5.3	142.6	3.9	174.0	-1.1
1995	-	-	-	-	-	-	-	-	-	-	-	-	-	-	-	-

Source: U.S. Department of Labor, Bureau of Labor Statistics, Division of Consumer Prices and Price Indexes. - indicates no data collected for period.

St. Louis, MO-IL
Consumer Price Index - Urban Wage Earners
Base 1982-1984 = 100
Annual Averages

For 1917-1995. Columns headed % show percentile change in the index from the previous period for which an index is available.

Year	All Items		Food & Beverage		Housing		Apparel & Upkeep		Trans- portation		Medical Care		Entertain- ment		Other Goods & Services	
	Index	%	Index	%	Index	%	Index	%	Index	%	Index	%	Index	%	Index	%
1917	-	-	-	-	-	-	-	-	-	-	-	-	-	-	-	-
1918	15.0	-	-	-	-	-	-	-	-	-	-	-	-	-	-	-
1919	17.0	13.3	-	-	-	-	-	-	-	-	-	-	-	-	-	-
1920	20.1	18.2	-	-	-	-	-	-	-	-	-	-	-	-	-	-
1921	17.6	-12.4	-	-	-	-	-	-	-	-	-	-	-	-	-	-
1922	16.5	-6.3	-	-	-	-	-	-	-	-	-	-	-	-	-	-
1923	16.8	1.8	-	-	-	-	-	-	-	-	-	-	-	-	-	-
1924	17.0	1.2	-	-	-	-	-	-	-	-	-	-	-	-	-	-
1925	17.5	2.9	-	-	-	-	-	-	-	-	-	-	-	-	-	-
1926	17.7	1.1	-	-	-	-	-	-	-	-	-	-	-	-	-	-
1927	17.5	-1.1	-	-	-	-	-	-	-	-	-	-	-	-	-	-
1928	17.1	-2.3	-	-	-	-	-	-	-	-	-	-	-	-	-	-
1929	17.2	0.6	-	-	-	-	-	-	-	-	-	-	-	-	-	-
1930	16.9	-1.7	-	-	-	-	-	-	-	-	-	-	-	-	-	-
1931	15.1	-10.7	-	-	-	-	-	-	-	-	-	-	-	-	-	-
1932	13.6	-9.9	-	-	-	-	-	-	-	-	-	-	-	-	-	-
1933	12.9	-5.1	-	-	-	-	-	-	-	-	-	-	-	-	-	-
1934	13.4	3.9	-	-	-	-	-	-	-	-	-	-	-	-	-	-
1935	13.8	3.0	-	-	-	-	-	-	-	-	-	-	-	-	-	-
1936	14.0	1.4	-	-	-	-	-	-	-	-	-	-	-	-	-	-
1937	14.4	2.9	-	-	-	-	-	-	-	-	-	-	-	-	-	-
1938	14.1	-2.1	-	-	-	-	-	-	-	-	-	-	-	-	-	-
1939	13.9	-1.4	-	-	-	-	-	-	-	-	-	-	-	-	-	-
1940	14.0	0.7	-	-	-	-	-	-	-	-	-	-	-	-	-	-
1941	14.7	5.0	-	-	-	-	-	-	-	-	-	-	-	-	-	-
1942	16.3	10.9	-	-	-	-	-	-	-	-	-	-	-	-	-	-
1943	17.2	5.5	-	-	-	-	-	-	-	-	-	-	-	-	-	-
1944	17.5	1.7	-	-	-	-	-	-	-	-	-	-	-	-	-	-
1945	17.8	1.7	-	-	-	-	-	-	-	-	-	-	-	-	-	-
1946	19.3	8.4	-	-	-	-	-	-	-	-	-	-	-	-	-	-
1947	22.4	16.1	-	-	-	-	-	-	18.5	-	13.1	-	-	-	-	-
1948	24.1	7.6	-	-	-	-	-	-	20.1	8.6	13.9	6.1	-	-	-	-
1949	23.8	-1.2	-	-	-	-	-	-	21.2	5.5	14.3	2.9	-	-	-	-
1950	24.1	1.3	-	-	-	-	-	-	21.7	2.4	14.4	0.7	-	-	-	-
1951	26.1	8.3	-	-	-	-	-	-	23.9	10.1	15.3	6.3	-	-	-	-
1952	27.0	3.4	-	-	-	-	-	-	26.2	9.6	17.9	17.0	-	-	-	-
1953	27.2	0.7	-	-	-	-	45.0	-	27.2	3.8	18.3	2.2	-	-	-	-
1954	27.3	0.4	-	-	-	-	44.9	-0.2	26.4	-2.9	18.7	2.2	-	-	-	-
1955	27.2	-0.4	-	-	-	-	44.8	-0.2	26.5	0.4	19.3	3.2	-	-	-	-
1956	27.5	1.1	-	-	-	-	45.3	1.1	26.7	0.8	19.7	2.1	-	-	-	-
1957	28.4	3.3	-	-	-	-	45.9	1.3	28.5	6.7	21.3	8.1	-	-	-	-
1958	29.2	2.8	-	-	-	-	46.7	1.7	30.1	5.6	22.0	3.3	-	-	-	-
1959	29.6	1.4	-	-	-	-	47.1	0.9	32.1	6.6	23.1	5.0	-	-	-	-
1960	29.8	0.7	-	-	-	-	48.0	1.9	31.9	-0.6	23.5	1.7	-	-	-	-
1961	30.3	1.7	-	-	-	-	48.5	1.0	32.5	1.9	24.0	2.1	-	-	-	-

[Continued]

St. Louis, MO-IL
Consumer Price Index - Urban Wage Earners
Base 1982-1984 = 100
Annual Averages
[Continued]

For 1917-1995. Columns headed % show percentile change in the index from the previous period for which an index is available.

Year	All Items		Food & Beverage		Housing		Apparel & Upkeep		Trans- portation		Medical Care		Entertain- ment		Other Goods & Services	
	Index	%	Index	%	Index	%	Index	%	Index	%	Index	%	Index	%	Index	%
1962	30.6	1.0	-	-	-	-	48.5	0.0	32.9	1.2	25.3	5.4	-	-	-	-
1963	30.9	1.0	-	-	-	-	48.9	0.8	32.8	-0.3	25.5	0.8	-	-	-	-
1964	31.5	1.9	-	-	-	-	49.6	1.4	33.2	1.2	25.6	0.4	-	-	-	-
1965	32.0	1.6	-	-	-	-	50.1	1.0	33.6	1.2	26.5	3.5	-	-	-	-
1966	33.0	3.1	-	-	-	-	51.6	3.0	34.6	3.0	28.0	5.7	-	-	-	-
1967	34.0	3.0	-	-	-	-	53.4	3.5	35.8	3.5	29.4	5.0	-	-	-	-
1968	35.3	3.8	-	-	-	-	56.5	5.8	36.6	2.2	30.8	4.8	-	-	-	-
1969	37.1	5.1	-	-	-	-	59.3	5.0	37.8	3.3	32.7	6.2	-	-	-	-
1970	39.2	5.7	-	-	-	-	61.6	3.9	40.1	6.1	34.8	6.4	-	-	-	-
1971	40.7	3.8	-	-	-	-	63.6	3.2	42.8	6.7	36.3	4.3	-	-	-	-
1972	41.6	2.2	-	-	-	-	64.2	0.9	43.1	0.7	37.0	1.9	-	-	-	-
1973	43.9	5.5	-	-	-	-	65.7	2.3	44.5	3.2	38.2	3.2	-	-	-	-
1974	48.3	10.0	-	-	-	-	69.3	5.5	48.2	8.3	41.4	8.4	-	-	-	-
1975	53.1	9.9	-	-	-	-	72.2	4.2	52.3	8.5	45.9	10.9	-	-	-	-
1976	56.1	5.6	62.5	-	51.0	-	75.7	4.8	57.0	9.0	49.7	8.3	72.4	-	56.8	-
1977	60.0	7.0	66.8	6.9	54.5	6.9	80.8	6.7	60.5	6.1	55.0	10.7	76.6	5.8	60.0	5.6
1978	64.7	7.8	72.5	8.5	59.9	9.9	80.9	0.1	63.1	4.3	59.5	8.2	82.3	7.4	64.2	7.0
1979	73.2	13.1	81.5	12.4	68.9	15.0	84.4	4.3	73.3	16.2	65.1	9.4	86.2	4.7	68.7	7.0
1980	83.4	13.9	87.4	7.2	81.0	17.6	90.5	7.2	85.6	16.8	73.5	12.9	93.6	8.6	75.5	9.9
1981	90.9	9.0	93.6	7.1	88.7	9.5	95.3	5.3	94.5	10.4	82.2	11.8	96.3	2.9	82.6	9.4
1982	97.1	6.8	97.1	3.7	97.8	10.3	97.5	2.3	97.8	3.5	93.4	13.6	96.5	0.2	90.6	9.7
1983	100.3	3.3	99.8	2.8	100.8	3.1	101.0	3.6	99.1	1.3	100.7	7.8	101.4	5.1	101.4	11.9
1984	102.6	2.3	103.2	3.4	101.3	0.5	101.5	0.5	103.2	4.1	105.9	5.2	102.1	0.7	108.0	6.5
1985	107.1	4.4	105.6	2.3	109.1	7.7	104.1	2.6	105.3	2.0	111.0	4.8	105.1	2.9	114.6	6.1
1986	108.2	1.0	109.8	4.0	111.9	2.6	102.4	-1.6	99.2	-5.8	119.8	7.9	109.2	3.9	121.1	5.7
1987	111.8	3.3	114.0	3.8	113.9	1.8	107.7	5.2	103.2	4.0	127.5	6.4	112.9	3.4	126.8	4.7
1988	115.4	3.2	117.8	3.3	116.6	2.4	112.6	4.5	105.8	2.5	135.2	6.0	117.1	3.7	135.7	7.0
1989	121.5	5.3	125.8	6.8	122.0	4.6	118.5	5.2	110.1	4.1	145.6	7.7	121.3	3.6	144.7	6.6
1990	127.5	4.9	134.8	7.2	126.7	3.9	121.2	2.3	115.5	4.9	158.3	8.7	123.3	1.6	153.7	6.2
1991	131.5	3.1	139.6	3.6	129.5	2.2	122.8	1.3	117.2	1.5	170.6	7.8	132.9	7.8	165.4	7.6
1992	134.3	2.1	140.2	0.4	131.9	1.9	122.1	-0.6	121.0	3.2	180.0	5.5	135.7	2.1	175.4	6.0
1993	136.9	1.9	140.3	0.1	135.2	2.5	123.0	0.7	124.6	3.0	190.5	5.8	135.3	-0.3	175.9	0.3
1994	140.7	2.8	144.3	2.9	138.9	2.7	125.9	2.4	129.2	3.7	200.1	5.0	140.7	4.0	170.4	-3.1
1995	-	-	-	-	-	-	-	-	-	-	-	-	-	-	-	-

Source: U.S. Department of Labor, Bureau of Labor Statistics, Division of Consumer Prices and Price Indexes. - indicates no data collected for period.

St. Louis, MO-IL
Consumer Price Index - All Urban Consumers
Base 1982-1984 = 100
All Items

For 1917-1995. Columns headed % show percentile change in the index from the previous period for which an index is available.

Year	Jan Index	%	Feb Index	%	Mar Index	%	Apr Index	%	May Index	%	Jun Index	%	Jul Index	%	Aug Index	%	Sep Index	%	Oct Index	%	Nov Index	%	Dec Index	%
1917	-	-	-	-	-	-	-	-	-	-	-	-	-	-	-	-	-	-	-	-	-	-	13.7	-
1918	-	-	-	-	-	-	-	-	-	-	-	-	-	-	-	-	-	-	-	-	-	-	16.0	16.8
1919	-	-	-	-	-	-	-	-	-	-	16.2	1.3	-	-	-	-	-	-	-	-	-	-	18.4	13.6
1920	-	-	-	-	-	-	-	-	-	-	21.1	14.7	-	-	-	-	-	-	-	-	-	-	18.8	-10.9
1921	-	-	-	-	-	-	-	-	17.2	-8.5	-	-	-	-	-	-	17.2	0.0	-	-	-	-	16.7	-2.9
1922	-	-	-	-	16.3	-2.4	-	-	-	-	16.5	1.2	-	-	-	-	16.2	-1.8	-	-	-	-	16.4	1.2
1923	-	-	-	-	16.5	0.6	-	-	-	-	16.6	0.6	-	-	-	-	16.9	1.8	-	-	-	-	16.8	-0.6
1924	-	-	-	-	16.7	-0.6	-	-	-	-	16.7	0.0	-	-	-	-	16.7	0.0	-	-	-	-	16.9	1.2
1925	-	-	-	-	-	-	-	-	-	-	17.3	2.4	-	-	-	-	-	-	-	-	-	-	17.7	2.3
1926	-	-	-	-	-	-	-	-	-	-	17.6	-0.6	-	-	-	-	-	-	-	-	-	-	17.6	0.0
1927	-	-	-	-	-	-	-	-	-	-	17.6	0.0	-	-	-	-	-	-	-	-	-	-	17.1	-2.8
1928	-	-	-	-	-	-	-	-	-	-	16.9	-1.2	-	-	-	-	-	-	-	-	-	-	16.9	0.0
1929	-	-	-	-	-	-	-	-	-	-	17.1	1.2	-	-	-	-	-	-	-	-	-	-	17.2	0.6
1930	-	-	-	-	-	-	-	-	-	-	16.8	-2.3	-	-	-	-	-	-	-	-	-	-	16.0	-4.8
1931	-	-	-	-	-	-	-	-	-	-	14.9	-6.9	-	-	-	-	-	-	-	-	-	-	14.2	-4.7
1932	-	-	-	-	-	-	-	-	-	-	13.4	-5.6	-	-	-	-	-	-	-	-	-	-	12.9	-3.7
1933	-	-	-	-	-	-	-	-	-	-	12.6	-2.3	-	-	-	-	-	-	-	-	-	-	12.9	2.4
1934	-	-	-	-	-	-	-	-	-	-	13.2	2.3	-	-	-	-	-	-	-	-	13.3	0.8	-	-
1935	-	-	-	-	13.6	2.3	-	-	-	-	-	-	13.7	0.7	-	-	-	-	13.7	0.0	-	-	-	-
1936	13.8	0.7	-	-	-	-	13.7	-0.7	-	-	-	-	13.9	1.5	-	-	14.1	1.4	-	-	-	-	13.9	-1.4
1937	-	-	-	-	14.2	2.2	-	-	-	-	14.3	0.7	-	-	-	-	14.5	1.4	-	-	-	-	14.3	-1.4
1938	-	-	-	-	14.0	-2.1	-	-	-	-	14.0	0.0	-	-	-	-	14.0	0.0	-	-	-	-	13.8	-1.4
1939	-	-	-	-	13.8	0.0	-	-	-	-	13.6	-1.4	-	-	-	-	14.0	2.9	-	-	-	-	13.8	-1.4
1940	-	-	-	-	13.8	0.0	-	-	-	-	13.8	0.0	-	-	-	-	13.9	0.7	13.9	0.0	13.9	0.0	14.1	1.4
1941	14.1	0.0	14.0	-0.7	14.1	0.7	14.2	0.7	14.2	0.0	14.5	2.1	14.5	0.0	14.6	0.7	15.0	2.7	15.1	0.7	15.3	1.3	15.4	0.7
1942	15.6	1.3	15.7	0.6	16.0	1.9	16.1	0.6	16.1	0.0	16.2	0.6	16.2	0.0	16.3	0.6	16.2	-0.6	16.4	1.2	16.5	0.6	16.7	1.2
1943	16.6	-0.6	16.7	0.6	16.9	1.2	17.1	1.2	17.3	1.2	17.2	-0.6	17.1	-0.6	17.1	0.0	17.1	0.0	17.1	0.0	17.1	0.0	17.1	0.0
1944	17.1	0.0	17.0	-0.6	17.1	0.6	17.2	0.6	17.3	0.6	17.3	0.0	17.5	1.2	17.4	-0.6	17.4	0.0	17.3	-0.6	17.4	0.6	17.4	0.0
1945	17.5	0.6	17.4	-0.6	17.4	0.0	17.4	0.0	17.6	1.1	17.7	0.6	17.7	0.0	17.7	0.0	17.6	-0.6	17.7	0.6	17.6	-0.6	17.9	1.7
1946	17.9	0.0	17.8	-0.6	17.9	0.6	18.0	0.6	18.0	0.0	18.3	1.7	19.5	6.6	19.9	2.1	19.9	0.0	20.4	2.5	21.0	2.9	21.1	0.5
1947	21.1	0.0	21.1	0.0	21.7	2.8	21.6	-0.5	21.5	-0.5	21.7	0.9	-	-	-	-	23.1	6.5	-	-	-	-	23.4	1.3
1948	-	-	-	-	23.4	0.0	-	-	-	-	24.0	2.6	-	-	-	-	24.4	1.7	-	-	-	-	23.9	-2.0
1949	-	-	-	-	23.6	-1.3	-	-	-	-	23.7	0.4	-	-	-	-	23.6	-0.4	-	-	-	-	23.4	-0.8
1950	-	-	-	-	23.4	0.0	-	-	-	-	23.5	0.4	-	-	-	-	24.2	3.0	-	-	-	-	24.9	2.9
1951	-	-	-	-	25.8	3.6	-	-	-	-	25.8	0.0	-	-	-	-	25.9	0.4	-	-	-	-	26.5	2.3
1952	-	-	-	-	26.5	0.0	-	-	-	-	26.8	1.1	-	-	-	-	26.8	0.0	-	-	-	-	26.7	-0.4
1953	-	-	-	-	26.6	-0.4	-	-	-	-	26.9	1.1	-	-	-	-	27.2	1.1	-	-	-	-	27.2	0.0
1954	-	-	-	-	27.2	0.0	-	-	-	-	27.3	0.4	-	-	-	-	26.9	-1.5	-	-	-	-	26.8	-0.4
1955	-	-	-	-	26.9	0.4	-	-	-	-	26.9	0.0	-	-	-	-	27.1	0.7	-	-	-	-	27.0	-0.4
1956	-	-	-	-	26.9	-0.4	-	-	-	-	27.2	1.1	-	-	-	-	27.4	0.7	-	-	-	-	27.7	1.1
1957	-	-	-	-	27.9	0.7	-	-	-	-	28.1	0.7	-	-	-	-	28.3	0.7	-	-	-	-	28.4	0.4
1958	-	-	-	-	28.9	1.8	-	-	-	-	28.9	0.0	-	-	-	-	29.1	0.7	-	-	-	-	29.2	0.3
1959	-	-	-	-	29.3	0.3	-	-	-	-	29.4	0.3	-	-	-	-	29.4	0.0	-	-	-	-	29.4	0.0
1960	-	-	-	-	29.4	0.0	-	-	-	-	29.6	0.7	-	-	-	-	29.6	0.0	-	-	-	-	29.7	0.3
1961	-	-	-	-	30.0	1.0	-	-	-	-	30.0	0.0	-	-	-	-	30.0	0.0	-	-	-	-	30.1	0.3

[Continued]

St. Louis, MO-IL
Consumer Price Index - All Urban Consumers
Base 1982-1984 = 100
All Items
[Continued]

For 1917-1995. Columns headed % show percentile change in the index from the previous period for which an index is available.

Year	Jan Index	%	Feb Index	%	Mar Index	%	Apr Index	%	May Index	%	Jun Index	%	Jul Index	%	Aug Index	%	Sep Index	%	Oct Index	%	Nov Index	%	Dec Index	%
1962	-	-	-	-	30.2	0.3	-	-	-	-	30.1	-0.3	-	-	-	-	30.4	1.0	-	-	-	-	30.6	0.7
1963	-	-	-	-	30.5	-0.3	-	-	-	-	30.4	-0.3	-	-	-	-	30.7	1.0	-	-	-	-	30.9	0.7
1964	-	-	-	-	31.0	0.3	-	-	-	-	31.0	0.0	-	-	-	-	31.3	1.0	-	-	-	-	31.4	0.3
1965	-	-	-	-	31.4	0.0	-	-	-	-	31.7	1.0	-	-	-	-	31.7	0.0	-	-	-	-	32.2	1.6
1966	-	-	-	-	32.3	0.3	-	-	-	-	32.8	1.5	-	-	-	-	33.1	0.9	-	-	-	-	33.1	0.0
1967	-	-	-	-	33.3	0.6	-	-	-	-	33.6	0.9	-	-	-	-	33.9	0.9	-	-	-	-	34.3	1.2
1968	-	-	-	-	34.6	0.9	-	-	-	-	35.0	1.2	-	-	-	-	35.4	1.1	-	-	-	-	35.6	0.6
1969	-	-	-	-	36.2	1.7	-	-	-	-	36.6	1.1	-	-	-	-	37.2	1.6	-	-	-	-	37.7	1.3
1970	-	-	-	-	38.2	1.3	-	-	-	-	38.7	1.3	-	-	-	-	39.3	1.6	-	-	-	-	39.6	0.8
1971	-	-	-	-	39.8	0.5	-	-	-	-	40.4	1.5	-	-	-	-	40.6	0.5	-	-	-	-	40.7	0.2
1972	-	-	-	-	40.7	0.0	-	-	-	-	41.0	0.7	-	-	-	-	41.6	1.5	-	-	-	-	41.6	0.0
1973	-	-	-	-	42.5	2.2	-	-	-	-	43.1	1.4	-	-	-	-	44.5	3.2	-	-	-	-	45.0	1.1
1974	-	-	-	-	46.5	3.3	-	-	-	-	47.5	2.2	-	-	-	-	49.1	3.4	-	-	-	-	50.0	1.8
1975	-	-	-	-	51.3	2.6	-	-	-	-	52.8	2.9	-	-	-	-	53.5	1.3	-	-	-	-	54.0	0.9
1976	-	-	-	-	54.8	1.5	-	-	-	-	55.6	1.5	-	-	-	-	56.3	1.3	-	-	-	-	56.6	0.5
1977	-	-	-	-	58.3	3.0	-	-	-	-	59.7	2.4	-	-	-	-	60.4	1.2	-	-	-	-	60.8	0.7
1978	-	-	-	-	61.9	1.8	-	-	63.8	3.1	-	-	65.0	1.9	-	-	66.0	1.5	-	-	67.1	1.7	-	-
1979	68.5	2.1	-	-	70.2	2.5	-	-	71.1	1.3	-	-	73.0	2.7	-	-	74.8	2.5	-	-	76.0	1.6	-	-
1980	78.3	3.0	-	-	80.2	2.4	-	-	81.4	1.5	-	-	82.5	1.4	-	-	85.0	3.0	-	-	85.4	0.5	-	-
1981	86.1	0.8	-	-	87.3	1.4	-	-	90.2	3.3	-	-	90.7	0.6	-	-	92.0	1.4	-	-	92.2	0.2	-	-
1982	93.7	1.6	-	-	94.5	0.9	-	-	96.2	1.8	-	-	97.7	1.6	-	-	99.0	1.3	-	-	97.6	-1.4	-	-
1983	98.0	0.4	-	-	98.7	0.7	-	-	99.5	0.8	-	-	100.8	1.3	-	-	101.7	0.9	-	-	100.9	-0.8	-	-
1984	101.3	0.4	-	-	101.9	0.6	-	-	102.8	0.9	-	-	103.9	1.1	-	-	104.8	0.9	-	-	104.1	-0.7	-	-
1985	105.5	1.3	-	-	105.8	0.3	-	-	106.4	0.6	-	-	107.7	1.2	-	-	108.3	0.6	-	-	108.3	0.0	-	-
1986	108.5	0.2	-	-	107.5	-0.9	-	-	107.3	-0.2	-	-	109.6	2.1	-	-	109.7	0.1	-	-	109.0	-0.6	-	-
1987	110.0	0.9	-	-	110.7	0.6	-	-	111.3	0.5	-	-	112.7	1.3	-	-	114.3	1.4	-	-	113.1	-1.0	-	-
1988	113.4	0.3	-	-	114.2	0.7	-	-	114.1	-0.1	-	-	116.0	1.7	-	-	117.3	1.1	-	-	118.3	0.9	-	-
1989	118.4	0.1	-	-	119.4	0.8	-	-	121.5	1.8	-	-	123.1	1.3	-	-	123.9	0.6	-	-	123.1	-0.6	-	-
1990	125.1	1.6	-	-	127.2	1.7	-	-	126.7	-0.4	-	-	128.0	1.0	-	-	129.9	1.5	-	-	130.4	0.4	-	-
1991	131.0	0.5	-	-	130.7	-0.2	-	-	131.3	0.5	-	-	132.7	1.1	-	-	133.5	0.6	-	-	133.2	-0.2	-	-
1992	132.5	-0.5	-	-	132.6	0.1	-	-	134.0	1.1	-	-	135.7	1.3	-	-	136.6	0.7	-	-	136.0	-0.4	-	-
1993	135.9	-0.1	-	-	136.1	0.1	-	-	136.8	0.5	-	-	138.8	1.5	-	-	138.4	-0.3	-	-	138.1	-0.2	-	-
1994	138.6	0.4	-	-	139.7	0.8	-	-	140.0	0.2	-	-	141.9	1.4	-	-	143.4	1.1	-	-	143.3	-0.1	-	-
1995	142.9	-0.3	-	-	144.5	1.1	-	-	144.6	0.1	-	-	145.6	0.7	-	-	147.1	1.0	-	-	145.7	-1.0	-	-

Source: U.S. Department of Labor, Bureau of Labor Statistics, Division of Consumer Prices and Price Indexes. - indicates no data collected for period.

St. Louis, MO-IL
Consumer Price Index - Urban Wage Earners
Base 1982-1984 = 100
All Items

For 1917-1995. Columns headed % show percentile change in the index from the previous period for which an index is available.

Year	Jan Index	%	Feb Index	%	Mar Index	%	Apr Index	%	May Index	%	Jun Index	%	Jul Index	%	Aug Index	%	Sep Index	%	Oct Index	%	Nov Index	%	Dec Index	%
1917	-	-	-	-	-	-	-	-	-	-	-	-	-	-	-	-	-	-	-	-	-	-	13.9	-
1918	-	-	-	-	-	-	-	-	-	-	-	-	-	-	-	-	-	-	-	-	-	-	16.2	16.5
1919	-	-	-	-	-	-	-	-	-	-	16.4	1.2	-	-	-	-	-	-	-	-	-	-	18.6	13.4
1920	-	-	-	-	-	-	-	-	-	-	21.3	14.5	-	-	-	-	-	-	-	-	-	-	18.9	-11.3
1921	-	-	-	-	-	-	-	-	17.4	-7.9	-	-	-	-	-	-	17.4	0.0	-	-	-	-	16.9	-2.9
1922	-	-	-	-	16.5	-2.4	-	-	-	-	16.6	0.6	-	-	-	-	16.3	-1.8	-	-	-	-	16.5	1.2
1923	-	-	-	-	16.6	0.6	-	-	-	-	16.7	0.6	-	-	-	-	17.1	2.4	-	-	-	-	17.0	-0.6
1924	-	-	-	-	16.9	-0.6	-	-	-	-	16.9	0.0	-	-	-	-	16.9	0.0	-	-	-	-	17.1	1.2
1925	-	-	-	-	-	-	-	-	-	-	17.5	2.3	-	-	-	-	-	-	-	-	-	-	17.9	2.3
1926	-	-	-	-	-	-	-	-	-	-	17.8	-0.6	-	-	-	-	-	-	-	-	-	-	17.7	-0.6
1927	-	-	-	-	-	-	-	-	-	-	17.8	0.6	-	-	-	-	-	-	-	-	-	-	17.2	-3.4
1928	-	-	-	-	-	-	-	-	-	-	17.1	-0.6	-	-	-	-	-	-	-	-	-	-	17.1	0.0
1929	-	-	-	-	-	-	-	-	-	-	17.2	0.6	-	-	-	-	-	-	-	-	-	-	17.4	1.2
1930	-	-	-	-	-	-	-	-	-	-	17.0	-2.3	-	-	-	-	-	-	-	-	-	-	16.1	-5.3
1931	-	-	-	-	-	-	-	-	-	-	15.1	-6.2	-	-	-	-	-	-	-	-	-	-	14.3	-5.3
1932	-	-	-	-	-	-	-	-	-	-	13.5	-5.6	-	-	-	-	-	-	-	-	-	-	13.0	-3.7
1933	-	-	-	-	-	-	-	-	-	-	12.7	-2.3	-	-	-	-	-	-	-	-	-	-	13.1	3.1
1934	-	-	-	-	-	-	-	-	-	-	13.4	2.3	-	-	-	-	-	-	-	-	13.5	0.7	-	-
1935	-	-	-	-	13.8	2.2	-	-	-	-	-	-	13.8	0.0	-	-	-	-	13.8	0.0	-	-	-	-
1936	14.0	1.4	-	-	-	-	-	-	13.8	-1.4	-	-	14.0	1.4	-	-	14.2	1.4	-	-	-	-	14.0	-1.4
1937	-	-	-	-	14.3	2.1	-	-	-	-	14.5	1.4	-	-	-	-	14.6	0.7	-	-	-	-	14.4	-1.4
1938	-	-	-	-	14.1	-2.1	-	-	-	-	14.1	0.0	-	-	-	-	14.1	0.0	-	-	-	-	14.0	-0.7
1939	-	-	-	-	13.9	-0.7	-	-	-	-	13.7	-1.4	-	-	-	-	14.1	2.9	-	-	-	-	13.9	-1.4
1940	-	-	-	-	13.9	0.0	-	-	-	-	14.0	0.7	-	-	-	-	14.0	0.0	14.1	0.7	14.0	-0.7	14.2	1.4
1941	14.2	0.0	14.2	0.0	14.2	0.0	14.3	0.7	14.3	0.0	14.6	2.1	14.7	0.7	14.8	0.7	15.2	2.7	15.3	0.7	15.4	0.7	15.5	0.6
1942	15.7	1.3	15.9	1.3	16.1	1.3	16.2	0.6	16.2	0.0	16.4	1.2	16.3	-0.6	16.5	1.2	16.4	-0.6	16.6	1.2	16.6	0.0	16.9	1.8
1943	16.8	-0.6	16.9	0.6	17.1	1.2	17.3	1.2	17.4	0.6	17.4	0.0	17.3	-0.6	17.3	0.0	17.2	-0.6	17.3	0.6	17.3	0.0	17.3	0.0
1944	17.3	0.0	17.2	-0.6	17.2	0.0	17.4	1.2	17.4	0.0	17.5	0.6	17.7	1.1	17.6	-0.6	17.6	0.0	17.5	-0.6	17.6	0.6	17.6	0.0
1945	17.7	0.6	17.6	-0.6	17.6	0.0	17.6	0.0	17.8	1.1	17.9	0.6	17.9	0.0	17.9	0.0	17.8	-0.6	17.8	0.0	17.8	0.0	18.0	1.1
1946	18.1	0.6	18.0	-0.6	18.0	0.0	18.2	1.1	18.2	0.0	18.5	1.6	19.6	5.9	20.1	2.6	20.1	0.0	20.6	2.5	21.2	2.9	21.3	0.5
1947	21.3	0.0	21.3	0.0	21.9	2.8	21.8	-0.5	21.8	0.0	21.9	0.5	-	-	-	-	23.3	6.4	-	-	-	-	23.6	1.3
1948	-	-	-	-	23.6	0.0	-	-	-	-	24.2	2.5	-	-	-	-	24.6	1.7	-	-	-	-	24.1	-2.0
1949	-	-	-	-	23.8	-1.2	-	-	-	-	23.9	0.4	-	-	-	-	23.8	-0.4	-	-	-	-	23.6	-0.8
1950	-	-	-	-	23.6	0.0	-	-	-	-	23.7	0.4	-	-	-	-	24.4	3.0	-	-	-	-	25.1	2.9
1951	-	-	-	-	26.0	3.6	-	-	-	-	26.0	0.0	-	-	-	-	26.2	0.8	-	-	-	-	26.8	2.3
1952	-	-	-	-	26.8	0.0	-	-	-	-	27.1	1.1	-	-	-	-	27.1	0.0	-	-	-	-	27.0	-0.4
1953	-	-	-	-	26.9	-0.4	-	-	-	-	27.2	1.1	-	-	-	-	27.5	1.1	-	-	-	-	27.4	-0.4
1954	-	-	-	-	27.4	0.0	-	-	-	-	27.5	0.4	-	-	-	-	27.1	-1.5	-	-	-	-	27.1	0.0
1955	-	-	-	-	27.1	0.0	-	-	-	-	27.2	0.4	-	-	-	-	27.3	0.4	-	-	-	-	27.2	-0.4
1956	-	-	-	-	27.1	-0.4	-	-	-	-	27.4	1.1	-	-	-	-	27.7	1.1	-	-	-	-	27.9	0.7
1957	-	-	-	-	28.2	1.1	-	-	-	-	28.4	0.7	-	-	-	-	28.6	0.7	-	-	-	-	28.7	0.3
1958	-	-	-	-	29.2	1.7	-	-	-	-	29.2	0.0	-	-	-	-	29.4	0.7	-	-	-	-	29.5	0.3
1959	-	-	-	-	29.5	0.0	-	-	-	-	29.6	0.3	-	-	-	-	29.6	0.0	-	-	-	-	29.7	0.3
1960	-	-	-	-	29.6	-0.3	-	-	-	-	29.8	0.7	-	-	-	-	29.9	0.3	-	-	-	-	30.0	0.3
1961	-	-	-	-	30.3	1.0	-	-	-	-	30.3	0.0	-	-	-	-	30.3	0.0	-	-	-	-	30.4	0.3

[Continued]

St. Louis, MO-IL
Consumer Price Index - Urban Wage Earners
Base 1982-1984 = 100
All Items
[Continued]

For 1917-1995. Columns headed % show percentile change in the index from the previous period for which an index is available.

Year	Jan Index	%	Feb Index	%	Mar Index	%	Apr Index	%	May Index	%	Jun Index	%	Jul Index	%	Aug Index	%	Sep Index	%	Oct Index	%	Nov Index	%	Dec Index	%
1962	-	-	-	-	30.5	0.3	-	-	-	-	30.4	-0.3	-	-	-	-	30.7	1.0	-	-	-	-	30.9	0.7
1963	-	-	-	-	30.8	-0.3	-	-	-	-	30.7	-0.3	-	-	-	-	31.0	1.0	-	-	-	-	31.2	0.6
1964	-	-	-	-	31.3	0.3	-	-	-	-	31.3	0.0	-	-	-	-	31.6	1.0	-	-	-	-	31.7	0.3
1965	-	-	-	-	31.7	0.0	-	-	-	-	32.1	1.3	-	-	-	-	32.0	-0.3	-	-	-	-	32.5	1.6
1966	-	-	-	-	32.6	0.3	-	-	-	-	33.1	1.5	-	-	-	-	33.4	0.9	-	-	-	-	33.4	0.0
1967	-	-	-	-	33.6	0.6	-	-	-	-	33.9	0.9	-	-	-	-	34.3	1.2	-	-	-	-	34.6	0.9
1968	-	-	-	-	35.0	1.2	-	-	-	-	35.3	0.9	-	-	-	-	35.7	1.1	-	-	-	-	35.9	0.6
1969	-	-	-	-	36.5	1.7	-	-	-	-	36.9	1.1	-	-	-	-	37.6	1.9	-	-	-	-	38.0	1.1
1970	-	-	-	-	38.5	1.3	-	-	-	-	39.0	1.3	-	-	-	-	39.6	1.5	-	-	-	-	40.0	1.0
1971	-	-	-	-	40.2	0.5	-	-	-	-	40.8	1.5	-	-	-	-	41.0	0.5	-	-	-	-	41.1	0.2
1972	-	-	-	-	41.1	0.0	-	-	-	-	41.4	0.7	-	-	-	-	42.0	1.4	-	-	-	-	42.0	0.0
1973	-	-	-	-	42.9	2.1	-	-	-	-	43.5	1.4	-	-	-	-	45.0	3.4	-	-	-	-	45.5	1.1
1974	-	-	-	-	47.0	3.3	-	-	-	-	48.0	2.1	-	-	-	-	49.6	3.3	-	-	-	-	50.5	1.8
1975	-	-	-	-	51.8	2.6	-	-	-	-	53.3	2.9	-	-	-	-	54.0	1.3	-	-	-	-	54.5	0.9
1976	-	-	-	-	55.3	1.5	-	-	-	-	56.2	1.6	-	-	-	-	56.8	1.1	-	-	-	-	57.2	0.7
1977	-	-	-	-	58.9	3.0	-	-	-	-	60.3	2.4	-	-	-	-	60.9	1.0	-	-	-	-	61.4	0.8
1978	-	-	-	-	62.5	1.8	-	-	63.9	2.2	-	-	64.9	1.6	-	-	66.2	2.0	-	-	67.2	1.5	-	-
1979	68.5	1.9	-	-	70.4	2.8	-	-	71.5	1.6	-	-	73.9	3.4	-	-	75.6	2.3	-	-	76.9	1.7	-	-
1980	79.4	3.3	-	-	81.1	2.1	-	-	82.5	1.7	-	-	83.6	1.3	-	-	85.9	2.8	-	-	86.4	0.6	-	-
1981	87.0	0.7	-	-	88.2	1.4	-	-	91.2	3.4	-	-	91.5	0.3	-	-	92.8	1.4	-	-	92.8	0.0	-	-
1982	94.2	1.5	-	-	94.9	0.7	-	-	96.7	1.9	-	-	98.3	1.7	-	-	99.6	1.3	-	-	98.2	-1.4	-	-
1983	97.0	-1.2	-	-	99.7	2.8	-	-	99.9	0.2	-	-	100.8	0.9	-	-	101.7	0.9	-	-	101.7	0.0	-	-
1984	100.9	-0.8	-	-	101.1	0.2	-	-	101.1	0.0	-	-	102.4	1.3	-	-	104.7	2.2	-	-	104.4	-0.3	-	-
1985	105.5	1.1	-	-	105.7	0.2	-	-	106.4	0.7	-	-	107.6	1.1	-	-	108.3	0.7	-	-	108.3	0.0	-	-
1986	108.5	0.2	-	-	107.1	-1.3	-	-	106.8	-0.3	-	-	109.0	2.1	-	-	109.0	0.0	-	-	108.4	-0.6	-	-
1987	109.4	0.9	-	-	110.2	0.7	-	-	110.9	0.6	-	-	112.5	1.4	-	-	114.1	1.4	-	-	112.7	-1.2	-	-
1988	113.0	0.3	-	-	113.8	0.7	-	-	113.7	-0.1	-	-	115.7	1.8	-	-	117.1	1.2	-	-	117.8	0.6	-	-
1989	118.0	0.2	-	-	119.1	0.9	-	-	121.2	1.8	-	-	122.8	1.3	-	-	123.5	0.6	-	-	122.6	-0.7	-	-
1990	124.6	1.6	-	-	126.5	1.5	-	-	126.0	-0.4	-	-	127.3	1.0	-	-	129.3	1.6	-	-	129.9	0.5	-	-
1991	130.3	0.3	-	-	130.1	-0.2	-	-	130.6	0.4	-	-	132.0	1.1	-	-	133.0	0.8	-	-	132.7	-0.2	-	-
1992	132.0	-0.5	-	-	132.0	0.0	-	-	133.6	1.2	-	-	135.4	1.3	-	-	136.5	0.8	-	-	135.6	-0.7	-	-
1993	135.4	-0.1	-	-	135.5	0.1	-	-	136.4	0.7	-	-	138.3	1.4	-	-	137.6	-0.5	-	-	137.5	-0.1	-	-
1994	137.7	0.1	-	-	138.7	0.7	-	-	139.2	0.4	-	-	141.4	1.6	-	-	143.0	1.1	-	-	142.9	-0.1	-	-
1995	142.3	-0.4	-	-	143.9	1.1	-	-	144.2	0.2	-	-	145.2	0.7	-	-	146.5	0.9	-	-	145.0	-1.0	-	-

Source: U.S. Department of Labor, Bureau of Labor Statistics, Division of Consumer Prices and Price Indexes. - indicates no data collected for period.

St. Louis, MO-IL
Consumer Price Index - All Urban Consumers
Base 1982-1984 = 100
Food and Beverages

For 1975-1995. Columns headed % show percentile change in the index from the previous period for which an index is available.

Year	Jan Index	%	Feb Index	%	Mar Index	%	Apr Index	%	May Index	%	Jun Index	%	Jul Index	%	Aug Index	%	Sep Index	%	Oct Index	%	Nov Index	%	Dec Index	%
1975	-	-	-	-	-	-	-	-	-	-	-	-	-	-	-	-	-	-	-	-	-	-	62.0	-
1976	-	-	-	-	61.8	-0.3	-	-	-	-	62.6	1.3	-	-	-	-	62.9	0.5	-	-	-	-	62.8	-0.2
1977	-	-	-	-	65.4	4.1	-	-	-	-	67.9	3.8	-	-	-	-	67.9	0.0	-	-	-	-	67.8	-0.1
1978	-	-	-	-	70.1	3.4	-	-	72.6	3.6	-	-	74.2	2.2	-	-	74.2	0.0	-	-	74.6	0.5	-	-
1979	77.6	4.0	-	-	79.5	2.4	-	-	81.3	2.3	-	-	82.4	1.4	-	-	82.1	-0.4	-	-	81.7	-0.5	-	-
1980	83.7	2.4	-	-	84.1	0.5	-	-	85.3	1.4	-	-	86.9	1.9	-	-	89.9	3.5	-	-	90.8	1.0	-	-
1981	91.2	0.4	-	-	92.3	1.2	-	-	92.7	0.4	-	-	94.2	1.6	-	-	94.6	0.4	-	-	94.8	0.2	-	-
1982	95.5	0.7	-	-	95.7	0.2	-	-	96.7	1.0	-	-	98.0	1.3	-	-	98.1	0.1	-	-	98.1	0.0	-	-
1983	98.2	0.1	-	-	99.5	1.3	-	-	99.8	0.3	-	-	99.7	-0.1	-	-	100.2	0.5	-	-	100.0	-0.2	-	-
1984	101.3	1.3	-	-	102.3	1.0	-	-	102.2	-0.1	-	-	103.8	1.6	-	-	104.3	0.5	-	-	104.3	0.0	-	-
1985	105.0	0.7	-	-	106.1	1.0	-	-	105.0	-1.0	-	-	105.4	0.4	-	-	106.7	1.2	-	-	105.7	-0.9	-	-
1986	107.3	1.5	-	-	107.6	0.3	-	-	108.1	0.5	-	-	110.0	1.8	-	-	111.9	1.7	-	-	112.1	0.2	-	-
1987	113.4	1.2	-	-	113.7	0.3	-	-	114.1	0.4	-	-	114.2	0.1	-	-	115.0	0.7	-	-	113.3	-1.5	-	-
1988	113.9	0.5	-	-	114.3	0.4	-	-	115.8	1.3	-	-	118.3	2.2	-	-	120.5	1.9	-	-	121.8	1.1	-	-
1989	121.3	-0.4	-	-	124.4	2.6	-	-	125.4	0.8	-	-	125.3	-0.1	-	-	127.2	1.5	-	-	128.4	0.9	-	-
1990	132.8	3.4	-	-	133.6	0.6	-	-	134.0	0.3	-	-	134.2	0.1	-	-	135.3	0.8	-	-	137.6	1.7	-	-
1991	139.8	1.6	-	-	139.1	-0.5	-	-	139.4	0.2	-	-	139.5	0.1	-	-	139.6	0.1	-	-	140.4	0.6	-	-
1992	140.5	0.1	-	-	139.2	-0.9	-	-	140.6	1.0	-	-	139.7	-0.6	-	-	139.9	0.1	-	-	140.8	0.6	-	-
1993	139.8	-0.7	-	-	138.9	-0.6	-	-	138.8	-0.1	-	-	140.0	0.9	-	-	140.9	0.6	-	-	141.1	0.1	-	-
1994	143.9	2.0	-	-	143.6	-0.2	-	-	143.6	0.0	-	-	143.6	0.0	-	-	143.8	0.1	-	-	145.2	1.0	-	-
1995	145.7	0.3	-	-	145.7	0.0	-	-	147.5	1.2	-	-	146.3	-0.8	-	-	147.2	0.6	-	-	148.3	0.7	-	-

Source: U.S. Department of Labor, Bureau of Labor Statistics, Division of Consumer Prices and Price Indexes. - indicates no data collected for period.

St. Louis, MO-IL
Consumer Price Index - Urban Wage Earners
Base 1982-1984 = 100
Food and Beverages

For 1975-1995. Columns headed % show percentile change in the index from the previous period for which an index is available.

Year	Jan Index	%	Feb Index	%	Mar Index	%	Apr Index	%	May Index	%	Jun Index	%	Jul Index	%	Aug Index	%	Sep Index	%	Oct Index	%	Nov Index	%	Dec Index	%
1975	-	-	-	-	-	-	-	-	-	-	-	-	-	-	-	-	-	-	-	-	-	-	62.0	-
1976	-	-	-	-	61.8	-0.3	-	-	-	-	62.6	1.3	-	-	-	-	62.9	0.5	-	-	-	-	62.8	-0.2
1977	-	-	-	-	65.4	4.1	-	-	-	-	67.9	3.8	-	-	-	-	67.9	0.0	-	-	-	-	67.8	-0.1
1978	-	-	-	-	70.1	3.4	-	-	72.3	3.1	-	-	73.1	1.1	-	-	74.2	1.5	-	-	74.5	0.4	-	-
1979	77.3	3.8	-	-	79.7	3.1	-	-	80.8	1.4	-	-	83.0	2.7	-	-	83.3	0.4	-	-	83.1	-0.2	-	-
1980	84.7	1.9	-	-	84.5	-0.2	-	-	85.0	0.6	-	-	87.2	2.6	-	-	90.5	3.8	-	-	91.1	0.7	-	-
1981	91.6	0.5	-	-	92.3	0.8	-	-	93.0	0.8	-	-	94.2	1.3	-	-	95.0	0.8	-	-	94.9	-0.1	-	-
1982	95.3	0.4	-	-	95.7	0.4	-	-	96.6	0.9	-	-	97.9	1.3	-	-	98.1	0.2	-	-	98.1	0.0	-	-
1983	98.3	0.2	-	-	99.6	1.3	-	-	99.9	0.3	-	-	99.8	-0.1	-	-	100.4	0.6	-	-	100.1	-0.3	-	-
1984	101.2	1.1	-	-	102.3	1.1	-	-	102.2	-0.1	-	-	103.8	1.6	-	-	104.2	0.4	-	-	104.3	0.1	-	-
1985	104.9	0.6	-	-	105.9	1.0	-	-	104.9	-0.9	-	-	105.3	0.4	-	-	106.5	1.1	-	-	105.6	-0.8	-	-
1986	107.1	1.4	-	-	107.6	0.5	-	-	108.1	0.5	-	-	109.9	1.7	-	-	112.0	1.9	-	-	112.2	0.2	-	-
1987	113.6	1.2	-	-	113.8	0.2	-	-	114.0	0.2	-	-	114.2	0.2	-	-	115.1	0.8	-	-	113.5	-1.4	-	-
1988	114.0	0.4	-	-	114.5	0.4	-	-	115.7	1.0	-	-	118.3	2.2	-	-	120.5	1.9	-	-	121.9	1.2	-	-
1989	121.2	-0.6	-	-	124.3	2.6	-	-	125.3	0.8	-	-	125.3	0.0	-	-	127.3	1.6	-	-	128.6	1.0	-	-
1990	132.6	3.1	-	-	133.6	0.8	-	-	134.1	0.4	-	-	134.3	0.1	-	-	135.3	0.7	-	-	137.4	1.6	-	-
1991	139.6	1.6	-	-	139.1	-0.4	-	-	139.3	0.1	-	-	139.5	0.1	-	-	139.8	0.2	-	-	140.3	0.4	-	-
1992	140.5	0.1	-	-	139.3	-0.9	-	-	140.6	0.9	-	-	140.0	-0.4	-	-	140.1	0.1	-	-	140.8	0.5	-	-
1993	140.0	-0.6	-	-	139.1	-0.6	-	-	139.1	0.0	-	-	140.3	0.9	-	-	141.1	0.6	-	-	141.3	0.1	-	-
1994	143.9	1.8	-	-	143.9	0.0	-	-	144.1	0.1	-	-	144.1	0.0	-	-	144.2	0.1	-	-	145.4	0.8	-	-
1995	145.7	0.2	-	-	145.9	0.1	-	-	147.7	1.2	-	-	146.4	-0.9	-	-	147.2	0.5	-	-	148.1	0.6	-	-

Source: U.S. Department of Labor, Bureau of Labor Statistics, Division of Consumer Prices and Price Indexes. - indicates no data collected for period.

St. Louis, MO-IL
Consumer Price Index - All Urban Consumers
Base 1982-1984 = 100
Housing

For 1975-1995. Columns headed % show percentile change in the index from the previous period for which an index is available.

Year	Jan Index	%	Feb Index	%	Mar Index	%	Apr Index	%	May Index	%	Jun Index	%	Jul Index	%	Aug Index	%	Sep Index	%	Oct Index	%	Nov Index	%	Dec Index	%
1975	-	-	-	-	-	-	-	-	-	-	-	-	-	-	-	-	-	-	-	-	-	-	48.7	-
1976	-	-	-	-	50.1	2.9	-	-	-	-	50.5	0.8	-	-	-	-	51.1	1.2	-	-	-	-	51.3	0.4
1977	-	-	-	-	52.8	2.9	-	-	-	-	53.9	2.1	-	-	-	-	55.1	2.2	-	-	-	-	55.7	1.1
1978	-	-	-	-	56.9	2.2	-	-	58.5	2.8	-	-	59.6	1.9	-	-	61.0	2.3	-	-	62.3	2.1	-	-
1979	63.7	2.2	-	-	65.4	2.7	-	-	65.3	-0.2	-	-	67.4	3.2	-	-	70.6	4.7	-	-	72.2	2.3	-	-
1980	75.4	4.4	-	-	77.2	2.4	-	-	78.4	1.6	-	-	79.7	1.7	-	-	83.1	4.3	-	-	82.9	-0.2	-	-
1981	82.6	-0.4	-	-	83.1	0.6	-	-	88.7	6.7	-	-	88.7	0.0	-	-	90.5	2.0	-	-	89.4	-1.2	-	-
1982	92.4	3.4	-	-	94.3	2.1	-	-	96.9	2.8	-	-	98.0	1.1	-	-	100.5	2.6	-	-	97.1	-3.4	-	-
1983	97.8	0.7	-	-	98.9	1.1	-	-	99.3	0.4	-	-	102.0	2.7	-	-	103.0	1.0	-	-	100.6	-2.3	-	-
1984	101.3	0.7	-	-	100.9	-0.4	-	-	102.7	1.8	-	-	104.4	1.7	-	-	104.8	0.4	-	-	101.9	-2.8	-	-
1985	106.2	4.2	-	-	105.2	-0.9	-	-	105.9	0.7	-	-	109.5	3.4	-	-	110.0	0.5	-	-	109.4	-0.5	-	-
1986	109.3	-0.1	-	-	108.5	-0.7	-	-	108.2	-0.3	-	-	114.2	5.5	-	-	112.9	-1.1	-	-	108.8	-3.6	-	-
1987	109.9	1.0	-	-	110.3	0.4	-	-	110.8	0.5	-	-	114.1	3.0	-	-	114.5	0.4	-	-	112.3	-1.9	-	-
1988	112.8	0.4	-	-	113.7	0.8	-	-	112.8	-0.8	-	-	115.8	2.7	-	-	116.1	0.3	-	-	117.1	0.9	-	-
1989	117.8	0.6	-	-	117.2	-0.5	-	-	118.4	1.0	-	-	122.5	3.5	-	-	124.3	1.5	-	-	120.6	-3.0	-	-
1990	121.6	0.8	-	-	124.5	2.4	-	-	123.9	-0.5	-	-	126.4	2.0	-	-	126.4	0.0	-	-	125.6	-0.6	-	-
1991	125.6	0.0	-	-	126.4	0.6	-	-	127.1	0.6	-	-	129.8	2.1	-	-	129.5	-0.2	-	-	127.4	-1.6	-	-
1992	126.5	-0.7	-	-	126.8	0.2	-	-	128.0	0.9	-	-	132.1	3.2	-	-	133.1	0.8	-	-	130.4	-2.0	-	-
1993	131.0	0.5	-	-	131.3	0.2	-	-	131.1	-0.2	-	-	135.4	3.3	-	-	135.6	0.1	-	-	132.7	-2.1	-	-
1994	133.8	0.8	-	-	135.7	1.4	-	-	135.2	-0.4	-	-	138.8	2.7	-	-	139.0	0.1	-	-	137.0	-1.4	-	-
1995	137.0	0.0	-	-	138.9	1.4	-	-	137.3	-1.2	-	-	141.1	2.8	-	-	142.1	0.7	-	-	139.7	-1.7	-	-

Source: U.S. Department of Labor, Bureau of Labor Statistics, Division of Consumer Prices and Price Indexes. - indicates no data collected for period.

St. Louis, MO-IL
Consumer Price Index - Urban Wage Earners
Base 1982-1984 = 100
Housing

For 1975-1995. Columns headed % show percentile change in the index from the previous period for which an index is available.

Year	Jan Index	%	Feb Index	%	Mar Index	%	Apr Index	%	May Index	%	Jun Index	%	Jul Index	%	Aug Index	%	Sep Index	%	Oct Index	%	Nov Index	%	Dec Index	%
1975	-	-	-	-	-	-	-	-	-	-	-	-	-	-	-	-	-	-	-	-	-	-	49.1	-
1976	-	-	-	-	50.5	2.9	-	-	-	-	51.0	1.0	-	-	-	-	51.6	1.2	-	-	-	-	51.8	0.4
1977	-	-	-	-	53.3	2.9	-	-	-	-	54.3	1.9	-	-	-	-	55.6	2.4	-	-	-	-	56.2	1.1
1978	-	-	-	-	57.4	2.1	-	-	58.8	2.4	-	-	60.0	2.0	-	-	61.7	2.8	-	-	63.1	2.3	-	-
1979	64.2	1.7	-	-	66.2	3.1	-	-	66.4	0.3	-	-	68.6	3.3	-	-	71.5	4.2	-	-	73.3	2.5	-	-
1980	76.5	4.4	-	-	78.4	2.5	-	-	80.0	2.0	-	-	81.2	1.5	-	-	84.1	3.6	-	-	84.1	0.0	-	-
1981	83.5	-0.7	-	-	84.0	0.6	-	-	90.1	7.3	-	-	89.8	-0.3	-	-	91.8	2.2	-	-	90.4	-1.5	-	-
1982	93.5	3.4	-	-	95.4	2.0	-	-	98.1	2.8	-	-	99.2	1.1	-	-	101.9	2.7	-	-	98.3	-3.5	-	-
1983	95.6	-2.7	-	-	101.4	6.1	-	-	100.4	-1.0	-	-	101.6	1.2	-	-	102.3	0.7	-	-	102.6	0.3	-	-
1984	100.4	-2.1	-	-	99.4	-1.0	-	-	98.5	-0.9	-	-	100.6	2.1	-	-	104.4	3.8	-	-	103.2	-1.1	-	-
1985	107.4	4.1	-	-	106.3	-1.0	-	-	107.0	0.7	-	-	110.6	3.4	-	-	111.4	0.7	-	-	110.8	-0.5	-	-
1986	110.8	0.0	-	-	110.0	-0.7	-	-	109.7	-0.3	-	-	115.6	5.4	-	-	114.4	-1.0	-	-	110.4	-3.5	-	-
1987	111.7	1.2	-	-	112.1	0.4	-	-	112.5	0.4	-	-	116.2	3.3	-	-	116.4	0.2	-	-	113.8	-2.2	-	-
1988	114.4	0.5	-	-	115.3	0.8	-	-	114.3	-0.9	-	-	117.6	2.9	-	-	117.9	0.3	-	-	118.7	0.7	-	-
1989	119.4	0.6	-	-	118.9	-0.4	-	-	120.1	1.0	-	-	124.4	3.6	-	-	126.2	1.4	-	-	122.1	-3.2	-	-
1990	123.3	1.0	-	-	126.3	2.4	-	-	125.5	-0.6	-	-	128.4	2.3	-	-	128.5	0.1	-	-	127.5	-0.8	-	-
1991	127.4	-0.1	-	-	128.1	0.5	-	-	128.8	0.5	-	-	131.7	2.3	-	-	131.6	-0.1	-	-	129.3	-1.7	-	-
1992	128.5	-0.6	-	-	128.9	0.3	-	-	130.1	0.9	-	-	134.6	3.5	-	-	135.5	0.7	-	-	132.6	-2.1	-	-
1993	133.2	0.5	-	-	133.4	0.2	-	-	133.2	-0.1	-	-	137.9	3.5	-	-	137.9	0.0	-	-	134.8	-2.2	-	-
1994	136.0	0.9	-	-	137.8	1.3	-	-	137.4	-0.3	-	-	141.2	2.8	-	-	141.4	0.1	-	-	139.1	-1.6	-	-
1995	139.1	0.0	-	-	141.0	1.4	-	-	139.3	-1.2	-	-	143.4	2.9	-	-	144.2	0.6	-	-	141.6	-1.8	-	-

Source: U.S. Department of Labor, Bureau of Labor Statistics, Division of Consumer Prices and Price Indexes. - indicates no data collected for period.

St. Louis, MO-IL
Consumer Price Index - All Urban Consumers
Base 1982-1984 = 100
Apparel and Upkeep

For 1952-1995. Columns headed % show percentile change in the index from the previous period for which an index is available.

Year	Jan Index	%	Feb Index	%	Mar Index	%	Apr Index	%	May Index	%	Jun Index	%	Jul Index	%	Aug Index	%	Sep Index	%	Oct Index	%	Nov Index	%	Dec Index	%
1952	-	-	-	-	-	-	-	-	-	-	-	-	-	-	-	-	-	-	-	-	-	-	43.8	-
1953	-	-	-	-	43.9	0.2	-	-	-	-	44.0	0.2	-	-	-	-	44.5	1.1	-	-	-	-	44.3	-0.4
1954	-	-	-	-	44.0	-0.7	-	-	-	-	44.1	0.2	-	-	-	-	43.9	-0.5	-	-	-	-	43.8	-0.2
1955	-	-	-	-	44.0	0.5	-	-	-	-	43.8	-0.5	-	-	-	-	43.9	0.2	-	-	-	-	44.1	0.5
1956	-	-	-	-	44.2	0.2	-	-	-	-	44.4	0.5	-	-	-	-	44.6	0.5	-	-	-	-	44.8	0.4
1957	-	-	-	-	45.0	0.4	-	-	-	-	44.8	-0.4	-	-	-	-	45.1	0.7	-	-	-	-	45.4	0.7
1958	-	-	-	-	45.9	1.1	-	-	-	-	45.7	-0.4	-	-	-	-	46.0	0.7	-	-	-	-	45.9	-0.2
1959	-	-	-	-	45.9	0.0	-	-	-	-	45.9	0.0	-	-	-	-	46.5	1.3	-	-	-	-	46.6	0.2
1960	-	-	-	-	46.8	0.4	-	-	-	-	46.9	0.2	-	-	-	-	47.5	1.3	-	-	-	-	47.5	0.0
1961	-	-	-	-	47.7	0.4	-	-	-	-	47.6	-0.2	-	-	-	-	47.6	0.0	-	-	-	-	47.4	-0.4
1962	-	-	-	-	47.5	0.2	-	-	-	-	47.6	0.2	-	-	-	-	47.8	0.4	-	-	-	-	47.5	-0.6
1963	-	-	-	-	47.6	0.2	-	-	-	-	48.0	0.8	-	-	-	-	48.3	0.6	-	-	-	-	48.7	0.8
1964	-	-	-	-	48.5	-0.4	-	-	-	-	48.5	0.0	-	-	-	-	48.8	0.6	-	-	-	-	48.9	0.2
1965	-	-	-	-	48.8	-0.2	-	-	-	-	48.9	0.2	-	-	-	-	49.6	1.4	-	-	-	-	49.7	0.2
1966	-	-	-	-	49.9	0.4	-	-	-	-	50.7	1.6	-	-	-	-	51.2	1.0	-	-	-	-	51.4	0.4
1967	-	-	-	-	52.1	1.4	-	-	-	-	52.2	0.2	-	-	-	-	52.6	0.8	-	-	-	-	53.4	1.5
1968	-	-	-	-	54.7	2.4	-	-	-	-	54.8	0.2	-	-	-	-	56.5	3.1	-	-	-	-	56.8	0.5
1969	-	-	-	-	57.5	1.2	-	-	-	-	57.9	0.7	-	-	-	-	58.8	1.6	-	-	-	-	59.1	0.5
1970	-	-	-	-	59.3	0.3	-	-	-	-	60.1	1.3	-	-	-	-	61.6	2.5	-	-	-	-	61.3	-0.5
1971	-	-	-	-	61.8	0.8	-	-	-	-	61.9	0.2	-	-	-	-	63.4	2.4	-	-	-	-	63.3	-0.2
1972	-	-	-	-	63.0	-0.5	-	-	-	-	62.6	-0.6	-	-	-	-	63.4	1.3	-	-	-	-	63.1	-0.5
1973	-	-	-	-	63.2	0.2	-	-	-	-	63.3	0.2	-	-	-	-	66.5	5.1	-	-	-	-	66.0	-0.8
1974	-	-	-	-	66.1	0.2	-	-	-	-	67.5	2.1	-	-	-	-	69.8	3.4	-	-	-	-	70.0	0.3
1975	-	-	-	-	70.2	0.3	-	-	-	-	70.6	0.6	-	-	-	-	71.3	1.0	-	-	-	-	72.0	1.0
1976	-	-	-	-	73.5	2.1	-	-	-	-	73.8	0.4	-	-	-	-	75.4	2.2	-	-	-	-	75.7	0.4
1977	-	-	-	-	78.8	4.1	-	-	-	-	79.0	0.3	-	-	-	-	80.0	1.3	-	-	-	-	80.9	1.1
1978	-	-	-	-	79.6	-1.6	-	-	78.0	-2.0	-	-	77.9	-0.1	-	-	80.6	3.5	-	-	84.1	4.3	-	-
1979	81.8	-2.7	-	-	87.3	6.7	-	-	85.4	-2.2	-	-	81.4	-4.7	-	-	86.9	6.8	-	-	87.5	0.7	-	-
1980	85.4	-2.4	-	-	92.0	7.7	-	-	92.9	1.0	-	-	91.0	-2.0	-	-	94.4	3.7	-	-	93.2	-1.3	-	-
1981	91.6	-1.7	-	-	96.2	5.0	-	-	94.1	-2.2	-	-	95.4	1.4	-	-	97.7	2.4	-	-	95.9	-1.8	-	-
1982	94.1	-1.9	-	-	99.2	5.4	-	-	97.5	-1.7	-	-	97.6	0.1	-	-	99.4	1.8	-	-	97.1	-2.3	-	-
1983	97.4	0.3	-	-	103.3	6.1	-	-	100.9	-2.3	-	-	100.5	-0.4	-	-	102.0	1.5	-	-	100.5	-1.5	-	-
1984	98.0	-2.5	-	-	102.5	4.6	-	-	100.0	-2.4	-	-	99.8	-0.2	-	-	105.3	5.5	-	-	103.8	-1.4	-	-
1985	99.6	-4.0	-	-	106.9	7.3	-	-	107.4	0.5	-	-	104.3	-2.9	-	-	105.2	0.9	-	-	103.9	-1.2	-	-
1986	98.0	-5.7	-	-	103.5	5.6	-	-	103.2	-0.3	-	-	99.2	-3.9	-	-	104.7	5.5	-	-	106.1	1.3	-	-
1987	102.0	-3.9	-	-	107.1	5.0	-	-	107.1	0.0	-	-	100.2	-6.4	-	-	114.6	14.4	-	-	113.1	-1.3	-	-
1988	109.1	-3.5	-	-	115.1	5.5	-	-	110.6	-3.9	-	-	107.4	-2.9	-	-	116.1	8.1	-	-	116.2	0.1	-	-
1989	111.5	-4.0	-	-	119.6	7.3	-	-	121.0	1.2	-	-	118.5	-2.1	-	-	119.3	0.7	-	-	119.0	-0.3	-	-
1990	118.7	-0.3	-	-	128.6	8.3	-	-	119.2	-7.3	-	-	116.7	-2.1	-	-	121.2	3.9	-	-	121.0	-0.2	-	-
1991	119.1	-1.6	-	-	124.6	4.6	-	-	121.4	-2.6	-	-	119.1	-1.9	-	-	125.8	5.6	-	-	124.6	-1.0	-	-
1992	121.4	-2.6	-	-	122.6	1.0	-	-	119.7	-2.4	-	-	118.0	-1.4	-	-	124.5	5.5	-	-	123.9	-0.5	-	-
1993	120.9	-2.4	-	-	122.8	1.6	-	-	126.0	2.6	-	-	122.6	-2.7	-	-	121.2	-1.1	-	-	123.5	1.9	-	-
1994	120.8	-2.2	-	-	123.1	1.9	-	-	123.7	0.5	-	-	121.4	-1.9	-	-	131.3	8.2	-	-	130.7	-0.5	-	-
1995	120.5	-7.8	-	-	120.7	0.2	-	-	117.9	-2.3	-	-	117.5	-0.3	-	-	123.0	4.7	-	-	116.4	-5.4	-	-

Source: U.S. Department of Labor, Bureau of Labor Statistics, Division of Consumer Prices and Price Indexes. - indicates no data collected for period.

St. Louis, MO-IL
Consumer Price Index - Urban Wage Earners
Base 1982-1984 = 100
Apparel and Upkeep

For 1952-1995. Columns headed % show percentile change in the index from the previous period for which an index is available.

Year	Jan Index	%	Feb Index	%	Mar Index	%	Apr Index	%	May Index	%	Jun Index	%	Jul Index	%	Aug Index	%	Sep Index	%	Oct Index	%	Nov Index	%	Dec Index	%
1952	-	-	-	-	-	-	-	-	-	-	-	-	-	-	-	-	-	-	-	-	-	-	44.6	-
1953	-	-	-	-	44.8	0.4	-	-	-	-	44.9	0.2	-	-	-	-	45.4	1.1	-	-	-	-	45.2	-0.4
1954	-	-	-	-	44.9	-0.7	-	-	-	-	44.9	0.0	-	-	-	-	44.7	-0.4	-	-	-	-	44.6	-0.2
1955	-	-	-	-	44.9	0.7	-	-	-	-	44.6	-0.7	-	-	-	-	44.8	0.4	-	-	-	-	44.9	0.2
1956	-	-	-	-	45.1	0.4	-	-	-	-	45.2	0.2	-	-	-	-	45.5	0.7	-	-	-	-	45.6	0.2
1957	-	-	-	-	45.8	0.4	-	-	-	-	45.6	-0.4	-	-	-	-	46.0	0.9	-	-	-	-	46.3	0.7
1958	-	-	-	-	46.8	1.1	-	-	-	-	46.6	-0.4	-	-	-	-	46.8	0.4	-	-	-	-	46.7	-0.2
1959	-	-	-	-	46.8	0.2	-	-	-	-	46.7	-0.2	-	-	-	-	47.4	1.5	-	-	-	-	47.5	0.2
1960	-	-	-	-	47.7	0.4	-	-	-	-	47.8	0.2	-	-	-	-	48.4	1.3	-	-	-	-	48.4	0.0
1961	-	-	-	-	48.6	0.4	-	-	-	-	48.5	-0.2	-	-	-	-	48.5	0.0	-	-	-	-	48.3	-0.4
1962	-	-	-	-	48.4	0.2	-	-	-	-	48.5	0.2	-	-	-	-	48.7	0.4	-	-	-	-	48.4	-0.6
1963	-	-	-	-	48.5	0.2	-	-	-	-	48.9	0.8	-	-	-	-	49.2	0.6	-	-	-	-	49.6	0.8
1964	-	-	-	-	49.4	-0.4	-	-	-	-	49.5	0.2	-	-	-	-	49.8	0.6	-	-	-	-	49.8	0.0
1965	-	-	-	-	49.7	-0.2	-	-	-	-	49.8	0.2	-	-	-	-	50.6	1.6	-	-	-	-	50.7	0.2
1966	-	-	-	-	50.9	0.4	-	-	-	-	51.6	1.4	-	-	-	-	52.2	1.2	-	-	-	-	52.4	0.4
1967	-	-	-	-	53.1	1.3	-	-	-	-	53.2	0.2	-	-	-	-	53.6	0.8	-	-	-	-	54.5	1.7
1968	-	-	-	-	55.7	2.2	-	-	-	-	55.8	0.2	-	-	-	-	57.6	3.2	-	-	-	-	57.8	0.3
1969	-	-	-	-	58.6	1.4	-	-	-	-	59.0	0.7	-	-	-	-	59.9	1.5	-	-	-	-	60.2	0.5
1970	-	-	-	-	60.5	0.5	-	-	-	-	61.2	1.2	-	-	-	-	62.8	2.6	-	-	-	-	62.4	-0.6
1971	-	-	-	-	63.0	1.0	-	-	-	-	63.1	0.2	-	-	-	-	64.6	2.4	-	-	-	-	64.5	-0.2
1972	-	-	-	-	64.2	-0.5	-	-	-	-	63.8	-0.6	-	-	-	-	64.6	1.3	-	-	-	-	64.4	-0.3
1973	-	-	-	-	64.4	0.0	-	-	-	-	64.5	0.2	-	-	-	-	67.8	5.1	-	-	-	-	67.3	-0.7
1974	-	-	-	-	67.3	0.0	-	-	-	-	68.8	2.2	-	-	-	-	71.1	3.3	-	-	-	-	71.4	0.4
1975	-	-	-	-	71.5	0.1	-	-	-	-	71.9	0.6	-	-	-	-	72.7	1.1	-	-	-	-	73.4	1.0
1976	-	-	-	-	74.9	2.0	-	-	-	-	75.2	0.4	-	-	-	-	76.8	2.1	-	-	-	-	77.2	0.5
1977	-	-	-	-	80.3	4.0	-	-	-	-	80.5	0.2	-	-	-	-	81.5	1.2	-	-	-	-	82.4	1.1
1978	-	-	-	-	81.1	-1.6	-	-	79.3	-2.2	-	-	79.4	0.1	-	-	82.1	3.4	-	-	82.0	-0.1	-	-
1979	80.3	-2.1	-	-	85.3	6.2	-	-	84.7	-0.7	-	-	81.2	-4.1	-	-	86.6	6.7	-	-	87.1	0.6	-	-
1980	85.6	-1.7	-	-	90.3	5.5	-	-	90.7	0.4	-	-	89.3	-1.5	-	-	93.1	4.3	-	-	92.3	-0.9	-	-
1981	92.1	-0.2	-	-	97.0	5.3	-	-	95.2	-1.9	-	-	95.2	0.0	-	-	96.7	1.6	-	-	95.3	-1.4	-	-
1982	93.1	-2.3	-	-	98.9	6.2	-	-	96.9	-2.0	-	-	97.5	0.6	-	-	99.4	1.9	-	-	98.0	-1.4	-	-
1983	97.5	-0.5	-	-	102.8	5.4	-	-	101.4	-1.4	-	-	101.3	-0.1	-	-	102.5	1.2	-	-	100.6	-1.9	-	-
1984	97.4	-3.2	-	-	101.1	3.8	-	-	98.6	-2.5	-	-	100.5	1.9	-	-	106.0	5.5	-	-	104.9	-1.0	-	-
1985	99.9	-4.8	-	-	106.0	6.1	-	-	106.9	0.8	-	-	103.3	-3.4	-	-	105.2	1.8	-	-	104.1	-1.0	-	-
1986	99.0	-4.9	-	-	102.6	3.6	-	-	102.1	-0.5	-	-	99.0	-3.0	-	-	105.1	6.2	-	-	105.9	0.8	-	-
1987	101.9	-3.8	-	-	107.2	5.2	-	-	107.4	0.2	-	-	100.7	-6.2	-	-	114.5	13.7	-	-	112.9	-1.4	-	-
1988	109.6	-2.9	-	-	115.3	5.2	-	-	110.8	-3.9	-	-	107.1	-3.3	-	-	116.4	8.7	-	-	116.1	-0.3	-	-
1989	111.8	-3.7	-	-	119.4	6.8	-	-	120.7	1.1	-	-	119.0	-1.4	-	-	119.2	0.2	-	-	119.4	0.2	-	-
1990	119.1	-0.3	-	-	129.6	8.8	-	-	119.2	-8.0	-	-	116.8	-2.0	-	-	121.4	3.9	-	-	121.0	-0.3	-	-
1991	119.6	-1.2	-	-	125.0	4.5	-	-	121.4	-2.9	-	-	119.0	-2.0	-	-	126.3	6.1	-	-	125.2	-0.9	-	-
1992	121.8	-2.7	-	-	123.1	1.1	-	-	119.9	-2.6	-	-	118.2	-1.4	-	-	125.3	6.0	-	-	124.7	-0.5	-	-
1993	121.0	-3.0	-	-	123.4	2.0	-	-	126.3	2.4	-	-	122.5	-3.0	-	-	120.9	-1.3	-	-	124.3	2.8	-	-
1994	120.6	-3.0	-	-	123.1	2.1	-	-	123.7	0.5	-	-	122.4	-1.1	-	-	133.0	8.7	-	-	132.7	-0.2	-	-
1995	120.7	-9.0	-	-	120.9	0.2	-	-	117.7	-2.6	-	-	118.3	0.5	-	-	124.0	4.8	-	-	117.1	-5.6	-	-

Source: U.S. Department of Labor, Bureau of Labor Statistics, Division of Consumer Prices and Price Indexes. - indicates no data collected for period.

St. Louis, MO-IL
Consumer Price Index - All Urban Consumers
Base 1982-1984 = 100
Transportation

For 1947-1995. Columns headed % show percentile change in the index from the previous period for which an index is available.

Year	Jan Index	%	Feb Index	%	Mar Index	%	Apr Index	%	May Index	%	Jun Index	%	Jul Index	%	Aug Index	%	Sep Index	%	Oct Index	%	Nov Index	%	Dec Index	%
1947	17.7	-	17.7	0.0	17.9	1.1	18.0	0.6	18.0	0.0	18.0	0.0	-	-	-	-	18.4	2.2	-	-	-	-	18.9	2.7
1948	-	-	-	-	19.2	1.6	-	-	-	-	19.6	2.1	-	-	-	-	20.4	4.1	-	-	-	-	20.4	0.0
1949	-	-	-	-	20.7	1.5	-	-	-	-	20.7	0.0	-	-	-	-	20.7	0.0	-	-	-	-	21.5	3.9
1950	-	-	-	-	21.3	-0.9	-	-	-	-	21.1	-0.9	-	-	-	-	21.4	1.4	-	-	-	-	21.6	0.9
1951	-	-	-	-	23.5	8.8	-	-	-	-	23.4	-0.4	-	-	-	-	23.7	1.3	-	-	-	-	24.3	2.5
1952	-	-	-	-	25.6	5.3	-	-	-	-	25.6	0.0	-	-	-	-	26.3	2.7	-	-	-	-	26.1	-0.8
1953	-	-	-	-	26.9	3.1	-	-	-	-	26.8	-0.4	-	-	-	-	26.8	0.0	-	-	-	-	26.7	-0.4
1954	-	-	-	-	26.7	0.0	-	-	-	-	26.7	0.0	-	-	-	-	24.5	-8.2	-	-	-	-	25.6	4.5
1955	-	-	-	-	26.4	3.1	-	-	-	-	26.4	0.0	-	-	-	-	25.7	-2.7	-	-	-	-	26.2	1.9
1956	-	-	-	-	25.9	-1.1	-	-	-	-	26.2	1.2	-	-	-	-	26.3	0.4	-	-	-	-	27.3	3.8
1957	-	-	-	-	27.6	1.1	-	-	-	-	28.0	1.4	-	-	-	-	28.3	1.1	-	-	-	-	28.6	1.1
1958	-	-	-	-	28.9	1.0	-	-	-	-	29.1	0.7	-	-	-	-	30.1	3.4	-	-	-	-	31.3	4.0
1959	-	-	-	-	31.7	1.3	-	-	-	-	31.7	0.0	-	-	-	-	31.3	-1.3	-	-	-	-	32.0	2.2
1960	-	-	-	-	31.6	-1.2	-	-	-	-	31.6	0.0	-	-	-	-	31.2	-1.3	-	-	-	-	30.6	-1.9
1961	-	-	-	-	32.0	4.6	-	-	-	-	32.2	0.6	-	-	-	-	32.0	-0.6	-	-	-	-	32.5	1.6
1962	-	-	-	-	32.1	-1.2	-	-	-	-	31.8	-0.9	-	-	-	-	32.8	3.1	-	-	-	-	33.2	1.2
1963	-	-	-	-	32.7	-1.5	-	-	-	-	31.3	-4.3	-	-	-	-	32.2	2.9	-	-	-	-	32.8	1.9
1964	-	-	-	-	32.7	-0.3	-	-	-	-	32.1	-1.8	-	-	-	-	32.9	2.5	-	-	-	-	33.3	1.2
1965	-	-	-	-	33.0	-0.9	-	-	-	-	32.9	-0.3	-	-	-	-	32.7	-0.6	-	-	-	-	33.5	2.4
1966	-	-	-	-	33.5	0.0	-	-	-	-	34.4	2.7	-	-	-	-	34.4	0.0	-	-	-	-	34.4	0.0
1967	-	-	-	-	34.8	1.2	-	-	-	-	35.2	1.1	-	-	-	-	35.7	1.4	-	-	-	-	36.0	0.8
1968	-	-	-	-	36.0	0.0	-	-	-	-	36.1	0.3	-	-	-	-	36.1	0.0	-	-	-	-	35.9	-0.6
1969	-	-	-	-	36.9	2.8	-	-	-	-	37.3	1.1	-	-	-	-	37.4	0.3	-	-	-	-	37.7	0.8
1970	-	-	-	-	37.4	-0.8	-	-	-	-	39.4	5.3	-	-	-	-	40.3	2.3	-	-	-	-	42.2	4.7
1971	-	-	-	-	41.2	-2.4	-	-	-	-	42.7	3.6	-	-	-	-	42.0	-1.6	-	-	-	-	42.6	1.4
1972	-	-	-	-	41.2	-3.3	-	-	-	-	42.3	2.7	-	-	-	-	42.9	1.4	-	-	-	-	43.3	0.9
1973	-	-	-	-	43.5	0.5	-	-	-	-	44.3	1.8	-	-	-	-	43.9	-0.9	-	-	-	-	43.6	-0.7
1974	-	-	-	-	45.5	4.4	-	-	-	-	47.9	5.3	-	-	-	-	49.0	2.3	-	-	-	-	49.2	0.4
1975	-	-	-	-	49.5	0.6	-	-	-	-	51.3	3.6	-	-	-	-	53.1	3.5	-	-	-	-	53.5	0.8
1976	-	-	-	-	54.0	0.9	-	-	-	-	56.5	4.6	-	-	-	-	57.4	1.6	-	-	-	-	58.3	1.6
1977	-	-	-	-	58.7	0.7	-	-	-	-	60.3	2.7	-	-	-	-	59.8	-0.8	-	-	-	-	60.0	0.3
1978	-	-	-	-	59.9	-0.2	-	-	63.4	5.8	-	-	64.4	1.6	-	-	65.2	1.2	-	-	66.5	2.0	-	-
1979	67.4	1.4	-	-	68.9	2.2	-	-	72.0	4.5	-	-	76.3	6.0	-	-	76.7	0.5	-	-	78.4	2.2	-	-
1980	80.9	3.2	-	-	83.3	3.0	-	-	84.8	1.8	-	-	85.5	0.8	-	-	86.0	0.6	-	-	88.1	2.4	-	-
1981	90.3	2.5	-	-	92.5	2.4	-	-	94.1	1.7	-	-	94.8	0.7	-	-	95.4	0.6	-	-	97.6	2.3	-	-
1982	96.9	-0.7	-	-	94.6	-2.4	-	-	97.1	2.6	-	-	100.0	3.0	-	-	99.2	-0.8	-	-	99.0	-0.2	-	-
1983	97.6	-1.4	-	-	95.8	-1.8	-	-	99.0	3.3	-	-	100.3	1.3	-	-	100.9	0.6	-	-	101.2	0.3	-	-
1984	100.5	-0.7	-	-	101.3	0.8	-	-	103.0	1.7	-	-	103.4	0.4	-	-	103.9	0.5	-	-	104.6	0.7	-	-
1985	103.9	-0.7	-	-	103.8	-0.1	-	-	106.0	2.1	-	-	105.8	-0.2	-	-	105.4	-0.4	-	-	106.5	1.0	-	-
1986	106.1	-0.4	-	-	100.7	-5.1	-	-	99.7	-1.0	-	-	99.3	-0.4	-	-	97.7	-1.6	-	-	99.8	2.1	-	-
1987	101.4	1.6	-	-	102.1	0.7	-	-	103.2	1.1	-	-	104.7	1.5	-	-	105.7	1.0	-	-	105.7	0.0	-	-
1988	105.2	-0.5	-	-	104.0	-1.1	-	-	105.8	1.7	-	-	106.5	0.7	-	-	106.7	0.2	-	-	107.1	0.4	-	-
1989	107.2	0.1	-	-	107.4	0.2	-	-	113.3	5.5	-	-	112.0	-1.1	-	-	109.2	-2.5	-	-	111.6	2.2	-	-
1990	115.4	3.4	-	-	114.0	-1.2	-	-	115.1	1.0	-	-	114.8	-0.3	-	-	120.9	5.3	-	-	122.6	1.4	-	-
1991	121.6	-0.8	-	-	115.8	-4.8	-	-	118.2	2.1	-	-	117.2	-0.8	-	-	118.9	1.5	-	-	120.3	1.2	-	-

[Continued]

St. Louis, MO-IL
Consumer Price Index - All Urban Consumers
Base 1982-1984 = 100
Transportation
[Continued]

For 1947-1995. Columns headed % show percentile change in the index from the previous period for which an index is available.

Year	Jan		Feb		Mar		Apr		May		Jun		Jul		Aug		Sep		Oct		Nov		Dec	
	Index	%	Index	%	Index	%	Index	%	Index	%	Index	%	Index	%	Index	%	Index	%	Index	%	Index	%	Index	%
1992	118.8	-1.2	-	-	119.0	0.2	-	-	122.7	3.1	-	-	122.6	-0.1	-	-	122.7	0.1	-	-	124.8	1.7	-	-
1993	122.8	-1.6	-	-	123.5	0.6	-	-	126.0	2.0	-	-	125.8	-0.2	-	-	125.1	-0.6	-	-	127.1	1.6	-	-
1994	124.7	-1.9	-	-	125.8	0.9	-	-	127.0	1.0	-	-	130.8	3.0	-	-	132.3	1.1	-	-	132.9	0.5	-	-
1995	131.4	-1.1	-	-	135.3	3.0	-	-	137.8	1.8	-	-	136.6	-0.9	-	-	136.9	0.2	-	-	136.1	-0.6	-	-

Source: U.S. Department of Labor, Bureau of Labor Statistics, Division of Consumer Prices and Price Indexes. - indicates no data collected for period.

St. Louis, MO-IL
Consumer Price Index - Urban Wage Earners
Base 1982-1984 = 100
Transportation

For 1947-1995. Columns headed % show percentile change in the index from the previous period for which an index is available.

Year	Jan Index	%	Feb Index	%	Mar Index	%	Apr Index	%	May Index	%	Jun Index	%	Jul Index	%	Aug Index	%	Sep Index	%	Oct Index	%	Nov Index	%	Dec Index	%
1947	18.0	-	18.0	0.0	18.2	1.1	18.3	0.5	18.3	0.0	18.2	-0.5	-	-	-	-	18.7	2.7	-	-	-	-	19.2	2.7
1948	-	-	-	-	19.5	1.6	-	-	-	-	19.9	2.1	-	-	-	-	20.7	4.0	-	-	-	-	20.7	0.0
1949	-	-	-	-	21.1	1.9	-	-	-	-	21.1	0.0	-	-	-	-	21.0	-0.5	-	-	-	-	21.9	4.3
1950	-	-	-	-	21.7	-0.9	-	-	-	-	21.4	-1.4	-	-	-	-	21.8	1.9	-	-	-	-	22.0	0.9
1951	-	-	-	-	23.8	8.2	-	-	-	-	23.8	0.0	-	-	-	-	24.1	1.3	-	-	-	-	24.7	2.5
1952	-	-	-	-	26.0	5.3	-	-	-	-	26.1	0.4	-	-	-	-	26.7	2.3	-	-	-	-	26.5	-0.7
1953	-	-	-	-	27.3	3.0	-	-	-	-	27.3	0.0	-	-	-	-	27.3	0.0	-	-	-	-	27.2	-0.4
1954	-	-	-	-	27.1	-0.4	-	-	-	-	27.1	0.0	-	-	-	-	24.9	-8.1	-	-	-	-	26.0	4.4
1955	-	-	-	-	26.9	3.5	-	-	-	-	26.9	0.0	-	-	-	-	26.1	-3.0	-	-	-	-	26.6	1.9
1956	-	-	-	-	26.3	-1.1	-	-	-	-	26.6	1.1	-	-	-	-	26.7	0.4	-	-	-	-	27.7	3.7
1957	-	-	-	-	28.0	1.1	-	-	-	-	28.5	1.8	-	-	-	-	28.8	1.1	-	-	-	-	29.1	1.0
1958	-	-	-	-	29.4	1.0	-	-	-	-	29.5	0.3	-	-	-	-	30.5	3.4	-	-	-	-	31.8	4.3
1959	-	-	-	-	32.3	1.6	-	-	-	-	32.2	-0.3	-	-	-	-	31.8	-1.2	-	-	-	-	32.5	2.2
1960	-	-	-	-	32.1	-1.2	-	-	-	-	32.1	0.0	-	-	-	-	31.7	-1.2	-	-	-	-	31.1	-1.9
1961	-	-	-	-	32.5	4.5	-	-	-	-	32.7	0.6	-	-	-	-	32.5	-0.6	-	-	-	-	33.0	1.5
1962	-	-	-	-	32.6	-1.2	-	-	-	-	32.3	-0.9	-	-	-	-	33.4	3.4	-	-	-	-	33.7	0.9
1963	-	-	-	-	33.2	-1.5	-	-	-	-	31.8	-4.2	-	-	-	-	32.7	2.8	-	-	-	-	33.3	1.8
1964	-	-	-	-	33.2	-0.3	-	-	-	-	32.6	-1.8	-	-	-	-	33.5	2.8	-	-	-	-	33.9	1.2
1965	-	-	-	-	33.5	-1.2	-	-	-	-	33.4	-0.3	-	-	-	-	33.2	-0.6	-	-	-	-	34.1	2.7
1966	-	-	-	-	34.0	-0.3	-	-	-	-	34.9	2.6	-	-	-	-	35.0	0.3	-	-	-	-	35.0	0.0
1967	-	-	-	-	35.3	0.9	-	-	-	-	35.8	1.4	-	-	-	-	36.2	1.1	-	-	-	-	36.6	1.1
1968	-	-	-	-	36.6	0.0	-	-	-	-	36.6	0.0	-	-	-	-	36.7	0.3	-	-	-	-	36.5	-0.5
1969	-	-	-	-	37.5	2.7	-	-	-	-	37.9	1.1	-	-	-	-	38.0	0.3	-	-	-	-	38.3	0.8
1970	-	-	-	-	38.0	-0.8	-	-	-	-	40.0	5.3	-	-	-	-	40.9	2.3	-	-	-	-	42.9	4.9
1971	-	-	-	-	41.8	-2.6	-	-	-	-	43.4	3.8	-	-	-	-	42.7	-1.6	-	-	-	-	43.3	1.4
1972	-	-	-	-	41.9	-3.2	-	-	-	-	43.0	2.6	-	-	-	-	43.6	1.4	-	-	-	-	44.0	0.9
1973	-	-	-	-	44.2	0.5	-	-	-	-	45.0	1.8	-	-	-	-	44.6	-0.9	-	-	-	-	44.3	-0.7
1974	-	-	-	-	46.3	4.5	-	-	-	-	48.7	5.2	-	-	-	-	49.8	2.3	-	-	-	-	50.0	0.4
1975	-	-	-	-	50.3	0.6	-	-	-	-	52.1	3.6	-	-	-	-	54.0	3.6	-	-	-	-	54.4	0.7
1976	-	-	-	-	54.9	0.9	-	-	-	-	57.4	4.6	-	-	-	-	58.3	1.6	-	-	-	-	59.3	1.7
1977	-	-	-	-	59.6	0.5	-	-	-	-	61.2	2.7	-	-	-	-	60.8	-0.7	-	-	-	-	61.0	0.3
1978	-	-	-	-	60.9	-0.2	-	-	62.2	2.1	-	-	63.4	1.9	-	-	64.3	1.4	-	-	65.3	1.6	-	-
1979	66.4	1.7	-	-	67.8	2.1	-	-	71.3	5.2	-	-	76.3	7.0	-	-	76.5	0.3	-	-	78.1	2.1	-	-
1980	81.2	4.0	-	-	83.5	2.8	-	-	85.4	2.3	-	-	86.3	1.1	-	-	86.6	0.3	-	-	88.4	2.1	-	-
1981	90.6	2.5	-	-	92.8	2.4	-	-	94.3	1.6	-	-	94.9	0.6	-	-	95.5	0.6	-	-	97.7	2.3	-	-
1982	96.9	-0.8	-	-	94.3	-2.7	-	-	96.9	2.8	-	-	100.1	3.3	-	-	99.2	-0.9	-	-	99.0	-0.2	-	-
1983	97.3	-1.7	-	-	95.3	-2.1	-	-	98.7	3.6	-	-	100.2	1.5	-	-	101.0	0.8	-	-	101.3	0.3	-	-
1984	100.5	-0.8	-	-	101.5	1.0	-	-	103.4	1.9	-	-	103.8	0.4	-	-	104.2	0.4	-	-	104.9	0.7	-	-
1985	103.8	-1.0	-	-	103.7	-0.1	-	-	106.1	2.3	-	-	105.9	-0.2	-	-	105.3	-0.6	-	-	106.3	0.9	-	-
1986	105.8	-0.5	-	-	99.9	-5.6	-	-	98.6	-1.3	-	-	98.2	-0.4	-	-	96.4	-1.8	-	-	98.3	2.0	-	-
1987	99.6	1.3	-	-	100.7	1.1	-	-	102.3	1.6	-	-	104.4	2.1	-	-	105.5	1.1	-	-	105.4	-0.1	-	-
1988	105.0	-0.4	-	-	103.9	-1.0	-	-	105.6	1.6	-	-	106.2	0.6	-	-	106.6	0.4	-	-	106.8	0.2	-	-
1989	106.9	0.1	-	-	107.4	0.5	-	-	112.9	5.1	-	-	111.7	-1.1	-	-	109.2	-2.2	-	-	111.0	1.6	-	-
1990	114.0	2.7	-	-	112.0	-1.8	-	-	113.1	1.0	-	-	113.1	0.0	-	-	118.9	5.1	-	-	120.7	1.5	-	-
1991	119.4	-1.1	-	-	114.4	-4.2	-	-	116.8	2.1	-	-	116.1	-0.6	-	-	117.9	1.6	-	-	119.2	1.1	-	-

[Continued]

St. Louis, MO-IL
Consumer Price Index - Urban Wage Earners
Base 1982-1984 = 100
Transportation
[Continued]

For 1947-1995. Columns headed % show percentile change in the index from the previous period for which an index is available.

Year	Jan Index	%	Feb Index	%	Mar Index	%	Apr Index	%	May Index	%	Jun Index	%	Jul Index	%	Aug Index	%	Sep Index	%	Oct Index	%	Nov Index	%	Dec Index	%
1992	117.5	-1.4	-	-	117.2	-0.3	-	-	121.3	3.5	-	-	122.1	0.7	-	-	122.4	0.2	-	-	124.2	1.5	-	-
1993	122.2	-1.6	-	-	122.3	0.1	-	-	125.2	2.4	-	-	125.5	0.2	-	-	125.0	-0.4	-	-	126.9	1.5	-	-
1994	124.3	-2.0	-	-	124.7	0.3	-	-	126.6	1.5	-	-	130.9	3.4	-	-	132.8	1.5	-	-	134.0	0.9	-	-
1995	133.1	-0.7	-	-	136.5	2.6	-	-	139.9	2.5	-	-	139.1	-0.6	-	-	138.9	-0.1	-	-	138.4	-0.4	-	-

Source: U.S. Department of Labor, Bureau of Labor Statistics, Division of Consumer Prices and Price Indexes. - indicates no data collected for period.

St. Louis, MO-IL
Consumer Price Index - All Urban Consumers
Base 1982-1984 = 100
Medical Care

For 1947-1995. Columns headed % show percentile change in the index from the previous period for which an index is available.

Year	Jan Index	%	Feb Index	%	Mar Index	%	Apr Index	%	May Index	%	Jun Index	%	Jul Index	%	Aug Index	%	Sep Index	%	Oct Index	%	Nov Index	%	Dec Index	%
1947	12.9	-	12.9	0.0	13.0	0.8	13.0	0.0	13.0	0.0	13.0	0.0	-	-	-	-	13.4	3.1	-	-	-	-	13.7	2.2
1948	-	-	-	-	13.8	0.7	-	-	-	-	13.8	0.0	-	-	-	-	14.3	3.6	-	-	-	-	14.4	0.7
1949	-	-	-	-	14.5	0.7	-	-	-	-	14.4	-0.7	-	-	-	-	14.4	0.0	-	-	-	-	14.5	0.7
1950	-	-	-	-	14.5	0.0	-	-	-	-	14.5	0.0	-	-	-	-	14.6	0.7	-	-	-	-	14.7	0.7
1951	-	-	-	-	15.0	2.0	-	-	-	-	15.0	0.0	-	-	-	-	15.1	0.7	-	-	-	-	17.7	17.2
1952	-	-	-	-	17.8	0.6	-	-	-	-	18.1	1.7	-	-	-	-	18.1	0.0	-	-	-	-	18.3	1.1
1953	-	-	-	-	18.4	0.5	-	-	-	-	18.5	0.5	-	-	-	-	18.5	0.0	-	-	-	-	18.6	0.5
1954	-	-	-	-	18.7	0.5	-	-	-	-	18.7	0.0	-	-	-	-	18.9	1.1	-	-	-	-	19.4	2.6
1955	-	-	-	-	19.5	0.5	-	-	-	-	19.5	0.0	-	-	-	-	19.5	0.0	-	-	-	-	19.5	0.0
1956	-	-	-	-	19.5	0.0	-	-	-	-	19.5	0.0	-	-	-	-	19.9	2.1	-	-	-	-	21.2	6.5
1957	-	-	-	-	21.4	0.9	-	-	-	-	21.4	0.0	-	-	-	-	21.5	0.5	-	-	-	-	21.7	0.9
1958	-	-	-	-	22.0	1.4	-	-	-	-	22.0	0.0	-	-	-	-	22.1	0.5	-	-	-	-	23.1	4.5
1959	-	-	-	-	23.2	0.4	-	-	-	-	23.3	0.4	-	-	-	-	23.5	0.9	-	-	-	-	23.7	0.9
1960	-	-	-	-	23.7	0.0	-	-	-	-	23.6	-0.4	-	-	-	-	23.6	0.0	-	-	-	-	23.8	0.8
1961	-	-	-	-	24.0	0.8	-	-	-	-	24.0	0.0	-	-	-	-	24.2	0.8	-	-	-	-	25.3	4.5
1962	-	-	-	-	25.4	0.4	-	-	-	-	25.5	0.4	-	-	-	-	25.6	0.4	-	-	-	-	25.6	0.0
1963	-	-	-	-	25.7	0.4	-	-	-	-	25.7	0.0	-	-	-	-	25.8	0.4	-	-	-	-	25.8	0.0
1964	-	-	-	-	25.8	0.0	-	-	-	-	25.7	-0.4	-	-	-	-	25.9	0.8	-	-	-	-	26.0	0.4
1965	-	-	-	-	26.5	1.9	-	-	-	-	26.9	1.5	-	-	-	-	27.0	0.4	-	-	-	-	27.1	0.4
1966	-	-	-	-	27.6	1.8	-	-	-	-	28.2	2.2	-	-	-	-	28.7	1.8	-	-	-	-	29.1	1.4
1967	-	-	-	-	29.5	1.4	-	-	-	-	29.5	0.0	-	-	-	-	30.0	1.7	-	-	-	-	30.3	1.0
1968	-	-	-	-	30.9	2.0	-	-	-	-	30.9	0.0	-	-	-	-	31.4	1.6	-	-	-	-	31.7	1.0
1969	-	-	-	-	32.6	2.8	-	-	-	-	33.1	1.5	-	-	-	-	33.4	0.9	-	-	-	-	33.5	0.3
1970	-	-	-	-	34.7	3.6	-	-	-	-	35.3	1.7	-	-	-	-	35.6	0.8	-	-	-	-	35.7	0.3
1971	-	-	-	-	36.4	2.0	-	-	-	-	36.8	1.1	-	-	-	-	37.1	0.8	-	-	-	-	36.8	-0.8
1972	-	-	-	-	37.2	1.1	-	-	-	-	37.4	0.5	-	-	-	-	37.5	0.3	-	-	-	-	37.6	0.3
1973	-	-	-	-	38.2	1.6	-	-	-	-	38.3	0.3	-	-	-	-	38.8	1.3	-	-	-	-	39.7	2.3
1974	-	-	-	-	40.7	2.5	-	-	-	-	41.2	1.2	-	-	-	-	42.7	3.6	-	-	-	-	44.1	3.3
1975	-	-	-	-	45.2	2.5	-	-	-	-	46.2	2.2	-	-	-	-	47.4	2.6	-	-	-	-	47.5	0.2
1976	-	-	-	-	49.1	3.4	-	-	-	-	50.1	2.0	-	-	-	-	50.7	1.2	-	-	-	-	52.4	3.4
1977	-	-	-	-	54.4	3.8	-	-	-	-	55.2	1.5	-	-	-	-	56.5	2.4	-	-	-	-	57.2	1.2
1978	-	-	-	-	58.9	3.0	-	-	59.1	0.3	-	-	60.1	1.7	-	-	60.3	0.3	-	-	60.5	0.3	-	-
1979	62.4	3.1	-	-	62.5	0.2	-	-	63.5	1.6	-	-	65.6	3.3	-	-	65.7	0.2	-	-	66.8	1.7	-	-
1980	70.7	5.8	-	-	71.2	0.7	-	-	72.1	1.3	-	-	73.4	1.8	-	-	73.4	0.0	-	-	75.1	2.3	-	-
1981	77.7	3.5	-	-	79.6	2.4	-	-	81.2	2.0	-	-	81.6	0.5	-	-	83.0	1.7	-	-	84.6	1.9	-	-
1982	90.2	6.6	-	-	91.5	1.4	-	-	92.1	0.7	-	-	93.7	1.7	-	-	94.5	0.9	-	-	95.9	1.5	-	-
1983	99.9	4.2	-	-	100.0	0.1	-	-	100.0	0.0	-	-	101.2	1.2	-	-	101.1	-0.1	-	-	101.7	0.6	-	-
1984	104.6	2.9	-	-	105.1	0.5	-	-	105.3	0.2	-	-	105.6	0.3	-	-	106.2	0.6	-	-	106.8	0.6	-	-
1985	108.6	1.7	-	-	109.5	0.8	-	-	110.3	0.7	-	-	111.3	0.9	-	-	111.5	0.2	-	-	112.6	1.0	-	-
1986	117.4	4.3	-	-	118.4	0.9	-	-	119.2	0.7	-	-	121.4	1.8	-	-	121.3	-0.1	-	-	122.1	0.7	-	-
1987	124.5	2.0	-	-	126.5	1.6	-	-	127.0	0.4	-	-	128.6	1.3	-	-	129.3	0.5	-	-	129.8	0.4	-	-
1988	132.4	2.0	-	-	133.4	0.8	-	-	134.0	0.4	-	-	136.5	1.9	-	-	136.6	0.1	-	-	138.8	1.6	-	-
1989	140.5	1.2	-	-	142.3	1.3	-	-	143.7	1.0	-	-	146.9	2.2	-	-	148.4	1.0	-	-	148.9	0.3	-	-
1990	152.4	2.4	-	-	156.5	2.7	-	-	158.7	1.4	-	-	159.6	0.6	-	-	160.5	0.6	-	-	162.3	1.1	-	-
1991	168.0	3.5	-	-	169.5	0.9	-	-	170.0	0.3	-	-	172.9	1.7	-	-	173.6	0.4	-	-	174.1	0.3	-	-

[Continued]

St. Louis, MO-IL
Consumer Price Index - All Urban Consumers
Base 1982-1984 = 100
Medical Care

[Continued]

For 1947-1995. Columns headed % show percentile change in the index from the previous period for which an index is available.

Year	Jan		Feb		Mar		Apr		May		Jun		Jul		Aug		Sep		Oct		Nov		Dec	
	Index	%	Index	%	Index	%	Index	%	Index	%	Index	%	Index	%	Index	%	Index	%	Index	%	Index	%	Index	%
1992	177.1	1.7	-	-	178.8	1.0	-	-	179.4	0.3	-	-	182.4	1.7	-	-	183.1	0.4	-	-	182.9	-0.1	-	-
1993	186.3	1.9	-	-	188.7	1.3	-	-	190.2	0.8	-	-	192.0	0.9	-	-	194.3	1.2	-	-	195.0	0.4	-	-
1994	197.5	1.3	-	-	199.2	0.9	-	-	199.9	0.4	-	-	202.5	1.3	-	-	204.2	0.8	-	-	204.6	0.2	-	-
1995	207.0	1.2	-	-	208.3	0.6	-	-	210.6	1.1	-	-	210.0	-0.3	-	-	210.6	0.3	-	-	211.1	0.2	-	-

Source: U.S. Department of Labor, Bureau of Labor Statistics, Division of Consumer Prices and Price Indexes. - indicates no data collected for period.

St. Louis, MO-IL
Consumer Price Index - Urban Wage Earners
Base 1982-1984 = 100
Medical Care

For 1947-1995. Columns headed % show percentile change in the index from the previous period for which an index is available.

Year	Jan Index	%	Feb Index	%	Mar Index	%	Apr Index	%	May Index	%	Jun Index	%	Jul Index	%	Aug Index	%	Sep Index	%	Oct Index	%	Nov Index	%	Dec Index	%
1947	12.8	-	12.8	0.0	12.9	0.8	12.9	0.0	12.9	0.0	12.9	0.0	-		-		13.2	2.3	-		-		13.6	3.0
1948	-	-	-	-	13.7	0.7	-	-	-	-	13.7	0.0	-		-		14.2	3.6	-		-		14.2	0.0
1949	-	-	-	-	14.3	0.7	-	-	-	-	14.3	0.0	-		-		14.3	0.0	-		-		14.3	0.0
1950	-	-	-	-	14.4	0.7	-	-	-	-	14.4	0.0	-		-		14.4	0.0	-		-	-	14.5	0.7
1951	-	-	-	-	14.9	2.8	-	-	-	-	14.9	0.0	-		-		14.9	0.0	-		-		17.6	18.1
1952	-	-	-	-	17.7	0.6	-	-	-	-	17.9	1.1	-		-		17.9	0.0	-		-		18.2	1.7
1953	-	-	-	-	18.2	0.0	-	-	-	-	18.3	0.5	-		-		18.3	0.0	-		-		18.4	0.5
1954	-	-	-	-	18.5	0.5	-	-	-	-	18.6	0.5	-		-		18.7	0.5	-		-		19.2	2.7
1955	-	-	-	-	19.3	0.5	-	-	-	-	19.3	0.0	-		-		19.3	0.0	-		-		19.3	0.0
1956	-	-	-	-	19.3	0.0	-	-	-	-	19.4	0.5	-		-		19.7	1.5	-		-		21.0	6.6
1957	-	-	-	-	21.3	1.4	-	-	-	-	21.3	0.0	-		-		21.3	0.0	-		-		21.5	0.9
1958	-	-	-	-	21.8	1.4	-	-	-	-	21.8	0.0	-		-		21.9	0.5	-		-		22.9	4.6
1959	-	-	-	-	23.0	0.4	-	-	-	-	23.0	0.0	-		-		23.3	1.3	-		-		23.5	0.9
1960	-	-	-	-	23.5	0.0	-	-	-	-	23.4	-0.4	-		-		23.4	0.0	-		-		23.6	0.9
1961	-	-	-	-	23.8	0.8	-	-	-	-	23.8	0.0	-		-		24.0	0.8	-		-		25.1	4.6
1962	-	-	-	-	25.1	0.0	-	-	-	-	25.3	0.8	-		-		25.3	0.0	-		-		25.3	0.0
1963	-	-	-	-	25.5	0.8	-	-	-	-	25.5	0.0	-		-		25.5	0.0	-		-		25.6	0.4
1964	-	-	-	-	25.6	0.0	-	-	-	-	25.5	-0.4	-		-		25.7	0.8	-		-		25.8	0.4
1965	-	-	-	-	26.3	1.9	-	-	-	-	26.7	1.5	-		-		26.7	0.0	-		-		26.9	0.7
1966	-	-	-	-	27.3	1.5	-	-	-	-	28.0	2.6	-		-		28.4	1.4	-		-		28.8	1.4
1967	-	-	-	-	29.2	1.4	-	-	-	-	29.2	0.0	-		-		29.7	1.7	-		-		30.0	1.0
1968	-	-	-	-	30.6	2.0	-	-	-	-	30.7	0.3	-		-		31.1	1.3	-		-		31.5	1.3
1969	-	-	-	-	32.3	2.5	-	-	-	-	32.8	1.5	-		-		33.1	0.9	-		-		33.2	0.3
1970	-	-	-	-	34.4	3.6	-	-	-	-	34.9	1.5	-		-		35.3	1.1	-		-		35.4	0.3
1971	-	-	-	-	36.0	1.7	-	-	-	-	36.4	1.1	-		-		36.8	1.1	-		-		36.5	-0.8
1972	-	-	-	-	36.8	0.8	-	-	-	-	37.1	0.8	-		-		37.1	0.0	-		-		37.3	0.5
1973	-	-	-	-	37.9	1.6	-	-	-	-	38.0	0.3	-		-		38.4	1.1	-		-		39.3	2.3
1974	-	-	-	-	40.4	2.8	-	-	-	-	40.8	1.0	-		-		42.3	3.7	-		-		43.7	3.3
1975	-	-	-	-	44.8	2.5	-	-	-	-	45.8	2.2	-		-		47.0	2.6	-		-		47.1	0.2
1976	-	-	-	-	48.6	3.2	-	-	-	-	49.6	2.1	-		-		50.2	1.2	-		-		51.9	3.4
1977	-	-	-	-	53.9	3.9	-	-	-	-	54.7	1.5	-		-		56.0	2.4	-		-		56.7	1.3
1978	-	-		-	58.4	3.0	-	-	59.0	1.0	-	-	59.6	1.0	-		60.2	1.0	-	-	61.3	1.8	-	-
1979	62.8	2.4	-	-	63.2	0.6	-	-	63.7	0.8	-		65.2	2.4	-		65.9	1.1	-	-	67.8	2.9	-	-
1980	70.9	4.6	-	-	72.3	2.0	-	-	72.6	0.4	-		73.7	1.5	-	-	74.0	0.4	-	-	75.8	2.4	-	-
1981	78.1	3.0	-	-	80.7	3.3	-	-	81.4	0.9	-		81.8	0.5	-	-	83.3	1.8	-	-	85.0	2.0	-	-
1982	90.4	6.4	-	-	91.6	1.3	-	-	92.1	0.5	-		93.7	1.7	-	-	94.4	0.7	-	-	95.8	1.5	-	-
1983	99.5	3.9	-	-	99.7	0.2	-	-	99.8	0.1	-		101.2	1.4	-	-	101.2	0.0	-	-	101.8	0.6	-	-
1984	104.6	2.8	-	-	105.1	0.5	-	-	105.3	0.2	-		105.7	0.4	-	-	106.4	0.7	-	-	107.0	0.6	-	-
1985	108.8	1.7	-	-	109.6	0.7	-	-	110.3	0.6	-		111.3	0.9	-	-	111.5	0.2	-	-	112.5	0.9	-	-
1986	117.2	4.2	-	-	118.1	0.8	-	-	118.9	0.7	-		121.0	1.8	-	-	120.7	-0.2	-	-	121.5	0.7	-	-
1987	123.9	2.0	-	-	126.0	1.7	-	-	126.7	0.6	-		128.3	1.3	-	-	129.1	0.6	-	-	129.3	0.2	-	-
1988	131.9	2.0	-	-	132.9	0.8	-	-	133.6	0.5	-		136.1	1.9	-	-	136.3	0.1	-	-	138.5	1.6	-	-
1989	140.4	1.4	-	-	142.2	1.3	-	-	143.6	1.0	-		147.1	2.4	-	-	148.6	1.0	-	-	148.8	0.1	-	-
1990	152.4	2.4	-	-	156.0	2.4	-	-	158.1	1.3	-		158.9	0.5	-	-	159.7	0.5	-	-	161.3	1.0	-	-
1991	167.0	3.5	-	-	168.4	0.8	-	-	169.0	0.4	-		171.8	1.7	-	-	172.4	0.3	-	-	172.9	0.3	-	-

[Continued]

St. Louis, MO-IL
Consumer Price Index - Urban Wage Earners
Base 1982-1984 = 100
Medical Care
[Continued]

For 1947-1995. Columns headed % show percentile change in the index from the previous period for which an index is available.

Year	Jan Index	Jan %	Feb Index	Feb %	Mar Index	Mar %	Apr Index	Apr %	May Index	May %	Jun Index	Jun %	Jul Index	Jul %	Aug Index	Aug %	Sep Index	Sep %	Oct Index	Oct %	Nov Index	Nov %	Dec Index	Dec %
1992	175.9	1.7	-	-	177.8	1.1	-	-	178.4	0.3	-	-	181.6	1.8	-	-	182.2	0.3	-	-	182.0	-0.1	-	-
1993	185.3	1.8	-	-	187.9	1.4	-	-	189.2	0.7	-	-	190.8	0.8	-	-	193.2	1.3	-	-	193.8	0.3	-	-
1994	196.2	1.2	-	-	197.7	0.8	-	-	198.3	0.3	-	-	200.8	1.3	-	-	202.5	0.8	-	-	202.9	0.2	-	-
1995	205.2	1.1	-	-	206.5	0.6	-	-	208.9	1.2	-	-	208.3	-0.3	-	-	208.8	0.2	-	-	209.5	0.3	-	-

Source: U.S. Department of Labor, Bureau of Labor Statistics, Division of Consumer Prices and Price Indexes. - indicates no data collected for period.

St. Louis, MO-IL
Consumer Price Index - All Urban Consumers
Base 1982-1984 = 100
Entertainment

For 1975-1995. Columns headed % show percentile change in the index from the previous period for which an index is available.

Year	Jan Index	%	Feb Index	%	Mar Index	%	Apr Index	%	May Index	%	Jun Index	%	Jul Index	%	Aug Index	%	Sep Index	%	Oct Index	%	Nov Index	%	Dec Index	%
1975	-	-	-	-	-	-	-	-	-	-	-	-	-	-	-	-	-	-	-	-	-	-	65.1	-
1976	-	-	-	-	65.4	0.5	-	-	-	-	66.5	1.7	-	-	-	-	66.8	0.5	-	-	-	-	67.5	1.0
1977	-	-	-	-	68.6	1.6	-	-	-	-	70.3	2.5	-	-	-	-	71.0	1.0	-	-	-	-	72.7	2.4
1978	-	-	-	-	75.1	3.3	-	-	76.2	1.5	-	-	78.6	3.1	-	-	79.9	1.7	-	-	80.0	0.1	-	-
1979	80.8	1.0	-	-	80.4	-0.5	-	-	80.6	0.2	-	-	80.5	-0.1	-	-	81.4	1.1	-	-	84.5	3.8	-	-
1980	83.8	-0.8	-	-	86.4	3.1	-	-	87.4	1.2	-	-	89.2	2.1	-	-	89.8	0.7	-	-	89.9	0.1	-	-
1981	93.9	4.4	-	-	94.0	0.1	-	-	94.2	0.2	-	-	91.7	-2.7	-	-	94.7	3.3	-	-	94.7	0.0	-	-
1982	95.6	1.0	-	-	96.4	0.8	-	-	93.9	-2.6	-	-	95.6	1.8	-	-	97.3	1.8	-	-	97.9	0.6	-	-
1983	99.9	2.0	-	-	101.4	1.5	-	-	101.0	-0.4	-	-	101.3	0.3	-	-	102.7	1.4	-	-	101.4	-1.3	-	-
1984	100.4	-1.0	-	-	100.8	0.4	-	-	101.9	1.1	-	-	102.0	0.1	-	-	103.0	1.0	-	-	105.1	2.0	-	-
1985	105.3	0.2	-	-	104.8	-0.5	-	-	104.5	-0.3	-	-	105.6	1.1	-	-	106.4	0.8	-	-	108.6	2.1	-	-
1986	108.4	-0.2	-	-	109.8	1.3	-	-	110.4	0.5	-	-	109.2	-1.1	-	-	110.3	1.0	-	-	111.9	1.5	-	-
1987	112.4	0.4	-	-	111.7	-0.6	-	-	112.7	0.9	-	-	114.3	1.4	-	-	115.5	1.0	-	-	116.0	0.4	-	-
1988	115.8	-0.2	-	-	117.8	1.7	-	-	116.8	-0.8	-	-	117.0	0.2	-	-	118.8	1.5	-	-	119.8	0.8	-	-
1989	120.6	0.7	-	-	121.0	0.3	-	-	122.8	1.5	-	-	123.0	0.2	-	-	123.6	0.5	-	-	123.0	-0.5	-	-
1990	120.3	-2.2	-	-	122.1	1.5	-	-	121.9	-0.2	-	-	124.3	2.0	-	-	128.4	3.3	-	-	127.7	-0.5	-	-
1991	127.5	-0.2	-	-	132.6	4.0	-	-	133.9	1.0	-	-	136.4	1.9	-	-	137.4	0.7	-	-	136.9	-0.4	-	-
1992	137.3	0.3	-	-	137.8	0.4	-	-	139.5	1.2	-	-	139.5	0.0	-	-	136.6	-2.1	-	-	135.9	-0.5	-	-
1993	137.3	1.0	-	-	137.3	0.0	-	-	135.4	-1.4	-	-	137.7	1.7	-	-	136.4	-0.9	-	-	139.5	2.3	-	-
1994	138.1	-1.0	-	-	137.6	-0.4	-	-	144.7	5.2	-	-	140.5	-2.9	-	-	142.0	1.1	-	-	148.9	4.9	-	-
1995	153.2	2.9	-	-	154.3	0.7	-	-	154.5	0.1	-	-	152.4	-1.4	-	-	159.0	4.3	-	-	157.7	-0.8	-	-

Source: U.S. Department of Labor, Bureau of Labor Statistics, Division of Consumer Prices and Price Indexes. - indicates no data collected for period.

St. Louis, MO-IL
Consumer Price Index - Urban Wage Earners
Base 1982-1984 = 100
Entertainment

For 1975-1995. Columns headed % show percentile change in the index from the previous period for which an index is available.

Year	Jan Index	%	Feb Index	%	Mar Index	%	Apr Index	%	May Index	%	Jun Index	%	Jul Index	%	Aug Index	%	Sep Index	%	Oct Index	%	Nov Index	%	Dec Index	%
1975	-	-	-	-	-	-	-	-	-	-	-	-	-	-	-	-	-	-	-	-	-	-	71.0	-
1976	-	-	-	-	71.4	0.6	-	-	-	-	72.5	1.5	-	-	-	-	72.9	0.6	-	-	-	-	73.7	1.1
1977	-	-	-	-	74.8	1.5	-	-	-	-	76.7	2.5	-	-	-	-	77.5	1.0	-	-	-	-	79.3	2.3
1978	-	-	-	-	81.9	3.3	-	-	82.3	0.5	-	-	81.7	-0.7	-	-	83.1	1.7	-	-	83.4	0.4	-	-
1979	83.3	-0.1	-	-	83.2	-0.1	-	-	85.8	3.1	-	-	86.0	0.2	-	-	87.0	1.2	-	-	90.5	4.0	-	-
1980	88.6	-2.1	-	-	92.1	4.0	-	-	94.9	3.0	-	-	94.7	-0.2	-	-	95.7	1.1	-	-	93.3	-2.5	-	-
1981	98.0	5.0	-	-	97.5	-0.5	-	-	96.2	-1.3	-	-	94.5	-1.8	-	-	97.0	2.6	-	-	95.5	-1.5	-	-
1982	96.2	0.7	-	-	96.6	0.4	-	-	93.8	-2.9	-	-	95.8	2.1	-	-	97.6	1.9	-	-	98.0	0.4	-	-
1983	100.1	2.1	-	-	101.6	1.5	-	-	101.0	-0.6	-	-	101.5	0.5	-	-	102.9	1.4	-	-	101.3	-1.6	-	-
1984	100.4	-0.9	-	-	100.7	0.3	-	-	101.7	1.0	-	-	101.5	-0.2	-	-	102.3	0.8	-	-	105.0	2.6	-	-
1985	105.1	0.1	-	-	103.8	-1.2	-	-	103.7	-0.1	-	-	104.6	0.9	-	-	105.2	0.6	-	-	107.4	2.1	-	-
1986	107.3	-0.1	-	-	108.6	1.2	-	-	109.2	0.6	-	-	108.4	-0.7	-	-	109.8	1.3	-	-	111.0	1.1	-	-
1987	111.4	0.4	-	-	110.8	-0.5	-	-	111.8	0.9	-	-	113.3	1.3	-	-	114.5	1.1	-	-	114.9	0.3	-	-
1988	115.1	0.2	-	-	117.3	1.9	-	-	115.7	-1.4	-	-	116.4	0.6	-	-	117.9	1.3	-	-	118.8	0.8	-	-
1989	119.9	0.9	-	-	120.0	0.1	-	-	122.2	1.8	-	-	122.0	-0.2	-	-	122.6	0.5	-	-	121.6	-0.8	-	-
1990	118.9	-2.2	-	-	120.7	1.5	-	-	120.8	0.1	-	-	123.0	1.8	-	-	127.5	3.7	-	-	126.9	-0.5	-	-
1991	126.7	-0.2	-	-	131.5	3.8	-	-	132.2	0.5	-	-	134.5	1.7	-	-	135.7	0.9	-	-	134.9	-0.6	-	-
1992	135.1	0.1	-	-	135.8	0.5	-	-	137.4	1.2	-	-	137.4	0.0	-	-	134.8	-1.9	-	-	134.0	-0.6	-	-
1993	135.0	0.7	-	-	134.8	-0.1	-	-	133.4	-1.0	-	-	135.7	1.7	-	-	134.7	-0.7	-	-	137.9	2.4	-	-
1994	136.6	-0.9	-	-	137.3	0.5	-	-	142.4	3.7	-	-	138.9	-2.5	-	-	139.9	0.7	-	-	146.1	4.4	-	-
1995	149.8	2.5	-	-	150.6	0.5	-	-	150.2	-0.3	-	-	148.3	-1.3	-	-	154.1	3.9	-	-	152.2	-1.2	-	-

Source: U.S. Department of Labor, Bureau of Labor Statistics, Division of Consumer Prices and Price Indexes. - indicates no data collected for period.

St. Louis, MO-IL
Consumer Price Index - All Urban Consumers
Base 1982-1984 = 100
Other Goods and Services

For 1975-1995. Columns headed % show percentile change in the index from the previous period for which an index is available.

Year	Jan Index	%	Feb Index	%	Mar Index	%	Apr Index	%	May Index	%	Jun Index	%	Jul Index	%	Aug Index	%	Sep Index	%	Oct Index	%	Nov Index	%	Dec Index	%
1975	-	-	-	-	-	-	-	-	-	-	-	-	-	-	-	-	-	-	-	-	-	-	55.7	-
1976	-	-	-	-	56.1	0.7	-	-	-	-	57.0	1.6	-	-	-	-	58.0	1.8	-	-	-	-	58.8	1.4
1977	-	-	-	-	59.2	0.7	-	-	-	-	60.1	1.5	-	-	-	-	61.4	2.2	-	-	-	-	62.6	2.0
1978	-	-	-	-	63.2	1.0	-	-	63.4	0.3	-	-	64.8	2.2	-	-	66.1	2.0	-	-	66.5	0.6	-	-
1979	66.8	0.5	-	-	67.0	0.3	-	-	67.8	1.2	-	-	68.6	1.2	-	-	70.3	2.5	-	-	70.4	0.1	-	-
1980	71.1	1.0	-	-	72.5	2.0	-	-	73.5	1.4	-	-	74.2	1.0	-	-	78.0	5.1	-	-	77.3	-0.9	-	-
1981	77.9	0.8	-	-	78.7	1.0	-	-	81.2	3.2	-	-	81.8	0.7	-	-	84.0	2.7	-	-	86.3	2.7	-	-
1982	86.7	0.5	-	-	88.3	1.8	-	-	87.6	-0.8	-	-	88.5	1.0	-	-	92.8	4.9	-	-	96.6	4.1	-	-
1983	98.3	1.8	-	-	99.7	1.4	-	-	98.8	-0.9	-	-	99.8	1.0	-	-	102.9	3.1	-	-	104.6	1.7	-	-
1984	105.8	1.1	-	-	106.2	0.4	-	-	106.5	0.3	-	-	107.5	0.9	-	-	111.5	3.7	-	-	111.6	0.1	-	-
1985	112.7	1.0	-	-	113.7	0.9	-	-	113.0	-0.6	-	-	114.6	1.4	-	-	117.0	2.1	-	-	119.5	2.1	-	-
1986	120.2	0.6	-	-	120.3	0.1	-	-	120.3	0.0	-	-	121.1	0.7	-	-	123.6	2.1	-	-	125.4	1.5	-	-
1987	126.6	1.0	-	-	125.9	-0.6	-	-	126.7	0.6	-	-	126.9	0.2	-	-	129.9	2.4	-	-	131.0	0.8	-	-
1988	133.7	2.1	-	-	135.1	1.0	-	-	134.7	-0.3	-	-	136.2	1.1	-	-	138.8	1.9	-	-	140.5	1.2	-	-
1989	141.8	0.9	-	-	143.1	0.9	-	-	143.7	0.4	-	-	145.9	1.5	-	-	146.7	0.5	-	-	149.2	1.7	-	-
1990	150.2	0.7	-	-	150.9	0.5	-	-	151.1	0.1	-	-	154.1	2.0	-	-	155.6	1.0	-	-	157.1	1.0	-	-
1991	159.7	1.7	-	-	160.6	0.6	-	-	158.1	-1.6	-	-	163.7	3.5	-	-	166.3	1.6	-	-	169.7	2.0	-	-
1992	169.9	0.1	-	-	169.9	0.0	-	-	170.9	0.6	-	-	171.6	0.4	-	-	175.0	2.0	-	-	174.8	-0.1	-	-
1993	177.4	1.5	-	-	176.6	-0.5	-	-	179.6	1.7	-	-	178.8	-0.4	-	-	170.3	-4.8	-	-	173.7	2.0	-	-
1994	174.1	0.2	-	-	172.8	-0.7	-	-	171.5	-0.8	-	-	168.8	-1.6	-	-	177.0	4.9	-	-	178.6	0.9	-	-
1995	179.0	0.2	-	-	178.6	-0.2	-	-	179.6	0.6	-	-	178.9	-0.4	-	-	183.0	2.3	-	-	182.4	-0.3	-	-

Source: U.S. Department of Labor, Bureau of Labor Statistics, Division of Consumer Prices and Price Indexes. - indicates no data collected for period.

St. Louis, MO-IL
Consumer Price Index - Urban Wage Earners
Base 1982-1984 = 100
Other Goods and Services

For 1975-1995. Columns headed % show percentile change in the index from the previous period for which an index is available.

Year	Jan Index	%	Feb Index	%	Mar Index	%	Apr Index	%	May Index	%	Jun Index	%	Jul Index	%	Aug Index	%	Sep Index	%	Oct Index	%	Nov Index	%	Dec Index	%
1975	-	-	-	-	-	-	-	-	-	-			-	-	-	-	-	-	-	-	-	-	55.3	-
1976	-	-	-	-	55.7	0.7	-	-	-	-	56.6	1.6	-	-	-	-	57.6	1.8	-	-	-	-	58.3	1.2
1977	-	-	-	-	58.8	0.9	-	-	-	-	59.7	1.5	-	-	-	-	60.9	2.0	-	-	-	-	62.1	2.0
1978	-	-	-	-	62.7	1.0	-	-	63.3	1.0	-	-	64.8	2.4	-	-	64.9	0.2	-	-	65.7	1.2	-	-
1979	67.7	3.0	-	-	67.3	-0.6	-	-	68.2	1.3	-	-	68.3	0.1	-	-	69.8	2.2	-	-	69.9	0.1	-	-
1980	71.8	2.7	-	-	73.0	1.7	-	-	74.3	1.8	-	-	74.7	0.5	-	-	78.3	4.8	-	-	78.9	0.8	-	-
1981	79.5	0.8	-	-	80.0	0.6	-	-	82.2	2.8	-	-	82.8	0.7	-	-	83.0	0.2	-	-	86.2	3.9	-	-
1982	86.4	0.2	-	-	88.5	2.4	-	-	87.8	-0.8	-	-	88.7	1.0	-	-	92.8	4.6	-	-	96.5	4.0	-	-
1983	98.6	2.2	-	-	100.5	1.9	-	-	99.3	-1.2	-	-	100.6	1.3	-	-	103.1	2.5	-	-	104.3	1.2	-	-
1984	105.8	1.4	-	-	106.0	0.2	-	-	106.2	0.2	-	-	107.5	1.2	-	-	110.5	2.8	-	-	110.5	0.0	-	-
1985	111.9	1.3	-	-	112.9	0.9	-	-	112.1	-0.7	-	-	114.2	1.9	-	-	116.4	1.9	-	-	118.5	1.8	-	-
1986	119.4	0.8	-	-	119.5	0.1	-	-	119.5	0.0	-	-	120.7	1.0	-	-	121.9	1.0	-	-	123.8	1.6	-	-
1987	125.2	1.1	-	-	124.5	-0.6	-	-	125.4	0.7	-	-	125.8	0.3	-	-	128.6	2.2	-	-	129.5	0.7	-	-
1988	132.1	2.0	-	-	133.7	1.2	-	-	133.6	-0.1	-	-	135.5	1.4	-	-	138.1	1.9	-	-	139.1	0.7	-	-
1989	141.3	1.6	-	-	142.2	0.6	-	-	143.0	0.6	-	-	145.3	1.6	-	-	145.9	0.4	-	-	148.5	1.8	-	-
1990	149.7	0.8	-	-	150.4	0.5	-	-	150.8	0.3	-	-	154.8	2.7	-	-	155.6	0.5	-	-	157.9	1.5	-	-
1991	161.4	2.2	-	-	162.8	0.9	-	-	160.1	-1.7	-	-	165.3	3.2	-	-	168.0	1.6	-	-	172.3	2.6	-	-
1992	172.5	0.1	-	-	172.5	0.0	-	-	174.6	1.2	-	-	174.7	0.1	-	-	179.0	2.5	-	-	177.0	-1.1	-	-
1993	181.1	2.3	-	-	178.7	-1.3	-	-	182.4	2.1	-	-	180.3	-1.2	-	-	165.6	-8.2	-	-	170.2	2.8	-	-
1994	170.4	0.1	-	-	169.5	-0.5	-	-	168.5	-0.6	-	-	166.7	-1.1	-	-	172.6	3.5	-	-	173.9	0.8	-	-
1995	174.2	0.2	-	-	173.9	-0.2	-	-	174.9	0.6	-	-	174.2	-0.4	-	-	177.6	2.0	-	-	177.0	-0.3	-	-

Source: U.S. Department of Labor, Bureau of Labor Statistics, Division of Consumer Prices and Price Indexes. - indicates no data collected for period.

Washington, DC-MD-VA
Consumer Price Index - All Urban Consumers
Base 1982-1984 = 100
Annual Averages

For 1914-1995. Columns headed % show percentile change in the index from the previous period for which an index is available.

Year	All Items		Food & Beverage		Housing		Apparel & Upkeep		Trans- portation		Medical Care		Entertain- ment		Other Goods & Services	
	Index	%	Index	%	Index	%	Index	%	Index	%	Index	%	Index	%	Index	%
1914	-	-	-	-	-	-	-	-	-	-	-	-	-	-	-	-
1915	10.6	-	-	-	-	-	-	-	-	-	-	-	-	-	-	-
1916	11.4	7.5	-	-	-	-	-	-	-	-	-	-	-	-	-	-
1917	13.8	21.1	-	-	-	-	-	-	-	-	-	-	-	-	-	-
1918	16.3	18.1	-	-	-	-	-	-	-	-	-	-	-	-	-	-
1919	17.8	9.2	-	-	-	-	-	-	-	-	-	-	-	-	-	-
1920	20.0	12.4	-	-	-	-	-	-	-	-	-	-	-	-	-	-
1921	17.6	-12.0	-	-	-	-	-	-	-	-	-	-	-	-	-	-
1922	16.7	-5.1	-	-	-	-	-	-	-	-	-	-	-	-	-	-
1923	16.9	1.2	-	-	-	-	-	-	-	-	-	-	-	-	-	-
1924	16.9	0.0	-	-	-	-	-	-	-	-	-	-	-	-	-	-
1925	17.3	2.4	-	-	-	-	-	-	-	-	-	-	-	-	-	-
1926	17.5	1.2	-	-	-	-	-	-	-	-	-	-	-	-	-	-
1927	17.0	-2.9	-	-	-	-	-	-	-	-	-	-	-	-	-	-
1928	16.9	-0.6	-	-	-	-	-	-	-	-	-	-	-	-	-	-
1929	16.8	-0.6	-	-	-	-	-	-	-	-	-	-	-	-	-	-
1930	16.5	-1.8	-	-	-	-	-	-	-	-	-	-	-	-	-	-
1931	15.5	-6.1	-	-	-	-	-	-	-	-	-	-	-	-	-	-
1932	14.3	-7.7	-	-	-	-	-	-	-	-	-	-	-	-	-	-
1933	13.9	-2.8	-	-	-	-	-	-	-	-	-	-	-	-	-	-
1934	14.3	2.9	-	-	-	-	-	-	-	-	-	-	-	-	-	-
1935	14.6	2.1	-	-	-	-	-	-	-	-	-	-	-	-	-	-
1936	14.7	0.7	-	-	-	-	-	-	-	-	-	-	-	-	-	-
1937	15.0	2.0	-	-	-	-	-	-	-	-	-	-	-	-	-	-
1938	14.7	-2.0	-	-	-	-	-	-	-	-	-	-	-	-	-	-
1939	14.6	-0.7	-	-	-	-	-	-	-	-	-	-	-	-	-	-
1940	14.7	0.7	-	-	-	-	-	-	-	-	-	-	-	-	-	-
1941	15.3	4.1	-	-	-	-	-	-	-	-	-	-	-	-	-	-
1942	17.0	11.1	-	-	-	-	-	-	-	-	-	-	-	-	-	-
1943	18.1	6.5	-	-	-	-	-	-	-	-	-	-	-	-	-	-
1944	18.4	1.7	-	-	-	-	-	-	-	-	-	-	-	-	-	-
1945	18.9	2.7	-	-	-	-	-	-	-	-	-	-	-	-	-	-
1946	20.6	9.0	-	-	-	-	-	-	-	-	-	-	-	-	-	-
1947	23.2	12.6	-	-			-	-	19.1	-	12.4	-	-	-	-	-
1948	24.6	6.0	-	-	-	-	-	-	21.2	11.0	12.8	3.2	-	-	-	-
1949	24.6	0.0	-	-	-	-	-	-	22.8	7.5	13.1	2.3	-	-	-	-
1950	24.9	1.2	-	-	-	-	-	-	23.3	2.2	13.2	0.8	-	-	-	-
1951	26.6	6.8	-	-	-	-	-	-	24.2	3.9	14.0	6.1	-	-	-	-
1952	27.3	2.6	-	-	-	-	-	-	25.8	6.6	14.8	5.7	-	-	-	-
1953	27.5	0.7	-	-	-	-	40.5	-	26.9	4.3	15.0	1.4	-	-	-	-
1954	27.5	0.0	-	-	-	-	40.3	-0.5	26.8	-0.4	15.0	0.0	-	-	-	-
1955	27.4	-0.4	-	-	-	-	40.0	-0.7	27.2	1.5	15.3	2.0	-	-	-	-
1956	27.7	1.1	-	-	-	-	41.1	2.8	27.5	1.1	16.0	4.6	-	-	-	-
1957	28.6	3.2	-	-	-	-	41.3	0.5	28.9	5.1	16.8	5.0	-	-	-	-
1958	29.3	2.4	-	-	-	-	41.1	-0.5	29.5	2.1	17.9	6.5	-	-	-	-

[Continued]

Washington, DC-MD-VA
Consumer Price Index - All Urban Consumers
Base 1982-1984 = 100
Annual Averages
[Continued]

For 1914-1995. Columns headed % show percentile change in the index from the previous period for which an index is available.

Year	All Items		Food & Beverage		Housing		Apparel & Upkeep		Trans- portation		Medical Care		Entertain- ment		Other Goods & Services	
	Index	%	Index	%	Index	%	Index	%	Index	%	Index	%	Index	%	Index	%
1959	29.4	0.3	-	-	-	-	41.7	1.5	30.4	3.1	19.1	6.7	-	-	-	-
1960	29.7	1.0	-	-	-	-	42.1	1.0	30.7	1.0	19.7	3.1	-	-	-	-
1961	30.1	1.3	-	-	-	-	42.8	1.7	31.0	1.0	20.4	3.6	-	-	-	-
1962	30.4	1.0	-	-	-	-	44.1	3.0	31.3	1.0	21.5	5.4	-	-	-	-
1963	30.9	1.6	-	-	-	-	44.3	0.5	31.6	1.0	22.4	4.2	-	-	-	-
1964	31.4	1.6	-	-	-	-	44.6	0.7	32.4	2.5	23.0	2.7	-	-	-	-
1965	31.9	1.6	-	-	-	-	44.9	0.7	32.7	0.9	23.7	3.0	-	-	-	-
1966	33.0	3.4	-	-	-	-	46.4	3.3	32.9	0.6	24.9	5.1	-	-	-	-
1967	33.9	2.7	-	-	-	-	48.7	5.0	34.1	3.6	27.0	8.4	-	-	-	-
1968	35.5	4.7	-	-	-	-	52.3	7.4	35.4	3.8	29.6	9.6	-	-	-	-
1969	37.7	6.2	-	-	-	-	55.7	6.5	37.1	4.8	31.9	7.8	-	-	-	-
1970	39.8	5.6	-	-	-	-	58.2	4.5	39.7	7.0	34.3	7.5	-	-	-	-
1971	41.6	4.5	-	-	-	-	59.9	2.9	42.1	6.0	36.9	7.6	-	-	-	-
1972	43.0	3.4	-	-	-	-	60.8	1.5	42.2	0.2	37.8	2.4	-	-	-	-
1973	45.7	6.3	-	-	-	-	63.7	4.8	43.0	1.9	39.0	3.2	-	-	-	-
1974	50.8	11.2	-	-	-	-	68.5	7.5	47.6	10.7	43.5	11.5	-	-	-	-
1975	54.7	7.7	-	-	-	-	70.5	2.9	51.8	8.8	48.5	11.5	-	-	-	-
1976	58.0	6.0	62.5	-	55.2	-	72.7	3.1	55.6	7.3	53.4	10.1	68.6	-	58.4	-
1977	62.0	6.9	66.8	6.9	59.4	7.6	74.3	2.2	59.8	7.6	58.3	9.2	73.8	7.6	62.1	6.3
1978	66.7	7.6	73.4	9.9	64.6	8.8	78.0	5.0	63.4	6.0	62.2	6.7	74.9	1.5	65.6	5.6
1979	74.0	10.9	81.8	11.4	71.9	11.3	83.5	7.1	71.8	13.2	68.3	9.8	78.6	4.9	70.0	6.7
1980	82.9	12.0	88.0	7.6	81.0	12.7	90.2	8.0	84.8	18.1	74.2	8.6	84.7	7.8	75.8	8.3
1981	90.5	9.2	92.6	5.2	90.1	11.2	90.5	0.3	94.4	11.3	80.1	8.0	88.9	5.0	83.4	10.0
1982	95.5	5.5	97.2	5.0	95.4	5.9	94.7	4.6	97.0	2.8	90.6	13.1	94.1	5.8	91.3	9.5
1983	99.8	4.5	99.8	2.7	99.7	4.5	100.6	6.2	99.3	2.4	101.5	12.0	99.1	5.3	101.0	10.6
1984	104.6	4.8	103.0	3.2	104.9	5.2	104.7	4.1	103.7	4.4	107.9	6.3	106.7	7.7	107.7	6.6
1985	109.0	4.2	106.1	3.0	110.1	5.0	109.9	5.0	105.6	1.8	114.7	6.3	113.7	6.6	114.5	6.3
1986	112.2	2.9	110.1	3.8	114.8	4.3	108.7	-1.1	103.8	-1.7	122.6	6.9	116.5	2.5	121.9	6.5
1987	116.2	3.6	113.6	3.2	118.9	3.6	116.3	7.0	105.9	2.0	129.1	5.3	121.5	4.3	129.4	6.2
1988	121.0	4.1	119.2	4.9	123.4	3.8	123.1	5.8	108.1	2.1	137.8	6.7	124.8	2.7	138.4	7.0
1989	128.0	5.8	126.1	5.8	129.3	4.8	134.9	9.6	114.4	5.8	146.4	6.2	127.5	2.2	152.2	10.0
1990	135.6	5.9	133.4	5.8	136.6	5.6	139.4	3.3	120.7	5.5	162.4	10.9	135.6	6.4	165.4	8.7
1991	141.2	4.1	137.7	3.2	140.8	3.1	142.4	2.2	126.2	4.6	176.4	8.6	142.7	5.2	178.6	8.0
1992	144.7	2.5	140.9	2.3	143.9	2.2	139.6	-2.0	129.9	2.9	186.3	5.6	147.6	3.4	186.9	4.6
1993	149.3	3.2	142.8	1.3	148.0	2.8	144.4	3.4	134.9	3.8	195.3	4.8	151.0	2.3	199.4	6.7
1994	152.2	1.9	144.2	1.0	150.9	2.0	141.5	-2.0	137.0	1.6	203.5	4.2	155.9	3.2	208.8	4.7
1995	-	-	-	-	-	-	-	-	-	-	-	-	-	-	-	-

Source: U.S. Department of Labor, Bureau of Labor Statistics, Division of Consumer Prices and Price Indexes. - indicates no data collected for period.

Washington, DC-MD-VA
Consumer Price Index - Urban Wage Earners
Base 1982-1984 = 100
Annual Averages

For 1914-1995. Columns headed % show percentile change in the index from the previous period for which an index is available.

Year	All Items		Food & Beverage		Housing		Apparel & Upkeep		Trans-portation		Medical Care		Entertain-ment		Other Goods & Services	
	Index	%	Index	%	Index	%	Index	%	Index	%	Index	%	Index	%	Index	%
1914	-	-	-	-	-	-	-	-	-	-	-	-	-	-	-	-
1915	10.5	-	-	-	-	-	-	-	-	-	-	-	-	-	-	-
1916	11.2	6.7	-	-	-	-	-	-	-	-	-	-	-	-	-	-
1917	13.6	21.4	-	-	-	-	-	-	-	-	-	-	-	-	-	-
1918	16.1	18.4	-	-	-	-	-	-	-	-	-	-	-	-	-	-
1919	17.6	9.3	-	-	-	-	-	-	-	-	-	-	-	-	-	-
1920	19.7	11.9	-	-	-	-	-	-	-	-	-	-	-	-	-	-
1921	17.4	-11.7	-	-	-	-	-	-	-	-	-	-	-	-	-	-
1922	16.4	-5.7	-	-	-	-	-	-	-	-	-	-	-	-	-	-
1923	16.7	1.8	-	-	-	-	-	-	-	-	-	-	-	-	-	-
1924	16.7	0.0	-	-	-	-	-	-	-	-	-	-	-	-	-	-
1925	17.1	2.4	-	-	-	-	-	-	-	-	-	-	-	-	-	-
1926	17.3	1.2	-	-	-	-	-	-	-	-	-	-	-	-	-	-
1927	16.8	-2.9	-	-	-	-	-	-	-	-	-	-	-	-	-	-
1928	16.7	-0.6	-	-	-	-	-	-	-	-	-	-	-	-	-	-
1929	16.6	-0.6	-	-	-	-	-	-	-	-	-	-	-	-	-	-
1930	16.3	-1.8	-	-	-	-	-	-	-	-	-	-	-	-	-	-
1931	15.3	-6.1	-	-	-	-	-	-	-	-	-	-	-	-	-	-
1932	14.1	-7.8	-	-	-	-	-	-	-	-	-	-	-	-	-	-
1933	13.7	-2.8	-	-	-	-	-	-	-	-	-	-	-	-	-	-
1934	14.1	2.9	-	-	-	-	-	-	-	-	-	-	-	-	-	-
1935	14.4	2.1	-	-	-	-	-	-	-	-	-	-	-	-	-	-
1936	14.5	0.7	-	-	-	-	-	-	-	-	-	-	-	-	-	-
1937	14.8	2.1	-	-	-	-	-	-	-	-	-	-	-	-	-	-
1938	14.5	-2.0	-	-	-	-	-	-	-	-	-	-	-	-	-	-
1939	14.4	-0.7	-	-	-	-	-	-	-	-	-	-	-	-	-	-
1940	14.5	0.7	-	-	-	-	-	-	-	-	-	-	-	-	-	-
1941	15.1	4.1	-	-	-	-	-	-	-	-	-	-	-	-	-	-
1942	16.8	11.3	-	-	-	-	-	-	-	-	-	-	-	-	-	-
1943	17.8	6.0	-	-	-	-	-	-	-	-	-	-	-	-	-	-
1944	18.1	1.7	-	-	-	-	-	-	-	-	-	-	-	-	-	-
1945	18.6	2.8	-	-	-	-	-	-	-	-	-	-	-	-	-	-
1946	20.3	9.1	-	-	-	-	-	-	-	-	-	-	-	-	-	-
1947	22.9	12.8	-	-	-	-	-	-	19.1	-	11.9	-	-	-	-	-
1948	24.3	6.1	-	-	-	-	-	-	21.1	10.5	12.3	3.4	-	-	-	-
1949	24.2	-0.4	-	-	-	-	-	-	22.7	7.6	12.5	1.6	-	-	-	-
1950	24.6	1.7	-	-	-	-	-	-	23.3	2.6	12.6	0.8	-	-	-	-
1951	26.2	6.5	-	-	-	-	-	-	24.1	3.4	13.4	6.3	-	-	-	-
1952	26.9	2.7	-	-	-	-	-	-	25.7	6.6	14.1	5.2	-	-	-	-
1953	27.1	0.7	-	-	-	-	36.4	-	26.8	4.3	14.3	1.4	-	-	-	-
1954	27.1	0.0	-	-	-	-	36.2	-0.5	26.7	-0.4	14.4	0.7	-	-	-	-
1955	27.0	-0.4	-	-	-	-	36.0	-0.6	27.1	1.5	14.6	1.4	-	-	-	-
1956	27.3	1.1	-	-	-	-	37.0	2.8	27.5	1.5	15.4	5.5	-	-	-	-
1957	28.2	3.3	-	-	-	-	37.2	0.5	28.9	5.1	16.1	4.5	-	-	-	-
1958	28.8	2.1	-	-	-	-	37.0	-0.5	29.4	1.7	17.1	6.2	-	-	-	-

[Continued]

Washington, DC-MD-VA
Consumer Price Index - Urban Wage Earners
Base 1982-1984 = 100
Annual Averages
[Continued]

For 1914-1995. Columns headed % show percentile change in the index from the previous period for which an index is available.

Year	All Items		Food & Beverage		Housing		Apparel & Upkeep		Trans-portation		Medical Care		Entertain-ment		Other Goods & Services	
	Index	%	Index	%	Index	%	Index	%	Index	%	Index	%	Index	%	Index	%
1959	29.0	0.7	-	-	-	-	37.5	1.4	30.4	3.4	18.2	6.4	-	-	-	-
1960	29.3	1.0	-	-	-	-	37.9	1.1	30.6	0.7	18.9	3.8	-	-	-	-
1961	29.7	1.4	-	-	-	-	38.5	1.6	30.9	1.0	19.5	3.2	-	-	-	-
1962	30.0	1.0	-	-	-	-	39.7	3.1	31.3	1.3	20.6	5.6	-	-	-	-
1963	30.5	1.7	-	-	-	-	39.8	0.3	31.5	0.6	21.4	3.9	-	-	-	-
1964	31.0	1.6	-	-	-	-	40.1	0.8	32.3	2.5	22.0	2.8	-	-	-	-
1965	31.4	1.3	-	-	-	-	40.4	0.7	32.6	0.9	22.7	3.2	-	-	-	-
1966	32.5	3.5	-	-	-	-	41.8	3.5	32.9	0.9	23.8	4.8	-	-	-	-
1967	33.4	2.8	-	-	-	-	43.8	4.8	34.0	3.3	25.8	8.4	-	-	-	-
1968	35.0	4.8	-	-	-	-	47.0	7.3	35.3	3.8	28.3	9.7	-	-	-	-
1969	37.1	6.0	-	-	-	-	50.1	6.6	37.0	4.8	30.5	7.8	-	-	-	-
1970	39.3	5.9	-	-	-	-	52.4	4.6	39.6	7.0	32.8	7.5	-	-	-	-
1971	41.0	4.3	-	-	-	-	53.8	2.7	42.0	6.1	35.3	7.6	-	-	-	-
1972	42.4	3.4	-	-	-	-	54.7	1.7	42.1	0.2	36.2	2.5	-	-	-	-
1973	45.1	6.4	-	-	-	-	57.3	4.8	42.9	1.9	37.3	3.0	-	-	-	-
1974	50.1	11.1	-	-	-	-	61.6	7.5	47.5	10.7	41.6	11.5	-	-	-	-
1975	54.0	7.8	-	-	-	-	63.4	2.9	51.7	8.8	46.4	11.5	-	-	-	-
1976	57.1	5.7	61.6	-	55.7	-	65.4	3.2	55.5	7.4	51.1	10.1	58.3	-	56.3	-
1977	61.1	7.0	65.8	6.8	59.8	7.4	66.8	2.1	59.6	7.4	55.8	9.2	62.6	7.4	59.8	6.2
1978	66.2	8.3	72.4	10.0	65.8	10.0	68.3	2.2	62.8	5.4	61.1	9.5	68.4	9.3	65.4	9.4
1979	73.4	10.9	79.7	10.1	73.1	11.1	72.2	5.7	70.9	12.9	68.5	12.1	75.8	10.8	70.0	7.0
1980	82.2	12.0	85.6	7.4	81.9	12.0	80.8	11.9	83.0	17.1	74.7	9.1	82.7	9.1	76.6	9.4
1981	90.3	9.9	91.8	7.2	90.5	10.5	89.2	10.4	92.9	11.9	79.8	6.8	88.0	6.4	84.3	10.1
1982	95.8	6.1	97.3	6.0	96.2	6.3	94.1	5.5	96.6	4.0	90.3	13.2	94.5	7.4	91.3	8.3
1983	99.8	4.2	99.7	2.5	99.5	3.4	102.8	9.2	99.3	2.8	101.4	12.3	99.2	5.0	101.3	11.0
1984	104.4	4.6	103.0	3.3	104.3	4.8	103.2	0.4	104.2	4.9	108.4	6.9	106.3	7.2	107.5	6.1
1985	108.6	4.0	106.0	2.9	109.6	5.1	108.7	5.3	106.1	1.8	115.6	6.6	111.9	5.3	112.7	4.8
1986	111.0	2.2	109.9	3.7	114.3	4.3	104.0	-4.3	104.3	-1.7	123.6	6.9	112.7	0.7	119.1	5.7
1987	115.4	4.0	113.9	3.6	118.2	3.4	114.6	10.2	108.0	3.5	130.5	5.6	118.0	4.7	125.7	5.5
1988	120.3	4.2	119.3	4.7	122.6	3.7	120.8	5.4	111.2	3.0	139.5	6.9	121.8	3.2	134.6	7.1
1989	127.3	5.8	126.5	6.0	128.4	4.7	133.4	10.4	117.9	6.0	148.2	6.2	124.6	2.3	148.5	10.3
1990	134.5	5.7	133.8	5.8	135.0	5.1	137.0	2.7	124.6	5.7	163.5	10.3	132.0	5.9	160.6	8.1
1991	139.7	3.9	137.8	3.0	139.0	3.0	141.2	3.1	129.8	4.2	176.8	8.1	138.7	5.1	172.5	7.4
1992	143.0	2.4	141.0	2.3	141.7	1.9	140.0	-0.8	133.3	2.7	186.8	5.7	143.7	3.6	180.5	4.6
1993	147.1	2.9	142.8	1.3	145.3	2.5	143.7	2.6	137.8	3.4	195.9	4.9	146.6	2.0	192.5	6.6
1994	149.8	1.8	144.4	1.1	148.1	1.9	141.1	-1.8	140.4	1.9	204.1	4.2	151.0	3.0	199.5	3.6
1995	-	-	-	-	-	-	-	-	-	-	-	-	-	-	-	-

Source: U.S. Department of Labor, Bureau of Labor Statistics, Division of Consumer Prices and Price Indexes. - indicates no data collected for period.

Washington, DC-MD-VA
Consumer Price Index - All Urban Consumers
Base 1982-1984 = 100
All Items

For 1914-1995. Columns headed % show percentile change in the index from the previous period for which an index is available.

Year	Jan Index	%	Feb Index	%	Mar Index	%	Apr Index	%	May Index	%	Jun Index	%	Jul Index	%	Aug Index	%	Sep Index	%	Oct Index	%	Nov Index	%	Dec Index	%
1914	-	-	-	-	-	-	-	-	-	-	-	-	-	-	-	-	-	-	-	-	-	-	10.7	-
1915	-	-	-	-	-	-	-	-	-	-	-	-	-	-	-	-	-	-	-	-	-	-	10.8	0.9
1916	-	-	-	-	-	-	-	-	-	-	-	-	-	-	-	-	-	-	-	-	-	-	12.0	11.1
1917	-	-	-	-	-	-	-	-	-	-	-	-	-	-	-	-	-	-	-	-	-	-	15.1	25.8
1918	-	-	-	-	-	-	-	-	-	-	-	-	-	-	-	-	-	-	-	-	-	-	17.6	16.6
1919	-	-	-	-	-	-	-	-	-	-	17.3	-1.7	-	-	-	-	-	-	-	-	-	-	18.8	8.7
1920	-	-	-	-	-	-	-	-	-	-	20.9	11.2	-	-	-	-	-	-	-	-	-	-	19.1	-8.6
1921	-	-	-	-	-	-	-	-	17.4	-8.9	-	-	-	-	-	-	17.5	0.6	-	-	-	-	17.1	-2.3
1922	-	-	-	-	16.6	-2.9	-	-	-	-	16.7	0.6	-	-	-	-	16.5	-1.2	-	-	-	-	16.7	1.2
1923	-	-	-	-	16.6	-0.6	-	-	-	-	17.0	2.4	-	-	-	-	17.2	1.2	-	-	-	-	17.0	-1.2
1924	-	-	-	-	16.8	-1.2	-	-	-	-	16.8	0.0	-	-	-	-	16.8	0.0	-	-	-	-	17.0	1.2
1925	-	-	-	-	-	-	-	-	-	-	17.3	1.8	-	-	-	-	-	-	-	-	-	-	17.6	1.7
1926	-	-	-	-	-	-	-	-	-	-	17.5	-0.6	-	-	-	-	-	-	-	-	-	-	17.4	-0.6
1927	-	-	-	-	-	-	-	-	-	-	17.1	-1.7	-	-	-	-	-	-	-	-	-	-	16.9	-1.2
1928	-	-	-	-	-	-	-	-	-	-	16.9	0.0	-	-	-	-	-	-	-	-	-	-	16.8	-0.6
1929	-	-	-	-	-	-	-	-	-	-	16.9	0.6	-	-	-	-	-	-	-	-	-	-	16.8	-0.6
1930	-	-	-	-	-	-	-	-	-	-	16.6	-1.2	-	-	-	-	-	-	-	-	-	-	16.2	-2.4
1931	-	-	-	-	-	-	-	-	-	-	15.4	-4.9	-	-	-	-	-	-	-	-	-	-	15.1	-1.9
1932	-	-	-	-	-	-	-	-	-	-	14.3	-5.3	-	-	-	-	-	-	-	-	-	-	13.9	-2.8
1933	-	-	-	-	-	-	-	-	-	-	13.7	-1.4	-	-	-	-	-	-	-	-	-	-	14.2	3.6
1934	-	-	-	-	-	-	-	-	-	-	14.3	0.7	-	-	-	-	-	-	-	-	14.5	1.4	-	-
1935	-	-	-	-	14.5	0.0	-	-	-	-	-	-	14.5	0.0	-	-	-	-	14.6	0.7	-	-	-	-
1936	14.7	0.7	-	-	-	-	14.5	-1.4	-	-	-	-	14.7	1.4	-	-	14.8	0.7	-	-	-	-	14.7	-0.7
1937	-	-	-	-	15.0	2.0	-	-	-	-	15.1	0.7	-	-	-	-	15.2	0.7	-	-	-	-	15.0	-1.3
1938	-	-	-	-	14.7	-2.0	-	-	-	-	14.7	0.0	-	-	-	-	14.7	0.0	-	-	-	-	14.7	0.0
1939	-	-	-	-	14.5	-1.4	-	-	-	-	14.5	0.0	-	-	-	-	14.7	1.4	-	-	-	-	14.5	-1.4
1940	-	-	-	-	14.7	1.4	-	-	-	-	14.7	0.0	-	-	-	-	14.7	0.0	-	-	-	-	14.7	0.0
1941	-	-	-	-	14.8	0.7	-	-	-	-	15.2	2.7	-	-	-	-	15.7	3.3	16.0	1.9	16.0	0.0	16.2	1.3
1942	16.3	0.6	16.5	1.2	16.7	1.2	16.7	0.0	16.9	1.2	17.0	0.6	17.1	0.6	17.2	0.6	17.3	0.6	17.3	0.0	17.4	0.6	17.5	0.6
1943	17.6	0.6	17.6	0.0	17.9	1.7	18.1	1.1	18.3	1.1	18.3	0.0	18.2	-0.5	18.2	0.0	18.2	0.0	18.3	0.5	18.2	-0.5	18.2	0.0
1944	18.3	0.5	18.2	-0.5	18.1	-0.5	18.2	0.6	18.3	0.5	18.4	0.5	18.4	0.0	18.5	0.5	18.5	0.0	18.5	0.0	18.6	0.5	18.6	0.0
1945	18.6	0.0	18.6	0.0	18.6	0.0	18.7	0.5	18.9	1.1	19.0	0.5	19.0	0.0	19.0	0.0	19.1	0.5	19.0	-0.5	19.1	0.5	19.2	0.5
1946	19.3	0.5	19.2	-0.5	19.4	1.0	19.4	0.0	19.4	0.0	19.8	2.1	20.8	5.1	21.1	1.4	21.4	1.4	21.8	1.9	22.2	1.8	22.5	1.4
1947	22.5	0.0	22.4	-0.4	22.9	2.2	22.9	0.0	22.9	0.0	23.1	0.9	-	-	23.5	1.7	-	-	-	-	23.9	1.7	-	-
1948	-	-	24.1	0.8	-	-	-	-	24.7	2.5	-	-	-	-	25.0	1.2	-	-	-	-	24.7	-1.2	-	-
1949	-	-	24.4	-1.2	-	-	-	-	24.6	0.8	-	-	-	-	24.7	0.4	-	-	-	-	24.8	0.4	-	-
1950	-	-	24.4	-1.6	-	-	-	-	24.5	0.4	-	-	-	-	25.1	2.4	-	-	-	-	25.5	1.6	-	-
1951	-	-	26.4	3.5	-	-	-	-	26.5	0.4	-	-	-	-	26.6	0.4	-	-	-	-	27.2	2.3	-	-
1952	-	-	27.0	-0.7	-	-	-	-	27.2	0.7	-	-	-	-	27.6	1.5	-	-	-	-	27.5	-0.4	-	-
1953	-	-	27.3	-0.7	-	-	-	-	27.4	0.4	-	-	-	-	27.6	0.7	-	-	-	-	27.6	0.0	-	-
1954	-	-	27.6	0.0	-	-	-	-	27.4	-0.7	-	-	-	-	27.6	0.7	-	-	-	-	27.4	-0.7	-	-
1955	-	-	27.3	-0.4	-	-	-	-	27.4	0.4	-	-	-	-	27.5	0.4	-	-	-	-	27.4	-0.4	-	-
1956	-	-	27.4	0.0	-	-	-	-	27.6	0.7	-	-	-	-	27.9	1.1	-	-	-	-	28.0	0.4	-	-
1957	-	-	28.4	1.4	-	-	-	-	28.3	-0.4	-	-	-	-	28.8	1.8	-	-	-	-	28.9	0.3	-	-
1958	-	-	29.1	0.7	-	-	-	-	29.3	0.7	-	-	-	-	29.3	0.0	-	-	-	-	29.3	0.0	-	-

[Continued]

Washington, DC-MD-VA
Consumer Price Index - All Urban Consumers
Base 1982-1984 = 100
All Items
[Continued]

For 1914-1995. Columns headed % show percentile change in the index from the previous period for which an index is available.

Year	Jan Index	%	Feb Index	%	Mar Index	%	Apr Index	%	May Index	%	Jun Index	%	Jul Index	%	Aug Index	%	Sep Index	%	Oct Index	%	Nov Index	%	Dec Index	%
1959	-	-	29.3	0.0	-	-	-	-	29.4	0.3	-	-	-	-	29.5	0.3	-	-	-	-	29.4	-0.3	-	-
1960	-	-	29.4	0.0	-	-	-	-	29.7	1.0	-	-	-	-	29.7	0.0	-	-	-	-	29.9	0.7	-	-
1961	-	-	30.1	0.7	-	-	-	-	30.0	-0.3	-	-	-	-	30.2	0.7	-	-	-	-	30.3	0.3	-	-
1962	-	-	30.2	-0.3	-	-	-	-	30.3	0.3	-	-	-	-	30.5	0.7	-	-	-	-	30.6	0.3	-	-
1963	-	-	30.7	0.3	-	-	-	-	30.9	0.7	-	-	-	-	31.1	0.6	-	-	-	-	31.1	0.0	-	-
1964	-	-	31.2	0.3	-	-	-	-	31.3	0.3	-	-	-	-	31.6	1.0	-	-	-	-	31.7	0.3	-	-
1965	-	-	31.6	-0.3	-	-	-	-	31.8	0.6	-	-	-	-	31.9	0.3	-	-	-	-	32.1	0.6	-	-
1966	-	-	32.6	1.6	-	-	-	-	32.8	0.6	-	-	-	-	33.2	1.2	-	-	-	-	33.3	0.3	-	-
1967	-	-	33.5	0.6	-	-	-	-	33.6	0.3	-	-	-	-	34.1	1.5	-	-	-	-	34.2	0.3	-	-
1968	-	-	34.6	1.2	-	-	-	-	35.2	1.7	-	-	-	-	35.8	1.7	-	-	-	-	36.3	1.4	-	-
1969	-	-	36.7	1.1	-	-	-	-	37.5	2.2	-	-	-	-	38.0	1.3	-	-	-	-	38.4	1.1	-	-
1970	-	-	39.1	1.8	-	-	-	-	39.7	1.5	-	-	-	-	40.1	1.0	-	-	-	-	40.4	0.7	-	-
1971	-	-	41.0	1.5	-	-	-	-	41.4	1.0	-	-	-	-	41.8	1.0	-	-	-	-	42.1	0.7	-	-
1972	-	-	42.2	0.2	-	-	-	-	42.5	0.7	-	-	-	-	43.3	1.9	-	-	-	-	43.9	1.4	-	-
1973	-	-	44.3	0.9	-	-	-	-	45.2	2.0	-	-	-	-	46.2	2.2	-	-	-	-	47.2	2.2	-	-
1974	-	-	48.8	3.4	-	-	-	-	50.0	2.5	-	-	-	-	51.7	3.4	-	-	-	-	52.9	2.3	-	-
1975	-	-	53.5	1.1	-	-	-	-	54.2	1.3	-	-	-	-	55.3	2.0	-	-	-	-	56.0	1.3	-	-
1976	-	-	56.6	1.1	-	-	-	-	57.6	1.8	-	-	-	-	58.6	1.7	-	-	-	-	59.0	0.7	-	-
1977	-	-	60.3	2.2	-	-	-	-	61.5	2.0	-	-	-	-	62.6	1.8	-	-	-	-	63.5	1.4	-	-
1978	64.3	1.3	-	-	64.7	0.6	-	-	65.8	1.7	-	-	67.0	1.8	-	-	68.0	1.5	-	-	69.1	1.6	-	-
1979	70.7	2.3	-	-	72.0	1.8	-	-	73.2	1.7	-	-	74.7	2.0	-	-	75.5	1.1	-	-	76.3	1.1	-	-
1980	78.5	2.9	-	-	80.9	3.1	-	-	81.7	1.0	-	-	83.7	2.4	-	-	84.4	0.8	-	-	85.9	1.8	-	-
1981	87.1	1.4	-	-	88.8	2.0	-	-	89.7	1.0	-	-	90.5	0.9	-	-	92.1	1.8	-	-	93.3	1.3	-	-
1982	94.2	1.0	-	-	94.4	0.2	-	-	94.3	-0.1	-	-	95.3	1.1	-	-	97.0	1.8	-	-	97.0	0.0	-	-
1983	98.0	1.0	-	-	98.0	0.0	-	-	99.2	1.2	-	-	100.6	1.4	-	-	100.7	0.1	-	-	101.2	0.5	-	-
1984	102.9	1.7	-	-	103.3	0.4	-	-	103.5	0.2	-	-	104.4	0.9	-	-	106.0	1.5	-	-	106.7	0.7	-	-
1985	106.6	-0.1	-	-	108.1	1.4	-	-	108.3	0.2	-	-	109.5	1.1	-	-	109.6	0.1	-	-	110.7	1.0	-	-
1986	112.2	1.4	-	-	111.5	-0.6	-	-	111.6	0.1	-	-	111.5	-0.1	-	-	112.6	1.0	-	-	113.1	0.4	-	-
1987	113.7	0.5	-	-	114.5	0.7	-	-	115.3	0.7	-	-	116.2	0.8	-	-	117.8	1.4	-	-	118.5	0.6	-	-
1988	118.3	-0.2	-	-	119.2	0.8	-	-	120.1	0.8	-	-	120.7	0.5	-	-	122.8	1.7	-	-	123.2	0.3	-	-
1989	124.3	0.9	-	-	126.1	1.4	-	-	127.1	0.8	-	-	127.8	0.6	-	-	130.1	1.8	-	-	130.5	0.3	-	-
1990	132.0	1.1	-	-	133.8	1.4	-	-	134.0	0.1	-	-	135.7	1.3	-	-	138.0	1.7	-	-	138.4	0.3	-	-
1991	139.1	0.5	-	-	139.3	0.1	-	-	140.9	1.1	-	-	140.9	0.0	-	-	143.3	1.7	-	-	142.6	-0.5	-	-
1992	142.9	0.2	-	-	143.0	0.1	-	-	143.2	0.1	-	-	144.8	1.1	-	-	146.0	0.8	-	-	146.9	0.6	-	-
1993	147.8	0.6	-	-	148.5	0.5	-	-	149.2	0.5	-	-	149.2	0.0	-	-	149.7	0.3	-	-	150.9	0.8	-	-
1994	150.9	0.0	-	-	151.5	0.4	-	-	151.4	-0.1	-	-	151.8	0.3	-	-	153.7	1.3	-	-	153.0	-0.5	-	-
1995	153.8	0.5	-	-	155.1	0.8	-	-	154.7	-0.3	-	-	156.1	0.9	-	-	156.2	0.1	-	-	155.2	-0.6	-	-

Source: U.S. Department of Labor, Bureau of Labor Statistics, Division of Consumer Prices and Price Indexes. - indicates no data collected for period.

Washington, DC-MD-VA
Consumer Price Index - Urban Wage Earners
Base 1982-1984 = 100
All Items

For 1914-1995. Columns headed % show percentile change in the index from the previous period for which an index is available.

Year	Jan Index	%	Feb Index	%	Mar Index	%	Apr Index	%	May Index	%	Jun Index	%	Jul Index	%	Aug Index	%	Sep Index	%	Oct Index	%	Nov Index	%	Dec Index	%
1914	-	-	-	-	-	-	-	-	-	-	-	-	-	-	-	-	-	-	-	-	-	-	10.5	-
1915	-	-	-	-	-	-	-	-	-	-	-	-	-	-	-	-	-	-	-	-	-	-	10.6	1.0
1916	-	-	-	-	-	-	-	-	-	-	-	-	-	-	-	-	-	-	-	-	-	-	11.8	11.3
1917	-	-	-	-	-	-	-	-	-	-	-	-	-	-	-	-	-	-	-	-	-	-	14.9	26.3
1918	-	-	-	-	-	-	-	-	-	-	-	-	-	-	-	-	-	-	-	-	-	-	17.3	16.1
1919	-	-	-	-	-	-	-	-	-	-	17.1	-1.2	-	-	-	-	-	-	-	-	-	-	18.5	8.2
1920	-	-	-	-	-	-	-	-	-	-	20.6	11.4	-	-	-	-	-	-	-	-	-	-	18.9	-8.3
1921	-	-	-	-	-	-	-	-	17.1	-9.5	-	-	-	-	-	-	17.3	1.2	-	-	-	-	16.9	-2.3
1922	-	-	-	-	16.4	-3.0	-	-	-	-	16.5	0.6	-	-	-	-	16.3	-1.2	-	-	-	-	16.5	1.2
1923	-	-	-	-	16.4	-0.6	-	-	-	-	16.8	2.4	-	-	-	-	16.9	0.6	-	-	-	-	16.8	-0.6
1924	-	-	-	-	16.6	-1.2	-	-	-	-	16.6	0.0	-	-	-	-	16.6	0.0	-	-	-	-	16.8	1.2
1925	-	-	-	-	-	-	-	-	-	-	17.0	1.2	-	-	-	-	-	-	-	-	-	-	17.4	2.4
1926	-	-	-	-	-	-	-	-	-	-	17.3	-0.6	-	-	-	-	-	-	-	-	-	-	17.2	-0.6
1927	-	-	-	-	-	-	-	-	-	-	16.9	-1.7	-	-	-	-	-	-	-	-	-	-	16.7	-1.2
1928	-	-	-	-	-	-	-	-	-	-	16.7	0.0	-	-	-	-	-	-	-	-	-	-	16.5	-1.2
1929	-	-	-	-	-	-	-	-	-	-	16.6	0.6	-	-	-	-	-	-	-	-	-	-	16.6	0.0
1930	-	-	-	-	-	-	-	-	-	-	16.4	-1.2	-	-	-	-	-	-	-	-	-	-	16.0	-2.4
1931	-	-	-	-	-	-	-	-	-	-	15.2	-5.0	-	-	-	-	-	-	-	-	-	-	14.9	-2.0
1932	-	-	-	-	-	-	-	-	-	-	14.1	-5.4	-	-	-	-	-	-	-	-	-	-	13.7	-2.8
1933	-	-	-	-	-	-	-	-	-	-	13.5	-1.5	-	-	-	-	-	-	-	-	-	-	14.0	3.7
1934	-	-	-	-	-	-	-	-	-	-	14.1	0.7	-	-	-	-	-	-	-	-	14.3	1.4	-	-
1935	-	-	-	-	14.3	0.0	-	-	-	-	-	-	14.3	0.0	-	-	-	-	14.4	0.7	-	-	-	-
1936	14.5	0.7	-	-	-	-	14.3	-1.4	-	-	-	-	14.5	1.4	-	-	14.6	0.7	-	-	-	-	14.5	-0.7
1937	-	-	-	-	14.8	2.1	-	-	-	-	14.9	0.7	-	-	-	-	15.0	0.7	-	-	-	-	14.8	-1.3
1938	-	-	-	-	14.5	-2.0	-	-	-	-	14.5	0.0	-	-	-	-	14.5	0.0	-	-	-	-	14.5	0.0
1939	-	-	-	-	14.3	-1.4	-	-	-	-	14.3	0.0	-	-	-	-	14.5	1.4	-	-	-	-	14.3	-1.4
1940	-	-	-	-	14.5	1.4	-	-	-	-	14.5	0.0	-	-	-	-	14.5	0.0	-	-	-	-	14.5	0.0
1941	-	-	-	-	14.6	0.7	-	-	-	-	15.0	2.7	-	-	-	-	15.5	3.3	15.7	1.3	15.8	0.6	15.9	0.6
1942	16.1	1.3	16.2	0.6	16.5	1.9	16.5	0.0	16.7	1.2	16.8	0.6	16.9	0.6	17.0	0.6	17.0	0.0	17.1	0.6	17.2	0.6	17.3	0.6
1943	17.4	0.6	17.3	-0.6	17.6	1.7	17.8	1.1	18.0	1.1	18.0	0.0	17.9	-0.6	17.9	0.0	18.0	0.6	18.1	0.6	18.0	-0.6	18.0	0.0
1944	18.0	0.0	17.9	-0.6	17.8	-0.6	17.9	0.6	18.1	1.1	18.1	0.0	18.1	0.0	18.2	0.6	18.2	0.0	18.2	0.0	18.3	0.5	18.3	0.0
1945	18.4	0.5	18.4	0.0	18.3	-0.5	18.4	0.5	18.6	1.1	18.7	0.5	18.8	0.5	18.8	0.0	18.8	0.0	18.8	0.0	18.9	0.5	18.9	0.0
1946	19.1	1.1	19.0	-0.5	19.1	0.5	19.2	0.5	19.2	0.0	19.5	1.6	20.5	5.1	20.8	1.5	21.1	1.4	21.5	1.9	21.9	1.9	22.2	1.4
1947	22.2	0.0	22.1	-0.5	22.6	2.3	22.6	0.0	22.5	-0.4	22.7	0.9	-	-	23.2	2.2	-	-	-	-	23.6	1.7	-	-
1948	-	-	23.8	0.8	-	-	-	-	24.3	2.1	-	-	-	-	24.7	1.6	-	-	-	-	24.4	-1.2	-	-
1949	-	-	24.0	-1.6	-	-	-	-	24.2	0.8	-	-	-	-	24.4	0.8	-	-	-	-	24.4	0.0	-	-
1950	-	-	24.1	-1.2	-	-	-	-	24.2	0.4	-	-	-	-	24.8	2.5	-	-	-	-	25.2	1.6	-	-
1951	-	-	26.0	3.2	-	-	-	-	26.1	0.4	-	-	-	-	26.2	0.4	-	-	-	-	26.8	2.3	-	-
1952	-	-	26.6	-0.7	-	-	-	-	26.8	0.8	-	-	-	-	27.2	1.5	-	-	-	-	27.1	-0.4	-	-
1953	-	-	26.9	-0.7	-	-	-	-	27.0	0.4	-	-	-	-	27.2	0.7	-	-	-	-	27.2	0.0	-	-
1954	-	-	27.2	0.0	-	-	-	-	27.0	-0.7	-	-	-	-	27.2	0.7	-	-	-	-	27.0	-0.7	-	-
1955	-	-	26.9	-0.4	-	-	-	-	27.0	0.4	-	-	-	-	27.1	0.4	-	-	-	-	27.0	-0.4	-	-
1956	-	-	27.0	0.0	-	-	-	-	27.2	0.7	-	-	-	-	27.5	1.1	-	-	-	-	27.6	0.4	-	-
1957	-	-	28.0	1.4	-	-	-	-	27.9	-0.4	-	-	-	-	28.3	1.4	-	-	-	-	28.4	0.4	-	-
1958	-	-	28.6	0.7	-	-	-	-	28.8	0.7	-	-	-	-	28.8	0.0	-	-	-	-	28.9	0.3	-	-

[Continued]

Washington, DC-MD-VA
Consumer Price Index - Urban Wage Earners
Base 1982-1984 = 100
All Items
[Continued]

For 1914-1995. Columns headed % show percentile change in the index from the previous period for which an index is available.

Year	Jan Index	%	Feb Index	%	Mar Index	%	Apr Index	%	May Index	%	Jun Index	%	Jul Index	%	Aug Index	%	Sep Index	%	Oct Index	%	Nov Index	%	Dec Index	%
1959	-	-	28.8	-0.3	-	-	-	-	29.0	0.7	-	-	-	-	29.0	0.0	-	-	-	-	29.0	0.0	-	-
1960	-	-	29.0	0.0	-	-	-	-	29.3	1.0	-	-	-	-	29.3	0.0	-	-	-	-	29.5	0.7	-	-
1961	-	-	29.7	0.7	-	-	-	-	29.6	-0.3	-	-	-	-	29.8	0.7	-	-	-	-	29.9	0.3	-	-
1962	-	-	29.8	-0.3	-	-	-	-	29.9	0.3	-	-	-	-	30.1	0.7	-	-	-	-	30.2	0.3	-	-
1963	-	-	30.3	0.3	-	-	-	-	30.4	0.3	-	-	-	-	30.6	0.7	-	-	-	-	30.7	0.3	-	-
1964	-	-	30.8	0.3	-	-	-	-	30.8	0.0	-	-	-	-	31.2	1.3	-	-	-	-	31.2	0.0	-	-
1965	-	-	31.2	0.0	-	-	-	-	31.4	0.6	-	-	-	-	31.4	0.0	-	-	-	-	31.7	1.0	-	-
1966	-	-	32.1	1.3	-	-	-	-	32.3	0.6	-	-	-	-	32.7	1.2	-	-	-	-	32.9	0.6	-	-
1967	-	-	33.0	0.3	-	-	-	-	33.2	0.6	-	-	-	-	33.6	1.2	-	-	-	-	33.8	0.6	-	-
1968	-	-	34.1	0.9	-	-	-	-	34.7	1.8	-	-	-	-	35.3	1.7	-	-	-	-	35.8	1.4	-	-
1969	-	-	36.2	1.1	-	-	-	-	36.9	1.9	-	-	-	-	37.5	1.6	-	-	-	-	37.8	0.8	-	-
1970	-	-	38.6	2.1	-	-	-	-	39.2	1.6	-	-	-	-	39.5	0.8	-	-	-	-	39.8	0.8	-	-
1971	-	-	40.4	1.5	-	-	-	-	40.8	1.0	-	-	-	-	41.2	1.0	-	-	-	-	41.5	0.7	-	-
1972	-	-	41.6	0.2	-	-	-	-	41.9	0.7	-	-	-	-	42.6	1.7	-	-	-	-	43.3	1.6	-	-
1973	-	-	43.6	0.7	-	-	-	-	44.5	2.1	-	-	-	-	45.5	2.2	-	-	-	-	46.5	2.2	-	-
1974	-	-	48.1	3.4	-	-	-	-	49.3	2.5	-	-	-	-	51.0	3.4	-	-	-	-	52.1	2.2	-	-
1975	-	-	52.7	1.2	-	-	-	-	53.4	1.3	-	-	-	-	54.6	2.2	-	-	-	-	55.2	1.1	-	-
1976	-	-	55.8	1.1	-	-	-	-	56.8	1.8	-	-	-	-	57.8	1.8	-	-	-	-	58.2	0.7	-	-
1977	-	-	59.4	2.1	-	-	-	-	60.7	2.2	-	-	-	-	61.7	1.6	-	-	-	-	62.6	1.5	-	-
1978	63.1	0.8	-	-	63.7	1.0	-	-	65.5	2.8	-	-	67.0	2.3	-	-	67.7	1.0	-	-	68.6	1.3	-	-
1979	69.9	1.9	-	-	71.3	2.0	-	-	72.7	2.0	-	-	74.1	1.9	-	-	74.9	1.1	-	-	75.7	1.1	-	-
1980	77.8	2.8	-	-	79.9	2.7	-	-	80.8	1.1	-	-	83.0	2.7	-	-	84.1	1.3	-	-	85.4	1.5	-	-
1981	86.6	1.4	-	-	88.2	1.8	-	-	89.4	1.4	-	-	90.6	1.3	-	-	92.1	1.7	-	-	93.3	1.3	-	-
1982	94.1	0.9	-	-	94.8	0.7	-	-	94.6	-0.2	-	-	95.6	1.1	-	-	97.5	2.0	-	-	97.4	-0.1	-	-
1983	97.9	0.5	-	-	98.4	0.5	-	-	99.4	1.0	-	-	100.3	0.9	-	-	100.6	0.3	-	-	101.2	0.6	-	-
1984	102.9	1.7	-	-	102.9	0.0	-	-	103.1	0.2	-	-	103.8	0.7	-	-	106.1	2.2	-	-	106.6	0.5	-	-
1985	106.1	-0.5	-	-	107.6	1.4	-	-	107.9	0.3	-	-	108.8	0.8	-	-	109.3	0.5	-	-	110.4	1.0	-	-
1986	111.1	0.6	-	-	110.4	-0.6	-	-	110.3	-0.1	-	-	110.3	0.0	-	-	111.7	1.3	-	-	112.2	0.4	-	-
1987	112.7	0.4	-	-	113.6	0.8	-	-	114.6	0.9	-	-	115.3	0.6	-	-	117.1	1.6	-	-	117.9	0.7	-	-
1988	117.6	-0.3	-	-	118.5	0.8	-	-	119.3	0.7	-	-	119.9	0.5	-	-	122.3	2.0	-	-	122.6	0.2	-	-
1989	123.7	0.9	-	-	125.6	1.5	-	-	126.6	0.8	-	-	127.3	0.6	-	-	129.5	1.7	-	-	129.6	0.1	-	-
1990	131.1	1.2	-	-	132.9	1.4	-	-	132.8	-0.1	-	-	134.6	1.4	-	-	136.9	1.7	-	-	137.2	0.2	-	-
1991	137.7	0.4	-	-	137.9	0.1	-	-	139.6	1.2	-	-	139.2	-0.3	-	-	141.8	1.9	-	-	141.1	-0.5	-	-
1992	141.3	0.1	-	-	141.3	0.0	-	-	141.6	0.2	-	-	143.3	1.2	-	-	144.2	0.6	-	-	145.1	0.6	-	-
1993	145.6	0.3	-	-	146.2	0.4	-	-	147.0	0.5	-	-	147.0	0.0	-	-	147.5	0.3	-	-	148.5	0.7	-	-
1994	148.3	-0.1	-	-	148.9	0.4	-	-	149.2	0.2	-	-	149.4	0.1	-	-	151.5	1.4	-	-	150.6	-0.6	-	-
1995	151.2	0.4	-	-	152.4	0.8	-	-	152.3	-0.1	-	-	153.5	0.8	-	-	153.5	0.0	-	-	152.5	-0.7	-	-

Source: U.S. Department of Labor, Bureau of Labor Statistics, Division of Consumer Prices and Price Indexes. - indicates no data collected for period.

Washington, DC-MD-VA
Consumer Price Index - All Urban Consumers
Base 1982-1984 = 100
Food and Beverages

For 1975-1995. Columns headed % show percentile change in the index from the previous period for which an index is available.

Year	Jan Index	%	Feb Index	%	Mar Index	%	Apr Index	%	May Index	%	Jun Index	%	Jul Index	%	Aug Index	%	Sep Index	%	Oct Index	%	Nov Index	%	Dec Index	%
1975	-	-	-	-	-	-	-	-	-	-	-	-	-	-	-	-	-	-	-	-	61.5	-	-	-
1976	-	-	61.5	0.0	-	-	-	-	61.7	0.3	-	-	-	-	63.5	2.9	-	-	-	-	63.0	-0.8	-	-
1977	-	-	65.1	3.3	-	-	-	-	66.4	2.0	-	-	-	-	67.5	1.7	-	-	-	-	68.3	1.2	-	-
1978	69.3	1.5	-	-	70.7	2.0	-	-	72.9	3.1	-	-	74.9	2.7	-	-	74.8	-0.1	-	-	75.4	0.8	-	-
1979	78.2	3.7	-	-	80.4	2.8	-	-	82.0	2.0	-	-	82.4	0.5	-	-	83.3	1.1	-	-	83.1	-0.2	-	-
1980	84.1	1.2	-	-	85.3	1.4	-	-	85.7	0.5	-	-	88.5	3.3	-	-	90.3	2.0	-	-	91.9	1.8	-	-
1981	93.0	1.2	-	-	93.6	0.6	-	-	90.7	-3.1	-	-	91.1	0.4	-	-	93.1	2.2	-	-	93.5	0.4	-	-
1982	95.0	1.6	-	-	96.2	1.3	-	-	97.0	0.8	-	-	97.9	0.9	-	-	98.5	0.6	-	-	97.6	-0.9	-	-
1983	98.4	0.8	-	-	99.7	1.3	-	-	100.9	1.2	-	-	100.3	-0.6	-	-	99.5	-0.8	-	-	99.2	-0.3	-	-
1984	101.8	2.6	-	-	103.4	1.6	-	-	102.5	-0.9	-	-	102.9	0.4	-	-	103.5	0.6	-	-	103.5	0.0	-	-
1985	104.2	0.7	-	-	105.7	1.4	-	-	105.9	0.2	-	-	106.0	0.1	-	-	106.4	0.4	-	-	107.3	0.8	-	-
1986	109.4	2.0	-	-	109.2	-0.2	-	-	110.9	1.6	-	-	110.5	-0.4	-	-	110.7	0.2	-	-	109.4	-1.2	-	-
1987	111.6	2.0	-	-	111.9	0.3	-	-	113.6	1.5	-	-	114.2	0.5	-	-	114.5	0.3	-	-	114.8	0.3	-	-
1988	116.0	1.0	-	-	116.7	0.6	-	-	117.9	1.0	-	-	120.5	2.2	-	-	121.3	0.7	-	-	121.1	-0.2	-	-
1989	122.7	1.3	-	-	124.4	1.4	-	-	126.5	1.7	-	-	126.4	-0.1	-	-	126.8	0.3	-	-	127.8	0.8	-	-
1990	131.7	3.1	-	-	133.3	1.2	-	-	132.8	-0.4	-	-	133.9	0.8	-	-	133.9	0.0	-	-	133.8	-0.1	-	-
1991	135.9	1.6	-	-	137.3	1.0	-	-	137.1	-0.1	-	-	137.7	0.4	-	-	138.1	0.3	-	-	139.0	0.7	-	-
1992	140.5	1.1	-	-	142.3	1.3	-	-	141.3	-0.7	-	-	140.2	-0.8	-	-	140.1	-0.1	-	-	140.9	0.6	-	-
1993	141.8	0.6	-	-	142.2	0.3	-	-	144.0	1.3	-	-	142.4	-1.1	-	-	141.9	-0.4	-	-	144.1	1.6	-	-
1994	143.8	-0.2	-	-	144.6	0.6	-	-	144.3	-0.2	-	-	143.0	-0.9	-	-	144.7	1.2	-	-	144.6	-0.1	-	-
1995	146.1	1.0	-	-	146.7	0.4	-	-	147.6	0.6	-	-	147.9	0.2	-	-	146.9	-0.7	-	-	147.4	0.3	-	-

Source: U.S. Department of Labor, Bureau of Labor Statistics, Division of Consumer Prices and Price Indexes. - indicates no data collected for period.

Washington, DC-MD-VA
Consumer Price Index - Urban Wage Earners
Base 1982-1984 = 100
Food and Beverages

For 1975-1995. Columns headed % show percentile change in the index from the previous period for which an index is available.

Year	Jan Index	%	Feb Index	%	Mar Index	%	Apr Index	%	May Index	%	Jun Index	%	Jul Index	%	Aug Index	%	Sep Index	%	Oct Index	%	Nov Index	%	Dec Index	%
1975	-	-	-	-	-	-	-	-	-	-	-	-	-	-	-	-	-	-	-	-	60.6	-	-	-
1976	-	-	60.6	0.0	-	-	-	-	60.8	0.3	-	-	-	-	62.6	3.0	-	-	-	-	62.0	-1.0	-	-
1977	-	-	64.1	3.4	-	-	-	-	65.4	2.0	-	-	-	-	66.5	1.7	-	-	-	-	67.3	1.2	-	-
1978	68.2	1.3	-	-	69.4	1.8	-	-	72.8	4.9	-	-	74.3	2.1	-	-	73.8	-0.7	-	-	73.9	0.1	-	-
1979	76.4	3.4	-	-	78.2	2.4	-	-	80.2	2.6	-	-	80.4	0.2	-	-	81.2	1.0	-	-	80.6	-0.7	-	-
1980	81.6	1.2	-	-	82.6	1.2	-	-	82.5	-0.1	-	-	85.7	3.9	-	-	88.0	2.7	-	-	90.8	3.2	-	-
1981	91.7	1.0	-	-	92.1	0.4	-	-	89.6	-2.7	-	-	90.5	1.0	-	-	92.7	2.4	-	-	93.3	0.6	-	-
1982	95.0	1.8	-	-	96.3	1.4	-	-	97.0	0.7	-	-	98.1	1.1	-	-	98.8	0.7	-	-	97.9	-0.9	-	-
1983	98.5	0.6	-	-	99.7	1.2	-	-	100.6	0.9	-	-	100.2	-0.4	-	-	99.2	-1.0	-	-	99.0	-0.2	-	-
1984	101.9	2.9	-	-	103.3	1.4	-	-	102.5	-0.8	-	-	102.8	0.3	-	-	103.5	0.7	-	-	103.5	0.0	-	-
1985	104.0	0.5	-	-	105.7	1.6	-	-	105.9	0.2	-	-	105.9	0.0	-	-	106.3	0.4	-	-	107.2	0.8	-	-
1986	108.9	1.6	-	-	108.8	-0.1	-	-	110.5	1.6	-	-	110.2	-0.3	-	-	110.7	0.5	-	-	109.6	-1.0	-	-
1987	112.0	2.2	-	-	112.2	0.2	-	-	114.0	1.6	-	-	114.6	0.5	-	-	114.7	0.1	-	-	114.9	0.2	-	-
1988	116.2	1.1	-	-	116.9	0.6	-	-	118.1	1.0	-	-	120.6	2.1	-	-	121.4	0.7	-	-	121.2	-0.2	-	-
1989	123.0	1.5	-	-	124.7	1.4	-	-	126.7	1.6	-	-	126.6	-0.1	-	-	127.3	0.6	-	-	128.2	0.7	-	-
1990	132.2	3.1	-	-	134.3	1.6	-	-	133.1	-0.9	-	-	134.2	0.8	-	-	134.2	0.0	-	-	134.0	-0.1	-	-
1991	136.1	1.6	-	-	137.5	1.0	-	-	137.2	-0.2	-	-	137.9	0.5	-	-	138.3	0.3	-	-	138.9	0.4	-	-
1992	140.5	1.2	-	-	142.4	1.4	-	-	141.2	-0.8	-	-	140.3	-0.6	-	-	140.1	-0.1	-	-	141.0	0.6	-	-
1993	141.8	0.6	-	-	142.3	0.4	-	-	144.2	1.3	-	-	142.3	-1.3	-	-	141.9	-0.3	-	-	143.8	1.3	-	-
1994	143.8	0.0	-	-	144.7	0.6	-	-	144.2	-0.3	-	-	143.2	-0.7	-	-	145.0	1.3	-	-	144.7	-0.2	-	-
1995	146.3	1.1	-	-	146.6	0.2	-	-	147.8	0.8	-	-	148.2	0.3	-	-	147.0	-0.8	-	-	147.6	0.4	-	-

Source: U.S. Department of Labor, Bureau of Labor Statistics, Division of Consumer Prices and Price Indexes. - indicates no data collected for period.

Washington, DC-MD-VA
Consumer Price Index - All Urban Consumers
Base 1982-1984 = 100
Housing

For 1975-1995. Columns headed % show percentile change in the index from the previous period for which an index is available.

Year	Jan Index	%	Feb Index	%	Mar Index	%	Apr Index	%	May Index	%	Jun Index	%	Jul Index	%	Aug Index	%	Sep Index	%	Oct Index	%	Nov Index	%	Dec Index	%
1975	-	-	-	-	-	-	-	-	-	-	-	-	-	-	-	-	-	-	-	-	53.0	-	-	-
1976	-	-	53.8	1.5	-	-	-	-	54.9	2.0	-	-	-	-	55.7	1.5	-	-	-	-	56.4	1.3	-	-
1977	-	-	57.6	2.1	-	-	-	-	58.7	1.9	-	-	-	-	60.0	2.2	-	-	-	-	61.2	2.0	-	-
1978	62.2	1.6	-	-	62.4	0.3	-	-	63.4	1.6	-	-	64.6	1.9	-	-	66.0	2.2	-	-	67.0	1.5	-	-
1979	69.5	3.7	-	-	70.2	1.0	-	-	70.8	0.9	-	-	72.9	3.0	-	-	72.7	-0.3	-	-	73.6	1.2	-	-
1980	76.5	3.9	-	-	79.0	3.3	-	-	80.2	1.5	-	-	82.5	2.9	-	-	81.8	-0.8	-	-	83.9	2.6	-	-
1981	85.3	1.7	-	-	87.5	2.6	-	-	89.3	2.1	-	-	90.6	1.5	-	-	91.8	1.3	-	-	93.8	2.2	-	-
1982	94.7	1.0	-	-	94.6	-0.1	-	-	94.1	-0.5	-	-	94.7	0.6	-	-	97.0	2.4	-	-	96.6	-0.4	-	-
1983	98.2	1.7	-	-	97.8	-0.4	-	-	98.6	0.8	-	-	101.2	2.6	-	-	100.3	-0.9	-	-	101.1	0.8	-	-
1984	103.3	2.2	-	-	103.5	0.2	-	-	103.2	-0.3	-	-	104.2	1.0	-	-	106.5	2.2	-	-	107.4	0.8	-	-
1985	107.4	0.0	-	-	109.1	1.6	-	-	108.9	-0.2	-	-	111.6	2.5	-	-	110.4	-1.1	-	-	111.4	0.9	-	-
1986	114.4	2.7	-	-	114.0	-0.3	-	-	114.5	0.4	-	-	113.9	-0.5	-	-	114.7	0.7	-	-	116.3	1.4	-	-
1987	117.1	0.7	-	-	116.7	-0.3	-	-	117.7	0.9	-	-	118.8	0.9	-	-	121.0	1.9	-	-	121.0	0.0	-	-
1988	121.1	0.1	-	-	121.2	0.1	-	-	122.3	0.9	-	-	124.7	2.0	-	-	125.3	0.5	-	-	124.4	-0.7	-	-
1989	125.9	1.2	-	-	127.6	1.4	-	-	128.1	0.4	-	-	129.5	1.1	-	-	131.7	1.7	-	-	131.2	-0.4	-	-
1990	134.1	2.2	-	-	134.8	0.5	-	-	134.6	-0.1	-	-	138.4	2.8	-	-	138.8	0.3	-	-	137.7	-0.8	-	-
1991	138.2	0.4	-	-	138.9	0.5	-	-	142.0	2.2	-	-	141.8	-0.1	-	-	142.9	0.8	-	-	140.2	-1.9	-	-
1992	142.1	1.4	-	-	142.2	0.1	-	-	142.4	0.1	-	-	144.9	1.8	-	-	146.0	0.8	-	-	145.2	-0.5	-	-
1993	145.2	0.0	-	-	145.9	0.5	-	-	147.3	1.0	-	-	149.2	1.3	-	-	149.4	0.1	-	-	149.6	0.1	-	-
1994	150.5	0.6	-	-	150.4	-0.1	-	-	150.1	-0.2	-	-	151.5	0.9	-	-	152.6	0.7	-	-	150.0	-1.7	-	-
1995	151.3	0.9	-	-	152.5	0.8	-	-	152.0	-0.3	-	-	154.7	1.8	-	-	154.7	0.0	-	-	152.8	-1.2	-	-

Source: U.S. Department of Labor, Bureau of Labor Statistics, Division of Consumer Prices and Price Indexes. - indicates no data collected for period.

Washington, DC-MD-VA
Consumer Price Index - Urban Wage Earners
Base 1982-1984 = 100
Housing

For 1975-1995. Columns headed % show percentile change in the index from the previous period for which an index is available.

Year	Jan Index	%	Feb Index	%	Mar Index	%	Apr Index	%	May Index	%	Jun Index	%	Jul Index	%	Aug Index	%	Sep Index	%	Oct Index	%	Nov Index	%	Dec Index	%
1975	-	-	-	-	-	-	-	-	-	-	-	-	-	-	-	-	-	-	-	-	53.4	-	-	-
1976	-	-	54.3	1.7	-	-	-	-	55.4	2.0	-	-	-	-	56.2	1.4	-	-	-	-	56.8	1.1	-	-
1977	-	-	58.1	2.3	-	-	-	-	59.1	1.7	-	-	-	-	60.5	2.4	-	-	-	-	61.7	2.0	-	-
1978	62.6	1.5	-	-	62.9	0.5	-	-	64.6	2.7	-	-	66.4	2.8	-	-	67.8	2.1	-	-	68.3	0.7	-	-
1979	70.5	3.2	-	-	71.5	1.4	-	-	72.2	1.0	-	-	73.9	2.4	-	-	74.0	0.1	-	-	74.8	1.1	-	-
1980	77.5	3.6	-	-	79.7	2.8	-	-	81.2	1.9	-	-	83.4	2.7	-	-	83.0	-0.5	-	-	84.5	1.8	-	-
1981	86.1	1.9	-	-	87.8	2.0	-	-	89.6	2.1	-	-	91.0	1.6	-	-	92.3	1.4	-	-	94.2	2.1	-	-
1982	95.1	1.0	-	-	95.1	0.0	-	-	95.1	0.0	-	-	95.7	0.6	-	-	98.1	2.5	-	-	97.7	-0.4	-	-
1983	98.0	0.3	-	-	98.6	0.6	-	-	98.9	0.3	-	-	100.0	1.1	-	-	99.5	-0.5	-	-	100.6	1.1	-	-
1984	103.2	2.6	-	-	102.5	-0.7	-	-	102.6	0.1	-	-	103.1	0.5	-	-	106.4	3.2	-	-	106.9	0.5	-	-
1985	106.6	-0.3	-	-	108.3	1.6	-	-	108.5	0.2	-	-	111.1	2.4	-	-	110.1	-0.9	-	-	111.2	1.0	-	-
1986	113.8	2.3	-	-	113.5	-0.3	-	-	114.1	0.5	-	-	113.4	-0.6	-	-	114.2	0.7	-	-	115.9	1.5	-	-
1987	116.7	0.7	-	-	116.1	-0.5	-	-	117.0	0.8	-	-	118.0	0.9	-	-	120.1	1.8	-	-	120.3	0.2	-	-
1988	120.4	0.1	-	-	120.5	0.1	-	-	121.5	0.8	-	-	123.9	2.0	-	-	124.7	0.6	-	-	123.5	-1.0	-	-
1989	125.2	1.4	-	-	126.9	1.4	-	-	127.2	0.2	-	-	128.7	1.2	-	-	130.9	1.7	-	-	129.8	-0.8	-	-
1990	133.0	2.5	-	-	133.2	0.2	-	-	132.8	-0.3	-	-	136.9	3.1	-	-	137.3	0.3	-	-	135.8	-1.1	-	-
1991	136.4	0.4	-	-	137.2	0.6	-	-	140.5	2.4	-	-	139.6	-0.6	-	-	141.1	1.1	-	-	138.5	-1.8	-	-
1992	140.1	1.2	-	-	140.0	-0.1	-	-	140.3	0.2	-	-	142.8	1.8	-	-	143.4	0.4	-	-	142.9	-0.3	-	-
1993	142.4	-0.3	-	-	143.1	0.5	-	-	144.6	1.0	-	-	146.7	1.5	-	-	146.9	0.1	-	-	146.9	0.0	-	-
1994	147.3	0.3	-	-	147.2	-0.1	-	-	147.5	0.2	-	-	148.7	0.8	-	-	150.4	1.1	-	-	147.5	-1.9	-	-
1995	148.5	0.7	-	-	149.5	0.7	-	-	149.5	0.0	-	-	151.8	1.5	-	-	152.1	0.2	-	-	150.3	-1.2	-	-

Source: U.S. Department of Labor, Bureau of Labor Statistics, Division of Consumer Prices and Price Indexes. - indicates no data collected for period.

Washington, DC-MD-VA
Consumer Price Index - All Urban Consumers
Base 1982-1984 = 100
Apparel and Upkeep

For 1952-1995. Columns headed % show percentile change in the index from the previous period for which an index is available.

Year	Jan Index	%	Feb Index	%	Mar Index	%	Apr Index	%	May Index	%	Jun Index	%	Jul Index	%	Aug Index	%	Sep Index	%	Oct Index	%	Nov Index	%	Dec Index	%
1952	-	-	-	-	-	-	-	-	-	-	-	-	-	-	-	-	-	-	-	-	40.1	-	-	-
1953	-	-	40.3	0.5	-	-	-	-	40.5	0.5	-	-	-	-	40.5	0.0	-	-	-	-	40.6	0.2	-	-
1954	-	-	40.5	-0.2	-	-	-	-	40.3	-0.5	-	-	-	-	40.0	-0.7	-	-	-	-	40.2	0.5	-	-
1955	-	-	39.8	-1.0	-	-	-	-	39.8	0.0	-	-	-	-	40.0	0.5	-	-	-	-	40.4	1.0	-	-
1956	-	-	40.7	0.7	-	-	-	-	41.1	1.0	-	-	-	-	41.2	0.2	-	-	-	-	41.2	0.0	-	-
1957	-	-	41.3	0.2	-	-	-	-	41.3	0.0	-	-	-	-	41.4	0.2	-	-	-	-	41.2	-0.5	-	-
1958	-	-	41.1	-0.2	-	-	-	-	41.1	0.0	-	-	-	-	41.2	0.2	-	-	-	-	41.2	0.0	-	-
1959	-	-	41.3	0.2	-	-	-	-	41.6	0.7	-	-	-	-	42.0	1.0	-	-	-	-	42.0	0.0	-	-
1960	-	-	41.7	-0.7	-	-	-	-	42.0	0.7	-	-	-	-	42.2	0.5	-	-	-	-	42.3	0.2	-	-
1961	-	-	42.4	0.2	-	-	-	-	42.6	0.5	-	-	-	-	42.6	0.0	-	-	-	-	43.7	2.6	-	-
1962	-	-	43.9	0.5	-	-	-	-	43.9	0.0	-	-	-	-	44.0	0.2	-	-	-	-	44.7	1.6	-	-
1963	-	-	44.2	-1.1	-	-	-	-	44.3	0.2	-	-	-	-	43.9	-0.9	-	-	-	-	44.5	1.4	-	-
1964	-	-	44.4	-0.2	-	-	-	-	44.7	0.7	-	-	-	-	44.6	-0.2	-	-	-	-	44.7	0.2	-	-
1965	-	-	44.3	-0.9	-	-	-	-	45.2	2.0	-	-	-	-	44.5	-1.5	-	-	-	-	45.3	1.8	-	-
1966	-	-	45.5	0.4	-	-	-	-	46.5	2.2	-	-	-	-	46.3	-0.4	-	-	-	-	47.5	2.6	-	-
1967	-	-	47.7	0.4	-	-	-	-	48.6	1.9	-	-	-	-	48.5	-0.2	-	-	-	-	49.7	2.5	-	-
1968	-	-	50.2	1.0	-	-	-	-	52.3	4.2	-	-	-	-	52.6	0.6	-	-	-	-	54.1	2.9	-	-
1969	-	-	54.3	0.4	-	-	-	-	55.9	2.9	-	-	-	-	55.7	-0.4	-	-	-	-	57.0	2.3	-	-
1970	-	-	57.0	0.0	-	-	-	-	58.5	2.6	-	-	-	-	58.0	-0.9	-	-	-	-	59.5	2.6	-	-
1971	-	-	58.8	-1.2	-	-	-	-	60.0	2.0	-	-	-	-	59.7	-0.5	-	-	-	-	61.1	2.3	-	-
1972	-	-	60.0	-1.8	-	-	-	-	61.0	1.7	-	-	-	-	60.3	-1.1	-	-	-	-	61.9	2.7	-	-
1973	-	-	62.2	0.5	-	-	-	-	64.1	3.1	-	-	-	-	63.7	-0.6	-	-	-	-	64.8	1.7	-	-
1974	-	-	66.3	2.3	-	-	-	-	68.2	2.9	-	-	-	-	69.2	1.5	-	-	-	-	70.5	1.9	-	-
1975	-	-	70.1	-0.6	-	-	-	-	70.5	0.6	-	-	-	-	69.9	-0.9	-	-	-	-	71.4	2.1	-	-
1976	-	-	70.6	-1.1	-	-	-	-	73.3	3.8	-	-	-	-	73.1	-0.3	-	-	-	-	73.8	1.0	-	-
1977	-	-	72.4	-1.9	-	-	-	-	74.1	2.3	-	-	-	-	74.6	0.7	-	-	-	-	75.8	1.6	-	-
1978	75.6	-0.3	-	-	76.8	1.6	-	-	78.2	1.8	-	-	76.5	-2.2	-	-	79.8	4.3	-	-	80.6	1.0	-	-
1979	77.3	-4.1	-	-	81.6	5.6	-	-	83.3	2.1	-	-	81.4	-2.3	-	-	87.2	7.1	-	-	87.7	0.6	-	-
1980	86.7	-1.1	-	-	91.5	5.5	-	-	89.9	-1.7	-	-	87.9	-2.2	-	-	91.8	4.4	-	-	93.0	1.3	-	-
1981	89.7	-3.5	-	-	89.7	0.0	-	-	90.8	1.2	-	-	87.6	-3.5	-	-	93.4	6.6	-	-	91.8	-1.7	-	-
1982	90.7	-1.2	-	-	95.5	5.3	-	-	93.7	-1.9	-	-	92.2	-1.6	-	-	96.6	4.8	-	-	97.8	1.2	-	-
1983	97.0	-0.8	-	-	100.4	3.5	-	-	102.6	2.2	-	-	103.0	0.4	-	-	100.9	-2.0	-	-	99.0	-1.9	-	-
1984	99.9	0.9	-	-	101.1	1.2	-	-	104.4	3.3	-	-	103.4	-1.0	-	-	109.8	6.2	-	-	108.6	-1.1	-	-
1985	104.8	-3.5	-	-	110.4	5.3	-	-	109.4	-0.9	-	-	106.7	-2.5	-	-	113.8	6.7	-	-	114.3	0.4	-	-
1986	106.2	-7.1	-	-	105.3	-0.8	-	-	104.4	-0.9	-	-	104.5	0.1	-	-	115.6	10.6	-	-	115.4	-0.2	-	-
1987	110.7	-4.1	-	-	113.0	2.1	-	-	115.0	1.8	-	-	112.1	-2.5	-	-	122.0	8.8	-	-	123.5	1.2	-	-
1988	116.4	-5.7	-	-	124.9	7.3	-	-	122.3	-2.1	-	-	111.6	-8.7	-	-	130.8	17.2	-	-	131.0	0.2	-	-
1989	125.0	-4.6	-	-	135.6	8.5	-	-	135.7	0.1	-	-	130.8	-3.6	-	-	142.1	8.6	-	-	139.7	-1.7	-	-
1990	128.2	-8.2	-	-	141.9	10.7	-	-	140.4	-1.1	-	-	135.0	-3.8	-	-	147.0	8.9	Oct	-	141.1	-4.0	Dec	-
1991	138.9	-1.6	-	-	138.8	-0.1	-	-	139.3	0.4	-	-	135.2	-2.9	-	-	153.3	13.4	-	-	149.9	-2.2	-	-
1992	136.5	-8.9	-	-	138.4	1.4	-	-	134.5	-2.8	-	-	136.2	1.3	-	-	145.3	6.7	-	-	144.8	-0.3	-	-
1993	145.7	0.6	-	-	150.6	3.4	-	-	146.4	-2.8	-	-	136.4	-6.8	-	-	144.3	5.8	-	-	145.2	0.6	-	-
1994	137.5	-5.3	-	-	143.7	4.5	-	-	144.9	0.8	-	-	137.0	-5.5	-	-	144.9	5.8	-	-	141.4	-2.4	-	-
1995	135.8	-4.0	-	-	149.1	9.8	-	-	143.6	-3.7	-	-	140.9	-1.9	-	-	142.5	1.1	-	-	133.5	-6.3	-	-

Source: U.S. Department of Labor, Bureau of Labor Statistics, Division of Consumer Prices and Price Indexes. - indicates no data collected for period.

Washington, DC-MD-VA
Consumer Price Index - Urban Wage Earners
Base 1982-1984 = 100
Apparel and Upkeep

For 1952-1995. Columns headed % show percentile change in the index from the previous period for which an index is available.

Year	Jan Index	%	Feb Index	%	Mar Index	%	Apr Index	%	May Index	%	Jun Index	%	Jul Index	%	Aug Index	%	Sep Index	%	Oct Index	%	Nov Index	%	Dec Index	%
1952	-		-		-		-		-		-		-		-		-		-		36.0	-	-	-
1953	-		36.3	0.8	-		-		36.4	0.3	-		-		36.5	0.3	-		-		36.6	0.3	-	-
1954	-		36.4	-0.5	-		-		36.2	-0.5	-		-		35.9	-0.8	-		-		36.2	0.8	-	-
1955	-		35.8	-1.1	-		-		35.8	0.0	-		-		36.0	0.6	-		-		36.3	0.8	-	-
1956	-		36.6	0.8	-		-		37.0	1.1	-		-		37.1	0.3	-		-		37.0	-0.3	-	-
1957	-		37.2	0.5	-		-		37.1	-0.3	-		-		37.3	0.5	-		-		37.1	-0.5	-	-
1958	-		37.0	-0.3	-		-		37.0	0.0	-		-		37.0	0.0	-		-		37.1	0.3	-	-
1959	-		37.1	0.0	-		-		37.4	0.8	-		-		37.8	1.1	-		-		37.7	-0.3	-	-
1960	-		37.5	-0.5	-		-		37.8	0.8	-		-		38.0	0.5	-		-		38.1	0.3	-	-
1961	-		38.1	0.0	-		-		38.3	0.5	-		-		38.4	0.3	-		-		39.3	2.3	-	-
1962	-		39.4	0.3	-		-		39.5	0.3	-		-		39.6	0.3	-		-		40.2	1.5	-	-
1963	-		39.8	-1.0	-		-		39.9	0.3	-		-		39.5	-1.0	-		-		40.1	1.5	-	-
1964	-		39.9	-0.5	-		-		40.2	0.8	-		-		40.1	-0.2	-		-		40.2	0.2	-	-
1965	-		39.9	-0.7	-		-		40.7	2.0	-		-		40.1	-1.5	-		-		40.7	1.5	-	-
1966	-		40.9	0.5	-		-		41.8	2.2	-		-		41.7	-0.2	-		-		42.7	2.4	-	-
1967	-		42.9	0.5	-		-		43.7	1.9	-		-		43.6	-0.2	-		-		44.7	2.5	-	-
1968	-		45.1	0.9	-		-		47.0	4.2	-		-		47.3	0.6	-		-		48.6	2.7	-	-
1969	-		48.9	0.6	-		-		50.3	2.9	-		-		50.1	-0.4	-		-		51.3	2.4	-	-
1970	-		51.3	0.0	-		-		52.6	2.5	-		-		52.1	-1.0	-		-		53.5	2.7	-	-
1971	-		52.9	-1.1	-		-		54.0	2.1	-		-		53.7	-0.6	-		-		55.0	2.4	-	-
1972	-		53.9	-2.0	-		-		54.9	1.9	-		-		54.2	-1.3	-		-		55.7	2.8	-	-
1973	-		55.9	0.4	-		-		57.7	3.2	-		-		57.3	-0.7	-		-		58.3	1.7	-	-
1974	-		59.7	2.4	-		-		61.4	2.8	-		-		62.2	1.3	-		-		63.4	1.9	-	-
1975	-		63.0	-0.6	-		-		63.4	0.6	-		-		62.9	-0.8	-		-		64.3	2.2	-	-
1976	-		63.5	-1.2	-		-		65.9	3.8	-		-		65.7	-0.3	-		-		66.4	1.1	-	-
1977	-		65.1	-2.0	-		-		66.6	2.3	-		-		67.1	0.8	-		-		68.2	1.6	-	-
1978	65.9	-3.4	-		66.6	1.1	-		68.2	2.4	-		67.9	-0.4	-		70.2	3.4	-		70.9	1.0	-	-
1979	67.6	-4.7	-		70.4	4.1	-		71.4	1.4	-		71.4	0.0	-		75.3	5.5	-		75.5	0.3	-	-
1980	75.7	0.3	-		78.4	3.6	-		78.7	0.4	-		78.3	-0.5	-		86.5	10.5	-		85.3	-1.4	-	-
1981	84.1	-1.4	-		87.1	3.6	-		90.1	3.4	-		90.0	-0.1	-		93.0	3.3	-		90.1	-3.1	-	-
1982	88.3	-2.0	-		98.0	11.0	-		90.8	-7.3	-		89.0	-2.0	-		97.1	9.1	-		99.0	2.0	-	-
1983	97.7	-1.3	-		102.8	5.2	-		105.6	2.7	-		105.9	0.3	-		104.2	-1.6	-		99.6	-4.4	-	-
1984	100.4	0.8	-		99.4	-1.0	-		99.1	-0.3	-		97.5	-1.6	-		111.9	14.8	-		110.1	-1.6	-	-
1985	103.5	-6.0	-		109.2	5.5	-		106.0	-2.9	-		103.3	-2.5	-		116.1	12.4	-		114.7	-1.2	-	-
1986	100.8	-12.1	-		98.5	-2.3	-		96.3	-2.2	-		97.2	0.9	-		116.1	19.4	-		113.8	-2.0	-	-
1987	108.3	-4.8	-		111.1	2.6	-		114.0	2.6	-		109.1	-4.3	-		120.6	10.5	-		123.1	2.1	-	-
1988	113.8	-7.6	-		123.5	8.5	-		119.9	-2.9	-		107.5	-10.3	-		127.8	18.9	-		130.5	2.1	-	-
1989	123.2	-5.6	-		134.1	8.8	-		133.7	-0.3	-		129.5	-3.1	-		141.5	9.3	-		138.3	-2.3	-	-
1990	124.8	-9.8	-		139.5	11.8	-		138.7	-0.6	-		130.8	-5.7	-		145.1	10.9	-		140.7	-3.0	-	-
1991	136.2	-3.2	-		137.6	1.0	-		138.0	0.3	-		133.0	-3.6	-		152.0	14.3	-		150.1	-1.2	-	-
1992	137.1	-8.7	-		139.6	1.8	-		134.8	-3.4	-		136.9	1.6	-		145.4	6.2	-		144.9	-0.3	-	-
1993	143.7	-0.8	-		149.2	3.8	-		145.2	-2.7	-		135.8	-6.5	-		144.7	6.6	-		145.0	0.2	-	-
1994	137.8	-5.0	-		143.7	4.3	-		144.7	0.7	-		135.2	-6.6	-		144.7	7.0	-		140.7	-2.8	-	-
1995	136.1	-3.3	-		150.0	10.2	-		143.2	-4.5	-		140.7	-1.7	-		142.2	1.1	-		131.9	-7.2	-	-

Source: U.S. Department of Labor, Bureau of Labor Statistics, Division of Consumer Prices and Price Indexes. - indicates no data collected for period.

Washington, DC-MD-VA
Consumer Price Index - All Urban Consumers
Base 1982-1984 = 100
Transportation

For 1947-1995. Columns headed % show percentile change in the index from the previous period for which an index is available.

Year	Jan Index	%	Feb Index	%	Mar Index	%	Apr Index	%	May Index	%	Jun Index	%	Jul Index	%	Aug Index	%	Sep Index	%	Oct Index	%	Nov Index	%	Dec Index	%
1947	18.0	-	18.0	0.0	18.1	0.6	18.3	1.1	19.1	4.4	19.3	1.0	-	-	19.6	1.6	-	-	-	-	19.8	1.0	-	-
1948	-	-	20.2	2.0	-	-	-	-	20.4	1.0	-	-	-	-	21.5	5.4	-	-	-	-	22.6	5.1	-	-
1949	-	-	22.7	0.4	-	-	-	-	22.8	0.4	-	-	-	-	22.8	0.0	-	-	-	-	22.9	0.4	-	-
1950	-	-	22.9	0.0	-	-	-	-	22.9	0.0	-	-	-	-	23.7	3.5	-	-	-	-	23.8	0.4	-	-
1951	-	-	23.8	0.0	-	-	-	-	24.0	0.8	-	-	-	-	24.1	0.4	-	-	-	-	24.7	2.5	-	-
1952	-	-	25.3	2.4	-	-	-	-	25.3	0.0	-	-	-	-	25.9	2.4	-	-	-	-	26.8	3.5	-	-
1953	-	-	26.7	-0.4	-	-	-	-	26.8	0.4	-	-	-	-	27.1	1.1	-	-	-	-	27.0	-0.4	-	-
1954	-	-	26.9	-0.4	-	-	-	-	26.7	-0.7	-	-	-	-	26.3	-1.5	-	-	-	-	27.2	3.4	-	-
1955	-	-	27.1	-0.4	-	-	-	-	27.0	-0.4	-	-	-	-	27.1	0.4	-	-	-	-	27.6	1.8	-	-
1956	-	-	27.4	-0.7	-	-	-	-	27.1	-1.1	-	-	-	-	27.4	1.1	-	-	-	-	28.4	3.6	-	-
1957	-	-	28.4	0.0	-	-	-	-	28.6	0.7	-	-	-	-	29.0	1.4	-	-	-	-	29.8	2.8	-	-
1958	-	-	29.0	-2.7	-	-	-	-	29.0	0.0	-	-	-	-	29.4	1.4	-	-	-	-	30.6	4.1	-	-
1959	-	-	30.2	-1.3	-	-	-	-	30.2	0.0	-	-	-	-	30.6	1.3	-	-	-	-	30.8	0.7	-	-
1960	-	-	30.7	-0.3	-	-	-	-	30.7	0.0	-	-	-	-	30.8	0.3	-	-	-	-	30.7	-0.3	-	-
1961	-	-	30.4	-1.0	-	-	-	-	30.8	1.3	-	-	-	-	31.3	1.6	-	-	-	-	31.4	0.3	-	-
1962	-	-	31.1	-1.0	-	-	-	-	31.3	0.6	-	-	-	-	31.4	0.3	-	-	-	-	31.5	0.3	-	-
1963	-	-	31.0	-1.6	-	-	-	-	31.5	1.6	-	-	-	-	31.7	0.6	-	-	-	-	32.2	1.6	-	-
1964	-	-	32.2	0.0	-	-	-	-	32.2	0.0	-	-	-	-	32.3	0.3	-	-	-	-	32.7	1.2	-	-
1965	-	-	32.7	0.0	-	-	-	-	32.7	0.0	-	-	-	-	32.5	-0.6	-	-	-	-	32.7	0.6	-	-
1966	-	-	32.6	-0.3	-	-	-	-	32.9	0.9	-	-	-	-	32.9	0.0	-	-	-	-	33.3	1.2	-	-
1967	-	-	33.3	0.0	-	-	-	-	34.1	2.4	-	-	-	-	34.3	0.6	-	-	-	-	34.7	1.2	-	-
1968	-	-	35.0	0.9	-	-	-	-	35.2	0.6	-	-	-	-	35.5	0.9	-	-	-	-	36.0	1.4	-	-
1969	-	-	36.4	1.1	-	-	-	-	36.9	1.4	-	-	-	-	37.3	1.1	-	-	-	-	38.0	1.9	-	-
1970	-	-	38.3	0.8	-	-	-	-	39.4	2.9	-	-	-	-	40.4	2.5	-	-	-	-	40.7	0.7	-	-
1971	-	-	41.8	2.7	-	-	-	-	42.5	1.7	-	-	-	-	42.3	-0.5	-	-	-	-	42.1	-0.5	-	-
1972	-	-	41.8	-0.7	-	-	-	-	42.0	0.5	-	-	-	-	42.4	1.0	-	-	-	-	42.6	0.5	-	-
1973	-	-	42.6	0.0	-	-	-	-	42.9	0.7	-	-	-	-	43.0	0.2	-	-	-	-	43.6	1.4	-	-
1974	-	-	45.1	3.4	-	-	-	-	47.1	4.4	-	-	-	-	48.8	3.6	-	-	-	-	49.4	1.2	-	-
1975	-	-	49.9	1.0	-	-	-	-	51.2	2.6	-	-	-	-	52.8	3.1	-	-	-	-	53.5	1.3	-	-
1976	-	-	53.7	0.4	-	-	-	-	55.3	3.0	-	-	-	-	56.6	2.4	-	-	-	-	56.8	0.4	-	-
1977	-	-	58.1	2.3	-	-	-	-	59.9	3.1	-	-	-	-	60.6	1.2	-	-	-	-	60.7	0.2	-	-
1978	61.0	0.5	-	-	61.3	0.5	-	-	62.3	1.6	-	-	64.0	2.7	-	-	64.5	0.8	-	-	65.9	2.2	-	-
1979	66.3	0.6	-	-	67.5	1.8	-	-	70.1	3.9	-	-	72.9	4.0	-	-	74.5	2.2	-	-	76.3	2.4	-	-
1980	79.1	3.7	-	-	82.5	4.3	-	-	83.5	1.2	-	-	85.4	2.3	-	-	87.2	2.1	-	-	88.3	1.3	-	-
1981	90.4	2.4	-	-	92.8	2.7	-	-	94.2	1.5	-	-	95.0	0.8	-	-	95.7	0.7	-	-	96.5	0.8	-	-
1982	97.1	0.6	-	-	95.2	-2.0	-	-	95.2	0.0	-	-	98.2	3.2	-	-	98.0	-0.2	-	-	98.0	0.0	-	-
1983	97.5	-0.5	-	-	96.0	-1.5	-	-	98.6	2.7	-	-	99.9	1.3	-	-	100.8	0.9	-	-	102.1	1.3	-	-
1984	102.3	0.2	-	-	102.2	-0.1	-	-	103.7	1.5	-	-	104.5	0.8	-	-	104.5	0.0	-	-	104.6	0.1	-	-
1985	104.1	-0.5	-	-	104.6	0.5	-	-	105.8	1.1	-	-	106.0	0.2	-	-	105.7	-0.3	-	-	107.0	1.2	-	-
1986	107.3	0.3	-	-	104.8	-2.3	-	-	103.2	-1.5	-	-	103.4	0.2	-	-	102.4	-1.0	-	-	102.6	0.2	-	-
1987	103.8	1.2	-	-	105.4	1.5	-	-	104.9	-0.5	-	-	107.2	2.2	-	-	106.4	-0.7	-	-	107.1	0.7	-	-
1988	106.0	-1.0	-	-	106.2	0.2	-	-	107.5	1.2	-	-	107.9	0.4	-	-	108.4	0.5	-	-	111.2	2.6	-	-
1989	112.5	1.2	-	-	112.3	-0.2	-	-	113.8	1.3	-	-	114.8	0.9	-	-	114.4	-0.3	-	-	117.0	2.3	-	-
1990	118.1	0.9	-	-	117.8	-0.3	-	-	117.9	0.1	-	-	118.7	0.7	-	-	122.3	3.0	-	-	127.1	3.9	-	-
1991	127.4	0.2	-	-	123.9	-2.7	-	-	124.8	0.7	-	-	124.7	-0.1	-	-	127.1	1.9	-	-	128.7	1.3	-	-

[Continued]

Washington, DC-MD-VA
Consumer Price Index - All Urban Consumers
Base 1982-1984 = 100
Transportation
[Continued]

For 1947-1995. Columns headed % show percentile change in the index from the previous period for which an index is available.

Year	Jan		Feb		Mar		Apr		May		Jun		Jul		Aug		Sep		Oct		Nov		Dec	
	Index	%	Index	%	Index	%	Index	%	Index	%	Index	%	Index	%	Index	%	Index	%	Index	%	Index	%	Index	%
1992	129.6	0.7	-	-	127.5	-1.6	-	-	129.0	1.2	-	-	130.9	1.5	-	-	127.8	-2.4	-	-	133.1	4.1	-	-
1993	135.5	1.8	-	-	134.8	-0.5	-	-	135.2	0.3	-	-	135.2	0.0	-	-	132.4	-2.1	-	-	136.3	2.9	-	-
1994	135.7	-0.4	-	-	136.0	0.2	-	-	135.6	-0.3	-	-	136.9	1.0	-	-	136.9	0.0	-	-	139.9	2.2	-	-
1995	140.6	0.5	-	-	139.7	-0.6	-	-	140.5	0.6	-	-	141.2	0.5	-	-	139.6	-1.1	-	-	140.1	0.4	-	-

Source: U.S. Department of Labor, Bureau of Labor Statistics, Division of Consumer Prices and Price Indexes. - indicates no data collected for period.

Washington, DC-MD-VA
Consumer Price Index - Urban Wage Earners
Base 1982-1984 = 100
Transportation

For 1947-1995. Columns headed % show percentile change in the index from the previous period for which an index is available.

Year	Jan Index	%	Feb Index	%	Mar Index	%	Apr Index	%	May Index	%	Jun Index	%	Jul Index	%	Aug Index	%	Sep Index	%	Oct Index	%	Nov Index	%	Dec Index	%
1947	18.0	-	18.0	0.0	18.0	0.0	18.3	1.7	19.1	4.4	19.2	0.5	-	-	19.6	2.1	-	-	-	-	19.8	1.0	-	-
1948	-	-	20.2	2.0	-	-	-	-	20.4	1.0	-	-	-	-	21.4	4.9	-	-	-	-	22.5	5.1	-	-
1949	-	-	22.6	0.4	-	-	-	-	22.8	0.9	-	-	-	-	22.7	-0.4	-	-	-	-	22.8	0.4	-	-
1950	-	-	22.9	0.4	-	-	-	-	22.9	0.0	-	-	-	-	23.6	3.1	-	-	-	-	23.7	0.4	-	-
1951	-	-	23.8	0.4	-	-	-	-	24.0	0.8	-	-	-	-	24.0	0.0	-	-	-	-	24.7	2.9	-	-
1952	-	-	25.2	2.0	-	-	-	-	25.2	0.0	-	-	-	-	25.9	2.8	-	-	-	-	26.7	3.1	-	-
1953	-	-	26.6	-0.4	-	-	-	-	26.7	0.4	-	-	-	-	27.0	1.1	-	-	-	-	26.9	-0.4	-	-
1954	-	-	26.9	0.0	-	-	-	-	26.6	-1.1	-	-	-	-	26.2	-1.5	-	-	-	-	27.1	3.4	-	-
1955	-	-	27.0	-0.4	-	-	-	-	27.0	0.0	-	-	-	-	27.1	0.4	-	-	-	-	27.5	1.5	-	-
1956	-	-	27.3	-0.7	-	-	-	-	27.0	-1.1	-	-	-	-	27.3	1.1	-	-	-	-	28.3	3.7	-	-
1957	-	-	28.4	0.4	-	-	-	-	28.6	0.7	-	-	-	-	28.9	1.0	-	-	-	-	29.7	2.8	-	-
1958	-	-	28.9	-2.7	-	-	-	-	28.9	0.0	-	-	-	-	29.3	1.4	-	-	-	-	30.5	4.1	-	-
1959	-	-	30.2	-1.0	-	-	-	-	30.1	-0.3	-	-	-	-	30.5	1.3	-	-	-	-	30.7	0.7	-	-
1960	-	-	30.6	-0.3	-	-	-	-	30.6	0.0	-	-	-	-	30.7	0.3	-	-	-	-	30.6	-0.3	-	-
1961	-	-	30.3	-1.0	-	-	-	-	30.7	1.3	-	-	-	-	31.3	2.0	-	-	-	-	31.3	0.0	-	-
1962	-	-	31.0	-1.0	-	-	-	-	31.2	0.6	-	-	-	-	31.3	0.3	-	-	-	-	31.5	0.6	-	-
1963	-	-	30.9	-1.9	-	-	-	-	31.4	1.6	-	-	-	-	31.6	0.6	-	-	-	-	32.1	1.6	-	-
1964	-	-	32.1	0.0	-	-	-	-	32.1	0.0	-	-	-	-	32.2	0.3	-	-	-	-	32.6	1.2	-	-
1965	-	-	32.6	0.0	-	-	-	-	32.6	0.0	-	-	-	-	32.4	-0.6	-	-	-	-	32.6	0.6	-	-
1966	-	-	32.5	-0.3	-	-	-	-	32.8	0.9	-	-	-	-	32.9	0.3	-	-	-	-	33.3	1.2	-	-
1967	-	-	33.3	0.0	-	-	-	-	34.0	2.1	-	-	-	-	34.2	0.6	-	-	-	-	34.6	1.2	-	-
1968	-	-	34.9	0.9	-	-	-	-	35.1	0.6	-	-	-	-	35.4	0.9	-	-	-	-	35.9	1.4	-	-
1969	-	-	36.3	1.1	-	-	-	-	36.8	1.4	-	-	-	-	37.2	1.1	-	-	-	-	37.9	1.9	-	-
1970	-	-	38.2	0.8	-	-	-	-	39.3	2.9	-	-	-	-	40.3	2.5	-	-	-	-	40.6	0.7	-	-
1971	-	-	41.7	2.7	-	-	-	-	42.4	1.7	-	-	-	-	42.2	-0.5	-	-	-	-	42.0	-0.5	-	-
1972	-	-	41.7	-0.7	-	-	-	-	41.8	0.2	-	-	-	-	42.3	1.2	-	-	-	-	42.5	0.5	-	-
1973	-	-	42.5	0.0	-	-	-	-	42.8	0.7	-	-	-	-	42.9	0.2	-	-	-	-	43.4	1.2	-	-
1974	-	-	45.0	3.7	-	-	-	-	47.0	4.4	-	-	-	-	48.7	3.6	-	-	-	-	49.3	1.2	-	-
1975	-	-	49.8	1.0	-	-	-	-	51.1	2.6	-	-	-	-	52.7	3.1	-	-	-	-	53.4	1.3	-	-
1976	-	-	53.5	0.2	-	-	-	-	55.1	3.0	-	-	-	-	56.4	2.4	-	-	-	-	56.7	0.5	-	-
1977	-	-	58.0	2.3	-	-	-	-	59.7	2.9	-	-	-	-	60.4	1.2	-	-	-	-	60.5	0.2	-	-
1978	60.6	0.2	-	-	60.8	0.3	-	-	62.0	2.0	-	-	63.3	2.1	-	-	63.6	0.5	-	-	65.5	3.0	-	-
1979	65.9	0.6	-	-	67.0	1.7	-	-	69.7	4.0	-	-	71.8	3.0	-	-	73.1	1.8	-	-	74.8	2.3	-	-
1980	77.8	4.0	-	-	80.9	4.0	-	-	81.5	0.7	-	-	84.2	3.3	-	-	85.3	1.3	-	-	86.0	0.8	-	-
1981	87.9	2.2	-	-	90.4	2.8	-	-	92.5	2.3	-	-	94.0	1.6	-	-	94.5	0.5	-	-	95.9	1.5	-	-
1982	96.4	0.5	-	-	94.8	-1.7	-	-	95.0	0.2	-	-	97.7	2.8	-	-	97.6	-0.1	-	-	97.5	-0.1	-	-
1983	97.3	-0.2	-	-	95.9	-1.4	-	-	98.4	2.6	-	-	99.7	1.3	-	-	100.8	1.1	-	-	102.3	1.5	-	-
1984	102.5	0.2	-	-	102.5	0.0	-	-	104.2	1.7	-	-	105.0	0.8	-	-	105.0	0.0	-	-	105.3	0.3	-	-
1985	104.8	-0.5	-	-	105.2	0.4	-	-	106.2	1.0	-	-	106.2	0.0	-	-	105.9	-0.3	-	-	107.3	1.3	-	-
1986	107.6	0.3	-	-	105.5	-2.0	-	-	103.5	-1.9	-	-	103.8	0.3	-	-	103.0	-0.8	-	-	103.3	0.3	-	-
1987	104.4	1.1	-	-	106.4	1.9	-	-	106.9	0.5	-	-	109.4	2.3	-	-	109.6	0.2	-	-	110.2	0.5	-	-
1988	108.9	-1.2	-	-	109.0	0.1	-	-	110.5	1.4	-	-	111.0	0.5	-	-	112.0	0.9	-	-	114.3	2.1	-	-
1989	115.6	1.1	-	-	115.6	0.0	-	-	117.5	1.6	-	-	118.5	0.9	-	-	117.9	-0.5	-	-	120.5	2.2	-	-
1990	121.9	1.2	-	-	121.3	-0.5	-	-	121.5	0.2	-	-	122.5	0.8	-	-	126.6	3.3	-	-	131.6	3.9	-	-
1991	131.4	-0.2	-	-	127.3	-3.1	-	-	128.5	0.9	-	-	128.5	0.0	-	-	130.7	1.7	-	-	132.4	1.3	-	-

[Continued]

Washington, DC-MD-VA
Consumer Price Index - Urban Wage Earners
Base 1982-1984 = 100
Transportation

[Continued]

For 1947-1995. Columns headed % show percentile change in the index from the previous period for which an index is available.

Year	Jan Index	%	Feb Index	%	Mar Index	%	Apr Index	%	May Index	%	Jun Index	%	Jul Index	%	Aug Index	%	Sep Index	%	Oct Index	%	Nov Index	%	Dec Index	%
1992	132.7	0.2	-	-	130.5	-1.7	-	-	132.4	1.5	-	-	134.5	1.6	-	-	131.9	-1.9	-	-	136.3	3.3	-	-
1993	138.6	1.7	-	-	137.5	-0.8	-	-	138.0	0.4	-	-	137.9	-0.1	-	-	135.6	-1.7	-	-	139.2	2.7	-	-
1994	138.2	-0.7	-	-	138.4	0.1	-	-	139.1	0.5	-	-	140.5	1.0	-	-	140.8	0.2	-	-	143.8	2.1	-	-
1995	144.3	0.3	-	-	143.3	-0.7	-	-	144.6	0.9	-	-	144.9	0.2	-	-	143.3	-1.1	-	-	143.9	0.4	-	-

Source: U.S. Department of Labor, Bureau of Labor Statistics, Division of Consumer Prices and Price Indexes. - indicates no data collected for period.

Washington, DC-MD-VA
Consumer Price Index - All Urban Consumers
Base 1982-1984 = 100
Medical Care

For 1947-1995. Columns headed % show percentile change in the index from the previous period for which an index is available.

Year	Jan Index	%	Feb Index	%	Mar Index	%	Apr Index	%	May Index	%	Jun Index	%	Jul Index	%	Aug Index	%	Sep Index	%	Oct Index	%	Nov Index	%	Dec Index	%
1947	12.3	-	12.4	0.8	12.4	0.0	12.4	0.0	12.3	-0.8	12.3	0.0	-	-	12.5	1.6	-	-	-	-	12.5	0.0	-	-
1948	-	-	12.6	0.8	-	-	-	-	12.8	1.6	-	-	-	-	12.8	0.0	-	-	-	-	13.0	1.6	-	-
1949	-	-	13.1	0.8	-	-	-	-	13.1	0.0	-	-	-	-	13.1	0.0	-	-	-	-	13.1	0.0	-	-
1950	-	-	13.1	0.0	-	-	-	-	13.0	-0.8	-	-	-	-	13.2	1.5	-	-	-	-	13.3	0.8	-	-
1951	-	-	13.7	3.0	-	-	-	-	13.9	1.5	-	-	-	-	14.2	2.2	-	-	-	-	14.4	1.4	-	-
1952	-	-	14.5	0.7	-	-	-	-	14.9	2.8	-	-	-	-	14.9	0.0	-	-	-	-	14.9	0.0	-	-
1953	-	-	14.9	0.0	-	-	-	-	15.0	0.7	-	-	-	-	15.0	0.0	-	-	-	-	15.0	0.0	-	-
1954	-	-	15.0	0.0	-	-	-	-	15.0	0.0	-	-	-	-	15.1	0.7	-	-	-	-	15.2	0.7	-	-
1955	-	-	15.1	-0.7	-	-	-	-	15.1	0.0	-	-	-	-	15.1	0.0	-	-	-	-	15.7	4.0	-	-
1956	-	-	15.7	0.0	-	-	-	-	15.8	0.6	-	-	-	-	16.3	3.2	-	-	-	-	16.4	0.6	-	-
1957	-	-	16.5	0.6	-	-	-	-	16.8	1.8	-	-	-	-	16.8	0.0	-	-	-	-	17.0	1.2	-	-
1958	-	-	17.5	2.9	-	-	-	-	17.5	0.0	-	-	-	-	17.9	2.3	-	-	-	-	18.8	5.0	-	-
1959	-	-	18.9	0.5	-	-	-	-	19.2	1.6	-	-	-	-	19.0	-1.0	-	-	-	-	19.2	1.1	-	-
1960	-	-	19.6	2.1	-	-	-	-	19.7	0.5	-	-	-	-	19.7	0.0	-	-	-	-	19.9	1.0	-	-
1961	-	-	20.2	1.5	-	-	-	-	20.3	0.5	-	-	-	-	20.5	1.0	-	-	-	-	20.6	0.5	-	-
1962	-	-	21.0	1.9	-	-	-	-	21.1	0.5	-	-	-	-	21.9	3.8	-	-	-	-	22.0	0.5	-	-
1963	-	-	22.2	0.9	-	-	-	-	22.4	0.9	-	-	-	-	22.4	0.0	-	-	-	-	22.6	0.9	-	-
1964	-	-	22.8	0.9	-	-	-	-	23.0	0.9	-	-	-	-	23.0	0.0	-	-	-	-	23.2	0.9	-	-
1965	-	-	23.4	0.9	-	-	-	-	23.5	0.4	-	-	-	-	23.8	1.3	-	-	-	-	24.0	0.8	-	-
1966	-	-	24.3	1.2	-	-	-	-	24.8	2.1	-	-	-	-	25.1	1.2	-	-	-	-	25.4	1.2	-	-
1967	-	-	26.3	3.5	-	-	-	-	26.8	1.9	-	-	-	-	27.0	0.7	-	-	-	-	28.0	3.7	-	-
1968	-	-	28.8	2.9	-	-	-	-	29.4	2.1	-	-	-	-	29.7	1.0	-	-	-	-	30.3	2.0	-	-
1969	-	-	31.3	3.3	-	-	-	-	31.6	1.0	-	-	-	-	32.2	1.9	-	-	-	-	32.3	0.3	-	-
1970	-	-	33.7	4.3	-	-	-	-	34.0	0.9	-	-	-	-	34.6	1.8	-	-	-	-	35.0	1.2	-	-
1971	-	-	36.4	4.0	-	-	-	-	36.8	1.1	-	-	-	-	37.4	1.6	-	-	-	-	37.0	-1.1	-	-
1972	-	-	37.3	0.8	-	-	-	-	37.8	1.3	-	-	-	-	38.0	0.5	-	-	-	-	38.2	0.5	-	-
1973	-	-	38.4	0.5	-	-	-	-	38.6	0.5	-	-	-	-	39.1	1.3	-	-	-	-	39.9	2.0	-	-
1974	-	-	41.1	3.0	-	-	-	-	42.6	3.6	-	-	-	-	44.8	5.2	-	-	-	-	45.6	1.8	-	-
1975	-	-	47.3	3.7	-	-	-	-	48.1	1.7	-	-	-	-	48.9	1.7	-	-	-	-	49.6	1.4	-	-
1976	-	-	51.7	4.2	-	-	-	-	52.6	1.7	-	-	-	-	53.9	2.5	-	-	-	-	55.4	2.8	-	-
1977	-	-	56.7	2.3	-	-	-	-	57.9	2.1	-	-	-	-	59.1	2.1	-	-	-	-	59.6	0.8	-	-
1978	61.0	2.3	-	-	61.2	0.3	-	-	60.9	-0.5	-	-	62.3	2.3	-	-	62.6	0.5	-	-	64.2	2.6	-	-
1979	65.2	1.6	-	-	66.8	2.5	-	-	67.1	0.4	-	-	68.1	1.5	-	-	70.2	3.1	-	-	70.7	0.7	-	-
1980	71.4	1.0	-	-	72.4	1.4	-	-	74.2	2.5	-	-	74.9	0.9	-	-	75.6	0.9	-	-	75.5	-0.1	-	-
1981	77.2	2.3	-	-	78.4	1.6	-	-	78.0	-0.5	-	-	80.7	3.5	-	-	81.8	1.4	-	-	82.9	1.3	-	-
1982	84.3	1.7	-	-	87.9	4.3	-	-	88.8	1.0	-	-	90.2	1.6	-	-	93.9	4.1	-	-	94.9	1.1	-	-
1983	98.9	4.2	-	-	99.5	0.6	-	-	100.1	0.6	-	-	99.7	-0.4	-	-	103.4	3.7	-	-	105.6	2.1	-	-
1984	107.0	1.3	-	-	106.3	-0.7	-	-	107.1	0.8	-	-	107.2	0.1	-	-	108.5	1.2	-	-	110.5	1.8	-	-
1985	110.1	-0.4	-	-	112.5	2.2	-	-	113.4	0.8	-	-	115.8	2.1	-	-	116.1	0.3	-	-	117.9	1.6	-	-
1986	119.4	1.3	-	-	121.1	1.4	-	-	122.7	1.3	-	-	123.0	0.2	-	-	123.6	0.5	-	-	124.5	0.7	-	-
1987	126.0	1.2	-	-	127.5	1.2	-	-	128.6	0.9	-	-	128.3	-0.2	-	-	129.4	0.9	-	-	132.4	2.3	-	-
1988	135.1	2.0	-	-	136.4	1.0	-	-	137.3	0.7	-	-	137.9	0.4	-	-	138.0	0.1	-	-	140.2	1.6	-	-
1989	142.6	1.7	-	-	144.1	1.1	-	-	145.4	0.9	-	-	146.4	0.7	-	-	147.2	0.5	-	-	149.6	1.6	-	-
1990	155.3	3.8	-	-	157.9	1.7	-	-	160.1	1.4	-	-	162.4	1.4	-	-	164.3	1.2	-	-	170.2	3.6	-	-
1991	173.0	1.6	-	-	175.3	1.3	-	-	175.9	0.3	-	-	176.6	0.4	-	-	176.3	-0.2	-	-	178.7	1.4	-	-

[Continued]

Washington, DC-MD-VA
Consumer Price Index - All Urban Consumers
Base 1982-1984 = 100
Medical Care

[Continued]

For 1947-1995. Columns headed % show percentile change in the index from the previous period for which an index is available.

Year	Jan Index	%	Feb Index	%	Mar Index	%	Apr Index	%	May Index	%	Jun Index	%	Jul Index	%	Aug Index	%	Sep Index	%	Oct Index	%	Nov Index	%	Dec Index	%
1992	184.1	3.0	-	-	181.9	-1.2	-	-	182.0	0.1	-	-	187.1	2.8	-	-	189.6	1.3	-	-	191.1	0.8	-	-
1993	192.6	0.8	-	-	193.6	0.5	-	-	194.3	0.4	-	-	196.1	0.9	-	-	197.0	0.5	-	-	196.8	-0.1	-	-
1994	198.5	0.9	-	-	199.9	0.7	-	-	202.1	1.1	-	-	204.5	1.2	-	-	205.6	0.5	-	-	207.7	1.0	-	-
1995	208.5	0.4	-	-	209.0	0.2	-	-	209.3	0.1	-	-	213.8	2.2	-	-	213.6	-0.1	-	-	216.0	1.1	-	-

Source: U.S. Department of Labor, Bureau of Labor Statistics, Division of Consumer Prices and Price Indexes. - indicates no data collected for period.

Washington, DC-MD-VA
Consumer Price Index - Urban Wage Earners
Base 1982-1984 = 100
Medical Care

For 1947-1995. Columns headed % show percentile change in the index from the previous period for which an index is available.

Year	Jan Index	Jan %	Feb Index	Feb %	Mar Index	Mar %	Apr Index	Apr %	May Index	May %	Jun Index	Jun %	Jul Index	Jul %	Aug Index	Aug %	Sep Index	Sep %	Oct Index	Oct %	Nov Index	Nov %	Dec Index	Dec %
1947	11.8	-	11.9	0.8	11.9	0.0	11.8	-0.8	11.8	0.0	11.8	0.0	-	-	11.9	0.8	-	-	-	-	11.9	0.0	-	-
1948	-	-	12.1	1.7	-	-	-	-	12.3	1.7	-	-	-	-	12.3	0.0	-	-	-	-	12.5	1.6	-	-
1949	-	-	12.5	0.0	-	-	-	-	12.5	0.0	-	-	-	-	12.6	0.8	-	-	-	-	12.6	0.0	-	-
1950	-	-	12.6	0.0	-	-	-	-	12.4	-1.6	-	-	-	-	12.6	1.6	-	-	-	-	12.7	0.8	-	-
1951	-	-	13.1	3.1	-	-	-	-	13.3	1.5	-	-	-	-	13.6	2.3	-	-	-	-	13.8	1.5	-	-
1952	-	-	13.9	0.7	-	-	-	-	14.2	2.2	-	-	-	-	14.3	0.7	-	-	-	-	14.2	-0.7	-	-
1953	-	-	14.2	0.0	-	-	-	-	14.3	0.7	-	-	-	-	14.4	0.7	-	-	-	-	14.4	0.0	-	-
1954	-	-	14.3	-0.7	-	-	-	-	14.3	0.0	-	-	-	-	14.4	0.7	-	-	-	-	14.5	0.7	-	-
1955	-	-	14.4	-0.7	-	-	-	-	14.5	0.7	-	-	-	-	14.5	0.0	-	-	-	-	15.0	3.4	-	-
1956	-	-	15.0	0.0	-	-	-	-	15.1	0.7	-	-	-	-	15.6	3.3	-	-	-	-	15.7	0.6	-	-
1957	-	-	15.8	0.6	-	-	-	-	16.1	1.9	-	-	-	-	16.1	0.0	-	-	-	-	16.3	1.2	-	-
1958	-	-	16.7	2.5	-	-	-	-	16.7	0.0	-	-	-	-	17.1	2.4	-	-	-	-	18.0	5.3	-	-
1959	-	-	18.1	0.6	-	-	-	-	18.3	1.1	-	-	-	-	18.1	-1.1	-	-	-	-	18.4	1.7	-	-
1960	-	-	18.8	2.2	-	-	-	-	18.8	0.0	-	-	-	-	18.9	0.5	-	-	-	-	19.0	0.5	-	-
1961	-	-	19.3	1.6	-	-	-	-	19.5	1.0	-	-	-	-	19.6	0.5	-	-	-	-	19.7	0.5	-	-
1962	-	-	20.1	2.0	-	-	-	-	20.2	0.5	-	-	-	-	21.0	4.0	-	-	-	-	21.1	0.5	-	-
1963	-	-	21.2	0.5	-	-	-	-	21.5	1.4	-	-	-	-	21.5	0.0	-	-	-	-	21.6	0.5	-	-
1964	-	-	21.8	0.9	-	-	-	-	22.0	0.9	-	-	-	-	22.0	0.0	-	-	-	-	22.2	0.9	-	-
1965	-	-	22.4	0.9	-	-	-	-	22.5	0.4	-	-	-	-	22.8	1.3	-	-	-	-	22.9	0.4	-	-
1966	-	-	23.3	1.7	-	-	-	-	23.7	1.7	-	-	-	-	24.0	1.3	-	-	-	-	24.3	1.2	-	-
1967	-	-	25.1	3.3	-	-	-	-	25.6	2.0	-	-	-	-	25.9	1.2	-	-	-	-	26.8	3.5	-	-
1968	-	-	27.6	3.0	-	-	-	-	28.1	1.8	-	-	-	-	28.4	1.1	-	-	-	-	29.0	2.1	-	-
1969	-	-	29.9	3.1	-	-	-	-	30.2	1.0	-	-	-	-	30.8	2.0	-	-	-	-	30.9	0.3	-	-
1970	-	-	32.3	4.5	-	-	-	-	32.5	0.6	-	-	-	-	33.1	1.8	-	-	-	-	33.5	1.2	-	-
1971	-	-	34.8	3.9	-	-	-	-	35.2	1.1	-	-	-	-	35.8	1.7	-	-	-	-	35.4	-1.1	-	-
1972	-	-	35.7	0.8	-	-	-	-	36.1	1.1	-	-	-	-	36.3	0.6	-	-	-	-	36.5	0.6	-	-
1973	-	-	36.7	0.5	-	-	-	-	37.0	0.8	-	-	-	-	37.4	1.1	-	-	-	-	38.1	1.9	-	-
1974	-	-	39.3	3.1	-	-	-	-	40.7	3.6	-	-	-	-	42.8	5.2	-	-	-	-	43.6	1.9	-	-
1975	-	-	45.3	3.9	-	-	-	-	46.0	1.5	-	-	-	-	46.8	1.7	-	-	-	-	47.5	1.5	-	-
1976	-	-	49.5	4.2	-	-	-	-	50.3	1.6	-	-	-	-	51.5	2.4	-	-	-	-	53.0	2.9	-	-
1977	-	-	54.2	2.3	-	-	-	-	55.4	2.2	-	-	-	-	56.6	2.2	-	-	-	-	57.0	0.7	-	-
1978	58.3	2.3	-	-	59.6	2.2	-	-	60.1	0.8	-	-	61.5	2.3	-	-	62.8	2.1	-	-	63.0	0.3	-	-
1979	63.9	1.4	-	-	67.1	5.0	-	-	67.9	1.2	-	-	68.4	0.7	-	-	70.3	2.8	-	-	71.2	1.3	-	-
1980	72.2	1.4	-	-	73.1	1.2	-	-	73.6	0.7	-	-	75.5	2.6	-	-	75.8	0.4	-	-	76.7	1.2	-	-
1981	77.4	0.9	-	-	78.0	0.8	-	-	77.9	-0.1	-	-	79.9	2.6	-	-	80.7	1.0	-	-	83.1	3.0	-	-
1982	84.5	1.7	-	-	88.0	4.1	-	-	88.5	0.6	-	-	89.7	1.4	-	-	93.3	4.0	-	-	94.2	1.0	-	-
1983	98.2	4.2	-	-	99.0	0.8	-	-	99.8	0.8	-	-	99.6	-0.2	-	-	103.6	4.0	-	-	105.9	2.2	-	-
1984	107.2	1.2	-	-	106.8	-0.4	-	-	107.5	0.7	-	-	107.8	0.3	-	-	109.0	1.1	-	-	111.0	1.8	-	-
1985	110.8	-0.2	-	-	113.4	2.3	-	-	114.3	0.8	-	-	116.7	2.1	-	-	116.9	0.2	-	-	118.8	1.6	-	-
1986	120.2	1.2	-	-	122.1	1.6	-	-	123.8	1.4	-	-	124.0	0.2	-	-	124.4	0.3	-	-	125.5	0.9	-	-
1987	127.2	1.4	-	-	128.7	1.2	-	-	129.9	0.9	-	-	129.7	-0.2	-	-	131.0	1.0	-	-	134.0	2.3	-	-
1988	136.9	2.2	-	-	137.9	0.7	-	-	138.9	0.7	-	-	139.5	0.4	-	-	139.8	0.2	-	-	142.2	1.7	-	-
1989	144.5	1.6	-	-	146.1	1.1	-	-	147.4	0.9	-	-	148.3	0.6	-	-	148.9	0.4	-	-	151.2	1.5	-	-
1990	156.9	3.8	-	-	159.4	1.6	-	-	161.3	1.2	-	-	163.4	1.3	-	-	165.2	1.1	-	-	170.7	3.3	-	-
1991	173.4	1.6	-	-	175.7	1.3	-	-	176.4	0.4	-	-	177.1	0.4	-	-	176.8	-0.2	-	-	179.0	1.2	-	-

[Continued]

Washington, DC-MD-VA
Consumer Price Index - Urban Wage Earners
Base 1982-1984 = 100
Medical Care
[Continued]

For 1947-1995. Columns headed % show percentile change in the index from the previous period for which an index is available.

Year	Jan Index	%	Feb Index	%	Mar Index	%	Apr Index	%	May Index	%	Jun Index	%	Jul Index	%	Aug Index	%	Sep Index	%	Oct Index	%	Nov Index	%	Dec Index	%
1992	184.5	3.1	-	-	182.1	-1.3	-	-	182.3	0.1	-	-	187.5	2.9	-	-	190.3	1.5	-	-	191.7	0.7	-	-
1993	193.3	0.8	-	-	194.0	0.4	-	-	194.8	0.4	-	-	196.9	1.1	-	-	197.7	0.4	-	-	197.5	-0.1	-	-
1994	199.1	0.8	-	-	200.4	0.7	-	-	202.9	1.2	-	-	205.2	1.1	-	-	206.2	0.5	-	-	208.2	1.0	-	-
1995	208.9	0.3	-	-	208.8	-0.0	-	-	208.9	0.0	-	-	213.7	2.3	-	-	213.6	-0.0	-	-	216.0	1.1	-	-

Source: U.S. Department of Labor, Bureau of Labor Statistics, Division of Consumer Prices and Price Indexes. - indicates no data collected for period.

Washington, DC-MD-VA
Consumer Price Index - All Urban Consumers
Base 1982-1984 = 100
Entertainment

For 1975-1995. Columns headed % show percentile change in the index from the previous period for which an index is available.

Year	Jan Index	%	Feb Index	%	Mar Index	%	Apr Index	%	May Index	%	Jun Index	%	Jul Index	%	Aug Index	%	Sep Index	%	Oct Index	%	Nov Index	%	Dec Index	%
1975	-	-	-	-	-	-	-	-	-	-	-	-	-	-	-	-	-	-	-	-	66.3	-	-	-
1976	-	-	67.3	1.5	-	-	-	-	68.3	1.5	-	-	-	-	68.7	0.6	-	-	-	-	70.0	1.9	-	-
1977	-	-	72.0	2.9	-	-	-	-	73.2	1.7	-	-	-	-	74.7	2.0	-	-	-	-	75.2	0.7	-	-
1978	74.8	-0.5	-	-	74.9	0.1	-	-	74.2	-0.9	-	-	74.4	0.3	-	-	74.4	0.0	-	-	76.4	2.7	-	-
1979	76.5	0.1	-	-	77.9	1.8	-	-	78.0	0.1	-	-	78.4	0.5	-	-	79.5	1.4	-	-	79.6	0.1	-	-
1980	83.8	5.3	-	-	83.0	-1.0	-	-	82.2	-1.0	-	-	86.0	4.6	-	-	86.8	0.9	-	-	85.7	-1.3	-	-
1981	87.0	1.5	-	-	86.1	-1.0	-	-	89.1	3.5	-	-	89.0	-0.1	-	-	90.2	1.3	-	-	90.9	0.8	-	-
1982	92.3	1.5	-	-	93.7	1.5	-	-	94.1	0.4	-	-	93.9	-0.2	-	-	94.6	0.7	-	-	95.3	0.7	-	-
1983	96.0	0.7	-	-	96.2	0.2	-	-	96.5	0.3	-	-	98.1	1.7	-	-	103.7	5.7	-	-	102.8	-0.9	-	-
1984	102.1	-0.7	-	-	104.3	2.2	-	-	102.9	-1.3	-	-	108.0	5.0	-	-	108.3	0.3	-	-	112.2	3.6	-	-
1985	112.8	0.5	-	-	112.4	-0.4	-	-	112.1	-0.3	-	-	113.6	1.3	-	-	114.2	0.5	-	-	116.0	1.6	-	-
1986	116.8	0.7	-	-	116.5	-0.3	-	-	115.2	-1.1	-	-	116.6	1.2	-	-	117.8	1.0	-	-	117.0	-0.7	-	-
1987	115.2	-1.5	-	-	121.8	5.7	-	-	122.1	0.2	-	-	123.6	1.2	-	-	121.3	-1.9	-	-	122.7	1.2	-	-
1988	125.4	2.2	-	-	126.5	0.9	-	-	127.5	0.8	-	-	122.1	-4.2	-	-	124.2	1.7	-	-	123.4	-0.6	-	-
1989	125.4	1.6	-	-	125.9	0.4	-	-	126.2	0.2	-	-	127.9	1.3	-	-	130.5	2.0	-	-	128.8	-1.3	-	-
1990	127.8	-0.8	-	-	131.1	2.6	-	-	136.9	4.4	-	-	137.0	0.1	-	-	139.6	1.9	-	-	139.0	-0.4	-	-
1991	137.2	-1.3	-	-	140.7	2.6	-	-	141.4	0.5	-	-	143.4	1.4	-	-	145.4	1.4	-	-	146.4	0.7	-	-
1992	143.4	-2.0	-	-	146.4	2.1	-	-	147.7	0.9	-	-	147.4	-0.2	-	-	149.3	1.3	-	-	149.8	0.3	-	-
1993	150.6	0.5	-	-	150.1	-0.3	-	-	148.3	-1.2	-	-	149.7	0.9	-	-	153.9	2.8	-	-	152.5	-0.9	-	-
1994	154.0	1.0	-	-	152.8	-0.8	-	-	151.6	-0.8	-	-	155.2	2.4	-	-	159.9	3.0	-	-	159.3	-0.4	-	-
1995	164.3	3.1	-	-	163.2	-0.7	-	-	161.2	-1.2	-	-	162.1	0.6	-	-	163.3	0.7	-	-	164.4	0.7	-	-

Source: U.S. Department of Labor, Bureau of Labor Statistics, Division of Consumer Prices and Price Indexes. - indicates no data collected for period.

Washington, DC-MD-VA
Consumer Price Index - Urban Wage Earners
Base 1982-1984 = 100
Entertainment

For 1975-1995. Columns headed % show percentile change in the index from the previous period for which an index is available.

Year	Jan Index	%	Feb Index	%	Mar Index	%	Apr Index	%	May Index	%	Jun Index	%	Jul Index	%	Aug Index	%	Sep Index	%	Oct Index	%	Nov Index	%	Dec Index	%
1975	-	-	-	-	-	-	-	-			-	-	-	-			-	-	-	-	56.3	-	-	-
1976	-	-	57.1	1.4	-	-	-	-	58.0	1.6	-	-	-	-	58.3	0.5	-	-	-	-	59.4	1.9	-	-
1977	-	-	61.1	2.9	-	-	-	-	62.1	1.6	-	-	-	-	63.4	2.1	-	-	-	-	63.8	0.6	-	-
1978	64.2	0.6	-	-	67.3	4.8	-	-	66.9	-0.6	-	-	69.0	3.1	-	-	69.2	0.3	-	-	71.7	3.6	-	-
1979	72.4	1.0	-	-	73.5	1.5	-	-	75.3	2.4	-	-	76.6	1.7	-	-	77.6	1.3	-	-	78.0	0.5	-	-
1980	79.3	1.7	-	-	80.3	1.3	-	-	83.3	3.7	-	-	84.2	1.1	-	-	83.6	-0.7	-	-	84.4	1.0	-	-
1981	84.2	-0.2	-	-	83.5	-0.8	-	-	86.6	3.7	-	-	89.5	3.3	-	-	90.7	1.3	-	-	91.1	0.4	-	-
1982	92.7	1.8	-	-	94.0	1.4	-	-	94.8	0.9	-	-	94.4	-0.4	-	-	95.2	0.8	-	-	95.2	0.0	-	-
1983	96.1	0.9	-	-	95.9	-0.2	-	-	96.8	0.9	-	-	98.0	1.2	-	-	103.6	5.7	-	-	103.3	-0.3	-	-
1984	102.7	-0.6	-	-	104.8	2.0	-	-	102.2	-2.5	-	-	107.4	5.1	-	-	107.6	0.2	-	-	110.6	2.8	-	-
1985	111.5	0.8	-	-	110.6	-0.8	-	-	110.2	-0.4	-	-	111.7	1.4	-	-	112.5	0.7	-	-	113.9	1.2	-	-
1986	114.8	0.8	-	-	113.9	-0.8	-	-	110.5	-3.0	-	-	111.6	1.0	-	-	114.4	2.5	-	-	113.1	-1.1	-	-
1987	110.8	-2.0	-	-	118.8	7.2	-	-	118.7	-0.1	-	-	120.0	1.1	-	-	117.3	-2.3	-	-	119.8	2.1	-	-
1988	122.0	1.8	-	-	123.1	0.9	-	-	124.0	0.7	-	-	119.1	-4.0	-	-	121.6	2.1	-	-	120.8	-0.7	-	-
1989	122.9	1.7	-	-	123.3	0.3	-	-	123.5	0.2	-	-	124.5	0.8	-	-	127.0	2.0	-	-	125.7	-1.0	-	-
1990	124.8	-0.7	-	-	127.7	2.3	-	-	133.2	4.3	-	-	133.2	0.0	-	-	135.9	2.0	-	-	135.1	-0.6	-	-
1991	133.5	-1.2	-	-	137.1	2.7	-	-	137.3	0.1	-	-	139.2	1.4	-	-	141.1	1.4	-	-	142.4	0.9	-	-
1992	139.6	-2.0	-	-	142.4	2.0	-	-	143.8	1.0	-	-	143.6	-0.1	-	-	145.5	1.3	-	-	145.8	0.2	-	-
1993	146.2	0.3	-	-	146.1	-0.1	-	-	144.6	-1.0	-	-	145.4	0.6	-	-	149.4	2.8	-	-	147.4	-1.3	-	-
1994	148.9	1.0	-	-	147.7	-0.8	-	-	146.7	-0.7	-	-	150.5	2.6	-	-	155.1	3.1	-	-	154.5	-0.4	-	-
1995	158.2	2.4	-	-	157.1	-0.7	-	-	155.1	-1.3	-	-	156.0	0.6	-	-	156.2	0.1	-	-	157.6	0.9	-	-

Source: U.S. Department of Labor, Bureau of Labor Statistics, Division of Consumer Prices and Price Indexes. - indicates no data collected for period.

Washington, DC-MD-VA
Consumer Price Index - All Urban Consumers
Base 1982-1984 = 100
Other Goods and Services

For 1975-1995. Columns headed % show percentile change in the index from the previous period for which an index is available.

Year	Jan Index	%	Feb Index	%	Mar Index	%	Apr Index	%	May Index	%	Jun Index	%	Jul Index	%	Aug Index	%	Sep Index	%	Oct Index	%	Nov Index	%	Dec Index	%
1975	-	-	-	-	-	-	-	-	-	-	-	-	-	-	-	-	-	-	-	-	54.9	-	-	-
1976	-	-	57.3	4.4	-	-	-	-	57.7	0.7	-	-	-	-	58.6	1.6	-	-	-	-	59.9	2.2	-	-
1977	-	-	60.6	1.2	-	-	-	-	61.4	1.3	-	-	-	-	61.9	0.8	-	-	-	-	64.4	4.0	-	-
1978	63.9	-0.8	-	-	64.4	0.8	-	-	64.6	0.3	-	-	65.2	0.9	-	-	67.1	2.9	-	-	67.3	0.3	-	-
1979	68.4	1.6	-	-	69.0	0.9	-	-	69.4	0.6	-	-	69.3	-0.1	-	-	71.3	2.9	-	-	71.5	0.3	-	-
1980	73.1	2.2	-	-	73.2	0.1	-	-	74.3	1.5	-	-	75.7	1.9	-	-	78.4	3.6	-	-	78.6	0.3	-	-
1981	79.2	0.8	-	-	81.1	2.4	-	-	81.7	0.7	-	-	82.1	0.5	-	-	86.5	5.4	-	-	87.6	1.3	-	-
1982	87.7	0.1	-	-	89.1	1.6	-	-	89.3	0.2	-	-	89.5	0.2	-	-	93.3	4.2	-	-	96.1	3.0	-	-
1983	98.9	2.9	-	-	99.1	0.2	-	-	98.9	-0.2	-	-	100.8	1.9	-	-	103.0	2.2	-	-	103.6	0.6	-	-
1984	105.4	1.7	-	-	105.4	0.0	-	-	106.1	0.7	-	-	106.9	0.8	-	-	109.4	2.3	-	-	111.5	1.9	-	-
1985	112.0	0.4	-	-	112.9	0.8	-	-	113.0	0.1	-	-	113.5	0.4	-	-	116.2	2.4	-	-	117.7	1.3	-	-
1986	119.0	1.1	-	-	119.2	0.2	-	-	119.6	0.3	-	-	121.4	1.5	-	-	124.1	2.2	-	-	126.2	1.7	-	-
1987	126.9	0.6	-	-	127.4	0.4	-	-	127.7	0.2	-	-	128.2	0.4	-	-	130.8	2.0	-	-	133.4	2.0	-	-
1988	135.1	1.3	-	-	134.9	-0.1	-	-	135.4	0.4	-	-	138.8	2.5	-	-	140.3	1.1	-	-	142.9	1.9	-	-
1989	146.2	2.3	-	-	147.1	0.6	-	-	148.4	0.9	-	-	150.5	1.4	-	-	157.7	4.8	-	-	160.0	1.5	-	-
1990	160.7	0.4	-	-	162.4	1.1	-	-	162.3	-0.1	-	-	164.4	1.3	-	-	168.3	2.4	-	-	170.7	1.4	-	-
1991	174.6	2.3	-	-	175.8	0.7	-	-	177.0	0.7	-	-	180.0	1.7	-	-	181.1	0.6	-	-	181.2	0.1	-	-
1992	181.2	0.0	-	-	181.5	0.2	-	-	183.9	1.3	-	-	184.7	0.4	-	-	193.2	4.6	-	-	193.3	0.1	-	-
1993	195.1	0.9	-	-	196.2	0.6	-	-	197.7	0.8	-	-	199.5	0.9	-	-	202.6	1.6	-	-	202.7	0.0	-	-
1994	206.0	1.6	-	-	206.3	0.1	-	-	207.2	0.4	-	-	207.3	0.0	-	-	212.2	2.4	-	-	212.2	0.0	-	-
1995	212.0	-0.1	-	-	211.5	-0.2	-	-	211.6	0.0	-	-	212.6	0.5	-	-	218.9	3.0	-	-	220.3	0.6	-	-

Source: U.S. Department of Labor, Bureau of Labor Statistics, Division of Consumer Prices and Price Indexes. - indicates no data collected for period.

Washington, DC-MD-VA
Consumer Price Index - Urban Wage Earners
Base 1982-1984 = 100
Other Goods and Services

For 1975-1995. Columns headed % show percentile change in the index from the previous period for which an index is available.

Year	Jan Index	%	Feb Index	%	Mar Index	%	Apr Index	%	May Index	%	Jun Index	%	Jul Index	%	Aug Index	%	Sep Index	%	Oct Index	%	Nov Index	%	Dec Index	%
1975	-		-		-		-		-		-		-		-		-		-		52.9		-	
1976	-		55.3	4.5	-		-		55.7	0.7	-		-		56.5	1.4	-		-		57.8	2.3	-	
1977	-		58.4	1.0	-		-		59.2	1.4	-		-		59.7	0.8	-		-		62.1	4.0	-	
1978	62.2	0.2	-		63.0	1.3	-		64.8	2.9	-		66.9	3.2	-		66.8	-0.1	-		67.2	0.6	-	
1979	67.8	0.9	-		68.5	1.0	-		68.7	0.3	-		70.2	2.2	-		71.3	1.6	-		72.1	1.1	-	
1980	73.7	2.2	-		74.4	0.9	-		75.5	1.5	-		76.9	1.9	-		78.1	1.6	-		79.3	1.5	-	
1981	80.0	0.9	-		82.2	2.8	-		83.8	1.9	-		83.7	-0.1	-		86.6	3.5	-		87.6	1.2	-	
1982	87.8	0.2	-		89.4	1.8	-		89.7	0.3	-		90.1	0.4	-		92.6	2.8	-		95.3	2.9	-	
1983	98.9	3.8	-		99.6	0.7	-		99.4	-0.2	-		101.9	2.5	-		103.1	1.2	-		103.1	0.0	-	
1984	105.6	2.4	-		105.4	-0.2	-		106.2	0.8	-		107.4	1.1	-		109.2	1.7	-		109.8	0.5	-	
1985	110.4	0.5	-		111.6	1.1	-		111.6	0.0	-		112.3	0.6	-		114.3	1.8	-		114.7	0.3	-	
1986	116.3	1.4	-		116.7	0.3	-		117.1	0.3	-		119.4	2.0	-		120.9	1.3	-		122.4	1.2	-	
1987	123.4	0.8	-		124.1	0.6	-		124.5	0.3	-		125.0	0.4	-		126.9	1.5	-		128.5	1.3	-	
1988	130.7	1.7	-		130.6	-0.1	-		131.3	0.5	-		135.4	3.1	-		137.3	1.4	-		139.6	1.7	-	
1989	142.7	2.2	-		144.0	0.9	-		145.5	1.0	-		147.6	1.4	-		153.4	3.9	-		154.7	0.8	-	
1990	155.7	0.6	-		157.9	1.4	-		157.6	-0.2	-		160.2	1.6	-		163.4	2.0	-		165.3	1.2	-	
1991	169.6	2.6	-		170.5	0.5	-		171.6	0.6	-		174.3	1.6	-		174.0	-0.2	-		174.2	0.1	-	
1992	174.2	0.0	-		174.4	0.1	-		178.1	2.1	-		178.8	0.4	-		186.8	4.5	-		187.0	0.1	-	
1993	189.1	1.1	-		190.8	0.9	-		191.8	0.5	-		192.8	0.5	-		194.1	0.7	-		194.3	0.1	-	
1994	197.6	1.7	-		198.1	0.3	-		198.8	0.4	-		198.1	-0.4	-		201.9	1.9	-		201.9	0.0	-	
1995	200.5	-0.7	-		200.2	-0.1	-		200.7	0.2	-		201.1	0.2	-		206.6	2.7	-		208.6	1.0	-	

Source: U.S. Department of Labor, Bureau of Labor Statistics, Division of Consumer Prices and Price Indexes. - indicates no data collected for period.

CHAPTER 7

PRODUCER PRICE INDEX

PRODUCER PRICE INDEX

The Producer Price Index (PPI) is a program of the Bureau of Labor Statistics (BLS), U.S. Department of Labor. In one of its publications, BLS describes the Producer Price Index (PPI) as follows:

> The Producer Price Index . . . measures average changes in selling prices received by domestic producers for their output. Most of the information used in calculating the Producer Price Index is obtained through the systematic sampling of virtually every industry in the mining and manufacturing sectors of the economy. The PPI program (also known as the industrial price program) includes some data from other sectors as well—agriculture, fishing, forestry, services, and gas and electricity. Thus the title "Producer Price Index" refers to an entire "family" or system of indexes. (Reference 1, p. 125.)

Description of the PPI

The PPI covers nearly 500 mining and manufacturing industries and about 8,000 specific products and product categories. More than 3,000 commodity prices are included, organized by type of product and end use. Data are reported by product groupings and sub-groups as well as in large aggregates.

Important aspects of the PPI include the definition of *price*, the selection of a *sample universe*, *data collection*, and the analytical management of the collected data, including the use of *weights*. Data are expressed as an index; the base year at present (1996) is 1982, meaning that prices for 1982 are indexed at 100.

Price. Price is defined as "the net revenue accruing to a specified producing establishment from a specified kind of buyer for a specified product shipped under specified transaction terms on a specified day of the month." (Reference 1). Under this definition, companies voluntarily providing pricing information to the BLS thus report on *actual* shipments in a given month rather than average price levels. Prices exclude taxes paid but reflect discounts, low-interest financing, and other forms of incentives, rebates, and the like.

Sampling. Samples are chosen from each industry surveyed using Unemployment Insurance System data for identifying establishments—because virtually all employers are required to report to the system. Establishments are stratified, meaning that they are assigned to groups with like characteristics within an industry. Within strata, units are ordered by size. The number of units required for the sample is selected within each stratum based on employment. Selection of each establishment is then accomplished systematically with a probability of selection proportionate to its size.

Data Collection. Data are collected by companies in the sample on a voluntary basis. Within each establishment, a portion of the transactions is selected by the BLS field representative; these transactions are then priced every month. The selection of the transactions is also made systematically so that the probability of a product or commodity being selected is proportional to its relative importance to the reporting unit.

Weights. In order to create price indexes for aggregations of products, price indexes for individual products/commodities must be combined to form a composite index. This is accomplished by giving each component a weight appropriate to its importance in the aggregate as a whole. Industrial products are weighted by their proportion of total industry shipments as measured by the Standard Industrial Classification (SIC) system and reported by the *Census of Manufactures*. Commodities are weighted based on gross value of shipments data.

Base of Index. The index shows prices relative to 1982, which is defined as 100. Changes in the index are usually expressed as increases or decreases in percent, derived by the following formula:

((Current Index / Previous Index) - 1) x 100.

If the current index is 220.5 and the last index is 219.7, the formula produces a 0.36% change. This is the actual price increase from the last measured index to the current index.

This brief description hides much of the complexity of the PPI. For more details, the reader is referred to Reference 1. In summary, the methodology used is designed to present an accurate picture of price movements. The accuracy of the index is dependent on voluntary reporting; however, price definitions, sampling, and analytical factors are designed to take into account producers of all sizes operating in all kinds of markets and geographies; prices are actual, excluding taxes but including sales incentives; industrial establishments as well as products and commodities are selected to reflect, in the index, in proportion to their relative importance overall.

History of the PPI

The PPI (then called the Wholesale Price Index or WPI), was first published in 1902 and covered the 1890-1901 period. The WPI was initially an average of prices. Weighting of components was first incorporated in 1914. Major sample expansions and reclassifications took place in 1952 and 1967. In 1978, the index was renamed Producer Price Index in recognition of the fact that the meaning of the word "wholesale"—which had been understood earlier to mean goods sold in large quantities—had come to mean prices charged by wholesalers, jobbers, and distributors. The PPI is based on prices received by producers from the party that makes the first purchase, be that a distributor, a retailer, or the final consumer. The last comprehensive revision of the PPI, begun in 1978, culminated in January 1986 with the introduction of the current methods of price definition, sampling, data collection, and analysis.

Uses of the PPI

The PPI is widely used by government, industry, labor organization, and in the academic sector. It is an early measure of inflation—because producer sales predate retail sales; the latter form the backbone of the Consumer Price Index (CPI). The CPI, however, does not mirror the movements of the PPI at some lag in time. The PPI excludes imported goods, the CPI does not; the CPI includes services, the PPI largely does not. The CPI does not directly include the prices of capital equipment (industrial tooling and the like);the PPI does. Sharp swings in the prices of goods and other items may not reflect in consumer prices in the same way—because distributors and retailers absorb price rises/drops rather than cause wide price swings at the consumer level. The PPI is used in the construction of the implicit GNP deflator. In addition to the use of the index for analytical purposes in industry, it is used in contracts in price escalation clauses and in inventory valuation.

Presentation of Data

Six summary tables of the Producer Price Index are presented in Chapter 4, Other Cyclic Indicators, in the section on Prices and Productivity. In this chapter, 120 detailed PPI tables are shown. The first four tables show annual averages for 15 major product and commodity groupings and 100 subdivisions from 1926 to

1995. Thereafter, monthly data, from 1913 or a later date to 1995 are shown, first by the major group ("Farm Products") and then followed by the next level of detail provided by the PPI ("Fruits & Melons, Fresh/Dry Vegetables & Nuts," "Grains," "Livestock," etc.). All tables show a 1982 base (1982 = 100). Percent changes in the index from month to month are precalculated.

Bibliography

1. U.S. Department of Labor, Bureau of Labor Statistics. *BLS Handbook of Methods*, Bulletin 2285, 1987. Washington, D.C.

Producer Price Index
Annual Averages, 1926-1934
Base 1982 = 100

Columns headed % show percentile change in the index from the previous period for which an index is available.

	1926		1927		1928		1929		1930		1931		1932		1933		1934	
	Index	%	Index	%	Index	%	Index	%	Index	%	Index	%	Index	%	Index	%	Index	%
Farm Products	25.3	-8.7	25.1	-0.8	26.7	6.4	26.4	-1.1	22.4	-15.2	16.4	-26.8	12.2	-25.6	13.0	6.6	16.5	26.9
Fruits & Melons, Fresh/Dry Vegetables & Nuts	27.0	-	25.8	-4.4	25.6	-0.8	25.7	0.4	25.8	0.4	18.5	-28.3	14.3	-22.7	15.5	8.4	16.9	9.0
Grains	33.7	-	34.0	0.9	36.0	5.9	32.8	-8.9	26.4	-19.5	17.9	-32.2	13.3	-25.7	17.9	34.6	25.1	40.2
Slaughter Livestock	18.8	-	18.8	0.0	20.0	6.4	20.0	0.0	16.8	-16.0	11.9	-29.2	8.9	-25.2	8.2	-7.9	9.8	19.5
Slaughter Poultry	102.5	-	91.9	-10.3	98.5	7.2	109.0	10.7	88.4	-18.9	75.4	-14.7	60.0	-20.4	47.4	-21.0	53.3	12.4
Plant and Animal Fibers	45.0	-	44.0	-2.2	48.0	9.1	45.6	-5.0	32.3	-29.2	21.2	-34.4	15.4	-27.4	19.8	28.6	26.3	32.8
Fluid Milk	19.5	-	19.9	2.1	20.3	2.0	21.2	4.4	20.6	-2.8	18.5	-10.2	13.6	-26.5	13.2	-2.9	16.2	22.7
Chicken Eggs	67.4	-	60.5	-10.2	63.7	5.3	70.3	10.4	54.1	-23.0	41.7	-22.9	37.5	-10.1	32.9	-12.3	39.1	18.8
Hay, Hayseeds and Oilseeds	29.5	-	26.2	-11.2	28.9	10.3	30.4	5.2	27.7	-8.9	21.1	-23.8	15.4	-27.0	16.0	3.9	23.3	45.6
Farm Products n.e.c.	13.2	-	13.1	-0.8	14.8	13.0	14.4	-2.7	9.7	-32.6	6.8	-29.9	6.0	-11.8	6.6	10.0	8.2	24.2
Processed Foods and Feeds	-	-	-	-	-	-	-	-	-	-	-	-	-	-	-	-	-	-
Cereal and Bakery Products	18.8	-	17.8	-5.3	17.6	-1.1	16.5	-6.3	15.3	-7.3	13.8	-9.8	12.5	-9.4	14.1	12.8	16.7	18.4
Meats, Poultry, and Fish	17.5	-	16.2	-7.4	18.7	15.4	19.1	2.1	17.2	-9.9	13.2	-23.3	10.2	-22.7	8.8	-13.7	11.0	25.0
Dairy Products	17.5	-	18.1	3.4	18.4	1.7	18.4	0.0	16.7	-9.2	14.3	-14.4	10.7	-25.2	10.6	-0.9	12.7	19.8
Processed Fruits and Vegetables	20.3	-	20.1	-1.0	21.5	7.0	22.4	4.2	21.0	-6.3	17.6	-16.2	15.7	-10.8	15.9	1.3	17.9	12.6
Sugar and Confectionery	19.3	-	20.7	7.3	19.5	-5.8	17.5	-10.3	16.1	-8.0	15.5	-3.7	13.8	-11.0	14.9	8.0	14.9	0.0
Beverages and Beverage Materials	-	-	-	-	-	-	-	-	-	-	-	-	-	-	-	-	-	-
Fats and Oils	-	-	-	-	-	-	-	-	-	-	-	-	-	-	-	-	-	-
Miscellaneous Processed Foods	-	-	-	-	-	-	-	-	-	-	-	-	-	-	-	-	-	-
Prepared Animal Feeds	-	-	-	-	-	-	-	-	-	-	-	-	-	-	-	-	-	-
Textile Products and Apparel	-	-	-	-	-	-	-	-	-	-	-	-	-	-	-	-	-	-
Synthetic Fibers	-	-	-	-	-	-	-	-	-	-	-	-	-	-	-	-	-	-
Processed Yarns and Threads	-	-	-	-	-	-	-	-	-	-	-	-	-	-	-	-	-	-
Gray Fabrics	-	-	-	-	-	-	-	-	-	-	-	-	-	-	-	-	-	-
Finished Fabrics	-	-	-	-	-	-	-	-	-	-	-	-	-	-	-	-	-	-
Apparel	-	-	-	-	-	-	-	-	-	-	-	-	-	-	-	-	-	-
Textile Housefurnishings	-	-	-	-	-	-	-	-	-	-	-	-	-	-	-	-	-	-
Miscellaneous Textile Products	-	-	-	-	-	-	-	-	-	-	-	-	-	-	-	-	-	-
Apparel & Other Fabricated Textile Products	-	-	-	-	-	-	-	-	-	-	-	-	-	-	-	-	-	-
Miscellaneous Textile Products/Services	-	-	-	-	-	-	-	-	-	-	-	-	-	-	-	-	-	-
Hides, Skins, Leather, and Related Products	17.1	-	18.4	7.6	20.7	12.5	18.6	-10.1	17.1	-8.1	14.7	-14.0	12.5	-15.0	13.8	10.4	14.8	7.2
Hides and Skins	20.5	-	24.6	20.0	30.4	23.6	23.0	-24.3	18.7	-18.7	12.3	-34.2	8.6	-30.1	13.6	58.1	14.0	2.9

Source: U.S. Department of Labor, Bureau of Labor Statistics, Division of Industry Prices and Price Indexes. n.e.c. stands for not elsewhere classified. - indicates no data collected for period or unavailable.

Producer Price Index
Annual Averages, 1935-1943
Base 1982 = 100

Columns headed % show percentile change in the index from the previous period for which an index is available.

	1935		1936		1937		1938		1939		1940		1941		1942		1943	
	Index	%	Index	%	Index	%	Index	%	Index	%	Index	%	Index	%	Index	%	Index	%
Farm Products	19.8	20.0	20.4	3.0	21.8	6.9	17.3	-20.6	16.5	-4.6	17.1	3.6	20.8	21.6	26.7	28.4	30.9	15.7
Fruits & Melons, Fresh/Dry Vegetables & Nuts	15.6	-7.7	18.4	17.9	18.9	2.7	14.2	-24.9	15.7	10.6	16.0	1.9	16.8	5.0	24.8	47.6	33.5	35.1
Grains	27.8	10.8	29.7	6.8	33.2	11.8	20.5	-38.3	19.8	-3.4	22.9	15.7	25.7	12.2	31.2	21.4	39.1	25.3
Slaughter Livestock	16.8	71.4	16.8	0.0	19.2	14.3	15.5	-19.3	13.7	-11.6	13.3	-2.9	18.0	35.3	23.7	31.7	25.4	7.2
Slaughter Poultry	71.1	33.4	70.9	-0.3	72.4	2.1	70.2	-3.0	58.5	-16.7	58.2	-0.5	74.9	28.7	86.1	15.0	97.8	13.6
Plant and Animal Fibers	25.7	-2.3	27.1	5.4	26.6	-1.8	20.4	-23.3	23.5	15.2	23.3	-0.9	29.9	28.3	38.7	29.4	40.3	4.1
Fluid Milk	17.0	4.9	17.0	0.0	16.4	-3.5	15.0	-8.5	14.2	-5.3	15.8	11.3	17.1	8.2	19.3	12.9	21.8	13.0
Chicken Eggs	50.7	29.7	48.6	-4.1	44.9	-7.6	44.1	-1.8	35.8	-18.8	38.1	6.4	50.4	32.3	64.5	28.0	76.8	19.1
Hay, Hayseeds and Oilseeds	23.0	-1.3	22.5	-2.2	26.8	19.1	22.4	-16.4	20.8	-7.1	20.5	-1.4	21.7	5.9	30.0	38.2	36.6	22.0
Farm Products n.e.c.	9.3	13.4	8.9	-4.3	10.7	20.2	8.9	-16.8	8.5	-4.5	7.7	-9.4	10.1	31.2	14.7	45.5	16.7	13.6
Processed Foods and Feeds	-	-	-	-	-	-	-	-	-	-	-	-	-	-	-	-	-	-
Cereal and Bakery Products	17.7	6.0	16.2	-8.5	16.5	1.9	14.8	-10.3	14.1	-4.7	14.7	4.3	15.2	3.4	16.8	10.5	17.6	4.8
Meats, Poultry, and Fish	16.5	50.0	15.3	-7.3	17.3	13.1	14.6	-15.6	13.5	-7.5	12.8	-5.2	15.8	23.4	19.6	24.1	19.3	-1.5
Dairy Products	13.9	9.4	14.6	5.0	14.5	-0.7	12.7	-12.4	12.0	-5.5	13.5	12.5	15.2	12.6	17.4	14.5	19.4	11.5
Processed Fruits and Vegetables	17.8	-0.6	17.5	-1.7	18.2	4.0	16.3	-10.4	15.7	-3.7	15.9	1.3	18.4	15.7	21.8	18.5	22.5	3.2
Sugar and Confectionery	16.3	9.4	16.8	3.1	16.4	-2.4	14.9	-9.1	15.2	2.0	14.4	-5.3	16.7	16.0	18.5	10.8	18.6	0.5
Beverages and Beverage Materials	-	-	-	-	-	-	-	-	-	-	-	-	-	-	-	-	-	-
Fats and Oils	-	-	-	-	-	-	-	-	-	-	-	-	-	-	-	-	-	-
Miscellaneous Processed Foods	-	-	-	-	-	-	-	-	-	-	-	-	-	-	-	-	-	-
Prepared Animal Feeds	-	-	-	-	-	-	-	-	-	-	-	-	-	-	-	-	-	-
Textile Products and Apparel	-	-	-	-	-	-	-	-	-	-	-	-	-	-	-	-	-	-
Synthetic Fibers	-	-	-	-	-	-	-	-	-	-	-	-	-	-	-	-	-	-
Processed Yarns and Threads	-	-	-	-	-	-	-	-	-	-	-	-	-	-	-	-	-	-
Gray Fabrics	-	-	-	-	-	-	-	-	-	-	-	-	-	-	-	-	-	-
Finished Fabrics	-	-	-	-	-	-	-	-	-	-	-	-	-	-	-	-	-	-
Apparel	-	-	-	-	-	-	-	-	-	-	-	-	-	-	-	-	-	-
Textile Housefurnishings	-	-	-	-	-	-	-	-	-	-	-	-	-	-	-	-	-	-
Miscellaneous Textile Products	-	-	-	-	-	-	-	-	-	-	-	-	-	-	-	-	-	-
Apparel & Other Fabricated Textile Products	-	-	-	-	-	-	-	-	-	-	-	-	-	-	-	-	-	-
Miscellaneous Textile Products/Services	-	-	-	-	-	-	-	-	-	-	-	-	-	-	-	-	-	-
Hides, Skins, Leather, and Related Products	15.3	3.4	16.3	6.5	17.9	9.8	15.8	-11.7	16.3	3.2	17.2	5.5	18.4	7.0	20.1	9.2	20.1	0.0
Hides and Skins	16.4	17.1	19.3	17.7	23.2	20.2	15.1	-34.9	17.3	14.6	18.8	8.7	22.2	18.1	24.1	8.6	23.5	-2.5

Source: U.S. Department of Labor, Bureau of Labor Statistics, Division of Industry Prices and Price Indexes. n.e.c. stands for not elsewhere classified. - indicates no data collected for period or unavailable.

Producer Price Index
Annual Averages, 1944-1952
Base 1982 = 100

Columns headed % show percentile change in the index from the previous period for which an index is available.

	1944		1945		1946		1947		1948		1949		1950		1951		1952	
	Index	%	Index	%	Index	%	Index	%	Index	%	Index	%	Index	%	Index	%	Index	%
Farm Products	31.2	1.0	32.4	3.8	37.5	15.7	45.1	20.3	48.5	7.5	41.9	-13.6	44.0	5.0	51.2	16.4	48.4	-5.5
Fruits & Melons, Fresh/Dry Vegetables & Nuts	33.4	-0.3	33.7	0.9	35.7	5.9	36.0	0.8	37.4	3.9	36.3	-2.9	33.4	-8.0	35.6	6.6	44.0	23.6
Grains	42.7	9.2	43.7	2.3	52.3	19.7	71.0	35.8	67.2	-5.4	54.0	-19.6	57.5	6.5	63.6	10.6	62.9	-1.1
Slaughter Livestock	24.8	-2.4	25.8	4.0	30.4	17.8	41.4	36.2	46.7	12.8	39.1	-16.3	42.7	9.2	50.8	19.0	44.1	-13.2
Slaughter Poultry	95.3	-2.6	100.7	5.7	108.9	8.1	111.8	2.7	128.7	15.1	105.6	-17.9	96.8	-8.3	106.4	9.9	101.4	-4.7
Plant and Animal Fibers	41.0	1.7	42.9	4.6	56.9	32.6	65.7	15.5	69.7	6.1	67.1	-3.7	78.4	16.8	97.1	23.9	77.7	-20.0
Fluid Milk	22.5	3.2	22.5	0.0	27.2	20.9	30.0	10.3	34.1	13.7	27.6	-19.1	27.1	-1.8	32.1	18.5	33.5	4.4
Chicken Eggs	67.8	-11.7	73.1	7.8	70.5	-3.6	85.1	20.7	92.2	8.3	88.7	-3.8	75.3	-15.1	95.7	27.1	84.9	-11.3
Hay, Hayseeds and Oilseeds	40.5	10.7	40.3	-0.5	43.5	7.9	55.5	27.6	56.9	2.5	43.2	-24.1	46.6	7.9	53.2	14.2	51.0	-4.1
Farm Products n.e.c.	17.5	4.8	17.2	-1.7	19.7	14.5	25.3	28.4	26.3	4.0	27.3	3.8	33.6	23.1	36.4	8.3	35.9	-1.4
Processed Foods and Feeds	-	-	-	-	-	-	33.0	-	35.3	7.0	32.1	-9.1	33.2	3.4	36.9	11.1	36.4	-1.4
Cereal and Bakery Products	17.9	1.7	17.9	0.0	21.5	20.1	28.7	33.5	29.2	1.7	27.7	-5.1	28.2	1.8	30.5	8.2	30.5	0.0
Meats, Poultry, and Fish	18.5	-4.1	18.8	1.6	25.3	34.6	35.3	39.5	41.0	16.1	35.8	-12.7	37.9	5.9	43.6	15.0	40.5	-7.1
Dairy Products	19.3	-0.5	19.4	0.5	25.4	30.9	28.0	10.2	31.3	11.8	28.2	-9.9	27.7	-1.8	31.5	13.7	33.1	5.1
Processed Fruits and Vegetables	22.8	1.3	23.0	0.9	24.4	6.1	31.7	29.9	31.6	-0.3	31.4	-0.6	31.6	0.6	33.3	5.4	33.2	-0.3
Sugar and Confectionery	18.6	0.0	18.5	-0.5	22.0	18.9	28.9	31.4	29.6	2.4	27.4	-7.4	27.9	1.8	30.3	8.6	31.1	2.6
Beverages and Beverage Materials	-	-	-	-	-	-	26.6	-	27.8	4.5	28.3	1.8	30.5	7.8	32.5	6.6	33.2	2.2
Fats and Oils	-	-	-	-	-	-	-	-	-	-	-	-	-	-	-	-	-	-
Miscellaneous Processed Foods	-	-	-	-	-	-	34.8	-	36.5	4.9	40.0	9.6	43.9	9.7	45.6	3.9	44.2	-3.1
Prepared Animal Feeds	-	-	-	-	-	-	55.3	-	56.0	1.3	49.0	-12.5	48.8	-0.4	53.7	10.0	57.7	7.4
Textile Products and Apparel	-	-	-	-	-	-	50.6	-	52.8	4.3	48.3	-8.5	50.2	3.9	56.0	11.6	50.5	-9.8
Synthetic Fibers	-	-	-	-	-	-	-	-	-	-	-	-	-	-	-	-	-	-
Processed Yarns and Threads	-	-	-	-	-	-	-	-	-	-	-	-	-	-	-	-	-	-
Gray Fabrics	-	-	-	-	-	-	-	-	-	-	-	-	-	-	-	-	-	-
Finished Fabrics	-	-	-	-	-	-	-	-	-	-	-	-	-	-	-	-	-	-
Apparel	-	-	-	-	-	-	95.1	-	97.0	2.0	89.9	-7.3	90.5	0.7	97.6	7.8	94.0	-3.7
Textile Housefurnishings	-	-	-	-	-	-	97.2	-	103.1	6.1	95.7	-7.2	99.9	4.4	111.5	11.6	100.8	-9.6
Miscellaneous Textile Products	-	-	-	-	-	-	-	-	-	-	-	-	-	-	-	-	-	-
Apparel & Other Fabricated Textile Products	-	-	-	-	-	-	-	-	-	-	-	-	-	-	-	-	-	-
Miscellaneous Textile Products/Services	-	-	-	-	-	-	-	-	-	-	-	-	-	-	-	-	-	-
Hides, Skins, Leather, and Related Products	19.9	-1.0	20.1	1.0	23.3	15.9	31.7	36.1	32.1	1.3	30.4	-5.3	32.9	8.2	37.7	14.6	30.5	-19.1
Hides and Skins	22.4	-4.7	23.9	6.7	30.3	26.8	47.6	57.1	44.5	-6.5	38.8	-12.8	45.0	16.0	51.9	15.3	27.5	-47.0

Source: U.S. Department of Labor, Bureau of Labor Statistics, Division of Industry Prices and Price Indexes. n.e.c. stands for not elsewhere classified. - indicates no data collected for period or unavailable.

Producer Price Index
Annual Averages, 1953-1961
Base 1982 = 100

Columns headed % show percentile change in the index from the previous period for which an index is available.

	1953		1954		1955		1956		1957		1958		1959		1960		1961	
	Index	%	Index	%	Index	%	Index	%	Index	%	Index	%	Index	%	Index	%	Index	%
Farm Products	43.8	-9.5	43.2	-1.4	40.5	-6.3	40.0	-1.2	41.1	2.8	42.9	4.4	40.2	-6.3	40.1	-0.2	39.7	-1.0
Fruits & Melons, Fresh/Dry Vegetables & Nuts	36.7	-16.6	36.3	-1.1	38.1	5.0	38.1	0.0	37.9	-0.5	41.0	8.2	37.6	-8.3	39.0	3.7	36.3	-6.9
Grains	57.8	-8.1	58.6	1.4	55.8	-4.8	55.8	0.0	53.9	-3.4	50.9	-5.6	49.5	-2.8	48.5	-2.0	49.2	1.4
Slaughter Livestock	37.5	-15.0	37.0	-1.3	31.8	-14.1	30.6	-3.8	35.3	15.4	41.6	17.8	38.2	-8.2	36.6	-4.2	36.0	-1.6
Slaughter Poultry	100.5	-0.9	81.8	-18.6	87.0	6.4	71.4	-17.9	66.4	-7.0	65.1	-2.0	59.4	-8.8	63.4	6.7	52.7	-16.9
Plant and Animal Fibers	69.8	-10.2	71.7	2.7	69.2	-3.5	69.4	0.3	70.2	1.2	68.6	-2.3	66.3	-3.4	63.6	-4.1	64.8	1.9
Fluid Milk	30.2	-9.9	27.9	-7.6	28.0	0.4	28.9	3.2	29.3	1.4	28.9	-1.4	28.9	0.0	30.0	3.8	30.2	0.7
Chicken Eggs	93.7	10.4	70.8	-24.4	76.0	7.3	72.6	-4.5	68.5	-5.6	72.5	5.8	58.1	-19.9	68.5	17.9	65.7	-4.1
Hay, Hayseeds and Oilseeds	46.8	-8.2	48.3	3.2	44.0	-8.9	42.9	-2.5	42.6	-0.7	39.9	-6.3	39.8	-0.3	38.8	-2.5	43.7	12.6
Farm Products n.e.c.	37.1	3.3	45.0	21.3	37.5	-16.7	38.6	2.9	38.0	-1.6	36.9	-2.9	34.9	-5.4	33.8	-3.2	34.1	0.9
Processed Foods and Feeds	34.8	-4.4	35.4	1.7	33.8	-4.5	33.8	0.0	34.8	3.0	36.5	4.9	35.6	-2.5	35.6	0.0	36.2	1.7
Cereal and Bakery Products	31.2	2.3	32.5	4.2	33.1	1.8	32.8	-0.9	33.3	1.5	33.6	0.9	34.0	1.2	34.7	2.1	35.4	2.0
Meats, Poultry, and Fish	34.7	-14.3	34.4	-0.9	31.7	-7.8	30.5	-3.8	34.4	12.8	39.9	16.0	36.7	-8.0	36.1	-1.6	35.3	-2.2
Dairy Products	32.3	-2.4	31.0	-4.0	31.0	0.0	31.7	2.3	32.6	2.8	32.9	0.9	33.4	1.5	34.6	3.6	35.4	2.3
Processed Fruits and Vegetables	33.1	-0.3	33.0	-0.3	33.3	0.9	34.1	2.4	32.8	-3.8	34.7	5.8	34.5	-0.6	33.8	-2.0	34.6	2.4
Sugar and Confectionery	31.3	0.6	32.2	2.9	31.6	-1.9	31.4	-0.6	32.4	3.2	33.1	2.2	32.9	-0.6	33.4	1.5	33.2	-0.6
Beverages and Beverage Materials	33.8	1.8	37.6	11.2	36.2	-3.7	37.1	2.5	37.1	0.0	36.3	-2.2	36.2	-0.3	36.1	-0.3	36.1	0.0
Fats and Oils	-	-	-	-	-	-	-	-	-	-	-	-	-	-	-	-	-	-
Miscellaneous Processed Foods	43.4	-1.8	38.3	-11.8	36.9	-3.7	35.9	-2.7	35.4	-1.4	35.8	1.1	35.9	0.3	37.9	5.6	37.8	-0.3
Prepared Animal Feeds	46.9	-18.7	51.3	9.4	40.5	-21.1	38.5	-4.9	36.0	-6.5	39.8	10.6	40.2	1.0	37.2	-7.5	40.4	8.6
Textile Products and Apparel	49.3	-2.4	48.2	-2.2	48.2	0.0	48.2	0.0	48.3	0.2	47.4	-1.9	48.1	1.5	48.6	1.0	47.8	-1.6
Synthetic Fibers	-	-	-	-	-	-	-	-	-	-	-	-	-	-	-	-	-	-
Processed Yarns and Threads	-	-	-	-	-	-	-	-	-	-	-	-	-	-	-	-	-	-
Gray Fabrics	-	-	-	-	-	-	-	-	-	-	-	-	-	-	-	-	-	-
Finished Fabrics	-	-	-	-	-	-	-	-	-	-	-	-	-	-	-	-	-	-
Apparel	93.4	-0.6	92.6	-0.9	92.6	0.0	93.6	1.1	93.6	0.0	93.4	-0.2	94.0	0.6	94.9	1.0	94.6	-0.3
Textile Housefurnishings	96.6	-4.2	94.3	-2.4	94.9	0.6	95.8	0.9	96.5	0.7	92.7	-3.9	93.8	1.2	96.1	2.5	96.6	0.5
Miscellaneous Textile Products	-	-	-	-	-	-	-	-	-	-	-	-	-	-	-	-	-	-
Apparel & Other Fabricated Textile Products	-	-	-	-	-	-	-	-	-	-	-	-	-	-	-	-	-	-
Miscellaneous Textile Products/Services	-	-	-	-	-	-	-	-	-	-	-	-	-	-	-	-	-	-
Hides, Skins, Leather, and Related Products	31.0	1.6	29.5	-4.8	29.4	-0.3	31.2	6.1	31.2	0.0	31.6	1.3	35.9	13.6	34.6	-3.6	34.9	0.9
Hides and Skins	29.8	8.4	24.1	-19.1	24.7	2.5	25.8	4.5	24.1	-6.6	25.1	4.1	39.6	57.8	29.7	-25.0	31.9	7.4

Source: U.S. Department of Labor, Bureau of Labor Statistics, Division of Industry Prices and Price Indexes. n.e.c. stands for not elsewhere classified. - indicates no data collected for period or unavailable.

Producer Price Index
Annual Averages, 1962-1970
Base 1982 = 100

Columns headed % show percentile change in the index from the previous period for which an index is available.

	1962		1963		1964		1965		1966		1967		1968		1969		1970	
	Index	%	Index	%	Index	%	Index	%	Index	%	Index	%	Index	%	Index	%	Index	%
Farm Products	40.4	1.8	39.6	-2.0	39.0	-1.5	40.7	4.4	43.7	7.4	41.3	-5.5	42.3	2.4	45.0	6.4	45.8	1.8
Fruits & Melons, Fresh/Dry Vegetables & Nuts	37.9	4.4	37.3	-1.6	40.1	7.5	39.5	-1.5	39.8	0.8	39.4	-1.0	42.0	6.6	43.4	3.3	44.0	1.4
Grains	50.8	3.3	52.4	3.1	48.4	-7.6	46.1	-4.8	50.0	8.5	47.4	-5.2	42.1	-11.2	42.8	1.7	46.8	9.3
Slaughter Livestock	37.4	3.9	34.2	-8.6	32.6	-4.7	38.6	18.4	42.2	9.3	38.8	-8.1	40.2	3.6	45.4	12.9	45.3	-0.2
Slaughter Poultry	54.3	3.0	53.9	-0.7	52.2	-3.2	55.0	5.4	58.2	5.8	52.1	-10.5	54.0	3.6	58.8	8.9	51.9	-11.7
Plant and Animal Fibers	67.3	3.9	68.7	2.1	67.2	-2.2	62.3	-7.3	56.2	-9.8	49.3	-12.3	51.5	4.5	45.9	-10.9	44.5	-3.1
Fluid Milk	29.4	-2.6	29.2	-0.7	29.6	1.4	30.1	1.7	34.2	13.6	35.4	3.5	37.5	5.9	39.2	4.5	40.8	4.1
Chicken Eggs	63.2	-3.8	62.4	-1.3	60.3	-3.4	62.1	3.0	71.6	15.3	56.0	-21.8	62.3	11.2	74.9	20.2	71.0	-5.2
Hay, Hayseeds and Oilseeds	42.9	-1.8	46.0	7.2	44.8	-2.6	46.0	2.7	50.0	8.7	47.0	-6.0	45.4	-3.4	44.5	-2.0	46.7	4.9
Farm Products n.e.c.	33.6	-1.5	32.7	-2.7	36.1	10.4	35.7	-1.1	37.1	3.9	36.4	-1.9	37.7	3.6	39.9	5.8	42.7	7.0
Processed Foods and Feeds	36.5	0.8	36.8	0.8	36.7	-0.3	38.0	3.5	40.2	5.8	39.8	-1.0	40.6	2.0	42.7	5.2	44.6	4.4
Cereal and Bakery Products	36.2	2.3	36.1	-0.3	36.3	0.6	36.7	1.1	38.8	5.7	39.4	1.5	39.8	1.0	40.5	1.8	42.4	4.7
Meats, Poultry, and Fish	36.6	3.7	34.5	-5.7	33.6	-2.6	37.3	11.0	40.8	9.4	38.8	-4.9	40.0	3.1	44.2	10.5	45.0	1.8
Dairy Products	35.2	-0.6	35.4	0.6	35.5	0.3	35.8	0.8	39.1	9.2	40.2	2.8	42.1	4.7	43.5	3.3	44.7	2.8
Processed Fruits and Vegetables	33.3	-3.8	35.3	6.0	35.6	0.8	34.7	-2.5	35.6	2.6	36.4	2.2	38.8	6.6	39.4	1.5	40.3	2.3
Sugar and Confectionery	33.5	0.9	38.9	16.1	36.7	-5.7	35.8	-2.5	36.3	1.4	37.1	2.2	38.1	2.7	40.8	7.1	42.9	5.1
Beverages and Beverage Materials	36.2	0.3	36.9	1.9	38.8	5.1	38.6	-0.5	38.7	0.3	38.9	0.5	40.0	2.8	41.3	3.2	44.0	6.5
Fats and Oils	-	-	-	-	-	-	-	-	-	-	46.5	-	44.8	-3.7	46.9	4.7	55.1	17.5
Miscellaneous Processed Foods	36.4	-3.7	37.3	2.5	38.9	4.3	40.6	4.4	40.7	0.2	40.2	-1.2	41.3	2.7	43.4	5.1	45.5	4.8
Prepared Animal Feeds	42.7	5.7	45.0	5.4	44.0	-2.2	44.9	2.0	48.9	8.9	47.3	-3.3	45.8	-3.2	45.7	-0.2	49.1	7.4
Textile Products and Apparel	48.2	0.8	48.2	0.0	48.5	0.6	48.8	0.6	48.9	0.2	48.9	0.0	50.7	3.7	51.8	2.2	52.4	1.2
Synthetic Fibers	-	-	-	-	-	-	-	-	-	-	-	-	-	-	-	-	-	-
Processed Yarns and Threads	-	-	-	-	-	-	-	-	-	-	-	-	-	-	-	-	-	-
Gray Fabrics	-	-	-	-	-	-	-	-	-	-	-	-	-	-	-	-	-	-
Finished Fabrics	-	-	-	-	-	-	-	-	-	-	-	-	-	-	-	-	-	-
Apparel	95.0	0.4	95.4	0.4	96.3	0.9	97.1	0.8	98.3	1.2	100.0	1.7	103.6	3.6	107.4	3.7	110.8	3.2
Textile Housefurnishings	98.3	1.8	97.1	-1.2	97.6	0.5	97.3	-0.3	98.5	1.2	100.0	1.5	104.2	4.2	100.8	-3.3	103.5	2.7
Miscellaneous Textile Products	-	-	-	-	-	-	-	-	-	-	-	-	-	-	-	-	-	-
Apparel & Other Fabricated Textile Products	-	-	-	-	-	-	-	-	-	-	-	-	-	-	-	-	-	-
Miscellaneous Textile Products/Services	-	-	-	-	-	-	-	-	-	-	-	-	-	-	-	-	-	-
Hides, Skins, Leather, and Related Products	35.3	1.1	34.3	-2.8	34.4	0.3	35.9	4.4	39.4	9.7	38.1	-3.3	39.3	3.1	41.5	5.6	42.0	1.2
Hides and Skins	31.4	-1.6	24.9	-20.7	25.9	4.0	32.9	27.0	41.7	26.7	27.9	-33.1	29.6	6.1	34.6	16.9	29.0	-16.2

Source: U.S. Department of Labor, Bureau of Labor Statistics, Division of Industry Prices and Price Indexes. n.e.c. stands for not elsewhere classified. - indicates no data collected for period or unavailable.

Producer Price Index
Annual Averages, 1971-1979
Base 1982 = 100

Columns headed % show percentile change in the index from the previous period for which an index is available.

	1971		1972		1973		1974		1975		1976		1977		1978		1979	
	Index	%	Index	%	Index	%	Index	%	Index	%	Index	%	Index	%	Index	%	Index	%
Farm Products	46.6	1.7	51.6	10.7	72.7	40.9	77.4	6.5	77.0	-0.5	78.8	2.3	79.4	0.8	87.7	10.5	99.6	13.6
Fruits & Melons, Fresh/Dry Vegetables & Nuts	47.3	7.5	50.3	6.3	66.3	31.8	75.8	14.3	72.4	-4.5	70.3	-2.9	75.8	7.8	85.3	12.5	90.3	5.9
Grains	47.8	2.1	48.8	2.1	87.1	78.5	122.3	40.4	106.2	-13.2	97.6	-8.1	78.2	-19.9	86.5	10.6	101.8	17.7
Slaughter Livestock	45.9	1.3	55.3	20.5	73.8	33.5	66.2	-10.3	72.9	10.1	67.2	-7.8	67.1	-0.1	85.4	27.3	100.9	18.1
Slaughter Poultry	52.2	0.6	54.2	3.8	93.5	72.5	82.0	-12.3	98.9	20.6	87.0	-12.0	91.4	5.1	104.1	13.9	101.2	-2.8
Plant and Animal Fibers	45.7	2.7	57.9	26.7	97.5	68.4	95.6	-1.9	75.5	-21.0	110.3	46.1	99.7	-9.6	95.3	-4.4	103.4	8.5
Fluid Milk	42.0	2.9	43.3	3.1	51.3	18.5	61.2	19.3	63.8	4.2	71.2	11.6	71.8	0.8	77.8	8.4	88.5	13.8
Chicken Eggs	56.4	-20.6	58.0	2.8	92.7	59.8	89.9	-3.0	89.4	-0.6	100.2	12.1	90.6	-9.6	88.7	-2.1	98.8	11.4
Hay, Hayseeds and Oilseeds	51.3	9.9	55.5	8.2	103.4	86.3	107.4	3.9	94.1	-12.4	98.9	5.1	110.1	11.3	101.4	-7.9	114.8	13.2
Farm Products n.e.c.	42.1	-1.4	45.5	8.1	53.7	18.0	59.9	11.5	61.8	3.2	81.4	31.7	118.7	45.8	100.2	-15.6	105.3	5.1
Processed Foods and Feeds	45.5	2.0	48.0	5.5	58.9	22.7	68.0	15.4	72.6	6.8	70.8	-2.5	74.0	4.5	80.6	8.9	88.5	9.8
Cereal and Bakery Products	44.0	3.8	45.2	2.7	53.0	17.3	67.5	27.4	70.1	3.9	67.8	-3.3	68.3	0.7	75.0	9.8	82.9	10.5
Meats, Poultry, and Fish	45.0	0.0	50.5	12.2	65.0	28.7	63.5	-2.3	74.2	16.9	70.5	-5.0	70.7	0.3	84.3	19.2	93.9	11.4
Dairy Products	46.5	4.0	47.7	2.6	52.7	10.5	58.8	11.6	62.6	6.5	67.7	8.1	69.7	3.0	75.7	8.6	84.9	12.2
Processed Fruits and Vegetables	41.7	3.5	43.6	4.6	47.2	8.3	56.3	19.3	61.9	9.9	62.0	0.2	68.3	10.2	73.8	8.1	80.9	9.6
Sugar and Confectionery	44.3	3.3	45.1	1.8	49.1	8.9	96.0	95.5	94.3	-1.8	70.8	-24.9	65.8	-7.1	73.3	11.4	79.6	8.6
Beverages and Beverage Materials	45.2	2.7	45.9	1.5	47.4	3.3	54.8	15.6	63.2	15.3	67.5	6.8	78.3	16.0	77.9	-0.5	82.0	5.3
Fats and Oils	58.6	6.4	54.6	-6.8	75.6	38.5	120.5	59.4	104.7	-13.1	82.8	-20.9	96.5	16.5	104.7	8.5	113.1	8.0
Miscellaneous Processed Foods	45.6	0.2	46.2	1.3	49.6	7.4	63.8	28.6	71.8	12.5	70.3	-2.1	76.5	8.8	80.1	4.7	87.1	8.7
Prepared Animal Feeds	49.4	0.6	54.9	11.1	94.0	71.2	87.1	-7.3	81.5	-6.4	92.0	12.9	96.8	5.2	93.4	-3.5	103.8	11.1
Textile Products and Apparel	53.3	1.7	55.5	4.1	60.5	9.0	68.0	12.4	67.4	-0.9	72.4	7.4	75.3	4.0	78.1	3.7	82.5	5.6
Synthetic Fibers	-	-	-	-	-	-	-	-	-	-	63.2	-	66.2	4.7	67.6	2.1	73.4	8.6
Processed Yarns and Threads	-	-	-	-	-	-	-	-	-	-	71.9	-	73.0	1.5	74.0	1.4	78.9	6.6
Gray Fabrics	-	-	-	-	-	-	-	-	-	-	73.0	-	72.1	-1.2	81.6	13.2	87.5	7.2
Finished Fabrics	-	-	-	-	-	-	-	-	-	-	81.2	-	83.3	2.6	83.3	0.0	86.2	3.5
Apparel	113.6	2.5	114.8	1.1	119.0	3.7	129.5	8.8	133.4	3.0	139.9	4.9	147.3	5.3	-	-	-	-
Textile Housefurnishings	104.9	1.4	109.2	4.1	113.3	3.8	143.1	26.3	151.9	6.1	159.3	4.9	171.3	7.5	-	-	-	-
Miscellaneous Textile Products	-	-	-	-	-	-	-	-	-	-	-	-	-	-	-	-	-	-
Apparel & Other Fabricated Textile Products	-	-	-	-	-	-	-	-	-	-	-	-	-	-	77.9	-	82.1	5.4
Miscellaneous Textile Products/Services	-	-	-	-	-	-	-	-	-	-	-	-	-	-	-	-	-	-
Hides, Skins, Leather, and Related Products	43.4	3.3	50.0	15.2	54.5	9.0	55.2	1.3	56.5	2.4	63.9	13.1	68.3	6.9	76.1	11.4	96.1	26.3
Hides and Skins	32.1	10.7	59.6	85.7	70.8	18.8	54.6	-22.9	48.6	-11.0	72.0	48.1	79.9	11.0	100.5	25.8	149.2	48.5

Source: U.S. Department of Labor, Bureau of Labor Statistics, Division of Industry Prices and Price Indexes. n.e.c. stands for not elsewhere classified. - indicates no data collected for period or unavailable.

Producer Price Index
Annual Averages, 1980-1988
Base 1982 = 100

Columns headed % show percentile change in the index from the previous period for which an index is available.

	1980 Index	%	1981 Index	%	1982 Index	%	1983 Index	%	1984 Index	%	1985 Index	%	1986 Index	%	1987 Index	%	1988 Index	%
Farm Products	102.9	3.3	105.2	2.2	100.0	-4.9	102.4	2.4	105.5	3.0	95.1	-9.9	92.9	-2.3	95.5	2.8	104.9	9.8
Fruits & Melons, Fresh/Dry Vegetables & Nuts	94.1	4.2	105.4	12.0	100.0	-5.1	103.3	3.3	109.6	6.1	102.7	-6.3	103.9	1.2	106.8	2.8	108.5	1.6
Grains	113.3	11.3	117.8	4.0	100.0	-15.1	114.0	14.0	113.7	-0.3	96.1	-15.5	79.3	-17.5	71.1	-10.3	97.9	37.7
Slaughter Livestock	98.0	-2.9	96.2	-1.8	100.0	4.0	94.3	-5.7	97.7	3.6	89.2	-8.7	91.8	2.9	102.0	11.1	103.3	1.3
Slaughter Poultry	105.3	4.1	104.8	-0.5	100.0	-4.6	107.6	7.6	125.4	16.5	117.9	-6.0	129.7	10.0	101.2	-22.0	121.5	20.1
Plant and Animal Fibers	133.6	29.2	119.2	-10.8	100.0	-16.1	111.9	11.9	112.6	0.6	97.5	-13.4	88.4	-9.3	106.5	20.5	98.4	-7.6
Fluid Milk	96.0	8.5	101.7	5.9	100.0	-1.7	99.8	-0.2	98.5	-1.3	93.7	-4.9	91.0	-2.9	91.9	1.0	89.4	-2.7
Chicken Eggs	95.7	-3.1	104.7	9.4	100.0	-4.5	-	-	117.9	17.9	95.7	-18.8	99.6	4.1	87.6	-12.0	88.6	1.1
Hay, Hayseeds and Oilseeds	116.1	1.1	128.8	10.9	100.0	-22.4	116.0	16.0	120.5	3.9	96.8	-19.7	92.9	-4.0	101.4	9.1	138.4	36.5
Farm Products n.e.c.	108.9	3.4	99.7	-8.4	100.0	0.3	102.8	2.8	104.1	1.3	103.1	-1.0	96.3	-6.6	94.4	-2.0	95.4	1.1
Processed Foods and Feeds	95.9	8.4	98.9	3.1	100.0	1.1	101.8	1.8	105.4	3.5	103.5	-1.8	105.4	1.8	107.9	2.4	112.7	4.4
Cereal and Bakery Products	93.0	12.2	100.7	8.3	100.0	-0.7	102.8	2.8	106.6	3.7	110.3	3.5	111.0	0.6	112.6	1.4	123.0	9.2
Meats, Poultry, and Fish	94.4	0.5	95.6	1.3	100.0	4.6	96.7	-3.3	98.8	2.2	95.9	-2.9	100.2	4.5	104.9	4.7	106.6	1.6
Dairy Products	92.7	9.2	98.7	6.5	100.0	1.3	100.7	0.7	101.1	0.4	100.2	-0.9	99.9	-0.3	101.6	1.7	102.2	0.6
Processed Fruits and Vegetables	83.3	3.0	95.2	14.3	100.0	5.0	101.1	1.1	107.3	6.1	108.0	0.7	104.9	-2.9	108.6	3.5	113.8	4.8
Sugar and Confectionery	119.6	50.3	102.3	-14.5	100.0	-2.2	108.6	8.6	111.7	2.9	107.9	-3.4	109.7	1.7	112.7	2.7	114.7	1.8
Beverages and Beverage Materials	90.7	10.6	96.5	6.4	100.0	3.6	102.6	2.6	106.3	3.6	107.7	1.3	114.6	6.4	112.5	-1.8	114.3	1.6
Fats and Oils	105.4	-6.8	105.7	0.3	100.0	-5.4	111.0	11.0	140.1	26.2	125.5	-10.4	96.5	-23.1	97.9	1.5	117.2	19.7
Miscellaneous Processed Foods	91.4	4.9	100.6	10.1	100.0	-0.6	102.5	2.5	111.8	9.1	114.1	2.1	116.2	1.8	119.8	3.1	122.5	2.3
Prepared Animal Feeds	107.3	3.4	109.0	1.6	100.0	-8.3	108.3	8.3	104.4	-3.6	90.1	-13.7	94.6	5.0	98.5	4.1	116.0	17.8
Textile Products and Apparel	89.7	8.7	97.6	8.8	100.0	2.5	100.3	0.3	102.7	2.4	102.9	0.2	103.2	0.3	105.1	1.8	109.2	3.9
Synthetic Fibers	83.1	13.2	96.5	16.1	100.0	3.6	96.7	-3.3	98.5	1.9	95.5	-3.0	92.5	-3.1	91.8	-0.8	97.3	6.0
Processed Yarns and Threads	88.6	12.3	99.8	12.6	100.0	0.2	100.1	0.1	103.2	3.1	102.1	-1.1	101.7	-0.4	103.8	2.1	108.0	4.0
Gray Fabrics	95.0	8.6	101.0	6.3	100.0	-1.0	101.2	1.2	105.8	4.5	104.4	-1.3	103.7	-0.7	107.2	3.4	114.0	6.3
Finished Fabrics	92.9	7.8	100.5	8.2	100.0	-0.5	98.9	-1.1	101.7	2.8	101.4	-0.3	101.4	0.0	104.2	2.8	109.4	5.0
Apparel	-		-		-		-		-		-		-		-		-	
Textile Housefurnishings	-		-		-		-		-		-		-		-		-	
Miscellaneous Textile Products	-		-		-		-		-		-		-		-		-	
Apparel & Other Fabricated Textile Products	88.7	8.0	95.8	8.0	100.0	4.4	101.0	1.0	102.8	1.8	104.2	1.4	105.5	1.2	107.3	1.7	110.4	2.9
Miscellaneous Textile Products/Services	-		-		-		-		-		-		96.4	-	98.7	2.4	105.3	6.7
Hides, Skins, Leather, and Related Products	94.7	-1.5	99.3	4.9	100.0	0.7	103.2	3.2	109.0	5.6	108.9	-0.1	113.0	3.8	120.4	6.5	131.4	9.1
Hides and Skins	103.4	-30.7	104.7	1.3	100.0	-4.5	109.8	9.8	143.8	31.0	126.1	-12.3	147.7	17.1	179.9	21.8	-	-

Source: U.S. Department of Labor, Bureau of Labor Statistics, Division of Industry Prices and Price Indexes. n.e.c. stands for not elsewhere classified. - indicates no data collected for period or unavailable.

892

Producer Price Index
Annual Averages, 1989-1995
Base 1982 = 100

Columns headed % show percentile change in the index from the previous period for which an index is available.

	1989		1990		1991		1992		1993		1994		1995					
	Index	%	Index	%	Index	%	Index	%	Index	%	Index	%	Index	%	Index	%	Index	%
Farm Products	110.9	5.7	112.2	1.2	105.7	-5.8	103.6	-2.0	107.1	3.4	106.3	-0.7	107.4	1.0				
Fruits & Melons, Fresh/Dry Vegetables & Nuts	114.6	5.6	117.5	2.5	114.7	-2.4	96.9	-15.5	106.9	10.3	104.6	-2.2	108.3	3.5				
Grains	106.4	8.7	97.4	-8.5	92.0	-5.5	97.3	5.8	94.5	-2.9	102.7	8.7	112.6	9.6				
Slaughter Livestock	106.1	2.7	115.6	9.0	107.9	-6.7	104.7	-3.0	107.0	2.2	96.4	-9.9	92.8	-3.7				
Slaughter Poultry	128.8	6.0	118.8	-7.8	111.2	-6.4	112.6	1.3	122.0	8.3	124.4	2.0	125.6	1.0				
Plant and Animal Fibers	107.8	9.6	117.8	9.3	115.1	-2.3	89.8	-22.0	91.3	1.7	120.7	32.2	155.3	28.7				
Fluid Milk	98.8	10.5	100.8	2.0	89.5	-11.2	96.1	7.4	94.1	-2.1	95.7	1.7	93.3	-2.5				
Chicken Eggs	119.6	35.0	117.6	-1.7	110.7	-5.9	94.1	-15.0	105.9	12.5	97.8	-7.6	104.1	6.4				
Hay, Hayseeds and Oilseeds	137.0	-1.0	122.1	-10.9	112.1	-8.2	111.2	-0.8	126.2	13.5	132.4	4.9	122.9	-7.2				
Farm Products n.e.c.	103.3	8.3	125.3	21.3	151.6	21.0	150.6	-0.7	149.6	-0.7	149.5	-0.1	-	-				
Processed Foods and Feeds	117.8	4.5	121.9	3.5	121.9	0.0	122.1	0.2	124.0	1.6	125.5	1.2	127.0	1.2				
Cereal and Bakery Products	131.1	6.6	134.2	2.4	137.9	2.8	144.2	4.6	147.6	2.4	151.1	2.4	154.7	2.4				
Meats, Poultry, and Fish	111.0	4.1	119.6	7.7	116.6	-2.5	112.2	-3.8	115.5	2.9	112.2	-2.9	111.7	-0.4				
Dairy Products	110.6	8.2	117.2	6.0	114.6	-2.2	117.9	2.9	118.1	0.2	119.4	1.1	119.7	0.3				
Processed Fruits and Vegetables	119.9	5.4	124.7	4.0	119.6	-4.1	120.8	1.0	118.2	-2.2	121.1	2.5	122.4	1.1				
Sugar and Confectionery	120.1	4.7	123.1	2.5	128.4	4.3	127.7	-0.5	127.9	0.2	132.5	3.6	134.1	1.2				
Beverages and Beverage Materials	118.4	3.6	120.8	2.0	124.1	2.7	124.4	0.2	124.8	0.3	127.7	2.3	133.8	4.8				
Fats and Oils	112.1	-4.4	119.4	6.5	112.0	-6.2	108.8	-2.9	116.9	7.4	135.8	16.2	138.6	2.1				
Miscellaneous Processed Foods	129.4	5.6	134.2	3.7	138.3	3.1	139.2	0.7	142.3	2.2	144.3	1.4	146.1	1.2				
Prepared Animal Feeds	116.6	0.5	107.4	-7.9	106.8	-0.6	108.3	1.4	111.0	2.5	111.3	0.3	109.1	-2.0				
Textile Products and Apparel	112.3	2.8	115.0	2.4	116.3	1.1	117.8	1.3	118.0	0.2	118.3	0.3	120.8	2.1				
Synthetic Fibers	104.8	7.7	106.7	1.8	105.3	-1.3	103.4	-1.8	103.6	0.2	104.1	0.5	109.1	4.8				
Processed Yarns and Threads	110.4	2.2	112.6	2.0	112.6	0.0	110.8	-1.6	107.8	-2.7	108.4	0.6	112.7	4.0				
Gray Fabrics	115.2	1.1	117.2	1.7	117.4	0.2	120.6	2.7	118.6	-1.7	116.8	-1.5	121.3	3.9				
Finished Fabrics	113.6	3.8	116.0	2.1	117.5	1.3	118.8	1.1	119.5	0.6	119.2	-0.3	121.6	2.0				
Apparel	-	-	-	-	-	-	-	-	-	-	-	-	-	-				
Textile Housefurnishings	-	-	-	-	-	-	-	-	-	-	-	-	-	-				
Miscellaneous Textile Products	-	-	-	-	-	-	-	-	-	-	-	-	-	-				
Apparel & Other Fabricated Textile Products	113.0	2.4	116.0	2.7	118.1	1.8	120.4	1.9	121.6	1.0	122.1	0.4	123.2	0.9				
Miscellaneous Textile Products/Services	111.8	6.2	114.0	2.0	113.5	-0.4	114.9	1.2	115.9	0.9	118.1	1.9	123.6	4.7				
Hides, Skins, Leather, and Related Products	136.3	3.7	141.7	4.0	138.9	-2.0	140.4	1.1	143.7	2.4	148.5	3.3	153.6	3.4				
Hides and Skins	212.9	-	217.9	2.3	174.2	-20.1	174.0	-0.1	184.2	5.9	206.3	12.0	215.5	4.5				

Source: U.S. Department of Labor, Bureau of Labor Statistics, Division of Industry Prices and Price Indexes. n.e.c. stands for not elsewhere classified. - indicates no data collected for period or unavailable.

Producer Price Index
Annual Averages, 1926-1934
Base 1982 = 100

Columns headed % show percentile change in the index from the previous period for which an index is available.

	1926		1927		1928		1929		1930		1931		1932		1933		1934	
	Index	%	Index	%	Index	%	Index	%	Index	%	Index	%	Index	%	Index	%	Index	%
Leather	16.2	-	17.7	9.3	20.4	15.3	18.3	-10.3	16.4	-10.4	13.9	-15.2	10.5	-24.5	11.5	9.5	12.1	5.2
Footwear	14.6	-	14.9	2.1	16.0	7.4	15.5	-3.1	14.9	-3.9	13.7	-8.1	12.6	-8.0	13.1	4.0	14.3	9.2
Leather and Related Products n.e.c.	-	-	-	-	-	-	-	-	-	-	-	-	-	-	-	-	-	-
Fuels and Related Products and Power	10.3	-	9.1	-11.7	8.7	-4.4	8.6	-1.1	8.1	-5.8	7.0	-13.6	7.3	4.3	6.9	-5.5	7.6	10.1
Coal	8.5	-	8.4	-1.2	7.9	-6.0	7.7	-2.5	7.6	-1.3	7.3	-3.9	7.1	-2.7	7.0	-1.4	7.7	10.0
Coke Oven Products	6.0	-	5.6	-6.7	5.0	-10.7	5.0	0.0	5.0	0.0	4.9	-2.0	4.6	-6.1	4.6	0.0	5.0	8.7
Gas Fuels	-	-	-	-	-	-	-	-	-	-	-	-	-	-	-	-	-	-
Electric Power	-	-	-	-	-	-	-	-	-	-	-	-	-	-	-	-	-	-
Utility Natural Gas	-	-	-	-	-	-	-	-	-	-	-	-	-	-	-	-	-	-
Crude Petroleum (Domestic Production)	-	-	-	-	-	-	-	-	-	-	-	-	-	-	-	-	-	-
Petroleum Products, Refined	-	-	-	-	-	-	-	-	-	-	-	-	-	-	-	-	-	-
Petroleum and Coal Products, n.e.c.	-	-	-	-	-	-	-	-	-	-	-	-	-	-	-	-	-	-
Chemicals and Allied Products	-	-	-	-	-	-	-	-	-	-	-	-	-	-	16.2	-	17.0	4.9
Industrial Chemicals	19.9	-	19.8	-0.5	19.6	-1.0	19.8	1.0	19.3	-2.5	17.9	-7.3	17.7	-1.1	17.3	-2.3	17.3	0.0
Paints and Allied Products	-	-	-	-	-	-	-	-	-	-	-	-	-	-	-	-	-	-
Drugs and Pharmaceuticals	-	-	-	-	-	-	-	-	-	-	-	-	-	-	-	-	-	-
Fats and Oils, Inedible	52.9	-	49.0	-7.4	50.5	3.1	47.1	-6.7	37.6	-20.2	25.9	-31.1	21.2	-18.1	20.9	-1.4	21.5	2.9
Agricultural Chemicals and Chemical Products	-	-	-	-	-	-	-	-	-	-	-	-	-	-	-	-	-	-
Plastic Resins and Materials	-	-	-	-	-	-	-	-	-	-	-	-	-	-	-	-	-	-
Chemicals and Allied Products n.e.c.	-	-	-	-	-	-	-	-	-	-	-	-	-	-	-	-	-	-
Rubber and Plastic Products	47.1	-	35.7	-24.2	28.3	-20.7	24.6	-13.1	21.5	-12.6	18.3	-14.9	15.9	-13.1	16.7	5.0	19.5	16.8
Rubber and Rubber Products	-	-	-	-	-	-	-	-	-	-	-	-	-	-	-	-	-	-
Plastic Products	-	-	-	-	-	-	-	-	-	-	-	-	-	-	-	-	-	-
Lumber and Wood Products	9.3	-	8.8	-5.4	8.5	-3.4	8.8	3.5	8.0	-9.1	6.5	-18.8	5.6	-13.8	6.7	19.6	7.8	16.4
Lumber	8.1	-	7.6	-6.2	7.3	-3.9	7.6	4.1	6.9	-9.2	5.6	-18.8	4.8	-14.3	5.7	18.8	6.8	19.3
Millwork	10.7	-	10.7	0.0	10.7	0.0	10.8	0.9	10.2	-5.6	8.5	-16.7	8.4	-1.2	8.8	4.8	9.2	4.5
Plywood	-	-	-	-	-	-	-	-	-	-	-	-	-	-	-	-	-	-
Wood Products n.e.c.	-	-	-	-	-	-	-	-	-	-	-	-	-	-	-	-	-	-
Logs, Bolts, Timber and Pulpwood	-	-	-	-	-	-	-	-	-	-	-	-	-	-	-	-	-	-
Prefabricated Wood Buildings & Components	-	-	-	-	-	-	-	-	-	-	-	-	-	-	-	-	-	-
Treated wood and contract Wood Preserving	-	-	-	-	-	-	-	-	-	-	-	-	-	-	-	-	-	-

Source: U.S. Department of Labor, Bureau of Labor Statistics, Division of Industry Prices and Price Indexes. n.e.c. stands for not elsewhere classified. - indicates no data collected for period or unavailable.

Producer Price Index
Annual Averages, 1935-1943
Base 1982 = 100

Columns headed % show percentile change in the index from the previous period for which an index is available.

	1935		1936		1937		1938		1939		1940		1941		1942		1943	
	Index	%	Index	%	Index	%	Index	%	Index	%	Index	%	Index	%	Index	%	Index	%
Leather	13.0	7.4	13.8	6.2	15.7	13.8	13.6	-13.4	14.2	4.4	15.0	5.6	15.8	5.3	16.4	3.8	16.4	0.0
Footwear	14.3	0.0	14.6	2.1	15.3	4.8	14.9	-2.6	15.0	0.7	15.7	4.7	16.5	5.1	18.3	10.9	18.4	0.5
Leather and Related Products n.e.c.	-	-	-	-	-	-	-	-	-	-	-	-	-	-	-	-	-	-
Fuels and Related Products and Power	7.6	0.0	7.9	3.9	8.0	1.3	7.9	-1.2	7.5	-5.1	7.4	-1.3	7.9	6.8	8.1	2.5	8.3	2.5
Coal	7.8	1.3	7.9	1.3	7.9	0.0	7.9	0.0	7.8	-1.3	7.8	0.0	8.3	6.4	8.7	4.8	9.2	5.7
Coke Oven Products	5.3	6.0	5.6	5.7	6.1	8.9	6.2	1.6	6.3	1.6	6.6	4.8	7.1	7.6	7.3	2.8	7.3	0.0
Gas Fuels	-	-	-	-	-	-	-	-	-	-	-	-	-	-	-	-	-	-
Electric Power	-	-	-	-	-	-	-	-	-	-	-	-	-	-	-	-	-	-
Utility Natural Gas	-	-	-	-	-	-	-	-	-	-	-	-	-	-	-	-	-	-
Crude Petroleum (Domestic Production)	-	-	-	-	-	-	-	-	-	-	-	-	-	-	-	-	-	-
Petroleum Products, Refined	-	-	-	-	-	-	-	-	-	-	-	-	-	-	-	-	-	-
Petroleum and Coal Products, n.e.c.	-	-	-	-	-	-	-	-	-	-	-	-	-	-	-	-	-	-
Chemicals and Allied Products	17.7	4.1	17.8	0.6	18.6	4.5	17.7	-4.8	17.6	-0.6	17.9	1.7	19.5	8.9	21.7	11.3	21.9	0.9
Industrial Chemicals	17.6	1.7	17.5	-0.6	17.5	0.0	17.2	-1.7	16.8	-2.3	16.9	0.6	17.4	3.0	19.2	10.3	19.2	0.0
Paints and Allied Products	-	-	-	-	-	-	-	-	-	-	-	-	-	-	-	-	-	-
Drugs and Pharmaceuticals	-	-	-	-	-	-	-	-	-	-	-	-	-	-	-	-	-	-
Fats and Oils, Inedible	32.7	52.1	33.5	2.4	40.7	21.5	26.2	-35.6	25.7	-1.9	23.6	-8.2	41.0	73.7	55.7	35.9	53.9	-3.2
Agricultural Chemicals and Chemical Products	-	-	-	-	-	-	-	-	-	-	-	-	-	-	-	-	-	-
Plastic Resins and Materials	-	-	-	-	-	-	-	-	-	-	-	-	-	-	-	-	-	-
Chemicals and Allied Products n.e.c.	-	-	-	-	-	-	-	-	-	-	-	-	-	-	-	-	-	-
Rubber and Plastic Products	19.6	0.5	21.1	7.7	24.9	18.0	24.4	-2.0	25.4	4.1	23.7	-6.7	25.5	7.6	29.7	16.5	30.5	2.7
Rubber and Rubber Products	-	-	-	-	-	-	-	-	-	-	-	-	-	-	-	-	-	-
Plastic Products	-	-	-	-	-	-	-	-	-	-	-	-	-	-	-	-	-	-
Lumber and Wood Products	7.5	-3.8	7.9	5.3	9.3	17.7	8.5	-8.6	8.7	2.4	9.6	10.3	11.5	19.8	12.5	8.7	13.2	5.6
Lumber	6.6	-2.9	7.0	6.1	8.1	15.7	7.1	-12.3	7.5	5.6	8.3	10.7	9.9	19.3	10.7	8.1	11.4	6.5
Millwork	9.1	-1.1	9.7	6.6	11.7	20.6	10.5	-10.3	10.3	-1.9	11.2	8.7	12.8	14.3	14.0	9.4	14.1	0.7
Plywood	-	-	-	-	-	-	-	-	-	-	-	-	-	-	-	-	-	-
Wood Products n.e.c.	-	-	-	-	-	-	-	-	-	-	-	-	-	-	-	-	-	-
Logs, Bolts, Timber and Pulpwood	-	-	-	-	-	-	-	-	-	-	-	-	-	-	-	-	-	-
Prefabricated Wood Buildings & Components	-	-	-	-	-	-	-	-	-	-	-	-	-	-	-	-	-	-
Treated wood and contract Wood Preserving	-	-	-	-	-	-	-	-	-	-	-	-	-	-	-	-	-	-

Source: U.S. Department of Labor, Bureau of Labor Statistics, Division of Industry Prices and Price Indexes. n.e.c. stands for not elsewhere classified. - indicates no data collected for period or unavailable.

Producer Price Index
Annual Averages, 1944-1952
Base 1982 = 100

Columns headed % show percentile change in the index from the previous period for which an index is available.

	1944		1945		1946		1947		1948		1949		1950		1951		1952	
	Index	%	Index	%	Index	%	Index	%	Index	%	Index	%	Index	%	Index	%	Index	%
Leather	16.4	0.0	16.5	0.6	20.7	25.5	31.4	51.7	29.9	-4.8	27.7	-7.4	31.8	14.8	37.0	16.4	26.6	-28.1
Footwear	18.4	0.0	18.4	0.0	20.4	10.9	25.8	26.5	27.6	7.0	27.2	-1.4	28.7	5.5	32.7	13.9	30.2	-7.6
Leather and Related Products n.e.c.	-	-	-	-	-	-	35.1	-	36.0	2.6	34.3	-4.7	34.5	0.6	39.5	14.5	35.4	-10.4
Fuels and Related Products and Power	8.6	3.6	8.7	1.2	9.3	6.9	11.1	19.4	13.1	18.0	12.4	-5.3	12.6	1.6	13.0	3.2	13.0	0.0
Coal	9.6	4.3	9.9	3.1	10.6	7.1	12.9	21.7	15.6	20.9	15.5	-0.6	15.6	0.6	15.9	1.9	16.0	0.6
Coke Oven Products	7.7	5.5	7.9	2.6	8.4	6.3	9.9	17.9	12.3	24.2	13.1	6.5	13.6	3.8	14.6	7.4	14.7	0.7
Gas Fuels	-	-	-	-	-	-	-	-	-	-	-	-	-	-	-	-	-	-
Electric Power	-	-	-	-	-	-	-	-	-	-	-	-	-	-	-	-	-	-
Utility Natural Gas	-	-	-	-	-	-	-	-	-	-	-	-	-	-	-	-	-	-
Crude Petroleum (Domestic Production)	-	-	-	-	-	-	-	-	-	-	-	-	-	-	-	-	-	-
Petroleum Products, Refined	-	-	-	-	-	-	9.7	-	12.2	25.8	10.7	-12.3	11.2	4.7	12.1	8.0	11.9	-1.7
Petroleum and Coal Products, n.e.c.	-	-	-	-	-	-	-	-	-	-	-	-	-	-	-	-	-	-
Chemicals and Allied Products	22.2	1.4	22.3	0.5	24.1	8.1	32.1	33.2	32.8	2.2	30.0	-8.5	30.4	1.3	34.8	14.5	33.0	-5.2
Industrial Chemicals	19.1	-0.5	19.1	0.0	19.8	3.7	23.3	17.7	24.7	6.0	22.7	-8.1	23.8	4.8	28.4	19.3	27.1	-4.6
Paints and Allied Products	-	-	-	-	-	-	-	-	-	-	-	-	-	-	-	-	-	-
Drugs and Pharmaceuticals	-	-	-	-	-	-	57.0	-	54.7	-4.0	50.7	-7.3	50.1	-1.2	51.8	3.4	50.1	-3.3
Fats and Oils, Inedible	54.0	0.2	54.0	0.0	63.4	17.4	97.6	53.9	88.7	-9.1	43.2	-51.3	52.5	21.5	67.9	29.3	38.3	-43.6
Agricultural Chemicals and Chemical Products	-	-	-	-	-	-	29.0	-	30.4	4.8	31.4	3.3	30.6	-2.5	32.5	6.2	33.1	1.8
Plastic Resins and Materials	-	-	-	-	-	-	37.4	-	37.2	-0.5	37.7	1.3	37.9	0.5	47.4	25.1	47.1	-0.6
Chemicals and Allied Products n.e.c.	-	-	-	-	-	-	31.7	-	32.5	2.5	28.6	-12.0	28.5	-0.3	31.8	11.6	29.7	-6.6
Rubber and Plastic Products	30.1	-1.3	29.2	-3.0	29.3	0.3	29.2	-0.3	30.2	3.4	29.2	-3.3	35.6	21.9	43.7	22.8	39.6	-9.4
Rubber and Rubber Products	-	-	-	-	-	-	-	-	-	-	-	-	-	-	-	-	-	-
Plastic Products	-	-	-	-	-	-	-	-	-	-	-	-	-	-	-	-	-	-
Lumber and Wood Products	14.3	8.3	14.5	1.4	16.6	14.5	25.8	55.4	29.5	14.3	27.3	-7.5	31.4	15.0	34.1	8.6	33.2	-2.6
Lumber	12.4	8.8	12.5	0.8	14.4	15.2	23.0	59.7	26.1	13.5	23.9	-8.4	27.9	16.7	30.2	8.2	29.4	-2.6
Millwork	14.6	3.5	14.7	0.7	16.6	12.9	21.3	28.3	25.7	20.7	26.3	2.3	28.0	6.5	31.7	13.2	31.0	-2.2
Plywood	-	-	-	-	-	-	47.1	-	53.5	13.6	46.8	-12.5	52.3	11.8	56.6	8.2	51.6	-8.8
Wood Products n.e.c.	-	-	-	-	-	-	-	-	-	-	-	-	-	-	-	-	-	-
Logs, Bolts, Timber and Pulpwood	-	-	-	-	-	-	-	-	-	-	-	-	-	-	-	-	-	-
Prefabricated Wood Buildings & Components	-	-	-	-	-	-	-	-	-	-	-	-	-	-	-	-	-	-
Treated wood and contract Wood Preserving	-	-	-	-	-	-	-	-	-	-	-	-	-	-	-	-	-	-

Source: U.S. Department of Labor, Bureau of Labor Statistics, Division of Industry Prices and Price Indexes. n.e.c. stands for not elsewhere classified. - indicates no data collected for period or unavailable.

Producer Price Index
Annual Averages, 1953-1961
Base 1982 = 100

Columns headed % show percentile change in the index from the previous period for which an index is available.

	1953		1954		1955		1956		1957		1958		1959		1960		1961	
	Index	%	Index	%	Index	%	Index	%	Index	%	Index	%	Index	%	Index	%	Index	%
Leather	27.7	4.1	25.3	-8.7	25.1	-0.8	27.1	8.0	26.8	-1.1	27.4	2.2	33.2	21.2	30.1	-9.3	30.9	2.7
Footwear	30.1	-0.3	30.1	0.0	30.2	0.3	32.1	6.3	32.6	1.6	32.9	0.9	34.9	6.1	35.8	2.6	35.9	0.3
Leather and Related Products n.e.c.	34.9	-1.4	34.1	-2.3	33.7	-1.2	34.6	2.7	34.4	-0.6	34.2	-0.6	38.3	12.0	37.2	-2.9	36.8	-1.1
Fuels and Related Products and Power	13.4	3.1	13.2	-1.5	13.2	0.0	13.6	3.0	14.3	5.1	13.7	-4.2	13.7	0.0	13.9	1.5	14.0	0.7
Coal	16.6	3.8	15.6	-6.0	15.4	-1.3	16.8	9.1	18.3	8.9	18.0	-1.6	18.0	0.0	17.9	-0.6	17.7	-1.1
Coke Oven Products	15.5	5.4	15.6	0.6	15.9	1.9	17.6	10.7	19.0	8.0	19.0	0.0	19.9	4.7	20.0	0.5	20.0	0.0
Gas Fuels	-	-	-	-	-	-	-	-	-	-	7.2	-	7.8	8.3	8.2	5.1	8.4	2.4
Electric Power	-	-	-	-	-	-	-	-	-	-	24.5	-	24.6	0.4	24.9	1.2	25.0	0.4
Utility Natural Gas	-	-	-	-	-	-	-	-	-	-	-	-	-	-	-	-	-	-
Crude Petroleum (Domestic Production)	-	-	-	-	-	-	-	-	-	-	-	-	-	-	-	-	-	-
Petroleum Products, Refined	12.2	2.5	11.8	-3.3	12.1	2.5	12.8	5.8	13.7	7.0	12.5	-8.8	12.4	-0.8	12.5	0.8	12.8	2.4
Petroleum and Coal Products, n.e.c.	-	-	-	-	-	-	-	-	-	-	-	-	-	-	-	-	-	-
Chemicals and Allied Products	33.4	1.2	33.8	1.2	33.7	-0.3	33.9	0.6	34.6	2.1	34.9	0.9	34.8	-0.3	34.8	0.0	34.5	-0.9
Industrial Chemicals	27.7	2.2	27.7	0.0	27.9	0.7	28.6	2.5	29.1	1.7	29.1	0.0	29.2	0.3	29.3	0.3	28.6	-2.4
Paints and Allied Products	-	-	-	-	-	-	-	-	-	-	-	-	-	-	-	-	-	-
Drugs and Pharmaceuticals	50.3	0.4	50.8	1.0	50.3	-1.0	49.9	-0.8	50.6	1.4	50.9	0.6	50.5	-0.8	50.7	0.4	49.8	-1.8
Fats and Oils, Inedible	40.3	5.2	44.2	9.7	43.3	-2.0	43.0	-0.7	46.9	9.1	47.9	2.1	43.3	-9.6	37.5	-13.4	40.3	7.5
Agricultural Chemicals and Chemical Products	33.0	-0.3	33.2	0.6	33.0	-0.6	32.5	-1.5	32.6	0.3	33.2	1.8	33.3	0.3	33.7	1.2	33.8	0.3
Plastic Resins and Materials	47.1	0.0	46.8	-0.6	44.6	-4.7	40.5	-9.2	40.6	0.2	40.0	-1.5	38.3	-4.2	38.2	-0.3	36.5	-4.5
Chemicals and Allied Products n.e.c.	29.7	0.0	31.2	5.1	31.5	1.0	32.4	2.9	33.6	3.7	34.3	2.1	34.6	0.9	34.7	0.3	35.0	0.9
Rubber and Plastic Products	36.9	-6.8	37.5	1.6	42.4	13.1	43.0	1.4	42.8	-0.5	42.8	0.0	42.6	-0.5	42.7	0.2	41.1	-3.7
Rubber and Rubber Products	-	-	-	-	-	-	-	-	-	-	-	-	-	-	-	-	-	-
Plastic Products	-	-	-	-	-	-	-	-	-	-	-	-	-	-	-	-	-	-
Lumber and Wood Products	33.1	-0.3	32.5	-1.8	34.1	4.9	34.6	1.5	32.8	-5.2	32.5	-0.9	34.7	6.8	33.5	-3.5	32.0	-4.5
Lumber	29.1	-1.0	28.6	-1.7	30.4	6.3	31.1	2.3	29.2	-6.1	28.8	-1.4	31.0	7.6	29.6	-4.5	28.1	-5.1
Millwork	32.1	3.5	31.8	-0.9	31.4	-1.3	31.5	0.3	31.3	-0.6	31.2	-0.3	33.1	6.1	33.3	0.6	32.5	-2.4
Plywood	53.8	4.3	50.7	-5.8	51.9	2.4	50.0	-3.7	47.4	-5.2	47.8	0.8	49.8	4.2	47.2	-5.2	46.2	-2.1
Wood Products n.e.c.	-	-	-	-	-	-	-	-	-	-	-	-	-	-	-	-	-	-
Logs, Bolts, Timber and Pulpwood	-	-	-	-	-	-	-	-	-	-	-	-	-	-	-	-	-	-
Prefabricated Wood Buildings & Components	-	-	-	-	-	-	-	-	-	-	-	-	-	-	-	-	-	-
Treated wood and contract Wood Preserving	-	-	-	-	-	-	-	-	-	-	-	-	-	-	-	-	-	-

Source: U.S. Department of Labor, Bureau of Labor Statistics, Division of Industry Prices and Price Indexes. n.e.c. stands for not elsewhere classified. - indicates no data collected for period or unavailable.

Producer Price Index
Annual Averages, 1962-1970
Base 1982 = 100

Columns headed % show percentile change in the index from the previous period for which an index is available.

	1962		1963		1964		1965		1966		1967		1968		1969		1970	
	Index	%	Index	%	Index	%	Index	%	Index	%	Index	%	Index	%	Index	%	Index	%
Leather	31.6	2.3	29.7	-6.0	30.0	1.0	31.5	5.0	35.3	12.1	32.1	-9.1	32.8	2.2	34.9	6.4	34.6	-0.9
Footwear	36.3	1.1	36.2	-0.3	36.3	0.3	37.0	1.9	39.5	6.8	40.8	3.3	42.8	4.9	44.7	4.4	46.2	3.4
Leather and Related Products n.e.c.	37.2	1.1	37.1	-0.3	36.8	-0.8	37.8	2.7	40.8	7.9	40.4	-1.0	40.2	-0.5	41.8	4.0	43.0	2.9
Fuels and Related Products and Power	14.0	0.0	13.9	-0.7	13.5	-2.9	13.8	2.2	14.1	2.2	14.4	2.1	14.3	-0.7	14.6	2.1	15.3	4.8
Coal	17.5	-1.1	17.5	0.0	17.5	0.0	17.5	0.0	17.9	2.3	18.7	4.5	19.4	3.7	21.1	8.8	28.1	33.2
Coke Oven Products	20.0	0.0	20.0	0.0	20.6	3.0	20.8	1.0	21.2	1.9	21.7	2.4	22.4	3.2	23.6	5.4	27.6	16.9
Gas Fuels	8.4	0.0	8.7	3.6	8.5	-2.3	8.7	2.4	9.1	4.6	9.4	3.3	8.7	-7.4	8.8	1.1	9.8	11.4
Electric Power	25.1	0.4	24.9	-0.8	24.7	-0.8	24.6	-0.4	24.5	-0.4	24.6	0.4	24.8	0.8	25.0	0.8	26.1	4.4
Utility Natural Gas	-	-	-	-	-	-	-	-	-	-	-	-	-	-	-	-	-	-
Crude Petroleum (Domestic Production)	-	-	-	-	-	-	-	-	-	-	-	-	-	-	-	-	-	-
Petroleum Products, Refined	12.6	-1.6	12.5	-0.8	11.9	-4.8	12.3	3.4	12.8	4.1	13.1	2.3	12.9	-1.5	13.1	1.6	13.3	1.5
Petroleum and Coal Products, n.e.c.	-	-	-	-	-	-	-	-	-	-	-	-	-	-	-	-	-	-
Chemicals and Allied Products	33.9	-1.7	33.5	-1.2	33.6	0.3	33.9	0.9	34.0	0.3	34.2	0.6	34.1	-0.3	34.2	0.3	35.0	2.3
Industrial Chemicals	28.1	-1.7	27.6	-1.8	27.4	-0.7	27.7	1.1	27.9	0.7	28.4	1.8	28.6	0.7	28.4	-0.7	28.6	0.7
Paints and Allied Products	-	-	-	-	-	-	-	-	-	-	-	-	-	-	-	-	-	-
Drugs and Pharmaceuticals	48.6	-2.4	48.2	-0.8	48.1	-0.2	47.8	-0.6	47.8	0.0	47.6	-0.4	47.3	-0.6	47.6	0.6	48.2	1.3
Fats and Oils, Inedible	35.1	-12.9	37.0	5.4	44.6	20.5	51.9	16.4	47.3	-8.9	37.4	-20.9	34.0	-9.1	40.9	20.3	49.7	21.5
Agricultural Chemicals and Chemical Products	33.6	-0.6	33.1	-1.5	32.9	-0.6	33.6	2.1	33.9	0.9	34.2	0.9	32.9	-3.8	29.6	-10.0	30.3	2.4
Plastic Resins and Materials	36.3	-0.5	35.6	-1.9	35.3	-0.8	35.0	-0.8	35.3	0.9	35.3	0.0	32.4	-8.2	31.9	-1.5	32.0	0.3
Chemicals and Allied Products n.e.c.	34.9	-0.3	35.3	1.1	35.6	0.8	36.0	1.1	36.4	1.1	37.0	1.6	37.6	1.6	38.6	2.7	40.2	4.1
Rubber and Plastic Products	39.9	-2.9	40.1	0.5	39.6	-1.2	39.7	0.3	40.5	2.0	41.4	2.2	42.8	3.4	43.6	1.9	44.9	3.0
Rubber and Rubber Products	-	-	-	-	-	-	-	-	-	-	37.3	-	38.6	3.5	39.3	1.8	41.1	4.6
Plastic Products	-	-	-	-	-	-	-	-	-	-	-	-	-	-	-	-	-	-
Lumber and Wood Products	32.2	0.6	32.8	1.9	33.5	2.1	33.7	0.6	35.2	4.5	35.1	-0.3	39.8	13.4	44.0	10.6	39.9	-9.3
Lumber	28.6	1.8	29.3	2.4	29.9	2.0	30.2	1.0	32.2	6.6	32.2	0.0	37.8	17.4	42.3	11.9	36.6	-13.5
Millwork	32.5	0.0	33.2	2.2	34.6	4.2	34.4	-0.6	35.1	2.0	35.8	2.0	37.9	5.9	42.2	11.3	41.5	-1.7
Plywood	44.6	-3.5	45.1	1.1	44.6	-1.1	44.6	0.0	44.8	0.4	43.1	-3.8	49.8	15.5	52.8	6.0	46.7	-11.6
Wood Products n.e.c.	-	-	-	-	-	-	-	-	41.6	-	42.3	1.7	44.4	5.0	47.7	7.4	49.7	4.2
Logs, Bolts, Timber and Pulpwood	-	-	-	-	-	-	-	-	-	-	-	-	-	-	-	-	-	-
Prefabricated Wood Buildings & Components	-	-	-	-	-	-	-	-	-	-	-	-	-	-	-	-	-	-
Treated wood and contract Wood Preserving	-	-	-	-	-	-	-	-	-	-	-	-	-	-	-	-	-	-

Source: U.S. Department of Labor, Bureau of Labor Statistics, Division of Industry Prices and Price Indexes. n.e.c. stands for not elsewhere classified. - indicates no data collected for period or unavailable.

Producer Price Index
Annual Averages, 1971-1979
Base 1982 = 100

Columns headed % show percentile change in the index from the previous period for which an index is available.

	1971		1972		1973		1974		1975		1976		1977		1978		1979	
	Index	%	Index	%	Index	%	Index	%	Index	%	Index	%	Index	%	Index	%	Index	%
Leather	36.2	4.6	45.1	24.6	51.4	14.0	49.6	-3.5	48.7	-1.8	60.4	24.0	64.6	7.0	76.6	18.6	114.6	49.6
Footwear	47.7	3.2	50.8	6.5	53.3	4.9	57.1	7.1	60.3	5.6	64.8	7.5	68.8	6.2	74.7	8.6	89.0	19.1
Leather and Related Products n.e.c.	43.8	1.9	47.6	8.7	52.5	10.3	55.2	5.1	57.0	3.3	61.8	8.4	66.0	6.8	71.5	8.3	82.9	15.9
Fuels and Related Products and Power	16.6	8.5	17.1	3.0	19.4	13.5	30.1	55.2	35.4	17.6	38.3	8.2	43.6	13.8	46.5	6.7	58.9	26.7
Coal	34.0	21.0	36.2	6.5	40.8	12.7	62.2	52.5	72.2	16.1	68.9	-4.6	72.8	5.7	80.4	10.4	84.3	4.9
Coke Oven Products	32.2	16.7	33.7	4.7	36.1	7.1	53.7	48.8	71.7	33.5	75.1	4.7	82.2	9.5	89.2	8.5	93.0	4.3
Gas Fuels	10.2	4.1	10.8	5.9	11.9	10.2	15.3	28.6	20.4	33.3	27.0	32.4	36.6	35.6	40.4	10.4	51.3	27.0
Electric Power	28.6	9.6	29.9	4.5	31.8	6.4	40.1	26.1	47.6	18.7	51.1	7.4	57.3	12.1	61.6	7.5	66.5	8.0
Utility Natural Gas	-	-	-	-	-	-	-	-	-	-	-	-	-	-	-	-	-	-
Crude Petroleum (Domestic Production)	-	-	-	-	-	-	-	-	-	-	-	-	-	-	-	-	-	-
Petroleum Products, Refined	14.1	6.0	14.3	1.4	16.9	18.2	29.3	73.4	33.8	15.4	36.3	7.4	40.5	11.6	42.2	4.2	58.4	38.4
Petroleum and Coal Products, n.e.c.	-	-	-	-	-	-	-	-	-	-	-	-	-	-	-	-	-	-
Chemicals and Allied Products	35.6	1.7	35.6	0.0	37.6	5.6	50.2	33.5	62.0	23.5	64.0	3.2	65.9	3.0	68.0	3.2	76.0	11.8
Industrial Chemicals	28.9	1.0	28.7	-0.7	29.3	2.1	43.0	46.8	58.7	36.5	62.2	6.0	63.5	2.1	64.0	0.8	74.9	17.0
Paints and Allied Products	39.5	-	-	-	-	-	-	-	60.5	53.2	64.3	6.3	68.5	6.5	71.4	4.2	78.5	9.9
Drugs and Pharmaceuticals	48.8	1.2	49.0	0.4	49.6	1.2	53.6	8.1	60.3	12.5	63.8	5.8	66.9	4.9	70.5	5.4	75.9	7.7
Fats and Oils, Inedible	50.0	0.6	43.4	-13.2	85.5	97.0	126.6	48.1	95.5	-24.6	93.6	-2.0	104.5	11.6	118.3	13.2	141.0	19.2
Agricultural Chemicals and Chemical Products	31.5	4.0	31.4	-0.3	33.0	5.1	47.1	42.7	69.6	47.8	64.4	-7.5	64.2	-0.3	67.8	5.6	73.3	8.1
Plastic Resins and Materials	31.3	-2.2	31.3	0.0	32.5	3.8	50.7	56.0	63.8	25.8	68.4	7.2	69.7	1.9	70.5	1.1	83.2	18.0
Chemicals and Allied Products n.e.c.	41.5	3.2	42.0	1.2	43.7	4.0	54.6	24.9	62.4	14.3	63.2	1.3	65.1	3.0	67.3	3.4	71.0	5.5
Rubber and Plastic Products	45.2	0.7	45.3	0.2	46.6	2.9	56.4	21.0	62.2	10.3	66.0	6.1	69.4	5.2	72.4	4.3	80.5	11.2
Rubber and Rubber Products	41.9	1.9	42.5	1.4	44.1	3.8	51.5	16.8	56.7	10.1	60.9	7.4	64.9	6.6	69.2	6.6	78.1	12.9
Plastic Products	48.5	-	-	-	-	-	-	-	68.7	41.6	71.5	4.1	74.5	4.2	-	-	83.1	11.5
Lumber and Wood Products	44.7	12.0	50.7	13.4	62.2	22.7	64.5	3.7	62.1	-3.7	72.2	16.3	83.0	15.0	96.9	16.7	105.5	8.9
Lumber	43.8	19.7	51.3	17.1	66.0	28.7	66.6	0.9	61.9	-7.1	75.0	21.2	89.0	18.7	103.7	16.5	114.0	9.9
Millwork	43.2	4.1	46.0	6.5	51.6	12.2	56.2	8.9	57.4	2.1	63.3	10.3	69.3	9.5	84.3	21.6	91.0	7.9
Plywood	49.4	5.8	56.3	14.0	66.9	18.8	69.4	3.7	69.4	0.0	80.6	16.1	91.4	13.4	101.5	11.1	107.9	6.3
Wood Products n.e.c.	50.3	1.2	52.8	5.0	63.4	20.1	70.5	11.2	68.5	-2.8	70.4	2.8	78.0	10.8	89.7	15.0	99.7	11.1
Logs, Bolts, Timber and Pulpwood	-	-	-	-	-	-	-	-	-	-	-	-	-	-	-	-	-	-
Prefabricated Wood Buildings & Components	-	-	-	-	-	-	-	-	-	-	-	-	-	-	-	-	-	-
Treated wood and contract Wood Preserving	-	-	-	-	-	-	-	-	-	-	-	-	-	-	-	-	-	-

Source: U.S. Department of Labor, Bureau of Labor Statistics, Division of Industry Prices and Price Indexes. n.e.c. stands for not elsewhere classified. - indicates no data collected for period or unavailable.

Producer Price Index
Annual Averages, 1980-1988
Base 1982 = 100

Columns headed % show percentile change in the index from the previous period for which an index is available.

	1980 Index	%	1981 Index	%	1982 Index	%	1983 Index	%	1984 Index	%	1985 Index	%	1986 Index	%	1987 Index	%	1988 Index	%
Leather	99.8	-12.9	102.7	2.9	100.0	-2.6	106.2	6.2	119.6	12.6	113.4	-5.2	122.9	8.4	140.9	14.6	167.5	18.9
Footwear	95.2	7.0	98.3	3.3	100.0	1.7	102.1	2.1	102.7	0.6	104.8	2.0	106.9	2.0	109.4	2.3	115.1	5.2
Leather and Related Products n.e.c.	88.3	6.5	97.7	10.6	100.0	2.4	102.2	2.2	106.6	4.3	110.3	3.5	110.3	0.0	113.0	2.4	119.1	5.4
Fuels and Related Products and Power	82.8	40.6	100.2	21.0	100.0	-0.2	95.9	-4.1	94.8	-1.1	91.4	-3.6	69.8	-23.6	70.2	0.6	66.7	-5.0
Coal	87.4	3.7	93.0	6.4	100.0	7.5	100.5	0.5	102.2	1.7	102.2	0.0	100.8	-1.4	97.1	-3.7	95.4	-1.8
Coke Oven Products	93.3	0.3	98.8	5.9	100.0	1.2	96.3	-3.7	94.5	-1.9	93.2	-1.4	88.0	-5.6	82.8	-5.9	84.9	2.5
Gas Fuels	71.7	39.8	88.6	23.6	100.0	12.9	108.1	8.1	104.5	-3.3	98.7	-5.6	83.2	-15.7	74.1	-10.9	71.4	-3.6
Electric Power	79.1	18.9	90.3	14.2	100.0	10.7	102.8	2.8	108.2	5.3	111.6	3.1	112.6	0.9	110.6	-1.8	111.2	0.5
Utility Natural Gas	-	-	-	-	-	-	-	-	-	-	-	-	-	-	-	-	-	-
Crude Petroleum (Domestic Production)	-	-	-	-	-	-	-	-	-	-	-	-	-	-	-	-	-	-
Petroleum Products, Refined	88.6	51.7	105.9	19.5	100.0	-5.6	89.9	-10.1	87.4	-2.8	83.2	-4.8	53.2	-36.1	56.8	6.8	53.9	-5.1
Petroleum and Coal Products, n.e.c.	-	-	-	-	-	-	-	-	-	-	100.5	-	77.1	-23.3	63.7	-17.4	66.4	4.2
Chemicals and Allied Products	89.0	17.1	98.4	10.6	100.0	1.6	100.3	0.3	102.9	2.6	103.7	0.8	102.6	-1.1	106.4	3.7	116.3	9.3
Industrial Chemicals	91.9	22.7	103.1	12.2	100.0	-3.0	97.3	-2.7	96.8	-0.5	96.0	-0.8	91.5	-4.7	95.5	4.4	106.8	11.8
Paints and Allied Products	89.7	14.3	-	-	100.0	11.5	100.5	0.5	105.1	4.6	106.7	1.5	105.7	-0.9	107.4	1.6	113.1	5.3
Drugs and Pharmaceuticals	83.0	9.4	92.1	11.0	100.0	8.6	107.6	7.6	114.2	6.1	122.0	6.8	130.1	6.6	139.1	6.9	148.4	6.7
Fats and Oils, Inedible	111.6	-20.9	110.7	-0.8	100.0	-9.7	106.9	6.9	139.1	30.1	110.6	-20.5	80.1	-27.6	92.7	15.7	110.9	19.6
Agricultural Chemicals and Chemical Products	87.9	19.9	97.4	10.8	100.0	2.7	95.9	-4.1	97.4	1.6	96.2	-1.2	94.2	-2.1	96.4	2.3	104.5	8.4
Plastic Resins and Materials	98.5	18.4	102.0	3.6	100.0	-2.0	102.8	2.8	108.9	5.9	107.5	-1.3	104.4	-2.9	110.3	5.7	132.4	20.0
Chemicals and Allied Products n.e.c.	83.1	17.0	94.1	13.2	100.0	6.3	101.3	1.3	102.7	1.4	105.2	2.4	105.8	0.6	107.0	1.1	111.9	4.6
Rubber and Plastic Products	90.1	11.9	96.4	7.0	100.0	3.7	100.8	0.8	102.3	1.5	101.9	-0.4	101.9	0.0	103.0	1.1	109.3	6.1
Rubber and Rubber Products	88.7	13.6	95.7	7.9	100.0	4.5	99.3	-0.7	99.4	0.1	98.7	-0.7	98.1	-0.6	99.4	1.3	103.6	4.2
Plastic Products	91.5	10.1	97.1	6.1	100.0	3.0	102.3	2.3	105.5	3.1	105.4	-0.1	106.1	0.7	107.3	1.1	115.0	7.2
Lumber and Wood Products	101.5	-3.8	102.8	1.3	100.0	-2.7	107.9	7.9	108.0	0.1	106.6	-1.3	107.2	0.6	112.8	5.2	118.9	5.4
Lumber	104.9	-8.0	104.6	-0.3	100.0	-4.4	113.5	13.5	112.5	-0.9	109.6	-2.6	110.5	0.8	118.2	7.0	122.1	3.3
Millwork	93.2	2.4	97.8	4.9	100.0	2.2	108.2	8.2	110.2	1.8	111.7	1.4	113.7	1.8	117.7	3.5	121.9	3.6
Plywood	106.2	-1.6	105.9	-0.3	100.0	-5.6	105.2	5.2	104.1	-1.0	99.6	-4.3	101.4	1.8	102.6	1.2	103.4	0.8
Wood Products n.e.c.	101.2	1.5	101.2	0.0	100.0	-1.2	97.6	-2.4	99.3	1.7	100.1	0.8	100.9	0.8	103.7	2.8	107.2	3.4
Logs, Bolts, Timber and Pulpwood	-	-	-	-	100.0	-	96.6	-3.4	97.0	0.4	96.0	-1.0	92.3	-3.9	101.8	10.3	117.7	15.6
Prefabricated Wood Buildings & Components	-	-	-	-	-	-	-	-	-	-	101.4	-	104.1	2.7	105.5	1.3	108.2	2.6
Treated wood and contract Wood Preserving	-	-	-	-	-	-	-	-	-	-	-	-	98.0	-	98.8	0.8	102.2	3.4

Source: U.S. Department of Labor, Bureau of Labor Statistics, Division of Industry Prices and Price Indexes. n.e.c. stands for not elsewhere classified. - indicates no data collected for period or unavailable.

Producer Price Index
Annual Averages, 1989-1995
Base 1982 = 100

Columns headed % show percentile change in the index from the previous period for which an index is available.

	1989		1990		1991		1992		1993		1994		1995					
	Index	%	Index	%	Index	%	Index	%	Index	%	Index	%	Index	%	Index	%	Index	%
Leather	170.4	1.7	177.5	4.2	168.4	-5.1	163.7	-2.8	168.6	3.0	179.6	6.5	191.2	6.5				
Footwear	120.8	5.0	125.6	4.0	128.6	2.4	132.0	2.6	134.4	1.8	135.5	0.8	139.1	2.7				
Leather and Related Products n.e.c.	123.1	3.4	128.9	4.7	132.6	2.9	134.9	1.7	136.3	1.0	136.8	0.4	138.9	1.5				
Fuels and Related Products and Power	72.9	9.3	82.3	12.9	81.2	-1.3	80.4	-1.0	80.0	-0.5	77.8	-2.8	77.9	0.1				
Coal	95.5	0.1	97.5	2.1	97.2	-0.3	95.0	-2.3	96.1	1.2	96.7	0.6	94.9	-1.9				
Coke Oven Products	89.9	5.9	91.4	1.7	93.9	2.7	91.3	-2.8	89.2	-2.3	88.6	-0.7	92.0	3.8				
Gas Fuels	75.3	5.5	78.4	4.1	77.0	-1.8	75.9	-1.4	78.5	3.4	72.8	-7.3	64.8	-11.0				
Electric Power	114.8	3.2	117.6	2.4	124.3	5.7	126.3	1.6	128.6	1.8	128.7	0.1	130.9	1.7				
Utility Natural Gas	-	-	-	-	97.2	-	98.6	1.4	104.1	5.6	104.4	0.3	98.8	-5.4				
Crude Petroleum (Domestic Production)	-	-	-	-	-	-	58.0	-	51.4	-11.4	47.1	-8.4	51.0	8.3				
Petroleum Products, Refined	61.2	13.5	74.8	22.2	67.2	-10.2	64.7	-3.7	62.0	-4.2	59.1	-4.7	60.6	2.5				
Petroleum and Coal Products, n.e.c.	65.0	-2.1	67.3	3.5	63.6	-5.5	58.8	-7.5	66.4	12.9	65.8	-0.9	69.8	6.1				
Chemicals and Allied Products	123.0	5.8	123.6	0.5	125.6	1.6	125.9	0.2	128.2	1.8	132.1	3.0	142.6	7.9				
Industrial Chemicals	114.8	7.5	113.2	-1.4	111.8	-1.2	109.3	-2.2	110.4	1.0	114.3	3.5	128.6	12.5				
Paints and Allied Products	122.6	8.4	128.5	4.8	131.6	2.4	131.0	-0.5	132.2	0.9	133.9	1.3	141.0	5.3				
Drugs and Pharmaceuticals	160.0	7.8	170.8	6.7	182.6	6.9	192.2	5.3	200.9	4.5	206.0	2.5	210.7	2.3				
Fats and Oils, Inedible	95.5	-13.9	88.1	-7.7	86.8	-1.5	93.0	7.1	95.6	2.8	110.6	15.7	126.8	14.6				
Agricultural Chemicals and Chemical Products	108.7	4.0	107.4	-1.2	111.7	4.0	110.3	-1.3	109.9	-0.4	119.9	9.1	130.0	8.4				
Plastic Resins and Materials	133.4	0.8	124.1	-7.0	120.0	-3.3	116.4	-3.0	117.1	0.6	122.4	4.5	143.9	17.6				
Chemicals and Allied Products n.e.c.	117.3	4.8	118.9	1.4	121.5	2.2	123.3	1.5	125.5	1.8	127.1	1.3	130.7	2.8				
Rubber and Plastic Products	112.6	3.0	113.6	0.9	115.1	1.3	115.1	0.0	116.0	0.8	117.6	1.4	124.3	5.7				
Rubber and Rubber Products	107.0	3.3	108.6	1.5	109.6	0.9	109.8	0.2	110.8	0.9	111.9	1.0	117.1	4.6				
Plastic Products	118.3	2.9	119.0	0.6	120.8	1.5	120.7	-0.1	121.6	0.7	123.5	1.6	131.0	6.1				
Lumber and Wood Products	126.7	6.6	129.7	2.4	132.1	1.9	146.6	11.0	174.0	18.7	180.0	3.4	178.2	-1.0				
Lumber	125.7	2.9	124.6	-0.9	124.9	0.2	144.7	15.9	183.4	26.7	188.4	2.7	173.7	-7.8				
Millwork	127.3	-4.4	130.4	2.4	135.5	3.9	143.3	5.8	156.6	9.3	162.4	3.7	163.8	0.9				
Plywood	115.9	12.1	114.2	-1.5	114.3	0.1	133.3	16.6	152.8	14.6	158.6	3.8	165.3	4.2				
Wood Products n.e.c.	113.1	5.5	114.7	1.4	118.6	3.4	124.5	5.0	135.3	8.7	137.7	1.8	143.6	4.3				
Logs, Bolts, Timber and Pulpwood	131.9	12.1	142.8	8.3	144.1	0.9	164.8	14.4	212.3	28.8	219.1	3.2	220.4	0.6				
Prefabricated Wood Buildings & Components	110.7	2.3	113.1	2.2	118.2	4.5	122.8	3.9	132.5	7.9	141.6	6.9	147.8	4.4				
Treated wood and contract Wood Preserving	109.7	7.3	112.6	2.6	115.6	2.7	123.5	6.8	138.1	11.8	149.0	7.9	149.2	0.1				

Source: U.S. Department of Labor, Bureau of Labor Statistics, Division of Industry Prices and Price Indexes. n.e.c. stands for not elsewhere classified. - indicates no data collected for period or unavailable.

Producer Price Index
Annual Averages, 1926-1934
Base 1982 = 100

Columns headed % show percentile change in the index from the previous period for which an index is available.

	1926		1927		1928		1929		1930		1931		1932		1933		1934	
	Index	%	Index	%	Index	%	Index	%	Index	%	Index	%	Index	%	Index	%	Index	%
Pulp, Paper, and Allied Products	-	-	-	-	-	-	-	-	-	-	-	-	-	-	-	-	-	-
Pulp, Paper, and Products, Ex. Building Paper	-	-	-	-	-	-	-	-	-	-	-	-	-	-	-	-	-	-
Building Paper & Building Board Mill Products	-	-	-	-	-	-	-	-	-	-	-	-	-	-	-	-	-	-
Publications, Printed Matter & Printing Materials	-	-	-	-	-	-	-	-	-	-	-	-	-	-	-	-	-	-
Metals and Metal Products	13.7	-	12.9	-5.8	12.9	0.0	13.3	3.1	12.0	-9.8	10.8	-10.0	9.9	-8.3	10.2	3.0	11.2	9.8
Iron and Steel	11.3	-	10.6	-6.2	10.6	0.0	10.7	0.9	10.1	-5.6	9.4	-6.9	9.0	-4.3	8.9	-1.1	9.8	10.1
Nonferrous Metals	16.5	-	15.3	-7.3	15.5	1.3	17.5	12.9	13.6	-22.3	10.2	-25.0	8.2	-19.6	9.8	19.5	11.2	14.3
Metal Containers	15.2	-	15.2	0.0	14.7	-3.3	14.9	1.4	14.7	-1.3	14.1	-4.1	13.5	-4.3	12.6	-6.7	14.5	15.1
Hardware	-	-	-	-	-	-	-	-	-	-	-	-	-	-	-	-	-	-
Plumbing Fixtures and Brass Fittings	26.2	-	23.4	-10.7	23.8	1.7	22.5	-5.5	21.3	-5.3	20.1	-5.6	16.4	-18.4	16.1	-1.8	16.8	4.3
Heating Equipment	-	-	-	-	-	-	-	-	-	-	-	-	-	-	-	-	-	-
Fabricated Structural Metal Products	-	-	-	-	-	-	-	-	-	-	-	-	-	-	-	-	-	-
Miscellaneous Metal Products	-	-	-	-	-	-	-	-	-	-	-	-	-	-	-	-	-	-
Metal Treatment Services	-	-	-	-	-	-	-	-	-	-	-	-	-	-	-	-	-	-
Machinery and Equipment	-	-	-	-	-	-	-	-	-	-	-	-	-	-	-	-	-	-
Agricultural Machinery and Equipment	14.1	-	14.1	0.0	14.0	-0.7	13.9	-0.7	13.4	-3.6	13.0	-3.0	12.0	-7.7	11.8	-1.7	12.7	7.6
Construction Machinery and Equipment	-	-	-	-	-	-	-	-	-	-	-	-	-	-	-	-	-	-
Metalworking Machinery and Equipment	-	-	-	-	-	-	-	-	-	-	-	-	-	-	-	-	-	-
General Purpose Machinery and Equipment	-	-	-	-	-	-	-	-	-	-	-	-	-	-	-	-	-	-
Electronic Computers and Computer Equipment	-	-	-	-	-	-	-	-	-	-	-	-	-	-	-	-	-	-
Special Industry Machinery and Equipment	-	-	-	-	-	-	-	-	-	-	-	-	-	-	-	-	-	-
Electrical Machinery and Equipment	-	-	-	-	-	-	-	-	-	-	-	-	-	-	-	-	-	-
Miscellaneous Instruments	-	-	-	-	-	-	-	-	-	-	-	-	-	-	-	-	-	-
Miscellaneous Machinery	-	-	-	-	-	-	-	-	-	-	-	-	-	-	-	-	-	-
Furniture and Household Durables	28.6	-	27.9	-2.4	27.2	-2.5	27.0	-0.7	26.5	-1.9	24.4	-7.9	21.5	-11.9	21.6	0.5	23.4	8.3
Household Furniture	22.9	-	22.3	-2.6	22.1	-0.9	21.7	-1.8	21.5	-0.9	20.1	-6.5	17.1	-14.9	17.2	0.6	18.1	5.2
Commercial Furniture	-	-	-	-	-	-	-	-	-	-	-	-	-	-	-	-	-	-

Source: U.S. Department of Labor, Bureau of Labor Statistics, Division of Industry Prices and Price Indexes. n.e.c. stands for not elsewhere classified. - indicates no data collected for period or unavailable.

Producer Price Index
Annual Averages, 1935-1943
Base 1982 = 100

Columns headed % show percentile change in the index from the previous period for which an index is available.

	1935		1936		1937		1938		1939		1940		1941		1942		1943	
	Index	%	Index	%	Index	%	Index	%	Index	%	Index	%	Index	%	Index	%	Index	%
Pulp, Paper, and Allied Products	-	-	-	-	-	-	-	-	-	-	-	-	-	-	-	-	-	-
Pulp, Paper, and Products, Ex. Building Paper	-	-	-	-	-	-	-	-	-	-	-	-	-	-	-	-	-	-
Building Paper & Building Board Mill Products	-	-	-	-	-	-	-	-	-	-	-	-	-	-	-	-	-	-
Publications, Printed Matter & Printing Materials	-	-	-	-	-	-	-	-	-	-	-	-	-	-	-	-	-	-
Metals and Metal Products	11.2	0.0	11.4	1.8	13.1	14.9	12.6	-3.8	12.5	-0.8	12.5	0.0	12.8	2.4	13.0	1.6	12.9	-0.8
Iron and Steel	9.8	0.0	9.9	1.0	11.1	12.1	11.1	0.0	10.8	-2.7	10.7	-0.9	10.9	1.9	11.0	0.9	11.0	0.0
Nonferrous Metals	11.3	0.9	11.8	4.4	14.8	25.4	12.0	-18.9	12.9	7.5	13.4	3.9	13.9	3.7	14.1	1.4	14.2	0.7
Metal Containers	14.4	-0.7	14.5	0.7	13.5	-6.9	14.4	6.7	13.8	-4.2	13.5	-2.2	13.6	0.7	13.8	1.5	13.8	0.0
Hardware	-	-	-	-	-	-	-	-	-	-	-	-	-	-	-	-	-	-
Plumbing Fixtures and Brass Fittings	14.7	-12.5	16.8	14.3	17.1	1.8	16.9	-1.2	16.9	0.0	17.9	5.9	18.3	2.2	20.3	10.9	19.7	-3.0
Heating Equipment	-	-	-	-	-	-	-	-	-	-	-	-	-	-	-	-	-	-
Fabricated Structural Metal Products	-	-	-	-	-	-	-	-	-	-	-	-	-	-	-	-	-	-
Miscellaneous Metal Products	-	-	-	-	-	-	-	-	-	-	-	-	-	-	-	-	-	-
Metal Treatment Services	-	-	-	-	-	-	-	-	-	-	-	-	-	-	-	-	-	-
Machinery and Equipment	-	-	-	-	-	-	-	-	14.8	-	14.9	0.7	15.1	1.3	15.4	2.0	15.2	-1.3
Agricultural Machinery and Equipment	13.2	3.9	13.3	0.8	13.3	0.0	13.5	1.5	13.2	-2.2	13.1	-0.8	13.2	0.8	13.7	3.8	13.7	0.0
Construction Machinery and Equipment	-	-	-	-	-	-	-	-	9.3	-	9.5	2.2	10.0	5.3	10.3	3.0	10.3	0.0
Metalworking Machinery and Equipment	-	-	-	-	-	-	-	-	-	-	-	-	-	-	-	-	-	-
General Purpose Machinery and Equipment	-	-	-	-	-	-	-	-	13.3	-	13.3	0.0	13.6	2.3	13.7	0.7	13.4	-2.2
Electronic Computers and Computer Equipment	-	-	-	-	-	-	-	-	-	-	-	-	-	-	-	-	-	-
Special Industry Machinery and Equipment	-	-	-	-	-	-	-	-	-	-	-	-	-	-	-	-	-	-
Electrical Machinery and Equipment	-	-	-	-	-	-	-	-	19.6	-	19.5	-0.5	19.6	0.5	19.6	0.0	19.5	-0.5
Miscellaneous Instruments	-	-	-	-	-	-	-	-	-	-	-	-	-	-	-	-	-	-
Miscellaneous Machinery	-	-	-	-	-	-	-	-	-	-	-	-	-	-	-	-	-	-
Furniture and Household Durables	23.2	-0.9	23.6	1.7	26.1	10.6	25.5	-2.3	25.4	-0.4	26.0	2.4	27.6	6.2	29.9	8.3	29.7	-0.7
Household Furniture	17.7	-2.2	17.8	0.6	19.7	10.7	19.0	-3.6	18.6	-2.1	18.7	0.5	20.2	8.0	22.3	10.4	22.4	0.4
Commercial Furniture	-	-	-	-	-	-	-	-	-	-	-	-	-	-	-	-	-	-

Source: U.S. Department of Labor, Bureau of Labor Statistics, Division of Industry Prices and Price Indexes. n.e.c. stands for not elsewhere classified. - indicates no data collected for period or unavailable.

Producer Price Index
Annual Averages, 1944-1952
Base 1982 = 100

Columns headed % show percentile change in the index from the previous period for which an index is available.

	1944		1945		1946		1947		1948		1949		1950		1951		1952	
	Index	%	Index	%	Index	%	Index	%	Index	%	Index	%	Index	%	Index	%	Index	%
Pulp, Paper, and Allied Products	-	-	-	-	-	-	25.1	-	26.2	4.4	25.1	-4.2	25.7	2.4	30.5	18.7	29.7	-2.6
Pulp, Paper, and Products, Ex. Building Paper	-	-	-	-	-	-	26.6	-	27.7	4.1	26.5	-4.3	27.1	2.3	32.2	18.8	31.4	-2.5
Building Paper & Building Board Mill Products	-	-	-	-	-	-	29.4	-	32.5	10.5	32.9	1.2	34.0	3.3	35.9	5.6	36.5	1.7
Publications, Printed Matter & Printing Materials	-	-	-	-	-	-	-	-	-	-	-	-	-	-	-	-	-	-
Metals and Metal Products	12.9	0.0	13.1	1.6	14.7	12.2	18.2	23.8	20.7	13.7	20.9	1.0	22.0	5.3	24.5	11.4	24.5	0.0
Iron and Steel	11.0	0.0	11.2	1.8	12.4	10.7	15.1	21.8	17.6	16.6	17.8	1.1	19.1	7.3	20.8	8.9	21.0	1.0
Nonferrous Metals	14.1	-0.7	14.1	0.0	16.3	15.6	22.4	37.4	24.8	10.7	23.1	-6.9	24.4	5.6	29.1	19.3	28.9	-0.7
Metal Containers	13.8	0.0	13.8	0.0	14.2	2.9	16.0	12.7	17.8	11.2	19.3	8.4	19.4	0.5	21.5	10.8	21.6	0.5
Hardware	-	-	-	-	-	-	17.2	-	18.7	8.7	19.6	4.8	21.1	7.7	23.3	10.4	23.2	-0.4
Plumbing Fixtures and Brass Fittings	19.0	-3.6	18.8	-1.1	20.1	6.9	24.0	19.4	26.1	8.7	26.1	0.0	27.4	5.0	31.1	13.5	29.8	-4.2
Heating Equipment	-	-	-	-	-	-	35.8	-	38.0	6.1	38.9	2.4	39.4	1.3	43.0	9.1	42.7	-0.7
Fabricated Structural Metal Products	-	-	-	-	-	-	22.6	-	23.9	5.8	23.5	-1.7	24.3	3.4	27.4	12.8	26.8	-2.2
Miscellaneous Metal Products	-	-	-	-	-	-	18.0	-	22.2	23.3	23.9	7.7	24.7	3.3	26.8	8.5	26.7	-0.4
Metal Treatment Services	-	-	-	-	-	-	-	-	-	-	-	-	-	-	-	-	-	-
Machinery and Equipment	15.1	-0.7	15.1	0.0	16.6	9.9	19.3	16.3	20.9	8.3	21.9	4.8	22.6	3.2	25.3	11.9	25.3	0.0
Agricultural Machinery and Equipment	13.7	0.0	13.8	0.7	14.8	7.2	17.1	15.5	19.2	12.3	20.5	6.8	21.0	2.4	22.8	8.6	23.0	0.9
Construction Machinery and Equipment	10.3	0.0	10.4	1.0	11.3	8.7	12.8	13.3	14.5	13.3	15.4	6.2	15.8	2.6	17.6	11.4	17.9	1.7
Metalworking Machinery and Equipment	-	-	-	-	-	-	14.3	-	15.4	7.7	16.2	5.2	17.2	6.2	19.2	11.6	19.5	1.6
General Purpose Machinery and Equipment	13.4	0.0	13.4	0.0	14.4	7.5	16.7	16.0	18.2	9.0	19.2	5.5	19.9	3.6	22.2	11.6	22.0	-0.9
Electronic Computers and Computer Equipment	-	-	-	-	-	-	-	-	-	-	-	-	-	-	-	-	-	-
Special Industry Machinery and Equipment	-	-	-	-	-	-	-	-	-	-	-	-	-	-	-	-	-	-
Electrical Machinery and Equipment	19.2	-1.5	19.3	0.5	22.0	14.0	26.9	22.3	28.1	4.5	28.8	2.5	29.8	3.5	34.1	14.4	33.6	-1.5
Miscellaneous Instruments	-	-	-	-	-	-	-	-	-	-	-	-	-	-	-	-	-	-
Miscellaneous Machinery	-	-	-	-	-	-	21.7	-	23.4	7.8	24.3	3.8	24.8	2.1	27.6	11.3	27.6	0.0
Furniture and Household Durables	30.5	2.7	30.5	0.0	32.4	6.2	37.2	14.8	39.4	5.9	40.1	1.8	40.9	2.0	44.4	8.6	43.5	-2.0
Household Furniture	23.1	3.1	23.4	1.3	25.0	6.8	29.9	19.6	32.2	7.7	31.8	-1.2	32.9	3.5	36.4	10.6	35.3	-3.0
Commercial Furniture	-	-	-	-	-	-	20.1	-	21.5	7.0	22.2	3.3	23.4	5.4	26.5	13.2	26.2	-1.1

Source: U.S. Department of Labor, Bureau of Labor Statistics, Division of Industry Prices and Price Indexes. n.e.c. stands for not elsewhere classified. - indicates no data collected for period or unavailable.

Producer Price Index
Annual Averages, 1953-1961
Base 1982 = 100

Columns headed % show percentile change in the index from the previous period for which an index is available.

	1953		1954		1955		1956		1957		1958		1959		1960		1961	
	Index	%	Index	%	Index	%	Index	%	Index	%	Index	%	Index	%	Index	%	Index	%
Pulp, Paper, and Allied Products	29.6	-0.3	29.6	0.0	30.4	2.7	32.4	6.6	33.0	1.9	33.4	1.2	33.7	0.9	34.0	0.9	33.0	-2.9
Pulp, Paper, and Products, Ex. Building Paper	31.2	-0.6	31.2	0.0	32.0	2.6	34.1	6.6	34.8	2.1	35.2	1.1	35.4	0.6	35.8	1.1	34.7	-3.1
Building Paper & Building Board Mill Products	38.4	5.2	40.4	5.2	41.4	2.5	43.3	4.6	44.8	3.5	45.3	1.1	46.3	2.2	46.1	-0.4	45.8	-0.7
Publications, Printed Matter & Printing Materials	-	-	-	-	-	-	-	-	-	-	-	-	-	-	-	-	-	-
Metals and Metal Products	25.3	3.3	25.5	0.8	27.2	6.7	29.6	8.8	30.2	2.0	30.0	-0.7	30.6	2.0	30.6	0.0	30.5	-0.3
Iron and Steel	22.1	5.2	22.4	1.4	23.7	5.8	26.1	10.1	28.0	7.3	28.4	1.4	29.0	2.1	28.6	-1.4	28.7	0.3
Nonferrous Metals	29.3	1.4	29.1	-0.7	33.5	15.1	36.6	9.3	32.2	-12.0	30.0	-6.8	31.9	6.3	32.6	2.2	31.5	-3.4
Metal Containers	22.6	4.6	23.2	2.7	23.6	1.7	25.1	6.4	26.8	6.8	27.6	3.0	27.2	-1.4	27.3	0.4	27.8	1.8
Hardware	24.5	5.6	25.7	4.9	27.1	5.4	28.8	6.3	30.5	5.9	31.6	3.6	32.0	1.3	32.2	0.6	32.5	0.9
Plumbing Fixtures and Brass Fittings	29.4	-1.3	30.0	2.0	31.8	6.0	34.0	6.9	33.0	-2.9	31.4	-4.8	33.0	5.1	33.5	1.5	33.5	0.0
Heating Equipment	43.1	0.9	42.9	-0.5	43.2	0.7	44.6	3.2	45.7	2.5	45.3	-0.9	45.5	0.4	44.6	-2.0	42.9	-3.8
Fabricated Structural Metal Products	27.0	0.7	27.3	1.1	28.5	4.4	30.9	8.4	31.2	1.0	31.2	0.0	31.1	-0.3	31.4	1.0	30.8	-1.9
Miscellaneous Metal Products	26.8	0.4	26.9	0.4	27.4	1.9	28.9	5.5	31.0	7.3	31.2	0.6	31.2	0.0	31.3	0.3	32.1	2.6
Metal Treatment Services	-	-	-	-	-	-	-	-	-	-	-	-	-	-	-	-	-	-
Machinery and Equipment	25.9	2.4	26.3	1.5	27.2	3.4	29.3	7.7	31.4	7.2	32.1	2.2	32.8	2.2	33.0	0.6	33.0	0.0
Agricultural Machinery and Equipment	23.2	0.9	23.1	-0.4	23.3	0.9	24.2	3.9	25.3	4.5	26.3	4.0	27.2	3.4	27.7	1.8	28.2	1.8
Construction Machinery and Equipment	18.4	2.8	18.7	1.6	19.5	4.3	21.1	8.2	22.7	7.6	23.6	4.0	24.5	3.8	25.0	2.0	25.4	1.6
Metalworking Machinery and Equipment	19.8	1.5	20.1	1.5	21.2	5.5	23.2	9.4	24.6	6.0	25.2	2.4	25.8	2.4	26.5	2.7	26.8	1.1
General Purpose Machinery and Equipment	22.6	2.7	23.1	2.2	24.1	4.3	26.5	10.0	28.4	7.2	28.8	1.4	29.7	3.1	30.0	1.0	29.8	-0.7
Electronic Computers and Computer Equipment	-	-	-	-	-	-	-	-	-	-	-	-	-	-	-	-	-	-
Special Industry Machinery and Equipment	-	-	-	-	-	-	-	-	-	-	-	-	-	-	-	-	26.5	-
Electrical Machinery and Equipment	34.5	2.7	35.2	2.0	35.8	1.7	38.7	8.1	41.6	7.5	42.5	2.2	43.1	1.4	43.0	-0.2	42.4	-1.4
Miscellaneous Instruments	-	-	-	-	-	-	-	-	-	-	-	-	-	-	-	-	-	-
Miscellaneous Machinery	28.3	2.5	29.0	2.5	29.8	2.8	31.6	6.0	33.5	6.0	34.2	2.1	34.5	0.9	34.7	0.6	35.1	1.2
Furniture and Household Durables	44.4	2.1	44.9	1.1	45.1	0.4	46.3	2.7	47.5	2.6	47.9	0.8	48.0	0.2	47.8	-0.4	47.5	-0.6
Household Furniture	35.6	0.8	35.5	-0.3	35.6	0.3	37.2	4.5	38.3	3.0	38.5	0.5	38.8	0.8	39.2	1.0	39.6	1.0
Commercial Furniture	26.6	1.5	27.0	1.5	28.1	4.1	30.2	7.5	32.1	6.3	32.9	2.5	33.1	0.6	33.4	0.9	33.2	-0.6

Source: U.S. Department of Labor, Bureau of Labor Statistics, Division of Industry Prices and Price Indexes. n.e.c. stands for not elsewhere classified. - indicates no data collected for period or unavailable.

Producer Price Index
Annual Averages, 1962-1970
Base 1982 = 100

Columns headed % show percentile change in the index from the previous period for which an index is available.

	1962		1963		1964		1965		1966		1967		1968		1969		1970	
	Index	%	Index	%	Index	%	Index	%	Index	%	Index	%	Index	%	Index	%	Index	%
Pulp, Paper, and Allied Products	33.4	1.2	33.1	-0.9	33.0	-0.3	33.3	0.9	34.2	2.7	34.6	1.2	35.0	1.2	36.0	2.9	37.5	4.2
Pulp, Paper, and Products, Ex. Building Paper	35.2	1.4	34.9	-0.9	34.9	0.0	35.2	0.9	36.2	2.8	36.6	1.1	37.0	1.1	38.1	3.0	39.7	4.2
Building Paper & Building Board Mill Products	44.2	-3.5	43.6	-1.4	42.7	-2.1	42.1	-1.4	42.1	0.0	41.8	-0.7	42.1	0.7	44.1	4.8	42.2	-4.3
Publications, Printed Matter & Printing Materials	-	-	-	-	-	-	-	-	-	-	-	-	-	-	-	-	-	-
Metals and Metal Products	30.2	-1.0	30.3	0.3	31.1	2.6	32.0	2.9	32.8	2.5	33.2	1.2	34.0	2.4	36.0	5.9	38.7	7.5
Iron and Steel	28.3	-1.4	28.2	-0.4	28.6	1.4	28.9	1.0	29.1	0.7	29.5	1.4	30.1	2.0	31.6	5.0	34.0	7.6
Nonferrous Metals	31.1	-1.3	31.1	0.0	33.2	6.8	36.2	9.0	37.9	4.7	37.9	0.0	39.3	3.7	43.1	9.7	47.3	9.7
Metal Containers	28.2	1.4	28.5	1.1	28.7	0.7	29.3	2.1	29.9	2.0	30.4	1.7	31.6	3.9	32.5	2.8	34.3	5.5
Hardware	32.6	0.3	32.6	0.0	32.9	0.9	33.2	0.9	34.4	3.6	35.7	3.8	36.6	2.5	37.9	3.6	39.8	5.0
Plumbing Fixtures and Brass Fittings	32.5	-3.0	32.5	0.0	32.8	0.9	33.5	2.1	35.2	5.1	35.9	2.0	37.1	3.3	38.5	3.8	39.9	3.6
Heating Equipment	42.4	-1.2	42.2	-0.5	41.8	-0.9	41.7	-0.2	42.1	1.0	42.2	0.2	43.3	2.6	44.4	2.5	46.6	5.0
Fabricated Structural Metal Products	30.6	-0.6	30.6	0.0	30.9	1.0	31.5	1.9	32.4	2.9	32.8	1.2	33.5	2.1	34.7	3.6	36.7	5.8
Miscellaneous Metal Products	32.3	0.6	32.7	1.2	33.8	3.4	34.0	0.6	34.7	2.1	35.4	2.0	36.1	2.0	38.0	5.3	40.5	6.6
Metal Treatment Services	-	-	-	-	-	-	-	-	-	-	-	-	-	-	-	-	-	-
Machinery and Equipment	33.0	0.0	33.1	0.3	33.3	0.6	33.7	1.2	34.7	3.0	35.9	3.5	37.0	3.1	38.2	3.2	40.0	4.7
Agricultural Machinery and Equipment	28.8	2.1	29.2	1.4	29.6	1.4	30.2	2.0	31.1	3.0	32.1	3.2	33.4	4.0	34.9	4.5	36.4	4.3
Construction Machinery and Equipment	25.4	0.0	25.9	2.0	26.5	2.3	27.2	2.6	28.1	3.3	29.1	3.6	30.7	5.5	32.1	4.6	33.7	5.0
Metalworking Machinery and Equipment	27.2	1.5	27.3	0.4	27.8	1.8	28.6	2.9	29.9	4.5	31.2	4.3	32.4	3.8	33.7	4.0	35.6	5.6
General Purpose Machinery and Equipment	29.9	0.3	30.1	0.7	30.2	0.3	30.4	0.7	31.8	4.6	32.9	3.5	34.0	3.3	35.2	3.5	37.4	6.3
Electronic Computers and Computer Equipment	-	-	-	-	-	-	-	-	-	-	-	-	-	-	-	-	-	-
Special Industry Machinery and Equipment	26.9	1.5	27.4	1.9	27.9	1.8	28.4	1.8	29.5	3.9	30.8	4.4	32.4	5.2	33.8	4.3	35.6	5.3
Electrical Machinery and Equipment	41.8	-1.4	41.3	-1.2	41.1	-0.5	41.1	0.0	42.0	2.2	43.2	2.9	43.7	1.2	44.4	1.6	45.9	3.4
Miscellaneous Instruments	-	-	-	-	-	-	-	-	-	-	-	-	-	-	-	-	-	-
Miscellaneous Machinery	35.2	0.3	35.3	0.3	35.6	0.8	35.8	0.6	36.3	1.4	37.3	2.8	38.9	4.3	40.3	3.6	42.0	4.2
Furniture and Household Durables	47.2	-0.6	46.9	-0.6	47.1	0.4	46.8	-0.6	47.4	1.3	48.3	1.9	49.7	2.9	50.7	2.0	51.9	2.4
Household Furniture	40.0	1.0	40.3	0.7	40.6	0.7	40.9	0.7	42.0	2.7	43.5	3.6	45.2	3.9	47.2	4.4	48.6	3.0
Commercial Furniture	33.4	0.6	33.5	0.3	33.7	0.6	33.9	0.6	34.5	1.8	36.3	5.2	37.7	3.9	39.2	4.0	41.6	6.1

Source: U.S. Department of Labor, Bureau of Labor Statistics, Division of Industry Prices and Price Indexes. n.e.c. stands for not elsewhere classified. - indicates no data collected for period or unavailable.

Producer Price Index
Annual Averages, 1971-1979
Base 1982 = 100

Columns headed % show percentile change in the index from the previous period for which an index is available.

	1971		1972		1973		1974		1975		1976		1977		1978		1979	
	Index	%	Index	%	Index	%	Index	%	Index	%	Index	%	Index	%	Index	%	Index	%
Pulp, Paper, and Allied Products	38.1	1.6	39.3	3.1	42.3	7.6	52.5	24.1	59.0	12.4	62.1	5.3	64.6	4.0	67.7	4.8	75.9	12.1
Pulp, Paper, and Products, Ex. Building Paper	40.4	1.8	41.6	3.0	44.8	7.7	55.9	24.8	62.9	12.5	66.2	5.2	68.6	3.6	71.6	4.4	80.6	12.6
Building Paper & Building Board Mill Products	42.9	1.7	44.4	3.5	47.1	6.1	51.6	9.6	53.1	2.9	57.9	9.0	65.6	13.3	78.2	19.2	76.2	-2.6
Publications, Printed Matter & Printing Materials	-	-	-	-	-	-	-	-	-	-	-	-	-	-	-	-	-	-
Metals and Metal Products	39.4	1.8	40.9	3.8	44.0	7.6	57.0	29.5	61.5	7.9	65.0	5.7	69.3	6.6	75.3	8.7	86.0	14.2
Iron and Steel	35.9	5.6	37.9	5.6	40.2	6.1	52.7	31.1	59.3	12.5	63.7	7.4	68.0	6.8	74.8	10.0	83.6	11.8
Nonferrous Metals	43.5	-8.0	44.3	1.8	51.2	15.6	71.0	38.7	65.1	-8.3	68.9	5.8	74.1	7.5	78.8	6.3	99.3	26.0
Metal Containers	37.1	8.2	39.2	5.7	41.0	4.6	50.1	22.2	58.5	16.8	61.5	5.1	66.4	8.0	74.1	11.6	81.9	10.5
Hardware	41.7	4.8	42.9	2.9	44.5	3.7	50.2	12.8	58.2	15.9	61.8	6.2	66.2	7.1	71.5	8.0	78.0	9.1
Plumbing Fixtures and Brass Fittings	41.8	4.8	43.0	2.9	45.1	4.9	53.5	18.6	58.2	8.8	62.5	7.4	67.0	7.2	71.4	6.6	77.9	9.1
Heating Equipment	48.6	4.3	49.8	2.5	50.8	2.0	56.9	12.0	63.5	11.6	66.6	4.9	69.8	4.8	73.5	5.3	78.9	7.3
Fabricated Structural Metal Products	38.8	5.7	40.2	3.6	41.8	4.0	52.9	26.6	62.0	17.2	63.6	2.6	67.8	6.6	74.3	9.6	81.6	9.8
Miscellaneous Metal Products	42.1	4.0	44.0	4.5	45.9	4.3	55.7	21.4	64.1	15.1	66.2	3.3	69.5	5.0	75.1	8.1	81.9	9.1
Metal Treatment Services	-	-	-	-	-	-	-	-	-	-	-	-	-	-	-	-	-	-
Machinery and Equipment	41.4	3.5	42.3	2.2	43.7	3.3	50.0	14.4	57.9	15.8	61.3	5.9	65.2	6.4	70.3	7.8	76.7	9.1
Agricultural Machinery and Equipment	37.8	3.8	39.3	4.0	40.5	3.1	46.2	14.1	54.2	17.3	58.8	8.5	63.6	8.2	68.5	7.7	74.6	8.9
Construction Machinery and Equipment	35.4	5.0	36.6	3.4	38.0	3.8	44.3	16.6	53.8	21.4	57.8	7.4	62.1	7.4	67.7	9.0	74.5	10.0
Metalworking Machinery and Equipment	36.7	3.1	37.5	2.2	39.1	4.3	45.8	17.1	53.5	16.8	56.9	6.4	61.9	8.8	67.6	9.2	75.2	11.2
General Purpose Machinery and Equipment	39.2	4.8	40.3	2.8	41.8	3.7	49.7	18.9	58.7	18.1	62.4	6.3	66.4	6.4	71.2	7.2	77.8	9.3
Electronic Computers and Computer Equipment	-	-	-	-	-	-	-	-	-	-	-	-	-	-	-	-	-	-
Special Industry Machinery and Equipment	37.2	4.5	38.0	2.2	40.0	5.3	46.4	16.0	53.8	15.9	58.0	7.8	62.3	7.4	68.6	10.1	76.0	10.8
Electrical Machinery and Equipment	47.1	2.6	47.7	1.3	48.5	1.7	54.0	11.3	60.7	12.4	63.4	4.4	66.6	5.0	71.2	6.9	77.2	8.4
Miscellaneous Instruments	-	-	-	-	-	-	-	-	-	-	-	-	-	-	-	-	-	-
Miscellaneous Machinery	43.7	4.0	44.8	2.5	46.2	3.1	52.0	12.6	60.5	16.3	64.1	6.0	67.3	5.0	72.5	7.7	77.8	7.3
Furniture and Household Durables	53.1	2.3	53.8	1.3	55.7	3.5	61.8	11.0	67.5	9.2	70.3	4.1	73.2	4.1	77.5	5.9	82.8	6.8
Household Furniture	50.0	2.9	51.0	2.0	53.5	4.9	59.4	11.0	63.6	7.1	66.8	5.0	70.6	5.7	75.5	6.9	81.0	7.3
Commercial Furniture	42.9	3.1	43.6	1.6	47.0	7.8	55.3	17.7	60.5	9.4	63.0	4.1	67.5	7.1	73.1	8.3	80.5	10.1

Source: U.S. Department of Labor, Bureau of Labor Statistics, Division of Industry Prices and Price Indexes. n.e.c. stands for not elsewhere classified. - indicates no data collected for period or unavailable.

Producer Price Index
Annual Averages, 1980-1988
Base 1982 = 100

Columns headed % show percentile change in the index from the previous period for which an index is available.

	1980		1981		1982		1983		1984		1985		1986		1987		1988	
	Index	%	Index	%	Index	%	Index	%	Index	%	Index	%	Index	%	Index	%	Index	%
Pulp, Paper, and Allied Products	86.3	13.7	94.8	9.8	100.0	5.5	103.3	3.3	110.3	6.8	113.3	2.7	116.1	2.5	121.8	4.9	130.4	7.1
Pulp, Paper, and Products, Ex. Building Paper	91.7	13.8	99.1	8.1	100.0	0.9	99.3	-0.7	107.3	8.1	106.9	-0.4	107.6	0.7	114.3	6.2	124.9	9.3
Building Paper & Building Board Mill Products	86.1	13.0	96.7	12.3	100.0	3.4	104.4	4.4	108.2	3.6	107.4	-0.7	108.8	1.3	111.2	2.2	113.3	1.9
Publications, Printed Matter & Printing Materials	-	-	91.4	-	100.0	9.4	106.3	6.3	112.7	6.0	118.7	5.3	123.3	3.9	128.1	3.9	134.7	5.2
Metals and Metal Products	95.0	10.5	99.6	4.8	100.0	0.4	101.8	1.8	104.8	2.9	104.4	-0.4	103.2	-1.1	107.1	3.8	118.7	10.8
Iron and Steel	90.0	7.7	98.5	9.4	100.0	1.5	101.3	1.3	105.3	3.9	104.8	-0.5	101.1	-3.5	104.6	3.5	115.7	10.6
Nonferrous Metals	115.7	16.5	108.4	-6.3	100.0	-7.7	104.7	4.7	105.1	0.4	99.6	-5.2	98.5	-1.1	108.8	10.5	133.2	22.4
Metal Containers	90.9	11.0	96.1	5.7	100.0	4.1	102.1	2.1	106.5	4.3	109.0	2.3	110.2	1.1	109.5	-0.6	110.2	0.6
Hardware	85.8	10.0	93.9	9.4	100.0	6.5	103.7	3.7	105.9	2.1	109.1	3.0	109.5	0.4	109.6	0.1	113.7	3.7
Plumbing Fixtures and Brass Fittings	88.5	13.6	96.0	8.5	100.0	4.2	103.8	3.8	108.6	4.6	111.9	3.0	115.5	3.2	119.7	3.6	128.7	7.5
Heating Equipment	87.0	10.3	94.5	8.6	100.0	5.8	102.7	2.7	106.6	3.8	109.5	2.7	113.0	3.2	115.5	2.2	119.2	3.2
Fabricated Structural Metal Products	88.8	8.8	96.9	9.1	100.0	3.2	99.6	-0.4	101.9	2.3	103.2	1.3	103.6	0.4	105.4	1.7	114.3	8.4
Miscellaneous Metal Products	88.5	8.1	95.8	8.2	100.0	4.4	100.5	0.5	104.6	4.1	107.1	2.4	107.0	-0.1	107.8	0.7	112.1	4.0
Metal Treatment Services	-	-	-	-	-	-	-	-	-	-	102.4	-	104.7	2.2	106.2	1.4	109.8	3.4
Machinery and Equipment	86.0	12.1	94.4	9.8	100.0	5.9	102.7	2.7	105.1	2.3	107.2	2.0	108.8	1.5	110.4	1.5	113.2	2.5
Agricultural Machinery and Equipment	83.3	11.7	92.7	11.3	100.0	7.9	104.9	4.9	108.0	3.0	108.7	0.6	109.2	0.5	109.6	0.4	112.7	2.8
Construction Machinery and Equipment	84.2	13.0	93.3	10.8	100.0	7.2	102.3	2.3	103.8	1.5	105.4	1.5	106.7	1.2	108.9	2.1	111.8	2.7
Metalworking Machinery and Equipment	85.5	13.7	93.9	9.8	100.0	6.5	101.7	1.7	104.1	2.4	106.6	2.4	108.4	1.7	110.1	1.6	113.5	3.1
General Purpose Machinery and Equipment	87.0	11.8	95.0	9.2	100.0	5.3	101.4	1.4	103.3	1.9	105.7	2.3	107.2	1.4	108.3	1.0	112.8	4.2
Electronic Computers and Computer Equipment	-	-	-	-	-	-	-	-	-	-	-	-	-	-	-	-	-	-
Special Industry Machinery and Equipment	84.8	11.6	94.7	11.7	100.0	5.6	103.7	3.7	107.3	3.5	110.8	3.3	114.2	3.1	117.3	2.7	121.7	3.8
Electrical Machinery and Equipment	87.1	12.8	95.1	9.2	100.0	5.2	103.7	3.7	107.4	3.6	109.6	2.0	111.2	1.5	112.6	1.3	114.5	1.7
Miscellaneous Instruments	-	-	91.9	-	100.0	8.8	105.3	5.3	106.6	1.2	109.8	3.0	112.7	2.6	115.7	2.7	118.9	2.8
Miscellaneous Machinery	85.7	10.2	94.1	9.8	100.0	6.3	102.1	2.1	102.2	0.1	103.3	1.1	104.2	0.9	105.7	1.4	108.6	2.7
Furniture and Household Durables	90.7	9.5	95.9	5.7	100.0	4.3	103.4	3.4	105.7	2.2	107.1	1.3	108.2	1.0	109.9	1.6	113.1	2.9
Household Furniture	89.1	10.0	95.4	7.1	100.0	4.8	102.1	2.1	105.3	3.1	108.5	3.0	110.3	1.7	113.0	2.4	117.6	4.1
Commercial Furniture	85.7	6.5	93.5	9.1	100.0	7.0	103.9	3.9	107.8	3.8	111.9	3.8	115.3	3.0	118.6	2.9	124.2	4.7

Source: U.S. Department of Labor, Bureau of Labor Statistics, Division of Industry Prices and Price Indexes. n.e.c. stands for not elsewhere classified. - indicates no data collected for period or unavailable.

Producer Price Index
Annual Averages, 1989-1995
Base 1982 = 100

Columns headed % show percentile change in the index from the previous period for which an index is available.

	1989		1990		1991		1992		1993		1994		1995					
	Index	%	Index	%	Index	%	Index	%	Index	%	Index	%	Index	%	Index	%	Index	%
Pulp, Paper, and Allied Products	137.8	5.7	141.2	2.5	142.9	1.2	145.2	1.6	147.3	1.4	152.5	3.5	172.2	12.9				
Pulp, Paper, and Products, Ex. Building Paper	132.4	6.0	132.9	0.4	129.8	-2.3	129.2	-0.5	127.6	-1.2	133.1	4.3	163.4	22.8				
Building Paper & Building Board Mill Products	115.6	2.0	112.2	-2.9	111.8	-0.4	119.6	7.0	132.7	11.0	144.1	8.6	145.3	0.8				
Publications, Printed Matter & Printing Materials	142.1	5.5	148.4	4.4	154.8	4.3	159.6	3.1	164.9	3.3	169.6	2.9	179.8	6.0				
Metals and Metal Products	124.1	4.5	122.9	-1.0	120.2	-2.2	119.2	-0.8	119.2	0.0	124.8	4.7	134.5	7.8				
Iron and Steel	119.1	2.9	117.2	-1.6	114.1	-2.6	111.5	-2.3	116.0	4.0	122.0	5.2	128.8	5.6				
Nonferrous Metals	141.5	6.2	133.8	-5.4	123.4	-7.8	120.9	-2.0	114.4	-5.4	126.6	10.7	149.6	18.2				
Metal Containers	111.5	1.2	114.0	2.2	115.5	1.3	113.9	-1.4	109.7	-3.7	108.1	-1.5	117.2	8.4				
Hardware	120.4	5.9	125.9	4.6	130.2	3.4	132.7	1.9	135.2	1.9	137.5	1.7	141.1	2.6				
Plumbing Fixtures and Brass Fittings	137.7	7.0	144.3	4.8	149.7	3.7	153.1	2.3	155.9	1.8	159.6	2.4	166.0	4.0				
Heating Equipment	125.1	4.9	131.6	5.2	134.1	1.9	137.3	2.4	140.4	2.3	142.5	1.5	147.5	3.5				
Fabricated Structural Metal Products	120.3	5.2	121.8	1.2	122.4	0.5	122.1	-0.2	123.2	0.9	127.3	3.3	135.0	6.0				
Miscellaneous Metal Products	117.0	4.4	119.4	2.1	120.4	0.8	121.4	0.8	122.3	0.7	123.6	1.1	125.9	1.9				
Metal Treatment Services	114.5	4.3	116.3	1.6	117.4	0.9	118.2	0.7	119.8	1.4	121.4	1.3	123.4	1.6				
Machinery and Equipment	117.4	3.7	120.7	2.8	123.0	1.9	123.4	0.3	124.0	0.5	125.1	0.9	126.5	1.1				
Agricultural Machinery and Equipment	117.7	4.4	121.7	3.4	125.7	3.3	129.5	3.0	133.6	3.2	137.0	2.5	142.6	4.1				
Construction Machinery and Equipment	117.2	4.8	121.6	3.8	125.2	3.0	128.7	2.8	132.0	2.6	133.7	1.3	136.7	2.2				
Metalworking Machinery and Equipment	118.2	4.1	123.0	4.1	127.6	3.7	130.9	2.6	133.5	2.0	136.5	2.2	139.9	2.5				
General Purpose Machinery and Equipment	119.0	5.5	123.7	3.9	127.8	3.3	129.9	1.6	132.2	1.8	134.8	2.0	139.0	3.1				
Electronic Computers and Computer Equipment	-	-	-	-	88.9	-	73.2	-17.7	62.2	-15.0	57.0	-8.4	52.2	-8.4				
Special Industry Machinery and Equipment	127.0	4.4	131.5	3.5	135.9	3.3	139.5	2.6	143.7	3.0	146.2	1.7	149.9	2.5				
Electrical Machinery and Equipment	117.5	2.6	119.3	1.5	120.8	1.3	121.3	0.4	122.5	1.0	123.4	0.7	124.2	0.6				
Miscellaneous Instruments	122.5	3.0	126.7	3.4	130.3	2.8	133.7	2.6	137.8	3.1	139.6	1.3	141.0	1.0				
Miscellaneous Machinery	112.7	3.8	116.7	3.5	120.3	3.1	121.7	1.2	122.7	0.8	124.7	1.6	127.0	1.8				
Furniture and Household Durables	116.9	3.4	119.2	2.0	121.2	1.7	122.2	0.8	123.7	1.2	126.1	1.9	128.1	1.6				
Household Furniture	121.8	3.6	125.1	2.7	128.0	2.3	130.0	1.6	133.4	2.6	138.0	3.4	141.8	2.8				
Commercial Furniture	129.0	3.9	133.4	3.4	136.2	2.1	138.1	1.4	140.5	1.7	144.7	3.0	148.2	2.4				

Source: U.S. Department of Labor, Bureau of Labor Statistics, Division of Industry Prices and Price Indexes. n.e.c. stands for not elsewhere classified. - indicates no data collected for period or unavailable.

Producer Price Index
Annual Averages, 1926-1934
Base 1982 = 100

Columns headed % show percentile change in the index from the previous period for which an index is available.

	1926		1927		1928		1929		1930		1931		1932		1933		1934	
	Index	%	Index	%	Index	%	Index	%	Index	%	Index	%	Index	%	Index	%	Index	%
Floor Coverings	31.7	-	30.3	-4.4	29.7	-2.0	29.7	0.0	30.0	1.0	25.4	-15.3	22.7	-10.6	23.6	4.0	25.8	9.3
Household Appliances	-	-	-	-	-	-	-	-	-	-	-	-	-	-	-	-	-	-
Home Electronic Equipment	-	-	-	-	-	-	-	-	-	-	-	-	-	-	-	-	-	-
Household Durable Goods n.e.c.	-	-	-	-	-	-	-	-	-	-	-	-	-	-	-	-	-	-
Nonmetallic Mineral Products	16.4	-	15.7	-4.3	16.2	3.2	16.0	-1.2	15.9	-0.6	14.9	-6.3	13.9	-6.7	14.7	5.8	15.7	6.8
Glass	-	-	-	-	-	-	-	-	-	-	-	-	-	-	-	-	-	-
Concrete Ingredients and Related Products	14.9	-	14.5	-2.7	16.4	13.1	16.5	0.6	16.6	0.6	15.1	-9.0	14.4	-4.6	15.6	8.3	16.6	6.4
Concrete Products	23.7	-	23.7	0.0	23.7	0.0	23.3	-1.7	23.6	1.3	22.3	-5.5	20.5	-8.1	20.9	2.0	20.9	0.0
Clay Construction Products Ex. Refractories	-	-	-	-	-	-	-	-	-	-	-	-	-	-	-	-	-	-
Refractories	-	-	-	-	-	-	-	-	-	-	-	-	-	-	-	-	-	-
Asphalt Felts and Coatings	21.2	-	20.0	-5.7	17.9	-10.5	15.8	-11.7	16.1	1.9	16.7	3.7	15.3	-8.4	15.7	2.6	16.9	7.6
Gypsum Products	-	-	-	-	-	-	-	-	-	-	-	-	-	-	-	-	-	-
Glass Containers	-	-	-	-	-	-	-	-	-	-	-	-	-	-	-	-	-	-
Nonmetallic Minerals	-	-	-	-	-	-	-	-	-	-	-	-	-	-	-	-	-	-
Transportation Equipment	-	-	-	-	-	-	-	-	-	-	-	-	-	-	-	-	-	-
Motor Vehicles and Equipment	16.7	-	16.0	-4.2	16.2	1.3	16.7	3.1	15.7	-6.0	14.9	-5.1	14.5	-2.7	13.9	-4.1	14.6	5.0
Aircraft and Aircraft Equipment	-	-	-	-	-	-	-	-	-	-	-	-	-	-	-	-	-	-
Ships and Boats	-	-	-	-	-	-	-	-	-	-	-	-	-	-	-	-	-	-
Railroad Equipment	-	-	-	-	-	-	-	-	-	-	-	-	-	-	-	-	-	-
Transportation Equipment, n.e.c.	-	-	-	-	-	-	-	-	-	-	-	-	-	-	-	-	-	-
Miscellaneous Products	-	-	-	-	-	-	-	-	-	-	-	-	-	-	-	-	-	-
Toys, Sporting Goods, Small Arms, etc.	-	-	-	-	-	-	-	-	-	-	-	-	-	-	-	-	-	-
Tobacco Products, Incl. Stemmed & Redried	-	-	-	-	-	-	-	-	-	-	-	-	-	-	-	-	-	-
Notions	-	-	-	-	-	-	-	-	-	-	-	-	-	-	-	-	-	-
Photographic Equipment and Supplies	-	-	-	-	-	-	-	-	-	-	-	-	-	-	-	-	-	-
Mobile Homes	-	-	-	-	-	-	-	-	-	-	-	-	-	-	-	-	-	-
Medical, Surgical & Personal Aid Devices	-	-	-	-	-	-	-	-	-	-	-	-	-	-	-	-	-	-
Industrial Safety Equipment	-	-	-	-	-	-	-	-	-	-	-	-	-	-	-	-	-	-
Mining Services	-	-	-	-	-	-	-	-	-	-	-	-	-	-	-	-	-	-
Miscellaneous Products n.e.c.	-	-	-	-	-	-	-	-	-	-	-	-	-	-	-	-	-	-

Source: U.S. Department of Labor, Bureau of Labor Statistics, Division of Industry Prices and Price Indexes. n.e.c. stands for not elsewhere classified. - indicates no data collected for period or unavailable.

Producer Price Index
Annual Averages, 1935-1943
Base 1982 = 100

Columns headed % show percentile change in the index from the previous period for which an index is available.

	1935		1936		1937		1938		1939		1940		1941		1942		1943	
	Index	%	Index	%	Index	%	Index	%	Index	%	Index	%	Index	%	Index	%	Index	%
Floor Coverings	26.2	1.6	26.3	0.4	29.5	12.2	28.2	-4.4	28.9	2.5	31.2	8.0	32.1	2.9	33.2	3.4	33.2	0.0
Household Appliances	-	-	-	-	-	-	-	-	-	-	-	-	-	-	-	-	-	-
Home Electronic Equipment	-	-	-	-	-	-	-	-	-	-	-	-	-	-	-	-	-	-
Household Durable Goods n.e.c.	-	-	-	-	-	-	-	-	-	-	-	-	-	-	-	-	-	-
Nonmetallic Mineral Products	15.7	0.0	15.8	0.6	16.1	1.9	15.6	-3.1	15.3	-1.9	15.3	0.0	15.7	2.6	16.3	3.8	16.4	0.6
Glass	-	-	-	-	-	-	-	-	-	-	-	-	-	-	-	-	-	-
Concrete Ingredients and Related Products	16.6	0.0	16.7	0.6	16.6	-0.6	16.7	0.6	16.7	0.0	16.6	-0.6	16.8	1.2	17.3	3.0	17.3	0.0
Concrete Products	19.0	-9.1	20.2	6.3	20.3	0.5	18.7	-7.9	18.6	-0.5	16.6	-10.8	19.2	15.7	19.9	3.6	19.9	0.0
Clay Construction Products Ex. Refractories	-	-	-	-	-	-	-	-	-	-	-	-	-	-	-	-	-	-
Refractories	-	-	-	-	-	-	-	-	-	-	-	-	-	-	-	-	-	-
Asphalt Felts and Coatings	17.7	4.7	17.4	-1.7	19.1	9.8	15.4	-19.4	15.9	3.2	17.4	9.4	17.9	2.9	17.5	-2.2	17.5	0.0
Gypsum Products	-	-	-	-	-	-	-	-	-	-	-	-	-	-	-	-	-	-
Glass Containers	-	-	-	-	-	-	-	-	-	-	-	-	-	-	-	-	-	-
Nonmetallic Minerals	-	-	-	-	-	-	-	-	-	-	-	-	-	-	-	-	-	-
Transportation Equipment	-	-	-	-	-	-	-	-	-	-	-	-	-	-	-	-	-	-
Motor Vehicles and Equipment	14.0	-4.1	13.9	-0.7	14.9	7.2	15.9	6.7	15.6	-1.9	16.1	3.2	17.2	6.8	18.8	9.3	18.8	0.0
Aircraft and Aircraft Equipment	-	-	-	-	-	-	-	-	-	-	-	-	-	-	-	-	-	-
Ships and Boats	-	-	-	-	-	-	-	-	-	-	-	-	-	-	-	-	-	-
Railroad Equipment	-	-	-	-	-	-	-	-	-	-	-	-	-	-	-	-	-	-
Transportation Equipment, n.e.c.	-	-	-	-	-	-	-	-	-	-	-	-	-	-	-	-	-	-
Miscellaneous Products	-	-	-	-	-	-	-	-	-	-	-	-	-	-	-	-	-	-
Toys, Sporting Goods, Small Arms, etc.																		
Tobacco Products, Incl. Stemmed & Redried	-	-	-	-	-	-	-	-	-	-	-	-	-	-	-	-	-	-
Notions	-	-	-	-	-	-	-	-	-	-	-	-	-	-	-	-	-	-
Photographic Equipment and Supplies																		
Mobile Homes																		
Medical, Surgical & Personal Aid Devices	-	-	-	-	-	-	-	-	-	-	-	-	-	-	-	-	-	-
Industrial Safety Equipment	-	-	-	-	-	-	-	-	-	-	-	-	-	-	-	-	-	-
Mining Services	-	-	-	-	-	-	-	-	-	-	-	-	-	-	-	-	-	-
Miscellaneous Products n.e.c.	-	-	-	-	-	-	-	-	-	-	-	-	-	-	-	-	-	-

Source: U.S. Department of Labor, Bureau of Labor Statistics, Division of Industry Prices and Price Indexes. n.e.c. stands for not elsewhere classified. - indicates no data collected for period or unavailable.

Producer Price Index
Annual Averages, 1944-1952
Base 1982 = 100

Columns headed % show percentile change in the index from the previous period for which an index is available.

	1944		1945		1946		1947		1948		1949		1950		1951		1952	
	Index	%	Index	%	Index	%	Index	%	Index	%	Index	%	Index	%	Index	%	Index	%
Floor Coverings	33.2	0.0	33.1	-0.3	36.8	11.2	43.6	18.5	46.4	6.4	46.6	0.4	52.3	12.2	62.7	19.9	55.9	-10.8
Household Appliances	-	-	-	-	-	-	51.5	-	54.0	4.9	53.7	-0.6	54.0	0.6	57.3	6.1	57.0	-0.5
Home Electronic Equipment	-	-	-	-	-	-	141.0	-	146.7	4.0	151.8	3.5	141.8	-6.6	136.2	-3.9	135.9	-0.2
Household Durable Goods n.e.c.	-	-	-	-	-	-	19.5	-	20.0	2.6	20.9	4.5	21.5	2.9	23.1	7.4	23.3	0.9
Nonmetallic Mineral Products	16.7	1.8	17.4	4.2	18.5	6.3	20.7	11.9	22.4	8.2	23.0	2.7	23.5	2.2	25.0	6.4	25.0	0.0
Glass	-	-	-	-	-	-	30.2	-	31.8	5.3	33.4	5.0	34.1	2.1	36.3	6.5	36.3	0.0
Concrete Ingredients and Related Products	17.5	1.2	18.0	2.9	18.7	3.9	20.5	9.6	22.4	9.3	23.2	3.6	23.5	1.3	24.9	6.0	24.9	0.0
Concrete Products	19.9	0.0	19.9	0.0	21.1	6.0	23.9	13.3	25.1	5.0	25.7	2.4	26.3	2.3	28.0	6.5	28.0	0.0
Clay Construction Products Ex. Refractories	-	-	-	-	-	-	23.9	-	25.7	7.5	26.5	3.1	27.6	4.2	29.9	8.3	29.8	-0.3
Refractories	-	-	-	-	-	-	14.3	-	15.8	10.5	16.5	4.4	18.2	10.3	19.6	7.7	19.8	1.0
Asphalt Felts and Coatings	17.6	0.6	18.0	2.3	18.8	4.4	21.4	13.8	23.5	9.8	23.4	-0.4	23.1	-1.3	23.9	3.5	23.4	-2.1
Gypsum Products	-	-	-	-	-	-	27.5	-	30.0	9.1	29.7	-1.0	30.4	2.4	34.1	12.2	34.2	0.3
Glass Containers	-	-	-	-	-	-	14.7	-	16.9	15.0	19.0	12.4	19.1	0.5	20.6	7.9	21.1	2.4
Nonmetallic Minerals	-	-	-	-	-	-	14.9	-	16.3	9.4	16.5	1.2	17.0	3.0	17.7	4.1	17.9	1.1
Transportation Equipment	-	-	-	-	-	-	-	-	-	-	-	-	-	-	-	-	-	-
Motor Vehicles and Equipment	18.9	0.5	19.2	1.6	22.3	16.1	25.5	14.3	28.2	10.6	30.1	6.7	30.0	-0.3	31.6	5.3	33.4	5.7
Aircraft and Aircraft Equipment	-	-	-	-	-	-	-	-	-	-	-	-	-	-	-	-	-	-
Ships and Boats	-	-	-	-	-	-	-	-	-	-	-	-	-	-	-	-	-	-
Railroad Equipment	-	-	-	-	-	-	-	-	-	-	-	-	-	-	-	-	-	-
Transportation Equipment, n.e.c.	-	-	-	-	-	-	-	-	-	-	-	-	-	-	-	-	-	-
Miscellaneous Products	-	-	-	-	-	-	26.6	-	27.7	4.1	28.2	1.8	28.6	1.4	30.3	5.9	30.2	-0.3
Toys, Sporting Goods, Small Arms, etc.	-	-	-	-	-	-	35.1	-	36.7	4.6	36.7	0.0	38.7	5.4	42.0	8.5	41.0	-2.4
Tobacco Products, Incl. Stemmed & Redried	-	-	-	-	-	-	20.5	-	21.3	3.9	22.3	4.7	22.8	2.2	23.5	3.1	23.6	0.4
Notions	-	-	-	-	-	-	37.8	-	37.9	0.3	34.2	-9.8	33.7	-1.5	37.0	9.8	34.4	-7.0
Photographic Equipment and Supplies	-	-	-	-	-	-	32.2	-	35.3	9.6	36.6	3.7	36.3	-0.8	37.5	3.3	38.0	1.3
Mobile Homes	-	-	-	-	-	-	-	-	-	-	-	-	-	-	-	-	-	-
Medical, Surgical & Personal Aid Devices	-	-	-	-	-	-	-	-	-	-	-	-	-	-	-	-	-	-
Industrial Safety Equipment	-	-	-	-	-	-	-	-	-	-	-	-	-	-	-	-	-	-
Mining Services	-	-	-	-	-	-	-	-	-	-	-	-	-	-	-	-	-	-
Miscellaneous Products n.e.c.	-	-	-	-	-	-	23.2	-	23.8	2.6	23.9	0.4	24.1	0.8	25.7	6.6	25.7	0.0

Source: U.S. Department of Labor, Bureau of Labor Statistics, Division of Industry Prices and Price Indexes. n.e.c. stands for not elsewhere classified. - indicates no data collected for period or unavailable.

Producer Price Index
Annual Averages, 1953-1961
Base 1982 = 100

Columns headed % show percentile change in the index from the previous period for which an index is available.

	1953		1954		1955		1956		1957		1958		1959		1960		1961	
	Index	%	Index	%	Index	%	Index	%	Index	%	Index	%	Index	%	Index	%	Index	%
Floor Coverings	56.8	1.6	56.0	-1.4	57.6	2.9	59.7	3.6	60.7	1.7	58.1	-4.3	58.3	0.3	59.3	1.7	58.6	-1.2
Household Appliances	57.5	0.9	58.1	1.0	56.7	-2.4	56.0	-1.2	56.0	0.0	55.6	-0.7	55.5	-0.2	54.0	-2.7	53.0	-1.9
Home Electronic Equipment	-	-	-	-	136.3	0.3	136.4	0.1	138.3	1.4	138.2	-0.1	135.9	-1.7	133.8	-1.5	131.0	-2.1
Household Durable Goods n.e.c.	24.2	3.9	25.0	3.3	25.9	3.6	27.3	5.4	28.7	5.1	29.8	3.8	30.2	1.3	30.8	2.0	30.8	0.0
Nonmetallic Mineral Products	26.0	4.0	26.6	2.3	27.3	2.6	28.5	4.4	29.6	3.9	29.9	1.0	30.3	1.3	30.4	0.3	30.5	0.3
Glass	38.4	5.8	39.6	3.1	40.7	2.8	42.4	4.2	43.1	1.7	43.0	-0.2	43.0	0.0	42.1	-2.1	41.7	-1.0
Concrete Ingredients and Related Products	25.8	3.6	26.6	3.1	27.5	3.4	28.7	4.4	29.9	4.2	30.6	2.3	30.9	1.0	31.3	1.3	31.3	0.0
Concrete Products	28.7	2.5	29.2	1.7	29.5	1.0	30.6	3.7	31.4	2.6	31.9	1.6	32.3	1.3	32.6	0.9	32.6	0.0
Clay Construction Products Ex. Refractories	30.4	2.0	30.9	1.6	32.1	3.9	33.8	5.3	34.3	1.5	34.5	0.6	35.4	2.6	35.9	1.4	36.1	0.6
Refractories	21.6	9.1	22.9	6.0	24.4	6.6	25.8	5.7	27.6	7.0	28.2	2.2	29.0	2.8	29.0	0.0	28.8	-0.7
Asphalt Felts and Coatings	24.4	4.3	23.7	-2.9	24.2	2.1	25.5	5.4	27.9	9.4	25.7	-7.9	26.5	3.1	24.4	-7.9	26.3	7.8
Gypsum Products	35.2	2.9	35.5	0.9	35.5	0.0	36.9	3.9	36.9	0.0	38.4	4.1	38.7	0.8	38.7	0.0	39.4	1.8
Glass Containers	22.7	7.6	23.8	4.8	24.1	1.3	25.4	5.4	26.8	5.5	28.3	5.6	28.3	0.0	27.6	-2.5	27.4	-0.7
Nonmetallic Minerals	18.6	3.9	19.1	2.7	19.3	1.0	19.6	1.6	20.4	4.1	20.9	2.5	21.1	1.0	21.4	1.4	21.2	-0.9
Transportation Equipment	-	-	-	-	-	-	-	-	-	-	-	-	-	-	-	-	-	-
Motor Vehicles and Equipment	33.3	-0.3	33.4	0.3	34.3	2.7	36.3	5.8	37.9	4.4	39.0	2.9	39.9	2.3	39.3	-1.5	39.2	-0.3
Aircraft and Aircraft Equipment	-	-	-	-	-	-	-	-	-	-	-	-	-	-	-	-	-	-
Ships and Boats	-	-	-	-	-	-	-	-	-	-	-	-	-	-	-	-	-	-
Railroad Equipment	-	-	-	-	-	-	-	-	-	-	-	-	-	-	-	-	27.9	-
Transportation Equipment, n.e.c.	-	-	-	-	-	-	-	-	-	-	-	-	-	-	-	-	-	-
Miscellaneous Products	31.0	2.6	31.3	1.0	31.3	0.0	31.7	1.3	32.6	2.8	33.3	2.1	33.4	0.3	33.6	0.6	33.7	0.3
Toys, Sporting Goods, Small Arms, etc.	41.1	0.2	40.9	-0.5	41.0	0.2	42.0	2.4	42.5	1.2	43.0	1.2	42.4	-1.4	42.8	0.9	43.1	0.7
Tobacco Products, Incl. Stemmed & Redried	25.3	7.2	25.6	1.2	25.6	0.0	25.6	0.0	26.7	4.3	27.7	3.7	27.9	0.7	27.9	0.0	27.9	0.0
Notions	34.2	-0.6	34.8	1.8	33.7	-3.2	34.9	3.6	35.6	2.0	35.7	0.3	35.6	-0.3	35.5	-0.3	35.2	-0.8
Photographic Equipment and Supplies	38.3	0.8	38.7	1.0	39.1	1.0	39.8	1.8	41.5	4.3	42.6	2.7	44.0	3.3	44.4	0.9	45.0	1.4
Mobile Homes	-	-	-	-	-	-	-	-	-	-	-	-	-	-	-	-	-	-
Medical, Surgical & Personal Aid Devices	-	-	-	-	-	-	-	-	-	-	-	-	-	-	-	-	-	-
Industrial Safety Equipment	-	-	-	-	-	-	-	-	-	-	-	-	-	-	-	-	-	-
Mining Services	-	-	-	-	-	-	-	-	-	-	-	-	-	-	-	-	-	-
Miscellaneous Products n.e.c.	25.7	0.0	26.0	1.2	26.1	0.4	26.5	1.5	27.2	2.6	27.4	0.7	27.5	0.4	27.9	1.5	28.0	0.4

Source: U.S. Department of Labor, Bureau of Labor Statistics, Division of Industry Prices and Price Indexes. n.e.c. stands for not elsewhere classified. - indicates no data collected for period or unavailable.

Producer Price Index
Annual Averages, 1962-1970
Base 1982 = 100

Columns headed % show percentile change in the index from the previous period for which an index is available.

	1962		1963		1964		1965		1966		1967		1968		1969		1970	
	Index	%	Index	%	Index	%	Index	%	Index	%	Index	%	Index	%	Index	%	Index	%
Floor Coverings	57.2	-2.4	57.0	-0.3	58.7	3.0	57.7	-1.7	57.2	-0.9	55.2	-3.5	55.9	1.3	55.4	-0.9	54.9	-0.9
Household Appliances	52.3	-1.3	51.1	-2.3	50.8	-0.6	49.7	-2.2	49.6	-0.2	50.2	1.2	51.1	1.8	51.7	1.2	52.9	2.3
Home Electronic Equipment	125.3	-4.4	121.8	-2.8	119.9	-1.6	117.1	-2.3	114.9	-1.9	113.6	-1.1	111.4	-1.9	107.4	-3.6	106.0	-1.3
Household Durable Goods n.e.c.	31.3	1.6	31.4	0.3	31.8	1.3	32.2	1.3	33.0	2.5	34.6	4.8	36.9	6.6	38.6	4.6	40.1	3.9
Nonmetallic Mineral Products	30.5	0.0	30.3	-0.7	30.4	0.3	30.4	0.0	30.7	1.0	31.2	1.6	32.4	3.8	33.6	3.7	35.3	5.1
Glass	41.8	0.2	42.3	1.2	44.1	4.3	43.4	-1.6	43.3	-0.2	-	-	-	-	-	-	-	-
Concrete Ingredients and Related Products	31.5	0.6	31.4	-0.3	31.3	-0.3	31.5	0.6	31.6	0.3	32.3	2.2	33.3	3.1	34.4	3.3	36.3	5.5
Concrete Products	32.7	0.3	32.4	-0.9	32.1	-0.9	32.3	0.6	32.8	1.5	33.6	2.4	34.5	2.7	35.8	3.8	37.7	5.3
Clay Construction Products Ex. Refractories	36.4	0.8	36.6	0.5	36.7	0.3	37.0	0.8	37.7	1.9	38.3	1.6	39.3	2.6	40.7	3.6	42.1	3.4
Refractories	28.7	-0.3	28.6	-0.3	28.8	0.7	29.1	1.0	29.3	0.7	29.7	1.4	31.7	6.7	32.5	2.5	35.9	10.5
Asphalt Felts and Coatings	25.3	-3.8	24.0	-5.1	23.7	-1.2	24.8	4.6	25.6	3.2	25.1	-2.0	25.9	3.2	25.8	-0.4	25.8	0.0
Gypsum Products	39.9	1.3	40.0	0.3	41.1	2.8	39.5	-3.9	38.9	-1.5	39.1	0.5	40.5	3.6	40.5	0.0	38.9	-4.0
Glass Containers	26.9	-1.8	26.9	0.0	27.0	0.4	27.3	1.1	27.8	1.8	28.1	1.1	30.2	7.5	32.3	7.0	33.9	5.0
Nonmetallic Minerals	21.2	0.0	21.1	-0.5	21.1	0.0	21.0	-0.5	21.1	0.5	21.2	0.5	21.9	3.3	22.7	3.7	23.8	4.8
Transportation Equipment	-	-	-	-	-	-	-	-	-	-	-	-	-	-	40.4	-	41.9	3.7
Motor Vehicles and Equipment	39.2	0.0	38.9	-0.8	39.1	0.5	39.2	0.3	39.2	0.0	39.8	1.5	40.9	2.8	41.7	2.0	43.3	3.8
Aircraft and Aircraft Equipment	-	-	-	-	-	-	-	-	-	-	-	-	-	-	-	-	-	-
Ships and Boats	-	-	-	-	-	-	-	-	-	-	-	-	-	-	-	-	-	-
Railroad Equipment	28.0	0.4	28.0	0.0	28.0	0.0	28.1	0.4	28.2	0.4	28.9	2.5	29.8	3.1	31.4	5.4	33.2	5.7
Transportation Equipment, n.e.c.	-	-	-	-	-	-	-	-	-	-	-	-	-	-	-	-	-	-
Miscellaneous Products	33.9	0.6	34.2	0.9	34.4	0.6	34.7	0.9	35.3	1.7	36.2	2.5	37.0	2.2	38.1	3.0	39.8	4.5
Toys, Sporting Goods, Small Arms, etc.	43.0	-0.2	43.1	0.2	43.1	0.0	43.8	1.6	44.4	1.4	45.2	1.8	46.2	2.2	47.6	3.0	49.5	4.0
Tobacco Products, Incl. Stemmed & Redried	28.0	0.4	28.7	2.5	29.1	1.4	29.1	0.0	30.1	3.4	31.0	3.0	31.6	1.9	33.1	4.7	35.2	6.3
Notions	35.2	0.0	35.2	0.0	35.3	0.3	35.3	0.0	35.8	1.4	36.1	0.8	36.1	0.0	37.2	3.0	39.1	5.1
Photographic Equipment and Supplies	46.1	2.4	46.0	-0.2	46.3	0.7	46.7	0.9	46.5	-0.4	47.5	2.2	48.6	2.3	48.7	0.2	49.9	2.5
Mobile Homes	-	-	-	-	-	-	-	-	-	-	-	-	-	-	-	-	-	-
Medical, Surgical & Personal Aid Devices	-	-	-	-	-	-	-	-	-	-	-	-	-	-	-	-	-	-
Industrial Safety Equipment	-	-	-	-	-	-	-	-	-	-	-	-	-	-	-	-	-	-
Mining Services	-	-	-	-	-	-	-	-	-	-	-	-	-	-	-	-	-	-
Miscellaneous Products n.e.c.	28.1	0.4	28.0	-0.4	28.1	0.4	28.4	1.1	28.8	1.4	29.6	2.8	30.3	2.4	30.9	2.0	32.1	3.9

Source: U.S. Department of Labor, Bureau of Labor Statistics, Division of Industry Prices and Price Indexes. n.e.c. stands for not elsewhere classified. - indicates no data collected for period or unavailable.

Producer Price Index
Annual Averages, 1971-1979
Base 1982 = 100

Columns headed % show percentile change in the index from the previous period for which an index is available.

	1971 Index	%	1972 Index	%	1973 Index	%	1974 Index	%	1975 Index	%	1976 Index	%	1977 Index	%	1978 Index	%	1979 Index	%
Floor Coverings	54.6	-0.5	54.4	-0.4	56.4	3.7	63.7	12.9	69.0	8.3	72.5	5.1	75.3	3.9	78.2	3.9	81.7	4.5
Household Appliances	54.0	2.1	54.0	0.0	54.5	0.9	59.2	8.6	66.5	12.3	69.9	5.1	72.9	4.3	76.8	5.3	80.8	5.2
Home Electronic Equipment	106.1	0.1	105.3	-0.8	104.4	-0.9	105.7	1.2	106.2	0.5	103.7	-2.4	99.6	-4.0	102.4	2.8	103.7	1.3
Household Durable Goods n.e.c.	41.8	4.2	43.4	3.8	45.1	3.9	51.4	14.0	58.3	13.4	61.9	6.2	65.7	6.1	70.2	6.8	78.9	12.4
Nonmetallic Mineral Products	38.2	8.2	39.4	3.1	40.7	3.3	47.8	17.4	54.4	13.8	58.2	7.0	62.6	7.6	69.6	11.2	77.6	11.5
Glass	55.6	-	-	-	-	-	-	-	62.8	12.9	67.7	7.8	72.6	7.2	78.0	7.4	83.0	6.4
Concrete Ingredients and Related Products	39.3	8.3	40.9	4.1	42.3	3.4	48.0	13.5	55.6	15.8	60.2	8.3	64.2	6.6	70.2	9.3	78.7	12.1
Concrete Products	40.5	7.4	42.2	4.2	44.2	4.7	50.9	15.2	57.3	12.6	60.5	5.6	64.4	6.4	71.9	11.6	82.0	14.0
Clay Construction Products Ex. Refractories	43.9	4.3	45.0	2.5	47.3	5.1	51.8	9.5	58.0	12.0	62.7	8.1	69.0	10.0	75.6	9.6	83.6	10.6
Refractories	37.6	4.7	38.3	1.9	40.4	5.5	42.6	5.4	49.2	15.5	54.6	11.0	59.2	8.4	64.2	8.4	70.2	9.3
Asphalt Felts and Coatings	31.5	22.1	32.9	4.4	34.0	3.3	49.2	44.7	56.7	15.2	59.8	5.5	63.5	6.2	73.3	15.4	81.7	11.5
Gypsum Products	42.7	9.8	44.8	4.9	47.2	5.4	53.7	13.8	56.2	4.7	60.3	7.3	71.7	18.9	89.5	24.8	98.5	10.1
Glass Containers	37.0	9.1	38.0	2.7	39.1	2.9	43.7	11.8	50.5	15.6	55.0	8.9	60.2	9.5	68.7	14.1	73.4	6.8
Nonmetallic Minerals	26.3	10.5	26.9	2.3	27.2	1.1	40.0	47.1	46.7	16.7	49.3	5.6	53.1	7.7	58.4	10.0	66.5	13.9
Transportation Equipment	44.2	5.5	45.5	2.9	46.1	1.3	50.3	9.1	56.7	12.7	60.5	6.7	64.6	6.8	69.5	7.6	75.3	8.3
Motor Vehicles and Equipment	45.7	5.5	47.0	2.8	47.4	0.9	51.4	8.4	57.6	12.1	61.2	6.3	65.2	6.5	70.0	7.4	75.8	8.3
Aircraft and Aircraft Equipment	36.6	-	-	-	-	-	-	-	48.5	32.5	54.5	12.4	59.3	8.8	64.1	8.1	69.9	9.0
Ships and Boats	-	-	-	-	-	-	-	-	-	-	-	-	-	-	-	-	-	-
Railroad Equipment	34.9	5.1	37.1	6.3	38.9	4.9	47.3	21.6	58.1	22.8	62.5	7.6	67.4	7.8	73.0	8.3	80.0	9.6
Transportation Equipment, n.e.c.	-	-	-	-	-	-	-	-	-	-	-	-	-	-	-	-	-	-
Miscellaneous Products	40.8	2.5	41.5	1.7	43.3	4.3	48.1	11.1	53.4	11.0	55.6	4.1	59.4	6.8	66.7	12.3	75.5	13.2
Toys, Sporting Goods, Small Arms, etc.	50.9	2.8	51.7	1.6	53.2	2.9	59.7	12.2	65.9	10.4	67.7	2.7	70.1	3.5	73.7	5.1	79.6	8.0
Tobacco Products, Incl. Stemmed & Redried	36.1	2.6	36.4	0.8	37.7	3.6	41.1	9.0	46.3	12.7	50.5	9.1	55.6	10.1	61.4	10.4	67.4	9.8
Notions	40.4	3.3	40.5	0.2	41.3	2.0	49.6	20.1	54.5	9.9	58.6	7.5	62.2	6.1	65.7	5.6	69.3	5.5
Photographic Equipment and Supplies	50.5	1.2	50.7	0.4	51.5	1.6	55.5	7.8	62.1	11.9	64.7	4.2	66.5	2.8	69.3	4.2	73.0	5.3
Mobile Homes	-	-	-	-	-	-	-	-	-	-	-	-	-	-	-	-	-	-
Medical, Surgical & Personal Aid Devices	-	-	-	-	-	-	-	-	-	-	-	-	-	-	-	-	89.5	-
Industrial Safety Equipment	-	-	-	-	-	-	-	-	-	-	-	-	-	-	-	-	83.3	-
Mining Services	-	-	-	-	-	-	-	-	-	-	-	-	-	-	-	-	-	-
Miscellaneous Products n.e.c.	33.3	3.7	34.3	3.0	37.1	8.2	42.0	13.2	46.0	9.5	45.2	-1.7	49.5	9.5	62.2	25.7	77.9	25.2

Source: U.S. Department of Labor, Bureau of Labor Statistics, Division of Industry Prices and Price Indexes. n.e.c. stands for not elsewhere classified. - indicates no data collected for period or unavailable.

Producer Price Index
Annual Averages, 1980-1988
Base 1982 = 100

Columns headed % show percentile change in the index from the previous period for which an index is available.

	1980 Index	%	1981 Index	%	1982 Index	%	1983 Index	%	1984 Index	%	1985 Index	%	1986 Index	%	1987 Index	%	1988 Index	%
Floor Coverings	90.0	10.2	98.7	9.7	100.0	1.3	102.4	2.4	105.6	3.1	105.6	0.0	108.3	2.6	110.7	2.2	114.7	3.6
Household Appliances	87.5	8.3	94.1	7.5	100.0	6.3	103.9	3.9	106.0	2.0	106.7	0.7	105.7	-0.9	105.6	-0.1	106.0	0.4
Home Electronic Equipment	103.8	0.1	101.3	-2.4	100.0	-1.3	97.8	-2.2	95.2	-2.7	90.8	-4.6	89.9	-1.0	88.8	-1.2	87.2	-1.8
Household Durable Goods n.e.c.	96.3	22.1	97.1	0.8	100.0	3.0	108.2	8.2	110.1	1.8	111.7	1.5	112.9	1.1	115.4	2.2	119.8	3.8
Nonmetallic Mineral Products	88.4	13.9	96.7	9.4	100.0	3.4	101.6	1.6	105.4	3.7	108.6	3.0	110.0	1.3	110.0	0.0	111.2	1.1
Glass	88.7	6.9	96.0	8.2	100.0	4.2	104.0	4.0	105.6	1.5	104.7	-0.9	107.4	2.6	109.4	1.9	112.3	2.7
Concrete Ingredients and Related Products	88.4	12.3	95.6	8.1	100.0	4.6	101.1	1.1	105.1	4.0	108.5	3.2	109.4	0.8	110.4	0.9	112.0	1.4
Concrete Products	92.0	12.2	97.8	6.3	100.0	2.2	101.4	1.4	103.9	2.5	107.5	3.5	109.2	1.6	109.4	0.2	110.0	0.5
Clay Construction Products Ex. Refractories	88.8	6.2	95.8	7.9	100.0	4.4	106.5	6.5	110.0	3.3	113.5	3.2	118.0	4.0	121.4	2.9	124.9	2.9
Refractories	78.5	11.8	89.7	14.3	100.0	11.5	101.2	1.2	107.1	5.8	109.7	2.4	110.2	0.5	110.5	0.3	113.8	3.0
Asphalt Felts and Coatings	99.6	21.9	102.3	2.7	100.0	-2.2	96.4	-3.6	100.3	4.0	102.6	2.3	97.9	-4.6	92.4	-5.6	94.7	2.5
Gypsum Products	100.1	1.6	100.1	0.0	100.0	-0.1	111.7	11.7	135.4	21.2	132.3	-2.3	137.0	3.6	125.2	-8.6	112.9	-9.8
Glass Containers	82.3	12.1	92.5	12.4	100.0	8.1	99.1	-0.9	101.4	2.3	106.8	5.3	111.9	4.8	113.0	1.0	112.3	-0.6
Nonmetallic Minerals	83.6	25.7	98.3	17.6	100.0	1.7	101.8	1.8	106.0	4.1	110.5	4.2	110.2	-0.3	110.3	0.1	112.9	2.4
Transportation Equipment	82.9	10.1	94.3	13.8	100.0	6.0	102.8	2.8	105.2	2.3	107.9	2.6	110.5	2.4	112.5	1.8	114.3	1.6
Motor Vehicles and Equipment	83.1	9.6	94.6	13.8	100.0	5.7	102.2	2.2	104.1	1.9	106.4	2.2	109.1	2.5	111.7	2.4	113.1	1.3
Aircraft and Aircraft Equipment	78.8	12.7	91.3	15.9	100.0	9.5	108.3	8.3	115.0	6.2	-	-	123.8	7.7	123.3	-0.4	126.0	2.2
Ships and Boats	-	-	-	-	100.0	-	103.0	3.0	107.3	4.2	110.3	2.8	113.4	2.8	114.1	0.6	115.1	0.9
Railroad Equipment	90.4	13.0	97.0	7.3	100.0	3.1	101.1	1.1	102.6	1.5	104.9	2.2	105.4	0.5	104.7	-0.7	107.5	2.7
Transportation Equipment, n.e.c.	-	-	-	-	-	-	-	-	-	-	-	-	100.2	-	102.0	1.8	106.1	4.0
Miscellaneous Products	93.6	24.0	96.1	2.7	100.0	4.1	104.8	4.8	107.0	2.1	109.4	2.2	111.6	2.0	114.9	3.0	120.2	4.6
Toys, Sporting Goods, Small Arms, etc.	89.7	12.7	95.7	6.7	100.0	4.5	101.7	1.7	102.6	0.9	104.5	1.9	106.6	2.0	107.8	1.1	111.8	3.7
Tobacco Products, Incl. Stemmed & Redried	76.0	12.8	83.1	9.3	100.0	20.3	113.1	13.1	123.3	9.0	132.5	7.5	142.5	7.5	154.7	8.6	171.9	11.1
Notions	78.4	13.1	93.8	19.6	100.0	6.6	101.1	1.1	102.3	1.2	102.9	0.6	103.7	0.8	105.2	1.4	107.9	2.6
Photographic Equipment and Supplies	96.4	32.1	99.8	3.5	100.0	0.2	102.5	2.5	102.0	-0.5	102.6	0.6	104.0	1.4	105.4	1.3	107.2	1.7
Mobile Homes	-	-	96.9	-	100.0	3.2	100.9	0.9	100.9	0.0	101.7	0.8	102.8	1.1	104.3	1.5	109.3	4.8
Medical, Surgical & Personal Aid Devices	93.3	4.2	97.2	4.2	-	-	103.8	6.8	108.3	4.3	109.0	0.6	111.8	2.6	117.0	4.7	118.9	1.6
Industrial Safety Equipment	89.6	7.6	95.3	6.4	100.0	4.9	103.0	3.0	106.9	3.8	111.3	4.1	121.0	8.7	129.1	6.7	136.7	5.9
Mining Services	-	-	-	-	-	-	-	-	-	-	-	-	91.3	-	87.3	-4.4	90.6	3.8
Miscellaneous Products n.e.c.	107.4	37.9	102.7	-4.4	100.0	-2.6	104.0	4.0	103.6	-0.4	103.4	-0.2	104.8	1.4	108.0	3.1	111.0	2.8

Source: U.S. Department of Labor, Bureau of Labor Statistics, Division of Industry Prices and Price Indexes. n.e.c. stands for not elsewhere classified. - indicates no data collected for period or unavailable.

Producer Price Index
Annual Averages, 1989-1995
Base 1982 = 100

Columns headed % show percentile change in the index from the previous period for which an index is available.

	1989		1990		1991		1992		1993		1994		1995					
	Index	%	Index	%	Index	%	Index	%	Index	%	Index	%	Index	%	Index	%	Index	%
Floor Coverings	117.6	2.5	119.0	1.2	120.4	1.2	120.3	-0.1	120.2	-0.1	121.5	1.1	123.2	1.4				
Household Appliances	108.7	2.5	110.8	1.9	111.3	0.5	111.4	0.1	112.9	1.3	112.8	-0.1	112.3	-0.4				
Home Electronic Equipment	86.9	-0.3	82.7	-4.8	83.2	0.6	82.0	-1.4	80.2	-2.2	80.3	0.1	78.7	-2.0				
Household Durable Goods n.e.c.	127.2	6.2	130.7	2.8	134.2	2.7	136.6	1.8	138.0	1.0	140.8	2.0	144.8	2.8				
Nonmetallic Mineral Products	112.6	1.3	114.7	1.9	117.2	2.2	117.3	0.1	120.0	2.3	124.2	3.5	129.0	3.9				
Glass	113.2	0.8	113.8	0.5	114.4	0.5	115.7	1.1	116.9	1.0	120.1	2.7	122.9	2.3				
Concrete Ingredients and Related Products	113.2	1.1	115.3	1.9	118.4	2.7	119.4	0.8	123.4	3.4	128.7	4.3	134.6	4.6				
Concrete Products	111.2	1.1	113.5	2.1	116.6	2.7	117.2	0.5	120.2	2.6	124.6	3.7	129.5	3.9				
Clay Construction Products Ex. Refractories	127.0	1.7	129.9	2.3	130.2	0.2	132.0	1.4	135.1	2.3	138.3	2.4	141.3	2.2				
Refractories	119.4	4.9	122.3	2.4	125.4	2.5	126.4	0.8	127.1	0.6	128.2	0.9	132.0	3.0				
Asphalt Felts and Coatings	95.8	1.2	97.1	1.4	98.2	1.1	96.2	-2.0	96.8	0.6	95.3	-1.5	100.0	4.9				
Gypsum Products	110.0	-2.6	105.2	-4.4	99.3	-5.6	99.9	0.6	108.3	8.4	136.1	25.7	154.5	13.5				
Glass Containers	115.2	2.6	120.4	4.5	125.4	4.2	125.1	-0.2	125.8	0.6	127.5	1.4	130.5	2.4				
Nonmetallic Minerals	114.2	1.2	116.0	1.6	118.4	2.1	116.4	-1.7	119.2	2.4	121.6	2.0	125.4	3.1				
Transportation Equipment	117.7	3.0	121.5	3.2	126.4	4.0	130.4	3.2	133.7	2.5	137.2	2.6	139.6	1.7				
Motor Vehicles and Equipment	116.2	2.7	118.2	1.7	122.1	3.3	124.9	2.3	128.0	2.5	131.4	2.7	133.0	1.2				
Aircraft and Aircraft Equipment	129.9	3.1	136.8	5.3	144.3	5.5	151.3	4.9	154.9	2.4	159.2	2.8	163.5	2.7				
Ships and Boats	120.1	4.3	125.4	4.4	130.3	3.9	137.4	5.4	143.3	4.3	145.4	1.5	147.9	1.7				
Railroad Equipment	114.0	6.0	118.6	4.0	122.2	3.0	123.7	1.2	125.2	1.2	129.2	3.2	134.8	4.3				
Transportation Equipment, n.e.c.	109.8	3.5	111.6	1.6	113.6	1.8	114.7	1.0	115.7	0.9	117.5	1.6	121.6	3.5				
Miscellaneous Products	126.5	5.2	134.2	6.1	140.8	4.9	145.3	3.2	145.4	0.1	141.9	-2.4	145.1	2.3				
Toys, Sporting Goods, Small Arms, etc.	116.7	4.4	119.6	2.5	122.6	2.5	124.6	1.6	125.5	0.7	127.0	1.2	129.0	1.6				
Tobacco Products, Incl. Stemmed & Redried	194.8	13.3	221.4	13.7	249.7	12.8	275.3	10.3	260.3	-5.4	224.7	-13.7	231.4	3.0				
Notions	112.4	4.2	115.8	3.0	117.9	1.8	119.3	1.2	120.5	1.0	121.8	1.1	123.8	1.6				
Photographic Equipment and Supplies	114.3	6.6	118.4	3.6	118.1	-0.3	118.6	0.4	117.9	-0.6	116.9	-0.8	118.3	1.2				
Mobile Homes	114.0	4.3	117.5	3.1	120.4	2.5	121.7	1.1	127.8	5.0	137.0	7.2	145.8	6.4				
Medical, Surgical & Personal Aid Devices	123.0	3.4	127.3	3.5	130.3	2.4	133.9	2.8	137.8	2.9	140.4	1.9	141.2	0.6				
Industrial Safety Equipment	144.2	5.5	149.7	3.8	157.7	5.3	163.6	3.7	166.5	1.8	172.6	3.7	178.6	3.5				
Mining Services	90.9	0.3	95.5	5.1	98.6	3.2	95.1	-3.5	100.0	5.2	102.9	2.9	104.4	1.5				
Miscellaneous Products n.e.c.	114.0	2.7	117.7	3.2	120.5	2.4	122.4	1.6	125.3	2.4	127.5	1.8	131.8	3.4				

Source: U.S. Department of Labor, Bureau of Labor Statistics, Division of Industry Prices and Price Indexes. n.e.c. stands for not elsewhere classified. - indicates no data collected for period or unavailable.

FARM PRODUCTS
Producer Price Index
Base 1982 = 100

For 1913-1995. Columns headed % show percentile change in the index from the previous period for which an index is available.

Year	Jan Index	%	Feb Index	%	Mar Index	%	Apr Index	%	May Index	%	Jun Index	%	Jul Index	%	Aug Index	%	Sep Index	%	Oct Index	%	Nov Index	%	Dec Index	%
1913	17.6	-	17.5	-0.6	17.6	0.6	17.5	-0.6	17.4	-0.6	17.6	1.1	18.1	2.8	18.2	0.6	18.8	3.3	18.8	0.0	18.9	0.5	18.5	-2.1
1914	18.4	-0.5	18.3	-0.5	18.2	-0.5	18.0	-1.1	18.0	0.0	18.1	0.6	18.0	-0.6	18.3	1.7	17.9	-2.2	17.2	-3.9	17.6	2.3	17.4	-1.1
1915	18.1	4.0	18.4	1.7	17.9	-2.7	18.2	1.7	18.2	0.0	17.7	-2.7	18.1	2.3	17.9	-1.1	17.5	-2.2	18.1	3.4	18.0	-0.6	18.4	2.2
1916	19.4	5.4	19.4	0.0	19.4	0.0	19.6	1.0	19.8	1.0	19.7	-0.5	20.3	3.0	21.7	6.9	22.6	4.1	23.7	4.9	25.3	6.8	25.0	-1.2
1917	26.2	4.8	27.2	3.8	28.6	5.1	31.6	10.5	33.6	6.3	33.8	0.6	34.0	0.6	34.6	1.8	34.3	-0.9	35.2	2.6	36.0	2.3	35.6	-1.1
1918	37.0	3.9	37.1	0.3	37.3	0.5	36.6	-1.9	35.4	-3.3	35.4	0.0	37.0	4.5	38.6	4.3	39.6	2.6	38.2	-3.5	38.0	-0.5	38.1	0.3
1919	38.9	2.1	37.5	-3.6	38.5	2.7	40.0	3.9	40.9	2.2	39.6	-3.2	41.5	4.8	41.3	-0.5	38.7	-6.3	38.5	-0.5	40.3	4.7	41.8	3.7
1920	43.0	2.9	41.2	-4.2	41.5	0.7	42.5	2.4	42.8	0.7	42.3	-1.2	40.5	-4.3	37.8	-6.7	36.4	-3.7	32.2	-11.5	30.0	-6.8	26.4	-12.0
1921	25.6	-3.0	23.4	-8.6	22.7	-3.0	20.9	-7.9	21.0	0.5	20.3	-3.3	21.8	7.4	22.5	3.2	22.7	0.9	22.7	0.0	22.1	-2.6	22.2	0.5
1922	22.2	0.0	24.0	8.1	23.6	-1.7	23.4	-0.8	23.8	1.7	23.4	-1.7	24.1	3.0	23.0	-4.6	23.3	1.3	23.8	2.1	24.7	3.8	25.0	1.2
1923	25.1	0.4	25.3	0.8	25.3	0.0	24.8	-2.0	24.4	-1.6	24.2	-0.8	23.7	-2.1	24.2	2.1	25.3	4.5	25.4	0.4	25.7	1.2	25.5	-0.8
1924	25.6	0.4	25.0	-2.3	24.2	-3.2	24.6	1.7	24.0	-2.4	23.8	-0.8	24.9	4.6	25.7	3.2	25.3	-1.6	26.0	2.8	26.2	0.8	27.3	4.2
1925	28.7	5.1	28.4	-1.0	28.5	0.4	27.1	-4.9	27.1	0.0	27.6	1.8	28.3	2.5	28.1	-0.7	27.7	-1.4	27.0	-2.5	27.3	1.1	26.6	-2.6
1926	27.1	1.9	26.5	-2.2	25.7	-3.0	26.0	1.2	25.8	-0.8	25.5	-1.2	24.9	-2.4	24.6	-1.2	25.1	2.0	24.7	-1.6	23.9	-3.2	24.0	0.4
1927	24.3	1.3	24.1	-0.8	23.8	-1.2	23.8	0.0	24.3	2.1	24.3	0.0	24.6	1.2	25.8	4.9	26.7	3.5	26.5	-0.7	26.3	-0.8	26.3	0.0
1928	26.8	1.9	26.4	-1.5	26.1	-1.1	27.1	3.8	27.7	2.2	26.9	-2.9	27.4	1.9	27.0	-1.5	27.5	1.9	26.1	-5.1	25.7	-1.5	26.2	1.9
1929	26.7	1.9	26.6	-0.4	27.1	1.9	26.5	-2.2	25.8	-2.6	26.1	1.2	27.1	3.8	27.1	0.0	26.9	-0.7	26.2	-2.6	25.5	-2.7	25.7	0.8
1930	25.5	-0.8	24.7	-3.1	23.9	-3.2	24.2	1.3	23.5	-2.9	22.5	-4.3	21.0	-6.7	21.4	1.9	21.5	0.5	20.8	-3.3	20.0	-3.8	19.0	-5.0
1931	18.4	-3.2	17.7	-3.8	17.8	0.6	17.7	-0.6	16.9	-4.5	16.5	-2.4	16.4	-0.6	16.1	-1.8	15.3	-5.0	14.8	-3.3	14.8	0.0	14.1	-4.7
1932	13.3	-5.7	12.8	-3.8	12.7	-0.8	12.4	-2.4	11.8	-4.8	11.6	-1.7	12.1	4.3	12.4	2.5	12.4	0.0	11.8	-4.8	11.8	0.0	11.1	-5.9
1933	10.8	-2.7	10.3	-4.6	10.8	4.9	11.2	3.7	12.7	13.4	13.4	5.5	15.2	13.4	14.6	-3.9	14.4	-1.4	14.1	-2.1	14.3	1.4	14.0	-2.1
1934	14.8	5.7	15.5	4.7	15.5	0.0	15.1	-2.6	15.1	0.0	16.0	6.0	16.3	1.9	17.6	8.0	18.5	5.1	17.8	-3.8	17.8	0.0	18.2	2.2
1935	19.6	7.7	20.0	2.0	19.7	-1.5	20.3	3.0	20.3	0.0	19.8	-2.5	19.5	-1.5	20.0	2.6	20.1	0.5	19.7	-2.0	19.6	-0.5	19.8	1.0
1936	19.7	-0.5	20.1	2.0	19.3	-4.0	19.4	0.5	19.0	-2.1	19.7	3.7	20.5	4.1	21.2	3.4	21.2	0.0	21.2	0.0	21.5	1.4	22.4	4.2
1937	23.1	3.1	23.1	0.0	23.8	3.0	23.3	-2.1	22.7	-2.6	22.3	-1.8	22.6	1.3	21.8	-3.5	21.7	-0.5	20.3	-6.5	19.1	-5.9	18.4	-3.7
1938	18.1	-1.6	17.6	-2.8	17.7	0.6	17.2	-2.8	17.0	-1.2	17.3	1.8	17.5	1.2	17.0	-2.9	17.2	1.2	16.8	-2.3	17.1	1.8	17.0	-0.6
1939	17.0	0.0	16.9	-0.6	16.6	-1.8	16.1	-3.0	16.1	0.0	15.7	-2.5	15.8	0.6	15.4	-2.5	17.3	12.3	16.9	-2.3	17.0	0.6	17.1	0.6
1940	17.4	1.8	17.3	-0.6	17.1	-1.2	17.5	2.3	17.1	-2.3	16.7	-2.3	16.8	0.6	16.5	-1.8	16.7	1.2	16.8	0.6	17.2	2.4	17.6	2.3
1941	18.1	2.8	17.7	-2.2	18.1	2.3	18.8	3.9	19.3	2.7	20.7	7.3	21.7	4.8	22.1	1.8	23.0	4.1	22.7	-1.3	22.9	0.9	23.9	4.4
1942	25.5	6.7	25.6	0.4	26.0	1.6	26.4	1.5	26.3	-0.4	26.3	0.0	26.6	1.1	26.8	0.8	27.2	1.5	27.5	1.1	27.9	1.5	28.7	2.9
1943	29.5	2.8	30.0	1.7	31.0	3.3	31.2	0.6	31.7	1.6	31.9	0.6	31.5	-1.3	31.2	-1.0	31.0	-0.6	30.9	-0.3	30.6	-1.0	30.7	0.3
1944	30.7	0.0	30.9	0.7	31.2	1.0	31.1	-0.3	31.0	-0.3	31.5	1.6	31.3	-0.6	30.9	-1.3	31.0	0.3	31.2	0.6	31.4	0.6	31.6	0.6
1945	31.9	0.9	32.1	0.6	32.1	0.0	32.5	1.2	32.8	0.9	32.9	0.3	32.5	-1.2	32.0	-1.5	31.4	-1.9	32.1	2.2	33.1	3.1	33.2	0.3
1946	32.7	-1.5	33.0	0.9	33.6	1.8	34.1	1.5	34.7	1.8	35.4	2.0	39.6	11.9	40.6	2.5	39.0	-3.9	41.7	6.9	42.8	2.6	42.4	-0.9
1947	41.6	-1.9	42.6	2.4	45.5	6.8	44.0	-3.3	43.6	-0.9	43.8	0.5	44.3	1.1	44.8	1.1	46.6	4.0	47.4	1.7	47.7	0.6	50.1	5.0
1948	51.2	2.2	47.7	-6.8	47.6	-0.2	48.3	1.5	49.4	2.3	50.4	2.0	50.2	-0.4	49.6	-1.2	48.8	-1.6	46.9	-3.9	46.3	-1.3	45.2	-2.4
1949	43.8	-3.1	42.0	-4.1	42.7	1.7	42.7	0.0	42.7	0.0	41.8	-2.1	41.7	-0.2	41.7	0.0	41.8	0.2	41.0	-1.9	40.9	-0.2	40.3	-1.5
1950	40.1	-0.5	41.0	2.2	41.7	1.7	41.5	-0.5	42.6	2.7	42.7	0.2	45.3	6.1	45.8	1.1	46.5	1.5	45.6	-1.9	47.1	3.3	48.8	3.6
1951	50.8	4.1	52.9	4.1	53.1	0.4	53.1	0.0	52.3	-1.5	51.5	-1.5	50.2	-2.5	49.9	-0.6	49.7	-0.4	50.4	1.4	50.6	0.4	50.3	-0.6
1952	49.7	-1.2	48.7	-2.0	48.9	0.4	49.1	0.4	48.8	-0.6	48.4	-0.8	49.8	2.9	49.7	-0.2	48.2	-3.0	47.4	-1.7	46.8	-1.3	44.8	-4.3
1953	45.0	0.4	44.2	-1.8	45.1	2.0	43.9	-2.7	44.2	0.7	43.1	-2.5	44.2	2.6	43.5	-1.6	44.3	1.8	43.0	-2.9	42.3	-1.6	42.7	0.9
1954	44.2	3.5	44.1	-0.2	44.4	0.7	44.9	1.1	44.2	-1.6	42.8	-3.2	43.4	1.4	43.3	-0.2	42.3	-2.3	42.0	-0.7	42.1	0.2	40.6	-3.6
1955	41.8	3.0	42.0	0.5	41.6	-1.0	42.5	2.2	41.2	-3.1	41.5	0.7	40.4	-2.7	39.8	-1.5	40.4	1.5	39.2	-3.0	38.0	-3.1	37.5	-1.3
1956	38.0	1.3	38.9	2.4	39.1	0.5	39.8	1.8	41.1	3.3	41.2	0.2	40.7	-1.2	40.3	-1.0	40.7	1.0	39.9	-2.0	39.7	-0.5	40.1	1.0
1957	40.4	0.7	40.1	-0.7	40.1	0.0	40.9	2.0	40.4	-1.2	41.1	1.7	41.9	1.9	42.0	0.2	41.1	-2.1	41.3	0.5	41.5	0.5	41.8	0.7

[Continued]

FARM PRODUCTS
Producer Price Index
Base 1982 = 100
[Continued]

For 1913-1995. Columns headed % show percentile change in the index from the previous period for which an index is available.

Year	Jan Index	%	Feb Index	%	Mar Index	%	Apr Index	%	May Index	%	Jun Index	%	Jul Index	%	Aug Index	%	Sep Index	%	Oct Index	%	Nov Index	%	Dec Index	%
1958	42.3	1.2	43.4	2.6	45.4	4.6	44.1	-2.9	44.5	0.9	43.2	-2.9	42.9	-0.7	42.1	-1.9	42.0	-0.2	41.7	-0.7	41.6	-0.2	40.9	-1.7
1959	41.3	1.0	41.2	-0.2	41.0	-0.5	41.8	2.0	41.0	-1.9	40.6	-1.0	39.9	-1.7	39.4	-1.3	40.1	1.8	39.1	-2.5	38.6	-1.3	38.8	0.5
1960	39.1	0.8	39.3	0.5	40.8	3.8	41.2	1.0	40.8	-1.0	40.2	-1.5	40.1	-0.2	39.1	-2.5	39.6	1.3	40.4	2.0	40.6	0.5	40.1	-1.2
1961	40.5	1.0	40.7	0.5	40.6	-0.2	40.0	-1.5	39.2	-2.0	38.5	-1.8	39.4	2.3	40.0	1.5	39.4	-1.5	39.4	0.0	39.6	0.5	39.7	0.3
1962	40.5	2.0	40.6	0.2	40.7	0.2	40.1	-1.5	39.8	-0.7	39.4	-1.0	39.9	1.3	40.4	1.3	41.6	3.0	40.8	-1.9	41.1	0.7	40.3	-1.9
1963	40.8	1.2	39.9	-2.2	39.5	-1.0	39.5	0.0	39.1	-1.0	39.3	0.5	40.1	2.0	39.9	-0.5	39.5	-1.0	39.4	-0.3	39.8	1.0	38.6	-3.0
1964	39.9	3.4	39.1	-2.0	39.4	0.8	39.1	-0.8	38.8	-0.8	38.6	-0.5	39.0	1.0	38.7	-0.8	39.6	2.3	38.8	-2.0	38.9	0.3	38.4	-1.3
1965	38.5	0.3	39.1	1.6	39.5	1.0	40.4	2.3	40.7	0.7	41.5	2.0	41.4	-0.2	41.0	-1.0	41.2	0.5	41.1	-0.2	41.5	1.0	42.6	2.7
1966	43.2	1.4	44.4	2.8	44.2	-0.5	44.0	-0.5	43.2	-1.8	43.1	-0.2	44.6	3.5	44.7	0.2	45.0	0.7	43.2	-4.0	42.4	-1.9	42.1	-0.7
1967	42.5	1.0	41.8	-1.6	41.3	-1.2	40.4	-2.2	41.7	3.2	42.4	1.7	42.5	0.2	41.1	-3.3	40.7	-1.0	40.2	-1.2	39.9	-0.7	41.0	2.8
1968	41.0	0.0	41.9	2.2	42.3	1.0	42.3	0.0	42.9	1.4	42.4	-1.2	43.0	1.4	42.0	-2.3	42.5	1.2	41.9	-1.4	42.7	1.9	42.8	0.2
1969	43.4	1.4	43.5	0.2	44.1	1.4	43.9	-0.5	45.9	4.6	46.2	0.7	46.0	-0.4	45.1	-2.0	44.9	-0.4	44.6	-0.7	46.0	3.1	46.4	0.9
1970	46.6	0.4	47.0	0.9	47.3	0.6	46.0	-2.7	45.9	-0.2	46.0	0.2	46.8	1.7	44.8	-4.3	46.3	3.3	44.5	-3.9	44.1	-0.9	44.2	0.2
1971	44.9	1.6	47.0	4.7	46.6	-0.9	46.6	0.0	47.0	0.9	47.9	1.9	46.8	-2.3	46.7	-0.2	45.6	-2.4	45.9	0.7	46.3	0.9	47.8	3.2
1972	48.6	1.7	49.8	2.5	49.4	-0.8	49.1	-0.6	50.4	2.6	51.1	1.4	52.8	3.3	52.9	0.2	53.1	0.4	51.8	-2.4	53.1	2.5	56.7	6.8
1973	59.5	4.9	62.3	4.7	66.4	6.6	66.3	-0.2	70.3	6.0	75.2	7.0	71.5	-4.9	88.0	23.1	82.7	-6.0	77.7	-6.0	75.9	-2.3	77.3	1.8
1974	83.6	8.2	84.8	1.4	81.3	-4.1	76.8	-5.5	74.6	-2.9	69.6	-6.7	74.6	7.2	78.1	4.7	75.4	-3.5	77.4	2.7	77.5	0.1	75.8	-2.2
1975	74.1	-2.2	72.1	-2.7	70.6	-2.1	73.3	3.8	76.1	3.8	76.8	0.9	79.9	4.0	79.7	-0.3	81.3	2.0	81.4	0.1	79.1	-2.8	80.0	1.1
1976	79.5	-0.6	78.7	-1.0	77.0	-2.2	79.6	3.4	79.5	-0.1	81.1	2.0	81.2	0.1	78.3	-3.6	79.2	1.1	77.0	-2.8	75.7	-1.7	79.1	4.5
1977	79.8	0.9	82.1	2.9	83.5	1.7	85.9	2.9	84.3	-1.9	79.5	-5.7	78.5	-1.3	75.0	-4.5	75.1	0.1	75.1	0.0	76.6	2.0	77.7	1.4
1978	79.3	2.1	82.1	3.5	84.2	2.6	88.2	4.8	89.0	0.9	90.6	1.8	90.7	0.1	86.8	-4.3	88.8	2.3	90.5	1.9	90.0	-0.6	91.9	2.1
1979	95.0	3.4	99.4	4.6	100.2	0.8	101.5	1.3	101.2	-0.3	100.2	-1.0	101.8	1.6	98.4	-3.3	99.5	1.1	98.9	-0.6	99.1	0.2	100.1	1.0
1980	97.6	-2.5	100.0	2.5	98.7	-1.3	94.5	-4.3	96.3	1.9	96.3	0.0	104.9	8.9	108.9	3.8	110.2	1.2	108.8	-1.3	109.3	0.5	109.5	0.2
1981	109.1	-0.4	108.3	-0.7	107.6	-0.6	108.7	1.0	107.1	-1.5	107.6	0.5	108.7	1.0	106.4	-2.1	103.6	-2.6	100.3	-3.2	97.9	-2.4	96.8	-1.1
1982	99.9	3.2	102.0	2.1	101.0	-1.0	103.4	2.4	105.8	2.3	104.3	-1.4	101.8	-2.4	99.4	-2.4	96.8	-2.6	94.6	-2.3	95.2	0.6	96.0	0.8
1983	96.2	0.2	99.3	3.2	99.6	0.3	103.4	3.8	103.3	-0.1	102.1	-1.2	100.8	-1.3	104.6	3.8	105.8	1.1	105.3	-0.5	103.6	-1.6	104.8	1.2
1984	108.7	3.7	107.9	-0.7	110.3	2.2	109.5	-0.7	107.6	-1.7	106.1	-1.4	106.7	0.6	104.5	-2.1	103.1	-1.3	99.1	-3.9	101.4	2.3	101.4	0.0
1985	100.4	-1.0	101.2	0.8	98.5	-2.7	97.7	-0.8	95.1	-2.7	94.7	-0.4	94.6	-0.1	90.0	-4.9	87.8	-2.4	90.7	3.3	95.1	4.9	95.8	0.7
1986	93.8	-2.1	91.5	-2.5	90.9	-0.7	90.2	-0.8	93.7	3.9	91.8	-2.0	94.3	2.7	93.7	-0.6	92.5	-1.3	93.8	1.4	95.0	1.3	93.8	-1.3
1987	91.1	-2.9	92.0	1.0	92.2	0.2	95.7	3.8	99.9	4.4	98.8	-1.1	97.9	-0.9	95.7	-2.2	96.1	0.4	94.9	-1.2	96.3	1.5	95.7	-0.6
1988	97.3	1.7	97.9	0.6	98.2	0.3	99.2	1.0	102.2	3.0	106.8	4.5	109.1	2.2	109.3	0.2	111.6	2.1	110.9	-0.6	107.9	-2.7	108.9	0.9
1989	112.0	2.8	110.8	-1.1	113.8	2.7	111.0	-2.5	115.1	3.7	111.8	-2.9	110.5	-1.2	109.3	-1.1	108.0	-1.2	107.8	-0.2	109.0	1.1	111.5	2.3
1990	114.9	3.0	115.7	0.7	115.3	-0.3	113.3	-1.7	113.7	0.4	113.6	-0.1	113.8	0.2	111.4	-2.1	109.2	-2.0	109.5	0.3	108.5	-0.9	107.2	-1.2
1991	106.9	-0.3	106.9	0.0	109.7	2.6	109.6	-0.1	110.4	0.7	109.1	-1.2	105.6	-3.2	102.9	-2.6	103.1	0.2	101.5	-1.6	101.6	0.1	100.6	-1.0
1992	102.8	2.2	105.5	2.6	106.4	0.9	103.2	-3.0	105.8	2.5	104.7	-1.0	102.5	-2.1	102.2	-0.3	101.6	-0.6	102.7	1.1	101.8	-0.9	103.7	1.9
1993	104.3	0.6	104.4	0.1	106.4	1.9	109.7	3.1	111.0	1.2	104.3	-6.0	105.4	1.1	106.6	1.1	106.3	-0.3	104.2	-2.0	110.1	5.7	113.0	2.6
1994	112.0	-0.9	112.3	0.3	112.8	0.4	111.5	-1.2	108.7	-2.5	107.2	-1.4	102.8	-4.1	101.0	-1.8	101.3	0.3	98.8	-2.5	101.4	2.6	105.5	4.0
1995	103.6	-1.8	104.9	1.3	105.1	0.2	104.8	-0.3	102.6	-2.1	104.2	1.6	106.2	1.9	105.1	-1.0	110.6	5.2	109.9	-0.6	115.1	4.7	116.4	1.1

Source: U.S. Department of Labor, Bureau of Labor Statistics, Division of Industry Prices and Price Indexes. n.e.c. stands for not elsewhere classified. - indicates no data collected for period or unavailable.

Fruits & Melons, Fresh/Dry Vegetables & Nuts
Producer Price Index
Base 1982 = 100

For 1926-1995. Columns headed % show percentile change in the index from the previous period for which an index is available.

Year	Jan Index	%	Feb Index	%	Mar Index	%	Apr Index	%	May Index	%	Jun Index	%	Jul Index	%	Aug Index	%	Sep Index	%	Oct Index	%	Nov Index	%	Dec Index	%
1926	29.4	-	28.9	-1.7	28.8	-0.3	32.4	12.5	29.7	-8.3	28.0	-5.7	24.1	-13.9	22.7	-5.8	24.4	7.5	26.1	7.0	25.1	-3.8	24.2	-3.6
1927	25.4	5.0	25.0	-1.6	23.6	-5.6	24.3	3.0	28.4	16.9	28.6	0.7	25.6	-10.5	26.3	2.7	24.7	-6.1	25.0	1.2	26.8	7.2	25.7	-4.1
1928	26.4	2.7	27.5	4.2	28.6	4.0	28.6	0.0	28.3	-1.0	26.7	-5.7	25.4	-4.9	25.0	-1.6	24.6	-1.6	22.6	-8.1	22.0	-2.7	21.8	-0.9
1929	22.5	3.2	21.5	-4.4	20.9	-2.8	21.3	1.9	22.6	6.1	25.3	11.9	28.1	11.1	29.6	5.3	29.6	0.0	29.3	-1.0	28.5	-2.7	28.9	1.4
1930	27.6	-4.5	27.4	-0.7	27.1	-1.1	29.8	10.0	30.3	1.7	30.2	-0.3	25.5	-15.6	23.1	-9.4	23.8	3.0	23.8	0.0	21.4	-10.1	19.0	-11.2
1931	19.6	3.2	18.6	-5.1	18.8	1.1	19.6	4.3	19.8	1.0	20.0	1.0	19.2	-4.0	19.0	-1.0	18.3	-3.7	17.3	-5.5	16.5	-4.6	15.9	-3.6
1932	15.5	-2.5	15.4	-0.6	15.5	0.6	15.5	0.0	15.2	-1.9	15.6	2.6	14.9	-4.5	13.6	-8.7	12.7	-6.6	12.5	-1.6	12.6	0.8	12.7	0.8
1933	12.9	1.6	12.7	-1.6	13.4	5.5	14.5	8.2	14.8	2.1	16.2	9.5	20.1	24.1	18.4	-8.5	16.8	-8.7	15.4	-8.3	15.1	-1.9	15.6	3.3
1934	17.2	10.3	18.4	7.0	18.3	-0.5	17.0	-7.1	17.1	0.6	17.7	3.5	17.0	-4.0	16.3	-4.1	16.2	-0.6	16.6	2.5	15.9	-4.2	14.9	-6.3
1935	15.0	0.7	15.3	2.0	15.1	-1.3	16.5	9.3	16.2	-1.8	17.1	5.6	16.0	-6.4	14.7	-8.1	14.6	-0.7	14.3	-2.1	15.7	9.8	15.9	1.3
1936	15.5	-2.5	15.5	0.0	16.3	5.2	17.2	5.5	18.6	8.1	22.0	18.3	21.1	-4.1	19.6	-7.1	18.1	-7.7	18.8	3.9	19.1	1.6	19.3	1.0
1937	21.5	11.4	23.4	8.8	23.0	-1.7	22.0	-4.3	22.2	0.9	22.2	0.0	17.9	-19.4	16.1	-10.1	15.7	-2.5	15.1	-3.8	14.8	-2.0	13.6	-8.1
1938	13.6	0.0	13.4	-1.5	13.2	-1.5	13.5	2.3	14.1	4.4	15.3	8.5	13.8	-9.8	13.6	-1.4	14.1	3.7	13.9	-1.4	16.0	15.1	15.5	-3.1
1939	15.5	0.0	15.9	2.6	16.2	1.9	16.5	1.9	16.3	-1.2	15.8	-3.1	15.7	-0.6	14.5	-7.6	15.8	9.0	14.9	-5.7	15.2	2.0	15.8	3.9
1940	15.0	-5.1	14.4	-4.0	14.5	0.7	16.9	16.6	18.1	7.1	19.6	8.3	17.9	-8.7	16.0	-10.6	15.3	-4.4	14.6	-4.6	15.1	3.4	15.4	2.0
1941	14.9	-3.2	14.7	-1.3	15.0	2.0	15.9	6.0	15.9	0.0	18.7	17.6	17.1	-8.6	17.1	0.0	17.3	1.2	18.8	8.7	18.2	-3.2	17.9	-1.6
1942	19.0	6.1	20.9	10.0	21.7	3.8	25.0	15.2	25.3	1.2	27.9	10.3	26.3	-5.7	26.0	-1.1	25.6	-1.5	25.7	0.4	26.9	4.7	27.7	3.0
1943	27.0	-2.5	29.0	7.4	31.4	8.3	33.9	8.0	38.7	14.2	40.6	4.9	38.7	-4.7	34.7	-10.3	31.7	-8.6	31.2	-1.6	32.3	3.5	32.6	0.9
1944	32.2	-1.2	33.0	2.5	33.9	2.7	34.9	2.9	35.0	0.3	38.6	10.3	36.0	-6.7	33.6	-6.7	31.3	-6.8	30.2	-3.5	30.6	1.3	31.4	2.6
1945	30.8	-1.9	32.0	3.9	31.3	-2.2	33.8	8.0	36.4	7.7	37.5	3.0	36.0	-4.0	34.1	-5.3	31.8	-6.7	31.4	-1.3	33.9	8.0	35.6	5.0
1946	34.5	-3.1	35.2	2.0	37.0	5.1	38.6	4.3	39.3	1.8	37.8	-3.8	35.8	-5.3	32.6	-8.9	30.9	-5.2	33.3	7.8	37.1	11.4	35.4	-4.6
1947	33.7	-4.8	35.4	5.0	38.2	7.9	38.2	0.0	39.3	2.9	37.1	-5.6	33.9	-8.6	34.5	1.8	34.0	-1.4	33.5	-1.5	37.1	10.7	37.2	0.3
1948	38.7	4.0	39.6	2.3	39.5	-0.3	42.1	6.6	43.5	3.3	38.2	-12.2	36.1	-5.5	35.4	-1.9	33.8	-4.5	33.9	0.3	34.7	2.4	33.9	-2.3
1949	37.6	10.9	38.2	1.6	37.8	-1.0	40.8	7.9	42.4	3.9	36.7	-13.4	36.0	-1.9	34.1	-5.3	33.0	-3.2	31.4	-4.8	33.8	7.6	33.4	-1.2
1950	33.0	-1.2	32.5	-1.5	33.3	2.5	35.4	6.3	35.2	-0.6	32.8	-6.8	34.9	6.4	32.9	-5.7	31.5	-4.3	30.6	-2.9	34.1	11.4	35.0	2.6
1951	33.2	-5.1	35.8	7.8	32.4	-9.5	36.0	11.1	38.0	5.6	34.5	-9.2	33.2	-3.8	32.7	-1.5	33.9	3.7	35.2	3.8	39.1	11.1	43.0	10.0
1952	44.4	3.3	41.2	-7.2	45.3	10.0	46.6	2.9	47.1	1.1	45.5	-3.4	46.9	3.1	45.5	-3.0	42.3	-7.0	40.8	-3.5	41.4	1.5	41.0	-1.0
1953	39.2	-4.4	37.4	-4.6	38.7	3.5	39.1	1.0	38.5	-1.5	40.2	4.4	34.7	-13.7	35.8	3.2	35.1	-2.0	34.5	-1.7	34.5	0.0	32.8	-4.9
1954	33.3	1.5	32.8	-1.5	32.8	0.0	35.6	8.5	38.2	7.3	35.4	-7.3	40.6	14.7	39.6	-2.5	36.5	-7.8	37.3	2.2	37.8	1.3	35.4	-6.3
1955	38.5	8.8	38.0	-1.3	38.2	0.5	44.2	15.7	43.4	-1.8	38.3	-11.8	36.1	-5.7	36.4	0.8	37.3	2.5	34.0	-8.8	37.5	10.3	35.0	-6.7
1956	38.4	9.7	35.9	-6.5	38.9	8.4	37.3	-4.1	40.9	9.7	44.0	7.6	40.9	-7.0	34.7	-15.2	34.8	0.3	35.7	2.6	38.2	7.0	37.5	-1.8
1957	36.8	-1.9	35.2	-4.3	34.4	-2.3	37.7	9.6	39.9	5.8	38.5	-3.5	39.5	2.6	38.9	-1.5	36.1	-7.2	39.4	9.1	38.9	-1.3	39.6	1.8
1958	44.2	11.6	46.4	5.0	52.1	12.3	47.3	-9.2	44.6	-5.7	37.3	-16.4	38.9	4.3	35.6	-8.5	35.8	0.6	37.1	3.6	35.9	-3.2	36.3	1.1
1959	37.5	3.3	38.7	3.2	34.2	-11.6	41.7	21.9	39.1	-6.2	36.9	-5.6	36.0	-2.4	33.9	-5.8	37.7	11.2	37.4	-0.8	37.8	1.1	39.5	4.5
1960	38.4	-2.8	36.7	-4.4	38.2	4.1	40.8	6.8	42.8	4.9	40.1	-6.3	41.3	3.0	36.1	-12.6	38.3	6.1	39.9	4.2	39.3	-1.5	36.4	-7.4
1961	37.9	4.1	36.5	-3.7	38.7	6.0	36.6	-5.4	37.1	1.4	37.8	1.9	38.2	1.1	35.6	-6.8	34.7	-2.5	34.6	-0.3	34.9	0.9	33.8	-3.2
1962	37.6	11.2	40.5	7.7	41.1	1.5	38.4	-6.6	41.5	8.1	38.3	-7.7	35.8	-6.5	35.3	-1.4	36.8	4.2	37.8	2.7	37.4	-1.1	34.3	-8.3
1963	40.4	17.8	37.4	-7.4	38.4	2.7	38.6	0.5	38.7	0.3	37.7	-2.6	37.6	-0.3	35.9	-4.5	34.1	-5.0	34.6	1.5	37.3	7.8	36.8	-1.3
1964	37.2	1.1	38.0	2.2	40.7	7.1	41.1	1.0	41.7	1.5	43.9	5.3	42.3	-3.6	38.0	-10.2	39.4	3.7	38.1	-3.3	41.9	10.0	38.4	-8.4
1965	38.2	-0.5	39.8	4.2	41.8	5.0	45.6	9.1	46.0	0.9	42.3	-8.0	40.3	-4.7	33.2	-17.6	37.3	12.3	37.1	-0.5	36.5	-1.6	35.8	-1.9
1966	37.8	5.6	38.0	0.5	39.5	3.9	43.1	9.1	40.1	-7.0	38.7	-3.5	41.5	7.2	37.9	-8.7	42.8	12.9	38.0	-11.2	40.4	6.3	39.3	-2.7
1967	39.5	0.5	40.6	2.8	38.3	-5.7	38.7	1.0	40.6	4.9	44.3	9.1	41.9	-5.4	37.5	-10.5	35.8	-4.5	35.6	-0.6	39.8	11.8	40.7	2.3
1968	41.9	2.9	43.5	3.8	44.3	1.8	43.4	-2.0	47.9	10.4	41.3	-13.8	42.0	1.7	37.8	-10.0	37.9	0.3	38.7	2.1	42.7	10.3	42.8	0.2
1969	43.8	2.3	42.8	-2.3	44.1	3.0	41.9	-5.0	49.7	18.6	44.2	-11.1	40.6	-8.1	41.5	2.2	40.2	-3.1	39.3	-2.2	48.6	23.7	43.6	-10.3
1970	45.3	3.9	45.6	0.7	45.9	0.7	43.7	-4.8	48.0	9.8	47.4	-1.2	43.6	-8.0	38.6	-11.5	44.0	14.0	39.7	-9.8	42.3	6.5	43.8	3.5

[Continued]

Fruits & Melons, Fresh/Dry Vegetables & Nuts
Producer Price Index
Base 1982 = 100
[Continued]

For 1926-1995. Columns headed % show percentile change in the index from the previous period for which an index is available.

Year	Jan Index	%	Feb Index	%	Mar Index	%	Apr Index	%	May Index	%	Jun Index	%	Jul Index	%	Aug Index	%	Sep Index	%	Oct Index	%	Nov Index	%	Dec Index	%
1971	45.6	4.1	46.6	2.2	49.3	5.8	47.6	-3.4	50.2	5.5	53.7	7.0	43.1	-19.7	45.7	6.0	40.9	-10.5	45.6	11.5	50.1	9.9	49.8	-0.6
1972	49.2	-1.2	50.3	2.2	44.5	-11.5	46.3	4.0	47.5	2.6	48.0	1.1	51.2	6.7	54.7	6.8	54.4	-0.5	48.4	-11.0	55.9	15.5	53.1	-5.0
1973	59.6	12.2	57.9	-2.9	62.5	7.9	69.4	11.0	73.3	5.6	77.9	6.3	74.0	-5.0	63.9	-13.6	58.7	-8.1	63.9	8.9	66.3	3.8	67.6	2.0
1974	72.7	7.5	84.6	16.4	83.0	-1.9	89.5	7.8	93.3	4.2	80.6	-13.6	73.7	-8.6	64.1	-13.0	64.3	0.3	65.5	1.9	73.7	12.5	64.5	-12.5
1975	69.0	7.0	66.6	-3.5	64.6	-3.0	72.3	11.9	72.2	-0.1	81.5	12.9	82.2	0.9	70.8	-13.9	72.0	1.7	72.2	0.3	70.5	-2.4	75.0	6.4
1976	76.8	2.4	74.6	-2.9	72.7	-2.5	76.9	5.8	70.6	-8.2	63.3	-10.3	64.9	2.5	62.8	-3.2	71.0	13.1	75.9	6.9	65.7	-13.4	68.8	4.7
1977	78.3	13.8	83.9	7.2	86.4	3.0	81.1	-6.1	79.6	-1.8	69.5	-12.7	71.8	3.3	69.6	-3.1	72.1	3.6	74.1	2.8	76.3	3.0	66.8	-12.5
1978	77.5	16.0	80.5	3.9	79.3	-1.5	89.6	13.0	86.8	-3.1	90.8	4.6	99.5	9.6	84.9	-14.7	82.0	-3.4	84.4	2.9	81.6	-3.3	87.3	7.0
1979	92.1	5.5	103.7	12.6	92.9	-10.4	94.2	1.4	90.0	-4.5	89.2	-0.9	89.4	0.2	95.3	6.6	82.1	-13.9	85.9	4.6	85.3	-0.7	83.1	-2.6
1980	86.3	3.9	87.0	0.8	86.1	-1.0	88.0	2.2	96.2	9.3	92.1	-4.3	99.4	7.9	100.1	0.7	104.9	4.8	95.0	-9.4	97.2	2.3	96.6	-0.6
1981	102.0	5.6	107.0	4.9	115.4	7.9	112.8	-2.3	108.5	-3.8	103.8	-4.3	104.7	0.9	101.7	-2.9	99.7	-2.0	98.1	-1.6	100.1	2.0	110.6	10.5
1982	114.0	3.1	114.4	0.4	101.4	-11.4	105.5	4.0	107.0	1.4	104.3	-2.5	94.3	-9.6	94.1	-0.2	87.1	-7.4	87.9	0.9	92.0	4.7	98.1	6.6
1983	89.7	-8.6	89.8	0.1	92.6	3.1	105.1	13.5	102.5	-2.5	104.2	1.7	101.8	-2.3	106.6	4.7	108.8	2.1	121.5	11.7	108.5	-10.7	108.9	0.4
1984	114.8	5.4	123.1	7.2	121.4	-1.4	104.0	-14.3	99.3	-4.5	107.9	8.7	111.1	3.0	115.8	4.2	114.4	-1.2	105.4	-7.9	99.0	-6.1	99.3	0.3
1985	102.1	2.8	114.1	11.8	109.6	-3.9	109.6	0.0	99.0	-9.7	100.2	1.2	108.7	8.5	103.0	-5.2	93.9	-8.8	92.2	-1.8	94.6	2.6	105.3	11.3
1986	101.1	-4.0	92.5	-8.5	93.5	1.1	103.8	11.0	108.1	4.1	102.8	-4.9	105.2	2.3	104.5	-0.7	105.7	1.1	113.4	7.3	109.7	-3.3	107.3	-2.2
1987	98.4	-8.3	101.9	3.6	108.3	6.3	105.1	-3.0	104.5	-0.6	110.3	5.6	112.2	1.7	99.5	-11.3	102.5	3.0	101.5	-1.0	124.1	22.3	113.8	-8.3
1988	118.2	3.9	100.5	-15.0	101.5	1.0	101.0	-0.5	101.2	0.2	100.8	-0.4	109.9	9.0	105.9	-3.6	117.4	10.9	111.3	-5.2	119.0	6.9	114.7	-3.6
1989	109.4	-4.6	123.8	13.2	118.7	-4.1	115.3	-2.9	128.9	11.8	122.3	-5.1	120.8	-1.2	109.7	-9.2	101.8	-7.2	114.3	12.3	102.9	-10.0	106.7	3.7
1990	139.1	30.4	156.9	12.8	133.3	-15.0	106.9	-19.8	103.6	-3.1	106.9	3.2	117.3	9.7	107.4	-8.4	104.0	-3.2	109.0	4.8	119.3	9.4	106.7	-10.6
1991	109.8	2.9	111.4	1.5	113.3	1.7	124.4	9.8	141.9	14.1	137.0	-3.5	124.8	-8.9	110.9	-11.1	108.1	-2.5	98.1	-9.3	108.5	10.6	88.7	-18.2
1992	99.6	12.3	106.9	7.3	104.6	-2.2	92.7	-11.4	91.3	-1.5	83.3	-8.8	85.2	2.3	95.9	12.6	89.3	-6.9	105.2	17.8	102.0	-3.0	106.3	4.2
1993	103.7	-2.4	105.2	1.4	101.6	-3.4	118.3	16.4	120.8	2.1	93.9	-22.3	97.5	3.8	99.7	2.3	102.3	2.6	94.6	-7.5	118.4	25.2	126.4	6.8
1994	113.3	-10.4	99.4	-12.3	100.0	0.6	96.6	-3.4	101.4	5.0	99.2	-2.2	100.3	1.1	95.3	-5.0	97.2	2.0	99.9	2.8	115.7	15.8	137.1	18.5
1995	110.9	-19.1	105.9	-4.5	107.7	1.7	118.9	10.4	117.0	-1.6	101.3	-13.4	101.5	0.2	96.9	-4.5	113.3	16.9	97.7	-13.8	113.4	16.1	115.3	1.7

Source: U.S. Department of Labor, Bureau of Labor Statistics, Division of Industry Prices and Price Indexes. n.e.c. stands for not elsewhere classified. - indicates no data collected for period or unavailable.

Grains
Producer Price Index
Base 1982 = 100

For 1926-1995. Columns headed % show percentile change in the index from the previous period for which an index is available.

Year	Jan Index	%	Feb Index	%	Mar Index	%	Apr Index	%	May Index	%	Jun Index	%	Jul Index	%	Aug Index	%	Sep Index	%	Oct Index	%	Nov Index	%	Dec Index	%
1926	37.9	-	36.5	-3.7	34.2	-6.3	34.7	1.5	33.7	-2.9	32.9	-2.4	33.9	3.0	32.2	-5.0	32.1	-0.3	32.8	2.2	31.5	-4.0	32.6	3.5
1927	32.3	-0.9	32.1	-0.6	31.3	-2.5	31.4	0.3	35.1	11.8	36.9	5.1	36.0	-2.4	36.5	1.4	34.7	-4.9	33.4	-3.7	33.6	0.6	34.4	2.4
1928	35.2	2.3	36.5	3.7	38.3	4.9	40.9	6.8	42.8	4.6	40.4	-5.6	37.5	-7.2	32.1	-14.4	32.8	2.2	32.6	-0.6	31.8	-2.5	31.8	0.0
1929	33.1	4.1	34.4	3.9	33.2	-3.5	31.8	-4.2	29.7	-6.6	30.6	3.0	34.4	12.4	33.4	-2.9	34.2	2.4	33.4	-2.3	32.0	-4.2	32.9	2.8
1930	31.6	-4.0	30.0	-5.1	28.1	-6.3	28.4	1.1	27.7	-2.5	26.4	-4.7	24.9	-5.7	27.1	8.8	25.9	-4.4	24.3	-6.2	21.5	-11.5	21.5	0.0
1931	21.1	-1.9	20.4	-3.3	20.0	-2.0	20.1	0.5	20.1	0.0	18.9	-6.0	16.5	-12.7	15.1	-8.5	14.8	-2.0	14.9	0.7	17.3	16.1	15.8	-8.7
1932	15.7	-0.6	15.5	-1.3	14.7	-5.2	15.0	2.0	14.4	-4.0	12.7	-11.8	12.3	-3.1	12.9	4.9	12.6	-2.3	11.6	-7.9	11.1	-4.3	10.7	-3.6
1933	11.0	2.8	11.0	0.0	12.1	10.0	15.1	24.8	17.7	17.2	19.3	9.0	24.8	28.5	21.8	-12.1	21.5	-1.4	19.6	-8.8	20.6	5.1	20.4	-1.0
1934	21.4	4.9	21.3	-0.5	20.9	-1.9	19.8	-5.3	21.5	8.6	24.4	13.5	25.1	2.9	29.0	15.5	29.7	2.4	28.6	-3.7	29.3	2.4	30.8	5.1
1935	29.9	-2.9	29.4	-1.7	27.9	-5.1	29.6	6.1	28.1	-5.1	25.9	-7.8	26.4	1.9	26.7	1.1	28.1	5.2	29.1	3.6	26.2	-10.0	25.8	-1.5
1936	26.6	3.1	26.3	-1.1	25.4	-3.4	24.9	-2.0	23.8	-4.4	24.6	3.4	29.9	21.5	34.5	15.4	34.4	-0.3	34.4	0.0	34.7	0.9	36.7	5.8
1937	38.1	3.8	37.6	-1.3	38.1	1.3	40.1	5.2	38.3	-4.5	35.5	-7.3	35.4	-0.3	31.0	-12.4	31.0	0.0	25.9	-16.5	23.3	-10.0	24.1	3.4
1938	25.3	5.0	24.6	-2.8	23.2	-5.7	22.2	-4.3	21.1	-5.0	21.1	0.0	19.6	-7.1	18.0	-8.2	17.9	-0.6	17.1	-4.5	17.1	0.0	18.3	7.0
1939	19.0	3.8	18.4	-3.2	18.3	-0.5	18.6	1.6	20.1	8.1	19.6	-2.5	17.6	-10.2	17.4	-1.1	21.9	25.9	20.8	-5.0	21.6	3.8	24.2	12.0
1940	24.8	2.5	24.5	-1.2	24.8	1.2	26.0	4.8	23.9	-8.1	21.7	-9.2	20.5	-5.5	20.0	-2.4	20.8	4.0	22.0	5.8	22.8	3.6	22.5	-1.3
1941	22.8	1.3	21.7	-4.8	22.8	5.1	23.9	4.8	25.1	5.0	25.6	2.0	25.7	0.4	26.8	4.3	28.7	7.1	27.4	-4.5	28.4	3.6	30.6	7.7
1942	32.3	5.6	32.1	-0.6	31.6	-1.6	30.8	-2.5	31.1	1.0	29.9	-3.9	30.0	0.3	30.3	1.0	31.5	4.0	30.8	-2.2	31.2	1.3	33.9	8.7
1943	36.1	6.5	36.6	1.4	37.8	3.3	37.8	0.0	38.1	0.8	38.3	0.5	39.1	2.1	39.4	0.8	40.3	2.3	41.3	2.5	41.5	0.5	43.2	4.1
1944	43.6	0.9	43.6	0.0	43.6	0.0	43.6	0.0	43.7	0.2	42.8	-2.1	42.2	-1.4	41.3	-2.1	41.0	-0.7	42.2	2.9	42.0	-0.5	43.0	2.4
1945	43.6	1.4	43.7	0.2	43.7	0.0	43.9	0.5	43.5	-0.9	43.8	0.7	43.3	-1.1	42.5	-1.8	42.7	0.5	43.8	2.6	44.8	2.3	44.9	0.2
1946	45.0	0.2	45.1	0.2	46.0	2.0	46.1	0.2	49.9	8.2	51.1	2.4	61.0	19.4	56.9	-6.7	57.4	0.9	58.7	2.3	55.7	-5.1	54.9	-1.4
1947	54.8	-0.2	57.7	5.3	68.9	19.4	67.9	-1.5	69.1	1.8	69.1	0.0	67.5	-2.3	70.0	3.7	77.2	10.3	81.4	5.4	83.2	2.2	85.5	2.8
1948	86.9	1.6	74.3	-14.5	73.5	-1.1	73.5	0.0	72.1	-1.9	69.9	-3.1	63.6	-9.0	60.1	-5.5	59.3	-1.3	57.5	-3.0	57.9	0.7	57.9	0.0
1949	56.8	-1.9	53.6	-5.6	55.5	3.5	55.9	0.7	54.6	-2.3	52.4	-4.0	52.0	-0.8	51.3	-1.3	53.5	4.3	53.4	-0.2	53.7	0.6	55.0	2.4
1950	54.8	-0.4	55.2	0.7	56.7	2.7	57.9	2.1	58.9	1.7	57.4	-2.5	58.8	2.4	56.9	-3.2	56.6	-0.5	56.6	0.0	58.5	3.4	61.5	5.1
1951	63.7	3.6	65.5	2.8	64.2	-2.0	64.2	0.0	63.0	-1.9	60.7	-3.7	60.4	-0.5	61.4	1.7	61.9	0.8	64.8	4.7	66.5	2.6	67.3	1.2
1952	66.3	-1.5	65.2	-1.7	65.3	0.2	64.6	-1.1	63.3	-2.0	61.1	-3.5	60.8	-0.5	62.1	2.1	62.1	0.0	60.8	-2.1	61.8	1.6	61.5	-0.5
1953	60.6	-1.5	59.7	-1.5	60.7	1.7	60.1	-1.0	59.8	-0.5	54.0	-9.7	54.7	1.3	55.4	1.3	56.6	2.2	56.3	-0.5	57.2	1.6	58.0	1.4
1954	58.5	0.9	58.7	0.3	59.6	1.5	59.5	-0.2	58.4	-1.8	55.4	-5.1	56.4	1.8	58.4	3.5	60.0	2.7	59.5	-0.8	59.9	0.7	59.2	-1.2
1955	59.9	1.2	59.7	-0.3	59.0	-1.2	58.3	-1.2	59.2	1.5	57.9	-2.2	55.5	-4.1	50.4	-9.2	52.2	3.6	52.8	1.1	51.1	-3.2	53.0	3.7
1956	52.2	-1.5	53.1	1.7	54.1	1.9	57.3	5.9	57.9	1.0	55.7	-3.8	56.6	1.6	56.9	0.5	58.1	2.1	53.8	-7.4	56.3	4.6	56.9	1.1
1957	57.3	0.7	55.8	-2.6	56.0	0.4	55.9	-0.2	54.7	-2.1	53.7	-1.8	53.0	-1.3	52.8	-0.4	52.0	-1.5	51.6	-0.8	51.8	0.4	51.6	-0.4
1958	50.6	-1.9	51.2	1.2	52.7	2.9	54.9	4.2	54.0	-1.6	52.1	-3.5	51.1	-1.9	49.5	-3.1	48.7	-1.6	49.2	1.0	48.2	-2.0	48.7	1.0
1959	48.7	0.0	49.3	1.2	49.8	1.0	51.1	2.6	50.4	-1.4	50.1	-0.6	50.1	0.0	49.8	-0.6	48.8	-2.0	48.5	-0.6	49.0	1.0	48.7	-0.6
1960	49.5	1.6	49.1	-0.8	50.1	2.0	50.9	1.6	49.8	-2.2	49.6	-0.4	48.4	-2.4	47.6	-1.7	48.0	0.8	47.0	-2.1	45.0	-4.3	46.6	3.6
1961	48.2	3.4	48.7	1.0	49.0	0.6	47.3	-3.5	47.9	1.3	47.5	-0.8	49.8	4.8	50.0	0.4	50.0	0.0	49.9	-0.2	50.8	1.8	50.6	-0.4
1962	50.0	-1.2	49.7	-0.6	50.1	0.8	50.6	1.0	51.9	2.6	51.4	-1.0	51.0	-0.8	50.5	-1.0	50.7	0.4	50.6	-0.2	51.2	1.2	52.0	1.6
1963	52.4	0.8	53.0	1.1	53.3	0.6	54.1	1.5	52.9	-2.2	52.2	-1.3	51.2	-1.9	50.6	-1.2	52.9	4.5	52.3	-1.1	51.6	-1.3	52.3	1.4
1964	53.4	2.1	52.4	-1.9	51.0	-2.7	53.1	4.1	53.1	0.0	46.2	-13.0	44.1	-4.5	44.1	0.0	46.4	5.2	45.7	-1.5	45.2	-1.1	46.3	2.4
1965	46.5	0.4	46.6	0.2	46.6	0.0	46.9	0.6	46.8	-0.2	46.1	-1.5	45.5	-1.3	45.4	-0.2	45.9	1.1	45.6	-0.7	45.0	-1.3	46.3	2.9
1966	47.5	2.6	47.8	0.6	46.7	-2.3	46.9	0.4	48.1	2.6	48.8	1.5	53.0	8.6	54.3	2.5	53.8	-0.9	50.9	-5.4	50.4	-1.0	52.2	3.6
1967	51.8	-0.8	49.3	-4.8	51.4	4.3	50.5	-1.8	50.4	-0.2	49.4	-2.0	47.6	-3.6	44.3	-6.9	44.0	-0.7	44.5	1.1	41.8	-6.1	43.9	5.0
1968	43.7	-0.5	44.4	1.6	43.8	-1.4	43.6	-0.5	44.4	1.8	42.2	-5.0	41.2	-2.4	38.6	-6.3	39.4	2.1	40.5	2.8	42.2	4.2	41.3	-2.1
1969	42.4	2.7	42.2	-0.5	42.0	-0.5	42.7	1.7	44.6	4.4	44.0	-1.3	43.1	-2.0	42.1	-2.3	42.9	1.9	43.6	1.6	42.0	-3.7	42.6	1.4
1970	44.2	3.8	44.2	0.0	44.0	-0.5	45.1	2.5	45.5	0.9	45.9	0.9	45.9	0.0	45.9	0.0	51.7	12.6	49.4	-4.4	49.4	0.0	51.2	3.6

[Continued]

Grains
Producer Price Index
Base 1982 = 100
[Continued]

For 1926-1995. Columns headed % show percentile change in the index from the previous period for which an index is available.

Year	Jan Index	%	Feb Index	%	Mar Index	%	Apr Index	%	May Index	%	Jun Index	%	Jul Index	%	Aug Index	%	Sep Index	%	Oct Index	%	Nov Index	%	Dec Index	%
1971	52.6	2.7	53.0	0.8	51.4	-3.0	50.7	-1.4	50.8	0.2	51.9	2.2	48.6	-6.4	44.0	-9.5	42.2	-4.1	41.9	-0.7	41.6	-0.7	45.3	8.9
1972	44.6	-1.5	44.1	-1.1	44.5	0.9	45.5	2.2	46.2	1.5	44.8	-3.0	45.7	2.0	47.3	3.5	51.9	9.7	51.8	-0.2	53.9	4.1	65.3	21.2
1973	64.3	-1.5	60.8	-5.4	59.8	-1.6	62.1	3.8	71.1	14.5	84.7	19.1	74.6	-11.9	126.3	69.3	109.8	-13.1	108.6	-1.1	104.7	-3.6	117.9	12.6
1974	128.4	8.9	131.9	2.7	124.7	-5.5	101.0	-19.0	99.8	-1.2	106.3	6.5	117.2	10.3	131.7	12.4	123.0	-6.6	138.1	12.3	134.4	-2.7	130.9	-2.6
1975	121.1	-7.5	115.2	-4.9	106.0	-8.0	103.6	-2.3	101.0	-2.5	96.4	-4.6	104.0	7.9	112.7	8.4	110.4	-2.0	107.8	-2.4	98.6	-8.5	97.5	-1.1
1976	99.8	2.4	101.6	1.8	103.3	1.7	99.1	-4.1	101.2	2.1	106.7	5.4	106.4	-0.3	98.5	-7.4	97.5	-1.0	88.5	-9.2	83.2	-6.0	85.7	3.0
1977	87.7	2.3	88.1	0.5	87.0	-1.2	87.4	0.5	81.2	-7.1	74.8	-7.9	71.7	-4.1	66.6	-7.1	68.4	2.7	68.6	0.3	78.0	13.7	79.3	1.7
1978	80.2	1.1	81.0	1.0	84.8	4.7	94.2	11.1	89.7	-4.8	89.2	-0.6	87.1	-2.4	84.8	-2.6	83.9	-1.1	86.3	2.9	89.6	3.8	87.6	-2.2
1979	87.4	-0.2	89.7	2.6	91.0	1.4	94.0	3.3	99.7	6.1	103.7	4.0	117.3	13.1	108.6	-7.4	106.4	-2.0	108.6	2.1	107.5	-1.0	108.1	0.6
1980	101.8	-5.8	105.9	4.0	103.3	-2.5	99.9	-3.3	103.8	3.9	102.1	-1.6	116.1	13.7	121.6	4.7	123.6	1.6	127.7	3.3	128.5	0.6	125.7	-2.2
1981	131.7	4.8	126.8	-3.7	124.1	-2.1	125.5	1.1	122.2	-2.6	121.9	-0.2	122.0	0.1	115.1	-5.7	107.7	-6.4	107.9	0.2	107.4	-0.5	101.3	-5.7
1982	106.8	5.4	105.8	-0.9	104.7	-1.0	107.1	2.3	108.2	1.0	107.0	-1.1	100.9	-5.7	93.5	-7.3	88.8	-5.0	86.9	-2.1	94.2	8.4	95.9	1.8
1983	97.8	2.0	105.4	7.8	107.8	2.3	115.6	7.2	114.8	-0.7	114.5	-0.3	112.2	-2.0	119.4	6.4	122.3	2.4	120.3	-1.6	122.1	1.5	115.5	-5.4
1984	116.4	0.8	111.6	-4.1	119.0	6.6	124.3	4.5	121.5	-2.3	122.3	0.7	118.0	-3.5	112.3	-4.8	109.7	-2.3	103.9	-5.3	104.2	0.3	100.8	-3.3
1985	103.1	2.3	103.0	-0.1	102.5	-0.5	104.6	2.0	101.5	-3.0	100.9	-0.6	97.2	-3.7	87.8	-9.7	85.9	-2.2	83.6	-2.7	91.0	8.9	92.8	2.0
1986	91.7	-1.2	91.8	0.1	90.8	-1.1	90.7	-0.1	94.6	4.3	86.4	-8.7	72.2	-16.4	65.9	-8.7	62.9	-4.6	63.9	1.6	69.4	8.6	71.0	2.3
1987	66.8	-5.9	66.7	-0.1	67.5	1.2	71.0	5.2	79.0	11.3	74.0	-6.3	68.8	-7.0	63.4	-7.8	69.5	9.6	72.8	4.7	74.9	2.9	78.9	5.3
1988	77.5	-1.8	83.5	7.7	80.6	-3.5	82.3	2.1	82.9	0.7	103.4	24.7	111.5	7.8	109.9	-1.4	112.9	2.7	114.2	1.2	107.4	-6.0	108.9	1.4
1989	115.2	5.8	111.3	-3.4	115.1	3.4	109.8	-4.6	114.1	3.9	105.8	-7.3	105.1	-0.7	100.3	-4.6	100.1	-0.2	98.2	-1.9	101.1	3.0	101.0	-0.1
1990	100.8	-0.2	100.4	-0.4	100.2	-0.2	107.2	7.0	108.6	1.3	110.4	1.7	103.1	-6.6	92.1	-10.7	88.3	-4.1	85.8	-2.8	85.1	-0.8	87.0	2.2
1991	85.9	-1.3	88.0	2.4	94.0	6.8	94.1	0.1	92.7	-1.5	90.2	-2.7	84.3	-6.5	93.2	10.6	92.4	-0.9	94.8	2.6	96.4	1.7	97.7	1.3
1992	103.1	5.5	106.2	3.0	108.5	2.2	102.7	-5.3	103.5	0.8	105.7	2.1	95.0	-10.1	88.5	-6.8	90.6	2.4	87.8	-3.1	86.6	-1.4	89.2	3.0
1993	89.9	0.8	88.1	-2.0	89.3	1.4	93.7	4.9	91.1	-2.8	85.3	-6.4	91.2	6.9	93.9	3.0	92.2	-1.8	96.4	4.6	106.1	10.1	116.4	9.7
1994	118.0	1.4	116.8	-1.0	112.5	-3.7	109.3	-2.8	106.8	-2.3	110.1	3.1	96.4	-12.4	90.2	-6.4	94.2	4.4	91.1	-3.3	91.2	0.1	95.3	4.5
1995	95.5	0.2	96.9	1.5	98.2	1.3	101.1	3.0	104.2	3.1	110.5	6.0	116.2	5.2	114.0	-1.9	119.3	4.6	126.2	5.8	131.1	3.9	137.6	5.0

Source: U.S. Department of Labor, Bureau of Labor Statistics, Division of Industry Prices and Price Indexes. n.e.c. stands for not elsewhere classified. - indicates no data collected for period or unavailable.

Slaughter Livestock
Producer Price Index
Base 1982 = 100

For 1926-1995. Columns headed % show percentile change in the index from the previous period for which an index is available.

Year	Jan Index	%	Feb Index	%	Mar Index	%	Apr Index	%	May Index	%	Jun Index	%	Jul Index	%	Aug Index	%	Sep Index	%	Oct Index	%	Nov Index	%	Dec Index	%
1926	-	-	-	-	-	-	-	-	-	-	-	-	-	-	-	-	-	-	-	-	-	-	-	-
1927	-	-	-	-	-	-	-	-	-	-	-	-	-	-	-	-	-	-	-	-	-	-	-	-
1928	-	-	-	-	-	-	-	-	-	-	-	-	-	-	-	-	-	-	-	-	-	-	-	-
1929	-	-	-	-	-	-	-	-	-	-	-	-	-	-	-	-	-	-	-	-	-	-	-	-
1930	-	-	-	-	-	-	-	-	-	-	-	-	-	-	-	-	-	-	-	-	-	-	-	-
1931	-	-	-	-	-	-	-	-	-	-	-	-	-	-	-	-	-	-	-	-	-	-	-	-
1932	-	-	-	-	-	-	-	-	-	-	-	-	-	-	-	-	-	-	-	-	-	-	-	-
1933	-	-	-	-	-	-	-	-	-	-	-	-	-	-	-	-	-	-	-	-	-	-	-	-
1934	-	-	-	-	-	-	-	-	-	-	-	-	-	-	-	-	-	-	-	-	-	-	-	-
1935	-	-	-	-	-	-	-	-	-	-	-	-	-	-	-	-	-	-	-	-	-	-	-	-
1936	-	-	-	-	-	-	-	-	-	-	-	-	-	-	-	-	-	-	-	-	-	-	-	-
1937	-	-	-	-	-	-	-	-	-	-	-	-	-	-	-	-	-	-	-	-	-	-	-	-
1938	-	-	-	-	-	-	-	-	-	-	-	-	-	-	-	-	-	-	-	-	-	-	-	-
1939	-	-	-	-	15.0	-	-	-	-	-	13.6	-9.3	-	-	12.8	-5.9	14.7	14.8	-	-	-	-	12.3	-16.3
1940	-	-	-	-	12.6	2.4	-	-	-	-	12.6	0.0	-	-	-	-	14.0	11.1	-	-	-	-	14.1	0.7
1941	-	-	-	-	15.7	11.3	-	-	-	-	17.9	14.0	-	-	-	-	19.4	8.4	-	-	-	-	19.0	-2.1
1942	-	-	-	-	22.2	16.8	-	-	-	-	23.7	6.8	-	-	-	-	24.3	2.5	-	-	-	-	24.4	0.4
1943	-	-	-	-	27.3	11.9	-	-	-	-	25.3	-7.3	-	-	-	-	25.3	0.0	-	-	-	-	23.4	-7.5
1944	-	-	-	-	24.8	6.0	-	-	-	-	24.6	-0.8	-	-	-	-	25.0	1.6	-	-	-	-	24.8	-0.8
1945	-	-	-	-	26.1	5.2	-	-	-	-	26.1	0.0	-	-	-	-	25.1	-3.8	-	-	-	-	25.8	2.8
1946	26.2	1.6	26.1	-0.4	26.5	1.5	26.6	0.4	26.6	0.0	27.0	1.5	31.8	17.8	34.2	7.5	28.8	-15.8	33.7	17.0	38.7	14.8	38.5	-0.5
1947	37.2	-3.4	39.6	6.5	41.6	5.1	38.6	-7.2	39.5	2.3	40.4	2.3	42.0	4.0	42.0	0.0	44.1	5.0	44.4	0.7	42.3	-4.7	45.1	6.6
1948	47.5	5.3	43.0	-9.5	42.9	-0.2	42.4	-1.2	45.7	7.8	49.7	8.8	51.9	4.4	51.8	-0.2	50.9	-1.7	47.0	-7.7	44.9	-4.5	42.7	-4.9
1949	40.4	-5.4	38.4	-5.0	40.1	4.4	39.1	-2.5	40.1	2.6	40.8	1.7	40.0	-2.0	39.3	-1.7	39.6	0.8	38.2	-3.5	36.8	-3.7	36.7	-0.3
1950	37.7	2.7	39.2	4.0	39.1	-0.3	38.8	-0.8	42.6	9.8	43.3	1.6	46.7	7.9	46.8	0.2	45.9	-1.9	43.4	-5.4	43.8	0.9	45.5	3.9
1951	49.1	7.9	52.4	6.7	53.1	1.3	53.2	0.2	51.9	-2.4	52.0	0.2	51.5	-1.0	51.4	-0.2	50.7	-1.4	50.3	-0.8	47.5	-5.6	46.8	-1.5
1952	46.0	-1.7	45.6	-0.9	45.4	-0.4	46.3	2.0	47.7	3.0	46.8	-1.9	46.9	0.2	45.9	-2.1	42.5	-7.4	40.6	-4.5	39.2	-3.4	36.9	-5.9
1953	39.4	6.8	38.7	-1.8	38.8	0.3	36.6	-5.7	38.9	6.3	37.0	-4.9	40.8	10.3	37.3	-8.6	38.6	3.5	34.9	-9.6	33.2	-4.9	36.2	9.0
1954	39.6	9.4	39.5	-0.3	39.8	0.8	41.1	3.3	40.5	-1.5	37.9	-6.4	35.8	-5.5	35.9	0.3	34.9	-2.8	33.5	-4.0	33.2	-0.9	32.2	-3.0
1955	34.0	5.6	34.2	0.6	33.0	-3.5	35.2	6.7	32.8	-6.8	35.0	6.7	33.4	-4.6	31.3	-6.3	31.5	0.6	30.3	-3.8	25.8	-14.9	24.6	-4.7
1956	26.3	6.9	28.4	8.0	28.0	-1.4	30.0	7.1	31.7	5.7	32.3	1.9	31.1	-3.7	33.0	6.1	33.2	0.6	32.0	-3.6	29.7	-7.2	31.2	5.1
1957	32.3	3.5	32.6	0.9	33.3	2.1	34.7	4.2	34.5	-0.6	36.7	6.4	38.0	3.5	38.2	0.5	36.1	-5.5	34.8	-3.6	35.1	0.9	36.9	5.1
1958	38.0	3.0	40.4	6.3	42.4	5.0	42.4	0.0	44.6	5.2	44.0	-1.3	43.4	-1.4	42.3	-2.5	41.4	-2.1	40.1	-3.1	40.7	1.5	39.7	-2.5
1959	40.5	2.0	39.5	-2.5	40.9	3.5	41.7	2.0	40.9	-1.9	40.4	-1.2	38.1	-5.7	37.5	-1.6	37.0	-1.3	35.3	-4.6	33.5	-5.1	33.0	-1.5
1960	34.5	4.5	35.5	2.9	38.1	7.3	37.9	-0.5	38.1	0.5	37.8	-0.8	37.4	-1.1	35.9	-4.0	35.1	-2.2	36.0	2.6	36.5	1.4	36.9	1.1
1961	37.6	1.9	37.6	0.0	36.8	-2.1	36.7	-0.3	34.9	-4.9	34.4	-1.4	34.4	0.0	36.8	7.0	35.9	-2.4	35.4	-1.4	35.3	-0.3	35.9	1.7
1962	37.0	3.1	36.5	-1.4	37.0	1.4	36.7	-0.8	35.6	-3.0	35.8	0.6	37.3	4.2	38.5	3.2	40.7	5.7	38.5	-5.4	38.4	-0.3	37.3	-2.9
1963	36.5	-2.1	34.2	-6.3	32.6	-4.7	33.7	3.4	33.4	-0.9	34.4	3.0	36.7	6.7	36.5	-0.5	34.3	-6.0	34.0	-0.9	33.7	-0.9	30.8	-8.6
1964	32.4	5.2	31.7	-2.2	32.2	1.6	31.6	-1.9	31.3	-0.9	31.6	1.0	33.8	7.0	34.2	1.2	35.3	3.2	33.2	-5.9	32.0	-3.6	32.0	0.0
1965	32.9	2.8	34.0	3.3	34.4	1.2	35.3	2.6	37.5	6.2	41.0	9.3	41.1	0.2	41.8	1.7	40.2	-3.8	40.5	0.7	40.8	0.7	42.9	5.1
1966	44.2	3.0	45.8	3.6	44.4	-3.1	44.0	-0.9	42.8	-2.7	42.2	-1.4	41.7	-1.2	43.0	3.1	41.9	-2.6	40.8	-2.6	37.7	-7.6	37.5	-0.5
1967	38.9	3.7	38.2	-1.8	37.3	-2.4	36.1	-3.2	39.4	9.1	40.3	2.3	41.2	2.2	40.8	-1.0	39.7	-2.7	39.1	-1.5	37.0	-5.4	37.5	1.4
1968	37.9	1.1	39.4	4.0	40.5	2.8	40.4	-0.2	40.5	0.2	40.7	0.5	42.0	3.2	40.7	-3.1	40.6	-0.2	39.9	-1.7	39.9	0.0	40.0	0.3
1969	40.7	1.7	41.9	2.9	43.2	3.1	43.7	1.2	47.2	8.0	50.0	5.9	48.6	-2.8	47.4	-2.5	45.7	-3.6	45.5	-0.4	44.7	-1.8	46.1	3.1
1970	45.0	-2.4	47.9	6.4	49.7	3.8	47.9	-3.6	46.9	-2.1	47.2	0.6	48.4	2.5	45.5	-6.0	44.1	-3.1	42.9	-2.7	39.2	-8.6	38.6	-1.5

[Continued]

Slaughter Livestock
Producer Price Index
Base 1982 = 100
[Continued]

For 1926-1995. Columns headed % show percentile change in the index from the previous period for which an index is available.

Year	Jan Index	%	Feb Index	%	Mar Index	%	Apr Index	%	May Index	%	Jun Index	%	Jul Index	%	Aug Index	%	Sep Index	%	Oct Index	%	Nov Index	%	Dec Index	%
1971	39.7	2.8	46.1	16.1	44.5	-3.5	45.3	1.8	46.1	1.8	46.1	0.0	47.0	2.0	47.0	0.0	46.2	-1.7	46.9	1.5	46.9	0.0	48.4	3.2
1972	51.3	6.0	54.1	5.5	53.0	-2.0	51.9	-2.1	54.2	4.4	56.8	4.8	59.1	4.0	57.4	-2.9	56.2	-2.1	55.9	-0.5	54.1	-3.2	59.2	9.4
1973	61.8	4.4	69.0	11.7	75.4	9.3	71.4	-5.3	73.2	2.5	75.2	2.7	77.3	2.8	94.4	22.1	80.4	-14.8	72.0	-10.4	69.8	-3.1	66.3	-5.0
1974	76.5	15.4	75.6	-1.2	70.2	-7.1	65.5	-6.7	61.7	-5.8	53.5	-13.3	67.3	25.8	71.6	6.4	65.4	-8.7	64.0	-2.1	60.7	-5.2	61.9	2.0
1975	60.5	-2.3	59.0	-2.5	60.3	2.2	67.3	11.6	76.8	14.1	78.5	2.2	81.9	4.3	78.7	-3.9	81.4	3.4	80.6	-1.0	75.0	-6.9	74.3	-0.9
1976	71.6	-3.6	69.6	-2.8	66.3	-4.7	74.6	12.5	72.5	-2.8	71.8	-1.0	68.2	-5.0	64.4	-5.6	62.7	-2.6	60.5	-3.5	59.9	-1.0	64.4	7.5
1977	64.4	0.0	64.5	0.2	63.4	-1.7	65.1	2.7	69.9	7.4	66.8	-4.4	70.0	4.8	68.0	-2.9	67.0	-1.5	68.8	2.7	66.5	-3.3	70.8	6.5
1978	73.0	3.1	78.4	7.4	80.8	3.1	84.6	4.7	89.3	5.6	91.6	2.6	87.9	-4.0	84.0	-4.4	88.0	4.8	91.2	3.6	86.3	-5.4	89.3	3.5
1979	95.9	7.4	103.4	7.8	107.0	3.5	110.2	3.0	108.8	-1.3	102.4	-5.9	99.3	-3.0	93.1	-6.2	99.4	6.8	97.6	-1.8	96.3	-1.3	97.9	1.7
1980	96.1	-1.8	99.7	3.7	97.7	-2.0	89.4	-8.5	90.5	1.2	93.1	2.9	101.0	8.5	106.9	5.8	103.5	-3.2	102.0	-1.4	98.8	-3.1	97.5	-1.3
1981	94.7	-2.9	94.9	0.2	92.8	-2.2	95.7	3.1	97.6	2.0	102.0	4.5	103.4	1.4	101.6	-1.7	99.8	-1.8	94.8	-5.0	89.6	-5.5	87.3	-2.6
1982	91.8	5.2	97.4	6.1	99.1	1.7	103.8	4.7	109.7	5.7	107.6	-1.9	104.8	-2.6	104.1	-0.7	100.4	-3.6	96.4	-4.0	92.7	-3.8	92.0	-0.8
1983	94.0	2.2	97.4	3.6	97.5	0.1	101.1	3.7	100.0	-1.1	97.6	-2.4	93.3	-4.4	93.9	0.6	89.8	-4.4	89.0	-0.9	85.5	-3.9	92.4	8.1
1984	97.2	5.2	97.7	0.5	101.2	3.6	101.1	-0.1	98.8	-2.3	97.0	-1.8	100.9	4.0	98.4	-2.5	95.0	-3.5	90.7	-4.5	96.1	6.0	97.8	1.8
1985	96.0	-1.8	96.8	0.8	91.8	-5.2	89.7	-2.3	88.3	-1.6	87.9	-0.5	86.9	-1.1	82.1	-5.5	77.0	-6.2	88.2	14.5	92.8	5.2	92.8	0.0
1986	90.2	-2.8	87.7	-2.8	85.4	-2.6	82.9	-2.9	88.9	7.2	87.3	-1.8	95.1	8.9	98.1	3.2	98.2	0.1	95.9	-2.3	96.6	0.7	95.6	-1.0
1987	93.1	-2.6	95.9	3.0	96.0	0.1	104.3	8.6	109.6	5.1	109.8	0.2	107.3	-2.3	106.5	-0.7	104.1	-2.3	102.6	-1.4	96.8	-5.7	98.1	1.3
1988	99.3	1.2	105.7	6.4	106.3	0.6	107.7	1.3	111.8	3.8	106.1	-5.1	99.7	-6.0	100.6	0.9	100.7	0.1	101.8	1.1	98.3	-3.4	101.0	2.7
1989	104.5	3.5	104.6	0.1	106.8	2.1	106.4	-0.4	107.4	0.9	106.0	-1.3	104.8	-1.1	108.8	3.8	103.7	-4.7	104.6	0.9	105.6	1.0	110.5	4.6
1990	110.7	0.2	113.2	2.3	117.0	3.4	117.9	0.8	120.5	2.2	117.8	-2.2	114.7	-2.6	117.8	2.7	113.3	-3.8	116.5	2.8	113.9	-2.2	114.3	0.4
1991	112.8	-1.3	113.9	1.0	117.1	2.8	115.8	-1.1	115.2	-0.5	112.8	-2.1	110.2	-2.3	100.7	-8.6	101.1	0.4	100.9	-0.2	96.6	-4.3	97.7	1.1
1992	100.0	2.4	106.0	6.0	107.0	0.9	106.7	-0.3	108.0	1.2	105.3	-2.5	103.7	-1.5	104.2	0.5	103.4	-0.8	104.2	0.8	101.8	-2.3	106.3	4.4
1993	108.3	1.9	110.0	1.6	112.6	2.4	113.0	0.4	112.8	-0.2	109.8	-2.7	105.0	-4.4	107.1	2.0	105.7	-1.3	100.0	-5.4	100.5	0.5	99.2	-1.3
1994	100.7	1.5	103.6	2.9	104.7	1.1	104.9	0.2	98.5	-6.1	92.4	-6.2	94.3	2.1	96.8	2.7	91.3	-5.7	88.1	-3.5	89.6	1.7	91.6	2.2
1995	96.4	5.2	100.5	4.3	96.9	-3.6	92.3	-4.7	87.4	-5.3	90.7	3.8	90.7	0.0	90.8	0.1	92.0	1.3	91.4	-0.7	91.9	0.5	92.3	0.4

Source: U.S. Department of Labor, Bureau of Labor Statistics, Division of Industry Prices and Price Indexes. n.e.c. stands for not elsewhere classified. - indicates no data collected for period or unavailable.

Slaughter Poultry
Producer Price Index
Base 1982 = 100

For 1926-1995. Columns headed % show percentile change in the index from the previous period for which an index is available.

Year	Jan Index	%	Feb Index	%	Mar Index	%	Apr Index	%	May Index	%	Jun Index	%	Jul Index	%	Aug Index	%	Sep Index	%	Oct Index	%	Nov Index	%	Dec Index	%
1926	-	-	-	-	-	-	-	-	-	-	-	-	-	-	-	-	-	-	-	-	-	-	-	-
1927	-	-	-	-	-	-	-	-	-	-	-	-	-	-	-	-	-	-	-	-	-	-	-	-
1928	-	-	-	-	-	-	-	-	-	-	-	-	-	-	-	-	-	-	-	-	-	-	-	-
1929	-	-	-	-	-	-	-	-	-	-	-	-	-	-	-	-	-	-	-	-	-	-	-	-
1930	-	-	-	-	-	-	-	-	-	-	-	-	-	-	-	-	-	-	-	-	-	-	-	-
1931	-	-	-	-	-	-	-	-	-	-	-	-	-	-	-	-	-	-	-	-	-	-	-	-
1932	-	-	-	-	-	-	-	-	-	-	-	-	-	-	-	-	-	-	-	-	-	-	-	-
1933	-	-	-	-	-	-	-	-	-	-	-	-	-	-	-	-	-	-	-	-	-	-	-	-
1934	-	-	-	-	-	-	-	-	-	-	-	-	-	-	-	-	-	-	-	-	-	-	-	-
1935	-	-	-	-	-	-	-	-	-	-	-	-	-	-	-	-	-	-	-	-	-	-	-	-
1936	-	-	-	-	-	-	-	-	-	-	-	-	-	-	-	-	-	-	-	-	-	-	-	-
1937	-	-	-	-	-	-	-	-	-	-	-	-	-	-	-	-	-	-	-	-	-	-	-	-
1938	-	-	-	-	-	-	-	-	-	-	-	-	-	-	-	-	-	-	-	-	-	-	-	-
1939	-	-	-	-	67.7	-	-	-	-	-	55.3	-18.3	-	-	56.3	1.8	60.8	8.0	-	-	-	-	52.5	-13.7
1940	-	-	-	-	60.0	14.3	-	-	-	-	54.9	-8.5	-	-	-	-	59.6	8.6	-	-	-	-	58.2	-2.3
1941	-	-	-	-	72.2	24.1	-	-	-	-	77.2	6.9	-	-	-	-	76.8	-0.5	-	-	-	-	73.8	-3.9
1942	-	-	-	-	89.3	21.0	-	-	-	-	77.6	-13.1	-	-	-	-	87.0	12.1	-	-	-	-	90.9	4.5
1943	-	-	-	-	98.8	8.7	-	-	-	-	99.8	1.0	-	-	-	-	96.5	-3.3	-	-	-	-	96.2	-0.3
1944	-	-	-	-	98.8	2.7	-	-	-	-	89.2	-9.7	-	-	-	-	94.8	6.3	-	-	-	-	98.2	3.6
1945	-	-	-	-	104.0	5.9	-	-	-	-	103.0	-1.0	-	-	-	-	97.3	-5.5	-	-	-	-	98.4	1.1
1946	102.6	4.3	104.3	1.7	103.2	-1.1	108.9	5.5	108.9	0.0	108.0	-0.8	110.6	2.4	103.9	-6.1	125.7	21.0	121.0	-3.7	101.9	-15.8	107.9	5.9
1947	103.7	-3.9	103.7	0.0	115.2	11.1	115.4	0.2	116.9	1.3	111.9	-4.3	110.6	-1.2	111.9	1.2	119.5	6.8	108.2	-9.5	107.4	-0.7	117.5	9.4
1948	128.5	9.4	119.1	-7.3	131.4	10.3	135.1	2.8	131.7	-2.5	133.2	1.1	129.2	-3.0	131.0	1.4	130.3	-0.5	119.4	-8.4	123.9	3.8	131.5	6.1
1949	123.9	-5.8	116.4	-6.1	122.8	5.5	120.5	-1.9	108.3	-10.1	97.8	-9.7	98.1	0.3	102.8	4.8	97.6	-5.1	95.5	-2.2	97.9	2.5	85.0	-13.2
1950	79.5	-6.5	97.3	22.4	105.9	8.8	102.6	-3.1	95.6	-6.8	92.5	-3.2	104.9	13.4	108.0	3.0	102.5	-5.1	92.4	-9.9	89.3	-3.4	90.5	1.3
1951	100.4	10.9	111.7	11.3	120.0	7.4	120.9	0.7	114.1	-5.6	111.9	-1.9	108.6	-2.9	106.3	-2.1	102.3	-3.8	94.1	-8.0	91.0	-3.3	95.1	4.5
1952	104.5	9.9	108.5	3.8	102.9	-5.2	97.9	-4.9	89.0	-9.1	92.7	4.2	101.0	9.0	105.1	4.1	105.2	0.1	98.2	-6.7	112.7	14.8	99.1	-12.1
1953	106.2	7.2	105.3	-0.8	107.4	2.0	110.8	3.2	106.0	-4.3	94.4	-10.9	106.7	13.0	102.6	-3.8	99.4	-3.1	93.1	-6.3	91.6	-1.6	82.7	-9.7
1954	91.2	10.3	87.9	-3.6	91.8	4.4	88.4	-3.7	84.3	-4.6	83.6	-0.8	83.0	-0.7	83.3	0.4	77.9	-6.5	72.2	-7.3	70.4	-2.5	66.8	-5.1
1955	79.8	19.5	86.5	8.4	100.5	16.2	96.9	-3.6	91.1	-6.0	92.4	1.4	89.8	-2.8	91.4	1.8	89.0	-2.6	78.6	-11.7	75.4	-4.1	72.1	-4.4
1956	74.1	2.8	78.1	5.4	80.9	3.6	76.1	-5.9	77.4	1.7	72.0	-7.0	75.2	4.4	69.2	-8.0	63.7	-7.9	63.0	-1.1	63.4	0.6	64.3	1.4
1957	63.9	-0.6	68.6	7.4	70.9	3.4	67.6	-4.7	67.7	0.1	69.3	2.4	71.3	2.9	70.8	-0.7	63.7	-10.0	60.2	-5.5	61.9	2.8	60.6	-2.1
1958	68.4	12.9	69.3	1.3	73.7	6.3	65.9	-10.6	71.4	8.3	73.5	2.9	67.7	-7.9	64.0	-5.5	58.2	-9.1	56.1	-3.6	58.4	4.1	55.5	-5.0
1959	62.4	12.4	63.6	1.9	63.0	-0.9	58.2	-7.6	59.0	1.4	58.7	-0.5	58.2	-0.9	54.7	-6.0	55.3	1.1	53.6	-3.1	56.3	5.0	69.1	22.7
1960	64.7	-6.4	66.1	2.2	68.4	3.5	67.8	-0.9	65.6	-3.2	64.7	-1.4	62.7	-3.1	60.1	-4.1	59.2	-1.5	60.1	1.5	60.0	-0.2	60.8	1.3
1961	64.3	5.8	67.4	4.8	63.6	-5.6	58.8	-7.5	56.9	-3.2	46.0	-19.2	46.6	1.3	46.8	0.4	41.3	-11.8	43.5	5.3	44.0	1.1	53.0	20.5
1962	56.2	6.0	57.6	2.5	56.7	-1.6	52.2	-7.9	50.6	-3.1	50.2	-0.8	53.3	6.2	54.0	1.3	57.8	7.0	54.4	-5.9	53.5	-1.7	54.7	2.2
1963	54.6	-0.2	57.7	5.7	57.0	-1.2	57.0	0.0	53.2	-6.7	53.8	1.1	53.8	0.0	51.9	-3.5	52.1	0.4	52.2	0.2	55.0	5.4	48.8	-11.3
1964	53.9	10.5	53.2	-1.3	52.7	-0.9	52.1	-1.1	49.8	-4.4	50.7	1.8	53.8	6.1	51.7	-3.9	52.7	1.9	51.6	-2.1	53.0	2.7	50.7	-4.3
1965	53.2	4.9	54.6	2.6	57.1	4.6	55.3	-3.2	53.7	-2.9	56.0	4.3	56.3	0.5	55.0	-2.3	54.3	-1.3	54.4	0.2	54.1	-0.6	55.5	2.6
1966	58.5	5.4	60.7	3.8	64.2	5.8	60.5	-5.8	64.5	6.6	60.8	-5.7	59.9	-1.5	57.1	-4.7	55.7	-2.5	52.9	-5.0	54.1	2.3	49.1	-9.2
1967	56.1	14.3	61.8	10.2	57.8	-6.5	56.6	-2.1	54.5	-3.7	54.5	0.0	56.6	3.9	49.2	-13.1	46.4	-5.7	47.0	1.3	41.7	-11.3	43.4	4.1
1968	49.8	14.7	55.3	11.0	51.8	-6.3	51.6	-0.4	54.4	5.4	57.0	4.8	59.7	4.7	55.9	-6.4	53.9	-3.6	50.4	-6.5	55.7	10.5	52.7	-5.4
1969	57.5	9.1	59.9	4.2	60.8	1.5	57.9	-4.8	62.7	8.3	61.9	-1.3	65.3	5.5	58.7	-10.1	56.5	-3.7	54.2	-4.1	54.9	1.3	55.2	0.5
1970	60.2	9.1	55.3	-8.1	57.7	4.3	52.7	-8.7	53.2	0.9	49.5	-7.0	52.1	5.3	49.2	-5.6	51.9	5.5	48.7	-6.2	49.6	1.8	41.8	-15.7

[Continued]

Slaughter Poultry
Producer Price Index
Base 1982 = 100
[Continued]

For 1926-1995. Columns headed % show percentile change in the index from the previous period for which an index is available.

Year	Jan Index	%	Feb Index	%	Mar Index	%	Apr Index	%	May Index	%	Jun Index	%	Jul Index	%	Aug Index	%	Sep Index	%	Oct Index	%	Nov Index	%	Dec Index	%
1971	50.1	19.9	52.0	3.8	52.1	0.2	51.8	-0.6	52.8	1.9	56.3	6.6	63.0	11.9	52.5	-16.7	53.5	1.9	48.6	-9.2	48.0	-1.2	45.4	-5.4
1972	49.1	8.1	54.9	11.8	56.1	2.2	49.1	-12.5	50.2	2.2	53.6	6.8	61.7	15.1	55.7	-9.7	58.5	5.0	54.1	-7.5	53.6	-0.9	54.0	0.7
1973	66.6	23.3	71.4	7.2	85.9	20.3	96.8	12.7	93.9	-3.0	96.1	2.3	98.7	2.7	140.5	42.4	118.0	-16.0	98.6	-16.4	80.5	-18.4	75.3	-6.5
1974	74.6	-0.9	93.7	25.6	86.6	-7.6	76.1	-12.1	76.5	0.5	69.2	-9.5	77.2	11.6	78.1	1.2	90.4	15.7	81.8	-9.5	93.2	13.9	87.2	-6.4
1975	90.5	3.8	92.1	1.8	88.6	-3.8	87.7	-1.0	92.5	5.5	99.3	7.4	114.2	15.0	105.5	-7.6	106.3	0.8	109.8	3.3	106.1	-3.4	94.5	-10.9
1976	88.1	-6.8	90.2	2.4	95.2	5.5	86.2	-9.5	90.8	5.3	91.1	0.3	95.9	5.3	93.3	-2.7	85.9	-7.9	78.4	-8.7	72.5	-7.5	75.9	4.7
1977	80.1	5.5	95.7	19.5	92.3	-3.6	95.0	2.9	95.4	0.4	95.2	-0.2	101.0	6.1	91.8	-9.1	94.7	3.2	88.8	-6.2	84.8	-4.5	82.2	-3.1
1978	88.7	7.9	98.4	10.9	97.9	-0.5	102.1	4.3	101.3	-0.8	115.5	14.0	128.5	11.3	106.7	-17.0	110.0	3.1	96.4	-12.4	100.2	3.9	103.5	3.3
1979	107.3	3.7	113.5	5.8	113.4	-0.1	109.1	-3.8	112.7	3.3	95.3	-15.4	95.8	0.5	89.6	-6.5	90.4	0.9	84.4	-6.6	101.9	20.7	101.4	-0.5
1980	101.7	0.3	96.2	-5.4	93.8	-2.5	89.6	-4.5	89.2	-0.4	86.8	-2.7	118.4	36.4	117.0	-1.2	125.6	7.4	116.2	-7.5	115.2	-0.9	114.0	-1.0
1981	111.1	-2.5	115.1	3.6	111.2	-3.4	101.8	-8.5	108.0	6.1	109.4	1.3	112.2	2.6	109.6	-2.3	102.5	-6.5	96.8	-5.6	91.2	-5.8	89.3	-2.1
1982	97.3	9.0	102.8	5.7	103.0	0.2	97.0	-5.8	100.4	3.5	108.0	7.6	110.7	2.5	98.7	-10.8	102.4	3.7	92.3	-9.9	94.6	2.5	92.7	-2.0
1983	92.3	-0.4	104.3	13.0	92.7	-11.1	89.0	-4.0	97.4	9.4	103.9	6.7	111.8	7.6	115.4	3.2	126.2	9.4	108.6	-13.9	124.3	14.5	125.7	1.1
1984	131.6	4.7	131.0	-0.5	134.6	2.7	125.5	-6.8	125.4	-0.1	118.7	-5.3	135.1	13.8	113.9	-15.7	124.9	9.7	114.3	-8.5	128.8	12.7	120.8	-6.2
1985	121.3	0.4	115.9	-4.5	112.3	-3.1	105.4	-6.1	111.8	6.1	116.5	4.2	118.6	1.8	112.6	-5.1	127.4	13.1	117.4	-7.8	132.8	13.1	122.5	-7.8
1986	110.9	-9.5	102.9	-7.2	108.9	5.8	110.1	1.1	113.7	3.3	123.3	8.4	154.6	25.4	177.2	14.6	145.7	-17.8	163.6	12.3	130.8	-20.0	114.5	-12.5
1987	110.6	-3.4	104.1	-5.9	104.0	-0.1	105.3	1.3	112.8	7.1	94.2	-16.5	102.3	8.6	111.2	8.7	100.3	-9.8	88.5	-11.8	93.9	6.1	87.7	-6.6
1988	99.1	13.0	86.9	-12.3	96.9	11.5	97.6	0.7	112.2	15.0	130.4	16.2	156.4	19.9	145.1	-7.2	142.7	-1.7	141.0	-1.2	128.0	-9.2	121.7	-4.9
1989	122.4	0.6	121.5	-0.7	138.5	14.0	138.4	-0.1	155.0	12.0	148.5	-4.2	135.5	-8.8	125.4	-7.5	134.9	7.6	109.0	-19.2	111.8	2.6	104.3	-6.7
1990	108.9	4.4	115.5	6.1	129.1	11.8	117.3	-9.1	128.2	9.3	118.5	-7.6	134.7	13.7	122.1	-9.4	128.9	5.6	110.2	-14.5	108.3	-1.7	104.2	-3.8
1991	110.4	6.0	103.1	-6.6	110.2	6.9	107.3	-2.6	113.9	6.2	112.7	-1.1	119.2	5.8	120.4	1.0	116.7	-3.1	109.1	-6.5	106.8	-2.1	105.1	-1.6
1992	106.9	1.7	102.8	-3.8	105.4	2.5	102.8	-2.5	116.1	12.9	110.7	-4.7	124.1	12.1	120.5	-2.9	111.8	-7.2	119.3	6.7	121.7	2.0	108.8	-10.6
1993	112.0	2.9	110.4	-1.4	116.1	5.2	116.5	0.3	132.3	13.6	118.9	-10.1	124.4	4.6	125.9	1.2	135.1	7.3	126.1	-6.7	127.2	0.9	118.4	-6.9
1994	110.9	-6.3	119.6	7.8	129.5	8.3	126.8	-2.1	138.2	9.0	135.2	-2.2	131.0	-3.1	119.9	-8.5	128.3	7.0	125.0	-2.6	114.4	-8.5	114.2	-0.2
1995	108.6	-4.9	109.3	0.6	113.1	3.5	109.1	-3.5	111.0	1.7	121.1	9.1	130.0	7.3	139.7	7.5	147.2	5.4	135.7	-7.8	150.3	10.8	132.5	-11.8

Source: U.S. Department of Labor, Bureau of Labor Statistics, Division of Industry Prices and Price Indexes. n.e.c. stands for not elsewhere classified. - indicates no data collected for period or unavailable.

Plant and Animal Fibers
Producer Price Index
Base 1982 = 100

For 1926-1995. Columns headed % show percentile change in the index from the previous period for which an index is available.

Year	Jan Index	%	Feb Index	%	Mar Index	%	Apr Index	%	May Index	%	Jun Index	%	Jul Index	%	Aug Index	%	Sep Index	%	Oct Index	%	Nov Index	%	Dec Index	%
1926	52.6	-	52.1	-1.0	48.5	-6.9	47.0	-3.1	46.4	-1.3	45.9	-1.1	46.2	0.7	48.3	4.5	43.6	-9.7	37.6	-13.8	36.4	-3.2	35.9	-1.4
1927	37.1	3.3	38.3	3.2	39.0	1.8	39.5	1.3	41.8	5.8	42.7	2.2	44.8	4.9	48.4	8.0	51.3	6.0	49.9	-2.7	48.4	-3.0	47.0	-2.9
1928	46.3	-1.5	45.6	-1.5	47.8	4.8	49.1	2.7	51.2	4.3	50.6	-1.2	50.9	0.6	46.8	-8.1	45.4	-3.0	47.1	3.7	47.5	0.8	48.2	1.5
1929	47.6	-1.2	47.7	0.2	48.9	2.5	47.2	-3.5	45.6	-3.4	45.2	-0.9	45.0	-0.4	45.4	0.9	45.6	0.4	44.7	-2.0	42.4	-5.1	41.7	-1.7
1930	41.3	-1.0	38.4	-7.0	37.3	-2.9	38.2	2.4	37.5	-1.8	33.1	-11.7	30.5	-7.9	28.7	-5.9	26.5	-7.7	25.6	-3.4	25.8	0.8	24.2	-6.2
1931	24.7	2.1	25.7	4.0	25.6	-0.4	24.2	-5.5	22.4	-7.4	22.0	-1.8	22.6	2.7	18.9	-16.4	17.5	-7.4	16.9	-3.4	17.3	2.4	16.5	-4.6
1932	16.7	1.2	16.8	0.6	16.4	-2.4	15.0	-8.5	13.7	-8.7	12.7	-7.3	13.6	7.1	16.6	22.1	17.8	7.2	15.9	-10.7	15.0	-5.7	14.3	-4.7
1933	14.5	1.4	13.9	-4.1	15.0	7.9	15.7	4.7	19.2	22.3	21.9	14.1	24.9	13.7	22.4	-10.0	22.5	0.4	22.1	-1.8	22.6	2.3	22.9	1.3
1934	24.7	7.9	26.7	8.1	26.7	0.0	26.0	-2.6	24.9	-4.2	26.2	5.2	26.7	1.9	27.4	2.6	27.0	-1.5	26.2	-3.0	26.5	1.1	26.8	1.1
1935	26.9	0.4	26.5	-1.5	24.4	-7.9	24.8	1.6	25.8	4.0	25.4	-1.6	25.7	1.2	25.1	-2.3	24.5	-2.4	25.7	4.9	27.2	5.8	26.9	-1.1
1936	26.7	-0.7	26.0	-2.6	26.1	0.4	26.2	0.4	26.0	-0.8	26.7	2.7	28.4	6.4	27.4	-3.5	27.4	0.0	27.3	-0.4	27.7	1.5	29.0	4.7
1937	29.8	2.8	29.9	0.3	31.9	6.7	31.6	-0.9	30.0	-5.1	28.9	-3.7	28.6	-1.0	24.9	-12.9	22.5	-9.6	20.8	-7.6	19.8	-4.8	20.0	1.0
1938	20.6	3.0	20.8	1.0	20.7	-0.5	20.5	-1.0	20.0	-2.4	19.8	-1.0	21.0	6.1	20.2	-3.8	19.5	-3.5	20.5	5.1	20.9	2.0	20.4	-2.4
1939	20.8	2.0	21.2	1.9	21.7	2.4	21.5	-0.9	23.1	7.4	23.5	1.7	23.3	-0.9	22.6	-3.0	24.0	6.2	25.3	5.4	26.3	4.0	29.3	11.4
1940	25.8	-11.9	25.0	-3.1	24.5	-2.0	24.0	-2.0	22.8	-5.0	23.5	3.1	22.9	-2.6	21.7	-5.2	21.7	0.0	22.0	1.4	22.8	3.6	23.0	0.9
1941	23.3	1.3	23.4	0.4	24.3	3.8	25.0	2.9	27.7	10.8	29.7	7.2	32.9	10.8	33.6	2.1	35.3	5.1	34.4	-2.5	34.1	-0.9	35.7	4.7
1942	38.7	8.4	38.7	0.0	39.5	2.1	40.4	2.3	40.3	-0.2	38.4	-4.7	39.0	1.6	37.3	-4.4	37.4	0.3	37.6	0.5	38.3	1.9	38.9	1.6
1943	40.1	3.1	40.6	1.2	41.2	1.5	41.3	0.2	41.2	-0.2	41.1	-0.2	40.7	-1.0	40.1	-1.5	40.1	0.0	39.6	-1.2	38.4	-3.0	38.5	0.3
1944	39.2	1.8	40.3	2.8	40.8	1.2	40.6	-0.5	40.7	0.2	41.5	2.0	41.7	0.5	41.1	-1.4	41.2	0.2	41.4	0.5	41.1	-0.7	41.4	0.7
1945	41.5	0.2	41.5	0.0	41.8	0.7	42.4	1.4	43.2	1.9	43.1	-0.2	42.6	-1.2	42.2	-0.9	42.4	0.5	43.5	2.6	44.9	3.2	45.3	0.9
1946	45.5	0.4	47.2	3.7	48.7	3.2	50.1	2.9	49.8	-0.6	52.1	4.6	63.1	21.1	67.5	7.0	68.7	1.8	67.7	-1.5	59.8	-11.7	61.9	3.5
1947	61.0	-1.5	62.9	3.1	65.6	4.3	66.3	1.1	67.5	1.8	69.3	2.7	70.3	1.4	65.7	-6.5	62.0	-5.6	62.7	1.1	65.9	5.1	69.5	5.5
1948	68.7	-1.2	65.7	-4.4	67.7	3.0	72.9	7.7	74.7	2.5	75.6	1.2	71.8	-5.0	67.8	-5.6	67.5	-0.4	67.1	-0.6	67.5	0.6	69.6	3.1
1949	70.7	1.6	70.6	-0.1	70.4	-0.3	70.8	0.6	69.4	-2.0	69.0	-0.6	67.1	-2.8	64.9	-3.3	63.6	-2.0	63.0	-0.9	62.0	-1.6	63.2	1.9
1950	65.0	2.8	67.4	3.7	67.1	-0.4	68.3	1.8	70.0	2.5	72.4	3.4	77.0	6.4	80.5	4.5	90.8	12.8	89.7	-1.2	94.7	5.6	98.0	3.5
1951	108.3	10.5	112.5	3.9	116.4	3.5	112.2	-3.6	107.9	-3.8	105.1	-2.6	92.6	-11.9	80.9	-12.6	77.0	-4.8	80.2	4.2	86.7	8.1	85.6	-1.3
1952	85.8	0.2	81.3	-5.2	80.2	-1.4	80.7	0.6	77.1	-4.5	80.1	3.9	77.9	-2.7	77.7	-0.3	76.5	-1.5	74.0	-3.3	72.3	-2.3	68.7	-5.0
1953	68.2	-0.7	69.3	1.6	70.6	1.9	69.8	-1.1	70.4	0.9	70.2	-0.3	70.9	1.0	70.1	-1.1	69.9	-0.3	69.6	-0.4	69.8	0.3	69.6	-0.3
1954	70.3	1.0	71.9	2.3	71.5	-0.6	71.2	-0.4	72.2	1.4	72.2	0.0	72.4	0.3	72.0	-0.6	72.5	0.7	72.3	-0.3	70.5	-2.5	70.9	0.6
1955	70.5	-0.6	70.4	-0.1	69.4	-1.4	69.3	-0.1	69.8	0.7	69.8	0.0	70.1	0.4	69.4	-1.0	68.1	-1.9	66.9	-1.8	68.2	1.9	68.1	-0.1
1956	68.7	0.9	71.4	3.9	71.2	-0.3	71.4	0.3	71.5	0.1	71.7	0.3	70.4	-1.8	66.3	-5.8	66.4	0.2	67.5	1.7	68.1	0.9	68.4	0.4
1957	69.4	1.5	70.1	1.0	70.2	0.1	70.4	0.3	70.4	0.0	70.8	0.6	70.9	0.1	70.2	-1.0	69.4	-1.1	69.7	0.4	70.7	1.4	70.0	-1.0
1958	69.8	-0.3	69.4	-0.6	68.6	-1.2	68.4	-0.3	68.6	0.3	68.7	0.1	68.7	0.0	68.7	0.0	68.0	-1.0	68.0	0.0	68.0	0.0	67.3	-1.0
1959	67.1	-0.3	66.9	-0.3	67.2	0.4	68.2	1.5	68.7	0.7	68.6	-0.1	67.5	-1.6	64.6	-4.3	64.5	-0.2	63.9	-0.9	63.9	0.0	64.6	1.1
1960	64.7	0.2	64.9	0.3	64.8	-0.2	65.0	0.3	65.2	0.3	65.3	0.2	65.1	-0.3	62.3	-4.3	62.2	-0.2	61.3	-1.4	61.3	0.0	61.3	0.0
1961	61.3	0.0	61.6	0.5	62.7	1.8	63.0	0.5	64.3	2.1	65.0	1.1	65.3	0.5	66.4	1.7	66.6	0.3	67.1	0.8	67.1	0.0	67.1	0.0
1962	67.0	-0.1	67.1	0.1	67.3	0.3	67.6	0.4	67.6	0.0	68.1	0.7	67.9	-0.3	67.3	-0.9	66.6	-1.0	66.6	0.0	66.7	0.2	67.1	0.6
1963	67.9	1.2	68.9	1.5	69.6	1.0	69.7	0.1	69.5	-0.3	69.3	-0.3	68.5	-1.2	68.1	-0.6	68.0	-0.1	68.0	0.0	68.2	0.3	69.3	1.6
1964	69.4	0.1	69.5	0.1	69.8	0.4	69.8	0.0	69.2	-0.9	69.2	0.0	68.0	-1.7	65.6	-3.5	64.5	-1.7	64.1	-0.6	64.2	0.2	63.3	-1.4
1965	63.2	-0.2	62.7	-0.8	62.6	-0.2	62.6	0.0	62.7	0.2	62.9	0.3	62.7	-0.3	61.8	-1.4	61.5	-0.5	61.5	0.0	61.4	-0.2	61.3	-0.2
1966	61.3	0.0	61.2	-0.2	61.3	0.2	61.5	0.3	61.7	0.3	61.7	0.0	61.8	0.2	49.4	-20.1	49.0	-0.8	48.8	-0.4	48.4	-0.8	48.5	0.2
1967	48.4	-0.2	48.0	-0.8	48.0	0.0	47.8	-0.4	47.8	0.0	48.4	1.3	48.4	0.0	48.8	0.8	49.5	1.4	49.5	0.0	51.2	3.4	55.2	7.8
1968	54.3	-1.6	52.3	-3.7	52.3	0.0	52.0	-0.6	51.8	-0.4	51.9	0.2	51.9	0.0	52.5	1.2	52.7	0.4	50.7	-3.8	48.7	-3.9	47.2	-3.1
1969	47.0	-0.4	46.3	-1.5	46.0	-0.6	46.0	0.0	46.3	0.7	46.3	0.0	46.3	0.0	45.7	-1.3	45.4	-0.7	45.2	-0.4	45.1	-0.2	44.9	-0.4
1970	44.6	-0.7	44.7	0.2	44.4	-0.7	44.7	0.7	44.8	0.2	44.9	0.2	45.2	0.7	45.2	0.0	44.4	-1.8	43.8	-1.4	43.3	-1.1	42.7	-1.4

[Continued]

Plant and Animal Fibers
Producer Price Index
Base 1982 = 100
[Continued]

For 1926-1995. Columns headed % show percentile change in the index from the previous period for which an index is available.

Year	Jan Index	%	Feb Index	%	Mar Index	%	Apr Index	%	May Index	%	Jun Index	%	Jul Index	%	Aug Index	%	Sep Index	%	Oct Index	%	Nov Index	%	Dec Index	%
1971	42.9	0.5	43.4	1.2	43.8	0.9	44.1	0.7	44.5	0.9	45.5	2.2	45.6	0.2	46.0	0.9	46.9	2.0	47.4	1.1	47.9	1.1	50.5	5.4
1972	54.0	6.9	55.8	3.3	56.3	0.9	60.2	6.9	64.1	6.5	62.7	-2.2	61.8	-1.4	59.4	-3.9	53.4	-10.1	52.1	-2.4	55.3	6.1	59.6	7.8
1973	66.1	10.9	69.0	4.4	75.2	9.0	76.2	1.3	84.5	10.9	87.6	3.7	91.9	4.9	112.6	22.5	132.0	17.2	131.3	-0.5	115.3	-12.2	127.8	10.8
1974	135.4	5.9	118.3	-12.6	108.1	-8.6	103.1	-4.6	96.7	-6.2	96.3	-0.4	92.6	-3.8	89.4	-3.5	83.6	-6.5	78.5	-6.1	74.3	-5.4	70.5	-5.1
1975	68.4	-3.0	66.7	-2.5	68.2	2.2	67.8	-0.6	75.5	11.4	71.7	-5.0	75.3	5.0	79.4	5.4	80.8	1.8	81.1	0.4	82.3	1.5	88.5	7.5
1976	95.3	7.7	91.9	-3.6	92.5	0.7	92.4	-0.1	99.3	7.5	116.2	17.0	132.6	14.1	116.1	-12.4	119.4	2.8	123.1	3.1	127.1	3.2	118.0	-7.2
1977	106.7	-9.6	118.3	10.9	124.4	5.2	123.0	-1.1	117.6	-4.4	97.3	-17.3	96.3	-1.0	88.8	-7.8	81.7	-8.0	82.3	0.7	80.9	-1.7	79.3	-2.0
1978	84.3	6.3	86.0	2.0	92.1	7.1	89.2	-3.1	94.5	5.9	95.1	0.6	93.6	-1.6	97.3	4.0	99.2	2.0	103.6	4.4	104.2	0.6	104.9	0.7
1979	105.3	0.4	101.1	-4.0	97.5	-3.6	97.5	0.0	102.3	4.9	108.2	5.8	102.3	-5.5	102.5	0.2	104.1	1.6	104.9	0.8	106.2	1.2	109.4	3.0
1980	117.8	7.7	132.8	12.7	125.6	-5.4	131.6	4.8	134.4	2.1	121.7	-9.4	131.6	8.1	138.4	5.2	145.5	5.1	137.2	-5.7	141.5	3.1	144.9	2.4
1981	140.0	-3.4	132.2	-5.6	133.1	0.7	135.1	1.5	127.3	-5.8	128.0	0.5	123.8	-3.3	114.6	-7.4	101.8	-11.2	104.3	2.5	97.8	-6.2	92.8	-5.1
1982	97.7	5.3	95.4	-2.4	98.3	3.0	102.2	4.0	105.5	3.2	100.1	-5.1	108.8	8.7	102.3	-6.0	97.0	-5.2	97.6	0.6	96.3	-1.3	98.8	2.6
1983	99.4	0.6	101.7	2.3	107.0	5.2	105.3	-1.6	110.3	4.7	113.2	2.6	113.5	0.3	118.6	4.5	117.6	-0.8	115.6	-1.7	120.1	3.9	120.3	0.2
1984	113.0	-6.1	114.7	1.5	123.4	7.6	124.3	0.7	127.7	2.7	124.5	-2.5	116.2	-6.7	104.2	-10.3	103.6	-0.6	100.0	-3.5	99.2	-0.8	100.1	0.9
1985	100.8	0.7	98.9	-1.9	98.8	-0.1	104.1	5.4	99.9	-4.0	98.1	-1.8	99.4	1.3	95.9	-3.5	94.2	-1.8	94.3	0.1	93.5	-0.8	91.9	-1.7
1986	96.8	5.3	97.8	1.0	101.9	4.2	103.8	1.9	106.2	2.3	108.2	1.9	108.7	0.5	46.5	-57.2	53.2	14.4	74.3	39.7	75.9	2.2	87.1	14.8
1987	94.7	8.7	93.1	-1.7	89.9	-3.4	98.4	9.5	108.7	10.5	116.1	6.8	120.1	3.4	123.4	2.7	118.5	-4.0	108.9	-8.1	105.1	-3.5	100.5	-4.4
1988	100.7	0.2	97.8	-2.9	103.2	5.5	103.6	0.4	103.7	0.1	107.6	3.8	99.4	-7.6	98.7	-0.7	89.6	-9.2	89.7	0.1	93.1	3.8	93.9	0.9
1989	95.8	2.0	94.8	-1.0	98.4	3.8	105.0	6.7	108.1	3.0	110.5	2.2	111.5	0.9	116.8	4.8	113.9	-2.5	116.9	2.6	115.3	-1.4	106.3	-7.8
1990	104.8	-1.4	108.7	3.7	114.7	5.5	118.7	3.5	121.9	2.7	125.9	3.3	129.4	2.8	125.1	-3.3	116.6	-6.8	116.4	-0.2	115.0	-1.2	116.9	1.7
1991	115.2	-1.5	126.3	9.6	129.1	2.2	134.0	3.8	139.2	3.9	130.8	-6.0	120.2	-8.1	106.7	-11.2	103.5	-3.0	96.3	-7.0	90.3	-6.2	89.7	-0.7
1992	85.4	-4.8	83.5	-2.2	84.7	1.4	89.0	5.1	93.4	4.9	96.2	3.0	102.0	6.0	96.6	-5.3	93.8	-2.9	82.8	-11.7	83.2	0.5	87.3	4.9
1993	89.5	2.5	89.5	0.0	94.2	5.3	91.5	-2.9	93.3	2.0	90.5	-3.0	90.8	0.3	88.5	-2.5	89.4	1.0	92.0	2.9	88.8	-3.5	98.1	10.5
1994	107.1	9.2	119.0	11.1	120.8	1.5	123.4	2.2	129.2	4.7	129.4	0.2	114.5	-11.5	118.7	3.7	122.1	2.9	111.1	-9.0	120.4	8.4	132.6	10.1
1995	143.5	8.2	149.4	4.1	180.2	20.6	175.2	-2.8	165.7	-5.4	178.9	8.0	163.5	-8.6	139.2	-14.9	147.6	6.0	142.6	-3.4	139.9	-1.9	137.9	-1.4

Source: U.S. Department of Labor, Bureau of Labor Statistics, Division of Industry Prices and Price Indexes. n.e.c. stands for not elsewhere classified. - indicates no data collected for period or unavailable.

Fluid Milk
Producer Price Index
Base 1982 = 100

For 1926-1995. Columns headed % show percentile change in the index from the previous period for which an index is available.

Year	Jan Index	%	Feb Index	%	Mar Index	%	Apr Index	%	May Index	%	Jun Index	%	Jul Index	%	Aug Index	%	Sep Index	%	Oct Index	%	Nov Index	%	Dec Index	%
1926	19.6	-	19.6	0.0	19.6	0.0	19.8	1.0	19.2	-3.0	18.9	-1.6	19.1	1.1	19.3	1.0	19.9	3.1	19.8	-0.5	19.7	-0.5	19.7	0.0
1927	19.6	-0.5	19.6	0.0	19.6	0.0	19.4	-1.0	19.2	-1.0	19.2	0.0	19.4	1.0	19.4	0.0	20.9	7.7	20.9	0.0	21.0	0.5	21.0	0.0
1928	20.8	-1.0	20.8	0.0	19.4	-6.7	19.3	-0.5	19.1	-1.0	19.1	0.0	20.0	4.7	20.9	4.5	21.1	1.0	21.0	-0.5	21.0	0.0	21.0	0.0
1929	21.2	1.0	21.1	-0.5	21.1	0.0	21.1	0.0	21.1	0.0	21.4	1.4	21.1	-1.4	21.1	0.0	21.2	0.5	21.4	0.9	21.4	0.0	21.4	0.0
1930	21.1	-1.4	21.1	0.0	21.1	0.0	21.1	0.0	19.8	-6.2	19.8	0.0	19.8	0.0	20.7	4.5	21.1	1.9	21.1	0.0	21.1	0.0	19.8	-6.2
1931	18.7	-5.6	18.5	-1.1	18.5	0.0	18.5	0.0	18.5	0.0	18.9	2.2	19.2	1.6	18.8	-2.1	18.8	0.0	18.8	0.0	17.5	-6.9	17.5	0.0
1932	14.7	-16.0	13.8	-6.1	13.8	0.0	13.8	0.0	13.8	0.0	13.5	-2.2	13.5	0.0	13.5	0.0	13.5	0.0	13.5	0.0	13.5	0.0	11.9	-11.9
1933	11.5	-3.4	11.0	-4.3	10.8	-1.8	10.8	0.0	12.0	11.1	13.5	12.5	13.9	3.0	14.7	5.8	14.7	0.0	14.8	0.7	15.2	2.7	15.5	2.0
1934	15.2	-1.9	14.6	-3.9	14.4	-1.4	14.3	-0.7	15.9	11.2	16.9	6.3	17.3	2.4	17.3	0.0	17.3	0.0	17.5	1.2	17.0	-2.9	17.0	0.0
1935	17.2	1.2	17.4	1.2	17.4	0.0	17.3	-0.6	17.1	-1.2	16.9	-1.2	16.9	0.0	17.1	1.2	16.8	-1.8	16.5	-1.8	16.5	0.0	16.6	0.6
1936	16.5	-0.6	16.6	0.6	15.9	-4.2	15.8	-0.6	15.8	0.0	15.8	0.0	16.4	3.8	17.1	4.3	18.2	6.4	18.3	0.5	18.4	0.5	18.4	0.0
1937	18.4	0.0	18.5	0.5	18.5	0.0	15.1	-18.4	13.3	-11.9	13.3	0.0	14.6	9.8	15.5	6.2	16.7	7.7	16.7	0.0	17.6	5.4	17.8	1.1
1938	16.4	-7.9	15.6	-4.9	15.4	-1.3	14.8	-3.9	14.2	-4.1	14.1	-0.7	14.3	1.4	14.2	-0.7	15.2	7.0	15.2	0.0	15.3	0.7	15.4	0.7
1939	15.2	-1.3	15.1	-0.7	13.0	-13.9	10.9	-16.2	10.9	0.0	11.1	1.8	13.2	18.9	14.6	10.6	15.9	8.9	16.9	6.3	16.9	0.0	16.7	-1.2
1940	16.7	0.0	16.6	-0.6	16.5	-0.6	16.5	0.0	14.8	-10.3	14.8	0.0	15.2	2.7	15.3	0.7	15.1	-1.3	15.4	2.0	16.4	6.5	16.2	-1.2
1941	16.1	-0.6	16.0	-0.6	16.1	0.6	15.5	-3.7	14.6	-5.8	15.4	5.5	16.8	9.1	17.7	5.4	18.2	2.8	19.3	6.0	19.4	0.5	19.4	0.0
1942	19.4	0.0	19.2	-1.0	19.0	-1.0	17.9	-5.8	17.6	-1.7	17.5	-0.6	18.7	6.9	19.0	1.6	20.0	5.3	20.2	1.0	21.1	4.5	21.3	0.9
1943	21.6	1.4	21.6	0.0	21.6	0.0	21.6	0.0	21.6	0.0	21.6	0.0	21.6	0.0	21.6	0.0	21.6	0.0	21.7	0.5	22.5	3.7	22.5	0.0
1944	22.6	0.4	22.6	0.0	22.5	-0.4	22.4	-0.4	22.3	-0.4	22.3	0.0	22.3	0.0	22.4	0.4	22.5	0.4	22.5	0.0	22.5	0.0	22.5	0.0
1945	22.5	0.0	22.5	0.0	22.5	0.0	22.5	0.0	22.4	-0.4	22.4	0.0	22.4	0.0	22.4	0.0	22.4	0.0	22.4	0.0	22.5	0.4	22.6	0.4
1946	22.6	0.0	22.7	0.4	22.7	0.0	22.8	0.4	22.9	0.4	24.8	8.3	28.9	16.5	29.8	3.1	30.5	2.3	32.9	7.9	33.2	0.9	32.8	-1.2
1947	32.3	-1.5	30.6	-5.3	29.8	-2.6	28.4	-4.7	25.8	-9.2	26.1	1.2	27.4	5.0	29.6	8.0	31.0	4.7	32.0	3.2	32.8	2.5	34.0	3.7
1948	35.3	3.8	34.8	-1.4	33.6	-3.4	33.9	0.9	34.0	0.3	35.0	2.9	36.3	3.7	36.2	-0.3	34.9	-3.6	32.6	-6.6	31.5	-3.4	31.4	-0.3
1949	29.7	-5.4	28.5	-4.0	27.6	-3.2	26.7	-3.3	26.3	-1.5	26.3	0.0	26.7	1.5	27.6	3.4	27.8	0.7	27.9	0.4	28.2	1.1	27.9	-1.1
1950	27.3	-2.2	27.2	-0.4	26.9	-1.1	25.9	-3.7	25.3	-2.3	25.0	-1.2	25.8	3.2	26.7	3.5	27.6	3.4	28.4	2.9	29.1	2.5	30.1	3.4
1951	32.5	8.0	32.7	0.6	32.5	-0.6	31.5	-3.1	30.8	-2.2	30.9	0.3	31.3	1.3	31.8	1.6	31.8	0.0	32.2	1.3	32.9	2.2	33.5	1.8
1952	33.7	0.6	33.9	0.6	33.7	-0.6	33.1	-1.8	31.9	-3.6	31.6	-0.9	32.7	3.5	33.7	3.1	34.8	3.3	35.1	0.9	34.5	-1.7	33.3	-3.5
1953	32.2	-3.3	31.5	-2.2	30.7	-2.5	29.6	-3.6	28.6	-3.4	28.5	-0.3	29.5	3.5	29.8	1.0	30.3	1.7	30.8	1.7	31.2	1.3	30.4	-2.6
1954	29.8	-2.0	29.0	-2.7	28.5	-1.7	27.0	-5.3	25.7	-4.8	25.6	-0.4	26.8	4.7	27.4	2.2	28.0	2.2	28.7	2.5	29.1	1.4	28.6	-1.7
1955	28.2	-1.4	28.1	-0.4	27.7	-1.4	27.6	-0.4	26.7	-3.3	26.6	-0.4	27.2	2.3	28.0	2.9	28.6	2.1	29.1	1.7	29.0	-0.3	28.9	-0.3
1956	28.7	-0.7	28.7	0.0	27.7	-3.5	27.5	-0.7	28.4	3.3	28.4	0.0	28.9	1.8	29.1	0.7	29.3	0.7	29.7	1.4	30.2	1.7	30.3	0.3
1957	30.0	-1.0	29.8	-0.7	29.2	-2.0	29.0	-0.7	28.2	-2.8	28.1	-0.4	28.5	1.4	29.0	1.8	29.6	2.1	30.2	2.0	30.4	0.7	30.3	-0.3
1958	30.1	-0.7	29.9	-0.7	29.2	-2.3	28.0	-4.1	27.7	-1.1	27.6	-0.4	28.1	1.8	28.6	1.8	29.3	2.4	29.4	0.3	29.5	0.3	29.4	-0.3
1959	29.2	-0.7	29.2	0.0	28.6	-2.1	28.1	-1.7	27.6	-1.8	27.5	-0.4	28.2	2.5	28.9	2.5	29.3	1.4	29.7	1.4	30.0	1.0	30.1	0.3
1960	30.3	0.7	30.3	0.0	29.9	-1.3	29.2	-2.3	28.4	-2.7	28.5	0.4	29.2	2.5	29.7	1.7	30.5	2.7	31.0	1.6	31.3	1.0	31.3	0.0
1961	30.9	-1.3	30.4	-1.6	30.2	-0.7	29.7	-1.7	29.2	-1.7	29.0	-0.7	30.0	3.4	30.1	0.3	30.4	1.0	30.7	1.0	30.8	0.3	30.6	-0.6
1962	30.6	0.0	30.4	-0.7	29.8	-2.0	28.7	-3.7	28.1	-2.1	28.2	0.4	29.0	2.8	29.3	1.0	29.5	0.7	29.8	1.0	29.7	-0.3	29.6	-0.3
1963	29.4	-0.7	29.3	-0.3	28.9	-1.4	28.5	-1.4	28.2	-1.1	28.4	0.7	29.0	2.1	29.2	0.7	29.6	1.4	29.8	0.7	30.0	0.7	30.0	0.0
1964	29.8	-0.7	29.7	-0.3	29.4	-1.0	28.9	-1.7	28.6	-1.0	28.7	0.3	29.2	1.7	29.6	1.4	30.1	1.7	30.3	0.7	30.6	1.0	30.5	-0.3
1965	30.2	-1.0	30.1	-0.3	29.1	-3.3	29.4	1.0	29.1	-1.0	29.2	0.3	29.7	1.7	30.2	1.7	30.4	0.7	30.8	1.3	31.2	1.3	31.4	0.6
1966	31.5	0.3	32.4	2.9	32.7	0.9	32.5	-0.6	32.2	-0.9	32.7	1.6	34.7	6.1	36.0	3.7	36.4	1.1	36.5	0.3	36.1	-1.1	36.0	-0.3
1967	35.8	-0.6	35.5	-0.8	34.5	-2.8	34.6	0.3	35.0	1.2	35.2	0.6	35.2	0.0	35.1	-0.3	35.9	2.3	35.9	0.0	35.9	0.0	36.1	0.6
1968	36.2	0.3	36.2	0.0	36.0	-0.6	36.7	1.9	37.5	2.2	37.6	0.3	37.9	0.8	37.9	0.0	38.1	0.5	38.4	0.8	38.4	0.0	38.4	0.0
1969	38.3	-0.3	38.5	0.5	38.5	0.0	38.8	0.8	38.9	0.3	39.1	0.5	39.2	0.3	39.2	0.0	39.5	0.8	39.7	0.5	40.0	0.8	40.8	2.0
1970	41.0	0.5	40.9	-0.2	40.6	-0.7	41.0	1.0	40.5	-1.2	40.5	0.0	40.6	0.2	40.5	-0.2	40.7	0.5	40.8	0.2	41.3	1.2	41.6	0.7

[Continued]

Fluid Milk
Producer Price Index
Base 1982 = 100
[Continued]

For 1926-1995. Columns headed % show percentile change in the index from the previous period for which an index is available.

Year	Jan Index	%	Feb Index	%	Mar Index	%	Apr Index	%	May Index	%	Jun Index	%	Jul Index	%	Aug Index	%	Sep Index	%	Oct Index	%	Nov Index	%	Dec Index	%
1971	41.6	0.0	41.7	0.2	41.9	0.5	42.1	0.5	42.0	-0.2	42.2	0.5	42.3	0.2	42.2	-0.2	42.2	0.0	42.2	0.0	42.1	-0.2	42.1	0.0
1972	42.7	1.4	42.6	-0.2	43.1	1.2	43.2	0.2	43.4	0.5	43.1	-0.7	43.2	0.2	43.2	0.0	43.5	0.7	43.8	0.7	43.7	-0.2	43.7	0.0
1973	44.8	2.5	45.5	1.6	46.1	1.3	46.2	0.2	47.0	1.7	47.2	0.4	47.2	0.0	50.8	7.6	56.2	10.6	59.6	6.0	62.7	5.2	62.7	0.0
1974	65.4	4.3	65.9	0.8	65.8	-0.2	65.3	-0.8	63.2	-3.2	58.3	-7.8	55.8	-4.3	56.0	0.4	56.4	0.7	58.8	4.3	61.8	5.1	61.2	-1.0
1975	60.9	-0.5	60.9	0.0	60.1	-1.3	59.3	-1.3	59.0	-0.5	58.6	-0.7	59.7	1.9	62.3	4.4	65.8	5.6	69.9	6.2	73.6	5.3	75.3	2.3
1976	75.2	-0.1	73.5	-2.3	71.4	-2.9	69.7	-2.4	68.7	-1.4	67.3	-2.0	68.4	1.6	71.0	3.8	72.1	1.5	73.2	1.5	72.3	-1.2	71.8	-0.7
1977	70.9	-1.3	70.2	-1.0	69.1	-1.6	70.0	1.3	70.2	0.3	70.6	0.6	71.7	1.6	72.6	1.3	73.2	0.8	74.2	1.4	74.3	0.1	74.4	0.1
1978	73.8	-0.8	74.2	0.5	74.7	0.7	75.1	0.5	75.1	0.0	75.1	0.0	76.6	2.0	78.1	2.0	80.0	2.4	82.1	2.6	83.5	1.7	85.4	2.3
1979	85.6	0.2	86.6	1.2	86.3	-0.3	85.8	-0.6	85.7	-0.1	86.3	0.7	87.7	1.6	88.5	0.9	91.5	3.4	92.3	0.9	92.9	0.7	93.5	0.6
1980	92.8	-0.7	93.4	0.6	93.1	-0.3	93.9	0.9	93.9	0.0	94.0	0.1	94.1	0.1	96.1	2.1	97.5	1.5	99.4	1.9	100.8	1.4	102.8	2.0
1981	102.1	-0.7	102.5	0.4	102.5	0.0	101.7	-0.8	100.4	-1.3	100.9	0.5	100.6	-0.3	100.9	0.3	101.7	0.8	104.2	2.5	102.0	-2.1	101.5	-0.5
1982	101.8	0.3	101.2	-0.6	100.0	-1.2	99.2	-0.8	98.7	-0.5	98.7	0.0	98.8	0.1	98.7	-0.1	99.8	1.1	100.9	1.1	101.2	0.3	101.1	-0.1
1983	100.7	-0.4	100.6	-0.1	100.1	-0.5	99.4	-0.7	99.0	-0.4	98.6	-0.4	98.7	0.1	99.7	1.0	100.7	1.0	100.6	-0.1	100.3	-0.3	99.6	-0.7
1984	98.8	-0.8	97.6	-1.2	97.1	-0.5	96.5	-0.6	96.2	-0.3	96.2	0.0	97.0	0.8	98.0	1.0	99.9	1.9	101.5	1.6	101.8	0.3	101.8	0.0
1985	100.7	-1.1	99.5	-1.2	98.5	-1.0	96.0	-2.5	93.8	-2.3	91.9	-2.0	90.7	-1.3	90.3	-0.4	90.6	0.3	90.6	0.0	91.1	0.6	90.3	-0.9
1986	90.3	0.0	90.2	-0.1	88.9	-1.4	87.9	-1.1	88.2	0.3	88.5	0.3	89.0	0.6	90.7	1.9	91.6	1.0	94.4	3.1	95.7	1.4	96.1	0.4
1987	96.1	0.0	94.6	-1.6	92.2	-2.5	90.7	-1.6	89.4	-1.4	88.1	-1.5	89.7	1.8	91.1	1.6	92.7	1.8	93.2	0.5	93.1	-0.1	91.5	-1.7
1988	90.5	-1.1	89.1	-1.5	86.7	-2.7	85.4	-1.5	85.3	-0.1	83.8	-1.8	84.9	1.3	88.1	3.8	91.2	3.5	94.3	3.4	96.5	2.3	97.0	0.5
1989	96.4	-0.6	94.7	-1.8	91.3	-3.6	90.2	-1.2	89.7	-0.6	91.0	1.4	93.7	3.0	98.1	4.7	103.1	5.1	107.6	4.4	113.1	5.1	116.2	2.7
1990	114.7	-1.3	105.1	-8.4	100.5	-4.4	98.0	-2.5	100.3	2.3	103.1	2.8	105.3	2.1	105.5	0.2	104.6	-0.9	95.4	-8.8	91.8	-3.8	85.8	-6.5
1991	84.4	-1.6	84.1	-0.4	83.1	-1.2	82.9	-0.2	83.4	0.6	85.1	2.0	88.1	3.5	91.8	4.2	94.3	2.7	98.1	4.0	99.3	1.2	99.6	0.3
1992	97.7	-1.9	93.8	-4.0	91.3	-2.7	91.7	0.4	95.3	3.9	98.0	2.8	99.6	1.6	100.1	0.5	99.5	-0.6	98.1	-1.4	95.4	-2.8	92.4	-3.1
1993	91.0	-1.5	89.1	-2.1	89.4	0.3	92.5	3.5	95.9	3.7	96.5	0.6	94.9	-1.7	92.6	-2.4	94.0	1.5	95.6	1.7	98.7	3.2	98.6	-0.1
1994	99.3	0.7	98.2	-1.1	99.3	1.1	99.7	0.4	95.3	-4.4	94.0	-1.4	90.9	-3.3	92.1	1.3	94.9	3.0	95.9	1.1	95.2	-0.7	93.5	-1.8
1995	92.1	-1.5	91.6	-0.5	92.8	1.3	90.7	-2.3	90.8	0.1	89.9	-1.0	89.3	-0.7	92.3	3.4	94.0	1.8	96.0	2.1	98.7	2.8	101.4	2.7

Source: U.S. Department of Labor, Bureau of Labor Statistics, Division of Industry Prices and Price Indexes. n.e.c. stands for not elsewhere classified. - indicates no data collected for period or unavailable.

Chicken Eggs
Producer Price Index
Base 1982 = 100

For 1926-1995. Columns headed % show percentile change in the index from the previous period for which an index is available.

Year	Jan Index	%	Feb Index	%	Mar Index	%	Apr Index	%	May Index	%	Jun Index	%	Jul Index	%	Aug Index	%	Sep Index	%	Oct Index	%	Nov Index	%	Dec Index	%
1926	-	-	-	-	-	-	-	-	-	-	-	-	-	-	-	-	-	-	-	-	-	-	-	-
1927	-	-	-	-	-	-	-	-	-	-	-	-	-	-	-	-	-	-	-	-	-	-	-	-
1928	-	-	-	-	-	-	-	-	-	-	-	-	-	-	-	-	-	-	-	-	-	-	-	-
1929	-	-	-	-	-	-	-	-	-	-	-	-	-	-	-	-	-	-	-	-	-	-	-	-
1930	-	-	-	-	-	-	-	-	-	-	-	-	-	-	-	-	-	-	-	-	-	-	-	-
1931	-	-	-	-	-	-	-	-	-	-	-	-	-	-	-	-	-	-	-	-	-	-	-	-
1932	-	-	-	-	-	-	-	-	-	-	-	-	-	-	-	-	-	-	-	-	-	-	-	-
1933	-	-	-	-	-	-	-	-	-	-	-	-	-	-	-	-	-	-	-	-	-	-	-	-
1934	-	-	-	-	-	-	-	-	-	-	-	-	-	-	-	-	-	-	-	-	-	-	-	-
1935	-	-	-	-	-	-	-	-	-	-	-	-	-	-	-	-	-	-	-	-	-	-	-	-
1936	-	-	-	-	-	-	-	-	-	-	-	-	-	-	-	-	-	-	-	-	-	-	-	-
1937	48.1	-	43.1	-10.4	44.3	2.8	43.3	-2.3	39.9	-7.9	39.4	-1.3	41.4	5.1	42.1	1.7	46.7	10.9	47.3	1.3	52.7	11.4	50.0	-5.1
1938	43.3	-13.4	35.1	-18.9	34.9	-0.6	35.2	0.9	39.6	12.5	39.7	0.3	42.2	6.3	44.1	4.5	50.5	14.5	52.8	4.6	57.2	8.3	54.3	-5.1
1939	38.6	-28.9	33.9	-12.2	33.2	-2.1	32.8	-1.2	31.7	-3.4	31.1	-1.9	31.8	2.3	32.0	0.6	37.3	16.6	40.9	9.7	46.8	14.4	39.3	-16.0
1940	40.7	3.6	43.4	6.6	33.2	-23.5	32.7	-1.5	32.7	0.0	31.4	-4.0	31.8	1.3	33.3	4.7	39.9	19.8	42.4	6.3	46.0	8.5	49.7	8.0
1941	37.8	-23.9	33.5	-11.4	36.1	7.8	42.5	17.7	44.5	4.7	49.3	10.8	51.8	5.1	54.1	4.4	57.7	6.7	61.0	5.7	69.4	13.8	66.7	-3.9
1942	65.0	-2.5	56.8	-12.6	54.6	-3.9	56.6	3.7	57.5	1.6	59.4	3.3	63.1	6.2	67.3	6.7	70.4	4.6	73.9	5.0	74.5	0.8	74.7	0.3
1943	74.0	-0.9	70.2	-5.1	72.9	3.8	71.6	-1.8	72.9	1.8	75.1	3.0	75.3	0.3	78.9	4.8	82.3	4.3	84.4	2.6	83.7	-0.8	80.2	-4.2
1944	72.6	-9.5	62.8	-13.5	60.2	-4.1	58.5	-2.8	57.5	-1.7	60.7	5.6	66.3	9.2	64.5	-2.7	70.3	9.0	74.5	6.0	82.4	10.6	83.8	1.7
1945	75.8	-9.5	68.2	-10.0	66.8	-2.1	67.0	0.3	67.0	0.0	68.3	1.9	69.9	2.3	74.0	5.9	67.5	-8.8	79.7	18.1	87.1	9.3	85.9	-1.4
1946	70.8	-17.6	65.8	-7.1	65.7	-0.2	64.5	-1.8	65.9	2.2	65.5	-0.6	65.3	-0.3	67.8	3.8	78.6	15.9	83.2	5.9	77.9	-6.4	75.2	-3.5
1947	76.0	1.1	74.5	-2.0	80.8	8.5	82.7	2.4	80.5	-2.7	82.0	1.9	86.6	5.6	84.5	-2.4	91.7	8.5	91.9	0.2	89.0	-3.2	100.7	13.1
1948	86.2	-14.4	83.3	-3.4	82.9	-0.5	83.3	0.5	81.9	-1.7	84.3	2.9	87.2	3.4	95.9	10.0	101.6	5.9	112.4	10.6	110.5	-1.7	96.5	-12.7
1949	85.1	-11.8	77.1	-9.4	79.8	3.5	85.6	7.3	86.0	0.5	87.2	1.4	95.2	9.2	100.6	5.7	108.7	8.1	101.2	-6.9	90.9	-10.2	67.9	-25.3
1950	58.9	-13.3	59.9	1.7	65.0	8.5	62.3	-4.2	58.5	-6.1	62.6	7.0	71.2	13.7	75.5	6.0	88.5	17.2	97.0	9.6	101.8	4.9	102.5	0.7
1951	79.9	-22.0	80.3	0.5	85.6	6.6	85.8	0.2	89.1	3.8	94.1	5.6	94.2	0.1	106.2	12.7	111.4	4.9	115.1	3.3	116.6	1.3	90.3	-22.6
1952	71.6	-20.7	65.9	-8.0	67.9	3.0	72.4	6.6	65.9	-9.0	71.8	9.0	100.1	39.4	101.2	1.1	99.8	-1.4	110.6	10.8	104.3	-5.7	88.3	-15.3
1953	83.3	-5.7	79.0	-5.2	89.2	12.9	90.9	1.9	87.5	-3.7	94.5	8.0	94.2	-0.3	100.9	7.1	108.6	7.6	112.0	3.1	99.0	-11.6	86.2	-12.9
1954	82.2	-4.6	79.5	-3.3	71.0	-10.7	69.1	-2.7	61.2	-11.4	62.8	2.6	74.8	19.1	76.6	2.4	68.5	-10.6	73.1	6.7	74.0	1.2	56.7	-23.4
1955	57.7	1.8	79.9	38.5	72.9	-8.8	69.1	-5.2	63.4	-8.2	66.0	4.1	69.8	5.8	84.6	21.2	91.3	7.9	82.1	-10.1	87.7	6.8	88.0	0.3
1956	76.2	-13.4	72.1	-5.4	75.3	4.4	70.8	-6.0	71.1	0.4	69.8	-1.8	72.8	4.3	68.9	-5.4	80.9	17.4	77.4	-4.3	70.3	-9.2	65.9	-6.3
1957	58.3	-11.5	58.8	0.9	56.6	-3.7	60.7	7.2	51.0	-16.0	54.1	6.1	67.6	25.0	70.7	4.6	80.9	14.4	91.8	13.5	88.7	-3.4	82.8	-6.7
1958	65.5	-20.9	65.8	0.5	83.0	26.1	68.4	-17.6	67.1	-1.9	66.4	-1.0	67.5	1.7	72.3	7.1	87.4	20.9	80.8	-7.6	76.7	-5.1	68.9	-10.2
1959	64.2	-6.8	61.4	-4.4	62.5	1.8	48.3	-22.7	45.3	-6.2	50.1	10.6	58.0	15.8	59.2	2.1	75.7	27.9	61.2	-19.2	56.2	-8.2	55.7	-0.9
1960	50.5	-9.3	51.8	2.6	67.3	29.9	71.1	5.6	61.7	-13.2	57.0	-7.6	58.0	1.8	67.8	16.9	75.8	11.8	87.7	15.7	95.9	9.4	77.8	-18.9
1961	66.7	-14.3	72.0	7.9	67.1	-6.8	58.9	-12.2	56.2	-4.6	56.2	0.0	67.0	19.2	71.6	6.9	67.9	-5.2	70.5	3.8	71.0	0.7	63.7	-10.3
1962	65.0	2.0	64.7	-0.5	60.3	-6.8	60.9	1.0	50.0	-17.9	53.1	6.2	57.2	7.7	65.1	13.8	73.5	12.9	68.4	-6.9	74.6	9.1	65.9	-11.7
1963	66.4	0.8	65.8	-0.9	66.3	0.8	53.9	-18.7	51.2	-5.0	52.6	2.7	58.1	10.5	63.7	9.6	71.6	12.4	65.0	-9.2	68.0	4.6	66.3	-2.5
1964	70.6	6.5	59.5	-15.7	60.1	1.0	52.8	-12.1	51.0	-3.4	58.9	15.5	58.0	-1.5	65.5	12.9	64.3	-1.8	64.9	0.9	60.8	-6.3	56.6	-6.9
1965	52.4	-7.4	50.9	-2.9	57.7	13.4	60.5	4.9	52.4	-13.4	54.4	3.8	56.2	3.3	66.4	18.1	70.3	5.9	69.8	-0.7	75.7	8.5	78.5	3.7
1966	66.3	-15.5	77.2	16.4	78.7	1.9	67.6	-14.1	57.7	-14.6	60.3	4.5	65.4	8.5	72.1	10.2	84.9	17.8	76.2	-10.2	80.9	6.2	72.4	-10.5
1967	66.4	-8.3	55.7	-16.1	60.3	8.3	51.1	-15.3	49.5	-3.1	50.5	2.0	57.1	13.1	54.5	-4.6	61.8	13.4	51.0	-17.5	53.6	5.1	60.3	12.5
1968	49.0	-18.7	53.1	8.4	53.7	1.1	54.9	2.2	48.2	-12.2	58.6	21.6	60.7	3.6	65.3	7.6	84.1	28.8	70.7	-15.9	71.4	1.0	78.2	9.5
1969	81.2	3.8	71.7	-11.7	73.6	2.6	64.6	-12.2	53.5	-17.2	57.0	6.5	77.7	36.3	66.7	-14.2	81.3	21.9	75.5	-7.1	92.8	22.9	103.4	11.4
1970	101.0	-2.3	90.9	-10.0	79.7	-12.3	63.0	-21.0	52.9	-16.0	56.6	7.0	73.8	30.4	59.5	-19.4	78.1	31.3	58.5	-25.1	65.9	12.6	71.2	8.0

[Continued]

Chicken Eggs
Producer Price Index
Base 1982 = 100
[Continued]

For 1926-1995. Columns headed % show percentile change in the index from the previous period for which an index is available.

Year	Jan Index	%	Feb Index	%	Mar Index	%	Apr Index	%	May Index	%	Jun Index	%	Jul Index	%	Aug Index	%	Sep Index	%	Oct Index	%	Nov Index	%	Dec Index	%
1971	63.4	-11.0	54.6	-13.9	56.6	3.7	58.4	3.2	51.7	-11.5	54.8	6.0	50.0	-8.8	61.6	23.2	60.3	-2.1	51.7	-14.3	49.5	-4.3	64.0	29.3
1972	51.8	-19.1	51.4	-0.8	60.3	17.3	48.8	-19.1	50.7	3.9	51.4	1.4	57.2	11.3	55.6	-2.8	64.3	15.6	55.4	-13.8	68.9	24.4	80.5	16.8
1973	88.5	9.9	72.8	-17.7	85.4	17.3	81.1	-5.0	76.7	-5.4	89.2	16.3	86.9	-2.6	117.3	35.0	107.2	-8.6	99.4	-7.3	101.4	2.0	106.6	5.1
1974	110.7	3.8	104.5	-5.6	93.9	-10.1	88.8	-5.4	70.5	-20.6	69.8	-1.0	73.8	5.7	83.7	13.4	95.0	13.5	93.9	-1.2	92.3	-1.7	101.3	9.8
1975	94.4	-6.8	90.9	-3.7	93.0	2.3	78.3	-15.8	81.4	4.0	77.1	-5.3	78.2	1.4	87.7	12.1	97.6	11.3	88.6	-9.2	98.4	11.1	107.6	9.3
1976	101.9	-5.3	99.0	-2.8	89.1	-10.0	91.0	2.1	96.0	5.5	92.8	-3.3	93.9	1.2	104.5	11.3	105.7	1.1	101.1	-4.4	107.9	6.7	119.5	10.8
1977	105.9	-11.4	109.0	2.9	97.1	-10.9	92.4	-4.8	80.8	-12.6	79.1	-2.1	87.6	10.7	90.7	3.5	91.4	0.8	77.0	-15.8	83.6	8.6	93.1	11.4
1978	81.2	-12.8	95.3	17.4	93.6	-1.8	85.2	-9.0	79.0	-7.3	71.3	-9.7	84.1	18.0	88.4	5.1	93.9	6.2	87.5	-6.8	99.6	13.8	105.7	6.1
1979	99.9	-5.5	98.9	-1.0	111.9	13.1	103.8	-7.2	91.7	-11.7	95.5	4.1	93.8	-1.8	93.3	-0.5	98.1	5.1	87.2	-11.1	100.0	14.7	111.0	11.0
1980	92.6	-16.6	84.2	-9.1	103.1	22.4	85.8	-16.8	78.6	-8.4	82.1	4.5	89.2	8.6	99.0	11.0	105.4	6.5	98.0	-7.0	108.6	10.8	121.7	12.1
1981	103.9	-14.6	103.4	-0.5	100.9	-2.4	109.8	8.8	92.3	-15.9	97.7	5.9	103.5	5.9	101.1	-2.3	108.1	6.9	108.4	0.3	117.3	8.2	109.4	-6.7
1982	104.7	-4.3	112.2	7.2	114.2	1.8	107.5	-5.9	91.9	-14.5	89.1	-3.0	96.1	7.9	96.1	0.0	97.0	0.9	99.5	2.6	96.5	-3.0	95.1	-1.5
1983	95.1	0.0	95.1	0.0	95.1	0.0	95.1	0.0	103.6	8.9	94.7	-8.6	99.2	4.8	106.0	6.9	112.0	5.7	-		96.5	-3.0	95.1	-1.5
1984	158.0	41.1	157.1	-0.6	132.0	-16.0	147.9	12.0	112.5	-23.9	99.5	-11.6	103.5	4.0	101.4	-2.0	99.4	-2.0	100.7	1.3	98.5	-2.2	104.9	6.5
1985	79.4	-24.3	90.4	13.9	93.8	3.8	98.0	4.5	84.0	-14.3	82.7	-1.5	91.8	11.0	94.5	2.9	105.4	11.5	106.9	1.4	109.2	2.2	111.9	2.5
1986	107.2	-4.2	98.5	-8.1	101.9	3.5	94.9	-6.9	90.7	-4.4	83.4	-8.0	93.6	12.2	107.1	14.4	101.3	-5.4	97.1	-4.1	110.4	13.7	108.5	-1.7
1987	99.0	-8.8	98.2	-0.8	89.7	-8.7	90.1	0.4	84.4	-6.3	80.1	-5.1	85.3	6.5	79.7	-6.6	100.6	26.2	81.1	-19.4	92.6	14.2	70.6	-23.8
1988	76.5	8.4	73.8	-3.5	79.7	8.0	73.1	-8.3	70.8	-3.1	77.1	8.9	95.7	24.1	107.0	11.8	102.1	-4.6	107.4	5.2	99.7	-7.2	100.3	0.6
1989	127.3	26.9	96.7	-24.0	135.8	40.4	110.8	-18.4	107.0	-3.4	104.8	-2.1	111.0	5.9	116.7	5.1	124.6	6.8	124.3	-0.2	134.5	8.2	141.3	5.1
1990	154.8	9.6	114.0	-26.4	128.9	13.1	127.9	-0.8	95.3	-25.5	100.4	5.4	91.6	-8.8	114.4	24.9	112.6	-1.6	121.6	8.0	125.0	2.8	124.5	-0.4
1991	140.0	12.4	110.5	-21.1	131.7	19.2	113.2	-14.0	94.6	-16.4	96.9	2.4	100.7	3.9	109.0	8.2	105.8	-2.9	105.0	-0.8	102.1	-2.8	118.7	16.3
1992	91.9	-22.6	94.1	2.4	92.8	-1.4	90.1	-2.9	86.4	-4.1	84.6	-2.1	83.9	-0.8	87.3	4.1	103.6	18.7	94.7	-8.6	112.4	18.7	107.7	-4.2
1993	102.9	-4.5	107.0	4.0	121.3	13.4	111.1	-8.4	101.6	-8.6	109.5	7.8	95.5	-12.8	110.5	15.7	93.2	-15.7	105.2	12.9	108.6	3.2	103.8	-4.4
1994	100.1	-3.6	109.1	9.0	112.3	2.9	99.0	-11.8	84.2	-14.9	91.1	8.2	89.3	-2.0	100.1	12.1	98.8	-1.3	89.2	-9.7	100.5	12.7	100.0	-0.5
1995	92.6	-7.4	95.8	3.5	97.1	1.4	97.1	0.0	85.4	-12.0	88.8	4.0	97.4	9.7	99.2	1.8	108.9	9.8	111.1	2.0	136.9	23.2	138.8	1.4

Source: U.S. Department of Labor, Bureau of Labor Statistics, Division of Industry Prices and Price Indexes. n.e.c. stands for not elsewhere classified. - indicates no data collected for period or unavailable.

Hay, Hayseeds and Oilseeds
Producer Price Index
Base 1982 = 100

For 1926-1995. Columns headed % show percentile change in the index from the previous period for which an index is available.

Year	Jan Index	%	Feb Index	%	Mar Index	%	Apr Index	%	May Index	%	Jun Index	%	Jul Index	%	Aug Index	%	Sep Index	%	Oct Index	%	Nov Index	%	Dec Index	%
1926	30.9	-	30.1	-2.6	30.1	0.0	31.9	6.0	31.3	-1.9	27.5	-12.1	28.2	2.5	28.7	1.8	29.0	1.0	28.8	-0.7	28.7	-0.3	28.9	0.7
1927	28.9	0.0	28.6	-1.0	27.6	-3.5	27.4	-0.7	27.3	-0.4	25.1	-8.1	24.0	-4.4	24.9	3.8	24.8	-0.4	25.3	2.0	24.8	-2.0	26.0	4.8
1928	27.0	3.8	26.9	-0.4	28.3	5.2	29.6	4.6	30.5	3.0	27.4	-10.2	26.9	-1.8	27.3	1.5	28.4	4.0	30.2	6.3	31.3	3.6	32.0	2.2
1929	33.1	3.4	33.3	0.6	33.1	-0.6	32.8	-0.9	30.1	-8.2	27.0	-10.3	27.3	1.1	28.1	2.9	29.7	5.7	30.8	3.7	30.4	-1.3	29.8	-2.0
1930	29.7	-0.3	28.7	-3.4	28.2	-1.7	29.0	2.8	28.4	-2.1	25.8	-9.2	25.6	-0.8	27.9	9.0	27.5	-1.4	27.6	0.4	27.6	0.0	26.7	-3.3
1931	25.8	-3.4	24.9	-3.5	24.5	-1.6	24.6	0.4	23.1	-6.1	20.3	-12.1	19.9	-2.0	18.4	-7.5	17.9	-2.7	17.3	-3.4	17.7	2.3	18.4	4.0
1932	18.3	-0.5	17.4	-4.9	18.0	3.4	18.0	0.0	16.2	-10.0	13.9	-14.2	13.5	-2.9	13.7	1.5	13.7	0.0	14.1	2.9	14.1	0.0	13.8	-2.1
1933	13.7	-0.7	13.3	-2.9	13.7	3.0	14.2	3.6	15.6	9.9	15.3	-1.9	16.5	7.8	17.9	8.5	18.0	0.6	17.5	-2.8	17.7	1.1	18.2	2.8
1934	18.8	3.3	19.2	2.1	19.2	0.0	19.7	2.6	20.0	1.5	21.2	6.0	23.3	9.9	26.4	13.3	28.3	7.2	27.6	-2.5	27.0	-2.2	28.3	4.8
1935	28.9	2.1	28.6	-1.0	28.1	-1.7	27.3	-2.8	26.0	-4.8	23.1	-11.2	19.8	-14.3	18.0	-9.1	18.6	3.3	19.3	3.8	19.4	0.5	19.1	-1.5
1936	19.3	1.0	19.3	0.0	18.9	-2.1	20.0	5.8	19.4	-3.0	18.4	-5.2	22.0	19.6	25.0	13.6	25.8	3.2	26.2	1.6	27.3	4.2	27.9	2.2
1937	28.9	3.6	28.9	0.0	28.4	-1.7	28.7	1.1	27.1	-5.6	25.6	-5.5	24.7	-3.5	24.8	0.4	25.5	2.8	26.4	3.5	26.0	-1.5	26.5	1.9
1938	26.8	1.1	26.4	-1.5	25.6	-3.0	24.7	-3.5	23.9	-3.2	22.4	-6.3	22.1	-1.3	20.5	-7.2	18.3	-10.7	19.1	4.4	19.5	2.1	20.1	3.1
1939	21.2	5.5	20.7	-2.4	20.8	0.5	20.7	-0.5	19.9	-3.9	19.6	-1.5	19.0	-3.1	21.5	13.2	20.6	-4.2	21.6	4.9	21.7	0.5	21.9	0.9
1940	22.3	1.8	22.4	0.4	22.1	-1.3	22.0	-0.5	21.8	-0.9	19.9	-8.7	19.4	-2.5	19.7	1.5	18.8	-4.6	18.8	0.0	19.0	1.1	19.4	2.1
1941	19.9	2.6	19.9	0.0	19.7	-1.0	19.9	1.0	20.3	2.0	20.6	1.5	20.9	1.5	21.2	1.4	22.3	5.2	23.5	5.4	25.3	7.7	26.5	4.7
1942	28.1	6.0	29.2	3.9	30.5	4.5	30.9	1.3	30.5	-1.3	29.7	-2.6	29.8	0.3	29.6	-0.7	29.4	-0.7	29.7	1.0	30.4	2.4	31.6	3.9
1943	32.8	3.8	34.3	4.6	35.5	3.5	36.4	2.5	36.5	0.3	34.9	-4.4	34.8	-0.3	34.9	0.3	36.4	4.3	38.9	6.9	41.5	6.7	42.2	1.7
1944	42.1	-0.2	41.7	-1.0	41.0	-1.7	41.0	0.0	41.6	1.5	38.6	-7.2	37.9	-1.8	38.1	0.5	38.7	1.6	41.4	7.0	42.1	1.7	42.2	0.2
1945	43.2	2.4	43.8	1.4	43.5	-0.7	44.4	2.0	41.8	-3.9	39.2	-6.2	39.4	0.5	39.1	-0.8	37.6	-3.8	37.7	0.3	38.3	1.6	39.7	0.0
1946	39.8	0.3	39.6	-0.5	40.4	2.0	40.2	-0.5	40.2	0.0	40.4	0.5	41.1	1.7	41.4	0.7	42.0	1.4	46.7	11.2	54.3	16.3	55.3	1.8
1947	55.7	0.7	55.8	0.2	61.8	10.8	60.2	-2.6	51.8	-14.0	50.9	-1.7	50.9	0.0	50.3	-1.2	51.7	2.8	55.7	7.7	58.8	5.6	61.7	4.9
1948	64.3	4.2	58.6	-8.9	59.4	1.4	60.9	2.5	61.7	1.3	62.1	0.6	59.5	-4.2	53.7	-9.7	51.7	-3.7	49.2	-4.8	50.8	3.3	50.9	0.2
1949	49.3	-3.1	45.9	-6.9	45.3	-1.3	44.7	-1.3	42.2	-5.6	40.8	-3.3	41.0	0.5	45.3	10.5	41.0	-9.5	40.4	-1.5	40.8	1.0	41.7	2.2
1950	42.1	1.0	41.5	-1.4	48.3	16.4	45.0	-6.8	45.3	0.7	45.4	0.2	46.5	2.4	48.1	3.4	46.7	-2.9	45.6	-2.4	51.1	12.1	53.3	4.3
1951	55.6	4.3	57.3	3.1	57.7	0.7	57.3	-0.7	56.3	-1.7	53.2	-5.5	49.7	-6.6	48.4	-2.6	48.5	0.2	50.2	3.5	52.4	4.4	52.9	1.0
1952	52.7	-0.4	52.4	-0.6	50.3	-4.0	49.5	-1.6	49.8	0.6	51.1	2.6	52.1	2.0	51.8	-0.6	50.0	-3.5	50.1	0.2	51.1	2.0	51.0	-0.2
1953	50.4	-1.2	49.2	-2.4	50.6	2.8	49.4	-2.4	48.6	-1.6	46.5	-4.3	44.4	-4.5	44.1	-0.7	42.1	-4.5	43.7	3.8	45.6	4.3	46.5	2.0
1954	46.9	0.9	47.5	1.3	48.4	1.9	50.0	3.3	49.4	-1.2	49.8	0.8	49.2	-1.2	48.8	-0.8	45.3	-7.2	47.6	5.1	47.7	0.2	48.6	1.9
1955	48.9	0.6	48.4	-1.0	48.3	-0.2	46.6	-3.5	46.0	-1.3	45.7	-0.7	44.4	-2.8	42.3	-4.7	38.9	-8.0	39.3	1.0	39.3	0.0	40.2	2.3
1956	40.9	1.7	41.7	2.0	42.8	2.6	45.0	5.1	46.7	3.8	45.3	-3.0	41.8	-7.7	41.5	-0.7	39.7	-4.3	40.7	2.5	43.6	7.1	44.3	1.6
1957	44.9	1.4	43.9	-2.2	44.1	0.5	44.2	0.2	43.8	-0.9	43.2	-1.4	42.7	-1.2	42.2	-1.2	40.4	-4.3	40.1	-0.7	40.2	0.2	40.7	1.2
1958	41.0	0.7	41.0	0.0	41.2	0.5	41.4	0.5	41.4	0.0	41.1	-0.7	39.5	-3.9	39.3	-0.5	37.4	-4.8	38.0	1.6	38.3	0.8	38.9	1.6
1959	39.6	1.8	40.4	2.0	40.7	0.7	41.2	1.2	41.6	1.0	40.4	-2.9	38.9	-3.7	37.9	-2.6	37.9	0.0	39.1	3.2	39.6	1.3	39.6	0.0
1960	40.2	1.5	40.0	-0.5	39.8	-0.5	39.6	-0.5	39.7	0.3	38.6	-2.8	38.1	-1.3	38.2	0.3	37.5	-1.8	37.4	-0.3	37.6	0.5	38.4	2.1
1961	41.2	7.3	42.2	2.4	45.3	7.3	50.0	10.4	47.7	-4.6	43.4	-9.0	43.4	0.0	43.0	-0.9	41.5	-3.5	41.4	-0.2	42.2	1.9	42.3	0.2
1962	42.4	0.2	42.6	0.5	43.0	0.9	43.8	1.9	43.8	0.0	43.3	-1.1	42.9	-0.9	42.9	0.0	40.7	-5.1	42.0	3.2	43.5	3.6	44.1	1.4
1963	45.6	3.4	46.2	1.3	46.3	0.2	45.1	-2.6	45.8	1.6	46.3	1.1	45.3	-2.2	45.3	0.0	45.0	-0.7	46.5	3.3	47.8	2.8	46.7	-2.3
1964	47.0	0.6	46.4	-1.3	45.1	-2.8	43.8	-2.9	42.7	-2.5	42.8	0.2	43.0	0.5	43.1	0.2	44.3	2.8	45.2	2.0	47.1	4.2	47.5	0.8
1965	48.5	2.1	49.1	1.2	48.5	-1.2	48.6	0.2	47.0	-3.3	46.7	-0.6	46.3	-0.9	43.4	-6.3	42.9	-1.2	41.8	-2.6	43.7	4.5	45.1	3.2
1966	46.2	2.4	47.5	2.8	47.1	-0.8	47.6	1.1	49.0	2.9	49.9	1.8	55.1	10.4	56.7	2.9	51.4	-9.3	49.5	-3.7	50.0	1.0	50.7	1.4
1967	50.3	-0.8	49.0	-2.6	49.1	0.2	48.2	-1.8	48.0	-0.4	47.5	-1.0	47.2	-0.6	45.4	-3.8	44.4	-2.2	44.2	-0.5	44.7	1.1	45.9	2.7
1968	46.0	0.2	46.0	0.0	46.5	1.1	46.4	-0.2	46.5	0.2	46.0	-1.1	46.1	0.2	46.0	-0.2	44.6	-3.0	42.9	-3.8	43.7	1.9	44.3	1.4
1969	45.4	2.5	45.8	0.9	45.8	0.0	46.3	1.1	46.9	1.3	45.0	-4.1	45.3	0.7	43.7	-3.5	43.1	-1.4	41.2	-4.4	42.1	2.2	42.8	1.7
1970	43.8	2.3	43.3	-1.1	43.3	0.0	44.7	3.2	45.3	1.3	45.9	1.3	47.6	3.7	47.5	-0.2	48.2	1.5	50.1	3.9	50.8	1.4	50.2	-1.2

[Continued]

Hay, Hayseeds and Oilseeds
Producer Price Index
Base 1982 = 100
[Continued]

For 1926-1995. Columns headed % show percentile change in the index from the previous period for which an index is available.

Year	Jan Index	%	Feb Index	%	Mar Index	%	Apr Index	%	May Index	%	Jun Index	%	Jul Index	%	Aug Index	%	Sep Index	%	Oct Index	%	Nov Index	%	Dec Index	%
1971	51.1	1.8	51.0	-0.2	50.5	-1.0	49.2	-2.6	50.1	1.8	51.6	3.0	53.7	4.1	53.7	0.0	51.1	-4.8	50.7	-0.8	51.4	1.4	51.3	-0.2
1972	51.1	-0.4	51.8	1.4	53.7	3.7	55.7	3.7	54.9	-1.4	54.9	0.0	54.9	0.0	54.5	-0.7	55.4	1.7	54.0	-2.5	58.6	8.5	66.5	13.5
1973	67.6	1.7	83.7	23.8	88.4	5.6	87.8	-0.7	114.2	30.1	140.9	23.4	88.1	-37.5	138.0	56.6	143.1	3.7	99.2	-30.7	91.3	-8.0	98.9	8.3
1974	101.9	3.0	102.5	0.6	102.9	0.4	92.3	-10.3	91.4	-1.0	89.9	-1.6	101.5	12.9	124.4	22.6	117.1	-5.9	126.9	8.4	122.7	-3.3	115.5	-5.9
1975	109.2	-5.5	99.4	-9.0	91.6	-7.8	100.6	9.8	94.1	-6.5	89.4	-5.0	96.2	7.6	100.2	4.2	93.2	-7.0	88.6	-4.9	83.3	-6.0	83.4	0.1
1976	85.3	2.3	86.7	1.6	84.9	-2.1	84.6	-0.4	89.0	5.2	103.1	15.8	112.0	8.6	105.5	-5.8	108.9	3.2	103.4	-5.1	109.0	5.4	113.9	4.5
1977	115.1	1.1	119.6	3.9	130.6	9.2	151.5	16.0	136.2	-10.1	127.0	-6.8	97.6	-23.1	92.1	-5.6	83.8	-9.0	84.0	0.2	90.9	8.2	92.5	1.8
1978	93.3	0.9	90.0	-3.5	98.5	9.4	101.8	3.4	103.2	1.4	103.6	0.4	104.6	1.0	101.2	-3.3	99.9	-1.3	104.0	4.1	107.0	2.9	110.0	2.8
1979	112.8	2.5	115.7	2.6	117.2	1.3	116.7	-0.4	113.1	-3.1	121.4	7.3	122.2	0.7	118.4	-3.1	113.2	-4.4	110.7	-2.2	108.0	-2.4	108.2	0.2
1980	102.5	-5.3	105.6	3.0	101.5	-3.9	96.4	-5.0	97.2	0.8	97.5	0.3	118.1	21.1	122.9	4.1	131.9	7.3	133.7	1.4	140.2	4.9	145.8	4.0
1981	146.5	0.5	138.6	-5.4	136.1	-1.8	139.2	2.3	140.5	0.9	134.1	-4.6	136.3	1.6	133.6	-2.0	125.5	-6.1	108.3	-13.7	103.9	-4.1	102.8	-1.1
1982	102.6	-0.2	102.3	-0.3	100.4	-1.9	104.7	4.3	106.8	2.0	103.1	-3.5	103.4	0.3	96.1	-7.1	94.8	-1.4	91.3	-3.7	96.2	5.4	98.2	2.1
1983	99.8	1.6	102.4	2.6	102.4	0.0	106.4	3.9	106.8	0.4	100.2	-6.2	106.8	6.6	123.5	15.6	139.9	13.3	135.7	-3.0	135.2	-0.4	132.6	-1.9
1984	135.0	1.8	124.7	-7.6	132.2	6.0	132.6	0.3	139.6	5.3	128.0	-8.3	115.5	-9.8	114.0	-1.3	107.3	-5.9	103.0	-4.0	106.8	3.7	106.9	0.1
1985	106.3	-0.6	100.8	-5.2	99.6	-1.2	100.5	0.9	100.3	-0.2	99.0	-1.3	97.2	-1.8	92.5	-4.8	91.3	-1.3	86.8	-4.9	94.0	8.3	93.7	-0.3
1986	94.3	0.6	95.2	1.0	96.0	0.8	91.1	-5.1	91.4	0.3	95.2	4.2	93.7	-1.6	89.4	-4.6	89.2	-0.2	88.0	-1.3	98.4	11.8	93.5	-5.0
1987	94.0	0.5	95.6	1.7	95.4	-0.2	97.7	2.4	104.3	6.8	106.4	2.0	105.1	-1.2	101.9	-3.0	99.7	-2.2	101.0	1.3	104.9	3.9	110.7	5.5
1988	113.7	2.7	114.7	0.9	114.2	-0.4	121.8	6.7	127.8	4.9	150.3	17.6	154.3	2.7	159.2	3.2	163.5	2.7	151.0	-7.6	142.8	-5.4	147.9	3.6
1989	153.2	3.6	144.2	-5.9	149.2	3.5	142.1	-4.8	149.7	5.3	143.8	-3.9	140.3	-2.4	129.8	-7.5	128.3	-1.2	118.2	-7.9	121.0	2.4	124.2	2.6
1990	121.0	-2.6	122.4	1.2	122.0	-0.3	122.6	0.5	116.8	-4.7	118.3	1.3	124.0	4.8	118.7	-4.3	121.4	2.3	128.3	5.7	123.1	-4.1	126.2	2.5
1991	121.3	-3.9	121.9	0.5	117.9	-3.3	116.1	-1.5	110.7	-4.7	114.4	3.3	104.5	-8.7	107.8	3.2	110.3	2.3	106.1	-3.8	106.8	0.7	106.8	0.0
1992	109.2	2.2	107.8	-1.3	111.7	3.6	109.3	-2.1	117.8	7.8	121.3	3.0	111.0	-8.5	107.2	-3.4	109.3	2.0	106.8	-2.3	109.0	2.1	114.5	5.0
1993	116.6	1.8	114.9	-1.5	118.3	3.0	123.2	4.1	128.1	4.0	119.7	-6.6	134.7	12.5	129.4	-3.9	127.3	-1.6	126.1	-0.9	132.9	5.4	142.7	7.4
1994	141.7	-0.7	141.7	0.0	144.7	2.1	143.3	-1.0	138.4	-3.4	141.8	2.5	130.0	-8.3	121.3	-6.7	122.4	0.9	117.2	-4.2	122.5	4.5	123.3	0.7
1995	121.2	-1.7	120.2	-0.8	119.3	-0.7	121.6	1.9	117.3	-3.5	117.4	0.1	120.5	2.6	114.2	-5.2	123.8	8.4	129.2	4.4	132.0	2.2	138.0	4.5

Source: U.S. Department of Labor, Bureau of Labor Statistics, Division of Industry Prices and Price Indexes. n.e.c. stands for not elsewhere classified. - indicates no data collected for period or unavailable.

Farm Products n.e.c.
Producer Price Index
Base 1982 = 100

For 1926-1995. Columns headed % show percentile change in the index from the previous period for which an index is available.

Year	Jan Index	%	Feb Index	%	Mar Index	%	Apr Index	%	May Index	%	Jun Index	%	Jul Index	%	Aug Index	%	Sep Index	%	Oct Index	%	Nov Index	%	Dec Index	%
1926	15.7	-	14.6	-7.0	12.8	-12.3	11.8	-7.8	12.3	4.2	12.5	1.6	12.6	0.8	12.6	0.0	12.9	2.4	12.9	0.0	13.6	5.4	14.2	4.4
1927	14.0	-1.4	12.9	-7.9	12.9	0.0	11.4	-11.6	11.0	-3.5	11.4	3.6	11.8	3.5	14.2	20.3	14.2	0.0	13.5	-4.9	13.3	-1.5	16.9	27.1
1928	18.1	7.1	16.8	-7.2	14.5	-13.7	14.4	-0.7	14.3	-0.7	12.4	-13.3	13.3	7.3	14.3	7.5	12.8	-10.5	14.3	11.7	13.3	-7.0	19.1	43.6
1929	20.3	6.3	18.0	-11.3	18.4	2.2	14.5	-21.2	14.2	-2.1	13.0	-8.5	12.8	-1.5	13.0	1.6	13.0	0.0	12.7	-2.3	11.9	-6.3	10.8	-9.2
1930	10.4	-3.7	10.2	-1.9	10.2	0.0	10.2	0.0	10.0	-2.0	9.9	-1.0	9.8	-1.0	9.6	-2.0	9.4	-2.1	9.5	1.1	8.7	-8.4	8.1	-6.9
1931	7.5	-7.4	7.3	-2.7	6.9	-5.5	6.8	-1.4	7.0	2.9	7.1	1.4	7.1	0.0	6.8	-4.2	6.6	-2.9	6.5	-1.5	6.5	0.0	6.3	-3.1
1932	5.9	-6.3	5.8	-1.7	5.8	0.0	5.9	1.7	5.9	0.0	5.8	-1.7	5.8	0.0	6.2	6.9	7.0	12.9	6.5	-7.1	6.1	-6.2	6.2	1.6
1933	6.2	0.0	6.3	1.6	6.3	0.0	6.2	-1.6	6.4	3.2	6.4	0.0	6.5	1.6	6.5	0.0	6.5	0.0	6.7	3.1	7.1	6.0	7.3	2.8
1934	7.6	4.1	7.9	3.9	7.9	0.0	7.8	-1.3	7.8	0.0	7.8	0.0	7.6	-2.6	8.0	5.3	8.5	6.3	9.2	8.2	9.4	2.2	9.4	0.0
1935	9.8	4.3	9.9	1.0	9.8	-1.0	9.7	-1.0	9.6	-1.0	9.5	-1.0	9.5	0.0	9.3	-2.1	8.9	-4.3	8.6	-3.4	8.4	-2.3	8.3	-1.2
1936	8.5	2.4	8.6	1.2	8.5	-1.2	8.4	-1.2	8.4	0.0	8.6	2.4	8.8	2.3	8.8	0.0	9.1	3.4	9.2	1.1	9.5	3.3	10.3	8.4
1937	10.9	5.8	11.1	1.8	11.0	-0.9	10.9	-0.9	10.8	-0.9	10.7	-0.9	10.7	0.0	10.8	0.9	10.7	-0.9	10.8	0.9	10.2	-5.6	9.8	-3.9
1938	9.2	-6.1	9.0	-2.2	8.9	-1.1	8.7	-2.2	8.7	0.0	8.7	0.0	8.9	2.3	9.1	2.2	9.1	0.0	9.0	-1.1	8.9	-1.1	8.8	-1.1
1939	8.8	0.0	8.9	1.1	8.7	-2.2	8.6	-1.1	8.6	0.0	8.6	0.0	8.6	0.0	8.5	-1.2	8.3	-2.4	7.8	-6.0	8.1	3.8	7.9	-2.5
1940	7.9	0.0	7.8	-1.3	7.9	1.3	7.9	0.0	7.7	-2.5	7.6	-1.3	7.5	-1.3	7.4	-1.3	7.5	1.4	7.7	2.7	7.8	1.3	8.1	3.8
1941	8.0	-1.2	8.2	2.5	8.7	6.1	9.0	3.4	9.4	4.4	9.7	3.2	9.8	1.0	10.4	6.1	11.3	8.7	11.8	4.4	12.2	3.4	13.1	7.4
1942	14.1	7.6	14.2	0.7	14.1	-0.7	14.1	0.0	14.1	0.0	14.1	0.0	14.1	0.0	14.5	2.8	15.1	4.1	15.7	4.0	15.9	1.3	16.3	2.5
1943	16.6	1.8	16.2	-2.4	16.3	0.6	16.6	1.8	16.6	0.0	16.6	0.0	16.7	0.6	16.8	0.6	17.0	1.2	16.9	-0.6	17.0	0.6	17.2	1.2
1944	17.4	1.2	17.5	0.6	17.5	0.0	17.5	0.0	17.5	0.0	17.5	0.0	17.4	-0.6	17.5	0.6	17.7	1.1	17.6	-0.6	17.7	0.6	17.7	0.0
1945	17.2	-2.8	17.1	-0.6	17.1	0.0	17.1	0.0	17.2	0.6	17.2	0.0	17.2	0.0	17.3	0.6	17.3	0.0	17.4	0.6	17.4	0.0	17.5	0.6
1946	17.8	1.7	17.7	-0.6	17.7	0.0	17.7	0.0	17.7	0.0	17.7	0.0	19.3	9.0	19.9	3.1	20.3	2.0	22.2	9.4	23.8	7.2	24.8	4.2
1947	25.4	2.4	25.1	-1.2	25.5	1.6	25.0	-2.0	24.2	-3.2	24.8	2.5	25.1	1.2	25.4	1.2	24.9	-2.0	25.7	3.2	25.9	0.8	26.2	1.2
1948	26.1	-0.4	25.9	-0.8	25.5	-1.5	25.2	-1.2	25.2	0.0	25.6	1.6	25.8	0.8	26.4	2.3	26.9	1.9	27.7	3.0	27.8	0.4	27.2	-2.2
1949	26.5	-2.6	26.0	-1.9	25.8	-0.8	25.6	-0.8	25.9	1.2	26.0	0.4	26.3	1.2	26.5	0.8	26.6	0.4	27.9	4.9	31.8	14.0	32.9	3.5
1950	32.4	-1.5	32.1	-0.9	31.3	-2.5	31.5	0.6	31.1	-1.3	32.2	3.5	34.0	5.6	35.2	3.5	36.8	4.5	35.5	-3.5	35.1	-1.1	36.0	2.6
1951	36.9	2.5	37.1	0.5	36.8	-0.8	36.8	0.0	36.7	-0.3	36.5	-0.5	36.1	-1.1	35.8	-0.8	35.7	-0.3	36.5	2.2	35.6	-2.5	36.3	2.0
1952	36.2	-0.3	36.4	0.6	36.4	0.0	35.9	-1.4	36.0	0.3	35.9	-0.3	36.3	1.1	36.2	-0.3	35.9	-0.8	35.7	-0.6	34.8	-2.5	35.4	1.7
1953	35.0	-1.1	35.3	0.9	37.5	6.2	36.0	-4.0	35.6	-1.1	35.9	0.8	37.0	3.1	37.9	2.4	39.2	3.4	38.4	-2.0	38.3	-0.3	38.9	1.6
1954	42.3	8.7	44.2	4.5	47.6	7.7	47.9	0.6	47.6	-0.6	47.7	0.2	48.3	1.3	44.4	-8.1	43.3	-2.5	42.0	-3.0	43.3	3.1	41.5	-4.2
1955	41.1	-1.0	36.7	-10.7	37.6	2.5	37.4	-0.5	36.4	-2.7	37.6	3.3	36.2	-3.7	36.4	0.6	38.4	5.5	38.2	-0.5	36.8	-3.7	36.5	-0.8
1956	36.7	0.5	38.3	4.4	37.7	-1.6	37.7	0.0	38.0	0.8	38.7	1.8	39.2	1.3	39.7	1.3	40.2	1.3	39.4	-2.0	38.7	-1.8	38.9	0.5
1957	39.1	0.5	38.9	-0.5	38.4	-1.3	38.0	-1.0	37.9	-0.3	38.3	1.1	37.6	-1.8	37.6	0.0	37.6	0.0	37.2	-1.1	37.9	1.9	37.5	-1.1
1958	37.7	0.5	37.4	-0.8	37.7	0.8	37.4	-0.8	37.3	-0.3	37.2	-0.3	36.8	-1.1	36.7	-0.3	36.1	-1.6	36.5	1.1	36.2	-0.8	35.8	-1.1
1959	35.3	-1.4	35.4	0.3	35.2	-0.6	35.1	-0.3	35.1	0.0	34.9	-0.6	34.8	-0.3	34.7	-0.3	35.0	0.9	34.6	-1.1	34.6	0.0	33.5	-3.2
1960	33.5	0.0	33.9	1.2	33.6	-0.9	33.8	0.6	33.7	-0.3	33.7	0.0	33.6	-0.3	33.0	-1.8	34.0	3.0	34.3	0.9	34.0	-0.9	34.3	0.9
1961	33.7	-1.7	34.1	1.2	34.1	0.0	34.0	-0.3	34.0	0.0	33.9	-0.3	34.0	0.3	34.0	0.0	34.5	1.5	34.2	-0.9	34.0	-0.6	34.6	1.8
1962	34.2	-1.2	34.2	0.0	34.2	0.0	34.1	-0.3	34.2	0.3	33.8	-1.2	33.8	0.0	32.9	-2.7	33.2	0.9	32.8	-1.2	33.0	0.6	32.6	-1.2
1963	32.0	-1.8	32.6	1.9	32.6	0.0	32.7	0.3	32.8	0.3	32.7	-0.3	32.6	-0.3	32.4	-0.6	32.6	0.6	33.1	1.5	33.2	0.3	33.2	0.0
1964	36.2	9.0	35.3	-2.5	36.8	4.2	36.4	-1.1	36.4	0.0	36.1	-0.8	36.0	-0.3	36.0	0.0	35.4	-1.7	36.3	2.5	36.0	-0.8	36.0	0.0
1965	34.9	-3.1	35.6	2.0	34.8	-2.2	35.0	0.6	34.7	-0.9	35.0	0.9	34.9	-0.3	36.0	3.2	36.9	2.5	36.6	-0.8	36.5	-0.3	37.9	3.8
1966	37.5	-1.1	37.4	-0.3	37.3	-0.3	37.5	0.5	37.1	-1.1	37.0	-0.3	37.1	0.3	37.5	1.1	37.4	-0.3	36.9	-1.3	36.1	-2.2	36.8	1.9
1967	36.4	-1.1	36.8	1.1	36.4	-1.1	36.3	-0.3	36.5	0.6	36.7	0.5	36.5	-0.5	36.3	-0.5	35.7	-1.7	35.6	-0.3	36.9	3.7	37.1	0.5
1968	37.2	0.3	37.0	-0.5	37.1	0.3	37.3	0.5	37.2	-0.3	37.2	0.0	37.2	0.0	37.7	1.3	38.1	1.1	38.1	0.0	39.1	2.6	39.4	0.8
1969	38.7	-1.8	38.9	0.5	39.1	0.5	38.8	-0.8	38.6	-0.5	38.8	0.5	39.1	0.8	40.0	2.3	40.7	1.7	42.7	4.9	42.4	-0.7	41.4	-2.4
1970	42.6	2.9	42.2	-0.9	42.0	-0.5	42.0	0.0	42.1	0.2	42.0	-0.2	42.6	1.4	43.3	1.6	43.4	0.2	42.8	-1.4	44.2	3.3	43.7	-1.1

[Continued]

Farm Products n.e.c.
Producer Price Index
Base 1982 = 100
[Continued]

For 1926-1995. Columns headed % show percentile change in the index from the previous period for which an index is available.

Year	Jan Index	%	Feb Index	%	Mar Index	%	Apr Index	%	May Index	%	Jun Index	%	Jul Index	%	Aug Index	%	Sep Index	%	Oct Index	%	Nov Index	%	Dec Index	%
1971	43.7	0.0	43.6	-0.2	42.3	-3.0	41.7	-1.4	41.4	-0.7	41.4	0.0	41.3	-0.2	41.8	1.2	42.1	0.7	42.1	0.0	41.2	-2.1	42.7	3.6
1972	43.0	0.7	42.5	-1.2	42.8	0.7	43.0	0.5	43.5	1.2	43.7	0.5	44.4	1.6	49.0	10.4	48.3	-1.4	48.2	-0.2	48.8	1.2	49.3	1.0
1973	49.7	0.8	51.2	3.0	52.2	2.0	51.8	-0.8	53.2	2.7	54.0	1.5	55.4	2.6	54.8	-1.1	55.8	1.8	56.3	0.9	55.6	-1.2	54.3	-2.3
1974	55.9	2.9	56.7	1.4	58.0	2.3	59.8	3.1	60.8	1.7	59.5	-2.1	58.3	-2.0	59.2	1.5	60.5	2.2	62.0	2.5	64.0	3.2	63.9	-0.2
1975	62.8	-1.7	63.6	1.3	62.3	-2.0	61.2	-1.8	60.2	-1.6	60.3	0.2	58.3	-3.3	61.2	5.0	61.9	1.1	63.7	2.9	62.8	-1.4	63.5	1.1
1976	64.8	2.0	66.0	1.9	65.6	-0.6	70.6	7.6	75.1	6.4	81.8	8.9	79.7	-2.6	82.9	4.0	92.1	11.1	93.6	1.6	98.8	5.6	105.9	7.2
1977	107.8	1.8	114.4	6.1	134.2	17.3	140.7	4.8	130.6	-7.2	124.5	-4.7	122.1	-1.9	106.4	-12.9	115.5	8.6	107.9	-6.6	110.5	2.4	110.2	-0.3
1978	103.7	-5.9	101.0	-2.6	100.1	-0.9	98.7	-1.4	98.9	0.2	99.3	0.4	97.7	-1.6	95.7	-2.0	103.3	7.9	100.7	-2.5	104.2	3.5	98.7	-5.3
1979	98.3	-0.4	92.4	-6.0	92.7	0.3	92.9	0.2	96.2	3.6	102.4	6.4	113.6	10.9	113.2	-0.4	115.1	1.7	114.2	-0.8	116.0	1.6	116.3	0.3
1980	109.7	-5.7	111.0	1.2	113.5	2.3	111.0	-2.2	113.3	2.1	112.7	-0.5	106.5	-5.5	103.0	-3.3	106.4	3.3	104.1	-2.2	108.1	3.8	107.8	-0.3
1981	107.9	0.1	107.5	-0.4	107.8	0.3	107.8	0.0	94.6	-12.2	88.4	-6.6	91.1	3.1	96.1	5.5	98.0	2.0	95.9	-2.1	99.5	3.8	102.1	2.6
1982	102.0	-0.1	99.7	-2.3	99.5	-0.2	99.9	0.4	99.8	-0.1	99.0	-0.8	96.7	-2.3	100.0	3.4	100.8	0.8	99.8	-1.0	100.7	0.9	102.1	1.4
1983	102.0	-0.1	102.4	0.4	102.1	-0.3	101.7	-0.4	102.4	0.7	103.6	1.2	102.9	-0.7	104.1	1.2	104.7	0.6	103.4	-1.2	103.3	-0.1	100.9	-2.3
1984	102.1	1.2	101.6	-0.5	101.2	-0.4	101.9	0.7	105.0	3.0	101.7	-3.1	101.1	-0.6	103.6	2.5	108.0	4.2	107.1	-0.8	108.5	1.3	107.0	-1.4
1985	105.5	-1.4	104.0	-1.4	104.1	0.1	103.4	-0.7	103.3	-0.1	103.3	0.0	103.2	-0.1	100.0	-3.1	103.0	3.0	102.9	-0.1	103.4	0.5	100.9	-2.4
1986	100.9	0.0	100.3	-0.6	99.1	-1.2	98.5	-0.6	97.9	-0.6	97.9	0.0	97.9	0.0	89.9	-8.2	94.8	5.5	91.1	-3.9	94.0	3.2	94.0	0.0
1987	93.5	-0.5	94.0	0.5	94.0	0.0	93.5	-0.5	93.5	0.0	93.5	0.0	92.0	-1.6	92.0	0.0	96.5	4.9	97.0	0.5	96.5	-0.5	96.5	0.0
1988	95.5	-1.0	95.5	0.0	95.5	0.0	91.5	-4.2	91.5	0.0	91.5	0.0	91.5	0.0	93.0	1.6	98.5	5.9	100.1	1.6	101.1	1.0	99.7	-1.4
1989	99.7	0.0	98.7	-1.0	98.7	0.0	99.2	0.5	99.2	0.0	99.2	0.0	98.7	-0.5	98.1	-0.6	101.2	3.2	114.2	12.8	114.5	0.3	117.8	2.9
1990	117.8	0.0	117.8	0.0	117.8	0.0	119.3	1.3	119.3	0.0	119.3	0.0	119.3	0.0	117.8	-1.3	117.3	-0.4	121.8	3.8	141.9	16.5	142.4	0.4	150.7	5.8
1991	151.6	0.6	151.6	0.0	151.2	-0.3	151.2	0.0	151.2	0.0	151.2	0.0	151.2	0.0	149.0	-1.5	154.3	3.6	142.7	-7.5	157.2	10.2	156.3	-0.6
1992	152.4	-2.5	152.4	0.0	169.9	11.5	140.8	-17.1	140.8	0.0	140.8	0.0	134.9	-4.2	143.7	6.5	158.2	10.1	157.3	-0.6	158.2	0.6	158.2	0.0
1993	156.3	-1.2	164.1	5.0	162.1	-1.2	145.6	-10.2	136.9	-6.0	136.9	0.0	136.9	0.0	138.8	1.4	150.5	8.4	152.4	1.3	157.3	3.2	157.3	0.0
1994	157.3	0.0	163.1	3.7	136.9	-16.1	147.6	7.8	147.6	0.0	147.6	0.0	130.1	-11.9	135.9	4.5	153.4	12.9	156.3	1.9	158.2	1.2	160.2	1.3
1995	164.7	2.8	167.8	1.9	149.5	-10.9	134.2	-10.2	-	-	-	-	154.3	15.0	152.1	-1.4	160.0	5.2	-	-	-	-	161.7	1.1

Source: U.S. Department of Labor, Bureau of Labor Statistics, Division of Industry Prices and Price Indexes. n.e.c. stands for not elsewhere classified. - indicates no data collected for period or unavailable.

PROCESSED FOODS AND FEEDS
Producer Price Index
Base 1982 = 100

For 1947-1995. Columns headed % show percentile change in the index from the previous period for which an index is available.

Year	Jan Index	%	Feb Index	%	Mar Index	%	Apr Index	%	May Index	%	Jun Index	%	Jul Index	%	Aug Index	%	Sep Index	%	Oct Index	%	Nov Index	%	Dec Index	%
1947	31.5	-	31.6	0.3	32.9	4.1	32.1	-2.4	31.5	-1.9	31.7	0.6	32.3	1.9	32.8	1.5	34.2	4.3	34.5	0.9	34.9	1.2	35.6	2.0
1948	36.7	3.1	35.0	-4.6	34.9	-0.3	35.4	1.4	35.7	0.8	35.9	0.6	36.1	0.6	35.8	-0.8	35.6	-0.6	34.5	-3.1	34.1	-1.2	33.6	-1.5
1949	32.9	-2.1	32.0	-2.7	32.1	0.3	32.0	-0.3	31.9	-0.3	31.9	0.0	32.1	0.6	32.5	1.2	32.2	-0.9	31.8	-1.2	31.6	-0.6	31.5	-0.3
1950	31.3	-0.6	31.5	0.6	31.7	0.6	31.7	0.0	32.4	2.2	32.4	0.0	34.2	5.6	34.7	1.5	34.9	0.6	34.1	-2.3	34.2	0.3	35.3	3.2
1951	36.4	3.1	37.2	2.2	37.0	-0.5	37.0	0.0	37.0	0.0	36.7	-0.8	36.6	-0.3	36.7	0.3	36.7	0.0	37.0	0.8	37.0	0.0	36.9	-0.3
1952	36.9	0.0	36.8	-0.3	36.6	-0.5	36.3	-0.8	36.4	0.3	36.3	-0.3	36.6	0.8	36.9	0.8	36.9	0.0	36.4	-1.4	36.0	-1.1	35.0	-2.8
1953	35.2	0.6	35.1	-0.3	34.8	-0.9	34.4	-1.1	34.8	1.2	34.2	-1.7	34.8	1.8	34.7	-0.3	35.2	1.4	34.7	-1.4	34.4	-0.9	34.9	1.5
1954	35.5	1.7	35.2	-0.8	35.4	0.6	36.0	1.7	36.2	0.6	35.4	-2.2	35.8	1.1	35.7	-0.3	35.3	-1.1	34.6	-2.0	34.7	0.3	34.6	-0.3
1955	34.7	0.3	34.5	-0.6	34.0	-1.4	34.2	0.6	33.9	-0.9	34.2	0.9	34.2	0.0	33.8	-1.2	33.6	-0.6	33.4	-0.6	32.8	-1.8	32.6	-0.6
1956	32.7	0.3	32.8	0.3	32.8	0.0	33.4	1.8	34.2	2.4	34.0	-0.6	33.8	-0.6	34.0	0.6	34.3	0.9	34.2	-0.3	34.3	0.3	34.2	-0.3
1957	34.6	1.2	34.4	-0.6	34.4	0.0	34.5	0.3	34.5	0.0	34.8	0.9	35.2	1.1	35.1	-0.3	35.0	-0.3	34.6	-1.1	34.8	0.6	35.1	0.9
1958	35.8	2.0	35.9	0.3	36.4	1.4	36.9	1.4	37.1	0.5	37.2	0.3	37.2	0.0	36.6	-1.6	36.4	-0.5	36.1	-0.8	36.1	0.0	36.3	0.6
1959	36.3	0.0	35.9	-1.1	35.8	-0.3	35.9	0.3	35.9	0.0	35.7	-0.6	35.6	-0.3	35.1	-1.4	35.4	0.9	35.2	-0.6	35.0	-0.6	34.9	-0.3
1960	35.2	0.9	35.1	-0.3	35.6	1.4	35.6	0.0	35.4	-0.6	35.5	0.3	35.8	0.8	35.5	-0.8	35.6	0.3	35.9	0.8	35.9	0.0	36.0	0.3
1961	36.5	1.4	36.6	0.3	36.5	-0.3	36.3	-0.5	36.1	-0.6	35.6	-1.4	35.9	0.8	36.0	0.3	36.0	0.0	35.9	-0.3	36.1	0.6	36.4	0.8
1962	36.7	0.8	36.6	-0.3	36.5	-0.3	36.2	-0.8	36.0	-0.6	36.0	0.0	36.5	1.4	36.6	0.3	37.3	1.9	36.7	-1.6	36.7	0.0	36.6	-0.3
1963	36.7	0.3	36.6	-0.3	36.1	-1.4	36.1	0.0	36.7	1.7	36.9	0.5	37.1	0.5	36.8	-0.8	36.9	0.3	37.2	0.8	37.2	0.0	36.7	-1.3
1964	37.3	1.6	36.8	-1.3	36.6	-0.5	36.5	-0.3	36.1	-1.1	36.3	0.6	36.6	0.8	36.5	-0.3	37.1	1.6	36.9	-0.5	36.6	-0.8	36.7	0.3
1965	37.1	1.1	37.0	-0.3	36.9	-0.3	37.1	0.5	37.3	0.5	38.3	2.7	38.5	0.5	38.5	0.0	38.5	0.0	38.5	0.0	38.9	1.0	39.3	1.0
1966	39.7	1.0	40.2	1.3	39.9	-0.7	39.7	-0.5	39.8	0.3	39.9	0.3	40.5	1.5	41.2	1.7	41.1	-0.2	40.6	-1.2	40.1	-1.2	40.2	0.2
1967	40.2	0.0	39.7	-1.2	39.4	-0.8	39.2	-0.5	39.4	0.5	40.1	1.8	40.3	0.5	39.9	-1.0	40.1	0.5	39.8	-0.7	39.5	-0.8	39.7	0.5
1968	40.0	0.8	40.3	0.7	40.2	-0.2	40.2	0.0	40.5	0.7	40.9	1.0	41.3	1.0	41.0	-0.7	41.0	0.0	40.7	-0.7	40.8	0.2	40.9	0.2
1969	41.3	1.0	41.4	0.2	41.5	0.2	41.8	0.7	42.5	1.7	43.3	1.9	43.5	0.5	43.3	-0.5	43.2	-0.2	43.3	0.2	43.3	0.0	43.7	0.9
1970	44.6	2.1	44.7	0.2	44.5	-0.4	44.5	0.0	44.2	-0.7	44.5	0.7	45.1	1.3	44.9	-0.4	45.0	0.2	44.5	-1.1	44.5	0.0	44.0	-1.1
1971	44.5	1.1	45.1	1.3	45.2	0.2	45.2	0.0	45.6	0.9	45.8	0.4	46.2	0.9	46.0	-0.4	45.7	-0.7	45.4	-0.7	45.5	0.2	46.1	1.3
1972	46.6	1.1	47.3	1.5	47.2	-0.2	46.8	-0.8	47.2	0.9	47.6	0.8	48.3	1.5	48.1	-0.4	48.5	0.8	48.5	0.0	48.9	0.8	51.5	5.3
1973	52.6	2.1	54.5	3.6	56.2	3.1	55.6	-1.1	57.7	3.8	60.3	4.5	58.3	-3.3	66.1	13.4	62.2	-5.9	60.9	-2.1	60.4	-0.8	61.9	2.5
1974	64.4	4.0	65.5	1.7	64.8	-1.1	63.3	-2.3	63.2	-0.2	62.6	-0.9	66.6	6.4	71.4	7.2	70.3	-1.5	73.0	3.8	75.4	3.3	74.8	-0.8
1975	74.1	-0.9	72.6	-2.0	70.5	-2.9	71.4	1.3	71.2	-0.3	71.5	0.4	73.4	2.7	74.1	1.0	74.0	-0.1	74.0	0.0	72.6	-1.9	72.0	-0.8
1976	71.3	-1.0	70.2	-1.5	69.9	-0.4	70.8	1.3	71.5	1.0	72.3	1.1	72.6	0.4	70.3	-3.2	70.5	0.3	69.6	-1.3	69.5	-0.1	71.2	2.4
1977	71.3	0.1	72.3	1.4	73.1	1.1	75.0	2.6	76.3	1.7	75.6	-0.9	74.4	-1.6	73.5	-1.2	73.3	-0.3	73.3	0.0	74.3	1.4	75.3	1.3
1978	76.2	1.2	77.5	1.7	78.3	1.0	79.6	1.7	80.5	1.1	81.4	1.1	81.2	-0.2	80.2	-1.2	81.7	1.9	83.1	1.7	82.8	-0.4	84.2	1.7
1979	85.6	1.7	87.1	1.8	87.7	0.7	88.4	0.8	88.3	-0.1	87.7	-0.7	88.8	1.3	87.7	-1.2	89.8	2.4	89.4	-0.4	90.3	1.0	91.2	1.0
1980	90.9	-0.3	92.7	2.0	92.1	-0.6	90.9	-1.3	92.7	2.0	93.0	0.3	96.1	3.3	99.2	3.2	99.3	0.1	101.8	2.5	102.3	0.5	100.0	-2.2
1981	100.7	0.7	99.5	-1.2	98.8	-0.7	98.4	-0.4	98.7	0.3	99.4	0.7	100.3	0.9	99.9	-0.4	99.0	-0.9	98.0	-1.0	97.2	-0.8	96.9	-0.3
1982	98.2	1.3	98.7	0.5	98.7	0.0	99.8	1.1	101.2	1.4	101.7	0.5	101.2	-0.5	100.8	-0.4	100.8	0.0	99.7	-1.1	99.5	-0.2	99.6	0.1
1983	100.1	0.5	101.3	1.2	101.2	-0.1	101.8	0.6	101.8	0.0	101.1	-0.7	101.2	0.1	101.6	0.4	103.2	1.6	102.5	-0.7	102.5	0.0	103.0	0.5
1984	104.9	1.8	104.7	-0.2	106.2	1.4	106.3	0.1	106.4	0.1	105.3	-1.0	106.3	0.9	105.3	-0.9	104.8	-0.5	104.4	-0.4	104.9	0.5	105.2	0.3
1985	105.1	-0.1	104.9	-0.2	104.3	-0.6	103.8	-0.5	103.4	-0.4	102.9	-0.5	103.3	0.4	102.3	-1.0	101.5	-0.8	102.5	1.0	103.9	1.4	104.5	0.6
1986	104.7	0.2	104.0	-0.7	103.7	-0.3	103.3	-0.4	104.3	1.0	104.7	0.4	106.1	1.3	107.2	1.0	107.0	-0.2	106.7	-0.3	106.5	-0.2	106.7	0.2
1987	106.1	-0.6	106.4	0.3	105.9	-0.5	107.2	1.2	109.1	1.8	109.0	-0.1	109.0	0.0	108.2	-0.7	108.9	0.6	108.7	-0.2	108.1	-0.6	108.2	0.1
1988	109.3	1.0	109.1	-0.2	109.6	0.5	110.1	0.5	111.2	1.0	113.5	2.1	115.0	1.3	114.5	-0.4	115.4	0.8	115.0	-0.3	114.8	-0.2	115.0	0.2
1989	116.6	1.4	116.6	0.0	117.5	0.8	117.2	-0.3	117.9	0.6	117.4	-0.4	118.1	0.6	117.9	-0.2	117.9	0.0	117.9	0.0	118.9	0.8	119.3	0.3
1990	120.2	0.8	120.0	-0.2	120.9	0.7	121.2	0.2	123.5	1.9	122.8	-0.6	123.2	0.3	123.0	-0.2	122.4	-0.5	122.2	-0.2	121.7	-0.4	121.7	0.0
1991	122.1	0.3	122.3	0.2	122.6	0.2	122.5	-0.1	122.3	-0.2	121.9	-0.3	121.6	-0.2	121.4	-0.2	121.1	-0.2	121.9	0.7	121.4	-0.4	121.4	0.0

[Continued]

PROCESSED FOODS AND FEEDS
Producer Price Index
Base 1982 = 100

[Continued]

For 1947-1995. Columns headed % show percentile change in the index from the previous period for which an index is available.

Year	Jan Index	%	Feb Index	%	Mar Index	%	Apr Index	%	May Index	%	Jun Index	%	Jul Index	%	Aug Index	%	Sep Index	%	Oct Index	%	Nov Index	%	Dec Index	%
1992	121.3	-0.1	121.7	0.3	121.8	0.1	122.0	0.2	122.5	0.4	123.0	0.4	122.4	-0.5	122.1	-0.2	122.1	0.0	121.8	-0.2	121.6	-0.2	122.4	0.7
1993	122.7	0.2	122.7	0.0	122.9	0.2	123.7	0.7	124.2	0.4	124.0	-0.2	124.3	0.2	124.3	0.0	124.3	0.0	124.5	0.2	124.8	0.2	125.4	0.5
1994	126.0	0.5	126.2	0.2	126.8	0.5	126.6	-0.2	126.1	-0.4	125.4	-0.6	124.9	-0.4	125.2	0.2	125.0	-0.2	124.5	-0.4	124.7	0.2	124.3	-0.3
1995	125.2	0.7	125.9	0.6	126.2	0.2	125.6	-0.5	125.0	-0.5	125.3	0.2	126.7	1.1	127.5	0.6	127.6	0.1	128.9	1.0	130.0	0.9	130.1	0.1

Source: U.S. Department of Labor, Bureau of Labor Statistics, Division of Industry Prices and Price Indexes. n.e.c. stands for not elsewhere classified. - indicates no data collected for period or unavailable.

Cereal and Bakery Products

Producer Price Index
Base 1982 = 100

For 1926-1995. Columns headed % show percentile change in the index from the previous period for which an index is available.

Year	Jan		Feb		Mar		Apr		May		Jun		Jul		Aug		Sep		Oct		Nov		Dec	
	Index	%	Index	%	Index	%	Index	%	Index	%	Index	%	Index	%	Index	%	Index	%	Index	%	Index	%	Index	%
1926	20.1	-	19.8	-1.5	19.5	-1.5	19.3	-1.0	18.9	-2.1	19.0	0.5	18.8	-1.1	18.3	-2.7	18.1	-1.1	18.3	1.1	18.0	-1.6	17.9	-0.6
1927	17.8	-0.6	17.8	0.0	17.6	-1.1	17.6	0.0	18.2	3.4	18.3	0.5	18.2	-0.5	18.0	-1.1	17.5	-2.8	17.5	0.0	17.4	-0.6	17.4	0.0
1928	17.6	1.1	17.6	0.0	17.9	1.7	18.6	3.9	18.9	1.6	18.4	-2.6	17.9	-2.7	17.1	-4.5	17.0	-0.6	16.9	-0.6	16.7	-1.2	16.7	0.0
1929	16.7	0.0	16.9	1.2	16.4	-3.0	16.2	-1.2	15.9	-1.9	16.0	0.6	17.2	7.5	17.0	-1.2	16.9	-0.6	16.6	-1.8	16.5	-0.6	16.5	0.0
1930	16.5	0.0	16.2	-1.8	16.0	-1.2	15.9	-0.6	15.8	-0.6	15.6	-1.3	15.2	-2.6	15.1	-0.7	14.8	-2.0	14.6	-1.4	14.3	-2.1	14.3	0.0
1931	14.3	0.0	14.2	-0.7	14.0	-1.4	13.9	-0.7	14.0	0.7	13.9	-0.7	13.5	-2.9	13.4	-0.7	13.2	-1.5	13.3	0.8	13.7	3.0	13.6	-0.7
1932	13.4	-1.5	13.1	-2.2	12.8	-2.3	12.8	0.0	12.8	0.0	12.6	-1.6	12.4	-1.6	12.4	0.0	12.4	0.0	12.1	-2.4	11.8	-2.5	11.6	-1.7
1933	11.5	-0.9	11.4	-0.9	11.8	3.5	12.4	5.1	13.0	4.8	13.3	2.3	15.7	18.0	16.0	1.9	16.0	0.0	16.0	0.0	16.2	1.3	16.0	-1.2
1934	16.2	1.3	16.2	0.0	16.0	-1.2	16.0	0.0	16.4	2.5	16.7	1.8	16.7	0.0	17.1	2.4	17.3	1.2	17.1	-1.2	17.1	0.0	17.3	1.2
1935	17.3	0.0	17.3	0.0	17.3	0.0	17.5	1.2	17.4	-0.6	17.1	-1.7	17.5	2.3	17.9	2.3	18.2	1.7	18.6	2.2	18.3	-1.6	18.3	0.0
1936	17.3	-5.5	16.7	-3.5	16.2	-3.0	15.8	-2.5	15.5	-1.9	15.4	-0.6	15.9	3.2	16.5	3.8	16.5	0.0	16.5	0.0	16.2	-1.8	16.4	1.2
1937	16.6	1.2	16.8	1.2	16.9	0.6	16.9	0.0	16.7	-1.2	17.0	1.8	17.4	2.4	16.5	-5.2	16.2	-1.8	15.9	-1.9	15.3	-3.8	15.4	0.7
1938	15.6	1.3	15.6	0.0	15.2	-2.6	15.1	-0.7	14.7	-2.6	15.1	2.7	14.9	-1.3	14.5	-2.7	14.3	-1.4	14.1	-1.4	13.9	-1.4	14.1	1.4
1939	13.8	-2.1	13.7	-0.7	13.6	-0.7	13.6	0.0	13.9	2.2	14.3	2.9	13.5	-5.6	13.5	0.0	14.9	10.4	14.7	-1.3	14.7	0.0	15.2	3.4
1940	15.1	-0.7	15.5	2.6	15.5	0.0	15.6	0.6	15.2	-2.6	14.6	-3.9	14.3	-2.1	14.1	-1.4	14.3	1.4	14.5	1.4	14.1	-2.8	13.9	-1.4
1941	14.1	1.4	13.9	-1.4	14.1	1.4	14.5	2.8	14.7	1.4	15.1	2.7	15.1	0.0	15.3	1.3	16.2	5.9	16.2	0.0	16.2	0.0	16.8	3.7
1942	17.1	1.8	17.2	0.6	17.1	-0.6	17.0	-0.6	16.7	-1.8	16.4	-1.8	16.4	0.0	16.5	0.6	16.7	1.2	16.8	0.6	16.9	0.6	16.8	-0.6
1943	17.1	1.8	17.4	1.8	17.6	1.1	17.6	0.0	17.6	0.0	17.6	0.0	17.6	0.0	17.6	0.0	17.8	1.1	17.9	0.6	17.9	0.0	17.9	0.0
1944	17.9	0.0	17.9	0.0	17.9	0.0	17.9	0.0	17.9	0.0	17.9	0.0	17.8	-0.6	17.7	-0.6	17.8	0.6	17.9	0.6	17.9	0.0	18.0	0.0
1945	17.9	0.0	17.9	0.0	17.9	0.0	17.9	0.0	18.0	0.6	18.0	0.0	17.9	-0.6	17.9	0.0	17.9	0.0	17.9	0.0	18.0	0.6	18.0	0.0
1946	18.0	0.0	18.1	0.6	18.1	0.0	18.7	3.3	18.9	1.1	19.2	1.6	23.5	22.4	23.4	-0.4	24.0	2.6	24.2	0.8	25.6	5.8	26.2	2.3
1947	26.6	1.5	26.8	0.8	27.9	4.1	28.4	1.8	28.2	-0.7	27.7	-1.8	28.4	2.5	28.4	0.0	29.1	2.5	30.3	4.1	31.2	3.0	31.1	-0.3
1948	31.1	0.0	29.8	-4.2	29.6	-0.7	29.5	-0.3	29.2	-1.0	29.1	-0.3	29.2	0.3	28.8	-1.4	28.6	-0.7	28.3	-1.0	28.4	0.4	28.4	0.0
1949	28.2	-0.7	28.0	-0.7	28.0	0.0	27.9	-0.4	27.8	-0.4	27.8	0.0	27.9	0.4	27.5	-1.4	27.3	-0.7	27.3	0.0	27.3	0.0	27.3	0.0
1950	27.3	0.0	27.5	0.7	27.6	0.4	27.6	0.0	27.6	0.0	27.5	-0.4	28.4	3.3	29.0	2.1	29.1	0.3	28.8	-1.0	28.8	0.0	29.4	2.1
1951	30.3	3.1	30.7	1.3	30.5	-0.7	30.5	0.0	30.5	0.0	30.3	-0.7	30.3	0.0	30.4	0.3	30.3	-0.3	30.5	0.7	30.7	0.7	30.8	0.3
1952	30.7	-0.3	30.6	-0.3	30.7	0.3	30.6	-0.3	30.5	-0.3	30.4	-0.3	30.3	-0.3	30.3	0.0	30.3	0.0	30.3	0.0	32.1	0.6	32.0	-0.3
1953	30.5	0.0	30.7	0.7	31.1	1.3	31.1	0.0	31.1	0.0	30.8	-1.0	30.9	0.3	30.9	0.0	31.6	2.3	31.9	0.9	33.2	1.8	33.3	0.3
1954	32.0	0.0	32.2	0.6	32.1	-0.3	32.3	0.6	32.3	0.0	32.4	0.3	32.5	0.3	32.3	-0.6	32.4	0.3	32.6	0.6	32.8	1.8	32.8	0.3
1955	33.3	0.0	33.1	-0.6	33.2	0.3	33.3	0.3	33.7	1.2	33.5	-0.6	33.5	0.0	32.8	-2.1	32.6	-0.6	32.7	0.3	32.8	0.3	32.9	-0.3
1956	32.8	0.0	32.9	0.3	32.9	0.0	32.9	0.0	32.9	0.0	32.9	0.0	32.7	-0.6	32.6	-0.3	32.7	0.3	32.9	0.6	33.0	0.3	32.9	-0.3
1957	33.0	0.3	33.1	0.3	33.3	0.6	33.3	0.0	33.2	-0.3	33.3	0.3	33.3	0.0	33.5	0.6	33.3	-0.6	33.3	0.0	33.5	0.6	33.7	0.6
1958	33.7	0.0	33.7	0.0	33.6	-0.3	33.8	0.6	33.6	-0.6	33.8	0.6	33.8	0.0	33.5	-0.9	33.3	-0.6	33.6	0.9	33.7	0.0	33.5	-0.6
1959	33.5	0.0	33.5	0.0	33.9	1.2	33.9	0.0	34.0	0.3	34.0	0.0	34.0	0.0	34.0	0.0	34.0	0.0	34.0	0.0	34.3	0.9	34.3	0.0
1960	34.4	0.3	34.4	0.0	34.4	0.0	34.4	0.0	34.6	0.6	34.6	0.0	34.9	0.9	34.8	-0.3	34.9	0.3	35.1	0.6	35.1	0.0	35.2	0.3
1961	35.2	0.0	35.2	0.0	35.2	0.0	35.2	0.0	35.2	0.0	35.3	0.3	35.3	0.0	35.3	0.0	35.4	0.3	35.7	0.8	35.7	0.0	35.7	0.0
1962	36.0	0.8	36.1	0.3	36.1	0.0	36.3	0.6	36.1	-0.6	36.2	0.3	36.3	0.3	36.3	0.0	36.2	-0.3	36.2	0.0	36.3	0.3	36.2	-0.3
1963	36.1	-0.3	36.5	1.1	36.3	-0.5	36.4	0.3	36.2	-0.5	36.0	-0.6	35.8	-0.6	35.7	-0.3	36.0	0.8	36.3	0.8	36.1	-0.6	36.0	-0.3
1964	36.0	0.0	36.1	0.3	35.9	-0.6	36.3	1.1	36.2	-0.3	36.3	0.3	36.5	0.6	36.4	-0.3	36.4	0.0	36.4	0.0	36.4	0.0	36.4	0.0
1965	36.4	0.0	36.3	-0.3	36.4	0.3	36.4	0.0	36.4	0.0	36.5	0.3	36.8	0.8	36.6	-0.5	36.7	0.3	36.8	0.3	37.2	1.1	37.4	0.5
1966	37.6	0.5	37.7	0.3	37.7	0.0	37.9	0.5	38.0	0.3	38.4	1.1	38.9	1.3	40.0	2.8	40.0	0.0	40.0	0.0	40.0	0.0	39.7	-0.7
1967	39.5	-0.5	39.5	0.0	39.4	-0.3	39.4	0.0	39.5	0.3	39.5	0.0	39.3	-0.5	39.3	0.0	39.3	0.0	39.3	0.0	39.4	0.3	39.4	0.0
1968	39.4	0.0	39.5	0.3	39.5	0.0	39.5	0.0	39.4	-0.3	39.4	0.0	39.8	1.0	40.2	1.0	40.0	-0.5	40.2	0.5	40.2	0.0	40.2	0.0
1969	40.2	0.0	40.2	0.0	40.2	0.0	40.2	0.0	40.2	0.0	40.3	0.2	40.4	0.2	40.5	0.2	40.6	0.2	40.8	0.5	41.0	0.5	41.1	0.2
1970	41.1	0.0	41.5	1.0	41.7	0.5	41.9	0.5	41.9	0.0	42.0	0.2	42.4	1.0	42.5	0.2	43.1	1.4	43.3	0.5	43.7	0.9	43.8	0.2

[Continued]

Cereal and Bakery Products
Producer Price Index
Base 1982 = 100
[Continued]

For 1926-1995. Columns headed % show percentile change in the index from the previous period for which an index is available.

Year	Jan Index	%	Feb Index	%	Mar Index	%	Apr Index	%	May Index	%	Jun Index	%	Jul Index	%	Aug Index	%	Sep Index	%	Oct Index	%	Nov Index	%	Dec Index	%
1971	44.0	0.5	44.0	0.0	44.1	0.2	44.1	0.0	44.1	0.0	44.1	0.0	43.9	-0.5	43.9	0.0	43.8	-0.2	43.9	0.2	43.9	0.0	44.0	0.2
1972	44.2	0.5	44.3	0.2	44.4	0.2	44.5	0.2	44.6	0.2	44.6	0.0	44.8	0.4	45.4	1.3	45.7	0.7	46.1	0.9	46.6	1.1	47.3	1.5
1973	47.7	0.8	47.6	-0.2	47.8	0.4	48.7	1.9	49.0	0.6	49.6	1.2	49.5	-0.2	53.7	8.5	58.2	8.4	59.3	1.9	61.5	3.7	63.1	2.6
1974	65.5	3.8	66.8	2.0	67.9	1.6	65.8	-3.1	65.8	0.0	65.4	-0.6	66.6	1.8	66.7	0.2	66.9	0.3	69.4	3.7	70.8	2.0	71.7	1.3
1975	71.8	0.1	72.3	0.7	71.7	-0.8	70.6	-1.5	69.4	-1.7	68.7	-1.0	69.6	1.3	69.3	-0.4	69.7	0.6	70.0	0.4	69.7	-0.4	68.8	-1.3
1976	69.0	0.3	69.1	0.1	68.8	-0.4	68.0	-1.2	68.3	0.4	68.5	0.3	68.4	-0.1	67.1	-1.9	66.9	-0.3	67.0	0.1	66.5	-0.7	66.4	-0.2
1977	66.4	0.0	67.0	0.9	67.6	0.9	67.6	0.0	67.8	0.3	67.4	-0.6	67.7	0.4	67.8	0.1	68.8	1.5	69.2	0.6	70.9	2.5	71.8	1.3
1978	72.6	1.1	72.9	0.4	73.4	0.7	74.4	1.4	74.2	-0.3	74.9	0.9	75.3	0.5	75.8	0.7	75.3	-0.7	76.2	1.2	77.3	1.4	77.5	0.3
1979	77.7	0.3	78.5	1.0	78.8	0.4	80.0	1.5	80.8	1.0	81.3	0.6	83.7	3.0	85.1	1.7	86.2	1.3	86.6	0.5	87.7	1.3	88.1	0.5
1980	88.8	0.8	90.6	2.0	91.3	0.8	91.6	0.3	92.5	1.0	91.9	-0.6	92.5	0.7	92.9	0.4	93.9	1.1	95.1	1.3	96.7	1.7	98.0	1.3
1981	99.1	1.1	99.4	0.3	99.4	0.0	100.0	0.6	101.0	1.0	101.0	0.0	101.8	0.8	101.5	-0.3	101.8	0.3	101.2	-0.6	101.1	-0.1	100.5	-0.6
1982	101.1	0.6	99.8	-1.3	99.8	0.0	99.9	0.1	99.6	-0.3	99.6	0.0	99.7	0.1	99.6	-0.1	100.1	0.5	99.7	-0.4	100.2	0.5	101.0	0.8
1983	101.4	0.4	101.2	-0.2	101.2	0.0	102.0	0.8	102.1	0.1	102.6	0.5	103.0	0.4	103.6	0.6	103.9	0.3	104.3	0.4	104.5	0.2	104.5	0.0
1984	105.1	0.6	105.3	0.2	105.4	0.1	105.7	0.3	105.9	0.2	106.9	0.9	107.3	0.4	107.1	-0.2	107.1	0.0	107.4	0.3	107.8	0.4	107.8	0.0
1985	109.0	1.1	109.4	0.4	109.5	0.1	109.9	0.4	109.6	-0.3	110.3	0.6	110.2	-0.1	110.3	0.1	110.8	0.5	111.4	0.5	111.3	-0.1	111.6	0.3
1986	111.6	0.0	111.6	0.0	111.6	0.0	111.4	-0.2	111.6	0.2	111.1	-0.4	110.7	-0.4	110.9	0.2	110.5	-0.4	110.6	0.1	110.5	-0.1	110.1	-0.4
1987	110.2	0.1	110.8	0.5	111.2	0.4	111.4	0.2	112.0	0.5	111.9	-0.1	111.9	0.0	112.6	0.6	113.0	0.4	114.5	1.3	115.3	0.7	116.7	1.2
1988	118.2	1.3	119.6	1.2	119.8	0.2	120.2	0.3	120.4	0.2	123.2	2.3	124.1	0.7	124.6	0.4	126.4	1.4	126.4	0.0	126.1	-0.2	126.5	0.3
1989	128.2	1.3	129.0	0.6	129.2	0.2	129.1	-0.1	130.8	1.3	131.2	0.3	132.1	0.7	132.9	0.6	132.8	-0.1	132.4	-0.3	132.4	0.0	133.3	0.7
1990	133.2	-0.1	133.8	0.5	133.9	0.1	134.6	0.5	135.1	0.4	134.7	-0.3	134.3	-0.3	134.2	-0.1	133.7	-0.4	134.2	0.4	134.2	0.0	134.6	0.3
1991	135.3	0.5	136.0	0.5	136.6	0.4	137.0	0.3	137.4	0.3	137.8	0.3	137.3	-0.4	138.3	0.7	138.6	0.2	139.9	0.9	140.0	0.1	141.0	0.7
1992	142.1	0.8	143.5	1.0	143.4	-0.1	143.5	0.1	144.0	0.3	145.3	0.9	144.8	-0.3	144.3	-0.3	144.6	0.2	144.9	0.2	145.1	0.1	144.7	-0.3
1993	145.7	0.7	146.5	0.5	146.1	-0.3	146.6	0.3	146.3	-0.2	146.4	0.1	146.6	0.1	147.6	0.7	147.1	-0.3	149.0	1.3	150.6	1.1	152.3	1.1
1994	152.0	-0.2	152.1	0.1	152.0	-0.1	151.5	-0.3	151.7	0.1	150.9	-0.5	150.0	-0.6	149.4	-0.4	150.4	0.7	151.0	0.4	151.1	0.1	151.0	-0.1
1995	151.2	0.1	151.4	0.1	151.1	-0.2	151.3	0.1	152.2	0.6	153.5	0.9	155.1	1.0	156.0	0.6	157.1	0.7	158.9	1.1	158.9	0.0	159.3	0.3

Source: U.S. Department of Labor, Bureau of Labor Statistics, Division of Industry Prices and Price Indexes. n.e.c. stands for not elsewhere classified. - indicates no data collected for period or unavailable.

Meats, Poultry, and Fish
Producer Price Index
Base 1982 = 100

For 1926-1995. Columns headed % show percentile change in the index from the previous period for which an index is available.

Year	Jan Index	%	Feb Index	%	Mar Index	%	Apr Index	%	May Index	%	Jun Index	%	Jul Index	%	Aug Index	%	Sep Index	%	Oct Index	%	Nov Index	%	Dec Index	%
1926	17.5	-	17.1	-2.3	17.2	0.6	17.4	1.2	17.5	0.6	17.9	2.3	17.7	-1.1	17.5	-1.1	17.8	1.7	17.7	-0.6	17.3	-2.3	17.2	-0.6
1927	15.6	-9.3	15.7	0.6	15.8	0.6	15.9	0.6	15.7	-1.3	15.5	-1.3	15.8	1.9	15.8	0.0	16.2	2.5	17.5	8.0	17.6	0.6	17.4	-1.1
1928	17.4	0.0	17.1	-1.7	16.6	-2.9	17.4	4.8	18.1	4.0	18.2	0.6	19.7	8.2	20.8	5.6	22.1	6.3	20.4	-7.7	19.0	-6.9	17.9	-5.8
1929	18.4	2.8	17.9	-2.7	19.0	6.1	19.5	2.6	19.5	0.0	19.5	0.0	20.4	4.6	20.3	-0.5	19.8	-2.5	18.6	-6.1	17.9	-3.8	18.1	1.1
1930	18.6	2.8	18.4	-1.1	18.2	-1.1	18.1	-0.5	17.7	-2.2	17.5	-1.1	16.0	-8.6	16.3	1.9	17.4	6.7	16.9	-2.9	16.0	-5.3	15.6	-2.5
1931	15.5	-0.6	14.6	-5.8	14.4	-1.4	14.0	-2.8	13.0	-7.1	12.5	-3.8	12.8	2.4	13.3	3.9	12.9	-3.0	12.5	-3.1	11.8	-5.6	11.1	-5.9
1932	10.8	-2.7	10.4	-3.7	10.7	2.9	10.5	-1.9	9.9	-5.7	9.8	-1.0	10.8	10.2	10.8	0.0	10.6	-1.9	9.9	-6.6	9.4	-5.1	8.6	-8.5
1933	8.7	1.2	8.8	1.1	8.9	1.1	8.8	-1.1	9.2	4.5	9.2	0.0	8.9	-3.3	8.9	0.0	9.0	1.1	8.9	-1.1	8.4	-5.6	8.0	-4.8
1934	8.5	6.3	9.4	10.6	9.9	5.3	10.0	1.0	10.5	5.0	10.9	3.8	11.1	1.8	12.2	9.9	13.4	9.8	12.2	-9.0	12.0	-1.6	12.0	0.0
1935	14.3	19.2	15.3	7.0	16.0	4.6	16.5	3.1	17.0	3.0	16.5	-2.9	16.3	-1.2	17.9	9.8	18.0	0.6	17.0	-5.6	16.5	-2.9	17.0	3.0
1936	16.6	-2.4	16.1	-3.0	15.7	-2.5	15.9	1.3	14.9	-6.3	14.9	0.0	14.8	-0.7	15.1	2.0	15.3	1.3	14.8	-3.3	14.9	0.7	15.2	2.0
1937	15.9	4.6	15.8	-0.6	16.1	1.9	16.6	3.1	16.8	1.2	17.2	2.4	18.5	7.6	19.6	5.9	19.8	1.0	18.8	-5.1	17.2	-8.5	15.5	-9.9
1938	14.4	-7.1	13.7	-4.9	14.3	4.4	14.4	0.7	14.4	0.0	14.8	2.8	15.7	6.1	15.0	-4.5	15.2	1.3	14.6	-3.9	14.3	-2.1	14.0	-2.1
1939	14.3	2.1	14.5	1.4	14.4	-0.7	14.2	-1.4	13.7	-3.5	13.2	-3.6	13.2	0.0	12.9	-2.3	14.2	10.1	13.1	-7.7	12.5	-4.6	12.0	-4.0
1940	12.2	1.7	12.0	-1.6	12.1	0.8	12.5	3.3	12.9	3.2	12.4	-3.9	12.8	3.2	13.3	3.9	13.8	3.8	13.2	-4.3	13.4	1.5	13.5	0.7
1941	14.5	7.4	14.6	0.7	14.6	0.0	15.0	2.7	15.2	1.3	15.9	4.6	16.4	3.1	17.0	3.7	17.4	2.4	16.4	-5.7	15.9	-3.0	16.7	5.0
1942	17.8	6.6	18.2	2.2	19.1	4.9	19.8	3.7	20.1	1.5	19.9	-1.0	19.8	-0.5	20.1	1.5	20.3	1.0	20.2	-0.5	19.6	-3.0	19.9	1.5
1943	20.2	1.5	20.2	0.0	20.2	0.0	20.3	0.5	20.3	0.0	19.5	-3.9	18.5	-5.1	18.5	0.0	18.5	0.0	18.6	0.5	18.6	0.0	18.5	-0.5
1944	18.5	0.0	18.5	0.0	18.5	0.0	18.6	0.5	18.6	0.0	18.5	-0.5	18.5	0.0	18.5	0.0	18.5	0.0	18.5	0.0	18.6	0.5	18.6	0.0
1945	18.6	0.0	18.6	0.0	18.8	1.1	18.9	0.5	19.0	0.5	18.9	-0.5	18.9	0.0	18.9	0.0	18.9	0.0	18.9	0.0	18.9	0.0	18.9	0.0
1946	18.9	0.0	18.9	0.0	19.2	1.6	19.3	0.5	19.3	0.0	19.3	0.0	29.7	53.9	34.6	16.5	22.9	-33.8	33.5	46.3	35.4	5.7	33.0	-6.8
1947	32.1	-2.7	32.8	2.2	34.5	5.2	33.1	-4.1	33.6	1.5	34.6	3.0	35.3	2.0	36.7	4.0	39.2	6.8	37.8	-3.6	36.4	-3.7	37.4	2.7
1948	40.3	7.8	37.8	-6.2	39.0	3.2	40.4	3.6	42.0	4.0	42.3	0.7	44.1	4.3	44.6	1.1	44.4	-0.4	41.0	-7.7	38.8	-5.4	37.7	-2.8
1949	36.6	-2.9	34.9	-4.6	36.5	4.6	36.6	0.3	36.7	0.3	36.8	0.3	36.2	-1.6	35.8	-1.1	36.8	2.8	35.3	-4.1	34.2	-3.1	33.4	-2.3
1950	33.7	0.9	34.6	2.7	34.4	-0.6	34.4	0.0	37.2	8.1	38.3	3.0	41.3	7.8	41.4	0.2	41.8	1.0	38.9	-6.9	38.8	-0.3	40.5	4.4
1951	41.9	3.5	43.9	4.8	43.8	-0.2	43.8	0.0	44.1	0.7	43.8	-0.7	43.7	-0.2	43.9	0.5	44.2	0.7	44.6	0.9	43.3	-2.9	42.4	-2.1
1952	42.4	0.0	41.4	-2.4	41.5	0.2	40.9	-1.4	41.9	2.4	41.2	-1.7	41.3	0.2	42.0	1.7	40.9	-2.6	38.9	-4.9	38.1	-2.1	35.1	-7.9
1953	37.1	5.7	36.7	-1.1	34.1	-7.1	33.3	-2.3	35.1	5.4	34.2	-2.6	36.2	5.8	35.0	-3.3	36.4	4.0	33.2	-8.8	32.2	-3.0	33.5	4.0
1954	36.0	7.5	34.7	-3.6	34.7	0.0	35.3	1.7	36.8	4.2	34.5	-6.3	35.2	2.0	34.4	-2.3	34.4	0.0	32.1	-6.7	32.2	0.3	31.8	-1.2
1955	32.7	2.8	32.5	-0.6	31.1	-4.3	32.1	3.2	32.0	-0.3	34.2	6.9	33.1	-3.2	32.2	-2.7	32.7	1.6	30.5	-6.7	29.1	-4.6	28.1	-3.4
1956	28.3	0.7	28.4	0.4	27.9	-1.8	29.7	6.5	30.7	3.4	31.1	1.3	31.3	0.6	31.8	1.6	33.4	5.0	32.0	-4.2	30.9	-3.4	30.5	-1.3
1957	31.7	3.9	31.4	-0.9	31.6	0.6	33.0	4.4	34.2	3.6	36.1	5.6	37.1	2.8	36.5	-1.6	35.8	-1.9	34.2	-4.5	35.0	2.3	35.7	2.0
1958	38.0	6.4	38.4	1.1	39.6	3.1	40.6	2.5	42.2	3.9	42.6	0.9	41.9	-1.6	40.5	-3.3	40.0	-1.2	38.7	-3.3	38.3	-1.0	37.9	-1.0
1959	38.6	1.8	37.7	-2.3	37.2	-1.3	37.7	1.3	37.9	0.5	38.1	0.5	37.1	-2.6	35.4	-4.6	37.3	5.4	35.5	-4.8	33.9	-4.5	33.8	-0.3
1960	34.6	2.4	34.8	0.6	36.6	5.2	36.1	-1.4	36.8	1.9	36.7	-0.3	37.2	1.4	36.1	-3.0	35.9	-0.6	36.6	1.9	36.1	-1.4	36.4	0.8
1961	36.8	1.1	37.2	1.1	35.9	-3.5	35.3	-1.7	34.3	-2.8	33.6	-2.0	34.6	3.0	35.4	2.3	35.3	-0.3	35.0	-0.8	34.6	-1.1	35.4	2.3
1962	36.7	3.7	36.5	-0.5	36.4	-0.3	35.3	-3.0	35.3	0.0	35.4	0.3	36.6	3.4	37.3	1.9	39.5	5.9	37.0	-6.3	37.0	0.0	36.8	-0.5
1963	36.2	-1.6	35.3	-2.5	33.9	-4.0	33.4	-1.5	34.0	1.8	34.8	2.4	35.6	2.3	35.2	-1.1	34.8	-1.1	34.5	-0.9	33.9	-1.7	32.4	-4.4
1964	33.9	4.6	32.9	-2.9	32.8	-0.3	32.7	-0.3	32.1	-1.8	33.3	3.7	34.5	3.6	34.5	0.0	35.5	2.9	34.5	-2.8	33.2	-3.8	32.8	-1.2
1965	34.0	3.7	34.0	0.0	34.2	0.6	34.6	1.2	36.1	4.3	39.0	8.0	39.3	0.8	39.3	0.0	38.9	-1.0	38.8	-0.3	39.0	0.5	40.8	4.6
1966	41.7	2.2	42.5	1.9	41.9	-1.4	41.0	-2.1	41.0	0.0	40.6	-1.0	40.7	0.2	41.1	1.0	41.5	1.0	40.0	-3.6	38.5	-3.8	38.6	0.3
1967	39.0	1.0	38.7	-0.8	37.6	-2.8	37.2	-1.1	38.4	3.2	40.0	4.2	40.6	1.5	39.7	-2.2	40.1	1.0	38.7	-3.5	37.8	-2.3	38.2	1.1
1968	39.1	2.4	39.8	1.8	39.6	-0.5	39.1	-1.3	39.5	1.0	40.6	2.8	42.0	3.4	40.6	-3.3	41.1	1.2	39.5	-3.9	39.8	0.8	39.7	-0.3
1969	41.1	3.5	41.2	0.2	41.5	0.7	42.2	1.7	44.7	5.9	46.8	4.7	47.1	0.6	46.0	-2.3	45.4	-1.3	44.5	-2.0	44.6	0.2	45.1	1.1
1970	46.6	3.3	46.2	-0.9	47.1	1.9	46.2	-1.9	45.3	-1.9	45.7	0.9	46.7	2.2	45.2	-3.2	44.7	-1.1	43.1	-3.6	42.2	-2.1	40.5	-4.0

[Continued]

Meats, Poultry, and Fish
Producer Price Index
Base 1982 = 100
[Continued]

For 1926-1995. Columns headed % show percentile change in the index from the previous period for which an index is available.

Year	Jan Index	%	Feb Index	%	Mar Index	%	Apr Index	%	May Index	%	Jun Index	%	Jul Index	%	Aug Index	%	Sep Index	%	Oct Index	%	Nov Index	%	Dec Index	%
1971	42.2	4.2	44.7	5.9	43.8	-2.0	44.0	0.5	45.2	2.7	45.3	0.2	46.4	2.4	45.7	-1.5	45.6	-0.2	45.4	-0.4	45.5	0.2	46.8	2.9
1972	48.7	4.1	50.7	4.1	49.4	-2.6	48.0	-2.8	49.2	2.5	51.0	3.7	52.7	3.3	51.3	-2.7	51.1	-0.4	50.6	-1.0	49.7	-1.8	52.9	6.4
1973	56.4	6.6	59.5	5.5	64.1	7.7	63.3	-1.2	63.1	-0.3	64.0	1.4	65.9	3.0	77.0	16.8	72.7	-5.6	66.1	-9.1	64.1	-3.0	64.0	-0.2
1974	69.0	7.8	69.8	1.2	64.3	-7.9	61.2	-4.8	59.5	-2.8	55.0	-7.6	64.9	18.0	65.9	1.5	64.3	-2.4	63.3	-1.6	62.3	-1.6	62.4	0.2
1975	64.3	3.0	63.9	-0.6	63.6	-0.5	67.7	6.4	74.0	9.3	77.5	4.7	81.4	5.0	79.4	-2.5	81.4	2.5	81.7	0.4	78.0	-4.5	76.9	-1.4
1976	75.0	-2.5	72.2	-3.7	70.1	-2.9	73.4	4.7	73.9	0.7	73.8	-0.1	71.9	-2.6	67.8	-5.7	68.4	0.9	65.4	-4.4	65.4	0.0	68.7	5.0
1977	68.6	-0.1	68.9	0.4	67.6	-1.9	67.9	0.4	71.3	5.0	71.2	-0.1	73.6	3.4	70.9	-3.7	71.0	0.1	71.7	1.0	71.2	-0.7	74.1	4.1
1978	75.2	1.5	79.8	6.1	79.5	-0.4	82.2	3.4	85.6	4.1	87.8	2.6	87.1	-0.8	83.8	-3.8	87.1	3.9	88.6	1.7	85.8	-3.2	89.0	3.7
1979	93.3	4.8	96.5	3.4	97.3	0.8	98.2	0.9	97.2	-1.0	93.7	-3.6	92.3	-1.5	87.6	-5.1	93.1	6.3	90.9	-2.4	92.9	2.2	94.3	1.5
1980	93.0	-1.4	93.0	0.0	92.9	-0.1	87.8	-5.5	87.1	-0.8	88.0	1.0	96.5	9.7	100.9	4.6	100.1	-0.8	99.4	-0.7	97.4	-2.0	96.3	-1.1
1981	96.3	0.0	94.6	-1.8	93.9	-0.7	92.8	-1.2	95.2	2.6	96.5	1.4	99.8	3.4	98.8	-1.0	98.3	-0.5	95.7	-2.6	93.2	-2.6	91.7	-1.6
1982	94.6	3.2	96.3	1.8	97.1	0.8	100.2	3.2	103.9	3.7	105.3	1.3	103.3	-1.9	101.8	-1.5	103.2	1.4	99.7	-3.4	97.7	-2.0	97.0	-0.7
1983	97.9	0.9	101.3	3.5	101.2	-0.1	100.6	-0.6	100.1	-0.5	97.1	-3.0	96.0	-1.1	94.4	-1.7	94.3	-0.1	92.0	-2.4	91.1	-1.0	94.1	3.3
1984	99.3	5.5	98.8	-0.5	102.6	3.8	101.6	-1.0	99.8	-1.8	96.1	-3.7	100.5	4.6	97.9	-2.6	96.9	-1.0	95.3	-1.7	97.2	2.0	99.4	2.3
1985	99.6	0.2	99.2	-0.4	97.0	-2.2	95.0	-2.1	94.7	-0.3	92.6	-2.2	94.4	1.9	92.9	-1.6	91.1	-1.9	94.5	3.7	99.1	4.9	100.5	1.4
1986	98.1	-2.4	95.1	-3.1	93.9	-1.3	92.4	-1.6	95.8	3.7	97.2	1.5	103.0	6.0	107.7	4.6	106.4	-1.2	105.2	-1.1	103.7	-1.4	103.6	-0.1
1987	101.9	-1.6	102.5	0.6	100.3	-2.1	104.5	4.2	109.7	5.0	108.9	-0.7	109.5	0.6	106.2	-3.0	108.0	1.7	106.1	-1.8	101.4	-4.4	99.9	-1.5
1988	103.8	3.9	102.7	-1.1	104.0	1.3	104.4	0.4	107.7	3.2	110.0	2.1	109.6	-0.4	107.8	-1.6	109.3	1.4	106.8	-2.3	106.0	-0.7	106.8	0.8
1989	109.8	2.8	109.9	0.1	111.8	1.7	111.4	-0.4	112.7	1.2	111.4	-1.2	111.6	0.2	111.3	-0.3	110.4	-0.8	109.6	-0.7	111.0	1.3	111.5	0.5
1990	114.0	2.2	114.9	0.8	116.9	1.7	118.4	1.3	124.1	4.8	121.5	-2.1	121.6	0.1	121.0	-0.5	119.5	-1.2	121.0	1.3	121.1	0.1	120.9	-0.2
1991	120.0	-0.7	119.6	-0.3	120.6	0.8	120.0	-0.5	121.0	0.8	119.1	-1.6	118.6	-0.4	114.4	-3.5	112.3	-1.8	113.3	0.9	110.9	-2.1	110.0	-0.8
1992	109.0	-0.9	110.8	1.7	112.2	1.3	113.5	1.2	113.7	0.2	113.5	-0.2	112.6	-0.8	111.8	-0.7	111.9	0.1	112.1	0.2	111.0	-1.0	113.8	2.5
1993	114.3	0.4	115.2	0.8	116.7	1.3	118.0	1.1	118.7	0.6	117.6	-0.9	115.0	-2.2	114.3	-0.6	115.2	0.8	114.4	-0.7	113.5	-0.8	112.5	-0.9
1994	113.9	1.2	114.2	0.3	116.7	2.2	116.1	-0.5	114.0	-1.8	112.0	-1.8	110.1	-1.7	112.3	2.0	110.8	-1.3	109.3	-1.4	109.1	-0.2	108.1	-0.9
1995	111.0	2.7	112.8	1.6	112.8	0.0	110.4	-2.1	108.5	-1.7	109.2	0.6	111.9	2.5	112.8	0.8	112.1	-0.6	112.8	0.6	113.6	0.7	112.2	-1.2

Source: U.S. Department of Labor, Bureau of Labor Statistics, Division of Industry Prices and Price Indexes. n.e.c. stands for not elsewhere classified. - indicates no data collected for period or unavailable.

Dairy Products
Producer Price Index
Base 1982 = 100

For 1926-1995. Columns headed % show percentile change in the index from the previous period for which an index is available.

Year	Jan Index	%	Feb Index	%	Mar Index	%	Apr Index	%	May Index	%	Jun Index	%	Jul Index	%	Aug Index	%	Sep Index	%	Oct Index	%	Nov Index	%	Dec Index	%
1926	17.9	-	17.7	-1.1	17.4	-1.7	17.0	-2.3	16.8	-1.2	16.6	-1.2	16.7	0.6	17.0	1.8	17.6	3.5	18.0	2.3	18.2	1.1	18.7	2.7
1927	18.4	-1.6	18.6	1.1	18.5	-0.5	18.3	-1.1	17.2	-6.0	17.0	-1.2	17.1	0.6	17.2	0.6	18.4	7.0	18.7	1.6	18.8	0.5	19.2	2.1
1928	18.8	-2.1	18.5	-1.6	18.2	-1.6	17.6	-3.3	17.4	-1.1	17.4	0.0	18.0	3.4	18.7	3.9	19.0	1.6	18.8	-1.1	19.0	1.1	19.2	1.1
1929	19.0	-1.0	19.1	0.5	19.0	-0.5	18.5	-2.6	18.2	-1.6	18.4	1.1	18.0	-2.2	18.2	1.1	18.5	1.6	18.5	0.0	18.1	-2.2	17.7	-2.2
1930	17.0	-4.0	17.0	0.0	17.2	1.2	17.3	0.6	16.1	-6.9	15.7	-2.5	16.0	1.9	17.0	6.3	17.4	2.4	17.2	-1.1	16.7	-2.9	15.5	-7.2
1931	14.6	-5.8	14.5	-0.7	14.6	0.7	14.1	-3.4	13.7	-2.8	13.7	0.0	14.1	2.9	14.3	1.4	14.7	2.8	15.0	2.0	14.1	-6.0	13.9	-1.4
1932	11.9	-14.4	11.2	-5.9	11.2	0.0	10.7	-4.5	10.4	-2.8	10.0	-3.8	10.2	2.0	10.5	2.9	10.6	1.0	10.6	0.0	10.8	1.9	10.4	-3.7
1933	9.6	-7.7	9.1	-5.2	8.9	-2.2	9.3	4.5	10.2	9.7	11.0	7.8	11.5	4.5	11.5	0.0	11.5	0.0	11.5	0.0	11.7	1.7	11.4	-2.6
1934	11.4	0.0	12.1	6.1	12.0	-0.8	11.6	-3.3	11.7	0.9	12.7	8.5	13.1	3.1	13.5	3.1	13.3	-1.5	13.5	1.5	13.7	1.5	13.9	1.5
1935	14.6	5.0	15.2	4.1	14.4	-5.3	14.8	2.8	13.6	-8.1	13.0	-4.4	12.9	-0.8	13.2	2.3	13.3	0.8	13.4	0.8	14.2	6.0	14.6	2.8
1936	14.7	0.7	14.9	1.4	14.0	-6.0	13.7	-2.1	13.1	-4.4	13.5	3.1	14.6	8.1	15.3	4.8	15.6	2.0	15.2	-2.6	15.4	1.3	15.5	0.6
1937	15.5	0.0	15.5	0.0	15.7	1.3	13.7	-12.7	12.7	-7.3	12.6	-0.8	13.3	5.6	13.9	4.5	14.8	6.5	14.9	0.7	15.5	4.0	15.7	1.3
1938	14.5	-7.6	13.7	-5.5	13.4	-2.2	12.5	-6.7	12.1	-3.2	12.0	-0.8	12.1	0.8	12.0	-0.8	12.4	3.3	12.5	0.8	12.7	1.6	12.9	1.6
1939	12.5	-3.1	12.5	0.0	11.3	-9.6	10.1	-10.6	10.2	1.0	10.5	2.9	10.4	-1.0	11.9	14.4	13.0	9.2	13.7	5.4	14.0	2.2	14.2	1.4
1940	14.3	0.7	13.9	-2.8	13.7	-1.4	13.5	-1.5	12.7	-5.9	12.6	-0.8	12.9	2.4	12.9	0.0	13.1	1.6	13.5	3.1	14.4	6.7	14.7	2.1
1941	14.0	-4.8	13.9	-0.7	14.0	0.7	14.1	0.7	14.2	0.7	14.7	3.5	15.3	4.1	15.7	2.6	16.2	3.2	16.6	2.5	16.8	1.2	16.7	-0.6
1942	16.8	0.6	16.6	-1.2	16.5	-0.6	16.4	-0.6	16.3	-0.6	16.1	-1.2	16.8	4.3	17.5	4.2	18.4	5.1	19.0	3.3	19.4	2.1	19.5	0.5
1943	19.8	1.5	19.8	0.0	19.8	0.0	19.8	0.0	19.7	-0.5	19.1	-3.0	19.0	-0.5	19.0	0.0	19.0	0.0	19.0	0.0	19.4	2.1	19.3	-0.5
1944	19.3	0.0	19.3	0.0	19.3	0.0	19.2	-0.5	19.2	0.0	19.2	0.0	19.2	0.0	19.3	0.5	19.3	0.0	19.3	0.0	19.3	0.0	19.3	0.0
1945	19.3	0.0	19.3	0.0	19.3	0.0	19.3	0.0	19.3	0.0	19.3	0.0	19.3	0.0	19.3	0.0	19.2	-0.5	19.3	0.5	19.7	2.1	19.8	0.5
1946	20.0	1.0	20.2	1.0	20.3	0.5	20.3	0.0	20.4	0.5	22.2	8.8	27.4	23.4	28.2	2.9	29.5	4.6	32.3	9.5	31.9	-1.2	31.4	-1.6
1947	28.7	-8.6	28.0	-2.4	27.4	-2.1	26.7	-2.6	26.1	-2.2	26.0	-0.4	26.9	3.5	27.8	3.3	28.5	2.5	29.3	2.8	30.3	3.4	30.9	2.0
1948	31.5	1.9	31.5	0.0	30.6	-2.9	30.9	1.0	30.8	-0.3	31.3	1.6	32.2	2.9	32.5	0.9	31.8	-2.2	31.3	-1.6	30.9	-1.3	30.5	-1.3
1949	29.8	-2.3	29.2	-2.0	28.3	-3.1	27.7	-2.1	27.3	-1.4	27.6	1.1	27.7	0.4	28.4	2.5	28.2	-0.7	28.2	0.0	28.0	-0.7	28.1	0.4
1950	27.4	-2.5	27.5	0.4	27.2	-1.1	26.9	-1.1	26.2	-2.6	26.3	0.4	27.0	2.7	27.7	2.6	28.5	2.9	28.9	1.4	29.0	0.3	29.5	1.7
1951	30.9	4.7	31.5	1.9	31.2	-1.0	30.9	-1.0	31.1	0.6	31.1	0.0	31.1	0.0	31.5	1.3	31.0	-1.6	31.7	2.3	32.4	2.2	33.0	1.9
1952	33.1	0.3	33.6	1.5	33.1	-1.5	32.7	-1.2	32.3	-1.2	32.1	-0.6	33.2	3.4	33.3	0.3	34.0	2.1	33.8	-0.6	33.7	-0.3	33.0	-2.1
1953	32.7	-0.9	32.4	-0.9	32.0	-1.2	31.7	-0.9	31.5	-0.6	31.5	0.0	32.1	1.9	32.3	0.6	32.5	0.6	32.9	1.2	33.3	1.2	32.5	-2.4
1954	31.9	-1.8	31.3	-1.9	31.0	-1.0	30.1	-2.9	29.7	-1.3	29.9	0.7	30.7	2.7	30.9	0.7	31.1	0.6	31.7	1.9	31.8	0.3	31.6	-0.6
1955	31.3	-0.9	31.3	0.0	31.3	0.0	31.2	-0.3	30.4	-2.6	30.5	0.3	30.9	1.3	31.5	1.9	30.5	-3.2	30.7	0.7	30.9	0.7	31.3	1.3
1956	31.0	-1.0	31.0	0.0	31.0	0.0	30.9	-0.3	31.5	1.9	31.5	0.0	31.5	0.0	31.8	1.0	32.0	0.6	32.4	1.3	33.1	2.2	32.9	-0.6
1957	32.8	-0.3	32.8	0.0	32.5	-0.9	32.5	0.0	32.3	-0.6	31.5	-2.5	31.6	0.3	32.2	1.9	32.8	1.9	33.2	1.2	33.4	0.6	33.5	0.3
1958	33.3	-0.6	33.3	0.0	33.1	-0.6	32.5	-1.8	32.3	-0.6	32.4	0.3	32.5	0.3	32.7	0.6	33.2	1.5	33.1	-0.3	33.1	0.0	33.1	0.0
1959	33.0	-0.3	33.0	0.0	33.0	0.0	32.7	-0.9	32.6	-0.3	32.7	0.3	33.3	1.8	33.5	0.6	33.9	1.2	34.1	0.6	34.4	0.9	34.5	0.3
1960	34.7	0.6	34.6	-0.3	34.4	-0.6	33.7	-2.0	33.5	-0.6	33.8	0.9	34.2	1.2	34.4	0.6	35.2	2.3	35.4	0.6	35.5	0.3	35.6	0.3
1961	35.4	-0.6	35.0	-1.1	35.2	0.6	35.0	-0.6	34.9	-0.3	35.0	0.3	35.1	0.3	35.3	0.6	35.6	0.8	36.1	1.4	36.1	0.0	36.3	0.6
1962	36.0	-0.8	36.0	0.0	35.6	-1.1	35.0	-1.7	34.4	-1.7	34.6	0.6	34.8	0.6	35.0	0.6	35.0	0.0	35.5	1.4	35.6	0.3	35.6	0.0
1963	35.5	-0.3	35.6	0.3	35.3	-0.8	35.2	-0.3	35.2	0.0	35.1	-0.3	35.4	0.9	35.6	0.6	35.6	0.0	35.4	-0.6	35.6	0.6	35.6	0.0
1964	35.6	0.0	35.4	-0.6	35.4	0.0	35.3	-0.3	35.1	-0.6	35.3	0.6	35.3	0.0	35.4	0.3	35.8	1.1	35.9	0.3	36.1	0.6	35.9	-0.6
1965	35.7	-0.6	35.5	-0.6	35.4	-0.3	35.4	0.0	35.2	-0.6	35.3	0.3	35.5	0.6	35.8	0.8	36.0	0.6	36.0	0.0	36.4	1.1	36.7	0.8
1966	36.6	-0.3	37.2	1.6	37.9	1.9	37.8	-0.3	37.9	0.3	38.4	1.3	39.5	2.9	40.9	3.5	40.9	0.0	41.0	0.2	40.4	-1.5	40.3	-0.2
1967	40.1	-0.5	39.9	-0.5	39.7	-0.5	39.6	-0.3	39.8	0.5	40.2	1.0	40.2	0.0	40.3	0.2	40.5	0.5	40.5	0.0	40.5	0.0	40.9	1.0
1968	40.8	-0.2	40.9	0.2	40.6	-0.7	41.5	2.2	42.5	2.4	42.4	-0.2	42.5	0.2	42.5	0.0	42.5	0.0	42.9	0.9	42.8	-0.2	43.0	0.5
1969	42.9	-0.2	42.9	0.0	43.0	0.2	43.3	0.7	43.6	0.7	43.8	0.5	43.8	0.0	43.8	0.0	44.1	0.7	43.1	-2.3	43.3	0.5	44.2	2.1
1970	44.2	0.0	44.3	0.2	43.9	-0.9	44.5	1.4	44.7	0.4	44.7	0.0	44.8	0.2	44.8	0.0	44.8	0.0	45.1	0.7	45.1	0.0	45.4	0.7

[Continued]

Dairy Products
Producer Price Index
Base 1982 = 100
[Continued]

For 1926-1995. Columns headed % show percentile change in the index from the previous period for which an index is available.

Year	Jan Index	%	Feb Index	%	Mar Index	%	Apr Index	%	May Index	%	Jun Index	%	Jul Index	%	Aug Index	%	Sep Index	%	Oct Index	%	Nov Index	%	Dec Index	%
1971	45.4	0.0	45.2	-0.4	46.2	2.2	46.4	0.4	46.7	0.6	46.7	0.0	46.7	0.0	46.8	0.2	46.8	0.0	46.8	0.0	46.7	-0.2	47.2	1.1
1972	47.1	-0.2	47.2	0.2	47.4	0.4	47.2	-0.4	47.2	0.0	46.3	-1.9	47.3	2.2	47.7	0.8	47.8	0.2	48.2	0.8	48.9	1.5	49.4	1.0
1973	49.7	0.6	49.8	0.2	51.0	2.4	51.1	0.2	50.8	-0.6	51.2	0.8	51.1	-0.2	52.8	3.3	55.1	4.4	56.1	1.8	56.2	0.2	57.2	1.8
1974	58.3	1.9	59.3	1.7	60.8	2.5	61.9	1.8	59.0	-4.7	57.4	-2.7	56.9	-0.9	57.2	0.5	58.2	1.7	58.8	1.0	59.0	0.3	59.0	0.0
1975	59.6	1.0	59.6	0.0	59.7	0.2	59.8	0.2	60.1	0.5	60.5	0.7	61.5	1.7	62.8	2.1	64.6	2.9	66.6	3.1	67.5	1.4	68.8	1.9
1976	68.2	-0.9	65.7	-3.7	67.0	2.0	67.4	0.6	67.2	-0.3	67.2	0.0	68.4	1.8	69.9	2.2	68.5	-2.0	68.2	-0.4	67.6	-0.9	67.2	-0.6
1977	67.0	-0.3	67.0	0.0	67.5	0.7	69.7	3.3	70.0	0.4	70.0	0.0	70.4	0.6	70.5	0.1	70.6	0.1	70.7	0.1	71.1	0.6	71.6	0.7
1978	71.5	-0.1	71.8	0.4	72.4	0.8	74.1	2.3	74.1	0.0	74.5	0.5	74.8	0.4	76.7	2.5	77.5	1.0	79.2	2.2	80.2	1.3	81.5	1.6
1979	81.8	0.4	81.6	-0.2	82.3	0.9	83.2	1.1	83.5	0.4	83.7	0.2	84.0	0.4	86.5	3.0	87.7	1.4	87.6	-0.1	88.1	0.6	88.3	0.2
1980	88.8	0.6	88.7	-0.1	89.6	1.0	91.4	2.0	91.8	0.4	92.2	0.4	92.4	0.2	93.5	1.2	93.9	0.4	95.6	1.8	96.5	0.9	97.4	0.9
1981	98.3	0.9	98.5	0.2	98.5	0.0	98.6	0.1	98.3	-0.3	98.5	0.2	98.5	0.0	98.5	0.0	98.6	0.1	99.2	0.6	99.2	0.0	99.3	0.1
1982	99.5	0.2	99.6	0.1	99.6	0.0	99.8	0.2	99.8	0.0	99.9	0.1	99.9	0.0	100.0	0.1	100.1	0.1	100.4	0.3	100.5	0.1	100.8	0.3
1983	100.7	-0.1	100.8	0.1	100.7	-0.1	100.8	0.1	100.8	0.0	100.6	-0.2	100.6	0.0	100.6	0.0	100.7	0.1	101.0	0.3	101.0	0.0	100.0	-1.0
1984	99.8	-0.2	99.8	0.0	100.0	0.2	100.0	0.0	100.0	0.0	100.3	0.3	101.0	0.7	100.9	-0.1	102.5	1.6	103.0	0.5	103.4	0.4	102.8	-0.6
1985	102.6	-0.2	102.1	-0.5	101.8	-0.3	101.0	-0.8	100.4	-0.6	100.2	-0.2	99.7	-0.5	99.2	-0.5	98.9	-0.3	98.8	-0.1	98.9	0.1	98.9	0.0
1986	98.8	-0.1	98.9	0.1	98.8	-0.1	98.8	0.0	99.2	0.4	99.2	0.0	99.5	0.3	100.3	0.8	100.6	0.3	101.2	0.6	101.8	0.6	102.1	0.3
1987	101.9	-0.2	101.4	-0.5	101.4	0.0	101.2	-0.2	100.9	-0.3	101.1	0.2	101.4	0.3	101.9	0.5	102.7	0.8	102.1	-0.6	102.0	-0.1	101.7	-0.3
1988	101.0	-0.7	100.5	-0.5	100.1	-0.4	100.0	-0.1	100.1	0.1	100.6	0.5	101.2	0.6	102.2	1.0	103.8	1.6	104.9	1.1	105.5	0.6	106.2	0.7
1989	107.1	0.8	106.5	-0.6	106.0	-0.5	105.6	-0.4	105.6	0.0	106.4	0.8	107.9	1.4	110.7	2.6	113.3	2.3	116.4	2.7	120.1	3.2	121.4	1.1
1990	120.5	-0.7	116.9	-3.0	116.1	-0.7	115.1	-0.9	116.6	1.3	118.0	1.2	119.5	1.3	120.2	0.6	119.0	-1.0	117.4	-1.3	114.8	-2.2	112.8	-1.7
1991	112.3	-0.4	112.0	-0.3	111.9	-0.1	111.5	-0.4	111.5	0.0	112.1	0.5	113.6	1.3	115.1	1.3	115.9	0.7	119.3	2.9	119.8	0.4	120.0	0.2
1992	118.3	-1.4	116.0	-1.9	115.0	-0.9	115.4	0.3	116.9	1.3	118.7	1.5	119.4	0.6	120.0	0.5	120.0	0.0	119.4	-0.5	118.7	-0.6	117.4	-1.1
1993	116.4	-0.9	115.4	-0.9	115.0	-0.3	117.2	1.9	118.5	1.1	119.5	0.8	119.2	-0.3	117.9	-1.1	118.4	0.4	119.0	0.5	120.3	1.1	121.0	0.6
1994	120.3	-0.6	119.9	-0.3	120.6	0.6	121.4	0.7	121.2	-0.2	118.7	-2.1	117.1	-1.3	118.2	0.9	118.8	0.5	119.2	0.3	119.4	0.2	118.6	-0.7
1995	117.1	-1.3	117.6	0.4	118.3	0.6	118.1	-0.2	117.7	-0.3	117.2	-0.4	118.0	0.7	119.0	0.8	120.5	1.3	122.6	1.7	125.1	2.0	125.0	-0.1

Source: U.S. Department of Labor, Bureau of Labor Statistics, Division of Industry Prices and Price Indexes. n.e.c. stands for not elsewhere classified. - indicates no data collected for period or unavailable.

Processed Fruits and Vegetables
Producer Price Index
Base 1982 = 100

For 1926-1995. Columns headed % show percentile change in the index from the previous period for which an index is available.

Year	Jan Index	%	Feb Index	%	Mar Index	%	Apr Index	%	May Index	%	Jun Index	%	Jul Index	%	Aug Index	%	Sep Index	%	Oct Index	%	Nov Index	%	Dec Index	%
1926	20.6	-	20.5	-0.5	20.3	-1.0	20.3	0.0	20.1	-1.0	20.2	0.5	20.3	0.5	20.1	-1.0	20.3	1.0	20.5	1.0	20.4	-0.5	20.2	-1.0
1927	20.1	-0.5	20.4	1.5	20.4	0.0	20.0	-2.0	20.0	0.0	20.0	0.0	20.0	0.0	20.0	0.0	19.7	-1.5	19.6	-0.5	20.3	3.6	20.5	1.0
1928	21.4	4.4	21.5	0.5	21.7	0.9	21.8	0.5	21.8	0.0	21.8	0.0	21.6	-0.9	21.0	-2.8	21.1	0.5	21.3	0.9	21.4	0.5	21.5	0.5
1929	21.4	-0.5	21.7	1.4	21.8	0.5	22.1	1.4	22.7	2.7	23.0	1.3	23.5	2.2	22.7	-3.4	22.5	-0.9	22.4	-0.4	22.3	-0.4	22.5	0.9
1930	22.7	0.9	22.6	-0.4	22.5	-0.4	22.2	-1.3	20.7	-6.8	20.5	-1.0	20.4	-0.5	20.4	0.0	20.6	1.0	20.3	-1.5	19.6	-3.4	19.2	-2.0
1931	19.0	-1.0	19.1	0.5	18.6	-2.6	18.3	-1.6	17.7	-3.3	17.5	-1.1	17.5	0.0	17.3	-1.1	17.1	-1.2	16.8	-1.8	16.3	-3.0	16.3	0.0
1932	16.2	-0.6	16.1	-0.6	16.4	1.9	16.4	0.0	16.3	-0.6	16.1	-1.2	15.5	-3.7	15.4	-0.6	15.0	-2.6	15.2	1.3	15.1	-0.7	15.0	-0.7
1933	14.9	-0.7	14.8	-0.7	14.8	0.0	14.9	0.7	15.4	3.4	15.6	1.3	15.9	1.9	16.4	3.1	17.1	4.3	17.2	0.6	17.1	-0.6	17.1	0.0
1934	17.2	0.6	17.5	1.7	17.6	0.6	17.7	0.6	17.6	-0.6	17.6	0.0	17.8	1.1	17.5	-1.7	18.0	2.9	18.7	3.9	18.5	-1.1	18.5	0.0
1935	18.5	0.0	18.7	1.1	18.7	0.0	18.5	-1.1	18.3	-1.1	18.2	-0.5	17.9	-1.6	17.1	-4.5	17.1	0.0	16.9	-1.2	16.8	-0.6	16.8	0.0
1936	16.6	-1.2	16.6	0.0	16.9	1.8	17.1	1.2	17.1	0.0	16.9	-1.2	17.1	1.2	18.1	5.8	18.3	1.1	18.2	-0.5	18.3	0.5	18.4	0.5
1937	18.5	0.5	18.5	0.0	18.5	0.0	18.5	0.0	18.5	0.0	18.7	1.1	18.3	-2.1	17.9	-2.2	17.8	-0.6	17.7	-0.6	17.9	1.1	17.8	-0.6
1938	17.7	-0.6	17.6	-0.6	17.5	-0.6	17.2	-1.7	16.9	-1.7	16.3	-3.6	15.9	-2.5	15.3	-3.8	15.2	-0.7	15.2	0.0	15.1	-0.7	15.1	0.0
1939	15.2	0.7	15.2	0.0	15.3	0.7	15.5	1.3	15.5	0.0	15.6	0.6	15.6	0.0	15.5	-0.6	16.1	3.9	16.4	1.9	16.3	-0.6	16.2	-0.6
1940	16.1	-0.6	16.1	0.0	15.9	-1.2	15.9	0.0	15.9	0.0	16.0	0.6	16.0	0.0	15.8	-1.2	15.7	-0.6	15.7	0.0	15.7	0.0	15.7	0.0
1941	15.9	1.3	16.3	2.5	16.4	0.6	16.8	2.4	17.1	1.8	17.6	2.9	18.9	7.4	19.9	5.3	19.8	-0.5	20.4	3.0	20.7	1.5	21.0	1.4
1942	21.1	0.5	21.2	0.5	21.4	0.9	21.5	0.5	21.5	0.0	22.0	2.3	21.8	-0.9	21.8	0.0	22.0	0.9	22.5	2.3	22.5	0.0	22.5	0.0
1943	22.5	0.0	22.5	0.0	22.5	0.0	22.5	0.0	22.5	0.0	22.5	0.0	22.5	0.0	22.4	-0.4	22.4	0.0	22.5	0.4	22.5	0.0	22.5	0.0
1944	22.6	0.4	22.6	0.0	22.6	0.0	22.6	0.0	22.6	0.0	22.6	0.0	22.6	0.0	22.8	0.9	23.1	1.3	23.0	-0.4	23.0	0.0	23.1	0.4
1945	23.0	-0.4	23.0	0.0	23.0	0.0	23.0	0.0	23.1	0.4	23.1	0.0	23.1	0.0	23.1	0.0	23.1	0.0	23.0	-0.4	23.1	0.4	23.0	-0.4
1946	23.0	0.0	23.0	0.0	23.0	0.0	23.2	0.9	23.4	0.9	23.7	1.3	23.7	0.0	23.4	-1.3	23.5	0.4	23.7	0.9	29.4	24.1	29.4	0.0
1947	31.9	8.5	31.8	-0.3	31.8	0.0	31.8	0.0	32.2	1.3	31.9	-0.9	31.7	-0.6	31.3	-1.3	31.6	1.0	31.6	0.0	31.6	0.0	31.5	-0.3
1948	31.6	0.3	31.6	0.0	31.4	-0.6	31.2	-0.6	31.2	0.0	31.3	0.3	31.5	0.6	32.1	1.9	32.2	0.3	31.8	-1.2	32.0	0.6	31.8	-0.6
1949	31.7	-0.3	31.8	0.3	31.8	0.0	31.8	0.0	32.0	0.6	31.7	-0.9	31.4	-0.9	31.3	-0.3	31.3	0.0	31.3	0.0	31.1	-0.6	30.0	-3.5
1950	30.6	2.0	31.0	1.3	31.0	0.0	30.8	-0.6	30.9	0.3	31.0	0.0	31.2	0.6	32.1	2.9	32.4	0.9	32.6	0.6	32.1	-1.5	32.6	1.6
1951	33.4	2.5	33.7	0.9	33.7	0.0	33.7	0.0	33.4	-0.9	33.0	-1.2	32.7	-0.9	32.6	-0.3	33.1	1.5	33.4	0.9	33.6	0.6	33.6	0.0
1952	33.4	-0.6	33.1	-0.9	33.2	0.3	33.1	-0.3	32.9	-0.6	32.7	-0.6	32.8	0.3	33.2	1.2	33.5	0.9	33.5	0.0	33.5	0.0	33.2	-0.9
1953	33.3	0.3	33.3	0.0	33.2	-0.3	33.0	-0.6	32.9	-0.3	32.8	-0.3	33.2	1.2	33.1	-0.3	33.1	0.0	33.2	0.3	33.1	-0.3	32.8	-0.9
1954	32.8	0.0	32.6	-0.6	32.6	0.0	32.6	0.0	33.0	1.2	33.1	0.3	33.1	0.0	33.1	0.0	33.2	0.3	33.3	0.3	33.3	0.0	33.5	0.6
1955	33.1	-1.2	33.0	-0.3	33.1	0.3	33.1	0.0	32.9	-0.6	33.0	0.3	33.1	0.3	33.2	0.3	33.7	1.5	34.0	0.9	34.0	0.0	34.1	0.3
1956	34.1	0.0	34.4	0.9	34.3	-0.3	34.4	0.3	34.5	0.3	34.7	0.6	34.5	-0.6	33.9	-1.7	33.7	-0.6	33.6	-0.3	33.6	0.0	33.4	-0.6
1957	33.4	0.0	33.5	0.3	33.5	0.0	33.2	-0.9	32.7	-1.5	32.2	-1.5	32.3	0.3	32.2	-0.3	32.4	0.6	32.7	0.9	32.8	0.3	33.1	0.9
1958	33.4	0.9	33.4	0.0	33.7	0.9	34.0	0.9	34.2	0.6	34.9	2.0	35.2	0.9	35.3	0.3	35.2	-0.3	35.4	0.6	35.7	0.8	35.7	0.0
1959	35.0	-2.0	34.9	-0.3	35.2	0.9	34.9	-0.9	34.9	0.0	35.1	0.6	34.9	-0.6	34.1	-2.3	33.8	-0.9	34.0	0.6	33.6	-1.2	33.1	-1.5
1960	33.0	-0.3	33.2	0.6	33.4	0.6	33.4	0.0	33.6	0.6	33.8	0.6	33.9	0.3	33.7	-0.6	34.0	0.9	34.4	1.2	34.6	0.6	34.8	0.6
1961	35.3	1.4	35.4	0.3	35.2	-0.6	35.1	-0.3	34.4	-2.0	34.4	0.0	34.5	0.3	34.0	-1.4	33.9	-0.3	34.1	0.6	34.1	0.0	34.1	0.0
1962	33.7	-1.2	33.9	0.6	33.7	-0.6	33.7	0.0	33.5	-0.6	33.7	0.6	33.6	-0.3	33.0	-1.8	32.8	-0.6	32.8	0.0	32.7	-0.3	32.5	-0.6
1963	34.0	4.6	33.9	-0.3	34.4	1.5	35.0	1.7	35.2	0.6	35.6	1.1	35.9	0.8	35.6	-0.8	35.8	0.6	36.0	0.6	36.2	0.6	36.3	0.3
1964	36.4	0.3	36.5	0.3	36.5	0.0	36.5	0.0	36.1	-1.1	36.1	0.0	35.7	-1.1	34.7	-2.8	34.7	0.0	34.9	0.6	34.8	-0.3	34.7	-0.3
1965	34.7	0.0	34.1	-1.7	34.2	0.3	34.3	0.3	34.1	-0.6	34.5	1.2	34.6	0.3	34.1	-1.4	34.6	1.5	35.6	2.9	35.8	0.6	35.7	-0.3
1966	35.6	-0.3	35.7	0.3	35.6	-0.3	35.6	0.0	35.8	0.6	35.7	-0.3	35.5	-0.6	34.8	-2.0	35.2	1.1	35.9	2.0	36.0	0.3	36.0	0.0
1967	36.0	0.0	35.4	-1.7	35.4	0.0	35.5	0.3	35.7	0.6	36.2	1.4	36.3	0.3	36.4	0.3	36.7	0.8	37.2	1.4	38.1	2.4	38.4	0.8
1968	38.6	0.5	38.7	0.3	38.9	0.5	39.0	0.3	39.1	0.3	39.1	0.0	39.1	0.0	38.6	-1.3	38.6	0.0	38.8	0.5	38.8	0.0	38.6	-0.5
1969	38.7	0.3	39.0	0.8	39.1	0.3	39.3	0.5	39.4	0.3	39.4	0.0	39.7	0.8	39.7	0.0	39.7	0.0	39.5	-0.5	39.6	0.3	39.6	0.0
1970	39.8	0.5	39.9	0.3	39.7	-0.5	39.9	0.5	40.2	0.8	40.3	0.2	40.5	0.5	40.7	0.5	40.8	0.2	40.5	-0.7	40.7	0.5	40.5	-0.5

[Continued]

Processed Fruits and Vegetables

Producer Price Index
Base 1982 = 100

[Continued]

For 1926-1995. Columns headed % show percentile change in the index from the previous period for which an index is available.

Year	Jan Index	%	Feb Index	%	Mar Index	%	Apr Index	%	May Index	%	Jun Index	%	Jul Index	%	Aug Index	%	Sep Index	%	Oct Index	%	Nov Index	%	Dec Index	%
1971	40.6	0.2	40.7	0.2	40.9	0.5	41.2	0.7	41.5	0.7	42.1	1.4	42.3	0.5	42.3	0.0	42.2	-0.2	42.0	-0.5	42.0	0.0	42.2	0.5
1972	42.3	0.2	42.3	0.0	42.5	0.5	43.1	1.4	43.4	0.7	43.5	0.2	43.6	0.2	43.8	0.5	43.7	-0.2	44.4	1.6	45.1	1.6	45.5	0.9
1973	45.7	0.4	45.9	0.4	46.0	0.2	46.1	0.2	46.4	0.7	46.6	0.4	46.5	-0.2	47.1	1.3	47.4	0.6	49.2	3.8	49.7	1.0	50.2	1.0
1974	50.7	1.0	51.3	1.2	51.5	0.4	52.0	1.0	52.9	1.7	54.0	2.1	57.5	6.5	59.3	3.1	60.3	1.7	61.9	2.7	62.3	0.6	62.0	-0.5
1975	62.4	0.6	62.3	-0.2	61.8	-0.8	62.2	0.6	62.3	0.2	62.3	0.0	61.7	-1.0	61.4	-0.5	61.4	0.0	61.7	0.5	61.6	-0.2	61.4	-0.3
1976	61.0	-0.7	60.6	-0.7	60.6	0.0	60.8	0.3	61.2	0.7	61.5	0.5	61.8	0.5	62.3	0.8	62.7	0.6	63.5	1.3	64.0	0.8	64.0	0.0
1977	63.8	-0.3	66.6	4.4	67.1	0.8	67.5	0.6	67.7	0.3	68.4	1.0	68.6	0.3	69.4	1.2	69.6	0.3	69.4	-0.3	70.4	1.4	70.8	0.6
1978	70.8	0.0	70.9	0.1	71.3	0.6	71.6	0.4	71.9	0.4	72.4	0.7	73.0	0.8	74.1	1.5	74.7	0.8	76.6	2.5	78.8	2.9	79.6	1.0
1979	79.6	0.0	80.0	0.5	80.0	0.0	80.3	0.4	80.7	0.5	80.7	0.0	81.5	1.0	81.8	0.4	82.0	0.2	81.4	-0.7	81.0	-0.5	81.1	0.1
1980	81.2	0.1	81.4	0.2	81.5	0.1	81.9	0.5	82.1	0.2	82.8	0.9	83.7	1.1	84.1	0.5	84.3	0.2	85.2	1.1	85.5	0.4	86.2	0.8
1981	86.9	0.8	88.8	2.2	93.0	4.7	94.0	1.1	94.5	0.5	95.6	1.2	96.9	1.4	97.4	0.5	98.4	1.0	99.0	0.6	98.6	-0.4	99.0	0.4
1982	99.5	0.5	100.7	1.2	100.5	-0.2	100.3	-0.2	99.8	-0.5	100.5	0.7	100.0	-0.5	99.9	-0.1	99.4	-0.5	99.6	0.2	99.4	-0.2	100.4	1.0
1983	100.1	-0.3	99.9	-0.2	100.2	0.3	99.7	-0.5	100.3	0.6	101.0	0.7	101.0	0.0	101.4	0.4	101.5	0.1	102.4	0.9	102.3	-0.1	103.1	0.8
1984	104.8	1.6	106.7	1.8	107.6	0.8	107.5	-0.1	108.5	0.9	108.6	0.1	107.9	-0.6	107.8	-0.1	106.3	-1.4	107.8	1.4	106.5	-1.2	106.9	0.4
1985	108.1	1.1	108.1	0.0	109.3	1.1	108.8	-0.5	108.6	-0.2	109.7	1.0	109.2	-0.5	109.3	0.1	107.5	-1.6	106.9	-0.6	105.2	-1.6	105.0	-0.2
1986	104.5	-0.5	104.6	0.1	104.7	0.1	104.1	-0.6	104.3	0.2	105.4	1.1	104.5	-0.9	105.1	0.6	105.1	0.0	104.6	-0.5	105.6	1.0	106.6	0.9
1987	107.3	0.7	107.5	0.2	108.4	0.8	108.3	-0.1	108.4	0.1	109.5	1.0	108.7	-0.7	109.3	0.6	108.5	-0.7	108.4	-0.1	108.8	0.4	110.1	1.2
1988	110.9	0.7	111.4	0.5	111.8	0.4	111.5	-0.3	111.7	0.2	111.6	-0.1	113.4	1.6	115.2	1.6	115.5	0.3	116.5	0.9	117.9	1.2	118.5	0.5
1989	119.0	0.4	118.8	-0.2	119.2	0.3	119.0	-0.2	119.8	0.7	120.5	0.6	120.8	0.2	121.2	0.3	120.7	-0.4	120.0	-0.6	119.9	-0.1	120.4	0.4
1990	122.4	1.7	125.7	2.7	126.9	1.0	126.9	0.0	127.0	0.1	126.5	-0.4	126.1	-0.3	125.8	-0.2	124.9	-0.7	123.6	-1.0	120.9	-2.2	120.2	-0.6
1991	120.0	-0.2	120.2	0.2	119.8	-0.3	119.2	-0.5	119.3	0.1	119.0	-0.3	119.6	0.5	118.7	-0.8	118.6	-0.1	119.2	0.5	120.4	1.0	121.6	1.0
1992	122.1	0.4	122.4	0.2	122.3	-0.1	122.0	-0.2	122.0	0.0	121.0	-0.8	120.6	-0.3	120.5	-0.1	119.8	-0.6	119.1	-0.6	118.9	-0.2	118.4	-0.4
1993	117.5	-0.8	117.0	-0.4	116.4	-0.5	116.1	-0.3	116.7	0.5	117.6	0.8	119.0	1.2	118.7	-0.3	118.9	0.2	119.5	0.5	120.3	0.7	120.4	0.1
1994	120.8	0.3	121.6	0.7	121.4	-0.2	121.7	0.2	122.0	0.2	122.0	0.0	121.9	-0.1	121.6	-0.2	120.6	-0.8	120.6	0.0	120.0	-0.5	119.6	-0.3
1995	120.2	0.5	120.7	0.4	121.3	0.5	120.7	-0.5	122.3	1.3	122.1	-0.2	122.7	0.5	122.9	0.2	122.9	0.0	123.1	0.2	124.2	0.9	125.0	0.6

Source: U.S. Department of Labor, Bureau of Labor Statistics, Division of Industry Prices and Price Indexes. n.e.c. stands for not elsewhere classified. - indicates no data collected for period or unavailable.

Sugar and Confectionery
Producer Price Index
Base 1982 = 100

For 1926-1995. Columns headed % show percentile change in the index from the previous period for which an index is available.

Year	Jan Index	%	Feb Index	%	Mar Index	%	Apr Index	%	May Index	%	Jun Index	%	Jul Index	%	Aug Index	%	Sep Index	%	Oct Index	%	Nov Index	%	Dec Index	%
1926	18.2	-	18.5	1.6	17.7	-4.3	18.3	3.4	19.0	3.8	18.8	-1.1	19.1	1.6	19.3	1.0	19.8	2.6	20.2	2.0	20.6	2.0	22.0	6.8
1927	22.0	0.0	21.4	-2.7	20.9	-2.3	20.9	0.0	21.2	1.4	21.0	-0.9	20.5	-2.4	19.8	-3.4	20.8	5.1	20.4	-1.9	20.1	-1.5	19.9	-1.0
1928	20.0	0.5	19.3	-3.5	20.1	4.1	20.4	1.5	20.5	0.5	20.4	-0.5	19.7	-3.4	19.2	-2.5	19.5	1.6	18.2	-6.7	17.8	-2.2	18.2	2.2
1929	17.7	-2.7	17.2	-2.8	17.0	-1.2	16.9	-0.6	16.9	0.0	16.8	-0.6	17.8	6.0	18.3	2.8	18.4	0.5	18.7	1.6	17.5	-6.4	17.5	0.0
1930	17.6	0.6	17.2	-2.3	16.8	-2.3	16.7	-0.6	16.0	-4.2	15.6	-2.5	15.8	1.3	15.2	-3.8	15.1	-0.7	15.5	2.6	16.1	3.9	15.7	-2.5
1931	15.8	0.6	15.5	-1.9	15.2	-1.9	15.3	0.7	14.9	-2.6	15.3	2.7	16.1	5.2	16.0	-0.6	15.6	-2.5	15.6	0.0	15.5	-0.6	14.6	-5.8
1932	14.3	-2.1	14.2	-0.7	13.5	-4.9	13.0	-3.7	12.5	-3.8	12.9	3.2	13.8	7.0	14.4	4.3	14.4	0.0	14.4	0.0	14.2	-1.4	13.8	-2.8
1933	13.1	-5.1	13.1	0.0	14.0	6.9	14.4	2.9	15.2	5.6	15.6	2.6	15.9	1.9	16.0	0.6	16.2	1.3	15.5	-4.3	15.1	-2.6	15.0	-0.7
1934	14.7	-2.0	15.3	4.1	14.9	-2.6	14.4	-3.4	13.8	-4.2	14.8	7.2	15.6	5.4	15.9	1.9	15.2	-4.4	15.1	-0.7	14.9	-1.3	14.6	-2.0
1935	14.2	-2.7	14.4	1.4	14.8	2.8	16.4	10.8	16.9	3.0	17.0	0.6	16.7	-1.8	16.7	0.0	17.0	1.8	17.5	2.9	17.2	-1.7	16.7	-2.9
1936	16.9	1.2	17.0	0.6	16.7	-1.8	17.1	2.4	17.1	0.0	17.1	0.0	16.7	-2.3	16.7	0.0	16.5	-1.2	16.0	-3.0	16.4	2.5	16.9	3.0
1937	17.4	3.0	16.9	-2.9	16.4	-3.0	16.4	0.0	16.3	-0.6	16.1	-1.2	16.3	1.2	16.3	0.0	16.8	3.1	16.0	-4.8	16.1	0.6	15.9	-1.2
1938	15.8	-0.6	15.5	-1.9	15.3	-1.3	14.8	-3.3	14.6	-1.4	14.3	-2.1	14.4	0.7	14.2	-1.4	15.0	5.6	15.3	2.0	15.0	-2.0	14.6	-2.7
1939	14.3	-2.1	14.2	-0.7	14.4	1.4	14.7	2.1	14.7	0.0	14.6	-0.7	14.5	-0.7	14.4	-0.7	18.5	28.5	17.2	-7.0	15.5	-9.9	15.2	-1.9
1940	14.6	-3.9	14.6	0.0	14.5	-0.7	14.6	0.7	14.5	-0.7	14.4	-0.7	14.3	-0.7	14.0	-2.1	14.1	0.7	14.2	0.7	14.4	1.4	14.5	0.7
1941	14.7	1.4	14.9	1.4	16.2	8.7	16.8	3.7	16.7	-0.6	16.8	0.6	16.9	0.6	17.8	5.3	17.7	-0.6	17.3	-2.3	17.3	0.0	17.4	0.6
1942	18.1	4.0	18.2	0.6	18.2	0.0	18.6	2.2	18.6	0.0	18.6	0.0	18.6	0.0	18.6	0.0	18.6	0.0	18.6	0.0	18.6	0.0	18.6	0.0
1943	18.6	0.0	18.6	0.0	18.6	0.0	18.6	0.0	18.6	0.0	18.6	0.0	18.6	0.0	18.6	0.0	18.6	0.0	18.6	0.0	18.6	0.0	18.6	0.0
1944	18.6	0.0	18.6	0.0	18.6	0.0	18.6	0.0	18.6	0.0	18.7	0.5	18.7	0.0	18.7	0.0	18.5	-1.1	18.5	0.0	18.5	0.0	18.5	0.0
1945	18.5	0.0	18.5	0.0	18.5	0.0	18.5	0.0	18.5	0.0	18.5	0.0	18.5	0.0	18.5	0.0	18.5	0.0	18.5	0.0	18.5	0.0	18.5	0.0
1946	18.5	0.0	19.5	5.4	20.2	3.6	20.2	0.0	20.2	0.0	20.2	0.0	20.7	2.5	20.8	0.5	23.5	13.0	26.1	11.1	26.6	1.9	27.2	2.3
1947	27.4	0.7	27.8	1.5	28.1	1.1	28.3	0.7	28.3	0.0	28.4	0.4	28.5	0.4	29.3	2.8	29.4	0.3	29.4	0.0	30.4	3.4	30.6	0.7
1948	30.3	-1.0	30.4	0.3	30.2	-0.7	30.1	-0.3	29.0	-3.7	28.7	-1.0	29.4	2.4	29.5	0.3	29.7	0.7	29.4	-1.0	29.6	0.7	29.2	-1.4
1949	29.4	0.7	28.7	-2.4	27.8	-3.1	27.3	-1.8	26.9	-1.5	26.9	0.0	26.7	-0.7	26.7	0.0	26.9	0.7	27.1	0.7	27.1	0.0	27.0	-0.4
1950	27.1	0.4	26.8	-1.1	26.5	-1.1	26.4	-0.4	26.7	1.1	26.9	0.7	27.7	3.0	28.6	3.2	29.7	3.8	29.6	-0.3	29.6	0.0	29.6	0.0
1951	29.6	0.0	29.6	0.0	29.6	0.0	29.5	-0.3	30.4	3.1	31.3	3.0	31.2	-0.3	30.7	-1.6	30.7	0.0	30.1	-2.0	30.2	0.3	30.1	-0.3
1952	30.1	0.0	30.2	0.3	30.5	1.0	31.2	2.3	31.1	-0.3	31.6	1.6	31.8	0.6	31.5	-0.9	31.5	0.0	31.6	0.3	31.3	-0.9	30.9	-1.3
1953	30.9	0.0	30.9	0.0	31.3	1.3	31.4	0.3	31.3	-0.3	31.4	0.3	31.4	0.0	31.5	0.3	31.4	-0.3	31.5	0.3	31.0	-1.6	31.1	0.3
1954	31.5	1.3	31.5	0.0	32.3	2.5	32.2	-0.3	32.4	0.6	32.4	0.0	32.6	0.6	32.7	0.3	32.3	-1.2	32.1	-0.6	32.1	0.0	31.9	-0.6
1955	31.9	0.0	32.2	0.9	31.7	-1.6	31.7	0.0	31.6	-0.3	31.6	0.0	31.7	0.3	31.5	-0.6	31.4	-0.3	31.5	0.3	31.4	-0.3	31.3	-0.3
1956	31.3	0.0	31.3	0.0	31.4	0.3	30.1	-4.1	31.4	4.3	31.3	-0.3	31.5	0.6	31.4	-0.3	31.5	0.3	31.7	0.6	32.0	0.9	32.1	0.3
1957	32.4	0.9	32.1	-0.9	32.1	0.0	32.1	0.0	32.3	0.6	32.5	0.6	32.7	0.6	32.6	-0.3	32.6	0.0	32.6	0.0	32.7	0.3	32.7	0.0
1958	32.8	0.3	32.7	-0.3	32.4	-0.9	32.7	0.9	33.0	0.9	33.3	0.9	33.3	0.0	33.2	-0.3	33.3	0.3	33.4	0.3	33.3	-0.3	33.5	0.6
1959	33.0	-1.5	32.6	-1.2	32.3	-0.9	32.1	-0.6	32.7	1.9	33.1	1.2	33.0	-0.3	33.0	0.0	33.3	0.9	33.6	0.9	33.4	-0.6	33.1	-0.9
1960	32.4	-2.1	32.6	0.6	32.9	0.9	33.0	0.3	33.1	0.3	33.1	0.0	33.9	2.4	33.9	0.0	34.1	0.6	33.9	-0.6	34.0	0.3	33.7	-0.9
1961	33.7	0.0	33.6	-0.3	33.4	-0.6	33.3	-0.3	33.6	0.9	33.7	0.3	33.3	-1.2	32.8	-1.5	32.7	-0.3	32.7	0.0	32.8	0.3	33.2	1.2
1962	33.2	0.0	33.4	0.6	33.4	0.0	33.6	0.6	33.5	-0.3	33.6	0.3	33.5	-0.3	33.7	0.6	33.5	-0.6	33.8	0.9	33.6	-0.6	33.7	0.3
1963	34.5	2.4	34.5	0.0	34.8	0.9	37.4	7.5	43.8	17.1	43.4	-0.9	39.5	-9.0	36.5	-7.6	36.9	1.1	41.2	11.7	43.1	4.6	41.0	-4.9
1964	42.8	4.4	40.3	-5.8	38.5	-4.5	37.9	-1.6	36.7	-3.2	35.5	-3.3	35.0	-1.4	34.9	-0.3	34.5	-1.1	34.7	0.6	34.4	-0.9	35.2	2.3
1965	36.1	2.6	36.1	0.0	35.5	-1.7	35.5	0.0	35.7	0.6	35.8	0.3	35.8	0.0	35.7	-0.3	35.7	0.0	35.9	0.6	35.8	-0.3	35.7	-0.3
1966	35.9	0.6	36.1	0.6	36.0	-0.3	35.9	-0.3	35.9	0.0	35.9	0.0	36.0	0.3	36.4	1.1	36.6	0.5	36.6	0.0	36.8	0.5	36.9	0.3
1967	37.1	0.5	37.0	-0.3	36.9	-0.3	36.7	-0.5	36.7	0.0	37.0	0.8	37.3	0.8	37.4	0.3	37.1	-0.8	37.2	0.3	37.4	0.5	37.0	-1.1
1968	37.2	0.5	37.3	0.3	37.3	0.0	37.4	0.3	37.8	1.1	38.5	1.9	38.6	0.3	38.5	-0.3	38.6	0.3	38.8	0.5	38.7	-0.3	38.9	0.5
1969	39.1	0.5	39.1	0.0	39.2	0.3	39.4	0.5	40.2	2.0	41.5	3.2	41.3	-0.5	41.7	1.0	41.8	0.2	41.9	0.2	42.0	0.2	41.7	-0.7
1970	42.3	1.4	41.9	-0.9	41.8	-0.2	42.2	1.0	42.5	0.7	42.8	0.7	43.5	1.6	43.5	0.0	43.8	0.7	44.0	0.5	43.8	-0.5	43.5	-0.7

[Continued]

Sugar and Confectionery
Producer Price Index
Base 1982 = 100
[Continued]

For 1926-1995. Columns headed % show percentile change in the index from the previous period for which an index is available.

Year	Jan Index	%	Feb Index	%	Mar Index	%	Apr Index	%	May Index	%	Jun Index	%	Jul Index	%	Aug Index	%	Sep Index	%	Oct Index	%	Nov Index	%	Dec Index	%
1971	43.7	0.5	44.2	1.1	44.5	0.7	44.2	-0.7	44.5	0.7	44.4	-0.2	44.5	0.2	44.5	0.0	44.5	0.0	43.7	-1.8	44.2	1.1	44.6	0.9
1972	44.5	-0.2	44.9	0.9	45.2	0.7	44.9	-0.7	44.8	-0.2	45.0	0.4	45.3	0.7	45.0	-0.7	45.1	0.2	45.8	1.6	45.1	-1.5	45.3	0.4
1973	45.0	-0.7	46.1	2.4	46.6	1.1	47.0	0.9	47.8	1.7	48.6	1.7	48.6	0.0	50.3	3.5	50.8	1.0	51.8	2.0	53.3	2.9	52.7	-1.1
1974	56.3	6.8	62.0	10.1	70.5	13.7	70.4	-0.1	80.0	13.6	89.3	11.6	91.5	2.5	100.3	9.6	110.5	10.2	116.9	5.8	155.7	33.2	148.8	-4.4
1975	132.8	-10.8	128.8	-3.0	112.4	-12.7	103.9	-7.6	88.8	-14.5	80.8	-9.0	84.7	4.8	90.2	6.5	81.4	-9.8	77.3	-5.0	77.0	-0.4	73.8	-4.2
1976	75.1	1.8	74.3	-1.1	76.8	3.4	75.1	-2.2	77.4	3.1	73.2	-5.4	74.6	1.9	68.6	-8.0	62.0	-9.6	65.4	5.5	63.6	-2.8	63.2	-0.6
1977	63.8	0.9	65.9	3.3	66.8	1.4	69.1	3.4	68.4	-1.0	65.4	-4.4	63.5	-2.9	66.3	4.4	64.6	-2.6	63.1	-2.3	66.2	4.9	66.4	0.3
1978	68.9	3.8	71.9	4.4	71.5	-0.6	72.7	1.7	72.8	0.1	73.1	0.4	72.6	-0.7	74.3	2.3	75.1	1.1	76.2	1.5	75.1	-1.4	75.8	0.9
1979	75.9	0.1	77.3	1.8	77.3	0.0	77.4	0.1	77.0	-0.5	78.3	1.7	80.0	2.2	80.9	1.1	80.6	-0.4	81.2	0.7	82.7	1.8	86.9	5.1
1980	87.1	0.2	106.6	22.4	98.0	-8.1	102.0	4.1	121.6	19.2	120.7	-0.7	116.3	-3.6	128.7	10.7	126.6	-1.6	150.1	18.6	151.7	1.1	126.0	-16.9
1981	127.8	1.4	119.9	-6.2	112.0	-6.6	105.5	-5.8	97.4	-7.7	101.9	4.6	98.6	-3.2	99.1	0.5	91.5	-7.7	91.5	0.0	90.5	-1.1	91.8	1.4
1982	95.2	3.7	95.4	0.2	94.6	-0.8	94.9	0.3	98.4	3.7	99.8	1.4	102.2	2.4	105.9	3.6	103.3	-2.5	102.5	-0.8	104.0	1.5	103.9	-0.1
1983	104.6	0.7	106.2	1.5	105.2	-0.9	106.6	1.3	107.5	0.8	109.8	2.1	109.9	0.1	110.8	0.8	111.3	0.5	110.5	-0.7	110.4	-0.1	110.3	-0.1
1984	111.2	0.8	111.4	0.2	111.7	0.3	111.9	0.2	112.6	0.6	112.8	0.2	113.1	0.3	112.6	-0.4	112.1	-0.4	111.2	-0.8	110.1	-1.0	109.7	-0.4
1985	108.8	-0.8	107.9	-0.8	108.5	0.6	108.8	0.3	109.2	0.4	109.2	0.0	108.9	-0.3	108.1	-0.7	107.6	-0.5	106.1	-1.4	105.8	-0.3	106.0	0.2
1986	108.0	1.9	108.4	0.4	109.2	0.7	108.8	-0.4	109.0	0.2	109.4	0.4	109.8	0.4	109.8	0.0	110.4	0.5	110.9	0.5	111.1	0.2	111.2	0.1
1987	110.8	-0.4	110.8	0.0	111.2	0.4	111.9	0.6	112.8	0.8	112.9	0.1	113.7	0.7	113.9	0.2	114.0	0.1	113.6	-0.4	113.5	-0.1	113.0	-0.4
1988	112.5	-0.4	112.8	0.3	113.0	0.2	113.3	0.3	113.1	-0.2	113.6	0.4	115.9	2.0	115.9	0.0	115.9	0.0	116.5	0.5	116.8	0.3	117.3	0.4
1989	117.8	0.4	118.3	0.4	118.6	0.3	119.2	0.5	119.6	0.3	120.7	0.9	122.0	1.1	121.3	-0.6	121.6	0.2	120.1	-1.2	120.5	0.3	121.0	0.4
1990	121.1	0.1	121.8	0.6	121.7	-0.1	122.6	0.7	122.8	0.2	123.0	0.2	123.9	0.7	123.7	-0.2	123.9	0.2	123.0	-0.7	124.8	1.5	124.7	-0.1
1991	126.3	1.3	128.4	1.7	127.8	-0.5	128.3	0.4	127.8	-0.4	127.6	-0.2	129.1	1.2	129.4	0.2	129.8	0.3	128.5	-1.0	128.6	0.1	128.8	0.2
1992	128.6	-0.2	127.7	-0.7	127.4	-0.2	127.6	0.2	127.8	0.2	127.7	-0.1	129.0	1.0	129.3	0.2	129.2	-0.1	126.0	-2.5	125.8	-0.2	125.9	0.1
1993	125.4	-0.4	124.5	-0.7	124.6	0.1	124.8	0.2	125.5	0.6	126.6	0.9	129.3	2.1	129.3	0.0	130.6	1.0	131.7	0.8	131.5	-0.2	130.7	-0.6
1994	130.6	-0.1	130.5	-0.1	131.3	0.6	133.2	1.4	133.6	0.3	134.6	0.7	134.7	0.1	134.3	-0.3	133.9	-0.3	130.9	-2.2	131.2	0.2	131.3	0.1
1995	132.0	0.5	133.0	0.8	133.2	0.2	133.5	0.2	133.8	0.2	133.8	0.0	134.6	0.6	134.3	-0.2	134.6	0.2	134.7	0.1	135.1	0.3	136.2	0.8

Source: U.S. Department of Labor, Bureau of Labor Statistics, Division of Industry Prices and Price Indexes. n.e.c. stands for not elsewhere classified. - indicates no data collected for period or unavailable.

Beverages and Beverage Materials
Producer Price Index
Base 1982 = 100

For 1947-1995. Columns headed % show percentile change in the index from the previous period for which an index is available.

Year	Jan Index	Jan %	Feb Index	Feb %	Mar Index	Mar %	Apr Index	Apr %	May Index	May %	Jun Index	Jun %	Jul Index	Jul %	Aug Index	Aug %	Sep Index	Sep %	Oct Index	Oct %	Nov Index	Nov %	Dec Index	Dec %
1947	26.3	-	26.5	0.8	26.6	0.4	26.6	0.0	26.4	-0.8	26.2	-0.8	26.2	0.0	26.4	0.8	26.7	1.1	26.8	0.4	27.0	0.7	27.3	1.1
1948	27.5	0.7	27.7	0.7	27.7	0.0	27.7	0.0	27.7	0.0	27.8	0.4	27.8	0.0	27.8	0.0	27.8	0.0	27.8	0.0	27.9	0.4	27.9	0.0
1949	27.9	0.0	27.9	0.0	27.9	0.0	27.8	-0.4	27.8	0.0	27.8	0.0	27.8	0.0	27.8	0.0	28.0	0.7	28.1	0.4	29.7	5.7	30.2	1.7
1950	30.2	0.0	30.1	-0.3	30.1	0.0	29.7	-1.3	29.6	-0.3	29.7	0.3	30.3	2.0	30.7	1.3	31.0	1.0	31.5	1.6	31.3	-0.6	32.0	2.2
1951	32.5	1.6	32.6	0.3	32.6	0.0	32.6	0.0	32.6	0.0	32.6	0.0	32.5	-0.3	32.5	0.0	32.5	0.0	32.5	0.0	32.5	0.0	32.5	0.0
1952	32.5	0.0	33.3	2.5	33.3	0.0	33.2	-0.3	33.2	0.0	33.2	0.0	33.2	0.0	33.2	0.0	33.2	0.0	33.2	0.0	33.2	0.0	33.2	0.0
1953	33.2	0.0	33.2	0.0	33.6	1.2	33.5	-0.3	33.3	-0.6	33.3	0.0	33.8	1.5	33.8	0.0	34.0	0.6	34.5	1.5	34.6	0.3	34.6	0.0
1954	35.2	1.7	35.6	1.1	36.6	2.8	38.7	5.7	38.7	0.0	38.7	0.0	39.0	0.8	38.7	-0.8	37.6	-2.8	37.6	0.0	37.2	-1.1	37.5	0.8
1955	37.5	0.0	36.6	-2.4	36.2	-1.1	36.2	0.0	36.2	0.0	35.8	-1.1	35.8	0.0	35.9	0.3	36.1	0.6	36.4	0.8	36.1	-0.8	36.1	0.0
1956	36.1	0.0	36.4	0.8	36.9	1.4	36.7	-0.5	36.6	-0.3	36.8	0.5	37.1	0.8	37.4	0.8	37.8	1.1	37.8	0.0	38.0	0.5	37.6	-1.1
1957	37.8	0.5	37.6	-0.5	37.5	-0.3	37.2	-0.8	37.2	0.0	37.2	0.0	37.2	0.0	37.2	0.0	36.9	-0.8	36.6	-0.8	36.6	0.0	36.7	0.3
1958	36.7	0.0	36.7	0.0	36.4	-0.8	36.4	0.0	36.4	0.0	36.4	0.0	36.4	0.0	36.2	-0.5	36.1	-0.3	36.1	0.0	36.2	0.3	36.1	-0.3
1959	35.9	-0.6	35.7	-0.6	36.4	2.0	36.3	-0.3	36.3	0.0	36.3	0.0	36.3	0.0	36.3	-0.3	36.2	0.0	36.2	0.0	36.2	0.0	36.2	0.0
1960	36.2	0.0	36.2	0.0	36.2	0.0	36.2	0.0	36.2	0.0	36.2	0.0	36.1	-0.3	36.1	0.0	36.1	0.0	36.1	0.0	36.1	0.0	36.1	0.0
1961	35.9	-0.6	36.0	0.3	36.0	0.0	35.9	-0.3	35.9	0.0	35.9	0.0	36.1	0.6	36.1	0.0	36.3	0.6	36.1	-0.6	36.2	0.3	36.2	0.0
1962	36.2	0.0	36.2	0.0	36.2	0.0	36.2	0.0	36.2	0.0	36.2	0.0	36.2	0.0	36.3	0.3	36.2	-0.3	36.1	-0.3	36.1	0.0	36.0	-0.3
1963	36.0	0.0	36.0	0.0	36.0	0.0	36.2	0.6	36.3	0.3	36.8	1.4	37.4	1.6	37.5	0.3	37.5	0.0	37.5	0.0	37.7	0.5	37.9	0.5
1964	38.3	1.1	38.5	0.5	38.8	0.8	38.8	0.0	38.9	0.3	38.9	0.0	38.9	0.0	38.9	0.0	38.9	0.0	38.9	0.0	38.9	0.0	38.9	0.0
1965	38.8	-0.3	38.8	0.0	38.5	-0.8	38.6	0.3	38.6	0.0	38.6	0.0	38.6	0.0	38.6	0.0	38.6	0.0	38.6	0.0	38.6	0.0	38.7	0.3
1966	38.7	0.0	38.6	-0.3	38.6	0.0	38.6	0.0	38.6	0.0	38.8	0.5	38.9	0.3	38.9	0.0	38.6	-0.8	38.6	0.0	38.6	0.0	38.7	0.3
1967	38.7	0.0	38.7	0.0	38.6	-0.3	38.7	0.3	38.8	0.3	38.9	0.3	38.9	0.0	39.0	0.3	39.0	0.0	39.2	0.5	39.2	0.0	39.4	0.5
1968	39.4	0.0	39.7	0.8	39.8	0.3	39.9	0.3	40.0	0.3	40.0	0.0	40.0	0.0	40.1	0.3	40.2	0.2	40.4	0.5	40.4	0.0	40.4	0.0
1969	40.5	0.2	40.6	0.2	40.7	0.2	40.7	0.0	40.9	0.5	41.1	0.5	41.2	0.2	41.2	0.0	41.3	0.2	42.1	1.9	42.4	0.7	42.5	0.2
1970	42.9	0.9	43.3	0.9	43.3	0.0	43.4	0.2	44.0	1.4	44.0	0.0	44.1	0.2	44.3	0.5	44.5	0.5	44.6	0.2	44.7	0.2	44.5	-0.4
1971	44.8	0.7	44.9	0.2	44.9	0.0	45.1	0.4	45.1	0.0	45.1	0.0	45.2	0.2	45.3	0.2	45.4	0.2	45.4	0.0	45.4	0.0	45.3	-0.2
1972	45.3	0.0	45.5	0.4	45.4	-0.2	45.6	0.4	45.6	0.0	45.8	0.4	45.9	0.2	46.3	0.9	46.4	0.2	46.2	-0.4	46.5	0.6	46.6	0.2
1973	46.6	0.0	46.7	0.2	47.0	0.6	47.3	0.6	47.5	0.4	47.3	-0.4	47.1	-0.4	47.2	0.2	47.3	0.2	47.9	1.3	48.2	0.6	48.4	0.4
1974	48.9	1.0	49.1	0.4	50.3	2.4	51.5	2.4	52.4	1.7	53.9	2.9	55.9	3.7	56.9	1.8	57.5	1.1	59.4	3.3	60.1	1.2	61.6	2.5
1975	63.3	2.8	63.2	-0.2	63.1	-0.2	63.0	-0.2	62.7	-0.5	62.4	-0.5	62.1	-0.5	62.9	1.3	63.3	0.6	64.3	1.6	64.3	0.0	64.4	0.2
1976	64.3	-0.2	65.1	1.2	65.1	0.0	65.9	1.2	67.1	1.8	67.3	0.3	68.5	1.8	68.4	-0.1	68.7	0.4	69.1	0.6	69.6	0.7	71.6	2.9
1977	71.7	0.1	73.7	2.8	77.7	5.4	78.7	1.3	80.2	1.9	80.9	0.9	79.7	-1.5	80.0	0.4	79.7	-0.4	79.8	0.1	78.5	-1.6	78.4	-0.1
1978	78.7	0.4	78.4	-0.4	77.9	-0.6	77.9	0.0	77.7	-0.3	77.9	0.3	77.3	-0.8	76.6	-0.9	77.0	0.5	78.3	1.7	78.4	0.1	78.3	-0.1
1979	78.2	-0.1	78.3	0.1	78.3	0.0	78.5	0.3	79.9	1.8	81.2	1.6	83.4	2.7	84.3	1.1	84.8	0.6	85.2	0.5	86.1	1.1	86.3	0.2
1980	87.2	1.0	87.5	0.3	88.0	0.6	88.7	0.8	90.0	1.5	91.2	1.3	91.3	0.1	92.3	1.1	91.9	-0.4	93.3	1.5	93.7	0.4	93.6	-0.1
1981	94.6	1.1	95.3	0.7	95.5	0.2	95.8	0.3	96.4	0.6	96.6	0.2	96.9	0.3	97.1	0.2	97.0	-0.1	97.3	0.3	97.9	0.6	98.1	0.2
1982	98.8	0.7	99.3	0.5	99.8	0.5	99.9	0.1	99.9	0.0	99.9	0.0	100.0	0.1	100.4	0.4	100.1	-0.3	100.4	0.3	100.6	0.2	100.8	0.2
1983	101.3	0.5	101.7	0.4	102.0	0.3	102.4	0.4	102.6	0.2	102.4	-0.2	102.7	0.3	102.7	0.0	102.9	0.2	103.3	0.4	103.7	0.4	103.7	0.0
1984	104.6	0.9	105.2	0.6	105.1	-0.1	105.7	0.6	106.5	0.8	106.2	-0.3	106.6	0.4	106.9	0.3	106.9	0.0	107.5	0.6	107.4	-0.1	107.3	-0.1
1985	107.4	0.1	108.0	0.6	107.9	-0.1	107.8	-0.1	107.8	0.0	107.3	-0.5	107.5	0.2	107.1	-0.4	107.1	0.0	107.6	0.5	107.9	0.3	109.0	1.0
1986	112.9	3.6	114.5	1.4	115.0	0.4	115.9	0.8	115.9	0.0	115.5	-0.3	115.5	0.0	114.0	-1.3	113.7	-0.3	114.2	0.4	113.9	-0.3	113.8	-0.1
1987	112.6	-1.1	112.8	0.2	112.9	0.1	113.3	0.4	113.2	-0.1	113.0	-0.2	112.1	-0.8	112.3	0.2	111.6	-0.6	112.3	0.6	112.0	-0.3	112.2	0.2
1988	112.5	0.3	113.0	0.4	113.9	0.8	114.1	0.2	114.1	0.0	114.1	0.0	113.8	-0.3	114.6	0.7	114.7	0.1	115.3	0.5	115.8	0.4	115.8	0.0
1989	116.5	0.6	117.7	1.0	118.7	0.8	119.2	0.4	119.7	0.4	119.6	-0.1	119.4	-0.2	118.3	-0.9	117.1	-1.0	118.1	0.9	118.4	0.3	118.4	0.0
1990	119.7	1.1	120.7	0.8	121.5	0.7	121.5	0.0	121.0	-0.4	120.8	-0.2	120.9	0.1	120.6	-0.2	120.8	0.2	120.3	-0.4	120.5	0.2	121.1	0.5
1991	125.5	3.6	125.5	0.0	125.3	-0.2	125.5	0.2	124.3	-1.0	124.2	-0.1	123.5	-0.6	123.2	-0.2	123.1	-0.1	123.0	-0.1	123.0	0.0	123.2	0.2

[Continued]

Beverages and Beverage Materials
Producer Price Index
Base 1982 = 100
[Continued]

For 1947-1995. Columns headed % show percentile change in the index from the previous period for which an index is available.

Year	Jan Index	%	Feb Index	%	Mar Index	%	Apr Index	%	May Index	%	Jun Index	%	Jul Index	%	Aug Index	%	Sep Index	%	Oct Index	%	Nov Index	%	Dec Index	%
1992	124.8	1.3	125.2	0.3	124.5	-0.6	124.6	0.1	125.1	0.4	125.7	0.5	124.4	-1.0	124.1	-0.2	123.8	-0.2	123.4	-0.3	123.5	0.1	124.0	0.4
1993	124.5	0.4	125.4	0.7	125.4	0.0	125.2	-0.2	125.0	-0.2	124.8	-0.2	124.4	-0.3	124.5	0.1	124.4	-0.1	124.5	0.1	124.3	-0.2	124.6	0.2
1994	125.5	0.7	126.0	0.4	125.2	-0.6	124.8	-0.3	124.8	0.0	125.3	0.4	129.9	3.7	129.7	-0.2	129.7	0.0	130.1	0.3	130.4	0.2	130.5	0.1
1995	131.8	1.0	133.4	1.2	133.8	0.3	134.3	0.4	134.1	-0.1	134.0	-0.1	134.2	0.1	134.4	0.1	133.6	-0.6	134.2	0.4	134.1	-0.1	134.2	0.1

Source: U.S. Department of Labor, Bureau of Labor Statistics, Division of Industry Prices and Price Indexes. n.e.c. stands for not elsewhere classified. - indicates no data collected for period or unavailable.

Fats and Oils
Producer Price Index
Base 1982 = 100

For 1967-1995. Columns headed % show percentile change in the index from the previous period for which an index is available.

Year	Jan Index	%	Feb Index	%	Mar Index	%	Apr Index	%	May Index	%	Jun Index	%	Jul Index	%	Aug Index	%	Sep Index	%	Oct Index	%	Nov Index	%	Dec Index	%
1967	48.8	-	48.3	-1.0	47.7	-1.2	47.7	0.0	47.6	-0.2	46.6	-2.1	45.3	-2.8	46.2	2.0	45.9	-0.6	44.8	-2.4	44.3	-1.1	44.3	0.0
1968	44.5	0.5	46.6	4.7	46.1	-1.1	45.4	-1.5	46.0	1.3	44.8	-2.6	44.3	-1.1	45.5	2.7	43.9	-3.5	42.3	-3.6	43.8	3.5	43.9	0.2
1969	45.1	2.7	46.6	3.3	46.6	0.0	45.8	-1.7	45.8	0.0	46.0	0.4	45.8	-0.4	45.9	0.2	45.9	0.0	48.6	5.9	50.8	4.5	49.8	-2.0
1970	49.5	-0.6	51.6	4.2	56.3	9.1	55.6	-1.2	54.4	-2.2	53.6	-1.5	53.4	-0.4	55.3	3.6	54.3	-1.8	57.5	5.9	60.7	5.6	58.2	-4.1
1971	57.7	-0.9	59.0	2.3	58.9	-0.2	56.8	-3.6	56.6	-0.4	57.3	1.2	60.2	5.1	62.9	4.5	60.3	-4.1	58.7	-2.7	58.8	0.2	56.4	-4.1
1972	55.6	-1.4	56.3	1.3	56.0	-0.5	56.3	0.5	55.4	-1.6	55.4	0.0	54.5	-1.6	53.5	-1.8	53.2	-0.6	53.2	0.0	52.7	-0.9	52.5	-0.4
1973	52.2	-0.6	57.4	10.0	63.3	10.3	64.0	1.1	68.0	6.3	73.9	8.7	74.2	0.4	103.3	39.2	84.2	-18.5	92.5	9.9	80.4	-13.1	93.7	16.5
1974	96.9	3.4	112.6	16.2	108.2	-3.9	101.3	-6.4	109.2	7.8	107.6	-1.5	119.3	10.9	145.4	21.9	128.0	-12.0	144.6	13.0	143.0	-1.1	129.9	-9.2
1975	127.9	-1.5	117.1	-8.4	110.3	-5.8	108.4	-1.7	98.7	-8.9	94.5	-4.3	108.3	14.6	113.3	4.6	103.5	-8.6	98.9	-4.4	92.0	-7.0	83.2	-9.6
1976	80.4	-3.4	79.8	-0.7	80.3	0.6	77.8	-3.1	76.8	-1.3	78.3	2.0	87.0	11.1	82.5	-5.2	89.8	8.8	85.2	-5.1	88.8	4.2	86.9	-2.1
1977	86.2	-0.8	91.4	6.0	98.3	7.5	109.8	11.7	111.1	1.2	107.1	-3.6	95.5	-10.8	92.5	-3.1	88.4	-4.4	90.2	2.0	90.9	0.8	96.6	6.3
1978	94.3	-2.4	94.5	0.2	104.9	11.0	107.0	2.0	107.9	0.8	105.7	-2.0	106.6	0.9	104.8	-1.7	111.3	6.2	108.2	-2.8	105.8	-2.2	105.8	0.0
1979	106.8	0.9	110.4	3.4	110.9	0.5	114.4	3.2	112.4	-1.7	113.2	0.7	117.7	4.0	117.0	-0.6	117.7	0.6	114.3	-2.9	112.4	-1.7	109.5	-2.6
1980	104.6	-4.5	105.2	0.6	103.5	-1.6	99.7	-3.7	98.5	-1.2	98.9	0.4	105.5	6.7	111.7	5.9	110.8	-0.8	107.4	-3.1	110.6	3.0	108.8	-1.6
1981	107.0	-1.7	106.1	-0.8	106.8	0.7	108.0	1.1	106.1	-1.8	105.7	-0.4	109.1	3.2	106.7	-2.2	104.3	-2.2	103.8	-0.5	102.9	-0.9	101.8	-1.1
1982	100.7	-1.1	100.7	0.0	99.4	-1.3	101.4	2.0	103.3	1.9	103.1	-0.2	102.9	-0.2	100.2	-2.6	98.2	-2.0	99.4	1.2	96.3	-3.1	94.3	-2.1
1983	93.8	-0.5	95.4	1.7	95.8	0.4	99.7	4.1	102.3	2.6	101.9	-0.4	103.3	1.4	114.2	10.6	141.1	23.6	130.9	-7.2	127.6	-2.5	126.3	-1.0
1984	129.4	2.5	127.0	-1.9	133.0	4.7	136.4	2.6	152.7	12.0	152.5	-0.1	145.4	-4.7	142.2	-2.2	138.8	-2.4	140.2	1.0	145.0	3.4	138.3	-4.6
1985	130.4	-5.7	132.6	1.7	135.0	1.8	140.8	4.3	137.6	-2.3	137.8	0.1	132.0	-4.2	118.4	-10.3	113.6	-4.1	110.6	-2.6	109.6	-0.9	106.8	-2.6
1986	107.3	0.5	103.8	-3.3	99.1	-4.5	97.8	-1.3	97.0	-0.8	95.5	-1.5	94.4	-1.2	92.8	-1.7	91.0	-1.9	93.4	2.6	92.9	-0.5	93.3	0.4
1987	95.3	2.1	95.8	0.5	95.6	-0.2	95.4	-0.2	99.2	4.0	97.9	-1.3	97.6	-0.3	96.4	-1.2	97.7	1.3	99.4	1.7	101.1	1.7	103.6	2.5
1988	110.6	6.8	111.1	0.5	109.3	-1.6	111.9	2.4	114.0	1.9	120.1	5.4	132.1	10.0	127.1	-3.8	122.7	-3.5	118.4	-3.5	114.3	-3.5	114.8	0.4
1989	114.1	-0.6	111.6	-2.2	114.7	2.8	113.7	-0.9	117.5	3.3	112.6	-4.2	112.5	-0.1	108.5	-3.6	108.9	0.4	108.3	-0.6	112.5	3.9	110.2	-2.0
1990	111.3	1.0	111.8	0.4	117.8	5.4	116.2	-1.4	124.6	7.2	126.0	1.1	124.6	-1.1	126.3	1.4	124.0	-1.8	118.5	-4.4	115.1	-2.9	116.9	1.6
1991	115.8	-0.9	115.8	0.0	118.2	2.1	116.9	-1.1	111.6	-4.5	110.5	-1.0	107.0	-3.2	110.8	3.6	111.2	0.4	109.8	-1.3	107.9	-1.7	108.9	0.9
1992	108.4	-0.5	108.8	0.4	111.1	2.1	108.6	-2.3	111.1	2.3	113.6	2.3	108.3	-4.7	104.2	-3.8	105.7	1.4	104.9	-0.8	108.5	3.4	111.9	3.1
1993	113.1	1.1	110.7	-2.1	111.5	0.7	112.9	1.3	113.7	0.7	111.4	-2.0	121.5	9.1	119.5	-1.6	118.7	-0.7	117.7	-0.8	120.2	2.1	132.1	9.9
1994	137.3	3.9	136.1	-0.9	137.1	0.7	136.2	-0.7	137.8	1.2	136.9	-0.7	128.5	-6.1	128.3	-0.2	133.6	4.1	132.2	-1.0	141.7	7.2	144.4	1.9
1995	144.3	-0.1	143.3	-0.7	143.2	-0.1	138.2	-3.5	134.3	-2.8	135.2	0.7	138.5	2.4	138.6	0.1	137.9	-0.5	138.8	0.7	136.6	-1.6	134.4	-1.6

Source: U.S. Department of Labor, Bureau of Labor Statistics, Division of Industry Prices and Price Indexes. n.e.c. stands for not elsewhere classified. - indicates no data collected for period or unavailable.

Miscellaneous Processed Foods
Producer Price Index
Base 1982 = 100

For 1947-1995. Columns headed % show percentile change in the index from the previous period for which an index is available.

Year	Jan Index	%	Feb Index	%	Mar Index	%	Apr Index	%	May Index	%	Jun Index	%	Jul Index	%	Aug Index	%	Sep Index	%	Oct Index	%	Nov Index	%	Dec Index	%
1947	35.5	-	35.7	0.6	35.6	-0.3	34.7	-2.5	33.9	-2.3	33.7	-0.6	33.8	0.3	33.9	0.3	34.3	1.2	35.5	3.5	35.7	0.6	35.2	-1.4
1948	35.2	0.0	35.0	-0.6	34.8	-0.6	35.1	0.9	35.3	0.6	35.9	1.7	36.2	0.8	37.3	3.0	38.1	2.1	39.0	2.4	38.1	-2.3	37.9	-0.5
1949	37.2	-1.8	36.8	-1.1	38.3	4.1	38.5	0.5	38.4	-0.3	39.6	3.1	40.3	1.8	42.3	5.0	42.0	-0.7	42.6	1.4	42.3	-0.7	42.1	-0.5
1950	41.1	-2.4	42.2	2.7	42.2	0.0	41.8	-0.9	41.4	-1.0	39.5	-4.6	44.2	11.9	52.2	18.1	48.2	-7.7	44.9	-6.8	43.6	-2.9	44.7	2.5
1951	46.1	3.1	47.4	2.8	45.2	-4.6	45.6	0.9	45.8	0.4	45.5	-0.7	45.3	-0.4	45.9	1.3	46.0	0.2	45.3	-1.5	45.1	-0.4	44.3	-1.8
1952	42.5	-4.1	42.8	0.7	43.0	0.5	40.0	-7.0	41.9	4.8	43.9	4.8	47.0	7.1	46.5	-1.1	47.4	1.9	46.1	-2.7	45.3	-1.7	43.4	-4.2
1953	41.9	-3.5	42.4	1.2	44.9	5.9	44.7	-0.4	45.1	0.9	44.6	-1.1	43.5	-2.5	43.3	-0.5	43.3	0.0	43.4	0.2	40.9	-5.8	42.3	3.4
1954	41.4	-2.1	40.4	-2.4	39.5	-2.2	38.2	-3.3	37.6	-1.6	35.9	-4.5	37.6	4.7	40.7	8.2	38.4	-5.7	37.0	-3.6	36.3	-1.9	36.5	0.6
1955	36.4	-0.3	37.4	2.7	37.4	0.0	37.5	0.3	37.5	0.0	37.6	0.3	37.3	-0.8	36.9	-1.1	36.4	-1.4	36.5	0.3	36.2	-0.8	36.3	0.3
1956	36.4	0.3	36.2	-0.5	36.2	0.0	36.3	0.3	36.2	-0.3	36.2	0.0	36.0	-0.6	35.6	-1.1	35.6	0.0	35.4	-0.6	35.5	0.3	35.5	0.0
1957	35.3	-0.6	35.5	0.6	35.3	-0.6	35.3	0.0	35.4	0.3	35.4	0.0	35.2	-0.6	35.3	0.3	35.6	0.8	35.6	0.0	35.8	0.6	35.7	-0.3
1958	35.4	-0.8	35.3	-0.3	35.8	1.4	36.0	0.6	35.9	-0.3	35.9	0.0	36.0	0.3	35.8	-0.6	35.9	0.3	36.0	0.3	36.2	0.6	35.9	-0.8
1959	35.7	-0.6	36.0	0.8	35.5	-1.4	35.4	-0.3	35.6	0.6	35.4	-0.6	35.6	0.6	35.8	0.6	35.9	0.3	35.9	0.0	36.5	1.7	37.1	1.6
1960	38.5	3.8	37.7	-2.1	37.7	0.0	38.1	1.1	37.9	-0.5	38.5	1.6	38.3	-0.5	37.7	-1.6	37.6	-0.3	37.3	-0.8	38.1	2.1	37.4	-1.8
1961	38.1	1.9	37.9	-0.5	38.3	1.1	38.0	-0.8	38.1	0.3	38.3	0.5	38.1	-0.5	37.9	-0.5	37.9	0.0	37.6	-0.8	36.9	-1.9	36.6	-0.8
1962	36.5	-0.3	36.4	-0.3	36.7	0.8	36.2	-1.4	36.0	-0.6	36.4	1.1	36.1	-0.8	36.1	0.0	36.7	1.7	37.4	1.9	36.2	-3.2	35.9	-0.8
1963	35.8	-0.3	36.2	1.1	36.2	0.0	36.2	0.0	36.4	0.6	37.1	1.9	37.3	0.5	38.1	2.1	38.1	0.0	38.8	1.8	38.5	-0.8	38.4	-0.3
1964	38.4	0.0	38.1	-0.8	38.5	1.0	39.3	2.1	38.9	-1.0	38.7	-0.5	38.9	0.5	38.9	0.0	39.1	0.5	39.0	-0.3	39.4	1.0	39.7	0.8
1965	40.9	3.0	40.9	0.0	40.2	-1.7	39.9	-0.7	40.1	0.5	40.3	0.5	40.5	0.5	41.0	1.2	40.8	-0.5	40.8	0.0	40.8	0.0	40.8	0.0
1966	40.7	-0.2	40.8	0.2	40.9	0.2	40.7	-0.5	40.4	-0.7	40.2	-0.5	40.7	1.2	40.8	0.2	40.8	0.0	41.1	0.7	41.0	-0.2	40.6	-1.0
1967	40.2	-1.0	39.8	-1.0	40.0	0.5	40.4	1.0	40.2	-0.5	40.2	0.0	40.4	0.5	40.1	-0.7	40.2	0.2	40.2	0.0	40.4	0.5	40.6	0.5
1968	40.8	0.5	40.8	0.0	40.8	0.0	40.8	0.0	40.7	-0.2	40.9	0.5	41.0	0.2	41.0	0.0	41.8	2.0	42.3	1.2	42.3	0.0	42.2	-0.2
1969	42.2	0.0	42.6	0.9	42.6	0.0	42.4	-0.5	42.4	0.0	42.4	0.0	42.7	0.7	42.8	0.2	43.3	1.2	47.0	8.5	45.5	-3.2	45.2	-0.7
1970	45.2	0.0	45.5	0.7	45.4	-0.2	44.9	-1.1	44.3	-1.3	45.3	2.3	45.8	1.1	45.9	0.2	46.3	0.9	45.9	-0.9	45.5	-0.9	45.3	-0.4
1971	45.0	-0.7	45.0	0.0	45.7	1.6	46.0	0.7	45.8	-0.4	45.8	0.0	45.8	0.0	45.8	0.0	45.5	-0.7	45.4	-0.2	45.5	0.2	45.5	0.0
1972	45.7	0.4	45.8	0.2	45.7	-0.2	45.8	0.2	46.3	1.1	46.0	-0.6	46.0	0.0	45.8	-0.4	46.8	2.2	47.0	0.4	46.7	-0.6	46.6	-0.2
1973	46.9	0.6	47.2	0.6	47.8	1.3	47.7	-0.2	47.8	0.2	48.3	1.0	49.7	2.9	51.7	4.0	51.5	-0.4	52.0	1.0	52.0	0.0	52.6	1.2
1974	54.0	2.7	56.3	4.3	59.1	5.0	60.1	1.7	61.5	2.3	63.0	2.4	64.5	2.4	66.4	2.9	68.5	3.2	69.0	0.7	71.1	3.0	72.1	1.4
1975	73.2	1.5	72.9	-0.4	72.3	-0.8	72.5	0.3	72.0	-0.7	71.4	-0.8	70.8	-0.8	71.6	1.1	71.8	0.3	71.3	-0.7	70.9	-0.6	70.4	-0.7
1976	69.5	-1.3	68.8	-1.0	68.8	0.0	69.8	1.5	69.9	0.1	69.5	-0.6	69.6	0.1	69.9	0.4	70.6	1.0	71.5	1.3	71.7	0.3	73.5	2.5
1977	73.3	-0.3	74.0	1.0	74.0	0.0	74.3	0.4	77.4	4.2	77.6	0.3	78.2	0.8	78.2	0.0	78.1	-0.1	78.0	-0.1	77.2	-1.0	77.2	0.0
1978	77.8	0.8	78.1	0.4	78.8	0.9	80.2	1.8	80.6	0.5	80.4	-0.2	81.5	1.4	79.2	-2.8	79.4	0.3	80.6	1.5	82.0	1.7	82.1	0.1
1979	83.1	1.2	83.7	0.7	87.5	4.5	88.2	0.8	88.6	0.5	84.9	-4.2	85.6	0.8	87.6	2.3	88.1	0.6	88.8	0.8	89.4	0.7	89.7	0.3
1980	90.7	1.1	89.9	-0.9	90.4	0.6	90.6	0.2	90.0	-0.7	89.9	-0.1	89.9	0.0	90.1	0.2	91.2	1.2	92.8	1.8	94.6	1.9	96.7	2.2
1981	98.2	1.6	99.8	1.6	100.2	0.4	100.6	0.4	101.0	0.4	101.2	0.2	101.5	0.3	101.4	-0.1	101.8	0.4	100.5	-1.3	100.6	0.1	100.6	0.0
1982	101.0	0.4	100.9	-0.1	100.4	-0.5	100.4	0.0	99.8	-0.6	100.0	0.2	99.8	-0.2	98.9	-0.9	99.4	0.5	99.7	0.3	99.7	0.0	100.0	0.3
1983	100.1	0.1	100.3	0.2	100.0	-0.3	100.5	0.5	100.5	0.0	101.2	0.7	102.6	1.4	101.7	-0.9	104.0	2.3	105.4	1.3	106.5	1.0	107.1	0.6
1984	107.3	0.2	110.8	3.3	110.7	-0.1	111.2	0.5	111.1	-0.1	112.6	1.4	113.2	0.5	112.8	-0.4	113.1	0.3	113.1	0.0	113.0	-0.1	113.0	0.0
1985	113.2	0.2	113.2	0.0	113.2	0.0	113.5	0.3	114.1	0.5	114.1	0.0	114.5	0.4	115.1	0.5	114.5	-0.5	114.5	0.0	114.6	0.1	114.6	0.0
1986	115.4	0.7	115.1	-0.3	115.2	0.1	115.1	-0.1	115.4	0.3	115.7	0.3	116.1	0.3	116.4	0.3	116.6	0.2	117.4	0.7	117.7	0.3	118.3	0.5
1987	118.9	0.5	119.5	0.5	119.8	0.3	120.0	0.2	120.0	0.0	119.5	-0.4	119.5	0.0	119.7	0.2	119.6	-0.1	119.9	0.3	120.3	0.3	120.5	0.2
1988	119.9	-0.5	120.5	0.5	120.7	0.2	121.4	0.6	121.5	0.1	121.3	-0.2	122.7	1.2	123.4	0.6	123.8	0.3	124.3	0.4	125.1	0.6	125.3	0.2
1989	126.2	0.7	127.5	1.0	128.1	0.5	128.6	0.4	129.3	0.5	129.3	0.0	129.4	0.1	130.0	0.5	130.3	0.2	130.6	0.2	131.1	0.4	131.8	0.5
1990	131.6	-0.2	132.2	0.5	132.9	0.5	133.1	0.2	133.8	0.5	133.7	-0.1	134.1	0.3	134.8	0.5	135.0	0.1	134.8	-0.1	136.7	1.4	137.4	0.5
1991	137.6	0.1	137.9	0.2	137.8	-0.1	138.2	0.3	137.3	-0.7	137.8	0.4	137.9	0.1	139.0	0.8	138.8	-0.1	139.2	0.3	138.9	-0.2	138.8	-0.1

[Continued]

Miscellaneous Processed Foods
Producer Price Index
Base 1982 = 100
[Continued]

For 1947-1995. Columns headed % show percentile change in the index from the previous period for which an index is available.

Year	Jan Index	%	Feb Index	%	Mar Index	%	Apr Index	%	May Index	%	Jun Index	%	Jul Index	%	Aug Index	%	Sep Index	%	Oct Index	%	Nov Index	%	Dec Index	%
1992	139.1	0.2	139.1	0.0	138.8	-0.2	138.7	-0.1	138.7	0.0	138.4	-0.2	138.9	0.4	139.4	0.4	139.5	0.1	139.4	-0.1	140.2	0.6	140.2	0.0
1993	140.7	0.4	141.2	0.4	141.8	0.4	141.9	0.1	142.1	0.1	142.2	0.1	142.5	0.2	143.1	0.4	142.8	-0.2	143.1	0.2	143.3	0.1	143.4	0.1
1994	143.5	0.1	144.2	0.5	144.1	-0.1	144.1	0.0	144.0	-0.1	144.1	0.1	144.2	0.1	144.3	0.1	144.3	0.0	144.7	0.3	145.0	0.2	145.3	0.2
1995	145.6	0.2	145.0	-0.4	145.2	0.1	145.4	0.1	145.3	-0.1	145.3	0.0	146.2	0.6	146.6	0.3	146.6	0.0	147.3	0.5	147.5	0.1	147.4	-0.1

Source: U.S. Department of Labor, Bureau of Labor Statistics, Division of Industry Prices and Price Indexes. n.e.c. stands for not elsewhere classified. - indicates no data collected for period or unavailable.

Prepared Animal Feeds
Producer Price Index
Base 1982 = 100

For 1947-1995. Columns headed % show percentile change in the index from the previous period for which an index is available.

Year	Jan Index	%	Feb Index	%	Mar Index	%	Apr Index	%	May Index	%	Jun Index	%	Jul Index	%	Aug Index	%	Sep Index	%	Oct Index	%	Nov Index	%	Dec Index	%
1947	45.3	-	42.0	-7.3	50.8	21.0	47.5	-6.5	48.7	2.5	52.8	8.4	57.3	8.5	58.4	1.9	65.4	12.0	63.8	-2.4	63.3	-0.8	67.9	7.3
1948	74.2	9.3	61.1	-17.7	60.2	-1.5	60.9	1.2	58.7	-3.6	60.3	2.7	55.4	-8.1	47.7	-13.9	48.5	1.7	44.9	-7.4	50.0	11.4	50.5	1.0
1949	49.5	-2.0	45.2	-8.7	47.4	4.9	50.5	6.5	48.7	-3.6	48.8	0.2	52.6	7.8	56.0	6.5	49.8	-11.1	47.5	-4.6	45.7	-3.8	46.5	1.8
1950	44.7	-3.9	43.8	-2.0	47.2	7.8	49.4	4.7	53.7	8.7	50.1	-6.7	56.7	13.2	49.2	-13.2	47.7	-3.0	45.5	-4.6	47.9	5.3	50.2	4.8
1951	51.4	2.4	52.7	2.5	52.9	0.4	54.4	2.8	51.7	-5.0	51.4	-0.6	52.4	1.9	51.2	-2.3	53.8	5.1	55.8	3.7	57.9	3.8	58.8	1.6
1952	60.2	2.4	60.7	0.8	58.5	-3.6	58.9	0.7	57.9	-1.7	57.7	-0.3	54.9	-4.9	58.5	6.6	57.9	-1.0	57.9	0.0	55.2	-4.7	54.6	-1.1
1953	52.3	-4.2	50.5	-3.4	50.8	0.6	47.4	-6.7	48.7	2.7	44.7	-8.2	44.2	-1.1	45.4	2.7	43.6	-4.0	43.3	-0.7	42.1	-2.8	49.3	17.1
1954	50.2	1.8	52.0	3.6	54.0	3.8	59.4	10.0	58.3	-1.9	53.8	-7.7	52.5	-2.4	50.9	-3.0	47.6	-6.5	45.1	-5.3	45.4	0.7	46.4	2.2
1955	45.3	-2.4	45.9	1.3	44.3	-3.5	42.8	-3.4	40.1	-6.3	37.8	-5.7	39.5	4.5	38.3	-3.0	38.8	1.3	39.9	2.8	36.3	-9.0	36.8	1.4
1956	37.3	1.4	36.4	-2.4	35.9	-1.4	39.8	10.9	43.7	9.8	40.6	-7.1	38.9	-4.2	38.5	-1.0	37.2	-3.4	36.4	-2.2	38.4	5.5	38.8	1.0
1957	39.8	2.6	38.9	-2.3	38.5	-1.0	38.0	-1.3	35.9	-5.5	33.9	-5.6	35.3	4.1	36.4	3.1	35.5	-2.5	33.7	-5.1	32.8	-2.7	33.2	1.2
1958	34.2	3.0	35.1	2.6	39.9	13.7	43.2	8.3	41.7	-3.5	39.2	-6.0	42.6	8.7	41.0	-3.8	38.2	-6.8	36.9	-3.4	38.8	5.1	46.2	19.1
1959	46.1	-0.2	43.9	-4.8	42.5	-3.2	44.3	4.2	40.9	-7.7	36.9	-9.8	38.6	4.6	37.8	-2.1	34.5	-8.7	37.6	9.0	39.4	4.8	39.6	0.5
1960	40.4	2.0	38.6	-4.5	39.1	1.3	40.4	3.3	36.3	-10.1	36.1	-0.6	36.0	-0.3	35.1	-2.5	36.2	3.1	35.4	-2.2	35.7	0.8	37.4	4.8
1961	39.9	6.7	39.6	-0.8	40.7	2.8	41.4	1.7	42.9	3.6	40.1	-6.5	39.9	-0.5	39.7	-0.5	39.7	0.0	38.0	-4.3	41.0	7.9	42.0	2.4
1962	42.4	1.0	41.6	-1.9	41.6	0.0	41.8	0.5	41.8	0.0	41.4	-1.0	42.9	3.6	42.6	-0.7	43.9	3.1	43.6	-0.7	44.4	1.8	44.7	0.7
1963	45.7	2.2	45.7	0.0	45.2	-1.1	43.2	-4.4	43.0	-0.5	43.3	0.7	44.9	3.7	45.5	1.3	46.0	1.1	45.5	-1.1	45.3	-0.4	46.2	2.0
1964	46.5	0.6	45.3	-2.6	44.5	-1.8	44.3	-0.4	42.7	-3.6	42.4	-0.7	42.8	0.9	42.6	-0.5	43.9	3.1	44.5	1.4	43.4	-2.5	45.0	3.7
1965	44.5	-1.1	44.2	-0.7	44.1	-0.2	44.6	1.1	43.6	-2.2	45.1	3.4	45.9	1.8	45.2	-1.5	45.1	-0.2	44.9	-0.4	46.3	3.1	45.8	-1.1
1966	47.0	2.6	48.2	2.6	46.2	-4.1	46.1	-0.2	47.6	3.3	47.9	0.6	51.2	6.9	51.6	0.8	51.1	-1.0	49.5	-3.1	49.6	0.2	51.0	2.8
1967	51.0	0.0	48.7	-4.5	48.2	-1.0	47.5	-1.5	45.9	-3.4	47.3	3.1	47.6	0.6	46.2	-2.9	47.0	1.7	46.6	-0.9	45.9	-1.5	46.2	0.7
1968	46.5	0.6	46.2	-0.6	46.0	-0.4	45.3	-1.5	45.5	0.4	46.2	1.5	46.2	0.0	45.8	-0.9	45.4	-0.9	45.4	0.0	45.3	-0.2	45.7	0.9
1969	45.7	0.0	45.4	-0.7	44.7	-1.5	45.8	2.5	44.4	-3.1	45.2	1.8	45.9	1.5	45.7	-0.4	46.1	0.9	46.4	0.7	46.2	-0.4	47.1	1.9
1970	51.0	8.3	50.9	-0.2	46.1	-9.4	46.9	1.7	46.3	-1.3	46.9	1.3	49.3	5.1	49.5	0.4	50.7	2.4	49.4	-2.6	50.0	1.2	51.7	3.4
1971	51.1	-1.2	49.7	-2.7	50.8	2.2	49.4	-2.8	49.5	0.2	50.9	2.8	50.6	-0.6	49.6	-2.0	48.0	-3.2	46.7	-2.7	47.5	1.7	49.5	4.2
1972	49.1	-0.8	49.1	0.0	51.4	4.7	51.3	-0.2	51.3	0.0	51.0	-0.6	52.5	2.9	52.9	0.8	55.8	5.5	55.1	-1.3	61.7	12.0	77.4	25.4
1973	78.7	1.7	86.4	9.8	86.3	-0.1	78.9	-8.6	100.0	26.7	122.0	22.0	93.3	-23.5	123.9	32.8	90.0	-27.4	87.3	-3.0	86.8	-0.6	95.1	9.6
1974	96.2	1.2	90.3	-6.1	85.7	-5.1	78.7	-8.2	73.4	-6.7	72.2	-1.6	73.9	2.4	102.8	39.1	87.4	-15.0	100.0	14.4	92.6	-7.4	92.1	-0.5
1975	87.8	-4.7	79.3	-9.7	75.4	-4.9	81.1	7.6	78.0	-3.8	80.0	2.6	80.2	0.3	84.0	4.7	83.9	-0.1	84.0	0.1	81.3	-3.2	82.6	1.6
1976	83.6	1.2	82.9	-0.8	82.9	0.0	82.2	-0.8	85.8	4.4	100.8	17.5	102.3	1.5	93.2	-8.9	100.1	7.4	94.6	-5.5	94.7	0.1	100.9	6.5
1977	103.6	2.7	103.6	0.0	105.0	1.4	115.0	9.5	113.3	-1.5	106.7	-5.8	89.1	-16.5	83.2	-6.6	82.7	-0.6	79.7	-3.6	91.7	15.1	88.6	-3.4
1978	92.0	3.8	88.4	-3.9	94.9	7.4	93.5	-1.5	91.7	-1.9	93.6	2.1	92.9	-0.7	89.9	-3.2	91.7	2.0	95.2	3.8	97.2	2.1	100.3	3.2
1979	100.0	-0.3	102.8	2.8	102.1	-0.7	102.0	-0.1	99.8	-2.2	104.3	4.5	111.2	6.6	102.3	-8.0	103.8	1.5	106.0	2.1	105.3	-0.7	106.5	1.1
1980	104.0	-2.3	104.0	0.0	102.5	-1.4	97.0	-5.4	98.0	1.0	97.0	-1.0	106.0	9.3	110.0	3.8	115.2	4.7	116.8	1.4	120.5	3.2	116.9	-3.0
1981	117.8	0.8	111.6	-5.3	109.4	-2.0	112.5	2.8	114.1	1.4	110.9	-2.8	109.9	-0.9	108.4	-1.4	105.5	-2.7	103.2	-2.2	101.6	-1.6	102.8	1.2
1982	102.9	0.1	101.7	-1.2	100.0	-1.7	102.4	2.4	102.9	0.5	102.4	-0.5	101.3	-1.1	98.2	-3.1	96.7	-1.5	94.6	-2.2	97.5	3.1	99.4	1.9
1983	100.2	0.8	100.5	0.3	100.5	0.0	105.5	5.0	104.8	-0.7	102.8	-1.9	104.1	1.3	110.3	6.0	118.0	7.0	117.7	-0.3	119.3	1.4	116.2	-2.6
1984	116.1	-0.1	109.4	-5.8	111.4	1.8	111.8	0.4	109.9	-1.7	106.7	-2.9	102.5	-3.9	101.3	-1.2	99.0	-2.3	95.8	-3.2	94.5	-1.4	94.1	-0.4
1985	93.7	-0.4	91.6	-2.2	89.7	-2.1	88.1	-1.8	86.3	-2.0	87.0	0.8	88.0	1.1	88.4	0.5	89.1	0.8	91.0	2.1	93.2	2.4	94.5	1.4
1986	95.6	1.2	94.1	-1.6	95.0	1.0	95.5	0.5	95.2	-0.3	95.5	0.3	94.4	-1.2	93.5	-1.0	95.7	2.4	92.5	-3.3	93.9	1.5	94.5	0.6
1987	93.8	-0.7	94.1	0.3	92.4	-1.8	93.8	1.5	98.4	4.9	99.9	1.5	99.4	-0.5	98.4	-1.0	99.9	1.5	100.3	0.4	104.8	4.5	107.3	2.4
1988	105.8	-1.4	102.9	-2.7	104.0	1.1	106.0	1.9	107.1	1.0	120.2	12.2	127.3	5.9	123.6	-2.9	125.4	1.5	125.5	0.1	123.3	-1.8	120.9	-1.9
1989	124.3	2.8	121.1	-2.6	122.0	0.7	119.0	-2.5	117.8	-1.0	114.9	-2.5	117.6	2.3	114.2	-2.9	115.3	1.0	112.3	-2.6	110.9	-1.2	110.3	-0.5
1990	110.7	0.4	106.1	-4.2	105.9	-0.2	106.2	0.3	109.1	2.7	107.4	-1.6	109.3	1.8	107.4	-1.7	107.7	0.3	108.0	0.3	105.6	-2.2	105.9	0.3
1991	104.5	-1.3	105.1	0.6	106.3	1.1	105.9	-0.4	105.8	-0.1	106.0	0.2	104.1	-1.8	107.9	3.7	109.0	1.0	108.7	-0.3	109.4	0.6	109.0	-0.4

[Continued]

Prepared Animal Feeds
Producer Price Index
Base 1982 = 100
[Continued]

For 1947-1995. Columns headed % show percentile change in the index from the previous period for which an index is available.

Year	Jan Index	%	Feb Index	%	Mar Index	%	Apr Index	%	May Index	%	Jun Index	%	Jul Index	%	Aug Index	%	Sep Index	%	Oct Index	%	Nov Index	%	Dec Index	%
1992	108.7	-0.3	108.9	0.2	109.3	0.4	107.9	-1.3	108.7	0.7	109.3	0.6	107.7	-1.5	106.9	-0.7	107.9	0.9	107.3	-0.6	107.3	0.0	109.6	2.1
1993	110.0	0.4	107.9	-1.9	107.0	-0.8	108.2	1.1	108.5	0.3	107.9	-0.6	113.2	4.9	114.9	1.5	112.6	-2.0	111.7	-0.8	113.3	1.4	116.2	2.6
1994	115.9	-0.3	116.6	0.6	116.0	-0.5	113.8	-1.9	113.2	-0.5	114.3	1.0	112.1	-1.9	109.4	-2.4	109.0	-0.4	107.1	-1.7	104.7	-2.2	103.9	-0.8
1995	104.1	0.2	102.8	-1.2	103.9	1.1	105.2	1.3	103.7	-1.4	104.7	1.0	105.7	1.0	108.4	2.6	110.2	1.7	114.8	4.2	120.9	5.3	125.3	3.6

Source: U.S. Department of Labor, Bureau of Labor Statistics, Division of Industry Prices and Price Indexes. n.e.c. stands for not elsewhere classified. - indicates no data collected for period or unavailable.

TEXTILE PRODUCTS AND APPAREL
Producer Price Index
Base 1982 = 100

For 1947-1995. Columns headed % show percentile change in the index from the previous period for which an index is available.

Year	Jan Index	%	Feb Index	%	Mar Index	%	Apr Index	%	May Index	%	Jun Index	%	Jul Index	%	Aug Index	%	Sep Index	%	Oct Index	%	Nov Index	%	Dec Index	%
1947	49.8	-	50.1	0.6	50.3	0.4	50.3	0.0	50.2	-0.2	50.0	-0.4	50.2	0.4	50.4	0.4	51.0	1.2	51.2	0.4	51.7	1.0	52.6	1.7
1948	53.2	1.1	53.5	0.6	53.4	-0.2	52.9	-0.9	53.1	0.4	52.8	-0.6	52.9	0.2	52.9	0.0	52.8	-0.2	52.6	-0.4	52.2	-0.8	52.1	-0.2
1949	51.0	-2.1	50.5	-1.0	49.8	-1.4	48.9	-1.8	47.8	-2.2	47.5	-0.6	47.3	-0.4	47.3	0.0	47.4	0.2	47.6	0.4	47.7	0.2	47.7	0.0
1950	47.7	0.0	47.8	0.2	47.7	-0.2	47.1	-1.3	47.0	-0.2	47.3	0.6	48.7	3.0	50.8	4.3	52.8	3.9	54.4	3.0	55.2	1.5	56.4	2.2
1951	58.0	2.8	58.6	1.0	58.7	0.2	58.5	-0.3	58.1	-0.7	57.2	-1.5	56.5	-1.2	54.9	-2.8	53.6	-2.4	52.6	-1.9	52.6	0.0	52.6	0.0
1952	52.3	-0.6	51.7	-1.1	50.9	-1.5	50.6	-0.6	50.3	-0.6	50.1	-0.4	50.1	0.0	50.2	0.2	50.4	0.4	50.2	-0.4	50.0	-0.4	49.8	-0.4
1953	50.1	0.6	49.9	-0.4	49.4	-1.0	49.3	-0.2	49.4	0.2	49.3	-0.2	49.4	0.2	49.4	0.0	49.1	-0.6	48.9	-0.4	48.7	-0.4	48.5	-0.4
1954	48.6	0.2	48.2	-0.8	48.1	-0.2	48.0	-0.2	48.0	0.0	48.1	0.2	48.2	0.2	48.2	0.0	48.2	0.0	48.3	0.2	48.2	-0.2	48.2	0.0
1955	48.2	0.0	48.2	0.0	48.2	0.0	48.1	-0.2	48.1	0.0	48.2	0.2	48.2	0.0	48.2	0.0	48.3	0.2	48.3	0.0	48.4	0.2	48.4	0.0
1956	48.4	0.0	48.6	0.4	48.5	-0.2	48.2	-0.6	48.1	-0.2	48.1	0.0	48.1	0.0	48.0	-0.2	48.0	0.0	48.2	0.4	48.3	0.2	48.4	0.2
1957	48.5	0.2	48.4	-0.2	48.3	-0.2	48.2	-0.2	48.3	0.2	48.3	0.0	48.3	0.0	48.3	0.0	48.3	0.0	48.2	-0.2	48.1	-0.2	48.1	0.0
1958	47.9	-0.4	47.7	-0.4	47.6	-0.2	47.5	-0.2	47.4	-0.2	47.3	-0.2	47.3	0.0	47.3	0.0	47.3	0.0	47.2	-0.2	47.2	0.0	47.3	0.2
1959	47.3	0.0	47.5	0.4	47.6	0.2	47.7	0.2	47.8	0.2	48.1	0.6	48.2	0.2	48.4	0.4	48.5	0.2	48.5	0.0	48.7	0.4	49.0	0.6
1960	48.9	-0.2	48.9	0.0	48.7	-0.4	48.7	0.0	48.7	0.0	48.7	0.0	48.7	0.0	48.6	-0.2	48.5	-0.2	48.5	0.0	48.3	-0.4	48.2	-0.2
1961	48.0	-0.4	48.0	0.0	47.8	-0.4	47.7	-0.2	47.6	-0.2	47.5	-0.2	47.6	0.2	47.7	0.2	47.8	0.2	48.0	0.4	48.0	0.0	48.1	0.2
1962	48.1	0.0	48.1	0.0	48.2	0.2	48.2	0.0	48.2	0.0	48.3	0.2	48.3	0.0	48.3	0.0	48.2	-0.2	48.2	0.0	48.2	0.0	48.2	0.0
1963	48.1	-0.2	48.1	0.0	48.0	-0.2	48.0	0.0	48.0	0.0	48.1	0.2	48.1	0.0	48.1	0.0	48.2	0.2	48.2	0.0	48.4	0.4	48.5	0.2
1964	48.5	0.0	48.5	0.0	48.5	0.0	48.4	-0.2	48.5	0.2	48.4	-0.2	48.4	0.0	48.5	0.2	48.5	0.0	48.6	0.2	48.6	0.0	48.6	0.0
1965	48.6	0.0	48.6	0.0	48.6	0.0	48.6	0.0	48.7	0.2	48.8	0.2	48.8	0.0	48.8	0.0	48.9	0.2	48.9	0.0	48.8	-0.2	48.9	0.2
1966	48.8	-0.2	48.9	0.2	48.9	0.0	49.0	0.2	49.0	0.0	49.0	0.0	49.1	0.2	49.1	0.0	49.0	-0.2	49.0	0.0	48.9	-0.2	48.8	-0.2
1967	48.9	0.2	48.9	0.0	48.8	-0.2	48.7	-0.2	48.6	-0.2	48.6	0.0	48.6	0.0	48.6	0.0	48.8	0.4	48.9	0.2	49.3	0.8	49.7	0.8
1968	50.0	0.6	50.1	0.2	50.2	0.2	50.2	0.0	50.3	0.2	50.5	0.4	50.7	0.4	50.9	0.4	51.1	0.4	51.3	0.4	51.5	0.4	51.4	-0.2
1969	51.6	0.4	51.5	-0.2	51.4	-0.2	51.4	0.0	51.4	0.0	51.7	0.6	51.9	0.4	52.1	0.4	52.1	0.0	52.2	0.2	52.3	0.2	52.2	-0.2
1970	52.4	0.4	52.3	-0.2	52.4	0.2	52.4	0.0	52.3	-0.2	52.4	0.2	52.4	0.0	52.4	0.0	52.4	0.0	52.3	-0.2	52.2	-0.2	52.2	0.0
1971	52.2	0.0	52.3	0.2	52.4	0.2	52.7	0.6	52.8	0.2	53.4	1.1	53.6	0.4	53.9	0.6	53.8	-0.2	53.8	0.0	53.9	0.2	54.3	0.7
1972	54.4	0.2	54.7	0.6	54.8	0.2	55.0	0.4	55.4	0.7	55.5	0.2	55.7	0.4	55.8	0.2	55.9	0.2	56.1	0.4	56.3	0.4	56.5	0.4
1973	57.0	0.9	57.4	0.7	58.2	1.4	59.0	1.4	59.8	1.4	60.5	1.2	60.7	0.3	61.2	0.8	62.0	1.3	62.8	1.3	63.5	1.1	64.2	1.1
1974	65.4	1.9	66.1	1.1	66.5	0.6	67.2	1.1	68.0	1.2	69.3	1.9	69.5	0.3	69.6	0.1	69.5	-0.1	68.7	-1.2	68.3	-0.6	67.7	-0.9
1975	67.2	-0.7	66.7	-0.7	65.7	-1.5	65.7	0.0	66.1	0.6	66.4	0.5	66.9	0.8	67.3	0.6	67.6	0.4	69.1	2.2	70.0	1.3	70.4	0.6
1976	71.2	1.1	71.5	0.4	71.7	0.3	72.0	0.4	72.0	0.0	72.5	0.7	72.8	0.4	73.1	0.4	72.8	-0.4	73.0	0.3	73.4	0.5	73.3	-0.1
1977	73.7	0.5	74.2	0.7	74.5	0.4	75.1	0.8	75.3	0.3	75.6	0.4	75.5	-0.1	75.6	0.1	75.8	0.3	75.9	0.1	75.9	0.0	76.2	0.4
1978	76.5	0.4	76.8	0.4	76.9	0.1	77.2	0.4	77.5	0.4	77.8	0.4	78.2	0.5	78.5	0.4	78.9	0.5	79.3	0.5	79.8	0.6	80.0	0.3
1979	80.2	0.3	80.3	0.1	80.8	0.6	81.4	0.7	81.7	0.4	82.3	0.7	82.8	0.6	83.4	0.7	83.7	0.4	84.1	0.5	84.5	0.5	84.6	0.1
1980	85.7	1.3	86.3	0.7	87.6	1.5	88.6	1.1	89.0	0.5	89.4	0.4	90.3	1.0	90.7	0.4	91.2	0.6	92.0	0.9	92.7	0.8	93.1	0.4
1981	94.4	1.4	94.8	0.4	95.4	0.6	96.6	1.3	97.4	0.8	97.8	0.4	98.4	0.6	98.9	0.5	99.2	0.3	99.7	0.5	99.5	-0.2	99.4	-0.1
1982	100.2	0.8	100.5	0.3	100.2	-0.3	100.4	0.2	100.4	0.0	100.2	-0.2	99.8	-0.4	99.8	0.0	99.9	0.1	99.8	-0.1	99.7	-0.1	99.0	-0.7
1983	99.1	0.1	99.0	-0.1	99.4	0.4	99.5	0.1	99.9	0.4	100.1	0.2	100.4	0.3	100.7	0.3	100.8	0.1	101.2	0.4	101.5	0.3	101.6	0.1
1984	101.8	0.2	102.5	0.7	102.6	0.1	102.6	0.0	102.9	0.3	102.8	-0.1	102.9	0.1	102.7	-0.2	103.0	0.3	102.9	-0.1	102.7	-0.2	102.6	-0.1
1985	102.8	0.2	103.0	0.2	102.9	-0.1	103.0	0.1	102.9	-0.1	102.8	-0.1	102.7	-0.1	102.9	0.2	102.8	-0.1	102.7	-0.1	102.9	0.2	103.0	0.1
1986	103.0	0.0	103.1	0.1	103.3	0.2	103.2	-0.1	103.2	0.0	103.2	0.0	103.3	0.1	103.2	-0.1	103.2	0.0	103.2	0.0	103.3	0.1	103.4	0.1
1987	103.6	0.2	103.7	0.1	103.9	0.2	104.2	0.3	104.4	0.2	104.8	0.4	105.3	0.5	105.6	0.3	106.0	0.4	106.4	0.4	106.6	0.2	107.0	0.4
1988	107.6	0.6	108.1	0.5	108.4	0.3	108.7	0.3	108.9	0.2	109.3	0.4	109.5	0.2	109.6	0.1	109.8	0.2	110.0	0.2	110.2	0.2	110.5	0.3
1989	111.0	0.5	111.3	0.3	111.2	-0.1	111.6	0.4	111.8	0.2	112.2	0.4	112.6	0.4	112.9	0.3	113.0	0.1	113.3	0.3	113.5	0.2	113.6	0.1
1990	114.6	0.9	114.6	0.0	114.7	0.1	114.9	0.2	114.8	-0.1	115.0	0.2	115.1	0.1	115.1	0.0	115.1	0.0	115.1	0.0	115.3	0.2	115.2	-0.1
1991	115.7	0.4	115.8	0.1	115.9	0.1	116.0	0.1	116.0	0.0	116.2	0.2	116.3	0.1	116.5	0.2	116.6	0.1	116.7	0.1	116.8	0.1	116.9	0.1

[Continued]

TEXTILE PRODUCTS AND APPAREL
Producer Price Index
Base 1982 = 100
[Continued]

For 1947-1995. Columns headed % show percentile change in the index from the previous period for which an index is available.

Year	Jan Index	%	Feb Index	%	Mar Index	%	Apr Index	%	May Index	%	Jun Index	%	Jul Index	%	Aug Index	%	Sep Index	%	Oct Index	%	Nov Index	%	Dec Index	%
1992	117.4	0.4	117.6	0.2	117.7	0.1	117.8	0.1	117.7	-0.1	117.9	0.2	117.8	-0.1	117.8	0.0	118.0	0.2	118.1	0.1	118.0	-0.1	118.0	0.0
1993	118.0	0.0	117.9	-0.1	117.9	0.0	118.1	0.2	118.0	-0.1	118.0	0.0	118.2	0.2	118.3	0.1	118.1	-0.2	118.1	0.0	118.0	-0.1	117.9	-0.1
1994	117.9	0.0	117.9	0.0	117.9	0.0	117.9	0.0	118.0	0.1	118.1	0.1	118.4	0.3	118.5	0.1	118.7	0.2	118.6	-0.1	118.6	0.0	118.8	0.2
1995	119.4	0.5	119.9	0.4	120.1	0.2	120.4	0.2	120.8	0.3	120.8	0.0	121.0	0.2	121.1	0.1	121.3	0.2	121.6	0.2	121.3	-0.2	121.5	0.2

Source: U.S. Department of Labor, Bureau of Labor Statistics, Division of Industry Prices and Price Indexes. n.e.c. stands for not elsewhere classified. - indicates no data collected for period or unavailable.

Synthetic Fibers
Producer Price Index
Base 1982 = 100

For 1975-1995. Columns headed % show percentile change in the index from the previous period for which an index is available.

Year	Jan Index	%	Feb Index	%	Mar Index	%	Apr Index	%	May Index	%	Jun Index	%	Jul Index	%	Aug Index	%	Sep Index	%	Oct Index	%	Nov Index	%	Dec Index	%
1975	-	-	-	-	-	-	-	-	-	-	-	-	-	-	-	-	-	-	-	-	-	-	61.7	-
1976	62.8	1.8	63.1	0.5	63.0	-0.2	63.5	0.8	63.4	-0.2	63.2	-0.3	63.3	0.2	63.7	0.6	63.6	-0.2	62.8	-1.3	62.7	-0.2	62.7	0.0
1977	63.2	0.8	63.8	0.9	63.7	-0.2	65.7	3.1	66.1	0.6	67.4	2.0	67.2	-0.3	67.4	0.3	67.5	0.1	67.4	-0.1	67.4	0.0	67.4	0.0
1978	67.9	0.7	67.8	-0.1	67.8	0.0	67.4	-0.6	67.6	0.3	67.2	-0.6	67.2	0.0	67.3	0.1	67.3	0.0	67.5	0.3	68.2	1.0	68.2	0.0
1979	69.7	2.2	70.0	0.4	70.1	0.1	71.0	1.3	72.4	2.0	73.1	1.0	73.8	1.0	74.4	0.8	76.2	2.4	76.9	0.9	76.6	-0.4	76.9	0.4
1980	78.4	2.0	78.5	0.1	79.6	1.4	80.5	1.1	82.2	2.1	83.0	1.0	83.9	1.1	84.8	1.1	86.1	1.5	86.5	0.5	86.8	0.3	86.9	0.1
1981	90.4	4.0	90.7	0.3	91.9	1.3	93.5	1.7	96.5	3.2	97.4	0.9	98.5	1.1	99.5	1.0	99.3	-0.2	100.4	1.1	99.7	-0.7	99.6	-0.1
1982	100.5	0.9	100.7	0.2	99.5	-1.2	100.6	1.1	100.8	0.2	100.5	-0.3	99.6	-0.9	100.1	0.5	100.3	0.2	99.4	-0.9	99.5	0.1	98.5	-1.0
1983	96.7	-1.8	94.5	-2.3	95.0	0.5	94.9	-0.1	96.0	1.2	96.2	0.2	97.7	1.6	97.2	-0.5	97.5	0.3	99.1	1.6	98.3	-0.8	97.5	-0.8
1984	98.3	0.8	99.6	1.3	99.2	-0.4	99.1	-0.1	99.1	0.0	99.0	-0.1	98.8	-0.2	98.7	-0.1	98.2	-0.5	97.6	-0.6	97.2	-0.4	97.3	0.1
1985	97.2	-0.1	97.2	0.0	96.6	-0.6	97.1	0.5	96.9	-0.2	96.5	-0.4	95.4	-1.1	95.5	0.1	95.6	0.1	92.4	-3.3	92.8	0.4	93.0	0.2
1986	93.6	0.6	93.5	-0.1	93.5	0.0	92.4	-1.2	92.3	-0.1	92.1	-0.2	92.5	0.4	92.3	-0.2	92.2	-0.1	91.7	-0.5	91.7	0.0	91.6	-0.1
1987	92.1	0.5	91.4	-0.8	91.3	-0.1	90.8	-0.5	90.8	0.0	91.0	0.2	91.4	0.4	91.7	0.3	91.9	0.2	92.8	1.0	93.3	0.5	93.6	0.3
1988	94.4	0.9	94.7	0.3	95.1	0.4	96.3	1.3	97.0	0.7	96.6	-0.4	97.6	1.0	98.0	0.4	98.6	0.6	99.4	0.8	99.4	0.0	99.9	0.5
1989	100.6	0.7	101.1	0.5	101.6	0.5	104.1	2.5	105.0	0.9	106.2	1.1	106.5	0.3	106.2	-0.3	105.9	-0.3	107.1	1.1	106.7	-0.4	106.9	0.2
1990	106.9	0.0	107.3	0.4	107.4	0.1	106.6	-0.7	106.7	0.1	106.4	-0.3	107.5	1.0	107.1	-0.4	107.2	0.1	105.4	-1.7	105.8	0.4	106.0	0.2
1991	106.8	0.8	106.9	0.1	106.6	-0.3	105.5	-1.0	105.3	-0.2	105.3	0.0	105.1	-0.2	105.0	-0.1	105.0	0.0	104.2	-0.8	104.0	-0.2	103.5	-0.5
1992	103.1	-0.4	103.6	0.5	103.5	-0.1	104.2	0.7	103.4	-0.8	103.9	0.5	103.9	0.0	103.6	-0.3	103.2	-0.4	103.3	0.1	102.4	-0.9	102.5	0.1
1993	102.6	0.1	102.3	-0.3	102.4	0.1	102.8	0.4	102.9	0.1	103.5	0.6	103.8	0.3	105.1	1.3	104.5	-0.6	104.4	-0.1	104.2	-0.2	104.2	0.0
1994	103.8	-0.4	103.5	-0.3	103.1	-0.4	103.0	-0.1	103.2	0.2	103.4	0.2	104.6	1.2	105.6	1.0	105.9	0.3	104.8	-1.0	104.2	-0.6	104.3	0.1
1995	106.8	2.4	107.0	0.2	106.4	-0.6	108.4	1.9	108.6	0.2	108.4	-0.2	109.6	1.1	111.0	1.3	110.5	-0.5	110.9	0.4	110.3	-0.5	111.6	1.2

Source: U.S. Department of Labor, Bureau of Labor Statistics, Division of Industry Prices and Price Indexes. n.e.c. stands for not elsewhere classified. - indicates no data collected for period or unavailable.

Processed Yarns and Threads
Producer Price Index
Base 1982 = 100

For 1975-1995. Columns headed % show percentile change in the index from the previous period for which an index is available.

Year	Jan Index	%	Feb Index	%	Mar Index	%	Apr Index	%	May Index	%	Jun Index	%	Jul Index	%	Aug Index	%	Sep Index	%	Oct Index	%	Nov Index	%	Dec Index	%
1975	-	-	-	-	-	-	-	-	-	-	-	-	-	-	-	-	-	-	-	-	-	-	72.3	-
1976	73.4	1.5	73.3	-0.1	72.8	-0.7	71.8	-1.4	71.6	-0.3	72.1	0.7	73.1	1.4	72.1	-1.4	71.5	-0.8	70.9	-0.8	70.5	-0.6	70.3	-0.3
1977	70.0	-0.4	70.5	0.7	71.4	1.3	73.4	2.8	74.0	0.8	74.8	1.1	74.8	0.0	74.3	-0.7	73.8	-0.7	73.2	-0.8	72.6	-0.8	72.7	0.1
1978	72.8	0.1	73.1	0.4	73.2	0.1	73.1	-0.1	73.0	-0.1	73.5	0.7	73.7	0.3	74.0	0.4	74.7	0.9	75.2	0.7	76.2	1.3	75.7	-0.7
1979	76.2	0.7	76.2	0.0	77.4	1.6	77.2	-0.3	78.0	1.0	78.5	0.6	79.2	0.9	80.0	1.0	80.8	1.0	81.0	0.2	81.4	0.5	81.5	0.1
1980	82.8	1.6	85.3	3.0	86.3	1.2	88.3	2.3	89.8	1.7	88.8	-1.1	88.5	-0.3	89.1	0.7	89.9	0.9	90.5	0.7	91.0	0.6	92.7	1.9
1981	93.9	1.3	94.2	0.3	97.3	3.3	97.6	0.3	100.2	2.7	100.7	0.5	101.5	0.8	102.7	1.2	102.9	0.2	104.4	1.5	101.5	-2.8	101.0	-0.5
1982	100.7	-0.3	101.7	1.0	101.6	-0.1	101.6	0.0	101.9	0.3	100.8	-1.1	98.3	-2.5	98.3	0.0	98.8	0.5	98.7	-0.1	98.9	0.2	98.9	0.0
1983	97.4	-1.5	97.7	0.3	98.2	0.5	98.3	0.1	99.3	1.0	99.5	0.2	100.2	0.7	101.4	1.2	101.4	0.0	102.2	0.8	102.5	0.3	103.3	0.8
1984	102.9	-0.4	104.1	1.2	104.1	0.0	103.8	-0.3	104.3	0.5	104.0	-0.3	103.9	-0.1	102.8	-1.1	102.8	0.0	102.3	-0.5	101.8	-0.5	101.8	0.0
1985	102.2	0.4	102.6	0.4	102.3	-0.3	102.2	-0.1	102.2	0.0	102.1	-0.1	102.2	0.1	101.9	-0.3	101.8	-0.1	101.8	0.0	101.8	0.0	101.6	-0.2
1986	101.3	-0.3	101.2	-0.1	101.3	0.1	101.9	0.6	101.7	-0.2	101.5	-0.2	101.7	0.2	102.1	0.4	102.3	0.2	101.9	-0.4	101.6	-0.3	102.1	0.5
1987	101.5	-0.6	101.3	-0.2	101.1	-0.2	101.6	0.5	102.6	1.0	103.4	0.8	104.3	0.9	104.8	0.5	105.3	0.5	106.2	0.9	106.4	0.2	106.9	0.5
1988	107.6	0.7	107.8	0.2	107.8	0.0	107.9	0.1	107.8	-0.1	108.1	0.3	108.2	0.1	108.0	-0.2	108.1	0.1	108.3	0.2	108.2	-0.1	108.5	0.3
1989	108.5	0.0	108.9	0.4	109.6	0.6	110.0	0.4	110.2	0.2	110.5	0.3	110.8	0.3	111.2	0.4	111.1	-0.1	111.4	0.3	111.7	0.3	111.4	-0.3
1990	113.1	1.5	113.4	0.3	113.4	0.0	113.6	0.2	113.6	0.0	113.8	0.2	112.4	-1.2	111.3	-1.0	111.2	-0.1	111.2	0.0	112.2	0.9	112.4	0.2
1991	112.8	0.4	112.7	-0.1	112.8	0.1	112.9	0.1	112.6	-0.3	113.1	0.4	113.1	0.0	112.4	-0.6	112.1	-0.3	112.0	-0.1	112.2	0.2	112.0	-0.2
1992	111.8	-0.2	111.6	-0.2	111.7	0.1	111.7	0.0	111.6	-0.1	111.7	0.1	110.1	-1.4	110.2	0.1	109.8	-0.4	109.7	-0.1	109.8	0.1	109.6	-0.2
1993	108.5	-1.0	108.2	-0.3	108.0	-0.2	107.9	-0.1	107.7	-0.2	107.9	0.2	107.9	0.0	107.7	-0.2	107.8	0.1	107.7	-0.1	107.3	-0.4	107.1	-0.2
1994	107.1	0.0	107.0	-0.1	107.1	0.1	107.2	0.1	107.3	0.1	108.4	1.0	109.1	0.6	108.9	-0.2	109.0	0.1	109.4	0.4	109.8	0.4	109.9	0.1
1995	110.6	0.6	111.1	0.5	112.0	0.8	112.2	0.2	113.1	0.8	113.2	0.1	112.9	-0.3	113.5	0.5	113.0	-0.4	113.6	0.5	113.8	0.2	113.6	-0.2

Source: U.S. Department of Labor, Bureau of Labor Statistics, Division of Industry Prices and Price Indexes. n.e.c. stands for not elsewhere classified. - indicates no data collected for period or unavailable.

Gray Fabrics
Producer Price Index
Base 1982 = 100

For 1975-1995. Columns headed % show percentile change in the index from the previous period for which an index is available.

Year	Jan Index	%	Feb Index	%	Mar Index	%	Apr Index	%	May Index	%	Jun Index	%	Jul Index	%	Aug Index	%	Sep Index	%	Oct Index	%	Nov Index	%	Dec Index	%
1975	-	-	-	-	-	-	-	-	-	-	-	-	-	-	-	-	-	-	-	-	-	-	68.8	-
1976	70.3	2.2	71.2	1.3	71.2	0.0	71.6	0.6	72.4	1.1	73.4	1.4	74.7	1.8	74.7	0.0	73.7	-1.3	73.9	0.3	75.1	1.6	74.1	-1.3
1977	73.0	-1.5	72.1	-1.2	71.9	-0.3	72.3	0.6	72.0	-0.4	71.9	-0.1	72.2	0.4	71.1	-1.5	70.9	-0.3	71.4	0.7	72.4	1.4	73.8	1.9
1978	75.0	1.6	75.7	0.9	77.2	2.0	78.4	1.6	80.7	2.9	81.1	0.5	82.0	1.1	83.2	1.5	85.5	2.8	87.1	1.9	87.2	0.1	86.7	-0.6
1979	86.4	-0.3	84.8	-1.9	84.7	-0.1	85.7	1.2	85.8	0.1	86.3	0.6	88.3	2.3	88.6	0.3	88.6	0.0	89.2	0.7	89.9	0.8	91.1	1.3
1980	91.3	0.2	91.1	-0.2	94.1	3.3	94.3	0.2	93.9	-0.4	92.7	-1.3	93.4	0.8	94.6	1.3	97.0	2.5	98.7	1.8	99.8	1.1	99.1	-0.7
1981	98.8	-0.3	99.1	0.3	99.6	0.5	100.9	1.3	100.4	-0.5	101.5	1.1	102.0	0.5	102.5	0.5	102.6	0.1	101.9	-0.7	101.4	-0.5	101.3	-0.1
1982	102.0	0.7	101.4	-0.6	100.9	-0.5	100.7	-0.2	100.4	-0.3	100.5	0.1	99.7	-0.8	99.5	-0.2	98.8	-0.7	98.9	0.1	98.5	-0.4	98.6	0.1
1983	99.4	0.8	99.3	-0.1	99.8	0.5	100.3	0.5	100.6	0.3	100.4	-0.2	100.6	0.2	101.0	0.4	101.4	0.4	102.9	1.5	104.2	1.3	104.6	0.4
1984	104.0	-0.6	105.2	1.2	105.4	0.2	105.3	-0.1	105.8	0.5	106.2	0.4	106.2	0.0	106.3	0.1	106.4	0.1	106.5	0.1	105.8	-0.7	106.0	0.2
1985	105.8	-0.2	105.0	-0.8	104.6	-0.4	104.4	-0.2	104.7	0.3	104.4	-0.3	104.0	-0.4	103.5	-0.5	103.5	0.0	104.0	0.5	104.2	0.2	104.3	0.1
1986	104.2	-0.1	104.1	-0.1	103.9	-0.2	104.1	0.2	103.9	-0.2	104.0	0.1	104.2	0.2	103.5	-0.7	102.9	-0.6	103.2	0.3	103.3	0.1	103.2	-0.1
1987	103.7	0.5	103.7	0.0	103.9	0.2	105.4	1.4	105.8	0.4	106.7	0.9	108.0	1.2	107.9	-0.1	109.3	1.3	110.3	0.9	110.8	0.5	111.1	0.3
1988	111.8	0.6	112.8	0.9	113.2	0.4	113.9	0.6	114.2	0.3	114.6	0.4	114.9	0.3	115.1	0.2	114.3	-0.7	114.2	-0.1	114.5	0.3	115.0	0.4
1989	115.5	0.4	113.9	-1.4	114.0	0.1	114.0	0.0	113.9	-0.1	114.5	0.5	115.5	0.9	115.7	0.2	115.8	0.1	116.5	0.6	116.5	0.0	116.7	0.2
1990	117.2	0.4	117.3	0.1	117.2	-0.1	117.3	0.1	117.2	-0.1	116.4	-0.7	117.6	1.0	117.2	-0.3	116.7	-0.4	116.8	0.1	117.5	0.6	117.8	0.3
1991	117.2	-0.5	116.7	-0.4	116.6	-0.1	116.6	0.0	116.8	0.2	116.6	-0.2	117.1	0.4	117.9	0.7	118.0	0.1	118.1	0.1	118.3	0.2	119.2	0.8
1992	119.8	0.5	120.2	0.3	120.3	0.1	120.7	0.3	121.2	0.4	121.5	0.2	121.5	0.0	121.2	-0.2	121.0	-0.2	120.5	-0.4	119.8	-0.6	120.1	0.3
1993	120.1	0.0	119.8	-0.2	119.5	-0.3	119.6	0.1	118.4	-1.0	119.0	0.5	118.8	-0.2	118.8	0.0	117.5	-1.1	118.1	0.5	117.0	-0.9	116.9	-0.1
1994	116.5	-0.3	116.3	-0.2	116.4	0.1	116.6	0.2	116.4	-0.2	116.4	0.0	116.3	-0.1	117.2	0.8	117.6	0.3	116.5	-0.9	117.2	0.6	117.7	0.4
1995	118.6	0.8	120.5	1.6	120.7	0.2	121.0	0.2	121.7	0.6	122.0	0.2	121.4	-0.5	121.4	0.0	123.5	1.7	121.8	-1.4	120.9	-0.7	121.6	0.6

Source: U.S. Department of Labor, Bureau of Labor Statistics, Division of Industry Prices and Price Indexes. n.e.c. stands for not elsewhere classified. - indicates no data collected for period or unavailable.

Finished Fabrics
Producer Price Index
Base 1982 = 100

For 1975-1995. Columns headed % show percentile change in the index from the previous period for which an index is available.

Year	Jan Index	%	Feb Index	%	Mar Index	%	Apr Index	%	May Index	%	Jun Index	%	Jul Index	%	Aug Index	%	Sep Index	%	Oct Index	%	Nov Index	%	Dec Index	%
1975	-	-	-	-	-	-	-	-	-	-	-	-	-	-	-	-	-	-	-	-	-	-	80.3	-
1976	79.8	-0.6	80.9	1.4	81.7	1.0	82.4	0.9	81.8	-0.7	81.4	-0.5	81.1	-0.4	81.2	0.1	80.7	-0.6	80.5	-0.2	81.4	1.1	81.5	0.1
1977	80.9	-0.7	81.7	1.0	82.7	1.2	83.7	1.2	84.3	0.7	84.2	-0.1	83.9	-0.4	83.9	0.0	83.8	-0.1	83.7	-0.1	83.1	-0.7	83.2	0.1
1978	83.2	0.0	83.3	0.1	82.7	-0.7	82.8	0.1	82.9	0.1	82.8	-0.1	82.9	0.1	83.0	0.1	83.6	0.7	83.9	0.4	84.2	0.4	85.1	1.1
1979	83.1	-2.4	83.6	0.6	84.6	1.2	85.0	0.5	85.9	1.1	86.4	0.6	86.9	0.6	87.5	0.7	87.6	0.1	87.4	-0.2	88.1	0.8	88.2	0.1
1980	88.7	0.6	89.2	0.6	90.9	1.9	91.9	1.1	92.6	0.8	93.0	0.4	93.6	0.6	93.8	0.2	93.9	0.1	95.0	1.2	95.6	0.6	96.5	0.9
1981	98.1	1.7	98.7	0.6	98.9	0.2	100.3	1.4	100.9	0.6	100.8	-0.1	101.1	0.3	101.8	0.7	101.8	0.0	101.7	-0.1	101.6	-0.1	100.8	-0.8
1982	101.8	1.0	102.1	0.3	100.8	-1.3	100.6	-0.2	100.5	-0.1	99.5	-1.0	99.4	-0.1	99.8	0.4	99.3	-0.5	98.9	-0.4	98.7	-0.2	98.6	-0.1
1983	98.1	-0.5	98.2	0.1	98.3	0.1	98.9	0.6	98.6	-0.3	98.3	-0.3	98.3	0.0	99.2	0.9	99.0	-0.2	99.4	0.4	99.9	0.5	100.2	0.3
1984	100.2	0.0	101.4	1.2	101.9	0.5	101.9	0.0	102.2	0.3	102.0	-0.2	101.9	-0.1	102.1	0.2	102.2	0.1	101.8	-0.4	101.7	-0.1	101.6	-0.1
1985	101.6	0.0	102.0	0.4	102.0	0.0	102.1	0.1	101.0	-1.1	100.9	-0.1	100.8	-0.1	101.1	0.3	101.3	0.2	101.3	0.0	101.2	-0.1	101.1	-0.1
1986	101.3	0.2	101.1	-0.2	101.3	0.2	101.3	0.0	101.5	0.2	101.5	0.0	101.6	0.1	101.6	0.0	101.4	-0.2	101.3	-0.1	101.3	0.0	101.3	0.0
1987	102.7	1.4	103.0	0.3	103.1	0.1	103.4	0.3	103.7	0.3	104.0	0.3	104.0	0.0	104.6	0.6	104.7	0.1	105.5	0.8	105.9	0.4	106.2	0.3
1988	106.9	0.7	108.2	1.2	109.0	0.7	109.2	0.2	109.3	0.1	109.6	0.3	109.4	-0.2	109.4	0.0	109.9	0.5	110.1	0.2	111.0	0.8	110.8	-0.2
1989	111.7	0.8	112.1	0.4	112.6	0.4	112.9	0.3	113.5	0.5	113.8	0.3	113.9	0.1	114.1	0.2	114.2	0.1	114.6	0.4	114.9	0.3	115.0	0.1
1990	115.5	0.4	115.6	0.1	115.7	0.1	116.0	0.3	115.9	-0.1	116.0	0.1	115.8	-0.2	115.8	0.0	115.8	0.0	116.4	0.5	116.4	0.0	116.5	0.1
1991	116.7	0.2	117.1	0.3	117.3	0.2	117.4	0.1	117.5	0.1	117.4	-0.1	117.6	0.2	117.8	0.2	118.0	0.2	117.9	-0.1	118.0	0.1	117.8	-0.2
1992	118.1	0.3	118.4	0.3	118.4	0.0	118.6	0.2	118.7	0.1	119.1	0.3	118.9	-0.2	119.0	0.1	119.0	0.0	119.2	0.2	119.3	0.1	119.2	-0.1
1993	119.4	0.2	119.4	0.0	119.4	0.0	119.5	0.1	120.0	0.4	119.8	-0.2	119.6	-0.2	119.5	-0.1	119.4	-0.1	119.4	0.0	119.3	-0.1	119.1	-0.2
1994	119.2	0.1	118.9	-0.3	118.9	0.0	119.2	0.3	119.2	0.0	119.2	0.0	119.1	-0.1	119.1	0.0	119.1	0.0	119.5	0.3	119.6	0.1	119.5	-0.1
1995	120.0	0.4	120.6	0.5	121.0	0.3	121.3	0.2	121.7	0.3	121.8	0.1	122.0	0.2	122.3	0.2	122.4	0.1	122.2	-0.2	122.1	-0.1	122.3	0.2

Source: U.S. Department of Labor, Bureau of Labor Statistics, Division of Industry Prices and Price Indexes. n.e.c. stands for not elsewhere classified. - indicates no data collected for period or unavailable.

Apparel & Other Fabricated Textile Products
Producer Price Index
Base 1982 = 100

For 1977-1995. Columns headed % show percentile change in the index from the previous period for which an index is available.

Year	Jan Index	%	Feb Index	%	Mar Index	%	Apr Index	%	May Index	%	Jun Index	%	Jul Index	%	Aug Index	%	Sep Index	%	Oct Index	%	Nov Index	%	Dec Index	%
1977	-	-	-	-	-	-	-	-	-	-	-	-	-	-	-	-	-	-	-	-	-	-	76.2	-
1978	76.5	0.4	76.7	0.3	76.9	0.3	77.1	0.3	77.3	0.3	77.8	0.6	78.2	0.5	78.4	0.3	78.3	-0.1	78.6	0.4	79.1	0.6	79.4	0.4
1979	80.1	0.9	80.4	0.4	80.8	0.5	81.4	0.7	81.4	0.0	82.1	0.9	82.2	0.1	82.8	0.7	83.1	0.4	83.4	0.4	83.8	0.5	83.7	-0.1
1980	85.0	1.6	85.6	0.7	86.6	1.2	87.5	1.0	87.6	0.1	88.6	1.1	89.7	1.2	90.0	0.3	90.1	0.1	90.6	0.6	91.3	0.8	91.6	0.3
1981	92.9	1.4	93.3	0.4	93.6	0.3	94.8	1.3	95.3	0.5	95.7	0.4	96.3	0.6	96.6	0.3	97.0	0.4	97.8	0.8	98.2	0.4	98.3	0.1
1982	99.3	1.0	99.6	0.3	99.8	0.2	100.1	0.3	100.1	0.0	100.3	0.2	100.1	-0.2	100.2	0.1	100.4	0.2	100.5	0.1	100.3	-0.2	99.4	-0.9
1983	100.0	0.6	100.1	0.1	100.5	0.4	100.3	-0.2	100.8	0.5	101.2	0.4	101.4	0.2	101.5	0.1	101.6	0.1	101.5	-0.1	101.8	0.3	101.7	-0.1
1984	102.2	0.5	102.4	0.2	102.5	0.1	102.6	0.1	102.8	0.2	102.6	-0.2	102.9	0.3	102.8	-0.1	103.3	0.5	103.3	0.0	103.4	0.1	103.2	-0.2
1985	103.5	0.3	103.7	0.2	103.8	0.1	104.0	0.2	104.0	0.0	104.0	0.0	104.2	0.2	104.5	0.3	104.4	-0.1	104.5	0.1	104.8	0.3	105.0	0.2
1986	105.0	0.0	105.3	0.3	105.6	0.3	105.4	-0.2	105.5	0.1	105.5	0.0	105.6	0.1	105.5	-0.1	105.6	0.1	105.8	0.2	105.9	0.1	105.9	0.0
1987	106.0	0.1	106.2	0.2	106.5	0.3	106.7	0.2	106.7	0.0	107.0	0.3	107.4	0.4	107.7	0.3	108.0	0.3	108.1	0.1	108.1	0.0	108.6	0.5
1988	109.1	0.5	109.3	0.2	109.6	0.3	109.7	0.1	109.9	0.2	110.4	0.5	110.7	0.3	110.8	0.1	111.1	0.3	111.2	0.1	111.3	0.1	111.6	0.3
1989	112.1	0.4	112.5	0.4	112.2	-0.3	112.4	0.2	112.5	0.1	112.6	0.1	113.0	0.4	113.4	0.4	113.6	0.2	113.7	0.1	114.0	0.3	114.2	0.2
1990	115.3	1.0	115.3	0.0	115.4	0.1	115.7	0.3	115.7	0.0	116.0	0.3	116.1	0.1	116.4	0.3	116.5	0.1	116.6	0.1	116.6	0.0	116.3	-0.3
1991	116.9	0.5	117.3	0.3	117.5	0.2	117.8	0.3	117.8	0.0	118.1	0.3	118.2	0.1	118.4	0.2	118.5	0.1	118.7	0.2	118.9	0.2	119.0	0.1
1992	119.8	0.7	120.0	0.2	120.2	0.2	120.2	0.0	120.1	-0.1	120.2	0.1	120.3	0.1	120.5	0.2	120.8	0.2	121.0	0.2	121.1	0.1	121.1	0.0
1993	121.3	0.2	121.3	0.0	121.4	0.1	121.5	0.1	121.6	0.1	121.3	-0.2	121.7	0.3	121.7	0.0	121.7	0.0	121.7	0.0	121.7	0.0	121.6	-0.1
1994	121.8	0.2	121.9	0.1	122.0	0.1	121.8	-0.2	122.0	0.2	121.8	-0.2	122.2	0.3	122.1	-0.1	122.2	0.1	122.3	0.1	122.2	-0.1	122.4	0.2
1995	122.6	0.2	122.8	0.2	123.1	0.2	122.9	-0.2	123.1	0.2	123.1	0.0	123.4	0.2	123.2	-0.2	123.4	0.2	124.1	0.6	123.6	-0.4	123.7	0.1

Source: U.S. Department of Labor, Bureau of Labor Statistics, Division of Industry Prices and Price Indexes. n.e.c. stands for not elsewhere classified. - indicates no data collected for period or unavailable.

Miscellaneous Textile Products/Services

Producer Price Index
Base June 1985 = 100

For 1985-1995. Columns headed % show percentile change in the index from the previous period for which an index is available.

Year	Jan Index	%	Feb Index	%	Mar Index	%	Apr Index	%	May Index	%	Jun Index	%	Jul Index	%	Aug Index	%	Sep Index	%	Oct Index	%	Nov Index	%	Dec Index	%
1985	-	-	-	-	-	-	-	-	-	-	100.0	-	99.7	-0.3	99.3	-0.4	99.2	-0.1	99.2	0.0	99.2	0.0	97.7	-1.5
1986	97.8	0.1	98.2	0.4	98.3	0.1	96.4	-1.9	96.6	0.2	96.5	-0.1	95.4	-1.1	94.1	-1.4	94.0	-0.1	95.2	1.3	96.2	1.1	97.5	1.4
1987	97.2	-0.3	97.8	0.6	97.8	0.0	97.8	0.0	97.7	-0.1	98.1	0.4	98.5	0.4	99.2	0.7	99.8	0.6	99.8	0.0	100.1	0.3	100.7	0.6
1988	102.7	2.0	103.4	0.7	104.3	0.9	104.9	0.6	105.0	0.1	105.2	0.2	105.3	0.1	105.3	0.0	105.2	-0.1	106.2	1.0	107.8	1.5	107.9	0.1
1989	109.3	1.3	109.8	0.5	109.6	-0.2	109.4	-0.2	109.5	0.1	110.9	1.3	113.6	2.4	113.8	0.2	113.9	0.1	113.7	-0.2	113.8	0.1	113.7	-0.1
1990	113.7	0.0	113.9	0.2	114.0	0.1	113.9	-0.1	113.6	-0.3	114.0	0.4	114.0	0.0	114.1	0.1	113.9	-0.2	113.9	0.0	114.3	0.4	114.3	0.0
1991	115.9	1.4	112.6	-2.8	112.0	-0.5	111.4	-0.5	111.7	0.3	111.9	0.2	111.7	-0.2	115.2	3.1	115.1	-0.1	114.6	-0.4	115.0	0.3	114.2	-0.7
1992	114.4	0.2	114.5	0.1	114.7	0.2	114.5	-0.2	114.7	0.2	114.8	0.1	114.8	0.0	114.8	0.0	115.3	0.4	115.3	0.0	115.3	0.0	115.3	0.0
1993	115.6	0.3	115.4	-0.2	115.5	0.1	115.9	0.3	115.7	-0.2	116.0	0.3	116.1	0.1	115.9	-0.2	116.2	0.3	116.4	0.2	116.2	-0.2	116.2	0.0
1994	116.4	0.2	116.6	0.2	117.1	0.4	117.0	-0.1	117.8	0.7	118.8	0.8	118.6	-0.2	118.3	-0.3	118.4	0.1	118.8	0.3	119.4	0.5	119.6	0.2
1995	120.2	0.5	120.8	0.5	122.2	1.2	123.0	0.7	124.1	0.9	124.1	0.0	124.3	0.2	124.6	0.2	124.5	-0.i	125.2	0.6	125.2	0.0	125.0	-0.2

Source: U.S. Department of Labor, Bureau of Labor Statistics, Division of Industry Prices and Price Indexes. n.e.c. stands for not elsewhere classified. - indicates no data collected for period or unavailable.

HIDES, SKINS, LEATHER, AND RELATED PRODUCTS
Producer Price Index
Base 1982 = 100

For 1926-1995. Columns headed % show percentile change in the index from the previous period for which an index is available.

Year	Jan Index	%	Feb Index	%	Mar Index	%	Apr Index	%	May Index	%	Jun Index	%	Jul Index	%	Aug Index	%	Sep Index	%	Oct Index	%	Nov Index	%	Dec Index	%
1926	17.6	-	17.3	-1.7	17.1	-1.2	16.9	-1.2	16.9	0.0	16.9	0.0	16.9	0.0	17.0	0.6	16.9	-0.6	17.2	1.8	17.1	-0.6	17.1	0.0
1927	17.2	0.6	17.1	-0.6	17.1	0.0	17.4	1.8	17.7	1.7	18.3	3.4	19.0	3.8	19.0	0.0	19.2	1.1	19.2	0.0	19.4	1.0	19.9	2.6
1928	20.6	3.5	21.1	2.4	21.1	0.0	21.6	2.4	21.5	-0.5	21.1	-1.9	21.1	0.0	20.6	-2.4	20.6	0.0	20.0	-2.9	19.7	-1.5	19.7	0.0
1929	19.3	-2.0	18.6	-3.6	18.4	-1.1	18.4	0.0	18.2	-1.1	18.4	1.1	18.6	1.1	18.7	0.5	18.9	1.1	18.8	-0.5	18.5	-1.6	18.4	-0.5
1930	17.9	-2.7	17.7	-1.1	17.6	-0.6	17.5	-0.6	17.5	0.0	17.5	0.0	17.2	-1.7	16.9	-1.7	17.0	0.6	16.5	-2.9	16.1	-2.4	15.6	-3.1
1931	15.1	-3.2	14.8	-2.0	14.9	0.7	14.9	0.0	14.9	0.0	15.0	0.7	15.3	2.0	15.1	-1.3	14.5	-4.0	14.1	-2.8	13.9	-1.4	13.6	-2.2
1932	13.5	-0.7	13.4	-0.7	13.2	-1.5	12.8	-3.0	12.4	-3.1	12.1	-2.4	11.7	-3.3	11.9	1.7	12.3	3.4	12.4	0.8	12.2	-1.6	11.9	-2.5
1933	11.8	-0.8	11.6	-1.7	11.6	0.0	11.8	1.7	13.1	11.0	14.1	7.6	14.7	4.3	15.6	6.1	15.8	1.3	15.2	-3.8	15.1	-0.7	15.2	0.7
1934	15.3	0.7	15.3	0.0	15.1	-1.3	15.2	0.7	15.0	-1.3	14.9	-0.7	14.7	-1.3	14.3	-2.7	14.4	0.7	14.3	-0.7	14.4	0.7	14.5	0.7
1935	14.7	1.4	14.7	0.0	14.6	-0.7	14.7	0.7	15.1	2.7	15.2	0.7	15.2	0.0	15.3	0.7	15.5	1.3	16.0	3.2	16.3	1.9	16.3	0.0
1936	16.6	1.8	16.4	-1.2	16.2	-1.2	16.1	-0.6	16.0	-0.6	16.0	0.0	16.0	0.0	16.0	0.0	16.1	0.6	16.3	1.2	16.5	1.2	17.0	3.0
1937	17.4	2.4	17.5	0.6	17.7	1.1	18.2	2.8	18.2	0.0	18.2	0.0	18.2	0.0	18.4	1.1	18.4	0.0	18.2	-1.1	17.3	-4.9	16.7	-3.5
1938	16.5	-1.2	16.2	-1.8	16.0	-1.2	15.7	-1.9	15.6	-0.6	15.4	-1.3	15.6	1.3	15.7	0.6	15.7	0.0	16.0	1.9	16.1	0.6	15.9	-1.2
1939	15.9	0.0	15.7	-1.3	15.6	-0.6	15.5	-0.6	15.6	0.6	15.8	1.3	15.8	0.0	15.8	0.0	16.8	6.3	17.9	6.5	17.7	-1.1	17.7	0.0
1940	17.7	0.0	17.5	-1.1	17.4	-0.6	17.4	0.0	17.3	-0.6	16.9	-2.3	16.9	0.0	16.5	-2.4	16.8	1.8	17.1	1.8	17.5	2.3	17.5	0.0
1941	17.5	0.0	17.4	-0.6	17.5	0.6	17.7	1.1	18.2	2.8	18.4	1.1	18.7	1.6	18.8	0.5	19.0	1.1	19.2	1.1	19.5	1.6	19.6	0.5
1942	19.6	0.0	19.7	0.5	19.9	1.0	20.4	2.5	20.3	-0.5	20.2	-0.5	20.2	0.0	20.2	0.0	20.1	-0.5	20.1	0.0	20.1	0.0	20.1	0.0
1943	20.1	0.0	20.1	0.0	20.1	0.0	20.1	0.0	20.1	0.0	20.1	0.0	20.1	0.0	20.1	0.0	20.1	0.0	20.1	0.0	19.9	-1.0	20.0	0.5
1944	20.0	0.0	20.0	0.0	20.0	0.0	20.0	0.0	20.0	0.0	19.9	-0.5	19.8	-0.5	19.8	0.0	19.8	0.0	19.8	0.0	19.8	0.0	20.0	0.0
1945	20.1	0.5	20.1	0.0	20.1	0.0	20.1	0.0	20.1	0.0	20.1	0.0	20.1	0.0	20.1	0.0	20.3	1.0	20.3	0.0	20.3	0.0	20.3	0.0
1946	20.4	0.5	20.4	0.0	20.4	0.0	20.4	0.0	20.6	1.0	20.9	1.5	24.1	15.3	23.7	-1.7	24.2	2.1	24.3	0.4	29.4	21.0	30.2	2.7
1947	30.1	-0.3	30.3	0.7	30.5	0.7	30.2	-1.0	30.0	-0.7	30.2	0.7	31.0	2.6	31.9	2.9	32.2	0.9	34.0	5.6	35.2	3.5	35.0	-0.6
1948	34.2	-2.3	32.6	-4.7	31.3	-4.0	31.7	1.3	32.2	1.6	32.1	-0.3	32.4	0.9	31.9	-1.5	31.6	-0.9	31.3	-0.9	31.9	1.9	31.6	-0.9
1949	31.5	-0.3	30.7	-2.5	30.2	-1.6	30.1	-0.3	30.0	-0.3	30.0	0.0	29.7	-1.0	30.0	1.0	30.4	1.3	30.7	1.0	30.8	0.3	30.7	-0.3
1950	30.2	-1.6	30.2	0.0	30.5	1.0	30.5	0.0	30.8	1.0	31.1	1.0	32.5	4.5	33.4	2.8	34.7	3.9	35.4	2.0	36.6	3.4	38.1	4.1
1951	39.9	4.7	40.1	0.5	39.8	-0.7	39.7	-0.3	39.6	-0.3	39.1	-1.3	38.4	-1.8	37.0	-3.6	37.0	0.0	35.7	-3.5	33.6	-5.9	33.0	-1.8
1952	32.1	-2.7	31.2	-2.8	30.8	-1.3	29.5	-4.2	29.7	0.7	30.1	1.3	30.2	0.3	30.3	0.3	30.3	0.0	30.3	0.0	30.7	1.3	31.1	1.3
1953	30.5	-1.9	30.8	1.0	30.8	0.0	30.7	-0.3	31.5	2.6	31.7	0.6	31.4	-0.9	31.4	0.0	31.3	-0.3	30.5	-2.6	30.5	0.0	30.0	-1.6
1954	29.9	-0.3	29.8	-0.3	29.7	-0.3	29.7	0.0	30.1	1.3	30.0	-0.3	29.8	-0.7	29.5	-1.0	29.2	-1.0	29.0	-0.7	29.1	0.3	28.8	-1.0
1955	28.8	0.0	29.0	0.7	28.9	-0.3	29.3	1.4	29.2	-0.3	29.2	0.0	29.4	0.7	29.4	0.0	29.5	0.3	29.9	1.4	30.2	1.0	30.3	0.3
1956	30.3	0.0	30.5	0.7	30.7	0.7	31.6	2.9	31.4	-0.6	31.4	0.0	31.4	0.0	31.4	0.0	31.4	0.0	31.3	-0.3	31.3	0.0	31.1	-0.6
1957	30.9	-0.6	30.8	-0.3	30.9	0.3	31.0	0.3	31.0	0.0	31.3	1.0	31.6	1.0	31.5	-0.3	31.4	-0.3	31.4	0.0	31.4	0.0	31.2	-0.6
1958	31.2	0.0	31.3	0.3	31.2	-0.3	31.3	0.3	31.4	0.3	31.5	0.3	31.5	0.0	31.5	0.0	31.4	-0.3	31.8	1.3	32.1	0.9	32.5	1.2
1959	32.7	0.6	33.1	1.2	34.1	3.0	37.0	8.5	37.2	0.5	37.3	0.3	37.5	0.5	37.6	0.3	37.4	-0.5	36.5	-2.4	35.1	-3.8	35.3	0.6
1960	35.4	0.3	35.1	-0.8	35.1	0.0	35.2	0.3	34.9	-0.9	34.6	-0.9	34.6	0.0	34.1	-1.4	33.9	-0.6	34.1	0.6	34.1	0.0	34.2	0.3
1961	34.0	-0.6	33.9	-0.3	34.3	1.2	34.5	0.6	34.8	0.9	34.6	-0.6	34.9	0.9	35.5	1.7	35.6	0.3	35.8	0.6	35.7	-0.3	35.6	-0.3
1962	35.6	0.0	35.4	-0.6	35.3	-0.3	35.1	-0.6	35.3	0.6	35.5	0.6	35.3	-0.6	35.2	-0.3	35.3	0.3	35.3	0.0	35.3	0.0	35.1	-0.6
1963	34.8	-0.9	34.6	-0.6	34.6	0.0	34.3	-0.9	34.5	0.6	34.3	-0.6	34.3	0.0	34.1	-0.6	33.9	-0.6	34.0	0.3	34.0	0.0	33.8	-0.6
1964	33.8	0.0	33.7	-0.3	33.7	0.0	34.3	1.8	34.4	0.3	34.5	0.3	34.6	0.3	34.7	0.3	34.6	-0.3	34.8	0.6	34.7	-0.3	34.6	-0.3
1965	34.5	-0.3	34.6	0.3	34.8	0.6	35.0	0.6	35.3	0.9	35.4	0.3	35.8	1.1	36.9	3.1	36.6	-0.8	37.2	1.6	37.4	0.5	37.7	0.8
1966	38.2	1.3	38.7	1.3	39.0	0.8	39.6	1.5	40.4	2.0	40.4	0.0	40.4	0.0	39.9	-1.2	39.4	-1.3	39.0	-1.0	38.6	-1.0	38.6	0.0
1967	38.8	0.5	38.8	0.0	38.5	-0.8	38.0	-1.3	37.9	-0.3	38.0	0.3	37.9	-0.3	37.5	-1.1	37.7	0.5	37.7	0.0	38.0	0.8	38.2	0.5
1968	38.3	0.3	38.4	0.3	38.8	1.0	38.9	0.3	39.1	0.5	39.0	-0.3	39.3	0.8	39.3	0.0	39.7	1.0	40.2	1.3	40.2	0.0	40.4	0.5
1969	40.6	0.5	40.6	0.0	40.6	0.0	41.5	2.2	41.5	0.0	41.3	-0.5	41.6	0.7	41.7	0.2	42.3	1.4	42.0	-0.7	42.0	0.0	41.8	-0.5
1970	42.0	0.5	42.0	0.0	42.0	0.0	42.3	0.7	42.1	-0.5	41.8	-0.7	41.8	0.0	41.8	0.0	41.8	0.0	42.0	0.5	42.2	0.5	42.0	-0.5

[Continued]

HIDES, SKINS, LEATHER, AND RELATED PRODUCTS
Producer Price Index
Base 1982 = 100
[Continued]

For 1926-1995. Columns headed % show percentile change in the index from the previous period for which an index is available.

Year	Jan Index	%	Feb Index	%	Mar Index	%	Apr Index	%	May Index	%	Jun Index	%	Jul Index	%	Aug Index	%	Sep Index	%	Oct Index	%	Nov Index	%	Dec Index	%
1971	42.6	1.4	42.8	0.5	42.8	0.0	43.4	1.4	43.6	0.5	43.5	-0.2	43.5	0.0	43.6	0.2	43.7	0.2	43.7	0.0	43.8	0.2	44.2	0.9
1972	44.9	1.6	45.4	1.1	46.8	3.1	48.4	3.4	49.3	1.9	49.8	1.0	50.1	0.6	51.3	2.4	51.7	0.8	53.2	2.9	54.8	3.0	54.1	-1.3
1973	54.8	1.3	55.2	0.7	54.6	-1.1	55.2	1.1	54.1	-2.0	53.6	-0.9	53.8	0.4	54.4	1.1	54.7	0.6	54.7	0.0	54.5	-0.4	54.0	-0.9
1974	54.3	0.6	54.6	0.6	54.6	0.0	55.4	1.5	55.7	0.5	55.6	-0.2	55.8	0.4	55.7	-0.2	56.4	1.3	55.3	-2.0	55.0	-0.5	54.5	-0.9
1975	54.1	-0.7	54.0	-0.2	54.5	0.9	56.2	3.1	56.2	0.0	56.6	0.7	56.8	0.4	56.9	0.2	57.6	1.2	58.0	0.7	58.8	1.4	58.9	0.2
1976	60.2	2.2	61.2	1.7	62.0	1.3	63.3	2.1	64.8	2.4	64.0	-1.2	64.9	1.4	65.3	0.6	66.1	1.2	65.1	-1.5	64.6	-0.8	65.3	1.1
1977	66.8	2.3	67.3	0.7	67.7	0.6	68.5	1.2	69.3	1.2	68.3	-1.4	68.5	0.3	68.6	0.1	68.4	-0.3	68.2	-0.3	68.5	0.4	69.1	0.9
1978	70.8	2.5	71.3	0.7	71.5	0.3	73.1	2.2	73.7	0.8	74.3	0.8	75.1	1.1	78.1	4.0	80.2	2.7	81.1	1.1	82.1	1.2	82.3	0.2
1979	85.1	3.4	88.4	3.9	96.5	9.2	98.6	2.2	102.6	4.1	102.0	-0.6	99.7	-2.3	98.2	-1.5	95.6	-2.6	96.7	1.2	94.8	-2.0	94.9	0.1
1980	97.3	2.5	95.5	-1.8	94.0	-1.6	92.7	-1.4	91.6	-1.2	91.7	0.1	93.3	1.7	95.7	2.6	94.3	-1.5	95.6	1.4	97.2	1.7	97.8	0.6
1981	98.3	0.5	98.1	-0.2	99.4	1.3	100.3	0.9	100.4	0.1	99.6	-0.8	99.4	-0.2	99.5	0.1	99.6	0.1	99.0	-0.6	98.9	-0.1	99.2	0.3
1982	99.7	0.5	99.6	-0.1	99.2	-0.4	100.3	1.1	100.2	-0.1	99.7	-0.5	100.2	0.5	99.8	-0.4	100.3	0.5	100.2	-0.1	100.2	0.0	100.6	0.4
1983	101.5	0.9	100.6	-0.9	100.9	0.3	101.8	0.9	102.6	0.8	103.3	0.7	103.7	0.4	104.6	0.9	104.5	-0.1	104.2	-0.3	105.5	1.2	105.6	0.1
1984	106.3	0.7	107.9	1.5	109.2	1.2	109.2	0.0	109.9	0.6	110.5	0.5	110.0	-0.5	109.9	-0.1	109.9	0.0	109.5	-0.4	108.1	-1.3	108.0	-0.1
1985	108.0	0.0	108.0	0.0	107.5	-0.5	108.4	0.8	108.2	-0.2	108.7	0.5	108.4	-0.3	109.0	0.6	109.3	0.3	109.9	0.5	110.4	0.5	111.3	0.8
1986	111.8	0.4	112.0	0.2	111.8	-0.2	112.3	0.4	112.9	0.5	113.4	0.4	113.2	-0.2	113.1	-0.1	112.9	-0.2	113.4	0.4	114.0	0.5	114.8	0.7
1987	114.9	0.1	115.0	0.1	116.5	1.3	118.3	1.5	120.7	2.0	120.2	-0.4	121.0	0.7	121.3	0.2	123.0	1.4	124.1	0.9	124.3	0.2	125.7	1.1
1988	128.4	2.1	129.1	0.5	132.6	2.7	134.2	1.2	134.6	0.3	131.2	-2.5	130.1	-0.8	131.6	1.2	132.5	0.7	131.9	-0.5	130.4	-1.1	130.1	-0.2
1989	131.2	0.8	133.2	1.5	136.8	2.7	136.1	-0.5	134.8	-1.0	135.2	0.3	136.9	1.3	137.2	0.2	138.0	0.6	138.2	0.1	138.0	-0.1	139.5	1.1
1990	138.9	-0.4	141.7	2.0	141.6	-0.1	142.9	0.9	143.7	0.6	143.0	-0.5	142.8	-0.1	142.2	-0.4	141.4	-0.6	140.9	-0.4	140.5	-0.3	140.6	0.1
1991	140.2	-0.3	140.0	-0.1	140.4	0.3	141.1	0.5	140.4	-0.5	140.0	-0.3	138.3	-1.2	138.1	-0.1	136.6	-1.1	136.3	-0.2	137.1	0.6	137.6	0.4
1992	138.6	0.7	139.0	0.3	139.8	0.6	139.9	0.1	140.7	0.6	140.8	0.1	140.1	-0.5	140.8	0.5	140.9	0.1	141.0	0.1	140.6	-0.3	142.0	1.0
1993	143.6	1.1	142.5	-0.8	142.9	0.3	143.6	0.5	143.8	0.1	143.7	-0.1	143.5	-0.1	143.9	0.3	144.1	0.1	143.7	-0.3	144.1	0.3	144.4	0.2
1994	145.1	0.5	143.8	-0.9	144.6	0.6	146.1	1.0	146.7	0.4	147.2	0.3	148.7	1.0	149.0	0.2	150.8	1.2	153.2	1.6	153.7	0.3	153.5	-0.1
1995	154.1	0.4	155.2	0.7	156.2	0.6	156.1	-0.1	157.8	1.1	155.0	-1.8	154.9	-0.1	153.2	-1.1	151.7	-1.0	150.5	-0.8	149.2	-0.9	149.4	0.1

Source: U.S. Department of Labor, Bureau of Labor Statistics, Division of Industry Prices and Price Indexes. n.e.c. stands for not elsewhere classified. - indicates no data collected for period or unavailable.

Hides and Skins
Producer Price Index
Base 1982 = 100

For 1926-1995. Columns headed % show percentile change in the index from the previous period for which an index is available.

Year	Jan Index	%	Feb Index	%	Mar Index	%	Apr Index	%	May Index	%	Jun Index	%	Jul Index	%	Aug Index	%	Sep Index	%	Oct Index	%	Nov Index	%	Dec Index	%
1926	23.1	-	21.3	-7.8	20.0	-6.1	18.7	-6.5	19.4	3.7	19.3	-0.5	19.9	3.1	20.6	3.5	19.6	-4.9	21.7	10.7	21.1	-2.8	21.1	0.0
1927	21.5	1.9	20.8	-3.3	20.9	0.5	22.1	5.7	23.4	5.9	25.3	8.1	27.3	7.9	26.8	-1.8	26.3	-1.9	26.2	-0.4	26.9	2.7	27.9	3.7
1928	30.9	10.8	32.4	4.9	32.2	-0.6	34.2	6.2	33.6	-1.8	31.7	-5.7	31.8	0.3	28.8	-9.4	29.0	0.7	26.6	-8.3	26.6	0.0	26.8	0.8
1929	25.4	-5.2	21.7	-14.6	22.1	1.8	22.1	0.0	21.4	-3.2	22.6	5.6	23.4	3.5	24.0	2.6	24.8	3.3	24.1	-2.8	22.3	-7.5	22.0	-1.3
1930	21.3	-3.2	20.2	-5.2	19.6	-3.0	19.6	0.0	19.8	1.0	20.2	2.0	19.2	-5.0	18.6	-3.1	19.2	3.2	17.1	-10.9	15.4	-9.9	14.1	-8.4
1931	13.2	-6.4	11.8	-10.6	12.7	7.6	12.7	0.0	12.8	0.8	13.4	4.7	14.9	11.2	14.1	-5.4	12.0	-14.9	10.2	-15.0	10.0	-2.0	10.0	0.0
1932	10.0	0.0	9.5	-5.0	9.1	-4.2	8.3	-8.8	7.3	-12.0	6.6	-9.6	6.9	4.5	8.0	15.9	9.9	23.7	10.1	2.0	9.5	-5.9	8.5	-10.5
1933	8.8	3.5	8.4	-4.5	8.5	1.2	9.4	10.6	13.8	46.8	16.6	20.3	18.1	9.0	18.7	3.3	17.2	-8.0	14.5	-15.7	14.4	-0.7	15.2	5.6
1934	15.8	3.9	16.0	1.3	15.0	-6.3	15.7	4.7	15.0	-4.5	14.3	-4.7	13.6	-4.9	11.7	-14.0	12.3	5.1	12.2	-0.8	12.9	5.7	13.8	7.0
1935	14.5	5.1	14.2	-2.1	13.6	-4.2	14.5	6.6	15.6	7.6	16.0	2.6	16.3	1.9	16.4	0.6	17.1	4.3	19.0	11.1	19.7	3.7	19.7	0.0
1936	20.6	4.6	19.8	-3.9	18.6	-6.1	18.4	-1.1	17.8	-3.3	18.2	2.2	17.9	-1.6	18.4	2.8	19.1	3.8	19.8	3.7	20.7	4.5	22.6	9.2
1937	23.7	4.9	23.5	-0.8	24.2	3.0	24.8	2.5	24.0	-3.2	23.4	-2.5	23.8	1.7	24.9	4.6	24.6	-1.2	24.0	-2.4	19.3	-19.6	17.5	-9.3
1938	16.8	-4.0	15.3	-8.9	14.2	-7.2	12.8	-9.9	13.0	1.6	12.8	-1.5	14.5	13.3	15.4	6.2	15.5	0.6	16.8	8.4	17.5	4.2	16.1	-8.0
1939	16.0	-0.6	14.9	-6.9	15.1	1.3	14.0	-7.3	14.7	5.0	15.4	4.8	15.8	2.6	15.8	0.0	19.9	25.9	23.0	15.6	21.3	-7.4	21.5	0.9
1940	21.0	-2.3	19.8	-5.7	19.3	-2.5	19.4	0.5	18.8	-3.1	16.7	-11.2	17.3	3.6	15.8	-8.7	17.2	8.9	19.2	11.6	20.7	7.8	20.3	-1.9
1941	20.2	-0.5	19.4	-4.0	20.3	4.6	21.4	5.4	22.6	5.6	23.0	1.8	23.0	0.0	22.9	-0.4	22.9	0.0	23.1	0.9	23.3	0.9	23.7	1.7
1942	23.6	-0.4	23.6	0.0	23.8	0.8	25.3	6.3	24.8	-2.0	24.2	-2.4	24.2	0.0	24.3	0.4	24.1	-0.8	23.7	-1.7	23.7	0.0	23.7	0.0
1943	23.7	0.0	23.7	0.0	23.7	0.0	23.7	0.0	23.7	0.0	23.7	0.0	23.7	0.0	23.7	0.0	23.7	0.0	23.7	0.0	22.2	-6.3	22.8	2.7
1944	23.1	1.3	22.7	-1.7	22.7	0.0	22.7	0.0	22.9	0.9	22.2	-3.1	21.9	-1.4	21.6	-1.4	21.7	0.5	22.0	1.4	21.9	-0.5	23.3	6.4
1945	23.5	0.9	23.6	0.4	23.8	0.8	23.9	0.4	23.9	0.0	24.0	0.4	24.0	0.0	24.1	0.4	24.1	0.0	24.0	-0.4	24.0	0.0	24.0	0.0
1946	24.0	0.0	24.0	0.0	24.0	0.0	24.0	0.0	24.7	2.9	24.8	0.4	34.6	39.5	31.8	-8.1	31.0	-2.5	31.3	1.0	45.2	44.4	44.2	-2.2
1947	40.6	-8.1	42.7	5.2	43.8	2.6	41.4	-5.5	39.9	-3.6	41.7	4.5	46.1	10.6	49.6	7.6	50.4	1.6	55.6	10.3	60.5	8.8	58.7	-3.0
1948	53.7	-8.5	46.8	-12.8	39.3	-16.0	42.0	6.9	45.0	7.1	44.6	-0.9	46.6	4.5	44.4	-4.7	42.9	-3.4	41.3	-3.7	44.6	8.0	43.1	-3.4
1949	43.2	0.2	38.7	-10.4	37.0	-4.4	37.2	0.5	37.2	0.0	37.7	1.3	36.0	-4.5	38.0	5.6	40.0	5.3	40.8	2.0	40.5	-0.7	38.9	-4.0
1950	37.4	-3.9	37.0	-1.1	38.4	3.8	38.1	-0.8	39.0	2.4	41.2	5.6	45.1	9.5	46.6	3.3	52.6	12.9	52.5	-0.2	54.7	4.2	57.1	4.4
1951	61.5	7.7	58.8	-4.4	58.5	-0.5	57.0	-2.6	56.8	-0.4	56.5	-0.5	54.1	-4.2	49.5	-8.5	48.6	-1.8	47.8	-1.6	38.2	-20.1	35.7	-6.5
1952	30.4	-14.8	27.8	-8.6	26.0	-6.5	21.7	-16.5	25.4	17.1	26.0	2.4	27.0	3.8	28.1	4.1	28.1	0.0	28.4	1.1	30.2	6.3	30.8	2.0
1953	27.1	-12.0	29.0	7.0	28.3	-2.4	29.0	2.5	32.6	12.4	33.3	2.1	32.0	-3.9	32.6	1.9	32.4	-0.6	28.1	-13.3	28.0	-0.4	25.2	-10.0
1954	24.8	-1.6	24.2	-2.4	24.4	0.8	24.6	0.8	27.3	11.0	26.5	-2.9	25.4	-4.2	24.4	-3.9	22.5	-7.8	21.6	-4.0	23.0	6.5	20.7	-10.0
1955	21.6	4.3	22.5	4.2	22.1	-1.8	24.8	12.2	23.2	-6.5	24.3	4.7	25.4	4.5	25.7	1.2	26.6	3.5	27.2	2.3	26.3	-3.3	26.7	1.5
1956	24.7	-7.5	25.4	2.8	25.5	0.4	27.0	5.9	25.8	-4.4	26.7	3.5	26.4	-1.1	26.4	0.0	27.6	4.5	25.2	-8.7	25.8	2.4	23.5	-8.9
1957	22.7	-3.4	21.9	-3.5	22.2	1.4	22.6	1.8	24.4	8.0	25.9	6.1	27.1	4.6	26.8	-1.1	25.4	-5.2	24.8	-2.4	23.5	-5.2	22.0	-6.4
1958	22.1	0.5	22.3	0.9	22.3	0.0	23.2	4.0	24.2	4.3	24.9	2.9	25.4	2.0	26.4	3.9	25.8	-2.3	27.0	4.7	28.4	5.2	29.0	2.1
1959	30.0	3.4	31.8	6.0	38.3	20.4	47.4	23.8	43.0	-9.3	46.6	8.4	47.0	0.9	46.6	-0.9	44.7	-4.1	38.2	-14.5	29.3	-23.3	32.2	9.9
1960	32.2	0.0	30.4	-5.6	31.4	3.3	32.1	2.2	31.8	-0.9	29.3	-7.9	29.7	1.4	27.8	-6.4	27.2	-2.2	28.0	2.9	28.7	2.5	28.3	-1.4
1961	26.9	-4.9	26.4	-1.9	30.0	13.6	29.7	-1.0	31.0	4.4	29.7	-4.2	33.3	12.1	36.2	8.7	36.0	-0.6	35.9	-0.3	34.7	-3.3	33.3	-4.0
1962	32.6	-2.1	31.2	-4.3	30.7	-1.6	30.6	-0.3	31.2	2.0	32.1	2.9	30.8	-4.0	31.1	1.0	32.8	5.5	32.2	-1.8	31.7	-1.6	30.1	-5.0
1963	28.2	-6.3	25.4	-9.9	26.1	2.8	25.1	-3.8	25.9	3.2	25.4	-1.9	24.7	-2.8	23.8	-3.6	22.9	-3.8	23.8	3.9	24.5	2.9	22.6	-7.8
1964	22.5	-0.4	21.9	-2.7	22.4	2.3	26.1	16.5	25.4	-2.7	26.7	5.1	27.4	2.6	28.4	3.6	28.3	-0.4	28.2	-0.4	26.8	-5.0	26.7	-0.4
1965	25.6	-4.1	26.7	4.3	27.3	2.2	28.5	4.4	31.3	9.8	30.5	-2.6	34.7	13.8	39.5	13.8	37.0	-6.3	37.2	0.5	37.4	0.5	39.1	4.5
1966	41.4	5.9	45.2	9.2	43.7	-3.3	44.0	0.7	48.2	9.5	47.6	-1.2	46.3	-2.7	41.8	-9.7	39.7	-5.0	35.7	-10.1	33.8	-5.3	32.3	-4.4
1967	32.6	0.9	31.9	-2.1	29.3	-8.2	26.1	-10.9	25.8	-1.1	28.4	10.1	27.7	-2.5	25.7	-7.2	27.6	7.4	25.7	-6.9	26.9	4.7	26.8	-0.4
1968	26.1	-2.6	26.8	2.7	29.7	10.8	28.3	-4.7	29.0	2.5	28.2	-2.8	30.0	6.4	30.4	1.3	31.6	3.9	31.2	-1.3	31.7	1.6	31.6	-0.3
1969	32.3	2.2	31.4	-2.8	32.3	2.9	37.2	15.2	36.3	-2.4	34.7	-4.4	36.4	4.9	36.4	0.0	38.1	4.7	34.9	-8.4	32.7	-6.3	32.2	-1.5
1970	30.4	-5.6	29.9	-1.6	29.4	-1.7	31.6	7.5	30.1	-4.7	27.8	-7.6	26.9	-3.2	27.4	1.9	27.8	1.5	28.8	3.6	30.4	5.6	28.4	-6.6

[Continued]

Hides and Skins
Producer Price Index
Base 1982 = 100
[Continued]

For 1926-1995. Columns headed % show percentile change in the index from the previous period for which an index is available.

Year	Jan Index	%	Feb Index	%	Mar Index	%	Apr Index	%	May Index	%	Jun Index	%	Jul Index	%	Aug Index	%	Sep Index	%	Oct Index	%	Nov Index	%	Dec Index	%
1971	27.6	-2.8	29.3	6.2	29.4	0.3	33.8	15.0	33.9	0.3	31.8	-6.2	31.8	0.0	31.9	0.3	32.8	2.8	32.7	-0.3	34.3	4.9	35.8	4.4
1972	37.9	5.9	41.5	9.5	48.5	16.9	52.6	8.5	55.8	6.1	56.9	2.0	59.2	4.0	67.7	14.4	68.0	0.4	75.5	11.0	80.0	6.0	71.1	-11.1
1973	76.4	7.5	76.0	-0.5	68.7	-9.6	75.3	9.6	70.7	-6.1	67.3	-4.8	68.7	2.1	72.9	6.1	71.7	-1.6	71.4	-0.4	66.8	-6.4	63.4	-5.1
1974	61.6	-2.8	61.9	0.5	56.2	-9.2	58.9	4.8	60.9	3.4	57.7	-5.3	60.1	4.2	57.0	-5.2	54.3	-4.7	44.9	-17.3	43.6	-2.9	38.1	-12.6
1975	34.8	-8.7	34.1	-2.0	38.6	13.2	48.5	25.6	47.6	-1.9	50.9	6.9	52.1	2.4	52.0	-0.2	53.6	3.1	56.0	4.5	58.3	4.1	57.2	-1.9
1976	62.6	9.4	64.0	2.2	66.8	4.4	75.4	12.9	79.7	5.7	72.8	-8.7	77.7	6.7	79.4	2.2	81.4	2.5	70.1	-13.9	64.6	-7.8	70.0	8.4
1977	77.8	11.1	78.8	1.3	79.7	1.1	85.0	6.6	87.3	2.7	80.5	-7.8	81.3	1.0	80.4	-1.1	76.5	-4.9	74.3	-2.9	76.2	2.6	81.4	6.8
1978	83.7	2.8	83.1	-0.7	82.5	-0.7	89.4	8.4	89.7	0.3	96.6	7.7	100.5	4.0	111.7	11.1	121.4	8.7	119.3	-1.7	116.2	-2.6	111.9	-3.7
1979	126.2	12.8	138.8	10.0	178.3	28.5	179.0	0.4	185.9	3.9	170.3	-8.4	157.9	-7.3	142.7	-9.6	129.7	-9.1	133.5	2.9	124.8	-6.5	123.7	-0.9
1980	130.7	5.7	112.9	-13.6	97.2	-13.9	91.6	-5.8	80.8	-11.8	88.0	8.9	99.4	13.0	111.1	11.8	99.3	-10.6	106.4	7.2	114.0	7.1	109.5	-3.9
1981	105.2	-3.9	102.4	-2.7	-	-	-	-	107.4	4.9	102.6	-4.5	100.8	-1.8	102.0	1.2	103.5	1.5	103.5	0.0	103.0	-0.5	105.9	2.8
1982	107.7	1.7	107.5	-0.2	102.4	-4.7	104.5	2.1	104.7	0.2	103.2	-1.4	99.3	-3.8	96.7	-2.6	95.6	-1.1	92.7	-3.0	90.2	-2.7	95.4	5.8
1983	95.3	-0.1	94.3	-1.0	94.5	0.2	99.3	5.1	109.2	10.0	109.1	-0.1	110.8	1.6	116.9	5.5	116.4	-0.4	115.1	-1.1	127.1	10.4	130.0	2.3
1984	134.1	3.2	141.4	5.4	146.3	3.5	145.8	-0.3	150.0	2.9	150.9	0.6	150.2	-0.5	149.1	-0.7	150.6	1.0	145.0	-3.7	129.7	-10.6	133.0	2.5
1985	125.4	-5.7	119.3	-4.9	114.3	-4.2	125.6	9.9	126.4	0.6	123.6	-2.2	120.5	-2.5	124.8	3.6	124.8	0.0	129.6	3.8	133.7	3.2	144.8	8.3
1986	144.4	-0.3	145.0	0.4	143.4	-1.1	148.3	3.4	149.7	0.9	151.6	1.3	150.0	-1.1	144.5	-3.7	142.0	-1.7	146.6	3.2	151.7	3.5	154.7	2.0
1987	152.5	-1.4	153.6	0.7	160.7	4.6	171.8	6.9	189.2	10.1	185.4	-2.0	182.9	-1.3	183.3	0.2	188.0	2.6	195.2	3.8	196.4	0.6	199.9	1.8
1988	210.2	5.2	208.7	-0.7	225.6	8.1	234.2	3.8	234.6	0.2	208.6	-11.1	188.8	-9.5	199.5	5.7	205.0	2.8	193.9	-5.4	181.9	-6.2	178.0	-2.1
1989	181.2	1.8	190.3	5.0	228.1	19.9	222.3	-2.5	207.8	-6.5	211.2	1.6	221.3	4.8	214.3	-3.2	217.1	1.3	218.8	0.8	216.9	-0.9	225.8	4.1
1990	203.8	-9.7	227.4	11.6	220.1	-3.2	234.4	6.5	233.0	-0.6	227.8	-2.2	227.4	-0.2	217.2	-4.5	210.3	-3.2	207.2	-1.5	204.0	-1.5	202.6	-0.7
1991	196.8	-2.9	190.6	-3.2	188.1	-1.3	198.1	5.3	184.0	-7.1	174.2	-5.3	166.6	-4.4	161.4	-3.1	152.1	-5.8	154.4	1.5	160.1	3.7	163.9	2.4
1992	164.5	0.4	168.5	2.4	168.4	-0.1	175.3	4.1	180.2	2.8	174.8	-3.0	171.5	-1.9	171.7	0.1	176.8	3.0	178.2	0.8	175.2	-1.7	183.0	4.5
1993	188.1	2.8	178.1	-5.3	180.6	1.4	185.8	2.9	186.6	0.4	181.6	-2.7	185.1	1.9	178.9	-3.3	187.1	4.6	183.9	-1.7	186.3	1.3	188.1	1.0
1994	184.6	-1.9	180.3	-2.3	183.4	1.7	196.4	7.1	199.1	1.4	198.1	-0.5	207.8	4.9	210.0	1.1	217.2	3.4	235.9	8.6	234.1	-0.8	229.1	-2.1
1995	227.1	-0.9	229.6	1.1	238.1	3.7	229.7	-3.5	243.0	5.8	222.6	-8.4	223.3	0.3	212.4	-4.9	204.9	-3.5	191.0	-6.8	181.6	-4.9	182.4	0.4

Source: U.S. Department of Labor, Bureau of Labor Statistics, Division of Industry Prices and Price Indexes. n.e.c. stands for not elsewhere classified. - indicates no data collected for period or unavailable.

Leather

Producer Price Index
Base 1982 = 100

For 1926-1995. Columns headed % show percentile change in the index from the previous period for which an index is available.

Year	Jan Index	%	Feb Index	%	Mar Index	%	Apr Index	%	May Index	%	Jun Index	%	Jul Index	%	Aug Index	%	Sep Index	%	Oct Index	%	Nov Index	%	Dec Index	%
1926	16.4	-	16.4	0.0	16.4	0.0	16.4	0.0	16.1	-1.8	16.1	0.0	16.0	-0.6	16.0	0.0	16.1	0.6	16.1	0.0	16.1	0.0	16.1	0.0
1927	16.1	0.0	16.1	0.0	16.2	0.6	16.2	0.0	16.7	3.1	17.4	4.2	18.3	5.2	18.5	1.1	18.7	1.1	18.9	1.1	18.9	0.0	19.8	4.8
1928	20.0	1.0	20.9	4.5	20.9	0.0	21.0	0.5	21.0	0.0	20.6	-1.9	20.8	1.0	20.8	0.0	20.4	-1.9	20.1	-1.5	19.2	-4.5	19.3	0.5
1929	19.5	1.0	18.9	-3.1	18.2	-3.7	18.0	-1.1	17.9	-0.6	17.9	0.0	18.1	1.1	18.0	-0.6	18.2	1.1	18.5	1.6	18.3	-1.1	17.9	-2.2
1930	17.5	-2.2	17.4	-0.6	17.4	0.0	17.0	-2.3	16.9	-0.6	16.6	-1.8	16.2	-2.4	16.2	0.0	15.9	-1.9	15.6	-1.9	15.1	-3.2	14.8	-2.0
1931	14.7	-0.7	14.4	-2.0	14.3	-0.7	14.3	0.0	14.2	-0.7	14.2	0.0	14.5	2.1	14.6	0.7	13.5	-7.5	13.0	-3.7	12.7	-2.3	12.7	0.0
1932	12.5	-1.6	12.4	-0.8	11.9	-4.0	10.9	-8.4	9.8	-10.1	9.5	-3.1	9.7	2.1	9.7	0.0	10.2	5.2	10.4	2.0	10.0	-3.8	9.5	-5.0
1933	9.2	-3.2	8.9	-3.3	9.0	1.1	9.2	2.2	11.0	19.6	12.0	9.1	12.6	5.0	13.3	5.6	13.8	3.8	13.5	-2.2	12.8	-5.2	12.9	0.8
1934	12.9	0.0	12.9	0.0	12.9	0.0	12.7	-1.6	12.3	-3.1	12.2	-0.8	12.1	-0.8	11.5	-5.0	11.4	-0.9	11.4	0.0	11.5	0.9	11.6	0.9
1935	12.0	3.4	12.0	0.0	12.0	0.0	12.1	0.8	12.9	6.6	13.0	0.8	13.0	0.0	13.0	0.0	13.4	3.1	14.0	4.5	14.2	1.4	14.2	0.0
1936	14.1	-0.7	13.9	-1.4	13.7	-1.4	13.6	-0.7	13.6	0.0	13.5	-0.7	13.4	-0.7	13.3	-0.7	13.6	2.3	13.8	1.5	14.3	3.6	15.0	4.9
1937	15.2	1.3	15.4	1.3	15.7	1.9	16.3	3.8	16.3	0.0	16.0	-1.8	16.0	0.0	16.2	1.3	16.0	-1.2	15.7	-1.9	15.0	-4.5	14.0	-6.7
1938	14.0	0.0	13.6	-2.9	13.5	-0.7	13.3	-1.5	13.3	0.0	13.2	-0.8	13.3	0.8	13.3	0.0	13.3	0.0	13.7	3.0	14.0	2.2	13.9	-0.7
1939	13.7	-1.4	13.6	-0.7	13.4	-1.5	13.4	0.0	13.4	0.0	13.6	1.5	13.6	0.0	13.6	0.0	14.9	9.6	15.8	6.0	15.8	0.0	15.4	-2.5
1940	15.5	0.6	15.2	-1.9	15.1	-0.7	15.1	0.0	15.1	0.0	14.9	-1.3	14.8	-0.7	14.3	-3.4	14.4	0.7	14.7	2.1	15.1	2.7	15.2	0.7
1941	15.3	0.7	15.3	0.0	15.3	0.0	15.4	0.7	15.7	1.9	15.8	0.6	15.9	0.6	15.9	0.0	16.2	1.9	16.3	0.6	16.4	0.6	16.4	0.0
1942	16.4	0.0	16.4	0.0	16.4	0.0	16.4	0.0	16.4	0.0	16.4	0.0	16.4	0.0	16.4	0.0	16.4	0.0	16.4	0.0	16.4	0.0	16.4	0.0
1943	16.4	0.0	16.4	0.0	16.4	0.0	16.4	0.0	16.4	0.0	16.4	0.0	16.4	0.0	16.4	0.0	16.4	0.0	16.4	0.0	16.4	0.0	16.4	0.0
1944	16.4	0.0	16.4	0.0	16.4	0.0	16.4	0.0	16.4	0.0	16.4	0.0	16.4	0.0	16.4	0.0	16.4	0.0	16.4	0.0	16.4	0.0	16.4	0.0
1945	16.4	0.0	16.4	0.0	16.4	0.0	16.4	0.0	16.4	0.0	16.4	0.0	16.4	0.0	16.4	0.0	16.8	2.4	16.8	0.0	16.8	0.0	16.8	0.0
1946	16.8	0.0	16.8	0.0	16.8	0.0	16.8	0.0	16.8	0.0	17.9	6.5	21.5	20.1	21.6	0.5	22.4	3.7	22.4	0.0	28.8	28.6	29.9	3.8
1947	29.2	-2.3	29.5	1.0	29.8	1.0	29.6	-0.7	29.2	-1.4	29.6	1.4	30.1	1.7	30.7	2.0	31.9	3.9	35.6	11.6	36.5	2.5	35.2	-3.6
1948	33.6	-4.5	30.5	-9.2	29.2	-4.3	29.7	1.7	30.3	2.0	30.4	0.3	30.4	0.0	29.1	-4.3	28.5	-2.1	28.5	0.0	29.8	4.6	29.2	-2.0
1949	29.2	0.0	27.9	-4.5	27.4	-1.8	27.1	-1.1	27.0	-0.4	27.1	0.4	26.7	-1.5	27.2	1.9	27.8	2.2	28.5	2.5	28.5	0.0	28.4	-0.4
1950	28.1	-1.1	27.9	-0.7	28.3	1.4	28.5	0.7	28.8	1.1	29.2	1.4	32.5	11.3	33.2	2.2	34.5	3.9	35.1	1.7	36.3	3.4	38.8	6.9
1951	40.8	5.2	40.9	0.2	40.9	0.0	40.9	0.0	40.8	-0.2	39.4	-3.4	37.9	-3.8	35.2	-7.1	35.7	1.4	32.7	-8.4	29.8	-8.9	29.3	-1.7
1952	28.8	-1.7	26.6	-7.6	26.0	-2.3	25.1	-3.5	25.1	0.0	26.4	5.2	26.5	0.4	26.5	0.0	26.5	0.0	26.7	0.8	26.8	0.4	27.6	3.0
1953	27.3	-1.1	27.3	0.0	27.7	1.5	27.5	-0.7	28.9	5.1	29.1	0.7	28.5	-2.1	28.2	-1.1	28.1	-0.4	26.8	-4.6	26.8	0.0	26.3	-1.9
1954	26.1	-0.8	26.0	-0.4	25.6	-1.5	25.5	-0.4	26.0	2.0	26.0	0.0	25.7	-1.2	25.1	-2.3	24.6	-2.0	24.4	-0.8	24.3	-0.4	24.2	-0.4
1955	24.1	-0.4	24.4	1.2	24.4	0.0	24.8	1.6	25.2	1.6	24.9	-1.2	25.3	1.6	25.2	-0.4	25.3	0.4	25.6	1.2	26.0	1.6	26.2	0.8
1956	26.6	1.5	26.7	0.4	27.0	1.1	28.1	4.1	27.6	-1.8	27.2	-1.4	27.2	0.0	27.0	-0.7	27.0	0.0	27.0	0.0	26.9	-0.4	27.0	0.4
1957	26.2	-3.0	26.0	-0.8	26.3	1.2	26.3	0.0	26.3	0.0	27.0	2.7	27.4	1.5	27.2	-0.7	27.2	0.0	27.1	-0.4	27.1	0.0	27.0	-0.4
1958	26.9	-0.4	26.9	0.0	27.0	0.4	27.0	0.0	27.0	0.0	27.3	1.1	27.2	-0.4	27.2	0.0	27.1	-0.4	27.6	1.8	28.1	1.8	29.5	5.0
1959	29.5	0.0	30.0	1.7	30.7	2.3	35.7	16.3	37.0	3.6	35.7	-3.5	35.2	-1.4	34.8	-1.1	34.8	0.0	33.3	-4.3	30.8	-7.5	30.7	-0.3
1960	31.3	2.0	31.1	-0.6	30.5	-1.9	31.1	2.0	30.7	-1.3	30.6	-0.3	30.4	-0.7	29.4	-3.3	28.9	-1.7	29.1	0.7	28.8	-1.0	29.5	2.4
1961	29.0	-1.7	28.9	-0.3	29.8	3.1	30.4	2.0	30.9	1.6	30.4	-1.6	30.4	0.0	31.6	3.9	32.0	1.3	32.5	1.6	32.2	-0.9	32.2	0.0
1962	32.3	0.3	32.2	-0.3	31.9	-0.9	31.9	0.0	32.2	0.9	32.0	-0.6	31.6	-1.2	31.1	-1.6	31.0	-0.3	31.0	0.0	31.1	0.3	30.9	-0.6
1963	30.6	-1.0	30.5	-0.3	30.2	-1.0	29.9	-1.0	30.1	0.7	29.8	-1.0	29.8	0.0	29.2	-2.0	29.0	-0.7	29.0	0.0	29.0	0.0	29.0	0.0
1964	29.0	0.0	29.0	0.0	29.0	0.0	29.7	2.4	30.4	2.4	30.1	-1.0	30.5	1.3	30.4	-0.3	30.3	-0.3	30.5	0.7	30.3	-0.7	30.3	0.0
1965	30.4	0.3	30.1	-1.0	30.8	2.3	30.2	-1.9	30.4	0.7	31.3	3.0	30.8	-1.6	32.8	6.5	32.3	-1.5	32.6	0.9	33.0	1.2	33.2	0.6
1966	33.9	2.1	34.4	1.5	35.9	4.4	35.6	-0.8	36.4	2.2	36.9	1.4	36.7	-0.5	36.4	-0.8	35.5	-2.5	34.2	-3.7	33.2	-2.9	33.8	1.8
1967	34.0	0.6	33.9	-0.3	33.4	-1.5	32.9	-1.5	32.3	-1.8	32.1	-0.6	31.9	-0.6	31.1	-2.5	30.7	-1.3	30.5	-0.7	31.0	1.6	31.8	2.6
1968	31.6	-0.6	31.7	0.3	32.1	1.3	32.5	1.2	32.8	0.9	32.9	0.3	33.1	0.6	33.1	0.0	33.2	0.3	33.5	0.9	33.1	-1.2	33.7	1.8
1969	34.0	0.9	33.9	-0.3	33.9	0.0	35.6	5.0	35.4	-0.6	35.4	0.0	35.3	-0.3	35.2	-0.3	35.4	0.6	35.0	-1.1	34.8	-0.6	34.8	0.0
1970	34.8	0.0	34.1	-2.0	34.4	0.9	35.1	2.0	35.1	0.0	34.9	-0.6	34.9	0.0	34.6	-0.9	34.0	-1.7	34.4	1.2	34.5	0.3	34.5	0.0

[Continued]

Leather
Producer Price Index
Base 1982 = 100
[Continued]

For 1926-1995. Columns headed % show percentile change in the index from the previous period for which an index is available.

Year	Jan Index	%	Feb Index	%	Mar Index	%	Apr Index	%	May Index	%	Jun Index	%	Jul Index	%	Aug Index	%	Sep Index	%	Oct Index	%	Nov Index	%	Dec Index	%
1971	34.8	0.9	34.9	0.3	34.9	0.0	35.6	2.0	36.3	2.0	36.7	1.1	36.7	0.0	36.7	0.0	36.6	-0.3	36.7	0.3	36.7	0.0	37.8	3.0
1972	38.5	1.9	38.7	0.5	41.3	6.7	44.4	7.5	44.3	-0.2	44.5	0.5	44.3	-0.4	45.1	1.8	46.1	2.2	49.2	6.7	52.2	6.1	52.1	-0.2
1973	52.3	0.4	52.3	0.0	52.8	1.0	51.8	-1.9	51.3	-1.0	50.2	-2.1	50.4	0.4	50.6	0.4	52.3	3.4	51.6	-1.3	51.5	-0.2	50.1	-2.7
1974	50.0	-0.2	49.8	-0.4	50.3	1.0	50.9	1.2	51.2	0.6	50.3	-1.8	49.9	-0.8	49.6	-0.6	49.9	0.6	48.7	-2.4	47.4	-2.7	46.7	-1.5
1975	45.3	-3.0	44.6	-1.5	45.5	2.0	48.7	7.0	49.2	1.0	49.2	0.0	49.0	-0.4	48.7	-0.6	49.5	1.6	49.8	0.6	52.2	4.8	52.3	0.2
1976	53.0	1.3	55.5	4.7	57.5	3.6	59.0	2.6	65.3	10.7	61.4	-6.0	61.7	0.5	63.1	2.3	63.4	0.5	62.0	-2.2	61.5	-0.8	61.6	0.2
1977	64.1	4.1	64.7	0.9	64.7	0.0	65.6	1.4	67.7	3.2	65.0	-4.0	63.8	-1.8	64.3	0.8	64.4	0.2	63.1	-2.0	63.2	0.2	64.4	1.9
1978	67.7	5.1	68.1	0.6	69.1	1.5	69.8	1.0	69.8	0.0	69.8	0.0	72.1	3.3	80.9	12.2	86.5	6.9	86.5	0.0	89.5	3.5	89.8	0.3
1979	94.0	4.7	99.3	5.6	119.4	20.2	126.4	5.9	137.9	9.1	133.2	-3.4	123.7	-7.1	117.5	-5.0	106.0	-9.8	110.3	4.1	102.7	-6.9	104.3	1.6
1980	111.6	7.0	109.3	-2.1	99.9	-8.6	95.6	-4.3	93.3	-2.4	91.3	-2.1	93.8	2.7	100.9	7.6	95.7	-5.2	97.0	1.4	101.9	5.1	106.8	4.8
1981	106.8	0.0	99.6	-6.7	103.6	4.0	108.5	4.7	106.0	-2.3	103.1	-2.7	102.4	-0.7	100.8	-1.6	100.6	-0.2	100.7	0.1	100.0	-0.7	100.3	0.3
1982	102.5	2.2	102.0	-0.5	100.6	-1.4	99.7	-0.9	99.5	-0.2	98.8	-0.7	98.7	-0.1	97.9	-0.8	99.3	1.4	99.4	0.1	100.5	1.1	101.0	0.5
1983	101.0	0.0	100.5	-0.5	101.6	1.1	102.9	1.3	104.9	1.9	107.9	2.9	108.5	0.6	110.3	1.7	109.0	-1.2	108.1	-0.8	109.4	1.2	110.5	1.0
1984	111.2	0.6	116.3	4.6	121.4	4.4	124.2	2.3	125.5	1.0	124.6	-0.7	123.1	-1.2	121.4	-1.4	119.3	-1.7	118.6	-0.6	115.5	-2.6	113.8	-1.5
1985	115.0	1.1	113.2	-1.6	111.9	-1.1	112.5	0.5	112.6	0.1	112.1	-0.4	112.0	-0.1	112.5	0.4	113.0	0.4	114.0	0.9	115.6	1.4	116.3	0.6
1986	118.4	1.8	118.4	0.0	118.5	0.1	118.9	0.3	123.2	3.6	126.6	2.8	125.4	-0.9	125.8	0.3	124.7	-0.9	122.7	-1.6	124.2	1.2	127.8	2.9
1987	128.1	0.2	129.4	1.0	131.9	1.9	137.5	4.2	140.5	2.2	143.1	1.9	142.3	-0.6	141.0	-0.9	145.6	3.3	148.6	2.1	149.6	0.7	153.0	2.3
1988	158.0	3.3	160.1	1.3	171.1	6.9	175.1	2.3	176.4	0.7	165.0	-6.5	165.7	0.4	168.2	1.5	168.8	0.4	170.7	1.1	166.0	-2.8	164.9	-0.7
1989	166.6	1.0	169.4	1.7	170.2	0.5	168.2	-1.2	166.7	-0.9	168.0	0.8	171.4	2.0	171.5	0.1	172.5	0.6	172.9	0.2	173.0	0.1	174.0	0.6
1990	176.6	1.5	178.0	0.8	177.7	-0.2	179.5	1.0	181.2	0.9	179.6	-0.9	179.0	-0.3	177.3	-0.9	176.5	-0.5	175.4	-0.6	174.9	-0.3	174.7	-0.1
1991	174.3	-0.2	173.7	-0.3	172.6	-0.6	172.1	-0.3	172.7	0.3	171.7	-0.6	167.7	-2.3	165.8	-1.1	163.4	-1.4	161.5	-1.2	162.4	0.6	162.8	0.2
1992	161.3	-0.9	161.8	0.3	163.4	1.0	162.8	-0.4	163.9	0.7	164.0	0.1	164.7	0.4	163.7	-0.6	164.8	0.7	165.1	0.2	164.0	-0.7	165.1	0.7
1993	166.6	0.9	169.0	1.4	169.0	0.0	168.3	-0.4	169.7	0.8	168.7	-0.6	167.2	-0.9	168.7	0.9	169.0	0.2	168.6	-0.2	168.9	0.2	169.1	0.1
1994	171.2	1.2	171.0	-0.1	172.9	1.1	173.6	0.4	174.9	0.7	178.5	2.1	180.7	1.2	181.2	0.3	184.4	1.8	186.8	1.3	189.4	1.4	190.4	0.5
1995	192.2	0.9	194.7	1.3	195.2	0.3	198.4	1.6	199.5	0.6	195.3	-2.1	193.9	-0.7	190.0	-2.0	186.0	-2.1	184.4	-0.9	182.5	-1.0	181.8	-0.4

Source: U.S. Department of Labor, Bureau of Labor Statistics, Division of Industry Prices and Price Indexes. n.e.c. stands for not elsewhere classified. - indicates no data collected for period or unavailable.

Footwear
Producer Price Index
Base 1982 = 100

For 1926-1995. Columns headed % show percentile change in the index from the previous period for which an index is available.

Year	Jan Index	%	Feb Index	%	Mar Index	%	Apr Index	%	May Index	%	Jun Index	%	Jul Index	%	Aug Index	%	Sep Index	%	Oct Index	%	Nov Index	%	Dec Index	%
1926	14.7	-	14.7	0.0	14.7	0.0	14.7	0.0	14.7	0.0	14.7	0.0	14.5	-1.4	14.5	0.0	14.5	0.0	14.5	0.0	14.5	0.0	14.5	0.0
1927	14.5	0.0	14.5	0.0	14.5	0.0	14.5	0.0	14.6	0.7	14.7	0.7	15.0	2.0	15.1	0.7	15.4	2.0	15.4	0.0	15.5	0.6	15.6	0.6
1928	15.8	1.3	15.9	0.6	16.0	0.6	16.1	0.6	16.1	0.0	16.2	0.6	16.2	0.0	16.2	0.0	16.2	0.0	16.1	-0.6	15.9	-1.2	15.8	-0.6
1929	15.6	-1.3	15.6	0.0	15.6	0.0	15.6	0.0	15.5	-0.6	15.5	0.0	15.5	0.0	15.5	0.0	15.5	0.0	15.5	0.0	15.5	0.0	15.5	0.0
1930	15.1	-2.6	15.1	0.0	15.1	0.0	15.1	0.0	15.1	0.0	15.0	-0.7	15.0	0.0	14.7	-2.0	14.7	0.0	14.7	0.0	14.7	0.0	14.3	-2.7
1931	13.9	-2.8	13.8	-0.7	13.8	0.0	13.8	0.0	13.8	0.0	13.8	0.0	13.6	-1.4	13.6	0.0	13.6	0.0	13.6	0.0	13.5	-0.7	13.0	-3.7
1932	12.9	-0.8	12.9	0.0	12.9	0.0	12.9	0.0	12.9	0.0	12.7	-1.6	12.3	-3.1	12.3	0.0	12.3	0.0	12.3	0.0	12.3	0.0	12.2	-0.8
1933	12.2	0.0	12.1	-0.8	12.1	0.0	12.1	0.0	12.2	0.8	12.4	1.6	12.9	4.0	14.0	8.5	14.4	2.9	14.4	0.0	14.4	0.0	14.4	0.0
1934	14.4	0.0	14.4	0.0	14.4	0.0	14.4	0.0	14.4	0.0	14.4	0.0	14.3	-0.7	14.3	0.0	14.3	0.0	14.3	0.0	14.2	-0.7	14.2	0.0
1935	14.1	-0.7	14.2	0.7	14.2	0.0	14.2	0.0	14.2	0.0	14.2	0.0	14.3	0.7	14.3	0.0	14.3	0.0	14.4	0.7	14.5	0.7	14.6	0.7
1936	14.7	0.7	14.7	0.0	14.7	0.0	14.7	0.0	14.6	-0.7	14.5	-0.7	14.5	0.0	14.5	0.0	14.5	0.0	14.5	0.0	14.5	0.0	14.5	0.0
1937	14.5	0.0	14.8	2.1	14.9	0.7	15.1	1.3	15.5	2.6	15.7	1.3	15.6	-0.6	15.6	0.0	15.7	0.6	15.7	0.0	15.6	-0.6	15.4	-1.3
1938	15.3	-0.6	15.2	-0.7	15.2	0.0	15.2	0.0	14.9	-2.0	14.9	0.0	14.8	-0.7	14.7	-0.7	14.7	0.0	14.7	0.0	14.7	0.0	14.7	0.0
1939	14.8	0.7	14.7	-0.7	14.8	0.7	14.8	0.0	14.8	0.0	14.8	0.0	14.7	-0.7	14.7	0.0	14.9	1.4	15.4	3.4	15.6	1.3	15.7	0.6
1940	15.7	0.0	15.8	0.6	15.8	0.0	15.8	0.0	15.8	0.0	15.8	0.0	15.6	-1.3	15.6	0.0	15.6	0.0	15.6	0.0	15.6	0.0	15.6	0.0
1941	15.6	0.0	15.6	0.0	15.6	0.0	15.8	1.3	16.0	1.3	16.3	1.9	16.7	2.5	16.9	1.2	17.1	1.2	17.3	1.2	17.6	1.7	17.6	0.0
1942	17.7	0.6	17.8	0.6	18.1	1.7	18.5	2.2	18.5	0.0	18.4	-0.5	18.4	0.0	18.4	0.0	18.4	0.0	18.4	0.0	18.4	0.0	18.4	0.0
1943	18.4	0.0	18.4	0.0	18.4	0.0	18.4	0.0	18.4	0.0	18.4	0.0	18.4	0.0	18.4	0.0	18.4	0.0	18.4	0.0	18.4	0.0	18.4	0.0
1944	18.4	0.0	18.4	0.0	18.4	0.0	18.4	0.0	18.4	0.0	18.4	0.0	18.4	0.0	18.4	0.0	18.4	0.0	18.4	0.0	18.4	0.0	18.4	0.0
1945	18.4	0.0	18.4	0.0	18.4	0.0	18.4	0.0	18.4	0.0	18.4	0.0	18.4	0.0	18.4	0.0	18.4	0.0	18.4	0.0	18.5	0.5	18.5	0.0
1946	18.7	1.1	18.7	0.0	18.7	0.0	18.7	0.0	18.8	0.5	18.9	0.5	20.5	8.5	20.5	0.0	21.1	2.9	21.1	0.0	23.8	12.8	24.8	4.2
1947	25.3	2.0	25.3	0.0	25.3	0.0	25.4	0.4	25.6	0.8	25.6	0.0	25.7	0.4	26.0	1.2	25.8	-0.8	26.1	1.2	26.5	1.5	27.2	2.6
1948	27.4	0.7	27.4	0.0	27.6	0.7	27.8	0.7	27.6	-0.7	27.5	-0.4	27.6	0.4	27.8	0.7	27.9	0.4	27.8	-0.4	27.5	-1.1	27.5	0.0
1949	27.4	-0.4	27.4	0.0	27.4	0.0	27.3	-0.4	27.1	-0.7	27.1	0.0	27.1	0.0	27.1	0.0	27.1	0.0	27.1	0.0	27.3	0.7	27.5	0.7
1950	27.3	-0.7	27.3	0.0	27.4	0.4	27.4	0.0	27.6	0.7	27.6	0.0	27.8	0.7	28.7	3.2	29.1	1.4	30.1	3.4	31.2	3.7	32.2	3.2
1951	32.9	2.2	33.5	1.8	33.1	-1.2	33.1	0.0	33.1	0.0	33.0	-0.3	32.9	-0.3	32.8	-0.3	32.8	0.0	32.1	-2.1	31.8	-0.9	31.3	-1.6
1952	31.2	-0.3	31.2	0.0	31.2	0.0	30.4	-2.6	29.9	-1.6	29.8	-0.3	29.8	0.0	29.8	0.0	29.8	0.0	29.8	0.0	29.8	0.0	30.1	1.0
1953	30.1	0.0	30.2	0.3	30.2	0.0	30.0	-0.7	30.0	0.0	30.0	0.0	30.0	0.0	30.1	0.3	30.1	0.0	30.0	-0.3	30.1	0.3	30.1	0.0
1954	30.1	0.0	30.1	0.0	30.1	0.0	30.1	0.0	30.1	0.0	30.1	0.0	30.1	0.0	30.1	0.0	30.1	0.0	30.1	0.0	30.0	-0.3	30.0	0.0
1955	30.0	0.0	30.0	0.0	30.0	0.0	30.0	0.0	30.0	0.0	30.0	0.0	30.0	0.0	30.0	0.0	30.0	0.0	30.5	1.7	31.1	2.0	31.1	0.0
1956	31.1	0.0	31.1	0.0	31.3	0.6	32.2	2.9	32.3	0.3	32.4	0.3	32.4	0.0	32.4	0.0	32.4	0.0	32.5	0.3	32.5	0.0	32.5	0.0
1957	32.5	0.0	32.5	0.0	32.5	0.0	32.6	0.3	32.5	-0.3	32.5	0.0	32.6	0.3	32.6	0.0	32.6	0.0	32.8	0.6	32.9	0.3	32.7	-0.6
1958	32.8	0.3	32.8	0.0	32.8	0.0	32.7	-0.3	32.8	0.3	32.8	0.0	32.8	0.0	32.8	0.0	32.8	0.0	33.0	0.6	33.1	0.3	33.1	0.0
1959	33.1	0.0	33.1	0.0	33.3	0.6	34.5	3.6	34.8	0.9	35.0	0.6	35.1	0.3	35.6	1.4	35.6	0.0	35.9	0.8	36.0	0.3	36.1	0.3
1960	36.1	0.0	36.1	0.0	36.1	0.0	35.9	-0.6	35.6	-0.8	35.6	0.0	35.6	0.0	35.6	0.0	35.6	0.0	35.6	0.0	35.6	0.0	35.6	0.0
1961	35.7	0.3	35.7	0.0	35.7	0.0	35.7	0.0	35.8	0.3	35.8	0.0	35.8	0.0	35.9	0.3	36.0	0.3	36.2	0.6	36.3	0.3	36.3	0.0
1962	36.3	0.0	36.3	0.0	36.3	0.0	36.3	0.0	36.3	0.0	36.3	0.0	36.4	0.3	36.4	0.0	36.4	0.0	36.2	-0.5	36.2	0.0	36.3	0.3
1963	36.2	-0.3	36.2	0.0	36.2	0.0	36.2	0.0	36.2	0.0	36.2	0.0	36.2	0.0	36.2	0.0	36.2	0.0	36.2	0.0	36.2	0.0	36.2	0.0
1964	36.2	0.0	36.2	0.0	36.2	0.0	36.2	0.0	36.2	0.0	36.2	0.0	36.2	0.0	36.2	0.0	36.2	0.0	36.5	0.8	36.5	0.0	36.5	0.0
1965	36.5	0.0	36.5	0.0	36.5	0.0	36.7	0.5	36.7	0.0	36.7	0.0	36.8	0.3	36.9	0.3	36.9	0.0	38.0	3.0	38.0	0.0	38.0	0.0
1966	38.3	0.8	38.5	0.5	38.6	0.3	39.5	2.3	39.8	0.8	39.8	0.0	39.8	0.0	39.8	0.0	39.8	0.0	40.2	1.0	40.2	0.0	40.2	0.0
1967	40.5	0.7	40.7	0.5	40.7	0.0	40.6	-0.2	40.6	0.0	40.6	0.0	40.6	0.0	40.5	-0.2	40.7	0.5	41.3	1.5	41.3	0.0	41.6	0.7
1968	42.0	1.0	42.0	0.0	42.0	0.0	42.3	0.7	42.5	0.5	42.5	0.0	42.6	0.2	42.5	-0.2	43.1	1.4	43.9	1.9	44.0	0.2	44.0	0.0
1969	44.2	0.5	44.2	0.0	44.0	-0.5	44.1	0.2	44.2	0.2	44.2	0.0	44.4	0.5	44.5	0.2	45.3	1.8	45.6	0.7	45.8	0.4	45.7	-0.2
1970	46.1	0.9	46.4	0.7	46.4	0.0	46.2	-0.4	46.1	-0.2	46.1	0.0	46.1	0.0	46.1	0.0	46.4	0.7	46.5	0.2	46.5	0.0	46.5	0.0

[Continued]

Footwear
Producer Price Index
Base 1982 = 100
[Continued]

For 1926-1995. Columns headed % show percentile change in the index from the previous period for which an index is available.

Year	Jan Index	%	Feb Index	%	Mar Index	%	Apr Index	%	May Index	%	Jun Index	%	Jul Index	%	Aug Index	%	Sep Index	%	Oct Index	%	Nov Index	%	Dec Index	%
1971	47.5	2.2	47.5	0.0	47.5	0.0	47.6	0.2	47.7	0.2	47.7	0.0	47.7	0.0	47.7	0.0	47.7	0.0	47.7	0.0	47.7	0.0	47.8	0.2
1972	48.2	0.8	48.4	0.4	49.0	1.2	50.0	2.0	50.9	1.8	51.4	1.0	51.6	0.4	51.6	0.0	51.7	0.2	51.8	0.2	52.4	1.2	52.5	0.2
1973	52.6	0.2	53.4	1.5	53.5	0.2	53.7	0.4	52.8	-1.7	52.8	0.0	52.9	0.2	52.9	0.0	53.2	0.6	53.5	0.6	53.8	0.6	54.1	0.6
1974	54.7	1.1	55.1	0.7	55.5	0.7	56.4	1.6	56.6	0.4	56.9	0.5	57.1	0.4	57.4	0.5	58.8	2.4	58.9	0.2	59.1	0.3	59.1	0.0
1975	59.3	0.3	59.6	0.5	59.6	0.0	59.9	0.5	59.9	0.0	60.0	0.2	60.1	0.2	60.2	0.2	61.0	1.3	61.3	0.5	61.3	0.0	61.4	0.2
1976	62.1	1.1	62.8	1.1	63.2	0.6	63.8	0.9	64.0	0.3	64.8	1.3	65.6	1.2	65.8	0.3	66.3	0.8	66.4	0.2	66.5	0.2	66.8	0.5
1977	67.1	0.4	67.5	0.6	67.9	0.6	68.2	0.4	68.6	0.6	68.6	0.0	69.3	1.0	69.4	0.1	69.4	0.0	69.9	0.7	70.0	0.1	70.1	0.1
1978	70.8	1.0	71.7	1.3	71.7	0.0	73.5	2.5	73.8	0.4	73.9	0.1	74.1	0.3	75.1	1.3	75.9	1.1	77.8	2.5	78.4	0.8	79.3	1.1
1979	80.2	1.1	82.8	3.2	85.7	3.5	86.6	1.1	88.3	2.0	90.3	2.3	90.5	0.2	92.0	1.7	92.6	0.7	92.9	0.3	93.0	0.1	93.0	0.0
1980	93.5	0.5	93.1	-0.4	94.6	1.6	94.7	0.1	94.7	0.0	94.7	0.0	95.0	0.3	95.4	0.4	96.1	0.7	96.6	0.5	97.0	0.4	96.7	-0.3
1981	97.3	0.6	98.2	0.9	98.1	-0.1	98.4	0.3	98.5	0.1	98.6	0.1	98.9	0.3	99.0	0.1	99.1	0.1	97.8	-1.3	97.9	0.1	98.0	0.1
1982	97.5	-0.5	97.4	-0.1	97.9	0.5	99.9	2.0	99.8	-0.1	99.7	-0.1	101.0	1.3	101.1	0.1	101.3	0.2	101.6	0.3	101.7	0.1	101.1	-0.6
1983	102.7	1.6	101.1	-1.6	101.3	0.2	102.1	0.8	101.5	-0.6	102.0	0.5	102.0	0.0	102.4	0.4	102.7	0.3	102.6	-0.1	102.6	0.0	102.2	-0.4
1984	102.4	0.2	103.1	0.7	103.5	0.4	102.7	-0.8	102.6	-0.1	102.3	-0.3	102.1	-0.2	102.4	0.3	102.8	0.4	102.9	0.1	103.0	0.1	103.1	0.1
1985	103.2	0.1	104.5	1.3	104.2	-0.3	104.1	-0.1	103.6	-0.5	104.9	1.3	104.9	0.0	105.3	0.4	105.7	0.4	105.7	0.0	105.5	-0.2	105.5	0.0
1986	105.9	0.4	106.3	0.4	106.8	0.5	107.1	0.3	106.8	-0.3	106.4	-0.4	106.5	0.1	106.8	0.3	107.0	0.2	107.5	0.5	107.5	0.0	107.8	0.3
1987	108.0	0.2	107.5	-0.5	108.4	0.8	108.2	-0.2	108.9	0.6	107.5	-1.3	109.7	2.0	110.3	0.5	111.0	0.6	110.9	-0.1	110.6	-0.3	111.4	0.7
1988	112.7	1.2	113.7	0.9	114.0	0.3	114.1	0.1	114.2	0.1	114.8	0.5	115.5	0.6	116.0	0.4	116.2	0.2	116.4	0.2	116.9	0.4	117.2	0.3
1989	118.1	0.8	119.5	1.2	119.8	0.3	120.0	0.2	119.9	-0.1	119.9	0.0	120.4	0.4	121.8	1.2	122.3	0.4	122.5	0.2	122.5	0.0	123.1	0.5
1990	124.2	0.9	125.3	0.9	125.5	0.2	125.4	-0.1	125.8	0.3	125.5	-0.2	125.6	0.1	126.0	0.3	126.1	0.1	126.2	0.1	125.9	-0.2	126.1	0.2
1991	126.3	0.2	127.1	0.6	128.0	0.7	128.3	0.2	128.7	0.3	128.8	0.1	129.2	0.3	129.3	0.1	129.5	0.2	129.1	-0.3	129.3	0.2	129.6	0.2
1992	130.6	0.8	131.8	0.9	131.4	-0.3	131.5	0.1	131.6	0.1	131.9	0.2	132.1	0.2	132.5	0.3	132.8	0.2	132.4	-0.3	132.4	0.0	133.3	0.7
1993	133.5	0.2	133.8	0.2	133.9	0.1	134.5	0.4	134.1	-0.3	134.2	0.1	134.8	0.4	134.8	0.0	134.9	0.1	134.7	-0.1	134.9	0.1	135.1	0.1
1994	135.5	0.3	135.1	-0.3	135.4	0.2	135.2	-0.1	135.4	0.1	135.2	-0.1	135.3	0.1	135.3	0.0	135.6	0.2	135.8	0.1	136.1	0.2	136.6	0.4
1995	137.5	0.7	138.6	0.8	138.7	0.1	138.8	0.1	138.9	0.1	139.0	0.1	139.2	0.1	139.3	0.1	139.1	-0.1	140.1	0.7	140.1	0.0	140.4	0.2

Source: U.S. Department of Labor, Bureau of Labor Statistics, Division of Industry Prices and Price Indexes. n.e.c. stands for not elsewhere classified. - indicates no data collected for period or unavailable.

Leather and Related Products n.e.c.
Producer Price Index
Base 1982 = 100

For 1947-1995. Columns headed % show percentile change in the index from the previous period for which an index is available.

Year	Jan Index	%	Feb Index	%	Mar Index	%	Apr Index	%	May Index	%	Jun Index	%	Jul Index	%	Aug Index	%	Sep Index	%	Oct Index	%	Nov Index	%	Dec Index	%
1947	35.0	-	34.4	-1.7	34.4	0.0	34.2	-0.6	33.6	-1.8	33.5	-0.3	34.5	3.0	35.0	1.4	35.4	1.1	36.0	1.7	37.6	4.4	37.8	0.5
1948	37.7	-0.3	37.2	-1.3	36.2	-2.7	35.7	-1.4	35.8	0.3	35.9	0.3	36.1	0.6	36.0	-0.3	35.5	-1.4	35.2	-0.8	35.3	0.3	35.6	0.8
1949	35.5	-0.3	35.4	-0.3	34.8	-1.7	34.3	-1.4	34.4	0.3	34.2	-0.6	34.0	-0.6	33.9	-0.3	33.8	-0.3	33.9	0.3	33.8	-0.3	34.0	0.6
1950	33.6	-1.2	33.6	0.0	33.6	0.0	33.6	0.0	33.7	0.3	33.5	-0.6	34.0	1.5	34.8	2.4	35.2	1.1	35.7	1.4	36.1	1.1	36.9	2.2
1951	40.0	8.4	40.6	1.5	40.6	0.0	40.9	0.7	40.7	-0.5	40.5	-0.5	40.1	-1.0	39.0	-2.7	39.0	0.0	37.6	-3.6	37.2	-1.1	37.2	0.0
1952	36.6	-1.6	36.3	-0.8	35.8	-1.4	35.2	-1.7	35.3	0.3	35.4	0.3	35.3	-0.3	35.2	-0.3	35.1	-0.3	34.8	-0.9	35.0	0.6	35.3	0.9
1953	34.8	-1.4	34.8	0.0	34.8	0.0	34.9	0.3	35.1	0.6	35.3	0.6	35.0	-0.8	35.0	0.0	34.8	-0.6	34.8	0.0	34.7	-0.3	34.5	-0.6
1954	34.5	0.0	34.4	-0.3	34.3	-0.3	34.2	-0.3	34.2	0.0	34.2	0.0	34.1	-0.3	34.0	-0.3	33.9	-0.3	33.8	-0.3	33.8	0.0	33.7	-0.3
1955	33.7	0.0	33.7	0.0	33.6	-0.3	33.7	0.3	33.4	-0.9	33.4	0.0	33.9	1.5	33.9	0.0	33.8	-0.3	33.8	0.0	33.8	0.0	34.0	0.6
1956	34.3	0.9	34.5	0.6	34.5	0.0	34.8	0.9	34.8	0.0	34.8	0.0	34.7	-0.3	34.8	0.3	34.6	-0.6	34.6	0.0	34.6	0.0	34.5	-0.3
1957	34.4	-0.3	34.2	-0.6	34.4	0.6	34.4	0.0	34.2	-0.6	34.2	0.0	34.6	1.2	34.5	-0.3	34.6	0.3	34.6	0.0	34.7	0.3	34.6	-0.3
1958	34.6	0.0	34.6	0.0	34.2	-1.2	34.3	0.3	34.2	-0.3	34.2	0.0	34.2	0.0	34.0	-0.6	34.0	0.0	34.2	0.6	34.2	0.0	34.5	0.9
1959	34.8	0.9	35.4	1.7	36.3	2.5	38.7	6.6	39.5	2.1	39.4	-0.3	40.0	1.5	40.1	0.3	40.0	-0.2	39.1	-2.3	38.4	-1.8	37.9	-1.3
1960	38.0	0.3	37.7	-0.8	37.7	0.0	37.7	0.0	37.5	-0.5	37.4	-0.3	37.1	-0.8	36.8	-0.8	36.5	-0.8	36.5	0.0	36.6	0.3	36.5	-0.3
1961	36.6	0.3	36.5	-0.3	36.4	-0.3	36.6	0.5	36.7	0.3	36.7	0.0	36.6	-0.3	36.9	0.8	37.0	0.3	36.9	-0.3	37.2	0.8	37.2	0.0
1962	37.4	0.5	37.3	-0.3	37.3	0.0	36.6	-1.9	36.3	-0.8	37.4	3.0	37.5	0.3	37.1	-1.1	37.1	0.0	37.4	0.8	37.5	0.3	37.6	0.3
1963	37.4	-0.5	37.4	0.0	37.4	0.0	37.3	-0.3	37.2	-0.3	37.2	0.0	37.1	-0.3	36.9	-0.5	36.9	0.0	36.9	0.0	36.8	-0.3	36.9	0.3
1964	36.3	-1.6	36.3	0.0	36.2	-0.3	37.0	2.2	36.9	-0.3	36.8	-0.3	37.1	0.8	37.0	-0.3	36.9	-0.3	36.9	0.0	37.1	0.5	37.1	0.0
1965	36.6	-1.3	36.7	0.3	36.7	0.0	37.2	1.4	37.4	0.5	37.4	0.0	37.6	0.5	38.8	3.2	39.0	0.5	38.9	-0.3	38.9	0.0	39.3	1.0
1966	39.4	0.3	39.8	1.0	40.1	0.8	40.8	1.7	41.2	1.0	41.3	0.2	41.6	0.7	41.4	-0.5	41.1	-0.7	41.2	0.2	41.1	-0.2	40.7	-1.0
1967	41.0	0.7	41.0	0.0	40.9	-0.2	40.9	0.0	40.8	-0.2	40.4	-1.0	40.3	-0.2	40.3	0.0	40.0	-0.7	39.9	-0.2	39.9	0.0	39.8	-0.3
1968	40.0	0.5	40.0	0.0	40.1	0.3	40.1	0.0	40.1	0.0	40.1	0.0	40.2	0.2	40.2	0.0	40.2	0.0	40.5	0.7	40.5	0.0	40.6	0.2
1969	41.0	1.0	41.0	0.0	41.2	0.5	41.5	0.7	41.7	0.5	41.8	0.2	42.0	0.5	41.9	-0.2	42.1	0.5	42.2	0.2	42.4	0.5	42.3	-0.2
1970	42.6	0.7	42.7	0.2	42.8	0.2	42.8	0.0	43.1	0.7	43.1	0.0	43.2	0.2	43.2	0.0	43.2	0.0	43.2	0.0	43.2	0.0	43.2	0.0
1971	43.4	0.5	43.5	0.2	43.5	0.0	43.5	0.0	43.6	0.2	43.7	0.2	43.8	0.2	44.0	0.5	44.1	0.2	44.1	0.0	44.1	0.0	44.4	0.7
1972	44.7	0.7	44.9	0.4	45.2	0.7	46.0	1.8	46.6	1.3	47.2	1.3	47.1	-0.2	48.0	1.9	48.7	1.5	50.0	2.7	51.4	2.8	51.9	1.0
1973	52.3	0.8	52.3	0.0	52.3	0.0	52.5	0.4	52.2	-0.6	52.1	-0.2	52.2	0.2	52.8	1.1	52.7	-0.2	52.8	0.2	52.6	-0.4	52.7	0.2
1974	53.3	1.1	53.8	0.9	54.8	1.9	54.7	-0.2	54.6	-0.2	55.3	1.3	55.4	0.2	55.4	0.0	56.3	1.6	56.0	-0.5	56.0	0.0	56.5	0.9
1975	56.6	0.2	56.4	-0.4	56.2	-0.4	56.2	0.0	56.4	0.4	56.8	0.7	57.0	0.4	57.2	0.4	57.3	0.2	57.4	0.2	58.0	1.0	58.3	0.5
1976	60.3	3.4	61.0	1.2	61.1	0.2	61.2	0.2	61.5	0.5	61.5	0.0	61.6	0.2	61.7	0.2	62.7	1.6	63.0	0.5	63.0	0.0	63.1	0.2
1977	64.5	2.2	65.3	1.2	65.7	0.6	66.0	0.5	66.2	0.3	66.2	0.0	66.2	0.0	66.4	0.3	66.5	0.2	66.5	0.0	66.6	0.2	66.6	0.0
1978	68.8	3.3	68.9	0.1	69.4	0.7	69.5	0.1	71.2	2.4	71.4	0.3	71.5	0.1	72.3	1.1	72.7	0.6	72.9	0.3	74.8	2.6	74.9	0.1
1979	77.1	2.9	77.7	0.8	79.2	1.9	81.2	2.5	84.5	4.1	85.8	1.5	85.7	-0.1	85.3	-0.5	84.9	-0.5	84.8	-0.1	84.3	-0.6	84.1	-0.2
1980	86.1	2.4	86.8	0.8	88.0	1.4	87.4	-0.7	87.9	0.6	87.3	-0.7	87.9	0.7	88.4	0.6	88.5	0.1	89.7	1.4	90.0	0.3	91.1	1.2
1981	93.0	2.1	95.8	3.0	96.4	0.6	96.4	0.0	98.7	2.4	98.8	0.1	98.2	-0.6	99.1	0.9	99.0	-0.1	99.0	0.0	99.2	0.2	99.2	0.0
1982	100.1	0.9	100.3	0.2	100.3	0.0	100.3	0.0	100.3	0.0	99.3	-1.0	99.8	0.5	99.0	-0.8	100.1	1.1	99.9	-0.2	99.9	0.0	100.7	0.8
1983	101.4	0.7	101.5	0.1	101.4	-0.1	101.5	0.1	101.7	0.2	101.7	0.0	102.5	0.8	102.6	0.1	102.5	-0.1	102.5	0.0	103.4	0.9	103.3	-0.1
1984	104.0	0.7	104.0	0.0	104.0	0.0	104.3	0.3	105.0	0.7	108.3	3.1	108.0	-0.3	108.2	0.2	108.2	0.0	108.4	0.2	108.3	-0.1	107.9	-0.4
1985	109.2	1.2	109.3	0.1	110.1	0.7	110.2	0.1	110.3	0.1	110.5	0.2	110.2	-0.3	110.2	0.0	110.6	0.4	110.8	0.2	111.3	0.5	111.3	0.0
1986	111.5	0.2	111.0	-0.4	109.7	-1.2	109.5	-0.2	109.5	0.0	109.9	0.4	109.9	0.0	110.0	0.1	110.2	0.2	111.0	0.7	111.0	0.0	111.1	0.1
1987	111.5	0.4	111.4	-0.1	111.6	0.2	111.6	0.0	112.2	0.5	112.5	0.3	112.9	0.4	113.4	0.4	114.2	0.7	114.4	0.2	114.8	0.3	115.2	0.3
1988	116.6	1.2	116.8	0.2	117.1	0.3	117.7	0.5	118.2	0.4	119.5	1.1	119.9	0.3	120.0	0.1	120.6	0.5	120.6	0.0	120.7	0.1	120.9	0.2
1989	121.4	0.4	121.9	0.4	122.2	0.2	122.4	0.2	123.2	0.7	122.9	-0.2	122.9	0.0	123.7	0.7	124.4	0.6	123.9	-0.4	123.7	-0.2	124.8	0.9
1990	126.0	1.0	126.3	0.2	127.9	1.3	127.6	-0.2	129.2	1.3	129.7	0.4	129.4	-0.2	130.6	0.9	130.1	-0.4	129.6	-0.4	130.0	0.3	130.8	0.6
1991	130.8	0.0	131.3	0.4	132.4	0.8	131.9	-0.4	132.7	0.6	134.4	1.3	132.4	-1.5	134.3	1.4	132.8	-1.1	132.8	0.0	132.9	0.1	133.0	0.1

[Continued]

Leather and Related Products n.e.c.
Producer Price Index
Base 1982 = 100
[Continued]

For 1947-1995. Columns headed % show percentile change in the index from the previous period for which an index is available.

Year	Jan Index	%	Feb Index	%	Mar Index	%	Apr Index	%	May Index	%	Jun Index	%	Jul Index	%	Aug Index	%	Sep Index	%	Oct Index	%	Nov Index	%	Dec Index	%
1992	135.7	2.0	133.7	-1.5	136.2	1.9	134.0	-1.6	134.4	0.3	136.2	1.3	134.2	-1.5	136.6	1.8	134.2	-1.8	134.3	0.1	134.6	0.2	134.6	0.0
1993	137.1	1.9	135.2	-1.4	135.3	0.1	135.7	0.3	135.8	0.1	137.8	1.5	135.9	-1.4	138.3	1.8	135.9	-1.7	136.1	0.1	136.1	0.0	136.1	0.0
1994	137.8	1.2	135.6	-1.6	135.8	0.1	136.0	0.1	136.2	0.1	136.3	0.1	136.4	0.1	136.5	0.1	137.5	0.7	137.6	0.1	137.8	0.1	137.6	-0.1
1995	138.2	0.4	138.0	-0.1	138.1	0.1	138.4	0.2	138.6	0.1	138.9	0.2	138.9	0.0	139.1	0.1	139.3	0.1	139.5	0.1	139.7	0.1	139.9	0.1

Source: U.S. Department of Labor, Bureau of Labor Statistics, Division of Industry Prices and Price Indexes. n.e.c. stands for not elsewhere classified. - indicates no data collected for period or unavailable.

FUELS AND RELATED PRODUCTS AND POWER
Producer Price Index
Base 1982 = 100

For 1926-1995. Columns headed % show percentile change in the index from the previous period for which an index is available.

Year	Jan Index	%	Feb Index	%	Mar Index	%	Apr Index	%	May Index	%	Jun Index	%	Jul Index	%	Aug Index	%	Sep Index	%	Oct Index	%	Nov Index	%	Dec Index	%
1926	10.2	-	10.2	0.0	10.2	0.0	10.1	-1.0	10.4	3.0	10.4	0.0	10.3	-1.0	10.4	1.0	10.4	0.0	10.4	0.0	10.5	1.0	10.2	-2.9
1927	10.1	-1.0	10.0	-1.0	9.4	-6.0	9.0	-4.3	8.9	-1.1	8.9	0.0	8.9	0.0	8.9	0.0	8.9	0.0	8.9	0.0	8.8	-1.1	8.7	-1.1
1928	8.6	-1.1	8.6	0.0	8.5	-1.2	8.6	1.2	8.6	0.0	8.7	1.2	8.7	0.0	8.9	2.3	8.9	0.0	8.9	0.0	8.9	0.0	8.8	-1.1
1929	8.7	-1.1	8.6	-1.1	8.5	-1.2	8.5	0.0	8.5	0.0	8.7	2.4	8.6	-1.1	8.5	-1.2	8.5	0.0	8.6	1.2	8.6	0.0	8.6	0.0
1930	8.4	-2.3	8.4	0.0	8.2	-2.4	8.2	0.0	8.3	1.2	8.2	-1.2	8.1	-1.2	8.0	-1.2	8.2	2.5	8.0	-2.4	7.8	-2.5	7.6	-2.6
1931	7.6	0.0	7.5	-1.3	7.0	-6.7	6.8	-2.9	6.7	-1.5	6.5	-3.0	6.5	0.0	6.9	6.2	7.0	1.4	7.0	0.0	7.2	2.9	7.0	-2.8
1932	7.0	0.0	7.0	0.0	7.0	0.0	7.2	2.9	7.3	1.4	7.4	1.4	7.5	1.4	7.4	-1.3	7.3	-1.4	7.3	0.0	7.4	1.4	7.2	-2.7
1933	6.8	-5.6	6.6	-2.9	6.5	-1.5	6.3	-3.1	6.2	-1.6	6.3	1.6	6.7	6.3	6.8	1.5	7.3	7.4	7.6	4.1	7.6	0.0	7.6	0.0
1934	7.5	-1.3	7.5	0.0	7.4	-1.3	7.4	0.0	7.5	1.4	7.5	0.0	7.6	1.3	7.7	1.3	7.7	0.0	7.7	0.0	7.7	0.0	7.6	-1.3
1935	7.5	-1.3	7.5	0.0	7.5	0.0	7.5	0.0	7.5	0.0	7.7	2.7	7.7	0.0	7.6	-1.3	7.5	-1.3	7.6	1.3	7.7	1.3	7.7	0.0
1936	7.8	1.3	7.8	0.0	7.9	1.3	7.9	0.0	7.8	-1.3	7.8	0.0	7.9	1.3	7.9	0.0	7.8	-1.3	7.9	1.3	7.9	0.0	7.9	0.0
1937	7.9	0.0	7.9	0.0	7.9	0.0	7.9	0.0	8.0	1.3	8.0	0.0	8.1	1.3	8.1	0.0	8.1	0.0	8.1	0.0	8.1	0.0	8.1	0.0
1938	8.1	0.0	8.1	0.0	8.0	-1.2	7.9	-1.2	7.9	0.0	7.9	0.0	7.9	0.0	7.9	0.0	7.9	0.0	7.8	-1.3	7.6	-2.6	7.6	0.0
1939	7.5	-1.3	7.5	0.0	7.5	0.0	7.6	1.3	7.6	0.0	7.5	-1.3	7.5	0.0	7.5	0.0	7.5	0.0	7.6	1.3	7.6	0.0	7.5	-1.3
1940	7.5	0.0	7.5	0.0	7.4	-1.3	7.4	0.0	7.4	0.0	7.4	0.0	7.3	-1.4	7.3	0.0	7.3	0.0	7.4	1.4	7.4	0.0	7.4	0.0
1941	7.4	0.0	7.4	0.0	7.4	0.0	7.5	1.4	7.8	4.0	8.0	2.6	8.1	1.3	8.2	1.2	8.2	0.0	8.2	0.0	8.1	-1.2	8.1	0.0
1942	8.1	0.0	8.0	-1.2	8.0	0.0	8.0	0.0	8.0	0.0	8.1	1.3	8.2	1.2	8.2	0.0	8.2	0.0	8.2	0.0	8.2	0.0	8.2	0.0
1943	8.2	0.0	8.2	0.0	8.3	1.2	8.3	0.0	8.3	0.0	8.4	1.2	8.4	0.0	8.4	0.0	8.4	0.0	8.4	0.0	8.4	0.0	8.5	1.2
1944	8.5	0.0	8.6	1.2	8.6	0.0	8.6	0.0	8.6	0.0	8.6	0.0	8.6	0.0	8.6	0.0	8.6	0.0	8.6	0.0	8.6	0.0	8.6	0.0
1945	8.6	0.0	8.6	0.0	8.6	0.0	8.6	0.0	8.6	0.0	8.7	1.2	8.7	0.0	8.8	1.1	8.7	-1.1	8.7	0.0	8.7	0.0	8.7	0.0
1946	8.8	1.1	8.8	0.0	8.8	0.0	8.9	1.1	8.9	0.0	9.1	2.2	9.3	2.2	9.8	5.4	9.7	-1.0	9.7	0.0	9.8	1.0	9.9	1.0
1947	10.1	2.0	10.2	1.0	10.5	2.9	10.8	2.9	10.8	0.0	10.8	0.0	11.2	3.7	11.4	1.8	11.5	0.9	11.6	0.9	11.9	2.6	12.4	4.2
1948	12.9	4.0	13.0	0.8	13.0	0.0	13.0	0.0	13.0	0.0	13.0	0.0	13.2	1.5	13.1	-0.8	13.1	0.0	13.2	0.8	13.2	0.0	13.1	-0.8
1949	13.1	0.0	12.9	-1.5	12.7	-1.6	12.4	-2.4	12.3	-0.8	12.2	-0.8	12.2	0.0	12.2	0.0	12.2	0.0	12.3	0.8	12.3	0.0	12.3	0.0
1950	12.4	0.8	12.4	0.0	12.4	0.0	12.3	-0.8	12.4	0.8	12.5	0.8	12.6	0.8	12.7	0.8	12.7	0.0	12.8	0.8	12.9	0.8	12.8	-0.8
1951	13.0	1.6	13.1	0.8	13.1	0.0	13.0	-0.8	13.0	0.0	13.0	0.0	13.0	0.0	13.0	0.0	13.0	0.0	13.0	0.0	13.0	0.0	13.1	0.8
1952	13.1	0.0	13.1	0.0	13.1	0.0	13.0	-0.8	12.9	-0.8	12.9	0.0	12.9	0.0	12.9	0.0	13.0	0.8	13.0	0.0	13.0	0.0	13.1	0.8
1953	13.1	0.0	13.2	0.8	13.2	0.0	13.1	-0.8	13.1	0.0	13.2	0.8	13.5	2.3	13.5	0.0	13.5	0.0	13.6	0.7	13.6	0.0	13.5	-0.7
1954	13.5	0.0	13.5	0.0	13.3	-1.5	13.2	-0.8	13.2	0.0	13.1	-0.8	13.0	-0.8	13.0	0.0	13.0	0.0	13.0	0.0	13.1	0.8	13.1	0.0
1955	13.2	0.8	13.3	0.8	13.2	-0.8	13.1	-0.8	13.0	-0.8	13.0	0.0	13.0	0.0	13.1	0.8	13.2	0.8	13.2	0.0	13.2	0.0	13.3	0.8
1956	13.5	1.5	13.6	0.7	13.5	-0.7	13.5	0.0	13.5	0.0	13.5	0.0	13.5	0.0	13.5	0.0	13.5	0.0	13.6	0.7	13.6	0.0	13.9	2.2
1957	14.2	2.2	14.6	2.8	14.5	-0.7	14.6	0.7	14.5	-0.7	14.3	-1.4	14.2	-0.7	14.2	0.0	14.2	0.0	14.1	-0.7	14.1	0.0	14.2	0.7
1958	14.2	0.0	13.8	-2.8	13.7	-0.7	13.5	-1.5	13.4	-0.7	13.5	0.7	13.6	0.7	13.9	2.2	13.9	0.0	13.8	-0.7	13.7	-0.7	13.8	0.7
1959	13.9	0.7	14.0	0.7	14.0	0.0	13.9	-0.7	13.8	-0.7	13.6	-1.4	13.5	-0.7	13.7	1.5	13.6	-0.7	13.6	0.0	13.6	0.0	13.6	0.0
1960	13.6	0.0	13.7	0.7	13.7	0.0	13.7	0.0	13.5	-1.5	13.7	1.5	13.9	1.5	14.1	1.4	14.2	0.7	14.2	0.0	14.2	0.0	14.2	0.0
1961	14.3	0.7	14.4	0.7	14.3	-0.7	14.1	-1.4	13.8	-2.1	13.9	0.7	14.0	0.7	14.0	0.0	13.9	-0.7	13.8	-0.7	13.9	0.7	14.0	0.7
1962	14.1	0.7	14.0	-0.7	13.8	-1.4	14.0	1.4	13.9	-0.7	13.9	0.0	13.9	0.0	13.8	-0.7	14.0	1.4	14.0	0.0	14.0	0.0	14.0	0.0
1963	14.0	0.0	14.0	0.0	14.0	0.0	14.0	0.0	14.0	0.0	14.1	0.7	14.0	-0.7	13.8	-1.4	13.8	0.0	13.8	0.0	13.6	-1.4	13.8	1.5
1964	13.8	0.0	13.8	0.0	13.5	-2.2	13.4	-0.7	13.4	0.0	13.4	0.0	13.5	0.7	13.4	-0.7	13.3	-0.7	13.5	1.5	13.6	0.7	13.7	0.7
1965	13.7	0.0	13.6	-0.7	13.6	0.0	13.6	0.0	13.7	0.7	13.7	0.0	13.7	0.0	13.8	0.7	13.8	0.0	13.8	0.0	14.0	1.4	14.0	0.0
1966	14.0	0.0	14.0	0.0	13.9	-0.7	13.9	0.0	14.0	0.7	14.1	0.7	14.1	0.0	14.2	0.7	14.2	0.0	14.3	0.7	14.3	0.0	14.3	0.0
1967	14.3	0.0	14.4	0.7	14.4	0.0	14.4	0.0	14.5	0.7	14.5	0.0	14.5	0.0	14.6	0.7	14.6	0.0	14.4	-1.4	14.3	-0.7	14.3	0.0
1968	14.2	-0.7	14.3	0.7	14.2	-0.7	14.3	0.7	14.3	0.0	14.4	0.7	14.4	0.0	14.3	-0.7	14.3	0.0	14.2	-0.7	14.2	0.0	14.2	0.0
1969	14.2	0.0	14.3	0.7	14.5	1.4	14.5	0.0	14.5	0.0	14.6	0.7	14.6	0.0	14.6	0.0	14.6	0.0	14.7	0.7	14.7	0.0	14.8	0.7
1970	14.7	-0.7	14.8	0.7	14.8	0.0	15.0	1.4	15.1	0.7	15.1	0.0	15.2	0.7	15.3	0.7	15.6	2.0	15.8	1.3	15.9	0.6	16.4	3.1

[Continued]

FUELS AND RELATED PRODUCTS AND POWER
Producer Price Index
Base 1982 = 100
[Continued]

For 1926-1995. Columns headed % show percentile change in the index from the previous period for which an index is available.

Year	Jan Index	%	Feb Index	%	Mar Index	%	Apr Index	%	May Index	%	Jun Index	%	Jul Index	%	Aug Index	%	Sep Index	%	Oct Index	%	Nov Index	%	Dec Index	%
1971	16.5	0.6	16.5	0.0	16.4	-0.6	16.4	0.0	16.6	1.2	16.6	0.0	16.7	0.6	16.8	0.6	16.8	0.0	16.7	-0.6	16.7	0.0	16.9	1.2
1972	16.7	-1.2	16.7	0.0	16.8	0.6	16.9	0.6	16.9	0.0	17.0	0.6	17.1	0.6	17.3	1.2	17.4	0.6	17.4	0.0	17.5	0.6	17.6	0.6
1973	17.6	0.0	18.2	3.4	18.4	1.1	18.6	1.1	18.9	1.6	19.2	1.6	19.4	1.0	19.5	0.5	19.8	1.5	20.1	1.5	20.8	3.5	21.9	5.3
1974	23.4	6.8	25.6	9.4	27.3	6.6	28.5	4.4	29.5	3.5	30.4	3.1	32.0	5.3	32.6	1.9	32.5	-0.3	33.0	1.5	32.8	-0.6	33.0	0.6
1975	33.5	1.5	33.5	0.0	33.6	0.3	34.1	1.5	34.4	0.9	35.0	1.7	35.6	1.7	36.4	2.2	36.8	1.1	37.0	0.5	37.1	0.3	37.2	0.3
1976	37.1	-0.3	36.9	-0.5	36.9	0.0	37.1	0.5	37.1	0.0	37.6	1.3	38.3	1.9	38.8	1.3	39.1	0.8	40.0	2.3	40.6	1.5	40.3	-0.7
1977	40.2	-0.2	41.7	3.7	42.4	1.7	43.1	1.7	43.6	1.2	43.9	0.7	44.3	0.9	44.7	0.9	44.7	0.0	44.8	0.2	44.8	0.0	45.0	0.4
1978	45.1	0.2	45.1	0.0	45.5	0.9	45.8	0.7	46.1	0.7	46.6	1.1	46.8	0.4	46.9	0.2	47.1	0.4	47.4	0.6	47.6	0.4	48.2	1.3
1979	48.8	1.2	49.4	1.2	50.6	2.4	52.2	3.2	54.5	4.4	56.8	4.2	59.4	4.6	62.4	5.1	65.6	5.1	67.6	3.0	68.8	1.8	70.4	2.3
1980	73.3	4.1	76.8	4.8	79.9	4.0	81.7	2.3	82.5	1.0	83.2	0.8	84.5	1.6	85.2	0.8	85.6	0.5	85.5	-0.1	86.6	1.3	88.8	2.5
1981	91.5	3.0	96.3	5.2	100.5	4.4	102.0	1.5	102.3	0.3	102.1	-0.2	101.7	-0.4	101.6	-0.1	101.5	-0.1	100.7	-0.8	100.7	0.0	101.3	0.6
1982	101.7	0.4	100.7	-1.0	99.5	-1.2	96.7	-2.8	95.5	-1.2	97.7	2.3	101.1	3.5	101.8	0.7	101.0	-0.8	100.8	-0.2	101.9	1.1	101.5	-0.4
1983	98.6	-2.9	96.5	-2.1	94.9	-1.7	93.0	-2.0	94.0	1.1	96.0	2.1	96.5	0.5	96.9	0.4	97.0	0.1	96.6	-0.4	95.7	-0.9	94.9	-0.8
1984	94.1	-0.8	94.6	0.5	95.0	0.4	94.4	-0.6	95.3	1.0	96.1	0.8	95.9	-0.2	94.9	-1.0	94.1	-0.8	94.4	0.3	94.5	0.1	93.6	-1.0
1985	91.9	-1.8	90.2	-1.8	90.2	0.0	91.4	1.3	93.4	2.2	92.4	-1.1	91.7	-0.8	90.5	-1.3	90.7	0.2	90.6	-0.1	91.6	1.1	92.3	0.8
1986	89.5	-3.0	81.8	-8.6	73.9	-9.7	69.6	-5.8	69.8	0.3	69.9	0.1	64.1	-8.3	63.2	-1.4	65.3	3.3	63.3	-3.1	63.3	0.0	63.4	0.2
1987	66.6	5.0	68.0	2.1	68.3	0.4	69.1	1.2	69.7	0.9	71.1	2.0	72.6	2.1	73.8	1.7	72.2	-2.2	71.1	-1.5	70.8	-0.4	69.5	-1.8
1988	67.2	-3.3	66.7	-0.7	65.9	-1.2	67.6	2.6	68.4	1.2	68.6	0.3	68.0	-0.9	67.6	-0.6	66.1	-2.2	64.5	-2.4	64.4	-0.2	65.6	1.9
1989	68.1	3.8	68.9	1.2	69.9	1.5	74.2	6.2	76.0	2.4	75.8	-0.3	75.5	-0.4	72.0	-4.6	73.9	2.6	73.7	-0.3	72.8	-1.2	73.7	1.2
1990	79.8	8.3	77.0	-3.5	74.6	-3.1	73.4	-1.6	74.1	1.0	72.8	-1.8	72.7	-0.1	82.4	13.3	91.3	10.8	101.0	10.6	97.4	-3.6	90.5	-7.1
1991	90.1	-0.4	83.0	-7.9	78.5	-5.4	78.1	-0.5	80.2	2.7	80.3	0.1	80.1	-0.2	81.3	1.5	81.4	0.1	81.3	-0.1	81.2	-0.1	79.1	-2.6
1992	76.3	-3.5	76.8	0.7	75.8	-1.3	77.1	1.7	79.7	3.4	83.2	4.4	83.3	0.1	82.8	-0.6	84.4	1.9	83.2	-1.4	82.1	-1.3	79.7	-2.9
1993	79.4	-0.4	79.2	-0.3	79.7	0.6	80.3	0.8	81.9	2.0	83.2	1.6	81.0	-2.6	80.2	-1.0	80.9	0.9	81.2	0.4	78.3	-3.6	74.7	-4.6
1994	75.4	0.9	75.4	0.0	76.0	0.8	76.4	0.5	77.2	1.0	79.5	3.0	80.6	1.4	82.0	1.7	79.9	-2.6	77.4	-3.1	77.5	0.1	76.6	-1.2
1995	76.8	0.3	76.8	0.0	76.8	0.0	78.5	2.2	80.0	1.9	81.0	1.3	79.2	-2.2	78.3	-1.1	78.3	0.0	76.3	-2.6	75.9	-0.5	77.2	1.7

Source: U.S. Department of Labor, Bureau of Labor Statistics, Division of Industry Prices and Price Indexes. n.e.c. stands for not elsewhere classified. - indicates no data collected for period or unavailable.

Coal
Producer Price Index
Base 1982 = 100

For 1926-1995. Columns headed % show percentile change in the index from the previous period for which an index is available.

Year	Jan Index	%	Feb Index	%	Mar Index	%	Apr Index	%	May Index	%	Jun Index	%	Jul Index	%	Aug Index	%	Sep Index	%	Oct Index	%	Nov Index	%	Dec Index	%
1926	8.7	-	8.4	-3.4	8.3	-1.2	8.1	-2.4	8.1	0.0	8.1	0.0	8.1	0.0	8.2	1.2	8.3	1.2	8.7	4.8	9.4	8.0	8.9	-5.3
1927	8.7	-2.2	8.5	-2.3	8.4	-1.2	8.3	-1.2	8.3	0.0	8.3	0.0	8.3	0.0	8.4	1.2	8.5	1.2	8.3	-2.4	8.2	-1.2	8.2	0.0
1928	8.1	-1.2	8.1	0.0	8.0	-1.2	7.8	-2.5	7.7	-1.3	7.8	1.3	7.7	-1.3	7.8	1.3	7.8	0.0	7.9	1.3	7.9	0.0	7.8	-1.3
1929	7.9	1.3	7.9	0.0	7.8	-1.3	7.5	-3.8	7.5	0.0	7.5	0.0	7.6	1.3	7.6	0.0	7.7	1.3	7.7	0.0	7.7	0.0	7.8	1.3
1930	7.7	-1.3	7.7	0.0	7.6	-1.3	7.5	-1.3	7.4	-1.3	7.4	0.0	7.4	0.0	7.5	1.4	7.5	0.0	7.6	1.3	7.5	-1.3	7.5	0.0
1931	7.5	0.0	7.4	-1.3	7.3	-1.4	7.2	-1.4	7.2	0.0	7.2	0.0	7.2	0.0	7.3	1.4	7.3	0.0	7.3	0.0	7.3	0.0	7.3	0.0
1932	7.4	1.4	7.3	-1.4	7.2	-1.4	7.1	-1.4	7.0	-1.4	7.0	0.0	7.0	0.0	7.0	0.0	7.0	0.0	7.0	0.0	7.0	0.0	7.0	0.0
1933	7.0	0.0	6.9	-1.4	6.9	0.0	6.7	-2.9	6.6	-1.5	6.6	0.0	6.8	3.0	7.0	2.9	7.1	1.4	7.4	4.2	7.5	1.4	7.5	0.0
1934	7.5	0.0	7.5	0.0	7.5	0.0	7.6	1.3	7.6	0.0	7.6	0.0	7.7	1.3	7.8	1.3	7.8	0.0	7.8	0.0	7.8	0.0	7.8	0.0
1935	7.8	0.0	7.8	0.0	7.8	0.0	7.6	-2.6	7.6	0.0	7.6	0.0	7.7	1.3	7.7	0.0	7.8	1.3	7.9	1.3	8.0	1.3	8.0	0.0
1936	8.0	0.0	8.1	1.3	8.0	-1.2	7.8	-2.5	7.7	-1.3	7.7	0.0	7.7	0.0	7.8	1.3	7.8	0.0	7.9	1.3	7.9	0.0	7.9	0.0
1937	7.9	0.0	7.9	0.0	7.8	-1.3	7.7	-1.3	7.8	1.3	7.8	0.0	7.8	0.0	7.9	1.3	7.9	0.0	7.9	0.0	7.9	0.0	8.1	2.5
1938	8.2	1.2	8.2	0.0	7.9	-3.7	7.8	-1.3	7.7	-1.3	7.7	0.0	7.8	1.3	7.8	0.0	7.9	1.3	7.9	0.0	7.9	0.0	7.9	0.0
1939	7.9	0.0	7.9	0.0	7.9	0.0	7.8	-1.3	7.8	0.0	7.6	-2.6	7.6	0.0	7.6	0.0	7.6	0.0	7.8	2.6	7.8	0.0	7.8	0.0
1940	7.9	1.3	7.9	0.0	7.8	-1.3	7.7	-1.3	7.6	-1.3	7.7	1.3	7.7	0.0	7.7	0.0	7.8	1.3	8.0	2.6	8.0	0.0	8.1	1.3
1941	8.1	0.0	8.1	0.0	8.0	-1.2	8.0	0.0	8.2	2.5	8.3	1.2	8.4	1.2	8.5	1.2	8.6	1.2	8.6	0.0	8.6	0.0	8.6	0.0
1942	8.7	1.2	8.7	0.0	8.7	0.0	8.6	-1.1	8.7	1.2	8.7	0.0	8.7	0.0	8.8	1.1	8.8	0.0	8.8	0.0	8.8	0.0	8.9	1.1
1943	9.0	1.1	9.1	1.1	9.2	1.1	9.2	0.0	9.2	0.0	9.2	0.0	9.3	1.1	9.3	0.0	9.3	0.0	9.3	0.0	9.3	0.0	9.5	2.2
1944	9.6	1.1	9.6	0.0	9.6	0.0	9.6	0.0	9.6	0.0	9.6	0.0	9.6	0.0	9.6	0.0	9.6	0.0	9.6	0.0	9.6	0.0	9.6	0.0
1945	9.6	0.0	9.6	0.0	9.6	0.0	9.6	0.0	9.8	2.1	9.9	1.0	10.0	1.0	10.0	0.0	10.0	0.0	10.0	0.0	10.0	0.0	10.1	1.0
1946	10.1	0.0	10.1	0.0	10.1	0.0	10.1	0.0	10.1	0.0	10.6	5.0	11.0	3.8	11.1	0.9	11.1	0.0	11.1	0.0	11.1	0.0	11.2	0.9
1947	11.5	2.7	11.5	0.0	11.5	0.0	11.6	0.9	11.6	0.0	11.6	0.0	13.5	16.4	14.3	5.9	14.4	0.7	14.5	0.7	14.5	0.0	14.6	0.7
1948	14.7	0.7	14.7	0.0	14.7	0.0	14.8	0.7	15.0	1.4	15.1	0.7	16.3	7.9	16.4	0.6	16.4	0.0	16.3	-0.6	16.3	0.0	16.3	0.0
1949	16.3	0.0	16.2	-0.6	16.0	-1.2	15.4	-3.8	15.2	-1.3	15.2	0.0	15.3	0.7	15.3	0.0	15.3	0.0	15.3	0.0	15.5	1.3	15.6	0.6
1950	15.7	0.6	15.8	0.6	16.0	1.3	15.5	-3.1	15.4	-0.6	15.4	0.0	15.4	0.0	15.5	0.6	15.6	0.6	15.6	0.0	15.6	0.0	15.6	0.0
1951	15.6	0.0	16.2	3.8	16.2	0.0	15.9	-1.9	15.8	-0.6	15.9	0.6	15.7	-1.3	15.8	0.6	15.9	0.6	16.0	0.6	16.0	0.0	16.0	0.0
1952	16.0	0.0	16.0	0.0	16.0	0.0	15.4	-3.8	15.4	0.0	15.5	0.6	15.6	0.6	15.6	0.0	15.8	1.3	16.6	5.1	16.7	0.6	17.0	1.8
1953	17.1	0.6	17.0	-0.6	16.8	-1.2	16.3	-3.0	16.3	0.0	16.3	0.0	16.4	0.6	16.4	0.0	16.5	0.6	16.5	0.0	16.5	0.0	16.5	0.0
1954	16.4	-0.6	16.3	-0.6	15.8	-3.1	15.3	-3.2	15.4	0.7	15.4	0.0	15.4	0.0	15.4	0.0	15.5	0.6	15.4	-0.6	15.4	0.0	15.4	0.0
1955	15.4	0.0	15.4	0.0	15.4	0.0	15.0	-2.6	14.7	-2.0	14.8	0.7	14.9	0.7	15.0	0.7	15.9	6.0	16.0	0.6	16.0	0.0	16.1	0.6
1956	16.1	0.0	16.1	0.0	16.2	0.6	16.4	1.2	16.4	0.0	16.5	0.6	16.6	0.6	16.7	0.6	16.8	0.6	17.8	6.0	17.9	0.6	18.1	1.1
1957	18.2	0.6	18.2	0.0	18.1	-0.5	18.1	0.0	18.1	0.0	18.1	0.0	18.2	0.6	18.3	0.5	18.3	0.0	18.4	0.5	18.5	0.5	18.5	0.0
1958	18.5	0.0	18.5	0.0	18.5	0.0	17.6	-4.9	17.6	0.0	17.7	0.6	17.8	0.6	17.9	0.6	18.0	0.6	18.2	1.1	18.2	0.0	18.2	0.0
1959	18.4	1.1	18.5	0.5	18.3	-1.1	17.5	-4.4	17.4	-0.6	17.6	1.1	17.8	1.1	17.9	0.6	18.0	0.6	18.1	0.6	18.2	0.6	18.2	0.0
1960	18.2	0.0	18.2	0.0	18.2	0.0	17.5	-3.8	17.4	-0.6	17.5	0.6	17.7	1.1	17.8	0.6	18.0	1.1	18.0	0.0	18.0	0.0	18.1	0.6
1961	18.1	0.0	18.1	0.0	18.0	-0.6	17.6	-2.2	17.2	-2.3	17.3	0.6	17.4	0.6	17.5	0.6	17.6	0.6	17.7	0.6	17.8	0.6	17.9	0.6
1962	17.9	0.0	17.9	0.0	17.9	0.0	17.3	-3.4	17.1	-1.2	17.1	0.0	17.3	1.2	17.3	0.0	17.5	1.2	17.6	0.6	17.7	0.6	17.8	0.6
1963	17.8	0.0	17.8	0.0	17.8	0.0	17.2	-3.4	17.1	-0.6	17.2	0.6	17.3	0.6	17.4	0.6	17.6	1.1	17.7	0.6	17.8	0.6	17.8	0.0
1964	17.8	0.0	17.8	0.0	17.6	-1.1	17.2	-2.3	17.2	0.0	17.3	0.6	17.4	0.6	17.5	0.6	17.6	0.6	17.7	0.6	17.7	0.0	17.8	0.6
1965	17.8	0.0	17.8	0.0	17.6	-1.1	17.1	-2.8	17.1	0.0	17.1	0.0	17.2	0.6	17.3	0.6	17.5	1.2	17.6	0.6	17.7	0.6	17.7	0.0
1966	17.8	0.6	17.8	0.0	17.7	-0.6	17.2	-2.8	17.5	1.7	17.6	0.6	17.7	0.6	17.8	0.6	18.0	1.1	18.2	1.1	18.4	1.1	18.5	0.5
1967	18.5	0.0	18.5	0.0	18.5	0.0	18.6	0.5	18.6	0.0	18.6	0.0	18.6	0.0	18.8	1.1	18.8	0.0	18.9	0.5	19.0	0.5	19.0	0.0
1968	19.0	0.0	19.0	0.0	19.1	0.5	19.2	0.5	19.1	-0.5	19.1	0.0	19.2	0.5	19.2	0.0	19.2	0.0	19.9	3.6	20.2	1.5	20.4	1.0
1969	20.4	0.0	20.4	0.0	20.4	0.0	20.6	1.0	20.5	-0.5	20.7	1.0	20.9	1.0	20.9	0.0	21.0	0.5	22.0	4.8	22.4	1.8	22.5	0.4
1970	22.7	0.9	23.8	4.8	24.1	1.3	26.4	9.5	26.6	0.8	27.8	4.5	28.4	2.2	28.8	1.4	30.1	4.5	32.8	9.0	32.9	0.3	32.9	0.0

[Continued]

Coal
Producer Price Index
Base 1982 = 100
[Continued]

For 1926-1995. Columns headed % show percentile change in the index from the previous period for which an index is available.

Year	Jan Index	%	Feb Index	%	Mar Index	%	Apr Index	%	May Index	%	Jun Index	%	Jul Index	%	Aug Index	%	Sep Index	%	Oct Index	%	Nov Index	%	Dec Index	%
1971	32.9	0.0	32.9	0.0	32.9	0.0	34.4	4.6	34.2	-0.6	34.1	-0.3	34.2	0.3	34.2	0.0	34.2	0.0	34.2	0.0	34.2	0.0	36.0	5.3
1972	36.0	0.0	36.0	0.0	36.0	0.0	35.8	-0.6	35.8	0.0	35.8	0.0	35.8	0.0	35.8	0.0	35.9	0.3	36.0	0.3	37.6	4.4	38.4	2.1
1973	38.4	0.0	38.7	0.8	38.8	0.3	40.0	3.1	40.1	0.3	40.2	0.2	40.0	-0.5	40.1	0.3	41.6	3.7	41.9	0.7	44.7	6.7	45.0	0.7
1974	46.6	3.6	47.3	1.5	48.5	2.5	56.8	17.1	57.6	1.4	60.1	4.3	64.3	7.0	66.9	4.0	69.5	3.9	73.7	6.0	74.4	0.9	80.1	7.7
1975	80.2	0.1	76.6	-4.5	72.6	-5.2	72.4	-0.3	72.8	0.6	72.2	-0.8	71.5	-1.0	70.7	-1.1	69.8	-1.3	69.4	-0.6	68.2	-1.7	69.4	1.8
1976	69.2	-0.3	69.0	-0.3	68.8	-0.3	68.7	-0.1	68.7	0.0	68.6	-0.1	68.8	0.3	68.8	0.0	68.8	0.0	68.9	0.1	69.0	0.1	69.9	1.3
1977	70.3	0.6	70.6	0.4	70.8	0.3	71.0	0.3	72.3	1.8	73.0	1.0	73.5	0.7	73.7	0.3	73.9	0.3	74.5	0.8	74.9	0.5	75.2	0.4
1978	75.5	0.4	75.7	0.3	76.1	0.5	79.7	4.7	80.9	1.5	81.3	0.5	81.7	0.5	82.6	1.1	82.8	0.2	83.0	0.2	82.7	-0.4	83.0	0.4
1979	83.0	0.0	83.0	0.0	83.3	0.4	83.6	0.4	84.3	0.8	84.5	0.2	84.6	0.1	84.9	0.4	84.6	-0.4	85.0	0.5	85.1	0.1	85.8	0.8
1980	85.9	0.1	86.0	0.1	86.3	0.3	87.0	0.8	87.2	0.2	87.2	0.0	87.4	0.2	87.6	0.2	88.1	0.6	88.0	-0.1	88.9	1.0	88.9	0.0
1981	89.4	0.6	89.9	0.6	90.0	0.1	90.9	1.0	91.1	0.2	91.9	0.9	94.5	2.8	94.8	0.3	95.4	0.6	95.5	0.1	95.9	0.4	96.4	0.5
1982	98.2	1.9	99.1	0.9	99.0	-0.1	99.6	0.6	99.9	0.3	99.8	-0.1	100.6	0.8	100.8	0.2	100.7	-0.1	100.6	-0.1	100.9	0.3	100.7	-0.2
1983	100.2	-0.5	99.7	-0.5	100.7	1.0	100.6	-0.1	100.1	-0.5	99.9	-0.2	100.0	0.1	100.3	0.3	100.6	0.3	100.7	0.1	101.4	0.7	101.7	0.3
1984	101.2	-0.5	101.9	0.7	102.1	0.2	101.4	-0.7	102.4	1.0	101.8	-0.6	102.5	0.7	102.9	0.4	102.7	-0.2	102.7	0.0	102.6	-0.1	102.4	-0.2
1985	102.5	0.1	102.8	0.3	102.6	-0.2	102.4	-0.2	102.5	0.1	102.4	-0.1	102.8	0.4	102.9	0.1	102.6	-0.3	101.7	-0.9	100.6	-1.1	101.1	0.5
1986	101.3	0.2	100.9	-0.4	101.5	0.6	101.1	-0.4	100.9	-0.2	100.8	-0.1	100.9	0.1	100.7	-0.2	100.5	-0.2	100.5	0.0	100.1	-0.4	100.0	-0.1
1987	100.1	0.1	99.3	-0.8	99.0	-0.3	97.2	-1.8	96.8	-0.4	96.5	-0.3	96.1	-0.4	96.1	0.0	95.8	-0.3	96.0	0.2	96.4	0.4	95.9	-0.5
1988	95.6	-0.3	96.3	0.7	95.8	-0.5	95.5	-0.3	95.2	-0.3	95.2	0.0	95.7	0.5	95.1	-0.6	95.4	0.3	95.5	0.1	94.7	-0.8	94.6	-0.1
1989	94.1	-0.5	93.6	-0.5	93.6	0.0	94.2	0.6	94.6	0.4	94.9	0.3	96.2	1.4	96.6	0.4	96.5	-0.1	97.1	0.6	97.7	0.6	97.2	-0.5
1990	97.8	0.6	96.3	-1.5	96.4	0.1	96.7	0.3	97.7	1.0	97.9	0.2	98.0	0.1	96.9	-1.1	97.5	0.6	98.2	0.7	98.8	0.6	97.9	-0.9
1991	98.5	0.6	98.2	-0.3	97.4	-0.8	97.3	-0.1	97.1	-0.2	98.0	0.9	97.6	-0.4	96.6	-1.0	96.6	0.0	95.9	-0.7	97.1	1.3	96.3	-0.8
1992	93.7	-2.7	94.5	0.9	93.8	-0.7	94.8	1.1	95.0	0.2	96.0	1.1	95.3	-0.7	95.1	-0.2	95.1	0.0	95.7	0.6	94.8	-0.9	96.5	1.8
1993	95.6	-0.9	94.9	-0.7	94.9	0.0	94.6	-0.3	94.1	-0.5	94.1	0.0	94.4	0.3	95.5	1.2	97.8	2.4	100.3	2.6	99.5	-0.8	97.5	-2.0
1994	97.3	-0.2	96.1	-1.2	96.2	0.1	96.5	0.3	96.8	0.3	95.5	-1.3	95.6	0.1	96.2	0.6	97.8	1.7	98.4	0.6	98.3	-0.1	95.5	-2.8
1995	91.9	-3.8	94.6	2.9	96.9	2.4	95.9	-1.0	93.9	-2.1	94.3	0.4	96.0	1.8	95.3	-0.7	94.0	-1.4	96.5	2.7	94.6	-2.0	94.8	0.2

Source: U.S. Department of Labor, Bureau of Labor Statistics, Division of Industry Prices and Price Indexes. n.e.c. stands for not elsewhere classified. - indicates no data collected for period or unavailable.

Coke Oven Products

Producer Price Index
Base 1982 = 100

For 1926-1995. Columns headed % show percentile change in the index from the previous period for which an index is available.

Year	Jan Index	%	Feb Index	%	Mar Index	%	Apr Index	%	May Index	%	Jun Index	%	Jul Index	%	Aug Index	%	Sep Index	%	Oct Index	%	Nov Index	%	Dec Index	%
1926	6.8	-	6.8	0.0	6.1	-10.3	5.6	-8.2	5.5	-1.8	5.6	1.8	5.6	0.0	5.6	0.0	5.7	1.8	5.7	0.0	6.3	10.5	6.1	-3.2
1927	5.8	-4.9	5.7	-1.7	5.7	0.0	5.7	0.0	5.6	-1.8	5.6	0.0	5.6	0.0	5.6	0.0	5.6	0.0	5.6	0.0	5.5	-1.8	5.5	0.0
1928	5.1	-7.3	5.0	-2.0	5.0	0.0	4.9	-2.0	5.0	2.0	5.0	0.0	5.0	0.0	5.0	0.0	5.0	0.0	5.0	0.0	5.0	0.0	5.0	0.0
1929	5.0	0.0	5.0	0.0	5.1	2.0	5.0	-2.0	5.0	0.0	5.0	0.0	5.0	0.0	5.0	0.0	5.0	0.0	5.0	0.0	5.0	0.0	5.0	0.0
1930	5.0	0.0	5.0	0.0	5.0	0.0	5.0	0.0	5.0	0.0	5.0	0.0	5.0	0.0	5.0	0.0	5.0	0.0	5.0	0.0	5.0	0.0	5.0	0.0
1931	5.0	0.0	5.0	0.0	5.0	0.0	5.0	0.0	5.0	0.0	4.9	-2.0	4.9	0.0	4.9	0.0	4.9	0.0	4.9	0.0	4.8	-2.0	4.8	0.0
1932	4.8	0.0	4.8	0.0	4.8	0.0	4.7	-2.1	4.6	-2.1	4.6	0.0	4.5	-2.2	4.6	2.2	4.6	0.0	4.6	0.0	4.5	-2.2	4.5	0.0
1933	4.5	0.0	4.5	0.0	4.5	0.0	4.5	0.0	4.5	0.0	4.5	0.0	4.5	0.0	4.6	2.2	4.7	2.2	4.9	4.3	5.0	2.0	5.0	0.0
1934	5.0	0.0	5.0	0.0	5.0	0.0	5.0	0.0	5.0	0.0	5.0	0.0	5.1	2.0	5.1	0.0	5.1	0.0	5.1	0.0	5.1	0.0	5.1	0.0
1935	5.1	0.0	5.3	3.9	5.3	0.0	5.3	0.0	5.3	0.0	5.3	0.0	5.3	0.0	5.3	0.0	5.3	0.0	5.3	0.0	5.3	0.0	5.3	0.0
1936	5.5	3.8	5.6	1.8	5.6	0.0	5.6	0.0	5.6	0.0	5.6	0.0	5.6	0.0	5.6	0.0	5.6	0.0	5.8	3.6	5.8	0.0	5.8	0.0
1937	5.8	0.0	5.8	0.0	5.8	0.0	6.1	5.2	6.2	1.6	6.2	0.0	6.2	0.0	6.2	0.0	6.2	0.0	6.2	0.0	6.3	1.6	6.3	0.0
1938	6.3	0.0	6.3	0.0	6.3	0.0	6.3	0.0	6.3	0.0	6.2	-1.6	6.2	0.0	6.2	0.0	6.2	0.0	6.2	0.0	6.2	0.0	6.2	0.0
1939	6.2	0.0	6.2	0.0	6.2	0.0	6.2	0.0	6.2	0.0	6.2	0.0	6.2	0.0	6.2	0.0	6.2	0.0	6.4	3.2	6.6	3.1	6.5	-1.5
1940	6.5	0.0	6.5	0.0	6.5	0.0	6.5	0.0	6.5	0.0	6.5	0.0	6.5	0.0	6.5	0.0	6.5	0.0	6.5	0.0	6.7	3.1	6.8	1.5
1941	6.8	0.0	6.8	0.0	6.8	0.0	6.8	0.0	7.1	4.4	7.3	2.8	7.3	0.0	7.3	0.0	7.3	0.0	7.3	0.0	7.3	0.0	7.3	0.0
1942	7.3	0.0	7.3	0.0	7.3	0.0	7.3	0.0	7.3	0.0	7.3	0.0	7.3	0.0	7.3	0.0	7.3	0.0	7.3	0.0	7.3	0.0	7.3	0.0
1943	7.3	0.0	7.3	0.0	7.3	0.0	7.3	0.0	7.3	0.0	7.3	0.0	7.3	0.0	7.3	0.0	7.3	0.0	7.3	0.0	7.4	1.4	7.4	0.0
1944	7.5	1.4	7.8	4.0	7.8	0.0	7.8	0.0	7.8	0.0	7.8	0.0	7.8	0.0	7.8	0.0	7.8	0.0	7.8	0.0	7.8	0.0	7.8	0.0
1945	7.8	0.0	7.8	0.0	7.8	0.0	7.8	0.0	7.8	0.0	7.8	0.0	7.8	0.0	8.0	2.6	8.0	0.0	8.0	0.0	8.0	0.0	8.0	0.0
1946	8.0	0.0	8.0	0.0	8.0	0.0	7.9	-1.2	7.9	0.0	7.9	0.0	8.8	11.4	8.8	0.0	8.8	0.0	8.8	0.0	8.8	0.0	8.8	0.0
1947	9.1	3.4	9.2	1.1	9.2	0.0	9.3	1.1	9.3	0.0	9.4	1.1	9.6	2.1	10.4	8.3	10.7	2.9	10.7	0.0	10.8	0.9	10.9	0.9
1948	11.3	3.7	11.4	0.9	11.4	0.0	11.5	0.9	12.1	5.2	12.4	2.5	12.6	1.6	12.9	2.4	12.9	0.0	12.9	0.0	12.9	0.0	12.9	0.0
1949	13.1	1.6	13.2	0.8	13.2	0.0	13.2	0.0	13.1	-0.8	13.1	0.0	13.1	0.0	13.1	0.0	13.1	0.0	13.1	0.0	13.1	0.0	13.1	0.0
1950	13.1	0.0	13.3	1.5	13.5	1.5	13.6	0.7	13.6	0.0	13.6	0.0	13.6	0.0	13.6	0.0	13.6	0.0	13.8	1.5	14.2	2.9	14.3	0.7
1951	14.5	1.4	14.5	0.0	14.5	0.0	14.6	0.7	14.6	0.0	14.6	0.0	14.6	0.0	14.6	0.0	14.6	0.0	14.6	0.0	14.6	0.0	14.6	0.0
1952	14.6	0.0	14.6	0.0	14.6	0.0	14.6	0.0	14.6	0.0	14.6	0.0	14.6	0.0	14.6	0.0	14.6	0.0	14.6	0.0	14.6	0.0	15.2	4.1
1953	15.5	2.0	15.5	0.0	15.5	0.0	15.5	0.0	15.5	0.0	15.5	0.0	15.5	0.0	15.5	0.0	15.5	0.0	15.6	0.6	15.6	0.0	15.6	0.0
1954	15.6	0.0	15.6	0.0	15.6	0.0	15.6	0.0	15.6	0.0	15.6	0.0	15.6	0.0	15.6	0.0	15.6	0.0	15.6	0.0	15.6	0.0	15.6	0.0
1955	15.6	0.0	15.6	0.0	15.6	0.0	15.7	0.6	15.7	0.0	15.7	0.0	15.7	0.0	16.2	3.2	16.1	-0.6	16.3	1.2	16.3	0.0	16.3	0.0
1956	17.1	4.9	17.1	0.0	17.1	0.0	17.1	0.0	17.1	0.0	17.1	0.0	17.1	0.0	18.0	5.3	18.4	2.2	18.4	0.0	18.4	0.0	18.4	0.0
1957	18.7	1.6	19.1	2.1	19.0	-0.5	19.0	0.0	19.0	0.0	19.0	0.0	19.0	0.0	19.0	0.0	19.0	0.0	19.0	0.0	19.0	0.0	19.0	0.0
1958	19.0	0.0	19.0	0.0	19.0	0.0	19.0	0.0	19.0	0.0	19.0	0.0	19.0	0.0	19.0	0.0	19.0	0.0	19.0	0.0	19.0	0.0	19.0	0.0
1959	19.2	1.1	20.0	4.2	20.0	0.0	20.0	0.0	20.0	0.0	20.0	0.0	20.0	0.0	20.0	0.0	20.0	0.0	20.0	0.0	20.0	0.0	20.0	0.0
1960	20.0	0.0	20.0	0.0	20.0	0.0	20.0	0.0	20.0	0.0	20.0	0.0	20.0	0.0	20.0	0.0	20.0	0.0	20.0	0.0	20.0	0.0	20.0	0.0
1961	20.0	0.0	20.0	0.0	20.0	0.0	20.0	0.0	20.0	0.0	20.0	0.0	20.0	0.0	20.0	0.0	20.0	0.0	20.0	0.0	20.0	0.0	20.0	0.0
1962	20.0	0.0	20.0	0.0	20.0	0.0	20.0	0.0	20.0	0.0	20.0	0.0	20.0	0.0	20.0	0.0	20.0	0.0	20.0	0.0	20.0	0.0	20.0	0.0
1963	20.0	0.0	20.0	0.0	20.0	0.0	20.0	0.0	20.0	0.0	20.0	0.0	20.0	0.0	20.0	0.0	20.0	0.0	20.0	0.0	20.0	0.0	20.0	0.0
1964	20.0	0.0	20.0	0.0	20.0	0.0	20.5	2.5	20.8	1.5	20.8	0.0	20.8	0.0	20.8	0.0	20.8	0.0	20.8	0.0	20.8	0.0	20.8	0.0
1965	20.8	0.0	20.8	0.0	20.8	0.0	20.8	0.0	20.8	0.0	20.8	0.0	20.8	0.0	20.8	0.0	20.8	0.0	20.8	0.0	20.8	0.0	20.8	0.0
1966	20.8	0.0	20.8	0.0	20.8	0.0	20.8	0.0	20.8	0.0	21.2	1.9	21.7	2.4	21.7	0.0	21.7	0.0	21.7	0.0	21.7	0.0	21.7	0.0
1967	21.7	0.0	21.7	0.0	21.7	0.0	21.7	0.0	21.7	0.0	21.7	0.0	21.7	0.0	21.7	0.0	21.7	0.0	21.7	0.0	21.7	0.0	21.7	0.0
1968	21.7	0.0	21.7	0.0	21.7	0.0	22.6	4.1	22.6	0.0	22.6	0.0	22.6	0.0	22.6	0.0	22.6	0.0	22.6	0.0	22.6	0.0	23.3	3.1
1969	23.3	0.0	23.3	0.0	23.3	0.0	23.3	0.0	23.3	0.0	23.3	0.0	23.3	0.0	23.3	0.0	23.3	0.0	24.5	5.2	24.5	0.0	24.5	0.0
1970	24.5	0.0	24.5	0.0	24.5	0.0	27.0	10.2	27.0	0.0	27.0	0.0	27.3	1.1	27.3	0.0	27.3	0.0	31.6	15.8	31.6	0.0	31.6	0.0

[Continued]

Coke Oven Products
Producer Price Index
Base 1982 = 100
[Continued]

For 1926-1995. Columns headed % show percentile change in the index from the previous period for which an index is available.

Year	Jan Index	%	Feb Index	%	Mar Index	%	Apr Index	%	May Index	%	Jun Index	%	Jul Index	%	Aug Index	%	Sep Index	%	Oct Index	%	Nov Index	%	Dec Index	%
1971	31.6	0.0	31.6	0.0	31.6	0.0	31.6	0.0	32.2	1.9	32.6	1.2	32.6	0.0	32.6	0.0	32.6	0.0	32.6	0.0	32.6	0.0	32.6	0.0
1972	32.6	0.0	33.6	3.1	33.6	0.0	33.6	0.0	33.6	0.0	33.6	0.0	33.6	0.0	33.6	0.0	33.6	0.0	34.0	1.2	34.0	0.0	34.6	1.8
1973	35.2	1.7	35.7	1.4	35.7	0.0	36.2	1.4	36.2	0.0	36.2	0.0	36.2	0.0	36.2	0.0	36.2	0.0	36.2	0.0	36.2	0.0	36.8	1.7
1974	37.7	2.4	37.6	-0.3	40.1	6.6	46.6	16.2	52.4	12.4	53.9	2.9	55.4	2.8	58.5	5.6	60.8	3.9	66.1	8.7	67.2	1.7	67.6	0.6
1975	71.6	5.9	71.6	0.0	71.6	0.0	72.0	0.6	72.0	0.0	72.0	0.0	71.4	-0.8	71.1	-0.4	71.7	0.8	71.7	0.0	71.7	0.0	71.7	0.0
1976	71.6	-0.1	74.9	4.6	75.0	0.1	75.0	0.0	75.0	0.0	75.0	0.0	75.0	0.0	75.0	0.0	75.0	0.0	75.8	1.1	75.8	0.0	78.7	3.8
1977	79.6	1.1	79.6	0.0	79.6	0.0	80.8	1.5	81.3	0.6	83.6	2.8	83.6	0.0	83.6	0.0	83.6	0.0	83.6	0.0	83.6	0.0	83.6	0.0
1978	84.1	0.6	86.8	3.2	86.8	0.0	86.8	0.0	90.7	4.5	90.7	0.0	90.7	0.0	90.7	0.0	90.7	0.0	90.7	0.0	90.7	0.0	90.7	0.0
1979	91.2	0.6	91.8	0.7	92.8	1.1	93.2	0.4	93.3	0.1	93.3	0.0	93.3	0.0	93.3	0.0	93.3	0.0	93.4	0.1	93.4	0.0	93.4	0.0
1980	93.3	-0.1	93.3	0.0	93.3	0.0	93.3	0.0	93.3	0.0	93.3	0.0	93.3	0.0	93.3	0.0	93.3	0.0	93.3	0.0	93.3	0.0	93.2	-0.1
1981	93.2	0.0	93.2	0.0	93.2	0.0	93.2	0.0	101.3	8.7	101.7	0.4	101.7	0.0	101.7	0.0	101.7	0.0	101.7	0.0	101.7	0.0	101.7	0.0
1982	101.7	0.0	101.7	0.0	101.3	-0.4	101.3	0.0	101.3	0.0	100.1	-1.2	99.7	-0.4	99.4	-0.3	99.6	0.2	98.0	-1.6	98.0	0.0	98.0	0.0
1983	97.7	-0.3	97.7	0.0	96.9	-0.8	96.9	0.0	95.0	-2.0	95.0	0.0	93.5	-1.6	98.3	5.1	98.3	0.0	98.1	-0.2	98.3	0.2	90.0	-8.4
1984	90.6	0.7	94.8	4.6	95.1	0.3	95.9	0.8	95.6	-0.3	95.8	0.2	95.7	-0.1	94.7	-1.0	94.4	-0.3	93.7	-0.7	93.7	0.0	94.2	0.5
1985	95.2	1.1	95.2	0.0	93.8	-1.5	93.2	-0.6	93.0	-0.2	93.0	0.0	92.8	-0.2	92.8	0.0	92.8	0.0	92.5	-0.3	92.5	0.0	91.8	-0.8
1986	90.2	-1.7	90.4	0.2	90.3	-0.1	89.1	-1.3	89.0	-0.1	88.1	-1.0	88.0	-0.1	87.9	-0.1	88.0	0.1	87.4	-0.7	84.0	-3.9	84.0	0.0
1987	81.9	-2.5	80.9	-1.2	82.3	1.7	83.2	1.1	84.0	1.0	82.5	-1.8	82.4	-0.1	82.5	0.1	82.3	-0.2	83.5	1.5	83.5	0.0	84.2	0.8
1988	84.3	0.1	84.6	0.4	85.0	0.5	85.0	0.0	85.0	0.0	85.0	0.0	85.0	0.0	85.0	0.0	85.0	0.0	85.0	0.0	85.0	0.0	85.0	0.0
1989	88.8	4.5	88.9	0.1	89.1	0.2	88.5	-0.7	90.5	2.3	90.4	-0.1	90.6	0.2	90.8	0.2	90.7	-0.1	91.0	0.3	89.8	-1.3	89.8	0.0
1990	90.4	0.7	94.1	4.1	91.1	-3.2	90.9	-0.2	90.7	-0.2	90.9	0.2	90.1	-0.9	91.2	1.2	91.0	-0.2	92.7	1.9	92.3	-0.4	91.7	-0.7
1991	90.7	-1.1	93.7	3.3	94.5	0.9	95.0	0.5	94.6	-0.4	94.6	0.0	94.6	0.0	93.1	-1.6	94.1	1.1	93.9	-0.2	94.2	0.3	93.8	-0.4
1992	94.4	0.6	94.3	-0.1	92.1	-2.3	91.8	-0.3	90.9	-1.0	89.5	-1.5	90.5	1.1	90.3	-0.2	90.1	-0.2	90.1	0.0	91.1	1.1	90.9	-0.2
1993	91.3	0.4	88.6	-3.0	88.7	0.1	88.8	0.1	88.2	-0.7	88.0	-0.2	88.7	0.8	89.8	1.2	90.7	1.0	89.7	-1.1	88.5	-1.3	88.9	0.5
1994	87.9	-1.1	88.3	0.5	88.7	0.5	90.4	1.9	90.1	-0.3	90.1	0.0	90.3	0.2	87.7	-2.9	87.5	-0.2	87.9	0.5	87.3	-0.7	87.0	-0.3
1995	87.9	1.0	91.7	4.3	91.7	0.0	91.5	-0.2	91.9	0.4	92.3	0.4	91.6	-0.8	91.8	0.2	93.0	1.3	93.3	0.3	93.1	-0.2	93.8	0.8

Source: U.S. Department of Labor, Bureau of Labor Statistics, Division of Industry Prices and Price Indexes. n.e.c. stands for not elsewhere classified. - indicates no data collected for period or unavailable.

Gas Fuels
Producer Price Index
Base 1982 = 100

For 1958-1995. Columns headed % show percentile change in the index from the previous period for which an index is available.

Year	Jan Index	%	Feb Index	%	Mar Index	%	Apr Index	%	May Index	%	Jun Index	%	Jul Index	%	Aug Index	%	Sep Index	%	Oct Index	%	Nov Index	%	Dec Index	%
1958	7.1	-	7.2	1.4	7.1	-1.4	6.9	-2.8	6.9	0.0	6.9	0.0	6.9	0.0	7.2	4.3	7.3	1.4	7.5	2.7	7.5	0.0	7.6	1.3
1959	7.9	3.9	7.9	0.0	8.0	1.3	7.7	-3.8	7.7	0.0	7.5	-2.6	7.5	0.0	7.7	2.7	8.0	3.9	7.8	-2.5	8.0	2.6	8.1	1.3
1960	8.2	1.2	8.1	-1.2	8.2	1.2	8.2	0.0	7.9	-3.7	7.9	0.0	8.1	2.5	8.2	1.2	8.5	3.7	8.5	0.0	8.5	0.0	8.5	0.0
1961	8.5	0.0	8.6	1.2	8.6	0.0	8.3	-3.5	8.4	1.2	8.1	-3.6	8.2	1.2	8.2	0.0	8.2	0.0	8.4	2.4	8.4	0.0	8.4	0.0
1962	8.3	-1.2	8.6	3.6	8.4	-2.3	8.1	-3.6	8.2	1.2	8.0	-2.4	8.4	5.0	8.3	-1.2	8.5	2.4	8.7	2.4	8.6	-1.1	8.7	1.2
1963	8.5	-2.3	9.0	5.9	9.0	0.0	8.7	-3.3	8.5	-2.3	8.5	0.0	8.5	0.0	8.5	0.0	8.6	1.2	8.6	0.0	8.6	0.0	8.8	2.3
1964	8.8	0.0	8.9	1.1	8.7	-2.2	8.5	-2.3	8.2	-3.5	8.2	0.0	8.5	3.7	8.5	0.0	8.4	-1.2	8.5	1.2	8.7	2.4	8.7	0.0
1965	8.6	-1.1	8.7	1.2	8.7	0.0	8.6	-1.1	8.6	0.0	8.7	1.2	8.6	-1.1	8.7	1.2	8.8	1.1	8.9	1.1	8.9	0.0	9.1	2.2
1966	9.0	-1.1	9.1	1.1	9.0	-1.1	9.1	1.1	9.0	-1.1	9.1	1.1	9.0	-1.1	9.1	1.1	9.1	0.0	9.2	1.1	9.2	0.0	9.3	1.1
1967	9.5	2.2	9.5	0.0	9.5	0.0	9.5	0.0	9.5	0.0	9.5	0.0	9.3	-2.1	9.4	1.1	9.4	0.0	9.4	0.0	9.4	0.0	9.4	0.0
1968	9.2	-2.1	9.4	2.2	8.9	-5.3	8.8	-1.1	8.7	-1.1	8.7	0.0	8.5	-2.3	8.5	0.0	8.5	0.0	8.5	0.0	8.5	0.0	8.6	1.2
1969	8.7	1.2	8.8	1.1	8.8	0.0	8.6	-2.3	8.6	0.0	8.6	0.0	8.6	0.0	8.7	1.2	8.7	0.0	9.1	4.6	9.1	0.0	9.3	2.2
1970	9.3	0.0	9.5	2.2	9.6	1.1	9.6	0.0	9.6	0.0	9.7	1.0	9.7	0.0	9.7	0.0	10.1	4.1	10.0	-1.0	10.1	1.0	10.3	2.0
1971	10.2	-1.0	10.3	1.0	10.4	1.0	10.1	-2.9	10.1	0.0	10.1	0.0	10.1	0.0	10.2	1.0	10.3	1.0	10.3	0.0	10.3	0.0	10.4	1.0
1972	10.4	0.0	10.4	0.0	10.5	1.0	10.6	1.0	10.7	0.9	10.6	-0.9	10.7	0.9	10.8	0.9	11.0	1.9	11.1	0.9	11.2	0.9	11.2	0.0
1973	11.2	0.0	11.2	0.0	11.2	0.0	11.3	0.9	11.4	0.9	12.1	6.1	12.1	0.0	12.3	1.7	12.5	1.6	12.6	0.8	12.5	-0.8	13.0	4.0
1974	12.9	-0.8	13.8	7.0	14.0	1.4	14.0	0.0	14.1	0.7	14.3	1.4	17.7	23.8	17.9	1.1	15.7	-12.3	15.8	0.6	16.5	4.4	16.7	1.2
1975	17.1	2.4	17.8	4.1	17.7	-0.6	19.5	10.2	20.6	5.6	20.7	0.5	21.3	2.9	21.4	0.5	21.8	1.9	21.8	0.0	22.2	1.8	23.1	4.1
1976	23.0	-0.4	23.3	1.3	24.0	3.0	25.1	4.6	25.2	0.4	26.0	3.2	26.1	0.4	27.0	3.4	27.3	1.1	31.2	14.3	34.4	10.3	31.8	-7.6
1977	30.4	-4.4	34.3	12.8	35.0	2.0	35.7	2.0	36.8	3.1	36.4	-1.1	36.9	1.4	37.8	2.4	38.2	1.1	38.3	0.3	39.0	1.8	39.8	2.1
1978	39.6	-0.5	39.4	-0.5	40.0	1.5	40.4	1.0	40.4	0.0	40.4	0.0	40.6	0.5	40.1	-1.2	40.7	1.5	40.5	-0.5	40.9	1.0	41.9	2.4
1979	42.4	1.2	43.2	1.9	44.4	2.8	45.0	1.4	47.8	6.2	49.2	2.9	51.7	5.1	54.0	4.4	56.9	5.4	58.4	2.6	60.0	2.7	62.4	4.0
1980	63.9	2.4	67.6	5.8	67.5	-0.1	68.8	1.9	70.2	2.0	70.6	0.6	71.8	1.7	72.8	1.4	74.1	1.8	75.6	2.0	77.8	2.9	79.6	2.3
1981	80.8	1.5	83.1	2.8	83.9	1.0	85.6	2.0	88.0	2.8	90.0	2.3	91.4	1.6	89.5	-2.1	92.1	2.9	91.0	-1.2	92.7	1.9	94.6	2.0
1982	93.1	-1.6	93.1	0.0	93.4	0.3	93.6	0.2	94.4	0.9	96.9	2.6	99.4	2.6	101.3	1.9	104.8	3.5	106.5	1.6	112.2	5.4	111.3	-0.8
1983	108.1	-2.9	108.8	0.6	111.2	2.2	109.0	-2.0	109.0	0.0	108.9	-0.1	108.3	-0.6	108.0	-0.3	108.1	0.1	106.4	-1.6	105.8	-0.6	105.6	-0.2
1984	105.9	0.3	105.4	-0.5	102.8	-2.5	103.9	1.1	104.1	0.2	104.6	0.5	104.7	0.1	105.3	0.6	104.1	-1.1	104.9	0.8	105.0	0.1	104.0	-1.0
1985	101.2	-2.7	100.6	-0.6	98.4	-2.2	98.9	0.5	101.7	2.8	99.7	-2.0	99.0	-0.7	96.7	-2.3	97.2	0.5	97.4	0.2	96.5	-0.9	97.1	0.6
1986	97.5	0.4	94.0	-3.6	94.2	0.2	88.6	-5.9	86.8	-2.0	85.2	-1.8	79.4	-6.8	76.3	-3.9	73.2	-4.1	74.4	1.6	74.9	0.7	73.6	-1.7
1987	73.6	0.0	73.0	-0.8	76.2	4.4	75.5	-0.9	74.4	-1.5	74.0	-0.5	74.1	0.1	74.8	0.9	75.4	0.8	73.1	-3.1	71.6	-2.1	73.8	3.1
1988	73.3	-0.7	71.7	-2.2	72.3	0.8	74.5	3.0	72.0	-3.4	69.8	-3.1	71.1	1.9	68.7	-3.4	69.0	0.4	71.7	3.9	70.5	-1.7	71.7	1.7
1989	75.2	4.9	77.3	2.8	74.0	-4.3	75.2	1.6	77.1	2.5	76.3	-1.0	76.2	-0.1	72.8	-4.5	75.4	3.6	73.7	-2.3	74.2	0.7	76.0	2.4
1990	82.5	8.6	81.8	-0.8	76.8	-6.1	74.3	-3.3	73.9	-0.5	71.8	-2.8	76.4	6.4	71.8	-6.0	76.5	6.5	80.7	5.5	85.9	6.4	88.4	2.9
1991	86.8	-1.8	80.5	-7.3	78.3	-2.7	74.6	-4.7	77.2	3.5	75.0	-2.8	73.2	-2.4	74.2	1.4	71.5	-3.6	74.3	3.9	78.4	5.5	80.6	2.8
1992	76.1	-5.6	73.7	-3.2	70.5	-4.3	70.1	-0.6	71.0	1.3	70.2	-1.1	75.9	8.1	75.3	-0.8	81.0	7.6	78.7	-2.8	86.2	9.5	82.5	-4.3
1993	82.2	-0.4	75.8	-7.8	74.0	-2.4	75.0	1.4	81.3	8.4	85.9	5.7	77.1	-10.2	75.7	-1.8	78.6	3.8	81.1	3.2	77.9	-3.9	77.5	-0.5
1994	82.7	6.7	75.6	-8.6	80.3	6.2	78.0	-2.9	72.7	-6.8	72.4	-0.4	69.1	-4.6	71.7	3.8	69.8	-2.6	66.1	-5.3	65.3	-1.2	70.3	7.7
1995	69.6	-1.0	66.0	-5.2	64.3	-2.6	65.2	1.4	66.0	1.2	67.8	2.7	65.5	-3.4	59.2	-9.6	60.2	1.7	62.9	4.5	65.5	4.1	65.5	0.0

Source: U.S. Department of Labor, Bureau of Labor Statistics, Division of Industry Prices and Price Indexes. n.e.c. stands for not elsewhere classified. - indicates no data collected for period or unavailable.

Electric Power
Producer Price Index
Base 1982 = 100

For 1958-1995. Columns headed % show percentile change in the index from the previous period for which an index is available.

Year	Jan Index	%	Feb Index	%	Mar Index	%	Apr Index	%	May Index	%	Jun Index	%	Jul Index	%	Aug Index	%	Sep Index	%	Oct Index	%	Nov Index	%	Dec Index	%
1958	24.4	-	24.5	0.4	24.5	0.0	24.4	-0.4	24.4	0.0	24.5	0.4	24.5	0.0	24.6	0.4	24.6	0.0	24.6	0.0	24.6	0.0	24.6	0.0
1959	24.6	0.0	24.6	0.0	24.6	0.0	24.6	0.0	24.6	0.0	24.6	0.0	24.6	0.0	24.6	0.0	24.6	0.0	24.6	0.0	24.6	0.0	24.7	0.4
1960	24.7	0.0	24.9	0.8	24.9	0.0	24.9	0.0	24.8	-0.4	24.9	0.4	24.9	0.0	24.9	0.0	24.9	0.0	24.9	0.0	25.0	0.4	25.0	0.0
1961	25.0	0.0	25.0	0.0	25.0	0.0	25.0	0.0	25.0	0.0	25.0	0.0	25.0	0.0	25.0	0.0	25.0	0.0	25.0	0.0	25.1	0.4	25.0	-0.4
1962	25.0	0.0	25.2	0.8	25.2	0.0	25.2	0.0	25.1	-0.4	25.1	0.0	25.1	0.0	25.1	0.0	25.1	0.0	25.1	0.0	25.1	0.0	25.1	0.0
1963	25.0	-0.4	25.0	0.0	25.0	0.0	25.0	0.0	25.0	0.0	25.0	0.0	24.9	-0.4	24.9	0.0	24.9	0.0	24.8	-0.4	24.7	-0.4	24.7	0.0
1964	24.7	0.0	24.7	0.0	24.3	-1.6	24.7	1.6	24.7	0.0	24.6	-0.4	24.6	0.0	24.8	0.8	24.8	0.0	24.8	0.0	24.8	0.0	24.7	-0.4
1965	24.7	0.0	24.6	-0.4	24.6	0.0	24.6	0.0	24.6	0.0	24.6	0.0	24.6	0.0	24.6	0.0	24.6	0.0	24.6	0.0	24.6	0.0	24.6	0.0
1966	24.5	-0.4	24.5	0.0	24.5	0.0	24.5	0.0	24.5	0.0	24.5	0.0	24.5	0.0	24.5	0.0	24.5	0.0	24.5	0.0	24.5	0.0	24.6	0.4
1967	24.6	0.0	24.6	0.0	24.6	0.0	24.6	0.0	24.6	0.0	24.6	0.0	24.6	0.0	24.6	0.0	24.6	0.0	24.6	0.0	24.6	0.0	24.7	0.4
1968	24.7	0.0	24.7	0.0	24.7	0.0	24.7	0.0	24.7	0.0	24.7	0.0	24.9	0.8	24.9	0.0	24.9	0.0	24.9	0.0	24.9	0.0	24.9	0.0
1969	24.8	-0.4	24.8	0.0	24.9	0.4	24.9	0.0	24.9	0.0	24.9	0.0	24.9	0.0	25.1	0.8	25.3	0.8	25.3	0.0	25.3	0.0	25.3	0.0
1970	25.3	0.0	25.3	0.0	25.3	0.0	25.3	0.0	25.5	0.8	25.6	0.4	26.0	1.6	26.2	0.8	26.6	1.5	26.9	1.1	27.0	0.4	27.4	1.5
1971	27.5	0.4	27.8	1.1	28.1	1.1	28.1	0.0	28.2	0.4	28.4	0.7	28.8	1.4	29.1	1.0	29.1	0.0	29.0	-0.3	29.1	0.3	29.8	2.4
1972	29.2	-2.0	29.5	1.0	29.5	0.0	29.6	0.3	29.8	0.7	29.9	0.3	30.0	0.3	30.0	0.0	30.2	0.7	30.3	0.3	30.2	-0.3	30.2	0.0
1973	30.5	1.0	31.0	1.6	31.2	0.6	31.4	0.6	31.5	0.3	31.6	0.3	31.7	0.3	31.8	0.3	32.2	1.3	32.5	0.9	32.8	0.9	33.4	1.8
1974	33.8	1.2	35.0	3.6	36.6	4.6	37.7	3.0	39.3	4.2	40.5	3.1	41.2	1.7	42.0	1.9	42.8	1.9	43.9	2.6	44.2	0.7	44.4	0.5
1975	45.1	1.6	45.9	1.8	47.0	2.4	47.9	1.9	47.4	-1.0	46.9	-1.1	47.4	1.1	48.0	1.3	48.6	1.3	49.1	1.0	49.0	-0.2	48.6	-0.8
1976	48.8	0.4	49.0	0.4	49.6	1.2	50.3	1.4	50.4	0.2	50.8	0.8	51.7	1.8	52.5	1.5	52.8	0.6	52.4	-0.8	52.6	0.4	52.0	-1.1
1977	52.6	1.2	54.0	2.7	55.0	1.9	56.4	2.5	56.7	0.5	57.6	1.6	58.8	2.1	60.2	2.4	59.7	-0.8	59.6	-0.2	58.5	-1.8	58.3	-0.3
1978	58.9	1.0	59.7	1.4	61.5	3.0	61.7	0.3	62.2	0.8	63.2	1.6	62.7	-0.8	62.4	-0.5	62.1	-0.5	62.2	0.2	61.6	-1.0	61.7	0.2
1979	61.7	0.0	61.8	0.2	63.3	2.4	64.1	1.3	65.4	2.0	66.4	1.5	67.6	1.8	68.6	1.5	69.0	0.6	69.7	1.0	69.3	-0.6	70.6	1.9
1980	71.5	1.3	73.6	2.9	75.2	2.2	76.3	1.5	77.9	2.1	80.2	3.0	81.5	1.6	82.1	0.7	83.2	1.3	83.0	-0.2	82.1	-1.1	83.1	1.2
1981	84.0	1.1	85.2	1.4	86.4	1.4	87.4	1.2	88.7	1.5	90.2	1.7	92.2	2.2	94.9	2.9	94.4	-0.5	93.1	-1.4	93.1	0.0	94.5	1.5
1982	96.6	2.2	96.6	0.0	99.3	2.8	99.9	0.6	100.1	0.2	99.8	-0.3	102.3	2.5	102.1	-0.2	102.1	0.0	100.6	-1.5	99.6	-1.0	100.8	1.2
1983	101.1	0.3	101.1	0.0	101.2	0.1	100.7	-0.5	101.4	0.7	103.2	1.8	104.9	1.6	105.1	0.2	105.3	0.2	104.2	-1.0	103.0	-1.2	102.7	-0.3
1984	103.4	0.7	104.3	0.9	105.0	0.7	106.2	1.1	106.6	0.4	109.9	3.1	111.6	1.5	112.4	0.7	112.3	-0.1	109.6	-2.4	109.0	-0.5	108.4	-0.6
1985	109.7	1.2	109.7	0.0	110.1	0.4	110.5	0.4	110.2	-0.3	113.2	2.7	113.7	0.4	114.0	0.3	113.7	-0.3	112.0	-1.5	111.4	-0.5	111.0	-0.4
1986	112.3	1.2	113.2	0.8	112.7	-0.4	111.5	-1.1	112.1	0.5	114.0	1.7	114.8	0.7	114.8	0.0	114.8	0.0	111.0	-3.3	110.2	-0.7	109.9	-0.3
1987	108.4	-1.4	108.3	-0.1	108.7	0.4	108.0	-0.6	109.9	1.8	113.2	3.0	114.8	1.4	114.6	-0.2	114.1	-0.4	110.4	-3.2	108.1	-2.1	108.4	0.3
1988	107.8	-0.6	108.0	0.2	107.7	-0.3	107.6	-0.1	107.6	0.0	115.6	7.4	116.8	1.0	116.8	0.0	117.1	0.3	112.8	-3.7	107.8	-4.4	109.1	1.2
1989	110.6	1.4	110.8	0.2	110.9	0.1	111.1	0.2	112.6	1.4	119.3	6.0	120.8	1.3	120.7	-0.1	120.7	0.0	115.2	-4.6	111.8	-3.0	112.6	0.7
1990	113.1	0.4	113.6	0.4	113.8	0.2	113.7	-0.1	115.5	1.6	121.7	5.4	121.9	0.2	122.1	0.2	122.4	0.2	119.1	-2.7	117.6	-1.3	116.8	-0.7
1991	120.5	3.2	120.4	-0.1	120.2	-0.2	120.2	0.0	123.1	2.4	128.8	4.6	130.4	1.2	130.4	0.0	130.5	0.1	124.7	-4.4	120.2	-3.6	121.9	1.4
1992	122.2	0.2	121.8	-0.3	122.1	0.2	121.4	-0.6	124.5	2.6	131.7	5.8	132.7	0.8	132.4	-0.2	132.7	0.2	127.4	-4.0	122.8	-3.6	123.7	0.7
1993	124.2	0.4	123.9	-0.2	124.0	0.1	124.6	0.5	125.7	0.9	134.8	7.2	135.1	0.2	135.3	0.1	135.8	0.4	129.7	-4.5	125.3	-3.4	125.1	-0.2
1994	125.2	0.1	125.2	0.0	125.1	-0.1	124.8	-0.2	125.7	0.7	133.0	5.8	133.9	0.7	134.1	0.1	134.1	0.0	128.6	-4.1	127.0	-1.2	127.4	0.3
1995	127.5	0.1	127.7	0.2	127.9	0.2	126.3	-1.3	129.6	2.6	135.9	4.9	137.0	0.8	137.0	0.0	135.6	-1.0	130.7	-3.6	128.1	-2.0	127.9	-0.2

Source: U.S. Department of Labor, Bureau of Labor Statistics, Division of Industry Prices and Price Indexes. n.e.c. stands for not elsewhere classified. - indicates no data collected for period or unavailable.

Utility Natural Gas
Producer Price Index
Base Dec. 1990 = 100

For 1990-1995. Columns headed % show percentile change in the index from the previous period for which an index is available.

Year	Jan		Feb		Mar		Apr		May		Jun		Jul		Aug		Sep		Oct		Nov		Dec	
	Index	%	Index	%	Index	%	Index	%	Index	%	Index	%	Index	%	Index	%	Index	%	Index	%	Index	%	Index	%
1990	-	-	-	-	-	-	-	-	-	-	-	-	-	-	-	-	-	-	-	-	-	-	100.0	-
1991	101.2	1.2	99.5	-1.7	97.7	-1.8	97.1	-0.6	96.2	-0.9	95.2	-1.0	95.0	-0.2	94.7	-0.3	95.1	0.4	96.2	1.2	98.6	2.5	99.8	1.2
1992	100.1	0.3	98.0	-2.1	96.9	-1.1	96.0	-0.9	95.5	-0.5	96.0	0.5	96.1	0.1	96.9	0.8	98.3	1.4	101.2	3.0	103.7	2.5	104.2	0.5
1993	104.0	-0.2	102.8	-1.2	102.2	-0.6	101.9	-0.3	103.9	2.0	103.5	-0.4	103.2	-0.3	104.0	0.8	105.0	1.0	104.9	-0.1	106.4	1.4	107.6	1.1
1994	107.6	0.0	107.7	0.1	108.1	0.4	106.7	-1.3	105.5	-1.1	103.0	-2.4	102.1	-0.9	102.2	0.1	101.9	-0.3	101.1	-0.8	103.1	2.0	103.7	0.6
1995	104.0	0.3	102.5	-1.4	101.2	-1.3	99.9	-1.3	97.5	-2.4	97.6	0.1	97.0	-0.6	96.2	-0.8	96.2	0.0	95.9	-0.3	97.7	1.9	100.5	2.9

Source: U.S. Department of Labor, Bureau of Labor Statistics, Division of Industry Prices and Price Indexes. n.e.c. stands for not elsewhere classified. - indicates no data collected for period or unavailable.

Crude Petroleum (Domestic Production)
Producer Price Index
Base 1982 = 100

For 1991-1995. Columns headed % show percentile change in the index from the previous period for which an index is available.

Year	Jan Index	%	Feb Index	%	Mar Index	%	Apr Index	%	May Index	%	Jun Index	%	Jul Index	%	Aug Index	%	Sep Index	%	Oct Index	%	Nov Index	%	Dec Index	%
1991	-	-	-	-	-	-	-	-	-	-	-	-	59.3	-	60.4	1.9	60.4	0.0	66.3	9.8	64.0	-3.5	55.1	-13.9
1992	51.3	-6.9	53.5	4.3	51.0	-4.7	56.0	9.8	59.2	5.7	64.3	8.6	61.9	-3.7	60.5	-2.3	63.1	4.3	63.4	0.5	58.5	-7.7	53.8	-8.0
1993	52.0	-3.3	56.1	7.9	58.1	3.6	57.7	-0.7	57.9	0.3	52.9	-8.6	50.2	-5.1	48.3	-3.8	46.5	-3.7	51.8	11.4	46.0	-11.2	38.9	-15.4
1994	39.3	1.0	37.8	-3.8	39.6	4.8	42.7	7.8	48.9	14.5	52.9	8.2	56.2	6.2	54.4	-3.2	48.3	-11.2	49.3	2.1	49.1	-0.4	47.1	-4.1
1995	48.4	2.8	51.0	5.4	50.6	-0.8	55.3	9.3	56.0	1.3	53.3	-4.8	48.3	-9.4	49.1	1.7	51.2	4.3	48.1	-6.1	48.9	1.7	52.0	6.3

Source: U.S. Department of Labor, Bureau of Labor Statistics, Division of Industry Prices and Price Indexes. n.e.c. stands for not elsewhere classified. - indicates no data collected for period or unavailable.

Petroleum Products, Refined
Producer Price Index
Base 1982 = 100

For 1947-1995. Columns headed % show percentile change in the index from the previous period for which an index is available.

Year	Jan Index	%	Feb Index	%	Mar Index	%	Apr Index	%	May Index	%	Jun Index	%	Jul Index	%	Aug Index	%	Sep Index	%	Oct Index	%	Nov Index	%	Dec Index	%
1947	8.3	-	8.4	1.2	9.0	7.1	9.6	6.7	9.6	0.0	9.7	1.0	9.9	2.1	10.1	2.0	10.1	0.0	10.2	1.0	10.7	4.9	11.3	5.6
1948	12.1	7.1	12.3	1.7	12.3	0.0	12.3	0.0	12.3	0.0	12.3	0.0	12.3	0.0	12.2	-0.8	12.1	-0.8	12.2	0.8	12.1	-0.8	11.9	-1.7
1949	11.7	-1.7	11.2	-4.3	11.0	-1.8	10.7	-2.7	10.5	-1.9	10.4	-1.0	10.3	-1.0	10.4	1.0	10.5	1.0	10.6	1.0	10.4	-1.9	10.4	0.0
1950	10.5	1.0	10.5	0.0	10.5	0.0	10.6	1.0	10.9	2.8	11.1	1.8	11.3	1.8	11.6	2.7	11.7	0.9	11.8	0.9	11.8	0.0	11.8	0.0
1951	12.0	1.7	12.0	0.0	12.1	0.8	12.1	0.0	12.0	-0.8	12.1	0.8	12.1	0.0	12.1	0.0	12.1	0.0	12.1	0.0	12.1	0.0	12.1	0.0
1952	12.1	0.0	12.0	-0.8	12.1	0.8	11.9	-1.7	12.0	0.8	11.9	-0.8	11.9	0.0	11.8	-0.8	11.8	0.0	11.8	0.0	11.7	-0.8	11.7	0.0
1953	11.7	0.0	11.6	-0.9	11.8	1.7	11.8	0.0	11.9	0.8	11.9	0.0	12.6	5.9	12.6	0.0	12.6	0.0	12.6	0.0	12.6	0.0	12.4	-1.6
1954	12.3	-0.8	12.2	-0.8	11.9	-2.5	12.0	0.8	12.0	0.0	11.9	-0.8	11.5	-3.4	11.6	0.9	11.7	0.9	11.6	-0.9	11.7	0.9	11.8	0.9
1955	11.9	0.8	11.9	0.0	12.0	0.8	11.9	-0.8	11.9	0.0	11.9	0.0	11.9	0.0	12.1	1.7	12.2	0.8	12.3	0.8	12.3	0.0	12.4	0.8
1956	12.6	1.6	12.7	0.8	12.6	-0.8	12.7	0.8	12.8	0.8	12.8	0.0	12.8	0.0	12.8	0.0	12.8	0.0	12.8	0.0	12.7	-0.8	13.1	3.1
1957	13.5	3.1	14.2	5.2	14.1	-0.7	14.1	0.0	14.0	-0.7	13.8	-1.4	13.6	-1.4	13.5	-0.7	13.5	0.0	13.4	-0.7	13.2	-1.5	13.2	0.0
1958	13.1	-0.8	12.6	-3.8	12.4	-1.6	12.2	-1.6	12.1	-0.8	12.2	0.8	12.4	1.6	12.7	2.4	12.7	0.0	12.5	-1.6	12.4	-0.8	12.4	0.0
1959	12.6	1.6	12.8	1.6	12.8	0.0	12.8	0.0	12.6	-1.6	12.2	-3.2	12.2	0.0	12.3	0.8	12.2	-0.8	12.2	0.0	12.1	-0.8	12.1	0.0
1960	12.2	0.8	12.2	0.0	12.2	0.0	12.3	0.8	12.0	-2.4	12.3	2.5	12.6	2.4	12.8	1.6	13.0	1.6	13.0	0.0	12.9	-0.8	13.0	0.8
1961	13.2	1.5	13.3	0.8	13.2	-0.8	12.8	-3.0	12.5	-2.3	12.7	1.6	12.8	0.8	12.7	-0.8	12.5	-1.6	12.3	-1.6	12.5	1.6	12.7	1.6
1962	12.8	0.8	12.6	-1.6	12.2	-3.2	12.7	4.1	12.6	-0.8	12.6	0.0	12.6	0.0	12.5	-0.8	12.8	2.4	12.7	-0.8	12.7	0.0	12.7	0.0
1963	12.6	-0.8	12.5	-0.8	12.6	0.8	12.6	0.0	12.7	0.8	12.8	0.0	12.7	-0.8	12.3	-3.1	12.3	0.0	12.3	0.0	12.1	-1.6	12.3	1.7
1964	12.4	0.8	12.2	-1.6	11.9	-2.5	11.7	-1.7	11.8	0.9	11.9	0.8	11.9	0.0	11.7	-1.7	11.5	-1.7	11.8	2.6	12.0	1.7	12.1	0.8
1965	12.2	0.8	12.1	-0.8	12.1	0.0	12.1	0.0	12.3	1.7	12.3	0.0	12.3	0.0	12.4	0.8	12.4	0.0	12.4	0.0	12.6	1.6	12.7	0.8
1966	12.6	-0.8	12.6	0.0	12.5	-0.8	12.6	0.8	12.7	0.8	12.9	1.6	12.8	-0.8	12.9	0.8	13.0	0.8	13.0	0.0	13.0	0.0	12.9	-0.8
1967	12.9	0.0	13.1	1.6	13.2	0.8	13.1	-0.8	13.3	1.5	13.3	0.0	13.3	0.0	13.4	0.8	13.4	0.0	13.0	-3.0	12.9	-0.8	12.8	-0.8
1968	12.7	-0.8	12.8	0.8	12.8	0.0	12.9	0.8	12.9	0.0	13.3	3.1	13.2	-0.8	13.0	-1.5	13.0	0.0	12.8	-1.5	12.8	0.0	12.7	-0.8
1969	12.7	0.0	12.8	0.8	13.1	2.3	13.2	0.8	13.2	0.0	13.3	0.8	13.3	0.0	13.2	-0.8	13.1	-0.8	13.1	0.0	13.1	0.0	13.1	0.0
1970	13.0	-0.8	13.0	0.0	13.0	0.0	13.0	0.0	13.3	2.3	13.1	-1.5	13.2	0.8	13.3	0.8	13.3	0.0	13.3	0.0	13.5	1.5	14.2	5.2
1971	14.2	0.0	14.1	-0.7	14.0	-0.7	13.8	-1.4	14.1	2.2	14.1	0.0	14.2	0.7	14.2	0.0	14.2	0.0	14.1	-0.7	14.0	-0.7	14.0	0.0
1972	13.9	-0.7	13.9	0.0	14.0	0.7	14.0	0.0	14.1	0.7	14.3	1.4	14.3	0.0	14.5	1.4	14.6	0.7	14.6	0.0	14.7	0.7	14.7	0.0
1973	14.7	0.0	15.6	6.1	15.9	1.9	16.1	1.3	16.4	1.9	16.8	2.4	17.1	1.8	17.1	0.0	17.2	0.6	17.6	2.3	18.4	4.5	19.9	8.2
1974	21.9	10.1	24.7	12.8	27.1	9.7	28.3	4.4	29.5	4.2	30.5	3.4	31.5	3.3	32.0	1.6	31.9	-0.3	32.1	0.6	31.3	-2.5	31.3	0.0
1975	31.8	1.6	31.6	-0.6	31.8	0.6	32.0	0.6	32.3	0.9	33.1	2.5	34.0	2.7	35.3	3.8	35.7	1.1	36.0	0.8	36.1	0.3	36.1	0.0
1976	35.8	-0.8	35.8	0.0	35.4	-1.1	35.1	-0.8	35.1	0.0	35.5	1.1	36.4	2.5	36.9	1.4	37.3	1.1	37.4	0.3	37.5	0.3	37.8	0.8
1977	38.0	0.5	38.8	2.1	39.7	2.3	40.3	1.5	40.8	1.2	41.0	0.5	41.2	0.5	41.1	-0.2	41.1	0.0	41.3	0.5	41.2	-0.2	41.2	0.0
1978	41.3	0.2	41.1	-0.5	40.8	-0.7	40.9	0.2	41.3	1.0	41.8	1.2	42.2	1.0	42.5	0.7	42.8	0.7	43.3	1.2	43.6	0.7	44.4	1.8
1979	45.2	1.8	46.0	1.8	47.3	2.8	49.7	5.1	52.5	5.6	55.6	5.9	59.1	6.3	63.4	7.3	67.5	6.5	70.1	3.9	71.7	2.3	72.9	1.7
1980	76.6	5.1	81.5	6.4	86.6	6.3	89.1	2.9	89.4	0.3	89.5	0.1	91.1	1.8	91.6	0.5	91.5	-0.1	90.7	-0.9	91.6	1.0	94.2	2.8
1981	96.8	2.8	101.1	4.4	108.4	7.2	110.5	1.9	109.7	-0.7	108.8	-0.8	107.2	-1.5	106.9	-0.3	105.9	-0.9	105.4	-0.5	104.9	-0.5	104.9	0.0
1982	105.3	0.4	103.7	-1.5	101.2	-2.4	96.4	-4.7	93.7	-2.8	97.1	3.6	102.0	5.0	102.7	0.7	100.0	-2.6	99.1	-0.9	99.6	0.5	99.1	-0.5
1983	94.7	-4.4	91.0	-3.9	87.6	-3.7	84.8	-3.2	86.6	2.1	89.9	3.8	90.5	0.7	91.3	0.9	91.3	0.0	91.5	0.2	90.4	-1.2	89.1	-1.4
1984	87.1	-2.2	88.0	1.0	89.4	1.6	87.6	-2.0	89.0	1.6	89.3	0.3	88.4	-1.0	86.0	-2.7	84.9	-1.3	86.1	1.4	86.9	0.9	85.7	-1.4
1985	83.5	-2.6	80.9	-3.1	81.5	0.7	83.6	2.6	86.4	3.3	84.3	-2.4	82.8	-1.8	81.5	-1.6	81.7	0.2	82.1	0.5	84.3	2.7	85.4	1.3
1986	79.9	-6.4	68.9	-13.8	56.7	-17.7	52.0	-8.3	53.3	2.5	53.3	0.0	44.7	-16.1	44.3	-0.9	48.2	8.8	45.4	-5.8	45.5	0.2	46.4	2.0
1987	50.8	9.5	53.9	6.1	52.9	-1.9	55.4	4.7	56.1	1.3	57.7	2.9	59.3	2.8	61.5	3.7	58.9	-4.2	59.0	0.2	59.8	1.4	56.8	-5.0
1988	53.7	-5.5	52.9	-1.5	52.1	-1.5	54.4	4.4	56.4	3.7	55.4	-1.8	55.3	-0.2	55.8	0.9	52.9	-5.2	51.1	-3.4	53.5	4.7	52.9	-1.1
1989	54.4	2.8	55.0	1.1	57.1	3.8	64.9	13.7	67.7	4.3	65.6	-3.1	63.1	-3.8	58.9	-6.7	61.4	4.2	63.0	2.6	61.6	-2.2	61.9	0.5
1990	71.8	16.0	64.5	-10.2	63.3	-1.9	65.1	2.8	65.3	0.3	63.9	-2.1	62.3	-2.5	74.5	19.6	86.7	16.4	96.9	11.8	96.4	-0.5	87.0	-9.8
1991	79.1	-9.1	71.5	-9.6	64.0	-10.5	63.6	-0.6	66.4	4.4	65.4	-1.5	63.3	-3.2	66.4	4.9	67.9	2.3	66.9	-1.5	67.8	1.3	63.4	-6.5

[Continued]

Petroleum Products, Refined
Producer Price Index
Base 1982 = 100
[Continued]

For 1947-1995. Columns headed % show percentile change in the index from the previous period for which an index is available.

Year	Jan Index	%	Feb Index	%	Mar Index	%	Apr Index	%	May Index	%	Jun Index	%	Jul Index	%	Aug Index	%	Sep Index	%	Oct Index	%	Nov Index	%	Dec Index	%
1992	57.7	-9.0	59.7	3.5	59.2	-0.8	61.9	4.6	66.2	6.9	69.9	5.6	68.1	-2.6	67.5	-0.9	68.6	1.6	68.5	-0.1	67.0	-2.2	62.1	-7.3
1993	61.6	-0.8	62.5	1.5	63.9	2.2	65.1	1.9	66.5	2.2	64.5	-3.0	62.0	-3.9	60.3	-2.7	61.1	1.3	63.1	3.3	60.5	-4.1	52.9	-12.6
1994	52.9	0.0	56.4	6.6	55.8	-1.1	57.0	2.2	58.1	1.9	59.3	2.1	62.0	4.6	66.1	6.6	63.0	-4.7	60.0	-4.8	61.6	2.7	57.5	-6.7
1995	58.1	1.0	58.2	0.2	59.0	1.4	63.1	6.9	66.1	4.8	64.8	-2.0	61.4	-5.2	60.9	-0.8	60.7	-0.3	58.2	-4.1	57.4	-1.4	59.8	4.2

Source: U.S. Department of Labor, Bureau of Labor Statistics, Division of Industry Prices and Price Indexes. n.e.c. stands for not elsewhere classified. - indicates no data collected for period or unavailable.

Petroleum and Coal Products, n.e.c.
Producer Price Index
Base Dec. 1984 = 100

For 1984-1995. Columns headed % show percentile change in the index from the previous period for which an index is available.

Year	Jan Index	%	Feb Index	%	Mar Index	%	Apr Index	%	May Index	%	Jun Index	%	Jul Index	%	Aug Index	%	Sep Index	%	Oct Index	%	Nov Index	%	Dec Index	%
1984	-	-	-	-	-	-	-	-	-	-	-	-	-	-	-	-	-	-	-	-	-	-	100.0	-
1985	100.0	0.0	99.9	-0.1	99.9	0.0	99.9	0.0	99.9	0.0	99.9	0.0	105.2	5.3	103.6	-1.5	103.1	-0.5	95.0	-7.9	100.2	5.5	99.2	-1.0
1986	95.2	-4.0	95.2	0.0	92.9	-2.4	90.8	-2.3	81.7	-10.0	78.7	-3.7	70.5	-10.4	70.8	0.4	63.4	-10.5	63.5	0.2	65.3	2.8	57.3	-12.3
1987	61.8	7.9	60.4	-2.3	63.7	5.5	63.6	-0.2	60.4	-5.0	62.4	3.3	62.8	0.6	63.7	1.4	64.6	1.4	65.6	1.5	66.0	0.6	69.9	5.9
1988	62.7	-10.3	70.8	12.9	62.6	-11.6	68.0	8.6	69.6	2.4	67.4	-3.2	69.4	3.0	69.9	0.7	68.1	-2.6	61.8	-9.3	63.7	3.1	62.7	-1.6
1989	59.1	-5.7	60.3	2.0	65.6	8.8	65.8	0.3	64.4	-2.1	63.5	-1.4	68.1	7.2	69.2	1.6	67.5	-2.5	67.1	-0.6	69.4	3.4	60.0	-13.5
1990	61.9	3.2	63.5	2.6	63.3	-0.3	64.2	1.4	67.6	5.3	68.3	1.0	66.6	-2.5	68.0	2.1	70.1	3.1	70.2	0.1	69.8	-0.6	74.2	6.3
1991	71.7	-3.4	76.3	6.4	67.0	-12.2	68.4	2.1	64.9	-5.1	68.4	5.4	61.4	-10.2	61.9	0.8	61.1	-1.3	61.9	1.3	55.9	-9.7	44.5	-20.4
1992	58.1	30.6	58.4	0.5	59.6	2.1	60.7	1.8	58.2	-4.1	54.7	-6.0	57.7	5.5	58.5	1.4	54.7	-6.5	61.1	11.7	63.1	3.3	60.5	-4.1
1993	67.0	10.7	66.8	-0.3	66.0	-1.2	69.3	5.0	68.0	-1.9	63.1	-7.2	69.0	9.4	65.8	-4.6	66.4	0.9	64.1	-3.5	67.3	5.0	64.0	-4.9
1994	65.0	1.6	65.2	0.3	61.6	-5.5	62.2	1.0	69.1	11.1	67.0	-3.0	68.4	2.1	65.3	-4.5	64.0	-2.0	66.5	3.9	68.1	2.4	66.9	-1.8
1995	67.5	0.9	67.9	0.6	68.1	0.3	76.7	12.6	71.8	-6.4	69.1	-3.8	69.5	0.6	70.9	2.0	73.6	3.8	71.6	-2.7	66.9	-6.6	63.5	-5.1

Source: U.S. Department of Labor, Bureau of Labor Statistics, Division of Industry Prices and Price Indexes. n.e.c. stands for not elsewhere classified. - indicates no data collected for period or unavailable.

CHEMICALS AND ALLIED PRODUCTS
Producer Price Index
Base 1982 = 100

For 1933-1995. Columns headed % show percentile change in the index from the previous period for which an index is available.

Year	Jan Index	%	Feb Index	%	Mar Index	%	Apr Index	%	May Index	%	Jun Index	%	Jul Index	%	Aug Index	%	Sep Index	%	Oct Index	%	Nov Index	%	Dec Index	%
1933	15.7	-	15.6	-0.6	15.7	0.6	15.7	0.0	16.0	1.9	16.2	1.3	16.6	2.5	16.7	0.6	16.6	-0.6	16.5	-0.6	16.5	0.0	16.6	0.6
1934	16.8	1.2	17.0	1.2	17.0	0.0	17.0	0.0	16.9	-0.6	16.9	0.0	16.9	0.0	16.9	0.0	17.0	0.6	17.1	0.6	17.0	-0.6	17.1	0.6
1935	17.2	0.6	17.3	0.6	17.6	1.7	17.6	0.0	17.7	0.6	17.8	0.6	17.6	-1.1	17.6	0.0	17.9	1.7	18.0	0.6	17.9	-0.6	17.9	0.0
1936	17.8	-0.6	17.7	-0.6	17.6	-0.6	17.6	0.0	17.4	-1.1	17.4	0.0	17.6	1.1	17.8	1.1	17.9	0.6	18.0	0.6	18.1	0.6	18.6	2.8
1937	18.9	1.6	19.0	0.5	19.0	0.0	19.0	0.0	18.7	-1.6	18.6	-0.5	18.7	0.5	18.6	-0.5	18.5	-0.5	18.4	-0.5	18.1	-1.6	17.9	-1.1
1938	18.1	1.1	18.1	0.0	18.0	-0.6	17.9	-0.6	17.7	-1.1	17.5	-1.1	17.5	0.0	17.6	0.6	17.6	0.0	17.6	0.0	17.6	0.0	17.5	-0.6
1939	17.5	0.0	17.4	-0.6	17.5	0.6	17.5	0.0	17.5	0.0	17.5	0.0	17.4	-0.6	17.3	-0.6	17.9	3.5	18.1	1.1	18.0	-0.6	18.1	0.6
1940	18.2	0.6	18.1	-0.5	18.1	0.0	18.3	1.1	17.9	-2.2	17.8	-0.6	17.8	0.0	17.7	-0.6	17.7	0.0	17.8	0.6	17.9	0.6	17.9	0.0
1941	18.1	1.1	18.1	0.0	18.4	1.7	18.8	2.2	19.2	2.1	19.4	1.0	19.7	1.5	19.9	1.0	20.3	2.0	20.6	1.5	20.6	0.0	20.8	1.0
1942	18.6	-10.6	21.9	17.7	22.1	0.9	22.1	0.0	22.1	0.0	22.0	-0.5	22.0	0.0	21.8	-0.9	21.9	0.5	21.9	0.0	21.8	-0.5	21.7	-0.5
1943	21.8	0.5	21.9	0.5	21.9	0.0	22.0	0.5	21.9	-0.5	21.9	0.0	21.9	0.0	22.0	0.5	22.0	0.0	22.0	0.0	22.0	0.0	22.0	0.0
1944	22.1	0.5	22.1	0.0	22.1	0.0	22.2	0.5	22.2	0.0	22.2	0.0	22.2	0.0	22.2	0.0	22.1	-0.5	22.2	0.5	22.2	0.0	22.2	0.0
1945	22.2	0.0	22.2	0.0	22.2	0.0	22.2	0.0	22.2	0.0	22.2	0.0	22.2	0.0	22.3	0.5	22.4	0.4	22.4	0.0	22.5	0.4	22.5	0.0
1946	22.5	0.0	22.5	0.0	22.5	0.0	22.5	0.0	22.6	0.4	22.6	0.0	23.5	4.0	23.3	-0.9	23.4	0.4	23.8	1.7	29.5	23.9	31.0	5.1
1947	32.1	3.5	32.4	0.9	32.9	1.5	32.8	-0.3	31.7	-3.4	31.2	-1.6	30.8	-1.3	30.5	-1.0	31.1	2.0	32.3	3.9	33.3	3.1	33.4	0.3
1948	33.8	1.2	33.3	-1.5	33.1	-0.6	33.0	-0.3	32.6	-1.2	32.8	0.6	32.9	0.3	32.7	-0.6	32.7	0.0	32.6	-0.3	32.4	-0.6	32.0	-1.2
1949	31.5	-1.6	31.1	-1.3	30.7	-1.3	30.1	-2.0	30.0	-0.3	29.9	-0.3	29.6	-1.0	29.6	0.0	29.5	-0.3	29.3	-0.7	29.3	0.0	29.2	-0.3
1950	29.2	0.0	29.1	-0.3	29.1	0.0	29.1	0.0	29.1	0.0	29.1	0.0	29.5	1.4	30.3	2.7	31.5	4.0	32.3	2.5	32.7	1.2	34.0	4.0
1951	35.2	3.5	35.6	1.1	35.4	-0.6	35.2	-0.6	35.2	0.0	34.8	-1.1	34.4	-1.1	34.3	-0.3	34.3	0.0	34.4	0.3	34.3	-0.3	34.3	0.0
1952	33.7	-1.7	33.5	-0.6	33.3	-0.6	33.1	-0.6	32.9	-0.6	32.9	0.0	32.9	0.0	32.9	0.0	32.9	0.0	32.8	-0.3	32.7	-0.3	32.6	-0.3
1953	32.7	0.3	32.7	0.0	32.9	0.6	33.4	1.5	33.4	0.0	33.4	0.0	33.6	0.6	33.6	0.0	33.7	0.3	33.7	0.0	33.9	0.6	33.9	0.0
1954	33.9	0.0	34.0	0.3	34.0	0.0	33.9	-0.3	33.9	0.0	33.8	-0.3	33.7	-0.3	33.8	0.3	33.8	0.0	33.8	0.0	33.8	0.0	33.8	0.0
1955	33.9	0.3	33.9	0.0	33.8	-0.3	33.9	0.3	33.8	-0.3	33.8	0.0	33.5	-0.9	33.5	0.0	33.5	0.0	33.7	0.6	33.7	0.0	33.7	0.0
1956	33.6	-0.3	33.6	0.0	33.7	0.3	33.8	0.3	33.8	0.0	33.9	0.3	33.9	0.0	33.9	0.0	33.9	0.0	34.0	0.3	34.2	0.6	34.2	0.0
1957	34.3	0.3	34.4	0.3	34.4	0.0	34.5	0.3	34.5	0.0	34.6	0.3	34.6	0.0	34.7	0.3	34.8	0.3	34.9	0.3	34.9	0.0	35.0	0.3
1958	35.0	0.0	35.0	0.0	35.0	0.0	35.1	0.3	35.0	-0.3	35.0	0.0	34.9	-0.3	34.8	-0.3	34.7	-0.3	34.8	0.3	34.8	0.0	34.8	0.0
1959	34.8	0.0	34.7	-0.3	34.7	0.0	34.8	0.3	34.8	0.0	34.8	0.0	34.7	-0.3	34.7	0.0	34.7	0.0	34.8	0.3	34.8	0.0	34.8	0.0
1960	34.7	-0.3	34.8	0.3	34.8	0.0	34.8	0.0	34.8	0.0	34.8	0.0	34.9	0.3	34.9	0.0	34.9	0.0	34.8	-0.3	34.8	0.0	34.8	0.0
1961	34.7	-0.3	34.8	0.3	34.8	0.0	34.8	0.0	34.7	-0.3	34.6	-0.3	34.4	-0.6	34.3	-0.3	34.2	-0.3	34.1	-0.3	34.1	0.0	34.1	0.0
1962	34.2	0.3	34.1	-0.3	34.1	0.0	34.0	-0.3	34.0	0.0	33.9	-0.3	33.8	-0.3	33.7	-0.3	33.7	0.0	33.8	0.3	33.7	-0.3	33.7	0.0
1963	33.7	0.0	33.6	-0.3	33.7	0.3	33.5	-0.6	33.5	0.0	33.5	0.0	33.4	-0.3	33.4	0.0	33.4	0.0	33.5	0.3	33.5	0.0	33.5	0.0
1964	33.5	0.0	33.5	0.0	33.6	0.3	33.6	0.0	33.6	0.0	33.6	0.0	33.6	0.0	33.6	0.0	33.6	0.0	33.7	0.3	33.8	0.3	33.8	0.0
1965	33.8	0.0	33.9	0.3	33.9	0.0	33.9	0.0	33.9	0.0	33.9	0.0	33.9	0.0	33.8	-0.3	33.8	0.0	33.9	0.3	33.9	0.0	33.9	0.0
1966	33.9	0.0	33.9	0.0	33.9	0.0	33.9	0.0	34.0	0.3	33.9	-0.3	34.0	0.3	34.0	0.0	34.1	0.3	34.0	-0.3	34.1	0.3	34.1	0.0
1967	34.2	0.3	34.2	0.0	34.2	0.0	34.3	0.3	34.3	0.0	34.2	-0.3	34.2	0.0	34.1	-0.3	34.0	-0.3	34.1	0.3	34.1	0.0	34.2	0.3
1968	34.1	-0.3	34.1	0.0	34.3	0.6	34.3	0.0	34.3	0.0	34.2	-0.3	34.1	-0.3	34.1	0.0	34.0	-0.3	34.0	0.0	34.0	0.0	34.0	0.0
1969	33.9	-0.3	34.0	0.3	34.1	0.3	34.0	-0.3	34.1	0.3	34.2	0.3	34.1	-0.3	34.3	0.6	34.4	0.3	34.3	-0.3	34.4	0.3	34.3	-0.3
1970	34.5	0.6	34.6	0.3	34.7	0.3	34.9	0.6	35.0	0.3	35.0	0.0	35.1	0.3	35.1	0.0	35.1	0.0	35.3	0.6	35.3	0.0	35.2	-0.3
1971	35.5	0.9	35.7	0.6	35.7	0.0	35.8	0.3	35.7	-0.3	35.7	0.0	35.7	0.0	35.6	-0.3	35.6	0.0	35.6	0.0	35.5	-0.3	35.4	-0.3
1972	35.4	0.0	35.4	0.0	35.4	0.0	35.6	0.6	35.7	0.3	35.7	0.0	35.6	-0.3	35.7	0.3	35.7	0.0	35.7	0.0	35.8	0.3	35.9	0.3
1973	36.0	0.3	36.1	0.3	36.5	1.1	36.8	0.8	37.4	1.6	37.8	1.1	37.9	0.3	38.0	0.3	38.1	0.3	38.6	1.3	38.8	0.5	39.6	2.1
1974	40.4	2.0	41.1	1.7	43.5	5.8	45.3	4.1	46.9	3.5	48.9	4.3	50.8	3.9	54.2	6.7	55.3	2.0	57.7	4.3	59.2	2.6	59.5	0.5
1975	60.2	1.2	60.9	1.2	62.2	2.1	62.4	0.3	62.3	-0.2	62.0	-0.5	62.1	0.2	62.3	0.3	62.3	0.0	62.4	0.2	62.6	0.3	62.7	0.2
1976	63.1	0.6	63.3	0.3	63.6	0.5	64.0	0.6	64.0	0.0	64.1	0.2	64.0	-0.2	64.3	0.5	64.5	0.3	64.5	0.0	64.5	0.0	64.4	-0.2
1977	64.6	0.3	65.0	0.6	65.4	0.6	66.0	0.9	66.4	0.6	66.4	0.0	66.2	-0.3	66.2	0.0	66.1	-0.2	66.3	0.3	66.4	0.2	66.4	0.0

[Continued]

CHEMICALS AND ALLIED PRODUCTS
Producer Price Index
Base 1982 = 100
[Continued]

For 1933-1995. Columns headed % show percentile change in the index from the previous period for which an index is available.

Year	Jan Index	%	Feb Index	%	Mar Index	%	Apr Index	%	May Index	%	Jun Index	%	Jul Index	%	Aug Index	%	Sep Index	%	Oct Index	%	Nov Index	%	Dec Index	%
1978	66.4	0.0	66.8	0.6	67.1	0.4	67.3	0.3	68.0	1.0	68.1	0.1	68.4	0.4	68.3	-0.1	68.5	0.3	69.0	0.7	69.2	0.3	69.2	0.0
1979	70.1	1.3	70.9	1.1	71.8	1.3	73.6	2.5	74.6	1.4	75.0	0.5	77.0	2.7	78.2	1.6	79.0	1.0	80.1	1.4	80.7	0.7	81.5	1.0
1980	84.2	3.3	85.1	1.1	86.5	1.6	88.9	2.8	89.8	1.0	89.9	0.1	90.1	0.2	90.5	0.4	90.1	-0.4	90.6	0.6	91.2	0.7	91.7	0.5
1981	93.9	2.4	95.0	1.2	95.9	0.9	97.8	2.0	98.7	0.9	99.4	0.7	99.7	0.3	100.3	0.6	100.4	0.1	100.1	-0.3	99.9	-0.2	99.8	-0.1
1982	100.2	0.4	100.5	0.3	100.8	0.3	100.7	-0.1	100.9	0.2	100.3	-0.6	99.7	-0.6	99.8	0.1	99.5	-0.3	99.2	-0.3	99.4	0.2	99.1	-0.3
1983	99.0	-0.1	99.4	0.4	99.2	-0.2	99.7	0.5	99.6	-0.1	99.5	-0.1	100.5	1.0	100.7	0.2	101.2	0.5	101.1	-0.1	101.4	0.3	101.9	0.5
1984	102.0	0.1	101.5	-0.5	102.7	1.2	103.3	0.6	103.6	0.3	103.4	-0.2	103.5	0.1	103.0	-0.5	103.0	0.0	103.1	0.1	103.2	0.1	102.9	-0.3
1985	103.2	0.3	103.4	0.2	103.5	0.1	103.8	0.3	103.7	-0.1	103.9	0.2	104.2	0.3	104.2	0.0	104.2	0.0	103.7	-0.5	103.5	-0.2	103.3	-0.2
1986	104.4	1.1	103.9	-0.5	104.0	0.1	102.7	-1.2	102.1	-0.6	102.1	0.0	102.1	0.0	101.6	-0.5	101.8	0.2	102.0	0.2	102.2	0.2	102.0	-0.2
1987	103.0	1.0	103.6	0.6	104.3	0.7	105.2	0.9	105.9	0.7	107.1	1.1	107.0	-0.1	107.1	0.1	107.5	0.4	108.2	0.7	108.8	0.6	109.1	0.3
1988	110.6	1.4	111.6	0.9	112.7	1.0	113.8	1.0	114.6	0.7	115.3	0.6	117.4	1.8	118.2	0.7	119.1	0.8	119.9	0.7	121.1	1.0	121.7	0.5
1989	123.7	1.6	124.3	0.5	124.5	0.2	124.9	0.3	124.9	0.0	124.1	-0.6	123.1	-0.8	121.9	-1.0	121.4	-0.4	121.4	0.0	121.0	-0.3	121.0	0.0
1990	121.2	0.2	121.7	0.4	121.8	0.1	121.9	0.1	122.3	0.3	122.2	-0.1	122.4	0.2	122.5	0.1	124.5	1.6	126.5	1.6	128.2	1.3	127.9	-0.2
1991	128.3	0.3	128.1	-0.2	126.0	-1.6	126.0	0.0	125.3	-0.6	125.0	-0.2	124.4	-0.5	124.5	0.1	124.5	0.0	124.9	0.3	124.9	0.0	125.0	0.1
1992	124.6	-0.3	124.5	-0.1	124.4	-0.1	124.8	0.3	125.2	0.3	126.0	0.6	126.4	0.3	126.7	0.2	127.0	0.2	127.1	0.1	127.5	0.3	127.0	-0.4
1993	127.6	0.5	128.1	0.4	127.8	-0.2	128.6	0.6	128.2	-0.3	128.5	0.2	128.2	-0.2	128.3	0.1	128.1	-0.2	128.2	0.1	128.5	0.2	127.9	-0.5
1994	128.3	0.3	128.2	-0.1	128.3	0.1	129.3	0.8	130.2	0.7	130.7	0.4	131.2	0.4	132.6	1.1	134.8	1.7	136.4	1.2	137.2	0.6	138.4	0.9
1995	140.4	1.4	141.8	1.0	142.5	0.5	144.1	1.1	144.4	0.2	143.8	-0.4	143.6	-0.1	142.9	-0.5	143.4	0.3	142.1	-0.9	141.6	-0.4	140.4	-0.8

Source: U.S. Department of Labor, Bureau of Labor Statistics, Division of Industry Prices and Price Indexes. n.e.c. stands for not elsewhere classified. - indicates no data collected for period or unavailable.

Industrial Chemicals
Producer Price Index
Base 1982 = 100

For 1926-1995. Columns headed % show percentile change in the index from the previous period for which an index is available.

Year	Jan Index	%	Feb Index	%	Mar Index	%	Apr Index	%	May Index	%	Jun Index	%	Jul Index	%	Aug Index	%	Sep Index	%	Oct Index	%	Nov Index	%	Dec Index	%
1926	-	-	-	-	-	-	-	-	-	-	-	-	-	-	-	-	-	-	-	-	-	-	-	-
1927	-	-	-	-	-	-	-	-	-	-	-	-	-	-	-	-	-	-	-	-	-	-	-	-
1928	-	-	-	-	-	-	-	-	-	-	-	-	-	-	-	-	-	-	-	-	-	-	-	-
1929	-	-	-	-	-	-	-	-	-	-	-	-	-	-	-	-	-	-	-	-	-	-	-	-
1930	-	-	-	-	-	-	-	-	-	-	-	-	-	-	-	-	-	-	-	-	-	-	-	-
1931	-	-	-	-	-	-	-	-	-	-	-	-	-	-	-	-	-	-	-	-	-	-	-	-
1932	-	-	-	-	-	-	-	-	-	-	-	-	-	-	-	-	-	-	-	-	-	-	-	-
1933	17.4	-	17.4	0.0	17.2	-1.1	17.2	0.0	17.3	0.6	17.3	0.0	17.2	-0.6	17.2	0.0	17.2	0.0	17.2	0.0	17.4	1.2	17.4	0.0
1934	17.4	0.0	17.4	0.0	17.4	0.0	17.3	-0.6	17.3	0.0	17.3	0.0	17.1	-1.2	17.2	0.6	17.2	0.0	17.2	0.0	17.2	0.0	17.3	0.6
1935	17.3	0.0	17.4	0.6	17.4	0.0	17.4	0.0	17.5	0.6	17.5	0.0	17.5	0.0	17.9	2.3	17.9	0.0	17.9	0.0	17.9	0.0	17.9	0.0
1936	17.8	-0.6	17.8	0.0	17.6	-1.1	17.6	0.0	17.5	-0.6	17.5	0.0	17.4	-0.6	17.3	-0.6	17.3	0.0	17.4	0.6	17.3	-0.6	17.4	0.6
1937	17.4	0.0	17.6	1.1	17.6	0.0	17.6	0.0	17.6	0.0	17.6	0.0	17.8	1.1	17.5	-1.7	17.5	0.0	17.4	-0.6	17.4	0.0	17.4	0.0
1938	17.4	0.0	17.4	0.0	17.3	-0.6	17.3	0.0	17.2	-0.6	17.2	0.0	17.2	0.0	17.1	-0.6	17.1	0.0	17.1	0.0	17.0	-0.6	17.0	0.0
1939	17.0	0.0	16.9	-0.6	16.8	-0.6	16.8	0.0	16.8	0.0	16.7	-0.6	16.7	0.0	16.7	0.0	16.8	0.6	17.0	1.2	17.0	0.0	17.0	0.0
1940	17.0	0.0	17.0	0.0	17.0	0.0	16.9	-0.6	17.0	0.6	17.0	0.0	16.9	-0.6	16.8	-0.6	16.8	0.0	16.9	0.6	17.0	0.6	17.0	0.0
1941	17.0	0.0	17.1	0.6	17.1	0.0	17.2	0.6	17.3	0.6	17.3	0.0	17.4	0.6	17.4	0.0	17.6	1.1	17.6	0.0	17.6	0.0	17.6	0.0
1942	18.9	7.4	19.2	1.6	19.2	0.0	19.2	0.0	19.2	0.0	19.2	0.0	19.2	0.0	19.2	0.0	19.2	0.0	19.2	0.0	19.2	0.0	19.1	-0.5
1943	19.3	1.0	19.3	0.0	19.2	-0.5	19.2	0.0	19.2	0.0	19.2	0.0	19.2	0.0	19.2	0.0	19.2	0.0	19.2	0.0	19.2	0.0	19.2	0.0
1944	19.2	0.0	19.2	0.0	19.2	0.0	19.2	0.0	19.2	0.0	19.2	0.0	19.2	0.0	19.2	0.0	19.1	-0.5	19.1	0.0	19.0	-0.5	19.0	0.0
1945	19.0	0.0	19.0	0.0	19.0	0.0	19.0	0.0	19.0	0.0	19.1	0.5	19.1	0.0	19.1	0.0	19.1	0.0	19.2	0.5	19.3	0.5	19.3	0.0
1946	19.3	0.0	19.3	0.0	19.3	0.0	19.3	0.0	19.5	1.0	19.5	0.0	19.6	0.5	19.6	0.0	19.6	0.0	19.7	0.5	21.2	7.6	22.2	4.7
1947	22.5	1.4	22.7	0.9	23.0	1.3	23.6	2.6	23.3	-1.3	23.4	0.4	23.2	-0.9	22.8	-1.7	23.0	0.9	23.6	2.6	24.1	2.1	24.2	0.4
1948	24.5	1.2	24.7	0.8	24.8	0.4	24.9	0.4	24.8	-0.4	24.8	0.0	25.2	1.6	24.9	-1.2	24.8	-0.4	24.9	0.4	24.4	-2.0	24.1	-1.2
1949	23.9	-0.8	23.3	-2.5	23.0	-1.3	22.6	-1.7	22.5	-0.4	22.4	-0.4	22.5	0.4	22.5	0.0	22.4	-0.4	22.3	-0.4	22.2	-0.4	22.2	0.0
1950	22.3	0.5	22.3	0.0	22.2	-0.4	22.4	0.9	22.4	0.0	22.7	1.3	23.1	1.8	23.7	2.6	24.8	4.6	26.1	5.2	26.3	0.8	27.5	4.6
1951	28.3	2.9	28.4	0.4	28.4	0.0	28.5	0.4	28.5	0.0	28.5	0.0	28.4	-0.4	28.4	0.0	28.4	0.0	28.5	0.4	28.5	0.0	28.4	-0.4
1952	27.8	-2.1	27.7	-0.4	27.5	-0.7	27.5	0.0	27.1	-1.5	27.1	0.0	27.0	-0.4	27.0	0.0	26.9	-0.4	26.8	-0.4	26.5	-1.1	26.4	-0.4
1953	26.5	0.4	26.6	0.4	26.8	0.8	27.5	2.6	27.8	1.1	28.1	1.1	28.3	0.7	28.3	0.0	28.3	0.0	28.2	-0.4	28.1	-0.4	27.9	-0.7
1954	27.9	0.0	27.9	0.0	27.8	-0.4	27.7	-0.4	27.6	-0.4	27.5	-0.4	27.6	0.4	27.7	0.4	27.7	0.0	27.7	0.0	27.7	0.0	27.7	0.0
1955	27.6	-0.4	27.7	0.4	27.7	0.0	27.8	0.4	27.7	-0.4	27.7	0.0	27.9	0.7	27.8	-0.4	27.9	0.4	28.0	0.4	28.1	0.4	28.1	0.0
1956	28.3	0.7	28.3	0.0	28.3	0.0	28.5	0.7	28.4	-0.4	28.5	0.4	28.8	1.1	28.8	0.0	28.7	-0.3	28.9	0.7	28.8	-0.3	28.8	0.0
1957	29.1	1.0	29.0	-0.3	29.0	0.0	29.1	0.3	29.1	0.0	29.2	0.3	29.1	-0.3	29.1	0.0	29.1	0.0	29.1	0.0	29.1	0.0	29.2	0.3
1958	29.2	0.0	29.1	-0.3	29.2	0.3	29.3	0.3	29.2	-0.3	29.1	-0.3	29.0	-0.3	28.9	-0.3	28.9	0.0	29.1	0.7	29.1	0.0	29.2	0.3
1959	29.2	0.0	29.2	0.0	29.1	-0.3	29.2	0.3	29.2	0.0	29.2	0.0	29.2	0.0	29.2	0.0	29.2	0.0	29.2	0.0	29.2	0.0	29.2	0.0
1960	29.2	0.0	29.3	0.3	29.3	0.0	29.3	0.0	29.4	0.3	29.4	0.0	29.4	0.0	29.4	0.0	29.3	-0.3	29.1	-0.7	29.1	0.0	29.1	0.0
1961	29.0	-0.3	29.0	0.0	29.0	0.0	29.0	0.0	28.9	-0.3	28.8	-0.3	28.5	-1.0	28.4	-0.4	28.4	0.0	28.3	-0.4	28.3	0.0	28.3	0.0
1962	28.3	0.0	28.2	-0.4	28.1	-0.4	28.1	0.0	28.1	0.0	28.0	-0.4	28.0	0.0	27.9	-0.4	27.9	0.0	28.0	0.4	27.9	-0.4	27.9	0.0
1963	28.0	0.4	27.7	-1.1	27.8	0.4	27.7	-0.4	27.7	0.0	27.7	0.0	27.6	-0.4	27.5	-0.4	27.5	0.0	27.4	-0.4	27.4	0.0	27.5	0.4
1964	27.5	0.0	27.4	-0.4	27.5	0.4	27.5	0.0	27.5	0.0	27.5	0.0	27.5	0.0	27.3	-0.7	27.3	0.0	27.5	0.7	27.4	-0.4	27.4	0.0
1965	27.5	0.4	27.6	0.4	27.5	-0.4	27.6	0.4	27.6	0.0	27.6	0.0	27.7	0.4	27.7	0.0	27.7	0.0	27.8	0.4	27.8	0.0	27.8	0.0
1966	27.7	-0.4	27.7	0.0	27.7	0.0	27.9	0.7	28.0	0.4	27.9	-0.4	27.9	0.0	27.9	0.0	27.9	0.0	27.9	0.0	28.0	0.4	28.1	0.4
1967	28.1	0.0	28.2	0.4	28.3	0.4	28.4	0.4	28.4	0.0	28.3	-0.4	28.3	0.0	28.3	0.0	28.3	0.0	28.6	1.1	28.6	0.0	28.6	0.0
1968	28.7	0.3	28.7	0.0	28.7	0.0	28.8	0.3	28.8	0.0	28.7	-0.3	28.6	-0.3	28.6	0.0	28.5	-0.3	28.5	0.0	28.5	0.0	28.5	0.0
1969	28.6	0.4	28.6	0.0	28.5	-0.3	28.2	-1.1	28.2	0.0	28.3	0.4	28.4	0.4	28.6	0.7	28.6	0.0	28.4	-0.7	28.5	0.4	28.5	0.0
1970	28.5	0.0	28.4	-0.4	28.3	-0.4	28.5	0.7	28.6	0.4	28.6	0.0	28.8	0.7	28.7	-0.3	28.7	0.0	28.8	0.3	28.8	0.0	28.7	-0.3

[Continued]

Industrial Chemicals
Producer Price Index
Base 1982 = 100
[Continued]

For 1926-1995. Columns headed % show percentile change in the index from the previous period for which an index is available.

Year	Jan Index	%	Feb Index	%	Mar Index	%	Apr Index	%	May Index	%	Jun Index	%	Jul Index	%	Aug Index	%	Sep Index	%	Oct Index	%	Nov Index	%	Dec Index	%
1971	28.9	0.7	28.9	0.0	29.0	0.3	28.9	-0.3	28.9	0.0	29.0	0.3	29.1	0.3	29.0	-0.3	29.1	0.3	29.1	0.0	28.8	-1.0	28.7	-0.3
1972	28.8	0.3	28.8	0.0	28.6	-0.7	28.8	0.7	28.8	0.0	28.8	0.0	28.8	0.0	28.7	-0.3	28.7	0.0	28.6	-0.3	28.6	0.0	28.6	0.0
1973	28.7	0.3	28.9	0.7	28.9	0.0	29.1	0.7	29.1	0.0	29.2	0.3	29.3	0.3	29.4	0.3	29.6	0.7	29.9	1.0	29.9	0.0	30.0	0.3
1974	30.7	2.3	31.3	2.0	34.6	10.5	37.1	7.2	39.2	5.7	41.7	6.4	44.1	5.8	47.6	7.9	49.5	4.0	51.6	4.2	53.9	4.5	55.2	2.4
1975	55.8	1.1	57.3	2.7	58.9	2.8	58.8	-0.2	59.2	0.7	58.7	-0.8	58.5	-0.3	58.8	0.5	59.1	0.5	59.3	0.3	59.7	0.7	59.9	0.3
1976	60.6	1.2	61.4	1.3	61.8	0.7	61.9	0.2	62.0	0.2	62.0	0.0	62.2	0.3	62.7	0.8	62.9	0.3	63.0	0.2	63.1	0.2	62.8	-0.5
1977	62.9	0.2	63.2	0.5	63.1	-0.2	63.4	0.5	63.6	0.3	63.6	0.0	63.7	0.2	63.7	0.0	63.6	-0.2	63.8	0.3	63.8	0.0	63.9	0.2
1978	63.6	-0.5	63.6	0.0	63.6	0.0	63.6	0.0	63.5	-0.2	63.5	0.0	63.8	0.5	64.2	0.6	64.2	0.0	64.7	0.8	64.5	-0.3	65.0	0.8
1979	66.4	2.2	67.3	1.4	68.0	1.0	70.4	3.5	72.5	3.0	73.5	1.4	76.7	4.4	78.6	2.5	79.4	1.0	81.0	2.0	81.8	1.0	82.9	1.3
1980	85.9	3.6	87.3	1.6	88.9	1.8	91.4	2.8	93.2	2.0	93.5	0.3	93.2	-0.3	93.6	0.4	92.9	-0.7	93.6	0.8	94.4	0.9	94.9	0.5
1981	97.7	3.0	99.9	2.3	100.5	0.6	102.8	2.3	104.5	1.7	104.9	0.4	105.1	0.2	105.4	0.3	105.5	0.1	104.3	-1.1	103.1	-1.2	102.9	-0.2
1982	102.9	0.0	102.7	-0.2	102.5	-0.2	101.5	-1.0	101.3	-0.2	99.6	-1.7	99.0	-0.6	99.0	0.0	98.3	-0.7	98.1	-0.2	97.9	-0.2	97.1	-0.8
1983	96.2	-0.9	96.5	0.3	96.1	-0.4	96.1	0.0	96.1	0.0	96.0	-0.1	98.4	2.5	98.6	0.2	98.0	-0.6	97.8	-0.2	98.2	0.4	99.1	0.9
1984	98.5	-0.6	95.8	-2.7	97.8	2.1	98.0	0.2	97.9	-0.1	98.0	0.1	98.0	0.0	96.7	-1.3	95.8	-0.9	95.3	-0.5	94.9	-0.4	95.0	0.1
1985	95.5	0.5	95.5	0.0	95.5	0.0	95.3	-0.2	95.5	0.2	96.3	0.8	96.4	0.1	97.5	1.1	97.1	-0.4	95.9	-1.2	95.4	-0.5	95.6	0.2
1986	96.9	1.4	95.0	-2.0	95.4	0.4	91.8	-3.8	90.2	-1.7	89.8	-0.4	89.7	-0.1	89.5	-0.2	89.9	0.4	90.2	0.3	89.8	-0.4	90.2	0.4
1987	92.0	2.0	92.8	0.9	93.7	1.0	94.1	0.4	95.2	1.2	97.8	2.7	96.3	-1.5	95.6	-0.7	95.5	-0.1	96.8	1.4	97.6	0.8	98.2	0.6
1988	99.4	1.2	100.3	0.9	102.1	1.8	103.3	1.2	104.3	1.0	105.8	1.4	108.6	2.6	109.4	0.7	110.0	0.5	111.4	1.3	112.8	1.3	114.2	1.2
1989	117.2	2.6	117.6	0.3	116.7	-0.8	117.5	0.7	117.8	0.3	115.6	-1.9	114.1	-1.3	113.4	-0.6	112.4	-0.9	112.5	0.1	111.7	-0.7	111.6	-0.1
1990	111.4	-0.2	111.3	-0.1	110.7	-0.5	110.4	-0.3	110.8	0.4	111.1	0.3	111.1	0.0	110.7	-0.4	114.9	3.8	118.4	3.0	120.1	1.4	117.8	-1.9
1991	117.5	-0.3	116.7	-0.7	113.2	-3.0	112.9	-0.3	111.9	-0.9	111.7	-0.2	109.7	-1.8	109.1	-0.5	109.7	0.5	109.7	0.0	109.7	0.0	109.9	0.2
1992	108.4	-1.4	107.3	-1.0	107.2	-0.1	107.5	0.3	107.7	0.2	109.9	2.0	110.2	0.3	110.5	0.3	111.0	0.5	110.7	-0.3	111.4	0.6	109.4	-1.8
1993	109.8	0.4	110.7	0.8	110.0	-0.6	111.9	1.7	111.1	-0.7	111.3	0.2	110.6	-0.6	110.4	-0.2	110.3	-0.1	110.2	-0.1	110.5	0.3	108.7	-1.6
1994	108.6	-0.1	108.1	-0.5	108.4	0.3	109.6	1.1	110.8	1.1	111.7	0.8	112.9	1.1	115.2	2.0	119.8	4.0	121.2	1.2	122.0	0.7	123.0	0.8
1995	125.6	2.1	127.9	1.8	128.5	0.5	131.5	2.3	132.0	0.4	130.3	-1.3	130.4	0.1	129.6	-0.6	130.9	1.0	127.8	-2.4	126.0	-1.4	123.0	-2.4

Source: U.S. Department of Labor, Bureau of Labor Statistics, Division of Industry Prices and Price Indexes. n.e.c. stands for not elsewhere classified. - indicates no data collected for period or unavailable.

Paints and Allied Products
Producer Price Index
Base 1982 = 100

For 1971-1995. Columns headed % show percentile change in the index from the previous period for which an index is available.

Year	Jan Index	%	Feb Index	%	Mar Index	%	Apr Index	%	May Index	%	Jun Index	%	Jul Index	%	Aug Index	%	Sep Index	%	Oct Index	%	Nov Index	%	Dec Index	%
1971	39.5	-	39.5	0.0	39.6	0.3	39.8	0.5	39.8	0.0	39.3	-1.3	39.4	0.3	39.4	0.0	39.4	0.0	39.4	0.0	39.4	0.0	39.6	0.5
1972	39.8	0.5	40.0	0.5	40.2	0.5	40.3	0.2	40.4	0.2	40.4	0.0	40.5	0.2	40.6	0.2	40.6	0.0	40.5	-0.2	40.5	0.0	40.7	0.5
1973	41.0	0.7	41.1	0.2	41.2	0.2	41.5	0.7	41.8	0.7	42.1	0.7	42.3	0.5	42.4	0.2	42.5	0.2	43.7	2.8	44.3	1.4	45.1	1.8
1974	46.1	2.2	46.5	0.9	47.9	3.0	49.3	2.9	49.6	0.6	52.2	5.2	53.9	3.3	54.5	1.1	55.3	1.5	56.8	2.7	59.2	4.2	59.2	0.0
1975	59.6	0.7	59.5	-0.2	60.4	1.5	60.3	-0.2	60.8	0.8	60.2	-1.0	60.4	0.3	60.3	-0.2	61.2	1.5	61.1	-0.2	61.0	-0.2	61.0	0.0
1976	60.8	-0.3	61.1	0.5	60.9	-0.3	64.1	5.3	64.2	0.2	64.3	0.2	65.0	1.1	65.5	0.8	66.1	0.9	66.2	0.2	66.6	0.6	66.6	0.0
1977	66.6	0.0	66.9	0.5	67.9	1.5	68.7	1.2	69.1	0.6	69.0	-0.1	68.9	-0.1	68.9	0.0	68.8	-0.1	68.6	-0.3	69.0	0.6	69.2	0.3
1978	69.0	-0.3	69.5	0.7	70.1	0.9	70.7	0.9	71.2	0.7	71.4	0.3	71.6	0.3	71.8	0.3	72.2	0.6	72.6	0.6	73.4	1.1	74.0	0.8
1979	74.3	0.4	75.2	1.2	75.7	0.7	76.7	1.3	77.1	0.5	77.7	0.8	79.6	2.4	79.8	0.3	80.6	1.0	81.0	0.5	82.0	1.2	82.3	0.4
1980	85.1	3.4	85.7	0.7	87.4	2.0	88.7	1.5	90.4	1.9	90.6	0.2	90.9	0.3	91.1	0.2	91.3	0.2	91.4	0.1	91.8	0.4	92.1	0.3
1981	92.9	0.9	94.0	1.2	94.6	0.6	95.7	1.2	96.9	1.3	-	-	-	-	-	-	-	-	98.4	1.5	99.1	0.7	99.0	-0.1
1982	99.6	0.6	99.6	0.0	99.7	0.1	99.6	-0.1	100.7	1.1	100.4	-0.3	100.3	-0.1	100.0	-0.3	100.1	0.1	100.1	0.0	100.0	-0.1	99.9	-0.1
1983	99.8	-0.1	99.5	-0.3	99.3	-0.2	99.6	0.3	99.6	0.0	99.5	-0.1	99.8	0.3	100.5	0.7	101.7	1.2	101.7	0.0	101.7	0.0	101.7	0.0
1984	102.0	0.3	102.6	0.6	102.5	-0.1	104.2	1.7	105.4	1.2	105.7	0.3	106.1	0.4	106.5	0.4	106.4	-0.1	106.6	0.2	106.6	0.0	106.8	0.2
1985	106.8	0.0	106.2	-0.6	106.4	0.2	106.7	0.3	107.0	0.3	107.2	0.2	107.1	-0.1	106.9	-0.2	106.5	-0.4	106.5	0.0	106.3	-0.2	106.6	0.3
1986	106.9	0.3	106.8	-0.1	107.0	0.2	105.4	-1.5	105.3	-0.1	105.3	0.0	105.9	0.6	105.5	-0.4	105.5	0.0	104.9	-0.6	105.0	0.1	105.1	0.1
1987	105.5	0.4	105.4	-0.1	105.7	0.3	106.8	1.0	106.9	0.1	107.9	0.9	108.1	0.2	108.7	0.6	108.8	0.1	108.8	0.0	107.6	-1.1	108.4	0.7
1988	109.6	1.1	109.8	0.2	110.6	0.7	111.2	0.5	111.5	0.3	112.2	0.6	113.7	1.3	114.1	0.4	114.7	0.5	115.4	0.6	117.0	1.4	117.2	0.2
1989	119.7	2.1	121.4	1.4	121.7	0.2	123.0	1.1	123.1	0.1	124.0	0.7	124.4	0.3	122.4	-1.6	123.0	0.5	123.3	0.2	122.2	-0.9	122.4	0.2
1990	122.8	0.3	125.3	2.0	125.5	0.2	126.1	0.5	126.4	0.2	127.0	0.5	127.3	0.2	127.5	0.2	131.8	3.4	132.3	0.4	134.7	1.8	134.7	0.0
1991	135.8	0.8	136.3	0.4	130.6	-4.2	130.7	0.1	130.7	0.0	131.3	0.5	131.4	0.1	131.3	-0.1	130.1	-0.9	130.1	0.0	130.5	0.3	130.4	-0.1
1992	130.3	-0.1	130.5	0.2	130.6	0.1	130.9	0.2	131.1	0.2	131.1	0.0	131.5	0.3	131.4	-0.1	131.2	-0.2	131.3	0.1	131.3	0.0	131.3	0.0
1993	131.7	0.3	132.0	0.2	131.9	-0.1	132.5	0.5	132.3	-0.2	132.2	-0.1	132.3	0.1	132.2	-0.1	132.2	0.0	132.1	-0.1	132.4	0.2	132.4	0.0
1994	132.6	0.2	133.0	0.3	133.1	0.1	133.1	0.0	133.3	0.2	133.5	0.2	133.8	0.2	134.1	0.2	134.4	0.2	134.7	0.2	135.3	0.4	135.8	0.4
1995	137.5	1.3	138.5	0.7	138.8	0.2	140.4	1.2	141.3	0.6	141.1	-0.1	141.5	0.3	142.1	0.4	142.8	0.5	143.1	0.2	142.6	-0.3	143.0	0.3

Source: U.S. Department of Labor, Bureau of Labor Statistics, Division of Industry Prices and Price Indexes. n.e.c. stands for not elsewhere classified. - indicates no data collected for period or unavailable.

Drugs and Pharmaceuticals
Producer Price Index
Base 1982 = 100

For 1947-1995. Columns headed % show percentile change in the index from the previous period for which an index is available.

Year	Jan Index	%	Feb Index	%	Mar Index	%	Apr Index	%	May Index	%	Jun Index	%	Jul Index	%	Aug Index	%	Sep Index	%	Oct Index	%	Nov Index	%	Dec Index	%
1947	59.3	-	59.3	0.0	58.7	-1.0	56.7	-3.4	56.8	0.2	56.5	-0.5	56.3	-0.4	55.6	-1.2	55.4	-0.4	55.6	0.4	56.5	1.6	57.5	1.8
1948	56.3	-2.1	56.3	0.0	55.4	-1.6	55.2	-0.4	55.0	-0.4	55.0	0.0	54.8	-0.4	55.3	0.9	54.6	-1.3	52.8	-3.3	52.9	0.2	52.9	0.0
1949	51.6	-2.5	51.9	0.6	51.5	-0.8	50.9	-1.2	50.9	0.0	50.9	0.0	50.5	-0.8	50.1	-0.8	50.1	0.0	50.1	0.0	50.0	-0.2	49.9	-0.2
1950	49.7	-0.4	49.5	-0.4	49.4	-0.2	49.4	0.0	49.4	0.0	49.4	0.0	49.5	0.2	50.2	1.4	50.5	0.6	50.8	0.6	51.3	1.0	51.7	0.8
1951	51.9	0.4	51.9	0.0	51.9	0.0	51.9	0.0	51.7	-0.4	51.8	0.2	51.7	-0.2	51.7	0.0	51.7	0.0	51.7	0.0	51.5	-0.4	51.6	0.2
1952	51.4	-0.4	50.6	-1.6	50.5	-0.2	50.2	-0.6	49.9	-0.6	49.9	0.0	49.9	0.0	49.9	0.0	49.9	0.0	49.8	-0.2	49.8	0.0	49.4	-0.8
1953	49.6	0.4	49.5	-0.2	49.6	0.2	50.4	1.6	50.5	0.2	50.5	0.0	50.7	0.4	50.6	-0.2	50.6	0.0	50.6	0.0	50.6	0.0	50.8	0.4
1954	50.8	0.0	50.8	0.0	50.8	0.0	50.9	0.2	50.9	0.0	50.9	0.0	50.9	0.0	50.9	0.0	50.9	0.0	50.7	-0.4	50.7	0.0	50.7	0.0
1955	50.7	0.0	50.6	-0.2	50.5	-0.2	50.5	0.0	50.5	0.0	50.4	-0.2	50.3	-0.2	50.0	-0.6	50.0	0.0	50.0	0.0	50.0	0.0	50.0	0.0
1956	50.1	0.2	49.8	-0.6	49.8	0.0	49.8	0.0	49.9	0.2	49.9	0.0	49.9	0.0	49.9	0.0	49.8	-0.2	49.8	0.0	50.0	0.4	50.1	0.2
1957	50.1	0.0	50.5	0.8	50.5	0.0	50.6	0.2	50.6	0.0	50.6	0.0	50.6	0.0	50.6	0.0	50.6	0.0	50.6	0.0	50.6	0.0	50.6	0.0
1958	50.7	0.2	50.7	0.0	50.9	0.4	50.9	0.0	51.1	0.4	51.2	0.2	51.1	-0.2	51.1	0.0	51.1	0.0	50.8	-0.6	50.5	-0.6	50.5	0.0
1959	50.5	0.0	50.5	0.0	50.3	-0.4	50.3	0.0	50.5	0.4	50.5	0.0	50.6	0.2	50.6	0.0	50.6	0.0	50.6	0.0	50.6	0.0	50.6	0.0
1960	50.6	0.0	50.6	0.0	50.6	0.0	50.7	0.2	50.9	0.4	51.1	0.4	51.1	0.0	51.1	0.0	50.7	-0.8	50.5	-0.4	50.3	-0.4	50.3	0.0
1961	50.2	-0.2	50.2	0.0	50.1	-0.2	50.1	0.0	50.0	-0.2	50.0	0.0	50.1	0.2	49.4	-1.4	49.1	-0.6	49.2	0.2	49.3	0.2	49.3	0.0
1962	49.2	-0.2	49.2	0.0	49.2	0.0	49.1	-0.2	49.1	0.0	49.1	0.0	48.2	-1.8	48.1	-0.2	48.1	0.0	48.2	0.2	48.2	0.0	48.0	-0.4
1963	48.2	0.4	48.2	0.0	48.2	0.0	48.2	0.0	48.2	0.0	48.2	0.0	48.2	0.0	48.1	-0.2	48.1	0.0	48.1	0.0	48.1	0.0	48.1	0.0
1964	48.3	0.4	48.3	0.0	48.2	-0.2	48.3	0.2	48.4	0.2	47.9	-1.0	48.0	0.2	47.9	-0.2	47.9	0.0	47.9	0.0	47.9	0.0	47.9	0.0
1965	47.8	-0.2	47.9	0.2	47.9	0.0	48.0	0.2	48.1	0.2	47.6	-1.0	47.6	0.0	47.6	0.0	47.6	0.0	47.6	0.0	47.9	0.6	47.9	0.0
1966	47.8	-0.2	47.8	0.0	47.8	0.0	47.6	-0.4	47.6	0.0	47.7	0.2	47.8	0.2	47.9	0.2	48.0	0.2	48.1	0.2	48.1	0.0	47.9	-0.4
1967	47.9	0.0	47.7	-0.4	47.8	0.2	47.6	-0.4	47.6	0.0	47.6	0.0	47.6	0.0	47.4	-0.4	47.4	0.0	47.4	0.0	47.5	0.2	47.5	0.0
1968	47.0	-1.1	47.1	0.2	47.3	0.4	47.3	0.0	47.3	0.0	47.4	0.2	47.3	-0.2	47.1	-0.4	47.0	-0.2	47.3	0.6	47.4	0.2	47.4	0.0
1969	47.4	0.0	47.4	0.0	47.4	0.0	47.5	0.2	47.6	0.2	47.5	-0.2	47.6	0.2	47.6	0.0	47.6	0.0	47.6	0.0	47.7	0.2	47.9	0.4
1970	47.8	-0.2	47.9	0.2	48.2	0.6	47.9	-0.6	48.0	0.2	48.1	0.2	48.2	0.2	48.4	0.4	48.1	-0.6	48.2	0.2	48.4	0.4	48.5	0.2
1971	48.5	0.0	48.7	0.4	48.8	0.2	48.6	-0.4	48.6	0.0	48.7	0.2	48.9	0.4	48.9	0.0	48.9	0.0	48.9	0.0	48.8	-0.2	48.8	0.0
1972	48.7	-0.2	48.7	0.0	48.8	0.2	48.8	0.0	48.9	0.2	49.1	0.4	49.1	0.0	49.2	0.2	49.1	-0.2	49.2	0.2	49.3	0.2	49.3	0.0
1973	49.3	0.0	49.3	0.0	49.4	0.2	49.4	0.0	49.5	0.2	49.7	0.4	49.7	0.0	49.7	0.0	49.8	0.2	49.8	0.0	49.9	0.2	50.0	0.2
1974	50.1	0.2	50.3	0.4	50.6	0.6	51.2	1.2	51.9	1.4	53.0	2.1	53.7	1.3	54.9	2.2	55.7	1.5	56.7	1.8	57.6	1.6	58.0	0.7
1975	58.9	1.6	59.1	0.3	59.3	0.3	59.9	1.0	59.9	0.0	60.2	0.5	60.7	0.8	60.7	0.0	60.6	-0.2	61.2	1.0	61.3	0.2	61.5	0.3
1976	62.3	1.3	62.7	0.6	62.9	0.3	63.3	0.6	63.4	0.2	64.0	0.9	64.1	0.2	64.3	0.3	64.5	0.3	64.5	0.0	64.7	0.3	64.9	0.3
1977	65.5	0.9	65.9	0.6	66.2	0.5	66.4	0.3	66.5	0.2	67.0	0.8	67.2	0.3	67.2	0.0	67.3	0.1	67.5	0.3	67.7	0.3	68.0	0.4
1978	68.6	0.9	69.0	0.6	69.2	0.3	69.6	0.6	69.8	0.3	70.3	0.7	70.7	0.6	70.9	0.3	71.2	0.4	71.5	0.4	72.4	1.3	72.9	0.7
1979	73.9	1.4	74.4	0.7	74.6	0.3	75.0	0.5	75.1	0.1	75.7	0.8	75.8	0.1	76.0	0.3	76.7	0.9	77.5	1.0	77.6	0.1	78.3	0.9
1980	79.3	1.3	79.8	0.6	80.4	0.8	82.2	2.2	82.3	0.1	83.0	0.9	83.6	0.7	83.8	0.2	84.2	0.5	84.9	0.8	86.2	1.5	86.9	0.8
1981	87.9	1.2	89.2	1.5	90.1	1.0	90.9	0.9	91.6	0.8	91.9	0.3	93.1	1.3	92.8	-0.3	94.2	1.5	94.5	0.3	94.3	-0.2	94.7	0.4
1982	96.2	1.6	97.3	1.1	98.0	0.7	99.4	1.4	99.9	0.5	99.8	-0.1	100.0	0.2	100.5	0.5	101.1	0.6	102.3	1.2	102.6	0.3	102.8	0.2
1983	104.1	1.3	105.7	1.5	106.1	0.4	107.2	1.0	107.2	0.0	107.2	0.0	108.3	1.0	108.2	-0.1	108.2	0.0	109.1	0.8	110.0	0.8	109.9	-0.1
1984	110.9	0.9	111.6	0.6	113.1	1.3	114.2	1.0	114.3	0.1	112.9	-1.2	114.5	1.4	114.6	0.1	114.1	-0.4	116.5	2.1	117.5	0.9	116.6	-0.8
1985	117.8	1.0	119.1	1.1	120.1	0.8	121.0	0.7	121.7	0.6	121.0	-0.6	123.6	2.1	122.9	-0.6	123.4	0.4	124.4	0.8	125.1	0.6	124.1	-0.8
1986	126.6	2.0	126.5	-0.1	128.0	1.2	129.2	0.9	129.6	0.3	129.8	0.2	130.3	0.4	130.7	0.3	131.5	0.6	132.5	0.8	133.2	0.5	133.2	0.0
1987	134.7	1.1	135.8	0.8	137.3	1.1	138.2	0.7	139.5	0.9	138.9	-0.4	139.2	0.2	139.5	0.2	141.0	1.1	140.0	-0.7	142.6	1.9	142.4	-0.1
1988	143.3	0.6	143.6	0.2	145.5	1.3	146.0	0.3	147.4	1.0	147.4	0.0	149.2	1.2	149.2	0.0	150.8	1.1	151.5	0.5	153.3	1.2	153.1	-0.1
1989	155.5	1.6	155.6	0.1	157.7	1.3	158.6	0.6	158.6	0.0	160.1	0.9	160.7	0.4	161.9	0.7	161.3	-0.4	162.3	0.6	163.6	0.8	164.3	0.4
1990	166.0	1.0	167.5	0.9	168.7	0.7	169.8	0.7	170.5	0.4	170.1	-0.2	171.0	0.5	171.7	0.4	171.6	-0.1	172.9	0.8	174.5	0.9	175.1	0.3
1991	176.3	0.7	178.0	1.0	178.3	0.2	181.1	1.6	181.7	0.3	182.6	0.5	184.7	1.2	185.5	0.4	184.0	-0.8	186.1	1.1	186.1	0.0	186.5	0.2

[Continued]

Drugs and Pharmaceuticals
Producer Price Index
Base 1982 = 100
[Continued]

For 1947-1995. Columns headed % show percentile change in the index from the previous period for which an index is available.

Year	Jan Index	%	Feb Index	%	Mar Index	%	Apr Index	%	May Index	%	Jun Index	%	Jul Index	%	Aug Index	%	Sep Index	%	Oct Index	%	Nov Index	%	Dec Index	%
1992	187.2	0.4	188.8	0.9	189.6	0.4	191.3	0.9	191.9	0.3	192.2	0.2	192.8	0.3	193.8	0.5	193.7	-0.1	194.8	0.6	194.6	-0.1	196.0	0.7
1993	197.9	1.0	199.1	0.6	199.2	0.1	200.5	0.7	200.3	-0.1	201.0	0.3	201.5	0.2	202.3	0.4	202.1	-0.1	202.6	0.2	202.2	-0.2	202.3	0.0
1994	204.6	1.1	204.5	-0.0	204.7	0.1	205.3	0.3	206.2	0.4	206.2	0.0	206.0	-0.1	206.3	0.1	206.6	0.1	206.4	-0.1	207.3	0.4	207.3	0.0
1995	207.8	0.2	208.9	0.5	208.9	0.0	210.4	0.7	210.4	0.0	210.2	-0.1	210.8	0.3	210.9	0.0	211.4	0.2	212.1	0.3	212.7	0.3	213.2	0.2

Source: U.S. Department of Labor, Bureau of Labor Statistics, Division of Industry Prices and Price Indexes. n.e.c. stands for not elsewhere classified. - indicates no data collected for period or unavailable.

Fats and Oils, Inedible
Producer Price Index
Base 1982 = 100

For 1926-1995. Columns headed % show percentile change in the index from the previous period for which an index is available.

Year	Jan Index	%	Feb Index	%	Mar Index	%	Apr Index	%	May Index	%	Jun Index	%	Jul Index	%	Aug Index	%	Sep Index	%	Oct Index	%	Nov Index	%	Dec Index	%
1926	-	-	-	-	-	-	-	-	-	-	-	-	-	-	-	-	-	-	-	-	-	-	-	-
1927	-	-	-	-	-	-	-	-	-	-	-	-	-	-	-	-	-	-	-	-	-	-	-	-
1928	-	-	-	-	-	-	-	-	-	-	-	-	-	-	-	-	-	-	-	-	-	-	-	-
1929	-	-	-	-	-	-	-	-	-	-	-	-	-	-	-	-	-	-	-	-	-	-	-	-
1930	-	-	-	-	-	-	-	-	-	-	-	-	-	-	-	-	-	-	-	-	-	-	-	-
1931	-	-	-	-	-	-	-	-	-	-	-	-	-	-	-	-	-	-	-	-	-	-	-	-
1932	-	-	-	-	-	-	-	-	-	-	-	-	-	-	-	-	-	-	-	-	-	-	-	-
1933	19.3	-	18.6	-3.6	18.8	1.1	19.1	1.6	22.2	16.2	23.4	5.4	23.0	-1.7	22.7	-1.3	21.0	-7.5	20.9	-0.5	21.1	1.0	20.3	-3.8
1934	19.5	-3.9	19.9	2.1	20.2	1.5	20.1	-0.5	20.4	1.5	19.8	-2.9	20.1	1.5	21.3	6.0	23.1	8.5	24.6	6.5	23.8	-3.3	25.4	6.7
1935	29.7	16.9	33.3	12.1	36.3	9.0	34.6	-4.7	35.3	2.0	33.0	-6.5	29.5	-10.6	29.4	-0.3	31.1	5.8	33.7	8.4	33.1	-1.8	32.8	-0.9
1936	32.8	0.0	31.8	-3.0	30.3	-4.7	29.4	-3.0	26.7	-9.2	27.4	2.6	30.8	12.4	32.6	5.8	36.8	12.9	37.6	2.2	39.8	5.9	45.7	14.8
1937	51.4	12.5	50.5	-1.8	50.1	-0.8	47.8	-4.6	42.8	-10.5	40.5	-5.4	39.4	-2.7	36.9	-6.3	34.4	-6.8	33.2	-3.5	31.2	-6.0	29.7	-4.8
1938	30.4	2.4	29.4	-3.3	28.5	-3.1	26.1	-8.4	25.2	-3.4	24.6	-2.4	26.1	6.1	25.6	-1.9	25.1	-2.0	25.0	-0.4	24.6	-1.6	24.5	-0.4
1939	24.6	0.4	24.3	-1.2	25.0	2.9	24.3	-2.8	24.7	1.6	24.5	-0.8	22.9	-6.5	21.5	-6.1	28.7	33.5	30.3	5.6	29.0	-4.3	28.2	-2.8
1940	27.8	-1.4	27.0	-2.9	25.4	-5.9	24.8	-2.4	24.4	-1.6	23.9	-2.0	22.8	-4.6	20.7	-9.2	21.1	1.9	21.0	-0.5	22.4	6.7	22.4	0.0
1941	24.5	9.4	24.8	1.2	29.5	19.0	36.7	24.4	42.7	16.3	42.7	0.0	44.4	4.0	46.2	4.1	48.4	4.8	49.4	2.1	49.2	-0.4	54.0	9.8
1942	56.3	4.3	57.3	1.8	57.6	0.5	57.7	0.2	57.5	-0.3	57.4	-0.2	55.2	-3.8	53.8	-2.5	53.8	0.0	53.8	0.0	53.8	0.0	53.8	0.0
1943	53.8	0.0	53.8	0.0	53.8	0.0	53.8	0.0	54.0	0.4	54.0	0.0	54.0	0.0	54.0	0.0	54.0	0.0	54.0	0.0	54.0	0.0	54.0	0.0
1944	54.0	0.0	54.0	0.0	54.0	0.0	54.0	0.0	54.0	0.0	54.0	0.0	54.0	0.0	54.0	0.0	54.0	0.0	54.0	0.0	54.0	0.0	54.0	0.0
1945	54.0	0.0	54.0	0.0	54.0	0.0	54.0	0.0	54.0	0.0	54.0	0.0	54.0	0.0	54.0	0.0	54.0	0.0	54.0	0.0	54.0	0.0	54.0	0.0
1946	53.8	-0.4	53.9	0.2	54.1	0.4	54.1	0.0	54.1	0.0	54.1	0.0	60.4	11.6	54.3	-10.1	54.7	0.7	58.8	7.5	101.1	71.9	107.5	6.3
1947	111.5	3.7	114.9	3.0	128.8	12.1	116.8	-9.3	86.3	-26.1	67.5	-21.8	64.5	-4.4	62.6	-2.9	82.4	31.6	103.6	25.7	121.2	17.0	111.0	-8.4
1948	120.6	8.6	96.0	-20.4	100.0	4.2	96.0	-4.0	85.6	-10.8	92.6	8.2	87.4	-5.6	77.9	-10.9	80.8	3.7	77.8	-3.7	79.0	1.5	70.2	-11.1
1949	56.2	-19.9	49.8	-11.4	44.8	-10.0	39.8	-11.2	42.0	5.5	40.1	-4.5	39.2	-2.2	46.1	17.6	41.7	-9.5	39.7	-4.8	39.7	0.0	39.9	0.5
1950	42.5	6.5	41.7	-1.9	43.4	4.1	43.3	-0.2	41.8	-3.5	37.3	-10.8	44.2	18.5	53.0	19.9	66.5	25.5	65.3	-1.8	71.5	9.5	80.1	12.0
1951	88.9	11.0	94.4	6.2	87.8	-7.0	82.3	-6.3	79.3	-3.6	67.7	-14.6	53.6	-20.8	53.8	0.4	55.8	3.7	54.9	-1.6	49.9	-9.1	47.0	-5.8
1952	43.4	-7.7	39.2	-9.7	36.2	-7.7	32.6	-9.9	36.1	10.7	39.8	10.2	38.1	-4.3	36.3	-4.7	37.4	3.0	39.0	4.3	40.6	4.1	40.4	-0.5
1953	40.9	1.2	40.3	-1.5	45.1	11.9	42.7	-5.3	38.2	-10.5	35.6	-6.8	35.7	0.3	35.9	0.6	39.1	8.9	40.8	4.3	44.4	8.8	44.8	0.9
1954	46.8	4.5	48.6	3.8	46.3	-4.7	45.7	-1.3	45.4	-0.7	42.6	-6.2	39.8	-6.6	40.9	2.8	41.3	1.0	43.2	4.6	44.2	2.3	45.4	2.7
1955	47.3	4.2	46.7	-1.3	42.4	-9.2	42.2	-0.5	40.7	-3.6	41.1	1.0	42.7	3.9	41.8	-2.1	42.7	2.2	44.5	4.2	44.1	-0.9	43.3	-1.8
1956	42.5	-1.8	41.6	-2.1	42.1	1.2	44.4	5.5	46.1	3.8	42.1	-8.7	41.1	-2.4	41.1	0.0	42.4	3.2	42.7	0.7	44.2	3.5	45.4	2.7
1957	44.9	-1.1	44.4	-1.1	44.3	-0.2	44.5	0.5	45.3	1.8	46.1	1.8	46.7	1.3	48.5	3.9	49.3	1.6	49.5	0.4	49.9	0.8	50.0	0.2
1958	48.3	-3.4	48.1	-0.4	49.1	2.1	47.6	-3.1	47.0	-1.3	47.3	0.6	47.8	1.1	47.8	0.0	47.2	-1.3	47.9	1.5	49.5	3.3	47.0	-5.1
1959	45.8	-2.6	45.0	-1.7	46.1	2.4	46.2	0.2	46.2	0.0	44.7	-3.2	42.3	-5.4	41.1	-2.8	42.1	2.4	41.7	-1.0	39.9	-4.3	38.9	-2.5
1960	37.6	-3.3	37.8	0.5	38.7	2.4	39.6	2.3	38.4	-3.0	36.6	-4.7	36.6	0.0	37.4	2.2	36.5	-2.4	36.6	0.3	37.4	2.2	37.1	-0.8
1961	38.4	3.5	41.8	8.9	44.1	5.5	47.5	7.7	47.0	-1.1	41.4	-11.9	39.9	-3.6	39.1	-2.0	37.3	-4.6	36.0	-3.5	35.2	-2.2	36.1	2.6
1962	38.2	5.8	35.5	-7.1	37.4	5.4	36.5	-2.4	35.5	-2.7	33.8	-4.8	33.9	0.3	33.6	-0.9	33.3	-0.9	35.3	6.0	35.0	-0.8	33.5	-4.3
1963	33.0	-1.5	33.5	1.5	34.3	2.4	35.8	4.4	36.2	1.1	37.1	2.5	37.5	1.1	37.6	0.3	37.4	-0.5	40.8	9.1	41.5	1.7	39.2	-5.5
1964	38.3	-2.3	38.3	0.0	39.5	3.1	40.2	1.8	40.8	1.5	42.9	5.1	44.2	3.0	46.7	5.7	48.9	4.7	49.6	1.4	51.9	4.6	53.8	3.7
1965	52.2	-3.0	54.5	4.4	54.7	0.4	55.8	2.0	53.7	-3.8	52.5	-2.2	50.8	-3.2	48.1	-5.3	49.9	3.7	50.7	1.6	49.1	-3.2	50.7	3.3
1966	52.1	2.8	50.7	-2.7	49.0	-3.4	47.9	-2.2	47.2	-1.5	46.8	-0.8	48.5	3.6	48.6	0.2	47.8	-1.6	43.5	-9.0	42.2	-3.0	43.8	3.8
1967	42.5	-3.0	41.0	-3.5	37.5	-8.5	39.3	4.8	38.2	-2.8	36.6	-4.2	35.5	-3.0	35.6	0.3	35.5	-0.3	36.2	2.0	35.9	-0.8	35.6	-0.8
1968	35.2	-1.1	35.3	0.3	36.8	4.2	37.2	1.1	36.1	-3.0	33.5	-7.2	31.8	-5.1	32.8	3.1	31.6	-3.7	32.2	1.9	33.8	5.0	32.2	-4.7
1969	33.3	3.4	33.9	1.8	37.0	9.1	38.6	4.3	38.4	-0.5	40.0	4.2	41.7	4.2	45.7	9.6	46.9	2.6	45.5	-3.0	46.3	1.8	42.7	-7.8
1970	43.8	2.6	43.4	-0.9	47.2	8.8	49.5	4.9	49.2	-0.6	49.8	1.2	49.6	-0.4	51.6	4.0	48.1	-6.8	54.1	12.5	56.7	4.8	53.8	-5.1

[Continued]

Fats and Oils, Inedible

Producer Price Index
Base 1982 = 100
[Continued]

For 1926-1995. Columns headed % show percentile change in the index from the previous period for which an index is available.

Year	Jan Index	%	Feb Index	%	Mar Index	%	Apr Index	%	May Index	%	Jun Index	%	Jul Index	%	Aug Index	%	Sep Index	%	Oct Index	%	Nov Index	%	Dec Index	%
1971	50.1	-6.9	53.4	6.6	54.0	1.1	53.6	-0.7	52.0	-3.0	49.4	-5.0	49.0	-0.8	50.2	2.4	49.8	-0.8	48.3	-3.0	46.9	-2.9	43.4	-7.5
1972	41.7	-3.9	41.4	-0.7	38.7	-6.5	42.0	8.5	43.4	3.3	43.4	0.0	42.4	-2.3	45.4	7.1	43.6	-4.0	43.9	0.7	46.1	5.0	48.0	4.1
1973	48.8	1.7	52.1	6.8	65.1	25.0	68.9	5.8	86.9	26.1	98.7	13.6	98.5	-0.2	102.3	3.9	104.7	2.3	102.2	-2.4	90.6	-11.4	107.1	18.2
1974	111.6	4.2	125.7	12.6	139.4	10.9	144.3	3.5	134.5	-6.8	135.3	0.6	130.1	-3.8	142.4	9.5	121.8	-14.5	122.9	0.9	112.8	-8.2	99.0	-12.2
1975	88.1	-11.0	86.7	-1.6	81.7	-5.8	97.9	19.8	93.8	-4.2	92.4	-1.5	97.5	5.5	107.0	9.7	108.5	1.4	99.0	-8.8	97.6	-1.4	96.3	-1.3
1976	92.3	-4.2	91.8	-0.5	95.9	4.5	91.2	-4.9	88.2	-3.3	91.2	3.4	97.0	6.4	93.4	-3.7	98.4	5.4	94.1	-4.4	94.1	0.0	95.3	1.3
1977	95.5	0.2	100.4	5.1	102.5	2.1	114.2	11.4	126.4	10.7	119.4	-5.5	105.6	-11.6	100.7	-4.6	92.4	-8.2	97.7	5.7	99.4	1.7	99.7	0.3
1978	98.6	-1.1	105.4	6.9	110.3	4.6	112.8	2.3	118.0	4.6	117.3	-0.6	125.7	7.2	117.2	-6.8	126.7	8.1	127.3	0.5	135.3	6.3	124.7	-7.8
1979	125.9	1.0	137.8	9.5	149.2	8.3	168.0	12.6	156.6	-6.8	140.1	-10.5	142.9	2.0	140.9	-1.4	142.3	1.0	137.4	-3.4	128.9	-6.2	122.5	-5.0
1980	121.9	-0.5	113.2	-7.1	112.3	-0.8	111.7	-0.5	110.4	-1.2	95.8	-13.2	97.4	1.7	115.2	18.3	114.0	-1.0	113.1	-0.8	115.4	2.0	118.8	2.9
1981	116.3	-2.1	108.5	-6.7	110.7	2.0	117.1	5.8	116.9	-0.2	113.5	-2.9	108.9	-4.1	114.4	5.1	106.9	-6.6	104.0	-2.7	105.8	1.7	105.0	-0.8
1982	102.1	-2.8	102.7	0.6	108.6	5.7	105.8	-2.6	108.0	2.1	107.6	-0.4	104.2	-3.2	95.2	-8.6	95.1	-0.1	90.7	-4.6	89.7	-1.1	90.2	0.6
1983	90.6	0.4	94.9	4.7	98.2	3.5	104.2	6.1	107.5	3.2	103.7	-3.5	97.7	-5.8	104.1	6.6	123.2	18.3	119.3	-3.2	120.4	0.9	119.4	-0.8
1984	125.2	4.9	130.7	4.4	137.3	5.0	143.5	4.5	149.5	4.2	155.1	3.7	141.8	-8.6	131.1	-7.5	134.6	2.7	136.7	1.6	142.3	4.1	141.1	-0.8
1985	129.7	-8.1	130.0	0.2	129.7	-0.2	130.7	0.8	124.0	-5.1	111.7	-9.9	104.8	-6.2	97.6	-6.9	92.6	-5.1	93.6	1.1	90.7	-3.1	91.9	1.3
1986	94.5	2.8	95.9	1.5	86.4	-9.9	81.6	-5.6	76.9	-5.8	71.5	-7.0	69.9	-2.2	71.2	1.9	72.2	1.4	76.9	6.5	80.2	4.3	84.1	4.9
1987	94.5	12.4	95.1	0.6	91.3	-4.0	83.0	-9.1	91.0	9.6	94.9	4.3	92.5	-2.5	93.0	0.5	95.5	2.7	94.8	-0.7	93.3	-1.6	93.4	0.1
1988	110.5	18.3	110.8	0.3	110.1	-0.6	109.6	-0.5	105.9	-3.4	115.1	8.7	123.0	6.9	122.0	-0.8	111.6	-8.5	107.2	-3.9	100.7	-6.1	103.7	3.0
1989	103.2	-0.5	102.4	-0.8	101.8	-0.6	99.1	-2.7	96.2	-2.9	99.2	3.1	94.5	-4.7	85.9	-9.1	86.8	1.0	93.9	8.2	92.2	-1.8	90.7	-1.6
1990	88.3	-2.6	94.2	6.7	90.6	-3.8	85.6	-5.5	86.8	1.4	88.5	2.0	88.4	-0.1	83.0	-6.1	82.4	-0.7	87.0	5.6	89.6	3.0	92.8	3.6
1991	96.6	4.1	89.5	-7.3	86.2	-3.7	86.5	0.3	83.5	-3.5	82.1	-1.7	80.5	-1.9	86.9	8.0	87.7	0.9	87.1	-0.7	88.3	1.4	87.0	-1.5
1992	88.9	2.2	86.5	-2.7	83.0	-4.0	84.6	1.9	87.2	3.1	91.7	5.2	94.7	3.3	98.1	3.6	99.4	1.3	98.8	-0.6	102.7	3.9	100.9	-1.8
1993	100.6	-0.3	97.5	-3.1	97.5	0.0	100.7	3.3	99.9	-0.8	96.5	-3.4	93.5	-3.1	94.7	1.3	91.2	-3.7	90.2	-1.1	90.1	-0.1	94.7	5.1
1994	99.9	5.5	102.8	2.9	101.7	-1.1	99.0	-2.7	99.3	0.3	105.0	5.7	106.6	1.5	112.6	5.6	116.1	3.1	118.4	2.0	125.2	5.7	140.2	12.0
1995	142.8	1.9	121.9	-14.6	124.1	1.8	122.0	-1.7	119.7	-1.9	121.8	1.8	125.7	3.2	124.8	-0.7	124.2	-0.5	126.1	1.5	133.9	6.2	134.5	0.4

Source: U.S. Department of Labor, Bureau of Labor Statistics, Division of Industry Prices and Price Indexes. n.e.c. stands for not elsewhere classified. - indicates no data collected for period or unavailable.

Agricultural Chemicals and Chemical Products
Producer Price Index
Base 1982 = 100

For 1947-1995. Columns headed % show percentile change in the index from the previous period for which an index is available.

Year	Jan Index	%	Feb Index	%	Mar Index	%	Apr Index	%	May Index	%	Jun Index	%	Jul Index	%	Aug Index	%	Sep Index	%	Oct Index	%	Nov Index	%	Dec Index	%
1947	28.3	-	28.3	0.0	28.9	2.1	29.0	0.3	29.0	0.0	28.8	-0.7	28.9	0.3	28.9	0.0	29.0	0.3	29.3	1.0	29.5	0.7	29.7	0.7
1948	29.9	0.7	29.8	-0.3	29.9	0.3	29.8	-0.3	29.7	-0.3	29.7	0.0	30.2	1.7	30.6	1.3	30.9	1.0	31.1	0.6	31.3	0.6	31.3	0.0
1949	31.6	1.0	31.5	-0.3	31.5	0.0	31.5	0.0	31.5	0.0	31.3	-0.6	31.5	0.6	31.4	-0.3	31.4	0.0	31.4	0.0	31.0	-1.3	30.9	-0.3
1950	30.8	-0.3	30.6	-0.6	30.7	0.3	30.8	0.3	30.8	0.0	30.1	-2.3	30.1	0.0	30.2	0.3	30.2	0.0	30.2	0.0	30.6	1.3	31.6	3.3
1951	32.1	1.6	32.1	0.0	32.1	0.0	32.1	0.0	32.1	0.0	31.9	-0.6	32.5	1.9	32.6	0.3	32.8	0.6	32.9	0.3	32.9	0.0	33.0	0.3
1952	33.0	0.0	33.1	0.3	33.3	0.6	33.3	0.0	33.5	0.6	32.9	-1.8	33.0	0.3	33.0	0.0	33.0	0.0	33.0	0.0	33.0	0.0	33.0	0.0
1953	32.9	-0.3	32.8	-0.3	32.8	0.0	32.9	0.3	33.0	0.3	32.7	-0.9	33.1	1.2	33.2	0.3	33.2	0.0	33.1	-0.3	33.3	0.6	33.4	0.3
1954	33.2	-0.6	33.4	0.6	33.4	0.0	33.4	0.0	33.4	0.0	33.1	-0.9	33.1	0.0	33.2	0.3	33.1	-0.3	33.0	-0.3	33.0	0.0	33.1	0.3
1955	33.2	0.3	33.2	0.0	33.2	0.0	33.1	-0.3	33.1	0.0	32.8	-0.9	32.9	0.3	33.0	0.3	32.9	-0.3	33.0	0.3	32.9	-0.3	32.9	0.0
1956	33.0	0.3	32.8	-0.6	32.8	0.0	32.8	0.0	32.3	-1.5	32.3	0.0	32.2	-0.3	32.3	0.3	32.2	-0.3	32.1	-0.3	32.3	0.6	32.3	0.0
1957	32.5	0.6	32.3	-0.6	32.3	0.0	32.5	0.6	32.4	-0.3	32.3	-0.3	32.3	0.0	32.5	0.6	32.7	0.6	32.8	0.3	32.8	0.0	33.1	0.9
1958	33.4	0.9	33.3	-0.3	33.4	0.3	33.6	0.6	33.6	0.0	33.6	0.0	33.4	-0.6	32.9	-1.5	32.8	-0.3	33.0	0.6	32.9	-0.3	32.9	0.0
1959	33.4	1.5	33.4	0.0	33.4	0.0	33.3	-0.3	33.2	-0.3	33.3	0.3	33.2	-0.3	33.0	-0.6	33.1	0.3	33.2	0.3	33.2	0.0	33.3	0.3
1960	33.4	0.3	33.5	0.3	33.5	0.0	33.5	0.0	33.5	0.0	33.5	0.0	33.7	0.6	33.7	0.0	33.8	0.3	34.0	0.6	34.0	0.0	33.9	-0.3
1961	34.0	0.3	34.0	0.0	34.0	0.0	34.0	0.0	34.0	0.0	33.8	-0.6	33.8	0.0	33.6	-0.6	33.8	0.6	33.4	-1.2	33.6	0.6	33.5	-0.3
1962	34.2	2.1	34.3	0.3	34.0	-0.9	34.0	0.0	33.9	-0.3	33.9	0.0	33.6	-0.9	33.2	-1.2	33.2	0.0	33.2	0.0	33.2	0.0	33.2	0.0
1963	33.4	0.6	33.2	-0.6	33.2	0.0	33.4	0.6	33.4	0.0	33.2	-0.6	33.1	-0.3	32.7	-1.2	32.8	0.3	32.8	0.0	32.9	0.3	32.7	-0.6
1964	32.8	0.3	32.9	0.3	32.9	0.0	32.9	0.0	32.9	0.0	32.9	0.0	33.0	0.3	32.8	-0.6	32.7	-0.3	32.8	0.3	33.0	0.6	33.0	0.0
1965	33.2	0.6	33.5	0.9	33.6	0.3	33.5	-0.3	33.5	0.0	33.6	0.3	33.7	0.3	33.6	-0.3	33.7	0.3	33.8	0.3	33.8	0.0	33.8	0.0
1966	33.8	0.0	33.9	0.3	33.9	0.0	34.1	0.6	34.2	0.3	34.0	-0.6	33.9	-0.3	33.6	-0.9	33.7	0.3	33.9	0.6	34.1	0.6	34.0	-0.3
1967	34.4	1.2	34.8	1.2	34.9	0.3	34.7	-0.6	34.7	0.0	34.7	0.0	34.2	-1.4	33.6	-1.8	33.4	-0.6	33.5	0.3	33.6	0.3	33.7	0.3
1968	32.8	-2.7	33.2	1.2	33.4	0.6	33.5	0.3	33.5	0.0	33.4	-0.3	33.4	0.0	32.7	-2.1	32.5	-0.6	32.3	-0.6	31.8	-1.5	31.8	0.0
1969	30.6	-3.8	30.4	-0.7	30.5	0.3	30.4	-0.3	30.4	0.0	30.4	0.0	29.2	-3.9	29.2	0.0	28.9	-1.0	28.5	-1.4	28.6	0.4	28.6	0.0
1970	28.9	1.0	30.2	4.5	30.4	0.7	30.5	0.3	30.3	-0.7	30.3	0.0	30.0	-1.0	30.2	0.7	30.4	0.7	30.6	0.7	30.6	0.0	30.6	0.0
1971	31.5	2.9	31.8	1.0	32.2	1.3	32.3	0.3	32.2	-0.3	32.2	0.0	31.5	-2.2	30.9	-1.9	30.9	0.0	30.9	0.0	30.9	0.0	30.9	0.0
1972	30.9	0.0	30.8	-0.3	31.0	0.6	31.5	1.6	31.5	0.0	31.6	0.3	31.4	-0.6	31.5	0.3	31.5	0.0	31.5	0.0	31.6	0.3	31.6	0.0
1973	31.8	0.6	31.8	0.0	32.0	0.6	32.3	0.9	32.4	0.3	32.5	0.3	33.1	1.8	32.8	-0.9	32.8	0.0	32.8	0.0	35.9	9.5	36.3	1.1
1974	38.4	5.8	38.7	0.8	40.4	4.4	40.4	0.0	40.4	0.0	41.1	1.7	44.8	9.0	48.6	8.5	49.7	2.3	58.3	17.3	61.9	6.2	62.3	0.6
1975	65.0	4.3	65.9	1.4	72.4	9.9	72.6	0.3	72.5	-0.1	72.2	-0.4	71.9	-0.4	70.6	-1.8	68.8	-2.5	68.4	-0.6	67.6	-1.2	67.7	0.1
1976	67.7	0.0	65.4	-3.4	65.1	-0.5	64.9	-0.3	64.9	0.0	64.3	-0.9	63.1	-1.9	63.7	1.0	63.9	0.3	63.9	0.0	63.0	-1.4	62.7	-0.5
1977	62.3	-0.6	62.9	1.0	64.0	1.7	64.6	0.9	64.5	-0.2	64.6	0.2	64.5	-0.2	64.8	0.5	65.0	0.3	65.0	0.0	64.4	-0.9	64.0	-0.6
1978	64.1	0.2	64.7	0.9	65.3	0.9	65.7	0.6	69.6	5.9	69.3	-0.4	69.1	-0.3	69.1	0.0	69.3	0.3	69.6	0.4	69.2	-0.6	69.1	-0.1
1979	69.0	-0.1	69.4	0.6	70.5	1.6	71.7	1.7	71.8	0.1	71.5	-0.4	72.2	1.0	73.6	1.9	75.0	1.9	76.7	2.3	78.5	2.3	79.6	1.4
1980	82.7	3.9	84.8	2.5	87.6	3.3	88.4	0.9	88.4	0.0	88.1	-0.3	88.5	0.5	88.9	0.5	89.1	0.2	89.1	0.0	89.3	0.2	90.0	0.8
1981	91.5	1.7	92.9	1.5	94.3	1.5	95.0	0.7	95.4	0.4	98.8	3.6	98.8	0.0	100.3	1.5	100.1	-0.2	100.2	0.1	101.1	0.9	100.8	-0.3
1982	101.5	0.7	101.9	0.4	101.6	-0.3	101.1	-0.5	100.8	-0.3	100.6	-0.2	99.7	-0.9	99.5	-0.2	99.1	-0.4	98.7	-0.4	98.0	-0.7	97.5	-0.5
1983	96.8	-0.7	96.9	0.1	97.2	0.3	96.7	-0.5	96.6	-0.1	96.0	-0.6	95.1	-0.9	94.8	-0.3	94.4	-0.4	94.5	0.1	95.9	1.5	96.4	0.5
1984	95.2	-1.2	97.7	2.6	98.5	0.8	98.6	0.1	98.1	-0.5	98.0	-0.1	97.4	-0.6	96.8	-0.6	97.4	0.6	97.6	0.2	96.6	-1.0	96.6	0.0
1985	96.7	0.1	96.3	-0.4	96.4	0.1	96.7	0.3	96.8	0.1	96.3	-0.5	96.4	0.1	96.5	0.1	96.4	-0.1	95.8	-0.6	95.7	-0.1	94.6	-1.1
1986	94.1	-0.5	95.1	1.1	95.6	0.5	95.5	-0.1	95.4	-0.1	95.7	0.3	95.1	-0.6	93.7	-1.5	93.5	-0.2	92.2	-1.4	92.4	0.2	92.2	-0.2
1987	92.1	-0.1	93.8	1.8	94.8	1.1	97.2	2.5	96.4	-0.8	96.5	0.1	96.8	0.3	97.3	0.5	97.8	0.5	97.7	-0.1	98.0	0.3	98.3	0.3
1988	101.1	2.8	103.1	2.0	104.3	1.2	104.5	0.2	103.9	-0.6	102.9	-1.0	103.4	0.5	103.8	0.4	104.4	0.6	105.5	1.1	107.6	2.0	109.2	1.5
1989	112.0	2.6	113.4	1.3	114.3	0.8	113.4	-0.8	112.2	-1.1	109.8	-2.1	106.5	-3.0	105.0	-1.4	104.7	-0.3	103.7	-1.0	104.4	0.7	104.5	0.1
1990	104.4	-0.1	105.8	1.3	105.7	-0.1	106.8	1.0	106.5	-0.3	105.3	-1.1	105.7	0.4	106.4	0.7	108.0	1.5	109.9	1.8	111.8	1.7	112.0	0.2
1991	112.0	0.0	112.3	0.3	112.3	0.0	112.2	-0.1	111.7	-0.4	111.2	-0.4	111.8	0.5	112.1	0.3	111.8	-0.3	111.5	-0.3	110.7	-0.7	110.9	0.2

[Continued]

Agricultural Chemicals and Chemical Products
Producer Price Index
Base 1982 = 100
[Continued]

For 1947-1995. Columns headed % show percentile change in the index from the previous period for which an index is available.

Year	Jan		Feb		Mar		Apr		May		Jun		Jul		Aug		Sep		Oct		Nov		Dec	
	Index	%	Index	%	Index	%	Index	%	Index	%	Index	%	Index	%	Index	%	Index	%	Index	%	Index	%	Index	%
1992	110.7	-0.2	110.9	0.2	111.2	0.3	111.3	0.1	111.7	0.4	111.6	-0.1	110.2	-1.3	109.3	-0.8	109.1	-0.2	109.3	0.2	109.4	0.1	109.3	-0.1
1993	110.6	1.2	110.2	-0.4	110.3	0.1	109.6	-0.6	109.3	-0.3	109.6	0.3	109.3	-0.3	107.7	-1.5	108.0	0.3	109.2	1.1	113.0	3.5	112.1	-0.8
1994	113.8	1.5	115.6	1.6	116.3	0.6	119.0	2.3	120.3	1.1	119.8	-0.4	120.5	0.6	120.1	-0.3	121.4	1.1	123.5	1.7	124.4	0.7	124.7	0.2
1995	126.9	1.8	129.6	2.1	131.5	1.5	132.5	0.8	132.1	-0.3	131.1	-0.8	129.4	-1.3	127.9	-1.2	127.8	-0.1	128.4	0.5	130.6	1.7	132.7	1.6

Source: U.S. Department of Labor, Bureau of Labor Statistics, Division of Industry Prices and Price Indexes. n.e.c. stands for not elsewhere classified. - indicates no data collected for period or unavailable.

Plastic Resins and Materials
Producer Price Index
Base 1982 = 100

For 1947-1995. Columns headed % show percentile change in the index from the previous period for which an index is available.

Year	Jan Index	%	Feb Index	%	Mar Index	%	Apr Index	%	May Index	%	Jun Index	%	Jul Index	%	Aug Index	%	Sep Index	%	Oct Index	%	Nov Index	%	Dec Index	%
1947	37.3	-	37.3	0.0	37.3	0.0	37.3	0.0	37.5	0.5	37.5	0.0	37.5	0.0	37.5	0.0	37.5	0.0	37.5	0.0	37.2	-0.8	37.2	0.0
1948	37.6	1.1	37.2	-1.1	36.6	-1.6	36.6	0.0	36.6	0.0	36.6	0.0	37.5	2.5	37.4	-0.3	37.5	0.3	37.6	0.3	37.6	0.0	37.6	0.0
1949	38.1	1.3	38.1	0.0	37.6	-1.3	37.6	0.0	37.6	0.0	37.6	0.0	37.6	0.0	37.6	0.0	37.6	0.0	37.6	0.0	37.7	0.3	37.7	0.0
1950	37.5	-0.5	38.0	1.3	37.5	-1.3	37.5	0.0	37.3	-0.5	37.3	0.0	37.3	0.0	37.3	0.0	38.4	2.9	38.5	0.3	39.2	1.8	39.3	0.3
1951	45.9	16.8	46.9	2.2	47.4	1.1	47.4	0.0	47.4	0.0	47.4	0.0	47.4	0.0	47.4	0.0	47.6	0.4	47.6	0.0	47.7	0.2	47.7	0.0
1952	47.7	0.0	47.2	-1.0	47.0	-0.4	47.0	0.0	47.0	0.0	46.9	-0.2	46.9	0.0	46.9	0.0	46.9	0.0	46.9	0.0	46.9	0.0	47.0	0.2
1953	47.0	0.0	47.0	0.0	47.0	0.0	47.0	0.0	47.0	0.0	47.0	0.0	47.0	0.0	47.2	0.4	47.4	0.4	47.4	0.0	47.4	0.0	47.4	0.0
1954	47.0	-0.8	46.8	-0.4	46.8	0.0	46.8	0.0	46.8	0.0	46.8	0.0	46.8	0.0	46.8	0.0	46.8	0.0	46.8	0.0	46.5	-0.6	46.5	0.0
1955	46.3	-0.4	46.3	0.0	46.3	0.0	46.3	0.0	46.3	0.0	46.3	0.0	42.9	-7.3	42.9	0.0	42.9	0.0	42.9	0.0	42.9	0.0	42.9	0.0
1956	40.7	-5.1	40.7	0.0	40.7	0.0	40.6	-0.2	40.6	0.0	40.6	0.0	40.6	0.0	40.6	0.0	40.3	-0.7	40.3	0.0	40.3	0.0	40.4	0.2
1957	40.4	0.0	40.6	0.5	40.6	0.0	40.6	0.0	40.6	0.0	40.5	-0.2	40.5	0.0	40.7	0.5	40.7	0.0	40.7	0.0	40.5	-0.5	40.7	0.5
1958	40.7	0.0	40.7	0.0	40.5	-0.5	40.5	0.0	40.5	0.0	40.5	0.0	40.2	-0.7	39.4	-2.0	39.4	0.0	39.4	0.0	39.4	0.0	38.9	-1.3
1959	38.9	0.0	38.9	0.0	38.2	-1.8	38.2	0.0	38.2	0.0	38.2	0.0	38.2	0.0	38.2	0.0	38.2	0.0	38.2	0.0	38.2	0.0	38.2	0.0
1960	38.2	0.0	38.2	0.0	38.2	0.0	38.2	0.0	38.2	0.0	38.2	0.0	38.2	0.0	38.2	0.0	38.2	0.0	38.2	0.0	38.2	0.0	38.1	-0.3
1961	36.5	-4.2	36.5	0.0	36.5	0.0	36.5	0.0	36.5	0.0	36.5	0.0	36.4	-0.3	36.4	0.0	36.4	0.0	36.3	-0.3	36.3	0.0	36.3	0.0
1962	36.3	0.0	36.3	0.0	36.3	0.0	36.3	0.0	36.3	0.0	36.3	0.0	36.3	0.0	36.3	0.0	36.3	0.0	36.3	0.0	36.3	0.0	36.3	0.0
1963	36.3	0.0	36.3	0.0	36.3	0.0	35.3	-2.8	35.3	0.0	35.3	0.0	35.3	0.0	35.3	0.0	35.3	0.0	35.3	0.0	35.3	0.0	35.3	0.0
1964	35.3	0.0	35.3	0.0	35.3	0.0	35.3	0.0	35.3	0.0	35.3	0.0	35.3	0.0	35.3	0.0	35.3	0.0	35.3	0.0	35.0	-0.8	35.0	0.0
1965	35.0	0.0	35.0	0.0	35.0	0.0	35.0	0.0	35.0	0.0	35.0	0.0	35.0	0.0	35.0	0.0	35.0	0.0	35.0	0.0	35.0	0.0	35.0	0.0
1966	35.0	0.0	35.0	0.0	35.0	0.0	35.0	0.0	35.0	0.0	35.0	0.0	35.0	0.0	35.3	0.9	35.6	0.8	35.7	0.3	35.7	0.0	35.7	0.0
1967	35.7	0.0	35.8	0.3	35.8	0.0	35.8	0.0	36.0	0.6	35.7	-0.8	35.6	-0.3	35.5	-0.3	34.7	-2.3	34.0	-2.0	34.3	0.9	34.4	0.3
1968	34.0	-1.2	33.0	-2.9	32.8	-0.6	32.9	0.3	32.5	-1.2	32.2	-0.9	32.0	-0.6	31.9	-0.3	32.0	0.3	32.1	0.3	32.0	-0.3	31.9	-0.3
1969	31.9	0.0	32.1	0.6	32.1	0.0	32.0	-0.3	32.0	0.0	32.0	0.0	31.8	-0.6	32.0	0.6	32.1	0.3	31.7	-1.2	31.5	-0.6	31.7	0.6
1970	31.7	0.0	31.9	0.6	31.9	0.0	32.1	0.6	31.8	-0.9	31.7	-0.3	32.1	1.3	32.0	-0.3	32.1	0.3	32.3	0.6	32.0	-0.9	31.8	-0.6
1971	31.6	-0.6	31.4	-0.6	30.8	-1.9	31.1	1.0	31.1	0.0	31.0	-0.3	31.2	0.6	31.4	0.6	31.5	0.3	31.7	0.6	31.4	-0.9	31.4	0.0
1972	31.3	-0.3	31.5	0.6	31.4	-0.3	31.2	-0.6	31.3	0.3	31.0	-1.0	31.0	0.0	31.1	0.3	31.4	1.0	31.5	0.3	31.6	0.3	31.5	-0.3
1973	31.6	0.3	31.8	0.6	31.9	0.3	32.2	0.9	32.6	1.2	32.7	0.3	32.9	0.6	32.9	0.0	32.9	0.0	32.6	-0.9	32.8	0.6	32.8	0.0
1974	33.1	0.9	34.0	2.7	40.9	20.3	43.7	6.8	45.2	3.4	49.7	10.0	52.0	4.6	56.7	9.0	61.6	8.6	63.2	2.6	64.0	1.3	64.6	0.9
1975	64.6	0.0	64.3	-0.5	64.2	-0.2	64.3	0.2	62.2	-3.3	62.1	-0.2	62.5	0.6	62.6	0.2	63.2	1.0	64.9	2.7	65.2	0.5	65.8	0.9
1976	66.1	0.5	67.2	1.7	67.1	-0.1	68.4	1.9	68.5	0.1	68.9	0.6	69.7	1.2	69.6	-0.1	69.1	-0.7	69.0	-0.1	68.9	-0.1	68.8	-0.1
1977	68.3	-0.7	68.1	-0.3	68.7	0.9	69.1	0.6	69.4	0.4	69.7	0.4	70.6	1.3	70.6	0.0	70.6	0.0	70.5	-0.1	70.4	-0.1	70.1	-0.4
1978	70.1	0.0	70.0	-0.1	70.2	0.3	70.2	0.0	70.8	0.9	70.9	0.1	71.0	0.1	70.6	-0.6	70.6	0.0	70.4	-0.3	70.3	-0.1	71.0	1.0
1979	72.1	1.5	72.8	1.0	74.4	2.2	77.8	4.6	80.6	3.6	81.2	0.7	86.3	6.3	88.2	2.2	88.9	0.8	91.7	3.1	92.2	0.5	92.6	0.4
1980	95.4	3.0	96.0	0.6	96.8	0.8	101.5	4.9	101.8	0.3	101.5	-0.3	100.8	-0.7	99.3	-1.5	97.6	-1.7	97.4	-0.2	97.5	0.1	96.7	-0.8
1981	96.9	0.2	97.4	0.5	98.6	1.2	100.6	2.0	101.6	1.0	102.3	0.7	104.4	2.1	105.0	0.6	104.7	-0.3	105.7	1.0	103.4	-2.2	103.8	0.4
1982	100.9	-2.8	101.4	0.5	100.7	-0.7	100.9	0.2	99.9	-1.0	99.5	-0.4	99.1	-0.4	99.6	0.5	99.3	-0.3	99.3	0.0	99.6	0.3	99.7	0.1
1983	100.2	0.5	99.9	-0.3	99.5	-0.4	100.7	1.2	101.6	0.9	102.0	0.4	102.8	0.8	103.6	0.8	106.8	3.1	105.5	-1.2	105.1	-0.4	106.4	1.2
1984	107.7	1.2	107.6	-0.1	108.0	0.4	108.6	0.6	109.6	0.9	109.8	0.2	109.6	-0.2	109.5	-0.1	110.0	0.5	109.2	-0.7	109.0	-0.2	108.1	-0.8
1985	107.7	-0.4	108.3	0.6	108.1	-0.2	108.0	-0.1	107.8	-0.2	108.4	0.6	108.5	0.1	108.1	-0.4	107.7	-0.4	106.1	-1.5	106.0	-0.1	105.6	-0.4
1986	106.2	0.6	106.7	0.5	106.5	-0.2	104.7	-1.7	104.3	-0.4	104.2	-0.1	104.7	0.5	103.9	-0.8	102.4	-1.4	103.4	1.0	104.1	0.7	102.4	-1.6
1987	102.6	0.2	102.4	-0.2	103.2	0.8	106.3	3.0	107.0	0.7	109.7	2.5	112.8	2.8	113.1	0.3	114.2	1.0	116.8	2.3	117.4	0.5	117.7	0.3
1988	121.5	3.2	123.5	1.6	124.4	0.7	127.6	2.6	130.1	2.0	131.2	0.8	134.8	2.7	136.9	1.6	138.9	1.5	139.8	0.6	140.2	0.3	140.1	-0.1
1989	140.3	0.1	141.1	0.6	140.6	-0.4	140.7	0.1	139.8	-0.6	138.0	-1.3	135.3	-2.0	127.7	-5.6	126.1	-1.3	124.7	-1.1	123.7	-0.8	123.3	-0.3
1990	122.2	-0.9	121.6	-0.5	122.2	0.5	123.0	0.7	123.5	0.4	123.0	-0.4	122.3	-0.6	122.3	0.0	122.0	-0.2	125.9	3.2	129.1	2.5	132.1	2.3
1991	131.1	-0.8	128.7	-1.8	126.1	-2.0	122.9	-2.5	120.6	-1.9	117.0	-3.0	115.0	-1.7	114.9	-0.1	114.9	0.0	116.4	1.3	116.4	0.0	116.0	-0.3

[Continued]

Plastic Resins and Materials
Producer Price Index
Base 1982 = 100
[Continued]

For 1947-1995. Columns headed % show percentile change in the index from the previous period for which an index is available.

Year	Jan		Feb		Mar		Apr		May		Jun		Jul		Aug		Sep		Oct		Nov		Dec	
	Index	%	Index	%	Index	%	Index	%	Index	%	Index	%	Index	%	Index	%	Index	%	Index	%	Index	%	Index	%
1992	115.5	-0.4	115.6	0.1	114.2	-1.2	114.2	0.0	114.7	0.4	115.2	0.4	116.9	1.5	117.7	0.7	118.0	0.3	118.2	0.2	118.1	-0.1	118.1	0.0
1993	118.3	0.2	118.0	-0.3	117.6	-0.3	117.1	-0.4	116.3	-0.7	116.9	0.5	116.9	0.0	117.6	0.6	117.4	-0.2	116.9	-0.4	116.2	-0.6	116.2	0.0
1994	115.0	-1.0	114.7	-0.3	114.5	-0.2	116.5	1.7	117.7	1.0	119.1	1.2	119.6	0.4	121.5	1.6	126.3	4.0	131.9	4.4	134.1	1.7	138.1	3.0
1995	142.5	3.2	145.8	2.3	146.1	0.2	148.5	1.6	149.0	0.3	148.9	-0.1	147.0	-1.3	144.8	-1.5	143.3	-1.0	140.5	-2.0	137.1	-2.4	133.9	-2.3

Source: U.S. Department of Labor, Bureau of Labor Statistics, Division of Industry Prices and Price Indexes. n.e.c. stands for not elsewhere classified. - indicates no data collected for period or unavailable.

Chemicals and Allied Products n.e.c.
Producer Price Index
Base 1982 = 100

For 1947-1995. Columns headed % show percentile change in the index from the previous period for which an index is available.

Year	Jan Index	%	Feb Index	%	Mar Index	%	Apr Index	%	May Index	%	Jun Index	%	Jul Index	%	Aug Index	%	Sep Index	%	Oct Index	%	Nov Index	%	Dec Index	%
1947	31.7	-	31.8	0.3	32.2	1.3	32.7	1.6	31.1	-4.9	30.8	-1.0	30.0	-2.6	30.0	0.0	30.1	0.3	32.1	6.6	33.4	4.0	34.2	2.4
1948	34.4	0.6	33.9	-1.5	33.2	-2.1	33.1	-0.3	32.2	-2.7	31.7	-1.6	32.1	1.3	32.2	0.3	32.1	-0.3	31.9	-0.6	31.8	-0.3	31.3	-1.6
1949	30.8	-1.6	30.0	-2.6	29.7	-1.0	29.0	-2.4	28.5	-1.7	28.5	0.0	28.0	-1.8	27.7	-1.1	27.8	0.4	27.8	0.0	27.8	0.0	27.7	-0.4
1950	27.3	-1.4	27.3	0.0	27.3	0.0	27.3	0.0	27.3	0.0	27.2	-0.4	27.2	0.0	28.5	4.8	29.7	4.2	30.2	1.7	30.7	1.7	32.0	4.2
1951	32.8	2.5	33.4	1.8	32.6	-2.4	32.4	-0.6	32.4	0.0	32.3	-0.3	31.7	-1.9	31.1	-1.9	30.7	-1.3	30.7	0.0	30.7	0.0	30.5	-0.7
1952	30.1	-1.3	30.1	0.0	30.1	0.0	29.7	-1.3	29.7	0.0	29.7	0.0	29.7	0.0	29.7	0.0	29.7	0.0	29.6	-0.3	29.5	-0.3	29.6	0.3
1953	29.6	0.0	29.5	-0.3	29.5	0.0	29.6	0.3	29.6	0.0	29.5	-0.3	29.5	0.0	29.4	-0.3	29.5	0.3	29.6	0.3	30.1	1.7	30.2	0.3
1954	30.4	0.7	31.0	2.0	31.4	1.3	31.4	0.0	31.4	0.0	31.3	-0.3	31.4	0.3	31.2	-0.6	31.3	0.3	31.4	0.3	31.4	0.0	31.5	0.3
1955	31.5	0.0	31.7	0.6	31.5	-0.6	31.4	-0.3	31.4	0.0	31.4	0.0	31.4	0.0	31.4	0.0	31.4	0.0	31.7	1.0	31.7	0.0	31.7	0.0
1956	31.8	0.3	31.8	0.0	31.7	-0.3	31.8	0.3	31.9	0.3	32.7	2.5	32.7	0.0	32.6	-0.3	32.6	0.0	32.8	0.6	33.0	0.6	33.0	0.0
1957	33.1	0.3	33.3	0.6	33.3	0.0	33.3	0.0	33.3	0.0	33.2	-0.3	33.5	0.9	33.5	0.0	34.1	1.8	34.1	0.0	34.1	0.0	34.2	0.3
1958	34.1	-0.3	34.1	0.0	34.1	0.0	34.4	0.9	34.4	0.0	34.4	0.0	34.4	0.0	34.4	0.0	34.5	0.3	34.4	-0.3	34.4	0.0	34.4	0.0
1959	34.6	0.6	34.5	-0.3	34.5	0.0	34.5	0.0	34.6	0.3	34.6	0.0	34.7	0.3	34.7	0.0	34.7	0.0	34.7	0.0	34.7	0.0	34.8	0.3
1960	34.6	-0.6	34.6	0.0	34.6	0.0	34.6	0.0	34.6	0.0	34.6	0.0	34.6	0.0	34.7	0.3	34.8	0.3	35.1	0.9	35.0	-0.3	35.0	0.0
1961	34.9	-0.3	35.0	0.3	35.0	0.0	35.0	0.0	35.1	0.3	35.1	0.0	35.1	0.0	34.9	-0.6	34.9	0.0	34.9	0.0	34.9	0.0	34.9	0.0
1962	34.9	0.0	34.8	-0.3	34.9	0.3	34.9	0.0	34.8	-0.3	34.9	0.3	34.9	0.0	34.8	-0.3	34.9	0.3	35.0	0.3	35.0	0.0	35.0	0.0
1963	35.1	0.3	35.1	0.0	35.2	0.3	35.3	0.3	35.3	0.0	35.3	0.0	35.3	0.0	35.4	0.3	35.4	0.0	35.5	0.3	35.5	0.0	35.5	0.0
1964	35.5	0.0	35.5	0.0	35.5	0.0	35.6	0.3	35.7	0.3	35.7	0.0	35.7	0.0	35.7	0.0	35.7	0.0	35.7	0.0	35.7	0.0	35.7	0.0
1965	35.8	0.3	35.9	0.3	35.9	0.0	35.9	0.0	35.9	0.0	35.9	0.0	35.9	0.0	36.0	0.3	36.1	0.3	36.2	0.3	36.3	0.3	36.2	-0.3
1966	36.4	0.6	36.4	0.0	36.4	0.0	36.4	0.0	36.4	0.0	36.3	-0.3	36.4	0.3	36.5	0.3	36.5	0.0	36.5	0.0	36.5	0.0	36.6	0.3
1967	36.8	0.5	36.8	0.0	36.8	0.0	37.1	0.8	37.1	0.0	37.1	0.0	37.1	0.0	37.2	0.3	37.1	-0.3	37.2	0.3	37.1	-0.3	37.1	0.0
1968	37.1	0.0	37.2	0.3	37.4	0.5	37.5	0.3	37.6	0.3	37.8	0.5	37.8	0.0	37.8	0.0	37.9	0.3	37.7	-0.5	37.7	0.0	37.7	0.0
1969	37.7	0.0	38.0	0.8	38.1	0.3	38.4	0.8	38.5	0.3	38.6	0.3	38.6	0.0	38.6	0.0	38.9	0.8	39.1	0.5	39.3	0.5	39.4	0.3
1970	39.5	0.3	39.5	0.0	39.8	0.8	39.9	0.3	40.2	0.8	40.3	0.2	40.5	0.5	40.5	0.0	40.5	0.0	40.5	0.0	40.5	0.0	40.4	-0.2
1971	41.1	1.7	41.2	0.2	41.3	0.2	41.3	0.0	41.5	0.5	41.6	0.2	41.6	0.0	41.6	0.0	41.6	0.0	41.6	0.0	41.6	0.0	41.6	0.0
1972	41.6	0.0	41.7	0.2	41.7	0.0	42.0	0.7	42.2	0.5	42.1	-0.2	41.9	-0.5	42.0	0.2	42.1	0.2	42.2	0.2	42.2	0.0	42.2	0.0
1973	42.2	0.0	42.3	0.2	42.6	0.7	43.1	1.2	43.6	1.2	43.7	0.2	43.7	0.0	43.8	0.2	43.8	0.0	44.9	2.5	45.2	0.7	46.1	2.0
1974	47.0	2.0	47.1	0.2	47.5	0.8	48.7	2.5	52.3	7.4	53.6	2.5	55.0	2.6	59.4	8.0	60.2	1.3	61.3	1.8	61.5	0.3	61.6	0.2
1975	62.8	1.9	63.1	0.5	63.1	0.0	62.2	-1.4	62.0	-0.3	62.0	0.0	61.9	-0.2	62.0	0.2	62.1	0.2	62.1	0.0	62.7	1.0	63.0	0.5
1976	63.5	0.8	63.4	-0.2	63.7	0.5	63.7	0.0	63.8	0.2	63.8	0.0	62.5	-2.0	62.6	0.2	62.7	0.2	62.9	0.3	62.9	0.0	62.7	-0.3
1977	63.8	1.8	64.2	0.6	64.6	0.6	64.9	0.5	65.1	0.3	65.2	0.2	65.1	-0.2	65.3	0.3	65.4	0.2	65.4	0.0	65.7	0.5	65.9	0.3
1978	66.1	0.3	66.8	1.1	67.1	0.4	67.2	0.1	67.3	0.1	67.5	0.3	67.6	0.1	67.1	-0.7	67.1	0.0	68.1	1.5	68.2	0.1	67.5	-1.0
1979	68.2	1.0	68.4	0.3	69.0	0.9	69.2	0.3	69.9	1.0	70.5	0.9	71.0	0.7	72.0	1.4	72.5	0.7	72.9	0.6	73.6	1.0	74.6	1.4
1980	77.5	3.9	78.2	0.9	79.6	1.8	82.6	3.8	83.2	0.7	84.0	1.0	84.6	0.7	84.8	0.2	84.8	0.0	85.5	0.8	86.0	0.6	86.7	0.8
1981	90.5	4.4	90.7	0.2	91.9	1.3	94.5	2.8	94.3	-0.2	94.9	0.6	94.3	-0.6	95.3	1.1	95.3	0.0	95.1	-0.2	96.2	1.2	96.2	0.0
1982	97.7	1.6	98.1	0.4	99.4	1.3	100.0	0.6	101.0	1.0	101.4	0.4	100.4	-1.0	100.8	0.4	100.4	-0.4	99.5	-0.9	100.8	1.3	100.7	-0.1
1983	101.0	0.3	101.6	0.6	100.7	-0.9	101.7	1.0	100.7	-1.0	100.9	0.2	101.5	0.6	101.5	0.0	101.6	0.1	101.6	0.0	101.4	-0.2	101.3	-0.1
1984	101.8	0.5	101.2	-0.6	101.9	0.7	102.6	0.7	102.6	0.0	102.1	-0.5	102.7	0.6	103.0	0.3	103.5	0.5	103.5	0.0	104.1	0.6	103.7	-0.4
1985	104.4	0.7	104.7	0.3	104.8	0.1	105.4	0.6	104.9	-0.5	105.4	0.5	105.5	0.1	105.1	-0.4	106.0	0.9	105.6	-0.4	105.5	-0.1	105.4	-0.1
1986	106.7	1.2	106.4	-0.3	105.5	-0.8	105.9	0.4	105.6	-0.3	106.0	0.4	105.8	-0.2	105.0	-0.8	105.5	0.5	105.8	0.3	105.8	0.0	105.3	-0.5
1987	105.9	0.6	106.0	0.1	106.2	0.2	106.1	-0.1	106.7	0.6	106.8	0.1	106.7	-0.1	107.4	0.7	107.7	0.3	107.9	0.2	108.2	0.3	108.1	-0.1
1988	108.6	0.5	109.3	0.6	109.4	0.1	110.1	0.6	110.6	0.5	111.0	0.4	112.5	1.4	113.4	0.8	114.2	0.7	114.1	-0.1	114.8	0.6	115.1	0.3
1989	115.7	0.5	116.1	0.3	116.8	0.6	117.1	0.3	117.3	0.2	117.6	0.3	117.7	0.1	118.0	0.3	118.0	0.0	118.1	0.1	117.6	-0.4	117.3	-0.3
1990	118.0	0.6	118.1	0.1	118.3	0.2	118.0	-0.3	118.1	0.1	118.1	0.0	118.5	0.3	118.8	0.3	119.6	0.7	119.7	0.1	120.4	0.6	120.6	0.2
1991	121.7	0.9	121.9	0.2	121.3	-0.5	121.4	0.1	121.1	-0.2	121.0	-0.1	120.9	-0.1	121.2	0.2	122.0	0.7	121.8	-0.2	122.1	0.2	122.1	0.0

[Continued]

Chemicals and Allied Products n.e.c.
Producer Price Index
Base 1982 = 100
[Continued]

For 1947-1995. Columns headed % show percentile change in the index from the previous period for which an index is available.

Year	Jan		Feb		Mar		Apr		May		Jun		Jul		Aug		Sep		Oct		Nov		Dec	
	Index	%	Index	%	Index	%	Index	%	Index	%	Index	%	Index	%	Index	%	Index	%	Index	%	Index	%	Index	%
1992	122.3	0.2	122.4	0.1	122.3	-0.1	122.7	0.3	123.0	0.2	123.1	0.1	123.3	0.2	123.4	0.1	123.8	0.3	124.0	0.2	124.4	0.3	124.3	-0.1
1993	124.9	0.5	125.3	0.3	125.1	-0.2	125.5	0.3	125.6	0.1	125.7	0.1	125.6	-0.1	125.6	0.0	125.5	-0.1	125.6	0.1	125.6	0.0	125.8	0.2
1994	126.0	0.2	126.1	0.1	125.9	-0.2	126.0	0.1	126.6	0.5	126.5	-0.1	126.6	0.1	127.9	1.0	127.6	-0.2	128.4	0.6	128.3	-0.1	129.1	0.6
1995	129.8	0.5	129.5	-0.2	130.6	0.8	130.5	-0.1	130.7	0.2	130.7	0.0	130.8	0.1	130.3	-0.4	131.2	0.7	130.8	-0.3	131.7	0.7	131.4	-0.2

Source: U.S. Department of Labor, Bureau of Labor Statistics, Division of Industry Prices and Price Indexes. n.e.c. stands for not elsewhere classified. - indicates no data collected for period or unavailable.

RUBBER AND PLASTIC PRODUCTS
Producer Price Index
Base 1982 = 100

For 1926-1995. Columns headed % show percentile change in the index from the previous period for which an index is available.

Year	Jan Index	%	Feb Index	%	Mar Index	%	Apr Index	%	May Index	%	Jun Index	%	Jul Index	%	Aug Index	%	Sep Index	%	Oct Index	%	Nov Index	%	Dec Index	%
1926	59.1	-	53.7	-9.1	52.8	-1.7	51.0	-3.4	50.5	-1.0	49.4	-2.2	44.0	-10.9	42.7	-3.0	42.6	-0.2	43.0	0.9	39.1	-9.1	37.0	-5.4
1927	36.6	-1.1	36.3	-0.8	36.9	1.7	36.8	-0.3	36.9	0.3	36.0	-2.4	35.6	-1.1	35.5	-0.3	35.2	-0.8	34.3	-2.6	33.8	-1.5	34.5	2.1
1928	34.3	-0.6	32.5	-5.2	31.5	-3.1	30.1	-4.4	29.7	-1.3	27.2	-8.4	26.3	-3.3	26.3	0.0	26.1	-0.8	25.6	-1.9	25.0	-2.3	24.9	-0.4
1929	25.2	1.2	25.6	1.6	25.7	0.4	25.1	-2.3	24.9	-0.8	24.7	-0.8	24.8	0.4	24.6	-0.8	24.5	-0.4	24.2	-1.2	23.2	-4.1	23.1	-0.4
1930	22.9	-0.9	23.0	0.4	22.9	-0.4	22.8	-0.4	22.7	-0.4	21.3	-6.2	21.0	-1.4	20.6	-1.9	20.2	-1.9	20.2	0.0	20.5	1.5	20.4	-0.5
1931	19.2	-5.9	19.0	-1.0	19.0	0.0	18.7	-1.6	18.7	0.0	18.4	-1.6	18.4	0.0	18.1	-1.6	18.1	0.0	18.1	0.0	17.9	-1.1	16.1	-10.1
1932	15.7	-2.5	15.5	-1.3	15.2	-1.9	15.1	-0.7	15.1	0.0	15.2	0.7	15.4	1.3	15.6	1.3	16.5	5.8	17.1	3.6	17.1	0.0	17.1	0.0
1933	17.0	-0.6	16.2	-4.7	15.8	-2.5	14.5	-8.2	14.9	2.8	16.1	8.1	17.1	6.2	17.5	2.3	17.5	0.0	17.6	0.6	17.9	1.7	17.9	0.0
1934	18.0	0.6	18.4	2.2	18.9	2.7	19.1	1.1	19.5	2.1	19.5	0.0	19.7	1.0	20.0	1.5	19.9	-0.5	19.6	-1.5	20.3	3.6	20.3	0.0
1935	20.3	0.0	20.3	0.0	19.7	-3.0	19.6	-0.5	19.3	-1.5	19.4	0.5	19.3	-0.5	19.3	0.0	19.2	-0.5	19.5	1.6	19.6	0.5	19.6	0.0
1936	19.9	1.5	20.1	1.0	20.2	0.5	20.3	0.5	21.1	3.9	21.2	0.5	21.3	0.5	21.3	0.0	21.3	0.0	21.3	0.0	22.5	5.6	23.0	2.2
1937	23.9	3.9	24.4	2.1	25.8	5.7	26.1	1.2	25.6	-1.9	25.2	-1.6	25.0	-0.8	24.9	-0.4	24.9	0.0	24.3	-2.4	24.0	-1.2	24.0	0.0
1938	24.3	1.3	24.3	0.0	24.1	-0.8	23.7	-1.7	23.6	-0.4	23.9	1.3	24.4	2.1	24.6	0.8	24.6	0.0	24.9	1.2	25.2	1.2	25.2	0.0
1939	25.1	-0.4	25.3	0.8	25.5	0.8	25.4	-0.4	25.5	0.4	25.5	0.0	25.5	0.0	25.5	0.0	27.0	5.9	26.4	-2.2	23.5	-11.0	24.4	3.8
1940	24.2	-0.8	24.0	-0.8	24.0	0.0	23.0	-4.2	23.5	2.2	23.8	1.3	23.7	-0.4	23.3	-1.7	23.1	-0.9	23.4	1.3	23.6	0.9	24.3	3.0
1941	24.2	-0.4	24.3	0.4	24.6	1.2	24.7	0.4	24.7	0.0	24.2	-2.0	24.5	1.2	25.8	5.3	25.7	-0.4	27.3	6.2	27.9	2.2	27.9	0.0
1942	27.8	-0.4	27.8	0.0	27.8	0.0	28.4	2.2	30.5	7.4	30.5	0.0	30.5	0.0	30.5	0.0	30.5	0.0	30.5	0.0	30.5	0.0	30.5	0.0
1943	30.5	0.0	30.5	0.0	30.5	0.0	30.5	0.0	30.5	0.0	30.5	0.0	30.5	0.0	30.5	0.0	30.5	0.0	30.5	0.0	30.5	0.0	30.5	0.0
1944	30.5	0.0	30.6	0.3	30.6	0.0	30.6	0.0	29.8	-2.6	29.8	0.0	29.8	0.0	29.8	0.0	29.8	0.0	29.8	0.0	29.8	0.0	29.8	0.0
1945	29.9	0.3	29.9	0.0	29.9	0.0	29.4	-1.7	28.9	-1.7	28.9	0.0	28.9	0.0	28.9	0.0	28.9	0.0	28.9	0.0	28.9	0.0	28.9	0.0
1946	28.9	0.0	28.9	0.0	28.9	0.0	28.9	0.0	28.9	0.0	29.2	1.0	29.5	1.0	29.6	0.3	29.7	0.3	29.7	0.0	29.7	0.0	29.9	0.7
1947	30.4	1.7	30.5	0.3	30.5	0.0	30.4	-0.3	29.9	-1.6	28.4	-5.0	27.8	-2.1	27.8	0.0	28.0	0.7	28.5	1.8	29.0	1.8	29.4	1.4
1948	29.6	0.7	29.5	-0.3	29.5	0.0	29.7	0.7	29.8	0.3	29.8	0.0	30.7	3.0	30.7	0.0	30.7	0.0	30.7	0.0	30.5	-0.7	30.3	-0.7
1949	30.2	-0.3	30.0	-0.7	30.0	0.0	29.7	-1.0	29.6	-0.3	28.8	-2.7	28.4	-1.4	28.3	-0.4	28.4	0.4	28.3	-0.4	28.8	1.8	29.5	2.4
1950	29.7	0.7	29.9	0.7	29.9	0.0	30.6	2.3	31.5	2.9	32.3	2.5	34.1	5.6	38.2	12.0	39.9	4.5	41.5	4.0	44.0	6.0	44.9	2.0
1951	45.2	0.7	45.0	-0.4	45.0	0.0	44.7	-0.7	44.6	-0.2	43.8	-1.8	42.6	-2.7	42.6	0.0	42.7	0.2	42.7	0.0	42.7	0.0	42.6	-0.2
1952	42.5	-0.2	42.3	-0.5	41.9	-0.9	41.5	-1.0	41.4	-0.2	39.4	-4.8	38.4	-2.5	37.7	-1.8	37.3	-1.1	37.2	-0.3	37.3	0.3	37.7	1.1
1953	37.6	-0.3	37.2	-1.1	37.1	-0.3	36.8	-0.8	37.0	0.5	36.9	-0.3	36.8	-0.3	36.4	-1.1	36.6	0.5	36.6	0.0	36.7	0.3	36.8	0.3
1954	36.8	0.0	36.8	0.0	36.9	0.3	36.9	0.0	36.9	0.0	37.2	0.8	37.4	0.5	37.3	-0.3	37.5	0.5	37.9	1.1	38.8	2.4	38.9	0.3
1955	40.4	3.9	41.5	2.7	40.7	-1.9	40.8	0.2	40.7	-0.2	41.4	1.7	42.3	2.2	43.9	3.8	44.7	1.8	43.6	-2.5	44.4	1.8	44.5	0.2
1956	43.8	-1.6	43.4	-0.9	43.1	-0.7	42.8	-0.7	42.3	-1.2	42.2	-0.2	42.3	0.2	43.3	2.4	43.0	-0.7	43.0	0.0	43.3	0.7	43.7	0.9
1957	42.8	-2.1	42.5	-0.7	42.6	0.2	42.6	0.0	42.7	0.2	42.8	0.2	42.8	0.0	43.3	1.2	43.2	-0.2	43.1	-0.2	42.7	-0.9	43.0	0.7
1958	42.8	-0.5	42.7	-0.2	42.7	0.0	42.6	-0.2	42.4	-0.5	42.6	0.5	42.7	0.2	42.7	0.0	42.9	0.5	43.2	0.7	43.3	0.2	43.0	-0.7
1959	42.8	-0.5	42.9	0.2	43.1	0.5	43.3	0.5	43.7	0.9	43.1	-1.4	43.1	0.0	41.5	-3.7	41.8	0.7	41.8	0.0	42.6	1.9	41.9	-1.6
1960	42.3	1.0	42.7	0.9	42.7	0.0	42.7	0.0	43.2	1.2	43.3	0.2	43.3	0.0	42.9	-0.9	42.8	-0.2	42.7	-0.2	42.4	-0.7	41.6	-1.9
1961	41.2	-1.0	41.2	0.0	41.3	0.2	41.3	0.0	41.4	0.2	41.2	-0.5	41.0	-0.5	41.1	0.2	41.2	0.2	41.1	-0.2	40.9	-0.5	40.4	-1.2
1962	40.2	-0.5	40.0	-0.5	40.0	0.0	39.7	-0.7	39.9	0.5	39.8	-0.3	39.7	-0.3	39.7	0.0	39.7	0.0	39.8	0.3	40.1	0.8	40.4	0.7
1963	40.3	-0.2	40.3	0.0	40.2	-0.2	40.2	0.0	39.9	-0.7	39.8	-0.3	39.8	0.0	40.1	0.8	39.9	-0.5	40.3	1.0	40.3	0.0	40.1	-0.5
1964	40.1	0.0	40.0	-0.2	40.1	0.3	39.8	-0.7	39.6	-0.5	39.2	-1.0	39.2	0.0	39.2	0.0	39.3	0.3	39.4	0.3	39.4	0.0	39.4	0.0
1965	39.5	0.3	39.4	-0.3	39.4	0.0	39.5	0.3	39.7	0.5	39.8	0.3	39.8	0.0	39.9	0.3	39.9	0.0	39.9	0.0	40.0	0.3	40.0	0.0
1966	40.1	0.3	40.2	0.2	40.3	0.2	40.8	1.2	40.8	0.0	40.8	0.0	40.6	-0.5	40.6	0.0	40.5	-0.2	40.4	-0.2	40.6	0.5	40.6	0.0
1967	40.9	0.7	41.0	0.2	41.0	0.0	41.0	0.0	40.9	-0.2	40.9	0.0	40.9	0.0	41.8	2.2	42.0	0.5	42.2	0.5	42.4	0.5	42.4	0.0
1968	42.4	0.0	42.5	0.2	42.5	0.0	42.5	0.0	42.6	0.2	42.7	0.2	42.9	0.5	43.1	0.5	43.1	0.0	43.2	0.2	43.2	0.0	43.3	0.2
1969	42.8	-1.2	43.0	0.5	43.1	0.2	43.3	0.5	43.2	-0.2	43.2	0.0	43.8	1.4	44.0	0.5	43.8	-0.5	44.2	0.9	44.5	0.7	44.5	0.0
1970	44.7	0.4	44.6	-0.2	44.6	0.0	44.5	-0.2	44.4	-0.2	44.4	0.0	45.0	1.4	45.2	0.4	45.2	0.0	45.2	0.0	45.2	0.0	45.2	0.0

[Continued]

RUBBER AND PLASTIC PRODUCTS
Producer Price Index
Base 1982 = 100
[Continued]

For 1926-1995. Columns headed % show percentile change in the index from the previous period for which an index is available.

Year	Jan Index	%	Feb Index	%	Mar Index	%	Apr Index	%	May Index	%	Jun Index	%	Jul Index	%	Aug Index	%	Sep Index	%	Oct Index	%	Nov Index	%	Dec Index	%
1971	44.9	-0.7	45.1	0.4	45.1	0.0	45.1	0.0	45.0	-0.2	45.0	0.0	45.3	0.7	45.5	0.4	45.4	-0.2	45.3	-0.2	45.3	0.0	45.3	0.0
1972	45.4	0.2	45.3	-0.2	45.1	-0.4	45.1	0.0	45.1	0.0	45.1	0.0	45.3	0.4	45.4	0.2	45.4	0.0	45.4	0.0	45.5	0.2	45.5	0.0
1973	45.6	0.2	45.6	0.0	45.7	0.2	45.8	0.2	46.2	0.9	46.6	0.9	46.8	0.4	46.9	0.2	46.7	-0.4	47.2	1.1	47.6	0.8	48.3	1.5
1974	48.8	1.0	49.6	1.6	51.3	3.4	53.6	4.5	55.4	3.4	56.2	1.4	57.8	2.8	59.4	2.8	60.3	1.5	61.1	1.3	61.5	0.7	61.9	0.7
1975	62.0	0.2	62.2	0.3	62.0	-0.3	61.9	-0.2	61.7	-0.3	61.6	-0.2	62.2	1.0	62.2	0.0	62.5	0.5	62.8	0.5	62.9	0.2	62.9	0.0
1976	63.1	0.3	63.9	1.3	64.4	0.8	64.9	0.8	65.1	0.3	65.1	0.0	65.6	0.8	66.7	1.7	67.9	1.8	68.2	0.4	68.3	0.1	68.2	-0.1
1977	68.2	0.0	68.0	-0.3	68.2	0.3	68.7	0.7	68.9	0.3	69.4	0.7	70.0	0.9	70.1	0.1	70.2	0.1	70.5	0.4	70.5	0.0	70.5	0.0
1978	70.5	0.0	70.5	0.0	71.0	0.7	71.6	0.8	72.0	0.6	72.3	0.4	72.5	0.3	72.8	0.4	73.2	0.5	73.8	0.8	74.3	0.7	74.4	0.1
1979	74.9	0.7	75.9	1.3	77.0	1.4	78.2	1.6	79.0	1.0	80.0	1.3	81.0	1.3	82.4	1.7	83.1	0.8	84.1	1.2	84.9	1.0	85.3	0.5
1980	86.1	0.9	87.3	1.4	88.1	0.9	88.7	0.7	89.1	0.5	90.0	1.0	90.7	0.8	91.3	0.7	92.0	0.8	92.3	0.3	92.6	0.3	92.5	-0.1
1981	93.2	0.8	93.8	0.6	94.6	0.9	95.6	1.1	96.1	0.5	96.7	0.6	96.2	-0.5	97.0	0.8	97.7	0.7	98.3	0.6	98.6	0.3	98.7	0.1
1982	98.3	-0.4	99.2	0.9	99.8	0.6	99.9	0.1	100.3	0.4	100.5	0.2	100.3	-0.2	100.5	0.2	100.5	0.0	100.4	-0.1	100.1	-0.3	100.3	0.2
1983	100.6	0.3	100.4	-0.2	100.2	-0.2	100.7	0.5	100.8	0.1	100.7	-0.1	100.8	0.1	101.0	0.2	100.8	-0.2	101.2	0.4	100.9	-0.3	101.0	0.1
1984	101.4	0.4	102.0	0.6	102.1	0.1	102.4	0.3	102.5	0.1	102.6	0.1	102.6	0.0	102.6	0.0	102.9	0.3	102.2	-0.7	102.0	-0.2	101.9	-0.1
1985	102.2	0.3	102.1	-0.1	102.1	0.0	102.2	0.1	102.1	-0.1	102.0	-0.1	101.9	-0.1	101.4	-0.5	101.5	0.1	101.6	0.1	101.7	0.1	101.9	0.2
1986	102.3	0.4	102.5	0.2	102.2	-0.3	102.2	0.0	102.0	-0.2	102.0	0.0	101.7	-0.3	102.0	0.3	101.8	-0.2	101.5	-0.3	101.3	-0.2	101.2	-0.1
1987	101.5	0.3	101.6	0.1	101.4	-0.2	101.8	0.4	102.0	0.2	102.3	0.3	102.9	0.6	103.2	0.3	103.7	0.5	104.4	0.7	105.1	0.7	105.5	0.4
1988	106.2	0.7	106.9	0.7	107.7	0.7	108.2	0.5	108.8	0.6	109.1	0.3	109.8	0.6	110.6	0.7	111.0	0.4	111.1	0.1	111.2	0.1	111.3	0.1
1989	111.9	0.5	112.2	0.3	112.7	0.4	113.0	0.3	113.0	0.0	112.8	-0.2	112.8	0.0	112.6	-0.2	112.7	0.1	112.5	-0.2	112.5	0.0	112.9	0.4
1990	113.2	0.3	112.9	-0.3	113.3	0.4	113.3	0.0	113.5	0.2	113.2	-0.3	113.1	-0.1	113.2	0.1	113.4	0.2	114.2	0.7	115.0	0.7	115.4	0.3
1991	116.0	0.5	116.0	0.0	115.8	-0.2	115.5	-0.3	115.2	-0.3	115.0	-0.2	114.8	-0.2	114.7	-0.1	114.6	-0.1	114.7	0.1	114.6	-0.1	114.7	0.1
1992	114.7	0.0	114.3	-0.3	114.3	0.0	114.6	0.3	114.9	0.3	115.0	0.1	115.2	0.2	115.3	0.1	115.5	0.2	115.7	0.2	115.8	0.1	115.7	-0.1
1993	115.7	0.0	115.7	0.0	115.6	-0.1	116.0	0.3	115.8	-0.2	115.9	0.1	115.9	0.0	116.0	0.1	116.4	0.3	116.5	0.1	116.4	-0.1	116.5	0.1
1994	116.2	-0.3	116.2	0.0	116.2	0.0	116.2	0.0	116.5	0.3	116.7	0.2	117.1	0.3	117.4	0.3	118.5	0.9	119.6	0.9	120.3	0.6	120.9	0.5
1995	122.1	1.0	122.7	0.5	123.4	0.6	124.1	0.6	124.7	0.5	125.1	0.3	125.2	0.1	125.3	0.1	125.2	-0.1	124.9	-0.2	124.7	-0.2	124.5	-0.2

Source: U.S. Department of Labor, Bureau of Labor Statistics, Division of Industry Prices and Price Indexes. n.e.c. stands for not elsewhere classified. - indicates no data collected for period or unavailable.

Rubber and Rubber Products
Producer Price Index
Base 1982 = 100

For 1967-1995. Columns headed % show percentile change in the index from the previous period for which an index is available.

Year	Jan Index	%	Feb Index	%	Mar Index	%	Apr Index	%	May Index	%	Jun Index	%	Jul Index	%	Aug Index	%	Sep Index	%	Oct Index	%	Nov Index	%	Dec Index	%
1967	36.9	-	36.9	0.0	37.0	0.3	37.0	0.0	36.9	-0.3	36.9	0.0	36.9	0.0	37.6	1.9	37.8	0.5	38.1	0.8	38.2	0.3	38.2	0.0
1968	38.2	0.0	38.3	0.3	38.3	0.0	38.3	0.0	38.4	0.3	38.5	0.3	38.7	0.5	38.8	0.3	38.8	0.0	38.9	0.3	38.9	0.0	39.0	0.3
1969	38.5	-1.3	38.8	0.8	38.9	0.3	39.0	0.3	38.9	-0.3	38.9	0.0	39.5	1.5	39.6	0.3	39.5	-0.3	39.8	0.8	40.1	0.8	40.1	0.0
1970	40.3	0.5	40.4	0.2	40.3	-0.2	40.4	0.2	40.4	0.0	40.4	0.0	41.3	2.2	41.7	1.0	41.9	0.5	42.0	0.2	42.0	0.0	42.0	0.0
1971	41.5	-1.2	41.5	0.0	41.5	0.0	41.4	-0.2	41.4	0.0	41.5	0.2	42.3	1.9	42.5	0.5	42.4	-0.2	42.3	-0.2	42.3	0.0	42.3	0.0
1972	42.4	0.2	42.2	-0.5	42.2	0.0	42.2	0.0	42.2	0.0	42.3	0.2	42.5	0.5	42.7	0.5	42.7	0.0	42.7	0.0	42.8	0.2	42.8	0.0
1973	42.9	0.2	43.0	0.2	43.1	0.2	43.2	0.2	43.7	1.2	44.1	0.9	44.3	0.5	44.4	0.2	44.2	-0.5	44.9	1.6	45.3	0.9	46.1	1.8
1974	46.6	1.1	47.4	1.7	49.1	3.6	49.7	1.2	50.7	2.0	51.1	0.8	52.4	2.5	53.5	2.1	53.8	0.6	54.4	1.1	54.6	0.4	55.2	1.1
1975	55.5	0.5	55.9	0.7	56.0	0.2	56.1	0.2	56.1	0.0	56.1	0.0	57.2	2.0	57.2	0.0	57.3	0.2	57.5	0.3	57.7	0.3	57.8	0.2
1976	58.0	0.3	58.4	0.7	59.2	1.4	59.3	0.2	59.4	0.2	59.5	0.2	59.9	0.7	62.1	3.7	63.4	2.1	64.0	0.9	64.0	0.0	64.0	0.0
1977	63.9	-0.2	63.0	-1.4	63.2	0.3	64.2	1.6	64.2	0.0	64.6	0.6	65.3	1.1	65.5	0.3	65.8	0.5	66.2	0.6	66.2	0.0	66.3	0.2
1978	66.5	0.3	66.5	0.0	66.9	0.6	68.0	1.6	68.9	1.3	69.3	0.6	69.5	0.3	69.8	0.4	70.2	0.6	71.1	1.3	71.9	1.1	72.0	0.1
1979	72.7	1.0	73.8	1.5	74.5	0.9	75.1	0.8	75.7	0.8	76.5	1.1	78.3	2.4	80.1	2.3	81.1	1.2	82.3	1.5	83.5	1.5	83.8	0.4
1980	84.5	0.8	86.4	2.2	86.5	0.1	87.1	0.7	87.6	0.6	88.4	0.9	89.3	1.0	89.7	0.4	90.6	1.0	91.3	0.8	91.5	0.2	91.5	0.0
1981	91.9	0.4	92.8	1.0	94.1	1.4	94.5	0.4	95.0	0.5	95.9	0.9	95.1	-0.8	95.9	0.8	97.2	1.4	98.2	1.0	98.7	0.5	98.8	0.1
1982	98.0	-0.8	99.3	1.3	99.6	0.3	99.6	0.0	100.5	0.9	100.6	0.1	100.4	-0.2	100.9	0.5	100.6	-0.3	100.4	-0.2	100.0	-0.4	100.2	0.2
1983	100.7	0.5	100.2	-0.5	99.8	-0.4	99.7	-0.1	99.7	0.0	99.2	-0.5	99.0	-0.2	99.0	0.0	98.5	-0.5	98.9	0.4	98.7	-0.2	98.8	0.1
1984	99.5	0.7	99.6	0.1	99.1	-0.5	99.8	0.7	99.4	-0.4	99.5	0.1	99.5	0.0	99.9	0.4	100.1	0.2	98.9	-1.2	98.5	-0.4	98.5	0.0
1985	98.7	0.2	99.1	0.4	99.0	-0.1	98.9	-0.1	99.0	0.1	98.7	-0.3	98.9	0.2	98.5	-0.4	98.6	0.1	98.5	-0.1	98.7	0.2	98.4	-0.3
1986	98.7	0.3	99.0	0.3	98.9	-0.1	98.8	-0.1	98.6	-0.2	98.5	-0.1	97.9	-0.6	97.8	-0.1	97.6	-0.2	97.6	0.0	97.0	-0.6	97.0	0.0
1987	97.5	0.5	97.5	0.0	97.4	-0.1	98.1	0.7	98.5	0.4	99.0	0.5	100.1	1.1	100.2	0.1	100.4	0.2	100.9	0.5	101.1	0.2	101.8	0.7
1988	102.3	0.5	102.5	0.2	102.6	0.1	102.9	0.3	102.6	-0.3	103.1	0.5	103.7	0.6	104.4	0.7	104.6	0.2	104.5	-0.1	104.5	0.0	104.9	0.4
1989	105.8	0.9	106.4	0.6	106.8	0.4	107.1	0.3	107.4	0.3	107.4	0.0	107.3	-0.1	107.1	-0.2	106.9	-0.2	107.2	0.3	107.4	0.2	107.7	0.3
1990	107.9	0.2	107.6	-0.3	108.5	0.8	108.1	-0.4	108.2	0.1	108.1	-0.1	108.1	0.0	108.5	0.4	108.6	0.1	109.2	0.6	110.1	0.8	110.4	0.3
1991	110.6	0.2	110.6	0.0	110.4	-0.2	109.9	-0.5	109.8	-0.1	109.7	-0.1	109.1	-0.5	108.8	-0.3	108.6	-0.2	109.1	0.5	109.1	0.0	109.0	-0.1
1992	109.2	0.2	109.1	-0.1	109.0	-0.1	108.9	-0.1	109.0	0.1	109.8	0.7	109.8	0.0	110.0	0.2	110.3	0.3	110.3	0.0	111.0	0.6	111.0	0.0
1993	110.4	-0.5	110.3	-0.1	110.4	0.1	110.9	0.5	110.9	0.0	111.0	0.1	111.0	0.0	110.9	-0.1	111.1	0.2	111.1	0.0	111.0	-0.1	111.0	0.0
1994	110.9	-0.1	110.8	-0.1	110.9	0.1	111.2	0.3	111.4	0.2	111.8	0.4	112.0	0.2	112.0	0.0	112.2	0.2	113.0	0.7	113.4	0.4	113.5	0.1
1995	114.5	0.9	115.1	0.5	116.1	0.9	116.5	0.3	116.9	0.3	117.7	0.7	118.2	0.4	118.3	0.1	118.4	0.1	118.3	-0.1	118.2	-0.1	117.5	-0.6

Source: U.S. Department of Labor, Bureau of Labor Statistics, Division of Industry Prices and Price Indexes. n.e.c. stands for not elsewhere classified. - indicates no data collected for period or unavailable.

Plastic Products
Producer Price Index
Base 1982 = 100

For 1971-1995. Columns headed % show percentile change in the index from the previous period for which an index is available.

Year	Jan Index	%	Feb Index	%	Mar Index	%	Apr Index	%	May Index	%	Jun Index	%	Jul Index	%	Aug Index	%	Sep Index	%	Oct Index	%	Nov Index	%	Dec Index	%
1971	48.4	-	49.3	1.9	49.2	-0.2	49.2	0.0	48.9	-0.6	48.8	-0.2	48.2	-1.2	48.2	0.0	48.2	0.0	48.1	-0.2	48.1	0.0	48.0	-0.2
1972	48.1	0.2	48.1	0.0	47.7	-0.8	47.6	-0.2	47.6	0.0	47.4	-0.4	47.5	0.2	47.5	0.0	48.4	0.0	48.5	0.2	48.7	0.4	49.1	0.8
1973	47.6	0.0	47.6	0.0	47.6	0.0	47.7	0.2	47.8	0.2	48.5	1.5	48.4	-0.2	48.4	0.0	48.4	0.0	48.5	0.2	48.7	0.4	49.1	0.8
1974	49.7	1.2	50.5	1.6	52.0	3.0	57.4	10.4	60.7	5.7	62.1	2.3	64.2	3.4	66.7	3.9	68.8	3.1	70.0	1.7	70.8	1.1	70.6	-0.3
1975	70.3	-0.4	70.0	-0.4	69.4	-0.9	68.9	-0.7	68.4	-0.7	67.9	-0.7	67.6	-0.4	67.4	-0.3	68.2	1.2	68.6	0.6	68.7	0.1	68.6	-0.1
1976	68.7	0.1	69.9	1.7	70.1	0.3	71.1	1.4	71.4	0.4	71.2	-0.3	71.8	0.8	71.9	0.1	72.8	1.3	72.8	0.0	72.9	0.1	72.9	0.0
1977	72.9	0.0	73.6	1.0	73.7	0.1	73.6	-0.1	74.0	0.5	74.6	0.8	75.1	0.7	75.2	0.1	75.1	-0.1	75.3	0.3	75.2	-0.1	75.1	-0.1
1978	74.9	-0.3	75.0	0.1	75.5	0.7	75.6	0.1	75.4	-0.3	75.6	0.3	75.7	0.1	76.1	0.5	76.6	0.7	76.7	0.1	77.0	0.4	77.1	0.1
1979	77.3	0.3	78.2	1.2	79.9	2.2	81.6	2.1	82.7	1.3	83.9	1.5	84.0	0.1	84.8	1.0	85.4	0.7	86.1	0.8	86.4	0.3	87.0	0.7
1980	87.9	1.0	88.2	0.3	89.9	1.9	90.4	0.6	90.7	0.3	91.8	1.2	92.2	0.4	93.1	1.0	93.5	0.4	93.4	-0.1	93.7	0.3	93.6	-0.1
1981	94.5	1.0	94.9	0.4	95.2	0.3	96.9	1.8	97.2	0.3	97.6	0.4	97.3	-0.3	98.1	0.8	98.2	0.1	98.5	0.3	98.5	0.0	98.7	0.2
1982	98.6	-0.1	99.0	0.4	100.0	1.0	100.3	0.3	100.1	-0.2	100.4	0.3	100.1	-0.3	100.2	0.1	100.3	0.1	100.3	0.0	100.3	0.0	100.5	0.2
1983	100.6	0.1	100.6	0.0	100.7	0.1	101.7	1.0	101.9	0.2	102.4	0.5	102.8	0.4	103.1	0.3	103.2	0.1	103.8	0.6	103.3	-0.5	103.4	0.1
1984	103.5	0.1	104.6	1.1	105.4	0.8	105.4	0.0	106.0	0.6	105.9	-0.1	106.0	0.1	105.6	-0.4	105.9	0.3	105.9	0.0	105.8	-0.1	105.7	-0.1
1985	106.1	0.4	105.4	-0.7	105.6	0.2	105.9	0.3	105.6	-0.3	105.7	0.1	105.2	-0.5	104.7	-0.5	104.8	0.1	105.0	0.2	105.1	0.1	105.8	0.7
1986	106.3	0.5	106.5	0.2	106.0	-0.5	106.0	0.0	105.9	-0.1	105.9	0.0	105.9	0.0	106.7	0.8	106.5	-0.2	105.9	-0.6	106.0	0.1	105.8	-0.2
1987	106.1	0.3	106.1	0.0	106.0	-0.1	106.1	0.1	106.2	0.1	106.4	0.2	106.7	0.3	107.3	0.6	107.9	0.6	108.7	0.7	109.6	0.8	109.9	0.3
1988	110.8	0.8	111.7	0.8	112.9	1.1	113.5	0.5	114.6	1.0	114.9	0.3	115.6	0.6	116.5	0.8	117.0	0.4	117.3	0.3	117.4	0.1	117.4	0.0
1989	117.8	0.3	118.0	0.2	118.5	0.4	118.8	0.3	118.7	-0.1	118.4	-0.3	118.4	0.0	118.2	-0.2	118.5	0.3	117.9	-0.5	117.9	0.0	118.3	0.3
1990	118.7	0.3	118.4	-0.3	118.5	0.1	118.7	0.2	119.0	0.3	118.6	-0.3	118.4	-0.2	118.4	0.0	118.7	0.3	119.5	0.7	120.3	0.7	120.8	0.4
1991	121.6	0.7	121.6	0.0	121.5	-0.1	121.2	-0.2	120.8	-0.3	120.6	-0.2	120.6	0.0	120.6	0.0	120.6	0.0	120.3	-0.2	120.3	0.0	120.5	0.2
1992	120.4	-0.1	119.8	-0.5	119.9	0.1	120.4	0.4	120.7	0.2	120.5	-0.2	120.8	0.2	120.9	0.1	121.1	0.2	121.3	0.2	121.3	0.0	121.0	-0.2
1993	121.3	0.2	121.3	0.0	121.2	-0.1	121.5	0.2	121.3	-0.2	121.3	0.0	121.3	0.0	121.5	0.2	122.0	0.4	122.1	0.1	122.1	0.0	122.2	0.1
1994	121.8	-0.3	121.9	0.1	121.8	-0.1	121.8	0.0	122.0	0.2	122.2	0.2	122.6	0.3	123.1	0.4	124.6	1.2	125.9	1.0	126.8	0.7	127.5	0.6
1995	129.0	1.2	129.5	0.4	130.2	0.5	131.0	0.6	131.6	0.5	131.9	0.2	131.9	0.0	132.0	0.1	131.7	-0.2	131.4	-0.2	131.1	-0.2	131.0	-0.1

Source: U.S. Department of Labor, Bureau of Labor Statistics, Division of Industry Prices and Price Indexes. n.e.c. stands for not elsewhere classified. - indicates no data collected for period or unavailable.

LUMBER AND WOOD PRODUCTS
Producer Price Index
Base 1982 = 100

For 1926-1995. Columns headed % show percentile change in the index from the previous period for which an index is available.

Year	Jan Index	%	Feb Index	%	Mar Index	%	Apr Index	%	May Index	%	Jun Index	%	Jul Index	%	Aug Index	%	Sep Index	%	Oct Index	%	Nov Index	%	Dec Index	%
1926	9.6	-	9.5	-1.0	9.5	0.0	9.4	-1.1	9.3	-1.1	9.2	-1.1	9.2	0.0	9.2	0.0	9.2	0.0	9.1	-1.1	9.3	2.2	9.2	-1.1
1927	9.0	-2.2	9.0	0.0	8.9	-1.1	8.9	0.0	8.9	0.0	8.9	0.0	8.8	-1.1	8.7	-1.1	8.6	-1.1	8.6	0.0	8.5	-1.2	8.4	-1.2
1928	8.4	0.0	8.4	0.0	8.4	0.0	8.3	-1.2	8.3	0.0	8.3	0.0	8.4	1.2	8.5	1.2	8.6	1.2	8.6	0.0	8.7	1.2	8.8	1.1
1929	8.7	-1.1	8.9	2.3	9.0	1.1	8.9	-1.1	8.8	-1.1	8.8	0.0	8.7	-1.1	8.8	1.1	8.9	1.1	8.9	0.0	8.6	-3.4	8.6	0.0
1930	8.6	0.0	8.6	0.0	8.6	0.0	8.6	0.0	8.4	-2.3	8.1	-3.6	7.8	-3.7	7.7	-1.3	7.7	0.0	7.5	-2.6	7.5	0.0	7.3	-2.7
1931	7.2	-1.4	6.9	-4.2	7.0	1.4	6.8	-2.9	6.6	-2.9	6.5	-1.5	6.4	-1.5	6.3	-1.6	6.3	0.0	6.1	-3.2	6.2	1.6	6.2	0.0
1932	6.2	0.0	6.0	-3.2	5.9	-1.7	5.8	-1.7	5.7	-1.7	5.5	-3.5	5.5	0.0	5.3	-3.6	5.4	1.9	5.4	0.0	5.4	0.0	5.4	0.0
1933	5.3	-1.9	5.4	1.9	5.5	1.9	5.5	0.0	5.7	3.6	6.4	12.3	7.1	10.9	7.4	4.2	7.7	4.1	7.9	2.6	8.1	2.5	8.1	0.0
1934	8.1	0.0	8.1	0.0	8.0	-1.2	8.1	1.3	8.0	-1.2	8.0	0.0	7.8	-2.5	7.6	-2.6	7.6	0.0	7.6	0.0	7.5	-1.3	7.5	0.0
1935	7.4	-1.3	7.5	1.4	7.4	-1.3	7.4	0.0	7.4	0.0	7.5	1.4	7.6	1.3	7.7	1.3	7.7	0.0	7.7	0.0	7.7	0.0	7.6	-1.3
1936	7.7	1.3	7.7	0.0	7.7	0.0	7.8	1.3	7.8	0.0	7.7	-1.3	7.8	1.3	7.8	0.0	8.0	2.6	8.0	0.0	8.1	1.3	8.4	3.7
1937	8.7	3.6	9.2	5.7	9.5	3.3	9.6	1.1	9.7	1.0	9.7	0.0	9.5	-2.1	9.4	-1.1	9.3	-1.1	9.2	-1.1	8.9	-3.3	8.9	0.0
1938	8.7	-2.2	8.6	-1.1	8.6	0.0	8.6	0.0	8.3	-3.5	8.3	0.0	8.3	0.0	8.4	1.2	8.5	1.2	8.4	-1.2	8.4	0.0	8.5	1.2
1939	8.6	1.2	8.6	0.0	8.6	0.0	8.5	-1.2	8.5	0.0	8.5	0.0	8.6	1.2	8.6	0.0	8.7	1.2	9.1	4.6	9.2	1.1	9.1	-1.1
1940	9.1	0.0	9.1	0.0	9.1	0.0	9.0	-1.1	9.0	0.0	9.0	0.0	9.0	0.0	9.3	3.3	10.1	8.6	10.7	5.9	11.0	2.8	11.1	0.9
1941	11.1	0.0	11.0	-0.9	11.0	0.0	11.0	0.0	11.0	0.0	11.0	0.0	11.4	3.6	11.9	4.4	12.0	0.8	12.2	1.7	12.1	-0.8	12.2	0.8
1942	12.4	1.6	12.5	0.8	12.5	0.0	12.4	-0.8	12.4	0.0	12.4	0.0	12.5	0.8	12.5	0.0	12.5	0.0	12.5	0.0	12.6	0.8	12.7	0.8
1943	12.7	0.0	12.8	0.8	12.8	0.0	12.8	0.0	12.9	0.8	13.0	0.8	13.1	0.8	13.5	3.1	13.7	1.5	13.7	0.0	13.8	0.7	13.8	0.0
1944	13.8	0.0	13.9	0.7	14.1	1.4	14.3	1.4	14.4	0.7	14.4	0.0	14.4	0.0	14.4	0.0	14.4	0.0	14.4	0.0	14.4	0.0	14.4	0.0
1945	14.4	0.0	14.4	0.0	14.4	0.0	14.4	0.0	14.4	0.0	14.4	0.0	14.5	0.7	14.5	0.0	14.5	0.0	14.5	0.0	14.5	0.0	14.6	0.7
1946	14.7	0.7	14.9	1.4	15.5	4.0	15.9	2.6	16.1	1.3	16.4	1.9	16.5	0.6	16.5	0.0	16.6	0.6	16.8	1.2	17.9	6.5	20.9	16.8
1947	23.4	12.0	23.9	2.1	24.7	3.3	25.4	2.8	25.5	0.4	25.4	-0.4	25.5	0.4	26.0	2.0	26.6	2.3	27.0	1.5	27.7	2.6	28.2	1.8
1948	28.7	1.8	28.9	0.7	29.2	1.0	29.3	0.3	29.6	1.0	29.8	0.7	30.0	0.7	30.2	0.7	30.1	-0.3	29.7	-1.3	29.5	-0.7	29.0	-1.7
1949	28.7	-1.0	28.3	-1.4	28.1	-0.7	27.8	-1.1	27.4	-1.4	27.0	-1.5	26.6	-1.5	26.3	-1.1	26.4	0.4	26.7	1.1	27.0	1.1	27.3	1.1
1950	27.7	1.5	28.3	2.2	28.9	2.1	29.3	1.4	30.3	3.4	30.9	2.0	31.7	2.6	33.1	4.4	34.3	3.6	34.0	-0.9	33.8	-0.6	33.9	0.3
1951	34.6	2.1	34.8	0.6	34.9	0.3	34.9	0.0	34.8	-0.3	34.3	-1.4	34.1	-0.6	33.7	-1.2	33.5	-0.6	33.5	0.0	33.4	-0.3	33.2	-0.6
1952	33.1	-0.3	33.2	0.3	33.2	0.0	33.3	0.3	33.3	0.0	33.1	-0.6	33.2	0.3	33.2	0.0	33.2	0.0	33.1	-0.3	33.0	-0.3	33.0	0.0
1953	33.2	0.6	33.4	0.6	33.5	0.3	33.7	0.6	33.6	-0.3	33.5	-0.3	33.4	-0.3	33.2	-0.6	32.8	-1.2	32.6	-0.6	32.3	-0.9	32.3	0.0
1954	32.2	-0.3	32.2	0.0	32.2	0.0	32.0	-0.6	32.0	0.0	32.1	0.3	32.8	2.2	32.8	0.0	32.9	0.3	33.0	0.3	33.0	0.0	33.1	0.3
1955	33.2	0.3	33.4	0.6	33.5	0.3	33.8	0.9	34.1	0.9	34.1	0.0	34.2	0.3	34.5	0.9	34.7	0.6	34.6	-0.3	34.5	-0.3	34.5	0.0
1956	34.8	0.9	34.9	0.3	35.3	1.1	35.4	0.3	35.3	-0.3	35.1	-0.6	34.9	-0.6	34.5	-1.1	34.1	-1.2	33.6	-1.5	33.5	-0.3	33.4	-0.3
1957	33.5	0.3	33.3	-0.6	33.1	-0.6	33.2	0.3	33.0	-0.6	33.0	0.0	32.9	-0.3	32.7	-0.6	32.5	-0.6	32.3	-0.6	32.2	-0.3	32.1	-0.3
1958	32.1	0.0	31.9	-0.6	31.8	-0.3	31.9	0.3	32.0	0.3	32.1	0.3	32.2	0.3	32.7	1.6	33.2	1.5	33.3	0.3	33.1	-0.6	33.0	-0.3
1959	33.2	0.6	33.8	1.8	34.2	1.2	34.8	1.8	35.3	1.4	35.5	0.6	35.4	-0.3	35.4	0.0	35.1	-0.8	34.8	-0.9	34.3	-1.4	34.4	0.3
1960	34.5	0.3	34.4	-0.3	34.3	-0.3	34.2	-0.3	34.1	-0.3	33.8	-0.9	33.5	-0.9	32.9	-1.8	32.8	-0.3	32.5	-0.9	32.2	-0.9	32.2	0.0
1961	31.9	-0.9	31.6	-0.9	31.8	0.6	32.5	2.2	32.4	-0.3	32.5	0.3	32.3	-0.6	32.0	-0.9	31.9	-0.3	31.6	-0.9	31.6	0.0	31.5	-0.3
1962	31.5	0.0	31.7	0.6	32.1	1.3	32.2	0.3	32.3	0.3	32.4	0.3	32.5	0.3	32.5	0.0	32.3	-0.6	32.2	-0.3	32.1	-0.3	31.9	-0.6
1963	32.0	0.3	32.0	0.0	32.2	0.6	32.3	0.3	32.5	0.6	32.8	0.9	33.9	3.4	34.2	0.9	33.3	-2.6	33.0	-0.9	33.0	0.0	33.0	0.0
1964	33.0	0.0	33.3	0.9	33.6	0.9	33.9	0.9	33.9	0.0	33.8	-0.3	33.7	-0.3	33.6	-0.3	33.5	-0.3	33.4	-0.3	33.2	-0.6	33.1	-0.3
1965	33.6	1.5	33.6	0.0	33.5	-0.3	33.5	0.0	33.5	0.0	33.4	-0.3	33.5	0.3	33.9	1.2	34.0	0.3	33.9	-0.3	33.9	0.0	34.0	0.3
1966	34.2	0.6	34.6	1.2	35.2	1.7	36.1	2.6	36.5	1.1	35.9	-1.6	35.5	-1.1	35.4	-0.3	35.3	-0.3	34.9	-1.1	34.3	-1.7	34.1	-0.6
1967	34.2	0.3	34.6	1.2	34.5	-0.3	34.7	0.6	34.7	0.0	34.9	0.6	35.1	0.6	35.4	0.9	36.2	2.3	35.7	-1.4	35.5	-0.6	35.9	1.1
1968	36.2	0.8	37.2	2.8	38.0	2.2	38.6	1.6	39.0	1.0	39.1	0.3	39.7	1.5	40.1	1.0	40.9	2.0	41.7	2.0	42.3	1.4	44.5	5.2
1969	45.9	3.1	48.2	5.0	49.8	3.3	47.8	-4.0	45.9	-4.0	43.3	-5.7	41.8	-3.5	41.3	-1.2	41.1	-0.5	40.9	-0.5	41.3	1.0	40.8	-1.2
1970	40.5	-0.7	40.0	-1.2	39.7	-0.7	40.0	0.8	40.3	0.7	40.0	-0.7	39.9	-0.2	40.1	0.5	40.1	0.0	39.7	-1.0	39.3	-1.0	39.0	-0.8

[Continued]

LUMBER AND WOOD PRODUCTS
Producer Price Index
Base 1982 = 100
[Continued]

For 1926-1995. Columns headed % show percentile change in the index from the previous period for which an index is available.

Year	Jan Index	%	Feb Index	%	Mar Index	%	Apr Index	%	May Index	%	Jun Index	%	Jul Index	%	Aug Index	%	Sep Index	%	Oct Index	%	Nov Index	%	Dec Index	%
1971	39.4	1.0	41.2	4.6	43.4	5.3	43.9	1.2	44.0	0.2	44.4	0.9	46.0	3.6	47.5	3.3	47.3	-0.4	46.4	-1.9	46.2	-0.4	46.7	1.1
1972	47.4	1.5	48.4	2.1	49.0	1.2	49.6	1.2	50.1	1.0	50.6	1.0	51.3	1.4	52.0	1.4	52.1	0.2	52.4	0.6	52.5	0.2	52.6	0.2
1973	53.0	0.8	56.5	6.6	60.8	7.6	63.9	5.1	65.6	2.7	64.3	-2.0	62.4	-3.0	62.8	0.6	63.9	1.8	63.3	-0.9	64.9	2.5	65.4	0.8
1974	64.5	-1.4	64.6	0.2	67.2	4.0	70.3	4.6	69.5	-1.1	67.5	-2.9	66.2	-1.9	64.5	-2.6	63.4	-1.7	59.5	-6.2	58.2	-2.2	58.1	-0.2
1975	57.9	-0.3	59.5	2.8	59.6	0.2	61.4	3.0	64.3	4.7	63.6	-1.1	63.1	-0.8	63.1	0.0	63.2	0.2	62.9	-0.5	62.6	-0.5	64.3	2.7
1976	67.0	4.2	68.9	2.8	71.1	3.2	71.4	0.4	71.1	-0.4	70.2	-1.3	71.5	1.9	72.9	2.0	74.7	2.5	75.0	0.4	75.3	0.4	77.3	2.7
1977	78.2	1.2	78.8	0.8	80.4	2.0	80.7	0.4	80.6	-0.1	80.3	-0.4	82.7	3.0	85.3	3.1	88.8	4.1	87.0	-2.0	85.5	-1.7	87.5	2.3
1978	90.0	2.9	92.6	2.9	93.5	1.0	94.7	1.3	96.0	1.4	97.8	1.9	97.4	-0.4	98.9	1.5	99.3	0.4	99.8	0.5	101.9	2.1	101.4	-0.5
1979	101.9	0.5	103.2	1.3	105.5	2.2	107.1	1.5	106.4	-0.7	105.3	-1.0	105.4	0.1	107.0	1.5	108.8	1.7	108.5	-0.3	105.0	-3.2	101.9	-3.0
1980	101.9	0.0	103.5	1.6	103.6	0.1	96.8	-6.6	95.5	-1.3	98.3	2.9	101.6	3.4	104.0	2.4	102.6	-1.3	101.5	-1.1	103.0	1.5	105.2	2.1
1981	104.1	-1.0	103.5	-0.6	103.4	-0.1	105.1	1.6	104.8	-0.3	104.7	-0.1	104.1	-0.6	103.4	-0.7	101.6	-1.7	99.8	-1.8	99.1	-0.7	100.2	1.1
1982	100.3	0.1	100.2	-0.1	100.2	0.0	100.6	0.4	99.9	-0.7	101.5	1.6	101.4	-0.1	99.8	-1.6	99.4	-0.4	98.1	-1.3	98.3	0.2	100.3	2.0
1983	103.0	2.7	106.4	3.3	107.4	0.9	107.9	0.5	108.2	0.3	110.6	2.2	110.5	-0.1	110.3	-0.2	107.3	-2.7	107.3	0.0	107.1	-0.2	108.4	1.2
1984	108.6	0.2	110.9	2.1	111.3	0.4	110.7	-0.5	108.3	-2.2	107.9	-0.4	106.9	-0.9	107.0	0.1	106.5	-0.5	105.5	-0.9	105.7	0.2	106.4	0.7
1985	106.9	0.5	106.5	-0.4	106.4	-0.1	105.9	-0.5	107.7	1.7	110.0	2.1	108.9	-1.0	107.3	-1.5	105.5	-1.7	105.2	-0.3	104.3	-0.9	104.7	0.4
1986	105.0	0.3	104.3	-0.7	105.8	1.4	108.4	2.5	108.2	-0.2	107.5	-0.6	107.8	0.3	107.9	0.1	108.4	0.5	107.9	-0.5	108.0	0.1	107.8	-0.2
1987	108.1	0.3	109.4	1.2	110.6	1.1	110.7	0.1	110.7	0.0	111.4	0.6	112.4	0.9	113.7	1.2	116.2	2.2	116.1	-0.1	116.9	0.7	117.1	0.2
1988	117.8	0.6	118.4	0.5	118.9	0.4	119.2	0.3	119.1	-0.1	119.3	0.2	120.0	0.6	118.8	-1.0	118.9	0.1	118.7	-0.2	118.8	0.1	119.0	0.2
1989	120.1	0.9	122.0	1.6	123.2	1.0	125.2	1.6	126.5	1.0	127.4	0.7	128.9	1.2	129.0	0.1	129.0	0.0	130.9	1.5	130.0	-0.7	128.5	-1.2
1990	129.0	0.4	129.7	0.5	130.5	0.6	132.4	1.5	132.0	-0.3	130.7	-1.0	131.3	0.5	130.2	-0.8	129.3	-0.7	127.5	-1.4	126.9	-0.5	126.8	-0.1
1991	127.6	0.6	127.2	-0.3	127.8	0.5	129.2	1.1	132.3	2.4	136.2	2.9	136.9	0.5	133.3	-2.6	133.4	0.1	133.2	-0.1	133.4	0.2	134.6	0.9
1992	137.6	2.2	142.9	3.9	145.7	2.0	147.5	1.2	147.6	0.1	146.3	-0.9	145.3	-0.7	145.4	0.1	148.7	2.3	148.7	0.0	149.5	0.5	154.4	3.3
1993	160.2	3.8	169.3	5.7	176.9	4.5	181.2	2.4	179.8	-0.8	174.1	-3.2	171.7	-1.4	171.1	-0.3	173.2	1.2	174.0	0.5	177.3	1.9	179.6	1.3
1994	184.6	2.8	183.3	-0.7	184.2	0.5	180.3	-2.1	178.2	-1.2	179.4	0.7	177.4	-1.1	177.7	0.2	178.3	0.3	177.8	-0.3	179.4	0.9	179.2	-0.1
1995	179.6	0.2	179.5	-0.1	180.6	0.6	180.4	-0.1	179.7	-0.4	178.0	-0.9	178.2	0.1	177.8	-0.2	179.3	0.8	177.6	-0.9	174.5	-1.7	173.6	-0.5

Source: U.S. Department of Labor, Bureau of Labor Statistics, Division of Industry Prices and Price Indexes. n.e.c. stands for not elsewhere classified. - indicates no data collected for period or unavailable.

Lumber
Producer Price Index
Base 1982 = 100

For 1926-1995. Columns headed % show percentile change in the index from the previous period for which an index is available.

Year	Jan Index	%	Feb Index	%	Mar Index	%	Apr Index	%	May Index	%	Jun Index	%	Jul Index	%	Aug Index	%	Sep Index	%	Oct Index	%	Nov Index	%	Dec Index	%
1926	8.3	-	8.3	0.0	8.3	0.0	8.2	-1.2	8.1	-1.2	8.0	-1.2	8.0	0.0	7.9	-1.2	7.9	0.0	7.9	0.0	8.1	2.5	8.0	-1.2
1927	7.9	-1.2	7.8	-1.3	7.7	-1.3	7.7	0.0	7.7	0.0	7.7	0.0	7.6	-1.3	7.5	-1.3	7.4	-1.3	7.4	0.0	7.3	-1.4	7.2	-1.4
1928	7.2	0.0	7.2	0.0	7.2	0.0	7.1	-1.4	7.1	0.0	7.2	1.4	7.2	0.0	7.3	1.4	7.4	1.4	7.5	1.4	7.5	0.0	7.6	1.3
1929	7.5	-1.3	7.7	2.7	7.8	1.3	7.7	-1.3	7.6	-1.3	7.6	0.0	7.5	-1.3	7.5	0.0	7.7	2.7	7.8	1.3	7.4	-5.1	7.4	0.0
1930	7.5	1.4	7.4	-1.3	7.4	0.0	7.4	0.0	7.2	-2.7	6.9	-4.2	6.8	-1.4	6.6	-2.9	6.6	0.0	6.4	-3.0	6.5	1.6	6.3	-3.1
1931	6.2	-1.6	6.0	-3.2	6.0	0.0	6.0	0.0	5.6	-6.7	5.6	0.0	5.4	-3.6	5.4	0.0	5.4	0.0	5.3	-1.9	5.3	0.0	5.3	0.0
1932	5.3	0.0	5.1	-3.8	5.0	-2.0	4.8	-4.0	4.8	0.0	4.7	-2.1	4.6	-2.1	4.5	-2.2	4.5	0.0	4.6	2.2	4.6	0.0	4.6	0.0
1933	4.5	-2.2	4.5	0.0	4.7	4.4	4.7	0.0	4.8	2.1	5.5	14.6	6.1	10.9	6.4	4.9	6.6	3.1	6.8	3.0	7.0	2.9	7.1	1.4
1934	7.1	0.0	7.1	0.0	7.0	-1.4	7.1	1.4	7.0	-1.4	7.0	0.0	6.9	-1.4	6.6	-4.3	6.7	1.5	6.6	-1.5	6.6	0.0	6.6	0.0
1935	6.4	-3.0	6.4	0.0	6.3	-1.6	6.3	0.0	6.5	3.2	6.7	3.1	6.9	3.0	6.9	0.0	6.8	-1.4	6.7	-1.5	6.6	-1.5	6.7	1.5
1936	6.8	1.5	6.8	0.0	7.0	2.9	7.1	1.4	7.1	0.0	7.1	0.0	7.0	-1.4	7.0	0.0	7.0	0.0	7.1	1.4	7.1	0.0	7.4	4.2
1937	7.8	5.4	8.3	6.4	8.6	3.6	8.6	0.0	8.5	-1.2	8.3	-2.4	8.1	-2.4	8.0	-1.2	8.0	0.0	7.8	-2.5	7.5	-3.8	7.2	-4.0
1938	7.1	-1.4	7.1	0.0	7.1	0.0	7.0	-1.4	7.0	0.0	6.8	-2.9	6.8	0.0	7.0	2.9	7.1	1.4	7.1	0.0	7.2	1.4	7.4	2.8
1939	7.4	0.0	7.4	0.0	7.4	0.0	7.4	0.0	7.3	-1.4	7.2	-1.4	7.2	0.0	7.3	1.4	7.6	4.1	8.0	5.3	8.1	1.3	8.0	-1.2
1940	8.0	0.0	7.9	-1.2	7.9	0.0	7.8	-1.3	7.8	0.0	7.7	-1.3	7.7	0.0	7.9	2.6	8.7	10.1	9.3	6.9	9.5	2.2	9.6	1.1
1941	9.6	0.0	9.5	-1.0	9.4	-1.1	9.4	0.0	9.4	0.0	9.5	1.1	9.9	4.2	10.3	4.0	10.5	1.9	10.5	0.0	10.4	-1.0	10.5	1.0
1942	10.6	1.0	10.7	0.9	10.7	0.0	10.7	0.0	10.6	-0.9	10.6	0.0	10.7	0.9	10.7	0.0	10.7	0.0	10.5	-1.9	10.9	3.8	10.9	0.0
1943	10.9	0.0	11.0	0.9	11.0	0.0	11.0	0.0	11.2	1.8	11.2	0.0	11.3	0.9	11.7	3.5	11.8	0.9	11.9	0.8	12.0	0.8	12.0	0.0
1944	12.0	0.0	12.1	0.8	12.2	0.8	12.5	2.5	12.5	0.0	12.5	0.0	12.5	0.0	12.5	0.0	12.5	0.0	12.5	0.0	12.5	0.0	12.5	0.0
1945	12.5	0.0	12.5	0.0	12.5	0.0	12.5	0.0	12.5	0.0	12.5	0.0	12.5	0.0	12.5	0.0	12.5	0.0	12.5	0.0	12.5	0.0	12.8	2.4
1946	12.8	0.0	12.9	0.8	13.6	5.4	13.9	2.2	14.0	0.7	14.2	1.4	14.4	1.4	14.4	0.0	14.4	0.0	14.4	0.0	15.5	7.6	18.4	18.7
1947	20.6	12.0	21.1	2.4	22.0	4.3	22.7	3.2	22.7	0.0	22.6	-0.4	22.8	0.9	23.2	1.8	23.9	3.0	24.2	1.3	24.9	2.9	25.4	2.0
1948	25.6	0.8	25.8	0.8	26.0	0.8	26.0	0.0	26.4	1.5	26.4	0.0	26.5	0.4	26.7	0.8	26.5	-0.7	26.2	-1.1	25.8	-1.5	25.5	-1.2
1949	25.2	-1.2	24.9	-1.2	24.7	-0.8	24.4	-1.2	24.0	-1.6	23.6	-1.7	23.3	-1.3	22.9	-1.7	23.0	0.4	23.3	1.3	23.6	1.3	23.9	1.3
1950	24.3	1.7	24.9	2.5	25.5	2.4	25.9	1.6	27.0	4.2	27.6	2.2	28.4	2.9	29.6	4.2	30.7	3.7	30.2	-1.6	30.1	-0.3	30.2	0.3
1951	30.6	1.3	30.8	0.7	30.9	0.3	30.9	0.0	30.8	-0.3	30.3	-1.6	30.0	-1.0	29.7	-1.0	29.5	-0.7	29.5	0.0	29.5	0.0	29.4	-0.3
1952	29.3	-0.3	29.4	0.3	29.4	0.0	29.6	0.7	29.5	-0.3	29.3	-0.7	29.4	0.3	29.4	0.0	29.4	0.0	29.3	-0.3	29.3	0.0	29.2	-0.3
1953	29.3	0.3	29.3	0.0	29.5	0.7	29.7	0.7	29.5	-0.7	29.4	-0.3	29.3	-0.3	29.1	-0.7	28.9	-0.7	28.6	-1.0	28.4	-0.7	28.4	0.0
1954	28.3	-0.4	28.2	-0.4	28.2	0.0	28.1	-0.4	28.1	0.0	28.2	0.4	28.9	2.5	28.9	0.0	29.0	0.3	29.2	0.7	29.2	0.0	29.2	0.0
1955	29.3	0.3	29.6	1.0	29.7	0.3	30.0	1.0	30.3	1.0	30.4	0.3	30.5	0.3	30.9	1.3	31.0	0.3	31.0	0.0	30.9	-0.3	30.8	-0.3
1956	31.2	1.3	31.3	0.3	31.7	1.3	31.9	0.6	31.9	0.0	31.6	-0.9	31.4	-0.6	31.0	-1.3	30.6	-1.3	30.2	-1.3	30.1	-0.3	29.9	-0.7
1957	30.0	0.3	29.8	-0.7	29.6	-0.7	29.6	0.0	29.4	-0.7	29.4	0.0	29.3	-0.3	29.2	-0.3	28.9	-1.0	28.7	-0.7	28.6	-0.3	28.4	-0.7
1958	28.5	0.4	28.3	-0.7	28.3	0.0	28.3	0.0	28.5	0.7	28.5	0.0	28.5	0.0	29.1	2.1	29.5	1.4	29.5	0.0	29.3	-0.7	29.3	0.0
1959	29.5	0.7	30.1	2.0	30.6	1.7	30.9	1.0	31.5	1.9	31.8	1.0	31.7	-0.3	31.8	0.3	31.6	-0.6	31.2	-1.3	30.7	-1.6	30.8	0.3
1960	30.8	0.0	30.8	0.0	30.7	-0.3	30.7	0.0	30.5	-0.7	30.1	-1.3	29.7	-1.3	29.1	-2.0	28.8	-1.0	28.4	-1.4	28.1	-1.1	28.1	0.0
1961	27.9	-0.7	27.7	-0.7	27.9	0.7	28.4	1.8	28.5	0.4	28.5	0.0	28.5	0.0	28.2	-1.1	28.1	-0.4	27.9	-0.7	27.8	-0.4	27.8	0.0
1962	27.9	0.4	28.2	1.1	28.4	0.7	28.7	1.1	28.9	0.7	29.0	0.3	29.1	0.3	29.0	-0.3	28.9	-0.3	28.7	-0.7	28.6	-0.3	28.4	-0.7
1963	28.5	0.4	28.5	0.0	28.7	0.7	29.0	1.0	29.2	0.7	29.4	0.7	30.3	3.1	30.5	0.7	29.9	-2.0	29.5	-1.3	29.5	0.0	29.4	-0.3
1964	29.4	0.0	29.8	1.4	30.1	1.0	30.3	0.7	30.3	0.0	30.2	-0.3	30.1	-0.3	30.0	-0.3	29.9	-0.3	29.8	-0.3	29.4	-1.3	29.4	0.0
1965	29.9	1.7	30.1	0.7	30.1	0.0	30.0	-0.3	30.0	0.0	30.0	0.0	30.1	0.3	30.4	1.0	30.6	0.7	30.6	0.0	30.6	0.0	30.7	0.3
1966	31.0	1.0	31.3	1.0	31.8	1.6	32.9	3.5	33.6	2.1	33.2	-1.2	32.8	-1.2	32.7	-0.3	32.5	-0.6	32.0	-1.5	31.3	-2.2	31.0	-1.0
1967	31.0	0.0	31.3	1.0	31.5	0.6	31.6	0.3	31.8	0.6	32.0	0.6	32.1	0.3	32.6	1.6	33.3	2.1	33.0	-0.9	32.8	-0.6	33.2	1.2
1968	33.9	2.1	34.8	2.7	35.7	2.6	36.7	2.8	37.2	1.4	37.1	-0.3	37.9	2.2	38.5	1.6	39.0	1.3	39.6	1.5	40.4	2.0	42.2	4.5
1969	43.9	4.0	46.3	5.5	48.9	5.6	49.0	0.2	46.3	-5.5	42.3	-8.6	39.6	-6.4	38.9	-1.8	38.5	-1.0	38.0	-1.3	38.4	1.1	38.1	-0.8
1970	37.7	-1.0	36.9	-2.1	36.5	-1.1	36.7	0.5	36.9	0.5	36.5	-1.1	36.2	-0.8	36.5	0.8	36.8	0.8	36.6	-0.5	36.1	-1.4	35.7	-1.1

[Continued]

Lumber

Producer Price Index
Base 1982 = 100

[Continued]

For 1926-1995. Columns headed % show percentile change in the index from the previous period for which an index is available.

Year	Jan Index	%	Feb Index	%	Mar Index	%	Apr Index	%	May Index	%	Jun Index	%	Jul Index	%	Aug Index	%	Sep Index	%	Oct Index	%	Nov Index	%	Dec Index	%
1971	36.4	2.0	38.7	6.3	41.5	7.2	42.5	2.4	42.9	0.9	43.5	1.4	46.1	6.0	47.6	3.3	47.5	-0.2	46.1	-2.9	45.8	-0.7	46.4	1.3
1972	47.3	1.9	48.4	2.3	49.0	1.2	49.9	1.8	50.5	1.2	51.2	1.4	52.0	1.6	52.8	1.5	53.1	0.6	53.5	0.8	53.7	0.4	54.0	0.6
1973	54.4	0.7	58.7	7.9	63.0	7.3	66.7	5.9	69.3	3.9	69.1	-0.3	67.4	-2.5	67.8	0.6	69.8	2.9	69.0	-1.1	67.9	-1.6	69.1	1.8
1974	68.6	-0.7	68.4	-0.3	71.2	4.1	74.3	4.4	73.1	-1.6	70.9	-3.0	68.9	-2.8	66.5	-3.5	64.2	-3.5	59.1	-7.9	57.3	-3.0	57.0	-0.5
1975	56.8	-0.4	58.3	2.6	58.7	0.7	60.9	3.7	64.6	6.1	64.2	-0.6	63.3	-1.4	63.7	0.6	63.3	-0.6	63.1	-0.3	62.1	-1.6	64.4	3.7
1976	67.6	5.0	70.7	4.6	74.1	4.8	74.2	0.1	73.1	-1.5	72.2	-1.2	74.4	3.0	76.0	2.2	78.6	3.4	79.0	0.5	78.6	-0.5	81.1	3.2
1977	83.0	2.3	83.5	0.6	85.7	2.6	86.5	0.9	86.3	-0.2	85.2	-1.3	88.8	4.2	92.1	3.7	97.1	5.4	94.1	-3.1	91.6	-2.7	93.6	2.2
1978	96.7	3.3	99.3	2.7	100.5	1.2	101.9	1.4	101.8	-0.1	103.2	1.4	102.7	-0.5	105.1	2.3	106.9	1.7	107.6	0.7	110.0	2.2	109.1	-0.8
1979	108.3	-0.7	109.4	1.0	112.8	3.1	114.3	1.3	114.2	-0.1	114.2	0.0	114.2	0.0	117.5	2.9	120.3	2.4	119.2	-0.9	114.4	-4.0	109.2	-4.5
1980	108.2	-0.9	109.9	1.6	109.6	-0.3	99.8	-8.9	97.0	-2.8	100.7	3.8	105.3	4.6	107.4	2.0	105.6	-1.7	103.2	-2.3	104.6	1.4	107.1	2.4
1981	106.6	-0.5	105.2	-1.3	104.9	-0.3	107.4	2.4	108.2	0.7	108.0	-0.2	107.0	-0.9	106.2	-0.7	103.0	-3.0	100.3	-2.6	98.7	-1.6	99.7	1.0
1982	99.7	0.0	99.1	-0.6	99.2	0.1	100.5	1.3	99.9	-0.6	101.6	1.7	102.7	1.1	100.3	-2.3	99.8	-0.5	98.3	-1.5	98.2	-0.1	100.6	2.4
1983	105.2	4.6	110.9	5.4	112.4	1.4	114.0	1.4	115.4	1.2	120.0	4.0	120.1	0.1	118.0	-1.7	111.5	-5.5	110.9	-0.5	110.3	-0.5	113.0	2.4
1984	113.5	0.4	117.4	3.4	119.2	1.5	118.9	-0.3	114.4	-3.8	112.8	-1.4	110.2	-2.3	110.1	-0.1	108.8	-1.2	107.6	-1.1	108.3	0.7	109.2	0.8
1985	110.4	1.1	110.4	0.0	110.7	0.3	109.4	-1.2	112.4	2.7	116.8	3.9	114.1	-2.3	110.0	-3.6	107.0	-2.7	105.3	-1.6	103.8	-1.4	104.8	1.0
1986	106.0	1.1	105.7	-0.3	108.3	2.5	113.3	4.6	113.0	-0.3	110.4	-2.3	111.1	0.6	111.3	0.2	112.9	1.4	111.1	-1.6	112.0	0.8	111.3	-0.6
1987	111.9	0.5	114.4	2.2	116.0	1.4	116.8	0.7	116.9	0.1	117.9	0.9	119.7	1.5	120.2	0.4	123.3	2.6	120.5	-2.3	120.4	-0.1	120.3	-0.1
1988	120.8	0.4	121.5	0.6	123.0	1.2	123.9	0.7	123.8	-0.1	124.4	0.5	125.1	0.6	123.2	-1.5	120.9	-1.9	120.0	-0.7	119.9	-0.1	118.8	-0.9
1989	119.8	0.8	122.3	2.1	123.4	0.9	126.5	2.5	128.5	1.6	128.7	0.2	130.0	1.0	128.8	-0.9	127.0	-1.4	127.3	0.2	123.2	-3.2	123.1	-0.1
1990	124.5	1.1	125.8	1.0	127.4	1.3	129.3	1.5	128.0	-1.0	125.9	-1.6	126.5	0.5	124.8	-1.3	123.5	-1.0	120.5	-2.4	119.4	-0.9	119.3	-0.1
1991	120.0	0.6	118.8	-1.0	119.6	0.7	121.6	1.7	125.2	3.0	132.7	6.0	133.2	0.4	125.1	-6.1	125.0	-0.1	124.5	-0.4	125.4	0.7	128.2	2.2
1992	132.3	3.2	140.9	6.5	146.4	3.9	148.6	1.5	148.7	0.1	144.1	-3.1	142.8	-0.9	142.0	-0.6	144.8	2.0	143.8	-0.7	146.9	2.2	155.5	5.9
1993	164.6	5.9	181.1	10.0	196.4	8.4	197.3	0.5	189.0	-4.2	178.7	-5.4	172.9	-3.2	175.9	1.7	179.0	1.8	181.5	1.4	188.6	3.9	195.9	3.9
1994	202.0	3.1	196.6	-2.7	197.4	0.4	188.2	-4.7	185.7	-1.3	189.7	2.2	184.4	-2.8	185.5	0.6	184.7	-0.4	181.4	-1.8	183.4	1.1	181.7	-0.9
1995	182.1	0.2	177.8	-2.4	179.3	0.8	175.7	-2.0	173.4	-1.3	169.9	-2.0	173.0	1.8	172.2	-0.5	175.4	1.9	172.5	-1.7	167.7	-2.8	166.0	-1.0

Source: U.S. Department of Labor, Bureau of Labor Statistics, Division of Industry Prices and Price Indexes. n.e.c. stands for not elsewhere classified. - indicates no data collected for period or unavailable.

Millwork
Producer Price Index
Base 1982 = 100

For 1926-1995. Columns headed % show percentile change in the index from the previous period for which an index is available.

Year	Jan Index	%	Feb Index	%	Mar Index	%	Apr Index	%	May Index	%	Jun Index	%	Jul Index	%	Aug Index	%	Sep Index	%	Oct Index	%	Nov Index	%	Dec Index	%
1926	10.7	-	10.7	0.0	10.7	0.0	10.7	0.0	10.7	0.0	10.7	0.0	10.7	0.0	10.7	0.0	10.7	0.0	10.7	0.0	10.7	0.0	10.7	0.0
1927	10.7	0.0	10.7	0.0	10.7	0.0	10.7	0.0	10.7	0.0	10.7	0.0	10.7	0.0	10.7	0.0	10.7	0.0	10.7	0.0	10.7	0.0	10.7	0.0
1928	10.7	0.0	10.7	0.0	10.7	0.0	10.7	0.0	10.7	0.0	10.7	0.0	10.7	0.0	10.7	0.0	10.7	0.0	10.7	0.0	10.7	0.0	10.7	0.0
1929	10.8	0.9	10.8	0.0	10.8	0.0	10.8	0.0	10.8	0.0	10.8	0.0	10.7	-0.9	10.7	0.0	10.7	0.0	10.7	0.0	10.7	0.0	10.7	0.0
1930	10.7	0.0	10.7	0.0	10.7	0.0	10.7	0.0	10.6	-0.9	10.6	0.0	9.9	-6.6	9.9	0.0	9.9	0.0	9.4	-5.1	9.4	0.0	9.1	-3.2
1931	8.9	-2.2	8.7	-2.2	8.7	0.0	8.7	0.0	8.7	0.0	8.7	0.0	8.7	0.0	8.7	0.0	8.4	-3.4	8.1	-3.6	8.1	0.0	8.1	0.0
1932	8.7	7.4	8.7	0.0	8.7	0.0	8.7	0.0	8.7	0.0	8.7	0.0	8.3	-4.6	8.3	0.0	8.3	0.0	7.8	-6.0	7.8	0.0	7.8	0.0
1933	7.8	0.0	7.8	0.0	8.3	6.4	8.3	0.0	8.3	0.0	8.4	1.2	8.9	6.0	9.7	9.0	9.7	0.0	9.7	0.0	9.7	0.0	9.5	-2.1
1934	9.5	0.0	9.5	0.0	9.5	0.0	9.6	1.1	9.7	1.0	9.7	0.0	9.2	-5.2	8.7	-5.4	8.7	0.0	8.7	0.0	8.7	0.0	8.7	0.0
1935	8.7	0.0	8.7	0.0	8.7	0.0	8.7	0.0	8.7	0.0	8.7	0.0	8.9	2.3	9.6	7.9	9.6	0.0	9.6	0.0	9.6	0.0	9.6	0.0
1936	9.6	0.0	9.6	0.0	9.6	0.0	9.6	0.0	9.6	0.0	9.8	2.1	9.8	0.0	9.8	0.0	9.8	0.0	9.8	0.0	9.8	0.0	10.1	3.1
1937	10.2	1.0	10.7	4.9	10.7	0.0	10.7	0.0	12.7	18.7	12.7	0.0	12.3	-3.1	12.1	-1.6	12.1	0.0	12.1	0.0	12.0	-0.8	11.9	-0.8
1938	11.1	-6.7	11.1	0.0	11.1	0.0	11.1	0.0	10.2	-8.1	10.2	0.0	10.1	-1.0	10.1	0.0	10.1	0.0	10.2	1.0	10.2	0.0	10.2	0.0
1939	10.2	0.0	10.2	0.0	10.2	0.0	10.2	0.0	10.2	0.0	10.2	0.0	10.2	0.0	10.2	0.0	10.2	0.0	10.2	0.0	10.7	4.9	10.7	0.0
1940	10.7	0.0	10.7	0.0	10.7	0.0	10.7	0.0	10.7	0.0	11.3	5.6	11.5	1.8	11.5	0.0	11.5	0.0	11.5	0.0	12.1	5.2	12.1	0.0
1941	12.1	0.0	12.1	0.0	12.2	0.8	12.3	0.8	12.5	1.6	12.5	0.0	12.6	0.8	12.8	1.6	12.8	0.0	13.9	8.6	14.0	0.7	14.0	0.0
1942	14.0	0.0	14.0	0.0	14.0	0.0	14.0	0.0	14.0	0.0	14.0	0.0	14.0	0.0	14.0	0.0	14.0	0.0	14.0	0.0	14.0	0.0	14.0	0.0
1943	14.0	0.0	14.0	0.0	14.0	0.0	14.0	0.0	14.0	0.0	14.0	0.0	14.0	0.0	14.0	0.0	14.4	2.9	14.4	0.0	14.4	0.0	14.4	0.0
1944	14.4	0.0	14.4	0.0	14.4	0.0	14.4	0.0	14.7	2.1	14.7	0.0	14.7	0.0	14.7	0.0	14.7	0.0	14.7	0.0	14.7	0.0	14.7	0.0
1945	14.7	0.0	14.7	0.0	14.7	0.0	14.7	0.0	14.7	0.0	14.7	0.0	14.7	0.0	14.7	0.0	14.7	0.0	14.7	0.0	14.7	0.0	14.7	0.0
1946	14.7	0.0	14.7	0.0	14.7	0.0	14.7	0.0	17.0	15.6	17.0	0.0	17.0	0.0	17.0	0.0	17.5	2.9	18.3	4.6	18.4	0.5	18.4	0.0
1947	19.5	6.0	19.9	2.1	20.1	1.0	20.3	1.0	20.6	1.5	21.0	1.9	21.4	1.9	21.6	0.9	22.2	2.8	22.8	2.7	23.0	0.9	23.0	0.0
1948	23.7	3.0	23.9	0.8	24.7	3.3	24.8	0.4	24.8	0.0	25.5	2.8	26.4	3.5	26.7	1.1	26.8	0.4	26.8	0.0	26.8	0.0	26.8	0.0
1949	26.6	-0.7	26.6	0.0	26.5	-0.4	26.4	-0.4	26.4	0.0	26.3	-0.4	26.2	-0.4	26.1	-0.4	26.0	-0.4	26.0	0.0	26.0	0.0	26.1	0.4
1950	26.4	1.1	26.6	0.8	26.6	0.0	26.8	0.8	26.9	0.4	27.1	0.7	27.6	1.8	28.4	2.9	29.5	3.9	29.8	1.0	29.9	0.3	29.9	0.0
1951	31.5	5.4	32.0	1.6	31.9	-0.3	32.0	0.3	32.0	0.0	31.9	-0.3	31.8	-0.3	31.6	-0.6	31.6	0.0	31.6	0.0	31.5	-0.3	31.4	-0.3
1952	31.0	-1.3	30.8	-0.6	30.9	0.3	30.8	-0.3	30.8	0.0	30.8	0.0	30.9	0.3	31.0	0.3	31.0	0.0	31.1	0.3	31.1	0.0	31.3	0.6
1953	31.5	0.6	32.1	1.9	32.1	0.0	32.2	0.3	32.2	0.0	32.2	0.0	32.1	-0.3	32.1	0.0	32.1	0.0	32.0	-0.3	32.0	0.0	32.0	0.0
1954	32.0	0.0	32.0	0.0	32.0	0.0	31.9	-0.3	31.9	0.0	31.9	0.0	31.9	0.0	31.6	-0.9	31.7	0.3	31.7	0.0	31.7	0.0	31.8	0.3
1955	31.8	0.0	31.5	-0.9	31.4	-0.3	31.5	0.3	31.5	0.0	31.3	-0.6	31.3	0.0	31.3	0.0	31.2	-0.3	31.2	0.0	31.2	0.0	31.4	0.6
1956	31.5	0.3	31.5	0.0	31.5	0.0	31.5	0.0	31.5	0.0	31.6	0.3	31.6	0.0	31.6	0.0	31.5	-0.3	31.4	-0.3	31.3	-0.3	31.3	0.0
1957	31.4	0.3	31.4	0.0	31.4	0.0	31.3	-0.3	31.3	0.0	31.3	0.0	31.3	0.0	31.3	0.0	31.3	0.0	31.3	0.0	31.2	-0.3	31.1	-0.3
1958	31.1	0.0	31.1	0.0	31.1	0.0	31.1	0.0	31.0	-0.3	31.0	0.0	31.0	0.0	30.9	-0.3	31.1	0.6	31.8	2.3	31.8	0.0	31.8	0.0
1959	31.7	-0.3	31.7	0.0	31.7	0.0	33.0	4.1	33.5	1.5	33.5	0.0	33.6	0.3	33.8	0.6	33.8	0.0	33.8	0.0	33.7	-0.3	33.6	-0.3
1960	33.6	0.0	33.6	0.0	33.6	0.0	33.4	-0.6	33.4	0.0	33.4	0.0	33.5	0.3	33.3	-0.6	33.0	-0.9	33.0	0.0	33.1	0.3	33.0	-0.3
1961	33.1	0.3	32.9	-0.6	32.9	0.0	32.9	0.0	32.5	-1.2	32.7	0.6	32.2	-1.5	31.9	-0.9	32.3	1.3	32.3	0.0	32.2	-0.3	32.2	0.0
1962	32.2	0.0	32.1	-0.3	32.2	0.3	32.3	0.3	32.5	0.6	32.5	0.0	32.6	0.3	32.7	0.3	32.6	-0.3	32.6	0.0	32.6	0.0	32.6	0.0
1963	32.6	0.0	32.6	0.0	32.7	0.3	32.7	0.0	32.7	0.0	32.9	0.6	33.2	0.9	33.5	0.9	33.7	0.6	33.9	0.6	33.9	0.0	33.9	0.0
1964	34.0	0.3	34.1	0.3	34.2	0.3	34.7	1.5	34.8	0.3	34.8	0.0	34.8	0.0	34.8	0.0	34.8	0.0	34.8	0.0	34.8	0.0	34.8	0.0
1965	34.4	-1.1	34.3	-0.3	34.3	0.0	34.3	0.0	34.4	0.3	34.4	0.0	34.4	0.0	34.4	0.0	34.4	0.0	34.4	0.0	34.4	0.0	34.4	0.0
1966	34.4	0.0	34.6	0.6	34.9	0.9	35.0	0.3	35.2	0.6	35.3	0.3	35.3	0.0	35.4	0.3	35.4	0.0	35.4	0.0	35.2	-0.6	35.2	0.0
1967	35.2	0.0	35.5	0.9	35.5	0.0	35.6	0.3	35.6	0.0	35.6	0.0	35.8	0.6	35.9	0.3	36.1	0.6	36.2	0.3	36.2	0.0	36.3	0.3
1968	36.4	0.3	36.6	0.5	36.9	0.8	37.2	0.8	37.6	1.1	37.8	0.5	37.8	0.0	38.0	0.5	38.5	1.3	38.8	0.8	39.2	1.0	39.5	0.8
1969	39.9	1.0	40.5	1.5	41.1	1.5	42.2	2.7	42.6	0.9	43.4	1.9	43.3	-0.2	43.1	-0.5	42.9	-0.5	42.7	-0.5	42.5	-0.5	42.0	-1.2
1970	41.9	-0.2	41.7	-0.5	41.7	0.0	41.7	0.0	41.8	0.2	41.8	0.0	41.8	0.0	41.8	0.0	41.4	-1.0	40.9	-1.2	40.9	0.0	40.8	-0.2

[Continued]

Millwork
Producer Price Index
Base 1982 = 100
[Continued]

For 1926-1995. Columns headed % show percentile change in the index from the previous period for which an index is available.

Year	Jan Index	%	Feb Index	%	Mar Index	%	Apr Index	%	May Index	%	Jun Index	%	Jul Index	%	Aug Index	%	Sep Index	%	Oct Index	%	Nov Index	%	Dec Index	%
1971	40.9	0.2	41.3	1.0	41.6	0.7	42.5	2.2	43.1	1.4	43.7	1.4	44.0	0.7	44.4	0.9	44.3	-0.2	44.3	0.0	44.3	0.0	44.5	0.5
1972	44.7	0.4	44.9	0.4	45.0	0.2	45.3	0.7	45.7	0.9	46.0	0.7	46.4	0.9	46.5	0.2	46.6	0.2	46.8	0.4	46.8	0.0	46.8	0.0
1973	47.0	0.4	47.7	1.5	48.3	1.3	50.5	4.6	52.4	3.8	52.9	1.0	53.1	0.4	53.1	0.0	53.3	0.4	53.5	0.4	53.5	0.0	53.8	0.6
1974	54.2	0.7	54.3	0.2	54.9	1.1	56.1	2.2	57.5	2.5	58.4	1.6	57.9	-0.9	57.7	-0.3	57.5	-0.3	56.2	-2.3	55.0	-2.1	54.9	-0.2
1975	55.1	0.4	55.5	0.7	55.5	0.0	56.0	0.9	57.4	2.5	57.9	0.9	58.3	0.7	58.4	0.2	58.5	0.2	58.7	0.3	58.7	0.0	59.0	0.5
1976	59.8	1.4	60.5	1.2	61.7	2.0	62.7	1.6	63.6	1.4	63.7	0.2	63.5	-0.3	63.8	0.5	64.5	1.1	65.0	0.8	65.5	0.8	65.5	0.0
1977	65.7	0.3	66.6	1.4	67.4	1.2	68.2	1.2	68.5	0.4	68.9	0.6	68.8	-0.1	69.7	1.3	70.8	1.6	71.8	1.4	72.5	1.0	73.1	0.8
1978	74.9	2.5	78.5	4.8	80.8	2.9	83.7	3.6	86.1	2.9	87.7	1.9	88.3	0.7	86.5	-2.0	86.0	-0.6	85.8	-0.2	86.4	0.7	86.5	0.1
1979	87.5	1.2	90.0	2.9	92.3	2.6	95.2	3.1	93.6	-1.7	92.7	-1.0	90.4	-2.5	89.3	-1.2	89.8	0.6	91.5	1.9	90.3	-1.3	89.6	-0.8
1980	90.9	1.5	92.3	1.5	93.8	1.6	92.2	-1.7	90.1	-2.3	90.5	0.4	91.6	1.2	93.2	1.7	94.6	1.5	94.7	0.1	96.6	2.0	97.8	1.2
1981	97.9	0.1	98.0	0.1	98.7	0.7	99.0	0.3	98.4	-0.6	97.4	-1.0	97.9	0.5	97.5	-0.4	97.1	-0.4	97.1	0.0	97.3	0.2	97.9	0.6
1982	99.2	1.3	99.7	0.5	98.9	-0.8	99.0	0.1	98.9	-0.1	100.4	1.5	101.0	0.6	100.3	-0.7	100.0	-0.3	99.7	-0.3	100.3	0.6	102.5	2.2
1983	105.1	2.5	107.5	2.3	108.8	1.2	108.4	-0.4	107.0	-1.3	105.5	-1.4	106.0	0.5	109.7	3.5	109.5	-0.2	110.0	0.5	110.2	0.2	110.4	0.2
1984	110.4	0.0	110.5	0.1	110.9	0.4	109.9	-0.9	108.9	-0.9	109.2	0.3	109.8	0.5	109.9	0.1	110.0	0.1	109.9	-0.1	110.8	0.8	111.5	0.6
1985	111.9	0.4	111.5	-0.4	111.0	-0.4	110.8	-0.2	111.1	0.3	111.6	0.5	112.2	0.5	112.3	0.1	112.3	0.0	112.0	-0.3	111.9	-0.1	111.8	-0.1
1986	111.6	-0.2	111.7	0.1	112.1	0.4	112.8	0.6	113.3	0.4	114.4	1.0	114.8	0.3	115.1	0.3	115.1	0.0	114.5	-0.5	114.2	-0.3	114.2	0.0
1987	114.7	0.4	115.0	0.3	116.1	1.0	116.9	0.7	117.4	0.4	118.1	0.6	118.5	0.3	118.8	0.3	118.9	0.1	119.3	0.3	119.4	0.1	119.5	0.1
1988	119.7	0.2	120.3	0.5	120.8	0.4	121.2	0.3	121.6	0.3	121.9	0.2	122.4	0.4	122.5	0.1	122.7	0.2	123.3	0.5	122.9	-0.3	123.0	0.1
1989	123.5	0.4	125.1	1.3	126.3	1.0	127.4	0.9	128.0	0.5	128.3	0.2	127.9	-0.3	128.0	0.1	127.9	-0.1	128.2	0.2	128.3	0.1	128.7	0.3
1990	128.9	0.2	129.5	0.5	130.0	0.4	130.6	0.5	130.9	0.2	130.4	-0.4	130.5	0.1	130.5	0.0	130.6	0.1	130.5	-0.1	130.8	0.2	131.0	0.2
1991	131.5	0.4	131.6	0.1	131.9	0.2	133.6	1.3	134.3	0.5	135.8	1.1	136.9	0.8	137.6	0.5	137.6	0.0	138.0	0.3	138.1	0.1	139.3	0.9
1992	140.3	0.7	142.2	1.4	142.9	0.5	144.0	0.8	144.0	0.0	144.0	0.0	143.3	-0.5	142.3	-0.7	143.3	0.7	143.6	0.2	143.7	0.1	145.7	1.4
1993	148.0	1.6	151.8	2.6	155.9	2.7	158.8	1.9	158.2	-0.4	156.6	-1.0	155.7	-0.6	156.1	0.3	158.7	1.7	159.1	0.3	159.9	0.5	160.7	0.5
1994	162.8	1.3	163.4	0.4	163.2	-0.1	162.4	-0.5	161.5	-0.6	161.7	0.1	161.5	-0.1	161.3	-0.1	161.6	0.2	162.6	0.6	163.3	0.4	163.3	0.0
1995	163.9	0.4	163.4	-0.3	163.8	0.2	163.8	0.0	163.7	-0.1	163.7	0.0	163.9	0.1	164.0	0.1	164.5	0.3	164.2	-0.2	163.8	-0.2	163.6	-0.1

Source: U.S. Department of Labor, Bureau of Labor Statistics, Division of Industry Prices and Price Indexes. n.e.c. stands for not elsewhere classified. - indicates no data collected for period or unavailable.

Plywood
Producer Price Index
Base 1982 = 100

For 1947-1995. Columns headed % show percentile change in the index from the previous period for which an index is available.

Year	Jan Index	%	Feb Index	%	Mar Index	%	Apr Index	%	May Index	%	Jun Index	%	Jul Index	%	Aug Index	%	Sep Index	%	Oct Index	%	Nov Index	%	Dec Index	%
1947	47.9	-	48.2	0.6	48.2	0.0	48.6	0.8	48.7	0.2	48.7	0.0	45.7	-6.2	45.7	0.0	45.7	0.0	45.7	0.0	45.8	0.2	46.9	2.4
1948	51.8	10.4	51.8	0.0	52.1	0.6	52.2	0.2	53.0	1.5	53.9	1.7	54.6	1.3	54.8	0.4	54.8	0.0	54.8	0.0	54.8	0.0	54.3	-0.9
1949	49.6	-8.7	49.0	-1.2	49.0	0.0	48.7	-0.6	47.0	-3.5	45.1	-4.0	44.5	-1.3	45.2	1.6	45.0	-0.4	45.5	1.1	46.1	1.3	47.0	2.0
1950	48.3	2.8	49.2	1.9	49.5	0.6	49.5	0.0	49.6	0.2	50.0	0.8	51.1	2.2	54.3	6.3	56.0	3.1	56.7	1.3	56.7	0.0	57.4	1.2
1951	57.7	0.5	57.9	0.3	57.9	0.0	57.9	0.0	57.9	0.0	57.9	0.0	57.5	-0.7	57.5	0.0	56.5	-1.7	56.2	-0.5	53.8	-4.3	50.5	-6.1
1952	51.2	1.4	51.5	0.6	51.9	0.8	51.9	0.0	51.9	0.0	52.0	0.2	52.0	0.0	52.1	0.2	52.1	0.0	52.2	0.2	50.3	-3.6	50.3	0.0
1953	53.4	6.2	54.5	2.1	55.1	1.1	55.1	0.0	55.3	0.4	55.3	0.0	55.4	0.2	55.3	-0.2	52.5	-5.1	51.5	-1.9	50.7	-1.6	51.1	0.8
1954	50.9	-0.4	51.6	1.4	50.6	-1.9	49.5	-2.2	49.8	0.6	49.0	-1.6	50.7	3.5	51.8	2.2	50.7	-2.1	51.3	1.2	51.3	0.0	51.3	0.0
1955	51.5	0.4	51.5	0.0	51.5	0.0	51.5	0.0	51.9	0.8	51.9	0.0	52.0	0.2	52.0	0.0	52.2	0.4	52.2	0.0	52.1	-0.2	52.0	-0.2
1956	52.8	1.5	52.8	0.0	52.8	0.0	52.6	-0.4	50.5	-4.0	49.6	-1.8	50.8	2.4	48.8	-3.9	48.8	0.0	47.2	-3.3	46.6	-1.3	46.5	-0.2
1957	47.7	2.6	47.4	-0.6	47.3	-0.2	47.5	0.4	47.6	0.2	48.0	0.8	47.6	-0.8	46.8	-1.7	46.6	-0.4	47.6	2.1	47.4	-0.4	47.0	-0.8
1958	47.0	0.0	46.0	-2.1	45.7	-0.7	46.4	1.5	45.4	-2.2	46.7	2.9	48.3	3.4	49.2	1.9	50.1	1.8	50.5	0.8	49.2	-2.6	48.7	-1.0
1959	49.0	0.6	51.0	4.1	51.1	0.2	52.4	2.5	52.4	0.0	51.7	-1.3	50.3	-2.7	49.6	-1.4	47.5	-4.2	47.4	-0.2	46.4	-2.1	47.8	3.0
1960	48.3	1.0	47.7	-1.2	47.1	-1.3	47.2	0.2	47.0	-0.4	47.0	0.0	47.0	0.0	46.6	-0.9	47.4	1.7	47.7	0.6	47.2	-1.0	46.7	-1.1
1961	45.1	-3.4	44.6	-1.1	45.2	1.3	48.7	7.7	47.8	-1.8	47.8	0.0	47.8	0.0	46.8	-2.1	46.1	-1.5	44.7	-3.0	45.0	0.7	44.8	-0.4
1962	44.5	-0.7	44.8	0.7	45.5	1.6	45.5	0.0	44.5	-2.2	44.8	0.7	44.6	-0.4	44.5	-0.2	44.5	0.0	44.4	-0.2	44.2	-0.5	43.6	-1.4
1963	43.7	0.2	43.7	0.0	44.0	0.7	43.9	-0.2	43.9	0.0	44.7	1.8	48.7	8.9	50.3	3.3	44.7	-11.1	44.6	-0.2	44.7	0.2	44.6	-0.2
1964	44.0	-1.3	44.5	1.1	45.7	2.7	45.8	0.2	45.5	-0.7	44.7	-1.8	44.6	-0.2	44.3	-0.7	44.3	0.0	44.0	-0.7	43.8	-0.5	43.6	-0.5
1965	45.6	4.6	44.9	-1.5	44.5	-0.9	44.4	-0.2	44.1	-0.7	43.7	-0.9	43.9	0.5	45.7	4.1	45.1	-1.3	44.2	-2.0	44.3	0.2	44.5	0.5
1966	45.4	2.0	45.4	0.0	47.2	4.0	49.5	4.9	48.4	-2.2	44.5	-8.1	44.2	-0.7	43.5	-1.6	43.1	-0.9	42.6	-1.2	42.0	-1.4	42.2	0.5
1967	42.2	0.0	43.1	2.1	42.3	-1.9	42.4	0.2	42.3	-0.2	42.3	0.0	43.2	2.1	43.9	1.6	46.2	5.2	43.4	-6.1	42.4	-2.3	43.6	2.8
1968	43.4	-0.5	45.7	5.3	47.0	2.8	47.0	0.0	47.0	0.0	47.4	0.9	48.9	3.2	49.2	0.6	51.5	4.7	54.0	4.9	54.4	0.7	62.3	14.5
1969	65.2	4.7	70.7	8.4	71.0	0.4	53.6	-24.5	50.0	-6.7	45.5	-9.0	45.4	-0.2	45.2	-0.4	45.6	0.9	46.4	1.8	48.1	3.7	46.8	-2.7
1970	45.9	-1.9	46.4	1.1	45.5	-1.9	47.0	3.3	47.9	1.9	47.4	-1.0	47.6	0.4	48.0	0.8	47.7	-0.6	46.5	-2.5	45.5	-2.2	45.1	-0.9
1971	45.2	0.2	48.4	7.1	51.8	7.0	49.9	-3.7	47.6	-4.6	47.5	-0.2	48.1	1.3	51.9	7.9	51.2	-1.3	49.9	-2.5	50.0	0.2	50.8	1.6
1972	51.8	2.0	53.9	4.1	55.5	3.0	55.5	0.0	56.1	1.1	56.7	1.1	57.3	1.1	58.5	2.1	58.0	-0.9	58.0	0.0	57.4	-1.0	57.0	-0.7
1973	57.8	1.4	64.4	11.4	76.2	18.3	78.6	3.1	76.6	-2.5	66.7	-12.9	59.4	-10.9	60.3	1.5	59.5	-1.3	58.0	-2.5	73.2	26.2	71.5	-2.3
1974	66.7	-6.7	68.0	1.9	73.6	8.2	81.5	10.7	77.3	-5.2	70.2	-9.2	69.4	-1.1	66.9	-3.6	68.1	1.8	63.4	-6.9	63.7	0.5	64.2	0.8
1975	63.1	-1.7	67.9	7.6	67.5	-0.6	71.1	5.3	74.4	4.6	69.9	-6.0	69.4	-0.7	68.3	-1.6	69.8	2.2	68.6	-1.7	70.2	2.3	73.1	4.1
1976	77.9	6.6	79.2	1.7	79.8	0.8	79.7	-0.1	78.8	-1.1	76.1	-3.4	78.0	2.5	80.8	3.6	82.5	2.1	82.0	-0.6	83.8	2.2	88.4	5.5
1977	88.2	-0.2	88.2	0.0	89.6	1.6	87.3	-2.6	86.2	-1.3	87.3	1.3	91.3	4.6	94.7	3.7	99.3	4.9	95.5	-3.8	92.0	-3.7	97.3	5.8
1978	99.9	2.7	100.5	0.6	97.5	-3.0	94.9	-2.7	98.4	3.7	101.7	3.4	99.7	-2.0	104.5	4.8	102.6	-1.8	103.5	0.9	107.7	4.1	107.3	-0.4
1979	110.9	3.4	110.8	-0.1	109.7	-1.0	108.7	-0.9	107.4	-1.2	102.8	-4.3	107.6	4.7	109.6	1.9	111.1	1.4	109.4	-1.5	104.3	-4.7	102.5	-1.7
1980	102.6	0.1	104.9	2.2	103.4	-1.4	94.7	-8.4	99.4	5.0	104.1	4.7	108.9	4.6	114.6	5.2	108.8	-5.1	109.0	0.2	110.6	1.5	113.5	2.6
1981	108.2	-4.7	108.2	0.0	107.2	-0.9	110.3	2.9	107.0	-3.0	108.4	1.3	106.7	-1.6	105.8	-0.8	103.8	-1.9	100.9	-2.8	100.6	-0.3	103.3	2.7
1982	102.3	-1.0	101.3	-1.0	101.9	0.6	100.8	-1.1	99.3	-1.5	103.0	3.7	100.1	-2.8	98.7	-1.4	98.4	-0.3	96.5	-1.9	98.2	1.8	99.6	1.4
1983	101.4	1.8	103.2	1.8	102.9	-0.3	103.1	0.2	103.9	0.8	110.1	6.0	108.8	-1.2	106.1	-2.5	104.3	-1.7	106.2	1.8	105.4	-0.8	106.5	1.0
1984	106.9	0.4	107.5	0.6	107.1	-0.4	104.9	-2.1	101.4	-3.3	101.8	0.4	102.2	0.4	106.0	3.7	104.9	-1.0	103.4	-1.4	101.2	-2.1	101.6	0.4
1985	100.9	-0.7	97.6	-3.3	96.3	-1.3	96.0	-0.3	100.1	4.3	102.2	2.1	102.0	-0.2	102.4	0.4	99.2	-3.1	100.8	1.6	99.0	-1.8	99.4	0.4
1986	98.9	-0.5	98.5	-0.4	100.6	2.1	105.3	4.7	103.3	-1.9	101.5	-1.7	101.6	0.1	101.3	-0.3	101.6	0.3	101.9	0.3	101.3	-0.6	100.6	-0.7
1987	100.5	-0.1	102.3	1.8	103.4	1.1	101.1	-2.2	99.3	-1.8	98.8	-0.5	100.3	1.5	102.8	2.5	107.4	4.5	104.6	-2.6	105.9	1.2	104.2	-1.6
1988	105.3	1.1	104.4	-0.9	103.4	-1.0	102.1	-1.3	100.3	-1.8	102.2	1.9	105.3	3.0	100.3	-4.7	106.3	6.0	103.1	-3.0	103.6	0.5	104.7	1.1
1989	105.9	1.1	109.9	3.8	111.1	1.1	111.3	0.2	113.4	1.9	113.4	0.0	118.4	4.4	115.2	-2.7	118.5	2.9	127.6	7.7	128.7	0.9	116.9	-9.2
1990	114.3	-2.2	115.8	1.3	116.1	0.3	125.3	7.9	122.7	-2.1	115.8	-5.6	117.6	1.6	112.6	-4.3	111.3	-1.2	106.8	-4.0	105.7	-1.0	106.7	0.9
1991	104.0	-2.5	102.7	-1.2	105.4	2.6	106.9	1.4	118.9	11.2	129.3	8.7	130.0	0.5	114.4	-12.0	116.2	1.6	112.6	-3.1	114.3	1.5	116.4	1.8

[Continued]

Plywood
Producer Price Index
Base 1982 = 100
[Continued]

For 1947-1995. Columns headed % show percentile change in the index from the previous period for which an index is available.

Year	Jan Index	%	Feb Index	%	Mar Index	%	Apr Index	%	May Index	%	Jun Index	%	Jul Index	%	Aug Index	%	Sep Index	%	Oct Index	%	Nov Index	%	Dec Index	%
1992	119.5	2.7	132.2	10.6	135.3	2.3	132.2	-2.3	130.1	-1.6	128.8	-1.0	125.2	-2.8	128.8	2.9	143.5	11.4	140.3	-2.2	138.0	-1.6	145.8	5.7
1993	154.9	6.2	164.8	6.4	168.9	2.5	158.7	-6.0	148.5	-6.4	144.0	-3.0	143.3	-0.5	146.4	2.2	149.6	2.2	147.9	-1.1	150.8	2.0	155.5	3.1
1994	159.7	2.7	153.8	-3.7	152.5	-0.8	147.8	-3.1	149.2	0.9	153.8	3.1	153.7	-0.1	157.6	2.5	165.7	5.1	164.6	-0.7	172.5	4.8	172.0	-0.3
1995	166.0	-3.5	162.8	-1.9	164.5	1.0	164.0	-0.3	165.2	0.7	159.3	-3.6	167.6	5.2	171.1	2.1	173.7	1.5	170.7	-1.7	161.4	-5.4	157.0	-2.7

Source: U.S. Department of Labor, Bureau of Labor Statistics, Division of Industry Prices and Price Indexes. n.e.c. stands for not elsewhere classified. - indicates no data collected for period or unavailable.

Wood Products n.e.c.
Producer Price Index
Base 1982 = 100

For 1966-1995. Columns headed % show percentile change in the index from the previous period for which an index is available.

Year	Jan Index	%	Feb Index	%	Mar Index	%	Apr Index	%	May Index	%	Jun Index	%	Jul Index	%	Aug Index	%	Sep Index	%	Oct Index	%	Nov Index	%	Dec Index	%
1966	-	-	-	-	-	-	-	-	-	-	-	-	-	-	-	-	-	-	-	-	-	-	41.6	-
1967	42.4	1.9	42.4	0.0	42.4	0.0	42.4	0.0	42.4	0.0	42.4	0.0	42.4	0.0	42.3	-0.2	42.1	-0.5	42.2	0.2	42.2	0.0	42.2	0.0
1968	42.5	0.7	44.0	3.5	44.0	0.0	44.1	0.2	44.2	0.2	44.2	0.0	44.3	0.2	44.3	0.0	44.7	0.9	44.8	0.2	45.4	1.3	45.9	1.1
1969	46.0	0.2	46.2	0.4	46.7	1.1	46.8	0.2	47.6	1.7	47.8	0.4	48.0	0.4	48.5	1.0	48.4	-0.2	48.5	0.2	48.5	0.0	49.2	1.4
1970	49.7	1.0	49.7	0.0	49.7	0.0	49.6	-0.2	49.6	0.0	49.6	0.0	49.7	0.2	49.7	0.0	49.6	-0.2	49.6	0.0	49.6	0.0	49.9	0.6
1971	49.9	0.0	50.0	0.2	50.1	0.2	50.5	0.8	50.5	0.0	50.4	-0.2	50.4	0.0	50.4	0.0	50.4	0.0	50.4	0.0	50.4	0.0	50.4	0.0
1972	50.6	0.4	50.8	0.4	50.9	0.2	51.3	0.8	51.9	1.2	52.2	0.6	53.2	1.9	53.7	0.9	54.0	0.6	54.3	0.6	55.1	1.5	55.2	0.2
1973	56.4	2.2	57.2	1.4	59.7	4.4	62.4	4.5	63.4	1.6	64.3	1.4	64.7	0.6	64.9	0.3	66.0	1.7	67.0	1.5	67.3	0.4	67.4	0.1
1974	67.4	0.0	68.5	1.6	69.2	1.0	69.5	0.4	70.8	1.9	71.3	0.7	71.6	0.4	71.8	0.3	72.1	0.4	71.7	-0.6	71.3	-0.6	71.1	-0.3
1975	70.4	-1.0	70.2	-0.3	69.5	-1.0	68.9	-0.9	68.7	-0.3	68.4	-0.4	68.0	-0.6	68.1	0.1	68.0	-0.1	67.8	-0.3	67.7	-0.1	66.9	-1.2
1976	67.8	1.3	68.7	1.3	68.9	0.3	69.2	0.4	69.3	0.1	70.0	1.0	70.3	0.4	70.4	0.1	71.9	2.1	72.1	0.3	72.5	0.6	73.0	0.7
1977	73.4	0.5	74.7	1.8	75.8	1.5	76.7	1.2	78.1	1.8	78.5	0.5	78.6	0.1	79.0	0.5	80.3	1.6	80.3	0.0	80.4	0.1	80.9	0.6
1978	82.4	1.9	84.3	2.3	85.6	1.5	86.7	1.3	88.4	2.0	90.6	2.5	92.0	1.5	92.0	0.0	92.8	0.9	93.4	0.6	93.8	0.4	94.0	0.2
1979	94.5	0.5	95.8	1.4	98.3	2.6	99.7	1.4	100.9	1.2	101.0	0.1	100.6	-0.4	100.5	-0.1	100.8	0.3	100.7	-0.1	101.6	0.9	101.8	0.2
1980	102.6	0.8	103.0	0.4	102.9	-0.1	102.3	-0.6	101.9	-0.4	101.1	-0.8	100.3	-0.8	100.0	-0.3	100.3	0.3	100.2	-0.1	100.2	0.0	100.0	-0.2
1981	101.0	1.0	100.8	-0.2	100.3	-0.5	100.9	0.6	100.9	0.0	101.5	0.6	101.9	0.4	101.5	-0.4	101.8	0.3	101.6	-0.2	101.3	-0.3	101.4	0.1
1982	100.9	-0.5	101.1	0.2	101.0	-0.1	100.7	-0.3	100.5	-0.2	99.9	-0.6	99.9	0.0	99.8	-0.1	99.8	0.0	99.8	0.0	98.7	-1.1	97.9	-0.8
1983	98.2	0.3	98.7	0.5	98.1	-0.6	97.7	-0.4	97.9	0.2	97.2	-0.7	97.3	0.1	97.1	-0.2	97.1	0.0	97.2	0.1	97.3	0.1	97.6	0.3
1984	97.4	-0.2	97.7	0.3	98.2	0.5	98.8	0.6	99.4	0.6	99.5	0.1	99.6	0.1	100.1	0.5	99.9	-0.2	100.2	0.3	100.2	0.0	100.8	0.6
1985	100.7	-0.1	100.7	0.0	101.0	0.3	101.2	0.2	100.1	-1.1	99.9	-0.2	99.9	0.0	99.7	-0.2	99.6	-0.1	99.7	0.1	99.5	-0.2	99.5	0.0
1986	99.7	0.2	99.6	-0.1	99.6	0.0	99.6	0.0	99.8	0.2	100.8	1.0	101.4	0.6	101.0	-0.4	101.1	0.1	102.0	0.9	102.7	0.7	102.9	0.2
1987	103.0	0.1	102.9	-0.1	103.0	0.1	103.2	0.2	103.3	0.1	103.5	0.2	103.5	0.0	103.8	0.3	104.1	0.3	104.6	0.5	104.6	0.0	105.0	0.4
1988	105.4	0.4	105.8	0.4	106.2	0.4	106.5	0.3	106.5	0.0	107.1	0.6	107.5	0.4	107.7	0.2	107.9	0.2	108.3	0.4	108.6	0.3	108.3	-0.3
1989	108.5	0.2	109.4	0.8	110.2	0.7	111.4	1.1	112.4	0.9	113.7	1.2	114.2	0.4	115.6	1.2	116.2	0.5	115.1	-0.9	115.2	0.1	114.9	-0.3
1990	114.6	-0.3	114.4	-0.2	114.1	-0.3	114.4	0.3	114.5	0.1	114.9	0.3	114.8	-0.1	115.1	0.3	115.0	-0.1	115.3	0.3	114.9	-0.3	114.8	-0.1
1991	115.4	0.5	116.1	0.6	117.0	0.8	117.9	0.8	118.3	0.3	119.1	0.7	120.4	1.1	119.3	-0.9	120.5	1.0	119.7	-0.7	119.9	0.2	119.9	0.0
1992	119.9	0.0	119.8	-0.1	121.7	1.6	122.4	0.6	125.1	2.2	125.6	0.4	125.4	-0.2	125.4	0.0	126.0	0.5	126.8	0.6	127.7	0.7	127.6	-0.1
1993	129.7	1.6	131.4	1.3	133.6	1.7	135.1	1.1	137.1	1.5	136.2	-0.7	136.4	0.1	135.6	-0.6	136.9	1.0	136.4	-0.4	136.4	0.0	138.1	1.2
1994	137.2	-0.7	137.7	0.4	137.6	-0.1	138.4	0.6	138.9	0.4	137.4	-1.1	137.8	0.3	137.5	-0.2	137.1	-0.3	137.8	0.5	138.0	0.1	137.5	-0.4
1995	139.0	1.1	141.5	1.8	141.6	0.1	141.8	0.1	144.0	1.6	142.8	-0.8	143.5	0.5	145.2	1.2	147.8	1.8	147.6	-0.1	144.5	-2.1	144.0	-0.3

Source: U.S. Department of Labor, Bureau of Labor Statistics, Division of Industry Prices and Price Indexes. n.e.c. stands for not elsewhere classified. - indicates no data collected for period or unavailable.

Logs, Bolts, Timber and Pulpwood
Producer Price Index
Base 1982 = 100

For 1981-1995. Columns headed % show percentile change in the index from the previous period for which an index is available.

Year	Jan Index	%	Feb Index	%	Mar Index	%	Apr Index	%	May Index	%	Jun Index	%	Jul Index	%	Aug Index	%	Sep Index	%	Oct Index	%	Nov Index	%	Dec Index	%
1981	-	-	-	-	-	-	-	-	-	-	-	-	-	-	-	-	-	-	-	-	-	-	103.1	-
1982	102.0	-1.1	103.3	1.3	104.4	1.1	104.8	0.4	103.3	-1.4	102.7	-0.6	99.8	-2.8	98.6	-1.2	97.1	-1.5	94.4	-2.8	93.7	-0.7	95.9	2.3
1983	94.8	-1.1	96.0	1.3	96.9	0.9	96.6	-0.3	96.2	-0.4	96.9	0.7	96.5	-0.4	97.3	0.8	97.9	0.6	96.2	-1.7	97.1	0.9	96.5	-0.6
1984	95.9	-0.6	100.8	5.1	96.9	-3.9	97.9	1.0	100.2	2.3	100.5	0.3	99.1	-1.4	94.7	-4.4	96.5	1.9	93.4	-3.2	93.7	0.3	93.8	0.1
1985	94.4	0.6	96.5	2.2	96.8	0.3	97.3	0.5	97.2	-0.1	97.5	0.3	96.5	-1.0	95.5	-1.0	94.4	-1.2	95.4	1.1	95.3	-0.1	95.3	0.0
1986	94.5	-0.8	90.6	-4.1	91.6	1.1	91.9	0.3	92.4	0.5	92.9	0.5	91.8	-1.2	92.3	0.5	92.0	-0.3	92.4	0.4	92.2	-0.2	92.6	0.4
1987	93.2	0.6	94.8	1.7	96.2	1.5	95.9	-0.3	96.0	0.1	97.3	1.4	98.5	1.2	102.1	3.7	107.2	5.0	111.0	3.5	114.0	2.7	115.6	1.4
1988	117.3	1.5	118.2	0.8	118.6	0.3	119.1	0.4	118.9	-0.2	117.5	-1.2	117.3	-0.2	116.6	-0.6	116.4	-0.2	116.8	0.3	117.4	0.5	118.7	1.1
1989	120.8	1.8	122.2	1.2	123.6	1.1	127.2	2.9	128.2	0.8	131.1	2.3	133.7	2.0	137.2	2.6	137.3	0.1	140.7	2.5	140.8	0.1	140.4	-0.3
1990	142.1	1.2	142.1	0.0	143.3	0.8	143.7	0.3	144.2	0.3	144.8	0.4	146.1	0.9	145.2	-0.6	143.3	-1.3	140.9	-1.7	139.5	-1.0	138.6	-0.6
1991	141.9	2.4	142.1	0.1	141.0	-0.8	141.6	0.4	144.3	1.9	144.0	-0.2	144.4	0.3	146.3	1.3	145.4	-0.6	147.5	1.4	145.8	-1.2	145.4	-0.3
1992	151.6	4.3	155.8	2.8	158.8	1.9	164.1	3.3	164.9	0.5	165.1	0.1	165.1	0.0	165.9	0.5	168.1	1.3	170.7	1.5	171.4	0.4	176.4	2.9
1993	183.2	3.9	193.8	5.8	200.9	3.7	222.6	10.8	233.5	4.9	224.9	-3.7	222.5	-1.1	212.6	-4.4	212.6	0.0	212.9	0.1	215.6	1.3	212.4	-1.5
1994	223.7	5.3	226.5	1.3	230.7	1.9	227.2	-1.5	220.7	-2.9	218.1	-1.2	215.5	-1.2	213.5	-0.9	212.6	-0.4	213.3	0.3	212.8	-0.2	214.5	0.8
1995	218.1	1.7	224.5	2.9	225.9	0.6	229.3	1.5	228.4	-0.4	228.8	0.2	219.9	-3.9	216.0	-1.8	215.9	-0.0	213.9	-0.9	211.6	-1.1	212.7	0.5

Source: U.S. Department of Labor, Bureau of Labor Statistics, Division of Industry Prices and Price Indexes. n.e.c. stands for not elsewhere classified. - indicates no data collected for period or unavailable.

Prefabricated Wood Buildings & Components
Producer Price Index
Base Dec. 1984 = 100

For 1984-1995. Columns headed % show percentile change in the index from the previous period for which an index is available.

Year	Jan Index	%	Feb Index	%	Mar Index	%	Apr Index	%	May Index	%	Jun Index	%	Jul Index	%	Aug Index	%	Sep Index	%	Oct Index	%	Nov Index	%	Dec Index	%
1984	-	-	-	-	-	-	-	-	-	-	-	-	-	-	-	-	-	-	-	-	-	-	100.0	-
1985	100.4	0.4	100.2	-0.2	100.6	0.4	100.7	0.1	101.1	0.4	101.6	0.5	101.9	0.3	102.1	0.2	102.2	0.1	102.2	0.0	102.1	-0.1	102.1	0.0
1986	102.7	0.6	103.1	0.4	103.3	0.2	104.1	0.8	104.4	0.3	104.4	0.0	104.3	-0.1	104.4	0.1	104.7	0.3	104.7	0.0	104.7	0.0	104.8	0.1
1987	104.8	0.0	104.9	0.1	104.5	-0.4	105.4	0.9	105.5	0.1	105.2	-0.3	105.7	0.5	105.8	0.1	105.8	0.0	105.8	0.0	106.1	0.3	106.1	0.0
1988	106.2	0.1	107.3	1.0	107.8	0.5	107.9	0.1	107.6	-0.3	108.1	0.5	108.5	0.4	108.5	0.0	108.5	0.0	109.2	0.6	109.2	0.0	109.2	0.0
1989	109.8	0.5	109.8	0.0	110.5	0.6	110.7	0.2	110.7	0.0	110.7	0.0	111.0	0.3	111.0	0.0	111.0	0.0	111.0	0.0	110.8	-0.2	111.0	0.2
1990	111.3	0.3	111.8	0.4	111.6	-0.2	111.9	0.3	112.8	0.8	113.1	0.3	113.2	0.1	113.8	0.5	113.9	0.1	114.7	0.7	114.7	0.0	114.7	0.0
1991	115.7	0.9	115.7	0.0	115.9	0.2	117.2	1.1	117.5	0.3	119.6	1.8	119.7	0.1	120.1	0.3	120.2	0.1	119.0	-1.0	118.9	-0.1	118.9	0.0
1992	119.3	0.3	120.3	0.8	120.6	0.2	122.8	1.8	122.9	0.1	123.0	0.1	122.9	-0.1	123.1	0.2	123.2	0.1	124.5	1.1	125.2	0.6	125.4	0.2
1993	125.7	0.2	128.3	2.1	130.1	1.4	132.1	1.5	134.7	2.0	134.4	-0.2	134.0	-0.3	133.2	-0.6	132.9	-0.2	133.6	0.5	134.5	0.7	136.3	1.3
1994	135.3	-0.7	138.5	2.4	139.6	0.8	141.8	1.6	141.9	0.1	142.4	0.4	142.5	0.1	142.7	0.1	143.1	0.3	144.0	0.6	143.9	-0.1	144.0	0.1
1995	145.3	0.9	146.1	0.6	146.5	0.3	148.2	1.2	148.5	0.2	148.8	0.2	148.4	-0.3	148.4	0.0	148.6	0.1	148.3	-0.2	148.3	0.0	148.3	0.0

Source: U.S. Department of Labor, Bureau of Labor Statistics, Division of Industry Prices and Price Indexes. n.e.c. stands for not elsewhere classified. - indicates no data collected for period or unavailable.

Treated wood and contract Wood Preserving
Producer Price Index
Base JUNE 1985 = 100

For 1985-1995. Columns headed % show percentile change in the index from the previous period for which an index is available.

Year	Jan Index	%	Feb Index	%	Mar Index	%	Apr Index	%	May Index	%	Jun Index	%	Jul Index	%	Aug Index	%	Sep Index	%	Oct Index	%	Nov Index	%	Dec Index	%
1985	-	-	-	-	-	-	-	-	-	-	100.0	-	99.5	-0.5	99.0	-0.5	99.0	0.0	98.9	-0.1	98.9	0.0	98.8	-0.1
1986	98.8	0.0	98.3	-0.5	98.9	0.6	98.1	-0.8	98.2	0.1	98.0	-0.2	97.7	-0.3	97.8	0.1	97.6	-0.2	97.7	0.1	97.3	-0.4	97.4	0.1
1987	97.0	-0.4	97.7	0.7	98.0	0.3	98.5	0.5	98.9	0.4	100.0	1.1	99.4	-0.6	99.5	0.1	99.4	-0.1	98.9	-0.5	98.9	0.0	99.1	0.2
1988	100.0	0.9	100.9	0.9	100.9	0.0	101.0	0.1	101.4	0.4	102.2	0.8	102.6	0.4	102.1	-0.5	101.8	-0.3	103.9	2.1	104.6	0.7	104.8	0.2
1989	106.6	1.7	107.9	1.2	108.3	0.4	108.9	0.6	110.6	1.6	110.9	0.3	111.2	0.3	111.1	-0.1	110.9	-0.2	110.1	-0.7	109.9	-0.2	110.0	0.1
1990	110.3	0.3	111.7	1.3	111.9	0.2	112.3	0.4	113.3	0.9	113.2	-0.1	113.5	0.3	113.6	0.1	112.7	-0.8	112.0	-0.6	113.3	1.2	113.3	0.0
1991	113.5	0.2	113.4	-0.1	114.4	0.9	114.8	0.3	114.6	-0.2	118.9	3.8	119.6	0.6	115.5	-3.4	115.3	-0.2	115.0	-0.3	115.9	0.8	116.7	0.7
1992	118.9	1.9	122.6	3.1	123.2	0.5	123.4	0.2	124.0	0.5	122.4	-1.3	122.2	-0.2	123.2	0.8	125.5	1.9	124.3	-1.0	124.4	0.1	127.6	2.6
1993	131.1	2.7	135.9	3.7	141.7	4.3	142.4	0.5	138.3	-2.9	132.4	-4.3	132.1	-0.2	134.3	1.7	136.7	1.8	139.2	1.8	146.1	5.0	147.3	0.8
1994	152.0	3.2	149.8	-1.4	151.4	1.1	148.2	-2.1	145.6	-1.8	149.2	2.5	148.4	-0.5	149.3	0.6	148.4	-0.6	147.0	-0.9	149.6	1.8	148.7	-0.6
1995	148.9	0.1	151.3	1.6	151.9	0.4	152.9	0.7	149.7	-2.1	147.5	-1.5	148.9	0.9	149.2	0.2	148.6	-0.4	147.4	-0.8	146.7	-0.5	147.1	0.3

Source: U.S. Department of Labor, Bureau of Labor Statistics, Division of Industry Prices and Price Indexes. n.e.c. stands for not elsewhere classified. - indicates no data collected for period or unavailable.

PULP, PAPER, AND ALLIED PRODUCTS
Producer Price Index
Base 1982 = 100

For 1947-1995. Columns headed % show percentile change in the index from the previous period for which an index is available.

Year	Jan Index	%	Feb Index	%	Mar Index	%	Apr Index	%	May Index	%	Jun Index	%	Jul Index	%	Aug Index	%	Sep Index	%	Oct Index	%	Nov Index	%	Dec Index	%
1947	24.5	-	24.7	0.8	24.8	0.4	25.1	1.2	25.1	0.0	25.1	0.0	25.1	0.0	25.2	0.4	25.3	0.4	25.5	0.8	25.5	0.0	25.8	1.2
1948	26.0	0.8	26.3	1.2	26.2	-0.4	26.1	-0.4	26.1	0.0	26.1	0.0	26.2	0.4	26.3	0.4	26.4	0.4	26.4	0.0	26.3	-0.4	26.3	0.0
1949	26.3	0.0	26.2	-0.4	26.0	-0.8	25.7	-1.2	25.3	-1.6	24.8	-2.0	24.5	-1.2	24.4	-0.4	24.5	0.4	24.5	0.0	24.6	0.4	24.6	0.0
1950	24.6	0.0	24.5	-0.4	24.5	0.0	24.5	0.0	24.4	-0.4	24.5	0.4	24.9	1.6	25.9	4.0	26.4	1.9	27.4	3.8	28.0	2.2	29.2	4.3
1951	30.6	4.8	30.7	0.3	30.7	0.0	30.5	-0.7	30.5	0.0	30.6	0.3	30.6	0.0	30.5	-0.3	30.4	-0.3	30.3	-0.3	30.2	-0.3	30.2	0.0
1952	30.1	-0.3	30.2	0.3	30.0	-0.7	29.9	-0.3	29.8	-0.3	29.7	-0.3	29.4	-1.0	29.5	0.3	29.5	0.0	29.4	-0.3	29.4	0.0	29.5	0.3
1953	29.5	0.0	29.4	-0.3	29.3	-0.3	29.4	0.3	29.4	0.0	29.5	0.3	29.5	0.0	29.6	0.3	29.8	0.7	30.0	0.7	29.9	-0.3	29.8	-0.3
1954	29.8	0.0	29.8	0.0	29.7	-0.3	29.6	-0.3	29.5	-0.3	29.5	0.0	29.6	0.3	29.6	0.0	29.6	0.0	29.6	0.0	29.6	0.0	29.5	-0.3
1955	29.6	0.3	29.7	0.3	29.8	0.3	29.9	0.3	30.0	0.3	30.2	0.7	30.3	0.3	30.5	0.7	30.7	0.7	31.3	2.0	31.4	0.3	31.5	0.3
1956	31.8	1.0	32.0	0.6	32.3	0.9	32.5	0.6	32.4	-0.3	32.5	0.3	32.5	0.0	32.6	0.3	32.6	0.0	32.7	0.3	32.6	-0.3	32.6	0.0
1957	32.8	0.6	32.8	0.0	32.8	0.0	32.8	0.0	32.9	0.3	32.9	0.0	33.0	0.3	33.1	0.3	33.2	0.3	33.4	0.6	33.4	0.0	33.4	0.0
1958	33.3	-0.3	33.3	0.0	33.3	0.0	33.3	0.0	33.3	0.0	33.3	0.0	33.4	0.3	33.4	0.0	33.6	0.6	33.6	0.0	33.6	0.0	33.5	-0.3
1959	33.5	0.0	33.6	0.3	33.6	0.0	33.7	0.3	33.6	-0.3	33.7	0.3	33.7	0.0	33.7	0.0	33.7	0.0	33.7	0.0	33.8	0.3	33.7	-0.3	33.7	0.0
1960	34.1	1.2	33.9	-0.6	33.9	0.0	33.9	0.0	34.0	0.3	34.0	0.0	34.0	0.0	33.9	-0.3	33.9	0.0	34.0	0.3	33.9	-0.3	33.7	-0.6
1961	33.7	0.0	33.7	0.0	33.5	-0.6	33.4	-0.3	32.1	-3.9	32.2	0.3	32.2	0.0	32.2	0.0	33.0	2.5	33.3	0.9	33.1	-0.6	33.3	0.6
1962	33.3	0.0	33.3	0.0	33.7	1.2	33.8	0.3	33.6	-0.6	33.5	-0.3	33.4	-0.3	33.3	-0.3	33.2	-0.3	33.1	-0.3	33.1	0.0	33.0	-0.3
1963	33.0	0.0	33.1	0.3	33.0	-0.3	33.0	0.0	33.1	0.3	33.2	0.3	33.0	-0.6	33.1	0.3	33.1	0.0	33.2	0.3	33.2	0.0	33.2	0.0
1964	33.3	0.3	33.3	0.0	33.1	-0.6	33.1	0.0	32.9	-0.6	32.9	0.0	32.9	0.0	32.9	0.0	32.9	0.0	33.1	0.6	33.0	-0.3	33.0	0.0
1965	33.0	0.0	33.0	0.0	33.2	0.6	33.3	0.3	33.4	0.3	33.4	0.0	33.3	-0.3	33.3	0.0	33.4	0.3	33.5	0.3	33.6	0.3	33.7	0.3
1966	33.8	0.3	33.8	0.0	34.0	0.6	34.2	0.6	34.3	0.3	34.4	0.3	34.4	0.0	34.4	0.0	34.4	0.0	34.4	0.0	34.4	0.0	34.4	0.0
1967	34.4	0.0	34.4	0.0	34.5	0.3	34.6	0.3	34.6	0.0	34.6	0.0	34.7	0.3	34.6	-0.3	34.6	0.0	34.7	0.3	34.8	0.3	34.9	0.3
1968	34.9	0.0	35.1	0.6	35.1	0.0	35.1	0.0	35.1	0.0	34.9	-0.6	35.0	0.3	34.9	-0.3	35.0	0.3	35.1	0.3	35.1	0.0	35.1	0.0
1969	35.4	0.9	35.6	0.6	35.8	0.6	35.9	0.3	36.0	0.3	36.0	0.0	36.0	0.0	36.2	0.6	36.3	0.3	36.4	0.3	36.5	0.3	36.6	0.3
1970	37.2	1.6	37.3	0.3	37.4	0.3	37.5	0.3	37.4	-0.3	37.4	0.0	37.5	0.3	37.4	-0.3	37.5	0.3	37.7	0.5	37.7	0.0	37.6	-0.3
1971	37.8	0.5	37.8	0.0	37.9	0.3	38.0	0.3	38.1	0.3	38.2	0.3	38.3	0.3	38.3	0.0	38.3	0.0	38.3	0.0	38.3	0.0	38.4	0.3
1972	38.4	0.0	38.7	0.8	38.9	0.5	39.1	0.5	39.2	0.3	39.3	0.3	39.4	0.3	39.5	0.3	39.6	0.3	39.7	0.3	39.8	0.3	39.9	0.3
1973	40.1	0.5	40.4	0.7	41.0	1.5	41.5	1.2	41.8	0.7	42.3	1.2	42.4	0.2	42.7	0.7	43.1	0.9	43.6	1.2	44.2	1.4	44.6	0.9
1974	45.6	2.2	46.0	0.9	47.5	3.3	50.0	5.3	50.8	1.6	51.1	0.6	53.1	3.9	56.4	6.2	56.9	0.9	57.5	1.1	57.8	0.5	57.9	0.2
1975	58.8	1.6	58.8	0.0	58.9	0.2	58.8	-0.2	58.8	0.0	58.8	0.0	58.9	0.2	58.9	0.0	59.0	0.2	59.2	0.3	59.3	0.2	59.9	1.0
1976	60.5	1.0	60.9	0.7	61.3	0.7	61.9	1.0	62.1	0.3	62.2	0.2	62.5	0.5	62.7	0.3	62.9	0.3	62.9	0.0	62.9	0.0	63.0	0.2
1977	63.4	0.6	63.4	0.0	63.6	0.3	64.2	0.9	64.5	0.5	64.9	0.6	65.0	0.2	65.1	0.2	65.2	0.2	65.3	0.2	65.2	-0.2	65.0	-0.3
1978	65.1	0.2	65.3	0.3	65.7	0.6	66.5	1.2	66.9	0.6	67.0	0.1	67.7	1.0	67.8	0.1	68.9	1.6	70.1	1.7	70.6	0.7	71.1	0.7
1979	71.7	0.8	72.3	0.8	73.5	1.7	74.5	1.4	74.9	0.5	75.0	0.1	75.6	0.8	77.0	1.9	77.2	0.3	78.8	2.1	79.5	0.9	80.3	1.0
1980	82.2	2.4	82.8	0.7	84.0	1.4	85.8	2.1	86.3	0.6	87.0	0.8	87.2	0.2	87.4	0.2	87.5	0.1	88.1	0.7	88.3	0.2	88.9	0.7
1981	91.6	3.0	92.5	1.0	93.2	0.8	94.0	0.9	94.3	0.3	94.5	0.2	95.2	0.7	95.6	0.4	96.2	0.6	96.7	0.5	97.1	0.4	97.3	0.2
1982	98.9	1.6	99.2	0.3	99.5	0.3	99.9	0.4	100.3	0.4	100.3	0.0	100.1	-0.2	100.2	0.1	100.2	0.0	100.4	0.2	100.4	0.0	100.6	0.2
1983	101.7	1.1	101.9	0.2	102.1	0.2	102.3	0.2	102.5	0.2	102.9	0.4	103.2	0.3	103.5	0.3	103.9	0.4	104.7	0.8	105.2	0.5	105.3	0.1
1984	107.0	1.6	108.1	1.0	108.8	0.6	109.5	0.6	110.1	0.5	110.3	0.2	110.8	0.5	111.3	0.5	111.5	0.2	111.9	0.4	112.2	0.3	112.3	0.1
1985	113.3	0.9	113.5	0.2	113.5	0.0	113.5	0.0	113.4	-0.1	113.3	-0.1	113.2	-0.1	113.2	0.0	113.1	-0.1	113.3	0.2	113.4	0.1	113.4	0.0
1986	114.5	1.0	114.7	0.2	114.7	0.0	115.3	0.5	115.6	0.3	115.8	0.2	116.1	0.3	116.5	0.3	117.0	0.4	117.6	0.5	117.9	0.3	118.1	0.2
1987	119.5	1.2	120.3	0.7	120.6	0.2	120.9	0.2	121.0	0.1	121.2	0.2	121.6	0.3	122.2	0.5	122.9	0.6	123.8	0.7	123.9	0.1	124.2	0.2
1988	126.6	1.9	127.3	0.6	128.0	0.5	128.9	0.7	129.6	0.5	130.0	0.3	131.0	0.8	131.3	0.2	132.1	0.6	132.8	0.5	133.1	0.2	133.5	0.3
1989	135.1	1.2	136.3	0.9	136.9	0.4	137.4	0.4	137.8	0.3	137.9	0.1	138.0	0.1	138.4	0.3	138.6	0.1	139.1	0.4	139.3	0.1	139.2	-0.1
1990	140.3	0.8	140.5	0.1	140.7	0.1	140.9	0.1	141.1	0.1	141.0	-0.1	141.1	0.1	141.1	0.0	141.3	0.1	142.0	0.5	142.3	0.2	142.3	0.0
1991	143.6	0.9	143.8	0.1	143.7	-0.1	143.2	-0.3	143.0	-0.1	142.7	-0.2	142.3	-0.3	142.2	-0.1	142.3	0.1	142.6	0.2	142.8	0.1	142.7	-0.1

[Continued]

PULP, PAPER, AND ALLIED PRODUCTS
Producer Price Index
Base 1982 = 100
[Continued]

For 1947-1995. Columns headed % show percentile change in the index from the previous period for which an index is available.

Year	Jan Index	%	Feb Index	%	Mar Index	%	Apr Index	%	May Index	%	Jun Index	%	Jul Index	%	Aug Index	%	Sep Index	%	Oct Index	%	Nov Index	%	Dec Index	%
1992	144.1	1.0	144.2	0.1	144.4	0.1	144.9	0.3	145.2	0.2	145.1	-0.1	145.2	0.1	145.4	0.1	145.8	0.3	146.1	0.2	145.9	-0.1	145.9	0.0
1993	147.0	0.8	147.1	0.1	147.3	0.1	147.7	0.3	147.7	0.0	147.1	-0.4	147.1	0.0	147.1	0.0	147.1	0.0	147.6	0.3	147.6	0.0	147.8	0.1
1994	148.6	0.5	148.8	0.1	149.2	0.3	149.4	0.1	150.1	0.5	151.0	0.6	152.0	0.7	153.1	0.7	154.5	0.9	156.2	1.1	158.0	1.2	159.5	0.9
1995	163.2	2.3	165.9	1.7	168.1	1.3	170.6	1.5	172.7	1.2	174.5	1.0	175.4	0.5	175.6	0.1	175.6	0.0	175.0	-0.3	175.1	0.1	174.5	-0.3

Source: U.S. Department of Labor, Bureau of Labor Statistics, Division of Industry Prices and Price Indexes. n.e.c. stands for not elsewhere classified. - indicates no data collected for period or unavailable.

Pulp, Paper, and Products, Ex. Building Paper
Producer Price Index
Base 1982 = 100

For 1947-1995. Columns headed % show percentile change in the index from the previous period for which an index is available.

Year	Jan Index	%	Feb Index	%	Mar Index	%	Apr Index	%	May Index	%	Jun Index	%	Jul Index	%	Aug Index	%	Sep Index	%	Oct Index	%	Nov Index	%	Dec Index	%
1947	25.8	-	26.0	0.8	26.2	0.8	26.6	1.5	26.5	-0.4	26.5	0.0	26.5	0.0	26.7	0.8	26.8	0.4	26.9	0.4	26.9	0.0	27.3	1.5
1948	27.5	0.7	27.7	0.7	27.7	0.0	27.6	-0.4	27.6	0.0	27.6	0.0	27.7	0.4	27.8	0.4	27.8	0.0	27.8	0.0	27.8	0.0	27.7	-0.4
1949	27.7	0.0	27.6	-0.4	27.5	-0.4	27.1	-1.5	26.6	-1.8	26.1	-1.9	25.8	-1.1	25.7	-0.4	25.8	0.4	25.8	0.0	25.9	0.4	25.9	0.0
1950	25.9	0.0	25.8	-0.4	25.8	0.0	25.8	0.0	25.7	-0.4	25.7	0.0	26.2	1.9	27.3	4.2	27.8	1.8	28.8	3.6	29.6	2.8	30.8	4.1
1951	32.4	5.2	32.5	0.3	32.4	-0.3	32.2	-0.6	32.2	0.0	32.4	0.6	32.4	0.0	32.2	-0.6	32.1	-0.3	32.0	-0.3	31.9	-0.3	31.9	0.0
1952	31.8	-0.3	31.8	0.0	31.7	-0.3	31.6	-0.3	31.5	-0.3	31.4	-0.3	31.0	-1.3	31.1	0.3	31.1	0.0	31.1	0.0	31.0	-0.3	31.1	0.3
1953	31.1	0.0	31.0	-0.3	30.9	-0.3	31.0	0.3	31.0	0.0	31.1	0.3	31.1	0.0	31.2	0.3	31.4	0.6	31.6	0.6	31.5	-0.3	31.4	-0.3
1954	31.4	0.0	31.4	0.0	31.3	-0.3	31.2	-0.3	31.1	-0.3	31.1	0.0	31.2	0.3	31.2	0.0	31.2	0.0	31.2	0.0	31.1	-0.3	31.1	0.0
1955	31.2	0.3	31.3	0.3	31.3	0.0	31.5	0.6	31.6	0.3	31.8	0.6	32.0	0.6	32.1	0.3	32.4	0.9	32.9	1.5	33.1	0.6	33.2	0.3
1956	33.5	0.9	33.7	0.6	34.1	1.2	34.2	0.3	34.2	0.0	34.2	0.0	34.3	0.3	34.4	0.3	34.3	-0.3	34.4	0.3	34.3	-0.3	34.4	0.3
1957	34.5	0.3	34.5	0.0	34.6	0.3	34.5	-0.3	34.6	0.3	34.6	0.0	34.7	0.3	34.9	0.6	35.0	0.3	35.1	0.3	35.2	0.3	35.2	0.0
1958	35.1	-0.3	35.1	0.0	35.0	-0.3	35.0	0.0	35.0	0.0	35.0	0.0	35.1	0.3	35.2	0.3	35.3	0.3	35.4	0.3	35.4	0.0	35.0	-1.1
1959	35.3	0.9	35.3	0.0	35.4	0.3	35.5	0.3	35.4	-0.3	35.5	0.3	35.5	0.0	35.5	0.0	35.5	0.0	35.5	0.0	35.5	0.0	35.5	0.0
1960	35.9	1.1	35.7	-0.6	35.7	0.0	35.7	0.0	35.8	0.3	35.8	0.0	35.9	0.3	35.7	-0.6	35.7	0.0	35.8	0.3	35.7	-0.3	35.5	-0.6
1961	35.5	0.0	35.4	-0.3	35.3	-0.3	35.1	-0.6	33.8	-3.7	33.9	0.3	33.8	-0.3	33.8	0.0	34.7	2.7	35.0	0.9	34.8	-0.6	35.0	0.6
1962	35.1	0.3	35.1	0.0	35.5	1.1	35.7	0.6	35.5	-0.6	35.4	-0.3	35.2	-0.6	35.1	-0.3	35.0	-0.3	34.9	-0.3	34.8	-0.3	34.8	0.0
1963	34.8	0.0	34.9	0.3	34.8	-0.3	34.8	0.0	34.8	0.0	35.0	0.6	34.8	-0.6	34.8	0.0	34.8	0.0	35.0	0.6	35.0	0.0	35.0	0.0
1964	35.1	0.3	35.2	0.3	35.0	-0.6	34.9	-0.3	34.7	-0.6	34.7	0.0	34.7	0.0	34.7	0.0	34.7	0.0	34.9	0.6	34.8	-0.3	34.8	0.0
1965	34.8	0.0	34.9	0.3	35.1	0.6	35.2	0.3	35.2	0.0	35.2	0.0	35.2	0.0	35.2	0.0	35.2	0.0	35.4	0.6	35.5	0.3	35.5	0.0
1966	35.7	0.6	35.7	0.0	35.9	0.6	36.1	0.6	36.2	0.3	36.3	0.3	36.4	0.3	36.4	0.0	36.4	0.0	36.3	-0.3	36.3	0.0	36.3	0.0
1967	36.3	0.0	36.4	0.3	36.5	0.3	36.6	0.3	36.6	0.0	36.6	0.0	36.7	0.3	36.6	-0.3	36.6	0.0	36.7	0.3	36.9	0.5	36.9	0.0
1968	37.0	0.3	37.1	0.3	37.0	-0.3	37.0	0.0	37.1	0.3	36.9	-0.5	37.0	0.3	36.9	-0.3	37.0	0.3	37.0	0.0	37.0	0.0	37.0	0.0
1969	37.4	1.1	37.6	0.5	37.8	0.5	37.9	0.3	37.9	0.0	38.0	0.3	38.1	0.3	38.3	0.5	38.4	0.3	38.5	0.3	38.7	0.5	38.7	0.0
1970	39.4	1.8	39.5	0.3	39.6	0.3	39.7	0.3	39.6	-0.3	39.6	0.0	39.7	0.3	39.7	0.0	39.7	0.0	39.9	0.5	39.9	0.0	39.9	0.0
1971	40.1	0.5	40.0	-0.2	40.1	0.3	40.2	0.2	40.3	0.2	40.5	0.5	40.6	0.2	40.6	0.0	40.6	0.0	40.6	0.0	40.6	0.0	40.6	0.0
1972	40.7	0.2	41.0	0.7	41.2	0.5	41.4	0.5	41.5	0.2	41.6	0.2	41.7	0.2	41.9	0.5	41.9	0.0	42.1	0.5	42.2	0.2	42.3	0.2
1973	42.5	0.5	42.8	0.7	43.4	1.4	44.0	1.4	44.3	0.7	44.8	1.1	44.9	0.2	45.3	0.9	45.7	0.9	46.2	1.1	46.8	1.3	47.2	0.9
1974	48.4	2.5	48.8	0.8	50.4	3.3	53.1	5.4	53.9	1.5	54.3	0.7	56.5	4.1	60.1	6.4	60.6	0.8	61.3	1.2	61.7	0.7	61.8	0.2
1975	62.7	1.5	62.8	0.2	62.8	0.0	62.7	-0.2	62.7	0.0	62.7	0.0	62.8	0.2	62.8	0.0	62.9	0.2	63.1	0.3	63.2	0.2	63.9	1.1
1976	64.6	1.1	64.9	0.5	65.3	0.6	65.9	0.9	66.2	0.5	66.2	0.0	66.6	0.6	66.7	0.2	67.0	0.4	67.0	0.0	66.9	-0.1	67.0	0.1
1977	67.4	0.6	67.5	0.1	67.7	0.3	68.3	0.9	68.6	0.4	69.0	0.6	69.1	0.1	69.0	-0.1	69.1	0.1	69.2	0.1	69.1	-0.1	68.8	-0.4
1978	68.9	0.1	69.0	0.1	69.3	0.4	70.2	1.3	70.6	0.6	70.7	0.1	71.5	1.1	71.7	0.3	72.9	1.7	74.2	1.8	74.8	0.8	75.3	0.7
1979	76.0	0.9	76.7	0.9	78.0	1.7	79.0	1.3	79.5	0.6	79.7	0.3	80.4	0.9	81.9	1.9	82.1	0.2	83.8	2.1	84.6	1.0	85.4	0.9
1980	87.5	2.5	88.1	0.7	89.3	1.4	91.3	2.2	91.7	0.4	92.4	0.8	92.6	0.2	92.9	0.3	93.0	0.1	93.6	0.6	93.8	0.2	94.4	0.6
1981	95.5	1.2	96.8	1.4	97.7	0.9	98.3	0.6	98.8	0.5	99.3	0.5	99.6	0.3	100.2	0.6	100.6	0.4	100.9	0.3	100.9	0.0	100.9	0.0
1982	101.0	0.1	101.3	0.3	101.3	0.0	100.8	-0.5	100.6	-0.2	100.3	-0.3	99.8	-0.5	99.6	-0.2	99.4	-0.2	98.9	-0.5	98.6	-0.3	98.4	-0.2
1983	98.4	0.0	98.4	0.0	98.4	0.0	98.3	-0.1	98.3	0.0	98.5	0.2	98.9	0.4	99.2	0.3	100.0	0.8	100.7	0.7	101.4	0.7	101.5	0.1
1984	102.8	1.3	104.3	1.5	105.5	1.2	106.7	1.1	107.1	0.4	107.4	0.3	108.2	0.7	108.5	0.3	108.9	0.4	109.6	0.6	109.7	0.1	109.4	-0.3
1985	109.1	-0.3	108.7	-0.4	108.2	-0.5	107.8	-0.4	107.4	-0.4	107.0	-0.4	106.3	-0.7	106.0	-0.3	105.7	-0.3	105.6	-0.1	105.4	-0.2	105.4	0.0
1986	105.4	0.0	105.5	0.1	105.9	0.4	106.3	0.4	106.7	0.4	106.9	0.2	107.6	0.7	108.2	0.6	108.7	0.5	109.3	0.6	109.8	0.5	110.0	0.2
1987	111.3	1.2	112.4	1.0	112.6	0.2	113.2	0.5	113.1	-0.1	113.4	0.3	114.0	0.5	114.8	0.7	115.7	0.8	116.7	0.9	117.1	0.3	117.6	0.4
1988	119.9	2.0	120.5	0.5	121.6	0.9	123.1	1.2	124.1	0.8	124.6	0.4	125.8	1.0	126.4	0.5	127.6	0.9	128.1	0.4	128.3	0.2	128.5	0.2
1989	129.5	0.8	131.1	1.2	131.8	0.5	132.4	0.5	132.9	0.4	132.8	-0.1	132.5	-0.2	132.8	0.2	132.8	0.0	133.6	0.6	133.6	0.0	133.4	-0.1
1990	133.4	0.0	133.3	-0.1	133.2	-0.1	133.4	0.2	133.1	-0.2	132.8	-0.2	132.6	-0.2	132.5	-0.1	132.3	-0.2	132.7	0.3	132.8	0.1	132.8	0.0
1991	132.6	-0.2	132.4	-0.2	131.8	-0.5	130.8	-0.8	129.8	-0.8	129.1	-0.5	128.6	-0.4	128.1	-0.4	128.5	0.3	128.4	-0.1	128.6	0.2	128.5	-0.1

[Continued]

Pulp, Paper, and Products, Ex. Building Paper
Producer Price Index
Base 1982 = 100
[Continued]

For 1947-1995. Columns headed % show percentile change in the index from the previous period for which an index is available.

Year	Jan		Feb		Mar		Apr		May		Jun		Jul		Aug		Sep		Oct		Nov		Dec	
	Index	%	Index	%	Index	%	Index	%	Index	%	Index	%	Index	%	Index	%	Index	%	Index	%	Index	%	Index	%
1992	128.5	0.0	128.6	0.1	128.6	0.0	129.4	0.6	129.5	0.1	129.4	-0.1	129.4	0.0	129.4	0.0	129.9	0.4	129.6	-0.2	129.2	-0.3	128.8	-0.3
1993	128.3	-0.4	128.0	-0.2	128.2	0.2	128.3	0.1	128.2	-0.1	128.0	-0.2	127.5	-0.4	127.0	-0.4	126.6	-0.3	126.9	0.2	126.9	0.0	126.9	0.0
1994	126.7	-0.2	127.0	0.2	127.3	0.2	127.9	0.5	128.6	0.5	130.5	1.5	132.3	1.4	134.2	1.4	136.3	1.6	139.5	2.3	142.0	1.8	144.4	1.7
1995	149.2	3.3	154.0	3.2	157.8	2.5	162.2	2.8	165.8	2.2	168.4	1.6	169.1	0.4	169.2	0.1	168.5	-0.4	166.9	-0.9	165.5	-0.8	164.0	-0.9

Source: U.S. Department of Labor, Bureau of Labor Statistics, Division of Industry Prices and Price Indexes. n.e.c. stands for not elsewhere classified. - indicates no data collected for period or unavailable.

Building Paper & Building Board Mill Products
Producer Price Index
Base 1982 = 100

For 1947-1995. Columns headed % show percentile change in the index from the previous period for which an index is available.

Year	Jan Index	%	Feb Index	%	Mar Index	%	Apr Index	%	May Index	%	Jun Index	%	Jul Index	%	Aug Index	%	Sep Index	%	Oct Index	%	Nov Index	%	Dec Index	%
1947	29.0	-	29.0	0.0	29.1	0.3	29.1	0.0	29.1	0.0	29.1	0.0	29.1	0.0	29.0	-0.3	29.0	0.0	29.5	1.7	30.9	4.7	30.9	0.0
1948	31.1	0.6	31.4	1.0	31.4	0.0	31.4	0.0	31.8	1.3	33.1	4.1	33.4	0.9	33.4	0.0	33.4	0.0	33.4	0.0	33.4	0.0	33.4	0.0
1949	33.3	-0.3	33.2	-0.3	33.2	0.0	33.2	0.0	32.9	-0.9	32.8	-0.3	32.8	0.0	32.8	0.0	32.8	0.0	32.8	0.0	32.8	0.0	32.8	0.0
1950	32.8	0.0	32.8	0.0	32.8	0.0	32.8	0.0	32.8	0.0	33.6	2.4	34.4	2.4	34.4	0.0	34.7	0.9	35.6	2.6	35.6	0.0	35.9	0.8
1951	35.9	0.0	35.9	0.0	35.9	0.0	35.9	0.0	35.9	0.0	35.9	0.0	35.9	0.0	35.9	0.0	35.9	0.0	35.9	0.0	35.9	0.0	35.9	0.0
1952	35.9	0.0	35.9	0.0	35.9	0.0	36.0	0.3	36.6	1.7	36.6	0.0	36.6	0.0	36.6	0.0	36.6	0.0	36.6	0.0	37.3	1.9	37.3	0.0
1953	37.3	0.0	37.3	0.0	37.3	0.0	37.3	0.0	38.9	4.3	38.9	0.0	38.9	0.0	38.9	0.0	38.9	0.0	38.9	0.0	38.9	0.0	38.9	0.0
1954	40.4	3.9	40.4	0.0	40.4	0.0	40.4	0.0	40.4	0.0	40.4	0.0	40.4	0.0	40.3	-0.2	40.3	0.0	40.3	0.0	40.3	0.0	40.3	0.0
1955	40.3	0.0	40.9	1.5	41.0	0.2	41.0	0.0	41.0	0.0	41.0	0.0	41.0	0.0	41.9	2.2	41.9	0.0	42.2	0.7	42.2	0.0	42.2	0.0
1956	42.2	0.0	42.2	0.0	42.2	0.0	43.7	3.6	43.7	0.0	43.7	0.0	43.7	0.0	43.7	0.0	43.7	0.0	43.7	0.0	43.7	0.0	43.7	0.0
1957	44.6	2.1	44.6	0.0	44.6	0.0	44.8	0.4	44.8	0.0	44.8	0.0	44.8	0.0	44.8	0.0	44.8	0.0	44.8	0.0	44.8	0.0	44.8	0.0
1958	44.8	0.0	44.8	0.0	45.1	0.7	45.6	1.1	45.6	0.0	45.6	0.0	45.3	-0.7	45.3	0.0	45.3	0.0	45.3	0.0	45.3	0.0	45.4	0.2
1959	45.5	0.2	45.6	0.2	45.6	0.0	45.8	0.4	46.4	1.3	46.4	0.0	46.6	0.4	46.7	0.2	46.7	0.0	46.7	0.0	46.7	0.0	46.7	0.0
1960	46.7	0.0	46.7	0.0	46.3	-0.9	45.9	-0.9	45.9	0.0	45.9	0.0	45.6	-0.7	46.0	0.9	45.9	-0.2	46.1	0.4	46.0	-0.2	46.0	0.0
1961	46.0	0.0	46.2	0.4	46.1	-0.2	45.9	-0.4	45.7	-0.4	45.8	0.2	45.8	0.0	45.8	0.0	45.8	0.0	45.8	0.0	45.5	-0.7	45.3	-0.4
1962	44.8	-1.1	44.7	-0.2	44.6	-0.2	44.5	-0.2	44.4	-0.2	43.4	-2.3	43.8	0.9	44.1	0.7	44.1	0.0	43.7	-0.9	43.8	0.2	43.6	-0.5
1963	43.3	-0.7	43.3	0.0	42.7	-1.4	43.3	1.4	43.6	0.7	44.2	1.4	44.2	0.0	44.2	0.0	44.3	0.2	43.9	-0.9	43.1	-1.8	43.2	0.2
1964	43.2	0.0	43.0	-0.5	42.5	-1.2	42.4	-0.2	42.8	0.9	42.8	0.0	42.8	0.0	42.7	-0.2	42.8	0.2	42.8	0.0	42.6	-0.5	42.3	-0.7
1965	42.3	0.0	41.8	-1.2	41.8	0.0	41.8	0.0	42.0	0.5	42.0	0.0	42.3	0.7	42.3	0.0	42.3	0.0	42.5	0.5	42.3	-0.5	42.0	-0.7
1966	42.0	0.0	42.0	0.0	42.0	0.0	42.0	0.0	42.0	0.0	42.0	0.0	42.1	0.2	42.2	0.2	42.1	-0.2	42.3	0.5	42.3	0.0	42.1	-0.5
1967	42.0	-0.2	42.2	0.5	41.9	-0.7	41.9	0.0	41.7	-0.5	41.5	-0.5	41.3	-0.5	41.5	0.5	41.8	0.7	41.8	0.0	41.8	0.0	41.7	-0.2
1968	41.7	0.0	41.6	-0.2	41.7	0.2	41.8	0.2	41.9	0.2	41.8	-0.2	41.8	0.0	42.3	1.2	42.4	0.2	42.5	0.2	42.6	0.2	43.0	0.9
1969	44.2	2.8	44.6	0.9	45.2	1.3	45.6	0.9	45.8	0.4	45.1	-1.5	43.5	-3.5	43.2	-0.7	43.2	0.0	42.9	-0.7	42.9	0.0	42.7	-0.5
1970	42.3	-0.9	42.2	-0.2	42.1	-0.2	42.4	0.7	42.3	-0.2	42.3	0.0	42.2	-0.2	42.1	-0.2	42.0	-0.2	42.0	0.0	42.0	0.0	41.8	-0.5
1971	41.7	-0.2	41.7	0.0	42.2	1.2	42.5	0.7	42.9	0.9	43.2	0.7	43.2	0.0	43.5	0.7	43.5	0.0	43.6	0.2	43.6	0.0	43.6	0.0
1972	43.7	0.2	43.7	0.0	44.1	0.9	44.3	0.5	44.5	0.5	44.5	0.0	44.6	0.2	44.7	0.2	44.8	0.2	44.8	0.0	44.8	0.0	44.8	0.0
1973	44.7	-0.2	45.1	0.9	45.3	0.4	45.6	0.7	46.3	1.5	46.7	0.9	46.8	0.2	47.1	0.6	48.4	2.8	49.2	1.7	49.6	0.8	50.2	1.2
1974	50.8	1.2	50.9	0.2	51.5	1.2	51.6	0.2	52.4	1.6	52.2	-0.4	51.9	-0.6	52.2	0.6	52.3	0.2	51.8	-1.0	50.5	-2.5	50.6	0.2
1975	51.8	2.4	51.9	0.2	51.6	-0.6	51.5	-0.2	52.5	1.9	52.7	0.4	53.2	0.9	53.3	0.2	53.8	0.9	54.8	1.9	54.9	0.2	55.0	0.2
1976	54.8	-0.4	55.6	1.5	57.2	2.9	56.9	-0.5	56.9	0.0	58.3	2.5	59.0	1.2	58.7	-0.5	59.2	0.9	58.9	-0.5	59.4	0.8	60.2	1.3
1977	60.6	0.7	60.3	-0.5	60.9	1.0	62.1	2.0	63.2	1.8	64.2	1.6	65.9	2.6	67.8	2.9	69.6	2.7	70.5	1.3	70.3	-0.3	71.3	1.4
1978	73.1	2.5	75.2	2.9	77.9	3.6	78.8	1.2	79.7	1.1	80.3	0.8	80.6	0.4	79.3	-1.6	78.1	-1.5	79.1	1.3	78.8	-0.4	77.9	-1.1
1979	76.9	-1.3	76.7	-0.3	76.2	-0.7	76.6	0.5	76.5	-0.1	75.5	-1.3	74.3	-1.6	74.8	0.7	76.3	2.0	76.6	0.4	76.7	0.1	77.1	0.5
1980	77.7	0.8	80.0	3.0	83.0	3.8	84.0	1.2	86.4	2.9	87.2	0.9	88.4	1.4	87.8	-0.7	87.8	0.0	88.8	1.1	90.4	1.8	91.7	1.4
1981	91.7	0.0	94.3	2.8	95.2	1.0	97.1	2.0	99.1	2.1	99.1	0.0	98.3	-0.8	97.8	-0.5	97.8	0.0	97.4	-0.4	96.9	-0.5	96.2	-0.7
1982	97.6	1.5	96.6	-1.0	100.1	3.6	98.7	-1.4	100.3	1.6	100.2	-0.1	100.1	-0.1	102.1	2.0	101.6	-0.5	101.1	-0.5	100.6	-0.5	101.1	0.5
1983	100.7	-0.4	100.8	0.1	102.0	1.2	103.1	1.1	104.1	1.0	106.8	2.6	107.0	0.2	105.3	-1.6	105.5	0.2	106.3	0.8	106.4	0.1	104.6	-1.7
1984	105.2	0.6	106.5	1.2	108.0	1.4	111.0	2.8	110.7	-0.3	110.7	0.0	109.8	-0.8	108.5	-1.2	108.3	-0.2	107.6	-0.6	105.9	-1.6	105.8	-0.1
1985	106.6	0.8	107.0	0.4	107.0	0.0	107.5	0.5	108.0	0.5	108.5	0.5	108.5	0.0	108.0	-0.5	108.6	0.6	106.5	-1.9	106.4	-0.1	105.9	-0.5
1986	105.8	-0.1	106.4	0.6	107.4	0.9	108.9	1.4	109.6	0.6	109.6	0.0	109.5	-0.1	109.5	0.0	109.7	0.2	110.7	0.9	109.7	-0.9	109.4	-0.3
1987	109.6	0.2	109.3	-0.3	109.2	-0.1	109.1	-0.1	109.8	0.6	110.2	0.4	111.1	0.8	112.2	1.0	113.2	0.9	113.8	0.5	113.4	-0.4	113.7	0.3
1988	113.7	0.0	114.0	0.3	113.1	-0.8	113.3	0.2	113.4	0.1	114.2	0.7	113.9	-0.3	112.7	-1.1	112.5	-0.2	112.5	0.0	112.7	0.2	113.3	0.5
1989	112.9	-0.4	113.8	0.8	114.2	0.4	115.1	0.8	115.5	0.3	115.8	0.3	116.4	0.5	116.2	-0.2	116.3	0.1	116.6	0.3	117.0	0.3	116.9	-0.1
1990	116.6	-0.3	116.0	-0.5	115.5	-0.4	113.7	-1.6	113.4	-0.3	111.9	-1.3	111.2	-0.6	110.3	-0.8	109.8	-0.5	109.4	-0.4	109.1	-0.3	108.9	-0.2
1991	109.3	0.4	109.8	0.5	111.3	1.4	112.7	1.3	113.5	0.7	113.4	-0.1	114.6	1.1	112.8	-1.6	112.2	-0.5	110.9	-1.2	110.6	-0.3	110.9	0.3

[Continued]

Building Paper & Building Board Mill Products
Producer Price Index
Base 1982 = 100
[Continued]

For 1947-1995. Columns headed % show percentile change in the index from the previous period for which an index is available.

Year	Jan Index	%	Feb Index	%	Mar Index	%	Apr Index	%	May Index	%	Jun Index	%	Jul Index	%	Aug Index	%	Sep Index	%	Oct Index	%	Nov Index	%	Dec Index	%
1992	112.5	1.4	117.1	4.1	119.2	1.8	118.5	-0.6	119.1	0.5	118.9	-0.2	118.8	-0.1	120.0	1.0	123.7	3.1	123.5	-0.2	121.8	-1.4	121.7	-0.1
1993	124.9	2.6	129.0	3.3	133.9	3.8	135.4	1.1	133.8	-1.2	132.0	-1.3	131.2	-0.6	131.6	0.3	134.7	2.4	133.8	-0.7	135.1	1.0	137.5	1.8
1994	138.7	0.9	139.2	0.4	140.4	0.9	140.9	0.4	142.3	1.0	142.9	0.4	143.2	0.2	146.0	2.0	148.6	1.8	146.9	-1.1	149.8	2.0	149.6	-0.1
1995	147.3	-1.5	148.0	0.5	147.3	-0.5	146.6	-0.5	145.4	-0.8	141.3	-2.8	141.4	0.1	142.3	0.6	147.1	3.4	147.8	0.5	147.2	-0.4	142.2	-3.4

Source: U.S. Department of Labor, Bureau of Labor Statistics, Division of Industry Prices and Price Indexes. n.e.c. stands for not elsewhere classified. - indicates no data collected for period or unavailable.

Publications, Printed Matter & Printing Materials
Producer Price Index
Base 1982 = 100

For 1980-1995. Columns headed % show percentile change in the index from the previous period for which an index is available.

Year	Jan Index	%	Feb Index	%	Mar Index	%	Apr Index	%	May Index	%	Jun Index	%	Jul Index	%	Aug Index	%	Sep Index	%	Oct Index	%	Nov Index	%	Dec Index	%
1980	-	-	-	-	-	-	-	-	-	-	-	-	-	-	-	-	-	-	-	-	-	-	84.5	-
1981	88.5	4.7	89.1	0.7	89.5	0.4	90.5	1.1	90.5	0.0	90.6	0.1	91.6	1.1	91.8	0.2	92.7	1.0	93.3	0.6	94.1	0.9	94.5	0.4
1982	97.2	2.9	97.5	0.3	98.2	0.7	99.3	1.1	100.1	0.8	100.2	0.1	100.4	0.2	100.6	0.2	100.9	0.3	101.5	0.6	101.7	0.2	102.4	0.7
1983	104.4	2.0	104.7	0.3	105.1	0.4	105.5	0.4	105.8	0.3	106.2	0.4	106.4	0.2	106.8	0.4	106.9	0.1	107.8	0.8	108.1	0.3	108.3	0.2
1984	110.5	2.0	111.1	0.5	111.4	0.3	111.8	0.4	112.3	0.4	112.6	0.3	112.8	0.2	113.6	0.7	113.7	0.1	113.9	0.2	114.4	0.4	114.7	0.3
1985	116.8	1.8	117.4	0.5	118.0	0.5	118.2	0.2	118.3	0.1	118.5	0.2	118.8	0.3	119.2	0.3	119.2	0.0	119.8	0.5	120.0	0.2	120.0	0.0
1986	122.0	1.7	122.2	0.2	122.1	-0.1	122.7	0.5	122.9	0.2	123.0	0.1	123.2	0.2	123.4	0.2	123.9	0.4	124.4	0.4	124.7	0.2	124.8	0.1
1987	126.4	1.3	127.0	0.5	127.3	0.2	127.4	0.1	127.6	0.2	127.8	0.2	128.0	0.2	128.4	0.3	128.8	0.3	129.5	0.5	129.4	-0.1	129.6	0.2
1988	132.2	2.0	132.8	0.5	133.3	0.4	133.6	0.2	134.0	0.3	134.3	0.2	135.1	0.6	135.2	0.1	135.6	0.3	136.5	0.7	136.9	0.3	137.3	0.3
1989	139.7	1.7	140.5	0.6	140.9	0.3	141.3	0.3	141.5	0.1	142.0	0.4	142.4	0.3	142.9	0.4	143.3	0.3	143.5	0.1	143.8	0.2	143.9	0.1
1990	146.0	1.5	146.6	0.4	147.0	0.3	147.4	0.3	148.0	0.4	148.0	0.0	148.4	0.3	148.7	0.2	149.3	0.4	150.2	0.6	150.7	0.3	150.9	0.1
1991	153.5	1.7	154.1	0.4	154.5	0.3	154.4	-0.1	154.9	0.3	155.0	0.1	154.7	-0.2	155.0	0.2	154.9	-0.1	155.5	0.4	155.8	0.2	155.7	-0.1
1992	158.4	1.7	158.3	-0.1	158.7	0.3	159.0	0.2	159.4	0.3	159.2	-0.1	159.5	0.2	159.8	0.2	160.1	0.2	161.0	0.6	161.0	0.0	161.3	0.2
1993	163.8	1.5	164.3	0.3	164.3	0.0	164.8	0.3	164.9	0.1	164.2	-0.4	164.5	0.2	165.1	0.4	165.2	0.1	166.0	0.5	165.9	-0.1	166.3	0.2
1994	168.0	1.0	168.1	0.1	168.5	0.2	168.5	0.0	169.0	0.3	169.1	0.1	169.3	0.1	169.6	0.2	170.3	0.4	170.8	0.3	171.8	0.6	172.6	0.5
1995	175.3	1.6	176.3	0.6	177.0	0.4	177.9	0.5	178.6	0.4	179.8	0.7	180.8	0.6	181.1	0.2	181.6	0.3	182.0	0.2	183.4	0.8	183.9	0.3

Source: U.S. Department of Labor, Bureau of Labor Statistics, Division of Industry Prices and Price Indexes. n.e.c. stands for not elsewhere classified. - indicates no data collected for period or unavailable.

METALS AND METAL PRODUCTS
Producer Price Index
Base 1982 = 100

For 1926-1995. Columns headed % show percentile change in the index from the previous period for which an index is available.

Year	Jan Index	%	Feb Index	%	Mar Index	%	Apr Index	%	May Index	%	Jun Index	%	Jul Index	%	Aug Index	%	Sep Index	%	Oct Index	%	Nov Index	%	Dec Index	%
1926	13.9	-	13.8	-0.7	13.8	0.0	13.7	-0.7	13.6	-0.7	13.6	0.0	13.6	0.0	13.7	0.7	13.8	0.7	13.8	0.0	13.7	-0.7	13.7	0.0
1927	13.2	-3.6	13.0	-1.5	13.0	0.0	13.0	0.0	12.9	-0.8	12.8	-0.8	12.8	0.0	12.9	0.8	12.8	-0.8	12.7	-0.8	12.7	0.0	12.7	0.0
1928	12.7	0.0	12.8	0.8	12.8	0.0	12.8	0.0	12.8	0.0	12.8	0.0	12.8	0.0	12.8	0.0	12.9	0.0	13.0	0.8	13.1	0.8	13.1	0.0
1929	13.2	0.8	13.3	0.8	13.7	3.0	13.6	-0.7	13.4	-1.5	13.4	0.0	13.3	-0.7	13.3	0.0	13.3	0.0	13.3	0.0	13.2	-0.8	13.1	-0.8
1930	12.9	-1.5	12.8	-0.8	12.8	0.0	12.5	-2.3	12.2	-2.4	11.9	-2.5	11.7	-1.7	11.6	-0.9	11.6	0.0	11.4	-1.7	11.4	0.0	11.4	0.0
1931	11.2	-1.8	11.2	0.0	11.2	0.0	11.1	-0.9	10.9	-1.8	10.8	-0.9	10.7	-0.9	10.6	-0.9	10.6	0.0	10.4	-1.9	10.4	0.0	10.3	-1.0
1932	10.2	-1.0	10.0	-2.0	9.9	-1.0	9.9	0.0	9.9	0.0	9.9	0.0	9.6	-3.0	9.8	2.1	10.0	2.0	10.1	1.0	9.9	-2.0	9.8	-1.0
1933	9.7	-1.0	9.5	-2.1	9.5	0.0	9.5	0.0	9.7	2.1	10.0	3.1	10.3	3.0	10.4	1.0	10.6	1.9	10.8	1.9	10.7	-0.9	10.9	1.9
1934	10.9	0.0	11.1	1.8	11.2	0.9	11.3	0.9	11.6	2.7	11.4	-1.7	11.2	-1.8	11.2	0.0	11.2	0.0	11.1	-0.9	11.1	0.0	11.1	0.0
1935	11.1	0.0	11.1	0.0	11.1	0.0	11.1	0.0	11.2	0.9	11.2	0.0	11.2	0.0	11.2	0.0	11.3	0.9	11.6	0.9	11.7	0.9	12.0	2.6
1936	11.3	0.0	11.3	0.0	11.2	-0.9	11.2	0.0	11.2	0.0	11.2	0.0	11.4	1.8	11.4	0.0	11.5	0.9	11.6	0.9	11.7	0.9	12.0	2.6
1937	12.3	2.5	12.4	0.8	13.4	8.1	13.5	0.7	13.3	-1.5	13.3	0.0	13.3	0.0	13.4	0.8	13.3	-0.7	13.1	-1.5	12.8	-2.3	12.7	-0.8
1938	12.8	0.8	12.6	-1.6	12.6	0.0	12.7	0.8	12.8	0.8	12.6	-1.6	12.4	-1.6	12.5	0.8	12.5	0.0	12.5	0.0	12.6	0.8	12.5	-0.8
1939	12.5	0.0	12.5	0.0	12.5	0.0	12.4	-0.8	12.3	-0.8	12.3	0.0	12.3	0.0	12.3	0.0	12.6	2.4	12.7	0.8	12.7	0.0	12.7	0.0
1940	12.7	0.0	12.6	-0.8	12.6	0.0	12.4	-1.6	12.4	0.0	12.4	0.0	12.4	0.0	12.4	0.0	12.5	0.8	12.6	0.8	12.6	0.0	12.6	0.0
1941	12.6	0.0	12.6	0.0	12.7	0.8	12.7	0.0	12.7	0.0	12.8	0.8	12.8	0.0	12.8	0.0	12.8	0.0	12.8	0.0	12.9	0.8	12.9	0.0
1942	12.9	0.0	12.9	0.0	13.0	0.8	13.0	0.0	13.0	0.0	13.0	0.0	12.9	-0.8	12.9	0.0	13.0	0.8	13.0	0.0	13.0	0.0	12.9	-0.8
1943	12.9	0.0	12.9	0.0	12.9	0.0	12.9	0.0	12.9	0.0	13.0	0.8	12.9	-0.8	12.9	0.0	12.9	0.0	12.9	0.0	12.9	0.0	12.9	0.0
1944	12.9	0.0	12.9	0.0	13.0	0.8	13.0	0.0	12.9	-0.8	12.9	0.0	12.9	0.0	12.9	0.0	12.9	0.0	12.9	0.0	12.9	0.0	12.9	0.0
1945	13.0	0.8	13.0	0.0	13.0	0.0	13.0	0.0	13.0	0.0	13.1	0.8	13.1	0.0	13.1	0.0	13.2	0.8	13.2	0.0	13.3	0.8	13.3	0.0
1946	13.3	0.0	13.5	1.5	13.9	3.0	14.0	0.7	14.1	0.7	14.7	4.3	15.0	2.0	15.1	0.7	15.1	0.0	15.2	0.7	15.7	3.3	16.4	4.5
1947	17.5	6.7	17.6	0.6	17.9	1.7	18.0	0.6	17.8	-1.1	17.9	0.6	18.1	1.1	18.5	2.2	18.6	0.5	18.7	0.5	18.8	0.5	18.9	0.5
1948	19.3	2.1	19.5	1.0	19.7	1.0	20.1	2.0	20.0	-0.5	20.1	0.5	20.5	2.0	21.6	5.4	21.8	0.9	21.9	0.5	22.0	0.5	22.1	0.5
1949	22.2	0.5	21.9	-1.4	21.7	-0.9	21.1	-2.8	20.6	-2.4	20.3	-1.5	20.3	0.0	20.4	0.5	20.5	0.5	20.5	0.0	20.6	0.5	20.6	0.0
1950	20.8	1.0	20.9	0.5	20.9	0.0	21.0	0.5	21.3	1.4	21.7	1.9	21.8	0.5	22.1	1.4	22.6	2.3	23.1	2.2	23.5	1.7	24.3	3.4
1951	24.7	1.6	24.7	0.0	24.6	-0.4	24.6	0.0	24.6	0.0	24.4	-0.8	24.4	0.0	24.3	-0.4	24.3	0.0	24.4	0.4	24.4	0.0	24.4	0.0
1952	24.4	0.0	24.4	0.0	24.4	0.0	24.4	0.0	24.3	-0.4	24.1	-0.8	24.3	0.8	24.7	1.6	24.8	0.4	24.7	-0.4	24.7	0.0	24.7	0.0
1953	24.7	0.0	24.8	0.4	25.0	0.8	24.9	-0.4	25.0	0.4	25.3	1.2	25.8	2.0	25.8	0.0	25.6	-0.8	25.5	-0.4	25.5	0.0	25.4	-0.4
1954	25.4	0.0	25.2	-0.8	25.2	0.0	25.3	0.4	25.3	0.0	25.3	0.0	25.5	0.8	25.6	0.4	25.7	0.4	25.9	0.8	25.9	0.0	25.9	0.0
1955	25.9	0.0	26.2	1.2	26.3	0.4	26.5	0.8	26.4	-0.4	26.4	0.0	27.3	3.4	27.8	1.8	28.3	1.8	28.4	0.4	28.5	0.4	28.7	0.7
1956	28.9	0.7	28.9	0.0	29.2	1.0	29.4	0.7	29.2	-0.7	29.1	-0.3	28.9	-0.7	29.9	3.5	30.3	1.3	30.3	0.0	30.3	0.0	30.4	0.3
1957	30.3	-0.3	30.2	-0.3	30.1	-0.3	29.9	-0.7	29.9	0.0	30.0	0.3	30.4	1.3	30.5	0.3	30.3	-0.7	30.1	-0.7	30.0	-0.3	30.0	0.0
1958	29.9	-0.3	29.9	0.0	29.9	0.0	29.6	-1.0	29.6	0.0	29.6	0.0	29.6	0.0	30.1	1.7	30.2	0.3	30.3	0.3	30.5	0.7	30.5	0.0
1959	30.5	0.0	30.6	0.3	30.6	0.0	30.5	-0.3	30.5	0.0	30.6	0.3	30.4	-0.7	30.5	0.3	30.6	0.3	30.8	0.7	31.1	1.0	30.9	-0.6
1960	31.0	0.3	30.9	-0.3	30.8	-0.3	30.8	0.0	30.7	-0.3	30.6	-0.3	30.6	0.0	30.6	0.0	30.6	0.0	30.5	-0.3	30.4	-0.3	30.3	-0.3
1961	30.3	0.0	30.4	0.3	30.4	0.0	30.4	0.0	30.5	0.3	30.5	0.0	30.5	0.0	30.6	0.3	30.6	0.0	30.5	-0.3	30.4	-0.3	30.4	0.0
1962	30.5	0.3	30.4	-0.3	30.4	0.0	30.3	-0.3	30.3	0.0	30.2	-0.3	30.2	0.0	30.2	0.0	30.2	0.0	30.1	-0.3	30.0	-0.3	30.0	0.0
1963	30.1	0.3	30.1	0.0	30.1	0.0	30.1	0.0	30.2	0.3	30.2	0.0	30.2	0.0	30.3	0.3	30.3	0.0	30.5	0.7	30.6	0.3	30.6	0.0
1964	30.8	0.7	30.8	0.0	30.9	0.3	30.9	0.0	30.9	0.0	30.9	0.0	31.0	0.3	31.2	0.6	31.2	0.0	31.4	0.6	31.6	0.6	31.7	0.3
1965	31.6	-0.3	31.6	0.0	31.7	0.3	31.8	0.3	32.0	0.6	32.0	0.0	32.0	0.0	32.1	0.3	32.1	0.0	32.2	0.3	32.3	0.3	32.3	0.0
1966	32.4	0.3	32.5	0.3	32.7	0.6	32.7	0.0	32.8	0.3	32.9	0.3	32.9	0.0	32.8	-0.3	32.8	0.0	32.9	0.3	33.0	0.3	33.0	0.0
1967	33.1	0.3	33.2	0.3	33.1	-0.3	33.0	-0.3	33.0	0.0	33.0	0.0	33.0	0.0	33.0	0.0	33.2	0.6	33.3	0.3	33.6	0.9	33.7	0.3
1968	34.0	0.9	34.3	0.9	34.4	0.3	34.2	-0.6	33.8	-1.2	33.8	0.0	33.7	-0.3	33.7	0.0	33.9	0.6	34.0	0.3	34.0	0.0	34.1	0.3
1969	34.6	1.5	34.8	0.6	35.0	0.6	35.2	0.6	35.5	0.9	35.7	0.6	35.9	0.6	36.4	1.4	36.8	1.1	37.0	0.5	37.1	0.3	37.5	1.1
1970	37.8	0.8	38.2	1.1	38.4	0.5	38.7	0.8	38.9	0.5	39.1	0.5	39.0	-0.3	38.9	-0.3	38.9	0.0	39.0	0.3	38.7	-0.8	38.5	-0.5

[Continued]

METALS AND METAL PRODUCTS
Producer Price Index
Base 1982 = 100
[Continued]

For 1926-1995. Columns headed % show percentile change in the index from the previous period for which an index is available.

Year	Jan Index	%	Feb Index	%	Mar Index	%	Apr Index	%	May Index	%	Jun Index	%	Jul Index	%	Aug Index	%	Sep Index	%	Oct Index	%	Nov Index	%	Dec Index	%
1971	38.6	0.3	38.5	-0.3	38.5	0.0	38.9	1.0	39.1	0.5	39.2	0.3	39.5	0.8	40.1	1.5	40.1	0.0	40.0	-0.2	40.0	0.0	39.9	-0.2
1972	40.3	1.0	40.6	0.7	40.9	0.7	40.9	0.0	41.0	0.2	41.0	0.0	40.9	-0.2	41.0	0.2	41.1	0.2	41.1	0.0	41.2	0.2	41.2	0.0
1973	41.6	1.0	42.1	1.2	42.8	1.7	43.3	1.2	43.7	0.9	43.9	0.5	44.0	0.2	44.3	0.7	44.5	0.5	45.1	1.3	45.9	1.8	47.0	2.4
1974	48.1	2.3	49.1	2.1	51.3	4.5	53.4	4.1	55.9	4.7	57.7	3.2	59.8	3.6	61.5	2.8	62.0	0.8	62.0	0.0	61.9	-0.2	61.2	-1.1
1975	61.5	0.5	61.8	0.5	61.7	-0.2	61.6	-0.2	61.4	-0.3	61.2	-0.3	60.8	-0.7	61.1	0.5	61.5	0.7	62.1	1.0	62.0	-0.2	62.0	0.0
1976	62.3	0.5	62.7	0.6	63.2	0.8	64.0	1.3	64.4	0.6	65.2	1.2	65.9	1.1	66.2	0.5	66.3	0.2	66.3	0.0	66.3	0.0	66.6	0.5
1977	67.0	0.6	67.4	0.6	68.5	1.6	69.0	0.7	69.1	0.1	68.9	-0.3	69.8	-1.3	70.2	0.6	70.5	0.4	70.2	-0.4	70.3	0.1	70.7	0.6
1978	71.4	1.0	72.6	1.7	73.3	1.0	74.2	1.2	74.5	0.4	74.9	0.5	75.4	0.7	76.6	1.6	76.7	0.1	77.6	1.2	78.1	0.6	78.5	0.5
1979	80.2	2.2	82.0	2.2	83.5	1.8	84.9	1.7	84.9	0.0	85.6	0.8	86.5	1.1	86.8	0.3	87.4	0.7	89.4	2.3	89.9	0.6	90.7	0.9
1980	94.3	4.0	95.8	1.6	95.1	-0.7	94.3	-0.8	93.4	-1.0	93.5	0.1	93.7	0.2	94.5	0.9	95.3	0.8	96.8	1.6	96.5	-0.3	96.4	-0.1
1981	97.5	1.1	97.5	0.0	98.3	0.8	99.1	0.8	99.2	0.1	98.9	-0.3	100.1	1.2	100.8	0.7	101.1	0.3	101.2	0.1	100.9	-0.3	100.5	-0.4
1982	101.0	0.5	100.9	-0.1	100.4	-0.5	100.5	0.1	100.4	-0.1	99.2	-1.2	99.3	0.1	99.2	-0.1	100.0	0.8	100.0	0.0	99.6	-0.4	99.4	-0.2
1983	99.6	0.2	101.0	1.4	100.9	-0.1	101.0	0.1	101.5	0.5	101.5	0.0	101.9	0.4	102.2	0.3	103.0	0.8	103.1	0.1	103.1	0.0	103.4	0.3
1984	103.7	0.3	104.4	0.7	105.0	0.6	105.4	0.4	105.2	-0.2	105.2	0.0	104.8	-0.4	104.8	0.0	104.7	-0.1	104.8	0.1	104.9	0.1	104.6	-0.3
1985	104.4	-0.2	104.6	0.2	104.6	0.0	105.0	0.4	104.9	-0.1	104.4	-0.5	104.3	-0.1	104.3	0.0	104.2	-0.1	104.2	0.0	103.9	-0.3	103.9	0.0
1986	103.1	-0.8	103.2	0.1	103.2	0.0	103.1	-0.1	103.0	-0.1	103.0	0.0	102.9	-0.1	103.1	0.2	103.3	0.2	103.4	0.1	103.4	0.0	103.3	-0.1
1987	103.7	0.4	103.8	0.1	104.0	0.2	104.4	0.4	105.2	0.8	105.8	0.6	106.7	0.9	107.7	0.9	108.8	1.0	110.8	1.8	111.7	0.8	112.9	1.1
1988	114.4	1.3	114.7	0.3	115.4	0.6	116.9	1.3	117.4	0.4	118.0	0.5	119.2	1.0	119.8	0.5	120.2	0.3	121.4	1.0	122.8	1.2	124.0	1.0
1989	125.3	1.0	125.1	-0.2	125.6	0.4	125.6	0.0	125.2	-0.3	124.0	-1.0	123.0	-0.8	123.0	0.0	123.7	0.6	123.9	0.2	122.8	-0.9	121.7	-0.9
1990	121.7	0.0	120.9	-0.7	122.0	0.9	122.9	0.7	123.1	0.2	122.6	-0.4	122.9	0.2	124.2	1.1	124.6	0.3	124.5	-0.1	123.3	-1.0	122.4	-0.7
1991	122.4	0.0	121.9	-0.4	121.5	-0.3	121.3	-0.2	120.5	-0.7	119.7	-0.7	119.6	-0.1	119.5	-0.1	119.5	0.0	119.3	-0.2	118.9	-0.3	118.7	-0.2
1992	118.2	-0.4	118.9	0.6	119.4	0.4	119.6	0.2	119.5	-0.1	119.6	0.1	120.0	0.3	120.2	0.2	119.6	-0.5	118.8	-0.7	118.2	-0.5	118.5	0.3
1993	118.9	0.3	119.2	0.3	119.0	-0.2	118.7	-0.3	118.4	-0.3	118.9	0.4	119.5	0.5	119.5	0.0	119.5	0.0	119.4	-0.1	119.6	0.2	120.2	0.5
1994	120.7	0.4	121.7	0.8	122.3	0.5	122.5	0.2	122.7	0.2	123.5	0.7	124.7	1.0	125.5	0.6	126.5	0.8	127.3	0.6	129.4	1.6	130.6	0.9
1995	133.4	2.1	134.6	0.9	134.7	0.1	135.2	0.4	134.7	-0.4	134.8	0.1	135.2	0.3	135.5	0.2	135.0	-0.4	134.1	-0.7	133.7	-0.3	133.3	-0.3

Source: U.S. Department of Labor, Bureau of Labor Statistics, Division of Industry Prices and Price Indexes. n.e.c. stands for not elsewhere classified. - indicates no data collected for period or unavailable.

Iron and Steel

Producer Price Index
Base 1982 = 100

For 1926-1995. Columns headed % show percentile change in the index from the previous period for which an index is available.

Year	Jan Index	%	Feb Index	%	Mar Index	%	Apr Index	%	May Index	%	Jun Index	%	Jul Index	%	Aug Index	%	Sep Index	%	Oct Index	%	Nov Index	%	Dec Index	%
1926	11.4	-	11.4	0.0	11.4	0.0	11.3	-0.9	11.3	0.0	11.2	-0.9	11.2	0.0	11.2	0.0	11.3	0.9	11.3	0.0	11.3	0.0	11.2	-0.9
1927	10.9	-2.7	10.7	-1.8	10.7	0.0	10.7	0.0	10.7	0.0	10.7	0.0	10.7	0.0	10.6	-0.9	10.6	0.0	10.6	0.0	10.5	-0.9	10.5	0.0	10.4	-1.0
1928	10.5	1.0	10.6	1.0	10.6	0.0	10.6	0.0	10.6	0.0	10.5	-0.9	10.5	0.0	10.5	0.0	10.5	0.0	10.6	1.0	10.6	0.0	10.7	0.9
1929	10.7	0.0	10.7	0.0	10.7	0.0	10.8	0.9	10.8	0.0	10.8	0.0	10.8	0.0	10.7	-0.9	10.7	0.0	10.7	0.0	10.6	-0.9	10.6	0.0
1930	10.4	-1.9	10.3	-1.0	10.3	0.0	10.2	-1.0	10.2	0.0	10.1	-1.0	10.0	-1.0	9.9	-1.0	9.9	0.0	9.9	0.0	9.8	-1.0	9.8	0.0
1931	9.6	-2.0	9.7	1.0	9.6	-1.0	9.5	-1.0	9.5	0.0	9.4	-1.1	9.4	0.0	9.3	-1.1	9.3	0.0	9.2	-1.1	9.2	0.0	9.1	-1.1
1932	9.0	-1.1	9.0	0.0	9.0	0.0	9.1	1.1	9.0	-1.1	9.0	0.0	8.7	-3.3	8.9	2.3	9.0	1.1	9.1	1.1	9.0	-1.1	8.9	-1.1
1933	8.8	-1.1	8.7	-1.1	8.6	-1.1	8.6	0.0	8.5	-1.2	8.6	1.2	8.8	2.3	8.9	1.1	9.1	2.2	9.3	2.2	9.2	-1.1	9.4	2.2
1934	9.4	0.0	9.7	3.2	9.8	1.0	9.9	1.0	10.2	3.0	10.0	-2.0	9.8	-2.0	9.8	0.0	9.8	0.0	9.7	-1.0	9.7	0.0	9.7	0.0
1935	9.7	0.0	9.7	0.0	9.7	0.0	9.7	0.0	9.8	1.0	9.9	1.0	9.8	-1.0	9.9	1.0	9.8	-1.0	9.8	0.0	9.8	0.0	9.8	0.0
1936	9.9	1.0	9.8	-1.0	9.8	0.0	9.8	0.0	9.7	-1.0	9.7	0.0	9.9	2.1	9.9	0.0	10.0	1.0	10.1	1.0	10.1	0.0	10.2	1.0
1937	10.4	2.0	10.4	0.0	11.0	5.8	11.2	1.8	11.2	0.0	11.2	0.0	11.3	0.9	11.3	0.0	11.3	0.0	11.2	-0.9	11.2	0.0	11.2	0.0
1938	11.2	0.0	11.2	0.0	11.2	0.0	11.3	0.9	11.5	1.8	11.4	-0.9	11.0	-3.5	11.0	0.0	11.0	0.0	10.9	-0.9	11.0	0.9	10.9	-0.9
1939	10.9	0.0	10.9	0.0	10.9	0.0	10.9	0.0	10.8	-0.9	10.7	-0.9	10.7	0.0	10.7	0.0	10.8	0.9	10.9	0.9	10.9	0.0	10.9	0.0
1940	10.9	0.0	10.9	0.0	10.9	0.0	10.6	-2.8	10.6	0.0	10.6	0.0	10.7	0.9	10.7	0.0	10.7	0.0	10.7	0.0	10.8	0.9	10.8	0.0
1941	10.8	0.0	10.8	0.0	10.8	0.0	10.8	0.0	10.9	0.9	10.9	0.0	10.9	0.0	11.0	0.9	11.0	0.0	11.0	0.0	11.0	0.0	11.0	0.0
1942	11.0	0.0	11.0	0.0	11.0	0.0	11.0	0.0	11.0	0.0	11.0	0.0	11.0	0.0	11.0	0.0	11.0	0.0	11.0	0.0	11.0	0.0	11.0	0.0
1943	11.0	0.0	11.0	0.0	11.0	0.0	11.0	0.0	11.0	0.0	11.0	0.0	11.0	0.0	11.0	0.0	11.0	0.0	11.0	0.0	11.0	0.0	11.0	0.0
1944	11.0	0.0	11.0	0.0	11.0	0.0	11.0	0.0	11.0	0.0	11.0	0.0	11.0	0.0	11.0	0.0	11.0	0.0	11.0	0.0	11.0	0.0	11.0	0.0
1945	11.1	0.9	11.1	0.0	11.1	0.0	11.1	0.0	11.1	0.0	11.2	0.9	11.2	0.0	11.2	0.0	11.2	0.0	11.3	0.9	11.3	0.0	11.4	0.9
1946	11.4	0.0	11.7	2.6	12.1	3.4	12.1	0.0	12.2	0.8	12.4	1.6	12.6	1.6	12.8	1.6	12.8	0.0	12.8	0.0	12.9	0.8	13.3	3.1
1947	14.4	8.3	14.5	0.7	14.7	1.4	14.7	0.0	14.4	-2.0	14.5	0.7	14.9	2.8	15.8	6.0	15.7	-0.6	15.9	1.3	15.9	0.0	16.0	0.6
1948	16.5	3.1	16.7	1.2	16.8	0.6	16.9	0.6	16.8	-0.6	16.8	0.0	17.2	2.4	18.5	7.6	18.5	0.0	18.6	0.5	18.7	0.5	18.8	0.5
1949	18.8	0.0	18.4	-2.1	18.3	-0.5	17.7	-3.3	17.4	-1.7	17.4	0.0	17.3	-0.6	17.4	0.6	17.7	1.7	17.8	0.6	17.9	0.6	18.1	1.1
1950	18.3	1.1	18.5	1.1	18.5	0.0	18.5	0.0	18.7	1.1	19.1	2.1	19.0	-0.5	19.2	1.1	19.3	0.5	19.4	0.5	19.6	1.0	20.6	5.1
1951	21.0	1.9	20.8	-1.0	20.7	-0.5	20.7	0.0	20.7	0.0	20.7	0.0	20.7	0.0	20.7	0.0	20.7	0.0	20.7	0.0	20.7	0.0	20.7	0.0
1952	20.7	0.0	20.8	0.5	20.8	0.0	20.7	-0.5	20.7	0.0	20.6	-0.5	20.6	0.0	21.4	3.9	21.5	0.5	21.4	-0.5	21.4	0.0	21.4	0.0
1953	21.4	0.0	21.5	0.5	21.5	0.0	21.5	0.0	21.7	0.9	22.0	1.4	22.9	4.1	22.9	0.0	22.7	-0.9	22.5	-0.9	22.5	0.0	22.4	-0.4
1954	22.2	-0.9	22.1	-0.5	22.0	-0.5	22.1	0.5	22.2	0.5	22.2	0.0	22.5	1.4	22.5	0.0	22.6	0.4	22.7	0.4	22.8	0.4	22.7	-0.4
1955	22.9	0.9	22.9	0.0	22.9	0.0	23.0	0.4	22.8	-0.9	22.9	0.4	24.1	5.2	24.4	1.2	24.4	0.0	24.5	0.4	24.6	0.4	24.8	0.8
1956	25.2	1.6	25.1	-0.4	25.2	0.4	25.4	0.8	25.4	0.0	25.2	-0.8	25.2	0.0	26.8	6.3	27.2	1.5	27.1	-0.4	27.4	1.1	27.5	0.4
1957	27.7	0.7	27.6	-0.4	27.6	0.0	27.3	-1.1	27.5	0.7	27.9	1.5	28.7	2.9	28.8	0.3	28.7	-0.3	28.3	-1.4	28.1	-0.7	28.1	0.0
1958	28.1	0.0	28.3	0.7	28.2	-0.4	28.1	-0.4	28.0	-0.4	28.1	0.4	28.1	0.0	28.9	2.8	28.9	0.0	28.9	0.0	29.0	0.3	28.9	-0.3
1959	29.0	0.3	29.1	0.3	29.0	-0.3	28.8	-0.7	28.7	-0.3	28.9	0.7	28.9	0.0	29.0	0.3	29.1	0.3	29.1	0.0	29.2	0.3	29.0	-0.7
1960	29.1	0.3	28.9	-0.7	28.7	-0.7	28.7	0.0	28.7	0.0	28.6	-0.3	28.6	0.0	28.6	0.0	28.6	0.0	28.4	-0.7	28.4	0.0	28.4	0.0
1961	28.5	0.4	28.6	0.4	28.7	0.3	28.8	0.3	28.7	-0.3	28.7	0.0	28.6	-0.3	28.7	0.3	28.8	0.3	28.7	-0.3	28.5	-0.7	28.5	0.0
1962	28.6	0.4	28.6	0.0	28.4	-0.7	28.3	-0.4	28.3	0.0	28.2	-0.4	28.2	0.0	28.2	0.0	28.2	0.0	28.1	-0.4	28.0	-0.4	28.1	0.4
1963	28.1	0.0	28.1	0.0	28.0	-0.4	28.1	0.4	28.3	0.7	28.2	-0.4	28.2	0.0	28.2	0.0	28.2	0.0	28.4	0.7	28.4	0.0	28.5	0.4
1964	28.5	0.0	28.5	0.0	28.5	0.0	28.5	0.0	28.6	0.4	28.6	0.0	28.7	0.3	28.8	0.3	28.6	-0.7	28.7	0.3	28.7	0.0	28.8	0.3
1965	28.9	0.3	28.8	-0.3	28.8	0.0	28.9	0.3	28.9	0.0	28.8	-0.3	28.9	0.3	28.9	0.0	28.8	-0.3	28.8	0.0	28.8	0.0	29.0	0.7
1966	29.1	0.3	29.1	0.0	29.1	0.0	29.1	0.0	29.0	-0.3	29.1	0.3	29.1	0.0	29.2	0.3	29.2	0.0	29.2	0.0	29.3	0.3	29.3	0.0
1967	29.4	0.3	29.4	0.0	29.5	0.3	29.4	-0.3	29.4	0.0	29.4	0.0	29.4	0.0	29.4	0.0	29.6	0.7	29.6	0.0	29.7	0.3	29.8	0.3
1968	30.1	1.0	30.1	0.0	30.0	-0.3	29.9	-0.3	29.9	0.0	29.9	0.0	29.9	0.0	29.9	0.0	30.4	1.7	30.4	0.0	30.2	-0.7	30.2	0.0
1969	30.6	1.3	30.7	0.3	30.9	0.7	31.0	0.3	31.3	1.0	31.4	0.3	31.6	0.6	32.1	1.6	32.2	0.3	32.4	0.6	32.4	0.0	32.5	0.3
1970	32.7	0.6	33.3	1.8	33.5	0.6	33.4	-0.3	33.9	1.5	34.3	1.2	34.3	0.0	34.2	-0.3	34.4	0.6	34.6	0.6	34.3	-0.9	34.3	0.0

[Continued]

Iron and Steel
Producer Price Index
Base 1982 = 100

[Continued]

For 1926-1995. Columns headed % show percentile change in the index from the previous period for which an index is available.

Year	Jan Index	%	Feb Index	%	Mar Index	%	Apr Index	%	May Index	%	Jun Index	%	Jul Index	%	Aug Index	%	Sep Index	%	Oct Index	%	Nov Index	%	Dec Index	%
1971	34.6	0.9	34.8	0.6	34.8	0.0	34.9	0.3	35.4	1.4	35.5	0.3	36.0	1.4	37.0	2.8	37.1	0.3	37.1	0.0	37.0	-0.3	37.0	0.0
1972	37.4	1.1	37.8	1.1	37.9	0.3	37.8	-0.3	37.8	0.0	37.8	0.0	37.8	0.0	37.9	0.3	38.0	0.3	38.0	0.0	38.1	0.3	38.2	0.3
1973	38.9	1.8	39.2	0.8	39.3	0.3	39.5	0.5	39.9	1.0	40.1	0.5	40.1	0.0	40.1	0.0	40.3	0.5	40.9	1.5	41.8	2.2	42.0	0.5
1974	42.7	1.7	43.9	2.8	46.5	5.9	48.6	4.5	49.9	2.7	52.5	5.2	56.2	7.0	57.7	2.7	58.4	1.2	58.7	0.5	58.9	0.3	58.0	-1.5
1975	58.8	1.4	59.1	0.5	59.2	0.2	59.3	0.2	59.2	-0.2	58.8	-0.7	58.2	-1.0	58.5	0.5	59.1	1.0	60.4	2.2	60.2	-0.3	60.3	0.2
1976	60.8	0.8	61.8	1.6	62.4	1.0	62.9	0.8	62.9	0.0	64.4	2.4	64.9	0.8	64.9	0.0	64.5	-0.6	64.5	0.0	64.6	0.2	65.7	1.7
1977	66.1	0.6	66.3	0.3	67.1	1.2	67.3	0.3	67.2	-0.1	66.9	-0.4	68.5	2.4	68.8	0.4	69.6	1.2	69.1	-0.7	68.9	-0.3	69.5	0.9
1978	70.2	1.0	72.2	2.8	73.0	1.1	74.3	1.8	74.3	0.0	74.5	0.3	74.9	0.5	76.3	1.9	76.3	0.0	76.7	0.5	77.2	0.7	77.6	0.5
1979	80.3	3.5	81.1	1.0	82.6	1.8	82.6	0.0	82.4	-0.2	83.5	1.3	84.6	1.3	84.4	-0.2	84.2	-0.2	85.3	1.3	86.1	0.9	86.4	0.3
1980	87.7	1.5	88.6	1.0	89.0	0.5	90.6	1.8	89.9	-0.8	89.5	-0.4	88.7	-0.9	89.3	0.7	89.8	0.6	91.6	2.0	92.2	0.7	93.3	1.2
1981	95.3	2.1	95.3	0.0	96.8	1.6	97.6	0.8	97.5	-0.1	97.4	-0.1	99.9	2.6	100.3	0.4	100.2	-0.1	100.7	0.5	100.3	-0.4	100.3	0.0
1982	101.2	0.9	101.1	-0.1	101.0	-0.1	101.1	0.1	100.7	-0.4	99.8	-0.9	99.5	-0.3	99.4	-0.1	99.3	-0.1	99.6	0.3	99.1	-0.5	98.2	-0.9
1983	98.3	0.1	100.3	2.0	100.8	0.5	100.7	-0.1	100.6	-0.1	100.7	0.1	100.9	0.2	101.2	0.3	102.7	1.5	102.8	0.1	103.1	0.3	103.5	0.4
1984	104.4	0.9	105.1	0.7	105.1	0.0	105.1	0.0	105.4	0.3	105.3	-0.1	105.4	0.1	105.4	0.0	105.6	0.2	105.7	0.1	105.5	-0.2	105.3	-0.2
1985	105.3	0.0	105.4	0.1	105.5	0.1	105.4	-0.1	105.0	-0.4	104.6	-0.4	104.5	-0.1	104.6	0.1	104.6	0.0	104.5	-0.1	104.1	-0.4	104.1	0.0
1986	101.0	-3.0	101.1	0.1	100.8	-0.3	101.0	0.2	101.2	0.2	101.1	-0.1	101.1	0.0	101.2	0.1	101.4	0.2	101.4	0.0	101.3	-0.1	101.3	0.0
1987	102.0	0.7	102.3	0.3	101.9	-0.4	101.9	0.0	102.2	0.3	102.5	0.3	103.1	0.6	103.7	0.6	105.4	1.6	109.5	3.9	110.4	0.8	109.9	-0.5
1988	110.9	0.9	113.0	1.9	113.6	0.5	114.8	1.1	115.0	0.2	114.9	-0.1	117.0	1.8	118.0	0.9	117.4	-0.5	118.3	0.8	117.6	-0.6	117.6	0.0
1989	119.7	1.8	120.6	0.8	120.7	0.1	120.8	0.1	120.6	-0.2	119.8	-0.7	119.0	-0.7	118.4	-0.5	118.1	-0.3	117.8	-0.3	116.9	-0.8	116.5	-0.3
1990	116.7	0.2	116.2	-0.4	116.5	0.3	117.1	0.5	117.9	0.7	117.4	-0.4	117.5	0.1	118.2	0.6	117.9	-0.3	117.5	-0.3	116.9	-0.5	116.8	-0.1
1991	117.0	0.2	116.6	-0.3	115.8	-0.7	115.4	-0.3	114.5	-0.8	113.5	-0.9	113.3	-0.2	113.0	-0.3	112.8	-0.2	112.4	-0.4	112.3	-0.1	112.3	0.0
1992	112.1	-0.2	112.3	0.2	112.7	0.4	112.3	-0.4	112.2	-0.1	111.4	-0.7	111.4	0.0	111.2	-0.2	111.0	-0.2	110.3	-0.6	110.1	-0.2	110.6	0.5
1993	111.9	1.2	113.1	1.1	113.4	0.3	113.5	0.1	114.2	0.6	115.6	1.2	116.5	0.8	116.7	0.2	117.3	0.5	119.0	1.4	119.9	0.8	120.8	0.8
1994	121.3	0.4	122.0	0.6	121.8	-0.2	121.4	-0.3	120.6	-0.7	118.8	-1.5	120.4	1.3	122.3	1.6	123.1	0.7	123.1	0.0	124.1	0.8	124.7	0.5
1995	127.2	2.0	128.4	0.9	129.1	0.5	129.8	0.5	129.9	0.1	129.7	-0.2	129.9	0.2	130.4	0.4	129.3	-0.8	128.4	-0.7	127.1	-1.0	126.4	-0.6

Source: U.S. Department of Labor, Bureau of Labor Statistics, Division of Industry Prices and Price Indexes. n.e.c. stands for not elsewhere classified. - indicates no data collected for period or unavailable.

Nonferrous Metals
Producer Price Index
Base 1982 = 100

For 1926-1995. Columns headed % show percentile change in the index from the previous period for which an index is available.

Year	Jan Index	%	Feb Index	%	Mar Index	%	Apr Index	%	May Index	%	Jun Index	%	Jul Index	%	Aug Index	%	Sep Index	%	Oct Index	%	Nov Index	%	Dec Index	%
1926	16.8	-	16.8	0.0	16.6	-1.2	16.2	-2.4	16.0	-1.2	16.1	0.6	16.5	2.5	16.8	1.8	16.8	0.0	16.6	-1.2	16.4	-1.2	16.0	-2.4
1927	15.7	-1.9	15.5	-1.3	15.8	1.9	15.5	-1.9	15.2	-1.9	15.0	-1.3	14.9	-0.7	15.4	3.4	15.1	-1.9	15.0	-0.7	15.1	0.7	15.4	2.0
1928	15.3	-0.6	15.1	-1.3	15.0	-0.7	15.2	1.3	15.3	0.7	15.4	0.7	15.4	0.0	15.4	0.0	15.6	1.3	15.9	1.9	16.2	1.9	16.2	0.0
1929	16.7	3.1	17.4	4.2	19.3	10.9	18.6	-3.6	17.4	-6.5	17.4	0.0	17.4	0.0	17.4	0.0	17.3	-0.6	17.3	0.0	17.0	-1.7	16.8	-1.2
1930	16.7	-0.6	16.7	0.0	16.4	-1.8	15.1	-7.9	13.5	-10.6	13.2	-2.2	12.4	-6.1	12.3	-0.8	12.1	-1.6	11.5	-5.0	11.6	0.9	11.8	1.7
1931	11.5	-2.5	11.3	-1.7	11.4	0.9	11.1	-2.6	10.4	-6.3	10.1	-2.9	10.1	0.0	9.9	-2.0	9.7	-2.0	9.1	-6.2	9.0	-1.1	8.9	-1.1
1932	9.1	2.2	8.7	-4.4	8.3	-4.6	8.1	-2.4	7.9	-2.5	7.9	0.0	7.7	-2.5	8.0	3.9	8.5	6.3	8.3	-2.4	8.1	-2.4	7.9	-2.5
1933	7.7	-2.5	7.6	-1.3	7.9	3.9	8.1	2.5	9.3	14.8	10.4	11.8	11.2	7.7	11.2	0.0	11.3	0.9	11.0	-2.7	11.2	1.8	11.0	-1.8
1934	10.9	-0.9	10.8	-0.9	10.9	0.9	11.2	2.8	11.2	0.0	11.3	0.9	11.3	0.0	11.3	0.0	11.3	0.0	11.3	0.0	11.2	-0.9	11.1	-0.9
1935	11.2	0.9	11.1	-0.9	11.1	0.0	11.2	0.9	11.4	1.8	11.4	0.0	10.9	-4.4	11.0	0.9	11.3	2.7	11.7	3.5	11.8	0.9	11.6	-1.7
1936	11.5	-0.9	11.5	0.0	11.5	0.0	11.6	0.9	11.7	0.9	11.5	-1.7	11.6	0.9	11.7	0.9	11.8	0.9	11.8	0.0	12.4	5.1	13.0	4.8
1937	14.0	7.7	14.8	5.7	16.7	12.8	16.0	-4.2	15.1	-5.6	15.1	0.0	15.3	1.3	15.4	0.7	15.3	-0.6	14.1	-7.8	12.9	-8.5	12.4	-3.9
1938	12.4	0.0	11.9	-4.0	11.8	-0.8	11.7	-0.8	11.3	-3.4	11.1	-1.8	11.8	6.3	12.0	1.7	12.1	0.8	12.6	4.1	12.8	1.6	12.7	-0.8
1939	12.6	-0.8	12.6	0.0	12.6	0.0	12.3	-2.4	12.1	-1.6	12.0	-0.8	12.1	0.8	12.3	1.7	14.0	13.8	14.1	0.7	14.0	-0.7	13.9	-0.7
1940	13.6	-2.2	13.0	-4.4	13.2	1.5	13.0	-1.5	13.2	1.5	13.4	1.5	13.4	0.0	13.0	-3.0	13.3	2.3	13.8	3.8	13.8	0.0	13.7	-0.7
1941	13.8	0.7	13.8	0.0	13.9	0.7	13.9	0.0	13.9	0.0	13.9	0.0	14.0	0.7	13.9	-0.7	13.9	0.0	13.9	0.0	14.0	0.7	14.0	0.0
1942	14.1	0.7	14.1	0.0	14.1	0.0	14.1	0.0	14.1	0.0	14.1	0.0	14.1	0.0	14.1	0.0	14.2	0.7	14.2	0.0	14.2	0.0	14.2	0.0
1943	14.2	0.0	14.2	0.0	14.2	0.0	14.2	0.0	14.2	0.0	14.2	0.0	14.2	0.0	14.2	0.0	14.2	0.0	14.2	0.0	14.2	0.0	14.2	0.0
1944	14.1	-0.7	14.1	0.0	14.1	0.0	14.1	0.0	14.1	0.0	14.1	0.0	14.1	0.0	14.1	0.0	14.1	0.0	14.1	0.0	14.1	0.0	14.1	0.0
1945	14.1	0.0	14.2	0.7	14.1	-0.7	14.1	0.0	14.1	0.0	14.1	0.0	14.1	0.0	14.1	0.0	14.1	0.0	14.1	0.0	14.1	0.0	14.1	0.0
1946	14.1	0.0	14.1	0.0	14.2	0.7	14.4	1.4	14.6	1.4	16.4	12.3	16.9	3.0	16.7	-1.2	16.7	0.0	16.8	0.6	19.5	16.1	21.3	9.2
1947	21.5	0.9	21.7	0.9	22.6	4.1	22.8	0.9	22.8	0.0	22.7	-0.4	22.5	-0.9	22.5	0.0	22.5	0.0	22.5	0.0	22.5	0.0	22.8	1.3
1948	23.0	0.9	23.2	0.9	23.2	0.0	23.6	1.7	23.6	0.0	23.9	1.3	24.6	2.9	26.1	6.1	26.1	0.0	26.3	0.8	27.0	2.7	27.1	0.4
1949	27.0	-0.4	26.8	-0.7	26.1	-2.6	24.4	-6.5	22.4	-8.2	21.2	-5.4	21.4	0.9	21.9	2.3	21.9	0.0	21.5	-1.8	21.7	0.9	21.4	-1.4
1950	21.4	0.0	21.3	-0.5	21.2	-0.5	21.4	0.9	22.4	4.7	23.9	6.7	24.1	0.8	24.9	3.3	26.4	6.0	27.9	5.7	28.9	3.6	29.1	0.7
1951	29.6	1.7	29.7	0.3	29.4	-1.0	29.5	0.3	29.4	-0.3	28.9	-1.7	28.5	-1.4	28.5	0.0	28.6	0.4	29.1	1.7	29.1	0.0	29.1	0.0
1952	29.1	0.0	29.3	0.7	29.3	0.0	29.3	0.0	28.6	-2.4	28.1	-1.7	29.1	3.6	29.2	0.3	29.2	0.0	28.8	-1.4	28.8	0.0	28.7	-0.3
1953	28.8	0.3	29.2	1.4	30.8	5.5	30.1	-2.3	29.7	-1.3	29.9	0.7	29.7	-0.7	29.2	-1.7	28.8	-1.4	28.6	-0.7	28.7	0.3	28.6	-0.3
1954	28.5	-0.3	28.1	-1.4	28.4	1.1	28.9	1.8	29.0	0.3	29.0	0.0	29.1	0.3	29.3	0.7	29.6	1.0	29.9	1.0	29.9	0.0	29.9	0.0
1955	30.0	0.3	31.4	4.7	31.5	0.3	32.4	2.9	32.3	-0.3	32.3	0.0	32.7	1.2	34.0	4.0	36.2	6.5	36.1	-0.3	36.1	0.0	36.6	1.4
1956	36.8	0.5	36.9	0.3	38.0	3.0	38.3	0.8	37.5	-2.1	37.1	-1.1	35.8	-3.5	36.5	2.0	36.3	-0.5	36.2	-0.3	35.1	-3.0	35.1	0.0
1957	34.9	-0.6	34.1	-2.3	33.6	-1.5	33.4	-0.6	32.8	-1.8	32.4	-1.2	31.5	-2.8	31.6	0.3	30.9	-2.2	30.5	-1.3	30.7	0.7	30.6	-0.3
1958	30.2	-1.3	30.0	-0.7	29.8	-0.7	29.1	-2.3	29.1	0.0	29.3	0.7	29.3	0.0	29.6	1.0	29.9	1.0	30.7	2.7	31.4	2.3	31.3	-0.3
1959	31.3	0.0	31.5	0.6	31.9	1.3	31.6	-0.9	31.9	0.9	31.9	0.0	31.4	-1.6	31.4	0.0	31.9	1.6	32.2	0.9	33.1	2.8	33.0	-0.3
1960	33.5	1.5	33.5	0.0	33.0	-1.5	32.9	-0.3	32.9	0.0	32.6	-0.9	32.5	-0.3	32.5	0.0	32.5	0.0	32.2	-0.9	31.8	-1.2	31.4	-1.3
1961	31.0	-1.3	31.0	0.0	31.0	0.0	31.1	0.3	31.5	1.3	31.7	0.6	31.9	0.6	31.9	0.0	32.0	0.3	31.7	-0.9	31.4	-0.9	31.6	0.6
1962	31.5	-0.3	31.5	0.0	31.4	-0.3	31.3	-0.3	31.3	0.0	31.1	-0.6	31.1	0.0	31.1	0.0	31.0	-0.3	30.7	-1.0	30.8	0.3	30.7	-0.3
1963	30.8	0.3	30.8	0.0	30.8	0.0	30.8	0.0	31.0	0.6	31.0	0.0	31.1	0.3	31.2	0.3	31.3	0.3	31.3	0.0	31.4	0.3	31.7	1.0
1964	31.8	0.3	31.9	0.3	32.2	0.9	32.6	1.2	32.6	0.0	32.6	0.0	32.8	0.6	33.2	1.2	33.6	1.2	34.6	3.0	35.1	1.4	35.5	1.1
1965	35.0	-1.4	35.1	0.3	35.2	0.3	35.6	1.1	36.2	1.7	36.5	0.8	36.2	-0.8	36.6	1.1	36.7	0.3	36.8	0.3	37.3	1.4	36.8	-1.3
1966	37.1	0.8	37.5	1.1	37.9	1.1	38.3	1.1	38.4	0.3	38.7	0.8	38.6	-0.3	37.8	-2.1	37.6	-0.5	37.7	0.3	38.0	0.8	37.8	-0.5
1967	38.2	1.1	38.4	0.5	38.0	-1.0	37.7	-0.8	37.3	-1.1	37.3	0.0	37.2	-0.3	37.3	0.3	37.5	0.5	38.0	1.3	39.0	2.6	39.5	1.3
1968	40.0	1.3	41.1	2.8	41.8	1.7	40.9	-2.2	38.8	-5.1	38.7	-0.3	38.3	-1.0	38.1	-0.5	38.0	-0.3	38.2	0.5	38.3	0.3	38.7	1.0
1969	39.8	2.8	40.4	1.5	40.7	0.7	41.5	2.0	42.0	1.2	42.5	1.2	42.6	0.2	43.7	2.6	45.0	3.0	45.4	0.9	45.9	1.1	47.0	2.4
1970	48.0	2.1	48.0	0.0	48.2	0.4	49.3	2.3	49.3	0.0	48.6	-1.4	47.8	-1.6	47.2	-1.3	46.4	-1.7	46.1	-0.6	45.0	-2.4	44.0	-2.2

[Continued]

Nonferrous Metals
Producer Price Index
Base 1982 = 100
[Continued]

For 1926-1995. Columns headed % show percentile change in the index from the previous period for which an index is available.

Year	Jan Index	%	Feb Index	%	Mar Index	%	Apr Index	%	May Index	%	Jun Index	%	Jul Index	%	Aug Index	%	Sep Index	%	Oct Index	%	Nov Index	%	Dec Index	%
1971	43.3	-1.6	42.8	-1.2	42.6	-0.5	44.0	3.3	43.9	-0.2	43.6	-0.7	43.7	0.2	43.9	0.5	43.7	-0.5	43.6	-0.2	43.5	-0.2	43.1	-0.9
1972	43.4	0.7	43.6	0.5	44.5	2.1	44.6	0.2	44.7	0.2	44.6	-0.2	44.3	-0.7	44.3	0.0	44.5	0.5	44.5	0.0	44.5	0.0	44.5	0.0
1973	44.7	0.4	45.9	2.7	48.7	6.1	49.8	2.3	50.5	1.4	51.2	1.4	51.5	0.6	52.3	1.6	52.6	0.6	53.4	1.5	55.0	3.0	59.0	7.3
1974	61.1	3.6	62.6	2.5	66.9	6.9	70.8	5.8	76.0	7.3	76.0	0.0	75.3	-0.9	76.0	0.9	74.7	-1.7	72.4	-3.1	71.0	-1.9	69.0	-2.8
1975	67.8	-1.7	66.8	-1.5	66.0	-1.2	65.3	-1.1	64.9	-0.6	64.2	-1.1	63.6	-0.9	64.2	0.9	64.8	0.9	64.8	0.0	64.5	-0.5	64.3	-0.3
1976	64.1	-0.3	64.4	0.5	65.2	1.2	67.4	3.4	68.9	2.2	69.5	0.9	71.0	2.2	71.3	0.4	72.0	1.0	71.5	-0.7	71.1	-0.6	70.2	-1.3
1977	70.7	0.7	71.9	1.7	74.3	3.3	75.9	2.2	76.2	0.4	74.8	-1.8	75.1	0.4	75.3	0.3	74.0	-1.7	73.4	-0.8	73.7	0.4	74.0	0.4
1978	75.1	1.5	75.8	0.9	76.3	0.7	77.0	0.9	77.1	0.1	77.9	1.0	78.1	0.3	80.1	2.6	80.2	0.1	82.4	2.7	82.8	0.5	83.1	0.4
1979	84.8	2.0	90.7	7.0	93.6	3.2	98.5	5.2	98.0	-0.5	98.5	0.5	99.5	1.0	99.8	0.3	102.2	2.4	107.4	5.1	107.8	0.4	110.7	2.7
1980	123.8	11.8	128.1	3.5	121.9	-4.8	113.2	-7.1	109.9	-2.9	109.6	-0.3	111.0	1.3	113.2	2.0	114.6	1.2	117.4	2.4	114.6	-2.4	111.3	-2.9
1981	110.8	-0.4	109.0	-1.6	108.7	-0.3	109.4	0.6	109.1	-0.3	107.9	-1.1	107.3	-0.6	109.0	1.6	109.8	0.7	108.3	-1.4	106.6	-1.6	105.1	-1.4
1982	104.1	-1.0	103.8	-0.3	101.4	-2.3	100.9	-0.5	100.0	-0.9	96.1	-3.9	97.3	1.2	97.0	-0.3	100.6	3.7	99.7	-0.9	99.3	-0.4	99.8	0.5
1983	101.3	1.5	104.6	3.3	102.6	-1.9	103.1	0.5	105.3	2.1	104.6	-0.7	105.6	1.0	106.1	0.5	107.0	0.8	106.0	-0.9	104.9	-1.0	105.5	0.6
1984	105.0	-0.5	106.3	1.2	108.6	2.2	109.7	1.0	107.8	-1.7	107.3	-0.5	105.1	-2.1	104.4	-0.7	103.1	-1.2	101.2	-1.8	102.2	1.0	100.9	-1.3
1985	99.9	-1.0	100.5	0.6	99.6	-0.9	101.8	2.2	101.7	-0.1	100.0	-1.7	99.2	-0.8	99.2	0.0	98.9	-0.3	98.6	-0.3	97.8	-0.8	97.6	-0.2
1986	98.5	0.9	98.6	0.1	99.3	0.7	98.5	-0.8	97.9	-0.6	98.2	0.3	97.6	-0.6	98.2	0.6	98.7	0.5	99.0	0.3	98.9	-0.1	98.5	-0.4
1987	99.1	0.6	99.1	0.0	100.2	1.1	101.8	1.6	104.6	2.8	106.0	1.3	109.1	2.9	112.0	2.7	114.2	2.0	116.7	2.2	118.5	1.5	124.1	4.7
1988	127.5	2.7	124.8	-2.1	125.7	0.7	128.9	2.5	129.3	0.3	131.7	1.9	132.8	0.8	132.9	0.1	134.8	1.4	137.8	2.2	144.0	4.5	148.3	3.0
1989	149.9	1.1	147.1	-1.9	148.2	0.7	147.2	-0.7	144.6	-1.8	140.1	-3.1	136.3	-2.7	136.9	0.4	139.5	1.9	140.2	0.5	136.5	-2.6	131.9	-3.4
1990	130.9	-0.8	127.9	-2.3	131.8	3.0	134.5	2.0	134.0	-0.4	132.1	-1.4	133.2	0.8	137.3	3.1	139.0	1.2	139.2	0.1	134.8	-3.2	130.6	-3.1
1991	129.6	-0.8	128.1	-1.2	127.2	-0.7	126.5	-0.6	124.2	-1.8	121.6	-2.1	120.9	-0.6	121.2	0.2	121.3	0.1	121.1	-0.2	120.2	-0.7	118.9	-1.1
1992	117.1	-1.5	119.4	2.0	121.0	1.3	121.5	0.4	121.6	0.1	122.8	1.0	124.0	1.0	125.2	1.0	122.9	-1.8	120.0	-2.4	117.6	-2.0	117.9	0.3
1993	119.1	1.0	118.8	-0.3	117.5	-1.1	115.7	-1.5	113.2	-2.2	113.5	0.3	114.6	1.0	114.7	0.1	113.4	-1.1	111.1	-2.0	110.2	-0.8	111.5	1.2
1994	112.8	1.2	116.2	3.0	118.5	2.0	119.1	0.5	120.5	1.2	125.2	3.9	128.1	2.3	128.8	0.5	131.2	1.9	134.0	2.1	140.5	4.9	144.5	2.8
1995	151.2	4.6	152.8	1.1	151.5	-0.9	152.1	0.4	149.1	-2.0	149.4	0.2	150.3	0.6	150.8	0.3	149.4	-0.9	146.8	-1.7	146.2	-0.4	145.4	-0.5

Source: U.S. Department of Labor, Bureau of Labor Statistics, Division of Industry Prices and Price Indexes. n.e.c. stands for not elsewhere classified. - indicates no data collected for period or unavailable.

Metal Containers
Producer Price Index
Base 1982 = 100

For 1926-1995. Columns headed % show percentile change in the index from the previous period for which an index is available.

Year	Jan Index	%	Feb Index	%	Mar Index	%	Apr Index	%	May Index	%	Jun Index	%	Jul Index	%	Aug Index	%	Sep Index	%	Oct Index	%	Nov Index	%	Dec Index	%
1926	15.2	-	15.2	0.0	15.2	0.0	15.2	0.0	15.2	0.0	15.2	0.0	15.2	0.0	15.2	0.0	15.2	0.0	15.2	0.0	15.2	0.0	15.2	0.0
1927	15.2	0.0	15.2	0.0	15.2	0.0	15.2	0.0	15.2	0.0	15.2	0.0	15.2	0.0	15.2	0.0	15.2	0.0	15.2	0.0	15.2	0.0	15.2	0.0
1928	14.7	-3.3	14.7	0.0	14.7	0.0	14.7	0.0	14.7	0.0	14.7	0.0	14.7	0.0	14.7	0.0	14.7	0.0	14.7	0.0	14.7	0.0	14.7	0.0
1929	14.9	1.4	14.9	0.0	14.9	0.0	14.9	0.0	14.9	0.0	14.9	0.0	14.9	0.0	14.9	0.0	14.9	0.0	14.9	0.0	14.9	0.0	14.9	0.0
1930	14.7	-1.3	14.7	0.0	14.7	0.0	14.7	0.0	14.7	0.0	14.7	0.0	14.7	0.0	14.7	0.0	14.6	-0.7	14.6	0.0	14.6	0.0	14.6	0.0
1931	14.2	-2.7	14.2	0.0	14.1	-0.7	14.1	0.0	14.1	0.0	14.1	0.0	14.0	-0.7	14.0	0.0	14.0	0.0	14.0	0.0	14.0	0.0	14.0	0.0
1932	13.5	-3.6	13.5	0.0	13.5	0.0	13.5	0.0	13.5	0.0	13.5	0.0	13.5	0.0	13.5	0.0	13.5	0.0	13.5	0.0	13.5	0.0	13.5	0.0
1933	12.6	-6.7	12.6	0.0	12.6	0.0	12.6	0.0	12.6	0.0	12.6	0.0	12.6	0.0	12.6	0.0	12.6	0.0	12.7	0.8	12.7	0.0	12.7	0.0
1934	14.4	13.4	14.4	0.0	14.4	0.0	14.5	0.7	14.5	0.0	14.5	0.0	14.5	0.0	14.5	0.0	14.5	0.0	14.5	0.0	14.5	0.0	14.5	0.0
1935	14.4	-0.7	14.4	0.0	14.4	0.0	14.4	0.0	14.4	0.0	14.4	0.0	14.4	0.0	14.4	0.0	14.4	0.0	14.4	0.0	14.4	0.0	14.4	0.0
1936	14.4	0.0	14.4	0.0	14.4	0.0	14.4	0.0	14.4	0.0	14.4	0.0	14.4	0.0	14.4	0.0	14.4	0.0	14.6	1.4	14.6	0.0	14.6	0.0
1937	13.4	-8.2	13.4	0.0	13.4	0.0	13.5	0.7	13.5	0.0	13.5	0.0	13.5	0.0	13.5	0.0	13.5	0.0	13.5	0.0	13.5	0.0	13.5	0.0
1938	14.4	6.7	14.4	0.0	14.4	0.0	14.4	0.0	14.4	0.0	14.4	0.0	14.4	0.0	14.4	0.0	14.4	0.0	14.4	0.0	14.4	0.0	14.4	0.0
1939	13.8	-4.2	13.8	0.0	13.8	0.0	13.8	0.0	13.8	0.0	13.8	0.0	13.8	0.0	13.8	0.0	13.8	0.0	13.8	0.0	13.8	0.0	13.8	0.0
1940	13.5	-2.2	13.5	0.0	13.5	0.0	13.5	0.0	13.5	0.0	13.5	0.0	13.5	0.0	13.5	0.0	13.5	0.0	13.5	0.0	13.5	0.0	13.5	0.0
1941	13.5	0.0	13.5	0.0	13.5	0.0	13.5	0.0	13.5	0.0	13.5	0.0	13.6	0.7	13.6	0.0	13.6	0.0	13.6	0.0	13.6	0.0	13.6	0.0
1942	13.8	1.5	13.8	0.0	13.8	0.0	13.8	0.0	13.8	0.0	13.8	0.0	13.8	0.0	13.8	0.0	13.8	0.0	13.8	0.0	13.8	0.0	13.8	0.0
1943	13.8	0.0	13.8	0.0	13.8	0.0	13.8	0.0	13.8	0.0	13.8	0.0	13.8	0.0	13.8	0.0	13.8	0.0	13.8	0.0	13.8	0.0	13.8	0.0
1944	13.8	0.0	13.8	0.0	13.8	0.0	13.8	0.0	13.8	0.0	13.8	0.0	13.8	0.0	13.8	0.0	13.8	0.0	13.8	0.0	13.8	0.0	13.8	0.0
1945	13.8	0.0	13.8	0.0	13.8	0.0	13.8	0.0	13.8	0.0	13.8	0.0	13.8	0.0	13.8	0.0	13.8	0.0	13.8	0.0	13.8	0.0	13.8	0.0
1946	13.8	0.0	13.8	0.0	13.8	0.0	13.8	0.0	14.3	3.6	14.3	0.0	14.3	0.0	14.3	0.0	14.3	0.0	14.3	0.0	14.3	0.0	14.3	0.0
1947	15.9	11.2	15.9	0.0	15.9	0.0	15.9	0.0	15.9	0.0	15.9	0.0	15.9	0.0	16.3	2.5	16.3	0.0	16.3	0.0	16.3	0.0	16.3	0.0
1948	17.8	9.2	17.8	0.0	17.8	0.0	17.8	0.0	17.7	-0.6	17.7	0.0	17.8	0.6	17.9	0.6	17.9	0.0	17.9	0.0	17.9	0.0	17.9	0.0
1949	19.3	7.8	19.3	0.0	19.3	0.0	19.3	0.0	19.3	0.0	19.3	0.0	19.3	0.0	19.3	0.0	19.3	0.0	19.3	0.0	19.3	0.0	19.3	0.0
1950	19.4	0.5	19.4	0.0	19.3	-0.5	19.3	0.0	19.3	0.0	19.3	0.0	19.3	0.0	19.3	0.0	19.3	0.0	19.3	0.0	19.3	0.0	19.6	1.6
1951	21.5	9.7	21.5	0.0	21.5	0.0	21.5	0.0	21.5	0.0	21.5	0.0	21.5	0.0	21.5	0.0	21.5	0.0	21.5	0.0	21.5	0.0	21.5	0.0
1952	21.4	-0.5	21.4	0.0	21.4	0.0	21.4	0.0	21.4	0.0	21.4	0.0	21.4	0.0	21.4	0.0	22.0	2.8	22.2	0.9	22.2	0.0	22.2	0.0
1953	22.2	0.0	22.2	0.0	22.2	0.0	22.4	0.9	22.4	0.0	22.4	0.0	22.8	1.8	22.8	0.0	22.8	0.0	22.8	0.0	22.8	0.0	22.8	0.0
1954	23.0	0.9	23.0	0.0	23.0	0.0	23.0	0.0	23.0	0.0	23.0	0.0	23.1	0.4	23.2	0.4	23.2	0.0	23.2	0.0	23.3	0.4	23.3	0.0
1955	23.3	0.0	23.3	0.0	23.3	0.0	23.3	0.0	23.3	0.0	23.3	0.0	23.3	0.0	23.5	0.9	23.5	0.0	23.5	0.0	24.4	3.8	24.4	0.0
1956	24.4	0.0	24.4	0.0	24.4	0.0	24.4	0.0	25.0	2.5	25.0	0.0	25.0	0.0	25.1	0.4	25.4	1.2	25.4	0.0	26.1	2.8	26.1	0.0
1957	26.1	0.0	26.1	0.0	26.2	0.4	26.2	0.0	27.0	3.1	27.0	0.0	27.1	0.4	27.1	0.0	27.1	0.0	27.1	0.0	27.1	0.0	27.1	0.0
1958	27.1	0.0	27.1	0.0	27.6	1.8	27.6	0.0	27.6	0.0	27.6	0.0	27.6	0.0	27.6	0.0	27.7	0.4	27.7	0.0	27.7	0.0	28.3	2.2
1959	27.7	-2.1	27.7	0.0	27.7	0.0	27.1	-2.2	27.1	0.0	27.1	0.0	27.1	0.0	27.1	0.0	27.1	0.0	27.1	0.0	27.1	0.0	27.1	0.0
1960	27.1	0.0	27.4	1.1	27.4	0.0	27.4	0.0	27.4	0.0	27.2	-0.7	27.2	0.0	27.2	0.0	27.2	0.0	27.2	0.0	27.2	0.0	27.2	0.0
1961	27.8	2.2	27.8	0.0	27.8	0.0	27.8	0.0	27.8	0.0	27.8	0.0	27.8	0.0	27.8	0.0	27.8	0.0	27.8	0.0	27.8	0.0	27.8	0.0
1962	28.2	1.4	28.2	0.0	28.2	0.0	28.2	0.0	28.2	0.0	28.2	0.0	28.2	0.0	28.2	0.0	28.2	0.0	28.2	0.0	28.2	0.0	28.2	0.0
1963	28.4	0.7	28.4	0.0	28.4	0.0	28.4	0.0	28.5	0.4	28.5	0.0	28.6	0.4	28.6	0.0	28.5	-0.3	28.5	0.0	28.5	0.0	28.5	0.0
1964	28.5	0.0	28.7	0.7	28.7	0.0	28.7	0.0	28.7	0.0	28.7	0.0	28.7	0.0	28.7	0.0	28.7	0.0	28.7	0.0	28.7	0.0	28.7	0.0
1965	28.8	0.3	28.8	0.0	28.8	0.0	28.8	0.0	29.5	2.4	29.5	0.0	29.5	0.0	29.5	0.0	29.5	0.0	29.5	0.0	29.5	0.0	29.9	1.4
1966	29.9	0.0	29.9	0.0	29.9	0.0	29.9	0.0	30.0	0.3	30.0	0.0	30.0	0.0	30.0	0.0	30.0	0.0	30.0	0.0	30.0	0.0	30.0	0.0
1967	30.3	1.0	30.3	0.0	30.3	0.0	30.4	0.3	30.4	0.0	30.4	0.0	30.4	0.0	30.4	0.0	30.4	0.0	30.4	0.0	30.7	1.0	30.7	0.0
1968	30.7	0.0	30.8	0.3	30.8	0.0	31.8	3.2	31.8	0.0	31.8	0.0	31.8	0.0	31.8	0.0	31.8	0.0	31.9	0.3	31.9	0.0	31.8	-0.3
1969	31.8	0.0	32.4	1.9	32.4	0.0	32.5	0.3	32.5	0.0	32.5	0.0	32.5	0.0	32.5	0.0	32.7	0.6	32.8	0.3	32.8	0.0	32.8	0.0
1970	32.8	0.0	34.0	3.7	34.0	0.0	34.0	0.0	34.0	0.0	34.0	0.0	34.3	0.9	34.3	0.0	34.3	0.0	35.2	2.6	35.2	0.0	35.2	0.0

[Continued]

Metal Containers
Producer Price Index
Base 1982 = 100
[Continued]

For 1926-1995. Columns headed % show percentile change in the index from the previous period for which an index is available.

Year	Jan Index	%	Feb Index	%	Mar Index	%	Apr Index	%	May Index	%	Jun Index	%	Jul Index	%	Aug Index	%	Sep Index	%	Oct Index	%	Nov Index	%	Dec Index	%
1971	35.2	0.0	35.2	0.0	35.2	0.0	37.5	6.5	37.5	0.0	37.5	0.0	37.5	0.0	37.8	0.8	37.8	0.0	37.8	0.0	37.8	0.0	37.8	0.0
1972	37.8	0.0	38.7	2.4	38.7	0.0	38.7	0.0	38.8	0.3	39.2	1.0	39.5	0.8	39.8	0.8	39.9	0.3	39.9	0.0	39.9	0.0	39.9	0.0
1973	39.9	0.0	39.8	-0.3	41.3	3.8	41.3	0.0	41.3	0.0	41.3	0.0	41.3	0.0	41.3	0.0	41.3	0.0	41.0	-0.7	41.0	0.0	41.0	0.0
1974	42.2	2.9	42.3	0.2	42.5	0.5	44.7	5.2	46.3	3.6	50.3	8.6	52.0	3.4	56.1	7.9	56.2	0.2	56.4	0.4	56.4	0.0	56.4	0.0
1975	56.4	0.0	60.0	6.4	59.6	-0.7	59.6	0.0	58.2	-2.3	58.2	0.0	58.2	0.0	58.1	-0.2	58.2	0.2	58.2	0.0	58.4	0.3	58.7	0.5
1976	58.6	-0.2	58.7	0.2	61.9	5.5	61.9	0.0	61.9	0.0	61.9	0.0	62.3	0.6	62.2	-0.2	62.2	0.0	62.2	0.0	62.3	0.2	62.3	0.0
1977	62.3	0.0	62.3	0.0	66.0	5.9	66.1	0.2	66.0	-0.2	66.0	0.0	66.2	0.3	66.4	0.3	68.5	3.2	69.0	0.7	69.1	0.1	69.1	0.0
1978	69.2	0.1	71.1	2.7	72.1	1.4	72.1	0.0	73.9	2.5	74.0	0.1	74.3	0.4	75.0	0.9	74.9	-0.1	77.5	3.5	77.5	0.0	77.4	-0.1
1979	78.2	1.0	78.2	0.0	80.5	2.9	82.2	2.1	81.7	-0.6	81.4	-0.4	81.3	-0.1	81.7	0.5	81.8	0.1	85.2	4.2	85.5	0.4	85.5	0.0
1980	86.2	0.8	86.6	0.5	87.8	1.4	91.6	4.3	92.1	0.5	92.1	0.0	92.2	0.1	92.3	0.1	92.3	0.0	92.7	0.4	92.3	-0.4	92.3	0.0
1981	94.8	2.7	95.5	0.7	95.6	0.1	95.6	0.0	95.6	0.0	95.6	0.0	96.0	0.4	97.0	1.0	97.0	0.0	96.9	-0.1	96.8	-0.1	96.4	-0.4
1982	98.7	2.4	99.3	0.6	99.6	0.3	100.5	0.9	100.5	0.0	100.4	-0.1	100.5	0.1	100.1	-0.4	100.1	0.0	100.3	0.2	100.1	-0.2	99.9	-0.2
1983	99.8	-0.1	100.8	1.0	100.9	0.1	101.0	0.1	102.6	1.6	102.7	0.1	102.4	-0.3	102.5	0.1	103.0	0.5	103.0	0.0	102.9	-0.1	103.6	0.7
1984	104.7	1.1	104.9	0.2	105.1	0.2	105.1	0.0	105.9	0.8	105.9	0.0	105.9	0.0	107.2	1.2	107.2	0.0	108.8	1.5	108.8	0.0	108.7	-0.1
1985	108.8	0.1	109.0	0.2	108.9	-0.1	108.9	0.0	109.0	0.1	109.0	0.0	109.0	0.0	108.9	-0.1	108.9	0.0	108.9	0.0	109.0	0.1	109.9	0.8
1986	110.2	0.3	110.1	-0.1	110.2	0.1	110.1	-0.1	110.0	-0.1	110.0	0.0	110.3	0.3	110.4	0.1	110.4	0.0	110.4	0.0	110.4	0.0	110.4	0.0
1987	109.9	-0.5	110.0	0.1	109.8	-0.2	109.8	0.0	109.6	-0.2	109.7	0.1	109.0	-0.6	109.1	0.1	109.8	0.6	109.6	-0.2	109.8	0.2	108.0	-1.6
1988	108.3	0.3	108.9	0.6	109.5	0.6	110.1	0.5	110.4	0.3	110.3	-0.1	110.1	-0.2	110.9	0.7	111.3	0.4	111.1	-0.2	111.0	-0.1	110.1	-0.8
1989	110.1	0.0	109.7	-0.4	109.7	0.0	110.3	0.5	111.3	0.9	111.5	0.2	112.5	0.9	112.0	-0.4	112.2	0.2	113.0	0.7	113.1	0.1	112.6	-0.4
1990	113.6	0.9	113.5	-0.1	113.8	0.3	113.8	0.0	114.2	0.4	114.1	-0.1	114.2	0.1	114.1	-0.1	114.2	0.1	114.1	-0.1	114.1	0.0	113.9	-0.2
1991	114.7	0.7	114.9	0.2	114.6	-0.3	114.7	0.1	114.9	0.2	114.9	0.0	116.1	1.0	116.3	0.2	116.2	-0.1	116.4	0.2	116.3	-0.1	116.2	-0.1
1992	113.8	-2.1	114.3	0.4	113.9	-0.3	114.0	0.1	113.8	-0.2	114.0	0.2	113.9	-0.1	113.7	-0.2	113.9	0.2	113.9	0.0	113.9	0.0	114.0	0.1
1993	109.9	-3.6	110.2	0.3	109.5	-0.6	109.2	-0.3	109.1	-0.1	109.1	0.0	109.2	0.1	108.8	-0.4	109.8	0.9	110.1	0.3	111.0	0.8	110.1	-0.8
1994	109.0	-1.0	108.5	-0.5	107.7	-0.7	108.0	0.3	108.0	0.0	106.6	-1.3	106.9	0.3	108.1	1.1	108.2	0.1	108.6	0.4	108.8	0.2	108.9	0.1
1995	109.6	0.6	117.8	7.5	117.8	0.0	118.1	0.3	118.1	0.0	118.3	0.2	118.0	-0.3	118.0	0.0	117.8	-0.2	117.9	0.1	117.7	-0.2	117.8	0.1

Source: U.S. Department of Labor, Bureau of Labor Statistics, Division of Industry Prices and Price Indexes. n.e.c. stands for not elsewhere classified. - indicates no data collected for period or unavailable.

Hardware
Producer Price Index
Base 1982 = 100

For 1947-1995. Columns headed % show percentile change in the index from the previous period for which an index is available.

Year	Jan Index	%	Feb Index	%	Mar Index	%	Apr Index	%	May Index	%	Jun Index	%	Jul Index	%	Aug Index	%	Sep Index	%	Oct Index	%	Nov Index	%	Dec Index	%
1947	16.7	-	16.9	1.2	16.9	0.0	16.9	0.0	17.0	0.6	17.0	0.0	17.1	0.6	17.2	0.6	17.4	1.2	17.6	1.1	17.7	0.6	17.7	0.0
1948	17.7	0.0	17.8	0.6	17.9	0.6	17.9	0.0	18.2	1.7	18.3	0.5	18.3	0.0	19.1	4.4	19.7	3.1	19.8	0.5	19.9	0.5	19.9	0.0
1949	19.9	0.0	19.9	0.0	19.9	0.0	19.7	-1.0	19.7	0.0	19.7	0.0	19.7	0.0	19.7	0.0	19.5	-1.0	19.2	-1.5	19.2	0.0	19.2	0.0
1950	19.6	2.1	20.1	2.6	20.2	0.5	20.3	0.5	20.5	1.0	20.6	0.5	20.9	1.5	21.4	2.4	21.8	1.9	22.2	1.8	22.9	3.2	23.2	1.3
1951	23.3	0.4	23.3	0.0	23.3	0.0	23.3	0.0	23.3	0.0	23.3	0.0	23.3	0.0	23.3	0.0	23.3	0.0	23.3	0.0	23.3	0.0	23.3	0.0
1952	23.3	0.0	23.3	0.0	23.4	0.4	23.4	0.0	23.4	0.0	22.9	-2.1	22.9	0.0	22.9	0.0	22.9	0.0	23.2	1.3	23.2	0.0	23.3	0.4
1953	23.3	0.0	23.3	0.0	23.3	0.0	23.7	1.7	24.7	4.2	24.9	0.8	24.9	0.0	25.1	0.8	25.3	0.8	25.4	0.4	25.4	0.0	25.4	0.0
1954	25.4	0.0	25.5	0.4	25.5	0.0	25.6	0.4	25.5	-0.4	25.5	0.0	25.5	0.0	25.7	0.8	26.0	1.2	26.2	0.8	26.3	0.4	26.3	0.0
1955	26.4	0.4	26.5	0.4	26.7	0.8	26.7	0.0	26.7	0.0	26.7	0.0	26.8	0.4	27.0	0.7	27.3	1.1	28.0	2.6	28.0	0.0	28.0	0.0
1956	28.0	0.0	28.0	0.0	28.3	1.1	28.5	0.7	28.5	0.0	28.6	0.4	28.7	0.3	29.3	2.1	29.3	0.0	29.5	0.7	29.6	0.3	29.6	0.0
1957	29.9	1.0	29.9	0.0	30.0	0.3	30.2	0.7	30.4	0.7	30.4	0.0	30.4	0.0	30.7	1.0	30.9	0.7	30.9	0.0	30.9	0.0	31.1	0.6
1958	31.2	0.3	31.2	0.0	31.2	0.0	31.3	0.3	31.6	1.0	31.8	0.6	31.8	0.0	31.8	0.0	31.8	0.0	31.8	0.0	31.9	0.3	31.9	0.0
1959	31.9	0.0	32.0	0.3	32.0	0.0	32.0	0.0	32.0	0.0	32.0	0.0	32.0	0.0	32.0	0.0	32.0	0.0	32.0	0.0	32.0	0.0	32.0	0.0
1960	32.1	0.3	32.1	0.0	32.1	0.0	32.2	0.3	32.2	0.0	32.3	0.3	32.3	0.0	32.3	0.0	32.3	0.0	32.3	0.0	32.3	0.0	32.3	0.0
1961	32.3	0.0	32.4	0.3	32.4	0.0	32.4	0.0	32.6	0.6	32.6	0.0	32.6	0.0	32.6	0.0	32.7	0.3	32.7	0.0	32.7	0.0	32.7	0.0
1962	32.8	0.3	32.7	-0.3	32.7	0.0	32.6	-0.3	32.6	0.0	32.7	0.3	32.5	-0.6	32.5	0.0	32.5	0.0	32.5	0.0	32.5	0.0	32.5	0.0
1963	32.5	0.0	32.6	0.3	32.6	0.0	32.6	0.0	32.6	0.0	32.6	0.0	32.6	0.0	32.6	0.0	32.7	0.3	32.7	0.0	32.7	0.0	32.7	0.0
1964	32.8	0.3	32.8	0.0	32.9	0.3	32.9	0.0	32.9	0.0	32.9	0.0	32.9	0.0	32.9	0.0	32.9	0.0	32.9	0.0	32.9	0.0	32.9	0.0
1965	32.9	0.0	32.9	0.0	33.0	0.3	33.0	0.0	33.2	0.6	33.2	0.0	33.3	0.3	33.4	0.3	33.4	0.0	33.5	0.3	33.5	0.0	33.6	0.3
1966	33.6	0.0	33.7	0.3	34.0	0.9	34.0	0.0	34.4	1.2	34.4	0.0	34.4	0.0	34.5	0.3	34.6	0.3	34.8	0.6	35.0	0.6	35.1	0.3
1967	35.0	-0.3	35.0	0.0	35.3	0.9	35.3	0.0	35.4	0.3	35.4	0.0	35.7	0.8	36.1	1.1	36.1	0.0	36.2	0.3	36.3	0.3	36.4	0.3
1968	36.4	0.0	36.6	0.5	36.5	-0.3	36.5	0.0	36.6	0.3	36.6	0.0	36.6	0.0	36.6	0.0	36.7	0.3	36.8	0.3	36.8	0.0	37.1	0.8
1969	37.3	0.5	37.4	0.3	37.5	0.3	37.5	0.0	37.6	0.3	37.6	0.0	37.8	0.5	37.8	0.0	37.9	0.3	38.4	1.3	38.6	0.5	38.6	0.0
1970	39.0	1.0	39.1	0.3	39.2	0.3	39.3	0.3	39.4	0.3	39.5	0.3	39.7	0.5	39.9	0.5	40.1	0.5	40.3	0.5	41.0	1.7	41.1	0.2
1971	41.2	0.2	41.3	0.2	41.3	0.0	41.3	0.0	41.3	0.0	41.4	0.2	41.7	0.7	42.0	0.7	42.0	0.0	42.0	0.0	42.1	0.2	42.2	0.2
1972	42.3	0.2	42.5	0.5	42.5	0.0	42.7	0.5	42.9	0.5	43.0	0.2	43.0	0.0	43.1	0.2	43.1	0.0	43.2	0.2	43.3	0.2	43.3	0.0
1973	43.4	0.2	43.5	0.2	43.6	0.2	43.8	0.5	44.0	0.5	44.3	0.7	44.4	0.2	44.4	0.0	45.2	1.8	45.6	0.9	45.7	0.2	46.1	0.9
1974	46.5	0.9	46.7	0.4	46.9	0.4	47.1	0.4	48.4	2.8	49.3	1.9	49.9	1.2	51.0	2.2	52.5	2.9	53.9	2.7	55.0	2.0	55.5	0.9
1975	56.0	0.9	56.5	0.9	57.7	2.1	57.7	0.0	58.1	0.7	58.2	0.2	58.3	0.2	58.4	0.2	58.6	0.3	59.3	1.2	59.5	0.3	59.6	0.2
1976	60.2	1.0	60.5	0.5	60.7	0.3	60.9	0.3	61.5	1.0	61.7	0.3	61.8	0.2	61.9	0.2	62.2	0.5	62.6	0.6	63.2	1.0	63.9	1.1
1977	64.8	1.4	65.1	0.5	65.4	0.5	65.5	0.2	65.6	0.2	65.9	0.5	66.7	1.2	66.7	0.0	66.9	0.3	66.7	-0.3	67.1	0.6	67.6	0.7
1978	69.0	2.1	69.2	0.3	69.4	0.3	70.2	1.2	70.7	0.7	70.8	0.1	71.5	1.0	71.9	0.6	72.2	0.4	73.5	1.8	74.4	1.2	75.2	1.1
1979	75.5	0.4	76.1	0.8	76.4	0.4	77.0	0.8	77.4	0.5	77.5	0.1	78.0	0.6	78.5	0.6	79.0	0.6	79.9	1.1	80.5	0.8	80.7	0.2
1980	81.4	0.9	82.2	1.0	82.6	0.5	84.7	2.5	85.1	0.5	85.8	0.8	86.6	0.9	86.8	0.2	87.7	1.0	88.0	0.3	89.1	1.3	89.8	0.8
1981	90.8	1.1	92.1	1.4	92.3	0.2	92.2	-0.1	92.6	0.4	92.6	0.0	94.1	1.6	94.7	0.6	95.6	1.0	96.2	0.6	96.9	0.7	97.1	0.2
1982	97.8	0.7	98.0	0.2	99.3	1.3	99.4	0.1	99.5	0.1	100.0	0.5	100.3	0.3	100.8	0.5	100.9	0.1	101.0	0.1	101.0	0.0	102.0	1.0
1983	102.5	0.5	102.7	0.2	102.8	0.1	103.0	0.2	103.0	0.0	104.0	1.0	104.2	0.2	104.3	0.1	104.4	0.1	104.5	0.1	104.6	0.1	104.7	0.1
1984	104.7	0.0	104.9	0.2	105.1	0.2	105.1	0.0	105.4	0.3	105.7	0.3	106.0	0.3	106.3	0.3	106.7	0.4	107.0	0.3	107.0	0.0	107.4	0.4
1985	108.0	0.6	108.2	0.2	108.8	0.6	109.1	0.3	109.1	0.0	109.1	0.0	109.2	0.1	109.4	0.2	109.4	0.0	109.6	0.2	109.7	0.1	109.9	0.2
1986	110.8	0.8	110.9	0.1	109.1	-1.6	109.2	0.1	109.3	0.1	109.3	0.0	109.4	0.1	109.5	0.1	109.2	-0.3	109.4	0.2	108.7	-0.6	108.9	0.2
1987	108.5	-0.4	108.9	0.4	109.0	0.1	109.2	0.2	109.6	0.4	109.8	0.2	109.6	-0.2	109.7	0.1	109.8	0.1	110.1	0.3	110.2	0.1	111.0	0.7
1988	111.5	0.5	111.9	0.4	112.2	0.3	112.8	0.5	113.0	0.2	112.9	-0.1	113.6	0.6	114.0	0.4	114.3	0.3	115.6	1.1	116.1	0.4	116.7	0.5
1989	117.3	0.5	118.4	0.9	119.1	0.6	119.2	0.1	119.7	0.4	119.9	0.2	120.5	0.5	120.7	0.2	121.2	0.4	122.3	0.9	122.8	0.4	123.2	0.3
1990	124.0	0.6	124.8	0.6	125.0	0.2	125.5	0.4	125.6	0.1	125.7	0.1	126.0	0.2	126.2	0.2	126.5	0.2	126.9	0.3	127.0	0.1	127.7	0.6
1991	129.4	1.3	129.7	0.2	129.9	0.2	129.9	0.0	130.0	0.1	130.1	0.1	130.1	0.0	130.2	0.1	130.3	0.1	130.7	0.3	130.6	-0.1	131.2	0.5

[Continued]

Hardware
Producer Price Index
Base 1982 = 100
[Continued]

For 1947-1995. Columns headed % show percentile change in the index from the previous period for which an index is available.

Year	Jan Index	%	Feb Index	%	Mar Index	%	Apr Index	%	May Index	%	Jun Index	%	Jul Index	%	Aug Index	%	Sep Index	%	Oct Index	%	Nov Index	%	Dec Index	%
1992	131.6	0.3	132.0	0.3	132.2	0.2	132.5	0.2	132.6	0.1	132.6	0.0	132.8	0.2	133.0	0.2	133.1	0.1	133.2	0.1	133.5	0.2	133.8	0.2
1993	134.1	0.2	134.3	0.1	134.6	0.2	134.8	0.1	134.8	0.0	135.2	0.3	135.3	0.1	135.5	0.1	135.6	0.1	135.7	0.1	135.9	0.1	136.2	0.2
1994	136.4	0.1	136.5	0.1	136.7	0.1	137.2	0.4	137.4	0.1	137.5	0.1	137.6	0.1	137.8	0.1	138.0	0.1	138.1	0.1	138.5	0.3	138.6	0.1
1995	139.4	0.6	139.7	0.2	140.4	0.5	140.8	0.3	140.9	0.1	141.4	0.4	141.5	0.1	141.6	0.1	141.7	0.1	141.8	0.1	141.9	0.1	142.2	0.2

Source: U.S. Department of Labor, Bureau of Labor Statistics, Division of Industry Prices and Price Indexes. n.e.c. stands for not elsewhere classified. - indicates no data collected for period or unavailable.

Plumbing Fixtures and Brass Fittings
Producer Price Index
Base 1982 = 100

For 1926-1995. Columns headed % show percentile change in the index from the previous period for which an index is available.

Year	Jan Index	%	Feb Index	%	Mar Index	%	Apr Index	%	May Index	%	Jun Index	%	Jul Index	%	Aug Index	%	Sep Index	%	Oct Index	%	Nov Index	%	Dec Index	%
1926	26.4	-	26.4	0.0	26.4	0.0	26.4	0.0	26.3	-0.4	25.9	-1.5	25.8	-0.4	26.0	0.8	26.2	0.8	26.2	0.0	26.1	-0.4	26.2	0.4
1927	26.2	0.0	25.5	-2.7	23.5	-7.8	23.5	0.0	23.1	-1.7	22.8	-1.3	22.8	0.0	22.8	0.0	22.9	0.4	22.9	0.0	22.9	0.0	22.7	-0.9
1928	22.7	0.0	22.7	0.0	23.4	3.1	23.5	0.4	23.6	0.4	24.3	3.0	24.3	0.0	24.3	0.0	24.3	0.0	24.3	0.0	24.4	0.4	24.4	0.0
1929	24.1	-1.2	22.4	-7.1	22.4	0.0	22.6	0.9	22.6	0.0	22.6	0.0	22.1	-2.2	22.5	1.8	22.5	0.0	22.1	-1.8	22.1	0.0	22.1	0.0
1930	22.1	0.0	22.7	2.7	23.0	1.3	24.1	4.8	24.1	0.0	20.8	-13.7	19.9	-4.3	19.9	0.0	19.8	-0.5	19.8	0.0	19.7	-0.5	20.5	4.1
1931	20.6	0.5	20.2	-1.9	20.2	0.0	20.2	0.0	20.2	0.0	20.2	0.0	20.2	0.0	20.2	0.0	20.0	-1.0	20.1	0.5	20.0	-0.5	19.3	-3.5
1932	16.4	-15.0	16.2	-1.2	15.6	-3.7	15.6	0.0	15.6	0.0	16.6	6.4	16.8	1.2	16.8	0.0	16.8	0.0	16.8	0.0	16.8	0.0	16.8	0.0
1933	14.5	-13.7	12.8	-11.7	12.8	0.0	12.8	0.0	13.8	7.8	16.2	17.4	16.7	3.1	16.9	1.2	19.1	13.0	19.1	0.0	19.1	0.0	19.0	-0.5
1934	19.0	0.0	18.8	-1.1	18.8	0.0	18.8	0.0	17.9	-4.8	16.9	-5.6	16.9	0.0	17.0	0.6	15.5	-8.8	14.0	-9.7	13.9	-0.7	13.9	0.0
1935	13.9	0.0	14.0	0.7	14.1	0.7	14.0	-0.7	14.0	0.0	14.0	0.0	14.9	6.4	15.5	4.0	15.5	0.0	15.5	0.0	15.5	0.0	15.5	0.0
1936	15.8	1.9	16.9	7.0	16.9	0.0	16.9	0.0	16.9	0.0	16.9	0.0	16.9	0.0	16.9	0.0	16.9	0.0	16.9	0.0	16.9	0.0	16.9	0.0
1937	16.9	0.0	16.9	0.0	17.0	0.6	17.2	1.2	17.2	0.0	17.2	0.0	17.2	0.0	17.2	0.0	17.2	0.0	17.2	0.0	17.2	0.0	17.2	0.0
1938	17.1	-0.6	17.1	0.0	17.0	-0.6	17.0	0.0	17.0	0.0	17.0	0.0	17.0	0.0	17.0	0.0	16.6	-2.4	16.6	0.0	16.6	0.0	16.6	0.0
1939	16.6	0.0	16.9	1.8	16.9	0.0	16.9	0.0	16.9	0.0	16.9	0.0	16.9	0.0	16.9	0.0	16.9	0.0	16.9	0.0	16.9	0.0	16.9	0.0
1940	17.0	0.6	17.2	1.2	18.1	5.2	18.1	0.0	18.1	0.0	18.1	0.0	18.1	0.0	18.1	0.0	18.1	0.0	18.1	0.0	18.1	0.0	18.1	0.0
1941	18.1	0.0	18.1	0.0	18.0	-0.6	18.0	0.0	18.0	0.0	18.0	0.0	18.1	0.6	18.3	1.1	18.5	1.1	18.6	0.5	18.7	0.5	19.2	2.7
1942	21.2	10.4	21.1	-0.5	20.5	-2.8	20.6	0.5	20.6	0.0	20.6	0.0	19.8	-3.9	19.8	0.0	19.8	0.0	19.7	-0.5	19.7	0.0	19.7	0.0
1943	19.8	0.0	19.8	0.0	19.8	0.0	19.8	0.0	19.8	0.0	19.8	0.0	19.8	0.0	19.8	0.0	19.7	-0.5	19.7	0.0	19.7	0.0	19.7	0.0
1944	19.7	0.0	19.7	0.0	19.7	0.0	19.7	0.0	18.6	-5.6	18.6	0.0	18.6	0.0	18.6	0.0	18.6	0.0	18.6	0.0	18.6	0.0	18.6	0.0
1945	18.6	0.0	18.6	0.0	18.6	0.0	18.7	0.5	18.7	0.0	18.7	0.0	18.7	0.0	18.9	1.1	19.1	1.1	19.1	0.0	19.1	0.0	19.1	0.0
1946	19.1	0.0	19.1	0.0	19.6	2.6	19.9	1.5	19.9	0.0	19.8	-0.5	19.8	0.0	20.0	1.0	20.4	2.0	20.4	0.0	20.4	0.0	22.8	11.8
1947	22.9	0.4	23.6	3.1	23.8	0.8	23.8	0.0	23.8	0.0	23.8	0.0	23.9	0.4	24.1	0.8	24.6	2.1	24.6	0.0	24.7	0.4	24.7	0.0
1948	25.2	2.0	25.7	2.0	25.7	0.0	25.7	0.0	25.7	0.0	25.7	0.0	25.8	0.4	26.6	3.1	26.7	0.4	26.7	0.0	26.7	0.0	26.6	-0.4
1949	26.5	-0.4	26.3	-0.8	26.2	-0.4	26.2	0.0	25.9	-1.1	25.9	0.0	25.9	0.0	25.9	0.0	25.9	0.0	25.9	0.0	25.9	0.0	25.8	-0.4
1950	25.8	0.0	25.8	0.0	25.8	0.0	25.9	0.4	26.2	1.2	26.2	0.0	26.2	0.0	27.8	6.1	28.1	1.1	29.6	5.3	30.8	4.1	31.3	1.6
1951	31.3	0.0	31.3	0.0	31.3	0.0	31.3	0.0	31.3	0.0	31.2	-0.3	31.1	-0.3	31.0	-0.3	30.9	-0.3	30.8	-0.3	30.8	0.0	30.7	-0.3
1952	29.6	-3.6	29.6	0.0	29.6	0.0	29.5	-0.3	29.4	-0.3	29.9	1.7	30.0	0.3	30.0	0.0	30.0	0.0	30.0	-0.3	30.0	0.0	30.0	0.0
1953	28.8	-4.0	29.0	0.7	29.0	0.0	28.9	-0.3	28.9	0.0	28.8	-0.3	29.5	2.4	30.1	2.0	30.1	0.0	30.1	0.0	30.1	0.0	30.1	0.0
1954	30.0	0.0	30.0	0.0	30.0	0.0	30.0	0.0	30.0	0.0	30.1	0.3	30.1	0.0	30.1	0.0	30.1	0.0	30.1	0.0	30.1	0.0	30.1	0.0
1955	30.1	0.0	30.1	0.0	31.2	3.7	31.3	0.3	31.3	0.0	31.3	0.0	31.3	0.0	32.5	3.8	32.5	0.0	32.8	0.9	33.8	3.0	33.8	0.0
1956	33.8	0.0	33.8	0.0	33.8	0.0	34.0	0.6	34.3	0.9	34.0	-0.9	34.0	0.0	34.0	0.0	34.0	0.0	34.0	0.0	34.0	0.0	34.0	0.0
1957	33.8	-0.6	33.8	0.0	33.5	-0.9	33.4	-0.3	33.0	-1.2	32.8	-0.6	32.8	0.0	32.7	-0.3	32.7	0.0	32.6	-0.3	32.6	0.0	32.6	0.0
1958	32.3	-0.9	31.9	-1.2	31.6	-0.9	31.4	-0.6	31.1	-1.0	31.1	0.0	30.4	-2.3	30.4	0.0	31.4	3.3	31.6	0.6	31.6	0.0	31.6	0.0
1959	31.7	0.3	31.9	0.6	32.8	2.8	32.9	0.3	33.2	0.9	33.2	0.0	33.2	0.0	33.2	0.0	33.2	0.0	33.1	-0.6	33.1	0.0	33.1	0.0
1960	34.0	0.6	34.0	0.0	34.0	0.0	33.5	-1.5	33.7	0.6	33.3	-1.2	33.3	0.0	33.3	0.0	33.3	0.0	33.1	-0.6	33.1	0.0	33.1	0.0
1961	33.2	0.3	33.2	0.0	33.2	0.0	33.2	0.0	33.3	0.3	33.5	0.6	33.6	0.3	33.8	0.6	33.8	0.0	33.9	0.3	33.9	0.0	33.8	-0.3
1962	33.8	0.0	33.8	0.0	33.7	-0.3	33.7	0.0	33.7	0.0	32.0	-5.0	31.5	-1.6	31.4	-0.3	31.4	0.0	31.5	0.3	31.6	0.3	31.6	0.0
1963	31.6	0.0	32.8	3.8	32.8	0.0	32.7	-0.3	32.7	0.0	32.6	-0.3	32.5	-0.3	32.5	0.0	32.5	0.0	32.5	0.0	32.5	0.0	32.5	0.0
1964	32.4	-0.3	32.4	0.0	32.3	-0.3	32.3	0.0	32.3	0.0	32.3	0.0	32.6	0.9	33.1	1.5	33.1	0.0	33.4	0.9	33.4	0.0	33.4	0.0
1965	33.3	-0.3	33.3	0.0	33.3	0.0	33.3	0.0	33.3	0.0	33.3	0.0	33.3	0.0	33.6	0.9	33.6	0.0	33.6	0.0	33.7	0.3	34.1	1.2
1966	34.0	-0.3	34.1	0.3	34.3	0.6	34.8	1.5	35.0	0.6	35.2	0.6	35.7	1.4	35.7	0.0	35.9	0.6	35.9	0.0	35.9	0.0	35.9	0.0
1967	35.9	0.0	36.0	0.3	36.0	0.0	36.0	0.0	36.0	0.0	36.0	0.0	35.7	-0.8	35.7	0.0	35.9	0.6	35.7	0.0	35.7	0.0	35.9	0.6
1968	36.0	0.3	37.0	2.8	37.1	0.3	37.2	0.3	37.2	0.0	37.0	-0.5	37.0	0.0	37.1	0.3	37.1	0.0	37.2	0.3	37.4	0.5	37.4	0.0
1969	37.6	0.5	37.7	0.3	37.8	0.3	37.8	0.0	38.0	0.5	38.3	0.8	38.8	1.3	38.8	0.0	39.1	0.8	39.2	0.3	39.6	1.0	39.4	-0.5
1970	39.2	-0.5	39.2	0.0	39.2	0.0	40.0	2.0	39.6	-1.0	39.8	0.5	40.0	0.5	39.8	-0.5	40.6	2.0	40.5	-0.2	40.4	-0.2	40.6	0.5

[Continued]

Plumbing Fixtures and Brass Fittings
Producer Price Index
Base 1982 = 100
[Continued]

For 1926-1995. Columns headed % show percentile change in the index from the previous period for which an index is available.

Year	Jan Index	%	Feb Index	%	Mar Index	%	Apr Index	%	May Index	%	Jun Index	%	Jul Index	%	Aug Index	%	Sep Index	%	Oct Index	%	Nov Index	%	Dec Index	%
1971	40.7	0.2	40.7	0.0	40.7	0.0	41.3	1.5	41.6	0.7	42.0	1.0	42.3	0.7	42.4	0.2	42.4	0.0	42.4	0.0	42.4	0.0	42.5	0.2
1972	42.4	-0.2	42.6	0.5	42.6	0.0	42.7	0.2	42.7	0.0	42.9	0.5	43.0	0.2	43.1	0.2	43.2	0.2	43.3	0.2	43.3	0.0	43.3	0.0
1973	43.4	0.2	43.6	0.5	44.2	1.4	44.8	1.4	45.1	0.7	45.3	0.4	45.3	0.0	45.4	0.2	45.6	0.4	45.8	0.4	46.3	1.1	46.7	0.9
1974	47.9	2.6	48.3	0.8	48.8	1.0	50.5	3.5	52.2	3.4	53.1	1.7	54.6	2.8	56.6	3.7	57.2	1.1	57.4	0.3	57.7	0.5	57.9	0.3
1975	58.3	0.7	58.4	0.2	58.7	0.5	58.3	-0.7	58.1	-0.3	58.0	-0.2	57.7	-0.5	57.6	-0.2	57.8	0.3	58.6	1.4	58.7	0.2	58.7	0.0
1976	59.0	0.5	60.4	2.4	60.5	0.2	60.9	0.7	61.4	0.8	62.8	2.3	63.8	1.6	63.8	0.0	64.2	0.6	64.2	0.0	64.3	0.2	64.3	0.0
1977	64.4	0.2	64.5	0.2	65.4	1.4	65.6	0.3	66.4	1.2	66.8	0.6	67.9	1.6	68.1	0.3	68.5	0.6	68.5	0.0	68.6	0.1	68.9	0.4
1978	69.0	0.1	69.9	1.3	70.3	0.6	70.9	0.9	71.1	0.3	71.4	0.4	71.7	0.4	72.2	0.7	72.4	0.3	72.6	0.3	72.6	0.0	73.1	0.7
1979	73.3	0.3	74.6	1.8	75.2	0.8	76.1	1.2	76.7	0.8	77.8	1.4	78.8	1.3	79.8	1.3	80.0	0.3	80.2	0.3	80.9	0.9	81.3	0.5
1980	83.5	2.7	84.9	1.7	87.0	2.5	87.5	0.6	88.8	1.5	89.2	0.5	89.6	0.4	89.9	0.3	89.9	0.0	89.9	0.0	90.5	0.7	91.5	1.1
1981	92.1	0.7	93.0	1.0	93.1	0.1	95.2	2.3	95.5	0.3	96.5	1.0	97.2	0.7	97.3	0.1	97.4	0.1	97.9	0.5	98.0	0.1	98.3	0.3
1982	98.5	0.2	99.2	0.7	100.2	1.0	100.6	0.4	100.8	0.2	101.4	0.6	101.6	0.2	98.5	-3.1	99.4	0.9	99.7	0.3	99.9	0.2	100.2	0.3
1983	100.7	0.5	101.7	1.0	102.5	0.8	103.2	0.7	103.7	0.5	104.3	0.6	104.2	-0.1	104.1	-0.1	104.9	0.8	105.0	0.1	105.5	0.5	105.5	0.0
1984	105.5	0.0	106.3	0.8	107.6	1.2	108.2	0.6	108.2	0.0	108.5	0.3	108.6	0.1	109.3	0.6	109.2	-0.1	109.9	0.6	110.9	0.9	111.0	0.1
1985	109.9	-1.0	110.1	0.2	110.4	0.3	111.7	1.2	112.1	0.4	112.3	0.2	112.3	0.0	112.4	0.1	112.6	0.2	113.0	0.4	113.0	0.0	112.9	-0.1
1986	113.0	0.1	113.5	0.4	115.7	1.9	115.8	0.1	115.9	0.1	116.3	0.3	116.2	-0.1	115.9	-0.3	116.1	0.2	115.9	-0.2	115.8	-0.1	115.6	-0.2
1987	116.2	0.5	118.4	1.9	118.3	-0.1	118.7	0.3	120.0	1.1	120.1	0.1	120.2	0.1	120.5	0.2	120.6	0.1	120.9	0.2	121.2	0.2	121.7	0.4
1988	121.9	0.2	123.6	1.4	127.6	3.2	127.9	0.2	128.4	0.4	128.7	0.2	129.0	0.2	130.6	1.2	130.8	0.2	131.6	0.6	131.8	0.2	132.2	0.3
1989	133.8	1.2	135.6	1.3	135.8	0.1	136.7	0.7	137.5	0.6	137.7	0.1	138.0	0.2	138.7	0.5	139.5	0.6	139.5	0.0	139.9	0.3	139.9	0.0
1990	141.2	0.9	141.9	0.5	142.7	0.6	143.5	0.6	144.0	0.3	144.1	0.1	144.3	0.1	144.5	0.1	145.9	1.0	146.3	0.3	146.5	0.1	146.6	0.1
1991	146.5	-0.1	149.0	1.7	149.4	0.3	150.0	0.4	150.1	0.1	150.1	0.0	150.3	0.1	150.3	0.0	150.0	-0.2	150.2	0.1	150.3	0.1	150.5	0.1
1992	150.7	0.1	151.0	0.2	152.1	0.7	153.4	0.9	153.7	0.2	153.9	0.1	154.1	0.1	154.2	0.1	152.9	-0.8	153.8	0.6	153.5	-0.2	153.8	0.2
1993	153.7	-0.1	153.3	-0.3	155.2	1.2	156.2	0.6	156.3	0.1	156.5	0.1	155.9	-0.4	156.5	0.4	156.5	0.0	156.8	0.2	156.9	0.1	156.8	-0.1
1994	157.4	0.4	157.8	0.3	158.6	0.5	159.2	0.4	159.3	0.1	160.3	0.6	159.7	-0.4	160.3	0.4	160.3	0.0	160.5	0.1	161.1	0.4	161.1	0.0
1995	161.7	0.4	164.8	1.9	165.7	0.5	165.9	0.1	166.5	0.4	166.5	0.0	166.5	0.0	166.7	0.1	166.8	0.1	166.9	0.1	166.7	-0.1	166.8	0.1

Source: U.S. Department of Labor, Bureau of Labor Statistics, Division of Industry Prices and Price Indexes. n.e.c. stands for not elsewhere classified. - indicates no data collected for period or unavailable.

Heating Equipment
Producer Price Index
Base 1982 = 100

For 1947-1995. Columns headed % show percentile change in the index from the previous period for which an index is available.

Year	Jan Index	%	Feb Index	%	Mar Index	%	Apr Index	%	May Index	%	Jun Index	%	Jul Index	%	Aug Index	%	Sep Index	%	Oct Index	%	Nov Index	%	Dec Index	%
1947	35.3	-	35.3	0.0	35.3	0.0	35.3	0.0	35.4	0.3	35.2	-0.6	35.5	0.9	35.7	0.6	36.3	1.7	36.5	0.6	36.6	0.3	36.7	0.3
1948	36.6	-0.3	36.8	0.5	36.8	0.0	37.0	0.5	37.1	0.3	37.1	0.0	37.2	0.3	38.6	3.8	39.7	2.8	39.7	0.0	39.7	0.0	39.7	0.0
1949	39.7	0.0	39.7	0.0	39.4	-0.8	39.3	-0.3	39.2	-0.3	38.9	-0.8	38.6	-0.8	38.5	-0.3	38.4	-0.3	38.4	0.0	38.3	-0.3	38.3	0.0
1950	38.2	-0.3	38.3	0.3	38.3	0.0	38.3	0.0	38.4	0.3	38.3	-0.3	38.6	0.8	39.6	2.6	40.3	1.8	41.2	2.2	41.5	0.7	42.4	2.2
1951	43.0	1.4	43.1	0.2	43.1	0.0	43.1	0.0	43.1	0.0	43.0	-0.2	42.9	-0.2	43.0	0.2	43.0	0.0	43.0	0.0	42.9	-0.2	43.0	0.2
1952	42.8	-0.5	42.8	0.0	42.8	0.0	42.7	-0.2	42.7	0.0	42.6	-0.2	42.7	0.2	42.7	0.0	42.7	0.0	42.7	0.0	42.7	0.0	42.7	0.0
1953	42.7	0.0	42.7	0.0	42.7	0.0	42.7	0.0	42.9	0.5	43.0	0.2	43.2	0.5	43.4	0.5	43.5	0.2	43.5	0.0	43.5	0.0	43.4	-0.2
1954	43.3	-0.2	43.1	-0.5	42.9	-0.5	43.0	0.2	42.7	-0.7	42.7	0.0	42.8	0.2	42.8	0.0	42.8	0.0	42.9	0.2	42.9	0.0	42.9	0.0
1955	42.7	-0.5	42.7	0.0	42.7	0.0	42.7	0.0	42.6	-0.2	42.6	0.0	42.7	0.2	43.5	1.9	44.0	1.1	44.0	0.0	44.1	0.2	44.0	-0.2
1956	44.0	0.0	44.0	0.0	44.0	0.0	44.0	0.0	44.0	0.0	44.1	0.2	44.3	0.5	44.7	0.9	45.4	1.6	45.7	0.7	45.8	0.2	45.8	0.0
1957	46.0	0.4	46.0	0.0	45.5	-1.1	45.5	0.0	45.4	-0.2	45.6	0.4	46.0	0.9	45.7	-0.7	45.7	0.0	45.7	0.0	45.7	0.0	45.5	-0.4
1958	45.4	-0.2	45.3	-0.2	45.1	-0.4	45.1	0.0	45.1	0.0	45.2	0.2	45.3	0.2	45.3	0.0	45.4	0.2	45.4	0.0	45.4	0.0	45.5	0.2
1959	45.5	0.0	45.6	0.2	45.5	-0.2	45.5	0.0	45.5	0.0	45.5	0.0	45.5	0.0	45.5	0.0	45.4	-0.2	45.4	0.0	45.4	0.0	45.4	0.0
1960	45.2	-0.4	44.9	-0.7	44.9	0.0	44.9	0.0	44.9	0.0	44.9	0.0	44.3	-1.3	44.4	0.2	44.6	0.5	44.6	0.0	44.3	-0.7	43.6	-1.6
1961	42.9	-1.6	42.9	0.0	42.7	-0.5	43.0	0.7	43.1	0.2	43.1	0.0	43.1	0.0	43.2	0.2	43.0	-0.5	42.9	-0.2	42.7	-0.5	42.9	0.5
1962	42.7	-0.5	42.7	0.0	42.6	-0.2	42.6	0.0	42.3	-0.7	42.2	-0.2	42.2	0.0	42.2	0.0	42.1	-0.2	42.2	0.2	42.2	0.0	42.4	0.5
1963	42.1	-0.7	42.0	-0.2	42.1	0.2	42.2	0.2	42.3	0.2	42.4	0.2	42.4	0.0	42.3	-0.2	42.3	0.0	42.3	0.0	42.2	-0.2	42.2	0.0
1964	41.8	-0.9	41.7	-0.2	41.9	0.5	41.9	0.0	41.8	-0.2	42.0	0.5	41.8	-0.5	41.7	-0.2	41.7	0.0	41.7	0.0	41.8	0.2	41.9	0.2
1965	41.5	-1.0	41.6	0.2	41.7	0.2	41.8	0.2	41.7	-0.2	41.8	0.2	41.7	-0.2	41.8	0.2	41.8	0.0	41.8	0.0	41.7	-0.2	41.7	0.0
1966	41.6	-0.2	41.7	0.2	41.7	0.0	41.9	0.5	41.9	0.0	42.1	0.5	42.2	0.2	42.1	0.0	42.2	0.2	42.4	0.5	42.5	0.2	42.5	0.0
1967	42.1	-0.9	41.8	-0.7	41.9	0.2	41.9	0.0	41.9	0.0	42.2	0.7	42.2	0.0	42.1	0.0	42.2	0.2	42.3	0.2	42.5	0.5	42.6	0.2
1968	42.5	-0.2	42.7	0.5	42.9	0.5	43.1	0.5	43.3	0.5	43.4	0.2	43.5	0.2	43.5	0.0	43.5	0.0	43.5	0.0	43.6	0.2	43.8	0.5
1969	43.7	-0.2	43.8	0.2	43.9	0.2	44.1	0.5	44.1	0.0	44.3	0.5	44.4	0.2	44.5	0.2	44.6	0.2	44.9	0.7	45.4	1.1	45.4	0.0
1970	45.4	0.0	45.5	0.2	45.7	0.4	46.1	0.9	46.2	0.2	46.6	0.9	47.0	0.9	47.0	0.0	47.1	0.2	47.4	0.6	47.6	0.4	47.7	0.2
1971	47.8	0.2	48.1	0.6	48.1	0.0	48.3	0.4	48.6	0.6	48.5	-0.2	48.8	0.6	49.0	0.4	49.0	0.0	49.0	0.0	49.0	0.0	49.0	0.0
1972	48.9	-0.2	49.0	0.2	49.3	0.6	49.7	0.8	49.8	0.2	50.0	0.4	50.2	0.4	50.2	0.0	50.3	0.2	50.2	-0.2	50.3	0.2	50.2	-0.2
1973	50.1	-0.2	50.3	0.4	50.4	0.2	50.8	0.8	50.7	-0.2	50.9	0.4	51.0	0.2	50.9	-0.2	50.9	0.0	50.9	0.0	51.0	0.2	51.3	0.6
1974	51.8	1.0	52.1	0.6	52.5	0.8	53.8	2.5	54.8	1.9	56.0	2.2	57.8	3.2	59.0	2.1	59.6	1.0	61.1	2.5	62.0	1.5	62.6	1.0
1975	62.5	-0.2	62.8	0.5	63.0	0.3	63.1	0.2	63.3	0.3	63.5	0.3	63.3	-0.3	63.4	0.2	63.4	0.0	64.1	1.1	64.5	0.6	65.4	1.4
1976	65.5	0.2	65.5	0.0	65.4	-0.2	65.7	0.5	66.1	0.6	66.2	0.2	66.8	0.9	67.2	0.6	67.6	0.6	67.5	-0.1	67.8	0.4	68.2	0.6
1977	68.7	0.7	68.8	0.1	69.0	0.3	68.9	-0.1	69.1	0.3	69.4	0.4	69.7	0.4	70.0	0.4	70.3	0.4	70.8	0.7	70.9	0.1	71.4	0.7
1978	72.2	1.1	72.0	-0.3	72.2	0.3	72.8	0.8	73.1	0.4	73.3	0.3	73.5	0.3	74.3	1.1	74.2	-0.1	74.6	0.5	74.7	0.1	75.5	1.1
1979	75.9	0.5	76.3	0.5	77.3	1.3	77.5	0.3	78.3	1.0	78.1	-0.3	78.4	0.4	79.3	1.1	80.7	1.8	81.0	0.4	81.4	0.5	82.4	1.2
1980	84.1	2.1	85.4	1.5	85.4	0.0	86.1	0.8	86.0	-0.1	86.4	0.5	86.9	0.6	87.7	0.9	88.0	0.3	88.8	0.9	89.4	0.7	90.2	0.9
1981	91.3	1.2	91.7	0.4	92.5	0.9	92.7	0.2	93.7	1.1	94.2	0.5	95.4	1.3	96.1	0.7	96.3	0.2	96.5	0.2	96.5	0.0	96.9	0.4
1982	98.4	1.5	98.3	-0.1	99.3	1.0	99.5	0.2	100.0	0.5	100.5	0.5	100.7	0.2	100.5	-0.2	100.8	0.3	100.5	-0.3	100.7	0.2	100.9	0.2
1983	101.5	0.6	101.5	0.0	101.6	0.1	102.2	0.6	102.3	0.1	102.4	0.1	103.2	0.8	103.3	0.1	104.0	0.7	103.4	-0.6	103.5	0.1	103.6	0.1
1984	104.2	0.6	104.6	0.4	104.8	0.2	105.5	0.7	106.4	0.9	106.5	0.1	107.6	1.0	107.7	0.1	107.8	0.1	107.9	0.1	107.9	0.0	108.1	0.2
1985	108.0	-0.1	108.5	0.5	108.6	0.1	108.7	0.1	109.4	0.6	109.5	0.1	109.6	0.1	110.0	0.4	110.3	0.3	110.2	-0.1	110.3	0.1	110.5	0.2
1986	111.6	1.0	111.7	0.1	111.6	-0.1	112.5	0.8	112.3	-0.2	113.0	0.6	113.1	0.1	113.5	0.4	113.4	-0.1	114.3	0.8	114.4	0.1	114.5	0.1
1987	115.3	0.7	115.4	0.1	115.7	0.3	115.6	-0.1	115.6	0.0	115.1	-0.4	115.5	0.3	115.6	0.1	115.5	-0.1	115.7	0.2	117.1	1.2	114.1	-2.6
1988	115.9	1.6	118.4	2.2	118.4	0.0	118.5	0.1	118.8	0.3	118.5	-0.3	119.9	1.2	120.1	0.2	120.0	-0.1	120.5	0.4	120.8	0.2	121.0	0.2
1989	121.8	0.7	123.2	1.1	123.7	0.4	124.6	0.7	124.7	0.1	124.3	-0.3	124.8	0.4	125.1	0.2	126.9	1.4	126.9	0.0	127.3	0.3	127.6	0.2
1990	129.9	1.8	130.8	0.7	130.9	0.1	130.7	-0.2	130.7	0.0	130.6	-0.1	131.7	0.8	131.8	0.1	132.0	0.2	133.3	1.0	133.3	0.0	133.3	0.0
1991	134.0	0.5	134.3	0.2	134.1	-0.1	133.2	-0.7	133.5	0.2	133.5	0.0	134.1	0.4	134.4	0.2	134.0	-0.3	134.8	0.6	134.8	0.0	134.6	-0.1

[Continued]

Heating Equipment
Producer Price Index
Base 1982 = 100
[Continued]

For 1947-1995. Columns headed % show percentile change in the index from the previous period for which an index is available.

Year	Jan Index	%	Feb Index	%	Mar Index	%	Apr Index	%	May Index	%	Jun Index	%	Jul Index	%	Aug Index	%	Sep Index	%	Oct Index	%	Nov Index	%	Dec Index	%
1992	136.2	1.2	136.6	0.3	137.2	0.4	137.1	-0.1	137.6	0.4	137.4	-0.1	137.6	0.1	137.4	-0.1	137.3	-0.1	137.6	0.2	137.0	-0.4	138.1	0.8
1993	139.2	0.8	139.3	0.1	139.4	0.1	140.6	0.9	140.7	0.1	141.2	0.4	140.9	-0.2	140.7	-0.1	140.4	-0.2	140.6	0.1	140.7	0.1	140.7	0.0
1994	141.2	0.4	141.8	0.4	142.1	0.2	142.4	0.2	142.6	0.1	142.4	-0.1	142.6	0.1	142.9	0.2	143.0	0.1	143.0	0.0	143.1	0.1	143.3	0.1
1995	145.3	1.4	146.5	0.8	147.0	0.3	147.2	0.1	147.4	0.1	147.6	0.1	147.7	0.1	148.1	0.3	148.3	0.1	148.4	0.1	148.4	0.0	148.0	-0.3

Source: U.S. Department of Labor, Bureau of Labor Statistics, Division of Industry Prices and Price Indexes. n.e.c. stands for not elsewhere classified. - indicates no data collected for period or unavailable.

Fabricated Structural Metal Products
Producer Price Index
Base 1982 = 100

For 1947-1995. Columns headed % show percentile change in the index from the previous period for which an index is available.

Year	Jan Index	%	Feb Index	%	Mar Index	%	Apr Index	%	May Index	%	Jun Index	%	Jul Index	%	Aug Index	%	Sep Index	%	Oct Index	%	Nov Index	%	Dec Index	%
1947	22.2	-	22.2	0.0	22.4	0.9	22.4	0.0	22.3	-0.4	22.3	0.0	22.3	0.0	22.3	0.0	22.9	2.7	23.0	0.4	23.1	0.4	23.1	0.0
1948	23.2	0.4	23.2	0.0	23.3	0.4	23.4	0.4	23.2	-0.9	23.2	0.0	23.4	0.9	24.5	4.7	24.7	0.8	24.7	0.0	24.7	0.0	24.7	0.0
1949	24.6	-0.4	24.5	-0.4	24.4	-0.4	24.0	-1.6	23.7	-1.2	23.4	-1.3	23.4	0.0	22.8	-2.6	22.7	-0.4	22.7	0.0	22.8	0.4	22.9	0.4
1950	23.0	0.4	23.4	1.7	23.4	0.0	23.3	-0.4	23.3	0.0	23.3	0.0	23.9	2.6	24.2	1.3	24.6	1.7	25.7	4.5	26.0	1.2	27.2	4.6
1951	27.6	1.5	27.8	0.7	27.7	-0.4	27.7	0.0	27.7	0.0	27.7	0.0	27.3	-1.4	27.1	-0.7	27.1	0.0	27.0	-0.4	27.0	0.0	27.0	0.0
1952	27.0	0.0	26.9	-0.4	26.9	0.0	26.9	0.0	26.9	0.0	26.9	0.0	26.9	0.0	26.9	0.0	26.9	0.0	26.6	-1.1	26.6	0.0	26.5	-0.4
1953	26.5	0.0	26.5	0.0	26.5	0.0	26.5	0.0	26.5	0.0	26.7	0.8	27.4	2.6	27.5	0.4	27.5	0.0	27.4	-0.4	27.4	0.0	27.3	-0.4
1954	27.4	0.4	27.2	-0.7	27.2	0.0	27.2	0.0	27.1	-0.4	27.0	-0.4	27.0	0.0	27.4	1.5	27.5	0.4	27.5	0.0	27.4	-0.4	27.5	0.4
1955	27.5	0.0	27.5	0.0	27.5	0.0	27.6	0.4	27.7	0.4	27.7	0.0	28.8	4.0	29.5	2.4	29.6	0.3	29.7	0.3	29.7	0.0	29.8	0.3
1956	30.0	0.7	30.0	0.0	30.2	0.7	30.6	1.3	30.1	-1.6	30.1	0.0	30.2	0.3	31.3	3.6	31.9	1.9	31.9	0.0	32.0	0.3	32.0	0.0
1957	31.2	-2.5	31.1	-0.3	31.1	0.0	30.9	-0.6	30.8	-0.3	30.7	-0.3	31.3	2.0	31.6	1.0	31.4	-0.6	31.4	0.0	31.4	0.0	31.4	0.0
1958	31.4	0.0	31.4	0.0	31.3	-0.3	31.3	0.0	31.3	0.0	31.2	-0.3	31.0	-0.6	31.1	0.3	31.0	-0.3	31.1	0.3	31.2	0.3	31.2	0.0
1959	31.2	0.0	31.2	0.0	30.8	-1.3	30.8	0.0	30.8	0.0	30.8	0.0	30.8	0.0	30.8	0.0	31.3	1.6	31.3	0.0	31.6	1.0	31.6	0.0
1960	31.6	0.0	31.6	0.0	31.7	0.3	31.5	-0.6	31.4	-0.3	31.4	0.0	31.4	0.0	31.4	0.0	31.3	-0.3	31.2	-0.3	31.2	0.0	31.2	0.0
1961	31.1	-0.3	31.1	0.0	30.9	-0.6	30.9	0.0	30.8	-0.3	30.8	0.0	30.8	0.0	30.8	0.0	30.7	-0.3	30.7	0.0	30.7	0.0	30.7	0.0
1962	30.6	-0.3	30.6	0.0	30.6	0.0	30.6	0.0	30.6	0.0	30.6	0.0	30.6	0.0	30.6	0.0	30.6	0.0	30.6	0.0	30.6	0.0	30.6	0.0
1963	30.6	0.0	30.5	-0.3	30.5	0.0	30.4	-0.3	30.5	0.3	30.6	0.3	30.6	0.0	30.6	0.0	30.7	0.3	30.7	0.0	30.8	0.3	30.8	0.0
1964	30.8	0.0	30.9	0.3	30.7	-0.6	30.8	0.3	30.7	-0.3	30.9	0.7	30.9	0.0	31.0	0.3	31.0	0.0	31.0	0.0	31.1	0.3	31.2	0.3
1965	31.3	0.3	31.2	-0.3	31.3	0.3	31.4	0.3	31.5	0.3	31.5	0.0	31.6	0.3	31.7	0.3	31.7	0.0	31.7	0.0	31.8	0.3	31.8	0.0
1966	31.9	0.3	32.0	0.3	32.1	0.3	32.3	0.6	32.3	0.0	32.4	0.3	32.5	0.3	32.5	0.0	32.5	0.0	32.6	0.3	32.6	0.0	32.7	0.3
1967	32.6	-0.3	32.6	0.0	32.6	0.0	32.7	0.3	32.7	0.0	32.7	0.0	32.8	0.3	32.9	0.3	32.9	0.0	33.0	0.3	33.0	0.0	33.0	0.0
1968	33.1	0.3	33.1	0.0	33.3	0.6	33.3	0.0	33.2	-0.3	33.5	0.9	33.5	0.0	33.7	0.6	33.8	0.3	33.9	0.3	33.9	0.0	34.0	0.3
1969	34.0	0.0	34.1	0.3	34.1	0.0	34.3	0.6	34.5	0.6	34.8	0.9	34.9	0.3	35.1	0.6	35.2	0.3	35.3	0.3	35.4	0.3	35.4	0.0
1970	35.6	0.6	35.8	0.6	36.2	1.1	36.3	0.3	36.5	0.6	36.8	0.8	37.1	0.8	37.2	0.3	37.3	0.3	37.3	0.0	37.3	0.0	37.5	0.5
1971	37.7	0.5	37.9	0.5	38.2	0.8	38.3	0.3	38.4	0.3	38.6	0.5	38.8	0.5	39.5	1.8	39.4	-0.3	39.4	0.0	39.4	0.0	39.4	0.0
1972	39.9	1.3	40.0	0.3	40.1	0.3	40.1	0.0	40.0	-0.2	40.1	0.3	40.1	0.0	40.2	0.2	40.2	0.0	40.4	0.5	40.4	0.0	40.5	0.2
1973	40.8	0.7	40.9	0.2	41.0	0.2	41.2	0.5	41.6	1.0	41.6	0.0	41.7	0.2	41.9	0.5	42.2	0.7	42.5	0.7	42.9	0.9	43.2	0.7
1974	44.4	2.8	44.9	1.1	46.0	2.4	47.2	2.6	49.8	5.5	52.1	4.6	54.2	4.0	57.5	6.1	59.0	2.6	59.7	1.2	59.9	0.3	60.0	0.2
1975	60.8	1.3	62.2	2.3	62.3	0.2	61.8	-0.8	61.9	0.2	61.9	0.0	61.8	-0.2	62.0	0.3	62.1	0.2	62.4	0.5	62.3	-0.2	62.6	0.5
1976	62.5	-0.2	62.4	-0.2	62.6	0.3	62.5	-0.2	62.6	0.2	63.0	0.6	63.5	0.8	64.1	0.9	64.6	0.8	64.8	0.3	65.0	0.3	65.3	0.5
1977	65.4	0.2	65.7	0.5	66.2	0.8	66.6	0.6	67.0	0.6	67.2	0.3	68.2	1.5	68.9	1.0	69.5	0.9	69.5	0.0	69.6	0.1	70.0	0.6
1978	70.4	0.6	71.8	2.0	72.6	1.1	73.7	1.5	73.9	0.3	74.1	0.3	74.8	0.9	75.5	0.9	75.7	0.3	76.0	0.4	76.2	0.3	76.6	0.5
1979	78.2	2.1	78.9	0.9	79.2	0.4	80.0	1.0	81.0	1.3	81.4	0.5	82.2	1.0	82.7	0.6	83.2	0.6	84.1	1.1	84.2	0.1	84.5	0.4
1980	84.9	0.5	85.2	0.4	87.0	2.1	88.3	1.5	88.5	0.2	88.6	0.1	89.3	0.8	89.6	0.3	89.9	0.3	90.9	1.1	91.2	0.3	91.6	0.4
1981	92.9	1.4	93.6	0.8	95.0	1.5	96.1	1.2	96.4	0.3	96.8	0.4	97.7	0.9	98.2	0.5	98.4	0.2	99.3	0.9	99.5	0.2	99.4	-0.1
1982	99.6	0.2	99.7	0.1	99.9	0.2	100.1	0.2	100.0	-0.1	100.2	0.2	99.7	-0.5	99.8	0.1	100.5	0.7	100.4	-0.1	100.2	-0.2	100.0	-0.2
1983	99.6	-0.4	99.4	-0.2	99.6	0.2	99.2	-0.4	99.1	-0.1	99.1	0.0	99.2	0.1	99.4	0.2	99.8	0.4	99.8	0.0	100.2	0.4	100.4	0.2
1984	100.6	0.2	100.7	0.1	101.2	0.5	101.5	0.3	101.9	0.4	102.1	0.2	102.3	0.2	102.4	0.1	102.4	0.0	102.9	0.5	102.6	-0.3	102.8	0.2
1985	102.9	0.1	102.9	0.0	103.2	0.3	103.2	0.0	103.2	0.0	103.2	0.0	103.2	0.0	103.4	0.2	103.3	-0.1	103.5	0.2	103.3	-0.2	103.3	0.0
1986	103.3	0.0	103.5	0.2	103.4	-0.1	103.4	0.0	103.3	-0.1	103.5	0.2	103.5	0.0	103.7	0.2	103.7	0.0	103.6	-0.1	104.1	0.5	103.8	-0.3
1987	103.6	-0.2	103.8	0.2	104.0	0.2	104.2	0.2	104.4	0.2	104.9	0.5	105.2	0.3	105.6	0.4	106.1	0.5	107.0	0.8	107.8	0.7	108.6	0.7
1988	110.2	1.5	110.8	0.5	111.7	0.8	112.9	1.1	113.8	0.8	114.4	0.5	115.4	0.9	115.8	0.3	116.2	0.3	116.5	0.3	116.8	0.3	117.4	0.5
1989	118.2	0.7	118.9	0.6	119.4	0.4	119.8	0.3	120.5	0.6	120.5	0.0	120.7	0.2	120.8	0.1	120.9	0.1	121.0	0.1	121.2	0.2	121.1	-0.1
1990	121.1	0.0	121.2	0.1	121.3	0.1	121.4	0.1	121.9	0.4	122.0	0.1	122.0	0.0	122.1	0.1	122.1	0.0	122.2	0.1	122.1	-0.1	122.4	0.2
1991	122.7	0.2	122.5	-0.2	122.5	0.0	122.9	0.3	122.7	-0.2	122.6	-0.1	122.5	-0.1	122.6	0.1	122.5	-0.1	122.0	-0.4	121.7	-0.2	121.7	0.0

[Continued]

Fabricated Structural Metal Products
Producer Price Index
Base 1982 = 100
[Continued]

For 1947-1995. Columns headed % show percentile change in the index from the previous period for which an index is available.

Year	Jan Index	%	Feb Index	%	Mar Index	%	Apr Index	%	May Index	%	Jun Index	%	Jul Index	%	Aug Index	%	Sep Index	%	Oct Index	%	Nov Index	%	Dec Index	%
1992	122.0	0.2	121.8	-0.2	122.0	0.2	122.2	0.2	122.0	-0.2	122.0	0.0	122.2	0.2	122.3	0.1	122.1	-0.2	122.2	0.1	122.2	0.0	122.2	0.0
1993	121.8	-0.3	122.1	0.2	122.4	0.2	122.7	0.2	122.9	0.2	123.1	0.2	123.4	0.2	123.6	0.2	123.8	0.2	124.1	0.2	124.4	0.2	124.6	0.2
1994	124.9	0.2	125.0	0.1	125.2	0.2	125.7	0.4	126.3	0.5	127.1	0.6	127.4	0.2	128.0	0.5	128.7	0.5	129.2	0.4	130.1	0.7	130.4	0.2
1995	131.9	1.2	132.5	0.5	133.6	0.8	134.4	0.6	134.6	0.1	135.2	0.4	135.8	0.4	136.0	0.1	136.5	0.4	136.6	0.1	136.8	0.1	136.7	-0.1

Source: U.S. Department of Labor, Bureau of Labor Statistics, Division of Industry Prices and Price Indexes. n.e.c. stands for not elsewhere classified. - indicates no data collected for period or unavailable.

Miscellaneous Metal Products

Producer Price Index
Base 1982 = 100

For 1947-1995. Columns headed % show percentile change in the index from the previous period for which an index is available.

Year	Jan Index	%	Feb Index	%	Mar Index	%	Apr Index	%	May Index	%	Jun Index	%	Jul Index	%	Aug Index	%	Sep Index	%	Oct Index	%	Nov Index	%	Dec Index	%
1947	17.4	-	17.4	0.0	17.7	1.7	17.9	1.1	17.9	0.0	18.0	0.6	18.1	0.6	18.2	0.6	18.2	0.0	18.5	1.6	18.6	0.5	18.6	0.0
1948	18.6	0.0	18.9	1.6	20.0	5.8	22.5	12.5	22.5	0.0	22.6	0.4	22.6	0.0	23.6	4.4	23.8	0.8	23.8	0.0	23.9	0.4	23.9	0.0
1949	23.9	0.0	23.9	0.0	23.9	0.0	24.0	0.4	24.0	0.0	23.9	-0.4	23.9	0.0	23.8	-0.4	23.8	0.0	23.8	0.0	23.7	-0.4	23.6	-0.4
1950	24.0	1.7	24.1	0.4	24.2	0.4	24.2	0.0	24.2	0.0	24.2	0.0	24.3	0.4	24.4	0.4	25.1	2.9	25.7	2.4	25.8	0.4	26.4	2.3
1951	26.9	1.9	26.9	0.0	26.9	0.0	26.9	0.0	26.9	0.0	26.9	0.0	26.9	0.0	26.8	-0.4	26.6	-0.7	26.6	0.0	26.6	0.0	26.6	0.0
1952	26.6	0.0	26.6	0.0	26.6	0.0	26.6	0.0	26.6	0.0	26.6	0.0	26.6	0.0	26.6	0.0	26.8	0.8	26.9	0.4	26.9	0.0	27.0	0.4
1953	27.0	0.0	27.1	0.4	26.1	-3.7	26.2	0.4	26.5	1.1	26.5	0.0	26.8	1.1	27.0	0.7	27.1	0.4	27.2	0.4	27.2	0.0	27.2	0.0
1954	27.2	0.0	27.0	-0.7	27.0	0.0	26.8	-0.7	26.8	0.0	26.8	0.0	26.8	0.0	26.9	0.4	26.9	0.0	26.9	0.0	27.0	0.4	26.9	-0.4
1955	26.9	0.0	26.9	0.0	26.9	0.0	26.9	0.0	26.9	0.0	26.9	0.0	27.1	0.7	27.7	2.2	27.9	0.7	28.1	0.7	28.2	0.4	28.3	0.4
1956	28.3	0.0	28.3	0.0	28.4	0.4	28.3	-0.4	28.3	0.0	28.3	0.0	28.3	0.0	28.5	0.7	29.3	2.8	30.2	3.1	30.2	0.0	30.2	0.0
1957	30.2	0.0	30.4	0.7	30.5	0.3	30.6	0.3	30.6	0.0	30.6	0.0	31.1	1.6	31.3	0.6	31.5	0.6	31.5	0.0	31.4	-0.3	31.6	0.6
1958	31.4	-0.6	31.3	-0.3	31.3	0.0	31.2	-0.3	31.2	0.0	31.0	-0.6	31.0	0.0	31.1	0.3	31.1	0.0	31.1	0.0	31.0	-0.3	31.0	0.0
1959	31.1	0.3	31.2	0.3	31.2	0.0	31.2	0.0	31.2	0.0	31.2	0.0	31.1	-0.3	31.0	-0.3	31.2	0.6	31.3	0.3	31.5	0.6	31.3	-0.6
1960	31.3	0.0	31.3	0.0	31.2	-0.3	31.2	0.0	31.2	0.0	31.2	0.0	31.2	0.0	31.2	0.0	31.2	0.0	31.2	0.0	31.3	0.3	31.7	1.3
1961	32.0	0.9	32.0	0.0	32.0	0.0	32.1	0.3	32.1	0.0	32.0	-0.3	31.9	-0.3	32.2	0.9	32.2	0.0	32.2	0.0	32.1	-0.3	32.1	0.0
1962	32.1	0.0	32.1	0.0	32.4	0.9	32.5	0.3	32.4	-0.3	32.3	-0.3	32.3	0.0	32.3	0.0	32.3	0.0	32.3	0.0	32.3	0.0	32.3	0.0
1963	32.2	-0.3	32.2	0.0	32.2	0.0	32.3	0.3	32.3	0.0	32.6	0.9	32.7	0.3	32.7	0.0	32.7	0.0	33.3	1.8	33.3	0.0	33.6	0.9
1964	34.0	1.2	34.0	0.0	33.9	-0.3	33.9	0.0	33.6	-0.9	33.7	0.3	33.6	-0.3	33.6	0.0	33.6	0.0	33.6	0.0	33.6	0.0	33.7	0.3
1965	33.7	0.0	33.9	0.6	33.9	0.0	34.0	0.3	34.0	0.0	34.0	0.0	33.9	-0.3	34.2	0.9	34.2	0.0	34.1	-0.3	34.1	0.0	34.1	0.0
1966	34.2	0.3	34.4	0.6	34.5	0.3	34.5	0.0	34.5	0.0	34.6	0.3	34.6	0.0	34.9	0.9	35.0	0.3	35.0	0.0	35.2	0.6	35.2	0.0
1967	35.3	0.3	35.3	0.0	35.3	0.0	35.3	0.0	35.3	0.0	35.3	0.0	35.4	0.3	35.5	0.3	35.5	0.0	35.5	0.0	35.5	0.0	35.6	0.3
1968	35.7	0.3	35.9	0.6	35.9	0.0	35.9	0.0	35.9	0.0	35.9	0.0	36.0	0.3	36.0	0.0	36.3	0.8	36.6	0.8	36.6	0.0	36.8	0.5
1969	37.2	1.1	37.4	0.5	37.5	0.3	37.5	0.0	37.5	0.0	37.6	0.3	38.0	1.1	38.5	1.3	38.7	0.5	38.7	0.0	38.7	0.0	38.8	0.3
1970	38.9	0.3	39.0	0.3	39.6	1.5	39.6	0.0	39.9	0.8	40.6	1.8	40.8	0.5	40.9	0.2	41.5	1.5	41.6	0.2	41.7	0.2	41.7	0.0
1971	41.6	-0.2	41.7	0.2	41.7	0.0	41.8	0.2	41.8	0.0	42.0	0.5	42.3	0.7	42.4	0.2	42.4	0.0	42.3	-0.2	42.3	0.0	42.8	1.2
1972	43.0	0.5	43.6	1.4	44.0	0.9	44.0	0.0	44.0	0.0	44.1	0.2	44.0	-0.2	44.2	0.5	44.2	0.0	44.2	0.0	44.2	0.0	44.2	0.0
1973	44.4	0.5	44.5	0.2	44.8	0.7	45.1	0.7	45.4	0.7	45.6	0.4	45.7	0.2	46.4	1.5	46.5	0.2	46.8	0.6	47.4	1.3	47.7	0.6
1974	48.5	1.7	49.1	1.2	49.5	0.8	50.7	2.4	53.2	4.9	54.6	2.6	57.1	4.6	59.0	3.3	60.5	2.5	61.7	2.0	62.2	0.8	62.6	0.6
1975	63.1	0.8	63.3	0.3	63.7	0.6	63.8	0.2	63.5	-0.5	64.3	1.3	64.5	0.3	64.5	0.0	64.5	0.0	64.6	0.2	64.7	0.2	64.7	0.0
1976	65.0	0.5	65.0	0.0	64.9	-0.2	65.2	0.5	65.5	0.5	65.7	0.3	66.3	0.9	67.0	1.1	67.2	0.3	67.4	0.3	67.7	0.4	67.5	-0.3
1977	67.8	0.4	68.0	0.3	68.1	0.1	68.1	0.0	68.3	0.3	68.9	0.9	69.7	1.2	70.2	0.7	70.8	0.9	71.0	0.3	71.4	0.6	71.6	0.3
1978	71.8	0.3	72.2	0.6	72.8	0.8	73.3	0.7	73.9	0.8	74.8	1.2	75.6	1.1	76.4	1.1	77.0	0.8	77.3	0.4	77.9	0.8	78.2	0.4
1979	78.6	0.5	79.1	0.6	79.8	0.9	80.4	0.8	80.9	0.6	81.5	0.7	82.1	0.7	83.4	1.6	83.8	0.5	84.5	0.8	84.5	0.0	84.7	0.2
1980	85.2	0.6	85.6	0.5	86.5	1.1	87.2	0.8	87.4	0.2	88.7	1.5	88.9	0.2	89.7	0.9	90.3	0.7	90.8	0.6	91.0	0.2	91.2	0.2
1981	92.3	1.2	93.2	1.0	93.8	0.6	94.6	0.9	95.5	1.0	95.4	-0.1	96.3	0.9	96.7	0.4	96.9	0.2	97.8	0.9	98.5	0.7	98.6	0.1
1982	99.6	1.0	98.7	-0.9	98.8	0.1	99.1	0.3	100.8	1.7	100.6	-0.2	100.3	-0.3	100.4	0.1	100.5	0.1	100.6	0.1	100.4	-0.2	100.3	-0.1
1983	98.9	-1.4	98.8	-0.1	99.3	0.5	99.4	0.1	99.5	0.1	100.4	0.9	100.5	0.1	100.6	0.1	100.7	0.1	102.3	1.6	102.6	0.3	102.6	0.0
1984	102.8	0.2	103.1	0.3	103.5	0.4	103.8	0.3	103.9	0.1	104.2	0.3	104.2	0.0	104.5	0.3	104.8	0.3	106.8	1.9	106.8	0.0	106.9	0.1
1985	106.9	0.0	107.0	0.1	107.0	0.0	107.0	0.0	107.0	0.0	107.2	0.2	107.3	0.1	107.2	-0.1	107.1	-0.1	107.0	-0.1	107.1	0.1	107.0	-0.1
1986	107.1	0.1	107.2	0.1	107.2	0.0	107.2	0.0	106.8	-0.4	106.8	0.0	106.6	-0.2	106.7	0.1	106.9	0.2	107.1	0.2	107.2	0.1	107.3	0.1
1987	107.5	0.2	107.6	0.1	107.6	0.0	107.5	-0.1	107.5	0.0	107.6	0.1	107.8	0.2	107.7	-0.1	107.7	0.0	108.2	0.5	108.4	0.2	108.8	0.4
1988	109.2	0.4	109.7	0.5	110.3	0.5	111.3	0.9	112.0	0.6	111.9	-0.1	112.3	0.4	113.1	0.7	113.4	0.3	113.8	0.4	114.2	0.4	114.5	0.3
1989	115.3	0.7	115.7	0.3	115.9	0.2	116.5	0.5	116.9	0.3	117.0	0.1	117.1	0.1	117.6	0.4	117.7	0.1	117.8	0.1	118.0	0.2	118.3	0.3
1990	118.6	0.3	118.8	0.2	118.9	0.1	119.1	0.2	119.2	0.1	119.4	0.2	119.3	-0.1	119.6	0.3	119.9	0.3	119.8	-0.1	119.9	0.1	119.8	-0.1
1991	120.1	0.3	120.1	0.0	120.2	0.1	120.1	-0.1	120.4	0.2	120.6	0.2	120.9	0.2	120.7	-0.2	120.7	0.0	120.6	-0.1	120.4	-0.2	120.6	0.2

[Continued]

Miscellaneous Metal Products
Producer Price Index
Base 1982 = 100
[Continued]

For 1947-1995. Columns headed % show percentile change in the index from the previous period for which an index is available.

Year	Jan Index	%	Feb Index	%	Mar Index	%	Apr Index	%	May Index	%	Jun Index	%	Jul Index	%	Aug Index	%	Sep Index	%	Oct Index	%	Nov Index	%	Dec Index	%
1992	120.9	0.2	121.0	0.1	121.1	0.1	121.2	0.1	121.2	0.0	121.2	0.0	121.3	0.1	121.3	0.0	121.5	0.2	121.9	0.3	121.9	0.0	121.9	0.0
1993	121.8	-0.1	122.0	0.2	122.0	0.0	122.2	0.2	122.3	0.1	122.3	0.0	122.5	0.2	122.3	-0.2	122.4	0.1	122.4	0.0	122.7	0.2	122.8	0.1
1994	123.0	0.2	123.0	0.0	123.2	0.2	123.3	0.1	123.4	0.1	123.5	0.1	123.5	0.0	123.6	0.1	123.8	0.2	124.0	0.2	124.2	0.2	124.4	0.2
1995	125.0	0.5	125.3	0.2	125.4	0.1	125.5	0.1	125.8	0.2	125.9	0.1	126.0	0.1	126.3	0.2	126.3	0.0	126.3	0.0	126.4	0.1	126.4	0.0

Source: U.S. Department of Labor, Bureau of Labor Statistics, Division of Industry Prices and Price Indexes. n.e.c. stands for not elsewhere classified. - indicates no data collected for period or unavailable.

Metal Treatment Services
Producer Price Index
Base Dec. 1984 = 100

For 1984-1995. Columns headed % show percentile change in the index from the previous period for which an index is available.

Year	Jan Index	%	Feb Index	%	Mar Index	%	Apr Index	%	May Index	%	Jun Index	%	Jul Index	%	Aug Index	%	Sep Index	%	Oct Index	%	Nov Index	%	Dec Index	%
1984	-	-	-	-	-	-	-	-	-	-	-	-	-	-	-	-	-	-	-	-	-	-	100.0	-
1985	100.4	0.4	100.9	0.5	100.8	-0.1	101.4	0.6	102.2	0.8	102.2	0.0	102.7	0.5	103.4	0.7	103.4	0.0	103.4	0.0	103.8	0.4	104.0	0.2
1986	104.5	0.5	104.2	-0.3	104.3	0.1	104.4	0.1	104.4	0.0	104.5	0.1	104.7	0.2	104.9	0.2	105.0	0.1	105.1	0.1	105.2	0.1	105.1	-0.1
1987	105.5	0.4	105.6	0.1	105.7	0.1	105.8	0.1	106.1	0.3	106.1	0.0	106.0	-0.1	106.5	0.5	106.2	-0.3	106.7	0.5	106.8	0.1	107.4	0.6
1988	107.5	0.1	107.7	0.2	107.8	0.1	108.7	0.8	108.3	-0.4	109.1	0.7	110.0	0.8	110.3	0.3	111.8	1.4	112.1	0.3	112.2	0.1	112.6	0.4
1989	113.3	0.6	113.6	0.3	114.0	0.4	114.6	0.5	114.6	0.0	114.7	0.1	114.6	-0.1	114.7	0.1	114.9	0.2	115.0	0.1	115.0	0.0	115.2	0.2
1990	115.5	0.3	115.6	0.1	115.7	0.1	115.7	0.0	115.8	0.1	115.9	0.1	116.7	0.7	116.8	0.1	116.9	0.1	117.1	0.2	116.9	-0.2	116.9	0.0
1991	117.5	0.5	117.6	0.1	117.5	-0.1	117.4	-0.1	117.3	-0.1	117.3	0.0	117.3	0.0	117.3	0.0	117.3	0.0	117.7	0.3	117.7	0.0	117.5	-0.2
1992	117.7	0.2	117.8	0.1	117.9	0.1	118.0	0.1	118.1	0.1	118.1	0.0	118.3	0.2	118.4	0.1	118.5	0.1	118.5	0.0	118.5	0.0	118.7	0.2
1993	119.1	0.3	119.3	0.2	119.4	0.1	119.6	0.2	119.6	0.0	119.7	0.1	119.9	0.2	120.1	0.2	120.1	0.0	120.3	0.2	120.3	0.0	120.3	0.0
1994	120.6	0.2	121.0	0.3	121.0	0.0	121.1	0.1	121.2	0.1	121.3	0.1	121.5	0.2	121.7	0.2	121.6	-0.1	121.6	0.0	122.2	0.5	122.2	0.0
1995	122.5	0.2	122.7	0.2	123.1	0.3	123.2	0.1	123.3	0.1	123.1	-0.2	123.6	0.4	123.6	0.0	123.7	0.1	123.8	0.1	124.2	0.3	124.3	0.1

Source: U.S. Department of Labor, Bureau of Labor Statistics, Division of Industry Prices and Price Indexes. n.e.c. stands for not elsewhere classified. - indicates no data collected for period or unavailable.

MACHINERY AND EQUIPMENT
Producer Price Index
Base 1982 = 100

For 1939-1995. Columns headed % show percentile change in the index from the previous period for which an index is available.

Year	Jan Index	%	Feb Index	%	Mar Index	%	Apr Index	%	May Index	%	Jun Index	%	Jul Index	%	Aug Index	%	Sep Index	%	Oct Index	%	Nov Index	%	Dec Index	%
1939	14.9	-	14.9	0.0	14.9	0.0	14.8	-0.7	14.8	0.0	14.8	0.0	14.8	0.0	14.8	0.0	14.8	0.0	14.8	0.0	14.8	0.0	14.8	0.0
1940	14.9	0.7	14.9	0.0	14.9	0.0	14.9	0.0	14.8	-0.7	14.9	0.7	14.9	0.0	14.9	0.0	14.9	0.0	14.9	0.0	14.9	0.0	14.9	0.0
1941	14.9	0.0	15.0	0.7	15.0	0.0	15.0	0.0	15.0	0.0	15.1	0.7	15.1	0.0	15.1	0.0	15.2	0.7	15.2	0.0	15.4	1.3	15.4	0.0
1942	15.4	0.0	15.4	0.0	15.4	0.0	15.4	0.0	15.4	0.0	15.4	0.0	15.4	0.0	15.3	-0.6	15.2	-0.7	15.2	0.0	15.2	0.0	15.2	0.0
1943	15.2	0.0	15.2	0.0	15.2	0.0	15.2	0.0	15.2	0.0	15.2	0.0	15.2	0.0	15.2	0.0	15.2	0.0	15.2	0.0	15.2	0.0	15.1	-0.7
1944	15.2	0.7	15.2	0.0	15.2	0.0	15.2	0.0	15.2	0.0	15.1	-0.7	15.1	0.0	15.1	0.0	15.1	0.0	15.1	0.0	15.1	0.0	15.1	0.0
1945	15.1	0.0	15.1	0.0	15.1	0.0	15.1	0.0	15.1	0.0	15.2	0.7	15.2	0.0	15.2	0.0	15.2	0.0	15.2	0.0	15.2	0.0	15.2	0.0
1946	15.3	0.7	15.4	0.7	15.4	0.0	15.6	1.3	16.3	4.5	16.6	1.8	16.9	1.8	17.1	1.2	17.4	1.8	17.5	0.6	17.9	2.3	18.4	2.8
1947	18.6	1.1	18.7	0.5	18.7	0.0	18.8	0.5	19.2	2.1	19.3	0.5	19.3	0.0	19.4	0.5	19.6	1.0	19.7	0.5	19.9	1.0	19.9	0.0
1948	20.1	1.0	20.1	0.0	20.2	0.5	20.2	0.0	20.2	0.0	20.4	1.0	20.7	1.5	21.2	2.4	21.6	1.9	21.8	0.9	21.9	0.5	22.0	0.5
1949	22.0	0.0	22.1	0.5	22.0	-0.5	22.0	0.0	21.9	-0.5	21.8	-0.5	21.8	0.0	21.8	0.0	21.8	0.0	21.7	-0.5	21.7	0.0	21.7	0.0
1950	21.7	0.0	21.7	0.0	21.7	0.0	21.8	0.5	21.8	0.0	22.0	0.9	22.2	0.9	22.8	2.7	23.2	1.8	23.6	1.7	23.9	1.3	24.8	3.8
1951	25.2	1.6	25.3	0.4	25.3	0.0	25.3	0.0	25.3	0.0	25.3	0.0	25.3	0.0	25.3	0.0	25.3	0.0	25.4	0.4	25.4	0.0	25.4	0.0
1952	25.4	0.0	25.4	0.0	25.4	0.0	25.4	0.0	25.4	0.0	25.3	-0.4	25.3	0.0	25.3	0.0	25.3	0.0	25.3	0.0	25.3	0.0	25.3	0.0
1953	25.3	0.0	25.3	0.0	25.4	0.4	25.6	0.8	25.7	0.4	25.9	0.8	26.0	0.4	26.2	0.8	26.3	0.4	26.3	0.0	26.3	0.0	26.3	0.0
1954	26.3	0.0	26.4	0.4	26.4	0.0	26.3	-0.4	26.3	0.0	26.3	0.0	26.3	0.0	26.3	0.0	26.3	0.0	26.3	0.0	26.4	0.4	26.4	0.0
1955	26.5	0.4	26.6	0.4	26.6	0.0	26.6	0.0	26.7	0.4	26.8	0.4	27.0	0.7	27.3	1.1	27.8	1.8	27.9	0.4	28.1	0.7	28.2	0.4
1956	28.3	0.4	28.4	0.4	28.5	0.4	28.8	1.1	29.1	1.0	29.1	0.0	29.2	0.3	29.4	0.7	30.0	2.0	30.3	1.0	30.6	1.0	30.7	0.3
1957	30.9	0.7	31.0	0.3	31.1	0.3	31.1	0.0	31.2	0.3	31.2	0.0	31.4	0.6	31.5	0.3	31.7	0.6	31.9	0.6	32.0	0.3	32.0	0.0
1958	32.1	0.3	32.0	-0.3	32.0	0.0	32.1	0.3	32.1	0.0	32.1	0.0	32.1	0.0	32.1	0.0	32.1	0.0	32.1	0.0	32.2	0.3	32.3	0.3
1959	32.4	0.3	32.4	0.0	32.5	0.3	32.5	0.0	32.6	0.3	32.7	0.3	32.9	0.6	33.0	0.3	33.0	0.0	33.0	0.0	33.1	0.3	33.1	0.0
1960	33.1	0.0	33.1	0.0	33.1	0.0	33.1	0.0	33.0	-0.3	33.0	0.0	33.0	0.0	33.0	0.0	33.0	0.0	33.0	0.0	33.0	0.0	33.0	0.0
1961	33.1	0.3	33.1	0.0	33.1	0.0	33.0	-0.3	33.0	0.0	33.0	0.0	33.0	0.0	32.9	-0.3	32.9	0.0	33.0	0.3	33.0	0.0	33.0	0.0
1962	33.0	0.0	33.0	0.0	33.1	0.3	33.1	0.0	33.1	0.0	33.0	-0.3	33.0	0.0	33.0	0.0	33.0	0.0	33.0	0.0	33.0	0.0	33.0	0.0
1963	33.0	0.0	33.0	0.0	32.9	-0.3	33.0	0.3	33.0	0.0	33.1	0.3	33.0	-0.3	33.0	0.0	33.1	0.3	33.1	0.0	33.2	0.3	33.3	0.3
1964	33.2	-0.3	33.3	0.3	33.3	0.0	33.4	0.3	33.4	0.0	33.3	-0.3	33.3	0.0	33.3	0.0	33.3	0.0	33.3	0.0	33.4	0.3	33.4	0.0
1965	33.5	0.3	33.5	0.0	33.5	0.0	33.6	0.3	33.6	0.0	33.7	0.3	33.6	-0.3	33.7	0.3	33.7	0.0	33.8	0.3	33.9	0.3	33.9	0.0
1966	34.0	0.3	34.2	0.6	34.3	0.3	34.4	0.3	34.6	0.6	34.7	0.3	34.8	0.3	34.8	0.0	34.9	0.3	35.1	0.6	35.4	0.9	35.5	0.3
1967	35.7	0.6	35.7	0.0	35.7	0.0	35.8	0.3	35.8	0.0	35.8	0.0	35.8	0.0	35.9	0.3	35.9	0.0	36.0	0.3	36.2	0.6	36.3	0.3
1968	36.6	0.8	36.7	0.3	36.7	0.0	36.9	0.5	37.0	0.3	37.0	0.0	37.1	0.3	37.1	0.0	37.2	0.3	37.3	0.3	37.4	0.3	37.5	0.3
1969	37.6	0.3	37.7	0.3	37.8	0.3	37.9	0.3	38.0	0.3	38.1	0.3	38.2	0.3	38.2	0.0	38.5	0.8	38.7	0.5	38.9	0.5	39.1	0.5
1970	39.4	0.8	39.4	0.0	39.5	0.3	39.6	0.3	39.7	0.3	39.8	0.3	40.0	0.5	40.0	0.0	40.2	0.5	40.4	0.5	40.6	0.5	40.8	0.5
1971	41.0	0.5	41.1	0.2	41.2	0.2	41.3	0.2	41.4	0.2	41.4	0.0	41.6	0.5	41.7	0.2	41.6	-0.2	41.6	0.0	41.6	0.0	41.7	0.2
1972	41.8	0.2	42.0	0.5	42.1	0.2	42.2	0.2	42.3	0.2	42.4	0.2	42.4	0.0	42.4	0.0	42.4	0.0	42.5	0.2	42.5	0.0	42.5	0.0
1973	42.6	0.2	42.8	0.5	43.0	0.5	43.3	0.7	43.6	0.7	43.7	0.2	43.8	0.2	43.9	0.2	44.0	0.2	44.2	0.5	44.4	0.5	44.7	0.7
1974	45.2	1.1	45.6	0.9	46.3	1.5	46.9	1.3	48.1	2.6	49.2	2.3	50.3	2.2	51.8	3.0	52.7	1.7	53.8	2.1	54.8	1.9	55.2	0.7
1975	56.2	1.8	56.6	0.7	57.0	0.7	57.3	0.5	57.5	0.3	57.7	0.3	58.0	0.5	58.2	0.3	58.5	0.5	58.9	0.7	59.3	0.7	59.5	0.3
1976	60.0	0.8	60.2	0.3	60.4	0.3	60.7	0.5	60.9	0.3	61.1	0.3	61.4	0.5	61.6	0.3	62.0	0.6	62.4	0.6	62.6	0.3	62.9	0.5
1977	63.4	0.8	63.7	0.5	63.9	0.3	64.2	0.5	64.6	0.6	64.8	0.3	65.2	0.6	65.6	0.6	65.9	0.5	66.6	1.1	67.0	0.6	67.3	0.4
1978	67.9	0.9	68.3	0.6	68.7	0.6	69.1	0.6	69.6	0.7	70.1	0.7	70.5	0.6	70.9	0.6	71.3	0.6	71.9	0.8	72.7	1.1	73.1	0.6
1979	73.6	0.7	74.1	0.7	74.6	0.7	75.2	0.8	75.8	0.8	76.2	0.5	77.0	1.0	77.5	0.6	78.1	0.8	78.9	1.0	79.4	0.6	80.1	0.9
1980	81.6	1.9	82.6	1.2	83.4	1.0	84.8	1.7	85.2	0.5	85.8	0.7	86.6	0.9	87.0	0.5	87.8	0.9	88.5	0.8	89.1	0.7	89.6	0.6
1981	90.9	1.5	91.6	0.8	92.4	0.9	93.1	0.8	93.5	0.4	94.0	0.5	95.0	1.1	95.5	0.5	96.2	0.7	96.6	0.4	97.0	0.4	97.6	0.6
1982	98.3	0.7	98.8	0.5	99.1	0.3	99.6	0.5	99.8	0.2	99.9	0.1	100.3	0.4	100.4	0.1	100.5	0.1	100.8	0.3	101.1	0.3	101.3	0.2
1983	101.6	0.3	102.0	0.4	102.1	0.1	102.4	0.3	102.6	0.2	102.7	0.1	103.1	0.4	103.1	0.0	103.3	0.2	103.2	-0.1	103.3	0.1	103.6	0.3

[Continued]

MACHINERY AND EQUIPMENT
Producer Price Index
Base 1982 = 100
[Continued]

For 1939-1995. Columns headed % show percentile change in the index from the previous period for which an index is available.

Year	Jan Index	%	Feb Index	%	Mar Index	%	Apr Index	%	May Index	%	Jun Index	%	Jul Index	%	Aug Index	%	Sep Index	%	Oct Index	%	Nov Index	%	Dec Index	%
1984	103.9	0.3	104.1	0.2	104.4	0.3	104.8	0.4	105.0	0.2	105.2	0.2	105.5	0.3	105.5	0.0	105.6	0.1	105.8	0.2	105.9	0.1	106.0	0.1
1985	106.5	0.5	106.8	0.3	106.8	0.0	106.9	0.1	107.1	0.2	107.2	0.1	107.3	0.1	107.5	0.2	107.6	0.1	107.6	0.0	107.7	0.1	107.8	0.1
1986	108.0	0.2	108.2	0.2	108.3	0.1	108.6	0.3	108.6	0.0	108.7	0.1	109.0	0.3	109.1	0.1	109.1	0.0	109.2	0.1	109.4	0.2	109.5	0.1
1987	109.8	0.3	109.9	0.1	110.0	0.1	110.0	0.0	110.2	0.2	110.1	-0.1	110.4	0.3	110.6	0.2	110.6	0.0	110.9	0.3	111.0	0.1	111.3	0.3
1988	111.9	0.5	112.2	0.3	112.3	0.1	112.5	0.2	112.9	0.4	112.9	0.0	113.2	0.3	113.6	0.4	113.9	0.3	114.2	0.3	114.5	0.3	114.8	0.3
1989	115.6	0.7	116.0	0.3	116.3	0.3	116.5	0.2	116.9	0.3	117.3	0.3	117.8	0.4	118.0	0.2	118.2	0.2	118.5	0.3	118.7	0.2	118.9	0.2
1990	119.6	0.6	119.7	0.1	120.0	0.3	120.2	0.2	120.4	0.2	120.5	0.1	120.8	0.2	120.9	0.1	121.2	0.2	121.4	0.2	121.7	0.2	122.0	0.2
1991	122.6	0.5	122.9	0.2	123.0	0.1	123.1	0.1	123.1	0.0	123.1	0.0	123.0	-0.1	123.0	0.0	123.0	0.0	123.0	0.0	123.1	0.1	123.2	0.1
1992	123.3	0.1	123.5	0.2	123.6	0.1	123.4	-0.2	123.4	0.0	123.2	-0.2	123.1	-0.1	123.2	0.1	123.2	0.0	123.3	0.1	123.4	0.1	123.5	0.1
1993	123.9	0.3	123.9	0.0	123.9	0.0	124.0	0.1	123.9	-0.1	124.0	0.1	124.0	0.0	124.0	0.0	124.1	0.1	124.2	0.1	124.2	0.0	124.2	0.0
1994	124.6	0.3	124.7	0.1	124.9	0.2	125.1	0.2	125.2	0.1	125.2	0.0	125.3	0.1	125.2	-0.1	125.2	0.0	125.2	0.0	125.3	0.1	125.4	0.1
1995	125.9	0.4	126.2	0.2	126.2	0.0	126.4	0.2	126.5	0.1	126.5	0.0	126.6	0.1	126.5	-0.1	126.7	0.2	126.8	0.1	127.0	0.2	127.0	0.0

Source: U.S. Department of Labor, Bureau of Labor Statistics, Division of Industry Prices and Price Indexes. n.e.c. stands for not elsewhere classified. - indicates no data collected for period or unavailable.

Agricultural Machinery and Equipment
Producer Price Index
Base 1982 = 100

For 1926-1995. Columns headed % show percentile change in the index from the previous period for which an index is available.

Year	Jan Index	%	Feb Index	%	Mar Index	%	Apr Index	%	May Index	%	Jun Index	%	Jul Index	%	Aug Index	%	Sep Index	%	Oct Index	%	Nov Index	%	Dec Index	%
1926	14.1	-	14.1	0.0	14.1	0.0	14.1	0.0	14.1	0.0	14.1	0.0	14.1	0.0	14.1	0.0	14.1	0.0	14.1	0.0	14.1	0.0	14.1	0.0
1927	14.1	0.0	14.1	0.0	14.1	0.0	14.1	0.0	14.1	0.0	14.1	0.0	14.1	0.0	14.1	0.0	14.1	0.0	14.0	-0.7	14.0	0.0	14.0	0.0
1928	14.0	0.0	14.0	0.0	14.0	0.0	14.0	0.0	14.0	0.0	14.0	0.0	14.0	0.0	14.0	0.0	14.0	0.0	14.0	0.0	14.0	0.0	14.0	0.0
1929	14.0	0.0	14.0	0.0	14.0	0.0	14.0	0.0	14.0	0.0	14.0	0.0	14.0	0.0	14.0	0.0	14.0	0.0	13.8	-1.4	13.8	0.0	13.7	-0.7
1930	13.7	0.0	13.7	0.0	13.5	-1.5	13.3	-1.5	13.3	0.0	13.3	0.0	13.3	0.0	13.3	0.0	13.3	0.0	13.3	0.0	13.3	0.0	13.3	0.0
1931	13.3	0.0	13.3	0.0	13.3	0.0	13.3	0.0	13.3	0.0	13.3	0.0	13.3	0.0	13.3	0.0	13.3	0.0	12.1	-9.0	12.1	0.0	12.1	0.0
1932	12.1	0.0	12.0	-0.8	12.0	0.0	12.0	0.0	12.0	0.0	12.0	0.0	12.0	0.0	12.0	0.0	12.0	0.0	12.0	0.0	12.0	0.0	11.9	-0.8
1933	11.9	0.0	11.7	-1.7	11.7	0.0	11.7	0.0	11.7	0.0	11.7	0.0	11.7	0.0	11.7	0.0	11.7	0.0	11.8	0.9	11.8	0.0	12.0	1.7
1934	12.0	0.0	12.0	0.0	12.0	0.0	12.0	0.0	12.9	7.5	12.9	0.0	13.0	0.8	13.0	0.0	13.0	0.0	13.0	0.0	13.0	0.0	13.1	0.8
1935	13.1	0.0	13.2	0.8	13.2	0.0	13.2	0.0	13.2	0.0	13.2	0.0	13.2	0.0	13.2	0.0	13.2	0.0	13.2	0.0	13.3	0.8	13.3	0.0
1936	13.3	0.0	13.4	0.8	13.3	-0.7	13.3	0.0	13.3	0.0	13.3	0.0	13.3	0.0	13.3	0.0	13.3	0.0	13.3	0.0	13.1	-1.5	13.1	0.0
1937	13.1	0.0	13.1	0.0	13.1	0.0	13.0	-0.8	13.2	1.5	13.3	0.8	13.3	0.0	13.3	0.0	13.3	0.0	13.3	0.0	13.6	2.3	13.6	0.0
1938	13.6	0.0	13.6	0.0	13.6	0.0	13.6	0.0	13.6	0.0	13.6	0.0	13.6	0.0	13.5	-0.7	13.5	0.0	13.5	0.0	13.2	-2.2	13.2	0.0
1939	13.2	0.0	13.1	-0.8	13.1	0.0	13.2	0.8	13.2	0.0	13.2	0.0	13.2	0.0	13.2	0.0	13.2	0.0	13.2	0.0	13.2	0.0	13.2	0.0
1940	13.2	0.0	13.2	0.0	13.2	0.0	13.2	0.0	13.1	-0.8	13.1	0.0	13.0	-0.8	13.0	0.0	13.1	0.8	13.1	0.0	13.1	0.0	13.1	0.0
1941	13.1	0.0	13.1	0.0	13.1	0.0	13.0	-0.8	13.1	0.8	13.1	0.0	13.1	0.0	13.1	0.0	13.2	0.8	13.2	0.0	13.6	3.0	13.6	0.0
1942	13.6	0.0	13.7	0.7	13.7	0.0	13.7	0.0	13.7	0.0	13.7	0.0	13.7	0.0	13.7	0.0	13.7	0.0	13.7	0.0	13.7	0.0	13.7	0.0
1943	13.7	0.0	13.7	0.0	13.7	0.0	13.7	0.0	13.7	0.0	13.7	0.0	13.7	0.0	13.7	0.0	13.7	0.0	13.7	0.0	13.7	0.0	13.7	0.0
1944	13.7	0.0	13.7	0.0	13.7	0.0	13.7	0.0	13.7	0.0	13.7	0.0	13.7	0.0	13.8	0.7	13.8	0.0	13.8	0.0	13.8	0.0	13.8	0.0
1945	13.8	0.0	13.8	0.0	13.8	0.0	13.8	0.0	13.8	0.0	13.8	0.0	13.8	0.0	13.8	0.0	13.8	0.0	13.8	0.0	13.9	0.7	13.9	0.0
1946	13.8	-0.7	13.8	0.0	13.8	0.0	13.9	0.7	14.4	3.6	14.8	2.8	14.8	0.0	15.2	2.7	15.3	0.7	15.3	0.0	15.8	3.3	16.7	5.7
1947	16.8	0.6	16.8	0.0	16.8	0.0	16.8	0.0	16.9	0.6	16.9	0.0	16.9	0.0	17.0	0.6	17.1	0.6	17.3	1.2	17.7	2.3	18.1	2.3
1948	18.2	0.6	18.3	0.5	18.4	0.5	18.5	0.5	18.6	0.5	18.8	1.1	19.1	1.6	19.3	1.0	20.0	3.6	20.3	1.5	20.5	1.0	20.5	0.0
1949	20.5	0.0	20.5	0.0	20.5	0.0	20.5	0.0	20.5	0.0	20.5	0.0	20.5	0.0	20.5	0.0	20.5	0.0	20.5	0.0	20.4	-0.5	20.4	0.0
1950	20.4	0.0	20.4	0.0	20.4	0.0	20.5	0.5	20.5	0.0	20.5	0.0	20.5	0.0	20.8	1.5	21.4	2.9	21.7	1.4	21.9	0.9	22.4	2.3
1951	22.4	0.0	22.8	1.8	22.8	0.0	22.8	0.0	22.8	0.0	22.8	0.0	22.8	0.0	22.8	0.0	22.8	0.0	22.8	0.0	22.8	0.0	22.8	0.0
1952	23.0	0.9	23.0	0.0	23.0	0.0	23.0	0.0	23.0	0.0	23.0	0.0	23.0	0.0	23.0	0.0	23.0	0.0	23.0	0.0	23.0	0.0	23.0	0.0
1953	23.0	0.0	23.0	0.0	23.1	0.4	23.2	0.4	23.2	0.0	23.2	0.0	23.2	0.0	23.2	0.0	23.2	0.0	23.2	0.0	23.2	0.0	23.2	0.0
1954	23.2	0.0	23.3	0.4	23.2	-0.4	23.2	0.0	23.2	0.0	23.2	0.0	23.2	0.0	23.1	-0.4	23.1	0.0	23.1	0.0	23.0	-0.4	23.0	0.0
1955	23.0	0.0	23.0	0.0	23.0	0.0	23.0	0.0	23.0	0.0	23.0	0.0	23.0	0.0	23.2	0.9	23.9	3.0	24.0	0.4	23.9	-0.4	23.9	0.0
1956	24.0	0.4	24.0	0.0	23.9	-0.4	23.9	0.0	23.9	0.0	24.0	0.4	24.0	0.0	24.0	0.0	24.1	0.4	24.5	1.7	24.8	1.2	24.8	0.0
1957	24.9	0.4	25.0	0.4	25.0	0.0	25.0	0.0	25.0	0.0	25.0	0.0	25.0	0.0	25.1	0.4	25.3	0.8	25.8	2.0	26.0	0.8	26.2	0.8
1958	26.2	0.0	26.2	0.0	26.2	0.0	26.2	0.0	26.2	0.0	26.2	0.0	26.2	0.0	26.1	-0.4	26.3	0.8	26.4	0.4	26.9	1.9	27.1	0.7
1959	27.1	0.0	27.1	0.0	27.1	0.0	27.1	0.0	27.2	0.4	27.2	0.0	27.2	0.0	27.2	0.0	27.2	0.0	27.2	0.0	27.3	0.4	27.3	0.0
1960	27.3	0.0	27.5	0.7	27.5	0.0	27.6	0.4	27.6	0.0	27.6	0.0	27.6	0.0	27.7	0.4	27.7	0.0	27.8	0.4	28.1	1.1	28.0	-0.4
1961	28.1	0.4	28.1	0.0	28.1	0.0	28.2	0.4	28.2	0.0	28.2	0.0	28.2	0.0	28.2	0.0	28.2	0.0	28.2	0.0	28.3	0.4	28.5	0.7
1962	28.6	0.4	28.7	0.3	28.7	0.0	28.7	0.0	28.7	0.0	28.8	0.3	28.8	0.0	28.7	-0.3	28.7	0.0	28.8	0.3	28.8	0.0	28.9	0.3
1963	29.1	0.7	29.1	0.0	29.2	0.3	29.1	-0.3	29.1	0.0	29.2	0.3	29.1	-0.3	29.1	0.0	29.1	0.0	29.2	0.3	29.3	0.3	29.4	0.3
1964	29.4	0.0	29.5	0.3	29.6	0.3	29.6	0.0	29.6	0.0	29.6	0.0	29.6	0.0	29.7	0.3	29.7	0.0	29.6	-0.3	29.9	1.0	30.0	0.3
1965	30.0	0.0	30.1	0.3	30.1	0.0	30.1	0.0	30.1	0.0	30.1	0.0	30.2	0.3	30.2	0.0	30.2	0.0	30.2	0.0	30.7	1.7	30.7	0.0
1966	30.8	0.3	30.9	0.3	31.0	0.3	31.0	0.0	31.1	0.3	31.1	0.0	31.1	0.0	31.1	0.0	31.1	0.0	31.1	0.0	31.6	1.6	31.7	0.3
1967	31.9	0.6	32.0	0.3	32.0	0.0	32.0	0.0	32.0	0.0	32.0	0.0	32.1	0.3	32.1	0.0	32.1	0.0	32.1	0.0	32.7	1.9	32.9	0.6
1968	33.0	0.3	33.1	0.3	33.1	0.0	33.1	0.0	33.1	0.0	33.2	0.3	33.3	0.3	33.4	0.3	33.5	0.3	33.7	0.6	34.0	0.9	34.2	0.6
1969	34.5	0.9	34.6	0.3	34.6	0.0	34.6	0.0	34.6	0.0	34.7	0.3	34.8	0.3	34.8	0.0	34.9	0.3	35.1	0.6	35.6	1.4	35.8	0.6
1970	35.9	0.3	36.1	0.6	36.1	0.0	36.1	0.0	36.2	0.3	36.1	-0.3	36.2	0.3	36.2	0.0	36.4	0.6	36.6	0.5	37.4	2.2	37.5	0.3

[Continued]

Agricultural Machinery and Equipment

Producer Price Index
Base 1982 = 100

[Continued]

For 1926-1995. Columns headed % show percentile change in the index from the previous period for which an index is available.

Year	Jan Index	%	Feb Index	%	Mar Index	%	Apr Index	%	May Index	%	Jun Index	%	Jul Index	%	Aug Index	%	Sep Index	%	Oct Index	%	Nov Index	%	Dec Index	%
1971	37.5	0.0	37.5	0.0	37.5	0.0	37.6	0.3	37.6	0.0	37.7	0.3	37.8	0.3	37.9	0.3	37.9	0.0	37.9	0.0	37.9	0.0	38.2	0.8
1972	38.5	0.8	39.1	1.6	39.2	0.3	39.3	0.3	39.3	0.0	39.4	0.3	39.4	0.0	39.5	0.3	39.4	-0.3	39.4	0.0	39.5	0.3	39.5	0.0
1973	39.7	0.5	40.0	0.8	40.1	0.3	40.1	0.0	40.2	0.2	40.3	0.2	40.3	0.0	40.4	0.2	40.4	0.0	41.0	1.5	41.4	1.0	41.6	0.5
1974	42.1	1.2	42.2	0.2	42.6	0.9	42.9	0.7	44.3	3.3	45.3	2.3	46.3	2.2	47.6	2.8	48.9	2.7	49.8	1.8	51.3	3.0	51.5	0.4
1975	52.6	2.1	52.8	0.4	53.4	1.1	53.6	0.4	53.8	0.4	53.9	0.2	54.2	0.6	54.3	0.2	54.4	0.2	55.1	1.3	56.0	1.6	56.3	0.5
1976	56.9	1.1	57.2	0.5	57.6	0.7	57.8	0.3	58.2	0.7	58.5	0.5	58.8	0.5	59.1	0.5	59.7	1.0	59.9	0.3	60.7	1.3	61.3	1.0
1977	61.8	0.8	62.2	0.6	62.5	0.5	62.6	0.2	62.8	0.3	63.0	0.3	63.2	0.3	63.8	0.9	64.4	0.9	64.7	0.5	66.0	2.0	66.3	0.5
1978	66.4	0.2	66.8	0.6	66.9	0.1	67.2	0.4	67.4	0.3	67.8	0.6	68.2	0.6	68.8	0.9	70.0	1.7	70.3	0.4	70.9	0.9	71.3	0.6
1979	71.6	0.4	72.0	0.6	72.3	0.4	72.8	0.7	73.4	0.8	73.7	0.4	74.3	0.8	75.0	0.9	76.3	1.7	77.1	1.0	78.2	1.4	78.5	0.4
1980	79.8	1.7	80.3	0.6	81.0	0.9	81.8	1.0	82.4	0.7	82.7	0.4	83.1	0.5	83.5	0.5	84.8	1.6	85.3	0.6	87.3	2.3	87.7	0.5
1981	88.8	1.3	89.5	0.8	90.0	0.6	90.8	0.9	91.8	1.1	92.2	0.4	92.6	0.4	93.3	0.8	94.1	0.9	95.0	1.0	96.7	1.8	97.3	0.6
1982	97.4	0.1	97.9	0.5	98.5	0.6	98.6	0.1	99.1	0.5	99.6	0.5	100.0	0.4	100.4	0.4	101.0	0.6	102.1	1.1	102.5	0.4	103.1	0.6
1983	103.6	0.5	103.9	0.3	104.0	0.1	104.1	0.1	104.9	0.8	104.9	0.0	105.1	0.2	105.2	0.1	105.6	0.4	105.4	-0.2	105.6	0.2	106.1	0.5
1984	106.4	0.3	106.5	0.1	107.0	0.5	107.9	0.8	108.7	0.7	108.6	-0.1	108.9	0.3	108.9	0.0	108.7	-0.2	108.4	-0.3	108.5	0.1	108.7	0.1
1985	108.8	0.3	108.7	-0.1	108.8	0.1	108.7	-0.1	108.8	0.1	108.9	0.1	108.9	0.0	108.7	-0.2	108.4	-0.3	108.5	0.1	108.6	0.1	108.7	0.1
1986	108.8	0.1	108.8	0.0	109.0	0.2	109.1	0.1	109.1	0.0	109.2	0.1	109.3	0.1	109.4	0.1	109.3	-0.1	109.6	0.3	109.7	0.1	109.6	-0.1
1987	108.9	-0.6	109.0	0.1	109.1	0.1	109.6	0.5	109.9	0.3	109.9	0.0	110.0	0.1	109.8	-0.2	109.7	-0.1	109.8	0.1	109.9	0.1	109.9	0.0
1988	111.4	1.4	111.5	0.1	112.2	0.6	112.3	0.1	112.5	0.2	111.8	-0.6	112.4	0.5	113.2	0.7	113.3	0.1	113.3	0.0	114.0	0.6	114.2	0.2
1989	114.2	0.0	116.5	2.0	116.5	0.0	116.9	0.3	117.7	0.7	117.6	-0.1	117.9	0.3	118.3	0.3	118.7	0.3	118.5	-0.2	119.5	0.8	120.1	0.5
1990	120.4	0.2	120.5	0.1	120.7	0.2	121.2	0.4	121.3	0.1	121.4	0.1	121.5	0.1	122.3	0.7	122.6	0.2	122.3	-0.2	122.8	0.4	123.4	0.5
1991	123.7	0.2	124.4	0.6	124.7	0.2	124.9	0.2	125.1	0.2	125.4	0.2	125.6	0.2	126.2	0.5	126.5	0.2	126.6	0.1	127.7	0.9	127.7	0.0
1992	127.9	0.2	128.3	0.3	128.5	0.2	128.7	0.2	128.7	0.0	128.8	0.1	128.9	0.1	129.1	0.2	131.3	1.7	131.4	0.1	131.4	0.0	131.5	0.1
1993	131.7	0.2	132.1	0.3	132.3	0.2	133.1	0.6	133.5	0.3	133.6	0.1	133.6	0.0	133.7	0.1	134.5	0.6	134.7	0.1	134.9	0.1	135.3	0.3
1994	135.8	0.4	136.0	0.1	136.1	0.1	136.4	0.2	136.5	0.1	136.6	0.1	136.7	0.1	136.8	0.1	137.5	0.5	138.2	0.5	138.4	0.1	139.0	0.4
1995	140.3	0.9	140.4	0.1	140.7	0.2	141.1	0.3	143.0	1.3	143.2	0.1	143.3	0.1	143.5	0.1	142.8	-0.5	143.4	0.4	144.3	0.6	144.4	0.1

Source: U.S. Department of Labor, Bureau of Labor Statistics, Division of Industry Prices and Price Indexes. n.e.c. stands for not elsewhere classified. - indicates no data collected for period or unavailable.

Construction Machinery and Equipment

Producer Price Index
Base 1982 = 100

For 1939-1995. Columns headed % show percentile change in the index from the previous period for which an index is available.

Year	Jan Index	%	Feb Index	%	Mar Index	%	Apr Index	%	May Index	%	Jun Index	%	Jul Index	%	Aug Index	%	Sep Index	%	Oct Index	%	Nov Index	%	Dec Index	%
1939	-	-	-	-	-	-	-	-	-	-	-	-	-	-	9.3	-	9.3	0.0	9.3	0.0	9.4	1.1	9.4	0.0
1940	9.4	0.0	9.4	0.0	9.4	0.0	9.4	0.0	9.4	0.0	9.4	0.0	9.5	1.1	9.5	0.0	9.5	0.0	9.5	0.0	9.5	0.0	9.5	0.0
1941	9.6	1.1	9.7	1.0	9.7	0.0	9.8	1.0	9.8	0.0	9.9	1.0	9.9	0.0	10.1	2.0	10.2	1.0	10.3	1.0	10.3	0.0	10.3	0.0
1942	10.3	0.0	10.3	0.0	10.3	0.0	10.3	0.0	10.3	0.0	10.3	0.0	10.3	0.0	10.3	0.0	10.3	0.0	10.3	0.0	10.3	0.0	10.3	0.0
1943	10.3	0.0	10.3	0.0	10.3	0.0	10.3	0.0	10.3	0.0	10.3	0.0	10.3	0.0	10.3	0.0	10.3	0.0	10.3	0.0	10.3	0.0	10.3	0.0
1944	10.3	0.0	10.3	0.0	10.3	0.0	10.3	0.0	10.3	0.0	10.3	0.0	10.3	0.0	10.3	0.0	10.3	0.0	10.3	0.0	10.3	0.0	10.4	1.0
1945	10.4	0.0	10.4	0.0	10.4	0.0	10.4	0.0	10.4	0.0	10.4	0.0	10.4	0.0	10.4	0.0	10.4	0.0	10.5	1.0	10.6	1.0	10.6	0.0
1946	10.6	0.0	10.7	0.9	10.7	0.0	11.0	2.8	11.2	1.8	11.4	1.8	11.4	0.0	11.4	0.0	11.5	0.9	11.7	1.7	11.7	0.0	12.0	2.6
1947	12.3	2.5	12.4	0.8	12.4	0.0	12.4	0.0	12.6	1.6	12.7	0.8	12.9	1.6	12.9	0.0	13.0	0.8	13.1	0.8	13.3	1.5	13.5	1.5
1948	13.6	0.7	13.7	0.7	13.8	0.7	13.9	0.7	13.9	0.0	14.2	2.2	14.4	1.4	14.8	2.8	15.2	2.7	15.4	1.3	15.4	0.0	15.5	0.6
1949	15.5	0.0	15.5	0.0	15.4	-0.6	15.4	0.0	15.4	0.0	15.4	0.0	15.4	0.0	15.4	0.0	15.4	0.0	15.4	0.0	15.4	0.0	15.4	0.0
1950	15.4	0.0	15.4	0.0	15.4	0.0	15.4	0.0	15.4	0.0	15.4	0.0	15.5	0.6	16.0	3.2	16.3	1.9	16.5	1.2	16.5	0.0	17.3	4.8
1951	17.5	1.2	17.6	0.6	17.6	0.0	17.6	0.0	17.6	0.0	17.6	0.0	17.6	0.0	17.6	0.0	17.6	0.0	17.6	0.0	17.6	0.0	17.6	0.0
1952	17.7	0.6	17.8	0.6	17.8	0.0	17.8	0.0	17.8	0.0	17.9	0.6	17.9	0.0	17.8	-0.6	17.9	0.6	17.9	0.0	18.0	0.6	18.0	0.0
1953	18.0	0.0	18.0	0.0	18.1	0.6	18.3	1.1	18.3	0.0	18.4	0.5	18.6	1.1	18.6	0.0	18.6	0.0	18.6	0.0	18.6	0.0	18.6	0.0
1954	18.7	0.5	18.7	0.0	18.7	0.0	18.7	0.0	18.7	0.0	18.7	0.0	18.7	0.0	18.7	0.0	18.7	0.0	18.7	0.0	18.7	0.0	18.9	1.1
1955	19.0	0.5	19.0	0.0	19.0	0.0	19.1	0.5	19.1	0.0	19.2	0.5	19.2	0.0	19.7	2.6	20.0	1.5	20.2	1.0	20.2	0.0	20.3	0.5
1956	20.4	0.5	20.4	0.0	20.4	0.0	20.6	1.0	20.8	1.0	20.8	0.0	21.0	1.0	21.3	1.4	21.5	0.9	22.0	2.3	22.1	0.5	22.2	0.5
1957	22.2	0.0	22.2	0.0	22.2	0.0	22.4	0.9	22.4	0.0	22.4	0.0	22.4	0.0	22.9	2.2	23.1	0.9	23.4	1.3	23.5	0.4	23.5	0.0
1958	23.5	0.0	23.5	0.0	23.5	0.0	23.5	0.0	23.5	0.0	23.5	0.0	23.5	0.0	23.5	0.0	23.6	0.4	23.7	0.4	23.9	0.8	24.2	1.3
1959	24.3	0.4	24.4	0.4	24.4	0.0	24.4	0.0	24.4	0.0	24.4	0.0	24.4	0.0	24.5	0.4	24.5	0.0	24.5	0.0	24.6	0.4	24.6	0.0
1960	24.7	0.4	24.7	0.0	24.8	0.4	24.9	0.4	24.9	0.0	24.9	0.0	25.0	0.4	25.1	0.4	25.1	0.0	25.1	0.0	25.2	0.4	25.2	0.0
1961	25.3	0.4	25.4	0.4	25.4	0.0	25.4	0.0	25.4	0.0	25.4	0.0	25.4	0.0	25.4	0.0	25.4	0.0	25.4	0.0	25.4	0.0	25.4	0.0
1962	25.4	0.0	25.4	0.0	25.4	0.0	25.4	0.0	25.4	0.0	25.4	0.0	25.4	0.0	25.4	0.0	25.4	0.0	25.5	0.4	25.5	0.0	25.6	0.4
1963	25.6	0.0	25.6	0.0	25.7	0.4	25.7	0.0	25.8	0.4	25.9	0.4	25.9	0.0	26.0	0.4	26.0	0.0	26.1	0.4	26.2	0.4	26.3	0.4
1964	26.4	0.4	26.4	0.0	26.4	0.0	26.5	0.4	26.5	0.0	26.5	0.0	26.5	0.0	26.5	0.0	26.5	0.0	26.5	0.0	26.8	1.1	26.8	0.0
1965	26.9	0.4	27.0	0.4	27.0	0.0	27.1	0.4	27.2	0.4	27.2	0.0	27.2	0.0	27.3	0.4	27.3	0.0	27.3	0.0	27.5	0.7	27.5	0.0
1966	27.6	0.4	27.7	0.4	27.8	0.4	28.0	0.7	28.1	0.4	28.1	0.0	28.1	0.0	28.1	0.0	28.2	0.4	28.3	0.4	28.5	0.7	28.6	0.4
1967	28.6	0.0	28.7	0.3	28.8	0.3	28.8	0.0	28.9	0.3	28.9	0.0	29.0	0.3	29.0	0.0	29.0	0.0	29.4	1.4	29.7	1.0	29.9	0.7
1968	30.2	1.0	30.3	0.3	30.4	0.3	30.5	0.3	30.6	0.3	30.6	0.0	30.6	0.0	30.6	0.0	30.9	1.0	31.1	0.6	31.4	1.0	31.4	0.0
1969	31.6	0.6	31.7	0.3	31.8	0.3	31.8	0.0	31.8	0.0	31.9	0.3	32.0	0.3	32.0	0.0	32.3	0.9	32.7	1.2	32.9	0.6	33.1	0.6
1970	33.1	0.0	33.2	0.3	33.2	0.0	33.2	0.0	33.4	0.6	33.4	0.0	33.4	0.0	33.6	0.6	33.7	0.3	34.4	2.1	34.7	0.9	35.0	0.9
1971	35.1	0.3	35.2	0.3	35.2	0.0	35.3	0.3	35.3	0.0	35.3	0.0	35.5	0.6	35.5	0.0	35.5	0.0	35.5	0.0	35.5	0.0	35.9	1.1
1972	36.1	0.6	36.3	0.6	36.3	0.0	36.5	0.6	36.5	0.0	36.6	0.3	36.6	0.0	36.7	0.3	36.7	0.0	36.7	0.0	36.7	0.0	36.7	0.0
1973	36.8	0.3	37.0	0.5	37.4	1.1	37.9	1.3	38.1	0.5	38.2	0.3	38.2	0.0	38.2	0.0	38.2	0.0	38.5	0.8	38.6	0.3	39.0	1.0
1974	39.4	1.0	39.8	1.0	40.3	1.3	40.7	1.0	42.2	3.7	43.3	2.6	44.0	1.6	46.9	6.6	47.5	1.3	48.6	2.3	49.1	1.0	49.4	0.6
1975	51.6	4.5	52.4	1.6	52.9	1.0	53.5	1.1	53.5	0.0	53.6	0.2	53.8	0.4	53.9	0.2	54.5	1.1	54.8	0.6	55.6	1.5	56.0	0.7
1976	56.2	0.4	56.6	0.7	56.7	0.2	56.8	0.2	57.1	0.5	57.5	0.7	58.1	1.0	58.3	0.3	58.4	0.2	58.9	0.9	59.5	1.0	59.9	0.7
1977	60.2	0.5	60.5	0.5	60.6	0.2	61.1	0.8	61.6	0.8	61.7	0.2	62.2	0.8	62.6	0.6	62.4	-0.3	63.2	1.3	64.2	1.6	64.9	1.1
1978	65.0	0.2	65.4	0.6	65.6	0.3	66.4	1.2	67.0	0.9	67.2	0.3	67.7	0.7	68.2	0.7	68.9	1.0	69.9	1.5	70.5	0.9	70.9	0.6
1979	71.4	0.7	72.1	1.0	72.3	0.3	73.2	1.2	73.8	0.8	73.9	0.1	74.7	1.1	75.2	0.7	75.3	0.1	76.7	1.9	77.2	0.7	78.2	1.3
1980	80.3	2.7	80.9	0.7	81.3	0.5	82.6	1.6	83.1	0.6	83.6	0.6	84.8	1.4	85.3	0.6	86.0	0.8	87.0	1.2	87.3	0.3	87.6	0.3
1981	88.9	1.5	90.1	1.3	90.9	0.9	92.2	1.4	92.6	0.4	93.1	0.5	94.2	1.2	94.5	0.3	94.9	0.4	95.5	0.6	95.9	0.4	96.5	0.6
1982	98.0	1.6	98.3	0.3	98.6	0.3	99.3	0.7	99.9	0.6	100.0	0.1	100.6	0.6	100.8	0.2	101.1	0.3	101.1	0.0	101.2	0.1	101.2	0.0
1983	101.3	0.1	101.6	0.3	101.7	0.1	102.0	0.3	102.4	0.4	102.5	0.1	102.6	0.1	102.6	0.0	102.8	0.2	102.8	0.0	102.9	0.1	102.8	-0.1

[Continued]

Construction Machinery and Equipment
Producer Price Index
Base 1982 = 100
[Continued]

For 1939-1995. Columns headed % show percentile change in the index from the previous period for which an index is available.

Year	Jan Index	%	Feb Index	%	Mar Index	%	Apr Index	%	May Index	%	Jun Index	%	Jul Index	%	Aug Index	%	Sep Index	%	Oct Index	%	Nov Index	%	Dec Index	%
1984	103.0	0.2	103.5	0.5	103.3	-0.2	104.0	0.7	104.0	0.0	104.1	0.1	104.2	0.1	103.8	-0.4	103.9	0.1	104.0	0.1	104.0	0.0	104.0	0.0
1985	105.3	1.3	105.6	0.3	105.4	-0.2	105.2	-0.2	105.2	0.0	105.3	0.1	105.3	0.0	105.4	0.1	105.5	0.1	105.6	0.1	105.7	0.1	105.7	0.0
1986	106.2	0.5	106.3	0.1	106.3	0.0	106.4	0.1	106.5	0.1	106.7	0.2	106.7	0.0	106.7	0.0	106.7	0.0	106.7	0.0	107.5	0.7	107.5	0.0
1987	107.7	0.2	107.9	0.2	108.4	0.5	108.5	0.1	109.2	0.6	109.2	0.0	109.1	-0.1	109.2	0.1	109.3	0.1	109.4	0.1	109.5	0.1	109.7	0.2
1988	110.6	0.8	111.0	0.4	111.0	0.0	111.1	0.1	111.1	0.0	111.2	0.1	111.9	0.6	112.3	0.4	112.3	0.0	112.3	0.0	113.0	0.6	113.2	0.2
1989	115.1	1.7	115.3	0.2	115.8	0.4	116.1	0.3	116.3	0.2	117.6	1.1	117.9	0.3	118.2	0.3	118.3	0.1	118.2	-0.1	118.5	0.3	118.6	0.1
1990	119.7	0.9	120.5	0.7	120.5	0.0	120.5	0.0	120.8	0.2	121.3	0.4	122.4	0.9	122.7	0.2	122.5	-0.2	122.6	0.1	122.8	0.2	123.1	0.2
1991	123.7	0.5	124.2	0.4	124.4	0.2	124.5	0.1	124.6	0.1	124.7	0.1	125.7	0.8	125.8	0.1	125.8	0.0	125.8	0.0	126.3	0.4	126.6	0.2
1992	126.8	0.2	127.3	0.4	127.4	0.1	127.7	0.2	127.7	0.0	128.2	0.4	129.4	0.9	129.6	0.2	129.7	0.1	129.8	0.1	130.2	0.3	130.5	0.2
1993	131.6	0.8	132.3	0.5	132.3	0.0	132.0	-0.2	132.1	0.1	132.2	0.1	132.2	0.0	132.3	0.1	131.4	-0.7	131.7	0.2	131.9	0.2	132.0	0.1
1994	133.4	1.1	133.4	0.0	133.3	-0.1	133.4	0.1	133.5	0.1	133.3	-0.1	133.6	0.2	133.6	0.0	133.8	0.1	134.1	0.2	134.3	0.1	134.6	0.2
1995	135.6	0.7	136.0	0.3	136.1	0.1	136.2	0.1	136.6	0.3	136.6	0.0	136.7	0.1	136.7	0.0	137.0	0.2	137.3	0.2	137.4	0.1	137.5	0.1

Source: U.S. Department of Labor, Bureau of Labor Statistics, Division of Industry Prices and Price Indexes. n.e.c. stands for not elsewhere classified. - indicates no data collected for period or unavailable.

Metalworking Machinery and Equipment
Producer Price Index
Base 1982 = 100

For 1947-1995. Columns headed % show percentile change in the index from the previous period for which an index is available.

Year	Jan Index	%	Feb Index	%	Mar Index	%	Apr Index	%	May Index	%	Jun Index	%	Jul Index	%	Aug Index	%	Sep Index	%	Oct Index	%	Nov Index	%	Dec Index	%
1947	13.9	-	13.9	0.0	13.9	0.0	14.0	0.7	14.2	1.4	14.3	0.7	14.3	0.0	14.5	1.4	14.5	0.0	14.7	1.4	14.8	0.7	14.8	0.0
1948	15.0	1.4	15.0	0.0	15.0	0.0	15.1	0.7	15.1	0.0	15.1	0.0	15.2	0.7	15.6	2.6	15.9	1.9	16.0	0.6	16.0	0.0	16.1	0.6
1949	16.2	0.6	16.2	0.0	16.2	0.0	16.2	0.0	16.2	0.0	16.2	0.0	16.2	0.0	16.1	-0.6	16.1	0.0	16.1	0.0	16.1	0.0	16.1	0.0
1950	16.3	1.2	16.3	0.0	16.3	0.0	16.6	1.8	16.7	0.6	16.7	0.0	16.9	1.2	17.4	3.0	17.7	1.7	17.9	1.1	18.2	1.7	18.8	3.3
1951	19.1	1.6	19.1	0.0	19.1	0.0	19.1	0.0	19.1	0.0	19.0	-0.5	19.0	0.0	19.0	0.0	19.2	1.1	19.4	1.0	19.5	0.5	19.6	0.5
1952	19.5	-0.5	19.5	0.0	19.5	0.0	19.5	0.0	19.5	0.0	19.5	0.0	19.5	0.0	19.5	0.0	19.5	0.0	19.5	0.0	19.5	0.0	19.5	0.0
1953	19.5	0.0	19.5	0.0	19.5	0.0	19.6	0.5	19.7	0.5	19.8	0.5	19.9	0.5	19.9	0.0	20.0	0.5	20.0	0.0	20.0	0.0	20.0	0.0
1954	20.0	0.0	20.1	0.5	20.1	0.0	20.0	-0.5	20.0	0.0	20.0	0.0	20.0	0.0	20.1	0.5	20.1	0.0	20.2	0.5	20.2	0.0	20.2	0.0
1955	20.3	0.5	20.4	0.5	20.4	0.0	20.5	0.5	20.8	1.5	21.2	1.9	21.5	1.4	21.6	0.5	21.7	0.5	21.8	0.5	21.9	0.5	22.0	0.5
1956	22.2	0.9	22.3	0.5	22.6	1.3	22.8	0.9	22.9	0.4	23.0	0.4	23.0	0.0	23.2	0.9	23.7	2.2	24.0	1.3	24.0	0.0	24.1	0.4
1957	24.1	0.0	24.2	0.4	24.3	0.4	24.3	0.0	24.3	0.0	24.3	0.0	24.5	0.8	24.6	0.4	24.8	0.8	25.1	1.2	25.2	0.4	25.2	0.0
1958	25.2	0.0	25.2	0.0	25.2	0.0	25.2	0.0	25.1	-0.4	25.1	0.0	25.1	0.0	25.1	0.0	25.1	0.0	25.2	0.4	25.2	0.0	25.2	0.0
1959	25.3	0.4	25.4	0.4	25.6	0.8	25.6	0.0	25.6	0.0	25.7	0.4	25.7	0.0	26.0	1.2	26.1	0.4	26.1	0.0	26.1	0.0	26.1	0.0
1960	26.1	0.0	26.2	0.4	26.3	0.4	26.3	0.0	26.4	0.4	26.5	0.4	26.5	0.0	26.5	0.0	26.6	0.4	26.7	0.4	26.8	0.4	26.8	0.0
1961	26.8	0.0	26.8	0.0	26.8	0.0	26.6	-0.7	26.6	0.0	26.6	0.0	26.6	0.0	26.6	0.0	26.7	0.4	26.8	0.4	26.9	0.4	27.0	0.4
1962	27.1	0.4	27.1	0.0	27.2	0.4	27.2	0.0	27.2	0.0	27.3	0.4	27.3	0.0	27.3	0.0	27.3	0.0	27.3	0.0	27.3	0.0	27.2	-0.4
1963	27.2	0.0	27.2	0.0	27.2	0.0	27.2	0.0	27.2	0.0	27.3	0.4	27.3	0.0	27.4	0.4	27.4	0.0	27.4	0.0	27.4	0.0	27.5	0.4
1964	27.5	0.0	27.5	0.0	27.5	0.0	27.6	0.4	27.7	0.4	27.8	0.4	28.0	0.7	28.0	0.0	28.0	0.0	28.1	0.4	28.1	0.0	28.1	0.0
1965	28.3	0.7	28.4	0.4	28.4	0.0	28.4	0.0	28.5	0.4	28.5	0.0	28.5	0.0	28.7	0.7	28.8	0.3	28.9	0.3	28.9	0.0	29.0	0.3
1966	29.1	0.3	29.3	0.7	29.4	0.3	29.4	0.0	29.7	1.0	29.9	0.7	29.9	0.0	30.1	0.7	30.3	0.7	30.5	0.7	30.6	0.3	30.7	0.3
1967	30.7	0.0	30.8	0.3	30.9	0.3	30.9	0.0	31.1	0.6	31.1	0.0	31.2	0.3	31.3	0.3	31.3	0.0	31.4	0.3	31.6	0.6	31.7	0.3
1968	31.8	0.3	31.9	0.3	32.0	0.3	32.2	0.6	32.3	0.3	32.3	0.0	32.5	0.6	32.6	0.3	32.7	0.3	32.7	0.0	32.8	0.3	32.9	0.3
1969	33.0	0.3	33.1	0.3	33.1	0.0	33.2	0.3	33.3	0.3	33.3	0.0	33.6	0.9	33.7	0.3	33.9	0.6	34.1	0.6	34.5	1.2	34.8	0.9
1970	35.1	0.9	35.2	0.3	35.3	0.3	35.3	0.0	35.7	1.1	35.8	0.3	35.9	0.3	35.5	-1.1	35.6	0.3	35.7	0.3	35.8	0.3	35.9	0.3
1971	36.0	0.3	36.2	0.6	36.2	0.0	36.4	0.6	36.6	0.5	36.8	0.5	36.9	0.3	37.0	0.3	37.0	0.0	37.0	0.0	37.0	0.0	37.0	0.0
1972	36.9	-0.3	37.1	0.5	37.2	0.3	37.3	0.3	37.4	0.3	37.4	0.0	37.5	0.3	37.6	0.3	37.7	0.3	37.8	0.3	37.8	0.0	37.8	0.0
1973	38.0	0.5	38.1	0.3	38.5	1.0	38.8	0.8	39.0	0.5	39.2	0.5	39.2	0.0	39.2	0.0	39.5	0.8	39.7	0.5	39.9	0.5	40.2	0.8
1974	40.9	1.7	41.2	0.7	41.8	1.5	42.6	1.9	43.9	3.1	45.1	2.7	46.5	3.1	47.6	2.4	48.6	2.1	49.8	2.5	50.4	1.2	50.8	0.8
1975	51.4	1.2	52.1	1.4	52.6	1.0	52.9	0.6	53.0	0.2	53.6	1.1	53.8	0.4	53.9	0.2	53.9	0.0	54.6	1.3	54.9	0.5	55.1	0.4
1976	55.5	0.7	55.7	0.4	55.9	0.4	56.3	0.7	56.5	0.4	56.7	0.4	56.9	0.4	57.2	0.5	57.5	0.5	57.9	0.7	58.4	0.9	58.8	0.7
1977	59.5	1.2	60.0	0.8	60.4	0.7	60.7	0.5	61.0	0.5	61.7	1.1	62.1	0.6	62.6	0.8	62.9	0.5	63.4	0.8	63.9	0.8	64.2	0.5
1978	64.9	1.1	65.3	0.6	65.7	0.6	66.1	0.6	66.7	0.9	67.2	0.7	67.5	0.4	68.0	0.7	68.7	1.0	69.7	1.5	70.5	1.1	71.1	0.9
1979	71.8	1.0	72.3	0.7	72.6	0.4	73.3	1.0	74.1	1.1	74.5	0.5	75.2	0.9	75.9	0.9	76.8	1.2	77.8	1.3	78.6	1.0	79.3	0.9
1980	80.7	1.8	81.6	1.1	82.3	0.9	84.2	2.3	85.0	1.0	85.8	0.9	86.6	0.9	86.9	0.3	87.3	0.5	88.0	0.8	88.5	0.6	89.0	0.6
1981	90.3	1.5	90.9	0.7	91.9	1.1	93.1	1.3	93.5	0.4	93.9	0.4	94.4	0.5	94.6	0.2	95.1	0.5	95.5	0.4	95.9	0.4	97.5	1.7
1982	98.4	0.9	98.9	0.5	99.0	0.1	99.6	0.6	99.9	0.3	100.1	0.2	100.5	0.4	100.6	0.1	100.7	0.1	100.7	0.0	100.8	0.1	100.8	0.0
1983	101.0	0.2	101.3	0.3	101.4	0.1	101.7	0.3	101.8	0.1	101.9	0.1	101.8	-0.1	101.7	-0.1	101.8	0.1	101.9	0.1	102.0	0.1	102.4	0.4
1984	102.6	0.2	102.9	0.3	103.0	0.1	103.6	0.6	103.9	0.3	103.9	0.0	104.1	0.2	104.3	0.2	104.6	0.3	105.0	0.4	105.4	0.4	105.5	0.1
1985	105.5	0.0	105.8	0.3	106.0	0.2	106.2	0.2	106.3	0.1	106.5	0.2	106.6	0.1	107.1	0.5	107.1	0.0	107.2	0.1	107.2	0.0	107.2	0.0
1986	107.6	0.4	107.8	0.2	107.9	0.1	108.1	0.2	108.2	0.1	108.5	0.3	108.7	0.2	108.7	0.0	108.7	0.0	108.9	0.2	109.0	0.1	109.2	0.2
1987	109.3	0.1	109.4	0.1	109.6	0.2	109.8	0.2	109.9	0.1	109.8	-0.1	110.3	0.5	110.3	0.0	110.5	0.2	110.6	0.1	110.8	0.2	111.0	0.2
1988	111.4	0.4	111.7	0.3	112.4	0.6	112.7	0.3	113.0	0.3	113.2	0.2	113.6	0.4	114.2	0.5	114.5	0.3	114.7	0.2	115.0	0.3	115.3	0.3
1989	116.0	0.6	116.4	0.3	116.9	0.4	117.4	0.4	117.8	0.3	118.1	0.3	118.5	0.3	118.8	0.3	119.0	0.2	119.3	0.3	119.9	0.5	120.1	0.2
1990	120.7	0.5	121.4	0.6	122.2	0.7	122.4	0.2	122.7	0.2	122.8	0.1	122.9	0.1	123.1	0.2	123.6	0.4	124.3	0.6	124.6	0.2	124.8	0.2
1991	126.4	1.3	126.7	0.2	127.1	0.3	127.2	0.1	127.3	0.1	127.8	0.4	128.0	0.2	128.0	0.0	128.1	0.1	128.2	0.1	128.4	0.2	128.5	0.1

[Continued]

Metalworking Machinery and Equipment
Producer Price Index
Base 1982 = 100
[Continued]

For 1947-1995. Columns headed % show percentile change in the index from the previous period for which an index is available.

Year	Jan Index	%	Feb Index	%	Mar Index	%	Apr Index	%	May Index	%	Jun Index	%	Jul Index	%	Aug Index	%	Sep Index	%	Oct Index	%	Nov Index	%	Dec Index	%
1992	129.4	0.7	129.7	0.2	130.2	0.4	130.6	0.3	130.8	0.2	130.8	0.0	131.0	0.2	131.5	0.4	131.6	0.1	131.7	0.1	131.6	-0.1	131.7	0.1
1993	132.4	0.5	132.5	0.1	133.0	0.4	132.8	-0.2	133.0	0.2	133.3	0.2	133.7	0.3	133.8	0.1	134.3	0.4	134.4	0.1	134.5	0.1	134.6	0.1
1994	134.8	0.1	135.0	0.1	135.4	0.3	136.5	0.8	136.7	0.1	136.5	-0.1	136.7	0.1	136.8	0.1	137.0	0.1	137.1	0.1	137.4	0.2	137.4	0.0
1995	137.9	0.4	138.6	0.5	138.9	0.2	139.2	0.2	139.7	0.4	139.8	0.1	140.4	0.4	140.5	0.1	140.7	0.1	140.9	0.1	141.1	0.1	141.0	-0.1

Source: U.S. Department of Labor, Bureau of Labor Statistics, Division of Industry Prices and Price Indexes. n.e.c. stands for not elsewhere classified. - indicates no data collected for period or unavailable.

General Purpose Machinery and Equipment
Producer Price Index
Base 1982 = 100

For 1939-1995. Columns headed % show percentile change in the index from the previous period for which an index is available.

Year	Jan Index	%	Feb Index	%	Mar Index	%	Apr Index	%	May Index	%	Jun Index	%	Jul Index	%	Aug Index	%	Sep Index	%	Oct Index	%	Nov Index	%	Dec Index	%
1939	13.4	-	13.3	-0.7	13.3	0.0	13.3	0.0	13.3	0.0	13.3	0.0	13.3	0.0	13.3	0.0	13.3	0.0	13.3	0.0	13.3	0.0	13.3	0.0
1940	13.3	0.0	13.3	0.0	13.3	0.0	13.3	0.0	13.3	0.0	13.3	0.0	13.3	0.0	13.3	0.0	13.3	0.0	13.3	0.0	13.3	0.0	13.3	0.0
1941	13.4	0.8	13.4	0.0	13.4	0.0	13.4	0.0	13.4	0.0	13.6	1.5	13.6	0.0	13.7	0.7	13.7	0.0	13.7	0.0	13.7	0.0	13.8	0.7
1942	13.9	0.7	13.8	-0.7	13.8	0.0	13.8	0.0	13.8	0.0	13.8	0.0	13.8	0.0	13.6	-1.4	13.6	0.0	13.6	0.0	13.5	-0.7	13.5	0.0
1943	13.5	0.0	13.5	0.0	13.5	0.0	13.5	0.0	13.4	-0.7	13.4	0.0	13.4	0.0	13.4	0.0	13.4	0.0	13.4	0.0	13.4	0.0	13.4	0.0
1944	13.4	0.0	13.4	0.0	13.4	0.0	13.4	0.0	13.4	0.0	13.4	0.0	13.4	0.0	13.4	0.0	13.4	0.0	13.4	0.0	13.4	0.0	13.4	0.0
1945	13.4	0.0	13.4	0.0	13.4	0.0	13.4	0.0	13.4	0.0	13.4	0.0	13.4	0.0	13.4	0.0	13.4	0.0	13.4	0.0	13.4	0.0	13.4	0.0
1946	13.4	0.0	13.5	0.7	13.5	0.0	13.5	0.0	13.8	2.2	14.0	1.4	14.4	2.9	14.7	2.1	15.2	3.4	15.3	0.7	15.6	2.0	16.0	2.6
1947	16.2	1.3	16.3	0.6	16.3	0.0	16.3	0.0	16.4	0.6	16.6	1.2	16.6	0.0	16.7	0.6	17.0	1.8	17.2	1.2	17.2	0.0	17.3	0.6
1948	17.4	0.6	17.4	0.0	17.5	0.6	17.5	0.0	17.6	0.6	17.6	0.0	17.9	1.7	18.5	3.4	18.8	1.6	19.1	1.6	19.1	0.0	19.1	0.0
1949	19.2	0.5	19.3	0.5	19.2	-0.5	19.2	0.0	19.2	0.0	19.2	0.0	19.1	-0.5	19.1	0.0	19.1	0.0	19.1	0.0	19.1	0.0	19.1	0.0
1950	19.0	-0.5	19.1	0.5	19.1	0.0	19.2	0.5	19.2	0.0	19.2	0.0	19.5	1.6	20.0	2.6	20.4	2.0	20.7	1.5	21.0	1.4	21.9	4.3
1951	22.2	1.4	22.2	0.0	22.2	0.0	22.2	0.0	22.2	0.0	22.2	0.0	22.2	0.0	22.2	0.0	22.2	0.0	22.3	0.5	22.3	0.0	22.2	-0.4
1952	22.2	0.0	22.2	0.0	22.1	-0.5	22.1	0.0	22.1	0.0	22.0	-0.5	22.0	0.0	22.0	0.0	22.0	0.0	21.9	-0.5	21.9	0.0	21.9	0.0
1953	21.9	0.0	21.9	0.0	22.0	0.5	22.2	0.9	22.3	0.5	22.5	0.9	22.6	0.4	22.8	0.9	23.0	0.9	23.1	0.4	23.1	0.0	23.1	0.0
1954	23.1	0.0	23.1	0.0	23.1	0.0	23.1	0.0	23.1	0.0	23.1	0.0	23.0	-0.4	23.0	0.0	23.1	0.4	23.1	0.0	23.1	0.0	23.1	0.0
1955	23.1	0.0	23.5	1.7	23.5	0.0	23.6	0.4	23.6	0.0	23.7	0.4	23.8	0.4	24.2	1.7	24.6	1.7	24.9	1.2	25.3	1.6	25.5	0.8
1956	25.5	0.0	25.5	0.0	25.7	0.8	25.9	0.8	26.3	1.5	26.2	-0.4	26.3	0.4	26.8	1.9	27.3	1.9	27.5	0.7	27.7	0.7	27.8	0.4
1957	28.0	0.7	28.0	0.0	28.1	0.4	28.1	0.0	28.1	0.0	28.2	0.4	28.3	0.4	28.4	0.4	28.5	0.4	28.7	0.7	28.9	0.7	28.9	0.0
1958	28.9	0.0	28.7	-0.7	28.7	0.0	28.7	0.0	28.7	0.0	28.8	0.3	28.7	-0.3	28.6	-0.3	28.7	0.3	28.8	0.3	29.1	1.0	29.2	0.3
1959	29.3	0.3	29.5	0.7	29.4	-0.3	29.3	-0.3	29.3	0.0	29.8	1.7	29.9	0.3	29.9	0.0	30.0	0.3	30.1	0.3	30.1	0.0	30.2	0.3
1960	30.1	-0.3	30.2	0.3	30.1	-0.3	30.2	0.3	30.1	-0.3	29.9	-0.7	29.9	0.0	29.9	0.0	30.0	0.3	29.9	-0.3	29.9	0.0	29.9	0.0
1961	29.9	0.0	29.9	0.0	29.9	0.0	29.8	-0.3	29.8	0.0	29.9	0.3	29.8	-0.3	29.7	-0.3	29.7	0.0	29.6	-0.3	29.7	0.3	29.7	0.0
1962	29.8	0.3	29.8	0.0	29.9	0.3	29.9	0.0	29.9	0.0	29.9	0.0	29.8	-0.3	29.9	0.3	30.0	0.3	30.0	0.0	30.0	0.0	30.1	0.3
1963	30.1	0.0	30.0	-0.3	29.9	-0.3	29.9	0.0	29.9	0.0	30.0	0.3	30.0	0.0	30.0	0.0	30.1	0.3	30.2	0.3	30.2	0.0	30.3	0.3
1964	30.3	0.0	30.3	0.0	30.4	0.3	30.3	-0.3	30.4	0.3	30.3	-0.3	30.2	-0.3	30.0	-0.7	30.0	0.0	30.3	1.0	30.3	0.0	30.4	0.3
1965	30.1	-1.0	30.2	0.3	30.2	0.0	30.2	0.0	30.3	0.3	30.3	0.0	30.3	0.0	30.5	0.7	30.6	0.3	30.8	0.7	30.9	0.3	30.9	0.0
1966	30.9	0.0	30.9	0.0	31.1	0.6	31.4	1.0	31.6	0.6	31.8	0.6	31.8	0.0	32.0	0.6	32.2	0.6	32.4	0.6	32.5	0.3	32.5	0.0
1967	32.7	0.6	32.8	0.3	32.8	0.0	32.8	0.0	32.8	0.0	32.7	-0.3	32.8	0.3	32.9	0.3	33.0	0.3	33.1	0.3	33.2	0.3	33.3	0.3
1968	33.4	0.3	33.6	0.6	33.7	0.3	33.8	0.3	33.9	0.3	34.0	0.3	34.0	0.0	34.1	0.3	34.2	0.3	34.3	0.3	34.2	-0.3	34.3	0.3
1969	34.4	0.3	34.5	0.3	34.7	0.6	34.8	0.3	34.9	0.3	35.1	0.6	35.2	0.3	35.3	0.3	35.6	0.8	35.8	0.6	35.9	0.3	36.2	0.8
1970	36.6	1.1	36.6	0.0	36.8	0.5	36.9	0.3	37.1	0.5	37.1	0.0	37.5	1.1	37.6	0.3	37.8	0.5	38.1	0.8	38.2	0.3	38.5	0.8
1971	38.5	0.0	38.6	0.3	38.8	0.5	39.0	0.5	39.2	0.5	39.3	0.3	39.5	0.5	39.6	0.3	39.6	0.0	39.6	0.0	39.6	0.0	39.7	0.3
1972	39.7	0.0	39.9	0.5	40.0	0.3	40.1	0.3	40.2	0.2	40.4	0.5	40.4	0.0	40.4	0.0	40.5	0.2	40.5	0.0	40.6	0.2	40.6	0.0
1973	40.7	0.2	40.9	0.5	41.1	0.5	41.3	0.5	41.6	0.7	41.8	0.5	41.9	0.2	41.9	0.0	42.0	0.2	42.2	0.5	42.9	1.7	43.0	0.2
1974	43.6	1.4	44.0	0.9	44.7	1.6	45.9	2.7	47.5	3.5	49.1	3.4	50.5	2.9	52.0	3.0	53.2	2.3	54.7	2.8	55.6	1.6	56.2	1.1
1975	56.8	1.1	57.2	0.7	57.5	0.5	57.9	0.7	58.4	0.9	58.6	0.3	59.1	0.9	59.3	0.3	59.6	0.5	59.8	0.3	60.1	0.5	60.4	0.5
1976	60.7	0.5	61.0	0.5	61.2	0.3	61.6	0.7	62.0	0.6	62.5	0.8	62.6	0.2	62.8	0.3	63.3	0.8	63.7	0.6	63.7	0.0	64.0	0.5
1977	64.4	0.6	64.7	0.5	65.0	0.5	65.2	0.3	65.9	1.1	66.4	0.8	66.7	0.5	67.0	0.4	67.3	0.4	67.6	0.4	68.0	0.6	68.2	0.3
1978	68.7	0.7	69.1	0.6	69.5	0.6	69.9	0.6	70.5	0.9	71.0	0.7	71.5	0.7	71.8	0.4	72.3	0.7	72.9	0.8	73.6	1.0	74.0	0.5
1979	74.5	0.7	74.9	0.5	75.8	1.2	76.5	0.9	77.0	0.7	77.3	0.4	78.0	0.9	78.4	0.5	79.0	0.8	79.9	1.1	80.3	0.5	81.4	1.4
1980	82.6	1.5	83.3	0.8	84.4	1.3	85.9	1.8	86.4	0.6	87.1	0.8	87.5	0.5	87.8	0.3	88.8	1.1	89.6	0.9	90.2	0.7	90.7	0.6
1981	91.6	1.0	92.2	0.7	92.9	0.8	93.5	0.6	94.1	0.6	94.4	0.3	95.6	1.3	96.1	0.5	96.7	0.6	97.1	0.4	97.4	0.3	98.0	0.6
1982	98.7	0.7	99.1	0.4	99.3	0.2	99.8	0.5	99.9	0.1	99.8	-0.1	100.3	0.5	100.3	0.0	100.3	0.0	100.6	0.3	100.8	0.2	101.0	0.2
1983	101.1	0.1	101.3	0.2	101.2	-0.1	101.4	0.2	101.5	0.1	101.5	0.0	101.5	0.0	101.3	-0.2	101.4	0.1	101.3	-0.1	101.5	0.2	101.9	0.4

[Continued]

General Purpose Machinery and Equipment
Producer Price Index
Base 1982 = 100
[Continued]

For 1939-1995. Columns headed % show percentile change in the index from the previous period for which an index is available.

Year	Jan Index	%	Feb Index	%	Mar Index	%	Apr Index	%	May Index	%	Jun Index	%	Jul Index	%	Aug Index	%	Sep Index	%	Oct Index	%	Nov Index	%	Dec Index	%
1984	102.2	0.3	102.3	0.1	102.5	0.2	103.0	0.5	103.0	0.0	103.3	0.3	103.7	0.4	103.8	0.1	103.9	0.1	103.9	0.0	104.1	0.2	104.2	0.1
1985	104.7	0.5	104.9	0.2	105.2	0.3	105.4	0.2	105.7	0.3	105.8	0.1	106.0	0.2	106.1	0.1	106.0	-0.1	106.1	0.1	106.2	0.1	106.2	0.0
1986	106.4	0.2	106.7	0.3	106.9	0.2	107.2	0.3	107.2	0.0	107.2	0.0	107.3	0.1	107.4	0.1	107.4	0.0	107.5	0.1	107.5	0.0	107.6	0.1
1987	107.8	0.2	107.8	0.0	107.9	0.1	107.9	0.0	108.0	0.1	108.1	0.1	108.2	0.1	108.3	0.1	108.6	0.3	108.6	0.0	108.9	0.3	109.4	0.5
1988	110.2	0.7	110.7	0.5	111.3	0.5	111.7	0.4	112.0	0.3	112.3	0.3	112.9	0.5	113.3	0.4	113.9	0.5	114.3	0.4	115.1	0.7	115.8	0.6
1989	116.6	0.7	117.0	0.3	117.7	0.6	118.0	0.3	118.6	0.5	119.1	0.4	119.3	0.2	119.6	0.3	120.2	0.5	120.5	0.2	120.7	0.2	121.0	0.2
1990	121.8	0.7	122.3	0.4	122.9	0.5	123.0	0.1	123.3	0.2	123.5	0.2	123.8	0.2	124.1	0.2	124.3	0.2	124.7	0.3	124.8	0.1	125.4	0.5
1991	126.3	0.7	126.9	0.5	127.2	0.2	127.3	0.1	127.7	0.3	128.0	0.2	128.0	0.0	128.1	0.1	128.2	0.1	128.4	0.2	128.5	0.1	128.6	0.1
1992	129.2	0.5	129.4	0.2	129.7	0.2	130.0	0.2	130.1	0.1	129.5	-0.5	129.8	0.2	130.0	0.2	130.2	0.2	130.2	0.0	130.3	0.1	130.3	0.0
1993	131.2	0.7	131.4	0.2	131.5	0.1	131.7	0.2	131.8	0.1	132.1	0.2	132.3	0.2	132.6	0.2	132.7	0.1	132.8	0.1	133.0	0.2	133.2	0.2
1994	133.6	0.3	133.7	0.1	134.1	0.3	134.2	0.1	134.3	0.1	134.6	0.2	134.9	0.2	135.1	0.1	135.2	0.1	135.7	0.4	135.9	0.1	136.1	0.1
1995	136.9	0.6	137.7	0.6	138.1	0.3	138.5	0.3	138.7	0.1	138.9	0.1	139.3	0.3	139.5	0.1	139.7	0.1	140.1	0.3	140.4	0.2	140.7	0.2

Source: U.S. Department of Labor, Bureau of Labor Statistics, Division of Industry Prices and Price Indexes. n.e.c. stands for not elsewhere classified. - indicates no data collected for period or unavailable.

Electronic Computers and Computer Equipment
Producer Price Index
Base Dec. 1990 = 100

For 1990-1995. Columns headed % show percentile change in the index from the previous period for which an index is available.

Year	Jan Index	%	Feb Index	%	Mar Index	%	Apr Index	%	May Index	%	Jun Index	%	Jul Index	%	Aug Index	%	Sep Index	%	Oct Index	%	Nov Index	%	Dec Index	%
1990	-	-	-	-	-	-	-	-	-	-	-	-	-	-	-	-	-	-	-	-	-	-	100.0	-
1991	97.9	-2.1	97.2	-0.7	96.2	-1.0	95.7	-0.5	93.1	-2.7	89.7	-3.7	86.1	-4.0	83.5	-3.0	83.2	-0.4	82.0	-1.4	81.6	-0.5	80.6	-1.2
1992	79.7	-1.1	78.9	-1.0	77.7	-1.5	75.7	-2.6	75.0	-0.9	73.1	-2.5	71.1	-2.7	70.8	-0.4	69.7	-1.6	68.9	-1.1	68.8	-0.1	68.6	-0.3
1993	67.6	-1.5	66.1	-2.2	64.9	-1.8	63.5	-2.2	62.9	-0.9	62.0	-1.4	61.3	-1.1	60.3	-1.6	60.3	0.0	59.2	-1.8	59.2	0.0	58.9	-0.5
1994	58.4	-0.8	57.8	-1.0	58.1	0.5	57.8	-0.5	57.5	-0.5	57.4	-0.2	57.0	-0.7	56.6	-0.7	56.7	0.2	55.8	-1.6	55.2	-1.1	55.2	0.0
1995	54.7	-0.9	53.8	-1.6	53.4	-0.7	53.5	0.2	53.2	-0.6	52.6	-1.1	52.2	-0.8	51.4	-1.5	50.8	-1.2	50.6	-0.4	50.4	-0.4	50.5	0.2

Source: U.S. Department of Labor, Bureau of Labor Statistics, Division of Industry Prices and Price Indexes. n.e.c. stands for not elsewhere classified. - indicates no data collected for period or unavailable.

Special Industry Machinery and Equipment
Producer Price Index
Base 1982 = 100

For 1961-1995. Columns headed % show percentile change in the index from the previous period for which an index is available.

Year	Jan Index	%	Feb Index	%	Mar Index	%	Apr Index	%	May Index	%	Jun Index	%	Jul Index	%	Aug Index	%	Sep Index	%	Oct Index	%	Nov Index	%	Dec Index	%
1961	26.4	-	26.4	0.0	26.4	0.0	26.4	0.0	26.5	0.4	26.5	0.0	26.5	0.0	26.5	0.0	26.5	0.0	26.5	0.0	26.5	0.0	26.6	0.4
1962	26.7	0.4	26.8	0.4	26.8	0.0	26.8	0.0	26.8	0.0	26.8	0.0	26.9	0.4	26.9	0.0	26.9	0.0	26.9	0.0	27.0	0.4	27.1	0.4
1963	27.1	0.0	27.2	0.4	27.2	0.0	27.4	0.7	27.4	0.0	27.4	0.0	27.4	0.0	27.5	0.4	27.6	0.4	27.6	0.0	27.6	0.0	27.7	0.4
1964	27.7	0.0	27.7	0.0	27.9	0.7	27.9	0.0	27.9	0.0	27.9	0.0	27.9	0.0	27.9	0.0	27.9	0.0	27.9	0.0	28.1	0.7	28.1	0.0
1965	28.3	0.7	28.3	0.0	28.4	0.4	28.4	0.0	28.4	0.0	28.4	0.0	28.4	0.0	28.4	0.0	28.5	0.4	28.5	0.0	28.7	0.7	28.7	0.0
1966	28.8	0.3	28.8	0.0	29.0	0.7	29.0	0.0	29.2	0.7	29.5	1.0	29.6	0.3	29.7	0.3	29.8	0.3	30.0	0.7	30.1	0.3	30.1	0.0
1967	30.4	1.0	30.5	0.3	30.5	0.0	30.5	0.0	30.7	0.7	30.7	0.0	30.7	0.0	30.8	0.3	30.8	0.0	31.2	1.3	31.2	0.0	31.4	0.6
1968	31.8	1.3	31.8	0.0	31.8	0.0	32.2	1.3	32.3	0.3	32.4	0.3	32.5	0.3	32.5	0.0	32.6	0.3	32.7	0.3	32.9	0.6	32.9	0.0
1969	33.0	0.3	33.3	0.9	33.4	0.3	33.5	0.3	33.6	0.3	33.7	0.3	34.0	0.9	34.0	0.0	34.1	0.3	34.2	0.3	34.4	0.6	34.9	1.5
1970	35.1	0.6	35.1	0.0	35.2	0.3	35.2	0.0	35.3	0.3	35.4	0.3	35.6	0.6	35.6	0.0	35.8	0.6	36.1	0.8	36.1	0.0	36.4	0.8
1971	36.7	0.8	36.8	0.3	36.8	0.0	36.9	0.3	37.0	0.3	37.2	0.5	37.4	0.5	37.4	0.0	37.5	0.3	37.5	0.0	37.5	0.0	37.5	0.0
1972	37.7	0.5	37.9	0.5	37.8	-0.3	37.9	0.3	38.0	0.3	38.1	0.3	38.1	0.0	38.1	0.0	38.1	0.0	38.2	0.3	38.3	0.3	38.3	0.0
1973	38.4	0.3	38.9	1.3	39.1	0.5	39.5	1.0	39.7	0.5	40.0	0.8	40.0	0.0	40.5	1.3	40.8	0.7	40.9	0.2	41.0	0.2	41.5	1.2
1974	41.8	0.7	42.5	1.7	43.6	2.6	44.1	1.1	45.2	2.5	45.8	1.3	46.2	0.9	48.0	3.9	48.8	1.7	49.8	2.0	50.4	1.2	51.0	1.2
1975	51.8	1.6	52.2	0.8	53.1	1.7	53.3	0.4	53.3	0.0	53.6	0.6	54.0	0.7	54.3	0.6	54.3	0.0	54.9	1.1	55.2	0.5	55.7	0.9
1976	56.3	1.1	56.5	0.4	56.8	0.5	57.5	1.2	57.5	0.0	57.8	0.5	58.3	0.9	58.4	0.2	58.7	0.5	59.0	0.5	59.0	0.0	59.6	1.0
1977	60.1	0.8	60.4	0.5	60.7	0.5	61.2	0.8	61.7	0.8	62.1	0.6	62.4	0.5	62.7	0.5	62.8	0.2	64.4	2.5	64.6	0.3	65.1	0.8
1978	65.7	0.9	65.9	0.3	66.6	1.1	67.1	0.8	67.4	0.4	68.3	1.3	68.7	0.6	69.2	0.7	69.8	0.9	70.8	1.4	71.6	1.1	71.9	0.4
1979	72.7	1.1	72.9	0.3	73.5	0.8	74.9	1.9	75.4	0.7	75.7	0.4	76.8	1.5	77.2	0.5	77.2	0.0	78.1	1.2	78.4	0.4	78.8	0.5
1980	80.1	1.6	80.9	1.0	81.6	0.9	83.6	2.5	84.0	0.5	84.4	0.5	85.1	0.8	85.2	0.1	87.0	2.1	88.0	1.1	88.5	0.6	89.5	1.1
1981	90.9	1.6	92.0	1.2	92.6	0.7	93.3	0.8	94.5	1.3	95.0	0.5	95.6	0.6	95.4	-0.2	96.2	0.8	96.8	0.6	96.9	0.1	97.3	0.4
1982	98.6	1.3	98.6	0.0	98.8	0.2	99.3	0.5	99.6	0.3	100.0	0.4	100.6	0.6	100.5	-0.1	100.5	0.0	100.8	0.3	101.2	0.4	101.5	0.3
1983	102.1	0.6	102.3	0.2	102.6	0.3	102.9	0.3	103.3	0.4	103.5	0.2	103.9	0.4	104.3	0.4	104.5	0.2	104.7	0.2	104.9	0.2	105.2	0.3
1984	105.2	0.0	105.5	0.3	106.0	0.5	106.7	0.7	107.1	0.4	107.2	0.1	108.2	0.9	108.5	0.3	108.0	-0.5	108.1	0.1	108.2	0.1	108.4	0.2
1985	109.4	0.9	109.8	0.4	110.0	0.2	110.2	0.2	110.4	0.2	110.7	0.3	111.0	0.3	111.2	0.2	111.4	0.2	111.5	0.1	111.8	0.3	112.2	0.4
1986	112.6	0.4	112.9	0.3	113.0	0.1	113.3	0.3	113.6	0.3	114.2	0.5	114.4	0.2	114.8	0.3	115.2	0.3	115.2	0.0	115.4	0.2	115.8	0.3
1987	116.2	0.3	116.6	0.3	116.7	0.1	116.8	0.1	117.0	0.2	117.0	0.0	117.3	0.3	117.3	0.0	117.5	0.2	118.1	0.5	118.4	0.3	118.8	0.3
1988	119.3	0.4	119.8	0.4	120.1	0.3	120.7	0.5	121.0	0.2	121.5	0.4	122.0	0.4	122.3	0.2	122.6	0.2	123.2	0.5	123.9	0.6	124.1	0.2
1989	124.7	0.5	125.4	0.6	125.7	0.2	126.2	0.4	126.7	0.4	127.1	0.3	127.3	0.2	127.6	0.2	127.9	0.2	128.1	0.2	128.3	0.2	128.6	0.2
1990	129.2	0.5	129.8	0.5	130.1	0.2	131.0	0.7	131.2	0.2	131.5	0.2	131.8	0.2	131.9	0.1	132.4	0.4	132.7	0.2	133.1	0.3	133.4	0.2
1991	134.7	1.0	134.9	0.1	135.2	0.2	135.6	0.3	136.0	0.3	136.1	0.1	136.1	0.0	136.1	0.0	136.4	0.2	136.7	0.2	136.8	0.1	136.9	0.1
1992	137.6	0.5	138.1	0.4	138.3	0.1	138.8	0.4	139.2	0.3	139.3	0.1	139.4	0.1	139.5	0.1	140.5	0.7	140.7	0.1	141.0	0.2	141.2	0.1
1993	141.9	0.5	142.6	0.5	143.0	0.3	143.3	0.2	143.4	0.1	143.7	0.2	143.9	0.1	143.9	0.0	144.1	0.1	144.5	0.3	144.7	0.1	144.7	0.0
1994	145.1	0.3	145.5	0.3	145.7	0.1	145.9	0.1	146.0	0.1	146.2	0.1	146.4	0.1	146.4	0.0	146.5	0.1	146.6	0.1	146.8	0.1	147.0	0.1
1995	148.1	0.7	148.6	0.3	149.0	0.3	149.3	0.2	149.7	0.3	150.0	0.2	150.2	0.1	150.3	0.1	150.6	0.2	150.6	0.0	151.0	0.3	151.1	0.1

Source: U.S. Department of Labor, Bureau of Labor Statistics, Division of Industry Prices and Price Indexes. n.e.c. stands for not elsewhere classified. - indicates no data collected for period or unavailable.

Electrical Machinery and Equipment
Producer Price Index
Base 1982 = 100

For 1939-1995. Columns headed % show percentile change in the index from the previous period for which an index is available.

Year	Jan Index	%	Feb Index	%	Mar Index	%	Apr Index	%	May Index	%	Jun Index	%	Jul Index	%	Aug Index	%	Sep Index	%	Oct Index	%	Nov Index	%	Dec Index	%
1939	19.6	-	19.6	0.0	19.6	0.0	19.6	0.0	19.6	0.0	19.6	0.0	19.5	-0.5	19.5	0.0	19.5	0.0	19.5	0.0	19.5	0.0	19.5	0.0
1940	19.5	0.0	19.5	0.0	19.5	0.0	19.5	0.0	19.5	0.0	19.5	0.0	19.5	0.0	19.5	0.0	19.5	0.0	19.5	0.0	19.5	0.0	19.5	0.0
1941	19.5	0.0	19.5	0.0	19.5	0.0	19.5	0.0	19.5	0.0	19.5	0.0	19.5	0.0	19.6	0.5	19.7	0.5	19.7	0.0	19.8	0.5	19.8	0.0
1942	19.8	0.0	19.8	0.0	19.7	-0.5	19.6	-0.5	19.6	0.0	19.6	0.0	19.6	0.0	19.6	0.0	19.6	0.0	19.6	0.0	19.5	-0.5	19.5	0.0
1943	19.5	0.0	19.5	0.0	19.5	0.0	19.5	0.0	19.5	0.0	19.5	0.0	19.5	0.0	19.4	-0.5	19.4	0.0	19.4	0.0	19.4	0.0	19.4	0.0
1944	19.4	0.0	19.4	0.0	19.4	0.0	19.4	0.0	19.4	0.0	19.1	-1.5	19.0	-0.5	19.0	0.0	19.0	0.0	19.0	0.0	19.0	0.0	19.0	0.0
1945	19.0	0.0	19.0	0.0	19.0	0.0	19.0	0.0	19.2	1.1	19.3	0.5	19.3	0.0	19.3	0.0	19.3	0.0	19.4	0.5	19.5	0.5	19.5	0.0
1946	19.6	0.5	19.6	0.0	19.6	0.0	20.5	4.6	21.9	6.8	22.3	1.8	22.5	0.9	22.6	0.4	22.8	0.9	23.3	2.2	24.4	4.7	25.3	3.7
1947	25.5	0.8	25.6	0.4	25.7	0.4	26.0	1.2	27.3	5.0	27.5	0.7	27.4	-0.4	27.5	0.4	27.6	0.4	27.5	-0.4	27.5	0.0	27.6	0.4
1948	27.4	-0.7	27.3	-0.4	27.3	0.0	27.3	0.0	27.2	-0.4	27.3	0.4	27.9	2.2	28.8	3.2	29.1	1.0	29.2	0.3	29.4	0.7	29.5	0.3
1949	29.7	0.7	29.8	0.3	29.8	0.0	29.2	-2.0	28.8	-1.4	28.5	-1.0	28.4	-0.4	28.4	0.0	28.4	0.0	28.4	0.0	28.4	0.0	28.4	0.0
1950	28.2	-0.7	28.0	-0.7	28.1	0.4	28.1	0.0	28.1	0.0	28.5	1.4	29.1	2.1	30.4	4.5	30.9	1.6	31.9	3.2	32.0	0.3	33.5	4.7
1951	34.0	1.5	34.0	0.0	34.0	0.0	34.0	0.0	34.0	0.0	34.0	0.0	34.2	0.6	34.1	-0.3	34.1	0.0	34.0	-0.3	34.1	0.3	34.0	-0.3
1952	33.9	-0.3	34.0	0.3	33.9	-0.3	33.8	-0.3	33.8	0.0	33.5	-0.9	33.5	0.0	33.5	0.0	33.4	-0.3	33.3	-0.3	33.4	0.3	33.4	0.0
1953	33.4	0.0	33.4	0.0	33.5	0.3	33.9	1.2	34.2	0.9	34.7	1.5	34.9	0.6	35.1	0.6	35.2	0.3	35.3	0.3	35.4	0.3	35.4	0.0
1954	35.4	0.0	35.4	0.0	35.4	0.0	35.3	-0.3	35.2	-0.3	35.2	0.0	35.2	0.0	35.1	-0.3	35.1	0.0	35.0	-0.3	35.4	1.1	35.4	0.0
1955	35.4	0.0	35.4	0.0	35.3	-0.3	35.3	0.0	35.3	0.0	35.3	0.0	35.4	0.3	35.7	0.8	36.5	2.2	36.5	0.0	36.7	0.5	36.9	0.5
1956	37.0	0.3	37.2	0.5	37.3	0.3	37.9	1.6	38.3	1.1	38.4	0.3	38.4	0.0	38.6	0.5	39.6	2.6	40.0	1.0	40.6	1.5	40.6	0.0
1957	40.8	0.5	41.1	0.7	41.2	0.2	41.3	0.2	41.4	0.2	41.4	0.0	41.8	1.0	41.8	0.0	42.2	1.0	42.1	-0.2	42.2	0.2	42.2	0.0
1958	42.2	0.0	42.2	0.0	42.2	0.0	42.4	0.5	42.5	0.2	42.6	0.2	42.6	0.0	42.7	0.2	42.7	0.0	42.7	0.0	42.5	-0.5	42.5	0.0
1959	42.5	0.0	42.5	0.0	42.7	0.5	42.7	0.0	43.0	0.7	43.0	0.0	43.5	1.2	43.4	-0.2	43.5	0.2	43.6	0.2	43.6	0.0	43.4	-0.5
1960	43.5	0.2	43.5	0.0	43.5	0.0	43.3	-0.5	42.8	-1.2	42.8	0.0	42.9	0.2	42.8	-0.2	42.7	-0.2	42.6	-0.2	42.6	0.0	42.6	0.0
1961	42.9	0.7	42.9	0.0	42.9	0.0	42.4	-1.2	42.4	0.0	42.4	0.0	42.4	0.0	42.0	-0.9	42.0	0.0	42.2	0.5	42.2	0.0	42.1	-0.2
1962	41.9	-0.5	41.9	0.0	41.9	0.0	41.8	-0.2	41.8	0.0	41.8	0.0	41.6	-0.5	41.6	0.0	41.8	0.5	41.8	0.0	41.6	-0.5	41.6	0.0
1963	41.5	-0.2	41.5	0.0	41.1	-1.0	41.2	0.2	41.4	0.5	41.5	0.2	41.2	-0.7	41.2	0.0	41.2	0.0	41.3	0.2	41.4	0.2	41.5	0.2
1964	41.0	-1.2	41.1	0.2	41.2	0.2	41.5	0.7	41.5	0.0	40.9	-1.4	40.9	0.0	41.0	0.2	40.9	-0.2	40.9	0.0	40.9	0.0	40.9	0.0
1965	41.0	0.2	41.1	0.2	41.1	0.0	41.2	0.2	41.2	0.0	41.1	-0.2	41.2	0.2	41.0	-0.5	41.0	0.0	41.0	0.0	40.9	-0.2	41.0	0.2
1966	41.2	0.5	41.5	0.7	41.7	0.5	41.8	0.2	42.0	0.5	41.9	-0.2	42.0	0.2	42.0	0.0	42.1	0.2	42.2	0.2	42.7	1.2	43.1	0.9
1967	43.2	0.2	43.2	0.0	43.2	0.0	43.2	0.0	43.2	0.0	43.2	0.0	43.2	0.0	43.1	-0.2	43.1	0.0	43.0	-0.2	43.1	0.2	43.4	0.7
1968	43.5	0.2	43.6	0.2	43.6	0.0	43.6	0.0	43.7	0.2	43.7	0.0	43.7	0.0	43.7	0.0	43.9	0.5	43.9	0.0	44.0	0.2	43.9	-0.2
1969	43.9	0.0	44.2	0.7	44.2	0.0	44.2	0.0	44.3	0.2	44.4	0.2	44.4	0.0	44.4	0.0	44.7	0.7	44.8	0.2	45.0	0.4	45.1	0.2
1970	45.3	0.4	45.2	-0.2	45.4	0.4	45.5	0.2	45.6	0.2	45.9	0.7	46.1	0.4	46.2	0.2	46.4	0.4	46.4	0.0	46.6	0.4	46.7	0.2
1971	46.9	0.4	47.1	0.4	47.2	0.2	47.1	-0.2	47.1	0.0	47.1	0.0	47.2	0.2	47.3	0.2	47.2	-0.2	47.2	0.0	47.1	-0.2	47.1	0.0
1972	47.3	0.4	47.5	0.4	47.6	0.2	47.6	0.0	47.7	0.2	47.8	0.2	47.8	0.0	47.8	0.0	47.7	-0.2	47.7	0.0	47.8	0.2	47.8	0.0
1973	47.9	0.2	47.9	0.0	48.1	0.4	48.2	0.2	48.5	0.6	48.7	0.4	48.7	0.0	48.7	0.0	48.7	0.0	48.8	0.2	48.9	0.2	49.2	0.6
1974	49.7	1.0	50.0	0.6	50.5	1.0	51.2	1.4	52.1	1.8	53.3	2.3	54.5	2.3	55.5	1.8	56.3	1.4	57.2	1.6	58.5	2.3	59.0	0.9
1975	59.6	1.0	59.9	0.5	60.1	0.3	60.2	0.2	60.5	0.5	60.6	0.2	60.8	0.3	60.9	0.2	61.2	0.5	61.5	0.5	61.8	0.5	61.8	0.0
1976	62.3	0.8	62.5	0.3	62.6	0.2	62.7	0.2	62.8	0.2	63.1	0.5	63.2	0.2	63.3	0.2	64.0	1.1	64.4	0.6	64.6	0.3	64.8	0.3
1977	65.1	0.5	65.4	0.5	65.6	0.3	65.7	0.2	66.0	0.5	66.1	0.2	66.5	0.6	66.7	0.3	67.2	0.7	67.9	1.0	68.2	0.4	68.2	0.0
1978	69.1	1.3	69.4	0.4	69.9	0.7	70.3	0.6	70.6	0.4	71.1	0.7	71.4	0.4	71.6	0.3	71.9	0.4	72.3	0.6	73.2	1.2	73.6	0.5
1979	73.9	0.4	74.6	0.9	75.1	0.7	75.6	0.7	76.2	0.8	76.7	0.7	77.7	1.3	78.2	0.6	78.8	0.8	79.6	1.0	79.8	0.3	80.6	1.0
1980	82.3	2.1	83.9	1.9	84.9	1.2	85.9	1.2	86.3	0.5	87.1	0.9	88.0	1.0	88.5	0.6	89.0	0.6	89.4	0.4	89.6	0.2	90.2	0.7
1981	91.5	1.4	92.3	0.9	93.3	1.1	93.9	0.6	93.9	0.0	94.7	0.9	95.5	0.8	96.2	0.7	96.8	0.6	97.3	0.5	97.6	0.3	98.0	0.4
1982	98.8	0.8	99.1	0.3	99.5	0.4	100.0	0.5	99.9	-0.1	100.0	0.1	100.0	0.0	100.1	0.1	100.1	0.0	100.5	0.4	100.9	0.4	101.2	0.3
1983	101.6	0.4	102.4	0.8	102.6	0.2	102.9	0.3	103.0	0.1	103.1	0.1	104.4	1.3	104.4	0.0	104.9	0.5	104.8	-0.1	104.9	0.1	105.3	0.4

[Continued]

Electrical Machinery and Equipment
Producer Price Index
Base 1982 = 100
[Continued]

For 1939-1995. Columns headed % show percentile change in the index from the previous period for which an index is available.

Year	Jan Index	%	Feb Index	%	Mar Index	%	Apr Index	%	May Index	%	Jun Index	%	Jul Index	%	Aug Index	%	Sep Index	%	Oct Index	%	Nov Index	%	Dec Index	%
1984	105.7	0.4	106.1	0.4	106.5	0.4	107.0	0.5	107.1	0.1	107.6	0.5	107.7	0.1	107.7	0.0	107.9	0.2	108.3	0.4	108.6	0.3	108.7	0.1
1985	109.3	0.6	109.6	0.3	109.6	0.0	109.3	-0.3	109.5	0.2	109.4	-0.1	109.6	0.2	109.7	0.1	109.8	0.1	109.9	0.1	109.8	-0.1	110.0	0.2
1986	110.3	0.3	110.6	0.3	110.8	0.2	111.0	0.2	111.0	0.0	110.9	-0.1	111.5	0.5	111.5	0.0	111.7	0.2	111.7	0.0	111.8	0.1	111.9	0.1
1987	112.3	0.4	112.4	0.1	112.3	-0.1	112.2	-0.1	112.3	0.1	112.2	-0.1	112.7	0.4	112.9	0.2	112.7	-0.2	113.1	0.4	113.2	0.1	113.4	0.2
1988	113.7	0.3	114.1	0.4	113.7	-0.4	113.8	0.1	114.4	0.5	114.2	-0.2	114.4	0.2	114.7	0.3	114.8	0.1	115.1	0.3	115.2	0.1	115.4	0.2
1989	116.2	0.7	116.6	0.3	116.7	0.1	116.8	0.1	117.0	0.2	117.5	0.4	117.9	0.3	118.0	0.1	117.9	-0.1	118.4	0.4	118.3	-0.1	118.4	0.1
1990	118.9	0.4	118.6	-0.3	118.9	0.3	119.0	0.1	119.0	0.0	119.2	0.2	119.5	0.3	119.4	-0.1	119.5	0.1	119.6	0.1	119.8	0.2	119.9	0.1
1991	120.5	0.5	120.6	0.1	120.7	0.1	120.9	0.2	120.7	-0.2	120.8	0.1	120.9	0.1	120.9	0.0	120.8	-0.1	120.8	0.0	120.9	0.1	120.9	0.0
1992	120.9	0.0	121.2	0.2	121.4	0.2	121.2	-0.2	121.3	0.1	121.2	-0.1	121.2	0.0	121.2	0.0	121.2	0.0	121.4	0.2	121.6	0.2	121.7	0.1
1993	122.0	0.2	122.2	0.2	122.2	0.0	122.6	0.3	122.4	-0.2	122.4	0.0	122.4	0.0	122.5	0.1	122.6	0.1	122.7	0.1	122.8	0.1	122.7	-0.1
1994	123.1	0.3	123.2	0.1	123.3	0.1	123.6	0.2	123.7	0.1	123.7	0.0	123.8	0.1	123.5	-0.2	123.4	-0.1	123.2	-0.2	123.4	0.2	123.4	0.0
1995	123.9	0.4	124.2	0.2	124.1	-0.1	124.2	0.1	124.2	0.0	124.1	-0.1	124.0	-0.1	124.0	0.0	124.3	0.2	124.2	-0.1	124.5	0.2	124.4	-0.1

Source: U.S. Department of Labor, Bureau of Labor Statistics, Division of Industry Prices and Price Indexes. n.e.c. stands for not elsewhere classified. - indicates no data collected for period or unavailable.

Miscellaneous Instruments
Producer Price Index
Base 1982 = 100

For 1980-1995. Columns headed % show percentile change in the index from the previous period for which an index is available.

Year	Jan Index	%	Feb Index	%	Mar Index	%	Apr Index	%	May Index	%	Jun Index	%	Jul Index	%	Aug Index	%	Sep Index	%	Oct Index	%	Nov Index	%	Dec Index	%
1980	-	-	-	-	-	-	-	-	-	-	86.1	-	86.4	0.3	86.3	-0.1	87.4	1.3	89.1	1.9	90.3	1.3	91.6	1.4
1981	89.9	-1.9	89.1	-0.9	88.5	-0.7	88.8	0.3	88.9	0.1	89.8	1.0	91.0	1.3	94.4	3.7	95.8	1.5	95.2	-0.6	95.8	0.6	95.8	0.0
1982	96.2	0.4	98.7	2.6	98.2	-0.5	99.3	1.1	99.4	0.1	99.3	-0.1	99.6	0.3	98.0	-1.6	100.8	2.9	103.1	2.3	101.9	-1.2	105.4	3.4
1983	106.1	0.7	107.1	0.9	106.9	-0.2	106.3	-0.6	105.9	-0.4	104.7	-1.1	104.6	-0.1	104.7	0.1	105.0	0.3	105.1	0.1	104.9	-0.2	104.6	-0.3
1984	104.9	0.3	105.4	0.5	105.6	0.2	105.0	-0.6	105.2	0.2	105.7	0.5	106.5	0.8	108.1	1.5	108.4	0.3	108.3	-0.1	108.0	-0.3	108.8	0.7
1985	109.4	0.6	109.5	0.1	109.0	-0.5	108.3	-0.6	108.8	0.5	109.6	0.7	110.5	0.8	110.1	-0.4	110.4	0.3	110.6	0.2	110.9	0.3	110.8	-0.1
1986	111.4	0.5	111.7	0.3	111.4	-0.3	111.7	0.3	111.9	0.2	112.3	0.4	113.2	0.8	113.7	0.4	113.7	0.0	113.9	0.2	114.0	0.1	114.2	0.2
1987	114.8	0.5	115.3	0.4	115.3	0.0	115.4	0.1	115.5	0.1	115.1	-0.3	115.7	0.5	115.9	0.2	116.1	0.2	116.3	0.2	116.4	0.1	116.8	0.3
1988	117.6	0.7	118.2	0.5	118.9	0.6	118.6	-0.3	118.6	0.0	118.6	0.0	118.9	0.3	119.2	0.3	119.2	0.0	119.3	0.1	119.9	0.5	119.9	0.0
1989	121.0	0.9	121.4	0.3	121.5	0.1	121.9	0.3	122.1	0.2	122.4	0.2	122.8	0.3	123.1	0.2	123.2	0.1	123.1	-0.1	123.4	0.2	123.9	0.4
1990	125.0	0.9	125.5	0.4	125.9	0.3	126.1	0.2	126.5	0.3	126.2	-0.2	126.9	0.6	127.1	0.2	127.2	0.1	127.5	0.2	128.1	0.5	128.3	0.2
1991	129.1	0.6	129.5	0.3	129.5	0.0	129.8	0.2	129.7	-0.1	129.9	0.2	130.5	0.5	130.6	0.1	130.8	0.2	131.4	0.5	131.3	-0.1	131.5	0.2
1992	132.4	0.7	132.6	0.2	132.6	0.0	132.9	0.2	132.9	0.0	133.4	0.4	134.0	0.4	134.2	0.1	134.4	0.1	135.0	0.4	135.1	0.1	135.2	0.1
1993	136.7	1.1	136.8	0.1	136.9	0.1	137.5	0.4	137.5	0.0	137.8	0.2	138.2	0.3	138.3	0.1	138.3	0.0	138.4	0.1	138.3	-0.1	138.5	0.1
1994	138.9	0.3	139.1	0.1	139.2	0.1	139.4	0.1	139.5	0.1	139.6	0.1	139.8	0.1	140.0	0.1	139.8	-0.1	139.8	0.0	140.1	0.2	139.6	-0.4
1995	139.9	0.2	140.2	0.2	140.2	0.0	140.4	0.1	140.6	0.1	140.9	0.2	141.6	0.5	141.3	-0.2	141.5	0.1	141.6	0.1	141.7	0.1	142.0	0.2

Source: U.S. Department of Labor, Bureau of Labor Statistics, Division of Industry Prices and Price Indexes. n.e.c. stands for not elsewhere classified. - indicates no data collected for period or unavailable.

Miscellaneous Machinery
Producer Price Index
Base 1982 = 100

For 1947-1995. Columns headed % show percentile change in the index from the previous period for which an index is available.

Year	Jan Index	%	Feb Index	%	Mar Index	%	Apr Index	%	May Index	%	Jun Index	%	Jul Index	%	Aug Index	%	Sep Index	%	Oct Index	%	Nov Index	%	Dec Index	%
1947	21.2	-	21.3	0.5	21.4	0.5	21.4	0.0	21.5	0.5	21.6	0.5	21.6	0.0	21.7	0.5	21.8	0.5	22.0	0.9	22.2	0.9	22.4	0.9
1948	22.5	0.4	22.6	0.4	22.7	0.4	22.8	0.4	22.8	0.0	22.9	0.4	23.4	2.2	23.8	1.7	24.0	0.8	24.2	0.8	24.3	0.4	24.3	0.0
1949	24.3	0.0	24.3	0.0	24.3	0.0	24.3	0.0	24.3	0.0	24.3	0.0	24.3	0.0	24.3	0.0	24.3	0.0	24.3	0.0	24.3	0.0	24.2	-0.4
1950	24.2	0.0	24.3	0.4	24.3	0.0	24.3	0.0	24.3	0.0	24.3	0.0	24.4	0.4	24.9	2.0	25.2	1.2	25.5	1.2	25.8	1.2	26.5	2.7
1951	27.5	3.8	27.5	0.0	27.5	0.0	27.5	0.0	27.5	0.0	27.5	0.0	27.6	0.4	27.6	0.0	27.6	0.0	27.6	0.0	27.6	0.0	27.8	0.7
1952	27.8	0.0	27.8	0.0	27.6	-0.7	27.6	0.0	27.5	-0.4	27.5	0.0	27.5	0.0	27.5	0.0	27.5	0.0	27.6	0.4	27.6	0.0	27.6	0.0
1953	27.6	0.0	27.8	0.7	27.8	0.0	27.8	0.0	28.2	1.4	28.3	0.4	28.5	0.7	28.7	0.7	28.7	0.0	28.7	0.0	28.7	0.0	28.8	0.3
1954	28.8	0.0	28.8	0.0	28.9	0.3	28.9	0.0	28.9	0.0	29.0	0.3	29.0	0.0	29.0	0.0	29.1	0.3	29.1	0.0	29.1	0.0	29.1	0.0
1955	29.2	0.3	29.2	0.0	29.3	0.3	29.3	0.0	29.4	0.3	29.4	0.0	29.4	0.0	30.1	2.4	30.5	1.3	30.7	0.7	30.8	0.3	30.8	0.0
1956	30.8	0.0	30.9	0.3	31.0	0.3	31.0	0.0	31.2	0.6	31.3	0.3	31.6	1.0	31.7	0.3	32.1	1.3	32.5	1.2	32.8	0.9	32.9	0.3
1957	32.9	0.0	33.0	0.3	33.1	0.3	33.2	0.3	33.2	0.0	33.2	0.0	33.4	0.6	33.8	1.2	34.0	0.6	34.1	0.3	34.2	0.3	34.3	0.3
1958	34.4	0.3	34.4	0.0	34.4	0.0	34.4	0.0	34.1	-0.9	34.1	0.0	34.1	0.0	34.1	0.0	34.1	0.0	34.1	0.0	34.2	0.3	34.3	0.3
1959	34.3	0.0	34.4	0.3	34.5	0.3	34.5	0.0	34.5	0.0	34.5	0.0	34.5	0.0	34.6	0.3	34.5	-0.3	34.6	0.3	34.6	0.0	34.6	0.0
1960	34.6	0.0	34.6	0.0	34.7	0.3	34.7	0.0	34.7	0.0	34.7	0.0	34.7	0.0	34.7	0.0	34.7	0.0	34.7	0.0	34.8	0.3	34.9	0.3
1961	34.9	0.0	34.9	0.0	34.9	0.0	35.0	0.3	35.0	0.0	35.0	0.0	35.1	0.3	35.1	0.0	35.1	0.0	35.0	-0.3	35.0	0.0	35.1	0.3
1962	35.1	0.0	35.1	0.0	35.2	0.3	35.1	-0.3	35.1	0.0	35.2	0.3	35.2	0.0	35.3	0.3	35.2	-0.3	35.2	0.0	35.2	0.0	35.2	0.0
1963	35.2	0.0	35.2	0.0	35.4	0.6	35.2	-0.6	35.2	0.0	35.2	0.0	35.2	0.0	35.2	0.0	35.3	0.3	35.3	0.0	35.4	0.3	35.4	0.0
1964	35.5	0.3	35.5	0.0	35.6	0.3	35.6	0.0	35.6	0.0	35.6	0.0	35.7	0.3	35.7	0.0	35.8	0.3	35.8	0.0	35.8	0.0	35.5	-0.8
1965	35.8	0.8	35.8	0.0	35.8	0.0	35.9	0.3	35.9	0.0	36.0	0.3	35.8	-0.6	35.8	0.0	35.8	0.0	35.8	0.0	35.9	0.3	35.9	0.0
1966	35.9	0.0	36.0	0.3	36.1	0.3	36.0	-0.3	36.1	0.3	36.1	0.0	36.3	0.6	36.3	0.0	36.4	0.3	36.6	0.5	36.7	0.3	36.8	0.3
1967	37.0	0.5	37.1	0.3	37.1	0.0	37.1	0.0	37.1	0.0	37.2	0.3	37.2	0.0	37.2	0.0	37.3	0.3	37.4	0.3	37.6	0.5	37.7	0.3
1968	38.2	1.3	38.4	0.5	38.5	0.3	38.6	0.3	38.9	0.8	38.9	0.0	38.9	0.0	38.9	0.0	39.0	0.3	39.3	0.8	39.3	0.0	39.4	0.3
1969	39.5	0.3	39.6	0.3	39.7	0.3	39.9	0.5	40.1	0.5	40.1	0.0	40.3	0.5	40.4	0.2	40.6	0.5	40.8	0.5	41.0	0.5	41.2	0.5
1970	41.3	0.2	41.4	0.2	41.6	0.5	41.9	0.7	41.8	-0.2	41.9	0.2	41.9	0.0	41.9	0.0	42.3	1.0	42.5	0.5	42.7	0.5	43.1	0.9
1971	43.3	0.5	43.3	0.0	43.4	0.2	43.7	0.7	43.8	0.2	43.7	-0.2	43.8	0.2	44.0	0.5	43.9	-0.2	43.9	0.0	43.9	0.0	44.0	0.2
1972	44.1	0.2	44.3	0.5	44.3	0.0	44.6	0.7	44.8	0.4	45.0	0.4	45.0	0.0	45.0	0.0	45.0	0.0	45.1	0.2	45.0	-0.2	45.1	0.2
1973	45.1	0.0	45.3	0.4	45.6	0.7	45.9	0.7	46.4	1.1	46.4	0.0	46.4	0.0	46.5	0.2	46.6	0.2	46.6	0.0	46.8	0.4	47.0	0.4
1974	47.6	1.3	47.9	0.6	48.7	1.7	49.3	1.2	50.0	1.4	51.0	2.0	52.0	2.0	53.5	2.9	54.0	0.9	55.7	3.1	56.9	2.2	57.1	0.4
1975	58.9	3.2	59.1	0.3	59.0	-0.2	59.7	1.2	60.2	0.8	60.2	0.0	60.3	0.2	60.8	0.8	61.5	1.2	61.8	0.5	62.1	0.5	62.2	0.2
1976	62.9	1.1	63.2	0.5	63.5	0.5	63.7	0.3	63.7	0.0	63.8	0.2	64.2	0.6	64.1	-0.2	64.4	0.5	65.0	0.9	65.0	0.0	65.2	0.3
1977	65.6	0.6	65.9	0.5	66.1	0.3	66.3	0.3	66.8	0.8	67.0	0.3	67.3	0.4	67.8	0.7	68.3	0.7	68.6	0.4	69.0	0.6	69.3	0.4
1978	70.1	1.2	70.5	0.6	71.2	1.0	71.4	0.3	71.8	0.6	72.3	0.7	72.9	0.8	73.3	0.5	73.6	0.4	73.9	0.4	74.6	0.9	74.7	0.1
1979	75.5	1.1	75.8	0.4	76.0	0.3	76.5	0.7	77.1	0.8	77.3	0.3	78.1	1.0	78.1	0.0	79.0	1.2	79.6	0.8	80.1	0.6	80.6	0.6
1980	82.1	1.9	82.4	0.4	83.2	1.0	84.7	1.8	84.7	0.0	85.0	0.4	86.1	1.3	86.5	0.5	87.0	0.6	88.1	1.3	88.9	0.9	89.3	0.4
1981	90.7	1.6	91.3	0.7	92.0	0.8	92.6	0.7	92.7	0.1	93.2	0.5	94.7	1.6	95.4	0.7	96.3	0.9	96.5	0.2	96.8	0.3	97.0	0.2
1982	97.4	0.4	98.4	1.0	98.7	0.3	99.2	0.5	99.8	0.6	100.1	0.3	100.4	0.3	100.9	0.5	101.1	0.2	101.2	0.1	101.4	0.2	101.5	0.1
1983	101.7	0.2	101.6	-0.1	102.0	0.4	102.1	0.1	102.6	0.5	102.5	-0.1	102.5	0.0	102.6	0.1	102.3	-0.3	101.8	-0.5	102.0	0.2	102.0	0.0
1984	102.7	0.7	102.2	-0.5	102.3	0.1	102.3	0.0	102.0	-0.3	102.1	0.1	102.2	0.1	102.1	-0.1	102.3	0.2	102.2	-0.1	102.4	0.2	102.3	-0.1
1985	102.5	0.2	102.6	0.1	102.6	0.0	103.1	0.5	103.0	-0.1	103.5	0.5	103.5	0.0	103.6	0.1	103.7	0.1	103.6	-0.1	103.7	0.1	103.7	0.0
1986	103.8	0.1	103.7	-0.1	103.8	0.1	104.2	0.4	104.3	0.1	104.3	0.0	104.3	0.0	104.3	0.0	104.0	-0.3	104.2	0.2	104.3	0.1	104.6	0.3
1987	105.1	0.5	105.2	0.1	105.4	0.2	105.5	0.1	105.6	0.1	105.4	-0.2	105.3	-0.1	105.9	0.6	105.9	0.0	106.1	0.2	106.6	0.5	106.9	0.3
1988	107.5	0.6	107.5	0.0	107.7	0.2	107.9	0.2	108.0	0.1	108.1	0.1	108.5	0.4	109.1	0.6	109.5	0.4	109.5	0.0	109.7	0.2	110.2	0.5
1989	110.7	0.5	110.8	0.1	111.1	0.3	111.3	0.2	111.7	0.4	112.2	0.4	113.1	0.8	113.5	0.4	114.2	0.6	114.4	0.2	114.6	0.2	114.7	0.1
1990	115.7	0.9	115.7	0.0	115.9	0.2	116.0	0.1	116.1	0.1	116.2	0.1	116.3	0.1	116.8	0.4	117.5	0.6	117.6	0.1	118.4	0.7	118.3	-0.1
1991	119.1	0.7	119.4	0.3	119.8	0.3	119.8	0.0	120.0	0.2	120.1	0.1	120.4	0.2	120.8	0.3	121.0	0.2	120.9	-0.1	121.0	0.1	121.2	0.2

[Continued]

Miscellaneous Machinery
Producer Price Index
Base 1982 = 100
[Continued]

For 1947-1995. Columns headed % show percentile change in the index from the previous period for which an index is available.

Year	Jan Index	%	Feb Index	%	Mar Index	%	Apr Index	%	May Index	%	Jun Index	%	Jul Index	%	Aug Index	%	Sep Index	%	Oct Index	%	Nov Index	%	Dec Index	%
1992	121.5	0.2	121.5	0.0	121.4	-0.1	121.3	-0.1	121.5	0.2	121.6	0.1	121.7	0.1	121.9	0.2	121.9	0.0	121.9	0.0	122.0	0.1	122.0	0.0
1993	122.3	0.2	122.4	0.1	122.5	0.1	122.4	-0.1	122.5	0.1	122.4	-0.1	122.6	0.2	122.9	0.2	123.0	0.1	123.2	0.2	123.1	-0.1	123.3	0.2
1994	123.9	0.5	124.2	0.2	124.2	0.0	124.2	0.0	124.2	0.0	124.4	0.2	124.5	0.1	124.7	0.2	125.2	0.4	125.5	0.2	125.6	0.1	125.7	0.1
1995	126.2	0.4	126.4	0.2	126.4	0.0	126.6	0.2	126.7	0.1	126.8	0.1	127.2	0.3	127.2	0.0	127.3	0.1	127.6	0.2	127.6	0.0	127.7	0.1

Source: U.S. Department of Labor, Bureau of Labor Statistics, Division of Industry Prices and Price Indexes. n.e.c. stands for not elsewhere classified. - indicates no data collected for period or unavailable.

FURNITURE AND HOUSEHOLD DURABLES
Producer Price Index
Base 1982 = 100

For 1926-1995. Columns headed % show percentile change in the index from the previous period for which an index is available.

Year	Jan Index	%	Feb Index	%	Mar Index	%	Apr Index	%	May Index	%	Jun Index	%	Jul Index	%	Aug Index	%	Sep Index	%	Oct Index	%	Nov Index	%	Dec Index	%
1926	28.8	-	28.8	0.0	28.8	0.0	28.7	-0.3	28.6	-0.3	28.6	0.0	28.6	0.0	28.6	0.0	28.5	-0.3	28.5	0.0	28.5	0.0	28.2	-1.1
1927	28.0	-0.7	28.0	0.0	27.9	-0.4	27.9	0.0	27.9	0.0	28.0	0.4	27.9	-0.4	27.9	0.0	27.6	-1.1	27.8	0.7	27.9	0.4	27.9	0.0
1928	27.6	-1.1	27.6	0.0	27.4	-0.7	27.3	-0.4	27.4	0.4	27.1	-1.1	27.1	0.0	27.1	0.0	27.1	0.0	26.9	-0.7	26.9	0.0	26.9	0.0
1929	26.9	0.0	26.8	-0.4	26.8	0.0	26.9	0.4	26.9	0.0	27.1	0.7	27.0	-0.4	27.0	0.0	27.0	0.0	27.1	0.4	27.1	0.0	27.1	0.0
1930	26.8	-1.1	26.8	0.0	26.8	0.0	26.8	0.0	26.8	0.0	26.8	0.0	26.6	-0.7	26.6	0.0	26.4	-0.8	26.4	0.0	26.2	-0.8	25.4	-3.1
1931	25.4	0.0	25.4	0.0	25.3	-0.4	25.3	0.0	24.9	-1.6	24.8	-0.4	24.6	-0.8	24.4	-0.8	23.7	-2.9	23.2	-2.1	23.2	0.0	22.5	-3.0
1932	22.3	-0.9	22.2	-0.4	22.1	-0.5	21.9	-0.9	21.4	-2.3	21.4	0.0	21.2	-0.9	21.2	0.0	21.1	-0.5	21.2	0.5	21.2	0.0	21.2	0.0
1933	20.8	-1.9	20.6	-1.0	20.6	0.0	20.5	-0.5	20.6	0.5	21.0	1.9	21.4	1.9	21.8	1.9	22.3	2.3	23.0	3.1	23.0	0.0	23.0	0.0
1934	23.1	0.4	23.2	0.4	23.3	0.4	23.4	0.4	23.6	0.9	23.6	0.0	23.5	-0.4	23.5	0.0	23.6	0.4	23.5	-0.4	23.4	-0.4	23.4	0.0
1935	23.2	-0.9	23.2	0.0	23.3	0.4	23.2	-0.4	23.3	0.4	23.2	-0.4	23.2	0.0	23.2	0.0	23.2	0.0	23.2	0.0	23.2	0.0	23.2	0.0
1936	23.5	1.3	23.5	0.0	23.5	0.0	23.5	0.0	23.5	0.0	23.5	0.0	23.4	-0.4	23.5	0.4	23.6	0.4	23.7	0.4	23.8	0.4	24.1	1.3
1937	25.4	5.4	25.7	1.2	25.8	0.4	25.9	0.4	26.1	0.8	26.1	0.0	26.4	1.1	26.6	0.8	26.6	0.0	26.6	0.0	26.4	-0.8	26.2	-0.8
1938	25.8	-1.5	25.8	0.0	25.8	0.0	25.7	-0.4	25.7	0.0	25.7	0.0	25.4	-1.2	25.4	0.0	25.3	-0.4	25.2	-0.4	25.2	0.0	25.3	0.4
1939	25.2	-0.4	25.2	0.0	25.2	0.0	25.2	0.0	25.2	0.0	25.3	0.4	25.3	0.0	25.3	0.0	25.5	0.8	25.9	1.6	25.9	0.0	25.9	0.0
1940	25.8	-0.4	25.9	0.4	25.9	0.0	26.0	0.4	26.0	0.0	26.0	0.0	26.0	0.0	26.0	0.0	26.0	0.0	26.0	0.0	26.0	0.0	26.1	0.4
1941	26.1	0.0	26.1	0.0	26.4	1.1	26.6	0.8	26.8	0.8	27.4	2.2	27.8	1.5	28.0	0.7	28.5	1.8	29.1	2.1	29.3	0.7	29.6	1.0
1942	29.8	0.7	29.8	0.0	29.8	0.0	29.9	0.3	29.9	0.0	29.9	0.0	29.9	0.0	29.9	0.0	29.9	0.0	29.9	0.0	29.9	0.0	29.9	0.0
1943	29.7	-0.7	29.7	0.0	29.7	0.0	29.7	0.0	29.7	0.0	29.7	0.0	29.7	0.0	29.7	0.0	29.7	0.0	29.7	0.0	29.7	0.0	29.7	0.0
1944	30.5	2.7	30.4	-0.3	30.4	0.0	30.4	0.0	30.4	0.0	30.4	0.0	30.4	0.0	30.5	0.3	30.5	0.0	30.5	0.0	30.5	0.0	30.5	0.0
1945	30.5	0.0	30.5	0.0	30.5	0.0	30.5	0.0	30.5	0.0	30.5	0.0	30.5	0.0	30.5	0.0	30.5	0.0	30.5	0.0	30.5	0.0	30.5	0.0
1946	30.8	1.0	30.9	0.3	31.0	0.3	31.2	0.6	31.6	1.3	32.2	1.9	32.4	0.6	32.5	0.3	32.9	1.2	33.2	0.9	34.2	3.0	35.9	5.0
1947	36.5	1.7	36.6	0.3	36.6	0.0	36.8	0.5	36.8	0.0	36.9	0.3	37.2	0.8	37.3	0.3	37.5	0.5	37.8	0.8	37.9	0.3	38.1	0.5
1948	38.4	0.8	38.4	0.0	38.5	0.3	38.8	0.8	38.8	0.0	38.9	0.3	39.2	0.8	39.5	0.8	40.0	1.3	40.8	2.0	40.9	0.2	40.9	0.0
1949	40.7	-0.5	40.7	0.0	40.6	-0.2	40.5	-0.2	40.3	-0.5	40.2	-0.2	39.8	-1.0	39.7	-0.3	39.6	-0.3	39.5	-0.3	39.6	0.3	39.7	0.3
1950	39.7	0.0	39.8	0.3	39.8	0.0	39.9	0.3	40.1	0.5	40.1	0.0	40.3	0.5	40.8	1.2	41.6	2.0	42.6	2.4	43.1	1.2	43.6	1.2
1951	44.4	1.8	44.6	0.5	44.7	0.2	44.9	0.4	44.8	-0.2	44.7	-0.2	44.5	-0.4	44.1	-0.9	44.0	-0.2	43.9	-0.2	43.8	-0.2	43.8	0.0
1952	43.7	-0.2	43.7	0.0	43.5	-0.5	43.6	0.2	43.4	-0.5	43.4	0.0	43.4	0.0	43.3	-0.2	43.5	0.2	43.5	0.0	43.6	0.2	43.7	0.2
1953	43.8	0.2	43.9	0.2	44.0	0.2	44.3	0.7	44.4	0.2	44.5	0.2	44.6	0.2	44.6	0.0	44.7	0.2	44.6	-0.2	44.7	0.2	44.7	0.0
1954	44.8	0.2	44.7	-0.2	44.7	0.0	44.9	0.4	44.9	0.0	44.9	0.0	44.8	-0.2	44.8	0.0	44.8	0.0	44.9	0.2	44.9	0.0	45.0	0.2
1955	44.9	-0.2	44.9	0.0	44.7	-0.4	44.7	0.0	44.7	0.0	44.8	0.2	44.9	0.2	45.1	0.4	45.3	0.4	45.5	0.4	45.6	0.2	45.6	0.0
1956	45.9	0.7	46.0	0.2	46.0	0.0	45.9	-0.2	45.9	0.0	46.0	0.2	46.0	0.0	46.3	0.7	46.5	0.4	47.0	1.1	47.1	0.2	47.1	0.0
1957	47.4	0.6	47.4	0.0	47.4	0.0	47.2	-0.4	47.3	0.2	47.3	0.0	47.5	0.4	47.6	0.2	47.5	-0.2	47.6	0.2	47.7	0.2	48.0	0.6
1958	48.1	0.2	48.0	-0.2	48.0	0.0	48.0	0.0	47.9	-0.2	47.8	-0.2	47.9	0.2	47.8	-0.2	47.8	0.0	47.8	0.0	47.7	-0.2	47.7	0.0
1959	47.9	0.4	47.9	0.0	48.0	0.2	48.0	0.0	48.0	0.0	48.0	0.0	48.1	0.2	48.0	-0.2	48.0	0.0	47.9	-0.2	47.9	0.0	47.9	0.0
1960	48.0	0.2	48.0	0.0	48.1	0.2	48.0	-0.2	47.9	-0.2	47.8	-0.2	47.8	0.0	47.8	0.0	47.7	-0.2	47.7	0.0	47.6	-0.2	47.6	0.0
1961	47.5	-0.2	47.5	0.0	47.5	0.0	47.6	0.2	47.6	0.0	47.6	0.0	47.5	-0.2	47.5	0.0	47.5	0.0	47.5	0.0	47.5	0.0	47.5	0.0
1962	47.5	0.0	47.4	-0.2	47.3	-0.2	47.3	0.0	47.3	0.0	47.3	0.0	47.2	-0.2	47.2	0.0	47.1	-0.2	47.1	0.0	47.1	0.0	47.0	-0.2
1963	47.0	0.0	46.9	-0.2	46.9	0.0	46.9	0.0	46.8	-0.2	46.9	0.2	46.8	-0.2	46.9	0.2	46.9	0.0	46.9	0.0	46.9	0.0	46.8	-0.2
1964	47.0	0.4	47.1	0.2	47.1	0.0	47.1	0.0	47.1	0.0	47.1	0.0	47.1	0.0	47.1	0.0	47.1	0.0	47.1	0.0	47.1	0.0	47.0	-0.2
1965	47.0	0.0	46.9	-0.2	47.0	0.2	46.8	-0.4	46.8	0.0	46.8	0.0	46.7	-0.2	46.7	0.0	46.7	0.0	46.7	0.0	46.8	0.2	46.9	0.2
1966	47.0	0.2	47.0	0.0	47.0	0.0	47.1	0.2	47.3	0.4	47.3	0.0	47.3	0.0	47.4	0.2	47.4	0.0	47.6	0.4	47.9	0.6	48.0	0.2
1967	48.0	0.0	48.0	0.0	48.0	0.0	48.1	0.2	48.2	0.2	48.2	0.0	48.2	0.0	48.3	0.2	48.4	0.2	48.6	0.4	48.8	0.4	48.9	0.2
1968	49.2	0.6	49.4	0.4	49.5	0.2	49.6	0.2	49.7	0.2	49.6	-0.2	49.7	0.2	49.8	0.2	49.8	0.0	49.9	0.2	49.9	0.0	50.1	0.4
1969	50.4	0.6	50.4	0.0	50.5	0.2	50.5	0.0	50.5	0.0	50.5	0.0	50.6	0.2	50.7	0.2	50.8	0.2	50.9	0.2	51.0	0.2	51.2	0.4
1970	51.4	0.4	51.6	0.4	51.6	0.0	51.8	0.4	51.7	-0.2	51.8	0.2	52.0	0.4	52.0	0.0	52.1	0.2	52.2	0.2	52.4	0.4	52.5	0.2

[Continued]

FURNITURE AND HOUSEHOLD DURABLES
Producer Price Index
Base 1982 = 100

[Continued]

For 1926-1995. Columns headed % show percentile change in the index from the previous period for which an index is available.

Year	Jan Index	%	Feb Index	%	Mar Index	%	Apr Index	%	May Index	%	Jun Index	%	Jul Index	%	Aug Index	%	Sep Index	%	Oct Index	%	Nov Index	%	Dec Index	%
1971	52.8	0.6	53.0	0.4	53.0	0.0	53.0	0.0	53.1	0.2	53.1	0.0	53.3	0.4	53.3	0.0	53.3	0.0	53.3	0.0	53.2	-0.2	53.2	0.0
1972	53.3	0.2	53.5	0.4	53.6	0.2	53.6	0.0	53.7	0.2	53.7	0.0	53.8	0.2	54.0	0.4	54.1	0.2	54.1	0.0	54.3	0.4	54.3	0.0
1973	54.4	0.2	54.6	0.4	54.8	0.4	55.1	0.5	55.6	0.9	55.7	0.2	55.7	0.0	56.0	0.5	56.1	0.2	56.3	0.4	56.6	0.5	56.8	0.4
1974	57.5	1.2	58.1	1.0	58.6	0.9	59.4	1.4	60.2	1.3	60.9	1.2	62.0	1.8	62.7	1.1	64.2	2.4	65.5	2.0	66.2	1.1	66.5	0.5
1975	67.1	0.9	67.2	0.1	66.9	-0.4	66.9	0.0	67.0	0.1	67.2	0.3	67.3	0.1	67.6	0.4	67.7	0.1	68.2	0.7	68.4	0.3	68.6	0.3
1976	69.3	1.0	69.4	0.1	69.6	0.3	69.8	0.3	70.0	0.3	70.2	0.3	70.4	0.3	70.6	0.3	70.9	0.4	71.1	0.3	71.3	0.3	71.5	0.3
1977	71.9	0.6	72.1	0.3	72.3	0.3	72.5	0.3	72.8	0.4	73.2	0.5	73.2	0.0	73.7	0.7	73.8	0.1	74.0	0.3	74.3	0.4	74.5	0.3
1978	75.6	1.5	75.7	0.1	76.2	0.7	76.5	0.4	76.9	0.5	77.1	0.3	78.0	1.2	78.2	0.3	78.3	0.1	78.7	0.5	79.0	0.4	79.5	0.6
1979	80.5	1.3	81.1	0.7	81.3	0.2	81.5	0.2	82.0	0.6	82.2	0.2	82.5	0.4	82.9	0.5	83.5	0.7	84.6	1.3	85.2	0.7	86.0	0.9
1980	88.6	3.0	89.7	1.2	89.7	0.0	89.1	-0.7	89.6	0.6	90.1	0.6	90.8	0.8	91.3	0.6	91.6	0.3	92.2	0.7	92.5	0.3	93.3	0.9
1981	93.7	0.4	94.3	0.6	94.6	0.3	94.9	0.3	95.4	0.5	95.3	-0.1	96.4	1.2	96.4	0.0	97.1	0.7	97.3	0.2	97.6	0.3	98.1	0.5
1982	98.3	0.2	98.9	0.6	99.3	0.4	99.6	0.3	99.8	0.2	100.0	0.2	100.0	0.0	100.5	0.5	100.7	0.2	101.0	0.3	100.9	-0.1	101.1	0.2
1983	101.8	0.7	102.7	0.9	102.6	-0.1	102.8	0.2	103.2	0.4	103.4	0.2	103.8	0.4	103.9	0.1	104.1	0.2	104.0	-0.1	104.2	0.2	104.2	0.0
1984	104.7	0.5	105.0	0.3	105.1	0.1	105.4	0.3	105.9	0.5	105.9	0.0	105.9	0.0	105.9	0.0	105.8	-0.1	105.9	0.1	106.3	0.4	106.3	0.0
1985	106.4	0.1	106.7	0.3	106.8	0.1	107.1	0.3	107.1	0.0	107.1	0.0	107.3	0.2	107.3	0.0	107.2	-0.1	107.2	0.0	107.4	0.2	107.5	0.1
1986	107.6	0.1	107.7	0.1	107.9	0.2	108.1	0.2	108.3	0.2	108.4	0.1	108.3	-0.1	108.4	0.1	108.3	-0.1	108.5	0.2	108.7	0.2	108.7	0.0
1987	109.0	0.3	109.1	0.1	109.2	0.1	109.6	0.4	109.8	0.2	109.9	0.1	110.0	0.1	110.3	0.3	110.3	0.0	110.5	0.2	110.7	0.2	110.9	0.2
1988	111.6	0.6	111.9	0.3	112.3	0.4	112.5	0.2	112.8	0.3	112.7	-0.1	113.1	0.4	113.4	0.3	113.7	0.3	113.9	0.2	114.3	0.4	114.5	0.2
1989	115.0	0.4	115.3	0.3	115.7	0.3	116.2	0.4	116.5	0.3	117.0	0.4	117.5	0.4	117.9	0.3	117.9	0.0	117.7	-0.2	117.8	0.1	117.9	0.1
1990	118.4	0.4	118.7	0.3	118.7	0.0	119.0	0.3	119.0	0.0	119.2	0.2	119.1	-0.1	119.2	0.1	119.3	0.1	119.5	0.2	119.8	0.3	120.0	0.2
1991	120.6	0.5	120.9	0.2	121.0	0.1	121.2	0.2	121.2	0.0	121.2	0.0	121.2	0.0	121.2	0.0	121.2	0.0	121.4	0.2	121.4	0.0	121.5	0.1
1992	121.8	0.2	121.8	0.0	121.9	0.1	122.0	0.1	122.1	0.1	122.2	0.1	122.2	0.0	122.2	0.0	122.4	0.2	122.3	-0.1	122.6	0.2	122.6	0.0
1993	122.6	0.0	122.9	0.2	123.0	0.1	123.2	0.2	123.4	0.2	123.6	0.2	123.8	0.2	124.0	0.2	124.0	0.0	124.5	0.4	124.8	0.2	124.8	0.0
1994	125.2	0.3	125.4	0.2	125.5	0.1	125.8	0.2	126.1	0.2	126.2	0.1	126.4	0.2	126.3	-0.1	126.2	-0.1	126.4	0.2	126.7	0.2	126.7	0.0
1995	127.2	0.4	127.5	0.2	127.5	0.0	127.8	0.2	128.0	0.2	128.1	0.1	128.2	0.1	128.4	0.2	128.4	0.0	128.5	0.1	128.9	0.3	128.9	0.0

Source: U.S. Department of Labor, Bureau of Labor Statistics, Division of Industry Prices and Price Indexes. n.e.c. stands for not elsewhere classified. - indicates no data collected for period or unavailable.

Household Furniture
Producer Price Index
Base 1982 = 100

For 1926-1995. Columns headed % show percentile change in the index from the previous period for which an index is available.

Year	Jan Index	%	Feb Index	%	Mar Index	%	Apr Index	%	May Index	%	Jun Index	%	Jul Index	%	Aug Index	%	Sep Index	%	Oct Index	%	Nov Index	%	Dec Index	%
1926	23.2	-	23.1	-0.4	23.1	0.0	23.0	-0.4	22.9	-0.4	22.8	-0.4	22.8	0.0	22.8	0.0	22.8	0.0	22.8	0.0	22.8	0.0	22.8	0.0
1927	22.4	-1.8	22.4	0.0	22.4	0.0	22.4	0.0	22.4	0.0	22.4	0.0	22.4	0.0	22.4	0.0	22.4	0.0	22.2	-0.9	22.3	0.5	22.2	-0.4
1928	22.3	0.5	22.3	0.0	22.2	-0.4	22.2	0.0	22.2	0.0	22.2	0.0	22.2	0.0	22.2	0.0	22.2	0.0	21.8	-1.8	21.8	0.0	21.8	0.0
1929	21.6	-0.9	21.6	0.0	21.6	0.0	21.6	0.0	21.6	0.0	21.8	0.9	21.8	0.0	21.8	0.0	21.8	0.0	21.5	-1.4	21.8	1.4	21.8	0.0
1930	21.7	-0.5	21.7	0.0	21.7	0.0	21.7	0.0	21.7	0.0	21.6	-0.5	21.5	-0.5	21.5	0.0	21.4	-0.5	21.4	0.0	21.4	0.0	21.1	-1.4
1931	21.1	0.0	21.1	0.0	21.1	0.0	21.1	0.0	20.7	-1.9	20.5	-1.0	20.4	-0.5	20.3	-0.5	19.4	-4.4	18.8	-3.1	18.8	0.0	18.4	-2.1
1932	18.2	-1.1	18.2	0.0	18.1	-0.5	17.7	-2.2	17.0	-4.0	16.9	-0.6	16.7	-1.2	16.6	-0.6	16.7	0.6	16.7	0.0	16.7	0.0	16.6	-0.6
1933	16.5	-0.6	16.4	-0.6	16.4	0.0	16.4	0.0	16.4	0.0	16.8	2.4	17.1	1.8	17.5	2.3	17.9	2.3	18.2	1.7	18.2	0.0	18.1	-0.5
1934	18.1	0.0	18.1	0.0	18.2	0.6	18.3	0.5	18.3	0.0	18.1	-1.1	18.0	-0.6	18.1	0.6	18.1	0.0	18.1	0.0	18.0	-0.6	17.9	-0.6
1935	17.9	0.0	17.7	-1.1	17.7	0.0	17.7	0.0	17.7	0.0	17.7	0.0	17.6	-0.6	17.6	0.0	17.6	0.0	17.6	0.0	17.7	0.6	17.7	0.0
1936	17.8	0.6	17.8	0.0	17.8	0.0	17.8	0.0	17.8	0.0	17.7	-0.6	17.7	0.0	17.7	0.0	17.8	0.6	17.9	0.6	18.1	1.1	18.2	0.6
1937	19.2	5.5	19.4	1.0	19.4	0.0	19.6	1.0	19.7	0.5	19.8	0.5	19.8	0.0	19.9	0.5	19.9	0.0	19.9	0.0	19.7	-1.0	19.7	0.0
1938	19.1	-3.0	19.1	0.0	19.1	0.0	19.1	0.0	19.1	0.0	19.1	0.0	18.8	-1.6	18.8	0.0	18.8	0.0	18.8	0.0	18.7	-0.5	18.7	0.0
1939	18.4	-1.6	18.4	0.0	18.4	0.0	18.5	0.5	18.5	0.0	18.5	0.0	18.5	0.0	18.5	0.0	18.6	0.5	18.7	0.5	18.8	0.5	18.8	0.0
1940	18.7	-0.5	18.7	0.0	18.7	0.0	18.7	0.0	18.7	0.0	18.7	0.0	18.7	0.0	18.7	0.0	18.7	0.0	18.7	0.0	18.7	0.0	18.8	0.5
1941	18.9	0.5	18.9	0.0	19.0	0.5	19.1	0.5	19.3	1.0	19.9	3.1	20.4	2.5	20.5	0.5	21.1	2.9	21.6	2.4	21.9	1.4	22.1	0.9
1942	22.3	0.9	22.3	0.0	22.3	0.0	22.3	0.0	22.3	0.0	22.3	0.0	22.3	0.0	22.3	0.0	22.3	0.0	22.3	0.0	22.3	0.0	22.3	0.0
1943	22.4	0.4	22.4	0.0	22.4	0.0	22.4	0.0	22.4	0.0	22.4	0.0	22.4	0.0	22.4	0.0	22.4	0.0	22.4	0.0	22.4	0.0	22.6	0.9
1944	22.9	1.3	23.1	0.9	23.1	0.0	23.1	0.0	23.1	0.0	23.1	0.0	23.1	0.0	23.1	0.0	23.1	0.0	23.1	0.0	23.2	0.4	23.2	0.0
1945	23.2	0.0	23.2	0.0	23.2	0.0	23.2	0.0	23.2	0.0	23.5	1.3	23.5	0.0	23.5	0.0	23.5	0.0	23.5	0.0	23.5	0.0	23.5	0.0
1946	23.9	1.7	24.0	0.4	24.0	0.0	24.1	0.4	24.5	1.7	24.8	1.2	24.9	0.4	25.2	1.2	25.4	0.8	25.8	1.6	26.3	1.9	26.9	2.3
1947	29.4	9.3	29.4	0.0	29.4	0.0	29.5	0.3	29.5	0.0	29.5	0.0	29.7	0.7	29.9	0.7	30.3	1.3	30.7	1.3	30.8	0.3	31.1	1.0
1948	31.9	2.6	31.9	0.0	31.9	0.0	32.0	0.3	31.9	-0.3	32.0	0.3	32.0	0.0	32.3	0.9	32.5	0.6	32.5	0.0	32.5	0.0	32.5	0.0
1949	32.3	-0.6	32.3	0.0	32.3	0.0	32.3	0.0	32.0	-0.9	31.9	-0.3	31.2	-2.2	31.3	0.3	31.3	0.0	31.3	0.0	31.3	0.0	31.4	0.3
1950	31.5	0.3	31.5	0.0	31.5	0.0	31.6	0.3	31.6	0.0	31.8	0.6	32.2	1.3	33.2	3.1	34.2	3.0	34.8	1.8	35.2	1.1	35.9	2.0
1951	36.7	2.2	36.8	0.3	36.8	0.0	36.8	0.0	36.7	-0.3	36.5	-0.5	36.2	-0.8	36.2	0.0	36.2	0.0	36.1	-0.3	36.2	0.3	36.0	-0.6
1952	35.5	-1.4	35.5	0.0	35.5	0.0	35.5	0.0	35.4	-0.3	35.2	-0.6	35.2	0.0	35.2	0.0	35.2	0.0	35.2	0.0	35.3	0.3	35.3	0.0
1953	35.4	0.3	35.5	0.3	35.5	0.0	35.6	0.3	35.6	0.0	35.7	0.3	35.6	-0.3	35.6	0.0	35.7	0.3	35.7	0.0	35.7	0.0	35.7	0.0
1954	35.7	0.0	35.6	-0.3	35.6	0.0	35.5	-0.3	35.5	0.0	35.4	-0.3	35.3	-0.3	35.3	0.0	35.3	0.0	35.3	0.0	35.3	0.0	35.3	0.0
1955	35.2	-0.3	35.2	0.0	35.2	0.0	35.3	0.3	35.4	0.3	35.3	-0.3	35.4	0.3	35.8	1.1	36.0	0.6	36.2	0.6	36.4	0.6	36.5	0.3
1956	36.7	0.5	36.7	0.0	36.8	0.3	36.9	0.3	36.9	0.0	36.9	0.0	37.3	1.1	37.4	0.3	37.6	0.5	37.8	0.5	37.9	0.3	37.9	0.0
1957	38.2	0.8	38.2	0.0	38.2	0.0	38.3	0.3	38.3	0.0	38.3	0.0	38.4	0.3	38.5	0.3	38.3	-0.5	38.3	0.0	38.4	0.3	38.4	0.0
1958	38.5	0.3	38.6	0.3	38.4	-0.5	38.4	0.0	38.4	0.0	38.3	-0.3	38.3	0.0	38.3	0.0	38.4	0.3	38.5	0.3	38.7	0.5	38.8	0.3
1959	38.8	0.0	38.8	0.0	38.8	0.0	38.6	-0.5	38.7	0.3	38.8	0.3	38.9	0.3	38.9	0.0	38.8	-0.3	38.9	0.3	38.9	0.0	38.9	0.0
1960	39.0	0.3	39.1	0.3	39.1	0.0	39.1	0.0	39.1	0.0	39.1	0.0	39.1	0.0	39.1	0.0	39.1	0.0	39.3	0.5	39.3	0.0	39.3	0.0
1961	39.5	0.5	39.5	0.0	39.5	0.0	39.5	0.0	39.6	0.3	39.6	0.0	39.6	0.0	39.6	0.0	39.6	0.0	39.7	0.3	39.9	0.5	39.8	-0.3
1962	39.9	0.3	39.9	0.0	39.9	0.0	39.9	0.0	40.0	0.3	40.0	0.0	40.1	0.3	40.1	0.0	40.0	-0.2	40.1	0.3	40.1	0.0	40.2	0.2
1963	40.3	0.2	40.3	0.0	40.3	0.0	40.2	-0.2	40.2	0.0	40.3	0.2	40.3	0.0	40.3	0.0	40.4	0.2	40.4	0.0	40.4	0.0	40.3	-0.2
1964	40.5	0.5	40.5	0.0	40.5	0.0	40.6	0.2	40.6	0.0	40.5	-0.2	40.6	0.2	40.6	0.0	40.6	0.0	40.6	0.0	40.7	0.2	40.7	0.0
1965	40.9	0.5	40.9	0.0	40.9	0.0	40.9	0.0	40.9	0.0	40.8	-0.2	40.8	0.0	40.9	0.2	40.9	0.0	41.0	0.2	41.1	0.2	41.1	0.0
1966	41.2	0.2	41.3	0.2	41.3	0.0	41.7	1.0	42.0	0.7	42.0	0.0	42.0	0.0	42.2	0.5	42.3	0.2	42.5	0.5	43.0	1.2	43.1	0.2
1967	43.1	0.0	43.2	0.2	43.3	0.2	43.3	0.0	43.3	0.0	43.3	0.0	43.4	0.2	43.6	0.5	43.6	0.0	43.7	0.2	44.0	0.7	44.0	0.0
1968	44.4	0.9	44.6	0.5	44.7	0.2	44.8	0.2	45.1	0.7	45.2	0.2	45.3	0.2	45.3	0.0	45.4	0.2	45.7	0.7	45.9	0.4	46.0	0.2
1969	46.6	1.3	46.7	0.2	46.8	0.2	46.8	0.0	47.0	0.4	47.1	0.2	47.4	0.6	47.4	0.0	47.5	0.2	47.6	0.2	47.7	0.2	47.6	-0.2
1970	47.9	0.6	48.3	0.8	48.4	0.2	48.4	0.0	48.6	0.4	48.6	0.0	48.7	0.2	48.8	0.2	48.8	0.0	48.8	0.0	48.9	0.2	49.0	0.2

[Continued]

Household Furniture

Producer Price Index

Base 1982 = 100

[Continued]

For 1926-1995. Columns headed % show percentile change in the index from the previous period for which an index is available.

Year	Jan Index	%	Feb Index	%	Mar Index	%	Apr Index	%	May Index	%	Jun Index	%	Jul Index	%	Aug Index	%	Sep Index	%	Oct Index	%	Nov Index	%	Dec Index	%
1971	49.2	0.4	49.7	1.0	49.7	0.0	49.7	0.0	50.1	0.8	50.1	0.0	50.2	0.2	50.3	0.2	50.3	0.0	50.3	0.0	50.0	-0.6	50.0	0.0
1972	50.5	1.0	50.8	0.6	50.8	0.0	50.9	0.2	51.0	0.2	51.0	0.0	51.1	0.2	51.3	0.4	51.2	-0.2	51.2	0.0	51.4	0.4	51.6	0.4
1973	51.8	0.4	51.9	0.2	52.2	0.6	53.0	1.5	53.2	0.4	53.6	0.8	53.6	0.0	53.8	0.4	54.1	0.6	54.5	0.7	55.1	1.1	55.3	0.4
1974	56.1	1.4	56.5	0.7	56.7	0.4	57.8	1.9	58.7	1.6	58.9	0.3	59.5	1.0	60.0	0.8	60.9	1.5	62.1	2.0	62.9	1.3	62.9	0.0
1975	63.3	0.6	63.3	0.0	63.2	-0.2	63.3	0.2	63.2	-0.2	63.2	0.0	63.3	0.2	63.3	0.0	63.6	0.5	64.3	1.1	64.6	0.5	65.1	0.8
1976	65.6	0.8	65.5	-0.2	65.6	0.2	65.8	0.3	66.1	0.5	66.6	0.8	66.8	0.3	66.9	0.1	67.4	0.7	68.1	1.0	68.5	0.6	69.0	0.7
1977	69.1	0.1	69.1	0.0	69.5	0.6	69.9	0.6	70.1	0.3	70.6	0.7	70.9	0.4	71.0	0.1	71.1	0.1	71.4	0.4	71.8	0.6	72.4	0.8
1978	73.2	1.1	73.4	0.3	73.7	0.4	73.9	0.3	74.3	0.5	75.0	0.9	76.0	1.3	76.4	0.5	76.6	0.3	77.4	1.0	77.8	0.5	78.0	0.3
1979	78.8	1.0	78.9	0.1	79.1	0.3	79.5	0.5	80.4	1.1	80.6	0.2	80.8	0.2	81.0	0.2	82.0	1.2	82.7	0.9	84.0	1.6	84.8	1.0
1980	85.9	1.3	86.4	0.6	86.6	0.2	87.2	0.7	88.3	1.3	88.8	0.6	89.8	1.1	90.5	0.8	90.7	0.2	91.3	0.7	91.8	0.5	92.3	0.5
1981	92.6	0.3	93.0	0.4	93.3	0.3	94.2	1.0	94.1	-0.1	95.1	1.1	95.7	0.6	96.0	0.3	96.7	0.7	96.9	0.2	97.9	1.0	98.6	0.7
1982	99.0	0.4	98.9	-0.1	99.0	0.1	99.9	0.9	100.1	0.2	100.2	0.1	100.1	-0.1	100.2	0.1	100.4	0.2	100.6	0.2	100.7	0.1	100.9	0.2
1983	100.9	0.0	101.2	0.3	100.6	-0.6	100.8	0.2	102.0	1.2	102.2	0.2	102.4	0.2	102.8	0.4	102.9	0.1	103.1	0.2	103.3	0.2	103.2	-0.1
1984	103.5	0.3	104.0	0.5	104.4	0.4	104.8	0.4	105.1	0.3	105.4	0.3	105.4	0.0	105.6	0.2	105.9	0.3	106.3	0.4	106.6	0.3	106.8	0.2
1985	107.4	0.6	107.7	0.3	107.7	0.0	108.3	0.6	108.8	0.5	109.0	0.2	108.7	-0.3	108.8	0.1	108.8	0.0	108.7	-0.1	108.9	0.2	109.0	0.1
1986	109.3	0.3	109.8	0.5	110.0	0.2	109.8	-0.2	110.3	0.5	110.2	-0.1	110.1	-0.1	110.6	0.5	110.4	-0.2	110.7	0.3	110.8	0.1	111.0	0.2
1987	111.2	0.2	111.7	0.4	112.0	0.3	112.5	0.4	112.8	0.3	112.8	0.0	112.8	0.0	113.1	0.3	113.6	0.4	113.6	0.0	114.2	0.5	115.2	0.9
1988	115.8	0.5	116.2	0.3	116.8	0.5	117.0	0.2	117.2	0.2	117.4	0.2	117.8	0.3	118.1	0.3	118.1	0.0	118.6	0.4	119.0	0.3	119.5	0.4
1989	119.6	0.1	120.2	0.5	120.7	0.4	121.3	0.5	121.6	0.2	121.7	0.1	121.9	0.2	122.3	0.3	122.5	0.2	123.1	0.5	123.4	0.2	123.5	0.1
1990	123.6	0.1	123.9	0.2	124.0	0.1	124.4	0.3	124.9	0.4	125.1	0.2	125.2	0.1	125.3	0.1	125.5	0.2	126.0	0.4	126.5	0.4	126.6	0.1
1991	126.9	0.2	127.3	0.3	127.7	0.3	127.8	0.1	127.9	0.1	127.9	0.0	128.0	0.1	128.1	0.1	128.3	0.2	128.7	0.3	128.9	0.2	128.9	0.0
1992	129.2	0.2	129.4	0.2	129.6	0.2	129.7	0.1	129.7	0.0	129.9	0.2	130.0	0.1	130.1	0.1	130.4	0.2	130.5	0.1	130.9	0.3	131.0	0.1
1993	131.2	0.2	131.6	0.3	131.7	0.1	132.2	0.4	132.6	0.3	133.0	0.3	133.2	0.2	133.3	0.1	133.6	0.2	135.8	1.6	136.4	0.4	135.8	-0.4
1994	136.1	0.2	136.9	0.6	137.2	0.2	137.4	0.1	137.8	0.3	138.0	0.1	138.1	0.1	138.1	0.0	138.6	0.4	138.9	0.2	139.2	0.2	139.4	0.1
1995	140.0	0.4	140.4	0.3	140.7	0.2	141.0	0.2	141.6	0.4	141.8	0.1	142.0	0.1	142.2	0.1	142.6	0.3	142.8	0.1	143.1	0.2	143.3	0.1

Source: U.S. Department of Labor, Bureau of Labor Statistics, Division of Industry Prices and Price Indexes. n.e.c. stands for not elsewhere classified. - indicates no data collected for period or unavailable.

Commercial Furniture

Producer Price Index
Base 1982 = 100

For 1947-1995. Columns headed % show percentile change in the index from the previous period for which an index is available.

Year	Jan Index	%	Feb Index	%	Mar Index	%	Apr Index	%	May Index	%	Jun Index	%	Jul Index	%	Aug Index	%	Sep Index	%	Oct Index	%	Nov Index	%	Dec Index	%
1947	19.5	-	19.5	0.0	19.6	0.5	20.1	2.6	20.3	1.0	20.3	0.0	20.3	0.0	20.3	0.0	20.4	0.5	20.5	0.5	20.5	0.0	20.7	1.0
1948	20.9	1.0	21.0	0.5	21.1	0.5	21.1	0.0	21.1	0.0	21.1	0.0	21.2	0.5	21.9	3.3	22.0	0.5	22.3	1.4	22.3	0.0	22.3	0.0
1949	22.3	0.0	22.3	0.0	22.3	0.0	22.3	0.0	22.2	-0.4	22.2	0.0	22.2	0.0	22.2	0.0	22.2	0.0	22.2	0.0	22.2	0.0	22.2	0.0
1950	22.2	0.0	22.2	0.0	22.2	0.0	22.2	0.0	22.5	1.4	22.6	0.4	23.0	1.8	23.7	3.0	23.8	0.4	24.5	2.9	25.4	3.7	26.0	2.4
1951	26.6	2.3	26.6	0.0	26.6	0.0	26.6	0.0	26.6	0.0	26.6	0.0	26.6	0.0	26.6	0.0	26.6	0.0	26.4	-0.8	26.1	-1.1	26.1	0.0
1952	26.1	0.0	26.1	0.0	26.2	0.4	26.2	0.0	26.2	0.0	26.2	0.0	26.2	0.0	26.1	-0.4	26.1	0.0	26.2	0.4	26.2	0.0	26.2	0.0
1953	26.2	0.0	26.2	0.0	26.2	0.0	26.2	0.0	26.5	1.1	26.8	1.1	26.8	0.0	26.8	0.0	26.8	0.0	26.8	0.0	26.9	0.4	26.9	0.0
1954	26.9	0.0	26.9	0.0	26.9	0.0	26.9	0.0	26.9	0.0	26.9	0.0	26.9	0.0	26.9	0.0	26.9	0.0	27.1	0.7	27.4	1.1	27.4	0.0
1955	27.4	0.0	27.4	0.0	27.4	0.0	27.4	0.0	27.4	0.0	27.6	0.7	27.7	0.4	28.6	3.2	29.0	1.4	29.2	0.7	29.2	0.0	29.2	0.0
1956	29.3	0.3	29.5	0.7	29.5	0.0	29.5	0.0	29.5	0.0	29.5	0.0	29.6	0.3	31.1	5.1	31.3	0.6	31.3	0.0	31.3	0.0	31.3	0.0
1957	31.3	0.0	31.3	0.0	31.3	0.0	31.4	0.3	31.4	0.0	31.4	0.0	32.7	4.1	32.7	0.0	32.7	0.0	32.7	0.0	32.8	0.3	32.8	0.0
1958	32.8	0.0	32.8	0.0	32.8	0.0	32.8	0.0	32.8	0.0	32.8	0.0	33.0	0.6	33.0	0.0	33.0	0.0	33.0	0.0	33.0	0.0	33.0	0.0
1959	33.0	0.0	33.0	0.0	33.0	0.0	33.0	0.0	33.0	0.0	33.0	0.0	33.1	0.3	33.1	0.0	33.1	0.0	33.1	0.0	33.1	0.0	33.1	0.0
1960	33.2	0.3	33.2	0.0	33.4	0.6	33.4	0.0	33.4	0.0	33.4	0.0	33.5	0.3	33.5	0.0	33.5	0.0	33.5	0.0	33.5	0.0	33.5	0.0
1961	33.2	-0.9	33.2	0.0	33.2	0.0	33.2	0.0	33.2	0.0	33.2	0.0	33.2	0.0	33.2	0.0	33.4	0.6	33.4	0.0	33.4	0.0	33.4	0.0
1962	33.4	0.0	33.4	0.0	33.4	0.0	33.4	0.0	33.4	0.0	33.4	0.0	33.5	0.3	33.5	0.0	33.5	0.0	33.5	0.0	33.5	0.0	33.4	-0.3
1963	33.4	0.0	33.4	0.0	33.4	0.0	33.4	0.0	33.4	0.0	33.6	0.6	33.6	0.0	33.7	0.3	33.7	0.0	33.7	0.0	33.7	0.0	33.7	0.0
1964	33.7	0.0	33.7	0.0	33.7	0.0	33.7	0.0	33.7	0.0	33.7	0.0	33.7	0.0	33.7	0.0	33.7	0.0	33.7	0.0	33.7	0.0	33.8	0.3
1965	33.8	0.0	33.8	0.0	33.8	0.0	33.8	0.0	33.9	0.3	33.9	0.0	33.9	0.0	33.9	0.0	33.9	0.0	33.9	0.0	34.0	0.3	34.0	0.0
1966	34.0	0.0	34.0	0.0	34.0	0.0	34.0	0.0	34.4	1.2	34.4	0.0	34.6	0.6	34.6	0.0	34.6	0.0	35.1	1.4	35.3	0.6	35.5	0.6
1967	35.5	0.0	35.7	0.6	35.7	0.0	35.7	0.0	36.6	2.5	36.6	0.0	36.6	0.0	36.6	0.0	36.6	0.0	36.6	0.0	36.7	0.3	36.8	0.3
1968	37.1	0.8	37.1	0.0	37.2	0.3	37.4	0.5	37.6	0.5	37.8	0.5	37.9	0.3	37.9	0.0	37.9	0.0	38.1	0.5	38.1	0.0	38.2	0.3
1969	38.2	0.0	38.3	0.3	38.5	0.5	38.5	0.0	38.9	1.0	39.0	0.3	39.1	0.3	39.1	0.0	39.8	1.8	40.0	0.5	40.5	1.3	40.5	0.0
1970	40.7	0.5	40.7	0.0	40.9	0.5	40.9	0.0	40.9	0.0	41.7	2.0	41.7	0.0	42.0	0.7	42.0	0.0	42.1	0.2	42.7	1.4	42.7	0.0
1971	42.7	0.0	42.9	0.5	42.9	0.0	42.9	0.0	42.9	0.0	42.9	0.0	42.9	0.0	42.9	0.0	42.9	0.0	42.9	0.0	42.9	0.0	42.9	0.0
1972	42.9	0.0	42.9	0.0	43.1	0.5	43.3	0.5	43.3	0.0	43.4	0.2	43.5	0.2	43.5	0.0	44.0	1.1	44.2	0.5	44.8	1.4	44.8	0.0
1973	44.9	0.2	44.9	0.0	44.9	0.0	44.9	0.0	47.4	5.6	47.4	0.0	47.4	0.0	48.0	1.3	48.2	0.4	48.5	0.6	48.6	0.2	48.6	0.0
1974	49.5	1.9	50.5	2.0	51.0	1.0	51.4	0.8	52.3	1.8	53.5	2.3	55.5	3.7	56.7	2.2	60.4	6.5	60.6	0.3	61.3	1.2	61.3	0.0
1975	60.5	-1.3	60.4	-0.2	60.3	-0.2	60.3	0.0	60.3	0.0	60.3	0.0	60.3	0.0	60.8	0.8	60.8	0.0	61.3	0.8	60.6	-1.1	60.6	0.0
1976	60.9	0.5	61.5	1.0	61.6	0.2	62.5	1.5	63.0	0.8	63.3	0.5	63.5	0.3	63.7	0.3	63.7	0.0	64.0	0.5	64.0	0.0	64.0	0.0
1977	64.3	0.5	64.7	0.6	64.9	0.3	66.5	2.5	67.1	0.9	67.8	1.0	66.9	-1.3	69.3	3.6	69.2	-0.1	69.2	0.0	69.8	0.9	69.8	0.0
1978	70.7	1.3	70.8	0.1	72.2	2.0	72.8	0.8	72.8	0.0	72.8	0.0	73.7	1.2	74.0	0.4	73.9	-0.1	74.2	0.4	74.4	0.3	75.2	1.1
1979	77.8	3.5	80.3	3.2	80.3	0.0	80.5	0.2	80.5	0.0	80.5	0.0	80.8	0.4	80.8	0.0	80.8	0.0	81.1	0.4	81.1	0.0	81.7	0.7
1980	82.4	0.9	84.0	1.9	84.5	0.6	84.8	0.4	84.9	0.1	85.5	0.7	86.1	0.7	86.1	0.0	86.3	0.2	87.6	1.5	87.9	0.3	88.0	0.1
1981	89.6	1.8	91.3	1.9	92.0	0.8	92.4	0.4	93.5	1.2	93.6	0.1	93.9	0.3	94.1	0.2	94.9	0.9	95.2	0.3	95.6	0.4	95.8	0.2
1982	96.8	1.0	98.4	1.7	99.3	0.9	99.5	0.2	99.9	0.4	100.2	0.3	100.7	0.5	100.9	0.2	101.0	0.1	101.0	0.0	101.1	0.1	101.1	0.0
1983	102.0	0.9	102.4	0.4	103.5	1.1	103.9	0.4	103.8	-0.1	104.1	0.3	104.3	0.2	104.0	-0.3	104.3	0.3	104.3	0.0	105.2	0.9	105.1	-0.1
1984	106.5	1.3	107.0	0.5	107.0	0.0	107.5	0.5	107.9	0.4	107.8	-0.1	108.2	0.4	108.3	0.1	108.0	-0.3	107.9	-0.1	109.1	1.1	108.8	-0.3
1985	109.0	0.2	109.9	0.8	110.2	0.3	111.2	0.9	111.4	0.2	111.7	0.3	112.5	0.7	112.9	0.4	113.1	0.2	112.9	-0.2	113.9	0.9	113.9	0.0
1986	114.2	0.3	114.2	0.0	114.2	0.0	114.9	0.6	114.9	0.0	115.3	0.3	115.5	0.2	115.4	-0.1	115.5	0.1	116.2	0.6	116.7	0.4	116.5	-0.2
1987	116.9	0.3	117.1	0.2	117.5	0.3	118.2	0.6	118.4	0.2	118.6	0.2	118.6	0.0	118.9	0.3	119.1	0.2	119.7	0.5	119.9	0.2	120.0	0.1
1988	121.2	1.0	121.4	0.2	122.7	1.1	123.5	0.7	123.8	0.2	123.8	0.0	125.0	1.0	125.2	0.2	125.8	0.5	125.7	-0.1	125.9	0.2	126.5	0.5
1989	126.9	0.3	126.9	0.0	127.4	0.4	127.7	0.2	128.2	0.4	128.6	0.3	129.3	0.5	130.1	0.6	130.8	0.5	130.6	-0.2	130.8	0.2	130.8	0.0
1990	131.8	0.8	132.4	0.5	132.4	0.0	132.7	0.2	133.2	0.4	133.4	0.2	133.5	0.1	133.7	0.1	133.9	0.1	134.3	0.3	134.6	0.2	135.4	0.6
1991	135.9	0.4	136.4	0.4	135.9	-0.4	135.8	-0.1	136.1	0.2	136.1	0.0	136.2	0.1	136.2	0.0	136.3	0.1	136.5	0.1	136.6	0.1	136.6	0.0

[Continued]

Commercial Furniture
Producer Price Index
Base 1982 = 100
[Continued]

For 1947-1995. Columns headed % show percentile change in the index from the previous period for which an index is available.

Year	Jan Index	%	Feb Index	%	Mar Index	%	Apr Index	%	May Index	%	Jun Index	%	Jul Index	%	Aug Index	%	Sep Index	%	Oct Index	%	Nov Index	%	Dec Index	%
1992	137.0	0.3	137.2	0.1	137.3	0.1	137.9	0.4	138.0	0.1	138.1	0.1	137.8	-0.2	138.2	0.3	138.5	0.2	138.5	0.0	139.1	0.4	139.3	0.1
1993	139.2	-0.1	139.8	0.4	139.6	-0.1	140.1	0.4	140.3	0.1	140.5	0.1	140.8	0.2	141.0	0.1	140.7	-0.2	140.8	0.1	141.0	0.1	141.8	0.6
1994	143.2	1.0	143.5	0.2	143.6	0.1	144.5	0.6	145.3	0.6	145.2	-0.1	145.6	0.3	145.3	-0.2	144.8	-0.3	144.5	-0.2	145.2	0.5	145.4	0.1
1995	146.2	0.6	146.6	0.3	146.6	0.0	147.8	0.8	147.4	-0.3	148.1	0.5	148.0	-0.1	148.9	0.6	148.8	-0.1	149.1	0.2	150.1	0.7	150.9	0.5

Source: U.S. Department of Labor, Bureau of Labor Statistics, Division of Industry Prices and Price Indexes. n.e.c. stands for not elsewhere classified. - indicates no data collected for period or unavailable.

Floor Coverings
Producer Price Index
Base 1982 = 100

For 1926-1995. Columns headed % show percentile change in the index from the previous period for which an index is available.

Year	Jan Index	%	Feb Index	%	Mar Index	%	Apr Index	%	May Index	%	Jun Index	%	Jul Index	%	Aug Index	%	Sep Index	%	Oct Index	%	Nov Index	%	Dec Index	%
1926	31.9	-	31.9	0.0	31.9	0.0	31.9	0.0	31.9	0.0	31.7	-0.6	31.7	0.0	31.7	0.0	31.7	0.0	31.7	0.0	31.7	0.0	30.3	-4.4
1927	30.3	0.0	30.3	0.0	30.1	-0.7	30.1	0.0	30.1	0.0	30.3	0.7	30.3	0.0	30.3	0.0	30.3	0.0	30.3	0.0	30.3	0.0	30.4	0.3
1928	30.4	0.0	30.4	0.0	30.4	0.0	30.4	0.0	30.4	0.0	29.1	-4.3	29.1	0.0	29.1	0.0	29.1	0.0	29.1	0.0	29.4	1.0	29.4	0.0
1929	29.4	0.0	29.4	0.0	29.4	0.0	29.4	0.0	29.4	0.0	29.4	0.0	29.7	1.0	29.7	0.0	29.7	0.0	30.2	1.7	30.2	0.0	30.3	0.3
1930	30.6	1.0	30.6	0.0	30.6	0.0	30.6	0.0	30.6	0.0	30.6	0.0	30.6	0.0	30.6	0.0	29.9	-2.3	29.9	0.0	29.9	0.0	25.6	-14.4
1931	25.6	0.0	25.6	0.0	25.6	0.0	25.6	0.0	25.6	0.0	25.6	0.0	25.6	0.0	25.6	0.0	25.6	0.0	25.6	0.0	25.6	0.0	22.7	-11.3
1932	22.7	0.0	22.7	0.0	22.7	0.0	22.7	0.0	22.9	0.9	23.0	0.4	22.8	-0.9	22.7	-0.4	22.7	0.0	22.7	0.0	22.7	0.0	22.7	0.0
1933	22.7	0.0	22.7	0.0	22.7	0.0	22.7	0.0	22.7	0.0	23.2	2.2	23.5	1.3	24.0	2.1	24.3	1.3	24.7	1.6	24.7	0.0	24.7	0.0
1934	24.7	0.0	24.7	0.0	24.7	0.0	24.7	0.0	25.4	2.8	26.7	5.1	26.7	0.0	26.7	0.0	26.7	0.0	26.1	-2.2	26.1	0.0	26.1	0.0
1935	26.2	0.4	26.2	0.0	26.2	0.0	26.2	0.0	26.2	0.0	26.2	0.0	26.2	0.0	26.2	0.0	26.2	0.0	26.2	0.0	26.2	0.0	26.2	0.0
1936	26.3	0.4	26.3	0.0	26.3	0.0	26.3	0.0	26.3	0.0	26.4	0.4	26.0	-1.5	26.0	0.0	26.1	0.4	26.3	0.8	26.3	0.0	27.1	3.0
1937	27.4	1.1	28.9	5.5	28.9	0.0	28.9	0.0	28.9	0.0	28.9	0.0	29.8	3.1	30.7	3.0	30.7	0.0	30.7	0.0	30.7	0.0	29.6	-3.6
1938	29.1	-1.7	29.1	0.0	28.7	-1.4	28.4	-1.0	28.4	0.0	28.4	0.0	28.2	-0.7	28.2	0.0	27.9	-1.1	27.0	-3.2	27.3	1.1	27.9	2.2
1939	28.1	0.7	28.1	0.0	28.1	0.0	28.1	0.0	28.1	0.0	28.1	0.0	28.0	-0.4	28.0	0.0	29.5	5.4	30.9	4.7	31.1	0.6	31.1	0.0
1940	30.8	-1.0	30.8	0.0	30.8	0.0	31.2	1.3	31.3	0.3	31.3	0.0	31.3	0.0	31.3	0.0	31.3	0.0	31.3	0.0	31.3	0.0	31.3	0.0
1941	31.3	0.0	31.3	0.0	31.5	0.6	32.0	1.6	32.2	0.6	32.5	0.9	32.5	0.0	32.5	0.0	32.5	0.0	32.5	0.0	32.5	0.0	32.5	0.0
1942	33.1	1.8	33.2	0.3	33.2	0.0	33.2	0.0	33.2	0.0	33.2	0.0	33.2	0.0	33.2	0.0	33.2	0.0	33.2	0.0	33.2	0.0	33.2	0.0
1943	33.2	0.0	33.2	0.0	33.2	0.0	33.2	0.0	33.2	0.0	33.2	0.0	33.2	0.0	33.2	0.0	33.2	0.0	33.2	0.0	33.2	0.0	33.2	0.0
1944	33.2	0.0	33.2	0.0	33.2	0.0	33.2	0.0	33.2	0.0	33.2	0.0	33.2	0.0	33.2	0.0	33.2	0.0	33.2	0.0	33.2	0.0	33.2	0.0
1945	33.1	-0.3	33.1	0.0	33.1	0.0	33.1	0.0	33.1	0.0	33.1	0.0	33.1	0.0	33.1	0.0	33.1	0.0	33.1	0.0	33.1	0.0	33.1	0.0
1946	34.3	3.6	34.8	1.5	35.3	1.4	36.3	2.8	37.0	1.9	37.0	0.0	37.0	0.0	37.0	0.0	37.3	0.8	37.4	-0.3	39.0	4.3	39.9	2.3
1947	42.7	7.0	42.7	0.0	42.8	0.2	42.9	0.2	42.9	0.0	43.1	0.5	44.0	2.1	44.0	0.0	44.1	0.2	44.1	0.0	44.1	0.0	45.3	2.7
1948	45.5	0.4	45.6	0.2	45.6	0.0	45.6	0.0	45.6	0.0	46.2	1.3	46.5	0.6	46.6	0.2	47.2	1.3	47.4	0.4	47.4	0.0	47.4	0.0
1949	47.8	0.8	47.9	0.2	48.0	0.2	47.3	-1.5	47.3	0.0	46.5	-1.7	45.6	-1.9	45.6	0.0	45.5	-0.2	45.6	0.2	46.0	0.9	46.8	1.7
1950	47.4	1.3	48.2	1.7	48.4	0.4	48.5	0.2	49.6	2.3	49.6	0.0	50.4	1.6	53.9	6.9	55.3	2.6	57.9	4.7	58.3	0.7	60.3	3.4
1951	63.0	4.5	64.0	1.6	66.6	4.1	68.0	2.1	68.0	0.0	66.9	-1.6	64.8	-3.1	60.8	-6.2	58.4	-3.9	57.7	-1.2	57.1	-1.0	57.5	0.7
1952	57.5	0.0	57.6	0.2	57.4	-0.3	57.7	0.5	55.0	-4.7	54.2	-1.5	54.2	0.0	54.1	-0.2	55.7	3.0	55.7	0.0	55.7	0.0	55.9	0.4
1953	56.5	1.1	56.5	0.0	56.5	0.0	56.5	0.0	56.9	0.7	56.8	-0.2	57.0	0.4	57.0	0.0	57.0	0.0	57.0	0.0	56.9	-0.2	56.8	-0.2
1954	55.8	-1.8	55.7	-0.2	55.8	0.2	55.8	0.0	55.8	0.0	55.8	0.0	55.9	0.2	56.2	0.5	56.6	0.7	56.4	-0.4	56.4	0.0	56.4	0.0
1955	56.5	0.2	56.6	0.2	56.6	0.0	56.9	0.5	56.9	0.0	57.5	1.1	57.7	0.3	57.7	0.0	58.3	1.0	58.6	0.5	58.6	0.0	58.8	0.3
1956	59.4	1.0	59.4	0.0	59.4	0.0	59.4	0.0	59.4	0.0	59.4	0.0	59.8	0.7	59.8	0.0	60.1	0.5	60.0	-0.2	60.1	0.2	60.1	0.0
1957	61.4	2.2	61.1	-0.5	61.1	0.0	60.9	-0.3	60.9	0.0	60.9	0.0	60.3	-1.0	60.3	0.0	60.3	0.0	60.3	0.0	60.3	0.0	60.3	0.0
1958	59.8	-0.8	59.1	-1.2	58.8	-0.5	58.5	-0.5	58.5	0.0	58.2	-0.5	57.7	-0.9	57.7	0.0	57.5	-0.3	57.4	-0.2	57.4	0.0	57.4	0.0
1959	57.4	0.0	57.5	0.2	57.9	0.7	58.1	0.3	58.1	0.0	58.3	0.3	58.5	0.3	58.5	0.0	58.7	0.3	58.8	0.2	58.8	0.0	58.7	-0.2
1960	59.0	0.5	59.0	0.0	59.5	0.8	59.5	0.0	59.5	0.0	59.5	0.0	59.5	0.0	59.5	0.0	59.4	-0.2	59.4	0.0	59.3	-0.2	59.3	0.0
1961	58.6	-1.2	58.5	-0.2	58.5	0.0	58.5	0.0	58.5	0.0	58.5	0.0	58.8	0.5	58.8	0.0	58.8	0.0	58.7	-0.2	58.7	0.0	58.6	-0.2
1962	58.4	-0.3	57.2	-2.1	57.2	0.0	57.2	0.0	57.2	0.0	57.2	0.0	57.1	-0.2	57.1	0.0	57.1	0.0	57.1	0.0	57.1	0.0	56.9	-0.4
1963	56.8	-0.2	56.6	-0.4	56.7	0.2	56.6	-0.2	56.5	-0.2	56.6	0.2	57.0	0.7	57.0	0.0	57.1	0.2	57.5	0.7	57.8	0.5	57.9	0.2
1964	59.1	2.1	59.1	0.0	59.1	0.0	59.1	0.0	58.9	-0.3	58.2	-1.2	58.5	0.5	58.5	0.0	58.5	0.0	58.5	0.0	58.5	0.0	58.5	0.0
1965	57.9	-1.0	57.9	0.0	57.8	-0.2	57.7	-0.2	57.7	0.0	57.7	0.0	57.7	0.0	57.6	-0.2	57.6	0.0	57.5	-0.2	57.5	0.0	57.6	0.2
1966	57.7	0.2	57.7	0.0	57.6	-0.2	57.6	0.0	57.6	0.0	57.4	-0.3	57.1	-0.5	57.0	-0.2	57.0	0.0	57.0	0.0	57.0	0.0	56.8	-0.4
1967	55.5	-2.3	55.0	-0.9	55.2	0.4	54.9	-0.5	54.9	0.0	54.9	0.0	54.5	-0.7	54.5	0.0	55.0	0.9	55.9	1.6	55.9	0.0	56.1	0.4
1968	56.1	0.0	56.0	-0.2	56.0	0.0	56.0	0.0	56.0	0.0	55.7	-0.5	55.8	0.2	56.0	0.4	55.9	-0.2	55.9	0.0	55.9	0.0	55.9	0.0
1969	56.3	0.7	56.4	0.2	56.3	-0.2	56.0	-0.5	55.8	-0.4	55.3	-0.9	54.9	-0.7	54.9	0.0	54.9	0.0	54.9	0.0	54.9	0.0	54.9	0.0
1970	55.1	0.4	55.1	0.0	55.0	-0.2	55.0	0.0	54.7	-0.5	54.5	-0.4	54.9	0.7	54.7	-0.4	54.7	0.0	54.9	0.4	54.9	0.0	55.0	0.2

[Continued]

Floor Coverings
Producer Price Index
Base 1982 = 100
[Continued]

For 1926-1995. Columns headed % show percentile change in the index from the previous period for which an index is available.

Year	Jan Index	%	Feb Index	%	Mar Index	%	Apr Index	%	May Index	%	Jun Index	%	Jul Index	%	Aug Index	%	Sep Index	%	Oct Index	%	Nov Index	%	Dec Index	%
1971	55.7	1.3	55.5	-0.4	55.4	-0.2	55.2	-0.4	55.2	0.0	54.2	-1.8	54.2	0.0	53.9	-0.6	53.9	0.0	53.9	0.0	53.9	0.0	54.1	0.4
1972	54.2	0.2	54.2	0.0	54.2	0.0	54.2	0.0	54.2	0.0	54.4	0.4	54.5	0.2	54.5	0.0	54.7	0.4	54.7	0.0	54.7	0.0	54.7	0.0
1973	55.0	0.5	55.7	1.3	55.8	0.2	56.1	0.5	56.6	0.9	56.7	0.2	56.7	0.0	56.7	0.0	56.6	-0.2	57.1	0.9	57.1	0.0	57.2	0.2
1974	58.6	2.4	59.0	0.7	59.4	0.7	61.0	2.7	61.4	0.7	63.2	2.9	64.0	1.3	65.8	2.8	67.6	2.7	68.1	0.7	68.2	0.1	68.6	0.6
1975	68.4	-0.3	68.2	-0.3	68.2	0.0	68.1	-0.1	67.9	-0.3	67.9	0.0	68.4	0.7	69.9	2.2	70.0	0.1	70.0	0.0	70.0	0.0	70.2	0.3
1976	72.1	2.7	72.4	0.4	72.4	0.0	72.4	0.0	72.4	0.0	72.5	0.1	72.5	0.0	72.6	0.1	72.6	0.0	72.6	0.0	72.6	0.0	72.8	0.3
1977	74.8	2.7	74.8	0.0	74.8	0.0	74.8	0.0	74.8	0.0	75.0	0.3	75.2	0.3	75.4	0.3	75.4	0.0	75.7	0.4	76.3	0.8	76.4	0.1
1978	77.2	1.0	77.2	0.0	77.3	0.1	78.2	1.2	78.3	0.1	78.6	0.4	78.7	0.1	78.7	0.0	78.6	-0.1	78.4	-0.3	78.4	0.0	78.5	0.1
1979	79.1	0.8	79.3	0.3	79.5	0.3	79.7	0.3	80.6	1.1	80.9	0.4	82.3	1.7	82.8	0.6	83.0	0.2	84.0	1.2	84.4	0.5	84.4	0.0
1980	87.8	4.0	87.5	-0.3	88.8	1.5	89.5	0.8	89.4	-0.1	89.5	0.1	90.1	0.7	90.4	0.3	90.5	0.1	90.7	0.2	91.4	0.8	94.2	3.1
1981	95.1	1.0	94.9	-0.2	96.1	1.3	96.8	0.7	99.1	2.4	99.8	0.7	100.9	1.1	100.4	-0.5	100.3	-0.1	99.9	-0.4	100.6	0.7	100.2	-0.4
1982	99.5	-0.7	99.7	0.2	99.7	0.0	100.0	0.3	100.1	0.1	100.4	0.3	100.0	-0.4	99.9	-0.1	100.2	0.3	100.2	0.0	100.1	-0.1	100.2	0.1
1983	100.6	0.4	100.5	-0.1	100.4	-0.1	100.6	0.2	100.5	-0.1	100.2	-0.3	103.0	2.8	104.3	1.3	104.6	0.3	104.6	0.0	104.5	-0.1	104.5	0.0
1984	103.9	-0.6	104.0	0.1	103.9	-0.1	103.9	0.0	105.8	1.8	106.4	0.6	106.4	0.0	106.3	-0.1	106.3	0.0	106.5	0.2	106.5	0.0	106.7	0.2
1985	106.9	0.2	106.2	-0.7	106.4	0.2	106.5	0.1	105.7	-0.8	104.8	-0.9	105.2	0.4	104.9	-0.3	105.2	0.3	104.9	-0.3	105.2	0.3	105.3	0.1
1986	107.4	2.0	107.7	0.3	107.7	0.0	107.8	0.1	108.1	0.3	108.6	0.5	108.1	-0.5	108.3	0.2	108.4	0.1	109.0	0.6	109.3	0.3	109.2	-0.1
1987	109.9	0.6	109.8	-0.1	109.2	-0.5	109.4	0.2	109.9	0.5	110.2	0.3	111.1	0.8	111.5	0.4	111.6	0.1	112.0	0.4	111.9	-0.1	111.6	-0.3
1988	112.7	1.0	113.1	0.4	112.9	-0.2	113.6	0.6	114.0	0.4	113.8	-0.2	114.7	0.8	115.4	0.6	116.0	0.5	116.5	0.4	117.1	0.5	117.0	-0.1
1989	117.5	0.4	116.7	-0.7	117.3	0.5	117.3	0.0	116.9	-0.3	117.9	0.9	118.6	0.6	119.0	0.3	117.5	-1.3	117.0	-0.4	117.4	0.3	117.7	0.3
1990	117.7	0.0	118.3	0.5	119.3	0.8	119.5	0.2	119.6	0.1	119.4	-0.2	119.4	0.0	119.2	-0.2	118.8	-0.3	118.6	-0.2	119.1	0.4	119.5	0.3
1991	120.3	0.7	121.4	0.9	120.9	-0.4	120.7	-0.2	120.5	-0.2	120.1	-0.3	120.1	0.0	120.1	0.0	119.9	-0.2	120.2	0.3	120.4	0.2	120.3	-0.1
1992	120.1	-0.2	120.1	0.0	119.5	-0.5	119.7	0.2	120.4	0.6	120.8	0.3	121.0	0.2	120.7	-0.2	120.5	-0.2	120.5	0.0	120.2	-0.2	120.2	0.0
1993	119.4	-0.7	119.5	0.1	119.5	0.0	119.4	-0.1	119.2	-0.2	119.1	-0.1	120.0	0.8	120.8	0.7	121.2	0.3	121.3	0.1	121.4	0.1	121.2	-0.2
1994	121.4	0.2	121.3	-0.1	120.9	-0.3	121.1	0.2	121.0	-0.1	121.3	0.2	121.9	0.5	121.8	-0.1	121.2	-0.5	121.7	0.4	122.4	0.6	122.2	-0.2
1995	122.6	0.3	122.9	0.2	122.7	-0.2	123.1	0.3	123.8	0.6	123.3	-0.4	123.5	0.2	123.6	0.1	123.3	-0.2	123.2	-0.1	123.4	0.2	123.4	0.0

Source: U.S. Department of Labor, Bureau of Labor Statistics, Division of Industry Prices and Price Indexes. n.e.c. stands for not elsewhere classified. - indicates no data collected for period or unavailable.

Household Appliances
Producer Price Index
Base 1982 = 100

For 1947-1995. Columns headed % show percentile change in the index from the previous period for which an index is available.

Year	Jan Index	%	Feb Index	%	Mar Index	%	Apr Index	%	May Index	%	Jun Index	%	Jul Index	%	Aug Index	%	Sep Index	%	Oct Index	%	Nov Index	%	Dec Index	%
1947	50.3	-	50.4	0.2	50.5	0.2	50.6	0.2	50.8	0.4	51.1	0.6	51.5	0.8	51.7	0.4	52.3	1.2	52.7	0.8	52.9	0.4	53.2	0.6
1948	53.1	-0.2	53.1	0.0	53.1	0.0	53.2	0.2	53.0	-0.4	53.1	0.2	54.0	1.7	54.3	0.6	54.7	0.7	55.4	1.3	55.5	0.2	55.5	0.0
1949	54.6	-1.6	54.6	0.0	54.4	-0.4	54.1	-0.6	53.7	-0.7	53.5	-0.4	53.4	-0.2	53.2	-0.4	53.2	0.0	53.1	-0.2	53.1	0.0	53.1	0.0
1950	53.1	0.0	53.0	-0.2	53.0	0.0	53.2	0.4	53.2	0.0	53.1	-0.2	53.2	0.2	53.8	1.1	54.7	1.7	55.5	1.5	56.0	0.9	56.7	1.3
1951	57.1	0.7	57.3	0.4	57.3	0.0	57.3	0.0	57.3	0.0	57.4	0.2	57.1	-0.5	57.1	0.0	57.3	0.4	57.3	0.0	57.3	0.0	57.4	0.2
1952	57.3	-0.2	57.3	0.0	57.0	-0.5	57.2	0.4	56.9	-0.5	56.7	-0.4	56.7	0.0	56.7	0.0	56.9	0.4	56.9	0.0	56.9	0.0	57.0	0.2
1953	57.0	0.0	57.0	0.0	57.3	0.5	57.3	0.0	57.4	0.2	57.4	0.0	57.8	0.7	57.8	0.0	57.9	0.2	57.9	0.0	57.9	0.0	57.9	0.0
1954	58.1	0.3	58.2	0.2	58.1	-0.2	58.3	0.3	58.3	0.0	58.3	0.0	58.2	-0.2	58.2	0.0	58.0	-0.3	58.1	0.2	57.9	-0.3	58.0	0.2
1955	57.7	-0.5	57.6	-0.2	56.9	-1.2	56.9	0.0	56.5	-0.7	56.5	0.0	56.5	0.0	56.6	0.2	56.4	-0.4	56.3	-0.2	56.4	0.2	56.2	-0.4
1956	56.0	-0.4	56.1	0.2	55.9	-0.4	55.8	-0.2	55.8	0.0	55.8	0.0	55.4	-0.7	55.8	0.7	56.0	0.4	56.5	0.9	56.5	0.0	56.2	-0.5
1957	56.5	0.5	56.7	0.4	56.7	0.0	55.9	-1.4	55.8	-0.2	55.8	0.0	55.7	-0.2	55.6	-0.2	55.5	-0.2	55.9	0.7	55.8	-0.2	55.9	0.2
1958	55.9	0.0	55.9	0.0	55.9	0.0	55.9	0.0	55.7	-0.4	55.7	0.0	55.7	0.0	55.6	-0.2	55.2	-0.7	55.3	0.2	55.1	-0.4	55.1	0.0
1959	55.8	1.3	55.8	0.0	55.8	0.0	55.8	0.0	55.8	0.0	55.8	0.0	55.4	-0.7	55.4	0.0	55.4	0.0	55.2	-0.4	55.3	0.2	55.0	-0.5
1960	54.8	-0.4	54.8	0.0	54.7	-0.2	54.7	0.0	54.2	-0.9	53.9	-0.6	53.9	0.0	53.6	-0.6	53.5	-0.2	53.5	0.0	53.4	-0.2	53.3	-0.2
1961	53.2	-0.2	53.2	0.0	53.1	-0.2	53.1	0.0	53.0	-0.2	52.9	-0.2	52.9	0.0	52.9	0.0	52.9	0.0	53.0	0.2	52.9	-0.2	52.8	-0.2
1962	52.9	0.2	52.9	0.0	52.8	-0.2	52.7	-0.2	52.5	-0.4	52.5	0.0	52.3	-0.4	52.0	-0.6	51.9	-0.2	51.8	-0.2	51.8	0.0	51.8	0.0
1963	51.4	-0.8	51.4	0.0	51.4	0.0	51.3	-0.2	51.2	-0.2	51.2	0.0	51.1	-0.2	51.1	0.0	50.9	-0.4	50.8	-0.2	50.8	0.0	50.7	-0.2
1964	50.9	0.4	51.1	0.4	51.1	0.0	51.0	-0.2	51.0	0.0	50.8	-0.4	50.8	0.0	50.8	0.0	50.7	-0.2	50.8	0.2	50.5	-0.6	50.4	-0.2
1965	50.2	-0.4	50.1	-0.2	50.1	0.0	49.8	-0.6	49.7	-0.2	49.8	0.2	49.7	-0.2	49.3	-0.8	49.3	0.0	49.3	0.0	49.3	0.0	49.4	0.2
1966	49.6	0.4	49.6	0.0	49.6	0.0	49.7	0.2	49.8	0.2	49.8	0.0	49.6	-0.4	49.4	-0.4	49.4	0.0	49.5	0.2	49.7	0.4	49.7	0.0
1967	49.9	0.4	50.0	0.2	50.0	0.0	50.1	0.2	50.0	-0.2	50.2	0.4	50.3	0.2	50.2	-0.2	50.3	0.2	50.4	0.2	50.6	0.4	50.6	0.0
1968	50.7	0.2	50.9	0.4	51.1	0.4	51.2	0.2	51.1	-0.2	51.0	-0.2	51.2	0.4	51.3	0.2	51.3	0.0	51.4	0.2	51.2	-0.4	51.3	0.2
1969	51.4	0.2	51.6	0.4	51.6	0.0	51.6	0.0	51.6	0.0	51.6	0.0	51.6	0.0	51.6	0.0	51.8	0.4	51.9	0.2	51.9	0.0	52.1	0.4
1970	52.7	1.2	52.6	-0.2	52.6	0.0	52.8	0.4	52.7	-0.2	52.7	0.0	52.8	0.2	52.9	0.2	52.9	0.0	53.2	0.6	53.3	0.2	53.3	0.0
1971	53.8	0.9	53.9	0.2	54.0	0.2	53.9	-0.2	53.9	0.0	53.9	0.0	54.1	0.4	54.2	0.2	54.2	0.0	54.2	0.0	54.1	-0.2	54.1	0.0
1972	53.7	-0.7	54.0	0.6	53.9	-0.2	54.0	0.2	53.9	-0.2	53.8	-0.2	53.9	0.2	54.1	0.4	54.3	0.4	54.2	-0.2	54.2	0.0	54.2	0.0
1973	54.1	-0.2	54.3	0.4	54.4	0.2	54.4	0.0	54.2	-0.4	53.9	-0.6	54.1	0.4	54.7	1.1	54.7	0.0	54.8	0.2	55.0	0.4	55.2	0.4
1974	55.9	1.3	56.1	0.4	56.5	0.7	56.9	0.7	57.3	0.7	58.0	1.2	58.6	1.0	59.4	1.4	60.7	2.2	62.8	3.5	63.7	1.4	64.6	1.4
1975	65.3	1.1	65.6	0.5	65.3	-0.5	65.6	0.5	65.8	0.3	66.4	0.9	66.4	0.0	66.5	0.2	67.1	0.9	67.4	0.4	68.0	0.9	68.2	0.3
1976	68.5	0.4	69.0	0.7	69.5	0.7	69.7	0.3	69.7	0.0	69.9	0.3	70.2	0.4	70.3	0.1	70.4	0.1	70.5	0.1	70.6	0.1	70.8	0.3
1977	71.0	0.3	71.4	0.6	71.8	0.6	72.0	0.3	72.0	0.0	72.7	1.0	73.2	0.7	73.6	0.5	74.1	0.7	74.2	0.1	74.3	0.1	74.3	0.0
1978	75.1	1.1	75.2	0.1	75.9	0.9	76.5	0.8	76.6	0.1	76.7	0.1	77.1	0.5	77.4	0.4	77.4	0.0	77.6	0.3	78.2	0.8	78.2	0.0
1979	78.9	0.9	79.5	0.8	79.8	0.4	79.7	-0.1	80.0	0.4	80.4	0.5	80.9	0.6	81.5	0.7	81.7	0.2	82.0	0.4	82.6	0.7	83.0	0.5
1980	83.6	0.7	84.8	1.4	85.3	0.6	85.9	0.7	87.0	1.3	88.1	1.3	88.3	0.2	88.5	0.2	89.0	0.6	89.2	0.2	89.6	0.4	90.1	0.6
1981	91.5	1.6	92.2	0.8	92.5	0.3	93.0	0.5	93.2	0.2	93.5	0.3	94.8	1.4	95.0	0.2	95.5	0.5	95.8	0.3	95.9	0.1	96.1	0.2
1982	97.1	1.0	98.1	1.0	99.1	1.0	99.3	0.2	99.9	0.6	100.2	0.3	100.6	0.4	101.0	0.4	101.1	0.1	101.1	0.0	101.1	0.0	101.3	0.2
1983	102.4	1.1	102.9	0.5	103.0	0.1	103.6	0.6	104.2	0.6	104.2	0.0	104.4	0.2	104.3	-0.1	104.5	0.2	104.3	-0.2	104.5	0.2	104.7	0.2
1984	105.4	0.7	105.8	0.4	106.0	0.2	105.9	-0.1	105.9	0.0	106.1	0.2	106.2	0.1	106.5	0.3	106.3	-0.2	106.0	-0.3	106.0	0.0	106.1	0.1
1985	106.1	0.0	106.1	0.0	106.3	0.2	106.5	0.2	106.7	0.2	106.8	0.1	107.1	0.3	107.2	0.1	107.0	-0.2	107.0	0.0	106.9	-0.1	106.6	-0.3
1986	105.5	-1.0	105.6	0.1	105.8	0.2	106.1	0.3	106.4	0.3	105.9	-0.5	105.9	0.0	105.6	-0.3	105.5	-0.1	105.4	-0.1	105.2	-0.2	105.0	-0.2
1987	105.2	0.2	105.3	0.1	105.6	0.3	105.7	0.1	105.8	0.1	105.8	0.0	106.0	0.2	105.8	-0.2	105.5	-0.3	105.4	-0.1	105.7	0.3	105.2	-0.5
1988	105.5	0.3	106.0	0.5	106.2	0.2	106.2	0.0	106.3	0.1	106.1	-0.2	105.6	-0.5	105.6	0.0	105.8	0.2	106.0	0.2	106.5	0.5	106.2	-0.3
1989	107.0	0.8	107.3	0.3	107.6	0.3	107.7	0.1	108.1	0.4	108.5	0.4	109.2	0.6	109.3	0.1	109.7	0.4	110.0	0.3	110.0	0.0	110.1	0.1
1990	110.5	0.4	110.6	0.1	110.7	0.1	110.9	0.2	110.4	-0.5	111.0	0.5	110.7	-0.3	110.8	0.1	110.9	0.1	110.9	0.0	111.0	0.1	110.9	-0.1
1991	111.6	0.6	111.3	-0.3	111.3	0.0	111.4	0.1	111.5	0.1	111.3	-0.2	111.3	0.0	111.4	0.1	111.3	-0.1	111.3	0.0	111.2	-0.1	111.0	-0.2

[Continued]

Household Appliances
Producer Price Index
Base 1982 = 100
[Continued]

For 1947-1995. Columns headed % show percentile change in the index from the previous period for which an index is available.

Year	Jan		Feb		Mar		Apr		May		Jun		Jul		Aug		Sep		Oct		Nov		Dec	
	Index	%	Index	%	Index	%	Index	%	Index	%	Index	%	Index	%	Index	%	Index	%	Index	%	Index	%	Index	%
1992	111.2	0.2	111.1	-0.1	111.1	0.0	111.4	0.3	111.3	-0.1	111.2	-0.1	111.2	0.0	111.2	0.0	111.3	0.1	111.6	0.3	112.3	0.6	111.8	-0.4
1993	112.0	0.2	112.3	0.3	112.5	0.2	112.8	0.3	113.0	0.2	113.4	0.4	113.4	0.0	113.4	0.0	113.4	0.0	113.0	-0.4	113.0	0.0	112.7	-0.3
1994	112.8	0.1	112.8	0.0	113.0	0.2	113.1	0.1	113.2	0.1	112.9	-0.3	112.9	0.0	112.7	-0.2	112.7	0.0	112.9	0.2	112.7	-0.2	112.4	-0.3
1995	112.3	-0.1	112.3	0.0	112.1	-0.2	112.4	0.3	112.4	0.0	112.2	-0.2	112.3	0.1	112.2	-0.1	112.1	-0.1	112.5	0.4	112.8	0.3	111.9	-0.8

Source: U.S. Department of Labor, Bureau of Labor Statistics, Division of Industry Prices and Price Indexes. n.e.c. stands for not elsewhere classified. - indicates no data collected for period or unavailable.

Home Electronic Equipment
Producer Price Index
Base 1982 = 100

For 1947-1995. Columns headed % show percentile change in the index from the previous period for which an index is available.

Year	Jan Index	%	Feb Index	%	Mar Index	%	Apr Index	%	May Index	%	Jun Index	%	Jul Index	%	Aug Index	%	Sep Index	%	Oct Index	%	Nov Index	%	Dec Index	%
1947	140.1	-	140.5	0.3	140.5	0.0	140.5	0.0	140.5	0.0	140.5	0.0	140.5	0.0	140.8	0.2	142.3	1.1	142.3	0.0	142.3	0.0	142.3	0.0
1948	142.1	-0.1	142.1	0.0	142.1	0.0	141.6	-0.4	141.6	0.0	143.8	1.6	143.8	0.0	143.8	0.0	152.6	6.1	155.5	1.9	155.5	0.0	155.3	-0.1
1949	154.6	-0.5	154.6	0.0	154.6	0.0	154.4	-0.1	154.4	0.0	154.2	-0.1	153.5	-0.5	149.9	-2.3	149.9	0.0	146.9	-2.0	146.9	0.0	146.7	-0.1
1950	146.2	-0.3	146.7	0.3	146.7	0.0	146.7	0.0	146.7	0.0	146.4	-0.2	141.8	-3.1	131.4	-7.3	134.9	2.7	139.1	3.1	139.0	-0.1	136.4	-1.9
1951	135.7	-0.5	135.7	0.0	135.7	0.0	135.7	0.0	135.7	0.0	135.7	0.0	137.1	1.0	136.5	-0.4	136.2	-0.2	136.3	0.1	136.3	0.0	136.3	0.0
1952	136.4	0.1	136.4	0.0	132.8	-2.6	132.8	0.0	132.8	0.0	137.3	3.4	137.3	0.0	137.2	-0.1	137.2	0.0	137.2	0.0	137.3	0.1	137.3	0.0
1953	-		-		-		-		-		-		-		-		-		-		-		-	
1954	-		-		-		-		-		-		-		-		-		-		-		-	
1955	137.0	-0.2	136.5	-0.4	136.4	-0.1	136.4	0.0	136.6	0.1	136.5	-0.1	136.4	-0.1	134.9	-1.1	135.7	0.6	135.8	0.1	135.9	0.1	136.4	0.4
1956	136.4	0.0	136.6	0.1	136.6	0.0	135.9	-0.5	135.7	-0.1	135.2	-0.4	136.2	0.7	136.5	0.2	137.2	0.5	137.0	-0.1	137.0	0.0	136.6	-0.3
1957	137.0	0.3	137.0	0.0	136.4	-0.4	136.4	0.0	136.4	0.0	136.8	0.3	138.9	1.5	140.1	0.9	140.1	0.0	140.1	0.0	140.1	0.0	140.4	0.2
1958	139.7	-0.5	138.8	-0.6	138.8	0.0	138.8	0.0	138.2	-0.4	137.2	-0.7	139.1	1.4	139.0	-0.1	139.0	0.0	139.0	0.0	135.8	-2.3	135.6	-0.1
1959	136.5	0.7	136.5	0.0	135.9	-0.4	135.9	0.0	135.9	0.0	136.2	0.2	138.2	1.5	136.6	-1.2	135.8	-0.6	134.9	-0.7	134.5	-0.3	134.6	0.1
1960	134.3	-0.2	134.5	0.1	134.5	0.0	134.3	-0.1	134.3	0.0	133.9	-0.3	133.9	0.0	133.5	-0.3	133.5	0.0	132.5	-0.7	132.5	0.0	133.7	0.9
1961	133.1	-0.4	132.5	-0.5	132.8	0.2	132.8	0.0	131.6	-0.9	131.8	0.2	131.8	0.0	129.9	-1.4	129.3	-0.5	128.8	-0.4	129.0	0.2	129.0	0.0
1962	127.1	-1.5	126.1	-0.8	125.7	-0.3	125.4	-0.2	126.8	1.1	124.9	-1.5	124.8	-0.1	124.8	0.0	124.7	-0.1	124.7	0.0	124.2	-0.4	124.2	0.0
1963	123.9	-0.2	123.9	0.0	122.9	-0.8	122.9	0.0	122.2	-0.6	122.2	0.0	120.6	-1.3	120.6	0.0	120.7	0.1	120.7	0.0	120.7	0.0	120.0	-0.6
1964	119.9	-0.1	119.9	0.0	119.9	0.0	120.0	0.1	120.0	0.0	120.0	0.0	120.0	0.0	120.0	0.0	120.0	0.0	120.0	0.0	119.9	-0.1	119.0	-0.8
1965	118.8	-0.2	118.1	-0.6	118.1	0.0	118.1	0.0	118.1	0.0	118.1	0.0	116.3	-1.5	116.1	-0.2	116.1	0.0	116.2	0.1	116.2	0.0	116.2	0.0
1966	115.4	-0.7	115.3	-0.1	114.8	-0.4	114.8	0.0	114.8	0.0	114.8	0.0	114.8	0.0	114.2	-0.5	114.5	0.3	115.3	0.7	115.3	0.0	115.3	0.0
1967	114.9	-0.3	114.5	-0.3	114.5	0.0	114.5	0.0	114.0	-0.4	112.8	-1.1	112.4	-0.4	112.4	0.0	112.2	-0.2	113.4	1.1	113.6	0.2	112.9	-0.6
1968	112.9	0.0	113.0	0.1	112.7	-0.3	112.3	-0.4	112.4	0.1	111.2	-1.1	110.9	-0.3	110.9	0.0	110.8	-0.1	110.3	-0.5	109.7	-0.5	109.7	0.0
1969	108.2	-1.4	108.2	0.0	108.1	-0.1	107.8	-0.3	107.2	-0.6	107.0	-0.2	107.0	0.0	107.0	0.0	107.0	0.0	107.0	0.0	106.6	-0.4	106.6	0.0
1970	105.8	-0.8	105.8	0.0	105.8	0.0	105.8	0.0	105.6	-0.2	105.5	-0.1	105.8	0.3	106.0	0.2	106.2	0.2	106.4	0.2	107.0	0.6	106.5	-0.5
1971	106.6	0.1	106.3	-0.3	106.2	-0.1	106.1	-0.1	106.1	0.0	106.2	0.1	106.3	0.1	105.9	-0.4	105.8	-0.1	105.8	0.0	105.8	0.0	105.8	0.0
1972	105.9	0.1	105.5	-0.4	105.6	0.1	105.4	-0.2	105.5	0.1	105.2	-0.3	104.9	-0.3	104.9	0.0	105.5	0.6	105.5	0.0	105.0	-0.5	104.8	-0.2
1973	104.9	0.1	104.9	0.0	104.7	-0.2	104.7	0.0	104.7	0.0	104.0	-0.7	104.0	0.0	104.4	0.4	103.9	-0.5	103.9	0.0	103.9	0.0	103.4	-0.5
1974	103.7	0.3	103.8	0.1	104.7	0.9	104.7	0.0	105.0	0.3	105.7	0.7	106.3	0.6	106.3	0.0	106.8	0.5	106.8	0.0	107.3	0.5	107.5	0.2
1975	108.3	0.7	108.6	0.3	108.4	-0.2	104.4	-3.7	104.4	0.0	105.6	1.1	105.9	0.3	107.4	1.4	105.4	-1.9	105.4	0.0	105.4	0.0	105.4	0.0
1976	104.8	-0.6	104.1	-0.7	103.7	-0.4	103.7	0.0	103.7	0.0	103.6	-0.1	103.6	0.0	103.6	0.0	103.6	0.0	103.6	0.0	103.3	-0.3	103.2	-0.1
1977	101.8	-1.4	101.5	-0.3	101.5	0.0	100.2	-1.3	100.3	0.1	100.4	0.1	98.6	-1.8	98.6	0.0	98.1	-0.5	97.9	-0.2	98.3	0.4	98.2	-0.1
1978	101.0	2.9	100.7	-0.3	101.1	0.4	100.7	-0.4	102.2	1.5	100.5	-1.7	103.2	2.7	103.1	-0.1	104.0	0.9	103.7	-0.3	103.9	0.2	104.9	1.0
1979	104.7	-0.2	104.8	0.1	104.8	0.0	104.8	0.0	105.0	0.2	105.4	0.4	102.4	-2.8	102.4	0.0	102.5	0.1	102.5	0.0	102.6	0.1	102.8	0.2
1980	103.3	0.5	103.5	0.2	103.6	0.1	103.8	0.2	104.5	0.7	104.3	-0.2	104.1	-0.2	103.7	-0.4	104.1	0.4	103.9	-0.2	103.6	-0.3	103.4	-0.2
1981	103.4	0.0	103.7	0.3	103.7	0.0	103.3	-0.4	103.1	-0.2	98.4	-4.6	99.3	0.9	99.4	0.1	99.7	0.3	100.0	0.3	99.9	-0.1	101.8	1.9
1982	101.4	-0.4	101.7	0.3	101.2	-0.5	99.8	-1.4	100.0	0.2	100.4	0.4	99.1	-1.3	99.9	0.8	99.2	-0.7	99.7	0.5	98.8	-0.9	98.9	0.1
1983	99.2	0.3	98.8	-0.4	98.8	0.0	98.3	-0.5	98.1	-0.2	98.2	0.1	97.6	-0.6	97.1	-0.5	97.4	0.3	97.4	0.0	96.7	-0.7	95.9	-0.8
1984	95.9	0.0	95.5	-0.4	95.4	-0.1	96.4	1.0	96.0	-0.4	95.3	-0.7	95.6	0.3	95.2	-0.4	94.3	-0.9	94.4	0.1	94.3	-0.1	93.9	-0.4
1985	91.8	-2.2	93.0	1.3	92.0	-1.1	91.8	-0.2	90.8	-1.1	90.1	-0.8	90.9	0.9	90.4	-0.6	89.7	-0.8	89.4	-0.3	89.4	0.0	90.3	1.0
1986	89.8	-0.6	89.8	0.0	89.8	0.0	89.8	0.0	89.8	0.0	90.5	0.8	90.1	-0.4	89.9	-0.2	89.9	0.0	89.9	0.0	89.9	0.0	89.9	0.0
1987	89.1	-0.9	88.5	-0.7	88.9	0.5	89.1	0.2	88.9	-0.2	88.8	-0.1	88.7	-0.1	89.0	0.3	88.9	-0.1	88.7	-0.2	88.7	0.0	88.7	0.0
1988	88.5	-0.2	89.0	0.6	88.2	-0.9	87.1	-1.2	87.2	0.1	86.3	-1.0	86.7	0.5	86.6	-0.1	86.7	0.1	86.6	-0.1	86.8	0.2	86.7	-0.1
1989	88.0	1.5	88.0	0.0	88.0	0.0	88.3	0.3	88.3	0.0	88.4	0.1	88.4	0.0	88.0	-0.5	87.5	-0.6	83.2	-4.9	83.2	0.0	83.0	-0.2
1990	83.0	0.0	82.9	-0.1	82.8	-0.1	82.7	-0.1	82.6	-0.1	82.6	0.0	82.6	0.0	82.6	0.0	82.6	0.0	82.6	0.0	82.7	0.1	82.8	0.1	82.8	0.0
1991	82.9	0.1	83.1	0.2	83.1	0.0	83.1	0.0	83.5	0.5	83.6	0.1	83.5	-0.1	83.0	-0.6	83.0	0.0	83.1	0.1	83.0	-0.1	83.0	0.0

[Continued]

Home Electronic Equipment
Producer Price Index
Base 1982 = 100
[Continued]

For 1947-1995. Columns headed % show percentile change in the index from the previous period for which an index is available.

Year	Jan Index	%	Feb Index	%	Mar Index	%	Apr Index	%	May Index	%	Jun Index	%	Jul Index	%	Aug Index	%	Sep Index	%	Oct Index	%	Nov Index	%	Dec Index	%
1992	83.0	0.0	82.8	-0.2	82.8	0.0	82.6	-0.2	82.3	-0.4	81.9	-0.5	81.9	0.0	81.9	0.0	81.6	-0.4	81.0	-0.7	80.8	-0.2	80.8	0.0
1993	80.6	-0.2	80.7	0.1	80.5	-0.2	80.4	-0.1	80.2	-0.2	79.9	-0.4	80.0	0.1	79.8	-0.2	79.4	-0.5	79.6	0.3	80.8	1.5	80.7	-0.1
1994	80.7	0.0	80.7	0.0	80.6	-0.1	80.7	0.1	80.1	-0.7	80.0	-0.1	80.0	0.0	80.0	0.0	79.9	-0.1	80.2	0.4	80.1	-0.1	80.1	0.0
1995	80.2	0.1	80.2	0.0	79.5	-0.9	79.1	-0.5	78.3	-1.0	78.3	0.0	78.4	0.1	78.4	0.0	77.9	-0.6	77.9	0.0	78.0	0.1	77.7	-0.4

Source: U.S. Department of Labor, Bureau of Labor Statistics, Division of Industry Prices and Price Indexes. n.e.c. stands for not elsewhere classified. - indicates no data collected for period or unavailable.

Household Durable Goods n.e.c.
Producer Price Index
Base 1982 = 100

For 1947-1995. Columns headed % show percentile change in the index from the previous period for which an index is available.

Year	Jan Index	%	Feb Index	%	Mar Index	%	Apr Index	%	May Index	%	Jun Index	%	Jul Index	%	Aug Index	%	Sep Index	%	Oct Index	%	Nov Index	%	Dec Index	%
1947	19.5	-	19.4	-0.5	19.5	0.5	19.5	0.0	19.5	0.0	19.5	0.0	19.4	-0.5	19.4	0.0	19.5	0.5	19.5	0.0	19.5	0.0	19.6	0.5
1948	19.5	-0.5	19.5	0.0	19.5	0.0	19.5	0.0	19.6	0.5	19.6	0.0	19.9	1.5	20.2	1.5	20.2	0.0	20.5	1.5	20.8	1.5	21.0	1.0
1949	21.1	0.5	21.1	0.0	21.1	0.0	21.1	0.0	21.0	-0.5	21.0	0.0	20.9	-0.5	20.9	0.0	20.8	-0.5	20.8	0.0	20.8	0.0	20.8	0.0
1950	21.0	1.0	21.0	0.0	21.0	0.0	21.0	0.0	21.0	0.0	21.1	0.5	21.2	0.5	21.4	0.9	21.7	1.4	22.0	1.4	22.3	1.4	22.7	1.8
1951	23.0	1.3	23.1	0.4	23.1	0.0	23.1	0.0	23.1	0.0	23.1	0.0	23.1	0.0	23.1	0.0	23.2	0.4	23.2	0.0	23.2	0.0	23.2	0.0
1952	23.2	0.0	23.2	-0.0	23.2	0.0	23.3	0.4	23.2	-0.4	23.2	0.0	23.3	0.4	23.3	0.0	23.3	0.0	23.3	0.0	23.3	0.0	23.4	0.4
1953	23.8	1.7	24.0	0.8	24.0	0.0	24.0	0.0	24.0	0.0	24.0	0.0	24.4	1.7	24.4	0.0	24.4	0.0	24.5	0.4	24.7	0.8	24.8	0.4
1954	24.9	0.4	24.9	0.0	24.9	0.0	25.0	0.4	25.0	0.0	25.0	0.0	25.0	0.0	25.0	0.0	25.0	0.0	25.2	0.8	25.3	0.4	25.3	0.0
1955	25.4	0.4	25.4	0.0	25.4	0.0	25.4	0.0	25.4	0.0	25.5	0.4	25.8	1.2	26.1	1.2	26.1	0.0	26.4	1.1	26.5	0.4	26.7	0.8
1956	26.9	0.7	27.1	0.7	27.1	0.0	27.0	-0.4	27.1	0.4	27.1	0.0	27.1	0.0	27.2	0.4	27.3	0.4	27.8	1.8	27.8	0.0	28.3	1.8
1957	28.3	0.0	28.4	0.4	28.4	0.0	28.4	0.0	28.6	0.7	28.7	0.3	28.7	0.0	28.7	0.0	28.8	0.3	28.9	0.3	29.0	0.3	29.3	1.0
1958	29.8	1.7	29.8	0.0	29.8	0.0	29.8	0.0	29.8	0.0	29.9	0.3	29.8	-0.3	29.8	-0.3	29.8	0.3	29.8	0.0	29.8	0.0	30.0	0.7
1959	30.0	0.0	30.1	0.3	30.1	0.0	30.1	0.0	30.2	0.3	30.2	0.0	30.3	0.3	30.2	-0.3	30.2	0.0	30.2	0.0	30.2	0.0	30.2	0.0
1960	30.7	1.7	30.8	0.3	30.8	0.0	30.8	0.0	30.8	0.0	30.8	0.0	30.9	0.3	30.9	0.0	30.9	0.0	30.9	0.0	30.9	0.0	30.9	0.0
1961	30.8	-0.3	30.7	-0.3	30.7	0.0	30.7	0.0	30.8	0.3	30.8	0.0	30.8	0.0	30.8	0.0	30.8	0.0	30.8	0.0	30.9	0.3	31.0	0.3
1962	31.3	1.0	31.2	-0.3	31.4	0.6	31.4	0.0	31.4	0.0	31.4	0.0	31.3	-0.3	31.2	-0.3	31.4	0.6	31.2	-0.6	31.2	0.0	31.2	0.0
1963	31.2	0.0	31.2	0.0	31.2	0.0	31.4	0.6	31.3	-0.3	31.5	0.6	31.6	0.3	31.5	-0.3	31.6	0.3	31.6	0.0	31.6	0.0	31.5	-0.3
1964	31.7	0.6	31.7	0.0	31.7	0.0	31.7	0.0	31.8	0.3	31.8	0.0	31.8	0.0	31.8	0.0	31.8	0.0	31.8	0.0	31.8	0.0	32.0	0.6
1965	32.2	0.6	32.2	0.0	32.2	0.0	32.2	0.0	32.2	0.0	32.2	0.0	32.2	0.0	32.1	-0.3	32.2	0.3	32.2	0.0	32.2	0.0	32.2	0.0
1966	32.5	0.9	32.6	0.3	32.6	0.0	32.6	0.0	32.6	0.0	32.6	0.0	33.1	1.5	33.1	0.0	33.3	0.6	33.6	0.9	33.6	0.0	33.7	0.3
1967	33.9	0.6	33.9	0.0	34.0	0.3	34.2	0.6	34.3	0.3	34.3	0.0	34.5	0.6	34.9	1.2	35.0	0.3	35.2	0.6	35.2	0.0	35.3	0.3
1968	36.5	3.4	36.6	0.3	36.7	0.3	36.8	0.3	36.7	-0.3	36.7	0.0	36.9	0.5	37.0	0.3	37.1	0.3	37.1	0.0	37.2	0.3	37.9	1.9
1969	38.1	0.5	38.2	0.3	38.3	0.3	38.4	0.3	38.4	0.0	38.5	0.3	38.7	0.5	38.7	0.0	38.8	0.3	38.9	0.3	38.8	-0.3	39.5	1.8
1970	39.5	0.0	39.9	1.0	39.8	-0.3	40.1	0.8	40.0	-0.2	40.1	0.3	40.1	0.0	40.1	0.0	40.4	0.7	40.3	-0.2	40.4	0.2	40.6	0.5
1971	41.2	1.5	41.4	0.5	41.4	0.0	41.5	0.2	41.5	0.0	41.5	0.0	42.1	1.4	42.2	0.2	42.2	0.0	42.1	-0.2	42.1	0.0	42.2	0.2
1972	42.3	0.2	42.9	1.4	43.0	0.2	43.0	0.0	43.2	0.5	43.4	0.5	43.7	0.7	43.8	0.2	43.9	0.2	43.9	0.0	43.9	0.0	43.9	0.0
1973	43.9	0.0	44.3	0.9	44.6	0.7	45.0	0.9	45.2	0.4	45.3	0.2	45.2	-0.2	45.2	0.0	45.1	-0.2	45.4	0.7	45.6	0.4	45.9	0.7
1974	46.3	0.9	47.2	1.9	48.1	1.9	49.2	2.3	50.2	2.0	50.8	1.2	52.3	3.0	52.6	0.6	53.3	1.3	55.1	3.4	55.5	0.7	56.1	1.1
1975	57.7	2.9	58.1	0.7	57.4	-1.2	58.1	1.2	58.1	0.0	58.1	0.0	58.1	0.0	58.0	-0.2	58.1	0.2	58.7	1.0	59.1	0.7	59.4	0.5
1976	60.6	2.0	60.9	0.5	61.0	0.2	61.1	0.2	61.4	0.5	61.4	0.0	61.7	0.5	62.1	0.6	62.9	1.3	62.9	0.0	63.2	0.5	63.4	0.3
1977	64.8	2.2	65.0	0.3	65.1	0.2	64.9	-0.3	65.5	0.9	65.6	0.2	65.9	0.5	66.1	0.3	66.1	0.0	66.3	0.3	66.5	0.3	66.9	0.6
1978	68.5	2.4	68.5	0.0	68.4	-0.1	68.4	0.0	69.3	1.3	69.9	0.9	70.9	1.4	70.7	-0.3	70.7	0.0	71.9	1.7	72.1	0.3	73.4	1.8
1979	74.7	1.8	74.9	0.3	75.3	0.5	75.6	0.4	75.9	0.4	76.3	0.5	77.3	1.3	78.3	1.3	79.8	1.9	84.9	6.4	85.8	1.1	87.9	2.4
1980	99.3	13.0	102.1	2.8	99.6	-2.4	92.4	-7.2	91.8	-0.6	92.1	0.3	93.8	1.8	95.4	1.7	95.5	0.1	97.4	2.0	97.2	-0.2	98.7	1.5
1981	96.4	-2.3	97.0	0.6	96.1	-0.9	95.2	-0.9	95.6	0.4	95.5	-0.1	97.5	2.1	97.1	-0.4	98.8	1.8	98.8	0.0	98.6	-0.2	98.9	0.3
1982	98.0	-0.9	98.1	0.1	98.5	0.4	98.8	0.3	98.7	-0.1	98.9	0.2	98.6	-0.3	100.9	2.3	101.4	0.5	102.5	1.1	102.7	0.2	103.1	0.4
1983	104.7	1.6	108.8	3.9	108.1	-0.6	107.8	-0.3	108.1	0.3	108.6	0.5	108.8	0.2	108.5	-0.3	108.7	0.2	108.5	-0.2	108.9	0.4	108.9	0.0
1984	109.9	0.9	109.5	-0.4	109.5	0.0	110.3	0.7	111.2	0.8	110.6	-0.5	110.1	-0.5	109.5	-0.5	109.5	0.0	109.8	0.3	110.8	0.9	110.8	0.0
1985	111.5	0.6	111.5	0.0	112.0	0.4	111.9	-0.1	111.7	-0.2	111.9	0.2	111.5	-0.4	111.4	-0.1	111.2	-0.2	111.9	0.6	111.8	-0.1	112.0	0.2
1986	112.6	0.5	112.1	-0.4	112.3	0.2	112.6	0.3	112.6	0.0	112.9	0.3	113.0	0.1	112.9	-0.1	113.1	0.2	113.1	0.0	113.3	0.2	113.6	0.3
1987	114.6	0.9	114.5	-0.1	114.7	0.2	114.7	0.0	115.2	0.4	115.3	0.1	115.6	0.3	115.8	0.2	115.8	0.0	116.2	0.3	116.3	0.1	116.6	0.3
1988	117.8	1.0	118.1	0.3	118.4	0.3	118.8	0.3	119.4	0.5	119.3	-0.1	119.8	0.4	120.5	0.6	120.9	0.3	121.2	0.2	121.4	0.2	121.8	0.3
1989	122.7	0.7	123.5	0.7	124.1	0.5	126.2	1.7	126.7	0.4	127.9	0.9	128.5	0.5	129.0	0.4	129.2	0.2	129.7	0.4	129.6	-0.1	129.7	0.1
1990	130.9	0.9	131.5	0.5	130.5	-0.8	131.1	0.5	130.7	-0.3	130.9	0.2	130.0	-0.7	130.4	0.3	130.7	0.2	130.8	0.1	130.7	-0.1	130.7	0.0
1991	132.1	1.1	132.6	0.4	133.5	0.7	134.6	0.8	134.5	-0.1	134.6	0.1	134.8	0.1	134.8	0.0	134.7	-0.1	134.7	0.0	134.8	0.1	135.2	0.3

[Continued]

Household Durable Goods n.e.c.
Producer Price Index
Base 1982 = 100
[Continued]

For 1947-1995. Columns headed % show percentile change in the index from the previous period for which an index is available.

Year	Jan Index	%	Feb Index	%	Mar Index	%	Apr Index	%	May Index	%	Jun Index	%	Jul Index	%	Aug Index	%	Sep Index	%	Oct Index	%	Nov Index	%	Dec Index	%
1992	136.1	0.7	136.6	0.4	137.2	0.4	136.1	-0.8	136.2	0.1	136.5	0.2	136.5	0.0	136.7	0.1	136.9	0.1	136.6	-0.2	136.5	-0.1	136.7	0.1
1993	137.3	0.4	137.4	0.1	137.8	0.3	137.9	0.1	137.8	-0.1	137.8	0.0	137.8	0.0	138.0	0.1	138.2	0.1	138.5	0.2	138.6	0.1	138.7	0.1
1994	139.4	0.5	139.4	0.0	139.7	0.2	139.6	-0.1	140.0	0.3	140.9	0.6	141.1	0.1	141.5	0.3	141.5	0.0	141.9	0.3	142.2	0.2	142.4	0.1
1995	143.4	0.7	144.1	0.5	144.5	0.3	144.5	0.0	144.8	0.2	144.8	0.0	145.0	0.1	145.1	0.1	145.2	0.1	145.3	0.1	145.6	0.2	145.7	0.1

Source: U.S. Department of Labor, Bureau of Labor Statistics, Division of Industry Prices and Price Indexes. n.e.c. stands for not elsewhere classified. - indicates no data collected for period or unavailable.

NONMETALLIC MINERAL PRODUCTS
Producer Price Index
Base 1982 = 100

For 1926-1995. Columns headed % show percentile change in the index from the previous period for which an index is available.

Year	Jan Index	%	Feb Index	%	Mar Index	%	Apr Index	%	May Index	%	Jun Index	%	Jul Index	%	Aug Index	%	Sep Index	%	Oct Index	%	Nov Index	%	Dec Index	%
1926	16.4	-	16.4	0.0	16.5	0.6	16.5	0.0	16.4	-0.6	16.4	0.0	16.4	0.0	16.3	-0.6	16.2	-0.6	16.4	1.2	16.4	0.0	16.4	0.0
1927	16.1	-1.8	15.9	-1.2	15.8	-0.6	15.8	0.0	15.8	0.0	15.8	0.0	15.8	0.0	15.7	-0.6	15.6	-0.6	15.6	0.0	15.3	-1.9	15.4	0.7
1928	15.5	0.6	15.4	-0.6	15.2	-1.3	16.0	5.3	16.3	1.9	16.6	1.8	16.6	0.0	16.6	0.0	16.6	0.0	16.6	0.0	16.6	0.0	16.3	-1.8
1929	16.1	-1.2	16.1	0.0	16.0	-0.6	16.1	0.6	16.1	0.0	16.0	-0.6	16.1	0.6	16.0	-0.6	15.8	-1.2	15.7	-0.6	15.8	0.6	16.1	1.9
1930	16.1	0.0	16.1	0.0	16.1	0.0	16.1	0.0	16.0	-0.6	15.7	-1.9	15.8	0.6	15.8	0.0	15.8	0.0	15.9	0.6	16.0	0.6	15.8	-1.2
1931	15.6	-1.3	15.6	0.0	15.3	-1.9	15.1	-1.3	15.0	-0.7	14.9	-0.7	14.5	-2.7	14.6	0.7	14.6	0.0	14.6	0.0	14.5	-0.7	14.3	-1.4
1932	14.1	-1.4	14.0	-0.7	14.0	0.0	13.9	-0.7	13.5	-2.9	13.4	-0.7	13.7	2.2	13.8	0.7	14.1	2.2	14.1	0.0	14.2	0.7	14.3	0.7
1933	14.2	-0.7	14.1	-0.7	14.1	0.0	14.1	0.0	14.2	0.7	14.4	1.4	14.8	2.8	15.1	2.0	15.2	0.7	15.5	2.0	15.6	0.6	15.6	0.0
1934	15.8	1.3	15.8	0.0	15.7	-0.6	15.6	-0.6	15.6	0.0	15.8	1.3	15.8	0.0	15.7	-0.6	15.7	0.0	15.7	0.0	15.7	0.0	15.7	0.0
1935	15.8	0.6	15.7	-0.6	15.7	0.0	15.7	0.0	15.8	0.6	15.8	0.0	15.8	0.0	15.7	-0.6	15.7	0.0	15.7	0.0	15.7	0.0	15.6	-0.6
1936	15.6	0.0	15.6	0.0	15.6	0.0	15.7	0.6	15.8	0.6	15.8	0.0	15.8	0.0	15.8	0.0	15.8	0.0	15.8	0.0	15.9	0.6	16.0	0.6
1937	16.0	0.0	16.1	0.6	16.1	0.0	16.2	0.6	16.3	0.6	16.2	-0.6	16.3	0.6	16.3	0.0	16.1	-1.2	16.1	0.0	16.0	-0.6	15.8	-1.2
1938	15.8	0.0	15.8	0.0	15.6	-1.3	15.6	0.0	15.6	0.0	15.6	0.0	15.7	0.6	15.6	-0.6	15.6	0.0	15.7	0.6	15.3	-2.5	15.4	0.7
1939	15.3	-0.6	15.3	0.0	15.3	0.0	15.4	0.7	15.3	-0.6	15.3	0.0	15.3	0.0	15.2	-0.7	15.3	0.7	15.3	0.0	15.3	0.0	15.4	0.7
1940	15.4	0.0	15.4	0.0	15.4	0.0	15.3	-0.6	15.3	0.0	15.3	0.0	15.3	0.0	15.3	0.0	15.3	0.0	15.3	0.0	15.3	0.0	15.3	0.0
1941	15.4	0.7	15.4	0.0	15.4	0.0	15.4	0.0	15.5	0.6	15.6	0.6	15.6	0.0	15.8	1.3	15.8	0.0	16.0	1.3	16.3	1.9	16.2	-0.6
1942	16.2	0.0	16.2	0.0	16.3	0.6	16.3	0.0	16.3	0.0	16.3	0.0	16.3	0.0	16.3	0.0	16.3	0.0	16.3	0.0	16.3	0.0	16.3	0.0
1943	16.3	0.0	16.3	0.0	16.3	0.0	16.3	0.0	16.3	0.0	16.3	0.0	16.3	0.0	16.3	0.0	16.5	1.2	16.5	0.0	16.5	0.0	16.5	0.0
1944	16.5	0.0	16.5	0.0	16.5	0.0	16.5	0.0	16.6	0.6	16.6	0.0	16.7	0.6	16.7	0.0	16.8	0.6	17.0	1.2	17.0	0.0	17.0	0.0
1945	17.2	1.2	17.3	0.6	17.3	0.0	17.3	0.0	17.3	0.0	17.3	0.0	17.4	0.6	17.4	0.0	17.5	0.6	17.6	0.6	17.7	0.6	17.7	0.0
1946	17.9	1.1	17.9	0.0	18.0	0.6	18.1	0.6	18.2	0.6	18.3	0.5	18.5	1.1	18.8	1.6	18.9	0.5	19.0	0.5	19.2	1.1	19.5	1.6
1947	20.0	2.6	20.1	0.5	20.4	1.5	20.6	1.0	20.6	0.0	20.6	0.0	20.7	0.5	20.7	0.0	20.8	0.5	21.0	1.0	21.2	1.0	21.4	0.9
1948	21.8	1.9	21.9	0.5	21.9	0.0	22.0	0.5	22.0	0.0	22.1	0.5	22.6	2.3	22.8	0.9	22.8	0.0	22.9	0.4	22.9	0.0	22.9	0.0
1949	23.0	0.4	23.0	0.0	23.0	0.0	23.0	0.0	23.0	0.0	23.0	0.0	22.9	-0.4	23.0	0.4	23.0	0.0	23.0	0.0	23.0	0.0	23.0	0.0
1950	23.1	0.4	23.1	0.0	23.2	0.4	23.2	0.0	23.1	-0.4	23.2	0.4	23.2	0.0	23.4	0.9	23.6	0.9	24.1	2.1	24.4	1.2	24.6	0.8
1951	25.0	1.6	25.0	0.0	25.0	0.0	25.0	0.0	25.0	0.0	25.0	0.0	25.0	0.0	25.0	0.0	25.0	0.0	25.0	0.0	25.0	0.0	24.8	-0.8
1952	24.9	0.4	24.9	0.0	24.9	0.0	24.8	-0.4	24.9	0.4	25.0	0.4	25.0	0.0	25.0	0.0	25.0	0.0	25.2	0.8	25.2	0.0	25.2	0.0
1953	25.2	0.0	25.2	0.0	25.3	0.4	25.7	1.6	25.8	0.4	26.0	0.8	26.3	1.2	26.3	0.0	26.5	0.8	26.5	0.0	26.6	0.4	26.6	0.0
1954	26.6	0.0	26.6	0.0	26.6	0.0	26.6	0.0	26.3	-1.1	26.2	-0.4	26.5	1.1	26.5	0.0	26.8	1.1	26.8	0.0	26.8	0.0	26.8	0.0
1955	26.9	0.4	26.8	-0.4	26.8	0.0	26.9	0.4	27.1	0.7	27.2	0.4	27.6	1.5	27.8	0.7	27.8	0.0	27.9	0.4	27.5	-1.4	27.6	0.4
1956	28.0	1.4	28.0	0.0	28.1	0.4	28.3	0.7	28.3	0.0	28.4	0.4	28.7	1.1	28.8	0.3	28.9	0.3	28.9	0.0	28.9	0.0	28.9	0.0
1957	29.0	0.3	29.2	0.7	29.3	0.3	29.6	1.0	29.7	0.3	29.7	0.0	29.8	0.3	29.8	0.0	29.8	0.0	29.8	0.0	29.8	0.0	29.9	0.3
1958	30.0	0.3	30.0	0.0	29.8	-0.7	29.8	0.0	29.8	0.0	29.8	0.0	29.8	0.0	29.8	0.0	30.1	1.0	30.1	0.0	30.1	0.0	30.1	0.0
1959	30.2	0.3	30.3	0.3	30.3	0.0	30.4	0.3	30.4	0.0	30.2	-0.7	30.3	0.3	30.2	-0.3	30.3	0.3	30.3	0.0	30.3	0.0	30.3	0.0
1960	30.4	0.3	30.4	0.0	30.4	0.0	30.4	0.0	30.3	-0.3	30.3	0.0	30.3	0.0	30.3	0.0	30.3	0.0	30.4	0.3	30.4	0.0	30.3	-0.3
1961	30.5	0.7	30.4	-0.3	30.5	0.3	30.5	0.0	30.5	0.0	30.4	-0.3	30.4	0.0	30.5	0.3	30.5	0.0	30.6	0.3	30.5	-0.3	30.4	-0.3
1962	30.5	0.3	30.6	0.3	30.6	0.0	30.7	0.3	30.6	-0.3	30.5	-0.3	30.4	-0.3	30.4	0.0	30.4	0.0	30.4	0.0	30.4	0.0	30.4	0.0
1963	30.4	0.0	30.4	0.0	30.4	0.0	30.4	0.0	30.3	-0.3	30.3	0.0	30.2	-0.3	30.2	0.0	30.3	0.3	30.3	0.0	30.3	0.0	30.3	0.0
1964	30.3	0.0	30.3	0.0	30.3	0.0	30.3	0.0	30.3	0.0	30.4	0.3	30.4	0.0	30.4	0.0	30.5	0.3	30.5	0.0	30.5	0.0	30.4	-0.3
1965	30.4	0.0	30.5	0.3	30.5	0.0	30.5	0.0	30.5	0.0	30.5	0.0	30.4	-0.3	30.4	0.0	30.4	0.0	30.4	0.0	30.4	0.0	30.4	0.0
1966	30.5	0.3	30.6	0.3	30.6	0.0	30.6	0.0	30.7	0.3	30.7	0.0	30.8	0.3	30.8	0.0	30.9	0.3	30.9	0.0	30.9	0.0	30.9	0.0
1967	31.1	0.6	31.1	0.0	31.1	0.0	31.2	0.3	31.0	-0.6	31.1	0.3	31.2	0.3	31.3	0.3	31.3	0.0	31.4	0.3	31.5	0.3	31.6	0.3
1968	31.9	0.9	32.0	0.3	32.2	0.6	32.2	0.0	32.3	0.3	32.4	0.3	32.5	0.3	32.5	0.0	32.5	0.0	32.6	0.3	32.7	0.3	32.7	0.0
1969	33.1	1.2	33.3	0.6	33.3	0.0	33.5	0.6	33.6	0.3	33.6	0.0	33.7	0.3	33.7	0.0	33.8	0.3	33.9	0.3	33.9	0.0	34.1	0.6
1970	34.8	2.1	34.9	0.3	34.9	0.0	35.3	1.1	35.1	-0.6	35.1	0.0	35.2	0.3	35.3	0.3	35.3	0.0	35.5	0.6	35.8	0.8	36.0	0.6

[Continued]

NONMETALLIC MINERAL PRODUCTS
Producer Price Index
Base 1982 = 100
[Continued]

For 1926-1995. Columns headed % show percentile change in the index from the previous period for which an index is available.

Year	Jan Index	%	Feb Index	%	Mar Index	%	Apr Index	%	May Index	%	Jun Index	%	Jul Index	%	Aug Index	%	Sep Index	%	Oct Index	%	Nov Index	%	Dec Index	%
1971	37.1	3.1	37.2	0.3	37.8	1.6	38.0	0.5	38.1	0.3	38.3	0.5	38.5	0.5	38.7	0.5	38.7	0.0	38.7	0.0	38.7	0.0	38.8	0.3
1972	38.8	0.0	38.9	0.3	39.0	0.3	39.2	0.5	39.3	0.3	39.3	0.0	39.4	0.3	39.6	0.5	39.6	0.0	39.7	0.3	39.8	0.3	39.8	0.0
1973	40.0	0.5	40.1	0.3	40.3	0.5	40.6	0.7	40.7	0.2	40.9	0.5	40.6	-0.7	40.6	0.0	40.6	0.0	40.9	0.7	41.1	0.5	41.4	0.7
1974	43.3	4.6	44.4	2.5	45.0	1.4	45.8	1.8	47.1	2.8	47.6	1.1	48.8	2.5	49.2	0.8	49.9	1.4	50.7	1.6	51.0	0.6	51.3	0.6
1975	52.6	2.5	53.2	1.1	53.4	0.4	54.0	1.1	54.1	0.2	54.1	0.0	54.6	0.9	54.9	0.5	55.0	0.2	55.3	0.5	55.5	0.4	55.6	0.2
1976	56.6	1.8	56.7	0.2	57.1	0.7	57.9	1.4	58.1	0.3	58.2	0.2	58.5	0.5	58.7	0.3	58.9	0.3	59.1	0.3	59.2	0.2	59.2	0.0
1977	60.1	1.5	60.5	0.7	60.9	0.7	62.0	1.8	62.2	0.3	62.6	0.6	63.0	0.6	63.3	0.5	63.8	0.8	64.1	0.5	64.2	0.2	64.5	0.5
1978	66.5	3.1	67.2	1.1	67.4	0.3	68.2	1.2	68.5	0.4	69.3	1.2	70.2	1.3	71.0	1.1	71.3	0.4	71.6	0.4	71.8	0.3	72.2	0.6
1979	74.4	3.0	75.1	0.9	75.2	0.1	76.0	1.1	76.7	0.9	77.1	0.5	77.9	1.0	78.1	0.3	79.5	1.8	80.0	0.6	80.4	0.5	81.1	0.9
1980	83.8	3.3	85.6	2.1	86.4	0.9	88.6	2.5	88.7	0.1	88.5	-0.2	88.9	0.5	89.3	0.4	89.6	0.3	90.1	0.6	90.2	0.1	90.9	0.8
1981	92.6	1.9	93.1	0.5	94.0	1.0	97.0	3.2	97.4	0.4	97.9	0.5	98.2	0.3	98.1	-0.1	97.8	-0.3	97.8	0.0	98.0	0.2	97.9	-0.1
1982	98.6	0.7	99.6	1.0	99.9	0.3	100.0	0.1	100.3	0.3	100.2	-0.1	100.3	0.1	100.1	-0.2	100.3	0.2	100.3	0.0	100.3	0.0	100.1	-0.2
1983	100.4	0.3	100.7	0.3	100.6	-0.1	101.2	0.6	101.2	0.0	101.4	0.2	101.5	0.1	101.9	0.4	102.2	0.3	102.4	0.2	102.7	0.3	102.7	0.0
1984	103.1	0.4	103.7	0.6	104.1	0.4	104.9	0.8	105.4	0.5	105.6	0.2	106.1	0.5	106.4	0.3	106.3	-0.1	106.2	-0.1	106.0	-0.2	106.2	0.2
1985	106.7	0.5	107.0	0.3	107.4	0.4	107.9	0.5	108.7	0.7	109.1	0.4	109.2	0.1	109.4	0.2	109.3	-0.1	109.5	0.2	109.5	0.0	109.6	0.1
1986	110.1	0.5	110.0	-0.1	110.1	0.1	110.2	0.1	110.4	0.2	110.2	-0.2	110.2	0.0	109.9	-0.3	109.7	-0.2	109.7	0.0	109.7	0.0	109.3	-0.4
1987	109.3	0.0	109.6	0.3	109.7	0.1	109.9	0.2	109.9	0.0	110.1	0.2	110.1	0.0	109.9	-0.2	110.0	0.1	110.4	0.4	110.5	0.1	110.4	-0.1
1988	110.8	0.4	110.9	0.1	110.9	0.0	111.0	0.1	111.2	0.2	111.3	0.1	111.1	-0.2	111.1	0.0	111.3	0.2	111.4	0.1	111.5	0.1	111.7	0.2
1989	111.8	0.1	111.8	0.0	112.0	0.2	112.6	0.5	112.7	0.1	112.8	0.1	112.8	0.0	112.8	0.0	112.9	0.1	113.0	0.1	113.1	0.1	113.2	0.1
1990	113.8	0.5	113.9	0.1	114.2	0.3	114.3	0.1	114.5	0.2	114.6	0.1	114.6	0.0	114.7	0.1	115.0	0.3	115.3	0.3	115.8	0.4	115.8	0.0
1991	116.9	0.9	117.2	0.3	117.4	0.2	117.3	-0.1	117.3	0.0	117.3	0.0	117.2	-0.1	117.1	-0.1	117.2	0.1	117.4	0.2	117.2	-0.2	117.1	-0.1
1992	117.2	0.1	117.1	-0.1	117.3	0.2	116.9	-0.3	116.9	0.0	117.0	0.1	117.1	0.1	117.4	0.3	117.4	0.0	117.4	0.0	117.7	0.3	117.8	0.1
1993	118.4	0.5	118.6	0.2	118.9	0.3	119.6	0.6	119.7	0.1	120.0	0.3	120.2	0.2	120.5	0.2	120.8	0.2	121.0	0.2	121.2	0.2	121.4	0.2
1994	121.8	0.3	122.2	0.3	122.9	0.6	123.4	0.4	123.7	0.2	124.3	0.5	124.5	0.2	124.8	0.2	125.1	0.2	125.5	0.3	125.8	0.2	126.0	0.2
1995	126.9	0.7	127.5	0.5	128.2	0.5	129.3	0.9	129.4	0.1	129.3	-0.1	129.3	0.0	129.4	0.1	129.6	0.2	129.6	0.0	129.7	0.1	129.7	0.0

Source: U.S. Department of Labor, Bureau of Labor Statistics, Division of Industry Prices and Price Indexes. n.e.c. stands for not elsewhere classified. - indicates no data collected for period or unavailable.

Glass

Producer Price Index
Base 1982 = 100

For 1947-1995. Columns headed % show percentile change in the index from the previous period for which an index is available.

Year	Jan Index	%	Feb Index	%	Mar Index	%	Apr Index	%	May Index	%	Jun Index	%	Jul Index	%	Aug Index	%	Sep Index	%	Oct Index	%	Nov Index	%	Dec Index	%
1947	28.9	-	28.9	0.0	30.0	3.8	30.5	1.7	30.5	0.0	30.5	0.0	30.5	0.0	30.5	0.0	30.5	0.0	30.5	0.0	30.5	0.0	30.5	0.0
1948	30.7	0.7	30.5	-0.7	30.5	0.0	30.7	0.7	30.5	-0.7	30.5	0.0	31.8	4.3	33.1	4.1	33.1	0.0	33.3	0.6	33.5	0.6	33.5	0.0
1949	33.5	0.0	33.5	0.0	33.4	-0.3	33.3	-0.3	33.3	0.0	33.3	0.0	33.3	0.0	33.3	0.0	33.3	0.0	33.3	0.0	33.3	0.0	33.3	0.0
1950	33.3	0.0	33.1	-0.6	33.9	2.4	34.0	0.3	33.6	-1.2	33.6	0.0	33.6	0.0	33.6	0.0	33.6	0.0	35.0	4.2	36.3	3.7	36.3	0.0
1951	36.3	0.0	36.3	0.0	36.3	0.0	36.3	0.0	36.3	0.0	36.3	0.0	36.3	0.0	36.3	0.0	36.3	0.0	36.3	0.0	36.3	0.0	36.3	0.0
1952	36.3	0.0	36.3	0.0	36.3	0.0	36.3	0.0	36.3	0.0	36.3	0.0	36.3	0.0	36.3	0.0	36.3	0.0	36.3	0.0	36.3	0.0	36.3	0.0
1953	36.3	0.0	36.3	0.0	37.0	1.9	37.0	0.0	37.0	0.0	39.1	5.7	39.6	1.3	39.6	0.0	39.6	0.0	39.6	0.0	39.6	0.0	39.6	0.0
1954	39.6	0.0	39.6	0.0	39.6	0.0	39.6	0.0	39.6	0.0	39.6	0.0	39.6	0.0	39.6	0.0	39.4	-0.5	39.4	0.0	39.4	0.0	39.4	0.0
1955	39.4	0.0	39.4	0.0	39.4	0.0	39.7	0.8	39.7	0.0	40.1	1.0	41.7	4.0	41.7	0.0	41.7	0.0	42.3	1.4	41.7	-1.4	41.7	0.0
1956	41.7	0.0	41.7	0.0	41.7	0.0	41.7	0.0	41.7	0.0	41.9	0.5	42.9	2.4	43.1	0.5	43.1	0.0	43.1	0.0	43.1	0.0	43.1	0.0
1957	43.1	0.0	43.1	0.0	43.1	0.0	43.1	0.0	43.1	0.0	43.1	0.0	43.1	0.0	43.1	0.0	43.1	0.0	43.1	0.0	43.1	0.0	43.1	0.0
1958	43.1	0.0	43.1	0.0	43.1	0.0	43.1	0.0	43.1	0.0	43.1	0.0	43.1	0.0	43.0	-0.2	42.9	-0.2	42.9	0.0	42.9	0.0	42.9	0.0
1959	42.9	0.0	42.9	0.0	42.9	0.0	42.9	0.0	42.9	0.0	43.0	0.2	43.0	0.0	43.0	0.0	43.0	0.0	43.0	0.0	43.0	0.0	43.0	0.0
1960	43.0	0.0	43.0	0.0	43.0	0.0	43.0	0.0	41.4	-3.7	41.4	0.0	41.4	0.0	41.4	0.0	42.0	1.4	42.0	0.0	42.0	0.0	42.0	0.0
1961	42.0	0.0	42.0	0.0	42.0	0.0	42.0	0.0	42.0	0.0	41.4	-1.4	41.4	0.0	41.4	0.0	41.4	0.0	41.4	0.0	41.4	0.0	41.4	0.0
1962	41.4	0.0	41.4	0.0	41.4	0.0	42.1	1.7	42.2	0.2	42.2	0.0	42.2	0.0	41.6	-1.4	41.6	0.0	41.6	0.0	41.6	0.0	41.6	0.0
1963	41.6	0.0	41.6	0.0	41.6	0.0	41.6	0.0	41.6	0.0	41.6	0.0	41.6	0.0	42.6	2.4	43.0	0.9	43.8	1.9	43.5	-0.7	43.5	0.0
1964	43.5	0.0	43.5	0.0	43.8	0.7	44.2	0.9	44.1	-0.2	44.1	0.0	44.1	0.0	44.4	0.7	44.4	0.0	44.4	0.0	44.4	0.0	43.9	-1.1
1965	43.9	0.0	43.8	-0.2	43.8	0.0	43.8	0.0	43.8	0.0	43.8	0.0	43.1	-1.6	43.1	0.0	43.0	-0.2	43.0	0.0	43.0	0.0	43.0	0.0
1966	43.0	0.0	43.0	0.0	42.7	-0.7	42.9	0.5	43.1	0.5	43.1	0.0	43.2	0.2	42.9	-0.7	43.3	0.9	43.9	1.4	44.5	1.4	44.5	0.0
1967	-		-		-		-		-		-		-		-		-		-		-		-	
1968	-		-		-		-		-		-		-		-		-		-		-		-	
1969	-		-		-		-		-		-		-		-		-		-		-		-	
1970	-		-		-		-		-		-		-		-		-		-		-		-	
1971	55.6	24.9	55.6	0.0	56.6	1.8	57.0	0.7	55.3	-3.0	55.3	0.0	55.3	0.0	55.3	0.0	55.3	0.0	55.3	0.0	55.3	0.0	55.4	0.2
1972	55.8	0.7	55.8	0.0	55.3	-0.9	54.7	-1.1	54.9	0.4	54.7	-0.4	55.0	0.5	55.5	0.9	55.5	0.0	55.3	-0.4	55.3	0.0	55.3	0.0
1973	55.3	0.0	55.3	0.0	56.0	1.3	56.0	0.0	56.2	0.4	55.2	-1.8	53.2	-3.6	53.2	0.0	53.4	0.4	53.4	0.0	54.5	2.1	55.8	2.4
1974	56.3	0.9	56.3	0.0	56.3	0.0	56.3	0.0	56.6	0.5	57.8	2.1	58.1	0.5	58.1	0.0	60.1	3.4	60.6	0.8	60.5	-0.2	60.9	0.7
1975	60.9	0.0	60.9	0.0	60.9	0.0	62.5	2.6	62.3	-0.3	61.4	-1.4	63.3	3.1	63.8	0.8	63.8	0.0	64.8	1.6	64.7	-0.2	64.7	0.0
1976	64.7	0.0	64.7	0.0	65.7	1.5	67.6	2.9	67.6	0.0	68.3	1.0	69.0	1.0	69.0	0.0	69.0	0.0	69.0	0.0	68.9	-0.1	68.9	0.0
1977	69.1	0.3	72.0	4.2	72.0	0.0	72.0	0.0	72.2	0.3	73.0	1.1	72.3	-1.0	72.8	0.7	72.8	0.0	73.4	0.8	74.1	1.0	76.0	2.6
1978	76.0	0.0	76.9	1.2	76.9	0.0	78.0	1.4	78.0	0.0	78.0	0.0	78.2	0.3	78.4	0.3	78.4	0.0	78.4	0.0	78.5	0.1	80.8	2.9
1979	81.8	1.2	82.7	1.1	82.7	0.0	82.7	0.0	82.7	0.0	83.1	0.5	83.1	0.0	83.1	0.0	83.3	0.2	83.4	0.1	83.7	0.4	84.2	0.6
1980	86.3	2.5	86.3	0.0	86.4	0.1	88.2	2.1	88.2	0.0	87.4	-0.9	87.7	0.3	90.1	2.7	90.2	0.1	90.6	0.4	91.7	1.2	91.7	0.0
1981	92.1	0.4	92.3	0.2	92.5	0.2	94.9	2.6	94.9	0.0	94.9	0.0	98.6	3.9	98.6	0.0	98.6	0.0	98.6	0.0	98.6	0.0	97.6	-1.0
1982	97.6	0.0	97.6	0.0	97.6	0.0	97.6	0.0	102.2	4.7	102.2	0.0	102.1	-0.1	99.8	-2.3	99.8	0.0	99.8	0.0	101.7	1.9	101.7	0.0
1983	103.7	2.0	103.7	0.0	103.7	0.0	103.7	0.0	103.7	0.0	103.7	0.0	103.7	0.0	103.7	0.0	103.8	0.1	104.5	0.7	104.8	0.3	104.7	-0.1
1984	107.0	2.2	107.1	0.1	106.8	-0.3	107.1	0.3	105.9	-1.1	106.0	0.1	106.0	0.0	103.9	-2.0	104.2	0.3	104.3	0.1	104.1	-0.2	104.2	0.1
1985	103.4	-0.8	103.3	-0.1	103.3	0.0	103.8	0.5	104.6	0.8	104.5	-0.1	105.1	0.6	105.4	0.3	105.2	-0.2	105.8	0.6	106.0	0.2	106.2	0.2
1986	106.8	0.6	106.8	0.0	106.8	0.0	107.0	0.2	106.9	-0.1	106.9	0.0	108.1	1.1	107.8	-0.3	107.8	0.0	107.8	0.0	108.1	0.3	108.2	0.1
1987	108.2	0.0	108.3	0.1	109.1	0.7	109.2	0.1	109.0	-0.2	109.5	0.5	109.7	0.2	109.8	0.1	109.6	-0.2	110.1	0.5	110.0	-0.1	110.7	0.6
1988	110.8	0.1	111.2	0.4	111.7	0.4	111.9	0.2	112.3	0.4	111.9	-0.4	112.3	0.4	112.7	0.4	113.1	0.4	113.0	-0.1	113.2	0.2	113.9	0.6
1989	113.4	-0.4	113.1	-0.3	112.6	-0.4	112.8	0.2	113.7	0.8	113.2	-0.4	113.3	0.1	113.0	-0.3	113.2	0.2	113.5	0.3	113.2	-0.3	113.7	0.4
1990	114.8	1.0	114.5	-0.3	114.3	-0.2	114.0	-0.3	114.1	0.1	113.9	-0.2	113.6	-0.3	113.2	-0.4	113.3	0.1	113.4	0.1	113.4	0.0	113.3	-0.1
1991	113.9	0.5	113.9	0.0	114.4	0.4	114.2	-0.2	114.3	0.1	113.7	-0.5	113.4	-0.3	114.0	0.5	115.0	0.9	115.8	0.7	115.2	-0.5	115.1	-0.1

[Continued]

Glass
Producer Price Index
Base 1982 = 100
[Continued]

For 1947-1995. Columns headed % show percentile change in the index from the previous period for which an index is available.

Year	Jan Index	%	Feb Index	%	Mar Index	%	Apr Index	%	May Index	%	Jun Index	%	Jul Index	%	Aug Index	%	Sep Index	%	Oct Index	%	Nov Index	%	Dec Index	%
1992	115.4	0.3	114.8	-0.5	114.9	0.1	115.3	0.3	115.3	0.0	115.2	-0.1	115.2	0.0	116.6	1.2	116.4	-0.2	116.0	-0.3	116.1	0.1	117.1	0.9
1993	116.3	-0.7	116.8	0.4	116.6	-0.2	116.9	0.3	117.0	0.1	117.1	0.1	117.0	-0.1	117.4	0.3	117.2	-0.2	116.5	-0.6	117.1	0.5	117.2	0.1
1994	117.6	0.3	118.2	0.5	118.6	0.3	118.7	0.1	119.7	0.8	120.5	0.7	120.7	0.2	121.1	0.3	120.8	-0.2	121.3	0.4	122.6	1.1	121.4	-1.0
1995	122.4	0.8	123.2	0.7	123.8	0.5	124.7	0.7	124.7	0.0	122.4	-1.8	122.6	0.2	122.3	-0.2	122.4	0.1	122.2	-0.2	122.0	-0.2	122.0	0.0

Source: U.S. Department of Labor, Bureau of Labor Statistics, Division of Industry Prices and Price Indexes. n.e.c. stands for not elsewhere classified. - indicates no data collected for period or unavailable.

Concrete Ingredients and Related Products
Producer Price Index
Base 1982 = 100

For 1926-1995. Columns headed % show percentile change in the index from the previous period for which an index is available.

Year	Jan Index	%	Feb Index	%	Mar Index	%	Apr Index	%	May Index	%	Jun Index	%	Jul Index	%	Aug Index	%	Sep Index	%	Oct Index	%	Nov Index	%	Dec Index	%
1926	15.0	-	15.0	0.0	15.0	0.0	14.9	-0.7	14.9	0.0	14.9	0.0	14.9	0.0	14.8	-0.7	14.8	0.0	14.9	0.7	14.9	0.0	15.0	0.7
1927	14.9	-0.7	14.6	-2.0	14.6	0.0	14.6	0.0	14.6	0.0	14.6	0.0	14.6	0.0	14.4	-1.4	14.4	0.0	14.4	0.0	14.4	0.0	14.5	0.7
1928	14.6	0.7	14.6	0.0	14.5	-0.7	16.5	13.8	17.1	3.6	17.1	0.0	17.0	-0.6	17.1	0.6	16.9	-1.2	16.8	-0.6	16.9	0.6	17.0	0.6
1929	17.0	0.0	17.0	0.0	16.7	-1.8	16.6	-0.6	16.6	0.0	16.6	0.0	16.6	0.0	16.4	-1.2	15.8	-3.7	15.7	-0.6	15.9	1.3	16.4	3.1
1930	16.5	0.6	16.7	1.2	16.6	-0.6	16.6	0.0	16.6	0.0	16.2	-2.4	16.6	2.5	16.6	0.0	16.6	0.0	16.6	0.0	16.6	0.0	16.5	-0.6
1931	16.5	0.0	16.2	-1.8	15.9	-1.9	15.6	-1.9	15.4	-1.3	15.2	-1.3	14.4	-5.3	14.6	1.4	14.6	0.0	14.5	-0.7	14.5	0.0	14.2	-2.1
1932	13.9	-2.1	13.9	0.0	13.9	0.0	13.7	-1.4	13.6	-0.7	13.8	1.5	14.7	6.5	14.8	0.7	14.8	0.0	14.8	0.0	14.9	0.7	15.1	1.3
1933	15.1	0.0	15.2	0.7	15.2	0.0	15.2	0.0	15.2	0.0	15.2	0.0	15.8	3.9	16.1	1.9	16.1	0.0	16.2	0.6	16.2	0.0	16.3	0.6
1934	16.6	1.8	16.7	0.6	16.6	-0.6	16.2	-2.4	16.2	0.0	16.6	2.5	16.6	0.0	16.6	0.0	16.6	0.0	16.6	0.0	16.6	0.0	16.6	0.0
1935	16.6	0.0	16.6	0.0	16.6	0.0	16.7	0.6	16.6	-0.6	16.6	0.0	16.6	0.0	16.6	0.0	16.6	0.0	16.6	0.0	16.7	0.6	16.7	0.0
1936	16.6	-0.6	16.7	0.6	16.6	-0.6	16.6	0.0	16.7	0.6	16.7	0.0	16.7	0.0	16.7	0.0	16.7	0.0	16.7	0.0	16.7	0.0	16.7	0.0
1937	16.7	0.0	16.6	-0.6	16.6	0.0	16.6	0.0	16.6	0.0	16.6	0.0	16.7	0.6	16.7	0.0	16.3	-2.4	16.7	2.5	16.7	0.0	16.7	0.0
1938	16.7	0.0	16.7	0.0	16.7	0.0	16.7	0.0	16.7	0.0	16.6	-0.6	16.8	1.2	16.7	-0.6	16.6	-0.6	16.7	0.6	16.9	1.2	16.9	0.0
1939	16.7	-1.2	16.7	0.0	16.7	0.0	16.7	0.0	16.7	0.0	16.7	0.0	16.7	0.0	16.7	0.0	16.7	0.0	16.7	0.0	16.7	0.0	16.7	0.0
1940	16.7	0.0	16.7	0.0	16.7	0.0	16.6	-0.6	16.6	0.0	16.6	0.0	16.6	0.0	16.6	0.0	16.6	0.0	16.6	0.0	16.6	0.0	16.6	0.0
1941	16.6	0.0	16.6	0.0	16.6	0.0	16.6	0.0	16.7	0.6	16.7	0.0	16.8	0.6	16.8	0.0	16.9	0.6	16.9	0.0	17.0	0.6	17.1	0.6
1942	17.1	0.0	17.2	0.6	17.2	0.0	17.3	0.6	17.3	0.0	17.3	0.0	17.3	0.0	17.3	0.0	17.3	0.0	17.3	0.0	17.3	0.0	17.3	0.0
1943	17.3	0.0	17.3	0.0	17.3	0.0	17.3	0.0	17.3	0.0	17.2	-0.6	17.2	0.0	17.3	0.6	17.3	0.0	17.2	-0.6	17.2	0.0	17.2	0.0
1944	17.2	0.0	17.2	0.0	17.2	0.0	17.3	0.6	17.6	1.7	17.6	0.0	17.6	0.0	17.6	0.0	17.6	0.0	17.7	0.6	17.7	0.0	17.7	0.0
1945	17.7	0.0	17.9	1.1	17.9	0.0	17.9	0.0	17.9	0.0	17.9	0.0	17.9	0.0	17.9	0.0	18.0	0.6	18.1	0.6	18.1	0.0	18.1	0.0
1946	18.4	1.7	18.4	0.0	18.5	0.5	18.5	0.0	18.5	0.0	18.6	0.5	18.7	0.5	18.9	1.1	19.0	0.5	19.0	0.0	19.1	0.5	19.2	0.5
1947	19.6	2.1	19.9	1.5	20.0	0.5	20.2	1.0	20.2	0.0	20.3	0.5	20.4	0.5	20.7	1.5	20.9	1.0	21.0	0.5	21.1	0.5	21.1	0.0
1948	21.7	2.8	21.9	0.9	22.0	0.5	22.1	0.5	22.1	0.0	22.2	0.5	22.7	2.3	22.7	0.0	22.8	0.4	22.8	0.0	22.9	0.4	23.0	0.4
1949	23.1	0.4	23.2	0.4	23.2	0.0	23.2	0.0	23.2	0.0	23.2	0.0	23.1	-0.4	23.1	0.0	23.1	0.0	23.2	0.4	23.2	0.0	23.2	0.0
1950	23.3	0.4	23.3	0.0	23.3	0.0	23.3	0.0	23.3	0.0	23.3	0.0	23.3	0.0	23.4	0.4	23.5	0.4	23.9	1.7	24.0	0.4	24.1	0.4
1951	24.9	3.3	24.9	0.0	24.9	0.0	24.9	0.0	24.9	0.0	24.9	0.0	24.9	0.0	24.9	0.0	24.9	0.0	24.9	0.0	24.9	0.0	24.9	0.0
1952	24.9	0.0	24.9	0.0	24.9	0.0	24.9	0.0	24.9	0.0	24.9	0.0	24.9	0.0	24.9	0.0	24.9	0.0	24.9	0.0	24.9	0.0	24.9	0.0
1953	24.9	0.0	24.9	0.0	25.0	0.4	25.9	3.6	26.0	0.4	26.0	0.0	26.0	0.0	26.1	0.4	26.3	0.8	26.3	0.0	26.3	0.0	26.3	0.0
1954	26.4	0.4	26.4	0.0	26.4	0.0	26.4	0.0	26.4	0.0	26.5	0.4	26.9	1.5	26.9	0.0	26.9	0.0	26.9	0.0	26.9	0.0	26.9	0.0
1955	27.1	0.7	27.3	0.7	27.3	0.0	27.5	0.7	27.5	0.0	27.5	0.0	27.5	0.0	27.6	0.4	27.6	0.0	27.6	0.0	27.6	0.0	27.7	0.4
1956	28.6	3.2	28.6	0.0	28.6	0.0	28.6	0.0	28.6	0.0	28.7	0.3	28.7	0.0	28.7	0.0	28.7	0.0	29.0	1.0	29.0	0.0	29.0	0.0
1957	29.6	2.1	29.7	0.3	29.7	0.0	29.8	0.3	29.8	0.0	29.9	0.3	30.0	0.3	30.0	0.0	30.1	0.3	30.1	0.0	30.1	0.0	30.1	0.0
1958	30.6	1.7	30.6	0.0	30.5	-0.3	30.6	0.3	30.6	0.0	30.6	0.0	30.6	0.0	30.6	0.0	30.6	0.0	30.6	0.0	30.6	0.0	30.6	0.0
1959	30.9	1.0	30.9	0.0	30.9	0.0	30.9	0.0	30.9	0.0	30.8	-0.3	30.9	0.3	30.9	0.0	30.9	0.0	30.9	0.0	30.9	0.0	30.9	0.0
1960	31.3	1.3	31.3	0.0	31.3	0.0	31.3	0.0	31.3	0.0	31.3	0.0	31.3	0.0	31.3	0.0	31.3	0.0	31.3	0.0	31.3	0.0	31.3	0.0
1961	31.3	0.0	31.3	0.0	31.4	0.3	31.4	0.0	31.4	0.0	31.4	0.0	31.4	0.0	31.4	0.0	31.4	0.0	31.4	0.0	31.2	-0.6	31.0	-0.6
1962	31.3	1.0	31.4	0.3	31.4	0.0	31.4	0.0	31.5	0.3	31.5	0.0	31.5	0.0	31.5	0.0	31.5	0.0	31.5	0.0	31.5	0.0	31.5	0.0
1963	31.3	-0.6	31.4	0.3	31.4	0.0	31.4	0.0	31.4	0.0	31.5	0.3	31.5	0.0	31.4	-0.3	31.4	0.0	31.4	0.0	31.4	0.0	31.4	0.0
1964	31.3	-0.3	31.3	0.0	31.3	0.0	31.3	0.0	31.3	0.0	31.3	0.0	31.3	0.0	31.3	0.0	31.3	0.0	31.3	0.0	31.4	0.3	31.4	0.0
1965	31.5	0.3	31.5	0.0	31.5	0.0	31.5	0.0	31.5	0.0	31.4	-0.3	31.4	0.0	31.5	0.3	31.5	0.0	31.5	0.0	31.5	0.0	31.5	0.0
1966	31.6	0.3	31.6	0.0	31.6	0.0	31.6	0.0	31.6	0.0	31.6	0.0	31.6	0.0	31.6	0.0	31.6	0.0	31.8	0.6	31.7	-0.3	31.8	0.3
1967	32.2	1.3	32.2	0.0	32.2	0.0	32.3	0.3	32.2	-0.3	32.2	0.0	32.2	0.0	32.3	0.3	32.3	0.0	32.4	0.3	32.4	0.0	32.5	0.3
1968	32.9	1.2	33.1	0.6	33.1	0.0	33.2	0.3	33.2	0.0	33.3	0.3	33.4	0.3	33.4	0.0	33.4	0.0	33.4	0.0	33.6	0.6	33.6	0.0
1969	34.3	2.1	34.2	-0.3	34.3	0.3	34.3	0.0	34.3	0.0	34.4	0.3	34.5	0.3	34.5	0.0	34.6	0.3	34.6	0.0	34.6	0.0	34.6	0.0
1970	35.9	3.8	36.1	0.6	36.1	0.0	37.1	2.8	36.2	-2.4	36.3	0.3	36.3	0.0	36.3	0.0	36.4	0.3	36.4	0.0	36.4	0.0	36.4	0.0

[Continued]

Concrete Ingredients and Related Products
Producer Price Index
Base 1982 = 100
[Continued]

For 1926-1995. Columns headed % show percentile change in the index from the previous period for which an index is available.

Year	Jan Index	%	Feb Index	%	Mar Index	%	Apr Index	%	May Index	%	Jun Index	%	Jul Index	%	Aug Index	%	Sep Index	%	Oct Index	%	Nov Index	%	Dec Index	%
1971	37.7	3.6	37.8	0.3	38.9	2.9	39.0	0.3	39.1	0.3	39.2	0.3	39.8	1.5	40.0	0.5	40.1	0.3	40.1	0.0	40.1	0.0	40.1	0.0
1972	40.1	0.0	40.2	0.2	40.2	0.0	40.8	1.5	40.9	0.2	40.9	0.0	40.9	0.0	41.3	1.0	41.4	0.2	41.4	0.0	41.4	0.0	41.4	0.0
1973	41.6	0.5	41.7	0.2	41.9	0.5	42.5	1.4	42.4	-0.2	42.5	0.2	42.5	0.0	42.5	0.0	42.5	0.0	42.6	0.2	42.6	0.0	42.6	0.0
1974	44.8	5.2	45.1	0.7	45.3	0.4	46.2	2.0	46.9	1.5	47.1	0.4	49.5	5.1	49.7	0.4	49.8	0.2	50.2	0.8	50.4	0.4	50.5	0.2
1975	53.9	6.7	54.4	0.9	54.7	0.6	55.3	1.1	55.5	0.4	55.6	0.2	56.1	0.9	56.1	0.0	56.5	0.7	56.4	-0.2	56.4	0.0	56.4	0.0
1976	58.2	3.2	58.4	0.3	58.6	0.3	60.3	2.9	60.4	0.2	60.5	0.2	60.9	0.7	60.9	0.0	61.0	0.2	61.1	0.2	61.0	-0.2	61.1	0.2
1977	62.6	2.5	62.7	0.2	63.0	0.5	64.0	1.6	64.4	0.6	64.5	0.2	64.7	0.3	64.8	0.2	64.9	0.2	64.9	0.0	65.0	0.2	65.0	0.0
1978	67.7	4.2	68.0	0.4	68.4	0.6	69.9	2.2	70.0	0.1	70.2	0.3	70.7	0.7	71.0	0.4	71.3	0.4	71.6	0.4	72.1	0.7	72.1	0.0
1979	76.1	5.5	76.9	1.1	77.4	0.7	78.1	0.9	78.2	0.1	78.5	0.4	79.1	0.8	79.3	0.3	79.6	0.4	80.1	0.6	80.5	0.5	81.0	0.6
1980	85.5	5.6	86.0	0.6	86.3	0.3	87.7	1.6	87.9	0.2	88.1	0.2	89.0	1.0	89.9	1.0	90.0	0.1	90.0	0.0	90.1	0.1	90.2	0.1
1981	93.5	3.7	94.0	0.5	94.4	0.4	96.0	1.7	96.0	0.0	96.0	0.0	96.1	0.1	96.1	0.0	96.3	0.2	96.3	0.0	96.3	0.0	96.4	0.1
1982	98.8	2.5	99.5	0.7	99.9	0.4	99.8	-0.1	100.8	1.0	100.9	0.1	100.6	-0.3	100.4	-0.2	100.3	-0.1	100.0	-0.3	100.0	0.0	98.9	-1.1
1983	99.1	0.2	100.0	0.9	99.5	-0.5	100.9	1.4	101.2	0.3	101.4	0.2	101.3	-0.1	102.1	0.8	102.3	0.2	102.2	-0.1	101.6	-0.6	101.5	-0.1
1984	101.8	0.3	103.2	1.4	104.6	1.4	104.6	0.0	105.8	1.1	105.4	-0.4	105.5	0.1	106.0	0.5	105.9	-0.1	105.7	-0.2	106.0	0.3	106.3	0.3
1985	106.8	0.5	107.6	0.7	108.2	0.6	108.5	0.3	109.3	0.7	109.3	0.0	108.9	-0.4	109.1	0.2	108.7	-0.4	108.6	-0.1	108.1	-0.5	108.4	0.3
1986	109.4	0.9	109.4	0.0	109.7	0.3	110.1	0.4	109.7	-0.4	109.5	-0.2	109.4	-0.1	109.3	-0.1	109.4	0.1	109.5	0.1	109.5	0.0	108.2	-1.2
1987	109.1	0.8	109.6	0.5	110.1	0.5	110.4	0.3	110.7	0.3	110.8	0.1	110.8	0.0	110.8	0.0	110.8	0.0	110.8	0.0	110.8	0.0	110.6	-0.2
1988	111.3	0.6	111.6	0.3	111.6	0.0	112.3	0.6	112.6	0.3	112.3	-0.3	112.1	-0.2	112.2	0.1	112.0	-0.2	111.9	-0.1	111.9	0.0	111.9	0.0
1989	112.3	0.4	112.3	0.0	112.3	0.0	113.1	0.7	113.3	0.2	113.3	0.0	113.3	0.0	113.2	-0.1	113.7	0.4	113.8	0.1	113.6	-0.2	113.6	0.0
1990	113.9	0.3	114.3	0.4	114.8	0.4	115.2	0.3	115.5	0.3	115.5	0.0	115.3	-0.2	115.5	0.2	115.8	0.3	115.8	0.0	116.0	0.2	115.9	-0.1
1991	117.1	1.0	118.3	1.0	118.3	0.0	118.6	0.3	118.8	0.2	118.9	0.1	118.7	-0.2	118.8	0.1	118.5	-0.3	118.5	0.0	118.3	-0.2	118.2	-0.1
1992	118.8	0.5	118.8	0.0	119.4	0.5	119.3	-0.1	119.4	0.1	119.4	0.0	119.4	0.0	119.5	0.1	119.4	-0.1	119.6	0.2	119.7	0.1	119.9	0.2
1993	120.9	0.8	121.1	0.2	121.4	0.2	123.2	1.5	123.2	0.0	123.5	0.2	123.7	0.2	123.8	0.1	124.5	0.6	125.5	0.8	125.2	-0.2	125.3	0.1
1994	126.2	0.7	126.6	0.3	127.0	0.3	128.4	1.1	128.4	0.0	129.0	0.5	129.2	0.2	129.7	0.4	129.8	0.1	130.2	0.3	130.2	0.0	130.2	0.0
1995	131.6	1.1	132.1	0.4	132.4	0.2	134.5	1.6	134.8	0.2	135.2	0.3	135.7	0.4	135.7	0.0	135.8	0.1	135.7	-0.1	135.8	0.1	135.8	0.0

Source: U.S. Department of Labor, Bureau of Labor Statistics, Division of Industry Prices and Price Indexes. n.e.c. stands for not elsewhere classified. - indicates no data collected for period or unavailable.

Concrete Products
Producer Price Index
Base 1982 = 100

For 1926-1995. Columns headed % show percentile change in the index from the previous period for which an index is available.

Year	Jan Index	%	Feb Index	%	Mar Index	%	Apr Index	%	May Index	%	Jun Index	%	Jul Index	%	Aug Index	%	Sep Index	%	Oct Index	%	Nov Index	%	Dec Index	%
1926	23.7	-	23.7	0.0	23.7	0.0	23.7	0.0	23.7	0.0	23.7	0.0	23.7	0.0	23.7	0.0	23.7	0.0	23.7	0.0	23.7	0.0	23.7	0.0
1927	23.7	0.0	23.7	0.0	23.7	0.0	23.7	0.0	23.7	0.0	23.7	0.0	23.7	0.0	23.7	0.0	23.7	0.0	23.7	0.0	23.7	0.0	23.7	0.0
1928	23.7	0.0	23.7	0.0	23.7	0.0	23.7	0.0	23.7	0.0	23.7	0.0	23.7	0.0	23.7	0.0	23.7	0.0	23.7	0.0	23.7	0.0	23.7	0.0
1929	23.7	0.0	23.7	0.0	23.7	0.0	23.7	0.0	23.7	0.0	23.7	0.0	23.0	-3.0	23.0	0.0	23.0	0.0	23.0	0.0	23.0	0.0	23.0	0.0
1930	23.0	0.0	23.0	0.0	23.0	0.0	23.0	0.0	22.6	-1.7	22.6	0.0	23.0	1.8	23.7	3.0	25.0	5.5	25.0	0.0	25.0	0.0	25.0	0.0
1931	24.6	-1.6	23.2	-5.7	22.6	-2.6	22.6	0.0	22.6	0.0	22.6	0.0	22.5	-0.4	21.3	-5.3	21.3	0.0	21.3	0.0	21.3	0.0	21.3	0.0
1932	21.3	0.0	21.2	-0.5	21.2	0.0	20.0	-5.7	20.0	0.0	20.0	0.0	20.0	0.0	20.0	0.0	20.0	0.0	20.9	4.5	20.9	0.0	20.9	0.0
1933	20.9	0.0	20.9	0.0	20.9	0.0	20.9	0.0	20.9	0.0	20.9	0.0	20.9	0.0	20.9	0.0	20.9	0.0	20.9	0.0	20.9	0.0	20.9	0.0
1934	20.9	0.0	20.9	0.0	20.9	0.0	20.9	0.0	20.9	0.0	20.9	0.0	20.9	0.0	20.9	0.0	20.9	0.0	20.9	0.0	20.9	0.0	20.9	0.0
1935	20.9	0.0	20.9	0.0	19.7	-5.7	18.6	-5.6	18.6	0.0	18.6	0.0	18.6	0.0	18.6	0.0	18.6	0.0	18.6	0.0	18.6	0.0	18.6	0.0
1936	20.9	12.4	20.9	0.0	20.9	0.0	20.9	0.0	20.9	0.0	20.9	0.0	20.9	0.0	20.9	0.0	20.4	-2.4	18.6	-8.8	18.6	0.0	18.6	0.0
1937	18.6	0.0	18.6	0.0	18.6	0.0	21.2	14.0	21.2	0.0	21.2	0.0	21.2	0.0	21.2	0.0	21.2	0.0	21.2	0.0	21.2	0.0	19.2	-9.4
1938	18.6	-3.1	18.6	0.0	18.6	0.0	18.6	0.0	18.6	0.0	18.6	0.0	18.6	0.0	18.6	0.0	18.6	0.0	18.6	0.0	18.6	0.0	19.9	7.0
1939	21.2	6.5	21.2	0.0	21.2	0.0	21.2	0.0	18.0	-15.1	15.9	-11.7	15.9	0.0	15.9	0.0	17.2	8.2	18.6	8.1	18.6	0.0	18.6	0.0
1940	18.6	0.0	18.6	0.0	16.6	-10.8	15.9	-4.2	15.9	0.0	15.9	0.0	15.9	0.0	15.9	0.0	15.9	0.0	15.9	0.0	15.9	0.0	18.0	13.2
1941	18.6	3.3	18.6	0.0	18.6	0.0	18.6	0.0	18.6	0.0	18.9	1.6	19.9	5.3	19.9	0.0	19.9	0.0	19.9	0.0	19.9	0.0	19.9	0.0
1942	19.9	0.0	19.9	0.0	19.9	0.0	19.9	0.0	19.9	0.0	19.9	0.0	19.9	0.0	19.9	0.0	19.9	0.0	19.9	0.0	19.9	0.0	19.9	0.0
1943	19.9	0.0	19.9	0.0	19.9	0.0	19.9	0.0	19.9	0.0	19.9	0.0	19.9	0.0	19.9	0.0	19.9	0.0	19.9	0.0	19.9	0.0	19.9	0.0
1944	19.9	0.0	19.9	0.0	19.9	0.0	19.9	0.0	19.9	0.0	19.9	0.0	19.9	0.0	19.9	0.0	19.9	0.0	19.9	0.0	19.9	0.0	19.9	0.0
1945	19.9	0.0	19.9	0.0	19.9	0.0	19.9	0.0	19.9	0.0	19.9	0.0	19.9	0.0	19.9	0.0	19.9	0.0	19.9	0.0	19.9	0.0	19.9	0.0
1946	19.9	0.0	19.9	0.0	19.9	0.0	19.9	0.0	20.2	1.5	21.2	5.0	22.0	3.8	21.2	-3.6	21.2	0.0	21.2	0.0	22.5	6.1	23.9	6.2
1947	23.9	0.0	23.9	0.0	23.9	0.0	23.9	0.0	23.9	0.0	23.9	0.0	24.0	0.4	23.8	-0.8	23.6	-0.8	24.0	1.7	24.2	0.8	24.2	0.0
1948	24.7	2.1	24.8	0.4	24.8	0.0	24.8	0.0	24.8	0.0	24.8	0.0	25.0	0.8	25.4	1.6	25.4	0.0	25.4	0.0	25.4	0.0	25.4	0.0
1949	25.4	0.0	25.4	0.0	25.6	0.8	25.6	0.0	25.6	0.0	25.6	0.0	25.6	0.0	25.8	0.8	25.8	0.0	25.8	0.0	25.8	0.0	25.8	0.0
1950	25.8	0.0	25.8	0.0	25.8	0.0	25.8	0.0	25.9	0.4	26.0	0.4	26.0	0.0	26.2	0.8	26.6	1.5	27.0	1.5	27.0	0.0	27.2	0.7
1951	27.9	2.6	28.0	0.4	28.0	0.0	28.0	0.0	28.0	0.0	28.0	0.0	28.0	0.0	28.0	0.0	28.0	0.0	28.0	0.0	28.0	0.0	28.0	0.0
1952	28.0	0.0	28.0	0.0	28.0	0.0	28.0	0.0	28.0	0.0	28.0	0.0	28.0	0.0	28.0	0.0	28.0	0.0	28.0	0.0	28.0	0.0	28.0	0.0
1953	28.1	0.4	28.1	0.0	28.1	0.0	28.4	1.1	28.7	1.1	28.7	0.0	28.8	0.3	28.9	0.3	29.2	1.0	29.2	0.0	29.2	0.0	29.1	-0.3
1954	29.1	0.0	29.2	0.3	29.2	0.0	29.2	0.0	29.2	0.0	29.2	0.0	29.3	0.3	29.3	0.0	29.3	0.0	29.3	0.0	29.2	-0.3	29.2	0.0
1955	29.0	-0.7	29.1	0.3	29.4	1.0	29.4	0.0	29.4	0.0	29.4	0.0	29.4	0.0	29.5	0.3	29.8	1.0	29.9	0.3	29.9	0.0	29.9	0.0
1956	30.2	1.0	30.2	0.0	30.2	0.0	30.3	0.3	30.3	0.0	30.3	0.0	30.6	1.0	30.7	0.3	31.1	1.3	31.1	0.0	31.2	0.3	31.2	0.0
1957	31.3	0.3	31.3	0.0	31.3	0.0	31.5	0.6	31.5	0.0	31.5	0.0	31.4	-0.3	31.4	0.0	31.4	0.0	31.5	0.3	31.5	0.0	31.6	0.3
1958	31.8	0.6	31.8	0.0	31.8	0.0	31.8	0.0	31.9	0.3	31.9	0.0	32.0	0.3	31.9	-0.3	31.8	-0.3	31.9	0.3	31.9	0.0	32.0	0.3
1959	32.0	0.0	32.1	0.3	32.2	0.3	32.2	0.0	32.3	0.3	32.3	0.0	32.3	0.0	32.3	0.0	32.4	0.3	32.4	0.0	32.4	0.0	32.4	0.0
1960	32.5	0.3	32.6	0.3	32.6	0.0	32.6	0.0	32.7	0.3	32.6	-0.3	32.6	0.0	32.6	0.0	32.6	0.0	32.6	0.0	32.6	0.0	32.6	0.0
1961	32.6	0.0	32.6	0.0	32.6	0.0	32.6	0.0	32.6	0.0	32.6	0.0	32.6	0.0	32.6	0.0	32.7	0.3	32.7	0.0	32.6	-0.3	32.6	0.0
1962	32.6	0.0	32.7	0.3	32.7	0.0	32.7	0.0	32.6	-0.3	32.6	0.0	32.7	0.3	32.7	0.0	32.7	0.0	32.7	0.0	32.7	0.0	32.6	-0.3
1963	32.6	0.0	32.6	0.0	32.6	0.0	32.6	0.0	32.5	-0.3	32.5	0.0	32.2	-0.9	32.2	0.0	32.3	0.3	32.3	0.0	32.3	0.0	32.3	0.0
1964	32.2	-0.3	32.2	0.0	32.1	-0.3	32.0	-0.3	32.0	0.0	32.1	0.3	32.1	0.0	32.1	0.0	32.2	0.3	32.2	0.0	32.2	0.0	32.2	0.0
1965	32.3	0.3	32.2	-0.3	32.2	0.0	32.3	0.3	32.3	0.0	32.4	0.3	32.4	0.0	32.3	-0.3	32.4	0.3	32.4	0.0	32.4	0.0	32.4	0.0
1966	32.5	0.3	32.5	0.0	32.6	0.3	32.7	0.3	32.7	0.0	32.8	0.3	32.8	0.0	32.9	0.3	33.0	0.3	33.0	0.0	33.0	0.0	33.1	0.3
1967	33.3	0.6	33.4	0.3	33.4	0.0	33.5	0.3	33.5	0.0	33.6	0.3	33.6	0.0	33.7	0.3	33.7	0.0	33.7	0.0	33.7	0.0	33.7	0.0
1968	33.9	0.6	34.0	0.3	34.1	0.3	34.3	0.6	34.3	0.0	34.5	0.6	34.5	0.0	34.6	0.3	34.6	0.0	34.8	0.6	34.8	0.0	34.9	0.3
1969	35.3	1.1	35.4	0.3	35.5	0.3	35.6	0.3	35.6	0.0	35.6	0.0	35.8	0.6	35.9	0.3	36.1	0.6	36.2	0.3	36.2	0.0	36.4	0.6
1970	37.0	1.6	37.1	0.3	37.3	0.5	37.3	0.0	37.4	0.3	37.6	0.5	37.7	0.3	37.8	0.3	38.1	0.8	38.1	0.0	38.2	0.3	38.4	0.5

[Continued]

Concrete Products
Producer Price Index
Base 1982 = 100
[Continued]

For 1926-1995. Columns headed % show percentile change in the index from the previous period for which an index is available.

Year	Jan Index	%	Feb Index	%	Mar Index	%	Apr Index	%	May Index	%	Jun Index	%	Jul Index	%	Aug Index	%	Sep Index	%	Oct Index	%	Nov Index	%	Dec Index	%
1971	39.3	2.3	39.5	0.5	39.8	0.8	40.1	0.8	40.1	0.0	40.3	0.5	40.8	1.2	41.2	1.0	41.1	-0.2	41.1	0.0	41.1	0.0	41.3	0.5
1972	41.4	0.2	41.6	0.5	41.8	0.5	42.0	0.5	42.0	0.0	42.1	0.2	42.3	0.5	42.3	0.0	42.4	0.2	42.7	0.7	42.7	0.0	42.8	0.2
1973	43.1	0.7	43.3	0.5	43.5	0.5	43.9	0.9	44.1	0.5	44.4	0.7	44.4	0.0	44.4	0.0	44.5	0.2	44.9	0.9	45.0	0.2	45.2	0.4
1974	47.0	4.0	47.8	1.7	48.6	1.7	48.8	0.4	49.6	1.6	50.3	1.4	52.1	3.6	52.5	0.8	52.8	0.6	53.6	1.5	53.9	0.6	54.3	0.7
1975	56.1	3.3	56.4	0.5	56.8	0.7	57.0	0.4	57.1	0.2	57.2	0.2	57.5	0.5	57.5	0.0	57.5	0.0	57.8	0.5	57.9	0.2	58.1	0.3
1976	59.6	2.6	59.8	0.3	59.8	0.0	59.9	0.2	60.2	0.5	60.3	0.2	60.8	0.8	60.9	0.2	60.9	0.0	60.9	0.0	61.2	0.5	61.5	0.5
1977	62.9	2.3	63.1	0.3	63.2	0.2	63.8	0.9	64.0	0.3	64.1	0.2	64.7	0.9	65.0	0.5	65.1	0.2	65.5	0.6	65.6	0.2	65.7	0.2
1978	68.1	3.7	68.9	1.2	69.2	0.4	69.8	0.9	70.4	0.9	71.1	1.0	72.0	1.3	73.8	2.5	74.4	0.8	74.6	0.3	74.8	0.3	75.3	0.7
1979	79.1	5.0	79.4	0.4	79.8	0.5	80.7	1.1	81.1	0.5	81.8	0.9	82.3	0.6	82.7	0.5	83.5	1.0	84.0	0.6	84.1	0.1	85.0	1.1
1980	89.1	4.8	89.6	0.6	90.3	0.8	91.6	1.4	92.4	0.9	92.6	0.2	92.6	0.0	92.7	0.1	93.1	0.4	93.2	0.1	93.3	0.1	93.2	-0.1
1981	96.1	3.1	96.2	0.1	96.3	0.1	97.3	1.0	97.8	0.5	98.5	0.7	98.5	0.0	98.5	0.0	98.4	-0.1	98.5	0.1	98.5	0.0	98.6	0.1
1982	99.2	0.6	99.3	0.1	99.5	0.2	100.0	0.5	100.1	0.1	100.2	0.1	100.3	0.1	100.4	0.1	100.3	-0.1	100.3	0.0	100.1	-0.2	100.2	0.1
1983	100.5	0.3	100.8	0.3	100.9	0.1	101.1	0.2	101.1	0.0	101.3	0.2	101.5	0.2	101.7	0.2	101.9	0.2	101.9	0.0	102.1	0.2	102.2	0.1
1984	102.4	0.2	102.7	0.3	102.8	0.1	103.7	0.9	103.9	0.2	104.1	0.2	104.3	0.2	104.5	0.2	104.7	0.2	104.8	0.1	104.7	-0.1	104.8	0.1
1985	105.6	0.8	105.6	0.0	106.0	0.4	106.3	0.3	107.5	1.1	107.9	0.4	107.9	0.0	108.4	0.5	108.5	0.1	108.4	-0.1	108.6	0.2	108.8	0.2
1986	109.1	0.3	109.1	0.0	109.1	0.0	109.6	0.5	109.6	0.0	109.3	-0.3	109.4	0.1	109.2	-0.2	109.1	-0.1	108.9	-0.2	108.9	0.0	109.1	0.2
1987	109.4	0.3	109.4	0.0	109.2	-0.2	109.3	0.1	109.4	0.1	109.3	-0.1	109.4	0.1	109.3	-0.1	109.4	0.1	109.4	0.0	109.6	0.2	109.4	-0.2
1988	109.7	0.3	109.8	0.1	109.8	0.0	109.7	-0.1	109.9	0.2	110.1	0.2	110.1	0.0	110.1	0.0	109.9	-0.2	109.9	0.0	110.2	0.3	110.3	0.1
1989	110.4	0.1	110.7	0.3	110.7	0.0	110.7	0.0	110.8	0.1	111.2	0.4	111.4	0.2	111.7	0.3	111.6	-0.1	111.6	0.0	111.6	0.0	111.9	0.3
1990	112.1	0.2	112.2	0.1	112.8	0.5	112.6	-0.2	113.1	0.4	113.3	0.2	113.7	0.4	113.9	0.2	114.2	0.3	114.2	0.0	114.8	0.5	115.0	0.2
1991	116.0	0.9	116.2	0.2	116.5	0.3	116.3	-0.2	116.5	0.2	116.9	0.3	117.0	0.1	116.9	-0.1	116.7	-0.2	116.7	0.0	116.7	0.0	116.9	0.2
1992	117.1	0.2	117.2	0.1	117.2	0.0	116.9	-0.3	117.1	0.2	117.0	-0.1	117.1	0.1	117.3	0.2	117.1	-0.2	117.2	0.1	117.7	0.4	118.0	0.3
1993	118.7	0.6	118.9	0.2	119.2	0.3	119.5	0.3	119.7	0.2	120.0	0.3	120.2	0.2	120.3	0.1	120.7	0.3	121.0	0.2	121.7	0.6	122.1	0.3
1994	122.5	0.3	122.7	0.2	123.4	0.6	123.7	0.2	124.0	0.2	124.2	0.2	124.7	0.4	125.1	0.3	125.3	0.2	125.8	0.4	126.5	0.6	127.0	0.4
1995	127.8	0.6	128.1	0.2	128.5	0.3	129.1	0.5	129.3	0.2	129.3	0.0	129.6	0.2	129.7	0.1	130.0	0.2	130.1	0.1	130.9	0.6	131.0	0.1

Source: U.S. Department of Labor, Bureau of Labor Statistics, Division of Industry Prices and Price Indexes. n.e.c. stands for not elsewhere classified. - indicates no data collected for period or unavailable.

Clay Construction Products Ex. Refractories
Producer Price Index
Base 1982 = 100

For 1947-1995. Columns headed % show percentile change in the index from the previous period for which an index is available.

Year	Jan Index	%	Feb Index	%	Mar Index	%	Apr Index	%	May Index	%	Jun Index	%	Jul Index	%	Aug Index	%	Sep Index	%	Oct Index	%	Nov Index	%	Dec Index	%
1947	23.5	-	23.5	0.0	23.6	0.4	23.6	0.0	23.7	0.4	23.7	0.0	23.7	0.0	24.0	1.3	24.2	0.8	24.3	0.4	24.5	0.8	24.5	0.0
1948	24.9	1.6	25.1	0.8	25.2	0.4	25.3	0.4	25.5	0.8	25.7	0.8	25.9	0.8	26.0	0.4	26.1	0.4	26.3	0.8	26.3	0.0	26.3	0.0
1949	26.5	0.8	26.5	0.0	26.5	0.0	26.5	0.0	26.5	0.0	26.5	0.0	26.5	0.0	26.4	-0.4	26.3	-0.4	26.3	0.0	26.4	0.4	26.4	0.0
1950	26.5	0.4	26.6	0.4	26.7	0.4	26.7	0.0	27.0	1.1	27.2	0.7	27.6	1.5	28.1	1.8	28.4	1.1	28.7	1.1	28.9	0.7	29.4	1.7
1951	29.8	1.4	29.9	0.3	29.9	0.0	29.9	0.0	29.9	0.0	29.9	0.0	29.9	0.0	29.9	0.0	29.9	0.0	29.9	0.0	29.9	0.0	29.9	0.0
1952	29.9	0.0	29.9	0.0	29.9	0.0	29.8	-0.3	29.9	0.3	29.9	0.0	29.8	-0.3	29.8	0.0	29.8	0.0	29.8	0.0	29.8	0.0	29.8	0.0
1953	29.8	0.0	29.8	0.0	29.9	0.3	30.1	0.7	30.1	0.0	30.3	0.7	30.4	0.3	30.6	0.7	30.8	0.7	30.8	0.0	30.8	0.0	30.8	0.0
1954	30.8	0.0	30.8	0.0	30.8	0.0	30.8	0.0	30.8	0.0	30.8	0.0	30.8	0.0	30.9	0.3	31.0	0.3	31.0	0.0	31.0	0.0	31.0	0.0
1955	31.2	0.6	31.3	0.3	31.5	0.6	31.6	0.3	31.7	0.3	31.9	0.6	32.0	0.3	32.3	0.9	32.8	1.5	33.0	0.6	33.0	0.0	33.1	0.3
1956	33.4	0.9	33.5	0.3	33.6	0.3	33.7	0.3	33.7	0.0	33.9	0.6	33.9	0.0	33.9	0.0	33.9	0.0	33.9	0.0	34.1	0.6	34.1	0.0
1957	34.2	0.3	34.2	0.0	34.3	0.3	34.3	0.0	34.3	0.0	34.4	0.3	34.4	0.0	34.3	-0.3	34.3	0.0	34.3	0.0	34.3	0.0	34.4	0.3
1958	34.5	0.3	34.5	0.0	34.5	0.0	34.5	0.0	34.5	0.0	34.5	0.0	34.5	0.0	34.5	0.0	34.6	0.3	34.6	0.0	34.7	0.3	34.9	0.6
1959	35.0	0.3	35.2	0.6	35.2	0.0	35.2	0.0	35.3	0.3	35.4	0.3	35.5	0.3	35.5	0.0	35.5	0.0	35.5	0.0	35.5	0.0	35.6	0.3
1960	35.8	0.6	35.9	0.3	35.9	0.0	35.9	0.0	35.9	0.0	35.9	0.0	35.9	0.0	36.0	0.3	36.1	0.3	36.1	0.0	36.1	0.0	36.1	0.0
1961	36.0	-0.3	36.0	0.0	36.0	0.0	36.0	0.0	36.1	0.3	36.1	0.0	36.1	0.0	36.2	0.3	36.2	0.0	36.3	0.3	36.3	0.0	36.3	0.0
1962	36.3	0.0	36.4	0.3	36.4	0.0	36.5	0.3	36.5	0.0	36.5	0.0	36.5	0.0	36.5	0.0	36.5	0.0	36.4	-0.3	36.4	0.0	36.4	0.0
1963	36.5	0.3	36.5	0.0	36.5	0.0	36.6	0.3	36.7	0.3	36.7	0.0	36.7	0.0	36.7	0.0	36.6	-0.3	36.6	0.0	36.7	0.3	36.7	0.0
1964	36.5	-0.5	36.7	0.5	36.7	0.0	36.8	0.3	36.8	0.0	36.7	-0.3	36.7	0.0	36.7	0.0	36.8	0.3	36.8	0.0	36.8	0.0	36.9	0.3
1965	36.9	0.0	36.9	0.0	36.9	0.0	36.9	0.0	36.9	0.0	36.9	0.0	36.9	0.0	37.1	0.5	37.2	0.3	37.2	0.0	37.2	0.0	37.3	0.3
1966	37.3	0.0	37.4	0.3	37.5	0.3	37.5	0.0	37.5	0.0	37.7	0.5	37.7	0.0	37.8	0.3	37.8	0.0	37.8	0.0	38.0	0.5	37.9	-0.3
1967	38.0	0.3	38.0	0.0	38.1	0.3	38.1	0.0	38.2	0.3	38.2	0.0	38.5	0.8	38.5	0.0	38.6	0.3	38.6	0.0	38.6	0.0	38.8	0.5
1968	38.9	0.3	38.9	0.0	39.0	0.3	39.0	0.0	39.2	0.5	39.0	-0.5	39.1	0.3	39.6	1.3	39.6	0.0	39.7	0.3	40.1	1.0	40.1	0.0
1969	40.3	0.5	40.3	0.0	40.3	0.0	40.6	0.7	40.6	0.0	40.6	0.0	40.6	0.0	40.7	0.2	40.9	0.5	41.0	0.2	41.2	0.5	41.2	0.0
1970	41.5	0.7	41.5	0.0	41.7	0.5	42.0	0.7	42.1	0.2	42.1	0.0	42.2	0.2	42.2	0.0	42.4	0.5	42.5	0.2	42.5	0.0	42.6	0.2
1971	43.0	0.9	43.5	1.2	43.8	0.7	44.0	0.5	44.0	0.0	44.1	0.2	44.1	0.0	44.3	0.5	44.0	-0.7	44.0	0.0	44.0	0.0	44.3	0.7
1972	44.0	-0.7	44.5	1.1	44.6	0.2	44.9	0.7	45.0	0.2	45.0	0.0	45.1	0.2	45.1	0.0	45.1	0.0	45.4	0.7	45.5	0.2	45.6	0.2
1973	46.1	1.1	46.6	1.1	46.9	0.6	47.2	0.6	47.4	0.4	47.5	0.2	47.5	0.0	47.5	0.0	47.5	0.0	47.8	0.6	47.8	0.0	47.9	0.2
1974	48.8	1.9	49.2	0.8	50.1	1.8	50.4	0.6	50.9	1.0	51.4	1.0	51.9	1.0	52.6	1.3	53.4	1.5	54.2	1.5	54.2	0.0	54.9	1.3
1975	55.7	1.5	56.3	1.1	56.3	0.0	57.0	1.2	57.2	0.4	57.9	1.2	58.0	0.2	58.4	0.7	59.1	1.2	59.7	1.0	59.9	0.3	59.9	0.0
1976	61.0	1.8	61.4	0.7	61.6	0.3	61.9	0.5	62.0	0.2	62.2	0.3	62.5	0.5	63.2	1.1	63.7	0.8	63.7	0.0	64.5	1.3	64.7	0.3
1977	65.2	0.8	64.6	-0.9	65.4	1.2	68.1	4.1	68.5	0.6	69.1	0.9	70.5	2.0	70.8	0.4	71.2	0.6	72.0	1.1	71.0	-1.4	71.2	0.3
1978	72.7	2.1	73.0	0.4	73.9	1.2	74.3	0.5	74.5	0.3	75.0	0.7	75.4	0.5	75.8	0.5	77.6	2.4	77.6	0.0	78.4	1.0	79.2	1.0
1979	80.4	1.5	80.8	0.5	81.6	1.0	82.4	1.0	82.7	0.4	83.0	0.4	84.5	1.8	85.3	0.9	85.8	0.6	84.8	-1.2	84.8	0.0	86.9	2.5
1980	88.0	1.3	88.6	0.7	88.7	0.1	90.1	1.6	88.2	-2.1	88.2	0.0	88.2	0.0	88.1	-0.1	88.2	0.1	89.5	1.5	89.6	0.1	89.6	0.0
1981	91.8	2.5	92.0	0.2	93.8	2.0	94.3	0.5	95.9	1.7	96.1	0.2	96.2	0.1	96.2	0.0	97.9	1.8	98.2	0.3	98.4	0.2	98.7	0.3
1982	98.7	0.0	98.8	0.1	98.8	0.0	99.0	0.2	99.2	0.2	99.3	0.1	99.4	0.1	101.2	1.8	101.2	0.0	101.2	0.0	101.5	0.3	101.5	0.0
1983	101.6	0.1	101.3	-0.3	103.8	2.5	105.7	1.8	106.5	0.8	107.9	1.3	108.3	0.4	108.3	0.0	108.3	0.0	108.7	0.4	108.9	0.2	109.0	0.1
1984	109.0	0.0	108.8	-0.2	109.0	0.2	109.3	0.3	109.5	0.2	109.8	0.3	109.8	0.0	110.5	0.6	111.0	0.5	111.0	0.0	111.0	0.0	111.1	0.1
1985	111.7	0.5	111.8	0.1	111.9	0.1	112.1	0.2	112.3	0.2	113.9	1.4	113.8	-0.1	114.2	0.4	114.5	0.3	114.7	0.2	114.9	0.2	115.8	0.8
1986	116.8	0.9	115.5	-1.1	116.8	1.1	117.6	0.7	117.7	0.1	118.3	0.5	119.2	0.8	119.0	-0.2	118.9	-0.1	119.6	0.6	118.6	-0.8	118.3	-0.3
1987	119.6	1.1	119.5	-0.1	119.8	0.3	120.9	0.9	121.4	0.4	121.8	0.3	121.5	-0.2	122.4	0.7	122.2	-0.2	122.5	0.2	122.7	0.2	122.7	0.0
1988	123.1	0.3	124.0	0.7	124.0	0.0	123.7	-0.2	124.4	0.6	125.4	0.8	125.9	0.4	125.1	-0.6	125.2	0.1	125.5	0.2	125.7	0.2	126.2	0.4
1989	126.1	-0.1	125.6	-0.4	126.3	0.6	126.5	0.2	125.7	-0.6	126.9	1.0	126.8	-0.1	127.5	0.6	127.7	0.2	127.9	0.2	128.2	0.2	128.6	0.3
1990	128.5	-0.1	128.6	0.1	129.4	0.6	129.4	0.0	129.6	0.2	130.0	0.3	130.5	0.4	130.4	-0.1	130.4	0.0	130.5	0.1	130.2	-0.2	130.7	0.4
1991	129.5	-0.9	129.7	0.2	129.9	0.2	130.4	0.4	130.6	0.2	130.2	-0.3	130.1	-0.1	130.0	-0.1	130.3	0.2	130.4	0.1	130.3	-0.1	130.4	0.1

[Continued]

Clay Construction Products Ex. Refractories
Producer Price Index
Base 1982 = 100
[Continued]

For 1947-1995. Columns headed % show percentile change in the index from the previous period for which an index is available.

Year	Jan Index	%	Feb Index	%	Mar Index	%	Apr Index	%	May Index	%	Jun Index	%	Jul Index	%	Aug Index	%	Sep Index	%	Oct Index	%	Nov Index	%	Dec Index	%
1992	130.3	-0.1	130.7	0.3	131.2	0.4	131.0	-0.2	132.0	0.8	132.4	0.3	132.5	0.1	132.7	0.2	132.6	-0.1	132.8	0.2	132.9	0.1	132.8	-0.1
1993	133.4	0.5	134.1	0.5	134.0	-0.1	134.7	0.5	134.9	0.1	135.3	0.3	135.5	0.1	135.8	0.2	135.9	0.1	136.1	0.1	136.1	0.0	135.7	-0.3
1994	135.9	0.1	136.7	0.6	138.2	1.1	138.1	-0.1	138.5	0.3	138.7	0.1	138.8	0.1	138.8	0.0	138.8	0.0	138.9	0.1	138.8	-0.1	138.9	0.1
1995	139.3	0.3	139.7	0.3	140.6	0.6	141.2	0.4	141.4	0.1	141.8	0.3	141.9	0.1	142.0	0.1	142.1	0.1	142.0	-0.1	142.1	0.1	142.1	0.0

Source: U.S. Department of Labor, Bureau of Labor Statistics, Division of Industry Prices and Price Indexes. n.e.c. stands for not elsewhere classified. - indicates no data collected for period or unavailable.

Refractories

Producer Price Index
Base 1982 = 100

For 1947-1995. Columns headed % show percentile change in the index from the previous period for which an index is available.

Year	Jan Index	%	Feb Index	%	Mar Index	%	Apr Index	%	May Index	%	Jun Index	%	Jul Index	%	Aug Index	%	Sep Index	%	Oct Index	%	Nov Index	%	Dec Index	%
1947	13.4	-	13.4	0.0	13.4	0.0	14.5	8.2	14.5	0.0	14.5	0.0	14.5	0.0	14.5	0.0	14.5	0.0	14.5	0.0	15.0	3.4	15.1	0.7
1948	15.1	0.0	15.1	0.0	15.1	0.0	15.1	0.0	15.1	0.0	15.1	0.0	16.1	6.6	16.5	2.5	16.5	0.0	16.5	0.0	16.5	0.0	16.5	0.0
1949	16.5	0.0	16.5	0.0	16.5	0.0	16.5	0.0	16.5	0.0	16.5	0.0	16.5	0.0	16.5	0.0	16.5	0.0	16.5	0.0	16.5	0.0	16.5	0.0
1950	17.6	6.7	17.8	1.1	17.8	0.0	17.8	0.0	17.8	0.0	17.8	0.0	17.8	0.0	17.8	0.0	17.8	0.0	19.1	7.3	19.6	2.6	19.6	0.0
1951	19.6	0.0	19.6	0.0	19.6	0.0	19.6	0.0	19.6	0.0	19.6	0.0	19.6	0.0	19.6	0.0	19.6	0.0	19.6	0.0	19.6	0.0	19.6	0.0
1952	19.6	0.0	19.6	0.0	19.6	0.0	19.6	0.0	19.6	0.0	19.6	0.0	19.6	0.0	19.6	0.0	19.6	0.0	20.5	4.6	20.5	0.0	20.5	0.0
1953	20.5	0.0	20.5	0.0	20.5	0.0	20.5	0.0	20.5	0.0	20.5	0.0	22.5	9.8	22.5	0.0	22.5	0.0	22.5	0.0	22.5	0.0	22.5	0.0
1954	22.5	0.0	22.5	0.0	22.5	0.0	22.5	0.0	22.5	0.0	22.5	0.0	22.5	0.0	22.5	0.0	23.6	4.9	23.6	0.0	23.6	0.0	23.6	0.0
1955	23.6	0.0	23.6	0.0	23.6	0.0	23.6	0.0	23.6	0.0	23.6	0.0	24.9	5.5	25.2	1.2	25.2	0.0	25.2	0.0	25.2	0.0	25.2	0.0
1956	25.2	0.0	25.2	0.0	25.2	0.0	25.2	0.0	25.2	0.0	25.2	0.0	26.2	4.0	26.5	1.1	26.5	0.0	26.5	0.0	26.5	0.0	26.5	0.0
1957	26.5	0.0	26.5	0.0	26.5	0.0	27.9	5.3	27.9	0.0	27.9	0.0	27.9	0.0	27.9	0.0	27.9	0.0	27.9	0.0	27.9	0.0	27.9	0.0
1958	27.9	0.0	27.9	0.0	27.9	0.0	27.9	0.0	27.9	0.0	27.9	0.0	27.9	0.0	27.9	0.0	29.0	3.9	29.0	0.0	29.0	0.0	29.0	0.0
1959	29.0	0.0	29.0	0.0	29.0	0.0	29.0	0.0	29.0	0.0	29.0	0.0	29.0	0.0	29.0	0.0	29.0	0.0	29.0	0.0	29.0	0.0	29.0	0.0
1960	29.0	0.0	29.0	0.0	29.0	0.0	29.0	0.0	29.0	0.0	29.0	0.0	29.0	0.0	29.0	0.0	29.0	0.0	29.0	0.0	29.0	0.0	29.0	0.0
1961	29.0	0.0	29.0	0.0	29.0	0.0	29.0	0.0	28.7	-1.0	28.7	0.0	28.7	0.0	28.7	0.0	28.7	0.0	28.7	0.0	28.7	0.0	28.7	0.0
1962	28.7	0.0	28.7	0.0	28.7	0.0	28.7	0.0	28.7	0.0	28.7	0.0	28.7	0.0	28.7	0.0	28.7	0.0	28.7	0.0	28.7	0.0	28.7	0.0
1963	28.7	0.0	28.7	0.0	28.7	0.0	28.7	0.0	28.7	0.0	28.7	0.0	28.4	-1.0	28.4	0.0	28.4	0.0	28.4	0.0	28.4	0.0	28.4	0.0
1964	28.4	0.0	28.4	0.0	28.4	0.0	28.9	1.8	28.9	0.0	28.9	0.0	28.9	0.0	28.9	0.0	28.9	0.0	29.0	0.3	29.1	0.3	29.1	0.0
1965	29.1	0.0	29.1	0.0	29.1	0.0	29.1	0.0	29.1	0.0	29.1	0.0	29.1	0.0	29.1	0.0	29.1	0.0	29.1	0.0	29.1	0.0	29.1	0.0
1966	29.1	0.0	29.1	0.0	29.1	0.0	29.2	0.3	29.4	0.7	29.4	0.0	29.4	0.0	29.4	0.0	29.4	0.0	29.4	0.0	29.4	0.0	29.4	0.0
1967	29.6	0.7	29.6	0.0	29.6	0.0	29.6	0.0	29.6	0.0	29.6	0.0	29.6	0.0	29.6	0.0	29.6	0.0	29.6	0.0	29.9	1.0	29.9	0.0
1968	30.1	0.7	31.7	5.3	31.8	0.3	31.8	0.0	31.8	0.0	31.8	0.0	31.8	0.0	31.8	0.0	31.8	0.0	31.8	0.0	31.8	0.0	31.8	0.0
1969	31.8	0.0	31.8	0.0	31.8	0.0	32.1	0.9	32.1	0.0	32.1	0.0	32.1	0.0	33.0	2.8	33.1	0.3	33.1	0.0	33.1	0.0	34.1	3.0
1970	34.9	2.3	35.3	1.1	35.4	0.3	35.6	0.6	35.6	0.0	35.5	-0.3	35.6	0.3	35.6	0.0	35.6	0.0	35.6	0.0	37.6	5.6	37.6	0.0
1971	37.6	0.0	37.6	0.0	37.6	0.0	37.6	0.0	37.6	0.0	37.7	0.3	37.7	0.0	37.7	0.0	37.7	0.0	37.7	0.0	37.7	0.0	37.7	0.0
1972	37.7	0.0	37.7	0.0	37.7	0.0	37.7	0.0	37.7	0.0	37.7	0.0	37.7	0.0	38.5	2.1	39.2	1.8	39.2	0.0	39.2	0.0	39.2	0.0
1973	40.4	3.1	40.4	0.0	40.4	0.0	40.4	0.0	40.4	0.0	40.4	0.0	40.4	0.0	40.4	0.0	40.4	0.0	40.4	0.0	40.4	0.0	40.4	0.0
1974	40.4	0.0	40.4	0.0	40.4	0.0	40.4	0.0	40.4	0.0	40.4	0.0	40.9	1.2	40.9	0.0	45.5	11.2	46.6	2.4	46.8	0.4	47.6	1.7
1975	47.8	0.4	48.4	1.3	48.5	0.2	48.5	0.0	48.6	0.2	48.6	0.0	48.6	0.0	48.6	0.0	48.7	0.2	48.7	0.0	52.5	7.8	53.3	1.5
1976	53.3	0.0	53.3	0.0	53.4	0.2	53.5	0.2	53.5	0.0	53.5	0.0	53.6	0.2	53.8	0.4	56.0	4.1	56.7	1.3	57.2	0.9	57.2	0.0
1977	57.3	0.2	57.3	0.0	57.3	0.0	57.3	0.0	57.6	0.5	58.3	1.2	58.5	0.3	58.9	0.7	61.4	4.2	61.8	0.7	62.1	0.5	62.1	0.0
1978	62.2	0.2	62.3	0.2	62.3	0.0	62.4	0.2	62.5	0.2	62.5	0.0	63.2	1.1	66.0	4.4	66.4	0.6	66.9	0.8	67.1	0.3	67.1	0.0
1979	67.5	0.6	67.6	0.1	67.7	0.1	67.8	0.1	67.8	0.0	69.0	1.8	71.4	3.5	71.7	0.4	71.9	0.3	72.6	1.0	73.4	1.1	73.6	0.3
1980	73.7	0.1	74.5	1.1	75.3	1.1	77.6	3.1	78.4	1.0	78.9	0.6	79.7	1.0	80.3	0.8	80.3	0.0	81.1	1.0	81.1	0.0	81.1	0.0
1981	83.8	3.3	87.1	3.9	87.9	0.9	87.9	0.0	90.2	2.6	91.1	1.0	91.1	0.0	91.1	0.0	91.1	0.0	91.3	0.2	91.6	0.3	92.4	0.9
1982	94.0	1.7	99.4	5.7	100.1	0.7	100.5	0.4	100.7	0.2	101.0	0.3	101.0	0.0	101.1	0.1	101.1	0.0	101.1	0.0	100.0	-1.1	100.0	0.0
1983	100.2	0.2	100.2	0.0	100.2	0.0	100.3	0.1	100.3	0.0	99.9	-0.4	100.3	0.4	100.7	0.4	100.9	0.2	102.3	1.4	104.8	2.4	104.8	0.0
1984	105.0	0.2	105.6	0.6	107.1	1.4	107.3	0.2	107.3	0.0	107.3	0.0	107.3	0.0	107.3	0.0	107.3	0.0	107.3	0.0	108.4	1.0	108.4	0.0
1985	108.6	0.2	108.6	0.0	108.9	0.3	109.5	0.6	110.1	0.5	110.1	0.0	110.1	0.0	110.1	0.0	110.1	0.0	110.1	0.0	110.1	0.0	110.2	0.1
1986	110.2	0.0	110.2	0.0	110.2	0.0	110.3	0.1	110.5	0.2	110.5	0.0	110.5	0.0	110.5	0.0	110.4	-0.1	109.9	-0.5	109.3	-0.5	109.7	0.4
1987	109.9	0.2	109.9	0.0	109.9	0.0	110.0	0.1	110.0	0.0	110.4	0.4	110.6	0.2	110.8	0.2	110.9	0.1	110.9	0.0	111.1	0.2	111.9	0.7
1988	112.6	0.6	112.6	0.0	112.5	-0.1	113.5	0.9	113.7	0.2	113.8	0.1	113.8	0.0	113.8	0.0	114.1	0.3	115.1	0.9	115.2	0.1	115.4	0.2
1989	118.1	2.3	119.0	0.8	119.2	0.2	119.6	0.3	119.6	0.0	119.6	0.0	119.8	0.2	119.3	-0.4	119.4	0.1	119.6	0.2	119.6	0.0	119.6	0.0
1990	120.3	0.6	120.9	0.5	121.5	0.5	122.0	0.4	122.1	0.1	122.8	0.6	122.8	0.0	122.9	0.1	122.7	-0.2	122.8	0.1	123.4	0.5	123.4	0.0
1991	124.7	1.1	125.1	0.3	125.3	0.2	125.4	0.1	125.8	0.3	125.3	-0.4	125.3	0.0	125.4	0.1	125.5	0.1	125.5	0.1	125.5	0.0	125.9	0.3

[Continued]

Refractories
Producer Price Index
Base 1982 = 100
[Continued]

For 1947-1995. Columns headed % show percentile change in the index from the previous period for which an index is available.

Year	Jan Index	%	Feb Index	%	Mar Index	%	Apr Index	%	May Index	%	Jun Index	%	Jul Index	%	Aug Index	%	Sep Index	%	Oct Index	%	Nov Index	%	Dec Index	%
1992	126.1	0.2	125.6	-0.4	126.8	1.0	126.7	-0.1	126.7	0.0	126.8	0.1	126.3	-0.4	127.6	1.0	126.3	-1.0	126.3	0.0	125.2	-0.9	125.8	0.5
1993	126.1	0.2	126.1	0.0	126.5	0.3	126.5	0.0	127.2	0.6	127.4	0.2	127.7	0.2	127.9	0.2	127.6	-0.2	127.9	0.2	127.5	-0.3	127.4	-0.1
1994	128.5	0.9	128.0	-0.4	127.7	-0.2	127.8	0.1	127.7	-0.1	127.9	0.2	128.3	0.3	127.8	-0.4	128.4	0.5	128.4	0.0	128.9	0.4	128.9	0.0
1995	128.8	-0.1	129.8	0.8	131.5	1.3	132.4	0.7	132.4	0.0	132.5	0.1	132.5	0.0	132.3	-0.2	132.9	0.5	132.7	-0.2	132.8	0.1	134.0	0.9

Source: U.S. Department of Labor, Bureau of Labor Statistics, Division of Industry Prices and Price Indexes. n.e.c. stands for not elsewhere classified. - indicates no data collected for period or unavailable.

Asphalt Felts and Coatings
Producer Price Index
Base 1982 = 100

For 1926-1995. Columns headed % show percentile change in the index from the previous period for which an index is available.

Year	Jan Index	%	Feb Index	%	Mar Index	%	Apr Index	%	May Index	%	Jun Index	%	Jul Index	%	Aug Index	%	Sep Index	%	Oct Index	%	Nov Index	%	Dec Index	%
1926	20.6	-	20.5	-0.5	20.8	1.5	21.0	1.0	21.2	1.0	21.3	0.5	21.4	0.5	21.4	0.0	21.4	0.0	21.4	0.0	21.4	0.0	21.3	-0.5
1927	20.8	-2.3	20.8	0.0	20.5	-1.4	20.1	-2.0	20.3	1.0	20.3	0.0	20.2	-0.5	20.3	0.5	20.3	0.0	20.3	0.0	17.7	-12.8	17.8	0.6
1928	18.0	1.1	17.6	-2.2	15.6	-11.4	15.8	1.3	15.8	0.0	18.9	19.6	19.2	1.6	19.2	0.0	19.3	0.5	19.4	0.5	19.4	0.0	15.9	-18.0
1929	14.4	-9.4	14.3	-0.7	14.3	0.0	15.4	7.7	16.1	4.5	16.2	0.6	16.4	1.2	16.4	0.0	16.4	0.0	16.4	0.0	16.4	0.0	16.4	0.0
1930	15.6	-4.9	15.6	0.0	15.6	0.0	15.6	0.0	15.6	0.0	15.6	0.0	15.6	0.0	15.8	1.3	16.4	3.8	17.3	5.5	17.3	0.0	17.3	0.0
1931	16.7	-3.5	16.7	0.0	16.7	0.0	16.7	0.0	16.7	0.0	16.7	0.0	16.7	0.0	16.7	0.0	16.7	0.0	16.7	0.0	16.7	0.0	16.7	0.0
1932	15.8	-5.4	15.3	-3.2	15.5	1.3	15.6	0.6	15.3	-1.9	14.3	-6.5	13.2	-7.7	13.6	3.0	15.1	11.0	16.1	6.6	17.0	5.6	16.9	-0.6
1933	15.7	-7.1	13.7	-12.7	13.8	0.7	13.9	0.7	15.1	8.6	15.8	4.6	16.0	1.3	16.4	2.5	16.5	0.6	16.9	2.4	17.1	1.2	17.1	0.0
1934	17.2	0.6	16.2	-5.8	15.2	-6.2	15.4	1.3	16.2	5.2	16.6	2.5	17.0	2.4	17.5	2.9	17.7	1.1	17.7	0.0	17.7	0.0	17.8	0.6
1935	17.9	0.6	17.8	-0.6	17.7	-0.6	17.7	0.0	18.0	1.7	18.1	0.6	18.0	-0.6	17.5	-2.8	17.5	0.0	17.7	1.1	17.8	0.6	16.7	-6.2
1936	16.5	-1.2	16.4	-0.6	16.4	0.0	17.2	4.9	17.5	1.7	17.5	0.0	17.5	0.0	17.6	0.6	17.7	0.6	18.3	3.4	18.4	0.5	18.4	0.0
1937	18.5	0.5	18.7	1.1	19.3	3.2	19.3	0.0	19.8	2.6	20.0	1.0	20.0	0.0	20.0	0.0	19.6	-2.0	19.1	-2.6	18.3	-4.2	16.3	-10.9
1938	16.1	-1.2	15.9	-1.2	15.0	-5.7	15.2	1.3	15.3	0.7	15.3	0.0	15.3	0.0	15.3	0.0	15.3	0.0	15.3	0.0	15.3	0.0	15.3	0.0
1939	15.5	1.3	15.5	0.0	15.5	0.0	15.6	0.6	15.9	1.9	15.9	0.0	15.9	0.0	16.0	0.6	16.2	1.3	16.3	0.6	16.3	0.0	16.6	1.8
1940	17.0	2.4	17.0	0.0	17.5	2.9	17.8	1.7	17.8	0.0	17.8	0.0	17.7	-0.6	17.4	-1.7	17.3	-0.6	17.1	-1.2	17.1	0.0	17.1	0.0
1941	17.2	0.6	17.2	0.0	16.9	-1.7	16.7	-1.2	17.0	1.8	17.5	2.9	18.0	2.9	18.5	2.8	18.8	1.6	19.5	3.7	19.5	0.0	18.3	-6.2
1942	17.5	-4.4	17.5	0.0	17.5	0.0	17.5	0.0	17.5	0.0	17.5	0.0	17.5	0.0	17.5	0.0	17.5	0.0	17.5	0.0	17.5	0.0	17.5	0.0
1943	17.5	0.0	17.5	0.0	17.5	0.0	17.5	0.0	17.5	0.0	17.5	0.0	17.5	0.0	17.5	0.0	17.5	0.0	17.5	0.0	17.5	0.0	17.5	0.0
1944	17.5	0.0	17.5	0.0	17.5	0.0	17.5	0.0	17.5	0.0	17.5	0.0	17.5	0.0	17.6	0.6	17.9	1.7	18.0	0.6	18.0	0.0	18.0	0.0
1945	18.0	0.0	18.0	0.0	18.0	0.0	18.0	0.0	18.0	0.0	18.0	0.0	18.0	0.0	18.0	0.0	18.0	0.0	18.0	0.0	18.0	0.0	18.0	0.0
1946	18.0	0.0	18.0	0.0	18.0	0.0	18.0	0.0	18.5	2.8	18.9	2.2	19.0	0.5	19.1	0.5	19.1	0.0	19.2	0.5	19.3	0.5	20.7	7.3
1947	20.5	-1.0	20.6	0.5	21.4	3.9	21.6	0.9	21.6	0.0	21.6	0.0	21.6	0.0	21.5	-0.5	21.5	0.0	21.5	0.0	21.5	0.0	22.6	5.1
1948	23.2	2.7	23.2	0.0	23.2	0.0	23.2	0.0	23.2	0.0	23.6	1.7	24.2	2.5	23.6	-2.5	23.6	0.0	23.6	0.0	23.6	0.0	23.6	0.0
1949	23.6	0.0	23.6	0.0	23.6	0.0	23.6	0.0	23.6	0.0	23.6	0.0	23.4	-0.8	23.4	0.0	23.4	0.0	23.2	-0.9	23.2	0.0	23.2	0.0
1950	23.2	0.0	23.2	0.0	23.2	0.0	22.9	-1.3	22.5	-1.7	22.5	0.0	22.5	0.0	22.9	1.8	22.9	0.0	23.2	1.3	24.0	3.4	24.0	0.0
1951	24.0	0.0	24.0	0.0	24.0	0.0	24.0	0.0	24.0	0.0	24.0	0.0	24.0	0.0	24.0	0.0	24.0	0.0	24.0	0.0	24.0	0.0	22.5	-6.3
1952	22.5	0.0	22.5	0.0	22.5	0.0	22.5	0.0	22.5	0.0	24.2	7.6	24.2	0.0	24.2	0.0	24.2	0.0	24.2	0.0	24.2	0.0	24.2	0.0
1953	24.2	0.0	24.2	0.0	24.2	0.0	24.2	0.0	24.2	0.0	24.2	0.0	24.1	-0.4	24.1	0.0	25.0	3.7	25.1	0.4	25.1	0.0	25.1	0.0
1954	25.1	0.0	25.1	0.0	25.1	0.0	24.7	-1.6	21.9	-11.3	21.5	-1.8	22.5	4.7	22.5	0.0	23.7	5.3	24.2	2.1	24.2	0.0	24.2	0.0
1955	24.2	0.0	22.9	-5.4	22.5	-1.7	22.5	0.0	24.1	7.1	24.3	0.8	25.3	4.1	26.1	3.2	26.1	0.0	26.1	0.0	23.0	-11.9	23.0	0.0
1956	22.7	-1.3	22.7	0.0	24.3	7.0	25.5	4.9	25.5	0.0	25.5	0.0	26.9	5.5	26.8	-0.4	26.8	0.0	26.8	0.0	26.1	-2.6	26.1	0.0
1957	25.4	-2.7	26.3	3.5	26.9	2.3	27.7	3.0	28.7	3.6	28.7	0.0	28.7	0.0	28.7	0.0	28.4	-1.0	28.4	0.0	28.4	0.0	28.4	0.0
1958	28.4	0.0	28.4	0.0	24.4	-14.1	24.4	0.0	24.2	-0.8	23.5	-2.9	23.5	0.0	23.5	0.0	27.0	14.9	27.0	0.0	27.0	0.0	27.0	0.0
1959	27.0	0.0	27.3	1.1	27.2	-0.4	28.8	5.9	28.8	0.0	25.9	-10.1	25.5	-1.5	25.5	0.0	25.3	-0.8	25.3	0.0	25.9	2.4	25.9	0.0
1960	25.9	0.0	24.5	-5.4	24.5	0.0	24.3	-0.8	24.3	0.0	24.3	0.0	24.3	0.0	24.3	0.0	24.3	0.0	24.3	0.0	24.3	0.0	24.3	0.0
1961	26.0	7.0	26.0	0.0	26.0	0.0	26.0	0.0	25.8	-0.8	25.8	0.0	26.0	0.8	26.0	0.0	26.0	0.0	27.5	5.8	27.5	0.0	27.5	0.0
1962	27.3	-0.7	27.1	-0.7	27.1	0.0	27.1	0.0	26.4	-2.6	25.5	-3.4	23.9	-6.3	23.9	0.0	23.9	0.0	23.9	0.0	23.9	0.0	23.9	0.0
1963	23.9	0.0	25.1	5.0	25.1	0.0	25.1	0.0	24.7	-1.6	23.8	-3.6	23.5	-1.3	23.5	0.0	23.5	0.0	23.3	-0.9	23.3	0.0	23.3	0.0
1964	23.3	0.0	23.3	0.0	23.1	-0.9	23.1	0.0	23.1	0.0	23.1	0.0	23.7	2.6	24.3	2.5	24.3	0.0	24.3	0.0	24.3	0.0	24.3	0.0
1965	24.3	0.0	24.3	0.0	24.5	0.8	24.6	0.4	24.6	0.0	24.6	0.0	24.6	0.0	24.6	0.0	25.4	3.3	25.3	-0.4	25.3	0.0	25.3	0.0
1966	25.3	0.0	25.3	0.0	25.3	0.0	25.3	0.0	25.2	-0.4	25.2	0.0	26.1	3.6	26.1	0.0	26.1	0.0	26.1	0.0	26.1	0.0	25.6	-1.9
1967	25.6	0.0	25.3	-1.2	25.3	0.0	25.3	0.0	23.6	-6.7	23.6	0.0	24.4	3.4	24.4	0.0	25.3	3.7	25.3	0.0	26.5	4.7	26.5	0.0
1968	26.6	0.4	26.2	-1.5	26.2	0.0	26.1	-0.4	26.1	0.0	25.8	-1.1	26.1	1.2	26.1	0.0	25.4	-2.7	25.4	0.0	25.4	0.0	25.4	0.0
1969	25.4	0.0	26.1	2.8	26.0	-0.4	26.0	0.0	25.6	-1.5	26.3	2.7	26.6	1.1	25.1	-5.6	25.1	0.0	25.1	0.0	25.1	0.0	27.1	8.0
1970	27.2	0.4	26.9	-1.1	26.1	-3.0	25.4	-2.7	25.4	0.0	24.5	-3.5	24.3	-0.8	24.9	2.5	25.4	2.0	25.6	0.8	26.5	3.5	26.9	1.5

[Continued]

Asphalt Felts and Coatings
Producer Price Index
Base 1982 = 100
[Continued]

For 1926-1995. Columns headed % show percentile change in the index from the previous period for which an index is available.

Year	Jan Index	%	Feb Index	%	Mar Index	%	Apr Index	%	May Index	%	Jun Index	%	Jul Index	%	Aug Index	%	Sep Index	%	Oct Index	%	Nov Index	%	Dec Index	%
1971	27.3	1.5	27.3	0.0	31.0	13.6	31.0	0.0	31.0	0.0	32.8	5.8	32.9	0.3	32.9	0.0	32.9	0.0	32.9	0.0	32.9	0.0	32.9	0.0
1972	32.9	0.0	32.9	0.0	32.9	0.0	32.9	0.0	32.9	0.0	32.9	0.0	32.9	0.0	32.9	0.0	32.9	0.0	32.9	0.0	32.9	0.0	32.9	0.0
1973	32.9	0.0	32.9	0.0	32.9	0.0	33.7	2.4	34.3	1.8	34.3	0.0	34.2	-0.3	34.2	0.0	34.2	0.0	34.3	0.3	35.1	2.3	35.1	0.0
1974	37.7	7.4	40.1	6.4	43.0	7.2	48.2	12.1	50.2	4.1	50.8	1.2	51.8	2.0	52.9	2.1	52.9	0.0	54.1	2.3	54.3	0.4	54.3	0.0
1975	54.3	0.0	54.7	0.7	54.7	0.0	57.2	4.6	57.2	0.0	57.2	0.0	57.5	0.5	56.9	-1.0	57.4	0.9	58.1	1.2	57.5	-1.0	57.5	0.0
1976	57.5	0.0	57.6	0.2	59.3	3.0	60.1	1.3	59.6	-0.8	59.6	0.0	59.6	0.0	62.1	4.2	61.6	-0.8	61.7	0.2	60.1	-2.6	58.9	-2.0
1977	57.9	-1.7	57.9	0.0	61.0	5.4	61.0	0.0	61.0	0.0	61.8	1.3	63.6	2.9	63.6	0.0	67.0	5.3	69.1	3.1	69.1	0.0	69.1	0.0
1978	69.6	0.7	69.6	0.0	69.7	0.1	72.2	3.6	72.2	0.0	72.6	0.6	74.2	2.2	74.7	0.7	74.8	0.1	76.6	2.4	76.6	0.0	76.6	0.0
1979	77.0	0.5	79.8	3.6	76.1	-4.6	79.4	4.3	79.8	0.5	81.1	1.6	82.4	1.6	81.8	-0.7	83.6	2.2	84.7	1.3	87.2	3.0	87.0	-0.2
1980	89.5	2.9	93.5	4.5	97.6	4.4	102.6	5.1	100.7	-1.9	100.6	-0.1	103.9	3.3	103.2	-0.7	102.4	-0.8	102.5	0.1	99.7	-2.7	99.1	-0.6
1981	99.1	0.0	97.8	-1.3	98.0	0.2	104.4	6.5	102.3	-2.0	107.6	5.2	105.9	-1.6	105.6	-0.3	100.8	-4.5	101.1	0.3	103.0	1.9	101.8	-1.2
1982	100.7	-1.1	100.5	-0.2	99.0	-1.5	97.1	-1.9	96.8	-0.3	99.5	2.8	100.4	0.9	100.4	0.0	103.8	3.4	102.1	-1.6	100.2	-1.9	99.6	-0.6
1983	98.8	-0.8	95.5	-3.3	94.0	-1.6	96.4	2.6	95.4	-1.0	95.3	-0.1	96.7	1.5	96.2	-0.5	97.2	1.0	97.4	0.2	97.3	-0.1	96.4	-0.9
1984	96.6	0.2	98.5	2.0	96.8	-1.7	99.4	2.7	100.1	0.7	99.0	-1.1	99.0	0.0	102.5	3.5	102.4	-0.1	102.7	0.3	102.9	0.2	103.4	0.5
1985	102.8	-0.6	102.3	-0.5	101.9	-0.4	103.4	1.5	103.6	0.2	103.0	-0.6	103.0	0.0	102.5	-0.5	102.1	-0.4	101.7	-0.4	102.7	1.0	102.2	-0.5
1986	101.8	-0.4	101.8	0.0	100.6	-1.2	99.3	-1.3	99.3	0.0	97.3	-2.0	97.1	-0.2	97.3	0.2	96.6	-0.7	95.6	-1.0	94.6	-1.0	94.0	-0.6
1987	91.8	-2.3	91.5	-0.3	90.8	-0.8	91.4	0.7	91.3	-0.1	90.9	-0.4	90.6	-0.3	92.8	2.4	93.4	0.6	94.4	1.1	94.9	0.5	94.8	-0.1
1988	93.8	-1.1	92.7	-1.2	93.4	0.8	92.7	-0.7	93.1	0.4	94.6	1.6	95.8	1.3	95.6	-0.2	96.3	0.7	97.1	0.8	96.0	-1.1	95.4	-0.6
1989	95.0	-0.4	94.9	-0.1	94.2	-0.7	96.0	1.9	95.7	-0.3	95.9	0.2	95.8	-0.1	95.7	-0.1	96.2	0.5	96.6	0.4	96.7	0.1	97.1	0.4
1990	97.1	0.0	95.8	-1.3	95.7	-0.1	96.0	0.3	95.6	-0.4	94.9	-0.7	94.3	-0.6	95.9	1.7	96.5	0.6	100.4	4.0	101.5	1.1	101.7	0.2
1991	100.5	-1.2	100.0	-0.5	100.4	0.4	99.3	-1.1	97.9	-1.4	98.4	0.5	98.4	0.0	97.0	-1.4	97.2	0.2	97.1	-0.1	96.5	-0.6	96.0	-0.5
1992	96.0	0.0	95.6	-0.4	95.4	-0.2	95.1	-0.3	95.6	0.5	95.9	0.3	96.3	0.4	96.2	-0.1	96.0	-0.2	97.1	1.1	98.1	1.0	97.8	-0.3
1993	98.2	0.4	97.3	-0.9	97.6	0.3	96.9	-0.7	96.7	-0.2	96.8	0.1	97.0	0.2	97.1	0.1	96.5	-0.6	96.1	-0.4	95.6	-0.5	95.8	0.2
1994	95.8	0.0	94.9	-0.9	94.5	-0.4	94.6	0.1	94.9	0.3	95.2	0.3	95.2	0.0	95.8	0.6	95.6	-0.2	95.7	0.1	95.8	0.1	95.8	0.0
1995	96.1	0.3	96.6	0.5	97.7	1.1	99.8	2.1	100.9	1.1	101.4	0.5	101.6	0.2	101.1	-0.5	101.1	0.0	101.3	0.2	101.1	-0.2	100.8	-0.3

Source: U.S. Department of Labor, Bureau of Labor Statistics, Division of Industry Prices and Price Indexes. n.e.c. stands for not elsewhere classified. - indicates no data collected for period or unavailable.

Gypsum Products

Producer Price Index
Base 1982 = 100

For 1947-1995. Columns headed % show percentile change in the index from the previous period for which an index is available.

Year	Jan Index	%	Feb Index	%	Mar Index	%	Apr Index	%	May Index	%	Jun Index	%	Jul Index	%	Aug Index	%	Sep Index	%	Oct Index	%	Nov Index	%	Dec Index	%
1947	26.9	-	26.9	0.0	26.9	0.0	26.9	0.0	26.9	0.0	26.9	0.0	26.9	0.0	26.9	0.0	26.9	0.0	28.6	6.3	29.4	2.8	29.4	0.0
1948	29.4	0.0	29.4	0.0	29.4	0.0	29.6	0.7	30.2	2.0	30.2	0.0	30.2	0.0	30.2	0.0	30.2	0.0	30.2	0.0	30.2	0.0	30.1	-0.3
1949	29.8	-1.0	29.7	-0.3	29.7	0.0	29.7	0.0	29.7	0.0	29.7	0.0	29.7	0.0	29.7	0.0	29.7	0.0	29.7	0.0	29.7	0.0	29.7	0.0
1950	29.7	0.0	29.7	0.0	29.7	0.0	29.7	0.0	29.7	0.0	29.7	0.0	29.7	0.0	30.4	2.4	31.1	2.3	31.1	0.0	31.1	0.0	32.9	5.8
1951	34.1	3.6	34.1	0.0	34.1	0.0	34.1	0.0	34.1	0.0	34.1	0.0	34.1	0.0	34.1	0.0	34.1	0.0	34.1	0.0	34.2	0.3	34.2	0.0
1952	34.2	0.0	34.2	0.0	34.2	0.0	34.2	0.0	34.2	0.0	34.2	0.0	34.2	0.0	34.2	0.0	34.2	0.0	34.2	0.0	34.2	0.0	34.2	0.0
1953	34.2	0.0	34.2	0.0	34.4	0.6	35.5	3.2	35.5	0.0	35.5	0.0	35.5	0.0	35.5	0.0	35.5	0.0	35.5	0.0	35.5	0.0	35.5	0.0
1954	35.5	0.0	35.5	0.0	35.5	0.0	35.5	0.0	35.5	0.0	35.5	0.0	35.5	0.0	35.5	0.0	35.5	0.0	35.5	0.0	35.5	0.0	35.5	0.0
1955	35.5	0.0	35.5	0.0	35.5	0.0	35.5	0.0	35.5	0.0	35.5	0.0	35.5	0.0	35.5	0.0	35.5	0.0	35.5	0.0	35.5	0.0	35.5	0.0
1956	36.9	3.9	36.9	0.0	36.9	0.0	36.9	0.0	36.9	0.0	36.9	0.0	36.9	0.0	36.9	0.0	36.9	0.0	36.9	0.0	36.9	0.0	36.9	0.0
1957	36.9	0.0	36.9	0.0	36.9	0.0	36.9	0.0	36.9	0.0	36.9	0.0	36.9	0.0	36.9	0.0	36.9	0.0	36.9	0.0	36.9	0.0	36.9	0.0
1958	36.9	0.0	36.9	0.0	38.7	4.9	38.7	0.0	38.7	0.0	38.7	0.0	38.7	0.0	38.7	0.0	38.7	0.0	38.7	0.0	38.7	0.0	38.7	0.0
1959	38.7	0.0	38.7	0.0	38.7	0.0	38.7	0.0	38.7	0.0	38.7	0.0	38.7	0.0	38.7	0.0	38.7	0.0	38.7	0.0	38.7	0.0	38.7	0.0
1960	38.7	0.0	38.7	0.0	38.7	0.0	38.7	0.0	38.7	0.0	38.7	0.0	38.7	0.0	38.7	0.0	38.7	0.0	38.7	0.0	38.7	0.0	38.7	0.0
1961	39.1	1.0	39.1	0.0	39.1	0.0	39.1	0.0	39.1	0.0	39.1	0.0	39.1	0.0	39.9	2.0	39.9	0.0	39.9	0.0	39.9	0.0	39.9	0.0
1962	39.9	0.0	39.9	0.0	39.9	0.0	39.9	0.0	39.9	0.0	39.9	0.0	39.9	0.0	39.9	0.0	39.9	0.0	39.9	0.0	39.9	0.0	39.9	0.0
1963	39.9	0.0	39.9	0.0	39.9	0.0	39.9	0.0	39.9	0.0	39.9	0.0	39.9	0.0	40.2	0.8	40.3	0.2	40.3	0.0	40.3	0.0	40.3	0.0
1964	40.3	0.0	41.2	2.2	41.2	0.0	41.2	0.0	41.2	0.0	41.2	0.0	41.2	0.0	41.2	0.0	41.2	0.0	41.2	0.0	41.2	0.0	40.5	-1.7
1965	40.5	0.0	40.9	1.0	41.2	0.7	41.1	-0.2	41.1	0.0	40.9	-0.5	40.1	-2.0	38.2	-4.7	38.0	-0.5	37.6	-1.1	37.5	-0.3	37.0	-1.3
1966	38.5	4.1	38.5	0.0	38.5	0.0	38.5	0.0	38.8	0.8	39.0	0.5	39.0	0.0	39.0	0.0	39.0	0.0	39.0	0.0	39.3	0.8	39.3	0.0
1967	39.4	0.3	39.4	0.0	38.9	-1.3	38.9	0.0	38.9	0.0	38.4	-1.3	38.3	-0.3	38.3	0.0	38.3	0.0	40.1	4.7	40.1	0.0	40.1	0.0
1968	40.1	0.0	40.5	1.0	40.5	0.0	40.5	0.0	40.5	0.0	40.5	0.0	40.5	0.0	40.5	0.0	40.5	0.0	40.3	-0.5	40.3	0.0	40.3	0.0
1969	40.3	0.0	40.3	0.0	40.3	0.0	40.3	0.0	41.7	3.5	40.2	-3.6	40.2	0.0	39.6	-1.5	40.2	1.5	40.9	1.7	41.6	1.7	39.5	-5.0
1970	40.7	3.0	41.2	1.2	40.6	-1.5	40.1	-1.2	39.5	-1.5	38.3	-3.0	38.1	-0.5	38.7	1.6	37.7	-2.6	37.9	0.5	37.5	-1.1	37.1	-1.1
1971	38.0	2.4	39.4	3.7	40.4	2.5	41.4	2.5	42.6	2.9	43.4	1.9	44.0	1.4	44.7	1.6	45.0	0.7	44.7	-0.7	44.1	-1.3	44.8	1.6
1972	44.3	-1.1	44.1	-0.5	45.0	2.0	44.9	-0.2	44.3	-1.3	44.5	0.5	45.2	1.6	45.4	0.4	45.0	-0.9	45.1	0.2	44.9	-0.4	44.9	0.0
1973	45.8	2.0	45.2	-1.3	46.1	2.0	46.7	1.3	47.0	0.6	48.5	3.2	48.0	-1.0	47.8	-0.4	47.6	-0.4	47.8	0.4	47.7	-0.2	48.1	0.8
1974	49.9	3.7	50.8	1.8	50.6	-0.4	51.8	2.4	52.1	0.6	53.7	3.1	54.2	0.9	55.8	3.0	56.9	2.0	56.5	-0.7	56.2	-0.5	56.4	0.4
1975	56.1	-0.5	56.1	0.0	56.9	1.4	56.2	-1.2	56.0	-0.4	56.0	0.0	55.0	-1.8	55.9	1.6	56.2	0.5	56.7	0.9	57.4	1.2	56.4	-1.7
1976	58.7	4.1	58.0	-1.2	58.7	1.2	58.9	0.3	60.0	1.9	59.9	-0.2	59.9	0.0	60.6	1.2	61.6	1.7	62.1	0.8	62.5	0.6	62.5	0.0
1977	62.8	0.5	63.5	1.1	64.1	0.9	67.2	4.8	68.7	2.2	73.1	6.4	72.9	-0.3	74.1	1.6	75.6	2.0	78.7	4.1	79.4	0.9	80.0	0.8
1978	81.9	2.4	84.3	2.9	84.8	0.6	86.4	1.9	89.1	3.1	89.9	0.9	91.4	1.7	92.1	0.8	92.2	0.1	92.5	0.3	94.5	2.2	94.8	0.3
1979	96.7	2.0	97.9	1.2	98.0	0.1	98.5	0.5	97.2	-1.3	98.2	1.0	98.3	0.1	98.5	0.2	99.6	1.1	99.7	0.1	100.1	0.4	99.6	-0.5
1980	99.7	0.1	102.4	2.7	104.5	2.1	103.1	-1.3	100.2	-2.8	100.4	0.2	98.9	-1.5	98.4	-0.5	98.3	-0.1	97.5	-0.8	98.9	1.4	98.7	-0.2
1981	101.4	2.7	100.5	-0.9	100.6	0.1	100.3	-0.3	102.0	1.7	101.8	-0.2	101.4	-0.4	99.7	-1.7	98.8	-0.9	98.6	-0.2	98.2	-0.4	97.5	-0.7
1982	97.8	0.3	99.6	1.8	101.8	2.2	102.8	1.0	101.3	-1.5	100.1	-1.2	99.9	-0.2	99.2	-0.7	99.2	0.0	99.6	0.4	99.6	0.0	99.2	-0.4
1983	102.7	3.5	104.4	1.7	103.9	-0.5	106.2	2.2	107.7	1.4	106.9	-0.7	107.8	0.8	113.0	4.8	116.3	2.9	122.2	5.1	123.1	0.7	126.0	2.4
1984	128.3	1.8	132.6	3.4	132.6	0.0	137.9	4.0	140.9	2.2	140.7	-0.1	140.5	-0.1	140.4	-0.1	138.8	-1.1	132.4	-4.6	130.6	-1.4	129.1	-1.1
1985	128.3	-0.6	134.5	4.8	131.4	-2.3	130.2	-0.9	130.1	-0.1	132.0	1.5	132.2	0.2	132.1	-0.1	129.4	-2.0	132.7	2.6	135.9	2.4	139.2	2.4
1986	140.7	1.1	141.4	0.5	137.4	-2.8	135.2	-1.6	140.7	4.1	138.3	-1.7	136.5	-1.3	134.3	-1.6	133.2	-0.8	134.0	0.6	137.0	2.2	135.7	-0.9
1987	133.9	-1.3	131.8	-1.6	127.1	-3.6	127.2	0.1	129.5	1.8	128.0	-1.2	124.0	-3.1	119.5	-3.6	118.8	-0.6	119.8	0.8	120.8	0.8	121.5	0.6
1988	120.9	-0.5	116.7	-3.5	113.3	-2.9	111.7	-1.4	112.7	0.9	110.4	-2.0	108.6	-1.6	108.0	-0.6	110.6	2.4	113.6	2.7	114.6	0.9	113.9	-0.6
1989	111.3	-2.3	110.8	-0.4	110.1	-0.6	110.3	0.2	110.6	0.3	110.4	-0.2	109.8	-0.5	107.9	-1.7	108.9	0.9	109.5	0.6	111.5	1.8	109.4	-1.9
1990	106.9	-2.3	106.0	-0.8	106.3	0.3	106.8	0.5	107.0	0.2	106.2	-0.7	105.4	-0.8	102.4	-2.8	104.0	1.6	103.4	-0.6	104.5	1.1	103.3	-1.1
1991	102.8	-0.5	105.4	2.5	104.8	-0.6	101.4	-3.2	100.3	-1.1	97.0	-3.3	96.0	-1.0	95.0	-1.0	97.5	2.6	98.2	0.7	96.8	-1.4	96.9	0.1

[Continued]

Gypsum Products

Producer Price Index
Base 1982 = 100

[Continued]

For 1947-1995. Columns headed % show percentile change in the index from the previous period for which an index is available.

Year	Jan Index	%	Feb Index	%	Mar Index	%	Apr Index	%	May Index	%	Jun Index	%	Jul Index	%	Aug Index	%	Sep Index	%	Oct Index	%	Nov Index	%	Dec Index	%
1992	94.8	-2.2	92.8	-2.1	96.0	3.4	96.6	0.6	100.5	4.0	100.4	-0.1	100.4	0.0	103.0	2.6	105.4	2.3	104.1	-1.2	104.0	-0.1	101.2	-2.7
1993	99.4	-1.8	102.0	2.6	103.4	1.4	108.8	5.2	108.2	-0.6	107.6	-0.6	106.7	-0.8	110.2	3.3	112.5	2.1	112.6	0.1	114.2	1.4	114.2	0.0
1994	113.0	-1.1	117.9	4.3	128.8	9.2	130.7	1.5	131.3	0.5	139.5	6.2	139.8	0.2	140.7	0.6	146.2	3.9	149.0	1.9	146.3	-1.8	149.4	2.1
1995	148.4	-0.7	151.9	2.4	157.6	3.8	161.2	2.3	159.9	-0.8	158.7	-0.8	154.8	-2.5	153.5	-0.8	152.6	-0.6	152.6	0.0	151.4	-0.8	150.9	-0.3

Source: U.S. Department of Labor, Bureau of Labor Statistics, Division of Industry Prices and Price Indexes. n.e.c. stands for not elsewhere classified. - indicates no data collected for period or unavailable.

Glass Containers
Producer Price Index
Base 1982 = 100

For 1947-1995. Columns headed % show percentile change in the index from the previous period for which an index is available.

Year	Jan Index	%	Feb Index	%	Mar Index	%	Apr Index	%	May Index	%	Jun Index	%	Jul Index	%	Aug Index	%	Sep Index	%	Oct Index	%	Nov Index	%	Dec Index	%
1947	14.1	-	14.5	2.8	14.5	0.0	14.5	0.0	14.5	0.0	14.5	0.0	14.9	2.8	14.9	0.0	14.9	0.0	14.9	0.0	14.9	0.0	14.9	0.0
1948	14.9	0.0	14.9	0.0	14.9	0.0	16.9	13.4	16.9	0.0	16.9	0.0	16.9	0.0	16.9	0.0	16.9	0.0	19.2	13.6	19.2	0.0	19.2	0.0
1949	19.2	0.0	19.2	0.0	19.2	0.0	19.2	0.0	19.2	0.0	19.0	-1.0	19.0	0.0	19.0	0.0	19.0	0.0	19.0	0.0	19.0	0.0	19.0	0.0
1950	18.7	-1.6	18.7	0.0	18.7	0.0	18.7	0.0	18.7	0.0	18.7	0.0	18.7	0.0	18.7	0.0	18.7	0.0	20.0	7.0	20.0	0.0	20.0	0.0
1951	20.6	3.0	20.6	0.0	20.6	0.0	20.6	0.0	20.6	0.0	20.6	0.0	20.6	0.0	20.6	0.0	20.6	0.0	20.6	0.0	20.6	0.0	20.6	0.0
1952	20.6	0.0	20.6	0.0	20.6	0.0	20.6	0.0	21.4	3.9	21.4	0.0	21.4	0.0	21.4	0.0	21.4	0.0	21.4	0.0	21.4	0.0	21.4	0.0
1953	21.4	0.0	21.4	0.0	21.4	0.0	23.2	8.4	23.2	0.0	23.2	0.0	23.2	0.0	23.2	0.0	23.2	0.0	23.0	-0.9	23.0	0.0	23.0	0.0
1954	23.0	0.0	23.0	0.0	23.0	0.0	24.1	4.8	24.1	0.0	24.1	0.0	24.1	0.0	24.1	0.0	24.1	0.0	24.1	0.0	24.1	0.0	24.1	0.0
1955	24.1	0.0	24.1	0.0	24.1	0.0	24.1	0.0	24.1	0.0	24.1	0.0	24.1	0.0	24.1	0.0	24.1	0.0	24.3	0.8	24.3	0.0	24.3	0.0
1956	24.9	2.5	24.9	0.0	24.9	0.0	24.9	0.0	24.9	0.0	24.9	0.0	24.9	0.0	24.9	0.0	24.9	0.0	26.7	7.2	26.7	0.0	26.7	0.0
1957	26.7	0.0	26.7	0.0	26.7	0.0	26.7	0.0	26.7	0.0	26.7	0.0	26.7	0.0	26.7	0.0	26.7	0.0	26.7	0.0	26.9	0.7	28.3	5.2
1958	28.3	0.0	28.3	0.0	28.3	0.0	28.3	0.0	28.3	0.0	28.3	0.0	28.3	0.0	28.3	0.0	28.3	0.0	28.3	0.0	28.3	0.0	28.3	0.0
1959	28.3	0.0	28.3	0.0	28.3	0.0	28.3	0.0	28.3	0.0	28.3	0.0	28.3	0.0	28.3	0.0	28.3	0.0	28.3	0.0	28.3	0.0	28.3	0.0
1960	28.2	-0.4	28.2	0.0	28.2	0.0	27.5	-2.5	27.5	0.0	27.5	0.0	27.5	0.0	27.5	0.0	27.5	0.0	27.0	-1.8	27.0	0.0	27.0	0.0
1961	27.0	0.0	27.0	0.0	27.0	0.0	27.8	3.0	27.8	0.0	27.8	0.0	27.4	-1.4	27.4	0.0	27.4	0.0	27.4	0.0	27.4	0.0	26.9	-1.8
1962	26.9	0.0	26.9	0.0	26.9	0.0	26.9	0.0	26.9	0.0	26.9	0.0	26.9	0.0	26.9	0.0	26.9	0.0	26.9	0.0	26.9	0.0	26.9	0.0
1963	26.9	0.0	26.9	0.0	26.9	0.0	26.9	0.0	26.9	0.0	26.8	-0.4	26.8	0.0	26.8	0.0	26.8	0.0	26.8	0.0	26.8	0.0	26.8	0.0
1964	26.8	0.0	26.8	0.0	26.8	0.0	27.1	1.1	27.1	0.0	27.1	0.0	27.1	0.0	27.1	0.0	27.1	0.0	27.1	0.0	27.1	0.0	27.1	0.0
1965	27.1	0.0	27.1	0.0	27.1	0.0	27.1	0.0	27.1	0.0	27.2	0.4	27.2	0.0	27.3	0.4	27.3	0.0	27.3	0.0	27.8	1.8	27.8	0.0
1966	27.8	0.0	27.9	0.4	27.8	-0.4	27.6	-0.7	27.6	0.0	27.6	0.0	27.6	0.0	27.6	0.0	27.6	0.0	28.1	1.8	28.1	0.0	28.1	0.0
1967	28.1	0.0	28.1	0.0	28.1	0.0	28.1	0.0	28.1	0.0	28.1	0.0	28.1	0.0	28.1	0.0	28.1	0.0	28.1	0.0	28.1	0.0	28.1	0.0
1968	29.3	4.3	29.6	1.0	29.6	0.0	29.6	0.0	30.5	3.0	30.5	0.0	30.5	0.0	30.5	0.0	30.5	0.0	30.7	0.7	30.7	0.0	30.7	0.0
1969	32.3	5.2	32.3	0.0	32.3	0.0	32.3	0.0	32.3	0.0	32.3	0.0	32.3	0.0	32.3	0.0	32.3	0.0	32.3	0.0	32.3	0.0	32.3	0.0
1970	33.6	4.0	33.6	0.0	33.6	0.0	33.6	0.0	33.6	0.0	33.6	0.0	33.6	0.0	33.6	0.0	33.6	0.0	33.6	0.0	35.0	4.2	35.0	0.0
1971	37.1	6.0	37.0	-0.3	37.0	0.0	37.0	0.0	37.0	0.0	37.0	0.0	37.0	0.0	37.0	0.0	37.0	0.0	37.0	0.0	37.0	0.0	37.0	0.0
1972	37.0	0.0	37.0	0.0	37.0	0.0	38.3	3.5	38.3	0.0	38.3	0.0	38.4	0.3	38.4	0.0	38.4	0.0	38.4	0.0	38.4	0.0	38.4	0.0
1973	38.4	0.0	38.4	0.0	38.4	0.0	38.5	0.3	38.5	0.0	39.8	3.4	38.6	-3.0	38.6	0.0	38.6	0.0	40.4	4.7	40.4	0.0	40.4	0.0
1974	40.4	0.0	40.4	0.0	41.0	1.5	41.3	0.7	44.2	7.0	44.3	0.2	44.3	0.0	44.3	0.0	44.3	0.0	46.7	5.4	46.7	0.0	46.7	0.0
1975	46.7	0.0	49.8	6.6	49.8	0.0	49.8	0.0	49.8	0.0	49.8	0.0	49.8	0.0	52.3	5.0	52.2	-0.2	52.2	0.0	52.2	0.0	52.2	0.0
1976	52.1	-0.2	52.1	0.0	52.1	0.0	55.3	6.1	55.5	0.4	55.5	0.0	55.5	0.0	55.5	0.0	55.5	0.0	56.8	2.3	56.8	0.0	56.8	0.0
1977	56.8	0.0	56.8	0.0	56.8	0.0	61.3	7.9	61.3	0.0	61.3	0.0	61.3	0.0	61.3	0.0	61.3	0.0	61.5	0.3	61.5	0.0	61.5	0.0
1978	66.5	8.1	66.5	0.0	66.5	0.0	66.5	0.0	66.5	0.0	70.0	5.3	70.0	0.0	70.5	0.7	70.5	0.0	70.5	0.0	70.5	0.0	70.5	0.0
1979	70.5	0.0	70.5	0.0	70.5	0.0	70.5	0.0	74.6	5.8	74.6	0.0	74.6	0.0	74.6	0.0	74.6	0.0	74.6	0.0	74.6	0.0	77.1	3.4
1980	77.1	0.0	77.1	0.0	77.1	0.0	82.8	7.4	82.8	0.0	82.8	0.0	82.8	0.0	82.8	0.0	82.8	0.0	86.1	4.0	86.1	0.0	87.6	1.7
1981	87.6	0.0	87.6	0.0	87.6	0.0	91.9	4.9	94.3	2.6	94.3	0.0	94.4	0.1	94.4	0.0	94.4	0.0	94.4	0.0	94.4	0.0	94.4	0.0
1982	94.3	-0.1	99.1	5.1	100.1	1.0	100.7	0.6	100.7	0.0	100.7	0.0	100.7	0.0	100.7	0.0	100.9	0.2	100.8	-0.1	100.6	-0.2	100.6	0.0
1983	100.3	-0.3	100.1	-0.2	99.6	-0.5	99.4	-0.2	99.0	-0.4	98.9	-0.1	98.9	0.0	98.8	-0.1	98.8	0.0	98.5	-0.3	98.5	0.0	98.6	0.1
1984	98.6	0.0	98.6	0.0	98.9	0.3	100.7	1.8	101.8	1.1	102.7	0.9	103.0	0.3	103.0	0.0	102.5	-0.5	102.6	0.1	102.4	-0.2	102.4	0.0
1985	102.3	-0.1	102.5	0.2	105.2	2.6	105.3	0.1	105.9	0.6	107.4	1.4	108.8	1.3	108.9	0.1	108.8	-0.1	109.2	0.4	108.8	-0.4	108.8	0.0
1986	109.5	0.6	109.5	0.0	111.0	1.4	111.1	0.1	112.2	1.0	112.6	0.4	112.8	0.2	113.1	0.3	113.1	0.0	112.7	-0.4	112.7	0.0	112.5	-0.2
1987	112.5	0.0	113.4	0.8	113.7	0.3	113.8	0.1	113.2	-0.5	113.3	0.1	113.0	-0.3	112.9	-0.1	112.9	0.0	112.7	-0.2	112.5	-0.2	112.5	0.0
1988	112.3	-0.2	112.2	-0.1	112.2	0.0	112.1	-0.1	112.1	0.0	112.2	0.1	112.2	0.0	112.5	0.3	112.3	-0.2	112.3	0.0	112.3	0.0	112.3	0.0
1989	112.3	0.0	112.3	0.0	113.8	1.3	116.9	2.7	116.4	-0.4	115.9	-0.4	115.9	0.0	115.9	0.0	115.7	-0.2	115.7	0.0	115.7	0.0	115.7	0.0
1990	118.9	2.8	119.5	0.5	120.0	0.4	120.2	0.2	120.4	0.2	120.7	0.2	120.7	0.0	120.7	0.0	121.0	0.2	121.0	0.0	121.0	0.0	121.0	0.0
1991	124.8	3.1	124.9	0.1	125.0	0.1	125.3	0.2	125.6	0.2	125.6	0.0	125.6	0.0	125.5	-0.1	125.7	0.2	125.7	0.0	125.7	0.0	125.7	0.0

[Continued]

Glass Containers
Producer Price Index
Base 1982 = 100
[Continued]

For 1947-1995. Columns headed % show percentile change in the index from the previous period for which an index is available.

Year	Jan Index	%	Feb Index	%	Mar Index	%	Apr Index	%	May Index	%	Jun Index	%	Jul Index	%	Aug Index	%	Sep Index	%	Oct Index	%	Nov Index	%	Dec Index	%
1992	125.5	-0.2	125.5	0.0	125.4	-0.1	125.3	-0.1	125.0	-0.2	125.1	0.1	125.1	0.0	125.0	-0.1	124.9	-0.1	124.9	0.0	124.7	-0.2	124.7	0.0
1993	124.5	-0.2	124.9	0.3	125.0	0.1	124.9	-0.1	125.4	0.4	126.0	0.5	126.4	0.3	126.5	0.1	126.7	0.2	126.7	0.0	126.6	-0.1	126.5	-0.1
1994	126.6	0.1	126.4	-0.2	126.4	0.0	126.4	0.0	127.9	1.2	127.9	0.0	127.9	0.0	127.9	0.0	128.2	0.2	128.2	0.0	128.2	0.0	128.3	0.1
1995	128.7	0.3	128.6	-0.1	130.1	1.2	129.9	-0.2	130.7	0.6	130.7	0.0	131.0	0.2	131.0	0.0	131.1	0.1	131.1	0.0	131.1	0.0	131.2	0.1

Source: U.S. Department of Labor, Bureau of Labor Statistics, Division of Industry Prices and Price Indexes. n.e.c. stands for not elsewhere classified. - indicates no data collected for period or unavailable.

Nonmetallic Minerals

Producer Price Index
Base 1982 = 100

For 1947-1995. Columns headed % show percentile change in the index from the previous period for which an index is available.

Year	Jan Index	%	Feb Index	%	Mar Index	%	Apr Index	%	May Index	%	Jun Index	%	Jul Index	%	Aug Index	%	Sep Index	%	Oct Index	%	Nov Index	%	Dec Index	%
1947	14.4	-	14.6	1.4	14.7	0.7	14.8	0.7	14.9	0.7	14.9	0.0	14.9	0.0	14.9	0.0	15.0	0.7	15.0	0.0	15.5	3.3	15.7	1.3
1948	15.9	1.3	16.0	0.6	16.0	0.0	16.1	0.6	16.1	0.0	16.3	1.2	16.6	1.8	16.6	0.0	16.6	0.0	16.6	0.0	16.5	-0.6	16.7	1.2
1949	16.6	-0.6	16.6	0.0	16.6	0.0	16.6	0.0	16.6	0.0	16.6	0.0	16.5	-0.6	16.4	-0.6	16.4	0.0	16.3	-0.6	16.3	0.0	16.3	0.0
1950	16.3	0.0	16.7	2.5	16.8	0.6	16.8	0.0	16.8	0.0	16.8	0.0	16.9	0.6	17.1	1.2	17.3	1.2	17.3	0.0	17.4	0.6	17.7	1.7
1951	17.7	0.0	17.7	0.0	17.7	0.0	17.7	0.0	17.7	0.0	17.7	0.0	17.7	0.0	17.7	0.0	17.7	0.0	17.7	0.0	17.7	0.0	17.7	0.0
1952	17.7	0.0	17.7	0.0	17.7	0.0	17.8	0.6	17.8	0.0	17.8	0.0	17.8	0.0	17.8	0.0	17.8	0.0	17.9	0.6	18.3	2.2	18.4	0.5
1953	18.4	0.0	18.4	0.0	18.4	0.0	18.4	0.0	18.4	0.0	18.5	0.5	18.7	1.1	18.8	0.5	18.8	0.0	18.8	0.0	18.9	0.5	18.9	0.0
1954	19.1	1.1	19.1	0.0	19.1	0.0	19.1	0.0	19.1	0.0	19.1	0.0	19.1	0.0	19.2	0.5	19.2	0.0	19.2	0.0	19.0	-1.0	19.0	0.0
1955	19.0	0.0	19.0	0.0	19.0	0.0	19.0	0.0	19.3	1.6	19.5	1.0	19.5	0.0	19.5	0.0	19.6	0.5	19.6	0.0	19.4	-1.0	19.4	0.0
1956	19.4	0.0	19.6	1.0	19.5	-0.5	19.6	0.5	19.6	0.0	19.6	0.0	19.7	0.5	19.7	0.0	19.7	0.0	19.8	0.5	19.8	0.0	19.8	0.0
1957	19.8	0.0	20.1	1.5	20.3	1.0	20.4	0.5	20.4	0.0	20.4	0.0	20.4	0.0	20.5	0.5	20.5	0.0	20.5	0.0	20.5	0.0	20.9	2.0
1958	20.9	0.0	20.9	0.0	20.9	0.0	20.9	0.0	20.9	0.0	20.9	0.0	20.9	0.0	20.9	0.0	20.9	0.0	20.9	0.0	20.9	0.0	20.9	0.0
1959	20.9	0.0	21.0	0.5	21.1	0.5	21.1	0.0	21.1	0.0	21.1	0.0	21.1	0.0	21.1	0.0	21.1	0.0	21.1	0.0	21.1	0.0	21.1	0.0
1960	21.1	0.0	21.3	0.9	21.3	0.0	21.4	0.5	21.4	0.0	21.4	0.0	21.4	0.0	21.4	0.0	21.4	0.0	21.5	0.5	21.3	-0.9	21.3	0.0
1961	21.3	0.0	21.2	-0.5	21.3	0.5	21.3	0.0	21.3	0.0	21.3	0.0	21.3	0.0	21.3	0.0	21.2	-0.5	21.2	0.0	21.2	0.0	21.1	-0.5
1962	21.1	0.0	21.4	1.4	21.4	0.0	21.4	0.0	21.2	-0.9	21.2	0.0	21.1	-0.5	21.1	0.0	21.1	0.0	21.2	0.5	21.3	0.5	21.3	0.0
1963	21.2	-0.5	21.1	-0.5	21.1	0.0	21.1	0.0	21.1	0.0	21.0	-0.5	21.0	0.0	20.9	-0.5	21.0	0.5	21.1	0.5	21.1	0.0	21.1	0.0
1964	21.0	-0.5	21.0	0.0	21.0	0.0	21.0	0.0	21.0	0.0	21.1	0.5	21.2	0.5	21.2	0.0	21.1	-0.5	21.1	0.0	21.1	0.0	21.0	-0.5
1965	21.0	0.0	21.0	0.0	21.1	0.5	21.1	0.0	21.1	0.0	21.1	0.0	21.1	0.0	21.1	0.0	21.0	-0.5	21.0	0.0	21.0	0.0	21.0	0.0
1966	21.2	1.0	21.1	-0.5	21.2	0.5	21.2	0.0	21.1	-0.5	21.0	-0.5	21.1	0.5	21.2	0.5	21.2	0.0	21.2	0.0	21.0	-0.9	21.0	0.0
1967	21.1	0.5	21.1	0.0	21.3	0.9	21.2	-0.5	21.2	0.0	21.2	0.0	21.2	0.0	21.2	0.0	21.1	-0.5	21.2	0.5	21.2	0.0	21.3	0.5
1968	21.6	1.4	21.6	0.0	21.6	0.0	21.6	0.0	21.6	0.0	21.9	1.4	22.0	0.5	22.0	0.0	22.0	0.0	22.2	0.9	22.2	0.0	22.2	0.0
1969	22.3	0.5	22.4	0.4	22.4	0.0	22.7	1.3	22.7	0.0	22.7	0.0	22.7	0.0	22.7	0.0	22.8	0.4	23.0	0.9	23.0	0.0	23.0	0.0
1970	23.0	0.0	23.1	0.4	23.4	1.3	23.6	0.9	23.6	0.0	23.6	0.0	23.7	0.4	23.8	0.4	23.8	0.0	24.4	2.5	24.4	0.0	24.9	2.0
1971	25.6	2.8	25.7	0.4	25.7	0.0	25.9	0.8	26.5	2.3	26.5	0.0	26.6	0.4	26.6	0.0	26.6	0.0	26.6	0.0	26.6	0.0	26.6	0.0
1972	26.6	0.0	26.7	0.4	26.8	0.4	26.8	0.0	27.2	1.5	27.0	-0.7	26.9	-0.4	26.9	0.0	27.0	0.4	27.0	0.0	27.0	0.0	27.0	0.0
1973	27.1	0.4	27.1	0.0	27.2	0.4	27.2	0.0	27.4	0.7	27.5	0.4	27.1	-1.5	27.1	0.0	27.0	-0.4	27.0	0.0	27.1	0.4	27.9	3.0
1974	31.9	14.3	35.4	11.0	36.2	2.3	37.5	3.6	40.1	6.9	40.4	0.7	41.4	2.5	42.0	1.4	42.8	1.9	43.1	0.7	44.4	3.0	44.5	0.2
1975	45.2	1.6	45.3	0.2	45.3	0.0	46.4	2.4	46.4	0.0	46.6	0.4	47.3	1.5	47.4	0.2	47.3	-0.2	47.7	0.8	47.6	-0.2	47.7	0.2
1976	48.5	1.7	48.5	0.0	49.3	1.6	49.0	-0.6	49.2	0.4	49.2	0.0	49.3	0.2	49.2	-0.2	49.7	1.0	49.8	0.2	49.8	0.0	49.8	0.0
1977	51.0	2.4	51.2	0.4	52.0	1.6	52.5	1.0	52.5	0.0	53.1	1.1	53.3	0.4	53.8	0.9	54.6	1.5	54.3	-0.5	54.3	0.0	54.5	0.4
1978	55.3	1.5	56.7	2.5	56.9	0.4	57.0	0.2	57.2	0.4	58.1	1.6	59.9	3.1	59.8	-0.2	59.8	0.0	60.0	0.3	60.1	0.2	60.1	0.0
1979	61.2	1.8	62.3	1.8	62.4	0.2	63.6	1.9	64.2	0.9	64.0	-0.3	65.8	2.8	65.7	-0.2	71.2	8.4	72.3	1.5	72.5	0.3	72.5	0.0
1980	74.6	2.9	80.9	8.4	82.0	1.4	84.7	3.3	84.9	0.2	83.7	-1.4	84.1	0.5	84.2	0.1	84.9	0.8	85.4	0.6	85.5	0.1	88.8	3.9
1981	88.7	-0.1	90.0	1.5	93.6	4.0	101.5	8.4	101.2	-0.3	101.1	-0.1	100.9	-0.2	100.7	-0.2	100.5	-0.2	100.3	-0.2	100.4	0.1	100.6	0.2
1982	100.6	0.0	101.5	0.9	101.6	0.1	101.5	-0.1	99.9	-1.6	98.6	-1.3	98.9	0.3	98.8	-0.1	99.1	0.3	99.7	0.6	99.9	0.2	99.8	-0.1
1983	99.9	0.1	100.9	1.0	101.0	0.1	101.5	0.5	101.4	-0.1	101.6	0.2	101.7	0.1	102.1	0.4	102.3	0.2	102.4	0.1	103.3	0.9	103.2	-0.1
1984	103.1	-0.1	103.4	0.3	104.0	0.6	104.1	0.1	104.9	0.8	105.8	0.9	107.5	1.6	108.4	0.8	108.0	-0.4	107.9	-0.1	107.2	-0.6	107.5	0.3
1985	109.0	1.4	109.0	0.0	109.0	0.0	110.0	0.9	110.9	0.8	111.0	0.1	111.0	0.0	111.1	0.1	111.1	0.0	111.5	0.4	111.0	-0.4	110.9	-0.1
1986	111.1	0.2	110.9	-0.2	110.8	-0.1	110.6	-0.2	111.0	0.4	111.0	0.0	110.4	-0.5	109.5	-0.8	109.3	-0.2	109.6	0.3	109.4	-0.2	109.0	-0.4
1987	108.6	-0.4	109.1	0.5	109.6	0.5	109.8	0.2	109.6	-0.2	110.3	0.6	110.9	0.5	110.1	-0.7	110.6	0.5	111.8	1.1	111.9	0.1	111.3	-0.5
1988	112.5	1.1	112.8	0.3	112.9	0.1	113.1	0.2	113.2	0.1	113.4	0.2	112.4	-0.9	112.3	-0.1	112.7	0.4	112.8	0.1	113.0	0.2	113.2	0.2
1989	113.6	0.4	113.5	-0.1	113.9	0.4	114.3	0.4	114.1	-0.2	114.2	0.1	114.5	0.3	114.4	-0.1	114.4	0.0	114.3	-0.1	114.5	0.2	114.7	0.2
1990	115.2	0.4	115.4	0.2	115.4	0.0	115.5	0.1	115.5	0.0	115.6	0.1	115.6	0.0	115.8	0.2	116.5	0.6	116.6	0.1	117.6	0.9	117.7	0.1
1991	118.5	0.7	118.4	-0.1	118.3	-0.1	118.5	0.2	118.6	0.1	118.5	-0.1	118.4	-0.1	118.4	0.0	118.4	0.0	118.5	0.1	118.5	0.0	118.1	-0.3

[Continued]

Nonmetallic Minerals
Producer Price Index
Base 1982 = 100
[Continued]

For 1947-1995. Columns headed % show percentile change in the index from the previous period for which an index is available.

Year	Jan Index	%	Feb Index	%	Mar Index	%	Apr Index	%	May Index	%	Jun Index	%	Jul Index	%	Aug Index	%	Sep Index	%	Oct Index	%	Nov Index	%	Dec Index	%
1992	117.8	-0.3	118.0	0.2	117.8	-0.2	116.1	-1.4	115.0	-0.9	115.5	0.4	115.8	0.3	116.0	0.2	116.0	0.0	116.0	0.0	116.2	0.2	116.3	0.1
1993	117.6	1.1	117.8	0.2	118.0	0.2	118.5	0.4	118.7	0.2	119.2	0.4	119.7	0.4	119.8	0.1	120.1	0.3	120.2	0.1	120.0	-0.2	120.3	0.3
1994	120.7	0.3	121.3	0.5	121.4	0.1	121.5	0.1	121.5	0.0	121.5	0.0	121.5	0.0	121.7	0.2	121.7	0.0	121.9	0.2	122.0	0.1	122.3	0.2
1995	123.6	1.1	124.3	0.6	124.7	0.3	125.4	0.6	125.1	-0.2	125.6	0.4	125.2	-0.3	125.9	0.6	126.7	0.6	126.4	-0.2	126.2	-0.2	126.2	0.0

Source: U.S. Department of Labor, Bureau of Labor Statistics, Division of Industry Prices and Price Indexes. n.e.c. stands for not elsewhere classified. - indicates no data collected for period or unavailable.

TRANSPORTATION EQUIPMENT
Producer Price Index
Base 1982 = 100

For 1969-1995. Columns headed % show percentile change in the index from the previous period for which an index is available.

Year	Jan Index	%	Feb Index	%	Mar Index	%	Apr Index	%	May Index	%	Jun Index	%	Jul Index	%	Aug Index	%	Sep Index	%	Oct Index	%	Nov Index	%	Dec Index	%
1969	40.1	-	40.1	0.0	40.1	0.0	40.1	0.0	40.1	0.0	40.2	0.2	40.2	0.0	40.1	-0.2	40.1	0.0	41.0	2.2	41.2	0.5	41.2	0.0
1970	41.3	0.2	41.2	-0.2	41.4	0.5	41.3	-0.2	41.4	0.2	41.4	0.0	41.4	0.0	41.5	0.2	41.5	0.0	43.3	4.3	43.5	0.5	43.5	0.0
1971	43.7	0.5	43.9	0.5	44.0	0.2	44.0	0.0	44.1	0.2	44.1	0.0	44.3	0.5	44.3	0.0	43.9	-0.9	44.4	1.1	44.4	0.0	45.2	1.8
1972	45.4	0.4	45.5	0.2	45.5	0.0	45.6	0.2	45.6	0.0	45.7	0.2	45.7	0.0	45.7	0.0	45.7	0.0	45.2	-1.1	45.3	0.2	45.7	0.9
1973	45.7	0.0	45.7	0.0	45.9	0.4	46.0	0.2	46.1	0.2	46.0	-0.2	46.1	0.2	46.1	0.0	45.9	-0.4	46.4	1.1	46.5	0.2	47.0	1.1
1974	47.5	1.1	47.6	0.2	47.7	0.2	47.8	0.2	48.6	1.7	49.2	1.2	50.1	1.8	50.8	1.4	51.1	0.6	53.8	5.3	54.1	0.6	54.9	1.5
1975	54.9	0.0	55.4	0.9	55.9	0.9	56.0	0.2	56.0	0.0	56.1	0.2	56.1	0.0	56.3	0.4	56.5	0.4	58.7	3.9	59.0	0.5	59.1	0.2
1976	59.6	0.8	59.6	0.0	59.7	0.2	59.7	0.0	59.7	0.0	59.8	0.2	59.8	0.0	60.2	0.7	60.5	0.5	62.5	3.3	62.6	0.2	62.9	0.5
1977	62.9	0.0	63.0	0.2	63.4	0.6	63.6	0.3	63.7	0.2	63.9	0.3	63.9	0.0	64.4	0.8	64.7	0.5	67.2	3.9	67.3	0.1	67.4	0.1
1978	67.7	0.4	67.9	0.3	67.9	0.0	68.3	0.6	68.9	0.9	69.1	0.3	69.2	0.1	69.3	0.1	69.5	0.3	71.8	3.3	72.1	0.4	72.3	0.3
1979	73.2	1.2	73.5	0.4	73.6	0.1	74.8	1.6	75.0	0.3	75.1	0.1	75.4	0.4	74.5	-1.2	74.8	0.4	77.8	4.0	78.0	0.3	78.3	0.4
1980	79.6	1.7	79.4	-0.3	79.6	0.3	81.4	2.3	81.1	-0.4	81.4	0.4	82.6	1.5	83.6	1.2	81.9	-2.0	87.1	6.3	87.2	0.1	89.8	3.0
1981	91.1	1.4	91.8	0.8	91.4	-0.4	92.9	1.6	93.6	0.8	93.8	0.2	94.1	0.3	94.5	0.4	92.8	-1.8	97.9	5.5	98.7	0.8	98.9	0.2
1982	99.6	0.7	98.2	-1.4	98.2	0.0	98.4	0.2	99.1	0.7	99.8	0.7	100.1	0.3	100.4	0.3	97.9	-2.5	102.5	4.7	102.6	0.1	103.1	0.5
1983	102.7	-0.4	102.5	-0.2	102.2	-0.3	102.4	0.2	102.5	0.1	102.6	0.1	102.6	0.0	102.9	0.3	100.3	-2.5	104.4	4.1	104.4	0.0	104.4	0.0
1984	104.8	0.4	105.0	0.2	105.1	0.1	105.2	0.1	105.1	-0.1	105.0	-0.1	105.1	0.1	105.0	-0.1	103.2	-1.7	106.1	2.8	106.4	0.3	106.2	-0.2
1985	106.9	0.7	107.4	0.5	107.2	-0.2	107.4	0.2	107.8	0.4	107.9	0.1	108.1	0.2	108.1	0.0	104.1	-3.7	110.2	5.9	110.2	0.0	109.8	-0.4
1986	109.5	-0.3	109.7	0.2	109.5	-0.2	110.3	0.7	110.2	-0.1	110.3	0.1	110.4	0.1	110.0	-0.4	107.5	-2.3	113.2	5.3	113.1	-0.1	112.8	-0.3
1987	113.1	0.3	112.1	-0.9	112.4	0.3	113.0	0.5	112.4	-0.5	112.3	-0.1	112.2	-0.1	111.9	-0.3	110.9	-0.9	113.8	2.6	113.5	-0.3	112.5	-0.9
1988	113.2	0.6	113.2	0.0	113.1	-0.1	113.5	0.4	113.7	0.2	114.0	0.3	113.9	-0.1	114.0	0.1	113.2	-0.7	116.6	3.0	116.3	-0.3	116.3	0.0
1989	116.8	0.4	117.1	0.3	116.8	-0.3	116.4	-0.3	117.2	0.7	117.6	0.3	116.9	-0.6	117.1	0.2	116.6	-0.4	120.0	2.9	120.0	0.0	119.8	-0.2
1990	119.7	-0.1	120.2	0.4	120.3	0.1	120.5	0.2	120.4	-0.1	121.0	0.5	121.2	0.2	121.1	-0.1	121.0	-0.1	124.0	2.5	124.2	0.2	124.2	0.0
1991	125.2	0.8	125.7	0.4	125.7	0.0	125.5	-0.2	125.6	0.1	125.6	0.0	125.7	0.1	126.0	0.2	125.2	-0.6	129.1	3.1	128.9	-0.2	129.0	0.1
1992	129.8	0.6	129.7	-0.1	130.0	0.2	130.2	0.2	130.2	0.0	130.1	-0.1	130.2	0.1	130.0	-0.2	128.5	-1.2	132.3	3.0	132.2	-0.1	132.1	-0.1
1993	132.7	0.5	133.1	0.3	133.3	0.2	133.4	0.1	133.3	-0.1	133.3	0.0	133.6	0.2	133.5	-0.1	131.7	-1.3	135.2	2.7	135.5	0.2	135.6	0.1
1994	136.5	0.7	136.6	0.1	136.6	0.0	136.7	0.1	137.1	0.3	137.0	-0.1	137.2	0.1	137.2	0.0	135.6	-1.2	138.5	2.1	138.3	-0.1	138.7	0.3
1995	139.6	0.6	139.6	0.0	139.4	-0.1	139.3	-0.1	139.3	0.0	139.0	-0.2	139.0	0.0	138.9	-0.1	137.0	-1.4	140.9	2.8	141.5	0.4	141.5	0.0

Source: U.S. Department of Labor, Bureau of Labor Statistics, Division of Industry Prices and Price Indexes. n.e.c. stands for not elsewhere classified. - indicates no data collected for period or unavailable.

Motor Vehicles and Equipment
Producer Price Index
Base 1982 = 100

For 1926-1995. Columns headed % show percentile change in the index from the previous period for which an index is available.

Year	Jan Index	%	Feb Index	%	Mar Index	%	Apr Index	%	May Index	%	Jun Index	%	Jul Index	%	Aug Index	%	Sep Index	%	Oct Index	%	Nov Index	%	Dec Index	%
1926	-	-	-	-	-	-	-	-	-	-	-	-	-	-	-	-	-	-	-	-	-	-	-	-
1927	-	-	-	-	-	-	-	-	-	-	-	-	-	-	-	-	-	-	-	-	-	-	-	-
1928	-	-	-	-	-	-	-	-	-	-	-	-	-	-	-	-	-	-	-	-	-	-	-	-
1929	-	-	-	-	-	-	-	-	-	-	-	-	-	-	-	-	-	-	-	-	-	-	-	-
1930	-	-	-	-	-	-	-	-	-	-	-	-	-	-	-	-	-	-	-	-	-	-	-	-
1931	-	-	-	-	-	-	-	-	-	-	-	-	-	-	-	-	-	-	-	-	-	-	-	-
1932	-	-	-	-	-	-	-	-	-	-	-	-	-	-	-	-	-	-	-	-	-	-	-	-
1933	-	-	-	-	-	-	-	-	-	-	-	-	-	-	-	-	-	-	-	-	-	-	-	-
1934	-	-	-	-	-	-	-	-	-	-	-	-	-	-	-	-	-	-	-	-	-	-	-	-
1935	-	-	-	-	-	-	-	-	-	-	-	-	-	-	-	-	-	-	-	-	-	-	-	-
1936	-	-	-	-	-	-	-	-	-	-	-	-	-	-	-	-	-	-	-	-	-	-	-	-
1937	14.4	-	14.4	0.0	14.4	0.0	14.5	0.7	14.5	0.0	14.5	0.0	14.5	0.0	15.0	3.4	15.2	1.3	15.4	1.3	15.9	3.2	15.9	0.0
1938	15.9	0.0	15.9	0.0	15.9	0.0	15.9	0.0	16.0	0.6	16.0	0.0	16.0	0.0	16.0	0.0	16.0	0.0	15.8	-1.2	15.6	-1.3	15.6	0.0
1939	15.6	0.0	15.6	0.0	15.6	0.0	15.6	0.0	15.5	-0.6	15.5	0.0	15.5	0.0	15.4	-0.6	15.4	0.0	15.6	1.3	15.8	1.3	15.8	0.0
1940	15.8	0.0	15.8	0.0	15.8	0.0	15.8	0.0	15.8	0.0	15.8	0.0	15.9	0.6	15.9	0.0	16.0	0.6	16.7	4.4	16.7	0.0	16.7	0.0
1941	16.7	0.0	16.6	-0.6	16.6	0.0	16.7	0.6	16.7	0.0	16.7	0.0	16.8	0.6	16.8	0.0	16.8	0.0	18.7	11.3	18.7	0.0	18.7	0.0
1942	18.7	0.0	18.7	0.0	18.8	0.5	18.8	0.0	18.8	0.0	18.8	0.0	18.8	0.0	18.8	0.0	18.8	0.0	18.8	0.0	18.8	0.0	18.8	0.0
1943	18.8	0.0	18.8	0.0	18.8	0.0	18.8	0.0	18.8	0.0	18.8	0.0	18.8	0.0	18.8	0.0	18.8	0.0	18.8	0.0	18.8	0.0	18.8	0.0
1944	18.8	0.0	18.8	0.0	18.8	0.0	18.8	0.0	18.8	0.0	18.9	0.5	18.9	0.0	18.9	0.0	18.9	0.0	18.9	0.0	19.0	0.5	19.0	0.0
1945	19.0	0.0	19.0	0.0	19.1	0.5	19.1	0.0	19.2	0.5	19.3	0.5	19.3	0.0	19.3	0.0	19.3	0.0	19.3	0.0	19.5	1.0	19.5	0.0
1946	19.7	1.0	20.1	2.0	20.4	1.5	20.9	2.5	21.9	4.8	22.6	3.2	22.6	0.0	23.1	2.2	23.4	1.3	23.6	0.9	24.3	3.0	24.8	2.1
1947	24.9	0.4	24.9	0.0	24.9	0.0	24.8	-0.4	24.9	0.4	25.0	0.4	25.0	0.0	25.9	3.6	26.4	1.9	26.4	0.0	26.5	0.4	26.6	0.4
1948	26.8	0.8	26.7	-0.4	26.7	0.0	26.7	0.0	26.8	0.4	27.8	3.7	28.5	2.5	29.4	3.2	29.6	0.7	29.6	0.0	29.7	0.3	29.9	0.7
1949	30.0	0.3	30.3	1.0	30.4	0.3	30.2	-0.7	30.1	-0.3	30.0	-0.3	30.1	0.3	30.1	0.0	30.1	0.0	30.1	0.0	30.1	0.0	30.1	0.0
1950	30.0	-0.3	29.9	-0.3	29.8	-0.3	29.8	0.0	29.9	0.3	29.9	0.0	29.9	0.0	29.9	0.0	30.1	0.7	30.1	0.0	30.1	0.0	30.4	1.0
1951	30.5	0.3	30.6	0.3	31.4	2.6	31.4	0.0	31.4	0.0	31.4	0.0	31.4	0.0	31.6	0.6	31.9	0.9	32.4	1.6	32.5	0.3	32.6	0.3
1952	32.7	0.3	33.5	2.4	33.5	0.0	33.5	0.0	33.5	0.0	33.5	0.0	33.5	0.0	33.5	0.0	33.5	0.0	33.5	0.0	33.5	0.0	33.5	0.0
1953	33.5	0.0	33.5	0.0	33.5	0.0	33.2	-0.9	33.2	0.0	33.2	0.0	33.2	0.0	33.2	0.0	33.2	0.0	33.2	0.0	33.2	0.0	33.2	0.0
1954	33.2	0.0	33.2	0.0	33.2	0.0	33.2	0.0	33.2	0.0	33.2	0.0	33.2	0.0	33.2	0.0	33.2	0.0	33.2	0.0	33.8	1.8	34.0	0.6
1955	34.0	0.0	34.0	0.0	34.0	0.0	34.1	0.3	34.1	0.0	34.1	0.0	34.1	0.0	34.1	0.0	34.1	0.0	34.9	2.3	35.3	1.1	35.4	0.3
1956	35.4	0.0	35.6	0.6	36.1	1.4	36.1	0.0	36.1	0.0	36.1	0.0	36.1	0.0	36.1	0.0	36.2	0.3	36.6	1.1	37.5	2.5	37.5	0.0
1957	37.5	0.0	37.6	0.3	37.6	0.0	37.7	0.3	37.7	0.0	37.7	0.0	37.7	0.0	37.7	0.0	37.7	0.0	37.9	0.5	38.8	2.4	38.9	0.3
1958	38.9	0.0	38.9	0.0	38.9	0.0	38.9	0.0	38.9	0.0	38.9	0.0	38.9	0.0	38.9	0.0	38.9	0.0	39.0	0.3	39.9	2.3	40.0	0.3
1959	40.0	0.0	40.0	0.0	40.0	0.0	40.0	0.0	40.0	0.0	40.0	0.0	40.0	0.0	40.0	0.0	40.0	0.0	39.6	-1.0	39.6	0.0	39.6	0.0
1960	39.6	0.0	39.6	0.0	39.6	0.0	39.6	0.0	39.6	0.0	39.6	0.0	39.6	0.0	39.6	0.0	39.6	0.0	37.9	-4.3	39.2	3.4	39.3	0.3
1961	39.4	0.3	39.2	-0.5	39.2	0.0	39.2	0.0	39.2	0.0	39.2	0.0	39.2	0.0	39.2	0.0	39.2	0.0	39.2	0.0	39.2	0.0	39.2	0.0
1962	39.2	0.0	39.1	-0.3	39.1	0.0	39.1	0.0	39.1	0.0	39.4	0.8	39.4	0.0	39.4	0.0	39.4	0.0	39.2	-0.5	39.2	0.0	39.2	0.0
1963	39.2	0.0	39.2	0.0	39.2	0.0	39.0	-0.5	38.9	-0.3	38.7	-0.5	38.9	0.5	38.8	-0.3	38.7	-0.3	38.9	0.5	38.9	0.0	38.9	0.0
1964	38.9	0.0	38.9	0.0	38.9	0.0	38.9	0.0	39.4	1.3	39.3	-0.3	39.3	0.0	39.2	-0.3	39.1	-0.3	39.2	0.3	39.2	0.0	39.2	0.0
1965	39.2	0.0	39.3	0.3	39.2	-0.3	39.2	0.0	39.2	0.0	39.2	0.0	39.2	0.0	39.2	0.0	39.1	-0.3	39.1	0.0	39.1	0.0	39.1	0.0
1966	39.1	0.0	39.1	0.0	39.0	-0.3	39.0	0.0	39.3	0.8	39.2	-0.3	39.2	0.0	39.1	-0.3	39.0	-0.3	39.6	1.5	39.6	0.0	39.6	0.0
1967	39.6	0.0	39.6	0.0	39.6	0.0	39.6	0.0	39.4	-0.5	39.5	0.3	39.4	-0.3	39.6	0.5	39.6	0.0	40.6	2.5	40.6	0.0	40.6	0.0
1968	40.7	0.2	40.7	0.0	40.7	0.0	40.7	0.0	40.6	-0.2	40.8	0.5	40.7	-0.2	40.7	0.0	40.7	0.0	41.6	2.2	41.6	0.0	41.6	0.0
1969	41.5	-0.2	41.5	0.0	41.4	-0.2	41.5	0.2	41.5	0.0	41.6	0.2	41.5	-0.2	41.4	-0.2	41.4	0.0	42.3	2.2	42.5	0.5	42.5	0.0
1970	42.5	0.0	42.5	0.0	42.7	0.5	42.5	-0.5	42.7	0.5	42.7	0.0	42.7	0.0	42.7	0.0	42.8	0.2	44.9	4.9	45.0	0.2	45.0	0.0

[Continued]

Motor Vehicles and Equipment
Producer Price Index
Base 1982 = 100
[Continued]

For 1926-1995. Columns headed % show percentile change in the index from the previous period for which an index is available.

Year	Jan Index	%	Feb Index	%	Mar Index	%	Apr Index	%	May Index	%	Jun Index	%	Jul Index	%	Aug Index	%	Sep Index	%	Oct Index	%	Nov Index	%	Dec Index	%
1971	45.2	0.4	45.4	0.4	45.5	0.2	45.6	0.2	45.6	0.0	45.7	0.2	45.8	0.2	45.8	0.0	45.3	-1.1	46.0	1.5	46.0	0.0	46.9	2.0
1972	46.9	0.0	47.0	0.2	46.9	-0.2	47.0	0.2	47.0	0.0	47.2	0.4	47.1	-0.2	47.1	0.0	47.1	0.0	46.5	-1.3	46.6	0.2	47.1	1.1
1973	47.0	-0.2	47.1	0.2	47.2	0.2	47.4	0.4	47.4	0.0	47.3	-0.2	47.4	0.2	47.4	0.0	47.1	-0.6	47.7	1.3	47.8	0.2	48.3	1.0
1974	48.9	1.2	49.0	0.2	49.0	0.0	49.1	0.2	49.7	1.2	50.2	1.0	51.1	1.8	51.8	1.4	52.0	0.4	55.0	5.8	55.3	0.5	56.0	1.3
1975	55.8	-0.4	56.3	0.9	56.9	1.1	56.9	0.0	56.9	0.0	57.0	0.2	56.9	-0.2	57.1	0.4	57.3	0.4	59.7	4.2	59.9	0.3	60.0	0.2
1976	60.2	0.3	60.2	0.0	60.4	0.3	60.4	0.0	60.3	-0.2	60.4	0.2	60.4	0.0	60.8	0.7	61.1	0.5	63.3	3.6	63.4	0.2	63.5	0.2
1977	63.4	-0.2	63.5	0.2	64.0	0.8	64.1	0.2	64.3	0.3	64.4	0.2	64.4	0.0	64.9	0.8	65.2	0.5	68.0	4.3	67.9	-0.1	68.0	0.1
1978	68.2	0.3	68.4	0.3	68.4	0.0	68.8	0.6	69.5	1.0	69.7	0.3	69.8	0.1	70.0	0.3	70.0	0.0	72.4	3.4	72.6	0.3	72.8	0.3
1979	73.6	1.1	74.0	0.5	74.1	0.1	75.4	1.8	75.6	0.3	75.7	0.1	76.0	0.4	74.7	-1.7	75.0	0.4	78.4	4.5	78.6	0.3	78.9	0.4
1980	79.9	1.3	79.6	-0.4	79.9	0.4	81.8	2.4	81.4	-0.5	81.7	0.4	83.0	1.6	84.2	1.4	81.8	-2.9	86.9	6.2	87.0	0.1	90.0	3.4
1981	91.1	1.2	91.9	0.9	91.4	-0.5	93.1	1.9	93.9	0.9	94.2	0.3	94.5	0.3	94.9	0.4	92.7	-2.3	98.6	6.4	99.1	0.5	99.3	0.2
1982	99.8	0.5	98.2	-1.6	98.2	0.0	98.4	0.2	99.2	0.8	99.9	0.7	100.3	0.4	100.6	0.3	97.4	-3.2	102.6	5.3	102.6	0.0	102.7	0.1
1983	102.3	-0.4	102.0	-0.3	101.7	-0.3	101.8	0.1	102.0	0.2	102.1	0.1	102.1	0.0	102.2	0.1	99.2	-2.9	103.7	4.5	103.7	0.0	103.7	0.0
1984	103.9	0.2	104.0	0.1	104.1	0.1	104.2	0.1	104.1	-0.1	103.9	-0.2	104.0	0.1	103.9	-0.1	101.6	-2.2	105.0	3.3	105.2	0.2	104.9	-0.3
1985	105.5	0.6	106.1	0.6	105.9	-0.2	106.0	0.1	106.4	0.4	106.5	0.1	106.5	0.0	106.5	0.0	101.4	-4.8	108.8	7.3	108.8	0.0	108.2	-0.6
1986	107.6	-0.6	107.8	0.2	107.5	-0.3	108.6	1.0	108.5	-0.1	108.7	0.2	108.8	0.1	108.3	-0.5	105.2	-2.9	113.1	7.5	113.0	-0.1	112.5	-0.4
1987	112.6	0.1	110.9	-1.5	111.1	0.2	112.3	1.1	111.8	-0.4	111.5	-0.3	111.4	-0.1	110.8	-0.5	108.9	-1.7	114.2	4.9	113.3	-0.8	111.8	-1.3
1988	112.0	0.2	111.9	-0.1	111.8	-0.1	112.0	0.2	112.3	0.3	112.4	0.1	112.6	0.2	112.8	0.2	110.9	-1.7	116.9	5.4	116.1	-0.7	116.0	-0.1
1989	116.2	0.2	116.5	0.3	115.5	-0.9	114.8	-0.6	115.6	0.7	115.9	0.3	114.5	-1.2	114.5	0.0	113.8	-0.6	119.6	5.1	118.8	-0.7	118.6	-0.2
1990	117.2	-1.2	117.3	0.1	117.0	-0.3	116.9	-0.1	116.6	-0.3	117.6	0.9	117.8	0.2	117.2	-0.5	116.7	-0.4	121.6	4.2	121.5	-0.1	121.5	0.0
1991	121.9	0.3	122.4	0.4	122.2	-0.2	121.5	-0.6	120.7	-0.7	120.6	-0.1	120.5	-0.1	120.6	0.1	119.2	-1.2	125.8	5.5	125.4	-0.3	124.9	-0.4
1992	124.8	-0.1	124.6	-0.2	124.9	0.2	124.8	-0.1	124.7	-0.1	124.3	-0.3	124.4	0.1	123.9	-0.4	121.3	-2.1	127.1	4.8	127.1	0.0	126.9	-0.2
1993	127.1	0.2	127.8	0.6	127.8	0.0	127.7	-0.1	127.6	-0.1	127.7	0.1	127.8	0.1	127.7	-0.1	124.9	-2.2	129.7	3.8	129.9	0.2	130.0	0.1
1994	130.7	0.5	130.9	0.2	130.8	-0.1	130.8	0.0	131.4	0.5	131.3	-0.1	131.5	0.2	131.6	0.1	129.0	-2.0	132.8	2.9	132.5	-0.2	133.0	0.4
1995	133.4	0.3	133.3	-0.1	133.1	-0.2	132.9	-0.2	132.7	-0.2	132.2	-0.4	132.2	0.0	131.9	-0.2	129.0	-2.2	134.6	4.3	135.5	0.7	135.4	-0.1

Source: U.S. Department of Labor, Bureau of Labor Statistics, Division of Industry Prices and Price Indexes. n.e.c. stands for not elsewhere classified. - indicates no data collected for period or unavailable.

Aircraft and Aircraft Equipment
Producer Price Index
Base 1982 = 100

For 1971-1995. Columns headed % show percentile change in the index from the previous period for which an index is available.

Year	Jan Index	%	Feb Index	%	Mar Index	%	Apr Index	%	May Index	%	Jun Index	%	Jul Index	%	Aug Index	%	Sep Index	%	Oct Index	%	Nov Index	%	Dec Index	%
1971	36.7	-	36.7	0.0	36.7	0.0	36.7	0.0	36.7	0.0	36.7	0.0	36.7	0.0	36.7	0.0	36.7	0.0	36.1	-1.6	36.1	0.0	37.0	2.5
1972	38.4	3.8	38.4	0.0	38.4	0.0	38.4	0.0	38.4	0.0	38.4	0.0	38.4	0.0	38.4	0.0	38.4	0.0	38.6	0.5	38.6	0.0	38.6	0.0
1973	38.6	0.0	38.8	0.5	39.0	0.5	39.0	0.0	39.0	0.0	39.0	0.0	39.0	0.0	39.0	0.0	39.0	0.0	39.0	0.0	39.1	0.3	39.2	0.3
1974	39.2	0.0	39.2	0.0	39.2	0.0	39.7	1.3	41.8	5.3	41.8	0.0	42.0	0.5	42.0	0.0	43.3	3.1	43.9	1.4	44.3	0.9	45.1	1.8
1975	46.1	2.2	46.1	0.0	46.3	0.4	48.2	4.1	48.2	0.0	48.2	0.0	48.2	0.0	48.2	0.0	49.4	2.5	50.9	3.0	50.9	0.0	50.9	0.0
1976	53.9	5.9	53.8	-0.2	53.8	0.0	53.8	0.0	53.8	0.0	53.8	0.0	53.8	0.0	53.8	0.0	54.7	1.7	55.7	1.8	55.7	0.0	57.6	3.4
1977	58.3	1.2	58.3	0.0	58.3	0.0	58.4	0.2	58.4	0.0	58.4	0.0	58.4	0.0	58.4	0.0	59.2	1.4	60.8	2.7	62.0	2.0	62.0	0.0
1978	63.1	1.8	63.1	0.0	63.1	0.0	63.1	0.0	63.1	0.0	63.1	0.0	63.1	0.0	63.1	0.0	64.3	1.9	65.9	2.5	67.3	2.1	67.4	0.1
1979	68.4	1.5	68.4	0.0	68.8	0.6	69.0	0.3	69.2	0.3	69.3	0.1	69.5	0.3	70.3	1.2	70.3	0.0	71.0	1.0	71.8	1.1	72.3	0.7
1980	75.3	4.1	75.3	0.0	75.3	0.0	75.9	0.8	75.9	0.0	75.9	0.0	76.1	0.3	76.1	0.0	78.9	3.7	87.0	10.3	87.0	0.0	87.4	0.5
1981	89.4	2.3	89.4	0.0	89.9	0.6	90.0	0.1	90.0	0.0	90.3	0.3	90.3	0.0	90.3	0.0	92.7	2.7	92.4	-0.3	95.5	3.4	95.5	0.0
1982	97.3	1.9	97.3	0.0	97.3	0.0	98.6	1.3	98.6	0.0	98.6	0.0	98.6	0.0	98.6	0.0	101.5	2.9	102.5	1.0	103.6	1.1	107.4	3.7
1983	106.3	-1.0	106.7	0.4	107.1	0.4	107.1	0.0	107.1	0.0	107.1	0.0	107.1	0.0	108.7	1.5	108.7	0.0	111.1	2.2	111.1	0.0	111.1	0.0
1984	112.5	1.3	114.4	1.7	114.4	0.0	114.4	0.0	114.4	0.0	114.4	0.0	114.6	0.2	114.6	0.0	116.1	1.3	116.2	0.1	117.2	0.9	117.2	0.0
1985	118.2	0.9	118.2	0.0	118.2	0.0	119.9	1.4	120.0	0.1	120.0	0.0	121.4	1.2	121.5	0.1	-		-		-		-	
1986	124.1	2.1	124.4	0.2	124.4	0.0	124.6	0.2	124.3	-0.2	124.3	0.0	124.5	0.2	124.6	0.1	122.6	-1.6	122.8	0.2	122.8	0.0	122.7	-0.1
1987	123.5	0.7	123.5	0.0	123.9	0.3	123.9	0.0	122.8	-0.9	122.9	0.1	122.9	0.0	122.9	0.0	123.1	0.2	123.1	0.0	123.4	0.2	123.3	-0.1
1988	125.1	1.5	125.2	0.1	125.3	0.1	126.2	0.7	126.0	-0.2	126.7	0.6	125.8	-0.7	126.0	0.2	126.4	0.3	126.3	-0.1	126.6	0.2	126.7	0.1
1989	127.9	0.9	128.1	0.2	128.9	0.6	129.3	0.3	129.4	0.1	129.6	0.2	129.9	0.2	130.4	0.4	130.4	0.0	130.7	0.2	132.0	1.0	132.2	0.2
1990	134.3	1.6	134.9	0.4	135.4	0.4	136.1	0.5	136.3	0.1	136.4	0.1	136.7	0.2	137.5	0.6	137.6	0.1	138.4	0.6	138.9	0.4	139.1	0.1
1991	141.7	1.9	142.0	0.2	142.3	0.2	142.8	0.4	144.2	1.0	144.3	0.1	144.7	0.3	145.5	0.6	145.6	0.1	146.0	0.3	146.2	0.1	146.4	0.1
1992	149.5	2.1	149.7	0.1	149.9	0.1	150.6	0.5	150.9	0.2	151.4	0.3	151.4	0.0	152.0	0.4	152.5	0.3	152.8	0.2	152.5	-0.2	152.6	0.1
1993	153.5	0.6	153.5	0.0	153.9	0.3	154.6	0.5	154.7	0.1	154.0	-0.5	154.7	0.5	155.1	0.3	154.8	-0.2	156.4	1.0	156.8	0.3	156.9	0.1
1994	158.4	1.0	158.6	0.1	158.5	-0.1	158.7	0.1	158.7	0.0	158.7	0.0	158.8	0.1	158.9	0.1	159.0	0.1	160.5	0.9	160.8	0.2	160.8	0.0
1995	163.1	1.4	163.1	0.0	162.9	-0.1	162.8	-0.1	163.0	0.1	163.3	0.2	163.4	0.1	163.5	0.1	163.3	-0.1	164.3	0.6	164.4	0.1	164.7	0.2

Source: U.S. Department of Labor, Bureau of Labor Statistics, Division of Industry Prices and Price Indexes. n.e.c. stands for not elsewhere classified. - indicates no data collected for period or unavailable.

Ships and Boats

Producer Price Index
Base 1982 = 100

For 1981-1995. Columns headed % show percentile change in the index from the previous period for which an index is available.

Year	Jan Index	%	Feb Index	%	Mar Index	%	Apr Index	%	May Index	%	Jun Index	%	Jul Index	%	Aug Index	%	Sep Index	%	Oct Index	%	Nov Index	%	Dec Index	%
1981	-	-	-	-	-	-	-	-	-	-	-	-	-	-	-	-	-	-	-	-	-	-	97.5	-
1982	98.1	0.6	98.9	0.8	99.2	0.3	99.7	0.5	99.8	0.1	100.3	0.5	100.1	-0.2	100.4	0.3	100.6	0.2	100.9	0.3	101.0	0.1	100.9	-0.1
1983	101.0	0.1	101.4	0.4	101.5	0.1	102.4	0.9	102.7	0.3	102.9	0.2	103.1	0.2	103.2	0.1	104.1	0.9	104.5	0.4	104.4	-0.1	105.2	0.8
1984	106.1	0.9	106.3	0.2	106.5	0.2	106.6	0.1	108.1	1.4	108.0	-0.1	108.6	0.6	108.0	-0.6	107.0	-0.9	107.3	0.3	107.6	0.3	108.1	0.5
1985	108.6	0.5	109.0	0.4	109.1	0.1	110.0	0.8	110.0	0.0	110.0	0.0	109.7	-0.3	110.4	0.6	110.5	0.1	111.6	1.0	112.0	0.4	112.4	0.4
1986	113.2	0.7	113.2	0.0	113.3	0.1	113.4	0.1	113.6	0.2	113.6	0.0	113.5	-0.1	113.4	-0.1	113.4	0.0	113.6	0.2	113.6	0.0	113.6	0.0
1987	113.8	0.2	113.9	0.1	114.0	0.1	114.1	0.1	114.1	0.0	114.1	0.0	114.1	0.0	114.1	0.0	114.2	0.1	114.2	0.0	114.2	0.0	114.3	0.1
1988	114.4	0.1	114.5	0.1	114.1	-0.3	114.1	0.0	114.2	0.1	114.2	0.0	114.5	0.3	114.6	0.1	116.5	1.7	116.3	-0.2	116.8	0.4	116.7	-0.1
1989	116.9	0.2	117.2	0.3	117.2	0.0	114.8	-2.0	119.9	4.4	122.1	1.8	122.4	0.2	124.0	1.3	122.1	-1.5	122.0	-0.1	122.1	0.1	120.6	-1.2
1990	120.9	0.2	123.5	2.2	125.0	1.2	125.1	0.1	125.1	0.0	125.2	0.1	125.3	0.1	125.9	0.5	127.0	0.9	127.4	0.3	127.2	-0.2	127.3	0.1
1991	127.5	0.2	127.7	0.2	128.7	0.8	128.7	0.0	130.6	1.5	130.6	0.0	130.8	0.2	130.8	0.0	130.8	0.0	131.3	0.4	131.3	0.0	134.9	2.7
1992	135.0	0.1	135.2	0.1	137.2	1.5	137.8	0.4	137.9	0.1	137.9	0.0	137.9	0.0	137.6	-0.2	137.9	0.2	137.9	0.0	138.0	0.1	138.1	0.1
1993	142.5	3.2	142.9	0.3	143.1	0.1	143.5	0.3	143.5	0.0	143.5	0.0	143.5	0.0	143.1	-0.3	143.4	0.2	143.5	0.1	143.5	0.0	143.5	0.0
1994	144.6	0.8	144.8	0.1	145.6	0.6	145.8	0.1	145.8	0.0	145.8	0.0	145.0	-0.5	145.1	0.1	145.3	0.1	145.5	0.1	145.5	0.0	145.6	0.1
1995	146.4	0.5	147.7	0.9	147.7	0.0	147.9	0.1	147.9	0.0	148.0	0.1	147.7	-0.2	147.8	0.1	149.5	1.2	148.2	-0.9	148.3	0.1	148.4	0.1

Source: U.S. Department of Labor, Bureau of Labor Statistics, Division of Industry Prices and Price Indexes. n.e.c. stands for not elsewhere classified. - indicates no data collected for period or unavailable.

Railroad Equipment
Producer Price Index
Base 1982 = 100

For 1961-1995. Columns headed % show percentile change in the index from the previous period for which an index is available.

Year	Jan Index	%	Feb Index	%	Mar Index	%	Apr Index	%	May Index	%	Jun Index	%	Jul Index	%	Aug Index	%	Sep Index	%	Oct Index	%	Nov Index	%	Dec Index	%
1961	27.9	-	27.9	0.0	27.9	0.0	27.9	0.0	27.9	0.0	27.9	0.0	27.9	0.0	27.9	0.0	27.9	0.0	28.0	0.4	28.0	0.0	28.0	0.0
1962	28.0	0.0	28.0	0.0	28.0	0.0	28.0	0.0	28.0	0.0	28.0	0.0	28.0	0.0	28.0	0.0	28.0	0.0	28.0	0.0	28.0	0.0	28.0	0.0
1963	28.0	0.0	28.0	0.0	28.0	0.0	28.0	0.0	28.0	0.0	28.0	0.0	28.0	0.0	28.0	0.0	28.0	0.0	28.0	0.0	28.0	0.0	28.0	0.0
1964	28.0	0.0	28.0	0.0	28.0	0.0	27.9	-0.4	27.9	0.0	27.9	0.0	28.0	0.4	28.0	0.0	28.0	0.0	28.0	0.0	28.0	0.0	28.0	0.0
1965	28.0	0.0	28.0	0.0	28.0	0.0	28.0	0.0	28.0	0.0	28.1	0.4	28.1	0.0	28.1	0.0	28.1	0.0	28.1	0.0	28.1	0.0	28.1	0.0
1966	28.1	0.0	28.1	0.0	28.1	0.0	28.1	0.0	28.1	0.0	28.1	0.0	28.1	0.0	28.1	0.0	28.1	0.0	28.1	0.0	28.1	0.0	28.6	1.8
1967	28.7	0.3	28.7	0.0	28.7	0.0	28.7	0.0	28.7	0.0	28.7	0.0	28.7	0.0	28.7	0.0	28.7	0.0	29.2	1.7	29.3	0.3	29.3	0.0
1968	29.4	0.3	29.4	0.0	29.4	0.0	29.4	0.0	29.4	0.0	29.4	0.0	29.8	1.4	29.9	0.3	29.9	0.0	30.3	1.3	30.3	0.0	30.3	0.0
1969	30.3	0.0	30.3	0.0	30.8	1.7	30.8	0.0	31.0	0.6	31.2	0.6	31.9	2.2	32.0	0.3	32.0	0.0	32.2	0.6	32.2	0.0	32.3	0.3
1970	32.7	1.2	32.8	0.3	33.0	0.6	33.1	0.3	33.1	0.0	33.2	0.3	33.2	0.0	33.2	0.0	33.3	0.3	33.5	0.6	33.5	0.0	33.7	0.6
1971	34.3	1.8	34.3	0.0	34.5	0.6	34.5	0.0	34.7	0.6	34.8	0.3	35.2	1.1	35.3	0.3	35.3	0.0	35.3	0.0	35.3	0.0	35.3	0.0
1972	35.7	1.1	35.8	0.3	36.7	2.5	37.1	1.1	37.4	0.8	37.4	0.0	37.6	0.5	37.6	0.0	37.6	0.0	37.6	0.0	37.6	0.0	37.8	0.5
1973	38.0	0.5	38.2	0.5	38.3	0.3	38.5	0.5	38.8	0.8	38.9	0.3	38.9	0.0	39.0	0.3	39.3	0.8	39.3	0.0	39.4	0.3	40.0	1.5
1974	40.5	1.3	40.7	0.5	41.8	2.7	42.9	2.6	44.4	3.5	47.2	6.3	48.5	2.8	50.4	3.9	51.4	2.0	52.2	1.6	53.1	1.7	54.2	2.1
1975	56.7	4.6	56.9	0.4	57.2	0.5	57.2	0.0	57.6	0.7	57.5	-0.2	58.4	1.6	58.2	-0.3	58.4	0.3	59.1	1.2	59.7	1.0	60.0	0.5
1976	60.4	0.7	61.2	1.3	61.2	0.0	61.7	0.8	61.7	0.0	62.2	0.8	62.6	0.6	63.2	1.0	63.2	0.0	64.3	1.7	64.3	0.0	64.4	0.2
1977	65.8	2.2	65.8	0.0	66.4	0.9	66.7	0.5	66.7	0.0	66.9	0.3	67.6	1.0	67.9	0.4	67.9	0.0	68.9	1.5	68.9	0.0	69.2	0.4
1978	70.3	1.6	70.6	0.4	70.6	0.0	72.2	2.3	72.4	0.3	72.4	0.0	73.2	1.1	73.4	0.3	74.1	1.0	75.1	1.3	75.5	0.5	75.6	0.1
1979	76.9	1.7	77.4	0.7	77.6	0.3	78.4	1.0	78.4	0.0	79.3	1.1	81.0	2.1	81.1	0.1	81.3	0.2	82.6	1.6	83.2	0.7	83.4	0.2
1980	85.9	3.0	86.4	0.6	87.2	0.9	89.4	2.5	89.6	0.2	90.1	0.6	91.3	1.3	91.8	0.5	92.4	0.7	93.3	1.0	93.4	0.1	93.5	0.1
1981	96.0	2.7	96.0	0.0	96.4	0.4	96.9	0.5	95.6	-1.3	95.7	0.1	97.6	2.0	97.8	0.2	97.8	0.0	97.8	0.0	98.5	0.7	98.2	-0.3
1982	99.8	1.6	99.8	0.0	99.9	0.1	99.1	-0.8	98.9	-0.2	98.9	0.0	98.9	0.0	100.4	1.5	100.4	0.0	101.2	0.8	101.2	0.0	101.2	0.0
1983	101.3	0.1	101.2	-0.1	101.1	-0.1	101.0	-0.1	101.1	0.1	101.0	-0.1	101.4	0.4	101.3	-0.1	101.2	-0.1	100.6	-0.6	100.6	0.0	101.2	0.6
1984	101.5	0.3	101.5	0.0	101.6	0.1	102.3	0.7	102.3	0.0	102.3	0.0	102.9	0.6	103.2	0.3	103.2	0.0	103.6	0.4	103.6	0.0	103.6	0.0
1985	103.9	0.3	104.4	0.5	104.7	0.3	104.8	0.1	104.6	-0.2	105.0	0.4	105.1	0.1	105.2	0.1	105.2	0.0	105.2	0.0	105.1	-0.1	105.2	0.1
1986	105.9	0.7	105.5	-0.4	105.6	0.1	105.6	0.0	105.3	-0.3	105.3	0.0	106.1	0.8	104.9	-1.1	105.2	0.3	105.2	0.0	105.2	0.0	105.3	0.1
1987	105.2	-0.1	104.6	-0.6	104.7	0.1	104.6	-0.1	104.5	-0.1	104.4	-0.1	104.7	0.3	104.8	0.1	104.8	0.0	104.6	-0.2	105.0	0.4	105.0	0.0
1988	105.3	0.3	104.8	-0.5	105.5	0.7	106.2	0.7	107.0	0.8	108.1	1.0	108.2	0.1	108.6	0.4	108.8	0.2	108.8	0.0	109.0	0.2	110.2	1.1
1989	111.8	1.5	112.2	0.4	112.2	0.0	114.2	1.8	114.2	0.0	114.3	0.1	114.6	0.3	114.6	0.0	114.7	0.1	114.8	0.1	114.9	0.1	115.6	0.6
1990	116.3	0.6	117.5	1.0	117.4	-0.1	117.6	0.2	117.7	0.1	118.5	0.7	118.5	0.0	118.5	0.0	119.9	1.2	119.9	0.0	120.9	0.8	120.9	0.0
1991	122.0	0.9	121.9	-0.1	122.2	0.2	122.1	-0.1	122.2	0.1	122.2	0.0	122.6	0.3	122.8	0.2	122.8	0.0	122.3	-0.4	121.9	-0.3	121.8	-0.1
1992	122.5	0.6	123.2	0.6	123.6	0.3	123.6	0.0	123.7	0.1	123.9	0.2	124.0	0.1	123.9	-0.1	124.2	0.2	124.2	0.0	123.8	-0.3	123.3	-0.4
1993	123.6	0.2	124.2	0.5	124.3	0.1	124.5	0.2	124.5	0.0	124.6	0.1	125.0	0.3	125.8	0.6	126.1	0.2	125.7	-0.3	125.7	0.0	127.6	1.5
1994	127.9	0.2	128.1	0.2	128.5	0.3	128.5	0.0	128.7	0.2	129.0	0.2	129.1	0.1	129.8	0.5	129.9	0.1	130.0	0.1	130.1	0.1	130.2	0.1
1995	130.9	0.5	132.7	1.4	133.2	0.4	134.2	0.8	134.7	0.4	135.2	0.4	135.5	0.2	135.7	0.1	135.7	0.0	135.8	0.1	136.6	0.6	137.0	0.3

Source: U.S. Department of Labor, Bureau of Labor Statistics, Division of Industry Prices and Price Indexes. n.e.c. stands for not elsewhere classified. - indicates no data collected for period or unavailable.

Transportation Equipment, n.e.c.
Producer Price Index
Base June 1985 = 100

For 1985-1995. Columns headed % show percentile change in the index from the previous period for which an index is available.

Year	Jan		Feb		Mar		Apr		May		Jun		Jul		Aug		Sep		Oct		Nov		Dec	
	Index	%	Index	%	Index	%	Index	%	Index	%	Index	%	Index	%	Index	%	Index	%	Index	%	Index	%	Index	%
1985	-	-	-	-	-	-	-	-	-	-	100.0	-	100.0	0.0	99.5	-0.5	99.3	-0.2	99.3	0.0	99.3	0.0	99.3	0.0
1986	99.0	-0.3	99.4	0.4	100.1	0.7	100.0	-0.1	99.9	-0.1	100.0	0.1	100.1	0.1	100.6	0.5	100.2	-0.4	100.3	0.1	101.1	0.8	101.1	0.0
1987	101.1	0.0	101.2	0.1	101.2	0.0	101.2	0.0	101.6	0.4	101.8	0.2	102.0	0.2	102.1	0.1	102.8	0.7	103.2	0.4	103.1	-0.1	103.1	0.0
1988	103.3	0.2	103.9	0.6	104.0	0.1	105.4	1.3	105.4	0.0	105.3	-0.1	106.5	1.1	106.6	0.1	108.0	1.3	108.0	0.0	108.3	0.3	108.2	-0.1
1989	108.7	0.5	109.0	0.3	109.1	0.1	109.4	0.3	109.4	0.0	109.2	-0.2	109.4	0.2	109.7	0.3	110.3	0.5	110.9	0.5	111.1	0.2	111.2	0.1
1990	111.2	0.0	111.2	0.0	111.0	-0.2	111.7	0.6	111.7	0.0	111.7	0.0	111.8	0.1	111.8	0.0	111.8	0.0	111.7	-0.1	112.0	0.3	111.8	-0.2
1991	112.4	0.5	112.6	0.2	113.1	0.4	113.3	0.2	113.7	0.4	113.8	0.1	113.8	0.0	113.9	0.1	114.3	0.4	114.2	-0.1	114.2	0.0	114.2	0.0
1992	114.8	0.5	114.9	0.1	114.7	-0.2	114.7	0.0	114.7	0.0	114.8	0.1	114.6	-0.2	114.6	0.0	114.6	0.0	114.8	0.2	114.8	0.0	114.8	0.0
1993	115.0	0.2	115.5	0.4	115.4	-0.1	115.5	0.1	115.5	0.0	115.5	0.0	115.6	0.1	115.8	0.2	116.0	0.2	115.8	-0.2	116.3	0.4	116.3	0.0
1994	116.4	0.1	116.6	0.2	116.6	0.0	116.8	0.2	117.1	0.3	117.4	0.3	117.5	0.1	117.5	0.0	117.8	0.3	118.3	0.4	118.4	0.1	119.0	0.5
1995	119.9	0.8	120.5	0.5	121.1	0.5	121.2	0.1	121.1	-0.1	121.3	0.2	121.2	-0.1	121.6	0.3	122.3	0.6	122.8	0.4	123.1	0.2	122.9	-0.2

Source: U.S. Department of Labor, Bureau of Labor Statistics, Division of Industry Prices and Price Indexes. n.e.c. stands for not elsewhere classified. - indicates no data collected for period or unavailable.

MISCELLANEOUS PRODUCTS
Producer Price Index
Base 1982 = 100

For 1947-1995. Columns headed % show percentile change in the index from the previous period for which an index is available.

Year	Jan Index	%	Feb Index	%	Mar Index	%	Apr Index	%	May Index	%	Jun Index	%	Jul Index	%	Aug Index	%	Sep Index	%	Oct Index	%	Nov Index	%	Dec Index	%
1947	26.5	-	26.5	0.0	26.5	0.0	26.6	0.4	26.7	0.4	26.6	-0.4	26.4	-0.8	26.6	0.8	26.6	0.0	26.6	0.0	26.8	0.8	26.8	0.0
1948	27.0	0.7	27.1	0.4	27.2	0.4	27.2	0.0	27.3	0.4	27.3	0.0	27.3	0.0	28.2	3.3	28.3	0.4	28.3	0.0	28.4	0.4	28.5	0.4
1949	28.5	0.0	28.5	0.0	28.5	0.0	28.2	-1.1	28.2	0.0	28.1	-0.4	28.1	0.0	28.0	-0.4	28.0	0.0	28.0	0.0	28.1	0.4	28.2	0.4
1950	28.1	-0.4	28.1	0.0	28.1	0.0	28.1	0.0	28.1	0.0	28.1	0.0	28.2	0.4	29.0	2.8	29.2	0.7	29.4	0.7	29.6	0.7	29.9	1.0
1951	30.3	1.3	30.3	0.0	30.3	0.0	30.4	0.3	30.4	0.0	30.3	-0.3	30.4	0.3	30.4	0.0	30.4	0.0	30.4	0.0	30.3	-0.3	30.3	0.0
1952	30.3	0.0	30.3	0.0	30.2	-0.3	30.2	0.0	30.2	0.0	30.1	-0.3	30.1	0.0	30.1	0.0	30.1	0.0	30.1	0.0	30.1	0.0	30.1	0.0
1953	30.1	0.0	30.1	0.0	31.1	3.3	31.1	0.0	31.1	0.0	31.1	0.0	31.1	0.0	31.1	0.0	31.1	0.0	31.1	0.0	31.1	0.0	31.1	0.0
1954	31.1	0.0	31.1	0.0	31.1	0.0	31.3	0.6	31.2	-0.3	31.3	0.3	31.3	0.0	31.3	0.0	31.3	0.0	31.3	0.0	31.3	0.0	31.3	0.0
1955	31.2	-0.3	31.1	-0.3	31.1	0.0	31.2	0.3	31.2	0.0	31.2	0.0	31.2	0.0	31.3	0.3	31.3	0.0	31.3	0.0	31.4	0.3	31.5	0.3
1956	31.6	0.3	31.6	0.0	31.6	0.0	31.7	0.3	31.7	0.0	31.7	0.0	31.7	0.0	31.7	0.0	31.8	0.3	31.8	0.0	31.9	0.3	31.9	0.0
1957	32.1	0.6	32.2	0.3	32.2	0.0	32.2	0.0	32.2	0.0	32.2	0.0	33.0	2.5	33.0	0.0	33.1	0.3	33.1	0.0	33.2	0.3	33.2	0.0
1958	33.2	0.0	33.2	0.0	33.2	0.0	33.2	0.0	33.2	0.0	33.4	0.6	33.3	-0.3	33.4	0.3	33.3	-0.3	33.3	0.0	33.3	0.0	33.3	0.0
1959	33.3	0.0	33.3	0.0	33.4	0.3	33.4	0.0	33.4	0.0	33.4	0.0	33.4	0.0	33.4	0.0	33.4	0.0	33.4	0.0	33.4	0.0	33.5	0.3
1960	33.6	0.3	33.6	0.0	33.6	0.0	33.6	0.0	33.6	0.0	33.6	0.0	33.6	0.0	33.7	0.3	33.7	0.0	33.7	0.0	33.7	0.0	33.7	0.0
1961	33.7	0.0	33.7	0.0	33.7	0.0	33.7	0.0	33.7	0.0	33.7	0.0	33.7	0.0	33.8	0.3	33.8	0.0	33.9	0.3	33.9	0.0	33.9	0.0
1962	33.8	-0.3	33.9	0.3	33.9	0.0	33.9	0.0	33.9	0.0	33.9	0.0	33.9	0.0	33.9	0.0	33.9	0.0	34.0	0.3	34.0	0.0	34.0	0.0
1963	34.0	0.0	34.0	0.0	33.9	-0.3	33.9	0.0	34.1	0.6	34.3	0.6	34.3	0.0	34.3	0.0	34.3	0.0	34.4	0.3	34.4	0.0	34.4	0.0
1964	34.4	0.0	34.4	0.0	34.4	0.0	34.4	0.0	34.4	0.0	34.4	0.0	34.4	0.0	34.5	0.3	34.5	0.0	34.5	0.0	34.5	0.0	34.5	0.0
1965	34.5	0.0	34.5	0.0	34.5	0.0	34.7	0.6	34.8	0.3	34.6	-0.6	34.8	0.6	34.8	0.0	34.8	0.0	34.8	0.0	34.8	0.0	34.8	0.0
1966	34.9	0.3	34.9	0.0	35.2	0.9	35.3	0.3	35.3	0.0	35.4	0.3	35.4	0.0	35.4	0.0	35.4	0.0	35.5	0.3	35.6	0.3	35.6	0.0
1967	35.7	0.3	35.7	0.0	35.7	0.0	35.7	0.0	35.8	0.3	36.3	1.4	36.4	0.3	36.4	0.0	36.5	0.3	36.6	0.3	36.6	0.0	36.7	0.3
1968	36.7	0.0	36.8	0.3	36.8	0.0	36.9	0.3	36.9	0.0	36.9	0.0	36.9	0.0	37.0	0.3	37.0	0.0	37.1	0.3	37.3	0.5	37.3	0.0
1969	37.3	0.0	37.3	0.0	37.3	0.0	37.4	0.3	37.4	0.0	38.2	2.1	38.4	0.5	38.5	0.3	38.6	0.3	38.7	0.3	38.7	0.0	38.7	0.0
1970	38.9	0.5	39.0	0.3	39.1	0.3	39.0	-0.3	39.2	0.5	40.1	2.3	40.2	0.2	40.2	0.0	40.3	0.2	40.3	0.0	40.3	0.0	40.4	0.2
1971	40.6	0.5	40.7	0.2	40.7	0.0	40.7	0.0	40.8	0.2	40.8	0.0	40.9	0.2	41.0	0.2	41.0	0.0	41.0	0.0	41.0	0.0	41.0	0.0
1972	41.1	0.2	41.2	0.2	41.3	0.2	41.3	0.0	41.3	0.0	41.3	0.0	41.6	0.7	41.6	0.0	41.7	0.2	41.6	-0.2	41.6	0.0	41.6	0.0
1973	41.9	0.7	42.4	1.2	42.7	0.7	42.9	0.5	43.2	0.7	43.5	0.7	43.7	0.5	43.8	0.2	43.8	0.0	43.8	0.0	43.9	0.2	44.0	0.2
1974	44.7	1.6	45.1	0.9	45.5	0.9	46.4	2.0	48.2	3.9	48.6	0.8	48.9	0.6	49.0	0.2	49.3	0.6	49.6	0.6	50.9	2.6	51.5	1.2
1975	52.6	2.1	52.9	0.6	53.1	0.4	53.3	0.4	53.3	0.0	53.4	0.2	53.4	0.0	53.4	0.0	53.6	0.4	53.4	-0.4	53.8	0.7	54.7	1.7
1976	54.9	0.4	55.1	0.4	55.2	0.2	55.2	0.0	55.2	0.0	55.8	1.1	55.6	-0.4	55.5	-0.2	55.7	0.4	55.7	0.0	56.4	1.3	56.8	0.7
1977	57.9	1.9	58.1	0.3	58.2	0.2	58.8	1.0	59.0	0.3	59.1	0.2	59.3	0.3	59.4	0.2	60.1	1.2	60.9	1.3	61.1	0.3	61.4	0.5
1978	62.1	1.1	62.0	-0.2	62.4	0.6	65.6	5.1	66.1	0.8	66.7	0.9	68.6	2.8	69.2	0.9	69.8	0.9	69.0	-1.1	68.4	-0.9	70.0	2.3
1979	71.5	2.1	72.3	1.1	72.6	0.4	72.9	0.4	73.6	1.0	74.2	0.8	74.9	0.9	75.6	0.9	77.1	2.0	79.2	2.7	80.1	1.1	82.3	2.7
1980	87.9	6.8	95.1	8.2	92.6	-2.6	91.4	-1.3	91.0	-0.4	93.3	2.5	94.6	1.4	94.1	-0.5	95.9	1.9	96.2	0.3	95.4	-0.8	96.0	0.6
1981	95.6	-0.4	95.8	0.2	95.5	-0.3	96.2	0.7	96.5	0.3	96.3	-0.2	95.2	-1.1	95.0	-0.2	96.6	1.7	97.1	0.5	96.8	-0.3	96.8	0.0
1982	97.1	0.3	98.9	1.9	98.7	-0.2	98.8	0.1	98.5	-0.3	98.2	-0.3	98.9	0.7	98.4	-0.5	101.1	2.7	103.3	2.2	103.1	-0.2	105.0	1.8
1983	103.3	-1.6	104.4	1.1	104.0	-0.4	104.0	0.0	103.8	-0.2	104.2	0.4	105.5	1.2	105.6	0.1	105.4	-0.2	105.5	0.1	105.5	0.0	105.9	0.4
1984	106.5	0.6	106.7	0.2	106.7	0.0	106.6	-0.1	106.4	-0.2	107.0	0.6	107.5	0.5	107.9	0.4	107.3	-0.6	107.2	-0.1	107.2	0.0	107.3	0.1
1985	108.2	0.8	108.8	0.6	108.7	-0.1	109.1	0.4	109.0	-0.1	109.0	0.0	109.8	0.7	109.8	0.0	109.9	0.1	110.0	0.1	110.1	0.1	109.9	-0.2
1986	111.2	1.2	111.0	-0.2	111.1	0.1	111.2	0.1	111.1	-0.1	111.0	-0.1	111.9	0.8	112.0	0.1	112.1	0.1	112.3	0.2	112.4	0.1	112.2	-0.2
1987	113.1	0.8	113.1	0.0	113.3	0.2	113.9	0.5	114.0	0.1	114.0	0.0	115.1	1.0	115.5	0.3	115.8	0.3	116.2	0.3	116.7	0.4	117.7	0.9
1988	118.7	0.8	119.2	0.4	119.1	-0.1	119.4	0.3	119.4	0.0	119.4	0.0	120.9	1.3	120.7	-0.2	120.7	0.0	121.1	0.3	121.2	0.1	122.6	1.2
1989	124.0	1.1	124.2	0.2	124.5	0.2	124.6	0.1	125.2	0.5	126.7	1.2	127.2	0.4	127.4	0.2	127.6	0.2	128.2	0.5	128.4	0.2	130.0	1.2
1990	131.2	0.9	131.9	0.5	132.0	0.1	132.3	0.2	133.2	0.7	134.4	0.9	134.6	0.1	134.9	0.2	135.3	0.3	135.9	0.4	136.9	0.7	138.2	0.9
1991	139.1	0.7	138.9	-0.1	139.4	0.4	140.0	0.4	140.1	0.1	140.9	0.6	141.8	0.6	141.7	-0.1	141.5	-0.1	141.4	-0.1	141.8	0.3	143.4	1.1

[Continued]

MISCELLANEOUS PRODUCTS
Producer Price Index
Base 1982 = 100
[Continued]

For 1947-1995. Columns headed % show percentile change in the index from the previous period for which an index is available.

Year	Jan Index	%	Feb Index	%	Mar Index	%	Apr Index	%	May Index	%	Jun Index	%	Jul Index	%	Aug Index	%	Sep Index	%	Oct Index	%	Nov Index	%	Dec Index	%
1992	143.9	0.3	143.9	0.0	144.0	0.1	144.8	0.6	146.4	1.1	146.2	-0.1	146.3	0.1	143.8	-1.7	145.3	1.0	145.5	0.1	145.8	0.2	147.3	1.0
1993	148.6	0.9	149.4	0.5	149.4	0.0	150.4	0.7	150.7	0.2	149.6	-0.7	149.6	0.0	138.9	-7.2	138.9	0.0	138.8	-0.1	139.1	0.2	140.9	1.3
1994	141.9	0.7	141.8	-0.1	141.6	-0.1	141.7	0.1	141.5	-0.1	141.6	0.1	141.8	0.1	141.8	0.0	141.8	0.0	142.0	0.1	142.4	0.3	142.4	0.0
1995	143.0	0.4	143.6	0.4	143.8	0.1	144.3	0.3	145.2	0.6	145.3	0.1	145.7	0.3	146.6	0.6	145.8	-0.5	145.6	-0.1	145.5	-0.1	146.8	0.9

Source: U.S. Department of Labor, Bureau of Labor Statistics, Division of Industry Prices and Price Indexes. n.e.c. stands for not elsewhere classified. - indicates no data collected for period or unavailable.

Toys, Sporting Goods, Small Arms, etc.
Producer Price Index
Base 1982 = 100

For 1947-1995. Columns headed % show percentile change in the index from the previous period for which an index is available.

Year	Jan Index	%	Feb Index	%	Mar Index	%	Apr Index	%	May Index	%	Jun Index	%	Jul Index	%	Aug Index	%	Sep Index	%	Oct Index	%	Nov Index	%	Dec Index	%
1947	34.8	-	34.8	0.0	34.9	0.3	35.1	0.6	35.1	0.0	35.1	0.0	35.3	0.6	35.3	0.0	35.1	-0.6	35.1	0.0	35.1	0.0	35.3	0.6
1948	36.0	2.0	36.1	0.3	36.3	0.6	36.5	0.6	36.6	0.3	36.6	0.0	36.6	0.0	37.0	1.1	37.0	0.0	37.0	0.0	37.1	0.3	37.1	0.0
1949	36.6	-1.3	36.8	0.5	36.9	0.3	36.9	0.0	36.8	-0.3	36.8	0.0	36.6	-0.5	36.5	-0.3	36.4	-0.3	36.5	0.3	36.9	1.1	36.9	0.0
1950	37.6	1.9	37.7	0.3	37.7	0.0	37.8	0.3	37.8	0.0	37.9	0.3	38.2	0.8	38.5	0.8	39.6	2.9	40.1	1.3	40.2	0.2	41.0	2.0
1951	41.8	2.0	42.0	0.5	42.2	0.5	42.2	0.0	42.2	0.0	42.2	0.0	42.1	-0.2	42.1	0.0	42.0	-0.2	42.0	0.0	41.7	-0.7	41.7	0.0
1952	41.5	-0.5	41.4	-0.2	41.1	-0.7	41.0	-0.2	41.0	0.0	41.0	0.0	41.0	0.0	40.9	-0.2	40.9	0.0	40.9	0.0	40.9	0.0	40.9	0.0
1953	40.8	-0.2	40.8	0.0	40.8	0.0	41.1	0.7	41.3	0.5	41.2	-0.2	41.2	0.0	41.2	0.0	41.2	0.0	41.2	0.0	41.2	0.0	40.9	-0.7
1954	40.9	0.0	40.9	0.0	40.9	0.0	41.0	0.2	41.0	0.0	41.0	0.0	41.0	0.0	41.0	0.0	41.0	0.0	40.8	-0.5	40.8	0.0	40.8	0.0
1955	40.9	0.2	40.9	0.0	40.9	0.0	40.9	0.0	40.9	0.0	40.9	0.0	40.9	0.0	41.0	0.2	41.0	0.0	41.1	0.2	41.3	0.5	41.6	0.7
1956	41.9	0.7	41.9	0.0	41.8	-0.2	41.9	0.2	41.9	0.0	41.9	0.0	41.8	-0.2	42.0	0.5	42.2	0.5	42.2	0.0	42.2	0.0	42.3	0.2
1957	42.4	0.2	42.4	0.0	42.4	0.0	42.4	0.0	42.4	0.0	42.4	0.0	42.4	0.0	42.6	0.5	42.7	0.2	42.6	-0.2	42.6	0.0	42.6	0.0
1958	43.2	1.4	43.2	0.0	43.1	-0.2	43.1	0.0	43.1	0.0	43.1	0.0	43.1	0.0	43.1	0.0	42.9	-0.5	42.9	0.0	42.9	0.0	42.9	0.0
1959	42.6	-0.7	42.6	0.0	42.4	-0.5	42.3	-0.2	42.3	0.0	42.3	0.0	42.4	0.2	42.5	0.2	42.5	0.0	42.5	0.0	42.5	0.0	42.6	0.2
1960	42.5	-0.2	42.6	0.2	42.6	0.0	42.8	0.5	42.8	0.0	42.8	0.0	42.9	0.2	42.9	0.0	42.9	0.0	42.9	0.0	42.9	0.0	42.9	0.0
1961	42.8	-0.2	42.8	0.0	43.0	0.5	43.0	0.0	43.0	0.0	43.0	0.0	43.0	0.0	43.3	0.7	43.2	-0.2	43.4	0.5	43.4	0.0	43.1	-0.7
1962	42.9	-0.5	42.8	-0.2	42.9	0.2	42.9	0.0	42.9	0.0	43.0	0.2	43.1	0.2	43.1	0.0	43.2	0.2	43.2	0.0	43.2	0.0	43.2	0.0
1963	43.2	0.0	43.2	0.0	42.9	-0.7	43.0	0.2	43.0	0.0	43.0	0.0	43.1	0.2	43.2	0.2	43.2	0.0	43.2	0.0	43.1	-0.2	43.2	0.2
1964	43.1	-0.2	43.1	0.0	43.2	0.2	43.0	-0.5	43.0	0.0	43.1	0.2	43.1	0.0	43.1	0.0	43.2	0.2	43.2	0.0	43.2	0.0	43.2	0.0
1965	43.6	0.9	43.6	0.0	43.6	0.0	43.7	0.2	43.8	0.2	43.8	0.0	43.9	0.2	43.8	-0.2	44.0	0.5	44.0	0.0	44.0	0.0	44.0	0.0
1966	44.0	0.0	44.1	0.2	44.1	0.0	44.3	0.5	44.3	0.0	44.3	0.0	44.6	0.7	44.8	0.4	44.8	0.0	44.8	0.0	44.8	0.0	44.8	0.0
1967	45.0	0.4	45.0	0.0	44.9	-0.2	45.0	0.2	45.0	0.0	45.1	0.2	45.2	0.2	45.2	0.0	45.3	0.2	45.4	0.2	45.4	0.0	45.4	0.0
1968	45.6	0.4	45.5	-0.2	46.1	1.3	46.1	0.0	46.2	0.2	46.2	0.0	46.3	0.2	46.4	0.2	46.5	0.2	46.5	0.0	46.6	0.2	46.6	0.0
1969	47.1	1.1	47.1	0.0	47.2	0.2	47.2	0.0	47.3	0.2	47.3	0.0	47.5	0.4	47.8	0.6	47.9	0.2	48.0	0.2	48.1	0.2	48.2	0.2
1970	48.9	1.5	49.0	0.2	49.6	1.2	49.1	-1.0	49.4	0.6	49.4	0.0	49.5	0.2	49.6	0.2	49.9	0.6	49.9	0.0	49.9	0.0	50.0	0.2
1971	50.8	1.6	50.8	0.0	51.0	0.4	50.8	-0.4	50.8	0.0	51.0	0.4	51.0	0.0	50.9	-0.2	50.9	0.0	50.9	0.0	51.0	0.2	51.0	0.0
1972	51.3	0.6	51.5	0.4	51.7	0.4	51.5	-0.4	51.5	0.0	51.6	0.2	51.7	0.2	51.7	0.0	51.8	0.2	51.9	0.2	51.9	0.0	52.0	0.2
1973	52.5	1.0	52.6	0.2	52.9	0.6	52.9	0.0	53.0	0.2	53.1	0.2	53.1	0.0	53.2	0.2	53.4	0.4	53.8	0.7	54.1	0.6	54.2	0.2
1974	56.2	3.7	57.0	1.4	57.5	0.9	57.8	0.5	58.4	1.0	59.0	1.0	59.6	1.0	61.3	2.9	61.8	0.8	62.4	1.0	63.0	1.0	63.0	0.0
1975	65.4	3.8	65.9	0.8	66.0	0.2	65.8	-0.3	65.8	0.0	65.9	0.2	65.9	0.0	65.9	0.0	65.9	0.0	66.1	0.3	66.3	0.3	66.3	0.0
1976	66.9	0.9	67.1	0.3	67.5	0.6	67.4	-0.1	67.6	0.3	67.9	0.4	68.0	0.1	67.9	-0.1	68.1	0.3	68.1	0.0	68.2	0.1	68.2	0.0
1977	69.4	1.8	69.6	0.3	69.8	0.3	69.7	-0.1	69.8	0.1	69.9	0.1	70.1	0.3	70.3	0.3	70.2	-0.1	70.7	0.7	70.8	0.1	70.9	0.1
1978	72.1	1.7	72.9	1.1	73.3	0.5	73.5	0.3	73.3	-0.3	73.7	0.5	73.7	0.0	74.0	0.4	74.1	0.1	74.5	0.5	74.6	0.1	74.4	-0.3
1979	76.9	3.4	77.2	0.4	77.5	0.4	78.2	0.9	78.7	0.6	78.9	0.3	79.9	1.3	80.2	0.4	81.2	1.2	81.8	0.7	81.8	0.0	82.6	1.0
1980	86.2	4.4	87.4	1.4	87.8	0.5	88.2	0.5	88.5	0.3	89.2	0.8	90.4	1.3	90.9	0.6	91.4	0.6	91.5	0.1	91.6	0.1	92.9	1.4
1981	94.1	1.3	95.1	1.1	95.3	0.2	95.4	0.1	95.4	0.0	95.4	0.0	96.3	0.9	96.0	-0.3	96.5	0.5	96.2	-0.3	96.1	-0.1	96.3	0.2
1982	98.6	2.4	99.4	0.8	99.6	0.2	99.8	0.2	100.2	0.4	100.2	0.0	100.3	0.1	100.9	0.6	100.1	-0.8	99.9	-0.2	100.0	0.1	101.0	1.0
1983	100.6	-0.4	101.7	1.1	101.9	0.2	102.2	0.3	102.1	-0.1	102.0	-0.1	101.3	-0.7	101.4	0.1	101.5	0.1	102.0	0.5	101.7	-0.3	101.7	0.0
1984	102.7	1.0	102.9	0.2	102.8	-0.1	102.3	-0.5	102.4	0.1	102.3	-0.1	102.3	0.0	102.3	0.0	102.5	0.2	102.7	0.2	102.8	0.1	102.8	0.0
1985	103.0	0.2	104.3	1.3	104.5	0.2	104.4	-0.1	104.4	0.0	104.3	-0.1	104.2	-0.1	104.2	0.0	104.4	0.2	105.7	1.2	105.9	0.2	105.2	-0.7
1986	105.7	0.5	106.1	0.4	106.3	0.2	106.4	0.1	106.5	0.1	106.6	0.1	106.8	0.2	106.9	0.1	106.8	-0.1	107.1	0.3	107.1	0.0	106.6	-0.5
1987	106.5	-0.1	107.3	0.8	107.1	-0.2	107.4	0.3	107.4	0.0	107.6	0.2	107.7	0.1	107.7	0.0	108.3	0.6	108.6	0.3	108.8	0.2	109.0	0.2
1988	110.1	1.0	110.9	0.7	111.0	0.1	111.1	0.1	111.2	0.1	111.5	0.3	112.0	0.4	112.2	0.2	112.3	0.1	112.7	0.4	112.9	0.2	113.2	0.3
1989	114.7	1.3	115.5	0.7	115.9	0.3	116.0	0.1	116.2	0.2	116.7	0.4	116.9	0.2	117.4	0.4	117.6	0.2	118.0	0.3	117.7	-0.3	118.1	0.3
1990	118.5	0.3	119.1	0.5	119.1	0.0	119.2	0.1	119.3	0.1	119.4	0.1	119.3	-0.1	119.6	0.3	119.5	-0.1	120.8	1.1	120.6	-0.2	120.8	0.2
1991	121.3	0.4	121.6	0.2	121.9	0.2	122.0	0.1	122.2	0.2	122.6	0.3	122.7	0.1	123.1	0.3	123.2	0.1	123.6	0.3	123.3	-0.2	123.2	-0.1

[Continued]

Toys, Sporting Goods, Small Arms, etc.
Producer Price Index
Base 1982 = 100
[Continued]

For 1947-1995. Columns headed % show percentile change in the index from the previous period for which an index is available.

Year	Jan Index	%	Feb Index	%	Mar Index	%	Apr Index	%	May Index	%	Jun Index	%	Jul Index	%	Aug Index	%	Sep Index	%	Oct Index	%	Nov Index	%	Dec Index	%
1992	123.8	0.5	124.1	0.2	123.9	-0.2	124.0	0.1	124.4	0.3	124.6	0.2	124.6	0.0	124.7	0.1	125.9	1.0	125.9	0.0	124.6	-1.0	124.2	-0.3
1993	125.0	0.6	125.2	0.2	125.1	-0.1	125.2	0.1	125.3	0.1	125.3	0.0	125.3	0.0	125.9	0.5	125.8	-0.1	126.0	0.2	125.9	-0.1	126.0	0.1
1994	126.5	0.4	126.5	0.0	126.4	-0.1	126.5	0.1	126.7	0.2	126.8	0.1	127.4	0.5	127.3	-0.1	127.3	0.0	127.2	-0.1	127.5	0.2	127.7	0.2
1995	128.1	0.3	128.5	0.3	128.7	0.2	129.0	0.2	128.8	-0.2	128.9	0.1	129.4	0.4	129.3	-0.1	129.0	-0.2	129.4	0.3	129.6	0.2	129.6	0.0

Source: U.S. Department of Labor, Bureau of Labor Statistics, Division of Industry Prices and Price Indexes. n.e.c. stands for not elsewhere classified. - indicates no data collected for period or unavailable.

Tobacco Products, Incl. Stemmed & Redried
Producer Price Index
Base 1982 = 100

For 1947-1995. Columns headed % show percentile change in the index from the previous period for which an index is available.

Year	Jan Index	%	Feb Index	%	Mar Index	%	Apr Index	%	May Index	%	Jun Index	%	Jul Index	%	Aug Index	%	Sep Index	%	Oct Index	%	Nov Index	%	Dec Index	%
1947	20.4	-	20.4	0.0	20.4	0.0	20.5	0.5	20.5	0.0	20.5	0.0	20.5	0.0	20.5	0.0	20.5	0.0	20.5	0.0	20.5	0.0	20.5	0.0
1948	20.5	0.0	20.5	0.0	20.5	0.0	20.5	0.0	20.5	0.0	20.5	0.0	20.6	0.5	22.3	8.3	22.3	0.0	22.3	0.0	22.3	0.0	22.3	0.0
1949	22.3	0.0	22.3	0.0	22.3	0.0	22.3	0.0	22.3	0.0	22.3	0.0	22.3	0.0	22.4	0.4	22.4	0.0	22.4	0.0	22.4	0.0	22.4	0.0
1950	22.4	0.0	22.4	0.0	22.4	0.0	22.4	0.0	22.4	0.0	22.4	0.0	22.4	0.0	23.3	4.0	23.3	0.0	23.4	0.4	23.4	0.0	23.4	0.0
1951	23.4	0.0	23.4	0.0	23.4	0.0	23.4	0.0	23.4	0.0	23.4	0.0	23.4	0.0	23.4	0.0	23.4	0.0	23.4	0.0	23.6	0.9	23.6	0.0
1952	23.6	0.0	23.6	0.0	23.6	0.0	23.6	0.0	23.6	0.0	23.6	0.0	23.6	0.0	23.6	0.0	23.6	0.0	23.6	0.0	23.6	0.0	23.6	0.0
1953	23.7	0.4	23.7	0.0	25.6	8.0	25.6	0.0	25.6	0.0	25.6	0.0	25.6	0.0	25.6	0.0	25.6	0.0	25.6	0.0	25.6	0.0	25.6	0.0
1954	25.6	0.0	25.6	0.0	25.6	0.0	25.6	0.0	25.6	0.0	25.6	0.0	25.6	0.0	25.6	0.0	25.6	0.0	25.6	0.0	25.6	0.0	25.6	0.0
1955	25.6	0.0	25.6	0.0	25.6	0.0	25.6	0.0	25.6	0.0	25.6	0.0	25.6	0.0	25.6	0.0	25.6	0.0	25.6	0.0	25.6	0.0	25.6	0.0
1956	25.6	0.0	25.6	0.0	25.6	0.0	25.6	0.0	25.6	0.0	25.6	0.0	25.6	0.0	25.6	0.0	25.6	0.0	25.6	0.0	25.6	0.0	25.7	0.4
1957	25.7	0.0	25.7	0.0	25.7	0.0	25.7	0.0	25.8	0.4	25.8	0.0	27.7	7.4	27.7	0.0	27.7	0.0	27.7	0.0	27.7	0.0	27.7	0.0
1958	27.7	0.0	27.7	0.0	27.7	0.0	27.7	0.0	27.7	0.0	27.7	0.0	27.7	0.0	27.7	0.0	27.7	0.0	27.7	0.0	27.7	0.0	27.7	0.0
1959	27.7	0.0	27.8	0.4	27.9	0.4	27.9	0.0	27.9	0.0	27.9	0.0	27.9	0.0	27.9	0.0	27.9	0.0	27.9	0.0	27.9	0.0	27.9	0.0
1960	27.9	0.0	27.9	0.0	27.9	0.0	27.9	0.0	27.9	0.0	27.9	0.0	27.9	0.0	27.9	0.0	27.9	0.0	27.9	0.0	27.9	0.0	27.9	0.0
1961	27.9	0.0	27.9	0.0	27.9	0.0	27.9	0.0	27.9	0.0	27.9	0.0	27.9	0.0	27.9	0.0	27.9	0.0	27.9	0.0	27.9	0.0	27.9	0.0
1962	27.9	0.0	27.9	0.0	27.9	0.0	27.9	0.0	27.9	0.0	27.9	0.0	27.9	0.0	27.9	0.0	27.9	0.0	28.0	0.4	28.0	0.0	28.0	0.0
1963	28.0	0.0	28.0	0.0	28.0	0.0	28.0	0.0	28.7	2.5	29.0	1.0	29.0	0.0	29.0	0.0	29.0	0.0	29.0	0.0	29.0	0.0	29.0	0.0
1964	29.0	0.0	29.0	0.0	29.1	0.3	29.1	0.0	29.1	0.0	29.1	0.0	29.1	0.0	29.1	0.0	29.1	0.0	29.1	0.0	29.1	0.0	29.1	0.0
1965	29.1	0.0	29.1	0.0	29.1	0.0	29.2	0.3	29.4	0.7	29.1	-1.0	29.1	0.0	29.1	0.0	29.1	0.0	29.1	0.0	29.1	0.0	29.1	0.0
1966	29.2	0.3	29.2	0.0	30.1	3.1	30.2	0.3	30.2	0.0	30.2	0.0	30.2	0.0	30.2	0.0	30.2	0.0	30.2	0.0	30.2	0.0	30.2	0.0
1967	30.2	0.0	30.2	0.0	30.2	0.0	30.2	0.0	30.2	0.0	31.5	4.3	31.5	0.0	31.5	0.0	31.5	0.0	31.5	0.0	31.5	0.0	31.5	0.0
1968	31.5	0.0	31.5	0.0	31.5	0.0	31.5	0.0	31.5	0.0	31.5	0.0	31.5	0.0	31.5	0.0	31.5	0.0	31.6	0.3	32.0	1.3	32.0	0.0
1969	32.0	0.0	32.0	0.0	32.0	0.0	32.1	0.3	32.1	0.0	33.8	5.3	33.9	0.3	33.9	0.0	34.0	0.3	34.0	0.0	34.0	0.0	34.0	0.0
1970	34.0	0.0	34.0	0.0	34.0	0.0	34.0	0.0	34.0	0.0	36.3	6.8	36.0	-0.8	35.9	-0.3	35.9	0.0	35.9	0.0	35.9	0.0	35.9	0.0
1971	36.0	0.3	36.1	0.3	36.1	0.0	36.1	0.0	36.1	0.0	36.1	0.0	36.1	0.0	36.1	0.0	36.1	0.0	36.1	0.0	36.1	0.0	36.1	0.0
1972	36.3	0.6	36.3	0.0	36.3	0.0	36.3	0.0	36.4	0.3	36.4	0.0	36.4	0.0	36.4	0.0	36.4	0.0	36.4	0.0	36.4	0.0	36.4	0.0
1973	36.4	0.0	37.5	3.0	37.7	0.5	37.7	0.0	37.9	0.5	37.9	0.0	37.9	0.0	37.9	0.0	37.9	0.0	38.0	0.3	38.0	0.0	38.1	0.3
1974	38.1	0.0	38.2	0.3	38.2	0.0	38.3	0.3	41.2	7.6	41.7	1.2	41.7	0.0	41.9	0.5	41.9	0.0	41.9	0.0	44.8	6.9	45.4	1.3
1975	45.6	0.4	45.8	0.4	45.9	0.2	46.0	0.2	46.0	0.0	46.0	0.0	46.0	0.0	46.0	0.0	46.1	0.2	46.2	0.2	46.8	1.3	49.2	5.1
1976	49.2	0.0	49.2	0.0	49.3	0.2	50.2	1.8	50.1	-0.2	50.1	0.0	50.1	0.0	50.1	0.0	50.2	0.2	50.3	0.2	53.3	6.0	53.3	0.0
1977	54.1	1.5	54.1	0.0	54.1	0.0	54.2	0.2	54.2	0.0	54.3	0.2	54.4	0.2	54.4	0.0	57.8	6.3	58.7	1.6	58.7	0.0	58.8	0.2
1978	59.0	0.3	59.2	0.3	59.2	0.0	59.3	0.2	59.3	0.0	61.3	3.4	63.6	3.8	63.6	0.0	63.6	0.0	63.1	-0.8	63.1	0.0	63.1	0.0
1979	66.1	4.8	66.1	0.0	66.2	0.2	66.4	0.3	66.4	0.0	66.4	0.0	66.5	0.2	68.5	3.0	68.7	0.3	68.8	0.1	68.8	0.0	70.1	1.9
1980	73.2	4.4	73.4	0.3	73.5	0.1	73.7	0.3	76.7	4.1	76.8	0.1	76.8	0.0	76.8	0.0	76.8	0.0	77.2	0.5	78.8	2.1	78.9	0.1
1981	78.9	0.0	79.3	0.5	79.3	0.0	83.2	4.9	83.2	0.0	83.2	0.0	83.2	0.0	83.2	0.0	85.0	2.2	86.1	1.3	86.1	0.0	86.1	0.0
1982	86.1	0.0	94.9	10.2	94.9	0.0	94.9	0.0	95.0	0.1	95.0	0.0	96.4	1.5	96.4	0.0	101.9	5.7	113.1	11.0	112.8	-0.3	118.5	5.1
1983	110.2	-7.0	110.3	0.1	109.5	-0.7	109.6	0.1	109.5	-0.1	109.0	-0.5	115.6	6.1	116.6	0.9	116.6	0.0	116.6	0.0	116.7	0.1	116.7	0.0
1984	120.5	3.3	120.8	0.2	120.8	0.0	120.8	0.0	120.9	0.1	123.9	2.5	126.5	2.1	125.9	-0.5	125.9	0.0	124.5	-1.1	124.6	0.1	124.7	0.1
1985	130.0	4.3	130.2	0.2	130.2	0.0	130.2	0.0	130.2	0.0	130.2	0.0	134.9	3.6	134.9	0.0	134.9	0.0	134.7	-0.1	134.8	0.1	134.8	0.0
1986	139.6	3.6	139.7	0.1	139.8	0.1	139.7	-0.1	139.8	0.1	139.8	0.0	145.2	3.9	145.2	0.0	145.2	0.0	145.2	0.0	145.2	0.0	145.2	0.0
1987	150.8	3.9	150.8	0.0	150.8	0.0	150.9	0.1	150.9	0.0	150.9	0.0	157.5	4.4	157.6	0.1	157.6	0.0	157.5	-0.1	157.6	0.1	163.3	3.6
1988	166.6	2.0	166.7	0.1	166.7	0.0	166.8	0.1	166.8	0.0	166.8	0.0	175.4	5.2	175.4	0.0	175.4	0.0	175.6	0.1	175.5	-0.1	184.7	5.2
1989	187.2	1.4	187.3	0.1	187.3	0.0	187.3	0.0	187.4	0.1	196.8	5.0	197.9	0.6	198.1	0.1	198.1	0.0	200.4	1.2	200.4	0.0	209.6	4.6
1990	212.3	1.3	212.8	0.2	212.8	0.0	212.8	0.0	217.4	2.2	224.1	3.1	224.3	0.1	224.3	0.0	225.0	0.3	224.9	-0.0	230.4	2.4	236.1	2.5
1991	237.4	0.6	237.4	0.0	239.6	0.9	243.3	1.5	243.4	0.0	249.1	2.3	254.4	2.1	255.0	0.2	254.9	-0.0	255.0	0.0	259.8	1.9	267.2	2.8

[Continued]

Tobacco Products, Incl. Stemmed & Redried
Producer Price Index
Base 1982 = 100
[Continued]

For 1947-1995. Columns headed % show percentile change in the index from the previous period for which an index is available.

Year	Jan Index	%	Feb Index	%	Mar Index	%	Apr Index	%	May Index	%	Jun Index	%	Jul Index	%	Aug Index	%	Sep Index	%	Oct Index	%	Nov Index	%	Dec Index	%
1992	268.1	0.3	268.2	0.0	268.2	0.0	273.7	2.1	283.2	3.5	283.2	0.0	283.4	0.1	265.9	-6.2	274.1	3.1	274.2	0.0	276.5	0.8	285.1	3.1
1993	291.8	2.4	292.2	0.1	292.2	0.0	296.2	1.4	296.9	0.2	289.2	-2.6	287.2	-0.7	213.3	-25.7	213.2	-0.0	213.5	0.1	213.6	0.0	224.2	5.0
1994	224.7	0.2	224.7	0.0	224.7	0.0	224.7	0.0	224.7	0.0	224.7	0.0	224.7	0.0	224.1	-0.3	224.9	0.4	224.6	-0.1	225.1	0.2	225.2	0.0
1995	225.4	0.1	226.0	0.3	228.1	0.9	228.5	0.2	233.7	2.3	233.6	-0.0	233.5	-0.0	233.6	0.0	233.9	0.1	233.5	-0.2	233.5	0.0	233.1	-0.2

Source: U.S. Department of Labor, Bureau of Labor Statistics, Division of Industry Prices and Price Indexes. n.e.c. stands for not elsewhere classified. - indicates no data collected for period or unavailable.

Notions
Producer Price Index
Base 1982 = 100

For 1947-1995. Columns headed % show percentile change in the index from the previous period for which an index is available.

Year	Jan Index	%	Feb Index	%	Mar Index	%	Apr Index	%	May Index	%	Jun Index	%	Jul Index	%	Aug Index	%	Sep Index	%	Oct Index	%	Nov Index	%	Dec Index	%
1947	37.9	-	37.9	0.0	37.9	0.0	37.9	0.0	37.9	0.0	37.9	0.0	37.9	0.0	37.9	0.0	37.6	-0.8	37.5	-0.3	37.5	0.0	37.5	0.0
1948	37.9	1.1	37.9	0.0	37.9	0.0	37.9	0.0	37.9	0.0	37.9	0.0	38.0	0.3	38.0	0.0	38.3	0.8	37.8	-1.3	37.8	0.0	37.5	-0.8
1949	37.5	0.0	37.5	0.0	37.1	-1.1	33.4	-10.0	33.0	-1.2	33.0	0.0	33.0	0.0	33.0	0.0	33.0	0.0	33.0	0.0	33.0	0.0	33.0	0.0
1950	33.0	0.0	33.0	0.0	33.0	0.0	33.0	0.0	32.5	-1.5	32.5	0.0	32.3	-0.6	33.6	4.0	34.6	3.0	34.9	0.9	35.8	2.6	36.1	0.8
1951	36.4	0.8	37.1	1.9	37.1	0.0	37.1	0.0	37.1	0.0	37.1	0.0	37.1	0.0	37.1	0.0	37.1	0.0	37.1	0.0	37.1	0.0	37.1	0.0
1952	36.7	-1.1	36.7	0.0	36.0	-1.9	35.2	-2.2	33.5	-4.8	33.5	0.0	33.5	0.0	33.2	-0.9	33.2	0.0	33.3	0.3	33.4	0.3	34.0	1.8
1953	34.0	0.0	34.0	0.0	34.5	1.5	34.1	-1.2	34.1	0.0	34.1	0.0	34.1	0.0	34.2	0.3	34.2	0.0	34.2	0.0	34.2	0.0	34.2	0.0
1954	34.2	0.0	34.2	0.0	34.2	0.0	34.2	0.0	34.2	0.0	35.2	2.9	35.2	0.0	35.2	0.0	35.1	-0.3	35.1	0.0	35.1	0.0	35.1	0.0
1955	35.1	0.0	33.8	-3.7	33.8	0.0	33.8	0.0	34.0	0.6	34.0	0.0	33.3	-2.1	33.3	0.0	33.3	0.0	33.3	0.0	33.3	0.0	33.3	0.0
1956	33.9	1.8	33.9	0.0	34.4	1.5	34.9	1.5	35.0	0.3	35.0	0.0	35.0	0.0	35.1	0.3	35.3	0.6	35.3	0.0	35.3	0.0	35.3	0.0
1957	35.4	0.3	35.4	0.0	35.4	0.0	35.6	0.6	35.6	0.0	35.6	0.0	35.6	0.0	35.6	0.0	35.6	0.0	35.6	0.0	35.8	0.6	36.0	0.6
1958	35.6	-1.1	35.7	0.3	35.7	0.0	35.7	0.0	35.7	0.0	35.7	0.0	35.7	0.0	35.7	0.0	35.7	0.0	35.7	0.0	35.7	0.0	35.7	0.0
1959	35.7	0.0	35.7	0.0	35.7	0.0	35.7	0.0	35.7	0.0	35.7	0.0	35.7	0.0	35.2	-1.4	35.2	0.0	35.7	1.4	35.7	0.0	35.7	0.0
1960	35.7	0.0	35.7	0.0	35.7	0.0	35.6	-0.3	35.3	-0.8	35.3	0.0	35.6	0.8	35.6	0.0	35.3	-0.8	35.3	0.0	35.3	0.0	35.3	0.0
1961	35.3	0.0	35.3	0.0	35.3	0.0	35.3	0.0	35.2	-0.3	35.2	0.0	35.2	0.0	35.2	0.0	35.2	0.0	35.2	0.0	35.2	0.0	35.2	0.0
1962	35.2	0.0	35.2	0.0	35.2	0.0	35.2	0.0	35.2	0.0	35.2	0.0	35.2	0.0	35.2	0.0	35.2	0.0	35.2	0.0	35.2	0.0	35.2	0.0
1963	35.2	0.0	35.2	0.0	35.2	0.0	35.2	0.0	35.2	0.0	35.2	0.0	35.2	0.0	35.2	0.0	35.3	0.3	35.3	0.0	35.3	0.0	35.3	0.0
1964	35.3	0.0	35.3	0.0	35.3	0.0	35.3	0.0	35.3	0.0	35.3	0.0	35.3	0.0	35.3	0.0	35.3	0.0	35.3	0.0	35.3	0.0	35.3	0.0
1965	35.3	0.0	35.3	0.0	35.3	0.0	35.3	0.0	35.3	0.0	35.3	0.0	35.3	0.0	35.3	0.0	35.3	0.0	35.3	0.0	35.3	0.0	35.3	0.0
1966	35.3	0.0	35.6	0.8	35.6	0.0	35.6	0.0	35.9	0.8	36.3	1.1	35.9	-1.1	35.9	0.0	35.9	0.0	35.9	0.0	35.9	0.0	35.9	0.0
1967	35.9	0.0	35.9	0.0	35.9	0.0	35.9	0.0	35.9	0.0	35.9	0.0	35.9	0.0	35.9	0.0	35.9	0.0	35.7	-0.6	37.0	3.6	37.0	0.0
1968	37.0	0.0	38.2	3.2	35.7	-6.5	35.7	0.0	35.7	0.0	35.7	0.0	35.7	0.0	35.8	0.3	35.8	0.0	36.0	0.6	36.0	0.0	36.0	0.0
1969	36.0	0.0	36.0	0.0	36.0	0.0	36.0	0.0	36.5	1.4	36.7	0.5	36.7	0.0	38.3	4.4	38.3	0.0	38.3	0.0	38.3	0.0	38.3	0.0
1970	38.3	0.0	39.0	1.8	39.0	0.0	38.8	-0.5	39.0	0.5	39.1	0.3	39.2	0.3	39.2	0.0	39.5	0.8	39.5	0.0	39.5	0.0	39.7	0.5
1971	40.4	1.8	40.4	0.0	40.4	0.0	40.4	0.0	40.4	0.0	40.4	0.0	40.4	0.0	40.4	0.0	40.4	0.0	40.4	0.0	40.4	0.0	40.4	0.0
1972	40.3	-0.2	40.3	0.0	40.3	0.0	40.3	0.0	40.3	0.0	40.3	0.0	40.3	0.0	40.3	0.0	40.8	1.2	40.8	0.0	40.8	0.0	40.8	0.0
1973	40.8	0.0	40.8	0.0	40.8	0.0	40.8	0.0	41.4	1.5	41.4	0.0	40.8	-1.4	41.0	0.5	41.0	0.0	41.7	1.7	42.3	1.4	42.6	0.7
1974	42.9	0.7	42.9	0.0	44.0	2.6	45.5	3.4	49.5	8.8	50.9	2.8	51.9	2.0	52.5	1.2	53.8	2.5	53.8	0.0	53.8	0.0	53.8	0.0
1975	54.2	0.7	54.2	0.0	54.2	0.0	54.2	0.0	54.2	0.0	54.2	0.0	54.2	0.0	54.2	0.0	54.2	0.0	54.7	0.9	55.7	1.8	56.5	1.4
1976	56.5	0.0	56.5	0.0	57.1	1.1	57.4	0.5	58.4	1.7	59.4	1.7	59.4	0.0	59.7	0.5	59.7	0.0	59.7	0.0	59.7	0.0	59.8	0.2
1977	61.3	2.5	62.3	1.6	62.3	0.0	62.3	0.0	62.3	0.0	62.3	0.0	62.3	0.0	62.4	0.2	62.4	0.0	62.4	0.0	62.4	0.0	62.4	0.0
1978	65.3	4.6	65.3	0.0	65.5	0.3	65.5	0.0	65.5	0.0	65.5	0.0	65.5	0.0	65.6	0.2	66.2	0.9	66.2	0.0	66.2	0.0	66.2	0.0
1979	67.9	2.6	67.9	0.0	68.7	1.2	68.7	0.0	68.8	0.1	68.8	0.0	69.3	0.7	69.3	0.0	69.3	0.0	70.6	1.9	70.7	0.1	71.0	0.4
1980	73.3	3.2	73.4	0.1	74.8	1.9	78.3	4.7	78.4	0.1	78.4	0.0	80.0	2.0	80.8	1.0	80.8	0.0	80.9	0.1	80.9	0.0	81.2	0.4
1981	82.0	1.0	89.3	8.9	89.3	0.0	89.7	0.4	96.7	7.8	96.7	0.0	96.6	-0.1	96.7	0.1	96.7	0.0	97.4	0.7	97.4	0.0	97.4	0.0
1982	97.6	0.2	97.6	0.0	98.0	0.4	98.0	0.0	101.1	3.2	101.1	0.0	101.1	0.0	101.1	0.0	101.1	0.0	101.1	0.0	101.0	-0.1	101.0	0.0
1983	101.3	0.3	101.3	0.0	101.3	0.0	101.2	-0.1	101.2	0.0	101.2	0.0	101.2	0.0	101.0	-0.2	101.0	0.0	101.0	0.0	100.9	-0.1	101.1	0.2
1984	101.6	0.5	101.9	0.3	101.9	0.0	102.2	0.3	102.5	0.3	102.5	0.0	102.5	0.0	102.5	0.0	102.5	0.0	102.3	-0.2	102.3	0.0	102.4	0.1
1985	102.4	0.0	102.6	0.2	102.6	0.0	103.1	0.5	103.1	0.0	103.1	0.0	103.1	0.0	103.0	-0.1	103.0	0.0	103.0	0.0	103.0	0.0	102.9	-0.1
1986	103.0	0.1	103.8	0.8	103.6	-0.2	103.8	0.2	103.9	0.1	103.8	-0.1	103.8	0.0	103.8	0.0	103.7	-0.1	103.7	0.0	103.9	0.2	103.9	0.0
1987	103.6	-0.3	104.8	1.2	105.0	0.2	105.0	0.0	105.1	0.1	105.2	0.1	105.5	0.3	105.7	0.2	105.7	0.0	105.8	0.1	105.5	-0.3	105.9	0.4
1988	106.3	0.4	106.6	0.3	106.5	-0.1	107.4	0.8	107.4	0.0	108.1	0.7	108.2	0.1	108.5	0.3	108.9	0.4	108.9	0.0	109.1	0.2	109.2	0.1
1989	109.9	0.6	110.6	0.6	111.1	0.5	111.5	0.4	112.0	0.4	112.2	0.2	112.1	-0.1	112.1	0.0	113.8	1.5	114.7	0.8	114.6	-0.1	114.7	0.1
1990	114.9	0.2	115.2	0.3	115.3	0.1	115.4	0.1	115.3	-0.1	115.7	0.3	115.7	0.0	115.7	0.0	115.9	0.2	116.5	0.5	116.5	0.0	116.9	0.3
1991	117.0	0.1	116.8	-0.2	116.9	0.1	116.9	0.0	117.5	0.5	118.2	0.6	118.4	0.2	118.7	0.3	118.5	-0.2	118.1	-0.3	118.2	0.1	119.1	0.8

[Continued]

Notions
Producer Price Index
Base 1982 = 100
[Continued]

For 1947-1995. Columns headed % show percentile change in the index from the previous period for which an index is available.

Year	Jan		Feb		Mar		Apr		May		Jun		Jul		Aug		Sep		Oct		Nov		Dec	
	Index	%	Index	%	Index	%	Index	%	Index	%	Index	%	Index	%	Index	%	Index	%	Index	%	Index	%	Index	%
1992	119.1	0.0	119.1	0.0	119.1	0.0	119.0	-0.1	119.3	0.3	119.4	0.1	119.6	0.2	119.0	-0.5	118.7	-0.3	119.4	0.6	120.1	0.6	119.3	-0.7
1993	119.6	0.3	120.4	0.7	119.8	-0.5	120.1	0.3	120.4	0.2	120.6	0.2	120.5	-0.1	120.4	-0.1	120.9	0.4	120.9	0.0	121.1	0.2	121.1	0.0
1994	121.0	-0.1	121.8	0.7	121.5	-0.2	121.6	0.1	121.9	0.2	121.9	0.0	121.5	-0.3	121.8	0.2	122.0	0.2	121.7	-0.2	122.1	0.3	122.4	0.2
1995	122.7	0.2	123.4	0.6	124.0	0.5	123.6	-0.3	123.6	0.0	123.3	-0.2	123.8	0.4	123.7	-0.1	123.7	0.0	124.4	0.6	124.4	0.0	124.9	0.4

Source: U.S. Department of Labor, Bureau of Labor Statistics, Division of Industry Prices and Price Indexes. n.e.c. stands for not elsewhere classified. - indicates no data collected for period or unavailable.

Photographic Equipment and Supplies
Producer Price Index
Base 1982 = 100

For 1947-1995. Columns headed % show percentile change in the index from the previous period for which an index is available.

Year	Jan Index	%	Feb Index	%	Mar Index	%	Apr Index	%	May Index	%	Jun Index	%	Jul Index	%	Aug Index	%	Sep Index	%	Oct Index	%	Nov Index	%	Dec Index	%
1947	31.5	-	31.5	0.0	31.6	0.3	31.6	0.0	31.8	0.6	31.9	0.3	31.9	0.0	32.9	3.1	32.9	0.0	32.9	0.0	33.0	0.3	33.4	1.2
1948	34.4	3.0	34.6	0.6	34.7	0.3	34.8	0.3	34.9	0.3	35.0	0.3	35.0	0.0	35.3	0.9	35.5	0.6	35.8	0.8	36.4	1.7	36.7	0.8
1949	36.7	0.0	37.5	2.2	37.1	-1.1	37.0	-0.3	36.7	-0.8	36.5	-0.5	36.5	0.0	36.5	0.0	36.5	0.0	36.3	-0.5	36.3	0.0	36.3	0.0
1950	36.3	0.0	36.2	-0.3	35.9	-0.8	35.9	0.0	36.0	0.3	36.0	0.0	36.0	0.0	36.0	0.0	36.4	1.1	36.9	1.4	36.9	0.0	37.1	0.5
1951	37.2	0.3	37.2	0.0	37.2	0.0	37.2	0.0	37.2	0.0	37.2	0.0	37.8	1.6	37.8	0.0	37.8	0.0	37.8	0.0	37.9	0.3	37.9	0.0
1952	37.7	-0.5	38.0	0.8	38.0	0.0	38.0	0.0	38.0	0.0	38.0	0.0	38.0	0.0	38.0	0.0	38.0	0.0	38.0	0.0	38.0	0.0	38.0	0.0
1953	38.0	0.0	38.0	0.0	38.1	0.3	38.1	0.0	38.2	0.3	38.4	0.5	38.4	0.0	38.3	-0.3	38.5	0.5	38.5	0.0	38.5	0.0	38.5	0.0
1954	38.5	0.0	38.5	0.0	38.5	0.0	38.7	0.5	38.7	0.0	38.7	0.0	38.8	0.3	38.7	-0.3	38.7	0.0	38.7	0.0	38.7	0.0	38.7	0.0
1955	38.6	-0.3	38.6	0.0	38.7	0.3	39.0	0.8	39.0	0.0	39.0	0.0	39.2	0.5	39.3	0.3	39.3	0.0	39.4	0.3	39.5	0.3	39.5	0.0
1956	39.6	0.3	39.7	0.3	39.7	0.0	39.6	-0.3	39.6	0.0	39.8	0.5	39.8	0.0	39.8	0.0	39.8	0.0	39.8	0.0	40.5	1.8	40.5	0.0
1957	41.1	1.5	41.1	0.0	41.2	0.2	41.3	0.2	41.3	0.0	41.3	0.0	41.3	0.0	41.8	1.2	42.2	1.0	42.2	0.0	42.2	0.0	42.3	0.2
1958	42.3	0.0	42.4	0.2	42.4	0.0	42.4	0.0	42.4	0.0	42.8	0.9	42.8	0.0	42.7	-0.2	42.7	0.0	42.7	0.0	42.8	0.2	42.8	0.0
1959	43.3	1.2	43.3	0.0	44.0	1.6	44.1	0.2	44.1	0.0	44.1	0.0	44.1	0.0	44.2	0.2	44.3	0.2	44.3	0.0	44.3	0.0	44.3	0.0
1960	44.2	-0.2	44.2	0.0	44.2	0.0	44.2	0.0	44.2	0.0	44.2	0.0	44.2	0.0	44.4	0.5	44.4	0.0	44.6	0.5	44.9	0.7	44.9	0.0
1961	44.8	-0.2	44.9	0.2	44.8	-0.2	44.8	0.0	44.5	-0.7	44.4	-0.2	44.5	0.2	45.0	1.1	45.2	0.4	45.4	0.4	45.5	0.2	45.7	0.4
1962	45.7	0.0	46.0	0.7	46.0	0.0	45.9	-0.2	46.0	0.2	46.1	0.2	46.1	0.0	46.2	0.2	46.1	-0.2	46.1	0.0	46.1	0.0	46.1	0.0
1963	46.2	0.2	46.2	0.0	45.9	-0.6	45.9	0.0	46.0	0.2	46.1	0.2	46.2	0.2	45.9	-0.6	45.8	-0.2	45.9	0.2	45.9	0.0	46.1	0.4
1964	46.2	0.2	46.2	0.0	46.2	0.0	46.2	0.0	46.2	0.0	46.2	0.0	46.3	0.2	46.3	0.0	46.3	0.0	46.5	0.4	46.5	0.0	46.5	0.0
1965	46.5	0.0	46.5	0.0	46.6	0.2	46.8	0.4	46.8	0.0	46.7	-0.2	46.7	0.0	46.7	0.0	46.7	0.0	46.7	0.0	46.7	0.0	46.7	0.0
1966	46.6	-0.2	46.6	0.0	46.6	0.0	46.5	-0.2	46.5	0.0	46.5	0.0	46.5	0.0	46.4	-0.2	46.3	-0.2	46.3	0.0	46.9	1.3	47.0	0.2
1967	47.1	0.2	47.1	0.0	47.1	0.0	47.1	0.0	47.1	0.0	47.1	0.0	47.1	0.0	47.6	1.1	47.7	0.2	48.6	1.9	48.6	0.0	48.6	0.0
1968	48.0	-1.2	48.6	1.3	48.6	0.0	48.6	0.0	49.0	0.8	49.0	0.0	48.5	-1.0	48.5	0.0	48.5	0.0	48.6	0.2	48.6	0.0	48.6	0.0
1969	48.4	-0.4	48.4	0.0	48.1	-0.6	48.2	0.2	48.4	0.4	48.4	0.0	48.7	0.6	48.7	0.0	49.0	0.6	49.1	0.2	49.2	0.2	49.3	0.2
1970	49.4	0.2	49.5	0.2	49.5	0.0	49.7	0.4	49.7	0.0	49.5	-0.4	50.1	1.2	50.2	0.2	50.1	-0.2	50.1	0.0	50.2	0.2	50.2	0.0
1971	50.3	0.2	50.4	0.2	50.4	0.0	50.4	0.0	50.4	0.0	50.5	0.2	50.6	0.2	50.6	0.0	50.6	0.0	50.6	0.0	50.6	0.0	50.6	0.0
1972	50.6	0.0	50.7	0.2	50.8	0.2	50.5	-0.6	50.5	0.0	50.5	0.0	50.5	0.0	50.8	0.6	50.8	0.0	50.8	0.0	50.8	0.0	50.8	0.0
1973	51.0	0.4	51.1	0.2	51.6	1.0	51.5	-0.2	51.4	-0.2	51.5	0.2	51.6	0.2	51.6	0.0	51.6	0.0	51.6	0.0	51.7	0.2	51.9	0.4
1974	51.9	0.0	52.3	0.8	52.5	0.4	52.6	0.2	55.6	5.7	55.6	0.0	56.4	1.4	56.4	0.0	57.4	1.8	57.6	0.3	58.0	0.7	59.9	3.3
1975	60.3	0.7	60.5	0.3	61.1	1.0	61.8	1.1	61.9	0.2	62.2	0.5	62.3	0.2	62.4	0.2	62.8	0.6	63.4	1.0	63.5	0.2	62.7	-1.3
1976	63.2	0.8	64.0	1.3	64.1	0.2	64.2	0.2	64.2	0.0	65.2	1.6	65.1	-0.2	65.1	0.0	65.1	0.0	65.1	0.0	65.2	0.2	66.2	1.5
1977	65.7	-0.8	65.8	0.2	65.8	0.0	65.6	-0.3	66.5	1.4	66.7	0.3	67.1	0.6	67.0	-0.1	66.8	-0.3	66.9	0.1	66.9	0.0	67.2	0.4
1978	67.6	0.6	67.8	0.3	67.8	0.0	68.7	1.3	68.8	0.1	69.4	0.9	69.4	0.0	69.6	0.3	70.2	0.9	70.7	0.7	70.7	0.0	70.7	0.0
1979	71.4	1.0	71.4	0.0	71.4	0.0	71.3	-0.1	71.6	0.4	72.1	0.7	72.2	0.1	72.3	0.1	73.3	1.4	74.8	2.0	76.6	2.4	78.1	2.0
1980	78.9	1.0	103.9	31.7	104.1	0.2	100.9	-3.1	94.9	-5.9	95.9	1.1	95.8	-0.1	95.5	-0.3	95.5	0.0	95.4	-0.1	98.2	2.9	98.2	0.0
1981	98.6	0.4	99.6	1.0	100.4	0.8	100.9	0.5	101.0	0.1	101.0	0.0	100.5	-0.5	98.4	-2.1	99.2	0.8	99.3	0.1	99.4	0.1	99.4	0.0
1982	99.8	0.4	100.0	0.2	100.8	0.8	101.8	1.0	100.1	-1.7	100.0	-0.1	99.3	-0.7	99.3	0.0	99.8	0.5	99.7	-0.1	99.7	0.0	99.8	0.1
1983	99.8	0.0	100.7	0.9	102.9	2.2	103.0	0.1	103.0	0.0	102.9	-0.1	102.9	0.0	102.9	0.0	102.9	0.0	103.0	0.1	103.0	0.0	103.0	0.0
1984	103.1	0.1	103.6	0.5	101.1	-2.4	101.5	0.4	101.5	0.0	101.5	0.0	101.6	0.1	102.4	0.8	102.4	0.0	102.5	0.1	101.2	-1.3	101.3	0.1
1985	101.5	0.2	101.6	0.1	102.6	1.0	102.6	0.0	102.5	-0.1	102.6	0.1	102.5	-0.1	102.5	0.0	103.0	0.5	103.0	0.0	103.1	0.1	103.2	0.1
1986	103.2	0.0	103.2	0.0	103.9	0.7	103.8	-0.1	104.7	0.9	104.1	-0.6	104.1	0.0	104.1	0.0	104.1	0.0	104.2	0.1	104.2	0.0	104.1	-0.1
1987	104.2	0.1	104.4	0.2	104.3	-0.1	105.4	1.1	105.6	0.2	105.7	0.1	105.7	0.0	105.7	0.0	105.9	0.2	106.1	0.2	106.1	0.0	105.8	-0.3
1988	105.8	0.0	105.8	0.0	105.8	0.0	106.5	0.7	106.5	0.0	107.1	0.6	107.1	0.0	107.3	0.2	107.3	0.0	108.9	1.5	109.1	0.2	108.7	-0.4
1989	111.8	2.9	111.9	0.1	112.7	0.7	113.1	0.4	114.4	1.1	114.4	0.0	114.4	0.0	114.5	0.1	115.8	1.1	116.2	0.3	116.2	0.0	116.2	0.0
1990	117.5	1.1	117.8	0.3	117.8	0.0	117.8	0.0	117.9	0.1	117.9	0.0	118.0	0.8	118.8	-0.1	119.0	0.2	118.9	-0.1	118.9	0.0	119.5	0.5
1991	119.6	0.1	117.6	-1.7	117.7	0.1	118.0	0.3	117.9	-0.1	117.9	0.0	117.9	0.0	117.9	0.0	117.9	0.0	118.3	0.3	118.4	0.1	118.5	0.1

[Continued]

Photographic Equipment and Supplies

Producer Price Index
Base 1982 = 100

[Continued]

For 1947-1995. Columns headed % show percentile change in the index from the previous period for which an index is available.

Year	Jan Index	%	Feb Index	%	Mar Index	%	Apr Index	%	May Index	%	Jun Index	%	Jul Index	%	Aug Index	%	Sep Index	%	Oct Index	%	Nov Index	%	Dec Index	%
1992	118.6	0.1	118.7	0.1	118.2	-0.4	118.2	0.0	118.4	0.2	118.7	0.3	118.7	0.0	118.7	0.0	118.9	0.2	118.8	-0.1	118.9	0.1	118.9	0.0
1993	117.7	-1.0	117.8	0.1	117.8	0.0	117.9	0.1	117.9	0.0	117.9	0.0	118.3	0.3	118.8	0.4	118.6	-0.2	117.1	-1.3	118.0	0.8	117.1	-0.8
1994	120.3	2.7	119.1	-1.0	118.0	-0.9	118.2	0.2	116.9	-1.1	116.2	-0.6	116.4	0.2	116.2	-0.2	114.5	-1.5	115.4	0.8	115.6	0.2	115.6	0.0
1995	116.6	0.9	117.9	1.1	117.6	-0.3	118.5	0.8	118.4	-0.1	118.5	0.1	119.5	0.8	120.0	0.4	119.7	-0.2	117.6	-1.8	117.1	-0.4	117.9	0.7

Source: U.S. Department of Labor, Bureau of Labor Statistics, Division of Industry Prices and Price Indexes. n.e.c. stands for not elsewhere classified. - indicates no data collected for period or unavailable.

Mobile Homes
Producer Price Index
Base 1982 = 100

For 1981-1995. Columns headed % show percentile change in the index from the previous period for which an index is available.

Year	Jan Index	%	Feb Index	%	Mar Index	%	Apr Index	%	May Index	%	Jun Index	%	Jul Index	%	Aug Index	%	Sep Index	%	Oct Index	%	Nov Index	%	Dec Index	%
1981	94.5	-	94.6	0.1	95.8	1.3	96.2	0.4	96.3	0.1	96.4	0.1	97.7	1.3	97.8	0.1	98.0	0.2	98.3	0.3	98.4	0.1	98.4	0.0
1982	98.5	0.1	98.6	0.1	100.0	1.4	100.2	0.2	100.4	0.2	100.3	-0.1	100.5	0.2	100.6	0.1	100.6	0.0	100.5	-0.1	99.9	-0.6	99.9	0.0
1983	100.0	0.1	99.9	-0.1	100.6	0.7	100.3	-0.3	100.3	0.0	100.8	0.5	101.0	0.2	101.2	0.2	101.5	0.3	101.8	0.3	101.9	0.1	102.0	0.1
1984	100.1	-1.9	100.3	0.2	100.4	0.1	101.2	0.8	101.1	-0.1	100.5	-0.6	100.7	0.2	100.8	0.1	101.1	0.3	101.1	0.0	101.6	0.5	101.5	-0.1
1985	101.5	0.0	101.6	0.1	101.5	-0.1	101.5	0.0	101.5	0.0	101.8	0.3	101.7	-0.1	101.8	0.1	102.0	0.2	101.8	-0.2	101.9	0.1	101.9	0.0
1986	102.2	0.3	100.9	-1.3	101.1	0.2	102.8	1.7	102.9	0.1	103.1	0.2	103.1	0.0	103.2	0.1	103.2	0.0	103.3	0.1	103.5	0.2	103.6	0.1
1987	103.7	0.1	103.7	0.1	103.7	0.0	103.5	-0.2	104.0	0.5	104.0	0.0	104.4	0.4	103.9	-0.5	104.7	0.8	105.0	0.3	105.1	0.1	106.2	1.0
1988	106.5	0.3	107.0	0.5	107.7	0.7	108.2	0.5	108.9	0.6	109.3	0.4	109.8	0.5	109.9	0.1	110.4	0.5	110.7	0.3	111.6	0.8	111.4	-0.2
1989	111.6	0.2	111.9	0.3	112.1	0.2	112.5	0.4	113.9	1.2	113.9	0.0	114.3	0.4	114.8	0.4	115.2	0.3	115.5	0.3	115.8	0.3	115.9	0.1
1990	115.9	0.0	116.2	0.3	116.2	0.0	116.4	0.2	116.9	0.4	117.5	0.5	117.7	0.2	118.0	0.3	118.2	0.2	118.4	0.2	119.3	0.8	119.3	0.0
1991	119.3	0.0	119.5	0.2	119.5	0.0	119.6	0.1	120.1	0.4	120.4	0.2	120.8	0.3	121.1	0.2	121.0	-0.1	121.0	0.0	121.2	0.2	121.2	0.0
1992	120.4	-0.7	120.4	0.0	120.4	0.0	120.9	0.4	121.3	0.3	121.4	0.1	121.7	0.2	122.0	0.2	122.1	0.1	123.0	0.7	123.5	0.4	123.5	0.0
1993	123.5	0.0	124.6	0.9	125.5	0.7	126.6	0.9	127.3	0.6	127.6	0.2	129.2	1.3	129.2	0.0	129.1	-0.1	129.3	0.2	130.7	1.1	131.1	0.3
1994	132.6	1.1	132.6	0.0	135.7	2.3	135.8	0.1	135.8	0.0	137.0	0.9	137.2	0.1	137.3	0.1	138.0	0.5	139.1	0.8	141.0	1.4	142.0	0.7
1995	143.9	1.3	144.7	0.6	144.7	0.0	144.9	0.1	144.9	0.0	145.9	0.7	146.1	0.1	144.9	-0.8	146.5	1.1	147.0	0.3	147.8	0.5	148.9	0.7

Source: U.S. Department of Labor, Bureau of Labor Statistics, Division of Industry Prices and Price Indexes. n.e.c. stands for not elsewhere classified. - indicates no data collected for period or unavailable.

Medical, Surgical & Personal Aid Devices
Producer Price Index
Base 1982 = 100

For 1978-1995. Columns headed % show percentile change in the index from the previous period for which an index is available.

Year	Jan Index	%	Feb Index	%	Mar Index	%	Apr Index	%	May Index	%	Jun Index	%	Jul Index	%	Aug Index	%	Sep Index	%	Oct Index	%	Nov Index	%	Dec Index	%
1978	-	-	-	-	-	-	-	-	-	-	86.5	-	86.4	-0.1	86.9	0.6	86.9	0.0	87.4	0.6	87.4	0.0	88.3	1.0
1979	88.6	0.3	88.6	0.0	88.6	0.0	88.6	0.0	89.1	0.6	89.6	0.6	89.8	0.2	90.2	0.4	90.2	0.0	90.2	0.0	90.3	0.1	90.3	0.0
1980	90.1	-0.2	90.5	0.4	92.9	2.7	92.9	0.0	94.2	1.4	94.2	0.0	94.2	0.0	94.2	0.0	94.7	0.5	93.8	-1.0	93.8	0.0	93.8	0.0
1981	93.8	0.0	94.0	0.2	94.9	1.0	97.4	2.6	98.2	0.8	98.2	0.0	98.2	0.0	98.2	0.0	98.2	0.0	98.2	0.0	98.2	0.0	98.2	0.0
1982	98.7	0.5	98.7	0.0	98.7	0.0	98.7	0.0	99.0	0.3	99.0	0.0	100.5	1.5	100.5	0.0	101.4	0.9	101.6	0.2	101.6	0.0	101.6	0.0
1983	102.7	1.1	101.7	-1.0	102.6	0.9	102.4	-0.2	102.6	0.2	102.8	0.2	104.4	1.6	104.7	0.3	104.5	-0.2	105.2	0.7	105.9	0.7	105.9	0.0
1984	107.6	1.6	107.7	0.1	107.8	0.1	108.3	0.5	108.2	-0.1	108.2	0.0	108.4	0.2	108.9	0.5	108.4	-0.5	108.6	0.2	108.7	0.1	108.7	0.0
1985	109.4	0.6	109.2	-0.2	109.3	0.1	109.2	-0.1	109.2	0.0	109.2	0.0	108.7	-0.5	108.7	0.0	108.7	0.0	108.9	0.2	108.9	0.0	109.0	0.1
1986	110.4	1.3	110.5	0.1	110.8	0.3	111.0	0.2	111.0	0.0	111.2	0.2	111.5	0.3	111.6	0.1	111.8	0.2	112.4	0.5	114.7	2.0	114.3	-0.3
1987	114.1	-0.2	114.2	0.1	114.6	0.4	117.8	2.8	117.6	-0.2	117.8	0.2	117.6	-0.2	117.9	0.3	117.7	-0.2	117.8	0.1	118.4	0.5	118.2	-0.2
1988	119.1	0.8	119.2	0.1	119.4	0.2	119.5	0.1	119.8	0.3	117.8	-1.7	118.0	0.2	118.1	0.1	118.1	0.0	119.3	1.0	119.4	0.1	119.4	0.0
1989	121.2	1.5	121.5	0.2	121.8	0.2	122.1	0.2	123.1	0.8	123.1	0.0	122.9	-0.2	123.0	0.1	123.8	0.7	124.4	0.5	124.5	0.1	124.8	0.2
1990	125.9	0.9	126.0	0.1	126.3	0.2	126.9	0.5	127.2	0.2	127.3	0.1	127.4	0.1	127.8	0.3	128.0	0.2	128.4	0.3	128.3	-0.1	128.5	0.2
1991	129.3	0.6	129.5	0.2	129.7	0.2	130.0	0.2	130.0	0.0	130.2	0.2	130.4	0.2	130.6	0.2	131.2	0.5	130.9	-0.2	131.1	0.2	130.9	-0.2
1992	132.4	1.1	132.8	0.3	133.5	0.5	133.6	0.1	133.8	0.1	133.9	0.1	133.5	-0.3	134.4	0.7	134.3	-0.1	134.8	0.4	134.7	-0.1	134.6	-0.1
1993	136.0	1.0	137.5	1.1	137.9	0.3	137.8	-0.1	138.5	0.5	137.9	-0.4	137.5	-0.3	138.3	0.6	137.7	-0.4	138.0	0.2	138.1	0.1	138.7	0.4
1994	139.3	0.4	140.3	0.7	140.6	0.2	140.4	-0.1	140.1	-0.2	140.3	0.1	140.7	0.3	140.5	-0.1	140.7	0.1	140.7	0.0	140.7	0.0	140.1	-0.4
1995	140.2	0.1	141.0	0.6	140.9	-0.1	140.6	-0.2	140.9	0.2	141.0	0.1	141.3	0.2	141.1	-0.1	141.2	0.1	142.1	0.6	141.9	-0.1	142.2	0.2

Source: U.S. Department of Labor, Bureau of Labor Statistics, Division of Industry Prices and Price Indexes. n.e.c. stands for not elsewhere classified. - indicates no data collected for period or unavailable.

Industrial Safety Equipment
Producer Price Index
Base 1982 = 100

For 1978-1995. Columns headed % show percentile change in the index from the previous period for which an index is available.

Year	Jan Index	%	Feb Index	%	Mar Index	%	Apr Index	%	May Index	%	Jun Index	%	Jul Index	%	Aug Index	%	Sep Index	%	Oct Index	%	Nov Index	%	Dec Index	%
1978	-	-	-	-	-	-	-	-	-	-	77.3	-	77.5	0.3	77.5	0.0	77.8	0.4	78.5	0.9	79.0	0.6	79.6	0.8
1979	80.2	0.8	81.0	1.0	81.6	0.7	82.5	1.1	82.9	0.5	83.1	0.2	83.7	0.7	83.9	0.2	84.2	0.4	84.5	0.4	86.3	2.1	86.1	-0.2
1980	87.4	1.5	88.2	0.9	88.6	0.5	89.0	0.5	89.5	0.6	89.9	0.4	90.2	0.3	90.2	0.0	90.2	0.0	90.5	0.3	90.5	0.0	91.1	0.7
1981	93.0	2.1	94.4	1.5	94.7	0.3	95.0	0.3	94.9	-0.1	94.9	0.0	95.7	0.8	96.1	0.4	96.1	0.0	96.3	0.2	96.4	0.1	96.6	0.2
1982	98.1	1.6	99.2	1.1	99.6	0.4	99.6	0.0	99.8	0.2	100.2	0.4	100.2	0.0	100.6	0.4	100.5	-0.1	100.7	0.2	100.7	0.0	100.7	0.0
1983	101.9	1.2	102.0	0.1	102.5	0.5	102.9	0.4	102.9	0.0	103.0	0.1	103.6	0.6	103.6	0.0	103.6	0.0	103.2	-0.4	103.2	0.0	104.2	1.0
1984	103.6	-0.6	103.6	0.0	103.6	0.0	103.6	0.0	103.8	0.2	109.5	5.5	108.1	-1.3	110.1	1.9	109.2	-0.8	109.2	0.0	109.0	-0.2	109.8	0.7
1985	111.1	1.2	111.2	0.1	111.0	-0.2	111.2	0.2	111.1	-0.1	110.9	-0.2	110.9	0.0	110.7	-0.2	111.1	0.4	111.1	0.0	112.1	0.9	113.4	1.2
1986	117.5	3.6	117.6	0.1	118.1	0.4	120.8	2.3	120.7	-0.1	120.7	0.0	120.8	0.1	121.7	0.7	121.9	0.2	123.2	1.1	124.4	1.0	125.0	0.5
1987	125.1	0.1	128.0	2.3	128.0	0.0	128.4	0.3	127.9	-0.4	128.7	0.6	129.3	0.5	130.0	0.5	130.2	0.2	130.9	0.5	131.0	0.1	131.1	0.1
1988	132.0	0.7	132.1	0.1	133.8	1.3	136.5	2.0	136.5	0.0	136.7	0.1	137.6	0.7	137.7	0.1	137.7	0.0	137.8	0.1	140.9	2.2	140.9	0.0
1989	140.9	0.0	140.9	0.0	142.0	0.8	144.6	1.8	144.6	0.0	144.8	0.1	144.9	0.1	144.9	0.0	144.8	-0.1	146.1	0.9	145.9	-0.1	146.0	0.1
1990	146.1	0.1	146.1	0.0	146.1	0.0	149.5	2.3	150.2	0.5	150.7	0.3	150.4	-0.2	150.4	0.0	151.0	0.4	151.5	0.3	151.2	-0.2	152.7	1.0
1991	154.6	1.2	153.7	-0.6	156.4	1.8	157.0	0.4	156.7	-0.2	156.9	0.1	158.5	1.0	159.9	0.9	159.8	-0.1	161.1	0.8	158.8	-1.4	159.5	0.4
1992	159.7	0.1	159.8	0.1	160.0	0.1	163.1	1.9	163.7	0.4	163.6	-0.1	166.3	1.7	166.3	0.0	165.5	-0.5	165.5	0.0	164.8	-0.4	164.7	-0.1
1993	165.0	0.2	166.0	0.6	165.3	-0.4	165.0	-0.2	165.5	0.3	166.0	0.3	166.1	0.1	166.7	0.4	166.6	-0.1	166.9	0.2	169.5	1.6	169.9	0.2
1994	169.9	0.0	172.1	1.3	172.2	0.1	172.2	0.0	172.4	0.1	172.6	0.1	173.2	0.3	173.2	0.0	173.2	0.0	173.7	0.3	173.7	0.0	172.9	-0.5
1995	173.6	0.4	173.7	0.1	179.6	3.4	179.7	0.1	179.7	0.0	180.4	0.4	180.4	0.0	180.3	-0.1	180.4	0.1	178.1	-1.3	178.4	0.2	178.3	-0.1

Source: U.S. Department of Labor, Bureau of Labor Statistics, Division of Industry Prices and Price Indexes. n.e.c. stands for not elsewhere classified. - indicates no data collected for period or unavailable.

Mining Services
Producer Price Index
Base June 1985 = 100

For 1985-1995. Columns headed % show percentile change in the index from the previous period for which an index is available.

Year	Jan Index	%	Feb Index	%	Mar Index	%	Apr Index	%	May Index	%	Jun Index	%	Jul Index	%	Aug Index	%	Sep Index	%	Oct Index	%	Nov Index	%	Dec Index	%
1985	-	-	-	-	-	-	-	-	-	-	100.0	-	99.6	-0.4	99.6	0.0	99.6	0.0	99.5	-0.1	99.2	-0.3	99.0	-0.2
1986	98.8	-0.2	97.0	-1.8	95.9	-1.1	93.7	-2.3	91.7	-2.1	90.7	-1.1	89.6	-1.2	88.8	-0.9	88.7	-0.1	87.6	-1.2	86.9	-0.8	86.7	-0.2
1987	86.5	-0.2	86.2	-0.3	86.4	0.2	86.5	0.1	86.5	0.0	86.3	-0.2	86.5	0.2	87.2	0.8	87.8	0.7	88.5	0.8	89.5	1.1	90.0	0.6
1988	90.6	0.7	91.6	1.1	91.1	-0.5	91.2	0.1	91.0	-0.2	91.0	0.0	90.9	-0.1	90.0	-1.0	89.9	-0.1	89.8	-0.1	89.8	0.0	89.8	0.0
1989	90.4	0.7	90.3	-0.1	90.3	0.0	90.0	-0.3	90.5	0.6	90.7	0.2	91.3	0.7	91.6	0.3	91.2	-0.4	91.4	0.2	91.7	0.3	91.9	0.2
1990	92.8	1.0	93.8	1.1	93.8	0.0	94.4	0.6	94.7	0.3	95.0	0.3	95.0	0.0	95.7	0.7	96.4	0.7	97.4	1.0	97.8	0.4	98.7	0.9
1991	99.6	0.9	99.6	0.0	99.8	0.2	99.5	-0.3	99.6	0.1	99.2	-0.4	99.0	-0.2	98.3	-0.7	97.9	-0.4	97.0	-0.9	96.3	-0.7	97.5	1.2
1992	97.0	-0.5	96.6	-0.4	96.8	0.2	95.6	-1.2	95.7	0.1	93.7	-2.1	94.2	0.5	93.3	-1.0	94.0	0.8	94.3	0.3	94.7	0.4	95.8	1.2
1993	96.3	0.5	98.4	2.2	98.3	-0.1	99.2	0.9	99.2	0.0	99.8	0.6	100.4	0.6	100.5	0.1	101.6	1.1	101.6	0.0	101.7	0.1	102.6	0.9
1994	103.3	0.7	103.3	0.0	102.2	-1.1	101.9	-0.3	101.7	-0.2	102.3	0.6	102.3	0.0	103.1	0.8	103.6	0.5	103.4	-0.2	104.1	0.7	103.9	-0.2
1995	103.6	-0.3	103.5	-0.1	102.7	-0.8	103.0	0.3	103.0	0.0	102.9	-0.1	103.1	0.2	109.0	5.7	103.6	-5.0	103.8	0.2	103.4	-0.4	111.1	7.4

Source: U.S. Department of Labor, Bureau of Labor Statistics, Division of Industry Prices and Price Indexes. n.e.c. stands for not elsewhere classified. - indicates no data collected for period or unavailable.

Miscellaneous Products n.e.c.
Producer Price Index
Base 1982 = 100

For 1947-1995. Columns headed % show percentile change in the index from the previous period for which an index is available.

Year	Jan Index	%	Feb Index	%	Mar Index	%	Apr Index	%	May Index	%	Jun Index	%	Jul Index	%	Aug Index	%	Sep Index	%	Oct Index	%	Nov Index	%	Dec Index	%
1947	23.2	-	23.2	0.0	23.2	0.0	23.4	0.9	23.4	0.0	23.1	-1.3	22.9	-0.9	22.9	0.0	23.0	0.4	23.2	0.9	23.4	0.9	23.4	0.0
1948	23.5	0.4	23.7	0.9	23.7	0.0	23.7	0.0	23.7	0.0	23.8	0.4	23.8	0.0	23.9	0.4	23.9	0.0	23.9	0.0	24.0	0.4	24.2	0.8
1949	24.2	0.0	24.2	0.0	24.2	0.0	23.8	-1.7	23.9	0.4	23.9	0.0	23.7	-0.8	23.7	0.0	23.7	0.0	23.7	0.0	23.9	0.8	23.9	0.0
1950	23.6	-1.3	23.6	0.0	23.6	0.0	23.7	0.4	23.7	0.0	23.6	-0.4	23.7	0.4	24.3	2.5	24.2	-0.4	24.6	1.7	24.7	0.4	25.2	2.0
1951	25.7	2.0	25.7	0.0	25.7	0.0	25.7	0.0	25.7	0.0	25.7	0.0	25.7	0.0	25.7	0.0	25.7	0.0	25.7	0.0	25.7	0.0	25.7	0.0
1952	25.7	0.0	25.7	0.0	25.7	0.0	25.7	0.0	25.7	0.0	25.7	0.0	25.7	0.0	25.7	0.0	25.7	0.0	25.7	0.0	25.7	0.0	25.7	0.0
1953	25.7	0.0	25.7	0.0	25.8	0.4	25.8	0.0	25.7	-0.4	25.7	0.0	25.7	0.0	25.7	0.0	25.7	0.0	25.7	0.0	25.7	0.0	25.7	0.0
1954	25.7	0.0	25.8	0.4	25.9	0.4	26.0	0.4	25.9	-0.4	26.0	0.4	26.0	0.0	26.0	0.0	26.0	0.0	26.1	0.4	26.1	0.0	26.1	0.0
1955	26.0	-0.4	26.0	0.0	26.0	0.0	26.0	0.0	26.0	0.0	26.0	0.0	26.1	0.4	26.2	0.4	26.2	0.0	26.2	0.0	26.3	0.4	26.4	0.4
1956	26.4	0.0	26.4	0.0	26.4	0.0	26.5	0.4	26.5	0.0	26.5	0.0	26.5	0.0	26.5	0.0	26.6	0.4	26.6	0.0	26.7	0.4	26.7	0.0
1957	27.0	1.1	27.1	0.4	27.1	0.0	27.1	0.0	27.1	0.0	27.0	-0.4	27.1	0.4	27.1	0.0	27.2	0.4	27.3	0.4	27.3	0.0	27.3	0.0
1958	27.2	-0.4	27.3	0.4	27.3	0.0	27.3	0.0	27.3	0.0	27.5	0.7	27.4	-0.4	27.4	0.0	27.4	0.0	27.4	0.0	27.4	0.0	27.5	0.4
1959	27.5	0.0	27.5	0.0	27.5	0.0	27.5	0.0	27.5	0.0	27.4	-0.4	27.4	0.0	27.5	0.4	27.5	0.0	27.5	0.0	27.5	0.0	27.7	0.7
1960	27.9	0.7	27.9	0.0	27.9	0.0	27.9	0.0	28.0	0.4	27.9	-0.4	28.0	0.4	28.0	0.0	28.0	0.0	28.0	0.0	27.9	-0.4	28.0	0.4
1961	28.1	0.4	28.1	0.0	28.0	-0.4	27.9	-0.4	28.0	0.4	28.0	0.0	28.0	0.0	28.1	0.4	28.1	0.0	28.1	0.0	28.1	0.0	28.1	0.0
1962	28.0	-0.4	28.0	0.0	28.0	0.0	28.1	0.4	28.1	0.0	28.1	0.0	28.1	0.0	28.1	0.0	28.1	0.0	28.1	0.0	28.2	0.4	28.1	-0.4
1963	28.1	0.0	28.1	0.0	28.1	0.0	28.0	-0.4	28.0	0.0	28.0	0.0	28.0	0.0	28.0	0.0	28.0	0.0	28.0	0.0	28.0	0.0	28.0	0.0
1964	28.1	0.4	28.0	-0.4	28.1	0.4	28.1	0.0	28.1	0.0	28.0	-0.4	28.2	0.7	28.2	0.0	28.2	0.0	28.2	0.0	28.2	0.0	28.2	0.0
1965	28.1	-0.4	28.1	0.0	28.1	0.0	28.1	0.0	28.1	0.0	28.3	0.7	28.6	1.1	28.6	0.0	28.6	0.0	28.6	0.0	28.6	0.0	28.6	0.0
1966	28.7	0.3	28.7	0.0	28.6	-0.3	28.7	0.3	28.7	0.0	28.7	0.0	28.8	0.3	28.9	0.3	28.9	0.0	28.9	0.0	29.0	0.3	29.0	0.0
1967	29.3	1.0	29.3	0.0	29.4	0.3	29.4	0.0	29.5	0.3	29.6	0.3	29.7	0.3	29.7	0.0	29.7	0.0	29.7	0.0	29.8	0.3	29.9	0.3
1968	30.1	0.7	30.1	0.0	30.1	0.0	30.2	0.3	30.2	0.0	30.2	0.0	30.3	0.3	30.4	0.3	30.5	0.3	30.6	0.3	30.6	0.0	30.6	0.0
1969	30.4	-0.7	30.4	0.0	30.5	0.3	30.5	0.0	30.6	0.3	30.9	1.0	31.2	1.0	31.2	0.0	31.3	0.3	31.4	0.3	31.4	0.0	31.4	0.0
1970	31.5	0.3	31.5	0.0	31.5	0.0	31.5	0.0	32.0	1.6	32.1	0.3	32.5	1.2	32.5	0.0	32.6	0.3	32.6	0.0	32.7	0.3	32.7	0.0
1971	32.9	0.6	33.0	0.3	32.9	-0.3	33.1	0.6	33.2	0.3	33.3	0.3	33.5	0.6	33.5	0.0	33.5	0.0	33.5	0.0	33.5	0.0	33.5	0.0
1972	33.7	0.6	33.8	0.3	33.8	0.0	34.0	0.6	34.0	0.0	34.1	0.3	34.7	1.8	34.8	0.3	34.8	0.0	34.6	-0.6	34.5	-0.3	34.6	0.3
1973	35.1	1.4	35.2	0.3	35.4	0.6	36.1	2.0	36.9	2.2	37.6	1.9	38.3	1.9	38.3	0.0	38.3	0.0	37.8	-1.3	37.9	0.3	38.0	0.3
1974	39.0	2.6	39.4	1.0	40.3	2.3	42.4	5.2	42.7	0.7	42.9	0.5	43.1	0.5	42.2	-2.1	42.5	0.7	42.9	0.9	43.1	0.5	43.6	1.2
1975	45.3	3.9	45.8	1.1	46.0	0.4	46.1	0.2	46.2	0.2	46.2	0.0	46.3	0.2	46.3	0.0	46.6	0.6	45.5	-2.4	45.5	0.0	45.8	0.7
1976	46.0	0.4	45.9	-0.2	45.9	0.0	45.0	-2.0	45.0	0.0	45.7	1.6	45.0	-1.5	44.6	-0.9	44.7	0.2	44.8	0.2	44.8	0.0	45.1	0.7
1977	47.4	5.1	47.6	0.4	47.9	0.6	49.4	3.1	49.4	0.0	49.4	0.0	49.4	0.0	49.5	0.2	49.6	0.2	51.2	3.2	51.5	0.6	51.7	0.4
1978	52.5	1.5	51.5	-1.9	52.5	1.9	61.0	16.2	62.3	2.1	62.4	0.2	66.9	7.2	68.1	1.8	69.3	1.8	66.6	-3.9	64.6	-3.0	69.4	7.4
1979	70.3	1.3	72.1	2.6	72.6	0.7	72.7	0.1	74.1	1.9	75.6	2.0	76.8	1.6	77.3	0.7	80.5	4.1	85.2	5.8	86.7	1.8	91.3	5.3
1980	103.9	13.8	111.8	7.6	103.8	-7.2	100.8	-2.9	100.6	-0.2	106.5	5.9	109.6	2.9	107.8	-1.6	112.9	4.7	113.3	0.4	108.5	-4.2	109.5	0.9
1981	107.4	-1.9	105.9	-1.4	103.8	-2.0	103.2	-0.6	103.3	0.1	102.6	-0.7	98.5	-4.0	98.9	0.4	102.1	3.2	103.0	0.9	101.9	-1.1	101.8	-0.1
1982	101.2	-0.6	100.8	-0.4	98.9	-1.9	98.7	-0.2	97.9	-0.8	97.1	-0.8	98.6	1.5	96.7	-1.9	102.0	5.5	102.0	0.0	102.0	0.0	103.9	1.9
1983	103.7	-0.2	106.4	2.6	103.6	-2.6	103.6	0.0	103.2	-0.4	104.5	1.3	104.5	0.0	104.3	-0.2	103.3	-1.0	103.2	-0.1	103.2	0.0	104.4	1.2
1984	103.7	-0.7	103.6	-0.1	104.7	1.1	104.0	-0.7	103.6	-0.4	103.5	-0.1	103.5	0.0	104.4	0.9	102.6	-1.7	103.0	0.4	103.4	0.4	103.5	0.1
1985	102.6	-0.9	103.7	1.1	103.0	-0.7	104.2	1.2	103.9	-0.3	103.7	-0.2	103.5	-0.2	103.4	-0.1	103.3	-0.1	103.4	0.1	103.5	0.1	103.1	-0.4
1986	103.7	0.6	103.9	0.2	104.2	0.3	104.4	0.2	104.5	0.1	104.5	0.0	104.6	0.1	105.1	0.5	105.5	0.4	106.1	0.6	106.0	-0.1	105.8	-0.2
1987	106.4	0.6	106.5	0.1	106.8	0.3	107.2	0.4	107.6	0.4	107.9	0.3	108.1	0.2	108.5	0.4	108.5	0.0	109.0	0.5	109.4	0.4	109.5	0.1
1988	110.0	0.5	109.8	-0.2	109.9	0.1	110.3	0.4	110.6	0.3	110.9	0.3	111.4	0.5	111.6	0.2	111.7	0.1	111.6	-0.1	111.9	0.3	112.1	0.2
1989	112.6	0.4	112.9	0.3	113.3	0.4	113.6	0.3	113.8	0.2	113.9	0.1	114.2	0.3	114.5	0.3	114.6	0.1	114.7	0.1	115.0	0.3	115.4	0.3
1990	116.5	1.0	117.0	0.4	117.4	0.3	117.2	-0.2	117.3	0.1	117.6	0.3	117.6	0.0	118.1	0.4	118.1	0.0	118.5	0.3	118.6	0.1	118.5	-0.1
1991	119.7	1.0	119.8	0.1	120.2	0.3	120.4	0.1	120.5	0.1	120.8	0.2	120.9	0.1	120.6	-0.2	120.4	-0.2	120.6	0.2	120.7	0.1	120.9	0.2

[Continued]

Miscellaneous Products n.e.c.
Producer Price Index
Base 1982 = 100
[Continued]

For 1947-1995. Columns headed % show percentile change in the index from the previous period for which an index is available.

Year	Jan Index	%	Feb Index	%	Mar Index	%	Apr Index	%	May Index	%	Jun Index	%	Jul Index	%	Aug Index	%	Sep Index	%	Oct Index	%	Nov Index	%	Dec Index	%
1992	121.6	0.6	121.6	0.0	121.7	0.1	122.2	0.4	122.3	0.1	122.4	0.1	122.5	0.1	122.7	0.2	122.6	-0.1	122.8	0.2	123.1	0.2	123.5	0.3
1993	123.9	0.3	124.2	0.2	124.2	0.0	124.9	0.6	125.3	0.3	125.3	0.0	125.8	0.4	126.0	0.2	125.8	-0.2	125.9	0.1	126.1	0.2	126.6	0.4
1994	126.8	0.2	126.6	-0.2	126.5	-0.1	127.0	0.4	127.3	0.2	127.4	0.1	127.7	0.2	127.7	0.0	127.8	0.1	128.0	0.2	128.4	0.3	128.9	0.4
1995	129.8	0.7	130.3	0.4	130.6	0.2	131.4	0.6	132.0	0.5	132.3	0.2	132.5	0.2	132.6	0.1	132.7	0.1	132.7	0.0	132.7	0.0	132.3	-0.3

Source: U.S. Department of Labor, Bureau of Labor Statistics, Division of Industry Prices and Price Indexes. n.e.c. stands for not elsewhere classified. - indicates no data collected for period or unavailable.

CHAPTER 8

SELECTED STOCK MARKET PRICE INDEXES

SELECTED STOCK MARKET PRICE INDEXES

This chapter presents stock market index data for the American Stock Exchange, the NASDAQ Stock Market, and the New York Stock Exchange. The Standard & Poors composite index, used by the Bureau of Economic Analysis (Department of Commerce) as a component of the composite index of leading indicators, is shown in Chapter 3.

General Concepts

Stock indexes measure the value of stocks traded on exchanges or in the over-the-counter (OTC) market.

Index Weightings. All the indexes presented here are so-called "market-value weighted" indexes, also called "capitalization-weighted" indexes. This means that the contribution of any one stock to the index is weighted by the stock's overall value—its price multiplied by the number of its shares outstanding.

A stock (Stock A) with a price of $100 per share and 50,000 shares outstanding has a capitalization of $5 million; another stock (Stock B), with a price of $50 and 30,000 shares outstanding has a capitalization of $1.5 million. If only these two stocks were present in a market, the total market would be valued at $6.5 million. Stock A's contribution to index changes would be 77% ($5 million as a percent of $6.5 million); Stock B's contribution would be 23%. Since prices and the number of shares outstanding are constantly changing—and the number of stocks traded is large—any one stock's contribution to an index is continuously in flux and relatively small.

Indexes are calculated so that the distorting effect of stock splits, mergers, and similar changes in corporate capitalization are eliminated.

Alternatives to the market-value weighted indexes are price-weighted indexes (none is shown in *EIH*). In these indexes, for example, in the American Stock Exchange's Major Market Index and the Dow Jones Industrial Average, high-priced stocks have a greater influence on the index than low-priced issues.

Market-value weighted indexes reflect overall market performance; price-weighted indexes tend to reflect the performance of important, leading stocks.

Index Basing. Index values are expressed in relation to a base—the value of the market on a given date. The *base index* may be any value but is 50 or 100 for the data shown here. Index values are calculated using the following formula:

(Market Today / Base Period Market) x Base Index

We can apply this formula to a situation where the base period market was $1,000, today's market is $1,050, and the base index is 100. The new index will be 105 (1,050 / 1,000 x 100). If a different base index is used, 50, for example, the same formula and values would yield a new index of 52.5.

The total market values ("market today" and "base period market") are obtained by adding, for each period, the capital value of all stocks: each stock's price multiplied by the number of shares of that stock outstanding. This, in effect, produces a market-value weighting of each stock.

Analytical Uses

The most common use of stock market indexes is to measure the performance of a given market or, by combining various indexes, measuring the performance of stocks as a whole. Investors can use stock market indexes to measure how well their portfolios are doing. The indexes included in this chapter are all broad composites; therefore, portfolios that under-perform these indexes may be overdue for review. Stock markets are sensitive indicators of anticipated economic conditions; the sustained rise or fall of composite indexes, therefore, can be used to forecast the future—the future as it is seen by all those buying and selling stocks.

Presentation

The composite indexes for the American, the NASDAQ, and the New York stock exchanges are presented for 1984-1995 side by side in the first table. All other tables are specific to one of these three stock markets.

American Stock Exchange. The AMEX Market Value Index is a broadly-based index reflecting the prices of more than 800 stocks. It is based on AMEX market value as of July 29, 1983, which was defined as 50. Unlike other stock indexes, this index includes the value of stock dividends paid. Two tables highlight the AMEX index; the first shows annual high, low, and close indexes for the 1969-1995 period; the second shows the Market Value Index and its sub-indexes for 1980 to 1995 by quarter, each item of data being the closing value of the quarter.

NASDAQ Stock Market. NASDAQ stands for the National Association of Security Dealers Automated Quotation System; NASDAQ reports the prices of more than 5,000 stocks traded over-the-counter (OTC); this is a relatively small subset of the more than 40 million OTC stock issues traded. The base period for the NASDAQ Price Index is February 5, 1971; the base index is 100. Two tables are included for the NASDAQ index; the first shows high, low, and close data for the 1971 to 1995 period; the second shows quarterly data for 1980 through 1995. In addition to the composite index, data for six sub-indexes are also included.

New York Stock Exchange. The New York Stock Exchange (NYSE) is the largest U.S. stock exchange, and the NYSE Composite Index reflects the share prices of more than 1,600 stocks traded on the exchange. The index base period is December 31, 1965 and the base index is 50. A single table summarizes the NYSE's performance. It shows annual high, low, and close data from 1966 through 1995.

Bibliography

1. Berlin, Howard M. *The Handbook of Financial Market Indexes, Averages, and Indicators*. Dow Jones-Irwin, Homewood, IL, 1990.

2. Downes, John and Jordan Elliot Goodman. *Dictionary of Finance and Investment Terms*. Barron's, New York, 1991.

AMEX, NASD, and NYSE Indexes
1984-1995

For 1984-1995. Index is the closing value at month end. Columns headed % show percentile change in each index from the previous period. The acronyms AMEX, NASD, and NYSE stand for American Stock Exchange, National Association of Securities Dealers (over the counter market), and New York Stock Exchange.

Year	Month	AMEX		NASD		NYSE	
		Index	%	Index	%	Index	%
1984	JAN	216.91	-2.7	268.43	-3.7	94.32	-0.9
	FEB	210.22	-3.1	252.57	-5.9	90.44	-4.1
	MAR	211.34	0.5	250.78	-0.7	91.67	1.4
	APR	210.42	-0.4	247.44	-1.3	91.98	0.3
	MAY	198.63	-5.6	232.82	-5.9	86.71	-5.7
	JUN	200.08	0.7	239.65	2.9	88.38	1.9
	JUL	188.67	-5.7	229.70	-4.2	86.73	-1.9
	AUG	215.41	14.2	254.64	10.9	95.86	10.5
	SEP	215.45	0.0	249.94	-1.8	95.77	-0.1
	OCT	208.18	-3.4	247.03	-1.2	95.74	-0.0
	NOV	204.27	-1.9	242.53	-1.8	94.30	-1.5
	DEC	204.26	-0.0	247.35	2.0	96.38	2.2
1985	JAN	224.07	9.7	278.70	12.7	103.75	7.6
	FEB	227.43	1.5	284.17	2.0	104.93	1.1
	MAR	229.59	0.9	279.20	-1.7	104.60	-0.3
	APR	227.44	-0.9	280.56	0.5	104.12	-0.5
	MAY	231.69	1.9	290.80	3.6	109.63	5.3
	JUN	230.89	-0.3	296.20	1.9	111.11	1.3
	JUL	233.92	1.3	301.29	1.7	110.47	-0.6
	AUG	234.25	0.1	297.31	-1.3	109.47	-0.9
	SEP	222.31	-5.1	280.33	-5.7	105.19	-3.9
	OCT	228.61	2.8	292.54	4.4	109.65	4.2
	NOV	242.26	6.0	313.95	7.3	116.55	6.3
	DEC	246.13	1.6	324.93	3.5	121.58	4.3
1986	JAN	243.87	-0.9	335.77	3.3	122.13	0.5
	FEB	257.35	5.5	359.53	7.1	130.74	7.0
	MAR	270.03	4.9	374.72	4.2	137.71	5.3
	APR	268.97	-0.4	383.24	2.3	135.75	-1.4
	MAY	282.60	5.1	400.16	4.4	142.06	4.6
	JUN	284.20	0.6	405.51	1.3	143.96	1.3
	JUL	261.56	-8.0	371.37	-8.4	135.89	-5.6
	AUG	273.85	4.7	382.86	3.1	145.32	6.9
	SEP	260.69	-4.8	350.67	-8.4	133.44	-8.2
	OCT	265.59	1.9	360.77	2.9	140.42	5.2
	NOV	264.81	-0.3	359.57	-0.3	142.57	1.5
	DEC	263.27	-0.6	348.83	-3.0	138.58	-2.8
1987	JAN	300.47	14.1	392.06	12.4	156.11	12.6
	FEB	321.76	7.1	424.97	8.4	162.01	3.8
	MAR	332.66	3.4	430.05	1.2	165.89	2.4
	APR	325.19	-2.2	417.81	-2.8	162.86	-1.8
	MAY	326.39	0.4	416.54	-0.3	163.48	0.4
	JUN	338.13	3.6	424.67	2.0	171.07	4.6
	JUL	358.03	5.9	434.93	2.4	178.63	4.4
	AUG	361.35	0.9	454.97	4.6	184.45	3.3
	SEP	358.45	-0.8	444.29	-2.3	180.24	-2.3
	OCT	260.36	-27.4	323.30	-27.2	140.80	-21.9
	NOV	242.39	-6.9	305.16	-5.6	129.69	-7.9
	DEC	260.35	7.4	330.47	8.3	138.23	6.6

[Continued]

AMEX, NASD, and NYSE Indexes
1984-1995
[Continued]

Year	Month	AMEX		NASD		NYSE	
		Index	%	Index	%	Index	%
1988	JAN	269.10	3.4	344.66	4.3	144.13	4.3
	FEB	288.46	7.2	366.94	6.5	150.46	4.4
	MAR	296.43	2.8	374.64	2.1	146.60	-2.6
	APR	303.14	2.3	379.23	1.2	147.87	0.9
	MAY	294.19	-3.0	370.34	-2.3	148.04	0.1
	JUN	309.25	5.1	394.66	6.6	154.47	4.3
	JUL	306.18	-1.0	387.33	-1.9	153.35	-0.7
	AUG	294.80	-3.7	376.55	-2.8	148.29	-3.3
	SEP	301.63	2.3	387.71	3.0	153.57	3.6
	OCT	300.95	-0.2	382.46	-1.4	156.94	2.2
	NOV	294.36	-2.2	371.45	-2.9	153.90	-1.9
	DEC	306.01	4.0	381.38	2.7	156.26	1.5
1989	JAN	323.02	5.6	401.30	5.2	166.63	6.6
	FEB	322.47	-0.2	399.71	-0.4	162.49	-2.5
	MAR	328.31	1.8	406.73	1.8	165.63	1.9
	APR	345.08	5.1	427.55	5.1	173.13	4.5
	MAY	356.66	3.4	446.17	4.4	178.85	3.3
	JUN	358.97	0.6	435.29	-2.4	177.90	-0.5
	JUL	376.56	4.9	453.84	4.3	192.41	8.2
	AUG	382.19	1.5	469.33	3.4	195.27	1.5
	SEP	388.76	1.7	472.92	0.8	193.97	-0.7
	OCT	370.58	-4.7	455.63	-3.7	188.24	-3.0
	NOV	373.84	0.9	456.09	0.1	191.30	1.6
	DEC	378.00	1.1	454.82	-0.3	195.04	2.0
1990	JAN	350.07	-7.4	415.81	-8.6	181.50	-6.9
	FEB	352.90	0.8	425.83	2.4	183.07	0.9
	MAR	361.75	2.5	435.54	2.3	186.84	2.1
	APR	343.10	-5.2	420.07	-3.6	181.49	-2.9
	MAY	363.06	5.8	458.97	9.3	196.94	8.5
	JUN	361.21	-0.5	462.29	0.7	195.48	-0.7
	JUL	353.60	-2.1	438.24	-5.2	194.60	-0.5
	AUG	323.39	-8.5	381.21	-13.0	176.97	-9.1
	SEP	307.72	-4.8	344.51	-9.6	167.85	-5.2
	OCT	287.79	-6.5	329.84	-4.3	166.17	-1.0
	NOV	301.79	4.9	359.06	8.9	176.06	6.0
	DEC	308.11	2.1	373.84	4.1	180.49	2.5
1991	JAN	317.54	3.1	414.20	10.8	187.59	3.9
	FEB	346.13	9.0	453.05	9.4	200.70	7.0
	MAR	359.20	3.8	482.30	6.5	205.30	2.3
	APR	360.76	0.4	484.72	0.5	205.37	0.0
	MAY	371.99	3.1	506.11	4.4	212.99	3.7
	JUN	358.12	-3.7	475.92	-6.0	203.47	-4.5
	JUL	388.28	8.4	502.04	5.5	212.34	4.4
	AUG	372.13	-4.2	525.68	4.7	216.69	2.0
	SEP	374.58	0.7	526.88	0.2	213.34	-1.5
	OCT	387.31	3.4	542.98	3.1	216.54	1.5
	NOV	370.68	-4.3	523.90	-3.5	207.75	-4.1
	DEC	395.05	6.6	586.34	11.9	229.44	10.4

[Continued]

AMEX, NASD, and NYSE Indexes
1984-1995
[Continued]

Year	Month	AMEX Index	AMEX %	NASD Index	NASD %	NYSE Index	NYSE %
1992	JAN	411.37	4.1	620.21	5.8	226.20	-1.4
	FEB	416.09	1.1	633.47	2.1	228.21	0.9
	MAR	395.04	-5.1	603.77	-4.7	223.25	-2.2
	APR	380.90	-3.6	578.68	-4.2	228.30	2.3
	MAY	394.90	3.7	585.31	1.1	228.87	0.2
	JUN	379.28	-4.0	563.60	-3.7	224.33	-2.0
	JUL	388.85	2.5	580.83	3.1	233.15	3.9
	AUG	380.78	-2.1	563.12	-3.0	228.03	-2.2
	SEP	376.72	-1.1	583.27	3.6	229.46	0.6
	OCT	381.72	1.3	605.17	3.8	230.57	0.5
	NOV	395.11	3.5	652.73	7.9	237.45	3.0
	DEC	399.23	1.0	676.95	3.7	240.21	1.2
1993	JAN	411.08	3.0	696.34	2.9	241.92	0.7
	FEB	406.84	-1.0	670.77	-3.7	244.08	0.9
	MAR	423.43	4.1	690.13	2.9	249.42	2.2
	APR	420.96	-0.6	661.42	-4.2	243.46	-2.4
	MAY	438.22	4.1	700.53	5.9	248.60	2.1
	JUN	434.24	-0.9	703.95	0.5	249.10	0.2
	JUL	437.00	0.6	704.70	0.1	248.49	-0.2
	AUG	458.60	4.9	742.84	5.4	256.88	3.4
	SEP	460.39	0.4	762.78	2.7	255.23	-0.6
	OCT	481.44	4.6	779.26	2.2	259.38	1.6
	NOV	460.03	-4.4	754.39	-3.2	254.79	-1.8
	DEC	477.15	3.7	776.80	3.0	259.08	1.7
1994	JAN	485.68	1.8	800.47	3.0	267.10	3.1
	FEB	471.34	-3.0	792.50	-1.0	259.23	-2.9
	MAR	443.11	-6.0	743.46	-6.2	247.06	-4.7
	APR	439.91	-0.7	733.84	-1.3	250.36	1.3
	MAY	440.45	0.1	735.19	0.2	252.24	0.8
	JUN	424.08	-3.7	705.96	-4.0	245.15	-2.8
	JUL	437.69	3.2	722.16	2.3	252.62	3.0
	AUG	454.34	3.8	765.62	6.0	261.99	3.7
	SEP	458.81	1.0	764.29	-0.2	255.52	-2.5
	OCT	458.57	-0.1	777.49	1.7	258.61	1.2
	NOV	433.86	-5.4	750.32	-3.5	248.41	-3.9
	DEC	433.67	-0.0	751.96	0.2	250.94	1.0
1995	JAN	435.36	0.4	755.20	0.4	255.93	2.0
	FEB	452.71	4.0	793.73	5.1	264.65	3.4
	MAR	464.41	2.6	817.21	3.0	271.04	2.4
	APR	477.56	2.8	843.98	3.3	277.31	2.3
	MAY	492.10	3.0	864.58	2.4	286.44	3.3
	JUN	500.19	1.6	933.45	8.0	291.84	1.9
	JUL	523.24	4.6	1001.21	7.3	301.32	3.2
	AUG	534.45	2.1	1020.11	1.9	302.00	0.2
	SEP	544.72	1.9	1043.54	2.3	313.26	3.7
	OCT	521.87	-4.2	1036.06	-0.7	309.61	-1.2
	NOV	537.37	3.0	1059.20	2.2	323.59	4.5
	DEC	548.23	2.0	1052.13	-0.7	329.51	1.8

Source: American Stock Exchange, private communication, for 1984-1995 and from the exchanges for later years.

American Stock Exchange Market Value Index
Yearly High, Low, and Close
1969-1995

For 1969 through December 1995. Dates indicate the date of high and low values reached in the year. Close is the last day of the year. Percent change is from previous year-end.

Year	High		Low		Close	% Change
	Index	Date	Index	Date	Index	
1969	84.50	1/2	57.23	7/29	60.01	
1970	62.77	1/5	36.10	5/26	49.21	-18.0
1971	60.86	4/28	49.09	1/4	58.49	18.9
1972	69.18	4/30	58.55	1/3	64.53	10.3
1973	65.06	1/2	42.61	12/24	45.17	-30.0
1974	51.01	3/14	29.13	12/9	30.16	-33.2
1975	48.43	7/15	31.10	1/2	41.74	38.4
1976	54.92	12/31	42.16	1/2	54.92	31.6
1977	63.95	12/30	54.81	1/12	63.95	16.4
1978	88.44	9/13	59.87	1/11	75.28	17.7
1979	123.54	12/31	76.02	1/2	123.54	64.1
1980	185.38	11/28	107.85	3/27	174.50	41.2
1981	190.18	8/13	138.38	9/25	160.32	-8.1
1982	170.93	11/11	118.65	8/12	170.30	6.2
1983	249.03	7/26	169.61	1/3	223.01	31.0
1984	227.73	1/16	187.16	7/25	204.26	-8.4
1985	246.13	12/31	202.06	1/8	246.13	20.5
1986	285.19	6/25	240.30	2/4	263.27	7.0
1987	365.01	8/13	231.90	12/4	260.35	-1.1
1988	309.59	7/5	262.76	1/12	306.01	17.5
1989	397.03	10/10	305.24	1/3	378.00	23.5
1990	382.45	1/5	287.79	10/31	308.11	-18.5
1991	393.01	11/11	368.51	10/9	395.05	28.2
1992	418.99	2/12	364.85	10/9	399.23	7.7
1993	484.28	11/2	395.84	1/8	477.15	19.5
1994	487.89	11/2	420.23	12/13	433.67	-9.1
1995	553.58	9/12	433.12	1/6	548.23	26.4

Source: American Stock Exchange, private communication.

American Stock Exchange Market Value Index
Quarterly Index and Sub-Indices

For 1980-1995 by Quarters. QTR stands for Quarter. MVI stands for Market Value Index.

QTR	Year	MVI	High Tech	Capital Goods	Consumer Goods	Services	Retail	Financials	Natural Resources	Housing, Constr., & Land
1	1980	116.52	155.94	111.47	69.37	115.58	98.33	93.74	129.69	95.65
2		146.81	175.24	127.44	80.55	145.54	113.08	113.76	172.95	119.20
3		165.78	254.94	147.45	103.90	173.14	131.88	135.77	178.76	142.85
4		174.50	316.74	158.66	118.35	189.03	126.55	143.93	177.80	145.93
1	1981	180.30	326.82	171.10	121.85	209.31	150.25	148.71	178.08	162.68
2		187.32	331.55	169.80	129.21	208.79	172.49	157.94	187.72	176.33
3		146.43	246.97	139.17	106.89	166.36	144.13	138.09	143.51	142.83
4		160.32	282.99	138.64	120.52	201.84	148.61	156.59	154.25	160.54
1	1982	130.06	247.33	116.40	117.06	191.02	145.78	153.81	112.19	137.17
2		125.40	246.12	115.08	116.94	199.25	162.72	151.48	101.18	137.11
3		141.59	294.16	121.71	132.79	222.22	190.77	168.52	115.47	158.10
4		170.30	426.62	143.92	166.10	287.16	242.20	214.39	119.37	249.39
1	1983	194.54	509.06	175.34	197.48	331.50	319.77	256.17	124.18	302.43
2		242.32	626.55	213.16	230.00	418.77	396.43	296.59	162.98	370.53
3		230.28	542.32	199.64	216.92	380.04	397.06	287.66	165.52	328.55
4		223.01	525.00	211.90	213.48	359.20	410.36	290.32	157.50	312.55
1	1984	211.34	421.50	196.45	195.92	356.41	378.47	294.33	157.53	304.48
2		200.08	404.96	190.39	190.47	362.42	404.01	299.35	140.14	282.72
3		215.45	402.27	210.07	207.47	384.28	458.05	325.85	155.40	300.47
4		204.26	374.87	202.84	195.49	403.65	465.89	351.54	135.60	305.48
1	1985	229.59	364.57	227.06	222.20	485.59	610.38	402.00	152.97	335.43
2		230.89	342.11	234.60	237.62	532.33	675.23	417.38	144.95	341.12
3		222.31	317.00	226.68	233.25	474.24	626.42	402.27	147.07	326.47
4		246.13	383.81	260.29	274.30	537.77	746.10	455.40	146.30	373.50
1	1986	270.03	417.26	299.49	332.93	654.23	877.42	538.73	128.63	456.82
2		284.20	423.69	314.92	379.02	747.81	975.06	586.47	120.16	442.97
3		260.69	384.57	264.95	341.27	656.11	794.23	504.62	127.11	398.50
4		263.27	349.26	273.28	335.83	662.25	769.80	478.49	137.94	390.10
1	1987	332.66	462.04	334.28	401.48	809.73	872.02	504.78	193.60	492.05
2		338.13	463.30	342.48	404.63	875.89	899.07	469.46	202.98	466.87
3		356.45	516.60	365.11	409.52	904.95	928.01	455.69	227.02	472.23
4		260.35	364.91	264.87	304.83	626.67	655.04	355.34	176.97	335.02
1	1988	296.43	378.96	300.67	357.99	718.63	772.42	382.89	200.20	377.01
2		309.25	423.65	332.08	374.30	709.98	885.87	396.24	201.52	414.99
3		301.63	375.48	315.42	368.91	701.25	982.95	386.82	190.88	435.53
4		306.01	368.83	321.55	393.07	710.63	949.31	378.49	202.21	429.99
1	1989	328.31	362.73	349.91	429.92	765.84	1050.22	378.37	221.40	452.81
2		358.97	378.65	377.86	466.48	909.00	1156.33	403.24	229.49	490.99
3		388.76	393.23	417.19	507.83	1002.04	1306.77	422.06	247.90	519.91
4		378.00	376.69	401.37	504.76	930.78	1193.34	407.45	258.52	446.11
1	1990	361.75	371.80	395.42	452.50	868.48	1178.63	400.54	253.99	416.85
2		361.21	390.96	413.50	459.92	890.36	1300.56	398.11	237.46	378.69
3		307.72	291.90	326.76	358.86	654.05	869.09	360.10	250.01	300.78
4		308.11	332.10	335.31	396.80	732.38	1000.70	351.31	215.22	230.58

[Continued]

American Stock Exchange Market Value Index
Quarterly Index and Sub-Indices
[Continued]

For 1980-1995 by Quarters. QTR stands for Quarter. MVI stands for Market Value Index.

QTR	Year	MVI	High Tech	Capital Goods	Consumer Goods	Services	Retail	Financials	Natural Resources	Housing, Constr., & Land
1	1991	359.20	454.92	396.58	515.93	852.89	1236.86	414.45	215.62	334.59
2		372.13	456.03	411.13	561.44	921.42	1225.14	435.31	219.56	286.58
3		374.58	466.42	411.43	579.21	931.05	1321.73	433.63	216.53	266.30
4		395.05	573.19	405.53	701.82	1034.14	1268.93	446.83	187.79	279.46
1	1992	395.04	543.87	438.78	740.29	1041.79	1293.46	484.44	172.89	341.48
2		379.28	422.20	399.87	537.19	872.35	1250.37	428.80	209.97	321.49
3		376.72	437.36	389.25	753.19	969.20	1107.57	471.52	187.71	282.47
4		399.23	486.10	410.73	805.70	1123.98	1334.84	500.65	164.56	344.25
1	1993	406.84	475.04	428.48	764.08	1111.29	1341.62	542.96	177.85	382.94
2		434.24	481.79	428.75	783.84	1196.67	1411.12	513.10	213.24	390.64
3		460.39	519.22	489.52	811.94	1386.74	1366.93	542.91	205.84	425.04
4		477.15	539.76	508.03	864.99	1468.54	1465.48	537.99	203.63	504.49
1	1994	443.11	516.52	511.70	807.05	1213.82	1400.93	526.58	197.66	513.03
2		424.08	457.32	485.52	734.44	1162.92	1226.52	531.49	195.58	522.48
3		458.81	541.73	515.77	804.34	1286.47	1272.14	528.93	215.54	561.23
4		433.67	519.61	491.08	792.00	1229.34	1222.97	487.37	201.64	519.29
1	1995	464.41	542.33	513.14	903.64	1312.08	1271.97	526.21	214.67	532.10
2		500.19	638.32	620.65	914.24	1386.64	1409.35	555.96	237.12	552.77
3		544.72	721.41	678.77	988.76	1568.74	1464.04	597.73	245.68	513.68
4		548.23	805.39	712.29	944.12	1518.63	1450.98	636.78	245.52	557.32

Source: American Stock Exchange, private communication.

NASDAQ Composite Index
Yearly High, Low, and Close
1971-1995

For 1971 through 1995. Dates indicate the date of high and low values reached in the year. Close is the last day of the year. Percent change is from previous year-end. The NASDAQ index began on February 5, 1971.

Year	High Index	Date	Low Index	Date	Close Index	% Change
1971	114.12	12/31	99.68	2/22	114.12	-
1972	135.15	12/8	113.65	1/3	133.73	17.2
1973	136.84	1/11	88.67	12/24	92.19	-31.1
1974	96.53	3/15	54.87	10/3	59.82	-35.1
1975	88.00	7/15	60.70	1/2	77.62	29.8
1976	97.88	12/31	78.06	1/2	97.88	26.1
1977	105.05	12/30	93.66	4/5	105.05	7.3
1978	139.25	9/13	99.09	1/11	117.98	12.3
1979	152.29	10/5	117.84	1/2	151.14	28.1
1980	208.15	11/28	124.09	3/27	202.34	33.9
1981	223.47	5/29	175.03	9/28	195.84	-3.2
1982	240.70	12/8	159.14	8/13	232.41	18.7
1983	328.91	6/24	230.59	1/3	278.60	19.9
1984	287.90	1/6	225.30	7/25	247.35	-11.2
1985	325.22	12/31	245.91	1/2	325.22	31.5
1986	411.16	7/3	323.01	1/9	348.83	7.3
1987	455.26	8/26	291.88	10/28	330.47	-5.3
1988	396.11	7/5	331.97	1/12	381.38	15.4
1989	485.73	10/9	378.56	1/3	454.82	19.3
1990	469.60	7/16	325.44	10/16	373.84	-17.8
1991	586.34	12/31	355.75	1/14	586.34	56.8
1992	676.95	12/31	547.84	6/26	676.95	15.5
1993	787.42	10/15	645.87	4/26	776.80	14.7
1994	803.93	3/18	693.79	6/24	751.96	-3.2
1995	1069.79	12/4	743.58 1	1/3	1052.13	40.0

Source: The NASDAQ Stock Market, Historical Data Services.

NASDAQ Stock Market Index
Quarterly Index and Sub-Indices

For 1980-1995 by Quarters. QTR stands for Quarter. Data show closing index for each period.

QTR	Year	Composite Index	Industrials	Banks	Insurance	Financials	Trans-portation	Computers
1	1980	131.00	155.70	93.29	133.26	109.84	105.28	-
2		157.78	185.74	108.34	158.94	136.35	125.10	-
3		187.76	233.90	114.87	176.90	148.74	160.17	-
4		202.34	261.36	118.39	166.81	154.07	164.19	-
1	1981	210.18	264.85	126.96	184.80	168.44	171.81	-
2		215.75	265.68	138.92	198.44	178.53	193.04	-
3		180.03	212.22	128.86	177.56	160.41	166.15	-
4		195.84	229.29	143.13	194.31	176.20	167.77	-
1	1982	175.65	199.05	136.66	188.09	165.00	148.10	-
2		171.30	196.33	130.61	172.49	158.52	151.46	-
3		187.65	213.35	134.16	201.84	177.31	172.50	-
4		232.41	273.58	156.37	226.40	207.50	195.48	-
1	1983	270.80	323.52	169.58	259.19	235.16	230.82	-
2		318.70	392.90	186.70	268.63	269.96	259.46	-
3		296.65	353.52	201.06	262.89	280.58	277.99	-
4		278.60	323.68	203.75	257.63	277.53	280.80	-
1	1984	250.78	283.34	204.09	254.19	270.20	228.19	-
2		239.65	270.65	194.48	244.26	258.28	203.71	-
3		249.94	275.16	209.23	271.59	281.23	224.99	-
4		247.35	260.73	229.77	283.11	298.62	239.29	-
1	1985	279.20	297.37	253.43	326.29	330.37	255.54	-
2		296.20	303.82	290.49	350.14	377.06	261.79	-
3		280.33	284.39	296.10	329.77	365.53	256.52	-
4		325.22	330.17	349.36	382.07	423.49	291.59	-
1	1986	374.72	375.91	403.25	455.06	499.73	340.56	-
2		405.51	409.96	450.45	452.72	543.95	362.92	-
3		350.67	344.16	403.70	425.20	482.84	322.95	-
4		348.83	349.33	412.53	404.14	460.64	348.84	-
1	1987	430.05	454.21	506.19	446.17	527.82	398.87	-
2		424.67	450.71	475.48	433.04	511.97	406.13	-
3		444.29	475.25	489.82	457.39	520.74	418.38	-
4		330.47	338.94	390.66	351.06	406.96	319.21	-
1	1988	374.64	383.67	448.77	397.65	456.39	373.51	-
2		394.66	411.48	455.91	398.36	468.43	374.07	-
3		387.71	388.19	456.94	435.45	473.20	390.74	-
4		381.38	378.95	435.31	429.14	459.34	395.81	-
1	1989	406.73	398.63	458.57	470.56	487.75	412.84	-
2		435.29	421.71	466.03	505.05	513.14	421.25	-
3		472.92	458.97	478.84	533.63	559.54	476.97	-
4		454.82	447.99	391.02	546.01	505.64	498.20	-
1	1990	435.54	450.51	366.25	502.65	466.36	476.70	-
2		462.29	499.01	335.71	506.31	446.61	488.28	-
3		344.51	368.46	249.25	406.56	340.34	389.31	-
4		373.84	406.05	254.91	451.84	359.13	417.07	-
1	1991	482.30	545.03	310.15	548.98	437.31	509.21	-
2		475.92	527.10	327.30	534.39	472.42	513.80	-
3		526.88	590.19	343.52	534.10	521.94	530.73	-
4		586.34	668.95	350.56	601.09	560.79	571.39	-

[Continued]

NASDAQ Stock Market Index
Quarterly Index and Sub-Indices
[Continued]

QTR	Year	Composite Index	Industrials	Banks	Insurance	Financials	Trans-portation	Computers
1	1992	603.77	676.05	396.32	617.46	621.85	604.09	-
2		563.60	601.65	442.93	623.26	666.02	551.92	-
3		583.27	620.85	462.50	705.60	687.31	567.47	-
4		676.95	724.94	532.93	803.91	788.81	634.10	-
1	1993	690.13	713.55	627.47	861.30	860.92	672.01	-
2		703.95	729.52	607.88	853.02	834.96	673.48	-
3		762.78	780.13	698.81	946.00	907.00	701.78	-
4		776.80	805.84	689.43	920.59	892.64	746.26	-
1	1994	727.41	760.80	662.57	864.59	860.68	734.19	201.48
2		706.85	715.83	761.83	880.94	931.59	690.03	188.43
3		760.88	773.25	767.81	942.65	931.93	706.39	212.27
4		743.58	743.47	702.95	921.12	861.99	657.00	229.99
1	1995	818.05	801.44	769.10	1021.77	944.26	701.26	269.10
2		934.53	886.49	849.88	1057.38	1033.25	777.65	336.69
3		1027.57	966.32	962.09	1171.88	1166.12	795.36	360.03
4		1052.13	964.68	1009.41	1292.64	1240.87	816.36	366.13

Source: The NASDAQ Stock Market, Historical Data Services.

New York Stock Exchange Composite Index
Yearly High, Low, and Close
1966-1995

For 1966 through 1995. Dates indicate the date of high and low values reached in the year. Close is the last day of the year. Percent change is from previous year-end.

Year	High		Low		Close	% Change
	Index	Date	Index	Date	Index	
1966	51.06	9/2	39.37	7/10	43.72	-12.6
1967	54.16	9/10	43.74	3/1	53.83	23.1
1968	61.27	29/11	48.70	5/3	58.90	9.4
1969	59.32	14/5	49.31	29/7	51.53	-12.5
1970	52.36	5/1	37.69	26/5	50.23	-2.5
1971	57.76	28/4	49.60	23/11	56.43	12.3
1972	65.14	11/12	56.23	3/1	64.48	14.3
1973	65.48	11/1	49.05	5/12	51.82	-19.6
1974	53.37	13/3	32.89	3/10	36.13	-30.3
1975	51.24	15/7	37.06	2/1	47.64	31.9
1976	57.88	31/12	48.04	2/1	57.88	21.5
1977	57.69	3/1	49.78	2/11	52.50	-9.3
1978	60.38	11/9	48.37	6/3	53.62	2.1
1979	63.39	5/10	53.88	27/2	61.95	15.5
1980	81.02	28/11	55.30	27/3	77.86	25.7
1981	79.14	6/1	64.96	25/9	71.11	-8.7
1982	82.35	9/11	58.80	12/8	81.03	14.0
1983	99.63	10/10	79.79	3/1	95.18	17.5
1984	98.12	6/11	85.13	24/7	96.38	1.3
1985	121.90	16/12	94.60	4/1	121.58	26.1
1986	145.75	4/9	117.75	22/1	138.58	14.0
1987	187.99	25/8	125.91	4/12	138.23	-0.3
1988	159.42	21/10	136.72	20/1	156.26	13.0
1989	199.34	9/10	154.98	3/1	195.04	24.8
1990	201.13	16/7	162.20	11/10	180.49	-7.5
1991	229.44	31/12	170.97	9/1	229.44	27.1
1992	242.08	18/12	217.92	8/4	240.21	4.7
1993	260.67	29/12	236.21	8/1	259.08	7.9
1994	267.71	2/2	243.14	4/4	250.94	-3.1
1995	331.17	12/13	250.73	1/3	329.51	31.3

Source: New York Stock Exchange Data Services.

KEYWORD INDEX

The *Keyword Index* is an alphabetical arrangement of the topics covered in the text and tables of *Economic Indicators Handbook*, 3rd edition. The table of contents (page v) provides an alternative means of locating tables. The primary reference numbers that follow subject index terms are page numbers. Cities cited in this index are metropolitan statistical areas (MSAs).

Numbers following p. or pp. are page references.

Keyword Index

Numbers following p. or pp. are page references.

Numbers following p. or pp. are page references.

Numbers following p. or pp. are page references.

Numbers following p. or pp. are page references.

Numbers following p. or pp. are page references.

Keyword Index

Numbers following p. or pp. are page references.